Y0-AAJ-990

The New York Public Library

The Research Libraries

Guide to *Festschriften*

The Retrospective *Festschriften* Collection of The New York Public Library: Materials Cataloged Through 1971

Volume 1

G. K. HALL & CO., 70 LINCOLN STREET, BOSTON, MASSACHUSETTS
1977

This publication is printed on permanent/durable acid-free paper.

ISBN 0-8161-0069-1

INTRODUCTION

The Research Libraries of the New York Public Library have a long history of extensive acquisition of *Festschriften* in all subject areas where the Library has been collecting materials. The *Festschriften* acquired by the Library include not only those collected essays in honor of scholars by colleagues, friends, and students, but also works of collected essays on the occasion of anniversaries of learned societies, institutions, and corporations. More than half of the *Festschriften* held by the Library are in foreign languages. The New York Public Library has extensive holdings of *Festschriften* in the humanities and the social sciences, but its holdings are especially strong in such specific fields as art, black studies, business, the dance, economics, finance, history, Judaica, linguistics, literature, literary history and criticism, music, Orientalia, philosophy, science and technology, Slavic studies, and the theatre.

Cataloging of *Festschriften* in The Research Libraries is traditionally very detailed. In many cases, extended notes consisting of names of contributors and titles of essays have been provided.

Festschriften in this guide have been arranged in two volumes. In the first volume, over 6,000 *Festschriften* collected by NYPL over a fifty-year period, ending in December 1971, have been arranged in alphabetic order by main entry.

The second volume of the Guide, which is computer produced, contains all *Festschriften* added to the NYPL collections since January 1972. Also represented in Volume 2 are all *Festschriften* presently available in the Library of Congress MARC data base (1968-1976). Volume 2 offers multiple access to the *Festschriften* cataloged by main entry, subject headings, and other secondary entries, all interfiled in dictionary format.

*C-4 p.v.543

A P. Romualdo Bizzarri, omaggio nel cinquantesimo del suo sacerdozio, e studio monografico sulla sua opera filosofica e critico-letteraria. [Siena, 1951] 61 p. illus. 25cm.

Bibliograhy, p. 49-61.

1. Bizzarri, Romualdo, 1878-

NN**R 4.55 OC,1b PC,1 SL (Z1,LC1,X1)

D-15
8815

ABC; DIARIO ILUSTRADO.

Homenaje de ABC a Gregorio Marañón [por Ramón Menéndez Pidal et al.] Madrid, Editorial Prensa española, 1960. 281 p. port. 23cm.

1. Marañón, Gregorio, 1887-1960. I. Menéndez Pidal, Ramón.

NN R 3.65 g/4 (OC)I OS PC,1,I SL (LC1, X1, Z1)

B-10
2114

A CHARLES VEILLON pour un anniversaire. [Zurich, Conzett & Huber, 1960] 253 p. illus. (part col.), facsims. 16cm.

Contributions in French, Italian or German.

1. Veillon, Charles, 1900- . 2. Literature--Collections.

NN R 5.62 e/4 OC, 1b PC, 1, 2 SL (LC1, X1, Z1)

GMB

Aaltonen, Esko, 1893-

Lounais- Hämeen entisyyttä. [Toimittaneet Esko Aaltosen 60-vuotispäiväksi Matti Aaltonen ja Päivikki Lyback] Forssa [Forssan kirjapaino] 1953. 184 p. port. 21cm.

Bibliography, p. 178-184.

1. Häme, Finland. I. Aaltonen, Matti, ed. II. Lybäck, Päivikki, ed. III. Aaltonen Matti. IV. Lybäck, Päivikki.

NN**R X 6.54 OC,I,II, IIIbo,IVbo PC,1,I,II SL (LC1,Z1,X1)

AN
(Ståhlberg, K.)

Aamun kannatusyhdistys r.y.

Kaarlo Juho Ståhlberg, juhlakirja 1940. Helsinki, Aamun kannatusyhdistys r.y. [1940] 323 p. illus. 29cm.

493422B. 1. Ståhlberg, Kaarlo Juho, pres. Finland, 1865-

N. Y. P. L. May 10, 1950

PPL

Aan P. van der Wielen, 1909-1934. [Amsterdam: D. B. Centen's Uitgevers-Maatschappij, N. V., 1934] 205 p. incl. tables. illus. (incl. charts), 3 pl., port. 25cm.

Autographed presentation copy by P. van der Wielen to the New York Public Library.

Essays contributed by Dutch chemists on various subjects pertaining to pharmaceutical chemistry.

Bibliographies included.

749191A. 1. Chemistry, Medical and pharmaceutical. I. Wielen, Pieter van der, 1872-

N. Y. P. L. June 17, 1935

STT
(Oslo)

AARS OG VOSS' SKOLE. Oslo.

Festskrift utgit i anledning av Aars og Voss' skoles femtiaars jubilæum ved Skolens bestyrelse med bidrag av forhenv. elever. Kristiania, Aschehoug, 1913. 333 p. illus., ports., maps. 22cm.

CONTENTS. --Aars og Voss' latin- og realskoles historie i femti aar, 1863-1913, ved A. Midsem. --Skolens programmer 1863-1913. --Skolens lærere 1863-1913. --Fortegnelse over de elever som... er utgaat... fra Aars og Voss' skole. --Bidrag av forhenværende elever: Solflekker, (Continued)

NN**R 2.56 a/4 OSs PCs, Is, Is SLs (LC1s, X1s, Z1s)

AARS OG VOSS' SKOLE. Oslo. Festskrift... (Card 2)

veir og mennesker, av A. Magelssen. Vort hjemsted, av I. Flood. Den antikke tid og det repræsentative system, av A. Ræder. Myten om Tor og Geirrød, av H. Falk. De virtuelle hastigheders' princip, av A. Thue. Om verdnernes tilblivelse, av K. Birkeland. Om arbeide og øvelsesutbytte, av K. B. -R. Aars. Om onsindet retsutøvelse (chichane) efter norsk ret, av U. A. Motzfeldt. Moral og religion, av O. Moe. Norsk realisme i 1830-aarene, av L. Heber. Meteor-krateret i Arizona, av W. Werenskiold. Archimedes's kvadratrotsberegning, av V. Brun. "Armauer Hansens"s første togt, av B. Helland-Hansen.

1. Education, Secondary--Norway--Oslo. I. Title.

OAC

Abb, Gustav, 1886- , editor.

Aus fuenfzig Jahren deutscher Wissenschaft; die Entwicklung ihrer Fachgebiete in Einzeldarstellungen; herausgegeben von Gustav Abb. Berlin: W. de Gruyter & Co., 1930. xi, 496 p. front. (port.) 4°.

"Seiner Excellenz Herrn Staatsministers D. Dr. Friedrich Schmidt-Ott zur Feier seines siebzigsten Geburtstages...überreicht von Walter von Dyck... [und Anderen]

(Continued)

N. Y. P. L. December 17, 1930

Abb, Gustav, 1886- , editor: Aus fuenfzig Jahren deutscher Wissenschaft... (Card 2)

Contents: HARNACK, A. VON. Geleitwort. SEEBERG, R. Friedrich Schmidt-Ott und die deutsche Wissenschaft. SCHREIBER, G. Auslandsbeziehungen der deutschen Wissenschaft. MILKAU, F. Bibliothekswesen. KATTENBUSCH, F. Evangelische Theologie. EHRHARD, A. Katholische Theologie. MAIER, H. Philosophie. SPRANGER, E. Pädagogik. HEYMANN, E. Rechtswissenschaft. SCHUMACHER, H. Staatswissenschaften. THILENIUS, G. Völkerkunde. MEYER, E. Geschichte und Kultur der Mittelmeerwelt. BRANDI, K. Mittlere und neue Geschichte. GOLDSCHMIDT, A. Kunstgeschichte. SCHRÖDER, E. Deutsche Philologie. BRIE, F. Englische Philologie. MEYER-LÜBKE, W. Romanische Philologie. VASMER, M. Slavische Philologie. LITTMANN, E. Semitische Philologie. HÄNISCH, E.

(Continued)

N. Y. P. L. December 17, 1930

Abb, Gustav, 1886– , editor: Aus fuenfzig Jahren deutscher Wissenschaft... (Card 3)

Sinologie. CARATHÉODORY, C. and W. VON DYCK. Mathematik. SCHENCK, R. Arbeitsgemeinschaft und Gemeinschaftsarbeit in Naturwissenschaft und Technik. PLANCK, M. Theoretische Physik. FRANCK, J. Experimentalphysik. ZENNECK, J. Technische Physik. HERGESELL, H. Physik des Erdkörpers. HABER, F. Chemie. STILLE, H. Geologie. LINCK, G. Mineralogie. PENCK, A. Maritime und geographische Expeditionen. DEFANT, A. Ozeanographie. WETTSTEIN, F. VON. Biologie. MÜLLER, F. VON. Medizin. KOLLE, W. Forschung und Forschungsinstitute auf dem Gebiet der experimentellen Medizin. MIESSNER, H. and J. PAECHTNER. Tiermedizin. NÄGEL, A. Maschinenwesen. THIERRY, G. DE. Bauingenieurwesen. SCHUMACHER, F. Entwicklung des Städtebaus. FALKE, F. Landwirtschaft. MÜNCH, E. Forstwissenschaft.

501674A. 1. Science—Hist.—Germany. 2. Learning and scholarship—Germany. 3. Schmidt-Ott, Friedrich, 1860– . I. Title.
N. Y. P. L. December 17, 1930

A p.v.449

Abb, Gustav, 1886– , editor.
Fritz Milkau zum Gedächtnis; Ansprachen, Vorträge und Verzeichnis seiner Schriften, herausgegeben von Gustav Abb. Leipzig: O. Harrassowitz, 1934. 54 p. incl. port. 24cm.

"Verzeichnis der Schriften Milkaus zusammengestellt von Curt Balcke," p. 49–[55].

Festschrift

743133A. 1. Milkau, Fritz, 1859–1934. I. Balcke, Curt, 1886– .
N. Y. P. L. January 24, 1935

MWES
(Petrolini, E.)

Abbasso Petrolini, di U. Ojetti [et al. Siena, tip. cooperativa, 192-] 238 p. illus., facsim. 19cm.

1. Petrolini, Ettore, 1886-1936. I. Ojetti, Ugo, 1871- .

NN••R 10.56 /b OCs,Is PCs,1,Is SLs (T3s, LC1s, X1s, Z1s)

XAN

Abhandlungen zur antiken Rechtsgeschichte; Festschrift für Gustav Hanausek zu seinem siebzigsten Geburtstage am 4. September 1925, überreicht von seinen Freunden und Schülern. Graz: J. Meyerhoff[, 1925]. vii, 159 p. 8°.

Bibliographical footnotes.
Contents: WENGER, L. Wandlungen im römischen Zivilprozessrecht. SAN NICOLO, M. Zur Entwicklung der babylonischen Urkundenformen. STEINWENTER, A. Neue Urkunden zum byzantinischen Libellprozess. LAUTNER, J. G. Zur interrogatio in iure nach klassischem Rechte. PFAFF, I. Zur Lehre vom Vermögen nach römischem Recht. KOSCHAKER, P. Bedingte Novation und pactum im römischen Recht.

1. Law, Roman. 2. Law, Byzantine. 3. Law, Assyrian and Babylonian. 4. Hanausek, Gustav, 1855– . 5. Title. Festschrift für Gustav Hanausek.
N. Y. P. L. January 12, 1927

ZDE

Abhandlungen aus dem gebiete der mittleren und neueren geschichte und ihrer hilfswissenschaften, eine festgabe zum siebzigsten geburtstag geh. rat prof. dr. Heinrich Finke gewidmet von schülern und verehrern des in- und auslandes ... Mit einem lichtbild Heinrich Finkes und 3 kunstdruckbeilagen. Münster i. W, Aschendorff, 1925. duplicate front (port.) inserted.
xi, 517 p. front. (port.) 3 facsim. 24½cm.
Half-title: Vorreformationsgeschichtliche forschungen. Supplementband.
Lettered: Finke-festschrift 1925.

318905A. 1. Finke, Heinrich, 1855– 2. Church history—~~Collections.~~ 3. Middle ages—Hist.—Collections. I. [series] Vorreformationsgeschichtliche forschungen. Supplementband. II. Title: Finkefestschrift.

Library of Congress BR141.A3 26–22903 (Over)
[2]

Write on slip class mark name, vol., and year of magazine. YAG

Abhandlungen zur geschichte der philosophie des mittelalters. Festgabe Clemens Baeumker zum 70 geburtstag (16 september 1923) dargebracht von seinen freunden und schülern ... Münster i. W., Aschendorff, 1923.
vii, [1], 269 p. 24cm. (*Added t.-p.:* Beiträge zur geschichte der philosophie des mittelalters ... Supplementband II)
"Vorwort" signed: Martin Grabmann.
CONTENTS.—Nikolaus Trivet, sein leben, seine Quolibet und Quaestiones ordinariae. Von kardinal F. Ehrle.—Der gedanke der erkenntnis des gleichen durch gleiches in antiker und patristischer zeit. Von prof. dr. A. Schneider.—Über die seelischen vorbedingungen der Plotinischen ekstase. Von prof. d. dr. G. Wunderle.—Die griechisch-lateinischen Metaphysikübersetzungen des mittelalters. Von prof. dr. F. Pelster.—Die logischen schriften des Nikolaus von Paris (Clm. 14460 und Vat. lat. 1311) und ihre stellung in der aristotelischen bewegung des 13. jahrhunderts. Von prof. dr. M.

(Continued on next card)
24–14895
[2]

YAG

Abhandlungen zur geschichte der philosophie des mittelalters ... 1923. (Card 2)

CONTENTS—Continued.

Grabmann.—Eine metaphysische frage zur differentiellen psychologie bei den mittelalterlichen scholastikern. Von lektor dr. P. R. Klingseis.—Zur einführung in das problem der evidenz in der scholastik. Von prof. dr. J. Geyser.—Stellung und bedeutung des voluntarium in der ethik des hl. Thomas von Aquin. Von prof. dr. M. Wittmann.—Zur allgemeinen kunstlehre des hl. Thomas. Von prof. geheimrat dr. A. Dyroff.—Der ethikkommentar des Johannes Pecham. Von dr. H. Spettmann.—Petrus de Trabibus. Seine spekulative eigenart oder sein verhältnis zu Olivi. Von dr. B. Jansen.—Das opusculum "De passionibus animae" Dionys' des Kartäusers. Von prof. dr. G. Heidingsfelder.

1. Philosophy, Medieval—Hist. 2. Philosophy—Collected works. 3. Baeumker, Clemens, 1853–

Library of Congress B720.B4 Suppl. 24–14895
[2]

Copy only words underlined & classmark-- RKKA

ABHANDLUNGEN zur niederdeutschen Philologie Conrad Borchling zum Gedächtnis. [Neumünster, K. Wachholtz, 1950] 351 p. port., map. 25cm. (Verein für niederdeutsche Sprachforschung, Hamburg. Jahrbuch. [no.] 71-73 (1948-50))

Half-title.
CONTENTS.--Conrad Borchling, von O. Lauffer.--Indogermanisch ā - urgermanisch ā, von W. Jungandreas.--Der christliche
(Continued)

NN R 11.59 1/b OC OI PC, 1 (LC2, X1, Z1)

ABHANDLUNGEN zur niederdeutschen Philologie Concrad Borchling zum Gedächtnis. (Card 3)

A. Hübner.--Der Wortschatz Georg Nicolaus Bärmanns, von K. Scheel.--Von den geistigen Grundlagen des Quickborn, von F. Pauli.--Elbostfälisch, von K. Bischoff.--Wortgeographische Untersuchungen zu K. F. A. Schellers Sassisch-Niederdeutschem Wörterbuch, von H. F. Rosenfeld.--Zur westfälischen Wortkunde, von F. Holthausen.--Einige Bemerkungen zum obigen Artikel, von E. Nörrenberg.--Vom Wortschatz des westfälischen Niederdeutschen, von E. Nörrenberg.--Zur Lage des Niederdeutschen in unserer Zeit, von W. Niekerken.

1. Borchling, Conrad August Johann Carl, 1872-1946.

VFC

Abir, David, *ed.*
Topics in applied mechanics; memorial volume to the late Professor Edwin Schwerin. Edited by David Abir, Franz Ollendorff [and] Markus Reiner. Amsterdam, New York, Elsevier Pub. Co., 1965.
xi, 318 p. illus., port. 23 cm.
Includes bibliographies.
CONTENTS.—Editorial foreword.—Professor Edwin Schwerin; biographical note, by M. Mittelman.—List of publications by Professor E. Schwerin (p. xi)—Instability of spherical shells subjected to external pressure, by T. von Kármán and A. D. Kerr.—A note on stress functions and compatibility equations in shell theory, by E. Reissner.—Elastically supported spherical segments under antisymmetrical loads, by M. G. Salvadori and S. Lichtenstein.—Buckling of circular
(Continued)

NN* R 7.65 g/ OC, 2b* PC, 1, 2 SL ST, 1t, 2 (LC1, X1, Z1)

4

ABIR, DAVID, ed. Topics in applied mechanics... (Card 2)

conical shells under combined torsion and external or internal pressure, by J. Singer and M. Baruch.—Approximate solution for the bending of a shallow circular paraboloidal shell, by L. Fisher.—On the theory of symmetrically heterogeneous plates having the same thickness variation of the elastic moduli, by Y. Stavsky.—The solid viscosity of mild steel, by D. Abir, H. Manor, and M. Reiner.—Field theory of self-excited influence machines, by F. Ollendorff.—Cross stresses in the flow of different gases, by A. Foux and M. Reiner.—The stability of viscous flow between two concentric counter-rotating cylinders, by P. Lieber and L. Rintel.—Flow between parallel boundaries in linear movement for two models of pseudoplastic flow with three rheological constants, by Z. Rotem.—Earthquakes and uplift in

(Continued)

ABIR, DAVID, ed. Topics in applied mechanics... (Card 3)

the elastic theory of triangular gravity dams, by S. Irmay.—The geomechanics of strains and stresses: theory and experiment, by I. Haber-Schaim.—Effective stresses in partly saturated soils, by Y. Alpan.—Theory of triaxial test specimens with high diameter-height ratio, by M. Livneh and E. Shklarsky.—Delayed cracking and fracture in cement mortars exposed to extreme hygrometric changes, by O. Ishai.—Performance of plastically designed reinforced concrete beams in the working stage, by A. Zaslavsky.—On the analysis of deformation and the strain tensors, by Z. Karni.—Mohr's circle as an aid to the transformation of symmetrical second-order tensors and to the solution of some other problems, by A. Werfel.—Nomograms for some algebraic equations, by L. Bonfiglioli.

(Continued)

ABIR, DAVID, ed. Topics in applied mechanics... (Card 4)

1. Mechanics, Applied. 2. Schwerin, Edwin, 1886-1959. t. 1965

---

*EI
A154
v.18

Åbo akademi, Turku, Finland.

Hyllningsskrift till Rolf Pipping, 1 juni 1949. Åbo, Åbo Tidnings och tryckeri aktiebolag, 1949. 358 p. illus., maps. 25cm. (In: Åbo akademi, Turku, Finland. Acta Academiae aboensis. Humaniora. 18)

"Tryckts i en separatuppl. av 300 exemplar."

CONTENTS.—Andersson, Otto. Framsades (reciterades) eller sjöngos de isländska rimorna?—Andersson, Sven. Sockennamnet Vårdö.—Colliander, Börje. Anteckningar om ordet 'nationalism'.—Dahlström, Svante. David Wilhelm af Grubbens.— Donner, H. W. De dödas uppror; ett omtvistat textställe i Macbeth (IV, i, 97).—Ekelund,

(Continued)

NN 1.53 (OC)I OS OI PC, 1, 2, 3, I (LC1, Z1, X1) ‹I›

Åbo akademi, Turku, Finland. Hyllningsskrift till Rolf Pipping ... (Card 2)

Erik. Karelsk exotism.—Gardberg, C.-R. Rikshistoriografen Jacob Wilde, Åbo domkapitel och de finska dialekterna.—Gardberg, John. Kommunala ärenden vid sockenstämman i Kimito 1747–1809.—Gyllenberg, Rafael. Den välklädda kvinnan; några synpunkter angående tolkningen av 1 Kor.11:10.—Hjärne, Erland. Sveriges holme och Bjärköarätten.—Hummelstedt, Eskil. Pejorativt neutrum i de finlandssvenska dialekterna.—Lagerborg Rolf. Honnör för Ruth Hedvall.—Lindblom, Johannes. Profetiskt bildspråk.—Pettersson, Björn. Anteckningar om prep. *på* i nusvenskan.—Ringbom, L.-I. Gallehushornens bilder.—Tegengren, Helmer. Smidda gravkors i Oravais; ur de österbottniska järnbrukens historia.—Wikman, K. R. V. Folkfolor—folkforor.—Wolf, Werner. Rainer Maria Rilke und die Liebenden.

1. Philosophy, 1901– . 2. Literature—Hist. and crit. 3. Pipping, Rolf, 1889– . I. Title.

E-14
240

Abram Mey tachtig jaar. Liber amicorum. Bussum, De Haan, 1970.

189 p. port. 25 cm.

Includes bibliographical references.

CONTENTS.—Abram Mey ter ere, door H. J. van der Schroeff.—Een kwart eeuw later, door E. Hijmans.—Ontmoetingen met Abram Mey, door J. Tinbergen.—Abram Mey en de Orde van organisatie-adviseurs, door H. van de Bunt.—Abram Mey as consultant to the State of Israel, by J. Hirsch.—Voorraadpolitiek bij simultane bestel-

(Continued)

NN R 1.71 e/z OC, I PC, 1, I SL E, 1, I (LC1, X1, Z1)

3

ABRAM MEY tachtig jaar. (Card 2)

lingen van verschillende artikelen, door J. F. Cahen.—Accounting and the public interest, by R. J. Chambers.—Les spontanéités de la création de monnaie depuis 1945, par L. H. Dupriez.—Current value accountancy within the progress of economic development, by J. H. Enthoven.—Van bedrijfsleer via bedrijfseconomie naar bedrijfskunde, door J. Goudriaan.—Tweeërlei arbeidsverhouding, door P. Kuin.—

(Continued)

ABRAM MEY tachtig jaar. (Card 3)

Welfare theory and the control of public expenditure, by K. S. Most.—On the unity of accounting, by G. G. Mueller.—Bedrijfseconomische aspecten van de groei, door P. A. M. van Philips.—La société de consommation, par A. Piettre.—Der Konzernabschluss in der Bundesrepublik Deutschland, von H. Rätsch.—De betekenis van de inlichtingen vanwege de gecontroleerde voor de accountantscontrole, door A. M. van Rietschoten.—De betekenis van internationale congressen voor het accountantsberoep, door A. F. Tempelaar.—Bibliografie van de publicaties van Abram Mey.

1. Accounting and bookkeeping--Addresses, essays, lectures. I. Mey, Abraham.

A p.v.768

Academia colombiana de historia, Bogota.

...Conferencias en homenaje al general Francisco de Paula Santander. [Bogota] Imprenta nacional, 1940. ix, 149 p. port. 25cm.

Festschrift

1. Santander, Francisco de Paula, pres. New Granada, 1792–1840.

N. Y. P. L. April 9, 1943

HBC

Academia Colombiana de Historia, Bogotá.

Homenaje al profesor Paul Rivet. Bogotá, Editorial A. B. C., 1958.

335 p. illus., map. 25 cm. (Biblioteca de antropología)

At head of title: Academia Colombiana de Historia. Fondo Eduardo Santos.

Includes bibliographies.

CONTENTS.—Paul Rivet, por L. Duque Gómez.—Paul Rivet, americanista y colombianista, por G. Hernández de Alba.—El profesor Rivet y sus corresponsales, por E. Rochereau.—Valor psicosociológico del análisis de la afectividad, por J. de Recasens y M. R. Mallol.—Trabajos científicos del profesor Paul Rivet sobre antropología colombiana, por S. Elías Ortiz.—Notas sobre la metalurgia prehistorica en el litoral caribe de Colombia, por G. Reichel-Dolmatoff.—Real cédula fechada en El Pardo el 18 de noviembre de 1718 sobre protec-

(Continued)

NN * 3.61 e/g OS, I, II PC, 1, 2 SL AH, 1, 2 (LC1, X1, Z1)
[S, NSCM]

Academia Colombiana de Historia, Bogotá. Homenaje al profesor Paul Rivet. (Card 2)

CONTENTS—Continued.

ción de los indios de la Provincia de Santa Marta, por V. A. Bedoya.—Alcohol y cultura en una clase obrera, Bogotá, por V. Gutiérrez de Pineda.—Apuntes sobre instrumentos musicales aborígenes hallados en Colombia, por J. C. Cubillos.—Vocabulario Opón-Carare, por R. Pineda Giraldo y M. Fornaguera.—Los indígenas del Cauca en la conquista y la colonia, por M. Chaves.—Etapas sagradas en la vida del chibcha, por A. Kipper.—Contribución a la arqueología y prehistoria del Valle de Tenza, por E. Silva Celis.—Notas históricas sobre la orfebrería indígena en Colombia, por L. Duque Gómez.

1. Rivet, Paul, 1876-1958. 2. Indians, S.A.--Reg. areas--Colombia. I. Academia colombiana de historia, Bogotá. Biblioteca de antropología. II. Biblioteca de antropología.

NQBC (Pereira Teixeira)

Academia de Coimbra.
A Teixeira de Pascoaes; homenagem da Academia de Coimbra, pela voz de escritores portugueses e brasileiros. [Figueira da Foz, 1951] 151 p. illus., ports. 22cm.

1. Pereira Teixeira de Vasconcellos, Joaquim, 1879- —Poetry. 2. Poetry, Portuguese—Collections. 3. Poetry, Brazilian—Collections. I. Title.
NN** 5.55 a/ (OC)I OS PC,1,2,3,I SL (LC1, X1,Z1)

Copy only words underlined & classmark— HPM

ACADEMÍA DOMINICANA DE LA HISTORIA, Trujillo Dominican Republic.
Homenaje a Mella. Santo Domingo, Editora del Caribe, 1964. 302 p. port. 24cm. (ITS: Publicaciones, [n. s.] v. 18)

"Centenario de la muerte de Mella, 1864-1964."
Bibliography, p. [287]-288.

1. Mella, Ramón, 1816-1861? I. Series.
NN 11.65 1/B OS, I PC, 1, I AH, 1, I (LC1, X1, Z1)

---

*C-4 p.v.602

Academia de la historia de Cuba, Havana.
Homenaje a Miguel Figueroa y García, por las Academias nacional de artes y letras, cubana de la lengua, y de la historia de Cuba. Discursos leídos en su elogio, en la sesión solemne conjunta celebrada el día 18 de diciembre de 1951. La Habana, Impr. "El Siglo XX," 1952. 32 p. port. 25cm. (Its: Publicaciones)

1. Figueroa y García, Miguel, 1853-1893. I. Title.
NN**R 4.56 (OC)I OS PC,1 SL AH,1 (Z1,LC1,X1)

F-10
6701

Academia portuguesa da histório, Lisbon.
Dois centenários. Lisboa, 1961. 165 p. 26cm.

1. Bensaúde Joaquim. 2. Queiros Velloso, José Maria de, 1860-1952.
3. Portugal—Hist.—Addresses, essays, lectures.
NN R 5.63 OS PC,1,2,3 SL (LC1,X1,Z1)

F-10
5520

Academia Republicii Populare Romîne.
Omagiu lui Constantin Daicoviciu cu prilejul împlinirii a 60 de ani. [Comitetul de inițiativă: Em. Condurachi et al. București] 1960.
xix, 576 p. illus., port., maps, diagrs., tables. 30 cm.
Contributions in Rumanian, French, German, Italian, or Russian; the Rumanian contributions have summaries in French and Russian.
Errata slip inserted.
"Bibliografia lucrărilor [academicianului Constantin Daicoviciu]": p. xv-xix.
Includes bibliographical references.

1. Archaeology--Addresses, essays, lectures. 2. Europe, Eastern--Archaeology. 3. Daicoviciu, Constantin, 1898-
NN* R 4.61 p/ OS PC, 1, 2, 3 SL (LCE1, LC1, X1, Z1)

TC

ACADEMISCHE ECONOMISCHE KRING, Tilburg, Netherlands.
Economische wetenschap en economische politiek; een bundel opstellen aangeboden aan de Academische senaat ter gelegenheid van het vijfentwintigjarig bestaan van de Katholieke economische hogeschool. Leiden, H. E. Stenfert Kroese, 1952. viii, 443 p. 25cm.

CONTENTS. — Enige beschouwingen over de samenhang tussen economische orde, economische wettelijkheid en economische politiek, door G. W. Groeneveld. — Enkele planhishoudkundige aspecten van de algemeen-economische politiek, door D. B. J. Schouten. —Sociologie van het economisch-politieke denken, door J. A. Ponsioen. — De problematiek der hedendaagse sociale politiek, door G. M. J.
(Continued)
NN ** R X 3.54 OS, (1b), I PC, 1, I SL E, 1, I (LC1, Z1, X1)

ACADEMISCHE ECONOMISCHE KRING, Tilburg, Netherlands.
Economische wetenschap en economische politiek... (Card 2)

Veldkamp. -- De Nederlandse loon- en prijspolitiek, door A. M. F. Smulders. — Collectieve loonbepaling, door T. B. C. Mulder. — Katholicisme- socialisme, door P. P. van Berkum. — Nationalisme en internationalisme in de betalingsbalanspolitiek, door H. J. Schings. - Perspectieven voor een buitenlands economisch beleid, door W. K. N. Schmelzer. — Problemen rond het monetaire evenwicht, door W. C. M. Mutsaers. -- Economische politiek, onzeherheid en ondernemingsfinanciering, door A. C. M. van Keep. --Industrie en handel, door J. A. Geertman. --De ondernemer in de branding, door J. B. L. Verster. —

(Continued)

ACADEMISCHE ECONOMISCHE KRING, Tilburg. Netherlands.
Economische wetenschap en economische politiek... (Card 3)

Enige notities over het klein- en middenbedrijf, door A. F. H. C. Schrijvers. --Evolutie der Nederlandse middenstandspolitiek in functionele richting, door C. A. Braun. -- Financieel centralisme, door L. J. G. de Mast. --De landbouwpolitiek in Nederland, door F. W. J. Kriellaars. — Enkele opmerkingen over de coördinatie van het binnenlandse goederenvervoer, door J. P. A. van Casteren. -- Transito-verkeerspolitiek, door J. Walter.

1. Economics, 1926- —Dutch authors. I. Roomsch Katholieke handelshoogeschool, Tilburg, Netherlands.

NNBC (Pontano)

Accademia pontaniana, Naples.
In onore di Giovanni Gioviano Pontano nel V centenario della sua nascita, l'Accademia pontaniana. Napoli: F. Sangiovanni & figlio, 1926. 161 p. facsim., plates, 2 ports. (incl. front.) 4°.

Bibliographical footnotes.
Contents: FILANGERI DI CANDIDA, R. Il tempietto di Gioviano Pontano in Napoli. PÈRCOPO, E. La biblioteca di Gioviano Pontano. SCHERILLO, M. Gioviano Pontano nel V centenario della nascità. PASCAL, C. Una lettera pontaniana del Summonte ed un autografo inedito del Pontano. PÈRCOPO, E. Nuove lettere di Gioviano Pontano a principi ed amici. La villa del Pontano ad Antignano.

387599A
1. Pontano, Giovanni Gioviano, 1426-1503.
N. Y. P. L. November 28, 1928

AN
(Osborn, C.)

An accolade for Chase S. Osborn; home, state, and national tributes on the occasion of Chase S. Osborn day October 4, 1939. Published by the City of Sault Ste. Marie, Michigan, for presentation to Governor Osborn in honor of his eightieth birthday, January 22, 1940. Edited by Stella Brunt Osborn; editorial committee: Paul Lincoln Adams, George Gordon Malcolm, John Paul Chandler [and others] ... Sault Ste. Marie, Mich., 1940–

v. 26cm.

"The beginning of a Chase S. Osborn bibliography": [v. 1], p. 573–588.

1. Osborn, Chase Salmon, 1860– I. Osborn, Stella Brunt, ed. II. Adams, Paul Lincoln. III. Malcolm, George Gordon. IV. Chandler, John Paul. V. Sault Ste. Marie, Mich.

41-1772

Library of Congress F566.O72
——— Copy 2.
Copyright A 147668 [3] 923.273

D–13
8507

Achinger, Hans, ed.
Neue Wege der Fürsorge; Rechtsgrundlagen, Arbeitsformen und Lebensbilder. Eine Festgabe für Herrn Professor Dr. Hans Muthesius zum 75. Geburtstag, hrsg. von Hans Achinger [et al.] Köln, C. Heymann, 1960. 317 p. port. 21cm. (Deutscher Verein für öffentliche und private Fürsorge. Schriften. Heft 214)

Bibliographical footnotes.

CONTENTS.—Hans Muthesius, von C. L. K. von Nidda.—Der soziale Bundesstaat, von A. Köttgen.—Zum verfassungsrechtlichen Begriff der Sozialversicherung, von W. Bogs.—Einige Bemerkungen zu einem Bundessozialhilfegesetz, von G. Scheffler.—Der Hilfesuchende als Rechtssubjekt, von J. Duntze.—Die persönliche Hilfe, von P. Collmer.—

(Continued)

NN R 8.63 OC (OS)I PC, 1, 2, 3, I SL E, 1, 2, 3, I (LC1, X1, Z1)

3

Achinger, Hans, ed. Neue Wege der Fürsorge... (Card 2)

Uber das Miteinander von Sozialhilfe und freier Wohlfahrtspflege heute, von W. Auerbach.—Familienverantwortung in Fürsorge und Sozialhilfe, von E. Weinbrenner.—Helfen wir genug, von E. Zillken.—Adoption als Schicksal, von G. von Mann-Tiechler.—Ermahnung und Verwarnug als erzieherische Aufgaben des Jugendrichters, von T. Würtenberger.—Sozialhilge und Gerichtshilfe, von W. Mollenhauer.— Krankenhausprobleme heute, von O. Ohl.—Ärztliches und soziales Denken, von W. Hagen.—Über die psychiatrische Begutachtung von Gesundheitsschäden aus der nationalsozialistischen Verfolgung, von W. R. von Baeyer.—Hygiene, Sozialhygiene, Psychohygiene und Sozialhilfe, von A. Rainer.—Das Problem der sozialen Fürsorge in Griechenland, von M. P. M. Goutos.—Zur Armutsbekämpfung in jungen und alten Industrieländern, von E. Lief-

(Continued)

Achinger, Hans, ed. Neue Wege der Fürsorge... (Card 3)

mann-Keil.—Eltern als Schicksal, von E. Simon.—Zur staatlichen Neufassung des sozialen Schulwesens, von H. Wollasch.—Arbeitsmarktpolitik und Fürsorge, von V. Siebrecht.—Das gefährliche Wort "sozial," von V. Muthesius.—Von der Einmaligkeit aller Menschen, von H. Achinger.

1. Charities, Public—Germany. 2. Social service—Germany. 3. Muthesius, Hans. I. Deutscher Verein für öffentliche und private Fürsorge.

L-11
3220
Bd. 1

ACHT Jahrhunderte Deutscher Orden in Einzeldarstellungen. (Festschrift zu Ehren Sr. Exzellenz P. Dr. Marian Tumler O. T. anlässlich seines 80. Geburtstages.) Hrsg. von Klemens Wieser. Bad Godesberg, Verlag Wissenschaftliches Archiv (1967).

xxi, 671 p. with illus., facsims. and maps., front. 24cm. (Quellen und Studien zur Geschichte des Deutschen Ordens. Bd. 1)

1. Teutonic Knights. I. Series. II. Tumler, Marian. III. Wieser, Klemens, ed.

NN 6.71 w/ OC,II,III (OS)I PC, 1,I,II,III G, 1,I,II,III S,1,II,III (LC1s, X1s, Z1)

E-19
8602

Acht Jahrhunderte Deutscher Orden in Einzeldarstellungen. (Festschrift zu Ehren Sr. Exzellenz P. Dr. Marian Tumler O. T. anlässlich seines 80. Geburtstages.) Hrsg. von Klemens Wieser. Bad Godesberg, Verlag Wissenschaftliches Archiv (1967).

xxi, 671 p. with illus., facsims. and maps., front. 24cm. (Quellen und Studien zur Geschichte des Deutschen Ordens, Bd. 1)

(Continued)

NN*R 5.70 v/ OC,I,II PC,1,I,II SL (LC1, X1,Z1)

2

ACHT Jahrhunderte Deutscher Orden in Einzeldarstellungen. (Card 2)

Bibliographical footnotes.

1. Teutonic Knights. I. Tumler, Marian. II. Wieser, Klemens, ed.

E-13
6876

Action and conviction in early modern Europe; essays in memory of E. H. Harbison. Editors: Theodore K. Rabb [and] Jerrold E. Seigel. Princeton, N. J., Princeton University Press, 1969.

xii, 463 p. illus., facsims., port. 25 cm. 13.50

Bibliographical footnotes.

CONTENTS.—Faith, reason, and the world of action. France: the

(Continued)

NN*R 12.69 v/ OC, I, II, IIIb* [I] PC, 1, 2, I, II SL (LC1, X1, Z1)

4

Action and conviction in early modern Europe ... (Card 2)

Holy Land, the chosen people, and the most Christian king, by J. R. Strayer. The Renaissance monarchy as seen by Erasmus, More, Seyssel, and Machiavelli, by J. R. Major. A matter of conscience, by L. B. Smith. James V and the Scottish Church, 1528–1542, by J. W. Ferguson. Utopia and Geneva, by J. H. Hexter. Religion and politics in the thought of Gasparo Contarini, by F. Gilbert. Sir Richard Maitland of Lethington: a Christian laird in the Age of Reformation, by M. Lee, Jr. The Puritans and the Convocation of 1563, by A. J. Carlson. Reform and counter reform: the case of the Spanish heretics, by P. J. Hauben. Francis Bacon and the re-

(Continued)

Action and conviction in early modern Europe ... (Card 3)

form of society, by T. K. Rabb.—Christians, scholars, and the world of thought. The iconography of *temperantia* and the virtuousness of technology, by L. White, Jr. Florence and its university, 1348–1434, by G. A. Brucker. The teaching of Argyropulos and the rhetoric of the first humanists, by J. E. Seigel. Talent and vocation in humanist and Protestant thought, by R. M. Douglas. Erasmus and Alberto Pio, Prince of Carpi, by M. P. Gilmore. Erasmus and the reformers on non-Christian religions and *salus extra ecclesiam*, by G. H. Williams. Inflation and witchcraft: the case of Jean Bodin, by E. W.

(Continued)

ACTION and conviction in early modern Europe... (Card 4)

Monter. History and politics: the controversy over the sale of offices in early seventeenth-century France, by D. Bitton. Reason and grace: Christian epistemology in Dante, Langland, and Milton, by R. M. Frye. John Locke and the new logic, by W. S. Howell.

1. Harbison, Elmore Harris, 1907-1964. 2. Renaissance--Addresses, essays, lectures. I. Seigel, Jerrold E., ed. II. Rabb, Theodore K., ed. III. Seigel, Jerrold E.

ADOLFU KELLNEROVI; sborník jazykovědných studif. (Card 3)

Jména Beskydy. --Stanislav, J. Po stopách Slezákov na Slovensku. --Jelínek, M. Ke stylu literárních prací Ludmily Hořké.

1. Kellner, Adolf. 2. Czech language. I. Králík, Stanislav, ed. II. Králík, Stanislav.

---

*QP

Adam Mickiewicz, poet of Poland; a symposium, edited by Manfred Kridl, with a foreword by Ernest J. Simmons. New York, Columbia univ. press, 1951. xii, 292 p. illus. 24cm. (Columbia Slavic studies)

Festschrift c.1.

1. Mickiewicz, Adam, 1798-1855. I. Kridl, Manfred, 1882- , ed.
N. Y. P. L. January 8, 1952

MAR p. v. 1667

ADOLPH GOLDSCHMIDT zum Gedächtnis, 1863-1944. [Herausgeber: Carl Georg Heise. Hamburg, Kommissionsverlag E. Hauswedell, 1963] 1 v. port. 25cm.

CONTENTS. --Vorwort des Herausgebers--Adolph Goldschmidt, von H. Jantzen. --Goldschmidt und die Wissenschaft der mittelalterlichen Buchmalerei, von O. Homburger. --Erinnerungen an Adolph Goldschmidt, von O. Freiherr von Taube. --Goldschmidts Humor, von E. Panofsky. --
(Continued)

NN R 10.66 r/ OC, I PC, 1, 2, I SL A, 1, 2, I (LC1, X1, Z1)

2

3-MAR p.v.823

Adolf Loos zum 60. Geburtstag am 10. Dezember 1930. Wien, R. Lanyi, 1930. 67 p. ports. 23cm.

Contributions by Peter Altenberg, Hermann Bahr, Anna Bahr-Mildenburg, and 41 others.
No. 355 of 1000 copies printed.

Festschrift

1. Loos, Adolf, 1870-1933.
N. Y. P. L. August 8, 1945

ADOLPH GOLDSCHMIDT zum Gedächtnis, 1863-1944. (Card 2)

Goldschmidt als Lehrer und Freund, von C. G. Heise. --Schriftenverzeichnis Adolph Goldschmidts in chronologischer Reihenfolge, von H. Ladendorf.

1. Goldschmidt, Adolph, 1863-1944. 2. Goldschmidt, Adolph, 1863-1944--Bibl. I. Heise, Carl Georg, 1890- , ed.

Copy only words underlined & classmark— *QVA

ADOLFU KELLNEROVI; sborník jazykovědných studif. [Redigoval Stanislav Králík] . Opava, Slezský studijní ústav, 1954. 191 p. port., fold. maps. 24cm. (Slezský studijní ústav, Opava. Publikace. sv. 8)

Bibliographical footnotes.

CONTENTS. --Králík, S. Vědecké dílo Adolfa Kellnera. --Kellnerová, A. Lidský profil Adolfa Kellnera. --Vážný, V. Soupis prací univ. prof. dr. Adolfa Kellnera. --Trávníček, F. Smíšená a přechodná nářečí. --Lamprecht, A. Z jazykového zeměpisu laššského. --Šlosar, D. Změna
(Continued)

NN R 7.58 m/ OC, I, IIbo OI PC, 1, 2, I S, 1, 2, I (LC1, X1, LCE1, Z1)

MAS

Adolph Goldschmidt zu seinem siebenzigsten geburtstag, am 15. januar 1933, dargebracht von allen seinen schülern, die in den jahren 1922 bis 1933 bei ihm gehört und promoviert haben. Berlin, Würfel verlag, 1935.

4 p. l., 174 p. illus. (incl. plan) xxxiii pl. (1 col.) 27cm.

On cover: Das siebente jahrzehnt; festschrift zum 70. geburtstag von Adolph Goldschmidt.

"Bibliographie der schriften Adolph Goldschmidts seit dem jahre 1923": p. 171-172.

"Bibliographie der doktor-dissertationen seit dem jahre 1923": p. 173-174.

CONTENTS.—Frühes mittelalter.—Deutsche kunst des 15. bis 17. jahrhunderts.—Italienische kunst des 13. bis 17. jahrhunderts.—Niederländische kunst des 16. und 17. jahrhunderts.—Allgemeine kunstwissenschaft.

1. Goldschmidt, Adolph, 1863- 2. Art—Addresses, essays, lectures.

Library of Congress N25.A4 [2] 36-15087 704

Festschrift

ADOLFU KELLNEROVI; sborník jazykovědných studif. (Card 2)

á >— o v laššském nářečí na Místecku. --Gregor, A. Citoslovečné věty v laššských nářečích. --Romportl, M. Příspěvek a melodie v nářečí na Těšínsku. --Bělič, J. Postavení moravské slovenštiny. --Skulina, J. Příspěvek k historické dialektologii Hranicka. --Vašek, A. Z jazykového zeměpisu Rožnovska a Valašskomeziříčska. --Svěrák, F. Charakteristika karlovického nářečí. --Habovštiak, A. Striednice za predhist. ɛ̨ b v oravských nárečiach. --Horák, G. "Pochýlené" samohlásky v nářečí Pohorelej a Lipt. Tepličky. --Chloupek, J. K otázce interdialektů. --Bauer J. Skladba v nářečních monografích. --Kopečný, F. O záhadě
(Continued)

AVB

Ætt og by, festskrift til S. H. Finne-Grønn om nordisk slektsforskning og Oslo byhistorie. [Oslo] Cammermeyers boghandel [1944] 236 p. port. 27cm.

Contributions in Danish, Norwegian or Swedish.

Festschrift

453265B. 1. Finne-Grønn, Stian Herlofsen, 1869- . 2. Scandinavia—Geneal. 3. Oslo—Hist.
N. Y. P. L. March 2, 1949

VPE

Agriculture in the twentieth century; essays on research, practice, and organization to be presented to Sir Daniel Hall. Oxford, Clarendon press, 1939.

x, 440 p. incl. tables, diagrs. front. (port.) 23cm.

"References to literature": p. 221.

CONTENTS.—Preface.—Dale, H. E. Agriculture and the civil service.—Venn, J. A. Agriculture and the state.—Ashby, A. W. Agricultural conditions and policies, 1910–1938.—Hanley, J. A. Agricultural education in college and county.—Watson, J. A. S. The art of husbandry.—Orwin, C. S. The farmer's business.—Russell, Sir E. J. Soil science in England, 1894–1938.—Stapledon, Sir R. G. Grassland.—Hunter, H. Developments in plant breeding.—Salaman, R. N. Outlines of the history of

(Continued on next card)

A 40-551

[3]

Agriculture in the twentieth century ... 1939. (Card 2)

CONTENTS—Continued.

plant virus research.—Fryer, J. C. F. Plant protection.—Hatton, R. G. Landmarks in the development of scientific fruit-growing.—Crowther, Charles. Some problems of animal nutrition.—Mackintosh, James. The evolution of milk-production.—Orr, Sir J. B. Agriculture and national health.

1. Agriculture—Addresses, essays, lectures. 2. Hall, Sir Alfred Daniel, 1864–

New York. Public library for Library of Congress

A 40-551

[3]

HWF

AITCHISON, J.H., ed.

The political process in Canada; essays in honour of R. MacGregor Dawson [Toronto] University of Toronto press [1963] vii, 193 p. 24cm.

Bibliographical footnotes.

1. Dawson, Robert MacGregor, 1895-1958. 2. Canada--Politics--Addresses, essays, lectures.

NN R 8.63 e/B OC PC, 1, 2 SL AH, 1, 2 (LC1, X1, Z1) [I]

---

*OKTO

AJATASHATRU Dr. ZAKIR HUSAIN; commemoration volume, first death-anniversary, May 3, 1970. [Editors: Yashpal Jain and Yatindra Bhatnagar. 1st ed.] Delhi, Chitra Kala Sangam, 1970. 1 v. (unpaged) illus. 29cm.

Hindi and English.

1. Zakir Husain. 2. Hindi literature--Collections.

NN R 1.71 e/j OC PC, 1, 2 SL O, 1, 2 (LC1, X1, Z1)

F-11
831

AKADEMIE FÜR STAATSMEDIZIN IN HAMBURG.

Zehn Jahre Akademie für Staatsmedizin in Hamburg, 1945-1955. Ten years review from the Akademie für Staatsmedizin in Hamburg, School of public health; annual report, 1955. Hrsg. von H. Harmsen und K.H. Weber. [Hamburg, 1956] 45 p. maps. 30cm.

German and English on opposite pages.

1. Hygiene, Public--Study and teaching--Germany--Hamburg. I. Harmsen, Hans, 1899- , ed. II. Weber, K. H. ed. III. Weber, K. H.

NN R 7.66 r/ (OC)I, II, IIIbo OS(Ib) PC, 1, I, II SL (LC1, X1, Z1)

D-12
953

Akademie der Wissenschaften, Göttingen.

Carl Friedrich Gauss, 1777–1855; Gedenkfeier der Akademie der Wissenschaften und der Georg-August-Universität zu Göttingen anlässlich seines 100ten Todestages. Göttingen, Musterschmidt-Verlag [c1955] 31 p. port. 21cm.

1. Gauss, Karl Friedrich, 1777–1855. I. Göttingen. Universität.

NN R X 9.60 OS,I PC,1,I SL (LC1,X1,Z1)

---

* EE
A332

Akademie der Wissenschaften, Göttingen.

Festschrift zur Feier des zweihundertjährigen Bestehens der Akademie der Wissenschaften in Göttingen... Berlin [etc.] Springer-Verlag, 1951. 2 v. in 1. illus. 25cm.

Bibliographies included.

CONTENTS.—[Bd.] 1. Mathematisch-physikalische Klasse: Smend R. Die Göttinger Gesellschaft der Wissenschaften. Born, M. Die Gültigkeitsgrenze der Theorie der idealen Kristalle und ihre Überwindung. Brix, P. und H. Kopfermann. Neuere Ergebnisse zum Isotopieverschiebungseffekt in den Atomspektren. Heisenberg, W. Paradoxien des Zeitbegriffs, in der Theorie der Elementarteilchen. Staudinger, H. Bedeu-

(Continued)

NN R 3.53 OS PC, 1, 2, 3 SL B ST, 4 (LC1, Z1, X1)

Akademie der Wissenschaften, Göttingen. Festschrift zur Feier des zweihundertjährigen Bestehens... (Card 2)

tung der makromolekularen Chemie für die Biologie. Stille, H. Einengungs- und Ausweitungsregionen beiderseits des Urkontinents Laurentia. Weizsäcker, C. F. v. Anwendungen der Hydrodynamik auf Probleme der Kosmogonie. Euler, H. v. Chlorophylldefekte Mutanten. Hedvall, J. A. Mineralographie, ein relativ neues Gebiet chemischer Forschung und technischer Anwendung. Siegel, C. L. Die Modulgruppe in einer einfachen involutorischen Algebra. Rellich, F. Über Lösungen nichtlinearer Differentialgleichungen. Nevanlinna, R. Über den Gauss-Bonnetschen Satz.—[Bd.] 2. Philologisch-Historische Klasse: Smend, R. Die Göttinger Gesellschaft der Wissenschaften. Eckhardt, K. A. Zur Entstehungszeit der Lex Salica. Pedersen, H. Weshalb

(Continued)

Akademie der Wissenschaften, Göttingen. Festschrift zur Feier des zweihundertjährigen Bestehens... (Card 3)

ist p ein unstabiler Laut? Littmann, E. Neuarabische Streitgedichte. Latte, K. Die Sirenen. Bissing, Fr. W. v. Ein christliches Amulett aus Ägypten. Holtzmann, W. Die Dekretalensammlungen des 12. Jahrhunderts. 1. Die Sammlung Tanner. Thomas, F. W. The Tibetan alphabet. Schneider, A. M. Die ältesten Denkmäler der Römischen Kirche.

1. Science—Essays and misc. lectures. 2. Philology—Addresses, essays, essays, lectures. 3. History—Addresses, essays, lectures. 4. Science—Essays and misc., 1951.

---

*QCB

AKADEMIYA NAUK.

220 лет Академии наук СССР [1725-1945] ; справочная книга. [Ответственный ред. Н.Г. Бруевич. Составители: В.С. Яблоков и Л.А. Плоткин] Москва, Изд-во Академии наук СССР, 1945. 326 p. illus., ports.(2 mounted) 27cm.

"Печатается по постановлению Президиума Всесоюзного комитета по проведению 220-летия Академии наук СССР".

Bibliography, p. 315-[319]

(Continued)

NN R 3.64 c/J (OC)I,II,III OS SL S,I,II,III,IV (LCR1,LC1,X1,Z1) 2

AKADEMIYA NAUK. 220 лет Академии наук СССР...
(Card 2)

Title transliterated: Dvesti dvadtzat' let Akademii nauk SSSR.

I. Yablokov, Vladimir Sergeyevich, 1901- , comp. II. Plotkin, L.A., comp. III. Bruyevich, Nikolaĭ Grigor'yevich., ed. IV. Title.

---

*QH

Akademiya nauk. Institut istorii nauki i tekhniki.
...Joseph Louis Lagrange, 1736–1936; recueil d'articles en commémoration du 200-me anniversaire du jour de sa naissance. Moscou [etc.] L'Acad. des sciences de l'URSS, 1937. 140 p. front., port. 25½cm.

At head of title: Académie des sciences de l'URSS. Travaux de l'Institut de l'histoire de la sciences [sic] et de la technique.
Added Russian t.-p.: ...Жозеф Луи Лагранж, 1736–1936; сборник статей к 200-летию со дня рождения. Москва [etc.] 1937.
Text in Russian. Table of contents in Russian and French.

(Continued)

N. Y. P. L. March 11, 1942

Akademiya nauk. Institut istorii nauki i tekhniki. ...Joseph Louis Lagrange, 1736–1936... (Continued)

CONTENTS.—Kryloff, A. N. Joseph Louis Lagrange.—Idelson, N. Sur la mécanique de Lagrange.—Soubbotin, M. F. Les travaux astronomiques de Lagrange.—Tchebotareff, N. G. Sur les travaux de Lagrange en algèbre et la théorie des nombres.—Polak, L. S. Lagrange et les principes variationnels en mécanique et en physique.

57924B. 1. Lagrange, Joseph Louis, comte, 1736–1813.
N. Y. P. L. March 11, 1942

---

*QH

Akademiya nauk U. S. R. R., Kiev. Instytut botaniky.
...Symposium dedicated to the memory of A. V. Fomin... Kiev, Ukr. SSR academy of sciences press, 1938. 377 p. illus. 26cm.

At head of title: Academy of sciences of the Ukrainian SSR. Institute of botany.
Added t.-p. in Ukrainian and Russian: ...Збірник праць присвячений пам'яті акад. О. В. Фоміна. Київ, 1938; ...Сборник работ посвященный памяти акад. А. В. Фомина. Киев, 1938.
Text in Russian or Ukrainian; summaries in English, French or German.
Bibliography at end of most articles.

(Continued)

Fest

N. Y. P. L. January 24, 1945

Akademiya nauk U. S. R. R., Kiev. Instytut botaniky. ...Symposium... (Continued)

CONTENTS.—Alexander Vassilyevich Fomin. Biographical essay.—Bordzilovsky, E. Review of the work of A. V. Fomin.—List of papers by A. V. Fomin.—Fedtschenko, V. Data on the flora of Afghanistan.—Shostenko-Dessiatova, N. Acinos fominii Shost.-Des. — une espèce nouvelle de la famille des Labiés de la RSS d'Ukraine.—Ilyin, M. A new Juncus species. Atriplex fominii Iljin.—Zoz, I. A new Juncus species for Southern Ukr. SSR and Northern Crimea.—Bordzilovsky, E. New plant species for Ukr. SSR; De plantis novis et rarioribus e Transcaucasia.—Palibin, I. Fossil tertiary pines of western Transcaucasia.—Krystofovich, A. The Miocene flora of the Ukraine and its connection by means of the Urals with the tertiary flora of Asia.—Tamamshian, Sophia. Carpobiological and carpological studies.—Korschikov, A. Algological notes.—Roll, J. Algological notes. III. Some new and rare algae.—

(Continued)

N. Y. P. L. January 24, 1945

Akademiya nauk U. S. R. R., Kiev. Instytut botaniky. ...Symposium... (Continued)

Milovtzova, M. Polyphagus fominii Milovtz. sp. n.—Illichevsky, S. Phytopathological data in the Ukrainian SSR.—Troitzky, N. La caractéristique de quelques phytocénoses des forêts de Transcaucasie.—Kotov, M. The vegetation of the Khomutovsky steppe in Budennovsky district.—Kossetz, N. Materials on the flora of parks in the Ukr. SSR.—Barbarich, A. Decorative plants of the right-bank Polessye Ukr. SSR and ways of supplementing the assortment.—Bilyk, G. New data on the vegetation and flora of the northernmost part of the Arabat headland.—Alexandrow, W. and M. Jakowlew. Ueber die morphologische Bedeutung der sackförmigen Zellen der Karyopse von Gramineen.—Moissejewa, M. On the anatomical structure of the leaves and wood of the Ukrainian pine.—Kostriukova, X. and M. Tchernoyarov. Observations on the germination of the pollen in Clivia miniata Hort. in vivo.—Bolsunov, I.

(Continued)

N. Y. P. L. January 24, 1945

Akademiya nauk U. S. R. R., Kiev. Instytut botaniky. ...Symposium... (Continued)

On the study of heterosis in Nicotiana rustica L. II. Reciprocal crossings.—Eremenko, V. Effect of the various elements of the mineral nutrition of wheat (N and P) on the duration of vegetation and on the yield.—Cholodny, N. A growth substance in carmine.—Sankewitsch, E. On the state of the protoplasm in hair cells of the immersed leaves of Salvinia natans.—Lichovitzer, V. On the resistance of some cherry varieties to Monilia cinerea.—Postrigan, S. Experiments in decorative planting on seacoast solonchaks.—Lipschitz, S. Materials on the history of Russian botanists.

289457B. 1. Fomin, Aleksandr Vasil'yevich, 1869–1935. 2. Fomin, Aleksandr Vasil'yevich, 1869–1935—Bibl. 3. Botany—Russia. I. Title. II. Title: Sbornik rabot posvyashchionnyĭ pamyati akad. A. V. Fomina.
N. Y. P. L. January 24, 1945

Akademiya nauk U.S.R.R., Kiev. Instytut botaniky. *QH
...Symposium dedicated to the memory of V. N. Lubimenko... Kiev, Ukr.SSR academy of sciences press, 1938. 478 p. illus. 26cm.

Added t.-p. in Russian and Ukrainian; Russian title: Сборник работ посвященный памяти академика В. Н. Любименко; Ukrainian title: Збірник праць присвячений пам'яті академіка В. М. Любименка.

Text in Russian or Ukrainian with summaries in English or French. Index in Russian and English.
"Список работ акад. В. Н. Любименко," p. 13–25.

Bibliographies at end of each chapter.

Festschrift

522442B. 1. Lyubimenko, Vladimir Nikolayevich, 1873–1937. 2. Botany—Essays and misc. I. Title.
N. Y. P. L. November 3, 1950

D-16
6382

AKTIONSGEMEINSCHAFT SOZIALE MARKTWIRTSCHAFT.
Wirtschaftsordnung und Menschenbild; Geburtstagsgabe für Alexander Rüstow. [Köln] Verlag für Politik und Wirtschaft [1960] 152 p. port. 22cm. (Aktionsgemeinschaft soziale Marktwirtschaft, Schriftenreihe, Heft 4)

Bibliographical footnotes.
CONTENTS.--Elemente der Weltanschauung in der Formation des Wirtschaftsdenkens, von G. Briefs.--Verständnis wecken
(Continued)

NN R 7.66 r/c OS, I PC, 1, 2, 3, II SI. E, 1, 2, 3, II (LC1, X1, Z1)
[NSCM]

AKTIONSGEMEINSCHAFT SOZIALE MARKTWIRTSCHAFT.
Wirtschaftsordnung und Menschenbild...
(Card 2)

für die Wirtschaftspolitik, von L. Erhard.--Einige Widersprüche in der Agrarpolitik, von H. Niehaus.--Bundesverfassungsgericht und Wirtschaftsverfassung, von H. C. Nipperdey.--Probleme der Vollbeschäftigungspolitik, von B. Pfister.--Agrarpolitik im Strukturwandel von Wirtschaft und Gesellschaft, von H. Priebe.--Europäische Demokratie oder supranationale Bürokratie?, von H. Reif.--Die politische Dimension der
(Continued)

AKTIONSGEMEINSCHAFT SOZIALE MARKTWIRTSCHAFT. Wirtschaftsordnung und Menschenbild... (Card 3)

Wirtschaftspolitik, von W. Röpke. --Das Bild vom Menschen in der neuen Sozialpolitik, von G. Schmölders. --Von den Interpreten der Marktwirtschaft, von O. Wesemann. --Alexander Rüstow, Persönlichkeit und Werk, von G. Eisermann.

1. Rüstow, Alexander, 1885- . 2. Economic policy--Germany. 3. Economic policy--Addresses, essays, lectures. I. Aktionsgemeinschaft soziale Marktwirtschaft. Schriftenreihe. II. Title.

TMB

AKTUELLE Betriebswirtschaft; Festschrift zum 60. Geburtstag von Konrad Mellerowicz, gewidmet von seinen Freunden, Kollegen und Schülern. Berlin, W. de Gruyter, 1952. 254 p. port. 24cm.

CONTENTS. — Grundlagen und Methodenprobleme: Methoden- und Entwicklungsprobleme der Betriebswirtschaftslehre, von W. Hasenack. Wissenschaft und Praxis, von J. Löffelholz. Personalverwaltung und Menschenführung im Betrieb, von G. Fischer. Zur Reform des Aktiengesetzes, von W. Koch. Über Wirtschaftlichkeit und Wirtschaftlichkeitsrechnung, von H. Seischab. — Kostenrechnung, Bewertung, Betriebsvergleich: Kosten und Kostenlehre, von H. Linhardt. (Continued)

NN*R 4.53 OC PC, 1, 2 SL E, 1, 2 (LC1, Z1, X1)

AKTUELLE Betriebswirtschaft... (Card 2)

Methoden zur Erreichung der optimalen Betriebsgrösse in der Industrie, von G. Thiede. Das Schwächebild des Betriebsvergleichs, von O. R. Schnutenhaus. Zur Praxis der Unternehmenswert-Ermittlung, von B. Hartmann. Kosten der Betriebseinrichtung im Jahresabschluss und in der Überschuldungsbilanz von Kapitalgesellschaften, von K. Schwantag. — Vertriebsprobleme: Distributionsprobleme, von K.C. Behrens. Zentrale Massnahmen zur Steigerung des Exports in ihrer Wirkung auf die verschiedenen Gruppen der Exportbetriebe, von C. Ruberz. — Unvollständige Bibliographie der Bücher, Beiträge zu Sammelwerken und Zeitschriftenaufsätze von Konrad Mellerowicz (p. 250-254)

1. Management, 1931- 2. Mellerowicz, Konrad, 1891-

M-10
4490
Bd.13

AKTUELLE Probleme geographischer Forschung; Festschrift für Joachim Heinrich Schultze aus Anlass seines 65. Geburtstages. Hrsg. von Klaus Achim Boesler und Arthur Kühn. Berlin, D. Reimer, 1970. 549 p. illus., port., maps (2 fold., issued in pocket) 24cm. (Berlin. Freie Universität. Geographisches Institut. Abhandlungen. Bd. 13)

(Continued)

NN 7.70 w/z OC, I, II, III (OS) IV PC, 1, I, II, III, IV (LC1, X1, Z1)

2

AKTUELLE Probleme geographischer Forschung... (Card 2)

German, French or English.
Bibliography of Schultze's works, p. 11-18.
Includes bibliographies.

1. Geography--Addresses, essays, lectures. I. Boesler, Klaus Achim, ed. II. Kühn, Arthur, ed. III. Schultze, Joachim Heinrich, 1903- . IV. Series.

AN
(Schweitzer, A.)

Albert Schweitzer; études et témoignages, publiés sous la direction de Robert Amadou, par André Siegfried... [et autres] [Paris] Éditions de la Main jetée [1951] 299 p. illus. 19cm.

600804B. 1. Schweitzer, Albert, 1875- . I. Amadou, Robert, ed. II. Siegfried, André, 1875-

N. Y. P. L. December 20, 1951

AN
(Schweitzer, A.)

The Albert Schweitzer jubilee book, edited by A. A. Roback ... with the co-operation of J. S. Bixler ... [and] George Sarton ... Cambridge, Mass., Sci-art [1945]

508 p. illus., ports. 23½cm.

1. Schweitzer, Albert, 1875- I. Roback, Abraham Aaron, 1890- ed.

Med 46-130

U. S. Army medical library for Library of Congress [W1045S413R 1945] [5]

AN
(Schweitzer, A.)

Albert Schweitzer, mannen och hans gärning; vänners hyllning till Lambarenesjukhusets 25-åriga tillvaro. Utgiven av Greta Lagerfelt. Uppsala, J. A. Lindblads bokförlag [1938] 252 p., 1 l. incl. front., illus. (incl. ports.) 21½cm.

The book also commemorates Albert Schweitzer's 60th birthday. cf. Förord.

CONTENTS.—Lagerfelt, Greta. Förord. — Fridrichsen, Anton. Albert Schweitzer; högtidstal på 60-årsdagen i Jakobs kyrka, Stockholm, den 14 januari 1935.—Stade, Frans. Albert Schweitzer: 1. Levnaden och verket. 2. Livsåskådningen och personligheten.—Fridrichsen, Anton. Albert Schweitzer som teolog.—Aster, Ernst von. Albert Schweitzers kulturfilosofi. — Bangert, Emilius. Albert Schweitzer som orgelkonstnär.—Krook, Oscar. Albert Schweitzers gärning som missionsläkare.—Holm, Stig. Två år som läkare vid sjukhuset i Lambarene.—Aurelius, Bengt. Kristus, läkaren; en skiss, tillägnad Albert Schweitzer. — Söderblom, (Continued on next card)

A C 39—3212

[a40c1]

Albert Schweitzer, mannen och hans gärning ... [1938] (Card 2)

CONTENTS—Continued.

Anna. Albert Schweitzer i Nathan Söderbloms hem. — Jonzon, Bengt. Några intryck av Albert Schweitzer. — Ekman, Henrik. Med Albert Schweitzer på konsert- och föredragsresa.—Dahl, Harald. Från Älvdalen till Landskrona. Glimtar från resor som tolk och registreringsbiträde åt Albert Schweitzer.—Stade, Frans. Människan Albert Schweitzer; minnen och intryck.—Oxenstierna, Bengt. Mina personliga minnen av Albert Schweitzer.—Lagerfelt, Greta. Hemma i Elsass; minnen från Strassburg och Günsbach, en miljöteckning.—Litteraturförteckning utarbetad av Karin Werner (p. [240]-250)—Svenska förbundet till stöd för Albert Schweitzers verksamhet.—Författarregister.

1. Schweitzer, Albert, 1875- 2. Lambarene, Gabon. 3. Missions, Medical. I. Lagerfelt, Greta Elizabeth (Berg) friherrinna, 1884- ed.

A C 39-3212

New York. Public library for Library of Congress [2]

D-15
3363

ALBERT SCHWEITZER: Mensch und Werk; eine kleine Festgabe zu seinem 85. Geburtstag, von Willy Bremi [et al.] Bern, P. Haupt [1959] 143 [5] p. port. 22cm.

Issued for the Hilfsverein für das Albert Schweitzer-Spital, Lambarene.

CONTENTS. --Albert Schweitzers theologische Arbeit im Rahmen seiner Biographie, von W. Bremi. --Albert Schweitzers "Weltanschauung der Ehrfurcht vor dem Leben" in philosophischer Sicht, von M. Werner. -- (Continued)

NN R 6.65 e/z OC, I PC, 1, I SL MU, 1, I (LC1, X1, Z1)

2

ALBERT SCHWEITZER: Mensch und Werk... (Card 2)

Albert Schweitzer als Musiker, von F. Morel. --Albert Schweitzer als Arzt, von H. Baur.

1. Schweitzer, Albert, 1875- . I. Breml, Willy.

AN
(Bernstein, A.)

Albion O. Bernstein memorial fund, New York.
Albion O. Bernstein memorial volume. New York, Albion O. Bernstein memorial fund, 1943. 1 v. illus. 24cm.

"Appraisals and tributes from...colleagues and teachers...also reprints of his own scientific writings, and reports of work inspired in part by his theories and research."
Bibliographies included.

291937B. 1. Bernstein, Albion Older, 1912–1940.
N. Y. P. L. Festschrift March 21, 1945

D-18
7809

Albrecht Goes zu seinem 60. Geburtstag am 22. März 1968. ⌊Frankfurt a. M.⌋ S. Fischer (1968).
43 p. port., facsims. 21cm.

Bibliography of the author's works: p. 35-43.

1. Goes, Albrecht, 1908-
NN * R 6.70 d/z OC PC, 1 SL (LC1, X1, Z1)

PTI

ALBRITTON, CLAUDE CARROL, 1913- , ed.
The fabric of geology. Prepared under the direction of a committee of the Geological Society of America, in commemoration of the society's 75th anniversary. Reading, Mass., Addison-Wesley pub. co. [1963]
x, 372 p. illus. 25cm.

Includes bibliographical references.
CONTENTS. --James Hutton and the philosophy of geology, by D. B. McIntyre. --Geologic laws, by W. H. Bradley. --Historical
(Continued)

NN * R 2.64 p/b OC, IIIb* (OS)I PC, 1, I, II SL ST, 1t, I, II (LC1, X1, Z1)
3

ALBRITTON, CLAUDE CARROL, 1913- , ed.
The fabric of geology. (Card 2)

science, by G. G. Simpson. --The theory of geology, by D. B. Kitts. --Geology as the study of complex natural experiments, by V. E. McKelvey. --Correlation by fossils, by A. O. Woodford. --Precision and resolution in geochronometry, by D. B. McIntyre. --Rational and empirical methods of investigation in geology, by J. H. Mackin. --Role of classification in geology, by M. L. Hill. --Simplicity in structural geology, by C. A. Anderson. --Association and indeterminacy in geomorphology, by L. B. Leopold and W. B. Langbein. --Geologic communication, by F. Betz, Jr. --The scientific
(Continued)

ALBRITTON, CLAUDE CARROL, 1913- , ed.
The fabric of geology. (Card 3)

philosophy of G. K. Gilbert, by J. Gilluly. --Nature and significance of geological maps, by M. M. Harrison. --Philosophical aspects of the geological sciences, by A. F. Hagner. --Geology in the service of man, by R. F. Legget. --Philosophy of geology: a selected bibliography and index, by C. C. Albritton, Jr. (p. 262-263)

1. Geology--Addresses, essays, lectures. I. Geological Society of America. II. Title. III. Albritton, Claude Carrol, 1913- t. 1963

3-MAS

Album discipulorum; aangeboden aan Professor Dr. J. G. van Gelder ter gelegenheid van zijn zestigste verjaardag, 27 Februari 1963. Utrecht. Haentjens Dekker & Gumbert ⌊1963⌋
205 p. plates, ports. 28 cm. (Orbis artium: Utrechtse kunsthistorische studiën, 7)
CONTENTS.—Een laat-Romeinse glazen beker uit Cuyk, door C. Isings.—La macchina dell'universo, di A. C. Esmeijer.—Twee kardinaalsportretten in het werk van Jan van Eyck, door J. Bruyn.—Het glorievolle rozenkransgeheim van Maria's kroning in de hemel door Geertgen tot Sint Jans, door J. H. A. Engelbregt.—De disharmonie van
(Continued)

NN * 11.65 e/ OC PC, 1, 2, 3 SL A, 1, 2, 3 (LC1, X1, Z1)
3

ALBUM discipulorum... (Card 2)

blauw en groen in oude schilderijen, door J. A. van de Graaf.—Drie figuren uit de fresco's in de Orsini-Kapel van Daniele da Volterra, door S. H. Levie.—Literaire bronnen voor Maarten de Vos' Ontvoering van Europa, door B. H. M. Mutsaers.—Drei unerkante Rottenhammer-zeichnungen in den Uffizien, von I. Jost.—Kanttekening bij Michael Maier's Atalanta Fugiens, door H. M. E. de Jong.—Linnen tafeldamast met de wapens en monogrammen van Frederik Hendrik en Amalia van Solms, door M.-C. Roodenburg.—The fountains designed for van Campen's Amsterdam town hall and Quellien's models for them, by K. Fremantle.—Twee "grootsmoediche" Haagse schilders, door E. K. J. Reznicek.—Natuur, onderwijzing en oefening: bij een drieluik van
(Continued)

ALBUM discipulorum... (Card 3)

Gerrit Dou, door J. A. Emmens.—Symboliek in een achttiende-eeuwse kloosterapotheek, door J. Schouten.—Berlage's Monument voor verleden en toekomst uit 1889, door P. Singelenberg.—Heinrich Campendonk en de moumentale kunst in Nederland, door B. Spaanstra-Polak.—De grafiek van Ap Sok, door J. N. van Wessem.—De mythe van Karel Appel's 'anrotzooien,' door L. Gans.—Lijst van geschriften over beeldende kunst van Professor Dr. J. G. van Gelder, door E. Verwey. (p. [187]-205)

1. Art--Essays and misc. 2. Gelder, Jan Gerrit van, 1903- .
3. Gelder, Jan Gerrit van, 1903- --Bibl.

GBXB

Album Dr. Jan Lindemans. Brussel, Drukkerij A. Hessens, 1951. 414 p. illus., port., map. 25cm.

Includes bibliographies. "Bibliographie van Dr. Jan Lindemans," p. 24-80.

1. Lindemans, Jan, 1888- . 2. Brabant—Hist.—Addresses, essays, lectures. 3. Geography—Names—Belgium—Brabant. 4. Names, Flemish.

NN** X 2.54 OC PC, 1, 2, 3, 4 SL G, 4 (LC1, Z1, X1)

E-10
709

ALBUM Dr. Louise Kaiser. Alphen aan den Rijn, N. Samson, 1951. 97 p. port. 25cm.

CONTENTS.—Bibliografie van de werken van Dr. L. Kaiser, door G. L. Meinsma. —Het numineuze element in de Nachtwacht, door J. C. Berntrop, jr. —Occlusief, explosief, etc., door E. Blancquaert. —Analyse van een Amsterdamse klankwet, door B. Faddegon. —Enkele para-phonetische mededelingen, door P. H. G. van Gilse. —Enige beschouwingen over de pathologie van taalgebruik en spraak, door F. Grewel. —Klankcultuur, (Continued)

NN * * 10.56 j/ OC PC, 1, 2 SL (LC1, X1, Z1) [I]

ALBUM Dr. Louise Kaiser. (Card 2)

door K. Heeroma. —Enkele opmerkingen over de uitspraak van de z, door A.R. Hol. —Een Nederlandse uitspraakleer van honderd jaar geleden, door P.J. Meertens. —Het gebaar, door G. van Rijnberk. —Taalafbraak bij de ziekten van Pick en Alzheimer, door V.W.D. Schenk. —De naam Bilderdijk, door M. Schönfeld. —Zin, spraak en taal, door C.F.P. Stutterheim. —Grenzen van de harmonische analyse, door R. Vermeulen. —Enkele socio-physiologische aantekeningen, door D. de Vries. —Pleidooi voor het accent, door J. Wils.

1. Kaiser, L. 2. Dutch language—Addresses, lectures etc.

F-11
1493

ALBUM Helen Maud Cam. Louvain, Publications universitaires, 1960-61. 2 v. port. 26cm. (International commission for the history of representative and parliamentary institutions. Studies, 23-24)

"Bibliography of Helen Maud Cam," v.1, p. 7-10. Bibliographical footnotes.

1. Cam, Helen Maud, 1885- 2. Government, Representative—Addresses, essays, lectures. I. Series.

NN 3.66 p/ OC (OS)I PC, 1, 2, I SL E, 1, 2, I (LC1, X1, Z1)

RAE
+

Album Kern; opstellen geschreven ter eere van Dr. H. Kern, hem aangeboden door vrienden en leerlingen op zijn zeventigsten verjaardag, den VI. April MDCCCIII. Leiden: E. J. Brill, 1903. xvii, 420 p. incl. table. diagrs., facsims., front. (port.), illus. (incl. map.) f°.

517614A. 1. Kern, Hendrik, 1833-1917. 2. Philology—Collections.
N. Y. P. L. April 25, 1931

Mr. Moth

* PWZ
+
(Berek)

Album pamiątkowy ku czci Berka Joselewicza, pułkownika wojsk polskich w 125-letnią rocznicę jego bohaterskiej śmierci, 1809–1934, pod redakcją profesora d-ra Majera Bałabana. Warszawa: Nakładem Biura wydawniczego "Tege" spółka z ogr. odp., 1934. 208 p. facsims., illus., plates, port. 31cm.

Cover-title: Księga pamiątkowa.
"Wydawnictwo Komitetu wileńskiego...ku uczczeniu pamięci Berka Joselewicza."
Bibliographies included.

828754A. 1. Berek Joselowicz, ca. 1765-1809. I. Bałaban, Majer, 1877- , ed.
N. Y. P. L. August 14, 1936

Festschrift

NIZ

Aleksis Kiven seura.
Kultanummi; Aleksis Kiven seuran juhlajulkaisu. Otto Manninen muistolle omistettu... Helsingissä, Otava [1951] 243 p. illus. 25cm.

1. Stenvall, Aleksis, 1834-1872. 2. Manninen, Otto, 1872- . 3. Poetry, Finnish—Hist. and crit.
NN

D-14
8680

ALEXY, DESIDER, ed.
Ein Leben für Kirche und Volk; zum 90. Geburtstag des Professors der Theologie, Dr. Roland Steinacker. Stuttgart, Hilfskomitee für die Ev.-Luth. Slowakeideutschen, 1960. 176 p. port. 22cm.

Caption title: Roland Steinacker Festschrift.
Includes bibliographies.

(Continued)

NN * R 2.64 e/ OC, 1bKG, I, IIb* PC, 1, 2, 3, I SL E, 3 S, 3 (LC1, X1, Z1) [I]

3

ALEXY, DESIDER, ed. Ein Leben für Kirche und Volk... (Card 2)

CONTENTS.--Melanchthon und die Slowakei, von A. Hudak.--Die Reformation auf der Schütt, von K. Kautz.--Tranoscius, der grösste lutherische Liederdichter der Slowakei, von W. Stökl.--Von evangelischer Kirchenmusik in der Slowakei, von K. Freitag.--Die Einheit im Glauben, von Z.A. Antony.--Die Wandlung des Volkstumsgedankens, von F. Spiegel-Schmidt.--Edmund Steinacker, 1839-1929, von H. Steinacker.--Jakob Glatz, 1776-1831 und die Entstehung des ungardeutschen Volksbewusstseins, von R. Steinacker.--Das Heidentor bei (Continued)

ALEXY, DESIDER, ed. Ein Leben für Kirche und Volk... (Card 2)

Petronell, von C.E. Schmidt.--Genus fidemque servabo, von K. Kautz.--Dr. Roland Steinacker achtzig Jahre alt, von R. Türke.--Lutherische Theologie im Dienste der Diaspora, von A. Hudak.

1. Steinacker, Roland, 1870- , 2. Evangelical Lutheran Church--Addresses, essays, lectures. 3. Germans in Slovakia. I. Title. II. Alexy, Desider.

NFD
(Doeblin)

Alfred Döblin zum 70. Geburtstag. [Hrsg. von Paul E. H. Lüth] Wiesbaden, Limes-Verlag, 1948.
175 p. illus., port., facsims. 24 cm.
"Bibliographie der Werke Alfred Döblins": p. 174–175.

1. Döblin, Alfred, 1878- I. Lüth, Paul E. H., 1919- ed.
PT2607.O35Z6 928.3 48-26687*
Library of Congress [1]

Festschrift.

NBC
(Meynell)

Alice Meynell centenary tribute, 1847–1947; a symposium opening an exhibition ⌈at Boston College⌉ of Alice Meynell manuscripts, letters, first and rare editions, here printed with a short-title list of her works; ed. by Terence L. Connolly. Boston, B. Humphries ⌈1948⌉

72 p. port. 21 cm.

CONTENTS.—Alice Meynell: a personal tribute, by R. F. Wilberforce.—Reminiscences of Mrs. Meynell through her prose, by A. K. Tuell.—Alice Meynell, poet of my delight, by Sister Mary Madeleva.—The Alice Meynell collection at Boston College, by T. L. Connolly.—Remarks concluding the symposium, by J. J. Wright.—Alice Meynell: a short-title list of published volumes, 1875–1947.

1. Meynell, Alice Christiana (Thompson) 1847–1922. I. Connolly, Terence Leo, 1888– ed. II. Boston College, Boston, Mass.

PR5021.M3A85 821.89 48–8730*

Library of Congress ⌈18⌉ Festschrift

E-14
1035

ALLEN, CHRISTOPHER, ed.
African perspectives; papers in the history, politics and economics of Africa presented to Thomas Hodgkin. Edited by Christopher Allen and R. W. Johnson. Cambridge, University press, 1970.
xx, 438 p. illus., maps. 24cm.

Bibliography, p. 427-430.
1. African studies--Collections. 2. Hodgkin, Thomas Lionel. I. Johnson, Richard William, joint ed. II. Allen, Christopher III. Johnson, Richard William.

NN R 4.71 e/ℓ OC, I, IIbo, IIIbBNB PC, 1, 2, I SL (LC1, X1, Z1, NWA1)

E-14
1293

Gli Allievi romani in memoria di Francesco Calasso. Scritti giuridici raccolti a cura del Gruppo studentesco europeo. Roma, Edizioni dell'Ateneo (Visigalli-Pasetti), 1967.
482 p. port. 25cm.

Bibliographical footnotes.
CONTENTS.—Continuando il colloquio con il Maestro, di C. A. Graziani.—Una vita per il diritto, di M. Bellomo.—Ateismo e libertà di religione, di O. Bucci.—La posizione degli istituti secolari nella legislazione canonica prima e dopo la codificazione, di M. Cavaniglia.—

(Continued)

NN * 5. 71 m/ OC, I PC, I, I SL (LC1, X1, Z1) 4

Gli ALLIEVI romani in memoria di Francesco Calasso. (Card 2)

Intorno ad alcune recenti teorie sulla natura e sui limiti del diritto di sciopero, di C. Ciampa.—Il terzo danneggiato e l'assicurazione della responsabilità civile, di E. Coglitore.—Sulla simulazione processuale, di M. Della Valle.—Brevi note sui problemi relativi all'iniziativa economica privata nella costituzione italiana, di M. Fedeli.—Il principio di uniformità e clausole più favorevoli al prestatore di lavoro, di A. Ferrari.—Distruzione, lacerazione, cancellazione del testamento olografo, di A. La Peccerella.—Alcune osservazioni sul concetto di di ritto, di P. Micara.—Note in tema di confessionismo, di

(Continued)

Gli ALLIEVI romani in memoria di Francesco Calasso. (Card 3)

C. Mirabelli.—Osservazioni in tema di buona fede in senso oggettivo nel diritto privato italiano, di E. Moscati.—Il problema costruttivo della frode alla legge e il principio tradizionale dell'irrilevanza del motivo, di G. Palermo.—La "causa legis" nelle fonti lombarde dell'età dell'assolutismo illuminato, di U. Petronio.—I soggetti del rapporto educativo familiare: genitore e figlio, di L. Poggi.—Figura giuridica del Pubblico Ministero nel processo civile, di D. Ruffino.—Le bolle istitutive del Maggiorasco e del Baliaggio Barberini, di A.

(Continued)

Gli ALLIEVI romani in memoria di Francesco Calasso. (Card 4)

Serafini.—Sul diritto di libertà religiosa nei nuovi Stati africani, di A. Sini.—Note intorno al problema della individuazione della domanda giudiziale, di S. Sorace.—Appunti sulla cosa giudicata, di C. M. Tardivo.—Accordo di riparto e riparto giudiziale nell'espropriazione singolare, di R. Vaccarella.

1. Law--Addresses, essays, lectures. I. Calasso, Francisco.

Copy only words underlined
& classmark—TB

The ALLOCATION of economic resources; essays in honor of Bernard Francis Haley, by Moses Abramovitz [and others] Stanford, Calif., Stanford university press, 1959. 244 p. 25cm. (Stanford university. Publications. University series: history, economics and political science. 17)

Includes bibliographies.
CONTENTS.--The welfare interpretation of secular trends in national income and product, by M. Abramovitz.--Costs and outputs, by

(Continued)

NN*R X 9.59 t/b OC, II (OS)I PC, 1, 2, 3, 4, I, II E, 1, 2, 3, 4, I, II (LC1, X1, Z1)

The ALLOCATION of economic resources... (Card 2)

A. Alchian.--Toward a theory of price adjustment, by K.J. Arrow.--Reflections on underconsumption, by P.A. Baran.--Unemployment compensation and the allocation of resources, by P.W. Cartwright.--The interdependence of investment decisions, by H.R. Chenery.--The theory of tax incidence applied to the gains of labor unions, by G.W. Hilton.--The scope and limits of futures trading, by H.S. Houthakker.--The handling of norms in policy analysis, by C.E. Lindblom.--Alternative theories of labor's share, by M. W. Reder.--Growth, balanced or unbalanced? By T. Scitovsky.--Monetary stability in a growing economy, by E. S. Shaw.--Factor inputs and international

(Continued)

The ALLOCATION of economic resources... (Card 3)

price comparisons, by L. Tarshis.

1. Income. 2. Prices. 3. Investments. 4. Haley, Bernard F. I. Series. II. Abramovitz, Moses, 1912-

---

PSO

Alpengeographische Studien. Aus dem Geographischen Institut der Universität Innsbruck. Zum 50. Geburtstag Prof. Dr. Hans Kinzl's. Innsbruck, Universitätsverlag Wagner, 1950. 210 p. illus., maps. 24cm. (Schlern-Schriften. 65)

Bibliographies included.

542585B. 1. Alps. 2. Kinzl, Hans, 1898- I. Ser. Festschrift
N. Y. P. L. October 11, 1950

SB p.v.4003
+

ALPHA A.-G., Nidau., Switzerland.
Festschrift zum 25- jahrigen bestehen der Alpha A.G. Nidau, 1928-1953. [Nidau, 1953. 27 p. illus. 30cm.

Cover-title: 25 Jahre Alpha A.-G. Nidau.

NN 10.58 p/$_S$ OS (1b) PC SL E (Z1, LC1, X1)

dd

RLB

ALTDEUTSCHES wort und wortkunstwerk. Georg Baesecke zum 65. geburtstage 13. januar 1941. Halle (Saale) M. Niemeyer, 1941. iv, 213 p., 1 l. 24cm.

Bibliographical foot-notes.

CONTENTS.—Schneider, F. J. Die anfänge germanistischer studien in und um Halle.—Brinkmann, Hennig. Theodiscus, ein beitrag zur frühgeschichte des namens "deutsch."—Frings, Theodor. Das wort deutsch.—Bögel, Theodor. Die überlieferung der germanischen namen und wörter bei Anthimus.—Wagner, Kurt. Zum problem einer althochdeutschen grammatik.—Specht, Franz. Zur ahd. stammbildung.—Karg-Gasterstädt

(Continued)

NN*R 11.52 OC PC,1,2,3 SL (LC1, Z1, X1)

ALTDEUTSCHES wort und wortkunstwerk... (Card 2)

Elisabeth. Zum wortschatz des Abrogans.—Schröbler, Ingeborg. Zu 'Himmel und hölle.'—Weyhe, Hans. Die heimat der riesen des Rother.—Voretzsch, Karl. Zum mittelhochdeutschen Reinhart Fuchs.—Schneider, Hermann. Morungens Elbenlied.—Leitzmann, Albert. Zur Vorauer novelle.—Rasch, Wolfdietrich. Realismus in der erzählweise deutscher versnovellen des 13. und 14. jahrhunderts.—Sperber, Hermann. Bibliographie Georg Baesecke 1936-1940 (p. [212]-213)

436209B. 1. Baesecke, Georg, 1876- . 2. Germanic languages. 3. German literature—Hist. and crit.

D-20
2864

Das Altertum und jedes neue Gute. Für Wolfgang Schadewaldt zum 15. März 1970. (Hrsg. von Konrad Gaiser.) Stuttgart, Berlin, Köln, Mainz, Kohlhammer (1970).

560 p. with illus. and map., front. 22 cm.

Includes bibliographical references.

I. Schadewaldt, Wolfgang, 1900- . II. Gaiser, Konrad, ed.

NN * R 2.71 b/ OC, I, II PC, I, II SL (LC1, X1, Z1)

Write on slip words underlined below and class mark—

* OAA

Altorientalische Studien; Bruno Meissner zum sechzigsten Geburtstag am 25. April 1928 gewidmet von Freunden, Kollegen und Schülern. Leipzig: O. Harrassowitz, 1928–29. 2 v. in 1. front. (port.), illus., plates. 25½cm. (Altorientalische Gesellschaft. Mitteil. Bd. 4, Heft 1–2.)

Paged continuously.

Partial contents: BAUER, T. Neues Material zur "Amoriter"-Frage. FRIEDRICH, J. Reinheitsvorschriften für den hethitischen König. GÖTZE, A. Die historische Einleitung des Aleppo-Vertrages. HOMMEL, F. Die "zwei verschwundenen Götter" der Adapa-Legende und Apokalypse. ROST, P. Miszellen: 1. Der Altar Ezechiels.

(Continued)

Festschrift

N. Y. P. L. May 16, 1933

Altorientalische Studien; Bruno Meissner zum sechzigsten Geburtstag am 25. April 1928 gewidmet... (Card 2)

2. Jesaja. SCHACHERMEYR, F. Zur staatsrechtlichen Wertung der hethitischen Verträge. TORCZYNER, H. Logisch-scholastische oder historisch-psychologische Sprachwissenschaft.

634144A. 1. Meissner, Bruno, 1868- . 2. Assyriology. 3. Assyria and Babylonia.
N. Y. P. L. May 16, 1933

MGO
+
(Ambrosi)

Ambrosi-Festschrift. Mit 52 Abbildungen und 18 Faksimiledrucken. Wien, Burgland-Verlag [1948] 47 p. illus. 36cm.

Includes contributions by Ambrosi.
At head of title: Die Fähre. Sonderdruck MCMXLVIII.

Fest

1. Ambrosi, Gustinus, 1893- .
N. Y. P. L. July 20, 1949

OAP

American Academy of Arts and Sciences, *Boston.*
Science and the modern mind; a symposium, edited by Gerald Holton. Boston, Beacon Press [1958]
ix, 110 p. 21 cm.

"These ... essays, and the ... [American] Academy [of Arts and Sciences] conference at which they were presented ... were assembled in honor of Dr. P. W. Bridgman and Dr. Philipp Frank on the occasion of their retirement from active teaching at Harvard University."

Includes bibliographical references.

CONTENTS.—Introduction, by G. Holton.—Three eighteenth-century social philosophers: scientific influences on their thought, by H. Guerlac.—Science and the human comedy: Voltaire, by H. Brown.—The seventeenth-century legacy: our mirror of being, by G. de Santillana.—Contemporary science and the contemporary world view, by P. Frank.—The growth of science and the structure of culture, by

(Continued)

NN * R 6.59 a/n (OC)I, II OS PC, 1, 2, 3, I, II SL ST, 1t, 2, 3, I, II (LC1, X1, Z1)

American Academy of Arts and Sciences, *Boston.* Science and the modern mind ... [1958] (Card 2)

CONTENTS—Continued.

R. Oppenheimer.—The Freudian conception of man and the continuity of nature, by J. S. Bruner.—Quo vadis, by P. W. Bridgman.—Prospects for a new synthesis: science and the humanities as complementary activities, by C. Morris.—A humanist looks at science, by H. M. Jones.

1. SCIENCE--PHILOSOPHY 2. BRIDGMAN, PERCY WILLIAMS, 1882- 3. FRANK, PHILIPP, 1884- I. Holton, Gerald James, ed. II. Science and the modern mind t. 1954

PPB

AMERICAN CHEMICAL SOCIETY. Biological chemistry, Division of.
Amino acids, proteins and cancer biochemistry. Papers presented at the Jesse P. Greenstein memorial symposium, Sept. 16, 1959. With a biographical article on Dr. Greenstein and a bibliography of his writings. Edited by John T. Edsall. Pref. by Sidney W. Fox and Julius Schultz. New York, Academic press, 1960. ix, 244 p. illus., port., diagrs., tables. 24cm.

(Continued)

NN*R 2.61 s/H (OC)I OS(1b+) PC, 1, 2, 3, 4, I SL ST, 1, 2t, 3t, I (LC1, X1, Z1)

AMERICAN CHEMICAL SOCIETY. Biological chemistry, Division of. Amino acids... (Card 2)

Includes bibliographies.

1. Greenstein, Jesse Philip, 1902-1959. 2. Acid, Amino. 3. Proteids and protein. 4. Cancer. I. Edsall, John Tileston, 1902- , ed. t. 1960.

E-12
5647

AMERICAN SCANDINAVIAN FOUNDATION.
Scandinavian studies; essays presented to Henry Goddard Leach on the occasion of his eighty-fifth birthday. Edited by Carl F. Bayerschmidt and Erik J. Friis. Seattle, University of Washington press [1965] vii, 458 p. port., maps. 25cm.

Bibliographical footnotes.

(Continued)

NN R 5.66 a/c (OC)I, II, III OS PC, 1, 2, 3, 4, I, II, III SL (LC1, X1, Z1) [I]

AMERICAN SCANDINAVIAN FOUNDATION. Scandinavian studies... (Card 2)

1. Leach, Henry Goddard, 1880- . 2. Scandinavian literature--Addresses, essays, lectures. 3. Scandinavian languages--Addresses, essays, lectures. 4. Scandinavia--Hist. --Addresses, essays, lectures. I. Bayerschmidt, Carl Frank, ed. II. Friis, Erik, J., ed. III. Title.

STE

AMERICAN COUNCIL ON EDUCATION.
American education faces the world crisis; addresses delivered at the thirty-third annual meeting of the American council on education, held in Chicago, May 5-6, 1950. Contributors: George F. Zook [and others] Washington, D. C. [1951] 72 p. port. 24cm.

"The American council on education issues this volume in honor of George F. Zook upon his retirement after more than sixteen years of distinguished service as president of the Council."

CONTENTS.—Dr. George F. Zook, president of the American council on education, by G. D. Stoddard.—Education for one world,

(Continued)

NN**R 4.54 (OC)I, II OS PC, 1, I, II SL (Z1, LC1, X1)

AMERICAN COUNCIL ON EDUCATION. American education faces the world crisis... (Card 2)

by G. F. Zook.—Scholary inquiry and the American tradition, by J. B. Conant.—Education faces the world crisis, by H. Benjamin.—The humanities face the world crisis, by C. E. Odegaard.—The natural sciences face the world crisis, by D. W. Bronk.—The social sciences face the world crisis, by W. Johnson.

1. Education—U. S., 20th cent. I. Zook, George Frederick, 1885- II. Title.

VIB

AMERICAN SOCIETY FOR METALS.
Utilization of heat resistant alloys; a symposium presented at the University of Michigan, Mar. 11 and 12, 1954, in honor of Albert Easton White on his 70th birthday for his pioneering and outstanding contributions to the research and development of alloys for high temperature service. Cleveland [1954] 288 p. illus., ports. 24cm.

Includes bibliographies.

(Continued)

NN ** R 4.55 p/+ (OC) I OS PC, 1, 2, 3, I SL ST, 1t, 2t, 3, I (LC1, X1, Z1)

AN
(Wells, H.)

American dental association. Horace Wells centenary committee.
Horace Wells, dentist, father of surgical anesthesia. Proceedings of centenary commemorations of Wells' discovery in 1844 and list of Wells memorabilia, including bibliographies, memorials and testimonials. Comp., by the editor, ₍William J. Gies₎ for the Horace Wells centenary committee of the American dental association. ₍Chicago?₎ 1948. xiii, 415 p. illus. 25cm.

Festschrift

1. Wells, Horace, 1815-1848. 2. Anesthetics. I. Gies, William John, 1872- , ed.

N. Y. P. L. February 5, 1952

AMERICAN SOCIETY FOR METALS. Utilization of heat resistant alloys... (Card 2)

CONTENTS.—Creep and fracture at elevated temperatures, by N. J. Grant.—Factors involved in using high temperature test date for selecting materials and proportioning parts, by C. L. Clark.—Alloys and their properties for elevated temperature service, by H. C. Cross.—Stress calculations for design for creep conditions, by P. F. Chenea.—Engineering practice for selecting materials and proportioning components operating at high temperatures in the steam power industry, by H. A. Wagner—Criteria in the selection of

(Continued)

PWR

AMERICAN JOURNAL OF SCIENCE.
Bowen volume. New Haven, 1952. 2 v. in 1 (viii, 627 p.) illus., port., maps. 24cm. (Carnegie institution of Washington. Geogphysical laboratory. Publication no. 1200)

This volume is dedicated tō Norman L. Bowen upon his retirement from the Geophysical laboratory.
Includes bibliographies.

1. Petrology. 2. Bowen, Norman Levi, 1887- I. Carnegie institution of Washington. Geophysical laboratory. t. 1952.

NN** 5.56 a/+OS, I PC, 1, 2, I SL ST, 1, 2t, I (U1, LC1, X1, Z1)

AMERICAN SOCIETY FOR METALS. Utilization of heat resistant alloys... (Card 3)

materials for aircraft gas-turbines, by H. Hanink and L. Luini.—Production and fabrication of heat resistant alloys from the producers' viewpoint, by C. T. Evans, jr.—Fabrication of high temperature alloy stell piping suitable for central station and oil refinery service, by R. W. Emerson.—Jets: from blueprint to engines, by W. E. Jones and A. J. Rosenberg.—Metallurgical variables influencing properties of heat resistant alloys, by J. W. Freeman, C. L. Corey and A. I. Rush.—Development of and acceptance testing procedures against specifications, by A. W. F. Green.— A chronological list of the

(Continued)

AMERICAN SOCIETY FOR METALS. Utilization of heat resistant
alloys... (Card 4)

publications of Albert Easton White, compiled by B. A. Uhlendorf.

1. Metals—Effect of temperature. 2. Alloys. 3. White, Albert
Easton, 1884- I. Title. t. 1954.

3-MAF

American University at Cairo. *Center for Arabic Studies.*
Studies in Islamic art and architecture in honour of Professor K. A. C. Creswell. Contributions by C. L. Geddes
[and others. Cairo] Published for the Center for Arabic
Studies by the American University in Cairo Press, 1965.

xx, 291 p. illus., plans (part fold.) port. 29 cm.

English, French, or German.
Includes bibliographical references.

NN*R 11.69 r/a (OC)I, II OS 4, I, II O, 1, 2, 3, 4, I, II (LC1, PC, 1, 2, 3, 4, I, II SL A, 1, 2, 3, X1, Z1) [I]
(Continued)

American University at Cairo. *Center for Arabic Studies.*
Studies in Islamic art and architecture ... (Card 2)

CONTENTS.—K. A. C. Creswell, by C. L. Geddes.—Bibliography of
the writings of K. A. C. Creswell (p. xiv–xix)—L'œuvre de K. A. C.
Creswell, by E. Combe.—Le Palais de Sedrata dans le Désert Saharien, by M. van Berchem.—Zum Bāb al-Wuzarā'(Puerta de San Este-
ban) der Hauptmoschee von Córdoba, by K. Brisch —Vorosmanische
Medresen und Imarets vom Medresentyp in Anatolien, by K. Erdmann.—Foundation-moulded leatherwork—a rare Egyptian technique
also used in Britain, by R. Ettinghausen.—A new inscription from
the Ḥaram al-Sharīf in Jerusalem, by O. Grabar.—Die Bauinschrift

(Continued)

American University at Cairo. *Center for Arabic Studies.*
Studies in Islamic art and architecture ... (Card 3)

der Moschee des Aḥmad ibn Ṭūlūn (265/879), by A. Grohmann.—
Dome decorations by means of pierced openings, by Ḥ. 'Abd al-
Wahhāb.—Die beiden Mosaikböden in Quṣayr 'Amra, by C. Kessler.—
Some notes on the façade of Mshattā, by E. Kühnel.—Sur les mo-
saïques de la Grande Mosquée de Cordoue, by G. Marçais.—The ṭirāz
institutions in medieval Egypt, by M. A. Marzouk.—Inscriptions on
the minarets of Saveh, Iran, by G. C. Miles.—Note on the aesthetic
character of the north dome of the Masjid-i-Jāmi' of Iṣfāhān, by
A. U. Pope.—The pottery of Byzantium and the Islamic world, by

---

AMERICAN UNIVERSITY AT CAIRO. Center for Arabic Studies. Studies in Islamic art and
architecture ... (Card 4)

D. T. Rice.— The Mashhad al-Juyūshī (archaeological notes and
studies), by F. Shāfe'ī.—An Ayyūbid basin of al-Ṣāliḥ Najm al-Dīn,
by W. 'Izzī.—La Mosquée de Kāfūr au Caire, by G. Wiet.—On Islamic
swords, by A. R. Zaky.

1. Creswell, Keppel Archibald Cameron, 1879- . 2. Creswell, Keppel Archibald Cameron, 1879- --Bibl. 3. Art, Muhammadan--Addresses, essays, lectures. 4. Architecture, Muhammadan--Addresses, essays, lectures. I. Geddes, Charles L. II. Title.

BAL

Amherst college
Teachers of history; essays in honor of
Laurence Bradford Packard, edited by H Stuart
Hughes with the collaboration of Myron P. Gilmore
and Edwin C. Rozwenc. Ithaca, N.Y., Cornell
university press [1954] vi, 372 p. port.
24cm.

Includes bibliographical references.
(Continued)

NN * R 3.55 s/4 (OC) I, II OS PC, 1, 2, I, II
SL (LC1 X1, Z1) [I]

Amherst college Teachers of history...
(Card 2)

Contents.--Introduction: Laurence Bradford
Packard, by C.W. Cole.--Individual figures:
Fides et eruditio: Erasmus and the study of
history, by M.P. Gilmore. The education of an
encyclopedist, by R. Bowen. The social theory
of Frédéric Le Play, by P. Farmer. An emperor
writes history. Napoleon III's Histoire de
Jules César, by M. Kranzberg. Pobedonostsev
(Continued)

Amherst college Teachers of history...
(Card 3)

as a historian, by R.F. Byrnes. Henry Adams
and the Federalists, by E.C. Rozwenc. Gaetano
Mosca and the political lessons of history, by
H.S. Hughes. Huizinga's approach to the Middle
Ages, by P.L. Ward.--Historiographic traditions:
The birth of Clio: a résumé and interpretation of
ancient Near Eastern historiography, by B.C.
Brundage. Spanish population thought before
(Continued)

Amherst college Teachers of history...
(Card 4)

Malthus, by R.S. Smith. Father Paisi and
Bulgarian history, by J.F. Clarke. Historiography
in Japan, by J.W. Hall.--Problems of interpreta-
tion: Trends, periods, and classes, by A. Gilmore.
War and the historian, by J. Bowditch. The Dred
Scott labyrinth, by F.S. Allis, jr.

1. History--Historiography. 2. Packard, Laurence
Bradford, 1887- . I. Hughes, Henry Stuart, 1916-
ed. II. Title.

---

*YIG

Amicitiæ corolla; a volume of essays presented to James Rendel
Harris...on the occasion of his eightieth birthday, edited by H. G.
Wood... London: Univ. of London Press, Ltd., 1933. xiii,
366 p. front. (port.) 22½cm.

CONTENTS.—Bakker, A. Testimony-influence in the Old-Latin Gospels.—Bartlet,
J. V. Papias's "Exposition": its date and contents.—Cadbury, H. J. Some Semitic
personal names in Luke-Acts.—Findlay, J. A. The first Gospel and the Book of Tes-
timonies.—Jackson, F. J. F. Newman's idea of a university.—Franks, R. S. The
interpretation of Holy Scripture in the theological system of Alexander of Hales.
—Hoskier, H. C. Concerning "AT" and its very special use in the Old Testament.
—Howard, W. F. John the Baptist and Jesus: a note on Evangelic chronology.—
Krappe, A. H. The Molionides.—Lake, K. The text of Mark in some dated lec-

(Continued)

N. Y. P. L. October 16, 1933

Amicitiæ corolla; a volume of essays presented to James Rendel Harris... (Card 2)

tionaries.—Levonian, L. Krikor Datewatzy and his treatise against Moslems.—Lietzmann, D. H. Der Sinn des Aposteldekretes und seine Textwandlung.—Naish, J. P. Some evidence of Egyptian influence on Hebrew civilisation.—Phillips, C. A. Some notes on Ephrem's Gospel-text.—Plooij, D. The baptism of Jesus.—Purdy, A. C. The purpose of the Epistle to the Hebrews in the light of recent studies in Judaism.—Robinson, T. H. The origin of the tribe of Judah.—Vogels, Dr. H. J. Der Codex Claromontanus der Paulinischen Briefe.—Wensinck, A. J. John VIII. 6, 8.—Windisch, Dr. H. Jesus und der Geist im Johannes-Evangelium.—Witt, R. E. Hypostasis.—Zwaan, J. de. Date and origin of the Epistle of the eleven Apostles.

667574A. 1. Harris, James Rendel, 1852- . 2. Bible. N. T.—Crit. 3. Bible—Essays and misc. I. Wood, Herbert George, 1879- , editor.

N. Y. P. L. October 16, 1933

AN
(Schweitzer, A.)

AMIS D'ALBERT SCHWEITZER.
Hommage à Albert Schweitzer. [Ont collaboré à cet Hommage: Henri Baruk et al. Paris] Diffusion "Le Guide" [1955] 141 p. port. 23cm.

"Deux textes inédits d'Albert Schweitzer: Discours sur Goethe, 1928 (extrait). Discours d'Oslo, 1954 (extrait)." p. 127-141.

I. Schweitzer, Albert, 1875- . II. Baruk, Henri, 1897- . III. Title.

NN** 1.57 t/b (OC)I, II, III OS (1b) PC, I, II, III SL (LC1, X1, Z1)

TB

Amsterdamsche kring van economen.
Bedrijfseconomische opstellen, aangeboden aan Prof. Th. Limperg jr. door den Amsterdamsche kring van economen ter gelegenheid van zijn 60e verjaardag, 21 December 1939. Groningen [etc.] P. Noordhoff [1939] 452 p. 24cm.

"Lijst van publicaties en artikelen van Th. Limperg jr.," p. 448-451.

Festschrift

337540B. 1. Limperg, Th., 1879- 2. Economics—Essays and misc. I. Title.

N. Y. P. L. May 24, 1946

F-10
6683

ANALECTA archaeologica; Festschrift Fritz Fremersdorf. Köln, Verlag der Löwe, 1960. 284 p. illus., 70 plates, port. 30cm.

Contributions in German, French, English and Italian.

1. Archaeology--Addresses, essays, lectures. 2. Fremersdorf, Fritz, 1894- .

NN R 7.62 g/ OC PC, 1, 2 SL (LC1, X1, Z1) [I]

---

*OAC

ANALECTA orientalia memoriae Alexandri Csoma de Körös dicata. Edendo operi praefuit L. Ligeti. Budapestini, Sumptibus Academiae litterarum hungaricae et Societatis a Csoma de Körös nominatae, 1942. 1 v. illus., port. 28cm. (Bibliotheca orientalis hungarica. [Nr.] 5)

Vol. 1.

CONTENTS. --v.1.: Beiträge zur hethitischen Grammatik, von O. Szemerényi. Das Volk der Sadagaren, von J. Harmatta.

(Continued)

NN** X 4.56 a/- OC, II (OS) I PC, 1, 2, I, II SL O, 1, 2, I, II (U1, LC1, X1, Z1)

ANALECTA orientalia memoriae Alexandri Csoma de Körös dicata. (Card 2)

Tibetan books and manuscripts of Alexander Csoma de Körös in the Library of the Hungarian academy of sciences, by L. J. Nagy. Probleme der türkischen Urzeit, von J. Németh. Die Tokuz-Oguz und die Köktürken, von F. László. Autour du codex Cumanicus, par G. Györffy. Monuments de la langue tatare de Kazan, par T. Halasi Kun. Mîrzâ Mehdis Darstellung der tschagataischen Sprache, von J. Eckmann.

1. Körösi-Csoma, Sándor, 1784-1842. 2. Oriental studies—Collections. I. Series. II. Ligeti, Lajos, ed.

---

*QD

ANALECTA slavica; a Slavonic miscellany, presented for his seventieth birthday to Bruno Becker, professor of Russian history, language and literature in the University of Amsterdam. Amsterdam, De Bezige bij, 1955. v, 223 p. 23cm.

Includes bibliographies.

CONTENTS. --De bronzen ruiter. A Dutch translation of Mednyj vsadnik by Puškin. by A. G. Schot. --Pierre Tolstoj et Pierre le Grand.

(Continued)

NN** 3.56 f/b OC PC, 1, 2 SL S, 1, 2 (LC1, X1, Z1)

ANALECTA slavica... (Card 2)

par A. Mazon. --Le conte de Bova Korolevič et le vocabulaire russe, par B. O. Unbegaun. --Neerlando-Polonica, door R. van der Meulen. --Die Anfänge der Kapuzinerniederlassungen in Russland, von P. Zacharias Anthonisse. --Willem de Clercq over Rusland, door T. J. G. Locher. --L'Onegin come diario lirico di Puškin, di E. Lo Gatto. --Dostoevskij visionnaire, par J. van der Eng. --Čechov, Melichovo and the peasants, by T. Eekman. --Lavrov and Russian literature, by J. M. Meijer. --

(Continued)

ANALECTA slavica... (Card 3)

L'intelligencija révolutionnaire vue à travers quelques œuvres soviétiques (1921-27). par J. van der Eng-Liedmeier. --Quelques héros dans les romans de Konstantin Fedin. par H. G. Schogt. --The Moscow fire of 1812 in Soviet historiography, by K. van het Reve. --Soviet agricultural policy (1953-54), by J. W. Bezemer. --The North-West Caucasian languages, by A. H. Kuipers. --On the meaning of the Russian cases, by C. L. Ebeling.

1. Becker, Bruno, 1885- . 2. Russian literature--Hist. and crit.

Write on slip, name, year, vol., page of magazine and class mark — PQA

Dem Andenken an Herrn Hofrat Ingenieur Josef Billek gewidment.

(Naturwissenschaftlicher Verein für Steiermark. Mitteil. Graz, 1929. 8° Bd.66, p.1-231. port.)

Biographical sketch, by A. Tornquist, p.5-8.

form 408a [ii-12-30 25m]

Copy only words underlined
& classmark-- STG

Ander, Oscar Fritiof, 1903- ed.
In the trek of the immigrants, essays presented to Carl Wittke, edited by O. Fritiof Ander. Rock Island, Ill., Augustana College Library, 1964.
xvi, 325 p. port. 24 cm. (Augustana college and theological seminary. Augustana library publications. no. 31)

Bibliographical references included in "Notes" (p. 266-299)
CONTENTS.—Preface, by C. W. Sorenson.—Introduction, by O. F.
(Continued)

NN R 3.65 g/3 OC (OS)I PC,1, 2,3,I E,1,2,3 (LC1,X1,Z1)
[I] 3

ANDER, OSCAR FRITIOF, 1903- , ed. In the trek of the immigrants... (Card 2)

Ander.—Carl Wittke, historian, by H. Wish.—Four historians of immigration, by O. F. Ander.—Immigration, emigration, migration, by C. C. Qualey.—Bibliography of works by Carl Wittke, by C. H. Cramer.—A forgotten theory of immigration, by E. P. Hutchinson.—Agrarian myths of English immigrants, by C. Erickson.—A brief history of immigrant groups in Ohio, by F. P. Weisenburger.—The German in American fiction, by J. T. Flanagan.—English migration to the American West, 1865-1900, by O. O. Winther.—Saga in steel and concrete, by K. O. Bjork.—Finnish immigrant farmers in New York, 1910-1960, by A. W. Hoglund.—The immigrant and the American national idea, by W. O. Forster.—British backtrailers: working-

(Continued)

ANDER, OSCAR FRITIOF, 1903- , ed. In the trek of the immigrants... (Card 3)

class immigrants return, by W. S. Shepperson.—Exodus U. S. A., by T. Saloutos.—The Negro in the old Northwest, by J. H. Rodabaugh.—The American Negro: an old immigrant on a new frontier, by J. I. Dowie.

1. Emigration and immigration--U.S. 2. Migration--U.S. 3. Wittke, Carl Frederick, 1892- . I. Series.

*PDG

ANDERSON, BERNHARD W., ed.
Israel's prophetic heritage; essays in honor of James Muilenburg, edited by Bernhard W. Anderson and Walter Harrelson. [1. ed.] New York, Harper [1962] xiv, 242 p. 22cm.

Bibliographical footnotes.
CONTENTS.--In the beginning, by W. Eichrodt.--The prophets and
(Continued)

NN R 1.64 e/r OC, I, IIb*, IIIb* PC, 1, 2, I SL J, 2, I (LC1, X1, Z1)
3

ANDERSON, BERNHARD W., ed. Israel's prophetic heritage... (Card 2)

the problem of continuity, by N.W. Porteous.--The lawsuit of God; a form-critical study of Deuteronomy 32, by G.E. Wright.--The background of Judges 17-18, by M. Noth.--The prophetic call of Samuel, by M. Newman.--The prophet as Yahweh's messenger, by J.F. Ross.--Amos and wisdom, by S. Terrien.--"Rejoice not, o Israel!" by D.W. Harvey.--Essentials of the theology of Isaiah, by T.C. Vriezen.--Nonroyal motifs in the royal eschatology, by W. Harrelson.--The king in the Garden of

(Continued)

ANDERSON, BERNHARD W., ed. Israel's prophetic heritage... (Card 3)

Eden; a study of Ezekiel 28: 12-19, by H.G. May.--Exodus typology in second Isaiah, by B.W. Anderson.--The promises of grace to David in Isaiah 55: 1-5, by O. Eissfeldt.--The Samaritan schism in legend and history, by H.H. Rowley.--Prophecy and the prophets at Qumrân, by M. Burrows.--A bibliography of James Muilenburg's writings, by R.L. Hicks (p. 233-241)

1. Muilenburg, James. 2. Prophets, Biblical. I. Harrelson, Walter J., joint ed. II. Anderson, Bernhard W. III. Harrelson, Walter J.

E-13
869

ANDERSON, HOWARD, ed.
Studies in criticism and aesthetics, 1660-1800; essays in honor of Samuel Holt Monk, edited by Howard Anderson and John S. Shea. Minneapolis, University of Minnesota Press [1967]

419 p. illus., port. 24 cm.

Includes bibliographical references.

(Continued)

NN *R1.68 1/LOC,I PC,1, 2,3,I SL A,3,I (LC1,X1,Z1) [I] 4

ANDERSON, HOWARD, ed. Studies in criticism and aesthetics, 1660-1800... (Card 2)

CONTENTS.—Introduction, by H. Anderson, and J. S. Shea.—When was neoclassicism? By B. H. Bronson.—Erminia in Minneapolis, by R. W. Lee.—Chaucer in Dryden's Fables, by E. Miner.—Shaftesbury and the age of sensibility, by E. Tuveson.—Addison on ornament and poetic style, by D. A. Hansen.—The watch of judgment: relativism and An essay on criticism, by P. Ramsey.—Sermon or satire: Pope's definition of his art, by L. Feder.—The cistern and the fountain; art and reality in Pope and Gray, by I. Ehrenpreis.—Thomson's poetry of space and time, by R. Cohen.—"The reach of art" in Augustan

(Continued)

ANDERSON, HOWARD, ed. Studies in criticism and aesthetics, 1660-1800... (Card 3)

poetic theory, by W. H. Halewood.—Philosophical language and the theory of beauty in the eighteenth century, by W. J. Hipple, Jr.—Hume's "Of criticism," by E. C. Mossner.—William Warburton as "new critic", by R. M. Ryley.—The naked science of language, 1747-1786, by S. Elledge.—Imlac and the business of a poet, by G. Tillotson.—The comic syntax of Tristram Shandy, by I. Watt.—Reynolds and the art of characterization, by R. E. Moore.—Gainsborough's Prospect, animated prospect, by E. Buchwald.—The Preface to Lyrical ballads: a revolution in dispute, by J. Scoggins.—A list of books, articles, and reviews published by Samuel Holt Monk (p. [401]-402)

(Continued)

ANDERSON, HOWARD, ed. Studies in criticism and aesthetics, 1660-1800... (Card 4)

1. Monk, Samuel Holt. 2. English literature—Addresses, essays, lectures. 3. Aesthetics—Addresses, essays, lectures. I. Shea, John S., joint ed.

E-12
3979

ANDREAE, BERND, ed.
Dem Verleger Richard Ulmer, Doktor honoris causa der Landwirtschaftlichen Hochschule Hohenheim und Inhaber des Grossen Verdienstkreuzes des Verdienstordens der Bundesrepublik Deutschland zu seinem 90. Geburtstag, am 4. Mai 1961 [Stuttgart, Verlag Eugen Ulmer, 1961] 110 p. port. 24cm.

1. Ulmer, Richard, 1871- . 2. Agriculture, 1901- . I. Title: Richard Ulmer.

NN R 6.66 r/c OC, I, Ib+ PC, 1, 2, I SL (LC1, X1, Z1)

AN
(Andreen, G.)

Andreen of Augustana, 1864–1940, tributes to Gustav Albert Andreen ... a loyal son of Augustana synod pioneers, third president of Augustana college and theological seminary, by associates, family and friends. Rock Island, Ill., Augustana book concern, 1942.

219 p. incl. front., illus. (incl. ports.) 20cm.

CONTENTS.—Boyhood years, by Daniel Nystrom.—Student days at Yale, by C. E. Seashore.—Years at Augustana, by Conrad Bergendoff.—Ambassador of good will, by O. N. Olson.—In the family circle, by Esther A. Albrecht.—In the classroom, by J. V. Nordgren.—The churchman, by P. O. Bersell.—The citizen, by J. W. Potter.—A college builder, by O. H. Pannkoke.—A tribute, by J. H. Hauberg.

1. Andreen, Gustav Albert, 1864–1940. I. Augustana college and theological seminary, Rock Island, Ill.

43-1041

Library of Congress LD271.A66517 1901

[3] 923.773

GDVW

Angelomontana; Blätter aus der Geschichte von Engelberg. Jubiläumsgabe für Abt Leodegar II. Gossau, St. G., J.G.Cavelti-Hangartner, 1914. 501 p. illus. 25cm.

Various contributors.
Includes music.

1. Scherer, Leodegar, 1840-1914. 2. Engelberg, Switzerland—Hist.

NN R 3.53 OC PC, 1, 2 SL (LC1, Z1, X1)

NCB

... **Anglica**; untersuchungen zur englischen philologie. Alois Brandl zum siebzigsten geburtstage überreicht ... Leipzig, Mayer & Müller, g. m. b. h., 1925.

2 v. front. (port.) fold. facsim. 23½cm. (Palaestra 147–148 ...)

Dedication signed: Wilhelm Dibelius, Hans Hecht, Wolfgang Keller.

CONTENTS.—bd. I. Sprache und kulturgeschichte.—bd. II. Literaturgeschichte.

1. English philology—Collections. 2. English literature—Hist. & crit.—Collections. 3. Brandl, Alois Leonhard, 1855–

246418A

Library of Congress PD25.P3 147-148 25-17575

[4]

Copy only words underlined
& Classmark-- NCB

ANGLISTISCHE Studien; Festschrift zum 70. Geburtstag von Professor Friedrich Wild, gesammelt und hrsg. von Karl Brunner, Herbert Koziol [und Siegfried Korninger. Wien, W. Braumüller [1958] x, 249 p. port. 24cm. (Wiener Beiträge zur englischen Philologie. Bd. 66)

Bibliographical footnotes.

CONTENTS.--Der Sprachlaut, von H. Aigner.--Zum Englischunterricht an der Mittelschule, von K. Baschiera.--Joseph Addisons umfassende Interessen, von K. Brunner.--The mythical method in the early
(Continued)

NN R 7.66 p/c OCs, Is, IIs, IIIs (OS)IV PCs, 1s, 2s, I, IIs, IIIs, IVs (LC1s, X1s, Z1s) 3

ANGLISTISCHE Studien... (Card 2)

poems of T.S. Eliot, by H. Foltinek.--Altenglische Wortgeographie, von O. Funke.--Ein Muttermal des deutschen Pyramus und die Spenserechos in A midsummer-night's dream, von K. Hammerle.--"actie"-"share," von H. Haschka. Moderne englische Wortbildungselemente, von O. Hietsch.--Change of emphasis as a factor in translation, by E. Koch-Emmery.--Wycherlys satirische Methode, von S. Korninger.--Zur Wortbildung im amerikanischen Englisch, von H. Koziol.--The bell-tower: Herman Melvilles Beitrag zur Roboterliteratur, von H.H. Kühnelt.--Zur Vorgeschichte von westsächsisch æ und zur Methode des Rekonstruierens, von H. Penzl.
(Continued)

ANGLISTISCHE Studien... (Card 3)

--"The man with three staves" in the structure of "The waste land," by E. Raybould.--G.M. Hopkins, W.B. Yeats, D.H. Lawrence und die Spontaneität der Dichtung, von F. Stanzel.--Das Zeitbewusstsein der englischen Romantik, von E. Stürzl.--Das Affektleben des Wertpapiermarktes im Spiegel der englischen Sprache, von J. Wirl.--Sidney in Austria, by R.W. Zandvoort.--Verzeichnis der Publikationen von Friedrich Wild (p. 246-249).

1. Wild, Friedrich, 1888- 2. English language--Addresses, essays, lectures. I. Brunner, Karl, 1887- , ed. II. Koziol, Herbert, ed. III. Korninger, Siegfried, ed. IV. Series.

D-12
8302

The ANGLO-SAXONS; studies in some aspects of their history and culture, presented to Bruce Dickins. Edited by Peter Clemoes. London, Bowes & Bowes [1959] 322 p. illus., port., maps. 23cm.

Bibliographical footnotes.

CONTENTS.--An early Mercian boundary in Derbyshire: the place-name evidence, by K. Cameron.--Edinburgh and the Anglican occupation of Lothian, by K.H. Jackson.--The East Anglian kings of the seventh
(Continued)

NN R 3.61 e/c OC, I PC, 1, 2, I SL (LC1, X1, Z1) [I] 3

The ANGLO-SAXONS... (Card 2)

century, by F.M. Stenton.--Æthelflæd, Lady of the Mercians, by F.T. Wainwright.--The dealings of the kings of England with Northumbria in the tenth and eleventh centuries, by D. Whitelock.--A Bromfield and a Coventry writ of King Edward the Confessor, by F.E. Harmer.--Legends of England in Icelandic manuscripts, by G. Turville-Petre.--An Icelandic account of the survival of Harold Godwinson, by M. Ashdown.--Some little-known aspects of English pre-Conquest churches, by H.M. Taylor.--A group of Anglo-Saxon amulet rings, by D.M. Wilson.--The monsters and Beowulf, by N.K. Chadwick. --Two notes on the Later
(Continued)

The ANGLO-SAXONS... (Card 3)

Genesis, by J.L. Young.--The chronology of Ælfric's works, by P.A.M. Clemoes.--The development of the colloquy, by G.N. Garmonsway.--Three Old English texts in a Salisbury pontifical, Cotton Tiberius, C.I, by N.R. Ker.--The relation between the textual and the linguistic study of Old English, by G.L. Brook.--The provenance of the Vespasian psalter gloss: The linguistic evidence, by R.M. Wilson.--Two notes on some West Yorkshire place-names, by A.H. Smith.--Bruce Dickins: a biographical note and list of books and papers (p. [316]-322)

1. Dickins, Bruce, 1889- . 2. Great Britain--Hist.--Anglo-Saxon period, 449-1066. I. Clemoes, Peter, ed.

Aníbal Fernandes Tomás; "In-memoriam" organizado por Eloy do Amaral e Cardoso Martha. Lisboa: A. Tavares, 1923. 239 p. 24cm.

"Dêste In-memoriam tiraram-se apenas cento e cinquenta exemplares."
"Bio-bibliografia," p. 141–171.

Festschrift.

150582B. 1. Fernandes Thomaz, Annibal, 1849–1911. I. Amaral, Eloy do, ed. II. Cardoso Martha, Manuel, jt. ed.
N. Y. P. L. June 25, 1942

Anniversary essays in mediaeval history, by students of Charles Homer Haskins ... 1929. (Card 3)

CONTENTS—Continued.

Angevin England, by J. C. Russell.—Taxation and representation in the middle ages, by Carl Stephenson.—Knight service in Normandy, by J. R. Strayer.—"Census de rebus" in the capitularies, by C. H. Taylor.—The use of the classics in the "Flores rhetorici" of Alberic of Monte Cassino, by H. M. Willard.—William of the white hands and men of letters, by J. R. Williams.

1. Haskins, Charles Homer, 1870– 2. Middle ages—Hist. 3. History—Addresses, essays, lectures. I. Taylor, Charles Holt, ed. II. La Monte, John Life, joint ed.

30-1411

Library of Congress D113.5.A6
~~Copy 2.~~
Copyright A 16725 [5]

Anna Seghers; Briefe ihrer Freunde. [Die Ausstattung der Festschrift besorgte Karl Gossow. Die Übersetzung der Briefe oblag Rudolf Krügel et al.] Berlin, Aufbau-Verlag, 1960. 106 p. 24cm.

"Diese Briefe...wurden anlässlich des sechzigsten Geburtstages der Autorin geschrieben und...veröffentlicht."

1. Radványi, Netty (Reiling), 1900– . 2. Authors—Correspondence, reminiscences, etc. 3. Letters, German. I. Gossow, Karl, ed. II. Gossow, Karl.
NN R 9.61 OC,I,IIbo PC,1,2,3,I SL (LC1,X1,Z1)

ANNIVERSARY volume on applied mechanics, dedicated to C. B. Biezeno by some of his friends and former students on the occasion of his sixty-fifth birthday, March 2, 1953. Haarlem, H. Stam [1953] 328 p. illus., port. 25cm.

Includes bibliographies.

CONTENTS. —Biographical outline. —Publications by C. B. Biezeno. —Triangles équilatères inscrits dans une conique donnée, par Boomstra. —Sur la théorie de Sturm-Liouville, par H. Bremekamp. —The thermal theory of constant pressure deflagration, by T. von Kármán and G. Millán. —Some remarks on detonation and deflagration problems in gases, by J. M. Burgers. —Some interference problems, by C. Koning. —
(Continued)

NN ** R X 10.53 OC, 2b PC, 1, 2 SL ST, 2, 3 (LC1, Z1, X1)

Annalen der Physik und Chemie.
...Jubelband, dem Hrsg. J.C.Poggendorff zur Feier fünfzig-jährigen Wirkens gewidmet... Leipzig: J.A. Barth, 1874. xix,685 p. incl. illus., tables. front.(port.), plates. 8°.

80443A. 1.Poggendorff, Johann Christian, 1796-1877. 2.Physics.—Collected essays. 3.Chemistry—Collected essays.

1923

ANNIVERSARY volume on applied mechanics... (Card 2)

A problem suggested by Saint-Venant's Mémoire sur la torsion des prismes, by R. V. Southwell and G. Vaisey. —Nichtlineare Schwingungen mit unendlich vielen Freiheitsgraden, von R. Grammel. —The d'Alembert principle, by R. J. Legger. —Compressive buckling of sandwich plates having various edge conditions, by F. J. Plantema and W. J. van Alphen. —La stabilité d'un dicône se déplaçant sur une voie en alignement droit, par A. D. de Pater. —The local instability of compression members, built up from flat plates, by A. van der Neut. —Stresses in corrugated diaphragms, by J. A. Haringx. —Ut tensio sic vis, by A. van Wijngaarden. —Shrink-fit used to transmit a torque, by D. Dresden. —On partially plastic
(Continued)

Anniversary essays in mediaeval history, by students of Charles Homer Haskins, presented on his completion of forty years of teaching. Boston and New York, Houghton Mifflin company, 1929.

x p., 1 l., 417 p. front. (port.) 24½cm.

Half-title: Haskins anniversary essays in mediaeval history, edited by Charles H. Taylor ... associate editor, John L. La Monte ...
"Bibliography of Charles Homer Haskins, compiled by George W. Robinson": p. [389]–398.

CONTENTS.—Libraries in the twelfth century: their catalogues and contents, by J. S. Beddie.—The English manors of La Trinité at Caen, by Jean Birdsall.—The claim of King Henry I to be called learned, by
(Continued on next card)

30-1411
[5]

Mr. H. Moth.

ANNIVERSARY volume on applied mechanics... (Card 3)

thick-walled tubes, by W. T. Koiter. —Some new elements in the calculation of flat slab floors, by C. G. J. Vreedenburgh.—Statistical problems in the code of practice for steel windows, by J. P. Mazure. —The Laboratory for applied mechanics at the Technological university of Delft, by J. J. Koch. —The design of diapragms for pressure measuring devices, based on the use of wire-electrical straingauges, by R. G. Boiten.

1. Mechanics, Applied. 2. Biezeno, Cornelis Benjamin, 1888-
3. Mechanics, Applied, 1953.

Anniversary essays in mediaeval history, by students of Charles Homer Haskins ... 1929. (Card 2)

CONTENTS—Continued.

C. W. David.—The legal significance of the Statute of praemunire of 1353, by E. B. Graves.—Greek visitors to England in 1455–1456, by H. L. Gray.—The communal movement in Syria in the thirteenth century, by J. L. La Monte.—Witnesses and oath helpers in old Norwegian law, by L. M. Larson.—Clerical tenths levied in England by papal authority during the reign of Edward II, by W. E. Lunt.—The anti-foreign movement in England, 1231–1232, by Hugh MacKenzie.—Henry V's policy of conciliation in Normandy, 1417–1422, by R. A. Newhall.—The Norman communes under Richard and John, 1189–1204, by S. R. Packard.—Alexander III, the "licentia docendi", and the rise of the universities, by Gaines Post.—The canonization of opposition to the king in
(Continued on next card)

30-1411
[5]

ANSCHAUUNG und Deutung; Willy Kurth zum 80. Geburtstag. [Herausgegeben von G. Strauss] Berlin, Akademie-Verlag, 1964. vi, 219 p. plates., port. 24cm. (Studien zur Architektur- und Kunstwissenschaft, 2)

Includes bibliographies.

CONTENTS: -Anschauung und Deutung, von G. Strauss. --Weltanschauung und künstlerische Methode des Velazquez, von T. P. Snamerowskaja. --Die Gemälde des Velazquez in der Eremitage, von U. Feist. --Dichtung und bilende Kunst. Vornehmlich am Beispiel Goethes, von J. Jahn. --
(Continued)

NN * 2.66 j/B OC, I (OS)II PC, 1, 2, I, II SL A, 1, 2, I, II (LC1, X1, Z1)

ANSCHAUUNG und Deutung; (Card 2)

Philipp Otto Runge und die Gedenkenwelt der Romantik, von H.G. Franz. --Über den Realismus bei Carl Blechen, von G. Strauss--Französischer Impressionismus und Neorokoko, von P.H. Feist. --Max Slevogt und die "Zauberflöte" von W.A. Mozart, von S. Gröger. --Zum Begriff "Naturalismus" in der Bildenden Kunst - Versuch einer Klärung, von H.-C. von der Gabelentz. --Zur Methodik der Kollwitz-Forschung, von G. Feist. --Die andere Front - Reinhard Schmidhagen (1941-1945), von D. Schmidt. --Das Problem des Modernen in der Malerei, von M.S. Kagan. --Die Anfänge der Ziergewölbe in Frankreich, von K.-H. Clasen. --Einige Mitteilungen über das Leben Jean de Bodts, von

(Continued)

ANSCHAUUNG und Deutung; (Card 3)

H. Weidhaas. --Über die Restaurierung des Schlosses Peters I. "Monplaisir" in Peterhof, von A.E. Gessen und M.A. Tichomirowa. --Zur Berlin-Potsdamer Architektur unter Friedrich II, von A. Dohmann. --Die ersten Entwürfe zur Terrassenanlage und zum Schloss Sanssouci, von G. Eckardt. --Der Londoner Glaspalast von 1851, von G. Münter. --Die Maschine in der deutschen Architekturtheorie des 19. und 20. Jahrhunderts, von K. Junghanns. --Die Münzkunst unter Erzbischof Wichmann von Madgeburg (1152-1192), von A. Suhle. -- Zur Geschichte des Gleiwitzer Eisenkunstgusses, von E. Schmidt. --Willy Kurth - Grusswort eines ehemaligen Schülers, von E. Jansen.

(Continued)

ANSCHAUUNG und Deutung; (Card 4)

1. Kurth, Willy, 1881- . 2. Art--Essays and misc., I. Strauss, Gerhard, 1908- , ed. II. Series.

JFD
71-84

Ansikt til ansikt. Oslo-journalisten i 18 portrett-intervjuer. ⸢Red. av⸣ Knut Eidem, Torleiv Opstad, Haavard Haavardsholm. Oslo, Gyldendal, 1969.

164 p. ports. 22 cm.

"Oslo Journalistklubb ... 75 år."

1. Norway--Biog. 2. Biography. 3. Oslo journalistklubb.

NN*R 1.71 m/z OC PC, 1, 2, 3 SL (LC1, X1, Z1)

YAR

Anteile; Martin Heidegger zum 60. Geburtstag. Frankfurt am Main, V. Klostermann ⸢1950⸣ 284 p. 22cm.

562946B. 1. Heidegger, Martin, 1889- . 2. Philosophy, 1901- . Festschrift.
2. Philosophy—Hist.
N. Y. P. L. February 9, 1951

MTE

Anthemon; scritti di archeologia e di antichità classiche in onore di Carlo Anti. Firenze, G. C. Sansoni, 1955. xv, 376 p. illus., 51 plates, fold. map. 25cm.

"Elenco cronologico degli scritti di Carlo Anti," p. [ix]-xii.

Contents.—Arte e antichità greche: Riflessioni sull'arte greca e romana a proposito di un lavoro di Miss Gisela M. A. Richter, di A. Boethius. La

(Continued)

NN**X 9.55 f/X OC PC, 1, 2, 3 SL A, 1, 3
(SR 1, LC1, Z1, X1)

Anthemon... (Card 2)

centauromachia del vaso François, di A. Minto. Documentazione numismatica e storia Syrakousana del V secolo a.c., di S. Mazzarino.—Who made the statues of Maussolos and Artemisia? By M. Bieber. Eine apulische Amphora in Bonn, von E. Langlotz.—Arte e antichità italiche e romane: Some observations on the tomb of Lars Porsena near Clusium, by A. W. Van Buren. L'asaroton del museo di Aquileia, di G. Brusin. Architekturfragment, von

(Continued)

Anthemon... (Card 3)

L. Curtius. I porti romani dell'Istria, di A. Degrassi. Ein kleiner Beitrag zur Markus-Säule, von R. Egger. Cavalli circensi del Catajo a Vienna, di G. Q. Giglioli. Vota publica, di O. U. Bansa.—Il teatro greco e romano: Dall'Edipo re di Sofocle, di M. Valgimigli. La data di pubblicazione della syngraphè di Anassagora, di C. Diano.—Un vaso inedito di Gela, di G. Libertini. Il teatro-ninfeo detto "Sepolcro di Agrippina" a Bacoli, di A. Maiuri. Les caryatides du

(Continued)

Anthemon... (Card 4)

théâtre de Vienne et les caryatides monumentales des théâtres occidenteaux, par C. Picard. Note sugli edifici teatrali della Cirenaica, di G. Caputo. La colimbetra del teatro di Ostie, di I. Gismondi. Theatralia, di B. Pace.—Arte del tardoantico: Il castello di Mschattà in Transgiordania nell'ambito dell'"arte di potenza" tardoantice, di S. Bettini. Ultime voci della Via Altinate, di G. Fiocco.

1. Anti, Carlo, 1889- 2. Archaeology, Classical—Addresses, essays, lectures. Art, Classical—Addresses, essays, lectures.

F-11
6266

ANTHROPICA; Gedenkschrift zum 100. Geburtstag von P. Wilhelm Schmidt. Gesammelte Aufsätze hrsg. vom Anthropos-Institut. St. Augustin bei Bonn, Verlag des Anthropos-Instituts, 1968. xii, 452 p. plates, ports., maps. 30cm. (Anthropos Institut, Fribourg, Switzerland. Studia Instituti Anthropos. v. 21)

Text in German, English, French, Dutch or Portuguese. Bibliographical footnotes.

(Continued)

NN R 5.70 e/L OC, II (OS)I, III PC, 1, I, II, III SL (LC1, X1, Z1)
[1] 2

ANTHROPICA; Gedenkschrift zum 100. Geburtstag von P. Wilhelm Schmidt. (Card 2)

1. Ethnology--Essays and misc. I. Series. II. Schmidt, Wilhelm, 1868-1954. III. Anthropos Institut, Fribourg, Switzerland.

L-10
3847
v. 8

'Αντίδωρον Hugoni Henrico Paoli oblatum; miscellanea philologica. [Genova] Istituto di filologia classica, 1956. 333 p. illus., port. 23cm. (Genoa (City). Università. Istituto di filologia classica. Pubblicazioni, 8)

Bibliographical footnotes.

(Continued)

NN R 1 8.60 1/ OC, 1b (OS)I PC, 1, 2, I (LC1, X1, Z1)

3

'Αντίδωρον Hugoni Henrico Paoli oblatum... (Card 2)

CONTENTS.--Ad collegas ianuenses, di H.H. Paoli.--Ugo Enrico Paoli, di M. Bonaria.--Studi corneliani, di L. Alfonsi.--I "Myrmidones" di Accio, di G. Barabino.--Arist. Plut. 566, di Q. Cataudella.--Frammento di stoffa antica, di T. Coco.--Suspiciones II, di F. Della Corte.--Pacuviana, di P. Frassinetti.--Sobre un proyecto de transliteración del griego clásico, por M. F. Galiano.--La morte di Tito, di F. Grosso.--Plaute, Mercator, vv. 16-17, par J. Heurgon.--La poetica dei poeti lirici arcaici, di G. Lanata.--Un'in-terpretazione di Omero, di V. Longo--Sall. Bell. Iug. 93-94, di T. Mantero.-- Σῆμος in

(Continued)

'Αντίδωρον Hugoni Henrico Paoli oblatum... (Card 3)

alcuni lirici, di A. Forti Messina.--Reminiscenze pindariche in Virgilio, di C. Nardi.--L'"epostracismo" in Minucio Felice, di A. Pastorino.--Lat. nummus, di V. Pisani.--È pitagorica la concezione dell'età dell'oro? Di N. Sacerdoti. Dell'aggettivo, di G. Scarpat.--Un ragionamento di Antonius Volscus, di G. Tibiletti.--L'iscrizione metrica per Felice, di A. Traversa.--Problemi senofanei, di M. [illegible] Untersteiner.

1. Paolo, Ugo Enrico, 1884- 2. Classical studies--Collections. I. Series. i. [Title] Antidōron.

Copy only words underlined
& Classmark-- *OBKQ

Antidoron Martino David oblatum miscellanea papyrologica. Collegerunt E. Boswinkel, B. A. van Groningen, P. W. Pestman. Lugdunum Batavorum, E. J. Brill, 1968.

168 p., 12 plates (facsims., port.) 28½ cm. (Papyrologica lugdano-batava. v.17)

English, French, German or Greek.
Includes bibliographical references.

CONTENTS.—Inventar und Einkünfte eines Ägyptischen Tempels, von E. Boswinkel.—Cives Romani und κατ' οἰκίαν ἀπογραφαί, von

(Continued)

NN*Ω. 70 r/c OC, II, III (OS)I PC, 1, I, II, III O, 1, I, II, III (LC1, X1, Z1)

3

ANTIDORON Martino David oblatum miscellanea papyrologica. (Card 2)

H. Braunert.—Urkundenfragment über eine Sklavin, von H. G. Gundel.—Loan of wine, by F. Hanemaayer.—Ein christlicher Prosahymnus des 4. Jhdt.s, von L. Koenen.—Two Greek Ostraka, by N. Lewis.—Instruction to track down murderers, by M. C. E. Mineur-Van Kassen.—Les préfets d'Égypte au début du règne d'Alexandre Sévère, par J. Modrzejewski.—Egyptianism in a late Ptolemaic document, by G. Mussies.—Acknowledgement of a debt concerning replacement of bad wine, by H. van Oyen.—Prolégomènes à une étude concernant le commandant de place lagide en dehors de l'Égypte, par W.

(Continued)

ANTIDORON Martino David oblatum miscellanea papyrologica. (Card 3)

Peremans et E. van 't Dack.—Eine Demotische Doppelurkunde, von P. W. Pestman.—L'engagement contractuel, ressort dramatique, par C. Préaux.—La lettre de Dios à Eutychidès, par J. Schwartz.—Eine Ptolemäische Eheurkunde der Kölner Sammlung, von E. Seidl.—Letter to Nemesion and his sons Apion and Herakleios, by H. W. van Soest.—Angabe an einen Nyktostrategen, von P. J. Sijpesteijn.—Archelaos, von E. G. Turner.

1. Papyri, Greek. I. Series. II. David, Martin, 1898- . III. Boswinkel, Ernst, 1913- , ed.

---

*GAH

ANTIKVARBOGHANDLERFORENINGEN, Copenhagen.
Mennesker og bøger, 46 skribenter om bogens betydning i vor tilværelse. Vignetter af Axel Nygaard. Redigeret af Volmer Rosenkilde og Eddie Salicath. København, Antikvarboghandlerforeningen, 1945. 270 p. illus. 22cm.

"Antikvarboghandlerforeningens 25-aars jubilæum den 16. december 1945."

1. Books and reading. I. Rosenkilde, Volmer, ed. II. Title.

NN OC, I, II PC, 1, I SL (PRII, LC1, Z1, X1)

F-10
3127

ANTI-REVOLUTIONAIRE PARTIJ.
Bene meritus, bundel opstellen uit dankbaarheid opgedragen aan Doctor Johannes Schouten, ere-voorzitter van de Anti-revolutionaire partij, ter gelegenheid van zijn vijf en zeventigste verjaardag. Kampen, J. H. Kok, 1958. 208 p. 26cm.

CONTENTS.—Bene meritus, door W. P. Berghuis.—De Anti-revolutionaire partij als christelijk-nationale partij, door J. A. H. S. Bruins Slot.—Verstarde beginselen in een veranderde wereld? Door W. P. Berghuis.—

(Continued)

NN R 3. 59 a/ (OC)I OS PC, 1, 2, I SL E, 1, 2, I (LC1, X1, Z1)

ANTI-REVOLUTIONAIRE PARTIJ. Bene meritus... (Card 2)

Reformatorische politiek in de lijn der historie, door J. Severijn.—De Anti-revolutionaire partij als politieke gestalte der gereformeerde gezindte, door C. J. Verplanke.—Kerk en politiek, door S. U. Zuidema.—Cultuur en politiek, door S. van Tuinen.—De school in de toekomst, door H. Algra.—Naar een verantwoordelijke maatschappij, door M. Ruppert.—Welvaartseconomie en welvaartspolitiek, door T. P. van der Kooy.—Europese economische integratie, door C. P. Hazenbosch.—De Verenigde naties: rechtsinstituut of politiek instrument? Door W. F. de Gaay Fortman.—Joahnnes Schouten 1883—

(Continued)

ANTI-REVOLUTIONAIRE PARTIJ. Bene meritus...
(Card 3)

12. aug. —1958, door K. Goren. —Kwartierstaat van Dr. Johannes Schouten, door D. van Baalen. —Afscheidsrede in de Deputatenvergadering van 22 juni 1955, door J. Schouten.

1. Schouten, Joannes, 1883- . 2. Christianity--Influence, Political and social--Netherlands. I. Title.

MW p.v.268

"APOLLO" KINO- UND THEATER-GES. M.B.H., Vienna.
Festschrift der Apollo Kino- und Theater-Ges. m. b. H. Hrsg, anlässlich des 50 jährigen Bestandes des "Apollo"- Theaters und zugleich des 25 jährigen Bestehens dieses Hauses als Film-Premieren-theater. Wien, 1954. 32 p. (p. 25-32 advertisements) illus., ports. 30cm.

CONTENTS.—Fünfzig Jahre "Apollo," ein Rückblick,
(Continued)

NN**R 2.58 l/ OS(lb+) PC,1 SL (T2,LC1,X1,Z1)

VBA p.v.1719

ANTONIO ZECCHETTIN DI CASTELLEONE. [Edito per volontà del "Consorzio di bonifica de Ariano" è stato curato dal giornalista Pino Bellinetti] [Padova? 1952] 42 p. illus. 25cm.

At head of title: Pionieri e bonificatori del Delta Padano.
Speeches, etc., in honor of A. Zecchettin di Castellone.

1. ZECCHETTIN DI CASTELLEONE, ANTONIO, 1858-1927
I. Bellinetti, Pino, ed. II. Consorzio di bonifica de Ariano
III. Bellinetti, Pino

NN**R X 12.57 v/ OC(1b) I, IIIbo (OS)II, IIb PC, 1, I, II SL ST, 1, I, II (Z1, LC1, X1)

"APOLLO" KINO- UND THEATER-GES. M.B.H., Vienna.
Festschrift der Apollo Kino- und Theater-Ges. m. b.H. (Card 2)

von J. Zak.--Ein grosser Mann und seine kleinen Schwächen; Erinnerungen an Ben Tieber, von R. Oesterreicher.--Aus dem Programm des "Apollo"-Theaters in der Jubiläumsspielzeit 1954/55.

1. Theatres--Austria--Vienna.
NN**R 2.58 l/ OS(lb+) PC,1 SL (T2,LC1,X1,Z1)

---

*QYN

Antons Benjamiņš, dzīvē un darbā; rakstu krājums, veltīts 75 g. šūpļa svētkos 1935. g. 13. jūlijā. Līgotņu Jēkaba [pseud.] redakcijā. Rigā: "Jaunāko ziņu," 1935. 248 p. facsim., illus., 2 col'd ports. (incl. front.) 27cm.

835038A. 1. Benjamiņš, Antons, 1860- . I. Roze, Jēkabs, 1874- , ed.
N. Y. P. L. August 24, 1936

WCL

Arbeiten über Tropenkrankheiten und deren Grenzgebiete. Bernhard Nocht zu seinem 70. Geburtstag von Freunden und Schülern gewidmet... Hamburg: L. Friederichsen & Co., 1927. x, 643 p. incl. tables. diagrs., map, port., plates (1 col'd). 4°. (Hamburg. Universitaet. Abhandl. aus dem Gebiet der Auslandskunde. Bd. 26.)

Contains bibliographies.

445695A. 1. Tropics—Diseases and hygiene. 2. Nocht, Albrecht Eduard Bernhard, 1857- . 3. Ser.
N. Y. P. L. December 27, 1929

YED

Applications of psychology; essays to honor Walter V. Bingham. Ed. by L. L. Thurstone... New York, Harper & bros. [1952] x, 209 p. 22cm.

Bibliographies included.
CONTENTS.—A look across the years, 1920 to 1950, by L. W. Ferguson.—Creative talent, by L. L. Thurstone.—Application of psychological principles and procedures to the military problem, by J. C. Flanagan.—Use of attitude surveys in personnel practice, by B. V. Moore.—Validation of measures of interests and temperament, by J. P. Guilford.—Should this student be at Harvard? By F. L. Wells.—Twenty-year follow-up of medical interests, by E. K. Strong, jr.—A tool for selection that has stood
(Continued)

NN* R 1.53 OC, I PC, 1, 2, I SL (LC1, Z1, X1)

NFD
(Panzer)

Arbeiten zur Volkskunde und zur deutschen Dichtung; Festgabe für Friedrich Panzer zum 60. Geburtstag... Unter Mitwirkung von Hans Teske herausgegeben von Eugen Fehrle. Bühl: Konkordia A. G., 1930. 96 p. front. (port.) 8°.

526711A. 1. Folk lore. I. Panzer, Friedrich, 1870- . II. Fehrle, Eugen, 1880- , editor. III. Teske, Hans, jt. editor.
N. Y. P. L. July 1, 1931

Applications of psychology... [1952] (Card 2)

the test of time, by M. A. Bills.—Identification and selection of teachers, by E. A. Lee.—Professional use of the clinical method in employee selection, by G. U. Cleeton.—A national scholarship program; methods, problems, results, by J. M. Stalnaker.

1. Psychology, Applied. 2. Bingham, Walter Van Dyke, 1880- . I. Thurstone, Louis Leon, 1887- , ed.

OAB

ARBEITSGEMEINSCHAFT FÜR FORSCHUNG DES LANDES NORDRHEIN-WESTFALEN.
Festschrift der Arbeitsgemeinschaft für Forschung des Landes Nordrhein-Westfalen zu Ehren des Herrn Ministerpräsidenten Karl Arnold anlässlich des fünfjährigen Bestehens der Arbeitsgemeinschaft für Forschung am 4. Mai 1955. Köln, Westdeutscher Verlag [1955] xii, 680 p. illus. 25cm.
(Continued)

NN**R 2.56 f/ (OC) I, II OS (lb) PC, 1, 2, I, II SL E, 3, I, II ST, 1t, 2t, I, II (LC1, X1, Z1)

ARBEITSGEMEINSCHAFT FÜR FORSCHUNG DES LANDES NORDRHEIN-WESTFALEN. Festschrift der Arbeitsgemeinschaft für Forschung des Landes Nordrhein-Westfalen... (Card 2)

On cover and spine: Karl Arnold Festschrift.
Includes bibliographies.
1. Research—Germany—North Rhine-Westphalia. 2. Science—Research—Germany—North Rhine-Westphalia. 3. Social sciences—Research—Germany—North Rhine-Westphalia. I. Title. II. Title: Karl Arnold Festschrift. t. 1955.

Copy only words underlined
& Classmark-- TB

ARBEITSGEMEINSCHAFT PLANUNGSRECHNUNG. Unternehmensplanung als Instrument der Unternehmensführung. Wiesbaden, T. Gabler [1965] 156 p. port. 24cm. (Arbeitsgemeinschaft Planungsrechnung. Schriftenreihe der AGPLAN. Bd. 9)

"Festgabe" for Josef Fuchs.
Bibliographical footnotes.
CONTENTS.--Ursprung und Ziele der AGPLAN, von J. D. Auffermann.
(Continued)
NN 7.66 p/c (OC)3b+ OS, I PC, 1, 2, 3, I E, 1, 2, 3, I (LC1, X1, Z1)

D-15
5475

ARBEITSGEMEINSCHAFT DER HOCHSCHULLEHRER FÜR WIRTSCHAFTSPÄDAGOGIK. Gedanken zur Wirtschaftspädagogik; Festschrift für Friedrich Schlieper zum 65. Geburtstag am 5. März 1962. Im Auftrage der Arbeitsgemeinschaft der Hochschullehrer für Wirtschaftspädagogik, hrsg. von Karl Abraham. Freiburg i. Br., Lambertus-Verlag [1962] 194 p. mounted port. 23cm.

Includes bibliographies.
(Continued)
NN R 10.64 j/b (OC)I, IIb* OS (1b+) PC, 1, 2, 3, I SL E, 1, 2, 3, I ST, 2t, I (LC1, X1, Z1)

ARBEITSGEMEINSCHAFT PLANUNGSRECHNUNG. Unternehmensplanung als Instrument der Unternehmensführung. (Card 2)

--Wesen, Objekt und Vollzug der Unternehmensplanung, von E. Grochla.--Ziele und Aufgaben der Unternehmensplanung aus der Sicht des Unternehmers, von C. Becker.--Zusammenhang von Unternehmenspolitik und Unternehmensplanung, von K. Lotz.--Möglichkeiten der Unternehmensplanung in Mittel- und Klein-betrieben, von R. Baudisch.--Unternehmungsplanung und Unternehmungsorganisation, von A. Meier.--Planungsrechnung und Entscheidungsmodelle des Operations Research, von W. Kilger.--Planung und Kontrolle des Erfolges im System einer geschlossenen Planungsrechnung.
(Continued)

ARBEITSGEMEINSCHAFT DER HOCHSCHULLEHRER FÜR WIRTSCHAFTS PÄDAGOGIK. Gedanken zur Wirtschaftspädagogik... (Card 2)

CONTENTS.--Die gegenwärtige Kultursituation und die Wirtschaftspädagogik, von K. Abraham.--Der Einfluss der Wirtschaftspädagogik auf die praktische Berufserziehung, von H.-J. von Worgitzky.--Der Zusammenhang von Wirtschaft und Erziehung zur Zeit des Merkantilismus, von F. Urbschat.--Berufspädagogik-Sozialpädagogik-Wirtschaftspädagogik, von J. Baumgardt.--Wirtschaftswissenschaft und Wirtschaftspädagogik, von A. Dörschel.--Probleme zwischen der Wirtschafts- und Sozialpädagogik und der Wirtschafts- und Sozial-
(Continued)

ARBEITSGEMEINSCHAFT PLANUNGSRECHNUNG. Unternehmensplanung als Instrument der Unternehmensführung. (Card 3)

von K. Schwantag.--Plankostenrechnung, Budgetierung, Unternehmensplanung, von P. Kreuzer.--Investitions- und Finanzplanung, von K. Siebert.--Managementplanung und Investition, von H. Wilde.--Krisenplanung von K. Bender --Die Bedeutung der Unternehmungsspiele für die Unternehmensplanung, von K. Hax.--Unternehmensplanung und zwischenbetriebliche Kooperation, von H. Rühle von Lilienstern.--Vergleichende Betrachtung der Planungssystematik in der öffentlichen Verwaltung und der Erwerbswirtschaft, von R. K. J. Badenhoop.
1. Management planning. 2. Accounting and bookkeeping. Cost. 3. Fuchs, Josef, 1905- I. Series

---

ARBEITSGEMEINSCHAFT DER HOCHSCHULLEHRER FÜR WIRTSCHAFTSPÄDAGOGIK. Gedanken zur Wirtschaftspädagogik... (Card 3)

andragogik, von C. Herzog.--Gedanken zur wissenschaftstheoretischen Grundlegung der Wirtschafts- und Berufspädagogik von der philosophischen Anthropologie her, von L. Kiehn.--Die Bedeutung der Wirtschaftspädagogik in der Erziehungspraxis der Gegenwart, von H. Krasensky.--Über berufsfördernde Erwachsenenbildung, von W. Löbner.--Entwicklungsphasen des Berufserziehungswesens in der Sowjetunion, von W. Stratenwerth.--Bibliographie Friedrich Schlieper.
(Continued)

---

*MFBR
(Germany)

ARBEITSGEMEINSCHAFT FÜR RHEINISCHE MUSIKGESCHICHTE. Studien zur Musikgeschichte des Rheinlandes II; Karl Gustav Fellerer zum 60. Geburtstag überreicht. Hrsg. von Herbert Drux, Klaus Wolfgang Niemöller und Walter Thoene. Köln, A. Volk, 1962. vi, 307 p. illus., music. 21cm. (Beiträge zur rheinischen Musikgeschichte. Heft 52)
1. Fellerer, Karl Gustav, 1902- . 2. Music--Germany--Rhine Province. 3. Germany--Rhine Province. I. Series. II. Drux, Herbert, ed. III. Title.
NN X 3.64 f/4 (OC)II OS, I PC, 1, 2, I, II, III SL MU, 1, 3, I, II, III (LC1, X1, Z1) [I]

ARBEITSGEMEINSCHAFT DER HOCHSCHULLEHRER FÜR WIRTSCHAFTS PÄDAGOGIK. Gedanken zur Wirtschaftspädagogik... (Card 4)

1. Commerce--Education. 2. Education, Industrial and technical. 3. Schlieper, Friedrich, 1897- . I. Abraham, Karl, 1904- , ed. II. Abraham, Karl, 1904- t. 1962.

SST

Arbetarnas bildningsförbund. En bok till Gunnar Hirdman. Stockholm, Arbetarnas bildningsförbund [1948] 157 p. illus. 23cm.

496408B. 1. Hirdman, Gunnar, 1888- 2. Working class—Education—Sweden. I. Title.
N. Y. P. L. June 19, 1950

*OAL
Archaeologica orientalia in memoriam Ernst Herzfeld. George C. Miles, ed. Editorial advisory committee René Dussaud...[and others] Locust Valley, N. Y., J. J. Augustin, 1952. 280 p. front., illus.,maps,36 pl. 29cm.

"Additions to the bibliography of Ernst Herzfeld," p. 279-280.

1. Herzfeld, Ernst Emil, 1879-1948. 2. Oriental studies. I. Miles, George Carpenter, 1904- , ed.
NN R 11.52 OC,I PC,1,2, I SL O,1,2,I (LC1,Z1,X1)

*PEB
Archäologie und Altes Testament. Festschrift f. Kurt Galling z. 8. Jan. 1970. Hrsg. von Arnulf Kuschke u. Ernst Kutsch. Tübingen, Mohr <Siebeck> 1970.
368 p. with illus., map., front. 24 cm.
German, English or French.
Includes bibliographical references, and a bibliography of K. Galling's works: p. [333]-347.
(Continued)
NN*R 4.71 d/L OC. I, II, III PC, 1, 2, I, II, III SL J, 1, 2, I, II, III (LC1, X1, Z1)
2

ARCHÄOLOGIE und Altes Testament. (Card 2)

1. Bible. O.T.--Archaeology. 2. Galling, Kurt, 1900- --Bibl. I. Galling, Kurt, 1900- . II. Kuschke, Arnulf, 1912- , ed. III. Kutsch, Ernst, ed.

MTI
+
Archaeologisches Institut des deutschen Reiches. Römisch-Germanische Kommission.
Fuenfundzwanzig Jahre Römisch-Germanische Kommission; zur Erinnerung an die Feier des 9.–11. Dezember 1927. Herausgegeben von der Römisch-Germanischen Kommission des Archäologischen Institut des deutschen Reiches... Berlin: W. de Gruyter & Co., 1930. ix, 113 p. front., illus. (incl. maps, plans), plates.

501655A. 1. Archaeology, Classical.
N. Y. P. L. January 6, 1931

AN
(Henderson, A.)
ARCHIBALD HENDERSON, the New Crichton; a composite portrait: authorized. Edited by Samuel Stevens Hood. New York, Beechhurst press [c1949] xviii, 252 p. ports., facsims. 22cm.

"Five hundred numbered copies." No. 110.
Bibliography of Archibald Henderson's writings," p. [219]-252.

1. Henderson, Archibald, 1877- . I. Hood, Samuel Stevens, ed. II. Hood, Samuel Stevens.
NN*R X 11.54 gk OC, I, IIbo PC, 1, I SL AH, 1, I ST, 1 (T3, Z1, LC1, X1)

TB
ARCHITECTS and craftsmen in history; Festschrift für Abbott Payson Usher. Tübingen, J. C. B. Mohr, 1956. xiii, 172 p. 24cm. (Friedrich List-Gesellschaft. Veröffentlichungen. [Neue Series] Bd. 2. [Reihe A: Historica])

In English.
Bibliographical references.
(Continued)
NN R X 12.59 l/ OC (OS)I PC, 1, 2, 3, 4, I SL E, 1, 3, 4, I (LC1, X1, Z1) [I]

ARCHITECTS and craftsmen in history... (Card 2)

CONTENTS.--Bibliography of Abbott Payson Usher (p.[x]-xiii)--Some heirs of Gustav von Schmoller, by F.C. Lane.--Sombart and the German approach, by E. Salin.--Michael I. Rostovtzeff, by C.B. Welles.--Marc Bloch, by L. Febvre.--Henri Pirenne, by C. Verlinden.--Henri Sée, by M.M. Knight.--Eli F. Heckscher, by A. Montgomery.--John H. Clapham, by W.H.B. Court.--Abbott Payson Usher, by W.N. Parker.

1. Economic history--Historiography. 2. Historians. 3. Usher, Abbott Payson, 1883- . 4. Economists. I. Series: Friedrich List-Gesellschaft. Veröffentlichungen. [Neue Serie] Bd. 2.

MQZ
+
(Korn)
ARCHITECTURAL ASSOCIATION, London.
Planning and architecture; essays presented to Arthur Korn by the Architectural Association. Edited by Dennis Sharp. [Contributors]: Walter Bor [and others] New York, George Wittenborn [1967] 169 p. illus.,plans.,ports. 31cm.

(Continued)
NN R 5.68 e/R(OC)I,Ibo II,III,IVbo OS PC,1,2, 3,I,II,III SL A,1,2,I, II,III E,1,3,I,II,III, ST,1,I,II,III (LC1,X1, Z1)
4

ARCHITECTURAL ASSOCIATION, London. Planning and architecture... (Card 2)

CONTENTS.--A question of urban identity, by W. Bor.--Density and traffic, by L. Hilberseimer.--On bird-and building-watchers by W. Holford.--The architect and regional planning, by L. Ginsburg.--Kranichstein New Town, by E. May.--Patrick Geddes, the Valley Section, by J. Tyrwhitt.--Urban form, by A. Ling.--Connell, Ward and Lucas, by B. Ward.--Le Corbusier and the coming generation, by S. Giedion.--The basic problem, by P. Oliver.--The
(Continued)

ARCHITECTURAL ASSOCIATION, London. Planning and architecture... (Card 3)

sensation of space, by E. Goldfinger.--Architecture in England in the 1930's by J. Pritchard.--Arthur Korn: man and teacher, by H. Morris and A. Derbyshire.--Arthur Korn and the English MARS Group, by M. Fry.--Arthur Korn: planner, by P. Johnson-Marshall--'Glas im Bau'-a prophetic book, by R. McGrath.--My recollections of Arthur Korn, Berlin, 1923-4, by R. Steiger.--Analytical and Utopian architecture, by A. Korn.--Extract from a letter to the Executive Committee of the MARS
(Continued)

ARCHITECTURAL ASSOCIATION, London. Planning and architecture... (Card 4)

Group.—The MARS plan.—Chronology of events and designs.—Writings by Arthur Korn.

1. Korn, Arthur. 2. Architecture, 20th cent. 3. Cities—Plans. I. Bor, Walter. II. Sharp, Dennis, ed. III. Title. IV. Sharp, Dennis.

E-10
7650

ARCHIVALIA et historia; Arbeiten aus dem Gebiet der Geschichte und des Archivwesens [Festschrift für Prof. Dr. Anton Largiadèr überreicht zum 65. Geburtstage am 17. Mai 1958 von Freunden, Kollegen und Schülern. Herausgeber: Dietrich Schwarz, Werner Schnyder] Zürich, Verlag Berichthaus, 1958. xxi, 353 p. illus., port., facsim. 25cm.

(Continued)

NN R 6. 59 m/$^{\rho}$OC, I, II PC, 1, 2, 3, 4, I, II SL E, 2, 4, I, II (LC1, X1) (Z/1)

ARCHIVALIA et historia... (Card 2)

Bibliographical footnotes.

CONTENTS. --Zur Frage der Wirtschafts- und Kulturarchive, von H. Nabholz. --Archiv und Rechtsgeschichte, von K. S. Bader. --Das altbernische Kanzleiarchiv und seine Zürichbücher, von R. von Fischer. --Das Bischöfliche Archiv Chur, von B. Hübscher. --Das Rheinauer Archiv in Einsiedeln, von R. Henggeler. --Paul Schweizers Gutachten und Archivplan des Jahres 1880 für das Staatsarchiv des Kantons Graubünden,

(Continued)

ARCHIVALIA et historia... (Card 3)

von R. Jenny. --Die Erschliessung des Kantonsarchivs Zug, von E. Zumbach. --Aufbau und Aufgaben des Stadtarchivs Zürich, von H. Waser. --Das Tschudische Familienarchiv, von J. Winteler. --Die Schicksale der Zürcher Zunftarchive, von W. Schnyder. --Abt Plazidus Tanner und das Stiftsarchiv Engelberg, von P. Gall Heer. --Bemerkungen zur Urkunde Kaiser Friedrichs I. für das Domkapitel von Citta di Castello von 1163 Nov. 6 (St. 3988a), von L. Santifaller. --Über eine landenbergische Gült auf dem Kirchensatz und Zehnten von Ulster, von A. Bauhofer. --Das

(Continued)

ARCHIVALIA et historia... (Card 4)

Schatzverzeichnis des Grossmünsters in Zürich aus dem Jahre 1333, von D. Schwarz. --Zu den althochdeutschen Sachwörtern in den lateinischen Urkunden der Schweiz, von S. Sonderegger. --Der Empfang des Königs im mittelalterlichen Zürich, von H. C. Peyer. --Zum Problem der Rechtfertigung der Eidgenössischen Befreiungstradition bei Ägidius Tschudi von M. Beck. --Die Frage der Kontinuität des Nikolausbrauches im nachreformatorischen Zürich, von R. Weiss. --Winterthurer Rechtsverhältnisse vor 1798, bon W. Ganz. --Die grossen italienischen Quellenpublika-

(Continued)

ARCHIVALIA et historia... (Card 5)

tionen des 18. und 19. Jahrhunderts und ihre Auswirkungen auf das Risorgimento, von E. Ulsteri. --Documents concernant la Suisse aux Archives nationales à Paris, par L. Junod. --Die Voraussetzungen des geschichtlichen Verständnisses Bismarcks, von L. von Muralt.

1. Largiadèr, Anton, 1893- . 2. Archives--Switzerland. 3. Switzerland --Hist. --Sources--Bibl. 4. Archives--Europe. I. Schwarz, Dietrich Wallo Hermann, 1913- , ed. II. Schnyder, Werner, 1899- ed.

NNR 6. 59 m/ OC, I, II PC, 1, 2, 3, 4, I, II SL E, 2, 4, I, II (LC1, X1, Z1)

---

*SAD

Archivstudien zum siebzigsten geburtstage von Woldemar Lippert; mit unterstützung der Wilhelm und Bertha v. Baensch stiftung hrsg. von Hans Beschorner. Mit einem bildnis und sechs abbildungen. Dresden, Buchdruckerei der Wilhelm und Bertha v. Baensch stiftung, 1931.

xi, 265, [1] p. front. (port.) plates. 25cm.

CONTENTS—Arras, P. Das stadtarchiv zu Bautzen.—Bässler, G. Die kriegstagebücher als geschichtlicher quellenstoff.—Beschorner, H. Risse und karten in den archiven.—Bittner, L. Zur neuorganisation des österreichischen archivwesens.—Boer, E. Der stadtschreiber Michael Weisse (1549–1566) und seine bedeutung für das Dresdner ratsarchiv.—Brabant, A. Das sächsische kriegsarchiv und seine neuordnung.—Bretholz, B. Fremde archivalien in archiven.—Butte, H. Archive und familienforschung.—Dersch, W. Die Meininger wachstafeln.—Engel, W.

(Continued on next card)

32-21339

[2]

Festschrift.

Archivstudien zum siebzigsten geburtstage von Woldemar Lippert ... 1931. (Card 2)

CONTENTS—Continued.

Territorialänderung und archivalienfolge.—Friedensburg, W. Die entstehung des staatsarchivs für die provinz Sachsen in Magdeburg.—Glasmeier, H. Die in den deutschen archiven verwendeten methoden zur aufbewahrung von urkunden.—Gröger, H. Neuzeitliche aufgaben grösserer stadtarchive.—Jecht, R. Der jahresanfang in der Görlitzer kanzlei bis 1550.—Kaiser, H. Das provenienzprinzip im französischen archivwesen.—Kretzschmar, H. Zentralismus oder regionalismus im sächsischen archivwesen.—Möllenberg, W. Die kursächsischen archivalien der preussischen staatsarchive.—Müller, G. H. Das massenproblem in den stadtarchiven.—Müsebeck, E. Grundsätzliches zur kassation moderner aktenbestände.—Naumann, R. Woldemar Lipperts schrifttum.—Oberdorffer, K. Aus dem archivwesen der sudetendeutschen

(Continued on next card)

32-21339

[2]

Archivstudien zum siebzigsten geburtstage von Woldemar Lippert ... 1931. (Card 3)

CONTENTS—Continued.

städte: Die archivlehrgänge.—Pietsch, E. Aus der praxis eines sächsischen stadtarchivars.—Redlich, O. R. Die fürsorge für nichtstaatliche archive und die archivberatungsstelle der Rheinprovinz.—Ruppersberg, O. Frankfurt und das archiv des Reichskammergerichts.—Schmidt-Ewald, W. Die drei kursächsischen archive zu Wittenberg.—Schultze, J. Gedanken zum "provenienzgrundsatze".—Tille, A. Soll das archiv gegenwartsstoff sammeln?—Tschirch, P. Das fragment aus dem XII. buche des Polybius. Eine Dresdener flugschrift aus der grossen krisis des jahres 1805.—Voges, H. Sollen die kirchenbücher in den archiven aufbewahrt werden?

1. Archives. 2. Archives—Germany. 3. Lippert, Woldemar, 1861– I. Beschorner, Hans Oskar, 1872– ed.

32-21339

Library of Congress CD931.A7

[2] 943.004

3-MAS

ARGO; Festschrift für Kurt Badt zu seinem 80. Geburtstag am 3. März 1970. Hrsg. Martin Gosebruch und Lorenz Dittmann. [Köln] M. DuMont Schauberg [1970] 536 p. 80 plates (138 figs.) ports. 25cm.

"Schriften Kurt Badts": p. 440-441.

1. Badt, Kurt, 1890- 2. Badt, Kurt, 1890- --Bibl. 3. Art--Essays and misc. I. Gosebruch, Martin, ed. II. Dittmann, Lorenz, ed. III. Title: Festschrift für Kurt Badt.

NN R 2. 72 e/$_{\Delta}$OC, I, II, III PC, 1, 2, 3, I, II, III SL A, 1, 2, 3, I, II, III (LC1, X1, Z1) [I]

3-MAS

ARKÆOLOGISKE og kunsthistoriske afhandlinger, tilegnede Frederik Poulsen, 7.3. 1941. [Redaktion: Ejnar Dyggve, Otto Koefoed-Petersen, Vagn Häger Poulsen, Haavard Rostrup. København, Gyldendalske boghandel, 1941. 126 p. plates(1 col.), ports, maps, plans. 30cm.

Includes bibliographical references.

(Continued)

NN S 3.67 l/ OC, I PC, 1, 2, I SL A, 1, 2, I (LC1, X1, Z1) 3

ARKÆOLOGISKE og kunsthistoriske afhandlinger... (Card 2)

CONTENTS.--De danske udgravninger i Lindos, af C. Blinkenberg.--Om den skopasiske stil, af P.J. Riis.--En landvinding, af O. Jørgensen.--Acheron og Styx, af P. Fossing.--En koptisk gravsten i Ny Carlsberg Glyptotek, af O. Koefoed-Petersen.--Impressionist-problemer, af H. Rostrup.--To lutroforer i antiksamlingen, af K.F. Johansen.--To alexandrinske hoveder, af N. Breitenstein.--Dodonæiske problemer, af E. Dyggve.--Et attisk skulpturfragment fra Fidias' tid, af V.H.

(Continued)

ARKÆOLOGISKE og kunsthistoriske afhandlinger... (Card 3)

Poulsen.--Portrætbuster af H.V. Bissen fra hans første ophold i Rom, af V. Thorlacius-Ussing.

1. Poulsen, Frederik, 1876-1950. 2. Art, Ancient--Essays and misc. I. Dyggve, Ejnar, 1887-1961, ed.

D-19
6002

ARISTE, PAUL, 1905-
Sõna sõna kõrvale; Paul Ariste teaduslikust tegevusest. Tallinn, 1965. 126 p. illus., port. 23cm. (Emakeele selts. Toimetised. [6])

Festschrift.
List of works, p. 23-60.

1. Esthonian language. I. Series.
NN R 12.69 v/l OC (OS)I PC, 1, I (LC1, X1, Z1)

YAR

Aristotelian Society for the Systematic Study of Philosophy, *London.*
Philosophical studies; essays in memory of L. Susan Stebbing. ⌊Written by friends and colleagues of Professor L. Susan Stebbing in the Aristotelian Society⌋ London, G. Allen & Unwin ⌊1948⌋

vii, 156 p. port. 22 cm.

CONTENTS.—Susan Stebbing, 1885–1943; an appreciation by J. Wisdom.—Moral ends and means, by H. B. Acton.—Reflections occasioned by ideals and illusions, by J. Laird.—The way of behaviour, by Beatrice Edgell.—Is there reason in history? By H. D. Oakeley.—The logic of elucidation, by C. A. Mace.—Philosophical analysis, by

(Continued on next card)
49–20171*

⌊1⌋

Aristotelian Society for the Systematic Study of Philosophy, *London.* Philosophical studies ... ⌊1948⌋ (Card 2)

CONTENTS—Continued.

A. C. Ewing.—The concert ticket, by Austin Duncan-Jones.—Logic and semantics, by Max Black.—The grounds of induction in Professor Whitehead's philosophy of nature, by R. L. Saw.—Epistemology and the ego-centric predicament, by L. J. Russell.—Susan Stebbing: Publications (p. 155–156)

1. Philosophy—Addresses, essays, lectures. 2. Stebbing, Lizzie Susan, 1885–1943. I. Title.

B21.S7 104 49—20171*

Library of Congress ⌊49b2⌋

E-13
6632

Arnold, Heinz Ludwig, ed.
Wandlung und Wiederkehr; Festschrift zum 70. Geburtstag Ernst Jüngers. Aachen, Verlag Text+Kritik ⌊1965⌋

245 p. port. 24 cm.

Includes bibliographical references.

CONTENTS.—Wandlung und Wiederkehr, von H. L. Arnold.—Rückzug des Geistes, von G. Hemmerich.—Lettre à Ernst Jünger. Ein

(Continued)

NN* 10.69 r/l OC, I PC, 1, 2, I, II SL (LC1, X1, Z1) 2

Arnold, Heinz Ludwig, ed. Wandlung und Wiederkehr ... ⌊1965⌋ (Card 2)

Gerechter, Stück in einem Akt. Nachwort zum Stück. Von G. Marcel.—Gedichte. Adam von Trott zu Solz. Von M. von Katte.—Hesiod: Der Mythos von den Zeitaltern, von A. von Schirnding.—Magischer Realismus, von V. Katzmann.—Der Arbeiter: Typus, Name, Gestalt, von S. Bein.—Ernst Jüngers Wende, von H. Plard.—Ernst Jüngers Rechtsentwurf zum Weltstaat, von R. Marcic.—Ein Mantrana zur Metaphysik Ernst Jüngers, von R. Immig.—Was wird aus dem Menschen? Aspekte der utopischen Romans. Von K. L. Tank.—Der Intellektuelle und die Politik, von R. Schroers.

1. Jünger, Ernst, 1895– 2. Literature—Addresses, essays, lectures. I. Jünger, Ernst, 1895– II. Title.

Copy only words underlined & classmark-- RNB

ARNOLD, ROLAND.
Bibliographie der Veröffentlichungen von S.B. Liljegren, anlässlich seines 70. Geburtstages am 8. Mai 1955 zusammengestellt; mit einem Portrait des Gelehrten von Magda Boalt-Liljegren, einer Einführung von F. Schubel, und drei Aufsätzen von S.B. Liljegren. Uppsala, Lundequistska bokhandeln; Cambridge, Harvard university press [1956] xxviii, 63 p. port. 25cm. (Upsala, Sweden. Universitet. Engelska seminariet. Essays and studies on English language and literature. 16)

(Continued)

NN 10.64 e/B OC(1bo)II (OS)I PC, 1, I, II (LC1, X1, Z1) 2

ARNOLD, ROLAND. Bibliographie der Veröffentlichungen von S.B. Liljegren... (Card 2)

1. Liljegren, Sten Bodvar, 1885- --Bibl. I. Series. II. Liljegren, Sten Bodvar, 1885- .

MQZ
(Arneberg)

ARNSTEIN ARNEBERG, 1882-6 juli-1952. [Illus. er utført av Arnstein Arneberg] Oslo, Gyldendal, 1952. 175 p. illus., col. front., port. 27cm.

CONTENTS.—Bare om løst og fast, av A. Rolfsen.—En generasjon og en vennehilsen, av H. Fett.—Til Arnstein, av M. Poulsson.—Episoder med Arnstein Arneberg, av H. Sørensen.—Utførbe byggverk.

I. Arneberg, Arnstein Rynning, 1882-

NN**R 6.53 OC,I PC,I SL A,I (LC1, Z1, X1)

MA

ARTE in Europa; scritti di storia dell'arte in onore di Edoardo Arslan [di Giulio Carlo Argan et al. Milano, Tip. Artipo, 1966. 2 v. illus., plans, plates, port. 25cm.

"Premessa" signed: Guido Mansuelli [and others].
Vol. 2 consists of plates.
"Bibliographia di Edoardo Arslan": p. 963-970.

1. Arslan, Edoardo. 2. Arslan, Edoardo--Bibl. 3. Art--Essays and misc. I. Argan, Giulio Carlo. II. Mansuelli, Guido Achille, ed.

NN R 6.69 v/L OC, I, II PC, 1, 2, 3, I, II SL A, 1, 2, 3, I, II (LC1, X1, Z1) [I]

Copy only words underlined & classmark— 3-MAA +

Arte veneta.
[Volume] dedicata al 70° compleanno di Giuseppe Fiocco. Venezia, 1954. 347 p. illus. (part col.) 32cm. (Annata 8)

Contributions in Italian, English, French or German.
Contents.—Per Giuseppe Fiocco, di R. Pallucchini.— (Continued)

NN R 8.55 j/3 OT (PC) 1,2,3,4 (A)1,2,3,4 (LC5, X1, Z1)

Copy only words underlined & classmark— 3-MAA +

Arte veneta. (Card 2)

Elenco delle pubblicazioni di Giuseppe Fiocco, a cura di C. Semenzato.—La tomba del Doge Marino Morosini nell'atrio di San Marco, di C. Anti.—I mosaici dell'atrio di San Marco e il loro seguito, di S. Bettini.—Capitelli veneziani del XII e XIII secolo, di G Mariacher.—Antico portale di Santa Giustina di Padova, di G. Nicco Fasola.--Intorno a qualche scultura romanica nel Veneto, di L. Coletti.—Maestro Paolo e la (Continued)

Copy only words underlined & classmark— 3-MAA +

Arte veneta. (Card 3)

pittura veneziana del suo tempo, di V. Lasareff.—Un'altra Madonna di Paolo Veneziano, di S. Moschini Marconi.—Due ritratti smarriti di Pisanello, di L. Venturi.—Di una pubblicazione su Pisanello e di altri fatti, di B. Degenhart.—La mosaïque à Venise et à Florence au XVe siècle par A. Chastel.—Aspetti della cultura figurativa di Padova e di Ferrara nella miniatura del primo rinascimento, di M. Salmi.—Un'opera poco nota (Continued)

Copy only words underlined & classmark— 3-MAA +

Arte veneta. (Card 4)

di Francesco Laurana, di S. Bottari.—Notes on Giorgione, by B. Berenson.—Spigolature giorgionesche, di W. Suida.—More about Giorgione's "Daniel and Susannah" at Glasgow, by P. Hendy.--Il mio Giorgione, di C. Gamba.--Esordi di Tiziano, di A. Morassi.—An early version of Titian's Danae, an analysis of Titian's replicas, by H. Tietze.—Un soffitto di Tiziano a Brescia ricordato in un disegno del Rubens, di E. Tietze-Conrat.— (Continued)

Copy only words underlined & classmark— 3-MAA +

Arte veneta. (Card 5)

Una citazione tizianesca nel Caravaggio, di R. Longhi.--Greco's Italian period, by M.S. Soria.—Un capolavoro del Tintoretto: La Madonna del Doge Alvise Mocenigo, di R. Pallucchini.--Peinture et musique à Venise vers la fin de la renaissance, par R. Jullian.--Una "vita" inedita del Muziano, di U. Procacci.—Notes brèves sur quelques tableaux vénitiens inconnus à Dallas, di C. Sterling.—I ritratti dell'Avogaria, di N. Ivanoff.—Domenico Maria Viani, von H. Voss.—Cinque (Continued)

Copy only words underlined & classmark— 3-MAA +

Arte veneta. (Card 6)

disegni veneti, di E. Arslan.--A Venetian settecento chapel in the English countryside, by F.J.B. Watson.—La Samaritana al pozzo di Sebastiano Ricci, di E. Berti Toesca.—Einige unbekannte Werke von Francesco Guardi, von O. Benesch.—Giacomo Leoni's edition of Palladio's "Quattro libri dell'architettura", by R. Wittkower.—The drawings of Francesco Fontebasso, by J.B. Shaw.--Tre dipinti di Francesco Fontebasso.—Il palazzo (Continued)

Copy only words underlined & classmark— 3-MAA +

Arte veneta. (Card 7)

Mocenigo di San Stae donato alla città di Venezia, di P. Zampetti.—Le "vedute veneziane" di Giovanni Migliara, di M. Pittaluga.

1. Art, Italian—Venice. 2. Fiocco, Giuseppe, 1884- 3. Giorgione, 1477-1510. 4. Tiziano Vecelli, 1477-1576

C-13
9594

ASCHBACH, JOSEPH.
Geschichte der Wiener Universität im Ersten Jahrhunderte ihres Bestehens. Wien, Verlag der K.K. Universität, 1865-88 [Farnborough, Hants, Eng., Gregg press, 1967] 3 v. illus., fold. plan. 20cm.

Vol. 2-3, edited by the K.K. Universität in Wien.
Pref. to v.3 signed: Adalbert Horawitz.
CONTENTS.--Bd.1. Festschrift zu ihrer fünfhundertjährigen Gründungs- (Continued)

NN R X 7.69 v/A OCs, I PCs, Is, I SL (LCls, Xls, [I], Zls)

2

ASCHBACH, JOSEPH. Geschichte der Wiener Universität im Ersten Jahrhunderte ihres Bestehens. (Card 2)

feier. --Bd. 2. Die Wiener Universität und ihre Humanisten im Zeitalter Kaiser Maximilians I. --Bd. 3. Die Wiener Universität und ihre Gelehrten 1520 bis 1565.

1. Vienna. Universität--Hist. I. Horawitz, Adalbert. i. Sub for 1865-88 ed.

ASLANAPA, OKTAY, ed. Beiträge zur Kunstgeschichte Asiens. (Card 2)

CONTENTS:--Possible Iranian contributions to the beginning of Gothic architecture, by A. U. Pope. Die Türbe der Isfendiyar Oglu in Sinop, von F. Taeschner Les mosquées a coupole à base hexagonale, par D. Kuban. La Mosquée-Zaviyah de Seyyid Mehmed Dede à Yenisehir, par S. Eyice. Wesenszüge Omayyadischer Schmuckkunst, von H. G. Franz. Decorations in the Seljukid style in the Church of Saint Sophia of Trebizond, by T. T. Rice. Die beiden türkischen Grabsteine im Türk ve Islâm Eserleri Müzesi in Istanbul, von K. Erdmann. Darstellungen des turco-islamischen Kunst, von K. chinesischen Tierzyklus in der Otto-Dorn. Einige Bemerkun-
(Continued)

D-13
3506

Aschendorffsche Verlagsbuchhandlung, Münster, Germany.
240 Jahre Aschendorff, 1720–1960. Werden und Wirken eines Buchverlages und seiner Druckerei. Münster in Westfalen [1960] 27 p. illus. 21cm.

"...wurde in Anlehnung an die Festschrift 'Die Aschendorffsche Presse, 1762–1912,' von Dr. Simon Peter Widmann zusammengestellt und bis auf die Gegenwart ergänzt von Dr. Gottfried Hasenkamp."

I. Hasenkamp, Gottfried, 1918– , ed. i. [Title] Zweihundertvierzig.
NN R 7.62 (OC)I OS PC,I SL (LC1,X1,Z1)

ASLANAPA, OKTAY, ed. Beiträge zur Kunstgeschichte Asiens. (Card 3)

gen zum Sternsystem in der Steinornamentik der anatolischen Seldschunken, von S. Ögel. Ein anatolischer Tierteppich vom ende des 15. Jahrhunderts, von O. Aslanapa. Zwei türkische Kilims, von S. Yetkin. Morgenländische und abendländische Seidenmuster in Mittelalter, von H. Schmidt. Chines representations of central Asian Turks, by R. Ettinghausen. An unpublished manuscript of the Gulistan of Sa'di, by B. W. Robinson. Four pages from a Turkish 16th century Shahnamah in the collection of the Metropolitan Museum of Art in New York, by E. J. Grube. Sur quelques illustrations de Kalila et Dimna, par J. David-Weill. An angel figure in the Miscellany Album H. 2152
(Continued)

OAC

ASHLEY-MONTAGU, MONTAGUE FRANCIS, 1905- , ed.
Studies and essays in the history of science and learning offered in homage to George Sarton on the occasion of his sixtieth birthday, 31 August 1944. New York, Schuman [1947] xiv, 594 p. illus., ports. 24cm.

Includes bibliographies.

1. Science--Hist. 2. Sarton, George Alfred Léon, 1884-1956. I. Title.
NN R 1.65 e/B OC PC, 1, 2, I SL ST, 1, 2, I (LC1, X1, Z1)

ASLANAPA, OKTAY, ed. Beiträge zur Kunstgeschichte Asiens. (Card 4)

of Topkapi, by E. Esin. Die Bronzeschale M. 31-1954 im Victoria and Albert Museum, von A. Grohmann. Die Burg der Magier, von L.-I. Ringbom. Eine keramische Werkstatt des 13. Jahrhunderts auf dem Takht-i Suleiman, von Rudolf Naumann. Die Ziegelreliefplatten vom Ta Ming Kung in Ch'ang an und der Westen von H. Fux. Cānakya's Aphorisms in the Pañcatantra, by L. Sternbach.

1. Art, Oriental--Addresses, essays, lectures. 2. Architecture, Oriental--Addresses, essays, lectures. 3. Diez, Ernst, 1878-1961. 4. Art, Turkish. I. Title. II. Title: Gedächtnisschrift: Ernst Diez.

---

*OAC

ASIATICA; Festschrift Friedrich Weller zum 65. Geburtstag gewidmet von seinen Freunden, Kollegen und Schülern. [Hrsg. von Johannes Schubert und Ulrich Schneider] Leipzig, O. Harrassowitz, 1954. xix, 902 p. illus., plates, port., maps (part fold., part col.) 30cm.

Includes bibliographies; "Verzeichnis der Arbeiten Friedrich Wellers," p. [xi]-xix.

1. Weller, Friedrich, 1889- 2. Indic studies. 3. Oriental studies. I. Schneider, Ulrich, ed. II. Schubert, Johannes, ed. III. Schneider, Ulrich.
NN * R 8. 55 p/ OC, I, II, IIIbo PC, 1, 2, 3, I, II SL O, 1, 2, 3, I, II (LC1, X1, Z1)

F-10
8542

ASOCIACION DE BIBLIOFILOS DE BARCELANO.
Homenaje de la Asociación de Bibliófilos de Barcelona a Marcelino Menéndez Pelayo en el centenario de su nacimiento. Barcelona, 1956. 52 p. illus., ports., facsim. 27cm.

CONTENTS.--Presentación, por la Asociacion de Bibliófilos de Barcelona, la Junta Directiva.--Discurs de gràcies de don Marcelino Menéndez Pelayo en els Jocs Florals de Barcelona de 1888.--Discurso de gracias de don Marcelino Menéndez Pelayo en los
(Continued)
NN * R 9.64 c/ (OC) I OS PC, I, I SL (LCL, X1, Z1) 2

3-MAF

ASLANAPA, OKTAY, ed.
Beiträge zur Kunstgeschichte Asiens. In memoriam Ernst Diez. [Istanbul, Baha Matbaasi, 1963] xv, 350 p. illus., plans. 25cm. (Constantinople. Istanbul Üniversitesi. Edebiyat fakültesi Sanat tarihi enstitüsu. [Yayinlari] 1)

Title on spine: Gedächtnisschrift: Ernst Diez.
"Bibliographie des Schriftums von Ernst Diez": p. [xiii]-xv.
Bibliographical footnotes.
(Continued)
NN R 11. 71 e/ OC, I, II PC, 1, 2, 3, 4, I, II A, 1, 2, 3, 4, I, II SL O, 1, 2, 3, 4, I, II (LC1, X1, Z1) 4

ASOCIACION DE BIBLIOFILOS DE BARCELONA.
de la Asociación de Bibliofilos de Barcelona a Marcelino Menéndez Pelayo en el centenario de su nacimiento. (Cont.)

Juegos Florales de Barcelona de 1888. Traducción del catalán por S. Sánchez Juan.--Menéndez Pelayo en els Jocs Florals de Barcelona, per O. Saltor.

1. Menéndez y Pelayo, Marcelino, 1856-1912. I. Menéndez y Pelayo, Marcelino, 1856-1912. Discurs de gràcies.

CBA

Aspects of archaeology in Britain and beyond; essays presented to O. G. S. Crawford, ed. by W. F. Grimes. London, H. W. Edwards, 1951. xvii,386 p. illus.,maps,22 pl. 25cm.

Bibliographies included.

1. Crawford, Osbert Guy Stanhope, 1886- . 2. Archaeology—Addresses, essays, lectures. 3. Great Britain—Archaeology. I. Grimes, William Francis, ed.

NN OC,I PC,1,2,3,I SL (LC1,Z1,X1)

E-10
8068

ASPECTS of liberty; essays presented to Robert E. Cushman. Edited by Milton R. Konvitz and Clinton Rossiter. Ithaca, N. Y., Cornell University Press [1958]
viii, 355 p. port. 24 cm. (Cornell studies in civil liberty)
Bibliographical footnotes.
CONTENTS.—Theoretical aspects: Ideas, institutions, and American liberty, by R. M. Hutchins. The pattern of liberty, by C. Rossiter. The state and human freedom, by J. Hart. On freedom, by G. E. G. Catlin.—Methodological aspects: The use of the intelligence in advancement of civil rights, by M. R. Konvitz. Social science in civil rights litigation, by J. Tanenhaus. Mediation and education for equal economic opportunity, by J. F. Cushman.—Historical aspects: American liberty: an examination of the "tradition" of freedom, by

(Continued)

NN*R 2.59 g/# OC, I, II (OS)III PC, 1, 2, 3, I, II SL E, 1, 2, 3, I, II (LC1, X1, Z1)

ASPECTS of liberty... (Card 2)

CONTENTS—Continued.
J. P. Roche. The Marshall Court and civil liberties, by D. G. Morgan.—International aspects: Freedom and human rights under international law, by O. Wright. The "rights of aliens" and international protection of human rights, by H. W. Briggs.—Comparative aspects: Observations by an American on English civil liberties, by R. K. Carr. Problems of freedom in postwar Europe, 1945–1957, by M. Einaudi.—Jurisdictional, institutional, and procedural aspects: The Bill of rights, the Fourteenth amendment, and the federal system, by W. Anderson. Procedural due process in the Fifth amendment, by R. F. Cushman. Congress: old powers, new techniques, by R. G. Whitesel. Robert Eugene Cushman: a bibliography, compiled by H. F. Way, Jr. (p. 349-355)

(Continued)

ASPECTS of liberty... (Card 3)

1. CIVIL RIGHTS 2. LIBERTY 3. CUSHMAN, ROBERT EUGENE, 1889-
I. Konvitz, Milton Ridvas, 1908- , ed.
II. Rossiter, Clinton Lawrence, 1917- , ed.
III. Cornell studies in civil liberty

E-12
4785

ASSMANN, DIETMAR, ed.
Volkskundliche Studien aus dem Institut für Volkskunde der Universität Innsbruck zum 50. Geburtstag von Karl Ilg. Innsbruck, Universitätsverlag Wagner, 1964. viii, 220 p. illus., maps, music. 24cm. (Schlern Schriften. 237)

Bibliographical footnotes.

CONTENTS.--Vergleichende Studien über Mensch und Siedlung in den Alphen und in Hochgebirgen Asiens, von C. Jentsch.--Über Vanänderungen

(Continued)

NN 11.65 p/# OC, IIbo (OS)I PC, 1, 2, I SL (LC1, X1, Z1)

3

ASSMANN, DIETMAR, ed. Volkskundliche Studien aus dem Institut für Volkskunde... (Card 2)

in der Flur des mittleren Inntals während der letzten dreihundert Jahre, von F. Fliri.--Gedanken zum ländlichen Siedlungsausbau während des 20. Jahrhunderts im mittleren Inntal, von H. Gschnitzer.--Siedlungsbewegungen und Wandel des Ortsbildes im innersten Pitztal, von L. Beyer.--Wohnsitten der Arbeiterschaft im Vorarlberger Rheintal, von A. Köhlmeier.--Almhütten im bayerischen und tirolischen Karwendel, von P. Fried.--Sitte und Brauch als bevölkerungsbiologische Faktoren, von A. Müller-Schuler.--Die Wallfahrt zu "Unserer Lieben Frau im Walde" in Landeck, von

(Continued)

ASSMANN, DIETMAR, ed. Volkskundliche Studien aus dem Institut für Volkskunde ... (Card 3)

D. Assmann.--Die Mirakelbilder der Wallfahrt Mariastein, von N.C. Kogler.--Motive der Malerien an Häusern des Wipptales, von K. Bleimfeldner.--Volkskundliches in Wolkensteins "Tirolischer Chronik," von E. Widmoser.--Zachäus im Tiroler Kirchweihlied, von N. Wallner.--Tracht in der Kleidung unserer Zeit, von K. Santner.--Wandlungen in der volkstümlichen Nahrungsweise im Paznauntal, von S. Magda.--Zur Situation der Bäuerin in Oberösterreich, von I. Loidl-Eckstein.--Die Bauweise der "cabane de pierre," von G. Grabner.

1. Ilg, Karl. 2. Folk lore--Austria. I. Series. II. Assmann, Dietmar.

PKH

Associazione italiana di chimica generale ed applicata, Rome.
Stanislao Cannizzaro; scritti vari e lettere inedite nel centenario della nascita. Roma: Tip. "Leonardo da Vinci," 1926. vii, 485 p. incl. tables. illus. (facsims.), ports. 8°.

Includes articles by E. Paternò, G. A. Cesareo, P. Giacosa and many others.

341.022A.

1. Cannizzaro, Stanislao, 1826-1910. 2. Chemistry—Essays and misc. 3. Letters.

N. Y. P. L. January 26, 1928

AN
(Medina, J.)

Atenea; revista mensual de ciencias, letras y bellas artes.
José Toribio Medina; homenaje en el centenario de su nacimiento. Colaboran: José Toribio Medina [et al. Santiago de Chile, Editorial Nascimento, 1952] 530 p. ports. 23cm.

Cover-title.
"Numero extraordinario de "Atenea."
Bibliographical footnotes.

(Continued)

NN**X 9.54 (OC)I,II OS PC,1,I,II SL AH,1, I,II (Z1,LC1,X1)

Atenea; revista mensual de ciencias, letras y bellas artes. José Toribio Medina... (Card 2)

Contents.—Viajes por Europa en 1876 y 1877, por J. T. Medina.—Medina, por G. Feliú Cruz.—Alrededor del centenario de don José Toribio Medina, por R. Hernández.—Medina, historiador de la literatura chilena, por R. Silva Castro.—José Toribio Medina y su afición a la lingüística y a la filología, por R. Oroz.—Los estudios de Medina sobre Ercilla, por S. Dinamarca.—J.T.Medina, traductor de Longfellow, por E. Pereira Salas.—

(Continued)

Atenea; revista mensual de ciencias, letras y bellas artes. José Toribio Medina... (Card 3)

Medina Cervantista, por J. Uribe-Echvarría.— Medina y la bibliografía, por J. Zamudio Z.

1. Medina, José Toribio, 1852-1930. I. Medina, José Toribio, 1852-1930. II. Title.

M-10
592
v. 12

ATLANTIC COLLOQUIUM. 2d, Groningen, 1964.
Neolithic studies in Atlantic Europe; proceedings of the second Atlantic colloquium, Groningen, 6-11 April, 1964. Presented to Albert Egges van Giffen for his 80th birthday. Groningen, J.B. Wolters, 1966 [i.e. 1967] 585 p. illus., port., maps. 27cm. (Palaeohistoria; acta et communicationes instituti bio-archaeologici Universitatis Groninganae. v. 12)

(Continued)

NN 12.68 k/ (OC)I OI PC, 1, 2, I (LC1, X1, Z1) 2

ATLANTIC COLLOQUIUM. 2d, Groningen, 1964.
Neolithic studies in Atlantic Europe...
(Card 2)

Edited by J.D. van der Waals.
In English, French or German.
Includes bibliographies.

1. Stone age. 2. Giffen, Albert Egges van, 1884- .
I. Waals, J.D., ed.

PRD

The ATMOSPHERE and the sea in motion; scientific contributions to the Rossby memorial volume, edited by Bert Bolin. New York, Rockefeller institute press, 1959. 509 p. illus., port. 28cm.

In English, except for two papers in German and one in French.
"Publications by Carl-Gustaf Rossby," p. 60-64.
Includes bibliographies.

1. Meteorology--Essays and misc. 2. Rossby, Carl Gustaf. I. Bolin, Bert, ed. II. Bolin, Bert. t. 1959.
NN R 7.60 l/A OC, I, IIbo PC, 1, 2, I SL ST, 1t, 2, I (LC1, X1, Z1)

E-12
6365

Aubin, Bernhard C H *ed.*
Festschrift für Otto Riese aus Anlass seines siebzigsten Geburtstages. Hrsg. von Bernhard Aubin [et al.] Karlsruhe, C. F. Müller, 1964.
527 p. port. 24 cm.
"Verzeichnis der Schriften von Otto Riese": p. [519]-527.

1. Riese, Otto. 2. Law--European economic community.
3. Riese, Otto--Bibl.
NN * R 8.66 l/c OC PC, 1, 2, 3 SL E, 1, 2, 3 (LC1, X1, Z1)

E-10
2591

AUFRECHT zwischen den Stühlen K. O. P.; Grüsse zum 50. Geburtstag am 23. November 1956 für Karl O. Paetel von Freunden in Deutschland und anderswo. [Zusammengestellt von Werner Wille, New York, und Heinrich Sperl, Nürnberg. Nürnberg, Druckhaus Nürnberg, 1956] 92 p. port. 25cm.

"Privatdruck, in 200 Exemplaren."

1. Paetel, Karl Otto, 1906- . I. Sperl, Heinrich, ed. II. Wille, Werner, 1907- ed.
NN R X 4.57 a/ OC, I, II, IIb PC, 1, I, II SL (LC1, X1, Z1, Y1)

RLB

Aufsätze zur Sprach- und Literaturgeschichte, Wilhelm Braune zum 20. Februar 1920 dargebracht von Freunden und Schülern. Dortmund, F. W. Ruhfus, 1920. vii, 402 p. 23cm.

532166B. 1. Braune, Theodor Wilhelm, 1850-1926. 2. German language. 3. German literature—Hist. and crit. 4. Heldensage.
N. Y. P. L. August 15, 1950

---

*MEC
(Mozart)

AUGSBURGER Mozart-Festsommer, 1956. [Herausgeber: Hans Meissner] [Augsburg] Städtische Bühnen Augsburg [1956] 14, [2] p. illus., ports., facsims. 21cm.

CONTENTS.—Die Mozart, Wurzel und Gipfel, von L. Wegele.—Augsburger Rokoko, von N. Lieb.—Das Wunder der Schönheit, von R. Benz.—Mozart als Europäer, von H.H. Stuckenschmidt.—Der Leidensweg des Genius.—Aufbruch des Genies, von W. Götze.—Le nozze di Figaro, von A. Greither.—Mozart, Don Juan, Kierkegaard und wir, von S. Melchinger.—Mozart der Gast, von A. Goes.— Quellen und Hinweise (p. [76]).

(Continued)

NN 5.58 e/ OC, I (OD)IIt, IIb (ED)IIt PC, 1, 2, I, II SL MU, 1, 2, 3, I, II (LC1, X1, Z1, Y1)

AUGSBURGER Mozart-Festsommer, 1956. (Card 2)

1. Mozart, Wolfgang Amadeus--Germany--Augsburg. 2. Mozart, Wolfgang Amadeus--Festivals, performances, etc. 3. Mozart, Wolfgang Amadeus. Operas. I. Meissner, Hans, ed. II. Augsburg, Germany. Städtische Bühnen. t. 1956.

Write on slip words underlined below and class mark—

RAA

August Leskien zum 4. Juli 1894, dem Tage seines 25 Jährigen Professor-Jubiläums, von seinen Schülern und Freunden. [Strassburg: K. J. Trübner, 1894] vi, 527 p. facsim., map. 23cm. (Indogermanische Forschungen. Bd. 4.)

1. Leskien, August, 1840-1916. Festschrift
N. Y. P. L. November 6, 1939

Copy only words underlined
& classmark-- STG

AUGUSTANA COLLEGE AND THEOLOGICAL SEMINARY, Rock Island, Ill.
Lincoln images; Augustana college centennial essays, by O. Fritiof Ander [and others] Edited by O. Fritiof ... Ander. Rock Island, Ill., Augustana college library, 1960. xiii, 161 p. illus., ports. 24cm. (Augustana college and theological seminary, Rock Island, Ill. Augustana library publications, no. 29)

(Continued)

NN*R 3.61 s/ (OC)I, II OS OI PC, 1, 2, I, II AH, 1, 2, I, II (LC5, X1, Z1)

AUGUSTANA COLLEGE AND THEOLOGICAL SEMINARY, Rock Island, Ill. Lincoln images... (Card 2)

Bibliography, p. 107-135. "Augustana Lincolniana," p. 139-151.

1. Lincoln, Abraham, 16th pres. U.S.--Addresses, sermons, etc. 2. Lincoln, Abraham, 16th pres. U.S.--Bibl. I. Ander, Oscar Fritiof, 1903- , ed. II. Title.

OAP

AUS der deutschen Forschung der letzten Dezennien Dr. Ernst Telschow zum 65. Geburtstag gewidmet 31. Oktober 1954. Hrsg. von B. Rajewsky und G. Schreiber. Stuttgart, G. Thieme, 1956. xii, 528 p. illus., port. 25cm.

Various contributors.
Includes bibliographies.
1. Science--Research--Germany. 2. Telschow, Ernst, 1889- I. Schreiber, Georg, 1882- , ed. II. Rajewsky, Boris, 1893- , ed. t. 1956.

NN **R X 9.56 j/b OC, 2b, I, II PC, 1, 2, I, II SL ST, 1t, 2, I, II (LC1, X1, Z1)

RRB

Aus den Forschungsarbeiten der Mitglieder des Ungarischen Instituts und des Collegium Hungaricum in Berlin; dem Andenken Robert Graggers gewidmet; herausgegeben vom Bund der ehemaligen Instituts- und Collegiumsmitglieder. Berlin: W. de Gruyter & Co., 1927. xi, 264 p. incl. tables. pl., port. 8°.

Bibliographical footnotes.
Contents: Vorspruch, [von] C. H. Becker [und] Graf K. Klebelsberg. MAGYARY, Z. Gragger, als Wissenschaftspolitiker. BRANDENSTEIN, A., FREIHERR VON. Die Schwierigkeiten der Metaphysik und die Richtlinien zu einem Versuch ihrer Lösung. PROHÁSZKA, L. Zur Theorie des Gegenstandes. MUZSNAI, D. Die "Projektion" in

(Continued)

Mr. Moth.

N. Y. P. L. February 19, 1930

Aus den Forschungsarbeiten der Mitglieder... (Card 2)

der Psychologie Karl Böhms. GÁL, J. Die Hauptperioden der Entwicklung der Kunstform. ÖHMANN, E. Sprachentwicklung und soziale Schichten. BANG, W. Aus Manis Briefen. RÁSONYI-NAGY, L. Valacho-turcica. KOSSÁNYI, B. Ephraim, Bischof von Cherson, Missionär der "Oyrpы." LEWY, E. Permisch-iranische Gleichungen. STOLL, W. Die deutschen Fremdworte des ungarischen Schusterhandwerkes. PUKÁNSZKY, B. Sebastian Tinódi und der deutsche Zeitungsgesang. FITZ, J. Georg Michaelis Cassai und seine Bibliothek. KOSZÓ, J. Ungarische Romantik. FARKAS, G. Reviczkys deutsche Dichtungen. BARTA, J. Franz Molnár als Dramatiker. LAJTI, S. Zu den griechischen Trauersitten. STEINITZ, W. Elchfang bei Germanen und Finnen. MOÓR, E. Über das Märchen von der verwünschten Königs-

(Continued)

N. Y. P. L. February 19, 1930

Aus den Forschungsarbeiten der Mitglieder... (Card 3)

tochter: Grimm Nr. 93. STRAUSZ, L. Über geologische Faciesstudien. SOÓ, R. VON. Zur Nomenklatur und Methodologie der Pflanzensoziologie. JENDRÁSSIK, L., and L. TESCHLER. Über die physiologische Unwirksamkeit des nicht isolierten Calciums.

452585A. 1. Gragger, Robert, 1887–1926. 2. Bund der ehemaligen Instituts- und Collegiumsmitglieder des Ungarischen Instituts und des Collegium Hungaricum, Berlin.
N. Y. P. L. February 19, 1930

Write on slip words underlined
and class mark- *OAA

Aus fünf jahrtausenden morgenländischer kultur; festschrift Max freiherrn von Oppenheim zum 70. geburtstage gewidmet von freunden und mitarbeitern. Berlin [E. F. Weidner] 1933.

2 p. l., 215 p., 1 l. front. (port.) illus. (incl. map, plans, facsims.) x pl. 27½ x 22cm. [Archiv für orientforschung, beiband I ... hrsg. von Ernst F. Weidner]
Printed in Belgium.
Bibliographical foot-notes.
CONTENTS.—Babinger, Franz. Die osmanischen statthalter von Damaskus.—Böhl, F. M. T. Vier antiken aus den assyriologischen sammlungen in Leiden und Groningen.—Bräunlich, Erich. Die bedeutung von [jāwaza 'l-ithnayni] — Dombart, Theodor. Die grabstele des Horus "schlange".—Ebeling, Erich. Aus den archiven von Uruk und Assur.—Grohmann, Adolf. Ein Qorra-brief vom jahre 90 D. H.—Hommel, Fritz.

(Continued on next card)

35-9775

[2]

Aus fünf jahrtausenden morgenländischer kultur ... 1933. (Card 2)

CONTENTS—Continued.

Oannes am sternhimmel. — Jensen, Peter. Mohammed. — Kahle, Paul. Ein Futuwwa-erlass des kalifen en-Nāṣir aus dem jahre 604 (1207).—Kühnel, Ernst. Zur tirāz-epigraphik der Abbasiden und Fatimiden.—Littmann, Enno. Ein arabischer text über die Nilschwelle.—Meissner, Bruno. Die keilschrifttexte auf den steinernen orthostaten und statuen aus dem Tell Ḥalāf.—Mordtmann, J. H. Jura per Anchialum.—Moritz, Bernhard. Arabische miszellen.—Prüfer, C. Bemerkungen zur jemenitischen frauentracht.—Rosen, Friedrich. Altpersische legende über die herkunft des weines. Aus einer neuentdeckten schrift Omar-i Khajjams. — Sarre, Friedrich. Eine frühislamische wanddekoration aus Nordmesopotamien. — Schmidt, Hubert. Zur buntkeramik des Susakreises.—Sobernheim, Moritz. Inschriftliche wirtschafts- und verwal-

(Continued on next card)

35-9775

[2]

Aus fünf jahrtausenden morgenländischer kultur ... 1933. (Card 3)

CONTENTS—Continued.

tungs-verordnungen der Mamluken-sultane aus der Omajjaden-moschee von Damaskus.—Unger, Eckhard. Kinematographische erzählungsform in der altorientalischen relief- und rund-plastik. — Ungnad, Arthur. Tierkapellen. — Caskel, Werner. Das farraschen-amt in Medina. — Guyer, S. Zwei spätantike grabmonumente Nordmesopotamiens und der älteste märtyrergrab-typus der christlichen kunst.—Herrmann, Albert. Die Saken und der Skythenzug des Dareios.—Landsberger, Benno. Die angebliche babylonische notenschrift.—Opitz, Dietrich. Altorientalische gussformen.

1. Oppenheim, Max Adrian Simon, freiherr von, 1860- 2. Oriental philology—Collections. 3. Asia, Western—Antiq. 4. Art, Oriental. I. Weidner, Ernst F., 1891- ed.

35-9775

Library of Congress DS42.4.A8

[2] 935.004

E-11
1852

AUS Geschichte und Landeskunde; Forschungen und Darstellungen, Franz Steinbach zum 65. Geburtstag gewidmet von seinen Freunden und Schülern. Bonn, L. Röhrscheid, 1960. 795 p. illus., ports. 25cm.

Bibliographical footnotes.
CONTENTS. --Politische Geschichte. --Allgemeine Verfassungsgeschichte. --Stadt- und Gemeindegeschichte. --

(Continued)

NN R 2.61 s/ OC PC, 1, 2, 3 SL (LC1, X1, Z1) [I]

AUS Geschichte und Landeskunde... (Card 2)

Wirtschafts- und Sozialgeschichte.--Sprach- und Kulturgeschichte.

1. Germany--Hist.--Addresses, essays, lectures. 2. Steinbach, Franz, 1895- . 3. German language--Addresses, essays, lectures.

M-10
4028
v.29

AUS kölnischer und rheinischer Geschichte; Festgabe Arnold Güttsches zum 65. Geburtstag gewidmet. Hrsg. von Hans Blum. Köln, H.Wamper, 1969. 367 p. plates, port. 24cm. (Kölnischer Geschichtsverein e.V. Veröffentlichungen. 29)

Bibliographical footnotes.

CONTENTS.--Zur Verwaltung des Kölner Erzstifts unter Erzbischof Walram von Jülich, 1332-1349, von W.Janssen.--Aus dem

(Continued)

NN 2.70 r/ℓOC, II, III, IIIb+ (OS)I PC, 1, 2, I, II, III (LC1, X1, Z1)

AUS kölnischer und rheinischer Geschichte...
(Card 2)

Brügge-Antwerpener Kontorsarchiv in Köln, von H.Thierfelder. Das älteste Kölner Stadtsiegel, von T.Diederich.--Johann Potken aus Schwerte, Propst von St.Georg in Köln, der erste Äthiopologe des Abendlandes, von A.D.von den Bricken.--Der Ordinarius des Stiftes St.Ursula in Köln, von G.Wegener.--Beiträge zur Wirtschaftsgeschichte des Klosters St.Panteleon in Köln, von E.Wisplinghoff.--Zur Geschichte einer rheinischen Handschrift, von W.Stüwer.--Die Brüder Adrian und Peter von Walenburch und der Erwerb eines Kanonikates am Kölner Dom,

(Continued)

AUS kölnischer und rheinischer Geschichte...
(Card 3)

von H.Wamper.--Die Rivalität der Universitätsstädte Köln und Bonn, von D.Höroldt.--Konrad Adenauer und das Kanzleramt während der Weimarer Zeit, von H.Stehkämper.--Die Töpferei in der Streitzeuggasse zu Köln, von F.Brill.--Das Rheinland in der Buchillustration des 19.Jahrhunderts, von H.Blum--Der Nachlass Fastenrath im Kölner Stadtarchiv, von W. Kienitz.--Die Strukturwardlungen der Kölner Stadtteile von St.Severin und St.Alban im Verlauf von acht Jahrhunderten, von H.Vogts.

(Continued)

AUS kölnischer und rheinischer Geschichte...
(Card 4)

1. Cologne--Hist.--Addresses, essays, lectures. 2. Rhine valley--Hist.--Addresses, essays, lectures. I. Series. II. Blum, Hans, ed. III. Güttsches, Arnold, 1904-

---

BAC

Aus politik und geschichte; gedächtnisschrift für Georg von Below. Berlin, Deutsche verlagsgesellschaft für politik und geschichte m. b. h., 1928.

x, 362 p. front. (port.) diagr. 24½cm.

"1. auflage."

CONTENTS.—Zum geleit.—Liste der spender.—Ahlhaus, J. Civitas und diözese.—Varges, W. Das herzogtum.—Kern, F. Der deutsche staat und die politik des Römerzuges.—Baethgen, F. Die promissio Albrechts I. für Bonifaz VIII.—Klaiber, L. Neues zum "königslager".—Voltelini, H. Der bericht über die rechte des herzogs von Kärnten in zwei handschriften des Schwabenspiegels.—Goldschmidt, H. Das erbkämmereramt im herzogtum Jülich 1331–1796.—Weigel, H. Die entstehung der sog. Reformation kaiser Sigmunds.—Meinecke, F. Petrus

(Continued on next card)

28-22716

[3]

Aus politik und geschichte ... 1928. (Card 2)

CONTENTS—Continued.

Valckeniers lehre von den interessen der staaten.—Redlich, O. Das angebliche politische testament eines ministers kaiser Leopolds I.—Hölzle, E. Justus Möser über staat und freiheit.—Rapp, A. Deutscher romantischer geist in verschiedenen politischen lagern.—Wahl, A. Methoden der verfassungsschöpfer im 19. jahrhundert.—Haering, H. Über Treitschke und seine religion.—Bächtold, H. Die entstehung von Jacob Burckhardt's "Weltgeschichtlichen betrachtungen".—Rothacker, E. Die grenzen der geschichtsphilosophischen begriffsbildung.—Spann, O. Über die einheit von theorie und geschichte.—Verzeichnis der schriften Georg von Belows, zusammengestellt von L. Klaiber (p. 338–362)

1. Below, Georg Anton Hugo von, 1858–1927. ~~2. Holy Roman empire—Hist.—Collections.~~ 3. Political science—~~Collections.~~ ~~4. History—Philosophy—Collections.~~

28-22716

Library of Congress D113.5.A8

Copyright A—Foreign 39009

[3]

ZEC

Aus Theologie und Philosophie. Festschrift für Fritz Tillmann zu seinem 75. Geburtstag (1. November 1949). Hrsg. von Theodor Steinbüchel† und Theodor Müncker. Düsseldorf, Patmos-Verlag [1950] 615 p. port. 24cm.

Bibliography at end of most chapters.

602575B. 1. Theology—Essays and misc. 2. Ethics, Christian. 3. Tillmann, Fritz, 1874- . I. Steinbüchel, Theodor, 1888- , ed. II. Müncker, Theodor, 1887- , ed.

N. Y. P. L. January 15, 1952

---

*PBS

Aus unbekannten Schriften; Festgabe für Martin Buber zum 50. Geburtstag. Berlin: L. Schneider, 1928. 245 p. 12°.

Contents: JOËL, K. Vom Unbekannten. BONUS, A. Australische Totemgesänge. JOËL, E. Eine Anamnese. DUMONT, L. Eine Upanishade des Veda. WEIZSÄCKER, V. v. Ein Spruch des Laotse. BEER-HOFMANN, R. Herakleitische Paraphrase. SCHMALENBACH, H. Das letzte Wort des Sokrates. SCHAEFFER, A. Ein lateinischer Spruch. BERGMANN, H. Ein Spruch aus dem Talmud. SIMON, E. Eine rabbinische Vorschrift. WITTIG, J. Aus dem Fragenbuche des Ambrosiasters. ROSENSTOCK, E. Ein Wort von Augustin und eins von Goethe. WOLFSKEHL, K. Das althochdeutsche Schlummerlied. ROTTEN, E. Aus den Offenbarungen der Schwester Mechtild von Magdeburg. BRAUN, F. Nach einem mystischen Spruch. GLENN, H. Um ein Wort Meister Eckeharts. THEIL, C. Nicolaus Cusanus: De Deo abscondito. MOMBERT, A. Ein unbekannter

(Continued)

Mr. Moth.

N. Y. P. L. January 4, 1929

Aus unbekannten Schriften... (Card 2)

persischer Dichter. SCHOLEM, G. Rabbi Abraham ben Elieser Halewi: Über den Tod der Märtyrer. BAECK, L. Samuel Laniado über III. M. 19, 18. STRAUSS, E. Zwei Sätze aus der Geschichte der Alchemie. GLATZER, N. N. Gleichnis des Pico della Mirandola. MAEDER, A. Paracelsus: Von Krankheit und gesundem Leben. HERRIGEL, H. Ein Bericht über das Marburger Religionsgespräch. PAQUET, A. Ein Quatrain des Nostradamus. SPOERRI, T. Ein französischer Entwicklungsroman vom Anfang des 17. Jahrhunderts. SPIRA, T. Ein Brief des George Fox an Cromwells Tochter. SUSMAN, M. Ein Wort aus Port-Royal. WILKER, K. Zwei Goethesche Paralipomena. MICHEL, W. Hölderlins Übersetzung eines Götternamens. STRAUSS, L. Ein Hymnenbruchstück Hölderlins. FRISCH, E. Aus Brentanos Godwi. KAHLER, E. v. Aus Ernst Moritz Arndts Vergleichender Völkergeschichte. EHRENBERG, R. Aus Carus: Von den

(Continued)

N. Y. P. L. January 4, 1929

Aus unbekannten Schriften... (Card 3)

Naturreichen. TRÜB, H. I. Ch. Blumhardt über unheimliche Hilfe. RAGAZ, L. Richard Rothe über Verweltlichung des Christentums. EHRENBERG, H. Hermann Oeser: Aus des Herrn Archemoros Gedanken über Irrende. LINDAU, H. Verschaeve über die Poesie der Psalmen. FRÄNKEL, J. Ein Gedicht von Gottfried Keller. STEHR, H. Ein Wort Emersons. BAUM, O. Aus J. J. David: Vom Schaffen. ZWEIG, A. Über ein unbekanntes, weltberümtes Buch. WOLFENSTEIN, A. Eine Strophe Shelleys. MELL, M. Ein Gedicht Franz Stelzhamers. HOLITSCHER, A. Aus Wilhelm Weitling: Die Menschheit, wie sie ist. OPPENHEIMER, F. Ein Wort Proudhons. MAYER, G. Aus einem Briefe Lassalles. KOHN, H. Gustav Landauer über Geistige und Volk. LAUFBAHN, I. Aus A. D. Gordons Nachlass. WELTSCH, R. A. D. Gordon über Erneuerung. SIMMEL,

(Continued)

N. Y. P. L. January 4, 1929

Aus unbekannten Schriften... (Card 4)

G. Aus Georg Simmels nachgelassener Mappe "Metaphysik." BROD, M. Aus Franz Kafkas Tagebüchern. RANG, B. Aus einem letzten Brief von Florens Christian Rang. THIEBERGER, F. Eine Erinnerung an Salomon Buber. ROSENZWEIG, F. Aus Bubers Dissertation. Nachwort.

386389A. 1. Essays, German—Collections. 2. Buber, Martin, 1878–
N. Y. P. L. January 4, 1929

Write on slip only words underlined and classmark:
*** HA**

Aus der Welt des Buches; Festgabe zum 70. Geburtstag von Georg Leyh, dargebracht von Freunden und Fachgenossen... Leipzig, O. Harrassowitz, 1950. 287 p. 24cm. (Zentralblatt für Bibliothekswesen. Beihefte. Heft 75)

"Verzeichnis der Schriften von Georg Leyh (1937–1950), zusammengestellt von Paul Schmid," p. 7–12.

1. Bibliography—Addresses, essays, lectures. 2. Libraries—Addresses, essays, lectures. 3. Leyh, Georg, 1877– . I. Ser.
NN 11.52 OC PC, 1, 2, 3 (LC1, X1)

MAF

AUS der Welt der islamischen Kunst. Festschrift für Ernst Kühnel zum 75. Geburtstag am 26.10.1957. [Hrsg. von Richard Ettinghausen] Berlin, Gebr. Mann [1959] 404 p. illus., port. 28cm.

Contributions in English, German, French or Italian.
Bibliographie des Schrifttums von Ernst Kühnel, zusammengestellt von Irene Kühnel-Kunze, " p. [388]-404.

1. Kühnel, Ernst, 1882- . 2. Art, Muhammadan. I. Ettinghausen, Richard, ed.
NN R 6.60 a/ OC, I PC, 1, 2, I SL A, 1, 2, I O, 1, 2, I (LC1, X1, Z1)

*** IIE**

Aus Wissenschaft und Antiquariat; Festschrift zum 500jährigen Bestehen der Buchhandlung Gustav Fock, G.m.b.H. Leipzig, 1929. 390 p. incl. tables. diagr., facsims., plates, port. 4°.

Contents: HELLPACH, W. Treue dem Buch. OSTWALD, W. Aus Vergangenem Künftiges. SCHULZE, F. Das deutsche Antiquariat in geschichtlicher Entwicklung. VAIHINGER, H. Die Weltanschauung des wissenschaftlichen Antiquars. GLAUNING, O. Das Antiquariat und die Geisteswissenschaften. MENZ, G. Der Antiquariatsbuchhandel als Wirtschaftsfaktor. HABER, F. Das Buch in der Chemie. RADBRUCH, G. Der Jurist und das Buch. SUDHOFF, K. Biologie und Medizin im Wandel der Zeiten. TROMMSDORFF, P. Die technischen Wissenschaften und das Antiquariat. WOLF, J. Antiquariat und Musikwissenschaft. ZIELINSKY, T.

(Continued)

N. Y. P. L. June 20, 1930

Aus Wissenschaft und Antiquariat... (Card 2)

Antiquariat und Antike. STEINMANN, E. Rariora und Curiosa der Michelangelo-Literatur. PAALZOW, H. Die deutschen wissenschaftlichen Bibliotheken und das Antiquariat. BUCHNER, M. Die chemische Industrie, die chemische Literatur und das Antiquariat. EBERT, O. E. Die deutsche Bücherei und das Antiquariat. LERCHE, O. Antiquariat und Volksbildung. HAEBLER, K. Antiquariat und Inkunabeln. WITKOWSKI, G. Antiquariat und Bibliophilie. JUNK, W. Der Antiquar und die beschreibenden Naturwissenschaften. FRAENKEL, S. M. Die Bewertung der Arbeit des Antiquars in der Öffentlichkeit und die Einschätzung seiner Persönlichkeit. LOEWE, J. R. Wissenschaftlicher Buchhandel und Auktionswesen in England. TRAUTZ, F. M. Japan-Bücher und japanische Bücher in Deutschland. GROSSMANN, P. Unsere geistigen Beziehungen zu den Vereinigten Staaten von Nordamerika. SCHULZE, F. Buchhandlung Gustav Fock G.m.b.H. 1879–1929.

479903A. 1. Fock, Gustav, firm, booksellers, Leipzig. 2. Booksellers and book trade.
N. Y. P. L. June 20, 1930

D-19
84

Ausblick und Rückblick. Erich R. Prölss zum 60. Geburtstag. Herausgeber: Emil Frey [u. a.] München, Beck, 1967.

xi, 315 p. front. 23 cm.
German, French or Italian.
Bibliographical footnotes.

1. Insurance--Jurisp. I. Prölss, Erich R., 1907- . II. Frey, Emil, ed.
NN 6.69 w/ OC, I, II PC, 1, I, II SL E, 1, I, II (LC1, X1, Z1)

MAWX
(Lanckoroński)

Ausgewählte Kunstwerke der Sammlung Lanckoroński. Mit 51 Tafeln und 23 Textabbildungen. Wien, 1918. 131 p. illus. 35cm.

"Seiner Exzellenz Dr. Karl Grafen Lanckoroński zu seinem siebzigsten Geburtstage von Freunden und Verehrern gewidmet."

446321B. 1. Lanckoroński, Karol, hrabia, 1848–1933. 2. Art—Collections, Private—Lanckoroński. 3. Art—Essays and misc.
N. Y. P. L. September 21, 1948

D-13
2455

AUSTIN, LLOYD JAMES, ed.
Studies in modern French literature presented to P. Mansell Jones by pupils, colleagues and friends. Edited by L. J. Austin, Garnet Rees and Eugène Vinaver. [Manchester] Manchester university press [1961] xix, 343 p. port., facsims. 23cm.

Contributions in English or French.
Includes bibliographies.

(Continued)
NN R 10.61 m/ OC, I, II, IIIbo PC, 1, 2, I, II SL (LC1, X1, Z1)
[I]

AUSTIN, LLOYD JAMES, ed. Studies in modern French literature presented to P. Mansell Jones by pupils... (Card 2)

1. French literature--Addresses, essays, lectures. 2. Jones, Percy Mansell. I. Rees, Garnet, joint ed. II. Vinaver, Eugène, 1899- , joint ed. III. Rees, Garnet.

PVW

AUSTRALASIAN INSTITUTE OF MINING AND METALLURGY.
F. L. Stillwell anniversary volume. [Melbourne, 1958] 302 p. illus., port., maps (part fold.) 22cm.

Includes bibliographies.

1. Stillwell, Frank Leslie, 1888- . 2. Geology--Australia.
3. Mineralogy--Australia. t. 1958.
NN 5. 59 t/℗ OS PC, 1, 2, 3 SL ST, 1, 2t, 3t (LC1, X1, Z1)

E-12
2132

AUSTRIA. Landwirtschaftlich-chemische Bundesversuchsanstalt, Linz.
Festschrift zum bojährigen Bestand der Landwirtschaftschaftlich-chemischen Bundesversuchsanstalt in Linz. Hrsg. von Egon Burggasser. Linz, 1959. 239. p. illus., ports. 24cm.

Includes bibliographies.
1. Agriculture, 1901- . 2. Chemistry, Agricultural.
I. Burggasser, Egon, ed. II. Burggasser, Egon. t. 1959.
NN R 10.65 l/B (OC)I, IIbo ODt (lb) EDt PC, 1, 2, I SL ST, 2t, I (LC1, X1, Z1)

---

* HZD
(Vienna)

Austria. National-Bibliothek, Vienna.
Festschrift der Nationalbibliothek in Wien; herausgegeben zur Feier des 200jährigen Bestehens des Gebäudes... Wien: Druck und Verlag der Österreichischen Staatsdruckerei, 1926. vii, 869 p. incl. tables. facsims., illus., map, plates, ports. 4°.

Bibliographies throughout.

1. No subject.
N. Y. P. L. September 14, 1927

---

*HZD
(Vienna)

Austria. National-Bibliothek, Vienna: Festschrift... (Continued)

Contents: Arnold, R. F. Widersprüche in Dichtungen. Ausserer, K. Die heraldischen Handschriften der Wiener Nationalbibliothek. Baumhackl, F. Die Grafen von Schaunberg und die Herrschaft Orth im Marchfeld. Beetz, W. Zur Geschichte der Porträtsammlung der Nationalbibliothek in Wien. Bick, J. Der unveröffentliche zweite Teil der Dilucida repraesentatio Bibliothecae Caesareae des S. Kleiner und J. J. Sedelmayr. Boehm, A. Edler von Boehmersheim. Zum Begriff und zum Verlauf der Loxodrome. Brechler, O. Kontagiosität des Geistes. Brotanek, R. Beschreibung der Handschrift 1409. (Suppl. 1776) der Nationalbibliothek in Wien. Doublier, O. Ein Vierteljahrhundert aus der Ge-

(Continued)

N. Y. P. L. August 25, 1927

Austria. National-Bibliothek, Vienna: Festschrift... (Continued)

schichte der Hofbibliothek 1891–1916. Dreger, M. Innsbrucher Dächer. Egger, H. Philipp von Stosch und die für seinen "Atlas" beschäftigten Künstler. Gamillscheg, E. Germanisches im Französischen. Gerstinger, H. Johannes Sambucus als Handschriftensammler. Glueck, G. Eine Vermutung über den Meister S. Gregor, J. Die Handzeichnungen der Sammlung Perera in der Wiener Nationalbibliothek. Groag, E. Zur Geschichte des Bücherankaufes in der Hofbibliothek. Grohmann, A. Bibliotheken und Bibliophilen im islamischen Orient. Haberditzl, F. M. Das Reiterdenkmal Kaiser Maximilians I. Haeusle, H. Franz Michael Felder. Hittmair, R. England im Spiegel der State — Poems. Hoeper, E. Zur Rolandssage. Koch, F. Fausts Gang zu den Müttern. Koenig, F. W. Mutter-

(Continued)

N. Y. P. L. August 25, 1927

Austria. National-Bibliothek, Vienna: Festschrift... (Continued)

recht und Thronfolge im alten Elam. Lach, R. Aus dem Handschriftenschatze der Musikaliensammlung der Wiener Nationalbibliothek. Leporini, H. Simon von Niederaltaich und Martin von Senging. Mantuani, J. Zu den Gemälden vom Meister der weiblichen Halbfiguren. Matzenauer, F. Hamsun, vorläufiges zu seiner Erkenntnis. Piesch, H. Meister Eckharts Lehre vom "Gerechten." Pirker, M. Die Komödie von den zum Edelmann gemachten Besenbinder und ihre Vorlage. Premerstein, A. V. M. Amand, Ritter von. Griechisch-heidnische Weise als Verkünder christlicher Lehre in Handschriften und Kirchenmalereien. Rathe, K. Ein Architektur-Musterbuch der Spätgotik mit graphischen Einklebungen. Roretz, K. von. Die Lebensauffassung des Rinascimento, ihre Wurzeln

(Continued)

N. Y. P. L. August 25, 1927

Austria. National-Bibliothek, Vienna: Festschrift... (Continued)

und Formen. Roettinger, H. Der Meister IB ist Jörg Pencz. Schmidl, M. Volkskundliche Studien in der Ebene von Sofia. Schoemer, R. Über die Quellen zu Vondels "Maeghden." Seif, T. Vom Alexanderroman. Smital, O. Miszellen zur Geschichte der Wiener Palatina. Sonnleithner, R. Die Mondseer Bruchstücke der ältesten hochdeutschen Evangelienübersetzung. Teichl, R. Der Wiegendruck im Kartenbild. Wallner, E. Wien zwischen Reich und Landesfürstentum unter Kaiser Friedrich II. Walzel, O. Vom Wesen des deutschen Klassizismus. Weixlgaertner, A. Perspektivische Spielereien bei Renaissancekünstlern. Winkler, E. Die textliche Stellung der Handschrift 2597 der Wiener Nationalbibliothek (René von Anjou, Livre du cuer d'amours espris).

N. Y. P. L. August 25, 1927

FHV
+

AUSTRIA. Österreichischer Rundfunk.
Kärnten; lebendiges Volkstum. Festschrift herausgegeben vom Österreichischen Rundfunk anlässlich der Arbeitstagung "Lebendiges Volkstum und Rundfunk" in Klagenfurt, Pfingsten 1954. [Klagenfurt] 1954. 60 p. illus. 30cm.

Includes bibliographies.
CONTENTS. — Der Loibl, von J. F. Perkonig. —Seltsame Kärntner
(Continued)

NN ** 5. 56 p/v ODt EDt PC, 1 SL (MU) 2, 3 (LC1, X1, Z1)

AUSTRIA. Österreichischer Rundfunk. Kärnten...
(Card 2)

Volksbräuche, von G. Graber. — Wiedersehn mit der Drau, von V. Haselbach. — Entwicklung der Singarten des Kärntnerliedes, von A. Anderluh. — Ländlicher Altar, von V. Haselbach. —Kärtner Brauchtumstänze, von F. Koschier. —Dar ålte Tradkåstn, von G. Glawischnig. — Vom Hochwald und von den Waldleuten, von A. Traunig. — Dorfschullehrer, von V. Haselbach. --Volkskunst in Kärnten, von O. Moser. --De ålte Truhgn, von G. Glawischnig. — Dar sege Måhda, von G. Glawischnig. — Geschichtliche Wahrzeichen in Kärntens Landschaft, von R. Wanner. — Dar Roahrbrunn, von G. Glawischnig. —Zur Entstehung des Kärntner Freilichtmuseums,
(Continued)

AUSTRIA. Österreichischer Rundfunk. Kärnten...
(Card 3)

von G. Moro. — Dar Röchnmåcha Hane, von G. Glawischnig. — Reise durch Kärnten, von V. Haselbach. — Aufn Kirchte, von G. Glawischnig.

1. Carinthia—Social life, 20th cent. 2. Folk songs, German—Austria—Carinthia. 3. Dancing—Austria—Carinthia. t. 1954.

D-13
1618

AUSTRIA. Unterricht, Bundesministerium für.
200 Jahre österreiche Unterrichtsverwaltung, 1760-1960; Festschrift. [Die Herausgabe besorgte Sektionsrat Anton Kolbabek] Wien, Österreichischer Bundesverlag für Unterricht, Wissenschaft und Kunst [1960] 111 p. illus., ports. 21cm.

1. Education--Austria. I. Kolbabek, Anton, ed. i. [Title] Zweihundert. t. 1960.
NN R 8.61 s/ø (OC)I ODt EDt PC, 1, I SL (LC1, [I], Z1, X1)

MGO
(Gemito)
Azienda autonoma di soggiorno cura e turismo, Naples.
Onoranze a Gemito, nel primo centenario della nascita, MCMLII. Napoli, 1953. 93 p. plates, ports. 22cm.

Various contributors.
"Elenco delle opere esposte," p.[79]-93.
1 Gemito, Vicenzo, 1852-1929.
NN** 3.55 f/k OS(1b) PC,1 SL A,1 (LC1, Z1, X1)

ZFB
AUTOUR de Michel Servet et de Sebastien Castellion; recueil publié sous la direction de B. Becker. Haarlem, H. D. Tjeenk Willink, 1953. vii, 302 p. 24cm.

Contributions in French, German, English or Italian.
Includes bibliographies.
CONTENTS. -- Das Geschichtsproblem der Toleranz, von J. Kühn. -- Michael Servetus and the trinitarian speculation of the Middle Ages, by R. H. Bainton. --Die Geschichte der Christianismi restitutio im Lichte ihrer Abschriften, von E. F. Podach. -- Michael Servetus and the lesser circulation of the blood through the lungs, by J. F. Fulton. --L'influence

(Continued)
NN ** R X 11.53 OC, I, Ib PC, 1, 2, I SL (LC1, Z1, X1)

G-10
1657
AZORIN; homenaje al maestro en su XC aniversario [por] Heliodoro Carpintero [et al.] Madrid, Editorial Prensa española, 1964. 310 p. ports. 33cm.

Issued by A B C in honor of Azorín's 90th birthday.
Bibliography, p. 293-298.
CONTENTS. --Retrato de Azorín, por H. Carpintero. --España en Azorín, por S. Riopérez y Milá. --El estilo de Azorín y su proyección en la literatura contemporánea, por J. A. Pérez-Rioja.
1. Martínez Ruíz, José, 1873- I. Carpintero, Heliodoro.
II. ABC; diario ilustrado.
NN R 4.65 a/ OC, I (OS)II PC, 1, I, II SL (LC1, X1, Z1)

AUTOUR de Michel Servet et de Sebastien Castellion... (Card 2)

de Servet sur le mouvement antitrinitarien en Pologne et en Transylvanie, par S. Kot. --L'affaire Servet dans les controverses sur la tolérance au temps de la révocation de l'Edit de Nantes, par J. Jacquot. -- La naturalisation de Michel Servet, par F. Rude. --Reinier Telle, traducteur de Castellion et de Servet, par H. de la Fontaine Verwey. --La place de Castellion dans l'histoire de l'esprit, par J. Lindeboom. --Castellio paedagogus, by H. W. F. Stellwag. --La langue de Castellion dans sa Bible française, par J. van Andel. --Die Frage nach einem hermeneutischen Prinzip bei Castellio, von H. Liebing. --Castellion, Jean Rouxel et les oracles sibyllins, par V. L. Saulnier. -- Note su alcuni

(Continued)

---

*KF
1965
B. W. HUEBSCH, 1876-1964. A record of a meeting of his friends at the Grolier club, New York City, on December 9, 1964. [New York] Privately printed [1965] 31 (1) p. port. 24cm.

"750 copies (not for sale) printed"
"Photography by Lotte Jacobi."

1. Huebsch, Benjamin W.

NN R 12.65 e/-OC PC, 1 SL R, 1 (RI 1, LC1, X1, Z1)

AUTOUR de Michel Servet et de Sebastien Castellion... (Card 3)

aspetti del misticismo del Castellione e della sua fortuna, di D. Cantimori. --Castellio's De arte dubitandi and the problem of religious liberty, by E. F. Hirsch. --Censured passages from Castellio's Defensio suarum translationum, by S. van der Woude. -- Sur quelques documents manuscrits concernant Castellion, par B. Becker.

1. Servetus, Michael, 1511-1553. 2. Châteillon, Sebastien, 1515-1563. I. Becker, B., historian, ed.

---

*OAC
+
BA SHIN, ed.
Essays offered to G.H. Luce by his collegues and friends in honour of his seventy-fifth birthday. Editors: Ba Shin, Jean Boisselier [and] A.B. Griswold. Ascona, Switzerland, Artibus Asiae, 1966. 2 v. illus., port., maps, plans. 32cm. (Artibus Asiae. Supplementum. 23)

Includes bibliographies.

(Continued)
NN R 10.68 v/A OC, Ibo, III SL A,3,4,III O,1, [I] III (OS)II PC,1,2,3,II, 2,3,II,III (LC1,X1,Z1)

---

*YNC
...Aux sources de la tradition chrétienne. Mélanges offerts à M. Maurice Goguel à la occasion de son soixante-dixième anniversaire. Neuchâtel [etc.] Delachaux & Niestlé [1950] xvi, 280 p. port. 24cm.

Bibliographical footnotes.

NN 1. Bible. N. T.—Criticism. 2. Goguel, Maurice, 1880-

BA SHIN, ed. Essays offered to G.H. Luce by his collegues and friends in honour of his seventy-fifth birthday. (Card 2)

CONTENTS.—v.1. Papers on Asian history, religion, languages, literature, music folklore, and anthropology.—v.2. Papers on Asian art and archaeology.
1.Luce, Gordon Hannington. 2. Oriental studies—Collections. 3, Luce, Gordon Hannington—Bibl.
4. Art, Oriental. I. Ba Shin. II.Series.
III. Title.

AN
(Singh, B.)
Baba Kharak Singh Abhinandan committee, New Delhi.
Baba Kharak Singh Abhinandan Granth, 86th birthday commemoration volume. New Delhi [1954] 247 p. illus.,ports. 29cm.

1. Singh, Baba Kharak, 1868-

NN**R 11.54 f/+ (OC)1b OS(1b+0) PC,1 SL 0,1 (LC1,Z1,X1)

MNR
Bäcksbacka, Leonard, 1892-
...St.Petersburgs juvelerare, guld- och silversmeder 1714-1870; ett bidrag till kännedom om deras verksamhet. Helsingfors, Konstsalongens förlag [1950] 548 p. illus. 25cm.

No. 304 of 500 copies.
"Källförteckning," p.547-548.

1. Jewelers—Russia—Leningrad. 2. Goldsmiths—Russia—Leningrad. 3. Silversmiths—Russia—Leningrad.
NN 12.52 OC PC,1,2,3. SL A,1,2,3 S,1,2,3 (LC1,Z1,X1)

E-12
3329
BACH, ADOLF, 1890-
Germanistisch-historische Studien; gesammelte Abhandlungen, dem Autor zum goldenen Doktorjubiläum am 27. Februar 1964. Hrsg. von Heinrich M. Heinrichs und Rudolf Schützeichel. Bonn, L. Röhrscheid, 1964. 839 p. illus., port., maps. 25cm.

Bibliography, p. [799]-815.

(Continued)
NN * R 5.65 e/ OC, I, II PC, 1, 2, 3, I, II SL (LC1, X1, Z1)

2

BACH, ADOLF, 1890- . Germanistisch-historische Studien... (Card 2)

1. German language--Addresses, essays, lectures. 2. Geography--Names--Germany. 3. Germany--Hist.--Addresses, essays, lectures.
I. Heinrichs, Heinrich Matthias, ed. II. Schützeichel, Rudolf, ed.

VPG
BADEN, GERMANY (DISTRICT). Staatliche landwirtschaftliche Versuchs- und Forschungsanstalt Augustenberg.
...Entwicklung und Wirken der Bad. Staatl. Landwirtschaftlichen Versuchs- und Forschungsanstalt Augustenberg; herausgegeben von Direktor Dr. H. Riehm. Grötzingen [1950] 173 p. illus. 24cm.

At head of title: 90 Jahre, 1859-1949.

591300B. 1. Riehm, H.

NN R 3.53 (OC)I OD ED PC, I SL (LC1, Z1, X1)

PKI
BADISCHE ANILIN-& SODA-FABRIK A.-G.
Festschrift Carl Wurster [Herrn Professor Dr. Ing. Dr. rer. nat.h.c., Dr.Ing.E.h. Carl Wurster zum 60. Geburtstag, 2.Dez. 1960. Wissenschaftliche Arbeiten aus den Laboratorien und Betrieben der Badischen Anilin- & Soda-Fabrik A.G.Gesamtherstellung: Johannes Weisbecker] Ludwigshafen am Rhein, 1960. 485 p. illus. 24cm.

Includes bibliographies.
1. Wurster, Carl, 1900- . 2. Chemistry--Essays and misc. I. Weisbecker, Johannes, ed. II. Title. III. Weisbecker, Johannes, t. 1960.
NN R 5.64 a/ (OC)Ib+, I, II, IIIb+ OS PC, 1, 2, I, II SL ST, 1, 2t, I, II (LC1, X1, Z1)

3-MNE
BADISCHE HANDWERKSKAMMER, FREIBURG IM BREISGAU, GERMANY.
Festschrift zum 50. Jahrestag der Errichtung der Badischen Handwerkskammer Freiburg im Breisgau. Im Auftrag des Vorstandes zusammengestellt von Egbert Keller. Freiburg i. Brg., Universitätsdruckerei Poppen & Ortmann, 1951. 160 p. (p. 128-160 advertisements) illus. 21cm.

1. Art industries and trade—Assoc. and org.—Germany—Freiburg im Breisgau. 2. Art industries and trade—Germany—Freiburg im Breisgau. I. Keller, Egbert.
NN** 4.54 (OC)I, Ibo OS PC. 1,2,I SL A,1,2,I (Z1, LC1, X1)

E-11
4377
BÄHR, HANS WALTER, ed.
Albert Schweitzer, sein Denken und sein Weg. Tübingen, J.C.B. Mohr, 1962. xiv, 578 p. port. 24cm.

Various contributors.
Bibliography, p. [xiii]-xiv.

1. Schweitzer, Albert, 1875-
NN R 3.62 p/p OC PC, 1 SL (LC1, X1, Z1)

---

*PBM p. v. 880
BAERWALD, HERMANN.
Dr. Hermann Baerwald, 1828-1907; selected papers, biographical and others (translated from the German), collected for the members of his family by his son, Paul Baerwald. With a bibliography of publications by and on Hermann Baerwald, prepared and annotated by Guido Kisch. New York City, 1950. 48 l. port. 28cm.

"For private circulation. Number 41."
Various contributors.

(Continued)
NN R 6.65 a/B OC, I, IIbo PC, I, I SL J, 2, I (LC1, X1, Z1)

2

BAERWALD, HERMANN. Dr. Hermann Baerwald, 1828-1907... (Card 2)

1. Jews in Germany--Hist.--Addresses, essays, lectures. 2. Germany--Hist.--Addresses, essays, lectures. I. Baerwald, Paul, ed. and tr. II. Baerwald, Paul.

L-11
2830
v. 30

BÄUMER, REMIGIUS.
Martin Luther und der Papst. Münster, Verlag Aschendorff [1970] 100 p. 23cm. (Katholisches Leben und Kirchenreform im Zeitalter der Glaubensspaltung. 30)

Festschrift in honor of H. Jedin.
Bibliographical footnotes.
1. Luther, Martin. 2. Papacy. 3. Jedin, Hubert, 1900- . I. Series.
NN 4.71 e/z OC(1bo) (OS)I PC, 1, 2, 3, I (LC1, X1, Z1)

P-10
5567

BAGGE, POVL, 1902- , ed.
Højesteret, 1661-1961; udg. på Højesterets foranstaltning i trehundreåret for udstedelsen af Forordning om dend Høyeste rettis administration i Danmarck den 14. Februar 1661 af Povl Bagge, Jep Lauesen Frost [og] Bernt Hjejle. København, Gads Forlag, 1961.
2 v. illus., ports. 26cm.
Bibliographical references included in "Noter" at end of articles.
Bibliography, p [542]
(Continued)
NN R 5.61 p/D OC. I. Ib,II. III. IV (OD)Vt (ED)Vt PC. 1. I. II. III. IV. V SL E. 1. I. II. III. IV RC. 1 (LC1, X1, Z1)

2

BAGGE, POVL, 1902- Højesteret, 1661-1961... (Card 2)

"Stat. af Arild Falk-Jensen og H. Hjorth-Nielsen: øverste tilforordnede, justitiarier og præsidenter, tilforordnede, ordinære assessorer og dommere, justitssekretærer, ekstraordinære assessorer, auskultanter, prokuratorer, advokater, sagførere, rigsadvokater, statsadvokater ved Højesteret." v. 2, p. [257]-541.

1. Lawyers--Denmark. I. Frost, Jep Lauesen, 1894- , joint ed. II. Hjejle, Bernt, joint ed. III. Falk-Jensen, Arild, 1886- IV. Hjorth-Nielsen, Henning, 1878- V. Denmark. Courts. Højesteret. t. 1961

E-11
3731

BAHNER, WERNER, ed.
Literaturgeschichte als geschichtlicher Auftrag. Werner Krauss zum 60. Geburtstag Festgabe von seinen Leipziger Kollegen und Schülern. [1. Aufl.] Berlin, Rütten & Loening [1961] 293 [1] p. 25cm.

Bibliographical references included in "Anmerkungen," p. 235-[294].
CONTENTS. --Der historisch-gesellschaftliche Standort der Ideen Mablys, von W. Bahner. --Epentheorie und Zeitgeschichte, von A. Dessau. --
(Continued)
NN R 12.61 a/P OC PC, 1, 2 SL (LC1, X1, Z1) [I]

3

BAHNER, WERNER., ed. Literaturgeschichte als geschichtlicher Auftrag. (Card 2)

Wandlungen Arkadiens: die Marcela-Episode des "Don Quijote," von E. Köhler. --Babeuf in Deutschland, von W. Markov. --Faust, Aufklärung, Sturm und Drang, von H. Mayer. --Rationalismus und Sensualismus in der Diskussion über die Wortstellung, von U. Ricken. --Dom Léger-Marie Deschamps, 1716-1774: La vérité ou le vrai système, von K. Schnelle. --Brissot und die Kritik am Eigentum in der zweiten Hälfte des 18. Jahrhunderts, von W. Techtmeier. --Prometheus: unmittelbare und mittelbare Produktion

(Continued)

BAHNER, WERNER, ed. Literaturgeschichte als geschichtlicher Auftrag. (Card 3)

der Geschichte, von C. Träger. --Bibliographie der Publikationen von Werner Krauss bis 1960, von H. Schäfer und E. Richter, p. 227-[231].

1. Literature--Addresses, essays, lectures. 2. Krauss, Werner, 1900-

D-14
3766

Bains, J S , ed.
Studies in political science. New York, Asia Pub. House [1961]
xv, 448 p. 23 cm.
"For Dr. C. J. Chacko ... on his sixtieth birthday."
Bibliographical footnotes.
CONTENTS.—International law and relations: The challenge to international law, by P. C. Jessup. Sovereignty and international cooperation, by Q. Wright. Changing balance of power: the "neutral" nations in the United Nations, by N. D. Palmer. The sociological approach to international relations, by B. Landheer. The discriminatory
(Continued)
NN* R 6.63 g/A OC PC, 1, 2, 3, 4 SL E, 1, 2, 3, 4 O, 3, 4 (LC1, X1, Z1)

4

Bains, J S ed. Studies in political science. [1961] (Card 2)

CONTENTS—Continued.

clause in South Asian treaties in the seventeenth and eighteenth centuries. Domestic jurisdiction and international law: a theoretical analysis, by J. S. Bains.—Political theory and research: Next steps in research in comparative electoral systems, by J. K. Pollock. Emergent areas of social science research, by P. Bradley. Politicians and generals, by W. H. Morris-Jones. The concept of force in the political theory of ancient India, by N. Singh. Synthesists or culturists: a study of Indian political thought, by P. S. Muhar. The problem of

(Continued)

Bains, J S ed. Studies in political science. [1961] (Card 3)

CONTENTS—Continued.

surveyability in the modern democratic process, by G. N. Dhawan. T. H. Green on political obligation, by B. S. Sharma. St. Thomas's conception of secular authority, by J. S. Bains. The philosophy of Sarvodaya, by B. S. Sharma.—Public administration: The political control of nationalized industries in Britain, by W. A. Robson. Relations between the political and the permanent executive in India, by G. N. Singh. Fundamental rights and the Constitution of India, by H. Singh. Development administration in India, by R. Dwarkadas. Accountability of public enterprises, by M. V. Pylee. Parliamentary procedure in India, by R. N. Mathur. Bureaucracy in action, by S. R. Nigam.

(Continued)

BAINS, J. S., ed. Studies in political science. [1961] (Card 4)

1. Political science--Addresses, essays, lectures. 2. International relations. 3. India--Govt., 1947- . 4. Chacko, Chirakaikaran Joseph, 1899-

* Z-925
Film Reproduction

BALINGER VOLKSFREUND.
700 [i.e. Siebenhundert] Jahre Stadt Balingen. Sonderbeilage des "Balinger Volksfreund" im Jubiläumsjahr 1955. [Balingen, 1955] 72 p. illus., port. 31cm.

Film reproduction. Negative.

1. Balingen, Germany.
NN R 1.61 g/ OS PC, 1   SL (UM 1, LC1, X1, Z1)

---

* MEC
(Nielsen)-C

Balzer, Jürgen, 1906– *ed.*
Carl Nielsen; centenary essays. Copenhagen, Nyt nordisk forlag, 1965.
127 p. illus., music, ports. 26 cm.

1. Nielsen, Carl, 1865–1931.
NN* R 2.66 g/ OC PC, 1   SL MU, 1 (LC1, X1, Z1)

SGN

BAMBERG, GERMANY. Stadtarchiv.
150 [i.e. Hundertfünfzig] Jahre Bürgerspital Bamberg auf dem Michaelsberg. Festschrift zur 150-Jahrfeier der Verlegung der Vereinigten Katharinen- und Elisabethen-Spitäler in die Gebäude der vormaligen Benediktiner-Abtei Michaelsberg. Bamberg, 1954.
19 p. illus., facsims. 25cm.

CONTENTS.—Das Alter des "Bürgerspitals."—Das Katharinen-Spital bei (Alt-) Sankt Martin. — Stifter und Ausstattung. -- Name und Zweck. — Spital-Gebäude. —Stiftungsverwaltung. —Das
(Continued)
NN** 6.55 g/, ODt(Ib+)   EDt PC, 1 SL (E)1 (Z1, LC1, X1)

BAMBERG, GERMANY. Stadtarchiv. 150 [i.e. Hundertfünfzig]...
(Card 2)

Elisabethen-Spital am Sand. — Die Vereinigung des Elisabethen-mit dem Katharinen-Spital. — Das Benediktinerabtei Sankt Michael. — Die Verlegung der Vereinigten Spitäler auf den Michaelsberg. — Das Schicksal der bisherigen Spitalgebäude. --Dr. Adalbert Friedrich Marcus und die Spital-Reform. — Die Reorganisation der Stiftungsverwaltung. — Seit der Rückkehr des Bürgerspitals unter städtische Verwaltung.
1. Almshouses— Germany—Bamberg.   t. 1954.

TG p.v.299

Bank- und Kreditwesen in Österreich... Wien: Österreichischer Wirtschaftsverlag, 1933. 80 p. front. (port.) 24cm. (Betriebswirtschaftliche Blätter. Sonderreihe. Heft 3.)

"Sonderdruck der Festnummer für Julius Ziegler zum 70. Geburtstage."
CONTENTS.—Meithner, K. Zur neueren Entwicklung des österreichischen Kreditbankwesens.—Kerschagl, R. Etappen der Notenbankpolitik in Österreich.—Zaglits, O. Entwicklung und Lage des Pfandbriefkredites in Österreich.—Stigleitner, H. Das Sparkassenwesen in Österreich.—Berger-Vösendorf, A. V. Probleme staatlicher und halbstaatlicher Banken in Österreich.—Gutmann, H. Rationalisierungsmassnahmen im

(Continued)

N. Y. P. L.   May 12, 1936

Bank- und Kreditwesen in Österreich... (Card 2)

österreichischen Bankwesen.—Swoboda, W. Das industrielle Bankgeschäft in Österreich.—Sprung, B. Die künftige Auslandsarbeit der österreichischen Banken.—Schlesinger, M. Die allgemeinen Geschäftsbedingungen der österreichischen und der deutschen Banken.

821375A. 1. Banks and banking—Austria. 2. Ziegler, Julius, 1863– . I. Meithner, Karl, 1892– . II. Kerschagl, Richard, 1896– . III. Zaglits, Oskar. IV. Ser.
N. Y. P. L.   May 12, 1936

D-16
5732

BANKS, CHARLOTTE, ed.
Στεφανος ; studies in psychology presented to Cyril Burt, edited by Charlotte Banks and P. L. Broadhurst. London, University of London press [1965]
283 p. port. 23cm.

Title transliterated: Stephanos.
Includes bibliographies.
CONTENTS. --Cyril Burt: a biographical sketch and appreciation, by C. Valentine. --Causal explanations in psychology, by C. A. Mace.
(Continued)
NN R 5.66 p/ OC, I, IIbo, IIIbo   PC, 1, 2, I SL (LC1, X1, Z1)
[1]   3

BANKS, CHARLOTTE, ed. Γτεφανος ; studies in psychology presented to Cyril Burt...
(Card 2)

--Neurology and free will, by J.S. Wilkie. --Motivation: a biased review, by A. Koestler. --The personality system, by P.E. Vernon. --Social ascent in England today, by T.H. Pear. --Implications of research on creativity, by J.P. Guilford. --The nature of man, by G. Murphy. --Prediction in practice, by M. Hamilton. --Intelligence testing of full-term and premature children by repeated assessments, by J.A. Frader Roberts and E. Sedgley. --The psychological assessment of the children from the Island of Tristan da Cunha, by G. Keir. --Boys in detention centres, by C. Banks.
(Continued)

BANKS, CHARLOTTE, ed. Στεφανος: studies in psychology presented to Cyril Burt...
(Card 3)

Emotionality in the rat; a problem of response specificity, by P.L. Broadhurst and H.J. Eysenck --Higher order factor structures and reticular-vs.-hierarchical formulae for their interpretation, by R.B. Cattell.

1. Burt, Sir Cyril Lodowic, 1883- 2. Psychology--Addresses, essays, lectures. I. Broadhurst, P.L., joint ed. II. Broadhurst, P.L. III. Banks, Charlotte.

L-11
698

BARCELONA (City). Universidad. Filosofía y letras, Facultad de.
Homenaje a Jaime Vicens Vives. Barcelona, 1965. 1 v. illus., maps (1 fold.), facsims. 25cm.

Articles in several languages.
Publicaciones de Vicens Vives [por] Pilar Galera Cuff, p. xix-xxxiv.
Bibliographical footnotes.
1. Vicens Vives, Jaime. 2. History—Historiography.
NN R 5.67 r/L OS PC, 1, 2 SL (LC1, X1, Z1)

TB

BARI, Italy (City). Università. Economia e commercio, Facoltà di.
Studi in memoria di Rodolfo Benini. Bari, 1956. 236 p. port. 26cm.

CONTENTS. --In memoria di Rodolfo Benini, di P. Mazzoni e G. Lasorsa. --Caratteri generali delle imprese di navigazione marittima, di A. Amaduzzi. --Rappresentazione della popolazione irlandese dal 1836 al 1856, di L. Amoroso. --La crisi finanziaria di un comune veronese del sec. XVI:
(Continued)

NN 9.60 a// OS PC, 1, 2 SL E, 1, 2 (LC1, X1, Z1)

3

Copy only words underlined & classmark-- CA

BARNES, PATRICIA M., ed.
A medieval miscellany for Doris Mary Stenton. General editors Patricia M. Barnes [and] C.F. Slade. London, Print. for the Pipe roll society, by J.W. Ruddock & sons, 1962. xii, 345 p. 26cm. (Pipe roll society. Publications, v. 76)

A list of the published writings of Doris Mary Stenton, p. [269]-273.
1. Great Britain--Hist.--Medieval period, 1066-1485. 2. Great Britain--Geneal. 3. Stenton, Doris Mary (Parsons), lady. I. Slade, C.F., joint ed. II. Series.
NN R 10.63 f/B OC, I (OS)II PC, 1, 2, 3, I, II G, 2, 3, II (LC1, X1, Z1)

BARI, Italy (City). Università. Economia e commercio, Facoltà di. Studi in memoria di Rodolfo Benini. (Card 2)

Porto di Legnano, di G. Barbieri. --Indici unilaterali e bilaterali di connessione, di C.E. Bonferroni. --Aspetti concreti della previsione economica in un scritto poco noto di R. Benini, di G. Capodaglio. --Metodologia contabile e metodologia statistica, di P.E. Cassandro. --Sulla ripartizione dei patrimoni ereditari, di R. D'Addario. --Dello stato fattore di produzione, di G. di Nardi. --Per la programmazione lineare nella finanza pubblica, di E. Fossati. --Postille in margine a due lettere di R. Benini sulle relazioni tra redditi e patrimoni, di G. Lasorsa. --Sulla
(Continued)

AN
(Bartels, A.)

Bartels-Bund.
Festgabe zum sechzigsten Geburtstag von Adolf Bartels, mit Beiträgen von Friedrich Andersen, Richard Behm, Theobald Bieder... [und anderen] Hrsg. vom Bartels-Bund... Leipzig: H. Haessel, 1922. 192 p. front. 22cm.

232299B. 1. Bartels, Adolf, 1862-
N. Y. P. L. June 30, 1943

Fest.

BARI, Italy (City). Università. Economia e commercio, Facoltà di. Studi in memoria di Rodolfo Benini. (Card 3)

distribuzione dei redditi, di P. Mazzoni. --La pubblicità delle società commerciali secondo il diritto (c.d.) transitorio, di G. Minervini. --"Tipi sociali" e "generi di vita" nel Molise, di L. Ranieri. --La imposta complementare e la imposta di famiglia nei comuni capoluoghi di provincia, di F.A. Répaci. --Sullo spopolamento dell'Appenino tosco-emiliano, di V. Ricchioni. --La geografia politica ed economica in Italia, di U. Toschi. --Rodolfo Benini dantista. --Teoria e pratica dei costi comuni, di F. Vinci.
1. Benini, Rodolfo, 1862-1956. 2. Economica--Essays and misc.

F-10
377

Barth, Germany. Rat.
Festschrift zur 700-Jahrfeier der Stadt Barth, vom 1. bis 10. Juli 1955. [Barth, 1955] 126 p. illus., ports., facsims. 30cm.

1. Barth, Germany—Hist. I. Title. t. 1955.
NN**R 3.58 ODt(1b+) EDt PC,1,I SL (LC1,X1,Z1)

C-13
1067

BARING, MARTIN, ed.
Aus 100 Jahren Verwaltungsgerichtsbarkeit; Festschrift Köln, C. Heymann, 1963. 172 p. illus., ports, map. 20cm.

Includes bibliographical references
CONTENTS--Paul Persius, der Schöpfer der preussischen Verwaltungsgerichtsbarkeit, von H. Egidi. --Verwaltungsrechtspflege in Bayern von 1863 bis 1960, von J. Widtmann. --Die Verwaltungsrechtspflege in Sachsen; Ereignisse und Gestalten, von M. Baring. --Über die württembergische Verwaltungsgerichtsbarkeit, von H.W. Zinser. --
(Continued)
NN 4.66 p/c OC PC, 1, 2 SL E, 1, 2 (LC1, X1, Z1)

2

IKL

BARTLETT, NAPIER, 1836-1877.
Military record of Louisiana, including biographical and historical papers relating to the military organizations of the State. Baton Rouge, Louisiana State University press [1964] xv, 259 p. 23cm.

1. United States--Hist.--Civil war--Personal narratives. 2. United States--Hist.--Civil war--Military--Regt. hist.--Louisiana.
NN *R 6.64 p/ OC PC, 1, 2 SL AH, 1, 2 (LC1, X1, Z1)

BARING, MARTIN, ed. Aus 100 Jahren Verwaltungsgerichtsbarkeit... (Card 2)

100 Jahre Verwaltungsgerichtsbarkeit in Baden, von E. Walz. --Karl Dugend, der Begründer der oldenburgischen Verwaltungsgerichtsbarkeit, von M. Sellmann. --36 Jahre thüringisches Oberverwaltungsgericht, 1912-1948, von H. Loening.

1. Law, Administrative--Germany. 2. Administrative courts--Germany.

---

*MEC
(Wagner, Wolfgang)

BARTH, HERBERT, ed.
Wolfgang Wagner zum 50. Geburtstag, mit Beiträgen von Martin Gregor-Dellin, Jim Ford und Paul-André Gaillard. Bayreuth, Edition Musica [1969] 26 p. illus. 20cm.

Title also in English and French.
Essays in German, English or French.

1. Wagner, Wolfgang. I. Gregor-Dellin, Martin.
NN 3.71 b/z OC, I PC, 1, I SL MU, 1, I (LC1, X1, Z1)

Copy only words underlined
& Classmark-- KAA

BARTHEL, HELLMUTH, ed.
Landschaftsforschung; Beitrage zur Theorie und Anwendung. Gotha, H. Haack, 1968. 279 p. illus., port., maps(7 fold. col., issued in pocket) 25cm. (Petermanns (Dr. A.) Mitteilungen aus Justus Perthes' geographischer Anstalt. Ergänzungshefte. Nr. 271)

"Neef-Festschrift."
Papers in German; summaries in German, Russian and English.
Includes bibliographies.
CONTENTS.--Historische Prinzipien in der geographische
(Continued)

NN R 8.69 k/ℓOC (OS)I PC, 1, 2, I (LC1, X1, Z1)

BARTHEL, HELLMUTH, ed. Landschaftsforschung...
(Card 2)

Raumforschung, von E. Lehmann. --Beitrag zum Modell des Geokomplexes, von H. Richter. --Grossmassstäbliche Landschaftsanalyse im Spiegel eines Modells, von K. Herz. --Pedon und Pedotop--Bemerkungen zu Grundfragen der regionalen Bodengeographie, von G. Haase. --Der Vergleich landschaftsökologischer Typen des nordsächsischen Flachlandes und ein Vorschlag zu ihrer Klassifikation, von H. Hubrich und R. Schmidt. --Beispiel einer Standortkarte im Massstab 1:25000 und die Möglichkeit ihrer Auswertung für die agrarische Praxis, von A. Bernhardt. --Zur Frage der landschaftsökologischen Erkundung in den Braunkohlenrevieren unter besonderer Berücksichtigung der Grundwassererneuerung in den Kippflächen, von H. Barthel. --Der Einfluss der Boden auf

(Continued)

BARTHEL, HELLMUTH, ed. Landschaftsforschung...
(Card 3)

die Grundwasserneubildung im Pathe-Gebiet, von M. Thomas-Lauckner und R. Spengler. --Geländebedingte Kaltluftverteilung in Strahlungsnächten im Elbsandsteingebirge--eine Diskussion der Methode von Schuepp und Uhlig, von G. Andreas. --Gedanken zur Frage der Bewertung des landschaftlichen Erholungspotentials, von E. Hartsch. --Modellvorstellungen der Entwicklung von Zentralortssystemen, von G. Kind. --Standortfragen und Entwicklungsprobleme der Leipziger Kleinindustrie, von D. Scholz. --Die Bedeutung vollständiger Netze topographischer Elemente für die Landeskenntnis, von W. Stams. --Einheitliche Gestaltungsprinzipien und Generalisierungswere bei der Schaffung geomorphologischer Karten verschiedener Massstäbe, von H. Kugler.
1. Geography--Addresses, essays, lectures. 2. Neef, Ernst. I. Series.

E-11
5394

BARTMUSS, HANS JOACHIM, ed.
Die Volksmassen, Gestalter der Geschichte; Festgabe für Prof. Dr. h. c. Leo Stern zu seinem 60. Geburtstag, hrsg. von Hans-Joachim Bartmuss [et al.] Berlin, Rütten & Loening, 1962. 576 p. port. 25cm.

CONTENTS.—Karolingische Reichsidee und die Anfänge eines nationalen Bewusstseins im Spiegel althochdeutscher Sprachbezeichnungen, von B. Schreyer-Mühlpfordt.— Zum Charakter der "staufischen"
(Continued)

NN R 10.62 g/B OC, I, IIbo PC, 1, 2, I SL (LC1, X1, Z1)
[I]

BARTMUSS, HANS JOACHIM, ed. Die Volksmassen, Gestalter der Geschichte... (Card 2)

Städtepolitik, von E. Voigt.—Über das Verhalten der unternehmerischen Gewerken zum sogenannten Direktionsprinzip im sächsischen Silberbergbau im 15. bis 16. Jahrhundert, von M. M. Smirin.—Der Pinzgauer Bauernkrieg von 1526 und Michael Gaismair, von J. Macek.—Die Martin-Luther-Universität Halle-Wittenberg und Ungarn, von E. Selbmann.—Die Geschichte der deutsch-russischen Wissenschaftsbeziehungen im 18. Jahrhundert und Frankreich, von E. Winter.—Bemerkungen über die soziale und nationale Bedeutung der preussischen Reformbewegung unter dem Ministerium des Freiherrn vom Stein, von K. Obermann.—
Continued)

BARTMUSS, HANS JOACHIM, ed. Die Volksmassen, Gestalter der Geschichte... (Card 3)

Die Volksagitation in der Freien Stadt Frankfurt nach dem Wachensturm vom April 1833, von W. Kowalski.—Zur Geschichte der demokratischen Linken in der revolutionären Bewegung des Jahres 1848 in Halle, von E. Neuss.—Der Kampf der deutschen Bauern und Landarbeiter um eine Bodenreform (1848-1918-1945), von H. Hübner.—Quellen und Methoden zur Erforschung der Herausbildung und Strukturwandlung des Deutschen Industrie-Proletariats im letzten Drittel des 19. Jahrhunderts, von E. Engelberg.—Der deutsche Imperialismus und die diplomatische
(Continued)

BARTMUSS, HANS JOACHIM, ed. Die Volksmassen, Gestalter der Geschichte... (Card 4)

Vorbereitung der internationalen Intervention in China im Jahre 1900, von A. S. Jerussalimski.—Hans Baluschek, ein Maler des Werktätigen Berlins (1870-1935), von M. Steinmetz.—Die Verbreitung der Ideen der Grossen Sozialistischen Oktoberrevolution unter den Volksmassen Siebenbürgens, von V. Cherestesiu.—Die Stellung Frankreichs zum deutschen Imperialismus und Militarismus am Ende des ersten Weltkrieges, von L. Zsigmond.—Anfänge und Entwicklung der KPD im mitteldeutschen Industriegebiet zur Massenpartei in den Jahren 1919/20, von E. Stein.—Der antifaschistische
(Continued)

BARTMUSS, HANS JOACHIM, ed. Die Volksmassen, Gestalter der Geschichte... (Card 5)

Volksaufstand im Bulgarien im September 1923, von D. Kosseff.—Die "Friedens" bedingungen der imperialistischen Mächte und die Welles-Reise (Februar/März 1940), von G. Hass.—Zur Deutschlandpolitik der Westmächte während des zweiten Weltkrieges (1941-1945), von J. Böhm.—Die Partisanenrepubliken Ossola und Carnia, von W. Markov.—Die zunehmande Zersetzung der Franco-Diktatur, von J. Galán.—Entwicklung end Ergebnisse der kubanischen Revolution (1953-1960), von W. Basler.—Bibliographie Leo Stern (p. 559-572).
1. Germany--Hist.--Addresses, essays, lectures. 2. Stern, Leo. I. Title. II. Bartmuss, Hans Joachim.

E-11
9032

BASANTA KUMAR MALLIK: a garland of homage from some who knew him well [by] S. Radhakrishnan [and others] with a biography [by Winifred Lewis] London, V. Stuart [1961] xi, 192 p. illus., ports. 25cm.

1. Mallik, Basanta Kumar. I. Radhakrishnan, Sir Sarvepalli, 1888- . II. Lewis, Winifred.
NN R 2.64 e/ℓOC, I, II, IIbo PC, 1, I, II SL O, 1, I, II (LC1, X1, Z1)

E-11
8527

BASANTA KUMAR MALLIK; a garland of homage from some who knew him well, with a biography. [Contributions by] S. Radhakrishnan [and others] London. V. Stuart [1961] xi, 192 p. illus., ports. 25cm.

1. Mallik, Basanta Kumar.
NN R 12.63 a/ℓOC PC, 1 SL O, 1 (LC1, X1, Z1)

QPH

Basel (City). Museum für Völkerkunde.
Südseestudien; Études sur l'Océanie; South seas studies. Gedenkschrift zur Erinnerung an Felix Speiser; hrsg. vom Museum für Völkerkunde und schweizerischen Museum für Volkskunde Basel. Basel, 1951. viii,422 p. illus. 25cm.

Contributions in German, French or English.
Bibliographies included.

1. Ethnology—Oceanica. 2. Speiser, Felix, 1880-1949. I. Title.
NN R 9.53 OCs PCs, 1,2s,Is SLs (Z/Is,LCls, Xls)

C-10
338

BASEL-STADT (Canton). Regierungsrat.
Basel; Denkschrift zur Erinnerung an die vor 2000 Jahren erfolgte Gründung der Colonia Raurica, 44. V. Chr.-1957 N. Chr. Basel, Urs Graf-Verlag [1957] xii, 331 p. illus., plates (49 col.), ports., maps. 31cm.

1. BASEL 2. ART--COLLECTIONS--SWITZERLAND--BASEL 3. ART, SWISS--BASEL t. 1957

NN R 5.58 g/ ODts EDt PCs, Is SL As, 2s, 3s (LCls, Xls, Z/s, Cls, Yls)

TLV

Basel, Switzerland (City). **Universität.** Juristische Fakultät.
Beiträge zum Handelsrecht; Festgabe zum siebzigsten Geburtstage von Carl Wieland; herausgegeben von der Juristischen Fakultät der Universität Basel. Basel: Helbing & Lichtenhahn, 1934. xi, 460 p. 25cm.

Edited by August Simonius and Robert Haab.

Festschrift

791395A. 1. Commerce—Jurisp., 1934. 2. Wieland, Carl Albert, 1864– . I. Simonius, August, 1885– , ed. II. Haab, Robert, 1865– , ed. III. Title.
N. Y. P. L. March 31, 1936

ZDN

Basel, Switzerland (city). **Universität.** Theologische Fakultät.
Aus fünf jahrhunderten schweizerischer Kirchengeschichte; zum sechzigsten Geburtstag von Paul Wernle herausgegeben von der Theologischen Fakultät der Universität Basel. Basel: Helbing und Lichtenhahn, 1932. viii, 474 p. 25cm.

CONTENTS.—Schweizer, J. Zur Vorgeschichte der Basler Universität.—Köhler, W. Zwingli und Italien.—Camenisch, E. Der erste Bündner Katechismus 1537.—Barth, P. Calvins Lehre vom Staat als providentieller Lebensordnung.—Vischer, E. Das Collegium Alumnorum in Basel.—Aubert, L. Neuchâtel et le Consensus Helveticus.—Hartmann, B. Daniel Willi und die Anfänge des Pietismus in Graubünden.—Hoffmann, H. Das Christentum David Müslins.—Gauss, K. Die Kirche des Basel-

(Continued)

Festschrift

N. Y. P. L. August 26, 1933

Basel, Switzerland (city). **Universität.** Theologische Fakultät: Aus fünf jahrhunderten schweizerischer Kirchengeschichte... (Card 2)

biets während der Zeit der Mediation und Restauration.—Staehelin, E. Die Basler Kirche in den Basler Revolutionswirren von 1830–1833.—Strasser, O. E. Ein Typus bernischer Frömmigkeit: Joseph Burkhalter.—Burckhardt, P. Aus der Korrespondenz von A. E. Biedermann.—Pfisterer, K. Die schweizerischen protestantisch-kirchlichen Hilfsvereine und ihre Patronatsgemeinden in der Schweiz.—Liechtenhan, R. Die soziale Frage vor der schweizerischen Prediger-Gesellschaft.—Guisan, R. Le journal "Évangile et liberté" 1880–1894, Étude d'histoire religieuse vaudoise.—Schmidt, P. Verzeichnis der Veröffentlichungen von Professor Dr. theol. et phil. Paul Wernle.

651820A. 1. Wernle, Paul, 1872– . 2. Church history—Switzerland. I. Title.
N. Y. P. L. August 26, 1933

---

* ORD

BASTIN, JOHN, ed.
Malayan and Indonesian studies; essays presented to Sir Richard Winstedt on his eighty-fifth birthday, edited by John Bastin and R. Roolvink. Oxford, Clarendon press [1964] xii, 357 p. illus., port., maps, facsim., general tables. 23cm.

Bibliographical footnotes.
Sir Richard Winstedt's writings, p. 10-23.
CONTENTS.—A possible interpretation of the inscription (Continued)

NN R 12.64 g/B OC, I PC, I, 2, I O, I, 2, I (LCl, Xl, Z) SL

4

BASTIN, JOHN, ed. Malayan and Indonesian studies... (Card 2)

at Kĕdukan Bukit (Palembang), by G. Coedès.—Desultory remarks on the ancient history of the Malay peninsula, by P. Wheatley.—Takuapa; the probable site of a pre-Malaccan entrepot in the Malay peninsula, by A. Lamb.—The opening of relations between China and Malacca, 1403-5, by Wang, G.—The Achinese attack on Malacca in 1629, as described in contemporary Portuguese sources, by C.R. Boxer.—British commercial and strategic interest in the Malay peninsula during the late eighteenth century, by D.K. Bassett.—Problems of personality in the (Continued)

BASTIN, JOHN, ed. Malayan and Indonesian studies... (Card 3)

reinterpretation of modern Malayan history, by J. Bastin.—A Kedah letter of 1839, by C. Skinner.—The origins of British control in the Malay states before colonial rule, by C.M. Turnbull.—The Colonial office and the protected Malay states, by E. Sadka.—Migration and assimilation of rural Chinese in Trengganu, by L.A.P. Gosling.—Hikayat raja-raja Pasai and Sejarah Melayu, by A. Teeuw.—The character of the Malay annals, by P.E. De Josselin de Jong.—Two new 'old' Malay manuscripts, by R. Roolvink.—A Malay scriptorium, by P. Voorhoeve.—The Balinese sengguhu-priest, a shaman, but not a sufi, a saiva, and a vaisnava, by C. Hooykaas.—'Internal (Continued)

BASTIN, JOHN, ed. Malayan and Indonesian studies... (Card 4)

conversion' in contemporary Bali, by C. Geertz.—Amir Hamzah; Malay prince, Indonesian poet, by A.H. Johns.—Sumbangan Sir Richard Winstedt dalam pĕnyĕlidekan pĕngajian Mĕlayu, by Zainal-'Abidin bin Ahmad.

1. Winstedt, Sir Richard Olaf, 1878- . 2. Malay studies. I. Roolvink, Roelof, joint ed.

QCN

Battle Creek sanitarium, Battle Creek, Mich.
...Special issue in honor of the eightieth birthday of Professor Ivan P. Pavlov, with papers by his pupils, friends and admirers. Battle Creek, Mich.: The Medical faculty of the Battle Creek sanitarium, 1929. 222 p. incl. diagrs., tables. front., illus. (incl. ports.) 25cm. (Its: Bulletin... v. 24, no. 4.)

Cover-title.
Also paged continuously with series.

Festschrift

104063B. 1. Pavlov, Ivan Petrovich, 1849–1936. 2. Physiology.
N. Y. P. L. RUSSIAN HISTORICAL ARCHIVES. May 22, 1941

E-13
3327

BATTS, M.S., ed.
Essays on German literature in honour of G. Joyce Hallamore, edited by Michael S. Batts and Marketa Goetz Stankiewicz. [Toronto] University of Toronto press [1968] viii, 255 p. port. 24cm.

Bibliographical footnotes.
CONTENTS.--The votive masses of the Holy Spirit in Middle High German literature, by E. Egert.--Allegory and symbol
(Continued)

NN R 10.68 1/OC, I, IIbo PC, 1, 2, I SL (LC1, X1, Z1)
[I]

BATTS, M.S., ed. Essays on German literature in honour of G. Joyce Hallamore... (Card 2)

in Hartmann's Gregorius, by R. Picozzi.--Opitz' Schäfferey von der Nimfen Hercinie in seventeenth-century literature, by U. Maché.--Poetic imagination and external reality in Tieck, by R. Belgardt.--The grotesque in Barlach's work, by B.R. Anderson.--Narrator and narrative in Goethe's Die Wahlverwandtschaften, by G. Marahrens.--Ferdinand Raimund's Gutenstein poems, by F. Krügel.--The tailor and the sweeper: a new look at Wilhelm Raabe, by M.G. Stankiewicz.--The professing Christian and the ironic humanist: a comment
(Continued)

BATTS, M.S., ed. Essays on German literature in honour of G. Joyce Hallamore... (Card 2)

on the relationship of Alfred Döblin and Thomas Mann after 1933, by A.W. Riley.--Myth and morality: reflections on Thomas Mann's Doktor Faustus, by L.L. Miller.--"Das Gestische" and the poetry of Brecht, by G.L. Tracy.--Observations on Otto Flake, by H. Boeschenstein.

1. Hallamore, Gertrude Joyce. 2. German literature--Addresses, essays, lectures. I. Stankiewicz, Marketa Goetz, joint ed. II. Stankiewicz, Marketa Goetz.

* C-2 p.v.140

Batty Weber im Spiegel seiner Zeitgenossen; zu seinem zehnten Todestag 15. Dezember 1950 hrsg. von Emma Weber-Brugmann. Luxemburg, P. Linden [1950] 102 p. illus. 19cm.

"Verzeichnis der literarischen Werke," p. 99-102.

1. Weber, Batty, 1860-1940. I. Weber-Brugmann, Emma, ed.
NN R 3.53 OC, I PC, 1, I SL (LC1, Z1, X1)

C-12
4240

BAUDREXEL, JOSEF, ed.
Erwachsenenbildung heute und morgen; Festschrift für Karl Witthalm hrsg. von Josef Baudrexel, Anton Fingerle [und] Hans Lamm. München, Olzog Verlag [1962] 279 p. illus., ports. 20cm.

1. Education, Adult--Addresses, essays, lectures. 2. Witthalm, Karl. I. Fingerle, Anton, joint ed. II. Lamm, Hans, joint ed. III. Fingerle, Anton.
NN R 9.63 e/ OC, I, II, 2b+, IIIbo PC, 1, 2, I, II SL (LC1, X1, Z1)

TAH

Bauer, Clemens, 1899-
Gesammelte Aufsätze zur Wirtschafts- und Sozialgeschichte. Dem Verfasser zum 65. Geburtstag am 16. Dezember 1964 von Freunden, Kollegen und Schülern als Festgabe dargebracht. Mit einem Titelbild. Freiburg (i. Br.) Basel, Wien, Herder, 1965.
x, 527 p. 24 cm. DM 65.-

Includes bibliographies. "Veröffentlichungen von Clemens Bauer": p. 516-518.

1. Economic history, 476-1700. 2. Historians, German.
NN*R 12.66 a/ OC PC, 1, 2 SL E, 1 (LC1, X1, Z1)

E-11
8724

BAUER, WALTER, ed.
Ich glaube eine heilige Kirche; Festschrift für D. Hans Asmussen zum 65. Geburtstag am 21. August 1963, hrsg. von Walter Bauer [et al.] Stuttgart, Evangelisches Verlagswerk, 1963. 249 p. port. 25cm.

"Bibliographie der Veröffentlichungen... Hans Asmussen, p. [229]-240.
1. Asmussen, Hans, 1898- . 2. Evangelical Lutheran Church. 3. Church and state--Germany, 20th cent.
NN R 1.64 j/ OC PC, 1, 2, 3 SL E, 3 (LC1, X1, Z1)

E-12
8865

Bauer, Clemens, 1899- *ed.*
Speculum historiale. Geschichte im Spiegel von Geschichtsschreibung und Geschichtsdeutung. (Johannes Spörl aus Anlass seines 60. Geburtstages, dargebracht von Weggenossen, Freunden und Schülern.) Hrsg. von Clemens Bauer, Laetitia Boehm [und] Max Müller. Freiburg, München, Alber (1965)
xvi, 783 p. with front. 25 cm.
(Continued)
NN*R 5.67 g/ OC PC, 1, 2 SL (LC1, X1, Z1)
[I]

BAUER, CLEMENS, 1899- , ed. Speculum historiale. (Card 2)

Bibliographical footnotes.

1. Spörl, Johannes, 1904- . 2. History—Historiography—Addresses, essays, lectures.

*MGA

BAUM, RICHARD, 1902- , ed.
Musik und Verlag; Karl Vötterle zum 65. Geburtstag am 12. April 1968. Hrsg. von Richard Baum und Wolfgang Rehm. Kassel, New York, Bärenreiter, 1968. 624 p. illus., facsims., music. 24cm.

Includes bibliographical footnotes.
"Karl Vötterle: Bibliographie": p. [593]-599.

1. Vötterle, Karl, 1903- . Voetterle, Cassel. I. Rehm, 2. Bärenreiter-Verlag, Karl Wolfgang, 1929- , ed.
NN R 2.70 w/ OC, I PC, 1, 2, I SL MU, 1, 2, I (LC1, X1, Z1)

*C-4 p.v. 464

Bavaria. Staatsbibliothek, Munich.
Festgabe der Bayerischen Staatsbibliothek; Emil Gratzl zum 75. Geburtstag. Wiesbaden, O. Harrassowitz, 1953. 123 p. port.,facsims., plan. 25cm.

Pref. signed: Gustav Hofmann.
Contents.—Schmeller als Bibliothekar, von P. Ruf.—Der Humanist Johann Albrecht Widmanstetter (1506-57) als klassischer Philologe, von H. Striedl.— (Continued)

NN* 1.55 j/ (OC)I ODi EDi PC,1,2,3,I SL (Z, LC1,X1)

Bavaria. Staatsbibliothek, Munich. Festgabe der Bayerischen Staatsbibliothek... (Card 2)

Ein Bibliophiles Gedicht von Wang an Shi (1019-86) von F.J. Meier.

1. Gratzl, Emil, 1877- . 2. Schmeller, Johann Andreas 1785-1852. 3. Widmanstetter, Johann Albrecht, d. 1557. I. Title. i. 1953

D-14 3172

BECK, Horace Palmer, 1920- ,ed.
Folklore in action; essays for discussion in honor of MacEdward Leach. Philadelphia, The American folklore society, 1962. 210 p. illus. 23cm. (American folk-lore society. Bibliographical and special series. v. 14)

1. Folk lore--Addresses, essays, lectures. 2. Leach, MacEdward. I. Series. i.Subs. for main entry: B-, H-P.

NN R L.65 c/ OCs (OS)Is PCs, 1s, 2s, Is SLs (AH)Is (LC1s, [i], X1s, Z1s) [II].

D-17 8194

Beckett at 60: a festschrift. London, Calder & Boyars, 1967.
vii, 100 p. front., 4 plates (incl. ports.). 21 cm.

CONTENTS.—Introduction, by J. Calder.—The thirties, by A. J. Leventhal.—A bloomlein for Sam, by M. Jolas.—First meeting with Samuel Beckett, by J. Lindon.—My collaboration with Samuel Beckett, by M. Mihalovici.—Working with Samuel Beckett, by J. MacGowran.—The first night of Waiting for Godot, by H. (Continued)

NN* R 11.67 g/ OC PC, 1 SL (LC1, X1, Z1)

2

BECKETT at 60... (Card 2)

Hobson.—In search of Beckett, by J. Fletcher.—Waiting for Beckett, by A. Schneider.—Samuel Beckett's poems, by M. Esslin.—Progress report 1962-65, by H. Kenner.—Beckett the magnificant, by M. Renaud.—My dear Sam, by R. Pinget.—Beckett, by H. Pinter.—Personal note, by C. Monteith.—In connection with Samuel Beckett, by F. Arrabal.—*A propos* Samuel Beckett, by P. Staib.—Tribute, by A. Higgins.—All the livelong way, by M. Hutchinson.—Samuel Beckett, by A. Simpson.—A letter, by J. Herbert.—Last tribute, by G. Devine.

1. Beckett, Samuel, 1906-

TPQ

[Beckh, Max,]
Deutschlands erste Eisenbahn, Nürnberg-Fürth; ein Werk von Tatkraft und Gemeinsinn. Nürnberg: J. L. Schrag, 1935. 353 p. illus. (incl. facsims.), ports. 25½cm.

"Festschrift zur Jahrhundertfeier."
On verso of t.-p.: Im Auftrag der Oberbürgermeister der Städte Nürnberg und Fürth, und der Ludwigseisenbahn-Gesellschaft verfasst von Stadtoberamtmann Dr. Max Beckh.

807217A. 1. Railways—Germany—Indiv.—Ludwigs-Eisenbahn. I. Fürth, Germany (Bavaria). Oberbürgermeister. II. Ludwigs-Eisenbahn. III. Nuremberg. Oberbürgermeister. IV. Title.
N. Y. P. L. April 29, 1936

E-12 1366

BECKSCHE, C.H., VERLAGSBUCHHANDLUNG OSKAR BECK, Munich.
Festschrift zum zweihundertjährigen Bestehen des Verlages C.H.Beck, 1763-1963. [München, 1963] vi, 296 p. illus. 25cm.

NN R 10.64 a/OS PC SL (LC1, X1, Z1)

MA

BEER, ELLEN J., ed.
Festschrift Hans R. Hahnloser, zum 60. Geburtstag 1959, hrsg. von Ellen J. Beer, Paul Hofer [und] Luc Mojon. Basel, Birkhäuser, 1961. vii, 441 p. 27cm.

Contributions chiefly in German, with a few in French or Italian.
Includes bibliographies.

1. Hahnloser, Hans Robert, 1899- . 2. Art--Essays and misc. I. Hofer, Paul, 1909- , joint ed. II. Mojon, Luc, joint ed. III. Title.

NN R 8.61 v/ OC, I, II PC, 1, 2, I, II, III SL A, 1, 2, I, II, III (LC1, X1, Z1) [I]

* MYM

BEETHOVEN, LUDWIG VAN, 1770-1827.
[DUET, VIOLA & VIOLONCELLO, K. 32]
Duett mit zwei obligaten Augengläsern; Sonatensatz für Viola und Violoncello. Für die Aufführung eingerichtet und hrsg. von Fritz Stein. Leipzig, C.F. Peters [1952, 1912] Pl. no. 9665. score (10 p.) 32cm. (Edition Peters. Nr. 3375)

"Herausgegeben aus Anlass des 125. Todestages von Ludwig van Beethoven im Auftrag der Staatlichen Kommission für Kunstangelegenheiten." (Continued)

NN 10.60 g/ OC, I (OD)IIt (ED)IIt (OAF 1) SL MUg, Ig, IIg (U1, Z1, LC1, X1)

BEETHOVEN, LUDWIG VAN, 1770-1827. [DUET, VIOLA & VIOLONCELLO, K. 32] Duett mit zwei obligaten Augengläsern... (Card 2)

1. Viola and violoncello. I. Stein, Fritz, 1879- , ed. II. Saxony. Kunstangelegenheiten, Staatliche Kommission für. t. 1952.

AN
(Heuss, T.)

Begegnungen mit Theodor Heuss. [Gruss der Freunde zum siebzigsten Geburtstag am 31.Januar 1954] Hrsg. von Hans Bott und Hermann Leins. [Tübingen, R. Wunderlich, 1954] 494 p. port. 22cm.

1. Heuss, Theodor, pres. Germany (Federal republic), 1884- . I. Bott, Hans, ed. II. Leins, Hermann, ed.

NN**R X 3.54 OC,I, II,IIb PC,1,I,II SL LC1,Z1,X1)

OIN

Behnke, Heinrich, 1898– , *ed.*

Festschrift zur Gedächtnisfeier für Karl Weierstrass 1815–1965. Hrsg. von Heinrich Behnke und Klaus Kopfermann. Köln u. Opladen, Westdeutscher Verlag, 1966. 612 p. 25 cm. (Arbeitsgemeinschaft für Forschung des Landes Nordrhein-Westfalen. Wissenschaftliche Abhandlungen, Bd. 33)

Includes bibliographies.

CONTENTS.—Karl Weierstrass und seine Schule, von H. Behnke.—

(Continued)

NN*R 12.70 r/z OC, I, II, III, Vb* (OS)IV PC, 1, 2, I, II, III, IV SL ST, 1t, 2, I, II, III (LC1, X1, Z1)

6

Behnke, Heinrich, 1898– *ed.* Festschrift ... 1966. (Card 2)

Die Berufung von Weierstrass nach Berlin, von K. R. Biermann.—Aus dem Briefwechsel von G. Mittag-Leffler, von O. Frostman.—Karl Weierstrass als Schüler des Theodorianischen Gymnasiums zu Paderborn, von F. G. Hohmann.—Die "100-Jahr-Feier" von Weierstrass' Geburtstag in Münster in Westfalen im Jahre 1925, von R. König.—Weierstrass' Vorlesung zur Funktionentheorie, von K. Kopfermann.—Entwicklung der Theorie der eindeutigen analytischen Funktionen einer komplexen Veränderlichen seit Weierstrass, von R. Nevan-

(Continued)

Behnke, Heinrich, 1898– *ed.* Festschrift ... 1966. (Card 3)

linna.—Der Weierstrassche Satz der algebraischen Abhängigkeit von Abelschen Funktionen und seine Verallgemeinerungen, von W. Thimm.—Sur le théorème de préparation de Weierstrass, par H. Cartan.—Der Weierstrassche Satz und die Anfänge der Werteverteilungstheorie, von A. Dinghas.—Entwicklungslinien der Variationsrechnung seit Weierstrass, von E. Hölder, R. Klötzler, S. Gähler [und] S. Hildebrandt.—Uniformization in a p-cyclic extension of a two dimensional regular local domain of residue field characteristic p, by S. S. Abhyankar.—Integrated forms derived from non-

(Continued)

Behnke, Heinrich, 1898– *ed.* Festschrift ... 1966. (Card 4)

integrated forms of value distribution theorems under analytic and quasi-conformal mappings, by K. Noshiro [and] L. Sario.—Die Cauchy-Weil'sche Integraldarstellung für Schnitte in kohärenten analytischen Garben, von H. Röhrl.—Saturationsklassen und asymptotische Eigenschaften Trigonometrischer singulärer Integrale, von P. L. Butzer [und] E. Görlich.—Nichtarchimedische Funktionentheorie, von H. Grauert [und] R. Remmert.—Ein n-dimensionales Analogon des Schwarz-Pickschen Flächensatzes für holomorphe Abbildungen der komplexen Einheitskugel in eine Kähler-Mannigfaltigkeit, von A.

(Continued)

BEHNKE, HEINRICH, 1898- ed. Festschrift... 1966. (Card 5)

Dinghas.—Bemerkungen über holomorphe Abbildungen komplexer Räume, von N. Kuhlmann.—About the convergence of a power series, by W. Stoll.—Einsetzen analytischer Flächenstücke in Zyklen auf Komplexen Räumen, von W. Rothstein [und] H. Sperling.—Über die untere Ordnung der ganzen Funktion f(z)e^{az}, von A. Hyllengren.—Über die Konstruktion von meromorphen Funktionen mit gegebenen Wertzuordnungen, von R. Nevanlinna.—Elliptische Differentialoperatoren auf Mannigfaltigkeiten, von F. Hirzebruch.—Analytische Funktionen, von K. Menger.

BEHNKE, HEINRICH, 1898- ed. Festschrift... 1966. (Card 6)

1. Functions. 2. Weierstrass, Karl Theodor Wilhelm, 1815-1897. I. Weierstrass, Karl Theodor Wilhelm, 1815-1897. II. Kopfermann, Klaus, joint ed. III. Title. IV. Series. V. Kopfermann, Klaus. t.1966

E-12
435

BEHRENDT, RICHARD FRITZ WALTER, 1908- , ed.

Strukturwandlungen der schweizerischen Wirtschaft und Gesellschaft, Festschrift für Fritz Marbach zum 70. Geburtstag; hrsg. im Namen seiner Freunde und Kollegen von R.F. Behrendt [et al.] Bern, Stämpfli, 1962. xvii, 618 p. port., diagrs., tables. 25cm.

Texts in German or French.
Includes bibliographies.
"Bibliographie Marbach", p. [611]-618.

1. Economic history--Switzerland. 2. Marbach, Fritz, 1892- . I. Title.

NN R 7.64 e/B OC, I PC, 1, 2, I SL E, 1, 2, I (LC1, X1, Z1)

Write on slip, name, year, vol., page of magazine and class mark— RFA

Behrens Festschrift.

(Zeitschrift für französische Sprache und Literatur. Supplementheft. Jena,1929. 8°. Heft [13],p.1-327.)

form 400a [viii-10-28 25m]

E-11
6724

BEHRENS, KARL CHRISTIAN, ed.

Der Handel heute; in Memoriam Julius Hirsch. Tübingen, J.C.B. Mohr, 1962. xvi, 322 p. port. 24cm.

Bibliographical footnotes.

CONTENTS.--Von der Art und dem Erfolg des Lebens und wissenschaftlichen Schaffens des Julius Hirsch, von B. Rogowsky.--Persönliche Erinnerungen an Julius Hirsch, von W. Le Coutre.--Julius Hirsch,

(Continued)

NN R 3.63 p/ OC PC, 1, 2 SL E, 1, 2 (LC1, X1, Z1)

4

BEHRENS, KARL CHRISTIAN, ed. Der Handel heute... (Card2)

der Begründer der Forschungsstelle für den Handel, von J. Tiburtius. --Professor Hirsch in Dänemark, von G. Thrane. --Zwischen der alten und der neuen Welt, von E. Hirsch. --Julius Hirsch in den USA, von N. D. Warren. --Würdigung der Persönlichkeit von Dr. Julius Hirsch, von D. Bloomfield. --Welthandelsdynamik und Unternehmer, von K. Oberparleiter. --Der moderne Grosshandel, von R. Nieschlag. --Versuch einer Systematisierung der Betriebsformen des Einzelhandels, von K.C. Behrens. --Dynamik im Handel, von G. Duttweiler. -- Einkaufsverbände des Handels

(Continued)

VFC

Beiträge zur angewandten Mechanik, von H. Beer...und 28 anderen, Hrsg. aus Anlass des 65. Geburtstages von Prof. Dr. Karl Federhofer...und des 60. Geburtstages von Prof. Dr. Karl Girkmann... Wien, F. Deuticke, 1950. xiv, 413 p. illus. 28cm.

"Federhöfers wissenschaftliche Veröffentlichungen," p. ii–viii; "Girkmanns wissenschaftliche Veröffentlichungen," p. xii–xiv.
Bibliographical footnotes.

1. Mechanics, Applied. 2. Federhofer, Karl, 1885- . 3. Girkmann, Karl. I. Beer, Hans.
N. Y. P. L.

BEHRENS, KARL CHRISTIAN, ed. Der Handel heute ... (Card 3)

im Umbruch, von E. H. Weinwurm-Wenkhoff. --Vom Verbraucher erzwungene Risiken des Einzelhandelsbetriebes, von C. Ruberg. --Probleme der Selbstbedienung, von F. Priess. --Im Handel von morgen: Einsatz elektronischer Geräte, von R. Hirsch. --Der Betriebsvergleich im modernen Handel, von W. Fleck. --Konsumgenossenschaften heute und morgen, von J. Thygesen. --Der Beitrag der Bildung zur Gewinnung des Nachwuchses für den Einzelhandel, von J. Tiburtius. --Aufgaben und Möglichkeiten der Wirtschaftsprüfung in internationaler Sicht, von .

(Continued)

E-10
8926

BEITRÄGE zum Arbeits-, Handels- und Wirtschaftsrecht; Festschrift für Alfred Hueck zum 70. Geburtstag 7.Juli 1959, hrsg. von Rolf Dietz, Hans Carl Nipperdey [und] Eugen Ulmer. München, C.H. Beck, 1959. ix, 574, [1] p. port. 24cm.

"Verzeichnis der Schriften von Alfred Hueck, 1913-1959," p. 565-[575]
1. Labor--Jurisp.--Germany. 2. Commerce--Jurisp.--Germany. 3. Corporations--Jurisp.--Germany. 4. Legislation, Economic--Germany. 5. Hueck, Alfred, 1889- . I. Dietz, Rolf, ed.
NN 10.59 t/A OC, I PC, 1, 2, 3, 4, 5, I SL E, 1, 2, 3, 4, 5, I (LC1, X1, Z1)

BEHRENS, KARL CHRISTIAN, ed. Der Handel heute ... (Card 4)

H. Jeppesen. --Grönland-ein Beispiel kurzfristiger Planung und Entwicklung von primitivem Tausch zu modernen Produktions- und Vertriebsformen, von H.C. Christiansen.

1. Commerce. 2. Hirsch, Julius, 1882-1962.

D-12
9989

BEITRÄGE zur Bildung der Person, Alfred Petzelt zum 75. Geburtstag, gewidmet von seinen Schülern. [Hrsg. von] Marian Heitger [und] Wolfgang Fischer. Freiburg i. Br., Lambertus-Verlag [1961] 206 p. port. 23cm.

Includes bibliographies.
CONTENTS. --Grussadresse im Namen der Schüler, von W. Fischer. --Zum Werk Alfred Petzelts, von M. Heitger. --Eine philosophisch-pädagogische Betrachtung zum Liebesbegriff bei Bonaventura,

(Continued)

NN R 4.61 e/J OC, I, II, IIIbo, IVbo PC, 1, 2, I, II SL (LC1, X1, Z1)

3

AN
(Carpenter, E.)

Beith, Gilbert, editor.
Edward Carpenter, in appreciation; edited by Gilbert Beith ... London: G. Allen & Unwin, Ltd.[, 1931.] 246 p. 2 ports. (incl. front.) 8°.

Contents: Editor's preface. BISHOP, H. Edward Carpenter as I knew him. CRAMP, C. T. My earliest teacher. DENT, E. J. Angels' wings. DICKINSON, G. L. Edward Carpenter as a friend. ELLIS, H. [Edward Carpenter.] ELLIS, Mrs. H. Personal impressions of Edward Carpenter. FERRANDO, G. Edward Carpenter as I knew him. FORSTER, E. M. Some memories. GLASIER, K. B. Edward Carpenter's influence. GODFREY, W. J. A worker's friendship in the last years. GRÖNDAHL, I. A Norwegian appreciation. HOUSMAN, L. A peaceful penetrator. HYETT, I. G.

(Continued)

N. Y. P. L. September 29, 1931

BEITRÄGE zur Bildung der Person, Alfred Petzelt zum 75. Geburtstag... (Card 2)

von A. Senftle. --"Nur Liebe und Wahrheit erziehen", zur Frage nach dem Wesen des Erziehers bei J.M. Sailer, von A. Regenbrecht. --Die Selbstbespiegelung als Fehlform der Selbstbetrachtung, zum Thema "Selbsterziehung", von G.L. Vogel. --Über die Bedeutung der Personalität im pädagogischen Verhältnis, von M. Heitger. --Kritische Gedanken zur Theorie der funktionalen Erziehung, von W. Fischer. --Über das pädagogische Fragen und seine Grenzen, von K.G. Pöppel. --Lieb und Seele, Gedanken zu den Voraussetzungen einer personalen Bildung, von O. Grupe. --

(Continued)

Beith, Gilbert, editor: Edward Carpenter, in appreciation... (Card 2)

From the family point of view. INIGAN, E. The last years. IVES, G. A pilgrimage to Derbyshire. MACDONALD, J. R. The living man. MAYERS, C. Edward Carpenter's work and life. MINSHALL, R. H. Edward Carpenter at home. MONROE, W. S. Walt Whitman and other American friends of Edward Carpenter. MUIRHEAD, R. F. Memories of Edward Carpenter. NEVINSON, H. W. Work and freedom. PICTON, H. Edward Carpenter as man and scientific thinker. SALT, H. S. A sage at close quarters. SENARD, M. A Frenchwoman's tribute. SEWARD, W. A very small tribute to a very great friend. SHARP, E. Towards the end of life. SIXSMITH, C. F. Edward as I knew him. UNWIN, R. Edward Carpenter and Towards democracy. Farewell message left by Edward Carpenter to be read over his grave.

547475A. 1. Carpenter, Edward, 1844-1929. I. Title.
N. Y. P. L. September 29, 1931

BEITRÄGE zur Bildung der Person, Alfred Petzelt zum 75. Geburtstag... (Card 3)

Entwicklung und Bildung, Deutungsversuch anlässlich der Dichtungen Adalbert Stifters, von K.G. Fischer. --Bemerkungen und Materialien zum Problem des Überzeitlichen in der geistig-seelischen Entwicklung, von W. Fischer. --Bildungsaufgaben der Volksschule in dieser Zeit, von R. Hülfshoff.

1. Petzelt, Alfred. 2. Education--Addresses, essays, lectures. I. Heitger, Marian, ed. II. Fischer, Wolfgang, ed. III. Heitger, Marian. IV. Fischer, Wolfgang.

SDB

Beiträge zur deutschen statistik; festgabe für Franz Žižek zur 60. wiederkehr seines geburtstages ... herausgegeben von Paul Flaskämper und Adolf Blind. Leipzig, Hans Buske verlag, 1936.

viii, 288 p. incl. tables. 23½cm.

Bibliographical foot-notes.

CONTENTS. — Allgemeine gegenwartsfragen der deutschen statistik: Gegenwarts- und zukunftsaufgaben der statistik in Deutschland, von P. Flaskämper. Der ganzheitscharakter der volkswirtschaft und die statistik, von A. Blind. Statistik und wirtschaftspraxis, von C. Lüer. Deutschlands mitarbeit an der internationalen statistik, von F. Zahn.—

(Continued on next card)

A C 36-2228

[3]

Beiträge zur deutschen statistik; festgabe für Franz Žižek ... 1936. (Card 2)

CONTENTS—Continued.

Zur theorie der statistik: Die wesensform als systembildender unterscheidungsgrund? Von W. Winkler. Die standardisierungs- und die tafelmethode im dienste der statistischen praxis, von F. Burkhardt. Geordnete und nichtgeordnete merkmale von statistischen einheiten, von K. Jörges.—Zur organisation der amtlichen statistik: Unterweisung und schulung der erhebungsorgane in der deutschen amtlichen statistik, von E. Lind. Die gemeindestatistik in Deutschland, von W. Morgenroth.—Einzelzweige der bevölkerungs-, kultur- und wirtschaftsstatistik: Geburtenhäufigkeit, sterblichkeit und abwanderung der bäuerlichen bevölkerung in Baden in den jahren 1852–1925, von M. Hecht. Zur geschichte des statistischen unterrichts an den deutschen universitäten im 19. und 20. jahrhun-

(Continued on next card)

A C 36-2228

[3]

Beiträge zur deutschen statistik; festgabe für Franz Žižek ... 1936. (Card 3)

CONTENTS—Continued.

dert, von M. Meyer. Historische hochschulstatistik als hochschulgeschichte, von J. Müller. Neue aufgaben der aussenhandelsstatistik, von W. Grävell. Regelmässigkeiten und wandlungen des verbrauchs in der häuslichen wirtschaft, von W. Gerloff. Verbrauchsforschung in qualitativer hinsicht, von W. Vershofen. Die gemeindliche wohnungsstatistik unter neuem blickpunkt, von K. Seutemann. Entwicklungsstand und problematik der betriebswirtschaftlichen statistik, von E. Schäfer. Der betriebsvergleich, von F. Henzel.

1. Statistics — Addresses, essays, lectures. 2. Germany — Statistics. 3. Žižek, Franz, 1876– I. Flaskämper, Paul, 1886– ed. II. Blind, Adolf, 1906– joint ed.

A C 36-2228

Title from N. Y. Pub. Libr. Printed by L. C.

[3]

E-10
7550

BEITRÄGE zur Einheit von Bildung und Sprache im geistigen Sein; Festschrift zur 80. Geburtstag von Ernst Otto. Hrsg. von Gerhard Haselbach und Günter Hartmann. Berlin, W. de Gruyter, 1957. 445 p. port. 24cm.

"Bibliographie aller Schriften Ernst Ottos," p. [437]-445.

1. Otto, Ernst, 1877- . 2. Philology--Addresses, essays, lectures. I. Haselbach, Gerhard, ed. II. Hartmann, Günter, ed. III. Haselbach, Gerhard. IV. Hartmann, Günter.

NN R 9. 59 t/{OC, I, II, IIIbo, IVbo PC, 1, 2, I, II SL (LC1, X1, Z1)

[I]

TIA

Beitraege zur Finanzwissenschaft.
Bd. 1- 2.

Tübingen: J. C. B. Mohr (P. Siebeck), 1928 8°.
2v. ports.

Editor : Bd. 1- 2. H. G. Teschemacher.
Contents:
Bd. 1-2. Festgabe für Georg von Schanz zum 75. Geburtstag 12 März, 1928. 1928.

1. Finance—Per. and soc. publ.
N. Y. P. L. February 7, 1929

TID

BEITRÄGE zur Finanzwissenschaft und zur Geldtheorie; Festschrift für Rudolf Stucken. Hrsg. von Fritz Voigt. Göttingen, Vandenhoeck & Ruprecht, 1953. 312 p. illus., port. 25cm.

Bibliographical footnotes.

CONTENTS.--Vom Wesen der Besteuerung, von F. Neumark.--Theoretische Darstellungsmethoden des Problems der unterschiedlichen Erfassbarkeit der Steuerobjekte bei direkter Besteuerung, von E. d'Albergo.--

(Continued)

NN R 1. 61 m/{OC, I PC, 1, 2, I SL E, 1, 2, I (LC1, X1, Z1)

BEITRÄGE zur Finanzwissenschaft und zur Geldtheorie... (Card 2)

Der monetäre Staatskredit, von H. Moeller.--Steuern im Sozialismus, von H. Timm.--Das private und der öffentliche Wirtschaftsbereich, von H. Laufenburger.--Finanzwirtschaftliche Probleme der protestantischen Missionskirchen, von E. Egner.--Das Budget im Lichte der Modernen Wirtschaftstheorie, von P. Senf.--Betrachtungen zum "Oberen Wendepunkt" im bekannten Halmschen Konjunkturmodell, von E. Lukas.--Der Einfluss der Keynesschen Volkswirtschaftslehre auf die USA, von A. H. Hansen.--

(Continued)

BEITRÄGE zur Finanzwissenschaft und zur Geldtheorie... (Card 3)

Über die Grenzen der modernen Finanztheorie. Aufgezeigt am Beispiel der Flüchtlingsfrage von K. E. Mössner.--Der Bundeshaushalt der Vereinigten Staaten, von K. E. Poole.--Finanzwirtschaft und Wirtschaftsordnung in der Finanzwirtschaftslehre und der staats wirtschaftlichen Praxis in USA, von B. Seidel.--Die deutsche Kriegsfinanzierung im ersten und zweiten Weltkrieg, von F. Lütge.--Die Bedeutung der Theorie der Konjunkturverändernden Momente für die Weiterentwicklung der Finanzwissenschaft, von W. Ehrlicher.-- Der öffentliche Haushalt im

(Continued)

BEITRÄGE zur Finanzwissenschaft und zur Geldtheorie... (Card 4)

Wirtschaftskreislauf, von F. Voigt.--Bibliographie der Veröffentlichungen Rudolf Stuckens (p. 302-304)

1. Finance--Addresses, essays, lectures. 2. Stucken, Rudolf, 1891- I. Voigt, Fritz, ed.

TF

Beiträge zur Geld- und Finanztheorie; Wilhelm Gerloff zum siebzigsten Geburtstag, hrsg. von Fritz Neumark und Heinz Sauermann. Tübingen, J. C. B. Mohr, 1951. xix,145 p. port. 24cm.

Contributions by various authors.
Bibliographical footnotes.

1. Money, 1933- 2. Finance. 3. Gerloff, Wilhelm, 1880- . I. Neumark, Fritz, ed. II. Sauermann, Heinz, ed.

NN

EAS

BEITRÄGE zur Gelehrtengeschichte des siebzehnten Jahrhunderts. Festschrift zur Begrüssung der 48. Versammlung deutscher Philologen und Schulmänner zu Hamburg im Jahre 1905, dargebracht von Edmund Kelter, Erich Ziebarth [und] Carl Schultess. Hamburg, Gedruckt bei Lütcke & Wulff, 1905. 206 p. map. 26cm.

At head of title: Wilhelm-Gymnasium zu Hamburg.

CONTENTS. —Der Briefwechsel zwischen Matthias Bernegger und Johann Freinsheim (1629, 1633-1636), von Edmund Kelter. —Heinrich Lindenbruch und Joseph Justus Scaliger, von Erich Ziebarth. — Aus dem

(Continued)

NN*R X 10.56 /r OCs, FCs,Js,Is,II SLs (LC1s Is (OD)IIts (ED)IIts X1s,~~Z1s~~) [J]

BEITRÄGE zur Gelehrtengeschichte des siebzehnten Jahrhunderts...
(Card 2)

Briefwechsel des französischen Philologen und Diplomaten Jacques Bongars (1554-1612) von Carl Schultess.

1. Learning and scholarship—Germany. I. Kelter, Edmund. II. Hamburg. Wilhelm Gymnasium. t.1905.

NARF

Beiträge zur Geschichte des zürcherischen Zeitungswesens. Vorwort, von Dr. Oscar Wettstein. Aus der Geschichte des Vereins der schweizerischen Presse, von Dr. A. Hablützel. Die zürcherische Presse bis zur Helvetik, von Dr. A. Jacob. Die zürcherische Presse in der Zeit der Helvetik, von S. Markus. Die zürcherische Presse im Anfange des 19. Jahrhunderts, von Dr. M. Uebelhör. Zürich: A. Raustein, 1908. xxvii, 239 p. 24cm.

(Continued)

N. Y. P. L. May 7, 1935

Beiträge zur Geschichte des zürcherischen Zeitungswesens...
(Card 2)

Cover-title: Festschrift zur Vierteljahrhundertfeier des Vereins der schweizerischen Presse 4. und 5. Juli 1908 in Zürich.

"In diesem Sommer...hat die journalistische Abteilung der Universität Zürich ihren zehnten Semesterring angesetzt... Ich bin...dem Verein 'Zürcher Presse' und dem 'Zürcher Pressverband'...dankbar, dass sie durch die Herausgabe dieser Festschrift dem jungen Institut Gelegenheit gaben, zu zeigen, was es anstrebt... Die drei Monographien, die sich mit der Geschichte der zürcherischen Presse beschäftigen, sind Arbeiten ehemaliger Schüler der journalistischen Abteilung der Hochschule Zürich, die

(Continued)

N. Y. P. L. May 7, 1935

Beiträge zur Geschichte des zürcherischen Zeitungswesens...
(Card 3)

erste und dritte...als Dissertationen...die zweite ist ein Auszug aus einer Dissertation." —*Vorwort.*

DR. ADOLF KOCH JOURNALISM COLL.

700532A. 1. Journalism—Switzerland—Zürich—Hist. 2. Verein der schweizerischen Presse. I. Hablützel, Albert, 1865– . Geschichte des Vereins der schweizerischen Presse. II. Jacob, Adolf. Die zürcherische Presse bis zur Helvetik. III. Markus, Samuel. Die zürcherische Presse während der Helvetik. IV. Uebelhör, Max, 1881– . Die zürcherische Presse zu Anfang des 19. Jahrhunderts. V. Verein "Zürcher Presse." VI. Zürcher Pressverband.

N. Y. P. L. May 7, 1935

E-11
2269

BEITRÄGE zur geschichtlichen Landeskunde Tirols. [Festschrift für Universitätsprofessor Dr. Franz Huter anlässlich der Vollendung des 60. Lebensjahres, dargebracht von Kollegen, Schülern und dem Verlag. Besorgt von Ernest Troger und Georg Zwanowetz] Innsbruck, Universitätsverlag Wagner, 1959. viii, 398 p. illus., port., fold. maps, facsims. 24cm. (Schlern-Schriften, 207)

(Continued)

NN X 3, 61 s/X OC, I, II, IVbo (OS)III PC, 1, 2, I, II, III SL (LC1, X1, Z1) [I]

2)

BEITRÄGE zur geschichtlichen Landeskunde Tirols.
(Card 2)

1. Huter, Franz, 1899- . 2. Tyrol--Hist.--Addresses, essays, lectures. I. Troger, Ernest, ed. II. Zwanowetz, Georg, ed. III. Series. IV. Zwanowetz, Georg.

3-MAS

Beiträge für Hans Gerhard Evers anlässlich der Emeritierung im Jahre 1968. J. A. Schmoll gen. Eisenwerth: Der alte Pan. Zum Spätwerk Rodins. [Mitarbeiter:] Hans-Christoph Hoffmann [u. a.] Darmstadt, Justus von Liebig Verlag, 1968.
106 p. with illus. 20 cm. (Darmstädter Schriften, 22)

"Herausgegeben im Auftrag des Magistrats der Stadt Darmstadt."

(Continued)

NN*2.70 1/ OC (OD)It (ED)It PC, 1, 2, 3, I SL A, 1, 2, 3, I (LC1, X1, Z1)

2

BEITRÄGE für Hans Gerhard Evers anlässlich der Emeritierung im Jahre 1968. (Card 2)

CONTENTS.—Professor liberatus, von L. Engel.—Der alte Pan, von J. A. Schmoll gen. Eisenwerth.—Notizen zu Eduard von der Nüll und August Sicard von Sicardsburg, von H.-C. Hoffmann.—Zur Bedeutung der geometrischen Bild- und Zeichensprache, von H. Knell.—Repräsentationsstil und Historienbild in der römischen Malerei um 1600, von H. Röttgen.—'Der Jüngling und der Tod.' von M. Wenzel.—Bibliographie Hans Gerhard Evers (p. 101-106)

1. Evers, Hans Gerhard, 1900- . 2. Evers, Hans Gerhard, 1900- .--Bibl. 3. Art--Essays and misc. I. Darmstadt, Germany. Magistrat. t. 1968.

FID

BEITRÄGE zur Heimatkunde des nordöstlichen Tirol. Festschrift zum 70. Geburtstag Matthias Mayer's. Innsbruck, Universitätsverlag Wagner, 1954. 273 p. illus., ports., maps. 25cm (Schlern-Schriften. 138)

Includes bibliographies.

CONTENTS. —Geleitwort des Landeshauptmanns von Tirol. —Geleitwort des Präsidenten des Tiroler Landtags. —Matthias Mayer, Lebenslauf und Würdigung, von E. Widmoser. —Vorspruch von Matthias Mayer. —Ausgrabung in Klein-Söll, von L. Franz. —

(Continued)

NN ** X 6. 56 s/3OC, Ib (OS)I PC, 1, 2, I SL (U1, LC1, X1, ~~Z1~~) [I]

BEITRÄGE zur Heimatkunde des nordöstlichen Tirol.
(Card 2)

Nordosttirols geschichtliche Besonderheiten, von O. Stolz. –Zur Frage der Beutellehen im Gericht Itter, von H. Klein. –Klein-Söll, zur Geschichte der Besiedlung und Entstehung seiner Kirche, von H. Bachmann. –Seelsorge im Winkel bei St. Johann, von F. Dörrer. –Zur Geschichte der Pfarre Steinberg, von K. Schadelbauer. –Die Urpfarre St. Johann und ihre wirtschaftliche Grundlage, von E. Widmoser. –Erl, Arbeit und Brauch, von A. Dörrer. –Das Fischerhäusel in Kössen, von K. Ilg. –Zwei Notburga-Spiele aus dem bayerischen Inntal, von H. Moser. –Votivbild-Notizen in den Wallfahrten rings um

(Continued)

Copy only words underlined
& classmark— *OHM

BEITRÄGE zur indischen Philologie und Altertumskunde, Walther Schubring zum 70. Geburtstag dargebracht von der deutschen Indologie.
Hamburg, Cram, De Gruyter, 1951. 217 p. illus., port. 29cm. (Alt- und neu-indische Studien. [Nr.] 7)

CONTENTS. – paṇ, von P. Thieme. – Die Zusammensetzung bei den Infinitiven und Gerundien im Rigveda, von J. A. Durr. -- Die angebliche Wurzel bhreṣ, von K. Hoffmann. – Vedische Skizzen, von H. Lommel. –

(Continued)

NN **6.57 p/ OC (OS)I PC, 1, 2, I O, 1, 2, I (U1, LC1, Z1, X1)
[I]

BEITRÄGE zur Heimatkunde des nordöstlichen Tirol.
(Card 3)

das Kaisergebirge, von L. Schmidt. --Mysterium, Prophetie, Volksheilige im Bergbau, von G. Schreiber. –Die Barockbaumeister-Familie Singer, von E. Egg. –Die gotische Madonna in der Pfarrkirche von Ebbs, von J. Gritsch. --Unterinntaler Bildsäulen, von J. Weingartner. –Rudolf Kink (1822-1664) aus Kufstein, der Geschichtsschreiber der Universität Wien, von N. Grass. –Verzeichnis der Veröffentlichungen Matthias Mayer's, von E. Widmoser.

1. Mayer, Matthias, 1884- . 2. Tyrol–Hist. --Addresses, essays, lectures. I. Series.

BEITRÄGE zur indischen Philologie und Altertumskunde
(Card 2)

Der Aśvamedha und der Puruṣamedha, von W. Kirfel. – Nīrājanā, von H. Losch. –Neues von alten Jaina-Bibliotheken, von L. Alsdorf. – Jaina-Versionen der Sodāsa-Sage, von F. -R. Hamm. – Die Polemik der Buddhisten und Brahmanen gegen die Jainas, von H. von Glasenapp. – Vergleichende Analyse des Catuṣpariṣatsutra, von E. Waldschmidt. –Das Zauberbad der Göttin Sarasvatī, von J. Nobel. – Literarhistorische Bemerkungen zur Sekoddeśaṭīkā des Nadapada, von H. Hoffmann. – Amalavijñānam und Ālayavijñānam. Ein Beitrag zur Erkenntnislehre des Buddhismus, von E. Frauwallner. – Jayantabhatta und Vācaspatimiśra, ihre Zeit

(Continued)

KAT

Beitraege zur historischen Geographie, Kulturgeographie, Ethnographie und Kartographie, vornehmlich des Orients; under Mitarbeit von Karl Ausserer [und Anderen]...herausgegeben von Hans Mzik... Leipzig: F. Deuticke, 1929. 202 p. incl. geneal. table. front., illus. (incl. facsim.), maps, plates. 8°.

"Dr. Eugen Oberhummer zur Vollendung seines 70. Lebensjahres am 29. März 1929 überreicht."
Bibliographical footnotes.
Contents: AUSSERER K. Der "Atlas Blaeu der Wiener National-- Bibliotek." JANSKY, H.
(Continued)

BEITRÄGE zur indischen Philologie und Altertumskunde
(Card 3)

und ihre Bedeutrung für die Chronologie des Vedānta, von P. Hacker. – Die Lehre vom Handeln in der Bhagavadgītā, von W. Ruben. – Metrica, von H. Weller. – Ein nicht identifiziertes Gāndhāra-Relief, von O. Hansen. – Ein indisches Soldatenlied aus dem letzten Kriege, von W. Rau. – Indische Seitenstücke zu zwei europäischen Anekdoten, von J. C. Tavadia. – Verzeichnis der bis zum 10. Dezember 1951 erschienenen Schriften von Walter Schubring, zusammengestellt von F. R. Hamm (p. 215-217).

1. Indic studies. 2. Schubring, Walther, 1881- I. Series.

Beitraege zur historischen Geographie...
(Card 2)

Das Meer in Geschichte und Kultur des Islams. KAHLE, P. Piri Re'is und seine Bahrije. ROHR v. DENTA, C. FREIIN v. Neue Quellen zu den Entdeckungsfahrten der Portugiesen im Indischen Ozean. TAESCHNER, F. Der Bericht des arabischen Geographen Ibn al-Wardi über Konstantinopel. NÉMETH, J. Magna Hungaria. HUESING, G. Panchaia. HERRMANN, A. Irrtümliche Namensversetzungen. KRAUS, K. Über die Grundlagen der Ter- minologie in der

(Continued)

SLA
(Monatsschrift)

Beitraege zur Kriminalpsychologie und Strafrechtsreform, Festgabe zum 60. Geburtstage von Gustav Aschaffenburg; herausgegeben von A. Graf zu Dohna und K. von Lilienthal. Heidelberg: C. Winter, 1926. 106 p. 8°. (Monatsschrift für Kriminalpsychologie und Strafrechtsreform. Beiheft [Nr.] 1.)

Bibliographical footnotes.
Contents: LILIENTHAL, K. v. Rechtsstrafe und Sicherungsstrafe und der Entwurf 1925. HEIMBERGER, J. Die Schuld im Strafrecht des Codex iuris canonici. HIPPEL, R. v. Die mildernden Umstände in den Entwürfen. GRUHLE, H. W. Der Unterricht in der Kriminalpsychologie. MITTERMAIER, W. Aus der Lehre der Zurechnungsfähig-

(Continued)

N. Y. P. L. January 7, 1929

Beitraege zur historischen Geographie...(Card 3)

"Geographie" des Ptolemaeus. HEINE-GELDERN, R. Freiherr v. Orissa und die Mundavölker im "Periplus des Erythräischen Meeres. Mžik, H.v. Parageographische Elemente in den Berichten der arabischen Geographen über Sudostasien.

442453A. 1. Geography--Essays and misc. 2. Oberhummer, Eugen, 1859- . 3. Mžik, Hans von, 1876- , editor.

Beitraege zur Kriminalpsychologie und Strafrechtsreform...
(Card 2)

keit. ROSENFELD, E. H. Grundsätzliches zur Bestrafung des Inzestes. LIEPMANN, M. Die Problematik des "Progressiven Strafvollzugs." WETZEL, A. Persönlichkeit und Kriminalität. FREUDENTHAL, B. Die unbestimmte Verurteilung im künftigen deutschen Strafgesetzbuche. DOHNA, A. GRAF ZU. Die reichsrechtliche Regelung der bedingten Strafaussetzung. GRÜNHUT, M. Gefährlichkeit als Schuldmoment. HENTIG, H. v. Zur Psychologie der Ausrede.

1. Criminals—Psychology. 2. Criminal law. 3. Aschaffenburg, Gustav, 1866- . 4. Dohna-Schlodien, Alexander Georg Theobald, Burggraf u. Graf zu, 1876- , editor. 5. Lilienthal, Karl von, 1853- , editor. 6. Ser.
N. Y. P. L. January 7, 1929

QOI

Beiträge zur Kulturgeschichte; Festschrift Reinhold Bosch zu seinem sechzigsten Geburtstag. Aarau, H. R. Sauerländer, 1947. 221 p. illus. 23cm.

"Herausgegeben...von Dr. Walter Drack und Dr. Peter Fischer."

CONTENTS.—Haefeli, Fritz. Ein Vierteljahrhundert Heimatforschung im Seetal.—Kuhn, Emil. Paläontologie und Prähistorie.—Vogt, Emil. Zum Problem des urgeschichtlich-völkerkundlichen Vergleiches.—Bandi, H. G. Altsteinzeitliche Funde aus Südsyrien und dem Libanon.—Tschumi, Otto. Zur Frage einer alteuropäischen Kupferzeit.—Gessner, Verena. Vom Problem der spätbronzezeitlichen Glasperlen.—Drack, Walter. Der Bönistein ob Zeiningen, eine spätbronzezeitliche und späthall-

(Continued)

N. Y. P. L. April 23, 1948

Beiträge zur Kulturgeschichte... (Card 2)

stättische Höhensiedlung des Juras.—Pelichet, Edgar. Contribution à l'étude de l'occupation du sol de la Colonia Julia Equestris.—Laur-Belart, Rudolf. Spätrömische Gräber in Kaiseraugst.—Poeschel, Erwin. Die 'gemurete Letzi' und 'das stainine pild' bei Chur.—Bouffard, Pierre. Problèmes d'iconographie burgonde.—Ammann, Hektor. Wirtschaft und Lebensraum einer aargauischen Kleinstadt im Mittelalter. —Reinle, Adolf. Die Schönauer Kreuze zu Stein.—Bibliographie von Reinhold Bosch (p. 210–220).

429395B. 1. Bosch, Reinhold, 1887– . 2. Archaeology, Prehistoric. I. Drack, Walter, 1917– , ed. II. Fischer, Peter, ed.

N. Y. P. L. April 23, 1948

KGE

BEITRÄGE zur Landeskunde von Schleswig-Holstein [Oskar Schmieder zum 60. Geburtstag, 27. I. 1951, gewidmet von seinen Freunden und Schülern] Hrsg. von Carl Schott. Kiel, F. Hirt, 1953. 268 p. illus., maps (part fold.) 25cm. (Kiel, Germany. Universität. Geographisches Institut. Schriften. Sonderband)

1. Schleswig-Holstein—Geography, Physical. 2. Schleswig-Holstein—Economic geography. 3. Schmieder, Oscar, 1891- . 4. Schleswig-Holstein—Geography, Physical, 1953. I. Kiel, Germany. Universität. Geographisches Institut. Schriften. Sonderband. II. Schott, Carl, ed.

NN**X 10.53 OC, II (OS)I PC, 1, 2, 3, I, II SL E, 2, 3, I, II ST, 4, I, II (Z1, LC1, X1)

D-15
6749

BEITRÄGE zur Landeskunde Südtirols; Festgabe zum 60. Geburtstag von Dr. F. Dörrenhaus, hrsg. von einem Freunderkreis des Jubilars. [Neustadt a.d. Aisch, P.C.W. Schmidt] 1962. 204 p. illus., maps(part fold.) 21cm.

Includes bibliographies.

CONTENTS.--Fritz Dörrenhaus als Geograph, von K. Kayser.--Mittler zwischen Nord und Süd, von F. Volgger.--Die jüngste Entwicklung der Frage

(Continued)

NN 9.65 s/ OC PC, 1, 2, 3 SL (LC1, X1, Z1)

BEITRÄGE zur Landeskunde Südtirols... (Card 2)

Südtirols, von F. Gschnitzer.--Graubünden und Tirol; zur wechselvollen Geschichte des alten Rätien, von L. Uffer.--Die Südtiroler Gemeinden im heutigen Italien, von T. Karner.--Die Entwicklung von Bauerntum und Höferecht in Südtirol, von P. Brugger.--Südtirols Bedeutung für den Alpinismus, von R. Rungaldier.--Die romanischen Namen in Schnals und Passeierals Zeugen für das Alter des Deutschtums, von K. Finsterwalder.--Tiroler Etschtal und Kaschmir-Becken, von H. Uhlig.--Bozen im Bewegungsfeld der Binnenwanderung. Südtirols, von A. Leidlmair.--Laas im Vinschgau, von K. Hermes.--Die Marillenkulturen im Vinschgau, von H. Becker.--Beiträge zu einer Bevölkerungs-und Sozialgeographie der Stadt Bruneck im Pustertal, von C. Jentsch.

(Continued)

BEITRÄGE zur Landeskunde Südtirols... (Card 3)

1. Dörrenhaus, Fritz. 2. Adige river and valley--Civilization. 3. Tyrol--Civilization.

D-19
9589

Beiträge zur Lehre von der Unternehmung. Festschrift für Karl Käfer. Hrsg. von Otto Angehrn und Hans Paul Künzi. Stuttgart, Poeschel, 1968.

835 p. port. 23 cm.

Bibliographical footnotes.

CONTENTS.—Karl Käfer zum 70. Geburtstag, von J. Auf der Maur.—Sur quelques aspects de l'œuvre du Professeur Karl Käfer, par P. Lauzel.—Absatzwirtschaft als Gegenstand wissenschaftlicher

(Continued)

NN*R 8.70 v/OC, I, II, III PC, 1, 2, I, II, III SL E, 1, 2, I, II, III (LC1, X1, Z1)

BEITRÄGE zur Lehre von der Unternehmung. (Card 2)

Forschung, von O. Angehrn.—Strukturwandel des landwirtschaftlichen Betriebes, von W. Bickel.—Zur kybernetischen Betrachtungsweise in der Betriebswirtschaftslehre, von L. L. Illetschko.—Mathematische Optimierung grosser Systeme, von H. P. Künzi.—Steuerfragen bei der Unternehmungsentwicklung, von R. Borkowsky.—Prognosepublizität von Aktiengesellschaften, von W. Busse von Colbe.—Some developments in industrial cost accounting in the United States since 1945, by R. I. Dickey.—New frontiers in management accounting education with emphasis on international developments, by P. Garner.—Was ist betriebswirtschaftlich notwendige Abschreibung? Von K. Hax.—Audit response to enterprise developments in America,

(Continued)

BEITRÄGE zur Lehre von der Unternehmung. (Card 3)

by R. K. Mautz.—Verrechnung innerbetrieblicher Leistungen mit Hilfe des Matrizenkalküls, von H. Münstermann.—Zur Entwicklung der Theorie der Unternehmungsorganisation, von W. Hill.—Probleme der inner- und ausserbetrieblichen Schulung kaufmännischer Führungskräfte, von E. Kilgus.—Grundzüge einer betriebswirtschaftlichen Entscheidungslehre, von E. Rühli.—Führungskonzeption und Unternehmungsorganisation, von H. Ulrich.—Langfristige Planung in der Unternehmung, von K. Weber.—Veröffentlichungen von Karl Käfer, von J. Auf der Maur [und] R. Moosmann (p. 331–335)

(Continued)

BEITRÄGE zur Lehre von der Unternehmung. (Card 4)

1. Management--Addresses, essays, lectures. 2. Accounting and bookkeeping, Cost. I. Käfer, Karl, 1898- . II. Angehrn, Otto, ed. III. Künzi, Hans Paul, 1924- , ed.

XAV

BEITRÄGE zum Recht des neuen Deutschland. [Festschrift für Franz Schlegelberger zum 60. Geburtstage] Hrsg. von Erwin Bumke, J. Wilhelm Hedemann [und] Gustav Wilke. Berlin, F. Vahlen, 1936. xiv, 455 p. port. 25cm.

CONTENTS.—Das Antlitz des Gesetzgebers, von J. W. Hedemann—Der Heimweg des Rechts in die völkische Sittenordnung, von R. Freisler.—Partei und Staat, von Dr. Stuckart.—Die Auswirkungen der Justizverreichlichung, von F. Sauer.—Vom personellen Aufbau der einheitlichen (Continued)

NN**R 2.56 d/ OC, I. II, III, IVbo PC, 1, 2, I, II, III SL (LC1, X1, Z1)

BEITRÄGE zum Recht des neuen Deutschland. (Card 2)

Reichsjustizverwaltung, von O. Wagner.—Gegenwartsfragen des deutschen Gemeinderechts, von Dr. Goerdeler.—Die Stellung der Revision im künftigen Strafverfahren, von E. Schäfer.—Die Wahrheitspflicht im Zivilprozess, von H. Titze.—Auswertung der Neuerungen der Vergleichsordnung für eine Weiterbildung des Konkursrechts, von W. Vogels.—Vermögensverbrechen im Wandel der Rechtsprechung und der Gesetzgebung, von E. Kohlrausch.—Die Entwicklung des Erbhofrechts in der Rechtsprechung des Reichserbhofgerichts, von Dr. Volkmar.—Der Durchbruch erbpflegerischen Denkens in der deutschen Rechtspflege von (Continued)

BEITRÄGE zum Recht des neuen Deutschland. (Card 3)

A. Gütt.—Gegenwartsfragen des Ehe- und Kindschaftsrechts, von Dr. Bergmann.—Grundbuch und materielles Recht, von Dr. Hesse.—Das arbeitsrechtliche Ruhegehaltsverhältnis als Teil des Arbeitsvertrages, von Graf von der Goltz.—Das Recht des schöpferischen Menschen- ein neues Ehrenrecht, von Dr. Waldmann.—Verwandtes und Gegensätzliches im Urheberrecht und Erfinderrecht, von Dr. v. Knieriem.—Der gewerbliche Rechtsschutz in Deutschland und Italien, von G. Klauer.—Aktienrechtliche Formen der Kapitalbeschaffung, von L. Quassowski.—Treupflicht des Aktionärs? von F. Klausing. (Continued)

BEITRÄGE zum Recht des neuen Deutschland. (Card 4)

1. Schlegelberger, Franz, 1876- . 2. Law—Germany—Addresses, essays, lectures. I. Hedemann, Justus Wilhelm, 1878- , ed. II. Wilke, Gustav, ed. III. Bumke, Erwin, 1874- , ed. IV. Wilke, Gustav.

D-13
2264

Beiträge zum Recht der Wasserwirtschaft und zum Energierecht; Festschrift zum 70. Geburtstag von Dr. jur. Paul Gieseke ... Dargebracht von Kollegen, Freunden und Schülern. Karlsruhe, C. F. Müller, 1958.

xvii, 400 p. port. 23 cm.

Preface signed: Hermann Conrad.
Bibliographical footnotes.

1. Water--Jurisp. 2. Power resources--Jurisp. 3. Gieseke, Paul Ferd, K.O., 1888- I. Conrad, Hermann, 1904- ed. t. 1958

NN* 9.61 g/ OC, I PC, 1, 2t, 3, I (LC1, X1, Z1) 2, 3, I SL E, 1, 2, 3, I ST, 1t,

E-13
7605

BEITRÄGE zur schlesischen. Kirchengeschichte; Gedenkschrift für Kurt Engelbert. Hrsg. von Bernhard Stasiewski. Köln, Böhlau Verlag, 1969. xii, 695 p. fold. maps (1 col., issued in pocket) 25cm. (Forschungen und Quellen zur kirchen- und Kulturgeschichte Ostdeutschlands. Bd. 6)

Bibliographical footnotes.

1. Engelbert, Kurt. 2. Church history--Silesia. I. Series. II. Stasiewski, Bernhard, ed.

NN R 2.70 e/ OC, II (OS)I PC, 1, 2, I, II SL S, 2 (LC1, X1, Z1)

E-10
4731

BEITRÄGE zur Sozialversicherung; Festgabe für Dr. Johannes Krohn zum 70. Geburtstag mit einem Vorwort von Maximilian Sauerborn, hrsg. von W. Rohrbeck. Berlin, Duncker & Humblot [1954] xii, 331 p. port. 24cm.

CONTENTS.—Gedanken zur Sozialpolitik, von W. Adler.—Die Errichtung von Betriebskrankenkassen nach dem Selbstverwaltungsgesetz und dem Sozialgerichtsgesetz, von K. Alexander.—Die Bedeutung der Selbstverwaltung für die Weiterentwicklung der gesetzlichen (Continued)

NN R 2.58 a/ OC, 2b, I PC, 1, 2, I SL E, 1, 2, I (LC1, X1, Z1, C1)

BEITRÄGE zur Sozialversicherung... (Card 2)

Krankenversicherung, von H. A. Aye.—Zur Rechtsnatur der Versorgungseinrichtungen freier Berufe, von W. Bogs.—Aus dem Leben der Land- und der Innungskrankenkassen, von O. Estenfeld.—Praeventive Medizin: Standort, Umfang und Zuständigkeit, von H. Gaumitz.—25 Jahre Berufsgenossenschaftliche Schiedsstellen, von G. Gravenhorst.—Die Neuordnung der Beziehungen zwischen Ärzten und Krankenkassen als Teilproblem der Reform der deutschen Krankenversicherung, von K. Haedenkamp.—Der Staatsbeitrag in der Rentenversicherung, in seiner Entwicklung und als Finanzierungselement, von F. Heinze.—Die soziale Sicherung (Continued)

BEITRÄGE zur Sozialversicherung... (Card 3)

der Selbständigen, von W. Heyn.—Grenzen und Gefahren staatlicher Sozialpolitik, von M. Kalinke.—Paritätische Selbstverwaltung in der Sozialversicherung, von G. Oberwinster—Probleme der deutschen Rentenversicherung, von A. Ostermayer.—Die gesetzliche Krankenversicherung in der Zeit der Weimarer Republik (1919 bis 1932), von P. Prange.—Zu der Mitwirkung von Laien in der Sozialgerichtsbarkeit, von E. Roehrbein.—Die Entwicklung der sozialen Sicherheit in England von 1948 bis 1953, von W. Rohrbeck.—Zur rechtlichen Idee der sozialen Unfallversicherung,

(Continued)

BEITRÄGE zur Sozialversicherung... (Card 4)

von H. Schrader.—Die deutsche soziale Unfallversicherung, Bewährung, Wandel und Ausblick, von H. Schraft.—Zum Rechtscharakter der Ersatzkassen, von E. Stolt.—Probleme der beamtenrechtlichen Unfallfürsorge, von A. Teutsch.—Die zusätzliche Alters- und Hinterbliebeneversicherung der Arbeitnehmer bei Bund, Ländern und Gemeinden, von F. Wieland.

1. Insurance, Workmen's—Germany. 2. Krohn, Johannes, 1884- I. Rohrbeck, Walter, 1885- ed.

E-11
7942

Beiträge zur Sozialversicherung. Festschrift für Kurt Hofmann aus Anlass seines 60. Geburtstages. (Hrsg. von: Arbeitsgemeinschaft der Knappschaften der Bundesrepublik Deutschland, Bochum, Bundesverband der Betriebskrankenkassen, Essen, Bundesverband der landwirtschaftlichen Berufsgenossenschaften, Kassel, Bundesversicherungsanstalt für Angestellte, Berlin [und] Hauptverband der gewerblichen Berufsgenossenschaften, Berlin, Bonn. Berlin) E. Schmidt [1964] 337 p., 2 l. of illus., front. 24cm.

(Continued)

NN*R 4.70 m/L OC,I,Ib+ PC,1,I SL E,1,I (LC1,X1,Z1)

BEITRÄGE zur Sozialverischerung. (1964) (Card 2)

Includes bibliographical references.

CONTENTS.—Lebenslauf von Kurt Hofmann, von R. Stössner.—Betriebskrankenkassen und Selbstverwaltung, von K. Alexander [und] K. Friede.—Internationale Entwicklungstendenzen im Leistungsrecht der Sozialen Sicherheit, von K. Jantz.—Die berufsgenossenschaftliche Unfallverhütung als gesetzliche Aufgabe, von P. Volkmann.—Die Arbeitsgemeinschaft für Arbeitssicherheit von P. Buss.—Die Unfallverhütung in der Seeschiffahrt, von B. Dieter.—Sinn und Aufgaben der Berufsgenossenschaftlichen Unfallkrankenhäuser, von A. Gridl.—Gedanken zum Territorialprinzip in der Sozialversicherung, von E. Wickenhagen.—Die Silikose im Bergbau der Bundesrepublik Deutschland aus der Sicht der Statistik betrachtet. von H.-A. Carganico.—

(Continued)

BEITRÄGE zur Sozialversicherung. (1964) (Card 3)

Verhütung und Bekämpfung der Silikose in der keramischen Industrie, von J. Kann.—Zur Frage der Verantwortlichkeit der Unfallversicherungsträger in der medizinischen Rehabilitation Unfallverletzter, von H. Lauterbach.—Gedanken über berufsgenossenschaftliche Heilbehandlungsmassnahmen, von W. Baetzner.—Die berufliche Rehabilitation bei den gewerblichen Berufsgenossenschaften, von W. Nickl.—Lassen sich seit dem UVNG Doppelentschädigungen für dasselbe Unfallereignis durch die Berufsgenossenschaften und dritte Schädiger vermeiden? von H. Münzel.—Die Nachkriegsentwicklung der gesetzlichen Unfallversicherung in Berlin, von H. Zilz.—Neue

(Continued)

BEITRÄGE zur Sozialversicherung. (1964) (Card 4)

Aspekte landwirtschaftlicher Sozialpolitik, von K. Noell.—Die landwirtschaftliche Unfallversicherung in der Neuregelung der gesetzlichen Unfallversicherung, von R. Breitbach.—Die Unfallverhütung in der Land- und Forstwirtschaft, von R. Gerstenberg.—Die finanzielle Entwicklung der Angestelltenversicherung seit der Errichtung der Bundesversicherungsanstalt für Angestellte, von E. Gaber.—Die Rehabilitation in der Rentenversicherung der Angestellten, von R. Schmidt.—Die Gesundheitsvorsorgekuren der Ruhrknappschaft, von E. Sudhaus.—Die Bedeutung des Änderungsgesetzes 1963 für die Altershilfe für Landwirte, von F. Baun.

1. Insurance, Workmen's--Germany. I. Hofmann, Kurt, 1904-

RAE

Beiträge zur Sprachwissenschaft und Volkskunde; Festschrift für Ernst Ochs zum 60. Geburtstag, hrsg. von Karl Friedrich Müller... Lahr, M. Schauenburg, 1951. 397 p. illus., maps. 23cm.

"Ernst-Ochs-Bibliographie," p. 374–382.

607748B. 1. Ochs, Ernst, 1888- . 2. Philology—Addresses, essays, lectures. I. Müller, Karl Friedrich, 1908- , ed.

N. Y. P. L. November 19, 1951

L-10
5104
Bd. 5

BEITRÄGE zur Sprachwissenschaft, Volkskunde und Literaturforschung. Wolfgang Steinitz zum 60. Geburtstag am 28. Februar 1965 dargebracht. (Herausgeber: A. V. Isačenko, W. Wissmann [und] H. Strobach] Berlin, Akademie-Verlag, 1965. 455 p. port. 24cm. (Deutsche Akademie der Wissenschaften, Berlin. Sprachwissenschaftliche Kommission. Veröffentlichungen. 5)

1. Steinitz, Wolfgang, 1905- . 2. Philology--Addresses, essays, lectures. 3. Folk lore--Addresses, essays, lectures. I. Series. II. Isačenko, Alexander V., ed.

NN R 10.65 a/3 (OS)I PC,1,2,3,I,II (LC1,X1,Z1) OC,II

E-10
9351

BEITRÄGE zur Theorie und Praxis des Wohnungsbaues; Arnold Knoblauch als Festschrift zum 80. Geburtstag gewidmet von seinen Freunden. Bonn, Domus-Verlag, 1959. 261 p. illus., port. 25cm.

CONTENTS.--Zum Geleit, von P. Lücke.--Entwicklungstendenzen im Wohnungsbau in der Bundesrepublik Deutschland, von H. Wandersleb.--Die Bedeutung Berlins für die Entwicklung des sozialen gemeinnützigen Wohnungsbaus, von E. Bodien.--Der Wohnungswirtschaftliche Beirat beim

(Continued)

NN R 12.59 1/ OC PC,1,2,3 SL E,1,2,3 (LC1,X1,Z1)

BEITRÄGE zur Theorie und Praxis des Wohnungsbauses... (Card 2)

Bundesministerium für Wohnungsbau, von O. von Nell-Breuning.--Wohnungswirtschaft gehört in die soziale Marktwirtschaft, von V. E. Preusker.--Der kurzfristige Baukredit im Wohnungsbau und die Deutsche Bau- und Bodenbank AG, von O. Kämper.--Der Realkredit in seiner Bedeutung für den Wohnungsbau, von K. Tornier.--Eingliederung der privaten Bausparkassen in den Realkredit, von G. Schloder.--Kapital- und Ertragssubventionen im öffentlich geförderten sozialen Wohnungsbau, von H. G. Pergande.--Grundlagen und Bedeutung der grossen Wohnungsunternehmen, von J. Brecht.--Betreuungsaufgaben

(Continued)

BEITRÄGE zur Theorie und Praxis des Wohnungsbauses... (Card 3)

im Wohnungsbau, von E. Schnell.--Kosten und Kostenrechnung in der Wohnungswirtschaft, von A. Flender.--Die Pflichtprüfung in der Wohnungswirtschaft, von K. Schneider.--Wegbereiter der Bausparkassen, von W. Lehmann.--Die gagfah im Auf und Ab der Wohnungspolitik, von G. Lange.--Lebensabriss Arnold Knoblauch.

1. Housing--Germany. 2. Real estate business--Fiance--Germany. 3. Knoblauch, Arnold, 1879-

---

EOB

Beitraege zur thüringischen und sächsischen Geschichte; Festschrift für Otto Dobenecker zum siebzigsten Geburtstage am 2. April 1929... Jena: G. Fischer, 1929. vi, 554 p. incl. geneal. table. diagr., front. (port.), plates. 8°.

Includes bibliographies.

Contents: EICHHORN, G. Die Entdeckung der Wallburg auf dem Jenzig durch Klopfleisch. WAEHLER, M. Die einstigen slawischen Nebensiedlungen in Thüringen. CARTELLIERI, A. Kaiser Otto II. DEVRIENT, E. Willigis und Jechaburg. TILLE, A. Die Anfänge der Stadt Weimar. LIPPERT, W. Das älteste Urkundenverzeichnis des thüringisch-meissnischen Archivs 1330. FÜSSLEIN, W. Die Thüringer Grafenfehde 1342–1346. WILLKOMM, B. Jenaer Klosterleben am Ende des XIV. Jahr-

(Continued)

N. Y. P. L. February 5, 1930

Beitraege zur thüringischen und sächsischen Geschichte...
(Card 2)

hunderts. Körner, F. Die Flurgrösse der Wüstungen in den Amtsgerichtsbezirken Apolda, Buttstädt... und Weimar. Schneider, F. Papst Nikolaus V. und Heinrich der Ältere. Brandis, C. G. Ein altes Bücherverzeichnis aus Mildenfurt. Kauffungen, K. v. Rechtssprüche der Schöffenstühle von Leipzig und Magdeburg für Zwickau. Weber, P. Eine Jenaer Altarwerkstatt am Ausgang des Mittelalters. Herrmann, R. Das Verfügungsrecht über die städtischen Pfarrstellen im Ernestinischen Thüringen. Biereye, J. Über die Wohnung Luthers. Koch, H. Die Jenaer Türkensteuer von 1542. Schmidt, B. Ein merkwürdiger Zwischenfall in der Schlacht bei Sievershausen. Arndt, G. Christoph Fischer und seine Tätigkeit.

(Continued)

N. Y. P. L. February 5, 1930

Beitraege zur thüringischen und sächsischen Geschichte...
(Card 3)

Engel, W. Ein bellum diplomaticum des 16. Jahrhunderts. Schmidt-Ewald, W. Die Bibliothek eines thüringischen Gelehrten. Goetz, G. Justus Lipsius und sein Dekanat. Beschorner, H. Öder und Thüringen. Lockemann, T. Ein Jenaer Universitäts-Bibliothekar des 18. Jahrhunderts. Mentz, G. Aus den Papieren des Grafen Görtz. Hagen, B. v. Die Balearen in der Schilderung eines reussischen Rheinbundoffiziers. Gerhardt, R. Die geschichtliche Entwicklung des Landtagswahlrechts in Sachsen-Weimar-Eisenach. Lundgreen, F. Friedrich Karl Hönniger. Anemüller, E. Paulinzeller Forschungen. Vollert, M. Die Berufung Rudolf Euckens nach Jena. Koch, H. Personen- und Ortsregister.

441018A. 1. Thuringia—Hist. 2. Saxony—Hist. 3. Dobenecker, Otto, 1859- .
N. Y. P. L. February 5, 1930

AN
(Ester, K.)

Beiträge zur Zeitungswissenschaft; Festgabe für Karl d'Ester zum 70. Geburtstage von seinen Freunden und Schülern. Münster, Westfalen, Aschendorff, 1952. 203 p. illus., port., facsims. 25cm.

"Karl d'Ester als Schriftsteller; Versuch einer Bibliographie (1899-1951)," p. 74-103.

Contents.—Karl d'Ester, der Mensch und sein Werk.—Beiträge zur Zeitungswissenschaft.

1. Ester, Karl d', 1881- .
2. Journalism—Hist.
NN*R 8.53 OC PC,1, 2 SL (LC1,Z1,X1)

AN
(Ester, K.)

Beiträge zur Zeitungswissenschaft. Festgabe für Karl d'Ester zum 70. Geburtstage von seinen Freunden und Schülern. Münster, Westfalen, Aschendorffsche Verlagsbuchhandlung, 1952. 203 p. illus. 24cm.

Bibliographies included.

1. Ester, Karl d', 1881- . 2. Journalism—Addresses, essays, lectures.

NN R 11.52 OC PC,1,2 SL (LC1,Z1,X1)

ZSB

BEKENNENDE KIRCHE; Martin Niemöller zum 60. Geburtstag. München, C. Kaiser, 1952. 328 p. port. 25cm.

"Kirche und Israel von Erica Küppers," pam. of 16 p., inserted.

1. Niemöller, Martin, 1892- . 2. Evangelical Lutheran church. 3. Theology—Essays and misc.
NN OC PC,1,2,3 SL (LC1,Z1,X1)

---

*Z-470
Film Reproduction

BEKENNTNIS zu Ernst Wiechert; ein Gedenkbuch zum 60. Geburtstag des Dichters. München, K. Desch [1947] 207 p. illus., port. 19cm.

Film reproduction. Negative. Original discarded.
"Bibliographie": p. 203-205.

1. Wiechert, Ernst Emil, 1887-1950.
NN *R X 6.58 j/POC PC,1 SL (UM1,LC1,X1,Z1)

VGC

BELGRADE. Muzej Nikole Tesle.
Tribute to Nikola Tesla, presented in articles, letters, documents [selected and prepared by Vojin Popović] Beograd, 1961. 1 v. (various pagings) illus., ports., facsims. 29cm.

Contributions in English, French, German, Russian or Polish.

1. Tesla, Nikola, 1856-1943. 2. Electric engineering--Addresses, essays, lectures. I. Popović, Vojin, ed. II. Popović, Vojin. t. 1961.
NN R 1.64 e/B (OC)I, IIb* OS PC,1,2,I SL S,1,2,I ST,1,2t, I (LC1,X1,Z1)

D-14
4301

BELL, H.E., ed.
Historical essays, 1600-1750, presented to David Ogg, edited by H.E. Bell & R. L. Ollard. London, Adam & C. Black [1963] 274 p. illus., port. 23cm.

Bibliographical footnotes.
CONTENTS: The northern borderland under the early Stuarts, by P. Williams. --Two Swedish financiers; Louis De Geer and Joel Gripenstierna, by
(Continued)

NN R 8.63 p/OC, I PC,1,2,I SL (LC1,X1,Z1) [I]
2

BELL, H.E., ed. Historical essays, 1600-1750...
(Card 2)

R. Carr. --Propagating the gospel, by C. Hill. --'A draught of Sir Phillip Sidney's Arcadia', by J. Buxton. --Scotland and the Puritan revolution, by H.R. Trevor-Roper. --Seventeenth century America, by B.D. Bargar. --Clayworth and Cogenhoe, by P. Laslett and J. Harrison. --King James II and the revolution of 1688, by M. Ashley. --The French privateering war, 1702-18, by J.S. Bromley. --The red priest, by H. K. Andrews. --A New college scandal of the seventeen-twenties, by H.E. Bell--A list of the books, articles and principal reviews written by David Ogg (p. 264-266)

1. Ogg, David, 1887- . 2. History--Addresses, essays, lectures. I. Ollard, R. L., joint ed.

Copy only words underlined
& classmark-- *OAC

BENDER, ERNEST, ed.
Indological studies in honor of W. Norman Brown. New Haven, American oriental society, 1962. xx, 253 p. illus., port. 26cm. (American Oriental series. v. 47)

CONTENTS.--Bibliography of W. Norman Brown's writings (p. ix-xx). --Gaurī, by V.S. Agrawala. --Namipavvajjā, by L. Alsdorf. --The prefession of prince Tcūṃ-ttehi, by H. W. Bailey. --Sanskrit āmoda-'fragance,perfume,' by T. Burrow. --Purāṇa-Apocrypha, by S.K. Chatterji. --Note on Khotanese poetry, by M.J. Dresden. --The manuscript of the
(Continued)

NN R 2.64 f/OC, IIbo (OS)I PC,1,2,I O,1,2,I (LC1,X1,Z1) [I]
3

BENDER, ERNEST, ed. Indological studies in honor of W. Norman Brown. (Card 2)

Rgveda of the M.A. Stein collection, by P.E. Dumont. --Atharva-veda, 13.1.10. by F. Edgerton. --New Brahui etymologies, by M.B. Emeneau. --Les dates du Bhāgavatapurāṇa et du Bhagavatamāhātmya, par J. Filliozat. --Rgveda 10.40.10, by J. Gonda. --Words for beauty in classical Sanskrit poetry, by D.H. Ingalls. --A special causative in Konkanī verbal bases, by S.M. Katre. --Two, its significance in the Rgveda, by S. Kramrisch. --The three strides of Viṣṇu, by F.B. J. Kuiper. --Der altindische kausative

(Continued)

BENDER, ERNEST, ed. Indological studies in honor of W. Norman Brown. (Card 3)

Aorist ajījanat, von M. Leumann. --Iranian feminines in *ī*, by G. Morgenstierne. --Du nouveau sur Rgveda 10.90?, par P. Mus. --The Vedanta as noticed in mediaeval Jain literature, by H. Nakamura. --Sur la forme des Brahmasūtra, par L. Renou. --Chess and backgammon in Sanskrit literature, by P. Thieme. --Humor in Indian and Southeast Asian art, by J.E van Lohuizen-deLeeuw. --Gharma and Oman in the Atri legend, by H.D. Velankar. --The Buddhist act of compassion, by R. W. Weiler.

1. Indic studies--Collections. 2. Brown, William Norman, 1892- . I. Series. II. Bender, Ernest.

D-19
7150

Bereitbleiben zur Tat. Zum siebzigsten Geburtstag von General a. D. Dr. Hans Speidel, 28. Oktober 1967. (Köln, Markus Verlagsgesellschaft m. b. H., 1967.) 79 p. front. 23cm.

CONTENTS.—Der Lebensweg eines deutschen Generals, von H. Rothfels.—Einem deutschen Freunde, von Sir R. Gale.—Die gemeinsame Sache des Friedens, des Fortschritts und der militärischen Sicherheit, von L. L. Lemnitzer.—Eine eindrucksvolle Persönlichkeit, ein bedeutender Soldat, von U. de Maizière.—Der Beginn einer neuen

(Continued)

NN*R 4.70 m/$_L$ OC PC,1 SL E,1 (LC1, X1, Z1)

2

BEREITBLEIBEN zur Tat. (Card 2)

Ära, von A. Béthouart.—General Speidel und die Schweiz, von E. Uhlmann.—Generalstab und Bildung, von H. Speidel.—Der Aufstand der Offiziere, von The Times, London.

1. Speidel, Hans, 1897-

F-11
2356

BERG, CHRISTIAN.

Stimmen aus der Ökumene; hrsg. ... in Verbindung mit Elisabeth Urbig... und Heinrich Hellstern... [Dankgabe an Willem Adolf Visser't Hooft] Berlin, Lettner-Verlag [1963] 279 p. ports. 27cm.

1. Visser't Hooft, Willem Adolf, 1900- . 2. Church unity. I. Urbig, Elisabeth, joint ed. II. Urbig, Elisabeth.

NN * R 2.67 r/$_c$ OC,Ib*,I, IIbo PC,1,2,I SL (LC1, X1, Z1)

SB

Berger, Morroe, ed.

Freedom and control in modern society [edited by] Morroe Berger, Theodore Abel [and] Charles H. Page. New York, Van Nostrand [1954] xii,326 p. 24cm. (The Van Nostrand series in sociology)

"This volume is written in honor of Robert Morrison MacIver."

Bibliographical footnotes.

Contents.—The internalization of social controls, by G. Murphy.—Friendship as social process: a substantive and methodological analysis, by

(Continued)

NN*R 10.54 f/$_t$ OC,I,II PC,1,2,3,I,II SL E,1,2,3,I,II (U 1,ZI,LC1,X1)

Berger, Morroe, ed. Freedom and control in modern society... (Card 2)

P. F. Lazarsfeld and R. K. Merton.—The problem of authority, by R. Bierstedt.—The political process in trade unions: a theoretical statement, by S. M. Lipset.—Social groups in the modern world, by F. Znaniecki.—Social structure and goals in group relations, by M. M. Gordon.—Ethnic groups in America: from national culture to ideology, by N. Glazer.—Individual liberty today: challenge and prospect,

(Continued)

Berger, Morroe, ed. Freedom and control in modern society... (Card 3)

by T. I. Cook.—America's changing capitalism: the interplay of politics and economics, by J. M. Clark.—The demographic foundations of national power, by K. Davis.—Social change in Soviet Russia, by A. Inkeles.—The utility of political science, by G. Catlin.—Robert M. MacIver's contributions to sociological theory, by H. Alpert.—Robert M. MacIver's contributions to political theory, by D. Spitz.

1. Sociology, 1945- 2. Liberty. 3. MacIver, Robert Morrison, 1882- I. Abel, Theodore Fred, 1896- , joint ed. II. Page, Charles Hunt, 1909- , joint ed.

EAG p.v.243

Bergzabern, Germany.

650 Jahre Stadt Bergzabern verbunden mit Heimattagen. Schirmherr: Gauleiter Bürckel. Festschrift zur Jubelfeier am 6., 7., 8. und 9. Juni 1936. Herausgegeben von der Kur- und Grenzstadt Bergzabern. Bergzabern: Pfeifer & Wessbecher [1936] xvi, 72 p. illus. (incl. plan), plates. 25cm.

1. Bergzabern, Germany—Hist.

N. Y. P. L. January 24, 1939

Festschrift

EIG

Berlin.

Geschichte der stadt Berlin. Festschrift zur 700-jahr-feier der reichshauptstadt. Im auftrage des oberbürgermeisters und stadtpräsidenten dargestellt von Max Arendt, Eberhard Faden [und] Otto-Friedrich Gandert. Berlin, Verlag von E. S. Mittler & sohn, 1937.

viii, [2] p., 1 l., 411, [1] p. illus. (incl. maps) xxxii (*i. e.* 33) pl. (1 fold.; incl. plans) on 17 l. 26cm.

Title vignette: Seal of the city of Berlin.

"Zum geleit" signed: Dr. Lippert, oberbürgermeister und stadtpräsident.

(Continued on next card)

A C 37-2955

[2]

Festschrift

Berlin. Geschichte der stadt Berlin ... 1937. (Card 2)

CONTENTS.—Gandert, O. F. Vorgeschichte.—Faden, Eberhard. Berlin im mitelalter. Die kurfürstlichen residenzstädte Berlin und Cölln an der Spree 1448–1648. Festung und hauptstadt unter dem Grossen kurfürsten und dem ersten könig. Das friderizianische Berlin—die stadt der soldaten und manufakturen.—Arendt, Max. Niederbruch und erhebung. Die biedermeierzeit. Die werdende weltstadt. Die kaiserstadt. Durch das inferno zur hauptstadt des dritten reiches.

1. Berlin—History. I. Arendt, Max, 1887– II. Faden, Eberhard. III. Gandert, Otto Friedrich. IV. Title. V. Title: Festschrift zur 700-jahr-feier der reichshauptstadt.

A C 37-2955

New York. Public library
for Library of Congress [2]

Copy only words underlined
& classmark— EAA

BERLIN. Freie Universität

Das Hauptstadtproblem in der Geschichte; Festgabe zum 90. Geburtstag Friedrich Meineckes, gewidmet vom Friedrich-Meinecke-Institut an der Freien Universität Berlin. Tübingen, M. Niemeyer, 1952. x, 308 p. port. 25cm. (Jahrbuch für Geschichte des Deutschen Ostens. Bd. 1)

Bibliographies included in "Anmerkungen."

CONTENTS. — Das Reich ohne Hauptstadt, von W. Berges. — Das Vorortproblem in der Frühzeit des Städtewesens im Gebiet der deutschen

(Continued)

NN ** R X 11.53 OS, I PC, 1, 2, 3, I, II (U1, LC1, Z1, X1)

BERLIN. Freie Universität. Das Hauptstadtproblem in der Geschichte... (Card 2)

Ostkolonisation, von H. Helbig. —Caput Marchionatus Brandenburgensis, Brandenburg und Berlin, von J. Schultze. —Die Idee des geistigen Mittelpunktes Europas im 17. und 18. Jahrhundert, von C. Hinrichs. — Von der Residenzstadt zur Weltstadt; Berlin vom Anfang des 19. Jahrhunderts bis zur Reichsgründung,von R. Dietrich. — Berlin als Kaiserstadt und Reichshaupstadt, 1871 bis 1945, von H. Herzfeld. — Der Kampf um die Selbstverwaltung in Berlin, von G. Kotowski. — Die städtebauliche Entwicklung Berlins, von E. Redslob. — Causa Imperii; Probleme Roms in Spätantike und Mittelalter, von P. Classen. —Haupstadt und Staat in Frankreich, von G. Roloff.

(Continued)

BERLIN. Freie Universität. Das Hauptstadtproblem in der Geschichte... (Card 3)

— Das englische Hauptstadtproblem in der Neuzeit, von P. Kluke. —Polens Haupstädte, ihr Wechsel im Laufe der Geschichte, von H. Jablonowski.

1. Capitals (Cities). 2. Berlin—Hist. 3. Meinecke, Friedrich, 1862- I. Series. II. Title.

F-10
1503

BERLIN. Freie Universität.

Veritas, iustitia, libertas; Festchrift zur 200-Jahrfeier der Columbia university, New York, überreicht von der Freien Universität Berlin und der Deutschen Hochschule für Politik, Berlin. Berlin, Colloquium-Verlag [c1954] 347 p. illus. 29cm.

Bibliographical footnotes.

CONTENTS. —Vorspruch, von E. Redslob. —Vorwort, von G. Rohde.. — Der Kampf um Berlins Univer- sität, von G. Kotowski. —

(Continued)

NN R 10. 57 j/ (OC)II OS, I PC, 1, I, II SL (LC1, X1, Z1)

BERLIN. Freie Universität. Veritas, iustitia, libertas... (Card 2)

Freiheit und Zwang in der politischen Willensbildung; Formen der demokratischen und der totalitären Meinungsführung, von E. Dovifat. — Von der Massenbewegung zur Managerorganisation: Die Evolution des Weltbolschewismus, von O. K. Flechtheim. —Freiheit und politisches Betätigungsrecht der Beamten in Deutschland und den USA, von E. Fraenkel. —Das Mitbestimmungsrecht der Arbeiter und Angestellten als Aufgabe der Wirtschaftspolitik und der Volksbildung, von O. H. von der Gablentz. —Staatsschutz und Grundrechte, von E. Heinitz. —Staat und Nation in der deutschen Geschichtsschreibung der Weimarer Zeit, von H. Herzfeld. —Die Freiheit von Forschung und Lehre

(Continued)

BERLIN. Freie Universität. Veritas, iustitia, libertas.... (Card 3)

als Problem der Theologie, von H. Köhler. —Vom Altern des Menschen, von H. Freiherr von Kress. —Das Problem der "Neuen Intelligenz" in der sowjetischen Besatzungszone, ein Beitrag zur politischen Soziologie der kommunistischen Herrschaftsordung, von M. G. Lange, E. Richert und O. Stammer. —Der deutsche Akademiker als soziologisches Problem, von H.-J. Lieber. —Die Stellung des Subjekts in der Quantentheorie, von G. Ludwig. —Vom Geist der Wissenschaft, von E. May. —Biologie und Totalitarismus, von H. Nachtsheim. —Zum Theorem des Gleichgewichts einer freien Verkehrswirtschaft, von A. Paulsen.

1. Columbia university— Centennial celebrations, etc., 1954. I. Hochschule für Politik, Berlin. II. Title.

M-10
4490
Bd. 5

Berlin. Freie Universität. Geographisches Institut.

Geomorphologische Abhandlungen, Otto Maull zum 70. Geburtstage gewidmet. Besorgt von E. Fels, H. Overbeck und J. H. Schultze. Berlin, D. Reimer, 1957. 72 p illus. 30cm. (Berlin. Freie Universität. Geographisches Institut. Abhandlungen. Bd. 5)

Summaries in English.
Includes bibliographies.

(Continued)

NN R X 12.60 (OC)II, III, IV, V OS, I PC, 1, 2, I, II, III, IV, V ST, 1t, 2, II, III, IV, V (LC1, X1, Z1)

Berlin. Freie Universität. Geographisches Institut. Geomorphologische Abhandlungen... 1957. (Card 2)

CONTENTS.—Zur Entstehung von Pingen, Oriçangas und Dellen in den feuchten Tropen, von J. P. Bakker.—"Verkarstungserscheinungen" in Silikatgesteinen, von W. Klaer.—Junge Erosion und Akkumulation in den Ostalpen, von S. Morawetz.—Untersuchungen an Blockströmen der Ötztaler Alpen, von W. Pillewizer.—Das mittlere Inntal und Silltal in der Schlernzeit, von H. Paschinger.—Formgestalt und Pflanzendecke der Niedertauern-Landschaft, von L. Koegel.—Klimamorphologische Beobachtungen in der Serra da Montiqueira und im Paraiba-Tal (Brasilien) von H. Lehmann.

1. Geography, Physical—Essays and misc. 2. Maull, Otto, 1887– I. Series. II. Fels, Edwin, 1888– , ed. III. Overbeck, Hermann, ed. IV. Schultze, Joachim Heinrich, 1903– , ed. V. Title. t. 1957.

STN
(Berlin)

Berlin. Friedrich Werder Gymnasium.

Festschrift zu der zweiten Säcularfeier des Friedrichs-Werderschen Gymnasiums zu Berlin, veröffentlicht von dem Lehrer-Kollegium des Friedrichs-Werderschen Gymnasiums. Berlin: Weidmann, 1881. 369 p. 8°.

Bibliographical footnotes.

Contents: BÜCHSENSCHÜTZ, B. Studien zu Aristoteles' Politik. MÜLLER, H. I. Symbolae ad emendandos scriptores Latinos. Particula II. MEWES, W. De codicis Horatiani, qui Blandinius vetustissumus (V) vocatur, natura atque indole. PAUL, W. F. Interprétation pratique des huits béatitudes tirées de l'évangile selon saint Mat-

(Continued)

N. Y. P. L. October 25, 1929

Berlin. Friedrich Werder Gymnasium: Festschrift zu der zweiten Säcularfeier des Friedrichs-Werderschen Gymnasiums . . . (Continued)

thieu, V, 3–10. KALLENBERG, H. Zur Quellenkritik von Diodors XVI. Buche. JACOBSEN, A. Ein Beitrag zur Evangelienkritik. NETTEBOHM, W. Die Preussisch-Türkische Defensivallianz (1763–65). SUPHAN, B. Goethe und Spinoza. 1783–86. SCHULZE, K. P. Catullforschungen. LASSER, H. Ueber die religiöse Lebensanschauung Walthers von der Vogelweide. SCHICHE, T. Zu Ciceros Briefen an Atticus. KRAUSE, A. Zu Adenets Cleomades. SIEGFRIED, E. Zur Metrik der kleineren gereimten althochdeutschen Gedichte. LÜBECK, G. Die Bewegung eines kugelförmigen Atoms in einem idealen Gase. HOFFMANN, O. Sertum plantarum Madagascariensium. WORPITZY, I. Zahl, Grösse, Messen. DIESTERWEG, G. Die Anwendung des inductiven und analytischen Verfahrens im Gymnasialunterricht.

1. No subject.
N. Y. P. L. October 25, 1929

Berlin. Universität. Rechts- und staatswissenschaftliche Fakultät. Festschrift... (cont'd.)

Mitgliedschaft bei der eingetragenen Genossenschaft, von L. Waldecker. Rechtsvergleichende Bemerkungen zur Stellung des Quittungsträgers, von F. K. Neubecker. Über die aufschiebenden Einreden des Erben, von T. Kipp. Polizei, Staat und Gemeinde in Preussen, von G. Anschütz. Positiver Kompetenzkonflikt nach Rechtskraft? von K. Dickel. Benedictus Levita decurtatus et excerptus, von E. Seckel. Die Entstehung des neuen Gotthardbahnvertrages vom 13. Oktober 1909, von F. von Martitz. Der Konviktorien-Beitrag der Landschaft Norder-Dithmarschen, von H. Triepel.

1. Law.—Essays. 2. Brunner, Heinrich, 1840– . 3. Title.
N. Y. P. L. June 22, 1915

F–10
5415

Berlin. Friedrich Werder Gymnasium.
Zweihundertfünfzig Jahre Friedrichs-Werdersches Gymnasium zu Berlin. [Berlin, 1931] 131 p. illus., ports. 28cm.

At head of title: 1681–1931.
Contributions by Ernst Pilch and others.

I. Pilch, Ernst. t. 1931.
NN R 9.61 (OC)I,Ibo ODt EDt PC,I SL (LC1,X1,Z1)

OAI

Berlin. Universität.
Forschen und Wirken; Festschrift zur 150-Jahr-Feier der Humboldt-Universität zu Berlin, 1810–1960. [Im Auftrage von Rektor und Senat hrsg. von Willi Göber und Friedrich Herneck] Berlin, Deutscher Verlag der Wissenschaften, 1960.

3 v. illus. (part mounted, part col.) ports., diagrs., facsims. 28 cm.
German or English.
Includes bibliographies.

(Continued)
NN * R 9. 61 m/ (OC)I, II, III, SL ST, It, I, II, III (LC1, X1, Z1) IVb* OS PC, 1, I, II, III

2

---

* MEC
(Wagner)

Berlin. Preussische Staatstheater. Opernhaus.
Richard Wagner und die Berliner Oper. Die Berliner Staatsoper dem Gedächtnis Richard Wagners. Herausgeber Julius Kapp. Berlin-Schöneberg: M. Hesse, 1933. 62 p. facsims., ports. 27½cm.

"Statistik der Aufführungen Rich. Wagnerscher Werke an der Berliner Staatsoper (abgeschlossen 13. Februar 1933)," p. 61–62.

663921A. 1. Wagner, Richard, 1813–1883. 2. Opera—Germany—Berlin. I. Kapp, Julius, 1883– , ed. II. Title.
N. Y. P. L. *Card revised* February 10, 1941

BERLIN. Universität. Forschen und Wirken... (Card 2)

CONTENTS.—Bd. 1. Beiträge zur wissenschaftlichen und politischen Entwicklung der Universität.—Bd. 2. Forschungsbeiträge aus den Gebieten der naturwissenschaftlichen Fakultäten.—Bd. 3. Forschungsbeiträge aus den Gebieten der gesellschaftswissenschaftlichen Fakultäten.

1. Science--Essays and misc. I. Herneck, Friedrich, ed. II. Göber, Willi, 1899- , ed. III. Title. IV. Göber, Willi, 1899- . t. 1960

---

* MG p.v.72

Berlin. Preussische Staatstheater. Opernhaus.
Richard Strauss und die Berliner Oper. Festschrift der Berliner Staatsoper zu des Meisters 70. Geburtstage. Herausgeber: Julius Kapp. Berlin-Schöneberg: M. Hesse, 1934. 48 p. facsims., plates, ports. (1 mounted.) 27cm.

"Statistik der Aufführungen Rich. Strauss'scher Werke an der Berliner Staatsoper (abgeschlossen 15. Juni 1934)," p. 47–48.

804371A. 1. Strauss, Richard, 1864– . 2. Opera—Germany—Berlin. I. Kapp, Julius, 1883– , ed. II. Title.
N. Y. P. L. *Card revised* February 10, 1941

E-13
8221

Berliner Festschift für Ernst E. Hirsch. Dargebracht von Mitgliedern der Juristischen Fakultät zum 65. Geburtstag. Berlin, Duncker & Humblot (1968). 265 p. front. 24cm.

Bibliographical footnotes.

CONTENTS.—Gewerbefreiheit der öffentlichen Hand, von K. A. Bettermann.—Zum relativen Verbot der Verfügung über Forderungen, von A. Blomeyer.—Zur Verfassungsmässigkeit der Strafbestimmung gegen den groben Unfug, von E. Heinitz.—Grundrechte und Gesellschaftspolitik, von R. Herzog.—Die Feststellung von Handelsbräuchen, von J. Limbach.—Korporative Versklavung deutscher Aktiengesell-

(Continued)
NN*R 4. 70 m/,OC, I PC, 1, I SL (LC1, X1) (Z1)

2

XAH

Berlin. Universität. Rechts- und staatswissenschaftliche Fakultät.
Festschrift für Heinrich Brunner, zum fünfzigjährigen Doktorjubiläum am 8. April 1914. Überreicht von der Juristenfakultät der Universität Berlin. München: Duncker & Humblot, 1914. iv, 554 p. 8°.

Glossenapparat des Vacarius Pragensis zu den Digestentiteln 43, 24, 25 und 39, 1, von A. Stölzel. Die Wurzeln des Dienstvertrages, von O. von Gierke. Die Petersburger Konvention vom 5.–17. Juni 1801 und das Seekriegsrecht, von R. Krauel. Zwei Beiträge zum materiellen Ziviljustizrecht, von J. Goldschmidt. Die rechtliche Natur des Arbeiterschutzes, von W. Kaskel. Ein Beweis- und Spruchtermin vor dem Königlichen Hofgericht im Jahre 1434, von J. Kohler. Der Begriff des militärischen Geheimnisses, von F. v. Liszt. Störung des religiösen Friedens und der Totenruhe, von W. Kahl. Über die Entstehung der (Continued)

N. Y. P. L. June 22, 1915

Berliner Festschrift für Ernst E. Hirsch. (1968) (Card 2)

schaften durch Beherrschungs- und Gewinnabführungsverträge gegenüber in- und ausländischen Unternehmen, von H. Meilicke.—Einflüsse der Wirtschaftsordnung auf die Rechtsfindung, von K. Pleyer.—Status—Kontrakt—Rolle, von M. Rehbinder.—Beweisregeln im Strafprozess, von W. Sarstedt.—Die Vererblichkeit von sozialversicherungsrechtlichen Ansprüchen, von K. Sieg.—Die Gegenseitigkeit von Rechtslagen im internationalen Privatrecht, von W. Wengler.—Das Bundesbaugesetz in der Bewährung, von F. Werner.—Sacheinlagen in der GmbH, von H. Wiedemann.

1. Law--Addresses, essays, lectures. I. Hirsch, Ernst E.

Berliner Volks-Chor. Gena-Guttmann-Stiftung.
Festschrift zum 25jährigen Bestehen des Berliner Volks-Chors. Den Mitgliedern und Freunden des Chors überreicht zum 8. Februar 1929 von der Gena-Guttmann-Stiftung. [Berlin: Buchdruckwerkstätte, G.m.b.H., 1929.] 64 p. plates, port., table. 8°.

On cover: Berliner Volks-Chor.

428722A. 1. Music—Assoc. and org.—Germany—Berlin. 2. Title.
N. Y. P. L. October 2, 1929

BERN (CITY). Burgerbibliothek.
Schätze der Burgerbibliothek Bern; hrsg. im Auftrag der burgerlichen Behörden der Stadt Bern anlässlich der 600-Jahr-Feier des Bundes der Stadt Bern mit den Waldstätten. Bern, H. Lang, 1953. 135 p. plates (part col., ports.), facsims (part col.) 29cm.

CONTENTS. — Die Handschriften der Burgerbibliothek als Spiegel der älteren bernischen Vergangenheit, von R. von Fischer. — Die Handschriften-sammlungen Gottlieb Emanuel von Hallers und der Familie von Mülinen, von H. Haeberli. — Jacques Bongars und seine Handschriftensammlung, von K. Müller. — Über die kunstgeschichtliche Bedeutung der Handschriften der Burgerbibliothek, von O. Homburger. — Bibliographische Hinweise (p. 131).
1. Manuscripts — Collections — Switzerland — Bern. I. 1953.

NN ** R 4. 54 ODi EDi PC, 1 SL (LC1, Z1, X1)

BERNDT, RONALD, ed.
Aboriginal man in Australia; essays in honour of emeritus professor A. P. Elkin, edited by Ronald M. Berndt and Catherine H. Berndt. Contributions by N. W. G. Macintosh [and others. Sydney] Angus and Robertson [1965] xviii, 491 p. illus., port., maps, music. 25cm.

Includes bibliographies.

(Continued)

NN R 11. 65 e/ OC, I PC, 1, 2, I SL (LC1, X1, Z1)

3

BERNDT, RONALD, ed. Aboriginal man in Australia ... (Card 2)

CONTENTS. --Foreword, by R. M. and C. H. Berndt. --A. P. Elkin, the man and the anthropologist, by R. M. and C. H. Berndt. --The physical aspect of man in Australia, by N. W. G. Macintosh. --The aboriginal past, by F. D. McCarthy. --Language in aboriginal Australia, by A. Capell. --Culture, social structure, and environment in aboriginal Central Australia, by T. G. H. Strehlow. --Marriage among the Walbiri of Central Australia, by M. J. Meggitt. --Law and order in aboriginal Australia, by R. M. Berndt. --Religion, totemism and symbolism, by W. E. H. Stanner.

(Continued)

BERNDT, RONALD, ed. Aboriginal man in Australia ... (Card 3)

--Women and the "secret life," by C. H. Berndt. --Australian aboriginal music, T. A. Jones. --The background of alien impact, by M. Reay. --The part-aborigines in New South Wales, by J. H. Bell. --The contemporary situation of change among part-aborigines in Western Australia, by R. A. Fink. --The problem of administration, by P. Hasluck. --Bibliography of A. P. Elkin (p. [455]-470).

1. Australian tribes. 2. Elkin, Adolphus Peter, 1891- . I. Berndt, Catherine, joint ed.

BERNA BERNENSIS.
Festschrift der akademischen Verbindung "Berna Bernensis", 1881-1956. [Bern, 1956] 64 p. illus., ports., facsims. 21cm.

1. Students--Assoc. and org.--Switzerland--Bern.

NN R 4. 66 r/ OS(1b+) PC, 1 SL (LC1, X1, Z1)

Write on slip words underlined below and class mark—

Berthold Delbrück zum siebzigsten Geburtstag am 26. Juli, 1912, von Freunden und Schülern. [Strassburg: K. J. Trübner, 1912–13] 534 p. 23cm. (Indogermanische Forschungen. Bd. 31, Heft 1–4.)

On series t.-p.: Festschrift für Berthold Delbrück.

556193. 1. Delbrück, Berthold, 1842–1922.
N. Y. P. L. October 31, 1939

Berti, Pietro, 1741–1813.
Pel solenne ingresso di Sua Eccellenza mss. Pietro Mocenigo k[r]. procuratore di S. Marco. Orazione del ab. Pietro Berti. [Venezia, S. Occhi? 1780] 2 p.l., xxviii p. incl. front. (port.) 36cm. (4°.)

Morazzoni: Libro illustrato veneziano del settecento, 274.
Illustrations: 31 copper engravings, comprising portrait of Mocenigo by Antonio Baratti after Andreas Compagnioni, title-page, 16 borders repeated to 28, and tailpiece. The t.-p. and borders are signed: Appresso. T. Viero Ven. One engraved initial.
Binding (unsigned), by James Macdonald, Inc., New York, of half red morocco with marbled paper sides.
With this is bound: Poesie pel solenne ingresso di... Pietro Mocenigo. Venezia, 1780.

1. Mocenigo, Pietro, b. ca. 1698.
N. Y. P. L. December 3, 1948

Bertine, Eleanor.
Jung's contribution to our time: the collected papers of Eleanor Bertine. Edited by Elizabeth C. Rohrbach. [New York] Published by Putnam for the C. G. Jung Foundation for Analytical Psychology [1968, °1967]
xvi, 271 p. port. 22 cm.

Published in honor of the author's eightieth birthday.
Bibliography: p. [267]-269.

(Continued)

NN*R 6. 69 v/ OC, II, IIIb* (OS)I PC, 1, 2, I, II SL (LC1, X1, Z1)

2

BERTINE, ELEANOR. Jung's contribution to our time... (Card 2)

1. Jung, Carl Gustav, 1875-1961. 2. Psychoanalysis--Addresses, essays, lectures. I. Jung Foundation for Analytical Psychology, New York. II. Rohrbach, Elizabeth C., ed. III. Rohrbach, Elizabeth C.

Beruff Mendieta, propulsor de la cultura (síntesis de un trienio de labor) marzo 25, 1936–1939; homenaje de las instituciones culturales de la Habana. La Habana, Molina y compañía [1939]

56 p. illus. (incl. plans) 23½cm.

1. Beruff Mendieta, Antonio. 2. Havana—~~Soc. life & cust.~~ ~~3. Havana—Intellectual life.~~ Civilization

Library of Congress F1799.H3B4 42-51307 [3] Festschrift ed.

BESKOUINGS oor poësie; 'n bundel opgedra aan G. Dekker op sy sestigste verjaarsdag 11 November 1957. Pretoria, J.L. van Schaik, 1957. 164 p. 24cm.

CONTENTS. —Die wakende droom in Die swart luiperd, van T. T. Cloete. —Leipoldt as versdramaturg, van P. du P. Grobler. —Die towenaar in die fles, van A. P. Grove. —Die digter as intellektueel, van N. P. van Wyk Louw. —Variasies op 'n tema, van W. E. G. Louw. —Probleme van die versdrama, van D. J. Opperman. —Die dans van die sluiers, van M. Scholtz. (Continued)

NN R 9. 59 a/ OC PC, 1, 2 SL (LC1, X1, Z1)

BESKOUINGS oor poësie... (Card 2)

—Georganiseerde geweld, van J. L. Steyn. —Vers en sin, van H. Venter. —Bibliografie van G. Dekker, 1926-1956 (p. 161-164)

1. Dekker, Gerrit, 1897- 2. Poetry, Afrikaans--Hist. and crit.

BESSON, WALDEMAR, ed.

Geschichte und Gegenwartsbewusstsein; historische Betrachtungen und Untersuchungen. Festschrift für Hans Rothfels zum 70. Geburtstag, dargebracht von Kollegen, Freunden und Schülern. Hrsg. von Waldemar Besson und Friedrich Frhr. Hiller v. Gaertringen. Göttingen, Vandenhoeck & Ruprecht [1963] 526 p. port. 25cm.

Contributions in German or English.

(Continued)

NN 4. 64 p/ OC, I PC, 1, 2, I SL (LC1, X1, Z1) [I] 4

BESSON, WALDEMAR, ed. Geschichte und Gegenwartsbewusstsein... (Card 2)

Bibliographical footnotes.

CONTENTS. --Geschichtliches Bewusstsein und politische Entscheidung von A. Bergstraesser. --The historian and the contemporary world, by J. Joll. --Geschichte und Gegenwartsverständnis, von J. Vogt. --Geschichte als politische Wissenschaft, von W. Besson. --Zeitkritik und Gegenwartsverständnis in Jacob Burckhardts Briefen aus den Jahren der Reichsgründung, von E. W. Zeeden. --Die russische Sozialdemokratie als parteigeschichtliches Problem, von D. Geyer. --"Dolchstoss"-Diskussion und "Dolchstosslegende" (Continued)

BESSON, WALDEMAR, ed. Geschichte und Gegenwartsbewusstsein... (Card 3)

im Wandel von vier Jahrzehnten, von F. Frhr. Hiller von Gaertringen. --Zur Problematik der Appeasement-Politik, von H. Herzfeld. --Vergleichende Geschichtsbetrachtung und Zeitgeschichte, von D. Gerhard. --Das Religiös-Humane als Grundlage der geschichtlichen Objektivität bei Herodot, von W. Schadewaldt. --Immanuel Kant über den Weg der Geschichte, von K. D. Erdmann. --Die inneren Wandlungen des Deutschen Ritterordens, von E. Maschke. --Die Unterwerfung Livlands und Estlands, 1710, von R. Wittram. -- Die Nation im östlichen Europa zur Zeit der französischen (Continued)

BESSON, WALDEMAR, ed. Geschichte und Gegenwartsbewusstsein... (Card 4)

Revolution, von H. Roos. --Der Beginn der deutschen Arbeiterbewegung, von W. Conze. --Italien und die Probleme des europäischen Nationalstaats im 19. Jahrhundert, von T. Schieder. --Holsteins grosses Spiel im Frühjahr 1887, von H. Krausnick. --Politische Form und Aussenpolitik des Nationalsozialismus, von H. Krausnick. --Pocolonial plans and policies, 1938-1942, von G. L. Weinberg. --Probleme der modernen Parteifinanzierung, von T. Eschenburg.

1. Rothfels, Hans, 1891- 2. History--Addresses, essays lectures. I. Hiller von Gaertringen, Friedrich, Freiherr, joint ed.

Der BESTÄNDIGE Aufbruch; Festschrift für Erich Przywara, hrsg. von Siegfried Behn. Nürnberg, Glock und Lutz [1959] 237 p. 25cm.

Includes bibliography.

CONTENTS. --Wer ist's, von S. Behn. --Die Bibliothek eines Gelehrten, von R. Adolph. --Zur Frage einer Evolution des menschlichen Gehirns während des Eiszeitalters, von P. Overhage. --Urleidenschaft und (Continued)

NN * R 3. 61 e/ OC, I PC, 1, 2, I SL (LC1, X1, Z1) 3

Der BESTÄNDIGE Aufbruch... (Card 2)

natürliche Gotteserkenntnis, von J. M. Hollenbach. --Grusswort an Erich Przywara, von K. Barth. --Anodische und kathodische Analogia entis, von J. Pienge. --"Analogia perfectionis" und die Methode der Aszetik, von G. Soballa. --Grussbrief an den Jubilar, von H. Heuvers. --Geschenk im Übermass, von G. von Le Fort. --Pathos und Naturalismus in der Diktion Shakespeares, von R. Flatter. --Besuch in Ronchamp, von K. A. P. Rohan. --Nomos--Nahme--Name, von C. Schmitt. --Zur Frage nach dem Wahrheitsgehalt von "Dialektik", von H. Ogiermann. --Natura und Creatura,

(Continued)

Der BESTÄNDIGE Aufbruch... (Card 3)

von S. Holm. --Franz Xaver Kraus und John Henry Newman, von H. Fries. --Newman and von Hügel, von H. Tristam. --Die Unterscheidung von Wesenheit und Sein, von J. B. Lotz. --Meister Eckhart als Mystiker und Metaphysiker, von A. Dempf. --Das Mehr, von M. Picard. --Über den Begriff des Geheimnisses in der katholischen Theologie, von K. Rahner. --Ignatius der Theologe, von H. Rahner.

1. Przywara, Erich, 1889- . 2. Theology--Essays and misc. I. Behn, Siegfried, 1884- , ed.

E-14
15

Betriebswirtschaftliche Forschung in internationaler Sicht. Festschrift für Erich Kosiol zum 70. Geburtstag. Hrsg. von Heinrich Kloidt. Berlin, Duncker u. Humblot (1969).

577 p., front. 24 cm.

German, English, or French.
Bibliography of E. Kosiol's works: p. ⌊569⌋-576.

1. Industrial organization. 2. Management--Addresses, essays, lectures. I. Kosiol, Erich, 1899- . II. Kloidt, Heinrich, ed.

NN * R 2.71 b/zOC, I, II PC, 1, 2, I, II SL E, 1, 2, I, II (LC1, X1, Z1)

E-13
9338

Betriebswirtschaftliche Strukturfragen. Beiträge zur Morphologie von erwerbswirtschaftlichen ⌊Unternehmungen und Genossenschaften. Festschrift zum 65. Geburtstag von Reinhold Henzler. Unter Mitwirkung von Karl Alewell ⌊u. a.⌋ Hrsg. von Karl Alewell. Wiesbaden, Betriebswirtschaftlicher Verlag Gabler (1967).

405 p. with illus. port. 25 cm. DM 49.70

(Continued)

NN * R 8.70 l/OC, I, II PC, 1, 2, I, II SL E, 1, 2, I, II (LC1, X1, Z1)

BETRIEBSWIRTSCHAFTLICHE Strukturfragen.
(Card 2)

Bibliographical footnotes.

CONTENTS.—Reinhold Henzler 65 Jahre, von K. Alewell.—Logische Bemerkungen über den Begriff "Genossenschaft," von G. Weisser.—Zum wirtschaftlichen Standpunkt und morphologischen Ansatz in der Betriebswirtschafts- und Genossenschaftslehre von W. Engelhardt.—Kommunistische Genossenschaftspolitik, von E. Boettcher.—Der Betriebswirt, der Jurist und die Mitbestimmung, von R. Reinhardt.—Zur Auslese von Unternehmungsleitern, von B. Bellinger.—Der Genossenschaftsleiter, von G. Draheim.—Die Bedeutung der Bildung von Betriebstypen für die Planung und Vorbereitung ex-

(Continued)

BETRIEBSWIRTSCHAFTLICHE Strukturfragen.
(Card 3)

terner Revisionen, von J. Stupka.—Die Betriebsverpachtung, von J. Fettel.—Finanzwirtschaftliches Gleichgewicht und ausländische Investitionen in Unternehmungen in der Bundesrepublik Deutschland, von H. Vormbaum.—Gedanken zur Frage einer weiteren Konzentration des kreditgenossenschaftlichen Verbundes, von K. Preiss.—Der Gestaltwandel der ländlichen Kreditgenossenschaften in Entwicklungsländern, von C. Eisfeld.—Die räumliche Struktur der Unternehmung, von K. Alewell.—Zur Standortwahl der Unternehmungen, von H. Jacob.—Der Einfluss der Transportkosten auf Produktions- und Verteilerstandorte, von O. Schneider.—Absatzpolitische Ent-

(Continued)

BETRIEBSWIRTSCHAFTLICHE Strukturfragen.
(Card 4)

scheidungen in Verkehrsbetrieben, von H. Diederich.—Beurteilung des Erfolges von Wirtschaftlichkeitsmassnahmen in Gross- und Einzelhandelsbetrieben, von C. Ruberg.—Strukturwandlungen der Edeka Genossenschaften unter dem Einfluss, von Marktveränderungen, von D. Lilienthal.—Lage und Leistung im Westberliner Aussenhandel, von K. C. Behrens und G. Willitzki.—Internationale Rohstoffabkommen und Importhandelsbetrieb, dargestellt am Beispiel des Internationalen Kaffee—Übereinkommens von 1962, von K. F. Roggenkamp.—Verzeichnis der Veröffentlichungen von Reinhold Henzler (p. ⌊381⌋-397).

(Continued)

BETRIEBSWIRTSCHAFTLICHE Strukturfragen.
(Card 5)

1. Business--Addresses, essays, lectures. 2. Co-operation--Addresses, essays, lectures. I. Henzler, Reinhold, 1902- . II. Alewell, Karl, ed.

---

* PBT

BETWEEN East and West; essays dedicated to the memory of Bela Horovitz, edited by A. Altmann. London, East and West library [printed at the Curwen press, Plaistow] 1958. 214 p. port., facsims. 25cm.

Bibliographical footnotes.

CONTENTS.—In memoriam Bela Horovitz, by M. Papo.—Hasidism and modern man, by M. Buber.—Hermann Cohen, by S. H. Bergman.—Franz Kafka and the tree of knowledge, by N. N. Glatzer.—Ahad Ha-Am and the future of the diaspora, by Sir Leon Simon.—The Hebrew university—a

(Continued)

NN R X 12.58 g/ OC, Ib+, I PC, 1, 2, I SL J, 1, 3, I (LC1, X1, Z1, RS1)

BETWEEN East and West... (Card 2)

link between East and West, by N. Bentwich.—The Dead sea scrolls type of Biblical exegesis among the Karaites, by N. Wieder.—An unpublished poem by Abraham Ibn Ezra, by S. M. Stern.—Maimonides' theory of miracle, by J. Heller.—An unidentified Hebrew incunable, by J. L. Teicher.—An early nineteenth-century Frankfurt benevolent society, by K. Wilhelm.—Moses Mendelssohn's concept of tolerance, by D. Patterson.—Modern anti-Semitism and its place in the history of the Jewish question, by A. Bein.—Franz Rosenzweig on history, by A. Altmann.

1. Horovitz, Bela, 1898-1955. 2. Essays, Jewish, in English 3. Essays, English. I. Altmann, Alexander, ed.

---

*PGF

BETZ, OTTO, ed.
Abraham unser Vater; Juden und Christen im Gespräch über die Bibel; Festschrift für Otto Michel zum 60. Geburtstag, hrsg. von Otto Betz, Martin Hengel, Peter Schmidt. Leiden, E.J. Brill, 1963. vi, 503 p. . port, 25cm. (Arbeiten zur Geschichte des Spätjudentums und Urchristentums. 5)

"Bibliographie der Schriften Otto Michels, zusammengestellt von

(Continued)

NN R 3.64 f/b OC, I, III, IVbo, Vbo (OS)II PC, 1, 2, 3, I, II, III SL J, 1, 2, 3, I, II, III, IVbo, Vbo (LC1, X1, Z1)

BETZ, OTTO, ed. Abraham unser Vater...
(Card 2)

Peter Schmidt," p. [484]-497.
Bibliographical footnotes.

1. Michel, Otto, 1903- . 2. Bible. N.T. and Jewish literature. 3. Bible--Criticism. I. Hengel, Martin, joint ed. II. Series. III. Schmidt, Peter, joint ed. IV. Betz, Otto. V. Hengel, Martin.

E-12
3793

Betz, Werner, *ed.*
Taylor Starck: Festschrift, 1964. Edited by Werner Betz, Evelyn S. Coleman ⌊and⌋ Kenneth Northcott. London, Mouton ⌊°1964⌋
276 p. port. 24 cm.
"Presented to Professor Emeritus Taylor Starck by his friends, colleagues, and pupils on the occasion of his seventy-fifth birthday."
Contributions in English or German.
Bibliographical footnotes.

NN * R 7.65 1/ OC PC, 1, 2, 3 SL (LC1, X1, Z1) [I] (Continued)

4

BETZ, WERNER, ed. Taylor Starck... (Card 2)

CONTENTS.—Taylor Starck: an appreciation, by A. Taylor.—Eine neue Hypothese vom schwachen Präteritum, by L. L. Hammerich.—Gothic spellings and phonemes: some current interpretations, by W. H. Bennett.—Die Phasen der althochdeutschen Lautverschiebung, by H. Penzl.—Das Alter des mittelfränkischen Glottisverschlusses, by W. Mitzka.—The origin of the German suffix *-heit*, by J. C. Wells.—On the etymology of "black," by W. P. Lehmann.—Althochdeutsch

(Continued)

Betz, Werner, *ed.* Taylor Starck ... ⌊°1964⌋ (Card 3)
CONTENTS—Continued.
iungiro, altsächsisch *iungro, iungaro*, by H. Eggers.—Supposed Anglicisms in 18th century German, by P. M. Palmer.—Zum Formenausgleich in der heutigen deutschen Hochsprache, by H. Moser.—Zum St. Galler Credo, by W. Betz.—Die Lehnbildungen in Notkers Übersetzungen, by E. S. Coleman.—The approach to mediaeval literature, by F. Norman.—Some heretical remarks on the Lay of Hiltibrant and Hadubrant, by E. A. Ebbinghaus.—Notkers Psalmenerklärung und Hieronymus, by P. W. Tax.—Paradisiacal love in Early Middle High German literature, by K. J. Northcott.—Der Arnsteiner Marienleich, by F. Maurer.—On Hartmann von Aue: Der arme Heinrich, v. 1010, by O. Springer.—Studies in the medieval scale of values: the virtues, by H. Adolf.—Zu Walthers Elegie (124, 1 ff.) by U. Pretzel.—Parzivals "Schwertleite," by J. Bumke.—Place names in Parzival and Willehalm, by C. E. Passage.—Three Skaldic passages: Sigvatr Þórðarson,

(Continued)

Betz, Werner, *ed.* Taylor Starck ... ⌊°1964⌋ (Card 4)
CONTENTS—Continued.
Bersøglisvísur 18; Þjóðólfr Arnórsson IV, 1 and III, 18, by L. M. Hollander.—Aus dem Freundeskreis der Brüder Grimm, by H. Schneider.—Tabula gratulatoria.

1. German language--Addresses, essays, lectures. 2. German literature--Addresses, essays, lectures. 3. Starck, Taylor, 1889-

---

E-11
9830

BEURON, Germany (Benedictine abbey).
Beuron, 1863-1963; Festschrift zum hundertjährigen Bestehen der Erzabtei St. Martin. Beuron/Hohenzollern, Beuroner Kunstverlag [1963] 566 p. illus., fold. col. map. facsims. 25cm.

CONTENTS.--Die monastischen Grundprinzipien nach Erzabt Dr. Maurus Wolter [1825-1890], von Reetz.--Ein Jahrhundert Beuroner

NN R 5.64 e/ OS PC SL (LC1, X1, Z1) (Continued)

2

BEURON, Germany (Benedictine abbey). Beuron, 1863-1963... (Card 2)

Geschichte, von V. Fiala.--Beurons Beitrag zur Gründung von St. Ottilien, von H.S. Brechter.--Beuron und die Anfänge des Studienkollegs St. Anselm in Rom, von G. Österle.--Beuron und die Restauration der Abteien in Brasilien, von M.E. Scherer.--Beurons Choralgesang, von C. Gindele.--Der Beitrag Beurons zur liturgischen Erneuerung, von D. Zähringer.--Zur Beuroner Kunst, von A. Dreher.--Hundert Jahre Bibliothek Beuron, von U. Engelmann.--Die theologische Schule der Beuroner Kongregation, von D. Helmecke.--Der Bruder im Beuroner Kloster, von M. Eckardt.--Der klösterliche Grundbesitz, 1863-1963, von L. Fischer.--Beuroner Glocken einst und jetzt, von G. Schwind.

MAMG

BEWAHREN und Gestalten; Festschrift zum siebzigsten Geburtstag von Günther Grundmann. [Hrsg. von Joachim Gerhardt, et al.] Hamburg, H. Christians [1962] 183 p. illus. 28cm.

"Verzeichnis der Veröffentlichungen Günther Grundmanns," by R. K. Gobert, p. 177-183.

1. Grundmann, Günther, 1892- --Bibl. 2. Art, German--Addresses, essays, lectures. 3. Architecture--Germany--Addresses, essays, lectures. I. Gerhardt, Joachim, ed.

NN R 2.64 e/ OC, I PC, 1, 2, 3, I SL A, 1, 2, 3, I (LC1, X1, Z1) [I]

Copy only words underlined & classmark— HTA

BEYER, HERMANN.
Obras completas. Recopiladas, traducidas y arregladas por Carmen Cook de Leonard. Mexico, 1965. 1 v. illus. 23cm. (El México antiguo. t.10)

Tomo 1.
Forms vol. 2 of: Tomo especial de homenaje consagrado a honrar la memoria del ilustre antropólogo Doctor Hermann Beyer, fundador de la Sociedad alemana mexicanista y de el México antiguo.

1. Indians, Mexican. 2. Indians, C.A. i. title: Collected works.

NN R 9.65 s/ OC OI PC, 1, 2 AH, 1, 2 (LC1, X1, [I], Z1)

BEYER, WILHELM R., ed. Homo, homini, homo. (Card 2)

CONTENTS.—Menschen- und Bürgerrechte bei Rousseau, Hegel und Marx, von K. Löwith.—Adalbert Stifters Gestalten, von M. Stefl.—Der Zwerg; Umriss eines Gottfried-Keller-Porträts, von W. Muschg.—Die Szenik bei Shakespeare, von G. Lukács.—Grenzland zwischen Einsamkeit und Gemeinschaft, von E. Goldstücker.—Kreatur und Kreator Mensch, von E. Schumacher.—Das Bild des Menschen bei

(Continued)

E-12
8972

Beyer, Wilhelm R., ed.
Homo, homini, homo. Festschrift für Joseph E. Drexel zum 70. Geburtstag. München, Beck, 1966.
327 p. 1 front. 25 cm.

Contributions chiefly in German, 1 in Italian, 1 in French.

NN * R 6.67 1/ OC PC, 1,2 SL (LC1, X1, Z1) [I] (Continued)

3

BEYER, WILHELM R., ed. Homo, homini, homo. (Card 3)

Hermann Broch, von W. Rothe.—Das Menschenbild Maxim Gorkis, von M. Girod.—Der Ort des Publikums im Theater, von H. Braun.—Der Schrecken; Gedichte aus den Jahren 1933-1948, von G. Anders.—Industriegesellschaft und Elite, von H. Maus.—Geschichtlichkeit und Toleranz, von E. Heintel.—Fondamenti d'un'etica umanistica, von M. Rossi.—Négation et dépassement de l'humanisme, von C. Bruaire.—Vom "alter Ego" zum "Wir," von W. R. Beyer.

1. Literature—Addresses, essays, lectures. 2. Drexel, Joseph, 1896- .

---

*OHM

Bhandarkar Oriental research institute, Poona, India.
...Commemorative essays presented to Professor Kashinath Bapuji Pathak... Poona: Bhandarkar Oriental researh [sic] institute, 1934. xxi, 488 p. facsims., plan, plates, port. 25cm. (Added t.-p.: Government Oriental series. Class B, no. 7.)

Series title also at head of title.
PARTIAL CONTENTS.—The Buddhist Pantheon and its classification, by B. Bhattacharyya.—Remains of a prehistoric civilisation in the Gangetic valley, by Dr. A. Banerji-Sastri.—A proposed interpretation of an Aśokan inscription, by R. K. Mookerji.—On the origin of Sanskrit and the Prakrits, by Prof. Devendrakumara Banerji.—The pronunciation of Sanskrit, by Prof. S. K. Chatterji.

966032A. 1. Pathak, Kashinath Bapu, 1850-1932. 2. India—Civilization. 3. India—Archaeology. I. Title. II. Ser.
N. Y. P. L. October 20, 1939

---

*OHMB

Bhandarkar Oriental Research Institute, *Poona, India. Post-graduate and Research Dept.*
Index to papers in commemoration volumes. Poona, 1963.
iv, 7, 647 p. 24 cm. (*Its* Post-graduate and Research Department series, no. 5)

Stamped on t. p.: Munshi Ram Manohar Lal, oriental & foreign book-sellers, Delhi.

1. Indic studies--Collections--Bibl. 2. Festschriften--Indexes.
I. Bhandarkar oriental research institute, Poona, India. Post-graduate and research department series.
NN 8.65 e/ OS(1b*), I PC, 1, 2 SL O, 1 (LC1, X1, Z1)
[S, NSCM]

NFD
(Wieland)

Biberach an der Riss, *Ger.*
Festschrift zum 200. geburtstag des dichters Christoph Martin Wieland, geb. 5. september 1733, gest. 26. januar 1813; mit 35 abbildungen. Herausgegeben von der Stadtgemeinde und dem Kunst- und altertumsverein Biberach/Riss. [Biberach] Im selbstverlag der herausgeber, 1933.
200, xx p. incl. 2 double geneal. tab. 32 pl. (incl. ports., facsims.) 27½cm.

Cover-title: Christoph Martin Wieland, 1733[-]1933.
"Zum geleit" signed: Die Stadtverwaltung, Bürgermeister Hammer; Kunst- und altertumsverein, Aichele.
"Die verantwortliche leitung der festschrift ward mir übertragen."—Vorwort, signed: Wilhelm Aichele.
(Continued on next card)
A C 33-4284
[3] Festschrift

Biberach an der Riss, *Ger.* Festschrift zum 200. geburtstag des dichters Christoph Martin Wieland ... 1933. (Card 2)

Genealogical tables compiled by Heinrich Werner.
"Bei der beschaffung des bildermaterials haben herr oberlandmesser Georg Grath ... und herr Julius Baur ... freundliche mithilfe geleistet."—p. xiii.
Sections II-IV contain short contributions by various authors, mostly in regard to Wieland.
PARTIAL CONTENTS.—I. Der dichter; kleine auswahl aus seinen schriften und briefen.—II. Der dichter und seine vaterstadt.—III. Schwäbische dichter und schriftsteller ihrem grossen landsmann.—IV. Gelehrte und forscher über Christoph Martin Wieland.
1. Wieland, Christoph Martin, 1733-1813. I. Kunst- und altertumsverein, Biberach an der Riss, Ger. II. Aichele, Wilhelm, ed. III. Title.
A C 33-4284
Title from N. Y. Pub. Libr. Printed by L. C.
[3]

---

*GAH

Bibliografiska bidrag tillägnade Carl Z. Hæggström på femtioårsdagen, den 14 April 1934. [Uppsala, 1934] 79 p. port. 27cm.

"Tryckt i sjuttiofem exemplar och utgöres av Avhandlingarna i Nordisk tidskrift för bok- och biblioteksväsen årg. 21 (1934): h. 1."
CONTENTS.—Collijn, I. Ett nyfunnet blad av Canon missæ 1458.—Madsen, V. Forening for Boghaandværk og dansk Bogtryk.—Munthe, W. Norsk forening for bokkunst.—Dahlberg, R. Ett nordiskt helgonstämpelband i Helsingfors universitetsbibliotek.—Adde, G. Brev från Zacharias Hæggström till P. A. Wallmark.—Wieselgren, O. En stambok från liturgistridens dagar.—Grape, A. Ett par märkliga inkunabelförvärv till Uppsala universitetsbibliothek.—Bring, S. Strinnholms båda arbeten om Magnus Sten-

(Continued)

N. Y. P. L. January 5, 1945

Bibliografiska bidrag tillägnade Carl Z. Hæggström... (Card 2)

bock.—Nelson, A. Om den svenska bondepraktikans ursprung.—Walde, O. Doktor Johann Copps bibliotek.—Carlsson, A. B. Ett svenskt 1500-talsexlibris och dess ägare.—Colliander, E. Några beslagtagne editioner av Sveriges rikes lag.—Holmberg, A. Pehr Wargentin och Kungl. Vetenskapsakademiens bibliotek.

288246B. 1. Hæggström, Carl Z., 1884- 2. Bibliography.
N. Y. P. L. January 5, 1945

---

*IT

Bibliografiska studier tillägnade friherre Johannes Rudbeck på hans femtioårsdag den 7 mars 1917. Stockholm, 1917. 92 p. incl. facsims., front. (port.) illus., plates (1 col'd). 30cm.

No. 5 of 150 copies printed.
"Detta arbete, som är redigeradt af Gustaf Rudbeck, är tryckt hos Almqvist & Wicksells boktryckeri-aktiebolag i Uppsala."
CONTENTS.—Tillägnan.—Collijn, I. En grupp Lübeckska inkunabelband.—Grape, A. Själfbiografiska anteckningar af Olof Rudbeck d. y.—Hannover, E. Roger Payne.—Hierta, P. Än ett Kristinaband.—Loubier, H. Hülleneinbände des ausgehenden Mittelalters.—Madsen, V. Nogle Oplysninger om et Bind af Johannes Richenbach.—Rudbeck, G. Två gamla bokband. Några boköden.—Sjögren, A. Ett par stilprof

(Continued)

Festschrift

N. Y. P. L. September 27, 1934

Bibliografiska studier...1917. (Card 2)

från Olof Rudbecks tid. Vandrande tryckare- och förläggaremärken.—Hierta, P. Förteckning öfver friherre Johannes Rudbecks utgifna skrifter.

694487A. 1. Rudbeck, Johannes Reinhold Gustaf, friherre, 1867- . 2. Bookbinding—Collections. 3. Rudbeck, Olof, 1630?-1702. 4. Payne, Roger, 1739-1797. I. Rudbeck, Gustaf, friherre, 1875- , editor.
N. Y. P. L. September 27, 1934

---

*GAH

Bibliographical essays; a tribute to Wilberforce Eames. [Cambridge, Mass., Printed at the Harvard university press] 1924.
xix p., 1 l., 440 p. incl. facsims., tables. front., port. 24½cm.

CONTENTS.—Wilberforce Eames, a bio-bibliographical narrative, by V. H. Paltsits.—Aids to the identification of American imprints, by Alice H. Lerch.—The Royal primer, by P. Merritt, with check list of Royal primers.—The New England primer, by W. C. Ford.—Chez Moreau de St-Méry, Philadelphie, by H. W. Kent, with publications of Moreau de St-Méry, 1795-1797.—Quienes fueron los autores, hasta ahora ignorados, de dos libros ingleses que interesan a America, by J. T. Medina.—The literary fair in the United States, by C. L. Nichols.—The ballad of Lovewell's fight, by G. L. Kittredge.—The first work with American types, by

(Continued on next card)
25-2291
[5]

Bibliographical essays ... 1924. (Card 2)
CONTENTS—Continued.
L. C. Wroth.—A Maryland tract of 1646, by L. C. Harper.—The surreptitious printing of one of Cotton Mather's manuscripts, by T. J. Holmes.—Elizabethan Americana, by G. W. Cole.—The Eliot Indian tracts, by G. P. Winship.—The New York printers and the celebration of the French revolution of 1830, by Ruth S. Granniss.—Wall-paper newspapers of the civil war; with checklist of issues, by C. S. Brigham.—Analytical methods in bibliography applied to Daniel Webster's speech at Worcester in 1832, by C. B. Clapp.—Mills Day's proposed Hebrew Bible, by O. Wegelin.—A translation of the Rosetta stone, by R. G. Adams.—Colonial American arithmetics, by L. C. Karpinski, with list of arithmetics published in America up to 1775.—Sixteenth-century Mexican imprints, by H. R. Wagner, with location table of Mexican sixteenth-century books.—The De Bry collector's painefull peregrination along the pleasant path-
(Continued on next card)
25-2291
[5]

Bibliographical essays ... 1924. (Card 3)
CONTENTS—Continued.
way to perfection, by H. N. Stevens.—A note on the laws of the republic of Vermont, by J. B. Wilbur, with list of Vermont laws, 1779-1791.—The promotion literature of Georgia, by V. W. Crane.—Books on architecture printed in America, 1775-1830, by A. J. Wall.—Isaac Eddy, printer-engraver, by H. G. Rugg, with bibliography of Eddy publications.—The first California laws printed in English, by C. M. Cate.—Ann Franklin of Newport, printer, 1736-1763, by H. M. Chapin.—The work of Hartford's first printer, by A. C. Bates, with list of Thomas Green's Hartford imprints, 1764-1768.—Writings of Rev. John Cotton, by J. H. Tuttle.—Some notes on the use of Hebrew type in non-Hebrew books, 1475-1520, by A. Marx.—The Fasciculus temporum, a genealogical survey of editions before 1480, by Margaret B. Stillwell.

399905A 1. Eames, Wilberforce, 1855- 2. Bibliography—Collections.

25—2291
Library of Congress Z1009.B51
[s25f5]

TB p.v.544

Bibliographie Jastrow. Verzeichnis sämtlicher Schriften von Dr. J. Jastrow, ordentlichem Professor der Staatswissenschaften an der Universität Berlin. Berlin, C. Heymann, 1929. 106 p. 21cm.

"Bearbeiter und Herausgeber ist Dr. Walter Taeuber."
"Die nachfolgende Bibliographie...wurde von einem Kreise dankbarer Schüler dem Lehrer zu seinem...70. Geburtstage dargebracht." — *Vorwort*, signed: Der Kreis ehemaliger Schüler.

Festschrift

487382A. 1. Jastrow, Ignaz, 1856-1937—Bibl. 2. Economics—Bibl. I. Taeuber, Walter, 1900- , ed.
N. Y. P. L.
Card revised
April 24, 1947

MA
+

BIBLIOTHECA HERTZIANA, Rome.
Miscellanea Bibliothecae hertzianae zu Ehren von Leo Bruhns, Franz Graf Wolff Metternich [und] Ludwig Schudt. München, A. Schroll [1961] 520 p. illus., diagrs., plans. 31cm. (Roemische Forschungen, hrsg. von der Bibliotheca Hertziana. Bd. 16)

Festschrift.
"Vorwort" signed Harald Keller.

(Continued)

NN R 11.65 g&(OC)II OS, I PC, 1, 2, 3, 4, I, II SL A, 1, 2, 3, 4, I, II (LC1, X1, Z1) [I]

2

BIBLIOTHECA HERTZIANA, Rome. Miscellanea Bibliothecae hertzianae zu Ehren von Leo Bruhns... (Card 2)

Bibliographical footnotes.

1. Bruhns, Leo, 1884-1957. 2. Wolff Metternich, Franz, Graf, 1893- . 3. Schudt, Ludwig. 4. Art--Essays and misc. I. Series. II. Title.

E-11
4408

BIBLIOTHEKAR-LEHRINSTITUT DES LANDES NORDRHEIN-WESTFALEN, Cologne.
Aus der Welt des Bibliothekars; Festschrift für Rudolf Juchhoff zum 65. Geburtstag, hrsg. von Kurt Ohly und Werner Krieg. Köln, Greven Verlag [1961] 478 p. illus., port., music. 25cm.

Contributions in German, English, or Dutch.

(Continued)

NN R 5. 62 e/4 (OC)I, II, IIIbo OS PC, 1, 2, 3, 4, I, II SL (LC1, X1, Z1) [I]

2

BIBLIOTHEKAR-LEHRINSTITUT DES LANDES NORDRHEIN-WESTFALEN, Cologne. Aus der Welt des Bibliothekars... (Card 2)

Includes bibliographies.

1. Juchhoff, Rudolf, 1894- . 2. Books--Hist. 3. Libraries--Hist. 4. Library science--Addresses, essays, lectures. I. Ohly, Kurt, 1892- , ed. II. Krieg, Werner, ed. III. Krieg, Werner.

Copy only words underlined
& Classmark-- *QAA

BIELFELDT, HANS HOLM, ed.
Slawistische Beiträge aus der Deutschen Demokratischen Republik. Zum 50. Jahrestag der grossen sozialistischen Oktoberrevolution. Hrsg. von H. H. Bielfeldt [et al.] Berlin, Akademie-Verlag, 1967. 296 p. 24cm. (Deutsche Akademie der Wissenschaften, Berlin. Forschungsinstitut für Slawistik. Veröffentlichungen. Nr. 48)

Includes bibliographical references.
1. Slavonic studies--Collections. I. Series. II. Title.
NN 7.68 r/A OC, II (OS)I PC, 1, I, II S, 1, I, II (LC1, X1, Z1)

BWO
+

Il **Biellese** e le sue massime glorie; scritti in onore di Benito Mussolini. Biella: Per deliberazione degli industriali biellesi coi tipi del Bertieri, 1938. xxiii, 777 p. incl. plates (part col'd, mounted), ports. map. 32½cm.

Map in pocket.
"Raccolta di scritti...per cura di Leone Garbaccio, con la collaborazione di A. Borello, L. Bubani, B. Buscaglia [ed altri]"

Festschrift.

69538B. 1. Biella, Italy. 2. Mussolini, Benito, 1883- . I. Garbaccio, Leone, ed. II. Biella, Italy. Industriali.
N. Y. P. L.
September 17, 1940

E-11
6902

Biermann-Ratjen, Hans Harder, 1901-
Kultur und Staat; Reden und Schriften aus den Jahren 1945-1959. [Zum 60. Geburtstag des Verfassers am 23. März 1961 hrsg. von W. Gramberg, C. G. Heise und J. Staubesand] Hamburg, E. Hauswedell, 1961.
237 p. 25 cm.

1. Essays, German. I. Gramberg, Werner, 1896- , ed.

NN *R 4.63 p/ OC(1b) I PC, 1, I SL (LC1, X1, Z1)

E-11
9113

BIEZAIS, HARALDS, ed.
Ieskatītais un atzītais; rakstu krājums veltīts prof. dr. phil. Teodoram Celman 70 gadu dzimumdienā, 1963. Gada 14. jūnijā. [Stockholm?] Daugava [1963] 304 p. illus. 25cm.

Includes bibliographies.

CONTENTS.--I. Filozofija un religija: Ziediņš, R. Pieredze un esamība. Ladusāns, S. Dažas gnozeologiskas refleksijas par
(Continued)

NN R 3.64 p/, OC PC, 1, 2, I SL S, 1, 2, I (LC1, X1, Z1)

BIEZAIS, HARALDS, ed. Ieskatītais un atzītais...
(Card 2)

indukciju. Biezais, H. Kristianisma vēsturiskā vide. Šmits, E. Ideāls ētiskā nozīme. --II. Psīchologija un sociologija: Reimanis, G. Anomija, tās cēloni un sekas. Picka, N. Introspektīvā metode atmiņas pētīšanā. Veidemanis, J. Imigrantu dzīves procesi Savienotajās Valstīs sociologiskā skatījumā. Siliņš, J. Vērtības un pārvērtības. --III. Vēsture un archaiologija: Ozols, J. Senbaltu ienākšana Latvijā. Ginters, V. Senlatviešu simbolikas problēmas. Bilkins, V. Daži avotu kritikas piemēri. Berkis, A. Kurzemes hercogu un Anglijas attiecības 17. g.s. vēstures dokumentu gaismā. Bokaladers, J. Krievijas ideologiskie stravojumi pirms pirmā pasaules kaŗa. --IV. Bibliografiia: Neulande, L. Teodora Celma raksti (p. [299]-304)

1. Essays, Lettish. 2. Celms, Teodors, 1893- I. Title.

D-14
4085

BIHLER, HEINRICH, ed.
Medium aevum romanicum; Festschrift für Hans Rheinfelder. Hrsg. von Heinrich Bihler und Alfred Noyer-Weidner. München, M. Hueber, 1963. xx, 411 p. illus., port., music. 22cm.

Contributions in German, French or Spanish.
Includes bibliographies.

1. Rheinfelder, Hans, 1898- 2. Romance literature--Addresses, essays, lectures. I. Noyer-Weidner, Alfred, joint ed.

NN R 7.63 a/ OC, I PC, 1, 2, I SL (LC1, X1, Z1) [I]

IAC

Billington, Ray Allen, 1903- *ed.*
The reinterpretation of early American history; essays in honor of John Edwin Pomfret. San Marino, Calif., Huntington Library, 1966.

viii, 264 p. port. 22 cm.

Includes bibliographical references.

CONTENTS.—John E. Pomfret: scholar-executive, by A. Nevins.—Jack Pomfret and the Huntington: a tribute, by A. L. Rowse.—A
(Continued)

NN * R 5.67 1/, OC, I PC, 1, 2, I SL AH, 1, 2, I (LC1, X1, Z1)

BILLINGTON, RAY ALLEN, 1903- , ed. The reinterpretation of early American history...
(Card 2)

bibliography of the writings of John Edwin Pomfret, by J. M. Steadman.—The historians of early New England, by E. S. Morgan.—The historians of the Middle Colonies by F. B. Tolles.—Historians and the Southern Colonies, by C. L. Ver Steeg.—Historians and the nature of the American Revolution, by M. Jensen.—"Experience must

(Continued)

BILLINGTON, RAY ALLEN, 1903- , ed. The reinterpretation of early American history...
(Card 3)

be our daily guide": history, democratic theory, and the United States Constitution, by D. G. Adair.—Changing interpretations of early American politics, by J. P. Green.—The imperial approach to early American history, by L. H. Gipson.—The international approach to early Angloamerican history, by L. J. Cappon.—Historic sites archaeology in the study of early American history, by W. M. Whitehill.

1. United States--Hist.--Historiography. 2. Pomfret, John Edwin, 1898- I. Pomfret, John Edwin, 1898-

---

AD-10
970

BIRDSALL, J. NEVILLE, ed.
Biblical and patristic studies in honor of Robert Pierce Casey, edited by J. Neville Birdsall and Robert W. Thomson. Freiburg, New York, Herder [1963] 269 p. illus., port., facsims. 23cm.

"Publication of the Vetus latina institute, Beuron."

CONTENTS.--A biography of Robert Pierce Casey.-- [Hebrew handwritten word] in the Old Testament, by D. W. Thomas.--MS 894: a collation and an analysis, by J. N. Birdsall.-- The quantitative relationships
(Continued)

NN R 10.64 c/5 OC, I, IIbo, [I, NSCM] IIbo PC, 1, 2, I SL (LC1, X1, Z1)

BIRDSALL, J. NEVILLE, ed. Biblical and patristic studies in honor of Robert Pierce Casey...(Card 2)

between ms. text-types, by E. C. Colwell and E. W. Tune.--Ein neuer Zeuge zum westlichen Text der Apostelgeschichte, von B. Fischer.--An eclectic study of the text of Acts, by G. D. Kilpatrick.--Explicit references in the works of Origen to variant readings in New Testament manuscripts, by B. M. Metzger.--Chicago studies in the Greek lectionary of the New Testament, by A. Wikgren.--Basile de Césaree et Damase de Rome, par E. A. de Mendieta.--Fragments de l'Ambroisienne de Milan à restituer aux mss. syriaques de Sinai 46 et 16.
(Continued)

BIRDSALL, J. NEVILLE, ed. Biblical and patristic studies in honor of Robert Pierce Casey...(Card 3)

par R. Draguet.--The fragments of the Greek apologists and Irenaeus, by R. M. Grant.--A homily on the raising of Lazarus and the harrowing of Hell, by S. Der Nersessian.--A note on the Anaphoras described in the liturgical homilies of Narsai, by E. C. Ratcliff.--The text of the Syriac Athanasian corpus, by R. W. Thomson.--Bibliography of R. P. Casey.

1. Casey, Robert Pierce, 1897-1959. 2. Bible--Criticism, Textual. I. Thomson, Robert W., joint ed. II. Birdsall, J. Neville. III. Thomson, Robert W.

CAB

BIRMINGHAM ARCHAEOLOGICAL SOCIETY, Birmingham, Eng.
Essays in honour of Philip B. Chatwin, prepared by the Birmingham archaeological society in collaboration with the Dugdale society. Oxford, Printed...by V. Ridler at the University press, 1962. 138 p. illus., port., maps, facsims. 26cm.

(Continued)

NN R 2.63 e/, OS, I PC, 1, 2, I [I] SL A, 1, I G, 2, I (LC1, X1, Z1)

BIRMINGHAM ARCHAEOLOGICAL SOCIETY, Birmingham, Eng. Essays in honour of Philip B. Chatwin... (Card 2)

CONTENTS.--The architectural work of Philip B. Chatwin, by A.B. Chatwin.--Bibliography of the writings of Philip B. Chatwin, by D.M. Norris.--The cathedral church of St. Mary, Coventry, by R. and J. Hemsley.--The Coventry guilds and trading companies with special reference to the position of women, by L. Fox.--The defences of Viroconium (Wroxeter), by G. Webster.--The diaries of Sir Roger Newdigate, 1751-1806, by A.C. Wood.--Documents concerning

(Continued)

BIRMINGHAM ARCHAEOLOGICAL SOCIETY, Birmingham, Eng. Essays in honour of Philip B. Chatwin... (Card 3)

Dr. William Johnston, physician, of Warwick, by R.A. Cohen.--Interim report on excavations at Weoley Castle, 1955-1960, by A. Oswald.--Royal arms in Staffordshire churches, by S.A. Jeavons.--The social structure of Kineton Hundred in the reign of Charles II, by P. Styles.--Some notes on the Bloxam family of Rugby, by H.T. Kirby.--The watermills of Edgbaston, Birmingham, by R.A. Pelham.

1. Chatwin, Philip B. 2. Great Britain--Hist., Local. I. Dugdale society.

AF-10
443

BISCHOFF (GOTTFRIED) K. G.
Weg und Arbeit der Gottfried Bischoff K. G. Essen, 1910-1960. [Text: F. Ress und F. Zierke. Illustrationen: Heinz Schubert. Essen, 1960]
66 p. illus., mounted 26cm.

NN R 4.65 c/ OS(1b+) PC SL E ST (LC1, X1, Z1)

E-11
5615

BISCHOFF, KARL, 1905- , ed.
Volk, Sprache, Dichtung: Festgabe für Kurt Wagner, hrsg. von Karl Bischoff und Lutz Röhrich. Giessen, W. Schmitz, 1960. 338 p. illus., port. 24cm. (Beiträge zur deutschen Philologie. Bd. 28)

Bibliographical footnotes.
CONTENTS.--Heldendichtung als Gattung der deutschen Literatur des

(Continued)

NN 10.62 e/ OC, I (OS)II PC, [I] 1, 2, 3, I, II SL (LC1, X1, Z1)

BISCHOFF, KARL, 1905- , ed. Volk, Sprache, Dichtung... (Card 2)

13. Jahrhunderts, von H. Rupp.--"Devotio" in der Kreuzzugspredigt des Mittelalters, von F.-W. Wentzlaff-Eggebert.--Herze und Lip in Friedrich von Hausens Gedicht MF 47, 9, von L. Baecker.--Idsteiner Sprüche der Väter, von F. Maurer.--Bemerkungen zur Sprache Gottfrieds von Strassburg, von W.-J. Schröder.--Oberammergau und das Mittelalter, von W. Flemming.--Gedanken über das lyrische Du, von F. Lockemann.--Scharf, von H. Kuhn.--Die älteste germanische Inschrift, von W. Krogmann.--Krise der Mundartforschung? von H. Moser.--

(Continued)

BISCHOFF, KARL, 1905- , ed. Volk, Sprache, Dichtung... (Card 3)

Altschlesische Vokabulare, von W. Mitzka.--Die Mundarten der schwäbisch alemannischen Siedlungen in Galizien, von J. Krämer.--Mundart, Urkundensprache und Schriftsprache, von R. Schützeichel.--Die Ortsnamen auf -angen im Westmoselfränkischen, von H. Engels.--Trappenberg, Wurmberg, Narrenberg, Bärenbach, von E. Christmann.--Die moselfränkischen Zunamen im Mittelalter, von W. Jungandreas.--Die Artikel vor deutschen Siedlungsnamen, von K. Bischoff.--Sprichwörtliche Redensarten aus Volskerzählungen, von L. Röhrich.--Vom

(Continued)

BISCHOFF, KARL, 1905- , ed. Volk, Sprache, Dichtung... (Card 4)

Sprichwört im Leben eines Dorfes, von F. Ohly.--Das Rad mit dem Speichenkreuz, von K. Rumpf.--Seetangwirtschaft und Tangfluren an der atlantischen Küste, von H. Becker.--Das literarisch-künstlerische Antlitz Schlesiens im Mittelalter, von L. Petry.

1. Wagner, Kurt, 1890- . 2. German literature--Addresses, essays, lectures. 3. German language--Addresses, essays, lectures. I. Röhrich, Lutz, joint ed. II. Series.

---

*MEC
(Götsch)

Bitterhof, Erich, 1905- ,ed.
Georg Götsch, Lebenszeichen. Zeugnisse eines Weges. Hrsg. von Erich Bitterhof. Wolfenbüttel, Zürich, Möseler (1969).

xxxiv, 356 p. with illus., front. 24 cm.
Bibliography of G. Götsch: p. xviii-xx.

1. Götsch, Georg. I. Bitterhof, Erich, 1905- .
NN*R 9.70 m/ OC, Ib+ PC, 1 SL MU, 1 (LC1, X1, Z1)

Write on slip words underlined below and class mark — PRA

Bjerknes-Festband.

(Beitraege zur Physik der freien Atmosphäre. Leipzig, 1932. Bd.19, p.i-vi, 1-310. diagrs., maps, port.)

form 400b [x-20-31 25m]

D-18
6291

Bjørnstad, Charles, 1885-1962.
Charles Bjørnstad. Husdikteren, vennen og kameraten. Redigert av Hans Johansen. Minneskrift utg. av Drammen typografiske forening. Drammen, Fremtidens trykkeri, 1966.
118 p. ports. 21 cm.

NN * 1.69 1/ OC(1b*) PC SL (LC1, X1, Z1)

BVL

Blanchet, Adrien, 1866- , and G. Millet, editors.
Mélanges offerts à M. Gustave Schlumberger... à l'occasion du quatre-vingtième anniversaire de sa naissance (17 octobre 1924)... Paris: P. Geuthner, 1924. 2 v. facsims., front. (port.), illus. (incl. mpa, plan), plates. 4°.

D-16
5724

BLAXLAND, GREGORY.
The story of the Queen's own Buffs, the Royal Kent regiment. [Canterbury, 1963] 91 p. illus., maps. 22cm.

1. Army, British--Regt. hist.--Queen's own Buffs (Royal Kent regiment).
NN * R 7.66 a/c OC(1b*) PC,1 SL (LC1, X1, Z1)

E-12
9579

BLIND, ADOLF, 1906- , ed.
Umrisse einer Wirtschaftsstatistik. Festgabe für Paul Flaskämper zur 80. Wiederkehr seines Geburtstages. Hamburg, Meiner (1966)
viii, 364 p. 24 cm.

Includes bibliographies.
CONTENTS.—Einführung in die Wirtschaftsstatistik, von A. Blind.—Die Nutzanwendung der Statistik für die Wirtschaftspolitik, von G.

(Continued)

NN R 7.67 1/✓OC PC,1, 2 SL E,1,2 ST,1t, 2 (LC1,X1,Z1) 3

BLIND, ADOLF, 1906- , ed. Umrisse einer Wirtschaftsstatistik... (Card 2)

Fürst.—Die statistischen Probleme der westeuropäischen Integration, von R. Wagenführ.—Statistik und Wirtshaftsprognose, von G. Menges.—Zum Konjunkturtest-Verfahren, von O. Anderson.—Die Statistik der Erwerbstätigkeit, von L. Herberger.—Die Landwirtschaftsstatistik, von H. Wirth.—Die Statistik der industriellen Produktion, von K. Werner.—Zur Aussenhandelsstatistik der Bundesrepublik

(Continued)

BLIND, ADOLF, 1906- , ed. Umrisse einer Wirtschaftsstatistik. (Card 3)

Deutschland, von P. Schmidt.—Indexzahlen für den Aussenhandel, von H. Hartwig.—Zum Preisbegriff und zur Methodik der Preisstatistik, von P. Deneffe.—Über die Konstruktion, den Sinn und die Zwecke von Preisindexzahlen, von W. Neubauer.—Einkommensstatistik, von H. Grohmann.—Die Statistik des Verbrauchs der privaten Haushalte, von A. Sobotschinski.—Statistik in der Marktforschung, von H. Proebsting.—Volkswirtschaftliche Gesamtrechnungen, von H. Bartels.—Die Produktionsverflechtung und ihre Darstellung, von G. Junior.—Die Finanzierungsrechnung im Rahmen der Volkswirtschaftlichen Gesamtrechnung, von M. Zucker.—Die Zahlungsbilanz, von F. Scholl.

1. Statistics. 2. Flaskämper, Paul, 1886- . t. 1966.

** MGA

Blume, Friedrich, 1893- , editor.
Gedenkschrift für Hermann Abert von seinen Schülern; herausgegeben von Friedrich Blume. Halle (Saale): M. Niemeyer Verlag, 1928. vi, 189 p. facsim. (music), front. (port.), illus. (music.) 8°.

"Beilage...Sebastian Sailer. Erschaffung des Adams und der Eva. Von Kain und Abel," 32 p., in pocket inside back cover.
Bibliographical footnotes.
Contents: Vorwort. Hermann Aberts Schriften, zusammengestellt von Ernst Laaff. BLUME, F. Hermann Abert und die Musikwissenschaft. BOETTCHER, H. Neues zu Sebastian Sailer. FELLERER, K. G. Das Credo in Palestrinas Messe "Ecce

(Continued)

N. Y. P. L. April 3, 1929

Blume, Friedrich, 1893- , editor: Gedenkschrift für Hermann Abert von seinen Schülern... (Card 2)

sacerdos." GERBER, R. Wort und Ton in den "Cantiones sacrae" von Heinrich Schütz. HAMEL, F., and A. RODEMANN. Unbekannte Musikalien im Braunschweiger Landestheater. KLEEMANN, P. Das Kompositionsprinzip Paul Hindemiths und sein Verhältnis zur Atonalität. LAAFF, E. Schuberts H-moll-Symphonie. OBERST, G. J. S. Bachs Englische und Französische Suiten. RATTAY, K. Das masurische Kirchenlied. SOUCHAY, M.-A. Zur Sonate Beethovens. SZABOLCSI, B. Die ungarischen Spielleute des Mittelalters. VETTER, W. Der Opernkomponist Georg Christoph Wagenseil und sein Verhältnis zu Mozart und Gluck. WICHMANN, H. Das Wesen der "Naturbewegung" und ihr Einfluss auf die französische Oper. Notenbeilagen: Sebastian Sailer: "Die Erschaffung des Adams und der Eva" und "Von Kain und Abel."

DREXEL MUSICAL FUND.

405267A. 1. Abert, Hermann, 1871- 1927. 2. Music—Essays. 3. Title.
N. Y. P. L. April 3, 1929

D-14
8589

BOCKEMÜHL, ERICH, 1885-
Das goldene Spinnrad; niederrheinische Sagen, Märchen und Legenden, neu erzählt. [Zeichnungen von Artur Schönberg] Duisburg, C. Lange [1960] 143 p. illus. 22cm.

"Herausgegeben vom Verein Linker Niederrhein als Ehrengabe für Erich Bockemühl."
Sources, p. 142.

1. Folk tales, German--Rhine valley. 2. Bockemühl, Erich, 1885- I. Verein Linker Niederrhein. II. Title.
NN R 2.64 p/c OC (OS)I PC, 1, 2, I, II SL (LC1, X1, Z1)

MDVF
+

Börsenverein der deutschen buchhändler. *Bibliothek.*
Aus der ex-libris sammlung der bibliothek des Börsenvereins der deutschen buchhändler. 65 meist unveröffentlichte blätter auf 50 tafeln. Leipzig, Verlag des Börsenvereins, 1897.
6 p. l., 65 facsim. on 50 pl. (part col.) 31cm.

Issued in portfolio.
"Herrn Dr. Albrecht Kirchhoff zur feier seines 70. geburtstages dargebracht am 30. januar 1897."

1. Book-plates. 2. Book-plates, German. 3. Kirchhoff, Albrecht, 1827–1902.

Library of Congress Z993.B59 5—27213
[31d1] Festschrift.

E-12
1208

BOETTCHER, ERIK, ed.
Entwicklungstheorie und Entwicklungspolitik; Gerhard Mackenroth zum Gedächtnis von seinen Freunden und Schülern, mit Beiträgen von Erik Boettcher [et al.] Tübingen, J.C.B. Mohr [1964] xii, 550 p. port. 24cm. (Die Einheit der Gesellschaftswissenschaft. Bd. 1)

Bibliography, p. 531-534. Bibliographical footnotes.

(Continued)

NN R 10.64 e/b OC (OS)I PC, 1, 2, 3, 4, I SL E, 1, 2, 3, 4, I (LC1, X1, Z1) 5

BOETTCHER, ERIK, ed. Entwicklungstheorie und Entwicklungspolitik... (Card 2)

CONTENTS.--Gedenkwort, von E. Boettcher.--Bevölkerung und Wirtschaft, von G. Mackenroth.--Die ursprüngliche europäische Haltung gegenüber anderen Kulturen und die Veränderung dieser Haltung im Zusammenhang mit der Auflösung der alten Kolonialreiche und der Hilfen für die Entwicklungsländer, von K.-H. Pfeffer.--Die amerikanische Entwicklungshilfe in historischer Sicht - Zur Veränderung der amerikanischen Haltung gegenüber anderen Kulturen, von D. Gerhard.--Politische Begründung und Methoden kommunistischer Entwicklungspolitik, von

(Continued)

NIT

Bogen om Thit Jensen; samlet og redigeret af Else Moltke. [København] Grafisk forlag, 1954. 222 p. illus.,ports, 24cm.

1. Jensen, Thit, 1876- . I. Moltke, Else (Moltke), grevinde, 1888- , ed.

NN**X 3.55 f/4 OC,I PC,1,I SL (LC1,Z1,X1)

BOETTCHER, ERIK, ed. Entwicklungstheorie und Entwicklungspolitik... (Card 3)

E. Boettcher.--Zur Theorie der wirtschaftlichen Entwicklung, von A. Predöhl.--Zur Wachstumspolitik der Entwicklungsländer, von K. Schiller.--Strukturwandel des Welthandels als Ergebnis der Eingliederung der Entwicklungsländer, von H. Jürgensen.--Entwicklungsprogrammierung und Programmbewertung. Zur Aufstellung und Bewertung von Entwicklungsplänen, von B. Knall.--Der Begriff der generativen Struktur als Instrument zur Analyse der Bevölkerungsbewegung der Entwicklungsländer, von K.M. Bolte.--Ansätze zu einem neuen bevölkerungsbiologischen

(Continued)

F-10
1284

En BOGENS tjener, Cai M. Woel. [På 60-årsdagen den 28. oktober 1955. Redaktion: Niels Th. Mortensen. Odense] Arnkrone, 1955. 168 p. illus., ports. 25cm.

CONTENTS.—En sommer i københave, af C. Stub-Jørgensen.—Tidsromanerne, af C. Stub-Jørgensen.—De historiske romaner, af P. Lauring.—Det gamle sogn, af N. P. Jensen.—Novellisten Cai M. Woel, af T. Kristensen.—Sange fra støvet; Cai M. Woels digte, af N. T. Mortensen.—Litteraturhistorikeren Cai M. Woel, af P. Hesselaa.—Woels forlag på Hauserplads, af L. Fischer.—Om at debutere på Woels forlag, af J. Wulff.—Woels forlag i omvendt perspektiv, af M. Zieler.—Organisationsmanden Cai M. Woel, af J. L. Hansen.— Om en olderman, af M. A. Hansen.

(Continued)

NN* R 9.57 c/ OC, I (OS)2b* PC, 1, 2, I SL (LC1, X1, Z1)

BOETTCHER, ERIK, ed. Entwicklungstheorie und Entwicklungspolitik... (Card 4)

Gleichgewicht, von H. Harmsen.--Die Ernährungsproblematik der Entwicklungsländer, von G. Hampel.--The impact of international minimum labor standards upon developing countries, by E.P. Hohman and H.F. Hohman.--Person- und Sozialstruktur bei Entwicklungsvölkern. Beiträge zur Theorie der Sozialisation und des sozialen Wandels, von G. Wurzbacher.--Die Unterrichtsplanung im Rahmen der allgemeinen Wirtschaftsplanung, von J. Tinbergen.--Das Bildungswesen als Entwicklungsfaktor, von H. von Recum.--Ausbildungshilfe - wohin? Zur Ausbildung von

(Continued)

En BOGENS tjener... (Card 2)

—Som ven, af Soya.—Punktet udenfor, af J. Bukdahl.—Bibliografi, af S. Lund (p. 159-167).

1. Woel, Cai Mogens, 1895- . 2. Woels forlag, a.s., Cophenhagen. I. Mortensen, Niels Theodor, 1909- , ed.

BOETTCHER, ERIK, ed. Entwicklungstheorie und Entwicklungspolitik... (Card 5)

Spezialisten und Führungskräften der Entwicklungsländer in der Bundesrepublik, von H.-D. Ortlieb.--Wirtschaftsprobleme der Indischen Union. Dargestellt am Beispiel des Dritten Fünfjahresplanes, von W.G. Hoffmann.--Die geschichtliche Situation des Kommunismus in Indien, von K.D. Erdmann.--The need of a critical view and a reorientation of our theoretical approaches in regard to the problems of underdeveloped countries, by G. Myrdal.--Schriften von Gerhard Mackenroth.

1. Economic development. 2. Community development. 3. Mackenroth, Gerhard, 1903-1955. 4. Underdeveloped areas. I. Series.

D-18
1504

BOHNSACK, ROLF, ed.

Gestalt, Gedanke, Geheimnis; Festschrift für Johannes Pfeiffer zu seinem 65. Geburtstag. Hrsg. von Rolf Bohnsack, Hellmut Heeger [und] Wolf Hermann. Berlin, Verlag Die Spur [1967] 416 p. port. 22cm.

"Bibliographie Johannes Pfeiffer," p. 401-409.

1. Pfeiffer, Johannes, 1902- . 2. Literature--Addresses, essays, lectures. I. Heeger, Hellmut, joint ed. II. Hermann, Wolf, joint ed. III. Bohnsack, Rolf. IV. Heeger, Hellmut.

NN R 5.68 r/ OC, I, II, IIIbo, IVbo PC, 1, 2, I, II SL (LC1, X1, Z1)

NIT

Bogen til Martin Andersen Nexø fra venner og kampfæller, 26. juni, 1949. København, Forlaget Tiden [1949] 192 p. illus. 25cm.

513476B. 1. Andersen Nexø, Martin, 1869-
N. Y. P. L. Festschrift February 27, 1950

---

*HB

...Bok- och bibliotekshistoriska studier tillägnade Isak Collijn på hans 50-årsdag. Uppsala: Almqvist & Wiksells boktryckeri-a.-b., 1925. xviii, 516 p. incl. front. (port.) facsims., illus., plates. 28½cm.

At head of title: 1875. 17/7. 1925.
No. 35 of 400 copies printed.
Edited by fil. dr. Axel Nelson.
CONTENTS.—Nelson, A. Förteckning över Isak Collijns intill den 17 juli 1925 utgivna skrifter.—Lehmann, P. Quot et quorum libri fuerint in libraria Fuldensi.—Nelson, A. Richard de Bury och Thomas a Kempis.—Jørgensen, E. Et Brudstykke af den hellige Ingrid af Skenninges Helgenproces.—Söderhjelm, W. Un manuscrit du

(Continued)

N. Y. P. L. Festschrift April 6, 1934

. . .**Bok-** och bibliotekshistoriska studier tillägnade Isak Collijn . . .
1925. (Card 2)

Roman de la Rose à la Bibliothèque royale de Stockholm.—Wieselgren, O. Två i Kungl. biblioteket befintliga miniatyrhandskrifter ur den Gent-Brüggeska skolan.—Haebler, K. Zwei Nürnberger Tonformen.—Polain, M.-L. Notes pour la collation des deux tirages de l'édition du Speculum doctrinale, s. ind. typ. <Strasbourg, Adolphe Rusch>.—Birkenmajer, A. Die Wiegendrucke der physischen Werke Johannes Versors.—Voullième, E. Zur Bibliographie Heinrich Knoblochtzers in Heidelberg. Der Totentanz.—Omont, H. Deux incunables imprimés à Tours le 7 mai 1496.—Rath, E. v. Zur Biographie Ludwig Hains.—Larsen, S. To danske Palæotyper trykte i Paris.—Madsen, V. Pergamenttryk i det Kongelige Bibliotek i København. Et Supplement.—Paulli, R. Bogfører-Dokumenter fra det 16. Aarhundrede.—Nielsen, L. Et sjældent

(Continued)

N. Y. P. L. April 6, 1934

. . .**Bok-** och bibliotekshistoriska studier tillägnade Isak Collijn . . .
1925. (Card 3)

Danicum.—Petersen, C. S. Dronning Sophie Amalies Bogsamling.—Munthe, W. Norske boksamlere i eldre tid.—Ljunggren, E. Fragment av en katolsk andaktsbok på svenska från 1525 (?).—Adde, G. Äldre finskspråkiga skrifter i svenska bibliotek.—Dahlberg, R. Gutterwitziana.—Rudbeck, G. Peter van Selow, stilgjutare och boktryckare i Stockholm 1618–1648.—Carlsson, A. B. Rester av Michael Agricolas boksamling i svenska bibliotek.—Walde, O. Johannes Bureus och den svenska bibelöversättningen under Gustaf II Adolfs tid.—Grape, A. Till frågan om J. G. Sparwenfeldts översättarverksamhet. Saavedra-verket.—Gobom, N. Eric Benzelius d.y:s Itineris eruditi album i Linköpings stiftsbibliotek.—Hulth, J. M. Studenten Carolus Linnæus' bibliotek.—Schmidt, A. Kölnische Einbände des vierzehnten Jahrhunderts in der

(Continued)

N. Y. P. L. April 6, 1934

. . .**Bok-** och bibliotekshistoriska studier tillägnade Isak Collijn . . .
1925 (Card 4)

Amploniana zu Erfurt.—Rudbeck, J. Några italienska bokband frå 1500-talet.—Loubier, H. Versuch einer Klassifizierung der Einbände für Jean Grolier.—Husung, M. J. Ein neuer signierter und datierter Badier, gefunden in der Preussischen Staatsbibliothek.—Milkau, F. Bibliothekwesen oder Bibliothekswesen.—Leyh, G. Zur Vorgeschichte des bibliothekarischen Berufes.—Lundgren, H. Diktare bland svenska biblioteksmän.—Sundström, E. Om tillkomsten av Kungl. bibliotekets svenska tryckavdelning.

684458A. 1. Collijn, Isak Gustaf Alfred, 1875- . 2. Books—Hist. 3. Libraries—Hist. I. Nelson, Axel Herman, 1880- , editor.
N. Y. P. L. April 6, 1934

NINA
(Edfelt)

En BOK till Johannes Edfelt [på femtioårsdagen den 21. dec. 1954 från vänner och beundrare] Stockholm, Bonnier [1954] 184 p. illus., port. 20cm.

"300 onumrerade exemplar."

1. Edfelt, Johannes, 1904-

NN ** 1.56 p/ OC PC, 1 SL (LC1, X1, Z1)

NGZ

BOLLERT, MARTIN, 1876-
. . . Gedichte, Reden, Sinnsprüche, zum 75. Geburtstag am 11. Oktober, 1951; ausgewählt und veröffentlicht von Hans Hofmann . . . [und anderen] Dresden, 1951. 64 p. port. 19cm.

I. Hofman, Hans, 1862- , jt. ed.

NN R 11.52 OC, I PC, I SL (LC1, Z1, X1)

---

*MFRB
(Germany)

Bollert, Werner, 1910- *ed.*
Sing-Akademie zu Berlin. Festschrift zum 175 jährigen Bestehen. (Mit 40 Abbildungen und Faksimiles) Berlin, Rembrandt Verlag (1966)

144 p. 1 front. 27 cm.

Includes bibliographies.

CONTENTS.—Vorwort, von W. Bollert.—Sing-Akademischer Alltag, von F. Herzfeld.—Rückschau auf denkwürdige Aufführungen ver-

(Continued)

NN*R 7.67 1/ OC (OS)I PC, I SL MU, I (LC1, X1, Z1)

BOLLERT, WERNER, 1910- , ed. Sing-Akademie zu Berlin. (Card 2)

gangener Zeit, von P. Wackernagel.—Die Musikbibliothek der Sing-Akademie, von F. Welter.—Zur Ästhetik der Berliner Sing-Akademie, von F. Milz.—Grundriss der Verfassung der Sing-Akademie von 1816.—Die Händelpflege der Sing-Akademie unter Zelter und Rungenhagen, von W. Bollert.—Auszüge aus den Tagebüchern der Sing-Akademie.—Eine Trauermusik der Sing-Akademie für Prinz Louis Ferdinand, von M. F. Schneider.—Frauen in der Geschichte der Sing-Akademie, von C. Auerbach-Schröder.—Ausstrahlungen der Sing-Akademie auf die Musikerziehung, von K. Rehberg.—Die Sing-Akademie unter Mathieu Lange, von E. Kroll.

I. Sing-Akademie, Berlin.

OE

BOLOGNA, Italy (City). Università. Economia e commercio, Facoltà di.
Scritti matematici in onore di Filippo Sibirani. Bologna, C. Zuffi, 1957. xix, 345 p. illus., port. 25cm.

"Pubblicato sotto gli auspici della facoltà di economia e commercio dell'Università degli studi di Bologna e a cura del suo Istituto di matematica finanziaria."

"Elenco delle pubblicazioni di Filippo Sibirani a cura di Giuseppe Varoli." p. [ix]-xix.

1. Mathematics--Addresses, essays, lectures. 2. Sibirani, Filippo, 1880- I. Title. t.1957.

NN * R 8.59 a/ (OC)2b*, I OS PC, 1, 2, I SL ST, 1t, 2, I (LC1, X1, Z1)

KAT

BOLOGNA, Italy (city). Università. Istituto di geografia.
Studi geografici in onore di Antonio Renato Toniolo. Milano, G. Principato [1952] 378 p. illus. 25cm.

CONTENTS. —Nuove osservazioni sulle variazioni di spiaggia del litorale della Versilia, di D. Albani. —Alcune notizie sopra un codice latino manoscritto del sec. XVII (1701) "De sphera" con particolare riguardo al capitolo "De globo geografico," di P. Frabetti. —La bonifica delle Valli Grandi veronesi ed Ostigliesi, d'E. Malesani. —Qualche considerazione geografica sulle comunicazioni stradali fra la Padania e la penisola attraverso l'Appennino tosco-emiliano, di G. Merlini. —Alcuni

(Continued)

NN ** 10.53 (OC) 1bo OS PC, 1, 2, 3 SL ST, 1, 4 (LC1, Z1, X1)

BOLOGNA, Italy (city). Università. Istituto di geografia. Studi geografici in onore di Antonio Renato Toniolo. (Card 2)

dati e osservazioni sul manto nevoso, di G. Morandini. -- Ricerche sull' insediamento in Dalmazia, di M. Ortolani. —Tipi di paesaggi e paesaggi tipici in Puglia e in Emilia, d'U. Toschi. —Andamento delle precipitazioni a Bologna dal 1813 al 1942, d'A. Capra. —Generalità geografico-fisiche sui bacini idrografici della Romagna, d'U. Buli. —L'Istituto di geografia dell' Università di Bologna, d'E. R. Armandi.

1. Toniolo, Antonio Renato. 2. Geography—Addresses, essays, lectures. 3. Italy—Geography, Physical. 4. Italy—Geography, Physical, 1952.

L-11
1022

BOLOGNA. Italy (City). Università. Scuola di perfezionamento in scienze amministrative.
Studi in onore di Silvio Lessona. Bologna, Zanichelli [1963] 1 v. 25cm.

Vol. 1.

1. Administration--Addresses, essays, lectures. 2. Law, Administrative--Addresses, essays, lectures. 3. Lessona, Silvio, 1887-

NN * 3.67 p/c OS (1b*) PC, 1, 2, 3 SL E, 1, 2, 3 (LC1, X1, Z1)

GDWP

Bonjour, Edgar, 1898–
...Basel und die Eidgenossen; Geschichte ihrer Beziehungen zur Erinnerung an Basels Eintritt in den Schweizerbund, 1501. Festschrift, herausgegeben im Auftrag des Regierungsrates des Kantons Basel-Stadt von der Historischen und antiquarischen Gesellschaft zu Basel. Basel, Birkhäuser [1951] 384 p. illus. 25cm.

At head of title: Edgar Bonjour. Albert Bruckner.
"Bibliographische Anmerkungen zu Basel im Schweizerbund," p. 368–379.
CONTENTS.—Bruckner, Albert. Basels Weg zum Schweizerbund.—Bonjour, Edgar. Basel im Schweizerbund.

1. Basel (City)—Hist. I. Bruckner, Albert Theophil, 1904– . II. Basel-Stadt, Switzerland (Canton). Regierungsrat. III. Historische und antiquarische Gesellschaft zu Basel.
NN

---

* MEC
(Beethoven)

Bonn, Germany. Beethoven-Haus.
Beethoven und die Gegenwart; Festschrift des Beethovenhauses Bonn, Ludwig Schiedermair zum 60. Geburtstag, in Verbindung mit Herbert Birtner, Ernst Bücken, Willi Kahl, Erich Schenk, Joseph Schmidt-Görg, Leo Schrade, herausgegeben von Arnold Schmitz. Berlin [etc.] F. Dümmler, 1937. xv, 342 p. 24cm.

Bibliography included in "Anmerkungen" (p. 294–342).
CONTENTS.—Birtner, Herbert. Zur deutschen Beethovenauffassung seit R. Wagner.—Schrade, Leo. Das französische Beethovenbild der Gegenwart.—Schmidt-Görg, Joseph. Stand und Aufgaben der Beethoven-Genealogie.—Bücken, Ernst. Das Wort-

(Continued)

N. Y. P. L. November 18, 1937

Bonn, Germany. Beethoven-Haus. Beethoven und die Gegenwart ... (Card 2)

Ton-Problem bei Beethoven.—Schenk, Erich. Barock bei Beethoven.—Kahl, Willi. Zu Beethovens Naturauffassung.—Schmitz, Arnold. Zur Frage nach Beethovens Weltanschauung und ihrem musikalischen Ausdruck.

BEETHOVEN ASSOCIATION FUND.

913275A. 1. Beethoven, Ludwig van. 2. Schiedermair, Ludwig, 1876– . I. Schmitz, Arnold, 1893– , ed. II. Title.
N. Y. P. L. November 18, 1937

D-17
7893

A Book of masques; in honour of Allardyce Nicoll. London, Cambridge U. P., 1967.

xv, 448 p. front., 48 plates. 23cm.

Includes bibliographical references. (B 67-9210)

CONTENTS.—The vision of the twelve goddesses, by S. Daniel, edited by J. Rees.—Oberon, the fairy prince, by B. Jonson, edited by R. Hosley.—Love freed from ignorance and folly, by B. Jonson, edited by N. Sanders.—The lord's masque, by T. Campion, edited by I. A. Shapiro.—The masque of the Inner Temple and Gray's Inn,

(Continued)

NN* R 11.67 p/ OC PC,1,2 SL (DC2,LC1,X1, Z1) [I]

A Book of masques ... 1967. (Card 2)

by F. Beaumont, edited by P. Edwards.—The masque of flowers, edited by E. A. J. Honigmann.—The masque of the Inner Temple (Ulysses and Circe) by W. Brown, edited by R. F. Hill.—Lovers made men, by B. Jonson, edited by S. Wells.—Pleasure reconciled to virtue, by B. Jonson, edited by R. A. Foakes.—The Inner Temple masque, or Masque of Heroes, by T. Middleton, edited by R. C. Bald.—The triumph of peace, by J. Shirley, edited by C. Leech.—The spring's glory, by T. Nabbes, edited by J. R. Brown.—Salmacida Spolia, by I. Jones and W. Davenant, edited by T. J. B. Spencer.—Cupid and death, by J. Shirley, edited by B. A. Harris.—"These pretty devices": a study of masques in plays, by Inga-Stina Ewbank.

1. Nicoll, Allardyce, 1894- 2. Masks (Plays), English--Collections.

PAH

BOPP, F., ed.
Werner Heisenberg und die Physik unserer Zeit; Beiträge von G. Beck [et al.] Braunschweig, Vieweg, 1961. xii, 310 p. port. 25cm.

"Herrn Professor Heisenberg... aus An lass seines sechzigsten Geburtstages."
Includes bibliographies.
CONTENTS.--Die Entstehung der Quantenmechanik, von N. Bohr.--Göttingen, Kopenhagen, Leipzig im Rückblick, von F. Hund.--Zur Physik

(Continued)

NN R 4.62 p/ OC, I PC, 1, 2, I SL ST, 1, 2t, I (LC1, X1, Z1)

BOPP, F., ed. Werner Heisenberg und die Physik unserer Zeit... (Card 2)

des Karlsruher Forschungsreaktors FR-2, von W. Häfele und K. Wirtz.--Die Einheit der Physik, von C. F. von Weizsäcker.--Zur Begründung der naturwissenschaftlichen Induktion, von H. Dolch.--Einige Probleme der allgemeinen Relativitätstheorie, von O. Klein.--Über den Ursprung der kosmischen Strahlung von L. Biermann.--Über die Darstellung der Lorentzgruppe mit Quaternionen, von P. Jordan.--Der quantenmechanische Messprozess und die Entropie, von E. Teller.--Zur Wirkung äusserer elektromagnetischer Felder auf kleine Systeme, von F. Bloch.--Bemerkungen zur

(Continued)

BOPP, F., ed. Werner Heisenberg und die Physik unserer Zeit... (Card 3)

statistischen Deutung der Quantenmechanik, von M. Born.--Dualismus, Wissenschaft und Hypothese, von A. Landé.--Statistische Mechanik bei Störung des Zustands eines physikalischen Systems durch die Beobachtung, von F. Bopp.--Gelöste und ungelöste Probleme des Messprozesses in der Quantenmechanik, von G. Ludwig.--Variationsmethoden in der Quantenstatistik, von H. Koppe.--Quasi-particles and transport phenomena, by G. Wentzel.--Über die Entartung des Grundzustandes in der Theorie der Supraleitung, von P. Mittelstaedt.--Beugungstheorie und n-Körperproblem,

(Continued)

BOPP, F., ed. Werner Heisenberg und die Physik unserer Zeit... (Card 4)

von G. Beck.--Der Einfluss der Ununterscheidbarkeit der Nukleonen auf die Struktur der Atomkerne, von K. Wildermuth.--Field theories with a degenerate vacuum, by B. Zumino.--The compound structure of elementary particles, by R. Oehme.--Teilchen und Antiteilchen, von G. Lüders.--Grundlagen und gegenwärtiger Stand der feldgleichungsfreien. Feldtheorie, von K. Symanzik.--Heisenbergs Theorie der Elementarteilchen, von H.-P. Dürr.

1. Heisenberg, Werner, 1901- 2. Physics--Addresses, essays, lectures. I. Beck, Guido. t. 1961.

M-11
3988
Bd. 6

BORGER, HUGO.
Beiträge zur Frühgeschichte des Xantener Viktorstiftes, von Hugo Borger und Friedrich Wilhelm Oediger. Düsseldorf, Rheinland-Verlag, 1969.
xii, 271 p. illus., plates, plans (part fold.) 27cm. (Rheinische Ausgrabungen. Bd. 6)

"Festgabe Herrn Prof. Dr. Walter Bader gewidmet.

(Continued)

NN R 7. 70 w/ OC(1bo), I, II OI PC, 1, 2, I, II A, 1, I, II (LC1, X1, Z/1)

BORGER, HUGO. Beiträge zur Frühgeschichte des Xantener Viktorstiftes... (Card 2)

Bibliography, p. [269]-271.

1. Christian archaeology and antiquities--Germany--Xanten. 2. Sankt Viktor, Xanten, Germany (Collegiate chapter of Augustinian canons) I. Oediger, Friedrich Wilhelm. II. Bader, Walter.

D-13
5759

Borgerhout, Belgium.
Gemeente Borgerhout, 1836–1961. [Borgerhout, 1961] 1 v. (unpaged) illus., plans, music. 21cm.

Cover title: Borgerhout 125 jaar.

1. Borgerhout, Belgium—Descr. t. 1961. 2. Borgerhout, Belgium—Hist.
NN R 10.62 ODt EDt PC,1,2 SL (LC1,X1,Z1)

D-20
4373

BORINSKI, FRITZ.
Gesellschaft, Politik, Erwachsenenbildung. Ausgewählte Aufsätze z. polit. Bildung u. Erziehung. Dokumente aus 4 Jahrzehnten. Von Fritz Borinski. Hrsg. von Johannes Ehrhardt [u. a.] Villingen, Neckar-Verl. (1969).
xiii, 227 p., front. 23 cm.

Bibliography of author's works: p. 221-227.

1. Education, Adult--Germany. 2. Education--Social and economic aspects--Germany. I. Ehrhardt, Johannes, ed. II. Ehrhardt, Johannes.
NN*R 6. 71 w/ OC, I, IIb* PC, 1, 2, I SL E, 1, 2, I (LC1, X1, Z1)

BGN

BOSE, SUBHAS CHANDRA, 1897-1945.
Life and work of Netaji Subhas Chandra Bose; a nation's homage. Editor-in-chief: P. D. Saggi. Foreword: Pattabhi Sitaramayya. Bombay, Overseas pub. house [195-?] 1 v. (various pagings) ports. 26cm.

Mainly composed of the thoughts, speeches, letters, articles, etc. of Subhas Chandra Bose.
1. India--Hist., 1919- . I. Saggi, Parshotam Das, 1913- ed.
NN **R X 11. 55 s/ OC, I PC, 1, I SL O, 1, I (LC1, X1, Z1)

NARL

Bote aus dem Riesengebirge, Hirschberg, Germany.
Festschrift des Boten aus dem Riesengebirge herausgegeben zur Hundertjahrfeier des Boten... [Hirschberg i. Schl., 1912] 112 p. illus. 31½cm.

CONTENTS.—Hundert Jahre Bote aus dem Riesengebirge. Von P. Werth.—Heimatschutz des Naturbildes im Riesengebirge. Von W. Bölsche.—Pressfreiheit. Geschichtliches aus vormärzlicher Zeit. Von dr. B. Ablass.—Unsere Heimat im Werden der neuen Zeit. Von O. Fiedler.—"Hans Sachs in seiner Werkstatt sass." Von G. Hauptmann.—Entwickelung des Naturgefühls und des Verkehrs im Riesengebirge. Von Dr. O. Baer.—Von der Handpresse zur Rotationsmaschine. Von A. Klein.—Wanderung durch das malerische Riesengebirge. Von K. E. Morgenstern.—Die grüssta Aperna. Eine traurig-lustige Buta-Geschichte. Von H. Hoppe.

735102A. 1. Newspapers—Germany—Breslau. 2. Riesengebirge, Germany. I. Title.
N. Y. P. L. October 24, 1935

MGO
(Pisano)

Bottari, Stefano.
Saggi su Nicola Pisano. Bologna, R. Pàtron. 1969.
xi, 103 p. 79 plates. 26 cm.

"La Facoltà di Lettere dell'Università di Bologna, per onorare la memoria di Stefano Bottari."
"Bibliografia degli scritti di Stefano Bottari": p. [55]-103.
Includes bibliographical references.

(Continued)

NN * R 7.71 b/ OC, II (OS)I PC, 1, 2, I, II SL A, 1, 2, I, II (LC1, X1, Z1)

2

BOTTARI, STEFANO. Saggi su Nicola Pisano. (Card 2)

1. Pisano, Niccolò, 1206-1280. 2. Bottari, Stefano--Bibl. I. Bologna, Italy (City). Università. Lettere e filosofia, Facoltà di. II. Title.

D-13
7667

BOYSON, EMIL, 1897- , ed.
Norsk poesi fra Henrik Wergeland til Nordahl Grieg; en antologi, ved Emil Boyson og Asbjørn Aarnes. [Tegninger ved Georg Barsgård. Oslo] Gyldendal [1961] 344 p. illus. 23cm.

1. Poetry, Norwegian--Collections. I. Aarnes, Asbjørn, joint ed. i. Subs. for B- , E- , 1890- .
NN R 1. 69 k/ OCs, Is PCs, 1s, Is SLs (PR1 1s, LC1s, [I], X1s, Z1s)

ITI

Bonner, James Calvin, 1904– *ed.*
Studies in Georgia history and government, edited by James C. Bonner and Lucien E. Roberts ... Athens, The University of Georgia press, 1940.
xiv, 284 p. 23½cm.
Bibliographical references in "Notes": p. 253-276.

1. Georgia—Hist. 2. Georgia—Pol. & govt. I. Roberts, Lucien Emerson, 1903– joint ed. II. Title.

40-29946

Library of Congress F286.B67
——— Copy 2.
Copyright [4] 975.8

Brahms-Fest, Königsberg, 1933.
Brahms-Fest zum 100. Geburtstag des Meisters (1833 — 7. Mai — 1933), veranstaltet vom Ostmarken-Rundfunk und der Stadt Königsberg, Pr. am 6. und 7 Mai 1933. ⌊Königsberg, Pr.: Ostmarken-Rundfunk G.m.b.H., 1933⌋ 47 p. front. (port.), illus. (incl. facsim., music.) 23cm.

On cover: Programmbuch.
Includes programmes with comments by Otto Besch, Herbert Sielmann and Hermann Killer, and articles about Brahms by Erwin Kroll, Joseph Müller-Blattau and Dr. Hermenau.

804349A. 1. Brahms, Johannes, 1833-1897. 2. Musical festivals. Königsberg. I. Ostmarken-Rundfunk G.m.b.H., II. Königsberg.
N. Y. P. L. April 8, 1936

Brandenburger Anzeiger.
...Fest-Nummer zur Feier des 100jährigen Bestehens. Brandenburg, 1909. 15 p. illus. (1 col'd, incl. facsims., ports.) 36 x 31 1/2 cm.

Caption-title.
At head of title: Brandenburger Anzeiger. 1809-1909.
Issue of the Brandenburger Anzeiger, Thursday, December 2, 1909.

1. Newspapers— Germany —Brandenburg.

Dr. Adolf Koch Journalism Coll
Festschr.

BRAND, CHARLES PETER, ed.
Italian studies presented to E.R. Vincent on his retirement from the Chair of Italian at Cambridge and edited by C.P. Brand, K. Foster, [and] U. Limentani. Cambridge, Heffer, 1962. x, 316 p. illus., ports. 22cm.

Contributions in English or Italian.
Includes bibliographies.
CONTENTS.--E.R. Vincent, by C. Foligno.--A bibliography of the published writings of Professor E.R. Vincent to September, (Continued)

NN * R 9.64 j/$_5$ OC(1b*), I PC, 1, 2, I SL (LC1, X1, Z1) [I] 4

Copy only words underlined & classmark-- *QVA

BRANISLAV Varsik. K Ŝest'desiatym narodeninám dňa 5 marca 1964. Bratislava, Slovenské pedagogické nakl., 1964. 385 p. illus., port, maps. 25cm. (Bratislava, Czechoslovakia. Univerzita. Filozofická fakulta. Sborník. Historica. roč. 15 (1964))

Contributions in Slovak, Czech, or Russian.
Table of contents also in Russian, German, French, and English.

(Continued)

NN R X 12.68 1/4 OI (PC)1, 2 (S)1, 2 (LC1, X1, Z1)
d.d. 2

BRAND, CHARLES PETER, ed. Italian studies presented to E.R. Vincent on his retirement... (Card 2)

1962, by B. Dickins (p. 9-14).--The teaching of Italian in Cambridge, by B. Dickins.--Nostalgia di Dante, by U. Bosco.--Beatrice or Medusa: the penitential element in Petrarch's 'Canzoniere', by K. Foster.--Dante and the Renaissance, by C. Grayson.--'Vox populi' in Antonio Pucci, by K. Speight.--Datazione della seconda centuria dei 'Miscellanea' di Angelo Poliziano, by V. Branca.--An unknown epigraphic tract by Annius of Viterbo, by R. Weiss.--Love and marriage in the 'Institutione' of Alessandro Piccolomini, by C. Fahy.--Stylistic trends in the 'Gerusalemme conquistata' by C.P. Brand.--Horace Mann in Florence, (Continued)

BRANISLAV Varsik. K Ŝest'desiatym narodeninám dňa 5 marca 1964. (Card 2)

Summaries in Russian, German, or Italian.
Includes bibliographical references.
"Bibliografia prác ... Branislava Varsika," p. 379-385.

1. Varsik, Branislav, 1904- . 2. Slovakia--Hist.--Addresses, essays, lectures.

BRAND, CHARLES PETER, ed. Italian studies presented to E.R. Vincent on his retirement... (Card 3)

1738-86, by B. Maloney.--Mr. Eustace and Lady Morgan, by J.H. Whitfield.--Antologie inglesi della letteratura italiana, by C. Dionisotti.--Il secondo biografo del Foscolo: Henry Stebbing, by U. Limentani.--Ugo Foscolo's 'Parallel between Dante and Petrarch' in two literary periodicals of 1821, by F. May.--El prestin di Scansc, le Grucce e gli Scanzi, by E.S. Legnani.--Note su alcune espressioni leopardiane, by F. Chiappelli.--Palmerston and Cavour: some English doubts about the risorgimento, 1859-60, by D. Mack Smith.--Some notes on William Young Ottley's collection of Italian primitives, by (Continued)

BRANN, MARCUS, 1849-1920, ed.
Gedenkbuch zur Erinnerung an David Kaufmann, hrsg. von M. Brann und F. Rosenthal. Breslau, S. Schottlaender, 1900. ii, lxxxvii, 682 p.; 112 p. port., fold. geneal. table. 25cm.

Added t.p. in Hebrew.
Text mainly in German with some contributions in English or French and a section in Hebrew.
Each article also paged separately. (Continued)

NN R 2.64 g/$_A$ OC, I, II PC, 1, 2, I, II SL J, 1, 3, I, II 2
(LC1, X1, Z1)

BRAND, CHARLES PETER, ed. Italian studies presented to E.R. Vincent on his retirement... (Card 4)

E.K. Waterhouse.--Il neo-realismo italiano e le sue origini, by M. Praz.--Profilittu 'e limba sarda, by M.F.M. Meiklejohn.

1. Italian literature--Addresses, essays, lectures. 2. Vincent, Eric Reginald Pearce, 1894- . I Title.

BRANN, MARCUS, 1849-1920, ed. Gedenkbuch zur Erinnerung an David Kaufmann... (Card 2)

Bibliographical footnotes.

SCHIFF COLLECTION

1. Kaufmann, David, 1852-1899. 2. Essays, Jewish. 3. Essays. I. Rosenthal, Ferdinand, 1839- , joint ed. II. Title.

*MF

Braun, Emil, 1870–
Geschichte des Orchesters des Musikvereins Lenzburg. Festschrift zur Feier des hundertjährigen Bestehens 1832–1932, von Emil Braun... Lenzburg: R. Müller, 1932. 97 p. illus. (incl. facsim., ports.) 23cm.

On cover: Herausgegeben vom Musikverein Lenzburg.
Bibliographical footnotes.

Feschrift

651232A. 1. Music—Assoc. and org. —Switzerland—Lenzburg. I. Musikverein Lenzburg.
N. Y. P. L. August 22, 1933

7-*MAA

Bremer Gesangverein, New York.
Denkschrift zum 25. Stiftungsfeste des Bremer Gesang-Verein von New York... New York City[,1910]. 22 l. illus.(incl. ports.) 26½cm.

Cover-title: Bremer Gesang-Verein, New York, Silbernes Jubiläum.
CONTENTS:—Festgruss zum Silber-Jubiläum des Bremer Gesang-Vereins am 27. November, 1910, von A.Baumann.—Geschichte des Vereins [von D. Leker].—Fest-Programm.
1.New York (city)— Societies, Musical.

1933 Festschrift

SEB

BRECHT, ARNOLD, 1884-
The political philosophy of Arnold Brecht, essays; edited by Morris D. Forkosch. New York [Exposition press] 1954. 178 p. port. 21cm.
Includes bibliographies.
"Presented to Arnold Brecht by his former and present students to commemorate the completion of twenty years of devoted service at the Graduate faculty of the New school for social research."
CONTENTS. — Foreword by Student's committee. — Signatures of the Graduate faculty members. — Faculty foreword. — Introduction: The life and political philosophy of Arnold Brecht. — Relative and absolute justice. —
(Continued)

NN*R X 7.54 OC,I,IIbo PC,1, 2,3,I SL E,1,3,I (Z1,LC1, X1)

D-17
1782

BREMNER, ROBERT HAMLETT, 1917- ,ed.
Essays on history and literature. [Columbus] Ohio state university press [1966] xi, 190 p. 22cm.

Bibliography, p. [161]-178.

1. Dulles, Foster Rhea, 1900- . 2. History--Historiography. 3. Literature--Hist. and crit. -- Historiography.
NN R 3.67 r/L OC PC,1,2,3 SL AH,1 (LC1,X1,Z1)

BRECHT, ARNOLD, 1884- The political philosophy of Arnold Brecht, essays;... (Card 2)

The rise of relativism in political and legal philosophy. — The search for absolutes in political and legal philosophy. — The myth of is and ought. — The impossible in political and legal philosophy. — The latent place of God in twentieth-century political theory. — Bibliography of books and articles by Arnold Brecht (p. [161]-174)— Biographical summary of Arnold Brecht.

1. Political science, 1918- 2. Law—Philosophy. 3. Brecht, Arnold, 1884- —Bibl. I. Forkosch, Morris D , ed. II. Forkosch, Morris D

TB

Brennan, Michael Joseph, 1928- ed.
Patterns of market behavior; essays in honor of Philip Taft, edited by Michael J. Brennan. Providence, Brown University Press, 1965.
viii, 258 p. illus. 25 cm. (Brown University bicentennial publications: studies in the fields of general scholarship)
Includes bibliographical references.
CONTENTS.—On the determination of prices in futures markets, by M. J. Beckmann.—Optimal programs for sequential investments, by D. Gale.—Some economic aspects of outdoor recreation, by E. S.
(Continued)

NN *R 10.65 e/ OC,I PC,1, 2,I SL E,1,2,I (LC1,X1,Z1)

3

AN
(Thaelmann,E.)

Bredel, Willi, 1901–
Ernst Thälmann; Beitrag zu einem politischen Lebensbild. Mit einem Vorwort von Wilhelm Pieck und einer Gedenkrede von Walter Ulbricht, gehalten am 18 August 1949. [4. erweiterte Aufl.] Berlin, Dietz, 1950 [°1948]
183 p. mounted port. 21 cm.

1. Thälmann, Ernst, 1886–1944.
DD247.T45B7 1950 51-31696

Festschrift

Library of Congress [3]

BRENNAN, MICHAEL JOSEPH, 1928- . Patterns of market behavior... (Card 2)

Mills.—A more general theory of resource migration, by M. J. Brennan.—Improved allocation of labor as a source of higher European growth rates, by E. F. Denison.—Time, work, and welfare, by J. N. Morgan.—Changes in occupational structure, by M. B. Schupack.—A commentary on some current issues in the theory of monetary policy, by P. Cagan.—The bills only doctrine in retrospect, by D. Carson.—The integration of simple growth and cycle models, by H. P. Minsky.—The effects of devaluation in a growing economy, by G. H. Borts.—Differential growth rates among open economies: theory and fact,
(Continued)

SB p.v.584

Bremen. Gesundheitsamt.
Das bremische Gesundheitswesen in Vergangenheit und Gegenwart; ein Festbeitrag zur Einweihung des Gesundheitsamtes in der Löningstrasse. Herausgegeben von Friedrich Kortenhaus. Bremen, 1937. 47 p. 21cm.

CONTENTS.—Zum Geleit, von T. Laue.—Die Entwicklung des bremischen Gesundheitswesens, von Dr. Tjaden.—Das Bremer Gesundheitsamt in der Gegenwart, von F. Kortenhaus.—Die rassenhygienischen Aufgaben des Gesundheitsamtes, von Dr. Schomburg.—Der Hafengesundheitsdienst in Bremen und Bremerhaven, von Dr. Wolf. —Die bremische Wasserversorgung, von Dr. Tjaden.

Festschrift

1. Hygiene, Public—Germany— Bremen. I. Kortenhaus, Friedrich, ed.
N. Y. P. L. June 30, 1941

BRENNAN, MICHAEL JOSEPH, 1928- . Patterns of market behavior... (Card 3)

by J. L. Stein.—Economic development and comparative advantage, by P. Hartland.—Bibliography of the writings of Philip Taft (p. 257-258)

1. Economics--Essays and misc. 2. Taft, Philip, 1902- . I. Title.

Copy only words underlined & classmark— * M A

BRENNECKE, DIETRICH.
Sprache des Lebens; Blick auf das Kammermusikschaffen von Leo Spies, zum 60. Geburtstag des Komponisten. (IN: Musik und Gesellschaft. Berlin. 26cm. Jahrg. 9, Heft 6 (Juni, 1959) p. 8-12. port., music)

Pages also numbered p. 328-332, continuing the paging of the preceding number.
List of works; p. 21.

1. Spies, Leo, 1899-
NN R 10. 59 t/A OI (MU)I (LC2, X1, Z1)

NFD (Keckeis)
Briefe, Erinnerungen und Beiträge zum siebzigsten Geburtstag von Gustav Keckeis. Zürich, Artemis Verlag [1954] 111, [3] p. 23cm.

"Cover-title: Dichterisch wohnet der Mensch.
Some text in French and English.
"Werke von Gustav Keckeis," p. [113]
"Tabula gratulatoria," ([3] p.) inserted.

(Continued)
NN** X 4.55 f/ OC PC,1 SL (LC1, Z1, X1)
[I]

* MGA

BRENNECKE, WILFRIED, ed.
Hans Albrecht in memoriam; Gedenkschrift mit Beiträgen von Freunden und Schülern. hrsg. von Wilfried Brennecke und Hans Haase. Kassel, New York, Bärenreiter, 1962. 290 p. illus., port., music. 24cm.

Bibliographical footnotes.
"Bibliographie der wissenschaftlichen Veröffentlichungen von Hans Albrecht," p. [16]-21.
1. Albrecht, Hans, 1902-1961. 2. Music--Essays. 3. Essays.
I. Haas, Hans, 1902- joint ed.
NN 5. 63 p/ OC, I PC, 1, 2, I SL MU, 1, 3, I (LC1, X1, Z1)

Briefe... (Card 2)

Partial Contents.—Die Stellung der Einzelperson im Völkerrecht, von Hans Nawiasky.—La littérature, facteur de la vie économique, par Otto Forst de Battaglia.—Die Bedeutung des Schweizer Lexikons, von Eduard Fueter.—Die Lexikographie des Humanismus am Oberrhein, von Hermann Sacher.

1. Keckeis, Gustav, 1884-
NN** X 4.55 f/ OC PC,1 SL (LC1, ZL, X1)
[I]

HCC p.v.214
Brepohl, Friedrich Wilhelm, 1879– , and W. Fugmann.
Die Wolgadeutschen im brasilianischen Staate Paraná; Festschrift zum Fünfzig-Jahr-Jubiläum ihrer Einwanderung; herausgegeben, im Auftrage des Festausschusses, von Friedrich Wilh. Brepohl und Wilhelm Fugmann... Stuttgart: Ausland und Heimat Verlags-Aktiengesellschaft, 1927. 100 p. illus. (map), plates. 8°.

Plates printed on both sides.

Mr. Math

384875A. 1. Germans in Russia. 2. Germans in Brazil—Paraná. 3. Paraná, Brazil. 4. Fugmann, Wilhelm, jt. au.
N. Y. P. L. December 5, 1928

E-11
7557
BRINGMANN, KARL, 1912- , ed.
Festschrift für Anton Betz [aus Anlass der Vollendung seines 70. Lebensjahres am 23 Februar 1963 hrsg. von Karl Bringmann, Max Nitzsche und Fritz Ramjoué] Düsseldorf, Rheinisch-bergische Druckerei- und Verlagsgesellschaft [1963] 339 p. illus. (part col.)port, facsims. 25cm.

CONTENTS.--Der Journalist und die Theologie, von M. Schmauss.--Die publizistische Persönlichkeit, von E. Dovifat.--Verleger,
(Continued)
NN R 2. 64 p/ OC, I, II, IIIbWi, IVbo PC, 1, I, II SL (LC1, X1, Z1)
[I]

C-10
1036
BREUER, ROBERT, 1878-1943.
Ein Meister der Feder: Robert Breuer. Hrsg. von Arno Scholz. Berlin, Arani [c1954] 111 p. port. 19cm.

Articles by author reprinted from various periodicals.
CONTENTS— Zeugnisse der Freunde. — Der politische Publizist; Anwalt der Kunst, von R. Breuer.

I. Scholz, Arno, ed.
NN **R 12. 56 p/ OC, I PC, I SL E, I (LC1, X1, Z1)

BRINGMANN, KARL, 1912- , ed. Festschrift für Anton Betz... (Card 2)

Redakteur, von W. Jänecke.--Dusseldorfer Zeitungen, 1945-1949, von E. Betz.--Presse und Fernsehen, von A. Springer.--Die Diskussionsreihe in der Tageszeitung, von P. Hübner.--Die Presse und ihr Recht, von K. Bringmann.--Die Kosten-und Erlösentwicklung der Zeitungsverlage, von F. Greiser.--Zur Bewertung des baierischen Barock im 19. und 20. Jahrhundert, von H. Schnell.--Personalität und Politik, von A. Schwan.--Eigentumspolitik aus christliche-demokratischer Sicht, von F. Burgbacher.--Die Wahrheit ist das Ganze, von P. Fleig.--Rechtliche Überlegungen
(Continued)

E-13
2728
BRICE, WILLIAM C., ed.
Europa; Studien zur Geschichte und Epigraphik der frühen Aegaeis. Festschrift für Ernst Grumach. Berlin, De Gruyter, 1967. xi, 349 p. illus., 28 plates. 24cm.

Papers in English, French or German.
Includes bibliographies.
"Schriftenverzeichnis von Ernst Grumach," p. [346]-349.
1. Grumach, Ernst. 2. Greek inscriptions. I. Title. II. Brice, William C.
NN S 7. 68 a/ OC, IIbo PC, 1, 2, I SL (LC1, X1, Z1)

BRINGMANN, KARL, 1912- , ed. Festschrift für Anton Betz... (Card 3)

zum Verhältnis Eltern-Schule, von W. Geiger.--Das nordrheinwestfälische Schulordnungsgesetz von 1952, von W. Schütz.--Der neue Schulbau, von G. Malbeck.--El camino de Santiago, von A. Dieterich.

1. Betz, Anton, 1893- I. Nitzsche, Max, joint ed. II. Ramjoue, Fritz, joint ed. III. Bringman, Karl, 1912- IV. Ramjoué, Fritz.

E-11
1619

BRITANNICA. Festschrift für Hermann M. Flasdieck. Hrsg. von Wolfgang Iser und Hans Schabram. Heidelberg, C. Winter, 1960. 270 p. port. 25cm.

Vita.
Includes bibliographical references.
CONTENTS.--Lexikalische Auswirkungen der englischen Herrschaft in Südwestfrankreich, 1152-1453, von K. Baldinger.--Chauces and the
(Continued)

NN R 12.60 m/ OC, I, II, IIIbo PC, 1, 2, 3, I, II SL (LC1, X1, Z1)
[I]

BRITANNICA. (Card 2)

Panthère d'amours, von A.C. Baugh.--Der Reim im frühen Mittelalter, von H. Brinkmann.--Almus altus agnus aptus, von W. Bulst.--Waltharius-Probleme, von G. Eis.--Das angelsächsische Element im französischen Wortschatz, von V. Günther and W. von Wartburg.--Über das englische understatement, von R. Haferkorn.--Lallans. Die künstliche Sprache der Scottish Renaissance, von W. Iser.--Some ghost-words in OED, by H. Kokeritz.--Bilingualism of occupation children in Germany, von W.F. Leopold.--Conceptions and images common to Anglo-Saxon poetry and
(Continued)

BRITANNICA. (Card 3)

the Kalevala, by F.P. Magoun, jr.--Eleven Beowulf notes, by K. Malone.--Die Literatur Neuseelands, von H. Oppel.--Referential prepositions, by S. Potter.--A hitherto unnoticed Anglo-Saxon sound-change, by A.S.C. Ross--The seasons for fasting 206 f. Mit einem Beitrag zur ae. Metrik, von H. Schabram.--Britannien und das "alteuropäische" Flussnamensystem, v. A. Scherer.--Bibliographie der wissenschaftlichen Veröffentlichungen von H.M. Flasdieck, von H. Zirker-Wolff, p. [251] -270.

1. Flasdieck, Hermann Martin, 1900- . 2. Philology--Addresses, essays, lectures. 3. English language--Adresses, essays, lectures.
I. Iser, Wolfgang, ed. II. Schabram, Hans, ed.
III. Schabram, Hans.

RNB

Britannica. Max Förster zum sechzigsten Geburtstage... Leipzig: B. Tauchnitz, 1929. 350 p. facsims., front. (port.) 8°.

Bibliographical footnotes.
Contents: KLAEBER, F. Eine germanisch-englische Formel: ein stilistisch-syntaktischer Streifzug. BRANDL, A. Der Saalkampf in Finns Burg. HOOPS, J. War Beowulf König von Dänemark? SCHICK, J. Die Urquelle der Offa-Konstanze-Sage. SIEVERS, E. Cædmon und Genesis. SCHÜCKING, L. L. Sōna im Beowulf. KELLER, W. Zur Worttrennung in den angelsächsischen Handschriften. MORSBACH, L. Umschriften ags. Urkunden in einer Pergamentrolle des späten 13. Jahrhunderts. JONES, T. G. Cerdd freuddwyd Gymraeg. MÜLLER, G. Wortkundliches aus mittelenglischen Medizinbüchern. PARRY-WILLIAMS, T. H. Fragments of English; Notes on two Welsh words. BOROWSKI, B. Die Rolle der Autologie im Lebenssystem des ausgehenden Mittelalters

(Continued)

N. Y. P. L. January 27, 1930

Britannica. Max Förster zum sechzigsten Geburtstage... (Card 2)

und der Renaissance in England. HAFERKORN, R. Quellen zur Erforschung des englischen Büchermarktes im achtzehnten Jahrhundert. DEUTSCHBEIN, M. Romantisch und Romanesk. SCHRÖER, A. Einiges über moderne Shakespeare-Aufführungen. SPINDLER, R. Die Arthursage in der viktorianischen Dichtung. FEHR, B. Expressionismus in der neuesten englischen Lyrik. HUSCHER, H. Über Eigenart und Ursprung des englischen Naturgefühls. WILDHAGEN, K. Die englische Sprache, ein Spiegelbild englischen Wesens. SCHÖFFLER, H. England in der deutschen Bildung. Verzeichnis der Schriften Max Försters.

435490A. 1. English language. 2. English literature—Hist. and crit. 3. Foerster, Max, 1869- .
N. Y. P. L. January 27, 1930

VMK

British Leather Manufacturers' Research Association.
Progress in leather science, 1920–1945. Issued in commemoration of the 25th anniversary of the formation of the British Leather Manufacturers' Research Association. London, 1948.

705 p. illus. 25 cm.

Includes bibliographies.

1. Leather. I. Title: Leather science, 1920–1945.

TS967.B87 675 49–52884*

Library of Congress [3]

ZHIY

British Museum. Manuscripts, Department of.
Miniatures from a French Horae; British Museum add. ms. 16997, fifteenth century. Reproduced in honour of John Alexander Herbert. [London: Waterlow and Sons, Ltd.,] 1927. 9 l. front. (port.), 19 pl. (1 col'd, mounted.) 8°.

357494A. 1. Hours, Book of. 2. Illumination of books and manuscripts—Specimens, reproductions, etc. 3. Herbert, John Alexander, 1862- . 4. Title.
N. Y. P. L. June 23, 1928

D-15
5761

BROWN, ARTHUR, ed.
Early English and Norse studies, presented to Hugh Smith in honour of his sixtieth birthday. Ed. by Arthur Brown and Peter Foote. London, Methuen, 1963. 225 p. illus. 23cm.

Bibliographical footnotes.
CONTENTS.—Some notes on medieval drama in York, by A. Brown.--Place-names and the geography of the past, by H.C. Darby.—
(Continued)

NN R 11.64 g/β OC, I PC, 1, 2, 3, I SL (LC1, X1, Z1) [I]

BROWN, ARTHUR, ed. Early English and Norse studies... (Card 2)

Sir Gawain's arrival in Wirral, by J.M. Dodgson.—The ending of Chaucer's Troilus, by E.T. Donaldson.—Some Continental Germanic personal names in England, by O. von Feilitzen.—Auðraeði, by P.G. Foote.—A Middle English metrical life of Job, by G.N. Garmonsway and R.M. Raymo.—The cult of Odin in Danish place-names, by K. Hald.—A newly discovered rune-stone in Törnevalla church, Ostergötland, by S.B.F. Jansson.—The Anglo-Saxon unicorn, by H. Kökeritz.—Béowulf B; a folk-poem on Béowulf's death, by F.P. Magoun.—Fjallið
(Continued)

BROWN, ARTHUR, ed. Early English and Norse studies... (Card 3)

Mikla, Áin i Dal, Millum Fjarða and Urð Mans, by C. Matras.—Poetic language and Old English metre, by R. Quirk.-- The name of the town Eslöv, by J. Sahlgren.—Uppsala, Iceland, and the Orient, by D. Strömbäck.—Whence the semicolon? By D. Thomas.-- A note on the Landdísir, by G. Turville-Petre.—The orthography and provenance of Henry Machyn, by R.M. Wilson.—Wing commander A.H. Smith, O.B.E., by R.V. Jones.
1. Smith, Hugh, 1903- . 2. English literature, Middle, 1100-1500--Addresses, essays, lectures. 3. Scandinavian literature--Addresses, essays, lectures. I. Foote, Peter, joint ed.

D-15
201

BRUNNER, OTTO, 1898- , ed.
Europa und Übersee; Festschrift für Egmont Zechlin. Herausgeber: Otto Brunner [und] Dietrich Gerhard. Hamburg, Hans Bredow-Institut [1961] 267 p. illus., port., facsim. 22cm.

Contributions in German or English.
Includes bibliographies.
CONTENTS.--Die "Welt" und "Europa"; Bemerkungen eines
(Continued)

NN R 4.64 f/ OC, I PC, 1, 2, 3, I SL (LC1, X1, Z1) [I]

3

*C-3 p.v.843

Brunswick, Germany (City).
Ina Seidel [zum fünfundsechzigsten Geburtstage am 15. September 1950 von der Stadt Braunschweig und der Literarischen Vereinigung Braunschweig E. V. Zusammengestellt von Ewald Lüpke]. [Braunschweig, 1950?] 31 p. illus. 20cm. (Ansprachen und Ehrungen in Braunschweig)

CONTENTS.—Zur Begrüssung und Einführung, von E. Hoppe.—Oberburgermeister Bennemann bei der Überreichung des Wilhelm-Raabe-Preises der Stadt Braunschweig. —Wortlauf der Urkunde. Ehrenmitgliedsbrief der Literarischen Vereinigung Braunschweig E. V.—Strophen an die Heimat; Kurzer Lebensbericht; Geduld, von I. Seidel. —Ina Seidels Werke.

1. Seidel, Ina (Seidel), 1885- . I. Literarische Vereinigung Braunschweig E. V. II. Lüpke, Ewald. i. 1950.
NN**R X 5.55 (OC)II ODi EDi (OS)I PC,1,I,II SL (Z1,LC1,X1)

BRUNNER, OTTO, 1898- , ed. Europa und Übersee...
(Card 2)

Mittelalter-Historikern, von O. Brunner.--Zum Problem der Periodisierung der europäischen Geschichte, von D. Gerhard.--Die Legende von der Aufsegelung Livlands durch Bremer Kaufleute, von P. Johansen.--Mittelasiens Ausscheiden aus der Weltgeschichte um 1500, von B. Spuler.--Zur Geschichte der Ausländer im spanischen Amerika, von I. Wolff.--Carl Schurz und Gottfried Kinkel, von E. Kessel.--Red rag and Gallic bull; the French decision for war, 1870, von W. L. Langer.--Das preussische Erbe, von H. Heffter.--Adolph Woerman
(Continued)

E-12
1464

BRUSSELS. Université libre. Droit, Faculté de. Etudes en hommage à René Marcq. Bruxelles, F. Larcier, 1957. 222 p. ports. (Université libre de Bruxelles. Faculté de droit. Travaux et conférences. 5)

Bibliographical footnotes.
CONTENTS.--Les nécessités présentes de l'enseignements du droit par R. Marcq.--Fondements théoriques d'une politique de plein emploi, par H. vander Eycken.--De bevoegdheidsverdeling tussen raad van state
(Continued)

NN 4.65 e/ (OC)I OS(1b*), II PC, 1, 2, I SL E, 2, I (LC1, X1, Z1)
[S, :NSCM]

BRUNNER, OTTO, 1898- , ed. Europa und Übersee... (Card 3)

Weltherrschaftsideen Hitlers, von G. Moltmann.--Die Pearl Harbor-Frage in der historischen Forschung, von J. Rohwer.--Egmont Zechlin: Verzeichnis seiner Schriften (p. 262-267).

1. Europe--Hist.--Addresses, essays, lectures. 2. History, Modern--Addresses, essays, lectures. 3. Zechlin, Egmont, 1896- . I. Gerhard, Dietrich, 1896- , joint ed.

BRUSSELS. Université libre. Droit, Faculté de. Études en hommage à René Marcq. (Card 2)

en rechterlijke macht, door A. Houtekier.--Les clauses de réserve de poids dans la jurisprudence congolaise, par J. Sace.--L'article 266-bis du Code civil peut-il être appliqué en matière de séparation de corps? Par J. de Gavre.--L'obligation de la femme séparée de biens aux charges du mariage et l'action des tiers créanciers en droit belge et en droit français, par P. van Ommeslaghe.--L'effet interruptif de la citation en conciliation devant le conseil de prud'hommes, par C. Draps.--La théorie de l'apparence,
(Continued)

TB

BRUNNER, OTTO, 1898-
Festschrift Hermann Aubin zum 80. Geburtstag. Hrsg. von Otto Brunner [et al.] Wiesbaden, F. Steiner, 1965. 2 v. (720 p.) 1 front. 24cm.

Bibliographical footnotes.

1. Aubin, Hermann, 1885- . 2. Economic history--Germany. 3. Germany--Hist.--Addresses, essays, lectures.
NN * 12.66 a/ OC PC, 1, 2, 3 SL E, 1, 2, 3 (LC1, X1, Z1)

BRUSSELS. Université libre. Droit, Faculté de. Études en hommage à René Marcq. (Card 3)

par L.A. Vincent.--La responsabilité des parents suivant l'article 1384 du Code civil, par W. Mathoux.--De geest van de nieuwe wetgeving op het handelsregister, door F. de Pauw.

1. Law--Addresses, essays, lectures. 2. Marcq, René. I. Title. II. Brussels. Université libre. Droit, Faculté de. Travaux et conférences.

NFD

Bruns, Max, 1876-
Max Bruns; sein Wesen und sein Werk. Mit Beiträgen von Fritz Droop, Hermann Eicke, Hanns Martin Elster, Karl A. Kuhlmann, Hanns Meinke, und Will Scheller; nebst einer Auswahl aus dem Gesamtwerk des Dichters. Minden, Westf: J.C. C. Bruns[,1926]. 123 p. 12°.

List of author's works at end.

500002A. 1.German literature—Music.

E-12
6145

BRYAN, ROBERT A., ed.
...All these to teach; essays in honor of C.A. Robertson. Edited by R.A. Bryan [and others] Gainesville, University of Florida press, 1965. x, 248 p. port. 24cm.

CONTENTS.--Charles Archibald Robertson; an appreciation by A.C. Morris.--Inkhornisms, fustian & current vogue words by T. Pyles.--The tavern scene in the Middle English Digby play of Mary Magdalene by R.H. Bowers.--Repetitions of a young prince--a note on thematic recurrence in
(Continued)

NN R 6.66 p/c OC (1bo) 1bDAS PC, 1, 2, I SL (LC1, X1, Z3)

3

BRYAN, ROBERT A., ed. All these to teach...
(Card 2)

Hamlet by F. A. Doggett. --A study of meaning in Antony & Cleopatra by T. W. Herbert. --The Hector-Achilles encounters in Shakespeare's Troilus & Cressida by C. P. Lyons. --A Macbeth of few words by A. C. Sprague. --The scenes in Shakespearean plays by T. B. Stroup.--Translation concepts in Donne's The progress of the soul by R. A. Bryan. --Darkness visible-notes on Milton's descriptive procedures in Paradise lost by A. Oras. --Notes on the organization of Locke's Essay by R. S. Crane. --Wit & Dryden by A. A. Murphree. --Alexander Pope's "knack" at versifying by A. L. Williams. --
(Continued)

BRYAN, ROBERT A., ed. All these to teach...
(Card 3)

--Peacock on the spirit of the age (1809-1860) by J. T. Fain. --Poe & John Nichol-notes on a source of Eureka by F. W. Connor. --Thackeray as Laocoon by W. Ruff.--The reconciliation of paganism & Christianity in Yeats' Unicorn from the stars by G. M. Harper--The mind & creative habits of Elizabeth Madox Roberts by H. E. Spivey.

1. Robertson, Charles Archibald, 1895- 2. English literature--Addresses, essays, lectures. I. Title.

ID

Bryce's American commonwealth, fiftieth anniversary, edited by Robert C. Brooks ... New York, The Macmillan company, 1939.

xii, 245 p. front. (port.) 22cm.

The first three papers in this collection were read at the Bryce memorial dinner sponsored by the American political science association, December 29, 1938, as one of the features of its thirty-fourth annual meeting. *cf.* Foreword.

"First printing."

CONTENTS.—Foreword, by R. C. Brooks.—James Bryce and American constitutional federalism, by C. G. Haines.—State and local governments in The American commonwealth: comparisons and contrasts with the present, by F. L. Reinhold.—American parties and politics, 1888 and 1938, by R. C. Brooks.—American public opinion as Bryce described it, and as it is today, by W. B. Graves.—Thoughts and afterthoughts on

(Continued on next card)

39-24463

[15]

Festschrift.

Bryce's American commonwealth, fiftieth anniversary ... 1939. (Card 2)

CONTENTS—Continued.

the future of democracy in America, by A. N. Holcombe.—How Bryce gathered his materials and what contemporary reviewers thought of the work, by F. W. Coker.—Bryce's American commonwealth: a review, by Woodrow Wilson. — Review of The American commonwealth, by Lord Acton.—"Such was the man"—the Bryce that I knew, by W. B. Munro.—Reference notes (p. 221-235).—Sales record of The American commonwealth.—Principal dates in connection with The American commonwealth.

1. Bryce, James Bryce, viscount, 1838-1922. The American commonwealth. 2. U. S.—Pol. & govt. I. Brooks, Robert Clarkson, 1874- ed.

Library of Congress JK246.B956 39-24463

~~Copy 2.~~

Copyright A 133501 [15] 342.73

NFD (Brehm)

Buch des dankes, Bruno Brehm zum fünfzigsten geburtstag. Karlsbad und Leipzig, A. Kraft [°1942]

371 p. front., illus. (incl. facsims.) plates, ports. 23cm.

"Festgabe der sudetendeutschen heimat ... herausgegeben von Ernst Schremmer."

1. Brehm, Bruno, 1892- I. Schremmer, Ernst, ed.

Library of Congress PT2603.R415Z55 46-34918

[2] 928.3

Festschrift

E-10
8379

BUCH des Dankes an Georg Simmel; Briefe, Erinnerungen, Bibliographie. Zu seinem 100. Geburtstag am 1. März 1958 hrsg. von Kurt Gassen und Michael Landmann. Berlin, Duncker & Humblot [1958] 371 p. illus., ports., facsim. 24cm.

CONTENTS. —Anfang einer unvollendeten Selbstdarstellung, von G. Simmel. —Bausteine zu Biographie, von M. Landmann. —Graphologische Analyse, von A. Gaugler. —Zur Dialektik der Simmelschen Konzeption
(Continued)

NN * R 8.59 a/ OC, I, II PC, 1, I, II SL E, 1, I, II (LC1, X1, Z1)

BUCH des Dankes an Georg Simmel... (Card 2)

einer formalen Soziologie, von H. J. Leiber und P. Furth. —Plan einer Gesamtausgabe der Werke Georg Simmels, von H. Müller. —Simmels Briefe. An P. Ernst [et al.]—Erinnerungen an Simmel, von P. Ernst [et al.]—Georg Simmel-Bibliographie, von K. Gassen (p. [313]-365)

1. Simmel, Georg, 1858-1918. I. Gassen, Kurt, 1892- , ed. II. Landmann, Michael, 1913- , ed.

NFF

Buch des Dankes für Hans Carossa. Dem 15. Dezember 1928. Leipzig: Insel-Verlag[, 1928]. 192 p. 3 pl. 8°.

"Zum 50. Geburtstage des Dichters."

Contents: SCHAEFFER, A. Hans Carossa zum 15. Dezember 1928 September. ALVERDES, P. Die Pfeiferstube. BACH, R. Ein Dank. BERTRAM, E. Sieben Gedichte. BILLINGER, R. Der Altar. BRANDENBURG, H. Lebenswanderlied. BRANDENBURG-POLSTER, D. Lichtdruck nach einer Radierung. BRAUN, F. Der Geist. CURTIUS, L. Beschreibung eines Bildes. GEIGER, W. Ein Brief. HEUSCHELE, O. Der Falke. HAUSENSTEIN, W. Hans Carossa. HOFMANNSTHAL, H. v. Hans Carossa. KIPPENBERG, K. Der Dichter und die Vögel. KUBIN, A. Zeichnung zu den Schlusszeilen des Gedichts "Selige Gewissheit." LAWRENCE, D. H. Kirchenlieder im Leben eines Mannes. MELL, M. Der Verzauberte. MOMBERT, A. Zwei Stimmen. PENZOLDT, E. Bildnis

(Continued)

N. Y. P. L. February 24, 1930

Buch des Dankes für Hans Carossa... (Card 2)

meines Vaters. PONTEN, J. Ein Brief. SCHOENBERNER, F. Gestalt und Gestaltung. STRAUSS, L. Vier Gedichte; Zehn Sprüche. SÜSKIND, W. E. Dank an Hans Carossa. ULLMANN, R. Kurze Betrachtung über das Kapitel "Das heimliche Gericht." RILKE, R. M. Ein Brief an Regina Ullmann. ZWEIG, S. Hans Carossa. Brief an einen französischen Freund.

457938A. 1. German literature—Collections. 2. Carossa, Hans, 1878- .
N. Y. P. L. February 24, 1930

NGO

Buch des Dankes für Hans Carossa, dem 15. Dezember 1928. Leipzig: Insel-Verlag[,1928]. 192 p. plates. 8°.

497290A. 1.Carossa, Hans, 1878-

N. Math

JFD
71-280

Das Buch in der dynamischen Gesellschaft; Festschrift für Wolfgang Strauss zum 60. Geburtstag. Hrsg. von Werner Adrian [et al.] Trier, Spee-Verlag, 1970.

308 p. port. 23 cm.
Includes bibliographical references.
CONTENTS.—Wolfgang Strauss und die Neuen Deutschen Hefte, von J. Günther.—Fromme Wünsche oder über die nachhaltige Wirkung von Büchern, von H. Weissgerber.—Von Linear B zur Informationsbank, von H. Widmann.—Die Wirkungsbereiche des Kinderbuchs, von K. Doderer.—Das Buch als Bildungsfaktor für den Jugendlichen, von R. Meyer.—Das Schulbuch—ein Hemmnis der Schul-

(Continued)

NN * R 4.71 b/zOC, I, II, IIIb* PC, 1, 2, I, II SL E, 2, I, II (LC1, X1, Z1) 3

Das BUCH in der dynamischen Gesellschaft; Festschrift für Wolfgang Strauss zum 60.
(Card 2)

reform, von I. Lichtenstein-Rother.—Zur Kritik des Sachbuches, von W. R. Langenbucher.—Gedruckte und verkaufte Studentenweisheit, von H.-J. Koppitz.—Dem Leser auf der Spur, von H. Steinberg.—Die Aufgaben der Zeit gegenüber der Literatur, von H. Göpfert.—Verlegerische Berufsideale und Leitmaximen, von P. Meyer-Dohm.—Der Verleger als Partner in der Bildungspolitik, von W. Adrian.—Vom Verlagsgesicht zum Image, von T. W. Dengler.—Wandlungen am Buchmarkt, von F. Hinze.—Wettbewerbsdynamik im amerikanischen

(Continued)

Das BUCH in der dynamischen Gesellschaft; Festschrift für Wolfgang Strauss zum 60.
(Card 3)

Bucheinzelhandel, von C. Uhlig.—Marketing und Marktforschung im Buchhandel, von R. Fröhner.—Der Leipziger Platz und seine Bedeutung für die buchhändlerische Ausbildung, von F. Uhlig.—Die Führung eines Berufsverbandes, von R. Mohn.—Wirtschaftsordnung und betriebliche Partnerschaft, von M. Köhnlechner.—Wahrheit und Tatsache, von G. Ehrhart.—Bibliographie Dr. phil. Wolfgang Strauss, von W. Klüvner.

1. Books and reading. 2. Booksellers and book trade. I. Strauss, Wolfgang. II. Adrian, Werner, 1915- , ed. III. Adrian, Werner, 1915- .

NFD
(Matzig)

BUCH der Freunde; eine Ehrengabe für Richard B. Matzig, Professor an der Kantonsschule St. Gallen, Privatdozent an der Handels-Hochschule St. Gallen und an der Universität Bern, 1904-1951. [Hrsg. von Lissy Matzig] St. Gallen, Tschudy-Verlag [1953] 194 p. mounted port. 22cm.

"Bücher und Schriften von Richard B. Matzig," p. 189-191.

1. Matzig, Richard Blasius, 1904- 1951. I. Matzig, Lissy, ed.

NN**R X 5.53 OC, I, Ib PC, 1, I SL (LC1, Z1, X1)

---

*QYN

Buch der Freundschaft. Zenta Maurina zum 70. Geburtstag. [Memmingen] Dietrich, 1967.

189 p. illus., front. 21 cm.

Bibliography of works by and about Zenta Maurina: p. 171-180.

1. Maurina, Zenta, 1897-
NN*R 5.68 1/R OC PC, 1 SL S, 1 (LC1, X1, Z1)

VMP

Buch und Papier; buchkundliche und papiergeschichtliche Arbeiten. Hans H. Bockwitz zum 65. Geburtstage dargebracht. Leipzig, O. Harrassowitz, 1949. 164 p. illus. 26cm.

"Herausgeber Horst Kunze."
One contribution in English.

550411B. 1. Paper. 2. Printing. 3. Bockwitz, Hans Heinrich, 1884- I. Kunze, Horst, 1909- , ed.
N. Y. P. L. December 22, 1950

D-13
8625

BUCHDRUCKEREI WINTERTHUR A.G.
Freundesgabe für Friedrich T. Gubler zum sechzigsten Geburtstag am 1. Juli 1960. [Winterthur, 1960] 180 p. illus., port. 21cm.

1. Gubler, Friedrich T., 1900-
NN * 10.64 e/& OS PC, 1 SL (LC1, X1, Z1) [I]
d.d.

F-11
3492

BUCHHOLTZ, AREND, 1857-
Geschichte der Buchdruckerkunst in Riga 1588-1888. Festschrift der Buchdrucker Rigas zur Erinnerung an die vor 300 Jahren erfolgte Einführung der Buchdruckerkunst in Riga. Nieuwkoop, B. de Graaf, 1965. viii,377 p. 6 facsims. 28cm.
Reprint of 1890 Riga ed.

1. Printing—Latvia—Riga i subs for 1890 ed.,*IPO
NN S 10.67 p/A OCs PCs,1 SL Ss,1 (LC1s, X1s,Z1s)

---

*OAC

Buckler, William Hepburn, 1867- , ed.
Anatolian studies presented to Sir William Mitchell Ramsay; edited by W.H. Buckler & W.M. Calder. Manchester: University Press, 1923. xxxviii, 479 p. front. (port.), illus. (incl. map), plates. 4°. (Victoria University, Manchester, Eng. Publications of the University of Manchester. no. 160.)
"A list of the writings of Sir William Mitchell Ramsay," p. xiii-xxxviii.

131219A. 1.Ramsay, Sir William Mitchell, 1851- . 2. Ramsay, Sir William Mitchell, 1851- .—Bibliography. 3. Asia Minor.—Archaeology. 4. Calder, William Moir, 1881- , jt. editor. 5. Title. 6. Series.
Festschrift

E-10
5580

BUDAPEST. TUDOMÁNY-EGYETEM. Nyomda.
A Királyi magyar egyetemi nyomda története 1577-1927, eredeti levéltári kutatások alapján összegyűjtötte és irta Iványi Béla és Gárdonyi Albert. A tárgy i emlékek ismertetésével kiegészitve szerk. Czakó Elemér. Budapest, [1927] 202 p. facsim. 25cm. (Könyvbarátok szövetsége sorozata)
"Alapitásának 350-ik ev fordulójára kiadta a Királyi magyar egyetemi nyomda, Budapest."

I. Iványi, Béla, 1878- II. Gárdonyi, Albert, 1874- III. Czakó, Elemér, 1876- ,ed. IV. Könyvbarátok szövetsége sorozata.
NN R 6.58 p/P (OC)I, II, III OS (1b) IV PC, I, II, III SL (LC1, X1, Z1) [NSCM]

VPE

Buenos Aires (City). **Universidad nacional.** Agronomía y veterinaria, Facultad de.

...La Facultad de agronomia y veterinaria en el XXV aniversario de su fundacion. (Trabajos de sus profesores). 1904 — 25 de septiembre — 1929. Buenos Aires: Impr. de la universidad, 1929. xvi, 355 p. incl. diagrs., tables. illus. (incl. charts, maps, plans). 26½cm.

CONTENTS.—Lahille, Fernando. Una hora entre los peces.—Wernicke, Raúl, y F. Modern. Acción oligodinámica de la plata.—Parodi, L. R. Observaciones sobre la vegetación de las islas cercanas al puerto de San Nicolás.—Reichert, Federico. Contribución al conocimiento de la madera de Coihue.—Paulsen, E. F. Ensayos sobre la influ-

(Continued)

N. Y. P. L. May 27, 1937

Buenos Aires (City). **Universidad nacional.** Agronomía y veterinaria, Facultad de. ...La Facultad... (Card 2)

encia de la concentración de los iones hidrógeno en la germinación y el primer período de vegetación del maíz.—Dankert, E. G. Taninos.—Rivas, J. G. La neutralización de las cremas destinadas a la elaboración de la manteca.—Marchionatto, J. B. La presencia de la Plasmodiophora brassicae en la República Argentina.—Grunberg, I. P. Contribución al estudio cultural de algunas especies forestales indígenas.—Girola, C. D. La yerba mate en la República Argentina.—Ortiz, A. A. Concepto climatérico del granizo en la República Argentina.—Carrasco, B. J. Observaciones generales sobre el problema del tráfico.—Conti, Marcelo. La organización científica, técnico-económica del trabajo en agricultura.—Coni, E. A. Una visita a la colonia "Baron Hirsch" de la Jewish Colonization Association en Rivera, F. C. S.—Soriano, S. Estudios sobre un

(Continued)

N. Y. P. L. May 27, 1937

Buenos Aires (City). **Universidad nacional.** Agronomía y veterinaria, Facultad de. ...La Facultad... (Card 3)

bacilo anaerobio enriador del lino.—Bórea, Domingo. Proyecto de creación de un banco agrario nacional.—Garbarini Islas, Guillermo. Síntesis del problema inmigratorio en el momento actual.—Trefolgi, Camilo. La glia perivascular de Andriezen.—Houssay, Bernardo, y L. Giusti. Las funciones de la hipófisis y la región infundíbulo-tuberiana en el sapo.—Laurino, L. F. Fuerza impulsiva del podofilo.—Quirós, A. B. de. Aeremia. —Rosenbusch, F. Ensayos de tratamiento combinado en el mal de caderas.

814556A. 1. Agriculture—Addresses, essays, lectures. I. Title.

N. Y. P. L. May 27, 1937

E-13
5548

BUENOS AIRES (City. Universidad nacional. Filosofia y letras, Facultad de.

Homenaje a Francisco Romero. [Buenos Aires, 1964]

323 p. port. 24 cm.

"La obra escrita de Francisco Romero ... elaborada por William F. Cooper en la biblioteca del profesor Romero": p. 221-288.

1. Romero, Francisco, profesor. I. Romero, Francisco, profesor.

NN° 6.69 √(OC)I OS PC,1,I SL(LC1,X1,Z1)

YBX
(Descartes)

Buenos Aires (City). **Universidad nacional.** Instituto de filosofía.

...Descartes. Homenaje en el tercer centenario del "Discurso del metodo." Tomo 1– Buenos Aires [Impr. de la Univ. de Buenos Aires] 1937– v. diagrs., plates. 24½cm.

1. Descartes, René, 1596–1650. I. Title.

N. Y. P. L. June 21, 1938

D-15
3242

BUHR, MANFRED, ed.

Wissen und Gewissen; Beiträge zum 200. Geburtstag Johann Gottlieb Fichtes, 1762-1814. Berlin, Akademie-Verlag, 1962. 291 p. 21cm.

At head of title: Deutsche Akademie der Wissenschaften zu Berlin, Institut für Philosophie.

CONTENTS.--Johann Gottlieb Fichte, Skizze seines Lebens und seiner

(Continued)

NN 8.64 e/f OC(1b*) (OS)I, Ib+ PC, 1, I SL (LC1, X1, Z1)

BUHR, MANFRED, ed. Wissen und Gewissen... (Card 2)

Philosophie, von D. Bergner.--Spekulation und Handeln, Grundthema der Philosophie Johann Gottlieb Fichtes, von M. Buhr.--Fichte und die Geschichte der deutschen Nation, von J. Streisand.--Die Dialektik in der Philosophie Johann Gottlieb Fichtes, von T.I. Oiserman.--Fichtes dialektischer Idealismus, seine synthetische Methode, Fichtes Kritik der metaphysischen Denkweise, von G. Stiehler.--Fichte als Agitator der Revolution. Uber Aufklärung und Jacobinismus in Deutschland, von C. Träger.--Der

(Continued)

BUHR, MANFRED, ed. Wissen und Gewissen... (Card 3)

"Atheismusstreit" und der streitbare Atheismus in den letzten Jahrzehnten des 18. Jahrhunderts in Deutschland, von A.W. Gulyga.--Fichtes ökonomische Anschauungen im "Geschlossenen Handelsstaat", von W. Krause.--Hegels ungenügendes Fichte-Bild, von W.R. Beyer.--Ein schweitzer Student über Fichtes Vorlesungen in Jena, von A. Rufer.

1. Fichte, Johann Gottlieb, 1762-1814. I. Deutsche Akademie der Wissenschaften, Berlin. Institut für Philosophie.

NHB

Bundel opstellen van oud-leerlingen aangeboden aan Prof. Dr. C. G. N. de Vooys, ter gelegenheid van zijn vijfentwintigjarig hoogleraarschap aan de Rijksuniversiteit te Utrecht. 1915 — 16 October — 1940. Met een bibliografie van Prof. Dr. C. G. N. de Vooys. Groningen [etc.] J. B. Wolters' uitg.-mij., 1940. 414 p. 25cm.

"Bibliografie," p. 383-414.

354287B. 1. Dutch literature—Hist. and crit. 2. Dutch language. 3. Vooys, Cornelis Gerrit Nicolaas de, 1873–

N. Y. P. L. January 28, 1947

E-12
1076

BUNGE, MARIO AUGUSTO, ed.

The critical approach to science and philosophy. Edited by Mario Bunge in honor of Karl R. Popper. [New York] Free Press of Glencoe [1964] xv, 480 p. port. 25cm.

Includes bibliographies. "Writings of Karl R. Popper": p. 473-480.

1. Popper, K. R. 2. Philosophy--Addresses, essays, lectures. 3. Science--Methods. 4. Logic, Symbolic and mathematical. t. 1964

NN *R 9.64 g/B OC PC, 1, 2, 3, 4 SL ST, 1, 3t (LC1, X1, Z1)

3-MDC p.v. 25

Busch, Wilhelm, 1832–1908.

Wilhelm Busch. Dem grossen deutschen humoristen zum 100. geburstage. ₍Leipzig, Buchdrucker-lehranstalt, 1932₎

1 p. l., 5–12 p., 1 l., 17–39 numb. l., 1 l. illus., 2 facsim. 22cm.

Portrait on t.-p.

"Zum gedenken des humorvollen meisters, anlässlich des 100. geburtstages, als gemeinschaftsarbeit von lehrern and schülern hergestellt in der Buchdrucker-lehranstalt, lehrlingsfachschule des Vereins Leipziger buchdruckerei-besitzer e. v. Den nachdruck 'Hans Huckebein' erlaubte gütig: Deutsche verlags-anstalt in Stuttgart und Berlin. Das lebensbild schrieb Hanns Zarn ... Strichätzung: Artur Bartmuss."

"Hans Huckebein, der unglücksrabe", by Wilhelm Busch: numb. leaves ₍16₎–39.

1. Wit and humor, Pictorial. I. Zarn, Hanns. II. Buchdrucker-lehranstalt, Leipzig.

A34–919

Title from N. Y. Pub. Libr. Printed by L. C.

₍2₎

SB p.v.492

Butte, Heinrich.

Festschrift zur Vierteljahrtausendfeier des Stadtwaisenhauses zu Dresden am 31. August/1. September. 1685/1935. Von Dr. Heinrich Butte und Dr. Gabriele Patzig... ₍Magdeburg: Enke & Schröder, 1935₎ 64 p. front., illus. 21cm.

1. Orphans—Asylums and homes—Germany—Dresden. I. Patzig, Gabriele. II. Dresden. Stadtwaisenhaus.

N. Y. P. L. April 1, 1940

Copy only words underlined & classmark— BVA

BYZANTINE INSTITUTE, INC.

Coptic studies in honor of Walter Ewing Crum. Boston, 1950. xi, 572 p. 36 plates (part col.) 29cm. (ITS: Bulletin, [no.] 2)

"A bibliography of Walter Ewing Crum," p. [vii]-xi.

1. Crum, Walter Ewing, 1865-1944. 2. Copts. I. Series. II. Title.

NN **6.57 p/10 (OC)II OS, I PC, 1, 2, I, II O, 1, 2, I, II (U1, Z1, LC1, X1) [I]

E-11
8332

CAEMMERER, ERNST VON, ed.

Vom deutschen zum europäischen Recht; Festschrift für Hans Dölle, hrsg. von Ernst von Caemmerer, Arthur Nikisch [und] Konrad Zweigert. Tübingen, J. C. B. Mohr, P. Siebeck, 1963. 2 v. port. 24cm.

CONTENTS.--Bd. 1. Deutsches Privat- und Zivilprozessrecht. Rechtsvergleichung.--Bd. 2. Internationales Recht, Kollisionsrecht und internationales Zivilprozessrecht. Europäisches Recht.

(Continued)

NN R 12.63 p/4 OC, I, II PC, 1, 2, 3, I, II SL E, 2, 3, I, II (LC1, X1, Z1)

CAEMMERER, ERNST VON, ed. Vom deutschen zum europäischen Recht... (Card 2)

Bibliographical footnotes.

1. Law--Germany. 2. Law, International, Private--Addresses, essays, lectures. 3. Law, International--Addresses, essays, lectures. I. Nikisch, Arthur, 1888- , joint ed. II. Zweigert, Konrad, joint ed.

---

* OHO

CALCUTTA UNIVERSITY. Ancient Indian history and culture, Dept. of. Alumni association.

J. N. Banerjea volume; a collection of articles by his friends and pupils presented on his retirement from Carmichael professorship of ancient Indian history and culture, University of Calcutta. [Calcutta, 1960] xiv, 352 p. illus., port. 23cm.

Includes a contribution in Bengali.

Includes bibliographies.

1. Banerjea, Jitendra Nath. 2. Indic studies--Collections.

NN R 11.65 p/8 OS(1b+) PC, 1, 2 SL O, 1, 2 (LC1, X1, Z1) [I]

Write on slip only words underlined and classmark: STG

California. University.

In honorem Lawrence Marsden Price; contributions by his colleagues and by his former students. Berkeley ₍etc.₎ Univ. of California press, 1952. 1 v. 23cm. (Its: Publications. Modern philology. v. 36)

"Bibliography," p. xi–xii.

CONTENTS.—The Meistersingerschule at Memmingen and its Kurtze Entwerffung, by C. H. Bell. Der leidende Dritte: Das Problem der Entsagung in bürgerlichen Romanen und Novellen, besonders bei Theodor Storm, by Marianne Bonwit.—The original model for Lessing's Der junge Gelehrte, by C. E. Borden.—The meaning of Snorri's categories, by A. B. Brodeur.—On education: John Locke, Christian Wolff,

(Continued)

NN R 4.53 OD, I ED, I PC, 1, I, II (LC1, Z1, X1)

California. University. In honorem Lawrence Marsden Price... (Card 2)

and the "Moral Weeklies," by F. A. Brown.—Ludwig Hohenwang's Von der Ritterschafft, by E. K. Heller.—Rilkes Duineser Elegien und die Einsamkeit, by A. O. Jászi.—The German theater in San Francisco, 1861–1864, by C. G. Loomis.—Hermann Hesse's Glasperlenspiel, by Joseph Mileck.—German works on America, 1492–1800, by P. M. Palmer.—Religious forms and faith in the Volksbuch, by S. B. Puknat.—Sebastian Brant, Ovid, and classical allusions in the Narrenschiff, by Eli Sobel.—Heinrich von Kleists Findling, by H. M. Wolff.

1. Price, Lawrence Marsden, 1881- . I. Series. II. Title.

Write on slip only words underlined and classmark: RNA

California. University. English dept.

Essays critical and historical dedicated to Lily B. Campbell, by members of the Departments of English, University of California. Berkeley, University of California Press, 1950. vii, 286 p. port. 24cm. (California. University. University of California publications. English studies: 1)

CONTENTS.—Wycliff and Chaucer on the contemplative life, by F. Towne.—Skelton's Colyn Cloute: the mask of Vox populi, by R. S. Kinsman.—Elizabethan portents: superstition or doctrine? By L. M. Buell.—Jean de Bordes' Maria Stuarta tragoedia:

(Continued)

NN*R 4.54 OCi, Ii EDi, Ii PC, 1, 2, I (Z1, LC1, X1)

California. University. Dept. of English. Essays critical and historical... 1950. (Card 2)

the earliest-known drama on the Queen of Scots, by J. E. Phillips.—Celtic antiquarianism in the Curious discourses, by L. Van Norden.—On editing Dryden's early poems, by H. T. Swedenberg, Jr.—The early poetical career of Samuel Woodforde: the heavenly muse in the age of reason, by E. N. Hooker.—Tarpaulin arabick in the days of Pepys, by W. Matthews.—John Locke as literary critic and Biblical interpreter, by G. G. Pahl.—Wycherley's Manly reinterpreted, by A. H. Chorney.—The genesis of Steele's The conscious lovers, by J. Loftis.—The 1737 editions of Alexander Pope's letters, by V. A. Dearing.—The mystery of Martin Chuzzlewit, by A. B. Nisbet.—Trollope on the novel, by B. A. Booth.—Henry James's romantic "vision of the real" in the 1870's, by R. P. Falk.—Notes.—Bibliography of Lily B. Campbell.

1. Campbell, Lily Bess, 1883- . 2. English literature—Hist. and crit. I. California. University. University at Los Angeles. English dept. II. Ser. i. 1950.

XAH

California. University. Law School Association.
Legal essays in tribute to Orrin Kip McMurray; edited by Max Radin and A. M. Kidd. Published for University of California Law School Association. Berkeley, Cal.: Univ. of California Press, 1935. x, 694 p. front. (port.) 24cm.

Two of the essays are in French.
"A partial list of the published writings of Orrin Kip McMurray," p. 693–694.
CONTENTS.—Some suggestions concerning the California law of riparian rights, by J. W. Bingham.—The reality of what the courts are doing, by F. H. Bohlen.—La "propriété commerciale," par H. Capitant.—The freedom of the miner and its influence on water law, by W. E. Colby.—Those protective trusts which are miscalled "spendthrift

(Continued)

N. Y. P. L. January 3, 1936

California. University. Law School Association. Legal essays in tribute to Orrin Kip McMurray... (Continued)

trusts" reëxamined, by G. P. Costigan, jr.—Jurisdiction following seizure or arrest in violation of international law, by E. D. Dickinson.—The story of the criminal jury in the civil law and in the common law, by the Hon. R. L. Henry.—Army courts-martial, by Captain H. D. Hoover.—International engagements and their interpretation by the Permanent Court of International Justice, by M. O. Hudson.—La protection des faibles par le droit, par L. Josserand.—Some recent subrogation problems in the law of suretyship and insurance, by S. I. Langmaid.—The constitution as an institution, by K. N. Llewellyn.—Our non-citizen nationals, who are they? By D. O. McGovney.—Growing lawlessness of trees, by S. MacNeil.—The constitution and the recovery legislation: the rôles of the document, doctrine, and judges, by D. B. Maggs.—Specific performance

(Continued)

N. Y. P. L. January 3, 1936

California. University. Law School Association. Legal essays in tribute to Orrin Kip McMurray... (Continued)

of contracts to deliver specific or ascertained goods under the English Sale of goods act and the American Sales act, by W. E. Masterson.—The criminal act, by J. Miller.—Instructing the jury upon presumptions and burden of proof, by E. M. Morgan.—More about the nature of law, by R. Pound.—A juster justice, a more lawful law, by M. Radin.—The law and morals of primitive trade, by F. J. Schechter.—The business relations of patron and freedman in classical Roman law, by A. A. Schiller.—The scientific rôle of consideration in contract, by J. H. Wigmore.—The American Law Institute, by H. E. Yntema.

789592A. 1. McMurray, Orrin Kip, 1869– . 2. Law—Essays and misc. I. Kidd, Alexander Marsden, 1879– , ed. II. Radin, Max, 1880– , ed.
N. Y. P. L. January 3, 1936

D-16
1880

CALLWEY (GEORGE D. W.) VERLAG, Munich.
Almanach des Verlages Georg D. W. Callwey, zum 75. Jahr. München, 1959. 150 p. illus., ports, facsims. 21cm.

Contributions by various authors.
Bibliography, p. 137-147.

NN R 5.66 p/ OS PC SL (LC1, X1, Z1)

F-11
1834

Cambridge essays in international law; essays in honour of Lord McNair. London, Stevens; Dobbs Ferry, N. Y., Oceana Publications, 1965.

186 p. 26 cm.

"Written in honour of Lord McNair in the year of his eightieth birthday."
Bibliographical footnotes.

(Continued)

NN • R 7.66 1/ OC PC, 1, 2 SL E, 1, 2 (LC1, X1, Z1)

3

CAMBRIDGE essays in international law...
(Card 2)

CONTENTS.—The International Disarmament Organisation, the United Nations, and the veto; some observations on problems of relationship and functioning, by D. W. Bowett.—Judicial innovation, its uses and its perils, as exemplified in some of the work of the International Court of Justice during Lord McNair's period of office, by Sir G. Fitzmaurice.—Unanimity, the veto, weighted voting, special

(Continued)

CAMBRIDGE essays in international law...
(Card 3)

and simple majorities and consensus as modes of decision in international organisations, by C. W. Jenks.—Nullity and effectiveness in international law, by R. Y. Jennings.—The legal effect of illegal acts of international organisations, by E. Lauterpacht.—The British consular conventions, by C. Parry.—The peaceful settlement of disputes, by Sir F. Vallat.

1. Law, International--Addresses, essays, lectures.
2. McNair, Sir Arnold Duncan, 1885-

E-11
9510

CAMDEN, CARROLL, 1903- , ed.
Restoration and eighteenth-century literature; essays in honor of Alan Dugald McKillop. [Chicago] Published for William Marsh Rice University by the University of Chicago press [1963] xi, 435 p. illus., port., facsims. 24cm. (Rice University semicentennial publications)

"The publications of Alan Dugald McKillop, compiled by Stuart Wilson": p. 429-435.

(Continued)

NN * R 4.64 p/ OC, III (OS)I, II PC, 1, 2, I, III SL (LC1, X1, Z1) [I, NSCM]

2

CAMDEN, CARROLL, 1903- , ed. Restoration and eighteenth-century literature...
(Card 2)

1. English literature--Addresses, essays, lectures. 2. McKillop, Alan Dugald. I. Rice university, Houston, Tex. II. Rice university, Houston, Tex. Semicentennial publications. III. Title.

E-10
9357

Caracas, Venezuela (City). Universidad central. Instituto de filosofia.
Homenaje a Ortega y Gasset. Caracas, 1958. 135 p. 24cm.

CONTENTS.—Pidiendo un Ortega Y Gasset desde dentro, por J. D. García Bacca.—El sistema de Ortega, por M. Granell.—Las fundaciones de Ortega y Gasset, por L. Luzuriaga.—Ortega y su ideología universitaria, por E. Mayz Vallenilla.—Ortega y Gasset: Lengua y estilo, por A. Rosenblat.

1. Ortega y Gasset, José, 1883–1955. I. García Bacca, Juan David, 1901- . II. Title.
NN R 8.60 (OC)I OS PC,1,I,II SL (LC1,X1,Z1)

E-12
1666

CARBONARA, CLETO, ed.
Il pensiero e l'opera di Guido della Valle... Napoli, Libreria scientifica editrice [presentazione 1957] 655 p. ports. 24cm.

"Un volume celebrativo...una raccolta di saggi di vari autori."
"Parte seconda: Mezzo secolo di lavoro di Guido della Valle [l'autobiografia]": p. [367]-636.
Includes bibliography.
1. Valle, Guido della, 1884- .
NN * 12.64 g/r OC PC,1 SL (LC1, X1, Z1)

Copy only words underlined & classmark— KAA

CARL RITTER zum Gedächtnis. Berlin, W. de Gruyter, 1959. [97]-254 p. port. 24cm. (Die Erde; Zeitschrift der Gesellschaft für Erdkunde zu Berlin. Jahrg. 90, Heft 2)

Cover title.
Includes bibliographies.
CONTENTS.--Carl Ritter zum Gedächtnis, von J.H. Schultze.--Carl Ritter, Hinweise und Versuche zu einer Deutung seiner Entwicklung, von E. Plewe.--C. Ritters "Vorhalle europäischer Völkergeschichten," von E. Kirsten.--Carl Ritters kartographische Leistung, von (Continued)
NN R X 12.59 t/b OI (PC)1 (MP)1 (LC2, X1, Z1)

M-11
1758

CARIAS REYES, MARCOS, 1905- ,ed.
Album morazánico; homenaje del gobierno... al General don Francisco Morazán con motivo del primer centenario de su fallecimiento. Textos seleccionados por Marcos Carías Reyes, colaboró Celeo Murillo. Tegucigalpa, Talleres tipográficos nacionales, 1942. 1 v. 27cm.

Tomo I.
(Continued)
NN R7.66 r/b OC, I, II PC, I, I, II SL AH, I, I, II (LC1, X1, Z1)

2

CARL RITTER zum Gedächtnis. (Card. 2)

E. Lehmann.--Carl Ritters Schriften zur Kunst, von W. Tichy.--Johann August Zeune in seinem Einfluss auf Carl Ritter, von H. Preuss.--Zeichnungen von Carl Ritter, von H. Beck.--Die Ritterforschungen Karl Simons, von H. Beck.--Beiträge zur Kenntnis der Literatur über Carl Ritter, von H. Beck (p.251-253).

1. Ritter, Karl, 1779-1859.

CARIAS REYES MARCOS, 1905- ,ed. Album morazánico... (Card 2)

Bibliographical footnotes.
CONTENTS.--t. 1. Biografía del General Francisco Morazán, por E. Martínez López. 3. ed. Vida de Morazán, por R. Reyes. 5. ed.

1. Morazán, Francisco, pres. Central America, 1792-1842. I. Martínez López, Eduardo. II. Title.

NFD
(Spitteler)

Carl Spitteler, in der Erinnerung seiner Freunde und Weggefährten. Gespräche, Zeugnisse, Begegnungen. Gesammelt und in biographischer Folge hrsg. von Leonhard Beriger. Zürich, Artemis-Verlag [1947] 318 p. illus. 21cm.

"Quellennachweis," p. 310–314.

Festschrift ed.

425754B. 1. Spitteler, Carl, 1845–1924. I. Beriger, Leonhard, ed.
N. Y. P. L. March 26, 1948

D-13
204

CARINTHIA.
Robert Musil; Leben, Werk, Wirkung; im Auftrag des Landes Kärnten und der Stadt Klagenfurt, hrsg. von Karl Dinklage. Zürich, Amalthea-Verlag [1960] 440 p. illus., ports. 21cm.

Collection of essays by various contributors, letters by Musil and pieces by him from Soldatenzeitung, issued in honor of his 80th birthday.

1. Musil, Robert, 1880-1942. I. Dinklage, Karl, ed. II. Klagenfurt, Austria. III. Title. t. 1960.
NN 5.61 p/b (OC)I. III ODt, IIt EDt, IIt PC, 1, I, II, III SL (LC1, X1, Z1)

Write on slip words underlined below and class mark- *EA

Carnegie institution of Washington.
Cooperation in research, by staff members and research associates, the Carnegie institution of Washington. Washington, D. C., The Carnegie institution of Washington, 1938.
ix, 782 p. front. (port.) illus., plates, maps (1 fold.) diagrs. 25½cm. (Carnegie institution of Washington. Publication no. 501)
A testimonial volume commemorating the retirement of John Campbell Merriam from the presidency of Carnegie institution of Washington. *cf.* Foreword.
Includes bibliographies.
CONTENTS.—Physical sciences.—Biological sciences.—History.—Palaeontology and geology.—Philosophy and interpretation.
1. Merriam, John Campbell, 1869– 2. Science—Collected works. 3. Research. I. Title.

39-4782

Library of Congress Q111.C27
——— ~~Copy 2.~~
——— ~~Copy 3.~~ AS32.A5 no. 501
[10] (508) 504

Festschrift.

AN
(Lindhagen, C.)

Carl Lindhagen tillägnas denna bok som en hyllning på sextioårsdagen, 19 20. [Stockholm, 1920] 276 p. illus. 25cm.

No. 109 of 125 copies.
"Bibliografi..." p. 226–272.

Festschrift

573773B. 1. Lindhagen, Carl Albert, 1860–1946.
N. Y. P. L. June 28, 1951

---

* EH

Carlsbergfondet, Copenhagen.
Carlsbergfondet, 1876–1926; et Jubilæumsskrift udgivet af Carlsbergsfondets Direktion... København: B. Lunos Bogtrykkeri A/S, 1930. 2 v. illus., plan, plates, ports., tables. 4°.

Contains also a matter relating to the two breweries "Gammel Carlsberg" and "Ny Carlsberg," the income from which forms the "Carlsbergfond."

525392-3A. 1. Breweries—Denmark—Copenhagen.
N. Y. P. L. May 28, 1931

HFS

CASTRO, JOSUÉ DE, 1908-
A cidade do Recife, ensaio de geografía urbana. [Ed. comemorativa do XXV ano de fundação da Casa do estudante do Brasil] Rio de Janeiro, Livraria-editôra da Casa do estudante do Brasil [1954] 166 p. illus., maps. 20cm.

Bibliographical footnotes.
1. Recife, Brazil—Descr. 2. Recife, Brazil—Hist. I. Casa do estudante do Brasil, Rio de Janeiro.
NN** 9.55 g/ OC (OS)I PC, 1, 2, I SL AH, 1, 2, I (LC1, X1)

E-12
4160

CELEBRAZIONI gianturchiane; centenario della nascita e cinquantenario della morte di Emanuele Gianturco. Napoli, Società di cultura "Aspetti letterari" e per la Lucania [1957] 80 p. 25cm. (Quaderni lucani)

1. Gianturco, Emanuele, 1857-1907.
NN R X 4.66 g/c OC PC, 1 SL (LC1, X1, Z1)

NKW

Cazamian, Louis François, 1877–
... Essais en deux langues. Paris, Henri Didier, éditeur, 1938.
xv, 318 p., 2 l. 22cm.
At head of title: Louis Cazamian.
Essays in French and English.
"Ce volume a été offert à m. Louis Cazamian, à l'occasion du trentième anniversaire de son enseignement à la Sorbonne, par ses amis, collègues et disciples, le 19 novembre 1938."
"Bibliographie": p. [301]–318.
CONTENTS.—Études de méthode et de théorie.—Le problème de l'humeur.—Romantisme, symbolisme et poésie.—Les lettres et la vie.
1. Literature—Addresses, essays, lectures. I. Title.

A C 39-206

Princeton univ. Library
for Library of Congress [2]

PPB

CELL chemistry; a collection of papers dedicated to Otto Warburg on the occasion of his 70th birthday; edited by Dean Burk. Amsterdam, Houston, Elsevier, 1953. 362 p. illus., port. 26cm.

"The original edition of this book appeared as an issue of Biochimica et biophysica acta, vol. 12, no. 1-2 (1953)."
Text in English, French or German; summary at end of each chapter in English, French and German.

(Continued)
NN ** R 7 55 p/ OCs, Is PCs, 1, 2s, Is SLs STs, 1t, 2s, Is (LC1s, X1s, Z1s)

Copy only words underlined & classmark— BWA

CECINI, NANDO, ed.
Studi storici bormiesi in memoria di Tullio Urangia Tazzoli. Milano A. Giuffrè, 1963. ports. 26cm. (Raccolta di studi storici sulla Valtellina, 20)

Includes bibliographies.
CONTENTS.--Profilo e bibliografia de Prof. Tullio Urangia Tazzoli (p. [1]-10). --Tullio Urangia Tazzoli e i suoi rapporti con la Società storica valtellinese, di E. Pedrotti. --Vicende bormiensi in un diario del 1813, di L. Varischetti. --Inventario delle carte antiche del comune di Bormio, di U. Cavallari. --Forma e funzione,
(Continued)
NN 3.66 r/ OC, II (OS)I PC, 1, 2, 3, I, II (LC1, X1, Z1s) 2

CELL chemistry; a collection of papers dedicated to Otto Warburg on the occasion of his 70th birthday... (Card 2)

Includes bibliographies.

1. Biochemistry—Addresses, essays, lectures. 2. Warburg, Otto Heinrich, 1883- I. Burk, Dean, ed. t. 1953.

CECINI, NANDO, ed. Studi storici bormiesi in memoria di Tullio Urangia Tazzoli. (Card 2)

struttura e folklore nell' architeturra alpina bormiese, di P. L. Gerosa. --Le tendenze artistiche delle alte valli dell'Adda, di G. B. Gianoli. --Troppo odore di zolfo intorno al Conte Diavolo, di R. Sertoli Salis. --Storia della parrocchia d'Isolaccia, di L. Bellotti. --Folclore di Valtellina, di L. R. Lombardini. --Dumno nell'isola Comacina e la dedicazione delle chiese regie lungo le vie transalpine, di O. Auteggi. --Notizie sulla stampa valtellinese dalle sue origini alla metà del secolo XIX, di N. Cecini.
1. Tazzoli, T. U. 2. Bormio, Italy. 3. Folk lore, Italian--Lombardy. I. Series. II. Title.

D-18
8942

Celtic studies: essays in memory of Angus Matheson, 1912–1962; edited by James Carney and David Greene. London, Routledge & K. Paul, 1968.
x, 182 p. port., map. 23cm.

"Publications of Professor Angus Matheson" (p. ix-x)
Includes bibliographies.

(Continued)
NN*R 5.69 a/ OC, I, II, III PC, 1, 2, I, II, III SL (LC1, X1, Z1) [I] 2

---

*C-5 p.v.264

A CELEBRATION for Wallace Stevens. Hartford, Conn., 1954. 48 p. illus., music. 28cm.

At head of title: The Trinity review...vol. VIII, May, 1954, no. 3. "Two new poems by Wallace Stevens," p. 5-8.

1. STEVENS, WALLACE, 1879- I. Trinity review
NN ** R 10.57 1/ OC (OS)I PC, 1, I SL (LC1, X1, Z1)

CELTIC studies. (Card 2)

1. Celtic language--Addresses, essays, lectures. 2. Celtic literature--Addresses, essays, lectures. I. Matheson, Angus. II. Carney, James, ed. III. Greene, David Herbert, 1913- ed.

AN
(Berthelot, P.)

. . . **Centenaire** de Marcel Berthelot. Paris₍: Imprimerie de Vaugirard₎, 1929. viii, 9–709 p. facsims. (part mounted), front., illus. (part col'd), plates, ports. f°.

At head of title: 1827–1927.
Printer's date: 1930.
"Œuvres, publications et communications scientifiques de Marcelin Berthelot," p. 21–52.

Mr. Moth.

570735A. 1. Berthelot, Pierre Eugène Marcellin, 1827–1907.
J. S. BILLINGS MEM. COLL.
N. Y. P. L. March 9, 1932

---

*OAC

Centenario della nascita di Michele Amari. Scritti di filologia e storia araba; di geografia, storia, diritto della Sicilia medievale; studi bizantini e giudaici relativi all' Italia meridionale nel medio evo; documenti sulle relazioni fra gli stati italiani ed il Levante. Palermo: Stabilimento tipografico Virzì, 1910. 2 v. fac., fold. maps, pl., port. 4°.

"Michele Amari," by G. Siragusa, p. ix–xliv.
"Le opere a stampa di Michele Amari," by G. Salvocozzo, p. xlv–cviii.

1. Amari, Michele, 1806–89. 2. Siragusa, Giovanni Battista, 1848– . 3. Salvo-Cozzo, Giuseppe, 1856– .
N. Y. P. L. July 20, 1916.

E-11
4281

CENTRAAL BOND VOOR INWENDIGE ZENDING EN CHRISTELIJK MAATSCHAPPELIJK WERK.
Mens en ontmoeting; enige facetten van het protestants - christelijk maatschappelijk werk. [Uitg. ter gelegenheid van het 60 - jarig bestaan van de Centraal bond voor inwendige zending en christelijk maatschappelijk werk]. Den Haag, van Keulen, 1961. 229 p. 24cm.

(Continued)

NN R 3.62 s/B (OC)I, Ibo, II OS(1b+) PC, 1, I, II SL E, 1, I, II (LC1, X1, Z1)

CENTRAAL BOND VOOR INWENDIGE ZENDING EN CHRISTELIJK MAATSCHAPPELIJK WERK. Mens en ontmoeting... (Card 2)

Contributions by P. S. Bakker and others.
Includes bibliographical references.

1. Church work, Social--Netherlands. I. Bakker, P. S. II. Title.

SHN

Centralförbundet för socialt arbete, Stockholm.
. . . Minnesskrift. Stockholm: O. Eklunds boktryckeri, 1928. 101 p. illus. (incl. ports.) 8°.

At head of title: 1903–1928.

Mr. Moth.

1. Social work—Sweden, 1903–1928.
N. Y. P. L. November 30, 1931

AN
(Rodó, J.)

Centro de estudiantes "Ariel", Montevideo.
Homenaje á José Enrique Rodó... Montevideo ₍1920₎ 224 p. illus. 19cm.

"Revista 'Ariel,' organo del Centro de estudiantes 'Ariel.' Febrero–mayo, 1920, año 1, no. 8–9."

273725B. 1. Rodó, José Enrique, 1872–1917. I. Title.
N. Y. P. L. August 10, 1944

AN
(Piedra Buena, L.)

Centro naval, Buenos Aires.
El capitán Luis Piedra Buena; su centenario. Homenaje del Centro naval á su memoria. ₍Buenos Aires₎ 1933. 335 p. illus. 20cm. (Biblioteca del oficial de marina. ₍v. 18₎)

298656B. 1. Piedra Buena, Luis, 1833–1883. I. Ser.
N. Y. P. L. March 27, 1945

3-MAR p.v. 1349

CERCLE SUÉDOIS, Paris.
Svenska klubben i Paris, en jubileumsskrift. Paris, 1952. 87 p. illus., ports. 28cm.

CONTENTS.--Inledning av Prins Wilhelm.--Klubbens öden av Sven Aurén.--Konstsamlingen av Gunnar W. Lundberg.--Katalog över Svenska klubbens i Paris konstsamling.--Hedersledamöter och styrelse.

1. Art, Swedish--Collections--France--Paris.
2. Swedes in France--Paris.
NN* R 6.57 v/ OS(1b) PC,1,2 SL A,1 E,2 (LC1, X1,Z1)

---

*QT

Česká akademie věd a umění, Prague.
Slovanská vzájemnost, 1836–1936; sborník prací k 100. výročí vydání rozpravy Jana Kollára o slovanské vzájemnosti. Uspořádal Jiří Horák. Praha: Nákl. České akademie věd a umění a Slovanského ustavu, 1938. 428 p. incl. facsims. port. 24½cm.

Added t.-p. in French: La réciprocité slave, 1836-1936; recueil des travaux publiés en mémoire du centenaire de l'édition de l'étude sur la réciprocité slave de Jan Kollár ... Praha, 1938.
Résumés in French.
Bibliographical footnotes.

(Continued)

Festschrift

N. Y. P. L. January 8, 1940

Česká akademie věd a umění, Prague. Slovanská vzájemnost, 1836–1936... (Continued)

CONTENTS.—Pastrnek, Fr. Úvodní projev.—Murko, M. Slovanská myšlenka před Kollárem.—Wollman, F. Kollárův mesianismus.—Georgijević, Krešimir. Kollárova ideja slovenske uzajamnosti kod Hrvata i Srba.—Heidenreich, Julius. Kollár a "nářečí illyrské."—Kidrič, Fr. Osnove za Kollárjev vpliv pri Slovencih do 1852.—Páta, Josef. Poznámka o bulharských vztazích ke Kollárovi.—Chernobayev, B. Ян Коллар в России.—Francev, V. A. Ohlasy Kollárovy

(Continued)

N. Y. P. L. January 8, 1940

Česká akademie věd a umění, Prague. Slovanská vzájemnost, 1836–1936... (Continued)

rozpravy "O literárni vzájemnosti" v ruské literatuře let třicátých a čtyřicátých.—Biletz'kyĭ, Leonid. Ян Коляр в українській літературі.—Vrtel-Wierczyński, St. Rozprawa Jana Kollára "O literackiej wzajemności Słowian" i jej odgłosy w ówczesnej Polsce.—Krejčí, Karel. Pokusy o sblížení českého a polského pravopisu.—Szyjkowski, Marjan. Polski przekład rozprawy "O wzajemności" i wiersza "Sławianin".—Wisłocki, W. T. Do stosunków Jana Kollára z Polakami.

(Continued)

N. Y. P. L. January 8, 1940

Česká akademie věd a umění, Prague. Slovanská vzájemnost, 1836–1936... (Continued)

—Páta, Josef. Jan Kollár a lužičtí Srbové.—Pražák, Albert. Kollárova myšlenka slovanské vzájemnosti a Slováci.—Štefánek, Ant. Kollárov nacionalizmus.—Seifert, Augustin. Pro převoz ostatků Jana Kollára z Vidně do Prahy r. 1893.

24807B. 1. Slavophilism. 2. Kollár, Jan, 1793–1852. I. Horák, Jiří, 1884– , ed. II. Slovanský ústav, Prague. III. Title.
N. Y. P. L. January 8, 1940

---

*QT
+

Česká vysoká škola technická, Brno, Czecho-Slovakia.
...Jubilejní vědecký sborník, 1899–1924. Brno: Nákl. Vysoké školy technické [1925] 190 p. incl. diagrs., tables. charts, illus., plates. 31½cm.

CONTENTS.—Rieger, J. Nové směry stavitelství betonového.—Smrček, Ant. Vědecké pokusy z oboru vodnich staveb a hydromechaniky.—Semerád, A. Konstanty aneroidu. Základní referenční bod a referenční elipsoid pro československou republiku.—Kladivo, B. Konstanty invarových kyvadel geodetického ústavu české techniky v Brně. Připojovací měření v Postupimi.—Mašík, Emil. Teoretický základ nového ručního přístroje k určení zemního tlaku v přírodě.—Jahn, J. Geologický podklad města Hodonína.—Kettner, Radim. O povaze ložisek měďnatých u Borovce na západní Moravě.—Šimek, Karel. Sborcené ložné plochy u spojovacích zdí zakřivených.—

(Continued)

Festschrift
N. Y. P. L. January 8, 1941

Česká vysoká škola technická, Brno, Czecho-Slovakia. ...Jubilejní (Card 2)

Záruba, Lad. O vlivu průřezové změny trámů a pilířů na průběch momentů ohybových některých nosníků rámových.—Zavadil, J. Vývin půdních typů.—Vlček, Bohumil. Za nejvyšší výkonností automatického stavu.—Elger, Zdeněk. Z tepelné laboratoře ústavu teoretické a obecné nauky o strojich.—Baborovský, J. Hydratace iontů.—Matějka, Jaroslav. Zařízení k samočinnému zapisování průtokové rychlosti plynů.—Ducháček, F. Mikrobi tuleního mléka z krajů polárních.—Vondráček, Rud. Fosilní dřevěné uhli.—Kubelka, Václav. Vliv koncentrace roztoku při určování nerozpustných látek v roztocích třislovin.—Novák, J. Příspěvek k otázce umělého stárnutí lihovin vlivem ozonu.—Veselý, Vítězslav. O reaktivnosti atomů vodíkových v methylskupině 1-methyl-2.4-dinitronaftalinu.—Mečíř, J. (Z ústavu analytické chemie) Příspěvek k elektroly-

(Continued)

N. Y. P. L. January 8, 1941

Česká vysoká škola technická, Brno, Czecho-Slovakia. ...Jubilejní (Card 3)

tyckému stanovení antimonu.—Kallauner, O. Státní výzkumný ústav pro průmysl silikatový.—Pelíšek, Mioslav. Sur l'hélicoïde gauche à noyau cylindrique à base néfroidique engendré par roulement cardioïdique et sur le cas plus général de cette surface.—Mašek, Vladimír. Poznámky ku ploše naplněné vrcholy hyperbolických paraboloïdů procházejících dvěma kolmými mimoběžkami.—Procházka, B. O zvláštním svazku kuželovíček.—Vojtěch, Jan. O základech geometrie projektivní.—Čupr, Karel. Přispěvek k numerickému řešení rovnic.—Caha, Jan. K úpravě studia práv na vysokých školách technických.—Loevenstein, Jan. Noetické základy vrchních pojmů hospodářské vědy.—Dominik, Rudolf. Vynálezy státních zaměstnanců.—Kostlivý, Stanislav. O vlivu subdiafragmatické vagotomie na hypertonický žaludek.

85454B. 1. Science—Essays and misc. I. Title.
N. Y. P. L. January 8, 1941

Copy only words underlined
& classmark-- * QVA

<u>ČESKOSLOVENSKÁ AKADEMIE VĚD, Prague. Sekce jazykověda a literatura.</u>
Studia antiqua Antonió Salač septuagenario oblata. Pragae, Sumptibus Academiae scientiarum bohemoslovenicae, 1955. 190 p. illus., 16 plates, port. fold. map. 25cm. (<u>ITS: Sborník filologický. [v.] 3 [no.] 1</u>)

Added t.p. in Czech.

1. ed., edited by L. Varcl. .

Articles by various authors in Czech, German, French, Greek, English or Latin. (Continued)

NN R 1.60 p/l (OC)II, IIIbo OS,I PC, 1, 2, I, II S, 1, 2, I, II (LCE1, LC1, X1, Z1)

<u>ČESKOSLOVENSKÁ AKADEMIE VĚD,</u> Prague. <u>Sekce jazykověda a literatura.</u> Studia antiqua Antonió Salae septuagenario oblata. (Cont.)

Some articles have summaries in English, Russian, or French.

Bibliographical footnotes.

Bibliography of works by A. Salač, p. 12-24.

1. Salač, Antonín. 2. Archaeology--Addresses, essays, lectures. I. Series. II. Varcl, Ladislav, ed. III. Varcl, Ladislav.

---

*QT
+

CESTAMI umění; sborník prací k poctě šedesátých narozenin Antonína Matějčka. Praha, Melantrich, 1949. 284 p. illus. 30cm.

"Za redakce O. J. Blažíčka a J. Květa."

By various authors.

"Soupis prací Antonína Matějčka," p. 215-228; bibliographical footnotes.

547821B. 1. Matějček, Antonín, 1889- . 2. Art, Bohemian. I. Blažíček, Oldřich J , ed. II. Květ, Jan, 1896- ed.
NN OC, I, II PC, 1, 2, I, II SL A, 1, 2, I, II S, 1, 2, I, II (LC1, Z1, X1)

---

* PWZ
(Weizmann)

CHAIM WEIZMANN; in memoriam. [n.p., Govt. Printer] 1952. 70, 38 p. illus., port. 28cm.

Added t.p.: לזכרו של חיים ויצמן

1. Weizmann, Chaim, Pres. Israel, 1874-1952.

NN* R 4.64 p/v OC PC, 1 SL I, 1 (LC1, X1, Z1)
dd

SSMC

Chalmers tekniska högskola, Gothenburg.
Chalmers tekniska högskola 1829-1954; minnesskrift utg. till högskolans 125-årsjubileum. Göteborg, Elanders boktryckeri, 1954. 194 p. illus., ports. (1 col.) 27cm.

Contents.—William Chalmers, av. G. Hössjer.—Chalmers' utveckling omkring och efter 100-års-jubileet 1929, av G. Hössjer.—Institutioner och forskning vid Chalmers tekniska högskola, av
(Continued)

NN**R 4.55 a/v OS PC, 1 SL E, 1 ST, 1t (LC1, X1, Z1)

Chalmers tekniska högskola, Gothenburg.
Chalmers tekniska högskola 1829-1954...
(Card 2)

O. Hedebrant.—Högskolans donationsfonder.—Carl Palmstedt och "Chalmers," av G. Bodman.—C.S., av H. Heyman.—Student- och kårliv vid Chalmers, av J. Forsberg.

1. Education, Industrial and technical—Indiv. inst.—Sweden—Gothenburg. t.1954.

AM-10
130
no. 7

CHARISTERIA IOHANNI KÕPP octogenario oblata. Holmiae, 1964. 304 p. port. 27cm. (Eesti usuteadlaste selts pagulsues. Toimetused. 7)

Edited by J. Aunver and A. Vööbus.
List of works by J. Kõpp, p. [297]-304.
Bibliographical footnotes.

1. Kõpp, Juhan 2. Theology--Essays and misc. I. Series. II. Aunver, J., ed. III. Vööbus, Arthur, ed. IV. Aunver, J

NN 7.68 p/R OC, II, III, IVbo (OS)I PC, 1, 2, I, II, III (LC1, X1, Z1)

D-18
1635

Chambers, Raymond J *ed.*
The accounting frontier: in honour of Sir Alexander Fitzgerald; editors R. J. Chambers, L. Goldberg, R. L. Mathews. Melbourne, London [etc.] F. W. Cheshire, [1965]
[13], 240 p. front., tables, diagrs. 22½ cm.

Bibliographical footnotes. "A list of writings by Sir Alexander Fitzgerald," p. 226-240.

(Continued)

NN * R 5.68 r/// OC, I, II PC, 1, 2, I, II SL E, 1, 2, I, II (LC1, X1, Z1)

2

NRD

Χαρίτες Friedrich Leo zum sechzigsten Geburtstag dargebracht. Berlin: Weidmannsche Buchhandlung, 1911. 4 p.l., 490 p., 8 pl. 4°.

1. Leo, Friedrich.

CHAMBERS, RAYMOND J , ed. The accounting frontier... (Card 2)

1. Fitzgerald, Adolph Alexander. 2. Accounting and bookkeeping--Addresses, essays, lectures. I. Goldberg, Louis, 1908- , joint ed. II. Mathews, Russell, joint ed.

Charites
* QCC p.v.536

Χαρίτες. Профессору Евгенію Александровичу Боброву признательные ученики въ честь четвертьвѣковой — 1888–1913 — его работы на поприщѣ науки и литературы. Варшава: тип. "Русскаго общества," 1913. viii, 123 p. port. 23cm.

"Труды профессора Е. А. Боброва," p. [i]–viii.

1. Bobrov, Yevgeniĭ Aleksandrovich, 1867- . 2. Philosophy— Festschrift.
Essays and misc.
N. Y. P. L. March 19, 1940

D-14
9428

CHAPMAN, ROBERT M., ed.
Studies of a small democracy; essays in honour of Willis Airey, edited by Robert Chapman and Keith Sinclair. [Auckland?] Paul's book arcade for the University of Auckland [1963] v, 288 p. illus., port. 23cm.

CONTENTS. —Willis Thomas Goodwin Airey. —Provincialism and centralism, 1853-1858, by D.G. Herron. —The Maori king movement, 1858-1885, by M.P.K. Sorrenson. —New Zealand promoters and British investors, 1860-1895, by H.J. Hanham. — Sir Robert Stout and the labour

(Continued)

NN R 3.64 a// OC, I PC, 1, 2, I SL E, 1, 2, I (LC1, X1, Z1)

2

AN
(Beard, C.)

CHARLES A. BEARD: an appraisal by Eric F. Goldman [and others] Howard K. Beale, ed. [Lexington] University of Kentucky press [1954] x, 312 p. port. 24cm.

Bibliographical references included in "Notes" (p. [293]-312)

CONTENTS. —Charles A. Beard: an impression, by E. F. Goldman. --Charles Beard: an English view, by H. J. Laski. —Charles Beard's political theory, by M. Lerner. —Beard and municipal reform, by L. Gulick. —Beard and the concept of planning, by G. Soule. —Charles Beard and the Constitution, by R. Hofstadter. —Fragments from the politics, by W. Hamilton. —Charles Beard: historian, by H. K. Beale. —Beard and foreign

(Continued)

NN * * R 8.54 OC, I PC, 1, I SL AH, 1, I (LC1, ~~Z1~~, X1)

CHAPMAN, ROBERT M., ed. Studies of a small democracy... (Card 2)

question, 1870-1893, by D.A. Hamer. —The significance of the Scarecrow ministry," 1887-1891, by K. Sinclair. —The fall of Reeves, 1893-1896, by R.T. Shannon. —The influence of political theories in the liberal period, 1890-1912; Henry George and John Stuart Mill, by F. Rogers. —The country party idea in New Zealand politics, 1901-1937, by B.D. Graham. —The unions and the arbitration system, 1900-1937 by R.C.J. Stone. —The response to labour and the question of parallelism of opinion, 1928-1960, by R. Chapman. —"References" (p. 255-280).

1. Airey, Willis Thomas Goodwin, 1897- . 2. New Zealand--Politics. I. Sinclair, Keith, 1922- , joint ed.

CHARLES A. BEARD: an appraisal by Eric F. Goldman [and others] Howard K. Beale, ed. (Card 2)

policy, by G. R. Leighton. —Beard as historical critic, by M. Curti. —Charles Beard, the teacher, by A. W. Macmahon. —Charles Beard, the public man, by G. S. Counts. —Beard's historical writings, by H. K. Beale. -- Bibliography of Beard's writings, by J. Frooman and E. D. Cronon. (p. 265-286). --Who's who in this volume.

1. Beard, Charles Austin, 1874-1948. I. Beale, Howard Kennedy, 1899- , ed.

D-15
9982

Charles Wendell David; scholar, teacher, librarian. ₍Edited by John Beverley Riggs₎ Philadelphia, 1965.

68 p. col. port. 23 cm.

CONTENTS.—Introduction, by J. F. Lewis, Jr.—The first half century, by C. Robbins. — The Union Library Catalogue, by E. E. Campion.—The peaceful revolution, by R. Hirsch and M. C. Nolan.—Bibliographical vision, by V. W. Clapp.—The library builder, by D. F. Cameron.—The Longwood achievement, by R. D. Williams.—The academic advisor, by H. C. Symons.—Mentor at Mystic, by R. G. Albion.

1. David, Charles Wendell, 1885- . I. Riggs, John Beverley, 1918- , ed.

NN* R 5.65 g/ OC, I PC, 1, I SL (LC1, X1, Z1)

E-12
6878

CHICAGO UNIVERSITY.

The Julius Rosenwald centennial; the Julius Rosenwald centennial observance at the University of Chicago, October 15, 1962. ₍Chicago, 1963₎

viii, 65 p. illus., ports., facsims. 24 cm.

1. Rosenwald, Julius, 1862-1932.

NN R 1.67 a/ OS PC, 1 SL (LC1, X1, Z1)

VDLA

Chemnitz, Germany. Wasserwerksamt.

Die Erweiterung des Wasserwerkes der Stadt Chemnitz. Als Festschrift herausgegeben zur feierlichen Einweihung der Wasserleitung Neunzehnhain-Einsiedel. ₍Chemnitz: J. C. F. Pickenhahn & Sohn, 1908₎ 57 p. plans, plates. 29cm.

Festschrift.

7934B. 1. Water supply—Chemnitz.
N. Y. P. L. October 8, 1940

Copy only words underlined & Classmark-- *OBF

CHICAGO UNIVERSITY. Oriental Institute.

Studies in honor of Benno Landsberger on his seventy-fifth birthday, April 21, 1965. Chicago [1965] viii, 448 p. illus., port. 30cm. (ITS: Assyriological studies, no. 16)

Bibliographical footnotes.

1. Oriental studies--Collections. 2. Landsberger, Benno, 1890- . I. Series.

NN 7.66 1/ OS, I PC, 1, 2, I O, 1, 2, I (LC1, X1, Z1) [I]

Copy only words underlined & classmark-- BXA

CHEVALIER, MAXIME, ed.

Mélanges offerts à Marcel Bataillon par les Hispanistes français et publiés par les soins de Maxime Chevalier, Robert Ricard [et] Noël Salomon. Bordeaux, Féret [1962] xxxii, 743 p. port. 25cm. (Bulletin hispanique. t. 56 bis (1962))

"Bibliographie des travaux de Marcel Bataillon," p. [ix]-xxxii.
Bibliographical footnotes.

1. Bataillon, Marcel. I. Title. II. Chevalier, Maxime.

NN 10.65 s/ OC, I, IIbo PC, 1, I (LC1, X1, Z1) [I]

NFF p.v.222

Chor um Schmidtbonn. Stuttgart ₍etc.₎ Deutsche Verlags-Anstalt, 1926. 76 p. front. 19cm.

"Zu Wilhelm Schmidtbonns 50. Geburtstage, 6. Februar 1926."

1. Schmidtbonn, Wilhelm August, 1876-
N. Y. P. L. Festschrift. March 24, 1948

NFGH

Chicago University.

Goethe centenary papers, read in observance of the one-hundredth anniversary of Goethe's death, March 22, 1832, at the University of Chicago, March 8 and 9, 1932. Edited by Martin Schütze. Chicago, London, The Open court publishing company, 1933.

2 p. l., ₍iii₎-vi, 174 p. illus. (incl. ports., facsims.) 23½cm.

Each paper preceded by leaf with half-title not included in the pagination (12 leaves)

CONTENTS.—Address of welcome, by R. M. Hutchins.—Goethe and the German spirit, by H. F. Simon.—Goethe in English literature, by R. M. Lovett.—Goethe's language, by G. O. Curme.—Goethe and France, by

(Continued on next card)

33-4477

₍5₎

Festschrift

---

*MGA

Chorerziehung und neue Musik. Für Kurt Thomas z. 65. Geburtstag. Hrsg. von Manfred Kluge. Wiesbaden, Breitkopf u. Härtel, 1969.

89 p. with illus., front. 24 cm.
Includes music.

CONTENTS.—Vorwort, von M. Kluge.—Erinnerungen eines Kurt-Thomas-Schülers aus dem Jahre 1930, von M. Schneider.—Das Chorklang-Ideal von Kurt Thomas in musikgeschichtlicher Bedeutung, von W. Blankenburg.—Methodik bei Kurt Thomas, von J. Uhde.—Gedanken über Laien, über die Frösche und anderes, von D. de la Motte.—

(Continued)

NN* 1.71 d/ OC, I PC, 1, 3, I SL MU, 1, 2, I (LC1, X1, Z1) 2

Chicago University. Goethe centenary papers ... 1933. (Card 2)

CONTENTS—Continued.

E. P. Daragan. Bibliography (p. 64)—On re-reading three thwarted romances: La nouvelle Héloïse, Die leiden des jungen Werthers, Iacopo Ortis, by W. L. Bullock.—Goethe and older German literature, by G. O. Arlt.—Goethe and present-day German writers, by A. W. Aron.—Emerson's Goethe, by Peter Hagboldt.—Goethe in Chicago, by Rose J. Seitz.—Goethe and philosophy, by E. L. Schaub.—Goethe as a lyrical poet, by Martin Schütze.

1. Goethe, Johann Wolfgang von — Addresses, essays, lectures. 2. Goethe, Johann Wolfgang von—Anniversaries, etc., 1932. I. Schütze, Martin, 1866- ed. II. Title.

33-4477

Library of Congress PT2139.B32C5

——— ~~Copy 2.~~

Copyright A 60328 ₍5₎ 928.3

CHORERZIEHUNG und neue Musik. (Card 2)

Siebenundsiebzig Intervalle, von M. Kluge.—Zum Problem des Mittelsatzes im 3. Brandenburgischen Konzert Bachs, von E. Platen.—Kurt Thomas als Thomas-Kantor, von A. Bode.—Eine improvisierte, kurze Geburtstagsrede, von W. Röhrig.

1. Thomas, Kurt, 1904- 2. Essays. 3. Music--Essays. I. Kluge, Manfred, ed.

ZBIE

Christiansen, Reidar Thoralf, 1886–
. . . Eventyr og sagn. Oslo, O. Norli, 1946. 168 p. front. 25cm.

CONTENTS.—Tabula gratulatoria Reidar Th. Christiansen på sekstiårsdagen 27. januar 1946.—Eventyr: Til studiet av nordiske folkeeventyr. Et irsk eventyr i Norge. Et norsk eventyr i Irland. Den heldige tigger. Yvon og Finette.—Sagn: Sagnstudier. Gårdvette og markavette. Til de norske sjøvetters historie. Vandring og stedegent.—Reidar Th. Christiansens forfatterskap (p. ₍161₎–168).

Festschrift

356039B. 1. Folk tales, Norwegian—Hist. and crit. 2. Folk tales, Irish Gaelic—Hist. and crit. 3. Sagas—Hist. and crit.
N. Y. P. L. January 20, 1947

3-MCZ
G155.C5

CHRISTINE GALLATI; kleine Festschrift zum 80. Geburtstag. [Einführung: O. Huber] Glarus, Kommissions-Verlag Baeschlin [1968] [3] p. 30 plates (ports. (part col.)) 28cm.

1. Gallati, Christine, 1888- . I. Huber, Otto.
NN 11.71 w/OC, I PC, 1, I SL A, 1, I B (LC1, X1, Z1)

---

*OVA

CHUNG-KUO tsao ch'uan. Zhongguo zao-chuan. Jan. 1963-date.
Shanghai, Chung-kuo tsao ch'uan ch'eng hsüeh hui. v. illus., charts, tables. 26cm.

中國造船

RECORD OF HOLDINGS UNDER MAIN ENTRY ONLY
Quarterly.

(Continued)
NN 9.66 r/c SL O, I, 2, I, II (UI, LCI, XI, Z1)

2

CHUNG-KUO tsao ch'uan. (Cont.)

Issued by Chung-kuo tsao ch'uan pien chi wei yüan hui.
From Jan. 1964, title also in English: Journal of shipbuilding of China.

1. Chinese literature--Per. and soc. publ. 2. Shipbuilding--China. I. Title: Zhongguo zao-chuan. II. Title: Journal of shipbuilding of China.

Write on slip words underlined and class mark—

Church historical society, Philadelphia. ZRA
Anglican evangelicalism, edited by Alexander C. Zabriskie, dean of the Virginia theological seminary. With foreword by the presiding bishop . . . Philadelphia, The Church historical society ₍1943₎ xiv p., 283 p. 24cm. (₍Church historical society, Philadelphia₎ Publication no. 13)

"These essays have been written and are published as a testimonial to Dr. Wallace E. Rollins."—*Foreword.*
CONTENTS.—Book 1. Historical: The rise and major characteristics of Anglican evangelicalism, by A. C. Zabriskie. The spiritual antecedents of the evangelicals, by C. W. Lowry, jr. The evangelicals and the Bible, by Stanley Brown-Serman.—Book 2.

(Continued)

N. Y. P. L. January 5, 1945

Church historical society, Philadelphia. Anglican evangelicalism . . . ₍1943₎ (Card 2)

Constructive theology: The situation and need of man, by C. W. Lowry, jr. Jesus Christ the Redeemer, by R. E. L. Strider. The body of Christ, by C. W. F. Smith.—Book 3. The practical application of evangelical principles: Evangelicals and missions, by H. S. G. Tucker and A. C. Zabriskie. Evangelicals and preaching, by W. R. Bowie. Evangelicals and the pastoral office, by E. H. Jones. Evangelicalism and Christian social ethics, by A. T. Mollegen.—Book 4. Bibliography (p. ₍263₎–275)—Book 5. Index of names.

1. Church of England—Movements and parties, Low and evangelical. 2. Protestant Episcopal church in the U. S. A.—Movements and parties, Low and evangelical. 3. Rollins, Wallace Eugene, 1870– . I. Zabriskie, Alexander Clinton, 1898– , ed. II. Protestant Episcopal theological seminary in Virginia, Alexandria, Va. III. Title. IV. Ser.
N. Y. P. L. January 5, 1945

ZEE

The **church** through half a century; essays in honor of William Adams Brown, by former students, John Coleman Bennett, Julius Seelye Bixler, B. Harvie Branscomb ₍and others₎ ... editors, Samuel McCrea Cavert, Henry Pitney Van Dusen. New York, London, C. Scribner's sons, 1936.
xii p., 3 l., 5–426 p. incl. front. (port.) 22½cm.
"References" at end of most of the chapters.
CONTENTS.—William Adams Brown: servant of the church of Christ, by S. M. Cavert.—Doctor Brown's contribution to the literature of religion, by A. C. McGiffert, jr.—The liberal movement in theology, by H. P. Van Dusen.—Science and theology, by W. M. Horton.—The social interpretation of Christianity, by J. C. Bennett.—Continental European theology, by H. E. Brunner, translated by Olive D. Doggett.—The philosophy of religion, by J. S. Bixler.—The study and interpretation of
(Continued on next card)
36–13441
₍7–5₎

The **church** through half a century ... 1936. (Card 2)
CONTENTS—Continued.
the Bible, by B. H. Branscomb.—Public worship, by H. S. Coffin.—Protestant preaching, by C. W. Gilkey.—Christian education, by Adelaide T. Case.—Theological education, by M. A. May.—The church's mission at home, by H. N. Morse.—The church and the community, by E. B. Chaffee.—The church and society, by P. P. Elliott.—The world task of the church, by D. J. Fleming.—Christian unity in America, by S. M. Cavert.—Ecumenical Christianity, by H. S. Leiper.—The writings of William Adams Brown, prepared by Maude M. Dolan (p. 395–406).—Chronology, William Adams Brown.—Contributors to this volume.
1. Brown, William Adams, 1865– 2. Church history—Modern period. 3. Christianity—20th cent. 4. U. S.—Church history. 5. Protestant churches—U. S. I. Cavert, Samuel McCrea, 1888– ed. II. Van Dusen, Henry Pitney, 1897– joint ed. III. Bennett, John Coleman, 1902–
36–13441
Library of Congress BR525.C5
Copyright A 96085 ₍7–5₎ 204

---

*QP

Cieniom Juliusza Słowackiego rycerza napowietrznej walki która się o narodowość naszą toczy uczniowie Wszechnicy lwowskiej. [Lwów, Gubrinowicz i syn, 1909] iv, 291 p. illus. 21cm.

Various contributors.
"Wydaniem kierował Stanisław Wasylewski."

464031B. 1. Słowacki, Juliusz, 1809-1849.
I. Wasylewski, Stanisław, 1885- , ed.
NN OC, I PC, 1, I SL S, 1, I (LC1, Z1, X1)

---

*QYN

ČIKAGAS BALTU FILOLOGU KOPA.
In honorem Endzelini. [Čikāgas baltu filologu kopas uzdevumā sakopojuši un rediģējuši E. Hauzenberga-Šturma] Chicago, 1960. 164 p. port., facsims. 25cm.

Foreword in Lettish and German.
Contributions in Lettish or German.
"Verzeichnis der Schriften J. Endzelins, zusammengestellt von B. Jēgers," p. [1]-24.

(Continued)
NN 11.60 s/X (OC) I, II OS PC, 1, 2, 3, I, II SL S, 1, 2, 3, I, II (LCE1, LC1, X1, Z1)

2

ČIKAGAS BALTU FILOLOGU KOPA. In honorem Endzelini. (Card 2)

1. Lettish language--Addresses, essays, lectures. 2. Baltic languages--Addresses, essays, lectures. 3. Endzelīns, Jānis, 1873- I. Hauzenberga-Šturma, Edite, 1901- , ed. II. Title.

---

*C

Cimbria; Beiträge zur Geschichte, Altertumskunde, Kunst und Erziehungslehre. Festschrift der phil.-hist. Verbindung Cimbria Heidelberg zu ihrem 50jährigen Bestehen. Dortmund: F. W. Ruhfus, 1926. viii, 226 p. illus., plates. 8°.

Contains bibliographies.

Contents: Schumacher, K. Urheidelberg. Gropengiesser, H. Zum Landschaftsbild am unteren Neckar in vor- und frühgeschichtlicher Zeit. Schuchhardt, C. Neue kelto-germanische Fragen. Hölk, C. Erinnerungen an Erwin Rohde. Stern, J. Eleusis. Hausrath, A. Kleinigkeiten zur griechischen Volkserzählung. Pfister, F. Der Wahnsinn des Weihepriesters. Bilabel, F. Ägyptische Thron-

(Continued)

N. Y. P. L. September 9, 1927

Cimbria; Beiträge zur Geschichte, Altertumskunde, Kunst und Erziehungslehre. (Continued)

besteigungsurkunden. Wattendorf, G. Die griechischen Altersbezeichnungen μεῖραξ und μειράχιον. Kramer, O., translator. Aus den Rittern des Aristophanes. Trenkel, P. Integer vitae. Hünnerkopf, R. Germanischer Totenglaube in heidnischer und christlicher Zeit. Hirsch, E. Glocke als Wetterzauber beim Friedberger Judenbad von 1260. Müller, O. A. Vom Wesen der Volkssage. Meisinger, O. St. Gertrud und Gertrudenminne. Schuhmacher, W. Volkslied und Soldatenlied. Stein, C. Zu Goethes Ballade "Die Braut von Korinth." Meisinger, O. Ein kleiner Hebelfund. Haas, H. Zur Weltanschauung Hans Thomas. Schatz, J. Antikes Gut in Hugo von Hofmannsthals "Tor und Tod." Höss, W.

(Continued)

N. Y. P. L. September 9, 1927

Cimbria; Beiträge zur Geschichte, Altertumskunde, Kunst und Erziehungslehre. (Continued)

Wandertage in Tirol und in der Südmark. Brandt, P. Eine Szene der Ilias von Genelli. Poppen, H. Alexanders Greifenfahrt am Freiburger Münster und die mittelalterlichen Kunsttypen der Alexanderfahrt. Weber, P. Die Burgen Thüringens. Löhr, A. v. Die Bedeutung der Numismatik als Sammeltätigkeit und wissenschaftliche Forschung. Marx, A. Senecas Apokolokyntosis im Unterricht. Reitz, E. Der Übergang von der Grundschule in die Höhere Schule. Müller, J. Die Bedeutung der Schülerheime. Bernays, U. Jugendbewegung und Romantik.

306163A. 1. No subject. 2. Heidelberg. Universitaet. Philologisch-historische Verbindung Cimbria.
N. Y. P. L. September 9, 1927

E-10
2555

Le CINQ-CENTIEME anniversaire de la prise de Constantinople, 1453-1953. Athènes, 1953. 287 p. illus., facsim. 25cm.

"L'Hellenisme contemporain, 2ème série, 7ème année, fasicule hors série."

CONTENTS. —La prise de Constantinople, par C. Amantos. —La prise de Constantinople selon les sources turques, par N. Moschopoulos. —Constantin Paléologue, le dernier défenseur de Constantinople, par G. Kolias. —Répercussion immédiate de la prise de Constantinople, par N. Tomadakis. —La prise de Constantinople et la fin du moyen age; La prise (Continued)

NN 5.57 c/B OC (OS)I PC, 1, 2, I SL (LCI, XI, Z1)

Le CINQ-CENTIEME anniversaire de la prise de Constantinople... (Card 2)

de Constantinople, tournant dans la politique et l'économie européennes, par D. Zakythinos. —Orientations idéologiques et politiques avant et après la chute de Constantinople, par G. Zoras. —La prise de Constantinople dans la poésie et la tradition populaires, par G. Megas. —La relation des Grecs asservis avec l'État musulman souverain, par N. Vlachos. —Les Grecs au service de l'empire ottoman, par P. A. Argyropoulos. —L'architecture religieuse en Grèce pendant la domination turque, par A. Orlandos. —Contribution à l'étude de la peinture post-byzantine, par M. Chatzidakis. —L'administration communale des Grecs pendant la domination

(Continued)

Le CINQ-CENTIEME anniversaire de la prise de Constantinople... (Card 3)

turque, par J. Visvisis. —L'école, facteur de réveil national, par J. Stephanopoli. —Aspects de l'organisation économique des Grecs dans l'empire ottoman, par A. Hadjimichali. —La grande idée, par J. Voyatzidis.

1. Constantinople--Siege, 1453. 2. Turkey--Hist. I. L'Hellenisme contemporain.

BWD

Cinquant' anni di vita intellettuale italiana, 1896–1946; scritti in onore di Benedetto Croce per il suo ottantesimo anniversario, a cura di Carlo Antoni e Raffaele Mattioli. Napoli, Edizioni scientifiche italiane, 1950. 2 v. 23cm.

575015B. 1. Learning and scholarship—Italy. 2. Croce, Benedetto, 1866– . I. Antoni, Carlo, ed. II. Mattioli, Raffaele, ed.
N. Y. P. L. May 9, 1951

HWF

CLARK, ROBERT M., ed.

Canadian issues; essays in honour of Henry F. Angus. [Toronto] Published for the University of British Columbia by University of Toronto press [1961] xx, 371 p. illus., port. 24cm.

CONTENTS:--Administration and democracy, by H. F. Angus.--Constitutional trends and federalism, by J. A. Corry.--The speakership of the Canadian house of commons, by J. H. Aitchison.--The Senate of Canada-political conundrum, by J. N. Turner.--Canada and (Continued)

NN R 5.62 p/OC (OS)I PC, 1, 2, 3, I AH, 1, I E, 2, 3, I (LCI, XI, Z1)

CLARK, ROBERT M., ed. Canadian issues... (Card 2)

"colonialism" in the United nations, by F. H. Soward.--Neighbour to a giant, by E. W. McInnis.--Some problems of Canadian trading policy, by J. D. Gibson.--Changing trends in world trade, by J. J. Deutsch.--The Royal commission on dominion-provincial relations; the report in retrospect, by R. M. Burns.--Government policy and the public lands, by A. D. Scott.--Some contrasts and similarities in Canadian, American, and British procedures for the examination of monopolistic situations, by A. S. Whiteley.--Telephone rates in Canada, by A. W. Currie.--

(Continued)

CLARK, ROBERT M., ed. Canadian issues...
(Card 3)

The export of electricity from Canada, by A.E. Dal Grauer. --The shrinkage in the value of money, by J. A. Crumb. --Trade unions and inflation; United States and Canada, by S. M. Jamieson. --Some reflections on economic security for the aged in Canada, by R. M. Clark. --Bibliography of publications by Henry F. Angus (p. [367]-371)

1. Canada--Govt., 1914- 2. Economic history--Canada, 1945- 3. Angus, Henry Forbes, 1891- I. British Columbia university, Vancouver, B. C.

E-12
6732

CLASSEN, PETER, ed.
Festschrift Percy Ernst Schramm zu seinem siebzigsten Geburtstag von Schülern und Freunden zugeeignet. [Hrsg. von Peter Classen und Peter Scheibert] Wiesbaden, F. Steiner, 1964. 2 v. illus., map, port. 25cm.

In English, German, Italian or Spanish.

"Veröffentlichungen von Professor Dr. Percy Ernst Schram": v. 2, p. [291]-321.

Bibliographical footnotes.

1. History--Addresses, essays, lectures. 2. Schramm, Percy Ernst, 1894- I. Scheibert, Peter, 1915- joint ed.

NN *R 10.66 p/ OC, I PC, 1, 2, I SL (LC1, X1, Z1) [I]

[illegible]C

Classical essays presented to James A. Kleist, S. J. Edited with an introduction by Richard E. Arnold, S. J. ... [St. Louis] The Classical bulletin, Saint Louis university [1946]

5 p. l., ix-xx, 122 p. front. (port.) facsims. 22½cm.

CONTENTS.—The Greek happy warrior, by W. R. Agard.—Honor, Fides and Fortuna in Horace, by W. H. Alexander.—The peaceful conquest of Gaul, by N. J. De Witt.—Sancti Eusebii Hieronymi Vita Malchi monachi captivi, by C. C. Mierow.—The didactic significance of erotic figures in Plato, by Clyde Murley.—The church's debt to Homer, by J. A. Scott.—Virgil's Mezentius, by F. A. Sullivan.

1. Classical philology—Addresses, essays, lectures. 2. Kleist, James Aloysius, 1873- I. Arnold, Richard Eugene, 1908- ed.

46—6914

Library of Congress PA26.K5

[a46d2] 880.4

RBG

Classical and mediæval studies in honor of Edward Kennard Rand, presented upon the completion of his fortieth year of teaching, edited by Leslie Webber Jones. New York city, Pub. by the editor [c1938]

ix, 310 p. front. (port.) facsims. 26cm.

CONTENTS.—The authorship of 'Quid sit ceroma', by C. H. Beeson.—Elementarunterricht und probationes pennae in der ersten hälfte des mittelalters, von B. Bischoff.—Horace: the beginning of the silver age, by J. Bridge.—Zur geschichte der Stiftsbibliothek von st. Peter zu Basel, von A. Bruckner.—The scriptorium of Reims during the archbishopric of Hincmar, by F. M. Carey.—The verbal 'ornament' (κόσμος) in Aristotle's Art of poetry, by L. Cooper.—L'Histoire des Longobards, comment fut-elle conçue et achevée? par Olga Dobiaš-Roždestvenskaja.—Varied strains in Martial, by J. W. Duff.—Acetabulum, by A. Ernout.—

(Continued on next card)

38-9259

[5]

Classical and mediæval studies in honor of Edward Kennard Rand ... [c1938] (Card 2)

CONTENTS—Continued.

Plutarch and Appian on Tiberius Gracchus, by R. M. Geer.—Note on Georgics IV, 491-493, by W. C. Greene.—Curatores tabularum publicarum, by M. Hammond.—A Latin medical manuscript, by H. B. Hoffleit.—The library of St. Aubin's at Angers in the twelfth century, by L. W. Jones.—Astronomy in Lucretius, by H. J. Leon.—In domo Rinucii, by D. P. Lockwood.—A manuscript of Alcuin in the script of Tours, by E. A. Lowe.—Modon—a Venetian station in mediaeval Greece, by S. B. Luce.—The De syllogismis categoricis and Introductio ad Syllogismos categoricos of Boethius, by A. P. McKinlay.—Tre dettati universitari dell' umanista Martino Filetico sopra Persio, Giovenale ed Orazio, di

(Continued on next card)

38-9259

[5]

Classical and mediæval studies in honor of Edward Kennard Rand ... [c1938] (Card 3)

CONTENTS—Continued.

Giovanni card. Mercati.—Da Prato's Saibantianus of Sulpicius Severus and its humanistic connections, by B. M. Peebles.—A magical text from Beroea in Macedonia, by D. M. Robinson.—The Eastern question in Lucan's Bellum ciuile, by Eva M. Sanford.—An old Irish version of Laodamia and Protesilaus, by J. J. Savage.—Abbreviations in clm. 6272 from Freising abbey, by A. Souter.—Ennodius and Pope Symmachus. Part I by W. T. Townsend; part II by W. F. Wyatt.—L'odyssée du manuscrit de San Pietro qui renferme les œuvres de saint Hilaire, par dom A. Wilmart.

1. Rand, Edward Kennard, 1871- 2. Classical philology—Collections. 3. Middle ages. I. Jones, Leslie Webber, 1900- ed.

38-9259

Library of Congress PA26.R3

[5] 480.4

F-10
7731

CLASSIFICATION RESEARCH GROUP.
The Sayers memorial volume; essays in librarianship in memory of William Charles Berwick Sayers. Edited by D.J. Foskett and B. I. Palmer for the Classification research group (London). London, Library association, 1961. 218 p. illus. 26cm.

Includes bibliographies.

(Continued)

NN R 5.63 f/ (OC)I, III OS, II PC, 1, 2, I, II, III SL (LC1, X1, Z1)

3

CLASSIFICATION RESEARCH GROUP. The Sayers memorial volume... (Card 2)

CONTENTS. --Sayers, by J.D. Stewart. --W.C. Berwick Sayers and children's libraries, by E. Colwell. --W.C. Berwick Sayers: his connection with the National central library and his contribution to library cooperation, by S.P.L. Filon. --The Library association in the twentieth century: selected aspects, by W.A. Munford. --"... Not for trafficking alone..." by R. Stokes. --Student and tutor, by R. Staveley. --Library classification on the march, by S.R. Ranganathan. --Points de vue retrospectiv et prospectif dans la classification, by E. de Grolier.

(Continued)

CLASSIFICATION RESEARCH GROUP. The Sayers memorial volume... (Card 3)

--Fundamental fallacies and new needs in classification, by J. Farradane. --Classification and integrative levels, by D. J. Foskett. --The classification of chemical substances; an historical survey, by B.C. Vickery. --Automation without fear, by J.H. Shera. --Classification and book-indexing, by D. Langridge. --Classification in the school curriculum, by B. Kyle. --Classification as a foundation study for librarians, by B. I. Palmer.

1. Sayers, William Charles Berwick, 1881-1960. 2. Libraries--Addresses, essays, lectures. I. Palmer, Bernard Ira, 1910- , ed. II. Library association. III. Foskett, Douglas John, ed.

G-10
2566

CLAUS, MARTIN, 1912- , ed.
Studien zur europäischen Vor- und Frühgeschichte. Hrsg. von Martin Claus, Werner Haarnagel [und] Klaus Raddatz. Neumünster, K. Wachholtz, 1968. 438 p. illus., 29 plates, maps. 31cm.

Festschrift for Herbert Jankuhn.
Includes bibliographies.

1. Jankuhn, Herbert. 2. Europe--Archaeology--Addresses, essays, lectures. I. Haarnagel, Werner, joint ed. II. Raddatz, Klaus, joint ed.

NN R 5.69 k/ OC, I, II PC, 1, 2, I, II SL (LC1, X1, Z1)

MDTT

CLAUSEN, ERNST, ed.
Billedet i bogen. [København] Grafisk cirkel, 1961. 201 p. illus. (part col.) 29cm. (Grafisk cirkel, Copenhagen. Publikation. nr. 100)

"Udgivet af Grafisk cirkel... i anledning af 25-års jubilaeet, februar 1961."
"300 eksemplarer er stillet til rådighed for boghandelen."
Bio-bibliography, p. 195-201.

1. Illustration of books, Danish, 20th cent. 2. Artists, Danish. I. Grafisk cirkel, Copenhagen.

NN R 5.62 e/ OC (OS)I PC, 1, 2, I SL A, 2, I PR, 1 RC, 2 (LC1, X1, Z1)

E-13
3798

Clauss, Herbert, ed.
Das Erzgebirge. Land und Leute. Hrsg. von Herbert Clauss. Unter Mitwirkung von zahlreichen Heimatforschern und Volkskundlern. Frankfurt (a. M.) Weidlich (1967).
307 p. with 63 illus. 24 cm.

"Erich Neubert zum 70. Geburtstag."

(Continued)

NN • R 12.68 1/ OC, Ib* PC, 1 SL (LC1, X1, Z1)

CLAUSS, HERBERT, ed. Das Erzgebirge. (Card 2)

Bibliography: p. 275-284.

1. Erzgebirge--Civilization. I. Clauss, Herbert.

E-12
8734

Claussen, Carsten Peter, *ed.*
Neue Perspektiven aus Wirtschaft und Recht. Festschrift für Hans Schäffer zum 80. Geburtstag am 11. April 1966. Mit Beiträgen von Hermann J. Abs [u. a.] ... Berlin, Duncker u. Homblot (1966)
536 p., 1 front. 24 cm.

1. Economics--Essays and misc. 2. Law--Addresses, essays, lectures. 3. Schäffer, Hans. I. Claussen, Carsten Peter. II. Abs, Hermann J. III. Title.

NN*R 4.67 a/ OC, Ib*, II, III PC, 1, 2, 3, II, III SL (LC1, X1, Z1)

M-10
6140
v.93

CLAVAL, PAUL.
Pour le cinquantenaire de la mort de Paul Vidal de la Blache; etudes d'histoire de la géographie par Paul Claval [et] Jean-Pierre Nardy. Paris, Les Belles lettres, 1968. 130 p. 24cm. (Besançon, France. Université. Annales littéraires. [sér. 2] v. 93)

Cahiers de géographie de Besançon, 16.
Includes bibliographies.

1. Geography--Hist. 2. Levasseur, Émile, 1828-1911. 3. Vidal de La Blache, Paul Marie Joseph 1845-1918. I. Series. II. Nardy, Jean-Pierre.

NN 1.69 d/ OC, II, IIbo (OS)I PC, I, 2, 3, I, II (LC1, X1, Z1)

YFH

The CLEAVAGE in our culture; studies in scientific humanism in honor of Max Otto. Ed. by Frederick Burkhardt. Boston, Beacon press [1952] ix, 201 p. port. 22cm.

CONTENTS.—The cleavage in our culture, by B. H. Bode.—Modern philosophy, by John Dewey.—Of truth, by H. M. Kallen.—Social philosophy: its method and purpose, by E. C. Lindeman.—Postulational methods in the social sciences, by Arnold Dresden.—Social planning, by H. S. Fries.—Toward an integrated ethics, by G. R. Geiger.—A biosocial approach to ethics, by Norman Cameron.—Religion down to earth, by A. E. Haydon.—The education of

(Continued)

NN*R 2.53 OC, I PC, 1, 2, I SL (LC1, Z1, X1)

The CLEAVAGE in our culture... (Card 2)

individuals, by Harold Taylor.—The integration of industrial society, by C. E. Ayres.—Max Otto: a biographical note, by G. C. Sellery.

1. Humanism, 20th cent. 2. Otto, Max Carl, 1876- . I. Burkhardt, Frederick Henry, 1912-

PSR

CLEMENTS, THOMAS, 1898- , ed.
Essays in marine geology in honor of K. O. Emery. Thomas Clements, ed., Robert E Stevenson and Dorothy M. Halmos, associate ed. Los Angeles, University of Southern California press, 1963. 201 p. illus., port. 25cm.

CONTENTS.--Dr. Kenneth Orris Emery, by T. Clements.--Published

(Continued)

NN R 12.63 e/ OC PC, 1, 2, 3 SL ST, 1t, 2t, 3 (LC1, X1, Z1)

3

CLEMENTS, THOMAS, 1898- , ed. Essays in marine geology in honor of K.O. Emery. (Card 2)

reports of K.O. Emery.--Thirty five thousand years of sea level, by F.P. Shepard.--Coastal erosion, northern Oregon, by J.V. Byrne.--Pleistocene history of Lake Chapola, Jalisco, Mexico, by T. Clements.--New evidence for a 40-foot shore line on Oahu, by W.H. Easton.--Oceanography of Apalachicola bay, Florida, by D.S. Gorsline.--Glauconite from the sea floor off southern California, by W.L. Pratt.--Size relationships of Eggerella advena to sediment and depth of substratum, by J.M. Resig.--

(Continued)

CLEMENTS, THOMAS, 1898- , ed. Essays in marine geology in honor of K.O. Emery. (Card 3)

Origin of adobe clays in the southwestern portion of the Los Angeles basin, by J.F. Riccio.--The summer fogs along the Yorkshire coast, England, by R. E. Stevenson.--Sediments of the Palos Verdes shelf, by E. Uchupi and R. Gaal.--Sediments of the Mainland shelf near Santa Barbara, California, by S. Wimberly.

1. Coasts. 2. Ocean bottom. 3. Emery, K.O. t. 1963.

NCB

Clifford, James Lowry, 1901- *ed.*
Pope and his contemporaries, essays presented to George Sherburn. Edited by James L. Clifford and Louis A. Landa. Oxford, Clarendon Press, 1949.
viii, 278 p. port. 23 cm.
"A list of the writings of George Sherburn": p. ⸢260⸣-262.

1. English literature—18th cent.—Hist. & crit. 2. Sherburn, George Wiley, 1884- I. Landa, Louis A., 1902- joint ed.

PR442.C6 820.4 50-2790

Library of Congress ⸢12⸣

E-10
2405

Club alpino italiano. Sezione di Modena.
In memoria di Fernando Malavolti; a cura del Comitato scientifico "F. Malavolti" della Sezione di Modena del Club alpino italiano. Modena, Società tip. editrice modense ⸢1956⸣ 145 p. illus., col. port., maps. 25cm.
Includes bibliographies.
CONTENTS.—Ricordo di Fernando Malavolti, di P. Graziosi.—Appunti sulla cuspide silicea di freccia eneolitica nella Valle Padana, di P. Barocelli.—Manufatti litici di tipo clactoniano del Preappennino emiliano e del promontorio Garganico, di R. Battaglia.—Vicende floristiche del pleistocene italiano in base ai reperti di macro e microfossili, di D. Bertolani-Marchetti.—Due ceramiche protostoriche del museo di Varese, di M. Bertolone.—Un amigdaloide del paleolitico inferiore rinvenuto nel torrente Nevola (Marche),
(Continued)

NN R 3.58 (OC)1bo OS(1b+) PC,1,2 SL (LC1,X1,Z1,Y1)

Club alpino italiano. Sezione de Modena. In memoria di Fernando Malavolti... (Card 2)

di C. Maviglia.—Come si è formato il Lago Maggiore (e gli altri laghi prealpini lombardi), di G. Nangeroni.—L'isola di Lagosta nella preistoria, di A. M. Radmilli.—Situla di bronzo di Valeggio sul Mincio, di F. Rittatore.—Ricerche sullo stato attuale della "Terramara" di Gorzano (Modena), di P. Severi.—I vasi a bocca quadrata dei livelli superiori del deposito quaternario di Quinzano veronese, di F. Zorzi.

1. Malavolti, Fernando. 2. Italy —Archaeology.

L-10
1575

COBURG mitten im Reich; Festgabe zum 900. Gedenkjahr der ersten Erwähnung der Ur-Coburg und ihres Umlandes; im Auftrag der Gesellschaft für Coburger Heimatkunde und Landesgeschichte hrsg. von Friedrich Schilling. Kallmünz, Opf., M. Lassleben, 1956-61. 2 v. illus. (part fold.), ports., maps (part col., part fold.) 25cm.

Includes bibliographies.
(Continued)

NN R 10.62 e/OCs, Is (OS)IIs PCs, 1s, Is, IIs SLs (LC1s, X1s, Z1s)

COBURG mitten im Reich... (Card 2)

1. Coburg, Germany. I. Schilling, Friedrich, historian, ed. II. Gesellschaft für Coburger Heimatkunde und Landesgeschichte.

---

* PWZ
(Marx)

Cohen, Boaz, 1899-
Professor Alexander Marx; a tribute upon his semi-centennial and a bibliography of his writings, by Boaz Cohen... New York, 1928. 16 p. illus. (port.) 23½cm.
"Reprinted from the United synagogue recorder, vol. VIII, no. 1."
"Bibliography of the works of Professor Alexander Marx," p. 9-16.

WILBERFORCE EAMES COLL.

105291B. 1. Marx, Alexander, 1870- —Bibliography. 2. Marx, Alexander, 1870-
N. Y. P. L. May 28, 1941

NPX

COLEGIO NACIONAL, Mexico.
La obra de Enrique Gonzalez Martinez. Estudios prologados por Antonio Castro Leal y reunidos por Jose Luis Martinez. Se publican con motivo del octogésimo aniversario del poeta. Homenaje del Colegio nacional a su miembro fundador. Mexico, Edicion del Colegio nacional, 1951.
xv, 286 p. port. 24cm.

"Bibliografia," p. xiii-xv.

1. González Martínez, Enrique, 1871- . I. Martínez, José Luis, ed. II. Title.

NN (OC), I, II OS PC, 1, I, II SL (LC1, Z1, X1)

AN
(Coleridge, S.)

Coleridge; studies by several hands on the hundredth anniversary of his death, edited by Edmund Blunden and Earl Leslie Griggs... London: Constable & Co. Ltd., 1934. viii, 243 p. front. (port.) 22½cm.

CONTENTS.—Biographical notes, being chapters of E. H. Coleridge's unpublished life of Coleridge, contributed by G. H. B. Coleridge.—Coleridge and Christ's Hospital, by E. Blunden.—Wordsworth, Coleridge, and the spy, by A. J. Eagleston.—Some contemporary allusions to Coleridge's death, by E. J. Morley.—A note on some early editions of Coleridge, by C. H. Wilkinson.—Coleridge the commentator, by J. L. Haney.—Gems of purest ray, by G. M. Harper.—The political thought of Coleridge, by H. Beeley.—Metaphysician or mystic? By J. H. Muirhead.—American comments on Coleridge a century ago, by A. D. Snyder.—The death of Coleridge ⸢by⸣ Mrs. H. N. Coleridge.

741773A. 1. Coleridge, Samuel Taylor, 1772-1834. I. Blunden, Edmund Charles, 1896- , ed. II. Griggs, Earl Leslie, ed.
N. Y. P. L. April 8, 1936

OLA

A Collection of papers in memory of Sir William Rowan Hamilton. New York, N. Y., Scripta mathematica, Yeshiva college, 1945.
82 p. illus. (facsims.) pl., port., diagr. 25½cm. (The Scripta mathematica studies, no. 2)
"References" at end of two papers.
CONTENTS.—Sir William Rowan Hamilton, by D. E. Smith.—The life and early work of Sir William Rowan Hamilton, by J. L. Synge.—Algebra's debt to Hamilton, by C. C. MacDuffee.—An elementary presentation of the theory of quaternions, by F. D. Murnaghan.—Two poems by Hamilton.—Hamilton's work in dynamics and its influence on modern thought, by H. Bateman.—Hamilton's contribution to mechanics, by E. B. Wilson.—The constancy of the velocity of light, by Vladimir Karapetoff.—The Hamilton postage stamp ⸢an announcement by the Irish minister of posts and telegraphs⸣
1. Hamilton, Sir William Rowan, 1805-1865. 2. Mathematics—Collections.

QA3.H27 510.4 46-22956

Library of Congress ⸢3⸣

E-12
7817

Collegium Philosophicum; Studien Joachim Ritter zum 60. Geburtstag, von Ernst-Wolfgang Böckenförde ⸢et al.⸣ Basel, Schwabe ⸢1965⸣
437 p. port. 25 cm.
Bibliographical footnotes.
CONTENTS.—Die Historische Rechtsschule und das Problem der Geschichtlichkeit des Rechts, von E.-W. Böckenförde.—Oblomowerei und Philosophie in Russland, von W. Goerdt.—Entstehungsgeschichtliche Voraussetzungen für Yorcks Frühschrift, von K. Gründer.—The
(Continued)

NN R 8.67 p/OC, I, II PC, 1, 2, 3, I, II SL (LC1, X1, Z1)

Collegium Philosophicum ... ,1965, (Card 2)

universe is more various, more Hegelian; zum Weltverständnis bei Hegel und Whitehead, von F. Kambartel.—Offene und verdeckte Urteilsgründe; zum Verhältnis von Philosophie und Jurisprudenz heute, von M. Kriele. — Zur Theorie der Entscheidung, von H. Lubbe. —

Glaube und Weltbild in der urchristlichen Überlieferung von Höllen- und Himmelfahrt Jesu, von U. Luck.—Der betrogene Deus iratus in Schillers Drama "Luise Millerin," von W. Malsch.—Zur Geschichte des philosophischen Begriffs "Anthropologie" seit dem Ende des 18. Jahrhunderts, von O. Marquard.—Zur Wirkungsgeschichte der platonischen Anamnesislehre, von L. Oeing-Hanhoff.—Lessing und Hamann; Prolegomena zu einem künftigen Gespräch, von W. Oelmüller—Aufklärung und Offenbarungsglaube, von G. Rohrmoser.—Zum Prob-

(Continued)

Collegium Philosophicum ... ,1965, (Card 3)

lem der Kontingenz bei Leibniz: die beste der möglichen Welten, von H. Schepers.—Aufklärung und Dramaturgie bei Lessing und Brecht, von H. J. Schrimpf.—Natürliche Existenz und politische Existenz bei Rousseau, von R. Spaemann.—Zum Verhältnis von Wissenschaft und Wahrheit, von E. Tugendhat.—Montesquieu in Deutschland; zur

Geschichte seiner Wirkung als politischer Schriftsteller im 18. Jahrhundert, von R. Vierhaus.

1. Ritter, Joachim, 1903- . 2. Philosophy—Addresses, essays, lectures. 3. German literatures. I. Böckenförde Ernst Wolfgang II. Title: Studien Joachim Ritter zum 60. Geburtstag.

---

*YIG
+

Colligere fragmenta; Festschrift Alban Dold zum 70. Geburtstag am 7.7.1952, hrsg. von Bonifatius Fischer und Virgil Fiala. Beuron in Hohenzollern, Beuroner Kunstverlag, 1952. xx,295 p. port., facsims.(part. col.) 31cm. (Beuron, Germany (Benedictine Abbey). Texte und Arbeiten. Abt. I. Beiheft 2)

Contributions by various authors in German,

(Continued)

NN** 5.54 OC,II,IIb, 3,I,II,III SL (U 1, III,IIIb (OS)I PC,1,2, LC1,~~Z1~~,X1)

Colligere fragmenta... (Card 2)

French, Italian or Catalan.
"Bibliographie von Alban Dold," p.[ix]-xx.

1. Dold, Alban, father, 1882- . 2. Bible—Essays and misc. 3. Christianity—Essays and misc. I. Series. II. Fischer, Bonifatius, father, ed. III. Fiala, Virgil, father, ed.

---

*ITE

Collin, Ernst, 1886-
Paul Kersten, von Ernst Collin. Berlin: Corvinus-Antiquariat E. Collin G.m.b.H.,1925. 81 p. (incl.plates.) front. (port.) 25cm.

679279A. 1. Kersten, Paul, 1865- . 2. Bookbinding. I. Jakob Krausse-Bund.

Festschrift

---

*OO

COLLINDER, BJÖRN, 1894-
Sprachverwandschaft und Wahrscheinlichkeit. ausgewählte Schriften neu veröffentlicht zum 70-. Geburtstag des Verfassers, 22. Juli 1964, zusammen mit einer Bibliographie der Werke von Björn Collinder, 1921-1964. Uppsala, 1964. 240 p. port. 25cm. (Acta Universitatis upsaliensis. Studia uralica et altaica upsaliensia. 1).

Papers in German or French.
Includes bibliographies.

1. Ural-Altaic languages. I. Series.
NN R 7.65 s/ OC (OS)I PC, 1, I SL O, 1, I &, 1, I (LC1, X1, Z1)

3-MCO
W15.C7

COLMAR, France. Musée d'Unterlinden.
Hommage à Charles Walch, 1898-1948. [Exposition] juillet-septembre 1968. [Colmar, Société Schongauer de Colmar, 1968] 53 p. illus. (part col.), port. 29cm.

Bibliography: p. 52-53.

1. Walch, Charles, 1898-1948. I. Title.
NN 11.71 m/ (OC)I OS PC,1,I SL A,1,I (LC1, X1, Z1) B

NAC p.v.435

Cologne. Universität. Deutsch-niederländisches Institut.
Joost van den Vondel, geboren zu Köln am 17 November 1587, gestorben zu Amsterdam am 5 Februar 1679. Festschrift zum 350 jährigen Geburtstag des Dichters. Jena: E. Diederichs [1937] 86 p. facsim., plates, ports. 22½cm. (Halftitle: Schriften des Deutsch-niederländischen Instituts, Köln. Heft 3.)

Published on occasion of the exhibition sponsored by the Deutsch-niederländische Gesellschaft, the city of Cologne, the Deutsch-niederländisches Institut an der Universität Köln, and the Wallraf-Richartz-Museum.

(Continued)

N. Y. P. L. Festschrift December 28, 1938

Cologne. Universität. Deutsch-niederländisches Institut. Joost van den Vondel... (Card 2)

"Katalog" of the exhibition, p. [61]-86, has special t.-p.: Der holländische Nationaldichter Joost van den Vondel und seine Welt...

CONTENTS.—Ehrenausschüsse der Vondel-Gedenkfeier.—Helffrich, E. Geleitwort.—Scholte, J. H. Hollands grösster Dichter.—Petri, Franz. Köln und die niederländischen Flüchtlinge.—Noordegraaf, W. G. Vondel und Köln.—Hechtle, M. Joost van den Vondel; sein Einfluss auf das deutsche Geistesleben.—May, H. Joost van den Vondel im Spiegel von Hollands Kunst und Kultur.—Katalog der Ausstellung.

960840A. 1. Vondel, Joost van den, 1587–1679. 2. German literature—Foreign influence on, Dutch. 3. Dutch literature—Foreign influence of. I. Cologne. II. Cologne. Wallraf-Richartz Museum der Stadt Köln. III. Deutsch-niederländische Gesellschaft, Cologne. IV. Title. V. Ser.
N. Y. P. L. December 28, 1938

E-11
3398

COLOGNE. Universität. Institut für Verkehrswissenschaft.
Der Verkehr in der wirtschaftlichen Entwicklung des Industriezeitalters. Festschrift zum 40-jährigen Jubiläum des Instituts für Verkehrswissenschaft an der Universität Köln. Hrsg. von Paul Berkenkopf. Düsseldorf, Verlag Handelsblatt, 1961. 203 p. diagrs., tables. 25cm.

Bibliographical footnotes.

(Continued)

NN R 10.61 a/ (OC)I OS PC, 1, I SL E, 1, I (LC1, X1, Z1)

3

COLOGNE. Universität. Institut für Verkehrswissenschaft. Der Verkehr in der wirtschaftlichen Entwicklung des Industriezeitalters. (Card 2)

CONTENTS. —Verkehrspolitik und Wirtschaftspolitik, von P. Berenkopf. —Wirtschaftssysteme und Verkehr, von A.-F. Napp.-Zinn. —Staatliche und private Unternehmung im Verkehr, von O. Most. —Der Staat und seine Eisenbahn, von Th. Kittel. —Industrialisierung und Weltverkehr, von A. Predöhl. —Die Entwicklung des Personenverkehrs der Eisenbahnen, von F. Niessen. —Die grosse Mengenstaffel und die Intensitätsstaffel als wichtigste Mittel zur Herbeiführung einer optimalen Aufgabenteilung im Verkehr, von P. Schulz-Kiesow. —Wasser- strassen- und Binnenhäfen-

(Continued)

COLOGNE. Universität. Institut für Verkehrswissenschaft. Der Verkehr in der wirtschaftlichen Entwicklung des Industriezeitalters. (Card 3)

Baupolitik, von W. Böttger. —Städtebau, Stadtverkehr, von E. Frohne. —Voraussetzungen für eine erfolgreiche Verkehrsplanung in den Städten, von J. Schlums. —Verkehrswirtschaftliche Fragen des Nahluftverkehrs, von W. Lambert. —Der moderne Nachrichtenverkehr als Mittel wirtschaftlicher Integration, von J. Lennertz. —Die Schweiz geht den Weg von der vertraglich gebundenen zur freien Konkurrenz im Güterverkehr auf Schiene und Strasse, von H.-R. Meyer.

1. Transportation--Social and economic relations. I. Berkenkopf, Paul, ed.

XAD

Cologne. Universität. *Rechtswissenschaftliche fakultät.*
Festschrift für Heinrich Lehmann zum sechzigsten geburtstag 20. juli 1936. Herausgegeben von der Kölner Rechtswissenschaftlichen fakultät. Berlin, Weidmannsche verlagsbuchhandlung, 1937.

4 p. l., 346 p. illus. (map) port. 24½cm.

Bibliographical foot-notes.

CONTENTS.—**Rechtsmethode und rechtserneuerung:** Coenders, Albert. Begriff und wirklichkeit in der rechtswissenschaft. Fehr, Hans. Die fortschritte des dynamischen rechts.—**Verfassungsrecht:** Freisler, Roland. Rationale staatsverfassung des liberalismus—völkische lebensordnung des nationalsozialismus.—**Rechtsgeschichte:** Planitz, Hans. Die schar-

(Continued on next card)

A C 37-3064

[2]

Cologne. Universität. *Rechtswissenschaftliche fakultät.*
Festschrift für Heinrich Lehmann ... 1937. (Card 2)

CONTENTS—Continued.

mannen von Prüm; ein beitrag zur wehrverfassung des mittelalters. Bohne, Gotthold. Die Magna charta von 1215 und das strafgesetzliche analogieverbot.—**Bürgerliches recht:** Blomeyer, Karl. Zur lehre von den rechten des einzelnen. Stoll, Heinrich. Der missbrauch der vertretungsmacht. Müller-Erzbach, Rudolf. Die interessen- und die machtlage beim kauf und deren haupteinwirkungen auf die rechtsgestaltung. Raape, Leo. Probleme der wandelung und minderung. Schmidt, Rudolf. Der ort der unerlaubten handlung im internationalen privatrecht.—**Handels- und wirtschaftsrecht:** Hedemann, J. W. Vom industrierecht zum wirtschaftsrecht. Gieseke, Paul. Alte und neue fragen aus dem industrierecht. Reinhardt, Rudolf. Der gerechte preis, ein bestandteil

(Continued on next card)

A C 37-3064

[2]

Cologne. Universität. *Rechtswissenschaftliche fakultät.*
Festschrift für Heinrich Lehmann ... 1937. (Card 3)

CONTENTS—Continued.

unserer rechtsordnung? Hueck, Alfred. Die stille beteiligung an handelsgesellschaften.—**Arbeitsrecht:** Nipperdey, H. C. Mindestbedingungen und günstigere arbeitsbedingungen nach dem arbeitsordnungsgesetz (ordnungsprinzip und leistungsprinzip) Dietz, Rolf. Der verdrängende stellvertreter des betriebsführers. Nikisch, Arthur. Vom arbeitsverhältnis.—**Strafrecht:** Gerland, Heinrich. Einige bemerkungen zum ehrenschutz im geltenden und künftigen strafrecht.—**Prozessrecht:** Schmidt, Richard. Prioritätsprinzip oder ausgleichsprinzip im künftigen deutschen vollstreckungsrecht.—Verzeichnis der schriften von Heinrich Lehmann (p. [343]-346)

1. Lehmann, Heinrich, 1876- 2. Law—Philosophy. 3. Law—Addresses, essays, lectures. I. Title.

A C 37-3064

New York. Public library
for Library of Congress

[2]

Write on slip only words underlined and classmark:

RGA

Colombia. Instituto Caro y Cuervo.
...Estudios de filología e historia literaria; homenaje al R. P. Félix Restrepo... Bogotá [1950] xii, 581 p. illus. 25cm. (Its: Boletin. Tomo 5, 1949.)

"Bibliografía," p. [481]-548.

CONTENTS.—Hatzfeld, Helmut. Ecclesiastical terms in Rumanian and their semantic implications.—Rosenblat, Angel. Vacilaciones y cambios de género motivados por el artículo.—Migliorini, Bruno. La metafora reciproca.—Tovar, Antonio. Semántica y etimología en el guaraní.—Bolinger, D. L. The sign is not arbitrary.—Ors, Alvaro d'. Papeletas semánticas.—Peruzzi, Emilio. Importanza e metodo dell' ermeneutica minoica.—Oroz, Rodolfo. Metáforas relativas a las partes del cuerpo humano

(Continued)

NN

Colombia. Instituto Caro y Cuervo. ...Estudios de filología e historia literaria; homenaje al R. P. Félix Restrepo... (Card 2)

en la lengua popular chilena.—González de la Calle, P. U. Advertencias al margen de una etimología griega de una palabra castellana.—Grases, Pedro. Locha, nombre de fracción monetaria en Venezuela.—Flórez, Luis. Cuestiones del español hablado en Montería y Sincelejo.—Padrón, A. F. Giros sintácticos usados en Cuba.—Robledo, Emilio. Orígenes castizos del habla popular de Antioquia y Caldas.—Selva, J. B. Sufijos americanos.—Malaret, Augusto. Antología de americanismos.—Ghisletti, L. V. Contribución a una semasiología nosológica.—Martínez, F. A. Un aspecto de la teoría estilística.—Bataillon, Marcel. Sur la genèse poétique du Cantique spirituel de Saint Jean de la Croix.—Blanco, M. G. Voces americanas en el teatro de Tirso de

(Continued)

NN

Colombia. Instituto Caro y Cuervo. ...Estudios de filología e historia literaria; homenaje al R. P. Félix Restrepo... (Card 3)

Molina.—Fugilla, J. G. Gil Polo y Sannazaro.—Peers, E. A. The religious verse of Pedro Espinosa.—Rubio, David. La fuente de La vida es sueño de Calderón.—Pellegrino, Michele. Di un manoscritto sconosciuto delle Confessioni.—Reyes, Alfonso. La nave de Demetrio Faléreo.—Espinosa, Pólit, Aurelio. La traducción como obra de arte. La métrica latinizante.—Leonard, I. A. Mateo Alemán en México.—Balaguer, Joaquín. Colón, precursor literario.—Hernández de Alba, Guillermo. José Celestino Mutis, poeta latino.—Restrepo, Roberto. Nuestro diccionario.—Forero, M. J. Hallarzo de un libro Jiménez de Quesada.—Rivas Sacconi, J. M. Una poesía de León XIII interpretada por Caro.—Grismer, R. L. Introduction to the classical influence on

(Continued)

NN

Colombia. Instituto Caro y Cuervo. ...Estudios de filología e historia literaria; homenaje al R. P. Félix Restrepo... (Card 4)

the literatures of Spain and Spanish America.—Ortega Torres, J. J. Cervantes en la literatura colombiana.—Kimsa, Antanas. Bibliografía del R. P. Félix Restrepo.—Restrepo, Félix. Explicación necesaria.—Flórez, Luis. Indice de materias y nombres propios.—Flórez, Luis. Indice de palabras.

1. Restrepo, Félix, 1887- 2. Philology—Addresses, essays, lectures.
NN

---

*C-5 p.v.98

Colonel Unni Nayar; commemoration volume, August 12, 1951. [Madras, P.A.S. press, 1951] 1 v. illus. 25cm.

Various contributors.

1. Nayar, Kesavan Unni, 1911-1950.

NN 12.52 OC PC,1 SL 0,1 (LC1,X1,X1)

Columbia university. Engineering, School of.
The School of engineering in commemoration of the seventy-fifth anniversary of the establishment of engineering education at Columbia university, 1864–1939. Edited by James Kip Finch... ₍New York₎ Columbia univ. press, 1940. 103 p. facsims., front., plates, tables. 25cm.

PARTIAL CONTENTS.—The anniversary lectures: "Strategic minerals".—Introduction, by C. K. Leith.—Antimony, by H. P. Henderson.—Chromium, by Enoch Perkins.—Manganese, by R. H. Sales.—Mercury, by C. S. Wehrly.—Nickel, by C. G. Fink.—Tin, by M. W. Tuthill.—Tungsten, by F. L. Hess.—Summary, by G. A. Roush.

Festschrift

1. Engineering—Education—U. S.—N. Y.—New York. 2. Engineering—Addresses, essays, lectures. I. Finch, James Kip, 1883– , ed.
N. Y. P. L. November 25, 1941

COLVIN, H.M., ed.
The country seat; studies in the history of the British country house, presented to Sir John Summerson on his sixty-fifth birthday, together with a select bibliography of his published writings. Edited by Howard Colvin and John Harris. [London] A. Lane, Penguin Press [1970] 295 p. 184 illus.(incl. plans) 28cm.

Continued

NN R 8.71 d/ OC, I, II PC, 1, 2, 3, 4, I, II SL A, 1, 2, 3, 4, I, II G, 2, 4, I, II (LC1, X1, Z1) 2.

COLVIN, H.M., ed. The country seat... (Card 2)

1. Architecture, Domestic--Gt. Br. 2. Historic houses--Gt. Br. 3. Summerson, Sir John Newenham, 1904- . 4. Summerson, Sir John Newenham, 1904- --Bibl. I. Harris, John, 1931- ed. II. Title.

Comisión nacional de homenaje a Ricardo Rojas.
La obra de Rojas, XXV años de labor literaria, Buenos Aires, 1903–1928. ₍Buenos Aires: Libreria "La Facultad" de J. Roldán y cia., 1928.₎ 591 p. illus. (ports.) 21cm.

"Este libro se imprimió...bajo los auspicios de la Comisión nacional de homenaje a Ricardo Rojas."—*Colophon*.
"La Comisión designó de su seno a Don Atilio Chiappori para prologar este libro."

Festschrift.

690694A. 1. Rojas, Ricardo, 1882- . I. Chiappori, Atilio, 1880- . II. Title.
N. Y. P. L. December 6, 1934

Comitato ariostesco dell' Ottava d'oro, *Ferrara.*
L'Ottava d'oro. La vita e l'opera di Ludovico Ariosto; letture tenute in Ferrara per il quarto centenario dalla morte del poeta, con due messaggi di Gabriele d'Annunzio. ₍Milano-Verona₎ A. Mondadori ₍1933₎

3 p. l., ₍ix₎–xvii p., 4 l., ₍3₎–921 p., 1 l. front., plates, ports., facsims. 23cm.

Illustrated cover.
Comprises addresses delivered from May, 1928, to January, 1933, under the auspices of the Comitato ariostesco dell' Ottava d'oro, edited and indexed by Paolo Rocca. *cf.* Premessa.

(Continued on next card)

A C 35–1594 ₍3₎

Festschrift

Comitato ariostesco dell' Ottava d'oro, *Ferrara.* L'Ottava d'oro ... ₍1933₎ (Card 2)

CONTENTS.—Baldini, Antonio. Premessa.—Annunzio, Gabriele d'. Due messaggi.—Balbo, Italo. Il volo di Astolfo.—Tumiati, Domenico. Il castello magico.—Bertoni, Giulio. Il linguaggio poetico di L. Ariosto.—Borgese, G. A. L'Ariosto nel mondo degli invisibili.—Galletti, Alfredo. "L'Orlando furioso" e l'epica medioevale.—Fatini, Giuseppe. La genesi del "Furioso".—Malaparte, Curzio. La pazzia d'Orlando.—Boschi, Gaetano. Diagnostica della pazzia d'Orlando.—Ravegnani, Giuseppe. Vita, morte e miracoli di Rodomonte.—Arcari, Paolo. Medoro.—Baldini, Antonio. La difesa di Angelica.—Momigliano, Attilio. Nell' isola di Alcina.—Bianchi, Fausto. Eterno femminino ariosteo.—Titta Rosa, Giovanni. L'Ariosto misogino.—Toffanin, Giuseppe. L'amore sacro e

(Continued on next card)

A C 35–1594 ₍3₎

Comitato ariostesco dell' Ottava d'oro, *Ferrara.* L'Ottava d'oro ... ₍1933₎ (Card 3)

CONTENTS—Continued.
l'amore profano nel "Furioso".—Lipparini, Giuseppe. Angelica e Medoro.—Turati, Augusto. Ruggiero e Bradamante.—Quilici, Nello. Fiordiligi e Brandimarte.—Pompeati, Arturo. La malinconia dell' Ariosto.—Fumagalli, Giuseppina. Paesaggi ariostei.—Bertú, Berto. Il mare nel l' "Orlando furioso".—Bontempelli, Massimo. L'Ariosto geografo.—Ferretti, Lando. Le artiglierie nell' "Orlando furioso".—Campanile, Achille. L'umorismo nell' Ariosto.—Marinetti, F. T. Una lezione di futurismo tratta dall' "Orlando furioso".—Rocca, Gino. Elementi di teatro nel l' "Orlando furioso".—Bragaglia, A. G. L'Ariosto come cineasta.—Toddi ₍i. e. P. S. Rivetta₎ De l'Ariosto abilissimo giocoliere.—Albini, Giuseppe. Riflessi virgiliani nell' "Orlando furioso".—Tambroni, Filippo.

(Continued on next card)

A C 35–1594 ₍3₎

Comitato ariostesco dell' Ottava d'oro, *Ferrara.* L'Ottava d'oro ... ₍1933₎ (Card 4)

CONTENTS—Continued.
Riflessi artistici della poesia ariostea.—Bodrero, Emilio. La vita prodigiosa di Ludovico Ariosto.—Bacchelli, Riccardo. Una difesa di messer Ludovico.—Marzio, Cornelio di. L'Ariosto diplomatico.—Catalano, Michele. Madonna Alessandra.—Cappa, Innocenzo. L'Italia ai tempi dell' Ariosto.—Agnelli, Giuseppe. Il "Furioso" nell' età nostra.—Farinelli, Arturo. L'estremo canto del "Furioso".—Tumiati, Gualtiero. Della poesia dell' Ariosto e della sua dizione.—Niccolini, Pietro. L'ultima ottava.—Indice dei personaggi e di cose notevoli.

1. Ariosto, Ludovico, 1474–1533. I. Rocca, Paolo, ed. II. Baldini, Antonio, 1889– III. Title.

A C 35–1594

Title from N. Y. Pub. Libr. Printed by L. C.

₍3₎

COMITATO LOMBARDO PER LE ONORANZE A MONSIGNOR GALBIATI.
Fragmenta dierum et vitae; bibliografia di Msgr. Giovanni Galbiati, cronologicamente disposta dal 1911 al 1961. 2.ed. ampliata. Milano, Allegretti di Campi, 1961. 164 p. illus., ports., facsim. 31cm.

At head of title: Fronde sparte.

(Continued)

NN 10.64 e/(OC)II, III OS(1b+)I PC, 1, I, II, III SL (LC1, X1, Z3) 2

COMITATO LOMBARDO PER LE ONORANZE A MONSIGNOR GALBIATI. Fragmenta dierum et vitae... (Card 2)

Continues the Bibliografia di Msgr. Giovanni Galbiati, issued by the Biblioteca Ambrosiana in 1941.

1. Galbiati, Giovanni, 1881- --Bibl. I. Biblioteca Ambrosiana, Milan. Bibliografia di Msgr. Giovanni Galbiati. II. Title. III. Title: Fronde sparte.

COMITATO PER LE ONORANZE A GIOVANNI MELI NEL II CENTENARIO DELLA NASCITA.

Studi su Giovanni Meli nel II centenario della nascita (1740-1940), contributo alla letteratura meliana promosso dal Comitato per le onoranze al poeta. [A cura della Biblioteca comunale di Palermo] Palermo, G. B. Palumbo [1942] xvi, 576 p. plates, ports., facsims. 28cm.

By various authors.

1. Meli, Giovanni, 1740-1815. I. Palermo, Italy (City). Biblioteca comunale. II. Title. t. 1942.

Commemoration of Nelson Timothy Stephens on commencement day 1932 at the University of Kansas in addresses by Dean Robert McNair Davis... Doctor Frank Strong... Chancellor Ernest Hiram Lindley... the Honorable Cyrus Crane... Judge Arthur Cornforth... upon the reception by the university of the portrait of Judge Stephens... New York ⌐The Tudor press⌐ 1933. 4 p.l., 7–38 p. 25cm.

Issued by "his daughter, Kate Stephens, and James McCrae Haughey, spokesman for other great-grandchildren of Judge Stephens."

(Continued)

N. Y. P. L. Festschrift January 4, 1943

Commemoration of Nelson Timothy Stephens... (Card 2)

"Other books speaking of Judge Stephens," p. 37–38.
With autograph of Kate Stephens.

203204B. 1. Stephens, Nelson Timothy. 2. Law—Study and teaching—U. S.—Kansas—Lawrence. I. Davis, Robert McNair, 1884–1940. II. Lindley, Ernest Hiram, 1869– . III. Strong, Frank, 1859–1934.

N. Y. P. L. January 4, 1943

Commemoration volume dedicated to Bundjirô Kotô...emeritus professor of geology in the Tokyo Imperial University, member of the Imperial Academy of Japan, by his pupils on the occasion of his seventieth birthday. Tokyo, 1925. 203 p. incl. tables. diagrs., front. (port.), illus., maps, plates. 4°.

The volume consists of reprints of papers published in the Journal of the Faculty of Science, Imperial University of Tokyo, and in the Japanese Journal of Geology and Geography.

352893A. Mr. Molle

1. Biology—Essays and misc. 2. Kotô, Bundjirô.

N. Y. P. L. January 9, 1928

COMMÉMORATION du voyage d'Alcide D'Orbigny en Amérique du Sud, 1826-1833. Paris, Masson, 1933. 108 p. illus., col. plate, port. 26cm. (Paris. Muséum national d'histoire naturelle. Publications. no. 3)

Microfilm.

CONTENTS.--Notice biographique sur Alcide Dessalines d'Orbigny (1802-1857), professeur de paléontologie au Muséum, par L. Roule.--D'Orbigny, ethnologue, par P. Rivet.--Les idées d'A. d'Orbigny et

(Continued)

 2

COMMÉMORATION du voyage d'Alcide D'Orbigny en Amérique du Sud, 1826-1833. (Card 2)

celles de H. Von Ihering sur la distribution géographique des mollusques marins côtiers de l'Amerique méridionale, par E. Lamy.--Les mollusques terrestres et fluviatiles dans l'œuvre d'Alcide d'Orbigny, par L. Germain.--Études de d'Orbigny sur les Céphalopodes, par L. Joubin.--D'Orbigny, ornithologiste, par J. Berlioz.--Plantes nouvelles de l'Amérique méridionale, par R. Benoist.--Le néopallium des Procyonidés, par R. Anthony et J. Botar.--L'Issiodoromys a-t-il des affinités avec les rongeurs sud-américains? Par M. Friant.

1. Orbigny, Alcide Dessalines d', 1802-1857. 2. South America--Descr. and trav., 1800-1850. I. Series.

Commemorative essays presented to Sir Ramkrishna Gopal Bhandarkar... Poona: Bhandarkar Oriental Research Institute, 1917. viii, 455 p. facsim., front, (port.), map, plates. 4°.

"This volume of essays...by his friends, pupils, and admirers from different lands is dedicated...to Sir Ramkrishna Gopal Bhandarkar upon the completion of his 80th year..."

1948

Commentationes in honorem Francisci Bvecheleri, Hermanni Vseneri; editae a Societate philologa bonnensi. Bonnae, apvd Adolphvm Marcvm, 1873.

2 p. l., 113, ⌐1⌐ p. fold. pl. 22½cm.

CONTENTS.—Observationes criticae ad L. Annaei Senecae opera minora: scripsit F. Schultess.—Qua vice Nestoris et Ulixis personae in arte rhetorica functae sint: scripsit C. Reinhardt.—Epigraphica: scripsit G. Kaibel.—Anecdoton lugdunense eclogas e tragoediis Senecae continens: edidit F. Leo.—Critica: scripsit H. Diels.—Quas rationes in hiatu vitando scriptor De sublimitate et Onesander secuti sint: scripsit H. de Rohden.—Observationes Plautinae et Terentianae: scripsit O. Brugman.—De pictura quadam eidem formae vasculari eadem fere semper inducta: scripsit F. de Duhn.

1. Buecheler, Franz, 1837–1908. 2. Usener, Hermann Karl, 1834–1905. 3. Classical philology—Collections. I. Societas philologa bonnensis.

Library of Congress PA26.B8 28—31234
⌐37b1⌐ Festschrift.

Commentationes philologicae in honorem professoris emeriti I. A. Heikel, ediderunt discipuli. ⌐Helsingforsiae, 1926.⌐ vi, 163 p. incl. map, tables. front. (port.) 8°.

Contents: AHLMAN, E. Zur Definition des Satzes. BIESE, Y. M. Bemerkungen zu einem τόπος in den Proömien der antiken Geschichtschreiber. FLINCK, E. Miscellanea critica. GULIN, E. G. Die Religion Epiktets und die Stoa. GUMMERUS, H. Cognomen und Beruf. GYLLENBERG, R. Zur Exegese von Hbr. 5, 11–6, 12. HAMMARSTRÖM, M. Zum lemnisch-phrygischen Alphabet. JAAKKOLA, K. De iteratis praepositionibus Zosimi. MALIN, A. Ein mittelalterliches Gedicht auf die hl Birgitta. REIN, E. De Danaa Euripidea. SALONIUS, A. H. Petroniana 1. Vorläufige Mitteilungen über Petrons Cena Trimalchionis. SUNDWALL, J. Über Menschenmotive auf italischen Hüttenurnen und Villanovavasen. TUDEER, L. O. T. Some maps attached to Ptolemy's Geography.

Mr. Molle

388730A. 1. Classical languages—Essays and misc. 2. Classical literature—Essays and misc. 3. Heikel, Ivar August, 1861– .

N. Y. P. L. December 22, 1928

Committee on the celebration of the eightieth birthday of Doctor William Henry Welch.

William Henry Welch at eighty; a memorial record of celebrations around the world in his honor, edited by Victor O. Freeburg. New York, Pub. for the Committee on the celebration of the eightieth birthday of Doctor William Henry Welch by the Milbank memorial fund, 1930.

230 p., 1 l. front., illus. (incl. facsims.) plates (1 col.) ports. 26½cm.

"This book is one of a limited edition of five hundred copies printed for presentation."

(Continued on next card)

A Second Copy ⌐5-5⌐ 31-5787

Mr. Molle

Committee on the celebration of the eightieth birthday of Doctor William Henry Welch. William Henry Welch at eighty ... 1930. (Card 2)

Simon Flexner, chairman, Executive committee.
"Copyright ... ₍by₎ William H. Welch medical library."
"List of books and the friends who gave them to Dr. Welch on the occasion of his eightieth birthday": p. 215-216.

1. Welch, William Henry, 1850- I. Freeburg, Victor Oscar, 1882- ed. II. Flexner, Simon, 1863- III. Milbank memorial fund. IV. Johns Hopkins university. William H. Welch medical library. V. Title.

31-5787

Library of Congress R154.W32C63

~~Copy 2~~

Copyright A 34506 ₍5-5₎ 926.1

MQE

CONCERNING architecture: essays on architectural writers and writing presented to Nikolaus Pevsner; edited by John Summerson. London, Allen Lane, 1968. xii,316 p. illus.,facsims., plans. 28cm.

"A select bibliography of the publications of Nikolaus Pevsner, by John Barr." Bibliographical footnotes.

(Continued)

NN*R 5.70 v/ OC,I PC, 1,2,3,I SL A,1,2,3,I (LC1,X1,Z1) [I] 2

Spencer Coll.
Ital. 1759

Componimenti poetici d'autori diversi in occasione dell'ingresso solenne di Sua Eccellenza il signor Girolamo Veniero procuratore di S. Marco per merito a Sua Eccellenza la signora Maria Veniero Contarini di lui figlia. Venezia, Appresso S. Coleti, 1759. 1 p.l., cvi p. illus. 31cm. (4°.)

Morazzoni: Libro illustrato veneziano del settecento, 281.
Includes a few poems in Latin and one in French.
Illustrations: numerous copper engravings, comprising title-vignette (portrait of the dedicatee) and head- and tailpieces (including portraits of Veniero and his wife), 4 signed by Francesco Bartolozzi. For reproductions, *cf. Morazzoni 110-111.*
Binding (unsigned), by James Macdonald, Inc., New York, of half green morocco with marbled paper sides.

1. Veniero, Girolamo—Poetry. 2. Poetry, Italian—Collections.
N. Y. P. L. December 3, 1948

CONCERNING architecture... (Card 2)

1. Pevsner, Sir Nikolaus, 1902- . 2.Architecture —Addresses, essays, lectures. 3. Pevsner, Sir Nikolaus, 1902- —Bibl. I. Summerson, Sir John Newenham, 1904- , ed.

Spencer Coll.
Ital.1764

Componimenti poetici per l'ingresso solenne alla dignità di proccuratore di S. Marco per merito di sua eccellenza il signor Lodovico Manin. ₍Venice, Albrizzi, 1764₎ Morazzoni: Libro illustrato
₍85₎ p. illus., port. 37 cm. veneziano del settecento,272.

Portrait dated 1764; Albrizzi's device on last page.
Frontispiece, portrait, borders, head and tail pieces are engravings by Francesco Bartolozzi. cf. L.C. Quarterly journal v.5, p.51. May 1948.
Original embossed paper binding. ~~Bookplate of Thomas Gaisford.~~
For reproductions, cf. Morazzoni 38-51, 56-57.

1. Manin, Lodovico, Doge of Venice, 1726-1802—Poetry. I. Bartolozzi, Francesco, 1727-1815, illus.

DG678.49.C6 Rosenwald Coll. 48-33231*

Library of Congress ₍1₎

NAD

Concinnitas; Beiträge zum Problem des Klassischen. Heinrich Wölfflin zum achtzigsten Geburtstag am 21. Juni 1944 zugeeignet. Basel, B. Schwabe & co. ₍1944₎ 231 p. illus. 23cm.

CONTENTS.—Burckhardt, C. J. Zum Begriff des Klassischen in Frankreich und in der deutschen Humanität.—Burckhardt, R. F. Über einige antike griechische Münzen.—Fiechter, Ernst. Raumgeometrie und Flächenproportion.—Gantner, Joseph. Jacob Burckhardts Urteil über Rembrandt und seine Konzeption des Klassischen.—

(Continued)

Festschrift.

N. Y. P. L. December 30, 1946

D-17
3442

Concepto humanista de la historia; ₍homenaje. Por₎ M. H. Alberti ₍et al.₎ Buenos Aires, Ediciones Líbera ₍1966₎

267 p. 21 cm.

CONTENTS.—Juan B. Justo en la historia y el pensamiento argentinos, por A. Solari.—Teoría y práctica de la historia, por M. H. Alberti.—La base biológica de la historia, por F. Escardó.—La técnica, por A. Justo.—La economía, por R. Bogliolo.—La guerra, por A. G. Rodríguez.—La política, por A. Ghioldi.—La lucha de clases, por R. Mondolfo.—El salariado, por M. Palacín.—Las formas

(Continued)

NN* 5.67 g/ OC,I,Ib* PC,1,2,I SL (LC1, X1,Z1) 2

Concinnitas... (Card 2)

Janner, Arminio. Il Castiglione e l'Ariosto a sostegno di Enrico Wölfflin.—Raymond, Marcel. Classique et baroque dans la poésie de Ronsard.—Salis, Arnold von. Klassische Komposition.—Speiser, Andreas. Die mathematische Betrachtung der Kunst.

356510B. 1. Classicism. 2. Art—Essays and misc. 3. Wölfflin, Heinrich, 1864-1946. 4. Burckhardt, Jakob, 1818-1897. 5. Rembrandt van Rijn, 1606-1669. 6. Castiglione, Baldassare, conte, 1478-1529. Il cortegiano. 7. Ariosto, Lodovico, 1474-1533. Orlando furioso. 8. Ronsard, Pierre de, 1524-1585.
N. Y. P. L. December 30, 1946

CONCEPTO humanista de la historia... (Card 2)

típicas del privilegio, por J. L. Pena.—El gremialismo proletario, por E. Frugoni.—La cooperación libre, por N. Repetto.—La democracia obrera, por L. Pan.—La religión, la ciencia, el arte, por R. Rivière.

1. Justo, Juan Bautista, 1865-1928. 2. History—Addresses, essays, lectures.
I. Alberti, M.H.

D-12
7560

CONFLICT in Stuart England; essays in honour of Wallace Notestein, edited by William Appleton Aiken and Basil Duke Henning. London, J. Cape [1960]

271 p. port. 23cm.

Includes bibliographical references.

CONTENTS.—Introductory. Wallace Notestein, by H. Simpson.—An analysis of major conflicts in seventeenth-century England, by W. H. Coates.—King James I and Anglo-Scottish unity, by D. H. Willson.—The procedure of the House of Commons against patents and monopolies, 1621-1624, by E. R. Foster.—Charles I and the Constitution, by H. Hulme.—"There are no remedies for many things but by a parliament": some opposition committees, 1640, by M. F. Keeler.—English pamphlet support for Charles I, November 1648-January 1649, by

(Continued)

NN * R 12. 60 m/ OC, I, II PC, 1, 2, I, II SL (LC1, X1, Z1) 2

CONFLICT in Stuart England... (Card 2)

W. L. Sachse.—"Of people either too few or too many"; the conflict of opinion on population and its relation to emigration, by M. Campbell.—The Admiralty in conflict and commission, 1679–1684, by W. A. Aiken.—The bishops in politics, 1688–1714, by F. G. James.—Bibliography of Wallace Notestein (p. 258–263)

1. Great Britain.--Hist.--Stuarts, 1603-1714--Addresses, essays, lectures. 2. Notestein, Wallace, 1879- I. Henning, Basil Duke, ed. 1907-1957, ed. II. Aiken, William Appleton,

---

E-13
3682

CONGRÈS DES ROMANISTES SCANDINAVES. 4th, Copenhagen, 1967.

Actes du quatrième congrès des romanistes scandinaves, Copenhague 8-11 août 1967; publiés à l'occasion du soixantième anniversaire, 19 juin 1967, de Holger Sten. Copenhague, Akademisk forlag, 1967. 255 p. port. 25cm. (Revue romane. Numéro spécial. 1)

In French, Spanish or Italian.
Bibliographical footnotes.

(Continued)

NN 12.68 1/LOS, I PC, 1, 2, I SL (LC1, X1, Z1)

6

CONGRÈS DES ROMANISTES SCANDINAVES. 4th, Copenhagen, 1967. Actes du quatrième congrès des romanistes scandinaves... (Card 2)

CONTENTS.--Bibliographie de travaux de Holger Sten.--Un sujeto indeterminado o general expresado por la segunda persona de singular: tú, por Gorosch, M.--Les modes d'action du verbe français-quelques réflexions, par Granberg, J.-H.--Les vertus devraient être soeurs, ainsi que les vices sont frères. Accord genre-sexe dans les figures généalogiques, par Hasselrot, B.--Les périphrases verbales du français moderne, par Henrichsen, A.-J.-- Observations sur les

(Continued)

CONGRÈS DES ROMANISTES SCANDINAVES. 4th, Copenhagen, 1967. Actes du quatrième congrès des romanistes scandinaves... (Card 3)

différentes disciplines de la linguistique descriptive, par Høybye, P.--Première phase de l'acquisition du système verbal français par Nina K., par Koefoed, O.--Remarques sémantiques sur les descendants romans de *brabus<barbarus, par Kræmer, E.v.--Un cas de synonymie en ancien français, par Laugesen, A.T.--Le rôle de la négation dans les exclamations introduites, par Nøjgaard, M.--Quelques réflexions sur le paradigme des pronoms interrogatifs, relatifs par Prebensen, H.--Facteurs

(Continued)

CONGRÈS DES ROMANISTES SCANDINAVES. 4th, Copenhagen, 1967. Actes du quatrième congrès des romanistes scandinaves... (Card 4)

déterminants de la combinaison sémantique d'éléments lexicaux, par Rasmussen, J.--Quelques périphrases passives du français moderne, par Spang-Hanssen, E.--Una congiunzione enigmatica: con ciò sia cosa che, per Ulleland, M.--Les études portugaises dans les pays scandinaves, par Sletsjøe, L.--La critique cornélienne des dernières années, par

(Continued)

CONGRÈS DES ROMANISTES SCANDINAVES. 4th, Copenhagen, 1967. Actes du quatrième congrès des romanistes scandinaves... (Card 5)

Gerlach-Nielsen, M.--Notes sur la structure de la Chartreuse de Parme, par Johansen, H.B.--Doina et saga. Parallèles épiques roumano-scandinaves, par Lozovan, E.--Le mythe de la "bourgeoisetė" dans les Mythologies de Roland Barthes, par Nykrog, P.--La reine de poissons, conte populaire ou création poétique, par Olsen, M.--L'origine des chansons de geste: Ami et Amile et Jourdain de Blaye, par Rasmussen,

(Continued)

CONGRÈS DES ROMANISTES SCANDINAVES. 4th, Copenhagen, 1967. Actes du quatrième congrès des romanistes scandinaves... (Card 6)

B.H.--Jacques-Louis David et la peinture néo-classique jugés par le auteurs français du XIXe siècle, par Verbraeken, R.--Nouvelle critique, ou trêve de polémique, par, Wewer, O.

1. Romance languages. 2. Romance literature--Addresses, essays, lectures. I. Revue romane.

E-10
8081

Congresso internazionale di filosofia Antonio Rosmini, *Stresa and Rovereto, 1955.*

Atti del Congresso internazionale di filosofia Antonio Rosmini, Stresa-Rovereto, 20–26 luglio 1955. A cura di Michele F. Sciacca e sotto gli auspici del Comitato nazionale per le onoranze centenarie. Firenze, G. C. Sansoni [1957]

2 v. (xxxiii, 1253 p.) 24 cm.

Italian, French, Spanish, German, or English.

1. ROSMINI SERBATI, ANTONIO, 1797-1855
I. Sciacca, Michele Federico, 1908- , ed.

NN 2.59 p/k (OC)I OS PC, 1 I SL (LC1, X1, Z1)

E-12
3649

CONNAISSANCE de l'étranger; mélanges offerts à la mémoire de Jean-Marie Carré. Paris. M. Didier, 1964. xx, 527 p. ports. 25cm. (Études de littérature étrangère et comparée. 50)

"L'oeurre de Jean-Marie Carrés," p. [xiii]-xviii.
Bibliographical footnotes.

1. Carré, Jean Marie, 1887- 2. Literature--Addresses essays, lectures. 3. French literature--Addresses, essays, lectures. I. Series.

NN 7.65 1/s OC (OS)I PC, 1, 2, 3, I (LC1, X1, Z1) SL [I]

Copy only words underlined & Classmark-- *GDM

Contributi alla storia del libro italiano. Miscellanea in onore di Lamberto Donati. Firenze, L. S. Olschki, 1969.

xxiii, 372 p. illus., port. 26cm. (La Bibliofilia. Biblioteca di bibliografia italiana. 57)

"Bibliografia di Lamberto Donati": p. [vii]-xxiii.

(Continued)

NN*R 3.72 e/l OC, II (OS)I PC, 1, 2, I, II (LC1, X1, Z1)

5

CONTRIBUTI alla storia del libro italiano.
(Card 2)

CONTENTS.—Bemerkungen su zwei Italienischen Inkunabeln (Hain 4942 und Hain 18883) von P. Amelung.—Intorno ad una rara edizione di Terenzio (Venezia 1506) e allo stampatore Alessandro Paganino, di L. Balasamo.—Derivazioni di frontespizi, di F. Barberi.—Alcuni incunabuli bresciani sconosciuti o poco noti, di U Baroncelli.—La tipografia di Mondovi dal 1470 al 1522, di L. Berra.—Note sulla tipografia Bevilacqua, di M. Bersano Begey.—Three Venetian editions of the Peregrinationes Terreae Sanctae, printed in the fifteenth century, by

(Continued)

CONTRIBUTI alla storia del libro italiano.
(Card 3)

C. F. Bühler.—Codici miniati a Napoli da Matteo Felice nel secolo xv, di T. De Marinis.—Apprendisti librai e operai tipografi in tre officini piemontesi del sec. xvi, di G. Dondi.—Su alcuni libri greci stampati a Venezia nella prima metà del Cinquecento, di E. Follieri.—Le Provanze di Aldo Manuzio il giovane, per essere ammesso nell'ordine dei Cavalieri di Santo Stefano, di T. Gasparrini Leporace.—Incunabuli italiani miniati o dipinti nella Biblioteca nazionale di Napoli, di G. Guerrieri.—Un libro scritto e miniato di Giulio Clovio, di M. Levi D'-Ancona.—Editori di incunabuli fiorentini, di B. Maracchi Biagia-

(Continued)

CONTRIBUTI alla storia del libro italiano.
(Card 4)
relli.—Osservazioni tipografiche sul Polifilo nelle edizione del 1499 e 1545, di G. Mardersteig.—Di alcune minuzie librarie, di L. Michelini Tocci.—Una edizione russa del 1823 delle Lettere di Jacopo Ortis, di O. Pinto.—Un tipografo ambulante e un nuovo luogo di stampa nel Cinquecento, di D. E. Rhodes.—Briciole bibliogiche, di R. Ridolfi.—Les différents colophons de l'Antiquae Urbis Romae cum Regionibus Simulachrum de 1532, par J. Ruysschaert.—Spigolature d'Archivio sull'arte libraria nel sec. xviii, di C. Santoro.—A sixteenth-century Bertochus, di V. Scholderer.—Quattro manifesti librari durante la repubblica romana del 1789–1799, di N. Vian.—Vdalricus Gallus de Bienna. Notizen zu einem Aufsatz von Lamberto Donati, von C. Wehmer.—Cesena ed il suo dilvio del 1525 in un poemetto poco note, di R. Weiss.

(Continued)

CONTRIBUTI alla storia del libro italiano. (Card 5)

1. Books--Hist.--Italy. 2. Donati, Lamberto--Bibl.
I. Series. II. Donati, Lamberto.

PSD

CONTRIBUTIONS in geophysics in honor of Beno Gutenberg. Editors: Hugo Benioff [and others] New York, Pergamon press, 1958. viii, 244 p. illus., tables. 22cm. (International series of monographs on earth sciences. v.1)

Includes bibliographies.

CONTENTS. -- The energies of seismic body waves and surface waves, by M. Båth. --Energy in earthquakes as computed from geodetic observations

(Continued)

NN R 6.59 m/P OC, II, IIIbo (OS)I PC, 1, 2, I, II SL ST, 1t, 2, I, II (LC1, X1, Z1)

CONTRIBUTIONS in geophysics in honor of Beno Gutenberg. (Card 2)

by P. Byerly and J. DeNoyer. --The variation of amplitude and energy with depth in love waves, by R. Stoneley. --About some phenomena preceding and following the seismic movements in the zone characterized by high seismicity, by P. Caloi. --Zur Mechanik and Dynamik der Erdbeben, by W. Hiller. --Direction of displacement in Western Pacific earthquakes, by J. H. Hodgson. --On seismic activities in and near Japan, by C. Tsuboi.--

(Continued)

CONTRIBUTIONS in geophysics in honor of Beno Gutenberg. (Card 3)

Solidity of the inner core, by K. E. Bullen. --On phases in earthquake records at epicentral distances of 105° to 115°, by I. Lehmann. --Quelques expériences sur la structure de la croûte terrestre en Europe Occidentale, by J. P. Rothe. --Seismic observations at one kilometer depth, by H. E. Tatel and M. A. Tuve. --Interpretation of the seismic structure of the crust in the light of experimental studies of wave velocities in rocks, by

(Continued)

CONTRIBUTIONS in geophysics in honor of Beno Gutenberg. (Card 4)

F. Birch. --The free oscillations of the earth, by C. L. Pekeris and H. Jarosch. --The geophysical history of a geosyncline, by F. A. Vening Meinesz. --Some recent studies on gravity formulas, by W. A. Heiskanen and U. A. Uotila. --Data processing in geophysics, by H. E. Landsberg. --Geomagnetic drift and the rotation of the earth, by W. Elsasser and W. Munk.
1. Geophysics. 2. Gutenberg, Beno, 1889- . I. Series. II. Benioff, Hugo, ed. III. Benioff, Hugo. t. 1958.

PBO

Contributions to the mechanics of solids dedicated to Stephen Timoshenko by his friends on the occasion of his sixtieth birthday anniversary. [New York, Boston, etc., The Macmillan company, 1938]
viii p., 1 l., 277 p. front. (port.) illus., diagrs. 24ᶜᵐ.
On cover: Stephen Timoshenko. 60th anniversary volume.
Contributions by J. M. Lessells, C. B. Biezeno and J. J. Koch, J. P. Den Hartog, L. H. Donnell, O. W. Ellis, Ludwig Föppl, J. N. Goodier, M. Hetényi, O. J. Horger, William Hovgaard, M. T. Huber, L. S. Jacobsen, G. B. Karelitz, Th. von Kármán, B. F. Langer, C. W. MacGregor, R. von Mises, A. Nadai, J. Ormondroyd, R. E. Peterson, L. Prandtl, C. R. Soderberg, R. V. Southwell, G. I. Taylor, A. M. Wahl, E. O. Waters, Stewart Way, E. E. Weibel, H. M. Westergaard.
Bibliography at end of some of the chapters.
1. Timoshenko, Stephen, 1878– 2. Mechanics, Applied.

39—234
Library of Congress QA801.C65 Festschrift
~~Copy 2.~~
Copyright A 123979 [39f5] 620.1

SDC

CONTRIBUTIONS to probability and statistics; essays in honor of Harold Hotelling. Edited by Ingram Olkin [and others] Stanford, Calif., Stanford university press, 1960. ix, 517 p. diagrs. 25cm. (Stanford studies in mathematics and statistics. 2)

Includes bibliographical references.

1. Statistics--Methods. 2. Probabilities. 3. Hotelling, Harld, 1895- . I. Olkin, Ingram, ed. II. Series. III. Olkin, Ingram. t. 1960
NN R X 4.61 g/& OC, I, IIIbo (OS)II PC, 1, 2, 3, I, II SL E, 1, 3, I ST, 1t, 2t, 3, I (LC1, X1, Z1)

E-12
5626
CONVEGNO DI STUDI PASCOLIANI, Bologna, 1958.
Studi per il centenario della nascita di Giovanni Pascoli pubblicati nel cinquantenario della morte. Bologna, Commissione per i testi di lingua, 1962. 3 v. 24cm. (Bologna, Italy (City). Biblioteca communale dell'archiginnasio. L'Archiginnasio. Numero speciale)

1. Pascoli, Giovanni, 1855-1912. I. Bologna, Italy (City). Biblioteca comunale dell'archiginnasio. L'Archiginnasio. II. Title.
NN*. 4.66 a/ (OD)I (ED)I PC, 1, I, II SL OS, II (LC1, X1, Z1)

AN
(Muratori, L.)
CONVEGNO DI STUDI STORICI IN ONORE DI L.A. MURATORI, MODENA, ITALY, 1950.
Miscellanea di studi muratoriani; atti e memorie del "Convegno di studi storici in onore di L. A. Muratori" tenuto in Modena 14-16 aprile 1950. Modena, Aedes muratoriana, 1951. 617 p. illus., facsim. 25cm.

At head of title: Deputazione di storia patria per le antiche provincie modenesi. Comitato per le onoranze a L.A. Muratori nel
(Continued)
NN** 1.55 g/ (OC)III OS(1b)I, II, IIb PC, 1, I, II, III
SL (MU)2, 3g (MUS1: Glorietur letabunda, Z1, LC1, X1)

CONVEGNO DI STUDI STORICI IN ONORE DI L.A. MURATORI, MODENA, ITALY, 1950. Miscellanea di studi muratoriani... (Card 2)

bicentenario dalla morte.
"S. Geminiano nella lirica della liturgia modenese [di] Giuseppe Vecchi," p. 524-538. "Glorietur letabunda," with music, v.p. following p. 536.
"Bibliografia muratoriana [di] Tommaso Sorbelli," p. [575]-609.
1. Muratori, Lodovico Antonio, 1672-1750. 2. Church music—Italy—Modena. 3. Sequences, Liturgical. I. Deputazione di storia patria per le antiche provincie modenesi. II. Comitato per le onoranze a L.A. Muratori nel bicentenario dalla morte. III. Title.

NRC
CONVIVIUM; Beiträge zur Altertumswissenschaft. Konrat Ziegler zum siebzigsten Geburtstag 12. Januar 1954. Stuttgart, A. Druckenmüller [1954] 186 p. port. 25cm.

CONTENTS.—"Ἔρως ἀνίκατε μάχαν", von L. Castiglioni. —Die Entstehung des Atomismus, von W. Kranz.—Die Inschriften im Geschichtswerk des Herodot, von H Volkmann—Clipeata imago und εἰκὼν ἔνοπλος, von W.H. Gross.—Der altrömische Staatskult im
(Continued)
NN**R 2.56 d/ OC PC, 1, 2 SL (LC1, X1, Z1) [I]

CONVIVIUM... (Card 2)

Spiegel Augusteischer und spätrepublikanischer Apologetik, von C. Koch.—Eine frühchristliche Arkadienvorstellung, von W. Schmid.—Von germanischer Waffenübung und Kriegskunst, von F. Miltner.—Goethe und der Historismus in der Altertumswissenschaft.

1. Classical studies—Collections. 2. Ziegler, Konrat Julius Fürchtegott, 1884- .

C-11
7841
COOK, WILLIAM, d.1824.
Memoirs of Samuel Foote, esq., with a collection of his genuine bon-mots, anecdotes, opinions, &c., mostly original, and three of his dramatic pieces, not published in his Works. London, Printed for R. Phillips, 1805. 3 v. in 1. port. 18cm.

"Three dramatic pieces... not published in his Works: The second act
(Continued)
NN**R X 6.61 m/OC PC, 1, 2 SL (LC1, X1, Z1)

2

COOK, WILLIAM, d.1824. Memoirs of Samuel Foote... (Card 2)

of The diversions of the morning [The trial of Samuel Foote, esq., for a libel on Peter Paragraph, and An occasional prelude]" v. 3, p. 113-159.

Laurie collection
1. Foote, Samuel, 1720-1777. 2. Drama, English.

QOL
+
COPENHAGEN. Nationalmuseet. Den Etnografiske samling.
Ethnographical studies, published on the occasion of the centenary of the Ethnographical department, National museum. København, Gyldendal, 1941. 250 p. illus., ports., map. 30cm. (Copenhagen. Nationalmuseet. Nationalmuseets skrifter: Etnografisk raekke. [v.] 1)
(Continued)
NN*R 12.55 g/ (OC)IIs OSs, Is PCs, Is, Is, IIs SL (U Is, LCIs, XIs, Z1s) [I]

COPENHAGEN. Nationalmuseet. Den Etnografiske samling. Ethnographical studies... (Card 2)

Includes bibliographies.
CONTENTS.—C.J. Thomsen and the founding of the Ethnographical museum, by V. Hermansen.—Brahmanistic temple sculpture from India in the National museum, by T. Thomsen.—Contributions to the history of some Oriental bazaar crafts, by C.G. Feilberg.—Some observations on the origin of Sino-Siberian animal bronzes, by W. Jacobsen.—Ashanti gold weights, by C. Kjersmeier.—Where did the Eskimo get their copper? By P. Bergsøe.—Early collections from the Pacific Eskimo, by K. Birket-Smith.—Had West Indian rock carvings a religious
(Continued)

COPHENGAGEN. Nationalmuseet. Den Etnografiske samling. Ethnographical studies... (Card 3)

significance? By G. Hatt.—Notes on Guatemala Indian costumes, by J. Yde.—Some ancient specimens from western and central Polynesia, by H. Larsen.

1. Ethnology—Essays and misc. I. Series. II. Title.

F-10
5877

Copland, *Sir* Douglas Berry, 1894- , *ed.*
Giblin, the scholar and the man; papers in memory of Lyndhurst Falkiner Giblin. Melbourne, F. W. Cheshire [1960]
vii, 228 p. port., map. 26 cm.
Bibliographical footnotes.
CONTENTS.—Biographical essays: An appreciation, by D. Copland. Giblin at Cambridge, by F. R. Earp. Giblin in north British Columbia, 1898-99, by C. Camsell. Giblin in politics and war, by F. C. Green. Giblin as Ritchie professor, by R. I. Downing. Giblin and the Grants Commission, by H. P. Brown. Giblin and the Commonwealth
(Continued)

NN* R 9.61 g/ OC PC, 1, 2 SL E, 1, 2 (LC1, X1, Z1)

COPLAND, Sir DOUGLAS BERRY, 1894- , ed.
Giblin, the scholar and the man... (Card 2)

Bank, by T. J. Bartley. Giblin and the arts, by A. E. Melville. Obituaries, by H. S. Nicholas and D. Copland.—Selected writings (extracts from Giblin's articles and letters)—Contributions to basic economic policy: Giblin as an economist, by T. Hytten. Giblin and the multiplier, by P. H. Karmel. Giblin and agriculture, by S. M. Wadham. Giblin as author; growth of a central bank, by W. B. Reddaway. Giblin and profit sharing, by S. Crawford. Giblin and the post war problem, by G. G. Firth. Giblin and John Smith, by J. M. Garland. L. F. Giblin bibliography, by M. Bourke (p. 223-228)

1. Giblin, Lyndhurst Falkiner, 1872-1951. 2. Economics--Essays and misc.

L-10
9574

CÓRDOBA, ARGENTINE REPUBLIC (City). Universidad nacional.
Homenaje jubilar a monseñor doctor Pablo Cabrera, 1857-1957. Córdoba, Dirección general publicidad, 1958. 1 v. port., maps. 24cm.

Parte 1.
"Revista de la Universidad nacional de Córdoba. Número especial."

1. Cabrera, Pablo, 1857-1936. 2. Argentine Republic--Hist. I. Córdoba, Argentine Republic (City). Universidad nacional. Revista Número especial.

NN 12.65 p/ OS, I PC, 1, 2, I SL AH, 1, 2 (LC1, X1, Z1)

3-MAH

Corolla. Ludwig Curtius zum sechzigsten geburtstag dargebracht ... Stuttgart, Verlag W. Kohlhammer, 1937.
2 v. plates, plans, diagrs. 32½cm.
Introductory letter signed: Heinrich Bulle.
Bibliographical foot-notes.
CONTENTS.—[v. 1] Text: Carossa, Hans. Ergänzungen; ein dank an Ludwig Curtius. Huch, Ricarda. Auf einen verwitterten grabstein im dom zu Mainz. Furtwängler, Wilhelm. Eine zeitgemässe betrachtung. Riezler, Walter. Das chorfinale. Klingner, Friedrich. Über Pindars drittes Pythisches gedicht. Curtius, E. R. Hofmannsthal und Calderon. Preetorius, Emil. Zum wesen ostasiatischer malerei. Schweitzer, Bernhard. Zum antiken künstlerbild. Kaschnitz-Weinberg, Guido. Zur struktur der griechischen kunst. Gerkan, Armin von. Die entwicklung des grossen tempels von Baalbek. Langlotz, Ernst. Eine eteokretische
(Continued on next card)
A C 38-855
[2]

Corolla. Ludwig Curtius zum sechzigsten geburtstag dargebracht ... 1937. (Card 2)
CONTENTS—Continued.
sphinx. Rodenwaldt, Gerhart. Metope aus Mykenai. Heidenreich, Robert. Über die bildungsgesetze einer archaischen statue. Schmidt, Eduard. Zur erzplastik des Phidias. Schrader, Hans. Zu den kopien nach dem schildrelief der Athena Parthenos. Sieveking, Johannes. Ein koroplasteneinfall. Wolters, Paul. Banausos. Horn, Rudolf. Ein bärtiger götterkopf aus Chios in Wien. Rupprecht, kronprinz von Bayern. Bronzestatuette eines Poseidon. Arndt, Paul. I. Bronzekopf eines Poseidon. II. Hypermnestra. Boehringer, Erich. Ein ring des Philetairos. Muthmann, Fritz. Der hängende Marsyas. Hahland, Walter. Zu den anfängen der attischen malerei. Technau, Werner. Eine amphora des Andokidesmalers in der sammlung des conte Faina zu Orvieto. Hampe,
(Continued on next card)
A C 38-855
[2]

Corolla. Ludwig Curtius zum sechzigsten geburtstag dargebracht ... 1937. (Card 3)
CONTENTS—Continued.
Roland. Rückkehr eines jünglings. Kraiker, Wilhelm. Eine attische pyxis. Bulle, Heinrich. Weihebild eines tragischen dichters. Salis, Arnold von. Sisyphos. Klauser, Theodor. Eine rätselhafte exultetillustration aus Gaëta. Klages, Ludwig. Bachofen als erneuerer des symbolischen denkens. Ranke, Hermann. Ägypter als götterkinder. Zimmer, Heinrich. Die vorarisch-altindische himmelsfrau. Schaeder, H. H. Gott und mensch in der verkündigung Zarathustras. Deubner, Ludwig. Der ithyphallische Hermes. Herbig, Reinhard. Herakles im Orient. Brendel, Otto. Die freidensgöttin. Crous, J. W. Roma auf waffen.—[v. 2] Tafeln.

1. Curtius, Ludwig, 1874- 2. Sculpture, Greek. 3. Pottery, Greek. I. Bulle, Heinrich, 1867-

A C 38-855

New York. Public library for Library of Congress [2]

MTE

Corolla archaeologica in honorem C. A. Nordman. Helsinki, 1952. xi, 289 p. illus., maps. 26cm.

Contributions in Danish, English, Finnish, German, Norwegian or Swedish.

1. Archaeology. 2. Nordman, Carl Axel, 1892-

NN R 3.53 OC PC, 1, 2 SL (LC1, Z1, X1)

Copy only words underlined & classmark -- FH

COROLLA memoriae Erich Swoboda dedicata. (Schriftleitung: Roksanda M. Swoboda-Milenović) [Mit Portrait und Werksverzeichnis] Graz, Köln, Böhlau, 1966. 237 p. xiv, p. of illus. 23cm. (Römische Forschungen in Niederösterreich. 5)

Bibliographical footnotes.
CONTENTS.--Erich Swoboda, von H. Wiesflecker.--In memoriam, von V. Ehrenberg.--Les thermes légionnaires de Gemellae, par J. Baradez.--Der "Hiltelberg" bei Carnuntum (Deutsch-Altenburg) .
(Continued)

NN* 8.68 p/ OC, II (OD)I (ED)I PC, 1, 2, 3, I, II (LC1, X1, Z1)

COROLLA memoriae Erich Swoboda dedicata. (Card 2)

von A. A. Barb.--Zur Geschichte der legio gemina, von A. Betz.--The duration of provincial commands under Antoninus Pius, by A. R. Birley.--Alae and cohortes milliariae, by E. Birley.--Ius Latii in den Stadtrechten von Salpensa und Malaca, von H. Braunert.--Le difese della romana Aquileia e la loro cronologia, di G. Brusin.--Beiträge zur Frage der ländlichen Bevolkerung in der römischen Dobrudscha, von E. Condurachi.--Der Giebel des Carnuntiner Fahnenheiligtums, von E. Diez.--Rom und die Völker jenseits der mittleren Donau, von J. Dobiáš.--Cäsarenwahnsinn,"
(Continued)

COROLLA memoriae Erich Swoboda dedicata. (Card 3)

von F. Hampl.--Die Begründung der Limesforschung in Deutschland, von J. Irmscher.--Julius Nepos and the Fall of the Western Empire, by J. P. C. Kent.--Hadrians Verhältnis zu Italica, von R. Nierhaus.--War Epidaurum colonia oder municipium? Von G. Novak.--Frühchristliche Silberlöffel, von H. v. Petrikovits.--Deux gouverneurs de la province de Cilicie de l'époque de Trajan à la lumiere de deux nouvelles inscriptions de Iotapé en Cilicie trachée, par H.-G. Pflaum.--Interpretation de la tombe de Vix, par A. Piganiol.--Keltisches portorium in den Ostalpen, von J. Šašel.--Zu den sogenannten Kulttheatern in Gallien, von W. Schleiermacher.--
(Continued)

COROLLA memoriae Erich Swoboda dedicata. (Card 4)

Zu den Statuenpreisen in der römischen Kaiserzeit, von J. Szilágyi.--Zur vorcaesarischen Siedlungsund Städtepolitik in Nordafrika, von F. Vittinghoff.--Schriftenverzeichnis Erich Swoboda (p. [235]-237)

1. Swoboda, Erich. 2. Rome--Provinces. 3. Rome--Archaeology--Addresses, essays, lectures. I. Series. II. Swoboda-Milenović, Roksanda M., ed.

CORONA amicorum. (Card 2)

bibliotek, av C. Davidsson.--"Bruns delineation af Constaninopel och locis Terrae Sanctae i Uppsala universitetsbibliotek, av A. Davidsson.--En gammal Uppsalgård, av N. Edling.--Bellmans ansikte enligt Sergelporträtten, av G. Ekholm.--Några handskrifter av svenskt interesse i Yale university library, av O. von Feilitzen.--Reprosektionen vid Uppsala universitetsbibliotek. Några drag ur verksamheten, av L. Grönberg.--Några Daliniana. Gustaf Ribbing om Olof von Dalin, av T. Hag- ström.--Uppsala

(Continued)

RAE

Corona; studies in celebration of the eightieth birthday of Samuel Singer, professor emeritus, University of Berne, Switzerland, edited by Arno Schirokauer & Wolfgang Paulsen. Durham, N.C.,Duke university press,1941.

ix, 282 p. 23½cm. (Half-title:Duke university publications)

Festschrift

CORONA amicorum. (Card 3)

universitetsbiblioteks första tryckta historia och dess kritiker, av G. Hornwall.--Ett latinskt ode över Bomarsunds fall, av L. Kjellberg.--Städer och borgerskap i äldre islamisk tid, av B. Lewin.--Eric Benzelius d.y:s naturvetenskapliga studier och biblioteksverksamhet, av A. Liljencrantz.--San Stefano dei Mori och de första etiopiska bibeltrycken, av O. Löfgren.--Något om de grekiska handskrifterna i Uppsal universitets- bibliotek, av S. Rudberg.--Skaras förste boktryckare, av H.

(Continued)

PQF

Corona amicorum; Emil Bächler zum 80. Geburtstag, 10. Februar 1948. St. Gallen, Tschudy-Verlag, 1948. 225 p. illus. 25cm.

"Herausgegeben von Emil Egli in Zusammenarbeit mit Georg Thürer und Walter Robert Corti."

Bibliographies included.

"Verzeichnis der Publikationen von Dr. Emil Bächler," p. 221-225.

CONTENTS.—Corti, W. R. Herz und Gehirn.—Hediger, H. Naturschutz und Heilaberglaube.—Vonwiller, Paul. Über moderne Auflichtmikroskopie in der Biologie.—Koch, Walo. Zur Pflanzengeographie der Kantone St. Gallen und Appenzell.—Keller-Tarnuzzer, Karl. Beitrag zur Konstruktion der Michelsberger Pfahlbauten.—

(Continued)

N. Y. P. L. July 12, 1948

CORONA amicorum. (Card 4)

Sallander.--Planeringen av läsesal--öppet magasin i Umeå universitetsbibliotek, av P. Sjögren.--Den dörflerska samlingen botanistbrev i Uppsala universitetsbibliotek av C.-O. von Sydow.--Uppsala universitets minnespenningar, av B. Waern.--Tönnes Klebergs tryckta skrifter, av G. Elvin.

1. Kleberg Tönnes. 2. Manuscripts--Addresses, essays, lectures. 3. Manuscripts--Sweden. I. Series.

Corona amicorum... (Card 2)

Gansser, August. Über die Archäologie des Leders.—Schmidt, W. Die Primitialopfer in der Urkultur.—Koppers, Wilhelm. Gottesglaube und Primitialopfer bei dem ethnologischen Altstamm der Chenchu im Dekkan.—Stuker, Peter. Wissenschaft als allgemeines Kulturgut.—Schmid, F. Oberhelfenschwil: eine Dämmerungsstudie.—Saxer, Friedrich. Alter und Dauer der Molassezeit.—Winkler, Otto. Über Lebensraum und Wirtschaft der freien Walser im st. gallischen Calfeisenthal.—Egli, Emil. Täler und Gemeinden.—Zürcher, Richard. Das Gebirge in Landschaftszeichnungen der Renaissance.—Kaegi, Werner. Aus Jacob Burckhardts erster Berliner Zeit.—Keller, Max. Schriftexpertise und Ausdruckskunde.—Voellmy, Samuel. Unbekannte Freundschaftsbriefe.—Thürer, Georg. Lesen und Leben.

450471B. 1. Bächler, Emil, 1868- . 2. Natural history—Addresses, essays, lectures. 3. Society, Primitive. I. Egli, Emil, ed.

N. Y. P. L. July 12, 1948

EBA
M8.Z8
v.6

Corona quernea, Festgabe Karl Strecker zum 80. Geburtstag dargebracht. Leipzig, K.W. Hiersemann, 1941.

viii, 428 p. port., facsims. 25 cm. (Schriften des Reichsinstituts für ältere Deutsche Geschichtskunde (Monumenta Germaniae historica)6)

Festschrift

F-11
4665

CORONA amicorum. Uppsala, 1968. 272 p. illus., port. 28cm. (Upsala, Sweden. Universitet. Bibliotek. Acta Bibliothecae R. Universitatis Upsaliensis. v. 15)

CONTENTS.--Supplement zu E. Rooths Katalog über die mittelalterlichen Handschriften der Universitätsbibliothek zu Uppsala, von M. Andersson-Schmitt.--Rodoslovnaja kniga. Två manuskript i svenska

(Continued)

NN 9.68 e/4 OC (OS)I PC,1,2,3,I SL (LC1, X1,Z1)

4

NPV

Correa, Luis, 1889-1940.

... Terra patrum, páginas de crítica y de historia literaria, prólogo de J. A. Cova. Caracas, Venezuela, Editorial Cecilio Acosta, 1941.

163 p., 2 l. incl. port. 20cm. (Biblioteca de escritores y asuntos venezolanos)

"Edición homenaje ... a la memoria de Luis Correa en el primer aniversario de su muerte."

CONTENTS.—Bello, Andrés. Una taza de café.—Baralt, R. M. En Bogotá.—González, J. V. Bolivarismo.—Acosta, Cecilio. Ideas políticas.—Yépez, J. R. Centenario.—Pardo, F. G. La musa extranjera.—Pérez Bonalde, J. A. Infancia en Puerto Rico.—Gutiérrez Coll, Jacinto. Su vida y su obra.—Tejera, Felipe. Serenidad.—Muñoz, G. E. Un poeta alejandrino.—Díaz Rodríguez, Manuel. Laude.—Epílogo: Los "inacabados."—La elegía del Cuzco.

1. Venezuelan literature—Hist. & crit. I. Title.

Library of Congress PQ8538.C6 41-26408
[2] 860.4

Il **Correggio**; raccolta di studi e memorie in onore di Antonio Allegri. Edita a cura di Aurea Parma nel IV. centenario della di lui morte, 1934. [Parma: La Bodoniana, 1934] 96 p. illus., plates. 25½cm. (Aurea Parma. Anno, 18, fasc. 2–3.)

Bibliographies included.
CONTENTS.—Copertini, Giovanni. "Il nostro messer Antonio Allegri."—Rigillo, Michele. Il pittore sacro.—Giorgi, Luigi de. La camera di San Paolo.—Copertini, Giovanni. La favola di Apollo, Marsia e Mida attribuita al Correggio.—Boselli, Antonio. Il Correggio giudicato da alcuni scrittori francesi.—Zorzanello, Pietro. La bibliografia del Correggio.—Mauceri, Enrico. Lorenzo Sabattini nella luce del Correggio.—Finzi, Riccardo. Documenti intorno al Correggio.—Foratti, Aldo. Influssi del Correggio sui Carracci.—Pettorelli L., Arturo. Il Correggio nella critica del Berenson.

834311A. 1. Correggio, Antonio Allegri, known as, 1494–1534. I. Aurea Parma.
N. Y. P. L. August 24, 1936

COST en baet... (Card 2)

CONTENTS.--De behandeling van vlottende en vaste kapitaalgoederen bij de winstbepaling, door R. Burgert.--Over de toerekening van prijsveranderingen aan oorzaken in geld- en goederensfeer, door W. Eizenga.--Fiscale concernwinst, door G. Slot.--Latente fiscale verplichtingen en aanspraken van de naamloze vennootschap, door L.J. Kegge.--Bedrijfseconomische aspecten van het investeringsbegrip, door A. Dek.--Recente waarderingen van "direct costing", door R. Slot.--Enige aspecten van een planningprobleem, door S. Schaap.--Kostprijs- en

(Continued)

Cosmic radiation, fifteen lectures edited by W. Heisenberg, translated by T. H. Johnson ... New York, Dover publications, 1946.

5 p. l., 192 p. illus., diagrs. 24cm.

A series of symposia, held in the years 1941 and 1942 in the Kaiser Wilhelm institut for physics, was published in Berlin in 1943 in commemoration of the 75th birthday of Arnold Sommerfeld. *cf.* Foreword.
"Published and distributed in the public interest by authority of the U. S. Alien property custodian."

CONTENTS.—Introduction: Review of the present state of our knowledge of cosmic radiation, by W. Heisenberg.—Cascades: The cascade theory, by W. Heisenberg. The large air showers, by G. Molière.—

(Continued on next card)
47-547
[10]

COST en baet... (Card 3)

resultatenberekening in ondernemingen met stukproduktie, door L.P.S. Gommers.--Enkele beschouwingen met betrekking tot kostprijsberekeningen in de zuivelindustrie, door W.F. Stutterheim.--Rentabiliteit, liquiditeit en solvabiliteit als financieringsgrondslagen, door J.C. Brezet.--Over investeringsbeslissingen en winstmaximalisatie, door F.H. Kruize.--Selectie van investeringsprojecten, door C.A. Buningh.--Rentabiliteitsvraagstukken bij de beoordeling van alternatieve financieringsmogelijkheden, door W.L.G.S. Hoefnagels.--Enkele opmerkingen over de begrippen risicodragend en risicomijdend in verband met beleggingsvraagstukken op lange termijn, door J.T. Groosmuller.--

(Continued)

Cosmic radiation ... 1946. (Card 2)

CONTENTS—Continued.

Mesons: The creation of mesons, by K. Wirtz. Showers with penetrating particles, by A. Klemm and W. Heisenberg. The absorption of mesons, by H. Voltz. Burst excitation by mesons, by C. F. v. Weizsäcker. Radioactive decay of the meson, by W. Heisenberg. The decay electrons of mesons, by F. Bopp. Theory of the meson, by C. F. v. Weizsäcker. Meson theory of the deuteron, by S. Flügge. Theory of explosion-like showers, by W. Heisenberg.—Nuclear particles: Nuclear disruptions and heavy particles in cosmic radiation, by E. Bagge. On the excitation of neutrons by cosmic rays and their distribution in the atmosphere, by S. Flügge.—Geomagnetic effects: Cosmic rays and the magnetic field of the earth, by J. Meixner.—References to the literature (p. [181]-186)

(Continued on next card)
47-547
[10]

COST en baet... (Card 4)

Levensverzekering in onze tijd, L.M. van Leeuwen.--Vraagstukken met betrekking tot de budgettering van de kosten, door J.C. Hoogheid.--Invloeden van seizoenen op de resultatenanalyse, door J. Kroeze.--Enkele beschouwingen over nationale- en internationale bedrijfsvergelijking, door J.F.P. Kreugel.--Enige macro-economische facetten van de verticale prijsbinding, door C. Brevoord.

1. Brands, J. 2. Economics, 1926--Dutch authors. 3. Economic policy--Addresses, essays, lectures.

Cosmic radiation ... 1946. (Card 3)

1. Sommerfeld, Arnold Johannes Wilhelm, 1868- 2. Cosmic rays. I. Heisenberg, Werner, 1901- ed. II. Johnson, Thomas Hope, 1899- tr.

QC485.C63 535 47-547
© 31Dec46; 2c 12Jan47; Dover book publishers, inc.; A9724.

Library of Congress [10]

COUNT, EARL WENDEL, 1899- , ed.
Fact and theory in social science. Earl W. Count [and] Gordon T. Bowles, editors. [Syracuse, N.Y.] Syracuse University Press, 1964. xvi, 253 p. 24cm.

Essays in honor of Douglas Haring presented in his seventieth year.
Includes bibliographical references.
CONTENTS.--Foreword, by S.K. Bailey.--Editors' preface, by E.W. Count and G.T. Bowles.--Douglas G. Haring, man and scholar: Earlier

(Continued)

NN * R 9.64 e/B OC, I PC, 1, 2, 3, I SL E, 1, 2, 3, I (LC1, X1, Z1)

4

COST en baet; opstellenbundel aangeboden aan Prof. Drs. J. Brands bij zijn afscheid als hoogleraar in de bedrijfshuishoudkunde aan de Nederlandsche economische hoogeschool op 28 november 1963. Leiden, H.E. Stenfert Kroese, 1963. xv, 282 p. port. 25cm.

Bibliographical footnotes.

(Continued)

NN R 6.64 e/B OC PC, 1, 2, 3 SL E, 1, 2, 3 (LC1, X1, Z1)

4

COUNT, EARL WENDEL, 1899- , ed. Fact and theory in social science. (Card 2)

years and scholarly career, by G.T. Bowles. The action-system theory of social behavior, by P. Meadows. Bibliography: the writings of Douglas G. Haring (p. 24-32)--Dimensions of sociological thought: Sociological and cultural-anthropological elements in the writings of Johann Gottfried von Herder, by W.C. Lehmann. Myth, theory, and value in cultural anthropology, questions and comments, by J.W. Bennett. Dimensions of fact in anthropology, by E.W. Count. Some issues of relevance of data for

(Continued)

COUNT, EARL WENDEL, 1899- , ed. Fact and theory in social science. (Card 3)

behavioral science, by R.E.L. Faris.--Developments in social theory: The uses of anthropological materials in political theory, by C.J. Friedrich. Recent trends in structural-functional theory, by T. Parsons. Societal complexity and limited alternatives, by J.F. Manfredi. The validity of "Oedipus complex" as an abstract scientific construct, by E. Becker.--Cultural relativity: Facts and their recognition among the Bella Coola, by T.F. McIlwraith. Cultural context and population control programs in village India, by M.E. Opler. Active vulcanism in Kau,

(Continued)

COUNT, EARL WENDEL, 1899- , ed. Fact and theory in social science. (Card 4)

Hawaii, as an ecological factor affecting native life and culture, by E.S.C. Handy. The American official overseas, by A.R. Hussey.

1. Haring, Douglas Gilbert, 1894- . 2. Social sciences--Addresses, essays, lectures. 3. Sociology--Addresses, essays, lectures. I. Bowles, Gordon Townsend, joint ed.

TAD

... **Cournot** nella economia e nella filosofia. **Padova, Cedam, 1939.**

3 p. l., [3]-243 p., 2 l. 24½cm. (Collana ca' Foscari. Facoltà di economia e commercio, Venezia)

At head of title: Amoroso, Baudin, Bordin ... [ed altri]

Bibliographical foot-notes.

CONTENTS.—La Harpe, J. de. Le rationalisme mathématique d'Antoine Augustin Cournot.—Baudin, L. La loi économique.—Lanzillo, A. "Caso" e vitalismo.—Roy, R. Cournot et la théorie mathématique des richesses.—Mises, L. von. Les hypothèses de travail dans la science économique.—Amoroso, L. La teoria matematica del programma economico.—Pietri-Tonelli, A. de. Generalizzazioni via via più larghe della soluzione data da Cournot al problema economico particolare dello scambio di beni economici fra i soggetti diversi in un tempo economico elementare.—Bordin, A. Le teorie economiche di A. Cournot e l'ordinamento corporativo.—Giacalone-Monaco, T. Nota biografica e bibliografica su A. A. Cournot (p. [227]-243)

1. Cournot, Antoine Augustin, 1801-1877.

Harvard univ. Library for Library of Congress [2] A C 40-386

---

*XM-2042

CRAIG, HARDIN, 1875- , ed.

The Parrot presentation volume; essays in dramatic literature. By pupils of Thomas Marc Parrott, published in his honor. Princeton, Princeton university press, 1935. 470 p. port. 24cm.

Microfiche (neg.) 10 sheets. 11 x 15cm. (NYPL FSN 10,265)

CONTENTS.--Thomas Marc Parrott, by J.D. Spaeth.--Published writings of Professor Parrott, by Harry Clemons (p. [13]-24)--Ethics in the

NN R 4.72 b/J OC PC, 1, 2 SL (UM1, LC1, X1, Z1, ZA1) (Continued)

CRAIG, HARDIN, 1875- , ed. The Parrot presentation volume; essays in dramatic literature. (Card 2)

Jacobean drama: the case of Chapman, by Hardin Craig.--Early sentimental comedy, by DeW. C. Croissant.--Political theory in the plays of George Chapman, by C.W. Kennedy.--For Shakespeare's Hamlet, by Huberths Cummings.--The greatest of Elizabethan melodramas, by Lacy Lockert.--Shakespeare's "Troilus and Cressida", yet deeper in its tradition, by W.B.D. Henderson.--A note upon William Shakespeare's use of Pliny, by T.W. Baldwin.--The drama in a frontier theater, by

(Continued)

CRAIG, HARDIN, 1875- , ed. The Parrot presentation volume; essays in dramatic literature. (Card 3)

G. R. Stewart, jr.--The scenes as Shakespeare saw them, by T.B. Hunt.--Shakespeare's portrayal of Shylock, by H.B. Walley.--Byron's "Werner" re-estimated: a neglected chapter in nineteenth century stage history, by T.H.V. Motter.--Sir Giles Mompesson and Sir Giles Overreach, by R. H. Ball.--A deep and sad passion, by D.A. Stauffer.--Milton and Euripides, by P.W. Timberlake.--The shipwreck, by William Huse.--Henry Nevil Payne, dramatist and Jacobite conspirator, by Willard Thorp.--Dryden's

(Continued)

CRAIG, HARDIN, 1875- , ed. The Parrot presentation volume; essays in dramatic literature. (Card 4)

"tagged" version of "Paradise lost", by P.S. Havens.--The influence of Shakespeare on Smollett, by G.M. Kahrl.--The verse lining of the first quarto of "King Lear", by Edward Hubler.--Jane Bell: printer at the East end of Christ-church, by Rudolf Kirk.--The philosophy of Hamlet, by J. E. Baker.

1. Parrott, Thomas Marc, 1866- . 2. Drama, English--Hist. and crit.

---

*MFG 71-26

Credo musicale. Komponistenporträts aus d. Arbeit d. Dresdener Kreuzchores. Festgabe zum 80. Geburtstag [v.] Rudolf Mauersberger. (Hrsg. im Auftr. d. Evang.-luth. Landeskirchenamtes Sachsens v. Ulrich von Brück.) Kassel, Basel, Bärenreiter-Verlag (1969).

217 p. with music, several plates, front. 25 cm.

NN*R 4. 71 w/J OC, I, II, IIIb* PC, 1, 3, I, II SL MU, 1, 2, 3, I, II (LC1, X1, Z1) (Continued)

CREDO musicale. Komponistenporträts aus d. Arbeit d. Dresdener Kreuzchores. (Card 2)

CONTENTS.—Wegbereiter der katholischen Kirchenmusik, von A. Kröhnert.—Wegweiser in die Zukunft? Von W. Steude.—Schein, ein hoher Mann, Schein, ein hoher Nam'! Von E.-O. Göring.—Sein Weg zum Thomaskantor, von H. Otto.—Omnia ad maiorem Dei gloriam, von H. Pflugbeil.—Romantik in der Kirche? Von W. Schönheit.—Blüh auf, gefrorner Christ! Von H. Collum.—Zwischen grossen Kirchenmusik und Gebrauchmusik, von H. Gadsch.—"Ahnung einer neuen Weltordnung," von E. Schmidt.—Lebendige Aussage, von L. Baumgärtel.—Bekenntnis zur Einheit des Glaubens, von H.-H. Albrecht.—

(Continued)

CREDO musicale. Komponistenporträts aus d. Arbeit d. Dresdener Kreuzchores. (Card 3)

Evangelische Kirchenmusik im Aufbruch, von K. Flämig.—"... wi ei ich die Möglichkeit der Tonalität noch nicht für erschöpft halte," von C. Albrecht.—In der Tradition zum Aufbruch, von V. Bräutigam.—Kirchenmusik und Jazz, von H.-G. Oertel.—Literatur (p. 215-[216])

1. Church music. 2. Essays. 3. Musicians. I. Mauersberger, Rudolf, 1889- . II. Brück, Ulrich von, ed. III. Brück, Ulrich von.

F-11
1456

Crisafulli, Alessandro S *ed.*
Linguistic and literary studies in honor of Helmut A. Hatzfeld, edited by Alessandro S. Crisafulli. Washington, Catholic University of America Press, 1964.
xii, 410 p. map, port. 26 cm.
Contributions in English, German, French, Italian, and Spanish.
"A bibliography of the writings of Helmut A. Hatzfeld": p. [1]-21.
Bibliographical footnotes.
1. Romance philology--Addresses, essays, lectures. 2. Literature--Addresses, essays, lectures. 3. Hatzfeld, Helmut, 1892- I. Crisafulli, Alessandro S.
NN* R 3.66 g/r OC, Ib* PC, 1, 2, 3 SL (LC1, X1, Z1) [I]

F-10
2219

CRITICA SOCIALE.
Esperienze e studi socialisti in onore di Ugo Guido Mondolfo, a cura di "Critica sociale." Firenze, La Nuova Italia editrice, 1957. xii, 342 p. port. 28cm.
1. Socialism, 1945- . 2. Socialism--Italy. 3. Mondolfo, Ugo Guido, 1875- . I. Title
NN 7.58 d/P(OC)3b+ OS PC, 1, 2, 3, I SL E, 1, 2, 3, I (LC1, X1, Z1, C1, Y1)

D-19
4433

Crisis in the "Great republic"; essays presented to Ross J. S. Hoffman. Edited by Gaetano L. Vincitorio, with the assistance of James E. Bunce, Elisa A. Carrillo, and Joseph F. X. McCarthy. New York, Fordham University Press, 1969.
xix, 322 p. port. 22 cm.
Bibliographical footnotes.
(Continued)
NN*R 6.70 w/l OC, I, II, IIIb* PC, 1, 2, I, II SL E, 2, I, II (LC1, X1, Z1)
4

E-13
2136

The Critical spirit; essays in honor of Herbert Marcuse. Edited by Kurt H. Wolff and Barrington Moore. With the assistance of Heinz Lubasz, Maurice R. Stein, and E. V. Walter. Boston, Beacon Press [1967]
xi, 436 p. 24 cm.
Bibliographical footnotes.
CONTENTS.—Introduction: What is the critical spirit?—Utopianism,
(Continued)
NN*R 5.68 v/R OC, I, II PC, 1, 2, 3, I, II SL E, 1, 2, 3, I, II (LC1, X1, Z1)
4

CRISIS in the "Great republic"... (Card 2)

CONTENTS.—Foreword, by R. I. Gannon.—An appreciation, by L. H. Gipson.—William Dowdeswell's Thoughts on the present state of public affairs, by M. F. De S. Boran.—Edmund Burke and the First Partition of Poland: Britain and the Crisis of 1772 in the Great republic, by G. L. Vincitorio.—The King's purse and the absentee's pocket in eighteenth-century Ireland, by S. J. Fanning.—The role of prudence in Burke's politics, by P. J. Stanlis.—The
(Continued)

The Critical spirit ... [1967] (Card 2)

ancient and modern, by M. I. Finley.—Primitive society in its many dimensions, by S. Diamond.—Manicheanism in the Enlightenment, by R. H. Popkin.—Schopenhauer today, by M. Horkheimer.—Beginning, in Hegel and today, by K. H. Wolff.—The social history of ideas; Ernst Cassirer and after, by P. Gay.—Policies of violence, from Montesquieu to the Terrorists, by E. V. Walter.—Thirty-nine articles; toward a theory of social theory, by J. R. Seeley.—History as private enterprise, by H. Zinn.—From Socrates to Plato, by H. Meyerhoff.—Rational society and irrational art, by H. Read.—The quest for the Grail; Wagner and Morris, by C. E. Schorske.—Valéry; Monsieur
(Continued)

CRISIS in the "Great republic"... (Card 3)

British career of a New York Federalist, by J. F. X. McCarthy.—The Whigs and the Invasion Crisis of 1779, by J. E. Bunce.—The forces of the Crown in Ireland, 1798, by W. D. Griffin.—"Young England" and its political debut, 1843, by N. Varga.—Napoleon III, Venetia, and the War of 1866, by J. W. Bush.—Crisis in East-central Europe: The Teschen dispute, by E. Kusielewicz.—Alcide De Gasperi: the view from the Vatican, 1929-1943, by E. A. Carrillo.—The new nationalism and the old: America and Europe, by C. R. Cleary.—Crisis and progress in postwar France, by J. N. Moody.—A select bibliography of the works of Ross J. S. Hoffman, by P. R. Ziegler (p. 309-315)
(Continued)

The Critical spirit ... [1967] (Card 3)

Teste, by L. Goldmann.—History and existentialism in Sartre, by L. Krieger.—German popular biographies; culture's bargain counter, by L. Lowenthal.—The Rechtsstaat as magic wall, by O. Kirchheimer.—Revolution from above; some notes on the decision to collectivize Soviet agriculture, by E. H. Carr.—Winston Churchill, power politician and counter-revolutionary, by A. J. Mayer.—Brahmins and business, 1870-1914; a hypothesis on the social basis of success in American history, by G. Kolko.—On the limits of professional thought, by M. R. Stein.—The limits of integration, by P. Mattick.—The society nobody wants; a look beyond Marxism and liberalism,
(Continued)

CRISIS in the "Great republic"... (Card 4)

1. History, Modern--Addresses, essays, lectures. 2. World politics, 1945- . I. Hoffman, Ross John Swartz, 1902- . II. Vincitorio, Gaetano L., ed. III. Vincitorio, Gaetano L.

The CRITICAL spirit... (Card 4)

by B. Moore.--Marcuse as teacher, by W. Leiss, J. D. Ober, and E. Sherover.--Marcuse bibliography, by W. Leiss, J. D. Ober, and E. Sherover (p. 427-433).

1. Social sciences--Addresses, essays, lectures. 2. Political science--Addresses, essays, lectures. 3. Marcuse, Herbert, 1898- . I. Wolff, Kurt H., 1912- , ed. II. Moore, Barrington, 1913- , ed.

CBA

Cronne, Henry Alfred, *ed.*

Essays in British and Irish history, in honour of James Eadie Todd. Edited by H. A. Cronne, T. W. Moody and D. B. Quinn. London, F. Muller [1949]

xv, 336 p. port. 23 cm.

Bibliographical footnotes.

1. Todd, James Eadie. 2. Gt. Brit.—Hist.—Addresses, essays, lectures. 3. Ireland—Hist.—Addresses, essays, lectures.

DA26.T6 942.004 50-3232

Library of Congress [2] Fest.

BAC

The Crusades and other historical essays ... 1928. (Card 2)

CONTENTS—Continued.

and the county of Edessa, by A. A. Beaumont, jr. The Genoese colonies in Syria, by E. H. Byrne. A twelfth century preacher—Fulk of Neuilly, by M. R. Gutsch. The crusading ardor of John of Garland, by L. J. Paetow.—pt. 2. Other historical essays: An exchequer reform under Edward I, by J. F. Willard. Lord Haldane's mission to Berlin in 1912, by Bernadotte E. Schmitt. Sources of diplomatic history and the control of foreign affairs, by W. E. Lingelbach. Rockbridge County, Virginia, in 1835: a study of ante-bellum society, by H. A. Kellar. List of the writings of Professor Dana C. Munro, 1894-1926, compiled by Marion P. West. List of patrons. Index, compiled by H. A. Kellar.

1. Munro, Dana Carleton, 1866- 2. Crusades. 3. History—Addresses, essays, lectures. I. Paetow, Louis John, 1880- ed.

Library of Congress D6.C7 28-8531

~~Copy 2.~~

Copyright A 1069395 [3-3]

E-12
4199

Cropsey, Joseph, *ed.*

Ancients and moderns; essays on the tradition of political philosophy in honor of Leo Strauss. New York, Basic Books [1964]

xiv, 330 p. illus. 24 cm.

Includes bibliographies.

CONTENTS.—Leo Strauss on his sixty-fifth birthday.—Preface, by J. Cropsey.—Sophocles' Oedipus tyrannus, by S. Benardete.—Human being and citizen: a beginning to the study of Plato's Apology of

(Continued)

NN* R 8.65 g/ OC PC,1,2, I SL E,1,2 (LC1,X1,Z1) 3

NPW

Cuba. Cultura, Dirección de.

Homenaje a Enrique Jose Varona en el cincuentenario de su primer curso de filosofía (1880–1930); miscelánea de estudios literarios, históricos y filosóficos. La Habana, Cuba: Secretaría de educación, Dirección de cultura, 1935. 591 p. facsims., front. (port.) 27cm.

"Bibliografía de Varona," p. 495-518.

770916A. 1. Varona y Pera, Enrique José, 1849-1933. 2. Varona y Pera, Enrique José, 1849-1933—Bibl. 3. Spanish America—Civilization.

N. Y. P. L. January 3, 1936

CROPSEY, JOSEPH, ed. Ancients and moderns... (Card 2)

Socrates, by G. Anastaplo.—Aristotle, an introduction, by J. Klein.—Aristotle's Poetics, by L. Berns.—Two horses and a charioteer, by P. H. Von Blanckenhagen.—The Emperor Julian and his art of writing, by A. Kojève.—Averroës on divine law and human wisdom, by M. Mahdi.—Natural law in Albo's Book of roots, by R. Lerner.—Bastards and usurpers: Shakespeare's King John, by H. B. White.—Grimmelshausen's laughter, by H. Speier.—Hobbes and the transition to modernity, by J. Cropsey.—An outline of Gulliver's travels, by A. Bloom.—Montesquieu and the classics: republican government in The spirit of the laws, by D. Lowenthal.—Mill's On liberty, by H.

(Continued)

HFE

Cultura política.

O pensamento político do presidente; separata de artigos e editoriais dos primeiros 25 números da revista "Cultura política" comemorativa do 60.° aniversário do Presidente Getúlio Vargas, 19 de abril de 1943. Rio de Janeiro [1943] 424 p. 23cm.

"Bibliografia sobre o estado nacional e o pensamento do presidente," p. [391]-424.

246599B. 1. Brazil—Politics, 1889- 2. Vargas, Getúlio, pres. Brazil, 1883- I. Title.

N. Y. P. L. December 15, 1943

CROPSEY, JOSEPH, ed. Ancients and moderns... (Card 3)

Gildin.—Political philosophy as the search for truth, by H. M. Magid.—The writings of Leo Strauss.—Index.

1. Political science--Addresses, essays, lectures. 2. Strauss, Leo--Bibl. I. Title

---

*MG p.v.370

Curjel, Hans.

Gedenkrede für Hermann Schechen 1891-1966. Zürich, Kommission Hug, [1967].

35 p. illus., facsim. 21 cm.

Reprinted from Generalprogramm 1967/68 des Musikkollegiums Winterthur.

1. Scherchen, Hermann, 1891 -1966.

NN R 4.72 e/k OC PC,1 SL MU,1 (LC1,X1,Z1)

BAC

The **Crusades** and other historical essays, presented to Dana C. Munro by his former students, edited by Louis J. Paetow. New York, F. S. Crofts & co., 1928.

x, 419 p. front. (port.) 23½cm.

"This edition is strictly limited to seven hundred and fifty copies printed from type, of which this is copy number ~~400~~." 355

CONTENTS.—pt. 1. History of the crusades: The great German pilgrimage of 1064-1065, by E. Joranson. The Pope's plan for the first crusade, by F. Duncalf. A neglected passage in the Gesta and its bearing on the literature of the first crusade, by A. C. Krey. Robert II of Flanders in the first crusade, by M. M. Knappen. Albert of Aachen

359332A (Continued on next card) 28-8531

[3-3]

E-11
7582

Curtiss, John Shelton, 1899- *ed.*

Essays in Russian and Soviet history, in honor of Geroid Tanquary Robinson. New York, Columbia University Press, 1963.

xx, 345 p. 25 cm.

Bibliographical footnotes.

CONTENTS.—Geroid Tanquary Robinson, by J. S. Curtiss.—Peter the Great and the church as an educational institution, by G. Bissonnette.—Radishchev and Catherine II: new gleanings from old archives, by D. M. Lang.—Alexander Herzen's parallel between the United States and Russia, by A. Kucherov.—N. K. Mikhailovskii's "What is

(Continued)

NN R 11.63 g/k OC PC,1,2 SL S,1,2 (LC1,X1,Z1)

Curtiss, John Shelton, 1899- *ed.* **Essays in Russian** and Soviet history ... 1963. (Card 2)

CONTENTS—Continued.

progress?" by F. B. Randall.—V. I. Semevskii (1848-1916): Russian social historian, by M. B. Petrovich.—Dostoevskii and Pobedonostsev, by R. F. Byrnes.—The form of government of the Russian Empire prior to the constitutional reforms of 1905-6, by M. Szeftel.—The first stage of Michurinism, by D. Joravsky.—Plekhanov and the Revolution of 1905, by S. H. Baron.—Lenin's "revolutionary democratic dictatorship of the proletariat and peasantry," by K. E. McKenzie.—Lenin on the "party" nature of science and philosophy, by M. W. Mikulak.—French socialism, German theory, and the flaw in the foun-

(Continued)

Curtiss, John Shelton, 1899- *ed.* Essays in Russian and Soviet history ... 1963. (Card 3)

CONTENTS—Continued.

dation of the socialist internationals, by B. D. Wolfe.—Russian industrialists look to the future: thoughts on economic development, 1906-17, by R. A. Roosa.—The Conference of Jassy: an early fiasco of the anti-Bolshevik movement, by R. H. McNeal.—Comintern policy toward the world trade-union movement: the first year, by A. Resis.—Zinoviev on the German revolution of October, 1923: a case study of a Bolshevik attitude toward revolutions abroad, by W. Korey.—Karl Radek and the Chinese Revolution, 1925-27, by W. Lerner.—M. N. Pokrovskii and the impact of the first five-year plan on Soviet historiography, by

(Continued)

CURTISS, JOHN SHELTON, 1899- , ed. Essays in Russian and Soviet history... 1963. (Card 4)

CONTENTS—Continued.

P. H. Aron.—Or the crises in the Russian polity, by T. H. von Laue.—How the Communists conquered a French trade union, by T. T. Hammond.

1. Russia--Hist.--Addresses, essays, lectures. 2. Robinson, Gerold Tanquary, 1892-

---

QOD

Custom is king; essays presented to R. R. Marett on his seventieth birthday, June 13, 1936. Edited by L. H. Dudley Buxton. London: Hutchinson's Scientific and Technical Publ. [1936] xiii, 325 p. incl. tables. front. (port.), illus. (charts), plates. 22½cm.

CONTENTS.—R. R. Marett, by L. H. D. Buxton.—An interesting Naga-Melanesian culture-link, by Henry Balfour.—Totemism and blood groups in West Africa, by R. S. Rattray.—Greeks and Northmen, by R. M. Dawkins.—The Wiro sky-god, by H. J. Rose.—The prehistory of the Canadian Indians, by Diamond Jenness.—The modern growth of the totem pole on the north-west coast, by Marius Barbeau.—The relation of physical anthropology to cultural anthropology, by E. A. Hooton.—A note on

(Continued)

N. Y. P. L. November 18, 1936

Custom is king... (Card 2)

rhytons, by C. G. Seligman.—Die religiöse Bedeutung der Paradiesmythen, von K. T. Preuss.—The chameleon and the sun-god Lisa on the West African slave-coast, by D. Westermann.—Snobbery, by A. M. Hocart.—Field work in Bougainville, by Beatrice Blackwood.—Western seaways, by O. G. S. Crawford.—The sea raiders, by L. H. D. Buxton.—Recht im Werden, von Leonhard Adam.—Kinship, incest and exogamy of the Northern Territories of the Gold Coast, by M. Fortes.—Bond-friendship in Tikopia, by Raymond Firth.—Zur Religion einiger hinterindischer Bergvölker, von Christoph von Fürer-Haimendorf.—Daily life of the Nuer in dry season camps, by E. E. Evans-Pritchard.—A bibliography of the scientific writings of R. R. Marett, edited by T. K. Penniman.

853929A. 1. Anthropology—Addresses, essays, lectures. 2. Marett, Robert Ranulph, 1866- . I. Buxton, Leonard Halford Dudley, ed.

N. Y. P. L. November 18, 1936

---

* C-4 p.v.297

Dabney, William M , ed.

...Dargan historical essays; historical studies presented to Marion Dargan by his colleagues and former students, University of New Mexico. Edited by William M. Dabney and Josiah C. Russell. Albuquerque, Univ. of New Mexico press, 1952. 118 p. illus. (port.) 22cm. (New Mexico. University. University of New Mexico publications in history. no. 4.)

"Marion Dargan: bibliography," p. 5.

(Continued)

NN 2.53 OC, I (OD)II (ED)II PC, 1, 2, I, II SL (LC1, Z1, X1)

Dabney, William M , ed. ...Dargan historical essays... (Card 2)

CONTENTS.—The date of Henry I's charter to London, by J. C. Russell.—Erasmus on learning, by J. E. Longhurst.—Inventories of church furnishings in some of the New Mexico missions, 1672, by F. V. Scholes and E. B. Adams.—The Royal society of London; retailer in experimental philosophy, 1666-1800, by R. P. Stearns.—John Robinson and the fall of the conservative Virginia oligarchy, by W. M. Dabney.—First theater in English in New Mexico, by Dorothy Woodward.—Precursors of the Union leagues, by G. W. Smith.—Albert Franklin Banta; a rolling stone, by F. D. Reeve.—Governor W. E. Lindsey: a progressive frontiersman, by I. C. Ihde.—J. Ramsay MacDonald, the monarchy, and republicanism, by Benjamin Sacks.

1. Dargan, Marion. 2. History—Addresses, essays, lectures. I. Russell, Josiah Cox, 1900- , jt. ed. II. Series.

D-16
2187

DAGENS NYHETER, Stockholm.

Festskrift: Harry Bjurström, 1905 2/7 1955. [Stockholm, 1955] 121 p. illus., ports. 23cm.

1. Bjurström, Harry, 1905- 2. Journalism--Sweden. I. Title.

NN 7.66 p/ (OC)1b+, I OS PC. 1, 2, I SL (LC1, X1, Z1)

F-10
9974

DAHL-IVERSEN, ERLING, 1892-

Vor kirurgiske arv, kirurgien i Danmark i det 19. århundrede. København, 1960. 348 p. illus., ports. 27cm.

Added t.-p.: Festskrift udgivet... i anledning af Deres Majestæter kong Frederik IX og dronning Ingrids sølvbryllup den 24. maj 1960...

Bibliography, p. [333]-335.

(Continued)

NN * R 2.65 e/5 OC (OS)I PC. 1, 2, I SL (LC1, X1, Z1)

DAHL-IVERSEN, ERLING, 1892- . Vor kirurgiske arv, kirurgien i Danmark i det 19. århundrede. (Card 2)

1. Surgery--Denmark. 2. Surgeons--Denmark. I. Copenhagen. Universitet Festskrift... i anledning af Deres Majestæter kong Frederik IX og dronning Ingrids sølvbryllup den 24. maj 1960.

NND
DAI dettatori al novecento; studi in ricordo di Carlo Calcaterra nel primo anniversario della sua morte. [Torino] Società editrice internazionale [1953] 280 p. ports. 26cm. (Convivium: raccolta nuova)

Includes music.

CONTENTS.--Umanità di un maestro, di F. Forti. —Le umane lettere di Carlo Calcaterra, di G. Marzot. —Bibliografia degli scritti di Carlo Calcaterra, a cura di M. Saccenti con la (Continued)

NN* 11.55 p/// OC (OS) I PC, 1, 2 SL (U1, LC1, X1, Z1)

DAI dettatori al novecento... (Card 2)

collaborazione di M. Belletti e R. di Sabatino (p. 26-57). —Scheda per Boncompagno, di V. Pini. -- Nota dantesca: "ritrarsi," di L. Serra. -- Ritrattistica petrarchesca, di E. Raimondi. —Nuove osservazioni intorno al petrarchismo di Juan Boscán, di M. Boni. —Ipotesi sul primo nucleo del De vita solitaria, di R. di Sabatino. —Melica medievale, "Ars nova" e lirica del Petrarca, di G. Vecchi. — (Continued)

DAI dettatori al novecento... (Card 3)

Le correzioni autografe al Torrismondo, di B. T. Sozzi. --Questioni dellavalliane, di P. Cazzani. -- Il Lucrezio di A. Marchetti nella crisi del seicento, di M. Saccenti. --L. A. Muratori e la poetica della meraviglia, di F. Forti. --Alfieri e Du Theil, di C. Jannaco. —Notre alfieriane, con documenti inediti, di L. Caretti. --Alessandro Manzoni e lo storicismo romantico, di U. Pirotti. —Una lettera inedita di Lodovico di Breme al Ginguené, di P. Camporesi. --Un testa- mento inedito del (Continued)

DAI dettatori al novecento... (Card 4)

Tommaseo e due note al suo "Carteggio" col Capponi, di M. Pecoraro. -- Ritmo e poesia nei contemporanei, di P. L. Contessi.

1. Italian literature—Addresses, essays, lectures. 2. Calcaterra, Carlo, 1884-1952. I. Convivium: raccolta nuova.

* OLY
DAIVAGNA choodamani vidyalankar shastri Rewashankar Becharbhai Trivedi abhinandana grantha (commemoration volume) presented to shastri Rewashankar Becharbhai Trivedi by sri Sankaracharya, sri Chandrasekharendra Saraswati swamiji of Kanchi Kamakoti Peetam. Madras, 1958. 1 v. (various pagings) illus., ports. 25cm.

Text in English, Gujarati or Sanskriti.

1. Trivedi, Rewashankar Becharbhai, 1892- 2. Hinduism.
NN X 12.58 p/// OC, 1b PC, 1, 2 SL O, 1, 2 (LC1, X1, Z1)

F-10
2784
DAMIANO, ANDREA.
Guido Donegani. [Firenze] Vallecchi [1957] 168 p. illus. (part col.), ports. 29cm.

"Questa pubblicazione è stata curata dalla Società Montecatini per ricordare il suo Presidente Guido Donegani nel decimo anniversario della morte."

1. Donegani, Guido, 1877-1947. I. "Montecatini," società generale per l'industria mineraria e chimica.
NN 10.58 d/γ OC, 1b+ (OS)I PC, 1, I SL (LC1, X1, Z1)

L-10
7749
Bd. 5
DANCKWORTT, DIETER, ed.
Internationale Beziehungen, ein Gegenstand der Sozialwissenschaft, bearb. von Dieter Danckwortt als Festgabe zum 70. Geburtstag von Dr. Walter Jacobsen. [Frankfurt a. M.] Europäische Verlagsanstalt [1966] 124 p. illus. 24cm. (Politische Psychologie. Bd. 5)
Includes bibliographies.
(Continued)
NN 8.66 p/lu OC (OS)I PC, 1, 2, I E, 1, 2, I (LC1, X1, Z1)

DANCKWORTT, DIETER, ed. Internationale Beziehungen... (Card 2)

CONTENTS.—Widmung für Dr. Walter Jacobsen. -Einführung, von D. Danckwortt. --Frieden und Friedensforschung, von J. Galtung. -Psychologische Forschungen zum Problem internationaler Konflikte, von H. Thomae.-Methoden zur Erforschung von Gruppenbeziehungen, von A. Karsten. -Gedanken zu Minoritätsfragen in der Schweiz, von H. Fischer. -Der Wechsel der Minoritäten beim Bevölkerungszuwachs von Helsinki, von K. von Fieandt. -Zur Soziologie und Sozialpsychologie kolonialer Abhängigkeitsverhältnisse, von G. Grohs. -Psychologische Probleme der Entwicklungshilfe, von D. Breitenbach. -Nationale Vorstellungen und internationale (Continued)

DANCKWORTT, DIETER, ed. Internationale Beziehungen... (Card 3)

Kontakte bei Auslandsurlaubern auf Mallorca, von E. E. Davis. -Multiplikatoren aus Frankreich an der Berliner Mauer, von E. V. Couchoud. -Der Beitrag der Sprachwissenschaft zum Problem der internationalen Erziehung, von W. Schmidt-Hidding.

1. Jacobsen, Walter, 1895- 2. International relations--Addresses, essays, lectures. I. Series.

E-10
9347
DANCWERC, opstellen aangeboden aan Prof. Dr. D. Th. Enklaar ter gelegenheid van zijn vijfenzestigste verjaardag. [De redactie: W. Jappe Alberts et al.] Groningen, J. B. Wolters, 1959. 362 p. illus., ports. 24cm.

Bibliographical footnotes.
CONTENTS.--Het begin van de Griekse kolonisatie in het Westen; geschiedenis en archaeologie, door L. Byvanck-Quarles van Ufford en (Continued)
NN R 12.59 t/ OC, I PC, 1, 2, I SL (LC1, X1, Z1)

DANC WERC... (Card 2)

A. W. Byvanck.--De laatste zeeslag tussen Carthago en Rome, door J.H. Thiel.--De stad in de geschiedenis van Azië, door W.P. Coolhaas.--Virgil of Salzburg versus "Aethicus Ister," by M. Draak.--Over de geboortedatum van Karel de Grote, door F.L. Ganshof.--De samantiek van Honor en de oorsprong van het heerlijk gezag, door J.F. Niermeyer.--De oorsprong van de rituele zalving der koningen; de stand van een probleem, door C.A. Bouman.--Scarmannen-Koningsvrijen, door J.M. van Winter.--Aux origines de Malines, par P. Bonenfant.--Bijdrage tot een nieuwe uitgave van de Annales gandenses, door H. van Werveke.--Opstand en revolutie in de Middeleuwen, door F.W.N. Hugenholtz.--
(Continued)

F-11
4744

Dannevig, Birger. 1921-
Farsunds sjøfarts historie. Utg. av Farsund sjømannsforening og Farsund kreds av Norges rederforbund. Farsund, 1967.

583 p. illus. 26 cm.

Issued in honor of Farsund sjømannsforenings 75th anniversary.
Bibliography: p. 564-567.

1. Shipping--Norway--Farsund. I. Farsund sjømannsforening.
t. 1967.
NN * R 10.68 1⁄c OC (OS)I, 1b* PC,1,I SL E,1,I ST,1t,I (LC1,X1,Z1)

DANC WERC... (Card 3)

Die Hanse in europaischer Sicht, von H. Sproemberg.--De Tolnaers als stadsklerken van Utrecht, door F. Ketner.--Afdamming van de Nederrijn, een plan uit 1447-'49, foor A.G. Jongkees.--Heerlijkheden in Overijssel onder het "Ancien regime", door G.J. ter Kuile jr.--Windesheim, Agnietenberg en Marienborn en hun aandeel in de Noordnederlandse boekverluchting, door G.I. Lieftinck.--Zuster Bertkens passieboekje, door.K. Meeuwesse.--Over een recente bijdrage tot de laatscholastieke natuurfilosofie, door E.J. Dijksterhuis.--Adriaan Florenzoon, familie, opleiding, door R.R. Post.--Karel V en de Nederlanden, door W. Jappe Alberts.--"Den Coninck van
(Continued)

M-11
4224
no.1

DANSK folkemuseum & Frilandsmuseet; history & activities. Axel Steensberg in honour of his 60th birthday 1st June 1966. [Copenhagen] 1966. 263 p. illus. 27cm. (Copenhagen. Nationalmuseet. Folkelivs studier. Studies of folklife. 1)

Edited by H. Rasmussen.
Includes bibliographies.
1. Copenhagen. Nationalmuseet. Dansk folkemuseum. 2. Copenhagen. Nationalmuseet. Frilandsmuseet. I. Series.
NNR 12.69 v⁄c OC (OS)I PC,1, 2,I A,1,2 (LC1,X1,Z1)

DANC WERC... (Card 4)

Hispaengien heb ick altijt geheert", door J.K. Oudendijk.--Wie schreef Protecteur Weerwolf? Dooe W. Asselbergs.--De familie-portretten uit de collectie De la Court, door J.H. Kernkamp.--Een postscriptum van De la Court, door P. Geyl.--Artem penetrat, door J.G. van Gelder.--"New history", door P.J. van Winter.--Lijst der geschriften van Prof. Dr. D. Th. Enklaar (p.330-355).

1. Enklaar, Diederik Theodorus, 1894- . 2. Europe--Hist.--Addresses, essays, lectures. I. Jappe Alberts, W., ed.

GHD

Dansk historisk fællesforening.
Festskrift til Knud Fabricius 13. august 1945 fra Dansk historisk fællesforening. København, 1945. 228 p. illus., maps. 27cm.

605082B. 1. Fabricius, Knud, 1875- . 2. Denmark.
N. Y. P. L.

---

* MEC
(Türk)

... Daniel Gottlob Türk; der Begründer der hallischen Händeltradition, aus Anlass der 125. Wiederkehr seines Todestages am 26. August 1938. Im Auftrage des Oberbürgermeisters herausgegeben vom Kulturamt der Händelstadt Halle. Wolfenbüttel [etc.] G. Kallmeyer, 1938. 64 p. facsims., front. (port.), illus. (incl. music), pl. 24cm. (Schriftenreihe des Händelhauses in Halle; Veröffentlichungen aus dem Musikleben Mitteldeutschlands. Heft 4.)

CONTENTS.—Vorwort.—Daniel Gottlob Türk, von Grete Thieme-Hedler.—Daniel Gottlob Türk; sein Weg vom Kantatenschöpfer zum Begründer einer Händeltradition, von Walter Serauky.—D. G. Türks Persönlichkeit; Abschnitte aus dem im Jahre 1814 in der Allgemeinen musikalischen Zeitung erschienenen Nekrolog.

1. Türk, Daniel Gottlob, 1750-1813. I. Ser.
N. Y. P. L. April 28, 1939

GHD

Den Danske historiske Forening, Copenhagen.
Festskrift til Kristian Erslev, den 28. Decbr. 1927, fra danske Historikere. Udgivet af den Danske historiske Forening. København: H. Hagerups Boghandel, 1927. 701 p. 4°.

370297A.
1. Erslev, Kristian Sofus August, 1852- . 2. Denmark—Hist. 3. Title.
N. Y. P. L. July 5, 1928

NGO

DANK und Erkenntnis; Paul Fechter zum 75. Geburtstag am 14. September 1955 [hrsg. von Joachim Günther. Gütersloh] C. Bertelsmann [1955] 135 p. port. 25cm.

1. Essays, German—Collections. 2. Fechter, Paul, 1880- . I. Günther, Joachim, ed.

NN **R 4.56 d⁄c OC,I PC, 1,2,I SL (LC1,X1,Z1)

VPQ

Danske Syrevækker-Laboratorium. Odense, Denmark.
Festskrift til Ære for Professor, Dr. Phil. & Scient. S. Orla-Jensen; i Anledning af hans Forskergerning gennem ⅓ Aarhundrede og hans Lærergerning gennem ¼ Aahundrede... Under Medvirken af...A. Simonsen Andersen...Chr. Barthel...P. Arne Hansen [and others]...udgivet af "Det Danske Syrevækker-Laboratorium." [Odense?, 1931.] 126 p. incl. front. illus. (ports.) 4°.

580633A. 1. Orla-Jensen, Sigurd, 1870- . 2. Milk—Bacteriology.
N. Y. P. L. June 15, 1932

NIV

꜀**Dansklærerforeningen,** Copenhagen꜁

Festskrift til Vilhelm Andersen fra Kolleger og Disciple, udgivet i Anledning af hans halvfjerdsaars Fødselsdag, den 16 Oktober 1934. København: Gyldendalske Boghandel, Nordisk Forlag, 1934. 392 p. front. (port.) 26½cm.

"Udgivet af Dansklærerforeningen, Universitets-Jubilæets danske Samfund, Selskab for nordisk Filologi ved Svend Norrild, Gunnar Knudsen, Paul Diderichsen ꜀og꜁ Paul V. Rubow. Med Understøttelse af Carlsbergfondet."

CONTENTS.—Vedel, V. Fra Indtryk til Udtryk.—Hald, K. Saxos Uffesagn.—Frandsen, E. Folkeviser og Folkeviseforskning.—Bukdahl, J. Prosaens Tegnér.—Plesner, K. F. P. O. Brøndsted som Kulturpersonlighed.—Galster, K. Carsten Hauch

(Continued)

N. Y. P. L. February 28, 1936

꜀**Dansklærerforeningen,** Copenhagen꜁ Festskrift til Vilhelm Andersen... (Card 2)

i Kiel.—Nørvig, J. Blicher og Delille.—Dahlerup, V. Et Par Småting om Poul Møller og Chr. Winther.—Ellekilde, H. Thieles Folkesagn.—Brix, H. Til J. L. Heiberg.—Jensenius, K. Myten om Søren Kierkegaards sædelige Fald.—Topsøe-Jensen, H. G. Mit Livs Eventyr.—Ilsøe, P. Litterære Forudsætninger for Schacks "Phantasterne" med særligt Henblik paa Parodierne.—Saxtorph, V. Billedsprog som Personkarakteristik.—Rubow, P. V. Holger Drachmanns Sangbøger.—Friis, O. Hans Sophus Vodskov som litterær Kritiker.—Borup, M. Vilhelm Andersen og "Rembrandttyskeren."

(Continued)

N. Y. P. L. February 28, 1936

꜀**Dansklærerforeningen,** Copenhagen꜁ Festskrift til Vilhelm Andersen... (Card 3)

—Hallar, S. Naturen i Tide-Bøgerne.—Thomsen, E. Gudindernes Strid.—Paludan, H. A. Studier over Lazarus-Motivet.—Aakjær, S. Jarl, Aar og Lev-Mand.—Knudsen, G. Provstens Hat, og andre Hatte.—Brøndum-Nielsen, J. Dækket direkte Tale.—Bang, C. Fortegnelse over Skrifter af Vilhelm Andersen, 1883–1934.

795793A. 1. Andersen, Vilhelm, 1864– . 2. Danish literature—Hist. and crit. I. Universitets-Jubilæets danske Samfund. II. Selskab for nordisk Filologi. III. Norrild, Svend. IV. Knudsen, Gunnar, 1886– . V. Diderichsen, Paul. VI. Rubow, Paul Victor, 1896– . VII. Bang, Christian. VIII. Title.

N. Y. P. L. February 28, 1936

D-20
4359

Da **Dante** al Novecento. Studi critici offerti dagli scolari a Giovanni Getto nel suo ventesimo anno di insegnamento universitario. Milano, U. Mursia, 1970.

628 p. 23cm.

Includes bibliographical references.

CONTENTS.—Dante, Purgatorio I, di E. Sanguineti.—Il topos dell'ineffabile nel Paradiso dantesco, di A. Jacomuzzi.—Divagazione su due solitari: Bellerofonte e Petrarca, di M. P. Stocchi.—Petrarca fra Abelardo ed Eloisa, di M. Guglielminetti.—La cornice del Decameron

(Continued)

NN*R 5.71 d/ℓOC, I PC, 1, I SL (LC1, X1, Z1) [I]

Da **Dante** al Novecento. 1970. (Card 2)

o il mito di Robinson, di G. B. Squarotti.—Il tumulto dei Ciompi in un cronista fiorentino del tardo Trecento, di F. Gabriele.—Appunti in margine alle Familiari del Caro, di S. Jacomuzzi.—Crisi delle strutture e strutture della crisi nella Venexiana, di R. Alonge.—Il narrato oggettuale del Lasca, di G. D. Bonino.—Appunti per una definizione della maschera barocca, di R. Tessari.—Il mondo alla rovescia nel Cane di Diogene, di B. Zandrino.—Mito e metafora del Conte Duca nella letteratura italiana del Seicento (con un memoriale inedito di F. Testi)—Aspetti e motivi del Redi prosatore, di R. Pavese.—Per un riesame dell'ellenismo italiano nel secondo Settecento: Melchior Cesa-

(Continued)

Da DANTE al Novecento. 1970. (Card 3)

rotti, di M. Cerruti.—La nuova Citèra e le isole felici, di C. Magris.—Strumenti del realismo portiano, di F. Portinari.—Silvio Pellico milanese, di R. Massano.—Leopardi e Guicciardini, di G. L. Beccaria.—La ribellione di Renzo tra Eden e storia, di G. Baldi.—Camerana prosatore inedito, di G. De Rienzo.—Da Coppée a Pascoli, di R. Agnes.—Esotismo di Gozzano, di L. Mondo.—Coscienza e struttura nella narrativa dell'ultimo Svevo, di M. Ricciardi.—Il teatro di Bontempelli dal grottesco al pirandellismo, di G. Livio.

1. Italian literature--Addresses, essays, lectures.
I. Getto, Giovanni.

---

*RB-*H

DANTON, JOSEPH PERIAM, 1908-

Index to festschriften in librarianship [by] J. Periam Danton with the assistance of Ottilia C. Anderson. New York, R.R. Bowker, 1970. xi,461 p. 26cm.

1. Library science--Bibl. 2. Festschriften--Indexes.

NN S 7.70 w/4 OC PC, 1, 2 SL MR, 1, 2 *R, 1, 2 (LC1, X1, Z1)

F-10
126

DARK-AGE Britain; studies presented to E. T. Leeds, with a bibliography of his works. Edited by D. B. Harden. London, Methuen [1956] xxii, 270 p. 58 illus. (incl. maps), 36 plates, port. 27cm.

"A bibliography of the works of E. T. Leeds," p. xvii-xxii.

Bibliographical footnotes.

CONTENTS. --The Roman and Celtic survival: Coinage in Britain in the fifth and sixth centuries, by C. H. V. Sutherland. Two Celtic heads in stone

(Continued)

NN**R 9.56 a/b OC, I PC, 1, 2, I SL A, 1, 3, 4, I (LC1, X1, Z1, Y1)

DARK-AGE Britain... (Card 2)

from Corbridge, Northumberland, by I. A. Richmond. Romano-Saxon pottery, by J. N. L. Myres. Some sub-Romano-British brooches from South Wales, by H. N. Savory. Imported pottery found at Tintagel, Cornwall, by C. A. Ralegh Radford. Irish enamels of the Dark Ages and their relation to the cloisonné techniques, by F. Henry. --The pagan Saxons: The Jutes of Kent, by C. F. C. Hawkes. The Anglo-Saxon settlement in eastern England, by T. C. Lethbridge. Anglo-Saxon cremation and inhuman in the upper Thames valley in pagan times, by J. R. Kirk. Glass vessels in Britain and Ireland, A. D. 400-1000, by D. B. Harden. --The Christian Saxon and the Viking age: Late Saxon disc-brooches, by R. L. S. Bruce-Mitford. The siting of the

(Continued)

DARK-AGE Britain... (Card 3)

monastery of St. Mary and St. Peter in Exeter, by Sir Cyril Fox. Trade relations between England and the continent in the late Anglo-Saxon period, by G. C. Dunning. Saxon Oxford and its region, by E. M. Jope.

1. Leeds, Edward Thurlow, 1877-1955. 2. Great Britain--Hist. --Anglo-Saxon period, 449-1066. 3. Art, British, Middle Ages. 4. Art, Anglo-Saxon.
I. Harden, Donald Benjamin, ed.

D-18
5020

DAU, HELMUT.
Bibliographie juristischer Festschriften und Festschriftenbeiträge; Deutschland, Schweiz, Österreich: 1962-1966. Bielefeld, K. Runge, 1967. 195 p. 23cm.

1. Festschriften--Bibl. 2. Law--Bibl.
NN 10.68 k/A OC PC, 1, 2 SL E, 2 (LC1, X1, Z1)

D-14
772

Dau, Helmut.
Bibliographie juristischer Festschriften und Festschriftenbeiträge, 1945-1961: Deutschland, Schweiz, Österreich. Karlsruhe, C. F. Müller, 1962. 166 p. 23cm.

1. Festschriften—Bibl. 2. Law—Bibl.
NN R 11.63 OC(1bo) PC,1,2 SL (LC1,X1,Z1)

D-16
7604

Daues, Vincent F *ed.*
Wisdom in depth; essays in honor of Henri Renard, S. J. Edited by Vincent F. Daues, Maurice R. Holloway [and] Leo Sweeney. Foreword by John Wright. Milwaukee, Bruce Pub. Co. [1966]
x, 260 p. port. 23 cm.
Bibliographical footnotes.
CONTENTS.—Henri J. Renard, S. J.: a sketch, by J. P. Jelinek.—The good as undefinable, by M. Childress.—Gottlieb Söhngen's sacramental

(Continued)
NN* R 6.66 g/c OC(Ib*), I, IIb* PC, 1, 2, 3, I SL (LC1, X1, Z1) 3

DAUES, VINCENT F., ed. Wisdom in depth... (Card 2)

doctrine on the mass, by J. F. Clarkson.—Christ's eucharistic action and history, by B. J. Cooke.—Objective reality of human ideas: Descartes and Suarez, by T. J. Cronin.—A medieval commentator on some Aristotelian educational themes, by J. W. Donohue.—God as sole cause of existence, by M. Holloway.—Knowledge, commitment, and the real, by R. O. Johann.—John Locke and sense realism, by H. R. Klocker.—The being of nonbeing in Plato's Sophist, by Q. Lauer.—Ethics and verification, by R. McInerny.—Analogy and the fourth way, by J. J. O'Brien.—Love and being, by W. L. Rossner.—

(Continued)

DAUES, VINCENT F., ed. Wisdom in depth... (Card 3)

Complexity in human knowledge: its basis in form/matter composition, by E. L. Rousseau.—Toward a more dynamic understanding of substance and relation, by J. M. Somerville.—The origin of participant and of participated perfections in Proclus' Elements of theology, by L. Sweeney.

1. Philosophy--Addresses, essays, lectures. 2. Theology--Essays and misc. 3. Renard, Henry, 1894- . I. Holloway, Maurice R., ed. II. Holloway, Maurice R.

AN
(Edwards,O.)

Davies, *Sir* Alfred Thomas, 1861- *ed.*
"O. M." (Sir Owen M. Edwards) a memoir edited by Sir Alfred T. Davies ... Cardiff & Wrexham, Hughes a'i fab for the Ceiriog memorial institute, Glynceiriog, Denbighshire, 1946.
2 p. l., [3]-98 p. front., plates, ports., facsims. 22½ᶜᵐ.

1. Edwards, Sir Owen Morgan, 1858-1920.
DA722.1.E2D3 923.2429 46-22147
Library of Congress [3]

D-15
6082

Davies, Hugh Sykes, 1909- *ed.*
The English mind; studies in the English moralists presented to Basil Willey. Edited by Hugh Sykes Davies and George Watson. Cambridge [Eng.] University Press, 1964.
viii, 302 p. 23 cm.
Bibliographical footnotes.
CONTENTS.—Basil Willey: a tribute, by H. Butterfield.—Francis Bacon, by A. Righter.—Thomas Hobbes, by R. L. Brett.—John Locke

(Continued)
NN* R 11.64 g/r OC, I PC, 1, 2, 3, 4, I SL (LC1, X1, Z1)

DAVIES, HUGH SYKES, 1909- , ed. The English mind... (Card 2)

and the rhetoric of the Second treatise, by T. Redpath.—Shaftesbury's horses of instruction, by J. B. Broadbent.—Berkeley and the style of dialogue, by D. Davie.—Joseph Butler, by G. Watson.—David Hume: reasoning and experience, by R. Williams.—Radical prose in the late eighteenth century, by M. Hodgart.—Wordsworth and the empirical philosophers, by H. S. Davies.—Coleridge and the Victorians, by G. Hough.—Newman and the romantic sensibility, by J. Beer.—John Stuart Mill, by N. Annan.—Matthew Arnold and the continental idea, by H. Straumann.—Joseph Conrad: alienation and commitment, by I. Watt.—English and some Christian traditions, by J. Holloway.

(Continued)

DAVIES, HUGH SYKES, 1909- ed. The English mind... (Card 3)

1. Philosophy, English. 2. Ethics, English. 3. English literature--Addresses, essays, lectures. 4. Willey, Basil, 1897- I. Watson, George, joint ed.

BTH

Davis, Henry William Carless, 1874-1928, editor.
Essays in history, presented to Reginald Lane Poole; edited by H. W. C. Davis. Oxford: Clarendon Press, 1927.
xiv, 483 p. incl. tables. facsims., front. (port.), col'd plan. 8°.

328840A. 1. Poole, Reginald Lane, 1857- . 2. Middle Ages—Hist.

E-11
9865

Davis, Richard Beale, *ed.*
Studies in honor of John C. Hodges and Alwin Thaler. ⌊Edited by Richard Beale Davis and John Leon Lievsay⌋ Knoxville, University of Tennessee Press, 1961.

209 p. ports. 24cm. (Tennessee studies in literature. Special number)

Includes bibliographical references.

CONTENTS.—Byron, Chênedollé, and Lermontov's Dying gladiator, by J. T. Shaw.—The critic and the ballad, by H. O. Nygard.—Some records of the Somyr play, by R. E. Parker.—Characterization through dreams in the drama of Shakespeare's day, by B. T. Stewart.—On the question of unity in Peele's David and Bethsabe, by C. Blair.—Magic

(Continued)

NN* R 6.64 g/ OC, I (OD)It (ED)It PC, 1, 2, 3, 4, I, II SL
(LC1, X1, Z1)

DAVIS, RICHARD BEALE, ed. Studies in honor of John C. Hodges and Alwin Thaler. (Card 2)

and morality in Comus, by T. Wheeler.—Political drama of the Salmasian controversy, by H. G. Merrill.—Johnson on literary texture, by R. W. Daniel.—Boswell's portrait of Goldsmith, by L. Morgan.—The library of Robert Southey, by K. Curry.—Browning's The statue and the bust once more, by B. R. Litzinger.—The road to the dark tower: an interpretation of Browning's Childe Roland, by C. R. Woodard.—Beauchamp's career: Meredith's acknowledgment of his debt to Carlyle, by J. W. Morris.—GBS as play director, by P. Soper.—The ignorance of Mr. Bloom, by E. C. McAleer.—Dylan Thomas' birthday

(Continued)

DAVIS, RICHARD BEALE, ed. Studies in honor of John C. Hodges and Alwin Thaler. (Card 3)

poems, by O. Evans.—The influence of Italy on The marble faun, by N. Wright.—Whitman's tally, put at random, by F. DeW. Miller.—Transvaluation in the poetics of Wallace Stevens, by J. Baird.—American literature in the universities of France, by P. G. Adams.—Quest for values: the pilgrimage of Joseph Wood Krutch, by D. da Ponte.—A bibliography of the published writings of Alwin Thaler (p. 199–203)—A bibliography of the published writings of John C. Hodges (p. 205–208)

(Continued)

DAVIS, RICHARD BEALE, ed. Studies in honor of John C. Hodges and Alwin Thaler. (Card 4)

1. English literature--Addresses, essays, lectures. 2. American literature--Addresses, essays, lectures. 3. Hodges, John Cunyus, 1892- . 4. Thaler, Alwin, 1891- . I. Lievsay, John Leon, joint ed. II. Tennessee studies in literature. t. 1961

QAS

De Beer, Gavin Rylands, 1899- *ed.*
Evolution; essays on aspects of evolutionary biology, presented to Professor E. S. Goodrich on his seventieth birthday. Edited by G. R. de Beer. Oxford, The Clarendon press, 1938.

viii, 350 p., 2 l. front. (port.) illus., II pl. on 1 l., diagrs. 23cm.

"References" at end of each essay except the first; "Scientific works of E. S. Goodrich": p. ⌊337⌋–340.

1. Evolution—Addresses, essays, lectures. 2. Biology—Addresses, essays, lectures. 3. Goodrich, Edwin Stephen, 1868-

38-30353

Library of Congress QH367.D33
⌊5⌋ 575.04

---

* GAH

De libris. Bibliofile Breve til Ejnar Munksgaard paa 50-Aarsdagen, 28. Februar. København ⌊V. Pedersen⌋ 1940. 233 p. facsims., plates, ports. (incl. front.) 20½cm.

"Trykt i 300 nummererede Eksemplarer... Dette Eksemplar har No. 256."

CONTENTS.—Gelsted, Otto. Tryllehaven.—Beattie, W. Ulric in personas.—Blöndal, Sigfus. Sjaldgæft íslenzk-sænskt brúðkaupsrit.—Christensen, Arthur. Orientalske Haandskrifter og Facsimileudgaver.—Collijn, Isak. Två danska bokband.—Finnbogason, Gudm. Örlög skinnbókanna.—Helgason, Jón. Smaating om Lucas Debes.—Hermannsson, Halldor. Íslenskar rímbækur og almanök.—Jolivet, J. La première traduction de Holberg en français.—Klose, Olaf. Die nordische Professur in Kiel in der

(Continued)

N. Y. P. L. April 24, 1941

De libris... (Card 2)

2. Hälfte des 19. Jahrhunderts.—Lange, H. O. Spændende Situationer i en Bibliotekmands Liv.—Leyen, Friedrich von der. Bücherfreunde, damals und heute.—Meiner, Annemarie. Bücherfreundschaften.—Munthe, W. I Holbergs Fotspor. Zacharias Conrad von Uffenbach i England 1710.—Myre, Olav. Bibliofil selvbiografi.—Nordal, Sigurður. Íslenzkir bókamenn.—Raabe, G. E. Litt om den første dansk-norske utgave av Snorre Sturlason.—Rubow, P. V. Om Læsning.—Rust, Werner. Bibliographie und Zeitschriftenverzeichnisse.—Viets, H. R. Smollett, 'the war of Jenkins's ear' and an account of the expedition to Carthagena, 1743.—Vries, Jan de. Het Snjófridlied van Harald Schoonhaar.—Wieselgren, O. När Strindberg sålde sin boksamling.—Wolf, E. C. J. En Hjertesag.

106449B. 1. Munksgaard, Ejnar, 1890- .
N. Y. P. L. April 24, 1941

D-19
1421

De Ronsard à Breton, recueil d'essais, hommages à Marcel Raymond. Paris, J. Corti, 1967.

317 p. illus. 23 cm.

French or English.
Includes bibliographical references.

1. Raymond, Marcel, 1897- 2. French literature--Addresses, essays, lectures.
NN*R 8.69 w/a OC PC, 1, 2 SL (LC1, X1, Z3)

Write on slip words underlined below and class mark— FTA

Deecke-Festschrift.

(Fortschritte der Geologie und Palaeontologie. Berlin, 1932. 8°. Bd. 11, p. i-xxvi, 1-532. port.)

Wilhelm Deeckes Wissenschaftliche Arbeiten, 1881-1891, p. vii-xx.

form 400b [x-20-31 25m]

Degras, Jane (Tabrisky) 1905- *ed.* TAH
Soviet planning; essays in honor of Naum Jasny. Edited by Jane Degras. With an introd. by Alec Nove. New York, Praeger ⌊1964⌋

xi, 225 p. illus., port. 22 cm. (Praeger publications in Russian history and world communism, 163)

Includes bibliographies.

CONTENTS.—Priorities and shortfalls in pre-war Soviet planning, by H. Hunter.—Plans to urbanize the countryside, 1950–61, by L. Rich-

(Continued)

NN* R 3.66 g/J OC PC, 1, 2 SL E, 1, 2 S, 1, 2 (LC1, X1, Z1)

DEGRAS, JANE (TABRISKY) 1905- , ed. Soviet planning... (Card 2)

ter.—The role of the state bank in Soviet planning, by G. Garvy.—The theory of international comparisons of economic volume, by P. Wiles.—Soviet planners in 1936–37, by J. Miller.—Welfare criteria in Soviet planning, by M. C. Kaser.—Development aid for development's sake, by W. Klatt.—Towards a theory of planning, by A. Nove.—Some statistical comparisons, by C. Clark.—Naum Jasny at eighty, by J. H. Richter.—Bibliography of the principal works of Naum Jasny (p. 221–224)

1. Jasny, Naum, 1883- . 2. Economic history--Russia, 1917- .

D-15
2821

DEGRAS, JANE (TABRISKY) 1905- , ed.
Soviet planning; essays in honour of Naum Jasny. Edited by Jane Degras and Alec Nove. Oxford, B. Blackwell, 1964. xi, 225 p. diagr., tables. 22cm.

Includes bibliographies.

CONTENTS.--Introduction, Naum Jasny, by A. Nove.--Priorities and shortfalls in prewar Soviet planning, by H. Hunter.--Plans to urbanize the countryside, 1950-61, by L. Richter.--The role of the state bank in

(Continued)

NN * R 7.64 e/ OC, I PC, 1, 2, I SL E, 1, 2, I (LC1, X1, Z1)

2

DEGRAS, JANE (TABRISKY) 1905- , ed. Soviet planning... (Card 2)

Soviet planning, by G. Garvy.--The theory of international comparisons of economic volume, by P. Wiles.--Soviet planners in 1936-37, by J. Miller.--Welfare criteria in Soviet planning, by M.C. Kaser.--Development aid for development's sake, by W. Klatt.--Towards a theory of planning, by A. Nove.--Some statistical comparisons, by C. Clark.--Naum Jasny at eighty, by J.H. Richter.--Bibliography of the principal works of Naum Jasny (p. 221-225)

1. Jasny, Naum, 1883- . 2. Economic policy--Russia.
I. Nove, Alec, joint ed.

3-MQW

Delftse studiën. Een bundel historische opstellen over de stad Delft, geschreven voor dr. E. H. ter Kuile naar aanleiding van zijn afscheid als hoogleraar in de geschiedenis van de bouwkunst. Assen, Van Gorcum, 1967.
x, 434 p. with illus. 25 cm. fl 43.50

Includes bibliographical references. (Ne 67-48)

CONTENTS.—Het Delftse stadsplan, door J. C. Visser.—Het tijnsboekje van 1461–1465, door M. Kossmann.—Middleleeuwse kapellen, door H. Janse.—Middeleeuwse stenen windmolens te Delft, door A. Bicker Caarten.—Delft als stad van zestiende-eeuwse woonhuizen,

(Continued)

NN * R 10.68 1/ OC, I PC, 1, 2, 3, 4, I SL A, 2, 3, 4, I E, 1, 4, I (LC1, X1, Z1)

3

DELFTSE studiën. Een bundel historische opstellen over de stad Delft... (Card 2)

door C. L. Temminck Groll.—Het Oost-Indisch huis, door P. van Dun.—Het Armamentarium, door G. Berends.—Het stadhuis van Hendrick de Keyser, door J. J. Terwen.—Het Klassicisme van 1620–1660, door R. Meischke.—Het Generaliteits-Kruitmagazijn aan de Schie, door J. K. van der Haagen.—De bomen op het marktveld, door E. A. Canneman.—De kaart figuratief, door S. J. Fockema Andreae.—Een onbekend werk van Johannes Blommendael, door A. Staring.—Interieur-decoratie in het tweede kwart van de achttiende eeuw, door H. M. van den Berg.—De fundatie der vrijvrouwe van Renswoude te Delft, door M. D. Ozinga.—De stadsfabriek in de tweede helft van de

(Continued)

DELFTSE studiën. Een bundel historische opstellen over de stad Delft... (Card 3)

achttiende eeuw, door C. A. van Swigchem.—Het werk van Pieter Adams in Delft, door J. A. C. Tillema.—De synagoge aan de Koornmarkt, door R. C. Hekker.—Sociëteit Phoenix, door J. J. F. W. van Agt.—De restauratie van het stadhuis 1963–1966, door J. Kruger.—De nieuwe aula van de Technische Hogeschool, door N. Luning Prak.—Engelbert Hendrik ter Kuile, door G. J. ter Kuile.—Publikaties van E. H. ter Kuile, door T. Kamstra.

1. Delft, Netherlands--Hist. 2. Architecture--Netherlands--Delft. 3. Historic houses--Netherlands--Delft. 4. Kuile, Engelbert Hendrik ter, 1900- --- Bibl. I. Kuile, Engelbert Hendrik ter, 1900-

---

Write on slip, name, year, vol., page of magazine and class mark — IEK

Dem Andenken von Karl Schurz.

(Deutsch Amerikanische Historische Gesellschaft von Illinois. Jahrb. Chicago, 1929. 8°. v.9, p.1-270. port.)

form 400a [vi-7-29 25m]

NFD
(Becher)

Dem Dichter des Friedens Johannes R. Becher zum 60. Geburtstag. Berlin, Aufbau-Verlag, 1951. 298 p. illus. 20cm.

"Bibliographie," p. 293-296.

607531B. 1. Becher, Johannes Robert, 1891- .
N. Y. P. L. November 21, 1951

TB

DEMARCO, DOMENICO, ed.
Studi in onore di Antonio Genovesi nel bicentenario della istituzione della cattedra di economia. Sotto gli auspici della Facoltà di economia e commercio della Università di Napoli e della Camera di commercio di Salerno. Napoli, L'Arte tipografica, 1956.
xvi, 346 p. illus., port., facsims. 26cm. (Istituto di storia economica e sociale della Università di Napoli. Serie 1: Miscellanee. 2)

(Continued)

NN R 8.63 e/ OC (OD)IIt (ED)IIt (OS)I PC, 1, 2, I, II SL E, 1, 2, I (LC1, X1, Z1)

5

DEMARCO, DOMENICO, ed. Studi in onore di Antonio Genovesi... (Card 2)

CONTENTS.--Le "Lezione di economia civile" di Antonio Genovesi viste attraverso una polemica del tempo suo, di F. Alderisio.--La panificazione a Napoli durante la carestia del 1764, in una memoria di Carlo Antonio Broggia, di A. Allocati.--I problemi della terra e l'influenza di Antonio Genovesi, di M. Bandini.--Una memoria inedita di Carlo Antonio Broggia, di L. dal Pane.--Influenze dottrinali, economiche-statistiche e sociologiche nel pensiero di Antonio Genovesi, di D. de Castro.

(Continued)

DEMARCO, DOMENICO, ed. Studi in onore di Antonio Genovesi... (Card 3)

--Attualità del pensiero di Antonio Genovesi sul problema del sviluppo delle economie arretrate, di M. de Luca.--Antonio Genovesi e il problema della popolazione, di M. de Vergottini.--La popolazione nel pensiero di Antonio Genovesi, di P. Fortunati.--La concezione mercantilista dell'intervento dello stato nell'economia, di G. Frisella Vella.--Le idee finanziarie di Antonio Genovesi, di L. Gangemi.--Modernità del pensiero economico di Antonio Genovesi, di A.G. Canina.--Le premesse filosofiche dell'"Economia civile" di Genovesi, di

(Continued)

DEMARCO, DOMENICO, ed. Studi in onore di Antonio Genovesi... (Card 4)

J. Griziotto Kretschmann.--Il pensiero demografico del Genovesi nel suo tempo, di G. Lasorsa.--Riflessi genovesiani nella rinascita economica e sociale del mezzogiorno ideata da Giuseppe Maria Galanti, di A. Petino.--Il posto di Antonio Genovesi fra gli economisti del secolo XVIII, di S. Scalfati.--La teoria della popolazione negli scritti di Antonio Genovesi, di G. Sensini.--Dialogo di un filosofo e di un forense sugli interessi del danaro, di A. Genovesi, a cura di L. Izzo.

(Continued)

DEMARCO, DOMENICO, ed. Studi in onore di Antonio Genovesi. (Card 5)

1. Genovesi, Antonio, 1712-1769. 2. Economics--Essays and misc. I. Naples (City). Università. Istituto di storia economica e sociale. II. Salerno, Italy (Province). Camera di commercio, industria e agricoltura. t. 1956.

Copy only words underlined & classmark-- TB

DEMARCO, DOMENICO, ed.
Studi in onore di Epicarmo Corbino. Milano, Giuffrè, 1961. 2 v. (cxii, 754 p.) port. 26cm. (Naples (City). Università. Istituto di storia economica e sociale. Biblioteca degli Annali. 3-4)

Bibliographical footnotes.

1. Corbino, Epicarmo, 1890- . 2. Economics--Essays and misc. I. Series.
NN X 7.63 g/ OC (OS)I PC, 1, 2, I E, 1, 2, I (LC1, X1, Z1)

E-13
4465

DEMETZ, PETER, 1922- , ed.
The disciplines of criticism; essays in literary theory, interpretation and history. Edited by Peter Demetz, Thomas Greene and Lowry Nelson, jr. New Haven, Yale university press, 1968. x, 616 p. 24cm.

"For René Wellek on the occasion of his sixty-fifth birthday, August 22, 1968."
Bibliographical footnotes.
1. Criticism, Literary--Addresses, essays, lectures.
I. Wellek, René.
NN R 3.69 v/ OC, I PC, 1, I SL (LC1, X1, Z1)

SFC

DEMOCRACY and the labour movement; essays in honour of Dona Torr, edited by John Saville. London, Lawrence & Wishart, 1954. 275 p. 23cm.

Bibliographical footnotes.
CONTENTS.--The Norman yoke, by C. Hill.--From hierarchy to evolution in the theory of biology, by S. F. Mason.--The Scottish contribution to Marxist sociology, by R. L. Meek.--The London corresponding society, by H. Collins.--The Christian socialists of 1848, by J. Saville.--Master and servant, by D. Simon.--The labour

(Continued)

NN**R 4.55 g/ OC, I PC, 1, 2, 3, 4, I SL E, 1, 2, 3, 4, I (LC1, X1, Z1)

DEMOCRACY and the labour movement... (Card 2)

aristocracy in 19th century Britain, by E. J. Hobsbawm.--Wordsworth and the people, by V. G. Kiernan.

1. Socialism--Gt. Br. 2. Labor--Gt. Br. 3. Democracy--Gt. Br. 4. Torr, Dona. I. Saville, John, ed.

E-11
6514

DEMOREST, JEAN.
Studies in seventeenth-century French literature presented to Morris Bishop. Ithaca, N.Y., Cornell university press [1962] 289 p. 24cm.

CONTENTS:--Common-sense remarks on the French Baroque, by H. Peyre.--Malherbe and his influence, by P.A. Wadsworth.--Saint-Amant, le poète sauve de eaux, by A Seznec.--Corneille's Horace: a study in tragic

(Continued)

NN R 2.63 p/ OC PC, 1, 2, I SL (LC1, X1, Z1)

2

DEMOREST, JEAN. Studies in seventeenth-century French literature presented to Morris Bishop. (Card 2)

and artistic ambivalence, by L.E. Harvey.--Attila redivius, by G. May.--Pascal's sophistry and the sin of poesy, by J.J. Demorest.--Human nature and institutions in Molière's plots, by J. Doolittle.--Futility and self-deception in Le misanthrope, by J.D. Hubert.--Les Yeux de César: the language of vision in Britannicus, by J. Brody.--Ariosto and La Fontaine: a literary affinity, by J.C. Lapp.--A'art poétique: "Long-temps plaire, et jamais ne lasser", by N. Edelman.--The literary arts of Longinus and Boileau, by H.M. Davidson.

1. French literature--Hist. and crit., 17th cent. 2. Bishop, Morris, 1893- I. Title.

E-11
8940

DEMPF, ALOIS, 1891- , ed.
Politische Ordnung und menschliche Existenz; Festgabe für Eric Voegelin zum 60. Geburtstag, hrsg. von Alois Dempf, Hannah Arendt [und] Friedrich Engel-Janosi. München, C.H. Beck, 1962. ix, 634 p. port. 24cm.

Text in English or German.
Bibliographical footnotes.

(Continued)

NN R 2.64 f/ OC, I PC, 1, 2, I SL E, 1, 2, I (LC1, X1, Z1)

2

DEMPF, ALOIS, 1891- , ed. Politische Ordnung und menschliche Existenz... (Card 2)

"Eric-Voegelin-Bibliographie," p. [607]-612.

1. Political science--Addresses, essays, lectures. 2. Voegelin, Erich, 1901- I. Arendt, Hannah, joint ed.

---

* MG p.v.17

Dessoir, Max, 1867–

Carl Stumpf zum 70. Geburtstag, von Max Dessoir... Berlin: Reuther & Reichard[, 1918?]. 5 p. front. (port.) 8°.

Repr.: Kant-Studien. Bd. 23, Heft 2/3, 1918.

Mr. Moth.

JUILLIARD FOUNDATION FUND.

493721A. 1. Stumpf, Karl, 1848– .
N. Y. P. L. September 10, 1930

Write on slip, name, year, vol., page of magazine and class mark — *EI

Den 2 Juni 1930 tillägnas Professor Emeritus Hans Wallengren detta band.

(Lund universitet. Acta. Avdelningen 2. Lund, 1930. 4°. N.F.bd.26.)

form 400a [ii-13-30 25m]

---

* OVA
+++

Deutsch-chinesische Nachrichten.

Dem Andenken Spinozas. [Tientsin-Peiping: Peiyang press, 1932] 20 p. illus. (incl. facsim., ports.) 46cm.

Issue of Deutsch-Chinesische Nachrichten, November 24, 1932.
Some of the articles are in Chinese.
"Sonderausgabe zum 24. November 1932 herausgegeben vom Deutschen Seminar der Pekinger Reichsuniversität."

1. Spinoza, Benedictus de, 1632–1677. I. National university, Peking. German seminar. II. Title.
N. Y. P. L. April 16, 1941

FIH
+

Denkbuch über die Anwesenheit Ihrer K. K. Majestäten Franz des Ersten und Caroline Auguste in Böhmen im Jahre 1833. Mit 81 lithographirten Blättern. Prag, 1836. xxii, 213 p. plates. 32cm.

Festschrift

595740B. 1. Francis I, emperor of Austria, 1768–1835. 2. Caroline Augusta, consort of Francis I, emperor of Austria.
N. Y. P. L. December 18, 1951

C-12
2686

DEUTSCHE AKADEMIE DER KÜNSTE, Berlin. Sektion Dichtkunst und Sprachpflege.

Arnold Zweig, ein Almanach; Briefe, Glückwünsche, Aufsätze. Berlin, Aufbau-Verlag, 1962. 199 p. 20cm.

Published in honor of Arnold Zweig's seventy-fifth birthday, November 10, 1962.

1. Zweig, Arnold, 1887-
NN R 3.63 f/ OS PC, 1 SL (LC1, X1, Z1)

E-12
5758

DESENVOLVIMENTO; problemas e soluções. Salvador, Livraria Progressa, 1960. 187 p. 24cm.

"Ensaios em homenagem a Pinto de Aguiar."
Includes bibliographical references.
CONTENTS.--Educação e desenvolvimento, por A. Ferreira.--As ideologias e o desenvolvimento, por A.L. Machado Neto.--A natureza dinâmica da distribuição da renda, por F.C. Pedrão.--O povo brasileiro e o desenvolvimento econômico, por Guerreiro Ramos.--Para melhor utilização dos recursos educacionais existente na mobilização de mão
(Continued)

NN R 7.66 p/, OC PC, 1, 2, 3 SL E, 1, 2, 3 (LC1, X1, Z1) 2

EAG p.v.278

Deutsche Akademie, Munich.

... Von deutscher Art. [München, 1939] 129 p. plates (part col'd), port. 22½cm.

"Dem Präsidenten der Deutschen Akademie Ludwig Siebert zum 65. Geburtstag gewidmet."
"Herausgegeben von Gustav Fochler-Hauke."
CONTENTS.—Von Sprache und Volksartung, von Georg Schmidt-Rohr.—Deutsche Dichtung, von L. F. Barthel.—Deutsches Bilden und Bauen, von Heinz Rosemann.—Vom Wesen deutscher Musik, von Roderich Mojsisovics.—Die Gestalt des Erziehers im neuen Staat, von Otto Kroh.—Deutsches Soldatentum, von Friedrich von Cochenhausen.—Der Deutsche und die Technik, von Fr. Hassler.—Deutsche Wirtschaftsführer, von Kurt Wiedenfeld.—Die deutsche Stadt, von Hans Fehn.—Vom Antlitz der deutschen Landschaft, von G. Fochler-Hauke.

Festschrift

1. Germany—Civilization. 2. Siebert, Ludwig, 1874– . I. Fochler-Hauke, Gustav, ed. II. Title.
N. Y. P. L. October 8, 1940

DESENVOLVIMENTO... (Card 2)

de obra, por J.F. Góes Filho.--Geografia e desenvolvimento economico, por M. Santos.--Democracia é desenvolvimento econômico, por N. de S. Sampaio.--A universidade e o desenvolvimento econômico, por O. Gomes.--Implicações culturais e estruturais do desenvolvimento, por T. de Azevedo.--A reforma agrária como exigência do século, por W.F. Oliveira.

1. Aguiar, Manoel Pinto de. 2. Economic development. 3. Economic policy--Brazil. 1945-

---

E-10
8467

DEUTSCHE AKADEMIE DER WISSENSCHAFTEN, Berlin. Alexander von Humboldt-Kommission.

Alexander von Humboldt, 14.9.1769-6.5.1859; Gedenkschrift zur 100. Wiederkehr seines Todestages. Berlin, Akademie-Verlag, 1959. 471 p. illus., ports. 25cm.

Includes bibliographies.

1. Humboldt, Alexander, Freiherr von, 1769-1859.
NN R X 8.59 g/ OS PC, 1 SL ST, 1 (LC1, X1, Z1)

E-10
9106

DEUTSCHE AKADEMIE DER WISSENSCHAFTEN, Berlin. Alexander von Humboldt-Kommission. Alexander von Humboldt, 14.9. 1769-6.5.1859; Gedenkschrift zur 100. Wiederkehr seines Todestages. Berlin, Akademie-Verlag, 1959. 471 p. illus., ports. 25cm.

Includes bibliographies.

CONTENTS. —Alexander von Humboldt und der Bergbau, von H. Baumgärtel. —Wilhelm Ludwig von Eschwege und Alexander von Humboldt, von H. Beck. — Graf Georg von Cancrin · und

(Continued)

NN R 11.59 a/ OS PC, 1 SL AH, 1 ST, 1 (LC1, X1, Z1)

DEUTSCHE AKADEMIE DER WISSENSCHAFTEN, Berlin. Alexander von Humboldt-Kommission. Alexander von Humboldt... (Card 2)

Alexander von Humboldt, von H. Beck. —Über die Förderung deutscher Mathematiker durch Alexander von Humboldt, von K. -R. Biermann. —Die Geschichte der (Alexander von) Humboldt-Stiftung für Naturforschung und Reisen, von G. Dunken. —Die wirtschaftlichen Lebensverhältnisse Alexander von Humboldts, von J. Eichhorn. —El Barón Alexander von Humboldt y su influencia en el desarrollo científico y económico de México, por J. González-Reyna y A. García-Rojas. —Alexander von Humboldt in seiner Stellung zur reinen Mathematik und ihrer Geschichte, von J. E. Hofmann. —

(Continued)

DEUTSCHE AKADEMIE DER WISSENSCHAFTEN, Berlin. Alexander von Humboldt-Kommission. Alexander von Humboldt... (Card 3)

Über Alexander von Humboldts Arbeiten zur Meteorologie und Klimatologie, von H. -G. Körber. —Alexander von Humboldt und Freiberg in Sachsen, von W. Schellhas. —Alexander von Humboldt und die Bedeutung seines wissenschaftlichen Werkes für die Hydrobiologie, von A. Steleanu. —Bildnisse Alexander von Humboldts, von F.G. Lange.

1. Humboldt, Alexander, Freiherr von, 1769-1859.

Copy only words underlined & classmark -- PTA

DEUTSCHE AKADEMIE DER WISSENSCHAFTEN, Berlin. Geotektonisches Institut. Gestein, Gebirgsbau und Zeit; Studien im Variszikum und Saxonikum Mitteldeutschlands [Festgabe hrsg. von] Serge von Bubnoff. Berlin, Akademie-Verlag, 1952. 134 p. illus. 24cm. (Geologica. [Heft] 11)

"Hans Stille zum 75sten Geburtstage gewidmet."
Bibliography at end of each chapter.

(Continued)

NN* * X 2.57 a/B (OC)II OS, I, Ib PC, 1, 2, I, II ST, 1, 3, I, II (U1, LC1, Z1, X1)

DEUTSCHE AKADEMIE DER WISSENSCHAFTEN, Berlin. Geotektonisches Institut. Gestein, Gebirgsbau und Zeit. (Card 2)

CONTENTS. --Tektonische Fazies und Bewegungsdifferentiation, von S. von Bubnoff. --Die Bewegungsvorgänge an der Finnestörung bei Bad Sulza, Eckartsberga und Rastenberg, von B. Dolezalek. --Die Ableitung der Bodenbewegungen aus der Feinstratigraphie der Baunkohle im mittleren Geiseltal, von H. Gallwitz. --Der "Florensprung" und die "Erzgebirgische Phase" Kossmats, von W. Gothan. --Die stratigraphische Parallelisierung des Rotliegenden am Südharz, von T. Kruckow. --Über den sog.

(Continued)

DEUTSCHE AKADEMIE DER WISSENSCHAFTEN, Berlin. Geotektonisches Institut. Gestein, Gebirgsbau und Zeit. (Card 3)

Kohlenkalk in Ostthüringen und Franken und die Devon-Karbongrenze am Bergaer Sattel, von K. -J. Müller. --Bemerkungen zur Stratigraphie der Ilfelder kohlenführenden Serie und Mitteilungen über einen Wirbeltier-fährtenrest. --Ichnium sp., von W. Remy. --Zur Tektonik des vogtländischen Variszikums bei Elsterberg, von R. Schönenberg. --Stratigraphie und Tektonik des Unterrotliegenden im südwestlichen Randgebiet des Thüringer Waldes bei Schleusingen und Hirschbach (Kr. Suhl), von A. Schreiber. --

(Continued)

DEUTSCHE AKADEMIE DER WISSENSCHAFTEN, Berlin. Geotektonisches Institut. Gestein, Gebirgsbau und Zeit. (Card 4)

Zur Grundgebirgsgeologie des Kyffhäuser, von A. Schüller. --Geologisches Auftreten und Entstehung der Kieselschiefer (Lydite), von W. Schwan.

1. Stille, Hans W., 1876- . 2. Geology--Germany. 3. Geology--Germany, 1952. I. Series. II. Bubnov, Sergyeĭ von, 1888- , ed.

L-10
2429
no. 11

Deutsche Akademie der Wissenschaften, Berlin: Institut für deutsche Sprache und Literatur.

Beiträge zur deutschen und nordischen Literatur; Festgabe für Leopold Magon zum 70. Geburtstag, 3. April, 1957. [Hrsg. von Hans Werner Seiffert] Berlin, Akademie-Verlag, 1958. 405 p. port., facsim., music. 24cm. (ITS: Veröffentlichungen. 11)

Bibliographical footnotes.

CONTENTS.—Die Viga-Glúms-Episode in der Reykdœla-Saga, von W. Baetke.—Nibelungensage und Gisla saga, von H. M. Heinrichs.—Schlüsselzahlen-Studie zur geistigen Durchdringung der Form in der deutschen Dichtung des Mittelalters, von

(Continued)

NN X 2.60 (OC)I,IIb,III OS,I PC,1,2,3,I,II,III (LC1,X1,Z1)

Deutsche Akademie der Wissenschaften, Berlin: Institut für deutsche Sprache und Literatur. Beiträge zur deutschen und nordischen Literatur... 1958. (Card 2)

F. Tschirch.—Idealismus und Realismus in der Novelle "Rittertreue," von H. Lenz.—Neue Faustsplitter, von K. Schreinert.—Hartmann Schenck, von H. G. Göpfert.—Nebel als Erscheinung und Symbol in deutschen Gedichten vom 18. bis zum 20. Jahrhundert, von E. Blühm.—Klopstock in Dänemark, von H. T. Betteridge.—Ein empfindsamer Briefwechsel, von H. W. Seiffert.—Goethe im Februar 1779. Ein Beitrag zur Chronik von Goethes Leben, von W. Flach.—Johann Georg Schlosser und die Familie Goethe, von I. Kreienbrink.—Interpretationen Goethescher Verskunst, von U. Pretzel.—Zu Goethes Stanzendichtung, von W. Simon.—Zu Goethes Timurgedicht, von J. Müller.—Georg Forster über die Humanität des Schauspielers, von G. Steiner.

(Continued)

Deutsche Akademie der Wissenschaften, Berlin: Institut für deutsche Sprache und Literatur. Beiträge zur deutschen und nordischen Literatur... 1958. (Card 3)

—Grundtvig und die deutsche Romantik, von S. Steffensen.—Der Danziger Aehrenleser, von H. Jacob.—Amalia von Helvig als Mittlerin zwischen Schweden und Deutschland, von A. Oberreuter.—Annette von Droste-Hülshoff und die nordische Literatur—gleichzeitig ein Beitrag zu dem Thema "Die Droste als Komponistin," von K. Schulte-Kemminghausen.—Aus Karl Goedekes Nachlass. Mit unbekannten Autographen von Mörike und Storm, von E. Rothe.—Über Otto Ludwigs Schaffensweise, von W. Meschke.—Der burde have været Roser; Jens Peter Jacobsen und die Überwindung des Naturalismus in Deutschland, von R. Schmidt-Wiegand.—Henri Bergson und das Problem des Komischen, von T. Barisch.—Zur holsteinischen Reimchronik, von H. Toldberg.

1. German literature—Addresses, essays, lectures. 2. Scandinavian literature—Addresses, essays, lectures. 3. Magon, Leopold, 1887- . I. Series. II. Seiffert, Hans Werner, 1920- , ed. III. Title.

E-11
2180
DEUTSCHE AKADEMIE DER WISSENSCHAFTEN, Berlin. Institut für deutsche Volkskunde.
Zwischen Kunstgeschichte und Volkskunde. Festschrift für Wilhelm Fraenger. Hrsg. vom Institut für deutsche Volkskunde durch Reinhard Peesch. Berlin, Akademie-Verlag, 1960. 238 [3] p. illus., plates (incl. facsims.), map. 25cm. (ITS: Veröffentlichungen. Bd. 27)

(Continued)

NN R X 3.61 e/ (OC)I OS, II PC, 1, 2, 3, I, II SL A, 1, 2, I, II (LC1, X1, Z1)

DEUTSCHE AKADEMIE DER WISSENSCHAFTEN, Berlin. Institut für deutsche Volkskunde. (Card 2)

"Die Aufsätze ... erscheinen gleichzeitig in Band VI/I. des Deutschen Jahrbuchs für Volkskunde."
Bibliographical footnotes.

1. Fraenger, Wilhelm, 1890- . 2. Art--Essays and misc. 3. Folk lore --Addresses, essays, lectures. I. Peesch, Reinhard, ed. II. Series.

Copy only words underlined & classmark-- ZE
DEUTSCHE AKADEMIE DER WISSENSCHAFTEN, Berlin. Spätantike Religionsgeschichte, Kommission für. Studien zum Neuen Testament und zur Patristik; Erich Klostermann zum 90. Geburtstag dargebracht. Berlin, Akademie-Verlag, 1961. viii, 378 p. port. 25cm. (Texte und Untersuchungen zur Geschichte der altchristlichen Literatur. Bd. 77)

Bibliographical footnotes.

(Continued)
NN 4.65 a/ OS, I PC, 1, 2, 3, I (LC1, X1, Z1)

DEUTSCHE AKADEMIE DER WISSENSCHAFTEN, Berlin. Spätantike Religionsgeschichte, Kommission für. Studien zum Neuen Testament und zur Patristik. (Card 2)

CONTENTS.—Todelot, von O. Eissfeldt.—Die Dauer des Census Augusti, von E. Stauffer.—Ein johanneischer Osterbericht, von O. Michel.—Das Bildwort vom Weizenkorn bei Paulus (zu I Cor 15), von H. Riesenfeld.—Die Hoffnung im Kolosserbrief, von G. Bornkamm.—Römer 13, von E. Barnikol.—Der Übermensch-Begriff in der Theologie der Alten Kirche, von E. Benz.—Bericht über eine neue Justinhandschrift auf dem Athos, von W. Eltester.—Der angebliche Chronograph

(Continued)

DEUTSCHE AKADEMIE DER WISSENSCHAFTEN, Berlin. Spätantike Religionsgeschichte, Kommission für. Studien zum Neuen Testament und zur Patristik... (Card 3)

Julius Cassianus, von N. Walter.—Der Logos-Christus als göttlicher Lehrer bei Clemens von Alexandrien, von E. Fascher.—Zur Hellenisierung des Christentums in den Sprüchen des Sextus, von G. Delling.—Origeniana: 1. Die Bücher gegen Celsus. 2. Zum Römerbriefkommentar, von L. Früchtel.—Origenes über das Paradies, von M. Rauer.—Eine altkirchliche Weihnachtspredigt, von H. Dörries.—Zu einer Kiewer Handschrift der

(Continued)

DEUTSCHE AKADEMIE DER WISSENSCHAFTEN, Berlin. Spätantike Religionsgeschichte, Kommission für. Studien zum Neuen Testament und zur Patristik... (Card 4)

Opuscula des Makarios, von K. Treu.—Die Arbeit am Makariustext des Typus I, von H. Berthold.—Φιλόχριστος πόλις, von J. Irmscher.—Der Einfluss des Pseudo-Dionysius Areopagita auf Maximus Confessor, von W. Völker.—Zur Problematik der russischen Bibelexegese, von R. A. Klostermann.
1. Bible. N.T.--Commentary and criticism. 2. Theology, Patristic--Hist. and crit. 3. Klostermann, Erich, 1870- . I. Series.

AE-10
879
DEUTSCHE BÜCHEREI, Leipzig.
Denkschrift zur Einweihungsfeier der Deutschen Bücherei des Börsenvereins der Deutschen Buchhändler zu Leipzig am 2. September 1916. Leipzig, Verlag des Börsenvereins der Deutschen Buchhändler zu Leipzig, 1916. 215 p. illus., ports. 24cm.

NN 6.67 p/ OS PC SL E (LC1, X1, Z1)

G-10
1233
DEUTSCHE BÜCHEREI, Leipzig.
Deutsche Bücherei, 1912-1962; Festschrift zum fünfzigjährigen Bestehen der Deutschen Nationalbibliothek. [Redaktion: Helmut Rötzsch, Gerhard Hesse, Hans-Martin Plesske] Leipzig, 1962. xxii, 400 p. illus., plates. 31cm.

Bibliography, p. [287]-367.
I. Rötzsch, Helmut, ed. II. Rötzsch, Helmut.
NN R 1.63 g/ (OC)I, IIbo OS PC, I SL (LC1, X1, Z1)

E-10
7517
DEUTSCHE BURSE, Marburg, Germany.
Weltweite Wissenschaft vom Volk: Volk—Welt—Erziehung; Johann Wilhelm Mannhardt zum 75. Geburtstag. Hrsg. von Karl Kurt Klein [et al.] Wien, R. M. Rohrer, 1958. 235, [1] p. port. 25cm.

CONTENTS.—Johann Wilhelm Mannhardt, von K. K. Klein.—Die Marburger Burse—ein Weg zu weltoffenem Deutschtum, von K. Ursin.—Volksbewusstsein als verpflichtendes Erbe. Soll und kann das

(Continued)
NN R 5.59 g/ (OC)I, II OS PC, 1, 2, I, II SL E, 1, 2, I, II (LC1, X1, Z1)

DEUTSCHE BURSE, Marburg, Germany. Weltweite Wissenschaft vom Volk: Volk—Welt—Erziehung ... (Card 2)

Volksbewusstsein wieder erweckt werden? Von J. W. Mannhardt.—Die religiose Begrundung des Volkstums, von A. Wustemann.—Erziehung zu Humanitas, von A. Lesky.—Bevolkerungsentwicklungen in den Grossräumen der Welt. Deutschland und Europa zwischen Ost und West, von H. Harmsen.—Heimatgedanke und Europabewusstsein, von F. H. Riedl.—Volk und Staat im Denken des Westens, von R. Blasig.—Das Rechtsgefuge im neuen Europa. Zur Frage der rechtlichen Ordnung der

(Continued)

DEUTSCHE BURSE, Marburg, Germany. Weltweite Wissenschaft vom Volk: Volk—West—Erziehung ... (Card 3.)

Beziehungen zwischen Volk und Staat, von H. Raschhofer. —Vereinigte Staaten in Amerika--Vereinigte Staaten in Europa, von A. Maurer. —Auslanddeutschtum heute und morgen, von J. W. Mannhardt. —Osterreichs europaische Funktion, von J. Klaus. —Volksgruppenfragen in Osterreich, von M. Straka. —Südtirol—eine Musterlandschaft europaischer Pragung, von A. Thaler. —Eine Sudtiroler Wahlrede 1958, von L. Sand. —Zum Erwachen des volklichen Denkens in Osteuropa. Die nationale Gedankenwelt der russischen Dekabristen, von

(Continued)

DEUTSCHE BURSE, Marburg, Germany. Weltweite Wissenschaft vom Volk: Volk—West—Erziehung ... (Card 4)

H. Lemberg. --Die Vertreibung der Konigstreuen aus den Neuenglandstaaten in Nordamerika. Ein geschichtliches Beispiel fur Volksgruppenaustreibung im 18. Jahrhundert, von E. Tscherne. —Zur Problematik der deutschen Volkssprache in Nordamerika, von R. C. Wood. —Zur Problematik des Deutschunterrichts in den Vereiningten Staaten von Nordamerika, von A. Maurer. —Begegnungen in USA und Kanada, von G. Rhode. —Staat und deutsches Volkstum in Chile, von R. F. Wilcke A. —Das Ende des kolonialen Zeitalters, von J. W. Mannhardt. —Die Veröffentlichungen Johann Wilhelm Mannardts, von

(Continued)

DEUTSCHE BURSE, Marburg, Germany. Weltweite Wissenschaft vom Volk: Volk—West—Erziehung ... (Card 5)

R. Wittmann (p. 231-[236])

1. Germans in foreign countries. 2. Mannhardt, Johann Wilhelm, 1883- . I. Klein, Karl Kurt, 1897- , ed. II. Title.

OX

DEUTSCHE GEODÄTISCHE KOMMISSION.
Festschrift zur Hundertjahrfeier der Internationalen Association für Geodäsie am 12. und 13. Oktober 1962 in München. Hrsg. von Max Kneissl im Auftrag der Internationalen Assoziation für Geodäsie. München, 1963. 149 p. illus. 22cm.

1. Geodesy--Assoc. and org.--Germany. 2. Distance--Measurement. I. Kneissl, M., ed. II. International geodetic and geophysical union. t. 1963
NN 2.64 g/b (OC)I OS, II PC, 1, 2, I, II SL ST, 1, 2t, I, II (LC1, X1, Z1)

---

*OSC

Deutsche Gesellschaft für Natur- und Völkerkunde Ostasiens, Tokio.
Jubiläumsband, hrsg. von der Deutschen Gesellschaft für Natur- und Völkerkunde Ostasiens anlässlich ihres 60 jährigen Bestehens, 1873–1933... Tôkyô: Im Selbstverlag der Gesellschaft, 1933. 2 v. illus. 26cm.

CONTENTS.—Teil 1. Zach, E. von. Aus dem Wên Hsüan. Bohner, H. "Ôsaka-Schloss" von Okamoto Kidô. Bohner, A. Spuren der Kirishitan in Iyo. Klautke, P. Beitrag zur Pflanzenwelt der Diamantberge Koreas. Shûzô Kure. Einfluss der fremden, insbesondere der deutschen Medizin auf die japanische seit Anfang des 18. bis gegen Ende des 19. Jahrhunderts. Ramming, M. Literarhistorische Bemerkungen über

(Continued)

N. Y. P. L. Festschrift. July 19, 1943

Deutsche Gesellschaft für Natur- und Völkerkunde Ostasiens, Tokio. Jubiläumsband... (Card 2)

die Kibyôshi der Tokugawazeit. Gubler, A. Rishiri und Rebun. Schurhammer, G. Die Jesuitenmissionare des 16. und 17. Jahrhunderts und ihr Einfluss auf die japanische Malerei. Kashiwa Ohyama. Yayoi-Kultur. Stübel, H. Vorläufiger Bericht über eine ethnologische Exkursion nach der Insel Hainan. Weidinger, K. Die Gründungssage des Sensôji (Asakusa-Kwannon-Tempels) im Lichte der japanischen Frühgeschichte. Laska, J. 7 Tankas aus der Sammlung Hyakunin-isshu für Altstimme, Flöte und Klavier. Haushofer, K. Die volkspolitische Dynamik Japans und ihre Antriebe und Hemmungen durch die Staatskultur. Goldschmidt, R. Einige Ergebnisse von Untersuchungen zum Evolutionsproblem, ausgeführt an japanischen Rassen des Schwammspinners. Irisawa, T. Ein Beitrag zur Statistik des Speiseröhrenkrebses. Trautz, F. M.

(Continued)

N. Y. P. L. July 19, 1943

Deutsche Gesellschaft für Natur- und Völkerkunde Ostasiens, Tokio. Jubiläumsband... (Card 3)

Eine japanische Natur- und Lebensschilderung aus der Zeit Engelbert Kämpfers. Hübotter, F. Über chinesische Arzneibehandlung. Fuchs, W. Was wussten die Chinesen von Deutschland im 17. Jahrhundert? Donat, W. Aus Saikaku; Fünf Geschichten von liebenden Frauen. 3. Bdchn.; Geschichte vom Kalendermacher. Barth, J. Kagekiyo. Kraus, J. B. Familiensystem und Wirtschaft im alten und neuen Japan. Biallas, F. X. Aus den "Neun Liedern" des K'ü Yüan.—Teil 2. Kowarz, A. Sachalin. Vogel, W. Das neue chinesische Familienrecht. Stieber, W. Netsuke-Schnitzer-Familien. Piper, Maria. Die Stellung des Kabuki-Theaters im modernen Japan. Paravicini, T. Seelische Erdbebenwirkungen. Meissner, K. Der alte japanische Handwebstuhl. Ohrt, E. Friedrich Wilhelm Grube's Reise nach Indien und China 1843 bis 1845. Hänisch, E. Chine-

(Continued)

N. Y. P. L. July 19, 1943

Deutsche Gesellschaft für Natur- und Völkerkunde Ostasiens, Tokio. Jubiläumsband... (Card 4)

sische Ladenschilder. Florenz, K. Die Elegie in der älteren japanischen Literatur. Wedemeyer, A. Erläuterung zu einer Dichtung von Hitomaro. Snellen, J. B. A few remarks on the subject of the Shoku Nihongi and the solar eclipses recorded therein. Schindler, B. Zum 44. Kapitel des Chou-Shu. Takeshi Nakamura. Die gegenwärtige Lage des japanischen Arbeitsrechts. Chôzô Mutô. Dr. Ph. Fr. von Siebold und sein erstes Projekt einer Schule für Handelswissenschaften in Nagasaki, Japan. Wakai, S. Meishô-Daishi, der Begründer der japanischen Jôdo Sekte. Gundert, W. Die Bananenstaude. Das Nôspiel "Bashô" von Konparu-Zenchiku. Weegmann, C. v. O-An Monogatari, O-Kiku Monogatari, Episoden aus Mädchenleben um 1600. Bonmarchand, G. Kôshoku-Ichidai-Onna, par Ibara Saikaku. Othmer, W. Die Lebensgeschichte des Feldherrn Sü Da (1332–1385). Petzold, B. Die Triratna.

223245–6B. 1. Japan—Civilization. 2. China—Civilization.
N. Y. P. L. July 19, 1943

E-10
5206

DEUTSCHE GESELLSCHAFT FÜR OSTEUROPAKUNDE.
Russland-Studien; Gedenkschrift für. Otto Hoetzsch, Aufsätze seiner Schüler anlässlich des 80. Jahrestages seiner Geburt und des 10. Jahrestages seines Todes. Stuttgart, Deutsche Verlags-Anstalt, 1957. 110 p. 24cm. (Schriftenreihe Osteuropa. Nr. 3)

Includes bibliographies.
CONTENTS. —Otto Hoetzsch als aussenpolitischer Kommentator

(Continued)

NN X 6.58 e/P (OC)II OS, I PC, 1, 2, I, II SL S, 1, 2, I, II (LC1, X1, Z1, Y1)

DEUTSCHE GESELLSCHAFT FUR OSTEUROPAKUNDE. Russland-Studien; Gedenkschrift für. Otto Hoetzsch... (Card 2)

während des Ersten Weltkrieges, von F. T. Epstein. —Ein russischer Exulant in XIX. Jahrhundert: Wladimir Petscherin, von V. Frank. —Die russischen Rechtsparteien 1905-1917, von H. Jablonowki. —Zur geschichtlichen Bedeutung de russischen "Intelligenzia," von W. Markert. —Die Sowjetpolitik in Turkestan, von K. Mehnert. —"Menschenrechte" und "Bürgerrechte" in der Verfassungsentwicklung Osteuropas bis zum XVI. Jahrhundert, von E. von Puttkamer. —Dobroljubows Jugend, von P. Scheibert. —Die Religionspolitik Alexanders III. im Lichte der zeitgenössischen Publizistik, von R. Stupperich.

1. Hoetzsch, Otto E. G., 1876-1946. 2. Russia--Civilization--Addresses, essays, lectures. I. Series. II. Title.

C-10
840

DEUTSCHE HAUSBÜCHEREI. Hamburg.
Die Sendung der Dichter; Festschrift [hrsg. von Lothar Schreyer] Hamburg [1956] 118 p. facsims. 20cm.

"Anlässlich des vierzigjährigen Bestehens der Deutschen Hausbücherei entstand diese Festschrift."

CONTENTS.--Warum dichte ich? von W. Bergengruen.--Eine notwendige Frage, von F. Griese.--Vom Beruf des Dichters, von E. Barth.--Der Weg hinter die Menschen und Dinge, von L. Tügel.--Traktat über Recht und Unrecht, von H. Risse --Das Gedicht als Tatsache,
(Continued)

NN** R 11.56 a/b (OC)I OS PC, 1, I SL (LC1, X1, Z1, Y1)

DEUTSCHE HAUSBÜCHEREI. Hamburg. Die Sendung der Dichter. (Card 2)

von W. Lehmann.--Die Kunst der kurzen Erzählung, von W. von Scholz.--Kleine Betrachtung über die Sendung des Dichters, von I. Seidel.--Der Dichter und der Wissenschaftler, von O. La Farge.--Der Anteil der Sprache, von G. Gunnarsson.--Glück und Elend des Übersetzers, von H. Rothe.--Aufgabe und Grenze der Illustration, von W. M. Busch.--Buch und Gemeinschaft, von E. Christlieb.

1. Literature--Addresses, essays, lectures. I. Schreyer, Lothar, 1886- , ed.

---

* MBA

DEUTSCHE HOCHSCHULE FÜR MUSIK, Berlin.
Zehn Jahre Deutsche Hochschule für Musik, Berlin; eine Festschrift, hrsg. vom Rektorat. Berlin, Henschel-verlag, 1960. 188 p. plates. 22cm.

NN 8.64 p/J OS (1b) PC SL MU (LC1, X1, Z1)

D-16
4412

DEUTSCHE KRIMINOLOGISCHE GESELLSCHAFT.
Zweihundert Jahre später. Caesare Bonasana. Marchese di Beccaria. "Dei delitti e delle pene." (1764); Jubiläums-Festschrift. [Hrsg. von Armand Mergen. Hamburg, Kriminalistik Verlag, 1965] 47 p. illus., ports. 23cm.

Addresses at the awarding of the Beccaria-medal of the Deutsche Kriminologische Gesellschaft, at Frankfurt a.M., Dec. 12, 1964.
(Continued)

NN 6.66 g/J (OC)I OS PC, 1, 2, I SL E, 1, 2, I (LC1, X1, Z1)

2

DEUTSCHE KRIMINOLOGISCHE GESELLSCHAFT.
Zweihundert Jahre später. (Card 2)

1. Beccaria, Cesare Bonesana, marchese di, 1738-1794. 2. Criminologists. I. Mergen, Armand, ed.

OAI

Deutsche Wissenschaft; Arbeit und Aufgabe. Leipzig: S. Hirzel, 1939. viii, 274 p. illus. (incl. charts, plan), 14 pl. 30½cm.

Collection of essays published in honor of Adolf Hitler's fiftieth birthday anniversary.
Dedication signed: Der Reichsminister für Wissenschaft, Erziehung und Volksbildung.
CONTENTS. — Geisteswissenschaften. — Rechts- und Wirtschaftswissenschaften. — Biologie, Landwirtschaft, Forstwissenschaft, Veterinärmedizin. — Medizin. — Naturwissenschaften. — Technik.

18222B. 1. Science—Germany. 2. Industrial arts—Germany. 3. Science—Essays and misc. 4. Hitler, Adolf, 1889- I. Germany. Wissenschaft, Erziehung und Volksbildung, Ministerium für.
N. Y. P. L. September 3, 1940

---

* MEC
(BACH)

DEUTSCHER BACH-AUSSCHUSS.
Bach-Probleme; Festschrift zur Deutschen Bach-Feier Leipzig 1950, anlässlich der 200. Wiederkehr des Todestages von Johann Sebastian Bach. Hrsg. von Hans-Heinz Draeger und Karl Laux im Auftrage des Deutschen Bach-Ausschusses 1950. Leipzig, C. F. Peters [c1950] 87 p. facsims., music. 30cm.

Bibliographical references included in "Anmerkungen" (p. 36-37, 50-51, 66)
CONTENTS.—Johann Sebastian Bach, von V. Gorodinskij.—Der
(Continued)

NN * R 1.54 (OC) I, II OS PC, 1, I, II, III SL MU, 1, 2, 3, 4, 5, 6, 7, I, II, III (LC1, Z1, X1)

DEUTSCHER BACH-AUSSCUSS Bach-Probleme; Festschrift zu Deutschen Bach-Feier Leipzig, 1950. (Card 2)

weltliche Charakter in Bachs Orgelwerken, von J. Hammerschlag.—Bach, die Volksmusik und das osteuropäische Melos, von B. Szabolcsi.—Bemerkungen zur Stilisierung der Volksmusik, besonders der Polonaisen, bei Bach, von D. Bartha.—Anfänge der Bachpflege in England, von H. F. Redlich.—Die gleichschwebende Temperatur, von H. H. Draeger.—Hätte Bach—, von E. Harich-Schneider.—Bachkonzerte mit Flügel oder Cembalo? von C. A. Martienssen.—Über das Problem des mehrstimmigen Spiels in J. S. Bachs Violinsonaten, von R. Schroeder.—Bach in Köthen, von W. Vetter.

(Continued)

DEUTSCHER BACH-AUSSCUSS Bach-Probleme; Festschrift zu Deutschen Bach-Feier Leipzig, 1950. (Card 3)

1. Bach, Johann Sebastian, 1685-1750. 2. Bach, Johann Sebastian. Organ music. 3. Bach, Johann Sebastian—Composition and style. 4. Bach, Johann Sebastian—England. 5. Bach, Johann Sebastian—Temperament. 6. Bach, Johann Sebastian—Instruments (Keyboard) 7. Bach, Johann Sebastian. Sonatas, Violin. I. Dräger, Hans Heinz, 1909- , ed. II. Laux, Karl, 1896- , ed. III. Title.

F-10
9083

DEUTSCHER GENOSSENSCHAFTSVERBAND (Schulze-Delitzsch)
Festschrift zur 100 Jahrfeier des Deutschen Genossenschaftsverbandes (Schulze-Delitzsch) e. V. [Wiesbaden, Deutscher Genossenschafts-Verlag, 1960] 249 p. illus. 28cm.

1. Cooperation--Germany.

NN * R 7.64 p/J OS PC, 1 SL E, 1 (LC1, X1, Z1)

F-10
3382
DEUTSCHER GENOSSENSCHAFTSVERBAND (SCHULZE-DELITZSCH)
Schulze-Delitzsch 1808-1958; Festschrift zur 150. Wiederkehr seines Geburtstages. Bonn, Herausgeber: Deutscher Genossenschaftsverband (Schulze-Delitzsch) e.V. in Zusammenarbeit mit dem Institut für Genossenschaftswesen an der Universität Marburg [1958] 167 p. mounted port. 28cm.
(Continued)
NN R 5.59 m/A OS, I, Ib PC, 1, 2, I SL E, 1, 2, I (LC1, X1, Z1)

EAM
Deutscher Staat und deutsche Parteien; Beiträge zur deutschen Partei- und Ideengeschichte. Friedrich Meinecke zum 60. Geburtstag dargebracht in Gemeinschaft mit Hermann Bächtold, Hans Fraenkel, Siegfried Kaehler... [und anderen] herausgegeben von Paul Wentzcke. München [etc.] R. Oldenbourg, 1922. 384 p. 23½cm.

744328A. 1. Meinecke, Friedrich, 1862- . 2. Political science—Germany. 3. Parties, Political—Germany. I. Wentzcke, Paul, 1879- , editor.
N. Y. P. L. February 8, 1935

DEUTSCHER GENOSSENSCHAFTSVERBAND (SCHULZE-DELITZSCH). Schulze-Delitzsch 1808-1958... (Card 2)

1. Schulze-Delitzsch, Franz Hermann, 1808-1883. 2. Co-operation--Germany. I. Marburg. Universität. Institut für Genossenschaftswesen.

VEH
DEUTSCHER STAHLBAU-VERBAND.
Beiträge aus statik und Stahlbau. Herr Prof. Dr.-Ing. Dr.-Ing. E.h. K. Klöppel zum 60. Geburtstag gewidmet von P. Boué [et al.] Köln, Stahlbau-Verlags-G.m.b.H. [c1961] 176 p. illus. 28cm.

Includes bibliographies.
CONTENTS.--Brandversuche mit Aussenstützen aus Stahl, von P. Boué. --Einfluss der Steifen-Exzentrizität auf Biegung und Stabilität orthotroper
(Continued)
NN R 9.64 p/S (OC) I, Ibo, II OS PC, 1, 2, 3, I, II SL ST, 1, 2t, 3t, I, II (LC1, X1, Z1) 2

F-10
5766
DEUTSCHER INDUSTRIE- UND HANDELSTAG.
Die Verantwortung des Unternehmers in der Selbstverwaltung. Hrsg. aus Anlass der 100-Jahr-Feier des Deutschen Industrie- und Handelstages. Frankfurt am Main, F. Knapp [1961] 415 p. illus., ports. 28cm.

NN R 7.61 e/o OS PC SL E (LC1, X1, Z1)

DEUTSCHER STAHLBAU-VERBAND. Beiträge aus statik und Stahlbau... (Card 2)

Platten, von E. Giencke. --Die Kaltverfestigung, ein Weg zur Steigerung der Wirtschaftlichkeit im Stahlbau, von O. Jungbluth. --Einflusszahlen in der Schwingungslehre, von K. Marguerre und H. T. Woernle. --Beitrag zur Berechnung längs- und querbelasteter Biegestäbe mit Hilfe von Konvergenzfaktoren, von H. Moppert. --Zum Problem der Gesamtstabilität des I-Trägers unter Querkraftbiegung, von W. Protte. --Elektronisches Rechnen im Stahlbau, von A. Walter und W. Barth. --Das Werkstoffverhalten unter verspröden-den Einflüssen, dargestellt an einigen Beispielen, von H. Wiegand. --Anwendung der Matrizenrechnung in der Statik, von R. Zurmühl.
1. Klöppel, Kurt. 2. Building, Iron and steel 3. Statics. I. Boué, P. II. Title. t. 1961.

C-12
1648
Deutscher Journalisten-Verband.
Zehn Jahre Deutscher Journalisten Verband. [Festschrift. Hrsg. anlässlich der Hauptversammlung des DJV vom 23. bis 27. März in Berlin. Für den Inhalt verantwortlich: Hans Dawill. Bonn, 1960] 119 p. illus. 20 x 21cm.

Cover title: Der Journalist in Tageszeitungen, in Illustrierten, in Rundfunk und Fernsehen, in Massenblättern, in Fachzeitschriften, in Werkseitungen, 1950-1960.
Contributions by various authors.

1. Journalism—Germany. I. Dawill, Hans, ed. II. Dawill, Hans.
NN R 9.63 (OC) I, IIbo OS PC, 1, I SL (LC1, Z1, X1)

SIE
Deutscher Verein für Versicherungs-Wissenschaft, Berlin.
Festgabe für Alfred Manes aus Anlass seiner 25 jährigen Tätigkeit als Vorstand des Deutschen Vereins für Versicherungs-Wissenschaft, dargebracht von Hanns Dorn...in Verbindung mit Joseph L. Cohen...Victor Ehrenberg...[und anderen.] Berlin: E. S. Mittler & Sohn, 1927. xi, 337 p. incl. tables. front. (port.) 4°.

On cover: 1902-1927.
Bibliographical footnotes.

359803A. 1. Manes, Alfred, 1877- . 2. Insurance. 3. Dorn, Hanns, 1878- .
N. Y. P. L. June 26, 1928

HKB
DEUTSCHER KLUB, Buenos Aires.
Geschichte des Deutschtums in Argentinien. Hrsg. vom deutschen Klub in Buenos Aires zur Feier seines 100 jährigen Bestehens, 18. Oktober 1955. [Buenos Aires, 1955] 385 p. illus. 23cm.

At head of title: Wilhelm Lütge, Werner Hoffmann [und] Wilhelm Körner.
"Anmerkungen und Quellenangaben," p. 379-385.
1. Germans in the Argentine Republic--Hist. I. Lütge, Wilhelm, d. 1954. II. Hoffmann, Werner, 1882- III. Körner, Karl Wilhelm.
NN* * R 1.57 a/b (OC) Ib+, II, III (OS) (Ib) PC, 1, I, II, III SL AH, 1, I, II, III (LC1, X1, Z1, Y1)

TAH
Deutsches Institut für Bankwissenschaft und Bankwesen.
Probleme des deutschen Wirtschaftslebens; Erstrebtes und Erreichtes. Eine Sammlung von Abhandlungen herausgegeben vom Deutschen Institut für Bankwissenschaft und Bankwesen. Berlin [etc.] W. de Gruyter & Co., 1937. xiv, 860 p. incl. tables. port. 25cm.

"Dr. Hjalmar Schacht zum vollendeten 60. Lebensjahre am 22. Januar 1937 gewidmet."
PARTIAL CONTENTS.—Die deutsche Reichsbahn, 1918-1936, von Julius Dorpmüller.—Die deutsche Reichspost, von Wilhelm Ohnesorge.—Das deutsche Bankwesen; Struk-
(Continued)

Festschrift
N. Y. P. L. August 25, 1937

Deutsches Institut für Bankwissenschaft und Bankwesen. Probleme des deutschen Wirtschaftslebens... (Card 2)

turwandlungen und Neubau, von O. C. Fischer.—Die deutschen Banken in der Krise, von Friedrich Reinhart.—Der deutsche Immobiliarkredit seit der Inflation, von Hermann Kissler.—Grundfragen der deutschen Absatzwirtschaft, von Carl Lüer.—Die deutschen Versicherungen, von Eduard Hilgard.—Die deutsche Energiewirtschaft, von Carl Krecke.—Die deutsche Seeschiffahrt im Wandel der Nachkriegsjahre bis 1936, von Karl Lindemann.—Die Etappen der Reparationspolitik, von H. F. Berger.—Reichsbank und Währung, von F. W. Dreyse.

897271A. 1. Economic history—Germany, 1918- . 2. Schacht, Hjalmar, 1877- . I. Title.
N. Y. P. L. August 25, 1937

EAH

Deutschkundliches; Friedrich Panzer zum 60. Geburtstage überreicht von Heidelberger Fachgenossen. Herausgegeben von Hans Teske... Heidelberg: C. Winter, 1930. 191 p. plates, port. 8°. (Beiträge zur neueren Literaturgeschichte. N. F., Heft 16.)

540405A. 1. Panzer, Friedrich, 1870- . I. Teske, Hans, editor. II. Ser.
N. Y. P. L. July 24, 1931

---

*RR-EAH

Deutschland und Europa; historische Studien zur Völker- und Staatenordnung des Abendlandes. Düsseldorf, Droste-Verlag [1951] 415 p. port. 25cm.

"Festschrift für Hans Rothfels, herausgegeben von Werner Conze."
"Verzeichnis der Veröffentlichungen von Hans Rothfels," p. 409–415.
Bibliographical footnotes.

1. Rothfels, Hans, 1891- . 2. Germany—Hist.—Addresses, essays, lectures. 3. Russia—Hist.—Addresses, essays, lectures. 4. History—Philosophy. 5. Europe—Politics. I. Conze, Werner, 1904- , ed.
NN

C-13
3819

DEUTSCHLAND, HEINZ.
Hermann Duncker und die russische revolutionäre Bewegung. Zum 90. Geburtstag Hermann Dunckers. Berlin, Verlag Tribüne, 1964. 50 p. ports. 20cm.

Bibliographical footnotes.

1. Duncker, Hermann. 2. Russia—Revolutionary movement.

NN^R 11.67 p/R OC(1b*) PC,1,2 SL E,1,2 S,1,2 (LC1,X1,Z1)

D-18
9461

Un Dialogue des nations, Albert Fuchs zum 70. Geburtstag. München, M. Hueber; Paris, C. Klinckspieck, 1967.
267 p. port. 22 cm.

On spine: Mélanges Albert Fuchs.
French or German.
Bibliographical footnotes.
CONTENTS.—Le mot, par J. Fourquet.—Une "lectio macaronica" chez Walter von der Vogelweide, par J. Charier.—Tellheim und Minna. Einige Bemerkungen zur Minna von Barnhelm, von B. von Wiese.—

(Continued)

NN*R 6.68 a/// OC, I, Ib*, II PC, 1, I, II SL (LC1, X1, Z1)
[I]

Un DIALOGUE des nations. Albert Fuchs zum 70. Geburtstag. (Card 2)

Réflexions sur Wieland et le classicisme, par R. Minder.—Les conceptions religieuses de Wieland dans le Miroir d'Or et l'Histoire des Abdéritains, par J. Murat.—Wieland, Napoleon und die Illuminaten. Zu einem bisher unbekannten Briefe, von F. Martini.—Napoléon dans l'opinion des Berlinois (1806), par P.-P. Sagave.—Réflexions sur quelques maximes de Goethe, par P. Grappin.—Klingsohr-Goethe? Par A. Schlagdenhauffen.—Karl Rosenkranz und sein Goethebuch, von H. Motekat.—Franz Grillparzer und die französische Tragödie, von E. Thurnher.—A propos d'Adriadne auf Naxos, par J.-J. Anstett.—

(Continued)

Un DIALOGUE des nations. Albert Fuchs zum 70. Geburtstag. (Card 3)

Hofmannsthal et le theâtre populaire viennois: Die Frau ohne Schatten, par R. Bauer.—Gestaltetes Leben: Friedrich Gundolfs kritische Grundhaltung in den Briefen, von A. Nivelle.—Les idées politiques de Hermann Hesse, par M. Colleville.—Aspekte des Stadtmotivs in der deutschen Dichtung, von W. Kohlschmidt.—Gedichte, von H. Adrian.—Bibliographie des travaux d'Albert Fuchs (p. 245–258).—Tabula gratulatoria.

1. German literature--Addresses, essays, lectures. I. Fuchs, Albert, 1896- . II. Title: Mélanges Albert Fuchs.

---

*PWZ
(Brod)

Dichter, denker, helfer: Max Brod zum 50. geburtstag. Herausgegeben von Felix Weltsch. Mähr.-Ostrau, Verlag von Julius Kittls nachfolger, Keller & co. [1934]

111 p. illus. (port., facsims.) 23cm.

CONTENTS.—Vorwort.—Politzer, H. M. B.—Mann, T. Festgruss.—Weltsch, F. Philosophie eines dichters.—Utitz, E. Platonismus.—Grab, H. Die schönheit hässlicher bilder.—Politzer, H. Der lyriker.—Ben-Chorin. Der novelist.—Bergmann, H. Die zweigeleisigkeit im chassidismus.—Lichtwitz, H. Dem zionisten.—Hellmann, A. Erinnerungen an gemeinsame kampfjahre.—Wiesenfeld, M. Begegnung mit ostjuden.—Engel, N. Die erste wirkungsstätte.—K., L. Ein hochmütiges be-

(Continued on next card)

A C 35-3155

[2]

Dichter, denker, helfer: Max Brod zum 50. geburtstag ... [1934] (Card 2)

CONTENTS—Continued.

kenntnis.—Werfel, F. Dem freunde.—Zweig, S. Die forderung der solidarität.—Kafka, F. Zwei briefe.—Haas, W. Auslegung eines aktes der freundschaft.—Leppin, P. Erste begegnung.—Baum, O. Max Bäuml.—Torberg, F. Die entdeckung.—Křička, J. Zum fünfzigsten.—Landes, Z. Künder tschechischer kunst.—Jacob, W. Der übersetzer.—Seidl, W. Der kritiker.—Jakobovits. Die abstammung.—Thieberger, F. Die stimme.—Fanta, O. Die handschrift.—Die werke.—Lebensdaten.

1. Brod, Max, 1884- I. Weltsch, Felix, 1884- ed.

A C 35-3155

Title from N. Y. Pub. Libr. Printed by L. C.

[2]

NGO

Dichtung und forschung; festschrift für Emil Ermatinger zum 21. mai 1933. Frauenfeld und Leipzig, Huber & co. aktiengesellschaft [1933]
2 p. l., [vii]–xii, 297 p., 1 l. front. (port.) 24cm.
"Herausgegeben von Walter Muschg und Rudolf Hunziker."
CONTENTS.—An Emil Ermatinger.—Cysarz, Herbert. Zwischen dichtung und philosophie; oder, Literaturhistorie als schicksal.—Spoerri, Theophil. Über einbildung.—Roedemeyer, Friedrichkarl. Gesprochene dichtung.—Petsch, Robert. Goethe und die naturformen der dichtung.—Wiget, Wilhelm. Die träume in Schillers Braut von Messina.—Weber, Marta. Schiller als kritiker.—Zinkernagel, Franz. Ein dramaturgischer aufsatz Hölderlins.—Muschg, Walter. Das dichterische im werk Jacob Grimms.—Koischwitz, Otto. Die literaturgeschichte des dichters Eichendorff.—Hirt, Ernst. Hegels geschichtsphilosophie und der geist der poesie.—Hunziker, Rudolf. Jeremias Gotthelf und Georg Wigand; ihr
(Continued on next card)
A C 33-3232

[3]

Dichtung und forschung: festschrift für Emil Ermatinger ... [1933] (Card 2)

CONTENTS—Continued.

briefwechsel.—Stodte, Hermann. Der konservative Hebbel.—Nussberger, Max. Das problem der historischen treue bei C. F. Meyer.—Bleyer, Jakob. Über geistige rezeption und nationales schrifttum. Ungarische literatur und deutscher einfluss.—Faesi, Robert. Rilke, der briefschreiber.—Helbling, Carl. Dichtung und literaturwissenschaft an der mittelschule.—Kriesi, Hans. Der weltkrieg in belletristik und fachliteratur.—Verzeichnis der wissenschaftlichen veröffentlichungen und der wichtigeren zeitungsaufsätze von Emil Ermatinger.

1. Ermatinger, Emil, 1873– 2. German literature—Addresses, essays, lectures. 3. German poetry—History and criticism. I. Muschg, Walter, 1898– ed. II. Hunziker, Rudolf, 1870– ed. III. Title: Festschrift für Emil Ermatinger.

A C 33-3232

Title from Columbia Univ. Printed by L. C.

[3]

NGO

Diederichs, Eugen, firm, publishers, Jena.

Das deutsche Gesicht; ein Weg zur Zukunft. Jena, E. Diederichs, 1926. 174 p. plates. 20cm.

On cover: Zum xxx. Jahr des Verlages Eugen Diederichs in Jena.
Various contributors.

1. Essays, German—Collections. I. Title.

NN 1.53 (OC)I OS PC, 1, I SL (LC1, Z1, X1)

ZDC

DIENST unter dem Wort; eine Festgabe für Helmuth Schreiner zum 60. Geburtstag am 2. März 1953. In Verbindung mit Walter Künneth und Carl Heinz Ratschow hrsg. von Karl Janssen. Gütersloh, C. Bertelsmann, 1953. 349 p. 23cm.

CONTENTS. — Stephanus und die Urgemeinde, von W. Foerster. —Die theologische Erklärung von Barmen und ihre Bedeutung für die Diakonissenmutterhäuser, von R. Frick. — Die Zukunft der Person, von E. Gerstenmaier. —Liebe und Gerechtigkeit, von T. Heckel. — Der 103. Psalm, von J. Herrmann. — Der Mund voll Lachens, von G. Holtz. —Was ist Praktische" Exegese? von R. Hupfeld. — Dämonie und Krankheit im Lichte der Erlösung, von P. Jacobs. —Die Familie bei Schleiermacher und Wichern, von K. Janssen. —Die Botschaft des Alten Testaments, von A. Jepsen. —

(Continued)

NN ** X 12.53 OC, I PC, 1, 2, I SL (LC1, Z1, X1)

DIENST unter dem Wort... (Card 2)

Evangelischer Offentlichkeitswille, von A. Köberle. — Die Heimatlosen, von H. Krimm. — Christologie und Rechtfertigung, von W. Künneth. — Der Mensch der Gegenwart und das Problem der Freiheit, von C. H. Ratschow. —Das Menschenbild des Alten Testaments, von W. Rudolph. — Das Namensrecht im Entwurf des Familienrechtsgesetzes, von F. K. Schumann. —Vom Glauben zum Tun, von C. G. Schweitzer. — Die Einheit des kirchlichen Handelns, von W. Stählin. —Die guten Werke in der Theologie Martin Luthers, von R. Stupperich. — Vom Menschenbild des Neuen Testaments, von H.-D. Wendland. —Der Heimgedanke in der Inneren Mission, von J. Wolff. --Bibliographie Helmuth Schreiner, von L. Schreiner. (p. 341-347)

1. Schreiner, Helmuth, 1893- 2. Christianity — Essays and misc. I. Janssen, Karl, 1898- ed.

---

* C p.v.3177

Diepenbach, Wilhelm, ed.

Das Mainzer Münzkabinett, 1784–1934; Beiträge zur mittelrheinischen Münz- und Wappenkunde. Festschrift, herausgegeben von Wilhelm Diepenbach. Mainz [Verlag der Numismatischen Gesellschaft Wiesbaden-Mainz] 1934. 57 p. map, col'd pl. 27cm.

Issued with the cooperation of the city of Mainz.
Bibliographical footnotes.

869913A. 1. Numismatics—Collections—Germany—Mainz. I. Mainz.
N. Y. P. L. January 28, 1937

E-13
2015

Dietse studies; bundel aangebied aan Prof. Dr. J. Du P. Scholtz by geleentheid van sy vyf-en-sestigste verjaardag, 14 Mei, 1965. [Assen] Van Gorcum [1965]

221 p. port. 24 cm.

Bibliographical footnotes.

CONTENTS.—Voorwoord.—Bredero se Brabander, deur R. Antonissen.—Heeft het Afrikaans zich uit het Hollands ontwikkeld? door B. van dem Berg.—Woordverschil uit d-verschil, door C. B. van Hae-

(Continued)

NN * R 4.68 c/R OC, I PC, 1, 2, I SL (LC1, X1, Z1)

3

DIETSE studies... (Card 2)

ringen.—De betekenis van de incunabelkunde voor de Nederlandistiek, door W. en L. Hellinga.—Die verbale hendiadis in Afrikaans, deur W. Kempen.—Na aanleiding van die eerste gepubliseerde Nama-leesboekie (1845) deur G. S. Nienaber.—De volgorde van verbogen verbale vormen in het Nederlands, door J. L. Pauwels.—Die bundel as eenheid, deur E. Raidt.—Enkele sintaktiese maneuwers by D. J. Opperman, deur M. Scholtz.—Rhijnvis Feith en del liefde van Julia, door W. A. P. Smit.—Sintaktiese verskynsels in die taal van Trichardt en tydgenote, deur J. Smuts.—'n Nederlandse adverbiale doeblet en die Afrikaanse taalsisteem, deur J. A. Verhage.—Aspekte van

(Continued)

DIETSE studies... (Card 3)

woordaksent, deur M. De Villiers. — Sleutelbegrippe van die Afrikaanse poësiekritiek, deur R. Wiehahn. — Curriculum vitae. — Bibliografie van prof. dr. J. du P. Scholtz.

1. Dutch language--Addresses, essays, lectures. 2. Afrikaans language--Addresses, essays, lectures. I. Scholtz, J. Du P.

D-17
3230

Dietz, Rolf, 1902- *ed.*

Festschrift für Hans Carl Nipperdey zum 70. Geburtstag, 21. Januar 1965. Hrsg. von Rolf Dietz und Heinz Hübner. München, Beck, 1965.

2 v. port. 23 cm.

On spine: Festschrift H. C. Nipperdey.
German, Spanish, Italian, French, or Dutch.
Includes bibliographical references.
"Bibliographie der veröffentlichungen von Hans Carl Nipperdey": v. 2, p. 937–[957]

(Continued)

NN * R 5.67 l/c OC, I, IIb* PC, 1, 2, 3, I SL E, 1, 2, 3, I (LC1, X1, Z1)

DIETZ, ROLF, 1902- , ed. Festschrift für Hans Carl Nipperdey zum 70. Geburtstag... (Card 2)

1. Nipperdey, Hans Carl, 1895- --Bibl. 2. Nipperdey, Hans Carl, 1895- . 3. Law--Addresses, essays, lectures. I. Hübner, Heinz, 1914- , joint ed. II. Hübner, Heinz, 1914-

IBD

Dietze, Gottfried, *ed.*
Essays on the American Constitution; a commemorative volume in honor of Alpheus T. Mason. Englewood Cliffs, N. J., Prentice-Hall [1964]

x, 245 p. port. 24 cm.

Bibliographical footnotes.

CONTENTS.—The chasm that separated Thomas Jefferson and John Marshall, by J. P. Boyd.—Representative equality: "political thicket" or voting right? by G. E. Baker.—Imperium in imperio revisited, by A. Hacker.—The influence of legal realism on William O. Douglas, by J. W. Hopkirk.—The amicus curiae brief: from friendship to ad-

(Continued)

NN*R 2.65 g/5 OC PC, 1, 2 SL AH, 1, 2 E, 1 (LC1, X1, Z1) 3

DIETZE, GOTTFRIED, ed. Essays on the American Constitution... (Card 2)

vocacy, by S. Krislov.—The lawyers need help with "the lawyer's clause," by H. W. Chase.—Intergovernmental cooperation and American federalism, by R. H. Leach.—Stateways versus folkways: critical factors in southern reactions to Brown v. Board of Education, by D. R. Matthews and J. W. Prothro.—Constitutional limitation and American foreign policy, by W. Howard.—Robert von Mohl, Germany's de Tocqueville, by G. Dietze.—Supreme Court biography and the study of public law, by J. W. Peltason.—Alpheus T. Mason, by

(Continued)

DIETZE, GOTTFRIED, e. Essays on the American Constitution... (Card 3)

J. Davies.—The art of precepting, by A. T. Mason.—Bibliography of Alpheus T. Mason (p. 239-248)—Lectureships and seminars.

1. United States. Constitution. 2. Mason, Alphaeus Thomas, 1899-

---

MCK
(Dilich)

Dilich, Wilhelm Schaeffer, called, d. 1655.
Wilhelm Dilichs Federzeichnungen erzgebirgischer und vogtländischer Orte aus den Jahren 1626-1629; mit einem Vorworte von Pfarrer Friedrich Hermann Löscher und einer Einleitung von Seminaroberlehrer i. R. Rich. Freytag; herausgegeben vom Erzgebirgsverein als Festgabe an seine Zweigvereine zur Fünfzig-Jahrfeier, 1928. Schwarzenberg, Sachsen: Glückauf-Verlag, 1928. xii, 52 p. illus. obl. 8°.

421390A. 1. Drawings, German. 2. Saxony—Views. 3. Erzgebirgsverein.
N. Y. P. L. August 20, 1929

D-18
9642

Discorrendo di Riccardo Bacchelli. Scritti di A. Andreoli [et al.] Milano, R. Ricciardi, 1966.

373 p. 22 cm.

Bibliographical footnotes.

CONTENTS.—C'era una volta, di A. Andreoli.—Riccardo Bacchelli bolognese, di G. Raimondi.—Bacchelli poeta, di S. Solmi.—I cinquant'anni dei "Poemi lirici," di F. Gavazzeni.—Appunti su Bacchelli teatrante, di E. F. Palmieri.—Bacchelli traduttore, di G. Contini.—Riccardo Bacchelli critico del Leopardi e del Manzoni, di L. Blasucci.—Occasione musicale di Bacchelli, di L. Ronga.—Preistoria di

(Continued)

NN* 6.€ v/4 OC, I, Ib* PC, 1, I SL (LC1, X1) (Z1) 2

DISCORRENDO di Riccardo Bacchelli. (Card 2)

"Non ti chiamerò più padre," di C. Segre.—Riccardo Bacchelli tra critica e poesia dal "Diavolo" al "Mulino": appunti di letture, di M. Fubini.—Bibliografia degli scritti di Riccardo Bacchelli, di M. Vitale (p. [253]-373)

1. Bacchelli, Riccardo, 1891- . I. Andreoli, Aldo.

D-20
7673

The Diversity of history: essays in honour of Sir Herbert Butterfield; edited by J. H. Elliott and H. G. Koenigsberger. Ithaca, N.Y., Cornell university press [1970] vii, 338 p., plate., port. 23cm.

Includes bibliographical references.

CONTENTS.—Sir Herbert Butterfield as a historian: an appreciation, by D. Brogan.—St Augustine, by D. Knowles.—Music and re-

(Continued)

NN*R 9.71 m/z OC, I, II, III PC, 1, 2, I, II, III SL (LC1, X1, Z1) 3

The DIVERSITY of history ... 1970.
(Card 2)

ligion in modern European history, by K. G. Koenigsberger.—Venetian diplomacy before Pavia: from reality to myth, by F. Gilbert.—The statecraft of Olivares, by J. H. Elliott.—Time, history and eschatology of the thought of Thomas Hobbes, by J. G. A. Pocock.—On the historical singularity of the scientific revolution of the seventeenth century, by A. R. Hall.—History and reform in the middle of the eighteenth century, by F. Venturi.—The Duke of Newcastle and the origins of the diplomatic revolution, by D. B. Horn.—Cavour and the Tuscan revolution of 1859, by D. M. Smith.—Bibliography

(Continued)

The DIVERSITY of history ... 1970.
(Card 3)

of Sir Herbert Butterfield's writings (to 1968), by R. W. K. Hinton (p. 315-325)

1. Europe--Hist.--Addresses, essays, lectures. 2. Butterfield, Sir Herbert, 1900- . I. Butterfield, Sir Herbert, 1900- . II. Elliott, John Huxtable, ed. III. Koenigsberger, Helmut G., ed.

E-12
2953

Dixey, Roger Nicholas, *ed.*
International explorations of agricultural economics. A tribute to the inspiration of Leonard Knight Elmhirst. Edited by Roger N. Dixey. Ames, Iowa State University Press, 1964.

ix, 306 p. illus., maps. 24 cm.

Includes bibliographies.

1. Agriculture--Economics. 2. Elmhirst, Leonard Knight, 1893-

NN* R 3.65 e/5 OC PC, 1, 2 SL E, 1, 2 (LC1, X1, Z1)

Dni žalu; památník o sklonku života, o nemoci, smrti a pohřbu presidenta Osvoboditele T. G. Masaryka. Praha: Čin [etc.] 1937. 169 p. illus., 80 pl. on 39 l. 38½cm.

"Redakční kruh, K. Č., Josef Kopta (hlavní redaktor), V. K. Škrach."

215207B. 1. Masaryk, Tomáš Garrigue, pres. Czecho-Slovakia, 1850-1937. I. Kopta, Josef, 1894- , ed. II. Škrach, Vasil K , 1891- , ed. III. Čapek, Karel, 1890-1938, ed.
N. Y. P. L. March 25, 1943

DOCUMENTA archaeologica. Wolfgang La Baume dedicata... (Card 2)

ehemaligen Westpreussen, von E. Šturms. --Bronze-und eisenzeitliche Varia, von O. Kleemann. --Der Schatzfund von Ossa, Kreis Löbau, von P. La Baume. --Germanische Goldnachprägung nach einem Denar des Caracalla aus der Umgebung von Danzig, von P. La Baume. --Völkerwanderungszeitliche Funde aus dem südlichen Ostpreussen, von O. Kleemann. --Das Problem der masurgermanischen Fibeln in Ostpreussen, von H. Kühn. --Samländische Funde und die Frage der ältesten Steigbügel, von O. Kleemann. --Einige Säbelschwerter im Ostseeraum, von P. Paulsen. --Wolfgang La Baume Curriculum vitae. -- Bibliographie.

1. East Prussia. --Archaeology. 2. La Baume, Wolfgang, 1885- I. Series. II. Kleemann, Otto, ed.

Dr. Modi memorial volume; papers on Indo-Iranian and other subjects, written by several scholars in honour of Shams-ul-Ulama Dr. Jivanji Jamshedji Modi... Ed. by the Dr. Modi memorial volume editorial board. Bombay, Fort prtg. press, 1930. xii, 774 p. illus. 25cm.

522136B. 1. Modi, Sir Jivanji Jamshedji, 1854-1933. 2. Indo-Iranian studies.
N. Y. P. L. August 15, 1950

DOERING, CARL, 1856 -
Hofrath Prof. Dr. ph. Julius Woldemar Zeibig; ein Lebensbild. Vortrag gehalten in Neu-Gersdorf zur XXXIII. Generalversammlung des Gesammtverein der Gabelsberger'schen Stenographenvereine im Königreich Sachsen. Dresden, G. Dietze, 1894. 12 p. port. 20cm. (Sammlung von Vorträgen aus dem Gebiete der Stenographie. No. 21)

John Robert Gregg Shorthand Coll.

1. Zeibig, Julius Woldemar, 1819-1905.
NN 3.71 w/J OC PC,1 SL (LC1, X1, Z1)

Dr. S. Krishnaswami Aiyangar commemoration volume. [Madras: The committee, 1936] 8, x-xxiv, 500 p. incl. tables (part geneal.). plates, port. 25cm.

"This volume...written by his friends, pupils and admirers is presented to...Dr. S. Krishnaswami Aiyangar...on his sixty-sixth birthday, 15th April, 1936."

"A committee consisting of Prof. V. Rangacharya, Prof. C. S. Srinivasachari and Mr. V. R. Ramachandra Dikshitar, was organised for editing the papers received." —*Foreword.*

PARTIAL CONTENTS.—The Sasanian conquest of the Indus region, by Jarl Charpentier.—Vedic monotheism, by A. K. Coomaraswamy.—Satiyaputra of Asoka's edict II, by M. G. Pai.—Al Ghazali, by Rahsid Ahmad.—Mahmud Gawan's political thought and administration, by H. K. Sherwani.—The committee system of village administration

(Continued)

N. Y. P. L. April 7, 1937

Dr. h.c. Hans Bernoulli, zum fünfundsiebzigsten Geburtstag am 17. Februar 1951 gewidmet von seinen Freuden. [Bern, Verlagsgenossenschaft Freies Volk, 1951] 103 p. illus. (incl. music), plates. 21 x 21cm.

"Dieses Buch wurde von Friedrich Salzmann erdacht und zusammengestellt."

606631B. 1. Bernoulli, Hans, 1876- . I. Salzmann, Friedrich, ed.
N. Y. P. L. November 19, 1951

Dr. S. Krishnaswami Aiyangar... (Card 2)

in Cola times, by A. Appadorai.—The capitals of Ceylon, ancient and modern, by Andreas Nell.—The pepper trade of India in early times, by P. J. Thomas.—South India as a centre of Pali Buddhism, by B. C. Law.—Asoka's Dhamma (Dharma), by Gurty Venkat Rao.—Camoens and his epic of India, by P. Seshadri.—The derivation of the word "Tamil," by K. N. S. Pillai.—The playhouse of the Hindu period, by P. K. Acharya.—The temple of Siva Nataraja at Chidambaram, by B. V. N. Naidu.—The rock-cut caves of Malabar, by M. D. Raghavan.—The evolution of the theory of music in the Vijayanagara empire, by N. S. Ramachandran.—Melody and harmony, by M. S. Ramaswami Aiyar.—A history of the Indian opera, by P. Sambamoorthy.—Hindu law in Java and Bali, by R. C. Majumdar.

869309A. 1. India—Hist.—Addresses, essays, lectures. 2. Aiyangar, Sakkottai Krishnaswami, 1871- . I. Rangāchārya, V., ed. II. Srinivasachari, C. S., ed. III. Dikshitar, V. R. Ramachandra, ed.
N. Y. P. L. April 7, 1937

Dr. Wilhelm Frick und sein Ministerium; aus Anlass des 60. Geburtstages des Reichs- und preussischen Ministers des Innern Dr. Wilhelm Frick am 12. März 1937 herausgegeben vom Staatssekretär im Reichs- und Preussischen Ministerium des Innern Hans Pfundtner. München: Zentralverlag der NSDAP., F. Eher Nachf., G.m.b.H., 1937. 202 p. incl. plates, ports. 29 x 22cm.

904281A. 1. Germany. Innern, Reichsamt des. 2. Prussia. Innern, Ministerium des. 3. Frick, Wilhelm, 1877- . 4. Germany—Politics, 1933- . I. Pfundtner, Hans, 1881- , ed.
N. Y. P. L. September 13, 1937

DOCUMENTA archaeologica. Wolfgang La Baume dedicata, 8.II. 1955. Hrsg. von Otto Kleemann. Bonn, L. Röhrscheid, 1956. 143 p. illus., port. map. 31cm. (Rheinische Forschungen zur Vorgeschichte. Bd. 5)

"Tafelbeilage" (33 plates, 1 fold. map) inserted.

Includes bibliographies.

CONTENTS. --Vor-und frühgeschichtlicher Bernsteinschmuck, von D. Bohnsack. --Der Bernsteinschmuck der östlichen Amphorenkultur, von E. Šturms. --Beispiele schnurkeramischer Irdenwaren aus Succase, von L. Kilian. --Tüllenbeile und Halsringe aus dem

(Continued)

NN X 12.57 m/J OC, II (OS)I PC, 1, 2, I, II SL (LC1, X1, Z1, C1, Y1)

Dole, Gertrude Evelyn, 1915- , *ed.*
Essays in the science of culture; in honor of Leslie A. White, in celebration of his sixtieth birthday and his thirtieth year of teaching at the University of Michigan. Edited by Gertrude E. Dole and Robert L. Carneiro. New York, Crowell [1960]

xlvi, 509 p. illus., port. 24 cm.

Includes bibliographies.

1. Civilization--Addresses, essays, lectures. 2. White, Leslie A., 1900- I. Carneiro, Robert Leonard, 1927- joint ed. II. Title. III. Dole, Gertrude Evelyn, 1915- IV. Carneiro, Robert Leonard, 1927-
NN*R 3.61 s/P OC, I, IIIb*, IVb* PC, 1, 2, I, II SL (LC1, X1, Z1)

Write on slip, name, year, vol., page of magazine and class mark — STT

Dolgozatok Dr. Entz Béla egyetemi tanári működésének 10-ik évfordulójára, irták tanítványai.

(Magyar király Erzsébet tudományehyetem, Pecs. Tanévi irataiból. Pécs,1928. 8°. 1927-28, füzet 5,p.1-321. illus.,front.port.)

form 400a [11-13-30 25m]

YBX
(Thomas Aquinas)

DOMINICANS IN FRANCE.

Mélanges thomistes,publiés a l'occasion du VIe centenaire de la canonisation de Saint Thomas d'Aquin (18 juillet 1323). Paris, J. Vrin, 1934. 408 p. 26cm. (Bibliothèque thomiste. 3)

Bibliographical footnotes.

1. Thomas Aquinas, Saint, 1225? -1274. I. Series.

NN **Z X5.55 p/ OS(1b)I PC, 1, I SL (U1, LC1, Z1, X1)

E-12
7653

Dommeyer, Frederick C *ed.*

Current philosophical issues; essays in honor of Curt John Ducasse. Compiled and edited by Frederick C. Dommeyer. Springfield, Ill., Thomas [1966]

xxv, 262 p. port. 24 cm. (American lecture series, publication no. 657. American lectures in philosophy)

Bibliographical footnotes.

(Continued)

NN * R 1.67 1/c OC, Ib* PC,1, 2 SL (LC1, X1, Z1)

DOMMEYER, FREDERICK C., ed. Current philosophical issues... (Card 3)

E. H. Madden.—A new look at the problem of evil, by C. Hartshorne.—Free will, the creativity of God, and order, by P. A. Bertocci.—Academic history of Curt John Ducasse.—Publications of Curt John Ducasse (p. 242-257)

1. Philosophy, Modern. 2. Ducasse, Curt John, 1881- I. Dommeyer, Frederick C.

DOMMEYER, FREDERICK C., ed. Current philosophical issues... (Card 2)

CONTENTS.—Standpoint commitments and the function of philosophy, by M. Farber.—Understanding philosophy, by M. Lazerowitz.—Metamorphoses of the principle of verifiability, by A. Ambrose.—Perception and sensation as presentational, by C. A. Baylis.—The principles of epistemic appraisal, by R. M. Chisholm.—A verdict of epiphenomenalism, by B. Blanshard.—The expressive theory of the mind-body relation, by H. H. Price.—Desires as causes of actions, by A. I. Melden.—Ducasse on "cause"—another look, by R. E. Santoni.—Pictures and maps, by V. Tomas.—The riddle of God and evil, by

(Continued)

L-10
3173
no.11

DOMONKOS, L.S., ed.

Studium generale; studies offered to Astrik L. Gabriel by his former students at the Mediaeval institute, University of Notre Dame, on the occasion of his election as an honorary doctor of the Ambrosiana in Milan. Edited by L.S. Domonkos [and] R.J. Schneider. Notre Dame, Ind., 1967. xxxi, 251 p. port., maps(part fold.), facsims. 26cm. (Texts and studies in the history of

(Continued)

NN R 7.69 v/ OC, II, III, Vbo, VIb+ (OS)I PC, 1, 2, I, II, III, IV (LC1, X1, Z1) [I]

DOMONKOS, L.S., ed. Studium generale... (Card 2)

mediaeval education. no. 11)

"Chronological bibliography of the works of A. L. Gabriel," p. xv-xxxi. Bibliographical footnotes.

CONTENTS.--The history of the Sigismundean foundation of the University of Obuda, Hungary, by L.S. Domonkos.--John de Martigny, principal and benefactor of the College of Burgundy, by P. A. Ford.--The unity of the mediaeval intellectual attitude, by B. A. Gendrau.--Jean Pain-et-Chair, c.1400-1473, principal of the College of Presles at the University of Paris, by F.K.

(Continued)

DOMONKOS, L.S., ed. Studium generale... (Card 3)

Jensen.--The university career of bishop Stephen Bodeker, 1384-1459 of Brandenburg, by J.J. John.--The early Franciscan studium at the University of Paris, by J.C. Murphy.--A "Mirror for princes" by Vincent de Beauvais, by R.J. Schneider.

1. Education--Hist., 476-1500. 2. Education--Addresses, essays, lectures. I. Series. II. Gabriel, Astrik Ladislas, 1907- . III. Schneider, Robert J., joint ed. IV. Title. V. Domonkos, L. S. VI. Schneider, Robert J.

G-10
961

DONATI, LAMBERTO, ed.

Studi e ricerche nella Biblioteca e negli Archivi vaticani in memoria del cardinale Giovanni Mercati, 1866-1957. Firenze, L.S. Olschki, 1959. viii, 360 p. illus., port., facasims. 32cm.

Contributions in Italian, German and French.

Bibliographical footnotes.

(Continued)

NN 8.61 e/ OC PC, 1, 2 SL (LC1, X1, Z1) [I]

DONATI, LAMBERTO, ed. Studi e ricerche nella Biblioteca e negli Archivi vaticani in memoria del cardinale Giovanni Mercati, 1866-1957. (Card 2)

CONTENTS.-- Proemio, di L. Donati.--Il vescovo di Barcellona Pietro Garsias bibliotecario della Vaticana sotto Alessandro VI, di A.M. Albareda.--Due liste di libri per la Biblioteca vaticana, di L. Berra.--La lettera di Walone abate di S. Arnolfo di Metz e di S. Remigio di Reims a Gregorio VIII (1073), di G.B. Borino.--Per il "Textus Evangelii" donato da Enrico II a Montecassino (Vat. Ottobon. lat. 74), di A. Campana.--Le fonti iconografiche di alcuni manoscritti urbinati della Biblioteca vaticana, di L. Donati. --I Registri vaticani e la loro

(Continued)

DONATI, LAMBERTO, ed. Studi e ricerche nella Biblioteca e negli Archivi vaticani in memoria del cardinale Giovanni Mercati, 1866-1957. (Card 3)

continuazione, di M. Giusti. --Der Amtsantritt des Rotarichters Bernardino Giraud, 1762-63, von H. Hoberg. --Enea Silvio Piccolominis Fortsetzung zum Liber Augustalis von Benvenuto Rambaldi aus Imola und ein ähnlicher zeitgenössischer Aufholversuch, von P. Künzle. --La traduction française du "Dizionario" de Gaetano Moroni, 1844-1862, par M. H. Laurent. --I due manoscritti urbinati dei privilegi dei Montefeltro, di L. Michelini Tocci. --Il clero della cattedrale di Lucca nei secoli XV e

(Continued)

DONATI, LAMBERTO, ed. Studi e ricerche nella Biblioteca e negli Archivi vaticani in memoria del cardinale Giovanni Mercati, 1866-1957. (Card 4)

XVI, di L. Nanni. --La riforma della segreteria di stato di Gregorio XVI, di L. Pásztor. --Recherche des deux bibliothèques romaines Maffei des XVe et XVIe siècles, par J. Ruysschaert. --Disavventure e morte di Vincent Raymond, miniatore papale, di N. Vian.

1. Mercati, Giovanni, cardinal, 1866-1957. 2. Bibliography--Addresses, essays, lectures.

MAMG

DONIN, RICHARD KURT, 1881-

Zur Kunstgeschichte Österreichs; gesammelte Aufsätze. [Richard Kurt Donin zum 70. Geburtstage überreicht. Herausgeber: Verein für Landeskunde von Niederösterreich und Wien, Gesellschaft für Vergleichende Kunstforschung, Verein für Geschichte der Stadt Wien] Wien, M. F. Rohrer, 1951. x, 495 p. illus., plates, port. 24cm.

"Richard Kurt Donin, von Karl Lechner, " p. 1-10.

"Verzeichnis der kunsthistorischen Arbeiten, " p. 459-465. Bibliographical footnotes

(Continued)

NN * R 7.53 OC (OS) I, II, III PC, 1, 2, I, II, III SL A, 1, 2, I, II, III (LC1, Z/, X1)

DONIN, RICHARD KURT, 1881- Zur Kunstgeschichte Österreichs... (Card 2)

1. Art, Austrian—Hist. 2. Architecture—Austria—Hist. I. Verein für Landeskunde und Heimatschutz von Nieder-Österreich und Wien. II. Gesellschaft für vergleichende Kunstforschung, Vienna. III. Verein für Geschichte der Stadt Wien.

---

*SAD

Donum Boëthianum; arkivvetenskapliga bidrag tillägnade Bertil Boëthius 31/1/1950. Stockholm, Norstedt [1950]

xx, 515 p. port. 22 cm.

"Festskriften har redigerats av Olof Jägerskiöld och Åke Kromnow."

1. Archives. 2. Archives—Sweden. 3. Boëthius, Bertil, 1885- I. Jägerskiöld, Olof, 1906- ed. II. Kromnow, Åke, 1914- ed.

A 51-5341

New York. Public Libr. for Library of Congress [1]

YAR

Donum lustrale, die natali vicesimo quinto Universitati Catholicae noviomagensi ab alumnis pristinis oblatum. Noviomagi [etc.] Dekker & van de Vegt, 1949. 518 p. maps. 25cm.

Bibliographical footnotes.

525908B. 1. Nimwegen, Netherlands. Roomsch Catholieke universiteit. 2. Philosophy—Essays and misc. 3. Theology—Essays and misc. 4. Law.

N. Y. P. L. July 6, 1950

---

* OAC

Donum natalicium H. S. Nyberg oblatum. [Edendum curaverunt Erik Gren et al. Uppsala] 1954.

218 p. illus., port., facsims. 25 cm.

Includes bibliographical footnotes and a bibliography (p. 216-218)

CONTENTS.—Bailey, H. W. Ariana.—Benveniste, E. Avestica.—Björkman, W. Ein türkischer Schenckungsbrief vom Jahre 1587.—Duchesne-Guillemin, J. V.-p. θarmiš "comble" et les noms iraniens en -mi-.—Dumézil, G. Karṇa et les Pāṇḍava.—Frye, R. N. An early Arabic script in eastern Iran.—Gerleman, G. Wort und Realität.—Hartman S. S. Yašts, jours et mois.—Kahle, P. The Ben Asher text of the Hebrew Bible.—Lentz, W. Das motivische Bild von Yasna 47.—Lévi-Provençal, E. A propos de l'ascète philosophe Ibn Massarra de Cordoue.—Lewin, B. La notion de muḥdat dans le kalām et dans la philosophie.—Littmann, E. Bilitterale Verba im Tigrē.—

(Continued)

NN * 10.58 p/ OC, I PC, 1, 2, I SL O, 1, 2, I (LC1, X1, Z1)

Donum natalicium H. S. Nyberg. 1954. (Card 2)

CONTENTS—Continued.

Lundman, B. Einige kritische Bemerkungen zur Anthropologie Vorderasiens.—Löfgren, O. Zur Charakteristik des "vormasoretischen" Jesajatextes.—Massignon, L. Qiṣṣat Ḥusayn al-Ḥallāj.—Menasce, J de. Le témoignage de Jayhānī sur le mazdéisme.—Mowinckel, S Die Gründung von Hebron.—Ringgren, H. Die Gottesfurcht im Koran.—Rowley, H. H. A recent theory on the Exodus.—Rundgren, F. Sillağdun=al-aḥāmira=al-Rūm nebst einigen Bemerkungen zu Ibn al-Sīrāfīs šarḥ abyāt iṣlāḥ al-manṭiq.

1. NYBERG, HENRIK SAMUEL, 1889-
2. ORIENTAL STUDIES—COLLECTIONS
I. Gren, Erik, 1904- , ed.

NAC p.v.357

Dortmunder Immermann-bund.

Julius Schwering zum 70. geburtstag. Kleine festgabe dargebracht im auftrage des Dortmunder Immermann-bundes und der Vereinigung von freunden der Stadt- und landesbibliothek Dortmund; herausgegeben von Erich Schulz. Dortmund, Verlag des Dortmunder Immermann-bundes, im kommission bei Max Thomas, 1933.

3 p. l., 87 p. front. (port.) 31cm.

CONTENTS.—Julius Schwering und sein lebenswerk [von] J. Risse.—Bei Maria Kahle [von] W. Uhlmann-Bixterheide.—4 briefe von Friedrich Leopold, graf zu Stolberg, an Johann Jakob Hess [hrsg. von] E.

(Continued on next card)

A C 34-1618

[3]

Dortmunder Immermann-bund. Julius Schwering zum 70. geburtstag ... 1933. (Card 2)

CONTENTS—Continued.

Reinhard.—Vollendung [von] H. Peitmann.—Der kleine rosengarten von Hermann Löns [von] W. Deimann.—Osnabrück vor 30 jahren [von] L. E. Schücking.—Wittekindsagen [von] W. Wenzel.—Die westfälische literatur in der schule [von] H. Woelbing.—Erlebnisse mit zwei Freiligrath-briefen [von] H. Uhlendahl.—Die schöngeistigen zeitschriften des Biedermeier in Westfalen [von] A. Wand.—Briefe von Levin Schücking, Annette von Droste-Hülshoff und Ferdinand Freiligrath [hrsg. von] E. Schulz.—Bildnisbeilage: Professor dr. Julius Schwering als rektor magnificus 1925/26; ölgemälde von Bernhard Pankok.

1. German literature—Addresses, essays, lectures. 2. Schwering, Julius, 1863- I. Vereinigung von freunden der Stadt- und landesbibliothek, Dortmund. II. Schulz, Erich Gustav Hermann, 1874- ed.

A C 34-1618

Title from N. Y. Pub. Libr. Printed by L. C.

[3]

Copy only words underlined
& Classmark-- ZSA

DOWIE, JAMES IVERNE, ed.
The immigration of ideas; studies in the North Atlantic community. Essays presented to O. Fritiof Ander. Edited by J. Iverne Dowie and J. Thomas Tredway. Rock Island, Ill., 1968. ix, 211 p. 25cm. (Augustana historical society, Rock Island, Ill. Publications. no. 21)

CONTENTS.--On the meaning of faith in the Great awakening and the Methodist revival, by R. Paulson.--Jacob Letterstedt and nordic

(Continued)

NN R 1.69 k/zOC, I, IIbo OI PC, 1, 2, 3, I AH, 1, 3, I (LC1, X1, Z1) 3

DOWIE, JAMES IVERNE, ed. The immigration of ideas... (Card 2)

cooperation, by F. Scott.--High churchmen in a hostile world, by T. Tredway.--O. E. Hagen, a pioneer Norwegian-American scholar, by T.C. Blegen.--The role of Augustana in the transplanting of culture across the Atlantic, by C. Bergendoff.--Ernst Skarstedt: a unique and free spirit, by E. Lindquist.--Edward Price Bell-Anglo-American spokesman, 1914-1917, by B.K. Zobrist.--Wilson Gladstone: Perils and parallels in leadership, by J.I. Dowie.--Fissures in the melting pot, by C. Wittke.--Sweden in the American social mind of the

(Continued)

DOWIE, JAMES IVERNE, ed. The immigration of ideas... (Card 3)

1930's, by M. Curti.--Recollections of a childhood and youth, by O.F. Ander.--One does not say goodbye to Gendalen, by B. Brodahl.--Bibliography of the published writings of O. Fritiof Ander, by E.M. Espelie.

1. Ander, Oscar Fritiof, 1903- . 2. Scandinavia--Cultural relations--United States. 3. United States--Cultural relations--Scandinavia. I. Tredway, J. Thomas, joint ed. II. Tredway, J. Thomas.

Copy only words underlined
& classmark-- ZSA

DOWIE, JAMES IVERNE, ed.
The Swedish immigrant community in transition; essays in honor of Dr. Conrad Bergendoff. Edited by J. Iverne Dowie and Ernest M. Espelie. Rock Island, Ill., Augustana historical society, 1963. x, 246 p. illus., port., map. 24cm. (Augustana historical society, Rock Island, Ill. Publications. no. 20)

Includes bibliographies.

(Continued)

NN R 9.64 g/J OC, I, IIbo OI PC, 1, 2, 3, I AH, 2, I E, 2, I (LC1, X1, Z1) [I] 3

DOWIE, JAMES IVERNE, ed. The Swedish immigrant community in transition... (Card 2)

CONTENTS.—Town and gown by the Mississippi, by J.I. Dowie.—The background of Swedish immigration, 1840-1850, by G. Westin.—The best americanizers, by C.E. Carlson.—The sacred music of the Swedish immigrants, by C.L. Nelson.—Prärieblomman: an immigrant community in central Kansas, by E. Lindquist.—Augustana and Gustavus, partners or competitors, by D.D. Lund.—The academies of the Augustana Lutheran church, by P.M. Lindberg.—Paul Peter Waldenström and Augustana, by K.A. Olsson.—Language in exile, by N. Hasselmo.—An immigrant community during the progressive

(Continued)

DOWIE, JAMES IVERNE, ed. The Swedish immigrant community in transition... (Card 3)

era, by O.F. Ander.—The Swedish-American press and isolationism, by F.H. Capps.—Primary sources in denominational historiography, by G.E. Arden.—Augustana, a people in transition, by C. Bergendoff.—Dr. Bergendoff, Christian scholar and educator, by E.M. Carlson.

1. Bergendoff, Conrad John Immanuel, 1895- . 2. Swedes in the U.S. 3. Evangelical Lutheran Augustana synod of North America. I. Espelie, Ernest M., joint ed. II. Espelie, Ernest M.

D-16
5060

DRASCHER, WARHOLD, 1892- , ed.
Ein Leben für Südwestafrika; Festschrift Dr. h.c. Heinrich Vedder; hrsg. von W. Drascher und H.J. Rust im Auftrage der S.W.A. Wissenschaftlichen Gesellschaft, Windhoek. v. 2., inhaltlich unveränderte Aufl. [Windhoek, S.W.A. Wissenschaftliche Gesellschaft, 1964?] 168 p. illus., port., maps. 22cm.

(Continued)

NN R 7.66 r/J OC, I, IIb* (OS)III PC, 1, 2, I, III SL (NWA1, LC1, X1, Z1) 2

DRASCHER, WARHOLD, 1892- , ed. Ein Leben für Südwestafrika... (Card 2)

Includes bibliographies.

1. Africa, Southwest. 2. Vedder, Heinrich. I. Rust, Hans Joachim, joint ed. II. Rust, Hans Joachim. III. South West African scientific society.

MW p.v.14

Drei Masken-Verlag A.-G., Berlin.
Frank Wedekind und das Theater; zusammengestellt und bearbeitet vom Drei Masken-Verlag G.m.b.H. Berlin, 1915. 84 p. plates, port. 23½cm.

CONTENTS.—Zur Einführung.—Wedekind-Statistik, von J. M. Jurinek.—Wedekind, von P. Block.—Frank Wedekinds Leben, von A. Kutscher.—Der fünfzigjährige Wedekind, von H. Kienzl.—Frank Wedekind als Bühnenautor, von A. Kutscher.—Frank Wedekind: Regisseur und Schauspieler, von A. Holzbock.—Wedekind; Romantiker, von W. Bolze.—Begegnung mit Josef Kainz; Die Furcht vor dem Tode, von F. Wedekind.

775516A. 1. Wedekind, Frank, 1864-1918. 2. Stage—Germany, 1897-1918.
N. Y. P. L. September 23, 1935

ZISF
(Drew)

Drew university, *Madison, N. J.*
The teachers of Drew, 1867-1942; a commemorative volume issued on the occasion of the 75th anniversary of the founding of Drew theological seminary, October 15, 1942, edited by James Richard Joy. Madison, N. J., Drew university, 1942.
xiii p., 1 l., 266 p. front., illus., plates, ports. 21½cm.

1. Drew university, Madison, N. J. Graduate school of theology. I. Joy, James Richard, 1863- ed. II. Title.

42-50725

Library of Congress BV4070.D759
[5] 207.749

E-12
5649

DRÖGEREIT, RICHARD, ed.
Erlebtes, Erzähltes, Erforschtes; Festgabe für Hans Wohltmann zur Vollendung des 80. Lebensjahres am 8. Dezember 1964. Hrsg. im Auftrag des Stader Geschichts- und Heimatvereins. [Stade] Selbstverlag des Stader Geschichts- und Heimatvereins, 1964.
271 p. illus., plates, port. 24cm. (Stader Geschichts- und Heimatvereins. Einzelschriften. Bd. 19)

1. Wohltmann, Hans. 2. Stade, Germany--Hist.
I. Series.
NN R 4.66 p/c OC (OS)I PC, 1, 2, I SL (LC1, X1, Z1)

E-12
7075

Le Droit pénal international; recueil d'études en hommage à Jacob Maarten van Bemmelen. Leiden, E. J. Brill, 1965.
xx, 257 p. port. 25 cm.
Bibliographical footnotes.
CONTENTS.—Jacob Maarten van Bemmelen, par D. Wiersma.—Bibliographie.—Des observations préliminaires, par A. Mulder.—Le principe de territorialité, par G. E. Langemeijer.—La compétence personnelle dans les législations de l'Europe occidentale, par Ch. J. Enschedé—La traité d'extradition en tant que sources de droits pour les individus, par H. F. van Panhuys.—The international dimensions of
(Continued)
NN* R 11.66 g/c OC PC, 1, 2, 3 SL E, 1, 2, 3 (LC1, X1, Z1)
3

Le Droit pénal international ... (Card 2)

the American antitrust laws, by H. Zwarensteyn.—Les conventions européennes et le traité Benelux d'entr'aide judiciaire en matière pénale et d'extradition, par A. L. Melai.—Transmission des poursuites pénales à l'état de séjour et exécution des décisions pénales étrangères, par L. H. C. Hulsman.—Collaboration au sein du Benelux pour la lutte contre les délits fiscaux et économiques, par W. Duk.—Consequences of international military co-operation, by H. H. A. de Graaff.—L'immunité devant le droit pénal, en particulier en ce qui concerne les infractions aux règles de la circulation, par H. G. Schermers.—International collaboration in the field of criminology,
(Continued)

Le DROIT pénal international... (Card 3)

by W. H. Nagel.—La fonction du psychiatre judiciaire en droit pénal international, par D. Wiersma.—Expertise en droit pénal international, par W. Froentjes.

1. Jurisdiction--Internat. law. 2. Bemmelen, Jacob Maarten van, 1898- . 3. Criminal law, International.

GHR
+

Dronning Anna Sophie. København, P. Haase & søn, 1951.
245 p. illus. 30cm.

"Udarbejdet som festskrift til lehnsbaron H. Berner Schilden Holsten i anledning af hans 70-årsdag 18. juli 1951."
"Noter og kildehenvisninger," p. 227-234.
CONTENTS.—Fabritius, A. Anna Sophie, slægt og personlighed.—Berner, H. Anna Sophie's vaabener og segl.—Langberg, H. Arkitektonisk baggrund.—Andrup, O. Anna Sophie's ikonografi.—Colding, T. H. Malerier og pretiosa.—Andersen, E. Anna Sophie's dragter.—Clemmensen, T. Anna Sophie's møbler.—Jensen, C. A. Anna Sophie's gravkapel i Roskilde domkirke.—Topsøe-Jensen, H. Eftermælet. En kronologisk oversigt.

1. Reventlow, Anna Sophie, 1693-1743. 2. Berner Schilden Holsten, Hans Heinrich, baron, 1881-
NN R 4.53 OC PC, 1, 2 SL (LC1, X1, Z1)

---

* PWZ
(Margolis)

DROPSIE COLLEGE FOR HEBREW AND COGNATE LEARNING, PHILADELPHIA. ALUMNI ASSOCIATION.
Max Leopold Margolis, scholar and teacher. [Robert Gordis, editor] Philadelphia, 5712-1952. xii, 124 p. port., facsim. 24cm.

CONTENTS. — Message, by E. A. Margolis. — Foreword by A. A. Neuman. — Preface. — The life of Professor Max Leopold Margolis: an appreciation, by R. Gordis. — The contributions of M. L. Margolis to the fields of Bible and rabbinics, by F. Zimmermann. — The contribution of Max Leopold Margolis to Semitic linguistics, by E. A. Speiser. — Margolis' work in the Septuagint, by H. M. Orlinsky. — Max L. Margolis'
(Continued)
NN * R X 1.54 (OC)I OS PC, 1, I SL J, 1, I (LC1, Z1, X1)

DROPSIE COLLEGE FOR HEBREW AND COGNATE LEARNING, PHILADELPHIA. ALUMNI ASSOCIATION. Max Leopold Margolis, scholar and teacher. (Card 2)

contribution to the history and philosophy of Judaism, by J. Bloch. — Bibliography of the works of Max L. Margolis, by J. Reider (p. 61-124)

1. Margolis, Max Leopold, 1866-1932. I. Gordis, Robert, 1908- , ed.

AN
(Tesla, N.)

Društvo za podizanje instituta Nikole Tesle, Belgrade.
...Nikola Tesla... Livre commémoratif à l'occasion de son 80ème anniversaire. Gedenkbuch anlässlich seines 80sten Geburtstages. Memorandum book on the occasion of his 80ieth birthday. Beograd: Édition de la Soc. pour la fondation de l'Institut Nikola Tesla, 1936. 519 p. incl. diagrs. illus. (incl. facsims., ports.) 25cm.

Title also in Serbian: Никола Тесла...Споменица поводом његове 80 годишњице...

(Continued)
Festschrift
N. Y. P. L. October 10, 1938

Društvo za podizanje instituta Nikole Tesle, Belgrade. ...Nikola Tesla... (Card 2)

Contributions in Serbian, Croatian, Bulgarian, Russian, French, English or German; the Slavonic articles accompanied by translations in French.
On cover: 1936-1937.
"La Société pour la fondation de l'Institut Nikola Tesla édite ce livre commémoratif comme sa première publication." — *Préf., p. 11.*
"Rédacteur: Ing. Slavko Boksan."
"The Tesla patents (U. S. A.)", p. 509.

947128A. 1. Tesla, Nikola, 1857- . I. Bokšan, Slavko, ed. II. Title.
N. Y. P. L. October 10, 1938

---

* QR

Duch Skargi w Polsce współczesnej; księga pamiątkowa obchodu czterechsetlecia urodzin księdza Piotra Skargi w Warszawie, 1536–1936, zestawił ks. J. Pawelski... Warszawa, Wydaw. Księży jezuitów, 1937. 264 p. illus. 25cm.

514558B. 1. Skarga, Piotr, 1536-1612. I. Pawelski, Jan, ed.
N. Y. P. L. July 25, 1950

Write on slip only words underlined and class mark — STG

Dudley memorial volume, containing a paper by William Russel Dudley, and appreciations and contributions in his memory by friends and colleagues... Stanford, The University, 1913. 137 p. illus. 25cm. (Stanford university. Publications. University series. no. [11])

"Publications of William Russel Dudley," p. [27]-28.

1. Dudley, William Russel, 1849-1911. 2. Botany—Essays. I. Ser.
N. Y. P. L. April 30, 1948

MQZ (Dudok)

DUDOK, WILLEM MARINUS, 1884-
Willem M. Dudok. [Amsterdam, G. van Saane, 1954] 168 p. illus.(part col.), port., plans. 29cm.

Profusely illustrated.
Illustrations of architectural works, quotations from speeches by and articles about Dudok, published in honor of his 70th birthday. Edited by R. M. H. Magnée.

I. Magnée, R. M. H., ed. II. Magnée, R. M. H.

NN ** R X 1.55 p/4 OC, I, IIbo PC, I SL A, I (Z1, LC1, X1)

EKZ

Duesseldorfer Geschichts-Verein.
Geschichte der Stadt Düsseldorf in zwölf Abhandlungen. Festschrift zum 600jährigen Jubiläum. Herausgegeben vom Düsseldorfer Geschichts-Verein. Düsseldorf: C. Kraus, 1888. 499 p. front. (plan), illus. 8°.

461754A. 1. Duesseldorf, Germany—Hist.
N. Y. P. L. March 26, 1930

IT

Duke university, Durham, N. C. Americana club.
American studies in honor of William Kenneth Boyd, by members of the Americana club of Duke university, edited by David Kelly Jackson. Durham, N. C., Duke university press, 1940.
ix, 377 p. front. (port.) 23½cm. (*Half-title:* Duke university publications)

Bibliographical foot-notes.

CONTENTS.—The political economy of Jefferson, Madison, and Adams, by J. J. Spengler.—Ante-bellum Cincinnati and its southern trade, by W. A. Mabry.—State geological surveys in the old South, by C. S. Syd-
(Continued on next card)

40-32285 [7]

Festschrift.

Duke university, Durham, N. C. Americana club. American studies in honor of William Kenneth Boyd ... 1940. (Card 2)

CONTENTS—Continued.

nor.—The natural history of agricultural labor in the South, by E. T. Thompson.—Literary nationalism in the old South, by J. B. Hubbell.—Charles Gayarré and Paul Hayne: the last literary cavaliers, by C. R. Anderson.—Philip Pendleton Cooke: Virginia gentleman, lawyer, hunter, and poet, by D. K. Jackson.—Some notes on the Unitarian church in the ante-bellum South: a contribution to the history of Southern liberalism, by Clarence Gohdes.

1. Boyd, William Kenneth, 1879-1938. 2. Southern states. I. Jackson, David Kelly, ed. II. Title.

40-32285
Library of Congress F209.D85
——— ——— Copy 2.
Copyright [7] 975.004

E-11
2398

DURHAM UNIVERSITY. King's college, Newcastle-upon-Tyne.
Essays presented to C. M. Girdlestone [Edited by E. T. Dubois and others] Newcastle-upon-Tyne, 1960. 360 p. port. 25cm.

1. Girdlestone, Cuthbert Morton, 1895- . 2. French literature—Addresses, essays, lectures. I. Dubois, Elfriede T., ed.
NN R 4. 61 m/4 (OC)I OS PC, 1, 2, I SL (LC1, X1, Z1)
[I]

D-14
1209

DUVAL, K. D. , ed.
Hugh MacDiarmid; a festschrift, edited by K. D. Duval and Sydney Goodsir Smith. Edinburgh, K. D. Duval, 1962. 221 p. illus., ports, facsims. 23cm.

CONTENTS.--MacDiarmid's lyrics, by N. MacCaig.--Hugh MacDiarmid and the Scottish renaissance, by W. Keir.--The early poems, by D. Daiches.--MacDiarmid's poetry in the 1930s, by W. Keir.--"Between any life and the sun," by G. Bruce.--The three hymns to Lenin,
(Continued)

NN R L.63 f/6 OC(1bo)I PC, 1, I SL (LC1, X1, Z1) 3

DUVAL, K. D. , ed. Hugh MacDiarmid...
(Card 2)

by S.G. Smith.--MacDiarmid the Marxist poet, by D. Craig.--The nationalism of Hugh MacDiarmid, by D. Young.--Hugh MacDiarmid and Gaelic literature, by D. Sealy.--Poetry and knowledge in MacDiarmid's later work, by E. Morgan--MacDiarmid, Joyce and Busoni, by R. Stevenson.--A great partnership, MacDiarmid and Francis George Scott, by A. T. Cunninghame.--Hugh MacDiarmid and the Scottish language, by A. Mackie.--Mainly domestics, being some personal reminiscences, by H.B. Cruickshank.--Angry influence; MacDiarmid in the 1940s,
(Continued)

DUVAL, K. D. , ed. Hugh MacDiarmid...
(Card 3)

by M. Lindsay.--A check list of the works of Hugh MacDiarmid, by W.R. Aitken (p. 213-221).

1. Grieve, Christopher Murray, 1892- I. Smith, Sydney Goodsir, 1915- , joint ed.

VOG

Dynamit Nobel Wien, Aktiengesellschaft.
Festschrift zu Ehren Alfred Nobels aus Anlass der Erteilung der ersten Sprengstoffpatente vor 100 Jahren. Hrsg. von der Aktiengesellschaft Dynamit Nobel Wien. (Autoren: Hanns Astegher [u. a.] Redaktion: Carl Hochstetter. Graphische Gestaltung: Ingrid Greiner) [Illustriert] (Wien, Montan-Verlag [1965])
199 p. 26 cm.

(Continued)
NN*R 10. 69 r/t (OC)I OS PC, 1, 2, I SL ST, It, 2, I
(LC1, X1, Z1) 4

Write on slip only words underlined and class mark — STG

Dudley memorial volume, containing a paper by William Russel Dudley, and appreciations and contributions in his memory by friends and colleagues... Stanford, The University, 1913. 137 p. illus. 25cm. (Stanford university. Publications. University series. no. ⌐11⌐)

"Publications of William Russel Dudley," p. ⌐27⌐-28.

1. Dudley, William Russel, 1849-1911. 2. Botany—Essays. I. Ser.

N. Y. P. L. April 30, 1948

E-11
2398

DURHAM UNIVERSITY. King's college, Newcastle-upon-Tyne.

Essays presented to C. M. Girdlestone [Edited by E. T. Dubois and others] Newcastle-upon-Tyne, 1960. 360 p. port. 25cm.

1. Girdlestone, Cuthbert Morton, 1895- . 2. French literature--Addresses, essays, lectures. I. Dubois, Elfriede T., ed.

NN R 4. 61 m/ (OC)I OS PC, 1, 2, I SL (LC1, X1, Z1)

[1]

MQZ
(Dudok)

DUDOK, WILLEM MARINUS, 1884-

Willem M. Dudok. [Amsterdam, G. van Saane, 1954] 168 p. illus.(part col.), port., plans. 29cm.

Profusely illustrated.

Illustrations of architectural works, quotations from speeches by and articles about Dudok, published in honor of his 70th birthday. Edited by R. M. H. Magnée.

I. Magnée, R. M. H., ed. II. Magnée, R. M. H.

NN ** R X 1.55 p/ OC, 1, IIbo PC, I SL A, I (Z1, LC1 X1)

D-14
1209

DUVAL, K. D. , ed.

Hugh MacDiarmid; a festschrift, edited by K. D. Duval and Sydney Goodsir Smith. Edinburgh, K. D. Duval, 1962. 221 p. illus., ports, facsims. 23cm.

CONTENTS.--MacDiarmid's lyrics, by N. MacCaig.--Hugh MacDiarmid and the Scottish renaissance, by W. Keir.--The early poems, by D. Daiches.--MacDiarmid's poetry in the 1930s, by W. Keir.--"Between any life and the sun," by G. Bruce.--The three hymns to Lenin, (Continued)

NN R 1.63 f/ OC(1bo)I PC, 1, I SL (LC1, X1, Z1)

3

EKZ

Duesseldorfer Geschichts-Verein.

Geschichte der Stadt Düsseldorf in zwölf Abhandlungen. Festschrift zum 600jährigen Jubiläum. Herausgegeben vom Düsseldorfer Geschichts-Verein. Düsseldorf: C. Kraus, 1888. 499 p. front. (plan), illus. 8°.

461754A. 1. Duesseldorf, Germany—Hist.

Mr. Math.

N. Y. P. L. March 26, 1930

DUVAL, K. D. , ed. Hugh MacDiarmid... (Card 2)

by S.G. Smith.--MacDiarmid the Marxist poet, by D. Craig.--The nationalism of Hugh MacDiarmid, by D. Young.--Hugh MacDiarmid and Gaelic literature, by D. Sealy.--Poetry and knowledge in MacDiarmid's later work, by E. Morgan--MacDiarmid, Joyce and Busoni, by R. Stevenson.--A great partnership, MacDiarmid and Francis George Scott, by A. T. Cunninghame.--Hugh MacDiarmid and the Scottish language, by A. Mackie.--Mainly domestics, being some personal reminiscences, by H.B. Cruickshank.--Angry influence; MacDiarmid in the 1940s, (Continued)

IT

Duke university, Durham, N. C. Americana club.

American studies in honor of William Kenneth Boyd, by members of the Americana club of Duke university, edited by David Kelly Jackson. Durham, N. C., Duke university press, 1940.

ix, 377 p. front. (port.) 23½cm. (*Half-title:* Duke university publications)

Bibliographical foot-notes.

CONTENTS.—The political economy of Jefferson, Madison, and Adams, by J. J. Spengler.—Ante-bellum Cincinnati and its southern trade, by W. A. Mabry.—State geological surveys in the old South, by C. S. Syd- (Continued on next card)

40-32285

⌐7⌐

Festschrift.

DUVAL, K. D. , ed. Hugh MacDiarmid... (Card 3)

by M. Lindsay.--A check list of the works of Hugh MacDiarmid, by W.R. Aitken (p. 213-221).

1. Grieve, Christopher Murray, 1892- I. Smith, Sydney Goodsir, 1915- , joint ed.

Duke university, Durham, N. C. Americana club. American studies in honor of William Kenneth Boyd ... 1940. (Card 2)

CONTENTS—Continued.

nor.—The natural history of agricultural labor in the South, by E. T. Thompson.—Literary nationalism in the old South, by J. B. Hubbell.—Charles Gayarré and Paul Hayne: the last literary cavaliers, by C. R. Anderson.—Philip Pendleton Cooke: Virginia gentleman, lawyer, hunter, and poet, by D. K. Jackson.—Some notes on the Unitarian church in the ante-bellum South: a contribution to the history of Southern liberalism, by Clarence Gohdes.

1. Boyd, William Kenneth, 1879-1938. 2. Southern states. I. Jackson, David Kelly, ed. II. Title.

40-32285

Library of Congress F209.D85

——— ~~Copy 2.~~

Copyright ⌐7⌐ 975.004

VOG

Dynamit Nobel Wien, Aktiengesellschaft.

Festschrift zu Ehren Alfred Nobels aus Anlass der Erteilung der ersten Sprengstoffpatente vor 100 Jahren. Hrsg. von der Aktiengesellschaft Dynamit Nobel Wien. (Autoren: Hanns Astegher ⌐u. a.⌐ Redaktion: Carl Hochstetter. Graphische Gestaltung: Ingrid Greiner) ⌐Illustriert⌐ (Wien, Montan-Verlag ⌐1965⌐) 199 p. 26 cm.

(Continued)

NN*R 10. 69 r/ (OC)I OS (LC1, X1, Z1) PC, 1, 2, I SL ST, 1t, 2, I

4

Dynamit Nobel Wien, Aktiengesellschaft. Festschrift zu Ehren Alfred Nobels ... ₍1965₎ (Card 2)

Includes bibliographies.

CONTENTS. — Alfred Nobel. — Die Entwicklung der Aktiengesellschaft Dynamit Nobel Wien und des Werkes St. Lambrecht, Steiermark, von H. Meal. — Sprengstoffe und Bergbau, von G. R. Fettweis.—Dynamit und Wasserkraft, von A. Kothbauer.—Alfred Nobel, sein Werk einst und heute, von J. Krische.—Die elektrische Zündung, von Schaffler & Co.—Die Entwicklung der Spreng- und Zündmittel in Österreich in den letzten 20 Jahren.—Die Entwicklung der Gesteinsbohrmaschinen für Sprengarbeiten, von O. P. Karpf und O. Fitz.—Die Geschichte der Sprengarbeit im Bergbau, von F. Kirn-

(Continued)

Dynamit Nobel Wien, Aktiengesellschaft. Festschrift zu Ehren Alfred Nobels ... ₍1965₎ (Card 3)

bauer.—Die Entwicklung der Bohr- und Sprengarbeit im Tagbau des Steirischen Erzberges seit 1914, von O. Klobassa.—Die Entwicklung der Sprengarbeit im Bergbau Bleiberg, von F. Jedlicka.—Einfluss der Mechanisierung im Abbau auf Leistung und Materialverbrauch, von M. Maczek.—Verbesserte Bohr- und Schiessarbeit als Voraussetzung für die Mechanisierung im Grubenbau des Magnesitbergbaus Hohentauern, von E. Luef.—Die Kohlegewinnung bei der Salzach-Kohlenbergbau-Gesellschaft m. b. H. Trimmelkam, von S. Pirklbauer.—Kohlengewinnung durch Schiessen, von H. Füreder.—Schiessen mit Katamerit im Tagbau Karlschacht der Graz-Köflacher Eisenbahn- und Bergbau-Gesellschaft, von R. Dorfmeister.—Die österreichische Granitindustrie im Schärdinger Raum, von O. Kufner.—Die Stein-

(Continued)

DYNAMIT NOBEL WIEN, AKTIENGESELLSCHAFT. Festschrift zu Ehren Alfred Nobels... (Card 4)

bruch für die Errichtung des Staudammes Gepatsch, von W. Reismann.—Die Entwicklung der Tiefbohrlochsprengung in Österreich, von H. Astegher.—Auflegersprengstoffe, ihre Entwicklung und ihre Prüfung, von J. Sinabell.—St. Barbara als Schutzpatronin der Bergleute und Artilleristen, von F. Kirnbauer.

1. Explosives—Addresses, essays, lectures. 2. Nobel, Alfred Bernhard, 1833-1896. I. Nobel, Alfred Bernhard, 1833-1896. II. Title. t.1965.

---

*I‡

E. R. Weiss zum fünfzigsten Geburtstage 12. Oktober 1925. ₍Leipzig: Insel-Verlag, 1925.₎ 106 p. front. (port.), illus. incl. music, plates (part col'd). f°.

Edited by Herbert Reichner.
no. 230 of 500 copies printed.
Contents: HOFER, C. Portrait E. R. Weiss. BLEI, F. Brief an E. R. Weiss. BUBER, M. Zwei Malergeschichten. DIEDERICHS, E. Vor dreissig Jahren. HAUPTMANN, G. Vaterland. HEIMANN, M. Elegie am Gardasee. WEISS, E. R. Antwort. LOERKE, O. Notiz zu Heimann und Weiss. LEVIN, J. Aus dem Roman: "Der bleierne Dämpfer." LOERKE, O. Ein Brief; Drei Gedichte. MOMBERT, A. An Emil Rudolf Weiss. RUPÉ, H. Aufstieg. Ein Gesang der Sappho. SIEMSEN, H.

(Continued)

N. Y. P. L. May 10, 1927

E. R. Weiss zum fünfzigsten Geburtstage 12. Oktober 1925. (Continued)

E. R. Weiss. STRAUSS, E. Totenfeier. ORLIK, E. Holzschnitt. WALSER, K. Ex libris E. R. W. MEIER-GRAEFE, J. E. R. Weiss. LOUBIER, H. Ein Blick in die Werkstatt von E. R. Weiss. BOGENG, G. A. E. Der Buchkünstler. JESSEN, P. Ein tapferer Buchdrucker. MORISON, S. On the typographical ornaments of Granjon, Fournier and Weiss. RODENBERG, J. Emil Rudolf Weiss. TAFELN: Buchschmuck. Initialen. Bücherzeichen. Signete. Druckschriften. Typographischer Schmuck. Buchumschläge. Buchtitel. Bucheinbände.

J. S. BILLINGS MEM. COLL.

290576A. 1. Weiss, Emil Rudolf, 1875- . 2. Books—Decoration. 3. Printing—Specimens. 4. Reichner, Herbert, editor.
N. Y. P. L. May 10, 1927

XBN

Earle, Edward Mead, 1894- , ed.
Nationalism and internationalism; essays inscribed to Carlton J. H. Hayes. New York, Columbia University Press, 1950. xvii, 510 p. 24cm.

Bibliographical footnotes.
CONTENTS.—Cultural nationalism and the makings of fame, by J. Barzun.—A secret agent's advice on America, 1797, by F. S. Childs.—"Big Jim" Larkin, a footnote to nationalism, by J. D. Clarkson.—The heavy hand of Hegel, by C. W. Cole.—H. G. Wells, British patriot in search of a world state, by E. M. Earle.—National sentiment in Klopstock's odes and Bardiete, by R. Ergang.—Arthur Young, British patriot, by J. G. Gazley.—French Jacobin nationalism and Spain, by B. F. Hyslop.—Nationalism

(Continued)

NN

Earle, Edward Mead, 1894- , ed. Nationalism and internationalism... (Card 2)

and history in the Prussian elementary schools under William II, by W. C. Langsam. —The Swiss pattern for a federated Europe, by C. Muret.—Sir John Seeley, pragmatic historian in a nationalistic age, by T. P. Peardon.—The Habsburgs and public opinion in Lombardy-Venetia, 1814-1815, by R. J. Rath.—American thought and the Communist challenge, by G. T. Robinson.—Friedrich Naumann, a German view of power and nationalism, by W. O. Shanahan.—Hitler and the revival of German colonialism, by M. E. Townsend.—The nationalism of Horace Greeley, by G. G. Van Deusen.—Scandinavia and the rise of modern national consciousness, by J. H. Wuorinen.

544705B. 1. Nationalism and nationality. 2. Internationalism. 3. Hayes, Carlton Joseph Huntley, 1882- . I. Title.
NN *

CDA

The early cultures of North-West Europe (H. M. Chadwick memorial studies). Ed. by Sir Cyril Fox and Bruce Dickins. Cambridge [Eng.] Univ. press, 1950. xv, 440 p. illus., maps, 12 pl. 26cm.

Bibliography, p. xv.

1. Great Britain—Archaeology. 2. Anglo-Saxon literature—Hist. and crit. 3. Chadwick, Hector Munro, d. 1947. I. Fox, Sir Cyril Fred, 1882- , ed. II. Dickins, Bruce, 1889- , ed.
NN

E-10
5812

The **Earth**: its crust and its atmosphere; geomorphological and geophysical studies presented to Professor Jacoba B. L. Hol on July 6th 1957. Leiden, E. J. Brill, 1957.

viii, 264 p. illus., maps (part fold.) 25 cm.

Articles in Dutch, English, French or German.
Includes bibliographies.

1. HOL, JACOBA BRIGITTA LOUISE 2. GEOGRAPHY, PHYSICAL--ESSAYS AND MISC. t. 1957

NN * R 7.58 a/5 OC, Ib* PC, 1, 2 SL ST, 1, 2t (LC1, X1, Z1)

MCZ
S12.C2

EBBE SADOLIN, en hilsen fra venner i anledning af tresårsdagen 19. feb. 1960. [Redigeret af Poul Carit Andersen. København] Carit Andersen [1960] 121, [3] p. illus. 27cm.

"Ebbe Sadolins tegninger er 'lånt' fra hans skitsebøger og fra trykte bøger."
"Bibliografi over bøger illustreret af Ebbe Sadolin, p. 117-[122]

1. Sadolin, Ebbe, 1900- . I. Carit Andersen, Poul, 1910- ed.
NN 7.60 1/P OC, I, Ib PC, 1, I SL A, 1, I PR, 1, I (LC1, X1, Z1) B

D-14
6181

ECKERT, GEORG, 1912- , ed.
Hermann Trimborn zum 60. Geburtstag von seinen Schülern gewidmet. [Hrsg. von Georg Eckert und Udo Oberem] Braunschweig, A. Limbach [1961] 176 p. illus., map. 22cm.

On cover: Kulturhistorische Studien.
Includes bibliographies.
CONTENTS.--Über eine kasachische Kolchose, von H. Bliss.--
(Continued)

ECKERT, GEORG, 1912- , ed. Hermann Trimborn zum 60. (Card 2)

Schädelamulette in Griechisch-Mazedonien, von G. Eckert.--Einige Bemerkungen über die Koma und ihre Medizinmänner, von H. Hilke.--Der Morgengesang der Sirionó, von H. Kelm.--Eingeborene als Arbeitskräfte auf den Viehstationen der südöstlichen Kimberley, vornehmlich auf Gordon Downs Station, von F.J. Mischa.--Uber die Omagua des Río Napo, von U. Oberem.--Die Nez Perce und die Plains, 1805-1877, von K.H. Schlesier.--Zur Geschichte des Bodenrechts bei mutterrechtlichen Stämmen in Nord-rhodesien. von R. Schott.
1. Anthropology--Addresses, essays, lectures. 2. Trimborn, Hermann, 1901- . I. Oberem, Udo, joint ed. II. Oberem, Udo.

D-18
2104

Eckhoff, Torstein Einang, 1916–
Rettferdighet og rettssikkerhet. [Av] Torstein Eckhoff. Artikler samlet i anledning professor Eckhoffs 50-årsdag 5. juni 1966. Redigert av Bjørn Smørgrav. Oslo, Tanum, 1966.
399 p. 23 cm.

Added t.p. in English.
(Continued)

ECKHOFF, TORSTEIN EINANG, 1916- . Rettferdighet og rettssikkerhet. (Card 2)

English or Norwegian. (N 66-24)
Bibliography: p. 398-[400]

1. Justice. 2. Rule of law--Addresses, essays, lectures.

Copy only words underlined & classmark-- TAA

ECONOMETRICA.
An issue in honor of Ragnar Frisch in the year of his sixty-fifth birthday; contributors K. Arrow [and others] Edited by R.H. Strotz and E. Malinvaud. [Amsterdam, 1960] 171-495 p. illus., port. 26cm. (Econometrica. v.28, no.2 (April, 1960))

Cover title.
Includes bibliographies.
(Continued)

ECONOMETRICA. An issue in honor of Ragnar Frisch in the year of his sixty-fifth birthday... (Card 2)

CONTENTS.--Salute to Professor Frisch.--Ragnar Frisch and the founding of the Econometric society, by A.J. Cowles.--The work of Ragnar Frisch, econometrician, by K.J. Arrow.--The foundations of utility, by J.S. Chipman.--Mathematical proofs of the breakdown of capitalism, by N. Georgescu-Roegen.--Additive preferences, by. H.S. Houthakker.--Rules of thumb for the expansion of industries in a process of economic growth, by L. Johansen.--Some theoretical
(Continued)

ECONOMETRICA. An issue in honor of Ragnar Frisch in the year of his sixty-fifth birthday... (Card 3)

issues in the measurement of capacity, by L.R. Klein.--Stationary ordinal utility and impatience, by T.C. Koopmans.--The output-investment ratio and input-output analysis, by O. Lange.--A method of fractile graphical analysis, by P.C. Mahalanobis.--Economic expansion and the interest rate in generalized von Neumann models, by M. Morishima.--A short note on the transmission of shocks in simultaneous models, by P. Norregaard Rasmussen.--An extension of the LeChatelier principle, by P.A. Samuelson.--Hans von Mangoldt on price theory: a contribution to the history of mathematical economics, by
(Continued)

ECONOMETRICA. An issue in honor of Ragnar Frisch in the year of his sixty-fifth birthday... (Card 4)

E. Schneider.--On a family of lag distributions, by R.M. Solow.--The durability of consumers' goods, by R. Stone and D.A. Rowe.--A triptych on casual systems: I. Recursive vs. nonrecursive systems, by R.H. Strotz and H.O.A. Wold. II. Interdependence as a specification error, by R.H. Strotz. III. A generalization of casual chain models, by H.O.A. Wold.--Best linear index numbers of prices and quantities, by H. Theil.--Optimum savings and utility maximization over time, by J. Tinbergen.--
(Continued)

ECONOMETRICA. An issue in honor of Ragnar Frisch in the year of his sixty-fifth birthday... (Card.5)

A note on Stochastic linear programming, by G. Tintner.

1. Frisch, Ragnar, 1895- . 2. Economics, Mathematical. I. Strotz, Robert H., ed. II. Malinvaud, Edmond, ed. III. Strotz, Robert H. IV. Malinvaud, Edmond.

TB

Economic essays in honor of Wesley Clair Mitchell, presented to him by his former students on the occasion of his sixtieth birthday. New York, Columbia university press, 1935.
ix, 519 p., 1 l. front. (port.) 23½cm.
CONTENTS.—Recent efforts of the federal government in the field of low-rental housing, by Asher Achinstein.—Genesis and import of the collective-bargaining provisions of the Recovery act, by P. F. Brissenden.—Long cycles in residential construction, by A. F. Burns.—Purchasing power of the masses and business depressions, by P. H. Douglas.—Obstacles to the statistical approach in economics and the social sciences with special reference to England, by P. S. Florence.—The Marxian right to the whole product, by A. L. Harris.—Some reflections on retail prices, by O. W. Knauth.—Relation between capital goods and finished products in the business cycle, by Simon Kuznets.—Some basic problems in
(Continued on next card)
35-798
[5] Festschrift.

Economic essays in honor of Wesley Clair Mitchell ... 1935. (Card 2)

CONTENTS—Continued.

index-number theory, by E. E. Lewis.—Urban decentralization, by R. J. McFall.—Some aspects of economic planning, by P. W. Martin.—On the changing structure of economic life, by F. C. Mills.—The rôle of the middle class in social development: fascism, populism, communism, socialism, by D. J. Saposs.—On the current skepticism toward systematic economics, by Horace Taylor.—Economic and social aspects of internal migrations: an exploratory study of selected Swedish communities, by Dorothy S. Thomas.—The problem of overcapacity, by W. L. Thorp.—Plateaus of prosperity and plains of depression, by Clark Warburton.

1. Economics—Addresses, essays, lectures. 2. Mitchell, Wesley Clair, 1874–

35–798

Library of Congress HB31.E33

——— Copy 2.

Copyright A 79036 [5] 330.4

TB

Economics and the public interest. [Essays written in honor of Eugene Ewald Agger] Robert A. Solo, editor. New Brunswick, N.J., Rutgers university press, 1955. xiv,318 p. port., diagrs., tables. 24cm.

Bibliographical footnotes.

Contents.—The method and purpose of economics: Economics as social philosophy, moral philosophy, (Continued)

NN*R 6.55 d/br OC,I, IIbo PC,1,2,I SL E,1, 2,I (LC1,X1,Z1)

Economics and the public interest. (Card 2)

and technology, by R.A. Solo. The task of institutionalism, by W.C. Bagley, Jr. The poverty of economics, by B. Mitchell.—Economics in the empirical analysis of modern society: The diffusion of business cycles, by G.H. Moore. Marketing's contribution to economics, by R.S. Alexander. Profits, a semantic problem child, by S.I. Simon. Forecasting automotive sales, by J. W. Sundelson. Economics and accounting, by R. Hoegstedt.—Economic policy and social control: The role of government in education, by M. Fried- (Continued)

Economics and the public interest. (Card 3)

man. Rain-making and monetary policy, by A. Murad. Public finance and the public interest, by A. Balinky. Public policy and union security, by M. Berkowitz. Managerial zones of reasonableness in public utility regulation, by L. Knappen. Economic systems and social size, by L. Kohr. The development of international commodity policy, by D. A. Morse.—Economic growth and development: Colonial experience and the social context of economic development programs, by H.D. Gideonse. (Continued)

Economics and the public interest. (Card 4)

Growth theory and the problem of economic stabilization, by K.K. Kurihara. Who bears the cost of economic development? By R.J.Alexander. Land tenure reform as an aspect of economic development in Asia, by R.R.Renne.

1. Economics—Essays and misc. 2. Agger, Eugene Ewald, 1879– . I. Solo, Robert A , ed. II. Solo, Robert A

TB

Economics, sociology & the modern world; essays in honor of T. N. Carver, edited by Norman E. Himes ... Cambridge, Harvard university press, 1935.

xii, 327, [2] p. front. (port.) diagrs. 24cm.

"This volume, consisting of eighteen papers by former students of Professor T. N. Carver, for thirty years (1902–1932) professor of political economy in Harvard university, is published on the occasion of his seventieth birthday (1865–1935)."

"Edition limited to 500 hand-numbered copies, of which 375 are for sale. This is copy number 237."

(Continued on next card)

35–36713

[7–5]

Economics, sociology & the modern world ... 1935. (Card 2)

CONTENTS.—pt. 1. Agricultural economics: Agricultural fundamentalism, by J. S. Davis. The Canadian wheat pool in prosperity and depression, by H. S. Patton. Overhead costs in agriculture: a problem in social control, by R. S. Vaile. The objectives of economic control, by E. J. Working.—pt. 2. Economic theory and history: Theoretical aspects of the scale of production, by M. M. Bober. Interest in work: some research problems, methods and results, by Z. C. Dickinson. The mercantilism of Gerónimo de Uztáriz: a reexamination by E. J. Hamilton. Pioneer life in western Kansas, by John Ise. On the chemical phase of the industrial revolution, by T. J. Kreps. Some propositions on interest, by R. S. Meriam. Some aspects of the theory of rent: von Thünen vs. Ricardo, by Bertil Ohlin. The nature of our program

(Continued on next card)

35–36713

[7–5]

Economics, sociology & the modern world ... 1935. (Card 3)

CONTENTS—Continued.

for national economic recovery, by C. J. Ratzlaff. Business cycles, by J. P. Wernette. The rationalization of production and of reproduction, by A. B. Wolfe. Bibliography (p. 243–244).—pt. 3. Sociology: Socialism in theory and in practice, by F. A. Bushee. Migration between city and country in the Buffalo metropolitan area, by Niles Carpenter. Cultural compulsives: the survival of dogma in the sciences, by W. H. Crook. New light on the causes of the declining birth rate, by N. E. Himes.

1. Carver, Thomas Nixon, 1865– 2. Economics—Addresses, essays, lectures. 3. Sociology—Addresses, essays, lectures. 4. Agriculture—Economic aspects. I. Himes, Norman Edwin, ed.

35–36713

Library of Congress HB31.E36

——— Copy 2.

Copyright A 89332 [7–5] 330.4

TAH

Economisch-historische opstellen. Geschreven voor Prof. Dr. Z. W. Sneller ter gelegenheid van zijn 25-jarig hoogleeraarsjubileum, 1922–5 April–1947. Amsterdam, H. J. Paris, 1947.

212 p. port. 25 cm.

Bibliographical footnotes.

CONTENTS.—Professor Dr Z. W. Sneller als hoogleeraar, 1922–1947, door P. J. Bouman.—Landbouw en handel in Friesland in de dertiende eeuw, door J. F. Niermeyer.—Dordrecht wordt geus, door T. S. Jansma.—Wat Cats, Bredero en anderen ons weten te vertellen over de geestesgesteldheid van de Nederlandsche kooplieden uit de Gouden Eeuw, door H. P. W. van Ravestijn.—Vrij schip, vrij goed, door C. Smit.—Rotterdam voor de omwenteling, door T. P. van der Kooy.—De droogmaking van den zuidplas in Schieland, door C. Wis-

(Continued on next card)

A 48–9962*

[1]

Economisch-historische opstellen ... 1947. (Card 2)

CONTENTS—Continued.

kerke.—De Nederlandsche Handel-Maatschappij en het emissiebedrijf, door D. C. Renooy.—Nederland en de wereldmarkt, 1860–1914, door T. T. L. M. Thurlings.—Socialisme in Nederland, 1878–1946, door P. J. Bouman.—Lijst van de belangrijkste geschriften en redevoeringen van Prof. Dr Z. W. Sneller. (p. [209]–212)

1. Netherlands—Econ. condit. 2. Netherlands—Comm. 3. Sneller, Zeger Willem, 1882– 4. Sneller, Zeger Willem, 1882– —Bibl.

A 48–9962*

Harvard Univ. Library for Library of Congress [1]

TB

ECONOMISCHE opstellen aangeboden aan Prof. Dr. C.A. Verrijn Stuart. Haarlem: De erven F. Bohn N.V., 1931. 349 p. front. (port.) 8°.

Festschrift

579676A. 1. Economics—Essays and misc. 2. Verrijn Stuart, Coenraad Alexander, 1865–

N. Y. P. L. April 26, 1932

TB

Economy, society, and government in medieval Italy; essays in memory of Robert L. Reynolds, edited by David Herlihy, Robert S. Lopez and Vsevolod Slessarev. ⌐Kent, Ohio.⌐ Kent State University Press ⌐1969⌐

ix, 270 p. ⌐port. 24cm.

Includes bibliographical references.

CONTENTS.—Bibliography of Robert L. Reynolds, by J. A. Leake.—Medieval "slavers," by C. Verlinden.—The cambium maritimum contract according to the Genoese notarial records of the twelfth and thirteenth centuries, by R. de Roover.—Stars and spices: the earliest Italian manual of commercial practice, by R. S. Lopez.—Italian

(Continued)

NN*R 1.71 m/c OC, I, II, III, IV PC, 1, 2, I, II, III, IV SL (LC1, X1, Z1) E, 1, 2, I, II, III IV

ECONOMY, society, and government in medieval Italy ... (Card 2)

merchants and the performance of Papal banking functions in the early thirteenth century, by G. Olsen.—The drapers of Lucca and the marketing of cloth in the mid-thirteenth century, by T. W. Blomquist.—Symon de Gualterio: a brief portrait of a thirteenth-century man of affairs, by R. D. Face.—The pound-value of Genoa's maritime trade in 1161, by V. Slessarev.—Italian bankers and Philip the Fair, by J. R. Strayer.—Some industrial price movements in medieval Genoa (1155–1255), by W. N. Bonds.—A Venetian naval expedition of 1224, by L. B. Robbert.—Notes on medieval English

(Continued)

ECONOMY, society, and government in medieval Italy ... (Card 3)

weights and measures in Francesco Balducci Pegolotti's "La pratica della mercatura," by R. E. Zupko.—The crossbow in the nautical revolution of the Middle Ages, by F. C. Lane.—Family solidarity in medieval Italian history, by D. Herlihy.—Patriapotestas, regia potestas, and Rex Imperator, by G. Post.—Direct taxation in a medieval commune: the Dazio in Siena, 1287–1355, by W. M. Bowsky.—The civic irresponsibility of the Venetian nobility, by D. E. Queller.—Civism and Roman law in fourteenth-century Italian society, by P. Riesenberg.

1. Commerce--Italy. 2. Italy--Soc. condit. I. Reynolds, Robert Leonard. II. Herlihy, David, ed. III. Lopez, Robert, ed. IV. Slessarev, Vsevolod, ed.

NID

EDDA, Skalden, Saga; Festschrift zum 70. Geburtstag von Felix Genzmer. Hrsg. von Hermann Schneider... Heidelberg, C. Winter, 1952. 335 p. 25cm.

CONTENTS.—Höfler, O. Das Opfer im Semnonenhain und die Edda.—Hunke, W. Odins Geburt.—Gutenbrunner, S. Versteckte Eddagedichte.—Leyen, F. v. d. Kleine Anmerkungen zu den Göttergeschichten der Edda.—Wolff, L. Eddisch-skaldische Blütenlese.—Schröder, F. R. Adynata.—Hempel, H. Sächsische Nibelungendichtung und sächsischer Ursprung der Thidrikssaga.—Boor, H. de. Kapitel 168 der Thidrekssaga.—Vries, J. de Bemerkungen zur Wielandsage.—Schneider, H. Die Geschichte

(Continued)

NN R 4.53 OC, I PC, 1, 2, 3, I SL (LC1, Z1, X1)

EDDA, Skalden, Saga... (Card 2)

vom Riesen Hrungnir.—Wais, K. Ullikummi, Hrungnir, Armilus und Verwandte.—Kuhn, H. Heldensage vor und ausserhalb der Dichtung.—Kuhn, H. Über nordische und deutsche Szenenregie in der Nibelungendichtung.—Naumann, H. Die altnordischen Verwandten des Ruodlieb-Romans.—Wais, K. Drei Jahre danach: Nachtrag 1951 zum Aufsatz über Ullikummi usw.—Dörr, H. Schriftenverzeichnis.

1. Edda Sæmundar. 2. Helden sage. 3. Genzmer, Felix, 1878- I. Schneider, Hermann, 1886- , ed.

ZISF

Eden Theological Seminary, St. Louis.

Festschrift zum goldenen Jubiläum des Predigerseminars der Evangelischen Synode von N. A., 1850–1900. St. Louis: Eden Pub. House⌐, 1900⌐. 42 p. incl. plates, ports. illus. obl. 8°.

Mr. Matis

1. No subject.
N. Y. P. L.

Revised September 16, 1931

---

*OPN

EDIRNE; Edirne'nin 600. fetih yildönümü armağan kitabı. Ankara, 1965. 349 p. plates, maps. 24cm. (Türk tarihi kurumu. Publications de la Société d'historie turque. Ser. 7, no.43)

Includes bibliographies.

1. Adrianople, Turkey--Hist. 2. Turkish literature--Hist. I. Series.
NN R 3.72 e/ OC (OS)I PC, 1, 2, I SL O, 1, 2, I (LC1, X1, Z1)

F-11
4916

Edschmid, Kasimir, 1890-

Italienische Gesänge. (Zum 75. Geburtstag des Dichters am 5. Oktober 1965) München, Wien, Basel, Desch (1965)

38 p. 26 cm.

I. Title.
NN * R 12.68 1/OC PC, I SL (LC1, X1, Z1)

E-11
1917

Eduard Paul Tratz. ⌐Festschrift. Salzburg, Etzendorfer, 1958⌐

56 p. illus., port. 24 cm.

Cover title.
"Veröffentlichungen von Prof. Tratz": p. 34-56.

1. Tratz, Eduard Paul.
NN*R 5.61 s/ OC PC, 1 SL (LC1, X1, Z1)

MDG
(Wiiralt)

EDUARD WIIRALT, 1898-1954; mälestusteos. [Lund] Eesti kirjanike kooperatiiv [1955] 80 p. illus., 43 plates, ports. 30cm.

Captions in Esthonian, English, French and German.
Bibliography, p. 77-80.

1. Wiiralt, Eduard, 1898-1954.

NN **R 12.56 p/, OC PC, 1 SL PR, 1 (LC1, X1, Z1)

A p.v.410

L'Église de l'Étoile, Paris.
...Eugène Bersier. Paris[,] 1931[]. iii, 7–124 p. port. 24cm. (Cahiers de Foi et vie.)

Cover-title.
"L'Église de l'Étoile, en 1931, a célébré le centenaire de son fondateur."—p. 87; "Un des pasteurs de l'Étoile a été invité à faire, entre ces morceaux détachés, les raccords indispensables."—*Avant-propos.*
CONTENTS.—Avant-propos.—Quelques souvenirs par H. Hollard.—Le prédicateur, par J. Monnier.—La réforme liturgique, par A. Schlemmer.—Bersier, critiques de lettres, par H. Dartigue.—Bersier et la liberté de conscience, par E. Soulier.—A propos du centenaire, par H. Monnier.—Annexe: La commune. Bibliographie des ouvrages d'Eugène Bersier, par H. Dartigue et A. Lods.

691939A. 1. Bersier, Eugène Arthur François, 1831–1889. I. Foi et vie.
N. Y. P. L. March 14, 1934

E-14
1365

EDWARD DAHLBERG; a tribute. Essays, reminiscences, correspondences, tributes, edited by Jonathan Williams. New York, D. Lewis [c1970] 196 p. illus., ports., facsim. 25cm. (A TriQuarterly book)

"This book first appeared as TriQuarterly 20, Fall 1970."

1. Dahlberg, Edward, 1900- . I. Dahlberg, Edward, 1900- .
II. Williams, Jonathan, 1929- , ed.
NNR 5.71 d/z OC, I, II PC, 1, I, II SL (LC1, X1, Z1)

ZAE p.v.782

Église réformée d'Alsace et de Lorraine. *Commission synodale.*
... Calvin à Strasbourg, 1538–1541; quatre études publiées à l'occasion du 400e anniversaire de l'arrivée de Calvin à Strasbourg par les soins de la Commission synodale de l'Église réf. d'Alsace et de Lorraine. Strasbourg, Éditions Fides [1938]
127, 4 p. illus., plates, ports. 23[cm]. Label of Éditions labor, Genève mounted on imprint.
At head of title: 1538–1938.
CONTENTS.—Calvin à Strasbourg, par J. D. Benoît.—Bucer et Calvin, par m. le professeur Courvoisier.—Calvin, der mann der kirche, und die bedeutung seines Strassburger aufenthalts, von herrn prof. Scherding.—Reformierte kirchen in und um Strassburg, von D. Kuntz.
1. Calvin, Jean, 1509–1564. I. Benoît, Jean D. II. Courvoisier, Jacques. III. Scherding, Pierre. IV. Kuntz, D. A. V. Title.

40-30599

Library of Congress BX9418.E4
[2] Festschrift 922.444

AN
(Seligman, E.)

Edwin Robert Anderson Seligman, 1861–1939; addresses delivered at the memorial meeting held on December the thirteenth, 1939, in the Low memorial library at Columbia university, to which are appended memorial tributes to Professor Seligman. Stamford, Conn.: Overbrook press, 1942. 101 p. front. (port.) 20½cm.

"Three hundred copies have been printed."

Festschrift.

202215B. 1. Seligman, Edwin Robert Anderson, 1861–1939.
N. Y. P. L. December 3, 1942

---

* OBKG

Egypt Exploration Society.
Studies presented to F. Ll. Griffith. London: Egypt Exploration Soc., 1932. xi, 502 p. front. (port.), illus., 74 pl. (incl. chart, facsims.) 29½cm.

Bibliography, p. 485–495.

Festschrift

620706A. 1. Egyptology—Collections. 2. Griffith, Francis Llewellyn, 1862– . I. Title.
N. Y. P. L. March 21, 1933

MA

EGBERT, DONALD DREW, 1902-
On arts in society; selections from the periodical writings of Donald Drew Egbert. [Compiled and edited by Alan Gowans] [Watkins Glen, N.Y., American Life Foundation for] University of Victoria [Dept. of History in Art], Victoria, British Columbia, 1970. 183 p. 7 plates, ports. 29cm. (History in the arts. 3)

Limited ed. of 500 copies.

(Continued)

NN R 3.71 b/a OC, I, IV (OS)II, III PC, 1, 2, 3, I, II, III, IV SL
A, 1, 2, 3, I, II, III, IV E, 1, I, II, IV (LC1, X1, Z1)

2

D-19
9098

Ehrengabe für Bruno Heusinger. Gewidmet von Mitgliedern des Bundesgerichtshofes, der Bundesanwaltschaft und der Rechtsanwaltschaft beim Bundesgerichtshof. Hrsg. von Roderich Glanzmann unter Mitwirkung von Hans Joachim Faller. München, Beck, 1968.

412 p. port. 23 cm.
Bibliographical footnotes.

(Continued)

NN * 5.70 d/z OC, I, II, III, IVb*, Vb* PC, 1, I, II, III
SL (LC1, X1, Z1) [I]

5

EGBERT, DONALD DREW, 1902- . On arts in society... (Card 2)

A Festschrift reader, compiled for presentation to the author by his former graduate students on the occasion of his retirement from the faculty of Princeton University.
Bibliographical footnotes.

1. Art--Economic and social aspects. 2. Art, U.S.--Addresses, essays, lectures. 3. Architecture--U.S.--Addresses, essays, lectures. I. Gowans, Alan, ed. and comp. II. Princeton University. III. Series. IV. Title.

Ehrengabe für Bruno Heusinger. (Card 2)

CONTENTS.—Geleitwort, von R. Glanzmann.—Das Ringen um ein Bundesgericht für den Deutschen Bund, von H. Kirchner.—Aus der Geschichte der Staatsanwaltschaft im Herzogtum Braunschweig, von R. Börker.—Voraussetzungen der richterlichen Unabhängigkeit in Deutschland, von W. Geiger.—Die Anonymität des Richters, von P. Möhring.—Die Bundesanwaltschaft beim Bundesgerichtshof, von L. Martin.—Die Anwaltschaft beim Reichsgericht und beim Bundesgerichtshof, von H. Schneider.—Der Syndikusanwalt, von F. Börtzler.—Contempt of court, von H.-J. Rinck.—Grenzfragen des Enteig-

(Continued)

Ehrengabe für Bruno Heusinger. (Card 3)

nungsrechts in der Rechtsprechung des Bundesgerichtshofes und des Bundesverwaltungsgerichts, von F. Kreft.—Praktische Probleme der Anschlusssicherungsübereignung, von J. Mormann.—Haftungsprobleme bei der GmbH & Co., von G. Kuhn.—Zum Anwendungsbereich des Territorialitätsprinzips und der lex rei (sitae) im internationalen Patent- und Lizenzrecht, von R. Nirk.—Gedanken zur Zulassungsrevision, von H. Arndt. — Revisionsrügen des Rechtsmittelgegners,

(Continued)

EHRENGABE für Bruno Heusinger. (Card 4)

von G. Rothe.—Über die Auswahl und Bestellung von Schiedsrichtern, von G. Heimann-Trosien.—10 Jahre Kartellsenat, von O. Löscher.—Zur Bedeutung der Marktstellung als Anknüpfungspunkt des Diskriminierungsverbots (§ 26 Abs. 2 GWB) in der Rechtsprechung des Bundesgerichtshofes, von H. Hill.—Zur Deliktsfähigkeit bei kartellrechtlichen Ordnungswidrigkeiten, von H. J. Faller.—Wandlungen des Strafrechts, von W. Sarstedt.—Wie soll die freiwillige Sterilisation künftig gesetzlich geregelt werden? Von E. Koffka.—Versäumte

(Continued)

EHRENGABE für Bruno Heusinger. (Card 5)

Gelegenheiten; zur Auslegung des § 338 Nr. 8 und des § 267 Abs. 1 Satz 2 StPO, von P. Baldus.—Wesen und Grenzen des Freibeweises, von G. Willms.

1. Law--Germany--Addresses, essays, lectures. I. Heusinger, Bruno. II. Glanzmann, Roderich, ed. III. Faller, Hans Joachim, 1915- ed. IV. Glanzmann, Roderich. V. Faller, Hans Joachim, 1915-

---

AN
(Seebach)

Ehrengabe dramatischer Dichter und Komponisten; Sr. Exzellenz dem Grafen Nikolaus von Seebach zum zwanzigjährigen Intendanten-Jubiläum. [Leipzig: K. Wolff,] 1914. 187 p. facsims. (music.) 4°.

Edited by Karl Zeiss.
"Als Manuskript gedruckt."
One of 600 copies printed.

JUILLIARD FOUNDATION FUND.

482512A. 1. Seebach, Nikolaus, Graf von, 1854- . 2. German literature—Collections. 3. Music—Facsimiles. I. Zeiss, Karl, editor.
N. Y. P. L. September 16, 1930

AN
(Schweitzer, A.)

EHRFURCHT vor dem Leben: Albert Schweitzer. Eine Freundesgabe zu seinem 80. Geburtstag. Bern, P. Haupt [1954] 268 p. port., facsim. 24cm.

Contributions in French or German.

1. Schweitzer, Albert, 1875-

NN * 4.56 p/o OC PC, 1 SL MU, 1 (LC1, X1, Z1)

---

*OHF

Ehrlich, Hugo.
Zur indogermanischen Sprachgeschichte. [Karl Brugmann zum fünfundzwanzigjährigen Professorenjubiläum dargebracht] Königsberg i. Pr., 1910. 82 p. 8°. (Königsberg. Altstädtisches Gymnasium. Jahresbericht: Beilage, Ostern, 1910.)

1. Indo-European languages. 2. Brugmann, Karl.
N. Y. P. L. May 4, 1911.

SSD p.v.477

Ehrlichsches Gestift, Dresden. Festausschuss.
Festschrift zum 250. Geburtstage Johann George Ehrlichs des Stifters des Ehrlichschen Gestifts in Dresden, herausgegeben von Stiftsdirektor Dr. Fr. Ludwig im Auftrage des Festausschusses. Dresden A.: Buchdr. A. Schütt [1927] 143 p. plates, ports. 23cm.

809595A. 1. Ehrlich, Johann George, 1677-1743. 2. Poor—Education—Germany—Dresden. I. Ludwig, Fr.
N. Y. P. L. April 17, 1936

AN
(Eichert)

Eichert, Franz, 1857-
Saenger und Prophet; Gedenkblätter zum 70. Geburtstage des Dichters Franz Eichert... Herausgegeben von den Bundesleitungen der katholischen deutschen Jugendverbände Österreichs und der Tschechoslowakei. Innsbruck: Verlagsanstalt Tyrolia[, 1927]. 239 p. front. (port.) 8°. (Franz Eicherts Lebenswerk. Bd. 2.)

"'Abendgebet' und 'Gefunden,' Worte von Eichert, Weise von Anton Orel," p. 236–239.

Contents: I. Franz Eichert: Mein Lebenslauf. II. Der Dichter spricht; eine Auslese aus Franz Eicherts Dichtungen. III. Stimmen berühmter Zeitgenossen; über das Werk und die Persönlichkeit Franz Eicherts.

343770A. 1. No subject.
N. Y. P. L. February 7, 1928

---

*MEC
W30.E25

EICHNER, WALTER, ed.
Weltdiskussion um Bayreuth; ein Querschnitt durch die ersten Festspiele nach dem Kriege... [Bayreuth?] Gesellschaft der Freunde von Bayreuth, 1952. 170 p. illus., ports. 27cm.

1. Wagner, Richard, 1813-1883— Performances— Bayreuth. I. Gesellschaft der Freunde von Bayreuth, e. V.

NN R OC (1b) (OS) I, Ib PC, 1, I SL MU, 1, I (LC1, Z1, X1)

M-11
2568

EIDGENÖSSISCHE TECHNISCHE HOCHSCHULE, Zürich. Betriebswissenschaftliches Institut.
Zwanzig Jahre Betriebswissenschaftliches Institut an der Eidgenössischen technischen Hochschule Zürich, 1929-1949. Festschrift zum siebzigsten Geburtstag von René de Vallière, ... am 23. März 1950, dargebracht von seinen Freunden, Schülern und Mitarbeitern. [Hrsg. von Walter Vogel et al. Zürich] 1950. 2 v.(404 p.) illus., ports. 30cm. (Industrielle

(Continued)

NN 6.67 1/OS, I PC, 1, 2, 3, I SL E, 1, 2, 3, I (LC1, X1, Z1)

2

EIDGENÖSSISCHE TECHNISCHE HOCHSCHULE, Zürich.
Betriebswissenschaftliches Institut.
Zwanzig Jahre Betriebswissenschaftliches Institut... (Card 2)

Organisation; Schweizerische Zeitschrift für Betriebswissenschaft. Jahrg. 19, Nr. 5-6)
Heft 2-3.
Cover title.
In German, French, or Italian.
1. Vallière, René de. 2. Industrial organization. 3. Management--Addresses, essays, lectures. I. Industrielle Organisation; Schweizerische Zeitschrift für Betriebswissenschaft.

STN
+

Eidgenössische technische Hochschule, Zürich.
Festschrift zum 75 jährigen Bestehen der Eidgenössischen technischen Hochschule in Zürich. Zürich, Orell Füssli, 1930.
plates. 31cm.

W.S.

N. Y. P. L. February 5, 1952

D-20
1392

Eighteenth century French studies: literature and the arts; edited by E. T. Dubois, Elizabeth Ratcliff ,and, P. J. Yarrow. Newcastle upon Tyne, Oriel P., 1969.
xii, 111 p. illus., music, port. 23 cm.
"Presented to Norman Suckling."
Includes bibliographical references.

(Continued)

NN*R 12.70 m/OC, I, II, III, IVb*, V PC, 1, 2, I, II, III, V SL A, 2, I, II, III, V (LC1, X1, Z1)

2

EIGHTEENTH century French studies ... (Card 2)

CONTENTS.—List of publications by Norman Suckling (p. xi-xii).—Reason and sentiment in eighteenth-century architecture, by B. Allsopp.—Pierre Bayle and the Chevalier Ramsay, by A. W. Fairbairn.—French influences on Bach, by E. Lockspeiser.—The Philosophes and the idea of progress, by J. Lough.—A Biblical 'conte philosophique': Voltaire's Taureau blanc, by H. T. Mason.—Tableaux mouvants as a technical innovation in Diderot's experimental novel, Jacques le fataliste, by R. Niklaus.—Le Brun-Pindare (1729-1807), by F. Scarfe.—'Nottes égales et inégales,' by C. Wood.

1. French literature--Addresses, essays, lectures. 2. Art, French. I. Suckling, Norman. II. Dubois, Elfriede T., ed. III. Ratcliff, Elizabeth, ed. IV. Ratcliff, Elizabeth. V. Yarrow, Philip John, ed.

F-11
7938

EIGHTEENTH-CENTURY studies in honor of Donald F. Hyde. Edited by W.H. Bond. New York, Grolier club, 1970. xv, 424 p. illus., port. 28cm.

Bibliographical footnotes.

1. English literature--Hist. and crit., 18th cent. 2. Johnson, Samuel, 1709-1784. I. Hyde, Donald F. 1915- , ed. II. Bond, William Henry, III. Grolier club, New York.
NN R 9.71 e/6 OC, I, II (OS)III PC, 1, 2, I, II, III SL (LC1, X1, Z1)

D-11
5841

EINO LEINO aikalaistensa silmin, lahikuvia, muistelmia, haastatteluja. Koonnut Aarre M. Peltonen. Helsingissä, Otava [1958] 262 p. 21cm.

"Ilmestyy Eino Leinon syntymän 80-vuotismuiston merkeissä."
Bibliography, p. 249-251.

1. Leino, Eino, 1878-1926. I. Peltonen, Aarre, ed.
NN R 2.59 g/I OC, I PC, 1, I SL (LC1, X1, Z1)

TB

EKONOMI och kultur; festskrift tillägnad Hugo E. Pipping 12.6.1955. [Redigerad av Eilif Appelberg et al.] Helsingfors, Söderström [1955] 325 p.
illus., port. 24cm.

Bibliography, p. [200]
CONTENTS.—Fogen mellan realkapital och kapital, av H. Björkqvist.—Kring den ekonomiska statsteorin, av J.-M. Jansson.—Om fastighetspriserna pa 1600-talent, av E. Jutikkala.—Kring intresserepresentationen i vår riksdag, av L. Krusius-Ahrenberg.—Undervisning i samhällsvetenskaper vid Helsingfors universitet, av M. Leppo.—En finländsk motsvarighet til striden
(Continued)
NN**X 10.56 d/ OC, I PC, 1, 2, 3, I SL E, 1, 2, 3, I (LC1, X1, Z1)

EKONOMI och kultur... (Card 2)

mellan Thibaut och Savigny, av S. Lindman.—Den statliga suveränitetens grundvalar, av N. Meinander.—Välfärds- och produktivitetsbegreppen som grund för indexberäkning vid differentierade priser, av G. Michwitz.—Förändringarna i arbetarfamiljernas levnadsnivå sedan sekelskiftet, av G. Modeen.—Utlåtande i skadeståndsfrågan våren 1944, av A. Montgomery.—Den privata sedelemissionen 1859-60, av O. Nikula.—Strövtåg i ett herrgårdsarkiv, av P. Nyberg.—Fattig och rik, av R. Pipping.—Vår instabila folkhushållning, av Br. Suviranta.—Om olika typer av beslut, av L. Törnqvist.—Familjekostnadernas utjämning som en regional inkom-
(Continued)

EKONOMI och kultur... (Card 3)

stöverföring i Finland, av H. Waris.—Familjens storlek och hushållsbudgeten, av K. Waris.—När ämbetsmännen skulle bli kooperatörer, av S.-E. Åström.—Hugo E. Pippings tryckta skrifter, av H. Schauman (p. [286]-325)

1. Economics—Essays and misc. 2. Economic history—Finland. 3. Pipping, Hugo Edvard, 1895- . I. Appelberg, Eilif, 1895- , ed.

TAH

Ekonomisk-historiska föreningen, Lund, Sweden.
Från Fugger till Kreuger; studier tillägnade Oscar Bjurling på hans 50-årsdag den 12. maj 1957. Lund, 1957.
141 p. facsim. 25 cm. (*Its* Skrifter, 2)
CONTENTS.—En Fugger-agent i Skåne år 1567, av L. Tomner.—Rutger Maclean som lanthushållare, av I. Svensson.—Uppkomsten av plattgårdar, av K. Björk.—Enskifte och socialvård, av P. E. Back.—Markegång och marknadspris vid 1800-talets mitt, av G. Fridlizius.—Svenska aktiebolag år 1859, av C. A. Nilsson.—"Feodalism" i de norrländska sågverksbolagens arrendekontrakt vid sekelskiftet, av O. Gerard.—Den officiella industristatistikens tillförlitlighet, av T. Fogelberg.—Företagare och arbetare under industrialismens genombrotts skede, av L. Jörberg.—Jordbrukspolitik och jordbruksproduktion från 1930 till 1940, av T. Ovesen.—Ett valutaproblem, av J. Strandh.
(Continued)
NN *5.62 p/A/(OC)I OS PC, 1, 2, I SL E, 1, 2, I (LC1, X1, Z1)

EKONOMISK-HISTORISKA föreningen. Lund, Sweden.
Från Fugger till Kreuger... (Card 2)

(ITS: Skrifter. v.2)

1. Economic history--Sweden. 2. Bjurling, Oscar, 1907-
I. Title.

NICC
Elias Wessén, 15 april 1954. Lund, C. Bloms boktryckeri, 1954. xi,255 p. illus.,port. 24cm.

Contents.—Sjundby och Sjundeå, av O. Ahlbäck.—Några äldre och nyare slanguttryck, av G. Bergman.—Beowulfskolier, av B. Collinder.—Om två ställen i den första grammatiska avhandlingen, av J. Helgason.—De medeltida lånorden i Siæ linna (Continued)

Elias Wessén... (Card 2)

thrøst, av S. Henning.—Vingolf eller Vingolf? av A. Holtsmark.—Noen folkeetymologier i østnorske stedsnavn av finsk opphav, av R. Iversen.—Pakkenelliker. En lexikografisk undersøgelse, av L. Jacobsen.—Ett uppländskt runstensfynd, av S.B.F. Jansson.—Nom. ack. sing. fem. och nom. ack. plur. neutr. av pronomenet den i fornsvenskan, av V. Jansson.—Ett eddaställe och ett ortnamn, av T. Johannisson.— (Continued)

Elias Wessén... (Card 3)

Ulimaroa, av G. Langenfelt.—Om dialekt i svensk skönlitteratur, av C. Larsson.—"Bokinæ bono." En detalj i Västgöta biskopskrönika, av K.G. Ljunggren.—Om det svenska personnamnsverket, av I. Modéer.—Sjá í vánarbug, av S. Nordal.—Skeðja grjóti, av M. Olsen.—Ordspråk i Peder Månssons svenska brev, av R. Pipping.—Binneberg, av J. Sahlgren.—De 12 patriarkers testamente på gammelnorsk, av D.A. Seip.—Af den danske (Continued)

Elias Wessén... (Card 4)

retskrivningsreforms forhistorie, av P. Skautrup.—Emporagrius och Torsåker, av D. Strömbäck.—Om förhållandet mellan Hälsingelagens texter, av C.I. Ståhle.—Vargens fiske. Efter branche III av le Roman de Renard, av G. Tilander.—Varm korvgubbe-vandrare i dimma, av E. Wellander.—Elias Wesséns bibliografi 1949-53, av M. Wessén (p. 251-254)

(Continued)

Elias Wessén... (Card 5)

1. Scandinavian languages. 2. Philology—Addresses, essays, lectures. 3. Wessén, Elias, 1889-

---

D-13
510

ELIZABETHAN government and society; essays presented to Sir John Neale. Edited by S. T. Bindoff, J. Hurstfield [and] C.H. Williams. [London] University of London, Athlone press, 1961. x, 423 p. illus., ports., facsims. 23cm.

Printed at the Curwen press, Plaistow.

CONTENTS.--In search of the queen, by C.H. Williams.--William Cecil and Elizabethan public relations, by C. Read.-- (Continued)

ELIZABETHAN government and society... (Card 2)

The making of the Statute of artificers, by S. T. Bindoff. --Place and patronage in Elizabethan politics, by W. T. MacCaffery. --John Field and Elizabethan puritanism, by P. Collinson. --The Elizabethan merchants of Exeter, by W. G. Hoskins. --Touching the writ of latitat; an act "of no great moment", by M. Blatcher. --The Elizabethan exchequer: War in the receipt, by G. R. Elton. --Mr. Myddelton the merchant of Tower street, by A. H. Dodd. --Foundations of Anglo-Scottish union, by G. Donaldson. --Ireland, Elizabeth I and the Counter-Reformation, by R. D. Edwards. --

(Continued)

ELIZABETHAN government and society... (Card 3)

Elizabethan war aims and strategy, by R. B. Wernham. --The succession struggle in late Elizabethan England by J. Hurstfield. --The historical writings of Sir John Neale.

1. Great Britain--Hist.--Elizabeth, 1558-1603. 2. Economic history--Gt. Br., 1461-1760. 3. Great Britain--Soc. condit., 1485-1700. 4. Neale, Sir John Ernest, 1890- . I. Bindoff, Stanky Thomas, 1908- , ed.

D-12
9394

Elizabethan and Jacobean studies; presented to Frank Percy Wilson in honour of his seventieth birthday. Oxford, Clarendon Press, 1959.

viii, 355 p. port., facsims., music. 23 cm.
Edited by Herbert Davis and Helen Gardner.
Bibliographical footnotes.

CONTENTS.—A mirror for magistrates revisited, by E. M. W. Tillyard.—Marlowe's light reading, by E. Seaton.—The complaint of Thomas Digges, by F. R. Johnson.—Harington's folly, by K. M. Lea.—Two notes: (I) When was Twelfth night? (II) Copyright in unauthorized texts, by W. W. Greg.—Classical myth in Shakespeare's plays, by D. Bush.—Shakespeare's reading in Chaucer, by N. Coghill.—On Venus and Adonis, by D. C. Allen.—Variations on a theme in Shakespeare's sonnets, by J. B. Leishman.—Shakespeare's use of popular

(Continued)

Elizabethan and Jacobean studies ... 1959. (Card 2)

CONTENTS—Continued.

song, by F. W. Sternfeld.—"Under which king, Bezonian?" By P. Alexander.—The rider on the winged horse, by M. Lascelles.—Sir Walter Ralegh's Instructions to his son, by A. M. C. Latham.—Elizabeth, Essex, and James, by J. McManaway.—Hume's history of the reign of James I, by G. Davies.—Some Jacobean catch-phrases and some light on Thomas Bretnor, by J. Crow.—The argument about "The ecstasy," by H. Gardner.—Donne's poetry in the nineteenth century, by K. Tillotson.—Memories of Harley Granville-Barker and two of his friends, by J. D. Wilson.—A select list of the writings of F. P. Wilson, by H. S. Bennett.

1. English literature--Addresses, essays, lectures. 2. Wilson, Frank Percy, 1889- I. Davis, Herbert, 1893- , ed.

E-12
9105

Elsener, Ferdinand, 1912- *ed.*

Festschrift Karl Siegfried Bader. Rechtsgeschichte, Rechtssprache, Rechtsarchäologie, rechtliche Volkskunde. Hrsg. von Ferdinand Elsener und W. H. Ruoff. Zürich, Schulthess; Köln, Graz, Böhlau, 1965.

xvi, 537 p. 8 plates. 25 cm.

(Continued)

NN * R 6.67 1/6 OC, I, IIb* PC, 1, 2, 3, I SL (LC1, X1, Z1)

ELSENER, FERDINAND, 1912- , ed. Festschrift Karl Siegfried Bader. (Card 2)

One contribution in French.
"Arbeiten von Karl Siegfried Bader": p. 503-544.
Bibliographical footnotes.

1. Law--Addresses, essays, lectures. 2. Law--Switzerland--Addresses, essays, lectures. 3. Bader, Karl Siegfried, 1905- . I. Ruoff, Wilhelm Heinrich, 1906- , joint ed. II. Elsener, Ferdinand, 1912-

---

Copy only words underlined & classmark-- *YIA

ELTESTER, WALTHER, ed.

Judentum, Urchristentum, Kirche; Festschrift für Joachim Jeremias. 2. viel fachberichtigte und ergänzte...Aufl. Berlin, A. Töpelmann, 1960. 259 p. illus., port. 25cm. (Zeitschrift für die neutestamentliche Wissenschaft und die Kunde des Urchristentums. Beihefte. 26)

CONTENTS.--Joachim Jeremias, by M. Black.--Bibliographie Joachim Jeremias, 1923-1963, von C. Burchard (p. [xix]-xxx).--Von Gott gezeugt, von O. Michel und O. Betz.--

(Continued)

NN * 7.65 s/ OC (OS)I PC, 1, 2, 3, 4, I I, 2, 3, 5 (LC1, X1, Z1)

ELTESTER, WALTHER, ed. Judentum... (Card 2)

Giljonim und sifre minim, von K.G. Kuhn.--Der siebenarmige Leuchter und der Titusbogen, von W. Eltester.--Jesu Worte über den Sabbat, von E. Lohse.--Er wird Nazoräer heissen, von E. Schweizer.--Quis et unde? An analysis of Mt 1-2, by K. Stendahl.--Die Stadt der Mörder, von K.H. Rengstorf.--Bethsaida und Gennesar, von H. Hegermann.--Marie-Madeleine et les disciples au tombeau selon Joh 20, 1-8, par P. Benoit.--Quellenanalyse und Kompositions-analyse in Act 15, von E. Haenchen.--Gottesdienst im Alltag der Welt, von E.

(Continued)

ELTESTER, WALTHER, ed. Judentum... (Card 3)

Käsemann.--Zur Leib-Christi-Vorstellung im Epheserbrief, von C. Colpe.--Sohnschaft und Leiden, von G. Bornkamm.--Zum Aufbau des Hebräerbriefes, von W. Nauck.--Unbekannte Gleichnisse Jesu aus dem Thomas-Evangelium, von C.H. Hunzinger.--Die Rücksicht auf die Reaktion der Nicht-Christen als Motiv in der altchristlichen Paränese, von W.C. van Unnik.--Die Beichte im alten Mönchtum, von H. Dörries.

(Continued)

ELTESTER, WALTHER, ed. Judentum... (Card 4)

Bibliographical footnotes.

1. Judaism--Addresses, essays, lectures. 2. Jeremias, Joachim, 1900- 3. Bible. N.T. and Jewish literature. 4. Church history--Primitive church, to 325. 5. Judaism --Essays. I. Series.

D-12
372

EMANUEL STICKELBERGER; Festgabe zum 75. Geburtstage 13. März 1959. [Die Herausgabe dieser Schrift besorgte Adrian Wolfgang Martin] Frauenfeld, Huber [1959] 197 p. illus., ports. 21cm.

Includes poems, some in dialect.

CONTENTS—Emanuel Stickelberger, Weg und Auftrag eines Schweizer Dichters, von A.W. Martin. —Bibliographie der Werke Emanuel Stickelbergers, von C. Vischer (p. 55-81). —Zeittafel. —Gedanken und Grüsse. —

(Continued)

NN R 10. 59 a/ OC, I PC, 1, I SL (LC1, X1, Z1)

EMANUEL STICKELBERGER... (Card 2)

Emanuel Stickelberger, von R.A. Schröder. —Zum dichterischen Werk Emanuel Stickelbergers, von H. Mast. —Besuch bei Emanuel Stickelberger, von D. Larese.

1. Stickelberger, Emanuel, 1884- I. Martin, Adrian Wolfgang, ed.

D-16
5280

The **Emerging** world. **Jawaharlal Nehru memorial volume.** New York, Asia Pub. House [1964]

xii, 268 p. port. 22cm.

CONTENTS.—The emerging world society, by S. Radhakrishnan.—Universities then and now, by Lord Adrian.—A balance-sheet for science and technology in Europe, by Sir E. Ashby.—Is peaceful change possible? By Earl Attlee.—The task of education, by V. Bhave.—Views on coexistence and the conflicts of our times, by W. Brandt.—"East" and "West," by N. Cousins.—Development planning in principle and practice, by J. K. Galbraith.—Some qualities of forthcoming changes, by R. B. Gregg.—The impact of the West on

(Continued)

NN* R 3.66 g/ OC PC, 1, 2 SL O, 2 (LC1, X1, Z1) [I]

The EMERGING world. (Card 2)

Indian traditions, by Humayun Kabir.—The future of non-violence, by O. Lacombe.—Religion and the problems of peace, by G. P. Malalasekera.—Europe and the developing countries, by P. Mendes-France.—The role of science and technology in the development of underdeveloped countries in South Asia, by G. Myrdal.—World morality and world peace, by L. Pauling.—Towards a wider conception of our common humanity, by Sir J. Plimsoll.—The essence of Hinduism, by C. Rajagopalachari.—Reflections on violence, by Sir H. Read.—Rich lands poor lands; recollections and reflections, by E. Reid.—Asia, Africa, and the world, by C. P. Romulo.—Secularism in India, by

(Continued)

The EMERGING world. (Card 3)

Sampurnanand.—The Zen language, by D. T. Suzuki.—Ancient contacts and relations between India and China, by T. Yun-Shan.—Towards one world by peaceful change, by A. Toynbee.—The creative individual, by G. Tucci.—Purpose in education, by Z. Husain.

1. Civilization, Modern—Addresses, essays, lectures. 2. Nehru, Jawaharlal, 1889-1964.

D-14
8112

EMGE, CARL AUGUST, 1886- , ed.
Kreise um Schopenhauer; Arthur Hübscher zum 65. Geburtstag am 3.1. 1962 und zum 25-Jahres-Jubiläum als Präsident der Schopenhauer-Gesellschaft im Oktober 1961. Festschrift. Wiesbaden, F.A. Brockhaus, 1962. 154 p. port. 23cm.

CONTENTS.--Zum Geleit, von C.A. Emge.--Omaggio ad Arthur Hübscher e alla Schopenhauer-Gesellschaft, di G. Del Vecchio.--

(Continued)

NN R 2.64 f/ OC PC, 1, 2 SL (LC1, X1, Z1)

3

EMGE, CARL AUGUST, 1886- , ed. Kreise um Schopenhauer... (Card 2)

Schopenhauer-Meditationen, von H. Glockner.--Actualité de Schopenhauer, par A. Baillot.--Schopenhauers Echo in Indien, von H. von Glasenapp.--Some significant aspects of Schopenhauer's philosophy, by E.F.J. Payne.--Der Begriff des Gewissens bei Schopenhauer, von F. Mockrauer.--Arthur Schopenhauer's concepts of salvation, by G. Stock.--Schopenhauer als philosophus christianissimus, von K. Pfeiffer.--Fr. Moltke Bugge und das Schulwesen Bayers, von Øverås.--Uber das Vorurteil, von M. Horkheimer.--

(Continued)

EMGE, CARL AUGUST, 1886- , ed. Kreise um Schopenhauer... (Card 3)

Geistiger Sinn und ästhetische Weltdeutung bei Goethe, von F.-J. von Rintelen.--Zu einer Theorie der Kunst, von E. Preetorius.--Warum Arbeitssoziologie? Von M. Rychner.--Glück des Sammelns, von F. Brahn.--Unordentliche Gedanken, von C.A. Emge.--Aphorismen zur Ethik und Metaphysik, von H. Margolius.--Sokratisches. Aphorismen, von L.F. Barthel.--Das Werk Arthur Hübschers, von F. Brahn.

1. Schopenhauer, Arthur, 1788-1860. 2. Hübscher, Arthur, 1897-

---

* OAC

Emlékkönyv Dr. Mahler Ede; a Budapesti kir. magyar Pázmány Péter tudományegyetem ny. nyilvános rendes tanárának nyolcvanadik születésnapjára kiadják barátai, tisztelöi és tanítványai. Dissertationes in honorem Dr. Eduardi Mahler, professoris emeriti Universitatis regiale scientiarum Budapestinensis de Petro Pázmány nominatae natali die octogesimo ab amicis, collegis et discipulis eius conscriptae et editae. Budapestini, 1937. 509, 35 p. incl. tables. front. (port.), illus. 22½cm.

(Continued)

N. Y. P. L. September 18, 1940

Emlékkönyv Dr. Mahler Ede... (Continued)

Added t.-p. in English: Jubilee volume in honour of Edward Mahler, Ph.D., professor of the Royal Hungarian Pázmány Péter university (retired); edited on his eightieth birthday by his friends, colleagues, and pupils...

"Szerkesztették: Dr. Somogyi József és Dr. Löwinger Sámuel."

Bibliographical footnotes.

Contents.—Balogh, Jenó. Mahler Ede, mint az Akadémia tagja.—Lukinich, Imre. Mahler Ede, mint tanár.—Wertheimer, Adolf. Mahler Ede.—Löwy, Adolf. Bibliographie der Schriften Prof. Dr. Eduard Mahlers (p. 12-36).—Aistleitner, Josef. Zum Verständnis des Ras-Schamra-Textes I.D.—Cassuto, Umberto. Il messaggio di Mot a Baal nella tavola I* AB di Ras Shamra.—David, Antoine. L'écriture sumérienne et l'écriture chinoise.—Dobrovits, Aladár. Harpokrates.—Éder-Szászy, Ladislaus. A hitherto unpublished martyr act of St. Victor of Alexandria.—Furlani,

(Continued)

N. Y. P. L. September 18, 1940

Emlékkönyv Dr. Mahler Ede... (Continued)

Giuseppe. Sulla confessione dei peccati presso gli Hittiti.—Goldziherné Freudenberg, Mária. Óegyiptomi reliefek.—Graf, Andreas. Der Sonnenlöwe.—Kováts, Ferenc. Korakapitalisztikus gazdasági válság magyarországon I. Mátyás király uralkodása alatt.—Kúnos, Ignácz. Olimpuszok alján.—Némethy, Ladislaus. Beobachtungen aus dem Gebiet der Urartu-Sprache.—Paulovits, István. Mithras-oltár és trák elemek Campona-ban.—Pálfi, Johann. Totenopfer und Opferformeln bei den Ägyptern der alten Zeit.—Pröhle, Wilhelm. Zur Frage der negativen Verbalformen in den Türksprachen.—Sidersky, D. Études sur la chronologie de la première dynastie babylonienne.—Somogyi, Joseph de. Biblical figures in ad-Damiri's Hayat al-hayawan.—Surányi-Unger, Tivadar. Gazdasági fellendülés és válságveszély.—Takács, Zoltán de. On the monument of the General Ho CH'ü-ping.—Waldapfel, Imre. Christophorus.—Wessetzky, Wilhelm. Herz und Skarabäus.—Wodetzky, Joseph. Über die Definition der Syzygien.

(Continued)

N. Y. P. L. September 18, 1940

Emlékkönyv Dr. Mahler Ede... (Continued)

—Büchler, Adolf. מפסע על ראשי עם קדוש.—Büchler, Sándor. Szerencsés Imre származása.—Guttman, Michael. Maimonides über das biblische "jus talionis".—Hahn, Stephan. Sifre Minim.—Heller, Bernát. Egyiptomi elemek az aggádában.—Kohlbach, Bertalan. A magyar nemzeti múzeum "beszámim"-tartói.—Krausz, Samuel. Rabbinische Nachrichten über das alte Aegypten.—Löw, Immanuel. Fényszóró drágakövek.—Marmorstein, Arthur. Egyptian mythology and Babylonian magic in Bible and Talmud.—Patai, Raphael. Some Hebrew sea legends.—Scheiber, Alexander. Das Problem des Ursprungs der Sprache im jüdischen Schrifttum.—Corrigenda.—Klein, Samuel. לחקר הכנויים והתוארים.—Löwinger, Samuel. הוספות על משלי שועלים.

11565B. 1. Mahler, Eduard, 1857- . 2. Mahler, Eduard, 1857- —Bibl. 3. Oriental studies. I. Somogyi, József, ed. II. Löwinger, Sámuel, ed. III. Title: Jubilee volume in honour of Edward Mahler.

N. Y. P. L. September 18, 1940

MQZ
+
(Lund)

En ARKITEKT morer seg; festskrift til Frederik Konow Lund i anledning 70-årsdagen 20. okt. 1959. [Redaksjonsutvalget: Kristian Bjerknes et al. Bergen, A. Garnaes boktr., 1959] 69 p. (chiefly illus.) port. 32cm.

1. Lund, Frederik Konow, 1889- . I. Bjerknes, Kristian, 1906-

NN 7.60 a/ OC, Ib, I PC, I, I SL A, I, I (LC1, X1, Z1)

NIT
En JYDSK kulturpersonlighed; en bog til Richardt Gandrup, 1885 22 jan., 1955 Aarhus, S Lund [1955] 175 p. port. 22cm.

CONTENTS.—Richardt Gandrup og den folkelige talerstol, av A. Andersen.--Den sprængte idyl, av J. Bomholt.—Jason og det gyldne skind: omkring Henrik Pontoppidanproblemet, av J. Bukdahl.—Nogle minder fra Århus, av. S. Elkjær.—Erfaring og eksempel, av E. Frederiksen.—Kuling
(Continued)
NN**X 10.55 g OC PC I SL (MU)I (LC1, X1, Z1)

En JYDSK kulturpersonlighed... (Card 2)

over Vandfuld herred, av M.A. Hansen.—Richardt Gandrup anmelder kunst, av P. Kirkegaard.--Richardt Gandrup; en biografisk skitse, av S. Lund.—Limfjordsdigtere, av H. Povlsen.—Richardt Gandrup og musikken, av T. Rasmussen.--Medarbejderen, av E. Schmidt.--Verset i hverdagen, av H. H. Seedorff Pedersen.—Richardt Gandrup, bidrag til en karakteristik, av E. Sejr.—Hanherredsmål hos Gandrup, en sproglig detalje, av P. Skautrup.
(Continued)

En JYDSK kulturpersonlighed... (Card 3)

--i stedet for, av E. Thomsen.—Digteren Richardt Gandrup, av H. Topsoe-Jensen.—I Hovedlandet: da den moderne kunst holdt sit indtog, av J. Voeler.

1. Gandrup, Richardt, 1885-

D-19
7684
L'Endurance de la pensée. Pour saluer Jean Beaufret. René Char. Martin Heidegger. Temps et être. Beda Allemann, Jean-Paul Aron ... ₍etc.₎ ₍Paris,₎ Plon, 1968.

360 p. plates. 21 cm. (Faits et thèmes)

Includes German text and French translation of Heidegger's Zeit und Sein (p. ₍12₎-71)
Includes bibliographical references.

1. Philosophy--Addresses, essays, lectures. 2. Literature—Addresses, essays, lectures. I. Beaufret, Jean. II. Char, René, 1907- III. Heidegger, Martin, 1889- Zeit und Sein.
NN*R 4.70 m/A OC, I, II, III PC, 1, 2, I, II, III SL (LC1, X1, Z1)

D-16
2490
ENGEL-JANOSI, FRIEDRICH.
Geschichte auf dem Ballhausplatz; Essays zur österreichischen Aussenpolitik, 1830-1945. [Graz] Verlag Styria [1963] 346 p. illus., ports. 22cm.

"Zur Feier des 70. Geburtstages von Universitätsprofessor Friedrich Engel-Janosi als Festgabe des Historischen Instituts, der Universität Wien... herausgegeben."
(Continued)
NN R 9.66 r/ OCs PCs, ls, 2s, SLs Es, ls, 2s (LCls, Xls, Zls, [1])

2

ENGEL-JANOSI, FRIEDRICH. Geschichte auf dem Ballhausplatz... (Card 2)

Includes bibliographical references.

1. Austria--Hungary--For. rel. 2. Austria--For. rel., 1918- . i. subs. for Engel- J-, F-, 1893- .

NCB
En engelsk bog tilegnet Kai Friis Møller. København, Gyldendal, 1948. 182 p. 20cm.

"Tilegnet Kai Friis Møller...paa hans 60 aars dag..."
"Redigeret af Kjeld Abell...₍og andre₎"

501005B. 1. Friis Møller, Kai, 1888- . 2. English literature—Hist. and crit. I. Abell, Kjeld, 1901- , ed.
N. Y. P. L. April 26, 1950

---

* C-4 p.v.665
Engelstad, Carl Fredrik, 1915-
Albert Schweitzer erobrer Norge; en liten bok om en stor opplevelse, redigert av Carl Fredrik Engelstad og Max Tau. Oslo, J. Grundt Tanum, 1954. 10 p., ₍52₎ p. of illus. (incl. ports.) 24cm.

1. Schweitzer, Albert, 1875- . —Iconography. II. Tau, Max, 1897- joint ed.
NN** 10.57 OC,I PC,I,I SL (LC1,X1,Z1)

D-15
6098
ENSAYOS filosóficos; homenaje al profesor Manuel Gonzalo Casas (1910-1961) por Guillermo Orce Remis [et al.] Buenos Aires, Ediciones Troquel [1963] 165 p. port. 21cm. (Colección Diálogos del Presente, 14)

Includes bibliographies.
CONTENTS.—Itinerario de Manuel Gonzalo Casas, de A. Caturelli.—La libertad interior y la problemática del acto libre, de M.F. Sciacca.—
(Continued)
NN R 4.65 g/ OC, I PC, 1, 2, I SL (LC1, X1, Z1)

2

ENSAYOS filosóficos... (Card 2)

La verdad en el ser, de M. Mindán.—Trascendencia o trascendentalidad, de O.N. Derisi.—Sobre la inteligibilidad de la naturaleza como forma y como regularidad, de C. Paris.—Existencia y existenciariedad en Heidegger, de D.F. Pró.—El último progreso de los tiempos modernos: la palabra violada, de M. Petit de Murat.—Posibilidad de la metafísica, de A. García Astrada.—Inteligencia e ideología como dos modos del ser de la vocación intelectual, de O.H. Travaglino.—La economía y lo jurídico social, de M. Herrera Figueroa.—Participación y libertad en la filosofía de Lavelle, de M. Santos Medina de Santos.—La obra de Manuel Gonzalo Casas de M. Yoshida (p. 137-165).
1. Gonzalo Casas, Manuel. 2. Philosophy--Addresses, essays, lectures. I. Orce Remis, Guillermo.

ZDC

Environmental factors in Christian history, edited by John Thomas McNeill, Matthew Spinka ₍and₎ Harold R. Willoughby. Chicago, Ill., The University of Chicago press ₍°1939₎

x, 417 p. front. (port.) 23½cm.

"Presented to Dr. Shirley Jackson Case ... as a tribute to his scholarship and leadership. The writers are his former colleagues and students."—Pref. Published, September, 1939.

CONTENTS.—The significance of John the Baptist for the beginnings of Christianity, by E. W. Parsons.—Religious healing in first-century Palestine, by S. V. McCasland.—The Hellenization of Jewish Messianism in early Christianity, by Clyo Jackson.—Popular reactions against Christianity in the Roman empire, by E. C. Colwell.—Roman religious survivals in Christianity, by G. J. Laing.—Current contributions from arche-

(Continued on next card)

39-31824

₍15₎

ZDC

Environmental factors in Christian history ... ₍°1939₎ (Card 2)

CONTENTS—Continued.

ology to early Christian history, by H. R. Willoughby.—The impact of gnosticism on early Christianity, by J. T. Carlyon.—Economic factors in the persecutions of the Christians to A. D. 260, by G. T. Oborn.—The sources of Christian asceticism, by M. M. Deems.—The effect of the barbarian invasions upon the liturgy, by M. H. Shepperd, jr.—The feudalization of the church, by J. T. McNeill.—Aristotelianism in western Christianity, by Richard McKeon.—The influence of medieval Judaism on Christianity, by A. E. Haydon.—The effect of the crusades upon eastern Christianity, by Matthew Spinka.—Renaissance culture and Christianity, by W. E. Garrison.—Nationalism and European Christianity, by

(Continued on next card)

39-31824

₍15₎

Environmental factors in Christian history ... ₍°1939₎ (Card 3)

CONTENTS—Continued.

Wilhelm Pauck.—The religion of early freemasonry, by C. H. Lyttle.—Christianity and the culture of India, by M. H. Harper.—Christianity in the modern Japanese environment, by D. C. Holtom.—Religious bearings on the modern scientific movement, by E. E. Aubrey.—The frontier in American Christianity, by W. W. Sweet.—Bibliography of the writings of Shirley Jackson Case, compiled by Allan Cabaniss (p. 399–407)

1. Case, Shirley Jackson, 1872– 2. Church history—Addresses, essays, lectures. 3. Christianity and other religions. I. McNeill, John Thomas, 1885– ed.

39-31824

Library of Congress BR141.E6

Copyright A 135168 ₍15₎ 270.04

L-10
3847
v. 2

EPICUREA in memoriam Hectoris Bignone; miscellanea philologica. [Genova] Istituto de filologia classica, 1959. 237 p. port. 23cm. (Genoa (City). Università. Istituto di filologia classica. Pubblicazioni. 2)

"Bibliografia epicurea di Ettore Bignone," p. [25]-27.

CONTENTS.--Ettore Bignone, di M. Untersteiner.--Il concetto del tempo nella fisica atomistica, di A. Barigazzi.--L'atomo come principio

(Continued)

NN R 9. 60 L/ OC (OS)I PC, 1, 2, 3, I (LC1, X1, Z1)

2

EPICUREA in memoriam Hectoris Bignone... (Card 2)

intelligibile, di V. E. Alfieri.--Nota su Democrito B 174, di A. Grilli.--Epicuro e le conquiste matematiche-astronomiche, di A. Barbieri.--Les épicuriens et la contemplation, par P. Boyancé.--Filodemo e l'autore dell'etica Comparetti, di M. Gigante.--Il finale (vv. 1440-1475) del V libro di Lucrezio, di P. Giuffrida.--L'epicureismo nella storia spirituale di Vergilio, di L. Alfonsi.--Aus der Arbeit an einem ethischen Traktat des Demetrios Lacon, von W. Schmid.--Plutarque et l'épicurisme, par R. Flacelière.--Ricerche sull'epicureismo del Quattrocento, di. E. Garin.

1. Bignone, Ettore, 1879-1953. 2. Epicurus. 3. Epicureanism. I. Series.

E-13
5271

EPIRRHOSIS; Festgabe für Carl Schmitt. Hrsg. von Hans Barion [et al.] Berlin, Duncker & Humblot [1968] 2 v.(778 p.). port. 24cm.

Bibliographical footnotes.

1. Political science--Addresses, essays, lectures. 2. Civilization--Addresses, essays, lectures. I. Barion, Hans, ed. II. Schmitt, Carl, 1888-

NN R 5. 69 k/A OC, I, II PC, 1, 2, I, II SL E, 1, I, II (LC1, X1, Z1)
[I]

IG

The era of the American revolution; studies inscribed to Evarts Boutell Greene, edited by Richard B. Morris. New York, Columbia university press, 1939.

xii, 415 p. 24½cm.

Second Copy

CONTENTS.—The effect of the Navigation acts on the thirteen colonies, by L. A. Harper.—Writs of assistance as a cause of the revolution, by O. M. Dickerson.—Labor and mercantilism in the revolutionary era, by R. B. Morris.—The American balance of power and European diplomacy, 1713–78, by Max Savelle.—The office of commander in chief: a phase of imperial unity on the eve of the revolution, by C. E. Carter.—The royal governors in the middle and southern colonies on the eve of the revolution: a study in imperial personnel, by Louise B. Dunbar.—The

(Continued on next card)

39-33070

₍35₎

The era of the American revolution ... 1939. (Card 2)

CONTENTS—Continued.

Sons of liberty in New Y. . by H. M. Morais.—Eliphalet Dyer: Connecticut revolutionist, by G. C. Groce, jr.—The patriot newspaper and the American revolution, by S. I. Pomerantz.—America and the Irish revolutionary movement in the eighteenth century, by Michael Kraus.—The Massachusetts conservatives in the critical period, by R. A. East.

1. U. S.—Hist.—Revolution. 2. U. S.—Hist.—Colonial period. 3. Greene, Evarts Boutell, 1870– I. Morris, Richard Brandon, 1904– ed.

39-33070

Library of Congress E203.E74

~~Copy 2.~~

Copyright A 134615 ₍35₎ 973.304

D-12
2797

The ERA of Goethe: essays presented to James Boyd, Taylor professor of the German language and literature. 1938-1959. Oxford, Blackwell, 1959. xvi, 193 p. front. (port.), 2 plates. 23cm.

CONTENTS.--Ambiguity in Die Wahlverwandtschaften, by H. G. Barnes. --The idea of 'Bildung' in Wilhelm von Humboldt's letters, by W. H. Bruford. --Unpublished Pestalozziana from the Renouard James papers, by L. Forster. --Auch eine Philosophie der Geschichte zur Bildung der Menschheit, by A. Gillies.--Some conjectures regarding Goethe's 'Erdgeist,'

(Continued)

NN R 3. 60 p/A OC PC, 1, 2 SL (LC1, X1, Z1) [I]

The ERA of Goethe... (Card 2)

by E. C. Mason.--Some words of Pylades, by R. Pascal.--Incompleteness and discrepancy in Die natürliche Tochter, by R. Peacock.--Hebbel's portrait of Goethe, by E. Purdie.--Hölderlin's idea of poetry, by E. L. Stahl. --Day and night symbolism in some poems of Mörike, by W. D. Williams. --Carlyle's conversion, by W. Witte.

1. Boyd, James, 1891- 2. German literature--Addresses, essays, lectures.

* KP
(Bremer)

Eranos. ⌊Eine Festschrift für Hugo von Hofmannsthal zum 1 Februar, 1924. München: Verlag der Bremer Presse, 1924.⌋ 3 p.l., xxxv, 159 p., 1 l. plates. 4°.

Colophon: Verlag der Bremer Presse, München, MCMXXIIII. Gesetzt in der Werkstatt des Verlages, gedruckt in 1050 Exemplaren von der Mandruck A. G. München. Den Druck der Radierung und der Lithographien haben Heinrich Wetteroth und Heinrich Eigner besorgt. Den Titel und die Initialen hat Anna Simons gezeichnet.

Contents: BORCHARDT, R. Brief. Der ruhende Herakles. BRECHT, W. Fragmentarische Betrachtung über Hofmannsthals Weltbild. HOFMANN, L. von. Radierung. BURDACH, K. Die deutschen wissenschaftlichen Akademien und der schöpferische nationale Geist. BEER-HOFMANN, R. Fragment aus "Die Historie von König David."

(Continued)

N. Y. P. L. January 23, 1930

Eranos. ⌊Eine Festschrift für Hugo von Hofmannsthal zum 1 Februar, 1924. (Card 2)

KASSNER, R. Gesichter. LIEBERMANN, M. Lithographie. MANN, T. Fragment aus dem Roman "Der Zauberberg." MURRAY, G. Griechische Elegie. MELL, M. Aus einem steirischen Tagebuch. NADLER, J. Altwiener Theater. RIEZLER, K. Die Krise des Geistes. SCHROEDER, R. A. Widmungen. ORLIK, E. Lithographie. VOSSLER, K. Spanischer Brief. WASSERMANN, J. "Achim," Fragment eines Gespräches über die Gerechtigkeit. ANDRIAN, L. Sonett.

454155A. 1. Hofmannsthal, Hugo Hofmann, Edler von, 1874–1929.
N. Y. P. L. January 23, 1930

RK

ERBE der Vergangenheit; germanistische Beiträge. Festgabe für Karl Helm zum 80. Geburtstage, 19. Mai 1951. Tübingen, M. Niemeyer, 1951. 272 p. 24cm.

Bibliographical footnotes.

CONTENTS. —Kimbren und Teutonen, von J. de Vries. —Erce und Fjorgyn, von F. R. Schröder. —Es gibt kein balder "Herr," von H. Kuhn. —Die nordische Swanhilddichtung, von H. de Boor. —Zur Frage des Alters der hochdeutschen Lautverschiebung, von W. Mitzka. —Der Waltharius Ekkehards und das Chronicon Novaliciense, von L. Wolff. —Der Weg der Nibelunge, von F. Panzer. — Das Wort keusch, von T. Frings

(Continued)

NN* 3.53 OC PC, 1, 2 SL (LC1, Z1, X1)

ERBE der Vergangenheit... (Card 2)

und G. Müller. —Der Streit um das ritterliche Tugendsystem, von E. Neumann. —Der Zwîvel bei Wolfram und anderweit, von H. Hempel. —Das 9. Buch des Parzival, von W. Henzen. —Hintersichwerfen als Kultritus, von H. Hepding. —Altdeutsches Wortgut in der heutigen Mundart, von L. Berthold. —Flurnamen als lebende Relikte für die Mundartgeographie. von B. Martin. —Über Rückbildung im heutigen Schwedisch, von T. Johannisson. —Verzeichnis der Schriften von Karl Helm, von E. -A. Ebbinghaus.

1. Germanic philology. 2. Helm, Karl, 1871-

BTC

Erdélyi férfiak egyesülete.
Jancsó Benedek emlékkönyv; az EFE "Jancsó Benedek társasága" megbízásából szerkesztette Asztalos Miklós. ⌊Budapest: Királyi magyar egyetemi nyomda, 1931.⌋ 413 p. front. (port.), illus., map, tables. 25cm.

Festschrift.

666249A. 1. Jancsó, Benedek, 1854– . 2. Europe, Central. I. Asztalos, Miklós, editor.
N. Y. P. L. July 20, 1934

3-MAS

Erffa, Hans Martin, *Freiherr* von, ed.
Festschrift für Harald Keller, zum sechzigsten Geburtstag, dargebracht von seinen Schülern. ⌊Hrsg. von Hans Martin Freiherrn von Erffa und Elisabeth Herget⌋ Darmstadt, E. Roether, 1963.

412 p. illus., facsims., maps (1 fold.) plans, ports. 28 cm.

Includes bibliographical references.

(Continued)

NN * R 10.68 1/A OC I, IIb* PC, 1, 2, 3, I SL A, 1, 2, 3, I
(LC1, X1, Z1) [I] 4

ERFFA, HANS MARTIN, Freiherr VON, ed.
Festschrift für Harald Keller... (Card 2)

CONTENTS.—Ziemlich viel Mut, von M.-L. Kaschnitz.—Ludiones Etruriae, von S. Haynes.—Hersfeld, Fulda und Erfurt als frühe Handelsniederlassungen, von W. Hess.—Zum Hauptstadtproblem im frühen Mittelalter, von C. Brühl.—Die Krone im hochmittelalterlichen Staatsdenken, von H. Hoffmann.—Die klugen und die törichten Jungfrauen und der Lettner des Magdeburger Doms, von F. Bellmann.—Das Bildnis in rechtlichen Zwangsmitteln, von W. Brückner.—Zum Neubau-Projekt von St. Peter unter Papst Nikolaus v., von G. Urban.—Imperator pedes papae deosculatur; ein Beitrag zur Bild-

(Continued)

ERFFA, HANS MARTIN, Freiherr VON, ed.
Festschrift für Harald Keller... (Card 3)

kunde des 16. Jahrhunderts, von K.-A. Wirth.—Venezianische Moscheeampeln in Istanbul, von R. Rückert.—Annotationes zu Michelangelos Mediceergräbern, von W. Goez.—Das Tintoretto-Bildnis der Kasseler Galerie, von L. Oehler.—Tintoretto und "I fatti di Cesare," von E. Herzog.—Wirkungen und Einflüsse des Palazzo del Te nördlich der Alpen, von E. Herget.—Der Lobkowitzsche Kaiserpokal und verwandte Arbeiten des Goldschmieds Hanns Reinhardt Taravell vom Prager Hof Ferdinands III, von G. Bott.—Die Ehrenpforten für den Possess der Päpste im 17. und 18. Jahrhundert, von H. M. Freiherr von Erffa.—Drei unbekannte Zeichnungen von Johann Paul Egell,

(Continued)

ERFFA, HANS MARTIN, Freiherr VON, ed.
Festschrift für Harald Keller... (Card 4)

von Baron L. Döry.—Streitfragen der Restaurierung, von W. Brücker.—Verzeichnis der Schriften von Harald Keller, zusammengestellt von W. Wenzel und K.-A. Wirth (p. 403–412)

1. Keller, Harald, 1903- . 2. Keller, Harald, 1903- --Bibl. 3. Art--Essays and misc. I. Herget, Elisabeth, 1923- , joint ed. II. Herget, Elisabeth, 1923-

---

D-18
9784

Erich Schairer zum Gedächtnis. (1887–1956.) Aus seinen Schriften, Würdigungen, Erinnerungen. (Hrsg. von Agathe Kunze.) (Stuttgart, Verlag Turmhaus, 1967.)

191 p. with illus. front. 21 cm.

1. Schairer, Erich. I. Schairer, Erich. II. Kunze, Agathe, ed. III. Kunze, Agathe.
NN* 6.69 v/L OC, I, II, IIIb+ PC, 1, I, II SL (LC1, X1, Z1)

GFZE

Erixon, Sigurd Emanuel, 1888-
Östgötska kulturbilder; en översikt med historiska aspekter på sentida miljöer och monument. På uppdrag av Östgöta gille i Stockholm framlagd vid firandet av dess 150-årsjubileum den 28 november 1953. [Stockholm, 1953] 31 p. 48 plates (92 figs.) 30cm.

1. Östergötland, Sweden—Civilization. 2. Architecture, Domestic—Sweden—Östergötland. I. Östgöta gille, Stockholm.
NN**R 5.55 d/ OCs (OS)I PCs,1s,2s,I SLs
As,2s,I (LC1s,X1s,Z1)

AN
(Schurz)

Erkelenz, Anton, 1878– , and F. Mittelmann, editors.
Carl Schurz, der Deutsche und der Amerikaner; zu seinem 100. Geburtstage am 2. März 1929; herausgegeben im Auftrage der Vereinigung Carl Schurz...von Anton Erkelenz... [und] Dr. Fritz Mittelmann... Berlin: Sieben Stäbe-Verlags- und Druckereigesellschaft m.b.H., 1929. 268 p. front., illus. (incl. facsims., ports.) 8°.

"Übersetzungen und Schriftleitung: Dr. Gertrud Ferber."
Contents: Geleitworte von Dr. Stresemann, Mr. J. J. Davis und Dr. von

(Continued)

Mr. Moth

N. Y. P. L. July 10, 1929

Erkelenz, Anton, 1878– , and F. Mittelmann, editors: Carl Schurz... (Card 2)

Prittwitz-Gaffron. METTERNICH, GRAF. Carl Schurz und seine deutsche Heimat. BRAUBACH, M. Carl Schurz als Bonner Student. FERBER, G. Carl Schurz und Gottfried Kinkel nach der Märzrevolution. SCHUMACHER, H. Carl Schurz. REIN, G. A. Deutschland und die Vereinigten Staaten. FRIEDRICH, C. J. Geschichtliche und wirtschaftliche Beziehungen zwischen Deutschland und den Vereinigten Staaten. BURGESS, J. W. Carl Schurz und Abraham Lincoln. VILLARD, O. G. Carl Schurz als Journalist. Aus Carl Schurz' Leben und Reden. FRANCKE, K. Carl Schurz und das Germanische Museum der Harvard Universität. Nachrufe und Totenfeiern.

413359A. 1. Schurz, Carl, 1829–1906. 2. Mittelmann, Fritz, 1886– , jt. editor. 3. Ferber, Gertrud, translator. 4. Vereinigung Carl Schurz.
N. Y. P. L. July 10, 1929

Write on slip words underlined below and class mark —
ELT

Erlangen. Universität. Bibliothek.
Zeugnisse fränkischer Kultur; Erinnerungsgabe der Universitätsbibliothek Erlangen zur 27. Versammlung deutscher Bibliothekare, 1931. Nürnberg: L. Spindler [1931] 118 p. front., 7 pl. (incl. facsim.) 24cm. (Fränkische Halbjahresschrift. Heft [1])

Bibliographical footnotes.
CONTENTS.—Aus der Geschichte der Nürnberger Stadtbibliothek. Von Friedrich Bock.—Die Erlanger Universitätsbibliothek im Spiegel der Reise- und Briefliteratur der

(Continued)

N. Y. P. L. September 20, 1938

Erlangen. Universität. Bibliothek. Zeugnisse fränkischer Kultur ... (Card 2)

Aufklärungszeit. Von Ernst Deuerlein.—Margarete Karteuserin, eine Nürnberger Klosterschreiberin des 15. Jahrhunderts. Von Karl Fischer.—Der sog. Ferdinand Neuberger-Codex in der Erlanger Universitätsbibliothek. Von Theodore Hampe.—Casus synodales. Ein bisher unbekannter Bamberger Incunabeldruck. Von Max Müller.—Wackenroders Erlanger Semester. Ein Beitrag zur Geistesgeschichte der Frühromantik. Von Fritz Redenbacher.—Zwei Geschenkbände von Heinrich Rantzau in der Universitätsbibliothek Erlangen. Von Eleonore Schmidt-Herrling.—Ein Erlanger Bibliothekenkenner des 18. Jahrhunderts: Friedrich Karl Gottlob Hirsching. Von Heinrich Schreiber.—Ein fränkischer Gnadenpfennig aus der Voit von Salzburg'schen Münzsammlung in der Erlanger Universitätsbibliothek. Von Willy Schwabacher.—Die Auflö-

(Continued)

N. Y. P. L. September 20, 1938

Erlangen. Universität. Bibliothek. Zeugnisse fränkischer Kultur ... (Card 3)

sung der Heilsbronner Universitätsbibliothek. Von Eugen Stollreither.—Kulturgeschichtliches im Spiegel einer alten Erlanger Liedersammlung. Von Ferdinand Weckerle.—Die orientalischen Münzen der Sammlung Will in der Universitätsbibliothek Erlangen. Von Eduard von Zambaur.—Hans Sebald Beham und sein Werkanteil an der Holzschnittsammlung der Erlanger Universitätsbibliothek. Von Hildegard Zimmermann.—Veröffentlichungen der Universitätsbibliothek Erlangen.

1. Libraries—Germany—Franconia. I. Title. II. Ser.
N. Y. P. L. September 20, 1938

F-10
5356

ERLANGEN. Universität. Institut für Ur- und Frühgeschichte.
Festschrift für Lothar Zotz; Steinzeitfragen der alten und neuen Welt. Hrsg. von Gisela Freund. Bonn, L.Röhrscheid, 1960. viii, 610 p. illus., port., maps. 30cm.

Contributions in German, French, Spanish, Italian or English.

(Continued)

NN R 3. 61 m/ (OC)I, Ib OS(1b) PC, 1, 2, 3, I SL AH, 2, 3, I
(LC1, X1, Z1) [I]

2)

ERLANGEN. Universität. Institut für Ur- und Frühgeschichte. Festschrift für Lothar Zotz... (Card 2)

Includes bibliographies.

1. Stone age. 2. America--Archaeology. 3. Zotz, Lothar Friedrich, 1899- . I. Freund, Gisela, 1920- , ed.

Write on slip, name, year, vol., page of magazine and class mark — YEA

Ernest Jones zum fünfzigsten Geburtstag.

(Internationale Zeitschrift für Psychoanalyse. Wien, 1929. 4°. Bd.15, Heft 2-3, p.147-346. port.)

Bibliography p.347-361.

form 400a [ri-7-29 25m]

TB

ERNST HEISSMANN 65 Jahre. Wiesbaden, Verlag Arbeit und Alter [1963] 108 p. ports., diagrs. 22cm.

At head of cover title: Beratungs- GmbH für Altersversorgung
CONTENTS--Rechnen oder Schätzen? Von E. Jaumann. --Zum Grundsatz der versicherungs-mathematischen Gleichverteilung, von K.O. Witzsche. --Ein Blick in die 'Werkstatt des Wirtschaftsmathematikers, von D. Breuer. --Wir rechnen elektronisch mit der IBM 1440, von W. Sperling. --Wirtschaftliche Betrachtungsweise im Steuerrecht der betrieblichen Altersversorgung,

(Continued)

NN6.65 p/ OC PC, 1, 2, 3 SL E, 1, 2, 3 (LC1, X1, Z1)

2

ERNST HEISSMANN 65 Jahre. (Card 2)

von H. Gottschalk. --Vom Wert der Kondurrenzklauseln in Ruhegeldzusagen, von R. Jung--Betriebliche Ruhegeldverpflichtungen oder Unterstützungskassen? Von R. Sieber. --Mit den Augen einer Frau gesehen von, E. Heissmann--Die Noble Lowndes Organisation in Grossbritannien und in der ganzen Welt, von C.G. Bloomfield. --So macht es das Ausland, von C. D. Sharp. --Ausgewählte Schriften von Ernst Heissmann 1950-1963, p. 90-107.

1. Heissmann, Ernst. 2. Economics, Mathematical--Addresses, essays, lectures. 3. Pensions, Old age.

NFD
(Uehli)

Ernst Uehli; Leben und Gestaltung. Festschrift zum siebzigsten Geburtstag überreicht von Freunden und Verehrern. 4. Mai 1945. Bern, Francke ₍1945₎

147 p. illus., ports. 25 cm.

CONTENTS.—Prolog. Aus meinem Leben. Epilog. Aus dem Roman "Ein Sohn des Schicksals." Der Kristall der sieben Einsamkeiten. Wandlung des Künstlers. Aus meinem Unterricht an den Oberklassen der freien Waldorfschule in Stuttgart. Von Ernst Uehli.—Waldorfschule; Aufsätze von Schülern.—Aus der Münchner Zeit, von A. Steffen.—Ernst Uehli in München. Die Tauben. Von W. Ueberwasser.—Erinnerungen an die Münchner, Einführungskurse von Ernst Uehli, von O. Dubach.—Ernst Uehli in Stuttgart, von P. Baumann.—Kunstgeschichte in der Waldorfschule, von W. Greiner.—Freundschafts-

(Continued on next card)

A 50-6366

₍2₎

Ernst Uehli; Leben und Gestaltung ... ₍1945₎ (Card 2)

CONTENTS—Continued.

Erinnerungen an Ernst Uehli, von J. Hugentobler.—Dank an Ernst Uehli, von H. B.—Am Ufer, von E. von Bodman.—"Ein Sohn des Schicksals," von O. Fränkl-Lundborg.—Eine neue Gralsuche, von G. Gamper.—"Die Geburt der Individualität aus dem Mythos als künstlerisches Erlebnis Richard Wagners," von H. Reinhart.—Ernst Uehli und die Urgeschichte von Erde und Mensch, von G. Wachsmuth.—An Elisabeth. Für Hans Reinhart. Von E. Uehli.—An Hans Reinhart (Komposition) Komposition für Ernst Uehli. Von R. Blum.—Werke von Ernst Uehli. Aus der publizistischen Tätigkeit. (p. 145–146)

1. Uehli, Ernst.

A 50-6366

New York. Public Libr.
for Library of Congress ₍2₎

NFC

Die **Ernte**; Abhandlungen zur Literaturwissenschaft, Franz Muncker zu seinem 70. Geburtstage überreicht, und in Verbindung mit Eduard Berend... ₍und anderen₎ hrsg. von Fritz Strich und Hans Heinrich Borcherdt. Halle an der Saale, M. Niemeyer, 1926. v, 413 p. plates. 24cm.

602065B. 1. German literature—Hist. and crit. 2. Stage—Hist. 3. Muncker, Franz, 1855— . I. Strich, Fritz, 1882— , ed. II. Borcherdt, Hans Heinrich, 1887— , ed.
N. Y. P. L. January 29, 1952

AD-10
987

ERSTE ÖSTERREICHISCHE MECHANISCHE KOKOSTEPPICH- UND MATTENFABRIK KARL EYBL, Krems, Austria.

Festreden anlässlich der 90- Jahrfeier der Ersten österr. mechanischen Kokosteppich- und Mattenfabrik Karl Eybl am 21. XI. 1958 im Parkhotel Krems a.d. Donau. [Krems/Donau, 1958] 32 p. illus., port. 21cm. (Continued)

NN 12.64 p/ OS (1b) PC SL E (LC1, X1, Z1)

ERSTE ÖSTERREICHISCHE MECHANISCHE KOKOSTEPPICH- UND MATTENFABRIK KARL EYBL, Krems, Austria. Festreden anlässlich der 90- Jahrfeier der Ersten österr. (Card 2)

Cover title: 90 Jahre [i.e. Neunzig] Erste österr. mechanische Kokosteppich-und Mattenfabrik Karl Eybl, Krems-Stein.

AN
(Serrano y Sanz,M.)

El **erudito español, d. Manuel Serrano y Sanz. (Notas bio-bibliográficas, apuntes sobre su personalidad, impresiones, recuerdos...) como contribución al homenaje que le rinde la ciudad de Sigüenza el 28 de julio de 1935, consagran este libro a la memoria del sabio alcarreño, sus admiradores F. Layna Serrano, J. M.ª Benavente, E. Cotarelo ₍y otros₎ ... 1. ed.—1.500 ejemplares. Madrid, Nuevas gráficas, 1935.**

161 p., 1 l. VIII pl. (incl. ports., facsims.) 25cm.

CONTENTS.—El pueblo natal, la familia, la vida y la obra de don Manuel Serrano Sanz (notas para una biografía) por F. Layna Serrano.—Publicaciones de don Manuel Serrano Sanz.—Estudio crítico

(Continued on next card)

36-13202

₍2₎

El **erudito** español, d. Manuel Serrano y Sanz ... 1935. (Card 2)

CONTENTS—Continued.

sobre una obra de Serrano Sanz, por F. Navarro Ledesma.—Sugestiones; de estudiante a catedrático, por J. M. Benavente.—Don Manuel Serrano Sanz, por E. Cotarelo.—Los hombres raros, por L. Cordavias.—En recuerdo de d. Manuel Serrano Sanz, por E. de Ibarra Rodríguez.—Don Manuel Serrano Sanz; su formación e ingreso en el Cuerpo de archiveros-bibliotecarios, por F. Gil Ayuso.—Del maestro al hombre, por J. M. Ramos Loscertales.—Recuerdos y evocaciones, por M. Lasso de la Vega, marqués del Saltillo.—Cómo conocí al viejo maestro, por J. de Entrambasaguas.—D. Manuel Serrano Sanz en Zaragoza, por M. Abizanda y

(Continued on next card)

36-13202

₍2₎

El **erudito** español, d. Manuel Serrano y Sanz ... 1935. (Card 3)

CONTENTS—Continued.

Broto.—D. Manuel Serrano en el Departamento de manuscritos en la Biblioteca nacional, por J. Paz.—D. Manuel Serrano Sanz en Sigüenza, por H. Yaben.—Así era d. Manuel ..., por P. Galindo Romeo.—Una gran figura alcarreña, por R. Catalina García.—A la memoria del maestro, por A. Millares Carlo.—El pleito sobre el autor de "La Celestina", por M. Artigas.—Curiosidad insaciable y fecunda, por Carlos Pereyra.—Un maestro del vivir, por J. F. Yela.—Post-scriptum, por A. R. Rodrígues Moñino.

1. Serrano y Sanz, Manuel, 1866–1932. I. Layna Serrano, Francisco.

36-13202

Library of Congress DP63.7.S43E7

——— Copy 2. ₍2₎ 928.6

F-10
1760

ERZIEHUNG zur Menschlichkeit; die Bildung im Umbruch der Zeit. Festschrift für Eduard Spranger zum 75. Geburtstag 27. Juni 1957 [Hrsg. von H. Walter Bähr et al] Tübingen, M. Niemeyer, 1957. viii, 638 p. 26cm.

1. Education--Addresses, essays, lectures. 2. Spranger, Eduard, 1882- . 3. Civilization--Addresses, essays, lectures. I. Bähr, Hans Walter, ed.
NN 2, 58 e/b OC, I PC, 1, 2, 3, I SL (LC1, X1, Z1, C1, Y1) [I]

D-18
7448
ERZIEHUNG in einer ökonomisch-technischen Welt. Festschrift für Friedrich Schlieper zum 70. Geburtstag. Hrsg. von Johannes Baumgardt. (Freiburg i. Br.) Lambertus-Verlag [1967] 193 p. port. 23cm.

Bibliographical footnotes.

CONTENTS.—Geleitwort, von R. Seyffert.—Die Probleme der Ausbildung für wirtschaftliche Berufe, von K. Abraham.—Die Bedeutung des Ideellen und Pragmatischen in Wirtschaft und Erziehung für die Wirtschaftserziehung, von J. Baumgardt.—Ansätze einer päda-

(Continued)

NN* 3.69 v/a OC, I, II, IIIb* PC, 1, 2, I, II SL E, 1, 2, I, II (LC1, X1, Z1)

ERZIEHUNG in einer ökonomisch-technischen Welt. (Card 2)

gogischen Theorie der Wirtschaftsberufe als Grundlage empirischer wirtschaftspädagogischer Forschung, von W. Buth.—Zur logischen Struktur einer empirischen Sozialpädagogik, von H. Heid.—Berufsausbildung und Erziehung durch Kunst, von K. Herberts.—Der Betriebspädagoge, von H. Krasensky-- Dienst am Mitarbeiter, von W. Löbner.—Anmerkungen zur Bildungsarbeit des Wirtschaftslehrers, von P. Luchtenberg.—Bemerkungen zur Weiterentwicklung der Terminologie Friedrich Schliepers, von J. Peege.—Stellung und Aufgabe des Lehrers in unserer Zeit, von H. Röhrs.—Erziehung zum Handeln, von M. Schmiel.

(Continued)

ERZIEHUNG in einer ökonomisch-technischen Welt. (Card 3)

1. Economics--Study and teaching. 2. Education--Psychology. I. Schlieper, Friedrich, 1897- . II. Baumgardt, Johannes, 1930- ed. III. Baumgardt, Johannes, 1930- .

D-12
9994
ERZIEHUNG und Politik; Minna Specht zu ihrem 80. Geburtstag. [Frankfurt a. M.] Verlag Öffentliches Leben [c1960] 413 p. port. 21cm.

Dedication signed: Hellmut Becker, Willi Eichler [und] Gustav Heckmann.

"Aus Reden und Schriften von Minna Specht," p. 369-400.

1. Education--Germany, 20th cent. 2. Education--Social and economic aspects--Germany. 3. Specht, Minna, 1879- . I. Becker, Hellmut, 1913- , ed. II. Becker, Hellmut, 1913- .

NN R 4.61 g/B OC, I, IIb+ PC, 1, 2, 3, I SL E, 2, 3, I (LC1, X1, Z1)

Copy only words underlined
& Classmark-- RNA

ESCH, ARNO.
Chaucer und seine Zeit; Symposion für Walter F. Schirmer. Tübingen, M. Niemeyer, 1968. 450 p. illus., port. 24cm. (Anglia. Zeitschrift für englische Philologie. Buchreihe. Bd. 14)

1. Chaucer, Geoffrey. 1888- . I. Series. 2. Schirmer, Walter Franz,

NN R 9.69 w/L OC (OS)I PC, 1, 2, I (LC1, X1, Z1)

E-11
8893
ESCHENBURG, THEODOR, ed.
Festgabe für Carlo Schmid zum 65. Geburtstag, dargebracht von Freunden, Schülern und Kollegen; hrsg. von Theodor Eschenburg, Theodor Heuss und Georg-August Zinn unter Mitwirkung von Wilhelm Hennis. Tübingen, J.C.B. Mohr (P. Siebeck), 1962. 311 p. port. 24cm.

Bibliographical footnotes.

(Continued)

NN R 2.64 e/B OC, I, II, III PC, 1, 2, I, II, III SL E, 1, 2, I, II, III (LC1, X1, Z1)

ESCHENBURG, THEODOR, ed. Festgabe für Carlo Schmid zum 65. Geburtstag... (Card 2)

CONTENTS.--Brief an Carlo Schmid zum 3. Dezember 1961, von T. Heuss.--Rechtsprechende Gewalt und Strafkompetenz, von A. Arndt.--"Can we be equal and excellent too?" Von H. Becker.--Indiens Eintritt in die moderne Welt, von M. Gräfin Dönhoff.--Aus den Anfängen des Landes Württemberg-Hohenzollern, von T. Eschenberg.--"Wider die Ächtung der Autorität," von E. Gerstenmaier.--Motive des Bürgersinns, von W. Hennis. --Le combat de dragon, de J. Hersch.--Zur Änderung des Wahlgesetzes,

(Continued)

ESCHENBURG, THEODOR, ed. Festgabe für Carlo Schmid zum 65. Geburtstag... (Card 3)

von R. Katz.--Zur Soziologie des ärztlichen Berufes, von A. Mitscherlich. --Zum Problem der Bundestreue im Bundesstaat, von H.G. Rupp.--Lebendige Demokratie. Der Basler Arbeitsrappen von 1936, von E. Salin.--Mass und Gerechtigkeit. Zu Albert Camus' Rechts- und Staatsauffassung, von P. Schneider.--The rights of man, by G. Schwarzenberger.--Zu den Grundlagen des Begriffs der politischen Partei, von W. Seuffert.--Die Verkündung und das Inkrafttreten der Gesetze in Frankreich 1789 und danach, von H. Wehrhahn.-- Zum richterlichen Charisma in einer ethisierten Rechtsordnung, von K. Zweigert.

(Continued)

ESCHENBURG, THEODOR, ed. Festgabe für Carlo Schmid zum 65. Geburtstag... (Card 4)

1. Germany--Govt.--Addresses, essays, lectures. 2. Schmid, Karl, 1896- . I. Heuss, Theodor, pres. Germany (Federal republic), 1884, joint ed. II. Zinn, Georg August, joint ed. III. Title.

---

*HZ
Escher, Hermann, 1857–
Ausgewählte Bibliothekswissenschaftliche Aufsätze von Dr. Hermann Escher, Direktor der Zentralbibliothek Zürich i.R. Zum 80. Geburtstage des Verfassers herausgegeben von der Zentralbibliothek Zürich und der Vereinigung schweizerischer Bibliothekare. Zürich: H. Rohr, 1937. 229 p. mounted port. 24cm.

Cover-title: Festgabe Hermann Escher zum 80. Geburtstage dargebracht.

CONTENTS.—Allgemeines und Bibliotheksverwaltung: Schweizerisches Bibliothekswesen (1929). Die Stellung der schweizerischen Bibliotheken zur Frage einer ein-

(Continued)

N. Y. P. L. January 26, 1939

Escher, Hermann, 1857– . Ausgewählte Bibliothekswissenschaftliche Aufsätze . . . (Card 2)

heitlichen Regelung der Katalogisierung (1912). Ein schweizerisches Gesamtzuwachsverzeichnis (1926). Der Schlagwortkatalog der Stadtbibliothek Zürich (1890–1897). Moderne Bibliotheksbestrebungen und Bibliotheksaufgaben mit besonderer Rücksicht auf die geplante zürcherische Zentralbibliothek (1912). Die Errichtung der Zentralbibliothek in Zürich (1915). Was es in einer Bibliothek zu tun gibt (Zentralbibliothek Zürich 1928). Die Schweizerische Landesbibliothek (1911). Die Schweizerische Volksbibliothek (1922). Das neue Pestalozzihaus in Zürich (1933). —Bibliotheksgeschichte: Die Bibliotheca universalis Konrad Gessners (1934). Konrad Gessner über Aufstellung und Katalogisierung von Bibliotheken (1937). Der

(Continued)

N. Y. P. L. January 26, 1939

Escher, Hermann, 1857– . Ausgewählte Bibliothekswissenschaftliche Aufsätze . . . (Card 3)

Bibliothecarius quadripartitus des Joh. Heinrich Hottinger (1934). Die schweizerischen Bibliotheken in der Zeit der Helvetik (1936). Ein amtlicher Bericht über die schweizerischen Bibliotheken aus der Zeit der Helvetik (1935).

928301A. 1. Libraries—Switzerland. I. Vereinigung schweizerischer Bibliothekare. II. Zürich (City). Zentralbibliothek. III. Title: Festgabe Hermann Escher zum 80. Geburtstage dargebracht.

N. Y. P. L. January 26, 1939

D-20
654

ESSAYS in American and English literature presented to Bruce Robert McElderry, Jr. Edited by Max F. Schulz, with William D. Templeman and Charles R. Metzger. Athens, O., Ohio university press [c1967] xiv, 334 p. port. 22cm.

Includes bibliographical references.

CONTENTS.--American literature: Melville's "geniality," by M.M. Sealts, Jr.--Mark Twain's search for identity, by J.C. Gerber.--

(Continued)

NNR 11.70 d/⁄ OC, I, II, III, IV PC, 1, 2, I, II, III, IV SL (LC1, X1, Z1) [I]

3

ESSAYS in American and English literature... (Card 2)

Walt Whitman and civil rights, by O. Cargill.--Henry Adams and the gossip mills, by E. Samuels.--Hamlin Garland's A son of the middle border, by D. Pizer.--Popular taste in 1899: Booth Tarkington's first novel, by J.L. Woodress, Jr.--Europe as catalyst for Thomas Wolfe, by C.H. Holman.--English literature: Current and recurrent fallacies in Chaucer criticism, by M. Thompson.--The morality of farce: The taming of the shrew, by I. Ribner.--The action of Samson Agonistes, by F. Fogle.--Milton's exalted man, by M.W. Bundy.--Rhetorical

(Continued)

ESSAYS in American and English literature... (Card 2)

patterns in Restoration prologues and epilogues, by E.L. Avery.--Image vs. abstraction: Coleridge vs. Pope and the tests of poetry, by H.R. Warfel.--The key poem of the Victorian age, by L. Stevenson.--Browning's debt to Meredith in James Lee's wife, by F.E. Faverty.--Two fires at Max Gate, by C.J. Weber.--Selected list of the scholarly publications of Bruce Robert McElderry, Jr. (p. [329]-334)

1. American literature--Addresses, essays, lectures. 2. English literature--Addresses, essays, lectures. I. McElderry, Bruce R. II. Schulz, Max F., ed. III. Templeman, William Darby, 1903- , ed. IV. Metzger, Charles Reid, 1921- , ed.

IAG

ESSAYS in American historiography; papers presented in honor of Allan Nevins. Edited by Donald Sheehan & Harold C. Syrett. New York, Columbia university press, 1960. x, 320 p. port. 25cm.

Includes bibliographies.

CONTENTS.--Allan Nevins, an appreciation, by J.A. Krout.--Scientific history in America: eclipse of idea, by E.N. Saveth.--Thoughts

(Continued)

NN R 12.60 s/A OC, I, II PC, 1, 2, I, II AH, 1, 2, I, II (LC1, X1, Z1) SL [I]

3

ESSAYS in American historiography... (Card 2)

on the Confederacy, by R.C. Black.--Radical Reconstruction, by D. Sheehan--The New South, by J.E. Cooke.--American historians and national politics from the Civil war to the First World war, by J.A. Rawley.--Reflections on urban history and urban reform, 1865-1915, by M.D. Hirsch.--The idea of the robber barons in American history, by H. Bridges.--Some aspects of European migration to the United States, by C.C. Qualey.--The evolution controversy, by J.A. Boromé.--Pragmatism in America, by S. Ratner.--Populism: its significance in American history, by E. Walters.--Imperialism and racism, by J.P. Shenton.--The muckrakers:

(Continued)

ESSAYS in American historiography... (Card 3)

in flower and in failure, by L. Filler.--A cycle of revisionism between two wars, by H.W. Baehr.--An interpretation of Franklin D. Roosevelt, by B. Bellush.

1. United States--Hist.--Historiography. 2. Nevins, Allan, 1890- . I. Syrett, Harold Coffin, 1913- , ed. II. Sheehan, Donald Henry, 1917- , ed.

HBC

Essays in anthropology presented to A. L. Kroeber in celebration of his sixtieth birthday, June 11, 1936. Berkeley, Calif., University of California press, 1936.

xxiii, 433 p. front. (port.) illus., 4 pl. on 2 l. fold. map. $26\frac{1}{2}^{cm}$.

Preface signed: Robert H. Lowie, editor.
Bibliography at end of some of the essays.

CONTENTS.—Alfred L. Kroeber: personal reminiscences and professional appreciation, by C. L. Alsberg and R. H. Lowie.—The army worm: a food of the Pomo Indians, by S. A. Barrett.—Problems in the study of Mixe marriage customs, by Ralph Beals.—The relations between physical and social anthropology, by Franz Boas.—Family, clan, and phratry

(Continued on next card)

36-14302

[5]

Essays in anthropology presented to A. L. Kroeber in celebration of his sixtieth birthday ... 1936. (Card 2)

CONTENTS—Continued.

in central Sumatra, by F. C. Cole.—Scapulimancy, by J. M. Cooper.—Papago nicknames, by Juan Dolores.—The wealth concept as an integrative factor in Tolowa-Tututni culture, by Cora Du Bois.—Estudillo among the Yokuts: 1819, by A. H. Gayton.—Californian balanophagy, by E. W. Gifford.—Loose ends of theory on the individual, pattern, and involution in primitive society, by A. A. Goldenweiser.—A preliminary report on the zöological knowledge of the Makah, by Erna Gunther.—Dreaming in relation to spirit kindred and sickness in Hawaii, by E. S. C. Handy.—Chemehuevi shamanism, by Isabel T. Kelly.—Speculations on new world prehistory, by A. V. Kidder.—The distribution and function of money in early societies, by E. M. Loeb.—Lewis H. Morgan in historical perspective, by R. H. Lowie.—The classification

(Continued on next card)

36-14302

[5]

Essays in anthropology presented to A. L. Kroeber in celebration of his sixtieth birthday ... 1936. (Card 3)

CONTENTS—Continued.

of the Sonoran languages (with an appendix by B. L. Whorf) by J. A. Mason.—Notes on the Santa Barbara culture, by N. C. Nelson.—Some trading customs of the Chilkat Tlingit, by R. L. Olson.—Wide-loom fabrics of the early Nazca period, by Lila M. O'Neale.—The house-clan complex of the Pueblos, by Elsie Clews Parsons.—Ojibwa and Ottawa puberty dreams, by Paul Radin.—Attitudes toward avoidance: a suggestion, by Gladys A. Reichard.—Hupa tattooing, by Edward Sapir.—American agricultural origins: a consideration of nature and culture, by Carl Sauer.—Donner und regenbogen beim höchsten wesen Yuki, by W. Schmidt.—The man petroglyph near Prince Rupert; or, The man who fell from heaven, by H. I. Smith.—Inland Eskimo bands of Labrador, by F. G. Speck.—The economic and social basis of primitive bands,

(Continued on next card)

36-14302

[5]

Essays in anthropology presented to A. L. Kroeber in celebration of his sixtieth birthday ... 1936. (Card 4)

CONTENTS—Continued.

by J. H. Steward.—Florida cultural affiliations in relation to adjacent areas, by M. W. Stirling.—Anthropological theory and archaeological fact, by W. D. Strong.—Early history of the eastern Siouan tribes, by J. R. Swanton.—Sozialpsychische abläufe im völkerleben, by R. C. Thurnwald.—Productive paradigms in Shawnee, by C. F. Voegelin.—The social configuration of magical behavior: a study of the nature of magic, by W. L. Warner.—The great world theater, by T. T. Waterman.—Bibliography of Alfred L. Kroeber (p. 423–432)

1. Anthropology — Addresses, essays, lectures. 2. Indians of North America. 3. Kroeber, Alfred Louis, 1876– I. Lowie, Robert Harry, 1883– ed.

36-14302

Library of Congress GN4.E7

~~Copy 2.~~

Copyright A 90097 [5] 572.04

PPB

ESSAYS in biochemistry. Samuel Graff, editor. New York, Wiley [1956] x, 345 p. illus., port., diagrs., tables. 24cm.

"Written in honor of Hans Thacher Clarke, on the occasion of his retirement as professor and chairman of the Department of biochemistry, College of physicians and surgeons, Columbia university."

Includes bibliographies.

1. Biochemistry—Addresses, essays, lectures. 2. Clarke, Hans Thacher, 1887- . I. Graff, Samuel, 1905- , ed. t. 1956.

NN *R X 5. 56 s/b OC, I PC, 1, 2, I SL ST, lt, 2, I (LC1, X1, Z1)

Write on slip words underlined and class mark- NAA

... Essays contributed in honor of President William Allan Neilson. Editors: Caroline B. Bourland, Hélène Cattanès, Paul G. Graham, Howard R. Patch, Margaret Rooke. Northampton, Mass., Smith college [1939]

vii, 269 p. pl., facsims. 23cm. (Smith college studies in modern languages. vol. XXI, no. 1-4, October, 1939 to July, 1940)

Bibliographical foot-notes.

CONTENTS.—The writer as partisan, by Newton Arvin.—Of men and angels, by Caroline B. Bourland.—Auguste Comte y "Marianela", by Joaquín Casalduero.—Remarques sur quelques emplois de l'imparfait en français moderne, by Hélène Cattanès.—Les derniers épigones de Jacques Copeau: la Compagnie des quinze et le Théâtre des quatre saisons, by Louise Delpit.—The Lord Chamberlain's company as portrayed in "Every man out of his humor", by S. A. Eliot, jr.—Hebbel's study of "King Lear", by P. G. Graham.—La question de la langue française dans les querelles

(Continued on next card)

39-16888

[5] Festschrift.

... Essays contributed in honor of President William Allan Neilson ... [1939] (Card 2)

CONTENTS—Continued.

musicales au XVIIIème siècle, by René Guiet.—"Hernani, ou L'honneur castillan", by Vincent Guilloton.—"Sin honra no hay valentía", by Ruth L. Kennedy.—Two new Icelandic manuscripts, by P. R. Lieder.—Thomas Hardy and Thomas Mann, by Helen Muchnic.—The first "electrical" flying machine, by Nora M. Mohler, Marjorie H. Nicolson.—Three medieval ideas, by H. R. Patch.—Parco di Velo, a hundred years of literature in an Italian garden, by Margaret L. Rooke.—The "baroque" epoch in German literature, by Martin Sommerfeld.—A case of secret language: the Benzorian language, by Marthe Sturm.—Paronomasia in John Heywood's plays, by Robert Withington.—Introduction to Castiglione and his "Courtier", by Ruth E. Young.—Algo sobre el "Libro del consejo e los consejeros" y sus fuentes, by Miguel Zapata y Torres.

1. Philology, Modern—Collections. 2. Neilson, William Allan, 1869– I. Bourland, Caroline Brown, 1871– ed.

39-16888

Library of Congress PB13.S6 vol. 21, no. 1/4

[5] (808) 404

E-13
3684

ESSAYS in divinity; Jerald C. Brauer, general editor. [Chicago, University of Chicago press, 1968] 3 v. 24cm.

Vol. 2-4.

Half title; each volume has special t.p.

Includes bibliographies.

Series of essays sponsored by the University of Chicago Divinity school to commemorate the hundreth anniversary of its founding.

(Continued)

NN R 12. 68 1/l OC, I PC, 1, 2, 3, 4, I SL (LC1, X1, Z1)

2

ESSAYS in divinity... (Card 2)

CONTENTS.--v. 2. The impact of the church upon its culture, edited by J.C. Brauer.--v.3. The dialogue between theology and psychology, edited by P. Homans.--v.4. Adversity and grace, edited by N.A. Scott, jr.

1. Religion in literature, American. 2. Philosophy and religion. 3. Christianity--Essays and misc. 4. Chicago university. Divinity school. I. Brauer, Jerald C., ed.

NCOD

Essays in dramatic literature; the Parrott presentation volume, by pupils of Professor Thomas Marc Parrott of Princeton university, published in his honor; edited by Hardin Craig ... Princeton, Princeton university press, 1935.

4 p. l., 470 p. front. (port.) 23½cm.

CONTENTS.—Thomas Marc Parrott, by J. D. Spaeth.—Published writings of Professor Parrott, by Harry Clemons (p. [13]–24)—Ethics in the Jacobean drama: the case of Chapman, by Hardin Craig.—Early sentimental comedy, by DeW. C. Croissant.—Political theory in the plays of George Chapman, by C. W. Kennedy.—For Shakespeare's Hamlet, by Hubertis Cummings.—The greatest of Elizabethan melodramas, by Lacy Lockert.—Shakespeare's "Troilus and Cressida", yet deeper in its tradition, by W. B. D. Henderson.—A note upon William Shakespeare's use of Pliny, by T. W. Baldwin.—The drama in a frontier theater, by G. R. Stewart, jr.—The scenes as Shakespeare saw them, by T. B. Hunt.—

(Continued on next card)

35-17523

[5]

Essays in dramatic literature ... 1935. (Card 2)

CONTENTS—Continued.

Shakespeare's portrayal of Shylock, by H. B. Walley.—Byron's "Werner" re-estimated: a neglected chapter in nineteenth century stage history, by T. H. V. Motter.—Sir Giles Mompesson and Sir Giles Overreach, by R. H. Ball.—A deep and sad passion, by D. A. Stauffer.—Milton and Euripides, by P. W. Timberlake.—The shipwreck, by William Huse.—Henry Nevil Payne, dramatist and Jacobite conspirator, by Willard Thorp.—Dryden's "tagged" version of "Paradise lost", by P. S. Havens.—The influence of Shakespeare on Smollett, by G. M. Kahrl.—The verse lining of the first quarto of "King Lear", by Edward Hubler.—Jane Bell: printer at the East end of Christ-church, by Rudolf Kirk.—The philosophy of Hamlet, by J. E. Baker.

1. English drama—Hist. & crit. 2. Shakespeare, William—Criticism and interpretation. 3. Parrott, Thomas Marc, 1866– I. Craig, Hardin, 1875– ed. II. Title: The Parrott presentation volume.

35-17523

Library of Congress PR627.E7

~~Copy 2.~~

Copyright A 85509 [5] 822.04

NCB

Essays on the eighteenth century, presented to David Nichol Smith in honour of his seventieth birthday. Oxford, The Clarendon press, 1945.

vi p., 1 l., 288 p. front. (port.) 22½cm.

Bibliographical foot-notes.

CONTENTS.—Addison, by C. S. Lewis.—The conciseness of Swift, by Herbert Davis.—Deane Swift, Hawkesworth, and The journal to Stella, by Harold Williams.—Pope at work, by George Sherburn.—The inspiration of Pope's poetry, by John Butt.—'Where once stood their plain homely dwelling,' by Collins Baker.—Some aspects of eighteenth-century prose, by James Sutherland.—Note on the composition of Gray's Elegy, by H. W. Garrod.—John Langhorne, by Hugh Macdonald.—Notes on some lesser poets of the eighteenth century, by W. L. Renwick.—The formal parts of Johnson's letters, by R. W. Chapman.—Mrs. Piozzi's letters, by

(Continued on next card)

[7] A 47-3607

Essays on the eighteenth century ... 1945. (Card 2)

CONTENTS—Continued.

J. L. Clifford.—The power of memory in Boswell and Scott, by F. A. Pottle.—Robert Burns, by R. Dewar.—Fanny Burney's novels, by Lord David Cecil.—Elegant extracts, by Edmund Blunden.—'The old Cumberland beggar' and the Wordsworthian unities, by H. V. D. Dyson.—Matthew Arnold and eighteenth-century poetry, by Geoffrey Tillotson.—A list of the writings of David Nichol Smith, 1896–1945, compiled by F. P. Wilson (p. 274–283)

1. Smith, David Nichol, 1875– 2. English literature—18th cent.—Hist. & crit.

A 47-3607

Harvard univ. Library
for Library of Congress [4]

QEL

Essays in geobotany in honor of William Albert Setchell, edited by T. H. Goodspeed. Berkeley, Calif., University of California press, 1936.

xxv, 319 p. incl. front. (port.) illus., diagrs. 22½cm.

Bibliography at end of most of the essays.

CONTENTS.—William Albert Setchell: a biographical sketch, by T. H. Goodspeed.—The rate of plant migration, by O. W. Arrhenius.—The origin of *Crepis* and related genera, with particular reference to distribution and chromosome relationships, by E. B. Babcock.—The succession and distribution of cenozoic floras around the northern Pacific basin, by R. W. Chaney.—The origin of the desert climax and climate,

(Continued on next card)

36-13844

[3]

Essays in geobotany in honor of William Albert Setchell ... 1936. (Card 2)

CONTENTS—Continued.

by F. E. Clements.—The strand and dune flora of the Pacific coast of North America: a geographic study, by W. S. Cooper.—The genetic phytogeography of the southwestern Pacific area, with particular reference to Australia, by Ludwig Diels.—The rôle of the terrestrial alga in nature, by F. E. Fritsch.—The plant as a metabolic unit in the soil-plant system, by D. R. Hoagland.—Malaysian phytogeography in relation to the Polynesian flora, by E. D. Merrill.—Plant communities of the world, by Eduard Rübel.—Antarctic plants in Polynesia, by Carl Skottsberg.—The published writings of William Albert Setchell (p. 313–319)

1. Botany—Geographical distribution. 2. Setchell, William Albert, 1864– I. Goodspeed, Thomas Harper, 1887– ed.

36-13844

Library of Congress QK101.E8
——— Copy 2.
Copyright A 95329 [3] 581.9

---

*C-4 p.v.376

Essays on German language and literature in honor of Theodore B. Hewitt; ed. by J. Alan Pfeffer. [Buffalo] University of Buffalo [1952] 87 p. 24cm. (Buffalo university. Studies. v. 20, no. 1 (May, 1952))

Bibliography [of works by T. B. Hewitt] p. 7-8.
Contents.—Universale Repraesantation bei Thomas Mann, von F. Kaufman.—The pronoun object in classical German, by C. C. D. Vail.—A. Goethean hymn? By J. A. Pfeffer.- Goethe's relation to

(Continued)

NN** X 9.53 OC, I PC, 1, 2, 3, I SL (LC1, ZX, X1)

Essays on German language and literature in honor of Theodore B. Hewitt... (Card 2)

music, by A. M. Sauerlander.—Clemens Brentano und Giovanni Battista, von M. Wagner.—A bibliography of Lessingiana Americana, by W. T. Daetsch.

1. Hewitt, Theodore Brown, 1881- . 2. German language—Word order. 3. German literature—Hist. and crit. I. Pfeffer, Jay Alan, 1907- , ed.

D-17
9693

ESSAYS in history and political theory in honor of Charles Howard McIlwain. New York, Russell & Russell [1967, c1964] x, 371 p. 22cm.

Preface signed: Carl Wittke.
Reprint of the edition published by Harvard university press, 1936.
Bibliographical footnotes.
CONTENTS.--God and the secular power, by S. Baldwin.--"Non obstante", a study of the dispensing power of English kings, by P. Birdsall.--

(Continued)

NN R 2.68 r/A OCs, Is PCs, 1, 2, 3s, Is SL Es, 2, 3s, Is (LC1s, [i], X1s, Z1) 3

ESSAYS in history and political theory in honor of Charles Howard McIlwain. (Card 2)

The attitude of the English clergy in the thirteenth and fourteenth centuries towards the obligation of attendance on convocations and parliaments, by D. B. Weske.--The struggle for the autonomy of the Church of England, by E. P. Chase.--Henry Parker and autonomy of the Church of England, by E. P. Chase.--Henry Parker and the theory of parliamentary sovereignty, by M. A. Judson.--The idea of majesty in Roman political thought, by F. S. Lear.--Attack of the common lawyers on the oath ex officio as administered

(Continued)

ESSAYS in history and political theory in honor of Charles Howard McIlwain. (Card 3)

in the ecclesiastical courts in England, by M. H. Maguire.--The concept of public opinion in political theory, by P. A. Palmer.--The trial of treason in Tudor England, by S. Rezneck.--The political and constitutional theory of Sir John Fortescue, by M. A. Shepard.--Parliamentary privilege in the empire, by C. Wittke.--The early history of written constitutions in America, by B. F. Wright, jr.

1. Great Britain--Hist.--Addresses, essays, lectures. 2. Political science--Addresses, essays, lectures. 3. McIlwain, Charles Howard, 1871- . I. Wittke, Carl Frederick, 1892- , ed.
i. subs. for 1936.

D-20
1605

ESSAYS in history: presented to Reginald Lane Poole. Edited by H. W. C. Davis. Oxford, Clarendon press [1927]; Freeport, N.Y., Books for libraries press [1967] xiv, 483 p. port., facsim. 22cm. (Essay index reprint series)

"A list of the published works of Reginald Lane Poole," p. [466]-477.
Bibliographical footnotes.

(Continued)

NN R 3.71 m/z OC, I, II PC, 1, 2, I, II SL (LC1, X1, Z1) 2

ESSAYS in history: presented to Reginald Lane Poole. (Card 2)

1. Poole, Reginald Lane, 1857-1939--Bibl. 2. Middle Ages--Hist. I. Poole, Reginald Lane, 1857-1939. II. Davis, Henry William Carless, 1874-1928, ed.

JFD
71-41

Essays in honor of Carl G. Hempel. A tribute on the occasion of his sixty-fifth birthday. Essays by Donald Davidson, Frederic B. Fitch, Adolf Grünbaum [and others] Edited by Nicholas Rescher on behalf of the editorial committee. Dordrecht, D. Reidel [1970]
viii, 280 p. port. 23 cm. (Synthese library)
Includes bibliographical references.

(Continued)

NN*R 2.71 d/&OC, I, II, III PC, 1, I, II, III SL (LC1, X1, Z1)

Essays in honor of Carl G. Hempel. (Card 2)

CONTENTS.—Reminiscences of Peter, by P. Oppenheim.—Natural kinds, by W. V. Quine.—Inductive independence and the paradoxes of confirmation, by J. Hintikka.—Partial entailment as a basis for inductive logic, by W. C. Salmon.—Are there non-deductive logics?, by W. Sellers.—Statistical explanation vs. statistical inference, by R. C. Jeffre.—Newcomb's problem and two principles of choice, by R. Nozick.—The meaning of time, by A. Grünbaum.—Lawfulness as mind-dependent, by N. Rescher.—Events and their descriptions: some considerations, by J. Kim.—The individuation of events, by D. Davidson.—On properties, by H. Putnam.—A method for avoiding the Curry paradox, by F. B. Fitch.—Publications (1934-1969) by Carl G. Hempel (p. [266]-270)

(Continued)

ESSAYS in honor of Carl G. Hempel. (Card 3)

1. Philosophy--Addresses, essays, lectures. I. Hempel, Carl Gustav, 1905- II. Davidson, Donald, 1917- III. Rescher, Nicholas, ed.

CBA

ESSAYS in honor of Conyers Read, ed. by Norton Downs... [Chicago] Univ. of Chicago press [1953] xxii, 304 p. port. 24cm.

Bibliographies included.

CONTENTS.—Bibliography of Conyers Read (p. xvii-xxii)—Some relationships between British inductive logic and French impressionist painting, by G. Haines IV.—The "official" scholar: a survey of certain research in American foreign policy, by R. Humphrey.—John Wesley and the American Revolution, by W. M. Wallace.—The Irish Republic, by S. M. Lough.—Notes on Scottish witchcraft cases, 1590-91,

(Continued)

NN*R 3.53 OC, I, Ib PC, 1, 2, I SL (LC1, Z1, X1) [I]

ESSAYS in honor of Conyers Read... (Card 2)

by H. Stafford.—Los Angeles diary, by E. C. Nef.—The role of the House of Commons in British foreign policy during the 1937-38 session, by M. L. Kenney.—Some aspects of London mercantile activity during the reign of Queen Elizabeth, by J. R. Jones.—The genesis of industrialism and of modern science (1560-1640) by J. U. Nef.

1. Great Britain—Hist.—Addresses, essays, lectures. 2. Read, Conyers, 1881- I. Downs, Norton, ed.

MA

ESSAYS in honor of Georg Swarzenski. Chicago, H. Regnery co. in cooperation with Verlag Gebr. Mann, 1951. illus. (part mounted), mounted ports. 26cm.

Bibliography of Georg Swarzenski's publications," p. 261-267.

1. Swarzenski, Georg, 1876- . 2. Art—Essays and misc.

NN R 11.54 g OC PC, 1, 2 SL A, 1, 2 (Z1, LC1, X1)

NRD

Essays in honour of Gilbert Murray... London: G. Allen & Unwin Ltd [1936] 308 p. 22½cm.

CONTENTS.—Pignus amicitiae, by H. A. L. Fisher.—G. M.—W. A., 1895-1924, by Charles Archer.—Gilbert Murray and Somerville, by Margery Fry.—Professor Murray and the amateur player, by John Masefield.—Gilbert Murray and some actors, by Sybil Thorndike.—The League of Nations Union and Gilbert Murray, by Lord Cecil.—Gladstone and the League of Nations mind, by J. L. Hammond.—The battle for open spaces, by Barbara Hammond.—Man and leviathan, by S. A. de Madariaga.—The machinery of indirect rule in Papua, by Sir Hubert Murray.—Post-war economic reconstruction: the story of a project, by Alfred Zimmern.—Rhetoric in the ancient world, by E. R. Bevan.—The invention of space, by F. M. Cornford.—On translating

(Continued)

N. Y. P. L. August 24, 1936

Essays in honour of Gilbert Murray... (Card 2)

Greek tragedy, by Harley Granville-Barker.—Some problems in the "Acta Judae Thomae," by D. S. Margoliouth.—The evidence for telepathy, by Mrs. W. H. Salter.—The present and future of classical scholarship, by J. A. K. Thomson.—The Greek door to the study of history, by A. J. Toynbee.

838627A. 1. Murray, Gilbert, 1866–

N. Y. P. L. August 24, 1936

YAR

Essays in honor of John Dewey, on the occasion of his seventieth birthday, October 20, 1929. New York, H. Holt and company [c1929]
xi, 425 p. front. (port.) 24cm.

CONTENTS.—Personality: how to develop it in the family, the school, and society, by Felix Adler.—Religious values and philosophical criticism, by E. S. Ames.—Evolution and time, by A. G. A. Balz.—Art, action, and affective states, by H. C. Brown.—Two basic issues in the problem of meaning and of truth, by Edwin Burtt.—Kant, Aquinas, and the problem of reality, by Cornelius Clifford.—A pragmatic approach to being, by W. F. Cooley.—Consolation and control. A note on the interpretation of philosophy, by J. J. Coss.—A philosophy of experience as a philosophy of art, by Irwin Edman.—Dimensions of uni-

(Continued on next card)

29-24486 [5]

Essays in honor of John Dewey ... [c1929] (Card 2)

CONTENTS—Continued.

versality in religion, by H. L. Friess.—A criticism of two of Kant's criteria of the aesthetic, by Kate Gordon.—A pragmatic critique of the historico-genetic method, by Sidney Hook.—Certain conflicting tendencies within the present-day study of education, by W. H. Kilpatrick.—Causality, by S. P. Lamprecht.—Externalism in American life, by M. T. McClure.—The empiricist and experimentalist temper in the middle ages. A prolegomenon to the study of mediaeval science, by Richard McKeon.—The nature of the past, by G. H. Mead.—A functional view of morals, by S. F. MacLennan.—A materialistic theory of emergent evolution, by W. P. Montague.—What is meant by social activity? By E. C. Moore.—The cult of chronology, by Helen H. Parkhurst.—Dualism in metaphysics and practical philosophy, by J. H.

(Continued on next card)

29-24486 [5]

Essays in honor of John Dewey ... [c1929] (Card 3)

CONTENTS—Continued.

Randall, jr.—Prolegomena to a political ethics, by A. K. Rogers.—Radical empiricism and religion, by H. W. Schneider.—The rôle of the philosopher, by T. V. Smith.—A methodology of thought, by John Storck.—Individualism and American life, by J. H. Tufts.—Looking to philosophy, by Matilde C. Tufts.—Some implications of Locke's procedure, by F. J. E. Woodbridge.

1. Philosophy—Collections. 2. Dewey, John, 1859-

29-24486

Library of Congress B29.E8

——— Copy 2.

Copyright A 15597 [5]

---

*PBN

Essays in honour of the Very Rev. Dr. J. H. Hertz, chief rabbi of the United Hebrew congregations of the British empire, on the occasion of his seventieth birthday, September 25, 1942 (5703) edited by I. Epstein, E. Levine and C. Roth. London, E. Goldston, 1943.

xi, 442 p.; 111 p. fronts. (ports.) 25cm.

Added t.-p.: ספר היובל לכבוד ... יוסף צבי הרץ ... למלאת לו שבעים שנה.

CONTENTS.—The Chief Rabbi, by Ephraim Levine.—Talmud manuscripts and editions, by E. N. Adler.—Gnostic themes in rabbinic cosmology, by Alexander Altmann.—Joseph da Veiga and stock exchange operations in the seventeenth century, by M. B. Amzalak.—Jewish languages, by Salomo Birnbaum.—The ethics of the rabbis, by Abraham Cohen.—The Chief Rabbis of Vilna, by Israel Cohen.—The meaning of "sacrifices" in the Psalms, by Samuel Daiches.—Collatio 2.6.5., by David Daube.—The so-called "science" movements and their relation to Judaism, by

(Continued on next card)

Festschrift

44-30227

[3]

Essays in honour of the Very Rev. Dr. J. H. Hertz, chief rabbi ... 1944 (Card 2)

CONTENTS—Continued.

Bernard Drachman.—The conception of the Commandments of the Torah in Aaron Halevi's Sefer ha-hinnuk, by Isidore Epstein.—Incunables about Jews and Judaism, by Aron Freimann.—Popular proverbs in the Jerusalem Talmud, by J. H. Greenstone.—Fasts and fasting, by A. W. Greenup.—Elisha ben Abujah, by R. T. Herford.—The fantastic career of Joshua Abraham Norton, by Louis Herrman.—A note on the sacred drum, by S. H. Hooke.—The childhood and youth of Moses, the messenger of God, by Benno Jacob.—Origins of the Balfour declaration: Dr. Hertz's contribution, by Samuel Landman.—The rationale of the Tiberian graphic accentuation (XXI books) by H. M. Lazarus.—The confession of sins for the Day of Atonement, by Arthur Marmorstein.—Some notes on the life of R. Yair Hayyim Bacharach, by Alexander Marx.—Franz Rosenzweig's

(Continued on next card)

44-30227

[3]

Essays in honour of the Very Rev. Dr. J. H. Hertz, chief rabbi ... 1944 (Card 3)

CONTENTS—Continued.

life and work, by Ignaz Maybaum.—Some observations on the language of the prayers, the benedictions and the Mishnah, by Eugen Mittwoch.—On Maimonides' "Sefer ha-madda," by Simon Rawidowicz.—Ibrahim al-'Ayyah, by Edward Robertson.—Sebastian Muenster's knowledge and use of Jewish exegesis, by I. I. J. Rosenthal.—The Chief Rabbinate of England, by Cecil Roth.—Foundations: Ezra IV, 12; V, 16; VI, 3, by Sidney Smith.—Phillipus Ferdinandus Polonus, by Siegfried Stein.—The religious basis for morality, by E. S. Waterhouse.—The Platonic, Aristotelian and Stoic theories of creation in Hallevi and Maimonides, by H. A. Wolfson.—צבת בצבת [by S. H. Bergmann]—פיוטים לר׳ יהודה בר אבון [by Simon Bern-

(Continued on next card)

44-30227

[3]

Essays in honour of the Very Rev. Dr. J. H. Hertz, chief rabbi ... 1944 (Card 4)

CONTENTS—Continued.

stein]—מעשה בני האלהים ובנות האדם [by Umberto Cassuto]—אזהרות [by Shem-tob Gaguin]—תורת האלהים של הרמב״ם [by Julius Guttmann]—שמעון הצדיק [by Isaac Herzog]—סידור ומחזור תימן כ״י [by Samuel Krauss]—כתבי״ד קראים [by I. D. Markon]—לתולדות הנביאים בישראל [by M. H. Segal]

1. Jewish literature—Addresses, essays, lectures. 2. Jews—Religion—Addresses, essays, lectures. 3. Hertz, Joseph Herman, 1872- I. Epstein, Isidore, ed. II. Levine, Ephraim, joint ed. III. Roth, Cecil, joint ed.

44-30227

Library of Congress BM40.H4

[3] 296.04

IAG

Essays in honor of William E. Dodd, by his former students at the University of Chicago; edited by Avery Craven. Chicago, Ill., The University of Chicago press [c1935]

ix, 362 p. 23½cm.

CONTENTS.—The southern backcountry on the eve of the revolution, by Philip Davidson.—George Washington and the French revolution—the first phase, by L. M. Sears.—Contemporary opinion in Virginia of Thomas Jefferson, by Maude H. Woodfin.—The apologia of American debtor states, by R. C. McGrane.—The fabric of Chicago's early society, by Bessie L. Pierce.—The reaper industry and midwestern agriculture, 1855-75, by W. T. Hutchinson.—Charles Sumner and the crisis of 1860-61, by Laura A. White.—America and the freedom of the seas, 1861-65,

(Continued on next card)

36-7460

[5]

Essays in honor of William E. Dodd ... [c1935] (Card 2)

CONTENTS—Continued.

by F. L. Owsley.—Some problems facing Joseph E. Johnston in the spring of 1863, by D. B. Sanger.—Salmon P. Chase and the nomination of 1868, by D. V. Smith.—The new South and the old crop (1865-80) by H. C. Nixon.—The ideology of American expansion, by J. W. Pratt.

1. U. S.—Hist.—Addresses, essays, lectures. 2. Dodd, William Edward, 1869- I. Craven, Avery Odelle, 1886- ed.

36-7460

Library of Congress E173.E785

——— Copy 2.

Copyright A 92453 [5] 973.04

E-13
7195

Essays in honour of William Gallacher. Supplement: Thomas Spence; the history of Crusonia and other writings. Berlin, Humboldt-Universität zu Berlin, 1966.

354 p. illus., facsims., ports. 25cm. (Life and literature of the working class)

Includes bibliographies.

1. English literature--Political and social relations. 2. Gallacher, William, 1881-1965. I. Spence, Thomas, 1750-1814. II. Life and literature of the working class.

NN*R 1. 70 r/. OC, I (OS)II PC, 1, 2, I SL E, 1, 2, I (LC1, X1, Z1) [I, NSCM]

---

*GBS

ESSAYS honoring Lawrence C. Wroth. Portland, [Anthoensen press] 1951. xxi, 515 p. port. 26cm.

CONTENTS.—Introduction [by W. S. Lewis]—Richard Eden's copy of the 1533 Decades of Peter Martyr, by E. Baer.—Columbus in sixteenth-century poetry, by L. Bradner.—American booksellers' catalogues, 1734-1800, by C. S. Brigham.—The river in the ocean, by L. A. Brown.—Novello Cattanio: Un viaggio fatto alli paesi del continente nuovo, by C. F. Bühler.—The first decade of the Federal act for copyright, 1790-1800, by F. R. Goff.—Not in Harrisse, by E. P. Goldschmidt.—The Historia

(Continued)

NN**R X 6.54 OC PC, 1, 2 SL (RS1, ~~Z1~~, LC1, X1)

ESSAYS honoring Lawrence C. Wroth. (Card 2)

de las Indias of Bartolomé de las Casas, by L. Hanke.—The melody of "The star spangled banner" in the United States before 1820, by R. S. Hill.—Tunc et nunc: or The Pepys and Taylor collections of early English books on navigation, by W. A. Jackson.—John Carter Brown and America, by G. Kubler.—William Bradford's book trade and John Bowne, Long Island Quaker, as his book agent, 1686-1691, by G. D. McDonald.—King James takes a collection, by J. G. McManaway.—The Browns and Brown university, by W. G. Roelker.—The Bibliographical press at Yale university, by C. P. Rollins.—The beginnings of systematic bibliography in America, 1642-1799, by J. H. Shera.—The Boston book trade, 1790-1799, by R. G. Silver.—Comparative

(Continued)

ESSAYS honoring Lawrence C. Wroth. (Card 3)

cartography exemplified in an analytical & bibliographical description of nearly one hundred maps and charts of the American continent published in Great Britain during the years 1600-1850, by H. Stevens and R. Tree. — The first printing in Providence, by B. F. Swan. —A half-century of Canadian life and print, 1751-1800, by M. Tremaine. — A patriotic pair of peripatetic printers; the up-state imprints of John Holt and Samuel Loudon, 1776-1783, by R. W. G. Vail. — Hispanic Americana in the John Carter Brown library, by H. R. Wagner. —Eighteenth-century American fiction, by L. H. Wright. — The first Maryland tract: a reconsideration of the date of printing of the Maryland charter, by J. C. Wyllie. — A list of published writings of Lawrence C. Wroth to December, 31, 1950, by M. W. Adams and J. D. Black.

(Continued)

ESSAYS honoring Lawrence C. Wroth. (Card 4)

1. Wroth, Lawrence Counselman, 1884- . 2. Bibliography—Addresses, essays, lectures.

Essays honoring Lawrence C. Wroth. Portland, Maine ⌊Anthoensen press⌋ 1951. xxi, 515 p. front. (port.) 26cm.

CONTENTS.—Introduction ⌊by W. S. Lewis⌋—Richard Eden's copy of the 1533 Decades of Peter Martyr, by Elizabeth Baer.—Columbus in sixteenth-century poetry, by Leicester Bradner.—American booksellers' catalogues, 1734–1800, by C. S. Brigham.—The river in the ocean, by L. A. Brown.—Novello Cattanio: Un viaggio fatto alli paesi del continente nuovo, by C. F. Bühler.—The first decade of the federal act for copyright, 1790–1800, by F. R. Goff.—Not in Harrisse, by E. P. Goldschmidt.—The Historia de las Indias of Bartolomé de las Casas, by Lewis Hanke.—The melody of "The star spangled banner" in the United States before 1820, by R. S. Hill.—Tunc et nunc: or The Pepys and Taylor collections of early English books on navigation, by W. A.

(Continued)

Essays honoring Lawrence C. Wroth. (Card 2)

Jackson.—John Carter Brown and America, by George Kubler.—William Bradford's book trade and John Bowne, Long Island Quaker, as his book agent, 1686–1691, by G. D. McDonald.—King James takes a collection, by J. G. McManaway.—The Browns and Brown university, by W. G. Roelker.—The Bibliographical press at Yale university, by C. P. Rollins.—The beginnings of systematic bibliography in America, 1642–1799; an exploratory essay, by J. H. Shera.—The Boston book trade, 1790–1799, by R. G. Silver.—Comparative cartography exemplified in an analytical & bibliographical description of nearly one hundred maps and charts of the American continent published in Great Britain during the years 1600 to 1850, by Henry Stevens and Roland Tree.—The first printing in Providence, by B. F. Swan.—A half-century of Canadian

(Continued)

Essays honoring Lawrence C. Wroth. (Card 3)

life and print, 1751–1800, by Marie Tremaine.—A patriotic pair of peripatetic printers; the up-state imprints of John Holt and Samuel Loudon, 1776–1783, by R. W. G. Vail.—Hispanic Americana in the John Carter Brown library, by H. R. Wagner.—Eighteenth-century American fiction, by L. H. Wright.—The first Maryland tract: a reconsideration of the date of printing of the Maryland charter, by J. C. Wyllie.—A list of published writings of Lawrence C. Wroth to December 31, 1950, by M. W. Adams and J. D. Black.

 1. Wroth, Lawrence Counselman, 1884- .

Essays in intellectual history, dedicated to James Harvey Robinson by his former seminar students. New York and London, Harper & brothers, 1929.

ix, 359 p. 24½cm.
"First edition."

CONTENTS.—Toleration, by D. S. Muzzey.—The philosophy of Anthony, third earl of Shaftesbury, by Emma P. Smith.—Occupational development of Roman society about the time of the elder Cato, by Ernest Brehaut.—Spengler, by J. T. Shotwell.—The three Arnolds and their Bible, by W. P. Hall.—The conquest of Algeria, a case of historical inertia, by M. M. Knight.—The inside of Germany's war politics, by C. A. Beard.—American Christianity and the world of everyday, by H. U. Faulkner.—Bayle's profanation of sacred history, by Howard

(Continued on next card)

 ⌊5⌋

A. Martin

Essays in intellectual history, dedicated to James Harvey Robinson ... 1929. (Card 2)

CONTENTS—Continued.

Robinson.—The Esquisse of Condorcet, by J. S. Schapiro.—The philosopher turned patriot, by C. J. H. Hayes.—The place of history among the sciences, by Preserved Smith.—Henri de Saint-Simon, by L. H. Jenks.—The fall of Constantinople symbolically considered, by Louise R. Loomis.—The economic determination of history: its value, status and limitations, by H. E. Barnes.—Baron von Holstein, the dark force of the German foreign office, by Maude A. Huttman.—History and the science of society, by J. W. Swain.—John Louis Vives: his attitude to learning and to life, by Lynn Thorndike.—A yardstick for civilization, by P. W. Slosson.

1. History—Addresses, essays, lectures. 2. Robinson, James Harvey, 1863-

ESSAYS on Jewish life and thought presented in honor of Salo Wittmayer Baron, edited by Joseph L. Blau [and others] New York, Columbia university press, 1959. xxx, 458 p. port. 25cm.

Various contributors.
"Bibliography of the writings of Salo Wittmayer Baron," p. [xv]-xxx.
Bibliographical footnotes.

1. Jews--Hist.--Addresses, essays, lectures. 2. History--Addresses, essays, lectures. 3. Baron, Salo Wittmayer, 1895- . I. Blau, Joseph Leon, 1909- , ed.

ESSAYS in labour history; in memory of G.D.H. Cole, 25 September 1889-14 January 1959. Edited by Asa Briggs and John Saville. With recollections of G.D.H. Cole by Ivor Brown [and others] London, Macmillan; New York, St. Martin's Press, 1960. vii, 363 p. port. 23cm.

Bibliographical footnotes.

CONTENTS.—G. D. H. Cole as an undergraduate, by I. Brown.—At Oxford in the twenties, by H. Gaitskell.—What Cole really meant, by S. K. Bailey.—Cole and Oxford, 1938–1958, by G. D. N. Worswick.—The language of "class" in early nineteenth-century England, by A. Briggs.—Nineteenth-century co-operation; from community building

(Continued)

ESSAYS in labour history... (Card 2)

to shopkeeping, by S. Pollard.—Custom, wages, and work-load in nineteenth-century industry, by E. J. Hobsbawm.—The socialists of the Polish "great emigration," by P. Brock.—The Bee-hive newspaper: its origin and early struggles, by S. Coltham. — Professor Beesly and the working-class movement, by R. Harrison. — The English branches of the First International, by H. Collins.—Homage to Tom Maguire, by E. P. Thompson.—Trade unions and free labour; the background to the Taff Vale decision, by J. Saville.

1. Socialism--Gt. Br., to 1923. 2. Labor--Gt. Br., 1851-1913. 3. Cole, George Douglas Howard, 1889-1959. I. Briggs, Asa, 1921- ed. II. Saville, John, ed.

Essays on the law and practice of governmental administration; a volume in honor of Frank Johnson Goodnow ... contributed by his students in grateful acknowledgment of his scholarly inspiration and counsel, edited by Charles G. Haines ... and Marshall E. Dimock ... Baltimore, The Johns Hopkins press, 1935.

xvii, 321 p. front. (port.) 22cm.

CONTENTS.—pt. I. Origin and meaning of public administration: Public administration and administrative law, by J. A. Fairlie.—pt. II. Executive leadership in administration: The President and federal administration, by James Hart. From political chief to administrative chief, by G. W. Spicer.—pt. III. Government in relation to industry: Judicial review of the findings and awards of industrial accident com-

(Continued on next card)

35-2938

[8]

Essays on the law and practice of governmental administration ... 1935. (Card 2)

CONTENTS—Continued.

missions, by C. G. Haines. Retirement or refunding of utility bonds, by M. R. Maltbie. The scope of the commerce power, by J. R. Powell.—pt. IV. Control of administration: State control of local finance in Indiana, by F. G. Bates. The inadequacies of the rule of law, by C. C. Thach. Forms of control over administrative action, by M. E. Dimock.

1. Goodnow, Frank Johnson, 1859– 2. U. S.—Pol. & govt.—Addresses, essays, lectures. 3. Administrative law—U. S.—Addresses, essays, lectures. I. Haines, Charles Grove, 1879– ed. II. Dimock, Marshall Edward, 1903– joint ed. III. Title: Governmental administration.

35-2938

Library of Congress JK421.E8

——— ~~Copy 2.~~

Copyright A 79658 [8] 353

Essays on Maimonides, an octocentennial volume, edited by Salo Wittmayer Baron ... New York, Columbia university press, 1941.

5 p. l., 316 p. 23½cm.

"The addresses given at the celebration [1935] held under the auspices of Columbia university and the essays ... written shortly thereafter ... appear here without any substantive alteration."—Pref.

"The Alexander Kohut memorial foundation has collaborated in the publication of this volume."

CONTENTS.—The celebration of the eight-hundredth anniversary of the birth of Moses Maimonides, Casa de las Españas, Columbia university, March 30, 1935: Introduction, by President N. M. Butler, chairman. Moses Maimonides, the philosopher, by Richard McKeon. Maimonides,

(Continued on next card)

41-7154

[8]

Essays on Maimonides ... 1941. (Card 2)

CONTENTS—Continued.

the scientist, by Richard Gottheil. Maimonides, the leader and lawgiver, by S. W. Baron.—Homage to Maimonides, by Etienne Gilson.—The literary character of the Guide for the perplexed, by Leo Strauss.—Maimonides' Treatise on resurrection: a comparative study, by Joshua Finkel.—A responsum of Maimonides, by Richard Gottheil.—The economic views of Maimonides, by S. W. Baron.—The medical work of Maimonides, by Max Meyerhof.—Index.

1. Moses ben Maimon, 1135-1204. I. Baron, Salo Wittmayer, 1895– ed. II. Columbia university.

41-7154

Library of Congress B759.M34E8

[8] 181.3

Essays mainly on the nineteenth century, presented to Sir Humphrey Milford. London, New York, Oxford Univ. Press, 1948.

vi, 160 p. port. 23 cm.

CONTENTS.—Introduction by G. F. J. Cumberlege.—The ruined cottage and The excursion, by Helen Darbishire.—Browning: a conversation, by Frederick Page.—'Say not the struggle nought availeth,' by A. L. P. Norrington.—The poetry of R. L. Stevenson, by H. W. Garrod.—A poet in Walton Street, by Simon Nowell-Smith.—Personal names in Trollope's political novels, by R. W. Chapman.—The diffusion of ideas, by R. C. K. Ensor.—The church in the nineteenth century, by R. H. Malden.—A minim's rest, by R. V. Williams.—Sporting writers of the nineteenth century, by Bernard Darwin.—The camel's

(Continued on next card)

A 48—5986*

[48d2]

Essays mainly on the nineteenth century ... 1948. (Card 2)

CONTENTS—Continued.

back; or, The last tribulation of a Victorian publisher, by Michael Sadleir.—The perfect author, by S. C. Roberts.

1. Milford, Sir Humphrey Sumner, 1877– 2. English literature—Addresses, essays, lectures. 3. Nineteenth century.

A 48-5986*

Yale Univ. Library
for Library of Congress [48d2]

Copy only words underlined
& Classmark-- QAA

ESSAYS in marine physiology. Presented to P.F. Scholander in honour of his sixtieth birthday. Oslo, Universitetsforlaget, 1965. 239 p. illus., charts. 28cm. (Hvalradets skrifter, Scientific results of marine biological research. Nr. 48)

Includes bibliographies.

CONTENTS.--Bibliography of written works by P.F. Scholander et al., by S.I. Scholander.--Field study of diving responses in the

(Continued)

NN 8.66 1/J OC (OD)I (ED)I PC,1,2,I (LC1,X1,Z1)

ESSAYS in marine physiology. (Card 2)

northern elephant seal, by R.L. Van Citters and others.--Heart rate response in forced versus trained experimental dives in pinnipeds, by R. Elsner.--Effect of brain stimulation on "diving" in ducks, by B. Folkow and E.H. Rubinstein.--Data on speed and underwater exhalation of a humpback whale accompanying ships, by C.L. Hubbs. --Physiology of a small cetacean, by J.W. Kanwisher and G. Sundnes. --Decompression sickness, by D.H. LeMessurier and B.A. Hills.--Salinity adaption in the mudskipper fish,

(Continued)

ESSAYS in marine physiology. (Card 3)

Periophthalmus sobrinus, by M.S. Gordon and others.--Dynamics of venous return in elasmobranch fishes, by K. Johansen.--Oxygen secretion in the isolated blood perfused swimbladder, by J.D. Steen and O. Iversen.--Crystalline hemoglobin from the marine annelid, Amphitrite ornata, by W.E. Love and E.E. Lattman.--Review of Ambilicaria Hoffm., and of the Lasallias, by G.A. Llamo.--The jack rabbit—A study in desert survival, by K. Schmidt-Nielsen and others.--Physiological basis of slothfulness in the sloth, by P. Stockfleth Enger and T. Holmes Bullock.--Tracer

(Continued)

ESSAYS in marine physiology. (Card 4)

studies of water and sodium transport in mangroves, by T. Enns.--Oxygen transport through hemoglobin solutions, by H.T. Hammel.--The effect of environmental pH and CO_2 concentration on mitochondrial ATPase activity of rabbit kidney cortex and medulla, by W.J. Longmore and others.--Some combination of the Scholander-Roughton capillary and van Slyke's gasometric techniques and their use in special haemoglobin problems, by F.J.W. Roughton and R.L.J. Lyster.--The initial enhancement of synaptic transmission in hypoxia, by Y. Loyning.--Physiological aspects of man's acclimatization to cold, by

(Continued)

ESSAYS in marine physiology. (Card 5)

K. Lange Andersen.--An analysis of Gloger's rule, by R.J. Hock.--A pulsatile pressure transport system across artificial membranes, by S. Lloyd Claff and A. A. Crescenzi.--Standard serum values in hospital chemistry, by O. Scott and others.

1. Scholander, Per Fredrik, 1905- . 2. Biology, Marine and freshwater--Addresses, essays, lectures. I. Series.

Copy only words underlined & classmark— SA

ESSAYS in modern European history, by students of the late William Thomas Morgan. Edited by John J. Murray. Bloomington, Indiana university [1951] 150 p. illus., port. 26cm. (Indiana. University. Indiana university publications. Social science series. no. 10)

Bibliographical footnotes. "Publications of Professor William T. Morgan." p. 145-147.

(Continued)

NN * * X 4. 56 s/ OC, II, (U1, LC1, X1, Z1) [I] IIIbo (OD)I (ED)I PC, 1, 2, I, II

E-13
6435

ESSAYS in medieval history presented to Bertie Wilkinson. Edited by T.A.Sandquist and M.R.Powicke. [Toronto, University or Toronto press, 1969] 405 p. port. 24cm.

Bibliographical footnotes.

CONTENTS.--Hadrian IV, the Byzantine empire, and the Latin Orient, by J.G.Rowe.--An unpublished letter by abbot Hugh II of Reading concerning Archbishop Hubert Walter, by G.Constable.--William de Montibus,

(Continued)

NN R 10.69 r/L OC, I, II, III, IVbo PC, 1, I, II, III SL (LC1, X1, Z1) [I]

Copy only words underlined & classmark— SA

ESSAYS in modern European history... (Card 2)

CONTENTS.—The tackers in the election of 1705, by D. M. Reed.—The British general election of 1713, by C. E. Langford.—Gallia frustra: Edward Russell and the attempted Jacobite invasion of 1696, by R. H. Irrmann.—Anglo-French naval skirmishing off Newfoundland, 1697, by J. J. Murray.—Antigua, 1710: Revolution in microcosm, by R. M. Bourne.—Tayllеyrand and the independence of Belgium, by J. E. Swain.—The Ruhr and French security as reflected by the British and French presses, 1923, by D. W. Trafford.

(Continued)

ESSAYS in medieval history presented to Bertie Wilkinson... (Card 2)

a medieval teacher, by H. Mackinnon.--The constitutional problem in thirteenth-century England, by F.Treharne.--Notes on the making of the Dunstable annals, AD 33 to 1242, by C.R.Cheney.--The Ordines of the Third Recension of the medieval English coronation order, by J.'Brückmann.--Matthew Paris and the Mongols, by J.J.Saunders.--A statue of Henry of Almain, by P.H.Brieger.--The commentary of Giles of Rome on the Rhetoric of Aristotle, by J.R.O'Donnell.--What made a medieval king constitutional? by B.Lyon.-- Statues of Edward I: Huntington library ms. H.M.25782, by V.H.Galbraith.--The letters of

(Continued)

Copy only words underlined & classmark— SA

ESSAYS in modern European history... (Card 3)

1. Morgan, William Thomas, 1883-1946. 2. Europe—Hist.—Addresses, essays, lectures. I. Series. II. Murray, John J., ed. III. Murray, John J.

ESSAYS in medieval history presented to Bertie Wilkinson... (Card 3)

John Mason: a fourteenth-century formulary from St. Augustine's, Canterbury, by W.A.Pantin.--Isabella and the bishop of Exeter, by F.D.Blackley.--The summons of the English feudal levy: 5 April 1327, by N.B.Lewis.--Parliament and the French war, 1336-40, by E.B.Fryde.--Some notes on Walter Burley's commentary on the Politics, by L.J.Daly.--The structure of commutation in a fourteenth-century village, by J.A.Raftis.--The wealth of Richard Lyons, by A.R.Myers.--The holy oil of St. Thomas of Canterbury, by T.A.Sandquist.--The Canterbury convocation of 1406, by E.F.Jacob.--Hermeneutics and history: the problem of Haec Sancta, by B.Tierney.--Lancastrian captains, by M.R.Powicke.

(Continued)

---

*SAB
(U.S. Library of Congress)

Essays offered to Herbert Putnam by his colleagues and friends on his thirtieth anniversary as librarian of Congress, 5 April 1929; edited by William Warner Bishop and Andrew Keogh. New Haven, Yale university press, 1929.

x p., 1 l., 555, [1] p. front., ports., maps. 24cm.

"600 copies printed in March 1929."

1. Putnam, Herbert, 1861– 2. U. S. Library of Congress. 3. Libraries—Addresses, essays, lectures. 4. Library science—Addresses, essays, lectures. I. Bishop, William Warner, 1871– ed. II. Keogh, Andrew, 1869– joint ed.

Library of Congress Z720.P9E7 29-9887

~~Copy 2.~~

Copyright A 7675 [4] Mr. Moth.

ESSAYS in medieval history presented to Bertie Wilkinson... (Card 4)

--The Huntingdonshire parliamentary election of 1450, by Sir J.G.Edwards.--Bibliography of the published works of Bertie Wilkinson, by M. Tyson.

1. Great Britain--Hist.--Medieval period, 1066-1485--Addresses, essays, lectures. I. Wilkinson, Bertie, 1898- . II. Sandquist, T.A., ed. III. Powicke, Michael, ed. IV. Sandquist, T.A.

---

*OKM

ESSAYS in philosophy presented to Dr. T.M.P. Mahadevan on his fiftieth birthday, contributed by fifty-two scholars, Eastern and Western. Madras, Ganesh, 1962. xvi, 527, a-c p. port. 25cm.

"Bibliography of the writings of T.M.P. Mahadevan," p. 515-527.

1. Mahadevan, Telliyavaram Mahadevan Ponnambalam, 1911- . 2. Philosophy, Indian. 3. Philosophy--Addresses, essays, lectures.

NN R 1.64 f/B OC PC, 1, 2, 3 SL O, 1, 2 (LC1, X1, Z1)

D-20
3048

ESSAYS & poems presented to Lord David Cecil. London, Constable [1970] x,204 p. 23cm.

On spine: Edited by W. W. Robson.
Bibliographical footnotes.
CONTENTS.--Preface, by W. W. Robson.--Lord David Cecil, by L. P. Hartley.--Religious attitudes in Beowulf, by A. D. Horgan.--The dream of the rood, by H. Gardner.--The former age, by N. Coghill.--Angelo and Andzhelo; Pushkin's version of Shakespeare's character, by
(Continued)

NN R 3.71 b/₄OC, I II PC, 1, I, II SL (LC1, X1, Z1) [I] 2

ESSAYS & poems presented to Lord David Cecil. (Card 2)

J. Bayley.--A note on characterization in Othello, by J. Wain.--Some reflections on Gibbon's Memoirs of my life, by R. Trickett.--Crabbe and the Augustan tradition, by D. H. Burden.--William Lisle Bowles and the riparian Muse, by J. D. Bamborough.--On reading Shelley, by J. Buxton.--Ward's Life of Newman; a great biography, by A. O. J. Cockshut.--The thought of George Tyrrell, by R. Chapman.--Existentialists and mystics, by I. Murdoch.--The art of reading in ignorance, by R. Pitter.

1. English literature--Addresses, essays, lectures. I. Cecil, Lord David, 1902- . II. Robson, William Wallace, ed.

*PBN

ESSAYS presented to Chief Rabbi Israel Brodie on the occasion of his seventieth birthday; edited by H. J. Zimmels, J. Rabbinowitz and I. Finestein. London, Soncino press [1967; v. 2, 1966] 2 v. illus., ports. 26cm. (Jews' college, London. Publications. New series. no. 3)

[Vol. 1] contains contributions in English, [v. 2.] contributions in Hebrew.
(Continued)

NN *R 9.69 r/₄OC, I, II, III (OS)IV PC, 1, 2, 4, I, II, III, IV SL J, 1, 3, 5, I, II, III, IV (LC1, X1, Z1) 2

ESSAYS presented to Chief Rabbi Israel Brodie on the occasion of his seventieth birthday... (Card 2)

Bibliographical footnotes.

1. Brodie, Israel. 2. Judaism--Addresses, essays, lectures. 3. Judaism--Essays. 4. Law, Jewish. 5. Law. I. Zimmels, Hirsch Jakob, ed. II. Rabbinowitz, Joseph, 1892- , ed. III. Finestein, Israel, 1921- , ed. IV. Series.

L-10
9263
v.8-9

ESSAYS presented to Jens Yde on his sixtieth birthday, April 3rd, 1966. København, Dansk etnografisk forening [1967] 428 p. 25cm. (Folk; dansk etnografisk tidsskrift. v. 8-9)

Includes bibliographies.

1. Yde, Jens, 1906-
NN R 10.68 v/₄ OI (PC)1 (AH)1 (LC1, X1, Z1) [I]

MA
+

ESSAYS presented to Rudolf Wittkower on his sixty-fifth birthday. Edited by Douglas Fraser, Howard Hibbard & Milton J. Lewine. [London] Phaidon Press [1967] 2 v. illus., facsims., plans, ports. 32cm.

In English, Italian, German and French.
Each part has individual t.p.
"The writings of Rudolf Wittkower" included at end
(Continued)

NN R 6.68 v/₄ OC, I PC, 1, 2, 3, 4, I SL A, 1, 2, 3, 4, I (LC1, X1, Z1) [I] 2

ESSAYS presented to Rudolf Wittkower on his sixty-fifth birthday. (Card 2)

of each volume.
Bibliographical footnotes.
CONTENTS.--[1] Essays in the history of architecture, with 26 contributions.--[2]. Essays in the history of art, with 39 contributions.
1. Art--Essays and misc. 2. Architecture--Addresses, essays, lectures. 3. Wittkower, Rudolf. 4. Wittkower, Rudolf, --Bibl. I. Fraser, Douglas, ed.

YED

Essays in psychology, dedicated to David Katz. Uppsala, Almqvist & Wiksell, 1951. x, 283 p. illus. 24cm.

Contributions in English, French or German.
Bibliographies included.

1. Katz, David, 1884- 2. Psychology, 1936-
NN R 5.53 OC PC, 1, 2 SL (LC1, Z1, X1)

E-10
415

ESSAYS in Roman coinage presented to Harold Mattingly, edited by R. A. G. Carson and C. H. V. Sutherland. [London] Oxford University press, 1956. xiv, 291 p. illus., maps. 25cm.

Bibliographical footnotes.
CONTENTS.—Bibliography of the works of Harold Mattingly (p. [1]-12)—Numismatics and history, by A. H. M. Jones.—Punic coins of Spain and their bearing on the Roman republican series, by E. S. G. Robinson.—
(Continued)

NN**R 8.56 d/₆ OC, I, II, IIIbBNB PC, 1, 2, I, II SL (LC1, X1, Z1, Y1)

ESSAYS in Roman coinage presented to Harold Mattingly... (Card 2)

Special coinages under the Triumviri monetales, by K. Pink.—The main aspects of political propaganda on the coinage of the Roman republic, by A. Alföldi.—The pattern of official coinage in the early principate, by M. Grant.—The behaviour of early imperial countermarks, by C. M. Kraay.—Greek mints under the Roman empire, by A. R. Bellinger.—The cistophoric series and its place in the Roman coinages, by A. M. Woodward.—Flexibility in the 'reformed' coinage of Diocletian, by C. H. V. Sutherland.—Gold coinage in the late Roman empire, by J. P. C. Kent.—
(Continued)

ESSAYS in Roman coinage presented to Harold Mattingly... (Card 3)

Picture-language in Roman art and coinage, by J.M.C. Toynbee. --System and product in the Roman mint, by R.A.G. Carson. --The Roman law of counterfeiting, by P. Grierson. --The numismatic evidence of Romano-British coin hoards, by A.S. Robertson.

1. Mattingly, Harold, 1884- . 2. Numismatics, Roman. I. Sutherland, Carol Humphrey Vivian, ed. II. Carson, Robert Andrew Glindinning, ed. III. Carson, Robert Andrew Glindinning.

NABM

Essays and studies in honor of Carleton Brown. New York, New York university press; London, H. Milford, Oxford university press, 1940.

xiii, 336 p. incl. front. (port.) pl.

"List ... of friends who join with New York university and the Modern language association in expressing their appreciation of Carleton Brown": p. ⌊335⌋-336.

CONTENTS.—Carleton Brown, by P. W. Long.—Hagbard and Ingeld, by Kemp Malone.—The 'Dream of the rood' as prosopopoeia, by Margaret Schlauch.—Medieval windows in romantic light, by Erika von Erhardt-Siebold.—Twelfth-century scholarship and satire, by Frederick Tupper.—Introduction to a study of the mediaeval French drama, by Grace Frank.—'Meditations on the life and passion of Christ': a note on its literary relationships, by Charlotte D'Evelyn.—Three Chaucer notes, by

(Continued on next card)

40-14963

⌊10⌋

Essays and studies in honor of Carleton Brown ... 1940. (Card 2)

CONTENTS—Continued.

Haldeen Braddy.—The tale of Melibeus, by W. W. Lawrence.—Chaucer and the Auchinleck MS: 'Thopas' and 'Guy of Warwick', by Laura H. Loomis.—Was Chaucer a Laodicean? by R. S. Loomis.—Some English words from the 'Fasciculus morum', by Frances A. Foster.—The dramatic unity of the 'Secunda pastorum', by H. A. Watt.—Richard Sellyng, by A. C. Baugh.—Wynkyn de Worde and a second French compilation from the 'Ancren riwle' with a description of the first (Trinity coll. Camb. MS 883), by Hope E. Allen.—Some notes on the circulation of lyric poems in sixteenth-century Italy, by W. Ll. Bullock.—Manuscripts of the 'Islands voyage' and 'Notes on the royal navy' (in relation to the printed versions in Purchas and in Ralegh's 'Judicious essayes'), by Helen E.

(Continued on next card)

40-14963

⌊10⌋

Essays and studies in honor of Carleton Brown ... 1940. (Card 3)

CONTENTS—Continued.

Sandison.—Shakespeare remembers his youth in Stratford, by C. F. T. Brooke.—Comedy versus opera in France, 1673-1700, by H. C. Lancaster.—The 'Memorias' of Felipe Fernández Vallejo and the history of the early Spanish drama, by J. E. Gillet.—Thomas Carlyle and Charles Butler of Wall street, by L. E. Kimball.—The mediaevalism of Henry Adams, by Oscar Cargill.—A bibliography of Carleton Brown's writings (p. ⌊330⌋-332)

1. Brown, Carleton Fairchild, 1869- 2. Literature—Addresses, essays, lectures. I. New York university. II. Modern language association of America.

40-14963

Library of Congress PN501.B7

~~Copy 2.~~ ⌊10⌋ 804

---

* PBN

Essays and studies in memory of Linda R. Miller; edited by Israel Davidson. New York: The Jewish theological seminary of America, 1938. 286 ⌊83⌋ p. front. (port.) 24cm.

Text and paging in Hebrew (83 p.) at end.
Bibliographical footnotes.

CONTENTS.—Editor's note.—Adler, Cyrus. Foreword.—Hurwitz, R. S. Linda R. Miller: An appreciation.—Baron, S. W. Freedom and constraint in the Jewish community.—Davidson, Israel. Wisdom and folly in mediaeval Hebrew proverbs.—Finkelstein, Louis. The ten martyrs.—Ginzberg, Louis. Beitraege zur Lexikographie des Juedisch-Aramaeischen, III.—Marcus, Joseph. Three hymns from the Genizah.—Marx, Alexander. The scientific work of some outstanding mediaeval Jewish scholars.—Roth, Cecil. The mediaeval conception of the Jew.—Weber, Max. Art conscious-

(Continued)

N. Y. P. L. November 30, 1938

Essays and studies in memory of Linda R. Miller... (Card 2)

ness.—Wolfson, H. A. The Aristotelian Predicables and Maimonides' Division of attributes.—Zeitlin, Solomon. The Pharisees and the Gospels.—דוידזון, ישראל.—חכמה וסכלות בפתגם העברי מימי הבינים.—לוין, ב. מ. לתולדות נר של שבת.—ריבקינד, יצחק. ענעלאוו הצעיר.

957795A. 1. Miller, Linda (Rosenberg), 1877-1936. 2. Essays, Jewish, in English—Collections. 3. Essays, Hebrew—Collections. I. Davidson, Israel, 1870- , ed.

N. Y. P. L. November 30, 1938

CS

Essays and studies presented to Professor Eoin MacNeill, D. LITT., on the occasion of his seventieth birthday, May 15th, 1938, edited by Reverend John Ryan ... Dublin, The sign of the Three candles, 1940.

xv, 593, ⌊1⌋ p. fronts. (incl. port.) illus. (incl. plans) plates, maps (1 fold.) diagrs. 26cm.

Added t.-p.: Féil-sgríbinn Eóin Mhic Néill.

Errata slip inserted.

"Bibliography of the publications of Professor MacNeill": p. 581-583.

CONTENTS.—Celtic languages.—Archaeology and prehistory.—Early and medieval Irish history.—Folklore.

1. Ireland—Antiq. 2. Celtic philology—Collections. 3. Ireland—Hist.—To 1603. 4. Folk-lore—Ireland. 5. MacNeill, John, 1868- I. Ryan, John, ed. II. Title (transliterated): Féil-sgríbhinn Eóin Mhic Néill.

42-10896

Library of Congress DA920.M23

⌊6⌋ 941.504

NDK

Essays and studies presented to Professor Tadhg Ua Donnchadha (Torna) on the occasion of his seventieth birthday, September 4th, 1944. Ed. by Séamus Pender... ⌊Corcaigh⌋ Cork univ. press, 1947. 258 p. illus. 25cm.

Added t.-p. in Gaelic: Féilscríbhinn Torna.
Contributions in English or Gaelic.
Bibliography, p. 227-258.

430923B. 1. Gaelic literature, Irish—Hist. and crit. 2. Gaelic literature, Scottish—Hist. and crit. 3. Gaelic language, Irish—Texts and translations—Collections. 4. Gaelic language, Scottish—Texts and translations—Collections. 5. O'Donoghue, Tadhg, 1874- . I. Pender, Séamus, ed. II. Féilscríbhinn Torna.

N. Y. P. L. March 3, 1948

---

*OAC

ESSAYS and studies presented to Stanley Arthur Cook; in celebration of his seventy-fifth birthday, 12 April 1948, by members of the faculties of Divinity and Oriental languages in the University of Cambridge. Edited by D. Winton Thomas. London, Taylor's foreign press, 1950. ix, 123 p. 26cm.

(Cambridge oriental series. no. 2)

CONTENTS. --Select bibliography of the writings of Stanley Arthur Cook, compiled by the editor (p. 1-13)--Prophetic influences in the sixth century B.C., by W.A.L. Elmslie. --"All Israel" in the Deuteronomic

(Continued)

NN **R 6.56 j/P OC, I (OS) II PC, 1, 2, I, II SL O, 1, 2, I, II (LC1, X1, ~~Z1~~)

ESSAYS and studies presented to Stanley Arthur Cook... (Card 2)

writers, by J.N. Schofield. --Early Hebrew script versus square Hebrew script, by D. Diringer. --Ostraca XIX-XXI from Tell ed-Duweir (Lachish), by the editor. --Notes on a Demotic papyrus from Thebes (B.M. 10026), by S.R.K. Glanville. --Some notes on late-Babylonian orthography, by C.P.T. Winckworth. --An examination of some Nestorian Kephalaia (Or. 1319, University library, Cambridge), by A.E. Goodman. --Laws of reason and laws of religion: a conflict in Toledo Jewry in the fourteenth century, by J.L. Teicher. --Edward Lively: Cambridge Hebraist, by E.I.J. Rosenthal. --Shahrastānī on pre-Islamic Arabia, by A.J. Arberry. --A Persian Solomon, by R. Levy. --A problem of the Kharoṣṭhī

(Continued)

ESSAYS and studies presented to Stanley Arthur Cook...
(Card 3)

script, by H. W. Bailey.

1. Cook, Stanley Arthur, 1873-1949. 2. Oriental studies—Collections.
I. Thomas, David Winton, 1901- , ed. II. Series.

RNC

Essays on the teaching of English in honor of Charles Swain Thomas. Cambridge, Mass., Harvard university press, 1940.
xxi, 286 p. front. (port.) 22cm.
Edited by R. M. Gay.
CONTENTS.—Introduction, by R. M. Gay.—Charles Swain Thomas and the teaching of English, by H. W. Holmes.—A modest caveat about the curriculum, by H. M. Jones.—The responsibility of the public schools for the maintenance of culture in America, by Dora V. Smith.—English and the social studies, by H. E. Wilson.—English as experience in secondary schools, by Angela M. Broening.—We dare to teach English, by Lou LaBrant.—Three question marks for the teacher of literature, by Reed Smith.—Can a sense of beauty be developed through the English class? By Phyllis Robbins.—College teaching and creative scholarship, by K. O. Myrick.—The teaching of English, by Mary E. Chase.—Yesterday, by A. M. Hitchcock.—A note on the writer's craft, by John Erskine.—How
(Continued on next card)
40-13235
[7]

Essays on the teaching of English in honor of Charles Swain Thomas ... 1940. (Card 2)
CONTENTS—Continued.
well can English teachers write? By Allan Abbott.—On saying what you mean, by J. E. Park.—Uneasy English, by Frances L. Warner.—Linguistics and the teaching of the English language, by R. C. Pooley.—The major in English composition, by Agnes C. Perkins.—Grammar in the elementary curriculum, by F. S. Hoyt.—The Commission on English and the present state of the comprehensive English examination, by E. S. Noyes.—A glimpse of English public schools, by C. M. Fuess.—Amateur spirit in Korean literature, by Younghill Kang.—Notes (p. [279]-284)—
Second Copy The contributors (p. [285]-286)

1. English language—Study and teaching. 2. Thomas, Charles Swain, 1868- I. Gay, Robert Malcolm, 1879- ed.

40-13235
Library of Congress PE1065.T5
~~Copy 2.~~
Copyright [7] 807

AG-10
107

ESSEN- & STAHLWERKE OEHLER & COMPAGNIE ARTIEN-GESELLSCHAFT, Aarau.
75 Jahre Eisen- und Stahlwerke Oehler & Co. Aktiengesellschaft, Aarau, 1881-1956. [Aarau, 1956]
57 p. illus., ports. 31cm.

1. [Title] Fünfundsiebzig.
NN R 9.66 a/ OSs PCs SL Es (LC1s, X1s, [I], Z1s)

JFE
70-74

Estudios de derecho civil en homenaje a Héctor Lafaille. Buenos Aires, Ediciones Depalma, 1968.
xvi, 780 p. port. 24 cm.

Running title: Homenaje a Héctor Lafaille.
Bibliographical footnotes.

1. Law--Argentine Republic--Addresses, essays, lectures.
2. Lafaille, Héctor. I. Lafaille, Héctor.
NN* 9.70 d/Z OC, I PC, 1, 2, I SL (LC1, X1, Z1)

E-12
6007

Estudios jurídicos en homenaje al profesor Luis Jiménez de Asúa. Buenos Aires, Abeledo-Perrot [1964]
829 p. mounted illus., mounted port. 24 cm.
Bibliographical footnotes.

1. Criminal law--Addresses, essays, lectures. 2. Jiménez de Asúa, Luis, 1889-
NN *R 5.66 a/ OC PC, 1, 2 SL E, 1, 2 (LC1, X1, Z1)

E-13
9489

Estudios jurídicos que en homenaje a Manuel Borja Soriano presenta la Universidad Iberoamericana. [1. ed.] México, Editorial Porrúa, 1969.
752 p. port. 24 cm.

Bibliographical footnotes.
CONTENTS.—En homenaje a don Manuel Borja Soriano, por M. Villoro Toranzo.—La obra jurídica de Manuel Borja Soriano, por A. García López.—Consecuencias jurídicas de la violación al derecho del
(Continued)

NN*R 10. 70 w/ OC, I (OS)II PC, 1, I, II SL E, 1, I, II (LC1, X1, Z1)

ESTUDIOS jurídicos que en homenaje a Manuel Borja Soriano presenta la Universidad Iberoamericana. (Card 2)

tanto, por L. Aguilar Carvajal.—Comentarios al artículo 161 del Código civil para el Distrito y Territorios Federales, por E. Baz W.—Los códigos civiles y la teoría general de los actos y de los hechos jurídicos, por M. Borja Covarrubia.—Validez jurídica de las cláusulas de estabilización monetaria contenidas en los contratos de mutuo, por F. Borja Martínez.—Análisis del efecto de la condición suspensiva sobre la obligación y sobre el negocio jurídico que le da origen, por M. Borja Martínez.—La responsabilidad objetiva y las obliga-
(Continued)

ESTUDIOS jurídicos que en homenaje a Manuel Borja Soriano presenta la Universidad Iberoamericana. (Card 3)

ciones reales, por J. Castro Estrada.—El consentimiento en el matrimonio de menores, por N. de Buen Lozano.—El reflejo del derecho civil sobre el derecho agrario, por A. de Ibarrola.—La declaración unilateral de la voluntad como fuente especial de obligaciones, por B. Flores Barroeta.—Algunas consideraciones sobre las acciones de filiación legítima, por J. López Noriega.—La estipulación a favor de tercero en derecho comparado, por J. Lozano y Romen.—Un caso de ilícito no previsto por el Código civil, por P. Macedo.—Sobre la
(Continued)

ESTUDIOS jurídicos que en homenaje a Manuel Borja Soriano presenta la Universidad Iberoamericana. (Card 4)

necesidad de llenar el endoso en blanco y sobre la identificación del cobrador del título, por A. Martínez Báez.—¿El mandato irrevocable se termina por la muerte del mandante? por R. R. Pacheco.—La administración de la herencia, por F. Puig Peña.—Los contratos aleatorios, por S. Rocha Díaz.—En defensa de los hijos naturales, por R. Rojina Villegas.— El daño moral, por J. Sànchez Cordero.

1. Law--Mexico--Addresses, essays, lectures. I. Borja Soriano, Manuel, 1873- 1967. II. Universidad Iberoamericana, Mexico.

M-10
7615
v.1

ESTUDIOS de lengua y literatura como humanidades, homenaje a Juan Uribe Echevarría [por] Felipe Alliende [et al.] Santiago de Chile, Seminario de humanidades [1960] 131 p. 27cm. (Santiago de Chile. Universidad de Chile. Seminario de humanidades. Ediciones, 1)

"Los autores... profesores del Departamento de castellano del Instituto pedagógico de la Universidad de Chile."

(Continued)

NN * 6.63 e/$_f$ OC, I, Ib (OS)II OI PC, 1, 2, 3, 4, I, II (LC1, X1, Z1)

3

ESTUDIOS de lengua y literatura como humanidades... (Card 2)

CONTENTS.--La misión humanística y social de nuestra universidad, por F. Martínez Bonati.--La novela chilena actual, por C. Goić.--Los estudios de literatura en la educación nacional, por J. Villegas Morales.--La poesía modernista chilena, por M. Rodríguez Fernández.--Hacia un sentido en el estudio de la gramática, por E. Camus Lineros.--El Purén indómito como obra literaria, por E. García Carroza.--Hijo de ladrón de Manuel Rojas, por N. Cortés Larrieu.--Las actuales promociones poéticas,

(Continued)

ESTUDIOS de lengua y literatura como humanidades... (Card 3)

por P. Lastra Salazar.--La enseñanza del latín en Chile, por F. Alliende González.

1. Uribe-Echevarría, Juan. 2. Chilean literature--Addresses, essays, lectures. 3. Spanish language--Addresses, essays, lectures. 4. Education --Chile--Addresses, essays, lectures. I. Alliende, Felipe. II. Santiago de Chile. Universidad de Chile. Instituto pedagógico.

BX I

Estudios sobre la monarquía asturiana; colección de trabajos realizados con motivo del XI centenario de Alfonso II el Casto, celebrado en 1942. Oviedo, 1949.

545 p. illus., maps. 31 cm.

At head of title: Diputación de Asturias. Instituto de Estudios Asturianos, del patronato José M.ª Quadrado (C. S. I. C.)
Spanish, Portuguese or French.
Bibliographical references in "Notas" at the end of most articles.

1. Alfonso II, el Casto, King of Asturias and Leon, 759-842.
2. Spain—Hist.—Arab period, 711-1492.

A 52-1270

New York. Public Libr.
for Library of Congress [3]

W. S

E-10
8896

An ÉTIENNE GILSON Tribute. An Étienne Gilson tribute presented by his North American students with a response by Étienne Gilson. Milwaukee, Marquette University Press [1959] x, 347 p. port. 24cm

Edited by Charles J. O'Neil.

Bibliographical footnotes.

CONTENTS.—Foreword, by C. J. O'Neil.—Is God's knowledge scientific? A study in Thomism, by J. F. Anderson.—Metaethics and Thomism, by V. J. Bourke.—John of Paris as a representative of Thomistic political philosophy, by M. F. Griesbach.—Two questions concerning the esse of creatures in the doctrine of Jean Quidort, by A. J. Heiman.—A phenomenological approach to realism, by R. J. Henle.—Some mediaeval doctrines on extrinsic titles to interest, by H. Johnston.—St. Thomas' treatment of the axiom, Omne agens agit propter finem, by G. P. Klubertanz.—Hugues de Saint-Victor et les

(Continued)

NN * R 10.59 m/$_A$ OC, I, IIbCUA PC, 1, 2, I SL (LC1, X1, Z1)

An ÉTIENNE GILSON Tribute. (Card 2)

conditions du savoir au moyen âge, by B. Lacroix.—Martin Heidegger: language and being, by L. Lynch.—The interpretation of the Heraclitean fragments, by J. Owens.—Some reflections on Summa contra Gentiles II, 56, by A. C. Pegis.—Thomas of Sutton's Critique on the doctrine of univocity, by J. J. Przezdziecki.—Intelligere intelligentibus est esse, by J. H. Robb.—The evidence grounding judgments of existence, by R. W. Schmidt.—Toward a metaphysical restoration of natural things, by K. Schmitz.—The sensibles and metaphysics, by G. Smith.—Doctrine of creation in Liber de causis, by L. Sweeney.—The universal in an anti-Ockhamist text, by E. A. Synan.—Presuppositions and realism, by L. H. Thro.—Concept formation in certain empiricist thinkers in America, by W. M. Walton.—Response: Amicus amicis, by E. Gilson.

1. Philosophy--Addresses, essays, lectures. 2. Gilson, Étienne Henry, 1884- . I. O'Neil, Charles Joseph, 1908- , ed. II. O'Neil, Charles Joseph, 1908-

---

SB

Études d'économie politique et sociale à la mémoire de Eugène Duthoit...par ses collègues, ses disciples et ses amis. Paris, Librairie générale de droit et de jurisprudence, 1949. 280 p. port. 25cm.

"Notice bibliographique," p. 9-12.

548255B. 1. Sociology, 1945- . 2. Economics, 1926- —French authors. 3. Duthoit, Eugène, 1869-1944.
N. Y. P. L.

April 6, 1951

GBD

Études d'histoire dédiées à la mémoire de Henri Pirenne, par ses anciens élèves. Bruxelles, Nouvelle société d'éditions, 1937.

ix, 502 p., 1 l. front. (port.) illus. (maps) facsims. 24ᶜᵐ.

CONTENTS.—Berben, H. Une guerre économique au moyen âge. L'embargo sur l'exportation des laines anglaises (1270-1274)—Bonenfant-Feytmans, A. M. Le plus ancien acte de l'abbaye d'Andenne.—Bourguignon, M. Claude de Genetaire, gouverneur d'Arlon (1624-1681)—Boyce, G. C. The controversy over the boundary between the English and Picard nations in the University of Paris (1356-1358)—Cate, J. L. The English mission of Eustace of Flay (1200-1201)—Denucé, J. De eerste nationale atlas van onze provinciën (België-Nederland) van 1586.—Dept, G. G. Étude critique sur une grande inondation marine à la côte flamande (19 novembre 1404)—Smet, A. de. L'origine des ports du Zwin: Damme, Mude, Monikerede, Hoeke et Sluis.—Smet, J.

(Continued on next card)

38-16965

[3]

Festschrift.

Études d'histoire dédiées à la mémoire de Henri Pirenne ... 1937. (Card 2)

CONTENTS—Continued.

de. Maître Nicolas de Biervliet l'aîné, clerc des échevins de la ville de Bruges (première moitié du XIIIe siècle-1293)—Feytmans, D. Actes d'aliénation suivis de notices de tradition. Documents inédits du IXe et du Xe siècle en Poitou.—Ganshof, F. L. Note sur les origines de l'union du bénéfice avec la vassalité.—Hansay, A. Note critique concernant l'histoire de la propriété foncière à Liège au moyen âge.—Lucas, H. S. A document relating to the marriage of Philippa of Hainault in 1327.—Nowé, H. La juridiction de Gand sur le canal du Sas.—Obreen, H. De oorsprong der Middelburgsche abdij. Een kerkhistorisch onderzoek.—Pirenne, J. Les trois cycles de l'histoire juridique et sociale de l'ancienne Égypte.—Quicke, F. Jean de Saint-Amand, chanoine de Cambrai,

(Continued on next card)

38-16965

[3]

Études d'histoire dédiées à la mémoire de Henri Pirenne ... 1937. (Card 3)

CONTENTS—Continued.

chapelain du pape, faussaire, traître et espion (13...-1368)—Reynolds, R. L. Genoese sources for the twelfth century history of Liège, with special attention to John of Liège.—Sabbe, E. Étude critique sur le diplôme d'Arnoul Ier, comte de Flandre, pour l'abbaye de Saint-Pierre à Gand (941, juillet 8)—Stragier, R. De Kreesers te Gent in 1539-1540.—Taylor, C. H. The Assembly of 1312 at Lyons-Vienne.—Unger, W. S. Aanteekening over den tol van Iersekeroord.—Linden, H. van der. La pacification de Gand et les États Généraux de 1576.—Vijver, A. van de. Clovis et la politique méditerranéenne.—Werveke, H. van. La banlieue primitive des villes flamandes.—Werveke, L. van. Het Gentsche Stadszegel tot bij den aanvang der XIVe eeuw.—Vercauteren-DeSmet, L.

(Continued on next card)

38-16965

[3]

Études d'histoire dédiées à la mémoire de Henri Pirenne ... 1937. (Card 4)

CONTENTS—Continued.

Étude sur les rapports politiques de l'Angleterre et de la Flandre sous le règne du comte Robert II (1093–1111)—Vercauteren, F. Étude sur les châtelains comtaux de Flandre, du XIe au début du XIIIe siècle.—Verlinden, Ch. Note sur l'esclavage à Montpellier au bas moyen âge (XIIIe–XVe siècles)—Sagher, H. de. Une enquête sur la situation de l'industrie drapière en Flandre à la fin du XVIe siècle.

1. History — Addresses, essays, lectures. 2. Netherlands — Hist. 3. Middle ages—Hist. I. Pirenne, Henri, 1862–1935.

Library of Congress D113.5.E78 38-16965
[3] 940.104

---

*VBE

ÉTUDES sur la propriété industrielle, littéraire, artistique; mélanges Marcel Plaisant. Paris, Sirey, 1960. xiii, 304 p. illus., port. 25cm.

"Principales publications," p. [ix]-x.

1. Patents--Jurisp. 2. Copyright--Jurisp. 3. Plaisant, Marcel, 1887- t. 1960.

NN R 1.65 e/B OC PC, 1, 2, 3 SL E, 2, 3 ST, 1t, 3 (LC1, X1, Z1)

Write on slip only words underlined and classmark: XAA

...**Études** d'histoire du droit, dédiées à M. Auguste Dumas, professeur honoraire à la Faculté de droit d'Aix correspondant de l'institut. Aix-en-Provence, Impr. d'Éditions provençales, 1950. 366 p. port. 26cm. (In: Université d'Aix-Marseille. Faculté de droit, Aix. Aix-en-Provence, 1950. n.s. no. 43)

Bibliographical footnotes.
"Bibliographie des travaux de M. Dumas," p. 13-16.

1. Law—Essays and misc. 2. Law—Hist. 3. Dumas, Auguste.
N. Y. P. L. November 29, 1951

RDV

Études romanes dédiées à Mario Roques par ses amis, collègues et élèves de France. Paris, E. Droz, 1946.

234 p., 2 l. incl. front. (port.) 25 cm. (*Half-title:* Société de publications romanes et françaises. [Publications] t. XXV)

Bibliographical foot-notes.

CONTENTS.—Pauphilet, Albert. La date du Roland.—Hoepffner, Ernest. Un ami de Bertrand de Born: mon Isembart.—Lecoy, Félix. Note sur le troubadour Raimbaut de Vaqueyras.—Frappier, Jean. Les discours dans la chronique de Villehardouin.—Jeanroy, Alfred. Un sirventés historique attribué à Peire Cardenal (1271)—Bossuat, Robert. Un débat d'amour dans le roman de Cassidorus.—Bastin, Julia. Le traité de Théodore Paléologue dans la traduction de Jean de Vignay.—Faral, Edmond. Guillaume de Digulleville, Jean Galloppe et Pierre

(Continued on next card)
A 47-5401
[3] Festschrift

D-16
36

ÉTUDES juridiques en hommage à Monsieur le juge Bernard Bissonnette par un groupe de professeurs et d'amis. Montréal, Les Presses de l'Université de Montréal, 1963. xiii, 547 p. 22cm.

Contributions in French or English.
Bibliographical footnotes.

1. Bissonnette, Bernard. 2. Law--Addresses, essays, lectures.

NN 5.65 1/J OC PC, 1, 2 SL (LC1, X1, Z1)

Études romanes dédiées à Mario Roques par ses amis ... 1946. (Card 2)

CONTENTS—Continued.

Virgin.—Vendryes, Joseph. Sur le suffixe *-is* du français.—Ernout, Alfred. Les noms latins en *-tūs*.—Brunel, Clovis. Le préfixe *ca* dans le vocabulaire picard.—Foulet, Lucien. Le "plus" quantitatif et le "plus" temporel.—Yvon, Henri. Étude sur notre vocabulaire grammatical: le mot *conditionnel*.—Bruneau, Charles. Esprit, essai d'un classement historique des sens.—Duraffour, Antonin. Dictionnaires français à mettre à jour et au jour.—Boutière, Jean. Quelques observations sur les cartes lexicologiques de l'Atlas linguistique de la Roumanie.—Wagner, R. L. Verbes, préfixes, adverbes complémentaires.—Matoré, G. En marge de Th. Gautier, notes lexicologiques.

(Continued on next card)
A 47-5401
[3]

---

*PBM p.v.678

Études orientales, à la memoire de Paul Hirschler, editées par O. Komlós. Budapest, 1950. 144; iv, 12 p. 21cm.

Added t. p. and section in Hebrew.
Bibliographical footnotes.
CONTENTS.—I. Benoschofsky, I. Hirschler Pál.—Heller, B. Jubileumi beszéd.—Csetényi, E. La situation speciale juridique des Juifs au Byzantium.—Vajda, G. Le manuscrit hebreu no. 815 de la Bibliotheque nationale de Paris.—Roth, C. Hungarian Protestants and English Jewry.—Telegdi, S. Sur les périphrases verbales dites "verbes composés" en persan.—Komlós, O. Jonah legends.—Löwinger, S. Tel Abib—Til Abūbi (Ezek. 3:15).—Strauss, E. The social isolation of Ahl adh-dhimma.—Scheiber, A. The role of the Tzitzit in agreements.—Somogyi, J. Chess and backgammon in Ad-

(Continued)

NN°°R 3.58 OC,I,IIbo PC,1,2,I SL J,1,3,I,IIbo (Z1,LC1,X1)

Études romanes dédiées à Mario Roques par ses amis ... 1946. (Card 3)

1. Roques, Mario Louis, 1875- 2. French literature—Old French—Addresses, essays, lectures. 3. French language—Addresses, essays, lectures.

A 47-5401

Harvard univ. Library for Library of Congress [3]

Études orientales, à la memoire de Paul Hirschler... 1950. (Card 2)

Damiri's Hayāt al-hayawān.—Hahn, S. Josephus on prayer in C.Ap.II, 197.—Roth, E. Does the Thorah punish impudence?—Trencsényi-Waldapfel, E. Defense de la version des Septante contre l'accusation d'apanthropie.—Komlós, O. Hirschler Pál irodalmi munkássága. II. Hebrew section.

1. Hirschler, Paul. 2. Essays, Jewish. 3. Essays. I. Komlós, Ottó, ed. II. Komlós, Ottó.

NGO

Eunusia. Festgabe für Ernst Howald zum sechzigsten Geburtstag am 20. April, 1947. Erlenbach-Zürich, E. Rentsch [1947] 207 p. 1 illus. 21cm.

CONTENTS.—Salis, A. von. Imagines illustrium.—Meyer, Ernst. Vom griechischen und römischen Staatsgedanken.—Wehrli, Fritz. Die Geschichtsschreibung im Lichte der antiken Theorie.—Risch, Ernst. Namensdeutungen und Worterklärungen bei den ältesten griechischen Dichtern.—Stoessl, Franz. Leben und Dichtung im Sparta des siebenten Jahrhunderts.—Bezzola, R. R. Olivier.—Straumann, Heinrich. Zur Auffassung vom Wesen der Tragödie in der englischen Literatur vor Shakespeare.—Spoerri, Theophil. Das Lächeln Molières.—Staiger, Emil. Goethes antike Versmasse.—Jedlicka, Gotthard. Grecos "Begräbnis des Grafen Orgaz" in Santo Tomé in Toledo.

444286B. 1. Howald, Ernst, 1887-
N. Y. P. L. October 28, 1948

E-10
8283

L'Europa e il diritto romano; studi in memoria di Paolo Koschaker. Milano, Giuffrè, 1954.

2 v. port. 25 cm.

German, English, Italian, Spanish or French.
Bibliographical footnotes.

1. Law, Roman--Addresses, essays, lectures. 2. Law, Roman--Reception--Addresses, essays, lectures. 3. Koschaker, Paul, 1879-1951
NN * 9. 59 g/// OC PC, 1, 2, 3 SL (LC1, X1, Z1) [I]

NPY

Euzko-Ikaskuntza.
Homenaje a D. Carmelo de Echegaray (Miscelánea de estudios referentes al País Vasco), acordado por la Excma. Diputación de Guipúzcoa con la cooperación de las de Alava y Vizcaya y organizado por la Sociedad de estudios vascos. San Sebastian: Diputación de Guipúzcoa, 1928. xii, 688 p. front. (port.), illus. (incl. maps), pl. 4°.

Mr. Moth.

1. Echegaray y Corta, Carmelo de, 1865- . 2. Basque provinces. 3. Basque literature. 4. Basque language. 5. Title.
N. Y. P. L. June 17, 1929

D-15
5237

EVANGELISCH-LUTHERISCHE KIRCHE IN OLDENBURG.
Auf dem wege; Beiträge zur Geschichte und Aufgabe der Evangelisch-lutherischen Kirche in Oldenburg. [Oldenburg, 1962?] 311 p. illus., map. 23cm.

"Bischof D. Gerhard Jacobi D. D. zu seinem 70. Geburtstag."
Bibliography, p. 47-48.
1. Jacobi, Gerhard, 1891- . I. Title.
NN R 10. 64 g/c (OC)I OS(1b+) PC, 1, I SL (LC1, X1, Z1)

---

* MFGM

EVANGELISCHE KIRCHE DER UNION.
Gestalt und Glaube; Festschrift für Vizepräsident Professor D. Dr. Oskar Söhngen zum 60. Geburtstag am 5. Dezember 1960, hrsg. von einem Freundeskreis. Witten, Luther-Verlag [c1960] 249 p. illus., facsim, music. 25cm.

"Bibliographie Oskar Söhngen," p. [224]-232.

1. Söhngen, Oskar, 1900- 2. Evangelical Lutheran church 3. Church music--Lutheran churches.
NN R 6. 63 p/B OS PC, 1, 2, 3 SL MU, 1, 3 (LC1, X1, Z1) [I]

BAC

ÉVENTAIL de l'histoire vivante; hommage à Lucien Febvre, offert par l'amitié d'historiens, linguistes, géographes, économistes, sociologues, ethnologues [à l'occasion de son 75e anniversaire] Paris, A. Colin, 1953. 2 v. illus., port., maps. 25cm.

Various contributors.
Bibliographical footnotes.
1. Febvre, Lucien Paul Victor, 1878- . 2. History--Addresses, essays, lectures.
NN**X 10. 55 g/v OC PC, 1, 2 SL (Z1, LC1, X1)

YEK

EXPLORATIONS in psychoanalysis; essays in honor of Theodor Reik, on the occasion of his sixty-fifth birthday, May 12, 1953. Robert Lindner, editor; Clement Staff, associate editor. Advisory editorial committee: Gisela Schwaetzer-Barinbaum [and others] New York, Julian press [c1953] xiii, 308 p. illus., port. 25cm.

Includes bibliographies. "Bibliography of Theodor Reik (1911-1952), compiled and annotated by Henry Walter Brann," p. 289-298.
CONTENTS.—Theodor Reik, by J. C. Gustin.—General and theoretical problems: Within the pleasure principle, by J. Nydes. Good
(Continued)
NN*R 8. 54 OC, I PC, 1, 2, I SL (Z1, LC1, X1)

EXPLORATIONS in psychoanalysis... (Card 2)

gifts to share, by R. P. Berkeley. Thought control and confession compulsion, by J. A. M. Meerloo. Psychodynamics and cognition, by E. Frenkel-Brunswik.—Special studies: On symbolism and the genesis of oramentation, by A. Garma. Recall and distortion of legendary material in the course of psychoanalysis, by M. S. Bergmann. Dame Holle, dream and folk take, by G. Roheim.—Literature and art: Reik and the interpretation of literature, by A. B. Feldman. The reader and the writer, by B. K. Ephron. On artistic production, by F. J. Hacker. The psychoanalyst looks at contemporary art, by F. Alexander.—Clinical and therapeutic studies: Psychological distance as a factor in the
(Continued)

EXPLORATIONS in psychoanalysis... (Card 3)

treatment of a schizophrenic patient by M. Wexler. Psychoanalytic notes on the paranoid personality, by C. F. Sulzberger. False confessions, by M. Frym. The psychodynamics of gambling, by R. Lindner.—Technique and training: Training the third ear, by M. Grotjahn. On current trends in psychoanalytic training, by R. Ekstein. Wir Schueler Reik's, by E. Frankel. Background and aims of the National psychological association for psychoanalysis, by G. Schwaetzer-Barinbaum.

1. Psychoanalysis. 2. Reik, Theodor, 1888- . I. Lindner, Robert Mitchell, 1914- , ed.

BAC

Exuli amico Huizinga historico amici non historici die VII mensis Decembris, anni MCMXLII. Haarlem, H. D. Tjeenk Willink & zoon, 1948. 223 p. illus. 24cm.

Bibliographies included.
CONTENTS.—Eysinga, W. J. M. van. De Internationale synode van Dordrecht, 13 November 1618 — 9 Mei 1619. — Groningen, B. A. van. Over het ordenend verband in Herodotus' historien.—Kalf, J. Wat uit de stadsrekeningen te lezen valt over den bouw van het Middelburgsche raadhuis. — Kan. J. van. Het recht van reden en rekenschap.—Leeuw, G. van der. Dans en beschaving.—Meijers, E. M. De St. Maartenslieden van Giethoorn.—Scholten, P. Over spel en ernst in het recht.—Vollgraff, C. W. De elve.

481341B. 1. Huizinga, Johan, 1872-1945. 2. History—Addresses, essays, lectures.
N. Y. P. L. August 18, 1949

OAP

FABER, ELMAR, ed.
Wissenschaft aus nationaler Verantwortung; Beiträge zum nationalen Kulturvorbild der Deutschen Demokratischen Republik auf dem Gebiet der Wissenschaft. Georg Mayer zum 70. Geburtstag herzlichst dediziert. [Herausgeber Elmar Faber, Rudolf Gehrke und Heinz Thiemig] Leipzig, Karl-Marx-Universität, 1963. 266 p. illus., port. 25cm.

(Continued)
NN R 11. 63 e/c OC, II, IIIbo (OS)I PC, 1, 2, 3, I, II SL E, 1, 2, 3, I, II ST, 1t, 2t, 3, I, II (LC1, X1, Z1)
2

FABER, ELMAR, ed. Wissenschaft aus nationaler Verantwortung... (Card 2)

Bibliographical footnotes.

1. Science--Social and economic aspects. 2. Science and state--Germany. 3. Mayer, Georg, 1892- . I. Leipzig. Universität. II. Title. III. Faber, Elmar. t. 1963.

FACIUS, FRIEDRICH, ed. Geistiger Umgang mit der Vergangenheit... (Card 2)

Beiträgen, p. 236-251.

CONTENTS. --Beginn der Oper in Frankreich, von K. F. Reinking. --Erinnerung an den Esprit des lois, von E. Hölzle. --Wilhelmsthal bei Eisenach, von F. Facius. --Christian Freidrich Schwan, 1733-1815, von L. W. Böhm. --Ein deutscher Michel, von W. Gunzert. --Aus dem klassischen Weimar, von W. Huschke. --André Chénier und die Französische Revolution, von B. Schütz-Sevin. --Rund um den Fürstenbund, von H. Tümmler. --Friedrich von Holstein und Paul Graf Wolff Metternich, (Continued)

PED

Fabry, Charles, 1867–

Charles Fabry. Œuvres choisies, publiées à l'occasion de son jubilé scientifique. Paris, Gauthier-Villars, 1938.

vi, 695, [1] p. incl. front. (port.) illus. diagrs., VII pl. 28cm.

"Il a été tiré de cet ouvrage 10 exemplaires sur pur fil Lafuma, non numérotés hors commerce; et 350 exemplaires sur papier de luxe numérotés de 1 à 350. no 73."

"J'y ai rassemblé une partie des œuvres publiées, depuis près de cinquante ans, soit par moi seul, soit en collaboration avec plusieurs autres physiciens, particulièrement avec mm. J. Macé de Lépinay, A. Perot et H. Buisson."—Préface.

(Continued on next card)

40-3264

[3]

Fest

FACIUS, FRIEDRICH, ed. Geistiger Umgang mit der Vergangenheit... (Card 3)

von W. Frauendienst. --Die gelben Gewerkschaften in der sozialen Bewegung am Beginn des 20. Jahrhunderts, von H. Angermeier. --Von den Zünften zu den Verbänden der Arbeitgeber und Arbeitnehmer der Gegenwart, von H. Schlick. --Schwankendes System der Gleichgewichtes, von W. W. Schütz. --Das Ressentiment in der deutschen Geschichte, von G. Böse.

1. Civilization--Addresses, essays, lectures. 2. Andreas, Willy, 1884- . I. Reinking, Karl Franz, joint ed. II. Schlick, Heinrich, joint ed. III. Schlick, Heinrich.

Fabry, Charles, 1867– Charles Fabry. Œuvres choisies ... 1938. (Card 2)

CONTENTS.—Interférences et applications.—Questions diverses d'optique. — Électricité. — Photométrie. Mesure des radiations. — Astrophysique. Géophysique. — Enseignement. Vulgarisation. — Liste des publications de Ch. Fabry (p. [669]–689)

1. Physics—Collected works. 2. Light. I. Macé de Lépinay, Jules Charles Antoine, 1851–1904. II. *Perot, Alfred, 1863–1925. III. *Buisson, Henri, 1873–

[Full name: Marie Paul Auguste Charles Fabry]

40-3264

Library of Congress QC3.F2

[3] 530.4

E-11
2406

FACOLTÀ VALDESE DI TEOLOGIA, Rome.

Ginevra e l'Italia; raccolta di studi promossa dalla Facoltà valdese di teologia di Roma a cura di Delio Cantimori [et al] Firenze, G.C. Sansoni [1959]

x, 769 p. 24cm. (Biblioteca storica Sansoni. Nuova ser. v. 34)

"All'Università di Ginevra nel IV centenario della sua fondazione."

Bibliographical footnotes.

CONTENTS. --I rapporti tra i valdesi franco-italiani e (Continued)

NN X 4.61 a/ (OC)II, III OS(lb) I PC, 1, 2, 3, I, II, III SL (LC1, X1, Z1)

4

E-13
6160

Fachliteratur des Mittelalters; Festschrift für Gerhard Eis, hrsg. von Gundolf Keil [et al.] Stuttgart, J. B. Metzler [1968]

[x, 584 p. facsims., port. 24 cm.

Papers in German, English, French of Dutch.

Includes bibliographies.

"Verzeichnis der Schriften von Gerhard Eis": p. 499-534.

1. Civilization, Medieval--Addresses, essays, lectures. I. Eis, Gerhard, 1908- II. Keil, Gundolf, ed.

NN*R 9.69 v/a OC, I, II PC, 1, I, II SL (LC1, X1, Z1) [I]

FACOLTÀ VALDESE DI TEOLOGIA, Rome. Ginevra e l'Italia... (Card 2)

i riformatori d'Oltralpe prima di Calvino, [di] G. Gonnet. --La colonia piemontese a Ginevra del sec. XVI [di] A. Pascal. --Bernardino Ochino esule a Ginevra (1542-1545) [di] B. Nicolini. --La "Impietas Valentini Gentilis" e il corruccio di Calvino [di] T. R. Castiglione. --Spigolature per la storia del nicodemismo italiano [di] D. Cantimori. --Libertà e dogma secondo Calvino e secondo i riformati italiani [di] V. Subilia. --Influenze franco-ginevrine nella formazione della discipline ecclesiastiche valdesi alla fine del XVI secolo [di] G. Peyrot. --Ginevra e la Riforma in Sicilia [di] S. Caponetto. -- La comunità evangelica (Continued)

E-11
8135

FACIUS, FRIEDRICH, ed.

Geistiger Umgang mit der Vergangenheit; Studien zur Kultur- und Staatengeschichte. Willy Andreas dargebracht von Schülern und Mitarbeitern, hrsg. von Friedrich Facius, Karl Franz Reinking [und] Heinrich Schlick. Stuttgart, C. Belser, 1962.

xiv, 251 p. port. 24cm.

Bibliography included in "Bemerkungen und Hinweise zu den (Continued)

NN R 11.63 g/ OC, I, II, IIIbo PC, 1, 2, I, II SL (LC1, X1, Z1) [I]

3

FACOLTÀ VALDESE DI TEOLOGIA, Rome. Ginevra e l'Italia... (Card 3)

italiana a Londra nel XVI secolo ed i suoi rapporti con Ginevra [di] L. Firpo. --La libertà politica di Ginevra agli inizi del seicento [di] L. Marini. --Riforma italiana e mediazioni ginevrine nella nuova Inghilterra puritana [di] G. Spini. --Il rifugio dei valdesi a Ginevra (1686-1690) [di] A. Armand-Hugon. --Il problema degli articoli fondamentali nel Nubes testium di Giov. Alfonso Turrettini [di] G. Miegge. --G. G. Burlamacchi e la storia costituzionale del settecento [di] M. M. Rossi. --Voltaire e Ginevra [di] P. Alatri. -- Il Sismondi e Napoleone [di] C. Pellegrini. --J. J. de Sellon (1782-1839) ed i fratelli (Continued)

FACOLTÀ VALDESE DI TEOLOGIA, Rome. Ginevra e l'Italia... (Card 4)

G. e C. di Cavour di fronte alla crisi politica europea del 1830 [di] E. Passerin d'Entrèves. --Vicende nizzarde e piemontesi di un professore di Ginevra, H. Dameth [di] F. Venturi. --La chiesa evangelica degli esuli italiani a Ginevra (1850-1855) [di] V. Vinay.

1. Reformation. 2. Reformers, Italian. 3. Waldenses--Hist. I. Series. II. Title. III. Cantimori, Delio, ed.

FACULTÉ DE THEOLOGIE DE L'ÉGLISE ÉVANGÉLIQUE LIBRE DU CANTON DE VAUD, Lausanne. Mélanges historiques offerts à monsieur Jean Meyhoffer... (Card 3)

des amis de la religion et de la patrie, à Vevey, 1799-1800, par M. Bonnard. -- Le débat sur l'église et sa composition au sein du réveil, par L. Rumpf. -- Liste des publications de M. Jean Meyhoffer.

1. Church history--Addresses, essays, lectures. 2. Meyhoffer, Jean, 1882-

---

F-10
1678

FACSIMILES of English royal writs to A.D. 1100 presented to Vivian Hunter Galbraith; edited by T.A.M. Bishop and P. Chaplais. Oxford, At the Clarendon press, 1957. xxiv, [50] p. 30 plates, port. 29cm.

"A select bibliography of the publications of V.H. Galbraith 1911-1957," p. [33]-[38].

1. Writs. 2. Great Britain--Hist.--Norman period, 1066-1154--Sources. 3. Galbraith, Vivian Hunter, 1889- . I. Bishop, T.A.M., ed. II. Chaplais, Pierre, ed. III. Bishop, T.A.M.

NN R 12.57 e/ OC, I, II, IIIbo PC, 1, 2, 3, I, II SL E, 1, I, II
(LC1, X1, C1, Y1, Z1)

ZDC

Facultés catholiques de Lyon. Memorial J. Chaine. Lyon, 1950. 408 p. illus., port. 26cm. (Bibliothèque de la Faculté catholique de théologie de Lyon. v.5)

"Bibliographie de M. Chaine," p. [25]-27. Bibliographical footnotes.

1. Chaine, Joseph, 1888- 2. Theology--Essays and misc. I. Title.

NN** 12 54 a/e (OC)I OS PC,1,2,I SL
(U1,LC1,X1,Z1)

TAH

Facts and factors in economic history; articles by former students of Edwin Francis Gay. Cambridge, Mass., Harvard university press, 1932.

x, 757 p. front. (port.) diagrs. $22\frac{1}{2}$cm.

"This volume ... [prepared] with the co-operation of the Graduate school of business administration, Harvard university."—Pref., signed: Arthur H. Cole, A. L. Dunham [and] N. S. B. Gras, committee in charge.

1. Economic conditions. 2. Gay, Edwin Francis, 1867- I. Cole, Arthur Harrison, 1889- II. Dunham, Arthur Louis. III. Gras, Norman Scott Brien, 1884- IV. Harvard university. Graduate school of business administration. V. Title: Economic history, Facts and factors in.

Library of Congress HC12.F3 33-2564
Copyright A 58959 [7] 330.4

SIO

Fællesforeningen for Danmarks Brugsforeninger.
Fællesforeningen for Danmarks Brugsforeninger, 1896–1946. København, Det danske Forlag [1946] 465 p. illus. 26cm.

"Hovedredaktør: A. Axelsen Drejer."
CONTENTS.—Poulsen, N. C. Ved halvtreds Aars Jubilæet.—Fynning, Andreas. De gamle Brugsforeninger.—Drejer, A. A. F. D. B. gennem halvtreds Aar.—Nielsen, Frederik. Retningslinier før og nu.—Vilstrup, V. F. D. B.s Produktionsvirksomheder. —Fabricius, Louis. Brugsforeningerne og F. D. B.—Arnfred, J. Th. Som Led af Helheden.

380420B. 1. Co-operation, Distributive—Denmark. I. Drejer, Aage Axelsen, 1889- , ed.
N. Y. P. L. April 8, 1947

ZDC

FACULTÉ DE THEOLOGIE DE L'ÉGLISE ÉVANGÉLIQUE LIBRE DU CANTON DE VAUD, Lausanne. Mélanges historiques offerts à monsieur Jean Meyhoffer docteur en théologie. Lausanne, 1952. 112 p. 24cm.

Includes bibliographies.
CONTENTS. — La conversion d'Augustin, par J. Barnaud. — La préhistoire de l'anabaptisme à Zurich (1523-1525) par F. Blanke. — L'histoire. (Continued)

NN 11.55 p/ OS PC, 1, 2 SL (Z1, LC1, X1)

AN
+
(Mannerheim)

Fältmarskalk Mannerheim, 75 år den 4 juni 1942; festskrift. Helsingfors, Suomen kirja [1942] 183 p. illus. 29cm.

"Festskriften har redigerats av Kaarlo Hildén, Ragnar Numelin, Birger Fagerström."

335019B. 1. Mannerheim, Gustaf, friherre, 1867- I. Hildén, Kaarlo Thorsten Oskar, 1893- , ed. II. Numelin, Ragnar, 1890- , ed. III. Fagerström, Birger, ed.
N. Y. P. L. September 24, 1947

FACULTÉ DE THEOLOGIE DE L'ÉGLISE ÉVANGÉLIQUE LIBRE DU CANTON DE VAUD, Lausanne. Mélanges historiques offerts à monsieur Jean Meyhoffer... (Card 2)

une discipline théologique, par J.-D. Burger. — Henri Fiot, traducteur de Jean Alphonse Turrettini (une traduction française du Nubes Testium) par J. Courvoisier. --Les martyrologes et la critique; contribution à l'étude du martyrologe protestant des Pays-Bas, par L.-E. Halkin. -- L'Église d'Anvers sous la terreur. Lettres inédites de Johannes Helmichius (1567) par H. Meylan. -- La Societé (Continued)

BWO

FAMÈJA BULGNÈISA.
Bologna. La Famèja bulgnèisa nel venticinquennio della fondazione, 1928-1953. [Questo volume, edito da "La Famèja bulgnèisa è stato diretto da Giuseppe Carlo Rossi] [Bologna, 1953] 208 p. illus., col. plates, ports. 25cm.

"La pubblicazione...esce ora grazie alla fattiva collaborazione dell'Ente provinciale per il turismo e della Camera di commercio, industria ed agricoltura di Bologna."

1. Bologna, Italy (City). 2. Bologna, Italy (City)—Views. I. Rossi, Giuseppe Carlo, ed. II. Turismo, Ente provinciale del. II. Bologna, Italy (Province). III. Title. i. 1953.

NN * * R 6.55 p/ (OC) I, III (OD) III (ED) III OS (1b) PC, 1, 2, I, II, III SL A, 2, I, II, III (LC1, Z1, X1)

*MEC
(Newman)
FANFARE for Ernest Newman; edited by Herbert van Thal. London, A. Barker, 1955. 191 [1] p. port., music. 22cm.

List of Newman's works, p. [192]
CONTENTS. --A letter to Ernest Newman from Professor Schweitzer. --Wagner's second thoughts, by G. Abraham. --Ernest Newman, by N. Cardus. --Giacomo Meyerbeer, by M. Cooper. --Bizet 'Ivan IV', by W. Dean. --
(Continued)

NN** R 6.56 a/>OC, I PC, 1, 2, 3, I SL MU, 2, 4, 5, 6, 7, I (LC1, X1, Z1)

FANFARE for Ernest Newman... (Card 2)

Donizetti: an Italian romantic, by E. Dent. --Words, words..., by C. Hassall. --Meditation, by P. Hope-Wallace. --Ernest Newman, the man, by St. John Nixon. --Ernest Newman, Manchester and the Hallé concerts, by J. F. Russell. --The new interest in Italian nineteenth-century opera by F. Toye. --A young person's appreciation of Ernest Newman, by P. Vincent. --Cherubino and the G minor symphony, by J. A. Westrup.

1. Music--Essays. 2. Newman, Ernest, 1868- . 3. Opera. 4. Essays. 5. Operas, 19th cent. 6. Autographs (Letters)--Schweitzer, A. --Facsimiles. 7. Librettos--Technique. I. Van Thal, Herbert Maurice, 1904- , ed.

*IDO
Federatie voor stenografie "Groote."
Leven en werken van A. W. Groote...ter gelegenheid van zijn 80ste verjaardag, 30 December 1939. Amsterdam: Federatie voor stenografie "Groote" [1939] 72 p., 48 l. incl. front. (port.) illus. (incl. facsims., map.) 27cm.

"Bijlage in stenografie; gedeelten uit het Tijdschrift in Nederlandsch alfabetisch kortschrift (door A. W. Groote geschreven)," 48 l. at end.

49177B. 1. Groote, A. W., 1859-1939. I. Groote, A. W., 1859- . 2. Shorthand—Systems, Dutch, Festschrift.
N. Y. P. L. April 22, 1940

E-10
783
FEESBUNDEL aangebied aan Doktor Barend Frederik Nel, hoogleraar in die pedagogiek aan die Universiteit Pretoria, by geleentheid van sy vyftigste verjaardag op 16 Desember 1955. Jubilee album dedicated to Doctor Barend Frederik Nel, professor of education in the University of Pretoria on the occasion of his fiftieth birthday on 16th December, 1955. Pretoria, J. L. van Schaik, 1955.
(Continued)

NN**R 10.56 g/a OC PC, 1, 2, 3 SL (LC1, X1, Z1, Y1)

FEESBUNDEL aangebied aan Doktor Barend Frederik Nel... (Card 2)

240 p. port. 23cm.

Title also in German and French.
Summaries in English, French or German.
Includes bibliography.
CONTENTS. --Die jubilaris en sy opvoedkundige arbeid, deur P. J. J. du Plessis. --Die verhouding tussen skool en staat in Transvaal, deur A. K. Bot. --Building healthy personalities in children, by C. Buhler. --About thought processes in children and schizophrenics,
(Continued)

FEESBUNDEL aangebied aan Doktor Barend Frederik Nel... (Card 3)

by K. and C. Buhler. --Die aard en betekenis van die skemabegrip of ordeningswete in die proses van sinsformulering, deur H. C. Castelyn. --L'Institut des sciences de l'éducation de l'Université de Genève et l'enseignement de la pédagogie, par R. Dottrens. --Die C. N. O. -stryd in Nederland en in Suid-Afrika. Ooreenkoms en verskil, deur J. J. du Toit. --The development of the ideal self, by R. J. Havighurst. --The importance of the Würzburg work to contemporary psychology, by G. Humphrey. --Over enkele kwesties, de verhouding van onderwijsstelsel en politica in enig land betreffende, door M. J. Langeveld. --'n Beskouing oor die gebruik van die fopspeen, deur
(Continued)

FEESBUNDEL aangebied aan Doktor Barend Frederik Nel... (Card 4)

A. B. Nel. --De van-zelf-sprekendheid en het onderwijs, door H. Nieuwenhuis. --Die teoretiese onderbou van en praktiese toepassing uit die pedagogiek, deur C. K. Oberholzer. --De opleiding en selectie van de leraars voor het middelbaar onderwijs in België, door R. L. Plancke. --Bijdrage tot de analyse van de traditionele aanpak van de didacticus in verband met de intellectuele vorming zijner leerlingen, door F. W. Prins. --Die "Schau" as metode van die begrypende sielkunde, deur P. R. Skawran. --Ergriffenheitsspiel und Bedeutungsverleihungsspiel, von E. Spranger. --Begaafdheid
(Continued)

FEESBUNDEL aangebied aan Doktor Barend Frederik Nel... (Card 5)

en bestemming, door I. C. van Houte. --Das Bewusstsein und die phänomenologische Methode in der Psychologie, von A. Wellek. --Ueber Irrationalismus und seine Antithesen in der Seelenlehre, von A. Willwoll. --Lys van publikasie van prof. dr. B. F. Nel (p. 235-239)--Review of the publications of prof. dr. B. F. Nel (p. 239-240).

1. Nel, Barend Frederik, 1905- . 2. Education--Psychology. 3. Education--Addresses, essays, lectures.

D-15
3173
FEESBUNDEL vir Prof. Dr. Jan Antonie Engelbrecht; 'n huldigingsblyk aan hom opgedra deur sy oud-studente ter geleentheid van sy vyf-en-sestigste verjaardag, 27 Augustus 1961. Johannesburg, Afrikaanse pers [1961] 93 p. port. 22cm.

CONTENTS. --Die benoeming van woordgroepe, deur J. Breed. --Verledetyd, subjunktief en konsekutief in Zoeloe, deur J. de Clercq. --Die affrikata van Noord-Sotho, deur T. M. H. Endemann. --Die gesnedenheid
(Continued)

NN R 8.64 e/b OC PC, 1, 2 SL (LC1, X1, Z1)
2

FEESBUNDEL vir Prof. Dr. Jan Antonie Engelbrecht... (Card 2)

van foneemverbindings in Sotho, deur J. A. Ferreira. --Die vergelykend-historiese literatuurwetenskap en sy bruikbaarheid in die geval van die Bantoetale, deur P. S. Groenewald. --Inleidende opmerkinge oor die predikatiewe woordgroepe in Tswana, deur C. J. H. Kruger. --Die dieresprokie by die Bantoe, deur J. D. N. Lotz. --Die gebruik van die objektskonkord in Zoeloe, deur B. I. C. van Eeden. --Die woordklasse van Noord-Sotho, deur E. B. van Wyk. --'n vergelykende benadering van die omskrywingskonstruksie in die Suidafrikaanse Bantoetale, deur D. Ziervogel.
1. African studies--Collections. 2. Engelbrecht, Jan Antonie.

E-10
5012

FEESTBUNDEL ter gelegenheid zijner veertigjarige ambtsbediening op den 28 November 1889 aangeboden aan Matthias de Vries door zijne leerlingen. Utrecht, J. L. Beijers, 1889. vi, 164 p. 25cm.

CONTENTS. — Het comisch intermezzo in Bredero's Rodderick ende Alphonsus, door H. J. Eymael. — Barwirdig of barwurdig, door J. H. Gallée. — Woordverklaringen, door W. L. van Helten. — Termino sacrum door G. Kalff. — Voorbeelden van klankkomzetting in Baltisch-Slawisch, door H. Kern. — Naar aanleiding van eene spreekwijze, door A. (Continued)

NN X 3.58 e/, OC PC, 1, 2 SL (LC1, X1, Z1, C1)

FEESTBUNDEL ter gelegenheid zijner veertigharige ambtsbediening... (Card 2)

Kluyver. — Rodenburgh en zijne Casandra, door H. E. Moltzer. — Over eenige gevallen van afwisseling tusschen i(y) en u(ui) in het Nederlandsch, door J. W. Muller. — Noode, door T. Nolen. — Over den tekst van het reisverhaal van Johannes de Hese, door G. Penon. — De la nonain qui mauga la fleur du chol, door J. J. Salverda de Grave. — Aanschenden, door F. A. Stoett. — Spreekwoorden en spreekwijzen, door J. Verdam. — De verhouding van ee en ei uit ai in het Nederlandsch, door J. te Winkel.

1. Vries, Matthias de, 1820-1892. 2. Dutch language--Addresses, essays, lectures.

AN
(Mackensen)

Feldmarschall v. Mackensen; eine Festschrift zu seinem 80 Geburtstage... Berlin: E. S. Mittler & Sohn, 1929. 56 p. facsims., front., plates, ports. 4°.

479579A. 1. Mackensen, Anton Ludwig Friedrich August von, 1849-
N. Y. P. L. June 25, 1930

M-11
4549

FELIÚ CRUZ, GUILLERMO, 1901- , comp.
Estudios sobre Andrés Bello [por] José Victorino Lastarria [et al.] Compilación y prólogo de Guillermo Feliú Cruz. Santiago de Chile, Fondo Andrés Bello, 1966. 1 v. 28cm.

Tomo 1.
Bibliography by Emilio Vaisse with additions by Guillermo Feliú Cruz (v. 1, p. 255-277) and by Eugenio Orrego Vicuña (v. 1, p. 279-290.)

1. Bello, Andrés, 1781-1865. 2. Bello, Andrés, 1781-1865--Bibl. I. Lastarria, José Victorino, 1817-1888. II. Title.
NN*4. 70m/A OC, I, II PC, 1, 2, I, II SL (LC1, X1, Z1)

A p.v.713

Félix F. Outes; nómina de sus publicaciones, 1897–1922. Edición privada, con motivo del XXV aniversario de su labor de publicista. Buenos Aires: Impr. y casa editora "Coni," 1922. 57 p. 22cm.

CONTENTS.—Sobre esta publicación.—Curriculum vitae.—Publicaciones.—Publicaciones editadas bajo la dirección de Félix F. Outes.

1. Outes, Félix Faustino, 1878-1939—Bibl.
N. Y. P. L. July 18, 1941

Write on slip words underlined below and class mark —
RAA

...Fem danske Studier tilegnet Vilh. Andersen den 16. Oktober 1934. København: P. Branner, 1934. 101 p. 21½cm. (Det Filologisk-historiske Samfund. Studier fra Sprog- og Oldtidsforskning. Nr. 167.)

"Skrifter udgivet af Litteraturvidenskabeligt Selskab. I."
CONTENTS.—Albeck, G. N. F. S. Grundtvigs Digtning om Peter Villemoes.—Henriques, A. Harald Haarfager, Oehlenschlägers første nordiske Drama.—Kruuse, J. Holberg og Swift.—Stangerup, H. J. L. Heiberg og Naturvidenskaberne.—Stevns, M. Kom i den sidste Nattevagt!

1. Andersen, Vilhelm, 1864- . 2. Danish literature—Hist. and crit. I. Ser.
N. Y. P. L. September 10, 1935

---

* PBN

Ferencz József országos rabbiképző intézet, Budapest.
...Festschrift zum 50jährigen Bestehen der Franz-Josef-Landesrabbinerschule in Budapest, herausgegeben von Ludwig Blau. Budapest, 1927. viii, 216, 97 p. front. 4°.

Added, Hungarian and Hebrew title-pages.
Text in English, German, Hungarian and Hebrew.
At head of title: Alexander Kohut Memorial Foundation.
Contents: BLAU, L. & M. KLEIN. A Ferenc József országos rabbiképző intézet első 50 éve. BLAU, L. Prosbol im Lichte der griechischen Papyri und der Rechtsgeschichte. FISCHER, J. Dr. Alexander Kohut. Ein Lebensbild. KOHUT, G. A. Con-

(Continued)

407823A
N. Y. P. L. February 25, 1929

Ferencz József országos rabbiképző intézet, Budapest: ...Festschrift... (Card 2)

cerning Alexander Kohut. Hebräische Abteilung: Abhandl. von B. Heller, S. Hevesi, A. Hoffer, B. Edelstein und M. Weisz.

1. Rabbinical seminaries—Hungary—Budapest. 2. Debt—Jews. 3. Sabbatical year. 4. Kohut, Alexander, 1842-1894. 5. Kohut, Alexander, 1842-1894.—Bibl. 6. Blau, Ludwig, 1861- , editor. 7. Alexander Kohut Memorial Foundation, New York.
N. Y. P. L. February 25, 1929

D-15
9400

Ferguson, Alan D *ed.*
Essays in Russian history; a collection dedicated to George Vernadsky, edited by Alan D. Ferguson and Alfred Levin. Hamden, Conn., Archon Books, 1964.
xxv, 317 p. port. 22 cm.
Chiefly essays by former students of Mr. Vernadsky published in appreciation of his high standards as a teacher, counselor, and friend.
"Bibliography of the works of George Vernadsky": p. [xiii]–xxv.
Includes bibliographical references.

(Continued)

NN* R 4.65 g/J OC, I, IIb* PC, 1, 2, I SL S, 1, 2, I (LC 1, X1, Z1) [I]

FERGUSON, ALAN D., ed. Essays in Russian history... (Card 2)

CONTENTS. — Dedication. — Bibliography of the works of George Vernadsky.—George Vernadsky as a historian of ancient and medieval Russia, by D. Obolensky.—The name Slav, by B. P. Lozinski.—Muscovite legal thought, the law of theft, and the problem of centralization, 1497–1589, by O. P. Backus.—La Piquetière's projected mission to Moscow in 1682 and the Swedish policy of Louis XIV, by A. Lossky.—The Russian military settlements, 1825–1866, by A. D. Ferguson.—A. S. Khomiakov on the agricultural and industrial problem in Russia, by P. K. Christoff.—The Russian national economy

(Continued)

FERGUSON, ALAN D., ed. Essays in Russian history... (Card 3)

and emancipation, by A. A. Skerpan.—June 3, 1907: action and reaction, by A. Levin.—Hitler's decision to attack the Soviet Union: the end of the grand design, by E. H. Boehm.

1. Russia--Hist.--Addresses, essays, lectures. 2. Vernadskii, Georgii Vladimirovich, 1887- I. Levin, Alfred, joint ed. II. Ferguson, Alan D.

AN (Castilho, W.)

A festa do Trianon em homenagem ao general Waldomiro Castilho de Lima. 15 de janeiro de 1933. São Paulo [Empresa gráfica da "Revista dos tribunais," 1933] 206 p. front. (port.) 19cm.

176684B. 1. Castilho de Lima, Waldomiro.
N. Y. P. L. December 29, 1942

BGP

Fergusson college, Poona, India. Historical and economic association.

Historical and economic studies. Published on the occasion of the silver jubilee of the Historical and economic association of the Fergusson college, Poona. Ed. by: D. G. Karve. [Poona] 1941. v, ii, 238, vi p. illus. 22cm.

"Dedicated to Prof. V. G. Kale...by the past and present members of the association."

CONTENTS.—Bajirao in the land of the brave Bundelas, by D. V. Potdar.—The evolutionary policy of Bajirao I, by D. V. Apte.—Gujerat and Maharashtra, by K. H.

(Continued)

N. Y. P. L. December 29, 1944

---

*IDT

Festbuch zur hundertjährigen Jubelfeier der deutschen Kurzschrift. Zur Mosengeilfeier... hrsg. von... Chr. Johnen. Berlin, F. Schrey, 1896. 207 p. illus. 22cm.

1. Shorthand—Hist. 2. Shorthand—Biog. I. Johnen, Christian, 1862- , ed.
NN 4.53 OC PC, 1, 2, I SL (LC1, X1, X1)

Fergusson college, Poona, India. Historical and economic association. Historical and economic studies... (Card 2)

Kamdar.—Some aspects of social life under Maratha rule, by R. V. Oturkar.—Where stands Clio? By S. R. Sharma.—Valabhi, the ancient Buddhist university, by M. G. Dikshit.—The state and the individual, by M. R. Palande.—What shall we do with our Indian states? By R. H. Kelkar.—Foundations of political science, by S. V. Kogekar.—Basic principles of minimum living wage, by S. G. Beri.—The problem of unemployment, by P. M. Limaye.—Bombay land revenue code (Amendment) act of 1939, by D. V. Divekar.—Population and progress, by D. G. Karve.—An approach to Indian economics, by J. J. Anjaria.—Civil aviation in India on the eve of war, by M. R. Dhekney and B. R. Dhekney.—Economics since Marshall, by T. M. Joshi.—The

(Continued)

N. Y. P. L. December 29, 1944

Write on slip, name, year, vol., page of magazine and class mark — BVA

Festgabe A. Heisenberg zum 60. Geburtstage gewidmet, hrsg. von Franz Dölger.

(Byzantinische Zeitschrift. Berlin, 1930. 8°. Bd.30, p.i-xiii, 1-681. plates.)

form 400a [ii-7-30 25m]

Ferguson college, Poona, India. Historical and economic association. Historical and economic studies... (Card 3)

building up of economics, by N. A. Mavlankar.—The educated middle class takes to industries, by S. V. Kale.—The competitive system, by S. G. Barve.—The future of foreign capital in India, by N. G. Abhyankar.—Towards national self-sufficiency, by R. C. Joshi.—Some aspects of local finance, by P. V. Agashe.

281974B. 1. India—Hist. 2. India—Govt., 1929- 3. Economic history—India. 4. Kale, Vaman Govind, 1876- I. Karve, Dattatraya Gopal, ed. II. Title.
N. Y. P. L. December 29, 1944

---

*YN

Festgabe für Adolf Jülicher zum 70. Geburtstag, 26. Januar 1927... Tübingen: J. C. B. Mohr, 1927. viii, 281 p. front. (port.), facsim. 8°.

Dedication signed R. Bultmann; H. v. Soden.

Contents: SATTLER, W. Die Anawim im Zeitalter Jesu Christi. BAUER, W. Jesu der Galiläer. MEYER, A. Die Entstehung des Markusevangeliums. CURTIS, W. A. The parable of the Labourers. RADE, M. Der Nächste. WETTER, G. P. Die Damaskusvision und das paulinische Evangelium. MUNDLE, W. Das Problem des Zwischenzustandes in dem Abschnitt 2. Kor. 5, 1-10. WINDISCH, H. Die fünf johanneischen Parakletsprüche. BULTMANN, R. Analyse des ersten Johannesbriefes. HOLL, K. Ein Bruchstück

(Continued)

N. Y. P. L. November 19, 1928

PCP

FERRARI, CARLO, ed.

High temperatures in aeronautics; proceedings of the symposium held in Turin to celebrate the 50th anniversary of the "Laboratorio di aeronautica," Politecnico di Torino, 10-12 September, 1962. Oxford, New York, Pergamon Press; Milano, Taburini editore, 1964.

xxiv, 446 p. illus. 25 cm. (International series of monographs in aeronautics and astronautics. Division IX: Symposia, v. 15)

International symposium organized by the Politecnico di Torino. English, French, or Italian.

Includes bibliographies.

1. Aerothermodynamics. 2. Building materials--Effect of temperature. 3. High temperatures. I. Turin. Politecnico. Laboratorio di Aeronautica. t. 1964
NN* R 10.65 g/ OC (OS)I, Ib* PC, 1, 2, 3, I SL ST, 1t, 2t, 3t, I (LC1, X1, Z1)

Festgabe für Adolf Jülicher... (Card 2)

aus einem bisher unbekannten Brief des Epiphanius. MÜLLER, K. Kanon 2 und 6 von Konstantinopel 381 und 382. SCHWARTZ, E. Die Kaiserin Pulcheria auf der Synode von Chalkedon. LIETZMANN, H. Ein liturgischer Papyrus des Berliner Museums. SODEN, H. v. Der lateinische Paulustext bei Marcion und Tertullian.

370950A. 1. Bible, N. T.—Misc. 2. Church history, Early. 3. Jülicher, Adolf, 1857- . 4. Bultmann, Rudolf, 1884- , editor. 5. Soden, Hermann, Freiherr von, 1852- , editor.
N. Y. P. L. November 19, 1928

3-MAI

Festgabe für Alois Fuchs zum 70. Geburtstage am. 19. Juni 1947, hrsg. von Dr. theol. Wilhelm Tack . . . Paderborn, F. Schöningh, 1950. xv, 533 p. illus., plates. 24cm.

Bibliographies included.

595529B. 1. Art, Christian—Germany. 2. Fuchs, Alois, 1877- I. Tack, Wilhelm, ed.
N. Y. P. L. November 29, 1951

Festgabe für bundesrat dr. h. c. Edmund Schulthess ... [1938] (Card 4)

CONTENTS—Continued.

Verschiedenes: Schirmer, August. Bundesrat Schulthess in seinen beziehungen zum schweizerischen gewerbestand. Ilg, Konrad. Die schweizerischen gewerkschaften in den letzten 25 jahren. Steiner, E. Das aargauische und das neue eidgenössische strafrecht. Wettstein, O. Regierungen und presse im wandel der zeiten.

1. Schulthess, Edmund, 1868- 2. Switzerland — Economic conditions. I. Mangold, Fritz, 1871-

A C 38-3000

New York. Public library for Library of Congress [2]

AN
+
(Ruppel, A.)

Festgabe Aloys Ruppel; zur Vollendung seines fünfzigsten Lebensjahres, 1882 * am 21. Juni * 1932. Dargebracht von seinen Freunden. Mainz: Zaberndruck, 1932. 67 p. illus. (part mounted, incl. facsim., port.) 29cm.

Contents: Introitus. Biographie. Grüsse aus Amerika. KEUNE, J. B. Erinnerungen an die Lothringer Zeit. KÖNIG, F. Wir Beide in Metz. THIELE, J. Zur Erinnerung an Fulda. EPPELSHEIMER, H. W. Ein Rückblick auf Mainz. MORI, G. Direktor Ruppel und die Gutenberg-Gesellschaft. RODENBERG, J. A Magonza da Roma. RUTZEN, F. Gott grüss die Kunst. ZANDERS, J. W. Papier und Druckkunst. Bibliographie der Arbeiten Ruppels. Die Namen der Mitarbeiter Ruppels. KLEUKENS, C. H. Die Gutenberg- und Goethe-Ehrung.

613738A. 1. Ruppel, Aloys Leonhard, 1882-
N. Y. P. L. April 25, 1933

MAR
+

Festgabe an Carl Hofer, zum siebzigsten Geburtstag, 11. Oktober 1948. [Potsdam, E. Stichnote, 1949] 60 p. illus. 31cm.

No. 149 of 250 copies.

553713B. 1. Hofer, Carl, 1878-

NN*

TAH

Festgabe für bundesrat dr. h. c. Edmund Schulthess zum siebzigsten geburtstag am 2. märz 1938, dargebracht von freunden und mitarbeitern. Zürich, Polygraphischer verlag a.-g. [1938]

534 p. incl. tables, diagrs. front. (mounted port.) 23cm.

Cover-title: Bundesrat Schulthess; festgabe 1938.

CONTENTS. — Mangold, Fritz. Zum geleit. — Schüpbach, Hermann. Ansprache in der Bundesversammlung.—Motta, Giuseppe. Dedica.—Lauchenauer, Eduard. Die politische herkunft.—Péquignot, Eugène. M. le conseiller fédéral E. Schulthess, homme d'état. — I. Allgemeine wirtschaftliche fragen: Renggli, P. Das recht auf handels- und gewerbefreiheit in der schweizerischen Bundesverfassung. Rappard, W. E. Des origines et de l'évolution de l'étatisme fédéral en Suisse. Stucki, Walter. 25 jahre schweizerische aussenhandelspolitik. Jöhr, Adolf.

(Continued on next card)

A C 38-3000

[2]

---

* PBS

Festgabe für Claude G. Montefiore; überreicht anlässlich der Tagung des Weltverbandes für religiös-liberales Judentum in Berlin. Berlin: Philo Verlag, G.m.b.H., 1928. 156 p. 8°.

Contents: An Claude G. Montefiore. BAECK, L. "Das Reich des Allmächtigen." BAYER, E. Hiob — Die Befreiung des Gottesbegriffs von dem Problem des Leids. BLAU, J. Jüdischkeit. DIENEMANN, M. "Die Überwindung der Erbsünde" im Judentum. ELBOGEN, I. Der Streit um die "positiv-historische Reform." FALKENBERG, H. "Erew." FREUDENTHAL, M. Ein liberales Gutachten als historisches Dokument. GALLINER, J. Häusliche Andacht. GOLDMANN, F. Die Grenzen des Liberalismus. GOTTSCHALK, B. Die Anfänge der deutschen Gebetsübersetzungen. GÖTZ, G. Vier Grundbegriffe des liberalen Judentums. HOLZMAN, M. Ein auf

(Continued)

N. Y. P. L. December 19, 1929

Festgabe für bundesrat dr. h. c. Edmund Schulthess ... [1938] (Card 2)

CONTENTS—Continued.

Die Schweiz und das transferproblem. Wetter, Ernst. Grundsätzliches zur revision der wirtschaftsartikel. Hotz, J. Zur schweizerischen zollpolitik der nachkriegszeit. Muller, Édouard. Le rôle de l'industrie alimentaire dans l'économie suisse. — II. Landwirtschaft: Käppeli, J. Unsere lebensmittelversorgung im kriegsfall. Laur, E. Die mitarbeit der landwirtschaftlichen verbände bei den staatlichen massnahmen zur erhaltung des schweizerischen bauernstandes. Flückiger, G. Eidgenössische tierseuchengesetzgebung.—III. Banken: Rossy, Paul. Monsieur Edmond Schulthess à la Commission fédérale des banques. Henggeler, J. Die verrechnung bei fälligkeitsaufschub und stundung gemäss dem Bundesgesetz über die banken und sparkassen vom 8. november

(Continued on next card)

A C 38-3000

[2]

Festgabe für Claude G. Montefiore... (Card 2)

die Septuaginta zurückgehender Übersetzungsfehler. KAHLBERG, A. Das Fahrverbot am Sabbat und an Festtagen. LEHMANN, J. Der "dritte Jesaia." LEVI, S. Maharils Stellung zur Gebetfassung. LEWKOWITZ, J. Wandlungen des Liberalismus. LILIENTHAL, A. Die jüdischen Gemeinden und der Staat. MAYBAUM, I. Geschichtlicher und eschatologischer Messianismus. NORDEN, J. Judentum und Völkerfrieden. OLLENDORF, P. Über soziale Arbeit. SALOMONSKI, M. Der kranke Gottesdienst und seine Heilung. SAMUEL, S. Unser Glaubensbesitz. SELIGMANN, C. Wandlungen jüdischer Frömmigkeit. STERN, H. Weg oder Umweg? VOGELSTEIN, H. Tradition. WIENER, M. Der Messiasgedanke in der Tradition. KOHUT, G. A. To Claude G. Montefiore on his seventieth birthday.

Bibliographical footnotes.

SCHIFF COLLECTION.

449091A. 1. Montefiore, Claude Joseph Goldsmid, 1858- . 2. Essays, Jewish—in German. 3. Judaism—Reform.
N. Y. P. L. December 19, 1929

Festgabe für bundesrat dr. h. c. Edmund Schulthess ... [1938] (Card 3)

CONTENTS—Continued.

1934 nebst den dazugehörigen verordnungen und ergänzungen. Jaberg, Paul. Krisenempfindlichkeit der banken und bankpolitik. — IV. Hotellerie: Ehrensperger, Fritz. Die umschichtungstendenzen im fremdenverkehr. Seiler, Franz. Das hotelhilfsinstitut des Bundes und seine tätigkeit. — V. Wasserwirtschaft und elektrizität: Villars, M. 50 jahre schweizerische elektrizitätswirtschaft. Keller, E. Ueber aargauische wasserwirtschafts- und elektrizitätspolitik. — VI. Sozialpolitik: Butler, Harold. Tendances modernes de la politique sociale. Kaufmann, M. Zur frage der durchführung internationaler konventionen. Schmidt, Dora. Die fabrikgesetzrevision von 1914. Giorgio, Hans. Die reform der schweizerischen krankenversicherung. — VII.

(Continued on next card)

A C 38-3000

[2]

F-11
471

FESTGABE dargebracht dem Verlage Otto Elsner zum 1. Juli 1921 [von] Walther v. Altrock [et al. Berlin, 1921] viii, 262 p. illus., facsims. 29cm.

CONTENTS. —Wissenschaft und Verlagsbuchhandlung im kaiserlichen Deutschland, von J. Hirschfeld. — Rechtswissenschaft. —Staats- und Sozialwissenschaft, Wirtschaftspolitik. —Kunst und Literatur. —Technik.

1. Elsner (Otto) Verlag. 2. Essays, German--Collections. I. Altrock, Walther Ferdinand Konstantin von, 1873-

NN R 6.65 a/ OC, I (OS)Ib PC, 1, 2, I SL (LC1, X1, Z1)

Write on slip words underlined below and class mark —
* OWB

Festgabe der Deutschen Gesellschaft für Natur- und Völkerkunde Ostasiens zum 70. Geburtstag von Prof. Dr. K. Florenz am 10. Januar 1935. Tokyo: Deutsche Gesellschaft für Natur- und Völkerkunde Ostasiens, 1935. 111 p. 24½cm. (Deutsche Gesellschaft für Natur- und Völkerkunde Ostasiens, Tokyo. Mittheilungen. Bd. 25 B.)

"Bibliographie der Schriften von Karl Florenz," p. 3–6, and bibliographical footnotes.

1. Florenz, Karl Adolf, 1865– . 2. Oriental studies. I. Ser.
N. Y. P. L. September 21, 1936

TIE

Festgabe für Dr. Hans Schorer, ordentlicher Professor für Finanzwissenschaft und Statistik an der Universität Freiburg (Schweiz). Zum siebzigsten Geburtstag, überreicht von Schülern, Freunden und Kollegen. Bern, A. Francke [1947] 268 p. 23cm.

CONTENTS.—Amonn, Alfred. Zur Grundlegung einer Theorie der öffentlichen Gemeinwirtschaft.—Britt, Josef. Die Entwicklung der Bundesbahnfinanzen im Weltkrieg, 1939–1945.—Grossmann, Eugen. Betrachtungen zum Problem der Staatsschuldentilgung. —Kellenberger, Eduard. Volkseinkommen, Steueraufkommen und Militärausgaben.—Kull, Ernst. Aspekte der Staatsverschuldung.—Leugger, Josef. Beitrag zum Problem

(Continued)

N. Y. P. L. December 12, 1947

Festgabe für Dr. Hans Schorer... (Card 2)

der Subventionen und zur Ausgabenlehre.—Meyer, Otto. Wirtschaft des Kleinstaates. —Casasus, Norbert. Über die quantitativen Beziehungen der lagebestimmten Mittelwerte zueinander und zu den errechneten Mittelwerten.—Ebneter, Guido. Armenstatistik unter besonderer Berücksichtigung gegenwärtiger schweizerischer Verhältnisse und allgemein methodischer Fragen.—Jenny, O. H. Über politische Statistik.—Kaufmann, Alois. Umsatz- und Lagerkontrolle im Detailhandelsgeschäft.—Krapf, Kurt. Der Fremdenverkehr als Erkenntnisgegenstand und Statistische Masse.

416139B. 1. Finance. 2. Statistics. 3. Schorer, Hans, 1876–
N. Y. P. L. December 12, 1947

L-13
5303

Festgabe für Dr. Walter Will, Ehrensenator der Universität München, zum 70. Geburtstag am 12. November 1966. (Herausgeber: Siegfried Lauffer. Redaktion: Friedrich Cornelius.) (Köln, Berlin, Bonn, München) Heymann (1966).

225 p. with illus. front. 24 cm.

Includes bibliographical references.

CONTENTS.—Verfassungsrecht vergeht, Reservatrecht besteht? Von O. Bachof. — Kulturgeschichtliche Gedanken, veranlasst durch den

(Continued)

NN*R 6.69 v/ OC, I, Ib*, II PC, 1, I, II SL (LC1, X1, Z1)
[I] .3

FESTGABE für Dr. Walter Will... (Card 2)

Fund eines Geigenglases, von W. Bremen. — Rechtsgedanken der Hethiter, von F. Cornelius.—Zwei altsumerische Schenkungsurkunden, von D. O. Edzard.—The Qantir Stela of the Vizier Rahotep and the statue "ruler of rulers," by L. Habachi.—Recht und konfuzianische Ethik, von H. Hammitzsch.—2000 Jahre deutsche Weinkultur, von H. Jung.—Zur Finanzpolitik der athenischen Demokratie, von S. Lauffer.—Ein Kopf von einem frühen Würfelhocker in der ägyptischen Staatssammlung München, von H. W. Müller. — Zur Bedeutung des Würfelhockers, von A. Eggebrecht. — Die Zerspanungstechnik in der metallverarbeitenden Industrie und ihre wissen-

(Continued)

FESTGABE für Dr. Walter Will... (Card 3)

schaftliche Bedeutung, von H. Schallbroch. — Die Paläontologie im Rahmen der Naturwissenschaften, von O. H. Schindewolf.—Ursprung und Wesen der Maat, der altägyptischen Göttin des Rechts, der Gerechtigkeit und der Weltordnung, von W. Westendorf.

1. Civilization--Addresses, essays, lectures. I. Will, Walter, 1896–
II. Lauffer, Siegfried, ed.

L-10
5407
Bd.3

FESTGABE für Ernst Christmann. [Schriftleitung: Friedrich Ludwig Wagner, Otterbach-Kaiserslautern, F. Arbogast] 1965. xxxiii,191 p. illus.,ports. 21cm. (Jahrbuch zur Geschichte von Stadt- und Landkreis Kaiserslautern. Bd. 3)

Includes bibliographical references. "Veröffentlichungen von Prof. Dr. Ernst Christmann," p. 179-190.

1. Christmann, Ernst, 1885-
NN 6.67 p/R OI (PC)1 (LC1,X1,Z1)

RDV

Festgabe Ernst Gamillscheg zu seinem fünfundsechzigsten Geburtstag, am 28. Oktober 1952, von Freunden und Schülern überreicht. Tübingen, M. Niemeyer, 1952. vi,260 p. port. 25cm.

Text in French or German.
Bibliographical footnotes.
Contents.—Compléments aux dictionnaires de l'ancien français, par M. Roques.—Euphémie et euphémisme, par C. Bruneau.—La langue des traduc-
(Continued)

NN**10.54 OC PC,1,2 SL (Z-1,LC1,X1) [I]

Festgabe Ernst Gamillscheg zu seinem fünfundsechzigsten Geburtstag, am 28. Oktober 1952... (Card 2)

teurs français au XVIe siècle, par R. Lebègue.—L'alexandrin ternaire et la césure féminine chez Mistral, par J. Boutière.—La déchéance d'un terme platonicien: "ma moitié," par G. Gougenheim.—Remarques sur la valeur des préverbes a- et en- (<in-) en ancien français, par R. L. Wagner.—Le préfixe inorganique es dans les noms propres en ancien français, par R. Louis.—Quelques mots
(Continued)

Festgabe Ernst Gamillscheg zu seinem fünfundsechzigsten Geburtstag, am 28. Oktober 1952... (Card 3)

de la langue de Maurice Scève, par V. L. Saulnier. —Die Artikel "fin" im altfranzösischen Wörterbuch, von E. Lommatzsch.—Pyxis im Galloromanischen, von W. von Wartburg.—Fränkische und frankoromanische Wanderwörter in der Romania, von G. Rohlfs.—Erwägungen zu iberoromanischen Substratetymologien, von H. Meier.—Rückläufige Bewegungen in der Entwicklung der romanischen Spra-
(Continued)

Festgabe Ernst Gamillscheg zu seinem fünfundsechzigsten Geburtstag, am 28. Oktober 1952... (Card 4)

chen zum analytischen Typus: dabis – dare habeo – darás, von H. Kuen.—Einige grundsätzliche Bemerkungen zum Vigesimalsystem, von G. Reichenkron.—Lexikalisches aus dem Altfrankoprovenzalischen, von H. Stimm.—Zum Verhältnis von Geschichte und Dichtung in den drei Girart-Epen, von K. Wais.—Der Streit um die Deutung der Sprachlaute, von M. Wandruszka.—Die Bedeutung des Abnormen in Diderots Wissenschaftslehre, von H. K. Weinert.—Sagesse, von J. Wilhelm.

1. Gamillscheg, Ernst, 1887- 2. Romance philology.

E-12
2161

FESTGABE für Friedrich Bülow zum 70. Geburtstag; hrsg. von Otto Stammer und Karl C. Thalheim. Berlin, Duncker & Humblot [1960] 428 p. port. 24cm.

"Schriften von Friedrich Bülow," p. [425]-428.
Includes bibliography.

1. Bülow, Friedrich, 1890- 2. Social sciences--Addresses, essays, lectures. I. Stammer, Otto, ed. II. Thalheim, Karl Christian, 1900- , joint ed.

NN R 1.65 p/ OC, I, II PC, 1, 2, I, II SL E, 1, 2, I, II (LC1, X1, Z1)

E-10
7745

Festgabe für Ernst Löpfe-Benz zu seinem 80. Geburtstag am 5. Februar 1958. [Rorschach, 1958?] 53 p. ports. 25cm.

1. Löpfe-Benz, Ernst, 1878-

NN 3.60 OC, 1b PC, 1 SL (LC1, X1, Z1)

D-16
9765

Festgabe für Friedrich Maurer; zum 70. Geburtstag am 5. Januar 1968. Hrsg. von Werner Besch, Siegfried Grosse und Heinz Rupp. [1. Aufl.] Düsseldorf, Pädagogischer Verlag Schwann [1968]

291 p. illus., maps, port. 21 cm.
"Tabula gratulatoria" ([7] p.) inserted.
Bibliographical footnotes.

CONTENTS.—Die "Grenze" der alemannischen Mundart am nördlichen Oberrhein in sprachhistorischer Sicht, von W. Kleiber.—Wort-

(Continued)

NN*R 6.69 v/ OC, I, II PC, 1, 2, I, II SL (LC1, X1, Z1)
[I]
3

L-10
8928
Bd. 15

FESTGABE des Friedberger Geschichtsvereins zum 750. Jahrestag der ersten Nennung der Burg Friedberg am 26. Oktober 1216. [Friedberg, Wetterau, 1966] 227 p. illus. 24cm. (Wetterauer Geschichtsblätter. Bd. 15)
Includes bibliographies.

(Continued)

NN 10.67 p/ OI (PC)1 (LC1, X1, Z1)
3

FESTGABE für Friedrich Maurer... (Card 2)

feld und Wortinhalt, von H. Rupp.—Mitteilungen ohne Verb, von S. Grosse.—Stilistik und Linguistik, von H. Singer.—Der Weg von der Stabreimlangzeile zum Endreimkurzvers, von S. Gutenbrunner.—Beobachtungen zur Form des deutschen Rolandsliedes, von W. Besch.—Spiel der Interpretation; der Erzähler in Hartmanns Iwein, von X. von Ertzdorff.—"gliete" bei Wolfram von Eschenbach, von G. Meissburger.—Parzivals Kämpfe, von H. Zutt.—Die Mönche von Kolmar; ein Beitrag zur Phänomenologie und zum Begriff des schwarzen Humors, von V. Schupp.—Seuses religiöse Sprache, von B. Boesch.—Eine Sammelhandschrift geistlicher Dichtungen des 12. und 13.

(Continued)

FESTGABE des Friedberger Geschichtsvereins zum 750. (Card 2)

CONTENTS.--Die Friedberger Gemarkung in urgeschichtlicher Zeit, von F. R. Hermann.--Friedberg in römischer und fränkischer Zeit von H. R. Schönberger.--Die Gründung und die Bedeutung der Burg Friedberg unter den Staufern von H. Roth.--Friedberg im Spätmittelalter (1250-1500) von W. H. Braun.--Friedberg in alten Ansichten. Versuch einer topographischen Auswertung von F.H. Herrmann.--Schulen und Bildungs-
(Continued)

FESTGABE für Friedrich Maurer... (Card 3)

Jahrhunderts (Wien 2696), von W. Fechter.—Zu einigen Fassungen der Veronika-Legende in der mittelhochdeutschen Literatur, von K.-E. Geith.—Bibliographie der Veröffentlichungen von Friedrich Maurer 1963-1967, zusammengestellt von S. Grosse (p. 289-291)

1. German language--Addresses, essays, lectures. 2. German literature, Middle High--Addresses, essays, lectures. I. Maurer, Friedrich, 1898- II. Besch, Werner, ed.

FESTGABE des Friedberger Geschichtsvereins zum 750. (Card 2)

möglichkeiten, Kunst und Wissenschaft in Friedberg. Beitrag zu einer Bestandsaufnahme, 1965 von E.R. Niederhoff.--Das Wetterau-Museum-Sinnbild unserer Landschaft, von W. Belz.

1. Friedberg, Germany (Hesse)--Hist.

BAC

Festgabe Friedrich von Bezold dargebracht zum 70. Geburtstag von seinen Schülern, Kollegen und Freunden. Bonn: K. Schroeder, 1921. 346 p. 8°.

Contents: DYROFF, A. Chronos. WIEDEMANN, A. Die aegyptische Geschichte in der Sage des Altertums. CICHORIUS, C. Ein Heiratsprojekt im Hause Caesars. LEVISON, W. Die Politik in den Jenseitsvisionen des frühen Mittelalters. KALLEN, G. Die angebliche Kölner Synode von 873. MEISSNER, R. Cuonio uuidi. HAMPE, K. Stilübungen zur Ketzerverfolgung unter Kaiser Friedrich II. AUBIN, H. Ein Gutachten über die Verbesserung der Kurkölnischen Zentralverwaltung von etwa 1440. SCHULTE, A. Die Deutschen und die Anfänge des Buchdrucks in Spanien. HASHAGEN, J. Erasmus und die Klevischen Kirchenordnungen von 1532/33.

(Continued)

N. Y. P. L. February 15, 1924.

Festgabe Friedrich von Bezold... (Continued)

Ellinger, G. Simon Lemnius als Lyriker. Küntzel, G. Der junge Friedrich und die Anfänge seiner Geschichtsschreibung. Beyerhaus, G. Der Kuchenheimer Religionsklub (1791/92). Bitterauf, T. Preussen und Bayern im Frühjahr 1813. Reuter, R. Ferdinand Röse (1815–1859). Platzhoff, W. Die Stellung der Rheinlande in der deutschen Geschichte. Luckwaldt, F. Die Vereinigten Staaten und Europa.

1. Bezold, Friedrich von, 1848–
N. Y. P. L. February 15, 1924.

XAH

Festgabe für Fritz Fleiner zum 60. Geburtstag, 24 Januar 1927... Tübingen: J. C. B. Mohr, 1927. viii, 431 p. front. (port.) 8°.

Prefatory note signed: Die Herausgeber: Zaccaria Giacometti; Dietrich Schindler.

Contents: Blumenstein, E. Die subjektive Seite der Zollhaftung im schweizerischen Recht. Bühler, O. Zur Theorie des subjektiven öffentlichen Rechts. Burckhardt, W. Eidgenössisches Recht bricht kantonales Recht. His, E. Eine historische Staatsteilung. Jèze, G. Le dogme de la volonté nationale et la technique politique. Im Hof, A. Die Entscheidungszuständigkeit der baselstädtischen Verwaltungsbehörden. Kelsen, H. Die Bundesexekution. Rappard, W. E. Des origines et de l'évolution de la Société des nations. Rothenbücher, K. Ueber einen Fall der

(Continued)

N. Y. P. L. October 13, 1927

Festgabe für Fritz Fleiner zum 60. Geburtstag 24 Januar 1927... (Continued)

Präventivpolizei und die Theaterzensur. Siotto-Pintór, M. La dottrina dell' immunità degli Stati esteri dalla giurisdizione interna e la recentissima giurisprudenza italiana. Stier-Somlo, F. Das Reichsrats- und Staatsratsproblem. Streit, G. Zur Frage über die Natur der zwischenprivatrechtlichen Anwendungsnormen. Werner, G. La notion judiciaire des contestations administratives. Giacometti, Z. Ueber das Rechtsverordnungsrecht im schweizerischen Bundesstaate. Schindler, D. Werdende Rechte.

1. Law—Essays and misc. 2. Law—Switzerland. 3. Switzerland—History. 4. Political science. 5. Fleiner, Fritz, 1867– . 6. Giacometti, Zaccaria, editor. 7. Schindler, Dietrich, jt. editor.
N. Y. P. L. October 13, 1927

AN
(Hanssen, G.)

Festgabe für Georg Hanssen zum 31. Mai 1889 von August Meitzen...[und 8 anderen] Tübingen, H. Laupp, 1889. 320 p. 26cm.

Bibliographical footnotes.

399488B. 1. Hanssen, Georg, 1809–1894. 2. Land—Germany. 3. Grain—Trade and stat.—Germany. 4. Village communities—Russia.
N. Y. P. L. June 21, 1951

Write on slip, name, year, vol., page of magazine and class mark — PWH

Festgabe für Gottlob Linck.

(Chemie der Erde. Jena,1930. 4°. Bd.5. port. front.)

Bibliography p.625-630.

form 400a [vi-7-29 25m]

---

* MEC
(Moser)

FESTGABE für Hans Joachim Moser zum 65. Geburtstag. 25. Mai 1954. Hrsg. von einem Freundeskreis. Kassel, Auslieferung: J.P. Hinnenthal [1954]
170 p. port. 24cm.

CONTENTS. — Bibliographie Hans Joachim Moser, von H. Wegener, p. [11]-108. —Selbstbericht des Forschers und Schriftstellers, von H. J. Moser. — Über den Sinn der Musikforschung, von H. J. Moser.

1. Moser, Hans Joachim, 1889- 2. Moser, Hans Joachim—Bibl. 3. Music-- Essays. 4. Essays. I. Wegener, Heinz. II. Moser, Hans Joachim, 1889-
NN * 1. 56 p/ OC, I, Ibo, II PC, 1, 2, 3, I, II SL MU, 1, 2, 4, I, II (LC1, X1, Z1)

ZMT

Festgabe Hans Nabholz zum siebzigsten Geburtstag. Aarau, H. R. Sauerländer & Co., 1944. xx,195 p. maps, port. 23cm.

"Bibliographie Hans Nabholz. Zusammengestellt vom Staatsarchiv Zürich," p. 185-195.

1. Monasteries—Switzerland. 2. Nabholz, Hans, 1874-

NN

E-13
4457

Festgabe Hans von Greyerz zum sechzigsten Geburtstag, 5. April 1967. (Hrsg.: Ernst Walder [u. a.] [Mit] Beiträgen von Gerhart Schürch [u. a.]) Bern, Lang (1967)

xx, 840 p. 6 plates. 24 cm.

Contributions also in French.
Bibliographical footnotes.

1. History--Addresses, essays, lectures. I. Greyerz, Hans von.
NN*R 3. 69 v/ OC, I PC, 1, I SL (LC1, X1, Z1) [I]

F-10
915

Festgabe für Heinrich Himmler. Darmstadt, L. C. Wittich, 1941.

4 p. l., 292 p., 1 l. illus. (map) 25½ x 19½ cm.

"Diese festgabe wurde für den reichsführer SS und chef der deutschen polizei Heinrich Himmler zu seinem 40. geburtstag verfasst und ihm am 5. jahrestag der übernahme der deutschen polizei am 17. juni 1941 überreicht."

Bibliographical foot-notes.

Contents. — Zentralgewalt, dezentralisation und verwaltungseinheit, von Wilhelm Stuckart.—Grundfragen einer deutschen grossraumverwaltung, von Werner Best.—Der kampf um die wiedergewinnung des deutschen ostens, erfahrungen der preussischen ostsiedlung 1886 bis 1914, von Reinhard Höhn und Helmut Seydel.—Das Fuldaer vasallengeschlecht vom Stein, von K. A. Eckhardt.—Eschwege, eine siedlungs- und verfassungsgeschichtliche untersuchung, von F. W. Zipperer.

1. Himmler, Heinrich, 1900-1945. 2. Pan-Germanism. 3. Stein, Von, family. 4. Eschwege, Germany.
NN *R 5. 57 d/ OC PC, 1, 2, 3, 4 SL E, 1, 2 G, 3 (LC1, X1, Z1)

TIN

Festgabe für Hermann Grossmann zum 60. geburtstage am 5. oktober 1932; herausgegeben von Paul Deutsch, unter mitarbeit von Herbert Dorn, Friedrich Geyler, Rolf Grabower, Johannes Popitz, Kurt Runge und Karl Senf. Steuerwirtschaftliche probleme der gegenwart. Berlin, Wien, Industrieverlag Spaeth & Linde [1932]

235 p. incl. tables. front. (mounted port.) 23½cm.

Bibliographical foot-notes.

1. Taxation—Germany. 2. Finance—Germany. 3. Grossmann, Hermann, 1872– I. Deutsch, Paul, 1901– ed.

A C 33-733

Title from N. Y. Pub. Libr. Printed by L. C.

[2]

Copy only words underlined & classmark— FHT

FESTGABE zur 150-Jahr-Feier der Wiederbesiedlung des Benediktinerstiftes St. Paul im Lavanttal durch die Mönche von St. Blasien im Schwarzwald. [Klagenfurt, Verlag des Geschichtsvereines für Kärnten, 1959.] 608 p. illus., ports. 24cm. (Carinthia I. Jahrg. 149, Heft 2/4)

Pages also numbered 315-920, continuing the paging of the preceding number.
Includes bibliographies.

1. Sankt Paul, Austria, Carinthia (Benedictine abbey).
NN X 6.60 g/P OI (PC)1 (A)1 (LC2, X1, Z1)

NRD

Festgabe für Martin von Schanz zur 70. Geburtstagsfeier (12. Juni 1912) in Dankbarkeit überreicht von ehemaligen Schülern. Würzburg: C. Kabitzsch, 1912. v(1) p., 2 l., (1)4-373 p. 4°.

[Edited by A. Dyroff.]

1. Schanz, Martin von. 2. Classical studies. 3. Dyroff, Adolf, editor.

RR

...Festgabe Josef Szinnyei zum 70. Geburtstag; herausgegeben vom Ungarischen Institut an der Universität Berlin. Berlin: W. de Gruyter, 1927. 153 p. front. (port.), illus. 4°. (Ungarische Bibliothek. Reihe 1, [Heft] 13.)

373414A.

1. No subject. 2. Szinnyei, József, 1857- . 2. Ser.
N. Y. P. L. June 29, 1928

SIE

Festgabe für Otto Prange...dargebracht von Berufskollegen, Freunden und Schülern. Beiträge zu Theorie und Praxis des Versicherungswesens... Berlin-Wilm: R. D. V., 1926. 324 p. 8°. (Reichsverband der deutschen Volkswirte. Schriften. Bd. 6, Reihe B, Heft 1–20.)

Bd. 6 of series called "Volkswirtschaft und Privatwirtschaft."
Contents: Widmung an Otto Prange. Argus, H. G. Die taxierte Police. Arnold, P. F. Notkassen und Rechtsanspruch. Ehrenzweig, A. Der zwangsrechtliche Schutz des Versicherungsanspruches. Golmick, M. Ursprung, Entwicklung und Leistung der Versichertenschutzbewegung. Heiss, C. Zur Reform der staatlichen Krankenversicherung. Heun, W. Die Auswirkungen der partiarischen Abrede bei

(Continued)

336545A

N. Y. P. L. October 21, 1927

---

*MEC
(Haas, J.)

Festgabe Joseph Haas; beiträge von seinen schülern, mitarbeitern und freunden, nebst einem verzeichnis seiner werke. Zum 60. geburtstage am 19. märz 1939. [Mainz, B. Schott's söhne, 1939]

2 p. l., 11–131, [1] p. mounted port., facsim. (music) 33 x 26cm.
"Herausgegeben von Max Gebhard, Otto Jochum und Hans Lang im namen der schüler und mitarbeiter von Joseph Haas ... Gedruckt in einer auflage von 600 exemplaren."—p. [132]
Principally musical compositions.
"Bildnis und bekenntnis: Der sechzigjährige Joseph Haas, von Karl Laux": p. 11–14.
"Verzeichnis der im druck erschienenen werke von Joseph Haas": p. 15–17.

1. Music (Collections) 2. Haas, Joseph, 1879- I. Gebhard, Max, ed. II. Jochum, Otto, 1898- joint ed. III. Lang, Hans, 1897- joint ed.

43-48226

Library of Congress M1.H15
[3] 780.82

Festgabe für Otto Prange...dargebracht von Berufskollegen...
(Continued)

den Rückversicherungs- und Retrozessionsverträgen auf die Geschäftsführung des Zedenten. Hoelemann, H. Volkswirtschaftliches aus dem Gebiete der Lebensversicherung. Jessen, G. Der privat- und tauschwirtschaftliche Begriff der Versicherung. Krüsel, E. Die steuerliche Behandlung der Versicherungsunternehmen auf Grund der Steuerreform. Luttenberger, K. Zur Frage einer deutschen Export-Kreditversicherung. Mildebrath, G. Allgemeines und Besonderes zur Frage der Kreditversicherung. Patzig, A. Die wirtschaftliche Bedeutung der privaten Lebensversicherung. Pintschovius, K. Wirtschaftskonjunktur und Delkredereverträge. Poszdzech, E. Wirtschaft und Versicherung in der Freien Stadt Danzig. Rech, H. Die historische Entwicklung der im Friedensvertrag für Versicherungsverträge getrof-

(Continued)

N. Y. P. L. October 21, 1927

---

* MGA

FESTGABE für Joseph Müller-Blattau zum 65. Geburtstag. 2. erweiterte Aufl., hrsg. von Walter Salmen. Saarbrücken, Universitäts- und Schulbuchverlag G.m.b.H., 1962. 130 p. illus., music. 26cm.

Bibliographical footnotes.

1. Müller-Blattau, Joseph, 1895- . 2. Music--Essays. 3. Essays.
I. Salmen, Walter, ed.
NN R 9.65 g/ OC, I PC, 1, 2, I SL MU, 1, 3, I (LC1, X1, Z1)

Festgabe für Otto Prange...dargebracht von Berufskollegen...
(Continued)

fenen Bestimmungen. Rocke, P. Öffentliche Lebensversicherung und Sparkassen. Stelzer, G. Die Einwirkung der Fusion von Versicherungs-Aktiengesellschaften auf bestehende Versicherungs- und Rückversicherungsverträge. Strusinski-Szeliga, W. Sind die Versicherungsvereine auf Gegenseitigkeit auch noch im 20. Jahrhundert lebensfähig? Vatke, H. Fortschritt in der Feuerversicherungstechnik. Volz, E. Pensionsverbände oder Pensionsversicherungen? Ein Beitrag zur Kritik der Umlagegemeinschaften.

1. Prange, Otto, 1865- . 2. Insurance. 3. Ser.
N. Y. P. L. October 21, 1927

Write on slip, name, year, vol., page of magazine and class mark — YAA

Festgabe für Ludwig Stein zum siebzigsten Geburtstag.

(Archiv für Philosophie und Soziologie. Abteil. II. Berlin, 1929. 8°. Bd.33, p.i-vi, 1-320. port.)

form 400a [vi-7-29 25m]

RLB

Festgabe Philipp Strauch, zum 80. geburtstage am 23. september 1932, dargebracht von fachkollegen und schülern, herausgegeben von Georg Baesecke und Ferdinand Joseph Schneider. Halle (Saale) Max Niemeyer verlag, 1932.

3 p. l., 157 p., 1 l. 23½cm. (*Added t.-p.:* Hermaea, ausgewählte arbeiten aus dem Deutschen seminar zu Halle ... XXXI)

Bibliographical foot-notes.

Contents.—Hempel, H. Über bedeutung und ausdruckswert der deutschen vergangenheitstempora.—Kisch, G. Die vorsiebenbürgische kulturentwicklung der Siebenbürger Sachsen im lichte der lehnworts.—Meier, J. Zum Hildebrandslied.—Baesecke, G. Über die verschollene

(Continued on next card)

A C 33-5
[2]

Festgabe Philipp Strauch ... 1932. (Card 2)

CONTENTS—Continued.

hälfte von Pa.—† Sievers, E. Zur inneren und äusseren chronologie der werke Hartmanns von Aue.—Pahncke, M. Materialien zu meister Eckeharts predigt über die armut des geistes.—Bihlmeyer, K. Die schwäbische mystikerin Elsbeth Achler von Reute († 1420) und die überlieferung ihrer Vita.—Schulte-Kemminghausen, K. Eberhard Tappe. Ein beitrag zur geschichte des westdeutschen humanismus.—Schneider, F. J. Zu Karl Ludwig von Knebels übersetzung der Elegien des Properz.—Unger, R. Zur geschichte der "Gesellschaft der freunde Kants" in Königsberg i. Pr.—Leitzmann, A. Zu Lachmanns briefen an Haupt.

1. German language. 2. German literature—Addresses, essays, lectures. 3. Jubilee publications. I. Strauch, Philipp, 1852– II. Baesecke, Georg, 1876– ed. III. Schneider, Ferdinand Josef, 1879– ed.

A C 33-5

Title from Illinois Univ. Printed by L. C.

[2]

Write on slip words underlined below
and class mark — EIX

Festgabe der rechts- und staatswissenschaftlichen Fakultät in Breslau für Paul Heilborn.

(Schlesische Gesellschaft für vaterlaendische Cultur. Abhandl...Geisteswissenschaftliche Reihe. Breslau,1931. 8°. Heft 5,p.1-203.)

form 100b [x-20-31 25m]

SLM

Festgabe für Reinhard von Frank; zum 70. Geburtstag, 16. August 1930... Tübingen: J. C. B. Mohr, 1930. 2 v. port., tables. 8°.

Added t.-p.: Beiträge zur Strafrechtswissenschaft...herausgegeben von August Hegler.

Bibliographical footnotes.

Contents: Bd. 1. GRÜNHUT, M. Methodische Grundlagen der heutigen Strafrechtswissenschaft. LOBE, A. Der Einfluss des bürgerlichen Rechts auf das Strafrecht. TESAR, O. Freiheitsidee und Strafrecht. WEGNER, A. Über den Geltungsbereich des staatlichen Strafrechts. RADBRUCH, G. Zur Systematik der Verbrechenslehre. HONIG, R. Kausalität und objektive Zurechnung. SAUER, W. Kausalität

(Continued)

N. Y. P. L. October 22, 1931

Festgabe für Reinhard von Frank... (Card 2)

und Rechtswidrigkeit der Unterlassung. FINGER, A. Begriff der Gefahr und Gemeingefahr im Strafrecht. HEGLER, A. Subjektive Rechtswidrigkeitsmomente im Rahmen des allgemeinen Verbrechensbegriffs. NAGLER, J. Der Begriff der Rechtswidrigkeit. OETKER, F. Notwehr und Notstand. HEIMBERGER, J. Arzt und Strafrecht. GOLDSCHMIDT, J. Normativer Schuldbegriff. WACHINGER, M. Der übergesetzliche Notstand nach der neuesten Rechtsprechung des Reichsgerichtes. MEZGER, E. Zurechnungsfähigkeit. HARTUNG, F. Die strafrechtliche Behandlung der Jugendlichen und Minderjährigen. EXNER, F. Fahrlässiges Zusammenwirken. MAYER, H. Der bindende Befehl im Strafrecht. Bd. 2. RITTLER, T. Strafbarkeitsbedingungen. KÖHLER, A. Zur Lehre vom Strafantrag im künftigen Recht. SCHOETENSACK, A. Verbrechensversuch. ALLFELD, P. Der Rücktritt vom Versuch nach gelten-

(Continued)

N. Y. P. L. October 22, 1931

Festgabe für Reinhard von Frank... (Card 3)

dem Recht und dem Entwurf eines allgemeinen Deutschen Strafgesetzbuchs von 1927 (Reichstagsvorlage). SCHMIDT, E. Die mittelbare Täterschaft. MERKEL, P. Anstiftung und Beihilfe. ROSENFELD, E. H. Mittäterschaft und Beihilfe bei subjektiv gefärbter Ausführungshandlung. BAUMGARTEN, A. Die Idealkonkurrenz. DOERR, F. Die Lehre vom fortgesetzten Delikt und R. von Franks Stellungnahme hierzu in seinem Komm. zum StGB. GERLAND, H. Bemerkungen zum Begnadigungsrecht. DOHNA, A. Graf. Der Hochverrat im Strafrecht der Zukunft. CALKER, F. VAN. Der Landesverrat, rechtspolitische Bemerkungen zum Entwurf von 1929. WEBER, H. VON. Der Schutz fremdländischer staatlicher Interessen im Strafrecht. KAHL, W. Strafrechtsreform und Religionsschutz. MANNHEIM, H. Fahrlässiger Falscheid. KERN, E. Die Beleidigung. KLEE, K. Das Recht auf Wahrheit als Grundprinzip des §

(Continued)

N. Y. P. L. October 22, 1931

Festgabe für Reinhard von Frank... (Card 4)

193 StGB. ENGELHARD, H. Zur Problematik des Erpressungstatbestandes. EBERMAYER, L. Urkundenfälschung. BOHNE, G. Kuppelei. WOLF, E. Die Stellung der Verwaltungsdelikte im Strafrechtssystem.

538470-1A. 1. Frank, Reinhard, 1860– . 2. Criminal law. I. Hegler, August, 1873– , editor. II. Title: Beiträge zur Strafrechtswissenschaft.

N. Y. P. L. October 22, 1931

XAV

Festgabe fuer Rudolph Sohm , dargebracht zum goldenen Doktorjubiläum, vom Freunden, Schülern und Verehrern. München: Duncker & Humblot, 1914. 3 p.l., 427 (1) p. 8°.

NFC

Festgabe Samuel Singer überreicht zum 12. Juli 1930 von Freunden und Schülern; herausgegeben von Harry Maync, unter Mitwirkung von Gustav Keller und Marta Marti, mit einem Bildnis von Samuel Singer... Tübingen: J. C. B. Mohr, 1930. 217 p. facsim., front. (port.) 8°.

Contents: BLOESCH, H. Aus der Frühzeit der Germanistik, Freiherr von Lassberg und Joh. Rud. Wyss d. j. FEHRLIN, H. Zwei deutsche Prosa-Handschriften der "Blumen der Tugend." GAUCHAT, L. Vom morphologischen Denken. JABERG, K. Spiel und Scherz in der Sprache. JELLINEK, M. H. Kudrun. KELLER, G. Die Persönlichkeit des Dichters und die Form der Kenning. KRAUS, C. v. Drei Märlein in der

(Continued)

N. Y. P. L. April 30, 1931

Festgabe Samuel Singer überreicht zum 12. Juli 1930 von Freunden und Schülern... (Card 2)

Parzivalhandschrift G. und das Exempel vom Armen Heinrich. MARTI, M. Berner Bruchstücke von Wolframs Willehalm. MAYNC, H. Ungedrucktes von deutschen Dichtern. STRICH, F. Byrons Manfred in Schumanns Vertonung. TUMARKIN, A. Die Überwindung der Mimesislehre in der Kunsttheorie des XVIII. Jahrhunderts. WIESSNER, E. Urkundliche Zeugnisse über Heinrich von Wittenwil. ZÜRICHER, G. Bernische Spiele mit Blumen und sonstigen Pflanzenteilen. ZWIERZINA, K. Die Innsbrucker Ferdinandeumhandschrift kleiner mhd. Gedichte. Verzeichnis der Schriften Samuel Singers, zusammengestellt von Marta Marti.

518509A. 1. Singer, Samuel, 1860– . 2. German literature—Hist. and crit. I. Maync, Harry Wilhelm, 1874– , editor. II. Keller, Gustav. III. Marti, Marta.

N. Y. P. L. April 30, 1931

Write on slip words underlined below
and class mark —

RDTA

Festgabe zum 60. Geburtstag Karl Vosslers (am 6. September 1932) überreicht, von Münchner Romanisten; Beiträge von Leo Jordan, Augusto de Olea, Theodor Ostermann [und anderen]... München: M. Hueber, 1932. 205 p. port. 24½cm. (Münchner romanistische Arbeiten. Heft 1.)

Includes bibliographies.

CONTENTS.—Pfandl, L. Spanische Prinzenhochzeit anno 1543.—Wilhelm, J. Louis Le Cardonnel.—Rheinfelder, H. Gloria.—Simon, J. Beiträge zur Erklärung von Rostands Cyrano und Aiglon.—Vincenti, L. Alfieri e lo Sturm und Drang.—

(Continued)

Festschrift.

N. Y. P. L. October 3, 1933

Festgabe zum 60. Geburtstag Karl Vosslers... (Card 2)

Rauhut, F. Das Dämonische in der "Celestina."—Jordan, L. Descartes' philosophischer Dilettantismus.—Olea, A. de. Sobre traducciones al alemán de novelas españolas modernas.—Ostermann, T. Bibliographie der Schriften Karl Vosslers 1897–1932.

1. Weddings, Royal—Spain. 2. Le Cardonnel, Louis, 1862– . 3. Gloria (word). 4. Rostand, Edmond, 1868–1918. 5. Alfieri, Vittorio, 1749–1803. 6. Rojas, Fernando de: La Celestina. 7. Descartes, René, 1596–1650. 8. Vossler, Karl, 1872– —Bibl. I. Ser.

N. Y. P. L. October 3, 1933

ELB

FESTGABE für Seine Königliche Hoheit Kronprinz Rupprecht von Bayern. [Herausgeber: Walter Goetz.] München, Verlag Bayerische Heimatforschung, 1953. 325 p. illus., port., maps (part fold.) 25cm.

CONTENTS.--Metternichs Pate erzählt, aus den Briefen des Prinzen Clemens Wenzeslaus von Sachsen, von Prinz Adalbert von Bayern.--Moderne Elemente in der ägyptischen Kunst, von F. W. v. Bissing.--Tizians "Danae," von O. Bock von Wülfingen.--Zum Malwerk des Meisters LCz, von E. Buchner.--Bronzefigur in der Sammlung Goethes,

(Continued)

NN**R X 11.56 g/ OC, I PC, 1, 2, I SL (Z/1, LC1, X1) [I]

FESTGABE für Seine Königliche Hoheit Kronprinz Rupprecht von Bayern. (Card 2)

von L. Curtius.--Auf dem Nürnberger Bürgermeisterstuhl im Weltkrieg, 1914-1918, von O. Gessler.--Römer und Italiener, von W. Goetz.--Das künstlerische Erbe der Kurfürsten Adelaide in ihren Kindern, Enkeln und Urenkeln, von E. J. Luin--Zwei Münchener Doktordiplome, von K. A. von Müller.--Die bayerische Herzogsurkunde als verfassungsgeschichtliche Aussage, von H. Rall.--Was ein Engländer 1687 in München gesehen hat, von H. Rheinfelder.--Die Pfalz in ihrem Verhältnis zum bayerischen Staat in der ersten Hälfte des 19. Jahrhunderts, von M. Spindler.--Kunstliebe

(Continued)

FESTGABE für Seine Königliche Hoheit Kronprinz Rupprecht von Bayern. (Card 3)

im Haus Wittelsbach, von H. Uhde-Bernays.--Bernhard von Waging, Reformer vor der Reformation, von P. Wilpert.--Feldmarschall Karl Philipp Fürst von Wrede, 1767-1838, von H. K. von Zwehl.

1. Rupert, crown prince of Bavaria, 1869- . 2. Bavaria--Hist.--Addresses, essays, lectures. I. Goetz, Walter Wilhelm, 1867- , ed.

3-MA

FESTGABE für Wilhelm Hausenstein zum 70. Geburtstag, 17. Juni 1952. [Hrsg. von W. E. Süskind] München, 1952. 278, [6] p. plates, port. 22cm.

"Wilhelm Hausenstein, Publikationen," p. [280]-[281]

1. Art—Essays and misc. 2. Hausenstein, Wilhelm, 1882- I. Süskind, Wilhelm Emmanuel, 1901- ed.

NN*R 4.53 OC, I PC, 1, 2, I SL A, 1, 2, I (LC1, Z/1, X1)

---

* PBM p.v.110

Festgabe zum zehnjährigen Bestehen der Akademie für die Wissenschaft des Judentums, 1919–1929. Berlin: Akademie-Verlag[, 1929]. 91 p. port. 8°.

Bibliographical footnotes.

Contents: Guttmann, J. Die Akademie für die Wissenschaft des Judentums. Baeck, L. Gustav Bradt. Cassirer, E. Die Idee der Religion bei Lessing und Mendelssohn. Cohen, H. Ein ungedruckter Vortrag Hermann Cohens über Spinozas Verhältnis zum Judentum. Eingeleitet von Franz Rosenzweig. Elbogen, I. Zum Problem der jüdischen Literaturgeschichte. Heinemann, I. Ursprung und Wesen des Antisemitismus im Altertum.

498729A. 1. Akademie für die Wissenschaft des Judentums, Berlin. 2. Bradt, Gustav, 1869–1928. 3. Lessing, Gotthold Ephraim, 1729–1781. 4. Mendelssohn, Moses, 1729–1786. 5. Spinoza, Benedictus de, 1632–1677. 6. Jewish literature—Hist. and crit. 7. Jews—Anti-Semitic movement.

N. Y. P. L. October 9, 1930

ZAE

Festgruss Bernhard Stade, zur Feier seiner 25jährigen Wirksamkeit als Professor dargebracht von seinen Schülern W. Diehl...[und anderen] Giessen, J. Ricker, 1900. 342 p. 24cm.

Contents.—Gall, August, Freiherr von. Zusammensetzung und Herkunft der Bileam-Perikope in Num. 22–24.—Weinel, Heinrich. Die Bildersprache Jesu in ihrer Bedeutung für die Erforschung seines innern Lebens.—Drescher, Richard. Das Leben Jesu bei Paulus.—Preuschen, Erwin. Die apokryphen gnostischen Adamschriften aus dem Armenischen übersetzt und untersucht.—Diehl, Wilhelm. Die Bedeutung der beiden Definitorialordnungen von 1628 und 1743 für die Geschichte des Darmstädter Definitoriums. Eine Studie zur Geschichte des hessischen Kirchenrechts.—Eger, Karl. Luthers Auslegung des Alten Testaments nach ihren Grundsätzen und ihrem Charakter an Hand seiner Predigten über das 1. und 2. Buch Mose (1524 ff.) untersucht.

239325B. 1. Stade, Bernard, 1848- 1906.

N. Y. P. L. March 15, 1948

Copy only words underlined & classmark-- *MA

FESTHEFT Willibald Gurlitt zum siebzigsten Geburtstag. Trossingen, Verlag Archiv für Musikwissenschaft, 1959. 259 p. illus., music. 24cm. (Archiv für Musikwissenschaft. Jahrg. 16, Heft 1/2)

Cover title.

Bibliographical footnotes.

(Continued)

NN R X 10.59 1/ OC OI PC, 1, 4 MU, 1, 2, 3 (LC1, X1, Z/1)

FESTHEFT Willibald Gurlitt zum siebzigsten Geburtstag. (Card 2)

CONTENTS.--Musikalische Beziehungen zwischen Deutschland und Spanien in der Zeit vom 5. bis 14. Jahrhundert, von H. Anglès.--Umgangsmusik und Darbietungsmusik im 16. Jahrhundert, von H. Besseler.--Der Harmonie-Begriff in der lutherisch-barocken Musikanschauung, von W. Blankenburg.--Zum Figur-Begriff der Musica poetica, von H. H. Eggebrecht.--Über Bach-Analysen am Beispiel einer Fuge aus dem Wohltemperierten Klavier, von H. Erpf.--Agrippa von Nettesheim und die Musik, von K. G. Fellerer.--Zur Entwicklung der italienischen Trecento-Notation, von K. von Fischer.-- Komposition als Unterricht,

(Continued)

FESTHEFT Willibald Gurlitt zum siebzigsten Geburtstag. (Card 3)

von W. Fortner.--Über Mozarts Klaviersatz, von W. Gerstenberg.--Instrumenta Hieronymi, von R. Hammerstein.--Sinn und Wesen der Tropen, von H. Husmann.--Der Ursprung der Musik, von J. Lohmann.--Grundsätze der Dispositionsgestalung des Orgelbauers Gottfried Silbermann, von C. Mahrenholz.--Die Musik in Guido von Arezzos Solmisationshymne, von C. A. Moberg.--Bachs Goldberg-Variationen, von J. Müller-Blattau.--Das Magnificat bei Josquin Desprez, von H. Osthoff.--Zur motettischen Passion des 16. Jahrhunderts, von A. Schmitz.--Deutung der Gegenwart, von H. H. Stuckenschmidt.

(Continued)

FESTHEFT Willibald Gurlitt zur siebzigsten Geburtstag. (Card 4)

1. Gurlitt, Willibald, 1889- . 2. Essays. 3. History and criticism. 4. Music--Essays.

---

*C-2 p.v.672

Festklänge. Herrn Elwin Paetel zum fünfundzwanzigjährigen Jubiläum, 14. März 1895, von Mitarbeitern der "Deutschen Rundschau" und Autoren seines Verlags. (Als Manuscript gedruckt.) [Altenburg, S. Geibel & Co., 1895] 107 p. music. 18cm.

A collection of tributes in prose and verse.

1. Paetel, Elwin.

NN R 4.53 OC PC,1 SL (LC1,Z1,X1)

Write on slip words underlined below and class mark— RAA

Festnummer. Otto Dempwolff.

(Zeitschrift für Eingeborenen-Sprachen. Berlin,1931. 8°. Bd.21,Heft 3,p.158-256. port.)

form 400b [11-13-31 25m]

RK

Festschrift. Eugen Mogk zum 70. Geburtstag 19. Juli 1924... Halle an der Saale: M. Niemeyer, 1924. lii, 652 p. front. (port.), illus., plates. 8°.

"Eugen Mogks Schriften," p. xi-xlviii.

232552A. 1. Mogk, Eugen, 1854- . 2. Mogk, Eugen, 1854- —Bibl.
N. Y. P. L. January 19, 1927

Write on slip, name, year, vol., page of magazine and class mark — IEK

Festschrift. Zur Feier des zweihundertjährigen Geburtstags von Baron Friedrich Wilhelm von Steuben,

(Deutsch-Amerikanische historische Gesellschaft von Illinois. Jahrb. Chicago,1930. 8°. v.30,p.1-207. port.)

form 400a [11-13-30 25m]

QOD

Festschrift; publication d'hommage offerte au P. W. Schmidt... Herausgeber (directeur) W. Koppers... Wien: Mechitharisten-Congregations-Buchdruckerei, 1928. xxix, 977 p. incl. map, tables. front., illus. (incl. music), plates, ports. 4°.
music), plates, ports. 4°.

391873A. 1. Schmidt, Wilhelm, 1868- . 2. Philology—Essays and misc. 3. Ethnology—Essays and misc. 4. Religion, Primitive. 5. Koppers, Wilhelm, 1886- , editor.
N. Y. P. L. February 27, 1929

Write on slip, name, year, vol., page of magazine and class mark —PKA

Festschrift. Rudolf Schenck. Zum 60. Geburtstage am 11. Marz 1930. Von seinen Freunden und Schülern gewidmet.

(Zeitschrift für anorganische und allgemeine Chemie. Leipzig,1930. 8°. Bd.188, p.1-408. diagrs.,illus.,tables.)

form 400a [11-7-29 25m]

BAC

Festschrift; Walther Judeich zum 70. Geburtstag überreicht von Jenaer Freunden. Weimar: H. Böhlaus Nachf., G.m.b.H., 1929. 290 p. front. (port.), pl. 8°.

Edited by Alexander Cartellieri, Albert Leitzmann and Theodor Meyer-Steineg. Bibliographical footnotes.

Contents: Dörpfeld, W. Die ältesten Stadtmauern Athens. Blumenthal, A. v. Anaxagoras und Demokrit. Pick, B. Die Neokorie-Tempel von Pergamon und der Asklepios des Phyromachos. Goetz, G. Varro de Re Rustica in indirekter Überlieferung. Preller, H. Paulus oder Seneca? Barwick, K. Zur Erklärung und Komposition des Rednerdialogs des Tacitus. Diehl, E. Zur Datierung lateinischer altchristlicher Inschriften. Zucker, F. Zur Landeskunde Ägyptens aus griechischen

(Continued)

N. Y. P. L. July 1, 1930

Festschrift; Walther Judeich... (Card 2)

und römischen Quellen. Meyer-Steineg, T. Arzt und Staat im Altertum. Staerk, W. Dei Gratia. Zur Geschichte des Gottesgnadentums. Cartellieri, A. Otto III., Kaiser der Römer. Brandis, C. G. Die Jenaer Handschriften des "Babiloth." Mentz, G. Ein Gutachten des Historikers Burcard Gotthelf Struve über die Gebrechen der Universität Jena und die Mittel zu ihrer Beseitigung aus dem Jahre 1722. Leitzmann, A. Wilhelm v. Humboldts Briefe an Gottfried Hermann. Schneider, F. Grossherzog Carl Alexander in Rom (1852).

481903A. 1. Judeich, Walther, 1859- . I. Cartellieri, Alexander, 1867- , editor. II. Leitzmann, Albert, 1867- , editor. III. Meyer-Steineg, Theodor, 1873- , editor.
N. Y. P. L. July 1, 1930

PMN

... Festschrift zum 80. geburtstag von hofrat prof. dr. Hans Molisch. Mit 1 bildnis, 1 tafel, 79 abbildungen im text und zahlreichen tabellen. Wien und Leipzig, Emil Haim & co., 1936.

viii, 454 p. front. (port.) illus., pl., tables, diagrs. $23\frac{1}{2}^{cm}$.

At head of title: Mikrochemie; internationale zeitschrift für deren gesamtgebiet.

Cover-title: Molisch festschrift.

Includes bibliographies.

CONTENTS.

Hans Molisch zum 6. dezember 1936.—Abderhalden, E. Anwendung der tüpfelreaktion bei der ausführung der ninhydrinprobe.—Benedetti-Pichler, A. A., and Spikes, W. F. Studies in qualitative separations on a micro scale. II. Separations in the ammonium sulfide group.

(Continued on next card)

A C 37-1747

[a38c1]

... **Festschrift** zum 80. geburtstag von hofrat prof. dr. Hans Molisch ... 1936. (Card 2)

CONTENTS—Continued.

Benedetti-Pichler, A. A., and Spikes, W. F. On methods of separation in the aluminum-chromium group.—Berg, R., Fahrenkamp, E. S., und Roebling, W. Die mikroanalytische verwendung des "thionalids".—Böttger, W. Über ausführung mikrochemischer reaktionen.—Denigès, G. Contribution à la microchimie des méthylxanthides (caféine, théobromine, théophylline).—Dubský, J. V., und Langer, A. Konstitution der verbindungen, die bei den mikroreaktionen nach Ardoino Martini entstehen.—Fischer, H. Chlorophyll.—Fischer, R., und Ehrlich, H. Zum nachweis des baptisins in radix baptisiae.—Fischer, R., und Ehrlich, H. Der nachweis des alantolaktons in radix enulae.—Frey-Wyssling, A. Über die optische unterscheidung der verschiedenen zellulosearten.

(Continued on next card)

A C 37-1747

[a38c1]

... **Festschrift** zum 80. geburtstag von hofrat prof. dr. Hans Molisch ... 1936. (Card 3)

CONTENTS—Continued.

Friedrich, A., und Sternberg, H. Über verfeinerung der mikro-kohlenstoff-wasserstoffbestimmung durch verbesserte wägetechnik.—Fritz, H. Die anwendung der elektrolytischen gleichrichtung von wechselstrom in der elektro-tüpfelanalyse.—Fuhrmann, F. Zur mikro-pH-messung mit chinhydron.—Gangl, J., und Liedl, E. Die bestimmung kleiner bleimengen in milch.—Gravestein, H., und Middelberg, A. W. F. Der nachweis kleiner mengen borsäure im glas.—Grünsteidl, E., und Stobiecky, T. Über eine neue mikrostatische methode zum nachweis von verfälschungen pulveriger substanzen, dargestellt an der verfälschung von gemahlenem schwarzen pfeffer mit pfefferschalen.—Györffy, I. Mooskapsel mit acrosyncarpia controversa aus der Hohen Tátra.—Halden, W., und Unger, G. K. Zur carotinbestimmung in kleinsten blutmengen.

(Continued on next card)

A C 37-1747

[a38c1]

... **Festschrift** zum 80. geburtstag von hofrat prof. dr. Hans Molisch ... 1936. (Card 4)

CONTENTS—Continued.

Heller, K., und Mayer, A. Versuche zur auffindung von ekacaesium.—Hellström, H., und Euler, H. v. Beobachtungen an chromosomen im dunkelfeld und im ultravioletten licht.—Hernler, F., und Pfenigberger, R. Abscheidung kleiner metallmengen aus grossem flüssigkeitsvolumen durch elektrolyse.—Höfler, K. Permeabilitätsunterschiede in verschiedenen geweben einer pflanze und ihre vermutlichen chemischen ursachen.—Iwanoff, N. N. Mikrochemische analyse von samen ohne verlust keimfähigkeit.—Kisser, J., und Kondo, Y. Der mikrochemische nachweis zwei- und drei-wertiger phenole mit hilfe von tüpfelreaktionen.—Kofler, L., und Müller, F. A. Über höher schmelzende kristalle aus pikrolonsäure-lösungen.—Kolthoff, I. M., and Lingane, J. J. The detection of copper with phenolphthalein-cyanide reagent.

(Continued on next card)

A C 37-1747

[a38c1]

... **Festschrift** zum 80. geburtstag von hofrat prof. dr. Hans Molisch ... 1936. (Card 5)

CONTENTS—Continued.

Kunze, R. Gravimetrische mikrobestimmung von acetoin und diacetyl.—Lieb, H., und Soltys, A. Erfahrungen aus der praxis der quantitativen organischen mikroanalyse.—Lindner, J. Über die haltbarkeit von titriersäuren und titrierlaugen. Verwendung von kupferflaschen.—Lohwag, K. Versuche zur haltbarmachung der gebräuchlichsten holzreaktionen.—Mika, J. Zur mikrotitration der sehr schwachen basen.—Nieuwenburg, C. J. van, and Brobbel, L. M. On the detection of malic acid by means of brucine.—Prát, S. Nachweis der schwermetalle in den pflanzen und die methode der chromospodogramme.—Richter, O. Der mikrochemische nachweis der zystolithen nach H. Molisch, ein mittel zum nachweis von durch UV-strahlen hervorgerufenen reduktionserscheinungen an zystolithen.

(Continued on next card)

A C 37-1747

[a38c1]

... **Festschrift** zum 80. geburtstag von hofrat prof. dr. Hans Molisch ... 1936. (Card 6)

CONTENTS—Continued.

Rosenthaler, L., und Beck, G. Über die zusammensetzung von drogenaschen II.—Roth, H. Ein neuer druckregler für die kohlenstoff-wasserstoff-bestimmung.—Roth, H. Stickstoff-bestimmung von diazokörpern.—Ruttner, F. Die bedeutung der mikrochemie für die limnologische forschung.—Sabalitschka, Th. Bestimmung des glutathiongehaltes medizinisch angewandter trockenhefen.—Soltys, A. Notizen zur präparativen behandlung kleiner substanzmengen.—Steiner, M. Histochemische notizen über das betulin.—Tischer, J. Zur mikrokolorimetrischen bestimmung des kaliums in pflanzenaschen.—Unterzaucher, J. Über die anwendung des normalschliffes beim mikro-Kjeldahl-apparat.—Vouk, V. Über eisenspeicherung bei blaualgen.—Weber, F. Doppelbrechung und grana der chloroplasten.—Werner, O. Kalziumoxalatanhäufung in stärkereichen zellen bei *Tradescantia fluminensis*.

1. Molisch, Hans, 1856–1937. 2. Microchemistry—Addresses, essays, lectures. 3. Plants—Chemical analysis. I. Mikrochemie.

[a38c1] A C 37-1747

QH221.M6 544.8

ELY (Bamberg. Historischer)

...**Festschrift** zur 800-Jahrfeier der ehemaligen Cistercienser-Abtei Ebrach... Bamberg: C. C. Buchner[, 1927]. 103 p. front., illus., map. 8°. (Historischer Verein zur Förderung der Geschichte des ehemaligen fuerstlichen Hochstifts in Bamberg. Heimatblätter. Jahrg. 6–7.)

1. Cistercians—Germany—Ebrach. 2. Monasteries—Germany—Ebrach. 3. Ser.

N. Y. P. L. May 5, 1928

NGO

Festschrift Adalbert Bezzenberger zum 14. April 1921 dargebracht von seinen Freunden und Schülern... Göttingen: Vandenhoeck & Ruprecht, 1921. 14, 172 p. front. (port.), illus., 10 pl. 24½cm.

Partial contents: DETHLEFSEN, R. Glockeninschriften. GERULLIS, G. Zur Sprache der Sudauer-Jatwinger. KROLLMANN, C. A. C. Lübecks Bedeutung für die Eroberung Preussens. MEISTER, K. Das Original der Asinaria des Plautus. SCHRÖDER, E. Ulfila.

601568A. 1. Bezzenberger, Adalbert, 1851–1922. 2. Germany—Hist.—Addresses, essays, lectures.

N. Y. P. L. September 15, 1932

MA

Festschrift für Adolph Goldschmidt zum 60. geburtstag am 15. januar 1923 ... Leipzig, E. A. Seemann, 1923.

4 p. l., 148 p. illus., 26 pl. (incl. ports.) on 16 l. 27cm.

Two of the plates each accompanied by three diagrammatic outlines on tissue paper.

CONTENTS.—Lebenslauf.—Börger, H. Das viergespann auf den münzen von Syrakus.—Gall, E. St. Georg in Limburg a. d. Lahn und die nordfranzösische frühgotik.—Bange, E. F. Eine unvollendete bayerische bilderhandschrift des XII. jahrhunderts im Berliner kupferstichkabinett.—Dirksen, V. Ein kruzifix im museum in Buxtehude.—Panofsky, E. Das Braunschweiger domkruzifix und das "Volto santo" von Lucca.—Burkhard, M. Ein katalanisches kästchen des XIV. jahrhunderts in der sammlung Apfelstädt-Münster.—Roosval, J. Eine kölnische marmorstatue in Wisby.—Jantzen, H. Der meister der madonna von St. Ulrich im Schwarzwald.—

(Continued on next card)

25-2631

[2]

Festschrift für Adolph Goldschmidt ... 1923. (Card 2)

CONTENTS—Continued.

Feigel, A. Gotische monumentalfiguren aus leder.—Swarzenski, G. Insinuationes divinae pietatis.—Wolters, A. Bemerkungen über einige eigentümlichkeiten spätgotischer bildgestaltung.—Baldass, L. Die anfänge des Joos van Cleve.—Homburger, O. Eine kreuzigungsgruppe aus der werkstatt Jörg Zürns.—Post, P. Über ein gotisches rossstirnschild im Berliner zeughaus.—Wichmann, H. Ein verschollener Rembrandt.—Kauffmann, H. Die farbenkunst des Aert van der Neer.—Zoege von Manteuffel, K. Jacob Jordaens' Meleager und Atalante im Pradomuseum und eine zeichnung dazu im Dresdener kupferstichkabinett.—Noack, W. Aufgaben und probleme architekturgeschichtlicher forschungen.—Eberlein, K. K. Johann Friedrich Böhmer und die kunstwissenschaft der Nazarener. Bibliographie der schriften Adolph Goldschmidts.—Bibliographie der doktordissertationen.

1. Art—Addresses, essays, lectures. 2. Goldschmidt, Adolph, 1863–
3. Dissertations, Academic—Germany—Bibl.

Library of Congress N25.F4 25-2631

[2]

BAC

FESTSCHRIFT Adolf Hofmeister, zum 70. Geburtstage am 9. August 1953 dargebracht von seinen Schülern, Freunden und Fachgenossen. Hrsg. von Ursula Scheil. Halle (Saale), M. Niemeyer, 1955. xvi, 342 p. illus., port. 25cm.

Includes bibliographical references.

CONTENTS.—Die Herkunft der sächsischen Pfalzgrafen und das Haus Goseck bis zum Jahre 1125, von R. Ahlfeld.—Ein rhythmisches Gedicht auf den heiligen Alexius, von E. Assmann.—Zu einer neuen These über die Konstantinische Schenkung, von R. Bork.—Über sino/desino im

(Continued)

NN* * R X 8. 56 a/ OC, I, IIbo PC, 1, 2, I SL (LC1, X1, Z1) [1]

FESTSCHRIFT Adolf Hofmeister. (Card 2)

Mittellatein, von N. Fickermann. –Die Borstel südlich der Niederelbe, von L. Fiesel. –Die auf den Namen Karls des Grossen gefälschte Urkunde für Beuron, von F. Herberhold. –Klassische Religionsbegründungen (Kant, Schleiermacher), von D. R. Hermann. –Siegel, Wappen und Farben der Stadt Harburg, von D. Kausche. –Gewerbe, Stand und Volkstum im Spiegel der Strassennamen von Stralsund, von H. Koeppen. –Das Triumphkreuz in der Nikolaikirche zu Spandau, von F. v. Lorentz. –Die Siegel der einheimischen wendischen Fürsten von Rügen, von U. Scheil. –Origines oder Etymologiae? Die Bezeichnung der Enzyklopädie des Isidor von Sevilla in den Handschriften des Mittelalters, von R. Schmidt. –Gens Francorum inclita. Zu Gestalt und Inhalt des längeren Prologes der Lex Salica,

(Continued)

FESTSCHRIFT Adolf Hofmeister. (Card 3)

von R. Schmidt-Wiegand. –Tedeschi lurchi, von F. Schneider. –Von der Trabea des römischen Kaisers, von P. E. Schramm. –Der ostfränkische Hof, Berengar v. Friaul und Ludwig v. Niederburgund, von F. Sielaff. –Über Ursprung, Zweck und Bedeutung der karlingischen Westwerke, von E. E. Stengel. –Vides quanta propter te sustinuerim? Ein Beitrag zum Verständnis des Naumburger Westlettners, von K. Wessel. –Verzeichnis der wissenschaftlichen Veröffentlichungen von Prof. Dr. A. Hofmeister (p. [325]-339).

1. Hofmeister, Adolf, 1883- 2. Middle Ages–Hist. –Addresses, essays, lectures. I. Scheil, Ursula, ed. II. Schiel, Ursula.

---

*MGA

Festschrift, Adolph Koczirz zum 60. Geburtstag; herausgegeben von Robert Haas und Josef Zuth. Wien:: E. Strache⌊, 1930⌋. 56 p. front. (port.) 24½cm.

Contents: ADLER, G. Persönliche Erinnerung. CAUCHIE, M. Maximilien Guilliaud. HAAS, R. Dreifache Orchesterteilung im Wiener Sepolcro. JUNK, V. Wendenschimpf. KOLETSCHKA, K. Esaias Reussner Vater und Sohn und ihre Choralbearbeitungen für die Laute. LACH, R. Das mittelalterliche Musikdrama im Spiegel der Kunstgeschichte. MALECEK, A. Anton Rotta. NETTL, P. Eine Wiener Tänzehandschrift um 1650. NOWAK, L. Paul Hofhaymers "Nach willen dein" in den Lautentabulaturen des 16. Jahrhunderts. OREL, A. Ein Verlegerbrief über eine Beethoven-Gesamtausgabe. PRUSIK, K. Die Sarabande in den Solopartien des

(Continued)

Festschrift

N. Y. P. L. May 3, 1933

Festschrift, Adolph Koczirz zum 60. Geburtstag... (Card 2)

Lautenisten Sylvius Leopold Weiss. TSCHERNITSCHEGG, E. Zu den Violintabulaturen im Germanischen Museum in Nürnberg. WELLESZ, E. Die Entwicklungsphasen der bysantischen Notation. WOLF, J. Ein Lautenkodex der Staatsbibliothek Berlin. ZUTH, J. Über Christian Gottlieb Scheidler.

1. Koczirz, Adolf, 1870- . 2. Music—Essays. 3. Lute music. I. Haas, Robert Maria, 1886- , editor. II. Zuth, Josef, 1879- , editor.

CARNEGIE CORPORATION OF NEW YORK.

N. Y. P. L. May 3, 1933

---

*PBN

Festschrift Adolf Schwarz zum siebzigsten Geburtstage, 15. Juli 1916, gewidmet von Freunden und Schülern. Unter Mitwirkung von V. Aptowitzer hrsg. von Samuel Krauss. Berlin: R. Löwit, 1917. iv, 577, 54 p. facsims. 4°.

19491A. 1.Schwarz, Adolf, 1846- . 2.Aptowitzer,V. 3.Krauss, Samuel, 1866- ,ed.

BTE

Festschrift Albert Brackmann dargebracht von freunden, kollegen und schülern; hrsg. von Leo Santifaller. Weimar, H. Böhlaus nachf., g. m. b. h., 1931.

6 p. l., 602 p. pl., facsims. (1 double) 24½cm.

CONTENTS.—Aus der altpäpstlichen diplomatie, von E. Caspar.—Der heilige Ingenuinus, von R. Heuberger.—Bischof Eberigisil von Köln, von W. Levison.—Eine Niederaltaicher privaturkunde aus dem 9. jahrhundert, von T. E. Mommsen.—Papsturkunden für domkapitel bis auf Alexander III., von L. Santifaller.—Εἰς τὸν ῥῆγα Σαξωνίας, von O. Meyer.—Das diplom Ottos I. für Herrenbreitungen, von H. Zatschek.—Kaiserbullen und papstbullen, von W. Erben.—Zur entstehung der verlorenen ältesten Halberstädter bistumschronik, von E. Kessel.—Verwandtschaftliche beziehungen des sächsischen adels zum russischen fürstenhause im XI. jahrhundert, von Raissa Bloch.—Der kampf um die reform des domkapitels in Lucca im 11. jahrhundert, von E. Kittel.—Das diplom Hein-

(Continued on next card)

32-24911

⌊3⌋

Festschrift

Festschrift Albert Brackmann dargebracht von freunden ... 1931. (Card 2)

CONTENTS—Continued.

richs IV. für Siegburg vom 4. oktober 1071 (St. 2747), von E. Weise.—Libelli de discordia inter monachos s. Remigii et s. Nicasii Remenses agitata tempore Paschalis II papae, von H. Meinert.—Guido von Monte Cassino und die "fortsetzung" der chronik Leos durch Petrus Diaconus, von W. Smidt.—Havelberg, Jerichow und Broda, von G. Wentz.—Die Translatio s. Alexandri von Ottobeuren, von Ina Friedlaender.—Ein beitrag zur geschichte Manuels I. von Byzanz, von W. Ohnsorge.—Zur entstehungszeit der fälschungen des klosters Peterlingen, von H. Hirsch.—Aus den briefsammlungen von st. Victor, von G. Laehr.—Die älteren papsturkunden der grossen karthause zu Farneta, von O. Vehse.—Beiträge zur kenntnis des geschäftsgangs der päpstlichen kanzlei im 13.

(Continued on next card)

32-24911

⌊3⌋

Festschrift Albert Brackmann dargebracht von freunden ... 1931. (Card 3)

CONTENTS—Continued.

jahrhundert, von R. v. Heckel.—Hessische wallfahrten im mittelalter, von W. Dersch.—Zum attentat von Anagni, von W. Holtzmann.—Andreas Horn, ein Londoner stadtkämmerer, von M. Weinbaum.—Über ein wiedergefundenes bruchstück der verlorenen jahrbücher von Asbach (Annales asbacenses maiores) von G. Leidinger.—Ludoviciana, von F. Bock.—Die vikare Karls IV. in Deutschland, von Lotte Hüttebräuker.—Die Defensorium ecclesiae des magister Adam, eine streitschrift gegen Marsilius von Padua und Wilhelm von Ockham, von M. Grabmann.—Landgraf Wilhelms IV. ökonomischer staat von Hessen, von L. Zimmermann.—Karl Widmers Pfäverser fälschungen, von E. E. Stengel.

1. Middle ages—Hist.—Collections. 2. Church history—Middle ages—Collections. 3. Brackmann, Albert, 1871- I. Santifaller, Leo, 1890- ed.

32-24911

Library of Congress D113.5.F4

⌊3⌋ 904

NFF p.v.117

Festschrift für Albert Leitzmann, herausgegeben von Ernst Vincent und Karl Wesle. Jena, Frommann (W. Biedermann) 1937.

2 p. l., 124 p., 1 l. 24cm. ⌊Jenaer germanistische forschungen. 2. sonderband⌋

CONTENTS. — Baesecke, Georg. Winileod. — Keferstein, Georg. Zur liebesauffassung in Wolframs "Parzival".—Stolte, Heinz. Walther von der Vogelweide und Goethe.—Deetjen, Werner. Die erwerbung Ossmannstedts durch Wieland.—Hecker, Max. Goethe und Schiller in ärztlicher behandlung. — Vincent, Ernst. Zwei gedichte des jungen Goethe.—Lockemann, Theodor. Schellings berufung nach Jena.—Maltzahn, Hellmuth, freiherr von. Ph. O. Runges erster brief an Goethe.—Wesle, Carl. Mörike, der junge dichter.

1. Leitzmann, Albert, 1867- 2. German literature—Addresses, essays, lectures. 3. Goethe, Johann Wolfgang von, 1749-1832. I. Vincent, Ernst, 1887- ed. II. Wesle, Carl, 1890- joint ed.

38-11510

Library of Congress PD25.J42 bd. 2

⌊5⌋ (439.082) 830.4

NAR

Festschrift Albert Oeri zum 21. september 1945. ⌊Basel, Buchdruckerei zum Basler berichthaus a. g. (Basler nachrichten) 1945⌋

373 p. illus. (ports., facsims.) plates. 22½cm.

Half-title: Umkreis und weite.

Bibliographical foot-notes.

1. Oeri, Albert, 1875- 2. Journalism—Addresses, essays, lectures. 3. Political science—Addresses, essays, lectures. I. Title: Umkreis und weite.

A 46-1950

Harvard univ. Library for Library of Congress ⌊2⌋

PKI

Festschrift für Alexander Tschirch zu seinem 70. Geburtstag am 17. Oktober 1926. Gewidmet von Freunden und Schülern. Leipzig: C. H. Tauchnitz, 1926. xi, 447 p. diagrs., front. (port.), illus., plates, tables. 4°.

Bibliographical footnotes.

316087A. 1. Tschirch, Alexander, 1856- . 2. Chemistry—Collected essays.
N. Y. P. L. September 19, 1927

3-MAH

Festschrift Andreas Rumpf, zum 60. Geburtstag dargebracht von Freunden und Schülern Köln im Dezember 1950. Krefeld, Scherpe-Verlag, 1952. 166 p. illus., 32 pl. 24cm.

Contributions in English or German.
"Herausgeber: Tobias Dohrn."

1. Rumpf, Andreas, 1890- . 2. Art, Greek.
I. Dohrn, Tobias, ed.

NN OC,I PC,1,2,I SL A,1,2,I (LC1,Z1,X1)

---

*PDB

Festschrift Alfred Bertholet zum 80. Geburtstag, gewidmet von Kollegen und Freunden. Hrsg. durch Walter Baumgartner [et al.] Tübingen, J.C.B.Mohr [1950] vii, 578 p. port. 25cm.

Contributions in German, English or French.
Bibliographical references included.
"Bibliographie A. Bertholet, von Verena Tamann-Bertholet," p. [564]-578.
1. Bertholet, Alfred, 1868- 2. Bible. O.T.—Essays and misc. I. Baumgartner, Walter, 1887- , ed.
NN** 8.54 OC,I PC, 1,2,I SL J,1,2,I (LC1, X1,Z1)

---

*MKK

Festschrift anlässlich der gemeinschaftlichen Gedenkfeier der Saiteninstrumentenmacher- (früh Geigenmacher-) Innung und der Saitenmacher-Innung zu Markneukirchen, zur Erinnerung an ihre Gründungsjahre 1677 und 1777, am 25. September 1927. Markneukirchen: Eigener Verlag der Innungen[, 1927]. 138 p. illus. (incl. facsims., ports.), tables. 8°.

Bibliographical footnotes.
Contents: Götz, B. Geschichte der Saiteninstrumentenmacher-Innung. Drechsel, F. A. Geschichte der Saitenmacher-Innung. Wild, E. Die Stadt Markneukirchen im Wandel der Zeiten. Bretschneider, Pfarrer. Die Kirche, das Exulantentum und die Innungen.

396430A
1. Violin makers. 2. Stringed instruments. 3. Saiteninstrumentenmacher-Innung, Markneukirchen. 4. Saitenmacher-Innung, Markneukirchen.
N. Y. P. L. December 21, 1928

PSD

Festschrift für Alfred Philippson zu seinem 65. Geburtstag; dargebracht von Schülern und Freunden. Leipzig: B. G. Teubner, 1930. 191 p. incl. tables. front. (port.), illus., map, plates. 8°.

Plates printed on both sides.
"Redaktionsausschuss: Karl Heck, Heinrich Müller-Miny [und] Otto Quelle."
Contents: Widmung. Veröffentlichungen von Alfred Philippson. Quelle, O. Die Bevölkerungsbewegung in Nordostbrasilien. Schmieder, O. Wandlungen im Siedlungsbilde Perus im 15. und 16. Jahrhundert. Waibel, L. Die wirtschaftsgeographische Gliederung Mexikos. Ponten, J. Bilder von den Strophaden. Tuckermann, W. Die ostniederländische Provinz Drente. Wenzel, H. Der

(Continued)

N. Y. P. L. March 19, 1931

VPH

Festschrift anlaesslich des siebzigsten Geburtstages von Julius Stoklasa...in Verbindung mit zahlreichen Mitarbeitern herausgegeben von Dr. Ing. Ernst Gustav Doerell...Dr. Ing. Jaroslav Křiženecký...Ing. Dr. Eduard Reich...[und] Ing. Bohuš Vláčil ... Berlin: P. Parey, 1928. 434 p. illus., col'd plates, ports. 4°.

Mr. Moth.

1. Stoklasa, Julius, 1857- . 2. Chemistry, Agricultural. 3. Doerell, Ernst Gustav, 1892- , editor. 4. Křiženecký, Jaroslav, jt. editor. 5. Reich, Eduard, jt. editor. 6. Vláčil, Bohuš, jt. editor.
N. Y. P. L. April 25, 1929

Festschrift für Alfred Philippson zu seinem 65. Geburtstag... (Continued)

Ostrand des rheinischen Schiefergebirges zwischen Dill und Diemel. Galladé, M. Die diluvialen Terrassen am Südabfall des westlichen Taunus. Zepp, P. Beitrag zur Frage der Rheinterrassen-, Löss- und Flugsandbildung auf Grund von Beobachtungen. Stickel, R. Der Westerwald. Müller-Miny, H. Bonn. Nussbaum, F. Uber die Schmutzbänderung der Gletscher. Olbricht, K. Gedanken zur Entwicklungsgeschichte der Grossstadt. Heck, K. Theorie und Praxis im heutigen Erdkundeunterricht. Tafelanhang.

514162A. 1. Philippson, Alfred, 1864- . 2. Geography, Physical. I. Heck, Karl, of Cologne. II. Mueller-Miny, Heinrich. III. Quelle, Otto Friedrich Jul. Rud., 1879- .
N. Y. P. L. March 19, 1931

---

*MGA
70-6

Festschrift aus Anlass des 100. [hundertsten] Geburtstags am 5. Mai 1969 und des 20. Todestags am 22. Mai 1969 von Hans Pfitzner. Hrsg. von Walter Abendroth in Zusammenarb. mit Karl-Robert Danler. München, Winkler (1969).

83 p. with illus. 25 cm.

Contents.—Annäherung an Pfitzner, von J. P. Vogel.—Über die Aktualität Hans Pfitzners, von K.-R. Danler.—Die musikalischen

(Continued)

NN* 9.70 d/A OC, I, II, IIb* PC, 1, 3, I, II SL MU, 1, 2, I, II (LC1, X1, Z1) 2

B-10
8296

FESTSCHRIFT fur Andreas Hermes zum 80. Geburtstag. [Neuwied/Rhein, Raiffeisendruckerei, 1958] 579 p. port. 24cm.

1. Credit, Agricultural. 2. Co-operation, Agricultural. 3. Agriculture--Economics. 4. Hermes, Andreas, 1878- .
NN R 7.59 m/B OC PC, 1, 2, 3, 4 SL E, 1, 2, 3, 4 (LC1, X1, Z1)

FESTSCHRIFT aus Anlass des 100. [hundertsten] (Card 2)

Zitate in Hans Pfitzners "Palestrina," von H. Rectanus.—Hans Pfitzners Naturgefühl, von H. W. v. Waltershausen.—Die gotischen Wesenszüge in der Tonwelt Hans Pfitzners, von R. Seebohm.—Erinnerungen (nach einem Vortrag) von K. Lewin.—Der Weg zu einer Freundschaft mit dem Meister, von M. Strub.—Im Zeichen Hans Pfitzners zur Geschichte und zum Schicksal zweier Vereinsgründungen, von H. Grohe.

1. Pfitzner, Hans Erich, 1869-1949. 2. Essays. 3. Music--Essays.
I. Abendroth, Walter, 1896- ed. II. Danler, Karl-Robert, ed. III. Danler, Karl-Robert.

*MOA

Festschrift Arnold Schering zum sechzigsten geburtstag, in verbindung mit Max Schneider und Gotthold Frotscher herausgegeben von Helmuth Osthoff, Walter Serauky, Adam Adrio. Berlin, A. Glas, 1937.

vii, 274 p., 1 l. front. (mounted port.) illus. (music) (incl. music) 24cm.

Bibliographical foot-notes.

D-14
8489

FESTSCHRIFT Arthur Baumgarten. Berlin, Deutscher Zentralverlag, 1960. 279 p. port. 22cm.

Bibliographical footnotes.

CONTENTS. — Der Weg Arthur Baumgartens zum Marxismus, von K. Polak. —Die Bedeutung der genossenschaftlichen Demokratie für die sozialistische Umgestaltung der Landwirtschaft, von R. Arlt. —Das Verschuldensproblem in der westdeutschen "Grossen Strafrechtsreform", von J. Lekschas. — Über die erste Etappe der Entwicklung des

(Continued)

NN R 1.64 g/ OC PC,1,2 SL E,1,2 (LC1,X1,Z1)

FESTSCHRIFT Arthur Baumgarten. (Card 2)

volksdemokratischen Staates in Deutschland, von W. Weichelt. — Von der proletarischen Revolution in der Staatstheorie, K.-H. Schöneburg. —Die westdeutsche Verfassungsjustiz als Mittel zur "rechtsstaatlichen" Verbrämung der imperialistischen Bonner Staatsgewalt, von R. Meister. — Bibliographie .

1. Germany--Constitutional law. 2. Baumgarten, Arthur, 1884- .

M-10
541
Bd. 11

FESTSCHRIFT für Balduin Saria, zum 70. Geburtstag. München, R. Oldenbourg, 1964. 513 p. illus., port. 25cm. (Südostdeutsche historische Kommission. Buchreihe. Bd. 11)

By various authors.

"Verzeichnis der Arbeiten von Balduin Saria, von Felix v. Schroeder," p. 493-513.

Bibliographical footnotes.

1. Saria, Balduin, 1893- 2. History--Addresses, essays, lectures. I. Series.

NN R 9.65 p/r (OS)I PC, 1, 2, I (LC1, X1, Z1) OC

SB

Festschrift für Carl Grünberg zum 70. Geburtstag, mit Beiträgen von Max Adler, Stephan Bauer, Max Beer...[und anderen.] Leipzig: C. L. Hirschfeld, 1932. 650 p. 24½cm.

CONTENTS.—Adler, M. Zur geistesgeschichtlichen Entwicklung des Gesellschaftsbegriffes.—Bauer, S. Der Verfall der metaphorischen Ökonomik.—Beer, M. Social foundations of pre-Norman England.—Blom, D. van. Über das Band zwischen historischem Materialismus und Klassenkampflehre und dessen Tragweite.—Bourgin, G. Le communiste Dezamy.—Brügel, F. Andreas Freiherr von Stifft.—Gerloff, W. Entwicklungstendenzen in der Besteuerung der Landwirtschaft.—Goldscheid, R. Die Zukunft der Gemeinschaft.—Grossmann, H. Die Goldproduktion im Reproduktionsschema von Marx und Rosa Luxemburg.—Horkheimer, M. Hegel und die Metaphysik.—Krzeczkowski, K. Daniel Defoe und John Vancouver als Vorläufer der

(Continued)

N. Y. P. L. July 21, 1933

Festschrift für Carl Grünberg... (Card 2)

Sozialversicherung.—Laskine, E. Socialisme, mouvement ouvrier et politique douanière. —Leichter, K. Vom revolutionären Syndikalismus zur Verstaatlichung der Gewerkschaften.—Leichter, O. Kapitalismus und Sozialismus in der Wirtschaftspolitik.—Menzel, A. J. P. Proudhon als Soziologe.—Michels, R. Eine syndikalistisch gerichtete Unterströmung im deutschen Sozialismus (1903–1907).—Mondolfo, R. Il concetto marxistico della "umwälzende Praxis" e suoi germi in Bruno e Spinoza.—Oppenheimer, F. Stadt und Land in ihren gegenseitigen Beziehungen.—Pollock, F. Sozialismus und Landwirtschaft.—Pribram, K. Das Problem der Verantwortlichkeit in der Sozialpolitik.—Szende, P. Nationales Recht und Klassenrecht.—Schneider, F. Zur sozialen Lage des freien Handwerks im frühen Mittelalter.—Sommer, L. Das geisteswissenschaftliche Phänomen des "Methodenstreits."—Wittfogel, K. A. Die Entstehung des Staates nach Marx und Engels.—Wittich, W. Der Schatz der bösen Werke.

638526A. 1. Grünberg, Karl, 1861- . 2. Sociology—Essays and misc.

N. Y. P. L. July 21, 1933

KAT

Festschrift für Carl Uhlig, zum sechzigsten geburtstag von seinen freunden und schülern dargebracht. Öhringen, Verlag der Hohenloheschen buchhandlung F. Rau, 1932.

345 p., 1 l. front. (port.) 16 pl. on 8 l., 4 fold. maps (in pocket) tables (1 fold.) diagrs. 25cm.

Contains bibliographies.

CONTENTS.—1. buch: Beiträge zur landeskunde von Afrika. Filzer, P. Nordafrikanische wüste und süddeutsche steppenheide, eine ökologische parallele. Hennig, E. Zur entstehungsgeschichte des Kongo-beckens. Jaeger, F. Zur morphologie der Fischflusssenke in Südwest-Afrika. Jessen, O. Lourenço Marques. Maull, O. Die kolonialgeographische struktur Französisch-Nordwestafrikas. Olpp, G. Die geographische verbreitung der tropenkrankheiten Afrikas. Reck, H. Über das alter der ostafrikanischen gräben und bruchstufen. Rupp-Gerdts, E. Gabes; kul-

(Continued on next card)

A C 33-3793

[2]

Festschrift für Carl Uhlig ... 1932. (Card 2)

CONTENTS—Continued.

turgeographische skizze einer tunesischen oase. Thorbecke, F. Natur- und kulturräume im Kameruner hochland. Uhden, R. Beckenformen und dünengebiete der Libyschen wüste.—2. buch: Beiträge zur kolonial- und auslanddeutschtumsgeographie. [illegible] E. Deutsch-Neuguinea im weltkriege. Hasenkamp, G. Das deutschtum in Irland. Holder, G. Bevölkerungsgeographische probleme des auslanddeutschtums. Krämer, A. Das kolonialproblem. Kuhn, W. Die regelmässigen flurformen der jungen deutschen sprachinseln. Werner, H. Nordqueensland als beispiel einer akklimatisation der weissen rasse im tropischen tiefland.—3. buch: Beiträge zur landeskunde von Südwestdeutschland. Huttenlocher, F. Die anfänge der geographie in Württemberg. Knödler, G. Drei bäuerliche siedlungen aus Gäu und Schwarzwald. Schrepfer, H. Aufgaben und ergebnisse der anthropogeographischen forschung im südwestlichen

(Continued on next card)

A C 33-3793

[2]

Festschrift für Carl Uhlig ... 1932. (Card 3)

CONTENTS—Continued.

badischen oberland. Wagner, G. Gestein und siedlung im westlichen Württemberg.—4. buch: Beiträge zur kartographie und klimatologie. Dieckmann, A. Kartographische darstellung klimatischer elemente. Geisler, W. Vom kartogramm zur wirtschaftskarte. Gradmann, R. Der einfluss der höhenlage auf die klimatische feuchtigkeit. Knoch, K. Das geographische moment in der mikroklimatologie. Lütgens, R. Wetter- und klimabeeinflussung, künstliches klima und wirtschaft. Schuon, G. Die kartographische behandlung des ungarländischen deutschtums.—5. buch: Varia geographica. Bader, G. Das stehende lichtbild im geographischen unterricht. Fels, E. Der einfluss des verkehrs auf naturlandschaft und lebewelt. Nopsca, F., baron. Topographie und stammesorganisation in Nord-Albanien. Obst, E. Die gliederung der tropenzonen nach ihren pflanzungserzeugnissen. Sapper, K. Indianer und Neger in Amerika. Seebass, F. Oberdalarne; eine schwedische landschaft.

1. Geography—Addresses, essays, lectures. 2. Uhlig, Carl Ludwig Gustav, 1872-

[2] A C 33-3793

Title from N. Y. Pub. Libr. Printed by L. C.

Copy only words underlined & classmark— *QAA

FESTSCHRIFT für Dmytro Čyževśkyj zum 60. Geburtstag am 23. März 1954. Berlin, In Kommission bei O. Harrassowitz, Wiesbaden, 1954. 306 p. port. 25cm. (Berlin. Freie Universität. Osteuropa-Institut. Slavistische Veröffentlichungen. Bd. 6)

Bibliographical footnotes.

CONTENTS. —Schriftenverzeichnis von D. I. Čyževśkyj (1912-1954), von D. Gerhardt (p. 1-34). —Stilistische Bemerkungen zu den Gedichten Janko Kráľs von G. Apel. —Zur Poetik der litauischen und ostslavischen

(Continued)

NN **R X 6.57 p/P OC (OS)I PC, 1, 2, I S, 1, 2, I (LC1, X1, Z1)

FESTSCHRIFT für Dmytro Čyževśkyj zum 60. Geburtstag am 23. März 1954. (Card 2)

Volksdichtung, von P. Arumaa. — Der Einfluss Tolstojs auf die kroatische dramatische Literatur, von J. Badalić. —Die Methodischen Voraussetzungen von Jagićs Literaturgeschichte des kroatischen und des serbischen Volkes, von A. Barac. — Die Beziehungen des August-Hermann-Francke-Kreises zu den Ostslawen, von E. Benz. —Ein Brief Johann Turgenevs an Caspar Lavater, von E. Dickenmann. —Der Nominativ als syntaktisch-elastische Einheit, von J. Ferrell. —Morphologische und etymologische Beiträge besonders aus baltischem und slavischem Gebiete, von E. Fraenkel. —Das Land ohne (Continued)

E-13
5304

FESTSCHRIFT für Edgar Mertner. Hrsg. von Bernhard Fabian und Ulrich Suerbaum. München, W. Fink, 1969. 356 p. illus., port. 25cm.

CONTENTS. --Runische Inschriftzeugnisse zum Stieropferkult der Angelsachsen, von K. Schneider. --Formen der Variation im Beowulf, von E. Standop. --Die altenglische Klage der Frau, von F. W. Schulze. --Kritische Bemerkungen zu Angaben über die Verbreitung altenglischer Wörter, von H. Schabram. --Unbekannte Einbände aus William Caxtons (Continued)

NN R 5.69 v/ OC, I, II PC, 1, 2, I, II SL (LC1, X1, Z1) [I]

3

FESTSCHRIFT für Dmytro Čyževśkyj zum 60. Geburtstag am 23. März 1954. (Card 3)

Apostel und seine Apostel, von D. Gerhardt. —Russisch burun und burunduk, von V. Kiparsky. — Zur Herkunft der slavischen Krjuki-Notation, von E. Koschmieder. —Die Struktur der lyrischen Gedichte von Julius Słowacki, von M. Kridl. — Das Bild der aetas aurea bei A. Del'vig, von W. Lettenbauer. — Zwei Bemerkungen über Gogol, von E. Lo Gatto. — Slavo-altajische Wortforschungen, von K. H. Menges. — Die nicht-hagiographische Quelle der Chronik-Erzählung von der Ermordung der Brüder Boris und Gleb und der Bestrafung ihres Mörders durch Jaroslav, von L. Müller. — Ukrainische (Continued)

FESTSCHRIFT für Edgar Mertner. (Card 2)

Werkstatt, von H. Schulte Herbrüggen. --The sacrifice of Serena: The faerie queene, V i. viii. 31-51, von W. F. McNeir. --Shakespeare's early use of wordplay: Love's labour's lost, von M Spevack. --Die Töchter von Harfleur; zu einer Emendation in Henry V, III. 3. 35, von E. Leisi. --Death in a cup of love. Middletons Women beware women; zur Funktion der Bankettszene im Drama, von D. Rolle. --The world as theatre; baroque variations on a traditional topos, von F. J. Warnke. --Die Synonymie bei Shaftesbury von E. Wolff. --Das Gasthaus zu Upton; zur Struktur von Fieldings Tom Jones. --The fourth part of logic; neue Quellen zur schottischen Schulrhetorik des achtzehnten (Continued)

FESTSCHRIFT für Dmytro Čyževśkyj zum 60. Geburtstag am 23. März 1954. (Card 4)

Dialekttexte, von Olesch. — Ein Anonymus der Tverer Publizistik im 15. Jahrhundert, von M. Philipp. —Kultur und Sprache der Hunnen, von O. Pritsak. — Zwei Briefe I. S. Turgenevs an Ludwig Pietsch, von A. Rammelmeyer. —Die Folgen des Falles von Konstantinopel, von W. Sas-Zaloziecky. — Dostojevskij und das Goldene Zeitalter, von V. Setschkareff. —Ein Kapitel aus der Geschichte der slovenischen erzählenden Prosa, von A. Slodnjak. —Helles Russland—Heiliges Russland, von A. Solovjev. —Die Ausnützung der Motive in den Bylinen, von C. Stief. —Bezeichnungen fremder Länder im Russischen, von M. Vasmer. — Virginität und (Continued)

FESTSCHRIFT für Edgar Mertner. (Card 3)

Jahrhunderts, von B. Fabian. --Der Leser als Komposition-element im realistischen Roman; wirkungsästhetische Betrachtung zu Thackerays Vanity fair, von W. Iser. --Geld und Traum; Scott Fitzgerald zwischen Cole Porter und Keats, von H. Viebrock. --Archibald MacLeish: You Andrew Marvell, von G. Blanke. --Zum Problem des Unsittlichen im literarischen Kunstwerk, von H. Mainusch. --Die veröffentlichungen Edgar Mertners.

1. Mertner, Edgar. 2. English literature--Addresses, essays, lectures. I. Fabian, Bernhard, ed. II. Suerbaum, Ulrich, ed.

FESTSCHRIFT für Dmytro Cyzevskyj zum 60. Geburtstag am 23. März 1954. (Card 5)

und Apathie als Höhepunkte asketischen Strebens bei Gregor von Nyssa, von W. Völker.

1. Chyzhevs'kyĭ, Dmytro, 1895- 2. Civilization—Addresses, essays, lectures. I. Series.

BTE

Festschrift Edmund E. Stengel zum 70. Geburtstag am 24. Dezember 1949 dargebracht von Freunden, Fachgenossen und Schülern. Münster [etc.] Böhlau-Verlag, 1952. xvi, 592 p. facsims., map, port. 28cm.

Bibliographical footnotes.

1. Europe—Hist.—Addresses, essays, lectures.
2. Stengel, Edmund Ernst Hermann, 1879-

NN 2.53 OC PC,1,2 SL (LC1,Z1,X1)

GDXA

Festschrift zum 300-jährigen Bestehen der Gemeinde Heiden, 1652-1952. [Heiden, Buchdruckerei R. Weber, 1952] 143 p. illus., ports., maps. 25cm.

"300 Jahre Kirchgemeinde Heiden haben die kirchlichen und politischen Behörden veranlasst, diese Feier in würdiger und bleibender Form zu begehen."

I. Heiden, Switzerland. i. 1952.

NN**R X 3.54 OCs PCs,Is SLs (RI ls, (OD)Iis (ED)Iis LC1s,Z1s,X1s)

Write on slip, name, year, vol., page of magazine and class mark— YAA

Festschrift Edmund Husserl zum 70. Geburtstag gewidmet.

(Jahrbuch für Philosophie und phänomenologische Forschung. Halle, a.S., 1929. 8°. Ergänzungsband, 1929, p.1-370.)

form 400a [viii-18-28 25m]

SLM

FESTSCHRIFT für Edmund Mezger zum 70. Geburtstag 15. 10. 1953. In Gemeinschaft mit Paul Bockelmann [et al.] hrsg. von Karl Engisch und Reinhart Maurach. München, Beck, 1954. xi, 521 p. port. 24cm.

"Bibliographie der Veröffentlichungen von Edmund Mezger"; p. 515-[520]

CONTENTS.--Zur ewigen Wiederkehr des Rechts-positivismus, von D. Lang-Hinrichsen.--Das Recht zu Strafen, von W. Preiser.--Die Grenzen des aktiven Personalitätsprinzips im internationalen Strafrecht, (Continued)

NN R 2.64 f/B OCs, Is, IIs PC, 1s, 2, Is, IIs SLs E, 1s, 2, Is, IIs (LC1s, X1s, Z1) 4

FESTSCHRIFT für Edmund Mezger zum 70. (Card 2)

von D. Oehler.--Gegenwartsfragen des internationalen Strafrechts, von A. Schönke.--Die beiden Tatbestandsbegriffe, von W. Sauer.--Die normativen Tatbestandselemente im Strafrecht, von K. Engisch.--Über die Abgrenzung von Tatbestands- und Verbotsirrtum, von R. Busch.--Negative Tatbestandsmerkmale, von H. von Weber.--Zur Rechtswidrigket der Kriegsverbrechen, von T. Würtenberger.--Zum Problem der Neufassung des 51, von E. Seelig.--Über die Leichtfertigkeit, Ein Vorschlag de lege ferenda, von K.A. Hall.--Zumutbarkeit und Unzumutbarkeit als regulatives Rechtsprinzip, von H. Henkel.-- (Continued)

FESTSCHRIFT für Edmund Mezger zum 70. (Card 3)

Pflichtenkollision als Schuldausschliessungsgrund, von W. Gallas.--Gilt die Strafrechtsordnung auch für und gegen Verbrecher untereinander? Von H-J. Bruns.--Die Behandlung unvollkommener Verbindlichkeiten im Vermögensstrafrecht, von P. Bockelmann.--Das Problem "Steuermoral und Steuerstrafrecht." von R. Goetzeler.--Die Busse und die Entschädigung des Verletzten, von E. Kern.--Gesetzliche und richterliche Strafzumessung von H. Schröder.--Das Ziel des Strafverfahrens, von U. Stock.--Der Sachverständige im Strafprozess, von H. Mayer.--Ein Beitrag zum Fehlurteil; Erfahrungen aus einem Lehrerprozess, von (Continued)

FESTSCHRIFT für Edmund Mezger zum 70. (Card 4)

K. Peters.--Der Stand der Rehabilitationsfrage in Deutschland, von F. Hartung.

1. Mezger, Edmund, 1883- . 2. Criminal law--Addresses, essays, lectures. I. Engisch, Karl, ed. II. Maurach, Reinhart, joint ed.

E-10
3354

FESTSCHRIFT für Edouard Tièche, ehemaligen Professor an der Universität Bern, zum 70. Geburtstage am 21. März 1947. Bern, H. Lang [1947] xv, 190 p. illus. 24cm. (Literarische Gesellschaft, Bern. Schriften. Heft 6)

Includes bibliographies.

CONTENTS.—Greifenvögel in Bern, von H. Bloesch.— Δημοχρατία, von A. Debrunner.—Christentum und Antike bei Adolf von Harnack und Ernest Troeltsch, von H. Hoffmann.—Elation und Komparation, (Continued)

NN X 8.57 d/ OC PC, 1, 2, 3 SL (LC1, X1, Z1) [I]

FESTSCHRIFT für Edouard Tièche... (Card 2)

von K. Jaberg.—῞Οτι δὴ τί μάλιστα, von A. Kuenzi.—Bemerkungen zur hippokratischen Psychologie, von W. Müri.—Thomas von Britannien und Gottfried von Strassburg, von S. Singer.—Über die Herausgabe gesammelter Werke, von F. Strich.—Der Dichter der Ilias, von W. Theiler.—Erinnerungen an eine Hellasfahrt, von O. Tschumi.—Die literarischen Beziehungen des Properz zu Horaz, von W. Willi.

1. Tièche, Édouard, 1877- . 2. Classical studies--Collections.
3. Literature--Addresses, essays, lectures.

QOD

FESTSCHRIFT Eduard Hahn zum LX. Geburtstag dargebracht von freunden und schülern, mit 1 titelbild, 1 tafel, 1 karte und 16 textabbildungen. Stuttgart, Strecker und Schröder, 1917. xi, 368 p. front. (port.) illus., fold. pl., fold. map, facsim. 24cm. (Studien und forschungen zur menschen-und völkerkunde... XIV)

On verso of t.-p.: Redaktionsausschuss: Hugo Mötefindt, Alfred Vierkandt, Walther Vogel.

CONTENTS.—Zueignung.—Verzeichnis der schriften von Eduard Hahn.—I. Haustiere: Fischer, E. Die sekundären geschlechtsmerkmale und das haustierproblem beim menschen. Hilzheimer, M. Der (Continued)

NN*R 11.52 OC, I PC, 1, 2, I SL (LC1, Z1, X1)

FESTSCHRIFT Eduard Hahn zum LX. geburtstag... (Card 2)

ur in Agypten.—II. Kulturpflanzen: Thies, H.E. über die entstehung des kulturroggens. Werth, E. Zur natur- und kulturgeschichte der banane.—III. Nahrung und wirtschaft: Vierkandt, A. Die vulgärpsychologie in der ethnologie und die anfänge der menschlichen ernährung. Knabenhans, A. Arbeitsteilung und kommunismus im australischen nahrungserwerb. Hambruch, P. Die kawa auf Ponape. Sieger, R. Die nation als wirtschaftkörper. Magnus, H. Neue städte in Norwegen.—IV. Landwirtschaft: Vogel, W. Pflugbau-Skythen und Hackbau-Skythen. Prietze, R. Landwirtschaftliche Haussa-lieder. Mielke, R. Das pfluggespann. Mötefindt, H. Der wagen im nordischen kulturkreise zur vor- und frühgeschichtlichen zeit.—V. Religion und mythos: Sartori, P. Der seelenwagen. Gressmann, H. (Continued)

FESTSCHRIFT Eduard Hahn zum LX. geburtstag... (Card 3)

Die reliquien der kuhköpfigen göttin in Byblos.—Bolte, J. Die dramatische busprozession zu Veurne, ein rest alter passionsspiele im heutigen Belgien.—VI. Volkskunde: Boehm, F. Das attische schaukelfest. Brunner, K. Die volkstümlichen deutschen schiffs fahrzeuge. Frobenius, L. Eine kabylische volkserzählung. Meyerhof, M. Ein beitrag zum volksheilglauben der heutigen Agypter. Ebermann, O. Bienensegen. Böhme, R. Volkskundliches bei Hebbel.—Register.

561658B. 1. Hahn, Eduard, 1856-1928. 2. Ethnology—Essays and misc.
I. Mötefindt, Hugo, ed. II. Ser.

XAH

Festschrift für Eduard Heilfron...zum 70. Geburtstage am 30. Juli 1930, dargebracht von Freunden und Verehrern. Berlin: Spaeth & Linde[, 1930]. 197 p. front. (port.) 8°.

Contents: Schiffer, E. Die Rechtsfremdheit des Volks und ihre Bekämpfung. Abegg, W. Eduard Heilfron und unsere juristische Jugend. Stern, J. Das Vorspiel der deutschen Freirechtsbewegung. Strupp, K. Das Londoner Flottenabkommen vom 22. April 1930. Honig, R. Zur Frage der Strafbarkeit der Unterlassung im römischen Recht. Koppe, F. Deutsche, englische und französische Verbrauchsteuern. Hollaender, A. Der Tankstellenvertrag. Eisner, A. Der Blutgruppenbeweis im Unterhaltsprozess. Leitner, F. Anmerkungen zur Pflichtrevision in der Aktienrechtsreform. Wertheimer, L. Zur Frage der Schadensberechnung bei Patent- und Gebrauchsmusterverletzungen. Elster, A. Schwierige Fragen bei der Entlehnung von Abbildungen. Kann, R. Justizreform.

528404A. 1. Heilfron, Eduard, 1860- . 2. Law—Essays and misc.
N. Y. P. L. June 10, 1931

Festschrift Eduard Sachau, zum siebzigsten Geburtstage gewidmet von Freunden und Schülern. In deren Namen hrsg. von Gotthold Weil. Berlin: G. Reimer, 1915. vi p., 1 l., 463(1) p., front. (port.), 1 fac., 3 pl. 4°.

1. Oriental literature.—Hist. and criticism 2. Sachau, Eduard, 1845- . 3. Weil, Gotthold, 1882- , editor.

...Festschrift zu Ehren Hermann Wopfners... Innsbruck, Wagner, 1947–48. 2 v. illus. 24cm. (Schlern-Schriften. Bd. 52–53)

On cover of v. 2: Geleitet von Karl Ilg.
Bibliographies included.
CONTENTS.—Teil 1. Beiträge zur Geschichte und Heimatkunde Tirols.—Teil 2. Beiträge zur Volkskunde Tirols.

1. Wopfner, Hermann, 1876- . 2. Tyrol—Hist. 3. Tyrol—Archaeology. I. Ser.
N. Y. P. L. September 26, 1949

Festschrift Eduard Seler, dargebracht zum 70. Geburtstag von Freunden, Schülern und Verehrern, hrsg. von Walter Lehmann... Stuttgart: Strecker und Schröder, 1922. vi, 654 p. front. (port.), illus., map, plates. 8°.

1. Seler, Eduard, 1849- 2. Indians. 3. America.—Archaeology. 4. Lehmann, Walter, 1878- , editor.

Write on slip, name, year, vol., page of magazine and class mark—

Festschrift zu Ehren Oswald Redlichs. Articles by Ignaz Philipp Dengel, and others.

(Ferdinandeum, Innsbruck. Veröffentlichungen. Innsbruck, 1928. 8°. Jahrg. 1928, Heft 8, p.i-xix, 1-632. fold. map, plates.)

form 400a [viii-10-28 25m]

Festschrift zu ehren von Georg Höckner; beiträge zur versicherungsmathematik und versicherungswirtschaft. Berlin, Verlag von E. S. Mittler & sohn, 1935.
viii, 174 p. front. (port.) 24cm.

"Dieser band wurde herausgegeben von dem Verein deutscher wissenschaftlicher und leitender praktischer versicherungs- und wirtschaftsmathematiker e. v. mit unterstützung einer grossen anzahl deutscher versicherungsanstalten. Die durchführung lag in den händen der herren Lorenz, Rose, Schönwiese und Schweer."—Verso of t.-p.

CONTENTS.—Georg Höckner 75 jahre alt, von R. Schönwiese.—Die bedeutung der Höcknerschen ideen für die sachversicherung, von P. Riebesell.—Allerlei "gewinnverbände" in lebensversicherungsbeständen,

(Continued on next card)

A C 36-2008

[2]

FESTSCHRIFT zu Ehren Richard Heuberger's, geleitet von Wilhelm Fischer. Innsbruck, Universitäts-verlag Wagner, 1960. 125 p. illus., port., map. 24cm. (Schlern-Schriften. 206)

Bibliographical footnotes.
CONTENTS.--Iuvavum oder Vianiomina? von A. Betz.--Bergisel, Burgeis und andere Namen als Unterscheidungsmerkmale indogermanischer Sprachen, von K. Finsterwalder.--Marc Aurel und die Völker jenseits der

(Continued)

NN 10.65 e/ OC, I (OS)II PC, 1, 2, I, II SL (LC1, X1, Z1)

2

Festschrift zu ehren von Georg Höckner ... 1935. (Card 2)

CONTENTS—Continued.

von J. Berger.—Betrachtungen über das bilanzdeckungskapital, von R. Dolezel.—Kurze überlegungen zu den begriffen individuelles und pseudoindividuelles deckungskapital, von E. Rose.—Die beitragsregelung in der gruppenversicherung, von A. Müller.—Über die säkulare sterblichkeitsabnahme, von H. Cramér.—Zur Lexisschen theorie der lebensdauer, von A. Timpe.—Ausgleichung einfacher beobachtungsreihen, von P. E. Böhmer.—Über die konstruktion von invaliditätstafeln, von J. F. Steffensen.—Ein beitrag zur analytischen ausgleichung von selektionstafeln, von W. Schweer.—Neue wege der mathematischen statistik, von P. Lorenz.—Die forderung versicherungstechnischer gerechtigkeit,

(Continued on next card)

A C 36-2008

[2]

FESTSCHRIFT zu Ehren Richard Heuberger's, geleitet von Wilhelm Fischer. (Card 2)

Donaugrenze, von F. Hampl.--Die Demission des Grafen Leopold Berchtold, von H. Hantsch.--Südtirol als Begabungslandschaft, von A. Helbok.--Beda Weber, 1798-1858 als Geograph, von H. Kinzl.--Zum Anonymus Leobiensis, von A. Lhotsky.--Eine Reliefplatte vom Tempel Hadrians in Ephesos, von F. Miltner.--Die Bibel und das mittellateinische Schrifttum, fon K. Pivec.--Urgeschichtliches zum Volkstum der Räter, von R. Pittioni.--Die Glocken im bäuerlichen Volksglauben Tirols, von H. Wopfner.

1. Heuberger, Richard, 1884- . 2. Austria--Hist.--Addresses, essays, lectures. I. Fischer, Wilhelm, 1886-1962, ed. II. Series.

Festschrift zu ehren von Georg Höckner ... 1935. (Card 3)

CONTENTS—Continued.

von D. Bischoff.—Die versicherung der kriegsgefahr in der lebensversicherung während des weltkrieges und ihre weitere entwicklung, von H. Nöbel.—Entwicklungslinien der mathematik der individualen krankheitskostenversicherung, von F. Rusam.—Über eine von Gauss erwähnte mischungsaufgabe und deren lösung aus einer Laplaceschen differenzengleichung mit ausgiebiger verwendung einer rechenmaschine, von W. Lorey.

1. Höckner, Georg, 1860- 2. Insurance—Addresses, essays, lectures. 3. Insurance—Mathematics. I. Verein deutscher wissenschaftlicher und leitender praktischer Versicherungs- und Wirtschaftsmathematiker e. V.

A C 36-2008

Title from Columbia Univ. Printed by L. C.

[2]

FESTSCHRIFT zur Ehrung von Heinrich Schütz (1585-1672). Hrsg. im Auftrage des Festausschusses zur "Heinrich-Schütz-Ehrung 1954"--anlässlich der Errichtung der Gedenkstätte zu Bad Köstritz--von Günther Kraft. Weimar, 1954. 104 p. illus., facsims., music. 25cm.

CONTENTS.--Zur Heinrich-Schütz-Ehrung 1954, von G. Kraft.--Zur sozialen Lage des Musikers der Schütz-Zeit, von R. Petzoldt.--

(Continued)

NN 3.57 j/ OC, I PC, 1, I SL MU, 1, I (LC1, X1, Z1)

FESTSCHRIFT zur Ehrung von Heinrich Schütz (1585-1672). (Card 2)

Reiseberichte über Italien als musikgeschichtliche Quellen für die Zeit Heinrich Schütz, von H. Müller. --Schütz und der Norden, von C. A. Moberg. --Schütz und Frankreich, von E. Borrel. -- Zur Neugestaltung der Heinrich-Schütz-Gedenkstätte in Bad Köstritz, von G. Kraft. --Schütz und Gera, von E. P. Kretzschmer. --Heinrich Schütz und Weimar, von A. Thiele. --Fortschritte der Schützkenntnis in den letzten zwanzig Jahren, von H. J. Moser. --Begegnungen mit Heinrich Schütz, von A. Werner. --Verzeichnis der erhaltenen Werke des Schütz-Schülers Johann Theile, von W. Maxton. --Was bedeutet Heinrich Schütz für unsere Zeit?

(Continued)

FESTSCHRIFT zur Ehrung von Heinrich Schütz (1585-1672). (Card 3)

Von K. Vötterle. --Motivsymbolik bei Heinrich Schütz, von W. S. Huber.

1. Schütz, Heinrich, 1585-1672. I. Kraft, Günther, 1907- , ed.

MAVY
(Hamburg)

FESTSCHRIFT für Erich Meyer zum sechzigsten Geburtstag 29. Oktober 1957; Studien zu Werken in den Sammlungen des Museums für Kunst und Gewerbe, Hamburg. [Hrsg. von Werner Gramberg et al.] [Hamburg, E. Hauswedell, 1959] 335 p. illus. 30cm.

Includes bibliography.

1. Meyer, Erich, 1897- . 2. Hamburg. Museum für Kunst und Gewerbe. I. Gramberg, Werner, 1896- ed.

NN R 10.60 d/x OC, I PC, 1, 2, I SL A, 1, 2, I (LC1, X1, Z1) [I]

A p.v.508

Festschrift zur erinnerung an die Gottlieb Daimler-ehrentage, 21. bis 23. april 1934. [Schorndorf, Daimler-ausschuss, 1934] 80 p. illus. (incl. ports.) fold. geneal. tables. 21cm.

Cover-title: Gottlieb Daimler zu ehren, 1834–1934; denkmalsweihe in Schorndorf Württemberg, 21.–23. april 1934.

Folded map laid in.

Contains advertising matter.

CONTENTS.—Festgruss des herrn reichsstatthalters Murr.—Ausschuss der Gottlieb-Daimler-ehrung. Festgruss der Gottlieb-Daimler-ehrung.—Beeg, Bürgermeister. Festgruss der stadt Schorndorf.—[Programm]—Ausflüge in die umgebung Schorndorfs.—Schloz, P. Gottlieb Daimler's schöpferjahre.—Daimler, P. Erinnerungen an meinen vater.—Oehler, Dr. Vorfahren Gottlieb Daimlers.—Rösler, Dipl.-ing. Die feststadt Schorndorf.—Hirschmann, Oberingenieur. Aus meiner Daimlerzeit.—Haushahn, C. Ein grosser mann kommt aus der kleinstadt. Die Schorndorfer industrie.

1. Daimler, Gottlieb, 1834–1900. 2. Daimler family. I. Ausschuss der Gottlieb-Daimler-ehrung, Schorndorf, Ger. [2]

A C 35–1537

Title from N. Y. Pub. Libr. Printed by L. C.

E-10
866

FESTSCHRIFT: Ernst Bloch zum 70. Geburtstag, hrsg. von Rugard Otto Gropp. Berlin, Deutscher Verlag der Wissenschaften, 1955. 304 p. port. 23cm.

CONTENTS. -- Verzeichnis der Schriften Ernst Blochs (p. 13-[15]. --Problem der Kausalität und der Freiheit, von A. Baumgarten. --Der französische Klassizismus in seinem Beziehungen zur Entwicklung Frankreichs im 17. und 18. Jahrhundert, von A. Cornu. --Vergil und die Arbeits-

(Continued)

NN **R 11.56 d/a OC, I, II, IIIbo PC, 1, 2, I, II SL (LC1, X1, Z1, Y1)

FESTSCHRIFT: Ernst Bloch zum 70. Geburtstag... (Card 2)

ethik, von F. Dornseiff. --Alexander Herzen über das Verhältnis von Philosophie und Naturwissenschaft, von R. O. Gropp. --Das Wesen metaphorischen Sprechens, von H. H. Holz. --Tschirnhaus, ein Beitrag zur Geschichte der deutschen Philosophie, von J. H. Horn. --Eine Besonderheit des dritten Grundzugs der marxistischen Dialektik, von G. Klaus. --Antikirchliche Aufklärung im 16. und 17. Jahrhundert, von H. Ley. --Über Schein, Irrtum, Lüge und Täuschung, von P. F. Linke. --Das ästhetische Problem des Besonderen in der Aufklärung und bei Goethe, von G. Lukács. --Die Utopia des Citoyen, von W. Markov. --Bermerkungen zu

(Continued)

FESTSCHRIFT: Ernst Bloch zum 70. Geburstag... (Card 3)

einer Maxime Ernst Jüngers, von H. Mayer. --Noch einmal die kopernikanische Wendung des historischen Bewusstseins, von G. Mende. --Ernst Bloch und die Utopie, von O. Morf. --Um die Prinzipien wissenschaftlicher Geschichtsphilosophie, von R. Schulz. --Über die Ethik Immanuel Kants, von H. Schwartze. --Zum Problem der Begriffsbestimmung der Gleichzeitigkeit, von V. Stern.

1. Bloch, Ernst, 1885- . 2. Philosophy--Addresses, essays, lectures. I. Gropp, Rugard Otto, ed. II. Title: Ernst Bloch zum 70. Geburtstag. III. Gropp, Rugard Otto.

XAI

Festschrift Ernst Heymann. Mit Unterstützung der Rechts- und Staatswissenschaftlichen Fakultät der Friedrich-Wilhelms-Universität zu Berlin und der Kaiser-Wilhelm Gesellschaft zur Förderung der Wissenschaften zum 70. Geburtstag am 6. April 1940. Überreicht von Freunden, Schülern und Fachgenossen ... Weimar, H. Böhlaus Nachf., 1940. 2 v. port. 27cm.

"Die Schriften Ernst Heymanns," v. 2, p. 233–263.

1. Law. 2. Heymann, Ernst, 1870- .

N. Y. P. L. February 7, 1952

E-10
8135

FESTSCHRIFT Ernst Kapp zum 70. Geburtstag am 21. Januar 1958 von Freunden und Schülern überreicht. Hamburg, M. von Schröder [1958] 143 p. port. 25cm.

CONTENTS. --Zu Hesiods Theogonieproömium, von E. Siegmann. --Dionysos oder Hephaistos? Von B. Snell. --Anaximander and the arguments concerning the apeiron at physics, von C. H. Kahn. --Nochmals: Überlieferung und Text der Schrift von der Umwelt, von H. Diller. --Lysias--

(Continued)

NN * R 9.59 m/J OC PC, 1, 2 SL (LC1, X1, Z1) [I]

FESTSCHRIFT Ernst Kapp zum 70. Geburtstag am 21. Januar 1958 von Freunden und Schülern überreicht. (Card 2)

Interpretationen, von H. Erbse. --Entstehung und Inhalt des neuten Kapitels von Aristoteles' Poetik, von K. von Fritz. --Aristotle on Hamartia and Sophocles' Oedipus Tyrannus, von M. Ostwald. --Die Region der Wolken bei Kallimachos, von P. von der Mühll. --Die Argo als Vogelscheuche, von H. Fränkel. --Der historische Ursprung des Naturgesetzbegriffs, Von K. Reich. --Eine Denkform bei Tacitus, von W. -H. Friedrich.

1. Kapp, Ernst, 1888- . 2. Classical literature--Addresses, essays, lectures.

F-11
5817

FESTSCHRIFT Ernst Kyriss; dem Bucheinbandforscher Dr. Ernst Kyriss in Stuttgart-Bad Cannstatt zu seinem 80. Geburtstag am 2. Juni 1961 gewidmet von seinen Freunden. Stuttgart, M. Hettler [1961] 493 p. illus., port. 26cm.

Contributions in German, English, French or Italian.
Includes bibliographies; "Veröffentlichungen von Ernst Kyriss," p. 487-493.

1. Kyriss, Ernst, 1881- . 2. Bookbinding--Addresses, essays, lectures.

NN R 8.61 g//OC PC, 1, 2 SL (LC1, X1, Z/1)

XAH

FESTSCHRIFT für Ernst Rabel. Tübingen, J. C. B. Mohr [1954] 2 v. port. 24cm.

Contributions in German, English or French.
Bibliographical footnotes.
Die Schriften Ernst Rabels... von Hans Peter des Coudres, v. 1, p. [685]-704.
CONTENTS. —Bd. 1. Rechtsvergleichung und internationales Privatrecht, hrsg. von H. Dölle, M. Rheinstein [und] K. Zweigert. —Bd. 2. Geschichte der antiken Rechte und allgemeine Rechtslehre, hrsg. von W. Kunkel und H. J. Wolff.

(Continued)

NN R X 10.57 p/ OCs, Is, II PCs, 1s, 2s, 3s, Is, II SLs Es, 2s, 3s, Is, II (LC1s, X1s, Z/1s)

FESTSCHRIFT für Ernst Rabel. (Card 2)

1. Law—Addresses, essays, lectures. 2. Law, International, Private. 3. Rabel Ernst, 1874- I. Dölle, Hans Heinrich Leonhard, 1893- , ed. II. Kunkel, Wolfgang, 1902- , ed.

RDV

Festschrift für Ernst Tappolet, professor der romanischen philologie an der Universität Basel. Basel, Benno Schwabe & co., 1935.

xvi, 278 p. incl. front. (port.) illus. 24½cm.
Bibliographical foot-notes.
CONTENTS.—Aebischer, Paul. Un point de phonétique historique du patois fribourgeois: La date approximative du changement *-st- > ş*.—Bally, Ch. *En été: au printemps. Croire en Dieu: croire au diable*.—Barth, Albert. Beiträge zur französischen lexikographie.—Becker, P. A. Eine versepistel Ronsards.—Bertoni, Giulio. La lingua della "scuola poetica siciliana".—Binz, Gustav. *Belp—Kehrsatz*?—Bloch, Oscar. Une frontière linguistique entre les Vosges et la Haute-Saône.—Bray, René. La nomination de Sainte-Beuve comme professeur honoraire à l'Académie de Lausanne.—Brunot, F. Sur la limite des dialectes du nord et du midi

(Continued on next card)

A C 37-171

[2]

Festschrift für Ernst Tappolet ... 1935. (Card 2)

CONTENTS—Continued.

de la France au temps du premier empire.—Dauzat, Albert. A propos de baragouin: Un type de sobriquet ethnique.—Dietschy, Charlotte. Natur und mensch in Gionos sprache.—François, Alexis. Lyrisme progressif chez Victor Hugo.—Gamillscheg, E. "Mirages phonétiques".—Gauchat, Louis. Interferenzen.—Glaser, Kurt. Edmond Scherer und die französische sprache.—Jaberg, K. Wie der hundedachs zum dachs und der dachs zum iltis wird.—Janner, Arminio. Il conflitto coniugale di Franco e Luisa in "Piccolo mondo antico".—Jeanjaquet, J. Une traduction de l'Évangile de Saint Matthieu en patois neuchâtelois de Fleurier (Val-de-Travers)—Keller, Oscar. *Gudazzo, guidazzo "padrino"* in den lombardischen mundarten.—Kohler, Pierre. Petites gloses sur la crise de l'histoire littéraire.—Kuen, H. Beobachtungen an einem kranken wort.—Lüdeke, H. Einiges zum thema: Chaucer und das romanische

(Continued on next card)

A C 37-171

[2]

Festschrift für Ernst Tappolet ... 1935. (Card 3)

CONTENTS—Continued.

formgefühl.—Merian-Genast, E. Corneilles wertgefühl im spiegel seiner bildersprache.—Niedermann, Max. Essais d'explication de quelques termes romans.—Raymond, Marcel. Entre le fidéisme et le naturalisme (à propos de l'attitude religieuse de Montaigne)—Roedel, Reto. Questione di critica foscoliana.—Roques, Mario. Un modèle de conversation pour la réception d'un envoyé royal au xve siècle.—Spoerri, Theophil. Ueber ein sonett Mallarmés.—Wartburg, W. von. Archaismus und regionalismus bei Chateaubriand.

1. Tappolet, Ernst, 1870- 2. Romance philology—Collections.

A C 37-171

Princeton univ. Library
for Library of Congress [2]

QEI

FESTSCHRIFT für Erwin Aichinger zum 60. Geburtstag. Hrsg. im Auftrage und mit Unterstützung des Landes Kärnten von Erwin Janchen. Wien, Springer-Verlag, 1954. 2 v. (xxxii, 1311 p.) illus., ports., maps. 24cm. (Angewandte Pflanzensoziologie. Sonderfoldge)

Contributions in English, French, German or Italian.

(Continued)

NN**X 11.55 g/ OC, 2b, I, 2, I, III SL (U1, LC1, X1, III (OD)It (ED)It (OS)II PC, Z/1) [SID, NSCM]

FESTSCHRIFT für Erwin Aichinger zum 60. (Card 2)

Italian.
Includes bibliographies. "Bisherige Veröffentlichungen Erwin Aichingers," p. xxix-xxxii.

1. Botany--Essays and misc. 2. Aichinger, Erwin. I. Carinthia. II. Angewandte Pflanzensoziologie. Sonderheft. III. Janchen, Erwin. t. 1954.

VWZ

FESTSCHRIFT Eugen Bircher. Aarau, H. R. Sauerländer & Co., 1952. 336 p. port. 23cm.

"Eugen Bircher... zum siebzigsten Geburtstag gewidmet von der Aargauischen vaterländischen Vereinigung, von Freunden, Kameraden und Mitarbeitern."
"Herausgegeben von Dr. iur. Hans Hemmeler."
List of patrons (35 p.) inserted.
"Bibliographie, zusammengestellt von H. R. Kurz," p. 332-336.

1. Bircher, Eugen, 1882- . 2. Army, Swiss. I. Hemmeler, Hans, ed. II. Aargauische vaterländische Vereinigung.

NN R 3.53 OC, I (OS)II PC, 1, 2, I, II SL (LC1, Z/1, X1)

YAM p.v.206

Festschrift für Eugen Kühnemann zum 28. Juli 1928. Breslau: Im Selbstverlag der Volkshochschule, 1928. 63 p. front. (port.) 8°. (Volkshochschule Breslau. Blätter. Jahrg. 7. [Nr.] 1.)

"Herausgegeben von Alfred Mann."
Contents: Eugen Kühnemann. SCHULEMANN, G. Philosophie als Wissenschaft und als Weisheit. GOLDMANN, F. Philosophie ist philosophisches Leben. MARCK, S. Das Gesetz, wonach Du angetreten! BORNHAUSEN, K. Die Schiller-Renaissance durch Eugen Kühnemann. SCHILLER, F. Der philosophische Kopf und der Brotgelehrte. MANN, A. Ursprünge. Bemerkungen zum Thema: "Alte und neue Volksbildung," Die Bücher, Abhandlungen, Ausgaben und Reden Eugen Kühnemanns.

472532A. 1. Kuehnemann, Eugen, 1868- . 2. Mann, Alfred Julius Wilhelm, 1889- , editor. 3. Volkshochschule, Breslau.
N. Y. P. L. May 7, 1930

*HB

Festschrift Eugen Stollreither zum 75. Geburtstage gewidmet, von Fachgenossen, Schülern, Freunden. Hrsg. von Fritz Redenbacher... Erlangen, Universitätsbibliothek, 1950. xii, 403 p. front., plan, 33 pl. 25cm.

Bibliographical footnotes.

1. Stollreither, Eugen, 1874- . 2. Library science—Addresses, essays, lectures. 3. Libraries—Germany—Erlangen. I. Redenbacher, Fritz, 1900- , ed.

NN 1.53 OC, I PÇ, 1, 2, 3, I SL (LC1, Z1, X1)

RAE

FESTSCHRIFT Franz Dornseiff zum 65.Geburtstag. Hrsg. von Horst Kusch. Leipzig, Bibliographisches Institut, 1953. 384 p. port. 24cm.

Bibliographical footnotes.

CONTENTS. — Verzeichnis der Schriften von Franz Dornseiff, von H. Kusch. — Einige rückschauende Bemerkungen, von F. Dornseiff. — Die Parascheneinteilung der Jesajarolle I von Qumrān, von H. Bardtke. -- Germanisches -- Römisches in Cäsars Bellum gallicum, von K. Barwick. — Karthago wurde erst 673-663 v. Chr. gegründet, von E. O. Forrer. —Der Kosmos Ovids, von W. H. Friedrich. — Über die Sowjetbyzantinistik, von J. Irmscher. -- Studien über Augustinus, von H. Kusch. —Die Toledoth in

(Continued)

NN ** R 10.54 OC, I, Ibo PC, 1, 2, I SL (Z1, LC1, X1)

FESTSCHRIFT Franz Dornseiff zum 65.Geburtstag. (Card 2)

Mt I, 1-17 und Lc 3, 23b ff., von M. Lambertz. —Griechisch-Irisches, von E. Lewy. -- Lord Byron and the Romaic language, by S. B. Liljegren. -- Charivari, von K. Meuli. — Wilamowitz und die klassische Philologie, von H. Patzer. --Sullat und Hanis, von M. Riemschneider. -- Sacra Scriptura -- Bemerkungen zur Inspirationslehre Augustins, von H. Sasse. — Der irische Seeroman des Brandan -- ein Ausblick auf die Kolumbus-Reise, von G. Schreiber. --Zur Vorgeschichte des Gewissensbegriffes im altgriechischen Denken, von O. Seel. — Zum juristischen Wortschatz der Alten Ägypter, von E. Seidl. --On two words in Homer (λύματα, ἀπολυμαντήρ) by T. A. Sinclair. -- Die Schallgefässe des antiken Theaters, von P. Thielscher.

(Continued)

FESTSCHRIFT Franz Dornseiff zum 65.Geburtstag. (Card 3)

-- Über eine für die Iliasanalyse wichtige Stelle, von P. Von der Mühll. -- Über den Fischnamen tecco bei Polemius Silvius und bei Anthimus sowie über andere semasiologisch analoge Süsswasserfischnamen, von R. Zaunick.

1. Philology -- Addresses, essays, lectures. 2. Dornseiff, Franz, 1888- I. Kusch, Horst.

SEC

Festschrift für Friedrich Giese zum 70. Geburtstag, 17. August 1952. Dargebracht von Freunden, Schülern und Fachkollegen. Frankfurt/Main, Verlag Kommentator [1953] 258 p. port. 25cm.

Preface signed: Friedrich Klein.

Bibliographical footnotes.

Contents.—Vorwort.—Stand und Aufgaben der Verwaltungswissenschaft, von [illegible] Becker.—Von der

(Continued)

NN**12.54 t/ OC, I PC, 1, 2, 3, I SL E, 1, 2, 3, I (Z1, LC1, X1)

Festschrift für Friedrich Giese zum 70. Geburtstag, 17. August 1952. (Card 2)

föderativen zur stärker unitarischen Gestaltung des Finanzwesens in der Bundesrepublik Deutschland, von F. Klein.—Über den Begriff und das Tatbestandsmerkmal der Öffentlichkeit, von F. List.—Rechtsformen der formalen Verfassungsänderung, von E. Menzel.—Evangelisches Kirchenrecht als bekennende Ordnung, von D. Oehler.—Der internationale Schutz der Menschenrechte, von W. Schätzel.—

(Continued)

Festschrift für Friedrich Giese zum 70. Geburtstag, 17. August 1952. (Card 3)

Der grundgesetzliche Schutz der Hochschullehrerrechte, von M. Wenzel.—Leben und Werk des Jubilars.—Schriftwerke und Reden des Jubilars. (p. 257-258)

1. Giese, Friedrich, 1882- 2. Political science--Addresses, essays, lectures. 3. Law, Constitutional--Germany. I. Klein, Friedrich, ed.

RK (Kluge)

Festschrift Friedrich Kluge zum 70. Geburtstage am 21. Juni 1926, dargebracht von O. Behaghel...[und anderen]. Tübingen: Verlag des Englischen Seminars, 1926. v, 164 p. front. (port.) 8°.

Contains bibliographies.

Contents: Behaghel, O. Zur Dauer der nhd. Endsilbenvokale. Bohnenberger, K. Zwischenformen. Dammann, O. Verzeichnis der Schriften Friedrich Kluges 1879–1926. Eckhardt, E. Gehört Shakespeare zur Renaissance oder zum Barock? Franz, W. Amerikanisches und britisches Englisch. Goetz, G. Aus lateinischen Glossaren. Götze, A. Alemannische Namenrätsel. Hoffmann-Krayer, E. Präterital-passivische Zusammensetzungen im Deutschen. Jellinek, M. H. Die

(Continued)

N. Y. P. L. March 30, 1927

Festschrift Friedrich Kluge zum 70. Geburtstage... (Continued)

angeblichen Beziehungen der gotischen zur kappadokischen Kirche. Karsten, T. E. Fi taika "Vorzeichen, Wahrsagung" und die Etymologie des Wortes Zeichen. Kieckers, E. Zum Dativus sympatheticus im Neuhochdeutschen. Kock, E. A. Dorthin, dort, von dort. Leumann, E. Eine Dissimilationsregel. Noreen, E. Einige Bemerkungen über den Ursprung des Stabreims in der altgermanischen Dichtung. Panzer, F. Bemme. Priebsch, R. Bruchstücke einer mittelfränkischen Ritternovelle. Schatz, J. Berg und deutsche Bergnamen in den Alpen. Schröer, A. Eventually. Stammler, W. Popularjurisprudenz und Sprachgeschichte im XV. Jahrhundert. Suolahti, H. Textkritische Bemerkungen zum König Rother. Teuchert, H. Niederfränkisches Sprachgut in der Mark Brandenburg. Wrede, A. Zur Geschichte des Sprachenkampfes in Köln um die Wende des 15. Jahrhunderts.

1. Kluge, Friedrich, 1856–1926.

N. Y. P. L. March 30, 1927

D-11 7980

Festschrift für Friedrich List zum 70. Geburtstag, 1. August 1957; dargebracht von Freunden, Schülen und Fachkollegen. Baden-Baden, Verlag für angewandte Wissenschaften, 1957. 203 p. 22cm.

Bibliographical footnotes.

Contents.—Leben und Werk des Jubilars.—Schriftwerke des Jubilars (p. 13–15)—Versorgungsentgelte in der Insolvenz des versorgten Abnehmers, von H. Bartholomeyczik.—Begriff und Bedeutung der Eisenbahnkonzession, von W. Böttger.—Die Autonomie der Deutschen Bundesbahn im Vergleich zu dem Verhältnis des Staates zum

(Continued)

NN R X 2.60 OC PC, 1 SL E, 1 (LC1, X1, Z1)

Festschrift für Friedrich List zum 70.... 1957. (Card 2)

Kraftverkehr und zur Binnenschiffahrt, von F. Busch.—Sinnvolle Begrenzung der Fahrgeschwindigkeit bei Wege- und Bahnkreuzungen, von F. Giese.—Grundfragen des Postverfassungsrechts, von L. Kämmerer.—Die Problematik eines "Rechts der Technik" und der Monopolsituation in der Energieversorgung, von H. F. Mueller.—Haftpflichtrecht und Persönlichkeitsrecht vor der neueren technischen Entwicklung, von K. Oftinger.—Die Beeinflussung von Fernmeldeanlagen der Deutschen Bundespost durch Energieversorgungsanlagen im Spiegel von Wirtschaftlichkeit, Recht und Sondervereinbarung, von H. Riedel.—Rechtsfragen um das Tonband, von G. Roeber.—Les deux projets de convention pour la protection des droits dits "voisins", par G. Straschnov.—Öffentlicher Dienst privater Betriebe, von H. Balser.

1. List, Friedrich, 1887- .

MAE

FESTSCHRIFT für Friedrich Matz. [Hrsg. von Nikolaus Himmelmann-Wildschütz und Hagen Biesantz] Mainz, P. von Zabern [1962] 124 p. illus., 39 plates. 28cm.

Bibliographical footnotes.

CONTENTS. --Some eminent Cretan gem-engravers, by V. E.G. Kenna.- Μια σφραγιστικη ιδιορρυθμια της προανακ-τορικης μινωικης περιοδου, ὑπο Ν. Πλατων.— Ἑνα σφραγισμα ἀπο την Πυλο, ὑπο Ἀ. Ξενακη-Σακελλαριου

(Continued)

NN R 6.63 p/ OC, I, II PC, 1, 2, I, II SL A, 1, 2, I, II (LC1, X1, Z1) [I] 3

FESTSCHRIFT für Friedrich Matz. (Cont.)

Technik der fotografischen Aufnahmen kretisch-mykenischer Siegel, von C. Albiker. -Erwähnen die Pylostafeln Herolde? von H. -G. Buchholz. -Zur Entstehung der griechischen Tempelringhalle, von H. Drerup. -Phrygische Fibeln, von U. Jantzen. -Der archaische Sarkophag mit Säulendekoration in Samos, von I. Kleemann. -Ein archaisierendes Grabrelief strengen Stils aus Krannon, von H. Biesantz. -Phidias und Perikles auf dem Schild der Athena Parthenos, von F. Eckstein. -Statuette einer Tänzerin aus Fianello Sabino, von B. Andreae. -Der Silberteller von Aquileja, von H. Möbius. -Roman Sarcophagi in America: a short inventory, by C. Vermeule. -

(Continued)

FESTSCHRIFT für Friedrich Matz. (Cont.)

Sarkophag eines gallienischen Konsuls, von N. Himmelmann-Wildschütz.

1. Art, Ancient--Addresses, essays, lectures. 2. Matz, Friedrich Ludwig Johannes, 1890- I. Himmelmann-Wildschütz, Nikolaus, ed. II. Biesantz, Hagen, ed.

E-12
6600

FESTSCHRIFT für Friedrich Smend zum 70. Geburtstag; dargebracht von Freunden und Schülern. Berlin, Verlag Merseburger [c1963] 99. [1] p. illus., ports., tables. 24cm.

Bibliographical footnotes.

CONTENTS. --Das Apollonorakel in Didyma . Pflege alter Musik im spätantiken Gottesdienst, von H. Hommel. --Hermeneutische Probleme der biblischen Urgeschichte, von R. Rendtorff. --

(Continued)

NN*R 9. 66 r/4 OC PC, 1 SL MU, 1 (LC1, X1, Z1) [I] 3

FESTSCHRIFT für Friedrich Smend zum 70. Geburtstag... (Card 2)

Die Perikope vom leeren Grabe Jesu in der nachmarkinischen Traditionsgeschichte, von U. Wilckens. --Ein Lied und seine Zeit; eine Frage im Anschluss an eine Stelle aus der Confessiones Augustini, von H. Vogel. --Begegnung mit dem Tode, von F. Dehn. --Drei Jahre Rektorat der Kirchlichen Hochschule Berlin, von C. Berg. --Aus glücklichen Zeiten der Preussischen Staatsbibliothek, von P. Wackernagel. --Ein zukunftweisender Bibliotheksbau, von J. Heydrich. --Vorläufiger Traumreise-

(Continued)

FESTSCHRIFT für Friedrich Smend zum 70. Geburtstag... (Card 3)

bericht aus Bibliopolis, von H. Steinberg. --Eine Auktions-Quittung J. S. Bachs, von H. Besch --Die Rastrierungen in den Originalhandschriften Joh. Seb. Bachs und ihre Bedeutung für die diplomatische Quellenkritik, von C. Wolff. --Nur ein Brief, von F. Schnapp. --Ein Jugendbrief von Felix Mendelssohn, von R. Elvers. --Bibliographie Friedrich Smend, von R. Elvers.

1. Smend, Friedrich, 1893- .

M-10
6315
Bd. 50

FESTSCHRIFT für Friedrich von Zahn, hrsg. von Walter Schlesinger. Köln, Böhlau Verlag, 1968. 1 v. illus., port., maps (3 fold., issued in pocket) 24cm. (Mitteldeutsche Forschungen. Bd. 50)

Bd. 1.

Bibliographical footnotes.

(Continued)

NN R 12. 69 w/4 OC, II, IIbo, III (OS)I PC, 1, I, II, III (LC1, X1, Z1) [I] 2

FESTSCHRIFT für Friedrich von Zahn, hrsg. von Walter Schlesinger. (Card 2)

CONTENTS. --Bd. 1. Zur Geschichte und Volkskunde Mitteldeutschlands.

1. Germany, Central--Hist.--Addresses, essays, lectures. I. Series. II. Zahn, Friedrich von. III. Schlesinger, Walter, 1908- ed.

---

*MGA

Festschrift, Fritz Stein zum 60. geburtstag überreicht von fachgenossen, freunden und schülern, herausgegeben von Hans Hoffmann und Franz Rühlmann. Braunschweig, H. Litolff, 1939.

213 p. front. (port.) illus. (music) fold. pl., facsims. (incl. music) fold. tab., diagrs. 25^{cm}.

"Anhang. [Das schaffensergebnis Fritz Steins zusammengestellt von Käte von Pein]": p. [197]-213.

CONTENTS.—Musikforschung und musikpraxis, von Friedrich Blume.—Max Regers sonatenform in ihrer entwicklung, von H. L. Denecke.—Beethovens Missa solemnis im erlebnis eines deutschen malers der gegenwart [Ewald Vetter] (mit 17 kohlezeichnungen) von Friedrich Mahling.—Brauchtümliches im Thüringer chorlied des frühbarock, von H. J. Moser.—Fünf briefe von Karl Stamitz, bruchstücke einer selbstbiographie,

(Continued on next card)

41-23500

[2]

Festschrift, Fritz Stein ... 1939. (Card 2)

CONTENTS—Continued.

von Arnold Schering.—Die Sperontes-lieder "Ich bin nun wie ich bin"—"Ihr schönen höret an" und Seb. Bach, von Max Seiffert.—Über die grundlagen der form bei Max Reger, von H. J. Therstappen.—Zur einheitlichen ausbildung des musikerziehers, von Eugen Bieder.—Vom einfluss des urheberrechts auf die musikpflege, von Alexander Elster.—Grundlagen einer bodenständigen musikpflege, von Karl Hasse.—Solmisationsmethoden im schulunterricht des 16. und 17. jahrhunderts, von Eberhard Preussner.—Zur chorleiter- und dirigentenerziehung, von Kurt Thomas.—Beethovens formale gestaltung als grundlage der interpretation, von Hans Hoffmann.—Über die werktreue und ihre grenzen, von Peter Raabe.—Zur wiederbelebung Glucks, von Franz Rühlmann.—Notenbild und werktreue, von Adolf Sandberger.—Werktreue bei der operninszenierung, von Fritz Tutenberg.—Anhang.

1. Music—Addresses, essays, lectures. 2. Stein, Fritz Wilhelm, 1879– I. *Hoffmann, Hans, 1902– ed. II. Rühlmann, Franz, 1896– joint ed. III. Pein, Käte von.

Library of Congress ML55.S83H6 41–23500
[2] 780.4

---

*IPF

Festschrift zum fünfhundertjährigen geburtstage von Johann Gutenberg, im auftrage der stadt Mainz, hrsg. von Otto Hartwig. Mainz [Kunstdr. von P. von Zabern]; Leipzig, Kommissionsverlag von O. Harrassowitz, 1900.

2 p. l., 455 p. illus., 35 pl. (part fold., part double, 1 col., incl. facsims.) 5 fold. geneal. tab. 30cm.

Issued also as Beihefte zum Centralblatt für bibliothekswesen ... 8. bd., hft. 23 (4 p. l., 584 p. and atlas of 35 pl. 24cm)

CONTENTS.—Hartwig, O. Zur einführung.—Schreiber, W. L. Vorstufen der typographie.—Falk, F. De stempeldruck vor Gutenberg und die stempeldrucke in Deutschland.—Schenk zu Schweinsberg, G., frhr. Genealogie des Mainzer geschlechtes Gänsfleisch.—Schorbach, K. Die urkundlichen nachrichten über Johann Gutenberg.—Falk, F. Die Mainzer Psalterien von 1457, 1459, 1490, 1502, 1515 und 1516 nach ihrer historisch-liturgischen seite.—Wallau, H. Die zweifarbigen initialen der

(Continued on next card)

33—4801

[35c1]

Festschrift zum fünfhundertjährigen geburtstage von Johann Gutenberg ... 1900. (Card 2)

CONTENTS—Continued.

Psalterdrucke von Johann Fust und Peter Schöffer.—Wyss, A. Der Türkenkalender für 1455. Ein werk Gutenbergs.—Velke, W. Zur frühesten verbreitung der druckkunst.—Labande, L. H. L'imprimerie en France au xve siècle.—Häbler, K. Deutsche buchdrucker in Spanien und Portugal.—Marzi, D. I tipografi tedeschi in Italia durante il secolo xv.—Schlusswort.

1. Printing—Hist.—Celebrations of invention. 2. Printing—Hist.—Origin and antecedents. 3. Gutenberg, Johann, 1397?–1468. 4. Incunabula. I. Hartwig, Otto, 1830–1903, ed. II. Schreiber, Wilhelm Ludwig, 1855–1932. III. Falk, Franz, 1840–1909. IV. *Schenk zu Schweinsberg, Gustav, freiherr, 1842–1922. V. Schorbach, Karl, 1851– VI. Wallau, Heinrich. VII. Wyss, Arthur Franz Wilhelm, 1852–1900. VIII. Velke, Wilhelm, 1854– IX. Labande, Léon Honoré, 1867– X. Haebler, Konrad, 1857– XI. Marzi, Demetrio, 1862–1920.

33—4801

Library of Congress Z127.C4F3
[a35c1] 655.12

---

*C–3 p.v.743

Festschrift zum 75. [i. e. fünfundsiebzigsten] Geburtstag des Sprechers der Sudetendeutschen, Rudolf Lodgman von Auen, hrsg. von Albert Karl Simon. München, Sudetendeutsche Landsmannschaft, 1953. 116 p. 21cm.

CONTENTS.—Rudolf Lodgman von Auen, von A. K. Simon.—Würdigung Dr. Lodgman von Auen, von L. Prchala.—Das Recht auf die Heimat, von H. C. Seebohm.—Die Landsmannschaftliche Aufgabe, von T. Oberländer.—Heimatvertriebene und Christentum, von E. J. Reichenberger.—Deutschland und der österreichische Staatsgedanke, von W. Weizäcker.—Regensburg, Patenstadt der Sudetendeutschen, von H. Hermann.—

(Continued)

NN**R X 8.55 OC,I,Ib PC,1,2,I SL E,1,2,I S,1 (Z1,LC1,X1)

Festschrift zum 75... 1953. (Card 2)

Die europäische Aufgabe des Donauraumes, von Otto von Habsburg.—Der europäische Weg, von M. Černák.—Die Durchsetzung des Selbstbestimmungsrechtes, eine Voraussetzung für die Fortentwicklung der Demokratie, von F. Dúrčansky.—Die ungarische Einstellung zur Zukunft des Donauraumes, von P. von Balla.—Die Kroaten als westliches Element, von S. Buć.—Die böhmische Frage, von K. A. Rohan.

1. Germans in Czecho-slovakia. 2. Lodgman von Auen, Rudolf, Ritter, 1877– . I. Simon, Albert Karl, ed.

---

*C-3 p.v.1067

Festschrift zum 75. Geburtstag des Sprechers der Sudetendeutschen Rudolf Lodgman von Auen, hrsg. von Albert Karl Simon. München, Sudetendeutsche Landsmannschaft, 1953. 116 p. 21cm.

CONTENTS.—Rudolf Lodgman von Auen, von A.K. Simon. —Würdigung Dr. Lodgman von Auen, von L. Prchala.— Das Recht auf die Heimat, von H.-C. Seebohm.—Die Landsmannschaftliche Aufgabe, von T. Oberländer.— Heimatvertriebene und Christentum, von E.J.

(Continued)

NN**R X 11.55 j/b OC,I, IIIb (OS)II,IIb+ PC,1 2,I,II SL S,1,2,I,II (Z1,LC1,X1)

Festschrift zum 75. Geburtstag des Sprechers der Sudetendeutschen Rudolf Lodgman von Auen... (Card 2)

Reichenberger.—Deutschland und der österreichische Staatsgedanke, von W. Weizsäcker.—Regensburg, Patentstadt der Sudetendeutschen, von H. Hermann.— Die europäische Aufgabe des Donauraumes, von O. von Habsburg.—Der europäische Weg, von M. Černák.—Die Durchsetzung des Selbstbestimmungsrechtes, eine Voraussetzung für die Fortentwicklung der Demokratie, von F. Ďurčansky.—Die

(Continued)

Festschrift zum 75. Geburtstag des Sprechers der Sudetendeutschen Rudolf Lodgman von Auen... (Card 3)

ungarische Einstellung zur Zukunft des Donauraumes, von P. von Balla.—Die Kroaten als westliches Element, von S. Buć.—Die böhmische Frage, von Prinz K.A. Rohan.

1. Lodgman von Auen, Rudolf, Ritter, 1877-
2. Europe, Eastern—Hist. I. Simon, Albert Karl, ed.
II. Sudetendeutsche Landsmannschaft.
III. Simon, Albert Karl.

---

* PBN

Festschrift zum 75jährigen Bestehen der Realschule mit Lyzeum der isr. Religionsgesellschaft Frankfurt am Main. Frankfurt am Main, 1928. 175, 59, vii p. facsims., front., ports., 2 pl., tables. 4°.

Commentar des Meiri zum Traktat Chagiga, is in Hebrew, with separate title-page and paging.

Bibliographical footnotes.

Contents: OCHSENMANN, K. Chronik. Die "jüdische" höhere Schule. FINK, E. Apologetisches. CARO, J. Bernard Shaw. SCHÜLER, M. Beiträge zur Kenntnis der alten jüdisch-deutschen Profanliteratur. MUNK, M. Zum Problem einer jüdischen

411709A

(Continued)

N. Y. P. L. February 25, 1929

Festschrift zum 75jährigen Bestehen der Realschule mit Lyzeum der isr... (Card 2)

Symbolik. ADLER, S. Der erste Plan zur Gründung einer jüdischen Schule mit profanem Unterricht in der Frankfurter Judengasse. LANGE, M. Commentar des Meiri zum Traktat Chagiga.

1. Education—Jews—Germany—Frankfurt am Main. 2. Bible. O. T.—Apologetics. 3. Bible—Natural history. 4. Shaw, Bernard, 1865– . 5. Judeo-German literature—Hist. and crit. 6. Symbolism, Jewish. 7. Talmud. Chagigah.

N. Y. P. L. February 25, 1929

RLB

FESTSCHRIFT zur 50 jährigen doktorjubelfeier Karl Weinholds am 14. januar 1896, von Oskar Brenner, Finnur Jónsson [etc.] Strassburg, K. J. Trübner, 1896. vi p., 1 l., 170 p. 23cm.

CONTENTS. —Brenner, O. Zum versbau der schnaderhüpfel. —Jónsson, F. Hogr. —Kluge, F. Deutsche suffixstudien. —Kossinna, G. Zur geschichte des volksnamens 'Griechen'. —Meisner, H. Die freunde der aufklärung. —Geschichte der Berliner Mittwochsgesellschaft. —Meyer, E. H. Totenbretter im Schwarzwald. —Pfaff, F. Märchen aus Lobenfeld. —Pietsch, P. Zur behandlung des nachvokalischen -n einsilbiger wörter in der schlesischen mundart. —Schröder, R. Marktkreuz und Rolandsbild. —Wunderlich, H.

(Continued)

NN*R 11.52 OC PC,1,2,3 SL (LC1, Z1, X1)

FESTSCHRIFT zur 50 jährigen doktorjubelfeier Karl Weinholds am 14. januar 1896... (Card 2)

Die deutschen mundarten in der Frankfurter Nationalversammlung. —Zingerle, O. v. Etzels burg in den Nibelungen.

594999B. 1. German language. 2. German literature. 3. Weinhold, Karl, 1823-1901.

---

*PDB

Festschrift Georg Beer zum 70. geburtstage. Unter mitwirkung von Albrecht Alt, Otto Eissfeldt, Johannes Hempel ... [u. a.] herausgegeben von Artur Weiser. Stuttgart, W. Kohlhammer, 1935.

4 p. l., 148 p. 23½[cm].

Bibliographical foot-notes.

CONTENTS.—Das Gottesurteil auf dem Karmel, von A. Alt.—Der geschichtliche hintergrund der erzählung von Gibeas schandtat (Richter 19–21) von O. Eissfeldt.—Berufung und bekehrung, von J. Hempel.—Jahwe und die vätergötter, von C. Steuernagel.—Der eschatologische glaube im Alten Testament, von P. Volz.—Glauben im Alten Testament, von A. Weiser.—Glaube und volkstum im Alten Testament, von A. Wendel.—Vom verstehen des Alten Testaments, von E. Würthwein.—Verzeichnis der schriften Georg Beers, von E. Würthwein (p. 147–148)

1. Bible. O. T.—Addresses, essays, lectures. 2. Bible—Addresses, essays, lectures—O. T. 3. Beer, Georg, 1865– I. Weiser, Artur, 1893– ed.

A C 36-2391

Title from N. Y. Pub. Libr. Printed by L. C.

[2]

---

*OAC

Festschrift Georg Jacob zum siebzigsten geburtstag 26. mai 1932 gewidmet von freunden und schülern, herausgegeben von Theodor Menzel. Mit dem bildnis G. Jacobs und 10 tafeln. Leipzig, O. Harrassowitz, 1932.

viii p., 1 l., 381 p. front. (port.) fold. col. plates, fold. plan, facsims. (1 fold., in pocket) 25[cm].

"Versuch einer Jacob-bibliographie": p. [369]–381.

1. Jacob, Georg, 1862– 2. Oriental philology—Collections. I. Menzel, Theodor, 1878– ed.

32-35091

Library of Congress PJ26.J3

[2] 490.4

---

*GAH

Festschrift für Georg Leidinger, zum 60. Geburtstag... München: H. Schmidt[, cop. 1930]. xiv, 324 p. facsims., front. (port.), plates (part col'd). 4°.

Edited by Albert Hartmann.

539778A. 1. Leidinger, Georg, 1870– . I. Hartmann, Albert, editor.

N. Y. P. L. July 24, 1931

---

*HB

Festschrift Georg Leyh, aufsätze zum bibliothekswesen und zur forschungsgeschichte dargebracht zum 60. geburtstage am 6. juni 1937 von freunden und fachgenossen. Leipzig, O. Harrassowitz, 1937.

vi, [3], [vii]–xxvi, 427 p. front., XXI pl. (incl. ports., plans, facsims.; 2 col.) 28[cm].

Vorwort signed: Ernst Leipprand.

CONTENTS.—Bibliographie: Raff, H. Verzeichnis der schriften von Georg Leyh.—Aufsätze: Bücher und handschriften aus mittelalter und renaissance: Eichler, F. Die renaissance des buches im 15. jahrhundert und ihre nachwirkung. Gerstinger, H. Ein bisher unbeachtetes verzeichnis griechischer handschriften der Vaticana aus dem jahre 1553. Jacobs, E. Büchergeschenke für sultan Mehemmed II. Nelson, A. Zum Wimpfeling-codex der universitätsbibliothek zu Uppsala. Bömer, A. Eine volkstümliche deutsche enzyklopädie eines Werdener bibliothekars

(Continued on next card)

38-3992

[5]

Festschrift Georg Leyh ... 1937. (Card 2)

CONTENTS—Continued.

aus dem jahre 1527. Preisendanz, K. Handschriftenausleihe in der Bibliotheca Palatina. Lehmann, P. Alte vorläufer des gesamtkatalogs. Christ, K. Karolingische bibliothekseinbände. Dold, P. A. Ein unbekanntes spezimen einer "Gunther-Zainer"-Bibel. Collijn, I. Zwei widmungsexemplare eines werkes des Valentinus Erythræus 1574.—Büchersammlungen: Diesch, C. Fürst Boguslav Radziwill und seine bücherschenkung an die Königsberger schlossbibliothek. Becker, J. Die bibliothek des Zacharias Konrad von Uffenbach. Fick, R. Der ankauf der Celler kirchenministerialbibliothek durch den Preussischen staat.—Bibliotheksgeschichte: Wieland, F. Früheste vorläufer der Vaticana. Craster, H. H. E. A note on the early history of libraries in Oxford. Teichl, R. Ein europäischer bibliothekenführer um das jahr 1780. Die handschrift des pfarrverwalters von Maria-Taferl Adalbert Blumenschein. Hilsenbeck, A. Die universitätsbibliothek Landshut-München und die

(Continued on next card)

38-3992

[5]

Festschrift Georg Leyh ... 1937. (Card 3)

CONTENTS—Continued.

säkularisation (1803). Buttmann, R. Beiträge zur baugeschichte der Bayerischen staatsbibliothek. Stollreither, E. Die universitätsbibliothek Erlangen zur zeit der praktikantentätigkeit August von Platens. Kindervater, J. Nachrichten von einer bibliotheksreise vor 100 jahren. Abb, G. Von der kollegialverfassung zum führerprinzip. Ein beitrag zur verfassungsgeschichte der Preussischen staatsbibliothek. Predeek, A. Antonio Panizzi und der alphabetische katalog des Britischen museums. Rath, E. von. Karl Schaarschmidt. Emler, J. Das neue im alten. Littmann, E. Ein arabisches lied über die ägyptische bibliothek in Kairo.—Bibliotheksverwaltung: Vorstius, J. Vergangenheit, gegenwart und zukunft des Deutschen gesamtkatalogs. Brown, C. H. Some similarities and differences in the administration of university libraries in the United States and Germany. Lemaître, H. Le libre accès au rayon. Munthe, W. Vom lesesaal ins magazin zurück. Koch, T. W.

(Continued on next card)

38-3992

[5]

Festschrift Georg Leyh ... 1937. (Card 4)

CONTENTS—Continued.

Notes on trends in library planning. Gratzl, E. Bedarfsberechnung an der Bayerischen staatsbibliothek 1932–1936.—Moderner druck: Rodenberg, J. Über zeitungs- und zeitschriftentypographie.—Buch und bibliothekar: Neuscheler, E. Buch und leben.—Wissenschaftsgeschichte: Wahl, A. Betrachtungen über die historiographie der vorgeschichte der französischen revolution. Wundt, M. Die überlieferung der deutschen philosophie.—Wirtembergicum: Frey, T. Nicolaus Ochsenbach, der kunstliebende und sammelnde schlosshauptmann auf Hohen-Tübingen (1562–1620)

1. Leyh, Georg, 1877– 2. Bibliography—Collections. 3. Library science—Addresses, essays, lectures. 4. Libraries—Addresses, essays, lectures. I. Leipprand, Ernst, 1905–

38-3992

Library of Congress Z1009.Z31.7

[5] 020.4

BTE

Festschrift für Gerhard Ritter zu seinem 60. Geburtstag. Tübingen, J. C. B. Mohr, 1950. 450 p. illus. 25cm.

"Herausgegeben von Richard Nürnberger."
Bibliographical footnotes.

562083B. 1. Ritter, Gerhard, 1888– . 2. Middle ages—Hist.—Addresses, essays, lectures. 3. Evangelical Lutheran Church—Hist. 4. Germany—Hist.—Addresses, essays, lectures. I. Nürnberger, Richard, 1912– , ed.

N. Y. P. L. March 12, 1951

Festschrift für Gert von der Osten. (Zum 60. Geburtstag am 17. Mai 1970 überreicht von seinem Mitarb. am Wallraf Richartz-Museum: Horst Keller u. a.) (Köln) DuMont Schauberg (1970).

202 p. with illus., port. 28cm.

Includes bibliographies.
"Bibliographie Gerd von der Osten": p. 281-291.

1. Osten, Gert von der, 1910- . 2. Osten, Gert von der, 1910- --Bibl. 3. Art--Essays, and misc. I. Cologne. Wallraf-Richartz-Museum der Stadt Köln.

Festschrift Gustav Binz, oberbibliothekar der Öffentlichen bibliothek der Universität Basel, zum 70. geburtstag am 16. januar 1935, von freunden und fachgenossen dargebracht. Basel, B. Schwabe & co., 1935.

320, [2] p. incl. illus., port. 2 facsim. (1 double col.) 25cm.

CONTENTS.—Zum 16. januar 1935.—Gratulanten- und subskribentenliste.—Glückwünsche der Universität, der kommission der Oeffentlichen bibliothek und der Vereinigung schweizerischer bibliothekare.—Diepenbach, W. Gustav Binz als direktor der Mainzer stadt-bibliothek.—Godet, M. M. Gustave Binz et la Bibliothèque nationale suisse.—Wackernagel, J. Zur wortfolge, besonders bei den zahlwörtern.—Vischer, E. Werenfelsiana.—Bruckner, W. Zur orthographie der althochdeutschen Isidorübersetzung und zur frage nach der heimat des denkmals.—Escher, D. H. Ein amtlicher bericht über die schweizerischen bibliotheken aus der zeit der Helvetik.—Bloesch, H. Ein englischer

(Continued on next card)

A C 35-575

[2]

Festschrift Gustav Binz ... zum 70. geburtstag am 16. januar 1935 ... 1935. (Card 2)

CONTENTS—Continued.

gönner der Berner stadtbibliothek im 18. jahrhundert.—Bruckner, A. Die anfänge des St. Galler stiftsarchivs.—Arbeiten der wissenschaftlichen beamten der universitätsbibliothek: Husner, F. Die handschrift der scholien des Erasmus von Rotterdam zu den Hieronymusbriefen.—Nidecker, H. The poetical prelude of Erasmus Darwin's second marriage.—Pfister, A. Vom frühsten musikdruck in der Schweiz.—Roth, C. Conrad Pfister, Basilius Iselin und die Amerbachische bibliothek.—Scherrer, P. Zum kampfmotiv bei Thomas Murner.—Schmidt, P. Die Bibelillustration als laienexegese.—Schwarber, K. Zentralistisch-politische reformvorschläge in der Schweiz im 18. jahrhundert.—Straub, H. Das kausalprinzip in der modernen physik.—Zehntner, H. Zur bewertung der wirtschaft in den anfängen der gesellschaftslehre in Deutschland.

1. Binz, Gustav, 1865- 2. Basel. Universität. Bibliothek. 3. Libraries—Addresses, essays, lectures.

Title from Yale Univ. Printed by L. C. A C 35-575

[2]

Festschrift für Gustav Boehmer. Dem Siebziger von Freunden und Kollegen dargebracht. Bonn, L. Röhrscheid, 1954. 176 p. port. 24cm.

Contents.—Über Wissen und Glauben im Kampf um das Rechtsgesetz, von J. Esser.—Auctoritas patrum und auctoritas senatus, von H. Siber.—Aufstieg, Blüte und Krisis der Kodifikationsidee, von F. Wieacker.—Das Recht auf Arbeit als allgemeines Menschenrecht, von J. W. Hedemann.—Vom Wesen des

(Continued)

Festschrift für Gustav Boehmer... (Card 2)

Geldes und seiner Einfügung in die Güterordnung des Privatrechts, von R. Reinhardt.—Der Begriff der actio im deutschen und italienischen Prozessrecht, von H. O. de Boor.—Nachträgliche Vereinbarung des Schuldstatuts, von L. Raape.—Privates und öffentliches Recht in den Lieferbeziehungen der Wasserversorgungsunternehmen, von P. Gieseke.—Zur Behandlung der bigamischen Ehe im internationalen Privatrecht, von H. Dölle.—

(Continued)

Festschrift für Gustav Boehmer... (Card 3)

Leistungsrückgewähr bei gutgläubigem Erwerb, von E. von Caemmerer.—Der dingliche Vertrag, von F. Beyerle.

1. Law—Addresses, essays, lectures. 2. Boehmer, Gustav, 1881-

Festschrift für Gustav Schwantes zum 65. Geburtstag, dargebracht von seinen Schülern und Freunden. Hrsg. von Karl Kersten. Neumünster, K. Wachholtz, 1951. vii, 233 p. illus., maps. 31cm.

Bibliographies included.

1. Germany—Archaeology. 2. Schwantes, Gustav, 1881- I. Kersten, Karl, ed.

FESTSCHRIFT für Hans Carl Nipperdey zum 60. Geburtstag, 21. Januar 1955, hrsg. von Rolf Dietz, Alfred Hueck [und] Rudolf Reinhardt. München, C.H. Beck, 1955. 319, [1] p. port. 24cm.

CONTENTS.—Allgemeines Zivilrecht: Zum Problem der Geschäftsgrundlage, von W. Schmidt-Rimpler. Berücksichtigung der für den Erwerb einer fremden Sache gemachten Aufwendungen bei der Bereicherungshaftung, von H. Lehmann. Internationales und interlokales

(Continued)

FESTSCHRIFT für Hans Carl Nipperdey zum 60. Geburtstag, 21. Januar 1955... (Card 2)

Privatrecht, von G. Beitzke.—Arbeitsrecht: Persönlichkeitsbild und Dienst am Arbeitsrecht, von W. Herschel. Dienstpflicht und Arbeitspflicht, von A. Nikisch. Zur Theorie des Urlaubs, von E. Molitor. Klage und Urteil im Kündigungsschutzstreit, von A. Hueck. Kollektivnorm und Individualrecht im Arbeitsverhältnis, von W. Siebert. Der Anspruch auf Abschluss einer Betriebsvereinbarung nach 56 BetrVG, von R. Dietz. Das zweiseitig kollek-

(Continued)

FESTSCHRIFT für Hans Carl Nipperdey zum 60. Geburtstag, 21. Januar 1955... (Card 3)

tive Wesen des Arbeitskampfes, von G.A. Bulla. Zur Neuordnung des Schlichtungswesens, von F. Sitzler. Die Bedeutung der Verwaltungsakte in der neue Entwicklung des Arbeitsrechts und der Sozialversicherung, von H. Dersch. Die für die Ordnung der Wirtschaft massgebenden Rechtsgrundsätze und die Rechtsform der Mitbestimmung, von R. Reinhardt.—Wirtschaftsrecht: Der Kontrahierungszwang Erinnerung und Ausblick, von J.W. Hedemann. Zur Lehre vom Gattungs-

(Continued)

FESTSCHRIFT für Hans Carl Nipperdey zum 60. Geburtstag, 21. Januar 1955... (Card 4)

kauf, von K. Ballerstedt. Der Anwendungsbereich des Wettbewerbsrechts, von W. Hefermehl. Bibliographie des Schrifttums von Hans Carl Nipperdey (p. 303-[320])

1. Nipperdey, Hans Carl, 1895- 2. Law—Addresses, essays, lectures. I. Hueck, Alfred, 1899- ,ed. II. Reinhardt, Rudolf,1902- ,ed. III.Dietz, Rolf, ed. IV. Dietz, Rolf.

F-13
3373

Festschrift für Hans G. Ficker. Zum 70. Geburtstag am 20. Juli 1967. Hrsg. von Murad Ferid. Frankfurt (a. M.), Berlin, Metzner, 1967.
506 p. front. 24 cm.

Bibliographical footnotes.

CONTENTS.—Der Jubilar, von H. Müller.—Über neuere Entwicklungen im Gebiete des Wohnungs-, Teil- oder Stockwerkeigentums im Ausland, von J. Bärmann.—Die subjektiven Merkmale der Willenserklärung, von H. Bartholomeyczik.—Zur rechtlichen Qualifikation

(Continued)

NN*R 10.68 v/OC,I PC,1,2,3,I SL E,1,3 (LC1,XY,Z1)

4

Festschrift für Hans G. Ficker. 1967. (Card 2)

der Verlöbnisfolgen, von G. Beitzke.—Leitende Angestellte als Aufsichtsratsmitglieder des Unternehmens, von H. Brox.—Arbitrage international ou Arbitrage étranger, par R. David.—Bemerkungen zu Art. 17 des Einheitsgesetzes über den Internationalen Kauf beweglicher körperlicher Gegenstände, von H. Dölle.—Interference with contractual relations und deliktsrechtlicher Schutz der Forderung, von H. C. Ficker.—Die Namensführung der geschiedenen Frau nach schweizerischem Recht, von E. Götz.—Die Interessen bei der Regelung der internationalen Zuständigkeit, von A. Heldrich.—Finanzrechtsprobleme der Europäischen Gemeinschaften, von K. M. Hettlage.—Auslandsmontage im Arbeitsrecht, von H. G. Isele.—Die nach-

(Continued)

Festschrift für Hans G. Ficker. 1967. (Card 3)

trägliche Heirat des französischen Rechts im deutschen IPR, von G. Kegel.—Certains aspects de l'évolution du droit contemporain, par M. Matteucci.—Zum räumlichpersönlichen Geltungsbereich Haager IPR Übereinkommen, insbesondere des Übereinkommens über das auf Unterhaltungsverpflichtungen gegenüber Kindern anzuwendende Recht v. 24. 10. 1956, von W. Müller-Freienfels.—Das Verhältnis von Auflösung und Annullierung der Ehe in rechtsvergleichender Sicht, von P. H. Neuhaus.—Bemerkenswerte Kapitel des ausländischen Personenstandsrechts, von E. Peters.—Marriage breakdown in Ticino and Comasco, by M. Rheinstein.—Verfolgung unlauteren Wettbewerbs im Allgemeininteresse, von G. Schwartz.—

(Continued)

FESTSCHRIFT fur Hans G. Ficker. 1967. (Card 4)

Österreichisches Staatsbürgerschaftsgesetz und internationales Privatrecht, von F. Freiherr von Schwind.—Bringt die französische Bodenregisterreform eine Annäherung an das deutsche Grundbuchrecht. Von F. Sturm.—Rechtsvergleichende Bemerkungen zur Entwicklung des ehelichen Güterrechts in Frankreich, von I. Zajtay.—Der Jurist in Frankreich und Deutschland, von K. Zweigert.

1. Ficker, Hans G. 2. Law—Addresses, essays, lectures. 3.Conflict of laws—Addresses, essays, lectures. I. Ferid, Murad,ed.

3-MA

FESTSCHRIFT für Hans Jantzen. Berlin, Gebr. Mann, 1951.
187 p. illus., plates, port. 26cm.

Vorwort signed Kurt Bauch.
Bibliographical footnotes.
CONTENTS. —Logos, von M. Heidegger. —Das Jahrtausend der Engel, von E. Buschor. —Die Bedeutung der Greifenprotomen aus dem Heraion von Samos, von U. Jantzen. —Der architektonische Ursprung der christlichen Basilika, von E. Langlotz. —Zwei St. Galler Fragmente, von A. Boeckler. —Deutsche Architekturdarstellung um das

(Continued)

NN*R 1.55 g/ OC,I PC, 1,2,I SL A,1,2,I (Z1,LC1, X1) [I]

FESTSCHRIFT für Hans Jantzen. (Card 2)

Jahr 1000, von W. Ueberwasser. —Zur Entstehung der sakralen Vollskulptur in der ottonischen Zeit, von H. Keller. —Ottonische Kapitelle im Chor der Kathedrale von Sens, von R. Hamann sen. —Trompe und Zwickel, von W. Rave. —Die Thanner Genesis und ihr Verhältnis zur gotischen Monumentalplastik Südwestdeutschlands, von O. Schmitt. — "Weicher Stil" am Oberrhein (Stand und Aufgaben der Forschung), von W. Noack —Donatello greift ein reimsisches Motiv auf, von W. Vöge. —Ein Beitrag zum Sterzinger Altar, von T. Müller. — Zur Entstehungsgeschichte der Felsgrottenmadonna in der Londoner National Gallery, von H. Beenken. —Bewegungsformen an Michelangelostatuen, von H. Kauffmann. — Michelangelos Juliusgrab im

(Continued)

FESTSCHRIFT für Hans Jantzen. (Card 3)

Entwurf von 1505 und die Frage seiner ursprünglichen Bestimmung, von H. von Einem. —Der Ruhm der Malkunst (Jan Vermeer "De schilderconst"), von H. Sedlmayr. — Zur Wesensbestimmung des österreichischen Barock, von D. Frey. —Inhaltsverzeichnis der Schülerfestschrift Jantzen.

1. Art—Essays and misc. 2. Jantzen, Hans, 1881- . I. Bauch, Kurt, 1887-

---

XBR

FESTSCHRIFT HANS LEWALD. Bei Vollendung des vierzigsten Amtsjahres als ordentlicher Professor im Oktober 1953, überreicht von seinen Freunden und Kollegen mit Unterstützung der Basler juristischen Fakultät. Basel, Helbing & Lichtenhahn, 1953. xv, 641 p. port. 25cm.

Bibliographical footnotes.

J. S. BILLINGS MEM. COLL.

1. Lewald, Hans, 1883- 2. Law, International, Private—Addresses, essays, lectures. 3. Law, Roman—Addresses, essays, lectures. I. Basel (City). Universität. Juristische Fakultät.

NN * * R 5.54 OC (OS) I, Ib+ PC, 1, 2, 3, I SL E, 2, I (LC1, Z1, X1)

BAC

Festschrift, Hans Nabholz. Zürich: A.-G. Gebr. Leemann & Co., 1934. xiv, 341 p. front. (port.) 24cm.

CONTENTS.—Koht, H. An Hans Nabholz.—Meyer, E. Über die Kenntnis des Altertums von der Schweiz in vorrömischer Zeit.—Hirsch, H. Die Urkundenfälschungen des Klosters Ebersheim.—Kehr, P. Die Belehnung der süditalienischen Normannenfürsten durch die Päpste.—Ammann, H. Die Froburger und ihre Städtegründungen.—Burckhardt, A. Untersuchungen zur Genealogie der Grafen von Tierstein.—Piaget, A. Jean de Fribourg et le meurtre de Jean sans Peur.—Muralt, L. von. Über den Ursprung

(Continued)

N. Y. P. L. August 5, 1935

Festschrift, Hans Nabholz . . . (Card 2)

der Reformation in Frankreich.—Berchem, V. von. Une prédication dans un jardin.—Gilliard, C. La rançon du Pays de Vaud.—Martin, P. E. Abraham Du Pan (1582–1665).—Pieth, F. Das Bündnis der III Bünde mit Zürich 1707.—Obser, K. Schweizerische Kunstsammlungen um 1760.—Burckhardt, C. J. Unveröffentlichte Briefe des Staatskanzlers Fürsten von Metternich.—Silberschmidt, M. Tendenzen der amerikanischen Entwicklung.—Bittner, L. Das Eigentum des Staates an seinen Archivalien nach dem österreichischem Allgemeinen bürgerlichen Gesetzbuch.—Largiadèr, A. Das abt.-st. gallische Archiv in Zürich.

758524A. 1. History—Addresses, essays, lectures. 2. Nabholz, Hans, 1874– .
N. Y. P. L. August 5, 1935

E-14
1204

Festschrift für Hans Schima zum 75. Geburtstag. Hrsg. v. Hans W[alter] Fasching [und] Winfried Kralik. [Mit Portr.] Wien, Manz, 1969.

422 p. port. 24cm.

German, English, or Italian.
Bibliography of the works of H. Schima: p. 13–16. Includes bibliographical references.

1. Procedure (Law)--Austria. 2. Law--Addresses, essays, lectures. I. Schima, Hans, 1894– II. Fasching, Hans Walter. III. Kralik, Winfried.

NN * R 4. 71 b/ OC, I, Ib*, II, IIb*, III, IIIb* PC, 1, 2, I, II, III SL E, 1, 2, I, II, III (LC1, X1, Z1)

L-11
299
Bd. 1

FESTSCHRIFT für Heinrich Friedrich Wiepking, hrsg. von Konrad Buchwald, Werner Lendholt [und] Konrad Meyer. Stuttgart, E. Ulmer [1963]

386 p. illus., ports., maps(part col.) 24cm. (Beiträge zur Landespflege. Bd. 1)

Includes bibliographies.

1. Wiepking-Jürgensmann, Heinrich Fr. 2. Landscape. 3. Natural resources--Conservation. I. Buchwald, Konrad, 1914– , ed. II. Buchwald, Konrad, 1914– . t. 1963.

NN R 10. 66 r/ (OC)I, IIbWWG OI (PC)1, 2, 3, I (E)3, I (ST)3t, I (LC1, X1, Z1) [I]

E-14
1501

Festschrift für Heinrich Kunnert. [Illustr.] Eisenstadt (Burgenländ. Landesarchiv) 1969.

205 p. 24 cm. (Burgenländische Forschungen. Sonderheft. 2)

"Schriften von Heinrich Kunnert, abgeschlossen am 15. 10. 1969": p. 197–205.
Includes bibliographies. (Continued)

NN*R 1. 72 w/ OC, I (OD)II (ED)II PC, 1, I, II SL (LC1, X1, Z1)

3

FESTSCHRIFT für Heinrich Kunnert. (Card 2)

CONTENTS.—Das Lebensbild Heinrich Kunnerts, von F. Probst.—Von vergessenen Grabstätten, von A. A. Barb.—Zur Auflösung des Burgenlandes im Jahre 1938, von A. Ernst.—Das Ministerium für Landeskultur und Bergwesen 1848–1853, von O. Guglia.—Mittelalterliche Schwerter im Burgenländischen Landesmuseum, von P. Krajasich.—Ur- und frühgeschichtliche Eisenverhüttung auf dem Gebiet Burgenlands, von A. J. Ohrenberger und K. Bielenin.—Kirtagsbräuche und Schützenwesen aus Burgenlands Vergangenheit, von C. Prickler.—Der Tabor von Unterloisdorf-Mannersdorf, von H. Prickler.—Das Bergland von Bernstein-Rechnitz und seine Bedeutung für

(Continued)

FESTSCHRIFT für Heinrich Kunnert. (Card 3)

den Landschafts- und Naturschutz, von F. Sauerzopf.—Die Sozialdemokratische Partei des Burgenlandes und der Anschluss des Landes an Österreich 1918–1921, von G. Schlag.—Die wissenschaftliche Voraussetzung zur wirtschaftlichen Nutzung von Mineralquellen, von H. Schmid.—Photographie und Museum, von P. Schubert.—Zur Urbarialregulierung nach 1848 im burgenländischen Raum, von H. Seedoch.

1. Burgenland--Hist. I. Kunnert, Heinrich. II. Series.

ENP

Festschrift für Heinrich Schrohe. [Mainz, Mainzer presse, 1934]

144, [7] p., 2 l. 1 illus., 12 pl., port. 25cm.
Half-title: Stadt und stift/beiträge zur Mainzer geschichte.
"Heinrich Schrohe ... anlässlich seines 70. geburtstages als festliche gabe dankbarer anerkennung von schülern, freunden und der vaterstadt."—p. [5]
Contains bibliographies.
CONTENTS.—Heinrich Schrohe, der schulmann und forscher, von H. Schmitt.—Die Dagobertlegende in Mainz, von W. Diepenbach.—Zur frühgeschichte von Altmünster, von R. Dertsch.—Der ursprung der ersten Mainzer kirchensteuer, von H. Knies.—Zur deutung der gewölbefigur am ehemaligen westlettner des Mainzer doms, von O. Schmitt.—Unsere liebe Frau vom hl. blute, von A. Feigel.—Über petitorien im

(Continued on next card)

A C 35-866

[2]

Festschrift für Heinrich Schrohe ... [1934] (Card 2)

CONTENTS—Continued.

erzstift Mainz am ausgang des mittelalters, von F. Herrmann.—Ein schreibfehler in der gründungsbulle der Mainzer universität, von H. Metzner.—Ein verabschiedeter Lübecker ratskellermeister als kläger vor kurmainzischen gerichten, 1686–91, von G. Fink.—Zur geschichte der besetzung und belagerung von Mainz 1688–89, von P. Krause.—Ein Muttergottesbild aus der werkstatt des Mainzer bildhauers Franz Mathias Hiernle, von E. Neeb.—Die berufung des Schweizer geschichtsschreibers und späteren staatsmannes Johannes von Müller zum bibliothekar der Universitätsbibliothek, von A. Kuppel.—Zur geschichte der Mainzer domstiftsfreiungen, von H. Burkard.—An Heinrich Schrohe, von H. Heidenheimer.

1. Mainz. 2. Art—Mainz. 3. Schrohe, Heinrich, 1864–

A C 35-866

Title from N. Y. Pub. Libr. Printed by L. C.

[2]

EAH

Festschrift für Hermann Reincke-Bloch zu seinem sechzigsten Geburtstage überreicht von seinen Schülern. Breslau: Trewendt & Granier, 1927. 168 p. 8°.

Bibliographical footnotes.
Contents: BELTZ, H. Der heutige Stand der Kulturkreislehre. NEUMANN, W. Päpstliche Reichsreformpläne im dreizehnten Jahrhundert. STEINMANN, P. Ein römisch-rechtliches Erachten (Konsilium) über die Steuerpflicht der Stadt Rostock gegenüber den mecklenburgischen Herzögen aus dem Jahre [1482]. BEHNCKE, W. Der Erbteilungsstreit der Herzöge Heinrich V. und Albrecht VII. von Mecklenburg 1518–1525 und die Entstehung der Union der mecklenburgischen Landstände von 1523. ENDLER, C. A. Beiträge zur älteren Geschichte des Rats in Neubrandenburg.

1. Reincke-Bloch, Hermann, 1867–
N. Y. P. L. January 30, 1929

PPB

Festschrift Herrn Emil Christoph Barell, doctor philosophiae, doctor medicinae h. c., Generaldirektor der F. Hoffmann-La Roche & Co. Aktiengesellschaft, am vierzigsten Jahrestage seiner Tätigkeit im Hause "Roche," überreicht von Freunden und Mitarbeitern. Basel [Gedruckt bei F. Reinhardt AG.] 1936. 575 p. incl. tables. front. (port.), illus. (incl. charts), plates. 24cm.

Bibliographies included.
CONTENTS.—Barger, George. From physostigmine to prostigmin.—Cloetta, M. Gedanken und Tatsachen über die biochemischen Grundlagen des Wachens und Schlafens.—Edlbacher, S. Untersuchungen über den Puringehalt der Organe bei Hunger und

(Continued)

N. Y. P. L. January 13, 1938

Festschrift Herrn Emil Christoph Barell... (Card 2)

einseitiger Ernährung.—Karrer, P. Konstitutionserforschung und Synthese des Lactoflavins.—Löffler, W. Helborsid als Herzmittel.—Mannich, C. Die Veredelung natürlicher Alkaloide auf chemischem Wege.—Reichstein, T., and V. Demole. Uebersicht über Chemie und biologische Wirkung der Ascorbinsäuregruppe.—Staehelin, Rud. Vitamine und Klinik.—Straub, W. Analyse der Darmwirkung der Folia Sennae.—Guggenheim, M. Grundlagen der Pharmakotherapie.—Preiswerk, E. Schlafmittelsynthese.—Schnider, Otto. Synthese von Schlafmitteln aus der Pyridinreihe.—Zumbrunn, R. Ueber 4, 4-Dialkyl-5-oxo-dihydro-pyrrole.—Spiegelberg, Hans. Eine einfache Synthese *a*-substituierter Crotonsäuren.—Klingenfuss, Max. Dihydroresorcin und Derivate.—Elger, Franz. Ueber die Umlagerung der *l*-Gulosonsäure in *l*-Ascorbinsäure.—Karrer, Walter. Untersuchungen über herzwirksame Glukoside.—Aeschlimann, J. A. The in-

(Continued)

N. Y. P. L. January 13, 1938

Festschrift Herrn Emil Christoph Barell... (Card 3)

fluence of alkylation on the pharmacological properties of urea and related compounds.—Warnat, K. Synthetische lobelinähnliche Analeptika.—Walter, M. Synthesen in der Gruppe der Oxydiphenyläther mit spezieller Berücksichtigung ihrer bakteriziden Fähigkeiten.—Blankart, A. Parasympathisch erregende und lähmende Wirkungen acetylcholinartiger Stoffe.—Wenner, Wilh. Ueber die Veresterung acetonierter Polyoxysäuren.—Winterstein, Alfred. Chemische Konstitution und physiologische Bedeutung krebserregender Substanzen.—Häussler, E. P. Ueber das Vorkommen des Follikelhormons in Organen und Organflüssigkeiten des Pferdes.—Anneler, Ernst. Ueber die Bestimmung von Codein, Narcotin, Papaverin und Thebain im Opium.—Kubli, Ulrich. Ueber die Stabilität von *l*-Ascorbinsäure.—Duschinsky, Robert. Le dédoublement spontané du monochlorhydrate d'histidine racémique.—Fromherz, K. Zur Analyse zentraler

(Continued)

N. Y. P. L. January 13, 1938

Festschrift Herrn Emil Christoph Barell... (Card 4)

narkotischer Wirkungen im Tierversuch.—Reinert, M. Zur Kenntnis des Bienengiftes.—Pfaltz, Hilde. Zur Kenntnis gonadotrop wirkender Hormone.—Silberschmidt, R. Biochemisches Verhalten und Wirkungsweise der Abführmittel der Phenolphthalein- und Diphenolindolinongruppe.—Gudernatsch, F. Endocrine and amino acid studies in the physiology of development.—Memmen, F. C. Ueber Hefe-Nucleinsäure und ihre Spaltstücke.—Fischer, Hugo. Beitrag zur Theorie der Drogenextraktion: Bestimmung der spezifischen Oberfläche des Extraktionsgutes.—Vetter, R. C. Neuere Probleme der Chininaufbereitung.—Wüest, H. M., and A. J. Frey. Opiate aus Mohnstroh.

923852A. 1. Barell, Emil Christoph. 2. Biochemistry.
N. Y. P. L. January 13, 1938

L-11
3822

FESTSCHRIFT zum hundertjährigen Bestehen der Berliner Gesellschaft für Anthropologie, Ethnologie und Urgeschichte, 1869-1969. Berlin [Berliner Gesellschaft für Anthropologie, Ethnologie und Urgeschichte; in Kommission bei B. Hessling] 1969-70. 2 v. plates. 23cm.

On cover: Hundert Jahre Berliner Gesellschaft für Anthropologie, Ethnologie und Urgeschichte, 1869-1969.

Edited by Hermann Pohle and Gustav Mahr.

(Continued)

NN R 2.72 w/cOCs, Is, IIs PCs, 1s, Is, IIs SLs (LC1s, X1s, Z1s)

FESTSCHRIFT zum hundertjährigen Bestehen der Berliner Gesellschaft für Anthropologie, Ethnologie und Urgeschichte, 1869-1969. (Card 2)

Bibliographical footnotes.

CONTENTS.--T. 1. Fachhistorische Beiträge.--T. 2. Fachwissenschaftliche Beiträge.

1. Berliner Gesellschaft für Anthropologie, Ethnologie und Urgeschichte. I. Pohle, Hermann, 1892- , ed. II. Mahr, Gustav, ed.

D-10
1460

FESTSCHRIFT zum hundertjährigen Bestehen der Wiener Stadtbibliothek, 1856-1956. Wien, Verlag für Jugend und Volk [1956]. 297 p. illus., port., facsims. 21cm. (Wiener Schriften, Heft 4)

1. Vienna. Stadtbibliothek. 2. Libraries--Austria--Vienna. I. Series.

NN* * X 12.56 t/// OC (OD)I, 1b (ED)I PC, 1, 2, I SL (LC1, X1, Z1)

VWE p.v.179, no.10

...**Festschrift** zur 125 jährigen Gründungs-Feier des Grenadier-Regts. König Karl (5. württembergisches) Nummer 123 am 17.–18. Mai 1924 in Ulm in Verbindung mit der Einweihung eines Denkmals für die im Weltkriege Gefallenen. Im Auftrag des Festausschusses bearbeitet von Hauptmann d.R.a.D. Richard Bechtle. Esslingen: O. Bechtle, 1924. 47 p. illus. 8°.

At head of title: 1799. 1924.

1. Army, German—Württemberg. Regt. hist.—Germany—Inf.—123d. 2. European war, 1914–1918—
3. Bechtle, Richard.
N. Y. P. L. October 27, 1927

*PBN

Festschrift für Jacob Rosenheim, anlässlich der vollendung seines 60. lebensjahres dargebracht von seinen freunden. Frankfurt am Main, J. Kauffmann, 1931.

3 p. l., 464 p., 3 p. l., 162 p. front. (port.) 2 pl. on 1 l., facsim. $24\frac{1}{2}$cm.

Contributions in Hebrew, forming the second part of the volume, have special t.-p.:

ספר היובל ליום מלאת ששים שנה לחיי מו"ה רבי יעקב רוזנהיים ... מֻקטר מֵעִם מאת אוהביו ומעריציו. פורטרט עם מ"ט. הוצאת י. קופמן, תרצ"ב.

The German part was edited by Heinrich Eisemann; the Hebrew, by Jakob Landau. *cf.* Pref.

Music: p. 451–458.

1. Rosenheim, Jacob, 1871– 2. Jews—Addresses, essays, lectures. I. Eisemann, Heinrich, ed. II. Landau, Jakob, ed.

Library of Congress BM40.R6 32-29721
[2] 296.04

*PBN

Festschrift dr. Jakob Freimann zum 70. geburtstag gewidmet von der Jüdischen gemeinde zu Berlin und dem Rabbinerseminar zu Berlin, sowie einem kreise seiner freunde und verehrer. Berlin [Buchdruckerei "Viktoria" gmbh] 1937.

xvi, 201, viii, 196 p. front. (port.) 24cm.

Contributions in Hebrew, forming the second part of the volume, have title:

אמת ליעקב. ספר יובל למלאות שבעים שנה למורנו ורבנו יעקב פריימאנן. מוגש על ידי ועד הקהלה ובית המדרש לרבנים בברלין מוקיריו וידידיו. יצא בהוצאת בהם לרבנים בשנת תרצ"ז.

Bibliographical foot-notes.

(Continued on next card)

A C 38-2439
[2]

Festschrift dr. Jakob Freimann zum 70. geburtstag ... 1937. (Card 2)

CONTENTS.—[pt. 1.] Levy, Harry. Der lebensweg. Schriften und aufsätze von dr. Jakob Freimann, zusammengestellt durch Alfred Freimann und Daniel Lewin. Altmann, Alexander. *Olam* und *aion*. Baeck, Leo. Drei alte lieder. Büchler, Adolf. Die Schammaiten und die levitische reinheit des עם הארץ. Elbogen, Ismar. Aus dem briefwechsel von Michael Sachs und Leopold Zunz. Freimann, Aron. Die hebräischen drucke in Rom im 16. jahrhundert. Heschel, Abraham. Der begriff des seins in der philosophie Gabirols. Horovitz, Jakob. Aus der Oxforder handscrift des Josif Omez. Kisch, Guido. Jüdisches recht und Judenrecht. Kober, Adolf. Vier generationen einer jüdischen familie am Rhein um 1400. Krauss, Samuel. Die namen der Königin von Saba. Landau, Maximilian. Der brief Hasdai ibn Šapruts an den

(Continued on next card)

A C 38-2439
[2]

Festschrift dr. Jakob Freimann zum 70. geburtstag ... 1937.
(Card 3)

CONTENTS—Continued.

Chazarenkönig Joseph. Lewin, Daniel Posener minhagim. Löw, Immanuel. Das zinn. Marx, Alexander. Zwei briefe berühmter gelehrter aus dem 14. jahrhundert. Posner, Arthur. Zwei bibliographien. Stern, Moritz. Der Wormser reichsrabbiner Jakob. Wiener, Max. Vorbemerkung zum religiösen verständnis der religionsphilosophischen attributenlehre.—[pt. 2] כתב ברכה. אלבעק, חנוך. רבא השני. אסף, שמחה. לשאלת הירושה של הבת. אפטוביצר, אביגדור. לחקר הלכה. בראדי, חיים. מי כמוכה בהלכה. טשמן, יחיאל מיכל. יסודות שייכות דתית ביחוסים שבין ישראל לעמים. גרינברג, שמואל. יִרְאָה-

(Continued on next card)

A C 38-2439

[2]

Festschrift dr. Jakob Freimann zum 70. geburtstag ... 1937.
(Card 4)

CONTENTS—Continued.

יִרְאָה ... הורודצקי, שמואל אבא. השפעת הרמב"ם על הרמ"א. הילדסהיימר, עוריאל. לחקר על ה,כלאי בתקופת הגאונים. לוין, בנימין מ. פירוש רבנו נסים לערובין. מרמרשטין, אברהם. המצב הכלכלי של היהודים בגליל בדורו של רבי יוחנן בר נפחא ובדור שלאחריו. מרקון, אברהם דוב. רבי אברהם הכהן רפאפורט וספרו ,איתן האורחי". פריימן, אברהם חיים. תשלום העיסור והמנהיג. קליין, שמואל. אסיא (עסיא). ראו, אהרן. קרובת ,אץ הסהר". ריבלין, אליעזר. חזקות של חצרות ובתים בירושלים. שלום, גרשם. תשובות המיוחסות לר' יוסף ג'יקאטילה. ויינברג, יחיאל יעקב. חקירת המקורות להלכה עידית.

1. Freimann, Jakob, 1866–1937. I. Berlin. Jüdische gemeinde. II. Berlin. Rabbiner-seminar für das orthodoxe Judenthum.

A C 38-2439

New York. Public library
for Library of Congress [2]

MAH
✚

Festschrift fuer James Loeb zum sechzigsten Geburtstag gewidmet von seinen archäologischen Freunden in Deutschland und Amerika... München: F. Bruckmann, A. G., 1930. 141 p. facsims., illus., 14 pl. (3 col'd.) 4°.

Bibliographical footnotes.

Contents: ARNDT, P. Der Kopf des Matteischen Amazonentypus. BULLE, H. Von griechischen Schauspielern und Vasenmalern. CHASE, G. H. Eight terracottas in the Museum of Fine Arts, Boston. CURTIUS, L. "Poenitentia." FOWLER, H. N. A marble head in Cleveland. GOLDMAN, H. Some votive offerings from the Acropolis of Halae. LUCE, S. B. A marble head of a goddess in the Rhode Island School of Design, Providence. RICHTER, G. M. A. Five Arretine stamps in the Metropolitan

(Continued)

N. Y. P. L. September 24, 1930

Festschrift fuer James Loeb... (Card 2)

Museum of Art, New York. SANBORN, A. R. The Amazon rhyton by Sotades in the Museum of Fine Arts, Boston. SIEVEKING, J. Archaische Bronze aus Tarent. SPIEGELBERG, W. Die demotischen Papyri Loeb der Universität München. WEICKERT, C. Maske eines Silens, Sammlung Loeb, Murnau. WOLTERS, P. Die goldenen Ähren, Sammlung Loeb, Murnau. ZAHN, R. Silber-Emblem, Sammlung Loeb, Murnau.

489777A. 1. Loeb, James, 1867– . 2. Art, Greek.
N. Y. P. L. September 24, 1930

Write on slip, name, year, vol., page of magazine and class mark — EK

Festschrift für Johannes Biereye zum 70. Geburtstage am 10. juni 1930.

(Verein für die Geschichte und Altertumskunde von Erfurt. Mitteil. Erfurt,1930. 8°. Heft 46,p.1-155. front.port.)

form 400a [11-13-30 25m]

** MGA
(Wolf)

...**Festschrift** für Johannes Wolf zu seinem sechzigsten Geburtstage; herausgegeben von Walter Lott, Helmuth Osthoff und Werner Wolffheim... Berlin: M. Breslauer, 1929. 221 p. diagr., facsims. (incl. music), front. (port.), illus. (music), plates. f°.

At head of title: Musikwissenschaftliche Beiträge.
no. 66 of 325 copies printed.
Bibliographical footnotes.

Contents: Widmung. Bibliographie der gedruckten Arbeiten von Johannes Wolf. ANGLÈS, H. Dos tractats medievals de música figurada. DAVID, H. Die Gesamtanlage

(Continued)

Mr. Moth.

N. Y. P. L. February 18, 1930

...**Festschrift** für Johannes Wolf zu seinem sechzigsten Geburtstage... (Continued)

von Bachs "H-moll"-Messe. DENT, E. J. William Byrd and the madrigal. EINSTEIN, A. Ein Emissär der Monodie in Deutschland: Francesco Rasi. FRIEDLAENDER, M. Ein unbekanntes Duett-Fragment Franz Schuberts. GOMBOSI, O. Die Musikalien der Pfarrkirche zu St. Aegidi in Bártfa. HAAS, R. Das Generalbassflugblatt Francesco Bianciardis. HELFERT, V. Die Jesuiten-Kollegien der Böhmischen Provinz zur Zeit des jungen Gluck. HIRSCH, P. Bibliographie der musiktheoretischen Drucke des Franchino Gafori. HORNBOSTEL, E. M. v. Tonart und Ethos. KROGH, T. Reinhard Keiser in Kopenhagen. LACH, R. Die musikalischen Konstruktionsprinzipien der altmexikanischen Tempelgesänge. LACHMANN, R. Die Weise vom Löwen und der pythische

(Continued)

N. Y. P. L. February 18, 1930

...**Festschrift** für Johannes Wolf zu seinem sechzigsten Geburtstage... (Continued)

Nomos. MAHLING, F. Das Farbe-Ton-Problem und die selbständige Farbe-Ton-[illegible]schung als Exponenten gegenwärtigen Geistesstrebens. MERSMANN, H. Sona[illegible]men in der romantischen Kammermusik. MEYER, K. Über Musikbibliog[illegible]. MOSER, H. J. Instrumentalismen bei Ludwig Senffl. NOACK, F. Die Musik zu d[illegible]lièreschen Komödie "Monsieur de Pourceaugnac von J. B. de Lully. NORLIND, [illegible] schwedische Hofkapelle in der Reformationszeit. OSTHOFF, H. Eine unbekannte [illegible]spielmusik Jacob Regnarts. PIRRO, A. Gilles Mureau, chanoine de Chartres. S[illegible]s, C. Zweiklänge im Altertum. SCHERING, A. Musikalisches aus Joh. Burckards "Liber Notarum." SCHNEIDER, M. Eine unbekannte Lautentabulatur aus den Jahren 1537–1544.

(Continued)

N. Y. P. L. February 18, 1930

...**Festschrift** für Johannes Wolf zu seinem sechzigsten Geburtstage... (Continued)

SCHUENEMANN, G. Ein Sing- und Spielbuch des 18.Jahrhunderts. SIMON, A. Ein Kanon aus Marco Scacchis "Cribrum musicum ad triticum Siferticum." TORREFRANCA, F. La prima opera francese in Italia? (L'Armida di Lulli, Roma 1690). VAN DEN BORREN, C. Le "Fragment de Gand." WAGNER, P. Ein versteckter Discantus. WERNER, T. W. Schuberts Tod. Versuch einer Deutung. WOLFFHEIM, W. Ein unbekannter Kanon von Joh. Seb. Bach.

DREXEL MUSICAL FUND.

465147A. 1. Wolf, Johannes, 1869– . 2. Music—Essays. 3. Lott, Walter, 1892– , editor. 4. Osthoff, Helmuth, jt. editor. 5. Wolffheim, Werner Joachim, 1877– , jt. editor.
N. Y. P. L. February 18, 1930

NABO

Festschrift für Jost Trier zu seinem 60. Geburtstag am 15. Dez. 1954, hrsg. von Benno von Wiese und Karl Heinz Borck. Meisenheim/Glan, Westkulturverlag, 1954. 518 p. port., music. 24cm.

Contents.—Sprach- und Literaturwissenschaft als Einheit? von H. Kuhn.—Die Sprachfelder in der geistigen Erschliessung der Welt, von L. Weisgerber.—Literaturwissenschaft als

(Continued)

NN**R 8.55 d/br OC,I, II,IIIbo PC,1,2,3,4,I, II SL (MU) 5,6 (MUS1: Quant li solleiz,LC1, XL,Z1)

Festschrift für Jost Trier zu seinem 60. Geburtstag am 15. Dez. 1954... (Card 2)

Auslegung und als Geschichte der Dichtung, von E. Trunz.—Zum altfranzösischen Assumptionstropus "Quant li solleiz", von H. Lausberg.—Ein niederrheinisches Liebesduett aus des Minnesangs Frühling, von T. Frings udn E. Linke.—Über das Verhältnis von rhythmischer Gliederung und Gedankenführung in den Strophen Heinrichs von Morungen, von F. Maurer.—Hilfe und Rat in Wolframs "Parzival", von W. Mohr.— Das Zeitgerüst des (Continued)

Festschrift für Jost Trier zu seinem 60. Geburtstag am 15. Dez. 1954... (Card 3)

"Fortunatus"-Volksbuchs, von G. Müller.—Prometheus und Pandora. Zu Goethes Metamorphose-Dichtungen, von C. Heselhaus.—Zur Sprache der "Wahlverwandtschaften", von H. Brinkmann.—Tagebuchaufzeichnungen des westfälischen Freiherrn Ludwig von Diepenborck-Grüter über Heinrich Heine, von K. Schulte-Kemminghausen.—Annette von Droste-Hülshoffs "Judenbuche" als Novelle, von B. von Wiese und Kaiserswal- dau.—Das Bild des Menschen im zeitgenö: sischen Drama, von (Continued)

Festschrift für Jost Trier zu seinem 60. Geburtstag am 15. Dez. 1954. (Card 4)

H.J. Schrimpf.—Ofen und Kamin, von J. Schepers.—Über das Verhältnis von Laut und Bedeutung in einigen indogermanischen Präpositionen, von B. Mergell.—Die niederländischen und westniederdeutschen Bezeichnungen des Klees, von W. Foerste.—Gaut, von H. Kuhn.—Lied und Licht, von H. Schwarz.—Zur Bedeutung der Wörter holz, wald, forst und witu im Althochdeutschen, von K.-H. Borck.—Jubel, von H. Grundmann.— Verzeichnis der (Continued)

Festschrift für Jost Trier zu seinem 60. Geburtstag am 15. Dez. 1954. (Card 5)

Schriften Jost Triers, von J.M. Giesbrecht. (p. 512-518)

1. Literature—Addresses, essays, lectures. 2. Philology—Addresses, essays, lectures. 3. German literature—Addresses, essays, lectures. 4. Trier, Jost. 5. Tropes. 6. Mary, Virgin (Assumption). I. Borck, Karl Heinz, , ed. II. Wiese, Benno von, 1903- , ed. III. Borck, Karl Heintz.

OAI

Festschrift Julius Elster und Hans Geitel, zum sechsigsten Geburtstag gewidmet von Freunden und Schülern... Braunschweig: F. Vieweg & Sohn, 1915. xi,719, 3 p. diagrs., illus., plates, tables (part fold.) 8°.

At head of title: Arbeiten aus den Gebieten der Physik, Mathematik, Chemie.
Vorwort signed: Karl Bergwitz.

889612.

1919

BAP

FESTSCHRIFT, JULIUS FRANZ SCHÜTZ, unter Mitwirkung der Steiermärkischen Landesbibliothek, hrsg. und redigiert von Berthold Sutter. Graz-Köln, H. Böhlaus Nachf., 1954. xvi, 493 p. plates, ports., plans. 23cm.

1. Schütz, Julius Franz, 1889- 2. Civilization—Addresses, essays, lectures. I. Styria, Austria. Landesbibliothek, Gratz. II. Sutter, Berthold, ed. III. Sutter, Berthold. t. 1954.
NN * * R X 7.55 p/s OC, II, IIIbo (OD) It (ED) It PC, 1, 2, I, II SL (LC1, X1, Z1)

3-MA

FESTSCHRIFT für Julius Schlosser zum 60. Geburtstage, hrsg. von Arpad Weixlgärtner und Leo Planiscig. Zürich, Amalthea-Verlag [1927] 289 p. 54 plates (112 figs.), port. 26cm.

CONTENTS.—'Εδιζησαμη 'εμεωυτόν , von H. Gomperz.—Il primo traduttore italiano di Enrico Heine, di B. Croce.—Über Vergleichung und Unvergleichlichkeit der Künste, von K. Vossler.—Musik und bildende Kunst im Rahmen der allgemeinen Kunstgeschichte, von C. Sachs.—Grillparzers Novelle "Der arme Spielmann" und die (Continued)

NN 6.57 c/ OC, I, II PC, 1, 2, 3, I, II SL A, 1, 2, 3, I, II (LC1, X1, Z1)

FESTSCHRIFT für Julius Schlosser zum 60... (Card 2)

Musikwissenschaft, von R. Lach.—"Arkadia," von E. Löwy.—Die Basilica des Junius Bassus und die Kirche S. Andrea cata Barbara auf dem Esquilin, von C. Huelsen.—Ein Porträtkopf aus merovingischer Zeit, von J. Banko.—Die byzantinische Buchmalerei der ersten nachikonoklastischen Zeit mit besonderer Rücksicht auf die Farbengebung, von J.J. Tikkanen.—Der romanische Epiphaniezyklus in Lambach und das lateinische Magierspiel, von K.M. Swoboda.—Über eine unbeachtete Wurzel der maniera moderna, von E.H. Buschbeck.—Von einigen Inkunabeln der Kölner Malerei, von B. Kurth.—Una "camera d'amore" nel castello di Avio, di A. Morassi.—"Aller Tugenden und Laster Abbildung," von F. Saxl.—Beiträge zur Andrea Bregno- Forschung, von H. Egger.— (Continued)

FESTSCHRIFT für Julius Schlosser zum 60... (Card 3)

Leonardos Porträte und Aristoteles, von L. Planiscig.—Ein ungedruckter Brief von Ludovico Buonarroti an seinen Sohn Michelangelo, von E. Steinmann.—Die Pietà von Ubeda, von E. Panofsky.—Alberto Duro, von A. Weixlgärtner.—Der Richter auf dem Fabeltier, von K. Rathe.—Ritterlich Spielzeug, von A. Gross.—Drei deutsche Bildhauerzeichnungen, von L. Baldass.—Original und Kopie, von G. Glück.—Georg Hoefnagel und der wissenschaftliche Naturalismus, von E. Kris.—Zwei unbekannte Büsten des Erzherzogs Leopold Wilhelm von Hieronymus Duquesnoy d. J. und François Dusart, von H.J. Hermann.— Maria Theresia von Paradis, von H. Ubell.—Bibliographie der bis zum 23. September 1926 erschienenen Schriften von Julius Schlosser, von H.R. Hahnloser (p. 274-284)
1. Schlosser, Julius, Ritter von, 1866-1938. 2. Schlosser, Julius, Ritter von, 1866-1938--Bibl. 3. Art--Essays and misc. I. Weixlgärtner, Arpád, ed. II. Planiscig, Leo, 1887- , ed.

XAD

Festschrift Justus Wilhelm Hedemann zum sechzigsten geburtstag am 24. april 1938. Herausgeber: Roland Freisler ... George Anton Löning ... [und] Hans Carl Nipperdey ... Jena, Fromannsche buchhandlung, W. Biedermann, 1938.

4 p. l., [3]-458 p. front. (port.) 24cm.
Bibliographical foot-notes.

CONTENTS.—Deutsche rechtsgeschichte: Fehr, H. Kraft und recht. Löning, G. A. Staat und wirtschaft unter Heinrich dem Löwen. Buchda, G. Wirtschaftsrecht in jüngeren thüringischen landesordnungen. Schultze von Lasaulx, H. A. Die krise des gemeinen Sachsenrechts. Meyer, H. Eine süddeutsche stammgutstiftung.—Allgemeine rechts-

(Continued on next card)

A C 38-2941

[3]

Festschrift Justus Wilhelm Hedemann ... 1938. (Card 2)
CONTENTS—Continued.

lehre und öffentliches recht: Schmidt-Rimpler, W. Zur gesetzgebungstechnik. Swoboda, E. Die rückkehr zu den grundgedanken des rechts. Kroellreutter, O. Führung und verwaltung. Jerusalem, F. W. Gesetzmässigkeit der verwaltung oder rechtmässigkeit der verwaltung? Brand, A. Die fürsorgepflicht des öffentlichen dienstherrn nach dem neuen deutschen beamtengesetz. Boehm, M. H. Volkstumswechsel und assimilierungspolitik.—**Richtertum und verfahren:** Freisler, R. Gerichtliche redekunst im strafverfahren. Dikoff, L. Abänderung von verträgen durch den richter. Blomeyer, K. Freiwillige gerichtsbarkeit und zivilprozess. Ekelöf, P. O. Das rechtliche interesse als interventionsgrund. Gerland, H. Ein fall zur blutgruppenlehre. — **Ausländisches zivilrecht und rechtsvergleichung:** Haataja, K. Geschichtliche

(Continued on next card)

A C 38-2041

[3]

Festschrift Justus Wilhelm Hedemann ... 1938. (Card 3)
CONTENTS—Continued.

grundzüge des finnischen bodenrechts. Molitor, E. Die familiengemeinschaft im entwurf des italienischen Sachsenrechts. Kaden, E. H. Zum problem der fahrnisübereignung im schweizerischen recht. Ionescu, O. L'influence de la législation allemande sur le projet du code civil roumain. Siebert, W. Die "faktische" gesellschaft. Ein rechtsvergleichender beitrag zur systematik des rechts der handelsgesellschaften und der gesellschaft des bürgerlichen rechts.—**Deutsches arbeitsrecht:** Nipperdey, H. C. Die regelung des anlernverhältnisses der jugendlichen. Hueck, A. Die pflicht des unternehmers zur fürsorge für den gefolgsmann nach dem gesetz zur ordnung der nationalen arbeit. Dietz, R. Die pflicht des ehemaligen beschäftigten zur verschwiegenheit über betriebsgeheimnisse. — **Recht und wirtschaft:** Köttgen, A. Zur lehre

(Continued on next card)

A C 38-2041

[3]

Festschrift Justus Wilhelm Hedemann ... 1938. (Card 4)

CONTENTS—Continued.

von den rechtsquellen des wirtschaftsrechts. Gieseke, P. Entschädigungspflicht bei marktordnenden massnahmen. Reinhardt, R. Grundsätzliches zum leistungswettbewerb. Ullrich, H. Ein beitrag zur reform des versicherungsvertragsrechts (Gedanken zu § 21 VVG) Lehmann, H. Die generalklausel des neuen aktiengesetzes. Hoffmann, W. Die deutsche seeschiffahrt in den nachkriegsjahren und ihre reorganisation. Scheuner, U. Die freien berufe im ständischen aufbau.—Verzeichnis der schriften Justus Wilhelm Hedemann's. Von referendar Wilhelm von Mutius.

1. Hedemann, Justus Wilhelm, 1878– 2. Law—Addresses, essays, lectures. I. Freisler, Roland, 1893– II. Löning, George Anton, 1900– III. Nipperdey, Hans Carl, 1895–

A C 38-2041

Yale univ. Library
for Library of Congress [3]

Write on slip words underlined below
and class mark —

RAA

...**Festschrift** für Karl Brugmann. Herausgegeben von Wilhelm Streitberg... Strassburg: K. J. Trübner, 1909. 2 v. front. (port.), pl. 23cm. (Indogermanische Forschungen. Bd. 25–26.)

CONTENTS.—Teil 1. Dittrich, O. Konkordanz und Diskordanz in der Sprachbildung. Rozwadowski, Jan von. Ein quantitatives Gesetz der Sprachentwicklung. Sütterlin, L. Der Schwund von idg. i und u. Baudouin de Courtenay, J. Zur 'Sonanten'-Frage. Garnier, Katharine von. Com- als perfektivierendes Präfix bei Plautus, sam- im Rigveda, ςυν- bei Homer. Behaghel, O. Beziehungen zwischen Umfang und Reihenfolge von Satzgliedern. Uhlenbeck, C. C. Etymologica. Holthausen, F. Etymologien. Ciardi-Dupré, G. Fruchtbäume und Baumfrüchte in den indogerm. Sprachen. Walde, A. Zu den indogerm. Wörtern für 'Milz'. Bartholomae, Chr. Arica XVI. Jackson,

(Continued)

N. Y. P. L. October 15, 1940

...**Festschrift** für Karl Brugmann... (Continued)

A. V. W. Indo-Iranian notes. Bloomfield, M. On some disguised forms of Sanskrit paçu 'cattle'. Zubatý, J. Zum Gebrauch von ved. víśvaḥ 'omnis'. Johansson, K. F. Zur mittelindischen Grammatik. Kern, H. Das Verbum āyūhati im Pāli. Bloch, J. Tamoul vāddyar: sanskrit upādhyāya. Charpentier, J. Kleine Beiträge zur armenischen Wortkunde. Buck, C. D. Greek notes. Danielsson, O. A. Zur Lehre vom homerischen Digamma. Hermann, E. Zur Behandlung der antispastischen Wörter im homerischen Epos. Sommer, F. Der Dativus pluralis der 3. Deklination im Nordwestgriechischen. Meister, R. Die äolischen Demonstrativa ὄνε, ὄνι, ὄνυ und die Partikel νι (νε) im Phrygischen. Wackernagel, J. Attische Vorstufen des Itazismus. Meltzer, H. Gibt es ein rein präsentisches Perfekt im Griechischen? Hatzidakis, G. N. Zum Gebrauch der verbalen Medialformen im Neugriechischen. Lagercrantz,

(Continued)

N. Y. P. L. October 15, 1940

...**Festschrift** für Karl Brugmann... (Continued)

O. Zwei griechische Fremdwörter. Grammont, M. Grec γυμνός 'nu'. Havers, W. Zur Etymologie von griech. φάρμακον. Krumbacher, K. Κτήτωρ.—Teil 2. Thumb, A. Altgriechische Elemente des Albanesischen. Cuny, A. Grec αἰγίλωψ 'espèce de chêne', latin īlex. Fay, E. W. αἷμων and imago. Niedermann, M. Zur griechischen und lateinischen Wortkunde. Persson, P. Zur lateinischen Grammatik und Wortkunde. Meister, K. Altes Vulgärlatein. Ernout, A. Note sur les thèmes en -u- latins. Günther, R. Die ursprüngliche Gestalt des lateinischen Präverbs re, red. Pokrowskij, M. Lateinische Zusammenrückungen. Solmsen, F. Zur lateinischen Etymologie. Postgate, J. P. Three Latin Etymologica. Stolz, Fr. Die Flexion von lavere und lavāre. Brugmann, O. Andes — Andicus. Thurneysen, R. Die irische Personalendung -enn -ann. Vendryes, J. À propos de la flexion du présent irlandais tiagu 'je

(Continued)

N. Y. P. L. October 15, 1940

...**Festschrift** für Karl Brugmann... (Continued)

vais'. Stokes, W. Irish etymologies. Bremer, O. Die germanische 'Brechung'. Helten, W. van. Zur pronominalen Flexion im Altgermanischen. Delbrück, B. Das schwache Adjektivum und der Artikel im Germanischen. Meillet, A. Sur le prétérito-présent got. lais. Loewe, R. Der Goldring von Pietroassa. Mogk, E. Die Halbvokale i̯ und u̯ in der isländischen Literatursprache. Noreen, A. Ein Paar altnordische Seenamen. Sievers, E. Angelsächsisch wēriȝ 'verflucht'. Karsten, T. E. Altdeutsche Kulturströmungen im Spiegel des finnischen Lehnworts. Kern, J. H. Zum Verhältnis zwischen Betonung und Laut in niederländisch-limbürgischen Mundarten. Wijk, N. van. Eine polnisch-niederländische Parallele. Schwyzer, E. Die Demonstrativpronomina des Schweizerdeutschen. Pedersen, H. Zum slavischen z. Mikkola, J. J. Zwei slavische Etymologien. Schrader, O. Der Hammelsonntag. Osten-Sacken,

(Continued)

N. Y. P. L. October 15, 1940

...**Festschrift** für Karl Brugmann... (Continued)

v. d. Zur Entwicklungsgeschichte der Nomins auf slavisch -ȝba, litauisch -ýbas -ýba -ỹbe, lettisch -ība. Leskien, A. Litauische Personennamen. Gauthiot, R. À propos des nominatifs pluriels lituaniens. Herbig, G. Indogermanische Sprachwissenschaft und Etruskologie. Streitberg, W. Kant und die Sprachwissenschaft. (Eine historische Skizze.) Anhang: Karl Brugmanns Schriften. 1871–1909 (p. 425–440).

1. Brugmann, Karl, 1849–1919. I. Streitberg, Wilhelm August, 1864–1925, ed.
N. Y. P. L. October 15, 1940

XAI

Festschrift Karl Haff zum siebzigsten Geburtstag dargebracht. Hrsg. von Dr. Kurt Bussmann...[und] Dr. Nikolaus Grass... Innsbruck, Wagner, 1950. 415 p. maps, plates. 24cm.

"Verzeichnis der wissenschaftlichen Veröffentlichungen von Karl Haff," p. 410–415.

585850B. 1. Law. 2. Haff, Karl, 1879– . I. Bussmann, Kurt. II. Grass, Nikolaus.
N. Y. P. L. December 13, 1951

YAR

Festschrift für Karl Joël zum 70. geburtstage (27. märz 1934) Basel, Helbing & Lichtenhahn, 1934.

3 p. l., [9]–267 p. 24cm.

CONTENTS.—Barth, Heinrich. Philosophie der zukunft.—Baumgarten, Arthur. Strafrecht und willensfreiheit. — Cohn, Jonas. Potenz und existenz. Eine studie über Schellings letzte philosophie.—Gauss, Hermann. Das problem der willensfreiheit bei Plato. — Griseback, Eberhard. Philosophie als beruf.—Groos, Karl. Die unsterblichkeit als philosophisches problem.—Häberlin, Paul. Zum "Ursprung der naturphilosophie aus dem geiste der mystik".—Hoffmann, Ernst. Die philosophischen erzieher Deutschlands im 19. jahrhundert. — Howald, Ernst. Noch einmal Leukippos.—Landmann-Kalischer, Edith. Die menschengestalt der homerischen götter.—Medicus, Fritz. Sittlichkeit und religion in ihrem verhältnis zur politik.—Schmalenbach, Herman. Das gewissen.—Stenzel, Julius. Zum aufbau des platonischen dialogs. — Tumarkin, Anna. Ein versuch, Diltheys leben aus ihm selbst zu verstehen.

1. Joël, Karl, 1864– 1934. 2. Philosophy—Addresses, essays, lectures.

A C 35-1953

Title from Columbia Univ. Printed by L. C. [2]

Copy only words underlined
& classmark— VHA

FESTSCHRIFT Karl Kegel zu seinem 80. Geburtstag am 19. Mai 1956. Berlin, Akademie-Verlag, 1957. 240 p. illus., port., diagrs. 25cm. (Freiberger Forschungshefte. Reihe A: Bergbau und Veredelung.60)

Bibliographical footnotes.
CONTENTS. —Grundlagen zum Entwerfen und Berechnen von Abschläg-gen beim Streckenvortrieb, von A. Ohnesorge. —Einige grundsätzliche Gedanken zur Mechanisierung des Weichbraunkohlentiefbaus, von G. Teufer. —Böschungsbewegungen im Lockergestein, von H. Härtig und
(Continued)

NN R X 7. 58 j/ OI (PC)1, 2 (ST)1, 2t (LC3, X1, Z1)

FESTSCHRIFT Karl Kegel zu seinem 80. Geburtstag am 19. Mai 1956. (Card 2)

H. Matschak. —Zur Geschichte der Theorie der bindemittellosen Brikettierung von Braunkohle, von E. Rammler. —Zur Theorie und Praxis der Braunkohlenverwertung um 1800, von H. Wilsdorf. —Zur Geschichte des erzgebirgischen Kohlenabbaus und seines Rechts bis 1542, von H. Löscher.

1. Kegel, Karl, 1876- 2. Mines and mining. t. 1957.

MA

Festschrift Karl M. Swoboda zum 28. Januar 1959. [Redaktionskomitee: Otto Benesch, et al.] Wien, R. M. Rohrer [°1959]

321 p. illus., plates, port., map. 25 cm.

Contributions in German except for one in French and two in Italian.
Bibliographical footnotes.

1. Art--Essays and misc. 2. Swoboda, Karl Maria, 1889- I. Benesch, Otto, 1896- , ed.

NN * R 11. 60 p/ OC, I X1, Z1) [I] PC, 1, 2, I SL A, 1, 2, I (LC1,

---

* MGA

Festschrift Karl Nef zum 60. Geburtstag (22. August 1933), dargebracht von Schülern und Freunden. Zürich [etc.] Kommissions-Verlag Gebrüder Hug & Co. [1933] 128, vii, 129–219 p. incl. front. (mounted port.) 22½cm.

Music, vii p.
Bibliographies included.
CONTENTS.—Mohr, E. Karl Nef und sein Werk.—Ehinger, H. Die Rolle der Schweiz in der "Allgemeinen musicalischen Zeitung" 1798–1848.—Geering, A. Homer Herpol und Manfred Barbarini Lupus.—Güldenstein, G. Die Gegenwertigkeit in der Musik.—Handschin, J. Die Schweiz, welche sang.—Hol, J. C. Cipriano de Rore.—Levy, E. Von der Synkope.—Lohr, I. Zur Wiederbelebung der geistlichen Monodie

(Continued)

N. Y. P. L. February 8, 1935

Festschrift Karl Nef zum 60. Geburtstag (22. August 1933)... (Card 2)

des Mittelalters im heutigen Chorkonzert.—Maag, O. Musik und Sprache.—Merian, W. Mozarts Klaviersonaten und die Sonatenform.—Refardt, E. Die Musik in den "Alpenrosen."—Rittmeyer-Iselin, D. Das Rebec.

Carnegie Corporation of New York.

740020A. 1. Nef, Karl, 1873- 2. Music—Essays. 3. Music—Switzerland.

N. Y. P. L. February 8, 1935

---

*HZ

Festschrift Karl Schwarber; Beiträge zur schweizerischen Bibliotheks-, Buch- und Gelehrtengeschichte. Zum 60. Geburtstag am 22. November 1949 dargebracht. Basel, B. Schwabe, 1949.

315 p. plate, port. 26 cm.
Bibliographical footnotes.
CONTENTS.—Die von Staalsche Historienbibel der Zentralbibliothek Solothurn, von L. Altermatt.—Quelques considérations sur les bibliothèques suisses dans la vie internationale, par P. Bourgeois.—Jacob Burckhardt in Rom, von M. Burckhardt.—Die rechtliche Natur des Bibliotheksbuches, von H. Flury.—Au temps de la "Respublica litterarum"; Jacob Christophe Iselin et Louis Bourguet, par M. Godet.—Die Zusammenarbeit der schweizerischen Bibliotheken, von H. Grosser.—Die editio princeps des "Corpus historiae Byzantinae,"

(Continued on next card)

[1] A 50–2402

Festschrift Karl Schwarber ... 1949. (Card 2)

CONTENTS—Continued.

Johannes Oporin, Hieronymus Wolf und die Fugger, von F. Husner.—Ein neues Bruchstück zu Liudprand von Cremona, von G. Meyer.—Wilhelm Wackernagel, Bücher und Freunde; ein Streifzug durch seine Bibliothek, von H. Nidecker.—Zur Sprachkunst des Germanisten Andreas Heusler, von T. Salfinger.—La Bulle d'excommunication de Georges de Supersaxo, par P.-E. Schazmann.—Über die sachliche Katalogisierung umfassender Werke, von P. Schmidt.—Die innerschweizerischen Handschriften der Bürgerbibliothek Luzern, von M. Schnellmann.—Christoph Martin Wieland an Johann III Bernoulli; ein unveröffentlichter Brief, von H. Straub.—Die Stammbücher der Universitätsbibliothek Basel, ein beschreibendes Verzeichnis, von C. Vischer.—Die Wundartzney von Felix Wirtz; das Rätsel ihrer Ver-

(Continued on next card)

A 50–2402

[1]

Festschrift Karl Schwarber ... 1949. (Card 3)

CONTENTS—Continued.

fasserschaft, von H. G. Wirz.—Die handschriftlichen Nachlässe von Schweizer Komponisten in der Universitätsbibliothek Basel, von H. Zehntner.

1. Basel. Universität. Bibliothek. 2. Libraries—Switzerland. 3. Schwarber, Karl.

Z1009.Z3S35 010.4 A 50–2402

Harvard Univ. Library for Library of Congress [1]

L-10
2846

FESTSCHRIFT Landesrat Professor Dr. Hans Gamper zur Vollendung seines 65. Lebensjahres. Hrsg. von Franz Grass. Innsbruck, Wagner, 1956-62. 3 v. ports. 25cm.

Title varies slightly.
Vol. 1 also published separately with title: Landesbewusstsein und Kulturpolitik Tirols in den letzten Jahrzehnten, von Franz Grass.
(Continued)

NN R 4. 63 p/ OCs, Is, IIs PCs, 1s, 2s, Is, IIs SLs Es, 1s, Is, IIs (LC1s, X1s, Z1s)

2

FESTSCHRIFT Landesrat Professor Dr. Hans Gamper zur Vollendung seines 65... (Card 2)

Includes bibliographies.

1. Gamper, Hans, 1890- 2. Tyrol--Civilization. I. Grass, Franz, ed. II. Gras, Franz. Landesbewusstsein und Kulturpolitik Tirols in den letzten Jahrzehnten.

XAA
(Leipziger)

...**Festschrift** der Leipziger Juristenfakultät für Dr. Victor Ehrenberg zum 30. März 1926. Leipzig: T. Weicher, 1927. iv, 395 p. 4°. (Leipziger rechtswissenschaftliche Studien. Heft 21.)

Bibliographical footnotes.

Contents: JACOBI, E. Betrieb und Unternehmen als Rechtsbegriffe. MOLITOR, E. Die Bestellung zum Vorstandsmitglied einer Aktiengesellschaft, ihre Voraussetzungen und Folgen. RICHTER, L. Die Einrichtungen der kassenärztlichen Selbstverwaltung. REHME, P. Stadtbücher des Mittelalters.

393604A- Mr. Watt

1. Ehrenberg, Victor, 1851– . 2. Business organization and management—Germany. 3. Corporations—Germany. 4. Insurance, Sickness—Germany. 5. Societies, Mutual aid—Germany. 6. Physicians. 7. Cities—Hist.—Germany—Bibl. 8. Municipal government—Germany—Bibl. 9. Ser.

N. Y. P. L. December 5, 1928

L-10
2529
Bd. 18/23, 24/29

FESTSCHRIFT Leopold G. Scheidl zum 60. Geburtstag. Im Auftrage des Vorstandes der Österreichischen Gesellschaft für Wirtschaftsraumforschung hrsg. von Heinz Baumgartner [et al.] Wien, F. Berger, 1965. 2 v. illus., port., maps (part fold., part issued in pocket) 25cm. (Wiener geographische Schriften. Bd. 18/23, 24/29)

Papers in German, English or French.

(Continued)

NN R 1.70 v/L OC, III, V, VIbo (OS)I, II, IV, IVb+ PC, 1, I, II, III, IV, V E, 1, I, II, III, IV, V (LC1, X1, Z1) [I] 2

FESTSCHRIFT Leopold G. Scheidl zum 60. (Card 2)

Includes bibliographies.

1. Geography, Economic--Addresses, essays, lectures. I. Series. Bd. 18/23. II. Series. Bd. 24/29. III. Scheidl, Leopold G, 1904- . IV. Österreichische Gesellschaft für Wirtschaftsraumforschung. V. Baumgartner, Heinz, ed. VI. Baumgartner, Heinz.

Copy only words underlined
& classmark— *OBKQ

FESTSCHRIFT für Leopold Wenger zu seinem 70. Geburtstag, dargebracht von Freunden, Fachgenossen und Schülern. München, C. H. Beck, 1944-45. 2 v. ports. 22cm. (Münchener Beiträge zur Papyrusforschung und antiken Rechtsgeschichte. Heft 34-35)

Bibliographical footnotes.

1. Wenger, Leopold. 2. Law, Roman. 3. Law—Hist., Ancient. I. Ser.

NN *R 4.53 OC PC, 1, 2, 3 O, 1, 3 (LC1, Z1, X1)

---

*Z-1861

FESTSCHRIFT für Lorenz Morsbach. Dargebracht von Freunden und Schülern. Redigiert von F. Holthausen und H. Spies. Halle a.S., M. Niemeyer, 1913. 721 p. ports., facsim. 8° (Studien zur englischen Philologie. 50)

Microfilm (Negative)

1. Morsbach, Lorenz, 1850- . 2. English literature--Hist. 3. English language--Hist. I. Holthausen, Ferdinand, 1860- , ed. II. Spies, Heinrich, 1873- , ed. III. Series. i. subs. for NCB.

NN R 1.69 e/L OCs, I, II (OS)IIs PCs, 1s, 2s, 3s, Is, IIs, III SL (UM1, LC1s, [i], X1, Z1s)

RDV

Festschrift Louis Gauchat. Aarau, H. R. Sauerländer & Co., 1926. xviii,522 p. illus., maps. 25cm.

1. Romance philology. 2. Gauchat, Louis, 1866-

NN WS

PAH

Festschrift Ludwig Boltzmann gewidmet zum sechzigsten Geburtstage 20. Februar 1904. Leipzig: J.A.Barth, 1904. xii,930 p., 2 pl., 1 port. 8°.

302741.

RAA

Festschrift für M. Blakemore Evans; herausgegeben von der redaktion der Monatshefte für deutschen unterricht und der Deutschen abteilung der Staatsuniversität von Ohio. Columbus, The Ohio state university press, 1945.

2 p. l., 207, [1] p. incl. front. (port.) illus. (incl. map, plan) diagrs. 25cm. [Ohio. State university, Columbus. Graduate school. Graduate school studies. Language and literature series. no. 1.]

"Appeared originally as the 'M. Blakemore Evans number' of the Monatshefte für deutschen unterricht (vol. XXXVII, nos. 4-5, April-May, 1945) in honor of Professor M. Blakemore Evans upon the occasion of his retirement from the chairmanship of the Department of German of the Ohio state university."

(Continued on next card)

A 45-2459

[3]†

Festschrift für M. Blakemore Evans ... 1945. (Card 2)

CONTENTS.—Professor M. Blakemore Evans, by Harlan Hatcher.—The probable source of the "Breisacher bulschaft," by G. O. Arlt.—On describing inflection, by Leonard Bloomfield.—Two Alsatian poets, by J. R. Breitenbucher.—Noch einmal Faust 1607ff, von Friedrich Bruns.—The chameleon image, a note on Goethe's Animula vagula, by Barker Fairley.—Philosophische motive im werk des jungen Hofmannsthal, von Ernst Feise.—Zur geschichte des wortes "innig" und seiner verwandten, von Wolfgang Fleischhauer.—Ein nochmaliger weg zu "Guiskard"; zum Kleist-problem, von Walter Gausewitz.—A note on the German-American newspapers of Cincinnati before 1860, by H. J. Groen.—Reue in Goethes "Faust," von A. H. Hohlfeld.—MHG ûf den plân treten and NHG auftreten, by G. J. Jordan.—The origin of the manuscript version of Niemand und jemand, by F. J. Kramer.—German relics in Pennsylvania English, by Hans Kurath.—Aus olims zeide, von A. C. Mahr.—Chronicle

(Continued on next card)

A 45-2459

[3]†

Festschrift für M. Blakemore Evans ... 1945. (Card 3)

CONTENTS—Continued.

and conte; a note on narrative style in Geoffrey of Villehardouin and Robert of Clari, by E. H. McNeal.—Der bühnenplan des Vigil Raber: ein beitrag zur bühnengeschichte des mittelalters, von Reinhold Nordsieck.—"As a tale that is told," by M. B. Ogle.—Um grundsätzliches in der märchenforschung, von E. A. Philippson.—The relation of Baculard d'Arnaud to German literature, by L. M. Price.—Die drei grossen tragödinnen des Burgtheaters im neunzehnten jahrhundert, von Franz Rapp.—Ost- und westpreuszens anteil am deutschen geistesleben, von R. O. Röseler.—Behaviorism in linguistics, by Hans Sperber.—A historical sketch of German bibliography to 1700, by Archer Taylor.—Miltonic words in the German poetic vocabulary: Empyreum, Hyazinthene locken, by J. A. Walz.—Marshall Blakemore Evans.—The colleagues of Professor M. Blakemore Evans at the Ohio state university.—Doctors of philosophy.—Publications of M. Blakemore Evans.

(Continued on next card)

A 45-2459

[3]†

*HB

Festschrift Martin Bollert zum 60. geburtstage. Dresden, Wolfgang Jess verlag [1936]

viii, 278 p. front., illus., plates (1 fold.) 25½cm.

"Herausgeber, dr. Hermann Neubert."

CONTENTS. — Benndorf, Gottfried, und Hofmann, Hans. Die Sächsische landesbibliothek 1920–36.—Ermisch, Hubert Georg. Landesbibliothek, Japanisches palais und denkmalpflege.—Boden, Charlotte. Der biographische katalog und das personalrepertorium der Sächsischen landesbibliothek.—Jatzwauk, Jakob. Kurzer abriss einer geschichte der sächsischen bibliographie.—Schunke, Ilse. Die Pariser büchersendung des Hubert Languet an kurfürst August von Sachsen 1566.—Beschorner, Hans. Johannes Nienborg.—Leyh, Georg. Ein brief Johann Michael

(Continued on next card)

A C 37-3172

[2]

Festschrift Martin Bollert zum 60. geburtstage ... [1936] (Card 2)

CONTENTS—Continued.

Franckes von 1748.—Schreiber, Heinrich. Friedrich Adolf Ebert und die Monumenta Germaniae.—Büscher, Alfred. Skandinavier, Dresden und die Landesbibliothek.—Schmidt, Ludwig. Die sächsischen bibliotheken im mittelalter.—Leppla, Rupprecht. Die landesbibliotheken als gattung.—Neubert, Hermann. Alphabetischer katalog—formalkatalog?—Schmieder, Wolfgang. Ein beitrag zur verwaltung von brief-autographen.—Wahl, Gustav. Statistisches über bibliotheksausstellungen.—Häbler, Konrad. Die Fuero-handschrift der Sächsischen landesbibliothek.—Fiebiger, Otto. Zwei unveröffentlichte briefe Heinrich Marschners.—Pietzsch, Gerhard. Mscr. Dresd. A 52.—Volkmann, Hans. Christoph

(Continued on next card)

A C 37-3172

[2]

Festschrift Martin Bollert zum 60. geburtstage ... [1936] (Card 3)

CONTENTS—Continued.

Transchel.—Glauning, Otto. Drei lederschnittbände von der wende des XIV. jahrhunderts aus Altzelle. — Kästner, Erhart. Scherenschnitt-illustration.—Thomsen, Peter. Die erste ausgabe von Johann Friedrich Naumanns Naturgeschichte der vögel. — Richter, Hubert. Heinrich Geffcken und seine veröffentlichung des tagebuchs kaiser Friedrichs.—Jammers, Ewald. Die barockmusik und ihre stellung in der entwicklungsgeschichte des rhythmus.

1. Bollert, Martin, 1876– 2. Libraries—Addresses, essays, lectures. 3. Library science—Addresses, essays, lectures. 4. Bibliography—Addresses, essays, lectures. 5. Dresden. Sächsische landesbibliothek. I. Neubert, Hermann, 1892– ed.

A C 37-3172

Columbia univ. Library for Library of Congress [2]

MAR

Festschrift für Max J. Friedländer zum 60. Geburtstage. Leipzig: E. A. Seemann, 1927. 351 p. front. (port.), illus. 4°.

no. 331 of 500 copies printed.
Bibliographical footnotes.
Contents: KRISTELLER, P. Holzschnitte des Meisters des Abendmahls in Ravenna. BOCK, E. Zeichnungen von Michael Pacher. HIND, A. M. An undescribed sheet of drawings by Nicolaus Alexander Mair of Landshut. PAULI, G. Dürers Monogramm. TIETZE, H. Aus der Werkstatt Dürers. BUCHNER, E. Der junge Schäufelein als Maler und Zeichner. GEISBERG, M. Burgkmairs St. Georg. ROMDAHL, A. L. Der Chorbau zu Linköping und seine kölnischen Baumeister. WINKLER, F. Neues von Hubert und Jan van Eyck. HULIN DE LOO, G. Le portrait du médailleur par Hans Memlinc: Jean de Candida et non Niccolo Spinelli. DODGSON,

(Continued)

N. Y. P. L. June 25, 1928

Festschrift für Max J. Friedländer zum 60. Geburtstage. (Continued)

C. Zwei unbeschriebene Holzschnitte des Lucas van Leyden. LUGT, F. Pieter Bruegel und Italien. GLÜCK, G. Van Dycks Apostelfolge. SCHNEIDER, H. Bildnisse des Adriaen Brouwer. BREDIUS, A. Rembrandt, Bol oder Backer? NEUMANN, C. Rembrandt-Legende. FALCK, G. Einige Bemerkungen über Ph. Konincks Tätigkeit als Zeichner. HOFSTEDE DE GROOT, C. Isack Koedijck. KAUFFMANN, H. Die Wandlung des Jacob Jordaens. HOLMES, SIR CHARLES. Three early Italian frescoes. MELLER, S. Eine unveröffentlichte Zeichnung Peruginos. SCHILLING, E. Eine Zeichnung Giorgiones. BERENSON, B. While on Tintoretto. VALENTINER, W. R. Zwei Predellen zu Raffaels frühestem Altarwerk. PANOFSKY, E. "Imago Pietatis." MEDER, J. Gedachtes und Erlebtes. STIX, A. Pariser Briefe des Adam Bartsch aus dem Jahre 1784.

351444A. 1. Art—Essays and misc. 2. Friedlaender, Max J., 1867– .
N. Y. P. L. June 25, 1928

*MGA

FESTSCHRIFT Max Schneider, zum achtzigsten Geburtstage. In Verbindung mit Franz von Glasenapp, Ursula Schneider und Walther Siegmund-Schultze hrsg. von Walther Vetter. Leipzig, Deutscher Verlag für Musik [1955] 363 p. port. 29cm.

Bibliographical footnotes.

1. Schneider, Max, 1875- . 2. Music--Essays. 3. Essays. I. Vetter, Walther, 1891- , ed. II. Glasenapp, Franz von, ed. III. Glasenapp, Franz.

NN**R 6.56 d/ OC, I, II, IIIbo PC, 1, 2, I, II SL MU, 1, 3, I, II (LC1, X1, Z1)

*MG

Festschrift Max Schneider zum 60. geburtstag überreicht von kollegen, freunden und schülern. In verbindung mit Arnold Schering, Walther Vetter, Hans Hoffmann, [und] Walter Serauky herausgegeben von Hans Joachim Zingel. Halle 1935. Eisleben-Lutherstadt, Druck und verlag: Ernst Schneider [1935]

3 p. l., 3–153, 7 p. front. (mounted port.) illus. (music) plates (music) 24cm.

"Notenbeilage: Fritz Koschinsky ... 'Der bauernhimmel', schlesisches volkslied zum singen mit instrumenten bearbeitet": 7 p. at end.
Bibliographical foot-notes.

(Continued on next card)

A C 36-3178

[2]

Festschrift Max Schneider zum 60. geburtstag ... [1935] (Card 2)

CONTENTS.—Schering, A. Widmung.—Hoffmann, H. Max Schneider, der lehrer.—Ludwig, H. Bibliographie der veröffentlichungen Max Schneiders.—Feldmann, F. Evangelische kirchenmusik in schlesischer landstadt; von der persönlichkeit und dem wirken J. Heinr. Quiels.—Gerber, R. Zu Luthers liedweisen.—Herrmann, J. Gibt es eine "schlesische musik"? Eine stilkritische problemstellung.—Hoffmann, H. Die gestaltung der evangelistenworte bei H. Schütz und J. S. Bach.—Martin, T. Wiedergeburt der sprache.—Müller-Blattau, J. In Gottes namen fahren wir; studie zur melodiegeschichte des altdeutschen fahrtenliedes.—Sander, H. A. Ein orgelbuch der Breslauer Magdalenen-kirche aus dem 17. jh.; ein beitrag zum aufführungsbrauch des späten 16. und

(Continued on next card)

A C 36-3178

[2]

Festschrift Max Schneider zum 60. geburtstag ... [1935] (Card 3)

CONTENTS—Continued.

17. jhs.—Schering, A. Aus der selbstbiographie eines deutschen kantors (Elias Nathusius, †1676)—Schmitz, A. Italienische quellen zur figuralpassion des 16. jhs.—Schröder, O. Zu Johann Walters choralpassionen.—Schünemann, G. Reichardts briefwechsel mit Herder.—Serauky, W. Andreas Werckmeister als musiktheoretiker.—Stein, F. Ein unbekannter evangelienjahrgang von Augustin Pfleger.—Vetter, W. Zur erforschung der antiken musik.—Zingel, H. J. Wandlungen im klang- und spielideal der harfe; zur geschichte des instruments im 19. jh.

1. Music—Addresses, essays, lectures. 2. Church music—Germany—History and criticism. 3. Schneider, Max, 1875– I. Zingel, Hans Joachim, 1904– ed.

A C 36-3178

Title from N. Y. Pub. Libr. Printed by L. C.

[2]

3-MAS

FESTSCHRIFT: Max Wegner zum sechzigsten Geburtstag. [Hrsg. von Dieter Ahrens] Münster, Aschendorff [1962] 168 p. plates (84 figs.), diagrams. 25cm.

"Bibliographie Max Wegner," p. 167-168.

CONTENTS.--Stillebenartige Bildelemente in der ägyptischen Flächenkunst, von M. Schmidt.--Minoische Porträts, von S. Marinatos.--Eine hethitische Statuette aus Kilikien, von R. Naumann. Eine attische Schale aus Etrurien, von E. Schumacher.-- Μειδιαμα σεμνον και λεληθος,

(Continued)

NN R 7.63 p/ OC, I PC, 1, 2, I SL A, 1, 2, I (LC1, X1, Z1)

FESTSCHRIFT... (Card 2)

von U. Jantzen. --Ein antiker Torso aus dem ehemaligen Provinzialmuseum in Mitau, von J. Ozols. --Facies decora - effigies Achillea, von J. Fink. --Das Vespasianmonument in Side, von A.R. Mansel. --Der Triumph des Titus, von G. Kleiner. --Der kompositorische Aufbau der Germania des Tacitus, von G. Bielefeld. -- Die Germania des Tacitus und das Fach der Vorgeschichte, von K. Tackenberg. --Observaciones sobre la estatua de Trajano, del Museo arqueológico de Sevilla, por C. Fernández-Chicarro y de Dios. --Doppelherme im Museo communale zu Rimini, von D. Ahrens. --Zu dem Münzbildnissen der Jahre 136-138, von P. Berghaus. --Una nuova

(Continued)

FESTSCHRIFT... (Card 3)

statua-ritratto di Antonino Pio, di G. Jacopi. --Un nouveau buste de Julia Mamaea au Musée du Louvre, par J. Charbonneaux. --Zur Wiederverwendung antiken Spolienmaterials an der Katherale von Sessa Aurunca, von K. Noehles. --Der Johannes Evangelist in der Neustädter Kirche zu Warburg, von G. Fiensch. --Nova Roma: Manierismus und Barock im römischen Stadtbau, von W. Hager. --Regie und Struktur in den letzen Gruppenbildnissen von Rembrandt und Frans Hals, von M. Imdahl. --Die Aphrodite von Melos und ihre russischen Verehrer, von H. -J. zum Winkel. --Erinnerungen an Italien, von M. Wackernagel. --Gedanken zum Ablauf des Weltgeschehens, von A. von Gerkan.

1. Wegner, Max, 1902- 2. Art--Essays and misc.
I. Ahrens, Dieter, ed.

RAE

Festschrift Meinhof. ⌜Glückstadt, etc.: J. J. Augustin, 1927⌝ 2 v. diagrs., illus. (music), port., tables. 27cm.

Paged continuously.

Prepared by a committee consisting of F. Boas, O. Dempwolff, G. Panconcelli-Calzia, A. Werner and D. Westermann.

Bibliographical footnotes.

Bibliographies included.

CONTENTS.—Beiträge zur afrikanischen Sprachwissenschaft: Vedder, H. Korana-Katechismus von C. F. Wuras. Delafosse, Maurice. Classes nominales en Wolof. Werner, Alice. A traditional poem attributed to Liongo fumo. Bleek, D. F. The distribution of Bushman languages in South Africa. Thomas, N. W. The Bantu languages of Nigeria. Dempwolff, Otto. Die Hervorhebung von Satzteilen als Anlass zur Verwendung besonderer Wortformen. Stumme, Hans. Eine sonderbare Anwendung

(Continued)

N. Y. P. L. April 7, 1937

Festschrift Meinhof. (Card 2)

von Akkusativkonfixen im Berberischen. Jones, Daniel. Words distinguished by tone in Sechuana. Cerulli, Enrico. Il gergo delle genti di bassa casta della Somali. Jensen, Hans. Negationspartikeln im Suaheli und in einigen anderen Bantusprachen. Laman, K. E. The musical tone of the Teke language. Wandres, C. Tiernamen in der Nama- und Bergdama-Sprache etymologisch erläutert. Klingenheben, August. Stimmtonverlust bei Geminaten. Trombetti, Alfredo. Le lingue dei Papua e gli'idiomi dell'Africa. Blessing Dahle, P. Eine Siegeshyme der Ama-Zulu. Doke, C. M. The significance of class I a of Bantu nouns. Czermak, Wilhelm. Die Lokalvorstellung und ihre Bedeutung für den grammatischen Aufbau afrikanischer Sprachen. Barlow, A. R. The use of the copula with the Kikuyu verb. Gutmann, Bruno. Grusslieder der Wadschagga. Roehl, K. Eine fast verloren gegangene Klasse des Ur-Bantu. Stevenson, M. S. Specimens of Kikuyu proverbs. Rossini, C. C. Sui linguaggi parlati a nord dei laghi Rodolfo e Stefania. Eiselen, Werner. Nasalverbindungen im Thonga.

(Continued)

N. Y. P. L. April 7, 1937

Festschrift Meinhof. (Card 3)

Heinitz, Wilhelm. Analyse eines abessinischen Harfenliedes. Beyer, Gottfried. Arzneipflanzen der Sotho-Neger. Bourquin, Walther. Die Sprache der Phuthi. Tiling, Maria v. Frauen- und Kinderlieder der Suaheli. Nekes, P. Herm. Zur Entwicklung der Jaunde-Sprache unter dem Einfluss der europäischen Kultur. Westermann, Diedrich. Laut, Ton und Sinn in westafrikanischen Sudansprachen. Hornbostel, E. M. v. Laut und Sinn.—Beiträge zur Sprachwissenschaft anderer Gebiete. Uhlenbeck, C. C. Die mit b anlautenden Körperteilnamen des Baskischen. Bogoroditzky, V. Experimentell-graphische Untersuchungen zwei- und dreisilbiger Wörter in der tartarischen Sprache. Zetterstéen, K. V. Über Abū Mahrama's تاريخ ثغر عدن. Adriani, N. Magische Sprache. Ray, S. H. The Papuan languages. Boas, Franz. Die Ausdrücke für einige religiöse Begriffe der Kwakiutl-Indianer. Bloomfield, Leonard. The word-stems of Central Algonquian. Michelson, Truman. Fox linguistic notes. Scheerer, Otto. Zur

(Continued)

N. Y. P. L. April 7, 1937

Festschrift Meinhof. (Card 4)

Sprachenkunde der Filipinen. Meriggi, Piero. Il problema della parentela dell'indeuropeo col semitico. Heider, E. Wortbildende Elemente in der samoanischen Sprache. Scripture, E. W. Analyse einer Aufnahme von Versen des Dichters von Schaukal. Panconcelli-Calzia, G. Über die Erweiterung des Relativitätsbegriffs der Stimmhaftigkeit. Meillet, A. Sur le degré de précision qu'admet la définition de la parenté linguistique. Schaade, A. Der Vokalismus der arabischen Fremdwörter im osmanischen Türkisch. Aichele, Walther. Altjavanische Beiträge zur Geschichte des Wunschbaumes.—Beiträge zu anderen Wissenschaften: Thilenius, G. Zum Problem des Animalismus. Danzel, T. W. Die psychologischen Grundlagen der Mythologie. Schlunk, Martin. Die Sprachenfrage in den Missionsschulen Afrikas. Cassirer, Ernst. Die Bedeutung des Sprachproblems für die Entstehung der neueren Philosophie.

864152A. 1. Philology—Addresses, essays, lectures. 2. Meinhof, Carl, 1857– . 3. African languages—Addresses, essays, lectures. I. Boas, Franz, 1858– . II. Dempwolff, Otto Heinrich, 1871– . III. Panconcelli-Calzia, Giulio, 1878– .

N. Y. P. L. April 7, 1937

---

*OHM

Festschrift Moriz Winternitz. 1863—23. dezember—1933. Hrsg. von Otto Stein und Wilhelm Gampert. Leipzig, Otto Harrassowitz, 1933.

xiv, 357 p. front. (port.) 25cm.

CONTENTS.—Sprache: Otto, E. Sinnhafte, sinnfreie und sinnlose sprachbetrachtung. Debrunner, A. Vedisch *neṣa* und *parṣa* und die vedischen "imperative" auf *-si*. Lesný, V. Die angeblichen dative der *a*-stämme auf *-āi* und das *asəm vohu*. Renou, L. Le suffixe *-ima-* en sanskrit. Alsdorf, L. Bemerkungen zu Pischels "Materialien zur kenntnis des Apabhraṃśa".—Literatur: Weller, H. Zu textkritik des Mahābhārata. Schrader, F. O. Rezensionen der Bhagavadgītā. Scheftelowitz, J. Varāhamihira's Bṛhat-Saṃh. c. 58 und das Bhaviṣya-Purāṇa. Meyer,

(Continued on next card)

A C 34-808

⌜3⌝

Festschrift Moriz Winternitz ... 1933. (Card 2)

CONTENTS—Continued.

J. J. Die baumzuchtkapitel des Agnipurāṇa in textgeschichtlicher beleuchtung. Schmidt, R. Ein monströses plagiat. Müller, R. F. G. Zur zusammensetzung des anfanges der Suśruta-Saṃhitā. Lalou, M. Les "Cent mille nāga". Johnson, H. M. Mūrkhaśataka. Gode, P. K. The date of Mahākṣapaṇaka's Anekārthadhvanimañjarī. Sarup, L. A queen poetess of Vijayanagara. Meyer-Benfey, H. Der könig der dunklen kammer. Körner, J. Indologie und humanität.—Religion: Shamasastry, R. The conception of sin in the Vedas. Hauer, J. W. Einige bruchstücke der Vrātya-spekulation. Rhys Davids, Mrs. C. A. F. A vanished Sakyan window. Thomas, E. J. Pre-Pāli terms in the Pātimokkha. Sieg, E. und Siegling, W. Bruchstück eines Udānavarga-kommentars (Udānālaṃkāra?) im tocharischen. Zachariae, T. Berichte über die

(Continued on next card)

A C 34-808

⌜3⌝

Festschrift Moriz Winternitz ... 1933. (Card 3)

CONTENTS—Continued.

Jainas bei autoren des 16. und 17. jahrhunderts. Krishnaswami Aiyangar, S. Pāñcarātra in classical Tamil literature. De, S. K. Pre-Caitanya Vaiṣṇavism in Bengal. Modi, Sir J. J. Who were the Persian magi, who influenced the Jewish sect of the Essenes?—Philosophie: Strauss, O. Scholastisches zum anfang der Iśā-Upaniṣad. Edgerton, F. Jñāna and vijñāna. Hiriyanna, M. What is Ananyatvam? Sharma, Har Dutt. The Sāṃkhya-teachers. Coomaraswamy, A. K. Parāvṛtti-transformation, regeneration, anagogy. Frauwallner, E. Dignāga und anderes. Tucci, G. Animadversiones indicae. Schayer, S. Über die methode der Nyāya-forschung. Tavadia, J. C. An Iranian text on the act of dreaming. A new parallel to Indian wisdom.—Kultur und geschichte: Paudler, F. Dātrākarṇa. Über den ursprung und die kulturgeschichtliche

(Continued on next card)

A C 34-808

⌜3⌝

Festschrift Moriz Winternitz ... 1933. (Card 4)

CONTENTS—Continued.

wichtigkeit der ohrmarken an haustieren. Steinmetzer, F. X. Ein verkannter berufsname. Fick, R. Die mischkaste der Ugras. Ein beitrag zur entwicklungsgeschichte der indischen kaste. Ehrenberg, V. Die opfer Alexanders an der Indusmündung. Adler, M. Ein zitat aus des Megasthenes 'Ινδικά bei Plutarch. Charpentier, J. Kleine bemerkungen zum fünften Säulenedikt des Aśoka. Geiger, W. Königsnamen in den Brāhmī-inschriften Ceylons. Brown, W. N. The identification of certain Indian reclining "mother and child" sculptures. Przyluski, J. Pradakṣina et prasavya en Indochine. Rypka, J. Über einen diplomatischen streit zwischen Śáhğahán und Stanbul. Jungbauer, G. Sartische und deutsche volksrätsel.

1. Winternitz, Moriz, 1863– 2. Indo-Aryan philology—Addresses, essays, lectures. 3. Civilization, Hindu—Addresses, essays, lectures. 4. India—Religion—Addresses, essays, lectures. I. Stein, Otto, 1893– ed. II. Gampert, Wilhelm, joint ed.

A C 34-808

Title from Columbia Univ. Printed by L. C.

⌜3⌝

E-13
5652

FESTSCHRIFT für Otto Höfler zum 65. Geburtstag. Hrsg. von Helmut Birkhan und Otto Gschwantler unter Mitwirkung von Irmgard Hansberger-Wilflinger. Wien, Verlag Notring, 1968. 2 v. (523 p.) illus., port. 24cm.

"Verzeichnis der Schriften Otto Höflers," v. 2, p. 519-523.
Bibliographical footnotes.

(Continued)

NN 7.69 v/4 OC, I, II, III, IVbo, Vbo PC, 1, 2, I, II, III SL (LC1, X1, Z1) [I]

FESTSCHRIFT für Otto Höfler zum 65. (Card 2)

1. Folk lore--Germanic races--Addresses, essays, lectures. 2. Germanic languages--Addresses, essays, lectures. I. Höfler, Otto, 1901- . II. Birkhan, Helmut, ed. III. Gschwantler, Otto, ed. IV. Birkhan, Helmut. V. Gschwantler, Otto.

*PDA

Festschrift Otto Procksch zum sechzigsten geburtstag am 9. august 1934 überreicht von Albrecht Alt / Friedrich Baumgärtel / Walther Eichrodt / Johannes Herrmann / Martin Noth / Gerhard von Rad / Leonhard Rost / Ernst Sellin. Leipzig, A. Deichert [etc.] 1934.
166 p. front. (port.) $24\frac{1}{2}$cm.

CONTENTS.—Die rolle Samarias bei der entstehung des Judentums, von Albrecht Alt.—Die Zehn gebote in der christlichen verkündigung, von Friedrich Baumgärtel.—Vorsehungsglaube und theodizee im Alten Testament, von Walther Eichrodt.—Der alttestamentliche urgrund des Vaterunsers, von Johannes Herrmann.—Erwägungen zur Hebräerfrage, von Martin Noth.—Die levitische predigt in den büchern der Chronik, von Gerhard von Rad.—Die bezeichnungen für land und volk im Alten Testament, von Leonhard Rost.—Das Deboralied, von Ernst Sellin.

1. Procksch, Otto, 1874- 2. Bible. O. T.—Addresses, essays, lectures. 3. Bible—Addresses, essays, lectures—O. T.

A C 34-4257

Title from Columbia Univ. Printed by L. C.
[2]

Festschrift.

EAS

FESTSCHRIFT für Otto Scheel; Beiträge zur deutschen und nordischen Geschichte. [Schleswig, J. Ibbeken] 1952. 359 p. illus. 25cm.

"Dr. Harald Thurau, Schleswig: Herausgeber."
Bibliographies at the end of each article.

1. Germany—Civilization. 2. Scandinavia—Civilization. 3. Scheel, Otto, 1876- . I. Thurau, Harald, ed.

NN R 10.52 OC, I PC, 1, 2, 3, I SL (LC1, Z1, X1)

MTE

Festschrift für Otto Tschumi zum 22. November 1948. Frauenfeld, Huber [1948]

165 p. illus., plates, ports., maps. 26 cm.

"Verzeichnis der Publikationen von Herrn Prof. Dr. Otto Tschumi, zusammengestellt von Walter Flükiger": p. [155]-165.

1. Archaeology—Collections. 2. Tschumi, Otto, 1878- I. Title.

GN705.T83 570.4 49-21999*

Library of Congress [1]

Festschrift

NFC

Festschrift Paul Kluckhohn und Hermann Schneider gewidmet zu ihrem 60. Geburtstag. Hrsg. von ihren Tübinger Schülern. Tübingen, J. C. B. Mohr, 1948.

vi, 539 p. 25 cm.

CONTENTS.—Vorzeitsaga und Heldenlied, von Felix Genzmer.—Die Schlacht von Ronceval in Einharts Leben Karls des Grossen, von Georg Baesecke.—Über die Dichtungen Gottschalks von Fulda, von Otto Herding.—Ruodlieb und Nibelungenlied, von Friedrich Panzer.—Kriemhilds Hort und Rache, von Hans Kuhn.—Heinrich von Veldeke, die Entwicklung eines Lyrikers, von Theodor Frings und Gabriele Schieb.—Erec, von Hugo Kuhn.—Wolframs Tagelieder, von Wolfgang Mohr.—Zu Begriff und Wesen der Klassik, von K. H. Halbach.—Erzählzeit und erzählte Zeit, von Günther Müller.—Die Persönlich-

(Continued on next card)

A 49-211*

[2]

Festschrift Paul Kluckhohn und Hermann Schneider gewidmet zu ihrem 60. Geburtstag ... 1948. (Card 2)

CONTENTS—Continued.

keit des Dichters, von Emil Ermatinger.—Ein Versuch über den Alexandriner, von Gerhard Storz.—C. M. Wieland und das 18. Jahrhundert, von Fritz Martini.—Von Wielands Epenfragmenten zum "Oberon," von Friedrich Sengle.—Der Osterspaziergang in Goethes "Faust," von Robert Petsch.—Die Bedeutung des Ursprungsgedankens für die Schicksalsauffassung in Hölderlins Jugendlyrik, von F. W. Wentzlaff-Eggebert.—Abschied und Wiederfinden, von Wolfgang Binder.—Bemerkungen zu Wilhelm Heinrich Wackenroders Religion der Kunst, von Gerhard Fricke.—Der Stammesgedanke im Schrifttum der Romantik und bei Ludwig Uhland, von Hugo Moser.—Der Wortschatz der Innerlichkeit bei Novalis, von Werner Kohlschmidt.—Unvor-

(Continued on next card)

A 49-211*

[2]

Festschrift Paul Kluckhohn und Hermann Schneider gewidmet zu ihrem 60. Geburtstag ... 1948. (Card 3)

CONTENTS—Continued.

greifliche Gedanken über den Sprachrhythmus, von Friedrich Beissner.—"Dienst" und "Reuelose Lebensbeichte" im lyrischen Werk Hermann Hesses, von Adolf Beck.—Alemannische Festtagsnamen, von Karl Bohnenberger.—Rugge und die Anfänge Reimars, von Hennig Brinkmann.—Zum Vortrag der Tristanverse, von Friedrich Ranke.

1. Kluckhohn, Paul, 1886- 2. Schneider, Hermann, 1886- 3. German literature—Addresses, essays, lectures. 4. German literature—Middle High German—Addresses, essays, lectures.

A 49-211*

Rochester, Univ. Libr. for Library of Congress PT36.K4
[2]

XAH

Festschrift Paul Koschaker, mit unterstützung der Rechts- und staatswissenschaftlichen fakultät der Friedrich-Wilhelms-universität Berlin und der Leipziger juristenfakultät, zum sechzigsten geburtstag überreicht von seinen fachgenossen ... Weimar, Verlag Hermann Böhlaus nachf., 1939.
3 v. port. 26cm.

CONTENTS.—bd. 1. Römisches recht. I. ALLGEMEINES, QUELLENGESCHICHTE UND METHODE DER QUELLENKRITIK: Beck, Alexander. Zur frage der religiösen bestimmtheit des römischen rechts. Buckland, W. W. Ritual acts and words in Roman law. Düll, Rudolf. Triginta dies. Bizoukides, P. K. Παρατηρήσεις τινες περὶ τῶν Γαϊαχῶν συγγραμμάτων καὶ τῶν ἐπιγραφῶν αὐτῶν. Solazzi, Siro. Sulle tracce di un commento alle Costituzioni di Caracalla. Collinet, Paul. Le Fr. 5, Dig., 19, 5, De

(Continued on next card)

A C 39-1702

[3]

Festschrift Paul Koschaker ... 1939. (Card 2)

CONTENTS—Continued.

praescr. verbis et in F. act.: Application de la méthode critique de décomposition des textes. Steinwenter, Artur. Utilitas publica—utilitas singulorum. Carolsfeld, L. S. von. *Repraesentatio* und *institutio.* Zwei untersuchungen über den gebrauch dieser ausdrücke in der römischen literatur. Citati, A. G. Supplemento II all' Indice delle parole, frasi e costrutti ritenuti; indizio di interpolazione nei testi giuridici romani. Erman, Heinrich. Zu Justinian.—II. STAAT UND VERWALTUNG: Siber, Heinrich. Die wahlreform des Tiberius. Wieacker, Franz. Protopraxie und "ius pignoris" im klassischen fiskalrecht.—III. ALLGEMEINE GRUNDSÄTZE DES PRIVATRECHTS: Lauria, Mario. Ius gentium. Manigk, Alfred. Privatautonomie. Betti, Emilio. Bewusste abweichung der parteiabsicht von der typischen zweckbestimmung (causa) des rechtsgeschäfts. Kaden, E. H. Die lehre vom vertragsschluss im klassischen römischen recht und

(Continued on next card)

A C 39-1702

[3]

Festschrift Paul Koschaker ... 1939. (Card 3)

CONTENTS—Continued.

die rechtsregel: Non videntur qui errant consentire. Simonius, August. Bemerkungen zur römischen irrtumslehre.—IV. PERSONEN- UND FAMILIENRECHT: Visscher, Fernand de. Aperçus sur les origines du postliminium. Noailles, Pierre. Junon, déesse matrimoniale des Romains. ·Harada, K. Zwei quellenstellen zum patronatsrecht. — V. SACHENRECHT: Cornil, Georges. Du mancipium au dominium. Kaser, Max. Geteiltes eigentum im älteren römischen recht. Erbe, Walter. Pfandverkauf und eviktion nach klassischem römischem recht.

bd. 2. Römisches recht (fortsetzung) VI. SCHULDRECHT: Kunkel, Wolfgang. Fides als schöpferisches element im römischen schuldrecht. Albertario, Emilio. I contratti a favore di terzi. Guarino, Antonio. Sul beneficium competentiae dell' extraneus "promissor dotis". Sachers, Erich.

(Continued on next card)

A C 39-1702

⌊3⌋

Festschrift Paul Koschaker ... 1939. (Card 4)

CONTENTS—Continued.

Die verschuldenshaftung des depositars. Lübtow, Ulrich von. Studien zum altrömischen kaufrecht. Arangio-Ruiz, Vincenzo. Diritto puro e diritto applicato negli obblighi del venditore romano. Vogt, Heinrich. Zur gefahrtragung beim sklavenkauf. Henle, Rudolf. Die rechtliche natur der in diem addictio beim kaufvertrage. Kreller, Hans. Das edikt de negotiis gestis in der geschichte der geschäftsbesorgung.—VII. ERBRECHT: Leifer, Franz. Altrömische studien VI: Suus heres und älteres libraltestament. Krüger, Hugo. Zum römischen pflichtteilsrecht. Bossowski, Franz von. Die Novelle 118 Justinians und deren vorgeschichte. Römische und orientalische elemente. Dénoyez, Joseph. La juris possessio dans la pétition d'hérédité en droit romain. Dulckeit, Gerhard. Voluntas und fides im vermächtnisrecht. Kübler, Bernhard. Das perlenhalsband

(Continued on next card)

A C 39-1702

⌊3⌋

Festschrift Paul Koschaker ... 1939. (Card 5)

CONTENTS—Continued.

der prinzessin Matidia.—VIII. PROZESS: Riccobono, Salvatore. Interdictum—actio. Ulp. LXIX ad Ed., fr. 1 § 4-9. D. 43, 17-Gai. IV 155.—IX. ZEITFRAGEN DER ROMANISTIK: Schönbauer, Ernst. Zur "Krise des römischen rechts".

bd. 3. Andere antike rechte und nachleben des römischen recht. Wenger, Leopold. Paulo Koschaker sexagenario.—I. ALTORIENTALISCHES RECHT: Lautner, J. G. Altbabylonische gesellschaftsverhältnisse. Studien zum miteigentum im altbabylonischen recht II. Klíma, Josef. Zur entziehung des erbrechtes im altbabylonischen recht. Eisser, Georg. Beiträge zur urkundenlehre der altassyrischen rechtsurkunden vom Kültepe. Korošec, Viktor. Einige beiträge zum hethitischen sklavenrecht.—II. GRIECHISCHES UND GRÄKO-ÄGYPTISCHES RECHT: Niedermeyer, Hans. Aristoteles und der begriff des nomos bei Lykophron. Simonétos,

(Continued on next card)

A C 39-1702

⌊3⌋

Festschrift Paul Koschaker ... 1939. (Card 6)

CONTENTS—Continued.

Georg. Das verhältnis von kauf und übereignung im altgriechischen recht. Pantazopoulos, N. J. Ein beitrag zur entwicklung der dialtesis im altgriechischen recht mit besonderer berücksichtigung des attischen rechts. Erdmann, Walter. Zum γάμος ἄγραφος der graeco-aegyptischen papyri. Hellebrand, Walter. Arbeitsrechtliches in den Zenonpapyri. Berneker, Erich. Zur rechtskraft im ptolemäischen prozessrecht. Eger, Otto. Eid und fluch in den maionischen und phrygischen sühne-inschriften.—III. BYZANTINISCHES RECHT: Seidl, Erwin. Die Basiliken des Patzes. Triantaphyllopoulos, K. Die Novelle 56 Leos des Weisen und ein streit über das meeresufer im 11. jahrhundert.—IV. MEDIÄVISTISCHES: Schwerin, Claudius, frh. von. Zur herkunft des schwertsymbols. Condanari-Michler, Slavomir. Bodem, pignus, ὑποθήκη.

(Continued on next card)

A C 39-1702

⌊3⌋

Festschrift Paul Koschaker ... 1939. (Card 7)

CONTENTS—Continued.

Eine rechtsgeschichtliche überlegung. Felgentraeger, Wilhelm. Zu den Formulae andecavenses. Genzmer, Erich. Eine anonyme kleinschrift de testibus aus der zeit um 1200. Coing, Helmut. Simulatio und fraus in der lehre des Bartolus und Baldus.—V. RECHTSGESCHICHTE UND RECHTSPHILOSOPHIE: Binder, Julius. Die einheit der praktischen gesetzgebung.

1. Koschaker, Paul, 1879- 2. Law—Addresses, essays, lectures. 3. Roman law—Addresses, essays, lectures. I. Berlin. Universität. Rechts- und staatswissenschaftliche fakultät. II. Leipzig. Universität. Juristen-fakultät.

A C 39-1702

Columbia univ. Library
for Library of Congress ⌊3⌋

PWF

Festschrift Paul Niggli, zu seinem 60. Geburtstag, den 26. Juni 1948, hrsg. von seinen Schülern, Mitarbeitern und Fachkollegen an den schweizerischen Hochschulen. Zürich, 1948. 568 p. illus. 24cm.

"Die wissenschaftlichen Beiträge erscheinen gleichzeitig als Heft 1, Band 28, der Schweizerischen mineralogischen und petrographischen Mitteilungen."
"Veröffentlichungen von P. Niggli," by J. Marquard and J. Schroeter, p. 555-568.
Bibliographies included.

500684B. 1. Niggli, Paul, 1888- . 2. Mineralogy.
N. Y. P. L. November 9, 1949

Write on slip words underlined below
and class mark—
EOT

Festschrift für Paul Zimmermann zur Vollendung seines 60. Lebensjahres von Freunden, Verehrern und Mitarbeitern... Wolfenbuettel: J. Zwissler, 1914. 318 p. facsims., illus., plates (1 col'd), ports. 24½cm. (Quellen und Forschungen zur braunschweigischen Geschichte. Bd. 6.)

Bibliographical footnotes.

1. Zimmermann, Paul, 1854- . I. Ser.
N. Y. P. L. August 19, 1932

F-10
3131

Festschrift für Peter Goessler. Tübinger Beiträge zur Vor- und Frühgeschichte. Stuttgart, Kohlhammer ⌊1954⌋

221 p. illus., mounted port., maps. 26 cm.

Bibliographical footnotes.

CONTENTS.—Das Alamannia-Relief in Nicaea (Bithyniae) von K. Bittel.—Zur Datierung der Gräber von Arkesine auf Amorgos, von E.-M. Bossert.—Zur Chronologie der jüngeren Latènezeit in Südwestdeutschland und in der Schweiz, von F. Fischer.—Zur Urnenfelderkultur in Südwesteuropa, von W. Kimmig.—Ein Grabhügel der jüngeren Urnenfelderkultur (Hallstatt B) auf der Schwäbischen Alb, von G. Krähe.—Zur Schichtenfolge des kleingerätigen Mesolithikums in

(Continued)

NN * 3, 59 a// OC PC, 1, 2 SL (LC1, X1, Z1)

Festschrift für Peter Goessler ... ⌊1954⌋ (Card 2)

CONTENTS—Continued.

Württemberg-Hohenzollern, von A. H. Nuber.—Zu einem spätneolithischen Gefäss aus Württemberg, von R. Pirling.—Ein frühalamannischer Grabfund aus Oberschwaben, von R. Roeren.—Ein Beitrag zur Kenntnis des Magdalénien in Südwestdeutschland, von O. Roller.—Das Hallstattgrab von Vilsingen, von S. Schiek.—Der Klimasturz um 800 v. Chr. und seine Bedeutung für die Kulturentwicklung in Südwestdeutschland, von G. Smolla.—Burg Dischingen. Ein Beitrag zur Burgenforschung im mittleren Neckarland, von G. Wein.

1. STONE AGE 2. GOESSLER, PETER, 1872-

Copy only words underlined
& classmark— ZOG

FESTSCHRIFT für Prof. D. Dr. Dr. Josef Bohatec. Wien, 1951. 236 p. illus. 24cm. (Gesellschaft für die Geschichte des Protestantismus Österreich. Jahrbuch. [no.] 67)

1. Bohatec, Josef, 1876-

NNR 9.53 OI (PC) 1 (LC2, Z1, X1)

VFK
Festschrift Prof. Dr. A. Stodola zum 70. Geburtstag, überreicht von seinen Freunden und Schülern; herausgegeben von E. Honegger. Zürich: O. Füssli, 1929. xxiii, 602 p. incl. tables. diagrs., front. (port.), illus. 8°.

"Prof. Dr. Aurel Stodola," by W. G. Noack, p. ix–xx.
Bibliography, p. xxi–xxiii.

454600A. 1. Stodola, Aurel, 1859– . 2. Turbines, Steam. 3. Honegger, Emil, 1892– , editor. 4. Noack, Walter G.
N. Y. P. L. February 24, 1930

MTE
FESTSCHRIFT für Rudolf Egger; Beiträge zur älteren europäischen Kulturgeschichte. [Schriftleitung: Gotbert Moro] Klagenfurt, Verlag des Geschichtsvereines für Kärnten, 1952-54. 3 v. illus., fold. plates (issued in pockets), fold maps (issued in pockets)

Also issued as Jahrg. 144, Heft 1-3 (1954) of Carinthia I.
Bibliographical footnotes.

(Continued)

NN**R 4.55 g/ OCs, Is, IIs, SLs As, 3s, Is, IIs, IIIs (LCIs, (OS)IIs PCs, Is, 2, 3s, Is, IIs, IIIs XIs, Z1s) [I]

PKI
FESTSCHRIFT. Prof. Dr. Arthur Stoll zum siebzigsten Geburtstag 8. Januar 1957; Arbeiten aus dem Gebiet der Naturstoffchemie. Basel, Birkhäuser, 1957. lv, 911 p. illus., port. 25cm.

Contributions chiefly in German or English; some in French or Italian.
Includes bibliographies.

1. Chemistry, Organic--Addresses, essays, lectures. 2. Stoll, Arthur. t. 1957.
NN R 7.59 m/3 OC PC, 1, 2 SL ST, 1t, 2 (LC1, X1, Z1)

FESTSCHRIFT für Rudolf Egger... (Card 2)

1. Egger, Rudolf, 1882- . 2. Europe—Archaeology—Addresses, essays, lectures. 3. Art—Essays and misc. I. Moro, Gotbert, ed. II. Geschichtsverein für Kärnten, Klagenfurt. III. Title: Beiträge zur älteren europäischen Kulturgeschichte.

---

*PBS
Festschrift, Professor Dr. Maybaum zum 70. Geburtstag (29. April 1914) gewidmet von seinen Schülern. Berlin: M. Poppelauer, 1914. v.p., 2 l., 208 p. 8°.

1. Maybaum, Siegmund, 1844- . 2. Sermons (Jewish) in German. 3. Jewish literature—Collections.

E-13
8280
Festschrift Rudolf Stamm. Zu seinem 60. Geburtstag am 12. April 1969. Hrsg. von Eduard Kolb und Jörg Hasler. Bern, München, Francke. (1969)
291 p. front. 24 cm.
English, French, or German.
CONTENTS.—Shaw and Shakespeare, by K. Muir.—Macbeth, by M. Lüthi.—King Lear in der Bildkunst, von H. Oppel.—King Lear and the Annesley case, by G. Bullough.—About the heart of Hamlet, by A. Bonjour.—Der deutsche Shakespeare, von U. Suerbaum.—Schillers Shakespeare-Verständnis, von P. A. Bloch.—Michelet et Shakespeare, par C. Pichois.—Now entertain conjecture of a time.

(Continued)

NN * R 5.70 d/ OC, I, II, III PC, 1, 2, I, II, III SL (LC1, X1, Z1)
[I]

TB
Festschrift Richard Thoma, zum 75. Geburtstag am 19. Dezember 1949 dargebracht von Freunden, Schülern und Fachgenossen. Tübingen, J. C. B. Mohr [1950] 276 p. port. 24cm.

"Verzeichnis der Schriften und Aufsätze von Richard Thoma, zusammengestellt mit Unterstützung von Herrn Geheimrat Thoma durch Bibliotheksrat Dr. Martin Kreplin," p. 271-276.
Bibliographical footnotes.

595020B. 1. Thoma, Richard, 1874- . 2. Economics, 1925– German and Austrian authors.
N. Y. P. L. October 16, 1951

Festschrift Rudolf Stamm. (1969). (Card 2)

Sprachliche Probleme, von E. Leisi.—Shakespeare's characters as parts for players, by A. C. Sprague.—Gordon Craig und Alfred Reucker. Zwei Zürcher Othello-Aufführungen, von P. Loeffler.—Shakespeare in his time and in ours, by R. Tschumi.—Englische und Spanische Soldateska im Zeitalter Shakespeares, von A. Guegg.—"Thus." Das demonstrative Adverb als verbales Signal für klimatische dramatische Gesen ... von H. Viebrock.—"Death" in Thomas Kyd's Spanish Tragedy, by S. Wyler.—Gedanken über Rationalität und Illusion, von A. Horn.—Gibbons Memoiren, von M. Wildi.—

(Continued)

ZAE
Festschrift Rudolf Bultmann zum 65. Geburtstag überreicht. Stuttgart [etc.] W. Kohlhammer [1949] vii, 251 p. 23cm.

"Bibliographia Bultmanniana," p. 241-251.

558605B. 1. Bultmann, Rudolf Karl, 1884-
2. Religion—Essays and misc.

NN

FESTSCHRIFT Rudolf Stamm. (Card 3)

Keats und die gläserne Wand, von H. Straumann.—Das Kathedralenmotiv in der modernen englischen Dichtung, von R. Fricker.—King Arthur in Flanders, by R. Derolez.—Blasphemy in literary criticism, by R. W. Zandvoort.—The language of art criticism, by M. Praz.—Tendenzen in den frühen amerikanischen Lyrik, von N. C. von Nagy.—Desire under the elms. A phase of Eugene O'Neill's philosophy, by R. Asselineau.—Bibliographie, von Jörg Hasler.

1. English literature--Addresses, essays, lectures. 2. Shakespeare, William--Commentaries and criticism--Collections. I. Stamm, Rudolf. II. Kolb, Eduard, 1924- ed. III. Hasler, Jörg, ed.

PMN

...**Festschrift** zum 60. Geburtstag von Hofrat Prof. Dr. Fritz Pregl... Wien [etc.] E. Haim & Co., 1929. xii, 340 p. incl. tables. front. (port.), illus. 23½cm.

At head of title: Mikrochemie; internationales Archiv für deren Gesamtgebiet.
"Literatur," p. 202–203; also bibliographical footnotes.
CONTENTS.—Fritz Pregl zum 3. September 1929.—Barrenscheen, H. K. und Margarete Frey. Zum Nachweis kleinster Wismutmengen im Harn.—Benedetti-Pichler, A. Beiträge zur Gewichtsanalyse mit der Mikrowaage von Kuhlmann.—Böttger, Wilhelm. Die Prüfung auf Natrium mit Kaliumantimonat.—Buchtala, J. Die Bedeutung der Mikrochemie in der forensischen Praxis.—De Crinis, Max. Eine Methode zur Bestimmung des spezifischen Gewichtes kleiner Organstücke.—Denigès, Georges. La céruléo-molybdimétrie méthode de micro-dosage des ions phosphoriques et arséniques.

(Continued)

N. Y. P. L. December 17, 1940

...**Festschrift** zum 60. Geburtstag... (Card 2)

—Egg, C., und A. Jung. Mikrochemischer Beitrag zur Bakterizidie von Silber und Kupfer.—Ehreneerg, Rudolf. Zur radiometrischen Mikroanalyse.—Euler, Hans von, Harry Hellström, und Margareta Rydbom. Bestimmung kleiner Mengen von Carotinoiden.—Feigl, F., und P. Krumholz. Beiträge zur qualitativen Mikroanalyse von Säuren. Flaschenträger, B. Verbesserte Darstellung des Grignard-Reagens zur Mikrobestimmung von OH-Gruppen nach Tschugaeff und Zerewitinoff; Mikrobestimmung von Glyzerin in Fetten mit der Methode von Zeisel und Fanto.—Friedrich, A. Über die quantitative mikroanalytische Bestimmung des Schwefels in organischen Substanzen auf massanalytischem Wege; Zentrifugenröhrchen mit abnehmbarer Kappe.—Fuchs, L., und A. Mayrhofer. Über Anwendungsmöglichkeiten verschiedener qualitativer Mikromethoden für die pharmazeutische (toxikologische) Analyse.—Hahn, F. L. Nachweis und Messung kleinster Magnesiummengen.—Hernler, Franz. Kurze Mittei-

(Continued)

N. Y. P. L. December 17, 1940

...**Festschrift** zum 60. Geburtstag... (Card 3)

lungen zur Mikro-Elementaranalyse nach Pregl; Beitrag zur Mikroanalyse organischer Quecksilberverbindungen.—Kimmelstiel, Paul. Eine Mikromethode zur Bestimmung der Cerebroside.—Kisser, Josef. Die Bedeutung der Methoden der botanischen Mikrotechnik für die pflanzliche Mikrochemie und Histochemie.—Klein, Gustav. Ein bewährter Mikroschmelzpunktsapparat.—Klein, Gustav, und Hans Linser. Zur Charakteristik und Analytik der Aldehydmethonverbindungen.—Lauer, W. M., and C. J. Sunde. An adaptation of Pregl's microcombustion to a semi-microcombustion method for the determination of nitrogen.—Lauer, W. M., and F. J. Dobrovolny. An adaptation of Pregl's microcombustion to a semi-microcombustion method for the determination of carbon and hydrogen.—Ledebur, J. von. Mikrorespirationsapparat zur gleichzeitigen Bestimmung von O_2 und CO_2.—Leipert, Theodor. Über die quantitative mikroanaly-

(Continued)

N. Y. P. L December 17, 1940

...**Festschrift** zum 60. Geburtstag... (Card 4)

tische Bestimmung von Jod in organischen Substanzen.—Lunde, Gulbrand, Karl Closs, und Jöns Böe. Beiträge zur Mikrojodbestimmung.—Moser, Ludwig. Eine einfache mikroanalytische Trennung von Chlor und Brom.—Pincussen, L., und W. Roman. Eine Methode zur quantitativen mikrochemischen Bestimmung des Silbers in Blut und Organen.—Rose, W. B., and C. J. Stucky. A micro method for the estimation of chlorides in blood.—Rosenthaler, L. Mikrochemischer Nachweis und Lokalisations-Ermittlung von Glykosiden.—Röttinger, A. C. Die Mikrobestimmung des Koffeins im Kaffee. Ein Apparat zur Mikrobestimmung der schwefeligen Säure in Luft.—Steenhauer, A. J. Zum Nachweis von Thallium.—Strebinger, R., und W. Reif. Die Mikrobestimmung des Magnesiums mit o-Oxychinolin und seine Trennung vom Calcium.—Szendrö, P., und G. Fleischer. Über eine quantitative Mikrobestimmung des Arsens in

(Continued)

N. Y. P. L. December 17, 1940

...**Festschrift** zum 60. Geburtstag... (Card 5)

Leichenteilen.—Vásárhelyi, Béla. Über die Brauchbarkeit der isomeren Aminonaphtholsulfosäuren für die kolorimetrische Phosphorbestimmung.—Zaribnicky, Franz. Untersuchungen über proteolytische Wirkung von Hefen.

470479A. 1. Pregl, Fritz, 1869–1930. 2. Microchemistry. I. Mikrochemie; internationales Archiv für deren Gesamtgebiet.

N. Y. P. L. *Card revised* December 17, 1940

Festschrift zum 60. geburtstag von Hans Stille. Stuttgart, Ferdinand Enke verlag, 1936.

4 p. l., 437 p. incl. illus., tables, diagrs. 28 pl. (part fold., incl. maps, profiles) mounted port. 25cm.

Errata slip inserted.
Some of the plates are preceded by leaf with descriptive letterpress.
Bibliographies interspersed.
CONTENTS.—Deutsches Variscikum: Schriel, Walter. Das Unterdevon im südlichen Sauerlande und Oberbergischen. Dahlgrün, Fritz. Die faziesverhältnisse im Silur und Devon des Kellerwaldes.—Kühne, Friedrich. Zur fazies des Karbons im westlichen Sauerlande.—Fiege, Kurt. Stratonomische beobachtungen in der grauwackenfazies des

(Continued on next card)

G S 37-31

[3]

Festschrift zum 60. geburtstag von Hans Stille ... 1936. (Card 2)

CONTENTS—Continued.

Harzer Kulms.—Petraschek, W. E. Sedimentation, vulkanismus und kupfererzführung im mittelschlesischen Rotliegend.—Kleinsorge, Hubert. Über die roten gesteine Schleswig-Holsteins.—Deutsches Saxonikum: Klingner, F.-E. Die tektonik der südlichen Korbacher Bucht und ihre paläogeographische entwicklung zur Zechsteinzeit.—Schröder, Eckart. Zur saxonischen struktur des Saargebietes.—Richter, Gerhard. Der sedimentationsraum des Unteren Keupers zwischen Harz und Thüringer wald.—Schmidt, Hermann. Die stratigraphische bedeutung der knollenstein-floren von Dransfeld und Münden.—Gallwitz, Hans. Die tektonische und morphologische entwicklung des Elbtalgrabens.—Junge bewegungen und morphologie: Gundlach, Kurt und Teichmüller, Rolf. Die postmiozäne verbiegung der nordalpinen saumtiefe.—Von Gaertner,

(Continued on next card)

G S 37-31

[3]

Festschrift zum 60. geburtstag von Hans Stille ... 1936. (Card 3)

CONTENTS—Continued.

H.-R. Morphologie am Ostabfall des Fichtelgebirges.—Selzer, Georg. Die gliederung des lösses im westlichen Eichsfeld und im talgebiet der oberen Leine.—Heck, H.-L. Art und auswirkung quartärer westperibaltischer tektonik.—Ashauer, Hans, Hollister, J. S. und Reed, R. D. Sedimentation und faltung im südlichen Kalifornien.—Misch, Peter. Ein gefalteter junger Sandstein im nordwest-Himalaya und seine gefüge.—Mittelmeerländer: Karrenberg, Herbert. Biostratigraphische studie im Koblenz der Westpyrenäen.—Quitzow, H. W. Faltung und vulkanismus im variscischen grundgebirge Korsikas.—Pilger, Andreas. Zur tektonik des provençalischen grundgebirges.—Trikkalinos, Johann. Über die schichtenfolge und den bau Attikas.—Arctis: Frebold, Hans. Zur stratigraphie des oberen Jungpaläozoikums und der älteren Eotrias Spitzbergens.

(Continued on next card)

G S 37-31

[3]

Festschrift zum 60. geburtstag von Hans Stille ... 1936. (Card 4)

CONTENTS—Continued.

bergens.—Salzgeologie: Lotze, Franz. Salzabscheidung und tektonik. Martini, H. J. Vorkommen und ursprung der sole von Bad Sulza.—Geohydrologie: Keller, Gerhard. Geohydrologische untersuchungen im zusammenhang mit dem bau des Baldeneysees im Ruhrtal in Essen.—Ozeanographie: Schott, Wolfgang. Rezente tiefseesedimente in ihrer abhängigkeit vom ozeanwasser.

1. Stille, Hans, 1876– 2. Geology—Addresses, essays, lectures. 3. Geology, Stratigraphic.

G S 37-31

U. S. Geol. surv. Library for Library of Congress 209 St5f [QE3]

[3]

STL

Festschrift zum 60. Geburtstag von Heinrich Hanselmann. Erlenbach-Zürich, Rotapfel-Verlag [°1945]

165 p. 24 cm.

CONTENTS.—Zurück ins Leben, von O. Baumgartner.—Heilpädagogik und Strafrecht, von E. Hauser.—Eine gemeinsame gewerbliche Berufsschule für die Taubstummen der deutschen Schweiz, von J. Hepp.—Die richtige Gattenwahl, von F. Keller.—Grundsätzliche Fragen der Organisation der Jugendhilfe in der Schweiz, von R. Loeliger.—Gebrechlichenhilfe und soziale Arbeit, von E. M. Meyer.—Umwelt, Mitwelt, Heimat, von P. Moor.—Verdrängen oder Beherrschen? Von L. Paneth.—Die musikalisch-rhythmische Erziehung im Dienste der Heilpädagogik, von M. Scheiblauer.—Gesinnungsbildung, von M.

(Continued on next card)

A 51-4036

[3]

Festschrift zum 60. Geburtstag von Heinrich Hanselmann. [c1945] (Card 2)

CONTENTS—Continued.

Schmid.—Die Erfassung des Kindes im Milieu der heutigen Schule, von M. Sidler.—Über Beziehung der Kinderpsychiatrie und Psychohygiene zur Heilpädagogik, von M. Tramer.—Zur Psychologie der Mittelbarkeit und Unmittelbarkeit, von T. Wagner-Simon.—Pädagogische Beobachtung und Aktenführung in der Erziehungsanstalt, von M. Zeltner.

1. Hanselmann, Heinrich, 1885- 2. Education—Switzerland.

A 51-4036

New York. Public Libr. for Library of Congress [3]

QGF

Festschrift zum 60. Geburtstage von Professor Dr. Embrik Strand ...enthaltend: dem Jubilar gewidmete Arbeiten ausländischer Zoologen und Palaeontologen. v. 1–3 Riga ["Latvija"], 1936–3[illegible]. 3 v. front., illus., plates, ports., tables. 24½cm.

Vol. 2 issued in 2 parts.
Contributions in German, French, English or Italian.
Imperfect: t.-p. of v. 2 wanting.
Bibliographies included.

1. Strand, Embrik, 1876- . 2. Zoology—Addresses, essays, lectures.
N. Y. P. L. March 2, 1938

MA
\+

FESTSCHRIFT zum sechzigsten Geburtstag von Paul Clemen, 31. Oktober 1926. [Hrsg. von Wilhelm Worringer, Heribert Reiners, Leopold Seligmann. Bonn, F. Cohen, 1926. 515 p. 32cm.

1. Art--Essays and misc. 2. Clemen, Paul, 1866-1947. I. Worringer, Wilhelm, 1881- , ed.
NN R 5. 58 a/V OC, I PC, 1, 2, I SL A, 1, 2, I (LC1, X1, Z1)

---

*PBS

Festschrift zum 70. Geburtstage von Moritz Schaefer zum 21. Mai, 1927; herausgegeben von Freunden und Schülern. Berlin: Philo Verlag[, 1927]. xvi, 273 p. front. (port.) 8°.

Contents: PINCZOWER, E. Psalm 24. NADEL, A. Psalm 24 für Männerchor. ARONSTEIN, P. Die Erklärung sprachlicher Erscheinungen. AUFRECHT, E. Willensfreiheit. BAECK, L. Natur und Weg. BRESLAUER, B. Erinnerung. BRESLAUER, W. Zum Recht der Eheschliessung und Ehescheidung der in Deutschland wohenden ausländischen Juden. ELBOGEN, I. Aus der Frühzeit der Vereine für jüdische Geschichte und Literatur. FEIST, S. Völker und Sprachen. GALLINER, J. Jugendgottesdienst. GLOGAUER, E. Konzentrationserscheinungen in der modernen deutschen Schriftsprache. GUDDAT, W. H. Heine und Verein für Kultur und Wissen-

(Continued)

Mr. Math.

376085A.
N. Y. P. L. October 3, 1928

Festschrift zum 70. Geburtstage von Moritz Schaefer... (Continued)

schaft der Juden. GÜTERBOCK, F. Roma aeterna und der moderne Fascismus. GUTMAN, J. Pestalozzis Forderung einer lebensnahen Erziehung. GUTSTEIN, M. Carl Weigert. HOLZMAN, M. Ein der Septuaginta zu verdankender Übersetzungsfehler. KELLERMANN, B. Die Ethik Spinozas. LASERSTEIN, B. Deutscher Geist und Judenhass. LEHMANN, J. Eine missverstandene Bibelstelle. MARKON, I. Wer ist der in einem Responsum des Natronai Gaon II erwähnte Karäer Daniel? MATZDORFF, C. Alte Sprachen und Naturgeschichte auf den höheren Schulen. NEUMANN, W. Ein nachdenklicher Fall aus der Fürsorge-Erziehung. PEYSER, A. Bevölkerungspolitik und Religionsgemeinde. PINCZOWER, E. Über den Kanon des Ibn Sina. PRESS, J. Die jüdische Besiedelung Palästinas während der letzten siebzig Jahre.

(Continued)

N. Y. P. L. October 3, 1928

Festschrift zum 70. Geburtstage von Moritz Schaefer... (Continued)

REISS, C. Erinnerungen. REISS, F. Ein Sederfest in Jerusalem im Jahre 1916. ROTHSTEIN, M. Aus einem Briefe Ciceros. SCHAEFER, E. Aus Fontanes Altersweisheit. SCHAEFER, R. Sind die Synagogengemeinden des preussischen Judengesetzes Körperschaften des öffentlichen Rechts? SPANIER, M. Heil und Friede küssen sich! STRAUSS, H. Probleme der Immunbiologie bei den Juden. TEITEL, J. Aus meinen Memoiren. TÜRK, M. Das erste Gemeindestatut und die Genossenschaft für Reform im Judentum. VOGELSTEIN, H. Gotteserkenntnis. WISCHNITZER, M. Aus einem Memoirenbuch des 18. Jahrhunderts. WISCHNITZER-BERNSTEIN, R. Jüdische Legendenstoffe bei Benozzo Gozzoli.

SCHIFF COLLECTION.

1. Essays, Jewish, in German—Collections. 2. Schaefer Moritz, 1857- .
N. Y. P. L. October 3, 1928

---

*C p.v.1894,no.6.
\+

Festschrift zum 70. Geburtstage 30. Mai 1927 und 40jährigen Dienstjubiläum 31. Mai 1927 des Herrn Professor Dr. H. H. Schauinsland... Bremen: Heilig & Bartels, 1927. 90 p. incl. tables. front. (mounted port.), illus., plates (1 col'd). f°.

Bibliographical footnotes.

Mr. Math.

1. Schauinsland, Hugo Hermann, 1857- . 2. Museums—Germany—Bremen.
N. Y. P. L. December 21, 1927

VRC

Festschrift zum 70. Geburtstage von Karl Eckstein... Mit Beiträgen von Fr. Beyer, K. Bugow, E. Contag [und Anderen]. Berlin: Verlag des Fischerei-Vereins für die Provinz Brandenburg e. V., 1929. 155 p. incl. tables. illus., port. 8°.

Mr. Math.

487502A. 1. Fish. I. Eckstein, Karl, 1859- .
N. Y. P. L. August 19, 1930

PMN

...**Festschrift** zum 70. Geburtstag von Hofrat Prof. Dr. Friedrich Emich... Wien: E. Haim & Co., 1930. xi, 288 p. diagrs., illus., plates, port., table. 8°.

At head of title: Mikrochemie; internationales Archiv für deren Gesamtgebiet.
Bibliography, p. 231–232; Bibliographical footnotes.
Contents: Friedrich Emich zum 5. September 1930. BENEDETTI-PICHLER, A., and F. SCHNEIDER. Gravimetric microanalysis of beryllium silicate rocks. BERG, R. Beiträge zur Auswertung chemischer Reaktionen für mikroanalytische Zwecke. BÖTTGER, W. Empfindlichkeitsstudien an chemischen Reaktionen. DONAU, J. Über eine neue Mikrowaage mit proportionalen Ausschlägen und Dämpfung der Schwingungen. EDER, R., and W. HAAS. Über Vakuummikrosublimation synthetischer

(Continued)

Mr. Math.

N. Y. P. L. August 14, 1931

...**Festschrift** zum 70. Geburtstag... (Card 2)

Arzneistoffe. HAAS, W. Kristalloptische Untersuchungen von Mikrosublimaten synthetischer Arzneistoffe. EHRENBERG, R. Zur radiometrischen Mikroanalyse, Sulfidbestimmung und Oxydimetrie. FEIGL, F. Beiträge zur Spurensuche. GRAVESTEIN, H. Bemerkungen über den Nachweis von Rubidium und Caesium mit gesättigter Kaliumplatinchloridlösung sowie über eine spezifische Caesiumreaktion. HAHN, F. L. Reagenskapillaren, ein neuer Behelf für die Mikroanalyse, und ihre Anwendung zum Nachweis von Nitrat und Nitrit. HERNLER, F. Beiträge zur C-H-Bestimmung nach Pregl. HETTERICH, H. Über die Anwendung mikrochemischer Methoden bei der Pigmentuntersuchung von Gemälden. HEVESY, G. v. Mikroanalyse auf röntgenspektroskopischem Wege. ITALLIE, L. VAN and A. J. STEENHAUER. Mikrochemische Erkennung einiger Barbitursäureverbindungen. KASSLER, J. Mitteilungen zur Mikro-

(Continued)

N. Y. P. L. August 14, 1931

...**Festschrift** zum 70. Geburtstag... (Card 3)

Stahlanalyse. KISSER, J. Die Verwendung von Jod-Phenol zum histochemischen Nachweis kleinster Stärkemengen. KOLTHOFF, I. M. Some color reactions for magnesium. LINDNER, J. and F. HERNLER. Massanalytische Bestimmung kleiner Mengen Kohlensäure. LUCAS, R. and F. GRASSNER. Über die Anwendung mikrochemischer Methoden bei der Bestimmung kleinster Mengen chemischer Stoffe. MOSER, L. and W. REIF. Die mikroanalytische Bestimmung des Thalliums und des Bleis. NIEDERL, J. B. AND OTHERS. Application of the dilution method to micro-analysis. PANETH, F. and W. D. URRY. Helium-Untersuchungen, VII. Mitteilung. PHILIPPI, E. and F. HERNLER. Zur Kenntnis der mikro-elektrolytischen Kupferbestimmung in organischen Substanzen. RAY, P. and P. B. SARKAR. Some new applications of urotropin, ammonia and hydrazine as microchemical reagents. ROSENTHALER, L.

(Continued)

N. Y. P. L. August 14, 1931

...**Festschrift** zum 70. Geburtstag... (Card 4)

Perjodate als charakteristische Kristallformen. SCHULEK, E. Jodometrisches Verfahren zur Bestimmung geringer Menge Silbers auch in Gegenwart von Chloriden, Bromiden und Cyaniden. SCHWARZ-BERGKAMPF, E. v. Eine neue Anwendung der Filterstäbchen. SOLTYS, A. Ein neuer Sublimationsapparat mit Glasfrittenmasse. ZEPF, K. and F. VETTER. Eine einfache Schnellmethode zur Bestimmung der schwefligen Säure in der Luft.

536611A. 1. Emich, Friedrich, 1860- . 2. Microchemistry. I. Mikrochemie; internationales Archiv für deren Gesamtgebiet.
N. Y. P. L. August 14, 1931

WPE

...**Festschrift** (honory [sic] publication — publication particulière) zum 70. Geburtstag von Prof. Dr. Otto Pötzl... Hrsg. von Prof. Dr. Hubert J. Urban... [Innsbruck, Universitätsverlag Wagner, 1949] 464 p. illus. 25cm.

Half-title: Pötzlfestschrift.
At head of title: Neurologie und Psychiatrie.
Contributions in German with summaries in German, English and French.
"Verzeichnis der wissenschaftlichen Arbeiten von Prof. O. Pötzl," p. 36–41.

496603B. 1. Pötzl, Otto, 1877- . I. Urban, Hubert J., ed.
N. Y. P. L. April 26, 1950

D–11
7783

Festschrift zum 70. Geburtstag für Adolph Freiherr von Gemmingen-Hornberg, Landrat a. D., am 8. September 1956. Hrsg. von Karl Diel. Frankfurt am Main, W. Kramer, 1957. 72 p. illus., port., facsim., geneal. table. 21cm.

Includes bibliographical references.
CONTENTS.—Weiprecht von Gemmingen, der Leiter der hessen-darmstädtischen Politik am Ende des 17. Jahrhunderts, von F. Knöpp.—Dieter von Gemmingen, ein Friedensstifter um 1400, von A. Brück.—Denkmal des Mainzer Erzbischofs Uriel von Gemmingen.—Biographische Nachrichten über Uriel von Gemmingen, Erzbischof von Mainz, 1508–1514, von H. Faulde.—Johann Konrad von Gemmingen, Fürstbischof von

(Continued)

NN R 2.60 OC,1b,I,IIbo PC,1,2, 3,I SL G,2,I (LC1,X1,Z1)

Festschrift zum 70. Geburtstag für Adolph Freiherr von Gemmingen-Hornberg... 1957. (Card 2)

Eichstätt (1595–1612).—Das religiössoziale Aufbauwerk des Mainzer Bischofs Wilh. Emmanuel Frhr. von Ketteler in den Pfarrbezirken des Odenwalds, von K. Diel.—Deutung einiger rätselhafter Namen im Odenwald, von W. Möller.—Epitaph des Friedrich Casimir Freiherrn von Gemmingen-Guttenberg in Dom zu Wetzlar.— Fränkisch-Crumbach als Bergungsort für Kunstwerke, von O. Müller.—Die Ruhestätten von zwei deutschen Zeitgenossen in den beiden deutschen Nationalkirchen zu Rom.—Spätgotische Grabmalplastik im Odenwald, von W. Hotz.—Humanas actiones intellegere, von K. Diel.—Aus der Frühzeit von Fränkisch-Crumbach, von T. Meisinger. —Groschlag in Wetzlar, von K. Diel.

1. Gemmingen-Hornberg, Adolph, Freiherr von, 1886- . 2. Gemmingen family. 3. Odenwald, Germany—Hist. I. Diel, Karl, ed. II. Diel, Karl.

E-10
5085

FESTSCHRIFT zum 70. Geburtstag von Dr. Hans Ehard; hrsg. von Hanns Seidel. München, Kommissionsverlag R. Pflaum [1957] 249 p. ports. 25cm.

CONTENTS. —Biographische Einleitung. —Wirtschaftspolitik und soziale Ethik, von H. Seidel. —Bayern im Rhythmus des Gestaltenwandels der deutschen staatsentwicklung, von K. Schwend. —Das Bund-Länder-Verhältnis in der Bayerischen Verfassung, von T. Maunz. —Ministerpräsidenten-Konferenzen seit 1949, von C. Leusser. — Die

(Continued)

NN R X 3. 58 g/ OC, I, IIbo PC, 1, 2, 3, I SL E, 1, 2, 3, I (LC1, X1, Z1, C1, Y1)

FESTSCHRIFT zum 70. Geburtstag von Dr. Hans Ehard... (Card 2)

gesamtdeutsche Aufgabe der Ministerpräsidenten während des Interregnums 1945-1949, von W. Strauss. —Föderalismus und die Notenbankverfassung, von C. Wagenhöfer. —Die Bereitschaftspolizeien der Länder, ihr Entstehen, ihre Bedeutung für die innere Sicherheit im Bundesgebiet von H. Ritter von Lex. —Aussenpolitik und Bundesrat, von B. Wegmann. — Die Versicherung von Atom (Kernenergie)-Risiken, von A. Alzheimer. —Entwicklung des Staatskirchenrechtes in Bayern in den Jahren 1947/54, von J. Maier. —Elternrecht, Schulfragen und Reichskonkordat im Palamentarischen Rat und in der Politik der deutschen

(Continued)

FESTSCHRIFT zum 70. Geburtstag von Dr. Hans Ehard... (Card 3)

Bundesrepublik und der Länder, von W. Böhler. --Vom Rechtsgedanken der nachkonstantinischen Zeit, eine Studie vom sog. Ambrosiaster, von O. Heggelbacher. —Kurfürst Lothar Franz von Schönborn inmitten der Geschichte seiner Zeit und seines Hauses, von O. Meyer. —Erzbischof Jacobus Hauck in der Kirchenpolitischen Entwicklung Deutschlands 1912-1943, von E. Deuerlein. —Bayern und die Ukraine, von J. Mirtschuk. — Das Schutzzeichen des Roten Kreuzes, seine geistesgeschichtlichen Wurzeln, Beschränkungen und Verheissungen, von P. P. Freiherr von und zu Egloffstein.

(Continued)

FESTSCHRIFT zum 70. Geburtstag von Dr. Hans Ehard... (Card 4)

1. Ehard, Hans. 2. Bavaria--Politics--Addresses, essays, lectures. 3. Germany--Politics, 1945- --Addresses, essays, lectures. I. Seidel, Hanns, ed. II. Seidel, Hanns.

TC

FESTSCHRIFT zum 70. Geburtstag von Walter G. Waffenschmidt, hrsg. von Karl Brandt. Meisenheim am Glan, A. Hain, 1958. 196 p. 23cm.

Bibliography, p. 195-196.
CONTENTS. --Grundlagen der Ökonometrie, von H. Peter. --Walter G. Waffenschmidt als Forscher und Lehrer, von K. Brandt. --Die Verrechnung innerbetrieblicher Leistungen in der Kostenstellenverrechnung, von A. Angermann. --Zur theoretischen Begründung linearer Kosten und

(Continued)

NN 6. 59 t/# OC, I PC, 1, 2, I SL E, 1, 2, I (LC1, X1, Z1)

FESTSCHRIFT zum 70. Geburtstag von Walter G. Waffenschmidt... (Card 2)

ihrer Wirkungen, von K. Brandt. --Zur volkswirtschaftlichen Gesamtrechnung, von H. Brenner. --Stationäre Gewinnmaximierung im grossen in der Theorie der Unternehmung, von H. Brenner und K. Förstner. --Wahrscheinlichkeitsbetrachtungen in der Theorie der Unternehmung, von K. Förstner. --Dynamische Aspekte der Lohntheorie, von R. Henn.

1. Economics, Mathematical. 2. Waffenschmidt, Walter Georg, 1887- I. Brandt, Karl, 1899- , ed.

Write on slip only words underlined and classmark: ESS

Festschrift zum siebzigsten Geburtstag Professor Dr. Heinrich Reinckes am 21. April 1951.

(Verein für hamburgische Geschichte. Zeitschrift. Hamburg, 1951. Bd. 41, p. 1-415)

1.Hamburg--Hist. 2.Reincke, Heinrich, 1881-

form 1004 [11-22-51 25m]

Write on slip, name, year, vol., page of magazine and class mark — QAA

Festschrift zum siebzigsten Geburtstag von Alfred Ploetz am 22 August 1930.

(Archiv für Rassen u. Gesellschafts-Biologie. München, 1930. 4°. Bd.24, p.i-xvii, 1-406. front.port.)

form 1004 [11-13-30 25m]

Copy only words underlined & classmark— VQN

FESTSCHRIFT zum siebzigsten Geburtstag von Prof. Dr. sc. techn. und Dr. h.c. Hans Burger, alt Direktor der Eidgenössischen Anstalt für das forstliche Versuchswesen, 11 Februar 1959. Herausgeber: A. Kurth. [Birmensdorf bei Zürich, 1959] 265 p. illus., port., diagrs. 25cm. (Schweizerische Anstalt für das forstliche Versuchswesen Mitteilungen, Bd. 35, Heft 1)

Summaries in French, Italian, English and/or German. Includes bibliographies.

(Continued)

NN 10. 59 t/4 OI (PC)1, 2 (LC1, XI, Z1)

WAF p.v.286

Festschrift zum siebzigsten geburtstage von herrn prof. dr. E. Zschokke in Zürich, gewidmet von schülern und freunden durch die veterinär-medizinische fakultät der Universität Zürich. Zürich, Art. institut Orell Füssli, 1925.

iv, 251 p. illus., diagrs. 23½cm.

Bibliographies at ends of some sections.

CONTENTS.—Keller, C. Die wanderwege unserer haustiere.—Moos, H. Die leistungsprüfung des rindes.—Giovanoli, G. Beitrag zur lehre der erblichen übertragungen von missbildungen und überzähliger körperanhänge.—Teiler, A. Das knochenfressen der rinder in Südafrika.—Martin, P. Die gekrösverhältnisse und lageveränderungen des hüft-blind-grimmdarmgebietes bei pferdeembryonen.—Zietzschmann, O. Der darm-

(Continued on next card)

Agr 26-23

[2]

FESTSCHRIFT zum siebzigsten Geburtstag von Prof. Dr. sc. techn. und Dr. h.c. Hans Burger... (Card 2)

CONTENTS.--Zum Geleit, von A. Kurth. --Schriftenverzeichnis von Prof. Dr. H. Burger (p. 4-7). --Some aspects of watershed management research in the United States, by B. Frank. --Vom wachsenden Wert der Wohlfahrtswirkungen der Wälder in Mitteleuropa, von E. Hornsmann. --Forest influences in world wide application, by C.R. Hursh. --Die Ordnung des Wasserhaushaltes im Mittelgebirge, von E. Kirwald. --Afforestation and water supplies in Britain, by L. Leyton and A. Carlisle. --Transmission of insolation

(Continued)

Festschrift ... 1925. (Card 2)

CONTENTS—Continued.

kanal der säugetiere, ein vergleichend-anatomisches und entwicklungsgeschichtliches problem. — Baer, H. Die rotlaufschutzimpfung im kanton Zürich 1902/1924.—Höhener, B. Die gefahr der ausbreitung der maul- und klauenseuche durch infizierte schlachttiere.—Stäheli, A. Über eierstocksimplantationen bei praesenilen kühen.—Grüter, F. Mitteilung über hodentransplantationen bei stieren.—Krupski, A. Über das vorkommen von bilirubin und urobilin in den nieren des kalbes.—Rubeli, O. Zur anatomie und mechanik des karpalgelenks der haustiere, speziell des pferdes.—Wyssmann, E. Weitere statistische mitteilungen über torsio uteri beim rind.—Duerst, U. Entwicklungsmechanische und physiologische betrachtungen über die ursachen der streifen- und fleckzeichnungen bei pferd und rind.—Huguenin, B. Über versprengte schilddrüsenkeime und ihre be-

(Continued on next card)

Agr 26-23

[2]

FESTSCHRIFT zum siebzigsten Geburtstag von Prof. Dr. sc. techn. und Dr. h.c. Hans Burger... (Card 3)

through pine forest canopy, as it affects the melting of snow, by D.H. Miller. --Remarques sur l'effet hydrologique d'une coupe à blanc, par L. Nys. --Von der Notwendigkeit einer zielbewussten Ordnung aller menschlichen Einwirkungen auf das Wasser, von M. Oesterhaus und E. Walser. --Some ecological considerations of forest influences, by J.D. Ovington. --Notes on the water balance of the Sperbelgraben and Rappengraben, by H.L. Penman. --Forest influences and watershed management in Indonesia, by M.H. Soedarma.

(Continued)

Festschrift ... 1925. (Card 3)

CONTENTS—Continued.

deutung für biologie und pathologie.—Ehrhardt, J. Zur prophylaxe der puerperalen erkrankungen.—Bürgi, O. Über gliedmassenlähmungen der haustiere.—Frei, W. Vitamine, avitaminosen und infektionskrankheiten bei tieren.—Schnyder, O. Fälle von zurückbleiben der nachgeburt beim rind.—Ackerknecht, E. Methodisches über den anatomischen unterricht im studium der tierheilkunde.—Pfenninger, W. Experimentelle beiträge zur genesis der fleckniere.—Heusser, H. Über das zustandekommen von hufdeformitäten, speziell des schiefen hufes.—Andres, J. Der einfluss des trächtigen uterus auf die lage der inneren organe direkt vor der geburt.

1. Veterinary anatomy. 2. Veterinary medicine. [1. Domestic animals—Anatomy and physiology] I. Zschokke, E.

Agr 26-23

Library, U. S. Dept. of Agriculture 41F42

[2]

FESTSCHRIFT zum siebzigsten Geburtstag von Prof. Dr. sc. techn. und Dr. h.c. Hans Burger... (Card 4)

--Wasserhaushalt und Landschaft in den südöstlichen Alpen, von H. Steinhäusser. --Vergleich der bisherigen Ergebnisse der Untersuchungen über den Wasserhaushalt und den Bodenabtrag im Harz mit den langfristigen Beobachtungen im Emmental in der Schweiz, von A. Wagenhoff und K. von Wedel. --Planning of catchment-management experiments in forest hydrological research, with reference to Southern Africa, by C.L. Wicht. --Soil and water conservation research in the United States with particular reference to arable land, by

(Continued)

FESTSCHRIFT zum siebzigsten Geburtstag von Prof. Dr. sc. techn. und Dr. h.c. Hans Burger... (Card 5)

P.J. Zwerman and G.R. Free.--Über Wald- und Wasserprobleme von ältesten Sickerungen zum vollen Strom, von K.A. Meyer.--30 Jahre Wassermesstationen im Emmental, von E. Casparis.--Die Wassermess-stationen im Flyschgebiet beim Schwarzsee (Kt. Freiburg), von W. Nägeli. --Über den Einfluss des Wasser- und Luftgehaltes im Boden auf das Wachstum von Fichtenkeimlingen, von F. Richard.

1. Burger, Hans, 1889- . 2. Forestry.

---

*PBN

Festschrift zu Simon Dubnows siebzigstem geburtstag (2. Tischri 5691). Hrsg. von Ismar Elbogen, Josef Meisl, Mark Wischnitzer. Berlin, Jüdischer verlag, 1930.

294, [2] p. 24cm.

CONTENTS.—Elbogen. Von Graetz bis Dubnow.—Steinberg. Die weltanschaulichen voraussetzungen der jüdischen geschichtsschreibung.—Rabin. Stoff und idee in der jüdischen geschichtsschreibung.—Rawidowicz. Nachman Krochmal als historiker.—Wischnitzer-Bernstein. Jüdische kunstgeschichtsschreibung.—Buber. Das Judentum und die neue weltfrage.—Bałaban. Hugo Grotius und die ritualmordprozesse in Lublin (1636)—Wischnitzer. Die stellung der Brodyer Juden im internationalen handel in der zweiten hälfte des XVIII. jahrhunderts.—Lewin. Die landessynode der grosspolnischen Judenschaft [nachträge)—Gelber. Die Juden und die Judenreform auf dem polnischen vierjährigen Sejm (1788–1792)—Tykocinski. Die stadt שלא während des ersten

(Continued on next card)

A 32–1488

[34b2]

Festschrift zu Simon Dubnows siebzigstem geburtstag ... 1930. (Card 2)

CONTENTS—Continued.

kreuzzuges.—Freimann. Zur geschichte der Juden in Xanten.—Wachstein. Zur biographie Löw b. Bezalels.—Roth. Joseph Saralvo.—Anchel. Les lettres patentes du 10 juillet 1784.—Ginsburger. Zwei unveröffentlichte briefe von Abbé Grégoire.—Posener. Lippmann Lippmann de Baccarat.—Kober. Abraham Geigers bemühungen um die organisation der jüdischen unterrichts- und kultursverhältnisse im ehemaligen herzogtum Nassau.—Meisl. Beiträge zur Damaskus-affäre (1840)—Jacobson. Eine aktion für die russischen grenzjuden in den jahren 1843/44.—Freund. Michael Sachs zur reform der preussischen Judengesetzgebung.—Goodman. Joseph Montefiore.—Schorr. Staatsseher und staatslehrer.—Meisl. Simon Dubnows abhandlungen und schriften (p. 266–[295])

1. Jews. 2. Jews—Hist. 3. Dubnov, Semen Markovich, 1860– ed. I. Elbogen, Ismar, 1874– ed. II. Meisl, Josef, joint ed. III. Vishnitser, Mark L'vovich, 1882– joint ed.

Title from Yale Univ. Printed by L. C. A 32–1488

[a34b2]

MW p.v. 221

FESTSCHRIFT der Städtischen Bühnen, Frankfurt am Main zur Eröffnung des Grossen Hauses im Dezember 1951. [Herausgeber: Harry Buckwitz; Schriftleitung: Rudolf Bach] [Frankfurt am Main, 1951] [48] p. illus., ports., facsims. 24cm.

"Festakt zur Eröffnung des 'Grossen Hauses'," [8] p., inserted.

CONTENTS. —Festgrüsse zur Eröffnung. —Das Theater wird bestehen, von G. Hauptmann. —Das neue Haus, von M. Wolf. —Aus der Chronik des Frankfurter Theaters, von R. Diehl. —Der alte Vorhang, von B. Reifenberg. —Die Entstehung der "Meistersinger," von Baudelaire, Nietzche, Thomas Mann. —Aus "Hans Sachsens poetische Sendung," von Goethe. —Zum

(Continued)

NN ** X 8.54 OC, I, Ib, II PC, 1, I, II SL MU, 2, I, II (T4, 21, LC1, X1)

FESTSCHRIFT der Städtischen Bühnen... (Cont.)

"Egmont," von F. Gundolf. —Aus "Dichtung und Wahrheit," von Goethe. —Hofmannsthal liest "Egmont," von C. J. Burckhardt. —Zauber der Operette, von T. Mann. —Wiener Presse 1874 über "Fledermaus." —Opfer der Zensur. —Brief aus Hietzing vom 19. Oktober 1868, von A. Strauss. —"Vergiss nicht, dass das Leben"...von F. Quevedo. —"Möge froh nach Angst und Grauen"..., von Goethe.

1. Theatres—Germany—Frankfurt am Main. 2. Opera houses—Germany—Frankfurt am Main. I. Buckwitz, Harry, ed. II. Bach, Rudolf, 1901- , ed.

YAM

Festschrift Th. G. Masaryk zum 80. Geburtstage. Teil 1– Bonn: F. Cohen, 1930– v. port. 4°.

Teil 1: "Ergänzungsband zur Zeitschrift 'Der russische Gedanke.'"

Pref. signed: B. Jakowenko.

Contents: Teil 1. ALIOTTA, A. Dell' esperimento scientifico e di quello metafisico. BRUNSCHVICG, L. Politique et philosophie. BULGAKOW, S. Was ist das Wort? CROCE, B. La grazia e il libero arbitrio. FISCHER, H. Der Realismus und das Europäertum. HESSEN, S. Der Zusammenbruch des Utopismus. HOOPER, S. E. Man and philosophy. JAKOWENKO, B. Die Philosophie in ihrem Verhältnisse zu den anderen Hauptgebieten der Kultur. KOZLOWSKI, W. M. L'idée de l'homogénéité de la science et les types des sciences. KRAUS, O. Zur Frage nach dem "Sinne der Geschichte." LAPSCHIN, I. Die Metaphysik Leo Tolstojs. LOSSKIJ, N. Die Lehre

(Continued)

N. Y. P. L. January 25, 1932

Festschrift Th. G. Masaryk zum 80. Geburtstage... (Card 2)

Wl. Solowjows von der Evolution. MARTINETTI, P. L'intelletto e la conoscenza noumenica in E. Kant. MICHALTSCHEW, D. Der Zufall als Bestandteil der Wirklichkeit. MILIUKOV, P. Eurasianism and Europeanism in Russian history. PETRONIEVICS, B. Ueber das Wesen der mathematischen Induktion. RÁDL, E. Natur und Geschichte. TSCHIŽEWSKIJ, D. "Uebermensch," "übermenschlich."

1. Masaryk, Tomáš Garrigue, pres. Czecho-Slovakia, 1850– .
2. Philosophy—Essays and misc.

N. Y. P. L. January 25, 1932

Write on slip words underlined below and class mark— *QCA

Festschrift Th. G. Masaryk zum 80. Geburtstage. Teil 1-2.

(Russischer Gedanke. Ergaenzungsband zur Zeitschrift "Der russische Gedanke." Bonn, 1930 4°. [Nr.] 1, p.i-vii, 1-269; Nr.2, p.i-xiii, 1-409. ports.)

Bibliography Nr.2, p.383-409.

form 460b [11-13-31 25m]

Copy only words underlined & classmark-- *DF

FESTSCHRIFT Theodor Frings. Bonn, L. Röhrscheid. 490 p. illus., maps. 26cm. (Rheinische Vierteljahrsblätter. Jahrg. 17 (1952))

1. Frings, Theodor, 1886- .

NN R 8.57 d/ OI (PC)1 (Z1, LC2, X1)

VWZ

Festschrift für Ulrich Wille zum 60. geburtstag. Zürich und Leipzig, Albert Müller verlag [1937]

255, [1] p. front. (port.) 23½cm.

"Für das ausland unter dem titel: 'Milizfragen'."

CONTENTS.—Widmung.—Aus Ulrich Willes gedankenwelt; zusammenstellung aus aufsätzen, befehlen und weisungen.—Vom inneren werden unserer armee, von Hans Berli.—La Suisse romande et son histoire avant la réforme, par Gonzague de Reynold.—La Suisse romande et la guerre, par Aymon de Mestral.—Il soldato ticinese, di Guglielmo Vegezzi.—Das problem der instruktionsoffiziere, von Gustav Däniker.—Vom wesentlichen in der ausbildung, von Georg Züblin.—Sport und militärische erziehung, von Franz Nager.—Ein beitrag zu den grundfragen

(Continued on next card)

A C 38–1840

[2]

Festschrift für Ulrich Wille ... [1937] (Card 2)

CONTENTS—Continued.

der offizierserziehung, von Werner Kobelt.—Pädagogische erinnerungen, von Fritz Ernst.—Der leutnant, von Oskar Frey.—Gedanken über die soldatische erziehung unserer jugend, von Hanspeter Brunner.—Der irrationale faktor in der truppenführung, von Hans Frick.—Führerentschluss und befehlsform, von Karl Brunner.—Le problème de l'histoire militaire, par Sven Stelling-Michaud.

1. Wille, Ulrich, 1877– 2. Switzerland—Army. I. Title: Milizfragen.

A C 38-1840

New York. Public library for Library of Congress [2]

STN

Festschrift zur Vierhundertjahrfeier des Alten Gymnasiums zu Bremen, 1528–1928... Bremen: G. Winter[, 1928]. vii, 476 p. incl. tables. diagrs., front., illus., 16 pl. 8°.

Contents: Vorwort. SPITTA, T. Zum Geleit. SCHRÖDER, R. A. Die dritte Satire des Horaz. ENTHOLT, H. Das Bremer Gymnasium und seine Lehrer. BOHM, W. Die Stellung des Alten Gymnasiums innerhalb des bremischen höheren Schulwesens... KURZ, K. Die Sonderstellung des Alten Gymnasiums... ACHELIS, T. O. Aus der Vorgeschichte des Hadersleben Johanneums. JORDAN, B. Das Prinzip der Zuordnung. THYSSEN, J. Über Triebe und Wertungen. VALENTINER, T. Zur Psychologie der Sextanerarbeit. KULENKAMPFF, D. Zur Frage der Willensfreiheit. HARMS, C., translator. "Abraham," von Hrotswitha von Gandersheim. MEIER, J. Alter Rechtsbrauch

(Continued)

N. Y. P. L. February 25, 1929

Festschrift zur Vierhundertjahrfeier des Alten Gymnasiums zu Bremen... (Card 2)

im bremischen Kinderlied. DIETZE, K. Manasse... HÄPKE, R. Bremen in der deutschen Geschichte. SCHÜSSLER, W. Beiträge zur Genealogie norddeutscher Herrengeschlechter. SCHWARTZE, E. Der Zusammenhang zwischen innerer und äusserer Politik bei Bismarck. WALDMANN, E. Das Experiment mit dem Spaten. SCHAAL, H. Flussschiffahrt und Flusshandel im Altertum. SCHUCHHARDT, C. Die Befestigung des achäischen Schiffslagers vor Troja. SCHUMACHER, F. Vom Schiffsbau. SCHUMACHER, H. Die Stellung der Börse in der Volkswirtschaft. HOFMANN, E. Die Bedeutung der elterlichen Blutsverwandtschaft. WILCKENS, O. Die deutschen Binnendünen. Verzeichnis der Tafeln.

398467A. 1. Education, Secondary—Germany—Bremen.
N. Y. P. L. February 25, 1929

---

*MGA

FESTSCHRIFT Walter Gerstenberg zum 60. Geburtstag. Im Namen seiner Schüler hrsg. von Georg von Dadelsen und Andreas Holschneider. Wolfenbüttel, Möseler Verlag [c1964] 175 p. music. 24cm.

CONTENTS.--Die Proportionen der Beethovenschen Tempi, von H. Beck.--Über das Wechselspiel von Musik und Notation, von G. von Dadelsen.--Auftakt und Taktschlag in der Musik

(Continued)

NN 2.70 e/ OC, I, II, III PC, 2, I, II, III SL MU, 1, I, II, III (LC1, X1, Z1)

3

FESTSCHRIFT Walter Gerstenberg zum 60. Geburtstag. (Card 2)

um 1600, von W. Dürr.--Musikdrucker, Musikalienhändler und Musikverleger in Berlin 1750 bis 1850, von R. Elvers.--Mozarts Duett, Bei Männern, welche Liebe fühlen, von A. Feil.--Zur Entstehung der Regenlieder von Brahms, von I. Fellinger.--Musik in Arkadien, von A. Holschneider.--Musik und Dichtung in Bogenform und Reprisenbar, von M. Just.--Zur Problematik einer temperierten Notation, von E. Karkoschka.--Dreiertakt und Zweiertakt als Eurhythmus und Ekrhythmus, von F. J. Machatius.--Musikgeschichtliche Vorstellungen des Niederländischen Zeitalters, von

(Continued)

FESTSCHRIFT Walter Gerstenberg zum 60. Geburtstag. (Card 3)

B. Meier.--Ein Beitrag zum Solfège aus den Anfängen der Schulmusik in Frankreich, von A. Palm.--Das Chorbuch Mus. ms. 40024 der Deutschen Staatsbibliothek Berlin, von G. Pätzig.--Bemerkungen zu einem missdeuteten Skizzenblatt Mozarts, von W. Plath.--Bericht von neuer Orgelmusik, von D. Schnebel.--Von Bachschen Modellen und Zeitarten, von U. Siegele.--Johann Walters Versuch einer Reform des gregorianischen Chorals, von J. Stalmann.

1. Essays. 2. Music--Essays. I. Dadelsen, Georg von, ed. II. Holschneider, Andreas, ed. III. Gerstenberg, Walter, 1904-

---

*MGA

FESTSCHRIFT für Walter Wiora zum 30. Dezember 1966. Hrsg. von Ludwig Finscher und Christoph-Hellmut Mahling. Kassel, New York, Bärenreiter, 1967. 677 p. front, illus., music. 24cm.

1. Essays. 2. Music--Essays. I. Finscher, Ludwig, ed. II. Mahling, Christoph Hellmut, ed. III. Wiora, Walter, 1906-

NN 2.70 e/ OC, I, II, III PC, 1, 2 I, II, III SL MU, 1, I, II, III (LC1, X1, Z1)

E-11
1918

FESTSCHRIFT für Walther Fischer. Heidelberg, C. Winter, 1959. viii, 332 p. plates, port. 25cm.

Bibliographical footnotes.

CONTENTS.--The Finn episode once again, by K. Malone.--Zu den Inschriften und Bildern des Franks Casket und einer ae. Version von Balders Tod, von K. Schneider.--The date of Walter of Bibbesworth's Traité, by A.C. Baugh.--Ariosto's Sospetto, Gascoigne's Suspicion, and

(Continued)

NN R 2.61 e/ OC PC, 1, 2 SL (LC1, X1, Z1) [I]

4

FESTSCHRIFT für Walther Fischer. (Card 2)

Spenser's Malbecco, by W.F. McNeir.--Ideale der Restaurationszeit, von L. Borinski.--Die dialektische Dichtung in der englischen Literaturtheorie des achtzehnten Jahrhunderts, von B. Fabian.--Thackerays Begriffe 'gentleman' und 'snob', von F. Schubel.--Dickens und Mark Twain in Italien, von K. Brunner.--A gossip from Florence: the diary of Elizabeth C.D. Stedman Kinney, by L. Leary.--Die amerikanische Literatur in Deutschland und das Problem der literarischen Wertung, von H. Oppel.--Anne Bradstreet, Du Bartas und Shakespeare im Zusammenhang kolonialer

(Continued)

FESTSCHRIFT für Walther Fischer. (Card 3)

Verpflanzung und Umformung europäischer Literatur: ein Forschungsbericht und eine Hypothese, von H. Galinsky.--Some sources of Irving's 'Italian banditti' stories, by W.A. Reichart.--Americanisms recorded by Duke Bernhard of Saxe-Weimar, by J.T. Krumpelmann.--Die Aufnahme und Verbreitung von E.A. Poes Werken im Deutschen, von H.H. Kühnelt.--Melvilles 'Billy Budd' und seine Quellen: eine Nachlese, von H.-J. Lang.--St. John Ervine on Eugene O'Neill, by H. Frenz.--Noah Webster and the dawn of linguistic science, by H.R. Warfel.--Die Sprache der englischen Kinderstube, von M. Lehnert.--"Neue Synthese" im

(Continued)

FESTSCHRIFT für Walther Fischer. (Card 4)

Gegenwartsenglisch, von G. Kirchner. --Die Veröffentlichungen Walther Fischers; zusammengestellt von E. Schuster und B. Fabian (p. [323]-332).

1. Fischer, Walther Paul, 1889- . 2. Literature--Addresses, essays, lectures.

GDD

Festschrift Walther Merz. Aarau: H. R. Sauerländer & Cie., 1928. 242 p. diagr., front. (port.), pl., tables. 4°.

"Herausgegeben unter Mitwirkung des Staates Aargau und der Städte Aarau, Baden und Zofingen."

Contents: Welti, F. E. Das Recht der Twingherrschaft Kehrsatz. Fleiner, F. Das Freianglerrecht im Aargau. Lehmann, H. Aus dem Wildegger Schlossarchiv. Tatarinoff, E. Ramelen ob Egerkingen. Hess, P. I. Die Pfarrgeistlichen von Sins, Auw und Abtwil im Kanton Aargau. Burckhardt, A. Die Herkunft von Beatrix, erster Ehefrau Graf Rudolfs III. von Tierstein. Türler, H. Das Burgernziel in Bern. Mittler, O. Die Anfänge des Johanniterordens im Aargau. Ammann, H. Die schweizerische Kleinstadt in der mittelalterlichen Wirtschaft. Frey, A. Einiges aus dem Sprachgut der aargauischen Rechtsquellen. Anhang: Verzeichnis der Schriften von Walther Merz.

1. Merz, Walther, 1868- .
N. Y. P. L. June 12, 1929

E-13
6524

FESTSCHRIFT Walther von Wartburg zum 80. Geburtstag. 18. Mai 1968. Hrsg. von Kurt Baldinger. Tübingen, Niemeyer, 1968. 2 v. 24cm.

Contributions in various languages.
Bibliography of works, since 1956, by W.v. Wartburg: v.2, p. [549]-558.
Bibliographical footnotes.

J.S. BILLINGS MEM. COLL.

1. Romance philology--Addresses, essays, lectures. 2. Romance literature--Addresses, essays, lectures. I. Wartburg, Walther von, 1888- II. Baldinger, Kurt, 1919- , ed.
NN*S 10.69 r/Λ OC, I, II PG, 1, 2, I, II SL (LC1, X1, Z1) [I]

3-MAS

FESTSCHRIFT Werner Hager. (Hrsg. von Günther Fiensch und Max Imdahl). Recklinghausen, Bongers (1966) 193 p. 31 l. of illus. 27cm.

Includes bibliographical references.

CONTENTS.--Ein sächsischer Bildnisgrabstein des 12. Jahrhunderts am Dom zu Münster, von H. Thümmler.--Die Kunst des Cosmaten und die Idee der Renovatio Rome, von K. Noehles.--Zum Stifterbildnis des Hugo van der Goes in Baltimore, von H. Schrade.

(Continued)

NN*R 3.71 d/2 OC, I, II PC, 1, 2, I, II SL A, 1, 2, I, II (LC1, X1, Z1) [I] 3

FESTSCHRIFT Werner Hager. (Card 2)

--Versuch, die Kupferstichpassion Martin Schongauers zeitlich zu ordnen, von G. Fiensch.--Dürerfragen, von G. Kauffmann.--Holbeins Venus und Lais in der Basler Öffentlichen Kunstsammlung, von H. Reinhardt.--Grabmal Arberini, von M. Wegner.--Jacques Callot--Das Welttheater in der Kavalierperspektive. Ein Essay, von J.A. Schmoll Gen. Eisenwerth.--Rembrandts Nachtwache. Überlegungen zur ursprünglichen Bildgestalt, von M. Imdahl.--Andrea Pozzos Kuppelzwickel von S. Ignazio in Rom, von B. Kerber.--Giuseppe Sardi e la

(Continued)

FESTSCHRIFT Werner Hager. (Card 3)

tradizione artigianale nel Settecento Romano, von P. Portoghesi.--Fläche, Welle, Ornament. Zur Deutung der nachimpressionistischen Malerei des Jugendstils, von W. Rasch.--Gedanken über die Darstellung des Sehens in der bildenden Kunst, von A. Neumeyer.--Kunstgeschichte und Musikwissenschaft. Eine vergessene musikhistorische Diskussion, von W.F. Korte.--Von Quellen und ihrer Fassung, von E.W. Eschmann.

1. Hager, Werner, 1900- . 2. Art--Essays and misc. I. Fiensch, Günther, ed. II. Imdahl, Max, joint ed.

RP
+

Festschrift Whitley Stokes zum siebzigsten geburtstage am 28. februar 1900 gewidmet, von Kuno Meyer, L. Chr. Stern, R. Thurneysen, F. Sommer, W. Foy, A. Leskien, K. Brugmann, E. Windisch. Leipzig, O. Harrassowitz, 1900.
vii, [1], 48 p. 28½cm.

Contents.—Meyer, K. Totenklage um könig Niall Nóigiallach.—Stern, L. C. Eine ossianische ballade aus dem xii. jahrhundert.—Thurneysen, R. Irisch *lith* und *cless*.—Sommer, F. Altirisch *bidu* "reus".—Foy, W. Die idg. langdipthonge im inselkeltischen.—Leskien, A. Pronominale prolepsis nominaler objecte.—Brugmann, K. Lateinisch *prope* und *proximus*.—Windisch, E. Ueber einige als *s*-aorist angesehene irische formen.

1. Stokes, Whitley, 1830-1909. 2. Celtic philology. i. *Meyer, Kuno, 1858-1919. ii. Stern, Ludwig Christian, 1846-1911. iii. Thurneysen, Rudolf, 1857- iv. *Sommer, Ferdinand, 1875- v. Foy, Willy, 1873-1929. vi. Leskien, August, 1840-1916. vii. *Brugmann, Karl, 1849-1919. viii. Windisch, Ernst Wilhelm Oskar, 1844-1918.
Library of Congress PR1002.S7 5—140
[a33b1]

MA

Festschrift Wilhelm Pinder zum sechzigsten geburtstage, überreicht von freunden und schülern. Mit einhundertsiebzig abbildungen. Leipzig, Verlag E. A. Seemann [1938]
444, [2] p. illus. (incl. plans, facsim.) 25½cm.
Includes bibliographies.
"Die werke von Wilhelm Pinder": p. [445]-[446]

Contents. — Geleitwort. — Vermutungen und fragen zur bestimmung der altfranzösischen kunst, von Hans Sedlmayr.—Vom plastischen in der malerei, von Theodor Hetzer.—"Fränkische kunstgeschichte", von Alexander freiherr v. Reitzenstein. — Die bedeutung des germanischen ornaments, von Hans Weigert.—Der figürliche kirchenschmuck des deutschen sprachgebiets in karolingischer, ottonischer und salischer zeit, von Wolfgang graf von Rothkirch.—Das bildprogramm an den mittelalterlichen kirchenportalen Frankreichs und Deutschlands, von Albert Walzer.—Zur mittelalterlichkeit der gotischen kathedrale, von Werner Gross — Aus-

(Continued on next card)
A C 39-11
[2]

Festschrift Wilhelm Pinder zum sechzigsten geburtstage ... [1938] (Card 2)

Contents—Continued.

strahlungen der Regensburger dombauhütte nach dem deutschen Südosten um 1300, von H. R. Rosemann.—Die risse der Orvietaner domopera und die anfänge der bildhauerzeichnung, von Harald Keller.—Die "Navicella" des Giotto, von Werner Körte.—Gedanken über Michelozzo di Bartolomeo, von L. H. Heydenreich.—Zur älteren Gmünder plastik, von Otto Schmitt. — Zur schwäbisch-bayrischen plastik der zeit Hans Multschers, von Theodor Müller. — Der meister des grafen von Kirchberg, von Wilhelm Vöge.—Das auge Dürers, von Wilhelm Niemeyer.—Die entwicklung der liegefiguren in der architekturplastik von Michelangelo bis zum klassizismus, von Kurt Reissmann.—"Vanitas"; die bedeutung mittelalterlicher und humanistischer bildinhalte in der niederländischen malerei des 17. jahrhunderts, von Herbert Rudolph.—Über Ulrich Pinder, von Georg Scheja.

1. Pinder, Wilhelm, 1878- 2. Art—Addresses, essays, lectures. 3. Art, Medieval—Addresses, essays, lectures.
A C 39-11

New York. Public library
for Library of Congress [2]

---

*Z-950
Film Reproduction

FESTSCHRIFT zum 2. Jahrestag der Gründung des Bayerischen Bauernverbandes, Passau, 7. September 1947. München, Bayerischer Landwirtschaftsverlag [1947] 44 p. 30cm.

Film reproduction. Negative.

1. Bayerischer Bauernverband. I. [Title] Festschrift zum zweiten.
NN R 3.65 e/k OC (OS)1b+ PC, 1 SL E, 1 (UM1, LC1, [I], X1, Z/1)

OAI

Festschriften Julius Elster und Hans Geitel, zum sechzigsten Geburtstag gewidmet von Freunden und Schülern... Braunschweig: F. Vieweg & Sohn, 1915. xi,719,3 p. diagrs., illus., plates, tables (part fold.) 8°.

At head of title: Arbeiten aus den Gebieten der Physik, Mathematik, Chemie.
Vorwort signed: Karl Bergwitz.

889612.

NIHC

Festskrift til Amund B. Larsen på hans 75-års fødselsdag 15. desember 1924. Kristiania: H. Aschehoug & Co., 1924. 246 p. front. (port.)

1. Larsen, Amund Bredesen, 1849- . 2. Norwegian language. 3. Norwegian language—Dialects.

YED

Festskrift til Anathon Aall på 70-årsdagen hans, 15. august 1937. Oslo, Forlagt av H. Aschehoug & co. (W. Nygaard) 1937.

5 p. l., 271 p. incl. 1 illus., tables. front. (port.) 25cm.
Bibliographical foot-notes.
CONTENTS. — Tabula gratulatoria. — Eriksen, Richard. Filosofi og psykologi. — Klausen, Sverre. Die transzendentale begründung des kausalprinzips bei Kant.—Marc-Wogau, Konrad. Om den dialektiska upplösningen av motsägelser.—Mie, Gustav. Raum und zeit in der physik.—Landmark, J. D. Kausalitet og ansvars-psykologi.—Jaensch, E. R. Die erneuerung der ethik und die psychologie.—Elmgren, John. Några psykologiska metodsynpunkter.—Katz, David. Die wahrnehmung des eigenen körpergewichts. — Tschermak-Seysenegg, Armin. Über chromatische mitverstimmung zwischen beiden augen. — Schjelderup, H. K. Følelsesfortrengning og virkelighetsoplevelse.—Skard, Å. G. Turfter og turftsenergi.—Havin, Henry. Alkohol og reaksjonssikkerhet.—
(Continued on next card)

A C 38-1994

[2]

Festskrift til Anathon Aall på 70-årsdagen hans ... 1937.
(Card 2)

CONTENTS—Continued.

Révész, G. Zur grundlegung der blindenpsychologie.—Stoeltzner, Wilhelm. Über den mongoloiden schwachsinn.—Eng, Helga. Eksperimentalismen—en retning i nutidens pedagogiske filosofi.—Barden, H. P. Opdragelse til arbeid.—Ribsskog, B. Elevenes alder og lærernes evnevurdering.—Lagerborg, Rolf. De tre stadiernas lag i vår moraluppfostran.—Drever, J. Examinations.—Guttmann, Alfred. Musik-psychologie und musik-pädagogik.—Holm, Sverre. Psychologie und soziologie der masse.—Brock-Utne, Albert. Eine studie zur psychologie der mythen-phantasie.—Beyer, Harald. Symbolene i "Brand".—Anathon Aall: skrifter (p. [268]–271)

1. Psychology—Addresses, essays, lectures. 2. Philosophy—Addresses, essays, lectures. 3. Aall, Anathon August Fredrik, 1867–

A C 38-1994

New York. Public library
for Library of Congress [2]

3-MA

Festskrift til Anders Bugge på 55 årsdagen, 1. mai, 1944. Redaksjonskomite: Missa Janicke [et al.] Oslo, Det Runde bords forlag, 1944. ii,159 l. illus. 31cm.

Cover-title: Flora ex Mensa rotunda.
"Trykt i 50 eksemplarer, hvorav dette er nr. 4."
Includes bibliographies.
Contents.—Drakt og smykker, av C. Thomas.—
(Continued)

NN**R X 11.55 d/ OC, 1,2,3,I,II SL A,2,I, I,IIbo (OS)II,IIb PC, II (LC1,X1,Z1)

Festskrift til Anders Bugge på 55 årsdagen...
(Card 2)

Kampen mellom pave og keiser fram til konkordatet i Worms, 1122. av M. Janicke.—Litt om natursyn og naturgjengivelse i mellomitaliensk quattrocentomaleri, av A. Liberg.—Renessansemåling frå taket av den gamle Suldalskyrkja, av S. Molaug.—Den norske barokkskje, av T. Krohn-Hansen.—"Drikk og syng med vivatskraal - ", av A. Buch.—Magi og ornamentikk, av H. Engelstad.—Et takkebrev, av R. Asker.—"Spinn, spinn dotter min," av
(Continued)

Festskrift til Anders Bugge på 55 årsdagen...
(Card 3)

.. Hoffmann.—17-mai-vester, av T. Sandal.—Når "man træder" etter Hanna Winsnes, av Aa. Bay.—Fra Dreier til Eckersberg, av R. Molaug.—Håv og håvdrætte, av T. Gjessing.—Et påtenkt kunstverk til Universitetet og et brev om dette fra Welhaven; et bidrag til den gamle festsals historie, av H. Gran.—En kunstbegivenhet i 1820-årenes Bergen, av J.H. Lexow.—En drammensisk hagestue, av H.Alsvik. —Norsk maleri igår og idag, av R.Revold.
(Continued)

Festskrift til Anders Bugge på 55 årsdagen...
(Card 4)

1. Bugge, Anders Ragnar, 1889- . 2. Art—Essays and misc. 3. Norway—Civilization. I. Janicke, Missa, ed. II. Det Runde bord, Oslo. III. Janicke, Missa.

---

*PBL

Festskrift i Anledning af Professor David Simonsens 70-aarige Fødselsdag. København: Hertz, 1923. 400, 55 p. 8°.

Added t.-p. and 55 pages of text in Hebrew.
Bibliography, p. [11-] 21.

1. Simonsen, David, 1853- .

AN
(Bergsgård, A.)

Festskrift til Arne Bergsgård på 60-årsdagen, 18. april 1946. Trondheim, 1946. 322 p. port. 27cm.

"Bergsgård-bibliografi, ved Ove Bakken," p. 118–128.

403151B. 1. Bergsgård, Arne, 1886– . 2. Education—Norway, 20th cent. 3. Bergsgård, Arne, 1886– —Bibl.
NN

NIC

Festskrift til Arnulf Øverland på sekstiårsdagen. Oslo, Aschehoug [1949] 98 p. port. 24cm.

"Lyrikkantologi."

538143B. 1. Øverland, Arnulf, 1889- . 2. Poetry, Scandinavian—Collections.
N. Y. P. L. September 5, 1950

F-10
6310

FESTSKRIFT till Arthur Thomson den 6 november 1961. [Redaktionskommitté: Sten Carlsson et al.] Stockholm, Almqvist & Wiksell [1961] 278 p. port., maps 27cm.

Bibliographical references included in "Noter" at end of articles.

CONTENTS. --Arthur Thomsons vetenskapliga författarskap, av S. Carlsson. --Tacitus kartbild av Norra Europa, av S. Bolin. --Skeppsvist och ledungslama, av G. Hafström-- Gedesbys skuld, av O. Biurling.

(Continued)

NN R 5.65 1/ OC, Ib*, I PC, 1, 2, 3, I SL (LC1, X1, Z1) [I]

FESTSKRIFT till Arthur Thomson den 6 november 1961. [Redaktionskommitté: (Card 2)

--Registrum regni, av J. Rosén. --Tillkomsten av regementsordningen för Västergötland den 9 april 1540, av A. Andrén. --Det gamla frälset, av S. A. Nilsson. --Det silfverskiöldska förslaget om gransikning av konsistoriernas protokoll, av C. E. Normann. --Begreppet "Volonté générale" hos Rousseau, av G. Heckscher. --Nagra episoder fran grundlagsriksdagen 1809-10, av E. Fahlbeck. --Kring Hans Järta och 1809 ars regeringsform, av E. Thermænius. --Förklaring av lag och förklaring av lagens rätta mening, av N. Stjernquist. --Begreppen statsreligion, statskyrka och folkkyrka, av S. Kjöllerström. -- Tomtebissen och husagan, av

(Continued)

FESTSKRIFT till Arthur Thomson den 6 november 1961. [Redaktionskommitté:... (Card 3)

H. Pleijel. --Brev fran Viktor Lennstrand, av C. A. Hessler. --Likt och olikt i nordisk offentlig rätt, av N. Herlitz. --Sociologiens systematik, av T. Segerstedt. --Om riksdagsmans immunitet, av H. G. F. Sundberg. --Utländska medborgare oche de svenska akademiska lärarbefattningarna, av J. Westerstahl.

1. Thomson, Arthur, 1891- 2. Sweden--Hist. --Addresses, essays, lectures. 3. Law--Addresses, essays, lectures. I. Carlsson, Sten, 1917- ed.

E-11
8948

FESTSKRIFT til Astrid Friis på halvfjerdsårsdagen den 1. august 1963. København, Rosenkilde og Bagger, 1963. 326 p. port. 24cm.

Bibliographical footnotes.

CONTENTS. --Nationalisme, antinationalisme og nationalfølelse i Danmark omkring 1900, af P. Bagge. --Det danske staendersamfunds epoker; et rids, af A. E. Christensen. --Bidrag til rentespørgsmaalets

(Continued)

NN R 2.64 f/ OC PC, 1, 2 SL (LC1, X1, Z1)

FESTSKRIFT til Astrid Friis pa halvfjerdsarsdagen den 1. august 1963. (Card 2)

historie i dansk senmiddelalder og reformationstid, af T. Dahlerup. --Reformationen pa Øresunds toldbod 1641, af S. Dalgard. --Flensborgkøbmanden Tile Petersen, af S. Ellehøj. --Frederik II. s. jyske råder, af S. Gissel. --Det aeldste danske kommercekollegium, af K. Glamann. --Valg og vurdering ved benyttelse af kompagniarkiver; et metodisk bidrag, af K. Glamann. --Bilantz 1660, adelsvaeldens bo, af J. Jørgensen. --Ripensiske patriciere, epitafieportraetter fra renaissancetiden, af O. Norn. --

(Continued)

FESTSKRIFT til Astrid Friis pa halvfjerdsarsdagen den 1. august 1963. (Card 3)

Et utrykt forord til "Grevens feide" og andre notater fra Caspar Paludan-Müllers hand i hans eget eksemplar af dette vaerk, af O. Olsen. --Omkring den gyldne bulle fra 1356, af E. L. Petersen. --Den danske konges kancelli i 1250'erne, af N. Skyum-Nielsen. --Fragtomkostningerne i den engelske ostindienshandel 1601-57, af N. Steensgaard. --C. St. A. Bille og det nordslesvigske spørgsmal, af K. Vohn. --Astrid Friis bibliografi ved N.-H. Jeppesen (p. [297]-312)

1. Friis, Astrid, 1893- 2. Denmark--Hist. --Addresses, essays, lectures.

VPP

Festskrift til Bernhard Bang, 1848 — 7. Juni — 1928. København: Kandrup & Wunsch Bogtrykkeri, 1928. xv, 389 p. facsim., front., illus. (incl. ports.), plates (part col'd), tables. 4°.

1. Bang, Bernhard Laurits Frederik, 1848- . 2. Veterinary medicine—Denmark.
N. Y. P. L. December 21, 1928

---

* C-4 p.v.30

Festskrift till Bertil Malmberg den 13. augusti 1949. Stockholm, Bonnier [1949] 79 p. 25cm.

CONTENTS.—Karin Boyes Linköpingsdikt, av M. Abenius.—Grillparzers estetiska grundåskådning, av A. Åhlberg.—Diktaren och det mobiliserade samhället, av W. Aspenström.—Marter vandrar du, av G. Björling.—Anima, av J. Edfelt.—Vaggsång, av G. Ekelöf.—Ur Agamemnons hemkomst, av R. Enckell.—Diktaren och döden, av H. Gullberg.—Vad hjälper musiken? Av Å. Janzon.—Ett prosafragment, av E. Johnson.—Dagboksblad, av O. Lagercrantz.—To dikt, av A. Larsen.—Bland offren för gryningens flyganfall märktes en hundraåring, av D. Thomas. Svensk tolkning av E. Lindegren.—Rop mot Rom, av F. Garcia Lorca. Tolkning, av A. Lundkvist.—Sex tyska dikter, i tolkning av P. E. Wahlund.

1. Malmberg, Bertil, 1889- . 2. Grillparzer, Franz, 1791-1872.
NN*R 3.54 OC PC, 1, 2 SL (Z1, LC1, X1)

Write on slip, name, year, vol., page of magazine and class mark — ZBA

Festskrift til Evald Tang Kristensen.

(Danmarks Folkeminder: København, 1917. 8°. no.17, p.1-259. front. illus.)

form 400a [ii-13-30 25m]

NIDC

Festskrift til Finnur Jónsson, 29. Maj 1928. København: Levin & Munksgaards Forlag, 1928. 501 p. 4°.

Udgivet med Understøttelse af Carlsbergfondet og Rask-Ørsted-Fondet.

1. Jónsson, Finnur, 1858–
N. Y. P. L. January 17, 1929

(Bjerre, P.)

Festskrift för Poul Bjerre, 24 maj 1946. Stockholm, Bokförlagsaktiebolaget Centrum [1946]

214 p. port. 24 cm.

Cover title: Festskrift till Poul Bjerres 70-årsdag.
Includes bibliographies.

CONTENTS.—En tak, av Johs. Borgen.—Den nordiske Psyke, av Olaf Brüel.—Institutet för medicinsk psykologi och psykoterapi och dess idé, av J. Tillgren.—Några praktiska detaljer vid det psykoterapeutiska arbetet, av Jakob Billström.—Dröm och lek, av Gösta Harding.—En detalj i den psykiska hälsovården, av R. Eeg-Olofsson.—Ett røn och dess tillämpning, av K. E. Törnqvist.—Sann och falsk religiositet, av Ivar Alm.—Om heligheten, av Rolf Lagerborg.—Om skuldproblemet, av Gösta Nordquist.—Poul Bjerre om religion och kristendom, av Giovanni Linde-

(Continued on next card)
Med 47–2555*
[2]

Festskrift för Poul Bjerre ... [1946] (Card 2)

CONTENTS—Continued.

berg. — Återuppståndelse, av Stig Ljunggren. — Kvarnen, krogen och hägringen, av Emilia Fogelklou.—Sammanträffanden med Poul Bjerre, av Ernst Norlind.—Poul Bjerre, världsmedborgaren, av Nils Simonsson.—Intervjuer med Poul Bjerre, av Signhild Forsberg.—Aforismer, av Arnulf Överland.

1. Bjerre, Poul Carl, 1876– ~~2. Psychiatry—Addresses, essays, lectures.~~ 3. Theology—~~Addresses, essays, lectures.~~

RC435.B54 616.804 Med 47–2555*

Library of Congress [2]

NIH

Festskrift til Francis Bull på 50 årsdagen. Oslo, Gyldendal, Norsk forlag, 1937.

5 p. l., 384, [4] p. front., illus. (incl. facsims) pl., ports., coats of arms. 27cm.

Bibliographical foot-notes.

NIG

Festskrift til Francis Bull på 50 årsdagen. Oslo, Gyldendal, Norsk forlag, 1937. 5 p.l., 384, [4] p. front., illus. (incl. facsims.) pl., ports., coats of arms. 27cm.

Text in French, Norwegian and Swedish.
Bibliographical footnotes.
CONTENTS.—Amundsen, Leiv. Hans Bull og A. G. Carstens.—Beyer, Harald. Om litteraturhistorie og litteraturgranskning med særlig henblikk på norske forhold.—Christophersen, H. O. Noen bemerkninger om idéhistoriens innhold og metode.—Ek, Sverker. Sanningsägarens roll hos Molière och Ibsen.—Fett, Harry. Et stamboksvers om å ville og kunne.—Foss, Kåre. Holberg selv i hans segl og våpen.—Grieg, Harald. Litt

(Continued)

NN*R 3.54 OC PC, 1, 2 SL (~~1~~, LC1, X1)

Festskrift til Francis Bull på 50 årsdagen... 1937. (Card 2)

om Knut Hamsun og hans forleggere.—Hamsun, Knut. Men glem ikke.—Hirn, Yrjö. Ett Bjørnson-brev, med några kommentarer.—Holtsmark, Anne. Sankt Olavs liv og mirakler.—Iversen, Ragnvald. Et nyfunnet bygdemålsdikt.—Jæger, Herman. "Wit, whither wilt?"—Laache, Rolv, ed. Tre brev om Norge og nordmennene.—Lamm, Martin. Kiellands Jacob och Zola.—Lescoffier, Jean. En écoutant Bjørnson.—Lie, Hallvard. Den glemsomme trellen i Eyrbyggja-saga.—Liestøl, Knut. Folkevisa um Gonge-Rolv.—Olsen, Magnus. Skålholts kirkedager i 12. århundre.—Bjørnson, Bjørnstjerne. Tre Bjørnson-breve om "Geografi og kærlighed" [udg. af] R. Paulli.—Petersen, C. S. Holbergs skrifter i samtidens bogsamlinger.—Seip, D. A. Om særnorske elementer i Holbergs skriftspråk.—Skard, Sigmund. Litt um rytmisk påverknad.—Smith,

(Continued)

Festskrift til Francis Bull på 50 årsdagen... 1937. (Card 3)

Emil. Orestes; fjellmannen, frondøren, flyktningen.—Thesen, Rolv. Arne Garborgs møte med Nietzsche.—Thiis, Jens. Minneord om Helge Rode.—Thomas, S. P. Tragedien "Octavia".—Trætteberg, Hallvard. Norges krone og våpen.—Tunold, Solveig. Norske forfattere i Peder Rafns visebok (1626–1630)—Zilliacus, Emil. Pindaros' hyllning till Chariterna.

1. Bull, Francis, 1887– 2. Norwegian literature—Hist. and crit.

ZB1E

Festskrift til H.F. Feilberg fra nordiske Sprog- og Folkemindeforskere på 80 Års Dagen den 6. August 1911. Udgivet af Svenska Landsmålen, Maal og Minne (Bymaalslaget, Kristiania), Universitetsjubilæets danske Samfund (Danske Studier). København: Gyldendal, 1911. 808,(1) 816-817 p. 2 l., 1 map, 1 port. illus. 8°.

EKD

Festskrift til H. P. Hanssen paa hans 70 Aars Dag den 21 Februar 1932. Aabenraa: Sønderjydske Aarboger, 1932. 501 p. incl. tables. 29 cm.

"Udgivet af Historisk Samfund for Sønderjylland, Sprogforeningen, og Sønderjydsk Skoleforening." - Verso of t.-p.

610505A.

BAC

Festskrift til Halvdan Koht på sekstiårsdagen 7de juli 1933. Oslo, H. Aschehoug & co., 1933.

5 p. l., 300 p. front. (port.) facsims. $26\frac{1}{2}$cm.

"~~Dette er av 225 nummererte eksemplarer nr. 84.~~"

CONTENTS.—Lhéritier, M. Histoire et causalité.—Eitrem, S. Das ende Didos in Vergils Aeneis.—Skard, E. Pater patriae.—Pirenne, H. Le trésor des rois mérovingiens.—Dopsch, A. Freilassung und wirtschaft im frühen mittelalter.—Vogel, W. Das emporium Reric.—Olsen, M. Fra Hávamál til Krákumál.—Schreiner, J. Slaget i Havsfjord.—Bergsgård, A. Skaldane um land og lands styring.—Indrebø, G. Rygjafylki—Ryfylke.—Paasche, F. Til erkebiskop Eysteins historie.—Seip, D. A. Seglremstudier.—Steinnes, A. Tiend-upgåvone i biskop Øysteins jordebok.—Liestøl, K. Det litterære grunnlaget for Sigurđar saga fóts ok Åsmundar Húnakongs.—Brandi, K. Machiavelli, humanismus und politik.—Hauser, H. De la valeur historique du Traité d'économie

(Continued on next card)
34–12775
[2]

BAC

Festskrift til Halvdan Koht på sekstiårsdagen 7de juli 1933 ... 1933. (Card 2)

CONTENTS—Continued.

politique d'Antoine de Montchrestien.—Steen, S. Hvordan en kjøpstad blev til. Kristiansand.—Hasund, S. Gardklasselikning og landsskatt i det 17. hundreåret.—Johnsen, O. A. Borgerlig selvstyre i Tønsberg under eneveldet.—Bull, F. Holberg og censuren.—Broch, O. Noen oplysninger om russernes Murman-fiske i 1760-årene.—Cahen, L. Les conditions générales du commerce parisien à la fin du 18e siècle.—Høverstad, T. Darre og Klæbu mot reaksjonen i 1840-åra.—Temperley, H. British secret diplomacy during the Palmerstonian period.—Skard, S. Forfattarskapet til "Andhrimner".—Thesen, R. Bjørnstjerne Bjørnson og Georg Brandes.—Lange, H. M. Internasjonale innslag i norsk arbeiderbevegelse i 90-årene.—Fostervoll, K. Optaket til sosialistisk jordpolitikk i Norge.—Ræstad, A. Historiske villfarelser i Grønlandsdommen.

1. History—Collected works. 2. Scandinavian literature—Hist. & crit. 3. Koht, Halvdan, 1873–

Library of Congress D6.K6 34–12775

[2] 904

AN (Grieg, H.)

Festskrift til Harald Grieg ved 25-års jubileet for Gyldendal norsk forlag 2. januar 1950. Oslo, 1950. 378 p. illus., ports., facsims. 29cm.

Most of the illustrative matter is folded.
List of contributors: Ingeborg Andersen [and others]
Errata slip inserted. "Ole Vollan; en skisse av Johannes Elgvin", p. 327–[370]

1. Grieg, Harald, 1894– . 2. Vollan, Ole Christiansen, 1837–1907. 3. Gyldendal, norsk forlag, a/s. I. Andersen, Ingeborg, 1887–

NN*R 4.53 OC, I PC, 1, 2, 3, I SL (LC1, Z1, X1)

NIGH (Krog)

Festskrift til Helge Krog på sekstiårsdagen. [Redaksjonskomité: Sigurd Hoel og Rolv Thesen] Oslo, Aschehoug [1949]

113 p. illus., plate, ports. 27 cm.

CONTENTS.—Helge Krogs diktning, av S. Hoel.—Lysvirkninger, av A. Øverland.—Dagboksblad, av J. Falkberget.—Johannes Edfelt.—Hakkespetten, av R. Thesen.—Et lite minne, av M. Kjaer.—Uredd mann, av T. Ørjasaeter.—Litteraturkritikeren Helge Krog, av P. Houm.—Drankeren, av T. Kristensen.—Litt om østers, av A. F. Mathiesen.—Denne Krog, av J. Borgen.—Parabel, av I. Hagerup.—På en dramatikers brygge, av A. Skouen.—Om opprør, av F. Havrevold.—Av en ung manns memoarer, av A. Moen.—13 år og fortapt,

(Continued on next card)

A 49–7948*

[3]

Festskrift til Helge Krog på sekstiårsdagen ... [1949] (Card 2)

CONTENTS—Continued.

av O. Solumsmoen.—Et radiospill, av O. Bang-Hansen.—Utkastet til "Underveis," av A. Stai.—Peter Egge.—H. Roeck Hansen.—Gerda Ring.—Halfdan Christensen.—August Oddvar.

1. Krog, Helge, 1889– 2. Norwegian literature—Addresses, essays, lectures. I. Hoel, Sigurd, 1890– ed. II. Thesen, Rolv, 1896– joint ed.

A 49–7948*

Minnesota. Univ. Libr. for Library of Congress [3]

BVE

Festskrift til J. L. Ussing i Anledning af hans 80-aarige Fødselsdag 10 April 1900. København: Gyldendal, 1900. 4 p.l., 276 p., 8 pl. (6 fold.) illus. 8°.

Z-13 5252

Festskrift til Jens Kruuse den 6. april 1968. Redaktion: Gustav Albeck, Hans Andersen, Jørgen Budtz-Jørgensen, Kristian Kjær og Chr. Ludvigsen. Aarhus, Universitetsforlaget; (D. B. K.) [1968].

25, 349 p. 5 plates. 25 cm.

CONTENTS.—EKKO Danmark, af K. Rifbjerg.—Herman Bang og Aarhus Teater, af G. Albeck.—Faderen: Om nogle træk i familien Dinesens liv og forfatterskaber, af H. Andersen.—Fragment af lidenskabens psykologi, af T. Bjørnvig.—Romantik og eksistensproblematik: Omkring Ragnhild Jølsen og hendes litterære baggrund,

(Continued)

NN*R 5.69 v/J OC, I PC, 1, 2, I SL (LC1, X1, Z1) [I]

FESTSKRIFT til Jens Kruuse den 6. april 1968. (Card 2)

af J. Bukdahl.—Om Mimoser til forsvar for litteraturhistorie, af E. M. Christensen.—Colonial style, af C. Elling.—Tre Hjalmar Gullbergmanuskript, av C. Fehrman.—Digtersfinxen: Et portræt af Sophus Claussen, af A. Henriksen.—"Kun en burleske af den værste art," af A. Henriques.—Fins deten moral i Ibsens skuespill? Af D. Håkonsen.—Om att være teaterkritiker, af J. Kistrup.—En fortolkning af Henrik Pontoppidans "Lykke-Per," af K. Kjær.—Stjernen fra Hinnerup, af S. Kragh-Jacobsen.—Jens af Odense og det levende ord, af P. G. Lindhardt.—Samuel Beckett og Theodor Fontane, af

(Continued)

FESTSKRIFT til Jens Kruuse den 6. april 1968. (Card 3)

C. Ludvigsen.—Litteraturvidenskabeligt selskab. Magnus Stevns. Af V. Ritsager.—Forskellig Holberglitteratur, af P. V. Rubow.—Litterær erosion: En betragtning tilegnet sprogelskeren og -revseren Jens Kruuse, af O. Sarvig.—Slaraffenland, af P. Seeberg.—Elmer: Uddrag af et kapitel fra forfatterens næste roman, af T. Skou-Hansen.—Valdemar Vedel—Redaktør af Tilskueren, af H. Stangerup.—Ridderen, der ikke var til, af H. Sørensen.—Til Jens Kruuse: For mange år siden og nu, af J. A. Schade.

1. Kruuse, Jens, 1908– . 2. Literature--Addresses, essays, lectures. I. Albeck, Gustav, 1906– .

ZEC

Festskrift til Jens Nørregaard den 16. maj 1947. København, G. E. C. Gad, 1947. 320 p. port. 25cm.

459430B. 1. Theology—Essays and misc. 2. Nørregaard, Jens, 1887–

NN

D-15 6101

FESTSKRIFT til Kaare Fostervoll på 70-årsdagen, 3. desember 1961. [Redaksjon: Einar Boyesen et al.] Oslo, Aschehoug, 1961. 110, [1] p. port. 23cm.

"Publikasjoner," p. [111]

1. Fostervoll, Kaare, 1891– . I. Boyesen, Einar, 1888– ed.

NN R 8.65 1/B OC, Ib+, I PC, 1, I SL E, 1, I (LC1, X1, Z1)

GGX

Festskrift til Konrad Nielsen på 70-årsdagen 28. august 1945. Oslo, A. W. Brøgger, 1945. 231 p. illus. 27cm. (Studia septentrionalia. 2)

Contributions in French, Norwegian, Lappish, or English.

1. Nielsen, Konrad Hartvig Isak Rosenvinge, 1875- . 2. Lapps—Norway. I. Ser.
NN R 5.53 OC PC, 1, 2 SL (LC1, Z1, X1)

RAE

Festskrift til L. L. Hammerich på tresårsdagen den 31. juli 1952. København, G. E. C. Gad [1952] xxiv, 271 p. port. 26cm.

1. Philology—Addresses, essays, lectures. 2. Hammerich, Louis Leonor, 1892-
NN R 4.53 OC PC, 1, 2 SL (LC1, Z1, X1)

VPW

...**Festskrift** til landbruksdirektör O. T. Bjanes. [Oslo, P. M. Bye & co., 1946] 352 p. illus. 25cm.

At head of title: 1906-1946.
Title on spine: Vårt landbruk; vekst og framtidsmål...

1. Agriculture—Norway. 2. Bjanes, Ole Taraldsen, 1875-
N. Y. P. L. January 15, 1953

NIC

Festskrift til Ludv. F. A. Wimmer ved hans 70 års Fødselsdag 7. Februar 1909. København: Gyldendalske Boghandel, Nordisk Forlag, 1909. 219 p. 22½cm.

"Nordisk Tidsskrift for Filologi XVII."
CONTENTS.—Andersen, V. Til Ewalds "Kong Christian."—Bertelsen, H. Pro scholis puerorum.—Dahlerup, V. Flensborg-Håndskriftet av Jyske Lov.—Falbe-Hansen, I. Rungsteds Lyksaligheder.—Guðmundsson, V. Sølvkursen ved År 1000.—Jakobsen, J. Streiflys over færøske Stednavne.—Jónsson, F. Versene i Hávarðarsaga.—Kristensen, M. Hvor hørte Rydårbogens Skriver hjemme?—Kålund, K. Bidrag til Digtningen på Island omkring 1500 fra Stockh. perg. 22, 4to, med Redegörelse for

(Continued)

N. Y. P. L. April 30, 1935

Festskrift til Ludv. F. A. Wimmer... (Card 2)

Membranens Marginalia.—Mortensen, K. Et Kapitel af dansk Versbygnings Historie i det 17. Århundrede.—Olrik, A. Danmarks ældste Kongegrav.—Olsen, B. M. Strøbemærkninger til Eddakvadene.—Petersen, C. S. Lavrids Kocks danske Grammatik.—Secher, V. A. Bandsættelse af ukendt Gærningsmand til en Forbrydelse.—Thorsen, P. K. Sprogforandringer.

720337A. 1. Wimmer, Ludvig Frands Adalbert, 1839-1920.
N. Y. P. L. April 30, 1935

GHI

Festskrift til museumforstander H. P. Hansen, Herning, på 70-årsdagen den 2.oktober 1949. København, Rosenkilde og Bagger, 1949. xxii, 406 p. illus., maps. 27cm.

3 tracing sheets issued in pocket.
"Bidrag til en bibliografi over H. P. Hansens trykte arbejder, ved Vagn Lindebo Hansen," p. 391-406.

(Continued)

NN

Festskrift til museumsforstander... (Card 2)

1. Hansen, Hans Peter, 1879- . 2. Denmark—Civilization. 3. Folk lore—Scandinavia. 4. Danish language—Dialects—Jutland.

NN

NIO
+

Festskrift til Niels Møller paa Firsaarsdagen, 11. December 1939. København, Munksgaard, 1939. xiii, 355 p. port. 29cm.

CONTENTS.—Gelsted, Otto. Tankens Sang.—Jespersen, Otto. En personlig Hilsen.—Saxild, Georg. Goethe og Fru v. Stein.—Andersen, Vilh. Med et Blad af Verdenslitteraturen.—Müller, T. A. Ærefuld Karakteristik af Holberg.—Vedel, Vald. Foreløbig Rekognoscering.—Jørgensen, Johannes. Grækeren fra det fyenske Arkipelag.—Poulsen, Frederik. Bondekultur og religiøs Digtning.—Schwanenflügel, Knud. Til den store Humanist.—Jacobsen, Lis. Stud. jur. Niels Møller.—Eckhoff, Lorentz. Molière og Le Misanthrope.—Bohr, Niels. Digter og Videnskabsmand.—Bull, Francis. En takk for "Verdenslitteraturen."—Pipping, Rolf. Fosterlandskänslan i Fänrik Ståls sägner.—Frisch, Hartvig. Ideologi og Virkelighed hos Thukydid.—Rubow, P. V. De tre

(Continued)

N. Y. P. L. May 18, 1948

Festskrift til Niels Møller paa Firsaarsdagen... (Card 2)

Fortællere i Pentateuchen.—Topsøe-Jensen, H. Anderseniana.—Plesner, K. F. Digterhumanisten Logan Pearsall Smith.—Jacobsen, Grete. Til den gamle Filosof.—Afzelius, Adam. Plutarchs Cato Minor som historisk Kilde.—Kruuse, Jens. Gaaseleverpostej og Basuner.—Koppel, H. D. Sang af Bakkantinder.—Iversen, Erik. Hölderlins Hyperion.—Eibe, M. L. Skrækromanens Indflydelse paa danske romantiske Værker.—Toldberg, Helge. Der staar et Slot i Vesterled.—Bøgh, Knud. Naar man blader i Niels Møllers Bøger.—Linneballe, Poul. Lessing i Danmark.—Herløv, Rasmus. Niels Møller og en gammel Emigrant.—Nielsen, K. M., and Ole Jacobsen. Bibliografi (p. 303-354.)

396094B. 1. Møller, Niels Lauritz, 1859- . 2. Literature—Hist. and crit.
N. Y. P. L. May 18, 1948

---

* HZD
(Oslo)

Festskrift til den Norske avdeling ved Universitetsbiblioteket på femtiårsdagen for loven om avgivelse av trykksaker, 1882—tyvende juni—1932; utgitt ved Francis Bull og Roar Tank. Oslo: Steenske forlag[, 1932]. 174 p. incl. tables. illus. (incl. facsims., ports.) 24½cm.

no. 78 of 100 copies printed.
Bibliographies included.
Contents: TANK, R. De femti år. NYGÅRD-NILSSEN, A. J. B. Halvorsen. AMUNDSEN, L. Hjalmar Pettersen. BULL, F. Norske avdeling og norsk bibliografi. HOLTSMARK, A. En side av norsk bokhistorie. SOLLIED, P. R. Relationer fra Christiania, Bergen og Trondhjem om smaae piecers censur. CHRISTIANSEN, R. T. Albrecht-

(Continued)

N. Y. P. L. August 26, 1933

Festskrift til den Norske avdeling ved Universitetsbiblioteket... (Card 2)

sons visesamling. LANDMARK, J. D. Bibliotekarer og assistenter ved Det Kgl. norske videnskabers selskabs bibliotek i Trondhjem 1766–1858. NISSEN, K. Den Werlauffske gave, en innholdsrik kartbunke i Universitetsbibliotekets kartsamling. SCHEEL, F. Latin i dommersproget.

633726A. 1. Oslo. Universitet. Bibliotek. I. Bull, Francis, 1887– , editor. II. Tank, Roar Nielsen, 1880– , editor.
N. Y. P. L. August 26, 1933

** MGA

Festskrift til O. M. Sandvik, 70-års dagen, 1875 — 9. mai — 1945. Oslo, H. Aschehoug & co., 1945. 268 p. front. (port.), illus. (music) 27cm.

CONTENTS. — Olsen, Sparre. O. M. Sandvik. — Sandvold, Arild. O. M. Sandvik i norsk kirkemusikk.—Eggen, Erik. Skalaen i Sinklar-marsjen.—Groven, Eivind. Det natursvarande i musikk-kjensla vår.—Gurvin, Olav. Norsk programmatisk folkemusikk. —Jeppesen, Knud. "Coralis Constantinus" som liturgisk dokument.—Kolsrud, Oluf. Korsongen i Nidarosdomen.—Krohn, Ilmari. Den lutherske koral i Finland.—Marstrander, Petter. De første kristenmenigheters gudstjenesteliv.—Moberg, C.-A. Musikforskningen och den praktiske musikodlingen.—Norlind, Tobias. Sång och harpespel under vikingatiden.—Platou, Olaf. Nutidens orgeltyper og våre to domkirkeorgler.—Winding-Sørensen, Dag. Carl Nilsen [i. e. Nielsen]—Sommerfeldt, W. P. Musiklivet i Christiania da Ole blev født.—Gaukstad, Øystein. Bibliografi (p. 247–258).

DREXEL MUSICAL FUND.

373924B. 1. Sandvik, Ole Mørk, 1875– 2. Music—Norway.
N. Y. P. L. July 28, 1950

---

*MGA

Festskrift til Olav Gurvin. (1893–1968) Red.: Finn Benestad og Philip Krømer. Drammen, Lyche [1968]

169 p. portr., music. 24 cm. (Edition Lyche)

Summaries in English.

CONTENTS.—Institutt for musikkvitenskap, Universitetet i Oslo, av F. Benestad.—Anteckningar om 20 sekunder svensk folkmusik, av I. Bengtsson.—Die "reine Stimmung" als musikalisches Problem, von C. Dahlhaus.—Noen særdrag ved Johan Svendsens instrumen-

(Continued)

NN R 1. 71 v/\ OC, I, II, IIIb* PC, 1, 3, I, II SL MU, 1, 2, I, II
(LC1, X1, Z1)

FESTSKRIFT til Olav Gurvin. (Card 2)

talstil, av Ø. Eckhoff.—Et orgeltabulatur-fragment i Det kgl. Bibliotek i København, av H. Glahn.—Hans Skramstad—et stebarn i norsk musikkhistorie, av N. Grinde.—Omkring tilblivelsen av en "Brorson-melodi"-tradition, av J. P. Larsen.—Breviariehymn och Laudasång, av C.-A. Moberg.—En "Musiqvens Elsker" i Risør omkring 1750, av H. H. Nystrøm.—Notater til et par Petter Dassmelodier, av N. Schiørring.—Kjerulfs fem sanger fra "Spanisches Liederbuch," av D. Schjelderup-Ebbe.—Noen metodologiske grunnproblemer i musikkforskningen, av K. Skyllstad.—Bibliografi over Olav Gurvins trykte arbeider, av N. Grinde (p. 168–[170])

(Continued)

FESTSKRIFT til Olav Gurvin. (Card 3)

1. Gurvin, Olav, 1893- . 2. Essays. 3. Music--Essays.
I. Benestad, Finn, ed. II. Krømer, Philip, ed. III. Krømer, Philip.

TB

Festskrift til professor, dr. polit. Jørgen Pedersen. Aarhus, Universitetsforlaget, 1951. 194 p. 25cm.

1. Pedersen, Jørgen, 1890- 2. Economics, 1926-

NN 12.52 OC PC,1, 2 SL E,1,2 (LC1,Z1, X1)

ZDR

Festskrift til Professor Dr. Theol. J. Oskar Andersen fra Fagfæller og Elever. København: G. E. C. Gad, 1936. 204 p. incl. front. (port.) 22cm.

"Særudgave af Teologisk Tidskrift 5, Række VII, Hefte 2–3."

CONTENTS.—Ammundsen, Valdemar. Varnæs-Salmebogens historiske Situation.—Becker, S. A. Et Bidrag til Menighedsraadenes Historie.—Bergmann, Lorenz. To katolske Missionsopraab fra Luthers Tid.—Haar, H. Fra Haderslev til Ribe.—Helgason, Jón. Personalhistorikeren Provst Jón Halldórsson til Hítadalur.—Kornerup, Bjørn. Bidrag til Oplysning om Katolikernes Retsstilling i Danmark i det 18. Aarhundrede.—Munck, Johannes. Billedet af Kætterne hos Irenæus.—Neiiendam, Michael. Et Brev fra Biskop J. P. Mynster til Kong Christian VIII.—Nørregaard, J. De ti engelske Religionsartikler fra 1536.—Pedersen, Johannes. "Forsamlinger" i København 1704–1706.

867729A. 1. Andersen, Johannes Oskar, 1866– . 2. Church history—Denmark. I. Teologisk Tidskrift.
N. Y. P. L. April 7, 1937

---

*EI
N867
1947

Festskrift til professor Olaf Broch på hans 80-årsdag fra venner og elever, ved Chr. S. Stang, Erik Krag og Arne Gallis. Oslo, I kommisjon hos J. Dybwad, 1947.

292 p. illus., port. 24 cm. (Avhandlinger utgitt av det Norske videnskaps-akademi i Oslo. II. Hist.-filos. klasse, 1947)

"Fremlagt i fellesmøtet den 2. mai 1947 av Chr. S. Stang."

CONTENTS.—Omring мы с тобой "vi med deg" (du og jeg), osv., av Knut Bergsland.—The Syriac phonematic vowel systems, av Harris Birkeland.—De prosodiske elementer i norsk, av C. H. Borgstrøm.—Stavingskontraksjon og tonelag, av Hallfrid Christiansen. — Der Stammvokal des deutschen Pronomens dieser, av Ingerid Dal.—Tallordenes syntaks i russisk, av Arne Gallis.—The White Huns and Tokharian, av Sten Konow.—Den historiske roman i Russland, Polen og Bøhmen, av Erik Krag.—Om neutrumsbøiningen i Nord-Gudbrands-

(Continued on next card)

A 48–7573*

[2]

Festskrift til professor Olaf Broch på hans 80-årsdag fra venner og elever ... 1947. (Card 2)

CONTENTS—Continued.

dal, av A. L. Fliflet.—Bredsideinnskriftene på Alstadstenen, av C. J. S. Marstrander.—Metathesis of liquids in Dardic, av Georg Morgenstierne.—Russiske og russisk-finske lånord i Finnmark-lappisk, av Asbjørn Nesheim.—En Finnmark-lappisk detalj, av Konrad Nielsen.—Runebrynet fra Holm på Helgeland, av Magnus Olsen.—Den unge Masaryk og Platon, av Olav Rytter.—Om suffikset -else i nordisk, av D. A. Seip.—Lydbuen, av E. W. Selmer.—On a Donegal verbal type with a dissylabic semanteme ending in a (:) av Alf Sommerfelt.—Adjectifs lituaniens en -is, av C. S. Stang.—Litt om fonetikk og fonologi, av Hans Vogt.

1. Broch, Olaf, 1867– 2. Philology—Collections. I. Stang, Christian Schweigaard, 1900– II. Krag, Erik, 1902– III. Gallis, Arne, 1908– (Series: Norske videnskaps-akademi i Oslo. Historisk-filosofisk klasse. Avhandlinger, 1947)

Minnesota. Univ. Libr. for Library of Congress A 48–7573*

[2]

Write on slip, name, year, vol., page of magazine and class mark— *F

Festskrift til Rektor J. Qvigstad.

(Tromsø Museum, Tromsø. Skrifter. Tromsø, 1928. 4°. v.2,p.i-xvi,1-376. illus., plates,front.port.)

Bibliography,p.xii-xv.

Contents:Bergfors,Georg. Ett par nordsvenska

(Continued)

form 406a [viii-10-28 25m]

Festskrift til Rektor J.Qvigstad. (Card 2).

varianter till H.C.Andersens "Lille Claus og store Claus". Bryn,Halfdan. Über den Ursprung des isländischen Volkes. Brøgger,A.W. Håløygenes Bjarmelandsferder. Christiansen,R.T. Norske eventyr fra de siste år. Demant Hatt, Emilie. Offerforestillinger og erindringer om troldtrommen hos nulevende lapper. Grundström, H. Ett lapskt ordstäv om pesten. Heika,H.O. Qvigstad samasjorggalam-barggo. Holmberg-Harva,
(Continued)

Festskrift til Rektor J.Qvigstad. (Card 3).

Uno. Skoltelapparnas "följeslagare". Indrebø, Gustav. Tjuvholmen. Itkonen,T.J. Fennoskandiaskienes oprinnelse. Johnsen,O.A. Norsk-dansk handelsforbindelse med Nord-Russland under Kristian IV. Kalima,Jalo. Onko suomen reuna balttilainen lainasana? Koht,Halvdan. Draumen um Nordland. Kristvik,Erling. Den nordnorske laereren.Vilkår for og krav til skulearbeidet i Nord-Norge. Krohn,Kaarle. "Auch die Lappenkinder singen." Lagercrantz,Eliel. Gesangs-
(Continued)

Festskrift til Rektor J.Qvigstad. (Card 4).

motive aus Nesseby. Lid,Nils. Vegetasjonsgudinne og vårplantar. Liestøl,Knut. Eit par nordnorske folkevisor. Mark,Julius. Zur lappischen Wortkunde. Nielsen,Konrad. Et tredelt bidrag. Nissen,Kristian. Nogen lappiske offerplasser i det indre av Finnmarken. Ohrt, F.Lemminkäinens fjender. Olsen,Magnus. Norske gårdnavn. Paulaharju,Samuli. Lemminjoki(Lakselv), Kuvaus suomalaisesta asutuksesta.Peter-

Festskrift til Rektor J.Qvigstad. (Card 5).

sen,T. Biskop Gunnerus's runebomme. Reuterskiöld,Edgar. Från guldhornen till lapptrumman. Rosberg,J.E. Kan en språklig sammanslutning bland lapparna tänkas? Raestad,Arnold. Lappeskatten og lappenes rettigheter i Norge før 1751. Seip,D.A. Om polemikken mellem Petter Dass og Ole Hansen Nysted. Selmer,E.W. Noen bemerkninger om den musikalske aksent i dens forhold til den sterkt og svakt skårne aksent.
(Continued)

Festskrift til Rektor J.Qvigstad. (Card 6).

Setälä,E.N. Virokannas. Smith,P.L. De svenske fogedregnskaper som kildemateriale for finnmarksk lokalhistorieforskning. Solem,Erik. Yngste sønns arverett hos lappene og andre folk. Toivonen,Y.H. Muutamista lapin sanoista. Wessel,A.B. Befolkningen i Sør-Varanger efter 1870. Wichmann,Yrjö. Etymologisches. Wiklund, K.B. Das lappische Verbaladverbium und einige andere Kasus des Verbalstammes. Äimä,F. Lapin
(Continued)

Festskrift til Rektor J.Qvigstad. (Card 7).

laiwask. Collinder,Björn. Die Wörter für fünf, sechs und sieben im Lappischen.

NIGH (Hoel)

Festskrift til Sigurd Hoel på 60 årsdagen. Oslo, Gyldendal, 1950. 299 p. ports. 27cm.

Contributions mainly in Norwegian, some in Danish, English or Swedish.

588225B. 1. Hoel, Sigurd, 1890-
N. Y. P. L. November 21, 1951

NIV

Festskrift til Soya paa halvtredsaarsdagen 30. oktober 1946. Fredericia, Nordiske landes bogforlag, 1946. 120 p. illus. 27cm.

514784B. 1. Soya, Carl Erik, 1896-
N. Y. P. L. February 27, 1950

NIO

Festskrift till Alma Söderhjelm. Stockholm, A. Bonnier, 1945.

123 p. illus., port. 26 cm.

CONTENTS.—Introduktion, av Karl Asplund.—På Clios tavla, av Bo Bergman.—Till Alma Söderhjelm, av Prins Eugen.—Språklig splittring och kulturell enhet, av Arthur Montgomery.—"Vägen till friheten," av Ragnar Hyltén-Cavallius.—Tervola, av Henning Söderhjelm.—Det Ehrenheimska "skrivfelet," av Arne Munthe.—Finsk mästare, av Gabriela Mistral; överssättning av Hjalmar Gullberg.—Ett dagboksblad, samt några reflexioner, av Joh. Lindblom.—Boulanger, revanschgeneralen, av Nils Forssell.—Helen Williams, av Lydia Wahlström.—Debuterande sol- och vårman, av Karl Asplund.—

(Continued on next card)

A 49-4355*

[1]

Festsskrift till Alma Söderhjelm ... 1945. (Card 2)

CONTENTS—Continued.

Kåsör, av Hasse Z.—Hon som upphävt naturlagarna, av Elsa Nyblom.—Alma Söderhjelm, av Olof Lagercrantz.—Kronprins Oscar som militär, av C. F. Palmstierna.—Två amerikaner i Oscar I:s Sverige, av Ingvar Andersson.—Till Alma, av Prins Wilhelm.—Illustrationer: Alma Söderhjelm. Teckning av Yngve Berg.—Skymning, Sanary. Målning av Hugo Zuhr.—Prinsessa vid spinnrocken. Teckning av Eric Grate.

1. Söderhjelm, Alma, 1870-

A 49-4355*

New York. Public Libr.
for Library of Congress [1]

YAR

...Festskrift till Anders Karitz. Uppsala [etc.] Almqvist & Wiksell [1946] 376 p. port. 24cm. (Föreningen för filosofi och specialvetenskap. Skrifter. 1)

517155B. 1. Philosophy—Essays and misc. 2. Karitz, Anders, 1881- . I. Ser.
N. Y. P. L. April 24, 1950

E-10
5109

FESTSKRIFT till Östen Undén den 25. augusti, 1956. [Redaktionskommitté: Åke Holmbäck, Sture Petrén [och] Uno Willers] Stockholm, Almqvist & Wiksell, 1956. 372 p. illus., port., map. 25cm.

CONTENTS.—De politiska förhållandena mellan Storbritannien och Uganda, av H. W. Ahlmann. —Ett spörsmål angående värdering vid expropriation, av A. Brunnberg. —Norge og Vestmaktene; en studie i sammenlignende statsrett, av F. Castberg. —Några randanteckningar kring

(Continued)

NN *R 7.58 p/v OC, I PC, 1, 2, 3, I SL E, 1, 2, 3, I (LC1, X1, Z1)
[I]

FESTSKRIFT till Östen Undén den 25. augusti, 1956. (Card 2)

den internationella skiljedomsidéns historia, av T. Gihl. —Ett spörsmål angående agarhypoteket, av N. Gärde. —The United nations; an appraisal, by D. Hammarskjöld. --Två källor till Atlantican, av Å. Holmbäck. --Sverige som immigrationsland, av K. Kock. —Åland i tysk utrikespolitik vinterhalvåret 1917-18, av Å. Kromnow. —Politics and economic theory in the Atlantic charter, by S. U. Palme. —Förutsättningarna för avtalsbunden organisations ansvar för olovlig stridsåtgärd, av S. Petrén. —"På nådigste befallning," av A. Thomson. --Demokrati och värdegemenskap, av E. Wigforss. --Med biblioteksylfen som riktrote, av U. Willers.

1. Undén, Östen, 1886- . 2. World politics, 1945- . 3. Social sciences—Addresses, essays, lectures. I. Holmbäck, Åke Ernst Vilhelm, 1889- , ed.

VDC

FESTSKRIFT till professor Carl Forssell. Stockholm, 1956. 111 l. illus., port. 21cm.

"[Carl Forssells] publikationer," l. 6-13.

CONTENTS.--Carl Forssell 75 år.--Garage-skyddsrum, Katarinavägen-Björns trädgård, av G. Aminoff.--Matrix formulation of hyperstatic analysis, by S. O. Asplund.--Lösning av Flügges homogena ekvationssystem för cirkulärcylindriska skal med generatrisbelastning, av S. Eggwertz.--Nockens deformation på skivkonstruktioner av sadeltakstyp, av S. Eriksson.--Scheitel-und Wandspannungen an Tunnelöffnungen mit reichteckigem

(Continued)

NN X 3.58 m/v OC, 2b PC, 1, 2 SL ST, 1t, 2 (LC1, X1, Z1, Y1)

FESTSKRIFT till professor Carl Forssell. (Card 2)

Nutzquerschnitt und kreisbogenförmiger Überwölbung, von R. Hiltscher.--Some aspects on the solution of linear integral equations, by E. Hogner.--Circular plates with an eccentric hole, by A. Holmberg.--Brandsäkerhet hos betongpelare med T-sektion, av A. L. Johnson.--Försök med tresidigt upplagda korsarmerade plattor, av S. Kinnunen.--Inverkan av sammantryckning i väggar på belastningsfördelning och deformationer i bjälklag, av H. Nylander.--Ett icke-konservativt knäckningsproblem, av O. Pettersson.--Betongens krypning och relaxation, av L. Östlund.

1. Engineering--Addresses, essays, lectures. 2. Forssell, Carl, 1881- . t. 1956.

GFG

...Festskrift till professor skytteanus Axel Brusewitz. Utgiven till 60-årsdagen den 9 juni 1941. Uppsala [etc.] Almqvist & Wiksell [1941] 506 p. port. 24cm. (Skrifter utgivna av Statsvetenskapliga föreningen i Uppsala. 12)

"Professor Axel Brusewitz' tryckta skrifter. Bibliografi sammanställd av... Sixten Björkblom," p. 499-506.

Festschrift.

348057B. 1. Brusewitz, Axel Karl Adolf, 1881- . 2. Sweden—Govt. 3. Scandinavia—Politics. 4. Press. I. Ser.
N. Y. P. L. October 10, 1951

KAT

Festskrift till Verner Söderberg, den 4 oktober 1932. Stockholm, Aktiebolaget Familjeboken [1932]

4 p. l., 214 p. front. (port.) illus. (incl. maps, plans, facsims.) 25cm.
Bibliographical foot-notes.

CONTENTS.—Heckscher, E. F. Svenskt och utländskt under Sveriges stormaktstid.—Almhult, A. Sverige i en ny rysk encyklopedi.—Björkbom, C. De nya fotografiska metoderna och de vetenskapliga biblioteken.—Brulin, H. Lybeckers dom och benådning.—Wåhlin, H. Lejonkyrkorna.—Lundquister, B. Indiska miniatyrer.—Roswall, G. Geografiska sjöforskningar i Jämtlands fjällområde.—Örström, O. Befolkningstillväxtens inflytande på länders utrikespolitik.—Sjögren, O. Mont Blanc och Kebnekaise.—Ahnlund, N. Gustav Adolf och det evangeliska väsendet.—Hildebrand, B. Anna Messenia och släkten Rechenberg.—

(Continued on next card)

A 33-2529
[3]

Festschrift.

Festskrift till Verner Söderberg ... [1932] (Card 2)

CONTENTS—Continued.

Lundmark, E. Klaraabbedissornas guldkedja och drottning Helvig.—Berg, R. G. Småplock ur Bernhard von Beskows dagbok.—Svahn, A. Magna charta i nyare forskning.—Lorents, Y. Till "svarta veckans" historia.—Laurent-Täckholm, V. Bibliographical notes to the flora of Egypt.—Rudeberg, G. Kvartärgeologien i malmgeologiens tjänst.

Festschrift.

1. *Soderberg, Verner, 1872- A 33-2529

Title from N. Y. Pub. Libr. Printed by L. C.
[3]

YAM

Festskrift tillägnad Axel Hägerström den 6 september 1928, av filosofiska och juridiska föreningarna i Uppsala. Uppsala: Almqvist & Wiksells boktryckeri-a.-b. [, 1928.] 336 p. front. (port.) 4°.

no. 357 of 500 copies printed.

Mr. Mohr

1. Hägerström, Axel Anders Theodor, 1868- .
N. Y. P. L. May 24, 1929

AN
(Herrlin, A.)

Festskrift tillägnad Axel Herrlin den 30 mars 1935. Studier och uppsatser överräckta på sextiofemårsdagen av kolleger, lärjungar och vänner. Lund, Carl Bloms boktryckeri, 1935.

6 p. l., [9]-464 p. incl. illus. (incl. map) tables, diagr. front. (port.) 25½cm.

"Denna festskrift är tryckt i 300 numrerade exemplar, varav detta är n:r 253."

"Redaktion: Alf Nyman, Elof Gertz, Herman Siegvald."—Verso of t.-p.

"Litteratur": p. 52; bibliographical foot-notes.

CONTENTS.—Gadelius, B. Några blad ur en "minnesbok".—Jørgensen, J. Videnskabernes logiske grundlag.—Freudenthal, G. Om enheternas konkurrens i övingssyntesen.—Aall, A. Om et mellemfolkelig

(Continued on next card)

A C 36-884
[2]

Festschrift.

Festskrift tillägnad Axel Herrlin den 30 mars 1935 ... 1935.
(Card 2)

CONTENTS—Continued.

samspråk.—Anderberg, R. Webers lag och uppfattningen av supraliminala retningsintervall.—Rydbeck, O. Arkeologiska hågkomster från Ö. Vemmenhög.—Aspelin, G. Det disjunktiva omdömet.—Hjelmqvist, T. Pontus Wikner och "Kapten Puff".—Ohlson, N. G. Daniel Boëthius som pedagogisk tänkare. — Bergqvist, B. J. Skolan — ett stridsämme. — Petrén, A. Om behandlingen av minderåriga lagövertrådare.—Liljeqvist, E. Vissa förbindelselinjer mellan Schleiermacher och Boström.—Rydsjö, D. Tegnér och folkundervisningen.—Larsson, H. Estetik och pedagogik.—Granat, H. Höijers betydelse för Geijers uppfostringsteori.—Orrgård, S. Till frågan om personlighetsfostrans filosofiska förutsättningar.—Holmberg, O. Dryaden, najaden och oreaden.—Gierow, A. Till minnets psykologi.—Gertz, H. Till elementarbegreppens analys.—Bergelt, R.

(Continued on next card)

A C 36–884

[2]

Festskrift tillägnad Axel Herrlin den 30 mars 1935 ... 1935.
(Card 3)

CONTENTS—Continued.

Några engelska musikestetiker under 1700-talet.—Marc-Wogau, K. Om skiljandet mellan primära och sekundära kvaliteter.—Nilsson, A. Balders död och återkomst.—Segerstedt, T. T. Apriorismen hos Cudworth.—Thunberg, T. Cellens maskineri och teknikens.—Nyman, A. Begåvningsklasser eller intellektuell demokrati?—Rubin, E. Lydforskydningsforsøg.—Gertz, E. En iakttagelse över assymetrisk bilateral perception.—Siegvald, H. Undersökningar rörande studentexamen.—Sydow, C. W. v. Ett bidrag till riternas psykologi.—Lundmark, K. On Greek cosmogony and astronomy.—Åkesson, E. Possibilitas erroris.

1. Herrlin, Per Axel Samuel, 1870– 2. Psychology — Addresses, essays, lectures. 3. Philosophy—Addresses, essays, lectures. 4. Education—Addresses, essays, lectures. I. Nyman, Alf Tor, 1884– ed. II. Gertz, Elof Martin, 1887– joint ed. III. *Siegvald, Herman, 1894– joint ed.

A C 36–884

Title from N. Y. Pub. Libr. Printed by L. C.

[2]

YBX

Festskrift tillägnad E.O. Burman på hans 65-års dag den 7 Oktober 1910. Uppsala: K.W. Appelberg, 1910. 5 p.l., 307 p., 1 port. 4°.

1.Burman, Erik Olof. 2.Philosophy.—Systems and works.

1911

XAI

Festskrift tillägnad f.d.presidenten, förutvarande statsrådet juris doktor Karl Schlyter den 21 december 1949. [Stockholm, 1949] 413 p. maps, port. 25cm.

"Utgiven av Svensk juristtidning."
"Förteckning över Karl Schlyters skrifter, 1907–1949...p. 396–413.

583747B. 1. Law. 2. Criminal law. 3. Schlyter, Karl, 1879– .
I. Svensk juristidning.
N. Y. P. L.

January 22, 1952

YAM

Festskrift tillägnad Hans Larsson, den 18 februari 1927; studier och uppsatser överräckta på sextiofemårsdagen av kolleger och lärjungar. Stockholm: A. Bonniers förlag[, 1927]. xii, 393 p. front. (port.) 4°.

no. 330 of 500 copies printed.
Edited by Alf Nyman.

1. Larsson, Hans, 1862– . 2. Philosophy—Collections.
3. Nyman, Alf, 1884– .
N. Y. P. L.

October 21, 1927

AN
(Béen, I.)

Festskrift tillägnad hovpredikanten Isaac Béen på hans sextioårsdag den sjätte juni MCMXLVIII av vänner i Finland. Helsingfors, 1948. 196 p. illus. 25cm.

Also issued in Finnish with title: Juhlakirja jonka ovat omistaneet hovisaarnaaja Isaac Been'ille...
Includes music.

517289B. 1. Béen, Isaac, 1888– .
N. Y. P. L.

December 11, 1950

NICC

Festskrift tillägnad Hugo Pipping på hans sextioårsdag den 5 november 1924. Helsingfors, 1924. xii, 607 p. port. 26cm. (Svenska litteratursällskapet i Finland, Helsingfors. Skrifter. 175)

"Hugo Pippings tryckta skrifter, förtecknade av Hugo E. Pipping," p. 588–607.

1. Scandinavian languages. 2. Philology—Addresses, essays, lectures. 3. Pipping, Hugo, 1864–1944. I. Pipping, Hugo Edvard, 1895– . II. Ser.
NN R 4.53 OC, I PC, 1, 2, 3, I SL (LC1, ~~Z1~~, X1)

OAP

Festskrift tillägnad J. Arvid Hedvall den 18 januari 1948. [Göteborg, 1948] 659 p. illus. 26cm.

"Redaktionskommitté: Erik Hemlin...[och 4 andra]"
Contributions in Swedish, English or German.
"J. Arvid Hedvalls bibliografi, av Erik Hemlin," p. [651]–659.

466505B. 1. Hedvall, Johann Arvid, 1888– . 2. Science—Essays and misc. I. Hemlin, Erik, 1897– , ed.
N. Y. P. L.

December 29, 1948

MWEL
+
(Finland)

Festskrift tillägnad professor Nicken Rönngren på hans sjuttioårsdag 2. XI. 1950. Helsingfors, 1950. 229 p. illus. 30cm.

1. Stage—Finland. 2. Stage, 1926– . 3. Rönngren, Nicken, 1880–
NN R 5.53 OC PC, 1, 2, 3 SL (T4, LC1, ~~Z1~~, X1)

PSD p.v.19, no. 10.

Festskrift tillägnad Professor Otto Pettersson den 12. Februari 1923. [Helsingfors, 1923.] 114 p. front. (port.) illus. (incl. diagrs., tables.) 4°.

1923

Festskrift tillägnad R. A. Wrede.

(Abo. Akademi. Acta academiae aboensis. Humaniora. Abo,1931. 8°. v.7, port.)

Festskrift tillägnad Rainer von Fieandt på hans sextioårsdag. Helsingfors, 1950. 248 p. 26cm.

Includes bibliographies.

585283B. 1. Economics, 1925- —Scandinavian authors. 2. Fieandt, Rainer, von, 1890- .
N. Y. P. L. January 29, 1953

Festskrift til Valdemar Vedel fra venner og elever, udgivet paa hans halvfjerdsaarsdag den 9. november 1935. København, Gyldendalske boghandel—Nordisk forlag, 1935.

382 p. front. (port.) 25cm.

"Udgivet med understøttelse af Carlsbergfondet. Under redaktion af K. F. Plesner."—Verso of t.-p.

CONTENTS. — Tilegnelse. — Andersen, Vilhelm. Italien i dansk digtning.—Bang, Yrsa. Lidt om tysk masseregle.—Bredsdorff, Morten. Schweiz--en midteuropæisk firklang.—Bukdahl, Jørgen. Humanisme og nationalromantik.—Budtz-Jørgensen, Jørgen. Chamisso's "Peter Schlemihl" og det romantiske eventyr.—Elfelt, Kjeld. J. P. Jacobsen–Stendhal.—Frederiksen, Emil. Til Johannes Jørgensens "Stemninger" 1892.—

(Continued on next card)

A C 36-2017

[2]

Festskrift til Valdemar Vedel ... 1935. (Card 2)

CONTENTS—Continued.

Hesselaa, Peder. Dickens' skæbne i den kritiske litteratur fra 1870 til vore dage.—Jørgensen, Johannes. Vald. Vedel og Italien.—Kruuse, Jens. Terents og Molière.—Møller, Margrete. Naturfølelse og naturskildring hos brødrene Goncourt.—Møller, Niels. Grækernes naturfølelse.—Normann, I. C. "Viola".—Paludan, Hans Aage. Sagn om borgtapeter.—Plesner, K. F. Kardinal Bernis.—Ranulf, Svend. Valdemar Vedel som sociolog.—Riisager, Vagn. Émile Verhaeren og Victor Hugo.—Saxild, Georg. An den mond.—Topsøe-Jensen, H. G. Om eventyrkomedien Ole Lukøie.—Werner, Hans. Danske kongers epigrammer.—Rimestad, Christian. Nogle ord om Valdemar Vedel.—Møller, Arne J. Fortegnelse over skrifter af Valdemar Vedel (p. [357]-382)

1. Vedel, Valdemar, 1865- 2. Literature, Modern—Addresses, essays, lectures. I. Plesner, Knud Frederik, 1898- ed.

A C 36-2017

Title from N. Y. Pub. Libr.
Library of Congress [PN506.F4]

[2] 804

Festskrift til Vilhelm Thomsen fra disciple; udgivet i anledning af hans femogtyveårige doktorjubilæum, 23 marts 1869–23 marts 1894. København: Gyldendal, 1894. 4 p.l., 368 p. 8°.

Contents: ANDERSEN, D.: Reduplikationsvokalen i verbernes perfektformer. ANDERSEN, V.: Sammenfald og berøring. BESTHORN, R.: Aristoteles og de arabiske grammatikere. DRACHMANN, A. B.: Skyld og nemesis hos Æschylus. GIGAS, E.: Det første udkast til et berømt værk. HEIBERG, J. L.: Bidrag til Georg Vallas biografi. HUDE, K.: Spredte iagttagelser i Thukydid. JESPERSEN, O.: Om subtraktionsdannelser. JÓNSSON, F.: Fremmede ords behandling i oldnordisk digtning. JØRGENSEN, C.: Bemærkninger om brugen af præsens på latin. KINCH, K. F.: Hellenske kolonier på den makedoniske halvø. LANGE, H. O.: En thebansk klosterforstanders testamente. NYROP, Kr.: Et afsnit af ordenes liv. OLRIK, A.: Nogle personnavne i Starkaddigtningen. PEDERSEN, H.: Bidrag til den albanesiske sproghistorie. SETÄLÄ, E. N.: Ueber einen "gutturalen" nasal im urfinni-

(Continued)

N. Y. P. L. November 20, 1915.

Festskrift til Vilhelm Thomsen fra disciple... (Continued)

schen. SØRENSEN, S.: Til spørgsmaalet om Āditya'erne. THORSEN, P. K.: Glidning og spring. TRIER, G.: Ordet "Laban"s oprindelse. ØSTRUP, J.: Topografiske bemærkninger til Xenofon.

1. Thomsen, Vilhelm Ludvig, 1842- . 2. Andersen, Dines, 1861- . 3. Andersen, Vilhelm, 1864- . 4. Besthorn, Rasmus Olsen, 1844- . 5. Drachmann, Anders Björn, 1860- . 6. Gigas, Emil Leopold, 1849- . 7. Heiberg, Johan Ludvig, 1854- . 8. Hude, Karl, 1860- . 9. Jespersen, Otto, 1860- . 10. Jónsson, Finnur, 1858- . 11. Jørgensen, Christian Peter Julius, 1851- . 12. Kinch, Karl Frederik, 1853- . 13. Lange, Hans Ostenfeldt, 1863- . 14. Nyrop, Kristoffer, 1858- . 15. Olrik, Axel, 1864- . 16. Pedersen, Holger, 1867- . 17. Setälä, Emil Nestor, 1864- . 18. Sørensen, Søren, 1848- . 19. Thorsen, Peder Kristian, 1851- . 20. Trier, Gerson. 21. Østrup, Johannes Elith, 1867- .

N. Y. P. L. November 20, 1915.

FETTEL, JOHANNES, ed.

Der Betrieb in der Unternehmung; Festschrift für Wilhelm Rieger zu seinem 85. Geburtstag, hrsg. von Johannes Fettel und Hanns Linhardt. Stuttgart, W. Kohlhammer, 1963. xii, 478 p. port. 24cm.

1. Management--Addresses, essays, lectures. 2. Rieger, Wilhelm, 1878- I. Linhardt, Hanns, 1901- joint ed.

NN R 12.64 a/OC, I PC, 1, 2, I SL E, 1, 2, I (LC1, X1, Z1)

FIELHAUER, HELMUT, ed.

Volkskunde und Volkskultur; Festschrift für Richard Wolfram...zum 65. Geburtstag. Wien, A. Schendl [1968] 431 p. illus. 23cm. (Vienna. Universität. Institut für Volkskunde. Veröffentlichungen. Bd.2)

1. Wolfram, Richard, 1901- 2. Folk lore--Addresses, essays, lectures.

NN 6.69 w/ OI (PC)1, 2 (LC1, X1, Z1)

Fierz, Markus, *ed.*

Theoretical physics in the twentieth century; a memorial volume to Wolfgang Pauli, edited by M. Fierz and V. F. Weisskopf. New York, Interscience Publishers 1960.

x, 328 p. port, diagrs. 24 cm.

Includes bibliographies.

CONTENTS. — Foreword, by N. Bohr. — The turning point, by R. Kronig.—Erinnerungen an die Zeit der Entwicklung der Quantenmechanik, by W. Heisenberg.—Quantum theory of fields, until 1947, by G. Wentzel. — Regularization and non-singular interactions in quantum field theory, by F. Villars.—Das Pauli-Prinzip und die

(Continued)

NN * R 9.61 e/ OC, I PC, 1, 2, I SL ST, 1, 2t, I (LC1, X1, Z1)

2

FIERZ, MARKUS, ed. Theoretical physics in the twentieth century... (Card 2)

Lorentz-Gruppe, by R. Jost.—Pauli and the theory of the solid state, by H. B. G. Casimir.—Quantum theory of solids, by R. E. Peierls.—Statistische Mechanik, by M. Fierz.—Relativity, by V. Bargmann.—Exclusion principle and spin, by B. L. van der Waerden.—Fundamental problems, by L. D. Landau.—The neutrino, by C. S. Wu.—Bibliography Wolfgang Pauli. by C. P. Ens.

1. Pauli, Wolfgang, 1900-1958. 2. Physics--Addresses, essays, lectures. I. Weisskopf, Viktor, 1908- joint ed. t. 1960.

E-12
8776

Fijalkowski, Jürgen, *ed.*
Politologie und Soziologie. Otto Stammer zum 65. Geburtstag. Köln u. Opladen, Westdeutscher Verlag (1965)
388 p. 1 front. 25 cm.

First published in Kölner Zeitschrift für Soziologie und Sozialpsychologie, Jahrg. 17, 1965.
Includes bibliographies.

(Continued)

NN * R 5.67 1/ OC,I PC,1,2,I SL E,1,2,I
(LC1,X1,Z1)
4

FIJALKOWSKI, JÜRGEN, ed. Politologie und Soziologie. (Card 2)

CONTENTS.—Otto Stammer, von J. Fijalkowski.—Notiz über sozialwissenschaftliche Objektivität, von T. W. Adorno. — Bemerkungen über die Klassifikation politischer Regime, von R. Aron.—Die vergleichende Analyse historischer Wandlungen, von R. Bendix.—Wissenschafts- und zeitgeschichtliche Probleme der politischen Wissenschaft in Deutschland, von K. D. Bracher.—Rationalität revidiert, von D. Claessens.—Politische Wissenschaft und politische Biographie, von L. J. Edinger.—Nationale und transnationale Zusammenhänge, von A. Grosser.—Max Webers Idealtypus der Bürokratie und

(Continued)

FIJALKOWSKI, JÜRGEN, ed. Politologie und Soziologie. (Card 3)

die Organisationssoziologie, von R. Mayntz.—Überlegungen zur Stellung der Politik unter den Sozialwissenschaften, von P. von Oertzen.—Der Begriff des "Politischen Systems," von C. B. Robson.—Die Bildung aktiver Minderheiten als Ziel demokratischer Erziehung, von F. Borinski.—Unterschiede im Wahlverhalten der Männer und Frauen in Italien, von M. Dogan.—Bemerkungen zur Theorie des Gesetzgebungsstaats, von M. Drath.—Die Struktur der sozialen Klassen in Deutschland, von G. Eisermann.—Die Anpassung der SPD: 1914, 1933 und 1959, von O. K. Flechtheim.—Zur Problematik christlich-sozialer Parteien, von O. H. von der Gablentz.—Die sozialen Bewegungen "ethnischer" Gruppen, von R. Heberle. — Ra-

(Continued)

FIJALKOWSKI, JÜRGEN, ed. Politologie und Soziologie. (Card 4)

tionale Legitimierung eines Staatsreiches als soziologisches Problem, von E. E. Hirsch.—Beruf und Industrie als Strukturprinzipien gewerkschaftlicher Organisation, von H. Kluth.—Kanada und die Vereinigten Staaten, von S. M. Lipset.—Zur entwicklungssoziologischen Analyse von Parteisystemen, von S. Rokkan.—Geschichte und Gesellschaft im Denken Diltheys, von H.-J. Lieber.—Max Weber—Das soziologische Werk, von J. Winckelmann.

1. Political science—Addresses, essays, lectures. 2. Stammer, Otto. I. Title.

L-10
4900
fasc. 18

FILOSOFINEN YHDISTYS, Helsingfors.
Studia logico-mathematica et philosophica, in honorem Rolf Nevanlinna die natali eius septuagesimo, 22. X. 1965. Helsinki, 1965. 320 p. port. 25cm. (Acta philosophica fennica. fasc. 18)

English, German or French.

Published by the society under its later name: Societas philosophica fennica.

(Continued)

NN 4. 66 r/c OS, I PC, 1, 2, 3, I ST, Ic, 3 (LC1, X1, Z1)
5

FILOSOFINEN YHDISTYS, Helsingfors. Studia logico-mathematica et philosophica... (Card 2)

Includes bibliographies.

CONTENTS. --Information and esthetic evaluation, by G. Elfving. --Zur arithmetischen Klassifikation reeller Zahlen, by G. Hasenjaeger. --On a combined system of inductive logic, by J. Hintikka. --Formal studies on the character of complete sets of basic vectors in a special quantum mechanical structure, by G. Järnefelt and P. Mattila. --Bemerkungen zu den sprachlichen und künstlerischen Symbolen, by R. Kauppi. --Die Ökonomie der Wissenschaft, by O. Ketonen. --Logical calculus and

(Continued)

FILOSOFINEN YHDISTYS, Helsingfors. Studia logico-mathematica et philosophica... (Card 3)

realizability, by S.C. Kleene. --Die klassische Analysis als eine konstruktive Theorie, by P. Lorenzen. --Bemerkungen zur Vektoranalysis, by I. Simo Louhivaara. --Sur deux principes généraux d'analyse mathématique et quelques applications, by A. Markouchevitch. --On models of Zermelo-Fraenkel set theory satisfying the axiom of constructibility, by A. Mostowski. --Versuch zur Überbrückung der Lücke in der Informationstheorie zwischen Datenverarbeitung und Bewusstseinsinhalt des Perzipienten, by Y.

(Continued)

FILOSOFINEN YHDISTYS, Helsingfors. Studia Logico-mathematica et philosophica... (Card 4)

Reenpää. --On the theory of normal families, by A. Robinson. --Nominalismus als Widerspruch, by U. Saarnio. --On some algebraic notions in the theory of truth-functions, by A. Salomaa. --On some relations between thought and hope, by M. Siirala. --On the number of dimensions of physical space, by E. Stenius. --A reconsideration of the highest intrinsic value in Kant, by J. Tenkku. --Evidential support, by H. Törnebohm. --Synthetische Urteile a priori, by B.L. van der Waerden. --"And next", by G.H. von Wright. --Verzeichnis der Veröffentlichungen von Rolf

(Continued)

FILOSOFINEN YHDISTYS, Helsingfors. Studia logico-mathematica et philosophica... (Card 5)

Nevanlinna, by I. Simo Louhivaara.

1. Logic, Symbolic and mathematical. 2. Philosophy--Addresses, essays, lectures. 3. Nevanlinna, Rolf Herman, 1895- . I. Series. t. 1965.

F-11
692

FILOSOFISKA studier tillägnade Konrad Marc-Wogan den 4 april 1962. [Redaktör: Ann-Mari Henschen-Dahlguist; i redaktionen: Ingemar Hedenius] Uppsala, 1962. 178 p. 30cm.

"Författarna till denna skrift...tillhör [alla] Filosofiska institutionen eller Filosofiska föreningen i Uppsala."

CONTENTS. --Sanning ovh sannolikhet i bevisvärderingen, av P.O. Ekelöf. --Värdenihilismens tillämpningsområde, av P. Ericson. --Beryllios och Andromenes eller Den egensindige

(Continued)

NN 8. 65 s/OC, III, IIIb, IV (OS)I, Ib+, II, IIb+ PC, 1, 2, I, II, III, IV SL (LC1, X 1, Z1)
3

FILOSOFISKA studier tillägnade Konrad Marc-Wogan den 4 april 1962... (Card 2)

resenären, av L. Gustafsson. --Några kommentarer om "mening," av E. Götlind. --A pragmatic approach to modal logic, by S. Halldén. --Om sanning i skönlitteraturen, av I. Hedenius. --Om epistemiska "kunna"-satser, av A.-M. Henschen-Dahlquist. --Mätning, av S. Kanger. --Det nya omröstningsförfarandet i tvistemål, några anmärkningar, av S. Larsson. --Om inneslutningsförhållandets karaktär av irreflexiv relation, av A.H.D. MacLeod. --Om formerna i Platons kunskapslära, av H. Morin. --Om innehallspykologi och funktionspsykologi samt

(Continued)

Write on slip words underlined below and class mark— PTI

Finsterwalder-Festschrift.

(Zeitschrift für Gletscherkunde. Leipzig, 1932. Bd.20, p.i-xxi, 1-199-543. diagrs., plates, map, port.)

Form 100b [ii-18-32 25m]

FILOSOFISKA studier tillägnade Konrad Marc-Wogan den 4 april 1962... (Card 3)

verkligmenande och verklighet, av F. Norström. --Inledning till en föreläsningsserie VT 1962 om sociologiens teori, av T. Segerstedt. --Ett förslag till en begränsning av uttrycksmedlen i predikatlogiken, av L. Svenonius. --Peirce's theory of meaning, by H. Wennerberg. --Interpretations of deontic logic, by L. Aqvist.

1. Marc-Wogau, Konrad, 1902- 2. Philosophy--Addresses, essays, lectures. I. Upsala, Sweden, Universitet. Filosofiska institutionen. II. Upsala, Sweden, Universitet. Filosofiska föreningen. III. Henschen-Dahlquist, Ann Mari, ed. IV. Hedenius, Ingemar, 1908- , ed.

*OAC

Fischel, Walter Joseph, 1902- *ed.*

Semitic and Oriental studies; a volume presented to William Popper, professor of Semitic languages, emeritus, on the occasion of his seventy-fifth birthday, October 29, 1949. Berkeley, University of California Press, 1951.

xii, 456 p. illus., port., fold. map. 26 cm. (University of California publications in Semitic philology, v. 11)

Bibliographical footnotes.

1. Oriental philology—Addresses, essays, lectures. 2. Semitic philology—Addresses, essays, lectures. 3. Oriental studies. 4. Popper, William, 1874- I. Title. (Series: California. University. University of California publications in Semitic philology, v. 11)

PJ3002.C3 vol. 11 495.04 A 51-9375

———— Copy 2. PJ26.P6

California. Univ. Libr. for Library of Congress [5]†

E-14
1647

Finanz- und Geldpolitik im Umbruch. Hrsg. von Heinz Haller und Horst Claus Recktenwald. Mainz, v. Hase u. Koehler (1969). 511 p. 24cm.

German or English.
Published on the occasion of Robert Nöll von der Nahmer's 70th birthday.

(Continued)

NN*R 6.71 w/ OC,I,II,III PC, 1,2,I,II,III SL E,1,2,I,II,III (LC1,X1,Z1)

2

D-14
8542

FISCHER, GEORG, 1897-
Volk und Geschichte; Studien und Quellen zur Sozialgeschichte und historischen Volkskunde. Festgabe dem Verfasser zum 65. Geburtstag dargebracht. Kulmbach, Freunde der Plassenburg, 1962. 395 p. 22cm. (Die Plassenburg. Schriften für Heimatkunde und Kulturpflege in Ostfranken. Bd.17)

Includes sources.

(Continued)

NN R 2.64 e/ OC (OS)I PC, 1, 2, 3, I, II SL E, 1, II (LC1, X1, Z1)

2

FINANZ- und Geldpolitik im Umbruch. (Card 2)

"Schrifttum von Robert Nöll von der Nahmer": p. 481-484.
"Über das 'Lehrbuch der Finanzwissenschaft,'" von H. C. Recktenwald: p. 485-499.
Bibliographical footnotes.

1. Finance--Addresses, essays, lectures. 2. Monetary policy. I. Nöll von der Nahmer, Robert. II. Haller, Heinz, ed. III. Recktenwald, Horst Claus, ed.

FISCHER, GEORG, 1897- . Volk und Geschichte... (Card 2)

Bibliographical references included in "Anmerkungen," p. 391-395.

1. Germany--Soc. condit. 2. Germany--Hist.--Addresses, essays, lectures. 3. Folk lore--Germany. I. Series. II. Title.

TIB

Finanza pubblica contemporanea. Studi di C. Arena ...[ed altri] in onore di Jacopo Tivaroni. Bari, G. Laterza & figli, 1950. 445 p. 21cm. (Biblioteca di cultura moderna. n. 469)

"Bibliografia cronologica degli scritti del Prof. Jacopo Tivaroni," p. 9-16.

1. Tivaroni, Jacopo, 1877- . 2. Finance. I. Arena, Celestino. II. Ser.

NN*R 6.53 OC,I PC,1,2,I SL E,1,2, I (LC1,~~Z1~~,X1)

TAH

Fisher, Frederick Jack, *ed.*

Essays in the economic and social history of Tudor and Stuart England, in honour of R. H. Tawney. Cambridge [Eng.] University Press, 1961.

235 p. port., tables. 23 cm.

Bibliographical footnotes.

CONTENTS.—Tawney's century, by F. J. Fisher.—Protestantism and the rise of capitalism, by C. Hill.—Habitation versus improvement: the debate on enclosure by agreement, by M. Beresford.—Industries in the countryside, by J. Thirsk.—The fruits of office: the case of Robert Cecil, first earl of Salisbury, 1596-1612, by L. Stone.—England

(Continued)

NN*R 11.61 g/ OC PC,1,2, 3 SL E,1,2,3 (LC1,X1,Z1)

2

Fisher, Frederick Jack, *ed.* Essays in the economic and social history ... 1961. (Card 2)

CONTENTS—Continued.

and the Mediterranean, 1570–1670, by R. Davis.—Charles I and the city, by R. Ashton.—The officers of the exchequer, 1625–42, by G. E. Aylmer.—The accounts of the Kingdom, 1642–49, by D. H. Pennington.—Sir John Banks, financier: an essay on Government borrowing under the later Stuarts, by D. C. Coleman.

1. Economic history--Gt. Br., 1461-1760. 2. Great Britain--Soc. condit., 1485-1700. 3. Tawney, Richard Henry, 1880- .

D-16
4653

FISHER, RUTH A., ed.

J. Franklin Jameson: a tribute. Edited by Ruth Anna Fisher [and] William Lloyd Fox. Washington, D. C., Catholic University of America Press [1965]

ix, 137 p. 22 cm.

Includes bibliographical references.

CONTENTS.—Introduction, by R. A. Fisher and W. L. Fox.—A tribute, by R. A. Fisher.—American religious history, by J. T. Ellis.—The List of doctoral dissertations in history, by W. L. Fox.—The

(Continued)

NN* R 2.66 g/ OC, I PC, 1, I SL AH, 1 (LC1, X1, Z1) 3

FISHER, RUTH A., ed. J. Franklin Jameson: a tribute. (Card 2)

origin of the National Historical Publications Commission, by W. G. Leland.—"Inevitably" the first incumbent, by V. W. Clapp.—The sage and the young man, by A. Nevins.—Hope for the young scholar, by M. R. Dearing.—Dr. Jameson's other side, by C. W. Garrison.—The Atlas of the historical geography of the United States, by J. K. Wright.—The Dictionary of American biography, by D. Malone.—The National Archives, by F. Shelley.—Jameson as editor, by B. C. Shafer.—J. F. H., by D. C. Mearns.—A bibliography of J. Franklin Jameson's writings, by D. H. Mugridge (p. 103–137)

(Continued)

FISHER, RUTH A., ed. J. Franklin Jameson: a tribute. (Card 3)

1. Jameson, John Franklin, 1859-1937. I. Fox, William Lloyd, joint ed.

HWB

Flenley, Ralph, *ed.*

Essays in Canadian history presented to George MacKinnon Wrong for his eightieth birthday; edited by R. Flenley. Toronto, The Macmillan company of Canada, limited, 1939.

x p., 1 l., 372 p. front. (port.) 22½ cm.

CONTENTS.—Professor G. M. Wrong and history in Canada, by Chester Martin.—Background and external influences: The British background, by Keith Feiling. The French revolution and French Canada, by R. Flenley. Canada and Ireland: a contrast in constitutional development, by D. J. McDougall. Two North American federations: a comparison, by Edgar McInnis.—Political and constitutional: The terms of the British North America act, by W. P. M. Kennedy. Edward Blake and Canadian liberal nationalism, by F. H. Underhill. Conservatism and national unity, by D. G. Creighton. The position of the lieutenant-governor in

(Continued on next card)

40-10106

[4] Festschrift

Flenley, Ralph, *ed.* Essays in Canadian history ... 1939. (Card 2)

CONTENTS—Continued.

British Columbia in the years following confederation, by W. N. Sage. Permanent factors in Canadian external relations, by G. P. de T. Glazebrook.—Social and economic: Geographical determinants in Canadian history, by A. R. M. Lower. The survival of Canada, by J. B. Brebner. Strathspey in the Canadian fur-trade, by W. S. Wallace. The policy of creating land reserves in Canada, by R. G. Riddell.—Cultural: The cultural development of New France before 1760, by R. M. Saunders. The formative period of the Canadian protestant churches, by G. W. Brown.

1. Canada—Hist.—Addresses, essays, lectures. 2. Wrong, George McKinnon, 1860- I. Title.

Library of Congress F1026.F56 40-10106

[4] 971.004

D-13
185

FLORILÈGE pour Albert Samain. [Commémoration du poète à Lille le 4 octobre, avec les discours prononcés à l'inauguration du monument et hommages de: Germaine Acremant, et al. Lille] Les "Amis de Lille," 1931. 1 v. illus., ports. 22cm.

Edited by Philippe Kah.

1. Samain, Albert Victor, 1858-1900. I. Acremant, Germaine (Poulain), 1898- . II. Amis de Lille. III. Kah, Philippe, ed. IV. Kah, Philippe. NN 5.61 a/4 OC, I, III, IVbo SL (OS)II, IIb PC, 1, I, II, III (LC1, X1, Z1)

NRE

FLORILEGIUM AMICITIAE. Till Emil Zilliacus, 1. IX. MCMLIII. [Helsingfors, H. Schildt, 1953] 219 p. illus., ports. 23cm.

1. Zilliacus, Emil, 1878- . 2. Greek literature—Addresses, essays, lectures.

NN**X 7.54 OC, PC, 1, 2 SL (LC1, Z1, X1)

GMB

Förbundet för svenskt församlingsarbete i Finland r.f., Helsingfors.

Borgå stift och dess herde; festskrift tillägnad biskop Max von Bonsdorff, 23 augusti 1952. Helsingfors, 1952. xxxii, 278 p. illus., ports. 25cm. (Lutherska litteraturstiftelsens svenska publikationer, n:o 6)

1. Bonsdorff, Max von, bp., 1882-
2. Borgå, Finland (Diocese). I. Title.
NN** X 10.53 (OC)1b, I OS, 2b PC, 1, 2, I SL (U 1, LC1, Z1, X1)

E-12
6755

FOERSTE, WILLIAM, ed.

Festschrift für Jost Trier zum 70. Geburtstag. Hrsg. von William Foerste und Karl Heinz Borck. Köln, Böhlau, 1964. 496 p. illus., port. 24cm.

Bibliographical footnotes.

CONTENTS.--Begriff und Vorkommen von Struktur in der Sprache, von P. Hartmann.--Zum Sinnbezirk des Geschehens im heutigen Deutsch, von L. Weisgerber.--Murmelspiel; ein Experiment, von W. Mohr.--

(Continued)

NN * R 10.66 r/c OC, I, IIbo PC, 1, 2, 3, I SL (LC1, X1, Z1)
[I] 4

FOERSTE, WILLIAM, ed. Festschrift für Jost Trier zum 70. Geburtstag. (Card 2)

Verschmitzt; von Leistung und Werden eines Wortinhalts im Sinnsprengel der Schlauheit,von H. Schwarz. --Bild; ein etymologischer Versuch, von W. Foerste. --Fechten, von D. Ader. --"Germanisch" $\bar{e}^2$ im Friesischen, von D. Hofmann. --Die Völkerschichtung Ostdeutschlands im Lichte der Ortsnamenforschung, von B. Schier. --Die Herkunft der Liudger-, Lebuin-, und Marklo-Überlieferung; ein brieflicher Vorbericht, von K. Hauck. --Mittelalterliche Texte als Aufgabe, von K. Stackmann. --Hraban und das Petrusbild der 37. Fitte im Heliand, von J. Rathofer. --(Continued)

---

*C-5 p.v. 164

Foncke, Robert

Feestbundel opgedragen aan Prof. Dr. Robert Foncke, ter gelegenheid van zijn zestigsten verjaardag, 1 Juli 1949. Aalst, G. Boeykens, 1950. 141 p. port. 28cm.

"Keurbladzijden uit het werk van Prof. Dr. Robert Foncke." p.[41]-135

"Bibliographie van Prof. Dr. Robert Foncke door Dr. Rob Roemans," p. 21-39.

Bibliographical foot- notes.

NN**R 11.54 j/ OC,I PC,1,2 SL (LC1,X1)

FOERSTE, WILLIAM, ed. Festschrift für Jost Trier zum 70. Geburtstag. (Card 3)

Die "Sprüche" Hergers; Artzugehörigkeit und Gruppenbildung, von H. Moser. --Zur Chronologie der Lieder Heinrichs von Morungen, von F. Maurer. --Walthers Lied Aller werdekeit ein füegerinne, von K. H. Borck. --Tristans Abschied; ein Vergleich der Dichtung Gotfrits von Strassburg mit ihrer Vorlage Thomas, von P. Wapnewski. --Apophthegmata teutsch; über Ursprung und Wesen der "Simplicianischen Scherzreden", von G. Weydt. --Vers ist tanzhafte Rede; ein Beitrag zur deutschen Prosodie aus dem achtzehnten Jahrhundert, von H. J. Schrimpf. --Eines (Continued)

3-MCZ
F44.F6

FONDATION LELO FIAUX, Lausanne.

Lélo Fiaux. [Réalisation: Edwin Engelberts et André Kuenzi. Textes de Réne Berger, et al.] Lausanne [Edition]: Fondation Lélo Fiaux; [Diffusion]: Editions Spes, 1967. 66 [7] p. illus., facsim., plates(7 col.), ports. 19cm.

Commemorative volume.

1. Fiaux, Lélo, 1909-1964. I. Engelberts, Edwin, ed. II. Kuenzi, André, joint ed. III. Title.

NN 12.69 k/(OC)I, II, III OS PC, 1, I, II SL A, 1, I, II B (LC1, X1, Z1)

FOERSTE, WILLIAM, ed. Festschrift für Jost Trier zum 70. Geburtstag. (Card 4)

matt geschliffnen Spiegels dunkler Widerschein. E. T. A. Hoffmanns Erzählkunst, von W. Preisendanz. --Thomas Manns Erzählung "Tristan", von W. Rasch. --Die Rezeption Swinburnes in der deutschen Literatur der Jahrhundertwende, von K.G. Just. --Verzeichnis der Schriften Jost Triers, von D. Ader.

1. German literature--Addresses, essays, lectures. 2. German language--Addresses, essays, lectures. 3. Trier, Jost. I. Borck, Karl Heinz, joint ed. II. Borck, Karl Heinz.

F-10
6981

Foote, B. P.

Denominational terms in Gregg shorthand. Washington, D. C., Home study institute, c1944. 35 l. 21 x 28cm.

John Robert Gregg Shorthand Collection

1. Shorthand, Religious.

NN R 8.63 OC PC,1 SL (LC1,X1,Z1)

D-16
9530

FOG, MOGENS, 1904-

Mogens Fog: sine meningers mod. Udsendt på 60 års dagen den 9. juni 1964 af en kreds af venner [Redaktion: Børge Houmann. København] Forlaget Sirius [1964] 246 p. 23cm.

1. Essays, Danish. I. Houmann, Børge, ed. II. Title: Sine meningers mod.

NN R 11.66 r/ OC,I PC,1,I, II SL (LC1, X1, Z1)

NCY

For Hilaire Belloc, essays in honor of his 71st birthday, edited by Douglas Woodruff. New York, Sheed & Ward, 1942.

vi, 218 p. 21½cm.

CONTENTS.—Hilaire Belloc and the counter-revolution, by Douglas Jerrold.—The man who tried to convert the Pope, by R. A. Knox.—On Newman, Chesterton, and exorbitance, by Douglas Woodruff.—Alpine mysticism and "cold philosophy," by Arnold Lunn.—The piety of Cicely, duchess of York: a study in late medieval culture, by C. A. J. Armstrong.—The meaning of Anthony Trollope, by Christopher Hollis.—Byzantium to Oxford, by Gervase Mathew.—The library at Naworth, by David Mathew.—André Chénier, by J. B. Morton.—The pre-conquest saints of Canterbury, by W. A. Pantin.—The myth of Arthur, by David Jones.

1. *Belloc, Hilaire, 1870- 2. English essays. 3. History—Addresses, essays, lectures. 4. Catholic literature—Hist. & crit. 5. Religious thought—Hist. I. Woodruff, Douglas, 1897- ed.

42-10264

Library of Congress AC5.F67 [10] Festschrift 042

---

*NCV

Folger Shakespeare Library, *Washington, D. C.*

Joseph Quincy Adams memorial studies, ed. by James G. McManaway, Giles E. Dawson [and] Edwin E. Willoughby. Washington, 1948.

x, 808 p. 7 plates, port. 25 cm.

"Bibliography, 1904–1946, of Joseph Quincy Adams": p. 13–20.

1. Shakespeare, William—Criticism and interpretation. 2. English literature—Early modern (to 1700)—Hist. & crit. 3. Adams, Joseph Quincy, 1881–1946. I. McManaway, James Gilmer, 1899- II. Title.

PR423.F6 820.903 48—10467*

Library of Congress [49n7] Festschrift card

---

*PBN
(Weinreich, M.)

FOR Max Weinreich on his seventieth birthday; studies in Jewish languages, literature, and society. London, Mouton, 1964. 527 p. port. 27cm.

Added t.p. in Yiddish.

Text in English with Yiddish summary or in Yiddish with English summary.

Bibliographical footnotes. Includes bibliography of Weinreich's works.

1. Judaism--Addresses, essays, lectures. 2. Judaism--Essays. 3. Weinreich, Max, 1894-

NN R 7.65 l/ OC PC, 1, 3 SL I, 2, 3 (LC1, X1, Z1) [I]

E-11
760

For Roman Ingarden; nine essays in phenomenology. 's-Gravenhage, M. Nijhoff, 1959.

viii, 179 p. 24 cm.

Bibliographical footnotes.

CONTENTS.—Editorial: the second phenomenology, by A. T. Tymieniecka.—Roman Ingarden, critique de Bergson, par J. M. Fataud.—Some remarks on the ego in the phenomenology of Husserl, by C. van Peursen.—The empirical and transcendental ego, by M. Natanson.—Rencontre et dialogue, par E. Minkowski.—Quelques thèmes d'une phénoménologie de rêve, par J. Héring.—Man and his life-world, by J. Wild.—Die Verwirklichung des Wesens in der Sprache der Dichtung: Gustave Flaubert, von F. Kaufmann.—Le langage de la poésie, par J. F. Mora.—L'analyse de l'idée et la participation, par A. T. Tymieniecka.

1. Ingarden, Roman, 1893- . 2. Phenomenalism--Addresses, essays, lectures. I. Tymieniecka, Anna Teresa.

NN * R 7. 60 m/ OC, I PC, 1, 2, I SL (LC1, X1, Z1)

STR

Foreningen for højskoler og landbrugsskoler.
Danmarks folkehøjskole, 1844–1944. Festskrift udgivet af Foreningen for højskoler og landbrugsskoler. København, Det Danske forlag, 1944. 593 p. illus. 26cm.

"Litteratur om folkehøjskolen," p. [594]

516713B. 1. People's high schools —Denmark. I. Title.
N. Y. P. L. August 29, 1950

NHS p.v.6

For Waling-om. 1821–1911. Oanbean oan Waling Dykstra op syn 90e jierdei troch ytlike Friezen en Friezinnen. Samler: F. J. de Zee. Ljouwert: W. A. Eisma cs. [1911] 157 p. incl. mounted front. mounted illus. (incl. ports.) 24cm.

"Eare-Muzyk" (organ or piano), p. [37–39]

CONTENTS.—Oanspraek oan Waling-om.—De stambeam fen Waling-om.—Doaitse mei de Noardske Balke.—Ho't yn 1821 de lytse Waling to boek steld is.—Lokwinsken fen selskippen ensf.—Bydragen fen skriuwers en skriuwsters.

1. Dykstra, Waling Gerritsz., 1821-1914. I. Zee, F. Jacob de, ed.
N. Y. P. L. July 13, 1938

E-12
7320

FORKOSCH, MORRIS D., ed.
Essays in legal history in honor of Felix Frankfurter. Indianapolis, Bobbs-Merrill co. [1966] xix, 647 p. port. 24cm.

"Published under the auspices of the Northeastern states branch of the American society for legal history."

Bibliographical footnotes.

1. Frankfurter, Felix, 1882-1965. 2. Law--Hist.

NN R 1.67 a/ OC PC,1,2 SL E,1 (LC1, X1, Z1)

---

* ITE

FORENING FOR BOGHAANDVAERK, Copenhagen.
Bogbinderen August Sandgren. [Redaktion: Henrik Park og Carl Thomsen. [København] 1952. 113 p. illus., port. 25cm.

Various contributors.
Bibliography, p. 112-113.

1. Sandgren, August, 1893-1934. 2. Bookbinding, Danish. I. Park, Henrik, 1918- , ed. II. Thomsen, Carl, 1894- , ed.

NN ** Z 12.54 (OC) I, II OS PC, 1, 2, I, II SL (LC1, Z1, X1)

MA

Form und Inhalt; kunstgeschichtliche Studien; Otto Schmitt zum 60. Geburtstag am 13. Dezember 1950, dargebracht von seinen Freunden. [Herausgeber: Hans Wentzel] Stuttgart, W. Kohlhammer [1951?] 351 p. illus. 27cm.

Bibliography, p. 347-350.

1. Schmitt, Otto, 1890-1951. 2. Art—Essays and misc. I. Wentzel, Hans , ed.

NN* 12.54 m/ OC,I PC,1,2,I SL A,1,2,I (Z1,LC1,X1)

Copy only words underlined & classmark— MWEG

FÖRENINGEN DROTTNINGHOLMSTEATERNS VÄNNER.
Teaterhistoriska studier. Uppsala, Almqvist & Wiksell boktr., 1940. 175 p. illus. 26cm. (Föreningen Drottningholmsteaterns vänner. Skrifter. 2)

"Hans Kunglig Höghet Prins Eugen. . . ägnas denna bok, 1. 8. 1940."
Text chiefly in Swedish, one article each in Danish and Norwegian.
Bibliography, p. 166-167; bibliographical footnotes.
CONTENTS. – Problem och arbetsuppgifter inom svensk teaterhistoria, av A. Beijer. – Teatermuseet ved Christiansborg, af R. Neiiendam. – Det Teaterhistoriske museum i Bergen, av S. Johannesen. – (Continued)

NN** R 5. 57 c/ (OC)II OS, I PC, 1, 2, 3, 4, I, II (T6, LC1, X1, Z1)

MAK

Formositas Romanica. Beiträge zur Erforschung der romanischen Kunst, Joseph Gantner zugeeignet. Frauenfeld, Huber [1958]

195 p. illus., plates. 23 cm.

Includes bibliographical references.

CONTENTS.—Die zwei Quellpunkte der romanischen Plastik Frankreichs: Toulouse und Cluny, von G. Paulsson.—Zur Stilbestimmung der figürlichen Kunst Deutschlands und des westlichen Europas im Zeitraum zwischen 1190 und 1250, von O. Homburger.—La troisième sculpture romane, par J. Baltrušaitis. — Vom ältesten Einsidler Gnadenbild, von L. Birchler.—Heidnisch oder christlich? Stammen die bekannten, in Arkona ausgegrabenen Mauerreste aus einem romanischen Baudenkmal? Von E. Dyggve.—Saalraum und Basilika

NN* R 9. 59 g/ OC PC, 1, 2 SL A, 1, 2 (LC1, X1, Z1) [1]

FÖRENINGEN DROTTNINGHOLMSTEATERNS VÄNNER.
Teaterhistoriska studier... (Card 2)

Teatermuseet på Drottningholm, av A. Beijer. – Ett finskt teaterjubileum, av H. Grevenius. – Ett svenskt direktörspar i Finland för 140 år sedan, av C. Deurell. – Bournonvillestudier, av S. Torsslow. – Förberedelser för en svensk talscen under 1700-talet, av L. Breitholtz. – Teater i Malmö och Lund i början av 1800-talet, av A. Baeckström -- Kring en gammal teatermålare, av H. Grevenius.

1. Stage--Sweden. 2. Stage--Finland. 3. Stage--Museums and collections--Scandinavia. 4. Eugene Napoleon Nicholas, prince of Sweden, 1865-1947. I. Series. II. Title.

Formositas Romanica ... [1958] (Card 2)

CONTENTS—Continued.

im frühen Mittelalter, von E. Lehmann. — Zisterzienser-Romanik: kritische Gedanken zur jüngsten Literatur, von J. A. Schmoll gen. Eisenwerth.—Architecture civile en Suisse à l'époque romane, par L. Blondel.

1. Art, Romanesque--Addresses, essays, lectures. 2. Gantner, Joseph, 1896-

E-10
7131

FORSCHUNGEN zu Staat und Verfassung; Festgabe für Fritz Hartung. [Hrsg. von Richard Dietrich und Gerhard Oestreich] Berlin, Duncker & Humblot [1958] 538 p. port. 24cm.

Bibliographical footnotes.

CONTENTS. — Kaisertum und Reichsteilung, zur Divisio regnorum von 806, von W. Schlesinger. -- Lehnrecht und Erbrecht in der brandenburgischen Territorialpolitik, von J. Schultze. — Zur Entwicklung der freien Landgemeinden im Mittelalter, Fehde, Land- frieden, Schiedsgericht,

(Continued)

NN 4.59 p/OC, I, II, IIIbo PC, 1, 2, 3, I, II SL E, 1, 2, 3, I, II (LC1, X1, Z1)

VDA
(Verein)

Forschungsarbeit; Festgabe Carl von Bach zum achtzigsten Geburtstag, dargebracht von R. Baumann, E. Berl, P. Goerens... [und Anderen]. Berlin: VDI-Verlag, G.m.b.H., 1927. 95 p. incl. diagrs., tables. front. (port.), illus. 4°. (Verein deutscher Ingenieure, Berlin. Forschungsarbeiten auf dem Gebiete des Ingenieurwesens. Heft 295.)

Bibliographical footnotes.

1. Bach, Carl von, 1847- . 2. Materials—Testing. 3. Ser.
N. Y. P. L. October 11, 1927

FORSCHUNGEN zu Staat und Verfassung... (Card 2)

von H. Aubin. — Drei lutherische Landesfürsten in Brandenburg; ein Beitrag zur Entstehung der märkischen Landeskirche, von W. Hoppe. — Die Stellung der Reichsstände zur Römischen Königswahl seit den Westfälischen Friedensverhandlungen, von G. Scheel. — Die deutsche Bundesakte und der schweizerische Bundesvertrag von 1815, von W. Näf. — Friedrich Meinecke als Kritiker der Bismarckschen Reichsverfassung, von G. Kotowski. — Jacobus Lampadius, seine Bedeutung für die deutsche Verfassungsgeschichte und Staatstheorie, von R. Dietrich. — Gottfried Wilhelm Leibniz und Hugo Grotius, von K. Müller. — Wandlungen der Tendenz in Leibniz' Bearbei-

(Continued)

OYM

FORTSCHRITTE der Uhrentechnik durch Forschung; vom Skisprung zum Skiflug. Festschrift für Herrn Dr.-Ing. ehrenhalber Reinhard Straumann. [Stuttgart, Druck und Kommissionsverlag von J. F. Steinkopf, 1952] 253 p. illus. (part col.), port. 25cm.

Bibliography at end of each chapter.

1. Clocks and watches, 1952. 2. Ski-running. 3. Straumann, Reinhard, 1892-

NN**R X 5.54 OC, 3b PC, 1, 2, 3 SL ST, 1, 3 (Z1, LC1, X1)

FORSCHUNGEN zu Staat und Verfassung... (Card 3)

tungen des Entretien 1677-1691? Von L. Knabe. — Die monarchische Regierungsform in Brandenburg-Preussen, von H. O. Meisner. — Die preussische Zentralverwaltung in den Anfängen Friedrich Wilhelms I, von C. Hinrichs. -- Provinz und Staat in der altpreussischen Finanzwirtschaft; Westpreussen unter Friedrich dem Grossen, von H. Haussherr. — Die Stadtvertretungen in Krefeld und Bochum im 19. Jahrhundert, ein Beitrag zur Geschichte der Selbstverwaltung der rheinischen und westfälischen Städte, von H. Croon. — Zur historischen und rechtlichen Problematik von Grenze und Flussgebiet in Nordamerika, von H. Binder Johnson. — État et commissaire; récherches sur la

(Continued)

F-10
8294

FOSTER, I. LL., ed.
Culture and evironment; essays in honor of Sir Cyril Fox. Edited by I. L. L. Foster and L. Alcock. London, Routledge & Kegan Paul [1963] 538 p. illus., plates, maps (part fold.), diagrs. (part fold.) plans. 26cm.

Includes bibliographies.

1. Fox, Sir Cyril Fred, 1882- 2. Wales--Archaeology. 3. Great Britain --Archaeology. 4. Architecture --Gt. Br. I. Alcock, Leslie, ed. II. Title. III. Foster, I. LL.

NN R 12.63 p/ OC, I, II, IIIbBNB PC, 1, 2, 3, 4, I, II SL A, 1, 4, I, II (LC1, X1, Z1) [I]

FORSCHUNGEN zu Staat und Verfassung... (Card 4)

creation des intendants des provinces (1634-1648), par R. Mousnier. — Johannes Popitz, ein Beitrag zur Geschichte des deutschen Beamtentums, von H. Herzfeld. — Das Problem des diplomatischen Nachwuchses im Dritten Reich, von H. G. Sasse. — Linksliberalismus und Arbeiterschaft in der preussischen Konfliktszeit, von E. Schraepler. — Des Zweiparteiensystem in der deutschen Politik, von T. Eschenburg. — Zur Heeresverfassung der deutschen Territorien von 1500-1800; ein Versuch vergleichender Betrachtung, von G. Oestreich. — Die Entlassung von Kameke und Stosch im Jahre 1883 ein Beitrag zur Geschichte der deutschen militärischen Institutionen,

(Continued)

MFA

Fotografiska föreningen, Stockholm.
...Fotografien i Sverige och Fotografiska föreningen, Stockholm; minnesskrift vid föreningens 50-årsjubileum. [Stockholm, 1938] 64 p. facsims., illus., plates, ports. 24cm.

At head of title: 1888-1938.
"Redaktör: Docent Helmer Bäckström."
Contributions by various authors.

Festschrift

18002B. 1. Photography—Assoc. and org.—Sweden. I. Bäckström, Helmer. II. Title.
N. Y. P. L. April 16, 1940

FORSCHUNGEN zur Staat und Verfassung... (Card 5)

von E. Kessel. — Reichskanzlei, 5 November 1937, Bemerkungen über "Politik und Kriegsführung" im Dritten Reich, von H. Gackenholz. — Holstein, Österreich-Ungarn und die Meerengenfrage im Herbst 1895, persönliches Regiment oder Regierungspolitik? Von H. Krausnick. — Zeitgeschichtliche Betrachtungen zum Problem der Realpolitik, von H. Rothfels. — Nachtrag zur Bibliographie Fritz Hartung, von W. Schochow (p. [537]-538)

1. Hartung, Fritz, 1883- 2. Law, Constitutional—Germany. 3. Germany—Govt. I. Dietrich, Richard, ed. II. Oestreich, Gerhard, ed. III. Dietrich, Richard.

OLA

FOX, RALPH HARTZLER, 1913- , ed.
Algebraic geometry and topology; a symposium in honor of S. Lefschetz. Edited by R. H. Fox, D. C. Spencer, A. W. Tucker for the Department of mathematics, Princeton university. Princeton, New Jersey, Princeton university press, 1957. 399 p. port. 24cm. (Princeton mathematical series. [v.] 12)

Includes bibliographies.

(Continued)

NN R 1.63 p/ OC, I, II, VbCBI O8, III, IIIb+, IV PC, 1, 2, 3, I, II, III, IV SL ST, 1t, 2t, 3, I, II, III, IV (LC1, X1, Z1)

2

FOX, RALPH HARTZLER, 1913- , ed.
Algebraic geometry and topology... (Card 2)

1. Geometry, Analytic. 2. Analysis situs. 3. Lefschetz, Solomon, 1884- I. Spencer, Donald Clayton, 1912- , joint ed. II. Tucker, Albert William, 1905- joint ed. III. Princeton university. Mathematics Dept. of. IV. Series. V. Fox, Ralph Hartzler, 1913- t. 1957

FRA il passato e l'avvenire... (Card 3)

Loddo Canepa.—Le riforme nel campo agricolo nel periodo sabaudo, di L. Bulferetti.—L'agricoltura sarda nel periodo sabaudo e il commercio dei prodotti agricoli, di C. Sole.—I Monti di soccorso in Sardegna, di L. Del Piano.

1. Agriculture--Economics--Italy--Sardinia. 2. Agriculture--Italy--Sardinia. I. Segni, Antonio, 1891- . II. Pampaloni, Enzo. III. Ente per la trasformazione fondiaria e agraria in Sardegna.

*IIW

Fra de gamle bøgers verden, festskrift fra en kreds af husets venner, udsendt i anledning af firmaet Herman H. J. Lynge & søns 100-aarige bestaaen som videnskabeligt antikvariat, 1853-1953. København, H. H. J. Lynge, 1953. 121 p. illus., ports. 23cm.

Contents.—Fra de gamle bøgers verden, af H. H. Seedorff Pedersen.—Herman H. J. Lynge & søn gennem tiderne, af A. Fabritius.—Tre generationer, af F.

(Continued)

NN** X 4.54 OC,2b (OS)I,Ib PC,1,2,3,I SL (LC1,Z1,X1)

E-11
9623

FRAENGER, WILHELM, 1890- , ed.
Jacob Grimm zur 100. Wiederkehr seines Todestages; Festschrift des Instituts für deutsche Volkskunde, hrsg. durch Wilhelm Fraenger und Wolfgang Steinitz. Berlin, Akademie-Verlag, 1963. 290 p. illus. (part issued in pocket) 24cm. (Deutsche Akademie der Wissenschaften, Berlin. Institut für deutsche Volkskunde. Veröffentlichungen. Bd. 32)

Bibliographical footnotes.

(Continued)

NN 4.64 f/bOC, I (OS)II, III PC, 1, I, II, III SL (LC1, X1, Z1) 2

Fra de gamle bøgers verden... (Card 2)

Lynge.—Kunde hos Lynge i en menneskealder, af E. Høeg.—Holbergske auktionspriser 1711-1760, af C. S. Petersen.—Det Thottske biblioteks sidste dage, af P. Birkelund.—En litteraturhistorie i bokrygger, af W. Munthe.—En hilsen, af J. Hersholt.—Summary.

1. Booksellers and book trade—Denmark. 2. Schweigaard, Johan, 1846-1919. 3. Thott, Otto, greve, 1703-1785. I. Lynge (Herman H.J.) & Søn, Copenhagen.

FRAENGER, WILHELM, 1890- , ed. Jacob Grimm zur 100. (Card 2)

1. Grimm, Jakob Ludwig Karl, 1785-1863. I. Steinitz, Wolfgang, 1905- joint ed. II. Series. III. Deutsche Akademie der wissenschaften, Berlin. Institut für deutsche Volkskunde.

E-13
9175

Fra il passato e l'avvenire; saggi storici sull'agricoltura sarda in onore di Antonio Segni. [Realizzato a cura dell'Ufficio stampa, pubblicazioni e divulgazione dell'E. T. F. A. S.] Padova, CEDAM, 1965.
xii, 422 p. illus., port. 25 cm.
Includes bibliographical footnotes.
CONTENTS.—L'agricoltura sarda tra il passato e l'avvenire, di E. Pampaloni.—Aspetti della vita curtense in Sardegna nel periodo altogiudicale, di A. Boscolo.—Agricoltura e pastorizia nella Sardegna

(Continued)

NN * 8. 70 1/4OC, I, II (OS)III, IIIb* PC, 1, 2, I, II, III SL E, 1, I, II, III (LC1, X1, Z1) 3

*QO

FRAGMENTY filozoficzne. Seria druga; księga pamiątkowa ku uczczeniu czterdziestolecia pracy nauczycielskiej w Uniwersytecie warszawskim profesora Tadeusza Kotarbińskiego. [Komitet redakcyjny: Janina Kotarbińska [et al.] 1. wyd.] Warszawa, Państwowe wydawn. naukowe, 1959. 330 p. port. 24cm.

Includes bibliography.

(Continued)

NN 1.60 t/4 OC PC, 1, 2, I SL S, 1, 2, I (LC1, LCE1, X1, Z1)

FRA il passato e l'avvenire... (Card 2)

pisana, di F. Artizzu.—Brevi cenni storici sul diritto agrario nel territorio di villa di Chiesa, di G. Zanetti.—L'importanza economica della Sardegna nel Medioevo, di F. Giunta.—Aspetti dell'agricoltura sarda nella legislazione del secolo XIV, di C. G. Mor.—Il commercio dei prodotti agricolo-pastorali sardi nel Medioevo e nell'età moderna, di I. Imberciadori.—Note sulla dimora rurale in Sardegna, di A. Terrosu Asole.—Aspetti dell'architettura rurale in Sardegna, di V. Mossa.—L'agricoltura sarda negli atti e voti parlamentari, di A. Marongiu.—Rapporti fra feudatari e vassalli in Sardegna, di F.

(Continued)

FRAGMENTY filozoficzne. Seria druga... (Card 2)

CONTENTS.--A. Grzegorczyk. O pewnych formalnych konsekwencjach reizmu.--H. Hiz. O rzeczach.--L. Kołakowski. Determinizm i odpowiedzialność.--J. Kotarbińska. Tak zwana definicja dejktyczna.--M. Ossowska. Norma prawna i norma moralna u Petrażyckiego.--S. Ossowski. Od "kodeksu natury" do "sprzysiężenia równych."--L. Lazari-Pawłowska. Tworzenie pojęć nauk humanistycznych według koncepcji Leona Petrażyckiego.--T. Pawłowski. Klasyfikacja sztuczna a klasyfikacja naturalna w biologii.--J. Pelc. Szkic analizy znaczeniowej terminu "ideologia dzieła literackiego."--E. Poznański.
(Continued)

FRAGMENTY filozoficzne. Sęria druga... (Card 3)

Operacjonalizm po trzydziestu latach.--M. Przełęcki. Postulat empiryczności terminów przyrodniczych.--T. Pszczołowski. Prakseologiczne pojecie pracy.--H. Stonert. Analiza logiczna teorii atomistycznej w klasycznej chemii.--K. Szaniawski. O indukcji eliminacyjnej.--M. Wallis. Koncepcje biologiczne w humanistyce.

1. Philosophy--Addresses, essays, lectures. 2. Kotarbinski, Tadeusz, 1886- . I. Kotarbińska, Janina, ed.

FRANCISCO JAVIER CISNEROS, homenaje del Gobierno nacional en el cincuentenario de su fallecimiento... (Card 2)

Cisneros, por E. Merchan. --Recuerdo de F. J. Cisneros, por S. Pérez Triana. --Francisco Javier Cisneros, por R. M. Merchan. --Cartas y telegramas.

1. CISNEROS, FRANCISCO JAVIER 2. RAILWAYS--COLOMBIA 3. RAILWAYS--COLOMBIA, 1948 I. Colombia t. 1948

VEB

FRÅN byggnadsforskningens front; festskrift till Hjalmar Granholm. [Redigerad av Sven Olof Asplund] Göteborg, Gumperts [1961] 301 p. illus., diagrs. 27cm. (Scandinavian university books)

Summary in English of most of the contributions.
Includes bibliographies.
"Förteckning över Hjalmar Granholms intill den 1 mars 1961 utgivna skrifter [av] Johnnie Svedin," p. 7-14.
1. Granholm, Hjalmar, 1900- . 2. Building--Research--Sweden. I. Asplund, Sven Olof, 1902- , ed. t. 1961.
NN R 8.61 e/P OC, I PC, 1, 2, I SL ST, 2t, I (LC1, X1, Z/1)

NGZ

FRANCK, HANS, 1879-
Das Herzgeschenk. Hans Franck zum 75. Geburtstag 30. Juli 1954. [Die Zusammenstellung besorgte Heinz Grothe. Hannover, A. Sponholtz, 1954] 55 p. illus., ports. 20cm.

CONTENTS. —Mein Leben und Schaffen. —Gründlich geheilt. —Nur ein Dichter. —Sonderbar. —Die Mütze. —Gekauft. —Das Herzgeschenk.—Bibliographie des Werkes (p. 41-49)
I. Grothe, Heinz, 1912- , ed. II. Title.
NN R 1.56 s/A OC, I, II PC, I, II SL (LC1, X1, Z1)

GEG

Från stenålder till rokoko; studier tillägnade Otto Rydbeck den 25 augusti 1937. Lund: C. W. K. Gleerup [1937] ix, 391 p. front. (port.), illus. (incl. plans.) 24½cm.

CONTENTS.—Gjessing, Gutorm. Mellom Komsa og Fosna.—Rydh, Hanna. Ett bidrag till frågan om snörornamentiken på stenåldersboplatsernas lerkärl.—Forssander, J. E. Bronsålderns guldornamentik.—Nilsson, M. P. Archaic Greek temples with fire-places in their interior.—Hanell, Krister. Äldre romerska bronsmynt i Lunds universitets Historiska museum.—Vifot, B. M. Brandgravar från Skånes äldre järnålder.—Nerman, Birger. Några skånska järnåldersfynd.—Arne, T. J. Ett skånskt fynd från folkvandringstiden.—Lidén, Oskar. Stenklubbor från tidig folkvandringstid.—Lindqvist, Sune. Från Skånes vendeltid.—Rasmusson, N. L. Kring de västerländska myn-

(Continued)

Festschrift

N. Y. P. L. June 3, 1938

TNK (Franck)

Franck und Kathreiner, firm, Ludwigsburg, Germany. Väter, Söhne, Sohnessöhne; ein Bilderbuch der letzten 125 Jahre, 1828-1953. [Ludwigsburg, 1953] [64 p.] col. illus. 30cm.

1. Inventions— Hist. I. Title.

NN**R 9.54 (OC)I OS(1b) PC,1,I SL E,I ST,1,I (Z1, LC1,X1)

Från stenålder till rokoko... (Card 2)

ten i Birka.—Thordeman, Bengt. Ett skånskt skattfynd med svensk runmynt.—Brøgger, A. W. Rékved.—Kjellberg, S. T. Primitivt fångstliv.—Curman, Sigurd. Två romanska träkonstruktioner.—Lundberg, Erik. Problemet Hegvald.—Mackeprang, M. Skaanske Fonte Vestensunds.—Ekholm, Gunnar. Broddestorpsaltaret.—Ugglas, C. R. af. Trydekrucifixet och Lund.—Romdahl, A. L. Magnus Ladulås' majestätssigill, ett höggotiskt mästerverk.—Nørlund, Poul. Det saakaldte "Erik af Pommerns Bælte."—Källström, O. Axmadonnan.—Rydbeck, Monica. Två renässansinventarier från Stora Råby och Bjällerups kyrkor i Skåne.—Josephson, Ragnar. Bouchardon, Bourguignon och Adrien Masreliez.—Tuneld, John. Bibliografi över professor Otto Rydbecks utgivna skrifter (p. [375]-391).

940108A. 1. Rydbeck, Otto Henrik, 1872- . 2. Sweden—Archaeology.
N. Y. P. L. June 3, 1938

AN (Wendel, F.)

François de Wendel, 1874–1949. [Metz, 1949] 104 p. port. 28cm.

564016B. 1. Wendel, François de, 1874-1949.
NN*R 2.53 OC PC, I SL E, I ST, I (LC1, Z1, X1)

---

* C-4 p. v. 687

FRANCISCO JAVIER CIZNEROS, homenaje del Gobierno nacional en el cincuentenario de su fallecimiento, julio 7, 1898-1948. [Bogotá, 1948] 73 p. port. 24cm.

CONTENTS. —Homenaje a Francisco Javier Cisneros, por M. Ospina Pérez. --Francisco J. Cisneros y su obra en Colombia, por A. Ortega Díaz. --Ley número 34 de 1907 (14 de junio) de honores al señor Francisco Javier Cisneros. --Decreto número 1827 de 1948 (mayo 31) por el cual se honra la memoria del ingeniero Francisco Javier Cisneros. --Francisco Javier

(Continued)

NN * * R X 10.57.v/ OC (OD)It (ED)It PC, 1, 2, I SL E, 2 ST, 3, I (LC1, X1, Z/1)

NKC (Rabelais)

François Rabelais: ouvrage publié pour le quatrième centenaire de sa mort, 1553-1953. Genève, E. Droz, 1953. 277 p. illus. 26cm. (Travaux d'humanisme et renaissance [no.] 7)

Bibliographical footnotes.
Contents.—Cinquante ans d'histoire de l'humanisme et de la renaissance en France, 1903-1953, par M. François.—La pensée politique de Rabelais, par Janeau.—Rabelais physicien, par P. Delaunay.—Un

(Continued)

NN** X 4.54 OC (OS)I PC,1,I SL (U 1,LC1,Z1, X1)

François Rabelais: ouvrage publié pour le quatrième centenaire de sa mort... (Card 2)

quatrième exemplaire des Grandes et inestimables cronicques, Lyon, 1532, par L. Scheler.—Rabelais et les chroniques gargantuines, par M. Françon.—Sur "un tas de prognostications de Lovain," par C. Perrat.—Les contemporains de Rabelais découvrirent-ils la "substantificque mouelle?" par M. De Grève.—Le livre des marchans d'Antoine Marcourt et Rabelais, par G. Berthoud.—En relisant l'Abbaye de Thélème,

(Continued)

François Rabelais: ouvrage publié pour le quatrième centenaire de sa mort... (Card 3)

Gargantua LI ss,par F. Desonay.—Thélème et la paulinisme érasmien: le sens de l'énigme en prophétie, Gargantua LVIII, par E. V. Telle.—Aspects de Panurge, par M. Roques.—A further study of Rabelais's position in the Querelle des femmes (Rabelais, Vivès, Bouchard Tiraqueau), par M. A. Screech.—Rabelais' satyrical Eulogy: the praise of borrowing, par C. A. Mayer.—La donation du Salmigondin, Tiers

(Continued)

François Rabelais; ouvrage publié pour le quatrième centenaire de sa mort... (Card 4)

livre II, par F. Dumont.—Le personnage de Pantagruel dans les Tiers et Quart livres, par R. Lebègue.—Les connaisances nautiques de Rabelais, Quart livre, par L. Denoix.—L'attitude de Rabelais devant le néoplatonisme et l'italianisme, Quart livre IX à XI, par R. Marichal.—Le roy sainct Panigon dans l'imagerie populaire du XVIe siècle, par A. Huon.—The andouilles of the Quart livre, par A. Krailsheimer --Le silence de Rabelais et le

(Continued)

François Rabelais: ouvrage publié pour le quatrième centenaire de sa mort... (Card 5)

mythe des paroles gelées, par V.-L. Saulnier.—La mort de Pierre Lamy, 1525, par H. Meylan.—Odet de Chastillon et la prétendue disgrace de Jean du Bellay en 1549, par M. Thomas.—Le testament de Sébastien Gryphius, 1556, par J. Tricou.

1. Rabelais, François, ca.1490-1553? I. Series.

*PPV

FRANK, JOSEPH, 1916- , ed.
Horizons of a philosopher, essays in honor of David Baumgardt. With a pref. in German by the editors: Joseph Frank, Helmut Minkowski[and] Ernest J. Sternglass. Leiden, E.J. Brill, 1963. vi, 425 p. 25cm.

Contributions in English, German, French or Italian.
Bibliographical footnotes.

(Continued)

NN R 2.64 f/ OC, 1b*, I, II, IVbo PC, 1, 2, I, II, III SL I, 1, 2, I, II, III (LC1, X1, Z1) [I]

2

FRANK, JOSEPH, 1916- , ed. Horizons of a philosopher, essays in honor of David Baumgardt. (Card 2)

1. Baumgardt, David, 1890- . 2. Philosophy--Addresses essays, lectures. I. Minkowski, Helmut, 1908- , joint ed. II. Sternglass, Ernest J., joint ed. III. Title. IV. Sternglass, Ernest J.

* OVC

FRANKE, HERBERT, ed.
Studia sino-altaica; Festschrift für Erich Haenisch zum 80. Geburtstag im Auftrag der Deutschen morgenländischen Gesellschaft hrsg. Wiesbaden, F. Steiner, 1961. vi, 223 p. illus., port. 25cm.

Contributions chiefly in German, some in French or English.
Includes bibliographies.
"Verzeichnis der Schriften von Erich Haenisch," p. 3-11.

(Continued)

NN 12.61 g/ OC (OS)I PC, 1, 2, 3, I SL O, 1, 2, 3, I (LC1, X1, Z1) [I]

2

FRANKE, HERBERT, ed. Studia sino-altaica... (Card 2)

1. Haenisch, Erich, 1880- . 2. Chinese studies--Collections. 3. Oriental studies--Collections. I. Deutsche morgenländische Gesellschaft.

F-11
982

FRANKFURT AM MAIN. Gymnasium.
Gymnasium francofurtanum, 1520-1920. Festgabe den Teilnehmern an der Vierhundertjahr-Feier am 26. und 27. August 1920 gewidmet vom Festausschuss. Frankfurt am Main, Druck der Kunstanstalt Wüsten, 1920. 70 p. illus., ports, facsims. 28cm.

Bibliographical footnotes.
CONTENTS.—Rückblick auf die Geschichte des Frankfurter Gymnasiums, 1520-1853, von R. Jung.--Johannes Classen, Direktor des Frankfurter Gymnasiums, 1853-1864, von F. Neubauer.—Tycho

(Continued)

NN R10.65 g/ (OC)I OS(1b) PC, 1, I SL (LC1, X1, Z1)

2

FRANKFURT AM MAIN. Gymnasium. Gymnasium francofurtanum, 1520-1920. (Card 2)

Mommsen und das Frankfurter Gymnasium 1864-1886, von O. Liermann.—Ehrentafel 1870-1871, 1914-1918.

1. Education, Secondary--Germany--Frankfurt am Main. I. Jung, Rudolf, 1859- .

QOA
+
(Abhandlungen)

Frankfurter Gesellschaft für Anthropologie, Ethnologie und Urgeschichte.
...Festschrift zur Feier des 25jährigen Bestehens der Frankfurter Gesellschaft für Anthropologie, Ethnologie und Urgeschichte...verfasst von Mitgliedern derselben. Frankfurt am Main: Kommissionsverlag der Gesellschaft, 1925. 140 p. col'd front., illus. (incl. ports.), plan, plates (part col'd). f°. (Abhandl. zur Anthropologie, Ethnologie und Urgeschichte. Bd. 2)

Contents: WEGNER, R. N. Frankfurts Anteil an der Rassen- und Völkerkunde:

(Continued)

(Over)

N. Y. P. L. September 12, 1927

Frankfurter Gesellschaft für Anthropologie, Ethnologie und Urgeschichte: ... Festschrift zur Feier... (Continued)

Multiple Exostosen und allgemeine Verdickung mehrerer Schädelknochen. BEHRMANN, W. Verkehrs- und Handelsgeographie eines Naturvolkes. POSNANSKY, A. Die erotischen Keramiken der Mochicas und deren Beziehungen zu occipital deformierten Schädeln. VATTER, E. Ein bemaltes Büffelfell und andere seltene amerikanische Ethnographica im Städtischen Völkermuseum zu Frankfurt a. M. LEHMANN, J. Beiträge zur Musikinstrumenten-Forschung: Literaturübersicht. LESER, P. Pflüge von Wehr. WARNER, E. H. Zum heutigen Stande der Erforschung der Taunusringwälle.

1. No subject. 2. Ser.
N. Y. P. L. September 12, 1927

3-MAAD

FRANKFURTER KÜNSTLERCHRONIK.
Festschrift zum fünfzigjährigen Stiftungsfeste der Frankfurter Künstlergesellschaft, 1857-1907. Frankfurt a.M., J. Maubach, 1907. 177 p. illus., ports. 24cm.

1. Art--Assoc., clubs, etc. --Germany--Frankfurt am Main. 2. Frankfurter Künstlergesellschaft. I. Title.
NN 1.72 d/(OC)I OS PC, 1, 2, I SL A, 1, 2, I (LC1, X1, Z1)

NINA
(Bengtsson)

FRANS G. BENGTSSON, en minnesbok under redaktion av Germund Michanek. Uppsala, J.A. Lindblad [1955] 285 p. illus., ports. 21cm.

1. Bengtsson, Frans Gunnar, 1894- I. Michanek, Germund, ed.

NN**R 3.56 j/ OC,I PC,1,I SL (LC1,X1,Z1)

Write on slip words underlined below and class mark — HBA

...Franz Boas, 1858-1942, by A. L. Kroeber, Ruth Benedict, Murray B. Emeneau [and others]... [Menasha, Wis.] American anthropological association [1943] 119 p. front (port.) illus. (port.) 24 1/2cm. (Memoir series of the American anthropological association, no. 61)

American anthropologist. New series, v. 45, no.3, pt. 2. July-September, 1943.

Festschrift

form 400b [viii-3-43 25m]

---

* MEC
(Philipp)

FRANZ-PHILIPP-GESELLSCHAFT.
Franz Philipp 70 Jahre; das Bild eines deutschen Musikers in Zeugnissen von Zeitgenossen. Gedruckt als Gabe seiner Freunde zum 70. Geburtstag 24. August 1960. [1. Aufl. Freiburg im Breisgau? 1960] 202 p. ports, facsims., music. 23cm.

"Verzeichnis der Werke," p. [161]-200.
Bibliography, p. 201.
1. Philipp, Franz, 1890-
NN R 2.61 p/ OS (1b) (OAF1) PC, 1 SL MU, 1 (LC1, X1, Z1)

---

*PWZ
+
(Rosenzweig)

Franz Rosenzweig; ein buch des gedenkens. Berlin, 1930.
1 p. l., 5-56, [3] p. 30½cm.

"Elfte publikation der Soncino-gesellschaft der freunde des jüdischen buches e. v. Herausgegeben von Herrmann Meyer. Gesetzt in italienischer antiqua. In 800 exemplaren gedruckt von Aldus druck, Berlin. Den druck stifteten Reinhold und Erich Scholem zur jahresversammlung in Berlin am 30. märz 1930."

CONTENTS.—Bertha Badt-Strauss. Wort des gedenkens.—Margarete Susman. Franz Rosenzweig.—Martin Buber. Für die sache der treue.—Ernst Simon. Versuch über Rosenzweig.—Jos. Prager. Begegnungen auf dem wege.—Victor Ehrenberg. Persönliches gedenken.—Hermann Badt. Erinnerungen.—Gerhard Scholem. Diwre Askara

1. Rosenzweig, Franz, 1886-1929. I. Meyer, Herrmann, ed. II. Soncino-gesellschaft der freunde des jüdischen buches e. v., Berlin.

A 33-791
Title from Columbia Univ. Printed by L. C.
[2]

D-20
4869

Franz Von Liszt zum Gedächtnis. Zur 50. Wiederkehr seines Todestages am 21. Juni 1919. Berlin, de Gruyter, 1969.
285 p. port. 23cm.

"Dieser Band erscheint zugleich als Band 81, Heft 3 der 'Zeitschrift für die gesamte Strafrechtswissenschaft.'"
Includes bibliographical references.

CONTENTS.—Persönliche Erinnerungen an Franz von Liszt, von E. Schmidt.—Das Menschenbild des Positivismus und die philosophische Anthropologie unserer Zeit, von R. Lange.—Franz von

(Continued)

NN * R 7.71 b/OC, I PC, 1, I SL E, 1, I (LC1, X1, Z1)

FRANZ VON LISZT zum Gedächtnis. (Card 2)

Liszt als Dogmatiker, von E. Heinitz.—Franz von Liszt und die kriminalpolitische Konzeption des allgemeinen Teils, von P. Bockelmann.—Franz von Liszt und die Kriminalpolitische Konzeption des Alternativentwurfs, von C. Roxin.—Franz von Liszt und die Reform des Strafvollzuges, von R. Sieverts.—Franz von Liszt als Österreicher, von R. Moos.—"Corsi e ricorsi"; Die Wiederkehr Franz von Liszts, von L. Jiménez de Asúa.—Franz von Liszt und die positive Strafrechtsschule in Italien, von S. Ranieri.—Der Einfluss Franz von Liszts auf die portugiesische Strafrechtsreform, von E. Correia.—Franz von Liszt und der Entwurf eines lateinamericanisch Strafgesetzbuches, von E. Novoa Monreal.—Die Ideen Franz von

(Continued)

FRANZ VON LISZT zum Gedächtnis. (Card 3)

Liszts im früheren und heutigen Jugoslawien, von B. Zlatarić.—Das Erbe Franz von Liszts und die gegenwärtige Reformsituation in der Schweiz, von H. Schultz.—Franz von Liszt und die Kriminologie, von G. Th. Kempe.—Franz von Liszt und die schwedische Strafrechtswissenschaft, von A. Nelson.

1. Criminal law--Addresses, essays, lectures. I. Liszt, Franz von, 1851-1919.

AN
(Miller,F.)

Fred J. Miller, a biography of a man who hoped never to grow so old that a new idea would shock him. New York, N. Y., The American society of mechanical engineers, 1941.

39 p. front. (port.) 21½cm.

"Prepared by a group of Fred Miller's friends and former associates consisting of Wallace Clark ... chairman, Morris L. Cooke ... Fred H. Colvin ... [and others] The Biography committee of the American society of mechanical engineers has decided to add this brochure to its ... list of ... biographies of eminent members of the society."—Foreword.

1. Miller, Fred J., 1857–1939. I. Clark, Wallace, 1880– II. American society of mechanical engineers. Biography committee.

42-5767
Library of Congress TJ140.M5F7 Festschrift
[2] 926.217

NBP

The **Fred Newton Scott** anniversary papers, contributed by former students and colleagues of Professor Scott and presented to him in celebration of his thirty-eighth year of distinguished service in the University of Michigan, 1888–1926. Chicago, Ill., The University of Chicago press [c1929]

ix, 319, [1] p. front. (port.) 24½cm.

Bibliography: p. 313–319.

CONTENTS.—Preface, by T. E. Rankin.—Half-lights, by Helen O. Mahin.—The approaches to literary theory, by C. E. Whitmore.—Origin and development of Herbert Spencer's principle of economy, by G. B.

(Continued on next card)

A Second Copy
SPINGARN COLLECTION
29-17756
[3]

The **Fred Newton Scott** anniversary papers ... [c1929] (Card 2)

CONTENTS—Continued.

Denton.—The meter of Christabel, by Ada L. F. Snell.—Mad Shelley, by E. S. Bates.—Shelley and the novels of Brown, by M. T. Solve.—The Cloisterham murder case, by E. S. Everett.—One stylistic feature of the 1611 English Bible, by C. C. Fries.—Allusion and style, by O. C. Johnson.—Grierson's suggested date for Milton's Ad patrem, by Harris Fletcher.—The aesthetic experience as illumination, by C. D. Thorpe.—The laughable in literature, by H. P. Scott.—The artist, by L. H. Conrad.—Artistry and dream, by H. S. Mallory.

1. Scott, Fred Newton, 1860– 2. Literature—Addresses, essays, lectures.

29-17756
Library of Congress PN36.S36
~~Copy 2.~~
Copyright A 12016 [3]

D-17
8536

FREEDMAN, MAURICE, ed.
Social organization; essays presented to Raymond Firth. [London] F. Cass, 1967. ix,300 p. port. 23cm.

Bibliography, p. 289-300.
CONTENTS.--Levels of change in Yugoslav kinship, by L. Barić.--Theoretical problems in economic anthropology, by C. S. Belshaw.--The equality
(Continued)

NN R 12.67 e/R OC PC,1, 2 SL (LC1,X1,Z1) [I]
3

FREEDMAN, MAURICE, ed. Social organization... (Card 2)

of the sexes in the Seychelles, by B. Benedict.--The Abelam artist, by A. Forge.--Ancestor worship: two facets of the Chinese case, by M. Freedman.--The plasticity of New Guinea kinship, by P. M. Kaberry.--The language of Kachin kinship; reflections on a Tikopia model, by E. Leach.--Voluntary associations in urban life, by K. Little.--Patrons and brokers; rural leadership in four
(Continued)

FREEDMAN, MAURICE, ed. Social organization... (Card 3)

overseas Indian communities, by A. C. Mayer.--Shamanism among the Oya Melanau, by H. S. Morris.--Reflections on Durkheim and aboriginal religion, by W. E. H. Stanner.--Economic concentration and Malay peasant society, by M. G. Swift.--Chinese fishermen in Hong Kong; their post-peasant economy, by B. E. Ward.
1. Ethnology--Essays and misc. 2. Firth, Reymond William, 1901-

---

ID

Freedom and reform; essays in honor of Henry Steele Commager. With contributions by Richard B. Morris [and others] Edited by Harold M. Hyman and Leonard W. Levy. [1st ed.] New York, Harper & Row [1967]

xi, 400 p. 22 cm.

Bibliographical references included in "Notes" (p. 313-367). "Bibliography of Henry Steele Commager": p. 369-385.

(Continued)

NN * R 11.68 l/A OC, I, II, III, IV PC, 1, I, II, III, IV SL AH, 1, I, II, III, IV (LC1, X1, Z1) [I]
3

FREEDOM and reform... (Card 2)

CONTENTS.—The view from the top of Fayerweather, by R. B. Morris.—Henry S. Commager as historian: an appreciation, by A. Nevins.—Accusatorial and inquisitorial systems of criminal procedure: the beginnings, by L. W. Levy.—The writ of habeas corpus: early American origins and development, by M. Cantor.—John Locke in the great Unitarian controversy, by W. Smith.—Libertarianism's loss: the case of Horace Holley and Transylvania University, by J. D. Wright, Jr.—Frederick Douglass' vision for America: a case study in nineteenth-century Negro protest, by A. Meier.—The narrow escape from a "Compromise of 1860": secession and the Constitution, by H. M. Hyman.—Some Catholic churchmen as Americanizers, by

(Continued)

FREEDOM and reform... (Card 3)

M. McKenna.—American socialists and the Russian Revolution of 1905–1906, by A. W. Thompson.—The enigma of poliomyelitis: 1910, by S. Benison.—Ben Lindsey: symbol of radicalism in the 1920's, by C. E. Larsen.—The case of the contentious commissioner: Humphrey's executor v. U. S., by W. E. Leuchtenburg.

1. United States--Politics--Addresses, essays, lectures. I. Commager, Henry Steele, 1902- . II. Morris, Richard Brandon, 1904- . III. Hyman, Harold Melvin, 1924- , ed. IV. Levy, Leonard William, 1923- , ed.

F-10
4883

FREEMAN, J. D., ed.
Anthropology in the South Seas; essays presented to H. D. Skinner. Edited by J. D. Freeman and W. R. Geddes. New Plymouth, Thomas Avery [1959] 267 p. illus., port., maps, diagrs., tables. 26cm.

Bibliographical footnotes. Bibliography at end of each section.
CONTENTS.--Henry Devenish Skinner: a memoir, by J. D. Freeman--Culture change in prehistoric New Zealand, by Jack Golson.--
(Continued)

NN R 8.60 l/ OC, I, II PC, 1, 2, 3, 4, I, II SL (LC1, X1, Z1)
3

FREEMAN, J. D., ed. Anthropology in the South Seas... (Card 2)

From moa-hunter to classic Maori in southern New Zealand, by Leslie Lockerbie. --Freestanding Maori images, by T. T. Barrow. --Neolithic adzes of eastern Polynesia, by Roger Duff. --Ritual adzes in Tikopia, by Raymond Firth. --Ascription of meaning in a ceremonial context, in the eastern central highlands of New Guinea, by Catherine H. Berndt. --The Joe Gimlet or Siovili cult: an episode in the religious history of early Samoa, by J. D. Freeman. --Fijian social structure in a period of transition, by W. R. Geddes--Maori and Polynesian: race and politics. The racial argument in support of New Zealand's interests in Polynesia, by Angus Ross--A modern Maori community, by John Booth. --The Maori population: a microcosm of new world, by
(Continued)

FREIBURG IM BREISGAU, Germany. Freiburg und seine Universität... (Card 2)

Universität in der Vergangenheit, von M. Kollofrath. --Der Freiburger und seine Universität, von F. Schneller. --Von den alten Gebäuden der Universität, von I. Schroth. --Der Oberried-Altar, seine Schicksale und Wiederherstellung, von P. Hübner. --Berühmte Wissenschaftler--berühmte Bürger. Die Verleihung des Ehrenbürgerrechts an Professoren der Albert-Ludwigs-Universität im 19. und 20. Jahrhundert, von F. Späth. --Der Vorbehalt der Stadt im Stiftungsbrief Erzherzog Albrechts, von T. Zwölfer. --Die Universität in der Baugeschichte der Stadt Freiburg von der Französischen Revolution bis zum ersten Weltkrieg, von G. Hirsch. --Die Vereinigten
(Continued)

FREEMAN, J. D., ed. Anthropology in the South Seas... (Card 3)

W. D. Borrie. --Bibliography of H. D. Skinner from 1912 to 1958, compiled by J. D. Freeman.

1. Ethnology--Polynesia. 2. Fijians. 3. Maoris. 4. Skinner, Henry Devenish. I. Geddes, W. R., joint ed. II. Title.

FREIBURG IM BREISGAU, Germany. Freiburg und seine Universität... (Card 3)

klinischen Universitätsanstalten, ein Gemeinschaftswerk von Land und Stadt, von A. Wild. --Die Armen der Stadt Freiburg und die ärztliche Wissenschaft, von F. Flamm. --Universität und Museum für Naturkunde der Stadt Freiburg im Breisgau, von M. Schneller. --Die wirtschaftlichen Beziehungen zwischen Stadt und Universität, von F. Kempf. --Der Einfluss der Universität auf den Freiburger Fremdenverkehr, von P. Ernst.

1. Freiburg im Breisgau, Germany. Universität. t. 1957.

AD-10
1336

FREEMASONS. Frankfurt am Main. Loge "Zur aufgehenden Morgenröthe." Frauenvereinigung.
Jubiläumsbericht der Frauenvereinigung der Frankfurt-Loge, 1903-1928, verfasst von Martha Schlesinger [Frankfurt a.M., 1928] 15 p. 22cm.

Cover title: 25 [i.e. fünfundzwanzig] Jahre Frauenvereinigung der Frankfurt-Loge.
1. Freemasons--Women.
NN 6.67 p/ OS PC,1 SL (LC1,X1,Z1)

F-10
7769

FREIBURG IM BREISGAU, Germany. Universität.
Festprogramm Seiner Königlichen Hoheit Grossherzog Friedrich zur Feier des siebzigsten Geburtstags, dargebracht von der Albrecht-Ludwigs-Universität zu Freiburg. Freiburg i. B., J. C. B. Mohr, 1896. 238 p. illus., maps (part col.) 28cm.

Bibliographical footnotes.

(Continued)

NN R 5.63 e/ OS PC, 1 SL (LC1, X1, Z1)

3

SKF

Freemasons. Oslo. Sankt Johanneslogen Kolbein til den oppgående sol.
St. Johs. [] Kolbein til den oppgående sol. 1891-1951, 60-års jubileumsskrift. [Oslo, Trykk: Dahl, Mathisen, 1951] 128 p. illus., ports. 31cm.

1. Freemasons. Lillehammer, Norway. Sankt Johanneslogen Kolbein til den oppgående sol.

NN** 12.54 m/ OS PC,1 SL (Z1,LC1,X1)

FREIBURG IM BREISGAU, Germany. Universität.
Festprogramm Seiner Königlichen Hoheit Grossherzog Friedrich zur Feier des siebzigsten Geburtstags... (Card 2)

CONTENTS.--Ferdinand Geminian Wanker, Professor zu Freiburg 1788-1824, Lebensbild eines Theologen der Uebergangszeit, von C. Krieg.--Der badische Hochzeitsbrauch des Vorspannens, von E. H. Meyer.--Badisches Staatsrecht um die Geburtszeit Grossherzog Friedrichs, von H. Rosin.--Ein Skulturwerk aus der Sammlung des Professor Dr. Franz Xaver Kraus.--Ueber freiherrliche Klöster in Baden: Reichenau, Waldkirch
(Continued)

F-10
1667

FREIBURG IM BREISGAU, Germany.
Freiburg und seine Universität; Festschrift der Stadt Freiburg im Breisgau zur Fünfhundertjahrfeier der Albert-Ludwigs-Universität. Hrsg. von der Stadtverwaltung. [Freiburg, 1957] 156 p. illus., ports., map. 26cm.

Includes bibliographical references.
CONTENTS. --Die Gegenwartsbeziehungen zwischen der Stadt Freiburg und ihrer Universität, von J. Brandel. --Stadtverwaltung und
(Continued)

NN R X 12.57 p/ ODt EDt PC, 1 SL (LC1, X1, Z1, C1, Y1)

FREIBURG IM BREISGAU, Germany. Universität.
Festprogramm Seiner Königlichen Hoheit Grossherzog Friedrich zur Feier des siebzigsten Geburtstags... (Card 3)

und Säckingen, von A. Schulte.--Die Veränderungen der Volksdichte im südlichen Schwarzwalde 1852-1895, von L. Neumann.--Die Spuren der letzten Eiszeit im hohen Schwarzwalde, von G. Steinmann.--Tierfährten im Tertiär des badischen Oberlandes, von G. Boehm.

1. Frederick William Louis, grand-duke of Baden, 1826-1907.

NFGS

Freies deutsches Hochstift, Frankfurt am Main.

...Ansprachen gehalten am 10. und 11. November, 1934, zur Feier des fünfundsiebzigjährigen Bestehens des Freien deutschen Hochstifts und zum hundertfünfundsiebzigsten Geburtstage Schillers. Im Auftrag der Verwaltung herausgegeben von Ernst Beutler. Halle an der Saale: M. Niemeyer, 1935. 49 p. mounted front. (port.) 24½cm.

CONTENTS.—Ansprache bei Enthüllung der Volger-Tafel gehalten von Alexander von Bernus.—Rede bei der Feier von Schillers hundertfünfundsiebzigstem Geburtstag gehalten von Ernst Beutler.

987166A. 1. Schiller, J. C. F. von. 1822–1897. I. Beutler, Ernst Rud., ander, Freiherr von, 1880– . 2. Volger, Georg Heinrich Otto, 1885– , ed. II. Bernus, Alex-

N. Y. P. L. December 29, 1939

NKW

The FRENCH mind; studies in honour of Gustave Rudler, edited by Will Moore, Rhoda Sutherland [and] Enid Starkie. Oxford, Clarendon press, 1952. viii, 355 p. illus. 23cm.

"Bibliography of the writings of Gustave Rudler," p. 347-351.

1. French literature—Hist. and crit. 2. Rudler, Gustave, 1872- . I. Moore, Will Grayburn, ed. II. Sutherland, Rhoda, ed. III. Starkie, Enid Mary, ed.

NN R 1.53 OC, I, II, (IIb), III PC, 1, 2, I, II, III SL (Z1, LC1, X1)

Copy only words underlined & classmark— BM

FRENCH WEST AFRICA. Afrique noir, Institute français d'.

Mélanges ichthyologiques dédiés à la mémoire d'Achille Valenciennes, 1794-1865, coauteur de l'Histoire naturelle des poissons, 1828-1849. Dakar, IFAN, 1963 [i.e. 1964] 485 p. illus., ports. 27cm. (ITS: Mémoires. no 68)

Includes bibliographies.

1. Fish. 2. Valenciennes, Achille, 1794-1865. I. Series. t. 1964.

NN 11.64 e/ ODt, I EDt, I PC, 1, 2, I (LC1, X1, Z1)

E-12
8254

Frenzke, Dietrich, *ed.*

Macht und Recht im kommunistischen Herrschaftssystem. (Boris Meissner zum 50. Geburtstag von seinen Schülern u. Mitarbeitern. Redaktion: Dietrich Frenzke und Alexander Uschakow) Köln, Verlag Wissenschaft u. Politik (1965)

334 p. with 1 map. 24cm.

Includes bibliographical references.

(Continued)

NN * R 3.67 1/ OC, I, IIb* PC, 1, 2, 3, I SL E, 1, 2, 3, I S, 2, 3, I (LC1, X1, Z1)

4

FRENZKE, DIETRICH, ed. Macht und Recht im kommunistischen Herrschaftssystem. (Card 2)

CONTENTS.—Zwecke und Mittel im Sowjetrecht, von H. Bahro.—Verwaltungsrechtspflege in Ungarn, von G. Brunner.—Der jugoslawische Reformkommunismus und seine internationale Ausstrahlung, von W. Eggers.—Das Verhältnis zwischen Völkerrecht und Landesrecht in der jugoslawischen Doktrin, von D. Frenzke.—Legenden um das Potsdamer Abkommen, von J. Hacker.—Der Kampf der Bolschewisten um die Bildung der ersten ukrainischen Sowjetregierung im

(Continued)

FRENZKE, DIETRICH, ed. Macht und Recht im kommunistischen Herrschaftssystem. (Card 4)

Rodingen.—Die territoriale Frage zwischen Japan und der Sowjetunion nach dem zweiten Weltkrieg, von H. Shibuya.—Die Stellung Polens im "Rat für gegenseitige Wirtschaftshilfe," von A. Uschakow.—Die Zadruga als Grundlage einer Militärverfassung in der Habsburger Monarchie, von U. Wagner.—Methodische Vorfragen der Ostrechtsforschung, von K. Westen.

1. Bolshevism--Jurisp. 2. Law--Europe, Eastern. 3. Meissner, Boris. I. Uschakow, Alexander, joint ed. II. Frenzke, Dietrich.

FRENZKE, DIETRICH, ed. Macht und Recht im kommunistischen Herrschaftssystem. (Card 3)

November/Dezember 1917, von D. Heinzig.—Die Aufnahme des "Grundsatzes der Selbstbestimmung der Völker" in die Satzung der Vereinten Nationen, von W. Koschorreck.—Unbewältigte Vergangenheit im sowjetischen Zivilrecht, von D. A. Loeber.—Die sowjetische Stellungnahme zur Finanzkrise der Vereinten Nationen, von H. H. Mahnke.—Die Gerichtsorganisation in der Volksrepublik Polen, von T. Pusylewitsch.—Die Wirtschaftsplanung in Ost und West, von H.

(Continued)

C-10
6909

Freundesgabe für Eduard Korrodi zum 60. geburtstag. [Zürich, Fretz & Wasmuth; etc., etc., 1945]

285 p., 1 l. 19½ cm.

"Herausgeber: Hans Barth, Fritz Ernst, Eduard Fueter ... [u. a.]"

1. KORRODI, EDUARD, 1885-
2. LITERATURE--ADDRESSES, ESSAYS, LECTURES
I. Barth, Hans, ed.

NN R X 4.58 g/ OC, I PC, 1, 2, I SL (LCEI, LC1, X1, Z1)

D-18
8340

Frey-Wehrlin, C T *ed.*

Festschrift zum 60. Geburtstag C. A. Meier, hrsg. von C. T. Frey-Wehrlin. Zürich, Rascher, 1965.

277 p. music, port. 21 cm.

Cover title: Spectrum psychologiae.
Bibliographical footnotes.

CONTENTS. — Mit Shakespeares xxx. Sonett (für Streichquartett) von M. Rothmüller. — Grund zur eleusinischen Vision, von K. Kerényi.—The Oedipus myth and the incest archetype, by R. M.

(Continued)

NN * R 4.69 1/a OC, I PC, 1, I, II SL (LC1, X1, Z1) [I]

4

FREY-WEHRLIN, C.T., ed. Festschrift zum 60. Geburtstag C.A. Meier. (Card 2)

Stein.—The birth of evil in Macbeth, by J. Kirsch.—Die verbrecherische Zerstörung der Einheit (zu Emersons Uriel) von H. K. Fierz.—Grundtrauer und Freudefrömmigkeit (zu Kellers Landvogt von Greifensee) von K. Schmid.—Fröbels mystische Beziehung zur Natur als Folge frühkindlichen Verlassenseins, von G. Hess.—Der Purzelbaum, von S. Marjasch.—Über den Zufall, von M. Fierz.—Health and conscience, by J. C. Aylward.—Jungian psychology and the Vedanta, by E. Thornton.—Philosophical roots of the psychothera-

(Continued)

FREY-WEHRLIN, C.T., ed. Festschrift zum 60. Geburtstag C.A. Meier. (Card 3)

pies of the West, by A. U. Vasavada.—Zur Rolle des Widerstandes in der Psychotherapie, von G. Zacharias.—Some implications of the transference, by J. M. Spiegelman.—Some dimensions of psychotherapy, by B. Klopfer and J. M. Spiegelman.—The child: his mind and his imagination, by H. Stone.—Owning, by D. L. Hart.—Reflections on psychotherapy among prisoners, by F. E. Smart.—Glossen zur Didaktik, von E. Diem.—The phenomenon of a poltergeist in a dream, by M. Zeller.—Ein prophetischer Traum, von C. T. Frey-

(Continued)

FREY-WEHRLIN, C.T., ed. Festschrift zum 60. Geburtstag C.A. Meier. (Card 4)

Wehrlin.—Varieties of paranormal cognition, by M. Rhally.—Herbstlied ("Blätterfall" von H. Leuthold) von M. Sturzenegger.—Publikationen von C. A. Meier (p. 272-275)

1. Psychology--Addresses, essays, lectures. I. Meier, Carl Alfred. II. Title: Spectrum psychologiae.

E-13
3576

FRIDTJOF-NANSEN-GEDÄCHTNIS-SYMPOSION ÜBER SPITZBERGEN, Würzburg, 1961. Vorträge des Fridtjof-Nansen-Gedächtnis-Symposion über Spitzbergen in Nansens 100. Geburtsjahr. Wiesbaden, F. Steiner, 1965. 85 p. 25cm. (Ergebnisse der Stauferland-Expedition 1959/60, Heft 3)

Symposium held April 3-11, 1961 in Würzburg, sponsored by the International geographical union.

(Continued)

NN R 2.69 l/ OS,I PC,1, 2,3,I SL ST,1t,3t (LC1,X1, Z1)

2

FRIDTJOF-NANSEN-GEDÄCHTNIS-SYMPOSION ÜBER SPITZBERGEN, Würzburg, 1961. Vorträge des Fridtjof-Nansen-Gedächtnis-Symposion über Spitzbergen in Nansens 100. (Card 2)

Bibliography, p. 84-85.

1. Geography, Physical--Congresses--Germany, 1961. 2. Nansen, Fridtjof, 1861-1930. 3. Spitsbergen--Geography, Physical. I. International geographical union. t. 1965.

ENB

Friedrich I. und Friedrich II., die letzten Grossherzöge von Baden; ein Gedenkbuch zum 25. Todestag Friedrich II. Hrsg. von Wilhelm Ilgenstein und Anna Ilgenstein-Katterfeld. Karlsruhe, C. F. Müller [1954] 192 p. illus.,ports. 21cm.

Bibliography, p. 189.

(Continued)

NN**R X 9.55 f/ OC, 1b,I II PC,1,2,I,II SL (LC1,Z1,X1)

Friedrich I. und Friedrich II... (Card 2)

1. Frederick William Louis, grand-duke of Baden, 1826-1907. 2. Frederick II, grand duke of Baden, 1857-1928. I. Ilgenstein, Wilhelm, ed. II. Ilgenstein-Katterfeld, Anna, ed.

SFC

Friedrich Engels der denker. Aufsätze aus der Grossen sowjet-enzyklopädie. Hauptdaten aus dem leben. Bibliographie. Basel, Mundus-verlag ag. [1945]

367 p., 2 l. front. (port.) 17½cm. [Erbe und gegenwart; schriftenreihe der vereinigung "Kultur und volk." 7]

"Diese aufsätze ... wurden folgender ausgabe entnommen: Friedrich Engels, der denker und revolutionär. Ring-verlag ag., Zürich, 1935 ... Der hier vorliegende text der neuausgabe folgt genau der oben erwähnten ausgabe mit ausnahme kleiner änderungen orthographischer, stilistischer und sachlicher natur."

"Diese neuausgabe der vereinigung 'Kultur und volk' erfolgt zum 50. todestag von Friedrich Engels 5, august 1945."

(Continued on next card)

A 46-4340

[2]

Fest

Friedrich Engels der denker ... [1945] (Card 2)

CONTENTS.—Haenisch, W. Hauptdaten aus dem leben von Friedrich Engels.—Czóbel, E. Die hauptetappen der politischen tätigkeit von Engels.—Mitin, M. Engels als philosoph.—Jegorschin, W. Engels und die naturwissenschaft.—Teleschnikow, F. Engels als theoretiker des historischen materialismus.—Rosenberg, D. Engels als ökonom.—Budkiewitsch, S. Engels und das kriegswesen.—Schiller, F. Engels als literaturkritiker.—Tschemodanow, N. und Schor, R. Engels und die fragen der sprachwissenschaft.—Seewann, F. L. Bibliographische angaben über veröffentlichungen von schriften von Engels und über Engels (p. [333]-351)—Anmerkungen.

1. Engels, Friedrich, 1820-1895.

A 46-4340

Harvard univ. Library for Library of Congress [2]

AN
(Muckermann, F.)

Friedrich Muckermann; ein Apostel unserer Zeit. [hrsg. von] Nanda Herbermann. Paderborn, F. Schoningh [1953] 188 p. 22cm.

Bibliographical footnotes.

CONTENTS.— Ein Apostel unserer Zeit, von O.F. de Battaglia.— Der lachelnde Gott, von F. Muckermann.— Friedrich Muckermann als Personlichkeit, von W. Vernekohl.— Aus den Aufzeichnungen eines Monches, von F. Muckermann.— Das literarische

(Continued)

NN**R X 9.54 OC,I,II PC,I,II SL (Z1,LC1,X1)

Friedrich Muckermann; ein Apostel unserer Zeit... (Card 2)

Schaffen, von N. Herbermann.—Der Monch an den Dichter, von F. Muckermann.— Friedrich Muckermanns Goethe Deutung, von P. Bauer.— Goethe-der Weise, von F. Muckermann.— Friedrich Muckermann und "Der Deutsche Weg," von J. Steinhage.— Die katholische Widerstandsbewegung, von F. Muckermann.— Unser Pater, von H. Engelfried.— Citta di Vaticano, von F. Muckermann.— Leben und Wirken in Rom, von O. Overhof.— Sacco di Roma, von F. Muckermann.—

(Continued)

Friedrich Muckermann; ein Apostel unserer Zeit... (Card 3)

Friedrich Muckermanns Begegnungen mit Solowjew, von W. Szylkarski.—Zwischen Russland und Europa, von F. Muckermann.— Friedrich Muckermanns Ende, von Dr. Gutzwiller.—Persönliche Erinnerungen, von F. Wagner.— Von der Ubermacht Gottes, von F. Muckermann.— Meine Begegnung mit einem uberragenden Menschen und Priester, von G. Schmitt.— Wir sind stolz auf diesen Mann, von R. Amelunxen.— Der Junger des hl. Ignatius, von Freiherr Clemens von Oer.
I. Muckermann, Friedrich, 1883-1946
II. Herbermann, Nanda, ed.

E-12
1210

FRIEDRICH-NAUMANN-STIFTUNG.
Gegenwartsaufgaben der Erwachsenenbildung; Festschrift zum 70. Geburtstag von Richard Freudenberg. Köln, Westdeutscher Verlag, 1962. 107 p. mounted port. 25cm.

CONTENTS.--Geleitwort, von P. Luchtenberg.--Probleme der Erwachsenenbildung, von W. Erbe.--Die verbindende Aufgabe der Erwachsenenbildung in Deutschland und in der Welt, von H. Becker.--Staatsbürgerliche
(Continued)

NN R 10.64 p/[?] (OC) 2b OS PC, 1, 2 SL E, 1, 2 (LC1, X1, Z1) 2

FRIEDRICH-NAUMANN-STIFTUNG. Gegenwartsaufgaben der Erwachsenenbildung... (Card 2)

Bildung heute, von K. Meissner.--Fernstudium als neuer Bildungsweg, von K.G. Schwier.--Die Aufgaben des Bibliothekars in der Erwachsenenbildung, von W. Möhring.--Universität und Erwachsenenbildung, von H. Plessner.--Berufsbildung und Volkshochschule, von P. Luchtenberg.

1. Education, Adult--Addresses, essays, lectures. 2. Freudenberg, Richard, 1892?-

---

VTZH

Frihet—sannhet; festskrift til Johan Scharffenberg, 70-årsdagen 23. november 1939. Oslo ͵Johansen & Nielsens boktrykkeri͵ 1939.

472 p. incl. front. (port.) tables, diagrs. 25cm.

"Redaksjonen og utgivelsen av dette festskriftet er forestått av professor, dr. med. Ragnar Vogt (formann), skoleinspektør Arne Braadland, direktør Johan Hvidsten, professor, dr. med. Otto Lous Mohr, fengselsdirektør Hartvig Nissen, sorenskriver Bj. Rognlien, redaktør Martin Tranmæl."—p. 13.

"Johan Scharffenberg: Skrifter og utvalg av artikler": p. 445-470.

CONTENTS.—Vogt, Ragnar. Åndsvirksomhet og alkohol.—Nissen, Hartvig. Psykiaternes innflytelse på strafferett og fangebehangling.—Arctander, Signy. Den sosiale forskning og kampen mot samfundssykdommene.—Hercod, Robert. Går alkoholismen i verden tilbake?—

(Continued on next card)

41-18952

͵2͵

Frihet—sannhet ... 1939. (Card 2)

CONTENTS—Continued.

Aalen, Leiv. Etikkens praktiske grunnproblem.—Marthinussen, Karl. Alkoholspørsmålet innenfor religionene.—Bergmann, Johan. Några ord om antikens alkoholfråga.—Steenhoff, G. Alkoholens roll som läkemedel genom tiderna och idag.—Nicolaysen, Ragnar. Alkohol og ernæring.—Hindhede, M. Spiritusforbrug og dødelighed.—Billstrom, Jakob. Tankar om prognosen av etylismus chronicus.—Tillgren, J. Alkoholsjukdomens vård på kroppssjukhus.—Kasa, Torgeir. Vår alkoholistforsorg og behandlingen av alkoholister.—Kristensen, K. J. Behandling av "åpenbar" beruselse og "jevnlig" alkoholmisbruk etter løsgjengerloven.—Ødegård, Ørnulv. Alkoholbruken blandt unge tilbakefallsforbrytere.—Sjövall, Einar. Några ord om alkohol och trafikkultur i anslutning till min erfarenhet som rättsobducent.—Tuovinen, P. J. Om alkoholens förhållande till människans arbetsförmåga særskilt i samband med trafikolyckorna.—Hallset, Lidvard. Den overbefolkede boligens innfly-

(Continued on next card)

41-18952

͵2͵

Frihet—sannhet ... 1939. (Card 3)

CONTENTS—Continued.

telse på alkoholmisbruk og kriminalitet.—Englund, Erik. Lag, forskning eller propaganda? Något om sambandet mellan och effektiviteten hos nykterhetsrörelsens olika medel.—Laurin, Ingvar. Till frågan om rusdryckslagstiftningens syfte.—Axelman, Ax. Om alkoholreklam.—Petersen, Kaare. Etterspørslen etter brennevin og vin.—Skaug, Arne. Økonomiske synspunkter i alkoholspørsmålet.—Dahlgren, Thorild. Några synpunkter på valet av innehåll vid nykterhetsundervisningen.—Lofthus, Johan. Alkoholspørsmålet i skoleundervisningen.—Abrahamsen, David. Den psykiatriskpsykologiske bakgrunn for et barnedrap begått av en vanfør.—Jacobsen, Rolf. Alkohol- og edruelighetslovgivningen i Norge.

1. Alcoholism. 2. Scharffenberg, Johan, 1869- I. Vogt, Ragnar, 1870- II. Title: Festskrift til Johan Scharffenberg.

Library of Congress RC367.S3F7 41-18952

͵2͵ 616.861

E-10
4232

FRITZ SAXL, 1890-1948; a volume of memorial essays from his friends in England, edited by D.J. Gordon. London, New York, T. Nelson [1957] xi, 369 p. plates, ports. 25cm.

Bibliographical footnotes.

CONTENTS.—Fritz Saxl, 1890-1948; a memoir, by G. Bing.—A statue of Iuno Regina from Chesters, by I.A. Richmond.—The implication of the term Sapiens as applied to Gildas. The comments of père Grosjean. By M. Deanesly.—Theodulf of Orleans and the problem of the Carolingian
(Continued)

NN R 2.58 p/ OC, I, IIbo PC, 1, 2, 3, I SL A, 1, 3, I (LC1, X1, Z1, C1, Y1) [I]

FRITZ SAXL, 1890-1948... (Card 2)

Renaissance, by H. Liebeschütz.—Prima clavis sapientiae: Augustine and Abelard, by B. Smalley.—The Sherborne "Chartulary", by F. Wormald.—King Edward I in fact and fiction, by F.M. Powicke.—The chronicle of Henry Knighton, by V. H. Galbraith.—The imagery of the Tree of Jesse on the west front of Orvieto cathedral, by A. Watson.—Some ideas on municipal progress and decline in the Italy of the Communes, by N. Rubinstein.—Notes and observations on the origin of humanistic book-decoration by O. Pächt.—A lost statue once in Thasos, by B. Ashmole.—The Latin classics known to Boston of Bury, by R.A.B. Mynors.—Humphrey, duke
(Continued)

FRITZ SAXL, 1890-1948... (Card 3)

of Gloucester and Tito Livio Frulovisi, by R. Weiss.—Lucian's Calumnia, by E.P. Goldschmidt.—Some classical and medieval ideas in Renaissance cosmography, by W. Oakeshott.—The confluence of humanism, anatomy and art, by C. Singer.—Notes on the genesis of Michelangelo's Leda, by J. Wilde.—Giannotti, Michelangelo and the cult of Brutus, by D.J. Gordon.—The office of devisor, by G. Webb.—An example of the theodicy-motive in antiquarian thought, by T. D. Kendrick.—The Précieux and French art, by A.F. Blunt.—Some renderings of Humanitas in German in the eighteenth century, by S. Purdie.—Painting in Ethiopia; a reflection of medieval practice, by D. Molesworth.

1. Saxl, Fritz, 1890-1948. 2. Civilization—Addresses, essays, lectures. I. Gordon, Donald James, ed. II. Gordon, Donald James. 3. Art—Essays and misc.

---

*IIV

Fritze, C. E., bokförlagsaktiebolag.

Fritzes, 1837-1937. Minnesskrift på uppdrag av C. E. Fritzes kungl. hovbokhandel utarbetad av Gunnar Mascoll Silfverstolpe. ͵Stockholm, Iduns tryckeri aktiebolag, Esselte ab.͵ 1938.

116 p. illus. (incl. ports., facsims.) 27 x 21½cm.

1. Publishers and publishing—Sweden. I. *Silfverstolpe, Gunnar Mascoll, 1893- ed.

New York. Public library for Library of Congress A C 39-2082

͵2͵

E-13
6446

FROM the Ancien Régime to the Popular Front; essays in the history of modern France in honor of Shepard B. Clough. Edited by Charles K. Warner. New York, Columbia university press, 1969. vii, 211 p. port. 25cm.

"Bibliography of Shepard B. Clough", p. [209-211]
Bibliographical footnotes.
CONTENTS.--The Encyclopédie as a business venture, by R.H.Bowen.

(Continued)

NN R 10.69 r/ OC, I, II PC, 1, 2, I, II SL E, 2, I, II (LC1, X1, Z1) [I]

FROM the Ancien Régime to the Popular Front...
(Card 2)

--The meaning of the Revolution: seven testimonies, by P.H.Beik.--French doctors face war, 1792-1815, by D.B.Weiner.--The growth of the French securities market, 1815-1870, by C.E.Freedeman.--The Journal d'Agriculture pratique and the peasant question during the July monarchy and the Second Republic, by C.K.Warmer.--The Alsace-Lorraine question in France, 1871-1914, by F.H.Seager.--The French colonial frontier, by R.F.Betts.--Edouard Herriot in Lyons: some aspects of his role as mayor, by S.Jessner.--French interwar stagnation revisited by, M. Wolfe.--Politics and economics in the 1930s: the balance sheets

(Continued)

FROM the Ancien Régime to the Popular Front...
(Card 3)

of the "Blum new deal", by J.Colton.

1. France--Hist.--Addresses, essays, lectures. 2. Economic history--France. I. Clough, Shepard Bancroft, 1901- . II. Warner, Charles K., ed.

E-10
7341

FROM Jane Austen to Joseph Conrad; essays collected in memory of James T. Hillhouse. Edited by Robert C. Rathburn and Martin Steinmann, Jr. Minneapolis, University of Minnesota Press, 1958.

xii, 326 p. 24 cm.

CONTENTS. — James Theodore Hillhouse, by T. Hornberger. — The makers of the British novel, by R. C. Rathburn.—The background of Mansfield Park, by C. Murrah.—Critical realism in Northanger Abbey, by A. D. McKillop.—Scott's Redgauntlet, by D. Daiches.—History on the Hustings: Bulwer-Lytton's historical novels of politics, by C. Dahl.—Thackeray, a novelist by accident, by J. Y. T. Greig.—A note on Dickens' humor, by D. Bush.—Self-help and the helpless in Bleak House, by G. H. Ford.—Form and substance in the Brontë novels, by

(Continued)

NN* R 4.59 g/l OC, I, II, IIIbo PC, 1, 2, I, II SL (LC1, X1, Z1)

FROM Jane Austen to Joseph Conrad... (Card 2)

CONTENTS—Continued.

M. R. Watson.—Charlotte Brontë's 'New' Gothic, by R. B. Heilman.—Elizabeth Cleghorn Gaskell, by Y. ffrench.—Trollope's Orley Farm: artistry Manqué, by B. A. Booth.—Anthony Trollope: the Palliser novels, by A. Mizener.—George Eliot's originals, by G. S. Haight.—Middlemarch, George Eliot's masterpiece, by S. J. Ferris.—Charles Reade's Christie Johnstone: a portrait of the artist as a young pre-Raphaelite, by W. Burns.—George Meredith's One of our conquerors, by F. Gudas.—Hardy's major fiction, by J. Holloway.—The spiritual theme of George Gissing's Born in exile, by J. Korg.—Samuel Butler and Bloomsbury, by W. V. O'Connor.—Apology for Marlow, by W. Y. Tindall.—The old novel and the new, by M. Steinmann, Jr.

(Continued)

FROM Jane Austen to Joseph Conrad... (Card 3)

1. FICTION, ENGLISH--HIST. AND CRIT., 19TH CENT.
2. HILLHOUSE, JAMES THEODORE, 1890-1956
I. Steinmann, Martin, 1915- , ed. II. Rathburn, Robert C., ed.
III. Rathburn, Robert C.

QAF

Frontiers in cytochemistry, the physical and chemical organization of the cytoplasm, ed. by Normand L. Hoerr... Lancaster, J. Cattell press, 1943. vii, 334 p. illus. 25cm. (Biological symposia. v. 10.)

Contributions, in expanded form, to a symposium held November 13, 1942, in honor of Dr. R. R. Bensley, on his seventy-fifth birthday. — *cf. Foreword.*

CONTENTS.—Foreword by N. L. Hoerr.—In appreciation of Professor R. R. Bensley, by E. V. Cowdry.—The chemical structure of cytoplasm as investigated in Professor Bensley's laboratory during the past ten years, by Arnold Lazarow.—Some considerations on the application of biological oxidation-reduction reaction systems to the study of cellular respiration, by E. S. Guzman Barron.—Ultracentrifugal studies on

(Continued)

N. Y. P. L. August 22, 1944

Frontiers in cytochemistry... (Card 2)

cytoplasmic components and inclusions, by H. W. Beams.—Electrolytic solutions compatible with the maintenance of Protoplasmic structures, by Robert Chambers.—Distribution of nucleic acids in the cell and the morphological constitution of cytoplasm, by Albert Claude.—Experimental epidermal methylcholanthrene carcinogenesis in mice, by E. V. Cowdry.—Histochemical analysis of changes in Rhesus motoneurons after root section, by Isidore Gersh and David Bodian.—Methods of isolation of morphological constituents of the liver cell, by N. L. Hoerr.—Electrolytes in the cytoplasm, by O. H. Lowry.—Fibrous nucleoproteins of chromatin, by A. E. Mirsky and A. W. Pollister.—The ultrastructure of protoplasmic fibrils, by F. O. Schmitt...[and others]—Mineral distribution in the cytoplasm, by G. H. Scott.—Studies on macromolecular particles endowed with specific biological activity, by K. G. Stern.—The chemistry of cytoplasm, by R. R. Bensley.

265768B. 1. Bensley, Robert Russell, 1867– 2. Cells. 3. Histology. 4. Biochemistry. I. Hoerr, Normand Louis, 1902– ed. II. Ser.
N. Y. P. L. August 22, 1944

E-10
4268

The FRONTIERS of social science; in honour of Radhakamal Mukerjee. Foreword by Sarvapalli Radhakrishnan; edited by Baljit Singh. London, Macmillan [1957] xi, 519 p. port., map, tables, diagr. 25cm.

Bibliographical footnotes.
1. Mukerjee, Radhakamal, 1889- . 2. Social sciences--Addresses, essays, lectures. I. Singh, Baljit, ed.
NN R X 12.57 g/P OC, I PC, 1, 2, I SL E, 1, 2, I (LC1, X1, Z1, C1, Y1)

GAXL

Fryske Akademy, ~~Leeuwarden~~.

Earebondel ta de tachtichste jierdei fan Dr. G. A. Wumkes op 4 Septimber 1949. Oanbean troch de Fryske Akademy. Boalsert, A. J. Osinga, 1950.

226 p. illus., ports., maps. 24 cm.

Contributions by various authors.
Bibliographies included.

1. Friesland—Hist.—Addresses, essays, lectures. 2. Wumkes, Geert Aeilco, 1869– I. Title.

A 51-5456

New York. Public Libr. for Library of Congress [3]

"Festschrift"

D-15
1630

FUCHS, ALBERT, professor, ed.
Stoffe, Formen, Strukturen; Studien zur deutschen Literatur. Hrsg. von Albert Fuchs und Helmut Motekat. Hans Heinrich Borcherdt zum 75. Geburtstag. München, M. Hueber [c1962] xvi, 521 p. port. 22cm.

1. Borcherdt, Hans Heinrich, 1887- . 2. German literature--Addresses, essays, lectures. I. Motekat, Helmut, joint ed.
NN * R 6.64 a/ OC, I PC, 1, 2, I SL (LC1, X1, Z1)

...50 Jahre Berliner Stadtbahn... (Card 2)

CONTENTS.—50 Jahre Berliner Stadtbahn, von Reichsbahnoberrat Hülsenkamp.—Die Auswechslung eiserner Brücken auf der Stadtbahn, von Reichsbahnrat K. Wehrmeister.—Die Verstärkung der Stadtbahnbögen, von Reichsbahnrat H. Böttcher.—Zahlen von der Berliner Stadtbahn.

730806A. 1. Railways, Elevated—Germany—Berlin. I. Blum, Otto, 1876– , editor. II. Baumann, Hans, 1888– , editor.
N. Y. P. L. October 9, 1934

E-12
8382

Führung und Bildung in der heutigen Welt; mit Geleitworten von Heinrich Lübke [et al.] Hsrg. zum 60. Geburtstag von Ministerpräsident Kurt Georg Kiesinger. Stuttgart, Deutsche Verlags-Anstalt, 1964.

498 p. 24 cm.

"Für die Forschungsbereiche und Themengebiete, die in diesem Buche vertreten sind, wurde die Sammlung der Beiträge von A. Bergstraesser, H. W. Bähr und G. Weng vorgenommen."

1. Education—Germany, 20th cent. 2. Kiesinger, Georg, 1904- . I. Bergsträsser, Arnold, 1896-1964, ed.
NN*R 3.67 a/c OC, I PC, 1, 2, I SL E, 2, I (LC1, X1, Z1)

STN
(Bochum)

Fünfzig Jahre höhere Schule Bochum-Langendreer, 1903-1953; Festschrift. Ein Beitrag zur Heimatgeschichte. Bearb. und hrsg. von Georg Frohberg. [Bochum-Langendreer, 1953] 256 p. (p. 228-256 advertisements) illus. 22cm.

Bibliography, p. 223.

1. Education—Germany—Bochum, 20th cent. I. Frohberg, Georg, ed. II. Frohberg, Georg.
NN**R X 4.54 OC, I IIbo PC, 1, I SL (LC1, Z1, X1)

AE-10
733

500 [i. e. **Fünfhundert**] Jahre Friedrichshütte. Festschrift zur Jubiläumsfeier am 2. August 1954. [Laasphe? 1954]

47 p. illus., ports. 25 cm.

Vorwort signed: Namens der Gesellschafter der Firma Carl von Wittgenstein.

CONTENTS. — Aus der Vorgeschichte der Friedrichshütte (1450-1799) von W. Hartnack.—Die neuere Zeit von 1799 an bis zur Gegenwart, von Friedrich Carl Freiherr von Wittgestein.

1. Friedrichshütte, Laasphe, Germany.
NN* R X 7.65 g/ OC (OS)Ib* PC, 1 E, 1 ST, 1 SL (LC1, X1, Z1)

QGH
+

Fünfzig
50 Jahre Leipziger Zoo; eine Festschrift...herausgegeben von Dr. Johannes Gebbing. Leipzig: Im Selbstverlag des Zoologischen Gartens, 1928. 141 p. incl. tables. diagrs., front., illus. (incl. facsims., ports.), plan. 4°.

On cover: 1878-1928.

404857A. 1. Zoological gardens—Germany—Leipzig. 2. Gebbing, Johannes, 1874– , editor.
N. Y. P. L. January 20, 1930

D-10
5560

50 [i. e. **Fünfzig**] Jahre AWF; 1918-1968. [Hrsg. vom Ausschuss für Wirtschaftliche Fertigung e. V. (AWF)] Freiburg im Breisgau, R. Haufe [1968]

160 p. illus. 22 cm.

Includes bibliographies.

1. Management--Addresses, essays, lectures. I. Ausschuss für wirtschaftliche Fertigung, Berlin.
NN*R 7.70 e/ OC (OS)I PC, 1, I SL E, 1, I (LC1, X1, Z1)

*PWZ
(Susman, M.)

Für MARGARETE SUSMAN; Auf gespaltenem Pfad [Hrsg. von Manfred Schlösser] Darmstadt, Erato-Presse [1964] 399 p. mounted ports., facsims. 26cm.

List of works of Margarete Susman, p. 383-395.

1. Susman, Margarete, 1874- . 2. Essays, Jewish, in German. 3. Essays, German. I. Schlösser, Manfred, ed. II. Title: Auf gespaltenem Pfad.
NN R 4.67 r/ OC, I PC, 1, 2, I, II SL J, 1, 3, I, II (LC1, X1, Z1)

TB p.v.769
+

...50 Jahre Berliner Stadtbahn, zum Jubiläum am 7. Februar 1932, herausgegeben von Professor Dr.-Ing. Blum...Reichsbahndirektor Dr.-Ing. Dr. rer. pol. Baumann... Berlin: O. Elsner Verlagsgesellschaft m.b.H., 1932. 32 p. incl. diagrs., tables. illus. (incl. plans.) 29½cm. (Technisch-wirtschaftliche Bücherei. Heft 51.)

Cover-title.
Printed in double columns.
"Sonderdruck aus der 'Verkehrstechnischen Woche,' Heft 5, 1932."
Bibliographical footnotes.

(Continued)

N. Y. P. L. October 9, 1934

TNK

FÜRSTLICH FÜRSTENBERGISCHE BRAUEREI AG. Donaueschingen.
Seit 250 Jahren Fürstenbergbräu [Text: Peter Berg. Zeichnungen: Erwin Maier] [Stuttgart, F. Vorwerk, 1955] 72 p. illus. 25cm.

1. Berg, Peter.
NN **R X 2.56 f/ (OC) I. Ibo OS (Ib) PC. I SL E. I (LC1. X1. Z1)

HCC

FUNDACIÓN VICENTE LECUNA.
Miscelánea Vicente Lecuna, homenaje continental. Caracas, Cromotip, 1959. 1v. port. 24cm.

Tomo I.
Includes bibliographies.
1. Lecuna, Vicente, 1870-1954. 2. Spanish America--Hist.--Addresses, essays, lectures. 3. History--Addresses, essays, lectures. I. Title.

NN 10.63 g/♧ (OC)I OS(1b+) PC,1,2,3,I SL AH,1,2,I (LC1,X1,Z1)

Copy only words underlined & classmark— NEQ

GAIMAR, GEOFFREY, 12th cent.
L'estoire des Engleis. Edited by Alexander Bell. Oxford, Published for the Anglo-Norman text society by B. Blackwell, 1960. lxxxiii, 307 p. facsim. 23cm. (Anglo-Norman texts. 14/16)

Bibliography, p. lxxxiii.

1. Great Britain--Hist.--Anglo-Saxon period, 443-1066--Sources. 2. Poetry, Anglo-Norman. I. Bell, Alexander, ed. II. Series.
NN R X 8.60 a/P OC, I (OS)II PC, 1, 2, I, II (LC1, X1)

NCC (Shaw)

G. B. S. 90; aspects of Bernard Shaw's life and work ₍by₎ Sir Max Beerbohm ... ₍and others₎ Edited by S. Winsten. London, New York ₍etc.₎ Hutchinson & co. ltd., 1946.
200 p. col. front., illus., plates (1 col.) ports., facsims. 23½ᶜᵐ.

CONTENTS.—Murray, Gilbert. A foreword.—Masefield, John. On the ninetieth birthday of Bernard Shaw.—Winsten, S. Introduction.—MacManus, M. J. Shaw's Irish boyhood.—Passfield, Lord. "Everywhere I gained something."—Housman, Laurence. G. B. S. and the Victorians.—Priestley, J. B. G. B. S., social critic.—Wells, H. G. A letter.—Beerbohm, Sir Max. A letter.—Joad, C. E. M. Shaw's philosophy.—Bridie, James. Shaw as dramatist (including a surrealist life of G. B. S.)—Dunsany, Lord. A permanent quality.—Bernal, J. D. Shaw the scientist.—Keynes, Lord. G. B. S. and Isaac Newton.—Inge, W. R. Shaw as a theologian.—Dent, E. J. Corno Di Bassetto.—Dobb, Maurice.

(Continued on next card)

46-8364

₍7₎

A p.v.691

Garden club of America.
Bulletin in memory of Mary Helen Wingate Lloyd. ₍New York₎ The Garden club of America, 1936.
4 p. l., 11-84, ₍3₎ p. incl. front. (port.) illus. 21½ᶜᵐ.
Half-title: Mary Helen Wingate Lloyd, 1868-1934.
CONTENTS.—Allgates.—Mrs. Lloyd's library.—Blue and mauve for the hardy garden, by Mary H. W. Lloyd.—Some decorative herbs, by Mary H. W. Lloyd.—Bermuda notes, by Mary H. W. Lloyd.—Mrs. Lloyd's quarry garden.—Bulletin articles by Mary H. W. Lloyd.

1. Lloyd, Mrs. Mary Helen (Wingate) 1868-1934. I. Title.

36-29878
Library of Congress SB454.G3
——— Copy 2.
Copyright A 92352 ₍3₎ 712

G. B. S. 90 ... 1946. (Card 2)

CONTENTS—Continued.
Bernard Shaw and economics.—Neill, A. S. Shaw and education.—Davies, A. E. G. B. S. and local government.—Jones, Daniel. G. B. S. and phonetics.—Trewin, J. C. Shaw as a wit.—Haley, Sir William. The stripling and the sage.—Gielgud, Val. Bernard Shaw and the radio.—Barnes, Sir Kenneth. G. B. S. and the R. A. D. A.—Limbert, Roy. The inspiration of Shaw.—Pascal, Gabriel. Shaw as a scenario-writer.—Hsiung, S. I. Through eastern eyes.—Huxley, Aldous. A birthday wish.

1. Shaw, George Bernard, 1856- I. Winsten, S., ed.

PR5366.G2 1946 928.2 46-8364
Library of Congress ₍7₎

---

*KP (Castle)

A GARLAND for Jake Zeitlin, on the occasion of his 65th birthday & the anniversary of his 40th year in the book trade. Edited by J.M. Edelstein. Los Angeles, Grant Dahlstrom & Saul Marks, 1967.
5 p.l., 3-131(1) p. port., 2 illus. 26cm.

One of "800 copies printed by Grant Dahlstrom at The Castle press."
"Typography by Saul & Lillian Marks, The Plantin press."
CONTENTS.--Jake, by C. McWilliams.--Vespasiano da Bisticci: a
(Continued)

NN * R 7.68 c/♧ OC, I PC, 1, I SL R, 1, I (RI 1, RS2, LC1, X1, Z1)
[I] 2

NPV

GABRIELA Mistral, premio Nobel. [Madrid, 1946] 126 p. port. 25cm.

Half-title: Homenaje a Gabriela Mistral. Madrid, 1946.
201 copies printed. "Ciento cincuenta ejemplares en papel Alfa ahuesado, numerados del 1 al 150." no. 108.
CONTENTS.—El cielo de Castilla, por G. Mistral.—Ante Gabriela Mistral, por I. de Ambia.—Surco de Gabriela Mistral, por C. Berges.—Imperfección y albricia, por G. Diego.—Luz-voz-de la poesía, por A. Espina.—Una sola vez, por G. Marañon.—Viento de cumbres, por C. Miró.—Proyección de Gabriela Mistral,—por A. Oliver Belmas.—
(Continued)

NN ** 9.53 OC PC,1 SL (LC1, Z1, X1)

A GARLAND for Jake Zeitlin... 1967. (Card 2)

great bookseller & his customers, by K. T. Steinitz.--The steam locomotive: a selective bibliography (p. 21-31), by E. L. DeGolyer.--Memo to Jake Zeitlin, by L. C. Powell.--Jake Zeitlin & the science vector, by B. Dibner.--The forgotten street of books, by W. Ritchie.--A day in Florence, by S. M. Malkin.--Jake Zeitlin: master at filling libraries, by E. Belt.--In it together, by W. A. Myers.--To be or not to be organized, by R. Vosper.--The telephone, by W. R. Howell.--Jake Zeitlin: a graphic appreciation, by E. M. Bloch.--Possibility theory & the bookshop, by P. Tuttle.--A bibliography of books published by the Primavera press (p. 117-131), by J. M. Edelstein.

1. Zeitlin, Jake. I. Edelstein, Jerome Melvin, 1924- , ed.

GABRIELA Mistral, premio Nobel... (Card 2)

Anticipo de un libro sobre Gabriela Mistral, por A. de la Rosa y G. de Albareda.—Daguerrotipos del recuerdo, por C. Zardoya.—A Gabriela Mistral, por V. Aleixandre.—Canción, por D. Alonso.—Dos poemas sobre la muerte, por C. Bousoño.—Canto a Gabriela Mistral, por C. Conde.—Ofrenda, por A. Valbuena Prat.—Bibliografía de Gabriela Mistral, por J. Romo Arregui.

1. Godoy Alcayaga, Lucila, 1889-

Write on slip words underlined below and class mark— *PZX

Eine Gartenstadt für Palästina; Festgabe zum siebzigsten Geburtstag von Max Nordau. Berlin: Jüdischer Verlag, 1920.
80 p. illus. 24cm. (Jewish national fund. Nationalfonds-Bibliothek. Nr. 5.)

CONTENTS.—Vorwort.—Adolf Friedemann: Max Nordau.—Max Nordau: Meine Selbstbiographie.—Franz Oppenheimer: Gartenstadt.—Alex Baerwald: Die Nordau-Gartenstadt.—Israel Cohen: Der Jüdische Nationalsfonds.

1. Garden cities—Palestine. 2. Nordau, Max Simon, 1849-1923.
N. Y. P. L. August 31, 1943

D-16
1116

Gaskill, Herbert S *ed.*
Counterpoint; libidinal object and subject. A tribute to René A. Spitz on his 75th birthday. New York, International Universities Press [1963]

200 p. port. 23 cm.

CONTENTS.—Foreword, by H. S. Gaskill.—A scientist's credo, by K. Lorenz.—Beyond and between the no and the yes: a tribute to Dr. René A. Spitz, by L. Rangell.—The evolution of a research project in psychoanalysis, by J. Fleming.—The central affective potential and its trigger mechanisms, by L. S. Kubie.—Further comments on some developmental aspects of anxiety, by J. D. Benjamin.—Life

(Continued)

NN* R 7.65 g/ OC, Ib* PC, 1, 2 SL (LC1, X1, Z1)

GASKILL, HERBERT S., ed. Counterpoint...
(Card 2)

and the dialogue, by R. A. Spitz.—Speeches at the banquet, by R. J. Glaser, G. Piers, H. S. Gaskill and R. A. Spitz. Publications by René A. Spitz.

Includes bibliographies.

1. Psychology--Addresses, essays, lectures. 2. Spitz., Rene Arpad, 1887-
I. Gaskill, Herbert S.

XAA
(Berlin)

Gedaechtnisschrift für Emil Seckel... Berlin: J. Springer, 1927. 494 p. front. (port.) 8°. (Berlin. Univ. Juristische Fakultaet. Abhandl. [Nr.] 4.)

Bibliographical footnotes.

Contents: GENZMER, E. Quare Glossatorum. SCHULZ, F. Der Irrtum im Beweggrund bei der testamentarischen Verfügung. LEVY, E. Verschollenheit und Ehe in antiken Rechten. JUNCKER, J. Haftung und Prozessbegründung im altrömischen Rechtsgang. HAMBURGER, G. Die Organgesellschaft. GRAU, W. Zusammenhängende Rechtsverhältnisse. GRAU, R. Diktaturgewalt und Reichsverfassung.

1. Seckel, Emil, 1864–1924. 2. Law— Essays and misc.
N. Y. P. L. October 21, 1927

E-12
9901

Gedächtnisschrift Hans Peters. Hrsg. von H. Conrad [et al.] Berlin, New York, Springer-Verlag, 1967.

xii, 983 p. port. 24 cm.

"Verzeichnis der Schriften und Aufsätze von Hans Peters": [977]-985.
Bibliographical footnotes.

1. Peters, Hans, 1896-1966. 2. Law--Addresses, essays, lectures. I. Conrad, Hermann, 1904- , ed.
NN * R 8.67 1/r OC, I PC, 1, 2, I SL (LC1, X1, Z1)

---

* C-6 p.v.1

[Gedenkalbum] 7 Januari 1937 – 7 Juli 1949. [Haarlem, Uitg. bij gelegenheid van het koperen huwelijksfeest van het koninklijk echtpaar door De Spaarnestad, 1949] [64] p. (chiefly illus., part col.) 36cm.

1. Juliana, Queen of the Netherlands, 1909- . 2. Orange-Nassau, House of. I. Title: 7 (i. e. Zeven) Januari 1937 – 7 Juli 1949.
NN*R 3.54 OC PC, 1, 2, I SL G, 2, I (Z1, LC1, X1)

D-12
1415

GEDENKBOEK C. M. van den Heever, 1902-1957 [door] P. J. Nienaber. Johannesburg, Afrikaanse pers-boekhandel, 1959. 392 p. ports. 21cm.

Bibliography, p. 371-392.

1. Heever, Christiaan Maurits van den, 1902-1957. I. Nienaber, Petrus Johannes, 1910- , ed.
NN R 12.59 g/P OC, I PC, 1, I SL (LC1, X1, Z1)

AN
(Junghuhn, F.)

Gedenkboek Franz Junghuhn 1809–1909. 's-Gravenhage, M. Nijhoff, 1910.

x, 361 p. front., illus., plates, facsims. (1 fold.) 25ᶜᵐ.

"De netto-opbrengst van het Junghuhn-gedenkboek komt geheel ten goede aan het Junghuhn-fonds. De Junghuhn-commissie."
"Junghuhn-bibliographie": p. [309]-356.

1. Junghuhn, Franz Wilhelm, 1809–1864.

10-24932

Library of Congress QK31.J8G5 Festschrift

E-10
3013

GEDENKBOEK Lode Zielens. 1901-1944. Brussel, Elsevier [1945] 98 p. ports. 25cm.

Cover title: In memoriam Lode Zielens...
CONTENTS.—Aanwezigheid, door R. Herreman.--Geen slag, door C. Huysmans.--Over Lode Zielens, door M. Gilliams.--Solidariteit, door R. Minne.--Waardoor komt het toch, door A. Mussche.--Een vriendschap, door F. Verschoren.--Herinneringen, door A. G.

(Continued)

NN*R 2.58 1/r OC, I PC, 1, I SL (LC1, X1, Z1)

GEDENKBOEK Lode Zielens. (Card 2)

Christiaens.--Lode Zielens, door F. V. Toussaint van Boelaere.--Precieser beeld van Lode Zielens, door G. Walschap.--Herinneringen aan Lode Zielens, door E. de Bom.--Lode Zielens, door K. Jonckheere.--In memoriam Lode Zielens, door M. J. Premsela.--Lode Zielens en de lezers van morgen, door R. Lissens.--Tegen sinecuren, voor loyaal Maecenaat, door G. Schmook.--Een bezoek, door F. de Backer.

1. Zielens, Lode, 1901- 1944. I. Title: In memoriam Lode Zielens.

E-10
6296

Gedenkboek voor Prof. Dr. Ph. A. Kohnstamm. Groningen, J. B. Wolters, 1957.

vi, 304 p. diagrs. 24 cm.

Includes bibliographies.

CONTENTS.—De leerstof voor rekenen op de lagere school en eakele motieven voor leerstofkeuze in het algemeen, door W. H. Brouwer.—Is er een natuurlijke drang tot leren? Door J. Bijl.—Die probleem van die openbare biblioteek en die denkpsigologie, door P. C. Coetzee.—De psychologie van het denken en het leren, door L. van Gelder en F. W. Prins.—Op het keerpunt der onderwijsgeschiedenis, door P. J. Idenburg.—Naar een nieuwe didactiek? Een verkenning, door J. Jonges.—De vernieuwing van de onderwijzersopleiding, door C. Kleywegt.—"Humanisering" mede in verband met "opvoeding"-, "kultuur,"

(Continued on next card)

NN * R 9.58 p//P OC PC, 1, 2 SL (LC1, X1, Z1)

Gedenkboek voor Prof. Dr. Ph. A. Kohnstamm. 1957. (Card 2)

CONTENTS—Continued.

door M. J. Langeveld.—Beskouinge oor 'n proefneming met die globale aanvangsleesmetode, door B. F. Nel.—Het onderwijs en de sociale pedagogiek (med. 61) door H. Nieuwenhuis.—Die mensbeeld by Viktor Frankl. Enkele opmerkinge, door C. K. Oberholzer.—De mondigheid van de onderwijzenden, door P. Post.—De toekomst van het personalisme, door H. van Praag.—Synidese. Enkele denkpsychologische beschouwingen over de functionele samenhang van waarnemings- en denkprocessen in verband met de didactiek, door H. W. F. Stellwag.—Paedagogiek en kunst, door S. Strasser.—Structuur en functie van het rijksschooltoezicht, door I. van der Velde.

1. EDUCATION—ADDRESSES, ESSAYS, LECTURES
2. Kohnstamm, Philipp Abraham, 1875-1951

---

*PXT

Gedenkbuch, herausgegeben zum 250. Jahrestag der Verheerung [sic] der Uh. Broder Judengemeinde am 20. Thamus 5443 (14. Juli 1683). Uh. Brod: Im Eigenverlage, 1936. 119, 41 p. facsims., plates. 20½cm.

Added t.-p. in Bohemian: Památník vydaný při 250 letém výročí vyplenění židovské obce Uherskeho Brodu od Uhrů, které se stalo dne 20. tamusu 5443 (14. července 1683).

Text in Bohemian and German.

"Z osudu židovského obyvatelstva v Uherském Brodě," p. [7]-37, by Ferdinand Prager.

"Kinah," [in Yiddish] p. [105]-111; "Seliḥot," [in Hebrew] 41 p., at end.

"Uebersetzung: Rudolf Kohn."

171132B. 1. Jews in Hungary—Brod. I. Prager, Ferdinand. II. Kohn, Rudolf, tr. III. Jews. Liturgy and ritual. Penitential prayers.

N. Y. P. L. September 28, 1942

XAA (Leipziger)

...**Gedenkschrift** für Ludwig Mitteis, verfasst von Mitgliedern der Leipziger Juristen-Fakultät. Leipzig: T. Weicher, 1926. 223 p. 4°. (Leipziger rechtswissenschaftliche Studien. Heft 11.)

Bibliographical footnotes.

Contents: Siber, H. Naturalis obligatio. Bohne, G. Zur Stellung der Frau im Prozess- und Strafrecht der italienischen Statuten. Apelt, W. Das Rechtsinstitut der öffentlichen Last und die Industriebelastung. Schmidt, R. Verfassungsausbau und Weltreichsbildung.

1. Mitteis, Ludwig, 1859–1921. 2. Obligations—Jurisp.—Rome. 3. Woman—Legal status—Italy. 4. European war, 1914–1918—Reparations. 5. Political science—Hist. 6. Ser.

N. Y. P. L. July 14, 1927

E-12
4065

GEDENKSCHRIFT für Margarete Eberhardt. [Hamburg, R. Meiner, 1961] 93 p. port. 24cm.

Cover title: Margarete Eberhardt, zum 18. August 1961.

1. Eberhardt, Margarete.

NN 5.66 g/ OC PC, 1 SL (LC1, X1, Z1)

E-13
7069

Gedenkschrift Martin Göhring; Studien zur europäischen Geschichte. Mit einem Geleitwort von Jacques Droz, hrsg. von Ernst Schulin. Wiesbaden, F. Steiner, 1968. x, 450 p. facsims., port. 25cm. (Institut für europäische Geschichte, Mainz. Veröffentlichungen. Bd. 50. Abteilung Universalgeschichte.)

German, English, or French.

"Schriftenverzeichnis Martin Göhring": p. [444]-445.

Bibliographical footnotes.

1. Göhring, Martin. 2. Europe--Hist.--Addresses, essays, lectures. I. Series. II. Schulin, Ernst, ed.

NN*R 1.70 r/ OC, II (OS)I PC, 1, 2, I, II SL (LC1, X1, Z/1) [I]

L-10
3690
Bd. 18

GEDENKSCHRIFT für William Foerste; hrsg. von Dietrich Hofmann, unter Mitarbeit von Willy Sanders. Köln, Böhlau, 1970. vii, 552 p. port., maps. 24cm. (Niederdeutsche Studien. Bd. 18)

"Verzeichnis der Schriften von William Foerste." p. [543]-552.

Bibliographical footnotes.

(Continued)

NN R 4.71 m/ OC, I, II (OS)III PC, 1, 2, I, II, III (LC1, X1, Z1) [I]

GEDENKSCHRIFT für William Foerste... (Card 2)

1. German language--Addresses, essays, lectures. 2. German literature--Addresses, essays, lectures. I. Foerste, William. II. Hofmann, Dietrich, ed. III. Series.

NABM

GEGENWART im Geiste; Festschrift für Richard Benz. [Hrsg. von Walther Bulst und Arthur v. Schneider] Hamburg, C. Wegner, 1954. 142 p. music. 21cm.

CONTENTS.—Zum 12. Juni 1954, von E. A. Herrmann.—Ein Brief mit der Eintrittskarte zur Zauberflöte, von H. Hesse.—Erinnerung an Leipziger Studienjahre, von H. Carossa.—Gruss an Richard Benz, von R. Minder.—Richard Benz: Deuter der Vergangenheit, Wegweiser in die Zukunft, von H. Günther.—Richard Benz und die deutsche Kunstgeschichte, von A. von Schneider.—Richard Benz und der Heidelberger Geist, von R. K. Goldschmit-Jentner.—Mythos und

(Continued)

NN**R X 2.55 g/ OC, I, II PC, 1, 2, 3, I, II SL (Z1, LC1, X1) [I]

GEGENWART im Geiste... (Card 2)

Vernunft, von H. G. Gadamer.—Tempelschlaf, Magnetismus, Mesmerismus, Hypnose, von H. W. Gruhle.—Das Daniel-Spiel, von W. Bulst.—Klärchen, von M. L. Kaschnitz.—Klang und Bild in der Stimmungslyrik der Romantik, von P. Böckmann.—'Das Wirtshaus' von Schubert und das Kyrie aus dem gregorianischen Requiem, von T. Georgiades.—Das Buch-Werk von Richard Benz (p. [136]-142).

1. Benz, Richard Edmund, 1884- . 2. Literature—Hist. and crit. 3. Philosophy—Addresses, essays, lectures. I. Schneider, Arthur von, 1886- , ed. II. Bulst, Walth ed.

NN**R X 2.55 g/ OC, I, II PC, 1, 2, 3, I, II SL (Z1, LC1, X1) [I]

---

*PXS

GEGENWART im Rückblick; Festgabe für die Jüdische Gemeinde zu Berlin, 25 Jahre nach dem Neubeginn. Hrsg. von Herbert A. Strauss und Kurt R. Grossmann. Heidelberg, L. Stiehm, 1970. 374 p. illus., ports., facsims., geneal. table in pocket. 25cm.

Includes bibliographies.

1. Jews in Germany--Berlin--Hist. 2. Berlin--Hist. I. Strauss, Herbert Arthur, ed. II. Grossmann, Kurt R., 1897- , ed. III. Berlin. Jüdische Gemeinde.

NN R 6.71 w/ OC, I, II (OS)III PC, 1, I, II, III SL J, 2, I, II, III (LC1, X1, Z1)

D-19
6338

GEGENWART und Tradition; Strukturen des Denkens. Eine Festschrift für Bernhard Lakebrink. Mit Beiträgen von Gerhart Baumann [et al.] Herausgeber: Cornelio Fabro. [1. Aufl.] Freiburg, Verlag Rombach [1969] 249 p. port. 23cm. (Sammlung Rombach. N.F. Bd.1)

Bibliographical footnotes.

CONTENTS.--Asebeia und Techne im 10. Buch der Nomoi, von

(Continued)

NN 1.70 I/A OC, I, II, III (OS)IV PC, 1, I, II, III SL (LC1, X1, Z1)
[S, NSCM]

GEGENWART und Tradition... (Card 2)

E. Fink.--Plotin: Das Eine und der Kosmos, von F.J. von Rintelin.--Die Zweite Begründung der kritisch-realistischen Metaphysik, von A. Dempf.--Naturrecht oder Vernunftrecht bei Thomas von Aquin? Von J. Hirschberger.--Die analogia attributionis intrinsecae und ihre Erkenntnis, von W. Hoeres.--Zusammenfall der Gegensätze und die Philosophie des Nichtwissens, von J. Stallmach.--Sicherheit als Mass der Freiheit? Von U. Hommes.--Die Rolle der Ästhetik in William von Humboldts Theorie der Bildung, von C. Menze.--Das Zeitalter

(Continued)

GEGENWART und Tradition... (Card 3)

ohne Menschenbild und die Dialektik der Befreiung, von L. Landgrebe.--Das Problem der Sonderwelten bei Husserl, von W. Marx.--Neuscholastik und Neuthomismus in Italien, von C. Fabro.--Das Geschichtliche und das Metaphysische in der Theologie, von M. Schmaus.--Historisch-objektivierende und existentiale Interpretation, von A. Vögtle.--Selbstgespräch, Selbstbewusstsein, Selbsterkenntnis, von G. Baumann.--Anmerkung über die mögliche Zukunft der Philosophie, von J. Pieper.

1. Philosophy--Addresses, essays, lectures. I. Fabro, Cornelio, ed. II. Lakebrink, Bernhard. III. Baumann, Gerhart. IV. Sammlung Rombach. N.F.

SLE

Gegenwartsfragen der strafrechtswissenschaft; festschrift zum 60. geburtstag von graf W. Gleispach, von Georg Dahm, Wilhelm Gallas, Friedrich Schaffstein, Erich Schinnerer, Karl Siegert, Leopold Zimmerl. Berlin und Leipzig, W. de Gruyter & co., 1936.

3 p. l., 187 p. 22½cm.

CONTENTS.—Der ehrenschutz der gemeinschaft, von Georg Dahm.—Zur kritik der lehre vom verbrechen als rechtsgutsverletzung, von Wilhelm Gallas.—Die unechten unterlassungsdelikte im system des neuen strafrechts, von Friedrich Schaffstein.—Erfolgshaftung, von Erich Schinnerer.—Berufung und revision im strafverfahren, von Karl Siegert.—Zur auslegung des §2 Stgb, von Leopold Zimmerl.

1. Gleispach, Wenzeslaus Karl Maximilian Maria, graf, 1876- 2. Criminal law—Addresses, essays, lectures. 3. Criminal law—Germany. I. Dahm, Georg, 1904- II. Gallas, Wilhelm, 1903- III. Schaffstein, Friedrich, 1905- IV. Schinnerer, Erich, 1908- V. Siegert, Karl, 1901- VI. Zimmerl, Leopold, 1899-

40-21936

Library of Congress [2]

E-11
2891

GEGENWARTSFRAGEN der Unternehmung; offene Fragen der Betriebswirtschaftslehre. [Festschrift zum 70. Geburtstag von Fritz Henzel] hrsg. von Bernhard Bellinger. Wiesbaden, T.Gabler [1961] 251 p. port. 25cm.

Bibliographical footnotes.

CONTENTS.--Offene Fragen der betrieblichen Substanzerhaltung, von B. Bellinger.--Zur Gliederungsproblematik der Gewinn- und Verlustrechnung,

(Continued)

NN R 7.61 p/A OC, I, IIbo PC, 1, 2, I SL E, 1, 2, I (LC1, X1, Z1)

GEGENWARTSFRAGEN der Unternehmung... (Card 2)

von W. le Coutre.--Die Problemstellung der betriebswirtschaftlichen Marktforschung, von P. Deutsch.--Das Problem der optimalen Unternehmungsplanung, von E. Grochla.--Die Betriebskosten der Versicherungsunternehmung, von M. Gürtler.--Das Unternehmen in der modernen Wettbewerbswirtschaft, von R. Henzler.--Einheit und Gliederung der Wirtschaftswissenschaften,' von A. Hertlein.--Leistungs- und kostentheoretische Korrelationen, von J.Kolbinger.--Probleme des Gestaltungsbereiches, von G. Krüger.--Unternehmer und Unternehmung, von A. Marx.--Marktmässige Gestaltung der Produktionsprogramme, von K. Mellerowicz.--Vermag die moderne Werbung den Menschen zu

(Continued)

GEGENWARTSFRAGEN der Unternehmung... (Card 3)

manipulieren"? von R. Nieschlag.--Die Problematik des industriellen Auftragsbestandes, von K. Oberparleiter.--Gliederung der Ergebnisse einer externen Bilanzänderungsrechnung, von C. Ruberg.--Beziehungen zwischen Abschreibungsmethoden, Abschreibungszinsen, kalkulatorischen Zinsen und Kapazitätserweiterungseffekt (der kalkulatorische Zinseffekt), von A. Schnettler.--Das Schwächebild der Werbeerfolgskontrolle, von O.R. Schnutenhaus.--Kapazitätsplanung und lineare Planungsrechnung, von K. Schwantag.--Verzeichnis der Schriften von Professor Dr. Fritz Henzel (p. [247]-251)

1. Management--Addresses, essays, lectures. 2. Henzel, Fritz. I. Bellinger, Bernhard, ed. II. Bellinger, Bernhard.

E-10
7999

Gegenwartsprobleme der Agrarökonomie: Festschrift für Fritz Baade zum 65. Geburtstag. [Schriftleitung: Anton Zottmann] Hamburg, Hoffmann & Campe, 1958.

482 p. illus., port., maps (1 fold.) tables. 24 cm.

Bibliographical footnotes.

CONTENTS.—Fritz Baade, von H. Paetzmann.—Die Agrarpolitik Belgiens, von V. von Arnim.—Die Umwälzungen in der Landwirtschaft Chinas, von M. Biehl.—Bestimmungsgründe des Handelsdüngerverbrauchs in Entwicklungsländern, von U. Ewald.—Die Landwirtschaft im Rahmen der Wirtschafspolitik der ostmitteleuropäischen und südosteuropäischen Staaten, von H. Gross.—Der Strukturwandel der Landwirtschaft dargestellt an Thünens "Landrentenformel," von H. H. Herlemann.—Über Zuverlässigkeit von Berechnungen in der Agrarwirtschaft, von G. Klauder.—Über Grundlagen der landwirtschaftlichen Marktlehre, von K. Langenheim.—Die Bodenreform in

(Continued)

NN*R 7.59 t/ OC, I PC, 1, 2, I SL E, 1, 2, I (LC1, X1, Z1)

Gegenwartsprobleme der Agrarökonomie ... 1958. (Card 2)

CONTENTS—Continued.

der sowjetischen Besatzungszone und ihre Auswirkungen auf die Landwirtschaft und Ernährungswirtschaft, von H. Liebe.—Die Rolle der Landwirtschaft in der Entwicklung des Mittleren Ostens, von A. Michaelis.—Die Desa und ihre Bedeutung für die wirtschaftliche Entwicklung Indonesiens, von K. Möbius.—Die Abwanderung aus der Landwirtschaft als Folge der geringen Elastizität des Nahrungsverbrauchs, von P. Quante.—Agriculture in Israel, by L. E. Samuel.—Die Landarbeiter in der internationalen Sozialpolitik, von G. Savelsberg.—Das sowjetische Agrarsystem: Modell für Entwicklungsländer? Von O. Schiller.—Das Produktivitätsproblem in der Landwirtschaft, von W. Schüttauf.—Indiens Bevölkerungs- und Nahrungsproblem, von R. Stisser.—Zum Aufstieg von Entwicklungsländern, von H. Wilbrandt.—Das Schrifttum von Fritz Baade. (p. 460-471)

1. AGRICULTURE--ECONOMICS 2. BAADE, FRITZ
I. Zottmann, Anton, ed.

D-10
6074

Gegenwartsprobleme der Betriebswirtschaft. [Hrsg. von Friedrich Henzel, in Verbindung mit Willi Bouffier [et al.] Baden-Baden, A. Lutzeyer [1955]

300 p. 21 cm.

"Gewidmet Herrn Prof. Dr. Dr. h. c. Le Coutre zu seinem 70. Geburtstage."

1. MANAGEMENT--ADDRESSES, ESSAYS, LECTURES
2. LE COUTRE, WALTER, 1885- I. Henzel, Fritz, ed.

NN* R 9.57 a/ OC, I PC, 1, 2, I SL E, 1, 2, I (LC1, X1, Z1)

ILH

GEIST einer freien Gesellschaft; Festschrift zu Ehren von Senator James William Fulbright aus Anlass der zehnjährigen Bestehens des Deutschen Fulbright-Programms. Heidelberg, Quelle & Meyer, 1962
391 p. illus., port., map. 23cm.

Added t.p. in English.
Bibliographical footnotes.
CONTENTS--Das Amerika-Bild von Claude-Henri de Saint-Simon und
(Continued)

NN R 7.63 p/ OC PC, 1, 2, 3 SL AH, 1, 3 (LC1, X1, Z1)
[I] 3

GEIST einer freien Gesellschaft... (Cont.)

seine Bedeutung für die Entwicklung der Europäischen Soziologie, von R. König. --Ferment of American freedom, by M. Abbott. --The self-interpretation of the South through reform, rebellion and reconstruction, by W. C. Harvard. --Recent trends in American social thought, by J.G. Sproat. --The American ideal of a world republic, by E. McNall Burns. --Temperaturschwankungen in den kalifornischen Küstengewässern und ihre Rückwirkungen auf die Sardinenfischerei Montereys [und] Die Goldrauschstädte der "Mother Lode" in Kalifornien, von H. Wilhelmy. --How ambiguous is Hawthorne?, by H.J. Lang. --Wege in die dichterische Welt Emily Dickinsons, von H.Galinsky --Symbolic action in the poetry of Robert Frost.
(Continued)

GEIST einer freien Gesellschaft... (Cont.)

by A. S. Ryan. --Young voices on the American literary scene, by M. Spevack. --Regionalism in American literature, by Cecil B. Williams

1. United States--Civilization, 20th cent. 2. American literature--Hist. and crit., 20th cent. 3. Fulbright, James William, 1905- .

ZKBK

Geistige Grundlagen römischer Kirchenpolitik. Stuttgart: W. Kohlhammer, 1937. xviii, 154, 123, viii, 162, iv, 90 p. 24cm. (Added t.-p.: Forschungen zur Kirchen- und Geistesgeschichte ... Bd. 11.)

Four studies, also issued as dissertations, collected and published in honor of Erich Caspar.
Bibliographies included.
CONTENTS.—Gmelin, Ulrich. Auctoritas. Römischer Princeps und päpstlicher Primat.—Roethe, Gerwin. Zur Geschichte der römischen Synoden im 3. und 4. Jahrhundert.—Pewesin, Wolfgang. Imperium, Ecclesia spiritualis, Rom.—Reinke, Arnold. Die Schuldialektik im Investiturstreit.

(Continued)

N. Y. P. L. July 9, 1940

Geistige Grundlagen... (Card 2)

966727A. 1. Church and state—Rome. 2. Church history—Undivided church, to 1054. 3. Catholic church, Roman—Councils and synods—Rome. 4. Catholic church, Roman—Influence, Political and social—Germany. 5. Investiture—Germany. 6. Caspar, Erich Ludwig Eduard, 1879–1935. I. Gmelin, Ulrich, 1912– . II. Roethe, Gerwin. III. Pewesin, Wolfgang. IV. Reinke, Arnold.
N. Y. P. L. July 9, 1940

TF

Geld- und kreditsystem der Schweiz; festgabe für Gottlieb Bachmann. 2. aufl. Zürich, Schulthess & co. a.-g., 1944.
viii, 449 p. front. (port.) diagrs. 22½cm.
Bibliographical foot-notes. Bibliography at end of some of the articles.
CONTENTS.—Wetter, E. Zum geleit.—Allgemeine grundlagen: Grossmann, E. Gestaltende kräfte in der schweizerischen geld- und kreditwirtschaft. Büchner, R. Geld- und kredittheorie im wandel des wirtschaftslebens. Egger, A. Ueber die verantwortlichkeit des bankiers. Oppikofer, H. Der nennwert des geldes im schweizerischen schuldrecht. Nabholz, H. Die anfänge des bankwesens in Zürich. Weisz, L. Der organisierte kredit in Zürich von der reformation bis zum jahre 1835.—Geldverfassung und kreditorganisation: Kellenberger, E. Die schweizerische münzpolitik im kriege. Ackermann, E. Banknote und giralgeld. Weber, E. Das kreditgeschäft der Schweizerischen nationalbank. Stampfli, A. Die banken in der schweizerischen kreditorgani-

(Continued on next card)

A 46–756

[2]

Geld- und kreditsystem der Schweiz ... 1944. (Card 2)

CONTENTS—Continued.

sation. Zollinger, W. Die private versicherung im rahmen des kreditsystems. Burri, J. Die ausbildung der bankbeamten.—Die finanzierung einzelner wirtschaftszweige: König, R. Probleme des agrarkredits. Keller, Th. Probleme der finanzierung von industrie, gewerbe und handel. Saitzew, M. Die finanzierung der schweizerischen elektrizitätswirtschaft.—Der öffentliche kredit: Rossy, P. Les besoins financiers de la confédération et leur couverture. Mosimann, E. Das eidgenössische schuldbuch als staatsschuldbuch des bundes.—Probleme der zahlungsbilanz: Borle, H. De l'exportation des capitaux et du circuit monétaire. Hirs, A. Der internationale zahlungsverkehr der Schweiz. Hotz, J. Clearing und aussenhandel. Schauwecker, C. Der private kompensationsverkehr.

1. Bachmann, Gottlieb, 1874– 2. Money—Switzerland. 3. Credit—Switzerland. 4. Banks and banking—Switzerland.

A 46–756

Harvard univ. Library
for Library of Congress [2]

GAXZ

Geleen. Netherlands.
Gedenkboek: Geleen, van dorp tot Mauritsstad. [Geleen, 1951] 249 p. illus. (part col.), plans. 27cm.

Issued in honor of F. A. L. M. Damen's thirty years as burgomaster of Geleen.
By various authors.
1. Geleen, Netherlands—Hist. 2. Economic history—Netherlands—Geleen. 3. Damen, Franciscus Antonius Ludovicus Maria, 1888- 1951. i.1951.
NN**R 2.54 (OC)3b OD1 ED1 PC,1,2,3 SL (E)2 (Z1,LC1,X1)

E-11
9079

GEMEINDE Gottes in dieser Welt; Festgabe für Friedrich-Wilhelm Krummacher zum sechzigsten Geburtstag. Berlin, Evangelische Verlagsanstalt [1961] 354 p. illus., facsims. 25cm.

Edited by Friedrich Bartsch and Werner Rautenberg.
Includes bibliographies.
CONTENTS.--Der Werdegang des Bischofs, von H. Faisst. --Blick
(Continued)

NN R 2.64 e/B OC, I, II, IIIb*, IVbo PC, 1, 2, I, II SL (LC1, X1, Z1) 4

GEMEINDE Gottes in dieser Welt... (Card 2)

auf den Dom in Greifswald, von B.-D. Krummacher. --Weinachten in St. Nicolai, Stralsund, von H. Faisst. --Zur Geschichte der ältesten pommerschen Agende, von H. Heyden. --Geschichte und Tradition als gestaltende Kräfte in der evangelischen Kirche, von H. Brunotte. --Der Katholizismus als Frage an uns, von E. Sommerlath. --Kann auch die Predigtverkündigung der Orthodoxen Kirche in der UdSSR einen Beitrag zur Überwindung unserer Predigtnot leisten? von F. Führ. --Über das Verhältnis der deutschen Geistlichen und des Adels in Estland, insbesondere im 17. Jahrhundert, von J. Kiivit. --Die Zukunftsaufgaben der
(Continued)

GEMEINDE Gottes in dieser Welt... (Card 3)

Protestantischen Kirchen Frankreichs, von G. Casalis.--Biblische Grundlage der evangelischen Abendmahlslehre, von J. Cullberg.--Haushalterschaft (stewardship) als ökumenischer Auftrag, von W. Rautenberg.--Brot für die Welt; von C. Berg.--Rilkes "Stunden-Buch", von H.-H. Krummacher.--Zur Quellenlage von Matthias Weckmanns geistlichen Vokalwerken, von F. Krummacher.--Die Musikauffassung des jungen Luther, von O. Söhngen.--Der Theologe, das Buch and die Rezension, von R. Stupperich.--Das Amt des Buches in der Gemeinde, von F. Bartsch.--Der katechetische Dienst in der Kirche, von H. Hafa.--Diakonie unter der

(Continued)

GEMEINDE Gottes in dieser Welt... (Card 4)

Weisung der Zehn Gebote, von R. Frick.--Die Chance der Rundfunkpredigt, von H. Wagner.

1. Krummacher, Friedrich Wilhelm, 1901- . 2. Christianity--Essays and misc. I. Bartsch, Friedrich, 1898- , ed. II. Rautenberg, Werner, ed. III. Bartsch, Friedrich, 1898- . IV. Rautenberg, Werner.

D-11
1372

Generālis Goppers kara un laika biedru atmiņās. Rakstu un materialu krājums pulkv. Kārļa Lobes un Mikeļa Goppera redakcijā. [Stockholm] Zelta ābele, 1951. 63 p. illus., ports. 23cm.

Caption title.
By various authors.

1. Goppers, Kārlis, 1876-1941. 2. Latvia—Hist., 1918- . I. Lobe, Kārlis, ed. II. Goppers, Mikelis, 1908- , ed. III. Lobe, Kārlis.
NN**R 8.59 OC,I,II,IIb,IIIbo PC,1,2,I,II SL S,1,2,I,II (LC1,X1,Z1)

Write on slip, name, year, vol., page of magazine and class mark — RBA

Genethliakon Wilhelm Schmid zum siebzigsten Geburtstag am 24. Februar 1929.

(Tuebinger Beitraege zur Altertumswissenschaft. Stuttgart,1929. 8°. Heft 5,p.1-464.)
Contents: F.Focke:Demosthenesstudien. J.Mewaldt: Fundament des Staates. J.Vogt: Herodot in Ägypten. C.Watzinger: Die griechische Grabstele und der Orient. O.Weinreich: Gebet und Wunder.

form 400a [vi-7-29 25m]

L-10
3847
v.16

GENOA (City). Università. Istituto di filologia classica.

Lanx Satura Nicolao Terzaghi oblata: miscellanea philologica. [Genova] 1963. 354 p. illus., port. 22cm. (ITS: Pubblicazioni. 16)

Bibliographical footnotes.
CONTENTS.--Nicola Terzaghi, di M. Bonaria.--Saggio di

(Continued)

NN 4.66 r/ OS,I PC,1,2,I (LC1,X1,Z1)

GENOA (City). Università. Istituto di filologia classica. Lanx Satura Nicolao Terzaghi oblata: miscellanea philologica. (Card 2)

bibliografia sul Dyscolos di Menandro, di G. Barabino.--La lettera prefatoria di Irzio all VIII libro del B.G., di G. Bartolini.--Ad alcuni frammenti saffici "incerti libri", di M. Bonaria.--I tre furi, di G. Brugnoli.--Il commento di Giovanni Tzetzes agli Halieutica di Oppiano, di A. Colonna.--Vindiciae archilochiae, di H. Della Casa.--I due proemi del De inventione, di P. Giuffrida.--Due proposte per il De Publio Cornelio Scipione Africano Maiore del Petrarca, di C.F. Goffis.--Marginalia Aesopica, di A. La Penna.--Deus ex

(Continued)

GENOA (City). Università. Istituto di filologia classica. Lanx Satura Nicolao Terzaghi oblata: miscellanea philologica. (Card 3)

machina e religione in Euripide, di V. Longo.--Horret et alget, di I. Mariotti.--Note ai Priapea, di S. Mariotti.--Noterelle su Matteo di Vendôme, di F. Munari.--Papiri inediti genovesi, di C. Pasqual.--De glossari "abolita" quadam glossa, di L. Strzelecki.--Per la critica testuale dell'Ephemeris di Ditti-Settimio, di S. Timpanaro.--Note a Petronio e al Marziale, di M. Zicari.

1. Literature--Addresses, essays, lectures. 2. Terzaghi, Nicola, 1880- . I. Series.

E-10
8102

GEOGRAPHISCHE Forschungen; Festschrift zum 60. Geburtstag von Hans Kinzl, dargebracht von Kollegen, Schülern und dem Verlag. Besorgt von Herbert Paschinger. Innsbruck, Wagner, 1958. 325 p. illus., port., maps (part fold.) 1 issued in pocket) 24cm. (Schlern-Schriften. 190)

Includes bibliographies.
CONTENTS. — Aus H. Kinzls Leben und Schaffen, von R. von

(Continued)

NN 2.59 g/[II] OC,I (OS)II PC,1,2,I,II SL (LC1,X1,Z1)

GEOGRAPHISCHE Forschungen... (Card 2)

Klebelsberg. — Teheran, von H. Bobek. —Über das Alter der Gebirge, von H. Boesch. — Lage und Materialbestimmtheit von Frostmusterböden, von W. Czajka. — Der Wiwiß-See in Thessalien, von E. Fels. — Die Landschaft des Simplonpasses, von H. Gutersohn. —Der Anteil der Stark- und Dauerniederschläge am Gesamtniederschlag im südlichen Deutschland nördlich der Alpen, von W. Hartke. —Beiträge zur Datierung alter Gletscherstände im Hochstubai (Tirol), von H. Heuberger und R. Beschel. —Die Städte von Schwäbisch-Österreich, von F. Huttenlocher. — Die Provinz Schensi (Nordchina), von G. Köhler. —

(Continued)

GEOGRAPHISCHE Forschungen... (Card 3)

Historische Gletscherschwankungen auf der Südhalbkugel, insbesondere auf Neuseeland, von A. Kolb. — Probleme der Agrarmeteorologie in Südtirol, von A. Leidlmair. —Der Bestrahlungsgang als Fundamentalerscheinung der geographischen Klimaunterscheidung, von H. Louis. — Das Weinland in Südtirol und im Elsass, von F. Metz. — Temperatursprünge, von S. Morawetz. — Firn und Gletschereis als Handelsgüter, von V. Paschinger. — Morphometrische Schotteranalysen im Quartär des alpinen Inntales, von H. Paschinger. — Studien über D. Anton Friedrich Büsching, von E. Plewe. — Das japanische

(Continued)

GEOGRAPHISCHE Forschungen... (Card 4)

Bevölkerungsproblem, von L. Scheidl. —Steiermark und Schlesien, von H. Schlenger. —Rezente und fossile Frosterscheinungen im Bereich der Gletscherlandschaft der Gurgler Ache (Ötztaler Alpen), von J. Schmid. —Frührezente und rezente Hochstände der Gletscher des kilikischen Ala Dag im Taurus, von H. Spreitzer. —Demnat, eine Berberstadt im Hohen Atlas, von K. Wiche. —Neue Lebensformen im tropischen Südamerika, von H. Wilhelmy. —Die Südgrenze der terra cognita von Juba und Plinius bis Ptolomäus, von H. v. Wissmann.

1. Kinzl, Hans, 1898- 2. Geography--Addresses, essays, lectures. I. Paschinger, Herbert, ed. II. Series.

PTK

Geological society of America.
...Application of geology to engineering practice. Berkey volume. Sidney Paige, chairman. Papers by John L. Savage ...[and 17 others] [New York] The society, 1950. xix, 327 p. illus., maps. 25cm.

Bibliography at end of most papers.

568446B. 1. Geology, Engineering. 2. Berkey, Charles Peter, 1867- . I. Paige, Sidney, 1880- , ed.
N. Y. P. L. March 12, 1951

PWR

GEOLOGICAL SOCIETY OF AMERICA.
Petrologic studies; a volume in honor of A. F. Buddington. A. E. J. Engel, Harold L. James, and B. F. Leonard, editors. [New York] 1962. xi, 660 p. illus., port. maps (part fold.) 25cm.

Includes bibliographies.

CONTENTS.--Iron-magnesium ratio in associated pyroxenes and olivines, by P. Bartholomé.--Pyroxenes and garnets from Charnockites and (Continued)

NN 3.63 p/3 (OC)I, II, III, IVbo, VbAMS, VIbAMS OS PC, 1, 2, I, II, III SL ST, 1t, 2, I, II, III (LC1, X1, Z1)

GEOLOGICAL SOCIETY OF AMERICA. Petrologic studies... (Card 2)

associated granulites, by A. P. Subramaniam.--Progressive metamorphism and amphibolite, Northwest Adirondack mountains, New York, by A. E. J. Engel and C. G. Engel.--Carbonatite problem in the Bearpaw mountains, Montana, by W. T. Pecora.--Isotopic composition and concentration of lead in some carbonate rocks, by J. M. Wampler and J. L. Kulp.--Lead-isotope studies in the Northern Rockies, U. S. A., by R. S. Cannon and others.--Tectonic-igneous sequence in Costa Rica, by G. Dengo.--Petrology of the Allard lake anorthosite suite, Quebec, by R. B. Hargraves. (Continued)

GEOLOGICAL SOCIETY OF AMERICA. Petrologic studies... (Card 3)

Origin and diagenetic alteration of the lower part of the John Day formation near Mitchell, Oregon, by R. L. Hay.--Oxygen isotope fractionation in metamorphosed iron formations of the Lake Superior region and in other iron-rich rocks, by H. L. James and R. N. Clayton.--Lead-isotope and potassium-argon studies in the East Kootenay district of British Columbia, by G. B. Leech and R. K. Wanless.--Origin of slaty and fracture cleavage in the Delaware Water Gap area, New Jersey and Pennsylvania, by J. C. Maxwell.--Faults and folds across Cordilleran trends at the headwaters of (Continued)

GEOLOGICAL SOCIETY OF AMERICA. Petrologic studies... (Card 4)

Leduc river, Northern British Columbia, by G. W. H. Norman.--Diatremes and uranium deposits in the Hopi Buttes, Arizona, by E. M. Shoemaker, and others.--Calderas and associated volcanic rocks near Beatty, Nye county, Nevada, by H. R. Cornwall.--Hypogene zoning and ore genesis, Central City district, Colorado, by P. K. Sims and P. B. Barton.--Sulphur Bank, California, a major hot-spring quicksilver deposit; by D. E. White and C. E. Roberson.--Effect of ionic substitution on the unit-cell dimensions of synthetic diopside, by L. C. Coleman.--Model for the evolution of the (Continued)

GEOLOGICAL SOCIETY OF AMERICA. Petrologic studies... (Card 5)

earth's atmosphere, by H. D. Holland.--Laramide comagmatic series in the Colorado front range: the feldspars, by G. Phair and F. G. Fisher.--Members of the Ludwigite-Vonsenite series and their distinction from ilvaite, by B. F. Leonard and others.--Stratigraphic interpretation of age measurements in Southern Africa, by L. O. Nicolaysen.--History of ocean basins, by H. H. Hess.

1. Petrology. 2. Buddington, Arthur Francis, 1891- I. Engle, A. E. J., ed. II. James, Harold Lloyd, 1912- , ed. III. Leonard, Benjamin Franklin, 1921- , ed. IV. Engle, A. E. J. V. James, Harold Lloyd, 1912- VI. Leonard, Benjamin Franklin, 1921- t. 1962.

NIT

GEORG BRANDES, 1842-1912; fra Norge paa syttiaarsdagen. [Bidragene samlet og utgit av Anders Krogvig og Einar Skavlan] [København] Gyldendal, 1912. 73 p. port. 25cm.

1. Brandes, Georg Morris Cohen, 1842-1927. I. Krogvig, Anders, 1880-1924, ed. II. Skavlan, Einar Kielland, 1882- , ed.

NN ** R 2.58 a/ OCs, Is, II PCs, Is, Is, IIs SLs (LCIs, XIs, ZIs)

3-MGQ +

Georg Habich zum 60. Geburtstag. München: Kress & Hornung, 1928. 122 p. mounted illus., 20 pl. sq. 4°.

Contents: Bechtold, A. Zu Dürers Radierung "Die grosse Kanone." Berliner, R. Der Schnitzer Matthias Loth in München. Bernhart, M. Zur Technik der Gussmedaille. Buchenau, H. Halbbrakteaten der Bischöfe Gebhard und Heinrich II. von Würzburg. Cahn, J. Das Vorbild zu einer Medaille Hans Reinharts. Drey, S. Kunstwissenschaft und Kunsthandel. Dworschak, F. Die Einflussphäre der Medaille. Gebhart, H. Die Statthalterguldener Friedrichs II. von der Pfalz. Gessert, O. Nachträge zur pfälzischen Medaillenkunde. Grotemeyer, P. Würz-

(Continued)

N. Y. P. L. May 24, 1929

Georg Habich zum 60. Geburtstag... (Card 2)

burger Sedisvakanzmedaillen nach den Entwurfen des Bildhauers Johann Wolfgang von der Auvera. Hampe, T. Splitter zur Jamnitzerforschung. Hill, G. F. Some Italian medals of the sixteenth century. Kris, E. Notizen zum Werk des Leone Leoni. Loehr, A. v. Die Medaille, Denkmal und Quelle der Kulturgeschichte. Neuhaus, A. Der Hochfürstlich Ansbachische Hofmedailleur Johann Christian Reich. Noss, A. Die Lincke's in Heidelberg als Münzstempelschneider. Regling, K. Drei neue Heraklesmünzen. Sauerlandt, M. Orpheus und Eurydice. Schwabacher, W. Zwei sizilische Tetradrachmen. Schwinkowski, W. Eine Prägemedaille mit Patrize, 1614. Sieveking, J. Zum Bildnis des Kaisers Vitellius. Stöcklein, H. Die Medaillen von Étienne Delaune in der Staatl. Münzsammlung, München. Wolters, P. Ein Bild der Kybele.

408604A. 1. Habich, Georg, 1868- . 2. Medals.
N. Y. P. L. May 24, 1929

D-12
2036

GEORG SIMMEL, 1858-1918; a collection of essays, with translations and a bibliography. Edited by Kurt H. Wolff. Columbus, Ohio state university press [1959] xv, 396 p. port. 22cm.

CONTENTS.--Preface to Georg Simmel's Fragments, posthumous essays, and publications of his last years, by G. Kantorowicz.--The structure of Simmel's social thought, by D.N. Levine.--Form and

(Continued)

NN R 1.60 m/ OC, I PC, 1, I E, 1, I (LC1, X1, Z1) SL

GEORG SIMMEL... (Card 2)

content in Simmel's philosophy of life, by R.H. Weingartner.--Formal sociology, by F.H. Tenbruck.--Simmel's image of society, by H.D. Duncan.--Some aspects of Simmel's conception of the individual, by M. Lipman.--Simmel's sociology of power: The architecture of politics, by E.V. Walter.--The time and thought of the young Simmel, by P. Honigsheim.--A note on Simmel's anthropological interests, by P. Honigsheim.--Simmel in German sociology, by H. Maus--

(Continued)

GEORG SIMMEL... (Card 3)

Georg Simmel's influence on Japanese thought, by M. Shimmei.--On Simmel's Philosophy of money, by H. Becker.--A note from a student of Simmel's, by A. Salz.----Translations [of] Letter from Simmel to Marianne Weber, The adventure, The ruin, The handle, The aesthetic significance of the face, On the nature of philosophy, The problem of sociology, How is society possible?--Bibliography of writings on Georg Simmel, by K. Gassen.--Bibliography of Simmel's books in German and his writings which are available in English, by K.H. Wolff.

1. Sociology--Addresses, essays, lectures. I. Wolff, Kurt H., 1912- , ed.

Write on slip, name, year, vol., page of magazine and class mark — ETA

Georg Wolfram...zur Feier seines siebzigsten Geburtstages.

(Elsass-Lothringisches Jahrb. Frankfurt a.M., 1929. 8°. Bd.8,p.i-xvi,1-452. port.)

Bibliography p.ix-xvi.

Form 400a [11-13-30 25m]

MW p.v.93

George Pierce Baker, a memorial. New York city, Dramatists play service, 1939.

46 p. incl. front. (port.) illus. 19½cm.

Text on p. [2] of cover.

CONTENTS.—The four Georges, George Pierce Baker at work, by J. M. Brown.—Professor G. P. Baker, a note and some communications, by Eugene O'Neill.—Mr. Baker in his theatre, by D. M. Oenslager.—G. P. B. of Harvard and Yale, by Sidney Howard.—First impression, by Allardyce Nicoll.—The Baker maps, by S. R. McCandless and Arthur Wilmurt.—Excerpt from a speech by Professor Baker.

1. Baker, George Pierce, 1866-1935.

Library of Congress PN1701.G45 40-6839

——— Copy 2.

Copyright A 136533 [2] 927.92

D-16
519

GERDES, HAYO, ed.

Wahrheit und Glaube; Festschrift für Emanuel Hirsch zu seinem 75. Geburtstag. Itzehoe, Verlag "Die Spur" [1963] 208 p. port. 22cm.

Includes bibliographies.

CONTENTS.--Der letzte Feind Christi, von E. Vogelsang.--Die Erforschung der Geschichte der alten Kirche, von H.G. Opiz.--Christologisches, von P. Althaus.--Eschatologie und Erfahrung, von H.-J. Birkner.

(Continued)

NN * R 6.65 e/s OC PC, 1, 2, I SL (LC1, X1, Z1)

2

GERDES, HAYO, ed. Wahrheit und Glaube... (Card 2)

--Karl Holl als Prediger, von W. Bodenstein.--Erneuerung der Frömmigkeit; Luthers Predigten, 1522-1524, von H. Bornkamm.--Tradition und Offenbarung, von R. Bring.--Die Frage von Gesetz und Evangelium in der gegenwärtigen theologischen Diskussion, von H. Gerdes.--Hamans Galgen und Christi Kreuz, von E. Haenchen.--Was nicht im Buche Hiob steht, von J. Hempel.--Das Recht des Glaubens auf theologischen Irrtum, von H. Kittel.--Der Protestantismus im 20.Jahrhundert, Rückgang oder Fortschritt? Von E. Mülhaupt.--Theologiegeschichte als Gewissensfrage, von U. Neuenschwander.--Die wirkliche Predigt, von W. Trillhaas.

1. Theology--Essays and misc. 2. Hirsch, Emanuel Arthur Friedrich Albert, 1888- . I. Title.

NFD
+
(Hauptmann)

Gerhart Hauptmann zum 80. Geburtstage am 15. November 1942. Breslau, Schlesien-Verlag [1942] 167 p. illus. (part col.) 34cm.

"Quellen und Benutztesschrifttum," p. 167.

CONTENTS.—Niekrawietz, Hans. "Der Dichter."—Merker, Paul. Ein reiches Leben.—Nadler, Josef. Sein Werk in der Gemeinschaft der Völker.—Bottai, Giuseppe. Gerhart Hauptmann und Italien.—Dirksen, Herbert von. Gerhart Hauptmann in Japan.—Krumbhermer, Christof. Die Erscheinung des Dichters als Vorwurf der bildenden Künste.—Hauptmann, Gerhart. Auszug aus "Iphigenie in Aulis."—Fridrich,

(Continued)

N. Y. P. L. January 8, 1947

Gerhart Hauptmann zum 80. Geburtstage... (Card 2)

Hans. Breslau im Leben Gerhart Hauptmanns.—Voigt, F. A. Gerhart Hauptmanns Werk im Spiegel der Welt.—Barthel, Gustav. Das Werk des Dichters in der bildenden Kunst.—Bischoff, Friedrich (also Kaergel, H. C., Ulitz, Arnold and Pohl, Gerhart) Für Gerhart Hauptmann.—Baumgart, Wolfgang. Gerhart Hauptmanns Mystik.—Aubin, Hermann. "Die Weber;" ein Spiegel schlesischer Volksgeschichte.—Klöpfer, Eugen. Gerhart Hauptmann und das Theater.—Sarneck, M. G. Gerhart Hauptmann auf den Bühnen Europas.—Knudsen, Hans. Grosse Schauspieler in Hauptmanns Dramen.—Pohl, Gerhart. Die Frau in Gerhart Hauptmanns Werk.—Behl, C. F. W. Über Schauspielkunst und Regie.—Glaeser, Edmund. Die Ahnen Gerhart Hauptmanns.

334364B. 1. Hauptmann, Gerhart, 1862-1946.
N. Y. P. L. January 8, 1947

NFC

German studies presented to Leonard Ashley Willoughby by pupils, colleagues and friends on his retirement. Oxford, Blackwell, 1952. xii,249 p. port. 22cm.

Contents.—List of Professor Willoughby's publications.—Stefan George and Ida Coblenz, by J. Bithell.—A footnote to "Wilhelm Meisters Lehrjahre," by W. H. Bruford.—Pandits and pariahs, by E. M. Butler.—Some expressions of the notions, "change" and "exchange" in the Germanic languages,

(Continued)

NN*R 10.53 OC PC,1, 2 SL (Z1,LC1,X1)
[I]

German studies presented to Leonard Ashley Willoughby... (Card 2)

by W. E. Collinson.—The modernity of Wilhelm Raabe, by B. Fairley.—Herder and Goethe, by A. Gillies.—"Ine Weiz": diplomatic ignorance on the part of medieval German poets, by A. T. Hatto.—Young Germany: a revaluation, by C. P. Magill.—Lenz as lyric poet, by R. Pascal.—Novalis and Schopenhauer: a critical transition in romanticism, by R. Peacock.—Some word-associations in the writings of Hamann and Herder, by E. Purdie.—

(Continued)

German studies presented to Leonard Ashley Willoughby... (Card 3)

Wolfram von Eschenbach and the paradox of the chivalrous life, by M. F. Richey.—The psychological approach to the study of literature, by W. Rose.—Tasso's tragedy and salvation, by E. L. Stahl.—Goethe's Irish enemy: Edward Kenealy, by G. Waterhouse.—The poet as thinker: On the varying modes of Goethe's thought, by E. M. Wilkinson.

1. German literature—Hist. and crit.
2. Willoughby, Leonard Ashley, 1885-

NFC

German studies presented to Professor H. G. Fiedler, M. V. O., by pupils, colleagues, and friends on his seventy-fifth birthday, 28 April 1937. Oxford: Clarendon press, 1938. viii, 507 p. front. (port.) 23cm.

Bibliographical footnotes.

CONTENTS.—The function of conversations and speeches in 'Witiko,' by H. G. Barnes.—The first French edition of 'Peter Schlemihl,' by L. A. Bisson.—Four prayers in Goethe's 'Iphigenie,' by J. Boyd.—Actor and public in Gottsched's time, by W. H. Bruford.—Formal values of the German lyric on the threshold of the 'baroque,' by August Closs.—Some German particles and their English equivalents: A study in the technique of conversation, by W. E. Collinson.—Paul Ernst's theory of the Novelle, by Kathleen Cunningham.—Some observations on Jean Paul, by H. C. Deneke.—Lutwin's Latin source,

(Continued)

N. Y. P. L. August 30, 1938

German studies presented... (Card 2)

by A. C. Dunstan.—Luther: Exegesis and prose style, by Walter Ettinghausen.—Wackenroder's apprenticeship to literature: His teachers and their influence, by A. Gillies.—The cadence in Germanic alliterative verse, by C. E. Gough.—Rilke and Rodin, by G. C. Houston.—Gottfried von Neifen's Minnelieder and ballads, by R. Marleyn.—A new reading of 'Wilhelm Tell,' by W. G. Moore.—The Germanic heroic poet and his art, by F. Norman.—The poetry of Novalis, by R. Peacock.—Friedrich von Matthisson on Gibbon, by L. F. Powell.—Some adventures of 'Pamela' on the continental stage, by E. Purdie.—Klinger's Medea dramas and the German fate tragedy, by F. E. Sandbach.—The genesis of Schiller's theory of tragedy, by E. L. Stahl.—A variation on the theme of Heusler's first lay of Brünhild, by R. A. Williams.—Wordsworth and Germany, by L. A. Willoughby.—Grillparzer's 'Sappho,' by Douglas Yates.

956790A. 1. Fiedler, Hermann Georg, 1862- . 2. German literature—Hist. and crit.
N. Y. P. L. August 30, 1938

D-14
8504

GERMAN studies, presented to Walter Horace Bruford on his retirement by his pupils, colleagues and friends. London, G.G. Harrap [1962] 240 p. port. 22cm.

Contributions in English, French or German.

Includes bibliographies.

CONTENTS.--Bildung and the division of labour, by R. Pascal.--The blind man and the poet; an early stage in Goethe's quest for form, by

(Continued)

NN R 2.64 p/ OC PC, 1, 2 SL (LC1, X1, Z1) [I]

GERMAN studies... (Card 2)

E. M. Wilkinson and L. A. Willoughby. --La philosophique politique et sociale de Goethe administrateur, 1776-1786, par A. Fuchs. --The paths and powers of Mestipholes, by E. C. Mason. --Der Gross-Cophta and the problem of German comedy, by C. P. Magill. --J. M. Turner and Goethe's colour-theory, by R. D. Gray. --Ottilie and "das innere Licht", by F. J. Stopp. --Goethe's thought in the context of to-day, by P. Roubiczek. --Schiller on poetry, by E. L. Stahl. --Some observations on Schiller's stage-directions, by H. B. Garland. --Das Hamlet-Motiv in den "Nachtwachen" des Bonaventura, von W. Kohlschmidt--Grillparzer's Vienna, by J. P. Stern.

(Continued)

GERMAN studies... (Card 3)

--Die Jüdin von Toledo, by E. A. Blackall. --Prolegomena to the study of Ludwig Anzengruber, by A. H. J. Knight. --Hofmannsthal's art of lyric concentration, by L. W. Forster.

1. Bruford, Walter Horace, 1894- 2. German literature--Addresses, essays, lectures.

EAH

Germanistische Abhandlungen zum LXX. Geburtstag Konrad von Maurers dargebracht, von Oscar Brenner, Finnur Jónsson, Felix Dahn...[und anderen] Göttingen: Dieterich, 1893. v, 554 p. front. (port.) 25cm.

CONTENTS.—Golther, W. Zur Færeyingasaga.—Lehmann, K. I. Das Bahrgericht. II. Kauffriede und Friedensschild.—Zorn, P. Die staatsrechtliche Stellung des preussischen Gesamtministeriums.—Ólsen, B. M. Sundurlausar hugleiðingar um stjórnarfar Íslendinga á þjóðveldistímanum.—Petersen, A. Om Indmaning i Danmark indtil Christian V's Danske Lov.—Brenner, O. Die Ueberlieferung der ältesten Münchener Ratssatzungen.—Gareis, C. Bemerkungen zu Kaiser Karl's des Grossen Capitulare de Villis.—Secher, V. A. Nogle meddelelser om skurdsmænd eller skursnævninger og

(Continued)

N. Y. P. L. April 30, 1935

Germanistische Abhandlungen... (Card 2)

om udmældelsen af ransnævninger på landet i Jylland.—Hertzberg, E. Lén og veizla i Norges sagatid.—Dahn, F. Zum merowingischen Finanzrecht.—Mayer, E. Zoll, Kaufmannschaft und Markt zwischen Rhein und Loire bis in das 13. Jahrhundert.—Jónsson, F. Um þulur og gátur.—Gudmunðsson, V. Manngjöld-hundrað.

722680A. 1. Maurer, Konrad von, 1823-1902.
N. Y. P. L. April 30, 1935

RKE

GERMANISCHE philologie; ergenbnisse und aufgaben; festschrift für Otto Behaghel, herausgegeben von Alfred Goetze, Wilhelm Horn [und] Friedrich Maurer. Heidelberg, C. Winter, 1934. viii, 573 p., 1 l. port. 23cm. (Added t.-p.: Germanische bibliothek... 1. abt.: Sammlung germanischer elementar- und handbücher. 1. reihe: Grammatiken. 19. bd.)

Bibliographical foot-notes.

"Otto Behagels schriften... 1924-1933. Zusammengestellt von Fritz Stroh": p. [531]-541.

(Continued)

NN*R 11.52 OC, I, II, III PC, 1, 2, I, II, III SL (LC1, Z1, X1)

GERMANISCHE philologie... (Card 2)

CONTENTS. —I. SPRACHE: Wagner, Kurt. Phonetik, rhythmik, metrik. Kuhn, Hans. Die altgermanische verskunst. Arntz, Helmut. Urgermanisch, gotisch, nordisch. Arntz, Helmut. Deutsche grammatik. Bach, Adolf. Deutsche mundartforschung. Will, Wilhelm. Deutsche namenforschung. Götze, Alfred. Deutsche wortforschung. Trier, Jost. Deutsche bedeutungsforschung. Maurer, Friedrich. Geschichte der deutschen sprache. Stroh, Fritz. Allgemeine sprachwissenschaft und sprachphilosophie. Horn, Wilhelm. Englische sprachforschung. Holthausen, Ferdinand. Friesisch. —II. LITERATUR: Ehrismann, Gustav. Die altdeutsche literaturwissenschaft in dem vergangenen halben jahrhundert. Spamer, Adolf. Die mystik. Berger, A. E.
(Continued)

TPG p.v.353

Germany. Reichsbahndirektion, Berlin.
Festschrift zur Jahrhundertfeier der Berlin-Potsdamer Eisenbahn. Herausgegeben von der Reichsbahndirektion Berlin. Leipzig: Konkordia-Verlag, 1938. 43 p. incl. front. facsims., illus. (incl. charts, plans.) 29½cm.

Cover-title: Hundert Jahre Eisenbahn Berlin-Potsdam.
"Quellennachweis," p. 43.
CONTENTS.—Die Geschichte der Berlin-Potsdamer Eisenbahn.—Das Reichsbahn-Ausbesserungswerk Potsdam 1838–1938.

1. Berlin-Potsdamer Eisenbahn.
N. Y. P. L. April 23, 1940

GERMANISCHE philologie... (Card 3)

Humanismus und reformation in geistesgeschichtlicher betrachtung. Kuhn, Hans. Die skaldendichtung. Fischer, Walther. Neuere deutsche Beowulfforschung. —III. VOLKSKUNDE: Spamer, Adolf. Allgemeines. Volkserzählung. Volkssprache. Volkskunst. Hoffmann-Krayer, Eduard. Volksglaube und volksbrauch. Helm, Rudolf. Volkstracht. Meixner, Liesel. Deutsche bauernhausforschung.

559983B. 1. Behaghel, Otto, 1854-1936. 2. Germanic languages. I. Goetze, Alfred August Woldemar, 1876- , ed. II. Horn, Wilhelm, 1876- , ed. III. Maurer, Friedrich, 1898- , ed. IV. Ser.

TPQ

Germany. Reichsbahndirektion, Wuppertal.
100 Jahre westdeutsche Eisenbahnen, 1838–1938. [Düsseldorf: Droste Verlag und Druckerei K. G., 1938?] 63 p. illus. (incl. charts, coats of arms, facsims., plan, ports.) 37cm.

Cover-title.
Printed in double columns.
"Überreicht von der Reichsbahndirektion Wuppertal zur Hundertjahrfeier der Eisenbahn Düsseldorf-Erkrath-Elberfeld."
"Im Auftrage der Reichsbahndirektion Wuppertal herausgegeben vom Bezirksverband der Eisenbahnvereine." — *p. 63.*

21642B. 1. Railways—Germany—Hist. I. Reichsverband der Eisenbahnvereine. Bezirksverband der Eisenbahnvereine im Reichsbahndirektionsbezirk Wuppertal.
N. Y. P. L. October 22, 1940

Write on slip, name, year, vol., page of magazine and class mark —
EAA

Germanisches Nationalmuseum, Nuremberg.
Das Germanische Museum von 1902–1927. Festschrift zur Feier seines 75jährigen Bestehens. Im Auftrag der Direktion verfasst von Professor Dr. Fritz Traugott Schulz... Nürnberg: Germanisches Museum, 1927. 97 p. illus. 4°. (Germanisches Nationalmuseum, Nuremberg. Anzeiger. Jahrg. 1926–1927.)

1. No subject. 2. Schulz, Fritz Traugott, 1875- .
N. Y. P. L. December 17, 1929

---

* MGA

GERSTEMBERG, WALTER, 1904-
Festschrift Otto Erich Deutsch zum 80. Geburtstag am 5. September 1963; hrsg. von Walter Gerstenberg, Jan LaRue and Wolfgang Rehm. Kassel, New York, Bärenreiter, 1963. 392 p. illus., ports., music. 23cm.

"Bibliographie der musikhistorischen Arbeiten von Otto Erich Deutsch," von Otto Schneider, p. [368]-390.
Bibliographical footnotes.

1. Deutsch, Otto Erich, 1883- 2. Music--Essays. 3. Essays.
NN 8.65 p/B OC PC, 1, 2 SL MU, 1, 3 (LC1, X1, Z1) [I]

KAT

Germanska namnstudier tillägnade Evald Lidén, den 3 oktober 1932. Uppsala: A.-B. Lundequistska bokhandeln, i distribution[, 1932]. 320 p. front. (port.), illus. (incl. charts.) 24½cm.

Bibliographical footnotes.

659804A. 1. Lidén, Evald, 1862- . 2. Geography—Names.
N. Y. P. L. October 13, 1933

---

*MGA

GERSTENBERG, WALTER, 1904-
Festschrift Otto Erich Deutsch zum 80. Geburtstag am 5. September 1963; hrsg. von Walter Gerstenberg. Jan LaRue and Wolfgang Rehm. Kassel, New York, Bärenreiter, 1963. 392 p. illus., ports., music. 23cm.

"Bibliographie der musikhistorischen Arbeiten von Otto Erich Deutsch," von Otto Schneider, p. [368]-390.
Bibliographical footnotes.
1. Deutsch, Otto Erich, 1883- . 2. Music--Essays. 3. Essays.
NN R 2.67 a/L OC PC, 1, 2 SL MU, 1, 3 (LC1, X1, Z1)
[I]

XMK

Germany. Justizministerium.
200 Jahre Dienst am Recht; Gedenkschrift aus Anlass des 200-jährigen Gründungstages des Preussischen Justizministeriums, herausgegeben von Reichsminister der Justiz Dr. h. c. Franz Gürtner. Berlin: R. v. Decker's Verlag, G. Schenk [1938] 431 p. illus. (incl. facsims., ports.) 28½cm.

"Schrifttumsverzeichnisse und Quellennachweise," p. 421–430.

990515A. 1. Justice—Administration—Germany. 2. Prussia. Justiz Ministerium. I. Gürtner, Franz, 1881- , ed.
N. Y. P. L. January 2, 1940

EAH

Gesamtdeutsche vergangenheit. Festgabe für Heinrich ritter von Srbik zum 60. geburtstag am 10. november 1938. München, F. Bruckmann [°1938]
ix, 414 p. front. (port.) pl. 24½cm.
Bibliographical foot-notes.
CONTENTS.—Brunner, O. Die südgrenze des alten Deutschen reiches und des Deutschen bundes zwischen Ortler und Quarnero.—Winter, E. Das Sudetendeutschtum als mittler zwischen Nord und Süd.—Uhlirz, M. Das deutsche gefolge Kaiser Ottos III. in Italien.—Hirsch, H. Konradin. Sein "prozess" und sein ende in gesamtdeutscher beleuchtung.—Mayer, T. Die Habsburger am Oberrhein im mittelalter.—Dopsch, A. Die weststaatspolitik der Habsburger im werden ihres grossreiches (1477–1526)—Brandi, K. Die versuchung des Pescara.—Kallbrunner, J. Philipp Melanchthon im deutschen Südosten.—Wostry, W. "Die römische krone
(Continued on next card)
A C 39-1001
[2]

Gesamtdeutsche vergangenheit. Festgabe für Heinrich ritter von Srbik ... [c1938] (Card 2)

CONTENTS—Continued.

gehört auf die böhmische."—Wandrufzka von Wanstetten, A. Vom begriff des "vaterlands" in der politik des dreissigjährigen krieges.—Wentzcke, P. Wiener beiträge zur geschichte vom fall Strassburgs (1680/81)—Lorenz, R. Ein jahrhundert oberrheinisch-österreichischer geschichte.—Sedlmayer, H. Die politische bedeutung des deutschen barocks (der "reichstil")—Redlich, O. Die tagebücher Kaiser Karls VI.—Voltelini, H.† Eine denkschrift des grafen Johann Anton Pergen über die bedeutung der römischen kaiserkrone für das haus Österreich.—Gross, L. Die panisbriefe Kaiser Josefs II. Ein beitrag zu seiner reichskirchenpolitik.—Ernstberger, A. Reichsheer und reich. Ein reformvorschlag 1794/95.—Meinecke, F. Schillers "Spaziergang".—Nadler, J. Goethes begriff der persönlichkeit.—Andreas, W. Napoleon in Karlsruhe. Ein brief

(Continued on next card)

A C 39-1001

[2]

Gesamtdeutsche vergangenheit. Festgabe für Heinrich ritter von Srbik ... [c1938] (Card 3)

CONTENTS—Continued.

der markgräfin Amalie von Baden an die herzogin Luise von Sachsen-Weimar.—Pleyer, K. Stein und Stadion.—Bauer, W. Zur Judenfrage als gesamtdeutscher angelegenheit zu beginn des 19. jahrhunderts.—Näf, W. Die Schweiz im "system" Metternichs.—Deutsch, W. Die mission von Hess und Radowitz 1840.—Küntzel, G. Heinrich v. Gagern und der grossdeutsche gedanke.—Reinöhl, F. v. Die frage der deutschen einheit und der Wien-Kremsierer reichstag.—Mayr, J. K. Der deutsch-österreichische postverein.—Müller, P. Das österreichische Parlament und die nationalen einheitsbewegungen in Europa zwischen Solferino und Königgrätz.—Meyer, A. O. Der preussische Kronrat vom 29. mai 1865.—Borodajkewycz, T. v. Leo Thun und Onno Klopp.—Frank, W. Friedrich und Viktoria.—Frauendienst, W. Bündniserörterungen zwischen Bis-

(Continued on next card)

A C 39-1001

[2]

Gesamtdeutsche vergangenheit. Festgabe für Heinrich ritter von Srbik ... [c1938] (Card 4)

CONTENTS—Continued.

marck und Andrássy im märz 1878.—Bilger, F. Heinrich von Treitschke und die österreichische literatur.—Bittner, L. Österreich-Ungarn und die deutsch-englischen bündnisverhandlungen im frühjahr 1898.—Uebersberger, H. Das friedensangebot der mittelmächte vom 12. dezember 1916 und Russland.—Raumer, K. v. Das ende von Helfferichs Moskauer mission 1918.—Hölzle, E. Saint-Germain. Das verbot des anschlusses.

1. Srbik, Heinrich, ritter von, 1878- 2. Germany—History—Addresses, essays, lectures. 3. Austria—History—Addresses, essays, lectures. I. Title: Festgabe für Heinrich ritter von Srbik.

A C 39-1001

Yale univ. Library
for Library of Congress [2]

L-10
717
v.16

GESCHICHTE und Altes Testament; Aufsätze von W.F. Albright [et al.] Tübingen, J.C.B. Mohr, 1953.
223 p. 25cm. (Beiträge zur historischen Theologie. 16)

"Albrecht Alt zum siebzigsten Geburtstag am 20. September 1953... dargebracht."

Bibliographical footnotes.

CONTENTS.—Dedan, by W.F. Albright.—Das alttestamentliche Geschehen als "heilsgeschichtliches" Geschehen, von F. Baumgärtel.—

(Continued)

NN R X 12.57 e/J OC, II (OS)I PC, I, 2, I, II J, I, 2, I, II (LC1, X1, Z1)

GESCHICHTE und Altes Testament; Aufsätze von W.F. Albright [et al.] (Card 2)

Weitere Briefe aus der Heiratskorrespondenz Ramses' II, von E. Edel.—Psalm 80, von O. Eissfeldt.—Die grossen Tempelsakristeien im Verfassungsentwurf des Ezechiel, von K. Elliger.—Der Gott Karmel und die Achtung der fremden Götter, von K. Galling.—Mari und Israel, von M. Noth.—Die Vorgeschichte der Gattung von 1. Kor. 13, 4-7, von G. von Rad.—Noah der Weinbauer, von L. Rost.—Ich bin Jahwe, von W. Zimmerli.—Bibliographie Albrecht Alt, von K.H. Mann (p. [211]-223).

(Continued)

GESCHICHTE und Altes Testament; Aufsätze von W.F. Albright [et al.] (Card 3)

1. Alt, Albrecht, 1883- . 2. Bible. O.T.--History in.
I. Series. II. Albright, William Foxwell, 1891- .

E-13
8293

Geschichte, Deutung, Kritik. Literaturwissenschaftliche Beiträge dargebracht zum 65. Geburtstag Werner Kohlschmidts. Hrsg. von Maria Bindschedler und Paul Zinsli. Bern, Francke, (1969).

282 p. illus. 24 cm.

Includes bibliographies.

CONTENTS.—Der Rotulus von Mülinen, von W. Henzen.—Bemerkungen zur Handschrift des Rotulus von Mülinen, von C. von Steiger.—Die Ehre im Menschenbild der deutschen Dichtung um

(Continued)

NN * R 5.70 d/J OC, I, II, III PC, I, I, II, III SL (LC1, X1, Z1)

Geschichte ... (1969). (Card 2)

1200, von F. Maurer.—Die Natur im mittelalterlichen Liede, von W. Mohr.—Iweins Erwachen, von M. Wehrli.—Gedanken zur Marienlyrik des Mittelalters und der Romantik, von M. Bindschedler.—Schönheit, Ausdruck und Charakter im ästhetischen Denken des 18. Jahrhunderts, von E. C. Mason.—Über Lichtenbergs Kurzformen, von R. Wildbolz.—Paris im Leben Goethes, von A. Fuchs.—Zu Goethes Marienbader Elegie, von L. Mittner.—Der Roman der Transsendentalpoesie in der Romantik, von P. Böckmann.—Kunst und Zeit

(Continued)

GESCHICHTE... (1969). (Card 3)

in Mörikes Maler Nolten, von J. Steiner.—Die Gnade sprach von Liebe, von H. Lehnert.—Thomas Mann e D'Annunzio, von V. Santoli.—Klingsor in Montagnola, von H. J. Lüthi.—Ein Dokument einstiger volkstümlich-deutscher Literatur am Südhang der Alpen, von P. Zinsli.—Bibliographie der Publikationen von Werner Kohlschmidt, zusammengestellt von Chr. Hostettler und R. Ramseyer. (p. [267]-282)

1. German literature--Addresses, essays, lectures. I. Kohlschmidt, Werner, 1904- II. Bindschedler, Maria, ed. III. Zinsli, Paul, ed.

BAC

GESCHICHTLICHE Kräfte und Entscheidungen; Festschrift zum fünfundsechzigsten Geburtstage von Otto Becker, hrsg. von Martin Göhring und Alexander Scharff.
Wiesbaden F. Steiner, 1954. 316 p. port. 25cm.

Bibliographical footnotes.

CONTENTS.—Geleitwort der Herausgeber.—Das Mittelalter und die deutsche Geschichte, von F. Rörig.—Heinrich der Löwe und Dänemark, von K. Jordan.—Der Schmalkaldische Bund und Schweden von G. Carlsson.—Calvin und Franz Hotman, von F. Kleyser

(Continued)

NN ** R X 9.55 p/A OC, I, II, IIIbo PC, 1, 2, I, II SL (LC1 X1, Z1)

GESCHICHTLICHE Kräfte und Entscheidungen... (Card 2)

Kaiserwahl und Rheinbund von 1658. Ein Höhepunkt des Kampfes zwischen Habsburg und Bourbon um die Beherrschung des Reiches, von M. Göhring. —Nationale Spannungen im Herzogtum Schleswig wäh - rend des 18. Jahrhunderts, von V. Pauls. —Eine Fehldeutung und Legende aus dem beginnenden Nationalitätenkampf im Herzogtum Schleswig, von O. Scheel.—Hans Christoph von Gagern und die Politik seiner Söhne 1848-1852, von H. Rössler. —König Friedrich Wilhelm IV., Deutschland und Europa im Frühjahr 1849, von A. Scharff. —Die Vereinigten Staaten und die eutsche (Continued)

GESCHICHTLICHE Landeskunde und Universalgeschichte... (Card 3)

der Balkanisierung Ostmitteleuropas, von E. Birke. —Mittelrhein und Schlesien als Brückenlandschaften der deutsche Geschichte, von L. Petry. —Hamburgisch-schlesische Handelsbeziehungen, von W. Jochmann. — Missionsbewegungen im Nordseeraum, von W. Trillmich.—Die niederländisch-nordwestdeutschen Siedlungsbewegungen des 16. und 17. Jahrhunderts, von W. Kuhn. —Deutsche Siedlung in Neuseeland, von G. Eichbaum. — Hermann Aubin: Verzeichnis seines Schrifttums, zusammengestellt von W. Jochmann.

1. Aubin, Hermann, 1885- 2. History—Addresses, essays, lectures.

GESCHICHTLICHE Kräfte und Entscheidungen... (Card 3)

Einheitsbewegung, von B. Siemers. —Das Geheimnis des Kaiserbriefes Ludwigs II, von W. Schüssler.—Rückversicherungsvertrag und Optionsproblem 1887-1890, von H. Krausnick. --Die englisch-russische Konvention von 1907 und die Meerengenfrage, von O. Hauser. Deutschland und die Wegscheide des ersten Weltkriegs, von E. Hölzle. -Argentinien und das deutsche Heer. Ein Beitrag zur Geschichte europäischer militarischer Einflüsse auf Südamerika, von F. Epstein. —Grenzen der Macht, von L. von Muralt. Verzeichnis der Schriften von O. Becker (p. [311]-316).

* KP (Gesellschaft)

Gesellschaft der Bibliophilen, Weimar.

Von Buechern und Menschen; Festschrift Fedor von Zobeltitz, zum 5. Oktober 1927, überreicht von der Gesellschaft der Bibliophilen. Weimar: Gesellschaft der Bibliophilen, 1927. 2 p.l., 377(1) p., 1 l. facsim., front. (port.), illus., plates. 4°.

Colophon: Diese Festschrift wurde im Auftrag der Gesellschaft der Bibliophilen gesammelt und herausgegeben von Conrad Höfer in Eisenach. Die Reihenfolge der Aufsätze im Buch ist durch das Los bestimmt worden. Das Bildnis radierte Hans U. Müller. Poeschel & Trepte druckten die dreihundert gezählten Stücke. Die Einbände lieferten Hübel & Denck, sämtlich in Leipzig. Dieses Stück trägt die Nummer 28.

346487A. 1. No subject. 2. Zobeltitz, Fedor Karl Maria Hermann August von, 1857- . 3. Hoefer, Conrad, 1872- , editor. 4. Title.
N. Y. P. L. July 10, 1928

GESCHICHTLICHE Kräfte und Entscheidungen... (Card 4)

1. Becker, Otto, 1885- 2. History—Addresses, essays, lectures. I. Scharff, Alexander, ed. II. Göhring, Martin. III. Scharff, Alexander.

.VIB

GESELLSCHAFT DEUTSCHER METALLHÜTTEN- UND BERGLEUTE. FACHAUSSCHUSS FÜR ERZAUFBEREITUNG.

Erzaufbereitungsanlagen in Westdeutschland; ein Führer durch die wichtigsten Betriebe für Aufbereitung von Erzen und anderen mineralischen Rohstoffen. [Festschrift] Schriftleitung: W. Gründer. Berlin, Springer, 1955. xv, 355 p. illus., map. 28cm.

(Continued)

NN**R 2.56 d/ (OC)I, IIbo OS PC, 1, I SL ST, 1t, I (LC1, X1, Z1)

BAC

GESCHICHTLICHE Landeskunde und Universalgeschichte; Festgabe für Hermann Aubin zum 23. Dezember 1950. [Hamburg, 1950] 283 p. port. 24cm.

CONTENTS. — Der Mensch als Geschichtsquelle, von I. Schwidetzky. —Die Geschichtliche Landeskunde im System der Wissenschaften, von H. Schlenger. —Die Herkunft des historischen Krisenbewusstseins, von W. Lammers. —Libertas. Der Begriff der Freiheit in den Germanenrechten (der Westgoten, Langobarden und Burgunden), von K. Jäkel. —Die angebliche Verleihung der Patriciuswürde an Boleslaw Chrobry, von H. (Continued)

NN*R 5.53 OC PC, 1, 2 SL (LC1, Z1, X1)

GESELLSCHAFT DEUTSCHER METALLHÜTTEN- UND BERGLEUTE. FACHAUSSCHUSS FÜR ERZAUFBEREITUNG. Erzaufbereitungsanlagen in Westdeutschland... (Card 2)

Includes bibliographies.

CONTENTS. —Die Blei-Zinkerz-Aufbereitungs-Anlage der Gewerkschaft Auguste Victoria in Marl in Westfalen, von F. Stolze. —Die Bleierz-Aufbereitungs-Anlage der Gewerkschaft Mechernicher Werke bei Mechernich in der Eifel, von E. Puffe. —Die Aufbereitungsanlagen des Erzbergwerks Grund der Preussischen Bergwerks- und Hütten-AG., Zweigniederlassung Harzer Berg- und (Continued)

GESCHICHTLICHE Landeskunde und Universalgeschichte... (Card 2)

Appelt. —Kolonisation und Gutsherrschaft in Ostdeutschland, von H. von zur Mühlen. —Über die Herkunft der Jenaer Studenten im 1. Jahrhundert des Bestehens der Universität, von E. E. Klotz. —Sozialgeschichtliche Zusammenhänge in der städtischen Besiedlung des Westerzgebirges im 16. Jahrhundert, von H. Kramm. —Aufstieg und Untergang der balkanslawischen Staatenwelt, von G Stadtmüller. —Schwedens Bemühungen um die deutsch-lutherische Gemeinde Bukarest, von E. Schieche. — Zwangsumsiedlungen in Osteuropa vor der Oktoberrevolution, von G. Rhode. —Russlands Orientpolitik, von B. Spuler. —Zur Vorgeschichte (Continued)

GESELLSCHAFT DEUTSCHER METALLHÜTTEN- UND BERGLEUTE. FACHAUSSCHUSS FÜR ERZAUFBEREITUNG. Erzaufbereitungsanlagen in Westdeutschland... (Card 3)

Hüttenwerke, Goslar in Bad Grund/Harz, von H.J. Salau. —Die Blei-Zinkerz-Aufbereitung Willibald der Stolberger Zink AG. für Bergbau und Hüttenbetrieb, Aachen, in Ramsbeck, Westfalen, von E. von Szantho. — Die Versuchsaufbereitung der Grube Maubacher Bleiberg der Stolberger Zink AG. für Bergbau und Hüttenbetrieb, Aachen, in Horm bei Gey, von H. Mehlbeer. —Die Zentralaufbereitung Ems der Stolberger Zink AG. für Bergbau und Hüttenbetrieb, Aachen, (Continued)

GESELLSCHAFT DEUTSCHER METALLHÜTTEN- UND BERGLEUTE. FACHAUSSCHUSS FÜR ERZAUFBEREITUNG. Erzaufbereitungsanlagen in Westdeutschland,.. (Card 4)

in Bad Ems (Lahn), von J. Hamann. —Die Blei Zinkerz-Aufbereitung der Grube Schauinsland-Kappel der Stolberger Zink AG. für Bergbau und Hüttenbetrieb, Aachen, in Bensberg, Bez. Köln, von O. Arnold. —Die Haldenerzaufbereitung Bensberg der Stolberger Zink AG. für Bergbau und Hüttenbetrieb, Aachen, in Bensberg, Bez. Köln, von O. Arnold. —Die Haldenerzaufbereitungs-Anlage Laurenburg der Stolberger Zink AG. für Bergbau und Hüttenbetrieb, Aachen, in Laurenburg (Lahn), von J. Hamann. —Die Aufbereitungs-
(Continued)

GESELLSCHAFT DEUTSCHE METALLHÜTTEN- UND BERGLEUTE. FACHAUSSCHUSS FÜR ERZAUFBEREITUNG. Erzaufbereitungsanlagen in Westdeutschland... (Card 5)

Anlagen des Erzbergwerks Rammelsberg der Unterharzer Berg- und Hüttenwerke GmbH., Oker bei Goslar, von E. Kraume, M. Clement, und H. Belka. —Die Aufbereitungs-Anlagen der Sachtleben AG., Abt. Schwefelkies- und Schwerspatbergbau, in Meggen (Lenne), von E. Goebel. —Die Aufbereitungs-Anlage der Kurhessischen Kupferschieferbergbau GmbH. in Sontra, von H. Triebel. —Die Anlage Kahlenberg der Barbara Erzbergbau AG., Bergverwaltung Süddeutschland, in Ringsheim, Kr. Lahr, von G. Sengfelder. —
(Continued)

GESELLSCHAFT DEUTSCHE METALLHÜTTEN- UND BERGLEUTE. FACHAUSSCHUSS FÜR ERZAUFBEREITUNG. Erzaufbereitungsanlagen in Westdeutschland... (Card 6)

Die Aufbereitungs-Anlage für sandige Doggererze der Gewerkschaft Eisensteinzeche Kleiner Johannes in Pegnitz (Ofr.), von G. Sengfelder und A. Goltz. —Die Aufbereitung der phosphorhaltigen Brauneisenerze der Grube Lengede-Broistedt der Hüttenwerke Ilsede-Peine AG., Eisenerzbergbau, Gross-Bülten, von K. Wiedelmann und E. Meinecke. —Die Erzaufbereitungs-Anlage Calbecht der Erzbergbau Salzgitter AG., von A. Goltz und K. Neumann. — Die Erzvorbereitung Watenstedt der Erzbergbau Salzgitter AG., von A. Goltz und K. Neumann.
(Continued)

GESELLSCHAFT DEUTSCHE METALLHÜTTEN- UND BERGLEUTE, FACHAUSSCHUSS FÜR ERZAUFBEREITUNG. Erzaufbereitungsanlagen in Westdeutschland... (Card 7)

—Die Aufbereitung der Siegerländer Erze, erläutert am Beispiel der Eisenerzgruben Füsseberg-Friedrich Wilhelm, Georg und Neue Haardt, von H. Gleichmann. —Die Flussspat-Aufbereitungs-Anlagen der Vereinigten Flussspatgruben GmbH. in Stulln und der Gewerkschaft Wölsendorf in Wölsendorf (Oberpfalz), von W.H. Finn. —Die Flussspat-Aufbereitungs-Anlage der Gewerkschaft Finstergrund, Baden-Baden, in Wieden/Utzenfeld (Schwarzwald), von G. Salzmann. —Die Flussspat-Aufbereitungs-Anlage der Fluor-Chemie GmbH. in
(Continued)

GESELLSCHAFT DEUTSCHER METALLHÜTTEN- UND BERGLEUTE. FACHAUSSCHUSS FÜR ERZAUFBEREITUNG. Erzaufbereitungsanlagen in Westdeutschland... (Card 8)

Karlsruhe, von G. Salzmann. —Die Schwerspat-Aufbereitungs-Anlage der Vereinigten Werke Dr. Rudolf Alberti & Co., Bad Lauterberg, von H. Götting. —Die Flotationsanlage der Kaliwerke Friedrichshall I/II der Kali-Chemie AG., Hannover, in Sehnde, von E. Risberg. —Die Flotationsanlage der Vereinigte Kaliwerke Salzdetfurth AG., Werk Sigmundshall, in Bokeloh über Wunstorf, von O. Karsten. —Die Flotationsanlage des Werkes Riedel der Burbach-Kaliwerke AG., Wolfenbüttel, in Hänigsen, von E.E. Buhe.
(Continued)

GESELLSCHAFT DEUTSCHER METALLHÜTTEN- UND BERGLEUTE. FACHAUSSCHUSS FÜR ERZAUFBEREITUNG. Erzaufbereitungsanlagen in Westdeutschland... (Card 9)

1. Ores—Dressing—Germany. I. Gründer, W., ed. II. Gründer, W. t. 1955.

*PBS

Gesellschaft zur Förderung der Wissenschaft des Judentums.
Festschrift Immanuel Löw zum 80. Geburtstage. Breslau: M. & H. Marcus, 1934. 256 p. front. (port.) 23cm.

Half-title: Immanuel Löw...widmen die Gesellschaft zur Förderung der Wissenschaft des Judentums und die Schriftleitung der Monatsschrift für Geschichte und Wissenschaft des Judentums dieses Heft als Festgabe zu seinem 80. Geburtstage.

"Für den Inhalt verantwortlich: Prof. Dr. I. Heinemann." — *p. 256.*

CONTENTS.—Köhler, L. Vom alttestamentlichen Wörterbuch.—Hess, J. J. Was bedeutet סבא Jesais 1^{22}? Ginzberg, L. Beiträge zur Lexikographie des Jüdisch-Aramäischen.—Elbogen, I. Bemerkungen Ignaz Goldzihers zu Levys neuhebräischem Wörterbuch.—Heller, B. Tierschätzung im Bibelwörterbuch.—Mahler, E. Zur Chronologie der

(Continued)

N. Y. P. L. May 7, 1935

Gesellschaft zur Förderung der Wissenschaft des Judentums.
Festschrift Immanuel Löw zum 80. Geburtstage... (Card 2)

Könige Judas und Israels.—Krauss, S. Die Landschaft im biblischen Hohenliede.—Epstein, J. N. Die Zeiten des Holzopfers.—Heinemann, I. Die Sektenfrömmigkeit der Therapeuten.—Goldziher, I. Erklärung einer Stelle in der Tefillah.—Blau, L. Ein Prinzip der Mischnaredaktion.—Büchler, A. Familienreinheit und Sittlichkeit in Sepphoris im 2. Jahrhundert.—Klein, S. Aus den Lehrhäusern Erez Israels im 2.-3. Jahrhundert.—Albeck, C. Einiges über Bereschit Rabba.—Guttmann, M. Berührungspunkte zwischen talmudischem und umweltlichem Denken.—Marmorstein, A. Das Motiv vom veruntreuten Depositum in der jüdischen Volkskunde.—Rawidowicz, S. Mendelssohns hand-

(Continued)

N. Y. P. L. May 7, 1935

Gesellschaft zur Förderung der Wissenschaft des Judentums.
Festschrift Immanuel Löw zum 80. Geburtstage... (Card 3)

schriftliche Glossen zum More Nebukim.—Mittwoch, E. Aus Briefen von W. Gesenius u. a. an Fr. S. Benary.—Kohut, G. A. Die Kohut-Löw-Steinschneider-Korrespondenz.—Jávorka, S. Vorgänger der "Flora der Juden."—Frenkel, E. Bibliographie der Schriften Immanuel Löws.—Epstein, J. N. Nachtrag zu S. 100.—Zeitschriftenschau.

726799A. 1. Essays, Jewish, in German. 2. Löw, Immanuel, 1854- . I. Heinemann, Isaac, 1876- , ed. II. Monatsschrift für Geschichte und Wissenschaft des Judenthums. III. Title.

N. Y. P. L. May 7, 1935

3-MAMG

GESELLSCHAFT ZUR FORDERUNG DES WURTEMBERGISCHEN LANDESMUSEUMS.
Beiträge zur schwäbischen Kunstgeschichte; Festschrift zum 60. Geburtstag von Werner Fleischhauer. Konstanz, J. Thorbecke [1964] 159 p. 74 illus. (incl. ports.) 24cm.

Includes bibliographical references.

CONTENTS.--Zu den Evangelistenbildern des Münchener Otto-
(Continued)

NN R 2.71 e/z (OC)I, II OS (LC1, X1) (Z1) PC, 1, 2, I, II SL A, 1, 2, I, II

3

GESELLSCHAFT ZUR FORDERUNG DES WÜRTEMBERG-ISCHEN LANDESMUSEUMS. Beiträge zur schwäbischen Kunstgeschichte... (Card 2)

Evangeliars, von H. Schrade. Zum Thema der schwäbischen Christus-Johannes-Gruppen an Hand nichtschwäbischer Beispiele, von H. Wentzel. Der Meister der Lautenbacher Altarflügel, von H. Haug. Noch einmal zur Darstellung der Maria im Ahrenkleid, von A. Walzer. Zur Konstanzer Plastik in der Mitte des 15. Jahrhunderts, von T. Müller. Eine oberrheinische Skulptur aus dem Kreis des Meisters der Dangolsheimer Maria, von R. Schnellbach. Eine (Continued)

GESELLSCHAFT ZUR FORDERUNG DES WURTEMBERG-ISCHEN LANDESMUSEUMS. Beiträge zur schwäbischen Kunstgeschichte... (Card 3)

Baldung-Zeichnung in Venedig, von H. T. Musper. Octavian Secundus Fugger (1549-1600), von N. Lieb. Das Anweil-Porträt des Württembergischen Landesmuseums, von H. Decker-Hauff. Verzeichnis der Mitarbeiter.

1. Art, German--Swabia. 2. Fleischhauer, Werner, 1903- . I. Title. II. Title: Festschrift zum 60. Geburtstag von Werner Fleischhauer.

3-MA

Gesellschaft zur Förderung des Württembergischen Landesmuseums.

Neue Beiträge zur Archäologie und Kunstgeschichte Schwabens. Julius Baum zum 70. Geburtstag am 9. April 1952 gewidmet. Stuttgart, W. Kohlhammer [1952] 246 p. plates. 26cm.

Contributions by various authors.

"Julius Baum, Schriften zur Kunstgeschichte [von] Konrat Baum," p. 240-246.

1. Art—Essays and misc. 2. Art, German—Swabia. 3. Baum, Julius, 1882-

NN* 10.54 OS(1b) PC,1, 2,3 SL A,1,2,3 (LC1,Z1,X1

9-* IPZ (Freunde)

Gesellschaft der Freunde der Deutschen Bücherei, Leipzig.

Seemannskost. Leipzig: Gesellschaft der Freunde der Deutschen Bücherei, 1919. 72 p. 28½cm.

"Dieses Buch wurde...in einer einmaligen in der Presse numerierten Auflage von 300 Exemplaren...gedruckt. Dieses Exemplar trägt die No 0219."

CONTENTS.—Ein Beitrag zum Körner-Göschenschen Verlagsunternehmen, von G. Minde-Pouet.—Ein russischer Dichter in Carl Alexanders Weimar, von A. Luther.—Wird Peer Gynt begnadigt? Von W. Frels.—Die naturphilosophisch-romantische Auffassung des Menschen als Vereinigung von Körper und Geist bei Heinrich Heine, von J. Thummerer.—Der junge van Gogh. Ein Präludium, von F. Riederer.

Festschrift

J. S. BILLINGS MEM. COLL.

1. Seemann, Artur, 1861-1925. I. Title.

N. Y. P. L. November 29, 1935

NFC

Gesellschaft Münchener Germanisten.

Abhandlungen zur deutschen Literaturgeschichte. Franz Muncker zum 60. Geburtstage dargebracht von Mitgliedern der Gesellschaft Münchener Germanisten; Eduard Berend...[und anderen] München, C. H. Beck, 1916. vi,264 p. 26cm.

586784B. 1. German literature—Hist. and crit. 2. Muncker, Franz, 1855- 1926. I. Title.

NN

C-14
3185

Gesicht des Menschen. Eine Festgabe zu Rudolf Felmayers 70. Geburtstag. (Hrsg. von Franz Richter.) Wien, Bergland Verl. (1968).

100 p. 20 cm.

1. Felmayer, Rudolf. 2. German literature--Collections. I. Felmayer, Rudolf. II. Richter, Franz, 1920- ed.

NN*R 5. 70 e/_J OC, I, II PC, 1, 2, I, II SL (LC1, X1, Z1)

E-10
1776

Der GESICHTSKREIS; Joseph Drexel zum sechzigsten Geburtstag. München, C.H. Beck'sche Verlagsbuchhandlung, 1956. vii, 218 p. port. 23cm.

CONTENTS.--Europäischer Nonkonformismus, von F. Heer.--Der Clerk, seine Gestalt und seine Funktion, von E. Niekisch.--Der schöpferische Prozess in der technischen Realität, von M. Bense.--Der Untergang der Utopie, von M. von Brück.--Asiens Rückkehr in die Weltpolitik, von H. Bechtoldt.--Hegel; Zeitungsverleger und Philosoph in Franken, von W. R. Beyer.--Drei Briefe, von T. Mann.--Thomas Manns Joseph- (Continued)

NN* * R 2. 57 a/* OC, Ib+ PC, 1 SL (LC1, X1, Z1, Y1)

Der GESICHTSKREIS... (Card 2)

Tetralogie, von J. Lesser.--Meisterschaft; eine Studie zu E. T. A. Hoffmanns Genieproblem, von M. Thalmann.--Bernard Shaw und die Ironie, von W. Puff.--Sprache als Aufklärung und Verschleierung, von H. H. Holz.

1. Drexel, Joseph, 1896-

E-11
560

GESTALTPROBLEME der Dichtung, hrsg. von Richard Alewyn, Hans-Egon Hass [und] Clemens Heselhaus. Bonn, H. Bouvier, 1957. ix, 337 p. port. 24cm.

"Günther Müller zu seinem 65. Geburtstag am 15. Dezember 1955." Includes bibliographies.

CONTENTS.--Der Gestaltwandel des Burgunderuntergangs von Prosper Aquitanus bis Magister Konrad, von W. Betz.--Obie und Meljanz; zum 7. Buch von Wolframs Parzival, von W. Mohr.--Bauformen der Waldleben-Episode in Gotfrids Tristan und Isold, von R. Gruenter.--Das (Continued)

NN R 7. 60 1/ OC, I PC, 1, 2, I SL (LC1, X1, Z1) [I]

GESTALTPROBLEME der Dichtung... (Card 2)

Zitat als Strukturelement in Rabelais' Erzählwerk, von H. Meyer.--Zur Struktur des "Standhaften Prinzen" von Calderón, von W. Kayser.--Werther-S udie, von H.-E. Hass.--Drei Goethesche Gedichte interpretiert, von K. May.--Über Brentanos "Geschichte vom braven Kasperl und dem schönen Annerl," von R. Alewyn.--Clemens Brentano "Die Abendwinde wehen," von E. Staiger.--Peter Schlemihls wundersame Geschichte; eine Studie zum Gestaltungsproblem des Novellen-Märchens, von B. von Wiese.--Drama und Roman im 19. Jahrhundert; Perspektiven auf ein Thema der Formengeschichte, von F. Martini.--Der Naturalismus Gerhart Hauptmanns, von P. Böckmann.--Zur Methode der (Continued)

GESTALTPROBLEME der Dichtung... (Card 3)

Strukturanalyse, von C. Heselhaus. --Darstellung, von E. L. Stahl. --Der Umfang als ein Problem der Dichtungswissenschaft, von F. Sengle. --Partnerschaft, von J. Trier. --Der Gestaltbegriff in Hegels "Phänomenologie des Geistes" und seine geistesgeschichtliche Bedeutung, von H. Schmiz. --Verzeichnis der wissenschaftlichen Schriften von Günther Müller, von H. Müller.

1. German literature--Addresses, essays, lectures. 2. Müller, Günther, 1890- . I. Alewyn, Richard, 1902- , ed.

E-11
141

GESTALTUNG, Umgestaltung; Festschrift zum 75. Geburtstag von Hermann August Korff. Hrsg. von Joachim Müller. Leipzig, Koehler & Amelang, 1957, 291 p. illus., port. 24cm.

Includes bibliographical references.

CONTENTS.—Frauenstrophe und Frauenlied in der frühen deutschen Lyrik, von T. Frings.—Ein Lied oder zwei Lieder? Über das Verhältnis von Ton und Lied bei Walther von der Vogelweide, von F. Maurer.—Die Selbstdarstellung Oswalds von Wolkenstein, von H. Emmel.—Die Pflege der gesprochenen deutschen Sprache durch Berthold von Regensburg, Meister Eckhart und Johannes Tauler, von I. Weithase.—Herzog Karl Eugen gründet ein Nationaltheater, von R. Buchwald.—Das "Märchen": Goethe und Gerhart Hauptmann, von H. Mayer.—Zu Goethes Auffassung von der Schauspielkunst, von L.

(Continued)

NN R 2. 61 m/ OC, I PC, 1, 2, I SL (LC1, X1, Z1) [I]

GESTALTUNG... (Card 2)

CONTENTS—Continued.

Scheithauer.—Goethe and Tschechow as liberal humanists, by W. H. Bruford.—Lunatscharski: "Faust und die Stadt," von R. Pascal.—Goethes Zeiterlebnis im "West-östlichen Divan," von J. Müller.—Goethes "West-östlicher Divan" und Rückerts "Östliche Rosen," von L. Magon.—Die Aufhebung der Zeit in Novalis' "Heinrich von Ofterdingen," von E. Haufe.—Die Struktur von Jean Pauls "Titan," von L. Markschies.—Das Geologenbild Adalbert Stifters, von E. Banitz.—W. B. Yeats: Der dichterische Symbolismus. Übersetzt und erläutert von W. Kayser.—Rilke und Stefan George, von E. C. Mason.—Österreichische Bewahrung in der Essayistik Hofmannsthals, von G. Konrad.

1. German literature--Addresses, essays, lectures. 2. Korff, Hermann August, 1882- . I. Müller, Joachim, 1906- , ed.

---

*POR

Get thee a teacher (from "The ethics of the fathers") ... Houston, Tex., 1945.

3 p. l., 5-31 p. illus. (port.) 27½cm.

"This volume, in which are contained some selections and excerpts from the teachings of reform Judaism, is dedicated to the memory of Israel Friedlander."

CONTENTS.—Dedication, by H. J. Schachtel.—Dr. David Philipson's "History and development of reform Judaism," edited by Israel Friedlander.—Selections from the writings of reform rabbis: Kaufman Kohler, H. G. Enelow, Henry Cohen, Samuel Goldenson.—Congregation Beth Israel and reform Judaism, by Israel Friedlander.—Memorial address, by W. H. Fineshriber.

1. Jews—Religion—Reform movements. 2. Friedlander, Israel, 1888-1944.

A 47-383

Harvard univ. Library
for Library of Congress [4]

TAH

Gewerbe und Wissenschaft. Festgabe Paul Gysler, 1953. St. Gallen, Zollikofer [1953?] xii,256 p. port. 25cm.

Contents.—Gewerbliche Gestaltungsprobleme, von E. Anderegg.—Möglichkeiten und Grenzen der Konjunkturpolitik, von E. Böhler.—Das Organisationsprinzip in der Inlandwirtschaft als Mittel der gegenseitigen Verständigung, von E. Feisst.—Voraussetzungen und Grenzen des freien Wettbewerbes, von A. Gutersohn.—Staatsgefüge, Wirtschaftsverbände

(Continued)

NN**R X 3.54 OC,2bo PC,1,2 SL E,1,2 (Z1, LC1,X1)

Gewerbe und Wissenschaft. Festgabe Paul Gysler, 1953. (Card 2)

und Betriebsleben in ihrer Gegenseitigkeit, von W. Heinrich.—Die Schweiz und die Probleme der Welthandelspolitik, von J. Hotz.—Vom Sinnwandel der Submission, von T. Keller.—Wesen und Wirken des Schweizerischen Gewerbeverbandes, von U. Meyer-Boller.—Die Strukturwandlungen der Handwerkswirtschaft, von K. Rössle.—Der geistige Standort des Gewerbes, von C. E. Scherrer.—Die Wirtschaftsartikel der BV und das Organisationsprinzip in der Wirtschaft, von E. von Steiger.

1. Industries,Small—Switzerland.I.Gysler,Paul.

F-11
287

GEWERKSCHAFT DER POLIZEI IM GEBIET DER DEUTSCHEN Bundesrepublik einschliesslich des Landes Berlin.

Beginn und Aufstieg; 10 Jahre Gewerkschaft der Polizei, 1950-1960. [Zusammengestellt und überarbeitet von Klaus Hübner] Hamburg, Verlag Deutsche Polizei [1961] 174 p. illus., ports. 27cm.

1. Trade unions, Police--Germany. I. Hübner, Klaus, ed. II. Hübner, Klaus.

NN R 5.65 p/B (OC)I, IIbo OS(1b*) PC, 1, I SL E, 1, I (LC1, X1, Z1)

PTI

GEYER, OTTO FRANZ, ed.

Festschrift Hermann Aldinger, zur Vollendung des 60. Lebensjahres am 1. Februar 1962, von seinen Schülern. Stuttgart, In Kommission bei E. Schweizerbart, 1962. 211 p. illus., port. 21cm.

Includes bibliographies.

CONTENTS. --Sedimentäre Eisenerzlagerstätten in Südwest-Angola, von G. Bauer. --Pleistozäner Bodenfrost und Klüftigkeit im nordschwarzwälder Buntsandstein, von K. Eissele. --Uber Schwammgesteine, von O. F. Geyer. --Uber alpine Tröge und Schwellen, von

(Continued)

NN 1.65 c/s OC, Ib*, II PC, 1, 2, I, II SL ST, 1t, 2 (LC1, X1, Z1)

GEYER, OTTO FRANZ, ed. Festschrift Hermann Aldinger... (Card 2)

M. P. Gwinner. --Bodenverfestigung als ingenieurgeologische Aufgabe, von H. W. Haag. --Onychoceras differens Wunstorf und die "Onychoceraten" K. Frentzen's, von W. Hahn. --Ein Profil des unteren Keupers (Lettenkeuper) von Stuttgart-Untertürkheim, von K. Hiller. --Baugeologische Untersuchungen im Bereich einer geplanten Strassenbrücke über die im Bau befindliche Biggetalsperre im Sauerland, von R. Klopp. --Drei Profile aus dem Grenzbereich Weissjura α/β bei Balingen (Württ.), von U. Koener. --Profil durch den Buntsandstein im Spessart, von M. Laemmlen. --Paläozoische und

(Continued)

GEYER, OTTO FRANZ, ed. Festschrift Hermann Aldinger... (Card 3)

mesozoische Fischfunde aus Alberta (Kanada), von K. O. A. Parsch. --Tertiär-Relikte auf Blatt Gammertingen (Schwäbische Alb), von W. Reiff. --Die Lagerungsverhältnisse im Kaliwerk Salzdetfurth (Hildesheimer-Wald-Sattel) und ihre Beziehungen zum Bau des Deckgebirges, von E. Schachl. --Der Einfluss der Sedimentmächtigkeit auf die Dispersion von Raleighwellen, von G. Schneider. --Der Jura in Erdölbohrungen des westlichen Molassetroges, von J. Schneider. --Die Erdgaslagerstätte

(Continued)

GEYER, OTTO FRANZ, ed. Festschrift Hermann Aldinger... (Card 4)

Emlichheim, von H. Söll. --Torbernit aus der Grube Clara bei Oberwolfach (Schwarzwald), von K. Walenta. --Jurassic Microfossils from Southern Alberta, Canada, von I. Weihmann. --Die Bedeutung der Cleveland-Eisenerze für die Frage nach der Entstehung von Eisenoolithen, von F. Werner.

1. Geology--Addresses, essays, lectures. 2. Aldinger, Hermann. I. Geyer, Otto Franz. II. Title. t.1962.

3-MLP

GINHART, KARL, 1888- , ed.
Gedenkbuch Bruno Grimschitz, hrsg. von Karl Ginhart und Gotbert Moro. Mit Beiträgen von Hermann Braumüller [et al.] Klagenfurt, Verlag des Geschichtsvereines für Kärnten, 1967. 206 p. illus., plans., ports. 24cm. (Kärtner Museumsschriften. 44)

"Die Datierung der Fresken in der Gurker Westempore, von Karl Ginhart": p. 9-174.

(Continued)

NN 8.68 a/ OC, II, III (OS)I PC, 1, 2, I, II, III SL A, 1, 2, II, III (LC1, X1, Z1)

3

E-13
591

Gilbert, Martin, 1936- *ed.*
A century of conflict, 1850-1950; essays for A. J. P. Taylor, edited by Martin Gilbert. [1st American ed.] New York, Atheneum, 1967 [°1966]
vi, 276 p. 24 cm.
English or French.
Bibliographical footnotes.
CONTENTS.—The man who likes to stir things up, by Lord Beaver-

(Continued)

NN * R 11.67 l/ OC PC, 1,2 SL (LC1,X1,Z1)

3

GINHART, KARL, 1888- , ed. Gedenkbuch Bruno Grimschitz... (Card 2)

"Verzeichnis der Bücher und Schriften von Bruno Grimschitz... zusammengestellt von H. Sedlmayr und K. Ginhart": p. 201-206.

1. Grimschitz, Bruno, 1892-1964--Bibl. 2. Painting, Mural--Austria--Gurk. I. Series. II. Moro, Gotbert, joint ed. III. Title.

GILBERT, MARTIN, 1936- , ed. A century of conflict, 1850-1950... (Card 2)

brook.—History teaching and the voter, by Sir N. Angell.—Reflections on the history of international relations, by F. H. Hinsley.—Patriotism, pledges, and the people, by B. Kemp.—European diplomacy and the expedition of the thousand; the conservative powers, by F. Valsecchi.—Queen Victoria's doctors, by E. Longford.—William I and the reform of the Prussian Army, by M. Howard.—Asquith: a new view, by A. Gollin.—Rathenau and Harden: a foot-

(Continued)

NNBC
(Gentile)

Giovanni Gentile, a cura di Vittorio Vettori. Scritti di Armando Carlini [et al.] Firenze, La Fenice [1954] 247 p. 22cm.

"Questo volume esce mentre ricorre il decimo anniversario della morte di Giovanni Gentile."

(Continued)

NN** X 4.55 a/ OC,I,II PC,1,I,II SL (LC1,X1,Z1)

GILBERT, MARTIN, 1936- , ed. A century of conflict, 1850-1950... (Card 3)

note to the history of Wilhelmine Germany, by J. Joll.—French military ideas before the First World War, by Sir B. L. Hart.—The special relationship: an Anglo-American myth, by M. Beloff.—Noel Buxton and A. J. P. Taylor's The trouble makers, by H. N. Fieldhouse.—Les leçons du Putsch de Hitler de 1923, by G. Bonnin.—Lewis Namier: a personal impression, by Sir I. Berlin.—The financial crisis of 1931, by P. Einzig.—Anarchist agrarian collectives in the Spanish Civil War, by H. Thomas.—Revisionism and reform in the Soviet Union since 1953, by E. Crankshaw.

1. Taylor, Alan John Percivale, 1906- 2. History, Modern--Addresses, essays, lectures.

Giovanni Gentile, a cura di Vittorio Vettori. (Card 2)

By various authors.

1. Gentile, Giovanni, 1875-1944. I. Vettori, Vittorio, ed. II. Carlini, Armando, 1878-

---

D-13
6677

GILDE, LUISE.
Friedrich von Schillers Geschichtsphilosophie; veranschaulicht in seinen Dramen. Zum 200. Geburtstage des Dichters. London [Im Selbstverlag] 1959-60. 2 v. 21cm.

Bibliography, v.1., p. 5-15.

1. Schiller, J.C.F. von, as a historian.
NN R 5.62 a/5 OC(1bo) PC, 1 SL (LC1, X1, Z1)

AN
(Porzio, G.)

A Giovanni Porzio nel LXXX compleanno. Napoli, Casa del lavoro tipografico V. Rappolla, 1954. 178p. ports. 25cm.

1. Porzio, Giovanni, 1873- .

NN ** X 6.55 s/ OC,1b PC,1 SL E,1 (Z1,LC1, X1)

E-10
9880

Gipper, Helmut, *ed.*
Sprache—Schlüssel zur Welt; Festschrift für Leo Weisgerber. Düsseldorf, Pädagogischer Verlag Schwann ₍1959₎
385 p. port. 24 cm.
Bibliographical footnotes.
CONTENTS.—Der philosophische Wahrheitsbegriff einer inhaltlich orientierten Sprachwissenschaft, von K. O. Apel.—Ontologische Voraussetzungen des Begriffs Muttersprache, von E. Rothacker.—Gegenstandskonstitution und sprachliches Weltbild, von E. Heintel.—Hegel und die Sprache, von J. Derbolav.—Die Leistung der Sprache für zwei Menschen, von H. Glinz.—Die Bedeutung Wilhelm v. Humboldts und Leo Weisgerbers für den Deutschunterricht in der Volksschule, von H. Schorer.—Einige Bemerkungen zu der Idee einer "inhaltbezogenen Grammatik," von J. Lohmann.—Strukturelle Syntax
(Continued)
NN * R 3. 60 m/V OC, I, IIb* PC, 1, 2, 2, I SL (LC1, X1, Z1)

EKZ
(Gladbach)
GLADBACH, Germany.
M. Gladbach; aus Geschichte und Kultur einer rheinischen Stadt. Im Auftrage der Stadtverwaltung zum 600 jährigen Stadtjubiläum hrsg. von Rudolf Brandts. [M. Gladbach, 1955] 1 v. illus., ports., facsims. 28cm.

[Bd. 1].
1. Gladbach, Germany—Hist. 2. Gladbach, Germany—Govt. 3. Art, German—Gladbach. I. Brandts, Rudolf. t. 1955.
NN * * R 6. 56 j/p (OC)I, Ibo ODt EDt PC, 1, 2, I SL A, 3, I (E)2, I (LC1, X1, Z1) [I]

Gipper, Helmut, *ed.* Sprache—Schlüssel zur Welt ... ₍1959₎ (Card 2)
CONTENTS—Continued.
und inhaltbezogene Grammatik, von J. Fourquet.—Offene Form, leere Form und Struktur, von P. Hartmann.—Die Einheit des Wortes, von W. Porzig.—Die Entstehung der deutschen dass-Sätze, von G. Müller und T. Frings.—Die "haben"-Perspektive im Deutschen, von H. Brinkmann.—Eigentümlichkeiten des Satzbaus in den Aussengebieten der deutschen Hochsprache (ausserhalb der Grenzen von 1939) von H. Moser.—Zur Geschichte der deutschen Kollektiva, von J. Erben.—Wonne, von J. Trier.—Leitmerkmale sprachlicher Felder, von H. Schwarz.—Die Lücke im sprachlichen Weltbild, von G. Kandler.—Sessel oder Stuhl? von H. Gipper.—Muttersprachliche Leistungen der Technik, von L. Mackensen.—Aufschlussreiche altenglische Wortin-
(Continued)

TAK
Glasfabriek "Leerdam" voorheen Jeekel, Mijnssen & Compagnie, Leerdam.
Vijftig jaar glasindustrie; gedenkboek uitgegeven ter gelegenheid van het 50-jarig bestaan der N. V. Glasfabriek "Leerdam" voorheen Jeekel Mijnssen & Co. te Leerdam. Rotterdam: W. L. & J. Brusse, 1928. 135 p. incl. front., plates, ports. 8°.
Plates printed on both sides.

451440A. 1. Glass—Trade and stat. —Netherlands—Leerdam.
N. Y. P. L. February 17, 1930

Gipper, Helmut, *ed.* Sprache—Schlüssel zur Welt ... ₍1959₎ (Card 3)
CONTENTS—Continued.
halte, von E. Leisi.—Synonymik nach Sinnbezirken im Englischen, von W. Schmidt-Hidding.—Der Sinnbezirk von 'Spiel' im Deutschen und im Schwedischen an Hand von Huibingas Homo ludens, von S. Öhman.—Ort und Richtung im Tscherkessischen, von G. Deeters.—Semantic patterns of the Navaho language, by H. Hoijer.—Bibliographie der Schriften Leo Weisgerbers (p. 374-385)

1. Language--Addresses, essays, lectures. 2. German language--Addresses, essays, lectures. 3. Weisgerber, Johann Leo, 1899- . I. Title. II. Gipper, Helmut.

NPBC
(Larreta)
La gloria de don Ramiro en veinticinco años de crítica; homenaje a don Enrique Larreta, 1908-1933 ... Buenos Aires, Ediciones Rosso, 1934-
v. 25½ᶜᵐ.
Bibliography of the editions of La gloria de don Ramiro: v. 1, p. 365-373.

1. Larreta, Enrique Rodríguez, 1875- La gloria de don Ramiro. I. Comisión de homenaje a Enrique Larreta. II. Title: Homenaje a don Enrique Larreta.
35-11520
Library of Congress PQ7797.L28G75
₍2₎ 863.6

*MGA
GISHFORD, ANTHONY, 1908- , ed.
Tribute to Benjamin Britten on his fiftieth birthday. London, Faber and Faber [1963] 195 p. illus. 23cm.

1. Britten, Benjamin, 1913- . I. Title.
NN R 1. 64 g/p OC PC, 1, I SL MU, 1, I (LC1, X1, Z1)
[I]

*MGA
GLOWACKI, JOHN M., ed.
Paul A. Pisk; essays in his honor. [Austin] College of fine arts, University of Texas [c1966] 294 p. illus., port., facsims., music. 26cm.

Includes bibliographies.
List of works by Paul Pisk, p. 283-294.

1. Pisk, Paul Amadeus, 1893- . 2. Music--Essays. 3. Essays.
NN R 11. 67 r/L OC(1bo) PC, 1, 2 SL MU, 1, 3 (LC1, X1, Z1)
[I]

A p.v.324
Giuseppe Peano... Collectione de scripto in honore de prof. G. Peano in occasione de suo 70° anno, edito per cura de interlinguistas, collegas, discipulos, amicos. Milano, 1928. 96 p. front. (port.), pl. 8°.
"Supplemento ad 'Schola et vita,' organo de Academia pro interlingua, Milano (Italia), 27 augusto, 1928."

497812A. 1. Peano, Giuseppe, 1858- . 2. Schola et vita.
N. Y. P. L. October 3, 1930

D-13
821
GODVILJENS mann, hilsen til Herman Smitt Ingebretsen på 70-ars-dagen. Oslo, J. Grundt Tanum, 1961. 202 p. port. 23cm.

1. Smitt Ingebretsen, Herman, 1891- .
NN 6.61 c/POC, 1b PC, 1 SL (LC1, X1, Z1)

D-20
4177

Göhler, Josef, 1911–
Eugen Eichhoff. Wegbereiter des Deutschen Turner-Bundes. Zu seinem 70. Geburtstag. Frankfurt/M., Limpert (1967).
175 p. with illus. and front. 23 cm.
[Bibliography of E. Eichhoff's works: p. 175–[176]

1. Eichhoff, Eugen, 1897- . 2. Gymnastics--Germany.
NN*R 11.71 w/ OC, 1b* PC, 1,2 SL (LC1, X1, Z1)

GÖTTING, FRANZ. Geschichte der Nassauischen Landesbibliothek zu Wiesbaden... (Card 2)

1. Libraries--Germany--Wiesbaden. I. Leppla, Rupprecht, 1900- , joint author. II. Series.

MHX

Goessler, Friedrich Peter, 1872– , editor.
Beiträge zur süddeutschen Münzgeschichte. Festschrift zum 25jährigen Bestehen des Württembergischen Vereins für Münzkunde, herausgegeben von Peter Goessler. Stuttgart: W. Kohlhammer, 1927. 131 p. illus., plates. 4°.

Mr Moth

329966A. 1. Numismatics—Assoc. and org.—Germany—Wurtemberg. 2. Numismatics, German—Hist. 3. Württembergischer Verein für Münzkunde.
N. Y. P. L. December 13, 1927

XAH

Göttinger Arbeitskreis.
Mensch und Staat in Recht und Geschichte; Festschrift für Herbert Kraus zur Vollendung seines 70. Lebensjahres dargebracht von Freunden, Schülern und Mitarbeitern. [Redaktion: Hans Kruse und Hans Günther Seraphim] Kitzingen/Main, Holzner-Verlag, 1954. viii, 468 p. port. 24cm.

"Verzeichnis der Veröffentlichungen und Gutachten von Herbert Kraus," p. 463-468.
(Continued)
NN**R 8.54 (OC)I,II, III SL E,2,3,I,II,III III OS PC,1,2,3,I,II, (LC1,Z1,X1)

NFGH

...Gœthe; études publiées pour le centenaire de sa mort (22 mars 1932) sous les auspices de la Faculté des lettres de l'Université de Strasbourg, par R. Ayrault, Ch. Beckenhaupt, G. Bianquis [et d'autres]... Paris: Les Belles lettres, 1932. xv, 474 p. 25½cm. (Strasbourg. Univ. Lettres, Faculté des. Publ. fasc. 57.)

Preface signed: E. V.
Includes bibliographies.
Contents: Avant-propos. La jeunesse de Gœthe: Vermeil, E. Gœthe à Strasbourg. Ayrault, R. Werther. Tronchon, H. Gœthe, Herder et Diderot.

(Continued)

Mr Moth

N. Y. P. L. October 10, 1932

Göttinger Arbeitskreis. Mensch und Staat in Recht und Geschichte... (Card 2)

1. Law—Addresses, essays, lectures. 2. Law, International, 1914- 3. Kraus, Herbert, 1884- I. Kruse, Hans, ed. II. Seraphim, Hans-Günther, ed. III. Title.

...Gœthe; études publiées pour le centenaire de sa mort... (Continued)

La philosophie de Gœthe: Loiseau, H. L'idée du "démonique" chez Gœthe. Beckenhaupt, C. Le quiétisme de Gœthe. Hauter, C. Gœthe et l'élite. Tonnelat, E. Le mot et l'idée de "Kultur" dans l'œuvre de Gœthe. L'esthétique de Gœthe: Will, R. Le génie visuel de Gœthe. Gérold, T. Gœthe et la musique. Rouge, J. La notion du symbole chez Gœthe. La politique de Gœthe: Redslob, R. Considérations sur l'état dans le Faust de Gœthe. Wittich, W. Gœthe et la guerre. Vullìod, A. Gœthe, l'Allemagne et l'Europe. Le testament poétique de Gœthe: Lichtenberger, H. Pandore. Bianquis, G. L'élégie de Marienbad. Gœthe, les contemporains, et la postérité: Fuchs, A. Gœthe et Wieland après les années d'Italie. Ehrhard, G. Gœthe et le comte de Pückler-Muskau. Dresch, J. Gœthe et la Jeune Allemagne. Pitrou, R. Storm et Goethe. Boucher, M. Gœthe inactuel.

601128A. 1. Goethe, Johann Wolfgang von. I. Vermeil, Edmond, 1878– , editor. II. Ser.
N. Y. P. L. October 10, 1932

D-12
1970

GÖTTINGER ARBEITSKREIS.
Preussenland und Deutscher Orden; Festschrift für Kurt Forstreuter zur Vollendung seines 60. Lebensjahres dargebracht von seinen Freunden. Würzburg, Holzner, 1958. vii, 381 p. 21cm. (Ostdeutsche Beiträge aus dem Göttinger Arbeitskreis. Bd. 9)

Der Göttinger Arbeitskreis. Veröffentlichung. Nr. 184.
"Staatsarchivdirektor Dr. Kurt Forstreuter: Verzeichnis seiner wissenschaftlichen Veröffentlichungen," von P. Buhl, p. 374-381.
1. Forstreuter, Kurt. 2. Teutonic knights. I. Series. II. Title.
NN R X 1.60 t/ (OC)II OS, I PC, 1, 2, I, II SL (LC1, X1, Z1)

Copy only words underlined & classmark-- EKL

GÖTTING, FRANZ.
Geschichte der Nassauischen Landesbibliothek zu Wiesbaden und der mit ihr verbundenen Anstalten 1813-1914. Festschrift zur 150-Jahrfeier der Bibliothek am 12. Oktober 1963 von Franz Götting und Rupprecht Leppla. Wiesbaden, Historischen Kommission für Nassau, 1963. 376 p. illus., ports., facsim. 25cm. (Verein für nassauische Altertumskunde und Geschichtsforschung, Wiesbaden. Historische Kommission für Nassau. Veröffentlichungen. 15)
(Continued)
NN R 5.64 g/ OC, I (OS)II PC, I, I, II (LC1, X1, Z1) 2

E-11
9243

GÖTTINGER ARBEITSKREIS.
Recht im Dienste der Menschenwürde; Festschrift für Herbert Kraus. Würzburg, Holzner [1964] x, 547 p. port. 24cm.

Bibliographical footnotes.
"Verzeichnis der Veröffentlichungen und Gutachten von Herbert Kraus. Fortsetzung des Verzeichnisses in 'Mensch und Staat in Recht und Geschichte', Kitzingen, 1954.", p. 545-547.
1. Kraus, Herbert, 1884- 2. Law, International--Addresses, essays, lectures.
NN R 3.64 f/ OS PC, 1, 2 SL E, 1, 2 (LC1, X1, Z1)

E-12
4780

Götze, Heinz, *ed.*
Dem Andenken an Reinhard Dohrn; Reden, Briefe und Nachrufe. Berlin, New York, Springer [1964]
70 p. illus., ports. (part col.) 25 cm.
English, French, German, or Italian.

1. Dohrn, Reinhard, 1880-1962. I. Götze, Heinz.
NN * R 11.65 e/ OC, 1bo, Ibo PC, 1 SL (LC1, X1, Z1)

E-13
1037

GOHDES, CLARENCE LOUIS FRANK, 1901- ,ed.
Essays on American literature in honor of Jay B. Hubbell. Durham, N.C., Duke university press, 1967. viii,350 p. 24cm.

Bibliographical footnotes.

1. American literature--Addresses, essays, lectures. 2. Hubbell, Jay Broadus, 1885-
NN R 2.68 e/ OC PC,1, 2 SL (LC1,X1,Z1)
[I]

D-12
2860

Golden, Herbert Hershel, 1919-
Modern Italian language and literature: a bibliography of homage studies, by Herbert H. Golden and Seymour O. Simches. Cambridge, Harvard University Press, 1959.
x, 207 p. 23 cm.

1. Festschriften--Bibl. 2. Festschriften--Indexes. 3. Italian language--Bibl. 4. Italian literature--Bibl. I. Simches, Seymour Oliver, 1919- , joint author.
NN* 3.60 1/3 OC, I PC, 1, 2, 3, 4, I SL (LC1, X1, Z1)

D-15
4231

GOODENOUGH, WARD H., ed.
Explorations in cultural anthropology; essays in honor of George Peter Murdock, edited by Ward H. Goodenough. New York, McGraw-Hill Book Co. [1964]
xiii, 635 p. illus., maps, port. 23 cm.
Includes bibliographies.
CONTENTS.—Introduction, by W. H. Goodenough.—Ethnogenealogical method, by H. C. Conklin.—Social structure of Santa Cruz Island, by W. Davenport.—Commercialization and political change in American Samoa, by M. Ember.—A structural description of Subanun "religious behavior," by C. O. Frake.—Semantic structure and social
(Continued)
NN* R 10.64 g/ OC PC, 1, 2 SL (LC1, X1, Z1) [I]

GOODENOUGH, WARD H., ed. Explorations in cultural anthropology... (Card 2)

structure: an instance from Russian, by P. Friedrich.—Culture and logical process, by T. Gladwin.—The Calusa: a stratified, nonagricultural society (with notes on sibling marriage) by J. M. Goggin.—Componential analysis of Könkämä Lapp kinship terminology, by W. H. Goodenough.—The Proto Central Algonquian kinship system, by C. F. Hockett.—Money, ecology, and acculturation among the Shipibo of Peru, by H. Hoffmann.—Survival of a cultural focus, by J. J. Honigmann.—Anthropology and non-Euro-American anthropologists: the situation in Indonesia, by Koentjaraningrat.—Snake-handling cult of the American Southeast, by W. La Barre.—A household survey of economic goods on Romonum Island, Truk, by F. M.

(Continued)

GOODENOUGH, WARD H., ed. Explorations in cultural anthropology... (Card 3)

LeBar.—The formal analysis of Crow- and Omaha-type kinship terminologies, by F. G. Lounsbury.—Law and societal structure among the Nunamiut Eskimo, by L. Pospisil.—The self-management of cultures, by J. M. Roberts.—Archeological approaches to cultural evolution, by I. Rouse.—Land and its manipulation among the Haitian peasantry, by F. W. Underwood.—Warfare and the integration of Crow Indian culture, by F. W. Voget.—Effects of climate on certain cultural practices, by J. W. M. Whiting.—The aboriginal location of the Kadohadacho and related tribes, by S. Williams.—Archeology and the "patriarchal age" of the Old Testament, by M. L. Zigmond.—Bibliography of George Peter Murdock (p. 599-603)

(Continued)

GOODENOUGH, WARD H., ed. Explorations in cultural anthropology... (Card 4)

1. Ethnology--Essays and misc. 2. Murdock, George Peter, 1897-

---

VOR

GORE, T.S., ed.
Recent progress in the chemistry of natural and synthetic colouring matters and related fields. Edited by T.S. Gore [and others] Dedicated to Professor K. Venkataraman in commemoration of his sixtieth birthday, 7 June, 1961. New York, Academic Press, 1962. xxvii, 659 p. port., diagrs., tables. 24cm.

Includes bibliographies.
PARTIAL CONTENTS.—Synthesis in the Brazilin group, by
(Continued)
NN *R 4.63 g/ OC, Ib* PC, 1, 2, 3 SL ST, It, 2t, 3 (LC1, X1, Z1)
4

GORE, T.S., ed. Recent progress in the chemistry of natural and synthetic colouring matters and related fields. (Card 2)

R. Robinson.—Ommochromes; by A. Butenandt and W. Schafer.—Bixdehy drocanthaxanthin, by H. Faigle and P. Karrer.—Azulenes from natural precursors, by S. Dev.—Naturally occurring phloroacylophenones, by W. Reidl.—Hooker's researches on lapachol, by L.F. Fieser.—The biflavonyl pigments, by W. Baker.—Anthocyanidin precursors, by K. Freudenberg.—A new synthesis of 5-hydroxycoumarin, by T. Nogradi, J. Swoboda and F. Wessely.—Naturally occurring phenylcoumarins, by N.R. Krishnaswamy and
(Continued)

GORE, T.S., ed. Recent progress in the chemistry of natural and synthetic colouring matters and related fields. (Card 3)

T.R. Seshadri.—Natural isoflavones and their glycosides, by L. Farkas.—A contribution to the chemistry of mangiferin, by B.J. Hawthorne, and others.—Chemistry of polyene antibiotics, by D.S. Bhate.—Some recent advances in diterpene chemistry, by V.P. Arya and H. Erdtman.—Alkaloids of the Indian rutaceae, by A. Ruegger.—The structure of chaksine, by G. Singh, and others.—Cobalt chelates of formazans, by H. Rudolf von Tobel and R. Wizinger.—Contribution to chemistry of
(Continued)

GORE, T.S., ed. Recent progress in the chemistry of natural and synthetic colouring matters and related fields. (Card 4)

formazans, by H. Wahl. and M. T. Le Bris. —Some problems of anthraquinone chemistry, by N.S. Dokunikhin. —Optical whitening agents, by D.A.W. Adams. —The desulphurization reaction, by G.M. Badger.

1. Dyes and dyeing--Chemistry. 2. Coal-tar colors. 3. Venkataraman, K. I. Gore, T.S. t. 1962

Gosudarstvennaya akademiya istorii material'noĭ kul'tury imeni N. Ya. Marra, Leningrad. Karl Marx et les sociétés des formations précapitalistes... (Continued)

Russian t.-p.: Карл Маркс и проблемы истории докапиталистических формаций; сборник к пятидесятилетию со дня смерти Карла Маркса. Москва ₍etc.₎ ОГИЗ, 1934.

Text in Russian; table of contents in Russian, French, English and German. Contributions by N. Y. Marr, A. G. Prigozhin, P. P. Yefimenko and others.

724851A. 1. Marx, Karl, 1818–1883. 2. History—Philosophy. I. Title. II. Title: Karl Marks i problemy istorii dokapitalisticheskikh formatzii. III. Ser.
N. Y. P. L. September 3, 1937

MA

Gosebruch, Martin, *ed.*
Festschrift Kurt Badt zum siebzigsten Geburtstage. Beiträge aus Kunst- und Geistesgeschichte. ₍Unter Mitarbeit von Rudolf Arnheim, et al.₎ Berlin, De Gruyter, 1961.
ix, 317 p. illus. (part mounted) plates (part col.) 23 cm.
Bibliographical footnotes.
CONTENTS.—Sokratischer und Sophokleischer Apollinismus, von R. Schottlaender.—A note on contemplation and creativity, by R. Arnheim.—The conceptual basis of archaic Greek sculpture, by P. Rawson.—Vom Aufragen der Figuren in Dantes Dichtung und Giottos Malerei, von M. Gosebruch.—Bemerkungen zum Kolorismus zweier
(Continued)

NN R 3.63 g/ OC PC,1,2,I SL A,1,2,I (PRW 1,LC1,X1,Z1)
[I]

Copy only words underlined & classmark-- NIMA

GOTHENBURG. Högskolan. Filologiska samfundet
Symbolae philologicae Gotoburgenses; minnesskrift utg. av Filologiska samfundet i Göteborg på femtioårsdagen av dess stiftande den 22. okt. 1950. Göteborg, Elanders boktr., 1950.
xxviii, 427 p. illus. 25 cm. (Gothenburg. Högskolan. Årsskrift. [bd.] 56 [no.] 3 (1950))
Includes bibliographies.

1. Philology--Addresses, essays, lectures. I. Title.
NN* 1.65 g/ (OC)I OS OI PC,1,I (LC1,X1,Z1)

GOSEBRUCH, MARTIN, ed. Festschrift Kurt Badt zum siebzigsten Geburtstage. (Card 2)

Gemälde der Münchener Pinakothek, von E. Strauss.—L. B. Albertis Langhaus von Sant Andrea in Mantua, von E. Hubala.—Albrecht Dürer: die vier Apostel, von A. M. Vogt.—Bruegels Verhältnis zu Raffael und zur Raffael-Nachfolge, von F. Grossmann.—Zur Bedeutung der Schrägsicht für die Deckenmalerei des Barock, von W. Schöne.—Ein Beitrag zu Meindert Hobbemas Allee von Middelharnis, von M. Imdahl.—Die Enthauptung des Dogen Marino Faliero von Eugène Delacroix, von G. Busch.—Zur Kunst Cézannes, von L. Dittmann.—Die Bilder van Goghs nach fremden Vorbildern, von F. Novotny.—Ungemalte Bilder von Vincent van Gogh, von E. Plüss.—Anton Bruckner und der Barock; Versuch einer vergleichenden

(Continued)

E-11
1948

GOTT und die Götter. Festgabe für Erich Fascher zum 60. Geburtstag. [Mitarbeiter Hans Bardtke et al.] Berlin, Evangelische Verlagsanstalt [1958] 157 p. 24cm.

Bibliographical footnotes.
CONTENTS. —Neutestamentliche Parallelen zu Láo-tsés Tao-te-king, von G. Lanczkowski. —Das Bild vom Kriege in der griechischen Welt, von J. Leitpoldt. —Biblos geneseōs, von O. Eissfeldt. —Zur Deutung des
(Continued)

NN 2.61 a/ OC,I PC,1,2,I SL (LC1,X1,Z1) [I]

3

GOSEBRUCH, MARTIN, ed. Festschrift Kurt Badt zum siebzigsten Geburtstage. (Card 3)

Künstebetrachtung, von W. Gross.—Theodor Hetzer, Gedanken zu seinem Werk, von G. Berthold.—Die Würdigung von Nietzsches Stil in der Hispania, von U. Rukser.—Herzchirurgie einst und jetzt, von G. J. Wittenstein.—Schriften Kurt Badts (p. 315–316)

1. Art--Essays and misc. 2. Badt, Kurt, 1890- . I. Title.

GOTT und die Götter. (Card 2)

Menschensohnes in Daniel 7, von L. Rost. —Wüste und Oase in den Hodajoth von Qumran, von H. Bardtke. —Der Tempel der goldenen Kuh, von O. Michel, O. Bauernfeind und O. Betz. —Zu Eigenart und Alter der messianisch-eschatologischen Zusätze im Targum Jeruschalmi I, von K.H. Bernhardt. —Nun aber sind sie heilig, von G. Delling. —Von jedem unnützen Wort? Von E. Stauffer. —Die Abschiedsreden Jesu. Ein Beitrag zur Frage der Komposition von Joh. 13,31-17,26, von J. Schneider. —Zur Exegese von I. Tim. 5,3-16, von J. Müller-Bardorff. —Das Apokryphon des Johannes, von W. Foerster. —Zur Bedeutung der lex, ihres Unvermögens und
(Continued)

Write on slip words underlined below and class mark —
*QCB

Gosudarstvennaya akademiya istorii material'noĭ kul'tury imeni N. Ya. Marra, Leningrad.
Karl Marx et les sociétés des formations précapitalistes; recueil d'études historiques à la mémoire de Karl Marx (1883–1933). Moscou ₍etc.₎ Les Éditions de l'état, Section sociale-économique, 1934. 766 p. front. (port.) 26cm. (Gosudarstvennaya akademiya istorii material'noĭ kul'tury imeni N. Ya. Marra, Leningrad. Известия. Выпуск 90.)

(Continued)

N. Y. P. L. September 3, 1937

GOTT und die Götter. (Card 3)

dennoch Bleibens, nach Luthers Antinomerthesen, von R. Hermann. —Johann Franz Buddeus und die Anfänge der historischen Auffassung des Alten Testaments, von K. Heussi.

1. Fascher, Erich, 1897- . 2. Theology--Collections. I. Bardtke, Hans.

GFD

GOTTFRID CARLSSON, 18. 12. 1952. Lund, C. W. K. Gleerup [1952] xi, 452 p. illus., port. 24cm.

"Signe Carlsson: Professor Gottfrid Carlssons skrifter, en bibliografi," p. 428-449.

1. Sweden—Hist. — Addresses, essays, lectures. 2. Carlsson, Gottfrid Henrik, 1887-

NN** 10. 53 OC PC, 1, 2 SL (Z/, LC1, X1)

E-13
2270

Gratulatio; Festschrift für Christian Wegner zum 70. Geburtstag am 9. September 1963. ₍Hamburg, Grossohaus Wegner, 1963₎

275 p. facsim., port. 24 cm.

"Die Herausgabe besorgten Maria Honeit und Matthias Wegner."
Includes bibliographical references.

CONTENTS.—Gruss zum 70. Geburtstag, von E. Trunz.—Hamburger Vorlesung 1945, von H. von Einem.—Die Utopie des Ästhetischen bei Schiller, von B. von Wiese.—Goethe, Spinoza, Jacobi, von H. Nicolai.—

(Continued)

NN * R 5. 68 1/R OC, I, II, IIIb* IVb* PC, 1, 2, I, II SL (LC1, X1, Z1) [I]

3

GRATULATIO; Festschrift für Christian Wegner zum 70. (Card 2)

Über die geschichtliche Bedeutung von Goethes Newton-Polemik und Romantik-Kritik, von H. J. Schrimpf.—Das Goethebild J. P. Eckermanns, von K. R. Mandelkow.—Die Formen der deutschen Lyrik in der Goethezeit, von E. Trunz.—Der "Gegner" in Hölderlins "Grund zum Empedokles," von D. Lüders.—Die Gestaltung des tragischen Geschehens in Kleists "Erdbeben in Chili," von J. Kunz.—Zu Kleists Aufsatz "Über die Rettung von Österreich," von R. Samuel—Prolegomena zu einer historisch-kritischen Büchner-Ausgabe, von W. R. Lehmann. — Expressionismus in Dichtung und Malerei, von K. L.

(Continued)

GRATULATIO; Festschrift für Christian Wegner zum 70. (Card 3)

Schneider.—Georg Trakl, "Nachtergebung," von W. Killy.—Musik in Steiermark, von R. Benz.—Über eine zeitgenössische Form der Landschaftsdarstellung; zu Radierungen von Karl Rohrmann, von R. Wankmüller.—Auf den Spuren der Niederländer in und um Hamburg, von G. Grundmann.

1. Wegner, Christian. 2. German literature--Addresses, essays, lectures. I. Honeit, Maria, ed. II. Wegner, Matthias, ed. III. Honeit, Maria. IV. Wegner, Matthias.

STT

Gratz, Austria. **Universität.**
Festschrift zur Feier des dreihundertfünfzigjährigen Bestandes der Karl-Franzens-Universität zu Graz; herausgegeben vom Akademischen Senat. Graz: Leuschner & Lubensky, 1936. 226 p. col'd front. (port.) 26½cm.

"Benütztes Schrifttum," p. 166-167.

Festschrift

935367A. 1. No subject.
N. Y. P. L. April 11, 1938

L-10
5132
Bd. 1

GRATZ, Austria. Universität. Philosophisches Seminar.
Meinong-Gedenkschrift; hrsg. mit Unterstützung des Bundesministeriums für Unterricht unter Mitwirkung von J.N. Findlay [et al.] Graz, "Styria," steirische Verlagsanstalt, 1952. 171 p. port. 24cm. (Graz, Austria. Universität. Schriften. Bd. 1)
Includes bibliographies.

(Continued)

NN 3.65 c/ (OC)I, II OS(1bo) OI PC, 1, 2, I, II (LC1, X1, Z1)

3

GRATZ, Austria. Universität. Philosophisches Seminar. Meinong-Gedenkschrift... (Card 2)

CONTENTS.--The influence of Meinong in Anglo-Saxon countries, by J. N. Findlay.--Die beiden Aspekte der Meinongschen Gegenstandstheorie, von R. Freundlich.--Das Problem der unvollkommenen Erkenntnisleistung in der Meinongschen Wahrnehmungslehre, von R. Kindlinger.--Zu Meinongs "unmöglichen Gegenständen", von F. Kröner. --Zu den logischen Paradoxien, von J. Mokre.--Meinongs Beziehungen zu den Grundlagen unserer Erkenntnistheorie und Weltanschauung, von K. Radaković.--Metaphysische Konsequenzen aus dem Persistenzgedanken Meinongs; Persönliches und Sachliches, von M.

(Continued)

GRATZ, Austria. Universität. Philosophisches Seminar. Meinong-Gedenkschrift... (Card 3)

Radaković.--Die Erkenntnistheorie Meinongs in der Grazer Schultradition, von A. Silva Tarouca.--Das Aussenweltproblem bei A. Meinong, von F. Weinhandl.--Die Entwicklung der Wertphilosophie in der Schule Meinongs, von K. Wolf.

1. Philosophy--Addresses, essays, lectures. 2. Meinong, Alexus, Ritter von Handschuchsheim, 1853-1920. I. Title. II. Findlay, John Niemayer.

D-15
512

GREAT BRITAIN. King's wardrobe.
Book of prests of the King's wardrobe for 1294-5. General editor: E.B. Fryde. Oxford, Clarendon press, 1962. lix, 266 p. port., facsim. 23cm.

"Presented to John Goronwy Edwards."
"A list of the writings of John Goronwy Edwards," p. 231-236.
Bibliographical footnotes.

(Continued)

NN R 4.64 f/ (OC)I ODt EDt PC, 1, 2, 3, I SL (E)3, I (LC1, X1, Z1)

2

GREAT BRITAIN. King's wardrobe. Book of prests of the King's wardrobe for 1294-5. (Card 2)

1. Edwards, Sir John Goronwy, 1891- . 2. Edward I, king of England, 1239-1307. 3. Royal households--Gt. Br. I. Fryde, E.B., ed. t. 1962

Greek poetry and life; essays presented to Gilbert Murray on his seventieth birthday, January 2, 1936. Freeport, N. Y., Books for Libraries Press [1967]
x, 399 p. illus., facsim., port. 22 cm. (Essay index reprint series)
CONTENTS.—The epilogue of the Odyssey, by J. W. Mackail.—Gold and ivory in Greek mythology, by H. L. Lorimer.—The date of Archilochus, by A. A. Blakeway.—Kynaithos, by H. T. Wade-Gery.—The ancient grief: a study of Pindar, Fr. 133 (Bergk), by H. J. Rose.—Μηδίζειν: μηδισμός, by J. L. Myres.—The Niobe of Aeschylus, by A. W. Pickard-Cambridge.—Lyric iambics in Greek drama, by J. D.

(Continued)

GREEK poetry and life... (Card 2)
Denniston.—The date of the Electra of Sophocles, by A. S. Owen.—The exodos of the Oedipus tyrannus, by Sir R. Livingstone.—Sophocles' Trachiniae, by T. B. L. Webster.—Lyrical clausulae in Sophocles, by A. M. Dale.—The elegiacs in Euripides' Andromache, by D. L. Page.—Who played "Dicaeopolis"? By C. Bailey.—Antistrophic variation in Aristophanes, by M. Platnauer.—Dramaturgical problems in the Ecclesiazusae, by E. Fraenkel.—On the treatment of disease in antiquity, by W. R. Halliday.—A tragic fragment, by E. Lobel.—Teliambi, by T. F. Higham.—Erinna's Lament for Baucis, by C. M. Bowra.—The Lock of Berenice: Callimachus & Catullus, by E. A. Barber.—Telepathy and clairvoyance in classical antiquity, by E. R. Dodds.

1. Greek literature--Hist. and crit. I. Murray, Gilbert, 1866-1957. i. Sub for 1936 ed.

The Greek political experience, studies in honor of William Kelly Prentice. Princeton, Princeton university press; London, H. Milford, Oxford university press, 1941.
x, 252 p. front. (port.) maps (1 double) 23½cm.
CONTENTS.—The people and the value of their experience, by N. T. Pratt, jr.—From kingship to democracy, by J. P. Harland.—Democracy at Athens, by G. M. Harper, jr.—Athens and the Delian league, by B. D. Meritt.—Socialism at Sparta, by P. R. Coleman-Norton.—Tyranny, by Malcolm MacLaren, jr.—Federal unions, by C. A. Robinson, jr.—Alexander and the world-state, by O. W. Reinmuth.—The Antigonids, by J. V. A. Fine.—Ptolemaic Egypt: a planned economy, by S. L. Wallace.—The Seleucids: the theory of monarchy, by Glanville Downey.—The political status of the independent cities of Asia Minor in the

(Continued on next card)

41-24541
[18]

The Greek political experience ... 1941. (Card 2)
CONTENTS—Continued.
Hellenistic period, by David Magie.—The ideal states of Plato and Aristotle, by W. J. Oates.—Epilogue, by A. C. Johnson.—Bibliography (p. [223]-233)—Index, by H. V. M. Dennis, III.

1. Greece—Pol. & govt. 2. Political science—Hist.—Greece. 3. Prentice, William Kelly, 1871-

41-24541

Library of Congress JC73.G78
[18] 320.938

Greenstreet, William John, 1861- , editor.
Isaac Newton, 1642–1727; a memorial volume edited for the Mathematical Association, by W. J. Greenstreet. London: G. Bell and Sons, Ltd., 1927. vii, 181 p. incl. diagrs., tables. front., illus. (facsims.), plates, ports. 8°.

325146A. 1. Newton, Sir Isaac, 1642–1727. 2. Science—Essays and misc. 3. Mathematical Association, London.
N. Y. P. L. October 10, 1927

GREIFENVERLAG, RUDOLSTADT, GERMANY.
Der Greifen Almanach. Zum 70. Geburtstag Lion Feuchtwangers und zum 35 jährigen Bestehen des Greifenverlags, hrsg. von Karl Dietz. Rudolstadt [1954?] 434 p. illus., ports., facsims. 22cm.

Various contributors.
"Unvollständiges Verzeichnis der Werke Lion Feuchtwangers," p. 123-124.

(Continued)

GREIFENVERLAG, RUDOLSTADT, GERMANY. Der Greifen Almanach. (Card 2)

1. Feuchtwanger, Lion, 1884- . 2. Graf, Oscar Maria, 1894- . 3. German literature—Collections. I. Title. II. Dietz, Karl, ed. t. Germany.

Greifswalder Studien. Theologische Abhandlungen, Hermann Cremer zum 25jährigen Professorenjubiläum dargebracht, von Samuel Oettli, Friedrich Giesebrecht, Adolf Schlatter... [und anderen] Gütersloh: C. Bertelsmann, 1895. 356 p. 24cm.

CONTENTS.—Der Kultus bei Amos und Hosea, von D. S. Oettli.—Grundlinien für die Berufsbegabung der alttestamentlichen Propheten, von F. Giesebrecht.—Zur Auslegung von Matth. 7, 21–23, von D. A. Schlatter.—Die Apostelgeschichte als Gegenstand höherer und niederer Kritik, von D. O. Zöckler.—Rolle und Codex, von V. Schultze.—Was versteht Paulus unter christlichem Glauben, von J. Haufsleiter.—Zur Paulinischen Erwählungslehre, von J. Dalmer.—Der Mensch aus dem Himmel, von W. Lügert.—Der Gedankeninhalt von Phil. 2, 12 u. 13, von E. Schaeder.—Der Glaube und die Thatsachen, von E. Cremer.—Gleichheit und Ungleichheit, von F. Lezius.—Zur Geschichte des Toleranzbegriffes, von D. M. v. Nathusius.

239323B. 1. Theology. 2. Cremer, Hermann, 1834-1903.
N. Y. P. L. August 13, 1943

GREISS, FRANZ, 1905- , ed.
Wirtschaft, Gesellschaft und Kultur; Festgabe für Alfred Müller-Armack, hrsg. von Franz Greiss und Fritz W. Meyer. Berlin, Duncker & Humblot [1961] xvii, 680 p. port. 24cm.

Includes bibliographies.

1. Economics--Essays and misc. 2. Social sciences--Addresses, essays, lectures. 3. European common market (1955-) 4. Müller-Armack, Alfred, 1901- I. Meyer, Fritz W., joint ed.

GRENOBLE. UNIVERSITÉ. Droit et des sciences économiques, Faculté de
Études historiques à la mémoire de Noël Didier. Publiées par la Faculté de droit et des sciences économiques de Grenoble. Paris, Éditions Montchrestien, 1960. xix, 361 p. port. 25cm.

Bibliographical footnotes.

1. France--Hist.--Addresses, essays, lectures. 2. Didier, Noël. I. Title.

KAT

Grenoble. Université. Institut de géographie alpine.
Mélanges géographiques offerts par ses élèves à Raoul Blanchard...à l'occasion du vingt-cinquième anniversaire de l'Institut de géographie alpine de Grenoble. Grenoble: Institut de géographie alpine, 1932. 665 p. incl. diagrs., tables. illus. (incl. charts), maps, plates, port. 25½cm.

"Cet ouvrage fait partie de la bibliothèque de l'Institut de géographie alpine."
"La plupart des articles du volume seront repris par la 'Revue de géographie alpine.'"
"Liste des travaux de Raoul Blanchard," p. 1-16.
Bibliographies included.

663220A. 1. Geography—Addresses, essays, lectures. 2. Anthropogeography. I. Blanchard, Raoul, 1877- . II. Title.
N. Y. P. L. October 10, 1933

AN
(Griese, F.)

Griese, Friedrich, 1890-
Kleine festliche Gabe Friedrich Griese, dargebracht als Zeichen des Dankes und der Freundschaft. [Schwerin i. M.:] Mecklenburgische Gesellschaft, 1931-32. 69 p. incl. mounted front., mounted plates, mounted ports. 25cm. (Mecklenburgische Gesellschaft. Veröffentlichung. Jahr 2, Bd. 4.)

One of 100 unnumbered copies.
Mainly selections of Griese's work.
"Zum 2. Oktober 1932 unter Mitarbeit von Paul Schurek, Reichskunstwart Dr. Redslob, Siegfried von der Trenck, herausgegeben von Ernst Metelmann."
"Friedrich Griese-Bibliographie," p. 67-69.

651212A. 1. No subject. I. Metelmann, Ernst, editor. II. Title. III. Ser.
N. Y. P. L. July 5, 1934

MW p.v.111

Grillparzer-Gesellschaft, Vienna.
Zu Adolf Wilbrandts 100. Geburtstag; Festschrift...hrsg. von der Grillparzergesellschaft, redigiert von Prof. Heinrich Glücksmann. [Horn, 1937] 115 p. port. 23cm.

"Beigabe zum 34. Jahrgang des Jahrbuchs der Grillparzergesellschaft."
CONTENTS.—Geleitwort, von Oswald Redlich.—Ein Idealist als Burgtheaterdirektor, von Karl Glossy.—Adolf Wilbrandt und wir, von Heinrich Glücksmann.—Aus Adolf Wilbrandts Burgtheater-Erinnerungen.—Aus den ersten Briefen Adolf Wilbrandts an seine spätere Gattin Auguste Baudius.

1. Wilbrandt, Adolf von, 1837-1911. I. Glücksmann, Heinrich, 1864-1943, ed. II. Title.
N. Y. P. L. April 21, 1947

E-12
924

GRIMME, ADOLF, 1889- , ed.
Kulturverwaltung der zwanziger Jahre; alte Dokumente und neue Beiträge, hrsg., in Gemeinschaft mit Wilhelm Zilius, von Adolf Grimme. [Stuttgart] W. Kohlhammer [1961] 140 p. 24cm.

"Für Dr. Otto Benecke zum 65. Geburtstag."
CONTENTS.--Zur Universitas; von C.H. Becker.--Offener Brief an Viscount Haldane über die Krisis in der deutschen Wissenschaft, von A. von
(Continued)

NN R 8.65 e/b OC, 3b+, I, IIbo PC, 1, 2, 3, I SL (LC1, X1, Z1) 3

GRIMME, ADOLF, 1889- , ed. Kulturverwaltung der zwanziger Jahre... (Card 2)

Harnack.--Die deutsche Studentenschaft in den ersten Jahren der Weimarer Republik, von T. Nipperdey.--Hochschule und öffentliches Leben in der Weimarer Republik, von T. Litt.--Die Bedeutung der wissenschaftlichen Pädagogik für das Volksleben, von E. Spranger.--Pädagogik auf der Universität und auf der Akademie, von C.H. Becker.--Schaffendes Schulvolk, von A. Reichwein.--Die Leipziger Büchereifeier.--Wesen und Aufgabe der städtischen Volkshochschule, von W. Picht.--Leitsätze der

(Continued)

GRIMME, ADOLF, 1889- , ed. Kulturverwaltung der zwanziger Jahre... (Card 3)

kommunalen Kulturarbeit, von A. Seeling.--Leitsätze zur kommunalen Kulturarbeit (Stuttgarter Richtlinien)--Die preussische Kunstpolitik und der Fall Schillings, von C.H. Becker.--Aus meiner Berliner Zeit, von H. Tietjen.--Dr. Otto Benecke.--Quellennachweise.

1. Education--Germany, 20th cent. 2. Germany--Civilization, 20th cent. 3. Benecke, Otto, 1896- . I. Zilius, Wilhelm, joint ed. II. Zilius, Wilhelm.

E-13
2559

GROB, GERALD N., ed.
Statesmen and statecraft of the modern West; essays in honor of Dwight E. Lee and H. Donaldson Jordan. Barre, Mass., Barre publishers, 1967. x,290 p. 24cm.

Includes bibliographical references.
CONTENTS.--The style of Russia's imperial policy and Prince G. A. Potemkin, by M. Raeff.--The Third
(Continued)

NN R 6.68 e/R OC,3b+ PC,1,2,3,I SL (LC1,X1, Z2) 2

GROB, GERALD N., ed. Statesmen and statecraft of the modern West... (Card 2)

French Republic in historical perspective, by S. M. Osgood.--Lord Roseberry, by W. G. Inman.--This time Germany is a defeated nation, by J. P. Glennon.--Konrad Adenauer, by E.Plischke.--John Foster Dulles and the Suez crisis, By C. B. Joynt.--Canada's role in the origin of NATO, by E. H. Miller.
1. Statesmen. 2. Lee, Dwight Erwin, 1898- . 3. Jordan, H. Donaldson. I. Title.

E-12
4224

GROCHLA, ERWIN, ed.
Organisation und Rechnungswesen. Festschrift für Erich Kosiol zu seinem 65. Geburtstag. Berlin, Duncker & Humblot [1964] 551 p. port. 24cm.

"Verzeichnis der wissenschaftlichen Veröffentlichungen von Eric Kosiol," p. [541]-551.
Bibliographical footnotes.
1. Kosiol, Erich, 1899- . 2. Management--Addresses, essays, lectures. i. subs. for Grochla, E- , ed.
NN R 9.66 r/u OCs PCs, ls, 2s SLs Es, ls, 2s (LCls, Xls, Zls[I])

3-MA

GROHMANN, WILL, 1887-1968.
Lieber Freund; Künstler schreiben an Will Grohmann. [Eine Sammlung von Briefen aus fünf Jahrzehnten] Hrsg. von Karl Gutbrod. Köln, M. DuMont Schauberg [1968] 223 p. illus., ports., facsims. 21cm. (DuMont Dokumente)

Title on spine: Künstler schreiben an Will Grohmann.
"Hommages an Will Grohmann": p. 9-224.
(Continued)

NN 2.71 d/i OC, I, II, IIIb* PC, 1, 2, I, II SL A, 1, 2, I, II (LC1, X1, Z1) 2

GROHMANN, WILL, 1887-1968. Lieber Freund... (Card 2)

"Will Grohmann: In eigener Sache": p. 25-31.
Bibliography, p. 215-223.

1. Artists--Correspondence, reminiscences, etc. 2. Grohmann, Will, 1887-1968--Bibl. I. Gutbrod, Karl, ed. II. Title. III. Gutbrod, Karl.

GRUNDPROBLEME des internationalen Rechts. (Card 2)

1. Law, International--Addresses, essays, lectures. 2. Spiropulos, Jean, 1895- I. Constantopoulos, Demetrios, S., 1916- , ed.

D-14
2975

GROSS, ELSE R., ed.
Karl Friedrich Reinhard, 1761-1827; ein Leben für Frankreich und Deutschland. Gedenkschrift zum 200. Geburtstag. Stuttgart, K. Wittwer [1961]
152 p. illus., ports., facsims. 21cm.

Bibliography, p. 123-130.

1. Reinhard, Charles Frédéric, comte, 1761-1837. I. Gross, Else R.
NN R 2.64 g/s OC, Ibo PC, 1 SL (LC1, X1, Z1)

MA

GSODAM, GERTRUDE, ed.
Festschrift W. Sas-Zaloziecky zum 60. Geburtstag. Graz, Akademische Druck- u. Verlagsanstalt, 1956.
212 p. illus., port. 25cm.

Includes bibliographies.

1. Art--Essays and misc. 2. Zalozetz'kyi, Volodymyr, 1896- . I. Title. II. Gsodam, Gertrude.
NN 2.64 f/J OC, I, IIbo PC, 1, 2, I SL A, 1, 2, I (LC1, X1, Z1) [I]

GFZE

... **Gruddbo** på Sollerön, en byundersökning. Tillägnad Sigurd Erixon, 19$\frac{26}{3}$38. Stockholm, Bokförlags aktiebolaget Thule [1938]

2 p. l., 583 p., 1 l. incl. illus., plates (1 col.) maps, plans, tables, diagrs. 2 fold. maps (in pocket) 28½cm. (Nordiska museets handlingar: 9)

Edited by Gösta Berg and Sigfrid Svensson.

Bibliography or bibliographical foot-notes at end of most of the articles.

CONTENTS.—Berg, Gösta. Inledning.—Lundqvist, G. Drag ur Solleröns geologi.—Öster, Johannes. Allmän översikt över naturförhållandena.—Gustawsson, K. A. Forntida bybebyggelse.—Granlund, John. Gruddbo by.—Granlund, John, and Homman, Olle. Beskrivning till kartan över Gruddbo by.—Granlund, John. Familj och gård. Fäbodlag. Bygdelag och byalag.—Nettelbladt, Sölve. Socknen och dess grannar.—Granberg, Gunnar. Bebyggelsesägner på Sollerön.—Homman, Olle. Byggnads-

(Continued on next card)

A 44-838

[3]

---

* GAH p.v.194

Guayaquil, Ecuador. Biblioteca de autores nacionales "Carlos A. Rolando."

XXV aniversario de la fundacion de la Biblioteca de autores nacionales "Carlos A. Rolando," 1913–1938. Guayaquil [Imprenta i talleres municipales, 1938] 104 p. 18½cm.

Foreword signed: Dr. Carlos A. Rolando.

1. Libraries—Ecuador—Guayaquil. I. Rolando, Carlos Alberto.
N. Y. P. L. August 21, 1941

... **Gruddbo** på Sollerön ... [1938] (Card 2)

CONTENTS—Continued.

skick.—Gustafsson, Gotthard. Eldhuset från Umsi.—Granlund, Ingalill. Stuga och bostad.—Jirlow, Ragnar. Jordbruket.—Svensson, Sigfrid. Notar och andra fiskeredskap.—Berg, Gösta. Djurfänge.—Trotzig, Dag. Laggningen på Sollerön.—Nilsson, Albert. Samfärdsel och fordon.—Zetterholm, D. O. Båtbyggeri.—Hazelius-Berg, Gunnel. Dräkt-tradition och modenyheter.—Strömberg, Elisabeth. Textil slöjd.—Campbell, Åke. Bröd och bak.—Svärdström, Svante. Bröllopsskildringar från Sollerön.—Boëthius, Gerda. S:t Laurentius kapell.—Wallin, Sigurd. Kaptensgården.—Lindén, Bror. Björkskipus och Skipustjärn.—Jansson, S. O. Runstavar.—Rehnberg, Mats. Bomärken.—Bannbers, Ola. Kass och kass-sticka.

1. Erixon, Sigurd Emanuel, 1888- 2. Sollerön, Sweden. 3. Gruddbo, Sweden. I. Berg, Gösta, 1903- ed. II. *Svensson, Sigfrid, 1901- ed.

A 44-838

Columbia univ. Libraries for Library of Congress [3]

TB p.v.416, no.5

Guenther, Adolf, 1881- , editor.

Eheberg-Festgabe; Beiträge zur Wirtschaftsgeschichte und Sozialtheorie. Carl Theodor von Eheberg zum 70. Geburtstage dargebracht, von G. Aubin...E. Lukas...E. Meier...H. Moeller ...C. L. Sachs...A. Günther...Herausgeber. Leipzig: W. Scholl, 1925. iv, 161 p. 8°.

Bibliographical footnotes.

Contents: AUBIN, G. Lübeck und München. GÜNTHER, A. Sozio-geographische Anwendungen der neueren Lebenshaltungsforschung. LUKAS, E. Erwägungen über

(Continued)

N. Y. P. L. March 10, 1927

E-10
3801

GRUNDPROBLEME des internationalen Rechts. Fundamental [sic] problems of international law. Festschrift für Jean Spiropoulas. Hrsg. von D. S. Constantopoulos, C. Th. Eustathiades [und] C. N. Fragistas. Bonn, Schimmelbusch [1957] xxxi, 471 p. port. 25cm.

Articles in German, English or French; title, preface and biographical sketch in all three languages.

(Continued)

NN 10.57 j/J OC, I PC, 1, 2, I SL E, 1, 2, I (LC1, X1, Z1, Y1)

Guenther, Adolf, 1881- , editor: Eheberg-Festgabe... (Cont'd)

die Bestimmungsgründe und die innere Verbundenheit des Angebotes und der Nachfrage, die den Kapitalzins begründen. MEIER, E. Systematische Prinzipienfragen der Statistik. MOELLER, H. Der Erkenntniswert der Tauschgleichung. SACHS, C. L. Die Nürnberger Girobank (1621–1827) im Rahmen der kontinentalen Bankgeschichte.

1. Lübeck—Hist. 2. Munich—Hist. 3. Hanseatic League. 4. Geography, Economic. 5. Supply and demand. 6. Interest. 7. Statistics. 8. Exchange (of wealth). 9. Banks and banking—Germany—Nuremberg. 10. Eheberg, Karl Theodor von, 1855- . 11. Aubin, Gustav Karl Will., 1881- . 12. Lukas, Eduard, 1890- . 13. Meier, Ernst. 14. Moeller, Hero, 1892- . 15. Sachs, Carl L., 1890- .
N. Y. P. L. March 10, 1927

MA

GULDAN, ERNST, ed.
Beiträge zur Kunstgeschichte; eine Festgabe für Heinz Rudolf Rosemann zum 9. Oktober 1960. [München] Deutscher Kunstverlag [1960] 361 p. illus. 28cm.

Includes bibliographies.
CONTENTS.--Zum Stil des Herimannkreuzes in Köln, von D. M. und R. Klessmann.--Eine unbekannte Madonnenstatue des 12. Jahrhunderts aus Niedersachsen, von S. Salzmann.--Grillenburg, Weisskirchen und Prag, (Continued)

NN R 8.61 p/POC, Ibo PC, 1, 2 SL A, 1, 2 (LC1, X1, Z1)

GULDAN, ERNST, ed. Beiträge zur Kunstgeschichte... (Card 2)

von W. Schadendorf.--Baugeschichtliche Untersuchungen an der Marktkirche in Hameln, von G. Kiesow.--Das Psalterium der Mechtild von Anhalt, von R. Kroos.--Christus in der Kelter, von A. Weckwerth.--Der Meister der Verkündigung in der Domopera zu Florenz, von M. Wundram.--Eine Braunschweiger Zeichnung von Agostino Veneziano, von B. Hedergott.--Studien zum Schlossbau des 16. Jahrhunderts in Mitteldeutschland, von G.F. Koch.--Hochaltar und Bischofsthron im Strassburger Münster, von E. Guldan.--Der Vertrag zum Hildesheimer Altar des Johann Paul Egell, (Continued)

GULDAN, ERNST, ed. Beiträge zur Kunstgeschichte... (Card 3)

von K. Lankheit.--Der Konsoltisch im Werk Joseph Effners, von R. und H. Jedding.--Ein "château triangulaire" des Maurizio Pedetti, von H. und K. Arndt.--Die Erfindung der Zeichenkunst, von H. Wille.--Die Thomakapelle der Karlsruher Kunsthalle, von K. Gallwitz.--Warnehaus und Späthistorismus, von H.G. Sperlich.--Zum zeichnerischen Werk des Österreichers Egon Schiele, von J. Reisner.--Zur Folge "Pâques" von Alfred Manessier, von P. Vogt.--Verzeichnis der angenommenen Göttinger Dissertationen.

1. Rosemann, Heinz Rudolf, 1900- 2. Art--Essays and misc. I. Guldan, Ernst.

E-12
2104

GUMMEL, HANS, 1891-
Hermann Allmers und die Altertumsforschung; Festschrift zur Wiedereröffnung des Morgensternmuseums, hrsg. von Magistrat der Stadt Bremerhaven. [Bremerhaven, 1961] 53 p. illus., port, facsims. 24cm.

Bibliography, p. 42-45.

1. Allmers, Hermann, 1821-1902. 2. Morgensternmuseum, Bremerhaven, Germany.
NN 11.65 g/B OC (OS) 2b PC, 1, 2 SL (LC1, X1, Z1)

---

*OLL

GUPTA, HARI RAM, ed.
Sir Jadunath Sarkar commemoration volume. [Hoshiarpur, Dept. of history, Panjab university, 1957-58] 2 v. illus., ports. 26cm.

Half-title; each volume has special t. p.
"Bibliography of Jadunath's works," v. 1, p. [108]-124.
Bibliographical footnotes.

(Continued)

NN R 6.61 e/OC, I, II (OS) III (LC1, X1, Z1) PC, 1, I, II, III SL O, 1, I, II, III

GUPTA, HARI RAM, ed. Sir Jadunath Sarkar commemoration volume. (Card 2)

CONTENTS.--1. Life & letters of Sir Jadunath Sarkar (Selections from Sarkar-Sardesai correspondence, 1907-1956).--2. Essays presented to Sir Jadunath Sarkar.

1. India--Hist.--Addresses, essays, lectures. I. Sarkar, Sir Jadunath, 1870- . II. Sardesai, Govind Sakharam, rao bahadur, 1865- . III. Panjab university, Chandigarh. History, Dept. of.

---

*MEC
(Mahler)

Gustav Mahler [von] Arnold Schönberg, Ernst Bloch, Otto Klemperer [u. a.] Tübingen, Rainer Wunderlich Verlag Hermann Leins (1966)

233 p. 22 cm.

1. Mahler, Gustav, 1860-1911. I. Schönberg, Arnold, 1874-1951.
NN R 5.67 a/ OC, I PC, 1, I SL MU, 1, I (LC1, X1, Z1)

---

*KAB

Gutenberg-Gesellschaft. Mainz.
Gvtenberg Festschrift, zvr Feier des 25iaehrigen Bestehens des Gvtenbergmvsevms in Mainz 1925. Heravsgegeben von A. Rvppel. Mainz: Verlag der Gvtenberg-Gesellschaft[,1925].
3 p.l., ix-xvi, 448 p., 5 l. facsims., illus., plates (part col'd). 29cm.

Advertisements, 5 l. at end.
Contents: Aus der Frühdruckzeit. Aus den vier Jahrhunderten 1500-1900. Heutige Buch- und Druckkunst. Verschiedene Forschungen. Organisationen.

E-11
6103

Guthke, Karl S., ed.
Dichtung und Deutung: Gedächtnisschrift für Hans M Wolff. Bern, Francke [1961]

166 p. port. 24 cm.

Includes bibliographies.

CONTENTS.--Hans M. Wolff (1912-1958)--A new etymology: Germanic erma/in(a)- reconsidered, by M. S. Beeler.--Jenseits von Sein und Nichtsein, von R. M. Chisholm.--Das schriftstellerische und wissenschaftliche Werk Max J. Wolffs, von K. S. Guthke.--The word and the world: some remarks on the difference between poetry and (Continued)

NN R 2.63 g/ OC PC, 1, 2, I SL (LC1, X1, Z1)
[I]

GUTHKE, KARL S., ed. Dichtung und Deutung... (Card 2)

prose, by A. O. Jaszi.--Zu Schillers Poetik, von V. Lange.--Zur Typenbildung der Lyrik, von B. Markwardt.--Volk, von der Aufklärung zur Romantik, von H. Meyer.--The Hohenstaufen dramas of C. D. Grabbe, by R. Nicholls.--Otto Ludwig's "Zwischen Himmel und Erde" and George Eliot's "Adam Bede," by L. M. Price.--Dichterrache, von F. R. Schröder.--Mensch und Natur in Goethes "Novelle," von D. W. Schumann.--Lessings Prosa. Eine Vorlesung, von E. Staiger.--Rilkes "Römische Sarkophage," von H. Weigand.--Die

(Continued)

GUTHKE, KARL S., ed. Dichtung und Deutung... (Card 3)

Veröffentlichungen Hans M. Wolffs, zusammengestellt von K. S. Guthke (p. [163]-166)

1. Wolff, Hans Matthias, 1912-1958. 2. Literature--Addresses, essays, lectures. I. Title.

GUYAN, WALTER ULRICH, ed. Im Dienste einer Stadt... (Card 3)

—Die kulturellen Aufgaben der Industrie, von C. Gasser. —Die Schaffhauser Bach-Feste, von W. Reinhart. —Zum Schaffhauser Stadttheater, von O. Wälterlin.

1. Schaffhausen, Switzerland (City)--Hist. 2. Bringolf, Walther. 3. Art, Swiss--Schaffhausen.

---

* C-3 p.v.596

Guxhagen, Germany.

1352 [i. e. Dreizehnhundertzweiundfünzig]-1952. Guxhagen, Kukushayn. Denkschrift zur Sechshundertjahrfeier der Gemeinde Guxhagen. Herausgeber: Gemeinde Guxhagen; Anzeigenteil: Gerhard Säwert. Melsungen, A. Bernecker [1952] 96 p. illus. 21cm.

On cover: Festschrift.

(Continued)

NN R 4.53 OD ED PC SL (LC1, Z1, X1)

Copy only words underlined & classmark— QPI

GUYAN, WALTER ULRICH, ed.

Das Pfahlbauproblem, von W.U. Guyan [et al.] Hrsg. zum Jubiläum des 100 jährigen Bestehens der schweizerischen Pfahlbauforschung. Basel, Birkhäuser, 1955. 334 p. illus., maps, charts (part fold.) 31cm. (Monographien zur Ur- und Frühgeschichte der Schweiz. Bd. 11)

Series edited by Schweizerische Gesellschaft für Urgeschichte.
Includes bibliographies.

(Continued)

NN**R X 3.57 d/b OC (OS)I PC, 1, I (U1, LC1, X1, Z1)

Guxhagen, Germany. 1352 [i. e. Dreizehnhundertzweiundfünzig]-1952. (Card 2)

CONTENTS.—Aus der Geschichte Guxhagens, von Dr. Christoph Weber.—Greben bzw. Bürgermeister der Gemeinde Guxhagen.—Das älteste Einwohnerverzeichnis von Guxhagen.—Wann und wie entstand Guxhagen? Von Adam Gerhold.—Verkehrsverbindungen Guxhagens durch Wasserstrasse und Schienenweg, von Karl Koch.—Entstehung und Bau der Reichsautobahn, von Adam Werner.— Die Schule in Guxhagen, von A. Elbrecht.—Daten aus der Geschichte des Klosters Breitenau.—Das Landesfürsorgeheim "Fuldatal," von Dr. Alter.—Der Maler Glinzer, ein Guxhagener Kind.—Von Sitte und Brauchtum, Feiern und Festen unserer Dorfheimat, von Fritz Riese.

GUYAN, WALTER ULRICH, ed. Das Pfahlbauproblem... (Card 2)

CONTENTS. —Pollenanalytische Untersuchungen zu einigen schweizerischen Pfahlbauproblemen, von J. Troels-Smith. —Pollenanlytische Untersuchungen über die neolithischen Siedlungsverhältnisse am Burgäschiesee, von M. Welten. —Beitrag zur Kenntnis der Vegetationsverhältnisse im schweizerischen Alpenvorland während der Bronzezeit, von W. Lüdi. —Datierung der Pfahlbausiedlung Egolzwil 3 mit Hilfe der Kohlenstoff-14-methode, von H. Levi und H. Tauber. —Pfahlbaustudien, von E. Vogt. —Das jungsteinzeitliche Moordorf von Thayngen-Weier, von

(Continued)

G-10
968

GUYAN, WALTER ULRICH, ed.

Im Dienste einer Stadt; Festschrift für Walther Bringolf. [Schaffhausen, 1960] 185 p. illus., port., facsims. 31cm.

PARTIAL CONTENTS. —Die Raumbildung in der Altstadt von Schaffhausen, von W. Henne. —Die Wiederherstellung der Fassadenmalerei des Hauses "Zum Ritter" in Schaffhausen, von P. Ganz. —Überlegungen zur Baugeschichte des Münsters: Die Bauetappen, von W. Drack. Versuche

(Continued)

NN R 8.61 g/B OC PC, 1, 2, 3 SL A, 3 (LC1, X1, Z1)

3

GUYAN, WALTER ULRICH, ed. Das Pfahlbauproblem... (Card 3)

W.U. Guyan. —Die Ausgrabungen in der spätbronzezeitlichen Ufersiedlung Zug-"Sumpf" von J. Speck.

1. Lake dwellings--Switzerland. I. Series.

GUYAN, WALTER ULRICH, ed. Im Dienste einer Stadt... (Card 2)

zur kunsthistorischen Auswertung, von A. Knoepfli. (Bibliography, p. 85). —Zwanzig Jahre Museum zu Allerheiligen, von W.U. Guyan. —Eröffnung der Ausstellung "Kunst und Kultur der Kelten" im Museum zu Allerheiligen in Schaffhausen am 1. August 1957, von M. Feldmann. —Fünfhundert Jahre venezianische Malerei, von G. Jedlicka. —Was die Naturforschende Gesellschaft der Stadt Schaffhausen zu danken hat, von A. Uehlinger. —Die Zürcher Kulturspende für Schaffhausen, von M. Fischer. —Das Stadtarchiv Schaffhausen, von A. Largiadèr.

(Continued)

E-14
863

Guyot, Charly, 1898-

De Rousseau à Marcel Proust. Recueil d'essais littéraires. Avant-propos de Marcel Raymond. Neuchâtel, (Éditions) Ides et Calendes, (1968).

235 p. 24 cm.

Published in honor of the author's 70th birthday.
Bibliography of the author's works, p. 227-232.
Includes bibliographical references.

1. French literature--Addresses, essays, lectures.

NN* 3.71 d/J OC PC, 1 SL (LC1, X1, Z1)

(NCC Yeats)

Gwynn, Stephen Lucius, 1864– *ed.*
Scattering branches; tributes to the memory of W. B. Yeats, edited by Stephen Gwynn. New York, The Macmillan company, 1940.
viii, 228, [1] p. 19½cm.
Printed in Great Britain.
CONTENTS.—Scattering branches, by Stephen Gwynn.—Yeats and Ireland, by Maud Gonne.—Yeats as a painter saw him, by William Rothenstein.—The man and the dramatist, by Lennox Robinson.—The poet and the actor, by W. G. Fay.—Without the twilight, by Edmund Dulac.—Yeats as Irish poet, by F. R. Higgins.—A note on W. B. Yeats and the aristocratic tradition, by C. D. Lewis.—William Butler Yeats, by L. A. G. Strong.
1. Yeats, William Butler, 1865–1939. I. Title.
41–9842
Library of Congress PR5906.G85
[7] 820.81

---

* IIV +

Gyldendal norsk forlag, 25 år, 1925–1950. [Oslo, Gyldendal norsk forlag, 1950] 1 v. (chiefly illus., ports., facsims.) 35cm.

I. Gyldendal, norsk forlag a/s.
NN*R 3.54 OC (OS)I PC, I SL E, I (LC1, Z1, X1)

Copy only words underlined & classmark-- IAA

GYLES, MARY FRANCIS, ed.
Laudatores temporis acti; studies in memory of Wallace Everett Caldwell, profesor of history at the University of North Carolina by his friends and students. [Edited] by Mary Francis Gyles and Eugene Wood Davis. Chapel Hill, University of North Carolina press, 1964. viii, 148 p. port. 24cm. (North Carolina. University. History dept. The James Sprunt studies in history and political science. v.46)
(Continued)
NN 12.65 a/c OC, I, IIIbo (OD) II (ED)II PC, 1, 2, I, II (AH)I 3
(LC1, X1, Z1) [I]

GYLES, MARY FRANCIS, ed. Laudatores temporis acti... (Card 2)

Bibliographical footnotes.
CONTENTS.— H[illegible] democracy and pleasure, by F.H. Bliss. —Some inscriptions on Attic pottery, by F.R. Immerwahr. --The beginning of coinage by Olynthian Chalcidians, by P.A. Clement. --The Persian battle plan at the Granicus, by E.W.Davis. --Cicero and his hoped-for triumph, by B.L. Ullman. --Cicero's Concordia in historical perspective, by H.C.Boren. --The unity of Propertius 2.34 and 3.20, by R.E. White. --Lucan and Caesar's crossing of the Rubicon, by R.J.Getty. --Speculum Caesaris, by R.E. Wolverton. --
(Continued)

GYLES, MARY FRANCIS, ed. Laudatores temporis acti... (Card 3)

Freedom of speech in the empire: Nero, by R.S. Rogers. --Effects of Roman capital investment in Britain under Nero, by M.F. Gyles. --Amber; an historical-etymological problem, by J.M. Riddle. --Tradition against independent investigation in pre-modern craniology, by L.C. MacKinney and T. Herndon. --The Sator-formula; an evaluation, by H.L. Bodman.

1. Caldwell, Wallace Everett, 1890- . 2. Classical studies--Collections. I. Davis, Eugene Wood, joint ed. II. Series. III. Davis, Eugene Wood.

E-11
9063

GYMNASIUM THOMAEUM, Kempen, Germany.
Festschrift des staatlichen altsprachlichen Gymnasium Thomaeum mit neusprachlichem Zweig zu Kempen-Niederrhein aus anlass seines 300 jährigen Bestehens als höhere Schule. [Herausgeber: Rudolf Knippen] Kempen-Niederrhein, 1959. 136 p. illus., ports. 25cm.
(Continued)
NN R 3.64 f/B (OC)I OS(1b) PC, I SL (LC1, X1, Z1) 2

GYMNASIUM THOMAEUM, Kempen, Germany.
Festschrift des staatlichen altsprachlichen Gymnasium Thomaeum... (Card 2)

Cover title: 300 Jahre Gymnasium Thomaeum, Kempen/Niederrhein, 1659-1959; Festschrift.
Bibliographical footnotes.

I. Knippen, Rudolf, 1886- , ed.

C-10
4254

H. A. Lorentz, impressions of his life and work. Edited by G.L. de Haas-Lorentz. [Translation by Joh.C. Fagginger Auer] Amsterdam, North-Holland pub. co., 1957. 172 p. illus., ports. 20cm.

CONTENTS. — H. A. Lorentz, his creative genius and his personality, by A. Einstein. — On the occasion of the undredth anniversary of the birth of Lorentz. H. A. Lorentz, by W. J. de Haas. —Reminiscences, by G. L. de Haas-Lorentz. —The scientific work, by A. D. Fokker. — Reminiscences (continued),
(Continued)
NN R X 8.57 p/ OC, I PC, 1, I SL ST, 1, I (LC1, X1, Z1, Y1)

H. A. Lorentz, impressions of his life and work. (Cont.)

by G. L. de Haas-Lorentz. —H. A. Lorentz and the bearing of his work on electromagnetic telecommunication, by B. van der Pol. — Enclosure of the Zuiderzee, by J. T. Thijsse. —Reminiscences (continued), by G. L. de Haas-Lorentz. — The influence of Lorentz' ideas on modern physics, by H. B. G. Casimir.

1. Lorentz, Hendrik Antoon, 1853-1928. I. Haas-Lorentz, G. L. de, ed.

JFD
71-129

Haan, Jacques den.
De buste van Beets wordt u persoonlijk aangeboden ⟨langs de hoofdspoorweglijn⟩. Bruna: 1868–1968. [Utrecht, A. W. Bruna, 1968].
144 p. illus., facsims., ports. 22 cm.
Published on the occasion of the 100th anniversary of Bruna N. V. and A. W. Bruna & Zoon's Uitgeversmaatschappij N. V.

1. Bruna N. V. 2. Bruna (A. W.) Uitgeversmaatschappij.
NN * R 2.71 b/B (OS)1b*, 2b* OC PC, 1, 2 SL E, 1, 2 (LC1, X1, Z1)

AL-10
363
Bd. 5

Haass, Robert, *ed.*
Zur Geschichte und Kunst im Erzbistum Köln; Festschrift für Wilhelm Neuss. Hrsg. von Robert Haass und Joseph Hoster. [1. Aufl.] Düsseldorf, L. Schwann [1960]
438 p. illus., ports., facsims, plans. 25 cm. (Studien zur Kölner Kirchengeschichte, Bd. 5)
"Bibliographie Wilhelm Neuss, 1902–1959": p. 425–437. Bibliographical footnotes.

(Continued)

NN* R 8.65 g/$_3$ OC, II, IIIb* (OS)I PC, 1, 2, 3, I, II A, 2, II (LC 1, X1, Z1)

2

HAASS, ROBERT, ed. Zur Geschichte und Kunst im Erzbistum Köln... (Card 2)

1. Cologne (Archdiocese)--Hist. 2. Art, Ecclesiastical--Germany--Cologne. 3. Neuss, Wilhelm, 1880- I. Series. II. Hoster, Joseph, joint ed. III. Hoster, Joseph.

M-10
9888

HABERLAND, EIKE, ed.
Festschrift für Ad. E. Jensen, hrsg. von Eike Haberland, Meinhard Schuster und Helmut Straube. München, K. Renner, 1964. 2 v. illus., port., maps. 28cm.

Contributions in German, some in French or English.
Includes bibliographies. "Veröffentlichungen von Ad. E. Jensen," T. 1, p. xi-xvi.

1. Jensen, Adolf Ellegard, 1899- . 2. Ethnology--Essays and misc.
NN R 10.65 s/ OCs PCs, 1s, 2s SLs (LC1s, X1s, Z1s) [I]

D-16
6705

HABERLAND, WOLFGANG.
Bibliographie der Arbeiten von Franz Termer aus den Jahren 1919-1964. Professor Dr. Franz Termer aus Anlass seines 70. Geburtstages am 5. Juli 1964, gewidmet von seinen Mitarbeitern. Zusammenstellung: Wolfgang Haberland. [n.p., 1964] 20 p. 21cm.

1. Termer, Franz, 1894- -- Bibl.
NN * R 9.66 1/d OC PC, 1 SL (LC1, X1, Z1)

---

* PWC p.v.29

Habonim. Germany.
Haboneh; Sammelschrift des Habonim anlässlich seines fünfjährigen bestehens. Dem Andenken von Seew Orbach. Berlin: Hechaluz-Verlag, 1938. 109 p. 22½cm.

Label: Hechaluz-Verlag Jüdischer Buchverlag und Buchvertrieb Berlin 1938, over original imprint.

1. Orbach, Seew. I. Title.
N. Y. P. L. December 9, 1940

E-12
518

HAFEMANN, DIETRICH, ed.
Mainzer geographische Studien; Festgabe zum 65. Geburtstag Professor Wolfgang Panzers am 16. Juni 1961 überreicht von seinen Schülern. Hrsg. von D. Hafemann, H. Kastrup [und] R. Klöpper. [Braunschweig] G. Westermann [1961] 176 p. port., maps, diagrs. 24cm.

Includes bibliographies.

(Continued)

NN R 6.65 e/$_4$ OC, Ib+ PC, 1, 2 SL (LC1, X1, Z1)

3

HAFEMANN, DIETRICH, ed. Mainzer geographische Studien... (Card 2)

CONTENTS.--Wolfgang Panzer; Versuch einer vorläufigen Porträtskizze, von H. Lehmann.--Die wissenschaftlichen Veröffentlichungen Wolfgang Panzers, p. 11-14.--Die letzteiszeitliche maximale Temperaturdepression in Europa, erschlossen aus der Depression der Schneegrenze, von W. Brauch.--Oklahoma; die Entwicklung vom Indianer-Reservat zur modernen Kulturlandschaft, von H. Rosenberg.--Der Eisenerzbergbau im mittleren Talgebiet der Sieg, seine Entwicklung und landschaftlichen Auswirkungen, von G. Hermann.-- Zur geschichtlichen Entwicklung

(Continued)

HAFEMANN, DIETRICH, ed. Mainzer geographische Studien... (Card 2)

des Obstbaues im nördlichen Rheinhessen, von M. Topp.--Zum Fremdenverkehr an der Hessischen Bergstrasse, von H. Häuser.--Beitrag zur Phänologie der Weinrebe, von H. E. May.--Über die Erosion von unter Eis fliessendem Wasser, von W. Tietze.--Die Auswirkungen der europäischen Fremdwirtschaft in Indonesien, von I. Wildförster.--Agrarklimatische Beobachtungen auf der Kanareninsel Lanzarote, von A. Hanle.--Zur Oberflächengestaltung des nördlichen Lanzarote, von H. Klug.

1. Panzer, Wolfgang, 1896- . 2. Geography--Addresses, essays, lectures. I. Hafemann, Dietrich.

AD-10
127

HAGEN (GOTTFRIED) A.-G.
125 [i.e. Hundertfünfundzwanzig] Jahre Gottfried Hagen Erzeugnisse; Werkgeschichte eines Familienunternehmens. [Köln-Kalk, 1952] 46 p. illus., ports. 21cm.

NN ** 3.59 a/ OC PC SL E (LC1, X1, Z1)

---

*MEC
(Fischer, E.)

HAID, HUGO, ed.
Dank an Edwin Fischer. Wiesbaden, F.A. Brockhaus, 1962 [c1961] 164 p. illus., ports., facsim. 20cm.

1. Fischer, Edwin, 1886-1960. 2. Fischer, Edwin--Iconography. I. Title. II. Haid, Hugo.
NN R 2.62 e/$_4$/OC, I, IIb+ PC, 1, I SL MU, 1, 2, I (LC1, X1, Z1)

Halle, Germany. Stadtarchiv.
Georg Friedrich Händel; Abstammung und Jugendwelt. Festschrift zur 250. Wiederkehr des Geburtstages Georg Friedrich Händel, mit einem Geleitwort von Oberbürgermeister Dr. Dr. Johannes Wiedemann. Beiträge ₍von₎ Richard Braütigan, Rolf Hünicken ₍und₎ Walter Serauky. Herausgegeben vom Stadtarchiv Halle. Halle: Gebauer-Schwetschke Druckerei und Verlag A.-G., 1935. xvi, 135 p. front (port.), 2 geneal. tables. 24cm.

Bibliographical footnotes.

788654A. 1. Handel, Georg Friedrich, 1685-1759. I. Bräutigam, Richard. II. Hünicken, Rolf. III. Serauky, Walter.
N. Y. P. L. January 14, 1936

HALLE, GERMANY. Universität. Kunstgeschichtliches Institut.
Deutschland-Italien: Beiträge zu den Kulturbeziehungen zwischen Norden und Süden; Festschrift für Wilhelm Waetzoldt zu seinem 60. Geburtstage 21. Februar 1940. Berlin, G. Grote, 1941. xlviii, 358 p. illus., port. 26cm.

Includes bibliographies.
CONTENTS.—Das Raumerlebnis in der deutschen und italienischen Malerei am Ende des 15. Jahrhunderts, von G. J. von Allesch.—Das Transzendente als Darstellungsvorwurf der Kunst des Abendlandes, von
(Continued)

NN**R 10.54 (OC)I OS(1b+) PC, 1, 2, I SL A, 1, 2, I (Z1, LC1, X1) [I]

HALLE, GERMANY. Universität. Kunstgeschichtliches Institut.
Deutschland-Italien:... (Card 2)

G. Weise.—Masaccio und Filippino Lippi, von R. Hamann.—Das Morgenländische in der Anbetung der Könige, von O. H. von Bockelberg.—Das Büchenstilleben in der Plastik, von K. Gerstenberg.—Zweimal "Trint," von E. Waldmann.—Italienische Majoliken, ihre deutschen Vorbilder und deutschen Besteller, von R. Schmidt.—Ein unbekanntes Bildnis Kardinal Albrechts von Brandenburg, von F.-K. Danneel.—Über ein unbekanntes Exemplar der "La petite Sainte Famille" genannten Raffael-Komposition, von C. E. von Liphart-Rathshoff.—Zum Stilproblem des Manierismus in der italienischen und deutschen
(Continued)

HALLE, GERMANY. Universität. Kunstgeschichtliches Institut.
Deutschland-Italien... (Card 3)

Malerei, von H. Lossow.—Shakespeare und die Bildende Kunst, von K. A. Laux.—Zu Wilhelm Heinses Antikenbeschreibung, von H. Koch.—Goethe als Liebhaber antiker Kleinkunst, von H. Börger.—E. T. A. Hoffmanns Künstlernovellen, von F. Baumgart.—Ein unveröffentlichter Brief des Peter Cornelius aus Rom, von H. von Einem.—Blechens italienische Skizzenbücher, von P. O. Rave.—Der Pfingstberg und seine italienischen Vorbilder, von F. Schreiber.— Karl Schuch in Olevano, von E. Ruhmer.
1. Waetzoldt, Wilhelm, 1880-1945. 2. Art—Essays and misc. I. Title.

Hallendorff, Barbro, 1904- comp.
800 [i.e. Åtta hundra] svenska facktidskrifter; bibliografisk sammanställning. Stockholm, Nordiska bokhandelns förlag, 1952. 84 p. 21cm.

1. Periodicals—Sweden—Direct.

NN*R 5.54 OC(1b) PC, 1 SL P,1 (LC1, Z1, X1)

Copy only words underlined & classmark— QOA
HALLOWELL, ALFRED IRVING, 1892-
Culture and experience. Philadelphia, University of Pennsylvania press, 1955. xvi, 434 p. 24cm. (Philadelphia anthropological society. Publications. v.4)

"This volume of selected papers celebrates the sixtieth birthday of Dr. A. Irving Hallowell, professor of anthropology in the University of Pennsylvania. It is a tribute to him from his friends and fellow anthropologists in Philadelphia."
(Continued)

NN**12.55 f/4 OC (OS) I PC, 1, 2, 3, I AH, 2, I E, 3, I (U 1, LC1, Z1, X1)

Copy only words underlined & classmark— QOA
HALLOWELL, ALFRED IRVING, 1892- . Culture and experience. (Card 2)

Bibliographical references included in "Notes" (p. 367-429); "Bibliography of A. Irving Hallowell." p. 430-434.

1. Society, Primitive. 2. Indians, American—Civilization. 3. Psychology, Social. I. Series.

HALLSTEIN, WALTER, ed.
Zur Integration Europas. Festschrift für Carl Friedrich Ophüls aus Anlass seines siebzigsten Geburtstages. Hrsg. von Walter Hallstein [und] Hans-Jürgen Schlochauer. Karlsruhe, C.F. Müller, 1965. 258 p. 1 front. 24cm.

"Verzeichnis der Veröffentlichungen von Carl Friedrich Ophüls" p. 257-258.
(Continued)

NN * R 6.67 r/A OC,1b*, I PC,1,2,3,I SL E,1,2, 3,I (LC1,X1,Z1) 4

HALLSTEIN, WALTER, ed. Zur Integration Europas. (Card 2)

Includes bibliographical references.
CONTENTS.—Zu den Grundlagen und Verfassungsprinzipien der Europäischen Gemeinschaften, von W. Hallstein.—Die fünfte Freiheit des Gemeinsamen Marktes: der freie Zahlungsverkehr, von B. Börner.—Zur Errichtung nachgeordneter Behörden der Kommission der Europäischen Wirtschaftsgemeinschaft, von U. Everling.—Das eigentum der Europäischen Atomgemeinschaft an Kernbrenstoffen, von H. Haedrich.—
(Continued)

HALLSTEIN, WALTER, ed. Zur Integration Europas. (Card 3)

Richtlinien-Ergebnisse, von H.P. Ipsen.—Die Supranationalität der Europäischen Gemeinschaften, von G. Jaenicke.—Die im Rat Vereinigten Vertreter der Regierungen der Mitgliedstaaten, von J.H. Kaiser.—Die Bemühungen um die politische Einigung Europas seit dem Scheitern der Europäischen Verteidigungsgemeinschaft, von N. Lang.—Der Briand-Plan, Vorbote der Europäischen Integration, von E. von Puttkamer.—Die Zuständigkeiten des Gerichtshofes der
(Continued)

HALLSTEIN, WALTER, ed. Zur Integration Europas.
(Card 4)

Europäischen Gemeinschaften, von H.J. Schlochauer.—Des traites de Rome a l'Europe politique, par, J.C. Baron Snoy et d'Oppuers.—Zur Nichtigkeit Wettbewerbsbeschränkender Abreden im Europäischen Gemeinschaftsrecht, von E. Steindorff.—Die Fusion der Organe der Europäischen Gemeinschaften, von O. Baron von Stempel.—Die Rechtsangleichung als Integrationsinstrument, von P.V. van Themaat.

1. Ophüls, Carl Friedrich, 1895- . 2. International agencies. 3. European federation, 1939- . I. Schlochauer, Hans Jürgen, joint ed.

D-14
1862

Halperin, Samuel William, *ed.*
Some 20th-century historians; essays on eminent Europeans. Contributors: James L. Cate ₍and others₎ Chicago₍ University of Chicago Press ₍1961₎
xxiv, 298 p. 23 cm.
Essays in honor of Bernadotte E. Schmitt.
"The writings of Bernadotte E. Schmitt": p. xvii-xxi. Bibliographical footnotes.
CONTENTS.—Introduction, by S. W. Halperin.—Henri Pirenne, by J. L. Cate.—George Macaulay Trevelyan, by H. R. Winkler.—Georges Lefebvre, by G. H. McNeil.—Herbert Butterfield, by H. T. Parker.—
(Continued)

NN * R 3.63 e/ OC PC, 1, 2 SL (LC1, X1, Z1)

2

HALPERIN, SAMUEL WILLIAM, ed. Some 20th-century historians... (Card 2)

Veit Valentin, by R. H. Bauer.—Pierre Renouvin, by S. W. Halperin.—Sir Charles Webster, by J. E. Fagg.—René Grousset, by D. F. Lach.—Erich Eyck, by W. H. Maehl.—George Peabody Gooch, by F. L. Hadsel.—Lucien Febvre, by P. A. Throop.

1. Historians, European. 2. Schmitt, Bernadotte Everly, 1886-

---

EST
*

Hamburg.
Hamburgs Weg zum Reich und in die Welt; Urkunden zur 750-Jahr-Feier des Hamburger Hafens. Hamburg, 1939. viii, 321 p. facsims. 30½cm.

Documents in Latin, German, French, Dutch or English, mostly followed by German translation.
Foreword signed: Professor Dr. Heinrich Reincke.

43514B. 1. Hamburg—Hist.—Sources. 2. Commerce—Germany—Hamburg. I. Reincke, Heinrich, 1881- . II. Title.
N. Y. P. L. July 1, 1941

AF-10
67

HAMBURG-BREMER FEUER-VERSICHERUNGS-GESELLSCHAFT.
100 [i.e. Hundert] Jahre Hamburg-Bremer Feuer-Versicherungs-Gesellschaft, Hamburg, 1854-1954. [Hamburg, 1954] 135 p. illus. (part col.), ports., maps 28cm.

NN R 11.58 g/ OS(Ib+) PC SL E (LC1, X1, Z1)

EST

HAMBURG, Grosstadt und Welthafen; Festschrift zum XXX. Deutschen Geographentag, 1.-5. August 1955, in Hamburg. Schriftleitung: W. Brünger. Kiel, F. Hirt, 1955. 326 p. illus., plans (1 fold.), diagrs. 25cm.

1. Hamburg. 2. Economic history—Hamburg. 3. Harbors—Germany—Hamburg. 4. Deutscher Geographentag. 30th, Hamburg, 1955. I. Brünger, Wilhelm, ed. t. 1955.

NN ** R 11.55 d/ OC, I PC, 1, 2, 3, 4, I SL E, 2, 3, I ST, 3t I (LC1, X1, Z1)

QOA

Museum für Voelkerkunde, Hamburg.
...Festschrift zum fünfzigjährigen Bestehn des Hamburgischen Museums für Völkerkunde. Hamburg: Selbstverlag des Museums für Völkerkunde, 1928. 267 p. col'd map, illus., plates. 4°. (Museum für Voelkerkunde, Hamburg. Mitteil. v. 13.)

7

1. Anthropology. 2. Ser.
N. Y. P. L. April 25, 1929

NFD
(Lessing)

Hamburg. Staats- und Universitaets-Bibliothek.
Lessing und Hamburg; Festgabe zur Zweihundertjahrfeier der Geburt des Dichters; dargebracht von der Hamburger Staats- und Universitäts-Bibliothek... Hamburg, 1929. 99 p. facsims., front. (port.), pl. 12°.

On cover: 1729–1929.
Bibliographical footnotes.
Contents: Verzeichnis der Tafeln. Vorbemerkung. BONDE, H. Die Übersetzer der in der "Hamburgischen Dramaturgie" behandelten französischen Theaterstücke. WAHL, G. Lessings Berufung nach Wien nach J. J. C. Bodes Brief an Klopstock vom 11. April 1769. Beschreibung der Lessing-Ausstellung. Namenverzeichnis.

453799A. 1. Lessing, Gotthold Ephraim, 1729–1781—Bibl.
N. Y. P. L. January 27, 1930

---

* OAC p.v.116

Hamburg. Staats- und Universitaetsbibliothek.
Orientalia Hamburgensia; Festgabe den Teilnehmern am Deutschen Orientalistentag Hamburg überreicht von der Hamburger Staats- und Universitäts-Bibliothek. Hamburg: Staats- und Universitäts-Bibliothek, 1926. vii, 96 p. plates, ports. 8°.

On cover: ...Festgabe den Teilnehmern am 4. Deutschen Orientalistentag, in Hamburg 28. Sept. bis 2. Okt. 1926 überreicht...
Contents: Vorwort. Beschreibung der ausgestellten Gegenstände. Abhandlungen: LUEDTKE, W. Die Uffenbachsche Evangelien-Harmonie. MUELLER, B. A. Der Dobrudscha-Bote.

407841A. 1. Orient—Bibl. 2. Deutscher Orientalistentag. 4th, Hamburg, 1926.
N. Y. P. L. May 9, 1929

OAI p.v.123

Hamburg. Universitaet.
...Beiträge zur Jungius-Forschung; Prolegomena zu der von der Hamburgischen Universität beschlossenen Ausgabe der Werke von Joachim Jungius...im Auftrage der Jungius-Kommission herausgegeben von Adolf Meyer. Hamburg: P. Hartung, 1929. 120 p. 4°.

At head of title: Festschrift der Hamburgischen Universität anlässlich ihres zehnjährigen Bestehens.
Bibliography, p. 88-93.

500192A. 1. Jungius, Joachim, 1587–1657. 2. Meyer, Adolf, 1893– , editor.
N. Y. P. L. October 29, 1930

KAT

HAMBURG. UNIVERSITAT. Geographisches Institut.
Festschrift zum 70. Geburtstag des ord. Professors der Geographie Dr. Ludwig Mecking, gewidmet von seinen Freunden und Schülern. Hrsg. vom Geographischen Institut der Universität Hamburg in Verbindung mit der Akademie für Raumforschung und Landesplanung. Bremen-Horn, W. Dorn, 1949. 272 p. port., maps, charts, diagrs. 21cm.

Includes bibliographies.
CONTENTS. --A: Vorwort. Zum 70. Geburtstag Ludwig Meckings, von N. Creutzburg. L. Meckings Schaffen und die Landesplanung, von K. Brüning. Liste der wissenschaft- lichen Veröffentlichungen nach
(Continued)

NN** X 8.53 OS,I PC,1, 2,I SL (Z/,LC1,X1)

HAMBURG. UNIVERSITAT. Geographische Institut. Festschrift zum 70. Geburtstag des ord. Professors der Geographie Dr. Ludwig Mecking...

Meckings60. Geburstag. --B. Physiogeographisch orientierte Probleme: Stabile und labile Erdräume, von W. Meinardus. Rumpffläche, Stufenlandschaft, alternierende Abtragung von H. Mortensen. Uber das subtropische Konvergenzgebiet im Südatlantischen Ozean, von A. Schumacher. Podsol-oder Bleicherdeerscheinungen in der Weserlandschaft zwischen Karlshafen und Holzminden und ihre geographischen Grundlagen, von W. Brünger. Meine Umsegelung des Nordostlandes von Spitzbergen, von W. Deege. --C. Kulturgeographisch ausgerichtete Themen: Erdbeben und Menschwerdung in Ostasien von S. Passarge. --Das Problem der
(Continued)

HAMBURG. UNIVERSITAT. Geographischen Institut. Festschrift zum 70. Geburtstag des ord. Professors der Geographie Dr. Ludwig Mecking...

Flussgrenze, von M. G. Schmidt. Verkehrsgeographische Entwicklungen und Probleme in Südamerika, von R. Lütgens. Kalifornien nach dem zweiten Weltkrieg, von G. Pfeifer. Pakistan und Indien, von E. Weigt. Vöden. Kulturgeographische Studie über eine Sonderform der Gemeinen Mark, von G. Niemeier. Landschaftswandel im hohen Böhmerwald, von O. F. Timmermann. Geestrandstädte der Niederelbe, von K. E. Fick. Voltaire und die Geographie im Zeitalter der Aufklärung, von H. Weinert. --D. Schulgeographische Fragen: Karten der neuen Schulatlanten und die Grenzen ihrer Verwend- barkeit, von E. Hinrichs.
1. Geography--Addresses, essays, lectures. 2. Mecking, Ludwig, 1879- I. Akademie für Raumforschung und Landesplanung.

E-12
1515

HAMBURG. Universität. Historisches Seminar.
Alteuropa und die moderne Gesellschaft; Festschrift für Otto Brunner. Göttingen, Vandenhoeck & Ruprecht [1963] 363 p. port. 25cm.

Bibliographical footnotes.
CONTENTS. --Randbemerkungen zu drei Aufsätzen über Sippe, Gefolgschaft und Treue, von W. Schlesinger. --Potens und Pauper; begriffsgeschichtliche Studien zur gesellschaftlichen Differenzierung
(Continued)

NN 12.64 e/ OS(1b*) PC, 1, 2 SL (LC1, X1, Z1) [I]

4

HAMBURG. Universität. Historisches Seminar.
Alteuropa und die moderne Gesellschaft... (Card 2)

im frühen Mittelalter und zum Pauperismus des Hochmittelalters, von K. Bosl. --Nationale Vorurteile und Minderwertigkeitsgefühle als sozialer Faktor im mittelalterlichen Livland, von P. Johansen. --Heldendichtung und Heldensage als Geschichtsbewusstsein, von K. Hauck. --Ein universales Geschichtsbild der Stauferzeit in Miniaturen; der Bilderkreis zur Chronik Ottos von Freising im Jenenser Codex Bose q. 6, von W. Lammers. --Die Weltmächte im Weltbild Altdeutschlands, von E. Hölzle.
(Continued)

HAMBURG. Universität. Historisches Seminar.
Alteuropa und die moderne Gesellschaft... (Card 3)

--Amtsträger zwischen Krongewalt und Ständen, ein europäisches Problem, von D. Gerhard. --Lorenz von Stein als Theoretiker der Bewegung von Staat und Gesellschaft zum Sozialstaat, von E.-W. Böckenförde. --Aristoteles-Tradition am Ausgang des 18. Jahrhunderts; zur ersten deutschen Übersetzung der Politik durch Johann Georg Schlosser, von M. Riedel. --Einige terminologische Auswirkungen des Aufschwungs der Industrie im 18. Jahrhundert in Frankreich, von K. Baldinger. --Koexistenz: Schlagwort,
(Continued)

HAMBURG. Universität. Historisches Seminar.
Alteuropa und die moderne Gesellschaft... (Card 4)

Sprach-und Menschenlenkung, von W. Betz. --Probleme der österreichischen Geschichtswissenschaft, von T. Mayer.

1. Brunner, Otto, 1898- . 2. Civilization--Addresses, essays, lectures.

WOE

... Dem **Hamburger** dermatologen P. G. Unna gewidmet von freunden und schülern zum sechzigsten geburtstage ... Hamburg und Leipzig, L. Voss, 1910.

2 v. front. (port.) illus., plates (partly col.) 24cm. (Dermatologische studien, bd. 20-21)

"Unter redaktion von dr. Ernst Delbanco—Hamburg."

~~1. Dermatology.~~ 2. Unna, Paul Gerson, 1850- I. Delbanco, Ernst, 1869- ed. 1. Skin-Diseases.

12-17562

Library of Congress RL36.D5 bd. 20-21 Card rev. 1941

E-12
3759

HAMMER, CARL, 1910- , ed.
Studies in German literature. Baton Rouge, Louisiana state university press, 1963. xviii, 172 p. 24cm. (Louisiana. State university and agricultural and mechanical college, Humanities series. no. 13)
"Presented to John T. Krumpelmann on his retirement from teaching at Louisiana state university in 1062."
Bibliographical references included in "Notes" (p. 149-164)
1. Krumpelmann, John T. 2. German literature--Addresses, essays, lectures. I. Series.
NN R 7.65 p/ OC (OD)I (ED)I PC, 1, 2, I SL (LC1, X1, Z1) [I]

Copy only words underlined & classmark— TB

HANDELSHOCHSCHULE, St. Gall, Switzerland. Juristische Abteilung.
Beiträge zum Wirtschaftsrecht; Festgabe für den schweizerischen Juristentag 1944 in St. Gallen. St. Gallen Verlag der Fehr'schen Buchhandlung, 1944. xi, 336 p. 25cm. (St. Galler wirtschaftswissenschaftliche Forschungen. Bd. 3).

Bibliographical footnotes.

1. Commerce--Jurisp.--Switzerland. 2. Schweizerischer Juristenverein. I. Series. II. Title.
NN R 7.65 s/ /(OC)II(OS(1b+)I PC, 1, 2, I, II E, 1, 2, I, II (LC1, X1, Z1)

AD-10
1335

HANNCKE, FRDR. jun., firm, Berlin.
Jubiläumsschrift zum 80 jährigen Bestehen der Firma Frdr. Hanncke jun. Fabrik für Ledertreibriemen und technische Lederartikel, 1842-1922. [Berlin, 1922] [12] p. 23cm.

NN 6.67 p/-OS PC SL E (LC1, X1, Z1)

E-13
6384

Hans Gerstinger. Festgabe zum 80. Geburtstag. Arbeiten aus dem Grazer Schülerkreis. [Mit Portrait] Graz, Akademische Druck- und Verlagsanstalt, 1966.
101 p. 25 cm.

Includes bibliographical references.
CONTENTS.—Verzeichnis der Schriften und Aufsätze (p. 6-15)—Zur profanen Bildung des Euagrios Pontikos, von W. Lackner.—Bilder und Vergleiche aus dem Sportwesen in der späten griechischen

(Continued)
NN *R 9.69 k/OC, I PC, 1, I SL (LC1, X1, Z1) 2

HANS GERSTINGER. Festgabe zum 80. Geburtstag. (Card 2)

Epik, von F. Lochner-Hüttenbach.—Die Gedankenfolge in Vergils "Heldenschau," von F. Loretto.—Non tutior ibis, von F. Quadlbauer.—Cum signo fidei, von H. Schmeja.—Nalopakhyana und Odyssee, von F. F. Schwarz.—Das Mus.-päd, Realgymnasium, von H. Trathnigg.

1. Classical studies--Collections. I. Gerstinger, Hans, 1885- .

AN
(Hedtoft, H.)

HANS HEDTOFT, liv og virke; redigeret af H. C. Hansen og Jul. Bomholt. København, Fremad, 1955.
251 p. illus., ports. 27cm.

Various contributors.

1. Hedtoft, Hans, 1903-1955. I. Bomholt, Julius, 1896- ed. II. Hansen, H.C., 1906- , ed.
NN** 4.56 a/ OC, I, II PC, 1, I, II SL E, 1, I, II (LC1, X1, Z1)

Copy only words underlined
& Classmark-- KAA

HANS-MORTENSEN-GEDENKSITZUNG, am 25. Mai 1965. Göttingen, Geographisches Institut der Universität Göttingen, 1965. 41 p. port. 24cm. (Göttinger geographische Abhandlungen, Heft 34)

CONTENTS.--Einführung, von H. Poser.—40 Jahre moderne Geomorphologie, von J. Hövermann.—Hans Mortensens Bedeutung für die deutsche Siedlungsgeographie, von G. Oberbeck.—Hans Mortensen und die deutsche geographische Ostforschung, von W. Wöhlke.—Das

(Continued)
NN 10.66 1/ OC (OS)I, II PC, 1, I, II (LC1, X1, Z1) 2

HANS-MORTENSEN-GEDENKSITZUNG, am 25. Mai 1965. (Card 2)

wissenschaftliche Werk Hans Mortensens, [Bibliographie] von E. Krause.—Biographien und Nachrufe.

1. Mortensen, Hans, 1894-1964. I. Series. II. Göttingen. Universität. Geographisches Institut.

E-11
6867

HANSEN, ROBERT LASSALLE, 1890- , ed.
I ideens tjeneste; udsendt som festskrift til Carl Thomsen ved hans afgang som biblioteksleder, 31. oktober 1962. København, Dansk bibliografisk kontor, 1962. iii, [1] p. port. 24cm.

CONTENTS. —Carl Thomsen, af H. Hvenegaard Lassen. —Bogen i det frie oplysningsarbejde, af B. Pihl. —Boghandelen og bibliotekerne, af V. Madsen. —Billigbogens betydning og udbredelse, af L. M. Olsen. —

(Continued)
NN R 4.63 g/ OC, II (OS)I PC, 1, 2, I, II SL (LC1, X1, Z1) 2

HANSEN, ROBERT LASSALLE, 1890- , ed. I ideens tjeneste... (Card 2)

Radio og fjernsyn—bog og bibliotek, af L. Thorsen. —Den praktiske bog, af B. Bramsen. —Biblioteksafgiften—vederlag for hvad og hvordan? Af H. Lyngby Jepsen. —Nyt dansk litteraturselskab, af R. L. Hansen. —Fortegnelse over artikler og bøger af Carl Thomsen (p. 105-[112])

1. Thomsen, Carl, 1894- . 2. Books and reading. I. Dansk bibliografisk kontor. II. Title.

Copy only words underlined
& classmark— TB

HANSEN, ULF KJÆR.
Danske jubilæumsskrifter; en bibliografi og et forsøg på en vurdering. København, Berlingske boktr., 1955.
196 [1] p. illus. 26cm. (Handelshøjskolen, Copenhagen. Instituttet for salgsorganisation og reklame. Skrifter. 18)

Handelshøjskolen, Copenhagen. Skriftraekke F.
"Bibliografi over udkomme danske jubilæumsskrifter til og med 1949": p. [55]-[197]

1. Festschriften—Bibl. 2. Bibliography, Danish. I. Series.
NN *R X 10.57 p/ OC (OS)I PC, 1, 2, I E, 1, I RC, 1, 2 (LC1, X1, Z1)

E-12
1124

DIE HANSISCHE ARBEITSGEMEINSCHAFT.
Hansische Studien; Heinrich Sproemberg zum 70. Geburtstag. Die wissenschaftliche Redaktion erfolgte im Auftrage der Hansischen Arbeitsgemeinschaft in der Deutschen Demokratischen Republik durch Gerhard Heitz und Manfred Unger. Berlin, Akademie-Verlag, 1961.
462 p. port., 3 maps. 25cm. (Forschungen zur mittelalterlichen Geschichte. Bd. 8)

(Continued)
NN R 9.64 e/ (OC)I, II, IVbo, Vbo OS(1b+)III PC, 1, 2, I, II, III SL E, 1, 2, I, II (LC1, X1, Z1) 2

DIE HANSISCHE ARBEITSGEMEINSCHAFT. Hansische Studien... (Card 2)

Includes bibliographies.

1. Hanseatic League. 2. Sproemberg, Heinrich, 1889- . I. Heitz, Gerhard, ed. II. Unger, Manfred, ed. III. Series. IV. Heitz, Gerhard. V. Unger, Manfred.

AN (Høffding, H.)

Harald Høffding in memoriam. Fire Taler holdt paa Københavns Universitet paa Harald Høffdings 89 Aars Dag, 11. Marts 1932, af Frithiof Brandt, Jørgen Jørgensen, Victor Kuhr ₍og₎ Edgar Rubin. Kronologisk Bibliografi over Harald Høffdings Arbejder, med Tillæg indeholdende Bibliografi over Skrifter om Høffding af Kalle Sandelin. København: Gyldendalske Boghandel, 1932. 111 p. front. (port.) 22cm.

"Udgivet af Selskabet for Filosofi og Psykologi, med Understøttelse af Carlsbergfondet."

647683A. 1. Høffding, Harald, 1843–1931. I. Brandt, Frithiof, 1892– . II. Jørgensen, Jørgen, 1894– . III. Kuhr, Victor, 1882– . IV. Rubin, Edgar, 1886– . V. Sandelin, Kalle. VI. Selskabet for Filosofi og Psykologi, Copenhagen.
N. Y. P. L. September 6, 1933

E-12
3546

HARIG, GERHARD, ed.
Lehre, Forschung, Praxis; die Karl-Marx-Universität, Leipzig, zum zehnten Jahrestag ihrer Namensgebung am 5. Mai, 1963, hrsg. im Auftrag von Rektor und Senat von Gerhard Harig und Max Steinmetz. Leipzig, Teubner [1963] 509 p. illus., ports., maps. 25cm.

Includes bibliographies.

1. Leipzig. Universität--Hist. I. Steinmetz, Max, 1912- joint ed. II. Title.

NN * R 6.65 a/ OC, I, II PC, 1, I, II SL (LC1, X1, Z1)

---

*MFSB (Germany)

HARMONIE-GESELLSCHAFT, Flensburg, Germany.
150 [i.e. Hundertfünfzig] Jahre Harmonie-Gesellschaft in Flensburg 1804-1954. Für die Mitglieder der Gesellschaft dargestellt von Klaus Witt. Flensburg, 1954. 86 p. illus. 24cm.

I. Witt, Arthur Nicolaus, 1890- .

NN **R X 1.56 s/ (OC)I OS (lb) PC, I SL MU, I (LC1, X1, Z1)

D-13
8373

Harr, Wilber Christian, 1908– ,ed.
Frontiers of the Christian world mission since 1938; essays in honor of Kenneth Scott Latourette. ₍1st ed.₎ New York, Harper ₍1962₎

viii, 310 p. 22 cm.

Bibliographical footnotes.

CONTENTS.—The Protestant enterprise in China, 1937-1949, by M. S. Bates.—The Christian mission since 1938: southeast Asia, by W. T. Thomas.—The Christian mission since 1938: the Pacific
(Continued)

NN * R 8.62 e/ OC, Ib* PC, 1, 2 SL (LC1, X1, Z1)

HARR, WILBER CHRISTIAN, 1908- , ed. Frontiers of the Christian world mission since 1938... (Card 2)

Islands, by J. L. Dunstan.—The Christian mission since 1938: Africa south of the Sahara, by W. C. Harr.—A study in the self-propagating church: Madagascar, by C. W. Forman.—The Christian mission since 1938: methods and techniques, by C. H. Reber, Jr.—Faith missions since 1938, by H. Lindsell.—Kenneth Scott Latourette: historian and friend, by E. T. Bachmann.—My guided life, by K. S. Latourette.—Select bibliography of Kenneth Scott Latourette, compiled by H. B. Uhrich, R. Norman, and R. P. Morris. (p. 295-305)

1. Missions, Foreign--Hist. 1884- . I. Harr, Wilber Christian, 1908- 2. Latourette, Kenneth Scott,

---

ZIY

Hartford seminary foundation. Hartford, Conn. Theological seminary. Alumni association.
Sermons for today, a tribute to Rockwell Harmon Potter, by former students, fellow teachers, church leaders, and ministers of the gospel, ed. by the Alumni association of Hartford theological seminary. Boston, Pilgrim press, 1946. viii, 247 p. front. 22cm.

441705B. 1. Potter, Rockwell Harmon, 1874- 2. Sermons—Collections. I. Title.
N. Y. P. L. June 28, 1948

E-11
6906

HARTMANN, KLAUS, 1925- , ed.
Lebendiger Realismus; Festschrift für Johannes Thyssen, hrsg. von Klaus Hartmann in Verbindung mit Hans Wagner. Bonn, H. Bouvier, 1962. 257 p. port. 24cm.

Includes bibliographies.
CONTENTS.--Zwei phänomenologische Betrachtungen zum Realismusproblem, von O. Becker.--Über den Weg zur
(Continued)

NN R 2.68 1/ OCs PCs, 1s, 2s SLs (LC1s, X1s, [i] Z1s) 3

HARTMANN, KLAUS, 1925- , ed. Lebendiger Realismus... (Card 2)

Begründung des Realismus, von H. Wagner.--Die Bedeutung des Realismus in der Erkenntnislehre des 19. Jahrhunderts, von F. Schneider.--Marxismus und Realismus, von J. Barion.--Das Realitätsproblem, von K. Hartmann.--Grenzen, von G. Funke.--Das Problem des Metasprachlichen in Platons "Kratylos", von J. Derbolav.--Der sprachliche Ausdruck des Seins, von
(Continued)

HARTMANN, KLAUS, 1925- , ed. Lebendiger Realismus... (Card 3)

V. Rüfner.--Asozial-Antisozial: Recht und Grenzen des Schuldprinzips in der Strafrechtsreform, von W. Schöllgen.--Bibliographie, zusammengestellt von E. Gerresheim (p. [249]-257)

1. Realism. 2. Thyssen, Johannes, 1892- i. m.e. Subs for H-, K- (no date).

AN
(Frisch, H.)

Hartvig Frisch; hans personlighed og gerning. Redigeret af Hans Hedtoft og M. K. Nørgaard. København, Forlaget Fremad, 1950. 171 p. illus. 27cm.

"Bibliografi," p. 169–₍172₎

572575B. 1. Frisch, Hartvig Marcus, 1893–1950. I. Hedtoft, Hans, 1903– , ed. II. Nørgaard, M. K., ed.
N. Y. P. L.
September 24, 1951

STG
(Harvard)

Harvard et la France; recueil d'études publié en l'honneur de l'Université Harvard et offert à cette université par le Comité français pour la célébration du troisième centenaire de Harvard. Paris: Édité par les soins de la Revue d'histoire moderne, 1936. 240 p. chart. 25½cm.

Bibliographical footnotes.

Contents.—Préambule: Lévis-Mirepoix, comte Emmanuel de. La première représentation de Harvard.—Présences et souvenirs: Doumic, René. Mon passage à l'Université Harvard. Tardieu, André. Les premiers conférenciers français à Harvard. Azan, Paul. Harvard pendant la Grande guerre.—Les grands hommes de Harvard et

(Continued)

N. Y. P. L.
June 8, 1937

Harvard et la France... (Card 2)

la France: Cestre, Charles. Emerson et la France. Le Breton, Maurice. Henry Adams et la France. Legouis, Émile. Barrett Wendell et la France. Chevalier, Jacques. William James et Bergson. Bergson, Henry. A Jacques Chevalier.—Les disciplines de Harvard et la France: Blache, Jules. La géographie à Harvard et les relations scientifiques franco-américaines. Lepaulle, Pierre. L'École de droit de Harvard et ses initiatives. Bréhier, Louis. L'Université Harvard et l'art français du moyen âge. Siegfried, André. L'École des sciences politiques de l'Université Harvard. Faÿ, Bernard. La langue française à Harvard.—Conclusion: Hazard, Paul. Harvard et la France.—Appendices: Fondation Hyde. Liste des étudiants de Harvard morts pour leur pays et pour la cause des Alliés pendant la Grande guerre.

874725A. 1. Harvard university—Hist. 2. United States—Civilization—French influence. 3. France—Civilization—American influence. I. Comité français pour la célébration du troisième centénnaire de Harvard. II. Revue d'histoire moderne.
N. Y. P. L.
June 8, 1937

E-13
5188

HARVARD UNIVERSITY. Law school.

The path of the law from 1967; proceedings and papers at the Harvard law school convocation, held on the one-hundred fiftieth anniversary of its founding, edited by Arthur E. Sutherland. Cambridge, Mass., distributed by Harvard university press, 1968. xiv, 223 p. illus., ports. 24cm.

On jacket: Harvard law school sesquicentennial papers.

1. Law--Addresses, essays, lectures. 2. Harvard university. Law school--Centennial celebrations, etc. I. Sutherland, Arthur E., ed. II. Title.
NN R 5.69 k/⁄(OC)I, II OS PC, 1, 2, I, II SL E, 1, 2, I, II (LC1, X1, Z1)

WAB

Harvey Cushing society.

A bibliography of the writings of Harvey Cushing; prepared on the occasion of his seventieth birthday April 8, 1939, by the Harvey Cushing society. ₍Springfield, Ill.₎ C. C. Thomas, 1939.

4 p. l., ₍xiii₎–xv, 108 p., 1 l. front. (port.) 23½cm.

"Papers from Dr. Cushing's clinics and laboratories": p. 61–89.

1. Cushing, Harvey Williams, 1869–1939—Bibl.

39–32331

Library of Congress Z8206.67.H33
——— ——— Copy 2. ₍3₎ [016.61] 012

E-12
9774

Haslinger, Adolf, *ed.*

Sprachkunst als Weltgestaltung. Festschrift für Herbert Seidler. ₍Mit Porträt und Werksverzeichnis₎ Salzburg, München, Pustet (1966)

415 p. 24 cm.

Bibliographical footnotes.

Contents.—Der komplexe Satz im deutschen Schrifttum der Gegenwart, von H. Brinkmann.—"Poesie des Stils" bei C. M. Wieland: Herkunft und Bedeutung, von O. Brückl.—Randbemerkungen zum Textbuch der "Zauberflöte," von M. Enzinger.—Aufgaben der deut-

(Continued)

NN*R 8.67 g/r OC, Ib*, PC, 1, 2 SL (LC1, X1, Z1)

Haslinger, Adolf, *ed.* Sprachkunst als Weltgestaltung. (Card 2)

schen Philologie heute, von J. Erben.—Wiederkehr und Variation. Bildkette und Bildgefüge in Heimito von Doderers Roman "Die Strudlhofstiege," von A. Haslinger.—Zu Neidhart 101,20—Bemerkungen zum 2. Preislied Neidharts auf Herzog Friedrich den Streitbaren von Österreich, von K. K. Klein.—Hermann Broch "Der Versucher." Versuchung und Erlösung im Bannkreis mythischen Erlebens, von D. Meinert.—Das Symbol der "Götin des Wortes" bei Josef Weinheber, von R. Mühlher.—"Meiner Wolke Tragewerk." Fausts Abschied von Helena, von J. Müller.—Ambivalenz in moderner Dich-

(Continued)

Haslinger, Adolf, *ed.* Sprachkunst als Weltgestaltung. (Card 3)

tung, von H. Pongs.—Zu Stil und Aufbau des Hildebrandsliedes, von I. Reiffenstein.—Hölderlins mythische Spiegelbilder, von J. Rosteutscher.—Zwei österreichische Schwankbücher: Die Geschichte des Pfarrers vom Kahlenberg. Neithart Fuchs, von H. Rupprich.—Raimund und Wieland, von E. Thurnher.—Robert Musils "Grigia," von K. Tober.—Adalbert Stifter: Der Waldgänger. Sinngefüge, Bau, Bildwelt und Sprachform, von W. Weiss.—Anmerkungen zur Men-

(Continued)

HASLINGER, ADOLF, ed. Sprachkunst als Weltgestaltung. (Card 4)

schenzeichnung in der modernen Epik, von W. Weizig.—Zu Gottfrieds literarischer Technik, von A. Wolf.—Verzeichnis der Schriften von Herbert Seidler (p. 411–414)

1. Seidler, Herbert, 1905- . 2. Philology--Addresses, essays, lectures. I. Haslinger, Adolf.

Write on slip, name, year, vol., page of magazine and class mark — RAA

Hatfield, James Taft, and others.
Curme volume of linguistic studies edited on the occasion of his seventieth birthday.

(Language monographs. Baltimore, 1930. 4°. No.7, p.1-178. port.)

form 406a [11-12-30 25m]

E-13
8495

HAUPTFRAGEN der Romanistik; Festschrift für Philipp August Becker zum 1. Juni 1922. Heidelberg, C. Winter, 1922. xxvii, 322 p. 25cm. (Sammlung romanischer Elementarbücher. Reihe V: Untersuchungen und Texte. [Bd.] 4)

Bibliographical footnotes.

"Verzeichnis der bis 1922 erschienenen Veröffentlichungen Philipp August Beckers," p. xi-xxiii.

(Continued)

NN 5. 70 e/k OC. I (OS)II PC. 1. 2. I. II SL (LC1, X1, Z1) [I]

3

HAUPTFRAGEN der Romanistik... (Card 2)

CONTENTS.--Die Rolle der Verba vicaria im poetischen Stil Lafontaines, von K. Ettmayer.--Zur Aussprache des lateinischen C vor hellen Vokalen von M. Friedwagner.--Zur sprachlichen Gliederung Frankreichs, von E. Gamillscheg.--Die verbale Negation bei Rabelais und die Methode psychologischer Einfühlung in der Sprachwissenschaft, von L. Jordan.--Die Aufgaben der romanischen Syntax, von E. Lerch.--Deiktische Elemente im Altfranzösischen, von E. Lommatzsch.--Zentripetale Kräfte im Sprachleben, von W. Meyer-Lübke.--Probleme des Kriegsfranzösischen, von G. Rieder.--Neue Denkformen im Vulgärlatein, von K. Vossler.--Literaturgeschichte und Sprachgeschichte,

(Continued)

HAUPTFRAGEN der Romanistik... (Card 3)

von J. Bruch.--Zur Charakterisierung der französischen Literatur des 19. Jahrhunderts, von H. Heiss.--Der fremde Dante, von V. Klemperer.--Französische Rokokoprobleme, von F. Neubert.--Das Kunstproblem der Tierdichtung, besonders der Tierfabel, von E. Winkler.

1. Romance languages--Addresses, essays, lectures. 2. Romance literature--Addresses, essays, lectures. I. Becker, Philipp August, 1862-1947. II. Series.

Write on slip only words underlined and classmark —
HOB

Havana (City). Ayuntamiento.
...La vida heroica de Antonio Maceo. Homenaje del Ayuntamiento de la Habana al glorioso lugarteniente general del ejercito Libertador Antonio Maceo en el centenario de su nacimiento, 1845–14 de junio–1945. Habana, 1945. 208 p. illus. 25cm. (Colección histórica cubana y americana. no. 6.)

CONTENTS.—Nota preliminar.—Atisbos en torno del ambiente y escenarios del héroe, por Gerardo Castellanos G.—En la Guerra del 68, por Gregorio Delgado

(Continued)

N. Y. P. L. January 20, 1947

Havana (City). Ayuntamiento. ...La vida heroica de Antonio Maceo... (Card 2)

Fernández.—Baraguá, por José Luciano Franco.—Ideologia político-revolucionaria, por Emilio Roig de Leuchsenring.—Apendice I: Cronologia de Antonio Maceo, por Leopoldo Horrego Estuch.—Apendice II: Bibliografía de Antonio Maceo, por Fermín Peraza y Sarausa.

1. Maceo, Antonio, 1845–1896. I. Peraza Sarausa, Fermín, 1907– II. Ser.
N. Y. P. L. January 20, 1947

RAE

Havana (City). Universidad.
Libro jubilar de homenaje al dr. Juan M. Dihigo y Mestre en sus cincuenta años de profesor de la Universidad de la Habana, 1890–1940... La Habana, 1941. 458 p. illus. 23cm.

With seal of the university on t.-p.
"Revista de la Universidad de la Habana (numero extraordinario)."
CONTENTS.—El dr. Juan M. Dihigo y Mestre, por Mercedes Labourdette.—Juan M. Dihigo y Mestre, pionero y fundador, por Luis de Soto.—Discurso del dr. Juan Miguel Dihigo y Mestre.—Bibliografía del dr. Juan Miguel Dihigo y Mestre.—La ética de Montalvo, por Roberto Agramonte.—Carta sobre el dr. Juan Miguel Dihigo, por Miguel Amunátegui Reyes.—Las ventajas del método histórico-comparativo en la enseñanza de la lengua latina, por Adolfo de Aragón.—Del grito á la razón, por L. A.

(Continued)

N. Y. P. L. October 11, 1944

Havana (City). Universidad. Libro jubilar... (Card 2)

Baralt.—Sobre la "S" psicológica, por A. Bernal.—La verdadera Safo de Lesbos, por Manuel Bisbé.—L'origine du nom de "Waterloo," par Emile Boisacq.—Rubén Darío, por Regino Boti.—El "Cantico di Frate Sole," por Aurelio Boza Masvidal.—Latin words in Athenaeus, by C. Burton Gulick.—Prólogo al "Léxico cubano" del dr. Juan M. Dihigo, por Julio Cejador y Frauca.—Heredia, traductor de Horacio, por J. M. Chacón y Calvo.—Sobre el origen del nombre de "Germanos," por Gustavo Du-Bouchet y Ramírez.—Apuntes caracterológicos sobre el Léxico cubano, por J. E. Entralgo.—Cantores del Niagara, por Antonio Gómez Restrepo.—La enseñanza del inglés en Cuba, por Inés Guiteras de Llorens.—El dr. Juan Miguel Dihigo, académico de la historia de Cuba, por Tomás de Jústiz.—Le dr. J. M. Dihigo et la phonetique experimentale, par abate Jean Larrasquet.—Teoría de los americanismos, por Raimundo Lazo.—Martí, hombre de fé, por D. M. Loynaz.—En torno á Capdevila, por Joaquín Llaverias.—González Prada y su obra, por Jorge Mañach.—Apuntes para el estudio

(Continued)

N. Y. P. L. October 11, 1944

Havana (City). Universidad. Libro jubilar... (Card 3)

de la religión de los indios de las Antillas, por Calixto Masó Vázquez.—La geografía en la obra de Dante, por Salvador Massip.—El lenguaje de los amerindios, por Aristides Mestre y Hevia.—En torno al bojeo de Cuba, por J. M. Pérez Cabrera.—El criollismo, por Herminio Portell Vilá.—French echoes from Antilles and tropical America, by W. A. Read.—El preceptismo literario en Cuba, por J. J. Remos.—Carta sobre el dr. Juan Miguel Dihigo, por Félix Restrepo.—Notas sobre la influencia del euskera en el idioma gallego, por J. Rubinos.—La retirada de Racine, por Salvador Salazar.—Conflictos y armonías en torno á la cubanidad, por Emeterio Santovenia.—Reformas necesarias en la enseñanza de idiomas en Cuba, por Roberto de la Torre.—La lingüística y sus relaciones con otras ciencias afines, por Isolina de Velasco de Millás.—Juicio del estudio Las siete partidas del dr. Juan M. Dihigo, por Valeriano Fernández Ferraz.

268945B. 1. Philology—Addresses, essays, lectures. 2. Dihigo y Mestre, Juan Miguel, 1866– . I. Title.
N. Y. P. L. October 11, 1944

---

*Z-1546
Film Reproduction

HAVERFORD essays; studies in modern literature, prepared by some former pupils of Professor Francis B. Gummere, in honor of the completion of the twentieth year of his teaching in Haverford College. Haverford, Pa., 1909. 303 p.

Film reproduction. Negative.

1. Literature--Addresses, essays, lectures. 2. Gummere, Francis Barton, 1855-1919.
NN R 12.65 1/f OCs PCs, 1,2 SL (UM1, LC1s, X1s, Z1)

ONK

Havinga, E., and others, editors.
Planetarium-boek, Eise Eisinga; dit boek uitgegeven op den honderdsten gedenkdag van zijn dood 27 Augustus 1928, onder de auspiciën van het Gemeentebestuur van Franeker en van het Friesch Genootschap van Geschied-, Oudheid- en Taalkunde te Leeuwarden is samengesteld door E. Havinga, W. E. van Wijk en J. F. M. G. d'Aumerie. Met een levensbericht en een bijvoegsel waarin vele onuitgegeven stukken van Eisinga en het planetarium, een lijst van in Nederland vervaardigde of aanwezige planetaria,

(Continued)

N. Y. P. L. June 5, 1929

Havinga, E., and others, editor: Planetarium-boek, Eise Eisinga ... (Card 2)

en een vertaling van Christiaan Huygens' automaton planetarii. Arnhem: Van Loghum Slaterus, 1928. viii, 416 p. incl. facsims., front., tables. diagr., illus. (incl. plan, ports.) 4°.

411470A. 1. Eisinga, Eise, 1744–1828. 2. Orrery, 17th–19th cent. 3. Wijk, W. E. van, jt. editor. 4. Aumerie, J. F. M. G. d', jt. editor. 5. Huygens, Christiaan, 1629–1695.
N. Y. P. L. June 5, 1929

---

*MEC
(Haydn)

Haydn festschrift zur Haydn-feier in Hainburg a. d. D. vom 2.–4. juli 1932. [Klosterneuburg, Augustinus-druckerei, 1932]
31 p. illus. (1 col.) 23ᶜᵐ.
Cover-title: Festschrift zur Haydn-feier in Hainburg a. d. D.
Advertising matter: p. 27–31.
CONTENTS.—Gruss an Haydn, von Josef Hiess.—Hainburg in geschichte und landschaft, von Johann Wenzel.—Joseph Haydn und Hainburg, von dr. E. F. Schmid-Tübingen.—Die Haydn-gedächtnisorgel, von prof. Vinzenz Goller.—Der Haydn-gedächtnisbrunnen, von Justine Mayer.—Sehenswürdigkeiten und spaziergänge in Hainburg und umgebung.—Festfolge anlässlich der einweihung der Haydn-gedächtnisorgel am 2. juli 1932.
1. Haydn, Joseph, 1732–1809—Anniversaries, etc., 1932. 2. Hainburg, Austria. I. Title: Festschrift zur Haydn-feier in Hainburg a. d. D.

35-7104
Library of Congress ML410.H4H32
[3] 927.8

---

* MEC
(Haydn)

...**Haydn**-Festschrift, 1932; enthält Führer durch die Haydn-Festwochen. Unveröffentlichte Musikstücke, Erstdrucke von Porträts, Gedenkstätten, Musikinstrumenten, Handschriften des Meisters u. a. ... [Wien, 1932.] 55 p. incl. pl. illus. (incl. facsims., music, ports.) 31cm.

Cover-title.
Issued as Osterreichische Kunst, Jahrg. 3, Heft 2/3, März–April, 1932.
Contents: CZERMAK, E. Geleitwort. Haydn-Feier der österreichischen Bundesregierung. KOBALD, K. Joseph Haydn. OREL, A. Haydns Sendung. REUTHER, H.

(Continued)

Festschrift

N. Y. P. L. June 23, 1933

...Haydn-Festschrift, 1932... (Card 2)

Joseph Haydn als Hausbesitzer. KELDORFER, V. Joseph Haydns "Hochgesang aller Deutschen." BOTSTIBER, H. War Antonio Polzelli Haydns Sohn? LEUX, I. Haydns Beziehungen zu Deutschland. DECSEY, E. Haydn in der Anekdote. HOFMANN, E. Joseph Haydns Leben und Wohnen. WELLESZ, E. Haydn und Oxford. KRAUS, H. Joseph Haydn und Spanien. CHANTAVOINE, J. Haydn et La France. SCHMID, E. F. Joseph Haydn und das Burgenland. GEIRINGER, K. Haydn und England. ISOZ, K. Haydnsche Musik in Ungarn. LUITHLEN, V. Haydn-Instrumente der Gesellschaft der Musikfreunde in Wien. HAYDN, J. Allegro con variazioni, für den praktischen Gebrauch eingerichtet von Dr. Karl Geiringer. HEGER, R. Die Musik zum Trauerspiel "König Lear." Marx, J., and F. BUXBAUM. Haydn als Erzieher. Programm der Haydn-Gedächtnisfeier der österreichischen Bundesregierung. Programm der in Niederösterreich...Haydn-Feierlichkeiten. Detail-Programm der Haydn-Feier in Rohrau... Programm der Haydn-Ehrungen...im Burgenland.

CARNEGIE CORPORATION OF NEW YORK

1. Haydn, Franz Joseph, 1732–1809. I. Title.
N. Y. P. L. June 23, 1933

---

*PXY

HEBREW UNION COLLEGE-JEWISH INSTITUTE OF RELIGION. American Jewish Archives.
Essays in American Jewish history, to commemorate the tenth anniversary of the founding of the American Jewish Archives under the direction of Jacob Rader Marcus. Cincinnati, 1958. xvii, 534 p. illus., port., facsim. 24cm. (ITS: Publications, no. 4)

"The writings of Jacob Rader Marcus": p. 493-512. Bibliographical footnotes.

(Continued)
NN*R 1.64 c/ OS, I PC, 1, 2, I SL (AH)I J, 1, 3, I (LC1, X1, Z/) 2

HEBREW UNION COLLEGE-JEWISH INSTITUTE OF RELIGION. American Jewish Archives. Essays in American Jewish history... (Card 2)

1. Marcus, Jacob Rader, 1896- . 2. Jews in the U.S.--Addresses, essays, lectures. 3. United States--Addresses, essays, lectures. I. Series.

OEG

HEBREW UNIVERSITY, Jerusalem.
Essays on the foundations of mathematics, dedicated to A.A. Fraenkel on his seventieth anniversary. Edited by Y. Bar-Hillel, E.I.J. Poznanski, M.O. Rabin, and A. Robinson. Jerusalem, Magnes press, Hebrew university, 1961. x, 351 p. 25cm.

Added t.p. in Hebrew.
Includes bibliographical references.

(Continued)
NN R 3.62 A/(OC)I OS PC, 1, 2, I SL J, 2, I ST, 1t, 2, I (LC1, X1, Z1) 4

HEBREW UNIVERSITY, Jerusalem. Essays on the foundations of mathematics... (Card 2)

CONTENTS.--Bibliography of A.A. Fraenkel (p. ix-x).--Zur Frage der Unendlichkeitsschemata in der axiomatischen Mengenlehre, von P. Bernays.--On some problems involving inaccessible cardinals, by P. Erdős and A. Tarski.--Comparing the axioms of local and universal choice, by A. Lévy.--Fraenkel's addition to the axioms of Zermelo, by R. Montague.--More on the axiom of extensionality, by D. Scott.--The problem of predicativity, by J.R. Shoenfield.--Grundgedanken einer typenfreien Logik, von W. Ackermann.--On the use of Hilbert's ε-operator in scientific theories, by R. Carnap.--Basic verifiability

(Continued)

HEBREW UNIVERSITY, Jerusalem. Essays on the foundations of mathematics... (Card 3)

in the combinatory theory of restricted generality, by H.B. Curry.--Uniqueness ordinals in constructive number classes, by H. Putnam.--On the construction of models, by A. Robinson.--Interpretation of mathematical theories in the first order predicate calculus, by Th. Skolem.--The elementary character of two notions from general algebra, by R. Vaught.--Axiomatic method and intuitionism, by A. Heyting.--On rank-decreasing functions, by G. Kurepa.--On non-standard models for number theory, by E. Mendelson.--Concerning the problem of axiomatizability

(Continued)

HEBREW UNIVERSITY, Jerusalem. Essays on the foundations of mathematics... (Card 4)

of the field of real numbers in the weak second order logic, by A. Mostowski.--Non-standard models and independence of the induction axiom, by M.O. Rabin.--Sur les ensembles raréfiés de nombres naturels, par W. Sierpiński.--Remarks on the paradoxes of logic and set theory, by E.W. Beth.--Logique formalisée et raisonnement juridique, par R. Feys.--Im Umkreis der sogenannten Raumprobleme, von H. Freudenthal.--Process and existence in mathematics, by H. Wang.

1. Mathematics--Addresses, essays, lectures. 2. Fraenkel, Abraham Adolf, 1891- . I. Bar-Hillel, Yehoshua, ed.
t. 1961.

MCZ

Hedemann-Gade, Hakon, 1891–
Pär Siegård [av] Hakon Hedemann-Gade och Carl Schill. [Redigerad av Torsten Mårtensson] [Hälsingborg] Hälsingborgs konstförening [i distribution: Killbergs bokhandel, 1948]
108 p. illus., 48 plates (part col.) port. 19 cm.
"Konstnären Pär Siegård tillägnas denna bok på sextioårsdagen den 28 december 1947 av Hälsingborgs konstförening."
1. Siegård, Pär, 1887– I. Schill, Carl Nicodemus, 1890– II. Mårtensson, Torsten, 1889– ed.
ND793.S5H4 48-26398*
Library of Congress [1] FESTSCHRIFT CAT.

HEIMAT und Welt, Sein und Leben... (Card 2)

Lebenskundliche Erkenntnisse aus der Schau auf den Menschen.
Contributions by various authors.
Preface and epilogue signed: R[iedl]

1. Moravia--Hist. 2. Germans in Moravia. 3. Oldřichovice, Czechoslovakia--Hist. I. Riedl, Franz, ed.

Copy only words underlined & classmark-- TB

HEGELAND, HUGO, ed.
Money, growth, and methodology, and other essays in economics in honor of Johan Åkerman, March, 31, 1961. Lund, C.W.K. Gleerup [1961] xii,509 p. -port. diagrs. 25cm. (Samhällsvetenskapliga studier, no. 20)

Contributions in English, French, German, Norwegian or Swedish, with English or German summaries of the Norwegian and Swedish texts.
(Continued)
NN R 1.62 e/LOC. (OS)I PC, 1, 2, 3, 4, I E, 1, 2, 3, 4, I (LC1, X1, Z1) 2

D-11
9058
Heimatbund der Männer vom Morgenstern.
Festschrift Robert Wiebalck, Amtsgerichtsrat a. D. in Dorum, zu seinem 80. Geburtstage am 27. Juli 1954. Bremerhaven, 1954. 82 p. map. 21cm.
"Die Veröffentlichungen Robert Wiebalcks," p. 4–7.
Includes bibliographies.

1. Wiebalck, Robert, 1874– 2. Hanover (Province)—Hist.
NN R 3.60 (OC)1b+ OS PC,1,2 SL (LC1,X1,Z1)

HEGELAND, HUGO, ed. Money, growth, and methodology, and other essays in economics in honor of Johan Akerman... (Card 2)

Includes bibliographies.

1. Economic development--Addresses, essays, lectures. 2. Economics--Methodology. 3. Money, 1933- . 4. Åkerman, Johan Henrik, 1896- . I. Series.

L-10
1977
Bd. 2
HEIMATKUNDE und Landesgeschichte; zum 65. Geburtstag von Rudolf Lehmann, hrsg. von Friedrich Beck. Weimar, H. Böhlaus, 1958. xv, 315 p. illus., port. 25cm. (Germany (Democratic republic, 1949-). Brandenburgisches Landeshauptarchiv, Potsdam. Veröffentlichungen. Bd. 2)

CONTENTS.--Bibliographie 1916-1957 (p. [xi]-xv).--Zur Geschichte der Lausitzen: Das ländliche Wirtschaftsleben einer Oberlausitzer Standesherrschaft bis zum Ausgange des 18. Jahrhunderts, von W. Boelcke.
(Continued)
NN R X 11.59 t/l OC, II (OD)I (ED)I PC, 1, 2, 3, I, II S, 1, 2, I, II (LC1, X1, Z1) [I]

VBA p.v. 2262
HEIDELBERG. Universität. Philipp-Lenard-Institut.
Naturforschung im Aufbruch, Reden und Vorträge zur Einweihungsfeier des Philipp Lenard-Instituts der Universität Heidelberg am 13. und 14. Dezember 1935. Hrsg. von August Becker, Leiter des Instituts. München, J.F. Lehmann, 1936. 80 p. illus., port. 25cm.
1. Science--Essays and misc. 2. Lenard, Philipp Eduard Anton, 1862-1879- , ed. t. 1936.
NN * R 6.66 1/ (OC)I OS PC, 1, 2, I SL ST, 1t, 2, I (LC1, X1, Z1)

HEIMATKUNDE und Landesgeschichte... (Card 2)

Das Volksschulwesen im Gubener Kreise um die Wende des 18. Jahrhunderts, von E. Müller. Soziale und nationale Zusammensetzung der Dorfbevölkerung am Beispiel eines Niederlausitzer Erbzinsregisters vom Jahre 1670, von F. Redlich. Metzker-Scharfenberg: "Abkontrafeitung der Stadt Görlitz im 1565 Jar" im Spiegel stadtgeschichtlicher Betrachtung, von M. Reuther. Zur Herkunft und Verbreitung des Niederlausitzer Adels im Mittelalter, von H. Schieckel.--Zur Geschichte der Nachbarlandschaften, insbesondere Brandenburgs und Sachsens: Die kommunalständischen Verhältnisse der Provinz Brandenburg in neuerer Zeit, von F. Beck. Zur Auflösung von Vermessungsangaben in geschichtlichen Quellen, von F. Bönisch. Zur
(Continued)

G-10
950
HEIMAT und Welt, Sein und Leben; Teile eines Ganzen. Versuch einer Darstellung dieses Zusammenhangs am Lebensgeschehen einer Landschaft an Hand ihrer allerlei geschichtlichen Vorgänge und einer daraus gewordenen Ausrichtung. [n.p.] 1960. 432 p. illus., maps, fold. charts. 31cm.

At head of title: Zum Denken an einer Zeiten- und Menschenwende.
(Continued)
NN R 7.61 m/ OC, I PC, 1, 2, 3, I SL E, 2, I S, 1, 2, 3, I (LC1, X1, Z1) 2

HEIMATKUNDE und Landesgeschichte... (Card 3)

Spruchpraxis der Juristenfakultät Frankfurt a.d.O., von J. Haalck. Dorfweber und Sozialstruktur in Langhennersdorf im 16. Jahrhundert, von G. Heitz. Das neumärkische Stift Soldin, von W. Hoppe. Die Messen zu Frankfurt an der Oder und ihre Bedeutung für den Ost-West-Handel, von L. Knabe. Geschichte der Stadt Braunschweig im Überblick, von R. Moderhack. Ein Norweger als Student zu Freiberg 1798/99, aus den Lebenserinnerungen von J. Aall. Von M. Rudolph. Landesteile und Zentralgewalt in Kursachsen zu Anfang des 19. Jahrhunderts, von G. Schmidt. Das "Markrecht" Markgraf Ottos II. von Brandenburg, von J. Schultze.
(Continued)

D-15
3354

HEIMATVEREIN SPIESEN.
Festschrift zur 750-Jahrfeier in Spiesen, vom 27. Juni bis 5. Juli 1953. [Textgestaltung Ewald Kohler Spiesen] Selbstverlag des Heimatvereins Spiesen, 1953. 88 p. illus., coats of arms. 21cm.

1. Spiesen, Germany--Hist. I. Kohler, Ewald.

NN R 10.65 p/ (OC)I, Ibo OS(1b) PC, 1, I SL (LC1, X1, Z1)

MCZ
+
D18.B5
Heinrich Danioth, eine Monographie; hrsg. zu seinem 50. Geburtstag von Freunden des Kunstlers... Zürich, Schweizer Spiegel Verlag [c1946] 31 p., 40 pl. (part col.) illus. 30cm.

CONTENTS.—Stieger, Hermann. Herkommen und Berufung.—Hilber, Paul. Die Stellung in der schweizer Kunst der Gegenwart.—Birchler, Linus. Die Gestaltungsweise.—Abbildungen.

374421B. 1. Danioth, Heinrich, 1896-
N. Y. P. L. January 20, 1947

E-11
4097

HEIMPEL, HERMANN, 1901-
Vier Kapitel aus der deutschen Geschichte. Festgabe zum 225 jährigen Bestehen des Verlages am 13. Februar 1960. Göttingen, Vandenhoeck & Ruprecht [1960] 88, 7 p. ports., facsim. 24cm.

"... sind einer Vorlesung entnommen, welche im Wintersemester 1954/55 und im Sommersemester 1958... ein Gesamtbild der deutschen Geschichte geben wollte."

(Continued)

NN R 1.62 p/ OC (OS)2b PC, 1, 2 SL (LC1, X1, Z1)

2

E-10
1316

HEINSBERG, Germany.
Heinsberg 700 Jahre Stadt; Beiträge zur Stadtgeschichte aus Anlass der 700 Jahrfeier 1956. Im Auftrage der Stadtverwaltung, Heinsberg. Schriftleitung: Hans-Peter Funken. Heinsberg, 1956. 170 p. illus. (part col.) map. 24cm.

CONTENTS. --Ursprung und Werden der Stadt Heinsberg im Mittelalter, von S. Corsten. --Urkunde vom Jahre 1255, in Welcher Heinsberg als Stadt erwähnt wird, Übersetzung, von A. Perey. --

(Continued)

NN* * 1.57 t/ (OC)I, Ibo ODt EDt PC, 1, I SL (LC1, X1, Z1, Y1)

HEIMPEL, HERMANN, 1901- Vier Kapitel aus der deutschen Geschichte. (Card 2)

"Nicht im Handel. Als Manuskript gedruckt."
CONTENTS. --Aachen. --Canossa. --Wittenberg. --Frankfurt.

1. Germany--Hist. --Addresses, essays, lectures. 2. Vandenhoeck & Ruprecht, Göttingen.

HEINSBERG, Germany. Heinsberg 700 Jahre Stadt... (Card 2)

Vom Werden und Wachsen der Herrschaft Heinsberg, von H. H. Deussen. — Die Pfarr- und Propsteigemeinde St. Gangolfus zu Heinsberg im Wandel der Jahrhunderte, von K.J. Kutsch. —Aus der Geschichte der evangelischen Kirchengemeinde zu Heinsberg, von H. H. Deussen. —Alt-Heinsburg; Erinnerungen an alte Häuser, Strassen und Plätze, von H. P. Funken. —Die Bürgermeister der Stadt Heinsberg von 1794-1945. —Heinsbergs Zerstörung und Wiederaufbau, von G. Laugs.

1. Heinsberg, Germany—Hist. I. Funken, Hans Peter, t. 1956.

NN* * 12.56 t/ (OC)I, Ibo ODt EDt PC, 1, I SL (LC1, X1, Z1, Y1)

*MEC
(Albert)

HEINRICH-ALBERT-FESTAUSSCHUSS.
Festschrift zur Ehrung von Heinrich Albert (1604-1651), hrsg. im Auftrag des Heinrich-Albert-Festausschusses von Günther Kraft. Weimar, 1954. 104 p. music. 21cm.

CONTENTS. —Zeittafel mit Werkverzeichnis. - Vorwort des Herausgebers. —Geleitwort des Vorsitzenden des Rates des Bezirkes Gera. —Neue Beiträge zur Albert-Forschung: Heinrich Albert und seine Zeit, von G. Kraft. Heinrich Albert und das weltliche Barocklied, von J. Müller-Blattau. Zur Kritik an der Heinrich-Albert-Ausgabe der

(Continued)

NN 5.58 e/P (OC)I, II, OS(1b) PC, 1, I, II SL MU, 1, 2, I, II (LC1, X1, Z1)

2

D-20
3202

Heinz Risse 70 Jahre. (30. März 1968.) (Krefeld, Scherpe, 1968.)
31 p. 28 cm.

CONTENTS.—Unerbetene Rezension, von J. Urzidil.—Heinz Risses kürzere Erzählungen, von H. M. Waldson.—Obwohl es keine Vollkommenheit gibt, von V. O. Hubba.—Risse, Heinz, von E. F. Bauer.—Das Problem der Gerechtigkeit bei Heinz Risse, von L. B. Foltin.

1. Risse, Heinz. I. Risse, Heinz.
NN*R 9.71 d/ OC PC, 1, I SL (LC1, X1, Z1)

HEINRICH-ALBERT-FESTAUSSCHUSS. Festschrift zur Ehrung von Heinrich Albert... (Card 2)

Denkmäler deutscher Tonkunst, von H. J. Moser. Der Stadtpfeifer und die Stadtkapelle in Lobenstein, von R. Haensel. Das Volkslied als Quelle des musikalischen Schaffens, von W. Rein. —Neue Beiträge zur zeitgenössischen Musikforschung: Georg Andreas Sorge, ein Lobensteiner Meister, von M. Frisch. Anonyme Bläsermusik des 17. Jahrhunderts, von F. von Glasenapp. Thüringer Meister im Umkreis von Heinrich Schütz und Heinrich Albert, von A. Thiele. Zur Ausstellung "Heinrich Albert und seine Zeit," von H. Jung.

1. Albert, Heinrich, 1604-1651. 2. Musicians, German--Thuringia. I. Kraft, Günther, 1907- , ed. II. Title.

MA

HEISE, CARL GEORGE.
Der gegenwärtige Augenblick; Reden und Aufsätze aus vier Jahrzehnten. [Zum 70. Geburtstag von Carl Georg Heise, hrsg. von Paul Ortwin Rave, Otto H. Hess und Marcus Bierich] Berlin, Gebr. Mann [1960] xii, 171, [1] p. 25cm.

Bibliographical references included in "Anmerkungen" p. 169-[172].

1. Essays, German. 2. Art, German, 20th cent. I. Rave, Paul Ortwin, 1893- , ed.
NN 5.61 e/ OC, I PC, 1, 2, I SL A, 2, I (LC1, X1, Z1)

E-11
8678

Die HEITERE Maske im ernsten Spiel; eine Freundesgabe für Volkmar Muthesius zum 19 März 1960. Frankfurt am Main, F. Knapp [1960] 118 p. mounted ports. 25cm.

Pref. signed: Hermann J. Abs [and others].

CONTENTS.--Muthesius ein Purist? Von H. J. Abs.--Meditieren und Musizieren; ein erdachtes Gespräch, von K. Dohrn.--Humor, Werkzeug einer freien Wirtschaft, von H. Gross.--Über die Relativität der Wahrheit,

(Continued)

NN R 1.64 f/ OC, I PC, 1, I SL E, 1, I (LC1, X1, Z1)

3

Die HEITERE Maske im ernsten Spiel... (Card 2)

von L. A. Hahn.-- "Muthesiana", Sprüche des Encyklopädisten Volkomar, von J. W. Hedemann.--Mythologie der Sitzung, von W. Hofmann.--Was ist Marktwirtschaft ? Von H. Ilau.--Bankologische Exzesse, von U. Klug.--Sybaris klagt die Götter an, von J. Lang.--Der nichtintellektuelle Intellektuelle, von L. Mellinger.--Ich weiss was auf wen, M. Müller-Jabusch.--Vom Warzenschwein-Scherz, Satire, Ironie und tiefere Bedeutung, von C. Plassmann.--Die Landschildkröte; eine furchtbare Entdeckung, von W. Röpke.--Forderungen an die Wirtschaftspublizistik,

(Continued)

Die HEITERE Maske im ernsten Spiel... (Card 2)

von W. Salewski.--Das Steuertrauma, von G. Schmölders.--Zum Thema intellektuelle Redlichkeit, von O. Veit.--Ein Trostbrief, von H. O. Wesemann.--Der alte Thyssen, von J. Winschuh.--Apostel der Marktwirtschaft, v. R. Zorn.

1. Muthesius, Volkmar. I. Abs, Hermann J., ed.

F-11
806

HELGAFELL, firm, Reykjavik.

Afmæliskveðjur heiman og handan; til Halldors Kiljans Laxness sextugs, Helgafell-Ragnar Jónsson, 23.4.62. [Reykjavík, 1962] 118 p. 26cm.

Contributions in Icelandic, Dutch, Norwegian, Gaelic, Swedish, English, Finnish, French, German, Japanese, Russian and Spanish.

1. Laxness, Halldor Kiljan, 1902- . I. Title. II. Ragnar Jónsson, ed. i [Title] Afmæliskvedjur.

NN R 5.66 g/ (OC)I, II, IIb OS(Ib) PC, 1, I, II SL (LC1, X1, Z1) [I]

F-10
169

Der HELLENISMUS in der deutschen Forschung, 1938-1948. [Pierre Jouguet in memoriam] Unter Mitwirkung zahlreicher Fachgelehrter hrsg. von Emil Kiessling. Wiesbaden, O. Harrassowitz, 1956. ix, 171 p. port. 26cm.

Bibliographical footnotes.

CONTENTS. --Literatur und literarische Papyruskunde, von F. Zucker. --Papyrusurkunden, von E. Kiessling. --Epigraphik, von G. Klaffenbach. --Orientalistik, von G. Fohrer. -- Religion, von H. Herter. --

(Continued)

NN** 4.57 c/ OC, I PC, 1, 2, I SL (LC1, X1, Z1, Y1)

Der HELLENISMUS in der deutschen Forschung, 1938-1948... (Card 2)

Philosophie, von W. Schmid. --Politische Geschichte, von H. Bengtson. --Recht, von E. Seidl. --Wirtschaft und Nationalökonomie, von F. Oertel. --Archäologie, von R. Horn. --Geographie, von E. Kirsten. --Grammatik und Linguistik, von H. J. Mette. --Rhetorik, von R. Güngerich. --Geschichte der Wissenschaften, von J. Mau. --Anhang: Numismatik. Metrologie.

1. Classical studies--Germany. 2. Jouguet, Pierre Felix Amédée, 1869-1949. I. Kiessling, Emil, 1896- , ed.

NGO

Hellpach, Willy Hugo, 1877–

Universitas litterarum, gesammelte Aufsätzte. ⌊Zum 70. Geburtstag im Namen von Freunden und Kollegen hrsg. von Gerhard Hess und Wilhelm Witte, mit Beiträgen von Curt Oehme, et al.⌋ Stuttgart, F. Enke, 1948.

381 p. illus. 24 cm.

CONTENTS.—Willy Hellpach und die praktische Heilkunde, von C. Oehme. — Arzt auf naturwissenschaftlichem Grenzland, von B. de Rudder.—Willy Hellpachs Werk als Psychologe, von A. Wellek.—Willy Hellpach als Denker, von W. Witte.—Religion. Philosophie, Geisteswissenschaften und Erziehung. Recht und Staat. Wirtschaft und Technik. Medizin und Naturwissenschaften. Psychologie. Logos und Pragma; eine Epikrise. Von W. Hellpach.—Bibliographie des wissenschaftlichen Schrifttums von Willy Hellpach (p. 376–381)

1. Medicine—Addresses, essays, lectures. 2. Psychology—Addresses, essays, lectures. I. Title.

R117.H46 A 51–1734

New York. Public Libr. for Library of Congress ⌊1⌋†

NIHC

Helsing til Olav Midttun på 50-årsdagen 8. april 1933. Oslo: Noregs boklag, 1933. 216 p. 25cm.

CONTENTS.—Bergsgård, A. Ætt og einmenne i norrøn vikingtid.—Indrebø, G. Tri norske stadnamn.—Skard, E. Hallvard Gunnarssons Chronicon regum Norvegiæ.—Skulerud, O. Av ordtilfanget på Sunnmøre.—Liestøl, K. Heimfesting av folkevisor.—Halland, N. Meteorologiske ord og ordelag i nokre Nordhordlands-bygder.—Skard, S. Eit Cervantes-motiv.—Lid, N. Um folkelivsgransking.—Øverås, A. Noko um grunnlaget for Bjørnsons forteljing "Faderen."— Kolsrud, S. Austlandsmål.

677670A. 1. Midttun, Olav, 1883- .
N. Y. P. L. November 17, 1933

E-13
3478

Helsingborg, *Sweden. Stadsfullmäktige.*

De hundra åren. Stadsfullmäktige i Hälsingborg 1862–1962. Minnesskrift utg. på Stadsfullmäktiges uppdrag av särskilda kommitterade. ⌊Redaktör: Krister Gierow⌋ Hälsingborg, 1965.

357, (1) p. illus. 25 cm.

CONTENTS.—För hundra år sedan, av K. Gierow.—Hälsingborgs stadsplan och bebyggelse, av G. Sundbärg.—Det nutida Hälsingborg,

(Continued)

NN * R 11.68 1/ (OC)I ODt EDt PC, 1, 2, I SL (E)1, 2 (LC1, X1, Z1)

5

HELSINGBORG, Sweden. Stadsfullmäktige. De hundra åren. Stadsfullmäktige i Hälsingborg 1862-1962. (Card 2)

av F. Andersson.—Hundra års kommunalval i Hälsingborg, av K. Gierow.—Pionjärerna, av A. Åberg.—Det sociala kapitlet, av A. Selge.—Hälsingborgs skolväsen under de sista hundra åren, av Å.

Ett sekels teater och musik i Hälsingborg, av L. Levin.—Kulturminnesvård och museiverksamhet, av T. Mårtensson.—Idrott och friluftsliv i Hälsingborg, av N. Carlius.—Kyrkolivet i Helsingborg genom hundra år, av A. Westin.—Militärstaden Hälsingborg, av K. Gierow.—Trafik, turism, utställningar, av G. Engfors.—Hälsingborgs-

(Continued)

HELSINGBORG, Sweden. Stadsfullmäktige. De hundra åren. Stadsfullmäktige i Hälsingborg 1862-1962. (Card 3)

bilder, av A. Anderberg.—Hälsingborg i litteraturen, av K. Gierow.—Statistiska uppgifter om Hälsingborg, 1863–1962, av A. M. Andersson.

1. Helsingborg, Sweden. Govt. 2. Economic history--Sweden--Helsingborg. I. Gierow, Krister, 1907- , ed.
t. 1965.

*QP

HENNEL, ROMAN, ed.
Ksiega pamiatkowa ku czci Karola Estreichera, 1827-1908; studia i rozprawy. [Komitet redakcyjny: Jan Baumgart et al.] Kraków, Wydawn. literackie, 1964. 433 p. ports., facsims. 25cm.

"Bibliografia prac Karola Estreichera i literatury o nim," p. [413]-433.

1. Estreicher, Karol Józef Teofil, 1827-1908.
NN S 4.65 e/5 OC PC, 1 SL S, 1 (LC1, X1, Z1)

GM

Helsingfors. Universitet. Nyliberala studentförbundet.
Finlandssvenskt frisinne; festskrift tillägnad John Österholm 5/10 1952. [Helsingfors] Nyliberala studentförbundet [1952] 159 p. port. 21cm.

CONTENTS.—Meinander, Nils. Jubilaren.—2. Valros, Fredrik. John Österholm som opinionsbildare.—Söderhjelm, J. O. JÖ och JO.—Meinander, Ragnar. Den kommunala självstyrelsens kris.—Åström, S.-E. Varför regionalism.—Jernström, Frank. Den "mänskliga faktorn" i opinionsbildningens tjänst.—Tallqvist, J. O. Nya Pressens start 1882 och männen kring tidningen.—Nordström, W. E. Myten som politiskt vapen.—Krusius-Ahrenberg, Lolo. Demokratin och den sinande idédebatten.—Bonsdorff, Göran von. Ideologiens ofrånkomlighet.—Dufholm, Lars. Etik och politik.—Jansson, J.-M. Reflexioner om jämlikhet.—Westerholm, Kurt. Socialpolitik och demokrati.—Gestrin, Kristian. Friheten och ansvaret i välfardsstaten.—Törnudd, Klaus. Har liberalerna en ljnje.

1. Finland—Politics. 2. Österholm, John, 1882- . I. Title.
NN R 5.53 (OC)I OS PC, 1, 2 SL E, 1, 2 (LC1, Z1, X1)

*OMA

HENNING, WALTER BRUNO HERMANN, ed.
A locust's leg; studies in honour of S.H. Taqizadeh [edited by W.B. Henning and E. Yarshater] London, Percy Lund, Humphries, 1962. vii, 250 p. illus., port. 23cm.

Contributions in English, French or German.
Bibliographical footnotes.

1. Taqizādeh, Hasan, sayyid. 2. Persian studies--Collections.
I. Yarshātir, Ihsān, joint ed.
NN R 3.63 e/6 OC, I PC, 1, 2, I SL O, 1, 2, I (LC1, X1, Z1)

Copy only words underlined
& Classmark-- V PA

HELSINGIN yliopiston rehtorin professori Erkki Kivisen juhlajulkaisu. Jubilee issue in honour of professor Erkki Kivinen rector of Helsinki university. Helsinki, 1971. 245 p. port., maps. 25cm. (Suomen maataloustieteellinen seura. Julkaisuja. N:o 123)

English, German or Finnish.
List of works by E. Kivinen, p. 242-245.
Includes bibliographical references.

1. Kivinen, Erkki, 1903- . 2. Peat. t. 1971.
NN 3.72 w/4 (OC)1b+ OI (PC)1, 2 (ST)2t (LC1, X1, Z1)

AN
(Pirenne, H.)

Henri Pirenne; hommages et souvenirs ... Bruxelles, Nouvelle société d'éditions, 1938.

2 v. xx pl. (incl. fronts., ports., facsim.) $23\frac{1}{2}$ cm.

Paged continuously.
Copies of the book were presented to subscribers to the commemoration exercises held in honor of Henri Pirenne May 18, 1938, at the Académie royale de Belgique. *cf.* p. [549]–556.
"L'ouvrage débute par la remarquable conférence ... par ... Jacques Pirenne ... A cette première partie succèdent les documents qui se rapportent aux différentes faces de l'activité d'Henri Pirenne."—Préf., signed: Jules Duesberg.
"A consulter ... outre les articles publiés dans ce volume": p. [263]–264.

(Continued on next card)

A C 39-2600

[2]

Festschrift

YDC

Henle, Paul, *ed.*
Structure, method, and meaning; essays in honor of Henry M. Sheffer, with a foreword by Felix Frankfurter. Edited by Paul Henle, Horace M. Kallen [and] Susanne K. Langer. New York, Liberal Arts Press, 1951.

xvi, 306 p. port. 24 cm.
Bibliographical footnotes.
CONTENTS.—Henry M. Sheffer: a bibliography (p. xv-xvi)—Structure: A formulation of the logic of sense and denotation, by A. Church. Notes on the logic of intension, by C. I. Lewis. The logic of terms, by J. W. Miller. Two-valued truth tables for modal functions, by H. S. Leonard. N-valued Boolean algebra, by P. Henle. Triangular matrices determined by two sequences, by L. L. Silverman. The ordered pair in number theory, by W. V. Quine.—

(Continued on next card) Fest

51-2957

[15]

Henri Pirenne; hommages et souvenirs ... 1938. (Card 2)

CONTENTS.—Préface, par le professeur J. Duesberg.—Henri Pirenne.—Quelques aspects de Henri Pirenne.—Chronologie de Henri Pirenne; bibliographie des travaux d'Henri Pirenne, par F.-L. Ganshof [e. a.] (p. [145]–164)—Henri Pirenne, écrivain.—Les hommages rendus à Henri Pirenne. — Nécrologie. — Commémoration professeur Henri Pirenne. — L'école de Henri Pirenne—ses élèves et leurs travaux (p. [591]–[639])

1. *Pirenne, Henri, 1862–1935. 2. *Pirenne, Henri, 1862–1935—Bibliography. I. Duesberg, Jules, 1881–

A C 39-2600

New York. Public library
for Library of Congress [2]

Henle, Paul, *ed.* Structure, method, and meaning ... 1951. (Card 2)

CONTENTS—Continued.
Method: Pure and applied mathematics, by N. Wiener. The importance of deductively formulated theory in ethics and social and legal science, by F. S. C. Northrop. Francis Bacon's philosophy of science, by C. J. Ducasse. The history of science versus the history of learning, by G. Sarton. The method of methodology, by C. H. Kaiser. Abstraction in science and abstraction in art, by S. K. Langer. Reflections on the nature and method of philosophy, by M. Farber.—Meaning: The meaning of mind, by C. C. Pratt. A note on neutralism, by R. B. Perry. The meanings of unity among the sciences, by H. M. Kallen. Strict and genetic identity; an illustration of the relations of logic to metaphysics, by C. Hartshorne. Field theory and judicial logic, by F. S. Cohen. The sea fight tomorrow, by D. C. Williams.

1. Logic, Symbolic and mathematical. 2. Sheffer, Henry Maurice. I. Title.

BC135.H35 160.4 51-2957
Library of Congress [15]

E-11
8175

Henry, Stuart Clark, *ed.*
A miscellany of American Christianity; essays in honor of H. Shelton Smith. Durham, N. C., Duke University Press, 1963.

viii, 390 p. port. 24 cm.
Bibliographical footnotes.
CONTENTS.—H. Shelton Smith: an appreciative memoir, by A. C. Outler.—Bishop Francis J. McConnell and the great Steel Strike of 1919–1920, by W. W. Benjamin.—The communitarian quest for perfection, by J. W. Chandler.—Some aspects of religion on the American frontier, by G. E. Finney. — A centennial appraisal of James

(Continued)

NN * R 11.63 a/ OC, Ib* PC, 1, 2 SL (LC1, X1, Z1) [I]

2

HENRY, STUART CLARK, ed. A miscellany of American Christianity... (Card 2)

Henley Thornwell, by P. L. Garber.—Puritan character in the witchcraft episode of Salem, by S. C. Henry.—John Caldwell, critic of the great awakening in New England, by B. L. Jones.—John Witherspoon: academic advocate for American freedom, by J. L. McAllister.—Bronson Alcott: Emerson's "tedious archangel," by H. B. Pannill.—Ontology and Christology: the apologetic theology of Paul Tillich, by J. Pemberton.—Jonathan Mayhew: American Christian rationalist, by M. S. Richey.—Solomon Stoddard and the theology of the revival, by T. A. Schafer.—Theology and architecture in America: a study of three leaders, by J. F. White

1. Smith, Hilrie Shelton, 1893- 2. Religion--U.S. I. Henry, Stuart Clark.

E-13
9907

Herbert Read: a memorial symposium; edited by Robin Skelton. London, Methuen, 1970.

264 p. plate. illus., facsims., ports. 25 cm.

Originally published as the ninth (Jan. 1969) number of 'The Malahat review'.

1. Read, Sir Herbert Edward, 1893-1968. I. Skelton, Robin, ed. II. The Malahat review.

NN*R 11.70 m/OC, I (OS)II PC, 1, I, II SL (LC1, X1, Z1)

E-11
8134

HERBRICH, ELISABETH.
Der Mensch als Persönlichkeit und Problem; philosophische Überlegungen und psychologische Erfahrungen. Gedenkschrift für Universitätsprofessor P. Dr. Ildefons Betschart OSB + zum 60. Geburtstag. Im Namen der Salzburger Psychologenrunde und anderer Betschart-Schüler hrsg. München, A. Pustet [1963]
463 p. illus., port., facsims. 25cm.

(Continued)

NN R 10.63 p/ OC, IIbo (OS)I, Ib+ PC, 1, 2, 3, I SL (LC1, X1, Z1) [I]

4

HERBRICH, ELISABETH. Der Mensch als Persönlichkeit und Problem... (Card 2)

Bibliographical footnotes.

CONTENTS.--Zur Problematik der Persönlichkeit als kulturintegraler Wirklichkeit, von T.V. Ziuraitis.--Das Phänomen des Schattens in der Tiefenpsychologie und in der christlichen Ethik, von I. Endres.--Die kommunistische Philosophie des Geistes, von W. Breitfuss.--Geistige Grundlagen des Maoismus in Theorie und Praxis, von N. v. Ostrowska.--Die ethischen Ziele des Taoismus und des Existentialismus, von I. Suppaner-Stanzel.--Der Begriff "Archeus" bei Paracelsus, von H. Danter.--Die

(Continued)

HERBRICH, ELISABETH. Der Mensch als Persönlichkeit und Problem... (Card 3)

Temperamentenlehre im Menschenbild des Paracelsus, von D. Brinkmann.--Lästerung und Lobpreisung des Paracelsus in Basel, von R. Blaser.--Augustinus und das psychologische Problem des freien Willens, von F. Haider.--Vom Wesen und von der Entwicklung des Gewissens, von E. Gollhammer.--Zur Psychologie des Vorurteils, von J. Steidl.--Die Verbindung von Bios und Logos bei Schopenhauer, von M. Kirchner-Hlavac v. Rechtwall.--Grösse und Grenze der Testmethoden, von E. Herbrich.--Alfred Kubin in kunstpsychologischer Sicht, von J. Brandauer.--Die begriffliche Erfassung der abstrakten Kunst des 20. Jahrhunderts, von

(Continued)

HERBRICH, ELISABETH. Der Mensch als Persönlichkeit und Problem... (Card 4)

L. Piekarz.--Das Dur-Moll-Problem und dessen Lösungen, von A. Heine.--Funktionsstörungen der Stimme in den verschiedenen Lebensaltern, von H. Weihs.--Überforderung und Überbelastung des Schulkindes als pädagogisch-psychologisches Problem, von E. Karas.--Film und Erlebnis, von A. Schibli.

1. Psychology--Addresses, essays, lectures. 2. Philosophy--Addresses, essays, lectures. 3. Betschart, Ildefons. I. Salzburger Psychologenrunde II. Herbrich, Elisabeth.

F-10
9355

HERDER-BLÄTTER; Faksimile-Ausgabe zum 70. Geburtstag von Willy Haas. [Hamburg] Freie Akademie der Künste in Hamburg, 1962. [4] p., facsim. (5 no.), xv p. port. 30cm.

Facsimile reproduction of a periodical published in Prague, Apr. 1911-Oct. 1912 (Jahrg. 1, no. 1-4/5), by the J.G. Herder-Vereinigung, organized by the Prague lodge of the B'nai B'rith.

(Continued)

NN R 9.64 e/ OS, I, II, IIb PC, 1, 2, I, II SL J, 2, I, II S, 1, 2, I, II (LC1, X1, Z1)

2

HERDER-BLÄTTER; Faksimile-Ausgabe zum 70. Geburtstag... (Card 2)

1. German literature--Czechoslovakia--Prague. 2. Haas, Willy, 1891- I. Freie Akademie der Künste, Hamburg. II. Johann Gottfried Herder-Vereinigung, Prague.

AN
(Ehlers, H.)

HERMANN EHLERS. [Hrsg. von Friedrich Schramm, Udo Schmidt und Johannes Schlingensiepen. Wuppertal, Jugenddienst-Verlag, 1955] 133 p. illus., ports., facsims. 22cm.

CONTENTS.—Die Sterben für Gewinn achten, sind schwer zu erschrecken, von T. Heuss.—Heimatboden und Kindheit, von F. Schramm.—Im Südwestgau von Berlin, von F. Schönfeld.—Studentische Verbindung, von E. Rosenbrock.—"Christus muss grösser werden!", von U. Smidt.—1945 - nach dem bitteren Ende,

(Continued)

NN** R X 5.55 p/ OC, Ib, I, IIbo PC, 1, I SL E, 1, I (LC1, X1, Z1)

HERMANN EHLERS. [Hrsg. von Friedrich Schramm, Udo Schmidt und Johannes Schlingensiepen. (Card 2)

von H. J. Schultz.—"Durch Bekenntnis wird die Wahrheit und das Recht offenbar", von K. Scharf.—Oberkirchenrat in Oldenburg, von E. Osterloh.—Aus publizistischer Arbeit, von K. H. Meyer.—Die Jahre des politischen Wirkens, von K. Lohmann.—Ein Gestalter des neuen Deutschland, von K. Adenauer.—Der getreue Eckart des Parlamentes, von C. Schmidt.—Das uns anvertraute Erbe, von A. Cillien.—Am Sarg auf dem heimatlichen Sattelhof, von U. Smidt.

1. Ehlers, Hermann, 1904-1954. I. Schramm, Friedrich, ed. II. Schramm, Friedrich.

C-11
4231
HERMANN KESTEN; ein Buch der Freunde, zum 60. Geburtstag am 28. Januar 1960. München, K. Desch [1960] 173 p. ports. 19cm.

Bibliography, p. 161-[172]

1. Kesten, Hermann, 1900-
NN R 3.60 c/ OC PC,1 SL (LC1,X1,Z1)

Write on slip words underlined below and class mark— RAA

Hermann Osthoff zum 29. Dezember 1902, dem Tage seines fünfundzwanzig-jährigen Jubiläums als ordentlicher Professor, von Freunden und Schülern. [Strassburg: K. J. Trübner, 1903] 558 p. 23cm. (Indogermanische Forschungen. Bd. 14.)

295886. 1. Osthoff, Hermann, 1847- 1909.
N. Y. P. L. October 31, 1939

E-11
1995
HERMANN SCHAFFT; ein Lebenswerk. [Hrsg. in Verbindung mit einem Freundeskreis von Werner Kindt] Kassel, J. Stauda-Verlag, 1960. 300 p. ports. 24cm.

Contributions by various authors.
Includes: "Lebensbericht, Predigten, Ansprachen" and Aus dem Schrifttum Hermann Schaffts, " p. [145]-267.
Bibliography, p. [271]-280.

I. Kindt, Werner, ed. II. Schafft, Hermann.
III. Kindt, Werner.
NN R 2.61 p/ OC, I, II, IIIbo PC, I, II SL (LC1, X1, Z1)

Write on slip words underlined below and class mark- KAA (Petermann)

Hermann Wagner gedächtnisschrift, ergebnisse und aufgaben geographischer forschung, dargestellt von schülern, freunden und verehrern des altmeisters der deutschen geographen ... Mit 1 titelbild, 13 abbildungen im text und 7 tafeln. Gotha, J. Perthes, 1930.

391, [1] p. incl. front. (port.) illus., diagrs. 7 fold. maps. 27½cm. (Ergänzungsheft nr. 209 zu "Petermanns mitteilungen")

Includes bibliographies.

1. •Wagner, Hermann, 1840- 2. Geography—Collections.
30-24020
Library of Congress G1.P44 no. 209
[2] (910.8) 910.8

F-11
4866
Hermansen, Sverre Fermann, 1889-
St. Andreas logen Oscar til den flammende stjerne. Festskrift i anledning 125-års jubileet 25. april 1841-25. april 1966. Oslo, 1966.

191 p. illus. 30 cm.

1. Freemasons. Oslo. Sankt Andreas logen Oscar til den flammende stjerne. i. Sankt.
NN • R 12.68 1/ OC(1b•) (OS)1b• PC, 1 SL (LC1, [i]X1,

NRC
Ἑρμηνεία; Festschrift Otto Regenbogen zum 60. Geburtstag am 14. Februar 1951 dargebracht von Schülern und Freunden. Heidelberg, C. Winter, 1952. 182 p. 13 plates. 25cm.

Title transliterated: Hermēneia.
Bibliographical footnotes.
Contents.— Die homerische Gleichniswelt und die kretisch-mykenische Kunst, von W. (Continued)
NN# R 2.54 OC PC,1 2 SL (Z1,LC1,X1)

Ἑρμηνεία; Festschrift Otto Regenbogen zum 60. Geburststag... (Card 2)

Schadewaldt.— Das Dämonische in der griechischen Kunst, von K. Schefold.— Eine attischrotfigurige Kotyle aus Heidelberger Privatbesitz, von R. Herbig.— Zur Eschatologie in Pindars zweiter olympischer Ode, von R. Hampe.— Das Tragikomische und das Wort νεανικῶς, von G. Björck.— Die Simonides-Interpretation in Platons Protagoras, von E.

(Continued)

Ἑρμηνεία; Festschrift Otto Regenbogen zum 60. Geburststag... (Card 3)

Gundert.— Diokles von Karystos und Aristoxenos von Tarent über die Prinzipien, von W. Jaeger.— Das Prooemium von Ciceros Tusculanen, von R. Harder.— Ohnmacht und Macht des musischen Menschen, von F. Klingner.— Horazens Willkommengruss an einen Spätheimkehrer, von V. Pöschl.— Stoische Haltung nach Mark Aurel, von W. Siegfried.— Frühe Apologetik und Platonismus, von W. Schmid.
1. Classical literature—Hist. and crit.
2. Regenbogen, Otto, 1891- i. [Title] Hermēneia.

E-12
4782
Herr, Richard, *ed.*
Ideas in history; essays presented to Louis Gottschalk by his former students. Edited by Richard Herr and Harold T. Parker. Durham, N. C., Duke University Press, 1965.
xx, 380 p. 25 cm.

Contents.—Introduction, by H. T. Parker.—The great inversion: America and Europe in the eighteenth-century revolution, by R. R. Palmer.—Utopia in modern Western thought: The metamorphosis of an idea, by L. C. Tihany.—Toward the history of the common (Continued)
NN • R 11.65 e/ OC, I PC, 1, 2, I SL (LC1, X1, Z1)
[I]

HERR, RICHARD, ed. Ideas in history... (Card 2)

man: Voltaire and Condorcet, by K. J. Weintraub.—A temperate crusade: The Philosophe campaign for Protestant toleration, by G. Adams.—French administrators and French scientists during the old regime and the early years of the Revolution, by H. T. Parker.—The legend of Voltaire and the cult of the Revolution, 1791, by R. O. Rockwood.—Robespierre, Rousseau, and representation, by G. H. McNeil.—Good, evil, and Spain's rising against Napoleon, by R. Herr.—The liberals and Madame de Staël in 1818, by E. Cappadocia.—The haunted house of Jeremy Bentham, by G. Himmelfarb.—Isabel II and the cause of constitutional monarchy, by J. E. Fagg.—The myth of counterrevolution in France, 1870-1914, by E. R. Tan- (Continued)

HERR, RICHARD, ed. Ideas in history... (Card 3)

nenbaum.—The dissolution of German historism, by G. G. Iggers.—Natural rights: The Soviet and the "Bourgeois" Diderot, by G. B. Carson, Jr.—Conclusion, by R. Herr.—Writings of Louis Gottschalk (p. [376]-380)

1. Gottschalk, Louis Reichenthal, 1899- . 2. History, Modern--Addresses, essays, lectures. I. Parker, Harold Talbot, 1907- , joint ed.

HERRMANN, JOHANNES, 1880- ed. Festschrift... (Card 2)

CONTENTS.—Ephod und Choschen, ein Beitrag zur Entwicklungsgeschichte des hohepriesterlichen Ornats, von K. Elliger.—Die Bewältigung heidnischer Vorstellungen u. Praktiken in der Welt des Alten Testaments, von J. Fichtner.—Überlieferung und Wandlung der Hioblegende, von G. Fohrer.—Palästinische Bezüge im Buche Kohelet, von H. W. Hertzberg.—Zur Frage der Wertung und der Geltung alttestamentlicher Texte, von F. Hesse.—Die Reform des Josia, von A. Jepsen.—Die Selbstliebe nach Leviticus 19, 18, von F. Maass.—Stilistische Bemerkungen zu einem angeblichen Auszug aus der "Geschichte der Könige von Juda," von R. Meyer.—"Siebzig Jahre," von O. Plöger.—

(Continued)

F-10
9495

Herrlau, Harry H 1896- *ed.*
Zeitenwende im Verkehr. [Festschrift für Dr. Wolfhart Schlichting zur Vollendung des 60. Lebensjahres am 1. März 1963] Hamburg, Deutscher Verkehrs-Verlag [1963]
304 p. 27 cm.
Bibliographical footnotes.
CONTENTS.—Zeitenwende im Verkehr, von H. H. Herrlau.—Grundsätze heutiger und zukünftiger Verkehrspolitik, von H.-C. Seebohm.—Auf Dem Wege zur Liberalisierung? Von P. Berkenkopf.—Die Stellung des deutschen Spediteurs im Wandel der Zeiten, von F. Gerlach.—Seehäfen und Seehafenverkehrswirtschaft in der wirtschaftlichen Entwicklung Europas, von L. L. V. Jolmes.—Der Umschichtungsprozess im Verkehr, von H. Jürgensen.—Die Emanzipation des Verkehrs, von W. Linden.—Vom nationalen zum Europas-Güter-
(Continued)

NN * R 11.64 c/5 OC, Ib* PC, 1, 2 SL E, 1, 2 ST, 1t, 2 (LC1, X1, Z1) 3

HERRMANN, JOHANNES, 1880- , ed. Festschrift... (Card 3)

Jesaja 14, 1-23, von G. Quell.—Die Wohnstätte des Zeugnisses, von L. Rost.—Jesaja 23, 1-14, von W. Rudolph.—Erwägungen zu Psalm 110 auf dem Hintergrund von 1. Sam. 21, von H. J. Stoebe.—Die Chronologie des Richterbuches, von W. Vollborn. — Bibliographie Friedrich Baumgärtel, von F. Hesse (p. [197]-200)

1. Bible. O.T. 2. Baumgärtel, Friedrich, 1888-

Herrlau, Harry H 1896- *ed.* Zeitenwende im Verkehr. [1963] (Card 2)

CONTENTS—Continued.

kraftverkehr, von O. Linder.—Soziale Marktwirtschaft und Verkehr, von O. Most.—Eine Europa-Eisenbahngesellschaft? Von H. M. Oefterlng.—Zukunftsfragen des Luftverkehrs, von H. Orlovius.—Der Mensch im Verkehr, von W. Pischel.—Verkehr, Schrittmacher der wirtschaftlichen Entwicklung, von A. Predöhl.—Internationale Spedition gestern, heute, morgen, von W. M. Rademacher.—Leben wir in einer Verkehrswende? Von H. St. Seidenfus.—Europäische Verkehrsintegration, von L. Schaus.—Zur Wettbewerbsordnung im Verkehr, von F. J. Schroiff.—Zu technisch neuen Ufern, eine Gemeinschaftsarbeit des Redaktionsstabes der DVZ mit Verkehrspraktikern.

(Continued)

Write on slip, name, year, vol., page of magazine and class mark — *EP

Herrn Dr. Fritz Sarasin zur Vollendung des siebenzigsten Lebensjahres am 3. Dezember 1929 gewidmet.

(Naturforschende Gesellschaft in Basel. Verhandlungen. Basel, 1929. 8°. Bd. 40, Teil 2, p. 1-625. plates, ports.)

form 400a [ii-7-29 25m]

HERRLAU, HARRY H., 1896- , ed. Zeitenwende im Verkehr. (Card 3)

1. Transportation--Social and economic relations. 2. Schlichting, Wolfhart. I. Herrlau, Harry H., 1896- t. 1963.

E-11
6934

HERZFELD, HANS, 1892-
Ausgewählte Aufsätze, dargebracht als Festgabe zum siebzigsten Geburtstage von seinen Freunden und Schülern. Berlin, W. de Gruyter, 1962. ix, 460 p. 24cm.

"Bibliographie Hans Herzfeld" (p. [417] -460) prepared by Werner Schochow.

1. Germany--Hist.--Addresses, essays, lectures. 2. Germany--Hist.--Historiography. 3. Berlin question (1945-). 4. Herzfeld, Hans, 1892- --Bibl. I. Schochow, Werner.

NN R 4.63 g/B OC, I, Ib+ PC, 1, 2, 3, 4, I SL E, 3, 4, I (LC1, X1, Z1)

AE-10
390

Herrmann, Johannes, 1880- *ed.*
Festschrift, Friedrich Baumgärtel zum 70. Geburtstag, 14. Januar 1958, gewidmet von den Mitarbeitern am Kommentar zum Alten Testament (KAT) Überreicht von Johannes Herrmann. Für den Druck hrsg. von Leonhard Rost. Erlangen [Universitätsbund Erlangen; Auslieferung: Universitätsbibliothek Erlangen] 1959.
200 p. 24 cm. (Erlanger Forschungen. Reihe A: Geisteswissenschaften, Bd. 10)
Bibliographical footnotes.

(Continued)

NN * 5.63 e/ OC PC, 1, 2 SL (LC1, X1, Z1) 3

E-11
9871

HESS, GERHARD, 1907- , ed.
Eine Freundesgabe der Wissenschaft für Ernst Hellmut Vits zur Vollendung seines 60. Lebensjahres am 19. September 1963, von Anton Antweiler [et al.] Frankfurt am Main, F. Knapp [1963] 279 p. illus., port. 25cm.

Bibliographical footnotes.
CONTENTS. —Der Fortschritt der Wissenschaft geht oft seltsame Wege.
(Continued)

NN R 5.64 g/A OC PC, 1, 2, 3 SL ST, 1, 3t (LC1, X1, Z1) [I] 4

HESS, GERHARD, 1907- , ed. Eine Freundesgabe der Wissenschaft für Ernst Hellmut Vits... (Card 2)

von O. Hahn. —Die Methode der Theologie, von A. Antweiler. —Zur Lage der naturwissenschaftlichen Forschung in der Bundesrepublik Deutschland, von A. Butenandt. —Verantwortung der Wissenschaft und Forschung, von G. Domagk. —Klinik und Forschung, von E. K. Frey. —Geist und Geld, von W. Gerlach. —Anpassung an die moderne technische Entwicklung, von W. Heisenberg. —Wissenschaft und Gesellschaft, von G. Hess. —Erziehungs-und Forschungsausgaben im wirtschaftlichen Wachstumsprozess, von W. G. Hoffmann. —Zweckbau und (Continued)

HESS, GERHARD, 1907- , ed. Eine Freundesgabe der Wissenschaft für Ernst Hellmut Vits... (Card 3)

Monument; zu Friedrich Schinkels Museum am Berliner Lustgarten, von H. Kauffmann. —Eine technische Entwicklung als gemeinsames Ziel, von K. Klöppel. —"Geld und Geist" im Kult des alten Israel, von M. Noth. —Mensch und informationsverarbeitender Automat, von H. Piloty. --Gedanken zur Verantwortung der Rechtswissenschaft, von L. Raiser. —Technik und biologisches Denken, von T. von Uexküll. —Die Verantwortung des Vorstandes der Aktiengesellschaft, von H. Westermann. (Continued)

HESS, GERHARD, 1907- , ed. Eine Freundesgabe der Wissenschaft für Ernst Hellmut Vits... (Card 4)

1. Vits, E. H., 1903- . 2. Civilization--Addresses, essays, lectures. 3. Science--Essays and misc. t. 1963

E-13
2281

Hess, Gerhard, 1907–
Gesellschaft, Literatur, Wissenschaft. Gesammelte Schriften 1938–1966. Hrsg. von Hans Robert Jauss und Claus Müller-Daehn. München, W. Fink, 1967.

xiv, 344 p. front. 25 cm.

Published to honor the author on the occasion of his 60th birthday.
"Schriftenverzeichnis Gerhard Hess": p. [345]–347.
Bibliographical footnotes.

1. Literature--Addresses, essays, lectures.

NN * 5.68 1/$_R$OC PC, 1 SL (LC1, X1, Z1) [I]

F-11
473

HEURLINSKA SKOLAN, Turku, Finland. Föreningen Heurlinska skolan i Åbo.
Heurlinska skolan i Åbo; en minnesskrift. [Åbo] 1961. 332 p. illus., ports. 26cm.

"Gunvor Söderling fick i uppdrag att författa och redigera...arbete[t]"
"Göta Tegengren: Matrikel över lärare och elever i Heurlinska skolan i Åbo," p. [105]-315.

(Continued)

NN 6.65 e/ (OC)I, Ib+, II, IIb+ OS(1b) PC, 1, 2, 3, I, II SL E, 2 RC, 2, 3 (LC1, X1, Z1)

HEURLINSKA SKOLAN, Turku, Finland. Föreningen Heurlinska skolan i Åbo. Heurlinska skolan i Åbo... (Card 2)

1. Woman--Education--Indiv. inst.--Finland--Turku. 2. Woman--Biog. --Finland. 3. Finland--Biog. I. Söderling, Gunvor Sigrid Maria, 1908- . II. Tegengren, Göta Maria (Hagerlund), 1909- .

HEUSS, THEODOR, pres. Germany (Federal republic) 1884- . Bei Gelegenheit... (Card 2)

"'Festgabe' der Papierfabrik des Bruderhauses in Reutlingen zu ihrem Hundertjahr-Jubiläum."

I. Kaufmann, Friedrich, ed. II. Leins, Hermann, ed. III. Papierfabrik zum Bruderhaus, Reutlingen.

D-15
4961

HEUSS, THEODOR, pres. Germany (Federal republic). 1884-
Bei Gelegenheit... "Ausseramtliche, gelöste, nebenstündliche Produkte." [Hrsg. von Friedrich Kaufmann und Hermann Leins. Tübingen, R. Wunderlich Verlag] 1961. 198 p. 22cm.

Collected speeches, essays, etc.

(Continued)

NN R 10.64 a/$_L$ OC, I, II (OS) III, IIIb+ PC, I, II, III SL E, III (LC1, X1, Z1)

---

*MGA

HEUSSNER, HORST, ed.
Festschrift Hans Engel zum siebzigsten Geburtstag. Kassel, New York, Bärenreiter-Verlag [1964] 464 p. music, port. 23cm.

"Hans Engel: Bibliographie": p. [11]-39.
Bibliographical footnotes.

1. Music--Essays. 2. Essays. 3. Engel, Hans, 1894- 4. Engel, Hans --Bibl.
NN S 3.68 a/$_R$OC PC, 1, 3, 4 SL MU, 2, 3, 4 (LC1, X1, Z1)

D-17
878

Hibbard, George Richard, *ed.*
Renaissance and modern essays. Presented to Vivian de Sola Pinto in celebration of his seventieth birthday. Edited by G. R. Hibbard, with the assistance of George A. Panichas and Allan Rodway. New York, Barnes & Noble [1966]

viii, 235 p. port. 23 cm.

Bibliographical footnotes.

1. English literature--Addresses, essays, lectures. 2. Pinto, Vivian de Sola, 1895-
NN * R 1.67 1/$_C$ OC PC, 1, 2 SL (LC1, X1, Z1)

E-11
5071

HIETSCH, OTTO, ed.
Österreich und die angelsächsische Welt; Kulturbegegnungen und Vergleiche. [Ministerialrat Dr. Karl Baschiera zum sechzigsten Geburtstag] Wien, W. Braumüller [1961] xii, 620 p. illus., ports., facsims. 24cm.

Contributions in German or English.
Bibliographical footnotes.
1. Baschiera, Karl. 2. Austria--Relations, General, with Gt. Br. 3. Great Britain--Relations, General, with Austria. I. Hietsch, Otto.
NN R 8.62 a/ OC, Ib+, Ib+ PC, 1, 2, 3 SL E, 2, 3 (LC1, X1, Z1) [I]

NIV

Hilsen til Jacob Paludan paa Halvtredsaarsdagen den 7. Februar 1946. Med en Bibliografi af Børge Benthien. København, S. Hasselbalch, 1946. 130 p. illus., port. 27cm.

"Redigeret af Orla Lundbo."

422320B. 1. Paludan, Jacob, 1896- . I. Benthien, Børge. II. Lundbo, Orla, 1909- , ed.
N. Y. P. L. February 17, 1948

E-12
4441

Hilles, Frederick Whiley, 1900- *ed.*
From sensibility to romanticism; essays presented to Frederick A. Pottle, edited by Frederick W. Hilles and Harold Bloom. New York, Oxford University Press, 1965.
vi, 585 p. illus., ports. 24 cm.
"Selected bibliography of Frederick A. Pottle": p. 561-566. Includes bibliographical references.
1. Poetry, English--Hist. and crit., 18th cent. 2. Poetry, English--Hist. and crit., 19th cent. 3. Romanticism in literature, English. 4. Pottle, Frederick Albert, 1897- . I. Bloom, Harold, joint ed. II. Title.
NN* R 10.65 g/ OC, I, II PC, 1, 2, 3, 4, I, II SL (LC1, X1, Z1) [I]

MCZ
L 32.M3

En Hilsen til Johannes Larsen paa 80-aars dagen. [Redigeret af Tage la Cour og Aage Marcus] København, Gyldendal, 1947.
121 p. illus., ports. (part col.) 25 cm.
"Litteratur": p. [64]

1. Larsen, Johannes, 1867- I. La Cour, Tage, ed.
N7023.L35L3 48-23919*
Library of Congress [1]

JFE
71-153

Hilsen til Hæstrup. 9. august 1969. Odense, Odense Universitetsforlag, 1969.
364 p. 24 cm.
Bibliographical footnotes.
CONTENTS.—Hilsen til Hæstrup, af P. Bagge.—Dansk illegal nyhetsförmedling till Sverige från 1940 till sommaren 1943, af G. Barke.—The First British Military Mission to Tito, by F. W. Deakin.—Sønner af de slagne, af T. Fink.—Holland og Auschwitz, af L. de Jong.—Antikominterndemonstrationerne i november 1941, af H.
(Continued)
NN * R 4.71 b/OC PC, 1, 2 SL (LC1, X1, Z1)

E-10
7297

HILSEN til Otto Gelsted [ved Kjeld Abell et al.; samlet og udg. af en kreds af venner i anledning af digterens 70 års dag den 4. nov. 1958. Redigeret af Børge Houmann og Hans Kirk. København, 1958]
165, [1] p. illus., port., music. 24cm.

Bibliography of Gelsted's works, p. [115-166]

1. Gelsted, Otto, 1888- . I. Houmann, Børge, ed. II. Kirk, Hans, 1898- , ed. III. Abell, Kjeld, 1901- .
NN 4.59 l/ OC, I, II, III PC, 1, I, II, III SL (LC1, X1, Z1)

HILSEN til Hæstrup. 9. august 1969. (Card 2)

Kirchhoff.—Adelige herregårdsregnskaber fra 1600-tallet, af E. L. Petersen.—USAs rekvisition af danske skibe i 1941, af F. Løkkegaard.—Omkring Bankkommissionen af 21. september 1922, af S. Mørch.—En fiktion bliver til, af H. S. Nissen.—Et vidne—en tolk—og 10 journalister, af H. Poulsen.—Jurisdiktionsspørgsmålet fra 9. april 1940 indtil sommeren 1942, af L. Rasmussen.—Folketingets beslutning af 19. januar 1940, af V. Sjøqvist.—Norge i stormaktsstrategien, af M. Skodvin.—Danmarks besættelse i efterkrigstidens historiebøger, af R. Skovmand.—Om Frit Danmark's opgaver ved besættelsestidens ophør, af H. Snitker.—Konvoj SL 125, af C. Tortzen.—Jødeforfølgelsens metoder, af L. Yahil.—Bibliografi (p. [352]-354)

1. Hæstrup, Jorgen, 1909- . 2. Denmark--Hist.--German occupation, 1940-1945.

E-12
4556

HILSMAN, ROGER, 1919- , ed.
Foreign policy in the sixties: the issues and the instruments; essays in honor of Arnold Wolfers, edited by Roger Hilsman and Robert C. Good. Baltimore, Johns Hopkins Press [1965]
xii, 299 p. port. 24 cm.
Bibliographical footnotes.
CONTENTS.—The contemporary arena: The cold war and the changing Communist world, by R. L. Garthoff. Europe and the future of
(Continued)
NN* R 10.65 g/ OC, I PC, 1, 2, 3, I SL E, 1, 2, 3, I (LC1, X1, Z1)

*C-4 p.v.140

Hilsen til J. Christian Bay paa firsaarsdagen, 12. oktober 1951. København, Rosenkilde og Bagger, 1951. 67 p. illus., map. 23cm.

Bibliographies included.

1. Bay, Jens Christian, 1871- 2. Steno, Nicolaus, bp., 1638-1686. 3. Caves. 4. Denmark. Det Kongelige bibliotek, Copenhagen.
NN OC PC, 1, 2, 3, 4 SL ST, 2 3 (LC1, Z1, X1)

HILSMAN, ROGER, 1919- , ed. Foreign policy in the sixties... (Card 2)

the Grand Alliance, by L. W. Martin. Colonial legacies to the postcolonial states, by R. C. Good. Nonalignment reassessed: the experience of India, by C. H. Heimsath. The changing United Nations, by H. K. Jacobson.—The instrumentalities of foreign policy: The foreign aid instrument: search for reality, by L. W. Pye. Political development: varieties of political change and U. S. policy, by W. H. Wriggins. The intelligence arm: the Cuban missile crisis, by F. Greene. The U. N. as a foreign policy instrument: the Congo crisis, by E. W. Lefever. The new diplomacy: the 1955 Geneva summit meeting, by P. C. Davis. Orchestrating the instrumentalities: the

(Continued)

HILSMAN, ROGER, 1919-   , ed. Foreign policy in the sixties... (Card 3)

case of Southeast Asia, by R. Hilsman.—Statecraft and moral theory: the perennial issues: Balance of power as a perennial factor: French motives in the Franco-Soviet Pact, by W. E. Scott. The role of political style: a study of Dean Acheson, by D. S. McLellan. Political necessity and moral principle in the thought of Friedrich Meinecke, by R. W. Sterling. National interest and moral theory: the "debate" among contemporary realists, by R. C. Good.

(Continued)

HILSMAN, ROGER, 1919-   , ed. Foreign policy in the sixties... (Card 4)

1. Wolfers, Arnold, 1892-   . 2. World politics, 1945-   . 3. International relations--Addresses, essays, lectures. I. Good, Robert Crocker, joint ed.

E-11
7229

HILTMANN, HILDEGARD, ed.
Dialektik und Dynamik der Person; Festschrift für Robert Heiss zum 60. Geburtstag am 22. Januar 1963 [hrsg. von Hildegard Hiltmann und Franz Vonessen. Köln] Kiepenheuer & Witsch, 1963. 314 p. illus., port. 24cm.

Includes bibliographical references.

(Continued)

NN 7.63 f/ OC, I, II, IIIbo PC, 1, 2, I, II SL (LC1, X1, Z1)
[I]

HILTMANN, HILDEGARD, ed. Dialektik und Dynamik der Person... (Card 2)

CONTENTS.--Zur Regelkreis-Dynamik psychischer Funktionen, von H. Selbach.--Die Intelligenz als psychodynamische Funktion, von K. J. Groffmann.--Die klinische Bedeutung der verbalen und der nichtverbalen Intelligenz, von H. Hiltmann und D. Bäseler.--Die "doppelte Darbietung" des Zullinger-Testes, von H. Zulliger.--Konflikt und Persönlichkeit, von K.-H. Wewetzer.--"Wunderheilungen" im affektiven Feld, von H. Bender.--Bewusstmachung, von C. Bondy.--Das dialektische Denken in der

(Continued)

HILTMANN, HILDEGARD, ed. Dialektik und Dynamik der Person... (Card 3)

Psychoanalyse, von W. Schraml.--Raum und Zeit als Valenzsysteme, von E. E. Boesch.--Personale Identität und das sogenannte brainwashing, von P. R. Hofstätter.--Psychoanalytische Anmerkungen über die Kultureignung des Menschen von A. Mitscherlich.--Kunstbilder und Bilder überhaupt, von C. Linfert.--Zum Phänomen und Begriff der Reflexion bei John Locke, von W. Brock.--Der Platonismus und die Hegelsche Metaphysik, von B. Lakebrink.--Seele und Idee, von K. H. Volkmann-Schluck.-Das Opfer der Götter, von F. Vonessen.--Die Sprache des Schweigens, von W. Weischedel.--Die

(Continued)

HILTMANN, HILDEGARD, ed. Dialektik und Dynamik der Person... (Card 4)

Schriften von Robert Heiss, zusammengestellt von A. Raschke und L. Michel (p. 305-312).

1. Heiss, Robert, 1903-   . 2. Psychology--Addresses, essays, lectures. I. Vonessen, Franz, joint ed. II. Title. III. Vonessen, Franz.

AN
(Hindenburg, P.)

Hindenburg-spende.
Paul von Hindenburg als mensch, staatsmann, feldherr, von Erich Marcks [und] Ernst von Eisenhart Rothe. Herausgegeben im namen der Hindenburg-spende, von Oskar Karstedt. Berlin, Verlagsanstalt Otto Stollberg, g m b h. [pref. 1932]

222 p., 1 l. incl. plates, ports., facsim. 24cm.
Pages 79-222 are plates.
Letterpress on versos facing the plates.
CONTENTS.—Geleitwort, von Oskar Karstedt.—Hindenburg als feldherr, von Ernst von Eisenhart Rothe.—Hindenburg als mensch und staatsmann, von Erich Marcks.—Sieben jahre reichspräsident.
1. Hindenburg, Paul von, pres. Germany, 1847-   2. Germany—Politics and government—1918-   I. Karstedt, Oskar, 1884-   ed. II. Marcks, Erich, 1861-   III. *Eisenhart Rothe, Ernst von, 1862-

A C 33-734

Title from N. Y. Pub. Libr. Printed by L. C.
[3]

M-11
673
no. 7

HINGST, HANS.
Denkmalschutz und Denkmalpflege in Deutschland. [Freiburg i Br., Staatliches Amt für Ur- und Frühgeschichte, 1964] 175 p. 30cm. (Badische Fundberichte. Sonderheft. 7)

"Karl Asal zum 75. Geburtstag."

1. Monuments--Preservation--Germany. 2. Asal, Karl, 1889-   . I. Series.
NN 10.65 s/ OC(Ibo) (OD)I (ED)I PC, 1, 2, I A, 1, 2 (LC1, X1, Z1)

F-11
1692

HIRANYAGARBHA; a series of articles on the archaeological work and studies of Prof. Dr. F. D. K. Bosch ... to which is added the address delivered by him at his retirement from the University Leiden. Published on the occasion of the 50th anniversary of his doctorate on 14th July 1964. The Hague, Mouton, 1964. 106 p. ports. 27cm.

(Continued)

NN * R 8.66 1/ OC PC, 1 SL O, 1 (LC1, X1, Z1)

HIRANYAGARBHA; a series of articles on the archaeological work and the studies of Prof. Dr. F. D. K. Bosch... (Card 2)

"Bibliographical list of books and articles published by F. D. K. Bosch": p. [95]-106.
Bibliographical footnotes.

1. Bosch, Frederik David Kan, 1887-   .

HCC

Hispanic American essays, a memorial to James Alexander Robertson, edited by A. Curtis Wilgus. Chapel Hill, The University of North Carolina press, 1942.

viii, 391 p. 23½cm.

CONTENTS.—Introduction: The life of James Alexander Robertson, by A. C. Wilgus. The published writings of James Alexander Robertson, by A. C. Wilgus.—The colonial era: Contribution to the history of the colonial ideas in Spain: unpublished documents, by Rafael Altamira. Early Mexican literature, by F. B. Steck. A great prelate and archaeologist, by P. A. Means. Spanish consulados, by C. E. Chapman. Argentine colonial economy, by Madaline W. Nichols. The foundation and early history of the Venezuelan intendencia, by W. W. Pierson. Juan Bautista de Anza in Sonora, 1777–1778, by A. B. Thomas. Spain and the Family compact, 1770–1773, by A. S. Aiton. Florida, frontier out-

(Continued on next card)

42–19322

[10]

Hispanic American essays ... 1942. (Card 2)

CONTENTS—Continued.

post of New Spain, by I. J. Cox.—The independent era: The odyssey of the Spanish archives of Florida, by Irene A. Wright. Diplomatic missions of the United States to Cuba to secure the Spanish archives of Florida, by A. J. Hanna. A Comanche constitutionalist: Miguel Ramos Arizpe, by Lillian E. Fisher. Federal intervention in Mexico, by J. L. Mecham. Justo Rufino Barrios, by J. F. Rippy. Indian labor in Guatemala, by C. L. Jones. Sarmiento and New England, by P. A. Martin. American marines in Nicaragua, 1912–1925, by R. R. Hill. Our present peril in historical perspective, by L. F. Hill.

1. Robertson, James Alexander, 1873–1939. 2. Spanish America—Hist.—Addresses, essays, lectures. I. Wilgus, Alva Curtis, 1897– ed.

42–19322

Library of Congress F1408.R7H5

[10] 980.04

EAH

Historische Aufsaetze; Aloys Schulte zum 70. Geburtstag gewidmet von Schülern und Freunden. Düsseldorf: L. Schwann, 1927. 336 p. front. (port.), illus., map. 8°.

Contains bibliographies.

Contents: Zum 2. August 1927. Verzeichnis der wichtigeren Schriften Aloys Schultes. WOLFRAM, G. Zur Geschichte der Einführung des Christentums. AUBIN, H. Zum Übergang von der Römerzeit zum Mittelalter. STEINBACH, F. Gewanndorf und Einzelhof. LEVISON, W. Zur Geschichte des Klosters Tholey. BEYERLE, K. Das Briefbuch Walahfrid Strabos. SANTE, G. W. Die deutsche Westgrenze im 9. und 10. Jahrhundert. AMMANN, H. Die wirtschaftliche Bedeutung der Schweiz im Mittelalter. TUMBÜLT, G. Gründung, Recht und Verfassung der Stadt Wolfach im

(Continued)

Mr. Moth

N. Y. P. L. June 21, 1928

Historische Aufsätze; Aloys Schulte zum 70. Geburtstag... (Continued)

Kinzigtal. KALLEN, G. Das Gandersheimer Vogtweistum von 1188. HASHAGEN, J. Gottesgnadentum und Kirchenregiment im Mittelalter. STRIEDER, J. Deutscher Metallwarenexport nach Westafrika im 16. Jahrhundert. VOLK, P. Das Seminar der Bursfelder Benediktinerkongregation zu Köln. RHEINDORF, K. Zur französischen Aussenpolitik des Jahres 1656. LUCKWALDT, F. Friedrichs des Grossen Anschauungen. BRAUBACH, M. Das Domkapitel zu Münster. WOHLERS, G. Der Flugschriftenkampf um das Rheinische Recht 1816–1817. SCHNÜTGEN, A. Die Frage der katholischen Feiertage in Rheinpreussen in der Ära Altenstein. HERRMANN, A. Regierung und Presse am Rhein im Vormärz. PLATZHOFF, W. Zum Frankfurter Frieden. BEYERHAUS, G. Bismarck und Kaiser Friedrichs Tagebuch. KIRCH, P. Der Marnefeldzug 1914.

351488A. 1. Schulte, Aloys, 1857– . 2. Germany—Hist.—Addresses, essays, lectures.

N. Y. P. L. June 21, 1928

F-10
5462

HISTORISCHE Forschungen und Probleme; Peter Rassow zum 70. Geburtstage dargebracht von Kollegen, Freundin und Schülern, hrsg. von Karl Erich Born. Wiesbaden, Franz-Steiner Verlag, 1961. 373 p. port. 26cm.

Bibliographical footnotes.

CONTENTS. --Theoderichs Gepidensieg im Winter 488/489, von H. Löwe. --Die rheinischen Lande an der Schwelle der deutschen Geschichte,

(Continued)

NN X 4, 61 p/# OC. I PC. 1, 2. I SL (LC1, X1, Z1)

4

HISTORISCHE Forschungen und Probleme... (Card2)

von T. Schieffer. --Mercaderes, artesanos y paños en Castilla (Segovia 1518-1550) por R. Carande. --Waldeck im Dreissigjährigen Kriege, von F. Seidel. --Die Moskauer Landesversammlung, von G. Stökl. --Das Bild des Bürgers in der Auseinandersetzung zwischen Christian Thomasius und August Hermann Francke, von C. Hinrichs. --"Le Diable;" ein Mentor Friedrichs des Grossen als Agent des Prinzen Eugen, von M. Braubach. --Der politische Ancient-Modern-Streit im England des 18. Jahrhunderts, von K. Kluxen. --Zwischen Berlin und Madrid. Preussisch-spanische Verbindungen im Zeitalter des aufgeklärten Absolutismus, von R. Konetzke. --

(Continued)

HISTORISCHE Forschungen und Probleme... (Card 3)

Ein „sehr wichtiger Brief," aus der Jugend Kaiser Leopolds II. von A. Wandruszka. --Vom aufgeklärten Absolutismus zum Liberalismus; die politischen Ideen des französischen Reformministers Turgot, von K. E. Born. --Über das Wesen der amerikanischen „Revolution," von E. C. Engel. --Schiller als Historiker, von T. Schieder. --Stein und Adam Smith, von G. Schmölders. --Ranke und die Politik, von O. Vossler. --Die asiatische Welt im Denken von Karl Marx und Friedrich Engels, von K. D. Erdmann. --Österreich, Preussen und die augustenburgische Presse in der zweiten Hälfte des Jahres 1865, von H. Segall. --Der Kulturbegriff Nietzsches, von H. M. Klinkenberg.

(Continued)

HISTORISCHE Forschungen und Probleme... (Card 4)

--Alexis de Tocqueville und die Vereinigten Staaten von heute, von D. Gerhard. --Pearl Harbor und der Eintritt der Vereinigten Staaten in den zweiten Weltkrieg, von J. Engel.

1. Rassow, Peter, 1889- 2. History--Addresses, essays, lectures. I. Born, Karl Erich, ed.

Copy only words underlined
& classmark-- GDXM

HISTORISCHE GESELLSCHAFT DES KANTONS AARGAU. Biographisches Lexikon des Aargaus, 1803-1957. Redaktion: Otto Mittler und Georg Boner. Aarau, H. R. Sauerländer, 1958. 936 p. 24cm. (ITS: Argovia; Jahreschrift der historischen Gesellschaft. Bd. 68/69)

"150 Jahre Kanton Aargau; Jubiläumsgabe der Historischen Gesellschaft. Bd. 2."

1. Aargau, Switzerland (Canton)--Biog.--Dictionaries. I. Mittler, Otto, ed. II. Boner, Georg, 1908- , ed. III. Title.

NN R 5.59 1/#(OC)I, II, III OS OI PC, 1, I, II, III (LC5, X1, Z1)

BAC

Historisch gezelschap, The Hague.

Historische opstellen, aangeboden aan J. Huizinga op 7 December 1942, door het Historisch gezelschap te 's-Gravenhage. Haarlem, H. D. Tjeenk Willink & zoon, 1948. 278 p. illus. 24cm.

Bibliographies included.

CONTENTS.—Brummel, L. Jacob Boehme en het 17e eeuwsche Amsterdam.—Bijlsma, R. Mr François Fagel, griffier der Staten-generaal, tijdens zijn laatste levensjaren (1743).—Rollin Couquerque, L. M. Hollands rechtspraak in strafzaken

(Continued)

N. Y. P. L. November 7, 1949

Historisch gezelschap, The Hague. Historische opstellen...
(Card 2)

ten tijde van de Republiek der Vereenigde Nederlanden.—Gelder, H. E. van. Bijkomstigheden.—Enno van Gelder, H. A. De vrede van Gent (8 November 1576).—Hille, G. E. W. van. Atheners en Macedoniërs.—Kan, J. van. Een vroegtijdig kampioen voor het inheemsch volksrecht.—Kuyk, J. van. Vorstelijke reizen in ouden tijd.—Locher, T. J. G. Rusland en het Westen in de ogen der oudere Slavophilen.—Martin, W. Een wetenschappelijk bloemstuk voor Leiden's Hortus.—Smit, H. J. De armenwet van 1854 en haar voorgeschiedenis.—Warnsinck, J. C. M. De memorie van Cornelis de Schepper van den 12-den Februari 1552 over de verdediging van Holland, Zeeland en Vlaanderen, in den oorlog tegen Frankrijk.

481660B. 1. Huizinga, Johan, 1872–1945. 2. History—Addresses, essays, lectures. I. Title.
N. Y. P. L. November 7, 1949

BAP

Historische kring, Leiden.
Varia historica, aangeboden aan professor doctor A.W. Byvanck ter gelegenheid van zijn zeventigste verjaardag door de Historische kring te Leiden. Assen, Van Gorcum, 1954. 285 p. illus.,port. 26cm.

Bibliographical footnotes.
Contents.--De Hebreeën in Egypte, van A. de Buck.—Over farao Bocchoris, van J.M.A. Janssen.—
(Continued)

NN**R 12.55 j/, OS (1b) PC,1,2,I SL (Z1, LC1,X1) [I]

Historische kring, Leiden. Varia historica...
(Card 2)

De Chaldeeuwse dynastie, van F.M. Th. de Liagre Bohl.—Over kunst en wereldbeschouwing der Kelten, van P. Lambrechts.--Het pronkzilver uit de eerste eeuw na Christus, van L. Byvanck-Quarles van Ufford.—Porphyrius als historicus in zijn strijd tegen het Christendom, van W. den Boer.—Iets over zeereizen der Chinezen, van J.J.L. Duyvendak.—"Les terreurs de l'an Mil,"van F.W.N. Hugenholtz.—Een verdwenen dorp? Zwieten bij Leiden, van S.J. Fockema Andreae.—
(Continued)

Historische kring, Leiden. Varia historica...
(Card 3)

Kruisridderburchten in het Midden-Oosten,van A. A. Kampman.—Bonaventura Vulcanius en Leiden, van J.N. Bakhuizen van den Brink.—Het Nederlands hulpeskader voor Portugal [1641], van T.H. Milo.—De reis van Sir Joshua Reynolds in de Nederlanden, van W.R. Juynboll.—Aantekeningen over de industriële revolutie in Engeland, van I.J. Brugmans.—Een schakel in de ontwikkeling van de cyclische geschiedopvatting, van Th. J.G. Locher.—De afstand der Nederlandse
(Continued)

Historische kring, Leiden. Varia historica...
(Card 4)

bezittingen ter kuste van Guinea aan Engeland in 1872, van A.M.P. Mollema.—Over Willem Pijper, Spel van emotie en intellect, van E.W. Schallenberg.—De illegale actie voor de eenheidsvakbeweging in historisch perspectief, van A.J.C. Rüter.

1. Byvanck, Alexander Willem, 1884- 2. Civilization—Addresses, essays, lectures. I. Title.

BAC

Historische Untersuchungen. Ernst Förstemann zum fünfzigjährigen Doctorjubiläum gewidmet von der Historischen Gesellschaft zu Dresden. Leipzig: B. G. Teubner, 1894. vi, 142 p. 8°.

Contents: DIESTEL, G. Anrede. BÜTTNER-WOBST, T. Der daphneische Apollo des Bryaxis. POLAND, F. Öffentliche Bibliotheken in Griechenland und Kleinasien. LINCKE, A. Wo lag Bechten? MELTZER, O. Der Kriegshafen in Karthago. HULTSCH, F. Das elfte Problem des mathematischen Papyrus von Akhmim. KAEMMEL, O. Zur Entwicklungsgeschichte der weltlichen Grundherrschaften in den deutschen Südostmarken während des 10. und 11. Jahrhunderts. MANITIUS, M. Über eine sächsische Geschichtstradition aus der Zeit Heinrichs IV. LIPPERT, W.

(Continued)

N. Y. P. L. January 30, 1931

Historische Untersuchungen... (Card 2)

Über das Geschützwesen der Wettiner im 14. Jahrhundert. LOBECK, O. Der X. Brief des Flavius Blondus. MÜLLER, G. Johann Erhard Kapp als Professor an der Universität Leipzig. RACHEL, P. Zur Belagerung von Danzig 1807. DIESTEL, G. Kurzgefasstes Jahrbuch der Historischen Gesellschaft zu Dresden; Mitgliederverzeichnis.

1. Foerstemann, Ernst Wilhelm, 1822–1906. 2. History—Addresses, essays, lectures. I. Historische Gesellschaft zu Dresden. II. Diestel, Gustav, editor.
N. Y. P. L. January 30, 1931

Write on slip words underlined below and class mark —
GDXD

Historischer Verein des Kantons St. Gallen.
Studien zur St. Gallischen Geschichte; Festschrift zur Feier seines 75jährigen Bestandes, herausgegeben vom Historischen Verein des Kantons St. Gallen. St. Gallen: Fehr, 1934. 326 p. illus. (facsims., maps), plates. 23½cm. (Its: Mitteilungen zur vaterländischen Geschichte. [Bd.] 39.)

Each contribution has also separate paging.
Bibliographies included.
Bibliographical footnotes.

(Continued)

N. Y. P. L. October 18, 1935

Historischer Verein des Kantons St. Gallen. Studien zur St. Gallischen Geschichte... (Card 2)

CONTENTS.—Der Historische Verein des Kantons St. Gallen, 1909–1934. Von W. Ehrenzeller.—Der Stand der prähistorischen Forschung im Kanton St. Gallen. Von H. Bessler.—Die Befreiungsgeschichte der drei Länder und der Appenzellerkrieg. Von T. Schiess.—Zur örtlichen und zeitlichen Bestimmung von Wittenweilers "Ring." Von H. Edelmann.—Athanas Gugger, 1608–1669, und die theatergeschichtliche Bedeutung des Klosters St. Gallen im Zeitalter des Barock. Von J. A. Bischof.—Briefe des Landammans Gallus Jakob Baumgartner zur Zeit des Sonderbundes von 1844–1848. Von E. Kind.—Die Buchdruckerei des Klosters St. Gallen 1633–1800. Von M. Grolig.

1. St. Gallen, Switzerland (Canton)—Hist. 2. Societies, Historical—Switzerland. I. Title. II. Ser.
N. Y. P. L. October 18, 1935

Copy only words underlined & classmark — FHP

HISTORISCHER VEREIN FÜR STEIERMARK, Gratz.
Luschin-Festschrift, hrsg. vom Ausschusse des Historischen Vereines für Steiermark mit Unterstützung durch das Bundesministerium für Unterricht, das Land Steiermark, die Landeshauptstadt Graz, die Rechts- und staatswissenschaftliche und die Philosophische Fakultät des Universität Graz, die Steiermark. Sparkasse und die Gemeindesparkasse Graz. Geleitet von Hans Pirchegger. Graz, Kommissions Verlag Leuschner & Lubensky, 1931. 314 p. illus., port. map. 23cm.
(Continued)

NN **R X 7.58 m/, (OC)I, II OS OI PC, 1, I, II (LC4, Z1, X1)

HISTORISCHER VEREIN FÜR STEIERMARK, Gratz.
Luschin-Festschrift... (Card 2)

(ITS: Zeitschrift. Jahrg. 26 (1931)).

"Arnold Luschin-Ebengreuth zum 90. Geburtstag (26. August 1931)."

1. Luschin von Ebengreuth, Arnold, 1841-1932. I. Pirchegger, Hans, 1875- , ed. II. Title.

L-10
2771
no. 8

HISTORISCHER VEREIN FÜR STEIERMARK, Gratz.
Schule und Heimat; Beiträge zur Geschichte und Methodik des Heimatgedankens in der Schule. Hofrat Dr. Anton Adalbert Klein, zur Vollendung des 70. Lebensjahres, dargebracht von seinen Freunden. Schriftleitung; Ferdinand Tremel. Graz, 1964. 104 p. illus., port. 23cm. (ITS: Zeitschrift. Sonderband. 8)

(Continued)

NN R 2.66 a/d (OC)I OS, II PC, 1, 2, 3, I, II E, 2, 3, I (LCl, X1, Z1)

2

HISTORISCHER VEREIN FÜR STEIERMARK, Gratz.
Schule und Heimat. (Card 2)

Bibliography, p. 12-16.

1. Education--Austria--Styria. 2. School and community--Austria--Styria. 3. Klein, Anton Adalbert. I. Tremel, Ferdinand, ed. II. Series.

Copy only words underlined & classmark— FHP

HISTORISCHER VEREIN FÜR STEIERMARK, Gratz.
Zeitschrift... Jahrg. 29, gewidmet vom Lande Steiermark dem verdienstvollen ehemaligen Direktor des Landesarchives Anton Mell zum 70. Geburtstage. Graz, Kommissionsverlag Leuschner & Lubensky, 1935. 263 p. port. 23cm. (ITS: Zeitschrift. Jahrg. 29 (1935))

CONTENTS. — Zur Geschichte der steirischen Masse (1.), von R. Baravalle. — Voitsberg, Schwanberg, von H. Pirchegger. — Zur Geschichte der Preise und Löhne in Steiermark, von F. Mensi. — Die steirische Arsenikesserei in

(Continued)

NN R 10.58 p/H OS OI PC, 1 E, 1 (Z1, LC2, X1)

HISTORISCHER VEREIN FÜR STEIERMARK, Gratz.
Zeitschrift... (Card 2)

geschichtlicher Betrachtung, von F. Byloff. — Der Amtmann und die Holden im Gösser Amte zu Seiersberg bei Strassgang um 1500, von A. Lang. — Die Bewegung der Fleischpreise in Österreich im 16. Jahrhundert, von F. Popelka. — Ausfuhr steirischer Zuchtrinder im 17. und 18. Jahrhundert, besonders nach Südböhmen, von A. Gstirner. — Meisterverzeichnis der steirischen Goldschmiede, von G. Wolfbauer. — Bücherbesprechungen. — Tätigkeitsbericht über das Jahr 1934.

1. Mell, Anton, 1865-

D-15
1487

HISTORISKA studier tillägnade Folke Lindberg, 27 augusti 1963. [Stockholm] Svenska bokförlaget [1963] 211, [1] p. port. 23cm. (Scandinavian university books)

Includes bibliographies.

(Continued)

NN R 5.65 1/B OC PC, 1, 2 SL (LCl, X1, Z1)

4

HISTORISKA studier tillägnade Folke Lindberg, 27 augusti 1963. (Card 2)

CONTENTS. --Biskop Henrik i Linköping och S:t Victor i Paris, av H. Schück. --Ödeläggelsen av Vadstena kungsgård, av B. Fritz. --Hamnskrån, Karl Knutssons och andra, av T. Söderberg. --Maximilian I av Habsburg och Sten Sture den äldre; kring några brev och anteckningar i det tyska riksregistraturet, av K. Kumlien. --Johan III övertar makten i Stockholm, av B. Lager. --Johan III och Hälsinglands landsköpmän år 1573, av R. Matz. --Consilium och consensus; några anteckningar i en statsrättshistorisk principfråga, av S. U. Palme. --De Militära transporterna över Östersjön under stora nordiska krigets första skede 1700-1708, av S. Grauers. --General Adam Ludvig Lewenhaupts berättelse om (Continued)

HISTORISKA studier tillägnade Folke Lindberg, 27 augusti 1963. (Card 3)

fälttåget i Ryssland 1708-09; några synpunkter, av G. T. Westin. --Den graderade röstskalans införande i Stockholm 1765, av T. Höjer. --Den statliga upplåningen i Sverige 1825-1854, av E. Söderlund. --Några avsnitt ur Bishop-Hillkoloniens historia, av K. Ankarberg. --De första folkmötena för en kommunal rösträttsreform, av E. Mellquist. --Adolf Hedin, upprustningsivrare i otakt med tiden, av A. Thulstrup. --Ett förebud till Järnbruksförbundet, av G. Utterström. --Hjalmar Branting och kommunalpolitiken, av U. Larsson. --Ellen Key och Afton-Tidningen; randanteckningar om Strindbergsstriden 1910, av J. Torbacke. --Särskilda (hemliga)

(Continued)

HISTORISKA studier tillägnade Folke Lindberg, 27 augusti 1963. (Card 4)

protokol i utrikesärenden, av A. Kromnow. --Handskriftssamlarna och de svenska arkiven, av B. Broomé. --Folke Lindberhs historia författarskap; bibliografi utarb. av B. Fritz (p. 199-[212])

1. Sweden--Hist. --Addresses, essays, lectures. 2. Lindberg, Folke, 1903-

---

GFD

Historiska studier tillägnade Nils Ahnlund, 23/8/1949. Stockholm, P. A. Norstedt & söner [1949] xxviii, 366 p. maps, port. 23cm.

"Nils Ahnlunds tryckta skrifter 1939-1949, av Wilhelm Odelberg," p. 340-366.

519006B. 1. Ahnlund, Nils Gabriel, 1889- . 2. Sweden—Hist.
N. Y. P. L. July 25, 1950

Historiska studier tillägnade Sven Tunberg den 1 februari 1942. [Uppsala, Almqvist & Wiksells boktryckeri a.-b., 1942] 2 p. l., ix–xxvii, 568 p., 1 l. incl. illus. (incl. maps) geneal. tab. front. (port.) 26½cm.

"Festskriften har redigerats av Adolf Schück och Åke Stille." Bibliographical references in "Noter" at end of each article.

CONTENTS.—Åberg, Nils. Romerska och germanska element i den frankiska kulturutvecklingen under merovingertid.—Hafström, Gerhard. Äldre Västgötalagens "landamæri."—Almquist, J. E. Om formerna för tingsfridens lysning i Sverige under äldre tid.—Kraft, Salomon. Schweiziska edsförbundets uppkomst.—Schück, Adolf. Ängelätten ett bidrag till den uppsvenska aristokratiens historia under folkungatiden.—Kumlien, Kjell. Svenskarna vid utländska universitet under medeltiden.—Tham, Wilhelm. Västra och östra bergen; en granskning av källor och

(Continued on next card)

A 46-3447

[2]

Historiska studier tillägnade Sven Tunberg den 1 februari 1942. [1942] (Card 2)

CONTENTS—Continued.

litteratur.— Ahnlund, Nils. Korner och Engelbrekt.—Sjödin, Lars. Gustav Vasas barndoms- och ungdómstid.—Lindberg, Folke. Daljunkern.—Seth, Ivar. Universitetsförhållanden i Greifswald vid 1600-talets slut.—Etzler, Allan. Zigenarna i svensk krigstjänst.—Fahlborg, Birger. Westaliska folkrättsprinciper och svensk jämviktspolitik.—Grauers, Sven Til belysning av Nystadsfredens verkningar.—Staf, Nils. Gustav III och Norge; Major F. A. U. Funcks resa till Norge 1785.—Forssell, Nils. En konspiratör mot Napoleonväldet; brigadgeneralen Claude-François Malet.—Palmstierna, C. F. Kronprins Oscar och tryckfriheten; en episod från "de menlösa tiderna."—Söderberg, Tom. Varför tilläts "ansvaringar"? En tolkning av bulvanskapets historia.—Almqvist, Daniel. Förborgade dokument.—Andreen, P. G. Till frågan om ett svenskt cen-

(Continued on next card)

A 46-3447

[2]

Historiska studier tillägnade Sven Tunberg den 1 februari 1942. [1942] (Card 3)

CONTENTS—Continued.

traluniversitet, en diskussion på 1820-talet.—Holm, Nils. Svensk försvarspolitik under den dansk-tyska krisen 1863–1864.—Willers, Uno. Den tyska socialdemokratien och kejsarfrågan under höstkrisen 1918.—Willers, Uno. Professor Sven Tunbergs tryckta historiska skrifter (p. [551]–568)

1. Tunberg, Sven August Daniel, 1882– 2. History—Addresses, essays, lectures. 3. Sweden — Hist. — Addresses, essays, lectures. I. Schück, Adolf, 1897– ed. II. Stille, Ake, ed.

A 46-3447

Harvard univ. Library for Library of Congress [2]

HJELMBORG, BJØRN, ed.
Natalicia musicologica, Knud Jeppesen septuagenario collegis oblata. Redigenda curaverunt Bjørn Hjelmborg & Søren Sørensen. Hafniae, W. Hansen, 1962.
318 p. illus., port., music. 27cm.

Contributions in English or German, some in Danish, Italian or French. "Bibliografi fortegnelse over Knud Jeppesens værker...," p. 309-318.

1. Jeppesen, Knud, 1892- 2. Music--Essays. 3. Essays. I. Sørensen, Søren, joint ed. II. Title

NN 7.64 p/OC, I, II PC, 1, 2, I SL MU, 1, 3, I (LC1, X1, Z1)
[I]

Hochschule für die Wissenschaft des Judentums, Berlin. Festschrift für Leo Baeck. Berlin: Schocken Verlag/Jüdischer Buchverlag, 1938. 181 p. port. 22½cm.

"Zum 25.Jahrestage seiner Tätigkeit an der Lehranstalt für die Wissenschaft des Judentums dargebracht von seinen Freunden und Mitarbeitern und herausgegeben im Auftrag der Lehranstalt für die Wissenschaft des Judentums zu Berlin."
Bibliographical footnotes.
CONTENTS.—Täubler, Eugen. Chazor in den Briefen von Tell el-Amarna.—Sister, Moses. Zu Motivproblemen in der Bibel.—Ormann, Gustav. Die Stilmittel im Deuteronomium.—Guttmann, Alexander. Der Minhag der Bibel im Spiegelbild des Talmuds.—Elbogen, Ismar. Die Überlieferung von Hillel.—Spanier, Arthur. Zur Analyse

(Continued)

N. Y. P. L. April 18, 1940

Hochschule für die Wissenschaft des Judentums, Berlin. Festschrift für Leo Baeck. (Card 2)

des Mischnatraktates Middot.—Liebeschütz, Hans. Bibel und klassisches Altertum im englischen Hochmittelalter.—Wiener, Max. Der Dekalog in Josef Albos dogmatischem System.—Friedländer, Hans. Vom ontologischen Gottesbeweis.—Caro, Friedrich. Schaffen und Schöpfung als rechtliche Kategorien.—Fischer, Jechiel. Zur Erklärung einiger jüdischer Namen.—Grumach, Ernst. Zur Herkunft des altsemitischen Alphabets.—Rosenthal, Franz. Zur Frage der Bildung des arabischen Elativs.

7553B. 1. Baeck, Leo, 1873– 2. Essays, Jewish, in German. I. Title.
N. Y. P. L. April 18, 1940

HOCHSTETTER, ERICH, ed.
Leibniz zu seinem 300. Geburtstag, 1646-1946. Mit Beiträgen von E. Benz [et al.] Berlin, W. de Gruyter, 1946-52. 8 pts. in 1 v. 24-25cm.

Microfiche (neg.) 10 sheets. 11 x 15cm. (NYPL FSN 13, 814)
Incomplete?
Bibliographical footnotes.

(Continued)

NN R 7.72 b/r OC PC, 1 SL ST, 1 (UM1, LC1, X1, Z1, ZA1)

2

HOCHSTETTER, ERICH, ed. Leibniz zu seinem 300. (Card 2)

CONTENTS.--Lfg. 1. Leibniz als Metaphysiker, von N. Hartmann.--Lfg. 2. Leibniz und Peter der Grosse, von E. Benz.--Lfg. 3. Zu Leibniz' Gedächtnis, von E. Hochstetter.--Lfg. 4. Leibniz' mathematische Studien in Paris, von J.E. Hofmann.--Lfg. 5. Leibniz' Forschungen im Gebiet der Syllogistik, von K. Dürr.--Lfg. 6. Leibniz als Historiker, von W. Conze.--Lfg. 7. Leibniz' Erkenntnislehre, von R. Zocher.--Lfg. 8. Leibniz und China, von R.F. Merkel.

1. Leibniz, Gottfried Wilhelm, Freiherr von, 1646-1716.

Hodeige, Fritz, *ed.*
Atlantische Begegnungen; eine Freundesgabe für Arnold Bergstraesser, von Carl J. Friedrich [et al.] Herausgeber: Fritz Hodeige [und] Carl Rothe. [1. Aufl.] Freiburg im Breisgau, Rombach [1964]
222 p. 23 cm. (Freiburger Studien zu Politik und Soziologie)
German or English.
Includes bibliographical references.
CONTENTS.—Brief an Arnold Bergstraesser, von H. Speidel.—Die Macht der Negation und das Verhängnis totaler Ideologie, von C. J.

(Continued)

NN* R 10.65 g/ OC, I PC, 1, 2, 3, I, II SL (LC1, X1, Z1)

3

HODEIGE, FRITZ, ed. Atlantische Begegnungen... (Card 2)

Friedrich.—Politik und Leidenschaft im mittelalterlichen Schachspiel, von H. M. Gamer.—Tendenzen und Kräfte in der sich wandelnden Welt, von E. Heimann.—Goethe and the unity of mankind, by R. M. Hutchins.—"Verstumm' Natur!" Zur Deutung der Sprache und Dichtung des jungen Schiller, von M. Jolles.—Die Ursprünge der modernen Wohltätigkeitspflege in England, von W. K. Jordan.—"Die Freiheit der Lehre entbindet nicht von der Treue zur Verfassung," von H. Kämpf.—Hofmannsthals Operntext "Die Ägyptische Helena," von M. McKenzie.—Religion und Nationalität, von H. Rothfels.—Gedanken zur Rolle der Publizistik, von H. Schelsky.—Die Prinzessin im

(Continued)

HODEIGE, FRITZ, ed. Atlantische Begegnungen...
(Card 3)

"Tasso" und Helene Altenwyl im "Schwierigen," von H. S. Schultz.—Staatskunst und moralische Entscheidungsfreiheit, von A. Wolfers.—Gleichberechtigung, Amerikas aufgeschobene Verpflichtung, von C. V. Woodward.

1. Bergsträsser, Arnold, 1896-1964. 2. German literature--Addresses, essays, lectures. 3. Civilization, Modern --Addresses, essays, lectures. I. Rothe, Carl, 1900- , joint ed. II. Title.

D-16
6105

Hodeige, Fritz, *ed.*
Das Recht am Geistesgut; Studien zum Urheber-, Verlags- und Presserecht. Eine Festschrift für Walter Bappert mit Beiträgen von Josef Knecht [et al. 1. Aufl.] Freiburg im Breisgau, Rombach [1964]

322 p. illus., port. 23 cm.

Bibliographical footnotes.

CONTENTS.—Walter Bappert, Gruss zum 70. Geburtstag, von J. Knecht.—Im Arbeits- und Dienstverhältnis geschaffene urheberrecht-

(Continued)

NN* R 5.66 g/ OC PC, 1, 2, 3 SL E, 1, 3 (LC1, X1, Z1) 4

Hodeige, Fritz, *ed.* Das Recht am Geistesgut ... [1964]
(Card 2)

liche Werke, von K. Bussmann.—Rechtsfragen zur Neubearbeitung wissenschaftlicher Werke verstorbener Autoren, von L. Delp.—Schriftbild und Urheberrecht, von E. Gerstenberg.—Zum Veröffentlichungsrecht der Wissenschaftlichen Assistenten, von L. Gieseke.—Optionsrechte des Verlegers, von H. G. Isele.—Über die Zulässigkeit der Herstellung von Vervielfältigungen geschützter Werke zum persönlichen Gebrauch, von H. Kleine.—Massenmedien, Presse, Zeitung und Zeitschrift als Rechtsbegriff, von M. Löffler.—Urheberrechtsverwertungsverträge in der Sicht der Urheberrechtsreform,

(Continued)

Hodeige, Fritz, *ed.* Das Recht am Geistesgut ... [1964]
(Card 3)

von P. Möhring.—Probleme der Musikverwertung in Gesetzgebung und Praxis, von M. Müller-Blattau.—Vorbehalt des Urheberrechts und Copyright Notice; Betrachtungen über den Schutz deutscher Werke in den USA, von H. L. Pinner.—Das Zeugnisverweigerungsrecht der Presse, von W. von Ramdohr.—Der Film in der deutschen Urheberrechtsreform, von G. Roeber.—Die Buchgemeinschaft und ihre Problematik, von K. Runge.—Die deutsche Urheberrechtsreform aus österreichischer Sicht, von F. Schönherr.—Originalität und Neuheit der Werke der Literatur und Kunst und der Geschmacksmuster,

(Continued)

HODEIGE, FRITZ, ed. Das Recht am Geistesgut...
[1964] (Card 4)

von A. Troller.—Originalwerk und Bearbeitung im internationalen Urheberrecht, von E. Ulmer.—Das Fernsehen in der Revidierten Berner Übereinkunft, von E. Wagner.—Walter Bappert, Bibliographie 1947 bis 1964.

1. Bappert, Walter, 1894- . 2. Copyright--Jurisp.--Germany. 3. Copyright, International.

---

*C-3 p v.1196

HOE het groeide op het Ellertsveld. Een geschiedenis in hoofdstukken, geschreven ter gelegenheid van Schoonoords eeuwfeest, door A.H.A. Canter Cremers [et al.] met een voorwoord van J. Cramer. Assen, "De Torenlaan" [1954] 124 p. illus. 22cm.

CONTENTS.—Wat is Schoonoord en omgeving?—Drentsche veen- en middenkanaal maatschappij, door A.H.A. Canter Cremers.—Naasting ven het Orangekanaal door het Rijk.—Kerk en school in Schoonoord, door

(Continued)

NN** X 2.56 j/ OC PC, 1 SL (LC1, X1, Z1)

HOE het groeide op het Ellertsveld. (Card 2)

I. Faber.—Over de geneeskundige voorziening van Schoonoord in het begin van 1900, door Th. A. van Reemst.—De gezondheidszorg in Schoonoord en omstreken, door F.A. Bol.—De ontwikkeling van de landbouw, door Ph. W. Loman.—Herinneringen van een Oudschoonoorder, door F. Siega.—En zij hebben moedig d'edele strijd volbracht, door W. Van Tellingen.

1. Schoonoord, Netherlands.

E-11
4647

HÖFLING, HELMUT, ed.
Beiträge zu Philosophie und Wissenschaft, Wilhelm Szilasi zum 70. Geburtstag. München, Francke [1960] 355 p. 24cm.

Bibliographical footnotes.

CONTENTS.--Imago, van K. Bauch.--Die Philosophie Wilhelm Szilasis und die psychiatrische Forschung, von L. Binswanger.--Zum

(Continued)

NN R 6.62 p/ OC, Ibo PC, 1, 2, 3 SL ST, 2t (LC1, X1, Z1) 3

HÖFLING, HELMUT, ed. Beiträge zu Philosophie und Wissenschaft... (Card 2)

philosolhischen Begriff der Funktion, von G. Freudenberg.--Zehn Sonette Petrarcas, verdeutscht, von H. Friedrich.--Unterricht oder Erfahrung der Philosophie?Von E. Grassi.--Was ist Leben? Von M. Hartmann.--Uber das naturwissenschaftliche Denken in der Medizin, von L. Heilmeyer.--Kants Ansätze zu einer Philosophie im Weltbegriff, von H. Höfling.-- Mudos in verbaler Form, von K. Kerényi.--Aus einer Psychotherapiestunde, von R. Kuhn.--Die Sprache als Vermittler von Mensch und Welt, von K. Löwith.--Positivismus und Phänomenologie (Mach und Husserl), von H. Lübbe.--

(Continued)

HÖFLING, HELMUT, ed. Beiträge zu Philosophie und Wissenschaft... (Card 3)

Heidegger und die Metaphysik, von W. Marx.--Die Epiphanie der ewigen Gegenwart, von G. Picht.--Uber Parästhesien, von H. Plügge.--Zum Problem der tierischen Erscheinung, von A. Portmann.--Mottostudien. Kierkegaards Motti, von W. Rehm.--Leiblichkeit und Hypochondrie, von H. Ruffin.--Das Problem der naturwissenschaftlichen Erfahrung, von T. von Uexküll.

1. Philosophy--Addresses, essays, lectures. 2. Science--Essays and misc. 3. Szilasi, Wilhelm I. Höfling, Helmut t.1960

Hölderlin; gedenkschrift zu seinem 100. todestag 7. juni 1943. Im auftrag der stadt und der Universität Tübingen, herausgegeben von Paul Kluckhohn.. 2. aufl. Tübingen, Mohr, 1944.

2 p. l., 324 p. facsims. (part fold.) 24^{cm}.

"Diese gedenkschrift stellt die erste jahresgabe der Hölderlin-gesellschaft dar. Die zweite auflage erscheint mit deren unterstützung."
Bibliographical references in "Anmerkungen" at end of most of the articles.

CONTENTS.—An Hölderlin; ode, von Josef Weinheber.—Zur einführung, von Paul Kluckhohn.—Hölderlins mythische welt, von Paul Böckmann.—Hölderlin und die antike, von H.-G. Gadamer.—Tiefe und abgrund in

(Continued on next card)

A 46–1353

[2]

Hölderlin ... 1944. (Card 2)

CONTENTS—Continued.

Hölderlins dichtung, von Walther Rehm.—Hölderlins und Goethes weltanschauung dargestellt am 'Hyperion' und 'Empedokles,' von Kurt Hildebrandt.—Hölderlin und Hegel in Frankfurt; ein beitrag zur beziehung von dichtung und philosophie, von Theodor Haering.—Die berufung des dichters, von W. F. Otto.—"So dacht'ich. Nächstens mehr." Die ganzheit des Hyperionromans. Von Wilhelm Böhm.—Zu den oden 'Abendphantasie' und 'Des morgens,' von Friedrich Beissner.—Deutung des elegischen bruchstücks 'Der gang aufs land,' von Friedrich Beissner.—'Andenken,' von Martin Heidegger.

1. *Hölderlin, Friedrich, 1770–1843. I. Kluckhohn, Paul, 1886– ed.

A 46–1353

Harvard univ. Library
for Library of Congress [2]

HOF, OTTO, ed.
Dienende Kirche; Festschrift für Landesbischof D. Julius Bender zu seinem 70. Geburtstag am 30. August 1963. Grussworte und Aufsätze, im Namen des Oberkirchenrats der Evangelischen Landeskirche in Baden hrsg. Karlsruhe, H. Thoma, 1963. 391 p. illus., port., music. 24cm.

Bibliographical footnotes.

(Continued)

NN R 5.64 e/3 OC, 1bo, IIbo (OS)I, Ib PC, 1, 2, I SL (LC1, X1, Z1) [I]

2

HOF, OTTO, ed. Dienende Kirche... (Card 2)

1. Bender, Julius. 2. Evangelical Lutheran Church--Germany. I. Evangelische Landeskirche in Baden. II. Hof, Otto.

HOFACKER, ERICH, 1898- , ed.
Studies in Germanic languages and literatures, in memory of Fred O. Nolte; a collection of essays written by his colleagues and his former students. Edited by Erich Hofacker and Liselotte Dieckmann. St. Louis, Washington university press, 1963. 159 p. port. 25cm.

(Continued)

NN R 2.64 f/(OC, I, IIbo PC, 1, 2, I SL (LC1, X1, Z1)

4

HOFACKER, ERICH, 1898- , ed. Studies in Germanic languages and literatures... (Card 2)

Contributions in English or German.
Bibliographical footnotes.
CONTENTS.--The Gothic character X, by E. Ebbinghaus.--The composition of Eddic verse, by W.P. Lehmann.--The views of Konrad Gesner on language, by G.J. Metcalf.--The languages of the world; a classification by G.W. Leibniz, by J.T. Waterman.--Another look at Lessing's Philotas, by B. Ulmer.-- A Gottschedian reply to

(Continued)

HOFACKER, ERICH, 1898- , ed. Studies in Germanic languages and literatures... (Card 3)

Lessing's seventeenth Literaturbrief, by R.R. Heitner.--José Ortega y Gassets Verhältnis zu Goethe, von E. Schwarz.--The character and function of Butler in Schiller's Wallenstein, by W. Silz.--Grillparzer as a critic of European literature, by F.D. Horvay.--Narrative and "musical" structure in Mozart auf der Reise nach Prag, by R. Immerwahr.--Faust ohne Transzendenz; Theodor Storms Schimmelreiter, von E. Loeb.--Symbols of isolation in some late nineteenth-century poets, by L. Dieckmann.--Das Motiv des "stirb und werde" bei Christian Morgenstern, von

(Continued)

HOFACKER, ERICH, 1898- , ed. Studies in Germanic languages and literatures... (Card 4)

E. Hofacker.

1. Nolte, Fred Otto, 1894- . 2. German literature--Addresses, essays, lectures. I. Dieckmann, Liselotte, joint ed. II. Dieckmann, Liselotte.

HOFFMANN-ERBRECHT, LOTHAR, ed.
Festschrift Helmuth Osthoff zum 65. Geburtstage, hrsg. von Lothar Hoffmann-Erbrecht und Helmut Hucke. Tutzing, H. Schneider, 1961. 237 p. illus., port., map, facsims., music. 21cm.

Bibliographical footnotes.
CONTENTS.--Bibliographie der Werke Helmuth Osthoffs (p. 5-14).--Zur Frühgeschichte der Laute, von W. Stauder.--Das Weihnachtslied In dulci

(Continued)

NN R 4.63 p/ OC, I PC, 1, 2, I, II SL MU, 1, 3, I, II (LC1, X1, Z1)

3

HOFFMANN-ERBRECHT, LOTHAR, ed. Festschrift Helmuth Osthoff zum 65... (Card 2)

iubilo und seine ursprügliche Melodie, von J. Smits van Waesberghe.--Senfliana, von W. Gerstenberg.--Datierungsprobleme bei Kompositionen in deutschen Musikhandschriften des 16. Jahrhunderts, von L. Hoffmann-Erbrecht.--Die Verbindung von Magnificat und Weihnachtsliedern im 16. Jahrhundert, von W. Kirsch.--Die Motetti, Madrigali, et Canzoni Francese Diminuiti des Giovanni Bassano, von E.T. Ferand.--Zur Lebens- und Familiengeschichte von Lambert de Sayve, von E. Schenk.--Tobias Michaels Musicalische Seelenlust, von A. Adrio.--Zur italienischen ChoralIehre im

(Continued)

HOFFMANN-ERBRECHT, LOTHAR, ed. Festschrift Helmuth Osthoff zum 65. (Card 3)

17-18. Jahrhundert, von K.G. Fellerer. --Verfassung und Entwicklung der alten neapolitanischen Konservatorien, von H. Hucke. --Hemiolenrhythmik bei Mozart, von K.P. Bernet-Kempers. --57 unveröffentlichte Briefe und Karten von Richard Strauss in der Stadt- und Universitätsbibliothek Frankfurt, Main, von W. Sschmieder. --Schönheit und Ausdruck, von H.C. Wolff. --Monteverdis Combattimento in deutscher Sprache und Heinrich Schütz, von W. Osthoff.

1. Osthoff, Helmuth, 1896- 2. Music--Essays. 3. Essays. I. Hucke, Helmut, 1926- joint ed. II. Title.

---

*MFPB (Germany)

HOFMEISTER, FRIEDRICH G. M. B. H., music publisher, Leipzig.
Tradition und Gegenwart; Festschrift zum 150 jährigen Bestehen des Musikverlages Friedrich Hofmeister. Leipzig, 1957. 101 p. port., facsim. (incl. music) 30cm.

1. Music--Publishing--Germany--Leipzig. 2. Music--Essays. 3. Publishers and publishing--Germany (Hofmeister). 4. Essays. I. Title.
NN R 1.61 a/// (OC)I OS PC, 1, 2, I SL MU, 3, 4, I (LC1, X1, Z1)
[I]

MWKF (Altona)

Hoffmann, Paul Theodor, 1891-
Die Entwicklung des Altonaer Stadttheaters; ein Beitrag zu seiner Geschichte. Festschrift zum fünfzigjährigen Bestehen des jetzigen Hauses im Auftrage der Altonaer Stadttheater-Aktiengesellschaft verfasst von Paul Th. Hoffmann. Mit Beiträgen von Franziska Ellmenreich [et al.] Altona-Elbe, H. W. Köbner, 1926. 316 p. illus., ports., facsims. 25cm.

(Continued)

NN**R X 8.54 OC, I, Ib+ (OS)II PC, 1, I, II SL MU, 2, 3, I, II (T 4, Z 1, LC1, X1)

Copy only words underlined & classmark-- *MA

HOHNER-STIFTUNG, Trossingen.
Wilibald Gurlitt zum siebzigsten Geburtstag [Festschrift. Trossingen, Verlag Archiv für Musikwissenschaft, 1959] 259 p. illus., music. 24cm.
(Archiv für Musikwissenschaft, Jahrg. 16, Heft 1-2)

Bibliographical footnotes.

(Continued)

NN 5.60 s/ (OC)I OS(1b+) OI MU, 1, 2, I (LC4, X1, Z1) 4

Hoffmann, Paul Theodor, 1891- Die Entwicklung des Altonaer Stadttheaters... (Card 2)

Bibliography, p. 293-306.

1. Stage—Germany—Altona. 2. Opera houses—Germany—Altona. 3. Operas—Germany—Altona. I. Title. II. Altonaer Stadttheater-Aktiengesellschaft.

HOHNER-STIFTUNG, Trossingen. Wilibald Gurlitt zum siebzigsten Geburtstag... (Card 2)

CONTENTS. --Musikalische Beziehungen zwischen Deutschland und Spanien in der Zeit vom 5. bis 14. Jahrhundert, von H. Anglès. --Umgangsmusik und Darbietungsmusik im 16. Jahrhundert, von H. Besseler. --Der Harmonie-Begriff in der lutherisch-barocken Musikanschauung, von W. Blankenburg. --Zum Figur-Begriff der Musica poetica, von H. H. Eggebrecht. --Über Bach-Analysen am Beispiel einer Fuge aus dem Wohltemperierten Klavier, von H. Erpf. --Agrippa von Nettesheim und die Musik, von K.G. Fellerer. --Zur Entwicklung der italienischen

(Continued)

---

*MGA

Hofmann, Erna Hedwig, *ed.*
Begegnungen mit Rudolf Mauersberger; Dankesgabe eines Freundeskreises zum 75. Geburtstag des Dresdner Kreuzkantors. [Hrsg. von Erna Hedwig Hofmann und Ingo Zimmermann] Berlin, Evangelische Verlagsanstalt [1963]
153 p. illus. (part mounted) ports. 25 cm.

(Continued)

NN R 5. 66 r/∫ OC, I, II, IIIb* PC, 1, 3, I, II, IV SL MU, 2, 3, I, II, IV (LC1, X1, Z1) 2

HOHNER-STIFTUNG, Trossingen. Wilibald Gurlitt zum siebzigsten Geburtstag... (Card 3)
Trecento-Notation, von K. von Fischer. --Komposition als Unterricht, von W. Fortner. --Über Mozarts Klaviersatz, von W. Gerstenberg. --Instrumenta Hieronymi, von R. Hammerstein. --Sinn und Wesen der Tropen, veranschaulicht an den Introitustropen des Weihnachtsfestes, von H. Husmann. --Der Ursprung der Musik, von J. Lohmann. --Grundsätze der Dispositionsgestaltung des Orgelbauers Gottfried Silbermann, von C. Mahrenholz. --Die Musik in Guido von Arezzos Solmisationshymne, von C.-A. Moberg. --Bachs Goldberg-Variationen, von J. Müller-Blattau. --Das Magnificat bei Josquin Desprez, von H. Osthoff. --Zur motettischen Passion des 16. Jahrhunderts, von A. Schmitz. -- Deutung der Gegenwart, von H.H. Stuckenschmidt.

(Continued)

HOFMANN, ERNA HEDWIG, ed. Begegnungen mit Rudolf Mauersberger... (Card 2)

1. Music--Essays. 2. Essays. 3. Mauersberger, Rudolf, 1889- . I. Mauersberger, Rudolf, 1889- . II. Zimmermann, Ingo, joint ed. III. Zimmermann, Ingo. IV. Title.

HOHNER-STIFTUNG, Trossingen. Wilibald Gurlitt zum siebzigsten Geburtstag... (Card 4)

1. Gurlitt, Wilibald, 1889- 2. Essays. I. Title.

HBC

HOHOKAM MUSEUMS ASSOCIATION.
For the dean; essays in anthropology in honor of Byron Cummings on his eighty-ninth birthday, September 20, 1950. Tucson, Ariz., Hohokam museums assoc. and the Southwestern monuments assoc., Sante Fe, N.M., 1950. 318 p. illus. 24cm.

"Erik K. Reed, and Dale S. King, editors."
Bibliographyies included.
CONTENTS.—Introduction: Our friend, Byron Cummings, by A.E. Douglass.—Annotated bibliography of papers, by Byron Cummings, comp. by G. Hill.—Pioneering in Southwestern archeology N.M. Judd.—A
(Continued)

NN*R 12.52 (OC)II, III OS, I PC, 1, 2, I, II, III SL AH, 1, 2, I, II, III (LC1, Z1, X1) [I]

HOHOKAM MUSEUMS ASSOCIATION. For the dean... (Card 2)

sequence of great kivas in the Forestdale valley, Arizona, by E.W. Haury.—Archeological survey of the Lake Mead area, by G.C. Baldwin.—Notes on the dragoon complex, by C. Tuthill.—Ceramic traits and the nature of culture contacts between Anasazi and Mogollon, by E.T. Hall, jr.—Hispanic pottery as a guide in historical studies, by L. Caywood.—Notes on Plains-Southwestern contacts in the light of archaeology, by W.R. Wedel.—Coral among Southwestern Indians, by C.L. Tanner.—Notes on Navaho astronomy, by S.P. Brewer.—Hogans vs. houses, by C. Lockett.—Mechanics of perpetuation of pueblo witchcraft, by F.M. Hawley.—A brief history of the Cocopa Indians, by D.S. Kelly.—The military orientation in Yaqui culture, by E.H. Spicer.
(Continued)

HOHOKAM MUSEUMS ASSOCIATION. For the dean... (Card 3)

—The physical status of the Papago, by N.E. Gabel.—Ethnic history of Tucson, Arizona, by H.T. Getty.—Growth trends in new world cultures, by G.R. Willey.—Gallery-patio type structures at Chichen Itza, by K. Ruppert.—Archeological excavations in El Salvador, by S.H. Boogs.—Pottery types from kitchen middens of Dutch New Guinea, by C.F. Miller.—Weighted traits and traditions, by J.C. McGregor.—The professional interpreter of science, by E. Jackson.

1. Cummings, Byron, 1861- . 2. Indians, American. I. Southwestern monuments association. II. Reed, Erik Kellerman, 1914- , ed. III. King, Dale Stuart, 1908- , ed.

E-12
5811

Holmes, Urban Tigner, 1900- *ed.*
French and Provençal lexicography; essays presented to honor Alexander Herman Schutz. Edited by Urban T. Holmes and Kenneth R. Scholberg. [Columbus] Ohio State University Press [1964]
viii, 278 p. 24 cm.
English or French.
Includes bibliographies.
CONTENTS.—Alexander Herman Schutz, by U. T. Holmes.—Lexicography and stylistics, by H. Hatzfeld.—The pucelle is not for burning,
(Continued)

NN* R 5.66 g/ OC, I PC, 1, 2, 3, 4, I SL (LC1, X1, Z1)

Holmes, Urban Tigner, 1900- *ed.* French and Provençal lexicography ... [1964] (Card 2)

by E. W. Bulatkin.—Les gloses françaises dans le Pentateuque de Raschi, by R. Levy.—The affective and expressive values of verb-complement compounds in romance, by F. Koenig.—Pleine sa hanste in the Chanson de Roland, by J. Harris.—Carestia, by H. and R. Kahane.—Quelques observations sur le texte des vidas and [sic] des razos dans les chansonniers provençaux AB et IK, by J. Boutière.—The name of the troubadour Dalfin d'Alvernhe, by S. C. Aston.—Three little problems of Old Provençal syntax, by K. Lewent.—Flamenca

(Continued)

HOLMES, URBAN TIGNER, 1900- , ed. French and Provencal lexicography... [1964] (Card 3)

gleanings, by E. B. Ham.—The lady from Plazensa, by F. M. Chambers.—The vocabulary of the New Testament in Provençal, by R. W. Linker.—Flux et réflux du vocabulaire français au XVIe siècle, by R. Lebègue.—Archaism in Ronsard's theory of a poetic vocabulary, by I. Silver.—Montaigne's later Latin borrowings, by W. L. Wiley.—The coins in Rabelais, by R. Harden.—Bibliography of Alexander Herman Schutz, by K. R. Scholberg.

(Continued)

HOLMES, URBAN TIGNER, 1900- , ed. French and Provençal lexicography... [1964] (Card 4)

1. Schutz, Alexander Herman. 2. French language--Addresses, essays, lectures. 3. French language--Lexicography. 4. Provençal language--Lexicography. I. Scholberg, Kenneth R., joint ed.

Write on slip only words underlined and classmark:
RDTA

Holmes, Urban Tigner, 1900- , ed.
Romance studies presented to William Morton Dey...on the occasion of his seventieth birthday by his colleagues and former students. Edited by Urban T. Holmes, jr., Alfred G. Engstrom and Sturgis E. Leavitt. Chapel Hill, 1950. 196 p. port. 23cm. (North Carolina. University. Studies in the Romance languages and literatures. no. 12.)

"Vita and bibliography," p. [7]-11. Includes bibliographical references.

1. Romance philology. 2. Dey, William Morton. I. Engstrom, Alfred G., jt. ed. II. Leavitt, Sturgis Elleno, 1880- , jt. ed. III. Ser.
NN

D-18
8704

Holmsen, Andreas, 1906-
Gard, bygd, rike. Festskrift i anledning Andreas Holmsens 60 års dag 5. juni 1966. Oslo, Universitetsforlaget, 1966.
247 p. maps, tables. 23 cm.
List of works, p. [238]-247.

1. Land--Norway.
NN*R 4.69 a/ OC PC, 1 SL E, 1 (LC1, X1, Z1)

E-11
5677

HOLMSTRÖM, BENGT, ed.
Idéer och resultat, nordiska biblioteksuppsatser tillägnade Ingeborg Heintze [den 30 december 1961. Redaktion: Bengt Holmström och Märta Sjögreen. Malmo] Allhem [1961] 278 p. illus. (part col., mounted) ports., facsims., music. 25cm.

CONTENTS.--Forudsætningerne for en ny dansk bibliotekslov, af
(Continued)

NN R 11.64 e/ OC, I, II, IIIbo, IVbo PC, 1, 2, I, II SL (LC1, X1, Z1) [I]

HOLMSTRÖM, BENGT, ed. Idéer och resultat...
(Card 2)

E. Allerslev Jensen.--Fragmenter av min svenske dagbok, av A. Andreassen. --Muhammed och berget; redogörelse för en experimentverksamhet i Sundbyberg, av B. Bianchini.--Henrik Reuterdahl som biblioteksman, av K. Gierow.--Svensk biblioteksdebatt omkring år 1860; ur en tidningsläsares citatsamling, av B. Hallvik.--Franske centralbiblioteker, av R.L. Hansen.--Samkatalogen i ny gestalt; ett förslag, av S.-O. Hellmér.--Lika möjligheter till lån; fragment av liktal över betänkande, av B. Hjelmqvist.--

(Continued)

HOLMSTRÖM, BENGT, ed. Idéer och resultat...
(Card 3)

Ett föregångsbibliotek i Stockholm, Gustav Vasa församlingsbibliotek 1909-1927, av G. Hornwall.--Två pionjärer för folkbiblioteksidén i Finland, av H. Kannila.--Ett decennium av gåvor; kring en utställning i Uppsala universitetsbibliotek, av T. Kleberg.--Biblioteksbenyttelsens intensivering of dens følger, av J. Lehm Laursen.--När vi började; minnen fran biblioteksksonsulenternas tidiga år, av G. Linder.--Om arbets- och ansvarsfördeling, av S. Möhlenbrock.--Bibliotek pa hjul; sommarsamhällets

(Continued)

HOLMSTRÖM, BENGT, ed. Idéer och resultat...
(Card 4)

bokförsörjning, av G. Nyman.--Kompetenskrav och utbildning vid de svenska universitetsbiblioteken, av G. Ottervik.--Bygherren, bygmesteren og bibliotekaren, af C. Thomsen.--Dag Hammarskjöld som bibliofil; föredrag vid invigningen av Dag Hammarskjöld memorial library den 17 nov. 1961, av U. Willers.--Stimulera individens strävan; om bibliotekens uppgift i samhället, av G. Östling.--Förteckning över uppsatser och skrifter av Ingeborg Heintze (p. [273]-278).

1. Libraries--Scandinavia. 2. Heintze, Ingeborg. I. Sjögreen, Märta, joint ed. II. Title. III. Holmström, Bengt. IV. Sjögreen, Märta.

E-10
1979

HOLTSMARK, ANNE, 1896-
Studier i norrøn diktning. Oslo, Gyldendal, 1956.
201 p. 25cm.

"[Anne Holtsmark] på 60-års dagen den 21. juni 1956."
Includes bibliographies.
CONTENTS.--En side av norsk bokhistorie.--Sankt Olavs liv og mirakler.--Litt om overleveringen i Hårvards saga.--Vitazgjafi.--Rosmofjóll rínar.--Isamkol.--Det norrøne ord luðr.--Bil og hjuke.--Myten om Idun og Tjatse

(Continued)

NN 3.57 a/tOC PC,1 SL (LC1,X1,Z1,Y1)

HOLTSMARK, ANNE, 1896- . Studier i norrøn diktning. (Card 2)

i Tjodolvs Haustlǫng.--Gevjons plog.--Olav den hellige og "seiersskjorten."--"Vefr darraðar."--Sarþuara--sárþvara.

1. Norse literature--Hist. and crit.

E-13
527

Holtzhauer, Helmut, *ed.*
Natur und Idee. Andreas Bruno Wachsmuth zugeeignet. Im Auftrage des Vorstands der Goethe-Gesellschaft in Weimar zum 30. November 1965. (Mit Titelbild und einer Tafel) Weimar, H. Böhlaus Nachfolger, 1966.

327 p. 25 cm.

Bibliographical footnotes.

(Continued)

.NN * R 2.68 1/OC,IIIb* (OS)I PC,1,2,I,II SL (LC1,X1,Z1) 4

HOLTZHAUER, HELMUT, ed. Natur und Idee.
(Card 2)

CONTENTS.—Vorwort, von Helmut Holtzhauer.—Iphigenie von der Antike bis zur Moderne, von L. Blumenthal.—Jenseits der Polarität, von E. Buchwald.—Zu Goethes Gedichten "Meeresstille" und "Glückliche Fahrt," von H. J. Geerdts.—Farbenlehre und kein Ende, von W. Gerlach.—Deutsche Klassik und literarische Tradition, von W. Girnus.—Zur Weimarer Hamlet-Inszenierung des Jahres 1809, von K.-H. Hahn.—Gesellschaft, Kultur und Kulturauffassung im klassischen Weimar, von H. Holtzhauer.—Welt und Geschichte in Hölderlins später Dichtung, von D. Lüders.—Goethes 'verfehlte' Lustspiele: "Die Mitschuldigen" und "Der Gross-Cophta," von F. Martini.—Goethes

(Continued)

HOLTZHAUER, HELMUT, ed. Natur und Idee.
(Card 3)

Terzinengedicht. Lyrische Bewegung, Gestaltcharakter und motivische Textur, von J. Müller.—Etappen einer italienischen Reise, von J. Rudolph.—Die "Wanderjahre" als "Hauptgeschäft" im Winterhalbjahr 1828/29, von E. Trunz.—Goethes Weimar am Vorabend der Befreiungskriege Aus den Berichten des französischen Gesandten Baron von Saint-Aignan 1812/13, von H. Tümmler.—Gottlob Heinrich Rapp (1761–1832). Ein Beitrag zur Geschichte der Kultur des Stuttgarter Bürgertums, von B. Zeller.

(Continued)

HOLTZHAUER, HELMUT, ed. Natur und Idee.
(Card 4)

1. German literature—Addresses, essays, lectures.
2. Wachsmuth, Bruno. I. Goethe Gesellschaft.
II. Title. III. Holtzhauer, Helmut.

---

*KF
1967

HOMAGE to a bookman. Essays on manuscripts, books and printing written for Hans P. Kraus on his 60th birthday, Oct. 12, 1967. Berlin, Gebr. Mann Verlag [1967] 271 p. illus. (part col.), facsims.(part col.), port. 28cm.

Edited by Hellmut Lehmann-Haupt.
Chiefly in English; some essays in German or Italian.
Bibliographical footnotes.

(Continued)

NN R 10.68 c/ OC,I PC,1,2,3,I SL R,1,2,3,I (RI 1,LC1,X1,Z1) [I] 4

HOMAGE to a bookman. [1967] (Card 2)

CONTENTS.--An early papyrus text of Isocrates, by A. E. Samuel.--The binding of the Glazier codex of the Acts of the Apostles, by J. S. Kebabian.--On the illumination of the Glazier codex, by H. Bober.--Some observations on Coptic influence in western early medieval manuscripts, by E. Rosenthal.--Codex arabicus (Sinai Arabic ms. no. 514) by A. S. Atiya.--More about medieval pouncing, by D. E. Miner.--The earliest known laws of an Italian city state, by T. E. Marston.--Di un codice di Petrarca da ritrovare, da Tommaro [sic] de Marinis.--Bildungsstand und ursprünglicher Beruf der deutschen Buchdrucker des 15. Jahrhunderts, von F. Geld-

(Continued)

HOMAGE to a bookman... [1967] (Card 3)

ner.--Remarks on the printing of the Augsburg edition (c. 1474) of Bishop Salomon's glossae, by C. F. Bühler.--Falsified dates in certain incunabula, by F. R. Goff.--Johannes Petreius, Nuremberg publisher of scientific works, 1524-1550, by J. C. Shipman.--Of martyrs, books and science, by B. Dibner.--Some reconsiderations of the origin of printing in sixteenth-century Mexico, by L. S. Thompson.--Two copies of the first book published in Brazil at the New York public library, by C. S. Smith.--Jonathan Carver's map of his travels, by J. Parker.--James Logan's correspondence with

(Continued)

HOMAGE to a bookman... [1967] (Card 4)

William Reading, by E. Wolf.--New Yorker illustrierte Bücher des 19. Jahrhunderts mit signierten Einbänden, von E. Kyriss.--Earliest Russian printing in the United States, by V. Lada-Mocarski.--Drawings for unidentified book illustrations by Tiepolo, by A. H. Mayor.--A checklist of books illustrated by Henry Alken, by W. Van Devanter.--Chorus mysticus, von M. Bodmer.

1. Kraus, Hans Peter, 1907- . 2. Manuscripts--Addresses, essays, lectures. 3. Printing--Addresses, essays, lectures. I. Lehmann-Haupt, Hellmut, 1903- , ed.

D-14
3741

HOMAGE to Charles Blaise Qualia. [John Clarkson Dowling, chairman, editorial committee] Lubbock, Texas tech. press, 1962. 148 p. port. 23cm.

Bibliography, p. 147-148.

1. Qualia, Charles Blaise, 1892- . 2. Literature--Addresses, essays, lectures.

NN 6.63 e/B OC, 1b+ PC, 1, 2 SL (LC1, X1, Z1) [I]

MCK
+
E71.S19

HOMAGE to Max Ernst. New York, Tudor [1971] 131 p. illus., col. plates, ports., facsims. 32cm.

Special issue of the XXe siècle review, edited by G. di San Lazzaro.

1. Ernst, Max, 1891- . I. San Lazzaro, Gualtieri di, ed. II. Vingtième siècle.

NN R 12.71 e/L OC, I (OS)II PC, 1, I, II SL A, 1, I, II (PRL1, LC1, X1, Z1) B

---

*MEC
(Paderewski)

Homage to Paderewski. Piano solo. New York [etc.] Boosey & Hawkes, inc. [1942] Publ. pl. no. U. S. Bk. no. 81. 63 [i. e. 67] p. ports. 31cm.

Corrected copy of Ernest Schelling's composition (p. 47-50) bound in.

CONTENTS.—Bartók, Béla. Three Hungarian folk-tunes.—Benjamin, Arthur. Elegiac mazurka.—Castelnuovo-Tedesco, Mario. Hommage à Paderewski.—Chanler, Theodore. Aftermath.—Goossens, Eugene. Homage.—Hammond, Richard. Dance.—Labuński, F. R. Threnody.—Martinů, Bohuslav. Mazurka.—Milhaud, Darius. Choral.—Nin-Culmell, J. In memoriam Paderewski.—Rathaus, Karol. Kujawiak.—Rieti, Vittorio. Allegro danzante.—Schelling, Ernest. [Last composition]—Stojowski, Sigismond. Cradle song.—Weinberger, Jaromír. Etude in G major.—Whithorne, Emerson. Hommage.

191625B. 1. Paderewski, Ignacy Jan, 1860-1941 [g] 2. Piano—Collections.

N. Y. P. L. October 2, 1942

Copy only words underlined & classmark— QPP

HOMENAJE a D. Isidro Ballester Tormo. Valencia, 1952-53. 2 v. illus. 29cm. (Valencia, Spain (Province). Investigación prehistórica, Servicio de. Archivo de prehistoria levantina. v. 3-4)

1. Ballester Tormo, Isidro, 1876-1950.

NN R X 2.57 d/B OC OI PC, 1 (Z1, LC2, X1) [I]

C-12
8104

HOMENAJE a D. José Miguel de Barandiarán; una jornada cultural en compañía del maestro. San Sebastián, Editorial Auñamendi [1963] 232 p. 19cm. (Colección Auñamendi, Anexa 4-5)

At head of title: La Academia errante.

1. Barandiarán, José Miguel de. 2. Basques.

NN 1.65 e/U OC PC, 1, 2 SL (LC1, X1, Z1)

AN
(Gamoneda, F.)

Homenaje a don Francisco Gamoneda, miscelánea de estudios de erudición, historia, literatura y arte. México, Imprenta universitaria, 1946.

581, [1] p., 1 l. illus., plates (part col.) ports., facsims. 24^cm.

"Organizadores del homenaje: dr. Alfonso Reyes, dr. Enrique González Martínez, Enrique Díez-Canedo [y otros]"—p. [5]

Includes music.

Includes bibliographies.

1. Gamoneda, Francisco, 1873- I. Reyes, Alfonso, 1889-

AC70.H6 47-22081

Library of Congress [1]

HCC

Homenaje a don José María de la Peña y Cámara. Madrid, Ediciones J. Porrúa Turanzas, 1969.

xi, 287 p. map, port. 26 cm. (Colección Chimalistac de libros y documentos acerca de la Nueva España. Serie José Porrúa Turanzas, 3)

Includes bibliographical references.

CONTENTS.—Nota preliminar, por E. J. Burrus y G. P. Hammond.—Presentación a don José María de la Peña y Cámara, por M. Bordonau y Mas.—Random thoughts on Spanish American letters, by I. A. Leonard.—Bandelier's manuscript sources for the study of the American

(Continued)

NN* 7.71 w/z OC (OS)I PC, 1, 2, 3, I SL AH, 1, 2, 3, I (LC1, X1, Z1) [I]

HOMENAJE a don José María de la Peña y Cámara.
(Card 2)

Southwest, by E. J. Burrus.— Lazos culturales entre California y España; las becas de los Natives Sons, por G. P. Hammond.– Catalogues and microfilm: the Louisiana Project of Loyola University (New Orleans) in the Archivo General de Indias, by C. E. O'Neill.— Viceroys, archivists, and historians, by L. Hanke.--La prohibición de casarse los oidores o sus hijos e hijas con naturales del distrito de la Audiencia, por R. Konetzke.—A research report on Consulado history, by R. S. Smith.—The illicit practice of medicine in the Spanish Empire in America, by J. T. Lanning.—The last days of Gonzalo de Sandoval, conquistador of New Spain, by F. V. Scholes.--Nuño de Guzmán and his "grand design" in New Spain, by D. E. Chipman.—

(Continued)

HOMENAJE a don José María de la Peña y Cámara.
(Card 3)

Sebastián Vizcaíno y los principios de la explotación comercial de California, por W. M. Mathes.--More about Gonzalo Méndez Canco, Governor of Florida (1596-1603), by C. W. Arnade.--Aspectos sociorracionales del proceso de poblamiento en la Audiencia de Quito durante los siglos XVI y XVII, port M. Mörner.

1. Latin America--Hist., to 1600. 2. Latin America--Hist., 1600-1830. 3. Peña y Cámara, José María de la. I. Series.

Copy only words underlined & classmark— *DR

HOMENAJE a Don Miguel de Unamuno. [Río Piedras] 1961. 636 p. illus., ports., fold. facsim. 24cm. (La Torre; revista general de la Universidad de Puerto Rico. año 9, núm. 35-36.)

"Bibliografía de Miguel de Unamuno," p. 601-636.

1. Unamuno y Jugo, Miguel de, 1864-1936.

NN 3.66 r/ OI (PC)1 (LC1, X1, Z1)

Copy only words underlined & classmark— HCA

HOMENAJE a Don Ramiro de Maeztu. (IN: Cuadernos hispanoamericanos. Madrid. 24cm. [no.] 33/34 (1952). 496 p. illus.)

Articles by various authors.
"Textos [por R. de Maeztu]" p. 173-235.
Bibliographies included.

1. Maeztu, Ramiro de. 1875-1936.

NN R 2.53 OI (PC)1 (LC1, Z1, X1)

L-10
7952

HOMENAJE a don Ramón Carande; artículos de Dámaso Alonso [et al.] Madrid, Sociedad de estudios y publicaciones, 1963. 1 v. port., facsim. 26cm.

[Tomo] 1.
Contributions in Spanish, German and Catalan.

1. Essays, Spanish. 2. Carande Thobar, Ramón. I. Alonso, Dámaso, 1898-
NN R 5.64 c/ OC PC, 1, 2, I SL (LC1, X1, Z1) [I]

Copy only words underlined & classmark— *MA

HOMENAJE a Eduardo Fabini. Montevideo 1960. (IN: Clave; voz de la juventud musical uruguaya. no. 37)

Includes discography and list of works.

1. Fabini, Eduardo, 1883-1950.
NN 12.61 e/ OI (MU)1 (LC2, Z1, X1)

D-20
1181

Homenaje a Franz Tamayo. La Paz, H. Municipalidad de La Paz, 1966.

197 p. illus., facsim., ports. 22 cm.

Edited by Alcira Cardona Torrico.

1. Tamayo, Franz, 1879-1956. I. Cardona Torrico, Alcira, ed.
NN*R 8.71 w/ OC, I PC, 1, I SL (LC1, X1, Z1)

Write on slip words underlined below and class mark— STZ (Nuestra Señora)

...Homenaje a Jaime Robledo Uribe. (In: Colegio de Nuestra Señora, Manizales, Colombia. Revista. Manizales, 1942, Tomo 2, núm. 9, p. 194–340. illus.)

1. Robledo Uribe, Jaime, 1903- 1942.
N. Y. P. L. July 28, 1943

Copy only words underlined & classmark— *DR

HOMENAJE a José Ortega y Gasset. [Río Piedras] 1956. 594 p. ports., facsim. 25cm. (La Torre; revista general de la Universidad de Puerto Rico. año 4, núm. 15-16)

Cover title.
Bibliography, p. 581-592.

1. Ortega y Gasset, José, 1883-1955.

NN 3.66 r/ OI (PC)1 (LC1, X1, Z1)

Copy only words underlined & classmark— *DR

HOMENAJE a Juan Ramón Jiménez. [Río Piedras] 1957. 414 p. col. illus., ports. 25cm. (La Torre; revista general de la Universidad de Puerto Rico. año 5, núm. 19-20)

Cover title.
Bibliography, p. 407-409.

1. Jiménez, Juan Ramón, 1881-1958.

NN 3.66 r/ OI (PC)1 (LC1, X1, Z1)

Copy only words underlined
& classmark— *DR

HOMENAJE a Luis Palés Matos. [Río Piedras] 1960.
336 p. ports., facsim. 24cm. (La Torre; revista general de la Universidad de Puerto Rico. año 8, núm. 29-30)

Bibliography, p. 331-336.

1. Palés Matos, Luis, 1898-1959.

NN 3.66 r/ OI (PC)1 (LC1, X1, Z1)

A p.v.1084

Homenaje a la memoria de don Miguel Luis Amunátegui en la traslación de sus restos al nuevo mausoleo erigido por su hijo D. Domingo Amunátegui Solar 29 de septiembre de 1945. Santiago, Prensas de la Universidad de Chile, 1945. 82 p. port. 23cm.

1. Amunátegui, Miguel Luis, 1828-1888.

NN R 4.53 OC PC,1 SL (LC1,Z1,X1)

Copy only words underlined
& classmark— HDA

HOMENAJE a la memoria de José María Restrepo Sáenz.
Bogotá, Academia colombiana de historia, 1952. [115]-221 p.
port. 25cm. (Boletín de historia y antigüedades. v. 39 no. 449-450)

PARTIAL CONTENTS.—En memoria de Don José María Restrepo Sáenz por A. Sánchez de Iriarte.—La muerte de un bogotano ilustre, por L. E. Nieto Caballero.—Don José María Restrepo Sáenz, colaborador honorario del Instituto Gonzalo Fernandez de Oviedo, por G. Hernández de Alba.—El sillón académico de José María Restrepo Sáenz, por R. Gómez Hoyes y D. Ortega Ricaurte.—Escritos de

(Continued)

NN R 12.53 OI (PC) 1 (AH) 1 (LC2, Z1, X1)

HOMENAJE a la memoria de José María Restrepo Sáenz. (Card 2)

José María Restrepo Sáenz.—Bibliografía de José María Restrepo Sáenz, por José Restrepo Posada (p. [208]-221)

1. Restrepo-Sáenz, José María.

NPV

Homenaje á Menéndez y Pelayo en el año vigésimo de su profesorado. Estudios de erudición española con un prólogo de d. Juan Valera ... Madrid, V. Suárez, 1899.

2 v. front. (port.) illus., pl., facsims. 23½cm.

Music: vol. II, p. [482–483]

CONTENTS.

Apráiz, J. Curiosidades cervantinas. t. I.
Asín, M. Mohidín. t. II.
Berlanga, M. R. de. Ilíberis. Examen de los documentos históricos genuinos iliberitanos. t. II.
Blanco García, F. Fr. Luis de León; rectificaciones biográficas. t. I.
Böhmer, E. Alfonsi Valdesii litteræ XL ineditæ. t. I.

(Continued on next card)

3—7011 [36e1] Fest.

Homenaje á Menéndez y Pelayo ... 1899. (Card 2)

CONTENTS—Continued.

Bofarull y Sans, F. de. Alfonso v de Aragón en Nápoles. t. I.
Cambronero, C. La torrecilla del Prado. t. I.
Campillo, T. del. El cancionero de Pedro Marcuello. t. I.
Canella y Secades, F. D. Carlos González de Posada (notas bio-bibliográficas) t. II.
Cañal y Migolla, C. Apuntes bio-bibliográficos acerca del P. Martín de Roa. t. I.
Carmena y Millán, L. El periodismo taurino. t. I.
Catalina García, J. El segundo matrimonio del primer marqués del Cenete. t. II.
Chabas, R. Arnaldo de Vilanova y sus yerros teológicos. t. II.
Cotarelo y Mori, E. Traductores castellanos de Molière. t. I.

(Continued on next card)

3—7011 [36e1]

Homenaje á Menéndez y Pelayo ... 1899. (Card 3)

CONTENTS—Continued.

Croce, B. Due illustrazioni al "Viaje del Parnaso" del Cervantes. t. I.
Cuervo, J. Fr. Luis de Granada y la inquisición. t. I.
De Haan, F. Picaros y ganapanes. t. II.
Eguílaz y Yanguas, L. Notas etimológicas á El ingenioso hidalgo Don Quijote de la Mancha. t. II.
Espinosa y Quesada. Pedro Perret, 1555–1639. t. I.
Estelrich, J. L. Poesías líricas de Schiller, traducidas. t. I.
Farinelli, A. Cuatro palabras sobre Don Juan y la literatura donjuanesca del porvenir. t. I.
Fernández Llera, V. Una etimología: "fatilado, fetillado". t. I.
Fitzmaurice-Kelly, J. Un hispanófilo inglés del siglo XVII [Leonard Digges] t. I.

(Continued on next card)

3—7011 [36e1]

Homenaje á Menéndez y Pelayo ... 1899. (Card 4)

CONTENTS—Continued.

Franquesa y Gomis, J. La venganza en el sepulcro, comedia inédita de d. Alonso de Córdoba Maldonado. t. I.
García, J. Antigüedades montañesas. t. I.
Gestoso y Pérez, J. Las industrias artísticas antiguas en Sevilla. t. I.
Gómez Imaz, M. El Príncipe de la Paz, la Santa Caridad de Sevilla y los cuadros de Murillo. t. I.
Hazañas, J. El analista Zúñiga, novelista y poeta. t. I.
Hinojosa, E. de. El derecho en el Poema del Cid. t. I.
Hinojosa, R. de. La jurisdicción apostólica en España y el proceso de d. Antonio de Covarrubias. t. II.
Hübner, E. Los más antiguos poetas de la Península. t. II.
Jerez, marqués de. Unas papeletas bibliográficas. t. II.
Lomba y Pedraja, J. R. El rey d. Pedro en el teatro. t. II.

(Continued on next card)

3—7011 [36e1]

Homenaje á Menéndez y Pelayo ... 1899. (Card 5)

CONTENTS—Continued.

Luanco, J. R. de. Clavis sapientiæ Alphonsi, regis Castellæ. t. I.
Menéndez Pidal, R. Notas para el Romancero del conde Fernán González. t. I.
Merimée, E. El ramillete de flores poéticas de Alejandro de Luna. t. I.
Michaelis de Vasconcellos, C. Uma obra inedita do condestavel d. Pedro de Portugal ["Tragedia de la insigne reyna doña Ysabel", preceded by introduction] t. I.
Miola, A. Un canzionero manoscritto Brancacciano. t. II.
Mir, M. Un gran trabajador ignorado [J. M. Sáenz del Prado] t. II.
Morel-Fatio, A. Cartas eruditas del marqués de Mondéjar y de Etienne Baluze, 1679–1690. t. I.
Paz y Melia, A. La Biblia puesta en romance por rabí Mosé Arragel, de Guadalfajara, 1422–1433 (Biblia de la casa de Alba) t. II.

(Continued on next card)

3—7011 [36e1]

Homenaje á Menéndez y Pelayo ... 1899. (Card 6)

CONTENTS—Continued.

Pedrell, F. Palestrina y Victoria. t. I.
Pereda, J. M. de. De cómo se celebran todavía las bodas en cierta comarca montañesa, enclavada en un repliegue de lo más enriscado de la cordillera cantábrica. t. II.
Pérez Pastor, C. Datos desconocidos para la vida de Lope de Vega. t. I.
Pons, F. Dos obras importantísimas de Aben-Hazam. t. I.
Rajna, P. A Roncisvalle; alcune osservazioni topografiche in servizio della Chanson de Roland. t. II.
Restori, A. Poesie spagnole appartenute a donna Ginevra Bentivoglio. t. II.
Ribera, J. Orígenes de la filosofía de Raimundo Lulio. t. II.
Roca, P. Orígenes de la Real academia de ciencias exactas, físicas y naturales. t. II.

(Continued on next card)

3—7011 [36e1]

Homenaje á Menéndez y Pelayo ... 1899. (Card 7)
CONTENTS—Continued.
Rodríguez Marín, F. Cervantes y la Universidad de Osuna. t. II.
Rodríguez Villa, A. D. Francisco de Mendoza, almirante de Aragón. t. II.
Rouanet, L. Un "auto" inédit de Valdivielso. t. I.
Rubió y Lluch, A. La lengua y la cultura catalanas en Grecia en el siglo XIV. t. II.
Schiff, M. La première traduction espagnole de la Divine comédie. t. I.
Serrano y Sanz, M. Dos canciones inéditas de Cervantes. t. I.
Viñaza, conde de la. Dos libros inéditos del maestro Gonzalo Correas. t. I.
Wulff, F. De las rimas de Juan de la Cueva, primera parte. t. II.
1. Menéndez y Pelayo, Marcelino, 1856–1912. 2. Spanish literature—Hist. & crit. I. Valera y Alcalá Galiano, Juan, 1824–1905. II. Title: Estudios de erudición española.
3—7011
Library of Congress PQ6004.M4
~~Copy 2.~~ [30e1]

HCC
HOMENAJE a Pablo Martínez del Río en el vigesimoquinto aniversario de la primera edición de Los orígenes americanos. México [Instituto nacional de antropología e historia] 1961. 520 p. illus. 25cm.

Contributions in Spanish or English.
Includes bibliographies.

1. Martínez del Río, Pablo, 1892- . 2. Latin America--Hist.--Addresses, essays, lectures. 3. Latin America--Archaeology--Addresses, essays, lectures. I. Mexico. Instituto nacional de. Antropología e historia.
NN * 12. 63 j/ OC (OD)It (ED)It PC,1,2,3,I SL AH,1,2,I (LC1,X1,Z1) [I]

Copy only words underlined & classmark— STZ (Panama)
HOMENAJE nacional al Dr. Ricardo J. Alfaro (IN: Universidad, Panamà. 23cm. no. 38 (1960) p. [128]-152)

1. Alfaro, Ricardo Joaquín, pres. Panama, 1882-
NN 10.65 1/B OI (PC)1 (AH)1 (LC1, X1, Z1)

F-11
4082
Homenaje al profesor Claudio Sánchez-Albornoz. [Buenos Aires, 1964]
308 p. ports. 27 cm.
Spanish, Italian, English, French, German, or Portuguese.
CONTENTS.—Presentación, por J. L. Romero.—Historia de un historiador, por H. Grassotti.—Bibliografía (p. [29]-52) —Palabras del maestro, por R. Menéndez Pidal.—Críticas y evocaciones de estudiosos
(Continued)
NN*R 4.68 a/R OC,I PC,1,I SL (LC1,X1, Z1)
2

AN
(Darío, R.)
...**Homenaje** de Nicaragua a Rubén Darío. León, Nicaragua: G. Alaniz, 1916. xv, 381 p. illus. 19cm.
At head of title: Darío Zúñiga Pallais.

201757B. 1. Darío, Rubén, 1867–1916. I. Zúñiga Pallais, Darío, ed.
N. Y. P. L. March 29, 1943

HOMENAJE al profesor Claudio Sánchez-Albornoz. (Card 2)

no españoles.—Críticas y evocaciones en lengua castellana.—Comentarios, recuerdos, juicios, adhesiones.—Instituciones culturales adheridas.—Adhesiones nominales de profesores y estudiosos.—Colofón: Sánchez-Albornoz en la Facultad de Filosofía y Letras, por D. Isola.—Adhesión de los colaboradores del Instituto de Historia de España.

1. Sánchez-Albornoz y Menduiña, Claudio, 1893-
I. Sánchez-Albornoz y Menduiña, Claudio, 1893-

RAE
Homenaje ofrecido a Menéndez Pidal; miscelánea de estudios lingüísticos, literarios e históricos... Madrid: Librería y casa editorial Hernando (s.a.), 1925. 3 v. facsims., front. (port.), illus., music, tables. 4°.

1. Menéndez Pidal, Ramón, 1869-
N. Y. P. L. September 19, 1927

AN
(Belou, P.)
Homenaje al profesor Pedro Belou de sus ex-colaboradores y miembros del personal docente y tecnico del Instituto de anatomia y 1.ª catedra de anatomia descriptiva de la Facultad de ciencias medicas de Buenos Aires en el 28.° año de su ejercicio docente en la catedra universitaria. Buenos Aires: G. Kraft ltda., 1941. 467 p. facsims., front., plates, ports. 21½cm.

177672B. 1. Belou, Pedro, 1884– I. Buenos Aires (City). Universidad nacional. Ciencias médicas, Facultad de.
N. Y. P. L. June 30, 1942

WAF
Homenaje ofrecido a Teófilo Hernando por sus amigos y discípulos. Madrid, Librería y casa editorial Hernando [1953] 592 p. illus., port. 27cm.

Bibliography at end of most chapters.
"Publicaciones," p. 587-590.

1. Medicine—Addresses, essays, lectures.
2. Hernando, Teófilo, 1881-

NN** 6.54 OC,2b PC,1,2 SL (LC1,Z1,X1)

F-11
3461
HOMENAJE a Rodríguez-Moñino; estudios de erudición que le ofrecen sus amigos o discípulos hispanistas norteamericanos. Madrid, Editorial Castalia [1966] 2 v. plates,port.,facsims. 28cm.

Contributions in Spanish or English.
Bibliography of Antonio Rodríguez Moñino, v.2, p. [329]-383.
(Continued)
NN R 10.67 p/R OC PC,1, 2,3 SL (LC1,X1,Z1) [I]
2

HOMENAJE a Rodríguez-Moñino... (Card 2)

Bibliographical footnotes.

1. Rodríguez Moñino, Antonio R., 1910- . 2. Spanish literature—Addresses, essays, lectures. 3. Spain—Civilization—Addresses, essays, lectures.

F-10
9615

HOMMAGE à Alfonso Reyes, 1889-1959 [par Jules Romains, et al. Cahors, 1960?] 36 p. port. 27cm.

1. Reyes, Alfonso, 1889-1959. I. Romains, Jules, 1885- .
NN R 4.66 r/c OCs, Is PCs, Is, Is SL (LCIs, XIs, Z1)

MCQ
V39.S7

HOMENAJE Vázquez Díaz; exposición. Madrid, junio, 1953. [Madrid, 1953] 91 p. 25 plates. 27cm.

"Este Homenaje ha sido patrocinado por la Dirección general de bellas artes."

Contributions by various authors.

1. Vázquez Díaz, Daniel, 1882- I. Spain. Bellas artes, Dirección general de. t. 1953.
NN* * 12.55 a/ OC (OD) It (ED) It PC, 1, I SL A, 1, I (LC1, X1, Z1)

NKC
(Gide)

Hommage à André Gide; études, souvenirs, témoignages, par Henry Bernstein, François Paul Alibert, Claude Aveline... Un portrait inédit et des feuillets d'André Gide. Paris: Éditions du Capitole[, 1928]. 235 p. front. (port.) 8°.

Bibliography, p. [203-]235.

417948A. 1. Gide, André Paul Guillaume, 1869- . 2. Gide, André Paul Guillaume, 1869- —Bibl.
N. Y. P. L. July 6, 1929

Write on slip words underlined below and class mark — *ET
S236

Homenaje à Vicuña Mackenna. [Articles by Luis Galdames and others].

(Santiago de Chile. Universidad de Chile. Anales. Santiago de Chile, 1931. Ser.3, año 1, tomo 1-2. ports.)

Includes bibliographies.

Festschrift

AN
(Spire, A.)

Hommage à André Spire. Paris, Librairie Lipschutz [°1939] 4 p. l., [5]-152, [2] p. front. (mounted photo) pl. (3 ports.) 26½cm.

CONTENTS.—Chanson. Le chien rit. Le chant du ski. Tu seras une ride. Pogromes. Exode. Mais vous. Anniversaire. Par André Spire.—Sur le passage, par Henri Hertz.—A Gabrielle Spire, par C. S.—Voici quelque quarante ans, par Daniel Halévy.—André Spire et le conflit des générations, par Édouard Dujardin.—A André Spire, par Robert de Souza.—La bataille des âmes, par Christian Sénéchal.—André Spire, le poète du fleuve, par Marcel Pobé.—Les grands thèmes lyriques, par Renée Aberdam.—André Spire, le technicien, par Georges Lote.—André Spire, poète juif, par Edmond Fleg.—André Spire et l'action juive, par Baruch Hagani.—André Spire et notre génération, par Armand Lunel.—André Spire et la jeunesse, par P.-L. Flouquet.—La poésie, danse religieuse, par Stanislaw Vincenz.—Homage to André Spire, by Stanley Burnshaw.—André Spire, par Alexandre Hérenger.—Témoignage, par Jean Cassou.—André Spire, par Paul Jamati.—Mon témoignage, par Joseph Milbauer.—Décorations, par André Spire.

1. Spire, André, 1868- I. Spire, André, 1868-
A C 40-1108
New York. Public library for Library of Congress [2]

D-19
8342

Homenajes al Dr. Bernardo A. Houssay, en ocasión de celebrarse el 80: aniversario de su nacimiento. [Buenos Aires, 1967]

45 p. ports. 22 cm.

"Edición especial dispuesta por la Secretaría de Estado de Cultura y Educación."

1. Houssay, Bernardo Alberto, 1887- . I. Houssay, Bernardo Alberto, 1887- .
NN *R6.71 b/OC, I PC, 1, I SL (LC1, X1, Z1)

Copy only words underlined & classmark— NAA

HOMMAGE à Arnold Reymond. (IN: Etudes de lettres. Lausanne. Tome 24, no. 5 (Oct., 1952) p. 1-25)

CONTENTS. — La philosophie en face de son histoire [par] P. Thévenaz. — Philosophie des sciences et sens cosmique [par] M. Gex. — La mission du philosophie [par] A. Reymond.

1. Philosophy, 1901- 2. Reymond, Arnold Frédéric, 1874-

NN R 2.53 OI (PC) 1, 2 (LC2, Z1, X1)

MDTT

HOMMAGE [à Werkman. Stuttgart, Auslieferung: Buchhandlung F. Eggert; New York, Alleinauslieferung für U.S.A.: G. Wittenborn, 1958] 1 v. (unpaged) illus. (part col.), plates(part. col.), facsims. 30cm.

German or Dutch with German translation.

On cover: The next call, 9.

Includes facsimiles of Werkman's clandestine publications, 1941-1944.

1. Werkman, Hendrik Nicolaas, 1882-1945. 2. World war, 1939-1945--Journalism, Clandestine, etc., Dutch. I. [Title] Hommage à Werkman.
NN R 6.61 m/ OC PC, 1, 2 SL PR, 1 (LC1, X1[1], Z1)

MGO
(Bourdelle)

HOMMAGE à Bourdelle; documents et dessins inédits d'Antoine Bourdelle. Avant-propos de Raymond Cogniat. [Paris] Plon [1961] iii, 175 p. plates, ports., facsims. 26cm.

1. Bourdelle, Émile Antoine, 1861-1929.
NN 10.62 c/OC PC, 1 SL A, 1 (LC1, X1, Z1)

Hommage à C.-F. Ramuz. Lausanne, V. Porchet & c^ie [1938]

4 p. l., 13–140 p., 1 l. incl. front., illus. (music) mounted ports., plates (part mounted) 22½cm.

"Cet ouvrage ... a été tiré à ... 750 exemplaires sur velin blanc numérotés de 1 à 750 ... Exemplaire n° 40."

CONTENTS. — Blanchet, A. Portrait de C.-F. Ramuz. — Ramuz, C.-F. Taille de l'homme. (Extraits)—Cingria, C. A., et Strawinsky, I. Petit ramusianum harmonique. — Martin, G. Portrait de C.-F. Ramuz. — Claudel, P. Du côté de chez Ramuz.—Cocteau, J. A Ramuz.—Maritain, J. Pour Ramuz.—Poulaille, H. Le nouveau signe.—Chiesa, P. Taille de l'homme.—Pourrat, H. Le laboureur.—Thérive, A. Psychanalyse d'un ramuzien.—Reymond, C. Buste de C.-F. Ramuz.—Valéry, P. Le dîner.—Mann, T. Henoch. — Auberjonois, R. Aline. — Barraud, M. Aline. — Zweig, S. Pour Ramuz.—Strawinsky, T. Le cirque.—Bovy, A. Lettre du jeudi.—Cingria, A. Méditations du peintre ambulant.—Cingria, A.

(Continued on next card)

A C 39-566

[2]

HOMMAGE à Edmond Appia. [Genève? 1961?]
1 v. of facsims. plates. 18 x 25cm.

Facsims. of testimonies by E. Ansermet and others.

1. Appia, Edmond, 1894- . 2. Autographs (Signatures, etc.)--Collections--Facsimiles.

NN 6.65 e/✓OC PC, 1 SL MU, 1, 2 (LC1, X1, Z1)

Hommage à C.-F. Ramuz ... [1938] (Card 2)

CONTENTS—Continued.

Joie dans le ciel.—Roud, G. Hommage.—Mermod, H. L. Portrait de C.-F. Ramuz.—Spiess, H. Printemps 1907.—Lansel, P. À Charles-Ferdinand Ramuz.—Chiesa, F. Tre quadri.—Severini, G. La beauté sur la terre.—Zahn, E. Jugendtage im Wallis.—Augsbourg, G. Une main.—Muret, A. Lettre.—Gos, E. Du côté de chez Ramuz.—Gagnebin, E. Lettre.—Ramuz, C.-F. L'exemple de Cézanne.—Cézanne. Joueurs de cartes.—Ansermet, E. Chanson des dragons (Paroles de C.-F. Ramuz)—Markewitch, I. Pour Ramuz (Paroles de Platon)

1. Ramuz, Charles Ferdinand, 1878-

A C 39-566

Yale univ. Library
for Library of Congress [2]

HOMMAGE à Edmond et Jules de Goncourt à l'occasion du cinquantième anniversaire de la mort d'Edmond de Goncourt. Textes de Lucien Descaves [et al. Paris] Flammarion [1946] 44 p. illus., ports. 22cm.

CONTENTS. — Les derniers jours d'Edmond de Goncourt, par L. Descaves. — Le document humain, par J.-H. Rosny jeune. -- Apparition de M. de Goncourt, par R. Dorgelès. — La maison d'un artiste, par L. Larguier. — La fille Elisa, par F. Carco. — Le cas Goncourt, par A. Billy. —

(Continued)

NN X 1.58 g/✓ OC, I PC, 1, 2, I SL (LC1, X1, Z1, C1)

Write on slip, name, year, vol., page of magazine and class mark —

Hommage à Charles Henry. [Articles by Paul Valéry, and others.]

(Cahiers de l'étoile. Paris, 1930. 8°. 1930, Jan.-Feb., p.1-159.)

Bibliography p.158-159.

form 400a [vi-7-29 25m]

HOMMAGE à Edmond et Jules de Goncourt... (Card 2)

Les Goncourt que je n'ai pas connus, par Colette.

1. Goncourt, Edmond Louis Antoine Huot de, 1822-1896. 2. Goncourt, Jules Alfred Huot de, 1833-1870. I. Descaves, Lucien, 1861-1949.

Hommage à Charles Péguy; Marcel Abraham, Julien Benda, Jacques Copeau... Textes inédits de Charles Péguy, reproduction de documents, bibliographie, illustrations de L. Deshairs, Roger Pierre, L. J. Soulas. Paris: Gallimard[, 1929]. 102 p. facsim., illus., port. [4. ed.] 8°.

"Les textes et les documents de cet Hommage à Charles Péguy ont été réunis... pour le douzième cahier de Mail."
Bibliography, p. [97–]102.

502773A. 1. Péguy, Charles Pierre, 1873–1914. I. Deshairs, Léon, 1874– , illustrator. II. Pierre, Roger, illustrator. III. Soulas, L. J., illustrator. IV. Le Mail.
N. Y. P. L. January 6, 1931

Hommage à Ernest Martinenche; études hispaniques et américaines. Paris, Éditions d'Artrey [1939?]

537, [1] p. incl. front. (port.) 26½cm.

Includes bibliographies.

CONTENTS.—Supervielle, J. Entre la France et l'Amérique du Sud.—Collet, H. Musique espagnole et musique russe.—Guinard, P. Zurbarán et la découverte de la peinture espagnole en France sous Louis-Philippe.—Lambert, E. La civilisation mozarabe. — Boussagol, G. Miscelánea hispánica.—Bayer, R. Les thèmes du néo-platonisme et la mystique espagnole de la renaissance.—Bédarida, H. De Foscolo à José Maria de Heredia: une adaptation cubaine des "sepolcri". — Carayon, M. Les

(Continued on next card)

A C 40—1182

[42c2]

Hommage des écrivains étrangers à Paul Valéry. Bussum: A. A. M. Stols, 1927. 242 p. front., illus. (incl. facsim.), plates, ports. 4°.

no. 257 of 1050 copies.

396360 A.

1. Valéry, Paul Ambroise, 1872–
N. Y. P. L. December 14, 1928

Hommage à Ernest Martinenche ... [1939?] (Card 2)

CONTENTS—Continued.

trois poèmes de Crashaw sur sainte Thérèse.—Castro, A. El don Juan de Tirso y el de Molière como personajes barrocos.—Gavel, H. De Pindare à Mistral en passant par Ronsard.—Kohler, E. Lope et Bandello.—Laplane, G. Les anciennes traductions françaises du Lazarillo de Tormes.—Le Gentil, G. Les thèmes de Gil Vicente dans les moralités, sotties et farces françaises.—Peixoto, A. Le "Bourgeois gentilhomme" et le "Gentilhomme apprenti".—Menéndez Pidal, R. Nota sobre una fábula de don Juan Manuel y de Juan Ruiz.—Riva Agüero, J. de la. Las influencias francesas en las obras dramáticas de d. Pedro de Peralta.—Serís, H. La segunda edad de oro de la literatura española.—Agnès, J. Sierras et Serranas.—Amade, J. Les chants du berceau en Espagne.—

(Continued on next card)

A C 40—1182

[42c2]

Hommage à Ernest Martinenche ... ⌊1939?⌋ (Card 3)

CONTENTS—Continued.

Lapesa, R. La poesia de Gutierre de Cetina.—Levillier, R. Herrera y Reissig y Leopoldo Lugones.—Salinas, P. El problema del modernismo en España ó un conflicto entre dos espiritus.—Thomas, R. Huit romances judéo-espagnols.—Aubrun, C. Sur les débuts du théâtre en Espagne.—Echagüe, J. P. Florencio Sánchez y su teatro.—Rumeau, A. Le théâtre à Madrid à la veille du romantisme.—Barbagelata, H. D. Apuntes sobre los primeros novelistas y cuentistas chilenos.—Bataillon, M. Salmacis y Trocho dans "l'Abencérage".—Delpy, G. En marge du don Quichotte.—Mas, A. Le thème de la "réalité oscillante" dans "Don Quichotte".—Pons, J. S. Le roman et l'histoire; De Galdós à Valle Inclán.—Denis, S. Caramba.—Fouché, P. Note de toponymie ibérique: à

(Continued on next card)

A C 40—1182

⌊42c2⌋

Hommage à Ernest Martinenche ... ⌊1939?⌋ (Card 4)

CONTENTS—Continued.

propos de l'aragonais Ibón.—Millardet, G. Leme; Essai de toponymie carioque.—Altamira, R. Felipe II y el tribunal de justicia internacional.—Duviols, M. Un reportage au XVIe siècle.—Lesca, C. Histoire d'une revue.—Levene, R. La estatua del Cid Campeador en la ciudad de Buenos-Aires.—Marañon, G. Los misterios de San Plácido.—Mérimée, P. Guevara, Santa Cruz et le "razonamiento" de Villabrájima.—Ronze, R. La prise de Martín García en 1838.—Sarrailh, J. Le voyage en Espagne du marquis de Custine (1831)—Schveitzer, M. N. Les vaqueiros de alzada (Asturies)—Viñas, A. Felipe II y la jornada de las Barricadas.

1. Martinenche, Ernest, 1869- 2. Spanish literature—Hist. & crit.

A C 40—1182

Wellesley college. Library
for Library of Congress ⌊42c2⌋

NFD
(Mann)

HOMMAGE de la France à Thomas Mann à l'occasion de son quatre-vingtième anniversaire. Paris, Flinker, 1955. 169 p. port. 24cm.

CONTENTS. --Gratitude personnelle, par J. Schlumberger. --Thomas Mann, un esprit libre, par F. Mauriac. --Humanisme de Thomas Mann, par M. Yourcenar. --Thomas Mann, citoyen du monde, par R. d'Harcourt. --Témoignage, par A. Schweitzer. --Rencontre avec Thomas Mann, par R. Schuman. --Thomas Mann et Nietzsche, par G. Marcel. --Présence du

(Continued)

NN ** 3.56 f/b OC PC,1 SL (LC1, X1, Z1)

HOMMAGE de la France à Thomas Mann à l'occasion de son quatre-vingtième anniversaire. (Card 2)

fantastique dans l'œuvre de Thomas Mann, par M. Brion. --Hommage à "Altesse royale," par J. Breitbach. --Hommage, par A. Maurois. --Le démon de la création par A. Vallentin. --Le domaine du diable, par E. Vermeil. --La rencontre avec le démon, par M. Blanchot. --Salut fraternel, par J. Cocteau. --L'Allemagne peut le remercier. . . , par J. Romains. --

(Continued)

HOMMAGE de la France à Thomas Mann à l'occasion de son quatre-vingtième anniversaire. (Card 3)

Docteur Faustus, chapitre 22, par P. Boulez. --Thomas Mann et la musique, par M. Schneider. --Hommage, par G. Duhamel. --En attendant un message d'espérance, par M. Boucher. --L'idée de l'état chez Thomas Mann, par P. P. Sagave. --André Gide et Thomas Mann, par M. Schlappner. --La spiritualité de Thomas Mann, par L. Leibrich. --Gratitude, par L. Servicen. --Thomas Mann et le problème de la solitude, par M. Flinker. --Bibliographie (p. 167-169).

E-11
8088

Hommage d'une génération de juristes au président Basdevant. Paris, A. Pedone, 1960.

xix, 561 p. port. 25 cm.

Bibliographical footnotes.

1. Law, International--Addresses, essays, lectures. 2. Basdevant, Jules, 1877-

NN* 10.63 g/R OC PC,1,2 SL E,1,2 (LC1,X1,Z1)

E-12
661

HOMMAGE a Grotius [le 16 février 1946 dans la salle du Sénat, Lausanne] Lausanne, F. Rouge & cie., 1946. 71 p. 24cm. (Études et documents pour servir à l'histoire de l'Université de Lausanne. fasc. 4)

CONTENTS.--Grotius et l'Université de Leyde, par D. van Berchem.--Grotius théologien, par H. Meylan.--Grotius et l'École du droit naturel, par Ph. Meylan.

1. Groot, Hugo de, 1583-1645. I. Series.

NN R 6.65 e/G OC (OS)I PC, 1, I SL E, 1 (LC1, X1, Z1)

Copy only words underlined & classmark— *DM

HOMMAGE À HENRI MARTINEAU, 1882-1958. [Paris, 1958] vii, 232 p. illus., ports. 20cm. (Le Divan: Année 50, no. 307)

1. Martineau, Henri, 1882-

NN R 6.60 c/N OI (PC)1 (LC2, X1, Z1)

---

*C-4 p.v. 447

Hommage à Henry Church. ⌊n. p.⌋ Mesures, 1948. 83 p. ports., facsim. 24cm.

CONTENTS.—I. Le souvenir d'Henry Church: A Henry Church, au milieu de ses amis, par J. Supervielle. Portrait, par W. Stevens. Souvenir, par B. de Schloezer. Il n'aimait pas la satisfaction, par H. Michaux. L'espérance, par E. Boissonnas.—II. Rencontres: Première, dernière image, par J. Wahl. Le dimanche des moulins, par H. Pourrat. Une journée à Marino, par G. Ungaretti. Les Hippopotames, par A. Remizov. En Amérique, par F. Auberjonois.—III. L'homme et l'œuvre: Un grand de ce monde, par A. Beucler. La maison de "Mesures," par R. Caillois. Le théâtre d'Henry Church, par M. Bernard. L'école de la modestie, par J. Paulhan. Lettre à propos du "Savant," par B. Groethuysen.—IV. Textes inédits: Tu es le père et l'amant tout ensemble, par H. Church. Du bien comme du mal, par H. Church. Incident sur la tour Eiffel, par H. Church.

1. Church, Henry. I. Mesures.

NN** R 6.57 a/ OCs (OS)Is PCs, Is, Is SLs (LCIs, XIs, ZIs)

3-MAS

HOMMAGE à Hermann Voss [di Giuseppe Fiocco. Comité de redaction: Vitale Bloch et al. Comité d'honneur: Colin Agnew, et al.] Strasbourg [Impr. Strasbourgeoise] 1966. 83[4] p. plates, port. 24cm.

"Cet hommage à Hermann Voss a été realisé grace à la generosité de ses amis strasbourgeois et de messieurs Thos. Agnew & Sons ltd., Londres [et al.]."

Verzeichnis der wissenschaftlichen Veröffentlichungen von Hermann Voss." by G. Ewald: p. 55-[68]

(Continued)

NN R 10.69 k/a OC, I, II PC, 1, 2, I, II SL A, 1, 2, I, II (LC1, X1, Z1)

2

HOMMAGE à Hermann Voss... (Card 2)

1. Voss, Hermann Georg August, 1884- . 2. Voss, Hermann Georg August, 1884- --Bibl. I. Fiocco, Giuseppe, 1884- II. Bloch, Vitale, ed.

Copy only words underlined
& classmark— BKA

HOMMAGE À JACQUES RICHARD-MOLARD, 1913-1951. Paris [1953] 382 p. 20cm. (Présence africaine. no. 15)

CONTENTS.--Ptie 1. Civilisations et sociétés ouest-africaines.--ptie. 2. La terre e l'homme en Afrique noire.--ptie. 3. L'Afrique nouvelle: bilan, transformations, perspectives.
Bibliographical footnotes.

1. Richard-Molard, Jacques. 2. Africa--Civilization. 3. African tribes--Africa, French, West.

NN R 2.57 j/8 OI (PC)1, 2, 3 (LC4, X1, Z1)

NKD p.v.365

Hommage à Jules Romains pour son soixantième anniversaire, 26 août 1945. [Paris] Flammarion [1945]

4 p. l., 7-139, [1] p. front. (port.) 23cm.

CONTENTS.—Cuisenier, André. Notice biographique.—Lecomte, Georges. Un retour attendu.—Billy, André. Les hommes de bonne volonté.—Arcos, René. Souvenirs.—Audisio, Gabriel. Le secret de Jules Romains.—Blanchart, Paul. Jules Romains, homme de théâtre.—Cazes, Albert. Jules Romains, homme libre.—Copeau, Jacques. Jules Romains au Vieux-Colombier.—Dullin, Charles. Un homme de théâtre.—Israël, Madeleine. Première rencontre avec Jules Romains.—Jouvet, Louis. Le dramaturge.—Lalou, René. La poésie chez Jules Romains.—Membré, Henri. Le théoricien, le critique.—Parigot, Hippolyte. Mon élève.—Pauphilet, Albert. Souvenirs de "Khagne."—Tinayre, Marcelle.

(Continued on next card)

47-18686

[3]

Festschrift

Hommage à Jules Romains pour son soixantième anniversaire ... [1945] (Card 2)

CONTENTS—Continued.

Que sont-ils devenus?—Vercors. L'ami.—Vildrac, Charles. Une page retrouvée.—Piérard, Louis. Hommage.—Reyes, Alfonso. L'esthétique de Jules Romains.—Hopkins, Geràrd. L'opinion du lecteur anglais.—Jules Romains et la Maison internationale des P. E. N. clubs.

1. *Romains, Jules, 1885-

PQ2635.O52Z65 928.4 47-18686

© 30Dec45; 1c 8May46; Ernest Flammarion; AF1341.

Library of Congress [3]

Copy only words underlined
& Classmark-- MAA

HOMMAGE à Julien Cain. Paris, 1966. 112 p. illus., ports. 28cm. (Gazette des beaux arts. ser. 6, v. 68, année 108, [no.] 1170-1171)

A collection of articles.
CONTENTS.--Julien Cain et les arts.--Julien Cain et les lettres.--Le bibliothèques; la Bibliothèque nationale.--Contributions étrangères. --L'amitié.

1. Cain, Julien, 1887- . 2. Bibliothèque nationale, Paris.

NN R 1.67 1/ OC OI PC, 1, 2 A, 1 PR, 1 (LC1, X1, Z1)

E-10
6788

EN hommage à Léon Graulich [par] ses anciens élèves. [Liège] Faculté de droit de Liège, 1957. xxiv, 726 p. port. 25cm.

Includes bibliographies.

1. Graulich, Léon. 2. Law--Addresses, essays, lectures. I. Liège. Université. Faculté de droit.

NN 12.58 m/ OC (OS)I, Ib+ PC, 1, 2, I SL E, 1, I (LC1, X1, Z1)

Copy only words underlined
& classmark — NAA

Hommage à M. Gottfried Bohnenblust. Lausanne, 1953. 47 p. 23cm. Etudes de lettres. t. 25, no.3; bull. no. 89)

Bibliographical footnotes.
Contents.—De l'unité de l'ésprit, par M. Reymond. —Arthur Schopenhauer en Suisse, par P. Bonard.—Nietzsche, lecteur des Essais de Montaigne, par C. Gagnebin.—Le silence de Prométhée, par J. Moser.—De Reinhold Lenz à Bertolt Brecht, par M. Dentan.—Spitteler et le génie de la France, par W. Stauffacher.

1. Bohnenblust, Gottfried, 1883-
NN R 3.54 OI (PC)1 (LC2, Z1, X1)

---

*MEC
(Massenet)

HOMMAGE a MASSENET, inédits études, témoignages d'hier et d'aujourd'hui...; plaquette du cinquantenaire de sa mort. [Fontainebleau, En vente chez Y. Leroux, 1963] 81 p. port. 22cm.

Cover title.
Dedication and "avertissement" signed: Y.L.
Includes bibliographies.

1. Massenet, Jules, 1842-1912. I. Leroux, Yves.
NN 6.65 e/ OC, I, Ib* PC, 1, I SL MU, 1, I (LC1, X1, Z1)

NKC
(Betz)

Hommage à Maurice Betz. [Paris] Émile-Paul frères [1949]
155 p. 5 pl. 24cm.

With 4 original lithographs.
No. 304 of 305 copies.
"Bibliographie," p. 153.

Festschrift

555464B. 1. Betz, Maurice, 1898- 1946.
N. Y. P. L. December 15, 1950

D-16
2199

HOMMAGE à Monique Saint-Hélier. [Sous le patronage de la ville de La Chaux-de-Fonds et de l'Institut neuchâtelois, le 25 octobre 1956. Neuchâtel (Suisse)] Éditions de la Baconnière [c1960] 49 p. port. 22cm. (Institut neuchâtelois, Neuchâtel, Switzerland. Cahiers. 6)

1. Saint-Hélier, Monique. I. Institut neuchâtelois, Neuchâtel, Switzerland.
NN * R 8.66 a/c OC (OS)I PC, 1, I SL (LC1, X1, Z1)

D-19
9054

Hommage für Peter Huchel, zum 3. April 1968. [Hrsg. von Otto F. Best] München, R. Piper [1968]

117, [1] p. front. 22 cm.

CONTENTS.—Hommage: Ein Essay des Vorbewussten nach vorwärts, von E. Bloch.—Drei Gedichte, von P. Celan.—Zeilen an Peter Huchel, von G. Eich.—An taube Ohren der Geschlechter, von W. Jens.—Für Peter Huchel, von H. Böll.—Die Verzauberte, von O. Schaefer.—Erinnerung an gemeinsame Jahre in Berlin, von H. Lange.—Sagen Schweigen Sagen/Schattengestalt, von H. Bienek.—

(Continued)

NN*R 9.70 m/ OC, I, II PC, 1, 2, I, II SL (LC1, X1, Z1)

2

HOMMAGE für Peter Huchel ... (Card 2)

Der Schwan, von N. Sachs.—Nicht gesagt, von M. L. Kaschnitz.—Ich will dich, von H. Domin.—Franz Werfel und S. L. Jacobowsky, von M. Reich-Ranicki.—Stunden-Gedicht (II), von K. Krolow.—Nach Potsdam, von W. Koeppen.—Materialien: Ein Mann namens Peter Huchel, von W. Haas.—Erinnerungen eines Mitarbeiters von "Sinn und Form," von H. Mayer.—Laudatio, von R. Hartung.—Natur und Geschichte in Huchels Gedicht, von H. E. Holthusen.—Über Peter Huchel, von C. Hohoff.—Das Gleichnis oder der Zeuge wider Willen, von G. Kalow.—Peter Huchel und sein lyrisches Werk, von I. Seidler.—Nachbemerkung und Lamento, von O. F. Best.—Lebensdaten.—Werke P. Huchels (p. 116)—Literatur über P. Huchel (p. 117-[118])

1. Huchel, Peter. 2. German literature--Collections. I. Huchel, Peter. II. Best, Otto F., ed.

Copy only words underlined
& classmark— NAA

EN HOMMAGE au Professeur Georges Bonnard. Lausanne, 1950. (Études de lettres. t. 23, no. 1)

CONTENTS.—Le problème du héros et la structure du Roi Jean de Shakespeare, par A. Bonjour.—L'évolution de la pensée de Shakespeare; la thèse de Max Deutschbein, par P. Cherix.—Note sur les premières traductions italiennes de Essais de Bacon, par E. Giddey.—Poésie naturaliste au xviie siecle, par A. Henchoz.—Willa Cather (1875-1947), par R. Rapin.

1. Bonnard, Georges Alfred, 1886- . 2. Literature—Hist. and crit.

NN R 3.53 OI (PC)1, 2 (LC2, Z1, X1)

Copy only words underlined
& classmark— RBA

Hommage au professeur J. Hammer. (IN: Latomus. Bruxelles. 29cm. t. 13, fasc. 3(juil.-sept., 1954) p. [337]-428)

Contents.—Cybèle aux Mégalésies, par P. Boyancé.—Les interpolations de la lettre de Pline sur les chrétiens, par L. Herrmann.—La légende de Péro et de Micon et l'allaitement symbolique, par W. Deonna.—Sur une plaque du chaudron de Gundestrup, par J.

(Continued)

NN R 4.55 s/ OI (PC) 1 (LC2, X1, Z1)

Copy only words underlined
& classmark— RBA

Hommage au professeur J. Hammer. (Card 2)

Gricourt.—Du chaudron de Gundestrup aux mythes classiques, par M. Renard.—II Carmen Fratrum Arvalium e il metodo archeologico, di S. Ferri.—Les consuls du césar-pharaon Caligula et l'héritage de Germanicus, par J. Colin.—L'exploration archéologique de Bavai, par H. Biévelet et R. Jolin.—Notes sur le Dialogus super auctoreus de

(Continued)

Copy only words underlined
& classmark— RBA

Hommage au professeur J. Hammer. (Card 3)

Conrad de Hirsau et le Commentaire sur Théodule de Bernard d'Utrecht, par R.B.C. Huygens.

1. Hammer, Jacob, 1894-

D-17
2097

HOMMAGE à René Maran. Paris, Présence africaine, 1965. 311 p. 23cm.

CONTENTS.—René Maran, précurseur de la negritude, par L. S. Senghor.—Mon ami René Maran, par R. Violaines.—Le cœur, l'esprit et la raison, par C. Kunstler.—Maran le poète, par C. Astruc.—Cet homme pareil aux autres, par A. Darnal.—La genèse de Batouala, par M. Gahisto.—Djogoni (texte) par R. Maran.—Maran-la-fidélité, par F. Raynal.—René Maran et Félix Eboué, une amitié, par A. Maurice.—A René Maran, en témoignage d'un amical souvenir, par

(Continued)

NN*R 4.67 a/ OC PC, 1 SL (LC1, X1, Z1)

2

HOMMAGE à René Maran. (Card 2)

J. Jacoulet.—René Maran, par P. Paraf.—Souvenirs, par C. Bareilley.—Hommage, par P. Tuffrau.—René Maran n'est plus ..., par M. Sinda.—René Maran, chevalier de l'amitié, par J. Portail.—René Maran, par A. Fraysse.—Ses amis les livres ... par F. Descœurs.—Le vrai René Maran, par O. Denys.—René Maran, journal présenté par M. Mercer Cook.

1. Maran, René, 1887-

NFV

Hommage à Ventura García Calderón. Paris, H. Lefebvre, 1947. 125 p. illus. 25cm.

Contributions by various authors.

562888B. 1. García Calderón, Ventura, 1886-

NN R 3.53 OC PC, 1 SL (LC1, Z1, X1)

Write on slip words underlined
and class mark —
*QCB

...**Hommage à W. Radloff**...à l'occasion de son 80-me anniversaire (1837–1917)... Leningrad, 1917–25. x, 740 p. illus. 30cm. (Akademiya nauk. Muzei antropologii i etnografii. Сборник. Том 5.)

Text and added t.-p. in Russian: ...Ко дню 80-тилетия академика Василия Васильевича Радлова... Ленинград, 1917–25.
Bibliographical footnotes.

287819A. 1. Ethnology—Essays and misc. 2. Ethnology—Siberia. 3. Radlov, Vasiliĭ Vasil'yevich, 1837–1918. I. Ser.
N. Y. P. L. April 6, 1944

E-11
2208

HOMMAGES a Georges Dumézil. Bruxelles, Latomus, 1960. xxiii, 237 p. illus. 25cm. (Collection Latomus. v. 45)

Chiefly in French, with some articles in English or German.
Bibliographical notes.
"Bibliographie des travaux de Georges Dumézil," p. [xi] -xxiii.

1. Literature--Addresses, essays, lectures. 2. Dumézil, Georges, 1898- I. Series.
NN X 3. 61 m/ OC (OS)I PC, 1, 2, I SL (LC1, X1, Z1)

F-10
5051

HOMMAGES à Léon Herrmann. Bruxelles, Latomus, 1960. xi, 804 p. illus. 26cm. (Collection Latomus. v. 44)

Chiefly in French, with a few contributions in Italian, English, Latin, Spanish or German.
Bibliographical footnotes.
"Bibliographie des travaux de Léon Herrmann, 1914-1959," par R. van Weddingen, p. [1] -59.

1. Herrmann, Léon. 2. Classical studies--Collections. I. Series.
NN X 11. 60m/ OC (OS)I PC, 1, 2, I SL (LC1, X1, Z1)

F-11
5767

HOMMAGES à Marcel Renard, édités par Jacqueline Bibauw. Bruxelles, Latomus, 1969. 3 v. illus., ports., maps (part fold.) 26cm. (Collection LATOMUS. v. 101-103)

Text in French, English or German.
Bibliographical footnotes.

1. Rome--Civilization--Addresses, essays, lectures. I. Series. II. Renard, Marcel. III. Bibauw, Jacqueline, ed. IV. Bibauw, Jacqueline.
NN 9. 69 v/ OC, II, III, IVbo (OS)I PC, 1, I, II, III SL (LC1, X1, Z1) [I]

F-11
7668

HOMMAGES à Marie Delcourt. Bruxelles, Latomus, 1970. xii, 442 p. illus., port. 26cm. (Collection Latomus. v. 114)

French, German or English.
"Bibliographie choisie des travaux de Marie Delcourt," p. [9]-19.
Bibliographical footnotes.

1. Classical studies--Collections. 2. Latin literature, Neo-Latin--Addresses, essays, lectures. I. Series. II. Delcourt, Marie.
NN 5. 71 e/z OC, II (OS)I PC, 1, 2, I, II SL (LC1, X1, Z1) [I]

F-10
1729

HOMMAGES à Waldemar Deonna. Bruxelles, Latomus, revue d'études latines, 1957. vii, 539 p. illus., 45 plates. 26cm. (Collection Latomus. v. 28)

Contributions chiefly in French; a few in German, Italian, English or Spanish.
Bibliographie des travaux de Waldemar Deonna, 1904-1956," p. [1]-48.

1. Deonna, Waldemar, 1880- . 2. Archaeology, Classical--Addresses, essays, lectures. 3. Classical studies--Collections. 4. Art, Classical--Addresses, essays, lectures. I. Series.
NN X 2. 58 m/o OC (OS)I PC, 1, 2, 3, 4, I SL A, 4, I (LC1, X1, Z1, C1, Y1)

E-14
1193

Honderd jaar rechtsleven. De Nederlandse Juristen-Vereniging 1870–1970. Zwolle, W. E. J. Tjeenk Willink, [1970].
x, 340 p. 25 cm.
Includes bibliographical references.

(Continued)

NN*R 4. 71 e/zOC (OS)I, Ib* PC, 1, I SL E, 1, I (LC1, X1, Z1) 3

HONDERD jaar rechtsleven. (Card 2)

CONTENTS.—Het leerstuk van de opgewekte schijn van volmacht en de Engels-Amerikaansrechtelijke leer van de 'apparent authority,' door H. C. F. Schoordijk.—Bezitloze zekerheid op roerende zaken, door W. Snijders.—De spanning van de contractsband in het bestaande en het komende recht, door A. L. de Wolf.—De invloed van de belangenverbreding op het handelen van de aandeelhouder, door J. L. P. Cahen.—De naamloze vennootschap als raakpunt van contraire belangen, door F. J. W. Löwensteyn.—Van werkman tot medewerker, door N. E. H. van Esveld.—Kentering in de opvattingen over de hoofdbeginselen van ons burgerlijk procesrecht tussen 1870–

(Continued)

HONDERD jaar rechtsleven. (Card 3)

1970, door W. L. Haardt.—In memoriam Dirkje Veldhuizen, door A. A. L. Minkenhof.—Strafrecht en publieke opinie toen en nu, door G. E. Mulder.—De overtuigingsdader, door J. Remmelink.—De magische lijn; verkenningen op de grens van publiek- en privaatrecht, door J. van der Hoeven.—De rol van de wetgever, door T. Koopmans.—De ontwikkeling van de rechtsbescherming tegen de overheid, door D. Simons.—Strijklicht over ons internationaal privaatrecht, door H. U. Jessurun d'Oliveira.—Individu en internationale gemeenschap, door A. M. Stuyt.—Europees recht en nationale soevereiniteit, door L. J. Brinkhorst.—Belastingbeginselen, door J. van Soest.

1. Law--Addresses, essays, lectures. I. Nederlandse juristen-vereniging.

D-17
1439

Honneur à Saint-John Perse, hommages et témoignages littéraires suivis d'une documentation sur Alexis Léger ... Paris, Gallimard, 1965.
819 p. plates. 23cm.
Bibliographical footnotes.

1. Léger, Alexis Saint-Léger, 1889- . I. Léger, Alexis Saint-Léger, 1889-
NN * 3. 67 1/3 OC, I PC, 1, I SL (LC1, X1, Z1)

E-13
9085

"An Honorable profession"; a tribute to Robert F. Kennedy. Edited by Pierre Salinger [and others. 1st ed.] Garden City, N. Y., Doubleday, 1968.
182 p. illus., facsims., ports. 24 cm.

1. Kennedy, Robert F., 1925-1968. I. Kennedy, Robert F., 1925-1968. II. Salinger, Pierre, ed.
NN*R 7. 70 v/zOC, I, II PC, 1, I, II SL AH, 1, I, II (LC1, X1, Z1)

E-12
3600

Horkheimer, Max, 1895– ed.
Zeugnisse, Theodor W. Adorno zum sechzigsten Geburtstag. Im Auftrag des Instituts für Sozialforschung. [Frankfurt am Main] Europäische Verlagsanstalt [1963]
501 p. music. 25 cm.
In German, French, or English.
Bibliographical footnotes.
1. Adorno, Theodor Wiesengrund, 1903– . 2. Civilization--Addresses, essays, lectures. I. Institut für Sozialforschung, Frankfurt am Main.
NN * R 6.65 e/ OC (OS)I PC, 1, 2, I SL (LC1, X1, Z1)

D-16
4633

HOWARD, MICHAEL, ed.
The theory and practice of war; essays presented to Captain B.H. Liddell Hart [on his seventieth birthday] London, Cassell [1965] x, 376,[1] p. 22cm.
Bibliography, p. 375-[377]
1. Liddell, Hart, Basil Henry, 1895– . 2. War--Addresses, essays, lectures. 3. Military art and science--Addresses, essays, lectures.
NN R 2.66 a/c OC PC, 1, 2, 3 SL (LC1, X1, Z1)

D-15
1632

HOROWITZ, IRVING LOUIS, ed.
The new sociology; essays in social science and social theory, in honor of C. Wright Mills. New York, Oxford University Press, 1964. xv, 512 p. 22cm.
Includes bibliographical references.
1. Social sciences--Addresses, essays, lectures. 2. Mills, Charles Wright.
NN * R 5.64 e/ OC PC, 1, 2 SL E, 1, 2 (LC1, X1, Z1)

..AN
(Whittemore, H.)

Howard Whittemore, 1864–1948; biographical note, letters & resolutions from organizations with which Mr. Whittemore was connected. Berkeley, Calif., 1950. 16 l. port. 24cm.
In ms. on t.-p.: Compiled by Norman Clark Whittemore.
596543B. 1. Whittemore, Howard, 1864–1948.
N. Y. P. L. November 21, 1951
Festschrift.

SSMC

HORTEN TEKNISKE SKOLE, Horten, Norway. Hortens-teknikernes forbund.
100 [i.e. Hundre] års biografisk jubileums-festskrift, Horten tekniske skole, 1855-1955. Skolens historie og de biografiske opplysninger over bestyrelsesmedlemmer, lærere og elever er utarb. av Styret i Horten teknikernes forbund i samarbeid med en redaksjonskomite. [Horten, 1955] 557 p. illus., ports. 28cm.
1. Education, Industrial and technical—Indiv. inst.—Norway—Horten.
2. Engineers—Norway. t. 1955.
NN * * R 6.56 j/ OS PC, 1, 2 SL RC, 2 ST, 1t, 2t (LC1, X1, Z1)

* MGA

HÜSCHEN, HEINRICH, ed.
Festschrift Karl Gustav Fellerer zum sechzigsten Geburtstag am 7. Juli 1962, überreicht von Freunden und Schülern. Regensburg, G. Bosse, 1962. xlv, 593 p. illus., port., music. 22cm.
Contributions in German, English or French, one in Spanish.
Bibliographical footnotes.
"Bibliographie des schrifttums von Karl Gustav Fellerer, zusammengestellt
(Continued)
NN R 2.63 p/ OC, I PC, 1, 2, 3, 5, 6, I SL MU, 1, 2, 4, 5, 6, I (LC1, X1, Z1) dd
2

AN
(Horthy, M.)

Horthy Miklós. [Budapest] Singer és Wolfner irodalmi intézet rt. kiadása [1939] 271 p. facsims., illus. (chart), plates, ports., geneal. table. 26cm.
Contents.—Herczeg Ferenc. Nagybányai Horthy Miklós.—Lukinich Imre. Húsz év krónikája.—Vitéz Ákosfalvi Szilágyi László. A Nagy-Bányai Horthy-család.—Harsányi Zsolt. A debreceni diák.—Norwalli Konek Emil. A tengerész.—Scholtz Andor. Ferenc József szárnysegéde.—Nemes Suhay Imre. A fővezér.—Kornis Gyula. Az államférfi.—Gróf Zichy Ráfaelné. A kormányzó felesége.—Gulácsy Irén. Az irodalom és művészet patrónusa.—Kállay Miklós. A kenderesi gazda.—Csathó Kálmán. A vadász.—Harsányi Zsolt. Hogyan él a kormányzó?—Hét kis történet.
Festschrift.
65196B. 1. Horthy, Miklós, nagybányai, 1868–
N. Y. P. L. July 19, 1940

HÜSCHEN, HEINRICH, ed. Festschrift Karl Gustav Fellerer zum sechzigsten Geburtstag... (Card 2)
von Klaus Wolfgang Niemöller." p. xv-xxxviii. "Verzeichnis der von Karl Gustav Fellerer betreuten Dissertationen, zusammengestellt von Jobst Peter Fricke," p. xxxix-xlv.
1. Fellerer, Karl Gustav, 1902– 2. Fellerer, Karl Gustav, 1902– --Bibl. 3. Music--Essays. 4. Essays. 5. Dissertations, Academic--Germany--Bibl. 6. Dissertations, Academic--Switzerland--Freiburg--Bibl. I. Title.

E-11
6201

Hosley, Richard, ed.
Essays on Shakespeare and Elizabethan drama in honor of Hardin Craig. Columbia, University of Missouri Press, 1962.
vi, 385 p. illus., port. 24 cm.
"A bibliography of the writings of Hardin Craig from 1940 to 1961": p. 369-374. Bibliographical footnotes.
1. Drama, English--Hist. and crit., 1500-1642. 2. Shakespeare, William--Commentaries and criticism. 3. Craig, Hardin, 1875–
NN * R 12.62 e/ OC PC, 1, 2, 3 SL (LC1, X1, Z1)

MAMG
+

HÜTTER, ELISABETH, ed.
Kunst des Mittelalters in Sachsen: Festschrift Wolf Schubert, dargebracht zum sechzigsten Geburtstag am 28. Januar 1963. [Herausgabe und redaktion: Elisabeth Hütter, Fritz Löffler [und] Heinrich Magirius, Dresden] Weimar, Herman Böhlaus Nachfolger, 1967. 343 p. 20 illus., 132 plates (part col.), plans (part fold.) 31cm.
Foreword signed Wolfgang Stier.
(Continued)
NN R 6.69 v/ OC, I, II, IIIbo PC, 1, 2, 3, 4, I, II SL A, 1, 2, 3, 4, I, II (LC1, X1, Z1) [I]
2

HÜTTER, ELISABETH, ed. Kunst des Mittelalters in Sachsen... (Card 2)

Folded col. plate in pocket.

1. Art, German--Saxony. 2. Art, German, Middle Ages. 3. Schubert, Wolf. 4. Polychromy. I. Title. II. Title: Festschrift Wolf Schubert. III. Hütter, Elisabeth.

HULDEBOEK Antoon vander Plaetse. (Card 2)

V. Verstegen. --Gesproken en geschreven algemene omgangstaal in Nederland, door C. Kops. --Gij en het toneel, door A. van de Velde. --Beschaafd Nederlands, door J. Grauls. --Proeve van overzicht van de moderne Vlaamse toneelletterkunde, door A Demedts. --Die beskaafde uitspraak van Afrikaans en die beskaafde Afrikaanse skrijftaal, deur T. H. le Roux. --Herinneringen aan het Vlaamse volkstoneel, door R. Jacobs. --De diepere betekenis van de toneelspeelkunst, door J. van Daele. --Zuidafrikaanse dramatiek voor het Nederlands toneel, door R. Antonissen. --Over het belang van zwijgen bij het voordragen. (Continued)

Write on slip, name, year, vol., page of magazine and class mark — *EE

Hugo de Vries; 6 Vorträge zur Feier seines 80. Geburtstages.

(Tuebinger naturwissenschaftliche Abhandlungen. Stuttgart, 1929. 8°. Heft 12, p. 1-62.)

Contents: Aus dem Leben und Wirken von Hugo de Vries von Theodor Stomps. Die Schlafbewegungen der Laubblätter von Walter Zimmermann. Die Entwicklung der Oenotheraforschung von Ernest Lehmann.

form 400a [vi-7-29 25m]

HULDEBOEK Antoon vander Plaetse. (Card 3)

door A. Fonteyne. --Het toneelleven in Vlaanderen, tot 1830 door G. van der Wiele.

1. Plaetse, Antoon vander, 1903- 2. Elocution. 3. Drama, Flemish--Hist. and crit.

---

(2)

Hugo de Vries;....

Die Ergebnisse der vergleichend zytologischen Untersuchungen an Onagraceen von Julius Schwemmle. Die Zytologie der Oenothera-Gruppe Biennis in ihrem Verhältnis zur Vererbungslehre von Raplh Cleland. Chromosomenbindung und Genetik bei Oenothera von Friedrich Oehlkers.

---

*GAH

Huldeboek Pater Dr Bonaventura Kruitwagen O. F. M. aangeboden op Sint Bonaventura 14 Juli 1949 ter gelegenheid van zijn gouden priesterfeest en zijn vijf en zeventigste verjaardag. 's-Gravenhage, M. Nijhoff, 1949. viii, 481 p. illus. 26cm.

"Lijst van de geschriften van Pater Dr B. Kruitwagen O. F. M.," p. 15-60.
Bibliographical footnotes.

J. S. BILLINGS MEM. COLL.

507103B. 1. Kruitwagen, Bonaventura, pater, 1874- . 2. Bibliography—Collections. 3. Bibliography—Rarities. 4. Libraries—Netherlands. 5. Printing—Netherlands.
N. Y. P. L. July 25, 1950

D-11
3181

VIIIe ,i e. Huitième, centenaire de la mort de Saint Bernard, abbé de Clairvaux, docteur de l'Église, 1153-1953. ,Colmar, 1953, 54 p. illus., ports. 22cm.

Text in French or German.
Includes: Lettre encyclique "Doctor Mellifluus" ,par, Pie XII, Pape.

1. Bernard de Clairvaux, Saint, 1091-1153. 2. Cistercians.
NN R X 7.59 OC PC,1,2 SL (LC1,X1,Z1)

E-11
2446

The HUMAN person and the world of values; a tribute to Dietrich Von Hildebrand by his friends in philosophy. Edited by Balduin V. Schwarz. New York, Fordham University press [1960]

xiii, 210 p. 24 cm. (The Orestes Brownson series on contemporary thought & affairs, no. 3)

Includes bibliographical references.

CONTENTS.—About Christian philosophy, by J. Maritain.—Von Hildebrand and Marcel: a parallel, by A. Jourdain.—Love and philosophy, by J. V. Walsh.—The concepts of cyclic and evolutionary time, by B. de Solages.—The sovereignty of the object; notes on truth and intellecutal humility, by A. Kolnai.—Authentic humanness and its existential primordial assumptions, by G. Marcel.—Individuality and (Continued)

NN * R X 4. 61 p/o OC, II, IIIb* (OS)I PC, 1, 2, I, II SL (LC1, X1, Z1) 2

NANL

HULDEBOEK Antoon vander Plaetse. Tielt, Lannoo, 1951. 202 p. ports. 25cm.

"Drie honderd genummerde en getekende exemplaren." No. 278.
CONTENTS. --Antoon vander Plaetse, apostel van het schone woord, door A. Verschuere. --Voordrachtkunst, door C. Verschaeve. --Proeve van karakteristiek van Antoon vander Plaetse, door W. Putman. --Voordragkuns in Suid-Afrika, deur A. Coetzee. --Spreek- en schrijftaal in Frans-Vlaanderen, door V. Celen. --De Kon. Vlaamse academie voor taal en letterkunde en het algemeen beschaafd, door (Continued)

NN** 12.55 a/o OC, 1b PC 1, 2, 3 SL (LC1, X1, Z1) [I]

The HUMAN person and the world of values... (Card 2)

CONTENTS—Continued.

personality, by M. F. Sciacca.—Can a will be essentially good? By H. de Lubac.—Reason and revelation on the subject of charity, by R. W. Gleason.—"Technique" of spiritualization and transformation in Christ, by J. A. Cuttat.—Some reflections on gratitude, by B. V. Schwarz.—Bibliography of the works of Dietrich Von Hildebrand (p. 195-210)

1. Philosophy--Addresses, essays, lectures. 2. Hildebrand, Dietrich von, 1889- I. Series. II. Schwarz, Balduin V., 1902- , ed. III. Schwarz, Balduin V., 1902-

E-13
4748
HUMANISME actif; mélanges d'art et de littérature offerts à Julien Cain. Préf. par Étienne Dennery. Lithographie de Chagall. Eau-forte d'André Dunoyer de Segonzac. [Paris] Hermann [1968] 2 v. illus., plates(1 col.), ports., facsims. 24cm.

"Jean Porcher... établi le plan de cet ouvrage. Après sa mort survenue... la mise au point de la publication ... assurée par... André Masson."
Bibliographical footnotes.

(Continued)

NN S 4.69 k/,OC, I, II, III PC, 1, 2, 3, 4, 5, I, II, III SL A, 1, 3, I, II, III PR, 1, I, II, III (PRET1, PRL1, LC1, X1, Z1) 2

D-16
5402
HUXLEY, Sir JULIAN SORELL, 1887- , ed. Aldous Huxley, 1894-1963; a memorial volume. London, Chatto & Windus, 1965. 174 p. ports. 23cm.

1. Huxley, Aldous Leonard, 1894-1963.
NN R 3.66 a/c OC PC, 1 SL (LC1, X1, Z1)

HUMANISME actif; mélanges d'art et de littérature offerts à Julien Cain. (Card 2)

CONTENTS.--1. Evocations et souvenirs. Littérature. Art et histoire. --2. Bibliothèques. Histoire du livre. Études et voyages.

1. Cain, Julien, 1887- . 2. French literature--Addresses, essays, lectures. 3. Art, French. 4. Books--Hist. 5. Libraries--Addresses, essays, lectures. I. Masson, André, 1900- ed. II. Porcher, Jean, ed. III. Dennery, Étienne.

MWES
(Schønberg, I.)
IB SCHØNBERG, en mindebog, skrevet af de der kendte ham. [Redigeret af Bent Schønberg og Kai Berg Madsen. Tegninger af Hans Bendix. København] C. Andersen [1955] 183 p. illus., ports. 23cm.

1. Schønberg, Ib, 1902-1955. I. Madsen, Kai Berg, 1903- , ed. II. Schønberg, Bent, ed. III. Schønberg, Bent.
NN** X 6.56 p/& OC, Ib, I, II, IIIbo PC, 1, I, II SL (T4, LC1, X1, Z1)

E-13
7726
HUMANIST und Politiker; Leo Wohleb, der letzte Staatspräsident des Landes Baden. Gedenkschrift zu seinem 80. Geburstag am 2. September 1968, hrsg. von Hans Maier und Paul-Ludwig Weinacht, in Verbindung mit Maria Wohleb [et al.] Heidelberg, F.H. Kerle [1969] 206 p. illus., port. 24cm.

I. Wohleb, Leo, 1888-1955. II. Maier, Hans, 1931- , ed. III. Weinacht, Paul Ludwig, ed. IV. Weinacht, Paul Ludwig.
NN R 3.70 v/& OC, I, II, III, IVbo PC, I, II, III SL E, I, II, III (LC1, X1, Z1)

D-16
2615
IDEARIO y presencia de Herminia Brumana [1. ed.] Buenos Aires, Edición Amigos de Herminia Brumana [1964] 176 p. illus., ports. 23cm.

Includes excerpts from Herminia C. Brumana's writings.

1. Brumana, Herminia C. 2. Argentine literature--Misc. 3. Education--Addresses, essays, lectures.
NN R 9.65 g/J OC PC, 1, 2, 3 SL (LC1, X1, Z1)

TAH

125 [*i. e.* **Hundertfünfundzwanzig**] Jahre Gewerbe- und Handelsverein von 1840 e. V., Oldenburg/Oldb; Jubiläumsfestschrift mit Chronik zum 10. April 1965. [Oldenburg, Buchdr. H. Prull, 1965]

311 p. illus., ports. 21 cm.

"Chronik des Oldenburgischen Gewerbe- und Handelsvereins, bearb. von Harry Colmsee": p. 21-175.

1. Economic history--Germany--Oldenburg (City). I. Colmsee, Harry. II. Gewerbe- und Handelsverein von 1840, Oldenburg, Germany.
NN*R 6.69 v/ OC, I, Ib* (OS)II PC, 1, I, II SL E, 1, I, II (LC1, X1, Z1)

E-13
7591
IDÉER och ideologier; sex studier utgivna till Statsvetenskapliga föreningens i Uppsala femtioårsdag den 7 november 1969. Stockholm, Almqvist & Wiksell [1969] 375 p. 24cm. (Statsvetenskapliga föreningen i Uppsala. Skrifter. 50)

Bibliographical footnotes.
CONTENTS.--Om demokrati och statsförvaltning, av S. Rylander --Den nya vänsterns idéer, av A.H. Eriksson.--22-marsrörelsen i

(Continued)

NN 2.70 l/OC (OS)I, II PC, 1, I, II SL E, 1, I, II (LC1, X1, Z1) 2

Write on slip words underlined below and class mark —
STL

Hunziker, Fritz, 1886–
Die Mittelschulen in Zürich und Winterthur, 1833–1933; Festschrift zur Jahrhundertfeier, herausgegeben vom Erziehungsrate des Kantons Zürich. Bearbeitet von Fritz Hunziker. Zürich: Erziehungsdirektion, 1933. 342 p. charts, plates, port. 25cm. (Zürich «Canton». Erziehungswesens, Direktion des. Die zürcherischen Schulen seit der Regeneration der 1830er Jahre. v. 2.)

"Anmerkungen und Quellennachweis," p. 306–310; "Beilagen zu den Jahresprogrammen," 1909–1915, p. 342.

71835B. 1. Education, Secondary—Switzerland—Zürich (Canton). 2. Education, Industrial and technical—Switzerland—Zürich (Canton).
N. Y. P. L. October 22, 1940

IDÉER och ideologier... (Card 2)

Frankrike, av I. Brandell.--Författarna och politiken i Tjeckoslovakien, av O. Kleberg.--Partibyråkrati och professionalism, av S. Söderlind.--A conceptual analysis of African nationalism, av W. Carlsnäs.--Statsvetenskapliga föreningen i Uppsala, av T. Petré.

1. Political science--Addresses, essays, lectures. I. Series. II. Statsvetenskapliga föreningen i Uppsala.

NCY

If by your art; testament to Percival Hunt. ⌈Editor, Agnes Lynch Starrett. Pittsburgh⌉ Univ. of Pittsburgh Press, 1948.
xiv, 293 p. illus., port. 24 cm.
"Five hundred copies ... printed ... on Worthy Permanent Book, all rag paper."
CONTENTS.—Percival Hunt, by J. G. Bowman.—Pericles, Prince of Tyre, by Hardin Craig.—Satan and the narrative structure of "Paradise lost," by P. F. Jones.—Origo crucis, by Henning Larsen.—George Meredith: an obscure comedian, by F. P. Mayer.—Searcher after truth, by E. L. Peterson.—A war for the arts, by E. G. Irvine.—Wisdom is a nut: or, The idols of Jonathan Swift, by Philip Sauers.—Standpoint of a republican radical, by J. W. Holmes.—Froude's "Life of Thomas Carlyle," by T. W. Brown.—Arnold Bennett, and after, by

(Continued on next card)
48-9005*
⌈5⌉

If by your art ... 1948. (Card 2)
CONTENTS—Continued.
F. D. Curtin.—Again that dear county, by W. L. Myers.—S. Thomas More's "Merye laughing harvest," by Sister M. Thecla.—Hazlitt's "Principles of human action" and the improvement of society, by W. P. Albrecht.—My demon poesy, by George Carver.—An unknown castigator of Christopher North, by N. S. Aurner.—Why can't they read and write? By A. M. Ellis.—What makes people read, by G. A. Yoakam.—Alexander Smith on the art of the essay, by Richard Murphy.—Freedom in restraint, by Elizabeth Johnston.—Political propaganda in ballad and masque, by M. M. Purdy.

1. Hunt, Percival, 1878– 2. English literature—Addresses, essays, lectures. I. Starrett, Agnes (Lynch) ed.

PR14.H8 820.4 48-9005*

Library of Congress ⌈5⌉

*QP

Ignacemu Chrzanowskiemu, uczniowie lubliniacy, 1910-1925. [Lublin, Gebethner i Wolff, 1926]
181 p. port. 25cm.

No. 66 of 500 copies printed.
Bibliographical footnotes.
Contents.—I. Chrzanowski. Synteza dziejów literatury staropolskiej.—F. Araszkiewicz. Ze spuścizny rękopiśmiennej Bolesława Prusa.—F. Gucwa. Przyroda w sielankach Woronicza.—L. Kamykowski. "Romantyczność" Mickiewicza.— J. Krzyżanowski.
(Continued)
NN** 4.54 OC PC,1,2 SL S,1,2 (Z-1,LC1,X1)

Ignacemu Chrzanowskiemu, uczniowie lubliniacy, 1910-1925. (Card 2)

Z dziejów "Sowizrzała" w Polsce.—Z. Kukulski. Lata szkolne Staszica.—J. Smieciuszewski. Kwiecie myśli z "Ogrodu" Wacława Potockiego.—Z. Tołwiński. "Pieśń świętojańska o sobótce "Jana Kochanowskiego.— Z. Bielska. Bibljografja prac Jana Chrzanowskiego (p. [167]-181).

1. Polish literature—Hist. and crit. 2. Chrzanowski, Ignacy, 1866-1940.

Copy only words underlined & classmark— GDTZ

ILDEFONS VON ARX, 1755-1833, Bibliothekar, Archivar Historiker zu St. Gallen und Olten; Gedenkschrift aus Anlass seines 200. Geburtstages [Hrsg. von Eduard Fischer] Olten, Walter [1957] 408 p. ports. facsim. 23cm. (Olten, Switzerland. Stadtarchiv. Publikationen. Nr. 4)

Bibliographical footnotes.

NN R X 6. 59 m/5 OC, I OI PC, 1, I (LC3, X1, Z1)

E-12
6662

ILLINOIS. State normal university, Normal. Social sciences, Dept. of.
Studies in history and the social sciences; essays in honor of John A. Kinneman. Normal, Ill. [1965]
x,135 p. port. 24cm.

Includes bibliographies.
CONTENTS.--The rise of historical studies in American colleges, by W.W. Dedman.--On the economics of education, by G.K. Brinegar
(Continued)
NN R 9.66 1/c ODt(1b+) EDt PC,1,2 SL (E)2 (LC1,X1,Z1)
3

ILLINOIS. State normal university, Normal. Social sciences, Dept. of. Studies in history and the social sciences... (Card 2)

--Occupation choice; expressive and instrumental types, by R.L. Meile.--Social studies preparation for tomorrow's citizens, by L.C. Stine.--A comparative study of political alienation and voting behavior in three suburban communities, by K. Janda.--A chief executive for urban counties: some recent developments with emphasis on elected chief executives, by T.D. Wilson.--Folklore on the
(Continued)

ILLINOIS. State normal university, Normal. Social sciences, Dept. of. Studies in history and the social sciences... (Card 3)

midwestern frontier, by W. Wyman.--The place of the negro in the defeated Confederacy, 1865, by P. Sowle.--Agree charges, innovation in transport prices, by B.J. McCamey.--A note on the role of member-bank borrowing in monetary control, by D.A. Berry.

1. Kinneman, John Albertus, 1895- . 2. Social sciences--Addresses, essays, lectures. t. 1965.

E-12
6662

ILLINOIS. State university, Normal. Social sciences, Dept. of.
Studies in history and the social sciences; essays in honor of John A. Kinneman. Normal, Ill. [1965]
x, 135 p. port. 24cm.

Includes bibliographies.
CONTENTS.--The rise of historical studies in American colleges, by W.W. Dedman.--On the economics of education, by
(Continued)
NN R 4.70 d/V ODt EDt PC,1,2 SL (E)2 (LC1, X1, Z1)
2

ILLINOIS. State university, Normal. Social sciences, Dept. of. Studies in history and the social sciences... (Card 2)

G.K. Brinegar.--Occupation choice; expressive and instrumental types, by R.L. Meile.--Social studies preparation for tomorrow's citizens, by L.C. Stine.--A comparative study of political alienation and voting behavior in three suburban communities, by K. Janda.--A chief executive for urban counties: some recent developments with emphasis on elected chief executives, by T.D. Wilson.--Folklore on the midwestern frontier, by W. Wyman.--The place of the negro in the defeated Confederacy, 1865, by P. Sowle.--Agree charges, innovation in transport prices, by B.J. McCarney.--A note on the role of member-bank borrowing in monetary control, by D.A. Berry.
1. Kinneman, John Albertus, 1895- 2. Social sciences--Addresses, essays, lectures. t. 1965.

E-10
8974

IM Dienste der Sprache; Festschrift für Victor Klemperer zum 75. Geburtstag am 9. Oktober 1956. Hrsg. von Horst Heintze und Erwin Silzer. Halle (Saale) M. Niemeyer, 1958.

452 p. port. 25 cm.

CONTENTS.—Verzeichnis der Veröffentlichungen Victor Klemperers, von H. Kunze (p. 1-40)—Südwestfrankreich am Vorabend der Französischen Revolution, von K. Baldinger. — Zwei frühe französische Zeugen für Arbeiterbewegung und Sozialismus, von H. Becker.—Zur Datierung von Ramon Lulls "Libre de Blanquerna," von R. Brummer. — Das humanistische Lebensideal in Alessandro Piccolominis Abhandlung "Della instituzione di tutta la vita dell'uomo nobile," von A. Buck.—Remarques à propos de la manière d'écrire de Jules Verne.

(Continued)

NN* R II. 59 m/ OC, I, II, IIIb*, IVb* PC, 1, 2, I, II SL (LC1, X1, Z1)
[I]

IM Dienste der Sprache...
(Card 2)

CONTENTS—Continued.

von M. Cohen.—Der Bergsonismus, von A. Cornu.—Les composants réalistes du Romantisme français, von Z. Czerny.—Die Pantomimik in einem italienischen Roman, von A. Franz.—Das sogenannte "Imparfait historique," von E. Gamillscheg.—Beredsamkeit und Rhetorik in der französischen Revolution, von H. Heintze.—Prolégomènes au régionalisme littéraire en France, von E. von Jan.—Les noms de métiers plaisants avant et après Rabelais, von H. Lewicka.—Soziale Problematik bei Giovanni Verga, von V. Macchi. — Brief aus der Bretagne, von H. Rheinfelder.—Hauptrichtungen in der modernen vergleichenden Literaturwissenschaft, von R. Schober. — François Belleforests Histoire Tragique d'Amleth, von F. W. Schulze.—Rumänisch-mittelhochdeutsche Parallelen, von E. Seidel.—Eugen Dühr-

(Continued on next card)

IM Dienste der Sprache...
(Card 3)

CONTENTS—Continued.

ing als Vorläufer der Nationalsozialisten, von I. Seidel. — "Une Soirée chez Molière," von E. Silzer.—Remarques Préliminaires à une étude de la langue de Jean Giono, von R. L. Wagner.—Motiv und Symbol der Rose in den Dichtungen von Paul Claudel, von J. Wilhelm.

1. Klemperer, Victor, 1881- . 2. Philology--Addresses, essays, lectures. I. Silzer, Erwin, ed. II. Heintze, Horst, ed. III. Silzer, Erwin. IV. Heintze, Horst.

D-11
9254

Im Dienste der Wahrheit: Paul Häberlin zum 80. Geburtstag. Bern, Francke [1958]

137 p. 23 cm.

Includes bibliographies.

CONTENTS.—Vorwort.—Brief, von L. Binswanger.—Brief, von W. Schohaus.—Paul Häberlin und die Stiftung Lucerna, von P. L. Sidler.—Hommage au professeur Haeberlin, par H. L. Miéville.—Erinnerungen ehemaliger Schüler: Dankbare Erinnerung, von M. Inglin. Der Wendepunkt, von H. Hiltbrunner. Nachklang, von N. Giamara.—Paul Häberlins Stellung innerhalb der deutschen Philosophie des zwanzigsten Jahrhunderts, von H. Gauss.—Das philosophische Spätwerk Paul Häberlins in biographischer Sicht, von P. Kamm.—Das Problem der Selbsterkenntnis bei Platon, Kant und Schopenhauer. von H. Zantop.—Vom Menschenbild bei Pestalozzi und

(Continued)

NN * 2. 60 p/ OC PC, 1, 2 SL (LC1, X1, Z1)

Im Dienste der Wahrheit: Paul Häberlin zum 80. Geburtstag. [1958] (Card 2)

CONTENTS—Continued.

Häberlin; eine Skizze zur philosophischen Anthropologie, von M. Simmen.— Philosophie et expression, par J. C. Piguet.— Foi et théologie, par G. Widmer.—Verzeichnis der Veröffentlichungen von Paul Häberlin. (p. 133-137)

1. Häberlin, Paul, 1878- 2. Philosophy—Addresses, essays, lectures.

Write on slip words underlined below and class mark —

YAM

...Immanuel Kant zum Gedächtnis, 22. April, 1924. Mit einem Jugendbildnis Immanuel Kants gezeichnet um das Jahr 1755 von der Gräfin Charlotte Amalia Keyserling, geb. Gräfin Truchsess-Waldburg. Herausgegeben von Paul Feldkeller. Darmstadt: O. Reichl, 1924. 479 p. incl. front. (port.) 20½cm. (Reichls philosophischer Almanach. [Bd. 2.])

J. S. BILLINGS MEM. COLL.

1. Kant, Immanuel, 1724-1804. I. Feldkeller, Paul, 1889- , ed. II. Ser.

N. Y. P. L. February 18, 1935

E-13
7467

Immer auf der Brücke. Eduard Schmidt-Ott gewidmet zum 70. Geburtstag. Köln, Deutsche Industrieverlagsgesellschaft. 1968.

80 p., front. 24 cm.

At head of title: Deutsches Industrieinstitut.

CONTENTS.—Eduard Schmidt-Ott—immer auf der Brücke, von L. Losacker. — Unternehmerische Öffentlichkeitsarbeit — ein Gebot der Stunde, von C. F. Schmidt-Ott.—Probleme unternehmerischer Öffentlichkeitsarbeit, von H.-J. Finkeldei.—Betreuung der Meinungsbildner, ·

(Continued)

NN*R 2. 70 v/OC, I (OS)II PC, 1, 2, I, II SL E, 1, 2, I, II
(LC1, X1, Z1)

2

IMMER auf der Brücke. (Card 2)

von H.-J. Reinicke.—Sein Presse-"Chef," von J. A. Simons.—Fast zehn Jahre, von W. Mühlbradt.—Interview mit dem Industrieinstitut, von W. Weisser. — Wer nicht "Hier!" ruft ... von K. Kunel. — Unternehmer und Rundfunk, von G. Triesch.—Lebensdaten.

1. Executives--Germany. 2. Business men--Germany. I. Schmidt-Ott, Eduard, 1898- II. Deutsches Industrieinstitut.

*RR NCC
(Hopkins)

Immortal diamond: studies in Gerard Manley Hopkins; ed. by Norman Weyand with the assistance of Raymond V. Schoder. Introd. by John Pick. New York, Sheed & Ward, 1949.

xxvi, 451 p. port. 22 cm.

"Conceived as an anniversary tribute to commemorate the one hundredth anniversary of the poet's birth on July 28, 1944."

CONTENTS.—Gerard Manley Hopkins and the Society of Jesus, by M. C. Carroll.—Hopkins and creative writing, by Arthur MacGillivray.—Greco-Roman verse theory and Gerard Manley Hopkins, by J. L. Bonn.—Hopkins' sprung rhythm and the life of English poetry, by W. J. Ong.—Gerard Manley Hopkins, poet of ascetic and aesthetic conflict, by C. A. Burns.—An interpretive glossary of difficult words in the poems, by R. V. Schoder.—Hopkins, poet of nature and of the

(Continued on next card)

49—8083*
[49k7]

Immortal diamond ... 1949. (Card 2)

CONTENTS—Continued.

supernatural, by M. B. McNamee.—The three languages of poetry, by W. T. Noon.—What does The Windhover mean? By R. V. Schoder.—The loss of the Eurydice, a critical analysis, by Youree Watson.—The thought structure of The wreck of the Deutschland, by R. R. Boyle.—Appendix: The historical basis of The wreck of the Deutschland and The loss of the Eurydice, by Norman Weyand.—A chronological Hopkins bibliography, comp. by Norman Weyand (p. 293-436)

1. Hopkins, Gerard Manley, 1844-1889. I. Weyand, Norman T., ed.

PR4803.H44Z65 821.89 49—8083*
Library of Congress [49k7]

Write on slip, name, year, vol., page of magazine and class mark — YEA

In commemoration of Dr. Ernest Jones' fiftieth birthday. [Articles by Paul Federn and others].

(International jour. of psycho-analysis. London, 1929. 4°. v.10, p.123-382. port., tables.)

Bibliography, p.363-382.

form 400a [xi-7-29 25m]

AN
(Francqui, É.)

In memoriam; hommage de l'Illustration congolaise au grand Belge, au grand colonial, Émile Francqui. [Anderlecht-Bruxelles, 1936?] 183 p. port. 33cm.

Cover-title: Émile Francqui, 1863-1935.

CONTENTS.—Note biographique.—Hommage des chambres législatives.—Hommage des universités et des académies.—Hommage de l'Union coloniale belge.—Hommage d'un ami. Un Bonaparte brabançon: Émile Francqui, par M. Paul Claudel.—Hommage de la presse belge.—Hommage de la presse étrangère.

382942B. 1. Francqui, Émile, 1863-1935. I. Illustration congolaise.
N. Y. P. L. April 25, 1947

D-15
4548

IN honor of Daniel Jones; papers contributed on the occasion of his eightieth birthday, 12 September 1961, edited by David Abercrombie [and others. London] Longmans [1964] xxi, 474 p. illus. 23cm.

Includes bibliographies.

1. Jones, Daniel, 1881- . 2. Phonetics--Addresses, essays, lectures. I. Abercrombie, David, ed.
NN R 9.64 e/ OC, I PC, 1, 2, I SL (LC1, X1, Z1) [I]

*ZAN-1282
v. 3
Film Reproduction

IN memoriam Achillis Beltrami; miscellanea philologica. [Genova] Istituto de filologia classica, 1954. 245 p. port. 22cm. (Genoa (City). Università. Istituto di filologia classica. Pubblicazioni. 3)

Film reproduction. Negative.

CONTENTS.--Achille Beltrami, di E. V. Marmorale.--Sull'Ad martyras di Tertulliano, di L. Alfonsi.--Congetture al testo dell'Apologia (Continued)

NN R X 9.60 1/ OC (OS)I PC, 1, 2, I (LC1, X1, Z1)

NBY

In honor of the ninetieth birthday of Charles Frederick Johnson, professor of English in Trinity college, 1883-1906; papers, essays, and stories by his former students, edited by Odell Shepard and Arthur Adams ... Hartford, Trinity college, 1928.

379 p. front. (port.) 23cm.

CONTENTS.—Charles Frederick Johnson: biographical, genealogical, by A. Adams.—Connecticut's place in colonial history, by C. M. Andrews.—How much social work can a community afford? by L. Purdy.—The natural history of dragons, by C. G. Child.—Observation and imagination in Coleridge and Poe: a contrast, by H. M. Belden.—The Platonic dialogue, by P. H. Frye.—What value Christianism? by the Rev. J. S. Littell.—Causes and prediction of earthquakes, by W (Continued on next card)

382717A 28-13594

[2]

Mr Moth

IN memoriam Achillis Beltrami... (Card 2)

di Apuleio, di Q. Cataudella.--Osservazioni su tre manoscritti del Bellum civile, di F. Cupaiuolo.--Suspiciones, di F. Della Corte.--Minucio Felice e le "Redazioni" dell'Apologeticum tertullianeo, di P. Frassinetti.--Tendenziosità dell'Agricola, di F. Grosso.--Addendum Chrysippeum? Di V. Longo.--Zwei griech.-röm. Klagen, von H. J. Mette.--Plauto, Rudens, v. 315, di U. E. Paoli.--Per il testo dell'Octavia, di L. Pedroli.--Plauto, Amphitruo, vv. 188-261, di M. Peyronel.--A proposito delle fonti di un passo di Porfirio, di N. Sacerdoti.--Cic. Or. 56-59, di G. Scarpat.--Notizie di papiri greci inediti, di A. Traversa.--Quanti drammi scrisse Eschilo, di M. Untersteiner.

1. Beltrami, Achille, 1868-1944. 2. Classical studies--Collections. I. Series.

In honor of the ninetieth birthday of Charles Frederick Johnson ... 1928. (Card 2)

CONTENTS—Continued.

Bowie.—The masterpiece of Luigi Capuana, by H. L. Cleasby.—The Christianity of the fourth Gospel, by the Rev. C. B. Hedrick.—Correctness, by the Rev. M. B. Stewart.—An optimistic realist, Ernst Zahn, by B. Q. Morgan.—The hermit story, as used by Voltaire and Mark Twain, by F. A. G. Cowper.—Thumbnail classics. Jack Harker at Yalevard, by P. Curtiss.—The man who heard everything, by W. Trumbull.—"Whiskey, bullets, and ..."—The novelist takes to real estate, by R. Wright.

1. Johnson, Charles Frederick, 1836- I. Shepard, Odell, 1884- ed. II. Adams, Arthur, 1881- joint ed.

28-13594

Library of Congress AC5.I 55

~~Copy 2.~~

Copyright A 1074623 [2]

*ZB-85
Film Reproduction

IN memoriam; Bernardo V. Moreira de Sá. Porto, Tavares Martins, 1947. 318 p. illus., ports. 23cm.

Film reproduction. Negative.

CONTENTS.--Moreira de Sá no espirito e na saudade de amigos e admiradores.--Notas biográficas.--Concertos em que Moreira de Sá actuon.

1. Moreira de Sá, Bernardo Valentim, 1853-
NN R 4.62 c/POC PC, 1 SL MU, 1 (MUF1, UM1, LC1, X1A Z1)

*Z-1880

IN Memoria di Napoleone Caix e Ugo Angelo Canello. Miscellanea di filologia e linguistica per G. I. Ascoli [et al.] Firenze, Succdssori Le Monnier, 1886. xxxviii, 478 p.

Microfilm.

1. Caix, Napoleone, 1845-1882. 2. Canello, Ugo Angelo, 1848-1883. 3. Philology--Addresses, essays, lectures. I. Ascoli, Graziadio Isaia, 1829-1907.
NN R 12.69 k/OC, I PC, 1, 2, 3, I SL (UM1, LC1, X1, Z1)

AN
(Castello, C.)

In memoriam de Camillo, coordenado por E. A. e V. A.; direcção artistica de Saavedra Machado. Lisboa: Casa Ventura Abrantes, 1925. 851 p. illus. (incl. facsims., ports.), plates, ports. (part col'd.) 34cm.

"Resenha bibliográfica das obras de Camilo Castelo Branco pela ordem cronológica da sua publicação," p. 773-808.

206761B. 1. Castello Branco, Camillo, 1825-1890. 2. Castello Branco, Camillo, 1825-1890—Bibl. 3. Castello Branco, Camillo, 1825-1890—Portraits. I. A., E., ed. II. A., V., ed.
N. Y. P. L. January 11, 1943

* C-6 p.v.58

IN memoriam Charles Nypels, 1893-1952. Amsterdam, 1953. 47 p. facsims. 33cm.

Text in Dutch or French.
Bibliography of works printed by Nypels, p. 21-26.
"Afbeeldingen," p. 27-47.

1. NYPELS, CHARLES, 1893-1952 2. PRINTING--SPECIMENS 3. TITLE-PAGES--SPECIMENS

NN ** R X 12.57 v/ OC PC, 1, 2, 3 SL (R1, RIB1, LC1, X1, Z1)

AN
(Brito Monteiro)

In memoriam de Delfim Guimarães. Organizado por Galino Marques. Lisboa: Livraria editora Guimarães & c.ª, 1934. 464 p. illus., plates, ports. 27cm.

No. 160 of 1000 copies printed.

151418B. 1. Brito Monteiro Guimarães, Delfim de, 1872-1933. I. Galino Marques.
N. Y. P. L. April 9, 1942

ZEC

In memoriam Ernst Lohmeyer, hrsg. von Werner Schmauch. Stuttgart, Evangelisches Verlagswerk [1951] 375 p. illus. 22cm.

Bibliographical footnotes.
CONTENTS.—"Mir ist gegeben alle Gewalt!" Von E. Lohmeyer.—Das Volksbegehren, von M. Buber.—Alttestamentliche Wurzeln der ersten Auferstehung, von L. Rost.—Jesus and first-century Galilee, by S. E. Johnson.—Christus, der Gnadenstuhl, von A. Nygren.—Opferbereitschaft für Israel, von O. Michel.—Nicht über das hinaus, was geschrieben steht! Von K. L. Schmidt.—A consideration of three passages in St. Mark's Gospel, by R. H. Lightfoot.—Die Verzögerung der Parusie, von G. Bornkamm.

(Continued)

NN * 1.53 OC, I PC, 1, 2, I SL (LC1, Z1, X1)

In memoriam Ernst Lohmeyer... (Card 2)

—Sabbat und Sonntag nach dem Johannesevangelium, von O. Cullmann.—Zur Frage der Komposition von Joh. 6, 27-58(59), von J. Schneider.—Zur Auslegung von Joh. 6 bei Luther und Zwingli, von H. Gollwitzer.—Sakrament und Wunder im Neuen Testament, von G. Fitzer.—Die kirchliche Redaktion des ersten Johannesbriefes, von R. Bultmann.—In der Wüste, von W. Schmauch.—Das Martyrium als theologisch-exegetisches Problem, von E. Esking.—Die Apostel in der Didache, von G. Sass.—Lehrerreihen und Bischofsreihen im 2. Jahrhundert, von H. von Campenhausen.—Vivit Deus, von E. Rosenstock-Huessy.—Moralismus und Nihilismus, von J. Konrad.—Die religiösen Kräfte in der Jugendfürsorge, von K. Peters.—Grundfragen des Städtebaues,

(Continued)

In memoriam Ernst Lohmeyer... (Card 3)

von H. Lohmeyer.—Die Problematik der modernen Physik, von C. Schaefer.—Physik und Glaube, von E. Fues.—Die Menschenrechte als theologisches Problem, von H. Vogel.—"Christlicher Humanismus?" Von E. Wolf.—Bibliographie: Ernst Lohmeyer (vom ihm selbst hinterlassen, vom Herausgeber ergänzt), p. 368-375.

1. Lohmeyer, Ernst, 1890-1946. 2. Theology—Essays and misc.
I. Schmauch, Werner, ed.

MAWC
(Franck)

In memoriam Fr. Franck. [Antwerpen, Gedrukt op de persen van het huis V. van Dieren & co., 1933] 72 p. 23 pl., 4 port. 29cm.

No. 110 of 350 copies.
"Schilderijen geschonken door Fr. Franck aan het Koninklijk museum van schoone kunsten, te Antwerpen," 23 pl. at end.

473092B. 1. Franck, Frans, 1872- 1932.
N. Y. P. L. April 26, 1950

NCC
(Joyce)

In Memoriam James Joyce; hrsg. von C. Giedion-Welcker. Zürich, Fretz & Wasmuth [1941] 55 p. illus. 25cm.

"Bibliographie der Hauptwerke von James Joyce," p. 55.

343264B. 1. Joyce, James, 1882-1941. I. Giedion-Welcker, Carola, ed.
N. Y. P. L. July 26, 1950

C-11
7430

IN memoriam Peter Suhrkamp. [Hrsg. von Siegfried Unseld. Frankfurt a.M., Suhrkamp Verlag, 1959] 162[5] p. illus., ports. 20cm.

Contributions by various authors.
"Vorläufige Bibliographie der Schriften von Peter Suhrkamp, zusammengestellt von Helene Ritzerfeld," p. 157-[163]

1. Suhrkamp, Peter, 1891-1959. I. Unseld, Siegfried, ed.
NN R 4.61 e/ OC, I PC, 1, I SL (LC1, X1, Z1)

D-16
8295

IN memory of J.R. Firth. Edited by C.E. Bazell [and others] [London] Longmans [1966] xi, 500 p. 23cm. (Longman's linguistics library)

Includes bibliographical notes.
"Bibliography; the writings of J.R. Firth," p. ix-xi.

1. Firth, John Rupert, 1890- 2. Philology--Addresses, essays, lectures. I. Bazell, Charles Ernest, ed.
NN R 8.66 p/ OC, I PC, 1, 2, I SL (LC1, X1, Z1)

Write on slip words underlined below and class mark —

NFD
(Herder)

... In piam memoriam Alexander von Bulmerincq; Gedenkschrift zum 5. Juni 1938, dem siebzigsten Geburtstage des am 29. März 1938 Entschlafenen, dargebracht von einem Kreise von Freunden und Kollegen. Riga: Akt.-Ges. "Ernst Plates," 1938. 231 p. front. (port.) 24½cm. (Herdergesellschaft, Riga. Abhandlungen der Herder-Gesellschaft und des Herder-Instituts zu Riga. Bd. 6, Nr. 3.)

CONTENTS.—Eine spätsyrische Überlieferung des Buches Ruth, von Rudolf Abramowski.—Der siebenarmige Leuchter und die Ölsöhne, von Hellmuth Frey.—Die Unmöglich-

(Continued)

N. Y. P. L. January 31, 1939

. . . **In** piam memoriam Alexander von Bulmerincq; Gedenkschrift zum 5. Juni 1938. . . (Card 2)

keit einer Theologie des Alten Testaments, von Rafael Gyllenberg.—Die "Schrift"-Prophetie, von Ivar Hylander.—Die Vergeltung Gottes im Buche Hiob, von Johannes Lindblom.—Jahwe und Baal im alten Israel, von Sven Linder.—Ein koptisch-arabischer Bauernkalender, von Enno Littmann.—Die Proklamation des Tab'alsohnes, von Uku Masing.—"Die mit des Gesetzes Werk umgehen, die sind unter dem Fluch," von Martin Noth.—Jesus der Gottesknecht, von Otto Procksch.—Gott und Geschichte im Alten Testament, von A. F. Puukko.—Die Gottesgewissheit der Pharisäer und die Verkündigung des Paulus, von Heinrich Seesemann.—Der alte lettische Gott Perkons, von Eduards Zicāns.—Die Wahlfahrt von Sichem nach Bethel, von Albrecht Alt.

1. Bulmerincq, Alexander von, 1868–1938. 2. Theology—Essays and misc. 3. Bible—Criticism. I. Ser.

N. Y. P. L. January 31, 1939

---

* KP
(Anthoensen)

In tribute to Fred Anthoensen, master printer. Portland, Me. ₍The Anthoensen press₎ 1952. x, 142 p., 1 l. illus., facsims. (part fold.) 21cm.

300 copies printed.

Compiled and printed by the staff of the Anthoensen press under the leadership of Ruth A. Chaplin.

CONTENTS.—A letter to Fred Anthoensen, esq., by P. A. Standard.—Portland printer, by C. J. Weber.—A trip to Subiaco, by C. R. Capon.—The Iconographic

(Continued)

NN*R 5.61 OC,I (OS)II PC,1,2,I,II SL R,1,2,I,II (RI 1,RS1, LC1,X1,Z1) ₍I₎

In tribute to Fred Anthoensen. . . 1952. (Card 2)

society, by W. M. Whitehill.—My anthology, by R. Ruzicka.—The Columbiad club of Connecticut, with a bibliography of keepsakes and club publications, by E. H. Hugo. —Que lire? An event in the story of books and reading, by E. F. Stevens.—The Thomas Johnston maps of the Kennebeck purchase, by L. C. Wroth.—Typographic debut: notes on the long s and other characters in early English printing, including ligatures, and punctuation marks, by P. A. Bennett.—Bowdoin of 1825. With an introductory note by Herbert R. Brown, by E. P. Mitchell.

1. Anthoensen, Fred, 1882– . 2. Bibliography—Addresses, essays, lectures. I. Chaplin, Ruth A. II. Anthoensen press, Portland, Me.

NHC
(Boudier-Bakker)

INA Boudier-Bakker, tachtig jaar; een album amicorum met bijdragen van C. J. A. de Ranitz [et al.] Amsterdam, P.N. van Kampen, 1955. 127 p. ports. 24cm.

Bibliography, p. 121-123.

CONTENTS. — Voorwoord, door C.J.A. de Ranitz. — Ter inleiding, door de uitgevers. -- In vriendelijke herinnering, door H. van Booven. -- Mevrouw Boudier-Bakker tachtig jaar,

(Continued)

NN**R 11.55 g/ OC PC,1 SL (LC1, X1, Z1)

INA Boudier-Bakker, tachtig jaar... (Card 2)

door N.A. Bruining. — De straat, door D. Coster. — Het motief en de greep, door A. Donker. — De schrijfster, door H. Edinga. — De dichter en de dalang, door B. van Eysselsteijn. — Herinnering aan een studente, door C.C. van de Graft. — Schrijfster en zangeres, door R. Houwink. — De schrijfster als spreekster, door J.C. van Ingen-Jelgersma. — De jaren, door K. de Josselin de Jong. — Herinnering van een fotograaf, door F. Kramer. — Onvergankelijk

(Continued)

INA Boudier-Bakker, tachtig jaar... (Card 3)

bekoorlijk, door C. Lennart. — Bij het kroonjaar van Ina Boudier-Bakker, door P.H. Ritter. — Persoonlijke herinneringen, door A. Salomons. — Het spiegeltje, door M. Scharten-Antink. --Een zelfportret van Ina Boudier-Bakker, door C. Serrurier. — Werkelijkheid, waarheid en wijsheid, door G. Stuiveling. -- Ina Boudier-Bakker, door F. van der Vooren-Kuyper. — Biografische aantekeningen.

1. Boudier-Bakker, Ina, 1875-

D-10
7250

INAMA VON STERNEGG, KARL THEODOR FERDINAND MICHAEL, 1843-1908.

Untersuchungen über das hofsystem im mittelalter, mit besonderer beziehung auf deutsches Alpenland. Von dr. Karl Theodor von Inama-Sternegg... Innsbruck, Wagner'schen universitäts-Buchhandlung, 1872. 2 p. 8., 129 p. 23cm.

"Festschrift zur 400 jährigen jubelfeier der Ludwigs-Maximilians- universität zu München."

(Continued)

NN X 11.57 e/ OC (OS)I PC, 1, I SL E, 1, I (LC1, X1, Z1)

INAMA VON STERNEGG, KARL THEODOR FERDINAND MICHAEL, 1843-1908. Untersuchungen über das hofsystem im mittelalter... (Card 2)

Bibliographical footnotes.

1. Manorial system--Germany. I. Munich. Universität.

PKI

Indian Chemical Society.

Sir Prafulla Chandra Rây seventieth birth day; commemoration volume. Calcutta: Indian Chemical Soc., 1933. v, 362 p. incl. tables. illus. (incl. charts), plates, port. 26cm.

Numerous contributors.

On cover: Journal of the Indian Chemical Society. Special number.

Bibliographies included.

Festschrift

707082A. 1. Chemistry—Essays and misc. 2. Ray, Sir Prafulla Chandra, 1861– .

N. Y. P. L. October 5, 1934

Write on slip words underlined below and class mark —

* OAA

Indian and Iranian studies presented to George Abraham Grierson on his eighty-fifth birthday, 7th January, 1936. ₍London₎ The School of Oriental studies (Univ. of London), 1936. vii, ₍297₎–881 p. incl. tables. facsims., front. (port.) 24½cm. (School of Oriental studies, London. Bulletin. v. 8, part 2–3.)

Edited by H. W. Bailey and R. L. Turner.

"Bibliography of the published writings of Sir George A. Grierson, compiled by Edith M. White," p. ₍297₎–318.

CONTENTS.—Alsdorf, L. The Vasudevahindi, a specimen of archaic Jaina-Māhārāṣṭrī.—Bailey, H. W. Yazdi.—Bailey, T. G. Does Kharī boli mean nothing more than rustic speech?—Barannikov, A. Modern literary Hindī.—Barr, K. Remarks on

(Continued)

N. Y. P. L. July 21, 1937

Indian and Iranian studies presented to George Abraham Grierson ... (Card 2)

the Pahlavi ligatures and .—Benveniste, E. Sur quelques dvandvas avestiques.—Bloch, Jules. La Charrue védique.—Burrow, T. The dialectical position of the Niya Prakrit.—Butlin, R. T. On the alphabetic notation of certain phonetic features of Malayalam.—Charpentier, Jarl. Śakadhūma.—Chatterji, S. K. Purāna legends and the Prakrit tradition in new Indo-Aryan.—Christensen, Arthur. Some new Awromānī material prepared from the collections of Åge Meyer Benedictsen.—Cuny, A. Les nasales en fin de mot en sanskrit (et latin).—Debrunner, Albert. Der Typus tudá-im altindischen.—Edgerton, Franklin. The Prakrit underlying Buddhistic hybrid Sanskrit.—Firth, J. R. Alphabets and phonology in India and Burma.—Geiger, Bernhard. Mittelpersisch vēnōk "Erbse (Linse?)."—Geiger, Wilhelm. Singhalesische Etymologien.—

(Continued)

N. Y. P. L. July 21, 1937

Indian and Iranian studies presented to George Abraham Grierson ... (Card 3)

Varma, K. G. The change of a to e in the Indo-Aryan loan words of Malayāḷam.—Gray, L. H. Observations on middle Indian morphology.—Hansen, Olaf. Sakische Etymologien.—Henning, W. Soghdische Miszellen.—Herzfeld, Ernst. Der Tod des Kambyses: hvāmršyuš amryatā.—Johnston, E. H. Bird-names in the Indian dialects.—Konow, Sten. Note on the ancient north-western Prakrit.—Kramers, J. H. The military colonization of the Caucasus and Armenia under the Sassanids.—Lévi, Sylvain. Māla vihāra.—Liebich, B. Nochmals mleccha.—Lorimer, D. L. R. Nugae Burushaskicae.—Lüders, Heinrich. Zur Schrift und Sprache der Kharoṣṭhī-Dokumente.—Morgenstierne, G. Iranian elements in Khowar.—Narasimhia, A. N. The history of p in Kanarese.—Nitti, Luigia. Grammairiens tardifs et dialectes du prākrit.—Oertel, Hanns.

(Continued)

N. Y. P. L. July 21, 1937

Indian and Iranian studies presented to George Abraham Grierson ... (Card 4)

The expressions for "The year consists of twelve months" and the like in Vedic prose.—Paṇḍit, B. S. Syntax of the past tense in old Rājasthānī.—Pisani, Vittore. Vedico yūḥ "se ipsum."—Printz, W. Neue singhalesische Lautregel.—Przyluski, J., and C. Régamey. Les noms de la moutarde et du sésame.—Rapson, E. J. Sanskrit sá and sáḥ.—Saksena, Baburam. Pāli bhūnaha.—Saldanha, Mariano. Historia de gramática concani.—Schaeder, H. H. Ein parthischer Titel im Sogdischen.—Schrader, F. O. On the "Uralian" element in the Drāviḍa and the Muṇḍā languages.—Stein, O. The numerals in the Niya inscriptions.—Thomas, E. J. Tathāgata and Tahāgaya.—Thomas, F. W. Some words found in Central Asian documents.—Turner, R. L. Sanskrit ā-kṣeti and Pali acchati in modern Indo-Aryan.—Tuttle, E. H. Some Dravidian prefixes.—Vogel,

(Continued)

N. Y. P. L. July 21, 1937

Indian and Iranian studies presented to George Abraham Grierson (Card 5)

J. P. Joan Josua Ketelaar of Elbing, author of the first Hindūstānī grammar.—Wackernagel, J. Altindische und mittelindische Miszellen.—Wüst, Walther. Wortkundliche Beiträge zur arischen Kulturgeschichte und Welt-Anschauung. II.—Zarubin, I. I. Two Yazghulāmī texts.

1. Grierson, Sir George Abraham, 1851– . 2. Oriental studies. 3. Iranian languages. I. Bailey, Harold Walter, ed. II. Turner, Ralph Lilley, 1888– , ed. III. Ser.

N. Y. P. L. July 21, 1937

STG

Indiana. University.

Studies in American history inscribed to James Albert Woodburn, PH. D., LL. D., professor emeritus of American history in Indiana university, by his former students. Bloomington, Ind., Indiana university, 1926.

ix, 455 p. illus. (maps) port. 25cm. (*Half-title:* Indiana university studies. vol. XII, study nos. 66–68. June, September, December, 1925)

CONTENTS.—The commerce between the United States and the Netherlands, 1783–1789, by A. L. Kohlmeier.—Relief legislation and the origin of the court controversy in Kentucky, by A. M. Stickles.—The fur trade in the Maumee-Wabash country, by P. C. Phillips.—National party politics, 1837–1840, by Lawrence Hurst.—The presidential campaign and election

(Continued on next card)

26-27235 [5]

Indiana, university. Studies in American history ... 1926. (Card 2)

CONTENTS—Continued.

of 1840, by Walter Prichard.—Americo-Canadian relations concerning annexation, 1846–1871, by J. M. Callahan.—Some inter-relationships in Canadian-American history, by W. P. Shortridge.—John Brown, by T. L. Harris.—The influence of railroad transportation on the civil war, by G. A. Barringer.—Indiana's care for her soldiers in the field, 1861–1865, by O. D. Morrison.—Indiana's part in reconstruction, by Charles Roll.—The territorial and economic roots of the Ruhr, by H. N. Sherwood.—History of the direct primary in the state of Maine, by O. C. Hormell.—Population movements in relation to the struggle for Kansas, by W. O. Lynch.—The political balance in the old Northwest, 1820–1860, by R. C. Buley.

1. U. S.—Hist.—Addresses, essays, lectures. I. Woodburn, James Albert, 1856–

Library of Congress AS36.I 4 vol. XII, nos. 66–68 26-27235 [5]

E-11
1625

INDOGERMANICA; Festschrift für Wolfgang Krause zum 65. Geburtstage am 18. September 1960 von Fachgenossen und Freunden dargebracht. Heidelberg, C. Winter, 1960. vi, 276 p. 25cm.

CONTENTS.--Zur Frage des süddeutschen Präteritumschwundes, von I. Dal.--Der Typus ocus é im Irischen, von H. Hartmann.--Zum Gebrauch der Partizipien in den Skeireins, von E. Hofmann.--Archäologisches zur frühen Falkenbeize im Norden, von H. Jankuhn.--Eine

(Continued)

NN R 12.60 s/4 OC PC, 1, 2 SL (LC1, X1, Z1) [I]

4

INDOGERMANICA... (Card 2)

syntaktische Entlehnung im Schwedischen, von T. Johannisson.--Der Flussname Aspa, von H. Krahe.-- von H. Kronasser.--Die alten germanischen Personennamen des Typs Hariso, von H. Kuhn.--The Indo-European labiovelars in Tocharian, by G.S. Lane.--Über religiöse Wurzeln des Epischen, von W. Lange.--Der Aufbau der vierten Darius-Inschrift von Persepolis, von W. Lentz.--Einige Gedanken über das Verhältnis von Sprachwissenschaft und Philologie, von J. Lohmann.--Kannte Layamon Runen? Von H. Marquardt.--Behistun I 91, von M. Mayrhofer.--Wie sprach Klopstock seine Laute aus?

(Continued)

INDOGERMANICA... (Card 3)

Von F. Neumann.--Zeitangebende Parenthesen im Hethitischen, von G. Neumann.--Sprache und Reim in den judendeutschen Gedichten des Cambridger Codex T.-S. 10.K.22, von H. Neumann.--Nhd. Aberglaube, ndd.-ndl. overgelôf, dän. overtro, schwed. övertro, von E. Öhmann.--Altitalische Sprachgeographie, von W. Porzig.--Der Monatsname mulseti, von D.A. Seip.--Zur Verwendung des tocharischen Verbalsubstantivs auf -r im Perlativ, von W. Thomas.--Die Interpretatio Romana der gallischen Götter, von J. de Vries.--Die Erleuchtung des Buddha, von E. Waldschmidt.--Zetazismus in niedersächsischen Flurnamen,

(Continued)

INDOGERMANICA... (Card 4)

von H. Wesche.--Zum althochdeutschen Tatian, von W. Wissmann.--Verzeichnis der Schriften von Wolfgang Krause (p. [268]-276).

1. Indo-European languages--Addresses, essays, lectures. 2. Krause, Wolfgang, 1895-

TAH

Industri og forskning; tilegnet J. Throne Holst på hans syttiårsdag. Oslo: J. G. Tanum, 1938. 231 p. incl. diagrs., tables. 26½cm.

Edited by Arvid Brodersen.
Bibliographies included.
CONTENTS.—Videnskapelig industriledelse: Industri og videnskap, av Arne Meidell. Rasjonaliseringen i industriens tjeneste, av R. Lowzow. Produksjonsrasjonaliseringen, av B. Hellern. Yrkesvalg og yrkesveiledning, Hygiene og industri, av Carl Schiøtz.—Bytteforholdet mellem forskning og industri: Kan vi hevde oss i en industrialisert verden? Av Sem Sæland. Forholdet mellem næringsmiddelproduksjon og forskning, av P. R. Sollied og Asbjørn Følling. Forskning i hermetikkindustrien, av Gulbrand Lunde. Papirindustrien og forskningen, av Sigurd Samuelsen. Som "Freia"-stipendiat

(Continued)

N. Y. P. L. October 10, 1939

Industri og forskning . . . (Card 2)

i U. S. A. våren 1927, av Olav Hanssen.—Den menneskelige faktor: Rasjonalisering og arbeidsglede, av Arvid Brodersen. Fritidsproblemer under industrialismen, av C. A. R. Christensen.—Fører industrialderen bort fra humanismen? Av H. O. Christophersen.—Norsk industri og forskning—fremtidslinjer: Norge i forskningsalderen, av V. Bjerknes. Om råstoffer og industrielle muligheter i Norge, av B. F. Halvorsen. Rekrutteringen til den høiere utdannelse, av Henrik Palmstrøm. Forskerens kår og forskningens fremtid, av Aa. W. Owe.

962769A. 1. Industry and science. 2. Industries—Norway. 3. Holst, Johan Throne, 1868– . I. Brodersen, Arvid, 1904– , ed.
N. Y. P. L. October 10, 1939

TB

INDUSTRIEBETRIEB und industrielles Rechnungswesen; neue Entwicklungstendenz. Eine Festschrift für Erwin Geldmacher. Köln, Westdeutscher Verlag [1961] 99 p. mounted port., diagrs., forms (part fold. (issued in pocket) 24cm.

Bibliographical footnotes.
CONTENTS. —Die Bedeutung der Abschreibungs- und Investitionspolitik für das Wachstum industrieller Unternehmungen, von K. Hax. —Die Grenz-Plankostenrechnung im industriellen Rechnungswesen, dargestellt an Beispielen aus der Textil- , industrie, von A. Hesse. —
(Continued)

NN * 3. 65 a/, OC PC, 1, 2, 3 SL E, 1, 2, 3 (LC1, X1, Z1)

INDUSTRIEBETRIEB und industrielles Rechnungswesen...
(Card 2)

Die Behandlung positiver und negativer Geschäftswerte bei der Verkehrswertermittlung von Betrieben, von A. Schmettler. —Optimalbedingungen am Arbeitsplatz und im Gesamtbetrieb, von E. Wedekind. —Erwin Geldmacher als Forscher und Lehrer, von H. H. Hohlfeld.

1. Business--Organization and management. 2. Accounting and bookkeeping for corporations. 3. Geldmacher, Erwin, 1885-

---

C-12
9798

INGEBORG BACHMANN; eine Einführung. München, R. Piper [1963] 57, [2] p. port. 19cm.

CONTENTS. --Ingeborg Bachmann, von J. Kaiser. --Literatur als Utopie, von Bachmann. --Die gestundete Zeit, von G. Blöcker. --Anrufung des Grossen Bären, von S. Unseld. --Eine Interpretation, von W. Rasch. --Der gute Gott von Manhattan, von W. Weber. --Das dreissigste Jahr, von H. Beckmann. --Biographisch-bibliographischer Abriss (p. 52-[58]). --Quellenangaben (p. [59]).
1. Bachmann, Ingeborg, 1926-
NN R 6. 66 r/ OC PC, 1 SL (LC1, X1, Z1)

Copy only words underlined
& classmark-- HAA

INNSBRUCK. Universität. Amerika-Institut.
Americana-Austriaca; Festschrift des Amerika-Instituts der Universität Innsbruck, anlässlich seines zehnjährigen Bestehens. Hrsg. im Auftrag des Amerika-Instituts von Klaus Lanzinger. Wien, W. Braumüller [1966]
301 p. illus. 23 cm. (Its Beiträge zur Amerikakunde, Bd. 1)
Bibliographical footnotes.
CONTENTS.—Das Amerika-Institut der Universität Innsbruck, von

(Continued)

NN* 6.67 g/ (OC)I OS OI PC,1,2,I AH,1,I
(LC1,X1,Z1)

INNSBRUCK. Universität. Amerika-Institut.
Americana-Austriaca... (Card 2)

K. Pivec.—Tätigkeit des Amerika-Instituts der Universität Innsbruck, 1956–1966, von K. Lanzinger.—The forward lookers of the New South, by C. Eaton.—The uniting of Europe and the United States precedent, by H. L. Mason.—The majoritarian principle challenges early American Republicanism, by H. Montgomery.—The political philosophy of John F. Kennedy, by N. Riemer.—The power of prestige: George Washington and the Federal Constitution, by R. A. Rutland.—Class and American fiction, by C. E. Eisinger.—What "South" are

(Continued)

INNSBRUCK. Universität. Amerika-Institut.
Americana-Austriaca... (Card 3)

they talking about in the U. S. A.? By C. Gohdes.—Herman Melville's major themes, by T. Hillway.—James Thurber and the art of fantasy, by C. S. Holmes.—The mystery of Melville's short stories, by L. Howard.—To make freedom real: James Baldwin and the conscience of America, by L. Langer.—Aspects of American fiction: a whale, a bear, and a marlin, by H. Wilner.—Thomas Jefferson: an essay on the Anglo-Saxon, by K. Brunner.—Zu den Bezeichnungsvorgängen im amerikanischen Englisch, von H. Koziol.—"Slave" und "Negro" im amerikanischen Englisch vor dem Bürgerkrieg, von K. Lanzinger.

(Continued)

INNSBRUCK. Universität. Amerika-Institut.
Americana-Austriaca... (Card 4)

1. United States--Hist.--Addresses, essays, lectures. 2. American literature--Addresses, essays, lectures. I. Lanzinger, Klaus, ed.

---

*OAA
+

... Die **Inschriften** vom Tell Halaf; keilschrifttexte und aramäische urkunden aus einer assyrischen provinzhauptstadt, hrsg. und bearb. von Johannes Friedrich, G. Rudolf Meyer, Arthur Ungnad, Ernst F. Weidner. Berlin, Im selbstverlage des herausgebers, 1940.

vi, 84 p., 1 l. front. (port.) 1 illus., 32 pl. on 16 l. 29cm. (Archiv für Orientforschung, hrsg. von Ernst F. Weidner. Beiheft 6)

On cover: Max freiherrn von Oppenheim zum 80. geburtstage.

CONTENTS.—I. Der kulturhistorische ertrag der keilschrifturkunden vom Tell Halaf, von E. F. Weidner.—II. Die keilschrifttexte vom Tell Halaf. 1. Das archiv des Mannu-ki-Aššur, von E. F. Weidner. 2. Spätassyrische und neubabylonische privaturkunden vom Tell Halaf, von

(Continued on next card)
A 44–839

[3]

... Die **Inschriften** vom Tell Halaf ... 1940. (Card 2)

CONTENTS—Continued.

Arthur Ungnad.—III. Denkmäler mit westsemitischer buchstabenschrift, von Johannes Friedrich.—Die personennamen, ortsnamen, götternamen und beamtentitel in den keilschrifttexten vom Tell Halaf, von G. R. Meyer.—Nummernregister zu den keilschrifttexten vom Tell Halaf.—Autographien der keilschrifttexte und aramäischen urkunden (tafel 1-32) von G. R. Meyer.

1. Oppenheim, Max Adrian Simon, freiherr von, 1860- 2. Cuneiform inscriptions. 3. Inscriptions, Aramaic. 4. Inscriptions—Mesopotamia. 5. Tell Halaf. I. Friedrich, Johannes, 1893- II. Meyer, G. Rudolf. III. Ungnad, Arthur, 1879- IV. Weidner, Ernst Friedrich, 1891- V. Title: Max freiherrn von Oppenheim zum 80. geburtstage.

A 44-839

Columbia univ. Libraries
for Library of Congress [3]

NFD
(Carossa)

Insel-Verlag, G.m.b.H., Leipzig.
Gruss der Insel an Hans Carossa. Dem 15. Dezember 1948. [Leipzig] Insel-Verlag [1948] 254 p. 21cm.

Prose and poetry.

500318B. 1. Carossa, Hans, 1878- I. Title.
N. Y. P. L. Fest. October 26, 1949

Copy only words underlined
& classmark-- * QAA

INSTITUT D'ÉTUDES SLAVES, Paris.
Mélanges en l'honneur de Jules Legras. Paris, Librairie Droz, 1939. xv, 276 p. 25cm. (ITS: Travaux, no. 19)

1. Legras, Jules, 1866- . 2. Slavonic studies--Collections. I. Ser. II. Title.
NN S 1.61 g/f (OC)II, OS PC, 1, 2, II S, 1, 2, II (LC1, X1, Z1)

BVL

INSTITUT FRANÇAIS D'ÉTUDES BYZANTINES, Bucharest.
...Mémorial Louis Petit; mélanges d'histoire et d'archéologie byzantines... Bucarest, 1948. xxviii, 426 p. illus. 25cm. (Archives de l'Orient chrétien. [v.] 1)

1. Petit, Louis, 1868-1927. 2. Byzantine studies. I. Series. II. Title.
NN R 3.53 (OC)II OS, I PC, 1, 2, I, II SL O, 1, 2, I, II (LC1, Z1, X1) [I]

C-12
1457

INSTITUT FÜR PSYCHOTHERAPIE UND TIEFEN-PSYCHOLOGIE.
Felix Schottlaender zum Gedächtnis; aus dem Arbeitskreis des Instituts für Psychotherapie und Tiefenpsychologie e.V., Stuttgart. Stuttgart, E. Klett [c1959] 186 p. 19cm.

300 copies issued also under title: Almanach 1959.

1. Psychotherapy--Addresses, essays, lectures. 2. Schottlaender, Felix, 1892- .
NN R 8.62 e/B OS PC, 1, 2 SL (LC1, X1, Z1)

SED

INSTITUT FÜR STAATSLEHRE UND POLITIK, Mainz.
Verfassung und Verwaltung in Theorie und Wirklichkeit; Festschrift für Herrn Geheimrat Professor Dr. Wilhelm Laforet anlässlich seines 75. Geburtstages. München, Isar Verlag, 1952. xix, 475 p. 25cm. (Institut für Staatslehre und Politik, e.V., Mainz. Veröffentlichungen. Bd. 3)

Includes bibliographical references.
CONTENTS.—Zur Metaphysik des römischen Staates, von E. von Hippel.—Der Kampf um der Verwaltungsstaat, von H. Peters.—
(Continued)

NN*R 4.54 OS(Ib)I PC, 1, 2, 3, I SL E, 1, 2, 3, I (U1, Z1, LC1, X1)

INSTITUT FÜR STAATSLEHRE UND POLITIK, Mainz. Verfassung und Verwaltung in Theorie und Wirklichkeit... (Card 2)

Zentralismus und Föderalismus, von F. W. Jerusalem.—Die Entwicklung des Verhältnisses von Bund und Ländern in der Bundesrepublik, von H. R. von Lex.—Staatsnotstand und Gesetzgebungsnotstand, von F. A. Freiherr von der Heydte.—Das Grundrecht der Kriegsdienstverweigerung, von H. Kipp.—Artikel 142 des Grundgesetzes und die Grundrechte in der bayerischen Verfassung, von J. Kratzer.—Starke und schwache Normen in der Verfassung, von T. Maunz.—Die staatsrechtliche Bedeutung der ministeriellen Gegenzeichnung im deutschen Reichsstaatsrecht, 1871-1945,
(Continued)

INSTITUT FÜR STAATSLEHRE UND POLITIK, Mainz. Verfassung und Verwaltung in Theorie und Wirklichkeit... (Card 3)

von R. Jaeger.—Grundgesetz und Bundesnotenbank, von A. Süsterhenn.—Die katholische Weltkirche und ihre Diplomatie, von F. T. Hollôs.—Über Eigenart und Methode verfassungsgerichtlicher Rechtsprechung, von J. Wintrich.—Die Bundesverfassungsgerichtsbarkeit in ihrem Verhältnis zur Landesverfassungsgerichtsbarkeit und ihre Einwirkung auf die Verfassungsordnung der Länder, von W. Geiger.—Die Verwaltungs- und Verfassungsgerichtsbarkeit in österreich, von G. J. Ebers.—Verwaltungsakt und innerdienstliche Weisung, von O. Bachof.—Die öffentlich-rechtliche Willenserklärung der Privatperson von G. Küchenhoff.—Die
(Continued)

INSTITUT FUR STAATSLEHRE UND POLITIK, Mainz. Verfassung und Verwaltung in Theorie und Wirklichkeit... (Card 4)

Privilegien und Immunitäten der internationalen Funktionäre, von E. Menzel.—Kommunalgesetzgebung und Finanzausgleich in Bayern, von L. Foohs.—Die Gemeindeordnung für den Freistaat Bayern vom 25. Januar 1952, von L. Gebhard.—Der gegenwärtige Verwaltungsaufbau in der Pfalz, von E. Becker.—Zur Entwicklung des Ausbildungs- und Prüfungswesens für Richteramt, höheren Verwaltungsdienst, Rechtsanwaltschaft und Notariat in Bayern, von O. Kollmann.

1. Law, Constitutional. 2. Law, Constitutional—Germany. 3. Laforet, Wilhelm, 1877- . I. Series.

BYR

Instituto de Coimbra.
Coimbra; colectânea de estudos organizada pelo Instituto de Coimbra e dedicada à memória do seu consócio honorário dr. Augusto Mendes Simões de Castro. [Coimbra] Gráfica de Coimbra, 1943. vi, 780 p. illus. 27cm.

294853B. 1. Coimbra, Portugal (City). 2. Mendes Simões de Castro, Augusto, 1845-1932.
N. Y. P. L. Festschrift January 31, 1945

AN
(Celso, A.)
Instituto histórico e geográfico brasileiro, Rio de Janeiro.
...Homenagem à memória do conde de Affonso Celso... Rio de Janeiro: Imprensa nacional, 1939. 307, ii p. illus. 24cm.

"Boletim do Instituto histórico."

242460B. 1. Celso de Assis Figueiredo, Affonso, conde, 1860-1938.
N. Y. P. L. September 13, 1943

A p.v.839

Instituto sanmartiniano, *Buenos Aires.*
... Don José de San Martín ... Homenajes realizados al cumplirse el 91 aniversario de su fallecimiento, 1850—17 agosto—1941. ₍Buenos Aires, 1941₎

112 p. illus. (incl. facsims.) 23ᶜᵐ.

"Conferencias irradiadas durante la 'Semana de San Martín,' comprendida entre los días 10 al 17 de agosto": p. ₍35₎-110.

1. San Martín, José de, 1778-1850.

A 42-5009

Stanford univ. Library
for Library of Congress ₍2₎

---

*QO

Instytut gospodarstwa społecznego, Warsaw.
...Ludwik Krzywicki; praca zbiorowa poświęcona jego życiu i twórczości. Warszawa [Drukarnia L. Nowaka] 1938. cxxxvi, 749 p. ports. 25 1/2cm.

Added t.-p. in French: Ludwik Krzywicki; travail collectif consacré à sa vie et à son oeuvre.
Résumé in French.
"Bibliografia prac Ludwika Krzywickiego," p. 249-306.

950926A. 1. Krzywicki, Ludwik, 1859-

Copy only words underlined
& classmark — *QPA

Inter arma; zbiór prac ofiarowanych prof. Kazimierzowi Nitschowi w siedemdziesiątą rocznicę urodzin (1,II,1944) przez przyjaciół, kolegów i uczniów. Kraków, Studium słowiańskie Uniwersytetu jagiellońskiego [1946] xix,129 p. port. 22cm. (Uniwersytet jagielloński, Cracow. Studium słowiańskie. Biblioteka. Seria A. nr. 1)

By various authors.

(Continued)

NN**R 3.54 OC (OS) I PC,1,2,I S,1,2,I (U 1, Z 1, LC1, X1)

Inter-arma; zbiór prac ofiarowanych prof. Kazimierzowi Nitschowi... (Card 2)

Contents.—Zurowska, W. Wykaz bibliograficzny prac naukowych Kazimierza Nitscha od r. 1934-44.—Grabowski, T. Stosunki Polski z Anglią w dziedzinie nauki, filozofii, literatury od średniowiecza do końca oświecenia (1800-1822).—Klemensiewicz, Z. O wyrazie jak z funkcją wskaźnika zespolenia zdań złożonych w gwarach ludowych.—Kowalski, T. Co oznacza kinsār w relacji Ibrāhīma o krajach sło-
(Continued)

Inter-arma; zbiór prac ofiarowanych prof. Kazimierzowi Nitschowi... (Card 3)

wiańskich?—Lehr-Spławiński, T. Kilka uwag o pierwotnych Wenetach.—Małecki, M. Czy św. Cyryl i Metody byli Grekami czy Słowianami?—Safarewicz, J. Dwa drobiazgi litewskie.—Semkowicz, W. Geneza im. Mieszko.—Sławski, F. Pol. kręzel, kądziel, konopie.—Stein, I. Czasowniki niedokonane i dokonane we współczesnym literackim języku polskim.—Urbańczyk, S. O imię pierwszego historycznego księcia Polski.—Wyka, K. Czas powieściowy.
1. Nitsch, Kazimierz, 1873- —Bibl. 2. Polish language. I. Series.

D-12
7928

INTERNAL Control durch Bewegungsbilanzen; Festschrift für Walter le Coutre zu seinem 75. Geburtstag. Hrsg. von Schülern und Freunden unter der Schriftleitung von Erich A. Weilbach. Stuttgart, Forkel-Verlag, 1960. 344 p. port., diagrs., tables. 21cm.

Includes bibliographical references.

(Continued)

NN R 1.61 e/ OC, I, IIbo PC, 1, 2, 3, 4, I SL E, 1, 2, 3, 4, I (LC1, X1, Z1)

3

INTERNAL Control durch Bewegungsbilanzen...
(Card 2)

CONTENTS.--Der Inhalt von Bewegungsbilanzen, von E. A. Weilbach.--Kontenordnung und Bewegungsbilanz, von M. Zimmermann.--Die Bewegungsbilanz als Grundlage der Liquiditätserfassung, -überwachung und -planung, von C. Voigtländer-Tetzner.--Bewegungsbilanzen und Erfolgsermittlung, von H. Roller.--Absatzanalyse durch Umsatzanalyse, von W. Fluch.--Kurzfristige Wirtschaftsrechnung mittels Bewegungsbilanzen, von W. Thoms.--Bewegungsbilanz und Bilanzpolitik,
(Continued)

INTERNAL Control durch Bewegungsbilanzen...
(Card 3)

von G. Kofahl.--Wirtschaftlichkeitskontrollen durch Mengenrechnungen, von K. Mehler.--Die Bedeutung der Bewegungsbilanz in der Revision, von J. Lenz.--Bewegungsbilanz und Organisationsprüfung, von H. Mechler.--Bewegungsbilanzen als Kontrollinstrument bei Streitkräften, von J. Gerber.--Verzeichnis der Veröffentlichungen von le Coutre, von H. Bussinger, p. [317]-344.

1. Financial statements. 2. Auditing. 3. Management--Controls. 4. Le Coutre, Walter, 1885- . I. Weilbach, Erich A., ed. II. Weilbach, Erich, A.

E-12
5319

INTERNATIONAL COMMISSION FOR THE HISTORY OF REPRESENTATIVE AND PARLIAMENTARY INSTITUTIONS.
Liber memorialis Antonio Era; studies presented to the International commission for the history of representative and parliamentary institutions, Cagliari, 1961. Bruxelles, D. Corten, 1963. xii, 230 p. port. 25cm. (ITS: Studies. 26)

(Continued)

NN 3.66 g/c (OC)Ib+ OS, I PC, 1, 2, I SL E, 1, 2, I (LC1, X1, Z1)

5

INTERNATIONAL COMMISSION FOR THE HISTORY OF REPRESENTATIVE AND PARLIAMENTARY INSTITUTIONS. Liber memorialis Antonio Era... (Card 2)

Text in English, French, German, Italian or Spanish.
Bibliographical footnotes.
CONTENTS. --Zu einer Geschichte der bäuerlichen Repräsentation in der deutschen Landgemeinde, von K. Bosl. --The political organisation of the Byzantine urban classes between 1204 and 1341, by C.P. Kyrris. --Doctrinas políticas manejadas en el parlamento sardo de 1481-1485, por F.E. de Tejada.
(Continued)

5

INTERNATIONAL COMMISSION FOR THE HISTORY OF REPRESENTATIVE AND PARLIAMENTARY INSTITUTIONS. Liber memorialis Sir Maurice Powicke... (Card 2)

Text in English, French or Italian.
Bibliographical footnotes.
CONTENTS. --Représentation et députation en Belgique du XIIIe au XVIe siècle, par H. Buch, P. Smets et M. Stroobant. --Note sulla deputazione nelle assemblee sabaude, di M.A. Benedetto. --Les pouvoirs des députés aux États généraux de France, par. Soule. --Representative government in early New England: the corporate
(Continued)

INTERNATIONAL COMMISSION FOR THE HISTORY OF REPRESENTATIVE AND PARLIAMENTARY INSTITUTIONS. Liber memorialis Antonio Era... (Card 3)

--Sulla nomina dei funzionari da parte del parlamento catalano, di J. Beneyto. --Una relazione cinquecentesca sulla "Forza del parlamento" in Sicilia, di R. de Mattei. --The problem of representation in the post-Renaissance Venetian state, by S.J. Woolf. --Sardegna 1624; gravami e voti parlamentari, di A. Marongiu. --Il primo donativo concesso dagli stamenti sardi ai Savoia, di G. Olla Repetto. --Nota sulla mancata convocazione del parlamento sardo nel secolo XVIII, di
(Continued)

INTERNATIONAL COMMISSION FOR THE HISTORY OF REPRESENTATIVE AND PARLIAMENTARY INSTITUTIONS. Liber memorialis Sir Maurice Powicke... (Card 3)

and the parliamentary traditions, by G.L. Haskins. --Discourse on the Parliament of England (1663), by le comte G.J.B. de Comminges, 1613-1679, ambassador of France in London, 1662-1665, by C. Robbins. --Problems of representation and delegation in the eighteenth century, by D. Gerhard. --La notion de représentation chez les révolutionnaires français, par J. Roels. --The powers of deputies in the Hungarian feudal diet, 1790-1848, by G. Bónis. --The private
(Continued)

INTERNATIONAL COMMISSION FOR THE HISTORY OF REPRESENTATIVE AND PARLIAMENTARY INSTITUTIONS. Liber memorialis Antonio Era... (Card 4)

M.A. Benedetto. --Protesti degli stamenti sardi contro l'attività del governo piemontese nella seconda metà del secolo XVIII, di G. Todde. --Gli stamenti e la crisi rivoluzionaria sarda della fine del XVIII secolo, di C. Sole. --La deputazione di storia patria e la raccolta degli atti parlamentari sardi, di F. Loddo Canepa. --Les assemblées spirituelles du clergé dans un diocèse de France aux XVIIe et XVIIIe siècles, par E. Appolis. --Antropologica fisica e sociale dei sardi, di C. Maxia.

INTERNATIONAL COMMISSION FOR THE HISTORY OF REPRESENTATIVE AND PARLIAMENTARY INSTITUTIONS. Liber memorialis Sir Maurice Powicke... (Card 4)

member of the House of Commons and foreign policy in the nineteenth century, by V. Cromwell. --The representatives and their powers in the Russian legislative chambers, 1906-1917, by M. Szeftel. --Le contentieux des élections parlementaires, par R. Villers.
1. Powicke, Sir Frederick Maurice, 1879-1963. 2. Government, Representative--Addresses, essays, lectures. I. Series.

INTERNATIONAL COMMISSION FOR THE HISTORY OF REPRESENTATIVE AND PARLIAMENTARY INSTITUTIONS. Liber memorialis Antonio Era ... (Card 5)

1. Era, Antonio. 2. Government, Representative--Addresses, essays, lectures. I. Series.

HBC

INTERNATIONAL CONGRESS OF AMERICANISTS. 31st, São Paulo, Brazil (City), 1954.
Miscellanea Paul Rivet; octogenario dicata. [México] Universidad nacional autónoma de México, 1958
2 v. illus., part fold., part ed., ports, maps (part col.) 23cm.

Vols. 2: Mexico (City). Universidad nacional. Instituto de historia. Publicaciones. Ser. 1, no. 50.
Contributions in Spanish, French, English, German, Italian or Portuguese.
(Continued)

NN 7.64 p/B OS, I PC, 1, 2, 3, I SL AH, 1, 2, 3, I (LC1, X1, Z1)

2

E-12
5320

INTERNATIONAL COMMISSION FOR THE HISTORY OF REPRESENTATIVE AND PARLIAMENTARY INSTITUTIONS.
Liber memorialis Sir Maurice Powicke; studies presented to the International commission for the history of representative and parliamentary institutions, Dublin, 1963. Louvain, Editions Nauwelaerts, 1965.
294 p. port. 25cm. (ITS: Studies. 27)
(Continued)

NN 2.66 g/c OS, I PC, 1, 2, I SL E, 1, 2, I (LC1, X1, Z1)

4

INTERNATIONAL CONGRESS OF AMERICANISTS. 31st, São Paulo, Brazil (City), 1954. Miscellanea Paul Rivet... (Card 2)

Includes bibliographies.

1. Rivet, Paul, 1876-1958. 2. Indians, American. 3. America--Archeology. I. Mexico (City) Universidad nacional Instituto de historia. Publicaciones. Ser. 1, no. 50

* PWZ
(Heller)

International ladies' garment workers' union.
Fiftieth anniversary celebration in honor of Jacob J. Heller... [New York, 1940] 51 l. illus. (ports.) 28cm.

Cover-title: Fifty years of life. In tribute to Jacob J. Heller. A life of service.
In spiral binder.

62489B. 1. Heller, Jacob J 1890?- .
N. Y. P. L. September 30, 1940

SST

International people's college, Elsinore, Denmark.
Adult education in the struggle for peace, by the International people's college, Elsinore. Miscellaneous articles on the environment and work of the International people's college, Elsinore, and other folk high schools in Denmark and elsewhere. Contributed by teachers, students and friends of the college on its 25th anniversary. Copenhagen, G. E. C. Gad, 1949. 400 p. illus. 25cm.

522465B. 1. Education, Adult.
N. Y. P. L. June 14, 1950

---

* MEC
(Bruckner)

INTERNATIONALE BRUCKNER-GESELLSCHAFT.
Bruckner-Studien. Leopold Nowak zum 60. Geburtstag. Wien, Musikwissenschaftlicher Verlag [°1964]

152 p. facsims., music, ports. 24 cm.

At head of title: Internationale Bruckner-Gesellschaft.
Hrsg. von Franz Grasberger.

1. Bruckner, Anton, 1824-1896. 2. Nowak, Leopold, 1904- . 3. Essays. I. Grasberger, Franz, ed.
NN 4.66 g/$_{5}$ (OC)I OS PC, 1,2,I SL MU,1,2,3,I
(LC1, X1, Z1)

NFC

Internationale forschungen zur deutschen literaturgeschichte. Julius Petersen zum 60. geburtstag, dargebracht von H. Cysarz ... A. R. Hohlfeld ... H. A. Korff ... [u. a.] Leipzig, Quelle & Meyer, 1938.
4 p. l., 218 p. port. 24cm.

Half-title: Festschrift für Julius Petersen.
Bibliographical foot-notes.

CONTENTS.—Zur poetik. Zur tongestaltung in der dichtung, von R. Petsch. — Zur geistesgeschichte. Die romantisierung des humanitätsideals, von H. A. Korff. Wurzeln und typen des deutschen realismus im 19. jahrhundert, von S. von Lempicki. Die deutsche dichtung unserer zeit, von J. Nadler.—Zu einzelnen dichtern. Grimmelshausen und

(Continued on next card)

A C 39-589
[2]

Internationale forschungen zur deutschen literaturgeschichte ... 1938. (Card 2)

CONTENTS—Continued.

das barock, von J. H. Scholte. Der pseudogoethische hymnus an die natur, von Fr. Schultz. Karl Ernst Schubarth und die anfänge der Fausterklärung, von A. R. Hohlfeld. Hölderlins liebeselegie, von K. Viëtor. Eichendorff und der mythos, von H. Cysarz. Justinus Kerner und Alexander von Württemberg, von L. A. Willoughby. "Traumland" und dichtung bei Isolde Kurz, von R. Unger.

1. Petersen, Julius, 1878- 2. German literature — Addresses, essays, lectures. I. Title: Festschrift für Julius Petersen.

A C 39-589

Yale univ. Library
for Library of Congress [2]

TLS

Der **internationale** kapitalismus und die krise; festschrift für Julius Wolf zum 20. april 1932, hrsg. von Siegfried v. Kardorff ... dr. Hans Schäffer ... professor dr. Götz Briefs [und] dr. Hans Kroner. Stuttgart, F. Enke, 1932.

xxvii, 383 p. front. (port.) diagr. 26cm.

Contributions in German, with the exception of one in French, and one in English.

1. Economic conditions — 1918- 2. Wolf, Julius, 1862- I. *Kardorff, Siegfried von, 1873- ed. II. Schäffer, Hans, joint ed. III. Briefs, Goetz, 1889- joint ed. IV. Kroner, Hans, joint ed. V. Title: Kapitalismus und die krise, Der internationale.

32-24152

Library of Congress HC57.I7
[3] 330.904

---

*PDB

INTERPRETATIONES ad Vetus Testamentum pertinentes Sigmundo Mowinckel Septuagenario missae. [Oslo] Forlaget Land og kirke [1955] 183 p. port. 23cm.

Includes bibliographies.
CONTENTS.—Notes on Psalms 68 and 134, by W. F. Albright.—Micha 2, 1-5, von A. Alt.—Some linguistic remarks on the Dead sea scrolls, by H. Birkeland.—The origin of baptism, by N. A. Dahl.—Zur Kompositionstechnik des Pseudo-Philonischen Liber antiquitatum Biblicarum, von O.

(Continued)

NN ** 7.56 j/$_{1}$ OC PC, 1, 2 SL J, 1, 2 (LC1, X1, Z1)

INTERPRETATIONES ad Vetus Testamentum pertinentes Sigmundo Mowinckel Septuagenario missae. (Card 2)

Eissfeldt.—Kultus und Offenbarung, von R. Gyllenberg.—Trois notes sur Genèse I, par P. Humbert.—The masseba and the holy seed, by F. Hvidberg.—Hesed and hāsîd, by A. R. Johnson.—King and fertility, by A. S. Kapelrud.—Der Eckstein in Jes. 28.16, von J. Lindblom.—The interpretation of Deutero-Isaiah, by C. R. North.—"Die Heiligen des Höchsten," von M. Noth.—The fall of man, by J. Pedersen.—Justin als Zeuge vom Glauben an den verborgenen und den leidenden Messias im Judentum, von E. Sjöberg.

1. Bible. O. T.—Essays and misc. 2. Mowinckel, Sigmund Olaf Plytt, 1884-

---

XAD

Interpretations of modern legal philosophies; essays in honor of Roscoe Pound, edited, with an introduction, by Paul Sayre. New York, Oxford university press, 1947.

ix, 807 p. front. (port.) diagrs. 24½cm.

Bibliographical references in "Notes" at the end of most of the chapters.

CONTENTS.—Justice and expediency, by C. K. Allen.—Note on Thomas Hobbes, by Elmér Balogh.—Kelsenism, by A. S. de Bustamante y Montoro.—Philosophy as jurisprudence, by Huntington Cairns.—On the nature of natural law, by A.-H. Chroust.—Phenomenology of the judgment, by Carlos Cossio.—Legal pragmatism and beyond, by T. A. Cowan.—Truth and untruth in morals and law, by Giorgio del Vecchio.—Legal development in a modern community, by F. W. Eggleston.—A sketch of an influence, by J. N. Frank.—The legal system of occupied Germany, by

(Continued on next card)

47-459
[8]

Interpretations of modern legal philosophies ... 1947. (Card 2)

CONTENTS—Continued.

Mitchell Franklin.—An apology for jurisprudence, by A. L. Goodhart.—The province of comparative law, by H. C. Gutteridge.—Integrative jurisprudence, by Jerome Hall.—Justice, law, and the cases, by W. E. Hocking.—Praise of law, by Werner Jaeger.—Cino da Pistoia, by J. W. Jones.—The metamorphoses of the idea of justice, by Hans Kelsen.—Roscoe Pound as a former colleague knew him, by Albert Kocourek.—Positive and 'natural' law and their correlation, by M. M. Laserson.—Law and justice: a criticism of the method of justice, by Vilhelm Lundstedt.—Some illustrations of the influence of unchanged names for changing institutions, by C. H. McIlwain.—On everlasting values of the Spanish school of natural law (F. de Vitoria) by Alfredo Mendizábal.—The tragedy of modern jurisprudence, by A. Meyendorff.—Law as fact, by

(Continued on next card)

47-459
[8]

Interpretations of modern legal philosophies ... 1947. (Card 3)

CONTENTS—Continued.
Karl Olivecrona.—Pound's theory of social interests, by E. W. Patterson.—Lask and the doctrine of the science of law, by Enrique Martinez Paz.—Ex facto ius: ex iure factum, by Max Radin.—Who watches the watchmen? By Max Rheinstein.—Ideas and historical conditioning in the realization of the juridical values, by Luis Recasens Siches.—Law and fact in the light of the pure theory of law, by Helen Silving.—The organized group (institution) and law-norms, by P. A. Sorokin.—Fallacies of the logical form in English law, by Julius Stone.—Petrazhitsky's philosophy of law, by N. S. Timasheff.—The judicial conception of legislation in Tudor England, by Arthur von Mehren.—A psychological theory of law, by Ranyard West.—Recent reforms of English private law, by P. H. Winfield.—Natural law and international law, by Lord Wright.

1. Law—Philosophy—Addresses, essays, lectures. 2. Pound, Roscoe, 1870- I. Sayre, Paul Lombard, ed.

Library of Congress [8] 47-459

---

*OREB

Iskandar, Nur Sutan, 1893-
Naraka dunia [oleh] N. St. Iskandar. Tjet. 6. Bukittinggi, Nusantara, 1964.

134 p. 22 cm.

1. Malay literature--Fiction. I. Title.
NN*R 11.67 g/ OC(1b*) PC,1,I SL O,1,I (LC1,X1,Z1)

---

*MG p.v.370

Interpreten über Harald Genzmer. Werkverzeichnis zum 60. Geburtstag, 9. Febr. 1969. (Frankfurt, C. F. Peters, 1969.)

89 p. 21 cm.

1. Genzmer, Harald--Bibl.
NN*R 4.72 e/OC PC,1 SL MU,1 (LC1,X1,Z1)

Write on slip words underlined below and class mark — *PBC

Ismar Elbogen zum 60. Geburtstage.

(Monatsschrift fur Geschichte und Wissenschaft des Judentums. Breslau, 1934. Jahrg.78, Heft 4,p.385-480. port.)

form 100b [xi-6-33 25m]

TB p.v.2329

IRAQ.
The Iraqi revolution; one year of progress and achievement, 1958-1959. [Baghdad] 14th July celebrations committee [1959] 126 p. port. 21cm.

1. Economic history--Iraq. 2. Iraq--Economic history. 3. Iraq--Soc. condit. t. 1959.
NN R 2.64 p/ ODt EDt PC,1, 3 SL (E)1,3 O,2,3 (LC1,X1,Z1)

TB

ISTITUTO TECNICO COMMERCIALE A INDIRIZZO MERCANTILE "EMANUELE FILIBERTO DUCA D'AOSTA." Florence.
Studi, in memoria di Enrico Bocci. Firenze, 1950. 330 p. port. 26cm.

Bibliographical footnotes.

1. Economics--Essays and misc. 2. Bocci, Enrico.
NN 12.59 1/ (OC)2bo OS(1b) PC,1,2 SL E,1,2 (LC1,X1,Z1)

---

*KP (Oriole)

Ishill, Joseph, editor.
Élisée and Élie Reclus, in memoriam, including: tributes, appreciations and essays by Élie Faure, Prof. Albert Heim, Jean Grave, Havelock Ellis, Dr. Max Nettlau, Bernard Lazare, Peter Kropotkin, Patrick Geddes, Jacques Mesnil, Anne Cobden-Sanderson and other important contributors, fragments, letters, and over sixty woodcuts by Louis Moreau; compiled, edited and printed by Joseph Ishill. Berkeley Heights, New Jersey: Published privately at the Oriole Press, 1927. xiv p., 1 l. 359(1) p. facsims., front., illus., plates, ports. 8°.

(Continued)

N. Y. P. L. February 17, 1930

E-12 7655

Istituto nazionale delle assicurazioni.
Studi sulle assicurazioni; raccolti in occasione del cinquantenario dell'Istituto nazionale delle assicurazioni. Roma, Edizione dell'Istituto nazionale delle assicurazioni; depositario Giuffrè, Milano, 1963.

616 p. 25 cm.

Italian, French, Spanish, German and/or English. Most articles have summaries: those with Italian text, in the other 4 languages; (Continued)

NN * R 1.67 1/c OS PC,1, 2 SL E,1,2 (LC1,X1,Z1)

Ishill, Joseph, editor: Élisée and Élie Reclus... (Card 2)

Title-page in red, blue and black.
Some portraits mounted.
Colophon: This book was hand-set throughout and printed on a little rusty, worn-out "Favorite" press which was abandoned in a wooden shed in the vicinity of Berkeley Heights, New Jersey. The Garamond type selected is cast by the American Type Founders. After each form the type was distributed and positively no plates made.
"This edition is limited to 290 copies of which only 230 are for sale. 40 copies are printed on Alexandra Japan. Copy number 153."
"Biblio-biographical data," p. 353-359.

J. S. BILLINGS MEM. COLL.
458943A. 1. Reclus, Élisée, 1830-1905. 2. Reclus, Élie, 1827-1904. 3. Moreau, Louis, illustrator.
N. Y. P. L. February 17, 1930

ISTITUTO NAZIONALE DELLE ASSICURAZIONI.
Studi sulle assicurazioni... (Card 2)

the rest, in the other 3 languages, excluding Italian.
Includes bibliographical references.

CONTENTS.—Diritto delle assicurazioni: Su talune recenti vedute circa la posizione giuridica dell'assicurazione contro gli infortuni, di A. Asquini. Le conducteur ou gardien autorisé en assurance-automobile, par A. Besson. Le imprese in posizione dominante secondo il primo regolamento di applicazione degli artt. 85 e 86 del Trattato di Roma e l'industria assicurativa italiana, di R. Bracco. Note sulla denuncia di aggravamento del rischio (art. 1898 Cod. civ.) di A. de

(Continued)

ISTITUTO NAZIONALE DELLE ASSICURAZIONI.
Studi sulle assicurazioni... (Card 3)
Gregorio. Economia, tecnica e diritto nell'assicurazione, di A. Donati. Interessi tecnici e pretese fiscali, di G. Fanelli. L'impresa nella struttura del contratto di assicurazione, di G. Ferri. El seguro de responsabilidad civil total en el derecho español, por J. Garrigues. Klassifikation der Privatversicherung, von H. Möller. La désignation d'une concubine comme bénéficiaire d'une assurance-décès, par M. Picard. La causa del contratto di assicurazione, di F. Santoro-

(Continued)

ISTITUTO NAZIONALE DELLE ASSICURAZIONI.
Studi sulle assicurazioni... (Card 4)
Passarelli.—Economia e finanza delle imprese d'assicurazione: È possibile difendere l'assicurato sulla vita contro il rischio della svalutazione monetaria? di L. Amoroso. Risparmio assicurativo e finanza pubblica, di C. Arena. Die Bedeutung des Eigenkapitals in der Versicherungswirtschaft, von P. Braess. The functions of private and of social insurance, by E. M. Burns. La finanza dell'impresa di assicurazione sulla vita, di C. Casali. Sulla formazione e determinazione del reddito di esercizio nell'impresa assicuratrice, di P. E. Cassandro. Insurance and measurement of risk, by B. A. Hedges.—Tecnica delle assicurazioni e matematica attuariale: Insurance termi-

(Continued)

ISTITUTO NAZIONALE DELLE ASSICURAZIONI.
Studi sulle assicurazioni... (Card 5)

nology, by R. H. Blanchard. Le assicurazioni di sopravvivenza, di R. Cultrera. Considerazioni sul premio scontato delle assicurazioni di risarcimento, di R. d'Addario. Sul divario tra valutazioni di probabilità per operazioni assicurative nei due sensi, di B. de Finetti. La teoria del rischio e il pieno di conservazione nelle assicurazioni vita, di G. Ottaviani. Aspetti attuariali di alcune formule sui momenti binomiali, di G. Santacroce.

1. Insurance. 2. Insurance-- Italy.

MWEF
(Hamburg)

ITALIAANDER, ROLF, 1913- , ed.
Mutter Courage und ihr Theater: Ida Ehre und die Hamburger Kammerspiele. Hamburg, Freie Akademie der Künste [1965] 64 p. illus., ports. 24cm.

"Zum 65. Geburtstag Ida Ehres und zum 20 jährigen Bestehen der Hamburger Kammerspiele."

1. Ehre, Ida, 1900- . 2. Stage--Germany--Hamburg. I. Freie Akademie der Künste, Hamburg.
NN * 2.68 1/A OC,1b* (OS)I PC,1,2,I SL T, 1,2,I (LC1,X1,Z1)

---

*C-4 p.v. 450

Italy. Archivio di stato, Lucca.
In memoria di Eugenio Lazzareschi, direttore dell' Archivio. Lucca, Stab. tipo-lito Lippi, 1952. 104 p. ports. 24cm.

"Bibliografia di Eugenio Lazzareschi, a cura di Domenico Corsi," p. 45-104.

1. Lazzareschi, Eugenio, 1882-1949—Bibl. i. 1952.

NN**R 3.54 ODi EDi PC,1 SL (Z/1,LC1,X1)

MCF
V7.C62

ITALY. Leonardo da Vinci nel quinto centenario della nascita. Comitato nazionale per le onoranze a.
Leonardo; saggi e ricerche. Presentazione di Achille Marazza. [Roma] Istituto poligrafico dello stato [1954] xxv, 604 p. 74 plates (part col.) 30cm.

Contributions in Italian, French or English.

1. Vinci, Leonardo da, 1452-1519. I. Marazza, Achille, 1894- , ed. t. 1954.

NN ** R 1.55 p/r (OC) I ODt (1b) EDt PC, 1, I SL A, 1, I B ST, 1, I (LC1, X1, Z1)

BWD

Italy. Luzio, Alessandro, Comitato esecutivo per l'onoranza ad.
Ad Alessandro Luzio. Gli Archivi di stato italiani; miscellanea di studi storici... Firenze: F. le Monnier, 1933. 2 v. fronts. (ports.) 28cm.

Issued by the Comitato esecutivo per l'onoranza ad Alessandro Luzio.—*cf. Presentazione.*

805662-3A. 1. Luzio, Alessandro, 1857- . 2. Italy—Hist.—Addresses, essays, lectures. I. Title.
N. Y. P. L. May 5, 1936

AN
(Esch, J.)

J. B. Esch in memoriam et in resurrectionem, in zusammenarbeit mit Freunden des verewigten, hrsg. von... Alphonse Turpel. Luxemburg, Sankt Paulus-Druckerei, 1951. 264 p. illus. 22cm.

1. Esch, Jean Baptiste, 1902-1942. I. Turpel, Alphonse, ed.

NN R OC,I PC,1,I SL (LC1, Z1, X1)

---

*QVZ

J.B. FOERSTER, jeho životní pouť a tvorba, 1859-1949. [Vydáno k poctě devadesátých narozenin národního umělce J.B. Foerstra na konci jubilejního roku 1949. Redakce slovesné části: Josef Bartoš, Přemysl Pražák a Josef Plavec. V Praze] Národní hudební vydavatelství Orbis [1949?] 420 p. illus., ports., facsims. 28cm.

Includes compositions by 13 Czechoslovakian composers.
"Seznam díla J.B. Foerstra, sestavil Jaromír Fiala," p. 363-393.
"Literatura o J.B. Foerstrovi," p. 394-402.

(Continued)

NN* * R X 8. 57 a/ OCs, Is PCs, Is, Is SLs As, Is, Is MUs, Is, 2s, Is Ss, Is, Is (LCEIs, LCIs, XIs, Z1s)

J.B. FOERSTER... (Card 2)

1. Foerster, Josef Bohuslav, 1859-1951. 2. Foerster, Josef Bohuslav--Iconography. I. Bartoš, Josef, 1887- , ed.

F-10
83

J.K. PAASIKIVI, valtakunnallinen elämäntyö. Toimittanut Kauko Kare. [Forssa] Kivi [1956] 134 p. illus., ports. 26cm.

CONTENTS.—Svento, R. Elämäntyö—muistomerkki.—Kare, K. Yrjö-Koskisen perintö.—Lähteenoja, K. Helmikuun manifestista Tarton rauhaan.—Laati, I. Tarton rauhasta Porkkalan palauttamiseen.—Leskinen, V. Mitä on 'Paasikiven linja'?—Tuura, J.W. Historiantutkija, lakimies, valtiomies.—Poukka, P. Talouspoliitikko J.K. Paasikivi.—Pekari, I. Lukulamppu, kävelykeppi, frakki.—Heikkilä, T.H. Isännän ääni.—Kurjensaari, M. 'Isänmaan isä'.

1. Paasikivi, Juho Kusti, 1870- . I. Kare, Kauko, ed.
NN * * R X 8. 56 s/o OC, 1b, I PC, 1, I SL E, 1, I (LC1, X1, Z1)

AN
(Byström, J.)

Jacob Byström, en minnesbok. Redaktion: Knut Lagerstedt och Arvid Svärd. Stockholm, Baptistmissionens bokförlag [1948] 246 p. illus. 23cm.

"Tryckta skrifter av Jakob Byström," p. 245-246.

1. Byström, Jakob Jakobsson, 1857-1947. I. Lagerstedt, Knut, ed.
NN R 4.53 OC, I PC, 1, I SL E, 1, I (LC1, Z1, X1)

E-11
2622

JAAN TÕNISSON; koguteos tema üheksakümnenda sünnipäeva tähistamiseks. [Koguteos väljaandmise toimkond: Evald Blumfeldt et al. Stockholm] Kirjastus Vaba Eesti [1960] 368 p. illus., ports, facsim. fold. geneal. table. 24cm.

Bibliographical footnotes.

1. Tõnisson, Jaan, 1868- . 2. Esthonia--Politics. I. Blumfeldt, Evald, 1902- , ed.
NN R 6.61 g/p OC, I PC, 1, 2, I SL E, 1, 2, I (LC1, X1, Z1)

C-12
9793

JACOB, HEINZ.
Otto Jespersen; his work for an international auxiliary language. Loughton, Essex, International language (Ido) society of Great Britain, 1943. 32 p. 19cm.

CONTENTS.--Jacob, H. Otto Jespersen.--Jespersen, O. History of our language, translated from the Ido original by Gilbert H. Richardson [English and Ido on opposite pages]--Comparative texts.--"The Times" on Otto Jespersen.

1. Language, Universal--Novial 2. Ido I. Jespersen, Otto, 1860-1934.
NN R 4.66 p/ OC, I PC, 1, 2, I SL (LC1, X1, Z1)

HAER

JACKSON, BRUCE, ed.
Folklore & society; essays in honor of Benj. A. Botkin. Hatboro, Pa., Folklore Associates, 1966. xii,192 p. port. 24cm.

Includes unacc. melodies.
Includes bibliographical references.
CONTENTS.--The folkness of the non-folk vs. the non-folkness of the folk, by C. Seeger.--Folk music
(Continued)

NN R 6.68 e/ OC PC,1, 2,3 SL AH,1,2 (LC1,X1, Z1)

3

*PNA

JACOB, PAUL, 1900- , ed.
Littera judaica; in memoriam Edwin Guggenheim. Ed.: Paul Jacob und Ernst Ludwig Ehrlich. [Frankfurt am Main] Europäische Verlagsanstalt [1964] 308 p. port. 20cm. (Bibliotheca judaica)

Bibliographical footnotes.

(Continued)

NN*R 12.69 r/ OC, Ib* (OS)II PC, 1, 2, 3, I SL J, 1, Ib*, 4, 5, I (LC1, X1, Z1) [NSCM]

2

JACKSON, BRUCE, ed. Folklore & society... (Card 2)

old and new, by W. Rhodes.--The question of folklore in a new nation, by R. M. Dorson.--The ballad scholar and the long-playing record, by K. S. Goldstein.--A sampling of bawdy ballads from Ontario, by E. Fowke.--Plugging, nailing, wedging, and kindred folk medicinal practices, by W. D. Hand.--Negro minstrelsy and Shakespearean burlesque, by C. Haywood.--John Henry, By M. Leach.--Some child ballads on hillbilly records, by J. McCulloh.--Slavic
(Continued)

JACOB, PAUL, 1900- , ed. Littera judaica...
(Card 2)

1. Guggenheim, Edwin, 1893- . 2. Judaism--Addresses, essays, lectures. 3. Jews--Hist. 4. Judaism--Essays. 5. History. I. Ehrlich, Ernst Ludwig, joint ed. II. Bibliotheca judaica.

JACKSON, BRUCE, ed. Folklore & society... (Card 3)

influences in Yiddish folksong, by R. Rubin.--Cents and nonsense in the urban folksong movement: 1930-1966, by E. Stekert.--Bibliography of the writings of Benjamin A. Botkin (p. 169-192)

1. Botkin, Benjamin Albert, 1901- . 2. Folk lore--U.S. 3. Folk lore--Addresses, essays, lectures.

D-11
7326

Jacob Saposnekow Memorial Volume Committee.
Essays in social science, in memory of Jacob Saposnekow. Editors: Henry Miller [and] Philip Shorr. [Brooklyn? 1958]
xiv, 157 p. port. 22 cm.

Bibliographical footnotes.

CONTENTS.--Biographical sketches: Youth and intellectual development, by J. Fox. Jacob Saposnekow at West Virginia university, by H. A. Gibbard. The teacher I knew, by Mrs. P. R. Datta.
(Continued)

NN*R 5.59 1/(OC)I, II, III, IIIb*, IVb* OS(1b) PC, 1, I, II, III SL E, 1, I, II, III (LC1, X1, Z1)

JACOB SAPOSNEKOW MEMORIAL VOLUME COMMITTEE.
Essays in social science... (Card 2)

A tribute from a former student, by J.L. McPherson. In memory of Jacob Saposnekow, by L.H. Taylor.--Articles by Professor Saposnekow: The independence of sociology. A critique of positivism in sociology. The emerging social theory. Is culture the locus of mathematical reality?--Essays and studies: The philosopher looks at the world, by A.H. Kamiat. Behavior, caloric intelligence, and knowledge, by F.E. Hartung. Psychological models and ethics: a proposal, by S. Skulsky. The crisis in education in our time, by P. Shoor. An approach to the teaching of social medicine in medical schools, by M.I. Roemer. The problem of school desegregation and integration in the North, by
(Continued)

E-11
3237

JAHN, RUDOLF, ed.
Zur Weltgeschichte der Leibesübungen; Festgabe für Erwin Mehl zum 70. Geburtstag. Frankfurt/M., W. Limpert [1960] 216, 136 p. illus., port. 24cm.

Contributions by various authors.
"Erwin Mehl: Ausgewählte Aufsätze aus vier Jahrzehnten, 1920-1960," p. [1]-135 of second group of pagings.

(Continued)
NN R 6.62 e/ OCs, I, II PC, Is, Is, IIs SLs (LC1s, X1s, Z1)

JACOB SAPOSNEKOW MEMORIAL VOLUME COMMITTEE.
Essays in social science... (Card 3)

H. Miller. A lover of books, by M.N. Cohen.

1. SOCIAL SCIENCES--ADDRESSES, ESSAYS, LECTURES
I. Miller, Henry, 1900- , ed. II. Shorr, Philip, 1898- , ed.
III. Saposnekow, Jacob, 1895-1956. IV. Miller, Henry, 1900-

JAHN, RUDOLF, ed. Zur Weltgeschichte der Leibesübungen... (Card 2)

"Verzeichnis der Schriften Erwin Mehls," p. 197-212.
Includes bibliographies.

1. Gymnastics--Hist. I. Mehl, Erwin. II. Title.

D-11
9577

JACQUES PRESSER; geschenk van vrienden bij zijn restigste verjaardag, 1899, 24 Februari, 1959. Amsterdam, J.M. Meulenhoff [1959] 68 p. port. 22cm.

Bibliography, p. 67-68.

1. Presser, Jacob, 1899- .
NN R 10.60 c/ OC PC, 1 SL (LC1, X1, Z1)

AN
(Maxwell, J.)

James Clerk Maxwell; a commemoration volume, 1831–1931. Essays by Sir J. J. Thomson, Max Planck, Albert Einstein [and others]... Cambridge[, England]: Univ. Press, 1931. 146 p. 2 ports. (incl. front.) 12°.

Contents: Thomson, Sir J. J. James Clerk Maxwell. Planck, M. K. E. L. Maxwell's influence on theoretical physics in Germany. Einstein, A. Maxwell's influence on the development of the conception of physical reality. Larmor, Sir J. The scientific environment of Clerk Maxwell. Jeans, Sir J. H. James Clerk Maxwell's method. Garnett, W. Maxwell's laboratory. Fleming, Sir A. Some memories. Lodge, Sir O. J. Clerk Maxwell and wireless telegraphy. Glazebrook, Sir R. T. Early days at the Cavendish Laboratory. Lamb, Sir H. Clerk Maxwell as lecturer.

571642A. 1. Maxwell, James Clerk, 1831–1879. I. Einstein, Albert, 1879– . II. Planck, Max Karl Ernst Ludwig, 1858– . III. Thomson, Sir Joseph John, 1856– .
N. Y. P. L. May 16, 1932

STN
(Osnabrück)

Jaeger, Julius, 1848–
Die Schola Carolina osnabrugensis. Festschrift zur elfhundertjahrfeier des Königlichen gymnasium Carolinum zu Osnabrück, von prof. dr. Julius Jaeger. Osnabrück, G. Pillmeÿer, 1904.
3 p. l., 127, [1] p. front., illus. (incl. ports.) 25cm.

1. Osnabrück. K. Gymnasium Carolinum. 1940

Library of Congress LF3195.O82J2 5-15330
[a30b1] Festschrift

---

* QO p.v.104

Janina Korolewicz-Waydowa; 35-lecie działalności. [Warszawa, 193–] 61 p. front. (port.), plates. 24cm.

"Komitet redakcyjny...prof. Stanisław Niewiadomski (przewodniczący)."

Festschrift

889812A. 1. Waydowa, Janina (Korolewicz), 1875– . I. Niewiadomski, Stanisław, 1859– , ed.
N. Y. P. L. June 21, 1937

Write on slip, name, year, vol., page of magazine and class mark — NIZ

Jahlajulkaisu Tohtori E. A. Tunkelon täyttäessä 60 vuotta.

(Suomalaisen kirjallisuuden seura. Suomi. Helsinki, 1930. 8°. Jakso 5, osa 10, p.1-429. port.)

form 400a [11-13 30 25m]

D-17
3035

Jarrett, Michael Grierson, *ed.*
Britain and Rome: essays presented to Eric Birley on his sixtieth birthday, edited by Michael G. Jarrett and Brian Dobson. Kendal (Westmoreland) Wilson [1966]
[7], 208 p. front. (port.), illus., 13 plates, plans, tables. 22 cm. unpriced

Bibliographical footnotes.

(Continued)
NN * R 4.67 1/ OC, I, IIb*, IIIb* PC, 1, I
SL (LC1, X1, Z1) 3

JARRETT, MICHAEL GRIERSON, ed. Britain and Rome ... (Card 2)

CONTENTS.—The South-West defences of the Fortress of Eboracum, by L. P. Wenham.—The Garrison of Maryport and the Roman Army in Britain, by M. G. Jarrett.—Three sherds of stamped ware from Aldborough, by D. Charlesworth.—Immunis Librarius, by G. R. Watson.—The origins of Gordian I, by A. R. Birley.—The Praefectus Fabrum in the Early Principate, by B. Dobson.—The vallum—its prob-

(Continued)

JARRETT, MICHAEL GRIERSON, ed. Britain and Rome ... (Card 3)

lems restated, by B. Heywood.—Roman Lancashire, by B. J. N. Edwards.—A Samian bowl from Eccles, Kent, by A. P. Detsicas.—City foundations in Gaul and Britain, by J. C. Mann.—Early fourth-century rebuilding in Hadrian's wall forts, by J. J. Wilkes.—Expleta Statione, by H. Lieb.—Dark Age dates, by J. Morris.

1. Birley, Eric. 2. Great Britain--Hist.--Roman period, B.C.55-A.D. 449. I. Dobson, Brian, joint ed. II. Dobson, Brian. III. Jarrett, Michael Grierson.

E-12
918

JAUSS, HANS ROBERT, ed.
Medium aevum vivum; Festschrift für Walther Bulst. Hrsg. von Hans Robert Jauss und Dieter Schaller. Heidelberg, C. Winter, 1960. 356 p. 25cm.

1. Bulst, Walther. 2. Civilization, Medieval--Addresses, essays, lectures. I. Schaller, Dieter, joint ed. II. Schaller, Dieter.
NN R 9.64 a/ OC, I, IIbo PC, 1, 2, I SL (LC1, X1, Z1) [I]

D-12
9885

Jean Soulairol (1892–1959); Témoignages, hommages, inédits. Paris, Éditions franciscaines [1960] 108 p. port., facsim. 22cm.

"Inédits," poems, p. [93]-[105]
Bibliography, p. 107–108.

1. Soulairol, Jean.
NN R 11.61 OC PC, 1 SL (LC1, X1, Z1)

D-16
1678

JEFFARES, ALEXANDER NORMAN, ed.
In excited reverie; a centenary tribute to William Butler Yeats, 1865-1939. Edited by A. Norman Jeffares and K. G. W. Cross. London, Macmillan; New York, St. Martin's press, 1965. viii, 353 p. port. 23cm.

Bibliographical footnotes.

1. Yeats, William Butler, 1865-1939. I. Cross, K. G. W., joint ed. II. Title. III. Cross, K. G. W.
NN R 8.65 p/ OC, I, IIIbo PC, 1, I, II SL (LC1, X1, Z1)

Copy only words underlined & Classmark-- * IIA

JENA. Universität. Bibliothek.
Weite Welt und breites Leben. Festschrift der Universitätsbibliothek der Friedrich-Schiller-Universität Jena zum 80. Geburtstag von Prof. Dr. phil. Karl Bulling am 24. Juli 1965. Leipzig, Bibliographisches Institut, 1966. 288 p. plates, port. facsims. 24cm. (Zentralblatt für Bibliothekswesen. Beiheft 82)

Includes bibliographical references. "Veröffentlichungen von Prof. Dr. Karl Bulling," p. 9-11.

NN 1.67 p/ (OC)II OS, I PC, 1, I, II (LC1, X1, Z1) (Continued)

JENA. Universität. Bibliothek. Weite Welt und breites Leben. (Card 2)

CONTENTS. --Das Schlagwortregister zum systematischen Katalog, von H. Beck--Schaubüchereien auch heute? von H. Becker.--Zur Anlage biographischer Schlüssel innerhalb systematischer Kataloge, von K. Bulling.--Aus dem ersten Jahr nach der Zerstörung der Universitätsbibliothek Jena 1945/46, von V. Burr.--Frau Dr. Šnimščikova, von C. Fleischhack.--Zehn Jahre Thüringer Zentralkatalog, von G. Pomassl. --Über den Stand beim Bau wissenschaftlicher Bibliotheken, von G. Schirrmeister. --Die Herstellung von Fachbibliographien, von E. Stein.--Geheimmte akademische Justiz, von W. Braun.--Zur Erwerbung des Papyrus Ebers, von D. Debes.

(Continued)

JENA. Universität. Bibliothek. Weite Welt und breites Leben. (Card 3)

--Hermann Ebels Selbstbiographie, von J. Dietze. --Die Bevölkerungsentwicklung schwarzburgischer Städte vom 15.-19. Jahrhundert, von H. Eberhardt. --Aus der Jenaer Aufklärung, von O. Feyl. --Handschriften von Johann Wolfgang Goethe im Autographenbestand der Universitätsbibliothek Jena, von G. Karpe. --Das "Rosenwunder" der Heiligen Elisabeth, von H. Koch. --Gegenseitige Beziehungen der Universitäten Leipzig und Krakau, von J. Müller. --Die Wüste Möblis bei Jena historisch und archäologisch, von G. Neumann.—Fünf Briefe J. B. Alxingers an Ch. F. Blankenburg,

(Continued)

JENA. Universität. Bibliothek. Weite Welt und breites Leben. (Card 4)

von H. Prokert. --Acht deutsche Übertragungen von Fabeln, von A. Rau. --Zur Melanchthonbibliographie, von E. Selbmann. --Johann Calvin, von M. Steinmetz. --Drei unbekannte Briefe Alexander V. Humboldts in der Universitätsbibliothek Leipzig, von F. Wustmann. --Aus einem Jenaer Studentenstammbuch des frühen 18. Jahrhunderts, von H. Ziegler.

1. Bulling, Karl. I. Series. II. Title.

XAH

Jena. Universität. *Rechts- und wirtschaftswissenschaftliche fakultät.*

Festschrift für Rudolf Hübner zum siebzigsten geburtstag, hrsg. von der Rechts- und wirtschaftswissenschaftlichen fakultät der Universität Jena. Jena, Frommann, 1935.

3 p. l., [5]-230 p. 23½cm.

CONTENTS.—Hedemann, J. W. Privatrechtsgeschichte der neuzeit.—Gerland, Heinrich. Die sicherungsverwahrung des § 42e St. g. b. und ihre voraussetzungen.—Fischer, H. A. Soziale organismen.—Koellreuter, Otto. Zur entwicklung der deutschen reichseinheit.—Hueck, Alfred. Der treuegedanke im recht der offenen handelsgesellschaft.—

(Continued on next card)

36-28793

[2]

Jena. Universität. *Rechts- und wirtschaftswissenschaftliche fakultät.* Festschrift für Rudolf Hübner ... 1935. (Card 2)

CONTENTS—Continued.

Blomeyer, Karl. Hat der bauer eigentum am erbhof?—Weber, Hellmuth von. Die verbrechen gegen den staat bei Anselm von Feuerbach.—Jerusalem, F. W. Das verwaltungsrecht und der neue staat.—Emge, C. A. Das aktuelle, ein dialog zur hinführung zu seinen problemen.—Boehm, M. H. Die krise des nationalitätenrechts.—Scheuner, Ulrich. Gesetz und einzelanordnung.—Buchda, Gerhard. Der hirtenschutt.

1. Hübner, Rudolf, 1864- 2. Law—Germany—Addresses, essays, lectures. I. Title.

36-28793

Library of Congress [2]

C-13
67

JESPERSEN, OTTO, 1860-1943.
Two papers on international language in English and Ido. 2. edition. [London, J. Warren Baxter] 1921 44 p. 19cm.

Cover title.

Title-page reads: Uniono por la linguo internaciona. Historio di nia linguo. History of our language. Composed in Ido by Otto Jespersen. And Artificala lingui pos la Mondmilito. Artificial languages (Continued)

NN R 7.66 1/ OC, I PC, 1, I SL (LC1, X1, Z1)

2

JESPERSEN, OTTO, 1860-1943. Two papers on international language in English and Ido. (Card 2)

after the World War. Composed in Danish by Dr. Otto Jespersen, translated into Ido by Miss Gunvar Mönster. With translation of both from the Ido into English by Gilbert H. Richardson.

English and Ido on opposite pages.

Mrs. Dave H. Morrison collection

1. Ido--Books in. I. Richardson, Gilbert H., tr.

YAG

Jesuit thinkers of the renaissance, essays presented to John F. McCormick, S. J., by his students on the occasion of the sixty-fifth anniversary of his birth. Edited by Gerard Smith ... Milwaukee, Wis., Marquette university press, 1939.
xvii, 254 p. front. (port.) diagr. 21½cm.

Tail-pieces.

CONTENTS.—Foreword, by Gerard Smith.—Biographical note.—Suarez and the organization of learning, by Clare C. Riedl.—Father Dominic Bouhours and neo-classical criticism, by V. M. Hamm.—Molina and human liberty, by A. C. Pegis.—Leonard Lessius, by C. H. Chamberlain.—Juan de Mariana, by G. K. Tallmadge.—Bellarmine and the dignity of man, by J. O. Riedl.—A Suarez bibliography (p. 227-238)—Bibliographical note on Molina (p. 239-241)—A Bellarmine bibliography (p. 242-254)

1. McCormick, John Francis, 1874- 2. Jesuits—Biog. 3. Jesuits—Bibl. I. Smith, Gerard ed.

39—14093

Library of Congress BX3755.J4
[a41g2] 271.5

---

* PBN

Jewish Institute of Religion, New York.
Jewish studies in memory of Israel Abrahams, by the faculty and visiting teachers of The Jewish Institute of Religion, published under the auspices of The Alexander Kohut Memorial Foundation. New York: Press of the Jewish Institute of Religion, 1927. lxvi, 458 p. facsims., front. (port.), illus. (incl. music.) 4 pl. 8°.

Printed in Austria.

Contents: The Alexander Kohut Memorial Foundations. Editor's preface. WISE, S. S. Foreword. WRIGHT, D. Select bibliography of the works of Israel

(Continued)

N. Y. P. L. September 18, 1928

Jewish Institute of Religion, New York: Jewish studies in memory of Israel Abrahams... (Continued)

Abrahams. HARRIS, M. H. Israel Abrahams and the Reform Jewish Movement in England. JACKSON, F. J. F. Israel Abrahams at Cambridge. KRASS, N. Israel Abrahams, master of homily. MONTEFIORE, C. G. Israel Abrahams and Liberal Judaism. ASKOWITH, D. Prolegomena. Baron, S. Azariah de Rossi's attitude to life. BINDER, A. W. V'shomru. BLOCH, J. Ὁ Σύρος and the Peshitta. DIESENDRUCK, Z. Maimonides' Lehre von der Prophetie. ELBOGEN, I. Einige neuere Theorien über den Ursprung der Pharisäer und Sadduzäer. GOTTHEIL, R. Tit-bits from the Genizah. GRESSMANN, H. Jewish life in ancient Rome. GUTTMANN, J. Elia del Medigos Verhältnis zu Averroës in seinem Bechinat ha-Dat. HERFORD, R. T. The separation of Christianity from Judaism. KOHUT, G. A. Royal Hebraists.

(Continued)

N. Y. P. L. September 18, 1928

Jewish Institute of Religion, New York: Jewish studies in memory of Israel Abrahams... (Continued)

LAKE, K. The Council of Jerusalem. LEVY, R. A collection of Yemenite piyyuṭim. LEWIS, H. S. The "golden mean" in Judaism. LYON, D. G. Text variations in some duplicate inscriptions of Adad-nirari. MARGOLIS, M. L. Specimen of a new edition of the Greek Joshua. MAXIMON, S. B. In the footsteps of the rabbis. MONTEFIORE, C. G. Religion and learning. MOORE, G. F. Simeon the Righteous. NEWMAN, L. I. Joseph ben Isaac Kimchi. OBERMANN, J. The death of Sisera. PERLES, F. Notes on some Midrashic texts. ROTH, C. Leone da Modena and the Christian hebraists of his age. TSCHERNOWITZ, C. The inheritance of illegitimate children

(Continued)

N. Y. P. L. September 18, 1928

Jewish Institute of Religion, New York: Jewish studies in memory of Israel Abrahams... (Continued)

according to Jewish law. VOGELSTEIN, H. Einige Probleme der jüdischen Geschichte der Zeit des zweiten Tempels. WOLFSON, H. A. Solomon Pappenheim on time and space. YELLIN, D. Forgotten meanings of Hebrew roots in the Bible. Additional notes.

369467A. 1. Essays, Jewish—Collections. 2. Abrahams, Israel, 1858-1925. 3. Alexander Kohut Memorial Foundation, New York.

N. Y. P. L. September 18, 1928

---

*PTZ
(Saadish)

The Jewish quarterly review. ~~New series.~~
Saadia studies, published by the Jewish quarterly review in commemoration of the thousandth anniversary of the death of Saadia Gaon, edited by Abraham A. Neuman and Solomon Zeitlin. Philadelphia, The Dropsie college for Hebrew and cognate learning, 1943.
2 p. l., 293 p. 24½cm.

Bibliographical foot-notes.

CONTENTS.—Saadia and his relation to Palestine, by A. A. Neuman.—Saadia's theory of knowledge, by Israel Efros.—A study of inflection in Hebrew from Saadia Gaon's grammatical work "Kutub al-lughah," by S. L. Skoss.—The double faith theory in Clement, Saadia, Averroes and St. Thomas, and its origin in Aristotle and the stoics by H. A. Wolfson.—

(Continued on next card)

43-5670

[4]

The Jewish quarterly review. ~~New series.~~ Saadia studies ... 1943. (Card 2)

CONTENTS—Continued.

The quest for certainty in Saadia's philosophy, by Abraham Heschel.—Saadia's Siddur, by Louis Ginzberg.—Saadia Gaon, champion for Jewish unity under religious leadership, by Solomon Zeitlin.

1. Saadiah ben Joseph, gaon, 892-942. I. Neuman, Abraham Aaron, 1890- ed. II. Zeitlin, Solomon, 1892- joint ed. III. Title.

43-5670

Library of Congress BM755.S2J4
[4] 922.96

*PBN

Jewish studies in memory of George A. Kohut, 1874–1933, edited by Salo W. Baron and Alexander Marx. New York, The Alexander Kohut memorial foundation, 1935.

xciii, 614 p., 2 l., קמה p. front. (port.) illus., facsims., tab. 24cm.

Studies in English, German and Hebrew. Hebrew section has title: מחקרים לזכרון ר' עמרם קאהוט ז"ל. י"ל ע"י שלום בארון ואלכסנדר מארכס. ניו־יורק, הוצאת המוסד לזכרון אלכסנדר קאהוט, התרצ"ה.

"A bibliography of George Alexander Kohut" compiled by E. D. Coleman: p. xii–xciii.

"Recent literature on Philo (1924–1934)" compiled by Ralph Marcus: p. 463–491.

1. Kohut, George Alexander, 1874–1933. 2. Jews—Addresses, essays, lectures. 3. Philo Judæus—Bibl. I. Baron, Salo Wittmayer, 1895– joint ed. II. Marx, Alexander, 1878– ed. III. Alexander Kohut memorial foundation, New York. IV. Coleman, Edward Davidson, 1891– V. Marcus, Ralph, 1900–

Library of Congress DS102.K6 36–4932

——— Copy 2.

Copyright A 91729 [5] 296.04

---

*PBN

JEWISH THEOLOGICAL SEMINARY OF AMERICA.

Alexander Marx; jubilee volume on the occasion of his seventieth birthday. English section. New York, Jewish theological seminary of America, 1950. xxiii, 667 p. 23cm.

Published simultaneously with a Hebrew section.

Bibliographical footnotes.

Contents.—Kohut, Rebekah. Prof. Alexander Marx.—Goldman, Solomon. The man of the book.—Cohen, Boaz. Bibliography of the writings of Prof. Alexander Marx (p. 35-59).—Albright, W. F. The

(Continued)

NN* OS PC, 1, 2 SL J, 2, 3 (LC1, Z1, X1)

JEWISH THEOLOGICAL SEMINARY OF AMERICA. Alexander Marx... (Card 2)

judicial reform of Jehoshaphat.—Baron, S. W. Moritz Steinschneider's contribution to Jewish historiography.—Bickerman, E. J. Some notes on the transmission of the Septuagint.—Cohen, Boaz. Antichresis in Jewish and Roman law.—Fischel, W. J. The region of the Persian gulf and its Jewish settlements in Islamic times.—Freimann, Aaron. Jewish scribes in medieval Italy.—Friedenwald, Harry. Themon Judaeus and his work.—Ginsberg, H. L. Judah and the Transjordan states from 734 to 582 B. C. E.—Gordis, Robert. Democratic origins in ancient Israel: The Biblical

(Continued)

NN* OS PC, 1, 2 SL J, 2, 3 (LC1, Z1, X1)

JEWISH THEOLOGICAL SEMINARY OF AMERICA. Alexander Marx... (Card 3)

'Ēdah.—Halkin, A. S. Ibn 'Aḳnīn's commentary on the Song of songs.—Kisch, Guido. The editio princeps of Pseudo-Philo's Liber antiquitatum biblicarum.—Marcus, J. R. A brief supplement to the standard Hebrew dictionaries of abbreviations.—Marx, Moses. On the date of appearance of the first printed Hebrew books.—Neuman, A. A. Josippon: history and pietism.—Roth, Cecil. Catalogue of manuscripts in the Roth collection.—Scheiber, Alexander. Piyyutim from the Geniza collection of David Kaufmann.—Sperber, Alexander. A new Bible translation.—Taeubler, E. Ḥabiru-'Ibhrim.—Torrey, C. C. The Hebrew of the Geniza

(Continued)

NN* OS PC, 1, 2 SL J, 2, 3 (LC1, Z1, X1)

JEWISH THEOLOGICAL SEMINARY OF AMERICA. Alexander Marx... (Card 4)

Sirach.—Wolfson, H. A. The veracity of scripture in Philo, Halevi, Maimonides, and Spinoza.—Zeitlin, Solomon. A note on the principle of intention in Tannaitic literature.

1. Essays, Jewish—Collections. 2. Marx, Alexander, 1878- 3. Essays—Collections.

NN* OS PC, 1, 2 SL J, 2, 3 (LC1, Z1, X1)

---

*PBL

Jewish theological seminary of America.

The Jewish theological seminary of America, semi-centennial volume, edited by Cyrus Adler. New York, The Jewish theological seminary of America, 1939.

v, 194 p. front., plates, ports. 23½cm.

CONTENTS.—Semi-centennial address, by Cyrus Adler.—Tradition in the making: the seminary's interpretation of Judaism, by Louis Finkelstein.—The beginnings of the seminary, by H. P. Mendes.—Sabato Morais, a pupil's tribute, by J. H. Hertz.—Memories of Solomon Schechter, by C. I. Hoffman.—The buildings of the seminary, by J. B. Abrahams.—The academic aspect and growth of the rabbinical department, the seminary proper, by Israel Davidson.—The library, by Alexander Marx.—

(Continued on next card)

39–31935

[3]

Jewish theological seminary of America. The Jewish theological seminary of America ... 1939. (Card 2)

CONTENTS—Continued.

The teachers institute and its affiliated departments, by M. M. Kaplan.—The seminary museum, by A. S. W. Rosenbach.—Directors of the seminary, by S. M. Stroock.—The seminary as a cultural center, by F. M. Warburg.—The seminary as a center of Jewish learning, by Louis Finkelstein.—The charter of the seminary: act of incorporation.—Directors of the library corporation.—Faculty, rabbinical department.—Faculty, teachers institute and seminary college of Jewish studies.—Faculty, Israel Friedlaender classes.

I. Adler, Cyrus, 1863– ed.

Library of Congress BM90.J565 1939 39–31935

——— Copy 2.

Copyright A 134001 [3] 296.07

---

*PBN

JEWISH THEOLOGICAL SEMINARY OF AMERICA.

Mordecai M. Kaplan; jubilee volume on the occasion of his seventieth birthday. English section. New York, 1953. ix, 549 p. port. 24cm.

Edited by Mosheh Davis.

Published simultaneously with a Hebrew section.

Bibliographical references included.

CONTENTS.—World religion and national religion, by L. Baeck.—Bibliography of the writings of M. M. Kaplan, by G. D. Cohen (p. 9-33)—

(Continued)

NN**R X 2, 54 (OC)I OS PC, 1, 3, I SL J, 2, 3, I (Z1, LC1, X1)

JEWISH THEOLOGICAL SEMINARY OF AMERICA. Mordecai M. Kaplan... (Card 2)

The teacher in Talmud and Midrash, by M. Arzt.—Church and State debates in the Jewish community of 1848, by S. W. Baron.—The Kehillah of New York, 1908-1922, by N. Bentwich.—"Outside books," by J. Bloch.—Letter and spirit in Jewish and Roman law, by B. Cohen.—Kaufmann Kohler, the reformer, by S. S. Cohon.—Israel Friedlaender's Minute book of the Achavah club (1909-1912), by M. Davis.—Prophecy, wisdom, and apocalypse, by I. Efros.—Judaism as a system of symbols, by L. Finkelstein.—Gleanings in First Isaiah, by H. L. Ginsberg.—Deuteronomy 23:8, 9, by N. Glueck.—The first chapter of Abot de Rabbi Nathan,

(Continued)

JEWISH THEOLOGICAL SEMINARY OF AMERICA. Mordecai M. Kaplan... (Card 3)

by J. Goldin.—The Song of songs, by R. Gordis.—The multiplication of the mitzvot, by S. Greenberg.—A Contra christianos by a Marrano, by A. S. Halkin.—The role of memory in Biblical history, by L. L. Honor.—Freedom and authority, by H. M. Kallen.—Defining Jewish art, by S. S. Kayser.—Educational abuses and reforms in Hanoverian England, by C. Roth.—Yidishkayt and Yidishkayt and Yiddish, by M. Weinreich.—Maimonides and Gersonides on divine attributes as ambiguous terms, by H. A. Wolfson.—Sociological analysis of Israel, by B. Wolman.

1. Essays, Jewish, in English—Collections. 2. Essays, American—Collections. 3. Kaplan, Mordecai Menahem, 1881- . I. Davis, Moshe, ed.

*PWZ
(Saadiah)

Jewish theological seminary of America.

Rab Saadia gaon: studies in his honor, edited by Louis Finkelstein. [New York] Jewish theological seminary of America, 1944.

xi p., 1 l., 191 p., 10 l. 21cm.

"Virtually all the material ... was prepared in connection with meetings held in honor of Rab Saadia gaon at the Jewish theological seminary of America, or under its auspices."—Pref.

CONTENTS.—Preface.—Foreword: The philosopher: architect of peace. On the significance of Rab Saadia gaon, by Louis Finkelstein.—Rab Saadia gaon, by Alexander Marx.—Saadia gaon, by R. P. McKeon.—Freedom: address for Saadia celebration, by A. H. Compton.—Saadia's exegesis and polemics, by A. S. Halkin.—Saadia as a philosopher of Judaism, by B. Z. Bokser.—Saadia in the light of today, by Robert

(Continued on next card)

44-24282

[3]

Jewish theological seminary of America. Rab Saadia gaon ... 1944. (Card 2)

CONTENTS—Continued.

Gordisp.—Appendices: I. Selected bibliography of Rab Saadia gaon (p. 185–191) by Boaz Cohen.—II. Hymn by Frederick Jacobi: words by Saadia gaon (882–942), for men's chorus.—III. Program of the assembly commemorating the life and works of Rabbi Saadia gaon (882–942), held at the Jewish theological seminary of America, March 24, 1942.—IV. Program of the convocation to commemorate the life and works of Rab Saadia gaon (882–942), held at Mandel hall of the University of Chicago, April 20, 1942.

1. Saadiah, ~~ben Joseph~~ gaon, 892–942. I. Finkelstein, Louis, 1895– ed.

44-24282

Library of Congress BM755.S2J43

[3] 922.96

Write on slip words underlined below and class mark—

*OKA

...Jhā commemoration volume; essays on Oriental subjects presented to Vidyāsāgara Mahāmahopādhyāya Paṇḍita Gaṅgānātha Jhā ... on his completing the 60th year on 25th September, 1932, by his pupils, friends and admirers. Poona: Oriental book agency, 1937. viii, x, 96, 472 p. facsims., front. (port.) 25cm. (Poona Oriental series. no. 39.)

"Select bibliography of the writings of Dr. Ganganatha Jha," p. 469–472; bibliographical footnotes.

"Papers in Sanskrit," p. 1–96.

59667B. 1. Oriental studies. 2. Jha, Gangānātha, 1872– . I. Ser.

N. Y. P. L. December 31, 1940

---

*Q p.v.1438

JIŘI WOLKER, příklad naší poesie; čtyři projevy [A.M. Píši, Jana Mukařovskeho, Miloše Tomčika a Viléma Závady] z wolkrovské konference [1954...k třicatému výroči básníkova úmrtí] Praha, Československý spisovatel, 1954. 79 p. 21cm. (Knihovnicka varu. sv. 52)

CONTENTS—Píša, A. M. Jiří Wolker, klasik české socialistické poesie. --Mukařovsky, J. Příklad Jiřího Wolkra a dnešní poesie. --Tomčík, M. Jiří Wolker a slovenská poézia. --Závada, V. Jiří Wolker po třiceti letech.

1. WOLKER, JIŘI, 1900-1924 I. Píša, Antonín M., 1902-

NN * * R X 10.57 1/, OC, I PC, 1, I SL S, 1, I (LCE1, LC1, X1, Z1)

AN
(Winterfeldt, J.)

Joachim von Winterfeldt zum sechzigsten Geburtstage, 15 . 5 . 1925. Berlin, Pontos-Verlag [1925] 180 p. illus. 25cm.

265224B. 1. Winterfeldt, Joachim von, 1865–

N. Y. P. L. April 26, 1944

JFE
70-279

Joast Hiddes Halbertsma, 1789–1869. Brekker en bouwer. Stúdzjes fan ûnderskate skriuwers oer syn persoan, syn libben en syn wurk, útjown ta gelegenheit fan de bitinking fan syn hûndertste stjerdei. Drachten, Laverman, 1969.

368 p. illus., ports. 24 cm. (Fryske Akademy. [Utjeften] nr. 342)

Dutch or Frisian.

"List fan publikaesjes fan Dr. J. H. Halbertsma" (p. 347–356)

Includes bibliographical references.

1. Halbertsma, Joost Hiddes, 1789-1869.

NN * R 1.71 b/2OC PC, 1 SL (LC1, X1, Z1)

Copy only words underlined
& classmark— GDWW

JOHANNES VON MÜLLER, 1752-1952; zum zweihundertsten Geburtstag des Geschichtschreibers. [Thayngen, K. Augustin, 1952] 221 p. illus., ports. 24cm. (Historischer Verein des Kantons Schaffhausen. Beiträge zur vaterländischen Geschichte. Bd. 29)

CONTENTS. — Zum Geleit, von K. Schib. —Johannes von Müllers Lebengeschichte, von ihm selbst beschrieben, 1806. —Johannes von Müller als Christ, nicht als Historiker, von H. Gelzer. —Johannes von Müller in Weimar, von W. Andreas. —Johannes von Müller, Autgabe und

(Continued)

NN R X 12.53 OC OI PC, 1, 2 (LC3, ~~Z1~~, X1)

JOHANNES VON MULLER, 1752-1952; zum zweihundertsten Geburtstag des Geschichtschreibers... (Card 2)

Schicksal, von P. Requadt. —Johannes von Müller und Erzherzog Johann von Oesterreich, von V. Theiss. —Genealogisches, von E. Rüedi. —Johannes von Müller-Andenken im Museum zu Allerheiligen, v. O. Stiefel. —Bildnisse Johannes von Müllers im Museum zu Allerheiligen, von Otto Stiefel. —Die Enststehung des Denkmals Johannes von Müllers, von A. Steinegger. —Johannes von Müller-Bibliographie, von E. Schellenberg (p. 161-209)

1. Müller, Johannes von, 1752-1809. 2. Müller, Johannes von, 1752-1809—Bibl.

MAD

Johnny Roosval, den 29 augusti 1929. Amici amico. Stockholm, 1929. 150 p. illus. (plans), plates. 25½cm. (Stockholm. Högskolan. Zornska institutet för nordisk och jämförande konsthistoria. Studier. [bd.] 6.)

On half-title: Konsthistoriska studier tillägnade Johnny Roosval den 29 augusti 1929.

"Summary" accompanies articles in Swedish.

CONTENTS.—Aubert, M. Les débuts de la sculpture gotique en Île-de France. Le portail de Saint-Loup de Naud.—Boëthius, G. Stavkyrkans ursprung och utveckling.—Cornell, H. Naturalismens möjligheter.—Goldschmidt, A. Der Zeichner des Jean de Waurin.—Lindblom, A. Ett apostolicum i nederländsk bildtolkning.—Lundberg, E.

(Continued)

Festschrift.

N. Y. P. L. April 6, 1934

Johnny Roosval, den 29 augusti 1929... (Card 2)

Den romanska katedralinteriören och vår uppfattning av medeltida arkitektur.—Meinander, K. K. Orientaliska drag i Finlands medeltida textilier.—Kingsley Porter, A. Notes on Irish crosses.—Romdahl, A. L. Ett pentimento i Linköpings domkyrka.—Rydbeck, O. Några småländska dopfuntar tillhörande Roosvals Bestiariusgrupp.—Seaver, E. I. The figure sculpture of the Scandinavian crosses on the Isle of Man.—Thordeman, B. En återfunnen Visbykyrka.—Ugglas, C. R. af. Till Vadstena klosters konsthistoria. En episod från vårt gotiska måleris utveckling.—Kjellin, H. Vergilius i korgen och som trollkarl.

654751A. 1. Art—Essays and misc. I. Roosval, Johnny August Emanuel, 1879– . II. Ser.

N. Y. P. L. April 6, 1934

TLH

JÖNKÖPINGS KÖPMANNAFÖRENING.

Köpenskap i Jönköping gennom tiderna. Minnesskrift i anledning av Jönköpings köpmannaförenings 50-åriga tillvaro, 1903-1953, skriven och redigerad av Eric Jonsson. [Jönköping, 1953] 276 p. (p. 235-276 advertisements) illus., ports. 25cm.

CONTENTS. -- Magnus Ladulås' privilegiebrev till Jönköping. -- Lojal tävlan har avlöst allas krig mot alla, av O. Ekblom. -- Köpenskap är värdeskapande, av O. Dahlbäck. --Samarbete inom Handelskammaren till näringarnas gagn, av T. Jung. --Samhället kräver organisation och

(Continued)

NN ** X 1.55 p/v (OC) I, IIbo OS (1b+) PC, 1, I SL E, 1, I (LC1, Z1, X1)

JÖNKÖPINGS KÖPMANNAFÖRENING. Köpenskap i Jönköpings gennom tiderna. (Card 2)

samgående, av G. Ekholm. -- Tacksamhet inför minnet av föreningens pionjärer, av G. Jonsson. -- Köpmannaandan är organisationens verk, av O. Lagerquist. --Gustav II Adolfs privilegiebrev till Jönköping. -- En köpstad med anor. Några anteckningar om handel och köpenskap i Jönköping från medeltiden till 1800-talets slut, av E. Jonsson. --Från köpmannaföreningens dagar.

1. Commerce-- Sweden-- Jönköping. I. Jonsson, Eric, ed. II. Jonsson, Eric.

NN ** X 1.55 p/v (OC) I, IIbo OS (1b+) PC, 1, I SL E, 1, I (LC1, Z1, X1)

F-10
8738

JOOST, SIEGFRIED, ed.

Bibliotheca docet; Festgabe für Carl Wehmer. [Unter Mitwirkung Heidelberger Bibliothekare hrsg.] Amsterdam, Verlag der Erasmus-Buchhandlung, 1963. 411 p. illus., port., facsims. 27cm.

On cover: Bibliotheca docet; Festschrift Carl Wehmer.
Contributions in German, English or Italian.
Includes bibliographies.

(Continued)

NN R 5.64 j/B OC(1bo) PC, 1, 2, 3, 4 SL (LC1, X1, Z1) [I]

2

JOOST, SIEGFRIED, ed. Bibliotheca docet... (Card 2)

J. S. Billings Mem. Coll.

1. Wehmer, Carl, 1903- . 2. Library science--Addresses, essays, lectures. 3. Bibliography--Addresses, essays, lectures. 4. Art--Essays and misc.

3-MQWK

JOPE, EDWARD MARTYN, ed.

Studies in building history; essays in recognition of the work of B.H. St. J. O'Neil. London, Odhams Press [1961] 287 p. illus., port., maps, diagrs., plans, tables. 27cm.

"Bibliography of the published works of B.H. St. J. O'Neil" : p. 275-279. Includes bibliographical references."

1. Architecture--Gt. Br. 2. Architecture--Restoration. 3. O'Neil, B.H. St. J. 4. Building--Gt. Br. I. Title. II. Jope, Edward Martyn. t.1961

NN * R 3.64 f/B OC, I, IIb* PC, 1, 2, 3, 4, I SL A, 1, 2, 3, I ST, 4t (LC1, X1, Z1) [I]

---

*KP
(St. Albert's)

JOSEPH DELTEIL; essays in tribute, by Eugène Louis Julien, Jacques Madaule, Henry Miller... [and others Aylesford, Kent] St. Albert's press, 1962. 4 p.l., 39 (1) p. 24cm.

No. 118 of "one hundred and fifty copies... reprinted... from The Aylesford review, volume IV, number 7, by the John Roberts press limited, London... for signature by Joseph Delteil and Henry Miller."

(Continued)

NN * R 10.65 e/J OC, I, II, III PC, 1, I, II, III SL R, 1, I, II, III (RA2, RI 2, RS1, LC1, X1, Z1)

2

JOSEPH DELTEIL; essays in tribute... 1962. (Card 2)

Contributions in English and French.
Foreword signed: Brocard Sewell.

1. Delteil, Joseph, 1894- . I. Julien, Eugène Louis Ernest, bp. of Arras, 1856-1930. II. Miller, Henry, 1891- . III. Sewell, Brocard.

---

*PWZ
(Jéhouda)

Josué Jéhouda, l'homme et l'oeuvre. [Les amis de la Revue juive à Josué Jéhouda pour ses 25 années d'activité littéraire, 1923-1948]. Préface de Jean Cassou. Paris, Éditions du centre [de documentation juive contemporaine, 1949] 288 p. port. 19cm. (Études et témoignages)

"Les 25 années d'activité littéraire de Josué

(Continued)

NN**Z X 11.55 d/ OC (OS)I, II, III PC, 1, I SL J, 1, I (U1, LC1, X1, Z1) [NSCM]

Josué Jéhouda... (Card 2)

Jéhouda," a bibliography, p. [19]-23.

1. Jéhouda, Josué. I. Centre de documentation juive contemporaine. II. Centre de documentation juive contemporaine. Études et témoignages. III. Études et témoignages.

---

*C-4 p.v.471

Journées nationales d'Aguesseau, 1951.

Le chancelier Henri-François d'Aguesseau, Limoges 1668-Fresnes 1751; journées d'etude tenues à Limoges à l'occasion du bicentenaire de sa mort (octobre 1951) Limoges, Aux dépens de la Société archéologique et historique du Limousin et de l'Académie de Poitiers, Librairie Desvilles, 1953. 151 p. illus. 26cm.

Includes bibliographies.
CONTENTS.—La vie et la personne: La naissance et la jeunesse du chancelier d'Aguesseau, par M. Gorceix; D'Aguesseau vu par Saint-Simon, par M. Vouin.—L'écri-

(Continued)

NN**R 8.55 (OC)I OS(1b+) PC,1,I SL E,1 (Z1, LC1, X1)

Journées nationales d'Aguesseau, 1951. Le chancelier... 1953. (Card 2)

vain, le philosophe, l'orateur: L'importance de d'Aguesseau pour son temps et pour le nôtre, par M. Carbonnier; D'Aguesseau écrivain, par M. Duchein; D'Aguesseau et l'humanisme, par R. P. Pierrot; D'Aguesseau, philosophe du droit, par M. Rigaud.—Le juriste, le législateur: L'opinion du chancelier Daguesseau [sic] sur l'unification du droit privé, par M. Garaud; D'Aguesseau, orateur et législateur, par M. Hoffmann, D'Aguesseau et le droit international privé, par M. Niboyet; D'Aguesseau, législateur ou jurisconsulte? par M. Villers.—Économie et finances: D'Aguesseau, économiste, par M. Bayart; Les "Considérations sur les monnaies" du chancelier d'Aguesseau, par M. Hubrecht.—Politique religieuse: D'Aguesseau et Fénelon, par M. Bellugou; D'Aguesseau et le jansénisme, par G. Rech.—Exposition: Catalogue, commenté par Mme M.-M. Gauthier.

1. Aguesseau, Henri François d', 1668–1751. I. Title.

AN

(Jovellanos, G.)

Jovellanos, su vida y su obra, por Luis Méndez Calzada [et al.] Homenaje del Centro Asturiano de Buenos Aires en el bicentenario de su nacimiento, con la adhesión de los Centros Asturianos de la Habana y México. [Ilustró Gori Muñoz. Buenos Aires, 1945]

703 p. illus., port. 24 cm.

CONTENTS.—Vida de Jovellanos, por Luis Méndez Calzada.—Jovellanos político, por Augusto Barcia Trelles.—Jovellanos jurista, por Angel Ossorio y Gallardo.—Jovellanos economista, por Jesús Prados Arrarte.—Jovellanos sociólogo, por Francisco Ayala.—Jovellanos magistrado, por Mariano Gómez.—Jovellanos literato, por Manuel Blasco Garzón.—Jovellanos y la reforma agraria, por Manuel

(Continued on next card)

A 49–1607*

[1]

Jovellanos, su vida y su obra ... [1945] (Card 2)

CONTENTS—Continued.

Serra Moret.—Jovellanos y la historia, por Claudio Sánchez Albornoz.—La obra asturianista de Jovellanos, por Clemente Cimorra.—Influencia de las ideas de Jovellanos en la gesta emancipadora argentina, por J. V. González.—Jovellanos en los orígenes de la nacionalidad cubana, por Ramón Infiesta.

1. Jovellanos, Gaspar Melchor de, 1744–1811. I. Méndez Calzada, Luis, 1888– II. Centro Asturiano de Buenos Aires.

A 49–1607*

New York. Public Libr. for Library of Congress [1]

---

*YN

The joy of study; papers on New Testament and related subjects presented to honor Frederick Clifton Grant. Ed. by Sherman E. Johnson. New York, Macmillan co., 1951. xii, 163 p. 21cm.

Bibliographical footnotes.

1. Bible, N. T.—Essays, etc. 2. Grant, Frederick Clifton, 1891- I. Johnson, Sherman Elbridge, 1908- , ed.

NN

---

*PXS

Jubilee volume dedicated to Curt C. Silberman. Edited by Herbert A. Strauss [and] Hanns G. Reissner. New York, American Federation of Jews from Central Europe, 1969.

xii, 132 p. port. 24 cm.

English or German.
Includes bibliographies.

CONTENTS.—Geleitwort des Präsidenten des Council of Jews from Germany, by S. Moses.—Editor's note, by H. A. Strauss.—The three

(Continued)

NN*R 5.70 r/L OC, I, Ib*, II, III (OS)IV PC, 1, I, II, III, IV SL J, 2, I, Ib*, II, III, IV (LC1, X1, Z1)

Jubilee volume dedicated to Curt C. Silberman. 1969. (Card 2)

regions of German-Jewish history, by W. J. Cahnman.—From Kiev via Brody to Pankow, by F. Grubel.—Facing the people, by M. Gruenewald.—Services to the Jewish aged in North America, by K. G. Herz.—Sacred tradition in Judaism, by J. Maier.—Germans and Jews—is there a bridge? By J. Prinz.—The American anti-Nazi boycott, by H. G. Reissner.—Missverstandenes Schlussgesetz, by A Schueler.—A note on the nature of ideal society—a rabbinic study, by S. Schwarzschild.—Nicht vom Winde verweht: Zwischenbilanz einer

(Continued)

JUBILEE volume dedicated to Curt C. Silberman. (Card 3)

Flüchtlingsgeneration, by H. Steinitz.—Immortality in the Bible, by H. Stransky.—Liberalism and conservatism in Prussian legislation for Jewish affairs, 1815–1847, by H. A. Strauss.

1. Jews in Germany--Hist. 2. Germany--Hist. I. Silberman, Curt C., 1908- . II. Strauss, Herbert Arthur, ed. III. Reissner, Hanns Günther, ed. IV. American Federation of Jews from Central Europe, inc.

---

* PBN

Jubilee volume in honour of Prof. Bernhard Heller on the occasion of his seventieth birthday. In collaboration with his friends, admirers and pupils, ed. by Alexander Scheiber... Budapest, 1941. 326, 132 p. illus. 24cm.

Added title-pages in Hungarian and Hebrew; Contributions in English, German, Hungarian or Hebrew (paged separately).

PARTIAL CONTENTS.—Goldziher, Ingaz. Ein orientalischer Ritter roman.—Graf, Andreas. Die Tataren im Spiegel der byzantinischen Literatur.—Bernstein, Béla. Graetz.—Büchler, Alexander. Das Judenprivilegium Bélas IV. vom Jahre 1251.—

(Continued)

N. Y. P. L. June 3, 1948

Jubilee volume in honour of Prof. Bernhard Heller... (Card 2)

Gaster, Moses. Beiträge zur vergleichenden Sagen- und Märchenkunde. Zu Paulis Schimpf und Ernst.—Heinemann, Isaak. Die Kontroverse über das Wunder im Judentum der hellenistischen Zeit.—Kohlbach, Berthold. Das Salz.—Levy, Raphael. Apostilles judéo-francaises.—Löw, Immanuel. Der Diamant.—Munkácsi, Ernest. Ancient and medieval synagogues in representations of the fine arts.—Naményi, Ernö. Ein ungarisch-jüdischer Kupferstecher der Biedermeierzeit (Markus Donath).—Nemoy, Leon. Al-Qirqisani on Liviticus 18.18.—Heller, Bernát. Goldziher Ignácz és a néprajz.

438715B. 1. Essays, Jewish—Collections. 2. Heller, Bernát, 1871– . I. Scheiber, Alexander, ed.
N. Y. P. L. June 3, 1948

---

* PBN

Juedische Studien, Josef Wohlgemuth zu seinem sechzigsten Geburtstage von Freunden und Schülern gewidmet. Frankfurt am Main: J. Kauffmann, 1928. 284, 39 p. incl. tables. facsims. 8°.

Bibliographical footnotes.

Contents: Widmung. AUERBACH, M. Der Streit zwischen Saadja Gaon und dem Exilarchen David ben Sakkai. BLAU, A. Ueber den Gegensinn der Worte im Hebräischen. CARLEBACH, J. Einleitung in das Buch Ruth. GRÜNBERG, S. מנחת שמואל. HILDESHEIMER, E. Die Komposition der Sammlungen von Responsen der Gaonen. HOROVITZ, J. Randglossen. KAATZ, S. Zu Psalm 115. KLEIN, S. Galiläa von der Makkabäerzeit bis 67. LEWIN, B. לחקר שאילתות רב אחאי גאון. MARKON, I. D. B.

(Continued)

N. Y. P. L. October 17, 1929

Juedische Studien... (Card 2)

Das Land Schabat in den Reisebemerkungen des Athanas Nikitin (1466–1472). MARMORSTEIN, A. Die Nachahmung Gottes (Imitatio Dei) in der Agada. UNNA, I. Die Stellung Schopenhauers zum Judentum.

SCHIFF COLLECTION.

429107A. 1. Wohlgemuth, Josef, 1867– . 2. Essays, Jewish—Collections.
N. Y. P. L. October 17, 1929

---

* PBN

Juedisch-theologisches Seminar, Breslau.
Festschrift zum 75-jährigen Bestehen des Jüdisch-theologischen Seminars Fraenckelscher Stiftung... Breslau: M. & H. Marcus, 1929. 2 v. facsims. 8°.

German and Hebrew.

492721–22A. 1. Rabbinical seminaries—Germany. 2. Essays—Collections.
N. Y. P. L. October 20, 1930

D-18
6155

JÜNGER, ERNST, 1895-
Grenzgänge [Zum siebzigsten Geburtstag des Autors 29. März, 1965] Olten, 1965. 61 p. 21cm. (Oltner liebhaber Druck. 6)

1. Essays, German.
NN R 12.68 d/A OC PC, 1 SL (LC1, X1, Z1)

Copy only words underlined & classmark— SA

JÜRGENSEN, HARALD, ed.
Gestaltsprobleme der Weltwirtschaft; Andreas Predöhl aus Anlass seines 70. Geburtstages gewidmet. Göttingen, Vandenhoek & Rupprecht [1964] 636 p. port. 25cm. (Jahrbuch fur sozialwissenschaft. Bd. 14, Heft 3)

Bibliographical footnotes.

1. Predöhl, Andreas, 1893- 2. Economic integration--Europe. 3. Economic policy, 1945-
NN 12.64 c/ OC OI PC, 1, 2, 3 E, 1, 2, 3 (LC1, X1, Z1)

F-11
1682

JUHLARKIRJA Eero K. Neuvoven täyttäessä 60 vuotta 31. päivänä heinäkuuta 1964. Turku, 1964. 216 p. illus., port. 26cm. (Turun yliopisto, Turku, Finland. Julkaisuja. Sarja B: Humaniora. Osa 91)

Contributions in Finnish, Swedish or French.
Bibliographical footnotes.

1. Neuvonen, Eero K. 2. Philology--Addresses, essays, lectures. I. Series.
NN R 8.66 1/ OC (OS)I PC, 1, 2, I SL (LC1, X1, Z1)

AN
(Béen, I.)

Juhlakirja jonka ovat omistaneet hovisaarnaaja Isaac Béen'ille hänen kuusikymmenvuotispäivänään kuudentena kesäkuuta MCMXLVIII ystävät Suomessa. Helsingissä, 1948. 198 p. illus. 25cm.

Also issued in Swedish with title: Festskrift tillägnad hovpredikanten Isaac Béen på hans sextioårsdag...
Includes music.

560194B. 1. Béen, Isaac, 1888– .
N. Y. P. L. January 15, 1951

AN
(Courmont, J.)

Jules Courmont, 1865-1917. [Macon: Protat frères, imprimeurs, 1917] 141 p. illus. 28cm.

"Liste chronologique des travaux scientifiques de Jules Courmont," p. [103]-125.

E-11
8392

JULIEN KUYPERS, vlaams europeeër. Antwerpen, Ontwikkeling, 1963. 112 p. 25cm.

Pref. signed: A. Molter.
CONTENTS.--Ten tijde van "La belle epoque," door R. Brulez.--Gedicht, door M. Coole.--Julien Kuypers in de B. R. T., door R. Declerck.--Ontmoetingen, door R. Herreman.--Hoe Julien Kuypers "factotum" werd in het Departement van onderwijs van 1925 tot 1927, door C. Huysmans.--
(Continued)

NN R 12.63 p/ OC, I PC, 1, I SL (LC1, X1, Z1)

2

JULIEN KUYPERS, vlaams europeeër. (Card 2)

Julien Kuypers, de meetrekker, door K. Jonckheere.--De les van een leven, door M. Lamberty.--Julien Kuypers, de historicus, door M. Oukhow.--Een jeugdvriend: Eugène Cantillon, door L. Picard.--Luister naar déze stem uit het graf, Julien Kuypers! Door G. Schmook.--Een mens, door H. Teirlinck.--Julien Kuypers, de onderwijsman, door H. de Vos.--Platenboo, door V.E. van Vriesland.--De morele marteling, door G. Walschap.

1. Kuypers, Julien, 1892- I. Molter, A.

AN
(Ofner, J.)

Julius Ofner zum 70ten Geburtstage. Wien [etc.] Anzengruber-verlag, Brüder Suschitzky [1915] 263 p. illus. 24cm.

"Beiträge zu einem Verzeichnisse über Aufsätze der Schriften Julius Ofners," p. [241]-263.

255099B. 1. Ofner, Julius, 1845–1924. 2. Ofner, Julius, 1845–1924—Bibl.
N. Y. P. L. June 12, 1944

YEK

JUNG-INSTITUT, Zürich.
Studien zur analytischen Psychologie C.G. Jungs. [Festschrift zum 80. Geburtstag von C.G. Jung. Zürich] Rascher [1955] 2 v. illus. (part col.) 24cm.

Contributions in German, English or French.
CONTENTS. --1. Beiträge aus Theorie und Praxis, von G. Adler [et al.] --2. Beiträge zur Kulturgeschichte, von K. Binswanger [et al.]

1. Psychoanalysis. 2. Jung, Carl Gustav, 1875- . I. Title: Festschrift zum 80. Geburtstag von C.G. Jung.

NN **R 3. 56 s/ (OC)I OS PC, 1, 2, I SL (LC1, X1, Z1)

*OMA

The K. R. Cama memorial volume; essays on Iranian subjects, written by various scholars in honour of Mr. Kharshedji Rustamji Cama on the occasion of his seventieth birth-day and edited by Jivanji Jamshedji Modi, B. A. Bombay, Fort prtg. press, 1270 A. Y., 1900. A–D, lxxvi, 323 p. illus. 22cm.

306823B. 1. Cama, Kharshedji Rustamji, 1831–1909. 2. Avesta. 3. Iranian literature—Hist. and crit. 4. Iranians. I. Modi, Sir Jivanji Jamshedji, 1854–1933, ed.
N. Y. P. L. *Card revised* May 14, 1946

VDY +

Junkers; Festschrift Hugo Junkers zum 70. Geburtstage gewidmet von A. Berson, A. Gramberg, A. Kessner, O. Mader, A. Nägel und seinen Mitarbeitern; überreicht vom Verein deutscher Ingenieure. Berlin: VDI-Verlag[, 1929]. 99 p. incl. tables. diagrs., illus. (incl. facsims.) 4°.

Contents: Vorwort. Das Werk, von Junkers' Mitarbeitern. Nägel, A. Der Junkersmotor. Gramberg, A. Junkers' wärmetechnische Arbeiten. Kessner, A. Konstruktion und Werkstoff. Mader, O. Vom Junkers-Flugzeugbau. Berson, A. Junkers in der Luftfahrt.

435467A. 1. Junkers, Hugo, 1859– . 2. Aeronautics—Motors—Type—Junkers, 1929.
N. Y. P. L. October 31, 1929

D-14 559

KÄSBAUER, MAX, ed.
Logik und Logikkalkül. [Herrn Professor Dr. Wilhelm Britzelmayr zum siebzigsten Geburtstag von seinen Freunden und Schülern gewidmet] Hrsg. von Max Käsbauer und Franz von Kutschera. Freiburg, K. Alber [1962] 248 p. port. 23cm.

Includes bibliographies.

(Continued)

NN R 1. 63 p/ OC, I, II, IIIbo, IVbo PC, 1, 2, I, II SL ST, 1t, 2, I, II (LC1, X1, Z1) 4

XAN

Juristforbundet, Copenhagen.
Festskrift til professor, dr. juris Vinding Kruse paa tresaarsdagen den 30. juli 1940. Under redaktion af Erik Reitzel-Nielsen, med bidrag af ...O. A. Borum...[og 14 andre] Udgivet af Juristforbundet. Kjøbenhavn, Nyt nordisk forlag, 1940. 329 p. port. 29cm.

Contributions in Danish, Norwegian or Swedish.
Contents.—Vinding Kruse.—Borum, O. A. Skyldbegrebet i skilsmisseretten.—Forchhammer, Olaf, Byplan.—Gjessing, Harald, and Svenning Rytter. Vinding Kruse og Tinglysningsloven.—Graae, Fr., and Torben Lund. Aandelig ejendomsret.—
(Continued)

N. Y. P. L. January 19, 1949

KÄSBAUER, MAX, ed. Logik und Logikkalkül.
(Card 2)

CONTENTS. --Über Jugend und Alter, von H. Scholz. --Drei Aporien der Identität, von H. Behmann.--Umformung einer abgeschlossenen deduktiven oder semantischen Tafel in eine natürliche Ableitung auf Grund der derivaten bzw. klassischen Implikationslogik, von E. W. Beth. --Eine Axiomatisierung der Mengenlehre, beruhend auf den Systemen von Bernays und Quine, von W. Stegmüller. --Logische Abgrenzungen der Transfiniten, von K. Schütte. --Bemerkungen zur logischen Analyse einiger rechtstheoretischer Begriffe und Behauptungen, von U. Klug. --Heteromorphe Zuordnung
(Continued)

Juristforbundet, Copenhagen. Festskrift til professor, dr. juris Vinding Kruse... (Card 2)

Granfelt, O. H. Förfarandet enligt finländsk rätt då inteckning sökes och fastställes i fastighet, inregistrerad tomtlegorätt eller anläggning och besittningsrätt till säkerhet för fordran, sytning (undantag) eller avgäld.—Hurwitz, Stephan. Om begrebet "retlig interesse" i procesretten.—Juul, Stig. Om permutationsretten.—Jørgensen, P. J. Begreberne tyveri og ran i de danske landskabslove.—Jørgensen, T. G. Betragtninger over ekspropriationsbestemmelserne i grundlovsforslaget af 1939.—Lindvik, Adolf. "Full verdi efter gangbar pris i egnen". Av den norske odelsrett.—Møller, Ejvind. Om naturfredning.—Popp-Madsen, Carl. Hvornaar "stiftes" pantretten efter et tinglyst skadesløsbrev i fast ejendom?—Ussing, Henry. Grænser for renten af laan i fast ejendom.—Reitzel-Nielsen, Erik, and Inger Vogt. Fortegnelse over Vinding Kruses skrifter (p. 311–329).

451094B. 1. Law—Scandinavian. 2. Economics—Essays and misc. 3. Kruse, Vinding, 1880– . I. Reitzel-Nielsen, Erik, 1908– , ed. II. Title.
N. Y. P. L. January 19, 1949

KÄSBAUER, MAX, ed. Logik und Logikkalkül.
(Card 3)

von Zeichen und Funktion in der Sprache, von E. Koschmieder. --Über die logische semantische Struktur implikativer Begriffe der natürlichen Sprache, von R. Freundlich. --Fragenfolgen, von G. Stahl. --Kaluzhnin graphs and Yanov writs, by E. M. Fels. --Bemerkungen zur Semantik quantifizierter mehrwertiger logistischer Systeme, von A. Wilhelmy. --Absolut unentscheidbare Sätze der Mathematik, von W. Hoering. --Frege und die Typentheorie, von H. D. Sluga. --Zum Deduktionsbegriff der klassischen Prädikatenlogik erster Stufe, von F. v Kutschera. --Logisches System mit Prädikatquantoren, von M. Käsbauer.
(Continued)

F-10 6337

K.-A. FAGERHOLM [31.12.1961] mies ja työkenttä, mannen och verket. [Toimituskunta: R.H. Oittinen et al. Helsinki, Tilgmann, 1961] 356 p. illus., ports. 28cm.

Text in Finnish or Swedish, captions in Finnish and Swedish.

1. Fagerholm, Karl August, 1901- . 2. Socialism--Finland. 3. Finland--Govt. I. Oittinen, Reino Henrik, 1912- , ed.

NN R 6.65 g/ OC, Ib+, I PC, 1, 2, 3, I SL E, 1, 2, 3, I (LC1, X1, Z1) [I]

KÄSBAUER, MAX, ed. Logik und Logikkalkül.
(Card 4)

1. Logic, Symbolic and mathematical. 2. Britzelmayr, Wilhelm I. Kutschera, Franz von, joint ed. II. Title. III. Käsbauer, Max. IV. Kutschera, Franz von t. 1962.

Kallinich, Günter, 1913–
Das Vermächtnis Georg Ludwig Claudius Rousseaus an die Pharmazie. Zweihundert Jahre Pharmazie an der Universität Ingolstadt-Landshut-München, 1760–1960; Festgabe zum zweihundertjährigen Bestehen des Münchener Instituts. München [Govi] 1960.

513 p. illus., ports., facsims. 29 cm.

Bibliography: p. 467–[477]

1. Rousseau, Georg Ludwig Claudius, 1724–1794. 2. Munich. Universität. Institut für Pharmazie und Lebensmittelchemie.

Karl Budde's Schrifttum bis zu seinem 80. Geburtstage am 13. April 1930. Eine Festgabe...

(Zeitschrift für die alttestamentliche Wissenschaft. Beihefte. Giessen, 1930. 8°. Nr.54, p.1-28. port.)

Ein Kampf um Wahrheit; Max Brod, zum 65. Geburtstag, hrsg. von Ernst F. Taussig. Tel-Aviv, "ABC" Verlag [1949?] 49 p. illus. 24cm.

One contribution in Herbrew.
Bibliography, p. 45–48.

1. Brod, Max, 1884– I. Taussig, Ernst, F., ed.

KARL HARTENSTEIN; ein Leben für Kirche und Mission. In Gemeinschaft mit einem Kreis von Freunden hrsg. von Wolfgang Metzger. Stuttgart, Evangelischer Missionsverlag [1953] 365 p. ports. 20cm.

CONTENTS. --Der Lebensgang, von H. und M. Hartenstein. --Direktor der Basler Mission, von H. Witschi. --Leiter der deutschen Heimatgemeinde der Basler Mission, von A. Dilger. --Prälat und Stiftsprediger in Stuttgart, von H. Thomä und K. Gottschick. --Mitarbeiter in der württembergischen Kirchenleitung und im Rat der Evangelischen Kirche in Deutschland, von W. Metzger, M. Haug und L. Kreyssig. -- Betreuer und Helfer der Diakonie, von

(Continued)

Kansas. University.
Studies in honor of Albert Morey Sturtevant. Lawrence, Univ. of Kansas press, 1952. 169 p. port. 23cm. (Kansas. University. Humanistic studies. no. 29.)

Bibliographies included.
CONTENTS.—The phonemes of modern Icelandic, by Kemp Malone.—The synonyms for "sea" in Beowulf, by Caroline Brady.—Compounds of the mann-skratti type, by Stefán Einarsson.—The runes of Kensington, by Erik Wahlgren.—Two unrecognized Celtic names, by L. M. Hollander.—The impact of English on American-Norwegian letter writing, by Einar Haugen.—On the original of the Codex regius of the Elder Edda, by D. A. Seip.—Melkólfs saga ok Salomons konungs, by J. H. Jackson.—Wilhelm Grimm's letters to Peter Erasmus Müller, by P. M. Mitchell.—The problem of Catholic sympathies in Swedish romanticism, by A. B. Benson.—Albert Morey Sturtevant: bibliography of publications, by L. R. Lind.

1. Sturtevant, Albert Morey, 1876– . 2. Scandinavian languages. 3. Scandinavian literature. I. Series.

KARL HARTENSTEIN; ein Leben für Kirche und Mission. (Card 2)

S. Schweickhardt, T. Lorch und H. Krimm. --Mitglied im Deutschen evangelischen Missionsrat und Missionstag und bei den Tagungen der Okumene, von W. Freytag, M. Warren und W. Metzger. --Doktor der Heiligen Schrift, von W. Metzger. --Aus dem Schrifttum von Karl Hartenstein.

1. Hartenstein, Karl, 1894-1952. I. Metzger, Wolfgang, 1899- , ed.

Kapp, Julius, 1883– , editor.
185 Jahre Staatsoper; Festschrift zur Wiedereröffnung des Opernhauses Unter den Linden am 28. April 1928. Mit 350 Abbildungen. Herausgegeben von Dr. Julius Kapp. Berlin: Atlantic-Verlag, G.m.b.H.[, 1928.] 192, 56 p. facsims., illus. (incl. plans, ports.), plates (part col'd). f°.

Plates most printed on both sides.
Contents: KAPP, J. Die Geschichte der Staatsoper. FÜRSTENAU, E. Das Opernhaus im Laufe der Zeiten. Die technischen Einrichtungen der Staatsoper:

(Continued)

KARL STRAUBE zu seinem 70. Geburtstag; Gaben der Freunde. Leipzig, Koehler & Amelang [1943] 385 p. ports., facsim. 23cm.

1. Straube, Karl, 1873-1950.

Kapp, Julius, 1883– , editor: 185 Jahre Staatsoper... (Card 2)

LINNEBACH, G. Die neue Bühne. TAUBERT, A. Die Heizungs- und Lüftungsanlage. GIESECKE, A. Bühne und Rundfunk. Empfehlungen aus Handel und Industrie... und Abbildungen von Solisten der Staatsoper.

DREXEL MUSICAL FUND.

400500A. 1. Opera—Germany—Berlin. 2. Opera houses—Germany—Berlin. 3. Singers.

Kārļa Ulmaņa 60 gadi. 1877, 4. septembris, 1937. Svētku raksti. [Rīgā: A/s. "Zemnieka domas," 1937] 370 p. 22cm.

"Grāmatu sakārtojis V. Cedriņš."
Contributions by various authors.

992720A. 1. Ulmanis, Kārlis, 1877– . I. Cedriņš, Vilis, comp.

KARLING, STEN INGVAR, 1906-
Nordisk medeltid; konsthistoriska studier tillägnade Armin Tuulse. [Redaktion: Sten Karling, Erland Lagerlöf, Jan Svanberg. Uppsala, Almqvist et Wiksells Boktryck, 1967] 342 p. illus., plans, port. 24cm. (Acta Universitatis stockholmiensis. Stockholm-studies in history of art. 13)

Festschrift.

(Continued)

2

KARLING, STEN INGVAR, 1906- . Nordisk medeltid... (Card 2)

Essays in Swedish, German or English; summaries in English or German.
Includes bibliographical references.

1. Tuulse, Armin. 2. Tuulse, Armin--Bibl. 3. Art, Medieval. 4. Architecture, Medieval. I. Series.

KARRENBERG, FRIEDRICH, ed.
Sozialwissenschaft und Gesellschaftsgestaltung; Festschrift für Gerhard Weisser, hrsg. von Friedrich Karrenberg und Hans Albert, unter Mitarbeit von Hubert Raupach. Berlin, Duncker & Humblot [1963] viii, 500 p. port. 24cm.

Bibliography, p. [495]-500.

1. Social sciences--Addresses, essays, lectures. 2. Weisser, Gerhard, 1898- I. Albert, Hans, joint ed. II. Title.

Copy only words underlined & classmark-- KAA

KARTOGRAPHISCHE studien, Haack- Festschrift, besorgt von Herman Lautensach und Hans-Richard Fischer. Gotha, H. Haack, 1957. 325 p. illus., port., maps (18 part fold., col., issued in pocket) 28cm. (Petermanns (Dr. A.) Mitteilungen aus Justus Perthes' geographischer Anstalt. Ergänzungshefte. Nr. 264)

Includes bibliographies.
CONTENTS. — Hermann Haack, geb. 29. Oktober 1872, von

(Continued)

KARTOGRAPHISCHE studien... (Card 2)

H. Lautensach. — Cristoforo Sorte, il primo grande cartografo e topografo della Repubblica di Venezia, di R. Almagià. — Über die Grundformen des kartographischen Ausdrucks, von H. Louis. — Grenzprobleme zwischen Originalkartographie und geographischer Kartographie, von T. Stocks. — Atlaskartographie, von W. Bormann. — Wirtschaftsatlanten, von E. Lehmann. — Generalisierung der Höhenkurven, von E. Imhof. — Zur Geländedarstellung in thematischen Karten, von F. Hölzel. — Über die Probleme der Darstellung der dritten Dimension in der Karte. — Unter Berücksichtigung der historischen Entwicklung, von

(Continued)

KARTOGRAPHISCHE studien... (Card 3)

E. Langer. — Praktische Farbenpsychologie in Karten, von H. Schiede. — Gedanken zur Schreibung geographischer Namen, von H. -R. Fischer. — Graphische Technik und Karte, von H. Bosse. — Kartometrie und Geographie, von N. M. Wolkow. — Wirkungsmöglichkeiten einer kartographischen Gesellschaft (nachgelassenes unvollendetes Manuskript), von K. Mair. — Über einige Fragen der deutschen Kartographie, von K. -H. Meine. — Nachwuchsprobleme in der Kartographie Westdeutschlands und Westberlins, von H. Heyde. — Die Entwicklung der Massstabe in Stielers Handatlas, von W. Horn. — Morphologische oder exakte

(Continued)

KARTOGRAPHISCHE studien... (Card 4)

Schichtlinien. Darstellungsfragen der Karte 1:25000, von R. Finsterwalder. — Gletscher und glaziale Formenwelt auf modernen Alpenkarten, von H. Paschinger. — Die naturnahe Karte in der Schweiz, von B. Carlberg. — Schwedische Kartographie von heute, von G. Lundqvist. — Die amtlichen spanischen Kartenwerke, von H. Lautensach. — Kartographische Ergebnisse von Luftkrokierungen in Nordgriechenland. Die morphologische Karte, von H. -P. Kosack. — Beschreibung und Kartenaufnahme der Krateroase Wau en-Namus in der zentralen Sahara, von W. Pillewizer und N. Richter. — A new four-sheet planning map of

(Continued)

KARTOGRAPHISCHE studien... (Card 5)

Antarctica for the International geophysical year 1957-1958, by W. Brisemeister. — Verzeichnis der wissenschaftlichen Veröffentlichungen von Hermann Haack (p. [323]-325)

1. Map making. 2. Haack, Hermann, 1872- I. Series. II. Fischer, Hans-Richard, ed. III. Lautensach, Hermann, 1886- , ed. IV. Fischer, Hans Richard.

KASER, DAVID, 1924- ed.
Books in America's past; essays honoring Rudolph H. Gjelsness. Charlottesville, Published for the Bibliographical Society of the University of Virginia [by] University Press of Virginia [1966] x,279 p. illus.,ports. 24cm.

Includes bibliographical references.
CONTENTS.--David Hall's bookshop and its British

(Continued)

KASER, DAVID, 1924- ed. Books in America's past... (Card 2)

sources of supply [by] R. D. Harlan.--The libraries of nineteenth-century college societies [by] R. Rouse.--French-language printing in the United States, 1711-1825 [by] S. J. Marino.--Children's books following the Civil War [by] R. L. Darling.--Periodical publishing in the Michigan Territory [by] W. J. Bonk.--Bernard Dornin, America's first Catholic bookseller [by] D. Kaser.--The

(Continued)

KASER, DAVID, 1924- ed. Books in America's past... (Card 3)

first printing press in Canada, 1751-1800 [by] O. B. Bishop.--Early handling of books at the University of Michigan [by] R. E. Bidlack.--James Rivington, Tory, printer [by] L. Hewlett.--The recurring emergence of American paperbacks [by] F. L. Schick.--Engravings in American magazines, 1741-1810 [by] B. M. Lewis.-- Antislavery publishing in Michigan [by] J. E. Kephart.--The library world of Norton's Literary gazette [by] (Continued)

KASER, DAVID, 1924- ed. Books in America's past... (Card 4)

D. W. Krummel.

1. Gjelsness, Rudolph H., 1894- . 2. Book industries--U.S. 3. Printing--U.S., 18th cent. 4. Printing--U.S., 19th cent. I. Virginia. University. Bibliographical society. t.1966.

---

* PBN

KASHER, MENACHEM MENDEL, ed.
The Leo Jung jubilee volume; essays in his honor on the occasion of his seventieth birthday 5722-1962, edited by Menahem M. Kasher, Norman Lamm [and] Leonard Rosenfeld. New York [Jewish center, 1962] 242 p.; 258 p. port. 24cm.

Added t.p. in Hebrew.
Contributions in English (1 in French) or in Hebrew.
Bibliographical footnotes.

(Continued)

NN R 3.64 g/ OC,I PC, 1,2,4,I SL J,1,3,4,I (LC1, X1, Z1)

2

KASHER, MENACHEM MENDEL, ed. The Leo Jung jubilee volume... (Card 2)

"Bibliography of the writings of Rabbi Leo Jung," p. 239-242 (English sectio).

1. Jung, Leo, 1892- . 2. Essays, Jewish, in English--Collections. 3. Essays, English--Collections. 4. Essays, Hebrew--Collections. I. Title.

NFD
(Edschmid)

Kasimir Edschmid; ein Buch der Freunde zu seinem 60. Geburtstage, hrsg. von Günter Schab. Düsseldorf, A. Bagel [1950] 95,[1] p. port. 20cm.

Contents.--Der Weg Kasimir Edschmids, von F. Thiess.--Die Gratulanten.--Die Anfänge; autobiographisches Fragment, von K. Edschmid.--Ein grosser Schriftsteller von G. Schab.--Das Werk Kasimir Edschmids [Bibliographie] (p. 93-[96])

1. Edschmid, Kasimir, 1890- I. Schab, Günter, ed. II. Schab, Günter
NN**R X 4.54 OC,I, IIbo PC,1,I SL (LC1, Z1,X1)

E-11
8969

KASTL, LUDWIG, ed.
Kartelle in der Wirklichkeit; Festschrift für Max Metzner zu seinem fünfundsiebzigsten Geburtstag. Köln, C. Heymanns Verlag, 1963. 469 p. port., facsim. 24cm.

"Veröffentlichungen von Dr. Max Metzner," p. [467]-469.

1. Metzner, Max, 1888- 2. Cartels--Germany.
NN R 2.64 a/B OC PC, 1, 2 SL E, 1, 2 (LC1, X1, Z1)

E-12
2184

KAUFMANN, EKKEHARD, ed.
Festgabe für Paul Kirn zum 70. Geburtstag dargebracht von Freunden und Schülern. [Berlin] E. Schmidt [1961] 256 p. illus., port. 24cm.

Bibliographical footnotes.
CONTENTS.—Komik und Satire in der griechischen Geschichtsschreibung, von H. Strasburger.—Der Antrag des Cato Uticensis, Caesar den Germanen auszuliefern, von M. Gelzer.—Gelehrte (Continued)

NN 1.65 g/ OC, Ibo PC, 1, 2 SL (LC1, X1, Z1) [I]

3

KAUFMANN, EKKEHARD, ed. Festgabe für Paul Kirn zum 70. (Card 2)

und Gelehrsamkeit im Lande der Chalifen, von R. Sellheim.—Comes Francorum und Pfalzgraf von Frankreich, von W. Kienast.—Zur Weltchronik des Bischofs Frechulf von Lisieux, von W. Goez.—West und Ost in der deutschen Verfassungsgeschichte des Mittelalters, von W. Schlesinger.—Die Haftung für rechtes Gericht, von A. Erler.--Canel contra Moschel; ein Schadensersatzprozess vor dem Ingelheimer Oberhof aus dem Jahre 1404, von E. Kaufmann.—Beiträge zur Geschichte des Frankfurter Oberhofes, von D. Andernacht.—Luther vor dem Reichstag (Continued)

KAUFMANN, EKKEHARD, ed. Festgabe für Paul Kirn zum 70. (Card 3)

in Worms 1521, von E. Kessel.—Die Aufhebung der oberhessischen Klöster in der Reformation, von F. Schunder.—Gottsbüren, das "hessische Wilsnack," von K. Köster.—"Federative power" und "consent" in der Staatslehre John Lockes, von O. Vossler.—Ein Dokument über grosshessische Umgliederungspläne in Sommer 1919, von P. Kluke.—Ein neues Bildnis Karls des Kühnen? Von H. Keller.—Bibliographie der Schriften Paul Kirns (p. 255-256).

1. Middle Ages--Hist.--Addresses, essays, lectures. 2. Kirn, Paul, 1890- . I. Kaufmann, Ekkehard.

MC
\+

KAUFFMANN, GEORG, ed.
Walter Friedlaender zum 90. Geburtstag; eine Festgabe seiner europäischer Schüler, Freunde und Verehrer [hrsg. von Georg Kauffmann und Willibald Sauerländer] Berlin, W. de Gruyter, 1965. 222 p. 48 plates, port. 32cm.

Bibliographical footnotes.

(Continued)

NN R 9.66 r/ OC, I, II, IIIbo, IVbo PC, 1, 2, I, II SL A, 1, 2, I, II (LC1, X1, Z1) [I]

4

KAUFFMANN, GEORG, ed. Walter Friedlaender zum 90. Geburtstag... (Card 2)

CONTENTS.--Poussins Landschaft mit Herkules und Cacus in Moskau, von M. Alpatov.--Delacroixs Gedanken über Leidenschaft und Vernunft (la vie et la raison) in den Künsten, von K. Badt.--Zu Tizian als Zeichner, von K. Bauch.--Neue Beiträge zum Werk des Rubens, von O. Benesch.--Mannerism and "vernacular" in Polish art, by J. Białostocki. --Poussin and his Roman patrons, by A. Blunt.--Bemerkungen zu Victor Orsel, von H. Brauer.--Guglielmo della Portas verlorene Propheten-statuen für San Pietro in Vaticano, von W. Gramberg.-- (Continued)

KAUFFMANN, GEORG, ed. Walter Friedlaender zum 90. Geburtstag... (Card 3)

Der Palazzo baronale der Colonna in Palestrina, von L. H. Heydenreich. --Poussins "Primavera", von G. Kauffmann.--Die Schützenbilder des Frans Hals, von H. Kauffmann.--A plea for Poussin as a painter, by D. Mahon.--Gellee-Deruet-Tassi-Onofri, von M. Röthlisberger.--Pathosfiguren im Oeuvre des Jean Baptiste Greuze, par W. Sauerländer.--Falconet, Diderot et le bas-relief, par J. Seznec.--Raphael's unexecuted projects for the Stanze, by J. Shearman.--Eustache le Sueur peintre de (Continued)

KAUFFMANN, GEORG, ed. Walter Friedlaender zum 90. Geburtstag... (Card 4)

portraits, par C. Sterling.--Ingres et le "Songe d'Ossian", par D. Ternois.--Les "Observations sur la peinture" de Charles Alphonse du Fresnoy, par J. Thuillier.--Zuschreibungen an François Perrier, von W. Vitzthum.--Bibliographie Walter Friedlaender, Zusammengestellt von H. Lietzmann.

1. Friedländer, Walter F., 1873-1966. 2. Friedländer, Walter F., 1873-1966--Bibl. I. Sauerländer, Willibald, joint ed. II. Title. III. Kauffmann, Georg. IV. Sauerländer, Willibald.

L-10
9624

KAULA, PRITHVI NATH, ed.
Library science today: Ranganathan Festschrift; papers contributed on the 71st birthday of Dr. S.R. Ranganathan, 12 August 1962. Bombay, New York, Asia pub. house [1965] 1 v. plates. 25cm. (Ranganathan series in library science. 14)

Vol. 1.
Includes bibliographies.
1. Ranganathan, Shiyali Ramamrita, 1892- . 2. Library science--Addresses, essays, lectures. I. Series.
NN R 11.65 e/∫ OC (OS)I PC, 1, 2, I SL (LC1, X1, Z1) [I]

---

*QY

KAZAKEVIČIUS, VYTAUTAS, ed.
Graži tu, mano brangi tėvyne; antologija. [Sudarė Vytautas Kazakevičius. Redakcinė komisija: Kazys Ambrasas et al.] Vilnius, Kultūrinių ryšių su užsienio lietuviais komitetas, 1967. 558 p. plates. 21cm.

Includes biographical sketches of the authors.
1. Lithuania--Poetry. 2. Poetry, Lithuanian--Collections. 3. Authors, Lithuanian. I. Title. II. Kazakevičius, Vytautas.
NN R 11.68 1/ OC, I, IIbo PC, 1, 2, 3, I SL RC, 3 S, 1, 2, 3, I (LC1, X1, Z1)

Copy only words underlined & Classmark-- RDTA

KELLER, JOHN ESTEN, ed.
Hispanic studies in honor of Nicholson B. Adams. Edited by John Esten Keller and Karl-Ludwig Selig. Chapel Hill, University of North Carolina press [1966] 197 p. port. 23cm. (North Carolina. University. Studies in the romance languages and literatures. no. 59)

"Biography and publications," p. [9]-[15].
CONTENTS.--Origen y semántica de la palabra "chévere", by J.J. Arrom.--El impacto del culteranismo en el teatro de la (Continued)
NN R 1.69 k/OC, II, III (OD)I (ED)I PC, 1, I, II, III (LC1, X1, Z1) [I]

KELLER, JOHN ESTEN, ed. Hispanic studies in honor of Nicholson B. Adams. (Card 2)

Edad de Oro, by J.A. Castañeda.--Reflección de los primeros párrafos de Niebla de Unamuno, by F.S. Escribano.--Melancholy and death in Cervante, by O.H. Green.--Attacks on Lope and his theatre in 1617-1621, by R.L. Kennedy.--Religious hispanisms in American Indian languages, by L.B. Kiddle.--Cracks in the Structure of Calderón's Alcalde de Zalamea, by S.E. Leavitt.--An unnoticed complement to "Concolorcorvo", by J.K. Leslie.--The Spanish sources of Paul Scarron's Jodelet duelliste, by R.R. MacCurdy.--Lope de Vega's Arte nuevo de hacer comedias: Post-centenary reflections, by J.H. Parker.--Cervantes and the (Continued)

KELLER, JOHN ESTEN, ed. Hispanic studies in honor of Nicholson B. Adams. (Card 3)

Amadís, by E.B. Place.--Some Baroque reflections on the Greek anthology in Lope de Vega, by I.P. Rothberg.--Cara y cruz de la novelística galdosiana, by W.H. Shoemaker.--The character of Don Juan of El burlador de Sevilla, by G.E. Wade.--Calderón's comedy and his serious sense of life, by B. W. Wardropper.

1. Spanish literature--Addresses, essays, lectures. I. Series. II. Selig, Karl Ludwig, 1926- , joint ed. III. Adams, Nicholson Barney, 1895- .

NAD

KELLNER, LORENZ, 1811-1892.
Materialien für den mündlichen und schriftlichen Gedankenausdruck in höheren Lehranstalten, bestehend in einer Sammlung von 210 Dispositionen zu leichteren und schwereren Aufsätzen, Vorträgen, Reden, Katechesen und Unterhaltungen. Hrsg. von L. Kellner. Altenburg: H.A. Pierer, 1883. vii(1), 232 p. 9. ed. 8°.

1. German language--Rhetoric and composition.
NN R 1.61 e/ OC PC, 1 SL (LC1, X1, Z1)

MA

KERN, WALTER, 1898- , ed.
J.P. Hodin, European critic; essays by various hands edited by Walter Kern and published as a tribute on his sixtieth birthday. London, Cory, Adams and Mackay [1965] ix, 201 p. illus., facsims. (music) 22cm.

CONTENTS.--The Russian avant-garde, by G.C. Argan. --Antico Desiderio--yearning for youth, by E. Greco.--The house martins, by M. Hamburger.--Rodin and some (Continued)
NN R 6.67 r/ OC, I PC, 1, 2, 3, I SL A, 1, 2, 3, I S, 1, 2, I (LC1, X1, Z1) [I]

KERN, WALTER, 1898- ,ed. J.P. Hodin, European critic... (Card 2)

archetypes of space, by A.M. Hammacher.--Greek diary: 1954-1964, by B. Hepworth.--Education and art, by B. Leach.--'Spiritual values' in the aesthetics of naturalism and supernaturalism, by T. Munro.--Art history and the arts, by G. Paulsson.--Art nouveau, by M. Praz.--The modern art book, by H. Read.--The problems of art criticism, by F. Roh.--The unity of visual experience, by L.L. Whyte.--Joseph Paul Hodin; (Continued)

KERN, WALTER, 1898- , ed. J.P. Hodin, European critic... (Card 3)

a biographical study, by V. Vanek.--A decade in Sweden, by R. Hoppe.--J.P. Hodin and Norway, by L. Østby.--Art criticism and Weltanschauung, by K. Mitchells.--List of works (p. 129-197)

1. Hodin, Josef Paul. 2. Hodin, Josef Paul--Bibl. 3. Art--Essays and misc. I. Title.

---

*ZM-2
Film Reproduction

Kestner-Gesellschaft, Hanover.
James Ensor. Festschrift zur ersten deutschen Ensor-Austellung veranstaltet von der Kestner Gesellschaft e.V., Hannover 1927. [Leiter der Austellung: Hanns Krenz. Hannover, 1927] 68 p. illus.,ports.

Film reproduction. Positive.

(Continued)

NN**R 6.55 j/ OS(1b) PC,1 SL A,1 (UM1,LC1, X1,Z1)

Kestner-Gesellschaft, Hanover. James Ensor. (Card 2)

Contents.--James Ensor, von A. Dorner.--Wie ich mit James Ensor und seinen Werken bekannt wurde. Aus Herbert von Garvens-Garvensburg, James Ensor 1913.--Die Kathedrale, von W. Fraenger.

1. Ensor, James, baron, 1860-1949.

Copy only words underlined & classmark-- KAA

KIEL, Germany. Universität. Geographisches Institut.
Beiträge zur Geographie der Neuen Welt. Hrsg. von Wilhelm Lauer. Kiel, Im Sebstverlag des Geographischen Instituts der Universität, 1961. 304 p. illus., maps. 24cm. (ITS: Schriften. Bd. 20)

"Oskar Schmieder zum 70. Geburtstag 27.1.1961 gewidmet."
Includes bibliographies.

(Continued)

NN 2.63 e/B (OC)II OS, I PC, 1, 2, I, II AH, 1, 2, II (LC1, X1, Z1) [I]

3

KIEL, Germany. Universität. Geographisches Institut.
Beiträge zur Geographie der Neuen Welt. (Card 2)

CONTENTS.--Oskar Schmieder zu seinem 70. Geburtstag, von W. Lauer.--Verzeichnis der Schriften von Oskar Schmieder.--Die Industrialisierung der Landwirtschaft am Beispiel Kanadas, von C. Schott.--Die Goldrauschstädte der "Mother Lode" in Kalifornien, von H. Wilhelmy.--Die gegenwärtigen Wandlungen in der Verbreitung von Gross- und Kleinbetrieben auf den Grossen Antillen, von H. Blume.--Das Valle General; landeskundliche Skizze eines jungen Rodungsgebietes in

(Continued)

KIEL, Germany. Universität. Geographisches Institut.
Beiträge zur Geographie der Neuen Welt. (Card 3)

Costa Rica, von G. Sandner.--Eisenerz in Venezolanisch-Guayana, von E. Dillner.--Llallauquén; Beispiel einer unterentwickelten ländlichen Gemeinde im Küstenbergland Mittelchiles, von D. Alaluf.--Wandlungen im Landschaftsbild des südchilenischen Seengebietes seit Ende der spanischen Kolonialzeit, von W. Lauer.--Die vulkanischen Schichten von Feuerland und Patagonien und das Zurückweichen der letzten Vergletscherung, von V. Auer.--Tiergeographische Betrachtungen an vorkolumbianischen Haustiere Südamerikas, von W. Herre.

1. America--Geography. 2. Schmieder, Oscar, 1891- ed. I. Series. II. Lauer, Wilhelm,

---

L-10
6065
Bd. 51

KIEL, Germany. Universität. Institut für internationales Recht.
Fünfzig Jahre Institut für internationales Recht an der Universität Kiel. Festakt am 12. 11. 1964, und wissenschaftliche Kolloquien mit Referaten von Max Sörensen [et al.] Lebensbilder und Bibliographien von Theodor Niemeyer, Walther Schücking [und] Hermann

(Continued)

NN R 9.66 1/c (OC)II, IIbo OS, I PC, 1, 2, 3, 4, I, II E, 1, 2, 3, 4, I, II (LC1, X1, Z1)

2

KIEL, Germany. Universität. Institut für internationales Recht. Fünfzig Jahre Institut für internationales Recht an der Universität Kiel. (Card 2)

v. Mangoldt. [Hamburg] Hanseatischer Gildenverlag, J. Heitmann [1965] 242 p. front. 24cm. (Kiel, Germany. Universität. Institut für internationales Recht. Veröffentlichungen. 51)

Includes bibliographies.
1. Law, International--Addresses, essays, lectures. 2. Niemeyer, Theodor, 1857-1939. 3. Schücking, Walther Max Adrian, 1875-1935. 4. Mangoldt, Hermann Hans von, 1895-1953. I. Series. II. Sorensen, Max.

---

*ZM-47

KIEL, Germany. Universität. Kunsthistorisches Institut.
Dagobert Frey, 1883-1962; eine Erinnerungsschrift. Hrsg. mit Unterstützung seiner Schüler, Kollegen und Freunde durch das Kunsthistorische Institut der Universität Kiel. Kiel, 1962. 39 p. ports.

Microfilm. Negative.
CONTENTS.--Bemerkungen zur "Wiener Schule der Kunstwissen-

(Continued)

NN * R 9.68 1/4 (OC)I, II, III OS PC, 1, I, II SL A, 1, I, II (LC1, X1, Z1, UM1)

3

KIEL, Germany. Universität. Kunsthistorisches Institut. Dagobert Frey, 1883-1962... (Card 2)

schaft, von D. Frey.--Dagobert Frey, von H. Tintelnot.--Die Veröffentlichungen Dagobert Freys (Bibliographie), von J. Schlick und H. Tintelnot.

1. Frey, Dagobert, 1883-1962--Bibl. I. Frey, Dagobert, 1883-1962. II. Tintelnot, Hans. III. Title.

---

*OCZE

KIENLE, RICHARD VON, 1908- , ed.
Festschrift Johannes Friedrich zum 65. Geburtstag am 27. August 1958 gewidmet. Hrsg. von R. von Kienle [et al.] Heidelberg, C. Winter, 1959. 505 p. illus., port. 21cm.

Articles in English, French, German, Italian, or Russian.
"Verzeichnis der wissenschaftlichen Veröffentlichungen von Johannes Friedrich": p. 487-505.

1. Hittite language. 2. Oriental studies--Collections. 3. Friedrich, Johannes, 1893-

NN * R 2.62 e/B OC PC, 1, 2, 3 SL O, 1, 2, 3 (LC1, X1, Z1) [I]

E-11
8759

KIESLICH, GÜNTER, ed.
Publizistik; Festschrift für Edgar Stern-Rubarth [Redaktion: Günter Kieslich und Walter J. Schütz] Bremen, B.C. Heye, 1963. 212 p. port., fold. map, facsims. 25cm.

Includes bibliographies.

1. Stern--Rubarth, Edgar, 1883- 2. Journalism--Addresses, essays, lectures. I. Schütz, Walter J., joint ed. II. Title.

NN R 3.64 p/ OC, I, II PC, 1, 2, I, II SL (LC1, X1, Z1) [I]

---

* MGA

KIRCHENMUSIK heute; Gedanken über Aufgaben und Probleme der Musica sacra, hrsg. von Hans Böhm. Berlin, Union Verlag, 1959. 186 p. illus., port. 22cm.

"So kam es zu diesem Essay-Band, der einem Repräsentanten der deutschen evangelischen Kirchenmusik, Rudolf Mauersberger, dem 25. evangelischen Kreuzkantor zu Dresden, anlässlich seines 70. Geburtstages zugedacht ist."

(Continued)

NN*R 1.61 g/ OC, I PC, 1, 2, 4, I SL MU, 1, 3, 4, I (LC1, X1, Z1)

2

KIRCHENMUSIK heute... (Card 2)

"Aus dem kompositorischen Schaffen Rudolf Mauersberger," p. 181-[182].
Bibliography, p. [185]

1. Mauersberger, Rudolf, 1889- . 2. Music--Essays. 3. Essays. 4. Church music, 20th cent. I. Böhm, Hans, ed.

Copy only words underlined & classmark— NIZ

KIRJALLISUUDENTUTKIJAIN SEURA.
Juhlakirja Rafael Koskimiehen täyttäessä 60 vuotta, 9.2. 1958. [Professori Rafael Koskimiehelle omistavat Kirjallisuudentutkijain seura, Suomalaisen kirjallisuuden seura ja Kustannusosakeyhtiö Otava. Toimituskunta Sulo Haltsonen, et al.] Helsingissä, Otava [1958] 316 p. port. 21cm. (Kirjallisuudentutkijain seuran vuosikirja. [Osa] 16)

(Continued)

NN X 5.60 s/ (OC)I, IV OS(1b) II, III OI PC, 1, 2, I, II, III, IV (LC7, X1, Z1) [I]

2

KIRJALLISUUDENTUTKIJAIN SEURA. Juhlakirja Rafael Koskimiehen täyttäessä 60 vuotta... (Card 2)

Summaries in French.
Bibliographical footnotes.

1. Koskimies, Rafael, 1898- 2. Finnish literature--Addresses, essays, lectures. I. Haltsonen, Sulo, ed. II. Suomalaisen Kirjallisuuden seura, Helsingfors. III. Kustannusosakeyhtiö Otava, Helsingfors. IV. Title.

AD-10
1743

Kirkens arv—kirkens fremtid. Festskrift til biskop Johannes Smemo på 70-årsdagen 31. juli 1968. Oslo, Land og kirke, 1968.

xxiv p., 2 l., 342 p. 23 cm.
Bibliography: p. 334-342.
CONTENTS.—Johannes Smemo, av K. Støylen.—Oslo biskop—primus inter pares, av A. Seierstad.—Det gamle Oslo og St. Hallvardsdomen, av F. Knudsen.—Kirken i drabantbyerne, av L. Sandsdalen.—Gudstjenestens rom—på en annen måte, av H. Fæhn.—

(Continued)

NN*R 12.69 v/ OC, 2b* PC, 1, 2 SL (LC1, X1, Z1)

3

KIRKENS arv--kirkens fremtid. (Card 2)

Kunsten—kirkens brysomme sannhetsvidne, av H. Stenstadvold.—Kyrkans inre frihet, av B. Giertz.—Förhållandet kyrka—stat såsom ett problem i vår tid, av M. Simojoki.—Kristen enhet—kirkens enhet, av F. A. Schiotz.—Bibelutgaver i oldkirken, av N. Alstrup Dahl.—Bibelordet i tidens språkdrakt, av A. Holter.—Teologi og forkyndelse, af H. Høgsbro.—Forkynnelsen under anklage, av S. Tschudi.—Presteidealet hos norske pastoralteologer, av B. O. Weider.—Våre konfirmasjonsordninger, av B. Hareide.—Kirke—skole, spenning eller samarbeid? av V. Hellern.—Olav Haraldsson som kongeideal i saga, kvad og legende, av C. F. Wisløff.—Konfesjon og misjon hos

(Continued)

KIRKENS arv-kirkens fremtid. (Card 3)

H. P. S. Schreuder, av O. G. Myklebust.—En islandsk salmedikter og hans verk, av S. Einarsson.—Ny psalm, av A. Frostenson.—Tradisjon og fornyelse i kirkemusikken, av A. Ølen.—Bibliografi. Bøker, skrifter og artikler av biskop Johannes Smemo, ved T.-L. Brekke (p. [334]-342)

1. Theology--Essays and misc. 2. Smemo, Johannes, 1898-

AN
(Lehtonen, A.)

Kirkon nuoriso.
Näkyjen mies; Aleksi Lehtosen muistokirja. Toimittanut Armo Nokkala. [Helsingissä] Kirkon nuoriso [1951] 156 p. illus. 22cm.

"Kirjallinen tuotanto," p. 153-156.

1. Lehtonen, Aleksi, abp., 1891-1951. I. Nokkala, Armo, ed.

NYPL

KLASSEN, WILLIAM, ed. Current issues in New Testament interpretation... (Card 3)

Matthias, by K.H. Rengstorf.--The existence of the church in history according to Apostolic and early Catholic thought, by L. Goppelt.--The theological vocabulary of the Fourth Gospel and of the Gospel of Truth, by C.K. Barrett.--The New Testament and gnosticism, by J. Munck.--The Apocalypse of John and the Epistles of Paul in the Muratorian fragment, by K. Stendahl.--A bibliography of books and articles by Otto A. Piper (p. 247-260)

1. Bible. N.T.--Interpretation. 2. Piper, Otto, 1891- . I. Snyder Graydon F., joint ed. II. Klassen, William. III. Snyder, Graydon F.

---

*IIV
+

Kisling, J. G., firm, printers, Osnabrück.
Festschrift zur Feier des 200jährigen Bestehens der Buchdruckerei J. G. Kisling zu Osnabrück. [Osnabrück] Druck von J. G. Kisling, 1909. 64 p. illus. (incl. ports.) 30 x 24½cm.

On cover: J. G. Kisling. Osnabrück. 1707-1907.
CONTENTS.—Geschichte der Firma Kisling, von H. Runge.—Die Osnabrückischen wöchentlichen Anzeigen und die Kislingsche Buchdruckerei, von H. Runge.—Rundgang durch den Betrieb der Firma J. G. Kisling, von F. Zumwinkel.

734875A. 1. Printing—Germany—Osnabrück. 2. Newspapers—Germany—Osnabrück—Osnabrücker Zeitung. I. Runge, Hermann, 1863- . II. Zumwinkel, Fritz.
N. Y. P. L. April 25, 1935

NFD
(Mann)

Klaus Mann; zum Gedächtnis. [Amsterdam] Querido Verlag, 1950. 201 p. port. 19cm.

"Die Heimsuchung des europäischen Geistes," by Klaus Mann, p. 177-201.
"Bücher von Klaus Mann," p. [202-204]

567157B. 1. Mann, Klaus, 1906-1949.
N. Y. P. L. March 7, 1951

Copy only words underlined & classmark— TB

KJAER-HANSEN, ULF.
Danske jubilæumsskrifter; en bibliografi og et forsøg på en vurdering. København, Berlingske boktr., 1955. 196[1]p. illus. 26cm. (Handelshøjskolen, Copenhagen. Institutet for salgsorganisation og reklame. Skrifter. 18)

Handelshøjskolen, Copenhagen. Skriftraekke F.
"Bibliografi over udkomme danske jubilæumsskrifter til og med 1949": p. [55]-[197]
1. Festschriften--Bibl. 2. Bibliography, Danish. I. Series.
NN 6.65 p/ OC (OS)I PC, 1, 2, I E, 1, I RC, 1, 2 (LC1, X1, Z1)

D-16
3275

KLEIN, HERBERT, 1900-
Beiträge zur Siedlungs-, Verfassungs- und Wirtschaftsgeschichte von Salzburg; gesammelte Aufsätze von Herbert Klein, Festschrift zum 65. Geburtstag. Mit einem Vorwort von Theodor Mayer. Salzburg, Hrsg. von der Gesellschaft für Salzburger Landeskunde, [1965] xxxi, 720 p. port., maps (part fold.) 23cm. (Gesellschaft für Salzburger Landeskunde. Mitteilungen. Ergänzungsband. 5)
Half title and cover: Festschrift für Herbert Klein.
(Continued)
NN R 11.65 p/ OC(1b+) (OS)I PC, 1, 2, I, II SL E, 2, II (LC1, X1, Z1) 2

AD-10
705

KLASSEN, WILLIAM, ed.
Current issues in New Testament interpretation; essays in honor of Otto A. Piper. Edited by William Klassen and Graydon F. Snyder [1.ed.] New York, Harper [1962] xiv, 302 p. 22cm.

Bibliographical references included in "Notes" (p. 261-302).
CONTENTS.--Otto Piper; an appreciation, by J.I. McCord.--Hebraic
(Continued)
NN R 12.63 e/ OC, I, IIb*, IIIb* PC, 1, 2, I SL (LC1, X1, Z1) 3

KLEIN, HERBERT, 1900- Beiträge zur Siedlungs- (Card 2)

Bibliographical footnotes.
"Schriften von Herbert Klein," p. 636-640.

1. Salzburg (Province) 2. Economic history--Austria--Salzburg. I. Series. II. Title.

KLASSEN, WILLIAM, ed. Current issues in New Testament interpretation... (Card 2)

and Greek thought-forms in the New Testament, by T. Boman.--The cosmology of the Apocalypse, by P.S. Minear.--New Testament hermeneutics today, by A.N. Wilder.--The Old Testament in Hebrews, an essay in Biblical hermeneutics, by M. Barth.--Biblical theology and the synoptic problem, by F.C. Grant.--The formal structure of Jesus' message, by J.M. Robinson.--The Gospel of life, a study of the Gospel of John, by F.V. Filson.--The Johannine Church and history, by N.A. Dahl.--Adam and Christ according to Romans 5, by R. Bultmann.--Two New Testament creeds compared, by E. Schweizer.--The election of
(Continued)

Copy only words underlined & classmark— *OPR

KLEINASIEN und Byzanz. Gesammelte Aufsätze zur Altertumskunde und Kunstgeschichte. Berlin, W. de Gruyter, 1950. 161 p. illus., 67 plates, maps (part col.) 29cm. (Istanbuler Forschungen. Bd. 17)

"Martin Schede zu seinem sechzigsten Geburstag am 20. Oktober 1943 im Manuskript überreicht."—Vorwort.
Bibliographical footnotes.
(Continued)
NN* R 11.57 e/ OC PC, 1, 2, 3 A, 1 O, 2 (LC1, X1, Z1) [I]

KLEINASIEN und Byzanz. (Card 2)

CONTENTS. —Die griechischen Säulenordnungen, von A. Walther. —Zur ältesten Besiedlungsgeschichte der unteren Kaikos-Ebene, von K. Bittel. —Fragen zum Kopfschmuck kleinasiatisch-jonischer Priesterinnen, von G. Bruns. —Zum Heiligtum des Apollon Delphinios in Milet, von A. von Gerkan. —Al-Ḥadaṯ al ḥamrā', von R. Hartmann. —Eine spätantike Statuette aus Tyrus, von J. Kollwitz. —Die Inschriften der Agora von Smyrna, von J. Keil. —Die Agora von Smyrna, von R. Naumann und S. Kantar. —Die Isa Bey Moschee in Ephesus,

(Continued)

KLEINASIEN und Byzanz. (Card 3)

von K. Otto-Dorn. —Stackelbergs Panorama von Konstantinopel, von G. Rodenwaldt. —Die Tonfriese von Pazarli, von K. Schefold. —Regionen und Quartiere in Konstantinopel, von A.M. Schneider. —Zwei oströmische Bildwerke, von M. Wegner.

1. Art, Ancient--Addresses, essays, lectures. 2. Levant--Archaeology. 3. Schede, Martin, 1883-1947. I. Ser.

D-18
7036

Kleine Bibliographie der Werke Karl Heinrich Waggerls; zum 70. Geburtstag des Dichters. Hrsg. vom Otto Müller Verlag. Salzburg [1967?]

14 p. 21 cm.
Cover title.

1. Waggerl, Karl Heinrich, 1897- --Bibl. I. Müller (Otto) Verlag, Salzburg.

NN * R 3. 69 d/ OC (OS)I PC, I, I SL (LC1, X1, Z1)

F-11
3106

Kleinsorge, Paul Lincoln, *ed.*

Public finance and welfare; essays in honor of C. Ward Macy, edited by Paul L. Kleinsorge. [Eugene] University of Oregon, 1966.

vii, 305 p. port. 27 cm.
Bibliographical footnotes.
CONTENTS. — Basic problems in taxation and welfare theory, by G. Babilot.—Welfare and the Federal income tax schedule of 1955, by P. B. Simpson.—The labor market, taxes, and public policy, by W. S.

(Continued)

NN * R 8.67 1/ OC,3b* PC,1,2,3 SL E,1,2,3 (LC1,X1,Z1) 3

KLEINSORGE, PAUL LINCOLN, ed. Public finance and welfare... (Card 2)

Hopkins. — Economic knowledge and government responsibility, by G. W. Mitchell and M. A. Grove. — National strategies and defense budgets, by L. B. McAllister.—Mercantilist elements in contemporary monetary thinking, by C. R. Whittlesey.—Value-added tax proposals in the United States, by J. F. Due. — Property tax reform: is this where we came in? By C. L. Harriss.—Taxation of capital gains at death, by H. M. Somers.—Old and new rules in tax depreciation, by R. B. Bangs. — On the positive theory of State and local expenditures, by B. N. Siegel.—Some unsettled issues in highway-cost allocation, by R. W. Harbeson. — Dollars for higher education, by H. R. Bowen. — The workability of competition in the lumber industry, by

(Continued)

KLEINSORGE, PAUL LINCOLN, ed. Public finance and welfare... (Card 3)

W. J. Mead.—Inflation and growth: observations from Latin America, by R. F. Mikesell.—Regional development and public finance in Venezuela, by R. L. Allen. — Tax incentives for development: Panama's experience, by M. C. Taylor.

1. Finance--Addresses, essays, lectures. 2. Finance--U.S., 1945- . 3. Macy, Charles Ward.

D-16
5864

KLINGMÜLLER, ERNST, ed.

Aktuelle Fragen der Individual- und der Sozialversicherung. Festgabe für Erich Roehrbein. Hrsg. im Auftrage der Gesellschaft für Versicherungswissenschaft und -gestaltung. Karlsruhe, Verlag Versicherungswirtschaft, 1962. 174 p. 23cm.

German or Italian.
Bibliographical footnotes.
CONTENTS. --Das Spannungsverhältnis persönlicher Entscheidungsfreiheit und sozialer Bindung im sozialen Rechtsstaat, von W. Adler. -

(Continued)

NN * R 4. 66 p/ OC (OS)I PC, 1, 2, I SL E, 1, 2, I (LC1, X1, Z1) 3

KLINGMÜLLER, ERNST, ed. Aktuelle Fragen der Individual- und der Sozialversicherung. (Card 2)

Zur Bindung der Versicherungsträger an fehlerhafte Verwaltungsakte, von W. Bogs. -Einige spezielle Belange des Akademikers in der gesetzlichen Angestelltenversicherung, von P. Braess. -Economia, tecnica e diritto nell' assicurazione, di A. Donati. -Das Recht auf Errichtung von Innungskrankenkassen, von O. Estenfeld. -Sozialreform in der Bundesrepublik Deutschland, von K. Jantz. -40 Jahre Sozialgerichtsbarkeit im Elsass, von R. Jung. -Zur Problematik wertbeständiger Renten, von E. Klingmüller. -Rechtliche und sozialpolitische Folgen aus der Rechtsnatur der Sozialversicherung, von

(Continued)

KLINGMULLER, ERNST, ed. Aktuelle Fragen der Individual- und der Sozialversicherung. (Card 3)

J. Krohn. -Grundzüge der Rehabilitation von Unfallverletzten durch die Berufsgenossenschaften, von H. Lauterbach. -Gemeinsame Grundbegriffe der Sozial- und Privatversicherung, von H. Möller. -Grenzen der Rückforderung überzahlter Arbeitsentgelte und Dienstbezüge, von H. Neumann-Duesberg. -Einige versicherungsrechtliche und -wirtschaftliche Bemerkungen zur norddeutschen Sturmflut des Jahres 1962, von R. Schmidt.

1. Roehrbein, Erich. 2. Insurance, Workmen's--Jurisp.--Germany. I. Gesellschaft für Versicherungswissenschaft und -gestaltung.

E-12
4375

KLINGNER, FRIEDRICH, 1894-

Studien zur griechischen und römischen Literatur [hrsg. von Klaus Bartels, mit einem Nachwort von Ernst Zinn] Zürich, Artemis Verlag [1964] 766 p. port. 24cm.

"Zum 70. Geburtstag des Autors, am 7. Juli 1964."
"Tabula gratulatoria" ([11] p.) inserted.

1. Classical literature--Hist. and crit.

NN * R 10. 65 a/ OC PC, 1 SL (LC1, X1, Z1)

F-10
9680

KLUG, ULRICH, ed.
Philosophie und Recht; Festschrift zum 70. Geburtstag von Carl August Emge. Wiesbaden, F. Steiner, 1960. 118 [1] p. port. 26cm.

CONTENTS.--Bemerkungen zum Problem der sogenannten Willensfreiheit und ihrer rechtlichen Bedeutung im Lichte einiger neuerer philosophischer Lehren, von H. Coing.--Der Wohlfahrtsstaat und das soziale Grundrecht, von F. Darmstaedter.--Über die verschiedenen Bedeutungen der Lehre vom Gesellschafts- vertrag, von G. del Vecchio.-- (Continued)

NN R 10.65 s/OC, I PC, 1, 2, I SL E, 1, 2, I (LC1, X1, Z1) 2

KLUG, ULRICH, ed. Philosophie und Recht... (Card 2)

Elite und Gemeinschaft, von P. Jordan.--Der Handlungsbegriff des Finalismus als methodologisches Problem, von U. Klug.--Aphorismen über die Ungeduld. Über den Intellektualismus. Von G. Radbruch.--Der Mensch als politisches Wesen, von H. Ryffel.--Das Gleichheitsproblem unter den Gesichtspunkten des Wissenschaftlichen und des Naiven im Recht, von H. Schröder.--Was heisst: Stand der Wissenschaft, von W. Szilasi.--Zwei Rechtsdogmatiken, von T. Viehweg.--Die letzten fünfzig Jahre der Geschichte der Soziologie, von L. von Wiese.--Verzeichnis der Hauptschriften von C.A. Emge, p. [119].

1. Law--Philosophy. 2. Emge, Carl August, 1886- . I. Title.

---

*KVM

KNER, IMRE, 1893-
A könyv művészete. [Budapest, Zrinyi nyomda, 1964] 170 p., 3 l. 47mm. (Nyomdászat dicsérete. 1.)

No. 23 of 100 numbered copies; 250 copies printed.
Festschrift on the occasion of György Haiman's 50th birthday in 1964.
Binding, publisher's, by János Erdélyi, of brown leather.

1. Haiman, György, 1914- . I. Nyomdászat dicsérete.

NN R 1.66 e/ OC, 1b+ (OS)I PC, 1 SL R, 1 (RB1, RI 1, LC1, X1, Z1) [NSCM]

L-10
9014
Heft 2

KNOCHE, ULRICH, 1902-
Vom Selbstverständnis der Römer; gesammelte Aufsätze anlässlich des 60. Geburtstages am 5. 9. 1962 hrsg. von Franz Bömer und Hans Joachim Mette. Heidelberg, C. Winter, 1962. 173 p. 4 plates 25cm. (Gymnasium; Zeitschrift für Kultur der Antike und humanistische Bildung. Beihefte. Heft 2)

Bibliographical footnotes.

1. Romans. 2. Rome--Civilization. I. Series. II. Bömer, Franz, 1911- , ed. III. Mette, Hans Joachim, 1906- , ed.

NN 9.65 s/OC, II, III (OS)I PC, 1, 2, I, II, III (LC1, X1, Z1)

AN
(Hamsun)

Knut Hamsun; festskrift til 70 aarsdagen, 4. august, 1929. [Oslo:] Gyldendal norsk forlag[, 1929]. 186 p. incl. port. f°.

Mr. Moth.

460803A. 1. Hamsun, Knut, 1859- .
N. Y. P. L. March 5, 1930

SKD

Københavns snedkerlaug.
Københavns snedkerlaug gennem fire hundrede år, 1554-1954. Teksten skrevet af Tove Clemmensen, Georg Nørregaard og Helge Søgaard. [København, J.H. Schultz, 1954] 335 p. illus. 26cm.

Includes bibliographies.

1. Gilds, Cabinet makers'—Denmark—Copenhagen. 2. Furniture, Danish. I. Clemmensen, Tove, 1915-

NN ** R 2.55 a/ (OC) I OS PC, 1, I SL A, 1, 2, I E, 1, I (LC1, X1, Z1)

L-11
2618
1960-1962

KOBUCH, MANFRED.
Bibliographie Hellmut Kretzschmar. Hellmut Kretzschmar zur Vollendung des 70. Lebensjahres am 12. Juli 1962 gewidmet. (IN: Sächsische Akademie der Wissenschaften, Leipzig. Jahrbuch. Berlin. 25cm. 1960-1962, p. 437-463)

1. Kretzschmar, Hellmut-- Bibl.
NN 7.69 k/ OI (PC)1 (LC1, X1, Z1)

E-11
7382

KOCH, HELMUT, 1919- , ed.
Zur Theorie der Unternehmung; Festschrift zum 65. Geburtstag von Erich Gutenberg. Unter Mitwirkung von Horst Albach [et al.] Wiesbaden, Th. Gabler [1962] 429 p. illus., port. 25cm.

Bibliographical footnotes.
CONTENTS.--Die Zielfunktion der Unternehmung, von E. Heinen.--Maximierung der Rentabilität als preispolitisches Ziel, von L. Pack.--Zur (Continued)

NN R 6.63 f/ OC, I, Ibo, IIIbKG PC, 1, 2, I, II SL E, 1, 2, I, II (LC1, X1, Z1) 2

KOCH, HELMUT, 1919- , ed. Zur Theorie der Unternehmung... (Card 2)

Verbindung von Produktionstheorie und Investitionstheorie, von H. Albach.--Productionsplanung und Kostentheorie, von H. Jacob.--Die quantitative Ableitung polypolistischer Preisabsatzfunktionen aus den Heterogenitätsbedingungen atomistischer Markte, von W. Kilger.--Das "Gesetz der Massenproduktion" in betriebswirtschaftlicher Sicht, von W. Lücke.--Über eine allgemeine Theorie des Handelns, von H. Koch.--Verzeichnis der bisherigen Veröffentlichungen von Erich Gutenberg (p. [427]-429)

1. Management--Addresses, essays, lectures. 2. Gutenberg, Erich. I. Albach, Horst. II. Title. III. Koch, Helmut, 1919-

---

VXV
+

KOCKUMS MEKANISKA VERKSTADS AB.
Från Hajen 1904 till Hajen 1954; minnesskrift till Ubåtsvapnets femtioårsjubileum, redigerad av Gustaf Halldin, utg. i anledning av ubåten Hajens sjösättning den 11 december 1954. [Malmö, 1954] 145, [4] p. illus., ports. 30cm.

Bibliography, p. [146]

1. Submarine boats--Hist. 2. Submarine boats, Swedish. I. Halldin, Gustaf Harold, 1882- , ed. t. 1954.

NN ** R X 6.55 p/ (OC)I OS (1b) PC, 1, 2, I SL ST, 1, 2t, I (LC1, X1, Z1)

*MGA

KÖLLNER, GEORG PAUL, ed.
Musicus-Magister; Festgabe für Theobald Schrems, zur Vollendung des 70. Lebensjahres. Regensburg, F. Pustet [1963] xxxi, 225 p. illus., ports. 22cm.

1. Schrems, Theobald, 1893- . 2. Church music--Catholic church, Roman. 3. Music--Essays. 4. Essays. I. Title. II. Köllner, Georg Paul.

NN R 8.63 e/p OC, IIbo PC, 1, 2, 3, I SL MU, 1, 2, 4, I (MUC16, LC1, X1, Z1)

AN
(Ohm, G.)

Kölnischer Geschichtsverein e. V.
Georg Simon Ohm als Lehrer und Forscher in Köln, 1817 bis 1826; Festschrift zur 150. Wiederkehr seines Geburtstages. Herausgegeben vom Kölnischen Geschichtsverein in Verbindung mit der Universität und dem Staatlichen Dreikönigs-Gymnasium in Köln. Köln: J. P. Bachem [1939] 328 p. incl. diagr. facsims., front., illus. (incl. chart, plans), plates, ports. 24½cm.

CONTENTS.—Köln zur Zeit Georg Simon Ohms, 1817–1826, von Hans Vogts.—Aus der Geschichte des Kölnischen Gymnasiums, von Wilhelm Limper.—Ohm in Köln; Beiträge zur Geschichte der Mathematik und Physik zu Beginn des 19. Jahrhunderts, von Jos. Schnippenkötter.—"Wissen und Handeln, Gelehrsamkeit und geistige Regsam-

(Continued)

N. Y. P. L. April 19, 1940

Kölnischer Geschichtsverein e. V. Georg Simon Ohm als Lehrer ... (Card 2)

keit;" ein Entwurf aus dem handschriftlichen Nachlasse George Simon Ohms, von Wilhelm Limper.—"Aber das hat Schweiss gekostet!" Von Georg Simon Ohms Fortschritten in der "mechanischen Profession," von Heinrich Ritter von Füchtbauer.—Die Entdeckung des Ohmschen Gesetzes, von Christian Füchtbauer.—Georg Simon Ohms Kampf um die Anerkennung der Gesetze der Stromstärke und des Spannungsgefälles, 1827–1837, von Carl Piel.—Ohm im mathematisch-naturwissenschaftlichen Gedankenkreis seiner Zeit, von Joseph Heinrichs.—Das Ohmsche Gesetz und die Technik, von Ulfilas Meyer.—Ohm und seine Leistung im Lichte der heutigen Physik, von Johannes Malsch.—Der Neubau des Physikalischen Instituts der Universität Köln, von F. Kirchner.—Übersicht über das Leben Georg Simon Ohms.

18952B. 1. Ohm, Georg Simon, 1789–1854. I. Cologne. Universität. II. Prussia. Dreikönigs-Gymnasium, Cologne.
N. Y. P. L. April 19, 1940

M-10
4028
v.25

Kölnischer Geschichtsverein e. V.
Im Schatten von St. Gereon. Erich Kuphal zum 1. Juli 1960. Köln, Verlag Der Löwe, 1960.
viii, 399 p. 8 plates (incl. ports., facsims.) map. 28 cm. (*Its* Veröffentlichungen, 25)
"Der Kölnische Geschichtsverein e. V. widmet diese 'Veröffentlichung' Stadtarchivdirektor Dr. Erich Kuphal zur Vollendung seines 65. Lebensjahres am 1. Juli 1960."
Bibliographical footnotes.

(Continued)

NN 3.65 c/OS, I PC, 1, 2, 3, I (LC1, X1, Z1)

4

KOLNISCHER GESCHICHTSVEREIN e.V. Im Schatten von St. Gereon. (Card 2)

CONTENTS.—Ludwig von Büllingen und seine Sammlungen, von H. Blum.—Über die Entwicklung des Namens M. Gladbach, von R. Brandts.—Der Heringshandel in der Reichsstadt Köln und seine museale Darbietung, x-FE, von F. Brill.—Die Universitäts- und Stadtbibliothek Köln im Zweiten Weltkriege, von H. Corsten.—Zur Geschichte und zur Frage der Rechtskraft der Bergheimer Dekanatsstatuten, von W. Corsten.—Kolpinggruft, Sacellum Conresheim und Marienaltar in der Minoritenkirche zu Köln, von H. Gerig.—Das sogenannte Overstolzenhaus in den Kölner Schreinsbüchern, von A. Güttsches.—Devotio moderna in der Stadt Köln im 15. und 16. Jahrhundert, von R. Haass.—Gedanken über die kulturellen Beziehungen zwischen Deutschland und Belgien im Wandel der Zeit, von J. A. van

(Continued)

KOLNISCHER GESCHICHTSVEREIN e. V. Im Schatten von St. Gereon. (Card 3)

Houtte.—Zur Überlieferung der Werke Konrads von Megenberg, von T. Kaeppeli.—Philipp von Heinsberg, von G. Kallen.—Aufgaben und Zukunft der Archive in der Bundesrepublik Deutschland, von H. Kownatzki.—Die Akten der Kölner Synoden von 1266 und 1322 nach einer unbekannten Handschrift, von G. G. Meersseman.—Lacomblet und das Stadtarchiv Köln, von F. W. Oediger.—Die neuere kommunale Selbstverwaltung Aachens, von B. Poll.—Die St. Annabruderschaft zu Koblenz, Bruderschaft der geistigen Arbeiter, von A. Schmidt.—Zum römischen Kataster von Orange, von H. Schmitz.—Die Glasmalereiwerkstatt von Friedrich Baudri in Köln, von H. Vogts.—Der Kölner Domscholaster Oliver und die Anfänge des Deutschen Ordens in Preussen, von E. Weise.—Bibliographie Erich Kuphal, von H. Blum (p. 395–399)

(Continued)

KOLNISCHER GESCHICHTSVEREIN e. V. Im Schatten von St. Gereon. (Card 4)

1. Kuphal, Erich. 2. Germany--Hist.--Addresses, essays, lectures. 3. Cologne--Hist. I. Series.

F-11
3430

Koenig, Duane, *ed.*
Historians and history; essays in honor of Charlton W. Tebeau. [Coral Gables, Fla.] University of Miami Press, 1966.
68 p. 27 cm.
Issued as a yearbook of Delta-Alpha Chapter of Phi Alpha Theta, national history honorary fraternity.
Includes bibliographical references.
CONTENTS.—Who were the great historians of the West? An invi-

(Continued)

NN * 10.67 1/r OC, Ib[s] PC, 1, 2 SL (LC1, X1, Z1)
[I]

2

KOENIG, DUANE, ed. Historians and history... (Card 2)

tation to a game, by B. C. Shafer.—Clio: muse or minion, by Sister Marie Carolyn.—Turner, the safety-valve, and social revolution, by W. Marina.—The historian and community service, by D. Koenig.—The Massachusetts conscience Whigs, by R. S. Ward.—The United States, Sweden, and the Mexican Empire: 1864–1865, by A. Blumberg.

1. History--Addresses, essays, lectures.
2. Tebeau, Charlton W. I. Koenig, Duane.

BAC p.v.284

König Ferdinand von Bulgarien zum 75. Geburtstag. Berlin: Phönix-Verlag C. Siwinna [1936] 99 p. front. (port.), illus. 27½cm.

CONTENTS.—Der König, von A. Zimmermann.—Die ersten Jahre auf bulgarischem Boden, von Paul Lindenberg.—Kriegstage in Bulgarien, von Generalfeldmarschall v. Mackensen.—Der Soldat, von Ewald v. Massow.—Der Politiker, von Kurt Freiherr v. Lersner.—Der Königs Stellung zu Kultur und Leben, von Ludwig Roselius und Ernst Roselius.—Der König als Mensch und Freund der Wissenschaft. Persönliche Erinnerungen aus zwei Jahrzehnten, von Hans v. Bötticher.—Der König und das Theater, von Paul v. Ebart.—Der Förderer des Verkehrs und der Technik, von Lüben Boschkoff.—Der König als Förderer von Finanzen, Handel und Wandel, von Dr. v. Stauss.—Zar Ferdinand und die bulgarische Armee, 1887 bis 1918, von General Jekoff.—Der zünftige Zoologe, Tierkenner und Tierpfleger, von Ludwig Heck.—Der Botaniker, von N. Stojanoff.—Der Entomologe, von Iwan Buresch.

897324A. 1. Ferdinand I, king of the Bulgarians, 1861– .
N. Y. P. L. April 28, 1938

*HSD
(Koenigsberg)

Koenigsberger Beitraege. Festgabe zur vierhundertjährigen Jubelfeier der Staats- und Universitätsbibliothek zu Königsberg, Pr. Königsberg, Pr.: Gräfe und Unzer, 1929. xii, 400 p. front., illus. (music), plates. 4°.

Edited by Carl Diesch.
Bibliographical footnotes.
Contents: Anderson, E. Vom Kneiphöfschen Rathaus zum Stadtgeschichtlichen Museum. Baltzer, U. Aus den Anfängen der Königsberger Kunstakademie. Bauer, H. Aus dem ersten Jahrhundert des Elbinger Gymnasiums und seiner Bibliothek. Brachvogel, E. Die Bibliotheken der geistlichen Residenzen des Ermlandes. Diesch, C. Crotus Rubeanus im Dienste des Herzogs Albrecht. Fischer, E. K. Königsberger

(Continued)

N. Y. P. L. January 24, 1930

Koenigsberger Beitraege... (Card 2)

Hartungsche Dramaturgie. Forstreuter, K. Die ersten Gemeinden der griechischen Kirche in Ostpreussen. Gaerte, W. Eine altertümliche Bauernhausform in Ostpreussen. Glasenapp, H. v. und H. H. Schäder. Zur Erinnerung an R. Otto Franke. Goldschmidt, G. Ein Beitrag zur ältesten Geschichte der Handschriftensammlung der Staats- und Universitäts-Bibliothek. Goldstein, L. Karl Rosenkranz und Alexander Jung. Gollub, H. Die beiden Buchdrucker und Erzpriester Maletius. Güttler, H. Die Gelegenheitskompositionen Georg Riedels. Hartmann, K. Ein medizingeschichtlicher Besitz der Staats- und Universitätsbibliothek. Hein, M. Ostpreussens wirtschaftlicher Zustand im 1. Jahrzehnt des Grossen Kurfürsten (1640–1650). Holstein, L. Wissenschaft und Presse. Killer, H. Zur Musik des deutschen Ostens im 18. Jahrhundert. Krollmann, C. Geistiges Leben in Königsberg während des 14. Jahrhunderts. Meyer,

(Continued)

N. Y. P. L. January 24, 1930

Koenigsberger Beitraege... (Card 3)

W. Nachklänge von der Dordrechter Nationalsynode. Müller-Blattau, J. Die Pflege der örtlichen musikgeschichtlichen Überlieferung. Preuss, H. Von älteren ostpreussischen Kalendern. Ranke, F. Eine neue Handschrift des gereimten Passionals. Rothfels, H. Bismarck und Johann Jacoby. Schwarz, F. Analyse eines Kataloges. Vanselow, O. Veraltete Literatur. Warda, A. Die Exlibris des Herzogs Albrecht von Preussen. Wermke, E. Friedrich August Gotthold und seine Bibliothek. Will, E. Zur Geschichte der Braunsberger Bibliotheken. Wreszinski, W. Eine altägyptische Haarnadel. Ziesemer, W. Zur Kenntnis des Bibliothekswesens Preussens im 15. Jahrhundert.

442316A. 1. Libraries—Germany—Königsberg. 2. Königsberg—Hist. 3. Diesch, Carl Hermann, 1880– , editor.
N. Y. P. L. January 24, 1930

PXR

Koenigswald, Gustav Heinrich Ralph von, 1902– *ed.*
Evolutionary trends in Foraminifera; a collection of papers dedicated to I. M. van der Vlerk on the occasion of his 70th birthday, edited by G. H. R. von Koenigswald [and others] Amsterdam, New York, Elsevier Pub. Co., 1963.

355 p. illus., port. 25 cm.

Includes bibliographies.

1. Vlerk, Isaäk Martinus van der, 1892– 2. Foraminifera, Fossil. I. Title. t. 1963.
NN * R 10.63 e/A OC, I PC, 1, 2, I SL ST, 1, 2t, I (LC1, X1, Z1)

D-14
98

KÖRBS, WERNER, ed.
Carl Diem; Festschrift zur Vollendung seines 80. Lebensjahres am 24 Juni 1962, von seinen Freunden und Schülern. Hrsg. von Werner Körbs, Heinz Mies [und] Klemens C. Wildt. Frankfurt/Main, W. Limpert [1962] 351 p. illus., port. 22cm.

Includes bibliographies.

(Continued)

NN 1.62 p/ OC, I, II, IIIbo, IVbo PC, 1, 2, I, II SL (LC1, X1, Z1)
[I]

KÖRBS, WERNER, ed. Carl Diem... (Card 2)

1. Sports--Addresses, essays, lectures. 2. Diem, Carl, 1882- I. Mies, Heinz, joint ed. II. Wildt, Klemens C., joint ed. III. Mies, Heinz IV. Körbs, Werner

E-13
3311

Kohlschmidt, Werner, 1904– *ed.*
Philologia Deutsch; Festschrift zum 70. Geburtstag von Walter Henzen. Hrsg. von Werner Kohlschmidt und Paul Zinsli. Bern, Francke, 1965.

167 p. illus., maps, port. 25 cm.

Bibliographical footnotes.

Contents.—Geleitwort, von W. Kohlschmidt und P. Zinsli.—Gattungsgeschichtliche Betrachtungen zum Ludwigslied, von M. Wehrli.—Landgraf Kingrimursel; zum achten Buch von Wolframs Parzival,

(Continued)

NN * R 10.68 l/A OC, I PC, 1, 2, 3, I SL (LC1, X1, Z1)
3

KOHLSCHMIDT, WERNER, 1904- , ed.
Philologia Deutsch... (Card 2)

von W. Mohr.—Zur Interpretation von Hartmanns Iwein, von K. Ruh.—Über die Rezeption von Vergangenem in mittelalterlicher Dichtung, von F. Maurer.—Heinrich Seuses Auffassung von der deutschen Sprache, von M. Bindschedler.—Zum Stilproblem in Heinrich Wittenwilers Ring, von B. Boesch.—Oswald von Wolkenstein: "Es ist ain altgesprochner Rat," von H. Rupp.—Bemerkungen zu Wackenroders und Tiecks Anteil an den Phantasien über die Kunst, von W. Kohlschmidt.—Frühe Übersetzungsschichten im Althochdeutschen, von S. Sonderegger.—Die schweizerdeutsche Hiatusdiph-

(Continued)

KOHLSCHMIDT, WERNER, 1904- , ed.
Philologia Deutsch... (Card 3)

thongierung in phonologischer Sicht, von W. G. Moulton.—Geographie und Geschichte des Numerusmodells von "Bruder" im Schweizerdeutschen, von R. Hotzenköcherle.—Cunéaz und andere entschwundene Walserkolonien am Südhang der Alpen, von P. Zinsli.

1. German language--Addresses, essays, lectures. 2. Henzen, Walter. 3. German literature--Addresses, essays, lectures. I. Zinsli, Paul, joint ed.

D-17
3925

Koktanek, Anton Mirko , ed.
Spengler-Studien; Festgabe für Manfred Schröter zum 85. Geburtstag. München, Beck [1965]

279 p. 21 cm.

Bibliographical footnotes.

Contents.—Vorwort, von A. M. Koktanek.—Begegnungen mit Oswald Spengler, von W. Drascher.—Eduard Spranger und Oswald Spengler, von L. Englert.—Spengler und Toynbee, von G. Schisch-

(Continued)

NN* 9.67 g/R OC, I PC, 1, 2, I SL (LC1, X1, Z1)
3

KOKTANEK, ANTON MIRKO, ed. Spengler-Studien... (Card 2)

koff.—Die Freundschaft zwischen Oswald Spengler und Paul Reusch, von B. Herzog.—Kulturmorphologie und Philosophie, von A. Baeumler.—Systemdenken und Intuition, von F. A. van Scheltema.—Hegel und die These vom "Verlust der Mitte," von D. Jähnig.— Die Lehre des Thukydides von der Zunahme geschichtlicher Grössenverhältnisse, von S. Lauffer.—Zur geschichtlichen Wesensbestimmung Europas, von H. E. Stier.—Wandlungen des Weltbilds—Wende der Zeiten? Von A. Wenzl.—Rom—die Macht der Idee in der Geschichte, von A. M. Koktanek.

(Continued)

KOKTANEK, ANTON MIRKO, ed. Spengler-Studien... (Card 3)

1. Spengler, Oswald, 1880-1936. 2. History--Addresses, essays, lectures. I. Schröter, Manfred, 1880- .

E-12
7703

KOLB, AEGIDIUS, ed.
Ottobeuren; Festschrift zur 1200-Jahrfeier der Abrei. Hrsg. von Aegidius Koln und Hermann Tüchle. Augsburg, Kommissionsverlag Winfried-Werk, 1964. viii, 416 p. plates (part col.), ports. 25cm.

1. Ottobeuren, Germany (Benedictine abbey) I. Tüchle, Hermann, joint ed.

NN R 2.67 r/c OC, I PC, 1, I SL A, 1, I (LC1, X1, Z1)

C-12
5554

KOLBENHEYER, ERWIN GUIDO, 1878-
Kolbenheyer-Heimat; E.G. Kolbenheyer zum 75. Geburtstag in dankbarer Treue [gestaltet von Otto Zerlik, hrsg. von] Der Bund der Eghalanda Gmoin. Geislingen (Steige), Egerland-Verlag [1953] 56 p. illus., ports., facsim. 20cm. (Bücher der Egerländer, Bd. 7)

CONTENTS.--Das Erbe, Gedicht.--Der Heimat, Gedicht.--Das Heimweh.--E.G. Kolbenheyers Blut und Erbe, von E. Reiniger.--

(Continued)

NN R 2.65 e/s OC, III (OS)I, II PC, 1, I, II, III SL (LC1, X1, Z1)

2

KOLBENHEYER, ERWIN GUIDO, 1878- . Kolbenheyer-Heimat... (Card 2)

Glaube an die Heimat.--Widmung, Gedicht.--Karlsbad, Bekenntnisworte. --Die Herkunft des Namens Kolbenheyer, von J. Hanika.--"Und Heimat tut Dir Not!" von E. Frank.--Einmal noch! Gedicht.--Rorate Coeli.-- 's Eghalånd taucht af.--Feierbend, Gedicht.--An Josef Hofmann, Zuruf.--Oin va mein Schöllbouwan ins Stammbölchl, von J. Hofmann.--Zeittafel der Werke Kolbenheyers in Erstdrucken (p. 51-52).--Werke von E.G. Kolbenheyer (p. 53).--Gesellschaft der Freunde des Werkes von E.G. Kolbenheyer e.V.

1. German language--Dialects--Egerland--Texts. I. Series. II. Bund der Eghalanda Gmoin. III. Zerlik, Otto, ed.

D-15
1427

KOLLEGIUM ST. FIDELIS, Stans, Switzerland.
Geist und Geschichte; Gedenkschrift zum 50jährigen Bestehen des Lyzeums am Kollegium St. Fidelis in Stans. Stans, 1959. 233 p. 23cm.

Contributions in German or French.
"Anmerkungen" (bibliographical): p. 208-230.
CONTENTS.--Geist und Geschichte, von L. Signer.--Der franziskanische

(Continued)

NN * R 6.64 p/√ OS (1b) PC, 1 SL (LC1, X1, Z1) [I]

2

KOLLEGIUM ST. FIDELIS, Stans, Switzerland. Geist und Geschichte... (Card. 2)

Geist unserer Studien, von H. Felder.--Ritter Melchior Lussy, von J. Wyrsch. --Ritter Melchior Lussy und die Kirche, von B. Niederberger.--P. Apollinaris und seine Freunde in Nidwalden, von B. Mayer.--P. Theodosius Florentini und die Schule, von A. Bünter.--P. Bernard Christen und das Kollegium St. Fidelis, von T. Graf.--P. Adelhelm Jann, Pionier der schweizerischen Missionswissenschaft und Missionsbewegung, von W. Bühlmann.--Le P. Christophe Favre, et son Lexique du parler de savièse, par T. Crettol.--P. Aurelian Roshardt, Kenner und Freund der Natur, von J. Koller.--Kirche, Vaterland, Menschheit, von P. Jäggi.

1. Catholic church, Roman--Switzerland.

AN
+
(Rumpf)

Koloniaal Museum, Haarlem.
Rumphius gedenkboek, 1702–1902... Haarlem, 1902. viii, 221 p. illus., plates (1 col'd). f°.

Contents: Greshoff, M. Inleiding. Heeres, J. E. Rumphius' levensloop. Haan, F. de Rumphius en Valentijn als geschiedschrijvers van Ambon. Verwijnen, J. J. Eene bladzijde uit de geschiedenis der vestiging van het Nederlandsch gezag in de Ambonsche kwartieren. Lotsy, J. P. Over de in Nederland aanwezige botanische handschriften van Rumphius. Goebel, K. Rumphius als botanischer naturforscher. Warburg, O. Die botanische Erforschung der Molukken seit Rumpf's Zeiten. Hartwich, C. Ueber in Rumphius' "Herbarium Amboinense" erwaehnte

(Continued)

Mr. Moth.

N. Y. P. L. September 14, 1927

Koloniaal Museum, Haarlem: Rumphius gedenkboek... (Continued)

amerikanische Pflanzen. Weber, M. Iets over Walvischvangst in den Indischen Archipel. Semon, R. Einige neue Ambonesische Raritäten. Man, J. G. de. Over de crustacea in Rumphius' rariteitkamer. Horst, R. Over de "Wawo" van Rumphius. Martens, E. von. Die Mollusken und die übrigen wirbellosen Thiere im Rumpf'schen Raritätkammer. Wichmann, A. Het aandeel van Rumphius in het mineralogisch en geologisch onderzoek van den Indischen Archipel. Rouffaer, G. P., and Muller, W. C. Eerste proeve van eene Rumphius-bibliographie.

1. Rumpf, Georg Eberhard, 1627–1702. 2. Rumpf, Georg Eberhard, 1627–1702—Bibl. 3. Natural history—East Indies, Dutch.

N. Y. P. L. September 14, 1927

SEV

Koloniale Studien; Hans Meyer zum siebzigsten Geburtstage am 22. März 1928, dargebracht von seinen Freunden, Verehrern und Schülern. Berlin: D. Reimer, 1928. xvi, 341 p. incl. tables. charts, diagrs., front. (port.), illus. (incl. maps), plates. 4°.

Plates printed on both sides.
Edited by Karl H. Dietzel and Hans Rudolphi.
Contains bibliographies.
Content: Zueignung. Zache, H. Weltwirtschaft und Kolonialpolitik. Schultze, E. Das Gesetz des Handelsbilanzumschwungs in der Kolonialwirtschaft. Obst, E. K. G. Die kulturpolitische Begründung des deutschen Kolonialbegehrens. Sander, E. Der Gestaltwandel Afrikas. Hahn, E. Zur Wirtschaftsgeschichte von

(Continued)

N. Y. P. L. July 8, 1929

Koloniale Studien... (Card 2)

Afrika. JAEGER, F. R. Das Windhuker Hochland. KRENKEL, E. Das Faltengebirge Ost- und Südafrikas. BOEHME, R. Die französische Somaliküste. HAUSHOFER, K. Zur Geopolitik des Pazifischen Ozeans. VOLZ, W. T. A. H. Der Mensch in der malaiischen Inselflur. GEISLER, W. Die Wirtschafts- und Lebensräume des Festlandes Australien. BEHRMANN, W. Beiträge zur Rassenkunde des Innern von Neuguinea. MAIER, H. Die Nordmandschurei als Kolonial- und Wirtschaftsgebiet. SCHMIEDER, O. Spuren spanischer Kolonisation in U. S. — amerikanischen Landschaften. DIETZEL, K. H. Südamerika als kolonialer Erdteil. HAUTHAL, R. Zur Entstehung und zum Formenschatz der Büsserschnees. WISSMANN, H. VON. Die Schriften Hans Meyers.

1. Meyer, Hans Heinrich Joseph, 1858- . 2. Colonies and colonization. 3. Dietzel, Karl Heinrich, editor. 4. Rudolphi, Hans, 1885- , editor.
N. Y. P. L. July 8, 1929

---

*QPK
+

Komitet jubileuszu Teatru Polskiego i Arnolda Szyfmana, Warsaw.
Teatr Polski, 1913-1948. Arnold Szyfman, 1908-1948. [Warszawa, Komitet jubileuszu Teatru Polskiego i Arnolda Szyfmana, 1948] 100 p. illus. 30cm.

Various contributors.

1. Theatres—Poland—Warsaw. 2. Szyfman, Arnold, 1882-
NN R X 3.54 OSs PCs,1s,2s SLs Ss,1s, 2s (T3s,Z1s,LC1s, X1s)

SEB

Kommission für Geschichte des Parlamentarismus und der politischen Parteien.
Aus Geschichte und Politik. Festschrift zum 70. Geburtstag von Ludwig Bergstraesser; hrsg. im Auftrag der Kommission für Geschichte des Parlamentarismus und der politischen Parteien von Alfred Herrmann. Düsseldorf, Droste [1954] 326 p. port. 26cm.

Contents.—Das Problem der "Hauptstadt Europas"
(Continued)

NN**R X 12.54 t/ (OC) I,II OS(1b) PC,1,2,3,I, II SL E,1,2,3,I,II (Z1,LC1,X1) [I]

Kommission für Geschichte des Parlamentarismus und der politischen Parteien. Aus Geschichte und Politik. (Card 2)

seit dem 17. Jahrhundert, von W. Treue.—Ein publizistischer Plan der Bonner Lesegesellschaft aus dem Jahre 1789. Ein Beitrag zu den Anfängen politischer Meinungsbildung, von M. Braubach.—Die Partei Gerlach-Stahl, von K. Buchheim.—Der Pakt Simon-Gagern und der Abschluss der Paulskirchenverfassung, von E. Bammel.—Die deutsche Sozialdemokratie und die Idee des internationalen Ausgleichs, von G. Schulz.—Der Untersuchungs-
(Continued)

Kommission für Geschichte des Parlamentarismus und der politischen Parteien. Aus Geschichte und Politik. (Card 3)

ausschuss für die Schuldfrage des ersten Weltkrieges, von E. Fischer-Baling.—Gustav Stresemann. Vom deutschen Nationalisten zum guten Europäer, von A. Herrmann.—Die Europa-Idee bei Briand und Coudenhove-Kalergi. Ein Vergleich, von W. Hagemann.—Objektivität und Subjektivität. Ein Prinzipienstreit in der amerikanischen Geschichtsschreibung, von F. Fischer.—Die Theorie der Partei im älteren deutschen Liberalismus, von
(Continued)

Kommission für Geschichte des Parlamentarismus und der politischen Parteien. Aus Geschichte und Politik. (Card 4)

T. Schieder.—Deutsche Geschichtsschreibung und Politik, von J. A. von Rantzau.—Der Mensch als homo politicus, von G. Weippert.—Politische Bildung. Ein Vortrag, von D. Sternberger.—Wahlsoziologie und Parteigeschichte. Neue französische Forschungen, von W. Conze.—Die Zukunft der amerikanischen Parteien, von O. K. Flechtheim.—Zum Begriff des demokratischen und sozialen Rechtsstaates im Grundgesetz der Bundesrepublik Deutschland, von W. Abendroth.—Von den
(Continued)

Kommission für Geschichte des Parlamentarismus und der politischen Parteien. Aus Geschichte und Politik. (Card 5)

tragenden Ideen der ersten deutschen Sozialpolitik, von L. Preller.—Die Problematik der Wirtschaftsordnung, von H. Sauermann.

1. Bergstraesser, Ludwig, 1883- . 2. Parties, Political—Germany. 3. Political science—Addresses, essays, lectures. I. Herrmann, Alfred Julius Moritz, 1879- ed. II. Title: Festschrift zum 70. Geburtstag von Ludwig Bergstraesser.

MAT

DET KONGELIGE AKADEMI FOR DE SKØNNE KUNSTER, Copenhagen.
Det kongelige akademi for de skønne kunster. 1904-1954. Med en kort udsigt over akademiets historie 1754-1904. København, Gyldendal, 1954. 525 p. illus. 24cm.

Edited by Aage Marcus.

CONTENTS.--Akademiets historie fra 1754 til 1904, af A. Rode. --Akademiets organisation og administration fra 1904 til 1931, af E. Spang-Hanssen.--Akademiets organisation efter 1931, af
(Continued)

1. Art—Education—Denmark—Copenhage. I. Marcus, Aage, 1888- , ed.
NN** 3.55 p/ (OC) I OS PC, 1, I SL A, 1, I (LC1, Z1, X1)

DET KONGELIGE AKADEMI FOR DE SKØNNE KUNSTER, Copenhagen.
Det kongelige akademi for de skønne kunster... (Card 2)

K. Millech.--Akademiets maler- og billedhuggerskoler efter 1900, af A. Rode.--Arkitekturskolens historie efter 1904, af K. Millech.--Akademiets bibliotek, af A. Marcus.--Fortegnelse over akademiets medlemmer, højere funktionaerer og modtagere af de større medailler fra 1904 til 1954, af E. Spang-Hanssen.

SSQ

Det Kongelige Døvstumme-Institut i Fredericia, Denmark.
Det Kongelige Døvstumme-Institut i Fredericia; 1880—22 Marts—1930. Festskrift ved Vilhelm Larsen. Fredericia: Fredericia Centraltrykkeri, 1930. 78 p. illus. (incl. ports.) 8°.

Festschrift

569917A. 1. Deaf—Hospitals and asylums—Denmark—Fredericia. I. Larsen, Vilhelm, 1868- .
N. Y. P. L. August 13, 1932

PAH

DET KONGELIGE NORSKE VIDENSKABERS SELSKAB; Trondheim.
Festskrift til Egil Hylleraas på sekstiårsdagen 15 de mai 1958. [Redigert av Harald Wergeland og Ole Peder Arvesen] Trondheim, i kommisjon hos F. Bruns bokhandel, 1958. 1 v. (various pagings) illus., port. 25cm.

"Særtrykk av Det Kongelige norske videnskabers selskabs forhandlinger." Includes bibliographies.

(Continued)

NN R 5.62 m/# OC)I, II, III OS PC, 1, 2, I, II, III SL ST, It, 2, I, II III (LC1, X1, Z1) 4

DET KONGELIGE NORSKE VIDENSKABERS SELSKAB; Trondheim. Festskrift til Egil Hylleraas på sekstiårsdagen 15 de mai 1958. (Card 2)

CONTENTS.--Egil A. Hylleraas, von M. Born.--Brownian motion of a particle in a linear chain, by P.C. Hemmer and H. Wergeland.--Exited states of helium, by G. Araki.--Physical inactivation of urease, by T. Langeland and Aa. Ore.--The use of the associated Laguerre functions in the method of configurational interaction, by E. Holøien.--Phenomenological eigenfunctions and potentials for the deuteron ground state, by L. Hulthén and L.T. Hedin.--An adiabatic invariance in quantum mechanics, by M. Kolsrud.--Die Polarisation eines Müonenstrahles beim

(Continued)

DET KONGELIGE NORSKE VIDENSKABERS SELSKAB; Trondheim. Festskrift til Egil Hylleraas på sekstiårsdagen 15 de mai 1958. (Card 3)

Pionenzerfall im Fluge, von J.H.D. Jensen und H. Øverås.--Foldy-Wouthuysen transformation in closed form for spin 1/2 particle in time-independent external fields, by E. Eriksen.--The Dirac theory of the electron in general relativity theory, by O. Klein.--Complementarity and statistics, by L. Rosenfeld.--Photoelectric effect from polarized photons, by H. Olsen.--Collective co-ordinates for nuclear rotation, by A. Bohr and B.R. Mottelson.-- The concepts of mass and

(Continued)

DET KONGELIGE NORSKE VIDENSKABERS SELSKAB; Trondheim. Festskrift til Egil Hylleraas på sekstiårsdagen 15 de mai 1958. (Card 4)

energy in the general theory of relativity, by C. Møller.--En praktisk metode til summering av konvergente og semikonvergente rekker, av Midtdal.--Berechnung der S-P-Matrixelemente des Helium-Atomes, von W. Romberg.--On the Schrödinger equation for the helium atom, by V. Fock.

1. Physics--Addresses, essays, lectures. 2. Hylleraas, Egil Andersen, 1898- I. Wergeland, Harald, ed. II. Arvesen, Ole Peder, 1895- ed. III. Title. t. 1958

E-10
7148

KONKRETE Vernunft; Festschrift für Erich Rothacker. Hrsg. von Gerhard Funke. Bonn, H. Bouvier, 1958 444 p. port. 24cm.

Bibliographical footnotes. "Erich Rothacker--Schriften, Vorträge und Herausgebertätigkeit, zusammengestellt von Jürgen Schmandt": p. 435-444.

1. Philosophy--Addresses, essays, lectures. 2. Rothacker, Erich, 1888- . I. Funke, Gerhard, ed.
NN*R 3.59 1/ OC, I PC, 1, 2, I SL (LC1, X1 Z1)

E-12
2831

KONSERVATIVE menn i Norges nyere historie, 15 politiske essays tilegnet C.J. Hambro i anledning av hans 75 års dag 5. januar 1960. Oslo, 1960. 282 p. ports. 25cm.

CONTENTS.--Herman Wedel Jarlsberg (1778-1840), av R. Norland.--Niels Wulfsberg (1775-1852), av R.A. Lorentzen.--A.M. Schweigaard (1808-1870), av R. Norland.--Frederik Stang (1808-1884), av J. Rivertz.--Frederik Stang, av P. Thyness.--Emil Stang (1834-1912), av A. Rygh.--

(Continued)

NN R 3.65 e/s OC PC, 1, 2, 3 SL E, 1, 3 (LC1, X1, Z1) 2

KONSERVATIVE menn i Norges nyere historie... (Card 2)

Francis Hagerup (1853-1921), av C.J. Hambro.--Otto B. Halvorsen (1872-1923), av H. Gram.--Thorstein Diesen (1862-1925), av B. Gotaas.--Nils Vogt (1859-1927), av O. Gjerlow.--E. Hagerup Bull (1855-1938), av J. Dannevig.--Jens Bratlie (1865-1939), av R. Halle.--I.E. Christensen (1872-1943), av E. Lauhn.--O.L. Bærøe (1877-1943), av C.I. Rieber-Mohn.--Ivar Lykke (1872-1949), av H. Torp.--Joh. H. Andresen (1888-1953), av T. Kandahl.

1. Norway--Politics. 2. Norway--Biog. 3. Hambro, Carl Joachim, 1885-1964.

* MBA

Konservatorium der Musik Klindworth-Scharwenka, Berlin.
Das Konservatorium der Musik Klindworth-Scharwenka, Berlin, 1881–1931. Festschrift aus Anlass des fünfzigjährigen Bestehens, verfasst von Dr. Hugo Leichtentritt. [Berlin, 1931.] 47 p. 24cm.

Festschrift

CARNEGIE CORPORATION OF NEW YORK.

1. Music—Conservatories—Germany—Berlin. I. Leichtentritt, Hugo, 1874- .
N. Y. P. L. August 18, 1933

MAAD

Konstnärsklubben, Stockholm.
Bohemer och akademister; skrift utg. av Konstnärsklubben vid dess 75-års-jubileum 1931. [Redaktionskommitté: Akke Kumlien (et al.)] Stockholm, Norstedt [1931] 135 p. illus., ports. 29cm.

Contents.—Förord, av E. Lindberg.—På 75-årsdagen, av G. Nordensvan.—Utdrag ur brev från 1890-talet, av Prins Eugen.—Ett huvud för sig, av Y. Berg.—Pirrin. Aapon Velis dödssång,

(Continued)

NN*12.54 t/ (OC)I OS(1b) PC,1,I SL A,1,I (Z 1,LC1,X1)

Konstnärsklubben, Stockholm. Bohemer och akademister... (Card 2)

av O. Elgström.—Minnen från Konstnärsklubben, av A. Engström.—"Polonus," av G. Kallstenius.—Till minne av min vän Axel Törneman, av R. Lindström.—En segling till Finland, av E. Schwab.—Rimbrev, av Stang.—Pa spännpapperets sträckbänk, av C. G. Laurin.—1906-1931. En återblick, av E. Lindberg.—En hälsning, av G. Cederström.—Enquête.—Till Erik Lindberg, av T. Strindberg.

1. Art—Assoc.,clubs, etc.—Sweden—Stockholm. I. Kumlien, Akke, 1884- ,ed.
NN**12.54 t/ (OC)I OS(1b) PC,1,I SL A,1,I (Z 1,LC1,X1)

E-13
2740

Kontakte mit der Wirtschaftspädagogik. Festschrift für Walther Löbner zum 65. Geburtstag. Hrsg. von Joachim Peege. Neustadt/Aisch, Schmidt, 1967.
208 p. 25 cm.

(Continued)

NN*R 7.68 e/ OC,I, IIb* PC,1,2,3,I SL
E,1,3,I (LC1,X1,Z1)

KONTAKTE mit der Wirtschaftspädagogik. (Card 2)

Includes bibliographical references

CONTENTS.—Das Recht als Kinderspielzeug. von H. Liermann.—Melanchthons Schola Privata, von W. Maurèr.—Die Hauswirtschaft unter dem Einfluss des Industrialisierungsprozesses, von E. Egner.—Anmerkungen zur Umwelt von Robert Owen, von F. W. Schoberth.—Die Nationalökonomie als Objekt der Bildung und Ausbildung, von E. Heuss. — Marginalien zur Reform des betriebswirtschaftlichen Studiums, von E. Leitherer.—Das Studium der romanischen Sprachen und Auslandswissenschaft an der Wirtschafts- und Sozialwissenschaftlichen Fakultät der Universität Erlangen-Nürnberg, von G.

(Continued)

KONTAKTE mit der Wirtschaftspädagogik. (Card 3)

Schiffauer.—Über Aufgabe und Ort der Didaktik heute, von H.-H. Groothoff.—Fragen der Soziologie an die Wirtschaftspädagogik, von G. Wurzbacher. — Maschinenbuchführung im Unterricht, von W. Kresse.—Schule und gemeindliche Integration durch den Lokalteil der Tageszeitung, von F. Ronneberger.—Erwachsenenbildung in unserer Zeit, von A. Reble.—Homo discens, von W. Loch.—Freiheit und Planung im Bildungswesen, von F. Pöggeler.—Wünsche aus der Wirtschaft and die Aus- und Fortbildung von kaufmännischen Führungskräften, von F. W. Hardach.—Die Ausbildung und Weiterbildung von Führungskräften, von H.-M. Schönfeld.—Die Ausweitung der Wirtschaftspädagogik, von J. Peege.

(Continued)

KONTAKTE mit der Wirtschaftspädagogik. (Card 4)

1. Löbner, Walther, 1902- . 2. Education--Addresses, essays, lectures.
3. Economics--Study and teaching--Germany.
I. Peege, Joachim, 1923- , ed.
II. Peege, Joachim, 1923-

NIDF
+

Konungs-skuggsjá.
Konungs skuggsiá. Speculum regale. De norske håndskrifter i faksimile. Festgave fra Universitetet i Oslo til H. M. kong Haakon VII på hans 75-årsdag 3. august 1947. [Oslo, Cammermeyers boghandel, 1947] 23 p., facsims.: 160 (i. e. 136), [30] p. 42cm.

"Det norske hovedhåndskriftet tilhører nå den Arnamagnæanske haandskriftsamling ved Universitetsbiblioteket i København, der det har nummer 243 b a, fol."

1. Manuscripts, Norse—Facsimiles. 2. Haakon VII, King of Norway, 1872- . I. Oslo. Universitet.
NN*R 5.54 OC (OS)I PC, 1, 2, I SL (LC1, Z1, X1)

SIO

Kooperativa förbundet. Bokförlaget.
Kooperation och kultur. Stockholm, Kooperativa förbundets bokförlag, 1952. 178 p. illus. 22cm.

"Denna bok tillägnas Harald Elldin."

CONTENTS.—Thedin, N. Den kooperativa upplysningen.—Silow, S. Konsument och formgivare.—Vylder-Widhe, E. de. Ett arbete i hemmens tjänst.—Sundahl, E. KF-arkitekternas verkstad.—Lundberg, B. Vi och litteraturen.—Stolpe, H. Boken som upplysnings- och bildningsmedel.—Cyrus, A. Från de sju grundsatserna till samhällsvetenskap.—Sjögren, C.-O. Pedagogiska hjälpmedel för bildningsarbete och skola.—Löfgren, Å. Riktiga bilderböcker.—Rabén, H. Läsning för de växande.—Löfgren, Å. Dynamit, opium och vida perspektiv.—Larson, I. Vad sker på Vår gård?—Fockstedt, S. Ett bildningsarbete för demokratin.—Norman, B. Debatten om folkrörelserna.

1. Co-operation—Sweden. 2. Education—Sweden, 20th cent.
3. Sweden—Civilization, 20th cent. 4. Elldin, Harald. I. Title.
NN R 3.53 (OC)I OS PC, 1, 2, 3, 4, I SL E, 1, I (LC1, Z1, X1)

---

*OT

KOREANICA; Festschrift Professor Dr. Andre Eckardt zum 75. Geburtstag, 21. September 1959. [Hrsg. von August Riekel] Baden-Baden, A. Lutzeyer, 1960. 184 p. (p. 183-184 advertisements). illus., port. 22cm.

CONTENTS. --Die Elementenlehre im chinesisch-koreanischen Denken, von A. Ott. --Beziehungen zwischen Korea und Japan in alter Zeit, von Tschö Hyonbä. --Yon-am Pak Chiwon und sein Ho-saeng chon, von F. Vos. --Zum Aufbau der Koreanischen Sprache, von Kim Yungyong. --Koreanische Lackarbeiten der Yi-Zeit, von F. Fontein. --Das koreanische Zahlensystem,

(Continued)

NN R 9.60 a/ OC, I PC, 1, 2, I SL O, 1, 2, I (LC1, X1, Z1)

KOREANICA... (Card 2)

von Kim Pogyom. --Entwicklungslinien im Hausbau Ostasiens, von B. Melchers. --Wesen und Struktur des koreanischen Rechts, von Tschon Pongdok. --Song-hoang Dang, das Tempelchen des Berggeistes, von Djong Bisok. --Literarische Arbeiten von Prof. Dr. A. Eckardt (p. 169-179).

1. Korean studies--Collections. 2. Eckardt, Andreas, 1884-
I. Riekel, August, 1897- , ed.

E-12
6166

KÕRESSAAR, VIKTOR, ed.
Estonian poetry and language; studies in honor of Ants Oras, edited by Viktor Kõressaar and Aleksis Rannit. [Stockholm] Kirjastus Vaba Eesti [for] Estonian learned society in America [1965] 298 p. port., maps, facsim. 24cm.

Articles in French, German, English, Finnish, or Estonian.
Includes bibliographies.

(Continued)

NN R 6.66 1/ OC, I, IIIbo (OS)II PC, 1, 2, 3, I, II SL
(LC1, X1, Z1) [I]

KÕRESSAAR, VIKTOR, ed. Estonian poetry and language... (Card 2)

CONTENTS. --Select list of publications by A. Oras. --Uneretk, by Under. --Ants Oras au coeur de son temps, par A. Aspel. --Ants Orasele, kirjutanud A. Rannit. --Translator and/or poet, by A. Raun. --Ein Dokument estnischen Geistes, von H. Stock. --Keelevabadused luules, kirjutanud J. Aavik. --Eine Analogie zu Iktus und Akzent im lateinischen Sprechvers, von V. Terras. --The role of agglutination in the development of Balto-Finnic case suffixes, by F.J. Oinas. --Zur

(Continued)

KÕRESSAAR, VIKTOR, ed. Estonian poetry and language... (Card 3)

Orthographie des Hauchlauts in der alten estnischen Schriftsprache, von M. Toomse. --Johannes Aavik's language reform 1912-1962, by V. Tauli. --English Christian names in Estonian anthroponymy, by H. Must. --Palatalization in Estonian: some acoustic observations, by I. Lehiste. --English railroad terms in Estonian, by G. Must. --Filles du soleil: folklore estonien et mythologie indieuropéenne, par J. Puhvel. --Die Wassergeister als Schutzwesen der Fische im Volksglauben der finnisch-ugrischen Völker, von I. Paulson. --Kalevanpojat (Continued)

KÕRESSAAR, VIKTOR, ed. Estonian poetry and language... (Card 4)

kirjoittanut H. Winter. --Zum Problem der Gelegenheitsdichtung, von O.A. Webermann. --Senitundmatut Koidula elust, kirjutanud A. Adson. --Kommunistlik kirjandusteooria ühel soome-ugri väikerahval, kirjutanud J. Mägiste. --The main tradition of Estonian poetry, by I. Ivask.

1. Oras, Ants, 1900- . 2. Esthonian literature--Addresses, essays, lectures. 3. Esthonian language--Addresses, essays, lectures. I. Rannit, Aleksis, joint ed. II. Estonian learned society in America. III. Kõressaar, Viktor.

E-12
1783

KORSHOLMS LANTHUSHÅLLNINGSSKOLORS ELEVFÖRBUND.

Korsholms skolor, 1859-1958; minnesskrift sammanställd av Knut von Schantz. [Korsholm, 1959] 287 p. illus., ports. 25cm.

"Elevmatrikeln," p. [139]-257.

1. Agriculture--Education--Institutions--Finland--Korsholm. 2. Finland--Biog. 3. Agriculture--Biog. I. Schantz, Knut von, ed. II. Schantz, Knut von.

NN X/9.65 1/J (OC)I, IIb+ OS(Ib+) PC, 1, 2, 3, I SL RC, 2, 3 (LC1, X1, Z1)

Copy only words underlined & classmark-- TB

KORTZFLEISCH, GERT VON, ed.

Aus der Praxis der kurzfristigen Erfolgsrechnung. Berlin, Duncker & Humblot [1964] 212 p. port. 24cm. (Cologne. Universität. Industrieseminar. Abhandlungen. Heft 18)

"Geburtstagsgeschenk für Herrn Professor Dr. Dr. h.c. Theodor Beste."

Bibliographical footnotes.

CONTENTS.--Kurzfristige Erfolgsrechnung mit dem Ziel der Ergebnis-Vorschau, von F. Krebs. --Überwachung überseeischer Bergbau-Beteiligungen mit Hilfe von Tageskostenrechnungen und monatlichen Erfolgsrechnungen, (Continued)

NN 8.65 s/S OC (OS)I PC, 1, 2, I, II E, 1, 2, I (LC1, X1, Z1) 4

KORTZFLEISCH, GERT VON, ed. Aus der Praxis der kurzfristigen Erfolgsrechnung... (Card 2)

von F. Feil. --Die kurzfristige Erfolgsrechnung in einem Unternehmen mit langfristiger Auftragsabwicklung, von E. Feuerbaum. --Die kurzfristige Erfolgsrechnung in einem mittelgrossen Unternehmen mit Einzelfertigung, von W. Hürfeld. --Die kurzfristige Erfolgsrechnung der Bauunternehmung. Aufgaben und Lösungsmöglichkeiten. von H. Schönnenbeck. --Kurzfristige Absatzerfolgsrechnung im Mineralölvertrieb, von J. Wibbe. --Ermittlung des Fabrikationserfolges in einem Chemie-Betrieb, von K.E. Bänsch. --Führungsprozesse als Gestalter des kurzfristigen Erfolgsrechnung in einem Unternehmen der Chemischen Industrie, von H. Rüschenpöhler. -- (Continued)

KORTZFLEISCH, GERT VON, ed. Aus der Praxis der kurzfristigen Erfolgsrechnung... (Card 3)

Die kurzfristige Kostenträger-Erfolgsrechnung in der Schraubenindustrie, von P. Römer. --Die kurzfristige Erfolgsrechnung in einem Filmtheaterunternehmen, von W. Wierichs. --Die Erfolgsbeteiligung der Geschäftsstellenleiter. Ein Beispiel der Praxis für die Anwendung der kurzfristigen Erfolgsrechnung in der Praxis, von G. Hundertmark. --Die kurzfristige Erfolgsrechnung auf der Grundlage der Grenz-Plankostenrechnung, von H.A. Heiner. --Entwicklungstendenzen der kurzfristigen Erfolgsrechnung, von G.v. Kortzfleisch. (Continued)

KORTZFLEISCH, GERT VON, ed. Aus der Praxis der kurzfristigen Erfolgsrechnung... (Card 4)

1. Accounting and bookkeeping, Cost. 2. Beste, Theodor, 1894- I. Series. II. Title.

Copy only words underlined & Classmark-- TB

KORTZFLEISCH, GERT VON, ed.

Die Betriebswirtschaftslehre in der zweiten industriellen Evolution. [Festgabe für Theodor Beste zum 75. Geburtstag] Berlin, Duncker & Humblot [1969] 354 p. diagrs., port. 24cm. (Cologne. Universität. Industrieseminar. Abhandlungen. Heft 25)

Includes bibliographical references.

CONTENTS.--Grundzüge der formalen Logik für den betriebswirtschaft- (Continued)

NN 10.69 r/a OC (OS)I PC, 1, I, II E, 1, I, II (LC1, X1, Z1) 3

KORTZFLEISCH, GERT VON, ed. Die Betriebswirtschaftslehre in der zweiten industriellen Evolution... (Card 2)

lichen Gebrauch, von H. Bergner. --Entscheidungsmodelle zur Auswahl von Produktideen, von H. Sabel. --Die Transformation von Kostenkategorien, von H. Kürpick. --Electronische Materialdisposition und Fertigungssteuerung einer Maschinenfabrik, von E. Feuerbaum. --Risikoanalyse von Markt-investitionen, von C. Grosche. --Die zwischenbetriebliche Kooperation in der Fertigungswirtschaft aus betriebswirtschaftlicher Sicht, von H.V. Kortzfleisch. --Kooperation in der Bauindustrie, von E. Bieger. --Die kalkulatorische Abschreibung in der modernen Kostenrechnung von H.A. Heiner. --Die Bilanzierung vorausberechneter (Continued)

KORTZFLEISCH, GERT VON, ed. Die Betriebswirtschaftslehre in der zweiten industriellen Evolution... (Card 3)

Kreditgebühren, von W. Hürfeld. --Der Geltungsbereich der aktienrechtlichen Bewertungsvorschriften für das materielle Umlaufvermögen, von A. Zybon. --Lohngestaltung als Führungsinstrument und Führungsaufgabe, von J. Wibbe. --Methoden der Stellenbesetzungskontrolle, von G. Struckmann. --Zur mikroökonomischen Problematik des technischen Fortschrittes, von G.V. Kortzfleisch. --Bibliographie [T. Beste], p. [351]-354.

1. Management--Addresses, essays, lectures. I. Series. II. Beste, Theodor, 1894-

3-MAS

KOSEGARTEN, ANTJE, ed.
Festschrift Ulrich Middeldorf. Hrsg. von Antje Kosegarten und Peter Tigler. Berlin, W. de Gruyter, 1968. 2 v. facsims., plans. 26cm.

Essays in German, Italian, English and French.
"Ulrich Middeldorf, Bibliographie 1923-1967": [v.1], p.[xiii]-xxiii.
Includes bibliographical references.
CONTENTS.--[Bd.1] Textband.--[Bd.2] Tafelband.

(Continued)

NN R 3.69 l/LOC, I, II, IIIbo PC, 1, 2, 3, 4, I, II SL A, 1, 2, 3, 4, I, II (LC1, X1, Z1) [I] 2

KOSEGARTEN, ANTJE, ed. Festschrift Ulrich Middeldorf. (Card 2)

1. Middeldorf, Ulrich Alexander, 1901- . 2. Middeldorf, Ulrich Alexander, 1901- --Bibl. 3. Art, Italian--Addresses, essays, lectures. 4. Art, Italian--Florence. I. Tigler, Peter, joint ed. II. Title. III. Kosegarten, Antje.

---

*C-4 p.v.622

Kraft und Innigkeit; Hans Ehrenburg als Gabe der Freundschaft im 70. Lebensjahr überreicht. [Hrsg. von Johannes Harder] Heidelberg, L. Schneider, 1953. 152 p. mount. port. 24cm.

"Die Schriften Hans Ehrenbergs," p. 151–152.
CONTENTS.—Wie studiere ich Philosophie? von H. J. Iwand.—Das neue Bild des Menschen in der Medizin, von W. Kütemeyer.—Du sollst nicht ehebrechen, von O. Hammelsbeck.—Vom echten Gespräch, von T. Kampmann.—Russlands Allmenschheitsidee, von N. von Bubnoff.—Dichtung als Dienst, von J. Harder.—Ergebnisse eines Goethebuches, von G. Schulz.—Über "Hiob, der Existentialist," von H. Demnitz.—Das Evangelium der Liebe, von J. Wittig.—Die Ungerechtigkeit der Welt und Gottes

(Continued)

NN*R 1.58 OC,I,IIbo PC,1,2,I SL (LC1,X1,Z1)

Kraft und Innigkeit; Hans Ehrenburg als Gabe der Freundschaft im 70. ... 1953. (Card 2)

Gerechtigkeit, von K. H. Rengstorf.—Die biblischen Feste im neuen Israel, von A. Waldstein.—Die unvergessene Stunde, von F. Stepun.—Sonett, von R. Ehrenberg.—Und das Licht wird auf deinem Wege scheinen, von W. Koch.—Drei Andachten aus dem KZ, von E. Wilm.—Brief an seine Mutter. Das Problem des Menschen in der Medizin, von V. von Weizsäcker.—Kleine Erinnerung, von R. Siebeck.—Brief aus England, von M. Belgion.—Reward, von G. Rupp.—Theologie vor dem Ausbruch des Bekenntniskampfes, von M. Berthold.—Vita, von L. Born.—Die Schriften Hans Ehrenbergs.—Notizen zur Biographie Hans Ehrenbergs.

1. Religion—Essays and misc. 2. Ehrenberg, Hans, 1883- I. Harder, Johannes ed. II. Harder, Johannes.

3-MCV
K89.K8

KRAMER, MILLIE, ed.
Kramer; Jacob Kramer, a memorial volume [by Sir Herbert Read and others. Foreword by Millie Kramer] Leeds, Privately printed for M. Kramer by E.J. Arnold & Son [1969] [7], 100 p. (p.[31]-94 plates) front., ports. 26cm.

1. Kramer, Jacob, 1892-1962. I. Read, Sir Herbert Edward, 1893-1968. II. Title. III. Kramer, Millie.
NN R 4.71 b/LOC, IbBNB, I, II, IIIb* PC, 1, I, II SL A, 1, I, II B J (LC1, X1, Z1)

D-20
1996

KRAUSSE, JOHANNES, 1909-
Gersthofen; 969-1969. Festschrift zur Tausendjahrfeier und Stadterhebung, 1969. In Zusammenarbeit mit Karl Kosel [et al.] Gersthofen, Im Selbstverlag der Stadt Gersthofen, 1969. 188 p. illus., maps., facsims. 22cm.

Includes bibliographical references.

1. Gersthofen, Germany--Hist. I. Gersthofen, Germany. t. 1969.
NNR 1.71 m/LOC (OD)It (ED)It PC, 1, I SL (LC1, X1, Z1)

AE-10
449

KRETSCHMAR, GEORG, ed.
Ecclesia und Res Publica. Unter Mitarbeit von Hans Beyer [et al.] hrsg. von Georg Kretschmar und Bernhard Lohse. Göttingen, Vandenhoeck & Ruprecht [1961] 204 p. 24cm.

"Kurt Dietrich Schmidt zum 65. Geburtstag."
Bibliographical footnotes.

(Continued)

NN R 1.64 e/LOC, I, IIbo PC, 1, 2, 3, I SL E, 2, I (LC1, X1, Z1)

2

KRETSCHMAR, GEORG, ed. Ecclesia und Res Publica. (Card 2)

1. Church history--Addresses, essays, lectures. 2. Church and state. 3. Schmidt, Kurt Dietrich. I. Lohse, Bernhard, joint ed. II. Lohse, Bernhard.

BAP

Kring konst och kultur. Helsingfors, Söderström & c:o [1948] 248 p. illus. 26cm.

"Studier tillägnade Amos Anderson, 3.IX.1948 av Otto Andersson... [och 13 andra]"
Bibliographies included.
CONTENTS.—Fagerholm, K. A. Företal.—Andersson, Otto. Orglar och organister i Åbo domkyrka intill slutet av 1600-talet.—Appelberg, Bertel. Om pekoral.—Carlson, Bengt. Klanger i svunnen tid.—Dahlström, Svante. C. G. Bonuviers teaterhus av 1817.—Hintze, Bertel. Till sekelminnet av vår konstskolas grundande.—Homén, Olaf. Förolyckade uttryck.—Huldén, J. J. Åboland i medaljkonsten.—Molander, Olof. Harald Molander går i landsflykt.—Nikander, Gabriel. De gamla järnbruken i Kimitobygden.—Ringbom, L.-I. Örnen och livsträdet.—Rosenqvist, G. O. Åbo akademi.—Rönngren, Nicken. Kring ett jubileum.—Sundwall, Joh. Medelhavets politiska nyckelställning genom tiderna.

517548B. 1. Anderson, Amos, 1878- I. Andersson, Otto, 1879-
N. Y. P. L. June 28, 1950

NIC p.v.244

Kristofer Uppdal; helsing på 60-årsdagen 19 februar 1938. Oslo: Det Norske samlaget, 1938. 91 p. incl. front. (port.) 21½cm.

"Dei fleste artiklane er serprent or 'Syn og segn,' hefte 2, 1938."
CONTENTS.—Strindberg, Axel. Ett norskt rallarepos.—Dalgard, Olav. Uppdal og norsk arbeidarrørsle.—Setrom, Ola. Kristofer Uppdal og lyrikken hans.—Krokann, Inge. Trønderlina hjå Kristofer Uppdal.—Ebbestad, A. H. Frå diktarverkstaden åt Uppdal.—Falkberget, Johan. Kristofer Uppdal.—Helsingar.

1. Uppdal, Kristofer, 1878- I. Det Norske samlaget.
N. Y. P. L. September 8, 1939

* MFBR
(Denmark)

KROGH, TORBEN THORBERG, 1895-
Musik og teater. [København] Munksgaard, 1955.
xv, 242 p. illus., music 29cm.

"Vi har... med anledning i 60 aars fødselsdagen den 21. april 1955, bedt Torben Krogh om tilladelse til at samle et stort udvalg af hans mindre arbejder. Professor Krogh har... foretaget et kritisk gennemsyn." — Efterskrift ([signed:] F. J. Billeskov Jansen, Henrik Nyrop-Christensen)
Includes various melodies set to the words Kong Christian stod ved højen
(Continued)

NN X 10.57 g/ OC, I, II PC, 1, 4, 5, I, II SL MU, 2, 3, I, II
(MUS 1, T 5, LC1, X1, Z1, C1, Y1)

KROYMANN, JÜRGEN, ed. Eranion; Festschrift für Hildebrecht Hommel... (Card 2)

CONTENTS.--Lukas und Paulus, von W. Eltester.--Das vierte Prooemium des Lukrez und die lukrezische Frage, von K. Gaiser.--Antikes und modernes Drama, von W. Jens.--Der Flussname Günz, von H. Krahe.--Römisches Sendungs- und Niedergangsbewusstsein, von J. Kroymann.--Torgötter, von F.G. Maier.--Die Wappnung des Eteokles; zu Aischylos' Sieben gegen Theben, von W. Schadewaldt.--Mythische Hochzeiten; zu den Epinetron des Eretria-Malers, von B. Schweitzer.--Alamannen im
(Continued)

KROGH, TORBEN THORBERG, 1895- . Musik og teater. (Card 2)

mast (p. [111]-123)
CONTENTS.--Optogsbilleder fra Christian IV's kroningsfest. — Har Christian IV set Shakespeare i England? — Hellig trekongers aften i musikalsk belysning. — En stor Shakespeareskuespiller og Danmark. — Det straffede brodermord. — Københavns første teater. — Prinsen morer sig. — Den dydige Susanne. — Omkring Grønnegadeteatret. — Holbergs forhold til operaen. — En Niels Klim-vise. — Holger Danske. — "Kong Christian stod ved højen mast."--Ukendte breve til J. P. E. Hartmann. — Nye bidrag til den tidlige italienske maskekomedies historie. — Den italienske komedie i
(Continued)

KROYMANN, JÜRGEN, ed. Eranion; Festschrift für Hidelbrecht Hommel... (Card 3)

römanischen Reichsdients, von K.F. Stroheker.--Heiden und Christen in der Familie Constantins des Grossen, von J. Vogt.--Singen und Sagen in der Dichtung des Horaz, von G. Willie.-- [Greek]; Horaz im Rettungsboot, von E. Zinn.--Verzeichnis der Schriften von Hildebrecht Hommel, von K. Gaiser.

1. Hommel, Hildebrecht, 1893- . 2. Classical studies--Collections. I. Title.

KROGH, TORBEN THORBERG, 1895- . Musik og teater. (Card 3)

Frankrig. — Don Juan og Faust som pantomimefigurer. — Den engelske pantomime. — Bibliografi over Torben Kroghs skrifter, ved H. Nyrop-Christensen (p. [231]-240)
Includes bibliographies.

1. Music--Denmark. 2. Operas--Denmark. 3. Denmark. 4. Stage--Addresses, essays, lectures. 5. Stage--Denmark--Copenhagen.
I. Jansen, Frederik Julius Billeskov, 1907- , ed.
II. Nyrop Christensen, Henrik, ed.

AD-10
788

KRÜGER, HANFRIED, ed.
Bis an das Ende der Erde; ökumenische Beiträge. Zum 70. Geburtstag von Martin Niemöller. München, Kaiser, 1962. 222 p. ports., facsim. 23cm.

1. Niemöller, Martin, 1892- I. Title.

NN R 3.64 p/ OC (1bo) PC, 1, I SL (LC1, X1, Z1)

Write on slip, name, year, vol., page of magazine and class mark— *DH

Kroonjaar Willem Kloos.

(Nieuwe gids. 's-Gravenhage, 1929. 8°. Jaarg. 44, Halfjaar 1, p. 489-641. port.)

form 400a [viii-10-28 25m]

VIR
+

Krupp'sche Gussstahlfabrik, Essen a. d. Ruhr.
Die chemischen Laboratorien der Fried. Krupp Aktiengesellschaft, Essen, im 75. Jahre ihres Bestehens und ihre Gefolgschaft. [Essen: Graphische Anstalt der Fried. Krupp Aktiengesellschaft, 1938] 39 p. illus. (incl. ports.) 24½ x 33cm.

23535B. 1. Metallurgy—Laboratories—Germany. Festschrift
N. Y. P. L. December 12, 1939

E-11
3612

KROYMANN, JÜRGEN, ed.
Eranion; Festschrift für Hildebrecht Hommel, dargebracht von seinen Tübinger Freunden und Kollegen. [Die Herausgabe der Festschrift besorgte Jürgen Kroymann unter Mitwirkung von Ernst Zinn] Tübingen, M. Niemeyer, 1961. 230 p. illus., port. 24cm.

Bibliographical footnotes.
(Continued)

NN R 12.61 e/OC, I PC, 1, 2, I SL (LC1, X1, Z1) [I]

3

*QR

Księga ku czci Oskara Haleckiego, wydana w XXV-lecie jego pracy naukowej. Warszawa: Nakładem uczniów, 1935. 319 p. port. 24½cm.

Bibliographies included.
CONTENTS.—Bibljografja prac prof. Oskara Haleckiego.—Brzeziński, S. Proces o testament prymasa Andrzeja Krzyckiego.—Dembińska, A. Projekt reformy skarbu w przededniu wielkich sejmów egzekucyjnych.—Herbst, S. Wojna Moskiewska 1507–8.—Jasnowski, J. Działalność antytrynitarzy włoskich w Polsce za czasów Zygmunta Augusta.—Kuczyński, S. M. Sine Wody.—Maciejewska, W. Wojciech Kryski.—Okniński, Z. Jan Kantakuzen.—Pajewski, J. Projekt przymierza polsko-tureckiego za Zygmunta Augusta.—Paszkiewicz, H. Z życia politycznego Mazowsza w XIII w.—Sobaniec, S. Zabiegi Henryka IV wrocławskiego o Kraków i jego usiłowania odnowie-
(Continued)

N. Y. P. L. June 9, 1936

Księga ku czci Oskara Haleckiego... (Card 2)

nia Królestwa.—Tomkiewicz, W. Polityka Francji wobec elektora brandenburskiego w czasie rokowań sztumdorfskich.—Wdowiszewski, Z. Uposażenie ks. Wigunta Olgerdowicza przez Władysława Jagiełłę.

815063A. 1. Halecki, Oskar, Ritter von, 1891- . 2. Poland—Hist., to 1773—Addresses, essays, lectures.
N. Y. P. L. June 9, 1936

Copy only words underlined & classmark-- * QPA

KSIĘGA ku czci Władysława Podlachy. [Redaktor tomu: Władysław Floryan] Wrocław, 1957. 269 p. illus., port. 26cm. (Wrocławskie towarzystwo naukowe. Komisja historii sztuki,. Rozprawy. t. 1)

Bibliographical footnotes.

CONTENTS. —Hornung Z. Władysław Podlacha. 1875-1951. —Podlacha, W. Bibliografia prac Władysława Podlachy (p. 23-27)—Podlacha, W. Scena Wieczerzy Pańskiej w malarstwie cerkiewnym

(Continued)

NN R X 9. 59 g/ OC, II (OS)I PC, 1, 2, I, II A, 1, 2, I, II S, 1, 2, I, II (LCE 1, LC1, K1, Z1)

KSIĘGA ku czci Władysława Podlachy. (Card 2)

XV i XVI wieku. —Orosz, J. Sztuka i ubiór. Wspólność założień w kształtowaniu. —Tatarkiewicz, W. Przezuty stylowe. —Majewski, K. Nowe formy kultu na Krecie na przełomie III i II tysiąclecia przed naszą erą. —Parnicki-Pudełko, S. Uwagi do genezy kolumny doryckiej. —Lepik-Kopaczyńska. W. Problem skiagrafii z czasów Platona. —Hawrot, J. Geneza formy kościoła św. Wojciecha w Krakowie o problem pastoforiów w Polsce. —Świechowski, Z. Drzewo życia w monumentalnej rzeźbie romańskiej Polski. —Hornung, Z. Czy Jan Maria zwany "Il Mosca" albo Padovano był klasycystą? Rudkowski, T. Renesansowy

(Continued)

KSIĘGA ku czci Władysława Podlachy. (Card 3)

zespół nagrobków w Szklarach Górnych. —Gębarowicz, M. Z dziejów przemysłu budowlanego XVI-XIX wieku. —Morelowski, M. Rysunki architektoniczne Samuela Suchodolca z roku 1672.—Blumowna, H. Na marginesie twórczości Leona Wyczółkowskiego.

1. Podlacha, Władysław. 2. Art--Essays and misc. I. Series. II. Floryan, Władysław, ed.

---

*QR

Księga pamiątkowa ku uczczeniu dwudziestopięcioletniej działalności naukowej prof. Marcelego Handelsmana, wydana staraniem i nakładem uczniów. Warszawa, 1929. 511 p. 25cm.

"Bibljografja prac prof. Marcelego Handelsmana, 1903–1928," by Halina Bachulska, p. 1–35.

Festschrift

338525B. 1. Handelsman, Marceli, 1882–1943. 2. Poland—Hist.—Addresses, essays, lectures.
NN

---

*QO

Księga pamiątkowa ku czci Leona Pinińskiego... Lwów: Nakładem Komitetu redakcyjnego, 1936. 2 v. fronts., plates, ports. 25½cm.

Bibliographies included.

CONTENTS.—Tom 1. Abraham, Władysław. Osobowość prawna biskupstw a statut łęczycki z r. 1180.—Adamus, Jan. O Lelewelu parę uwag.—Batowski, Zygmunt. Rembrandtowskie otoczenie i Polacy.—Bernacki, Ludwik. Sienkiewicz w Pieniakach.—Bigo, Tadeusz. Samorząd terytorjalny w nowej konstytucji.—Blumówna, Helena. O rzeźbie Karola Despiau.—Bochnak, Adam. "Opłakiwanie Chrystusa." Obraz w głównym ołtarzu kościoła parafjalnego w Bieczu.—Bossowski, Franz von. Das römische Recht und die vergleichende Rechtswissenschaft.—Brahmer, Mieczysław. Z dziejów polskiego kostjumu wśród obcych.—Bruchnalski, Wilhelm. Paralele niektóre między "Panem

(Continued)

N. Y. P. L. August 27, 1937

Księga pamiątkowa ku czci Leona Pinińskiego... (Card 2)

Tadeuszem" a "Męczennikami" Chateaubrianda.—Bujak, Franciszek. Oskar Żebrowski i jego pogląd na dzieje Polski.—Bulanda, Edmund. Venus Medici.—Chlamtacz, Marceli. Sposoby wynagrodzenia szkody w polskim kodeksie zobowiązań i w prawodawstwach nowożytnych.—Czuma, Ignacy. Wielość współczesnego prawa państwowego.—Dembiński, Bronisław. William Gardiner, ostatni minister W. Brytanji na dworze Stanisława Augusta.—Deryng, Antoni. Niektóre zagadnienia interpretacyjne z dziedziny prawa publicznego.—Dubanowicz, Edward. Ewolucja zadań i składu parlamentu.—Dyboski, Roman. Myśli o moralności życia publicznego w Anglji.—Fischer, Adam. Pierwiastki wierzeniowe w polskiem zdobnictwie ludowem.—Gębarowicz, Mieczysław. Nieznany portret króla Zygmunta III.—Gintowt, Edward. Czy z przekazanych w Digestach rozstrzygnięć konkurencji w obrębie prawa interdyktalnego można wysnuć wniosek o charakterze iudiciorum ex interdicto?—Głąbiński, Stanisław. Czy kryzys gospodarczy

(Continued)

N. Y. P. L. August 27, 1937

Księga pamiątkowa ku czci Leona Pinińskiego... (Card 3)

pobudzi ekonomikę do nowego życia?—Godlewski, Michał, bp. "Il Magnifico," sylwetka historyczna.—Handelsman, Marceli. Nieznany list M. Grabowskiego do ks. Adama.—Hejnosz, Wojciech. Deklaracja królewska z r. 1661.—Hilarowicz, Tadeusz. Znaczenie pewnych przepisów prawa kanonicznego dla ogólnej teorji prawa administracyjnego.—Hornung, Zbigniew. Pomnik ostatnich Jagiellonów w kaplicy zygmuntowskiej na Wawelu.—Jachimecki, Zdzisław. W kole zagadnień Bogurodzicy.—Keuprulian, B. (W.) Elementy ludowej rytmiki polskiej w muzyce Chopina.—Kleiner, Juljusz. Rola wyrazu "pielgrzym" w słownictwie Mickiewicza.—Komarnicki, Wacław. Określenie napastnika we współczesnem prawie narodów.—Koranyi, Karol. Przywileje dla miasta Krakowa i miasta Lwowa z r. 1444.—Tom 2. Koschembahr-Łyskowski, Ignacy. Uwzględnienie przez sędziego zwyczajów obrotu w prawie klasycznem rzymskiem.—Kozicki, Władysław. Mona Lisa.—Kutrzeba, Stanisław. Kilka uwag o recepcji w prawie.—Lancko-

(Continued)

N. Y. P. L. August 27, 1937

Księga pamiątkowa ku czci Leona Pinińskiego... (Card 4)

rońska, Karolina. Nieznany obraz Piazzetty na Wawelu.—Langrod, J. S. Nowe prądy w sądownictwie administracyjnem.—Lisowski, Zygmunt. Zamojski czy Sigonius? Notatka bibljograficzna.—Longchamps de Berier, Roman. Przelew dla zabezpieczenia.—Łapicki, Borys. Misericordia w prawie rzymskiem.—Mańkowski, Tadeusz. Pochodzenie ośiadłych we Lwowie budowniczych włoskich.—Osuchowski, Wacław. Znaczenie doktryny Aristona dla ochrony umów synallagmatycznych w prawie rzymskiem.—Pilch, Stanisław. Jak u starożytnych Germanów karano zdradę i wszeteczeństwo.—Piotrowski, Roman. "Zysk spekulacyjny."—Polaczkówna, Helena. Z przeszłości miasta Grzymałowa.—Rafacz, Józef. Z dziejów prawa rzymskiego w Polsce.—Skwarczyński, Paweł. O pojęciu korony w artykułach henrycjańskich.—Smolka, Franciszek. Kontrakt pożyczki z Dura-Europos.—Starzyński, Stanisław. Droga ustawodawcza.—Swiencickyj, Hilarjon.

(Continued)

N. Y. P. L. August 27, 1937

Księga pamiątkowa ku czci Leona Pinińskiego... (Card 5)

Forma pierwszych pomników dyplomatyki staroruskiej.—Śmiałek, Wincenty. Utopijne rojenia w starożytności.—Tatarkiewicz, Władysław. Historja i klasyfikacja.—Taubenschlag, Rafał. Egipskie kontrakty w greckich papyrusach.—Tretiak, Andrzej. Na marginesie lektury Dickensa.—Tymieniecki, Kazimierz. Okresy w dziejach ludności wieśniaczej w Polsce średniowiecznej.—Umiński, Józef. Andrzej, biskup zwierzyński w latach 1348–1356.—Walicki, Michał. Poliptyk olkuski i problem jego autorstwa.—Winiarski, Bohdan. "Obrona konieczna" w prawie narodów.—Witkowski, Stanisław. Cesarstwo bizantyńskie w powieści polskiej.—Wróblewski, Stanisław. Umowa o pracę pracowników umysłowych.—Wyszyński, Michał. Jak doszło w prawie kanonicznem do zasiedzenia beneficjum.—Zoll, Fryderyk. Znamienny objaw umoralnienia prawa w polskiej ustawie o prawie autorskiem.—Osuchowski, Wacław. Bibljografja prac prof. Pinińskiego.

880331-2A. 1. Piniński, Leon, hrabia, 1857- . 2. Law—Poland.
N. Y. P. L. August 27, 1937

*QR

Księga pamiątkowa ku czci profesora dra Wacława Sobieskiego. t. 1– Kraków, 1932– v. port. 25cm.

Added t.-p.: Mélanges Wacław Sobieski.
"Przedmowa" signed: Oskar Halecki.
"Bibljografja prac profesora dr Wacława Sobieskiego," by Karol Piotrowicz, p. ix-xvi.

1. Sobieski, Wacław, 1872–1935. 2. Poland—Hist.—Addresses, essays, lectures. I. Halecki, Oskar, 1891– , ed. II. Title: Mélanges Wacława Sobieski.
NN

3-MAŜ

Kühn, Margarete, *ed.*
Gedenkschrift Ernst Gall. Hrsg. von Margarete Kühn und Louis Grodecki. (München, Berlin) Deutscher Kunstverlag, 1965.

447 p. with illus. 26 cm.

Includes bibliographies.

CONTENTS.—Geleitwort, von H. Kauffmann.—Die Wandsysteme des Speyerer Domes, von H. A. Kubach.—Der salische Gründungsbau der

(Continued)

NN*R 5. 69 v/L OC, I, II PC, 1, 2, 3, 4, I, II SL A, 1, 2, 3, 4, I, II (LC1, X1, Z1)

4

KÜHN, MARGARETE, ed. Gedenkschrift Ernst Gall. (Card 2)

Siegburger Abteikirche und seine Nachfolge, von A. Verbeek.—A propos de l'église abbatiale de Saint-Lucien de Beauvais, par M. Aubert.—The inside of St.-Denis' west façade, by S. M. Crosby.—The transept of Cambrai Cathedral, by R. Branner.—A propos de la sculpture monumentale dans le nord de la France au XIIème siècle, par J. Vanuxem.—Origines des piles gothiques anglaises à fûts en délit, par J. Bony.—Die Entwicklung der gotischen Travée, von H. Reinhardt.—La famille monumentale de la cathédrale de Bourges et l'architecture de l'Europe au moyen âge, par P. Heliot.—Le maître de Saint-Eustache

(Continued)

KÜHN, MARGARETE, ed. Gedenkschrift Ernst Gall. (Card 3)

de la cathédrale de Chartres, par L. Grodecki.—Zur Baugeschichte der Kathedrale von Reims, von R. Hamann-MacLean.—Zur inneren Eingangswand der Kathedrale von Reims, von H. Keller.—Über einen Reimser Bildhauer in Cluny, von W. Sauerländer.—Die Ostteile des Meissner Domes, von E. Lehmann. — St. Nicolai in Visby, von H. Thümmler. — Das Berliner Schloss und Andreas Schlüter, von E. Hubala.—Die städtebauliche Einordnung des Berliner Schlosses zur Zeit des preussischen Absolutismus, von G. Peschken.—Kulturhistorische Ausstellungen in Heidelberg, von G. Poensgen.—Über den Denkmalschutz in den Vereinigten Staaten, von H. Huth.—Der Gemäl-

(Continued)

KÜHN, MARGARETE, ed. Gedenkschrift Ernst Gall. (Card 4)

debesitz der brandenburgisch-preussischen Schlösser, von M. Kühn.—Literaturverzeichnis zur Geschichte der Gemäldesammlungen in den brandenburgisch-preussischen Schlössern, von H. Börsch-Supan (p. 432–443)—Schriftenverzeichnis Ernst Gall, von H. Lietzmann (p. 444–447)

1. Gall, Ernst, 1888-1958. 2. Gall, Ernst, 1888-1958--Bibl. 3. Art, Gothic--Addresses, essays, lectures. 4. Architecture, Gothic--Addresses, essays, lectures. I. Grodecki, Louis, 1910- joint ed. II. Title.

L-10
2886
Bd. 35

KUEN, HEINRICH.
Romanistische Aufsätze, hrsg. vom Romanischen Seminar der Universität Erlangen-Nürnberg. Nürnberg, H. Carl, 1970. xi, 437 p. port., maps, facsims. 24cm. (Erlanger Beitrage zur Sprach- und Kunstwissenschaft. Bd. 35)

Issued in honor of the author's 70th birthday.
Bibliographical footnotes.
1. Romance languages--Addresses, essays, lectures. I. Erlangen. Universität. Romanisches Seminar. II. Series.
NN R 5. 71 e/L OC (OS)I, II PC, 1, I, II (LC1, X1, Z1)

E-12
8747

KUHN, HELMUT, 1899- , ed.
Interpretation der Welt; Festschrift für Romano Guardini zum achtzigsten Geburtstag. Hrsg. von Helmut Kuhn, Heinrich Kahlefeld und Karl Forster in Verbindung mit der Katholischen Akademie in Bayern. Würzburg, Echter-Verlag [1965] 722 p. port. 25cm.

1. Christianity. 2. Guardini, Romano, 1885-
NN * R 5.67 1/L OC PC, 1,2 SL (LC1,X1,Z1)
[I]

E-11
8722

KUHN, HUGO, ed.
Märchen, Mythos, Dichtung; Festschrift zum 90. Geburtstag Friedrich von der Leyens am 19. August 1963. Hrsg. von Hugo Kuhn und Kurt Schier. München, C.H. Beck [1963] xiv, 518 p. fold. plate, port., music. 24cm.

Contributions in German or English.
Bibliographical footnotes.
1. Leyen, Friedrich von der, 1873- . 2. Folk lore--Addresses, essays, lectures. I. Schier, Kurt, joint ed. II. Title. III. Schier, Kurt.
NN R 2. 64 a/L OC, I, IIIbo PC, 1 2, I, II SL (LC1, X1, Z1) [I]

---

* ZB-98
Film Reproduction

Der KULTISCHE Gesang der abendländischen Kirche; ein gregorianisches Werkheft aus Anlass des 75. Geburtstages von Dominicus Johner, in Verbindung mit zahlreichen Mitarbeiten, hrsg. von Franz Tack. Köln, J.P. Bachem, 1950. 126 p. port., music. 24cm.

Film reproduction. Negative.

1. Johner, Dominicus, father, 1874-1954. 2. Chant (Plain, Gregorian, etc.) 3. Church music. I. Tack, Franz, ed.
NN R 8. 62 p/S OC. I PC. 1, 2, I SL MU. 1, 2, 3, I (MUF1, LC1, UM1, X1, Z1)

QOD

Kultur und rasse. Otto Reche zum 60. geburtstag gewidmet von schülern und freunden; herausgegeben von Michael Hesch und Günther Spannaus. Mit 138 abbildungen und 7 karten. München/Berlin, J. F. Lehmanns verlag, 1939.
428 p. incl. illus. (incl. maps, plan) tables, diagrs. front. (port.) 26^{cm}.

Includes bibliographies.

CONTENTS.—Vorwort der herausgeber.—Verzeichnis der mitarbeiter.—I. Rassenkunde und vorgeschichte: Hesch, Michael. Otto Reche als rassenforscher. Kulz, Werner. Die politisch-weltanschauliche bedeutung der arbeiten Otto Reches. Grau, Rudolf. Die rassenkundlichen erhebungen des Instituts für rassen- und völkerkunde an der Universität Leipzig. Bellmann, Herbert. Bestandsaufnahme der in sächsischen museen befindlichen menschlichen schädel und skelette. Andree, Julius.

(Continued on next card)

A C 40-1111

(2)

Kultur und rasse. Otto Reche ... 1939. (Card 2)
CONTENTS—Continued.
Mittel- und Westeuropa als älteste kulturherde der nordischen rasse. Brückner, Werner. Die häufigkeit der thenar- und hypothenarmuster in der Leipziger bevölkerung. Davenport, C. B. The genetical basis of resemblance in the form of the nose. Eydt, Alfred. Grundsätzliches zur frage der rassen- und erbbiologischen ausrichtung der erziehungswissenschaft. Franz, Leonhard. Ein frühdeutscher fund aus dem Egerland. Geyer, Eberhard. Der stand der rassenkundlichen untersuchungen in der Ostmark. Grahmann, Rudolf. Bemerkungen über einige arbeitsweisen bei der herstellung von feuersteinartifakten. Helbok, A. Das staufische rittertum—eine auslese germanischen bauernblutes. Hoff, Richard v. Die aufgabe der geschichtlichen rassenseelenkunde. Hohlfeld, Johannes. Bismarcks ahnen und enkel; eine genealogische studie. Knorr, Wolfgang. Grundsätzliche bemerkungen zum
(Continued on next card)
A C 40-1111
[2]

Kultur und rasse. Otto Reche ... 1939. (Card 3)
CONTENTS—Continued.
asozialen-problem. Mjöen, J. A. Die biologische lebensauffassung und sippenpflege. Mollison, Theodor. Die sonderstellung des orang-utan im bau seines arteigenen eiweisses. Richter, Johannes. Wildrinderjagd in Alteuropa. Richthofen, Bolko, frhr. v. Die bronzezeitkultur mit streifenverzierter irdenware der polnischen forschung und die urslawenfrage. Routil, Robert. Von der erwartung des blutartlichen ausschlusses der vaterschaft bei verschiedenen völkern. Ruttke, Falk. Dr. Friedrich Lange (1852 bis 1917); ein vorkämpfer für den rassengedanken in schwerer zeit. Sachse, Peter. Zur siedlungsgeschichte und anthropologie des obererzgebirgischen dorfes Satzung (vorbericht) Schlaginhaufen, Otto. Ein melanesierschädel mit parietalia bipartita und anderen nahtvariationen. Stigler, Robert. Altersermittlung und alterserscheinungen bei Negern in Uganda. Streng, Oswald. Die verteilung der blutfaktoren M und N und ihre beziehungen zur verteilung der blut-
(Continued on next card)
A C 40-1111
[2]

Kultur und rasse. Otto Reche ... 1939. (Card 4)
CONTENTS—Continued.
gruppen. Tackenberg, Kurt. Ein doppeljoch aus dem Reitzenhainer moor bei Annaberg (Erzgebirge) Wastl, Josef. Prähistorische menschenreste aus dem muschelhügel von Bindjai-Tamiang in Nord-Sumatra. Weber, Elisabeth. Zwillingbefunde über die erbphysiologie der menschlichen haut; dermographismus und handfeuchtigkeit.—II. Völkerkunde und volkstumskunde: Spannaus, Günther. Otto Reche als völkerkundler. Bernatzik, H. A. Die kolonisation primitiver völker unter besonderer berücksichtigung des Mokenproblems. Böhme, H. H. Das problem des totemismus in Mikronesien. Damm, Hans. Zeremonialschemel vom Sepik (Kaiser-Wilhelmsland) Germann, Paul. Hand und elefantenrüssel in West-Afrika. Henning, Joachim. Zum leben der witwe in Melanesien; ein beitrag zur sozialen stellung der frau. Heydrich, M. Gustav Klemm und seine kulturhistorische sammlung. Hirschberg, Walter. Zur geschichte der afrikanischen kulturkrise. Klingen-
(Continued on next card)
A C 40-1111
[2]

Kultur und rasse. Otto Reche ... 1939. (Card 5)
CONTENTS—Continued.
heben, August. Züge der religion der Vai in Liberia. Körner, Theo. Historisch-kritisches zum Mongolenbegriff. Kötzschke, Rudolf. Die völkertafel Germaniens in der angelsächsischen Orosius-bearbeitung aus der zeit könig Alfreds von England. Krämer, Augustin. Die Matupiter; ein beitrag zur monographie. Lagercrantz, Sture. Zur verbreitung des klystiers in Negerafrika. Lehmann, F. R. Die gegenwärtige lage der mana-forschung. Lindblom, Gerhard. Der lasso in Afrika; einige ethnographisch-kulturgeschichtliche notizen. Plischke, Hans. Völkerkundliches zur entstehung von stammes- und völkernamen. Schilde, Willy. Die völker, sprachen und rassen am oberen Nil. Thurnwald, R. Methoden in der völkerkunde.
1. Reche, Otto, 1879- 2. Anthropology—Addresses, essays, lectures. 3. Germanic tribes. 4. Ethnology—Addresses, essays, lectures. 5. Europe—Antiquities. I. Hesch, Michael, ed. II. Spannaus, Günther, 1901- ed.
New York. Public library for Library of Congress
A C 40-1111
[2]

TB
KULTUR und Wirtschaft; eine Festgabe zum 70. Geburtstag von Wilhelm Vershofen. Hrsg. von Georg Bergler. [Detmold] A. Nauck & Co., 1949. 435 p. plates. 24cm.

Bibliographies included.
CONTENTS.—Der Dichter, von Winckler.—Mein Weg mit Wilhelm Vershofen, von Kneip.—Werkleute, von T. Rody.—Vor der Reise. Kind, von G. Engelke.—Der Priester, von H. Lersch.—Der Mensch in der Exzentrik, von W. Meridies.—Wilhelm Vershofen, der Philosoph des wirtschaftenden Menschen, von H. J. Schneider.—Aspekte zur Weltwende, von E. Diesel.—Empirische Wirtschafts-forschung im Rahmen der Gemeinwirtschaft, von R. Grünwald.—Das soziologische Gemeinschaftsprinzip,
(Continued)
NN 3.53 OC, I, Ib PC, 1, 2, I SL E, 1, 2, I (LC1, Z1, X1)

KULTUR und Wirtschaft... (Card 2)

von E. Rogner.—Über Meinungsforschung, von H. Proesler.—Einige Berichte über Gegenstand, Verfahren und Ergebnisse der Meinungsforschung in den Vereinigten Staaten von Amerika, von C. Hundhausen.—Humanistische Volkskunde als Mittel zur Wesensdeutung, von H. F. J. Kropff.—Deutschtum in den Vereingten Staaten von Amerika, von E. Brenner.—Die Bedeutung der Verbrauchsforschung in der Energiewirtschaft, von H. F. Mueller.—Verbraucherpolitik, von W. Trömel.—Das Menschliche als Schicksal und Aufgabe in Wirtschaft und Betrieb, von H. H. Meyer-Mark.—Die Lösung des Mitbesitzproblems durch die Konsumgenossenschaften, von F. Klein.—"Kriegsgewinnler"? von E. Fratz.—Die Schriften Wilhelm Vershofens, von G. Bergler und T. Olesch.
1. Vershofen, Wilhelm, 1878- 2. Economics, 1926—German and Austrian authors. I. Bergler, Georg, ed.

E-10
1937
KULTUROPTIMISME og folkeopplysning; festskrift til Arne Kildal på 70-års dagen, 10. desember 1955. [Redaksjonskomite: Ingeborg Lyche, Haakon M. Fiskaa og Didrik Arup Seip] Oslo, Aschehoug, 1956. 147 p. illus., port. 24cm.

CONTENTS.—Boka kom til barnet, av T. Vesaas.—Arne Kildals første bedrift som biblioteksmann, av G. Stoltz.—Kulturoptimisme, av M. Oftedal Broch.—Fra arbeidet "ute i marken," av M. Skancke.—Utflytterne i norsk
(Continued)
NN** 2.57 d/P OC, I, IIb+ PC, 1, 2, 3, 4, I SL AH, 4, I E, 4, I (LC1, X1, Z1, Y1) [I]

KULTUROPTIMISME og folkeopplysning... (Card 2)

litteratur, av D. Arup Seip.—Norske bøker i norsk-amerikanske hyller, av E. Haugen.—Åndsliv gjennom kiosklukene, av N.J. Rud.—Soldater og kulturfront, av D. Tveito.—Bibliotekaren og publikum, av Ø. Anker.—Det frivillige opplysningsarbeidets oppgaver i det moderne samfunnet av i dag, av I. Lyche.—Vår barndoms Inger Johanne, av R. Deinboll.—Staten og kulturlivet, av H. Sivertsen.—Bøker langs landeveien, av B. Rongen.—Det talte ord, av A. Kildal.
1. Kildal, Arne, 1885- . 2. Librarians--Norway. 3. Education--Norway. 4. Norwegians in the U.S. I. Lyche, Ingeborg, ed. II. Lyche, Ingeborg.

E-10
3082
KUNGLIGA GUSTAV ADOLFS AKADEMIEN FÖR FOLKLIVSFORSKNING, Upsala, Sweden.
Sed och sägen; festskrift till Edwin Berger den 13/5 1956. Uppsala, 1956. 132 p. illus., port. 25cm.

"Tryckt i 250 exemplar."
Includes bibliography and bibliographical footnotes.
CONTENTS.—"Gamla Fader vår," av N. Ahnlund.—Orden båg s. 'bluff' och båga v. 'bluffa', av E. Abrahamson.—Om allmogemål och språkvård, av B. Collinder.—Medan man lefwer i wärlden säll, en gammal
(Continued)
NN** R 7.57 c/B (OC)Ib, I OS PC, 1, I SL (LC1, X1, Z1) [I]

KUNGLIGA GUSTAV ADOLFS AKADEMIEN FÖR FOLKLIVSFORSKNING, Upsala, Sweden. Sed och sägen;... (Card 2)

sånglek, av N. Dencker.—Rock som namn på slåndarter, av M. Eriksson.—Moderna festseder, av S. Erixon.—Några folkvisor, av H. Gustavson.—Omöjlighetssymboler i finsk epik, av M. Haavio.—Plog och årder i Södermanland, av R. Jirlow.—Folkvisan om Herr Peder och Malfred, av J. Sahlgren.—Trollgädden; jämförelse mellan August Bondesons primärupptecknìng och den publicerade sagan, av A. Sandklef.—Några isländska folklekar från medeltiden, av D. Strömbäck.—Torvmossared och Tommered, av H. Ståhl.—Räven och bonden; efter branche XXV av Le roman de Renard, av Gunnar Tilander.

1. Berger, Edwin, 1871- I. Title.

XAH

Kunst und Recht, Festgabe für Hans Fehr, mit Beiträgen von Karl S. Bader [et al.] Karlsruhe, C. F. Müller, 1948.

235 p. 25 cm. (Arbeiten zur Rechtssoziologie und Rechtsgeschichte, Bd. 1)

1. Fehr, Hans Adolf, 1874- 2. Law—Addresses, essays, lectures. (Series)

48-25284*‡

Library of Congress [1]

MA

KUNSTGESCHICHTLICHE Studien für Hans Kauffmann. [Hrsg. von Wolfgang Braunfels] Berlin, Gebr. Mann [1956] 274 p. plates. 26cm.

Bibliographical footnotes.

" Schrifttumsverzeichnis Hans Kauffmann, zusammengestellt von Veronika von Below und Günter Bandmann, " p. 272-274.

1. Kauffmann, Hans, 1896- . 2. Kauffmann, Hans, 1896- --Bibl. 3. Art--Essays and misc. I. Braunfels, Wolfgang, 1911- , ed.

NN R 5.57 a/ OC, I PC, 1, 2, 3, I SL A, 1, 2, 3, I (LC1, X1, Z/ Y1)

[I]

E-11
4350

KURTH, GOTTFRIED, 1912- , ed.

Evolution und Hominisation; Festschrift zum 60. Geburtstag von Gerhard Heberer mit Beiträgen von A. A. Dahlberg [et al.] Stuttgart, G. Fischer, 1962. x, 228 p. illus. 24cm.

Added t.p. in English.
Includes bibliographies.

(Continued)

NN R 3.62 p/ OC, I PC, 1, 2, 3, I SL (LC1, X1, Z1)

KURTH, GOTTFRIED, 1912- , ed. Evolution und Hominisation... (Card 2)

CONTENTS.--Die wichtigsten Publikationen von Gerhard Heberer: Allgemeine Zoologie, Genetik und allgemeine Phylogenetik, Anthropologie und menschliche Phylogenetik.--Some cosmic aspects of organic evolution, by G. G. Simpson.--Zufall oder Plan; das Paradox der Evolution, von E. Mayr.--Zum phylogenetischen Pluripotenzbegriff, von W. Herre.--Bemerkungen zur Bergmannschen Regel, von M. Roehrs.--Ein Beitrag zur genetischen Basis der Quanten-Evolution, von T. Dobzhansky und W. Drescher.--The relative ages of the australopithecines of Transvaal and the pithecanthropines

(Continued)

KURTH, GOTTFRIED, 1912- , ed. Evolution und Hominisation... (Card 3)

of Java, by B. Kurtén.--The Middle Pleistocene fauna of the Near East, by D. A. Hooijer.--Zur relativen Chronologie ostasiatischer Mittelpleistozän-Faunen und Hominoidea-Funde, von H. H. Kahlke.--The Middle Pleistocene fauna of Java, by D. A. Hooijer.--Das absolut Alter des Pithecanthropus Erectus Dubois, von G. H. R. von Koenigswald.--The origin and adaptive radiation of the australopithecines, by J. T. Robinson.--The gradual appraisal of Australopithecus, by R. A. Dart.--The earliest tool-makers, by K. P. Oakley.--Stellung und Aussagewert der gegenwärtig bekannten mittelpleistozänen Hominidae, von G. Kurth. --Early members of the Genus

(Continued)

KURTH, GOTTFRIED, 1912- , ed. Evolution und Hominisation... (Card 4)

Homo in Africa, by P. Tobias.--On the teeth of early Sapiens, by A. A. Dahlberg.--Ein Endokranialausguss von einem frühmagdalenienzeitlichen Schädel aus Döbritz, Kreis Pössneck, Thüringen, von H. Grimm.--Menschenfunde an der Grenze von Mittel- und Jungpaläolithikum in Europa (einige chronologische Aspekte) von K. J. Narr.

1. Heberer, Gerhard. 2. Man, Prehistoric. 3. Evolution. I. Title.

---

* PDB

KUSCHKE, ARNULF, 1912- , ed.

Verbannung und Heimkehr; Beiträge zur Geschichte und Theologie Israels im 6. und 5. Jahrhundert v. Chr. Wilhelm Rudolph zum 70. Geburtstage dargebracht von Kollegen, Freunden und Schülern. Tübingen, J. C. B. Mohr, 1961. xii, 326 p. port. 24cm.

Bibliographical footnotes.

CONTENTS.--Zu den Gottesnamen in den Büchern Jeremia und Ezechiel, von F. Baumgärtel.--Jeremias Drohorakel gegen Ägypten und

(Continued)

NN R 2.64 p/ OC, I, IIb* PC, 1, 2, I SL J, 1, 2, I (LC1, X1, Z1)

KUSCHKE, ARNULF, 1912- , ed. Verbannung und Heimkehr... (Card 2)

gegen Babel, von O. Eissfeldt.--Zur Analyse des Sündopfergesetzes, von K. Elliger.--Jesaja 52, 7-10 in der christlichen Verkündigung, von J. Fichtner.--Serubbabel und der Wiederaufbau des Tempels in Jerusalem, von K. Galling.--Die "Abtrünnigen" und die "Vielen," ein Beitrag zu Jesaja 53, von H. W. Hertzberg.--Haggai, von F. Hesse.--Zwei Begriffe für Eigentum (Besitz): אֲחֻזָּה und נַחֲלָה, von F. Horst.--L'Étymologie du substantif Tô'ēbā, par P. Humbert.--Berith; ein Beitrag zur Theologie der Exilszeit, von A. Jepsen.--Jeremia 48, 1-8;

(Continued)

KUSCHKE, ARNULF, 1912- , ed. Verbannung und Heimkehr... (Card 3)

zugleich ein Beitrag zur historischen Topograhie Moabs, von A. Kuschke.--Die Bedeutung von Deuteronomium 32, 8f. 43 (4 Q) für die Auslegung des Moseliedes, von R. Meyer.--"Ich" und "Er" in der Ezrageschichte, von S. Mowinckel.--Jerusalem-Zion: the growth of a symbol, by N. W. Porteous. --Das Phänomen des Wunders im Alten Testament, von G. Quell.--Erwägungen zum Kyroserlass, von L. Rost.--Bibliographie Wilhelm Rudolph, von R. Hentschke (p. [309]-312).

1. Bible. O.T.--Essays and misc. 2. Rudolph, Wilhelm, 1891- I. Title. II. Kuschke, Arnulf, 1912-

---

GAE

Een kwart eeuw oudheidkundig bodemonderzoek in Nederland. Gedenkboek A. E. van Giffen, directeur van het Biologisch-archaeologisch instituut der Rijksuniversiteit te Groningen, 1922–17 Juni–1947. Meppel, J. A. Boom & zoon, 1947. 608 p. illus. 25cm.

"Samengesteld onder redactie van Dr H. E. van Gelder...[en anderen]"
"Publicaties van de hand van Prof. Dr A. E. van Giffen," p. 557–563.

419636B. 1. Netherlands—Archaeology—Assoc. and org.—Netherlands. 2. Archaeology. 3. Archaeology. 4. Giffen, Albert Egges van, 1884-

N. Y. P. L. December 29, 1947

Kyoto. Imperial University. Science Department. Chemical Institute.

The sexagint; being a collection of papers dedicated to Professor Yukichi Osaka by his pupils in celebration of his sixtieth birthday. Kyoto, 1927. 293 p. incl. tables. diagrs., front. (port.), illus. 8°.

356654A. 1. Osaka, Yukichi, 1867– . 2. Chemistry—Collected essays. 3. Title.
N. Y. P. L. October 26, 1928

Ladendorf, Heinz, ed.

Festschrift Dr. h. c. Eduard Trautscholdt zum siebzigsten Geburtstag am 13. Januar. 1963. Hamburg, E. Hauswedell, 1965.

209 p. illus., mounted port. 26 cm.

"Schriftenverzeichnis Eduard Trautscholdt": p.[219]-223.

(Continued)

NN*R 4.68 a/AOC,1b*,I PC,1,2,3,I SL A,1,2,3, I PR,1,2,I (LC1,X1,Z1) [I]

2

LADENDORF, HEINZ, ed. Festschrift Dr. h.c. Eduard Trautscholdt zum siebzigsten Geburtstag am 13. Januar. 1963. (Card 2)

Includes bibliographical references.

1. Trautscholdt, Eduard. 2. Trautscholdt, Eduard—Bibl. 3. Art—Essays and misc. I. Title.

The Labor movement: a re-examination; a conference in honor of David J. Saposs, January 14–15, 1966. Edited under the direction of Jack Barbash. [Madison, °1967]

vii, 162 p. port. 23 cm.

"Sponsored by the Industrial Relations Research Institute, Department of Economics [and the] Wisconsin State Historical Society." Bibliographical footnotes.

CONTENTS.—Labor statistics in the American economy, by E. Clague.—Limited and/or inclusive unionism: central contention in

(Continued)

NN*R 10.69 w/FOC, I, II (OD)IIIt, IVt (ED)IIIt, IVt (OS)V PC, 1, I, II, III, IV, V SL E, 1, 2, I, II (LC1, X1, Z1)

4

The LABOR movement: a re-examination... (Card 2)

organized labor, by J. B. S. Hardman.—Labor views on industrial democracy, 1865–1964; a sketch, by M. Derber.—The international posture of the American labor movement; the relevance of American experience to world labor problems, by A. H. Cook.—The relevance of the American labor movement's experience to Japanese labor problems, by P. L. Garman.—Conflict and integration in trade union development, by E. M. Kassalow.—A political theory of the labor movement, by G. Tyler.—American labor's origins and ideology, by P. Taft.—The labor movement; a look backward and forward, by D. J. Saposs.—David J. Saposs and the Wisconsin school, by J. Bar-

(Continued)

Copy only words underlined & Classmark-- STG

A LAND called Crete; a symposium in memory of Harriet Boyd Hawes, 1871-1945. Northampton, Mass., Smith college, 1967. 153 p. illus., port. 23cm. (Smith college studies in history. v. 45)

Bibliographical footnotes.

1. Crete--Archaeology. Minoan and Mycenaean. 2. Greece--Civilization. I. Series. II. Hawes, Harriet Ann (Boyd), 1871-1945.

NN 12.68 k/A OC, II (OS)I PC, 1, 2, I, II (LC1, X1, Z1)

The LABOR movement: a re-examination... (Card 3)

bash.—Research as a tool of administration: the contribution of David J. Saposs, by M. Weiss.—Introductory remarks, by A. M. Douty.—The economist and the labor union; then and now, by E. Oliver.—How far have we come in workers' education? by L. Rogin.—A piece of the action in the early 30's, by J. Herling.—Toward an understanding of "the public interest" in collective bargaining, by H. S. Roberts.—A bibliography of the works of David J. Saposs (p. 158–162)

(Continued)

LAND van mijn hart; Brabantse feestbundel voor Mgr Prof. Dr Th. J. A. J. Goossens op zijn zeventigste verjaardag (8 Febr. 1952) aangeboden door Prof. Dr L. G. J. Verberne en Dr A. Weijnen, namens vrienden en leerlingen. Tilburg, H. Bergman, 1952. 168 p. illus., port., map. 25cm.

Includes bibliographies.

CONTENTS. —Monseigneur Prof. Dr Th. Goossens zeventig jaar, door H. M. J. Blomjous. —Rector Goossens, door A. C. J. Commissaris. —Van wolhandelaar tot prelaat, door P. C. Boeren Stukken betreffende de kerkelijke toestand te Eindhoven en Heusden tijdens de godsdienst-troebelen in 1566 en 1567, (Continued)

NN**R X 1.54 OC, I, II PC, 1, 2, I, II SL (LC1, Z1, X1)

Laboratory of anthropology, inc., Santa Fé, N. M.

Mary Austin; a memorial...ed. and with a preface and check list of Mrs. Austin's works, by Willard Hougland. Santa Fe, Laboratory of anthropology, 1944. 63 p. 23cm.

One of 1000 copies.

1. Austin, Mary (Hunter), 1868–1934. I. Hougland, Willard.
N. Y. P. L. September 17, 1945

LAND van mijn hart... (Card 2)

door A. M. Frenken. —Nog eens: De VII Weeën, door P. J. M. van Gils... Van heilige varkens en maarschalken, door B. H. D. Hermesdorf. —Initialen en vignetten, door L. van Hoek. — August Sassen en de Brabantse cultuur, door H. H. Knippenberg. —Over de natuurpoëzie van Pater Dr Antoon Smoor, door K. Meeuwesse. —Middelnoordbrabants, door L. C. Michels. —Syntagma's met het type ge moet gij + het/et, door P. C. Paardekooper. —De zangers van het Onze Lieve Vrouwe gilde te Bergen op Zoom, door A. Piscaer. — Antwerpen, van Sonnius tot Torrentius of een kerk zonder herder (1576-1586), door F. Prims. —Adrian Poirters als lyrisch dichter in "Het duyfken in de steen-rotse" (1657), door E. Rombauts. —Huiden en pelzen op de jaarmarkt...

(Continued)

LAND van mijn hart... (Card 3)

van Bergen op Zoom, door K. Slootmans.—Oud arbeidsrecht in Noord-Brabant, door F. J. H. M. van der Ven. —Over de Noordbrabantse nijverheid in de eerste jaren na 1830, door L. G. J. Verberne. —De linnen- en katoenindustrie in de Bataafse en Franse tijd door F. B. A. M. Verhagen. —Oude Germaanse namen in de Meierij, door A. Weijnen. —Bbliografie van Mgr. Prof. Dr. Th. Goossens.

1. Goossens, Thomas, 1882- 2. Brabant—Hist.—Addresses, essays, lectures. I. Verberne, Louis Gerardus Josephus, 1889- , ed. II. Weijnen, Antonius Angelus, 1909-

---

BAC p.v.745

[Landlinger, Johann] ed.
Die alte Eisenstadt Waidhofen a.d.Ybbs. Festschrift zur Feier ihres 700jährigen Bestehens in der Heimatfestwoche 23. bis 31. July 1949. Waidhofen A.Y., L. Stummer, 1949. 117 p. illus. 24cm.

"Im Auftrage des Festausschusses herausgegeben von Dr. Johann Landlinger."
CONTENTS.—Landlinger, J. Stadtbild und Kunstdenkmäler.—Freiss, Edmund. Aus Waidhofens älterer Vergangenheit.—Mayr, Thomas. Kleine Waidhofner Chronik, 1797–1946.—Kornmüller, Josef. Die Landschaft und Wirtschaft.—Feuchtmüller-Wien, Rupert. Das Museum der Stadt Waidhofen a.d.Ybbs.—Mayr, Thomas. Die Zeller Hochbrücke.—Namen, die Bleiben.—Schweiger, Anton. Berühmte Gäste unserer Stadt.—Mayr, Thomas. Wie Waidhofen Schulstadt wurde.—Kohout, Leopold. Sport-stadt Waidhofen a.d.Ybbs.—Fried, Richard. Die Ybbstalbahn, ihre Geschichte und ihre Bedeutung.—Heimatfestwoche Waidhofen a.d.Ybbs.—Festleitung.

I. Waidhofen an der Ybbs, Austria. II. Title.
N. Y. P. L. June 14, 1951

BAC p.v.782

Landlinger, Johannes.
Ardagger: Stifts- und Pfarrgeschichte, 1049–1949, von Dr. Johannes Landlinger... [Ardagger] Gemeinde Stift Ardagger, 1949. 93 p. illus. 24cm.

"Literaturnachweis," p. 76.

Mr. Schreiber

NN 1. Ardagger, Austria--Hist. I. Ardagger, Austria.

---

*MFBH

LANDON, H. C. ROBBINS, ed.
Studies in eighteenth-century music; a tribute to Karl Geiringer on his seventieth birthday. Edited by H. C. Robbins Landon in collaboration with Roger E. Chapman. New York, Oxford university press, 1970. 425 p. port., music. 25cm.

Bibliographical footnotes.

(Continued)

NN R 3.71 w/(C OC, I PC, 2, 3, I SL MU, 1, 2, I (LC1, X1, Z1) 2

LANDON, H. C. ROBBINS, ed. Studies in eighteenth-century music... (Card 2)

1. History and criticism, 1750-1800. 2. Music--Hist. and crit.--Classical, 1750-1800. 3. Geiringer, Karl, 1899- . I. Chapman, Roger Eddington, 1916- , joint ed.

E-13
5547

Landwirtschaftliche Marktforschung in Deutschland. Arthur Hanau zum 65. Geburtstag. Mit einer Würdigung von Emil Woermann und Beiträgen von Hans Eberhard Buchholz [u. a.] Hrsg. von Günther Schmitt. München, Basel, Wien, Bayerischer Landwirtschaftsverlag (1967).
330 p. front. 25 cm.

Includes bibliographies.

(Continued)

NN*R 6.69 v/a OC, I, IIb*, II, IIIb*, III PC, 1, 2, I, II, III SL E, 1, 2, I, II, III (LC1, X1, Z1) 5

LANDWIRTSCHAFTLICHE Marktforschung in Deutschland. (Card 2)

CONTENTS.—Arthur Hanau, von E. Woermann.—Zur frühen Geschichte der landwirtschaftlichen Marktforschung in Deutschland, von G. Schmitt.—Landwirtschaftliche Marktforschung und Agrarpolitik, von C. von Dietze.—Marktwirtschaft und Betriebswirtschaft, von G. Weinschenck.—Dynamik der Anpassung in der Landwirtschaft, von T. Heidhues.—Welternährung und Marktforschung, von H. Wildbrandt.—Zusammenhänge zwischen Produktion und Markt in der Landwirtschaft der Entwicklungsländer, von H. Ruthenberg.—Aussenhandelstheorie und Landwirtschaft, von H. Richter-Altschäf-

(Continued)

LANDWIRTSCHAFTLICHE Marktforschung in Deutschland. (Card 3)

fer.—Gedanken zur Agrarmarktstrategie in der Massenkonsumgesellschaft, von H. Kötter.—Der landwirtschaftliche Haushalt im Umstrukturierungsprozess der Landwirtshaft, von H. Schmucker und R. von Schweitzer.—Angebotsschwankungen bei Agrarproduktion, von R. Plate.—Grundfragen zu Vorausschauen in der landwirtschaftlichen Marktforschung, von E. Wöhlken.—Marktstruktur und Absatzprobleme, von A. Weber.—Offene Fragen bei der Beurteilung der Wirkungen von Handelsspannen, von D. Hiss.—Interregionale Marktgleichgewichte, von H. E. Buchholz.—Produktivitätsberechnun-

(Continued)

LANDWIRTSCHAFTLICHE Marktforschung in Deutschland. (Card 4)

gen als Orientierungsmasstab für die Agrarpolitik, von D. Goeman und F.-C. Rustemeyer.—Marktforschung und Gemeinsame Agrarpolitik der EWG, von H.-B. Krohn.—Gedanken über die Beziehungen zwischen Agrarhandel und landwirtschaftlicher Marktforschung, von H.-J. Riecke.—Landwirtschaftliche Marktforschung, von G. Vogel.—Verzeichnis der wissenschaftlichen Veröffentlichungen von Arthur Hanau (p. 333–336)

(Continued)

LANDWIRTSCHAFTLICHE Marktforschung in Deutschland. (Card 5)

1. Agricultural products--Marketing--Germany. 2. Agricultural products--Trade and stat.--Germany. I. Hanau, Arthur, 1902- II. Buchholz, Hans Eberhard. III. Schmitt, Günther, ed.

E-13
3659

LANG, O.E., ed.
Contemporary problems of public law in Canada; essays in honour of dean F.C. Cronkite. [Toronto] Published for the College of law, University of Saskatchewan by University of Toronto press [1968] 171 p. port. 24cm.

CONTENTS.--Foundations of Canadian law in history and theory, by W.R. Jackett.-The Canadian bill of rights, by E.A. Driedger.-
(Continued)

NN R 11.68 1/ OC, I, IIbo PC, 1, 2, I SL E, 1, 2, I (LC1, X1, Z1)
2

LANG, O.E., ed. Contemporary problems of public law in Canada... (Card 2)

Freedom of the press, by E.A. Tollefson.- Crown immunity and the power of judicial review, by B.L. Strayer.- Judicial review of the proceedings of administrative tribunals in Saskatchewan, by M. Woods.- Legislative power to create corporate bodies and public monopolies in Canada, by W.R. Lederman.-Combines: the continuing dilemma, by D.G. Blair.- Rational solutions for labour problems, by O.E. Lang.

1. Law--Canada. 2. Law-- Addresses, essays, lectures. I. Cronkite, F.C. II. Lang, O.E.

QOV

Language, culture, and personality; essays in memory of Edward Sapir. Edited by Leslie Spier, A. Irving Hallowell [and] Stanley S. Newman. Menasha, Wis., Sapir memorial publication fund, 1941.

x, 298 p. front. (port.) illus. (maps) plates, diagrs. (1 fold.) 27 x 21ᶜᵐ.

Includes bibliographies.

1. Sapir, Edward, 1884–1939. 2. Indians of North America—Culture. 3. Indians of North America—Languages. I. Spier, Leslie, 1893– ed. II. Hallowell, Alfred Irving, 1892– joint ed. III. Newman, Stanley Stewart, 1905– joint ed.

Library of Congress E98.C9L25 42-2294
[30] 970.6

E-11
4767

LANGUAGE and society; essays presented to Arthur M. Jensen on his seventieth birthday. Copenhagen, Berlingske bogtrykkeri, 1961. 202 p. 24cm.

Contribution in English, French, German or Italian.

1. Jensen, Arthur M. 2. Philology--Addresses, essays, lectures.
NN 7.62 g/s OC, Ibo PC, 1, 2 SL (LC1, X1, Z1)

*MGA

LaRUE, JAN, ed.
Aspects of Medieval and Renaissance music; a birthday offering to Gustave Reese. Edited by Jan LaRue. Associate editors: Martin Bernstein, Hans Lenneberg, Victor Yellin. New York, W.W. Norton [1966] xvii, 891 p. illus., facsims. 25cm.

Includes music.
"Gustave Reese: A partial list of publications, compiled by
(Continued)

NN S 9.66 1/ OC PC, 1, 2, 3, 4, I SL MU, 1, 5, 6, 7, I (LC1, X1, Z1) [I]
2

LaRUE, JAN, ed. Aspects of Medieval and Renaissance music... (Card 2)

Frederick Freedman." p. 889-891.

1. Reese, Gustave, 1899- . 2. Music--Essays. 3. Music--Hist. and crit.--Medieval, 1000-1450. 4. Music--Hist. and crit.--Renaissance, 1450-1600. 5. Essays. 6. History and criticism, 1000-1450. 7. History and criticism, 1450-1600. I. Title.

C-12
41

LAUENAU, GERMANY.
Lauenau, Landkreis Springe, 1059-1959. Festschrift zur 900-Jahrfeier. [Springe, 1959] 80 p. (p.49-80 advertisements) illus. 21cm.

Cover title: 900 [i.e. Neunhundert] Jahre Lauenau. "Programm der Festwoche," p.39-49.

1. Lauenau, Germany--Hist. t.1959.
NN R 6.62 c/B0Dt EDt PC, 1 SL (LC1, X1, Z1)

Copy only words underlined & classmark— KAA

LAUER, WILHELM.
Oskar Schmieder zu seinem 70. Geburtstag. (IN: Kiel, Germany. Universität. Geographisches. Institut. Schriften. Kiel. 26cm. Bd. 20. p. 9-17)

1. Schmieder, Oskar, 1891-
NN 4.63 a/ OI (PC)1 (LC2, X1, Z1)

E-14
1421

LAUSANNE, Switzerland. Université. Droit, Faculté de.
Mélanges Philippe Meylan; recueil de travaux publiés [à l'occasion de son soixante-dixième anniversaire. Lausanne, Impr. centrale de Lausanne, 1963.

2 v. plates, port. 25 cm.

English, French, German or Italian.
Bibliographical footnotes. "Bibliographie des travaux de Philippe Meylan": v. 1, pt. xi-xv.
(Continued)

NN * R 6.71 b/(OC)I OS(1b*) PC, 1, 2, I SL (LC1, X1, Z1)
2

LAUSANNE, Switzerland. Université. Droit, Faculté de. Mélanges Philippe Meylan... (Card 2)

CONTENTS.—v. 1. Droit romain.—v. 2. Histoire du droit.

1. Law, Roman--Addresses, essays, lectures. 2. Law--Addresses, essays, lectures. I. Meylan, Philippe, 1893-

VDC

Lausanne, Switzerland. **Université.** École d'ingénieurs.
...Recueil de travaux; publiés à l'occasion du quatrième centenaire de la fondation de l'université, juin MCMXXXVII. Lausanne: F. Rouge & cie s. a. [1937] 269 p. incl. diagrs., tables. illus. (incl. charts.) 24cm.

CONTENTS.—Dumas, Gustave. La probabilité élémentaire et le paradoxe de Bertrand.—Mercier, Robert. L'ingénieur et les nouvelles mécaniques.—Perrier, Albert, and H. Favez. Installations nouvelles pour l'étude des propriétés physiques des solides sous contraintes mécaniques intenses.—Bolle, L. Quelques remarques au sujet du rôle de l'effort tranchant en résistance des matériaux.—Dumas, Antoine. Sur le régime des contraintes d'un organe de machine d'un type spécial (bâche de turbine spirale).—Hübner, F. Répartition des surcharges par les tabliers des ponts.—Paris, A. Efforts

(Continued)

N. Y. P. L. September 16, 1938

Lausanne, Switzerland. **Université.** École d'ingénieurs. ...
Recueil de travaux... (Card 2)

de solidarisation au contour des voiles formant fond, parois et couverture des réservoirs sur plan circulaire.—Bolomey, J. Contrôle des qualités des ciments.—Ansermet, A. De l'évolution des méthodes en aérotopographie.—Colombi, Charles. Notes relatives aux prises de vapeur pour préchauffage de l'eau d'alimentation d'une chaudière.—Oguey, Pierre. Le calcul du rendement de la roue dans la turbine Pelton.—Juillard, E. Étude des courants induits par un champ tournant dans un tube de cuivre.—Dutoit, Paul. Fabrication du ferro-phosphore au four électrique.—Goldstein, Henri. Contributions à l'étude des acides naphtoïques halogénés.—Fath, A. L'industrie et la préparation de l'ingénieur-chimiste à l'École d'ingénieurs de Lausanne.

958488A. 1. Engineering—Addresses, essays, lectures.
I. Title.
N. Y. P. L. September 16, 1938

GDD

Lausanne, Switzerland. **Université.** Lettres, Faculté des.
...Mélanges d'histoire et de littérature offerts à Monsieur Charles Gilliard, professeur honoraire de l'Université de Lausanne à l'occasion de son soixante-cinquième anniversaire. Lausanne, F. Rouge & cie, 1944. xxxii, 717 p. illus., maps. 26cm. (Université de Lausanne. Publications de la Faculté des lettres)

"Bibliographie des travaux de M. Charles Gilliard," p. xxi-xxxii. Also other bibliographies.

500526B. 1. Gilliard, Charles, 1879- . 2. Switzerland—Hist., Local.
3. History—Addresses, essays, lectures. I. Title.
N. Y. P. L. July 26, 1950

NKW

Lausanne, Switzerland. **Université.** Lettres, Faculté des.
...Recueil de travaux publiés à l'occasion du quatrième centenaire de la fondation de l'université. Lausanne: F. Rouge & cie s. a., 1937. 230 p. chart, plates. 24cm.

CONTENTS.—Reymond, A. De la méthode dans la recherche métaphysique.—Bonnard, A. Victor Bérard et les Cyclopes.—Olivier, F. À propos d'Aulus Hirtius et de sa lettre-préface.—Bray, R. Des genres littéraires, de leur hiérarchie.—Aebischer, P. Le théâtre dans le pays de Vaud à la fin du moyen âge.—Bohnenblust, G. Lob der Waadt in deutscher Dichtung.—Arcari, P. La dialettica del ricordo.—Bonnard, G. A. Note on the English translations of Crousaz' two books on Pope's "Essay on man."—Bovy, A. Corot et Théodore Rousseau devant les paysages du Léman.—Biermann, C. La maison du vigneron vaudois.—Miéville, H. L. Note sur l'unité de la raison.

941760A. 1. No subject. I. Title.
N. Y. P. L. July 5, 1938

OAI

Lausanne, Switzerland. **Université.** Sciences, Faculté des.
...Recueil de travaux publiés à l'occasion du quatrième centenaire de la fondation de l'université, juin MCMXXXVII. Lausanne: F. Rouge & cie. s. a. [1937] 223 p. incl. diagrs., tables. illus. (incl. charts.) 24cm.

Bibliographies included.
CONTENTS.—Dumas, Gustave. Maxima, minima, indicatrice.—Marchand, Jules. Géométrie du quadrilatère complet.—Goldstein, Henri. Oximation de quelques dérivés de la β-naphtoquinone.—Duboux, Marcel. La catalyse par les acides en rapport avec la concentration et l'activité des ions hydrogène.—Strzyzowski, Casimir. L'intoxication

(Continued)

N. Y. P. L. June 21, 1938

Lausanne, Switzerland. **Université.** Sciences, Faculté des.
...Recueil de travaux... (Card 2)

par le permanganate de potassium et son traitement.—Lugeon, Maurice, and E. Gagnebin. La géologie des collines de Chiètres.—Gagnebin, Élie. Les invasions glaciaires dans le bassin du Léman.—Déverin, Louis. Recherches cristallographiques sur les composés à formule symétrique dérivés du benzène par substitution triple ou sextuple.—Oulianoff, Nicolas. Superposition des tectoniques successives.—Maillefer, Arthur. Recherches en cours au Laboratoire de botanique systématique.—Cosandey, Florian. Recherches en cours au Laboratoire de botanique générale et de génétique.—Matthey, Robert. Aperçu sur l'activité du Laboratoire de zoologie et d'anatomie comparée durant les années 1930–36.

941925A. 1. Science—Essays and misc. I. Title.
N. Y. P. L. June 21, 1938

E-13
9336

LAW and justice; essays in honor of Robert S. Rankin. Edited by Carl Beck. Durham, N.C., Duke university press, 1970. xii,358 p. 24cm.

CONTENTS.--Preface, by C. Beck.--Robert S. Rankin, a biographical sketch, by R.T. Cole and J.H. Hollowell.--State and local government; scholar and participant, by F.M. Riddick.--Searchers seizures,
(Continued)

NN R 8.70 v/LOC,I,II PC,1,2,I,II SL E,1,
I,II (LC1,X1,Z1) 4

LAW and justice; essays in honor of Robert S. Rankin. (Card 2)

and military justice, by S.S. Ulmer.--Religion and the draft; Jehovah's Witnesses revisited, by C.H. Richards, Jr.--Constitutional casuistry; cases of conscience, by F. Canavan.--Patterns of voting on Mallory, Durham and other criminal procedural issues in Congress, by C.N. Stone.--And kids have rights too, by S.R. Gervin.--Equal protection of voting rights; the logic of "one person, one vote," by J.L. Bernd.--From Maxwell to
(Continued)

LAW and justice; essays in honor of Robert S. Rankin. (Card 3)

Duncan, progress of regression? by J.A. Morgan, Jr. --Bills of rights in new state constitutions, by A.L. Sturm.--Equality and social change, by F.D. Dallmayr.--Academic freedom in political context; the North Carolina speaker-ban law, by P.B. Secor. --A Negro candidate for mayor in the urban South, by A.O. Canon.--Some reflections on social change, by L.E. Noble, Jr.--Cigarettes and public policy; the inauguration of a new policy, by C.B. Hagan.--Fundamental
(Continued)

LAW and justice; essays in honor of Robert S. Rankin. (Card 4)

rights in the African Commonwealth, by R.E. Clute. --Civil rights and the Australian constitutional tradition, by E. Campbell.--Civil liberties in the Canadian community, by W.D.K. Kernaghan.--Publications of Robert Stanley Rankin.

1. Law and justice. 2. Law--Addresses, essays, lectures. I.Beck, Carl, 1930- ,ed. II. Rankin, Robert Stanley, 1899- .

D-17
4601

Lawlor, John, *ed.*
Patterns of love and courtesy; essays in memory of C. S. Lewis, edited by John Lawlor. Evanston, Ill., Northwestern University Press, 1966.

206 p. port. 23 cm.

Bibliographical footnotes.

(Continued)

NN*R 7.67 a/ OC PC, 1,2,3 SL (LC1,X1,Z1)

LAWLOR, JOHN, ed. Patterns of love and courtesy ... (Card 2)

CONTENTS.—The granz biens of Marie de France, by J. Stevens.—Dante and the tradition of courtly love, by C. Hardie.—Ideals of friendship, by G. Mathew.—Courtesy and the Gawain-poet, by D. D. Brewer.—Troilus and Criseyde: a reconsideration, by E. Salter.—Gower's 'Honeste love,' by J. A. W. Bennett.—On romanticism in the Confessio amantis, by J. Lawlor.—Love and 'Foul delight': some contrasted attitudes, by N. K. Coghill.—The worshipful way in Malory, by R. T. Davies.—Order, grace, and courtesy in Spenser's world, by P. C. Bayley.

1. Lewis, Clive Staples, 1898-1963. 2. Courtly love. 3. English literature, Middle, 1100-1500—Hist. and crit.

---

* PBN
(Peri)

Lazar, Moshe, 1928- *ed.*
Romanica et occidentalia; études dédiées à la mémoire de Hiram Peri (Pflaum) Jersualem, Magnes Press, Université hébraïque, 1963.

368 p. port. 25 cm.

Added t. p. in Hebrew.
French, Italian, English, German and/or Hebrew.

(Continued)

NN* R X 2,67 g/ OC PC,1, 2,I SL J,2 (LC1,X1,Z1)

LAZAR, MOSHE, 1928- , ed. Romanica et occidentalia... (Card 2)

"Bibliographie des écrits de Hiram Peri (Pflaum)": p. 17-22.
Bibliographical footnotes.

1. Literature—Addresses, essays, lectures. 2. Peri, Hiram, 1900-1962. I. Title.

E-11
4115

LAZAROWICZ, KLAUS, ed.
Unterscheidung und Bewahrung; Festschrift für Hermann Kunisch zum 60. Geburtstag 27. Oktober 1961. [Hrsg. von Klaus Lazarowicz und Wolfgang Kron] Berlin, Walter de Gruyter, 1961. viii, 397 p. port. 25cm.

Contributions by various authors.
Bibliographical footnotes.

1. Kunisch, Hermann, 1901- 2. German literature--Addresses, essays, lectures. I. Kron, Wolfgang, joint ed.

NN R 2.62 a/OC, I PC, 1, 2, I SL (LC1, X1, Z1)

E-11
4564

Ein LEBEN aus freier Mitte: Beiträge zur Geschichtsforschung. Festschrift für Prof. Dr. Ulrich Noack von seinen Kollegen, Schülern und Freunden zum 60. Geburtstag gewidmet. Göttingen, Musterschmidt-Verlag [1961] xxxii, 440 p. port. 25cm.

CONTENTS.—Ulrich Noack—ein Leben aus freier Mitte, von H. Euler.—Der einzelne vor Gott, von M. Mezger.—Das Lutherbild im

(Continued)

NN R 7.62 g/ OC PC, 1, 2 SL (LC1, X1, Z1) [I]

Ein LEBEN aus freier Mitte... (Card 2)

Wandel der Zeit, von M. Seidlmayer.—Bildungsreise und erste Heirat des Freiherrn Karl August von Hardenberg, von H. Haussherr.—Die elsässische Frage und das deutsch-französische Verhältnis im 19. Jahrhundert, von R. Buchner.—Die Anfänge des Bonapartismus in Frankreich (1815-1830), von H. Euler.—Lamartine und Deutschland—eine Episode, von H. Rheinfelder.—Die sozialpolitischen Bestrebungen des Reichsfreiherrn Friedrich Carl von Fechenbach in Franken, von H.-J. Schoeps.—Bismarcks Begegnungen mit Wilhelm II. nach seiner Entlassung, von H.J. Zeumer.—Skizzen aus Dalama, von H. Kellenbenz.

(Continued)

Ein LEBEN aus freier Mitte... (Card 3)

—Neusiedlung und institutionelles Erbe—zum Problem von Turners "frontier", eine vergleichende Geschichtsbetrachtung, von D. Gerhard.—Die politische Entwicklung des deutschen Studententums (1924-1931), von W. Zorn.—War Hitler geisteskrank? Von G. Schaltenbrand.—"Der Volksgenosse muss erfasst, ausgerichtet, gleichgeschaltet und eingesetzt werden"—ein sprachpsychologischer Versuch, von F. Rauhut.—Die Weltkriege als Folge der ungelösten sozialen Frage, von F. Wilken.—Elitebildung gestern und heute. Charisma, Dienst, Leistung, von K. Bosl.—Vom Sinn der Geschichte, von A. Wenzl.—Musik und Sprache—ein

(Continued)

Ein LEBEN aus freier Mitte... (Card 4)

Beitrag zum Problem der Epochengliederung in der Musikgeschichte, von H. Beck.—Die endzeitliche Botschaft Reinhold Schneiders, von E. Dörr.—Geschichte als Erziehungsmacht, von A. Dünisch.

1. Noack, Ulrich, 1899- . 2. History--Addresses, essays, lectures.

D-18
6931

Lebende Antike. Symposion für Rudolf Sühnel. Hrsg. von Horst Meller und Hans-Joachim Zimmermann. (Berlin) E. Schmidt (1967).

568 p. with illus., front. 28 cm.

German or English.
Includes bibliographies.

(Continued)

NN 2. 69 e/ OC, I, II, III, IVb*, Vb* PC, 1, 2, I, II, III SL (LC1, X1) (Z1)

LEBENDE Antike. (Card 2)

1. English literature--Addresses, essays, lectures. 2. Classicism. I. Meller, Horst, ed. II. Zimmermann, Hans-Joachim, ed. III. Sühnel, Rudolf. IV. Meller, Horst. V. Zimmermann, Hans-Joachim.

L-10
1428
v.4

LEBENDIGER Geist; Hans-Joachim Schoeps zum 50. Geburtstag von Schülern dargebracht, hrsg. von Hellmut Diwald. Leiden, E.J. Brill, 1959. 252 p. port. 25cm. (Zeitschrift für Religions- und Geistesgeschichte. Beihefte. 4)

Bibliographical footnotes.
CONTENTS.--'Herakles Charops', von C.M. Bruehl.--Σympolologia.

(Continued)
NN X 12.59 t/ OC, II (OS)I PC, I, I, II (LC1, X1, Z1)

LEBENDIGER Geist... (Card 2)

Briefe von Paul de Lagarde an Adolf Hilgenfeld aus den Jahren 1862-1887, von H.M. Pölcher.--Die gegenwärtige Täuferforschung.--Forschritt oder Dilemma? Von H. Hillerbrand.--Das verständnis der Geistesgeschichte in der zeitgenossischen evangelischen Theologie, von G.H. Huntemann.--Aimé Pallière--das Leben eines Noachiden, von M. Schwarze.--Nordmann.--Bernard Bolzano und der Bohemismus, von H. Diwald.--Das jüdisch-christliche Arbeitsethos und der Wandel der Einstellung zur Arbeit im 19. und 20. Jahrhundert, von D.A. Oberndörfer.--Geschichte als Gedanke und Tat? Von H. Speckner.-- 'Das Gewissen', von H.-J. Schwierskott.--Politische Vorstellungen und Versuche der
(Continued)

LEBENDIGER Geist... (Card 3)

'Deutschen Freischar', von H. Siefert.--Der autoritäre Staat, von J.H. Knoll.--Bemerkungen zur Entwicklung und Wandlung des deutsch-jüdischen Lebensgefühls, von H. Lamm.--'Le style c'est l'homme', von H. Fiebiger.--Bibliographie der wissenschaftlichen Publikationen von Hans-Joachim Schoeps bis 1958 (p.[243]-252).

1. Schopes, Hans Joachim, 1909- . I. Series. II. Diwald, Hellmut, ed.

BAC

Lebenskräfte in der abendländischen Geistesgeschichte. Dank- und Erinnerungsgabe an Walter Goetz zum 80. Geburtstage am 11. November 1947, dargebracht von Bernhard Bischoff...[und anderen] Marburg/Lahn, Simons-Verlag, 1948. 358 p. maps. 24cm.

"Herausgeber: Professor Dr. Wolfgang Stammler..."
Bibliographical footnotes.

507542B. 1. Goetz, Walter Wilhelm, 1867- . 2. Church history--Early and primitive church, to 325.
NN*
(Continued)

Lebenskräfte in der abendländischen Geistesgeschichte. (Card 2)

3. Johannes, of Mantua, fl. 1081. 4. Bible. O. T. Song of Solomon--Commentaries. 5. Cities--Plans--Germany--Bavaria. 6. Villani, Giovanni, d. 1348. 7. Physiognomy. 8. Slogans, German. 9. Gagern, Hans Christoph Ernst, Freiherr von, 1766-1852. 10. Germans in Palestine. 11. Stifter, Adalbert, 1805-1868. I. Stammler, Wolfgang, 1886- ed.
NN*

D-13
1545

Leclerc, Ivor, *ed.*
The relevance of Whitehead; philosophical essays in commemoration of the centenary of the birth of Alfred North Whitehead. London, Allen & Unwin; New York, Macmillan [1961]

383 p. 23 cm. (The Muirhead library of philosophy)

Bibliographical footnotes.

CONTENTS.—Whitehead and contemporary philosophy, by C. Hartshorne.—Some uses of reason, by W. A. Christian.—Sketch of a philosophy, by F. B. Fitch.—Metaphysics and the modality of existential judgments, by C. Hartshorne.—Whitehead on the uses of language,

(Continued)
NN * R 8.61 a/ OC PC, 1, 2 SL (LC1, X1, Z1) 2

LECLERC, IVOR, ed. The relevance of Whitehead... (Card 2)

by A. H. Johnson.—Time, value, and the self, by N. Lawrence.—Form and actuality, by I. Leclerc.—The approach to metaphysics, by V. Lowe.--Metaphysics as Scientia universalis and as Ontologia generalis, by G. Martin.—The relevance of "On mathematical concepts of the material world" to Whitehead's philosophy, by W. Mays.—Aesthetic perception, by E. Schaper.—In defence of the humanism of science: Kant and Whitehead, by H. Wein.—History and objective immortality, by P. Weiss.—Whitehead's empiricism, by W. P. D. Wightman.—Deity, monarchy, and metaphysics: Whitehead's critique of the theological tradition, by D. D. Williams.

1. Whitehead, Alfred North, 1861-1947. 2. Philosophy--Addresses, essays, lectures.

IC

Lee, Dwight Erwin, 1898- *ed.*
Essays in history and international relations, in honor of George Hubbard Blakeslee; ed. by Dwight E. Lee and George E. McReynolds. Worcester, Mass., Clark Univ., 1949.

xi, 324 p. port. 24 cm.
Bibliographical footnotes.
CONTENTS.—The shifting strategy of American defense and diplomacy, by S. F. Bemis.—The United States, paramount power of the Pacific, by R. H. Fifield.—The United States and Greece: the Truman doctrine in historical perspective, by L. S. Stavrianos.—Canada's Department of External Affairs, by H. L. Keenleyside.—Canada, the United States and Latin America, by E. H. Miller.—Sovereignty and imperialism in the polar regions, by Elmer Plischke.—United States

(Continued on next card)
49-4447*
[15]

Lee, Dwight Erwin, 1898- *ed.* Essays in history and international relations ... 1949. (Card 2)

CONTENTS—Continued.
immigration policy, 1882-1948, by J. P. Shalloo.—The two Paris Peace Conferences of the twentieth century, by F. L. Benns.—The Supreme Allied Command in Northern Europe, 1944-1945, by F. C. Pogue.—Influence of pro-Fascist propaganda on American neutrality, 1935-1936, by John Norman.—The nonapplication of sanctions against Japan, 1931-1932, by E. R. Perkins.—The United States and Chinese territorial integrity, 1908, by J. A. Miller.—England and the United States, 1897-1899, by N. M. Blake.—The Civil War blockade reconsidered, by E. B. Coddington.—The fall of protection in Britain, by A. H. Imlah.—Appendix: Bibliography of the works of George Hubbard Blakeslee, by Marion Henderson (p. [321]-324)
1. Blakeslee, George Hubbard, 1871- 2. U. S.—For. rel.—20th cent. 3. World politics. I. McReynolds, George E., joint ed.

E744.B58 327.73 49-4447*
Library of Congress [15]

F-11
1613

LEE, GEORGE WASHINGTON, 1894-
Confessions of an Esperantist. [Boston, 1926] p. [482]-487. 25cm.

Detached from: Stone and Webster public service journal, v. 39, no. 4, October, 1926.

MRS. DAVE H. MORRIS COLLECTION

1. Esperanto.
NN 7.66 p/ OC PC, 1 SL (LC1, X1, Z1)

*PBM p.v.607

LEIPZIG. ISRAELITISCHE RELIGIONSGEMEINDE.
Aus Geschichte und Leben der Juden in Leipzig; Festschrift zum 75 jährigen Bestehen der Leipziger Gemeindesynagoge, 1855-1930. Leipzig [1930] 88 p. illus., ports. 23cm.

Bibliographical footnotes.
CONTENTS.--Frühzeit und Übergang von G. Cohn.--Juden als Messgäste in Leipzig von M. Freudenthal.--Die Entstehung der israelitischen Religionsgemeinde von J. Jacobson.--Die Entwicklung der gottesdienstlichen
(Continued)
NN••R 8.57 1/J OS PC, 1, 3 SL J, 2, 3 (LC1, X1, Z1)

VDY

LEES, SIGNEY, ed.
Air, space and instruments; a collection of original contributions written in commemoration of the sixtieth birthday of Charles Stark Draper. New York, McGraw-Hill book co. [c1963] xi, 516 p. illus., port. 24cm.

"Draper anniversary volume."
Includes bibliographies.
1. Aeronautics--Instruments. 2. Astronautics--Instruments and apparatus. 3. Draper, Charles Stark. t. 1963
NN * R 11.64 a/B OC PC, 1, 2, 3 SL ST, 1t, 2t, 3 (LC1, X1, Z1)

LEIPZIG. ISRAELITISCHE RELIGIONSGEMEINDE. Aus Geschichte und Leben der Juden in Leipzig... (Card 2)

Verhältnisse bis zur Einweihung der Synagoge von G. Cohn.--Der Tempelbau von W. Haller.--Zahlen von G. Katzenstein.--Der Weg von G. C.--Der Charakter der Leipziger Gemeinde von F. Goldmann.--Wohlfahrtswesen und Vereine der Leipziger Gemeinde von F. Goldmann.

1. JEWS IN GERMANY--LEIPZIG 2. LEIPZIG
3. LEIPZIG--SYNAGOGUES--GEMEINDESYNAGOGE

XAS

LEGAL essays in honour of Arthur Moxon; edited by J. A. Corry, F. C. Cronkite & E. F. Whitmore. [Toronto] Published in co-operation with the University of Saskatchewan [by] University of Toronto press, 1953. xi, 262 p. port. 24cm.

Bibliographical footnotes.
CONTENTS. --Introduction, by F. C. Cronkite. --The retrospective operation of statutes, by E. A. Driedger. --Burland v. Earle; the liability of a vendor, by F. A. Sheppard. --The jurisdiction of the Canadian parliament in matters of labour legislation, by G. R. Schmitt. --Judicial control of union discipline: the Kuzych case, by E. F. Whitmore.
(Continued)
NN * * R 2.54 OC, 1bo, I, II, IIb, III, IIIb PC, 1, 2, I, II, III SL (LC1, Z1, X1)

*GY
+

Leipzig. Stadtbibliothek.
Die Bibliothek und ihre Kleinodien. Festschrift zum 250 jährigen Jubiläum der Leipziger Stadtbibliothek; herausgegeben von Johannes Hofmann. Leipzig: K. W. Hiersemann, 1927. 112 p. facsims, illus., plates, tables. sq. f°.

On cover: 1677-1927.
Partial contents: Hofmann, J. Die Leipziger Stadtbibliothek 1677-1927. Rath, E. von. Die Kupferstichillustration im Wiegendruckzeitalter. Leskien, E. Johann Gottlob Böhme. Glauning, O. Ein Beitrag zur Kenntnis der Einbände Johann Richenbachs.

340428A. 1. Libraries—Germany—Leipzig. 2. Hofmann, Johannes, 1888- , editor.
N. Y. P. L. August 31, 1928

LEGAL essays in honour of Arthur Moxon; edited by J. A. Corry. (Card 2)

--Law and labour relations, by H. J. Clawson. --Statutory powers, by J. A. Corry. --Sections 91 and 92 of the British North America act and Privy council, by W. R. Jackett. --Classification of laws and the British North America act, by W. R. Lederman. --The Crown and Res judicata, by D. W. Mundell.--Isolation, intention, and income, by G. F. Curtis.

1. Law--Canada. 2. Moxon, Arthur. I. Corry, James Alexander, 1899- , ed. II. Cronkite, F. C., ed. III. Whitmore, E. F., ed.

L-10
1788
Nr. 1

LEIPZIG. Universität. Institut für Vor- und Frühgeschichte.
Leipziger Beiträge zur Vor- und Frühgeschichte; Festschrift zum 70. Geburtstag von Friedrich Behn. Leipzig, J. A. Barth, 1955. vi, 167 p. illus., port., maps. 24cm. (Forschungen zur Vor- und Frühgeschichte. Nr. 1)

Bibliographical footnotes.
(Continued)
NN X 10.59 t/ (OC)I OS OI PC, 1, 2, I (LC1, X1, Z1)

*MEC
(Kahn)

LEIBOWITZ, RENÉ, 1913-
Erich Itor Kahn, un grand représentant de la musique contemporaine [par] René Leibowitz et Konrad Wolff. [Paris] Buchet/Chastel, Corrêa [c1958] 182 p. port., facsims., music. 23cm.

"Les écrits [de Kahn]" p. [83]-140.

1. Kahn, Erich Itor, 1905- . I. Wolff, Konrad, joint author.
NN * 4.64 f/J OC, I PC, 1, I SL MU, 1, I (LC1, X1, Z1)

LEIPZIG. Universität. Institut für Vor- und Frühgeschichte. Leipziger Beiträge zur Vor- und Frühgeschichte... (Card 2)

CONTENTS. --Prähistorische Belege für eine spätpleistozäne Besiedlung Nordamerikas, von R. Weinhold. --Die steinzeitlichen Funde im Heimatmuseum Rochlitz, von H. Hanitzsch. --Ein Verwahrfund aus der bandkeramischen Siedlung in der Harth bei Zwenkau, von Hans Quitta. --Das Hockergrab von Elstertrebnitz-Trautzschen, von R. Moschkau. --Sechs Gräber der jüngsten Bronzezeit aus Markkleeberg-Ost, Kreis Leipzig, von L. Langhammer. --Neue Funde von der Burker Höhe bei Bautzen,
(Continued)

LEIPZIG. Universität. Institut für Vor- und Frühgeschichte. Leipziger Beiträge zur Vor- und Frühgeschichte... (Card 3)

von J. Schneider.--Ein Brandgrab der frühen Eisenzeit von Dölzig, Kreis Leipzig, von H. Grünert.--Ein eisenzeitliches Gräberfeld aus der Altmark, von E. Hoffmann.--Die frühromischen Fibeln in Mecklenburg, von H. Schubart.--Eine thüringische Siedlung von Naumburg (Saale), von G. Mildenberger.--Mittelalterliche Sicheln aus Leipzig, von Hildegard Quitta.--Rekonstruktion einer spätgotischen Ofenkachel mit dem Leipziger Stadtwappen, von H. Küas.--Vorgeschichtliche und moderne Kunst, von H. Menz.

(Continued)

LEIPZIG. Universität. Institut für Vor- und Frühgeschichte. Leipziger Beiträge zur Vor- und Frühgeschichte... (Card 4)

1. Behn, Friedrich, 1883- . 2. Archaeology--Addresses, essays, lectures. I. Title.

Write on slip words underlined and class mark- XAA

Leipzig. Universität. *Juristen Fakultät.*

... Festschrift der Leipziger juristenfakultät für dr. Richard Schmidt zum 1. november 1934. Leipzig, T. Weicher, 1936.

v p., 1 l., 246 p. 25cm. (Leipziger rechtswissenschaftliche studien, hrsg. von der Leipziger juristen-fakultät. hft. 91)

CONTENTS.—Richter. Zum aufbau der sozialversicherung.—Schaffstein. Zum problematik des teleologischen begriffsbildung im strafrecht.—Oeschey. Über gewerbefreiheit in der gesetzgebung des dritten reichs.—Weider. Die beendigung der einmanngesellschaft in erleichterter form.—Busch. Betrug durch verschweigen.—Kühn. Der führergedanke in der neuen arbeitsverfassung—zugleich ein beitrag zu den rechtsformen der führerverfassung im allgemeinen.—Stock. Zur strafprozesserneuerung.—Langer. Der diktatfrieden.

1. Schmidt, Richard Karl Bernhard, 1862- 2. Law—Addresses, essays, lectures. I. Richter, Lutz, 1891- II. Title.

40-5451

Library of Congress [2]

Write on slip only words underlined and classmark: XAA

Leipzig. Universität. Juristische Fakultät.

...Festschrift der Leipziger Juristenfakultät für Dr. Heinrich Siber zum 10. April 1940. Bd. 2. Leipzig, T. Weicher, 1943. 1 v. 25cm. (Leipziger rechtswissenschaftliche Studien. Heft 124 [Teil 2])

Bibliographical footnotes.

CONTENTS.—Bd. 2. Haupt, G. Über faktische Vertragsverhältnisse.—deBoor, H. O. Zur Lehre vom Parteiwechsel und vom Parteibegriff.—Michaelis, K. Beiträge zur Gliederung und Weiterbildung des Schadensrechts.

1. Siber, Heinrich, 1870- . 2. Contracts—Jurisp.—Germany. 3. Procedure (Law)—Germany. 4. Damages—Jurisp.—Germany. I. Ser. II. Title.

NN R 3.53 (OC)II OS PC, 1, 2, 3, 4 E, 1, 2, 3, 4 (LC1, Z1, X1)

MA

Leipzig. Universität. *Kunsthistorisches Institut.*

Festschrift Johannes Jahn zum XXII. November MCMLVII. Leipzig, E. A. Seemann [1958]

438 p. illus. 32 cm.

"Johannes Jahn; Schriftenverzeichnis in sachlicher Folge," p. 343-349.

Includes bibliographical references.

1. Art--Essays and misc. 2. Jahn, Johannes, 1892- . 3. Jahn, Johannes, 1892- --Bibl.

NN * R 11.59 m/// OS PC, 1, 2 SL A, 1, 2, 3 (LC1, X1, Z1) [I]

RAE

Leipzig. Universität. Vereinigte sprachwissenschaftliche institute.

Streitberg festgabe, herausgegeben von der direktion der Vereinigten sprachwissenschaftlichen institute an der universität zu Leipzig. Leipzig, Markert & Petters verlag, 1924.

xv, 441 p. front. (port.) 2 double maps, double facsim. 24½cm.

"Tabulagratulatoria": p. [ix]–xiii.

CONTENTS.—Belić, A. Zur slavischen aktionsart.—Bloomfield, M. On vedic Agni Kravyavāhana and Agni Kavyavāhana.—Blümel, R. Grundbedingungen der quantitierenden und der akzentuirerenden dichtung.—Bremer, O. Vier und acht.—Buga, K. Die vorgeschichte der aistischen (baltischen) stämme im lichte der ortsnamenforschung.—Deutschbein, M. Das resultativum im neuenglischen.—Endzelin, J. Baltische beiträge.—

(Continued on next card)

A 33–2888

[a2]

Leipzig. Universität. Vereinigte sprachwissenschaftliche institute. Streitberg festgabe ... 1924. (Card 2)

CONTENTS—Continued.

Fischer, A. Ausdrücke per merismum im arabischen.—Förster, M. Ablaut in flussnamen.—Fraenkel, E. Zur griechischen, baltoslavischen und albanesischen grammatik und wortkunde.—Fraser, J. Λυχάβας.—Gerullis, G. Zur beurteilung des altpreussischen enchiridions.—Gombocz, Z. Ossetenspuren in ungarn.—Grammont, M. L'interversion.—Hatzidakis, G. Ἰυτοῖ.—Γιούχτας.—Heinze, R. Zum gebrauch des praesens historicum im Altlatein.—Hermann, E. Lateinisch *mi fili*.—Hertel, J. Sivadāsas vetālapañcavimśatikā.—Holthausen, F. Etymologische forschungen.—Jacobi, H. Über Visnu-Nārāyana Vāsudeva.—Jacobsohn, H Zum vokalismus der germanischen und litauischen lehnwörter im Ostseefinnischen.—Jokl, N. Thrakisches.—Keller, G. S.

(Continued on next card)

A 33–2888

[2]

Leipzig. Universität. Vereinigte sprachwissenschaftliche institute. Streitberg festgabe ... 1924. (Card 3)

CONTENTS—Continued.

Über ellipse im Ukrainischen.—Kettunen, L. Geschichtliches und phonetisches über die auslautenden konsonanten im Finnischen.—Kieckers, E. Zur 3. sing. ind. praes. pass. im Altirischen.—Krause, Ch. Eine neue Pañcatantra-Mischrezension in Alt-Gujarātī.—Lagercrantz, O. Die drei dorischen phylennamen.—Lidén, E. Griechische worterklärungen.—Liebich, B. Lateinisch campus als lehnwort im Indischen?—Maurenbrecher, B. Die lateinische ellipse, satzbegriff und satzformen.—Meillet, A. A propos du groupe lituanien de *beriù*.—Melich, J. Über den ungarischen flussnamen *Tisza* "Teiss".—Mikkola, J. Die verschärfung der intervokalischen *j* und *w* im Gotischen und Nordischen.—Mladenov, St. Zu den slavischen *nd*-Sätzen.—Mogk, E. Der machtbegriff im

(Continued on next card)

A 33–2888

[2]

Leipzig. Universität. Vereinigte sprachwissenschaftliche institute. Streitberg festgabe ... 1924. (Card 4)

CONTENTS—Continued.

altnordischen.—Olsen, M. Der runenstein von Varnum (Järsberg).—Pokorny, J. Etymologische miszellen.—Reichelt, H. Die indoiranischen benennungen des salzes.—Saran, Fr. Die quantitätsregeln der griechen und römer.—Schmid, H. F. Zur geschichte der bedeutungsentwicklung westslavischer lehnwörter für institutionen der lateinisch-germanischen kultur.—Schrijnen, Jos. "Silva lupus in Sabina."—Schröder, Fr. R. Deutsch *eren*.—Schwyzer, E. Ein indogermanischer rest im schweizerdeutschen wortschatz.—Thurneysen, R. Der akkusativ pluralis der geschlechtlichen *n*-stämme.—Trautmann, R. Über die sprachliche stellung der Schalwen.—Trubetzkoy, N. Zum urslavischen intonationssystem.—Vasmer, M. Iranisches aus Südrussland.—

(Continued on next card)

A 33–2888

[2]

Leipzig. Universität. Vereinigte sprachwissenschaftliche institute. Streitberg festgabe ... 1924. (Card 5)

CONTENTS—Continued.

Weissbach, F. H. Altpersische aufgaben.—Wengler, H. Noterellina dantesca. Zur inversion der objekts-pronomina in der Danteschen prosa.—Weyhe, H. Ae. *ēawis* "offenbar".—Wiget, W. Die endung der weiblichen germanischen lehnwörter im Finnischen.—Wijk, N. Van. Die grossrussische pronominale genitivendung-*vo*.—Wiklund, K. B. Zur frage vom germ. ē' in den lehnwörtern im Finnischen und Lappischen.—Zimmern, H. Der kampf des wettergottes mit der schlange Illujankas. Ein hettitischer mythus.

1. Germanic languages—Grammar. 2. Germanic languages—Grammar, Comparative. I. Streitberg, Wilhelm August, 1864–1925. II. Title.

A 33–2888

Title from Univ. of Virginia. Printed by L. C.

[2]

TB p.v. 1935

LEIPZIGER OKONOMISCHE SOZIETAT.
...Festschrift zum 150 jährigen Bestehen der Ökonomischen Sozietät zu Leipzig und der Ökonomischen Gesellschaft im Königreiche Sachsen zu Dresden. Leipzig, A. Edelmann [1914] 108 p.

At head of title: 1764-1914.
Bibliography, p. 104-105.

1. Economics—Assoc. and org.—Germany—Leipzig. 2. Economics—Assoc. and org.—Germany—Dresden. I. Oekonomische Gesellschaft in Sachsen, Dresden.
NN 3.53 OS, I PC, 1, 2, I SL E, 1, 2, I (LC1, Z1, X1)

NFD (Mann)

Lemke, Karl, 1895–
Heinrich Mann, zu seinem 75. Geburtstag. Berlin, Aufbau-Verlag, 1946.
71, [1] p. port. 20 cm.
"Das Werk Heinrich Manns (bis 1939)": p. [72]

1. Mann, Heinrich, 1871–
PT2625.A43Z7 830.81 A F 48-1662*
Yale Univ. Library for Library of Congress [1]†

L-10
1952
Nr. 5

LEIPZIGER Studien; Theodor Frings zum 70. Geburtstag. Halle (Saale), M. Niemeyer, 1957. 257 p. 24cm. (Deutsch-slawische Forschungen zur Namenkunde und Siedlungsgeschichte. Nr. 5)

Includes bibliographies.
CONTENTS.—Archäologisches zur slawischen Landnahme in Mitteldeutschland, von G. Mildenberger.—Namenkundliches und
(Continued)
NN R X 9.58 g/P OC (OS)I PC, 1, 2, I S, 1, 2, I (LC1, X1, Z1)

VOD

Leo Ubbelohde, sein bisheriges Lebenswerk; dargestellt und hrsg. von Schülern, Kollegen und Freunden. [Karlsruhe, 1952?] viii, 156 p. illus., ports., 22cm.

Includes bibliographies.

1. Chemical technology. 2. Ubbelohde, Leo, 1877- 3. Chemical technology, 1951.

NN**R X/8.53 OC PC, 1, 2 SL ST, 2, 3 (LC1, Z1, X1)

LEIPZIGER Studien... (Card 2)

Sprachgeschichtliches zum Hassegau, von M. Bathe.—Namenforschung und Sprachgeschichte im Meissnischen, von R. Grosse.—Orts- und Flurnamen des Rochlizter Landes in namengeographischer Sicht, von H. Walther.—Zu einigen slawischen Flussnamen des Saale- und Muldesystems, von E. Eichler.—Deutsche und slawische Siedlungen an der oberen Ilm im frühen Mittelalter, von K. Elbracht.—Zur Flurnamenforschung in den deutsch-sorbischen Gebieten der Oberlausitz, von L. Hoffmann.—Namen der Flurstücke hinter den Höfen in den sorbischen Dörfern des Kreises Kamenz, von W. Sperber.—Sorbische
(Continued)

NFD (Weismantel)

Leo Weismantel; Leben und Werk. Ein Buch des Dankes zu des Dichters 60. Geburtstag. Berlin, A. Nauck & Co., 1948. 238 p. 21cm.

"Verzeichnis der Schriften und Aufsätze Leo Weismantels," p. 229-238.

513696B. 1. Weismantel, Leo, 1888–
N. Y. P. L. Festschrift May 19, 1950

LEIPZIGER Studien... (Card 3)

Personennamen in der Niederlausitz aus der zweiten Hälfte des 17. Jhs., von F. Redlich.—Der Bergname Kotine, von J. Jejkal.—Die Ausdehnung des Gaues Chutici und seine spätere Entwicklung, von E. Müller.—Beiträge zur Auswertung des Hersfelder Zehntverzeichnisses, von S. A. Wolf.—Theodor Frings und die Namenforschung, von H. Protze.—Germanistische und slawistische Publikationen zur Namenforschung in der DDR, zusammengestellt von E. Eichler.
1. Geography--Names--Germany. 2. Frings, Theodor, 1886- I. Series.

NKC (Bloy)

... Léon Bloy. Ed. du centenaire augm. de textes inédits ... Neuchâtel, Éditions de la Baconnière, 1946.

222 p. incl. front. (port.) facsim. 19½ᶜᵐ. (Les Cahiers du Rhône. [Sér. bleue] 11)

First published in 1944 under title: Léon Bloy pour le vingt-sixième anniversaire de sa mort.
"La réimpression de ce Cahier pour le centenaire de Léon Bloy ajoute au texte primitif des lettres et fragments inédits ... et une étude de Stanislas Fumet."—p. 10.

CONTENTS.—Fumet, Stanislas. Les cent ans de Léon Bloy.—Termier, Pierre. A la table de Léon Bloy.—Maritain, Jacques. Le mendiant ingrat.—Cattaui, Georges. Bloy, témoin des promesses.—Emmanuel, Pierre. L'annonciateur du corps mystique.—Béguin, Albert. La pau-

(Continued on next card)
A 47-3042
[3]†

MAVZ (Leirvik)

LEIRVIK, Norway. Sunnhordland folkemuseum og sogelag.
Festskrift til Kristofer Sydnes på 80 årsdagen 6. august 1961. [Leirvik, 1961] 39 p. illus., ports., map. 25cm. (ITS: Sunnhordlands arv. 1)

1. Sydnes, Kristofer, 1881- . 2. Museums, Open air--Norway--Leirvik. 3. Folk art, Norwegian--Sunnhordland. 4. Architecture, Danish--Sunnhordland. I. Sunnhordlands arv. II. Leirvik, Norway. Sunnhordland folkemuseum og sogelag. Sunnhordlands arv.
NN 6.65 e/ (OC)1b+ OS(1b)I, II PC, 1, 2, 3, 4 SL A, 2, 3, 4 (LC1, X1, Z1) [SID, NSCM]

... Léon Bloy ... 1946. (Card 2)

CONTENTS—Continued.

vreté et l'argent.—Bollery, Joseph. Léon Bloy, avocat de la douleur.—Lobet, Marcel. Léon Bloy et la violence nécessaire.—Rouzet, Georges. Bloyiana.—Colleye, Hubert. La femme de Léon Bloy.—Maritain, Raïssa. Souvenirs.—Rouault, Georges. Lettre.—Boussac-Termier, Jeanne. Leçons de Léon Bloy.—Textes: Textes inédits. Lettres de jeunesse. Christophe Colomb. La femme pauvre. Méditations d'un solitaire. Dans les ténèbres. Le secret de la Salette.

1. Bloy, Léon, 1846-1917. I. Bloy, Léon, 1846-1917.
PQ2198.B18Z7 A 47-3042
Rochester. Univ. Library for Library of Congress [3]†

YBX
(Coimbra)

Leonardo Coimbra; testemunhos dos seus contemporâneos. Porto, Livraria Tavares Martins, 1950. 428 p. ports. 25cm.

Bibliography, p. 299–404.

564616B. 1. Coimbra, Leonardo, 1883–1936. 2. Coimbra, Leonardo, 1883–1936—Bibl.
N. Y. P. L. March 12, 1951

AN
(Sonnemann, L.)

Leopold Sonnemann's siebzigste Geburtstagsfeier. Am 29 Oktober 1901 in Frankfurt a.M. Den Theilnehmern zur freundlichen Erinnerung. [Frankfurt a.M.: Druck der Frankfurter Societäts-Druckerei, 1901] 87p. 20 1/2cm.

"Als Manuskript gedruckt nach den Berichten der Frankfurter Zeitung."

1. Sonnemann, Leopold, 1831-1909.
I. Frankfurter Zeitung.

3-MCZ
G39.L6

Lesezirkel Hottingen, Zürich.
Salomon Gessner, 1730–1930; Gedenkbuch zum 200. Geburtstag, hrsg. vom Lesezirkel Hottingen. Mit Unterstützung von Behörden und Literaturfreunden von Gessners Vaterstadt. Zürich, Lesezirkel Hottingen, 1930. 163 p. illus. 26cm.

Bibliography, p. 161–163.

452141B. 1. Gessner, Salomon, 1730–1788.
N. Y. P. L. August 11, 1949

TF

The **Lessons** of monetary experience; essays in honor of Irving Fisher, presented to him on the occasion of his seventieth birthday, by J. W. Angell ... D. B. Copland ... [and others] edited by A. D. Gayer. New York, Farrar & Rinehart, inc. [©1937]

xii, 450 p. front. (port.) diagrs. 21½cm.

CONTENTS.—Foreword, by A. D. Gayer.—**The United States:** Eccles, M. S. Controlling booms and depressions. William, J. H. International monetary organization and policy. Angell, J. W. The general objectives of monetary policy. Hansen, A. H. Monetary policy in the upswing. Rogers, J. H. Monetary initiative in a traditional world.—

(Continued on next card)

38—103

[38m5]

The **Lessons** of monetary experience ... [©1937] (Card 2)

CONTENTS—Continued.

Canada: Noble, S. R. The monetary experience of Canada during the depression.—**England:** Hawtrey, R. G. The credit deadlock. Keynes, J. M. The theory of the rate of interest. Strakosch, Sir Henry. The monetary tangle of the postwar period.—**Denmark:** Pedersen, Jørgen. Monetary policy and economic stability.—**Germany:** Schumacher, H. Germany's present currency system. Bibliography (p. 234–235)—**Holland:** Verrijn Stuart, G. M. The Netherlands during the recent depression.—**Italy:** Einaudi, Luigi. The medieval practice of managed currency.—**Poland:** Mlynarski, Feliks. Proportionalism and stabilization policy.—**Sweden:** Lindahl, Erik. International economic reconstruction realized through rational management of free currencies. Ohlin, Bertil.

(Continued on next card)

38—103

[38t5]

The **Lessons** of monetary experience ... [©1937] (Card 3)

CONTENTS—Continued.

Employment stabilization and price stabilization.—**India:** Shirras, G. F. The absorption of gold: a study in monetary policy.—**China:** Soong, T. V. Lessons of Chinese money policy. Kann, E. The currencies of China: old and new.—**Japan:** Fukai, Eigo. The recent monetary policy of Japan.—**Australia:** Copland, D. B. Australian monetary policy in the depression, 1930–1933. Bibliography (p. 423)—**Geneva:** Loveday, A. Collective behavior and monetary policy.—**Appendix:** Biographical sketch of Irving Fisher. Selected bibliography of the economic writings of Irving Fisher (p. 445–450)

1. Fisher, Irving, 1867– 2. Currency question. 3. Money. 4. Gold. 5. Economics—Addresses, essays, lectures. I. Gayer, Arthur David, 1903– ed. II. Title: Essays in honor of Irving Fisher.

38—103

Library of Congress HG255.L47

——— ~~Copy 2.~~

Copyright A 110684 [38m5] 332.404

D-13
8169

LETMATHE, Germany.
Letmathe, eine aufstrebende westfälische Stadt im Sauerland. Bearbeitung: Stadtdirektor Schossier. [Letmathe, Heimatverlag] 1961. 560 p. illus., ports., coats of arms, geneal. tables. 22cm.

Half title: Festbuch zur Jubiläumsfeier: "925 Jahre Dorf—25 Jahre Stadt Letmathe."
Contributions by various authors.
Includes bibliographical references.

1. Letmathe, Germany--Hist. I. Schossier, H., ed. t. 1961
NN R 8.62 a/B (OC)I, Ibo ODt EDt PC, 1, I SL (LC1, X1, Z1)

MAM
+

Λευκωμα 'Ελληνων καλλιτεχνων. Νικηφορος Λυτρας, 1832–1904. 'Εγραψε Ξενοφων Σωχος... 'Εν 'Αθηναις: Τυπογραφειον παρασκευα Λεωνη, 1929. 132 p. plates, ports. 32cm.

Cover-title: 'Ελληνες καλλιτεχναι. 'Εκατονταετηρις, 1821–1930... 1930.
Printed in double columns.

75890B. 1. Art, Greek, Modern. 2. Lytras, Nikēphoros, 1832–1904. I. Sōchos, Xenophōn, comp.
N. Y. P. L. January 29, 1941

Copy only words underlined
& Classmark-- ZAA

LIBER amicorum; studies in honour of C.J. Bleeker, published on the occasion of his retirement from the chair of the history of religions and the phenomenology of religion at the University of Amsterdam. Leiden, E.J. Brill, 1969. 324 p. port. 25cm. (Studies in the history of religions. (Supplements to Numen) 17)

(Continued)

NN R 1.70 m/ OC (OS)I PC, 1, I (LC1, X1, Z1) [I]

4

LIBER amicorum... (Card 2)

CONTENTS.--List of Prof. Bleeker's publications.--Professor C.J. Bleeker, a personal appreciation, by G. Widengren.--Are the Bororo parrots or are we? By Th. P. van Baaren.--Le professeur W.B. Kristensen et l'Ancien Testament, par M.A. Beek.--Pour l'histoire du dualisme: un coyote africain, le renard pâle, par U. Bianchi.--Saviour and judge, two examples of divine ambivalence, by S.G.F. Brandon.--Mitologia, contributo a un problema di fenomenologia religiosa, di A. Brelich.--

(Continued)

LIBER amicorum... (Card 3)

Sehen und hören, von K. A. H. Hidding. --Prasāda in the Rāmāyana, by D. J. Hoens. --The conception of creation in cosmology, by E. O. James.-- Der Schrecken Pharaos, von S. Morenz. --Jesus and Mani, a comparison, by L. J. R. Ort. --Light and darkness in Ancient Egyptian religion, by H. Ringgren.--Shāh 'Ināyat Shāhīd of Jhōk, a Sindhi mystic of the early 18th century, by Schimmel. --Pietism and enlightenment, by H. W. Schneider. --Ein Fragment zur Physiognomik und Chiromantik

(Continued)

LIBER amicorum ... (Card 4)

aus der Tradition der spätantiken jüdischen Esoterik, von G. Scholem. -- Histoire des religions, histoire du Christianisme, histoire de l'Eglise, par M. Simon. --Koranisches Religionsgespräch, eine Skizze, von J. D. J. Waardenburg. --Muhammad and the Qur'ān. Criteria for Muhammad's prophecy, by K. Wagtendonk. --Die Hymnen der Pistis Sophia und die gnostische Schriftauslegung, von G. Widengren. --The Book of gates, by J. Zandee.

(Continued)

1. Bleeker, C. Jouco. I. Series.

D-15
6498

LIBER amicorum, Albin Fringeli zu seinem 60. Geburtstage gewidmet von seinen Freunden. Breitenbach, Schwarzbueb-Verlag unter dem Patronat des Heimatmuseums Schwarbubenland, 1959. 51 p. illus., mounted port. 22cm.

1. Fringeli, Albin, 1899-

NN 5.66 p/c OC PC, 1 SL (LC1, X1, Z1)

---

*MGA

Liber amicorum Charles van den Borren. Anvers, Impr. L. Anversois, 1964.

223 p. illus., facsims., music, ports. 27 cm.

1. Music—Essays. 2. Essays. 3. Borren, Charles van den, 1874-
NN 5.67 1/ OC PC,1,3 SL MU,2,3 (LC1,X1,Z1)
[I]

AN
(Eeden, F.)

Liber amicorum, Dr. Frederik van Eeden aangeboden ter gelegenheid van zijn zeventigsten verjaardag, 3 April 1930... Amsterdam: N. V. Maatschappij tot Verspreiding van goede en goedkoope Lectuur, 1930. 212 p. facsim., mounted front., illus. (incl. music), plates, ports. 4°.

Some plates printed on both sides.
Music, "In Epiphania Domini ad 4 voces inaequales," Hendrik Andriessen, p. 11–13.

548909A. 1. Eeden, Frederik Willem van, 1860–
N. Y. P. L. October 26, 1931

RDB

Liber floridus; mittellateinische Studien, Paul Lehmann zum 65. Geburtstag am 13. Juli 1949 gewidmet von Freunden, Kollegen und Schülern. Hrsg. von Bernhard Bishoff und Suso Brechter. [St. Ottillien] Eos Verlag, 1950. xiv, 384p. illus. 24cm.

Bibliographical footnotes.

WC

... **Liber** gratulatorius in honorem Oluf Thomsen ante diem XII kal. sept. MCMXXXVIII ab amicis, discipulis et collegis editus. København, Levin & Munksgaard, E. Munksgaard, 1938.

631 p. front. (port.) illus., diagrs. 25cm. (Acta pathologica et microbiologica scandinavica. Supplementum XXXVII)

Edited by J. Engelbreth-Holm, T. Kemp and P. V. Marcussen.

"Index operum professoris Oluf Thomsen": p. [9]–32.

Bibliography at end of most articles.

CONTENTS.—Alsted, G. Studies on immunity in *Bartonella anæmia*.—Andersen, F. Lesions of the fetuses of rats after treatment of the mothers with gonadotropic hormones.—Andersen, O. Über vakzineimmunität.—Andersen, T. Die fähigkeit der kaninchen, antistoffe gegen

(Continued on next card)

A C 39–74

[6]

... **Liber** gratulatorius in honorem Oluf Thomsen ... 1938. (Card 2)

CONTENTS—Continued.

menschen-A-blutkörperchen und schafblutkörperchen zu bilden.—Castrèn, H. Rhabdomyom mit atypischer entwicklung.—Christensen, J. F. Über das verhältnis zwischen den A-antigenen in menschenblutkörperchen von gruppe A, schafblutkörperchen und meerschweinchenorganen.—Christiansen, T., and Rosling, E. A case of infantile myxoedema.—Clausen, J. On the fate of the red blood cells in intraperitoneal blood-transfusion.—Engelbreth-Holm, J., and Frederiksen, O. The reactivation of the fowl-leukosis agent after inactivation by oxydization.—Engelbreth-Holm, J., and Frederiksen, O. The transmission of mouse-leucaemia to healthy animals by means of cell-free substance.—Forssman, J. A contribution to the knowledge of late paralyses in rabbits following staphylococcus in-

(Continued on next card)

A C 39–74

[6]

... **Liber** gratulatorius in honorem Oluf Thomsen ... 1938. (Card 3)

CONTENTS—Continued.

fections (Studies in staphylococci, XII)—Friedenreich, V. On the relation between the human type antigens A and B and antigens in the animal kingdom.—Fölger, A. F. Über einige bemerkenswerte tuberkulöse primärkomplexe im darmkanal vom rind und schwein.—Gregersen, N. F. Angioma racemosum pedis.—Guldberg, E. Verschiedengeschlechtige eineiige zwillinge.—Hamburger, C. How early can anti-gonadotropic hormone be demonstrated?—Henschen, F. Über die verschiedenen formen von hyperostose des schädeldachs.—Jensen, E. Comparative bacteriological assay of some phenylmercuric compounds, including merfen.—Jensen, V., und Roth, H. Zur einwanderung der trichinenlarve in die quergestreifte muskelfaser.—Johansen, A. H. Hypoproteinaemia.—

(Continued on next card)

A C 39–74

[6]

... **Liber** gratulatorius in honorem Oluf Thomsen ... 1938. (Card 4)

CONTENTS—Continued.

Kemp, T. Heredity and the endocrine function.—Kissmeyer, A. Une nouvelle orientation dans le traitement de la blenorrhagie.—Kreyberg, L. The influence of extrinsic factors on the development of induced tumours in animals.—Kristensen, M. Studies on the sero-diagnosis of mononucleosis infectiosa.—Lindau, A. Are benign lymphogranuloma (Boeck's sarcoid) and uveoparotid fever of tuberculous origin or not?—Madsen, T., and Rasch, G. On immunization of rabbit groups.—Marcussen, P. V. The mechanism of incompatibility (the significance of antigen-antibody-reaction)—Møller-Christensen, E. Über kryptorchismus und seine behandlung mit sexualhormonen.—Nyberg, C. Zwei mit der zweiteilung nicht identische vermehrungsarten von bakterien.—Okkels, H. The his-

(Continued on next card)

A C 39–74

[6]

... Liber gratulatorius in honorem Oluf Thomsen ... 1938.
(Card 5)

CONTENTS—Continued.

tology of tomorrow.—Olesen, M. Über supravitalfärbung in salzwasser und monocyt/lymphocyt ratio. — Pedersen-Bjergaard, K., and Madsen, G. B. The effect of oestrogenic and androgenic hormone on the spontaneous muscular activity of gonadectomized male and female rats.—Plum, N. Tuberculosis abortion in cattle.—Poulsen, E. Über präzipitingehalt in eiweisspräzipitierenden seren. — Sievers, O. Das vorkommen von sog. Forssman-antigen in vogeleiern.—Sjövall, E., und Lundgren, N. Zur kenntnis des angioma simplex cerebri (Teleangiektasien)—Streng, K. O. Kann ein meerschweinchenorganismus M-antikörper bilden?—Streng, O. Zur kentniss der heterogenetischen und homologen antigene.—Thjøtta, T., and Sømme, O. M. The bacteriological flora of nor-

(Continued on next card)

A C 39-74

[6]

... Liber gratulatorius in honorem Oluf Thomsen ... 1938.
(Card 6)

CONTENTS—Continued.

mal fish, a preliminary report.—Thjøtta, T., and Böe, J. *Neisseria hemolysans*, a hemolytic species of *Neisseria trevisan*.—Thomsen, A. Contribution to elucidation of the question about the frequency of infectious abortion in cattle and its combating in Denmark.—Uhl, E. Active immunization of chickens against chicken leukosis with agent absorbed by aluminium hydroxide. — Wallgren, A. Studien über den amöboidismus der monozyten in normalem menschenblut. — Westman, A. Über den luteinisierungseffekt des gonadotropen chorionhormons auf die ovarien der frau. — Vogelsang, T. M. Séro-diagnostic de la syphilis dans les liquides céphalo-rachidiens.—Worsaae, E. Thomsens vier-gen-hypothese erläutert durch untersuchungen von familien mit neugeborenen kin-

(Continued on next card)

A C 39-74

[6]

... Liber gratulatorius in honorem Oluf Thomsen ... 1938.
(Card 7)

CONTENTS—Continued.

dern.—Wulff, F. On nosocomial catarrhal infection in children's departments.—Ørskov, J., and Andersen, E. K. Weitere untersuchungen über die bildungsstätten der virusneutralisierenden stoffe bei vaccineinfektion von kaninchen.

1. Thomsen, Oluf, 1878– 2. Pathology — Addresses, essays, lectures. 3. Bacteriology—Addresses, essays, lectures. I. Engelbreth-Holm, Julius, 1904– ed. II. Kemp, Tage, 1896– ed. III. Marcussen, Poul Vedel, 1907– ed.

A C 39-74

John Crerar library
for Library of Congress [6]

E-11
6771

LIBERALE gedachten, een bundel opstellen aangeboden aan Prof. Mr. P. J. Oud ter gelegenheid van zijn 75ste verjaardag. Rotterdam, Nijgh & van Ditmar [1962] 276 p. ports. 25cm.

Bibliographical references included in "Aantekeningen" at end of articles.
CONTENTS.--Opdracht, door H. A. Korthals.--Politiek portret van een groot parlementariër, door A. W. Abspoel.--Oud als schrijver over staatsrecht en staatkunde, door D. Simons.--Politieke partijen

(Continued)

NN R 3.63 p/ OC PC, 1, 2, 3, 4 SL E, 1, 2, 3, 4 (LC1, X1, Z1) 2

LIBERALE gedachten... (Cont.)

en beginsel in 1962, door H. van Riel.--Geestelijke vrijheid en verdraagzaamheid, door J. F. van Royen.--Hedendaags staatsrecht, door J. V. Rijpperda Wierdsma.--De toekomst van de rechtsstaat, door E. H. s'Jacob.--Territoriale decentralisatie in de tegenwoordige tijd, door E. H. Toxopeus.--De vrijheid in het sociaal-economische leven, door N. E. H. van Esveld.--Gelijkheid-ongelijkheid, door K. van Dijk.--Perspektieven der economische politiek, door H. J. Witteveen.--Over opvoeding en onderwijs, door J. F. Schouwenaar-Franssen.--De plaats van de liberale fractievorming in de Europese democratie, door F. G. van Dijk.

1. Liberalism. 2. Volkspartij voor vrijheid en democratie 3. Netherlands--Politics, 1940- 4. Oud, Pieter Jacobus, 1886-

---

BAC

Liberty and learning; essays in honour of Sir James Hight... Christchurch, Whitcombe and Tombs, 1950. vii, 328 p. port. 22cm.

"A bibliography of the writings of Sir James Hight," by the editor, R. S. Allan, p. 325-328.

544474B. 1. Hight, Sir James, 1870- . 2. History—Addresses, essays, lectures. 3. Political science, 1918- . I. Allan, Robin Sutcliffe, ed.
N. Y. P. L. October 16, 1951

E-13
5712

LIBRARIANSHIP in Canada, 1946-1967; essays in honour of Elizabeth Homer Morton; edited by Bruce Peel. Victoria, B.C., printed for the Canadian Library Association by the Morriss Printing Co., 1968. 205 p. 24cm.

Added t.p. in French: Le bibliothécariat au Canada de 1946 à 1967.
English or French.
Includes bibliographies.

1. Libraries--Canada. I. Morton, Elizabeth Homer. II. Peel, Bruce Braden, 1916- , ed.
NN * S 7.69 k/JOC, I, Ibo, II PC, 1, I, II SL (LC1, X1, Z1)

D-19
5640

LIBRARIANSHIP and literature; essays in honour of Jack Pafford, edited by A. T. Milne. [London] Athlone press, 1970. viii, 141 p. illus., port. 23cm.

Includes bibliographies.

1. Pafford, John Henry Pyle. 2. Library science--Addresses, essays, lectures. I. Milne, Alexander Taylor, ed.
NN S 7.70 e/£OC, I PC, 1, 2, I SL (LC1, X1, Z1)

E-12
6103

Libri e stampatori in Padova: miscellanea di studi storici in onore di mons. G. Bellini: tipografo, editore, libraio. [Il raccoglitore, Antonio Barzon] Padova, Tipografia antoniana, 1959.

xxxi, 468 p. illus., 2 col. plates, port., fold. map, facsims. 24 cm.

CONTENTS.—Mons. Giuseppe Bellini, di I. Daniele.—Il "Loco delle vergini" di Piazzola, di G. Saggiori.—La stamperia Volpi-Cominiana di Padova, di G. Aliprandi.—La stampa a Padova nei secoli XIX e XX, di E. Cavallini.—Nicolò Bettoni a Padova, di S. Cella.—L'illustrazione

(Continued)

NN* 6.66 g/e OC, I, 2b* PC, 1, 2, I SL A, 1, 2, I
(RIB 1, LC1, X1, Z1) [I] 3

LIBRI e stampatori in Padova... 1959. (Card 2)

nell'arte grafica, di A. Monticelli.—Anche di musica pubblicò la tipografia del Seminario di Padova, di A. Garbelotto.—La biblioteca dei canonici regolari di S. Agostino nel monastero di S. Giovanni da Verdara in Padova.—Documenti padovani sull'arte della stampa nel sec. XV, di A. Sartori. Documenti (p. 116-228)—Il codice miniato B 31 della Capitolare di Padova, di L. Montobbio.—Il movimento nazionale a Padova e il "Giornale euganeo," di G. Balasso.—Tracce di una scuola episcopale in Padova (dall' 800 al 1170) di A. Barzon.—La tipografia ebraica di Piove di Sacco, di S. Bassi e A. Barzon.—Saggi di rilegature (codici e incunabuli della Biblioteca capitolare) di A. Barzon.—Intorno ad un atlante manoscritto del Seminario di Padova (note

(Continued)

LIBRI e stampatori in Padova... 1959. (Card 3)

alla tavola delle Venezie) di E. Bevilacqua.—La libreria di un parroco di città in Padova nell'anno 1559 (Br.-Nota d'archivio)—I libri di Bartolomeo e Bono Astorelli, dottori giuristi (1421) di P. Sambin.—Un ignoto Dioscoride miniato (il codice greco 194 del Seminario di Padova) di E. Mioni.—Le opere a stampa del Guilandino, di G. E. Ferrari.

1. Printing--Italy--Padua. 2. Bellini, Giuseppe, 1888-1957.
I. Barzon, A., ed.

HOF

LIBRO homenaje al coronel Cosme de la Torriente en reconocimiento de sus grandes servicios a Cuba. La Habana, 1951.
514 p. illus., ports. 27cm.

1. Torriente y Peraza, Cosme de la, 1872- 2. Cuba—For. rel.

NN ** X 12.53 OC PC, 1, 2 SL AH, 1, 2 (LC1, Z1, X1)

F-11
5795

Libro de homenaje a **Luis Alberto Sánchez, en los 40 años de su docencia universitaria. Lima** [Tall. Gráf. P. L. Villanueva] 1967 [i.e. 1968]
xi, 646 p. illus. 26 cm.

Includes bibliographies. Bibliographical footnotes.

1. Sánchez, Luis Alberto, 1900- . I. Sánchez, Luis Alberto, 1900- .
NN * R 10.69 k/OC, I PC, 1, I SL (LC1, X1, Z1). [I]

E-11
6548

In LIBRO humanitas; Festschrift für Wilhelm Hoffmann zum sechzigsten Geburtstag, 21. April 1961. [Hrsg. von Ewald Lissberger, Theodor Pfizer und Bernhard Zeller] Stuttgart, E. Klett, 1962.
383, [3] p. illus., port., maps. 25cm.

1. Bibliography--Addresses, essays, lectures. 2. Hoffmann, Wilhelm, 1901- . I. Lissberger, Ewald, ed.
NN R 5.63 g/ OC, I PC, 1, 2, I SL (LC1, X1, Z1) [I]

E-10
6158

LIBRO jubilar de Emeterio S. Santovenia en su cincuentenario de escritor. La Habana, 1957 [i.e. 1958] 621 p. port. 24cm.

Introduction signed: Félix Lizaso.
Various contributors.
"Bibliografía activa del doctor Emeterio S. Santovenia, con notas adicionales sobre las obras relacionadas," p. 585-596.
"Bibliografía selecta de libros y folletos de Emeterio S. Santovenia," p. 597-609.

(Continued)

NN X 8.58 g/ OC, I PC, 1, I SL AH, 1, I (LC1, X1, Z1, Y1)

LIBRO jubilar de Emeterio S. Santovenia ... (Card 2)

1. Santovenia y Echaide, Emeterio Santiago, 1889- .
I. Lizaso, Félix, 1891- , ed.

YAR

Lichamelijkheid; wijsgerige beschouwingen door professoren in de philosophie van het Dominicanenklooster te Zwolle, uitg. bij gelegenheid van het vijftigjarig bestaan van het convent, 1901-1951. Utrecht, Heft Spectrum, 1951.
222 p. 22cm.

Summaries in French at end of each article.
Includes bibliographies.

(Continued)

NN** 11.55 j/ OC (OS)I, Ib PC, 1, 2, I SL (Z1, LC1, X1)

Lichamelijkheid... (Card 2)

Contents.—De lichamelijkheid bij Gabriel Marcel en Jean-Paul Sartre, door R.W. Thuijs.—Ben ik mijn lichaam of heb ik mijn lichaam? Door T.G. de Valk.—De bemiddeling van het lichaam, door C.B. Barendse.—Het aanvaarden van de lichamelijkheid, door A.J. Arntz.—Het lichamelijke in de voorstelling, door A.J. de Witte.—God eren met het lichaam, door C.F. Pauwels.
1. Mind and body. 2 Existentialism I. Zwolle, Netherlands. Dominicanenklooster.

E-11
4167

LIEB, IRWIN C.
Experience, existence, and the good; essays in honor of Paul Weiss. Carbondale, Southern Illinois university press [1961] x, 309 p. 25cm.

Includes bibliographies.
CONTENTS.--Experience and speculation, by C. W. Hendel.--Experience and philosophy, by R.O. Johann.--Creativity and otherness,

(Continued)

NN R 4.62 p/OC, Ibo PC, 1, 2 SL (LC1, X1, Z1) [I]

LIEB, IRWIN C. Experience, existence, and the good... (Card 2)

by I. S. Stearns.--Love and metaphysics, by W. Earle.--Purposes and words, by I. C. Lieb.--Man in nature, by C. Hartshorne.--The limits of reductionism, by R. M. Rorty.--Kinds of time, by R. S. Brumbaugh.--The elusive nature of the past, by M. Čapek.--Causality and time, by W. N. Clarke.--Is the word reality meaningful? By F. S. C. Northrop.--Time and action, by A.B. Gibson.--Existence and being, by R.F. Grabau.--The modes of law, by I. Jenkins.--The relation of fact and value, by A. Edel.--The objectivist view of human freedom, by J. Wild.--

(Continued)

LIEB, IRWIN C. Experience, existence, and the good... (Card 3)

Is there a primacy of practical reason? By N. Rotenstreich. --The analysis of the good, in Kierkegaard's Purity of heart, by L. Mackey. --The criterion of the good and the right, by W. H. Sheldon. --The metaphysics of liberty, by A. J. Reck.

1. Weiss, Paul, 1901- 2. Metaphysics--Addresses, essays, lectures. I. Lieb, Irwin C.

AN
(Irving, G.)

The life work of George Irving; experiences in witnessing for Christ. Ed. by David R. Porter. New York, Association press [1945] viii,146 p. illus. 21cm.

"Collection of contributions from many colleagues." Irving's Experiences in witnessing for Christ, p. 99-146.

I. Irving, George. Experiences in witnessing for Christ. II. Porter, David Richard, 1882- , ed.

NN OC,I,II PC,I,II SL (LC1,Z1,X1)

---

* MFHB
(Austria)

LIED und Brauch; aus der Kärntner Volksliedarbeit und Brauchforschung. [Anton Anderluh zur Vollendung seines 60. Lebensjahres dargebracht] Klagenfurt, Verlag des Landesmuseums für Kärnten, 1956. 167 p. illus., ports, music. 24cm. (Kärntner Museumsschriften. 8)

Includes music.
"Anton Anderluh-Bibliographie," p. 165-167.

1. Folk songs, German--Austria --Carinthia. 2. Anderluh, Anton, 1896- . I. Series.

NN X 11.60 p/X OC, 2b+ (OS)I PC, 1, 2, I SL MU, 1, 2 (LC1, X1, Z1)

E-13
8109

Linares, Julio.
Letras nicaragüenses. Managua, Nicaragua, 1966.
85 p. port. 25 cm.

Cover title.
"Homenaje al centenario de Darío, 1867-1967."

1. Nicaraguan literature—Addresses, essays, lectures. 2. Darío, Rubén, 1867-1916.

NN*R 8.70 e/ OC PC, 1, 2 SL (LC1, X1, Z1)

---

*QAA
(Deutsche)

Liewehr, Ferdinand, editor.
...Slavistische Studien; Franz Spina, zum sechzigsten Geburtstag von seinen Schülern. Redigiert von Ferdinand Liewehr. Reichenberg: Gebrüder Stiepel, Ges.m.b.H., 1929. 201 p. incl. diagr. front. (port.), plates. 8°. (Deutsche Univ., Prague. Slavistische Arbeitsgemeinschaft. Veröffentlichungen: Reihe 1: Untersuchungen. Heft 5.)

1. Bohemian literature—Hist. and crit. 2. Slavs. 3. Spina, Franz, 1868- . 4. Title. 5. Ser.
N. Y. P. L. April 18, 1930

AN
(Schweitzer, A.)

Lind, Emil, 1890–
...Albert Schweitzer zum 75. Geburtstage. Speyer, O. Dobbeck, 1950. 84 p. illus. 19cm. (Schriftenreihe: Albert Schweitzer. Heft 1)

586823B. 1. Schweitzer, Albert, 1875– . Festschrift
N. Y. P. L. November 27, 1951

E-10
3641

LIFE, language, law; essays in honor of Arthur F. Bentley. Edited by Richard W. Taylor. Yellow Springs, Ohio, Antioch press [1957] xii, 223 p. illus., port. 24cm.

Bibliographical references included in "Notes" at end of most chapters.
CONTENTS. —Life, language, law, by R. W. Taylor. —A. F. Bentley's inquiries into the behavioral sciences and the theory of scientific inquiry, by S. Ratner. —General system theory, by L. von Bertalanffy. —The coming revolution in the economic thought, by B. Gross. —
(Continued)

NN R 9.57 a/ OC, I, IIb* PC, 1, 2, I SL E, 1, 2, I (LC1, X1, Z1, Y1)

---

* OHP

LINGUISTIC SOCIETY OF INDIA.
Sir Ralph Turner jubilee volume, presented on the occasion of his seventieth birthday, 5th October, 1958, by members of the faculty of the schools of linguistics, Deccan college, Poona, jointly with Linguistic society of India. [Calcutta?] 1958. 1 v. port. 25cm.
[Vol.] 1.
On cover: Indian linguistics. Edited by Sukumar Sen.
A few articles in German

1. Turner, Sir Ralph Lilley, 1888- 2. Indic languages. I. Sen, Sukumar, ed. II. Title. III. Title: Indian linguistics.

NN 5.64 p/ (OC)I, II OS, III PC, 1, 2, I, II, III SL O, 1, 2, I, III (LC1, X1, Z1)

LIFE, language, law; essays in honor of Arthur F. Bentley. (Card 2)

Some characteristics of visual perception, by A. Ames, jr. —The group in political science, by C. B. Hagan. —Error, quantum theory, and the observer, by P. W. Bridgman. —The quest for "being" by S. Hook. —The illusion of rationality, by D. Calhoun. —Conflicting orientation in law and national policy, by G. A. Lundberg. —Human rights: an appeal to philosophers, by F. S. Cohen. —Epilogue, A. F. Bentley. —Arthur F. Bentley: a bibliography.

1. Bentley, Arthur Fisher, 1870- .2. Social sciences--Addresses, essays, lectures. I. Taylor, Richard Wirth, 1923- , ed. II. Taylor, Richard Wirth, 1923-

---

EMB

Lippert, Woldemar, 1861– , editor.
Meissnisch-sächsische Forschungen; zur Jahrtausendfeier der Mark Meissen und des Sächsischen Staates, herausgegeben von Woldemar Lippert. Dresden: W. und B. v. Baensch Stiftung, 1929. 254 p. facsims., illus. (incl. maps), plate. 8°.

Mr. Moth

452765A. 1. Saxony—Hist. 2. Title.
N. Y. P. L. January 27, 1930

* Q p.v.991

Listy filologické Oldřichu Hujerovi k šedesátým narozeninám, 25–XI–1940 z podnětu výboru jednoty českých filologů uspořádali J. M. Kořínek a V. Machek. [Praha, Nákladem Jednoty českých filologů, 1940] p. [131]–408. illus. 25cm.

"Zvláštní otisk z Listů filologických r.67., str.129–408.
By various authors.
Bibliographical footnotes.

1. Languages. 2. Slavonic languages. 3. Hujer, Oldřich, 1880–1942. I. Kořínek, Josef Miroslav, 1899– , ed. II. Machek, Vaclev, ed.

NN 1.53 OC, I, II PC, 1, 2, 3, I, II SL S, 1, 2, 3, I, II (LC1, Z1, X1)

---

*C-3 p. v. 531

LITERARISCHE VEREINIGUNG BRAUNSCHWEIG E. V.

Robert Jordan, zum fünfundsechzigsten Geburtstage, 11. September 1950, von der Literarischen Vereinigung Braunschweig E. V. [Braunschweig, 1950] 23 p. illus. 20cm.

Title-page on two pages.
"Zusammengestellt von Ewald Lüpke."
"Bibliographie.: p. 22-23.
CONTENTS. —Trapp, Albert. Robert Jordan, sein Wesen und seine Leistung. —Ernst, Heinrich. Robert Jordan und sein Verhältnis zur bildenden Kunst. —Keil, Arno. Offener Brief an ein Geburtstagskind. —Schmidtke, (Continued)

NN 11. 52 (OC)I, Ib OS(Ib) PC, 1, I SL (LC1, Z1, X1)

LITERARISCHE VEREINIGUNG BRAUNSCHWEIG E. V. Robert Jordan...
(Card 2)

Gotthard Die spitze Feder. —Wedemeyer, Max. Ein persönliches Bekenntnis zu Robert Jordan.

1. Jordan, Robert, 1885- . I. Lüpke, Ewald, , ed.

E-14
2082

Literatur und Sprache der Vereinigten Staaten. Aufsätze zu Ehren von Hans Galinsky. Hrsg. von Hans Helmcke, Klaus Lubbers und Renate Schmidt-v. Bardeleben. Heidelberg, C. Winter, 1969.

247 p. front. 25 cm.
English or German.
Includes bibliographical references.
CONTENTS.—Strophe, Vers und Reim in Edward Taylors "Meditations," von F. W. Schulze.—Das Tagebuch des kolonialen Südens, (Continued)

NN*R 11.71 w/OC, I, II PC, 1, I, II SL (LC1, X1, Z1)
[I]

LITERATUR und Sprache der Vereinigten Staaten.
(Card 2)

von R. Schmidt -v. Bardeleben.—William Bartrams bewegter Stil, von F. Busch.—The American Literary Declaration of Independence, by R. E. Spiller.—Die deutsche Siedlung in Louisiana im Spiegel des Amerika-Romans der Goethezeit, von H. Oppel.—The Blithedale Romance, by H.-J. Lang.—Metaphorical Patterns in Hawthorne's The House of the Seven Gables, by K. Lubbers.—Before Ellison and Baldwin, by G. Moore.—"A Momentary Stay Against Confusion," by F. Schulz.—Sherwood Anderson, by L. Leary.—"Tristitia" und "Nobiskrug," von R. Haas.—The writer in America, by C. R. Dolmetsch.—Das christliche Schauspiel T. S. Eliots, von F. H. Link.— (Continued)

LITERATUR und Sprache der Vereinigten Staaten.
(Card 3)

The American epic impulse and Thomas Wolfe, by C. H. Holman.—Das wüste Land bei T. S. Eliot und Thomas Wolfe, von H. Helmcke.—Intellectual und seine Synonyme im britischen und amerikanischen Englisch, von B. Carstensen.—Das Suffix -wise im heutigen amerikanischen und britischen Englisch, von W. Rahn.—Verzeichnis der Schriften von Hans Galinsky, von K. Lubbers (p. [242]–247)

1. American literature--Addresses, essays, lectures. I. Galinsky, Hans. II. Helmcke, Hans, ed.

E-11
8972

LITTELL, FRANKLIN H., ed.

Reformation studies; essays in honor of Roland H. Bainton. Richmond, Va., John Knox press [1962] 285 p. port. 25cm.

Includes bibliographies.
CONTENTS. — Roland H. Bainton: a bibliographical appreciation, by G. Harkness. —Faith and knowledge in Luther's theology, by N. A. Bendtz. —A reasonable Luther, by R. H. Fischer. —Anfechtung in Luther's (Continued)

NN R 3. 64 g/ OC PC,1,2,3 SL (LC1, X1, Z1) [I]

LITTELL, FRANKLIN H., ed. Reformation studies...
(Card 2)

Biblical exegesis, by C. W. Hovland. —Medieval consolation and the young Luther's despair, by J. von Rohr. —Luther's frontier in Hungary, by W. Toth. —The relation of God's grace to His glory in John Calvin, by H. Kuizenga. —Calvin's theological method and the ambiguity in his theology, by J. H. Leith. — Lefèvre d'Etaples: three phases of his life and work, by J. W. Brush. — Continental Protestantism and Elizabethan Anglicanism, 1570-1595, by J. M. Krumm. —New light on Butzer's significance, by F. H. Littell. —Reason and conversion in the thought of (Continued)

LITTELL, FRANKLIN H., ed. Reformation studies...
(Card 3)

Melanchthon, by C. L. Manschreck. —The strangers' "model churches" in sixteenth-century England, by F. A. Norwood. —Sectarianism and skepticism, the strange allies of religious liberty, by W. Beach. — Augsburg and the early Anabaptists; by P. J. Schwab. — Bernhard Rothmann's views on the early church, by F. J. Wray. —Fecund problems of eschatological hope, election proof, and social revolt in Thomas Müntzer, by L. H. Zuck. —A bibliography of Professor Bainton's writings on the Reformation period, by R. P. Morris. (Continued)

LITTELL, FRANKLIN H., ed. Reformation studies...
(Card 4)

1. Bainton, Roland Herbert, 1894- . 2. Reformation. 3. Protestantism--Addresses, essays, lectures.

F-11
6224

LITTERAE Hispanae et Lusitanae. Festschrift zum 50 Jährigen Bestehen des Ibero-Amerikanischen Forschungsinstituts der Universität Hamburg. Hrsg. von Hans Flasche. München, Hueber [1968]
vii, 511 p. 26cm.

1. Aufl.
Bibliographical footnotes.

(Continued)

NN R 4.70 l/₄OC, I (OS)II PC, 1, 2, I, II SL (LC1, X1, Z1)
[1] 2

LITTERAE Hispanae et Lusitanae. (Card 2)

1. Spanish language--Addresses, essays, lectures. 2. Portuguese language--Addresses, essays, lectures. I. Flasche, Hans, ed. II. Ibero-amerikanisches Institut, Hamburg.

---

*OAC

LITTMANN, ENNO, 1875-
Ein Jahrhundert Orientalistik; Lebensbilder aus der Feder von Enno Littmann und Verzeichnis seiner Schriften. Zum achtzigsten Geburtstage am 16. September 1955 zusammengestellt von Rudi Paret und Anton Schall. Wiesbaden, O. Harrassowitz, 1955.
ix, 194, [1] p. port. 25cm.

CONTENTS. —Lebensbilder von Orientalisten: August Dillmann.
(Continued)

NN **R 4.56 s/₄ OC, I, II, IIIbo PC, 1, 2, I, II SL O, 1, 2, I, II (LC1, X1, Z1)

LITTMANN, ENNO, 1875- . Ein Jahrhundert Orientalistik... (Card 2)

Johann Gottfried Wetzstein. Naffa ͨ wad ͨEtmân. Richard Sundström. Carl Bezold. Hermann Reckendorf. Franz Praetorius. Mark Lidzbarski. Theodor Nöldeke. Ignazio Guidi. Friedrich Rosen. Christiaan Snouck Hurgronje. Georg Jacob. Carlo Alfonso Nallino. Eugen Mittwoch. Max Meyerhof. —Verzeichnis der Schriften von Enno Littmann (p. [139]-[195]).

1. Orientalists. 2. Littmann, Enno, 1875- —Bibl. I. Paret, Rudi, 1901- , ed. II. Schall, Anton, ed. III. Schall, Anton.

---

*PBN

Livre d'hommage à la mémoire du Dr. Samuel Poznański (1864–1921), offert par les amis et les compagnons du travail scientifique. Varsovie: Édit par le Comité de la Grande Synagogue à Varsovie, 1927. xlvii, 216, 214 p. front. (port.) f°.

Articles in English, German, Polish and Hebrew; the last, 214 p., paged separately and with added Hebrew t.-p.
Added t.-p. in Polish.
Contents: Balaban, M. Dr. Samuel Poznański. Marx, A., et E. Poznanski. Bibliographie de tous les ouvrages et articles du Dr. Samuel Poznański (1889–1926). Abrahams, I. The words of Gad the Seer. Adler, E. N. The divan of El'azar ha Babli. Balaban, M. Studien und Quellen zur Geschichte der frankistischen Bewe-

(Continued)

N. Y. P. L. May 22, 1928

Livre d'hommage à la mémoire du Dr. Samuel Poznański... (Continued)

gung in Polen. Büchler, A. The induction of the bride and the bridegroom into the חופה in the first and the second centuries in Palestine. Duschinsky, C. The Yekum Purkan (יקום פורקן) Ginzberg, L. Die Haggada bei dën Kirchenvätern. Kokowzoff, P. The date of life of Bahya ibn Paqoda. Krauss, S. Beiträge zur Geschichte der Geonim. Marx, A. Der arabische Bustanai-Bericht und Nathan ha-Babli. Obermann, J. Drei Kontextglossen zum Deboraliede. Schorr, M. Les composés dans les langues sémitiques. Schwarz, A. Muss Lev. 16, 23 umgestellt werden? Seeligmann, S. Ein Originalbrief der Vierländersynode nach Amsterdam aus 1677. Simonsen, D. Vier arabische Gutachten des R. Mose ben Maimon.

347425A. 1. Poznanski, Samuel, 1864-1921. 2. Poznanski, Samuel—Bibl. 3. Essays, Jewish—Collections.
N. Y. P. L. May 22, 1928

KAT

Livre jubilaire offert à Maurice Zimmermann, professeur honoraire de géographie à l'Université de Lyon, par ses élèves et ses amis à l'occasion de ses quatre-vingts ans, 4 mars 1949. Géographie naturelle, géographie humaine générale, géographie régionale, géographie historique et divers. Lyon, Université de Lyon, Institut des études rhodaniennes, Institut de géographie, 1949.
xvii, 425 p. illus., ports., maps (part fold.) 30 cm.

"Bibliographie ... des principaux ouvrages et articles de M. Maurice Zimmermann, par M. Laferrère et J. Thibaudet": p. [xiii]-xvii.

1. Geography—~~Addresses, essays, lectures~~. 2. Zimmermann, Maurice, 1869–
G58.L55 910.04 A 51-1451
Harvard Univ. Library for Library of Congress [3]† FEST. CD

NKC (France)

Le livre d'or du centenaire d'Anatole France, 1844–1944... Paris, Calmann-Lévy [1949] 304 p. illus. 25cm.

"Établi sur l'initiative et par les soins de M. Claude Aveline."
"Bibliographie," p. 285–297.

526236B. 1. France, Anatole, 1844–1924. I. Aveline, Claude, 1901- , ed.
N. Y. P. L. July 26, 1950

VDY

Livre d'or de l'École nationale supérieure de l'aéronautique; cinquante années d'existence (1909–1959) [Rédigé par un groupe d'anciens élèves, sous la présidence de E. Ploix. Paris? 1959?]
197 p. illus., ports., facsims., plans. 28 cm.
Contents.—Le colonel Roche.—Hommage aux anciens élèves disparus.—L'École supérieure d'aéronautique et de construction mécanique (1909–1914)—Les ancêtres.—L'École supérieure d'aéronautique et de construction mécanique au lendemain de la Première Guerre mondiale (1918–1928)—M. A. Caquot et l'École nationale supérieure de l'aéronautique.—L'École de 1928 à 1939.—M. P. Du-
(Continued)

NN*R 7.63 g/₄ OC, I, Ib+ PC, 1, 2, I SL ST, 1t, 2, I
(LC1, X1, Z1) 2

LIVRE d'or de l'École nationale supérieure de l'aéronautique... (Card 2)

manois et l'École nationale supérieure de l'aéronautique.—L'École pendant la Seconde Guerre mondiale et l'immédiat après-guerre (1939–1953)—L'École en 1959.—Le rayonnement de l'École à l'extérieur.—Les anciens élèves de Sup'Aéro dans l'action.—L'Association des anciens élèves.— L'avenir.

1. Aeronautics--Education--France. 2. France. École nationale supérieure d'aéronautique, Paris. I. Ploix, Étienne. t. 1959

NHP

Lode Baekelmans ter eere, 1945... Antwerpen, De Sikkel, 1946. 2 v. illus. 26cm.

No. 21 of 300 copies.

604591-2B. 1. Bibliography. 2. Libraries. 3. Essays, Flemish—Collections. 4. Baekelmans, Lode, 1879-
NN

---

*ZP-456
Film Reproduction

LOEWINGER, SAMUEL, ed.
Jewish studies in memory of Michael Guttmann. [Bd.] 1. Budapest, 1946. 1, 418 p. port. 24cm.

Film reproduction. Positive.
Added t. p. in Hungarian.
Bibliographical footnotes.

1. Guttmann, Michael, 1872-1942. 2. Judaism--Addresses, essays, lectures. 3. Judaism--Essays.
NN R 2.67 r/ OC PC, 1, 2 SL J, 1, 3 (UM1, LC1, Z1, X1)

D-14
8537

LOGIC and language; studies dedicated to Professor Rudolf Carnap on the occasion of his seventieth birthday. Dordrecht, Holland, D. Reidel Pub. Co. [c1962] 246 p. 23cm. (Synthese library)

CONTENTS.--A prerequisite for rational philosophical discussion, by Y. Bar-Hillel.--Epistemology and logic, by A.A. Fraenkel.--Zur Rolle der Sprache in erkenntnistheoretischer Hinsicht, by P. Bernays.--Some
(Continued)

NN* R 2.64 f/ OC PC, 1, 2 SL (LC1, X1, Z1)

LOGIC and language... (Card 2)

remarks concerning languages, calculuses, and logic, by J. Jørgensen.--Carnap and logical truth, by W.V. Quine.--Extension and intension, by E.W. Beth.--The present situation in the philosophy of mathematics, by H. Mehlberg.--A counterpart of Occam's razor in pure and applied mathematics ontological uses, by K. Menger.--Towards a general theory of computability, by R. Montague.--Inductive inconsistencies, by C.G. Hempel.--Einige Beiträge zum Problem der Teleologie und der Analyse von Systemen mit zielgerichteter Organisation, von W. Stegmüller.--
(Continued)

LOGIC and language... (Card 3)

Beleuchtung von Anwendungen der Logistik in Werken von Rudolf Carnap, von K. Dürr.--Typology of questionnaires adopted to the study of expressions with closely related meanings, by A. Naess.--Permissible and impermissible locutions, by H. Tennessen.--Non-cognitive synonymy and the definability of "good," by D. Rynin.--On the history of the International encyclopedia of unified science, by C. Morris.

1. Carnap, Rudolf, 1891- . 2. Logical positivism.

F-10
5827

The LOGIC of personal knowledge; essays presented to Michael Polanyi on his seventieth birthday, 11th March 1961. London, Routledge & K. Paul [1961] 247 [1] p. illus., port. 26cm.

CONTENTS.--The Hungary of Michael Polanyi, by P. Ignotus.--An index to Michael Polanyi's contributions to science, by J. Polanyi.--Polanyi's contribution to the physics of metals, by E. Schmid.--Rates of reaction,
(Continued)

NN R 8.61 e/ OC PC, 1 SL ST, 1 (LC1, X1, Z1) [I]

The LOGIC of personal knowledge... (Card 2)

by H. Eyring.--The size and shape of molecules in their biological activity, by E.D. Bergmann.--Kepler and the psychology of discovery, by A. Koestler.--The scientists and the English Civil war, by C.V. Wedgwood.--Vibrating strings and arbitrary functions, by J.R. Ravetz.--The controversy on freedom in science in the nineteenth century, by J.R. Baker.--Max Weber and Michael Polanyi, by R. Aron.--Centre and periphery, by E.A. Shils.--The republic of science, by B. de Jouvenel.--Machiavelli and the profanation of politics, by I. Kristol.--Applied economics: the application
(Continued)

The LOGIC of personal knowledge... (Card 3)

of what? by E. Devons.--Some notes on "Philosophy of history" and the problems of human society, by D.M. Mackinnon.--Law-courts and dreams, by E. Sewell.--The logic of biology, by M. Grene.--Origin of life on earth and elsewhere, by M. Calvin.--The probability of the existence of a self-reproducing unit, by E.P. Wigner.--Bibliography, p. 239-[248].

1. Polanyi, Michael, 1891- .

D-20
1849

Logik, rätt och moral. Filosofiska studier tillägnade Manfred Moritz på 60-årsdagen den 4 juni 1969. Red.: Sören Halldén ... Lund. Studentlitteratur, 1969.
235 p. 22 cm.

CONTENTS.—Marx und die "bürgerliche" Nationalökonomie, von G. Aspelin.—Några textkritiska problem i Berkeleyforskningen, av B. Belfrage.—Några kommentarer till C. L. Stevensons teori om etisk oenighet, av L. Bergström.—Viljeteorins premisser, av J. Evers.—
(Continued)

NN* 1.71 d/J OC, 2b*, I PC, 1, 2, I SL (LC1, X1, Z1)

Logik, rätt och moral. 1969. (Card 2)

Axel Hägerströms analys av värdeupplevelsen, av L. Fröström.—On archetypical performatives, by M. Furberg.—The better something is, the worse its absence, by S. Halldén.—Ett slags representationsteorem för deontisk logik, av B. Hansson.—Om Platons "Euthyphron," av I. Hedenius.—Tolkningssatsernas logik, av G. Hermerén.—Är verkligheten motsägande? Ett dialektiskt argument, av K. Marc-Wogau.—Moral, amoral og indifferens, av H. Ofstad.—Begreppet "property" hos John Locke, av K. Olivecrona.—En skademodell, av U. Persson.—Objektivitet som kunskaps teoretiskt begrepp och som värderingsideal, av H. Regnéll.—Satsen "Flickan F är vacker," av E.
(Continued)

LOGIK, rätt och moral. (Card 3)

Ryding.—Lathund för lagläsare, av T. Strömberg.—Was the ether hypotheses refuted by the Michelsen-Morley experiment?, by H. Törnebohm.—Konsekvensprincipen i deontisk logik och frågan om deontiska satsers sanningsvärde, av A. Wedberg.—Bibliografi över Manfred Moritz' skrifter (p. 233-235)

1. Philosophy--Addresses, essays, lectures. 2. Moritz, Manfred, 1909- I. Halldén, Sören, ed.

TNK

LORENZ (C.) AKTIENGESELLSCHAFT.

75 [i.e. Fünfundsiebzig] Jahre Lorenz, 1880-1955. Festschrift der C. Lorenz Aktiengesellschaft. Stuttgart. [Stuttgart, 1955] 272 p. illus., ports., maps. 29cm.

I. Title.

NN **R X 12.55 f/ (OC)I OS(Ib) PC, I SL E, I (LC1, Z1, X1)

E-14
1843

LOH, GERHARD.

Arndt-Bibliographie; Verzeichnis der Schriften von und über Ernst Moritz Arndt. Festgabe zum 200. Geburtstage von Ernst Moritz Arndt, hrsg. von der Ernst-Moritz-Arndt Universität, Greifswald. [1. Aufl. Berlin] Deutscher Verlag der Wissenschaften [zu beziehen: Ernst-Moritz-Arndt-Universität] Greifswald, 1969. 307 p. 24cm.

1. Arndt, Ernst Moritz, 1769-1860--Bibl. I. Greifswald, Germany. Universität.

NN R 7.71 w/ OC(1b*) (OS)I PC, 1, I SL (LC1, X1, Z1)

MAMC

LOTZ, WOLFGANG, 1912- , ed.

Studien zur toskanischen Kunst; Festschrift für Ludwig Heinrich Heydenreich zum 23. März, 1963. [Hrsg. von Wolfgang Lotz und Lise Lotte Möller] München, Prestel-Verlag [1964] 319 p. illus. 27cm.

Text in German, English or Italian.

"Verzeichnis der Schriften von Ludwig H. Heydenreich, zusammengestellt von Peter Tigler," (Continued)

NN 6.67 g/i OC, I, II, III PC, 1, 2, 3, I, II, III SL A, 1, 2, 3, I, II, III (LC1, X1, Z1) [I] 2

E-12
1894

LOITLSBERGER, ERICH, ed.

Empirische Betriebswirtschaftslehre; Festschrift zum 60. Geburtstag von Leopold L. Illetschko. Unter Mitwirkung von Robert Buchner [et al.] Wiesbaden, Betriebswirtschaftlicher Verlag [c1963] 208 p. port. 25cm.

"Verzeichnis der Schriften von ... Leopold L. Illetschko," p. [203]-208. (Continued)

NN R 12.64 e/, OC, 1bo, I, Ibo, IIbo PC, 1, 2, I SL E, 1, 2, I (LC1, X1, Z1) 2

LOTZ, WOLFGANG, 1912- , ed. Studien zur toskanischen Kunst... (Card 2)

p. 315-319.
Bibliographical footnotes.

1. Heydenreich, Ludwig Heinrich, 1903- . 2. Heydenreich, Ludwig Heinrich, 1903- --Bibl. 3. Art, Italian--Tuscany. I. Möller, Lieselotte, joint ed. II. Title. III. Title: Festschrift für Ludwig Heinrich Heydenreich zum 23. März 1963.

LOITLSBERGER, ERICH, ed. Empirische Betriebswirtschaftslehre... (Card 2)

Bibliographical footnotes.

1. Illetschko, Leopold L. 2. Management--Addresses, essays, lectures. I. Buchner, Robert. II. Loitlsberger, Erich.

PAH

LOUIS DE BROGLIE, physicien et penseur. Paris, A. Michel [1953] xi, 497 p. port. 20cm. (Les Savants et le monde)

By various authors.

Two of the articles have text in the original language (German or English) with French translation.

1. Broglie, Louis, prince de, 1892- . 2. Physics—Addresses, essays, lectures. 3. Physics—Addresses, essays, lectures, 1953.

NN** X 10.53 OC PC, 1, 2 SL ST, 1, 3 (U1, Z1, LC1, X1)

NHS p.v.6

Lokwinsken fen Fryske skriuwers en skriuwsters oan Waling Dykstra to Holwert, op syn tachtichste jierdei. 14 Augustus 1821 — 14 Augustus 1901. Ljouwert: W. A. Eisma cz. [1901] 63 p. plates, port. 27½cm.

"Foarwird" signed: F. Jac. de Zee, M. Miedema, Sj. de Zee.
Short contributions by 35 Friesian authors, arranged alphabetically.

1. Dykstra, Waling Gerritsz., 1821-1914. I. Zee, F. Jacob de, ed. II. Miedema, Marcus, 1841-1911, ed. III. Zee, Sjouke de, 1867- , ed.
N. Y. P. L. July 18, 1938

AN
(Brouckère, L.)

Louis de Brouckère. [Bruxelles, L'Églantine, 1930?] 76 p. illus. 25cm.

Commemorative volume.
No. 83 of 100 copies.

532351B. 1. Brouckère, Louis de, 1870-
N. Y. P. L. September 11, 1950

Festschrift

*HB

Louis Round Wilson; papers in recognition of a distinguished career in librarianship. Chicago, Ill., The University of Chicago Press, 1942. 713 p.

E-11
7506

Luck, Georg, 1926- *ed.*
Horizonte der Humanitas. Eine Freundesgabe für Professer Dr. Walter Wili zu seinem 60. Geburtstag. Bern, P. Haupt ⌐1960⌐

197 p. port. 24 cm.

Includes bibliographical references.

CONTENTS.—Der Mythos und die Götter Griechenlands, von W. Theiler.—Das Prooemium des Diogenes Laertios, von O. Gigon.—Das Glück der Grossen, von E. Bickel.—Die Musen in der römischen Poesie, von G. Luck.—Plinio il giovane e la sua piccola patria, di L. Rusca.--
(Continued)

NN * R 7.63 e/₄ OC PC, 1, 2 SL (LC1, X1, Z1)

2

LUCK, GEORG, 1926- , ed. Horizonte der Humanitas.
(Card 2)

Über Perioden des lateinischen Schrifttums im Mittelalter, von P. Lehmann.—Walter Wili zum 60. Geburtstag, von R. Graf Coudenhove-Kalergi.—Römisches Recht in unserer Rechtsordnung, von A. Beck.—Banchieri, umanisti e mecenati, di E. Cello.--Les trois facteurs de la paix et leur nouvelle orientation, par N. Matcesco.—Le professeur docteur Walter Wili, par G. Pimienta.—Geburtstagsbrief, von R. A. Schröder.--Vier Gedichte, von C. Lauber.--Papilloten, von W. Lauber.

1. Classical studies--Addresses, essays, lectures. 2. Wili, Walter, 1900-

---

YED

Ludwig Klages, Erforscher und Künder des Lebens; Festschrift zum 75. Geburtstage des philosophen am 10. Dezember, 1947. Hrsg. von Herbert Hönel. Linz a.D., Osterreichischer Verlag für Belletristik und Wissenschaft[1947] 269 p. illus. 22cm.

Fest.

---

*QEB
(Tolstoi, L.N.)

LUDWIG, NADESCHDA, ed.
L.N. Tolstoi; Aufsätze und Essays zum 50. Todestag. Halle (Saale), Verlag Sprache und Literatur, 1960. 128 p. port. 22cm.

CONTENTS.--Zum Gedenken L.N. Tolstois. "Krieg und Frieden." Von N. Ludwig.--Gedanken zu "Anna Karenina." Die Aufnahme Tolstois in der zeitgenössischen deutschen Kritik. Von Ch. Stulz.--"Auferstehung," von E. Reissner.--"Die Macht der Finsternis." "Der lebende
(Continued)

NN R 2.64 f/₃ OC PC, 1 SL S, 1 (LC1, X1, Z1)

2

LUDWIG, NADESCHDA, ed. L.N. Tolstoi...
(Card 2)

Leichnam." Von W. Pieper.

1. Tolstoi, Lev Nikolayevich, graf, 1828-1910.

D-14
1930

Ludwig, Richard M., *ed.*
Aspects of American poetry; essays presented to Howard Mumford Jones. ⌐Columbus⌐ Ohio State University Press ⌐1963, °1962⌐

vi, 335 p. 23 cm.

Includes bibliography.

CONTENTS.—The meter-making argument, by E. Fussell.—Some varieties of inspiration, by G. F. Cronkhite.—Poe: journalism and the theory of poetry, by W. Charvat.—The problem of structure in some poems by Whitman, by M. Feiheim.—Ezra Pound's London years, by
(Continued)

NN R 3.63 g/ OC PC, 1, 2, I SL (LC1, X1, Z1) [1]

Ludwig, Richard M *ed.* Aspects of American poetry ... ⌐1963, °1962⌐ (Card 2)

R. M. Ludwig.— Robert Frost and man's "royal role," by C. M. Simpson.—Sherwood Anderson's Mid-American chants, by W. B. Rideout.—The bridge and Hart Crane's "span of consciousness," by A. Van Nostrand.—Wallace Stevens' ice-cream, by R. Ellmann.—"The situation of our time": Auden in his American phase, by F. P. W. McDowell.—Mr. Tate: whose wreath should be a moral, by R. Squires.—Deliberate exiles: the social sources of agrarian poetics, by W. W. Douglas.—A bibliography of Howard Mumford Jones (p. ⌐301⌐-335).

1. Poetry, American--Addresses, essays, lectures. 2. Jones, Howard Mumford, 1892- I. Title.

---

*OHM

Lüders, Heinrich, 1869-
Philologica indica; ausgewählte kleine Schriften von Heinrich Lüders. Festgabe zum siebzigsten Geburtstage am 25. Juni 1939 dargebracht von Kollegen, Freunden und Schülern... Göttingen, Vandenhoeck & Ruprecht, 1940. 812 p. illus. 26cm.

Bibliographical footnotes.

Festschrift

536234B. 1. Indic studies.
N. Y. P. L. December 4, 1950

---

*C-1 p.v.314

LUIGI CORRIDORI, studente universitario; nel decimo anniversario della morte. Verona, Editrice Nigrizia [1953] 63 p. port. 17cm.

"Appendice" (p.49-61) contains writings by Luigi Corridori.

I. Corridori, Luigi, 1922-1943.

NN** X 2.56 j/₄ OC, I, Ib PC, I SL (Z1, LC1, X1)

NINA
(Tegnér)

Lund, Sweden. **Universitet.**
Esaias Tegnér; studier til hans person och verk. Minnesskrift utgiven av Lunds universitet den 2 november 1946. Lund, C. W. K. Gleerup [1946] 1072 p. 25cm.

"Nils Palmborg: Bidrag til en förteckning över Esaias Tegnérs bevarade manuskript," p. 747–911; "Signe Carlsson: Bidrag til en förteckning över Esaias Tegnérs brev," p. 913–1072.

393321B. 1. Tegnér, Esaias, 1782–1846. I. Title.
N. Y. P. L. September 12, 1947

LYBERG, BENGT, ed. Festskrift tillägnad Carl Kempe 80 år... (Card 2)

1. Lumber--Trade and stat.--Sweden. 2. Kempe,Carl. I. Ulfsparre, Sixten, joint ed. II.Gyllensvärd, Bo Vilhelm,1916- joint ed. III. Lyberg, Bengt. IV. Ulfsparre, Sixten.

L–10
5287
bd. 14

Lund, Sweden. Universitet. Institutionen för nordiska språk.
Studier i nordisk språkvetenskap från Lunds universitets institution för nordiska språk och Landsmålsarkivet i Lund. Lund, C. W. K. Gleerup [1958] 182 p. illus. 25cm. (Lundastudier i nordisk språkvetenskap. 14)

Rev. ed. of a handwritten festschrift to Professor Karl Gustav Ljunggren from friends and colleagues at the Institutionen för nordiska språk och Landsmålsarkivet i Lund for his 50. birthday, Dec. 6, 1956; editor: Bertil Ejder.

(Continued)

NN R 8.62 (OC)III (OD)IIt,IIb (ED)IIt OS(1b+)I PC,1,2,I,II,III (LC1,X1,Z1) [I]

XAH

Lyons. Université. *Faculté de droit.*
Introduction à l'étude du droit comparé; recueil d'études en l'honneur d'Édouard Lambert ... Paris, Librairie de la Société anonyme du Recueil Sirey; [etc., etc.] 1938.
3 v. front. (port., v. 1) 25½cm.
"Ce recueil, préparé par la Faculté de droit de Lyon ... [est] formé de contributions écrites d'après un plan préconçu, par des universitaires et des spécialistes de tous pays, choisis pour leur autorité en droit comparé."—Préf., signed: Pierre Garraud.
"L'œuvre d'Édouard Lambert" (bibliography): v. 1, p. [7]–10.
"Les publications de l'Institut de droit comparé de Lyon": v. 1, p. [17]–21.
1. Comparative law. 2. Lambert, Édouard, 1866– I. Title. II. Title: Recueil d'études en l'honneur d'Édouard Lambert.

A C 38-3360

New York. Public library for Library of Congress [2] Festschrift.

Lund, Sweden. Universitet. Institutionen för nordiska språk. (Card 2)

CONTENTS.—Poesien i inskrifterna på Hällestad-stenarna, av I. Lindquist.—För en finare transkription av färöiskan, av P. Naert.—Ett anonymt prelatbrev från Sturetiden, av G. Lindblad.—Något om presens konjunktiv i nysvenskan, av A. Sundquist.—Den bibliska bilden och bibelkunskapen, av G. Mattsson.—Redgarn, av S. Ekbo.—Verner von Heidenstam och Pär Lagerkvist, av W. Åkerlund.—Ett försök att levandegöra et folkmål i ett hembygdsmuseum, av G. Sjöstedt.—Franska låneord i folkmålen, av I. Ingers.—Fonetisk och fonematisk kartläggning, av S. Benson.—Råset, Funderset et consortes, av B. Ejder.

1. Ljunggren, Karl Gustav, 1906– . 2. Swedish language—Addresses, essays, lectures. I. Series. II. Sweden. Landsmålsarkivet, Lund. III. Ejder, Bortil, ed. t. 1958.

D-19
4605

McComas, J Francis, *comp.*
Special wonder; the Anthony Boucher memorial anthology of fantasy and science fiction. Edited by J. Francis McComas. New York, Random House [1970]
xv, 410 p. 22 cm.
"Companion volume to Crimes and misfortunes; the Anthony Boucher memorial anthology of mysteries; edited by J. Francis McComas."

1. Science--Fiction--Collections. 2. Fantastic fiction--Collections. I. White, William Anthony Parker, 1911-1968. II. Title.
NN*R 6.70 m/OC, I PC, 1,2,I,II SL (LC1, X1, Z1)

ZOV

Luther, Martin. ~~1483–1546.~~
Luthers randbemerkungen zu Gabriel Biels Collectorium in quattuor libros sententiarum, und zu dessen Sacri canonis missae expositio, Lyon 1514, herausgegeben von Hermann Degering. Mit einer faksimilewiedergabe auf einer lichtdrucktafel. Weimar, H. Böhlaus nachf., 1933.
xii p., 1 l., 20 p. fold. facsim. 28cm.
Half-title: Festgabe der Kommission zur herausgabe der werke Martin Luthers zur feier des 450. geburtstages Luthers, 10. november 1933.
1. Biel, Gabriel, d. 1495. Collectorium in quattuor libros sententiarum. 2. Biel, Gabriel, d. 1495. Sacri canonis missae tam mystica, quam litteralis expositio. I. Degering, Hermann, 1866– ed. II. Kommission zur herausgabe der werke Martin Luthers. III. Title: Festgabe ... zur feier des 450. geburtstages Luthers.

34-17152
Library of Congress BR332.B5 Card rev. 1940
[2] 208.1

Write on slip only words underlined and classmark:
ZRA

McCulloch, Samuel Clyde, ed.
British humanitarianism; essays honoring Frank J. Klingberg, by his former doctoral students at the University of California, Los Angeles. Philadelphia, Church Historical Society [1950] x, 254 p. port. 24cm. (Church Historical Society [Philadelphia] Publication 32)

CONTENTS.—The Society for the Propagation of the Gospel's plantations and the emancipation crisis, by J. H. Bennet, Jr.—Convicts, colonists and progress in Australia, 1800–1850, by C. S. Blackton.—The S. P. G. and the foreign settler in the American Colonies, by W. A. Bultmann.—Early factory legislation; a neglected aspect of British

(Continued)

NN*R 3.54 OC, I PC, 1, 2, 3 E, 1 (U1, LC1, Z1, X1)

E-13
3509

Lyberg, Bengt, *ed.*
Festskrift tillägnad Carl Kempe 80 år, 1884–1964. [Redaktionskommitté: Bengt Lyberg, Sixten Ulfsparre och Bo Gyllensvärd. Uppsala, Almqvist & Wiksell, 1965]
985 p. illus. (part col.) maps, col. port. 25 cm.
Includes bibliographies.

(Continued)

NN*R 10.65 v/ OC,I,II IIIb*,IVb* PC,1,2,I, II SL E,1,2,I,II (LC1, X1,Z1)

2

McCulloch, Samuel Clyde, ed. British humanitarianism... [1950] (Card 2)

humanitarianism, by J. Duffy.—The Anglican Church in British North America; ecclesiastical government before 1688, by H. E. Kimball.—Thomas Bradbury Chandler, Anglican humanitarian in colonial New Jersey, by S. C. McCulloch.—Matthew Graves, Anglican missionary to the Puritans, by M. O'Neil.—James Ramsay, essayist, aggressive humanitarian, by J. A. Schutz.—The attempt of British humanitarianism to modify chattel slavery, by R. W. Smith.—Education and the children's hymn in eighteenth century England, by P. J. Wetherell.—Selected list of publications by Frank J. Klingberg (p. 200–204)—Bibliographical references (p. 205–235).

1. Social problems. 2. Humanitarianism—Gt. Br. 3. Klingberg, Frank Joseph, 1883– . I. Title. II. Ser.

*OAC

McCULLOUGH, W. S., ed.
The seed of wisdom; essays in honour of T. J. Meek. [Toronto] University of Toronto press [1964] xi, 200 p. 24cm.

Bibliographical footnotes.

CONTENTS.--The reign of Nebuchadnezzar I: a turning point in the history of ancient Mesopotamian religion, by W. C. Lambert.--Literature as a medium of political propaganda in ancient Egypt, by R. J. Williams.--The formal aspect of ancient Near Eastern law, by R. A. F. MacKenzie.--Yahweh the god of heavens, by D. K.

(Continued)

NN R 1.65c/ OC, Ibo PC, 1, 2 SL O, 1, 2 (LC1, X1, Z1) [1]

McCULLOUGH, W. S., ed. The seed of wisdom... (Card 2)

Andrews.--Proto-Septuagint studies, by J. W. Wevers.--The life and works of Joseph Ḥazzāyā, by E. J. Sherry.--Zeus in the Hellenic age, by F. W. Beare.--The molten sea of Solomon's temple, by G. Bagnani.--In search of the divine Denis, by J. M. Rist.--Mamluk Egypt at the eleventh hour, some eyewitness observations, by G. M. Wickens.--Avicenna's theory of prophecy in the light of Ash'rite theology, by M. E. Marmura.--A study of ancestor worship in ancient China, by C. C. Shih.

1. Meek, Theophile James, 1881- 2. Oriental studies--Collections. I. McCullough, W. S.

TG p.v.525

[McDonald, J C]
Propositions relating to Colombia, S. A. ... [New York?] 1916. 1 v. map. 29cm.

Seven reports, compiled for Fred Lavis, four of which are signed: JCM [i. e. J. C. McDonald]

1. Investments, Foreign—Colombia. 2. Debt, Public—Colombia—Bogota. 3. Railways—Finance—Colombia. I. Lavis, Fred, 1871-

N. Y. P. L. March 2, 1949

A p.v.303

Mack, Heinrich, 1867-
...Carl Friedrich Gauss und die Seinen; Festschrift zu seinem 150. Geburtstage; herausgegeben von Heinrich Mack... Braunschweig: E. Appelhans & Comp., 1927. xi, 130 p. facsims., front., geneal. tables, illus. (map), ports. 8°. (Werkstuecke aus Museum, Archiv und Bibliothek der Stadt Braunschweig. [Teil] 2.)

Contents: Einleitung. Aus dem Briefwechsel der Familie Gauss. Nachfahrentafeln Gauss.

428292A. 1. Gauss, Karl Friedrich, 1777–1855. 2. Letters, German. 3. Ser.

N. Y. P. L. September 9, 1929

D-18
7308

MACK, MAYNARD, 1909- , ed.
Imagined worlds; essays on some English novels and novelists in honour of John Butt. Edited by Maynard Mack and Ian Gregor. London, Methuen; [distributed in the U.S.A. by Barnes and Noble, 1968] xxv, 485, [1] p. port. 23cm.

CONTENTS.--Memorial address, 11 December 1965, by D. Hay.--British academy obituary, by J. Sutherland.--Congreve's Incognita and the contrivances of providence, by A. Williams.--Early theories of prose

(Continued)

NN R 2.69 k/, OC, I PC, 1, 2, 3, I, II SL (LC1, X1, Z3) [1]

MACK, MAYNARD, 1909- ed. Imagined worlds... (Card 2)

fiction: Congreve and Fielding, by I. Simon.--The relation of Defoe's fiction to his non-fictional writings, by J. Sutherland.--Gulliver and the gentle reader, by C. J. Rawson.--Art and artifice in Tom Jones, by F. W. Hilles.--In praise of Rasselas; four notes (converging) by W. K. Wimsatt.--Scott and the art of revision, by M. Lascelles.--Robert Smith Surtees, by B. Dobrée.--New readings in Dombey and son, by K. Tillotson.--Hard times and common things, by K. J. Fielding.--George Eliot's Klesmer, by G. S. Haight.--Authorial presence; some observations, by G. Tillotson.--The "sociological" approach to The Mayor of Casterbridge, by J. C. Maxwell.--Jude the obscure, by I. Gregor.--

(Continued)

MACK, MAYNARD, 1909- ed. Imagined worlds... (Card 3)

George Moore as historian of consciences, by P. Ure.--The other self; thoughts about character in the novel, by M. Price.--Conrad, James and Chance, by I. P. Watt.--The shaping of time: Nostromo and Under the volcano, by C. Leech.--Portrait of Miriam; a study in the design of Sons and lovers, by L. L. Martz.--The marble and the statue; the exploratory imagination of D. H. Lawrence, by M. Kinkead-Weekes.--Joyce's Ulysses, symbolic poem, biography or novel?, by C. Brooks.--Waugh's Sword of honour, by A. Rutherford.--Rayner Heppenstall and the nouveau roman, by S. Monod.--A list of the published writings of John Butt, compiled by G. D. Carnall (p. 477-[486]).

1. Fiction, English--Addresses, essays, lectures. 2. Butt, John Everett. 3. Butt, John Everett--Bibl. I. Gregor, Ian, joint ed. II. Title.

E-12
2040

MacLure, Millar, *ed.*
Essays in English literature from the Renaissance to the Victorian Age, presented to A. S. P. Woodhouse, 1964. Edited by Millar MacLure and F. W. Watt. [Toronto] University of Toronto Press [1964]

x, 339 p. facsim. 24 cm.

Bibliographical footnotes.

CONTENTS.—Introduction.—"Spenserus," by R. Tuve.—Spenser's

(Continued)

NN * R 12.64 e/ OC, I, IIb* PC, 1, 2, I SL (LC1, X1, Z1)

MacLURE, MILLAR, ed. Essays in English literature from the Renaissance to the Victorian Age... (Card 2)

Mutabilitie, by W. Blissett.—Ben Jonson's poems: notes on the ordered society, by H. MacLean.—Historical doubts respecting Walton's Life of Donne, by R. C. Bald.—Some aspects of self-revelation and self-portraiture in Religio medici, by N. J. Endicott.—Milton and east, by G. Bullough.—Satan and the "myth" of the tyrant, by M. Y. Hughes.—Milton and sacred history: books XI and XII of Paradise lost, by H. R. MacCallum.—Structural and doctrinal pattern in Milton's later poems, by A. E. Barker.—The correspondence of the Augustans, by H. Davis.—Pope and the great chain of being, by F. E. L. Priestley.—The three forms of The prelude, 1798–1805, by

(Continued)

MacLURE, MILLAR, ed. Essays in English literature from the Renaissance to the Victorian Age... (Card 3)

J. R. MacGillivray.—John Stuart Mill and James Bentham, with some observations on James Mill, by J. M. Robson.—The idea of reform in Newman's early reviews, by L. K. Shook.—Ruskin, Hooker, and "the Christian theoria," by M. M. Ross.—The problem of spiritual authority in the nineteenth century, by N. Frye.—A. S. P. Woodhouse: scholar, critic, humanist, by D. Bush.—Publications of A. S. P. Woodhouse, by M. H. M. MacKinnon (p. [334]–339)

1. English literature--Addresses, essays, lectures. 2. Woodhouse, Arthur Sutherland Pigott. I. Watt, Frank William, 1927- joint ed. II. Watt, Frank William, 1927-

D-14
1966

Madan, T N ed.
Indian anthropology; essays in memory of D. N. Majumdar. Edited by T. N. Madan and Gopāla Śarana. London , Asia Pub. House [1962]
x, 420 p. illus. (1 col.) port., maps (on lining-papers) tables. 23 cm.
Includes bibliographies.
1. Anthropology--Addresses, essays, lectures. 2. Majumdar, Dhirendra Nath. 3. Anthropology--India. I. Sarana, Gopāla.
NN* R 3.63 g/ OC, I, Ib PC, 1, 2, 3, I SL O, 2, 3, I (LC1, X1, Z1)

*OHO
Mahāmahōpādhyāya Prof. D. V. Potdar sixty-first birthday commemoration volume; studies in historical and Indological research... Ed.: Dr. Surendra Nath Sen... [Poona, M. M.] 1950. 1 v. illus. 25cm.
Contributions in English or Mahratta.
Bibliographical footnotes.
1. India—Hist.—Addresses, essays, lectures. 2. Indic studies. 3. Potdar, Datto Vaman, 1890- . 4. Mahrattas—History. I. Sen, Surendra Nath, 1890- , ed.
N. Y. P. L.

* MF
Maennerchor Rapperswil.
Jubilaeumsschrift zur Feier des 75-jährigen Bestandes, 1854–1929. Rapperswil: G. Meyer[, 1930]. 124 p. plates. 8°.
Contents: Gmür, A. Jubiläum. Oser, H. Entwicklung und Ziele des Männergesanges. Schnellmann, M. Zur Vorgeschichte des Männerchors. Chronik: 1854–1910, von A. Gmür; 1910–1929, von M. Hofmann.
Juilliard Foundation Fund.
583058A. 1. Music—Assoc. and org.—Switzerland—Rapperswil. I. Gmuer, Alfons. II. Oser, Hans, 1895- . III. Schnellmann, Meinrad, 1896- . IV. Hofmann, Moriz.
N. Y. P. L. June 6, 1932

AN
(Gandhi, M.)
Mahatma Gandhi; essays and reflections on his life and work, presented to him on his seventieth birthday, October 2nd, 1939, edited by S. Radhakrishnan. London, G. Allen & Unwin, ltd. [1939]
382 p., 1 l. front., port. group. 24½cm.
"First published in 1939."
1. Gandhi, Mohandas Karamchand, 1869- I. Radhakrishnan, Sir Sarvepalli, 1888- ed.
Library of Congress DS481.G3M25 40-8958
[7] 923.254

E-11
1510
MAGYAR NÉPRAJZI TÁRSASÁG, Budapest.
Opuscula ethnologica memoriae Ludovici Biró sacra [anniversario nativitatis eius centesimo. Redigerunt T. Bodrogi et L. Boglár] Budapest, Akadémiai kiadó, 1959. 472 p. illus., port. 25cm.
Contributions in German or English; biography of Biró (p. 470-472) in German and English.
Includes bibliographies.
(Continued)
NN R 12.60 g/ (OC)I, II, IVbo OS, III PC, 1, 2, I, II, III SL (LC1, X1, Z1)

Copy only words underlined
& Classmark-- *MG
MAHLING, CHRISTOPH HELLMUT, ed.
Zum 70. Geburtstag von Joseph Müller-Blattau. Im Auftrage des Musikwissenschaftlichen Instituts der Universität des Saarlandes hrsg. von Christoph Hellmut Mahling. Kassel, New York, Barenreiter, 1966. 340 p. illus., ports., music. 25cm. (Saarbrücker Studien zur Musikwissenschaft. Bd. 1)
1. Müller-Blattau, Joseph, 1895- . 2. Music--Essays. 3. Essays. I. Series. II. Saarbrücken. Universität des Saarlandes.
NN R 7.68 e/(OS)I, II PC, 1, 2, I, II MU, 1, 3, I, II (LC1, X1, Z1) OC

MAGYAR NÉPRAJZI TÁRSASÁG, Budapest. Opuscula ethnologica memoriae Ludovici Biró sacra... (Card 2)
1. Ethnology--Essays and misc. 2. Biró, Lajos. I. Bodrogi, Tibor, ed. II. Boglár, L., ed. III. Akademiai kiadó, Budapest. IV. Boglár, L.

Write on slip words underlined below
and class mark— *PBC
Maimonides-Festschrift. [Articles by I. Elbogen, Heinz Wolff and others.]
(Monatsschrift für Geschichte und Wissenschaft des Judentums. Breslau, 1935. Jahrg. 79, p. 66-194.)
form 466b [x 21-31 25m]

FOG
Magyar történelmi társulat.
Emlékkönyv Kossuth Lajos születésének 150. évfordulójára. Budapest, Akadémiai kiadó, 1952. 2 v. plates, ports., facsims. 24cm.
1. Kossuth, Lajos, 1802-1894. 2. Hungary—Hist.—Uprising of 1848-1849. I. Title.
NN**R X 11.53 (OC)I OS PC, 1, 2 SL (Z1, LC1, X1)

3-MAH
Mainz. Römisch-Germanisches Central-Museum.
Festschrift des Römisch-Germanischen Zentralmuseums in Mainz zur Feier seines hundertjährigen Bestehens, 1952. Mainz, 1952-53. 3 v. in 2. illus., plates, maps. 30cm.
Bd. 1-3.
Bibliographical footnotes.
1. Germany—Archaeology—Roman remains. 2. Art, Roman—Germany.
NN**R X 10.54 OSs PCs, 1s, 2s SLs As, 2s (LC1s, X1s, Z1s)

L-10
3063
no. 4
MAINZ. Universität. Institut für menschliche Stammesgeschichte und Biotypologie.
Festschrift für Frédéric Falkenburger, mit Beiträgen von W. Busanny-Caspari [et al.] Baden-Baden, Verlag für Kunst und Wissenschaft, 1955. 101 p. illus., port. 24cm. (Beiträge zur Anthropologie. Heft 4)

Includes bibliographies.

(Continued)
NN R X 2.60 1/4 (OC)2bo, II, III OS(1b+)I PC, 1, 2, I, II, III (LC1, X1, Z1) 2

MAINZ. Universität. Institut für menschliche Stammesgeschichte und Biotypologie. Festschrift für Frédéric Falkenburger... (Card 2)

CONTENTS.--Mischlingskinder in Westdeutschland; eine anthropologische Studie an farbigen Heimkindern, von R. Sieg.--Die verschiedenen Typen des Sulcus mylohyoideus bei Mensch und Anthropoiden, von W. Korn und P. Riethe.--Zur Frage der Konstitutionsbestimmung an der Leiche, von W. Busanny-Caspari.

1. Anthropology--Addresses, essays, lectures. 2. Falkenburger, Frédéric. I. Series. II. Busanny-Caspari, W. III. Title.

E-11
1990
MAINZ. Universität. Katholisch-theologische Fakultät.
Universitas, Dienst an Wahrheit und Leben; Festschrift für Bischof Dr. Albert Stohr. Im Auftrag der Katholisch-theologischen Fakultät der Johannes Gutenberg-Universität Mainz hrsg. von Ludwig Lenhart. Mainz, M. Grünwald [1960] 2 v. illus., ports. (1 col.), facsims. 25cm.

Includes bibliographical references.
1. Stohr, Albert, bp., 1890- 2. Theology--Essays and misc. ed. I. Lenhart, Ludwig, 1902-
NN R 2.61 a/X (OC)1b*, I OS(1b+) PC, 1, 2, I SL (LC1, X1, Z1)

D-17
7508
MALTUSCH, GOTTFRIED, ed.
100 Jahre innere Mission Hannover; Festschrift. Hannover, Lutherhaus-Verlag, 1965. 141 p. illus., ports. 22cm.

1. Landesverein für innere Mission, Hanover.
2. Evangelical Lutheran church--Charities. I. Maltusch, Gottfried. i. [Title] Hundert.
NN 8.68 v/4 OC, Ibo PC, 1, 2 SL (LC1, X1, Z1)

E-12
6873
MANIFESTATIONS d'hommage organisées à l'occasion du centenaire de la naissance de Paul Hymans. [Bruxelles, Presses universitaires de Bruxelles [1965?] 35 p. illus., ports. 24cm.

Cover title.
Addresses by F. J. de Weert, L. Cooremans, F. Leblanc, J. Rey, R. Fenaux, and P.-H. Spaak.

1. Hymans, Paul, 1865-1941. I. Brussels. Université libre.
NN R 3.67 1/- OC (OS)I PC, 1, I SL (LC1, X1, Z1)

PAH
Manne Siegbahn, 1886 [12] 1951. [Uppsala, Almqvist & Wiksell, 1951] 845 p. illus. 25cm.

Chiefly in English; some contributions in Swedish.

1. Siegbahn, Manne, 1886- 2. Physics--Addresses, essays, lectures.
NN

E-12
2836
Manners, Robert Alan, 1913- ed.
Process and pattern in culture, essays in honor of Julian H. Steward, edited by Robert A. Manners. Chicago, Aldine Pub. Co. [1964]
ix, 434 p. illus., maps, ports. 25 cm.
Includes bibliographies.

1. Steward, Julian Haynes, 1902- . 2. Anthropology--Addresses, essays, lecturers. 3. Indians, American--Culture.
NN* R 6.65 g/ OC PC, 1, 2, 3 SL AH, 1, 3 (LC1, X1, Z1)
[I]

---

*XM-108
MANNHEIMER SCHACHKLUB.
Wilhelm Gudehus, ein Meister des Schachspiels; Festschrift zu seinem 25 jährigen Jubiläum als Vorsitzender des Mannheimer Schachklubs 17. Oktober 1895-17. Oktober 1920. Im Auftrage des Mannheimer Schachklubs hrsg. von Herm. Römmig. [Mannheim, 1920] 88 p. illus. 22cm.

Microfiche (Negative). 2 sheets 11 x 15cm. (NYPL FSN 452)
(Continued)
NN R 9.68 p/4 (OC) 2bo, I, IIbo OS(1b+) PC, 1, 2, I SL (UM1, LC1, X1, Z1) 2

MANNHEIMER SCHACHKLUB. Wilhelm Gudehus... (Card 2)

1. Chess--Games played. 2. Gudehus, Wilhelm I. Römmig, Herm, ed. II. Römmig, Herm.

---

*C-4 p.v.380
The Maple's praise of Franklin Delano Roosevelt, 1882–1945; Canadian tributes by Robert J. C. Stead, Dorothy Dumbrille [and] Nathaniel A. Benson. Ottawa, Tower books, 1945. 18 p. 23cm.

CONTENTS—Franklin Delano Roosevelt, by R. J. C. Stead.—The traveller, by D. Dumbrille.—A Canadian elegy of remembrance, by N. A. Benson.—Prayer for V-E day, by N. A. Benson.

Franklin Delano Roosevelt Collection pres. U. S.
1. Roosevelt, Franklin Delano, 32d pres. U. S. I. Stead, Robert James Campbell, 1880- . II. Dumbrille, Dorothy. III. Benson, Nathaniel Anketell, 1903-
NN**R X 8.55 OC, I, II, III PC, 1, I, II, III SL AH, 1, I, II, III (Z1, LC1, X1)

AN
*
(Behring, E.)

Marburg, Germany. **Universität.**
Behring zum Gedächtnis; Reden und wissenschaftliche Vorträge anlässlich der Behring-Erinnerungsfeier. Marburg an der Lahn, 4. bis 6. Dez. 1940. Hrsg. von der Philipps-Universität... Berlin-Grunewald, B. Schultz [c1942] 200 p. plates. 30cm.

336674B. 1. Behring, Emil Adolf von, 1854-1917. 2. Immunity. 3. Tuberculosis. 4. Medicine, Biochemic. I. Title.
N. Y. P. L. July 12, 1946

Write on slip words underlined below and class mark —
EAA

Marburg, Germany. **Universität.** Institut für Grenz- und Auslanddeutschtum.
...Die evang. Landeskirche A. B. in Siebenbürgen, mit den angeschlossenen evang. Kirchenverbänden Altrumänien, Banat, Bessarabien, Bukowina, ungarisches Dekanat. Festschrift, herausgegeben vom Institut für Grenz- und Auslandsdeutschtum an der Universität Marburg, 1922. Mit einem Vorwort von Geh. Kirchenrat Professor D. F. Rendtorff... Jena: G. Fischer, 1923. vi, 140 p. incl. tables. front. (port.) 24½cm. (Marburg,

(Continued)

N. Y. P. L. February 23, 1938

Marburg, Germany. **Universität.** Institut für Grenz- und Auslanddeutschtum. ...Die evang. Landeskirche... (Card 2)

Germany. Universität. Institut für Grenz- und Auslanddeutschtum. Schriften. Heft 2.)

"Handschriftlich ist es [das vorliegende Werk]...als Ehrengabe zum siebenzigsten Geburtstag von seinen...Mitarbeitern dem Sachsenbischof D.Dr. Friedrich Teutsch überreicht."

CONTENTS.—Bischof D. Friedrich Teutsch, von G. A. Schuller.—Die evang. Landeskirche A. B. in Siebenbürgen, von Max Tschurl.—Die Diaspora der evang. Landeskirche A. B. in Siebenbürgen und die nach Amerika ausgewanderten Glaubensgenossen, von Berthold Buchalla.—Die deutsch-evang. Kirchengemeinden A. B. in Altrumänien, von

(Continued)

N. Y. P. L. February 23, 1938

Marburg, Germany. **Universität.** Institut für Grenz- und Auslanddeutschtum. ...Die evang. Landeskirche... (Card 3)

Max Tschurl.—Banater Kirchenbezirk and magy. evang. Gemeinden, von Wilhelm Melzer.—Die evang.-luth. Landeskirche Bessarabiens, von Hans Weprich.—Die evang. Kirche in der Bukowina, von Albert v. Hochmeister.—Die Schule, von Carl Albrich.—Die allg. Pensionsanstalt der evang. Landeskirche A. B. in Siebenbürgen, von Max Sigerus.—Das Landeskonsistorium und seine Ämter, von Karl Fritsch.

1. Evangelische Landeskirche in Rumania—Transylvania. I. Teutsch, Friedrich, bp., 1852-1933. II. Ser.
N. Y. P. L. February 23, 1938

K-10
208

MARBURG. Universität. Burschenschaft Arminia.
Die Toten der Marburger Burschenschaft Arminia, bearb. von Rudolf Bonnet. Frankfurt am Main, 1955. 1 v. 22cm.

Teil 3.
CONTENTS. —T. 3. 253 Lebensläufe; Festgabe zum 95. Stiftungsfest der M. B. Arminia.

1. Germany--Biog. I. Bonnet, Rudolf, 1889- , ed.
NN* * R 11. 57 a/P (OC)I OS(1b) PC, 1, I SL (LC1, X1, Z1)

D-19
4087

Marc-Wogau, Konrad, 1902-
Philosophical essays. History of philosophy. Perception. Historical explanation. [Edited by the Philosophical Society of Uppsala.] Lund, Gleerup; Copenhagen, E. Munksgaard, 1967.
xi, 278 p. port. 22cm. (Library of Theoria, no. 11)

"This volume is a collection of philosophical articles by Prof. Konrad Marc-Wogau, which has been edited [and translated] in celebration of his 65th birthday, 4th April, 1967."

(Continued)

NN*R 1. 70 r/L OC (OS)I PC, 1, 2, 3, I SL (LC1, X1, Z1)
2

MARC-WOGAU, KONRAD, 1902- . Philosophical essays... (Card 2)

"Writings of Konrad Marc-Wogau": p. 243-251.
Bibliographical references included in "Notes." (p. 253-273)

1. Philosophy--Hist. 2. Perception. 3. History--Philosophy. I. Upsala, Sweden. Universitet. Filosofiska föreningen.

AN
(Churchill, W.)

MARCHANT, Sir JAMES, 1867- , ed.
Winston Spencer Churchill, servant of Crown and Commonwealth; a tribute by various hands presented to him on his eightieth birthday. London, Cassell [1954] ix, 172 p. port. 22cm.

CONTENTS. —To W. S. C., by Viscount Norwich. —Prologue, by G. Murray. —The Churchill heritage, by Sir A. MacNalty. —The man of peace, by Viscount Cecil of Chelwood. —Churchill's use of English

(Continued)

NN**R 5. 55 g/L OC PC, 1 SL E, 1 (LC1, X1, Z1)

MARCHANT, Sir JAMES, 1867- , ed. Winston Spencer Churchill ... (Card 2)

speech, by Viscount Simon. —The politician, by C. Coote. —The Campbell-Bannerman-Asquith government, by Viscount Samuel. —Two great war leaders, by L. S. Amery. —Across the House, by C. Attlee. —Churchill and the Navy, by Lord Fraser of North Cape. —Churchill and the Commonwealth, by R. G. Menzies. —The master of words, by Sir A. Herbert. —The chronicler, by Sir C. Webster. —The artist, by Sir J. Rothenstein. —The sportsman, by H. H. the Aga Khan. —Winston Churchill—as I know him, by Lady V. B. Carter. —

(Continued)

MARCHANT, Sir JAMES, 1867- , ed. Winston Spencer Churchill ... (Card 3)

A birthday letter, by B. Baruch. —Epilogue, by A. Eden.

1. Churchill, Sir Winston Leonard Spencer, 1874-

* MGA

MARCKHL, ERICH, 1902-
Musik und Gegenwart; Ansprachen, Vorträge, Aufsätze. Hrsg. von den steiermärkischen Volks-Musikschulen mit Unterstützung der steiermärkischen Landesregierung. [Graz, 1962?]
173 p. port. 23cm.

Bibliography, p. 170-171.
1. Music--Essays. 2. Essays. 3. History and criticism, 1900- . (In German).
NN 4.65 g/c OC PC, 1 SL MU, 2, 3 (LC1, X1, Z1)

PBE

Marcolongo, Roberto, 1862–
... Memorie sulla geometria e la meccanica di Leonardo da Vinci. Napoli, S. I. E. M.—Stabilimento industrie editoriali meridionali, 1937.
1 p. l., [v]–xii, 364 p., 1 l. illus., diagrs. 25½cm.
Cover-title: Studi vinciani.
Issued to commemorate the retirement of the author from the University of Naples. *cf.* Prefatory note by Comitato onoranze prof. Roberto Marcolongo.
Includes articles published in periodicals, 1929–1935.
Bibliographical foot-notes.
CONTENTS.—Arte e scienza di Leonardo da Vinci.—Le ricerche geometrico-meccaniche di Leonardo da Vinci.—La meccanica di Leonardo da Vinci.—Il trattato di Leonardo da Vinci sulle trasformazioni del soldi; analisi del Codice Forster I. nel "Victoria a. Albert museum".
1. Leonardo da Vinci, 1452–1519. 2. Geometry. 3. Mechanics.
A C 39–161
New York. Public library for Library of Congress [2]

---

*PXR

Marcus Melchior. En mindebog. Red. af familien i forbindelse med forlaget. København, Thaning & Appel, [1970]

142 p. 8 plates. 22 cm.

CONTENTS.—Min far, af W. D. Melchior.—Til minde om en ven, af W. S. Jacobson.—Flygtning i Sverige, af P. Borchsenius.—Forholdet til efterkrigstidens Tyskland, af H. Sandbæk.—Danmark og Israel, af P. P. Rohde.—Jøde i Danmark, af V. Kampmann.—Spredte glimt fra Marcus Melchiors liv som taler, af N. Lind.—Overrabbinerens

(Continued)

NN* R 7.71 b/zOC, I PC, 1, 2, I SL J, 2, 3, I (LC1, X1, Z1)
2

MARCUS MELCHIOR. En mindebog. (Card 2)

virke i synagogen i København 1947-1969, af S. Friedman.—Rabbinergerning i det 20. århundrede, af I. Mowshowitz.—Kirke og synagoge, af H. Fuglsang-Damgaard.—Samtaler om religion, af H. Berger.—Min rebbes verden, af S. Besekow.—Ikke tidligere i bogform publicerede artikler og taler af Marcus Melchior: Jødedommen. Jødisk nytår 5723. Indvielsen af Samfundshuset i Oslo. Tolerance. En ny anmeldelse af en meget gammel tekst. Hjælp flygtningene. Optimisten af 1942.

1. Jews in Denmark. 2. Melchior, Marcus. 3. Denmark.
I. Melchior, Marcus.

YBX

Maréchal, Joseph, 1878–1944.
...Mélanges Joseph Maréchal... Bruxelles, L'Édition universelle [etc., etc.] 1950, 2 v. in 1. port. 23cm. (Museum Lessianum. Sect. philosophique. no. 31)

"Bibliographie du père J. Maréchal," v. 1, p. 47–71.
CONTENTS.—1. Oeuvres.—2. Hommages.

1. Philosophy, 1901– . I. Title.
NN 1.53 OC, I PC, 1 SL (LC1, Z1, X1)

Write on slip words underlined below and class mark — *DM

Le maréchal Lyautey (17 novembre 1854-28 juillet 1934). [Articles by M.-D. Forestier, R. Garric, and others.]

(Revue des jeunes. Paris, 1935. Année 26, juillet-aout, p.1-152.)

form 400b [x-21-34 25m]

Write on slip words underlined below and class mark —
YAGA

...The **Maritain** volume; dedicated to Jacques Maritain on the occasion of his sixtieth anniversary. New York, Sheed and Ward [1943] 360 p. 24cm. (The Thomist. New York, 1943. v. 5.)

Cover-title.
CONTENTS.—Jacques Maritain, a biographical impression, by H. L. Binsse.—On Maritain's political philosophy, by Waldemar Gurian.—The theological ingredients of peace, by J. C. Osbourn.—The virtue of social justice and international life, by F. E. McMahon.—The theory of oligarchy: Edmund Burke, by R. M. Hutchins.—Jacques Maritain: Est, est, non, non, by R. N. Anshen.—Maritain's philosophy of the sciences, by Y. R. Simon.—The role of dogma in Judaism, by Louis Finkelstein.—The Thomistic

(Continued)

N. Y. P. L. January 27, 1944

...The **Maritain** volume... (Card 2)

concept of culture, by R. E. Brennan.—To be—that is the answer, by Emmanuel Chapman.—Justice and friendship, by G. B. Phelan.—Claudel and the Catholic revival, by L. S. Bondy.—The demonstration of God's existence, by M. J. Adler.—Contemplation in America, by J. S. Middleton.—Providence, by W. R. Thompson.—A date in the history of epistemology, by Gerald Smith.—Dante and Thomism, by Daniel Sargent.—Matter, beatitude and liberty, by A. C. Pegis.—Art in France and England, 1540–1640, by J. U. Nef.—John Dewey and modern Thomism, by William O'Meara.—Motet: De ordinatione angelorum, by Arthur Lourié.—Bibliography of Jacques Maritain, 1910–1942, by Ruth Byrns.

247054B. 1. Maritain, Jacques, 1882– 2. Philosophy—Essays and misc.
N. Y. P. L. January 27, 1944

D-17
8718

Markedsføring i 70-årene. Et fremtidsrettet tverrsnitt av fagområdet markedsføring ved nordiske markedsøkonomer. Redaksjonskomité: Roald P. Aukner, Dag Coward, Ulf Johns[og] Ingar Tanum. Oslo, Tanum, 1967.
192 p. 1 port., tables, diagrs. 23 cm.

"Utsendt som hilsen til Leif Holbæk-Hanssen på 50-årsdagen."
Bibliographical footnotes.

(Continued)

NN* R 1.67 p/, OC, I, IIb* PC, 1, 2, I SL E, 1, 2, I (LC1, X1, Z1)
2

MARKEDSFØRING i 70-årene. (Card 2)

1. Holbaek-Hanssen, Leif 2. Marketing. I. Aukner, Roald P., ed. II. Aukner, Roald P.

D-12
8301

MARTIN HEIDEGGER zum siebzigsten Geburtstag: Festschrift. [Hrsg. von Günther Neske. Pfullingen] Neske [c1959] 347 p. illus.(part col., 1 mounted), mount. port. 21cm.

1. Philosophy--Addresses essays, lectures. 2. Literature--Addresses, essays, lectures. 3. Heidegger, Martin, 1889- . I. Neske, Günther, ed. II. Neske, Günther.
NN R 2. 61 m/$_{A}$/OC, I, IIb* PC, 1,2, 3, I SL (LC1, X1, Z1)
[1]

E-12
7355

Martin, Roscoe Coleman, 1903- *ed.*
Public administration and democracy; essays in honor of Paul H. Appleby. Roscoe C. Martin, editor. [1st ed. Syracuse, N. Y.] Syracuse University Press [1965]

vii, 355 p. 24 cm.

CONTENTS.—Paul H. Appleby and his administrative world, by R. C. Martin.—Reflections on institutions and their ways, by P. H. Appleby.—Public administration and culture, by D. Waldo.—Business as government, by E. S. Redford.—The budget and democratic govern-

(Continued)

NN* R 6. 66 g/$_{A}$ OC PC, 1, 2, 3 SL AH, 2, 3 E, 1, 3 3
(LC1, X1, Z1)

YBX
(Heidegger)

Martin Heideggers Einfluss auf die Wissenschaften; aus Anlass seines sechzigsten Geburtstages verfasst von Carlos Astrada ... [und 10 anderen] Bern, A. Francke, 1949. 174 p. 22cm.

Bibliographical footnotes.

Fest

588723B. 1. Heidegger, Martin, 1889- . I. Astrada, Carlos, 1894-
N. Y. P. L. October 10, 1951

MARTIN, ROSCOE COLEMAN, 1903- , ed.
Public administration and democracy...
(Card 2)

ment, by J. Burkhead.—The managers of national economic change, by B. M. Gross.—Some notes on reorganizations in public agencies, by F. C. Mosher.—The changing intergovernmental system, by G. S. Birkhead.—The citizen as administrator, by J. M. Gaus.—Responsibility and representativeness in advisory relations, by A. W. Macmahon.—Bureaucracy in a democratic society, by V. A. Thompson.—Conjectures on comparative public administration, by L. K. Caldwell.—Public administration and nation-building, by D. C. Stone.—

(Continued)

ZSC

Martin Luther-bund.
Lutherische kirche in bewegung. Festschrift für Friedrich Ulmer zum 60. geburtstag; herausgegeben von Gottfried Werner. Erlangen, Martin Luther-verlag [1937]

xi, 228 p. incl. tab. front. (port.) 23½cm.

"Der Martin Luther-bund [bietet] seinem ... leiter zum 60. geburtstage die vorliegende festschrift [dar]"—p. ix.
Bibliographical foot-notes.

CONTENTS.—Werner, Gottfried. Substantia ecclesiae est in Verbo Dei.—Pont, J. W. Die Niederlande und das Luthertum vor 1648.—Werner, Gottfried. Diasporafürsorge und unionismus im 17. jahrhun-

(Continued on next card)

A C 38-74

[2]

Festschrift

MARTIN, ROSCOE COLEMAN, 1903- , ed.
Public administration and democracy...
(Card 3)

Administration and policy in international technical assistance, by H. Emmerich.—Ethics and the public service, by S. K. Bailey.—Responsibility in administration: an exploratory essay, by R. Egger.—Public administration and democracy, by P. H. Appleby.—The writings of Paul H. Appleby: a classified list (p. 349-350)

1. Administration--Addresses, essays, lectures. 2. United States--Govt.--Addresses, essays, lectures. 3. Appleby, Paul Henson, 1891-1963.

Martin Luther-bund. Lutherische kirche in bewegung ... [1937] (Card 2)

CONTENTS—Continued.

dert.—Schmidt, Martin. Die anfänge der kirchenbildung bei den Salzburgern in Georgia.—Fritz, F. Die diasporafürsorge des lutherischen Württemberg bis zum anfange des 19. jahrhunderts.—Fleisch, Paul. Kirchenorganische diasporapflege der hannoverschen landeskirche in Südafrika.—Uhlhorn, Friedrich. Deutsche lutherische diasporaarbeit für Nordamerika.—Eppelein, Friedrich. Die anfänge der Neuendettelsauer diasporamission. — Schomerus, Chr. Die diasporafürsorge der Hermannsburger mission.—Mützelfeldt, Karl. Die Vereinigte ev.-luth. kirche in Australien und das deutsche volkstum. — Nagel, Gottfried. Der diasporacharakter der ev.-luth. freikirchen; dargestellt am beispiel der ev.-luth. kirche Altpreussens.—Jentsch, W. Die bedeutung des pre-

(Continued on next card)

A C 38-74

[2]

D-11
3494

Martinsdorf, Austria.
Festschrift zur Feier der Wiederverleihung des Marktrechtes und des 800jährigen Bestandes der Marktgemeinde Martisdorf. Zusammengestellt von Wilhelm Wenzel. [Martinsdorf, 1957] 36 p. illus., port. 23cm.

Bibliographical footnotes.

I. Wenzel, Wilhelm. t. 1957.
NN R X 9.59 (OC)I,Ibo ODt EDt PC,I SL (LC1,X1,Z1)

Martin Luther-bund. Lutherische kirche in bewegung ... [1937] (Card 3)

CONTENTS—Continued.

digerseminars "Eben Ezer" in Kropp für die Lutherische kirche in Nordamerika.—Teckhaus, H. U. Die bedeutung von Breklum für die Lutherische kirche Amerikas.—Cramer, Karl. Die deutschen kolonisten an der Wolga.—Elert, Werner. Erlangen und die Lutherische kirche.—Liermann, Hans. Die bedeutung der diaspora für die rechtsgestaltung in der Lutherischen kirche.—Preuss, Hans. Luther als kommunikant.—Pröhle, Karl. Das Luthertum in der krise des völkerlebens.—Schomerus, Hans. Die frage der kirche in der diaspora.

1. Ulmer, Friedrich, 1877- 2. Lutheran church—Addresses, essays, lectures. I. Werner, Gottfried, ed. II. Title. III. Title: Festschrift für Friedrich Ulmer zum 60. geburtstag.

A C 38-74

New York. Public library
for Library of Congress [2]

---

*QV

MASARYKOVA UNIVERSITA, Brno, Czechoslovakia. Filosofická fakulta.
Franku Wollmanovi k sedmdesátinám; sborník prací. [Redigoval Artur Závodský. Vyd. 1] Praha, Státní pedagogické nakladatelství, 1958. 691 p. illus., port. 25cm.

Contributions by various authors in Czech, Slovak or Russian.
Bibliographical footnotes.

(Continued)

NN R 7. 59 t/$_{A}$ (OC)I, IIbo OS PC, 1, 2, I SL S, 1, 2, I (LC1, X1, Z1, LCE1)

MASARYKOVA UNIVERSITA, Brno, Czechoslovakia. Filosofická fakulta. Franku Wollmanovi k sedmdesátinám... (Card 2)

"Soupis prací Franka Wollmana za léta 1948-1958," p.686-688.

1. Wollman, Frank. 2. Slavonic literature--Hist. and crit. I. Závodský, Artur, ed. II. Závodský, Artur.

RLB

MAURER, FRIEDRICH, 1898- , ed.
Angebinde, John Meier zum 85. Geburtstag am 14. Juni 1949 dargeboten von Basler und Freiburger Freunden und Kollegen. Lahr, M. Schauenburg [1949] 198 p. illus., port. 21cm.

Includes music.
Bibliographical footnotes.
CONTENTS. — Ein Basler Gesprächspiel aus dem Jahre 1778, von W. Altwegg. —Über das Verhältnis von Rechtsgeschichte und Volkskunde, von K. S. Bader. —Wortsinn und ursprüngliche Aufgabe der altfränkischen
(Continued)

NN*R 11.52 OC, I PC, 1, 2, 3, 4, 5, I SL A, 7, I MU, 6, 8, 9, I S, 8, I (MUS2: Donna Lombarda. Ich bin von Gott, LC1, Z1, X1)

---

*QT

MASARYKOVA UNIVERSITA, Brno, Czechoslovakia. Filosofická fakulta.
Studie ze slovanské jazykovědy; sborník k 70. narozeninám akademika Františka Trávníčka. [Redigovali: Václav Machek et al. Vyd. 1] Praha, Státní pedagogické nakladatelství, 1958. 493 p. port., 6 col. maps (in pocket) 25cm.

Contributions by various authors in Czech or Slovak.
(Continued)

NN R 7.59 t/ (OC)I OS PC, 1, 2, I SL S, 1, 2, I (LC1, X1, Z1, LCE1)

MAURER, FRIEDRICH, 1898- , ed. Angebinde... (Card 2)

Rachinburgen, von F. Beyerle. —Vom Hornussen, von P. Geiger. —Zur "Donna Lombarda," von W. Heiske. —Das Leid im Nibelungenlied, von F. Mauer. —"Ich bin von Gott, ich will wieder zu Gott," von F. Ranke. —Phidias und der Parthenon, von W. H. Schuchhardt. —Das slovenische Kiltlied, von E. Seemann. —Alpenländische Liedweisen der Frühzeit und des Mittelalters im Lichte vergleichender Forschung, von W. Wiora.

555533B. 1. Meier, John, 1864- . 2. German language—Dialects—Switzerland—Basel. 3. Law—Hist. 4. Frankish language—Words—Indiv.—Rachinburgen. 5. Ball—Switzerland. 6. Nibelungenlied. 7. Phidias, ca. B.C. 500-ca. B.C. 430. 8. Folk songs, Slovenian. 9. Folk songs. I. Title.

MASARYKOVA UNIVERSITA, Brno, Czechoslovakia. Filosoficka fakultá. Studie ze slovanské jazykovedy... (Card 2)

Includes bibliographies.
"Soupis prací akademika Františka Trávníčka za léta 1948-1958," p.469-476.

1. Trávníček František, 1888- . 2. Slavonic languages--Hist. I. Machek, Václav, ed.

Write on slip only words underlined and classmark:
RKA

Maurer, Friedrich, 1898- , ed.
Deutsche Wortgeschichte, hrsg. von Friedrich Maurer und Fritz Stroh. Berlin, W. de Gruyter, 1943. 3 v. 25cm. [Grundriss der germanischen Philologie, 17[1-3]]

Vol. 1-3.
"Festschrift für Alfred Götze zum 17. Mai, 1941."
"Druckfehlerberichtigung:" slip inserted in v. 1.
Includes bibliographies.

1. German language—Etymology. 2. German language—Hist. 3. Götze, Alfred August Woldemar, 1876- . I. Stroh, Fritz, 1898- , joint ed. II. Ser.
NN*R 5.54 OC, I PC, 1, 2, 3, I (U1, Z1, LC1, X1)

---

* QKK

MATICA HRVATSKA, Zagreb.
Spomen-cviečе iz hrvatskih i slovenskih dubrava. [Narodnomu dobrotvoru biskupu Josipu Jurju Strossmayeru u spomen pedesetgodišnjice njegova biskupovanja] Zagreb, 1900. xxxii, 657 p. illus., plates, ports. 25cm.

1. Strossmayer, Josip Juraj, bp. of Diakovo, 1815-1905. 2. Croatian literature—Collections. I. Title.

NN** R 9.53 OS PC, 1, 2, I SL S, 1, 2, I (LC1, Z1, X1)

---

*C-4 p.v.212
Maurice Gilliams, 1900-1950. [Antwerpen, 1950] 30 p. port. 24cm.

"Huldealbum...door...vrienden en bewonderaars...aan de feesteling [Maurice Gilliams] opgedragen."

1. Gilliams, Maurice, 1900-

NN 12.52 OC PC,1 SL (LC1, Z1, X1)

Copy only words underlined & classmark— *MA

MATTHIES, LUDWIG.
Sturm und Gesang; über Kurt Schwaens "Wartburg-Kantate" zu seinem 50. Geburtstag. (IN: Musik und Gesellschaft. Berlin. 26cm. Jahrg. 9, Heft 6 (Juni, 1959) p. 15-18. port., music)

Pages also numbered p. 335-338, continuing the paging of the preceding number.
List of works; p. 21-23.

1. Schwaen, Kurt.
NN R 10.59 t/ OI (MU)I (LC2, X1, Z1)

---

*MEC (Ravel)

Maurice Ravel, par quelques-uns de ses familiers: Colette, Maurice Delage, Léon-Paul Fargue ... [e. a.] Illustrations de Galanis, Luc-Albert Moreau, [et] Roger Wild. A Paris, Éditions du Tambourinaire, 1939.

3 p. l., ii, [1], 185, [1] p., 3 l. illus., ports., facsims. (music) 23 x 18½cm. [Collection musicale ... sous la direction de Roger Wild ... 4]

Head and tail pieces.
"Cet ouvrage a été réalisé sur l'initiative et sous le patronage de la Compagnie française Thomson-Houston et de la Société des établissements Ducretet."—1st prelim. leaf.

(Continued on next card)

A C 40-47

[2]

Maurice Ravel, par quelques-uns de ses familiers ... 1939. (Card 2)

CONTENTS.—Avertissement de l'éditeur.—L'œuvre de Maurice Ravel, par Émile Vuillermoz.—Les premiers amis de Ravel, par Maurice Delage.—Un salon de musique en 1900, par Colette.—L'époque Ravel, par Tristan Klingsor.—Des Valses à "La valse" (1911–1921) par Roland-Manuel.—Autour de Ravel, par Léon-Paul Fargue.—Ravel à Montfort-l'Amaury, par Hélène Jourdan-Morhange.—Souvenirs ravéliens, par Jacques de Zogheb.—Ravel et l'édition phonographique, par Dominique Sordet.

1. *Ravel, Maurice, 1875–1937. I. Compagnie française pour l'exploitation des procédés Thomson-Houston, Paris. II. Société des établissements Ducretet, Paris.

A C 40–47

New York. Public library for Library of Congress [2]

D-19
1429

Maurras, Charles, 1868–1952.
Critique et poésie. Paris, Libr. Académique Perrin, 1968.

285 p. 21 cm.

Published on the occasion of the 100th anniversary of my birth.

1. French literature--Addresses, essays, lectures.
NN*R 8.69 w/ OC PC, 1 SL (LC1, X1, Z1)

Write on slip, name, year, vol., page of magazine and class mark — RNA

Max Friedrich Mann... zum 70.Geburtstag...

(Anglia. Halle,1930. 8°. Bd.54,Heft 3.)

form 100a [11-13-30 25m]

3-MAR p.v.228

Max Laeuger; Festschrift zur Ausstellung des gesammelten Werks, vom 15. Dezember bis 2. Februar 1930 in der Städtischen Kunsthalle Mannheim, mit Beiträgen von: Karl Albiker, Hermann Esch, Otto Fiederlin, G. F. Hartlaub [und] Eberhard Zschimmer. [Mannheim, 1929.] 29 p. illus. 8°.

549525A. 1. Laeuger, Max, 1864– . I. Staedtische Kunsthalle, Mannheim.
N. Y. P. L. October 13, 1931

D-15
7425

MAX PICARD zum siebzigsten Geburtstag. [Hrsg. von Wilhelm Hausenstein und Benno Reifenberg. Erlenbach] E. Rentsch [1958] 201 p. port. 23cm.

"Bücher von Max Picard," p. 199-201.

1. Picard, Max, 1888- 2. Philosophy--Addresses, essays, lectures. I. Hausenstein, Wilhelm, 1882-1957, ed. II. Reifenberg, Benno, 1892- , ed.
NN R 1.65 p/ OC, I, II PC, 1, 2, I, II SL (LC1, X1, Z1)

PAH

MAX-PLANCK-FESTSCHRIFT 1958; mit Beiträgen von H. Alfvén [et al.] Hrsg. von B. Kockel, W. Macke [und] A. Papapetrou. Redigiert und bearb. von W. Frank. Berlin, Deutscher Verlag der Wissenschaften [1959] 412 p. illus., port. 28cm.

Papers in German, English or French.
Includes bibliographies.

(Continued)

NN R 7.59 t/ OC, I, II, IIb, III, IV, V, VIbo PC, 1, 2, I, II, III, IV, V SL ST, 1t, 2, I, II, III, IV, V (LC1, X1, Z1)

---

*ZX-1

Max Planck-Institut, Berlin.
Kosmische Strahlung; Vorträge gehalten im Max Planck-Institut, Berlin-Dahlem, von E. Bagge, F. Bopp, S. Flügge... [und andere] Hrsg. von Werner Heisenberg... Berlin, Springer-Verlag, 1943. vi, 173 p. illus.

Film reproduction of the original in Columbia university library. Positive.
"Arnold Sommerfeld zu seinem 75. Geburtstag am 5. Dezember 1943 gewidmet."
CONTENTS.—Einleitung: Übersicht über den jetzigen Stand der Kenntnisse von der kosmischen Strahlung, von Professor Dr. W. Heisenberg.—Kaskaden: Die Kaskadentheorie, von Professor Dr. W. Heisenberg. Die grossen Luftschauer, von Dr. G.

(Continued)

N. Y. P. L. March 25, 1947

Max Planck-Institut, Berlin. Kosmische Strahlung... (Card 2)

Molière.—Mesonen: Die Entstehung der Mesonen, von Dozent Dr. K. Wirtz. Schauer mit durchdringenden Teilchen, von Dr. A. Klemm und Professor Dr. W. Heisenberg. Die Absorbtion der Mesonen, von Dozent Dr. H. Volz. Stosserzeugung durch Mesonen, von Professor Dr. C. F. v. Weizsäcker. Der radioaktive Zerfall der Mesonen, von Professor Dr. W. Heisenberg. Die Zerfallselektronen der Mesonen, von Dozent Dr. F. Bopp. Theorie des Mesons, von Professor Dr. C. F. v. Weizsäcker. Mesontheorie des Deuterons, von Dozent Dr. S. Flügge. Theorie des explosionsartigen Schauer, von Professor Dr. W. Heisenberg.—Kernteilchen: Kernzertrümmerungen und schwere Teilchen in der kosmischen Strahlung, von Dr. E. Bagge. Über die Erzeugung und Neutronen durch die Höhenstrahlung und ihre Verteilung in der Atmosphäre, von Dozent Dr. S. Flügge.—Geomagnetische Effekte: Kosmische Strahlung und Magnetfeld der Erde, von Professor Dr. J. Meixner.—Literaturverzeichnis.

F3103. 1. Sommerfeld, Arnold Johannes Wilhelm, 1868– 2. Radiation, Cosmic. I. Heisenberg, Werner, 1901– , ed.
N. Y. P. L. March 25, 1947

---

*MEC
(Reger)

Max Reger Archiv, Meiningen, Germany.
Max Reger. Festschrift aus Anlass des 80. Geburtstages des Meisters am 19. März 1953, hrsg. vom Max-Reger-Archiv Meiningen in Verbindung mit dem Rat des Bezirkes Suhl. Beiträge zur Reger-Forschung. Leipzig, F. Hofmeister [1953] 90 p. ports., facsims. 21cm.

Contents.—Das Künstler- und Menschentum Regers im eigenen Wort, von J. Haas.—Max Regers musikalische Sendung, von K. Hasse.—Max Reger als Weggenosse Bachs

(Continued)

NN** X 10.54 a/+ OS(1b) PC,1 SL MU,1,2 (LC1,Z2,X1)

Max Reger Archiv, Meiningen, Germany. Max Reger... (Card 2)

und Beethoven, von H. Unger.—Max Regers Orchesterwerke, von H. J. Moser.—Die Orgelwerke Max Regers, von A. Kalkoff.—Max Regers Auseinandersetzung mit dem Lied, von G. Wehmeyer.—Über das Charakterische an Regers Tonsprache, von H. Poppen.—Regers Bedeutung für das gegenwärtige Schaffen, von H. Grabner.—Max Reger als Freund, von F. Stein.—Aus meinen Erinnerungen an Max Reger, von A. Schmid-Lindner.—Das Max Reger-Archiv in Meiningen, von O. Güntzel.
1. Reger, Max, 1873-1916. 2. Reger, Max—Museums, monuments, etc.

TAH

Max Weber. Im Kampf um die soziale Gerechtigkeit. Combat pour la justice sociale. Beiträge von Freunden und Auswahl aus seinem Werk. Contributions de ses amis et choix de ses oeuvres. (Max Weber zum 70. Geburtstag. 2. Aug. 1967. Hrsg. von Erich Gruner.) Bern, Lang, (1967).

399 p. 25 cm.

In French or German.

(Continued)

NN * R 10.68 l/ OC, I, II, III PC, 1, 2, 3, I, II, III SL E, 1, 2, 3, I, II, III (LC1, X1, Z1)

MAX WEBER. Im Kampf um die soziale Gerechtigkeit. (Card 2)

"Bibliographie Max Weber": p. [390]-396.

1. Economic history--Switzerland. 2. Switzerland--Social policy. 3. Weber, Max, 1897- . I. Weber, Max, 1897- . II. Gruner, Erich, 1915- , ed. III. Title: Im Kampf um die soziale Gerechtigkeit.

F-10
3990

MAXIMILIAN GESELLSCHAFT. Libris et litteris; Festschrift für Hermann Tiemann zum sechzigsten Geburtstag am 9. Juli 1959 [hrsg. von Christian Voigt und Erich Zimmermann] Hamburg [1959]
360 p. mounted illus., port., music. 27cm.

Includes bibliographies.

CONTENTS.—Aus Geschichte und Gegenwart der Bibliotheken.—Aus der Geschichte des Buches.—Zur Geistes- und Literaturgeschichte.—

(Continued)

NN R 12.59 t/, (OC)I, II, III OS PC, 1, 2, 3, 4, I, II, III SL (LC1, X1, Z1) [I]

MAXIMILIAN GESELLSCHAFT. Libris et litteris... (Card 2)

Verzeichnis der Veröffentlichungen, Vorlesungen, Vorträge und Referate Hermann Tiemanns, 1923-1959, von W. Kayser (p. 350-360).

1. Tiemann, Hermann, 1899- . 2. Libraries--Addresses, essays, lectures. 3. Bibliography--Addresses, essays, lectures. 4. Literature--Addresses, essays, lectures. I. Voigt, Christian. II. Zimmermann, Erich. III. Title.

E-10
5846

MAXIMILIEN ROBESPIERRE, 1758-1794; Beiträge zu seinem 200. Geburtstag. In Verbindung mit Georges Lefebvre hrsg. von Walter Markov. Berlin, Rütten & Loening, 1958. 628 p. port. 25cm.

CONTENTS.--À la mémoire de Maximilien Robespierre, par G. Lefebvre.--Robespierre, einige Fragezeichen, von H. Calvet.--Charlotte Robespierre, ihre Memoiren und ihre Freunde, von G. Pioro und P. Labracherie.--Beiträge zur Biographie Robespierres, von M. Eude.--Maximilien Robespierre und die Kolonialprobleme, von J. Bruhat.

(Continued)

NN R X 7.58 m/V OC, I, II PC, 1, I, II SL (LC1, X1, Z1, Y1)

MAXIMILIEN ROBESPIERRE, 1758-1794; Beiträge zu seinem 200. Geburtstag. (Card 2)

--Robespierristen und Jacquesroutins, von W. Markov.--Robespierre und der Hébertismus, von L. Jacob.--Robespierre und der General Boulanger, von R. C. Cobb.--Robespierre und die Volksgesellschaften, von A. Soboul.--Die Arbeiter und die Revolutionsregierung, von G. E. Rudé.--Schauspieler und Jakobiner, von K. Schnelle.--Zum Robespierrebild im Jahre III, von K. D. Tönnesson.--Amerikanische Freunde der Französischen Revolution, von S. Bernstein.--Die polnischen Jakobiner während des Aufstandes von 1794, von B. Leśnodorski.--Die Jakobiner in der tschechischen öffentlichen Meinung, von K. Mejdřická.--Die ungarischen

(Continued)

MAXIMILIEN ROBESPIERRE, 1758-1794; Beiträge zu seinem 200. Geburstag. (Card 3)

Jakobiner, von K. Benda.--Zum Prozess gegen die österreichische "Jakobiner-Verschwörung," von L. Stern.--Robespierres Reden im Spiegel der Publizistik Georg Friedrich Rebmanns, von H. Voegt.--Eine literarische Parallele zwischen Kant und Robespierre, von D. Cantimori.--Jakobinisches in Fichtes ursprünglicher Rechtsphilosophie, von M. Buhr.--Karl Marx' Stellung zur Französischen Revolution und zu Robespierre, von A. Cornu.--Literaturverzeichnis (p. 573-595).

1. Robespierre, Maximilien Marie Isidore de, 1758-1794. I. Markov, Walter M., ed. II. Lefebvre, Georges, 1874- , ed.

D-19
8352

Máximo Etchecopar en México. [Textos de] Antonio Acevedo Escobedo [et al.] México, Ecuador 0°0'0", 1968 [cover 1967]
60 p. ports. 23 cm.

"Homenaje de admiración y de cariño a Máximo Etchecopar."

1. Etchecopar, Máximo. I. Acevedo Escobedo, Antonio, 1909-

NN*R 10.70 d/ OC, I PC, 1, I SL AH, 1, I (LC1, X1, Z1)

HBC

The **Maya** and their neighbors. Limited ed. New York, London, D. Appleton-Century company, incorporated [c1940]
xxiii, 606 p. incl. illus. (incl. maps, charts, plans) tables. xx pl., fold. map. 24cm.

"To Alfred Marston Tozzer, his students and colleagues dedicate this volume, in recognition of his services to Middle American research and in appreciation of their debt to him as teacher, counsellor, and friendly critic."

CONTENTS.—pt. I. The background of the Maya: Howells, W. W. The origins of American Indian race types. Ricketson, O. G., jr. An outline of basic physical factors affecting Middle America. Linton, Ralph. Crops, soils, and culture in America. Kluckhohn, Clyde. The conceptual structure in Middle American studies. Mason, J. A. The native languages of Middle America. Johnson, Frederick. The lin-

(Continued on next card)

40-33305

[5]

Festschrift

The **Maya** and their neighbors ... [c1940] (Card 2)

CONTENTS—Continued

guistic map of Mexico and Central America.—pt. II. The Maya: Kidder, A. V. Archaeological problems of the highland Maya. Thompson, J. E. S. Archaeological problems of the lowland Maya. Morley, S. G. Maya epigraphy. Andrews, E. W. Chronology and astronomy in the Maya area. Spinden, H. J. Diffusion of Maya astronomy. Pollock, H. E. D. Sources and methods in the study of Maya architecture. Smith, A. L. The corbeled arch in the new world. Ruppert, Karl. A special assemblage of Maya structures. Wauchope, Robert. Domestic architecture of the Maya. Smith, R. E. Ceramics of the Peten. Butler, Mary. A pottery sequence from the Alta Verapaz, Guatemala. Longyear, J. M. The ethnological significance of Copan pottery. Hooton, E. A. Skeletons from the Cenote of sacrifice at Chichen Itzá. La Farge, Oliver. Maya ethnology: the sequence of cultures.—pt. III. The

(Continued on next card)

40-33305

[5]

The Maya and their neighbors ... [c1940] (Card 3)

CONTENTS—Continued

northern neighbors of the Maya: Vaillant, G. C. Patterns in Middle American archaeology. Noguera, Eduardo. Excavations at Tehuacan. Ekholm, G. F. The archaeology of northern and western Mexico. Roberts, F. H. H., jr. Pre-pottery horizon of the Anasazi and Mexico. Brew, J. O. Mexican influence upon the Indian cultures of the southwestern United States in the sixteenth and seventeenth centuries. Phillips, Philip. Middle American influences on the archaeology of the southeastern United States. Guthe, C. E. Sequence of culture in the eastern United States.—pt. IV. **The southern neighbors of the Maya:** Strong, W. D. Anthropological problems in Central America. Stone, Doris. The Ulua valley and lake Yojoa. Richardson, F. B.

(Continued on next card)

40-33305

[5]

The Maya and their neighbors ... [c1940] (Card 4)

CONTENTS—Continued

Non-Maya monumental sculpture of Central America. Lothrop, S. K. South America as seen from Middle America. Means, P. A. The philosophic inter-relationship between Middle American and Andean religions. Kidder, Alfred. South American penetrations in Middle America. Kroeber, A. L. Conclusions: The present status of Americanistic problems. Bibliography (p. 491-594)

1. Mayas—Antiq. 2. Mayas. 3. Mayas—Bibl. 4. Central America—Antiq. 5. Mexico—Antiq. 6. America—Antiq. 7. Archaeology—Addresses, essays, lectures. 8. Tozzer, Alfred Marston, 1877-

40-33305

Library of Congress F1435.M45

——— ~~Copy 2.~~

Copyright [5] 913.72

HBC

Los Mayas antiguos; monografías de arqueologia, etnografía y lingüística mayas, publicadas con motivo del centenario de la exploración de Yucatán por John L. Stephens y Frederick Catherwood en los años 1841-42. [México] El Colegio de México [1941] 361 p. illus., col'd plates. 23cm.

"Primera edición."

189 SIB.

1947

L-11
1461

MAYER-MALY, THEO, ed.

Festschrift für Hans Schmitz zum 70. Geburtstag. hrsg. von Theo Mayer-Maly, Albert Nowak [und] Theodor Tomandl. Wien, Verlag Herold [1967] 2 v. port. 25cm.

Includes bibliographies.

1. Schmitz, Hans. 2. Labor--Jurisp.--Austria. 3. Austria--Social policy.

NN R 8.69 k/ OCs PCs, 1s, 2s, 3s SLs Es, 1s, 2s, 3s (LC1s, X1s, Z1s)

---

*QAA
(Institut)

[Mazon, André,] 1881- , editor.

...Mélanges publiés en l'honneur de M. Paul Boyer. Paris: É. Champion, 1925. vi, 376 p. 4°. (Institut d'études slaves, Paris. Travaux. [no.] 2.)

Avant-propos signed: André Mazon.
Bibliographical footnotes.

1. Boyer, Paul, 1864- . 2. Slavs. 3. Slavonic languages. 4. Title. 5. Ser.

D-14
5688

Mazzeo, Joseph Anthony, 1923- *ed.*

Reason and the imagination; studies in the history of ideas, 1600-1800. New York, Columbia University Press, 1962.

viii, 321 p. plates. 23 cm.

The studies are in honor of Marjorie Hope Nicolson.

Bibliographical footnotes.

CONTENTS.—Noble numbers and the poetry of devotion, by M. K. Starkman.—Cromwell as Davidic king, by J. A. Mazzeo.—The isolation of the Renaissance hero, by D. Bush.—The humanistic defence of learning in the mid-seventeenth century, by R. F. Jones.--Some

(Continued)

NN * R 9. 63 e/k OC PC, 1, 2, 3 SL (LC1, X1, Z1)

MAZZEO, JOSEPH ANTHONY, 1923- , ed.
Reason and the imagination... (Card 2)

paradoxes in the language of things, by R. L. Colie.—Milton's dialogue on astronomy, by A. O. Lovejoy.—Music, mirth, and Galenic tradition in England, by G. L. Finney.—Eve and Dalila: renovation and the hardening of the heart, by M. A. N. Radzinowicz.—The bird, the blind bard, and the fortunate fall, by A. D. Ferry.—The tragedy of God's Englishman, by W. Haller.—The Augustan conception of history, by H. Davis.—The Houyhnhnms, the Yahoos, and the history of ideas, by R. S. Crane.—Locke and Sterne, by E. Tuveson.—Literary criticism and artistic interpretation: eighteenth-century English illustrations of "The seasons," by R. Cohen.—Bibliographical afterword (p. 307-310)

(Continued)

MAZZEO, JOSEPH ANTHONY, 1923- , ed.
Reason and the imagination... (Card 3)

1. Great Britain--Civilization, 17th-18th cent. 2. English literature--Hist. and crit., 17th-18th cent. 3. Nicolson, Marjorie Hope, 1894-

---

E-11
8398

MEASUREMENT in economics; studies in mathematical economics and econometrics in memory of Yehuda Grunfeld, by Carl F. Christ [and others] Stanford, Calif., Stanford University Press, 1963. xiv, 319 p. port., diagrs. 25cm.

Includes bibliographies.

CONTENTS.—Yehuda Grunfeld: in memoriam.—Bibliography of Yehuda Grunfeld (p. xiii-xiv)—Theory and measurement of consumption:

(Continued)

NN*R 12. 63 g/ OC,2b+,I,Ib* PC,1,2,I SL E,1,2,I(LC1,X1,Z1)

3

MEASUREMENT in economics... 1963 (Card 2)

Windfalls, the "horizon," and related concepts in the permanent-income hypothesis, by M. Friedman. Tests of the permanent-income hypothesis based on a reinterview savings survey, by N. Liviatan. Market prices, opportunity costs, and income effects, by J. Mincer. Demand curves and consumer's surplus, by D. Patinkin. --Theory and measurement of production: Capital stock in investment functions: some problems of concept and measurement, by Z. Griliches. Estimation of production and behavioral functions from a combination of cross-section and time-series data, by Y. Mundlak. Returns to scale in electricity supply, by M. Nerlove. —Theory and measurement of monetary

(Continued)

MEASUREMENT in economics... 1963 (Card 3)

phenomena: Interest rates and "portfolio selection" among liquid assets in the U.S., by C.F. Christ. The dynamics of inflation in Chile, by A.C. Harberger. —Econometric methodology: Tests based on the movements in and the comovements between m-dependent time series, by L.A. Goodman. Least-squares estimates of transition probabilities, by L.G. Telser. On the specification of mutivariate relations among survey data, by H. Theil.

1. Economics, Mathematical. 2. Grunfeld, Yehuda, 1930-1960. I. Christ, Carl F.

D-19
5969

Med lov skal land byggjast. Heiderskrift til Knut Robberstad. 70 år. Oslo, Universitetsforlaget, 1969.

248 p. 23 cm.

CONTENTS.—Knut Robberstad 70 år, av O. Lid.—Årsakssammenheng, adekvans, skyld og skadens omfang, av K. Andersen.—Kronprinsens giftermål, av F. Castberg.—Regjeringens adgang til å avskjedige embetsmenn, av T. Eckhoff.—Bygningsfredningsloven og fredningsarbeidets stilling, av R. Hauglid.—Nasjonal og internasjonal standardisering av stadnamn, av P. Hovda.—Gammal og ny rett,

(Continued)

NN*R 1.70 w/L OC, 1b* PC, 1, 2 SL (LC1, X1, Z1)

MED lov skal land byggjast. (Card 2)

av M. Nygard.—Lex Rinde, av N. Nygaard.—Internasjonale midler til å gjennomføre menneskerettene, av T. Opsahl.—Ekspropriasjon eller overdragelse og oppgjør etter avtale, av E. Sandene.—Ansvar for vannledningsskader i naboforhold, av T. Sandvik.—Forsikring av antikvariske verdier, av K. S. Selmer.—Kring norsk lovmål, av K. Skogen.—Kvifor er Common law case law, av H. Thue.—Inntektsskatt i forbindelse med bruksretter over fast eiendom, av M. Aarbakke.—Virkeområdet for forskjellige lover om arbeidervern og arbeidsavtaler, av H. Jakhelln.—Lista yver dei arbeid Knut Robberstad hev late prenta, av K. Haukaas.

1. Robberstad, Knut, 1899- 2. Law--Norway.

E-10
7877

MEDICUS Viator; Fragen und Gedanken am Wege Richard Siebecks; eine Festgabe seiner Freunde und Schüler zum 75. Geburtstag. Tübingen, J.C.B. Mohr (P.Siebeck), 1959. viii, 376 p. port. 24cm.

Includes bibliographies.

CONTENTS. —Therapeutische Katharsis und Logotherapie im Homerischen Epos, von P. Lain Entralgo. —Die Gestalt des Paracelsus, von H. Marx. —Ludolf von Krehl, von K. Hansen. —Die metaphysische und anthropolog-

(Continued)

NN R 7.59 p/A OC, 1bKG PC, 1, 2 SL (LC1, X1, Z1)

MEDICUS Viator; Fragen und Gedanken am Wege Richard Siebecks... (Card 2)

ische Bedeutung der Ausdrucksphänomene, von C. Oehme. —Über den Erfolg in der ärztlichen Tätigkeit, von K. Stoevesandt. —Die heilende Liebe, von P. Christian. —Krankheit und Geschichte in der anthropologischen Medizin: Richard Siebeck und Viktor von Weizsäcker, von D. Rössler. —Medizin in Bewegung, von W. Kütemeyer. —Klinische Heilungsphänomene, von H. Huebschmann. —Macht und Ohnmacht des Kranken, von W. Jacob. —Über die Bedeutung der Selbstverborgenheit in der Beurteilung und Behandlung von Kranken, von F. Schaeffer. —Arzt und Seelsorger in der Begegnung mit dem

(Continued)

MEDICUS Viator; Fragen und Gedanken am Wege Richard Siebecks... (Card 3)

leidenden Menschen, von E. Thurneysen. —Zum Gespräch des christlichen Glaubens mit der Naturwissenschaft, von E. Schlink. —Naaman, von G. von Rad. —Gewissheit des Glaubens, von G. Bornkamm. —Die abendländische Kultur des Gesprächs und ihr Verfall, von E. Metzke. —Die Heilungen Jesu und medizinizusammengestellt von K. Fink-Eitel (p. [365]-376)

1. Siebeck, Richard, 1883- 2. Medicine—Addresses, essays, lectures.

BTH

Medieval and historiographical essays in honor of James Westfall Thompson, edited by James Lea Cate and Eugene N. Anderson. Chicago, Ill., The University of Chicago press [1938]

x, 499 p. front. (port.) 23½cm.

CONTENTS.—Medieval essays: A critic of the fourteenth century: St. Birgitta of Sweden, by Conrad Bergendoff. The beginning of the struggle between the regular and the secular clergy, by Helen R. Bittermann. The church and market reform in England during the reign of Henry III, by J. L. Cate. The origin of the town of Subiaco, by Geneva Drinkwater. The Van der Molen, commission merchants of Antwerp: trade with Italy, 1538–44, by Florence Edler. The Palestine pilgrimage of Henry the Lion, by Einar Joranson. The south German reichsstaedte in the late middle ages, by Ernest Lauer. Medieval medical dictionaries and glossaries, by L. C. MacKinney. The emergence of

(Continued on next card)

38-3148

[8]

Medieval and historiographical essays in honor of James Westfall Thompson ... [1938] (Card 2)

CONTENTS—Continued.

conciliarism, by J. T. McNeill. A study of twelfth-century interest in the antiquities of Rome, by J. B. Ross. Bernward of Hildesheim, by F. J. Tschan. The long tradition: a study in fourteenth-century medical deontology, by Mary C. Welborn.—Historiographical essays: Meinecke's Ideengeschichte and the crisis in historical thinking, by E. N. Anderson. Justus Möser's approach to history, by W. J. Bossenbrook. Theodore Roosevelt, historian, by Raymond C. Miller. Kautsky and the materialist interpretation of history, by S. K. Padover. The Varangians in Russian history, by S. R. Tompkins.—Bibliography of the works of James Westfall Thompson (p. 493–499)

1. Thompson, James Westfall, 1869- 2. Middle ages—Hist.—Addresses, essays, lectures. 3. History—Historiography. I. Cate, James Lea, ed. II. Anderson, Eugene Nelson, joint ed.

38-3148

Library of Congress D113.5.M4

——— ~~Copy 2.~~

[8] 940.104

E-14
1803

Medieval literature and folklore studies; essays in honor of Francis Lee Utley. Edited by Jerome Mandel and Bruce A. Rosenberg. New Brunswick, N. J., Rutgers University Press [1970]

viii, 408 p. illus., port. 25 cm.

CONTENTS.—Preface, by J. Mandel and B. A. Rosenberg.—Beowulf: one poem or three? By A. G. Brodeur.—A symbolic word-group in Beowulf, by F. G. Cassidy.—A reading of Beowulf 3169–3182, by K.

(Continued)

NN*R 12.71 w/L OC, I, II, III, IVb* PC, 1, 2, I, II, III SL (LC1, X1, Z1) [I]

MEDIEVAL literature and folklore studies... (Card 2)

Malone.—Problems of communication in the romances of Chrétien de Troyes, by W. T. H. Jackson.—The suggestive use of Christian names in Middle English poetry, by T. F. Mustanoja.—Caxton and Malory; a defense, by W. Matthews.—Thomas Usk as translator, by M. Schlauch.—Some observations on King Herla and the Herlething, by H. Newstead.—Gawain's green chapel and the cave at Wetton Mill, by R. E. Kaske.—Convention and individuality in the Middle English romance, by A. C. Baugh.—From motive to ornament, by E. Vinaver.—Troilus and Criseyde; the art of amplification, by R. W. Frank, Jr.—Experience, language, and consciousness: Troilus and

(Continued)

MEDIEVAL literature and folklore studies...
(Card 3)

Criseyde, II, 596-931, by D. R. Howard.—The ordering of the Canterbury tales, by E. T. Donaldson.—The Miller's tale; an unBoethian interpretation, by M. W. Bloomfield.—Unfinished business: the folktale, by S. Thompson.—The anecdote: a neglected genre, by A. Taylor.—Paris og Helen i Trejeborg: a reduction to essentials, by W. E. Richmond.—Some notes on the nix in older Nordic tradition, by D. Strömbäck.—Etiological stories in Ireland, by S. Ó Súilleabháin.—A Bohemian medieval fable on the fox and the pot, by J. Jech.—A modern medieval story: "The soldier's deck of cards," by

(Continued)

MEDIEVAL liteature and folklore studies...
(Card 4)

D. K. Wilgus and B. A. Rosenberg.—Esthetic form in British and American folk narrative, by R. M. Dorson.—Hangmen, the gallows, and the dead man's hand in American folk medicine, by W. D. Hand.—Folk logic and the Bard: Act I of Macbeth, by T. Coffin.—Notes (bibliographical: p. 343-387)

1. Literature--Hist. and crit., Middle Ages. 2. Folk lore--Addresses, essays, lectures. I. Utley, Francis Lee, 1907- . II. Mandel, Jerome, ed. III. Rosenberg, Bruce A., ed. IV. Rosenberg, Bruce A.

RAE

Mediaeval studies in honor of Jeremiah Denis Matthias Ford, Smith professor of French and Spanish literature, emeritus, ed. by Urban T. Holmes, Jr. and Alex. J. Denomy. Cambridge, Harvard Univ. Press, 1948.

xxxii, 376 p. port., facsims. 22 cm.

Contents.—Vita.—A bibliography of the writings of J. D. M. Ford (p. xxiii-xxxii)—Provençal os "jambon," by Clovis Brunel.—Ancient Ireland and Spain, by T. P. Cross.—Avaler et descendre, by Lucien Foulet.—A postscript in textual criticism, by E. B. Ham.—A sketch of Joinville's prose style, by Helmut Hatzfeld.—On the Vulgar Latin of Roman Britain, by Kenneth Jackson.—The praefatio and versus

(Continued on next card)

48-9269*

[15]

Mediaeval studies in honor of Jeremiah Denis Matthias Ford ... 1948. (Card 2)

Contents—Continued.

associated with some Old-Saxon Biblical poems, by F. P. Magoun, Jr.—An Old Spanish life of Saint Dominic: sources and date, by W. F. Manning.—Considerations on the interchange of -ou-, -oi- in Portuguese, by L. G. Moffatt.—How did the Fisher King get his name? By W. A. Nitze.—Un viejo romance cantado por Sabbatai Cevi, by R. Menéndez Pidal.—The Irish marginalia in the Drummond Missal, by F. N. Robinson.—Insular Portuguese pronunciation: alleged Flemish influence, by F. M. Rogers.—Le manuscrit de Turin, aujourd'hui détruit, du lexique Abavus, by Mario Roques.—Lilium medicinae, by George Sarton.—The list of Norman names in the Auchinleck ms (Battle Abbey roll) by H. M. Smyser.—The history of diphthongization and metaphony in Rumanian, by L. F. Solano.—Unpublished Old

(Continued on next card)

48-9269*

[15]

Mediaeval studies in honor of Jeremiah Denis Matthias Ford ... 1948. (Card 3)

Contents—Continued.

High German glosses to Boethius and Prudentius, by Taylor Starck.—A colt's tooth, by B. J. Whiting.—Who named them rhétoriqueurs? By W. L. Wiley.—The meaning of ex nihilo in the church Fathers, Arabic and Hebrew philosophy and St. Thomas, by H. A. Wolfson.

1. Ford, Jeremiah Denis Matthias, 1873- 2. Philology—Collections. I. Holmes, Urban Tigner, 1900- ed.

P26.F6 404 48-9269*

Library of Congress [15]

MAK

Medieval studies in memory of A. Kingsley Porter; edited by Wilhelm R. W. Koehler ... Cambridge, Harvard university press, 1939.

2 v. front. (port.) illus. (incl. plans) plates, diagrs., facsims. 31cm. (*Half-title:* Harvard-Radcliffe fine arts series)

Paged continuously.

Contents.—I. A. Kingsley Porter, by Lucy K. Porter. Bibliography of the writings of A. Kingsley Porter (p. [xvii]-xxiv) General aspects of the middle ages: Das irreführende am begriffe "mittelalter", by Josef Strzygowski. Die mittelstellung der mittelalterlichen kunst zwischen antike und renaissance, by Hermann Beenken. Chivalric and dramatic imitations of Arthurian romance, by R. S. Loomis. Early Christian and Byzantine art: Early Christian art and the Far East, by E. W. Anthony. Per la storia del portale romanico, by Ugo Monneret de Villard. Eine illustrierte ausgabe der spätantiken Ravennater annalen, by Bernhard

(Continued on next card)

39-12282

[4]

Medieval studies in memory of A. Kingsley Porter ... 1939. (Card 2)

Contents—Continued.

Bischoff und Wilhelm Koehler. A fragment of a tenth-century Byzantine psalter in the Vatican library, by E. T. De Wald. Medieval art in Italy: A manuscript from Troia: Naples VI B 2, by Myrtilla Avery. Bemerkungen zu Galliano, Basel, Civate, by Julius Baum. Italian Gothic ivories, by C. R. Morey. The Barberini panels and their painter, by Richard Offner. Medieval art in Spain and Portugal: Changes in the study of Spanish Romanesque art, by W. M. Whitehill. Un chapiteau du xe siècle au cloître de Sant Benet de Bages, by J. Puiz i Cadafalch. Little Romanesque churches in Portugal, by Georgiana G. King. A Catalan wooden altar frontal from Farrera, by W. W. S. Cook. Sculptured columns from Sahagún and the Amiens style in Spain, by F. B. Deknatel. The Pedralbes master, by C. R. Post.—II. Medieval art in France: A.

(Continued on next card)

39-12282

[4]

Medieval studies in memory of A. Kingsley Porter ... 1939. (Card 3)

Contents—Continued.

Kingsley Porter et la Bourgogne, by Charles Oursel. The third church at Cluny, by K. J. Conant. The sculptures of Souillac, by Meyer Schapiro. Les traits originaux de l'iconographie dans la sculpture romane de l'Auvergne, by Louis Bréhier. Les statues du chœur de Saint-Martin d'Angers aujourd'hui au Musée d'art de l'Université Yale, by Marcel Aubert. Das tier in der romanischen plastik Frankreichs, by Richard Hamann. Quelques survivances de la sculpture romane dans l'art français, by Henri Focillon. An enameled reliquary from Champagnat, by M. C. Ross. Reintegration of a book of hours executed in the workshop of the "Maître des grandes heures de Rohan", by Erwin Panofsky. Medieval art in Germany and Switzerland: Die stellung der westtürme des Naumburger domes, by Paul Frankl. Untersuchungen zum stil der Base-

(Continued on next card)

39-12282

[4]

Medieval studies in memory of A. Kingsley Porter ... 1939. (Card 4)

Contents—Continued.

ler Galluspforte, by Otto Homburger. German late Gothic sculpture in the Gardner museum, Boston, by C. L. Kuhn. Medieval art in Scandinavia and the British isles: The sculptured stones of Wales, by R. A. S. Macalister. Some examples of Viking figure representation in Scandinavia and the British isles, by Esther I. Seaver. The canon tables of the Book of Kells, by A. M. Friend, jr. The psalter in the British museum, Harley 2904, by Charles Niver. Une voûte à nervures du xie siècle à Sigtuna, by Johnny Roosval. Some minor Irish cathedrals, by A. W. Clapham. English influence on medieval art of the continent, by Adolph Goldschmidt.

1. Porter, Arthur Kingsley, 1883-1933. 2. Art, Medieval. 3. Archaeology, Medieval. I. Köhler, Wilhelm Reinhold Walter, 1884- ed.

39-12282

Library of Congress N5975.M5
——— Copy 2.
Copyright A 129407 [4] 709.02

NAB

Medieval studies in memory of Gertrude Schoepperle Loomis. Paris: H. Champion, 1927. xv, 535 p. front. (port.) 8°.

Bibliography, p. x-xi.

Contents: Curriculum vitae G. S. Loomis. List of publications by G. S. Loomis. Beckwith, M. A note on Punjab legend in relation to Arthurian romance. Bergin, O. J. How the Dagda got his magic staff. Best, R. I. The birth of Brandub and of Aedan. Blondheim, D. S. Gleanings from the Bible of Alva. Brown, A. C. L. The Irish element in King Arthur and the Grail. Bruce, J. D. Mordred's incestuous birth. Brugger, E. Bliocadran, the father of Perceval. Foulet, L. Villon et Charles d'Orléans. Fraser, J. The alleged matriarchy of the Picts. Grandgent, C. Rime and rhetoric in the Divine comedy. Hamilton, G. L. The royal mark of the Merovingians and

(Continued)

N. Y. P. L. December 18, 1928

Medieval studies in memory of Gertrude Schoepperle Loomis.
(Card 2)

kindred phenomena. LOOMIS, L. H. Malory's book of Balin. HULL, E. The Helgi lay and Irish literature. HYDE, D. Mediaeval account of Antichrist. LEACH, H. G. Is Gibbonssaga a reflection of Partonopeus? LOOMIS, L. R. The Greek studies of Poggio Bracciolini. LOOMIS, R. S. The date of the Arthurian sculpture at Modena. LOT, F. De la valeur historique du De excidio et conquestu Britanniae de Gildas. LOT-BORODINE, M. Tristan et Lancelot. NITZE, W. A. The identity of Brons in Robert de Borron's Metrical Joseph. PATTERSON, F. Hymnal from Ms. Additional 34193, British Museum. PEEBLES, R. J. The children in the tree. RAJNA, P. Sono il De ortu Walwanii e L'historia Meriadoci opera di un medesimo autore? RANKE, F. Isoldes Gottesurteil. ROQUES,

(Continued)

N. Y. P. L. December 18, 1928

YAG

Mélanges Auguste Pelzer; études d'histoire littéraire et doctrinale de la scolastique médiévale offertes à Auguste Pelzer à l'occasion de son soixante-dixième anniversaire. Louvain, Bibliothèque de l'Université, Bureaux du "Recueil," 1947.

xix, 662 p. port. 25cm. (Université de Louvain. Recueil de travaux d'histoire et de philologie, 3. sér., 26. fasc.)

Medieval studies in memory of Gertrude Schoepperle Loomis.
(Card 3)

M. Correspondance de Karl Bartsch et Gaston Paris de 1865 à 1885. THOMAS, A. Sur une nouvelle étymologie de "Chantepleure." VENDRYES, J. Mellifont fille de Clairvaux. VINAVER, E. The love potion in the primitive Tristan romance. WEEKS, R. Le lai de l'oiselet.

375768A. 1. Schoepperle, Gertrude, 1882–1921. 2. Literature—Hist. and crit., Middle Ages.
N. Y. P. L. December 18, 1928

MAS

Mélanges Bertaux; recueil de travaux, dédié à la mémoire d'Emile Bertaux... Paris, E. de Boccard, 1924. 345 p. 21 pl. 26cm.

Contributions in French, Spanish or Italian.
Bibliographical footnotes.

556335B. 1. Art—Essays and misc. 2. Bertaux, Émile, 1869–1917.
N. Y. P. L. October 16, 1951

E-11
8115

MEIER, HARRI, 1905- , ed.
Worf und Text; Festschrift für Fritz Schalk [hrsg. von Harri Meier und Hans Sckommodau] Frankfurt am Main, V. Klostermann [1963]
xi, 531 p. port. 24cm.

Contributions in German, French, Italian or Spanish.
Bibliographical footnotes.
1. Literature--Addresses, essays, lectures. 2. Schalk, Fritz, 1902- I. Sckommodau, Hans, joint ed.
NN 10.63 g/B OC,I PC, 1,2,I SL (LC1,X1,Z1)
[I]

E-11
2112

MÉLANGES bibliques rédigés en l'honneur de André Robert. [Paris] Bloud & Gay [1957] 580 p. illus., port. 25cm. (Institut catholique, Paris. Travaux. 4)

Contributions in French, English, German or Spanish.
Bibliographical footnotes.
"Bibliographie de M. André Robert," p. [5]-10.

1. Robert, André. 2. Bible--Essays and misc. I. Series.
NN X 3.61 g/ OC (OS)I PC,1,2,I SL J,2 (LC1,X1,Z1)
[I]

MA

MEISS, MILLARD, ed.
De artibus opuscula XL; essays in honor of Erwin Panofsky. [New York, Pub. for the Institute for advanced study [by] New York university press [1961, c1960] 2 v. 177 plates, port. 32cm.

Vol. 2 consists of plates.
Chiefly in English; includes three essays in German, two in French and one in Italian.
(Continued)

NN R 4.63 p/ OC, I, III, IV (OS) II PC, 1, 2, 3, I, II, III, IV SL A, 1, 2, 3, I, II, III, IV (LC1, X1, Z1) [I]

Write on slip words underlined below and class mark —
*CA

...Mélanges Bidez. Bruxelles: Secrétariat de l'institut, 1934. 2 v. facsims., front. (port.), illus., plates. 25cm. (Bruxelles. Université libre. Institut de philologie et d'histoire orientales et slaves. Annuaire. Tome 2, fasc. 1–2.)

Paged continuously.
Contributions in French, English, Italian or German.
Bibliographical footnotes.

795147-8A. 1. Classical studies. 2. Oriental studies. 3. Philology—Collections. 4. Bidez, Joseph, 1867-
N. Y. P. L. December 29, 1939

MEISS, MILLARD, ed. De artibus opuscula XL...
(Card 2)

Bibliographical footnotes.
"Erwin Panofsky: bibliography to July 1960," v. 1, p. xiii-xxi.

1. Art--Essays and misc. 2. Panofsky, Erwin, 1892-
3. Panofsky, Erwin, 1892- --Bibl. I. Meiss, Millard, ed. Essays in honor of Erwin Panofsky. II. Institute for advanced study, Princeton, N.J. III. Title. IV. Title: Essays in honor of Erwin Panofsky

---

NMX

...**Mélanges** bretons et celtiques offerts à M. J. Loth... Rennes: Plihon et Hommay, 1927. vii, 428 p. front. (port.), illus. (plan), music. 4°.

At head of title: Volume hors série: Annales de Bretagne.
Bibliographical footnotes.

1. Breton literature—Hist. and crit. 2. Irish literature—Hist. and crit. 3. Loth, Joseph, 1847- . 4. Rennes. Université. Faculté des lettres. Annales de Bretagne.
N. Y. P. L. November 27, 1928

... **Mélanges** Ch. Appleton. Études d'histoire du droit, dédiées à M. Charles Appleton ... à l'occasion de son xxve anniversaire de professorat. Lyon, A. Rey; Paris, A. Rousseau, 1903.

4 p. l., vii, 655 p., 1 l. front. (port.) illus. 25cm. (Annales de l'Université de Lyon. Nouv. sér. II. Droit, lettres. fasc. 13)

"Exemplaire no. 84." 313

"Principales publications de M. Charles Appleton": p. iii–iv.

CONTENTS.—Caillemer, E. À M. Charles Appleton.—Audibert, A. L'évolution de la formule des actions familiae erciscundae et communi dividundo.—Blondel, G. Note sur les origines de la propriété.—Caillemer, E.

(Continued on next card)

4—20753

... **Mélanges** Ch. Appleton ... 1903. (Card 2)

CONTENTS—Continued.

Jean de Blanot.—Caillemer, R. Quelques observations sur l'histoire du douaire des enfants.—Coville, A. Flavius Afranius Syagrius.—Erman, H. D. (44, 2) 21 § 4: Études de droit classique et byzantin.—Fabia, P. Titi Livii loci qvi svnt de praeda belli romana.—Huvelin, P. La notion de l'"iniuria" dans le très ancien droit romain.—Lambert, E. L'histoire traditionnelle des XII tables et les critères d'inauthenticité des traditions en usage dans l'école de Mommsen.—Lameire, I. Les sources décentralisées de l'histoire.—Thaller, E. À propos du contrat estimatoire.

1. Law (Roman).

~~1. Appleton, Charles Louis, 1846-~~

~~Series.~~

4—20753

Library of Congress

Mélanges Charles de Harlez: recueil de travaux d'érudition offert à Mgr. C. de Harlez à l'occasion du vingt-cinquième anniversaire de son professorat à l'Université de Louvain, 1871-1896. Leyde: E.J. Brill, 1896. 4°.

Gift of Jacob H. Schiff

1. Orientalia—Collections. 2. Harlez, Charles Joseph.

1178

Mélanges dédiés à la mémoire de Félix Grat... Paris, Pecqueur-Grat, 1946–49. 2 v. illus., 24 pl. 25cm.

Bibliographical footnotes.

Festschrift

 1. Grat, Félix, 1898–1940. 2. History—Addresses, essays, lectures.

N. Y. P. L. August 13, 1951

Mélanges économiques et sociaux, offerts à Émile Witmeur. Paris, Librairie du Recueil Sirey, société anonyme, 1939.

2 p. l., [vii]–xv, [1], 382 p. incl. front. (port.) illus. (maps) diagrs. 25cm.

CONTENTS.—Notice biographique, par G. Dykmans.—L'économie des nouvelles lois de comptabilité et de contrôle du budget et du patrimoine public en Roumanie, par George Alesseano.—L'Europe et l'économie africaine, par E. Antonelli.—Une apologie des droits de douane par un libéral impénitent, par G.-H. Bousquet.—La signification de Max Weber dans les sciences sociales actuelles, par Carl Brinkmann.—De la nature monétaire du billet de banque, par F. Casters.—La crise structurelle de 1930 (Essai sur les conjonctures et la logique scientifique), par Laurent Dechesne.—Les accords intellectuels de la Belgique, par Fernand Dehousse.—La loi du marché et ses impératifs, par Georges De Leener.—Les tendances de l'économie congolaise, par F. Dellicour.—Une sociologie objective est-elle possible? Par Élie Diaconide.—La théorie des races en sociologie

(Continued on next card)

39—31145

[2]

Festschrift.

Mélanges économiques et sociaux ... 1939. (Card 2)

CONTENTS—Continued.

générale et en économie politique, par G. Dykmans.—Notes sur une source du socialisme moderne. La légende du bon sauvage au xvie siècle, par René Gonnard.—L'expression des émotions et la société, par Maurice Halbwachs.—Vers une théorie dynamique, par R. F. Harrod.—La politique du gouvernement au point de vue de la constitution de réserves de matières premières et de denrées alimentaires, par J. M. Keynes.—Quelques remarques sur la théorie du salaire, par M. Kurtschinsky.—Le rythme des méthodes économiques et l'historisme, par Émile Lasbax.—L'enseignement colonial, par N. Laude.—Quelques aspects du développement industriel et minier au Canada, par M. Legraye.—Le coefficient de corrélation, par Jules Lejeune.—Coûts et prix dans le monde économique contemporain (pour la science contre les systèmes), par Jean Lescure.—Les caractères de l'empire colonial français, par René Maunier.—Économie politique et "Économie de défense", par Raoul

(Continued on next card)

39-31145

[2]

Mélanges économiques et sociaux ... 1939. (Card 3)

CONTENTS—Continued.

Miry.—La mentalité primitive chez les peuples civilisés, par Achille Ouy.—Pour un approfondissement de la notion de structure, par François Perroux.—La réforme de l'état, par Jacques Pirenne.—Les divisions de l'économie politique, par Gaëtan Pirou.—Les phases socio-culturelles dans la culture euro-américaine au cours des cent dernières années, par P. A. Sorokin.—Capitaux errants, par Henri Truchy.—L'herbage dans l'agriculture belge, par O. Tulippe.—Quelques observations sur le rôle des banques dans la vie économique des Pays-Bas, par G. M. Verryn Stuart.—La compétence dans l'administration civile, par Daniel Warnotte.—Les fondements de la sociologie relationnelle, par Léopold von Wiese.

1. Witmeur, Émile, 1874- 2. Social sciences—Addresses, essays, lectures.

39-31145

Library of Congress H35.M4

[2] 304

Write on slip words underlined below and class mark —

... **Mélanges** Émile Boisacq. Bruxelles: Secrétariat des éditions de l'institut, 1937–38. 2 v. charts, facsims., front., maps, plates, ports., geneal. table. 25cm. (Brussels. Université libre. Institut de philologie et d'histoire orientales et slaves. Annuaire. Tome 5–6.)

Contributions in French, German, English, Italian or Greek.

"Bibliographie d'Émile Boisacq," v. 1, p. [vii]–xvi; "Addenda à la Bibliographie d'Émile Boisacq," v. 2, p. [427]

Bibliographical footnotes.

Festschrift

1. Philology—Collections. 2. Classical studies. 3. Greek literature—Hist. and crit. 4. Greek language. 5. Boisacq, Émile, 1865-

N. Y. P. L. December 29, 1939

Mélanges d'esthétique et de science de l'art offerts à Étienne Souriau, professeur à la Sorbonne, par ses collègues, ses amis et ses disciples. Paris, Nizet [1952] 277 p. illus., port. 26cm.

"Œuvres d'Étienne Souriau," p.[15]-16.

1. Art—Essays and misc. 2. Souriau, Étienne, 1892-

Write on slip only words underlined and classmark — TB

...Melanges d'etudes économiques et sociales, offerts à William E. Rappard... Precedes de l'allocution sur "L'universite et les temps actuels"...par le professeur W.E.Rappard... Geneve, Georg & cie., 1944. xx, 493 p. port. 23cm. (Geneva "City". Universite. Sciences économiques et sociales, Faculte des. Publications. v.8)

Bibliographical footnotes.

 1. Rappard, William Emmanuel, 1886- . 2. Economics, 1926- . 3. Sociology, 1945- . I. Ser.

form 400c [viii-8-50 25m]

BYC

... **Mélanges,** d'études luso-marocaines dédiés à la mémoire de David Lopes et Pierre de Cenival. Lisboa, Portugália editora [1945]

2 p. l., [7]–417 p., 1 l. plates, ports. 22cm. (Collection portugaise, pub. sous le patronage de l'Institut français au Portugal. 6. v.)

CONTENTS.—Ricard, Robert. David Lopes (1867–1942) Notice biographique. Bibliographie sommaire (p. 12–14)—Lopes, David. Pierre de Cenival (1888–1937) Notice biographique. Note bibliographique (p. 20–25)—Balão, António. Como o terceiro marquês de Vila Real recompensa os serviços em Ceuta dum fidalgo da sua casa.—Bataillon, Marcel. Le rêve de la conquête de Fès et le sentiment impérial portugais au XVIe siècle.—Cirot, Georges. "Gaita" et "Rhaita."—Colin, G. S. Des Juifs nomades retrouvés dans le Sahara marocain au XVIe siècle.—Evin, P.-A. Un musée portugais à Mazagan.—Figanier, Joaquim. Contribuição para

(Continued on next card)

46-20901

[3] Festschrift cd.

BYC

... **Mélanges** ... [1945] (Card 2)

CONTENTS—Continued.

o estudo da cultura arábica em Portugal.—Laranjo Coelho, P. M. Três figuras desaparecidas.—Machado, J. P. Os estudos arábicos em Portugal.—Marcy, G. L'origine du nom de l'île de Fer.—Santos, D. M. dos. A entrada dos jesuítas em Marrocos no século XVI.—Pires de Lima, Durval. Lisboa e os mouros.—Queiroz Velloso. O professor David Lopes.—Renaud, H. P. J. Recherches historiques sur les épidémies du Maroc. Les "pestes" des XVe et XVIe siècles, principalement d'après les sources portugaises.—Ricard, Robert. Sur les facteurs portugais d'Andalousie.—Terrasse, Henri. Note sur les contacts artistiques entre le Maroc et le Portugal, du XVe au XVIIe siècle.

1. Lopes, David de Melo, 1867–1942. 2. *Cenival, Pierre de, 1888–1937. 3. Portugal—Hist.—Addresses, essays, lectures. 4. Morocco—Hist.—Addresses, essays, lectures.

Library of Congress DP538.M43 46-20901

[3] 946.9004

Write on slip words underlined below and class mark- *CA

... **Mélanges** Franz Cumont. Bruxelles, Secrétariat de l'Institut, 1936.

2 v. plates, port., maps (1 fold.) facsims., diagrs. 25cm. (Brussels. Université libre. Institut de philologie et d'histoire orientales et slaves. Annuaire. t. IV (1936))

Paged continuously.

Vol. 2 has cover-title only.

"Liste des publications de Franz Cumont": v. 1, p. [vii]–xxxi.

Bibliographical foot-notes.

CONTENTS.—1. Aymard, A. Le rôle politique du sanctuaire fédéral achaien. Bayet, J. Présages figuratifs déterminants dans l'antiquité gréco-latine. Bickermann, É. Sur la version vieux-russe de Flavius-Josèphe. Bidez, J. Proclus: Περὶ τῆς ἱερατικῆς τέχνης. Blanchet, A. Le dieu Bacon de Cabillonum. Bonner, C. The homily on the passion by

(Continued on next card)

A C 37-2822

[38c2]

... **Mélanges** Franz Cumont ... 1936. (Card 2)

CONTENTS—Continued.

Melito, bishop of Sardis. Chantraine, P. Homérique μερόπων ἀνθρώπων Des Places, É. Platon et l'astronomie chaldéenne. Dussaud, R. Sur le chemin de Suse et de Babylone. Gagé, J. Le "templum urbis" et les origines de l'idée de "renovatio". Gernet, L. Dolon le Loup. Goguel, M. La conception jérusalémite de l'église et les phénomènes de pneumatisme. Gundel, W. Religiongeschichtliche lesefrüchte aus lateinischen astrologenhandschriften. Heuten, G. Le "soleil" de Porphyre. Honigmann, E. Un itinéraire arabe à travers le Pont. Janne, H. La lettre de Claude aux Alexandrins et le christianisme. Jeanmaire, H. Le règne de la femme des derniers jours et le rajeunissement du monde. Magnien, V. Le mariage chez les Grecs; conditions premières. Martin, C. Fragments palimpsestes d'un discours sur la pâque attribué à saint Hippolyte de Rome (Crypt. B. a. LV) Nilsson, M. P. Reflexe von

(Continued on next card)

A C 37-2822

[38c2]

... **Mélanges** Franz Cumont ... 1936. (Card 3)

CONTENTS—Continued.

dem durchbruch des individualismus in der griechischen religion um die wende des 5. und 4. jhts v. Chr. Seston, W. La vision païenne de 310 et les origines du chrisme constantinien. Seyrig, H. Inscription relative au commerce maritime de Palmyre. Simon, M. La polémique anti-juive de S. Jean Chrysostome et le mouvement judaïsant d'Antioch. Srebrny, S. Kult der thrakischen göttin Kotyto in Korinth und Sicilien. Toutain, J. L'évolution de la conception des Erinyes dans le mythe d'Oreste d'Eschyle à Euripide. Ussani, V. I miei studi su Flavio Giuseppe e alcune osservazioni su Gesù nel Giuseppe Slavo. Weinreich, O. Catulls Attisgedicht.—2. Adontz, N. Les vestiges d'un ancien culte en Arménie. Bertholet, D. A. Hesekielprobleme. Causse, A. L'humanisme juif et le conflit du judaïsme et de l'hellénisme. Cook, S. A. The development of the religion of Israel. Couvreur, W. Les

(Continued on next card)

A C 37-2822

[38c2]

... **Mélanges** Franz Cumont ... 1936. (Card 4)

CONTENTS—Continued.

désinenses [!] hittites ~ḫi, ~ti, ~i du présent et ~ta du prétérit. Delatte, A., et Delatte, L. Un traité byzantin de géomancie (Codex parisinus 2419) La Vallée Poussin, L. de. Le libre examen dans le bouddhisme. Desrousseaux, A. M. Le fragment 74B d'Alcman. Ruyt, F. de. À propos de l'interprétation du groupe étrusque Herclé-Mlacukh. Dhorme, É. À propos de la correspondance du clergé assyrien. Duchesne-Guillemin, J. Ahura Miθra. Forrer, E. O. Eine geschichte der [!] götterkönigtums aus dem Hattireiche. Goossens, R. Un conte égyptien: Pharaon, roi des phoques. Grégoire, H. L'Amazone Maximô. Herzfeld, E. Ušā—Eos. Hubaux, J., et Leroy, M. Le talisman de Phaon. Koppers, W. Le principe historique et la science comparée des religions. Leroy, M. La traduction arménienne d'Euclide. Lévy, I. Autour d'un roman mythologique égyptien. Lods, A. Les fouilles d'Aï et l'époque de

(Continued on next card)

A C 37-2822

[38c2]

... **Mélanges** Franz Cumont ... 1936. (Card 5)

CONTENTS—Continued.

l'entrée des Israélites en Palestine. Massé, H. Aspects du pèlerinage à la Mekke dans la poésie persane. Murphy, J. The development of individuality in the ancient civilization. Perdrizet, P. Atargatis. Pettazzoni, R. La confession des péchés dans l'histoire des religions. Pirenne, J. Le culte funéraire en Égypte sous l'ancien empire. Przyluski, J. Les trois hypostases dans l'Inde et à Alexandrie. Puech, H.-C. Fragments retrouvés de l'"Apocalypse d'Allogène". Stracmans, M. Origine et sémantique de quelques hiéroglyphes égyptiens. Chronique de l'institut. Notes et informations. Liste des souscripteurs.

1. Cumont, Franz Valery Marie, 1868– 2. Cumont, Franz Valery Marie, 1868– —Bibliography. 3. Classical antiquities—Collections. 4. Oriental antiquities—Collections.

Johns Hopkins univ. Libr. for Library of Congress [PJ4.B7 vol. 4] A C 37-2822

[38c2] (490.5)

*OGC

Mélanges Gaudefroy-Demombynes; mélanges offerts à Gaudefroy-Demombynes par ses amis et anciens élèves. Le Caire, Impr. de l'Institut français d'archéologie orientale, 1945. xii, 323 p. illus., port. 28cm.

"Principales publications de M. Gaudefroy-Demombynes," p. [xi]-xii.

1. Gaudefroy-Demombynes, Maurice, 1862- 2. Muhammadans—Civilization. 3. Muhammadans—Hist.

NN** X 3.55 a/ OC PC,1,2,3 SL 0,1,2,3 (LC1,X1,Z1) [I]

*OAC

Mélanges de géographie et d'orientalisme offerts à E.-F. Gautier, professeur honoraire à la Faculté des lettres d'Alger. Tours, Arrault et cie, maîtres imprimeurs, 1937.

xiv, 464 p. incl. illus. (incl. plan) tables, diagrs. front. (port.) IX pl., maps (part fold.) 25cm.

Bibliographical foot-notes.

CONTENTS.—Liste des travaux de E.-F. Gautier (p. [v]–xi)—Albertini, Eugène. Les loups de Carthage.—Allix, André. Le problème du bilan colonial et le privilège du conquérant.—Baulig, H. Captures fluviales et déversements.—Bel, Alfred. Les premiers émirs mérinides et l'Islam.—Blache, Jules. Les montagnes peintres.—Blanchard, Raoul. Les Méditerranéens à Grenoble.—Bourcart, Jacques. Les "pénéplaines" du Maroc et du Sahara.—Bourdarie, P. E.-F. Gautier "le Saharien".—Bowman, Isaiah. A new chapter in Pan-American cartography.—

(Continued on next card)

A C 38-3372

[2]

Mélanges de géographie et d'orientalisme offerts à E.-F. Gautier ... 1937. (Card 2)

CONTENTS—Continued.

Brockelmann, C. Arabische streitgedichte gegen das Christentum.—Capot-Rey, R. La région des dayas.—Célérier, J. La croisée des routes marocaines en Haute Moulouya.—Cohen, Marcel. Ponctuations du discours empruntées au français par l'arabe d'Algérie.—Colin, Elicio. La géographie dans l'enseignement secondaire en France—Deffontaines, Pierre. Notes sur la répartition des types de voiture.—Despois, Jean. Rendements en grains du Byzacium il y a 2.000 ans et aujourd'hui.—Dresch, J. De la Sierra Nevada au Grand Atlas, formes glaciaires et formes de nivation.—Faucher, D. Glaciaire pyrénéen et vallées sous-pyrénéennes.—Feghali, Michel. L'élève du ver à soie.—Gernet, Louis. De l'origine des Maures selon Procope.—Isnard, H. Le cantonnement des

(Continued on next card)

A C 38-3372

[2]

Mélanges de géographie et d'orientalisme offerts à E.-F. Gautier ... 1937. (Card 3)

CONTENTS—Continued.

indigènes dans le Sahel d'Alger (1852–1864)—Jaeger, Fritz. Limites d'aridité en Algérie.—Johnson, Douglas. "Cicatrices météoritiques" sur la côte des Carolines.—Joleaud, L. Les girafes du Sahara d'après les documents préhistoriques.—Kratchkovsky, Ignace. Daghestan et Yémen.—Larnaude, Marcel. Tentes et habitations fixes en Oranie.—Lefebvre, Th. Quelques aspects des modes de vie dans la Pologne occidentale.—Leschi, Louis. Un sacrifice pour le salut de Ptolémée, roi de Maurétanie.—Martino, Pierre. Quelques notes sur l'historie et la géographie dans le "Mahomet" de Voltaire.—Massé, Henri. Le voyage de Farhâd-Mirzâ (Turquie, Égypte, Hedjaz)—Maurette, Fernand. Niveaux de vie et genres de vie.—Monod, Théodore. Essai de synthèse structurale

(Continued on next card)

A C 38-3372

[2]

Mélanges de géographie et d'orientalisme offerts à E.-F. Gautier ... 1937. (Card 4)

CONTENTS—Continued.

de l'Ouest saharien.—Musset, René. Gallieni et Madagascar.—Noureddine, A. Un épisode de l'histoire de l'ancien Alger.—Pawlowski, Stanislas. Quelques remarques supplémentaires sur la morphologie des régions d'Algérie.—Pérès, Henri. Relations entre le Tafilalet et le Soudan à travers le Sahara, du XIIe au XIVe siècle.—Perret, Robert. L'Adrar des Ajjers et sa périphérie.—Russo, P. Gautier et les hauts plateaux marocaines.—Savornin, J. Interprétations graphiques de la structure géologique de l'Afrique du Nord.—Tinthoin, Robert. La plaine de l'Habra.—Vonderheyden, M. Le Harmel.

1. Gautier, Émile Félix, 1864–1937. 2. Oriental philology—Collections. 3. Geography—Collected works.

A C 38-3372

New York. Public library
for Library of Congress [2]

RBG

Mélanges Graux. Recueil de travaux d'érudition classique dédié à la mémoire de Charles Graux, né à Vérvins le 23 Novembre 1852, mort à Paris le 13. Janvier 1882. Paris: E. Thorin, 1884. lvi, 823 pp., 7 fac-sim, 1 pl., 1 port. 8°.

BTGP

Mélanges Gustave Glotz... Paris, Les Presses universitaires de France, 1932.
2 v. front. (port.) illus. (part mounted) plates, map. 25cm.

Paged continuously.
Eighty-one contributions to classical archaeology, philology and history, mainly in French; several in English; a few in German or Italian.
"Bibliographie des oeuvres de m. G. Glotz": v.1, p.[xix]-xxvii; bibliographical foot-notes.

NDK

Mélanges H. d'Arbois de Jubainville. Recueil de mémoires concernant la littérature et l'histoire celtiques. Dédié à M. H. d'Arbois de Jubainville à l'occasion du 78e anniversaire de sa naissance... Paris: A. Fontemoing, [1906?] vii, 287 p. il. 8°.

---

*OAC

Mélanges Hartwig Derenbourg (1844-1908); recueil de travaux d'érudition dédiés à la mémoire d'Hartwig Derenbourg par ses amis et ses élèves. Paris: E. Leroux, 1909. 2 p.l., ii, 466 p., 1 port. illus. 4°.

Schiff collection.

1. Derenbourg, Hartwig.

1912

---

* CA
B912
t. 9-12

MÉLANGES Henri Grégoire. Bruxelles, Secrétariat des Éditions de l'Institut, 1949-53. 4 v. illus., port. 25cm. (Brussels. Université libre. Institut de philologie et d'histoire orientales et slaves. Annuaire. t 9-12)

At head of title: Παγχάρπεια.
Articles in English, French, German, Greek, Italian or Latin.
Includes bibliographies.

1. Grégoire, Henri, 1881- I. Series.

NN **R 4.57 p/ OC (OS)I PC, 1, I (LC1, Z1, X1)

NRE

Mélanges Henri Weil. Recueil de mémoires concernant l'histoire et la littérature grecques dédié à Henri Weil... Paris: A. Fontemoing, 1898. 3 p.l. 465 pp., 1 pl., 1 port. 8°.

Frederick ...

TAH

MÉLANGES d'histoire économique et sociale en hommage au professeur Antony Babel à l'occasion de son soixante-quinzième anniversaire. Genève, 1963.
2 v. illus. 24cm.

Includes bibliographies.

1. Economic history--Addresses, essays, lectures. 2. Economic history--Switzerland. 3. Babel, Antony, 1888-

NN *R 5.66 p/ OC PC, 1, 2, 3 SL E, 1, 2, 3 (LC1, X1, Z1)

---

*MGA

MÉLANGES d'histoire et d'esthétique musicales offerts a Paul-Marie Masson par ses collègues, ses élèves et ses amis. Paris, R. Masse [c1955]
2 v. in 1 illus., port., music. 26cm. (Bibliothèque d'études musicales)

1. Masson, Paul Marie, 1882-

NN 12.70 d/ OC PC, 1 SL MU, 1 (LC1, X1, Z1)

NKB

MÉLANGES d'histoire littéraire et de bibliographie offerts à Jean Bonnerot, conservateur en chef honoraire de la Bibliothèque de la Sorbonne, par ses amis et ses collègues. Paris, Librairie Nizet, 1954. 551 p. illus., port. 25cm.

"Bio-bibliographie de Jean Bonnerot," p. [25]-53. Bibliographical footnotes.

1. Bonnerot, Jean, 1882- . 2. French literature—Hist. and crit. 3. Bibliography—Addresses, essays, lectures.

NN * 3. 56 s/y OC PC, 1, 2, 3 SL (LC1, X1, Z1)

F-10
6985

Mélanges d'histoire du livre et des bibliothèques offerts à Monsieur Frantz Calot, conservateur en chef honoraire de la Bibliothèque de l'Arsenal. Paris, Librairie d'Argences, 1960.

xxiii, 384 p. illus., 26 plates, port. 26 cm. (Bibliothèque elzévirenne, nouv. sér. Études et documents)

"Préface" by Julien Cain.
"Bibliographie des travaux de Frantz Calot": p. [xiii]-xviii.

1. Calot, Frantz. 2. Bibliography--Addresses, essays, lectures.

NN R 2. 63 g/ OC PC, 1, 2 SL (LC1, X1, Z1) [I]

NABM

Mélanges d'histoire littéraire générale et comparée offerts à Fernand Baldensperger... Paris: H. Champion, 1930. 2 v. front. (port.) 8°.

500073-4A. 1. Baldensperger, Fernand, 1871- . 2. Baldensperger, Fernand, 1871- —Bibl.
N. Y. P. L. December 17, 1930

BTE

Mélanges d'histoire offerts à Henri Pirenne par ses anciens élèves et ses amis à l'occasion de sa quarantième année d'enseignement à l'Université de Gand, 1886–1926... Bruxelles: Vromant & C°., 1926 2 v. diagr., front. (port.), illus. (maps), plates (facsims.), tables. sq. 8°.

Continuous paging.
Some plates printed on both sides.
Bibliographical footnotes.
"Bibliographie des travaux historiques de Henri Pirenne," p. xxv–xxxix.

1. Pirenne, Henri, 1862- . 2. Europe—Hist.—Addresses, essays, lectures.
N. Y. P. L. July 16, 1927

BTH

Mélanges d'histoire du moyen âge; offerts à M. Ferdinand Lot, par ses amis et ses élèves. Paris: E. Champion, 1925. xli, 770 p. facsims., front. (port.), illus., plates. 8°.

"Bibliographie méthodique des oeuvres de Ferdinand Lot," p [xvii-]xli.
Bibliographical footnotes.

286152A. 1. Middle Ages—Hist.—Addresses, essays, lectures. 2. Lot, Ferdinand, 1866–1910.
N. Y. P. L. March 30, 1927

BAC

Mélanges d'histoire offerts à M. Charles Bémont par ses amis et ses élèves à l'occasion de la vingt-cinquième année de son enseignement à l'École pratique des hautes études. Paris, F. Alcan, 1913.

2 p. l., vi, 666, [2] p. front. (port.) 25½cm.

1. Gt. Brit.—Hist. 2. France—Hist. 3. Bémont, Charles, 1848-

14-12568

Library of Congress D6.M5

B T H

Mélanges d'histoire du Moyen Age, dédiés à la mémoire de Louis Halphen. Préf. de Charles-Edmond Perrin. Paris, Presses universitaires de France, 1951.

xxiii, 713 p. port. 26 cm.

"Bibliographie des travaux de Louis Halphen": p. [xv]-xxiii.

1. Civilization, Medieval. 2. Middle Ages—Hist. 3. Halphen, Louis, 1880–1950.

Yale Univ. Library for Library of Congress [2] A 51-6389 Festschrift

---

F-11
7669

MÉLANGES d'histoire du XVIe siècle offerts à Henri Meylan. Genève, Droz, 1970. 195 p. port. 26cm. (Travaux d'humanisme et renaissance. 110)

Bibliographical footnotes.

CONTENTS.--Érasme, de Turin à Rome, par L. E. Halkin.--Bucer et la discipline ecclésiastique, par J. Courvoisier.--Six consultations populaires bernoises à l'époque de la Réforme, par L. E. Roulet.--La version française d'un célèbre manuel de controverse: (Continued)

NNR 5. 71 e/z OC, II (OS)I PC, 1, I, II SL E, 2, II (LC1, X1, Z1) [I]

JFF
71-25

Mélanges d'histoire littéraire (xvie-xviie siècle), offerts à Raymond Lebègue par ses collègues, ses élèves et ses amis. Paris, A.-G. Nizet, 1969.

399 p. music, plates. 26cm.

Bibliography: p. [377]-394.

1. French literature--Hist. and crit., 16th cent. 2. French literature--Hist. and crit., 17th cent. I. Lebègue, Raymond, 1895- .

NN*R 3. 71 d/z OC, I PC, 1, 2, I SL (LC1, X1, Z1)

MÉLANGES d'histoire du XVIe siècle offerts à Henri Meylan. (Card 2)

Les lieux communs de Jean Eckius, par P. Fraenkel.--Emblems and colours; the controversy over Gargantua's colours and devices, by M. A. Screech.--The deacons of the reformed church in Calvin's Geneva, by R. M. Kingdom.--Tournée zoologique à travers les dialogues de Pierre Viret, 1545, par M. Bossard.--Les Capita calumniarum de Zébédée et la réponse de Pierre Viret, par R. Centlivres--Le colloque de Poissy, par A. Dufour.--Le pasteur Antoine Mermet, par G. Berthoud.--Note sur le style de Roger Ascham dans The scholemaster, 1570, par E. Giddey.--Salaires des pasteurs de Genève au XVIe siècle, par J. F. Bergier.--Notes sur les anciennes papeteries (Continued)

MÉLANGES d'histoire du XVIe siècle offerts à Henri Meylan. (Card 3)

vaudoises, par L. Junod.

1. Europe--Hist., 1492-1648. 2. Europe--Intellectual life. I. Series. II. Meylan, Henri, 1900- .

E-13
3589

Mélanges en l'honneur de Jean Dabin, professeur émérite de l'Université catholique de Louvain, membre de l'Académie royale des sciences, des lettres et des beaux-arts de Belgique. Bruxelles, E. Bruylant, 1963.

2 v. (ii, 968 p.) port. 25 cm.

Bibliography of works by Jean Dabin: v. 1, p. xi-xx.
Bibliographical footnotes.

CONTENTS.—t. 1. Théorie générale du droit.—t. 2. Droit positif.

1. Law--Addresses, essays, lectures. I. Dabin, Jean, 1889- .

NN * 11. 68 d/, OC, I PC, 1, I SI E, 1, I (LC1, X1, Z1)

Copy only words underlined
& Classmark-- GDY

MÉLANGES d'histoire du XVIe siècle offerts à Henri Meylan. Lausanne, 1970. 195 p. port. 25cm. (Bibliothèque historique vaudoise. 43)

Bibliographical footnotes.

CONTENTS.--Érasme, de Turin à Rome, par L.E. Halkin.--Bucer et la discipline ecclésiastique, par J. Courvoisier.--Six consultations populaires bernoises à l'époque de la Réforme, par L.E. Roulet.--La version française d'un célèbre manuel de controverse: Les lieux communs
(Continued)

NN 8.71 d/ OC, II (OS)I PC, 1, 2, I, II E, 2, II (LC1, X1, Z1)

Copy only words underlined
& classmark— *QAA

MÉLANGES en l'honneur de Jules Legras. Paris, Droz, 1939. xxxi, 276 p. 25cm. (Institut d'études slaves, Paris. Travaux. 19)

Bibliographical footnotes.

CONTENTS.—Jules Legras voyageur, par H. Moysset.—La deuxième démission de Delcassé, par E. Fournol.—La pièce de deux lires, par A. Remisov.—La valeur de la science d'après Goethe, par H. Lichtenberger.—Le pédantisme de Lessing, par H. Loiseau.—Goethe au pays des Lazzaroni, par R. Michéa.—Reflexions sur les divers aspects de la pensée politique polonaise au XVIIIe siècle, par C. Backvis.—
(Continued)

NN X 8.58 e/OC PC, 1 S, 1 (LC1, X1, Z1)

MÉLANGES d'histoire du XVIe siecle offerts... (Card 2)

de Jean Ecklus, par P. Fraenkel.--Emblems and colours; the controversy over Gargantua's colours and devices, by M.A. Screech.--The deacons of the reformed church in Calvin's Geneva, by R.M. Kingdom.--Tournée zoologique à travers les dialogues de Pierre Viret, 1545, par M. Bossardi--Les Capita calumniarum de Zébédée et la réponse de Pierre Viret, par R. Centlivres.--Le colloque de Poissy, par A. Dufour.--Le pasteur Antoine Mermet, par G. Berthoud.--Note sur le style de Roger

(Continued)

MÉLANGES en l'honneur de Jules Legras. (Card 2)

Allemand "Herzog" en onomastique polonaise, par H. Grappin.—[illegible] Przybyszewski et l'Infemo de Strindberg, par M. Herman.—Christ et révolution dans la poésie russe et polonaise, par V. Lednicki.—Deux siècles et demi de luttes religieuses dans la Pologne méridionale (1339-1596), par C. Quénet.—Un problème de géopolitique: L'integration de l'économie slovaque dans le cadre de l'État tchécoslovaque, par A. Fichelle.—Ljutica Bogdan, par A. Vaillant.—Contribution au lexique des abréviations et mots conventionnels entrés dans l'usage russe depuis la Révolution de 1917, par L. Beaulieux.—Quelques observations sur le rythme de la poésie russe par M. Hoffmann.—Les prophéties de Dostoievski touchant la Russie, par N. Koulmann.— L'enseignement d' I.G. Schwartz,
(Continued)

MÉLANGES d'histoire du XVIe siecle offerts... (Card 3)

Asham dans The scholemaster, 1570, par E. Giddey.--Salaires des pasteurs de Genève au XVIe siècle, par J.F. Bergier.--Notes sur les anciennes papeteries vaudoises, par L. Junod.

1. Europe--Hist., 1492-1648. 2. Europe--Intellectual life. I. Series. II. Meylan, Henri, 1900- .

MÉLANGES en l'honneur de Jules Legras. (Card 3)

Rose-Croix, professeur à l'Université de Moscou, et son influence, par R. Larry.—La légende de Valdaj, par G. Lozinski.—Le conte du Coq d'Or: Pouchkine, Klinger et Irving, par A. Mazon.—Un zélateur du calvinisme auprès du tzar Mikhajl Fedorovič, par J.J. Mikkola.—Un pauvre homme, grand fondateur: Ephrem Potemkin, par P. Pascal.—Englishmen in Shakespeare's Muscovy or The victims of Jerome Horsey, by C. Sisson.—L'opposition morphologique de l'accent dans le substantif russe, par L. Tesnière.—Un point d'histoire de la politesse russe: tutoiement et vousoiement, par B. Unbegaun.

1. Legras, Jules, 1866- . I. Ser.

MWEC

Mélanges d'histoire du théâtre du moyen-age et de la renaissance, offerts à Gustave Cohen, professeur honoraire én Sorbonne, par ses collègues, ses élèves et ses amis. Paris, Librairie Nizet, 1950. 294 p. port. 25cm.

"Bibliographie des oeuvres de Gustave Cohen," p. 15-27.

1. Stage—Hist., Middle Ages. 2. Stage—Hist., 16th-18th cent. 3. Cohen, Gustave, 1879- .

NN*12.52 OC PC, 1, 2, 3, SL T, 1, 2, 3 (LC1, Z1, X1)

3-MAR

Mélanges Hulin de Loo [pseud.]. Bruxelles: Librairie nationale d'art et d'histoire, 1931. ix, 355 p. front. (port.), 47 pl. 4°.

Includes bibliographies.

Contents: BERGMANS, P. Introduction. AGAPITO Y REVILLA, J. El arte flamenco en Valladolid. ANGULO IÑIGUEZ, D. Bordados de estilo eyckyiano del sepulcro del cardenal Cervantes de la catedral de Sevilla. ARU, C. Il trittico di Clemente VII nel tesoro del duomo di Cagliari. BALDASS, L. Ein Madonnentüchlein aus der Nähe des Quinten Metsys. BAUTIER, P. La descente du Saint-Esprit de la collection Laurent Meeus à Bruxelles. BENESCH, O. Ein Spaetwerk von Hieronymus Bosch. BERTINI-CALOSSO, A. La vetrata di Hendrick van den Broeck nella cattedrale di Perugia. BURCHARD, L. "Sotte Cleef," était-il portraitiste? BURROUGHS, A. Jan van Eyck's portrait of his wife. BURROUGHS, B. Un portrait inédit attribué à Hugo

(Continued)

N. Y. P. L. July 29, 1932

Mélanges Hulin de Loo ₍pseud.₎. (Card 2)

van der Goës. BYVANCK, A. W. La miniature dans les anciens Pays-Bas pendant la première moitié du XVe siècle. DODGSON, C. Deux estampes d'après P. Bruegel l'Ancien. CONWAY, Sir ₍W.₎ M. The Wilton diptych. BRUYN, E. DE. La collaboration des frères van Eyck dans le retable de l' "Adoration de l' agneau." DELEN, A. J. J. Illustration de livres par Pierre Coecke d'Alost. MÉLY, F. DE. Nos premiers parents dans l'art; Adam, Ève, Lilith. DEMONTS, L. Le maitre de l'Annonciation d'Aix et Colantonio. DESTRÉE, J. Épisodes de la jeunesse de David; tapisseries bruxelloises de la première moitié du XVIe siècle. DESTRÉE, J. Le retable de Cambrai de Roger de la Pasture. DIMIER, L. Un tableau méconnu de Guillaume Key. DUVERGER, J. Jacopo de Barbari en Jan Gossart by Filips van Burgondie te Souburg (1515). FOERSTER, O. H. Scorels Grablegung Christi im Wallraf-Richartz-

(Continued)

N. Y. P. L. July 29, 1932

Mélanges Hulin de Loo ₍pseud.₎. (Card 3)

Museum zu Köln. FIGUEIREDO, J. DE. Metsys e Portugal. FRIEDLAENDER, M. J. Ueber die Frühzeit Jan Gossarts. GESSLER, J. Le peintre liégeois Dominique Lampsonius et son calvaire à Hasselt. GLUCK, G. Ein Gemaelde des Meisters der tiburtinischen Sibylle. GOFFIN, A. À propos du voyage de Roger de la Pasture (van der Weyden) en Italie. GUIFFREY, J. Note sur deux tableaux avignonnais. HOOGEWERFF, G. J. Jacob Claessoon et Jacob Nobel, peintres portraitistes d'Utrecht de la première moitié du XVIe siècle. JAMOT, P. Un tableau inconnu de Lodewyk Toeput dit Lodovico Pozzoserrato. LAES, A. Un paysagiste flamand de la fin du XVIe siècle: Kerstiaen de Keuninck. LEBEER, L. Une suite de gravures du "Maitre du martyre des dix mille." LEFÈVRE, P. ₍F.₎ À propos de Roger van der Weyden et d'un tableau peint par lui pour l'église Sainte-Gudule, à Bruxelles. LUGT, F. Italië

(Continued)

N. Y. P. L. July 29, 1932

Mélanges Hulin de Loo ₍pseud.₎. (Card 4)

en het Noorden. LYNA, F. Un livre de prières inconnu de Philippe le Hardi. MAQUET-TOMBU, J. Inspiration et originalité des tapisseries de l'Apocalypse d'Angers. MICHEL, É., WRITER ON BELGIAN MONASTERIES. Pierre Bruegel le Vieux et Pieter Coecke d'Alost. POPHAM, A. E. A Dutch designer for glass. REINACH, S. Un triptyque inédit de l'école d'Anvers. RICCI, S. DE. Le maitre de l'Exhumation de Saint-Hubert. ROGGEN, D. Drie schilderijen van Marten van Heemskerk, te Gent. ROLLAND, P. La double école de Tournai, peinture et sculpture. SERRA, L. Intorno ad una serie di Arazzi Fiamminghi. VAES, M. "Prospettiva di mare" de Paul Bril au musée de l'Ambrosienne à Milan. BASTELAER, R. VAN. Le paysage de la Parabole des aveugles de Pierre Bruegel. PUYVELDE, L. VAN. Peintures murales du XIVe siècle à Gand. VOGELSANG, W. Een vroeger navolger van Hieronymus Bosch.

(Continued)

N. Y. P. L. July 29, 1932

Mélanges Hulin de Loo ₍pseud.₎. (Card 5)

VUYK, J. Un portrait de femme par Anthonie Blocklandt de Montfort (1534–1583). WINKLER, F. Eine verschollene Kreuzigung des Dirk Bouts.

561957A. 1. Hulin, Georges Charles Nicolas Marie, 1862– . 2. Art—Essays and misc.
N. Y. P. L. July 29, 1932

*OHO

Mélanges d'indianisme à la mémoire de Louis Renou ... Paris, E. de Boccard, 1968. 800 p. port. 25cm. (Paris. Université. Institut de civilisation indienne. Publications. Série in-8°. fasc. 28)

At head of title: 40e anniversaire de la fondation de l'Institut de civilisation indienne de l'Université de Paris, 1967.

English, French, German, or Italian.

(Continued)

NN* 5. 71 w/⸗ OC, I (OS)II PC, 1, I, II SL O, 1, I, II (LC1, X1, Z1) 2

MÉLANGES d'indianisme à la mémoire de Louis Renou... (Card 2)

Bibliographie des travaux de Louis Renou, par Jean Filliozat": p. [xiii]-xxix. Bibliographical footnotes.

1. Indic studies--Collections. I. Renou, Louis, 1896-1966. II. Series.

*OHM

Mélanges d'indianisme, offerts par ses élèves à S. Lévi, le 29 janvier 1911 à l'occasion des vingt-cinq ans écoulés depuis son entrée à l'École Pratique des Hautes Études. Paris: E. Leroux, 1911. 4 p.l., 345 p. 4°.

1. Lévi, Sylvain.

NRC

...**Mélanges** Joseph de Ghellinck, S.J. ... Gembloux, J. Duculot, 1951. 2 v. illus. 26cm. (Museum Lessianum—Section historique no 13–14)

"Bibliographie du R. P. Joseph de Ghellinck, par Roger Demortier," v. 1, p. 41–112. Bibliographical footnotes.

1. Classical literature—Hist. and crit. 2. Latin literature, Neo-Latin—Hist. and crit. 3. Theology—Essays and misc. 4. Ghellinck, Joseph de, 1872–1950. I. Demortier, Roger. II. Museum Lessianum.
N. Y. P. L.

NKW

Mélanges Julien Havet. Recueil de travaux d'érudition dédié à la mémoire de Julien Havet (1853–1893). Paris: E. Leroux, 1895. xvi, 780 p. front. (port.), illus., plates (incl. facsims., part fold.). 25cm.

"Bibliographie des travaux de Julien Havet," p. xi–xvi.

CONTENTS.—Auvray, Lucien. Notices sur quelques cartulaires et obituaires français conservés à la bibliothèque du Vatican.—Batiffol, Pierre. Note sur un bréviaire cassinésien du XIe siècle. — Bémont, Ch. La date de la composition du *Modus tenendi parliamentum in Anglia.*—Berger, Ph. *Poseidôn Narnakios.*—Berger, Samuel. De quelques anciens textes latins des Actes des apôtres.—Chatelain, E. Notes tironiennes d'un manuscrit de Genève.—Cipolla, C. La tachygraphie ligurienne au XIe siècle.—

(Continued)

N. Y. P. L. July 29, 1912

Mélanges Julien Havet... (Card 2)

Couderc, C. Essai de classement des manuscrits des *Annales* de Flodoard.—Couraye du Parc, Joseph. Recherches sur la chanson de *Jehan de Lanson.*—Delaborde, H. F. Un arrière petit-fils de saint Louis, Alfonse d'Espagne.—Delaville le Roulx, J. Fondation du grand prieuré de France de l'ordre de l'Hôpital.—Delisle, L. Un nouveau manuscrit des livres des Miracles de Grégoire de Tours.—Derenbourg, Hartwig. Femmes musulmanes et chrétiennes de Syrie au XIIe siècle.—Duchesne, L. La passion de saint Denis.—Durrieu, P. L'origine du manuscrit célèbre, dit le *Psautier d'Utrecht.*—Fournier, Paul. Le *Liber Tarraconensis.*—Funck-Brentano, Frantz. Le traité de Marquette (septembre 1304).—Giry, A. La donation de Rueil à l'abbaye de Saint-Denis.—Grandmaison, L. de. Les bulles d'or de Saint-Martin de Tours.—Hauréau, B. Prévostin, chancelier de Paris (1206–1209).—Huet, Gédéon. La pre-

(Continued)

N. Y. P. L. July 29, 1942

Mélanges Julien Havet... (Card 3)

mière édition de la *Consolation* de Boèce en néerlandais.—Ingold, P. A. Les droits et priviièges d'un prieur clunisien en Alsace en 1448.—Jacob, Alfred. Notes sur les manuscr:ts grecs palimpsestes de la Bibliothèque nationale.—Jullian, Camille. Question de géographie historique; la cité des Boïens et le pays de Buch.—Krusch, Bruno. La falsification des vies de saints burgondes.—Labande, L. H. Un légiste du XIVe siècle: Jean Allarmet.—Ledos, E. G. L'imposition d'Auvergne en janvier 1357.—Lot, Ferdinand. La date de naissance du roi Robert II et le siège de Melun.—Merlet, René. Origine de Robert le Fort.—Molinier, A. Un diplôme interpolé de Charles le Chauve.—Molinier, Émile. A propos d'un ivoire byzantin inédit du Musée du Louvre. —Monod, G. Hilduin et les *Annales Einhardi*.—Morel-Fatio, A. Maitre Fernand de Cordoue et les humanistes italiens du XVe siècle.—Muehlbacher, E. Un diplôme

(Continued)

N. Y. P. L. July 29, 1942

Mélanges Julien Havet... (Card 4)

faux de Saint-Martin de Tours.—Müntz, E. La bibliothèque du Vatican pendant la Révolution française.—Nerlinger, Charles. Deux pamphlets contre Pierre de Hagenbach.—Nolhac, P. de. Vers inédits de Pétrarque.—Omont, H. Épitaphes métriques en l'honneur de différents personnages du XIe siècle, composées par Foulcoie de Beauvais.—Paoli, C. Un diplôme de Charles VIII en faveur de la seigneurie de Florence.—Paris, Gaston. La légende de Pépin le Bref.—Petit-Dutaillis, Ch. Une femme de guerre au XIIIe siècle: Nicole de la Haie.—Picot, Emile. Aveu en vers rendu par Regnault de Pacy à Pierre d'Orgemont (1415).—Pirenne, H. La chancellerie et les notaires des comtes de Flandre avant le XIIIe siècle.—Prou, Maurice. Les diplômes de Philippe Ier pour l'abbaye de Saint-Benoit-sur-Loire.—Raynaud, G. Une édition de Froissart projetée par Christophe Plantin (1563–1565).—Robert,

(Continued)

N. Y. P. L. July 29, 1942

Mélanges Julien Havet... (Card 5)

Ulysse. Note sur l'origine de l'*e* cédillé dans les manuscrits.—Schmitz, Wilhelm. *Tironianum*.—Schwab, Moïse. Transcription de mots européens en lettres hébraïques au moyen âge.—Sickel, Th. von. Nouveaux éclaircissements sur la prémière édition du *Diurnus*.—Tardif, Joseph. Un abrégé juridique des *Étymologies* d'Isidore de Séville.—Thomas, A. Sur un passage de la *Vita sancti Eptadii*.—Trudon des Ormes, A. Note sur un fragment de la règle latine du Temple.—Valois, N. La situation de l'église au mois d'octobre 1378.—Wattenbach, W. Sur les poésies attribuées à Philippe de Harvengt.

49384. 1. Havet, Julien Pierre Eugène, 1853–1893. 2. Philology—Addresses, essays, lectures. 3. History—Addresses, essays, lectures.

Card revised

N. Y. P. L. July 29, 1942

AN
(Couture)

Mélanges Léonce Couture; études d'histoire méridionale, dédiées à la mémoire de Léonce Couture (1832-1902). Toulouse: É. Privat, 1902. xliv, 360, viii p. front. (port.) 8°.

1.Couture, Léonce, 1832-1902. 2.France (Southern).—History. 3.Batiffol, Pierre, 1861-

---

*Z-811
Film Reproduction

MÉLANGES Léonce Couture; études d'histoire méridionale, dédiées à la mémoire de Léonce Couture (1832-1902). Toulouse, É. Privat, 1902. xliv, 360, viii p. port. 23cm.

Film reproduction. Negative.

CONTENTS.--M. Léonce Couture, par P. Batiffol.--Bibliographie des travaux de M. Léonce Couture. (p.[xxxvii]-xliv).-- Le préhistorique pyrénéen, Par E. Cartailhac.--La plus ancienne vie de saint Seurin de

(Continued)

NN R 1.60 1/POCs, Is PCs, 1, 2, Is SL (UM1, LC1, X1, Z1)

MÉLANGES Léonce Couture... (Card 2)

Bordeaux, par H. Quentin.--La societé d'acuêts entre époux sous les lois wisigothiques, par M. J. Brissaud.--L'origine méridionale des fausses généologies carolingiennes, par L. Saltet.--Chronologie des évêques de Tarbes, (506-1226) par G. Balencie.--Un sirventes historique de 1242, par A. Jeanroy.--Une chronique béarnaise inédite du quatorzième siècle, par H. Courteault.--Bernard Gasc, soi-disant évêque de Ganos, par J.-M. Vidal.--La chapellenie de Montgauzy (1347), par F. Pasquier.--L'abbaye de Lucq en Bearn, par V. Dubarat.--Deux textes gascons originaires de Montesquieu-Volvestre, par J. Ducamin.--L'élection de Bérenger Guillot, archevêque d'Auch,

(Continued)

MÉLANGES Léonce Couture... (Card 3)

par J. de Carsalade du Pont.--La fin du schisme d'Occident en Gascogne, par A. Degert.--L'art français en Navarre sous Charles le Noble (1361-1425), par E. Privat et D. Cau-Durban.--Étymologies gasconnes, par A. Thomas.--Du Bartas et Augier Gaillard, par L. Campistron.--L'aumône générale à Toulouse, par l'abbé Lestrade.--La publication de la bulle in "Cœna Domini", par le chanoine Torreille.--Garaison en 1791-1792, par l'abbé Rigaud.--Note sur les bustes antiques du Musée de Toulouse, par H. Graillot.--Les statues de la Vierge au Musée de Toulouse, par J. de Lahon-dès-Lafigère.--Le prétendu "Philippe de

(Continued)

MELANGES Léonce Couture... (Card 4)

Champagne" de l'église d'Asté, par P. Durrieu.--Naimeri-n Aimeric, par G. Paris.

1. Couture, Léonce, 1832-1902. 2. France--Hist.--Addresses, essays, lectures. I. Batiffol, Pierre, 1861-1929.

RDV

MÉLANGES de linguistique et de littérature romanes, offerts à Mario Roques par ses amis, ses collègues et ses anciens élèves de France et de l'étranger. Bade, Editions Art et science, 1950-53 [v. 4, 1952] 4 v. illus., port., maps. 25-27cm.

Tome 1-4

Vols. 3-4 have imprint: Paris, En dépot à la Librairie M. Didier.

"Cet ouvrage a été publié aus frais et par les soins de la Direction générale des affaires culturelles du Haut commissariat de la République Française en Allemagne."—v. 1

(Continued)

NN R 9. β1 e/ / OCs (OD)Its (ED)Its PCs, 1, 2s, Is SLs (LC1s, X1s, Z1s)

MÉLANGES de linguistique et de littérature romanes... (Card 2)

Includes bibliographies.

1. Romance philology. 2. Roques, Mario Louis, 1875- I. France. Haut commissariat en Allemagne. Affaires culturelles, Direction générale des. t. 1950.

RAE

Mélanges de linguistique offerts à Albert Dauzat, professeur à l'Ecole pratique des hautes-études, par ses élèves et ses amis. Paris, Éditions d'Artrey [1951] viii,399 p. map.,port. 25cm.

"Bibliographie des principales publications d'ordre linguistique," p. 2-10.

1. Languages—Addresses, essays, lectures.
2. Dauzat, Albert, 1877-

NN*OC PC,1,2 SL(LC1,Z1, X1)

RAE

Mélanges de linguistique offerts à Charles Bally sous les auspices de la Faculté des lettres de l'Université de Genève par des collègues, des confrères, des disciples reconnaissants. Genève, Georg et c^ie, s. a., 1939.

xii, 515, [1] p. front. (port.) diagrs. 26½^cm.

"Liste des principales publications de Charles Bally": p. [x]–xii.

CONTENTS.—Linguistique générale: Wartburg, W. von. Betrachtungen über das verhältnis von historischer und deskriptiver sprachwissenschaft. Sechehaye, A. Évolution organique et évolution contingentielle. Richter, E. Unterbewusste vorgänge im sprachleben. Vendryes, J. "Parler par économie". Real, W. Linguistique et pédagogie.—Grammaire gé-

(Continued on next card)

A C 40–162

[2]

RAE

Mélanges de linguistique offerts à Charles Bally ... 1939. (Card 2)

CONTENTS—Continued.

nérale: Trubetzkoy, N. Les rapports entre le déterminé, le déterminant et le défini. Ginneken, J. van. *Avoir* et *être*, du point de vue de la linguistique générale. Cuendet, G. Sur l'expansion de la particule relative. Boer, C. de. Un peu de "comparatisme". Groot, A. W. de. Les oppositions dans les systèmes de la syntaxe et des cas. Terracini, B. A. Analisi del sintagma un padre cappuccino. Considerazioni sul valore morfologico del segno linguistico. Jakobson, R. Signe zéro. Tesnière, L. Théorie structurale des temps composés. Frei, H. Sylvie est jolie des yeux.—Antiquités indo-européennes: Bonfante, G. Études sur le tabou dans les langues indo-européennes. Lommel, H. Kāvya Uçan. Lommel, H. Der welt-ei-mythos im Rig-Veda.—Langues slaves: Havránek, B. Aspects et temps du verbe en vieux slave. Karcevski, S. Remarques sur la psycho-

(Continued on next card)

A C 40–162

[2]

RAE

Mélanges de linguistique offerts à Charles Bally ... 1939. (Card 3)

CONTENTS—Continued.

logie des aspects en russe.—Langues romanes: Migliorini, B. Note sugli aggettivi derivati da sostantivi. Devoto, G. Il prefisso *s-* in italiano. Iordan, I. De quelques traits caractéristiques du roumain. Jaberg, K. Considérations sur quelques caractères généraux du romanche.—Dialectologie romane: Gauchat, L. Promenade étymologique. Jud, J. Zur herkunft des ortsnamens *Grabs*. Tappolet, E. Der typus *nous suis*-"*je suis*" in francoprovenzalischen mundarten.—Français: Ernout, A. Allaiter et sevrer. Brœndal, V. L'originalité des prépositions du français moderne. Lerch, E. Die inversion im modernen französisch. Ein beitrag zum studium der heutigen schriftsprache.—Stylistique: François, A. Précurseurs français de la grammaire affective. Hotzenköcherle, R. Schwedischer forschungsbericht. Grammont, M. "L'homme entre deux âges et ses deux

(Continued on next card)

A C 40–162

[2]

RAE

Mélanges de linguistique offerts à Charles Bally ... 1939. (Card 4)

CONTENTS—Continued.

maîtresses". Mathesius, V. Verstärkung und emphase. Marouzeau, J. Dire "non". Niedermann, M. Tendances euphoniques en latin. Jeanjaquet, J. Le problème de *par exemple*! Genèse et développement d'un gallicisme. Grégoire, A. Le style des chroniqueurs financiers. Ribi, A. Stilistische beobachtungen an den fischbenennungen des unterseegebietes.

1. Bally, Charles, 1865– 2. Language and languages—Collections. I. Geneva. Université. Faculté des lettres.

A C 40–162

Johns Hopkins univ. Libr. for Library of Congress

[2]

Write on slip words underlined below and class mark—

STT

...**Mélanges** linguistiques offerts à M. Holger Pedersen à l'occasion de son soixante-dixième anniversaire, 7 avril 1937. Aarhus: Universitetsforlaget [etc., etc.] 1937. xxvii, 549 p. illus., port. 25cm. (Aarhus, Denmark. Universitet. Acta Jutlandica; Aarsskrift. [Nr.] 9 [Afdeling] 1.)

"Louis Hjelmslev s'est chargé de la direction du travail administratif et rédactionnel." — *Pref.*

CONTENTS.—Tabula gratulatoria.—Bibliographie des publications de Holger Pedersen, rédigée par Hans Hendriksen.—Feist, Sigmund. Die Dialekte in der indogermanischen Ursprache.—Bonfante, G. Les isoglosses gréco-arméniennes. I. Faits

(Continued)

N. Y. P. L. May 11, 1938

...**Mélanges** linguistiques... (Continued)

phonétiques.—Hjelmslev, Louis. Quelques réflexions sur le système phonique de l'indo-européen.—Whatmough, Joshua. The development of the Indo-European labiovelars with special reference to the dialects of ancient Italy.—Sturtevant, E. H. Latin and Hittite substantive i-stems with lengthened grade in the nominative.—Schwyzer, Eduard. Griech. -άζω und got. -atja.—Kretschmer, Paul. Danuvius und das Geschlecht der altindogermanischen Flussnamen.—Lidén, Evald. Wortgeschichtliches.—Mladenov, Stefan. Zur armenischen und slavischen Etymologie.—Hamel, A. G. van. La racine u̯en- en celtique et en germanique.—Uhlenbeck, C. C. Über den Wert eskimoisch-indogermanischer Wortähnlichkeiten.—Leumann, Manu. Der altindische Typus kṛtavān.—Adjarian, Hratchia. Etymologie du mot arménien mełc.—Jokl, Norbert. Ein Beitrag zur Lehre von der alb. Vertretung der idg. Labiove-

(Continued)

N. Y. P. L. May 11, 1938

...**Mélanges** linguistiques... (Continued)

lare.—Tagliavini, Carlo. Albanesische Etymologien.—Holt, Jens. Remarques sur l'assibilation grecque.—Höeg, Carsten. Les syllabes longues par position en grec.—Debrunner, A. Homerica.—Chantraine, P. Grec μενεαίνω.—Cuny, A. Gr. βαθύς, hom. βένθος, cf. hom. βῆσσα (dor. βᾶσσα), βυθός (βυσσός) "Fond de la mer" et autres mots apparentés.—Devoto, Giacomo. Umbrica.—Pisani, Vittore. Über drei neue faliskische Inschriften.—Blatt, Franz. Wortumfang und Satzrhythmus im Latein.—Boisacq, Ém. L'étymologie de lat. proelium 'combat.'—Brøndal, Viggo. Omnis et totus: analyse et étymologie.—Sommer, Ferdinand. Trinum nundinum.—Sommerfelt, Alf. Les consonnes vélarisées de l'irlandais.—Bergin, Osborn. On the origin of modern Irish rhythmical verse.—Vendryes, J. Restes en celtique du thème verbal en -ē-.—Lewis, Henry. Some medieval Welsh prepositions.—Thurneysen, R. Zwei irische Etymologien.—Bloomfield, Leonard. Notes on Germanic com-

(Continued)

N. Y. P. L. May 11, 1938

...**Mélanges** linguistiques... (Continued)

pounds.—Broch, Olaf. Begriffsunterschied durch Intonationsunterschied in dem Ostnorwegischen.—Lindquist, Ivar. Aljamarkią.—Agrell, Sigurd. Die Runen auf dem Stein von Krogsta.—Lindroth, Hjalmar. Isl. sef, altschw. sæf, u. s. w., "Binse."—Hammerich, L. L. Über das Frisische.—Hermann, Eduard. Altfriesisches.—Møller, Christen. Zerfall und Aufbau grammatischer Distinktionen; die Feminina im Deutschen.—Wijk, N. van. La décadence et la restauration du système slave des quantités vocaliques.—Lehr-Spławiński, Tadeusz. Zu den slavischen ą- und u-Doubletten.—Kuryłowicz, Jerzy. La structure de l'imparfait slave.—Vasmer, M. Alte slavische Participia.—Stender-Petersen, Ad. Das russische part. praet. pass. von imperfektiven Verben.—Belic, A. Sur le développement des syntagmes adverbiaux.—Mikkola, J. J. Zum slavischen Suffix -dlo.—Ekblom, R. Le slave *kol-

(Continued)

N. Y. P. L. May 11, 1938

...**Mélanges** linguistiques... (Continued)

dęd'źь.—Endzelin, J. Baltische Streitfragen.—Arumaa, P. Sur les adjectifs en -i dans les langues baltiques.—Fraenkel, Ernst. Zur baltischen Wortforschung und Syntax.—Senn, Alfred. Lithuanian dỹkas and related words.—Petersen, Walter. Hethitische Lautprobleme.—Mansion, Jos. À propos de la déclinaison du hittite.—Goetze, Albrecht. Transfer of consonantal stems to the thematic declension in Hittite.—Benveniste, A. Hittite hatugi.—Hrozný, Bedřich. Sur une inscription "hittite"-hiéroglyphique.—Meriggi, P. Zur Xanthosstele.—Friedrich, Joh. Die urartäische Inschrift von Kolagran.—Fraser, J. Phrygian ιος νι.—Pokorny, J. Die illyrische Herkunft der westdeutschen apa-Namen.

1. Pedersen, Holger, 1867- . 2. Pedersen, Holger, 1867- —Bibl. 3. Philology—Addresses, essays, lectures. 4. Philology, Comparative. I. Hjelmslev, Louis, ed. II. Ser.

N. Y. P. L. May 11, 1938

Mélanges de linguistique et de philologie, Fernand Mossé in memoriam. Paris, Didier, 1959.

534 p. port. 28 cm.

Contributions in various languages.
Includes bibliographical references.

1. Philology—Addresses, essays, lectures. 2. Mossé, Fernand.

Mélanges linguistiques et philologiques offerts à M. Aleksandar Belić par ses amis et ses élèves à l'occasion du quarantième anniversaire de son activité scientifique. Beograd ₍Штампарија "Млада Србија"₎ 1937. xxxiii, 472 p. chart, illus. (facsims.), port. 26cm.

Added t.-p. in Serbian: Зборник лингвистичких и филолошких расправа. А. Белићу о четрдесетогодишњици његова научног рада посвећују његови пријатељи и ученици. Београд, 1937.

Cover-title: Зборник у част А. Белића.

(Continued)

N. Y. P. L. July 12, 1939

Mélanges linguistiques et philologiques... (Continued)

Contributions in Serbian, Croatian, German, French, Italian, Russian, Polish and Slovenian.

Partial contents.—Библиографија радова професора А. Белића. —Трубецкой, Н. С., князь. О притяжательных прилагательных (possessiva) староцерковнославянского языка.—Karcevskij, Serge. Sur la rationalisation de l'orthographe russe.—Якобсон, Роман. Спорный вопрос древнерусского правописания (дъжгь, дъжчь).—Alessio, Giovanni. Il nome di Ragusa.—Vasmer, Max. Der Name des ältesten Moskauer Bojaren.—Погодин, А. "Внѣшняя Россія"

(Continued)

N. Y. P. L. July 12, 1939

Mélanges linguistiques et philologiques... (Continued)

Константина Багрянороднаго.—Barbulescu, Ilje. Origine du nom de famille "Mic(ul)" et la nouvelle théorie sur la formation du peuple roumain et de sa langue.—Grivec, Fran. Prvo poglavje žitja Metodija.—Шкарић, Ђуро. Прилог за српскохрв. етимологију.—Čajkanović, Veselin. De numinibus apud Serbos coniugalibus.—Bartoli, Matteo. Ancora del carattere conservativo dello Slavo e del Baltico. —Милетић, Бранко. Утицај реченичке мелодије на интонацију речи.—Murko, M. Glagol knaditi.—Грујић, Р. М. Једно јеванђеље босанскога типа XIV–XV века у Јужној Србији.—Ginneken, Jac.

(Continued)

N. Y. P. L. July 12, 1939

Mélanges linguistiques et philologiques... (Continued)

van. Das Pronomen reflexivum der Balkansprachen.—Hjelmslev, Louis. La syllabation en slave.—Ердељановић, Јован. Стари Срби Зећани и њихов говор.—Ramovs, F. K razvoju ь in ъ v slovenskem jeziku.—Mazon, Andre. L'attribut en russe littéraire moderne.—Ляцкій, Ев. Нѣсколько замѣчаній къ тексту "Слова о полку Игоревѣ."—Розовъ, Владимиръ. Лѣтопись Нестора какъ памятникъ древнерусскаго юмора.—Milewski, Tadeusz. Kilka uwag o genezie aspektów słowianskich.

994723A. 1. Belić, Aleksandar, 1876– . 2. Philology—Addresses, essays, lectures. 3. Slavonic languages. I. Title: Zbornik lingvističkih i filoloških rasprava.

N. Y. P. L. July 12, 1939

Mélanges de linguistique romane offerts à m. Jean Haust, professeur de dialectologie wallonne à l'Université de Liège ... à l'occasion de son admission à l'éméritat. Liège, H. Vaillant-Carmanne, 1939.

439, ₍1₎ p. illus., port. 25cm.

"Il a été tiré de cet ouvrage 50 exemplaires sur papier d'arches numérotés à la main de 1 à 50."

Contents.—Bibliographie de Jean Haust (p. ₍7₎–19)—Bal, W. Sur le vocabulaire du jeu de balle dans l'ouest-wallon.—Barbier, P. Étymologie et historique de quelques mots français.—Bastin, J. En marge de l'anthroponymie malmédienne.—Bruneau, Ch. Les sobriquets modernes dans le village wallon de Chooz.—Carnoy, A. Le problème des Wavre.—Cohen, G. Un inventaire de meubles inédit du xvie siècle en dialecte romanche de la Haute-Engadine.—Dauzat, A. Un cas de désarroi morphologique: l'infinitif *avér* (*avoir*) dans le Massif Central.—Delbouille, M.

(Continued on next card)

A C 40-1373

₍2₎

Mélanges de linguistique romane offerts à m. Jean Haust ... 1939. (Card 2)

Contents—Continued.

Essai sur la genèse des nativités wallonnes de Chantilly et sur leur adaptation française du xviie siècle.—Dupire, N. L'*n* mouillé en ancien picard.—Duraffour, A. La reviviscence des atones dans le nord du domaine gallo-roman.—Gamillscheg, E. Autour des mots wallons d'origine germanique.—Gessler, J. Notes de lexicologie comparée (limbourgeoise et liégoise)—Grootaers, L. A propos de noms wallons du "fruit tapé".—Henry, A. Notes sur la phonétique de l'ancien liégeois.—Herbillon, J. La Vita sancti Evermari et la toponymie.—Jodogne, O. Notes sur la diphtongaison de l'*e* ouvert entravé en wallon liégeois.—Jud, J. Deux notes étymologiques.—Legros, E. Le joug et la charrue en Ardenne liégeoise.—Michel, L. *Saligot*, nom commun, dans un texte liégeois du xive siècle.—Piron, M. Formation de la langue litté-

(Continued on next card)

A C 40-1373

₍2₎

Mélanges de linguistique romane offerts à m. Jean Haust ... 1939. (Card 3)

Contents—Continued.

raire des écrivains liégeois.—Remacle, L. La langue écrite à Stavelot vers 1400. Contribution à l'étude de l'ancien wallon.—Renard, E. Expressions tautologiques dans l'ancien wallon.—Roques, M. Compléments aux dictionnaires de l'ancien français.—Rousseau, F. Fausses étymologies, créatrices de légendes.—Salverda de Grave, J. J. Un Livre des droits de Verdun du moyen âge.—Valkhoff, M. Individualité et interdépendance des vieux dialectes français.—Verdeyen, R. De *neppe* à *nozé* et *nifeter*.—Vincent, A. Les noms de lieux de la Belgique dans les langues étrangères.—Warland, J. Français *grimper*, wallon *griper*.—Wartburg, W. von. Problèmes relatifs aux mots romans d'origine germanique.—Comité de patronage et Comité organisateur.—Liste des souscripteurs.

1. Haust, Jean, 1868– 2. Romance languages—Addresses, essays, lectures. 3. Walloon dialect—Addresses, essays, lectures.

Newberry library for Library of Congress

A C 40-1373

₍2₎

Mélanges linguistiques offerts à M. Antoine Meillet par ses élèves D. Barbelenet, G. Dottin [and others] avec un avant-propos par P. Boyer. Paris: C. Klincksieck, 1902. vii, 131 pp., 12. 4°.

Gift of the Evening Post.

Mélanges de littérature, d'histoire et de philologie offerts à Paul Laumonier, professeur à la Faculté des lettres de Bordeaux, par ses élèves et ses amis. Paris, E. Droz, 1935.

xix, 682 p., 1 l. front. (port.) facsims. (1 fold.) 25½cm.

"Bibliographie des publications de P. Laumonier": p. ₍xi₎–xix.

Contents.—Littérature latine: Cousin, J. La femme dans la comédie latine. Boyancé, P. Virgile et le destin. Bégué, C. La polémique anti-juive de Commodien.—Littérature médiévale: Hoepffner, E. Les deux lais du Chèvrefeuille. Nitze, W. A. Un ex-libris médiéval. Remigereau, F. Le livre du roy Modus et de la royne Ratio. Cohen, G. Emblèmes moraux inédits du xve siècle. Doutrepont, G. L'extension de la prose au xve siècle.—XVIe siècle: Nolhac, P. de. Jean Second et Corneille de Lyon. Jourda, P. Les annonces de l'esprit et de l'âme fidèle. Lefranc, A. La descente d'Epistemon aux enfers et le Calendrier des bergers. Tilley, A. From Marot to Ronsard. Chamard, H. Une

(Continued on next card)

A C 35-2351

₍2₎

Mélanges de littérature ... offerts à Paul Laumonier ... 1935. (Card 2)

CONTENTS—Continued.

divinité de la renaissance: Les Hymnides. Vianey, J. La nature dans la poésie française au XVIe siècle. Perrotin, L. Pour Didon: sur quatre vers d'Ausone traduits par J. du Bellay. Étienne, S. Ronsard a-t-il su le grec? Leroy, A. Une amitié littéraire: Ronsard et du Bellay. Pimenta, A. P. de Ronsard foi Cavalleiro de Christo? Vergès, R. Ronsard et Florent Chrestien à propos d'un sonnet anonyme. Blum, L. Sur une épithète de Ronsard. Charlier, G. Les sonnets d'estat. Diller, G. E. Un amant de Catherine des Roches: Claude Pellejay. Courteault, P. La mère de Montaigne. Porteau, P. Sur un paradoxe de Montaigne. Cons, L. Montaigne et l'idée de justice. Plattard, J. Sur une source des Tragiques, le Pimandre. Coissac de Chavrebière, J.-B. Un projet de mariage scoto-navarrais: Catherine de Bourbon et Jacques

(Continued on next card)

A C 35-2351

[2]

Mélanges de littérature ... offerts à Paul Laumonier ... 1935. (Card 3)

CONTENTS—Continued.

VI. Cirot, G. Une élégie latine du p. Mariana avec la réponse.—**XVIIe et XVIIIe siècles:** Guillaumie, G. Quelques variantes du prince de Guez de Balzac. Cherel, A. Art littéraire et morale chez les classiques. Barrière, P. L'histoire en Périgord du XVIe siècle à 1789. Teulié, H. Projet d'une prétendue traduction des essais de Montaigne au XVIIIe siècle. Feugère, A. Un compte fantastique de Voltaire: 95 lettres anonymes attribuées à la Beaumelle. Delage, F. Le théâtre à Limoges au XVIIIe siècle. Carré, H. Quelques fêtes révolutionnaires à Poitiers de 1793 à 1799.—**XIXe et XXe siècles:** Fouilhé, A. René; ou, Le Beau Ténébreux. Bisson, L. A. Le préromantisme étranger à Bordeaux. Rudler, G. Comment un règne se prépare: Benjamin Constant et le Palais-royal. Salomon, P. Quel est l'auteur de la chanson de Sténio

(Continued on next card)

A C 35-2351

[2]

Mélanges de littérature ... offerts à Paul Laumonier ... 1935. (Card 4)

CONTENTS—Continued.

dans Lélia? Raymond, M. Note sur le "spirituel" baudelairien. Pitrou, R. Le "cas" Brunetière vu par un allemand. Thieme, H. P. F. Brunetière aux États-Unis en 1897. Bernard, A. Un poète de Gascogne, J. Larribau. Maupoint, M. Un romancier belge: André Baillon. Laumonier, A. L'Acropole d'Athènes dans la littérature française. Coindreau, M.-E. Actualité du XVIe siècle.—**Varia:** Cuny, A. Nasale gutturale palatale et nasale gutturale vélaire. Gavel, H. Le nom de Fontarable est-il d'origine gasconne? Lafon, R. Observations sur la place de l'accent dans quelques formes des parlers souletins. Feghali, M. La famille maronite catholique au Liban. Simon, A. Sonnets.

1. Laumonier, Paul, 1867- 2. French literature—Addresses, essays, lectures. 3. Latin literature—Addresses, essays, lectures.

Title from Yale Univ. Printed by L. C. A C 35-2351

[2]

ZFB

MÉLANGES MANDONNET; études d'histoire littéraire et doctrinale du moyen âge. Paris, J. Vrin, 1930. 2 v. facsims. 26cm. (Bibliothèque thomiste. 13-14)

Contributions by various authors in French, German, Italian, English or Spanish, with some "texts" in Latin.

Includes bibliographies.

"Bibliographie du R. P. Mandonnet," v.1, p. [7]-17.

1. Mandonnet, Pierre, 1858-1936. 2. Thomas Aquinas, Saint, 1225?-1274. 3. Literature—Hist. and crit.—Middle Ages. 4. Catholic church, Roman—Doctrine and discipline. I. Series.

NN* X 2.55 p/ OC (OS) I PC, 1, 2, 3, 4, I SL (U1, Z1, LC1, X1) [I]

BTGP

Mélanges Nicole. Recueil de mémoires de philologie classique et d'archéologie offerts à Jules Nicole, professeur à l'Université de Genève à l'occasion du XXXe anniversaire de son professorat. Avec un portrait... [etc.] Genève: W. Kündig & Fils, 1905. 4 p.l., 671(1) p. 1 facsim., 19pl., 1 port. 8°.

E-11
1886

MÉLANGES offerts à Étienne Gilson. Toronto, Pontifical institute of mediaeval studies; Paris, J. Vrin, 1959. 704 p. port. 25cm. (Études de philosophie médiévale. Hors série)

"The writings of Étienne Gilson chronologically arranged," p.[15]-58.

1. Gilson, Étienne Henry, 1884- . 2. Literature--Addresses, essays, lectures. I. Toronto university. St. Michael's college. Pontifical institute of mediaeval studies. II. Series.

NN 6.61 e/P OC (OS)I, II PC, 1, 2, I, II SL (LC1, X1, Z1) [I]

F-11
4439

Mélanges offerts à Léon-Éli Troclet. Thème: Droit social national et international. Bruxelles, Éditions de l'Institut de sociologie (de l')Université libre de Bruxelles, (1967).

xxx, 344 p. port., tables. 26 cm.

CONTENTS.—Avant-propos, par M. Charpentier et V. Pons.—Bibliographie des ouvrages et écrits de Léon-Éli Troclet.—Biographie, par E. Vogel-Polsky.—Les responsabilités de l'État dans les guerres civiles, par T. Alvarado-Garaioca.—Problèmes théoriques et prati-

(Continued)

NN * R 7.68 1/R OC, I PC, 1, I SL E, 1, I (LC1, X1, Z1)

3

MÉLANGES offerts à Léon-Éli Troclet. (Card 2)

ques de programmation sociale, par R. Consael.—Réflexions sur la réforme des juridictions du travail, par C. De Swaef.—La naissance des premières associations ouvrières; l'évolution du droit de coalition en France, en Angleterre et en Belgique, par A. Doucy.—Considérations sur la programmation, la planification et quelques méthodes en vue de mesurer les données macro-économiques, par P. Frantzen.—Point de vue français sur la réglementation des honoraires médicaux, par A. Gazier.—Pour une sociologie de la Sécurité sociale, par H. Janne.—Europe sociale et culture européenne, par V. Larock.—La réduction de la durée du travail et de la vie active dans le monde moderne, par P. Laroque.—Observations sur la notion de droit du

(Continued)

MÉLANGES offerts à Léon-Éli Troclet. (Card 3)

travail, sa nature et ses limites, par L. Levi-Sandri.—Le Plan Beveridge: vingt ans après, par V. Pons.—Quelques remarques sur les données nouvelles de la vie internationale, par J. Rey.—L'œuvre sociale de la C. E. C. A. dans la perspective de la fusion des Communautés européennes, par F. Vinck.—L'opinion publique internationale comme facteur de développement du droit social international: Le cas de l'Afrique du Sud à l'O. I. T., par E. Vogel-Polsky.—La Convention internationale sur la protection des artistes interprètes ou exécutants, des producteurs de phonogrammes et des organismes de radio-diffusion, par F. Wolf.—Quelques remarques sur les régimes spéciaux en agriculture, par E. Zelenka.

1. Legislation, Social. I. Troclet, Léon Éli.

D-16
8112

Mélanges offerts à Mademoiselle Christine Mohrmann. Utrecht, Spectrum, 1963.

xxxv, 281 p. illus., port. 23 cm.

English, French, German, Italian and Latin.

"Bibliographie de Christine Mohrmann," by T. N. Hamers and M. H. Kruse: p. xxi-xxxv.

Bibliographical footnotes.

1. Classical studies--Collections. 2. Mohrmann, Christine.

NN* R 8.66 g/c OC PC, 1, 2 SL (LC1, X1, Z1) [I]

NKB

Mélanges offerts à m. Abel Lefranc, professeur au Collège de France ... par ses élèves et ses amis. Paris, E. Droz, 1936.

2 p. l., [vii]-xxxv, 506 p. incl. front. (port.) illus. (incl. facsim.) 25cm.

Printed in Belgium.

"Publications de m. Abel Lefranc, par Jacques Lavaud": p. [xi]-xxxv.

CONTENTS.—Coville, A. Nicolas de Clamanges à l'index au XVIe siècle.—Livingston, C.-H. Rabelais et Ph. de Vigneulles.—Doutrepont, G. La légende du Chevalier au Cygne.—Espezel, P. d'. Un nouveau portrait du cardinal d'Amboise.—Vianey, J. L'art du vers chez Clément Marot.—Lebègue, R. La source d'un poème religieux de Marot.—Ruutz-Rees, C. Flower garlands of poets, Milton, Shakespeare, Spenser, Marot, Sannazaro.—François, Alexis. D'une préfiguration de la langue classique au XVIe siècle.—Delcourt, Marie. Le pouvoir du roi dans l'Utopie.—

(Continued on next card)

37-15824

[3]

Mélanges offerts à m. Abel Lefranc ... 1936. (Card 2)

CONTENTS—Continued.

Mann, Margaret. Autour du Paris d'Érasme.—Renaudet, A. Érasme économiste.—Holban, Marie. Le Miroir de l'âme pécheresse.—Jourda, Pierre. Lettres inédites de Victor Brodeau.—Pannier, Jacques. Notes sur la date d'une lettre de Calvin à la duchesse de Ferrare (1536)—Bourrilly, V.-L. Un correspondant provençal de Jean du Bellay, abbé de Lérins: Denys Faucher.—Marichal, Robert. Rabelais à l'Ile-Bouchard.—Herrmann, Léon. Qui était l'escholier limousin?—Delaunay, Paul. Les animaux venimeux dans Rabelais.—Pons, E. Rabelais et Swift. A propos du lilliputien.—Porcher, Jean. L'auteur des Songes drolatiques de Pantagruel.—Courteault, P. Le premier principal du Collège de Guienne.—Chamard, Henri. Le collège de Boncourt et les origines du théâtre classique.—Plattard, Jean. Un témoignage peu connu sur Hélène de Surgères.—Becker, P.-A. Du Bril.—Droz, E. Guillaume

(Continued on next card)

37-15824

[3]

Mélanges offerts à m. Abel Lefranc ... 1936. (Card 3)

CONTENTS—Continued.

Boni, de Saint-Flour en Auvergne, musicien de Ronsard.—Thibault, G. Antoine de Bertrand, musicien de Ronsard, et ses amis toulousains.—François, Michel. Denis Lambin et le conclave de 1559.—Hauser, Henri. La crise de 1557-1559 et le bouleversement des fortunes.—Busson, H. Consolation de Francesco Vimercati à Catherine de Médicis (1559)—Jasinski, R. Sur la composition des Regrets.—Samaran, C. Un document notarié sur Joachim du Bellay.—Espiner-Scott, J. G. Note sur le cercle de Henri de Mesmes et sur son influence.—Borch-Bonger, F. de. Un ami de Jacques Amyot: Henry Scringer.—Maugain, Gabriel. L'Italie dans l'Apologie pour Hérodote.—Laumonier, P. Madame de Montaigne, d'après les Essais.—Boase, Alan. Un lecteur hollandais de Montaigne: Pieter van Veen.—Lavaud, Jacques. Les dépenses extraordinaires d'un ambassadeur en 1574.—Hulubei, Alice. Sur l'Hydromance ou Pyro-

(Continued on next card)

37-15824

[3]

Mélanges offerts à m. Abel Lefranc ... 1936. (Card 4)

CONTENTS—Continued.

mance, poème d'incantation de Ph. Desportes.—Raymond, Marcel. Réflexions sur les poésies d'amour d'Agrippa d'Aubigné.—Boulenger, Jacques. Testament et codicille de Jacquette de Montbron, belle-sœur de Brantôme.—Courteault, Henri. La Faculté de théologie de Paris et la bibliothèque de l'infant d'Espagne en 1591.—Charlier, Gustave. J.-B. Chassignet, historien.—Hazard, Paul. Voltaire et la pensée philosophique de la renaissance italienne.—Clouzot, Henri. Le style renaissance en France au XIXe siècle.—Index des noms de lieux, de personnes et des principaux titres, par E. Droz.

1. French literature—16th cent.—Hist. & crit. 2. Lefranc, Abel Jules Maurice, 1863- I. Lavaud, Jacques.

37-15824

Library of Congress PQ233.M4

[3] 840.4

NKW

Mélanges offerts à M. Charles Andler, par ses amis et ses élèves. Strasbourg, 1924. 446 p. 4°. (Strassburg. Université. Lettres, Faculté des. Publ. fasc. 21.)

Festschrift

184767A

1. Andler, Charles Philippe Théodore, 1866- . 2. Ser.

N. Y. P. L. May 1, 1925

RBG (Mélanges)

Mélanges offerts à M. Emile Chatelain... par ses élèves et ses amis. 15 avril 1910. Paris: H. Champion, 1910. xvi, 668 p., 1 l., 33 facsim., 1 port. 4°.

No.411 of 501 copies printed.
Autograph of E. Chatelain.

1910

NKW

Mélanges offerts à M. Émile Picot, membre de l'Institut, par ses amis et ses élèves. Paris: É. Rahir, 1913. 2 v. front., illus., plates, ports. 4°.

no.220 of 500 copies printed.
Contributed on the occasion of the retirement of M. Picot from the École des langues orientales.

1. Picot, Émile, 1844-1918. 2. Picot, Émile, 1844-1918.—Bibliography.

3-MAA (Société)

Mélanges offerts à M. Henry Lemonnier ... par la Société de l'histoire de l'art français, ses amis et ses élèves. Préface de M. Ernest Lavisse ... Ouvrage illustré de 21 reproductions hors texte. Paris, E. Champion, 1913.

Soc. de histoire

xvi, 563, [1] p. front. (port.) illus., plates (1 fold.) 22½cm. (Archives de l'art français, ~~nouv. période, t. VII)~~ Paris. Nouvelles archives [illegible])

CONTENTS.—Les fresques de la chapelle Saint-Jean au palais des papes d'Avignon, par R. Michel.—Quelques noms d'ivoiriers des XIVe et XVe siècles, par R. Kœchlin.—La peinture dans la Haute-Toscane et les Marches. Piero della Francesca, Melozzo de Forli, par H. Marcel.—L'importance de Jacopo Bellini dans le développement de la peinture italienne, à propos de deux tableaux conservés à la galerie Barberini à Rome, par C. de Mandach.—Le secret de Scipion; essai sur les effigies de profil dans

(Continued on next card)

15-24627

Mr. Math

Mélanges offerts à M. Henry Lemonnier ... 1913. (Card 2)

CONTENTS—Continued.

la sculpture italienne de la renaissance, par É. Bertaux.—Un portrait de sultan par un émailleur limousin du XVIe siècle, par J. J. Marquet de Vasselot.—Note sur trois retables franco-flamands de la Flamengrie (Aisne) par C. G. Picavet.—Note sur les livres à gravures et la décoration de la renaissance en Normandie, par R. Schneider.—Quelques imitations de la gravure italienne par les peintres-verriers français du XVIe siècle, par É. Mâle.—Sur certains livres d'architecture du XVIe siècle, par C. Saunier.—La musique des Italiens, d'après les Remarques triennales de Jean Baptiste Duval (1607-1609) par A. Pirro.—Une vie inédite de François Perrier par le comte de Caylus et Mariette; par J. Laran.—Les derniers jours de Nicolas Poussin et les origines de l'Académie de France à Rome, par A. Fontaine.—Un érudit bolonais du XVIIe siècle, Carlo Cesare Malvasia

(Continued on next card)

15-24627

Mélanges offerts à M. Henry Lemonnier ... 1913. (Card 3)

CONTENTS—Continued.

(1616-1693) par G. Rouchès.—Traités du XVIIe siècle sur le dessin des jardins et la culture des arbres et des plantes, par Jules Guiffrey.—Les tapisseries de Colbert, par G. Macon.—Le cabinet d'estampes de Claude Boucot, par H. Martin.—Louis XIV et l'imagerie satirique pendant les dernières années du XVIIe siècle, par A. Blum.—Les arabesques de Watteau, par L. Deshairs.—Les bustes des trois Gabriel, par P. Vitry.—La lutte des critiques d'art contre les portraitistes au XVIIIe siècle, par J. Locquin.—Un projet de journal de critique d'art en 1759, par M. Tourneux.—Jean Dominique Tiépolo, graveur, par H. Focillon.—Notes sur quelques bustes de Houdon, par G. Brière.—La Société des beaux-arts de Montpellier (1779-1787) par H. Stein.—Les visites du monument de la Place des victoires (1687-1788) par A. Tuetey.—Un collectionneur rouennais au

(Continued on next card)

15-24627

Mélanges offerts à M. Henry Lemonnier ... 1913. (Card 4)

CONTENTS—Continued.

XVIIIe siècle. Le président Robert de Saint-Victor, par P. Ratouis de Limay.—Pierre Alexandre Wille le fils (1748–1821?) par L. Hautecœur.—La collection de dessins de Gabriel Lemonnier au musée de Rouen, par P. Marcel.—Les statues de la cour du château de Versailles; que faut-il en faire? Par P. Fromageot.—Un chapitre de l'histoire de la manufacture de Sèvres. Madame Victoire Jaquotot, peintre sur porcelaines, par R. Jean.—Les idées artistiques de Sainte-Beuve, par A. Roux.—Tableaux français conservés au musée de Boston et dans quelques collections de cette ville, par Jean Guiffrey.—Imagiers modernes, par A. Marty.

1. Lemonnier, Henry *i. e.* Joseph Henry, 1842– 2. Art—France. 3. Artists, French. I. Société de l'histoire de l'art français, Paris. II. Lavisse, Ernest, 1842–

15-24627

Library of Congress N6841.A9 4th ser., t. 7

3-MAA
(Société)

...Mélanges offerts à M. Jules Guiffrey... Paris: É. Champion, 1916. cxlv, 350 p. front., plates, ports. 8°. (Société de l'histoire de l'art français, Paris. Nouvelles archives de l'art français. nouv. période. Tome 8.)

1.Art, French, 2.Guiffrey, Jules Marie Joseph, 1840-1918— Bibl. 3.Ser.

RAE

...**Mélanges** offerts à M. Max Niedermann à l'occasion de son soixante-dixième anniversaire. Neuchâtel, Secrétariat de l'Université, 1944. 208 p. port. 24cm. (Université de Neuchâtel. Recueil de travaux publiés par la Faculté des lettres. fasc. 22)

1. Philology—Addresses, essays, lectures. 2. Niedermann, Max, 1874–

NN

NRE

Mélanges offerts à m. Octave Navarre par ses élèves et ses amis. Toulouse, É. Privat, 1935.

xxxi, 515 p. incl. front. (port.) illus. (incl. plans) diagrs. plates. 24^cm.

"Publications et travaux de m. Octave Navarre": p. [xxv]–xxxi.

CONTENTS.—Béquignon, G. Le théâtre de Larissa en Thessalie.—Berthelot, A. La côte méridionale de l'Iran d'après les géographes grecs.—Bidez, J. Plantes et pierres magiques d'après le ps. Plutarque De fluviis.—Bieber, M. Ein statuetten-torso in Fulda.—Bodin, L. Thucydide et la campagne de Brasidas en Thrace.—Castiglioni, L. Adnotationes variae.—Chantraine, P. L'épithète homérique Ἀργεϊφόντης.—Cloché, P. Remarques sur la réaction anti-oligarchique à Athènes en 411 et 410 avant J.-C.—Collart, P. Livres neufs ou vieux bouquins? (Platon, Apologie de Socrate, 26 d-e)—Cousin, J. Une prétendue preuve

(Continued on next card)

A C 35-1809

[2]

Mélanges offerts à m. Octave Navarre ... 1935. (Card 2)

CONTENTS—Continued.

de l'inauthenticité de la Rhétorique d'Aristote.—Cuny, A. Hittite lāman "nom", tokh. ñom.—Delage, É. Accius imitateur d'Apollonios de Rhodes.—Delatte, A. La méthode oniromantique de Blaise d'Athénien.—Demangel, R. Μέτωπον.—Des Places, Éd. Citations et paraphrases de poètes chez Démosthène et Platon.—Desrousseaux, A.-M. Sur quelques fragments des comiques.—Dörpfeld, W. Das proskenion des Kaisers Nero im Dionysos-theater von Athen.—Festa, N. Ortodossia e propaganda nello stoicismo antico.—Fiechter, E. Einige beobachtungen über die chronologie der rand-formen der griechischen orchestra.—Flickinger, R. C. The staging of the Aristophanes' Pax.—Gernet, L. La légende de Procnè et la date du Tèreus de Sophocle.—Gonçalves, F. R. O sonho no drama clássico.—Goossens, R. Un vers d'Eschyle

(Continued on next card)

A C 35-1809

[2]

Mélanges offerts à m. Octave Navarre ... 1935. (Card 3)

CONTENTS—Continued.

parodié dans le Cyclope et dans les Grenouilles.—Grégoire, H. Euripidea.—Groh, F. De scaena Sophoclis.—Hubaux, J. La déesse et le passeur d'eau.—Jouguet, P. Le roi nubien Hurgonaphor et les révoltes de la Thébaïde.—Lorentzatos, P. Miscellanea graeca.—Mathieu, G. Sur quelques variantes du texte d'Isocrate.—Mazon, P. Inscription chorégique d'Aixônê.—Méautis, G. L'apologétique de Delphes dans un traité de Plutarque.—Mirambel, A. Une difficulté de phonétique néo-grecque.—Picard, Ch. Dionysos Psilax.—Plassart, A. Locations de domaines sacrés à Thespies.—Puech, A. La langue d'Hermas.—Rattenbury, R. M. Six notes on the text of the Aethiopica of Heliodorus.—Roussel, L. Bel canto et Sophocle.—Roussel, P. Σιτών.—Séveryns, A. Thrène épicidie.—Tierney, M. Ὅροι ἄγων μυστήρια.—Tolstoï, J. Quelques

(Continued on next card)

A C 35-1809

[2]

Mélanges offerts à m. Octave Navarre ... 1935. (Card 4)

CONTENTS—Continued.

observations sur les prologues d'Euripide.—Van Daele, H. Création en latin de trois types de verbes en *-co*. Origine de l'indicatif imparfait en latin.—Vieillefond, J.-R. Les imitations d'Homère dans Daphnis et Chloé; ou, L'humanisme de Longus.—Witkowski, St. Die zahl der schatzmeister der Athena im IV. jahrhundert.—Zielinski, Th. L'envoûtement de la sorcière chez Horace.—Aymard, A. Le Zeus fédéral achaien Hamarios-Homarios.—Caster, M. La composition du Nigrinos et les intentions ironiques attribuées à Lucien.—Magnien, V. Sur le subjonctif du grec ancien.—Orsini, P. Observations sur la mise en scène du Prométhée enchaîné.

1. *Navarre, Octave, 1864– 2. Greek literature—History and criticism.

A C 35-1809

Title from Univ. of Mich. Printed by L. C.

[2]

Copy only words underlined
& classmark— GDYM

MÉLANGES offerts à M. Paul-E. Martin par ses amis, ses collègues [et] ses. élèves. [Genève, 1961] 677 p. illus. 24cm. (Société d'histoire et d'archéologie de Genève. Mémoires et documents. t. 40)

Contributions in French or German.

Bibliography of Martin's works, p. [665]-673.

1. Martin, Paul Edmond. 2. Switzerland--Hist.--Addresses, essays, lectures.

NN 4.62 e/ OC OI PC, 1, 2 (LC3, X1, Z1) [I]

NAC p.v.1464

Mélanges offerts à M. le professeur Victor Magnien. Toulouse, É. Privat, 1949. 83 p. illus., port. 26cm.

CONTENTS.—Hommage à Victor Magnien, par D. Faucher.—Sur Isocrate, IV (Panég.) 50, par A. Aymar.—Sur un passage du choeur des initiés dans les Grenouilles d'Aristophane, par F. Buffière.—Repères géographiques dans le recueil théognidéen, par J. Carrière.— Position de Clément d'Alexandrie, par M. Caster.—A propos de la Cité de Dieu, par L. Delaruelle.—Les circonstances de la mort dans les épitaphes grecques métriques, par G. Fohlen.—Pour le Grec, par J. Hémous.—Sur une statuette de Vénus d'inspiration classique trouvée à Montmaurin (Haute-Garonne) par M. Labrousse.—En marge de Synésios, par C. Lacombrade.—Mysticisme artémisiaque, par A. Laumonier.—A propos de l'astrologue de Properce, par R. Lucot.—Ἐν παραβύστῳ (Démosthène contre Timocrate, 47) par P. Orsini.—Jéhova, Βάκχος, Ἴακχος, par L. Roussel.—A propos de la fin de l'hexamètre dactylique classique, par P. Ruffel.

1. Magnien, Victor. 2. Greek literature—Hist. and crit.

NN*R 3.54 OC PC, 1, 2 SL (Z1, LC1, X1) [I]

E-11
201

MÉLANGES offerts à Octave et Melpo Merlier, à l'occasion du 25e anniversaire de leur arrivée en Grèce. Athènes, 1956-57. 3 v. plates. (Collection de l'Institut français d'Athènes. 92-94)

Contributions in various languages.

Includes bibliographical references.

1. Merlier, Octave. 2. Merlier, Melpo. 3. Byzantine studies--Collections. 4. Greek literature, Modern--Addresses, essays, lectures. I. Institut français d'Athènes.

NN * X 4.60 a/ OC (OS)I PC, 1, 2, 3, 4, I SL (LC1, X1, Z1)

Copy only words underlined & classmark— * OAC

MÉLANGES offerts au Père René Mouterde pour son 80e anniversaire. Beyrouth, Impr. catholique, 1960-62. 2 v. illus., plates (part col.) port. 26cm. (Université Saint-Joseph, Beirut, Syria. Mélanges, t. 37-38)

French or English.

"Bibliographie du Père René Mouterde, S.J.," t. 37, p. [1]-29. Bibliographical footnotes.

1. Mouterde, René. 2. Oriental studies--Collections.

NN 4.66 p/ OI (PC) 1, 2 (O)1, 2 (LC1, X1, Z1)

F-10
4974

MÉLANGES offerts par ses confrères étrangers à Charles Braibant, directeur général des Archives de France, président d'honneur du Conseil international des archives. Bruxelles, Comité des Mélanges Braibant, 1959. xx, 571 p. illus., ports., facsims. 26cm.

Contributions in French, Italian, Spanish, English or German. Includes bibliographies.

1. Braibant, Charles Maurice, 1889- . 2. Archives.

NN 10.60 a/ OC PC, 1, 2 SL E, 2 (LC1, X1, Z1) [I]

E-13
6648

Mélanges offerts à Polys Modinos ... Problèmes des droits de l'homme et de l'unification européenne. Paris, A. Pedone, 1968.

xxiv, 499 p. port. 25 cm.

Illustrated cover.
English, French, German, or Italian.
Bibliography: p. [xix]-xxi. Bibliographical footnotes.

1. Natural rights. 2. European federation, 1929- . I. Modinos, Polys, 1899-

NN*R 10.69 r/ OC, I, Ib+ PC, 1, 2, I SL E, 1, 2, I (LC1, X1, Z1)

XAP

Mélanges P.F. Girard; études de droit romain dédiées a Mr. P.F. Girard, professeur de droit romain à l'Université de Paris à l'occasion du 60e anniversaire de sa naissance (26 octobre 1912). Paris: A. Rousseau, 1912. 2 v. front. (port.) 4°.

1.Law (Roman). 2.Girard, Paul Frédéric, 1852- .

E-13
5527

MÉLANGES offerts à Rita Lejeune, professeur à l'Université de Liège. Gembloux, J. Duculot [1969] 2 v. (xxxii, 1762 p. illus., port., fold. map, facsims., music. 25cm.

Text in French, English, German, Spanish, Provençal or Catalan.

"Bibliographie des travaux de Madame Rita Lejeune," v. 1, p. xv-xxiv.

(Continued)

NN R 6.69 w/ OC, I PC, 1, 2, I SL (LC1, X1, Z1) [I]

2

NRC

MÉLANGES PAUL THOMAS; recueil de mémoires concernant la philologie classique dédié à Paul Thomas. Bruges, Impr. Sainte Catherine, 1930. lxvii, 757 p. illus., port. 26cm.

"Bibliographie des travaux de M. Paul Thomas," p. xxv-lxv.

1. Classical studies--Collections. 2. Thomas, Paul Louis Désiré, 1852-1937. 3. Thomas, Paul Louis Désiré, 1852-193'. --Bibl.

NN** 5.57 c/ OC PC, 1, 2, 3 SL (LC1, X1, Z1) [I]

MÉLANGES offerts a Rita Lejeune, professeur à l'Université de Liège. (Card 2)

Bibliographical footnotes.

1. Romance literature--Addresses, essays, lectures. 2. Literature--Hist. and crit., Middle ages. I. Lejeune, Rita.

MTN

Mélanges Perrot. Recueil de mémoires concernant l'archéologie classique, la littérature et l'histoire anciennes, dédié à Georges Perrot... à l'occasion du 50e anniversaire de son entrée à l'École normale supérieure... Paris: Thorin et Fils, 1903. 3 p.l., 343 p., 5 pl., 1 port. illus. 4°.

NKG

Mélanges offerts par ses amis et ses élèves à M. Gustave Lanson... Paris: Librairie Hachette, 1922. 534 p. 4°.

"Bibliographie des oeuvres de M. Lanson," p.7-21.

RFB

Mélanges de philologie et d'histoire littéraire; offerts à Edmond Huguet, professeur honoraire à la Faculté des lettres de l'Université de Paris, président de la Société des textes français modernes. Par ses élèves, ses collègues et ses amis. [Paris, Boivin & cie] 1940. xiii, 488 p. plates. 27cm.

"Publications de M. Edmond Huguet, par G. Saintville," p. xi-xiii.
Bibliographical footnotes.

499915B. 1. Huguet, Edmond Eugène Auguste, 1863- . 2. French language. 3. French literature—Hist. and crit.
N. Y. P. L. February 24, 1950

Write on slip words underlined below and class mark—

ZLF

...**Mélanges** de philologie et d'histoire publiés á l'occasion du cinquantenaire de la Faculté des lettres de l'Université catholique de Lille. Lille: Facultés catholiques, 1927. 318 p. 8°. (Facultés catholiques de Lille. Mém. et travaux. fasc. 32.)

1. No subject. I. Ser.
N. Y. P. L. February 29, 1932

F-11
4039

MÉLANGES de philologie et de linguistique offerts à Tauno Nurmela [comité de rédaction: Eero K. Neuvonen, Lauri Lindgren, Pirjo Mäkelä] Turku, Turun yliopisto, 1967. 167 p. port. 26cm. (Turun yliopisto, Turku, Finland. Julkaisuja. Seria B: Humaniora. Tom 103)

CONTENTS.--Tauno Nurmela-Homme de culture, par E. Krohn.--Publications et travaux de Tauno Nurmela, par
(Continued)

NN 3.28 1/1 OC,II (OS)I PC,1,2,I,II SL (LC1, X1,Z1) [I]

MÉLANGES de philologie et de linguistique offerts à Tauno Nurmela... (Card 2)

P. Mäkelä.--Ein deutscher Boccaccio im Knittelvers.--par H. Fromm.--Rôle de l'imitation dans les changements linquistiques, par A. Graur.--Gilbert Romme et son recit de voyage en Finland, par S. Haltsonen.--Sémantique de l'ancien français gab et gaber comparée à celle des termes correspondants dans d'autres langues romanes, par E. von Kraemer.--courtebarbe,
(Continued)

MÉLANGES de philologie et de linguistique offerts à Tauno Nurmela... (Card 3)

auteur des trois aveugles de Compiegne, est-il aussi l'auteur du fabliau du Chevalier à la robe vermeille, par L. Lindgren.--Les thèmes zéro, par P. Naert.--Dante et l'ascétique du XIIIe siècle, par G. Petrocchi.--Ugo Marescale, companh de Guillem de Saint-Didier, par A. Sakari.--De triginta notis mulierum, par V. Väänänen.--Ein deutscher Palästina-
(Continued)

MÉLANGES de philologie et de linguistique offerts à Tauno Nurmela... (Card 4)

Pilgerbericht als Quelle italienischer Seetermini, Par M. Wis.--Due lettere inedite en un ritratto di Paolina Leopardi, par R. Wis.--Sprache, Weltbild, Weltanschaung, par E. Öhmann.--Retouches au lexique du Roman du Thèbes, par G. Raynaud de Lage.

1. Nurmela, Tauno. 2. Philology--Addresses, essays, lectures. I. Series. II. Neuvonen, Ero K., ed.

RBC

Mélanges de philologie, de littérature et d'histoire anciennes, offerts à J. Marouzeau par ses collègues et élèves étrangers. Paris, Belles Lettres, 1948.

xv, 568 p. port. 26 cm.
Bibliographical footnotes.

1. Classical philology—Collections. 2. Marouzeau, Jules, 1878-

A 49-36*

Rochester. Univ. Libr. for Library of Congress PA26.M3 [8]

Festschrift c.d.

F-11
6125

MÉLANGES de philologie offerts à Alf Lombard à l'occasion de son soixante-cinquième anniversaire, par ses collègues et ses amis. Lund, C.W.K. Gleerup [1969] 252 p. illus., port. 26cm. (Études romanes de Lund. no.18)

Text in French, English, German or Italian.
Bibliographical footnotes

(Continued)

NN 4.70 r/1 OC, II (OS)I PC, 1, 2, I, II SL (LC1, X1, Z1) 2

MÉLANGES de philologie offerts à Alf Lombard à l'occasion de son soixante-cinquième anniversaire... (Card 2)

1. Romance languages--Addresses, essays, lectures. 2. Rumanian language--Addresses, essays, lectures. I. Series. II. Lombard, Alf.

RAE

Mélanges de philologie offerts à. m. Johan Melander. Uppsala, A.-b. Lundequistska bokhandeln [1943]
4 p. l., 305 p., 1 l. front. (port.) 24½cm.
Bibliographical foot-notes. Bibliography at end of some of the articles.
CONTENTS.—Sävborg, Torsten. Les sources de la préposition *dès*.—Kjellman, Hilding. Le miracle de la Sacristine; étude sur les versions métriques de l'ancien français.—Andolf, Sven. Une version bourguignonne du Dit de l'unicorne et du serpent.—Tilander, Gunnar. Vieux français, provençal, catalan *ades*, italien *adesso*, ancien espagnol *adieso*.—Michaëlsson, Karl. A propos de *fuiz*.—Ekblom, R. Die entwicklung der wörter vom typus spătulam > *épaule*.—Nilsson-Ehle, Hans. Sur les adverbes en *-ment* qui signifient "en qualité de ...," "à titre de ..."—Rooth, Erik. Das verb *cratmen* bei Goethe und seine stellung im system der verben mit *er-* präfix.—Falk, Paul. La valeur de *-que* dans *tresque* 'très.'—

(Continued on next card)

A 46-4638

[2]

Mélanges de philologie offerts à m. Johan Melander ... [1943] (Card 2)

CONTENTS—Continued.

Walberg, E. La vision de saint Foursi en vers français du XIVe siècle.—Liljegren, S. B. Voltaire et l'Angleterre d'après La princesse de Babylone.—Fahlin, Carin. Catalan *com* et *com a* dans les subordonnées comparatives.—Ringenson, Karin. Un type d'expressions de temps en français. *A cette époque—A ce moment*.—Ekwall, Eilert. Old English *ambyrne wind*.—Långfors, Arthur. L'arrièreban d'amours; poème du XIIIe siècle inspiré par le Bestiaire d'amour de Richard de Fournival.—Franzén, Torsten. *Ki en lui creit il n'a nul bon talent;* quelques observations sur l'emploi, en ancien français, des propositions relatives indépendantes et sur la structure de la principale qui suit.

1. Melander, Johan, 1878- 2. Philology—Collections.

A 46-4638

Harvard univ. Library for Library of Congress [2]

RAE

Mélanges de philologie offerts à M. Johan Vising par ses élèves et ses amis scandinaves à l'occasion du soixante-dixième anniversaire de sa naissance, le 20 avril 1925. Göteborg: N.J. Gumpert[, 1925]. xii, 419 p. front. (port.) 8°.

no. 210 of 250 copies printed.

1. Vising, Johan, 1855- . 2. Philology—Collections.

RDT

Mélanges de philologie romane et d'histoire littéraire offerts à M. Maurice Wilmotte, professeur à l'Université de Liége, à l'occasion de son 25e anniversaire d'enseignement... Pt.1-2. Paris: H. Champion, 1910. 2 v. illus. 8°.

Continuously paged.

RDV

Mélanges de philologie romane et de littérature medievale offerts à Ernest Hoepffner... par ses élèves et ses amis. Paris, Les Belles Lettres, 1949. xii,390 p. fold. plate. 26cm. (Publications de la Faculté des lettres de l'Université de Strassbourg. Fasc. 113)

"Bibliographie des travaux de M. Ernest Hoepffner, par Paul Imbs": p. [5]-12.

Bibliographical footnotes.

578450B. 1. Romance philology. 2. Hoepffner, Ernst, 1879- I. Ser.

NN*R 11.52 OC PC,1,2 SL (LC1,Z1,X1)

RDV

Mélanges de philologie romane offerts à M. Karl Michaëlsson par ses amis et ses élèves. Göteborg, 1952. [13] 481 p. port. 25cm.

Bibliographical footnotes.

"Bibliographie des publications de M. Karl Michaëlsson," 8th-13th prelim. page.

1. Michaëlsson, Karl, 1890- . 2. Romance philology.

NN** X 8.53 OC PC,1, 2 SL (LC1,Z1,X1)

F-10
1563

MÉLANGES de philosophie grecque offerts à Mgr Diès, membre de l'Institut de France, doyen honoraire de la Faculté des lettres d'Angers, par ses élèves, ses collègues, ses amis. Paris, J. Vrin, 1956. 243 p. 26cm.

CONTENTS. --Hommage à Mgr A. Diès. --Bibliographie de Mgr Diès (p. [17]-20). --Un fragment perdu du de aeternitate mundi de Proclus, par G. C. Anawati. --Autour de la noétique aristotélicienne. L'interprétation du témoignage de Théophraste par Averroès et Saint Thomas

(Continued)

NN 11.57 m/J OC PC,1,2 SL (LC1,X1,Z1,Y1)

MÉLANGES de philosophie grecque offerts à Mgr Diès... (Card 2)

d'Aquin, par E. Barbotin. --Trois noms grecs de l'Artisan, par P. Chantraine. --Timaeus 52 C 2-5, par Harold Cherniss--Introduction inédite à l'"Epictète chrétien", par A. Dain. --Eusèbe de Césarée juge de Platon dans la Préparation évangélique, par E. des Places. --Le Théorie aristotélicienne du lieu, par V. Goldschmidt. --Note sur la structure du Lachès, par P. Grenet. --La conception platonicienne de la liberté, par A. Jagu. --Observations sur le vocabulaire technique d'Aristote, par P. Louis. --L'objet de la science philosophique suprême d'après Aristote, Metaphysique, E. I, par A. Mansion. --Sur une lettre de Platon, par P. Mazon. --La vérité transcendantale du Socrate d'Aristophane, par

(Continued)

MÉLANGES de philosophie grecque offerts à Mgr Diès... (Card 3)

P. Mesnard. --L'idéalisme platonicien et la transcendance de l'être, par J. Moreau. --Espace et changement dans le Timée de Platon, par A. Rivaud. --The text of Aristotle's Topics and Sophistici Elenchi, par W. D. Ross. --L'univers spirituel de Pindare, par R. Schaerer. -- ΔΕΣΜΟΣ , par P. M. Schuhl. --La genèse du plaisir dans le Philèbe, par M. Vanhoutte.

1. Diès, Auguste. 2. Philosophy, Greek--Addresses, essays, lectures.

XAH

Mélanges R. Carré de Malberg. Paris, Librairie du Recueil Sirey (société anonyme) 1933.

viii, 536 p., 1 l. front. (port.) 24½cm.

Introduction signed: J. Duquesne ...

CONTENTS. — Introduction. — La conception matérielle de la fonction juridictionnelle, par Roger Bonnard.—Régimes parlementaires, par René Capitant.—Les doctrines politiques des physiocrates, par Ernest Chavegrin.—A propos du "positivisme juridique" de Carré de Malberg, par Paul Cuche.—Le pouvoir "lié" des tribunaux et les lois fiscales, par Joseph Delpech.—Esquisse d'une définition réaliste des droits publics individuels, par Paul Duez.—Sur la généralité de la loi, par Henri Dupeyroux.—L' "Esprit des lois" et la séparation des pouvoirs, par

(Continued on next card)

34-31562

[3]

Mélanges R. Carré de Malberg ... 1933. (Card 2)

CONTENTS—Continued.

Charles Eisenmann.—Le particularisme du droit fiscal, par François Geny.—Le pouvoir discrétionnaire et sa justification, par André Hauriou.—Le procès de la Commission des finances, par Joseph Barthélemy.—Le pouvoir réglementaire du président des États-Unis d'Amérique, par Julien Laferrière.—La constitution centrifuge, par Irénée Lameire.—Les privilèges des clercs dans les concordats récents, par Gabriel Le Bras.—Volonté générale et collaboration. Leur rôle dans le droit international public, par Louis Le Fur.—De la méthode dans l'enseignement du droit constitutionnel, par Henry Nézard.—La séparation des pouvoirs et les traités diplomatiques, par Jean-Paulin Niboyet.—L'enseignement du droit romain à l'ancienne Faculté de droit de Strasbourg (1806–

(Continued on next card)

34-31562

[3]

Mélanges R. Carré de Malberg ... 1933. (Card 3)

CONTENTS—Continued.

1870), par Christian Pfister.—La théorie de l'état dans le droit fasciste, par Marcel Prélot.—La reconnaissance de la nation tchécoslovaque pendant la guerre, par Robert Redslob.—Qu'est-ce que le droit constitutionnel? Le droit constitutionnel et la théorie de l'institution, par Georges Renard.—Le droit constitutionnel international, par Georges Scelle.—Positivisme philosophique, juridique et sociologique, par Marcel Waline.

1. *Carré de Malberg, Raymond, 1861- 2. Constitutional law—Collections. 3. Administrative law—Collections. 4. International law and relations—Collections. 5. Executive power—U. S. 6. Fascism—Italy. 7. Law—Philosophy. 8. Political science—Collections. 9. Strasbourg. Université. Faculté de droit et des sciences politiques.

34-31562

Library of Congress [3]

*EN

Mélanges Renier. Recueil de travaux publiés par l'École Pratique des Hautes Études, (section des sciences historiques et philologiques) en mémoire de son président Léon Renier. Paris: F. Vieweg, 1887. 4 p.l., iij, lx, 468 pp. 1 port. 8°. (École des Hautes Études.- Scie. Phil. et Hist. [v.33]. Fasc. 73.)

Copy only words underlined & classmark—

BAA

MÉLANGES Roger Goossens. Bruxelles, 1954. 24cm. (Nouvelle Clio. t. 6, no. 3-4)

Cover-title.

1. Goossens, Roger.

NN R 8.65 g/ OIs (PC)1s (LC1s, X1s, Z1)

---

*OFXA

Mélanges syriens offerts à Monsieur René Dussaud, secrétaire perpétuel de l'Académie des inscriptions et belles-lettres, par ses amis et ses élèves... Tome 1- Paris: P. Geuthner, 1939- v. front. (port.), illus. (incl. charts, plans), plates (part col'd). 29cm. (Half-title: Haut-commissariat de la République Française en Syrie et au Liban. Service des antiquités. Bibliothèque archéologique et historique. Tome 30)

Bibliographical footnotes.
"Travaux originaux de René Dussaud," v. 1, p. v–xvi.

(Continued)

N. Y. P. L. Festschrift December 28, 1939

Mélanges syriens... (Continued)

CONTENTS.—Tome 1. Un dieu supposé syrien, associé à Hérôn en Égypte, par Franz Cumont. Drogues de Canaan, d'Amurru et jardins botaniques, par G. Contenau. Tre sigilli neoassiri, par Giuseppe Furlani. Une monnaie présumée de Doura et la legio III Parthica, par Adrien Blanchet. ὁ Μυριανδικὸς κόλπος ὁ πρὸς Φοινίκῃ κείμενος, by Sydney Smith. Sur un vers de Baudelaire, par P. Perdrizet. Zur Einleitungsformel der ältesten phönizischen Inschriften aus Byblos, von Johannes Friedrich. Ḥrb de Ras Shamra-Ugarit, par Georges Chenet. Sur un cachet "hittite"-hiéroglyphique de Ras Shamra, par Bedřich Hrozný. Le "tell" d'Alep, par J. Sauvaget. Un paradis palestinién? Par Joh. de Groot. Une fable babylonienne? Par J. Nougayrol. Archéologie hittite, par Alfred Boissier. Onze Normands en Terre Sainte, par Seymour de Ricci. Sur une inscription grecque de Sidon, par E. Bikerman. Sur quelques symboles de Iahvé, par A. G. Barrois. Astarte plaques and

(Continued)

N. Y. P. L. December 28, 1939

Mélanges syriens... (Continued)

figurines from Tell Beit Mirsim, by W. F. Albright. Le maitre des animaux sur une gemme crétoise du M.M.I., par Pierre Demargne. Notes de géographie syrienne, par Ernest Honigmann. On a steatopygous stone figure from North Syria, by Leonard Woolley. Sur deux bulles de l'Orient latin, par le comte Chandon de Briailles. La leggenda di abbā Afṣē in Etiopia, par C. Conti Rossini. La statue Cabane, par F. Thureau-Dangin. Linos und Alijan, von Otto Eissfeldt. Le "Bon Pasteur" à propos d'une statue de Mari, par A. Parrot. Eski Hissar, ein römisches Lagerkastell im Gebiet von Edessa, par S. Guyer. Le roi Sahurê et la princesse lointaine, par Pierre Montet. La confession des péchés en Syrie aux époques préchrétiennes, par R. Pettazzoni. Lettre du roi de Kargamish au roi d'Ugarit, par E. Dhorme. Sur une statistique méconnue de l'armée romaine au début du IIIe siècle ap. J. C., par Jérome

(Continued)

N. Y. P. L. December 28, 1939

Mélanges syriens... (Continued)

Carcopino. Quelques remarques sur la carrière de L. Catilius Severus, légat de Syrie, par A. Merlin. Le roi sassanide Narsès, les Arabes et le manichéisme, par W. Seston. Alexandre en Syrie; les offres de paix que lui fit Darius, par Georges Radet. La légende de Kombabos, par E. Benveniste. Les adjectifs "zâr" et "nokri" et la "femme étrangère" des proverbes bibliques, par Paul Humbert. Les rites du balancement (tenoûphâh) et du prélèvement (teroûmâh) dans le sacrifice de communion de l'Ancien Testament, par Albert Vincent. Nāḫ et Rušpān, par Julius Lewy. La Susiane dans une inscription palmyrénienne, par Jean Cantineau. Le Gad de Doura et Séleucus Nicator, par M. Rostovtzeff. Un nouvel encensoir syrien et la série des objets similaires, par G. de Jerphanion. Nouveaux textes hiératiques de proscription, par G. Posener. Les frises historiées autour de la cella et devant l'adyton, dans le

(Continued)

N. Y. P. L. December 28, 1939

Mélanges syriens... (Continued)

temple de Bacchus à Baalbek, par C. Picard. Note sur l'histoire de la legio III Gallica, par E. Albertini. Le voyage en Syrie de W. R. Waddington [edité] par J. B. Chabot. Un monument d'Hiérapolis-Bambykè relatif à la paix "perpétuelle' de 532 ap. J. C., par P. Roussel. La représentation divine orientale archaïque, par L. H. Vincent. Le dieu syrien Op, par René Mouterde. Monnaies musulmanes et poids en verre inédits, par Djafar Abdel-Kader. Une tablette magique de la région du moyen Euphrate, par le comte du Mesnil du Buisson. Deux vases chypriotes du Musée du Louvre, par Maggie Rutten. Le cimetière des marins à Séleucie de Piérie, par Henri Seyrig. Une trouvaille de monnaies archaïques grecques à Ras Shamra, par C. F. A. Schaeffer.

(Continued)

N. Y. P. L. December 28, 1939

Mélanges syriens... (Continued)

J. S. BILLINGS MEM. COLL.

1. Oriental studies. 2. Dussaud, René, 1868- . I. Ser.

N. Y. P. L. December 28, 1939

D-19
4311

MEMOIRS of a modern Scotland, edited by Karl Miller. London, Faber and Faber [1970] 206 p. illus., ports. 23cm.

Published in honor of Hector MacIver.

CONTENTS.--Scottish nationalism since 1918, by A. Marwick.--The three dreams of Scottish Nationalism, by T. Nairn.--Satori in Scotland, by H. MacDiarmid.--The heart of the cabbage by L. Simpson.--The Scottish Renaissance of the 1930's, by G. Scott-

(Continued)

NN R 6.70 1/ OC, I, IIbo, III, IIIb+ PC, 1, 2, 3, I, III SL (LC1, X1, Z1)

MEMOIRS of a modern Scotland... (Card 2)

Moncrieff.--Strangers, by R. Taubman.--Romantic town, by K. Miller.--Old songs and new poetry, by S. Maclean.--The broken heraldry, by G.M. Brown.--What images return, by M. Spark.--Borderlines, by A. Reid.--Growing up in Langholm, by H. MacDiarmid.--Growing up in the west, by W. McIlvanney.--Scottish schoolmasters, by C. McAra.--The emergence of Scottish music, by R. Stevenson.--The backwardness of Scottish television, by S. Hood.

(Continued)

MEMOIRS of a modern Scotland... (Card 3)

1. Scotland--Civilization, 20th cent. 2. Scottish literature--Hist. and crit. 3. Scotland--Politics, 20th cent. I. Miller, Karl, ed. II. Miller, Karl. III. MacIver, Hector, 1910-1966.

OEG

Memoirs presented to the Cambridge Philosophical Society on the occasion of the jubilee of Sir George Gabriel Stokes, Bart.... Cambridge University Press, 1900. xxviii, il., 447 p., 19 pl., 1 port. sq.4°.

Also issued as v.18 of the Transactions of the Cambridge Philosophical Society.

211093. 1.Physics— Addresses, essays, lectures.

F-11
5226

Mémorial Alfred Bertrang. Arlon, Institut archéologique du Luxembourg, 1964.

296 p. illus., maps, ports. 25 cm.

Includes bibliographies.

CONTENTS.—In memoriam, par M. Bourguignon.—La répression de la sorcellerie dans le duché de Bouillon aux XVIe et XVIIe siècles; par P. Bodart.—Une famille arlonaise: les Lamock, par M. Bourguignon.—La charte d'affranchissement de Martué, par J. de Remont.—Le Mercure de Martelange, par G. Faider-Feytmans.—Recherches sur les sires de Cons, par Comte de Failly.—Quelques documents de l'année

(Continued)

NN ° 4.69 1/a OC, II (OS)I PC, 1, I, II SL (LC1, X1, Z1)

MEMORIAL Alfred Bertrang. (Card 2)

1815 relatifs à la région d'Arlon, par M. Fourneau.—Chasse en Ardenne au Moyen Age, par L. Hector.—Note sur l'introduction de la culture du topinambour à Saint-Léger, par F. Ladrier.—La crise religieuse dans la région de Bastgone pendant la Révolution française, par L. Lefebvre.—Forêts, affranchissement et légende dans le comté de Chiny et à Chassepierre, par J. Massonnet.—Les archives du Conseil de Luxembourg, par A. May.—Le Luxembourg méridional au Bas-Empire, par J. Mertens.—Bases anciennes dans la toponymie

(Continued)

MEMORIAL Alfred Bertrang. (Card 3)

luxembourgeoise, par J. Meyers.—Familles, reflets du temps, par P. Nothomb.—Priesmont, anciennes familles, anciennes maisons, par G. Remacle.—Manuels, leçons et concours publics au Collège des Jésuites et au Collège thérésien de Luxembourg, par A. Spruneck.—Les monnaies gauloises du Musée d'Arlon, par M. Thirion.—La justice à Saint-Hubert sous le régime français, par A. Vermer.

1. Luxembourg (Province)--Hist.--Addresses, essays, lectures. I. Institut archéologique de la province de Luxembourg, Arlon, Belgium. II. Bertrang, Alfred.

---

*OEZA

Mémorial André Basset, 1895–1956. Paris, A. Maisonneuve, 1957.

158 p. 26 cm.

Bibliographical footnotes.

CONTENTS.—Mots "berbères" dans le dialecte arabe de Malte, par G. S. Colin.—Notes détachées pour servir à l'étude de la syntaxe d'un parler, par J. M. Dallet.—Un cas particulier de phrase non verbale: "l'anticipation renforcée" et l'interrogation en berbère, par L. Galand.—Une tradition orale encore vivante: le Poème de Çabi, par P. Galand-Pernet.—El dialecto bereber del Rif, por E. Ibáñez.—Deux notes grammaticales sur le berbère de Ghadamès, par J. Lanfry.—Sur l'emploi du démonstratif *i* introduisant la proposition subordonnée relative dans le parler des Aït-Hichem, par G. Laoust-Chantréaux.—Réflexions sur la structure de la vie familiale chez les indigènes de l'Afrique du Nord, par P. Marçais.—Some properties of

(Continued)

NN * 4.60 m/2 OC PC, 1, 2 SL O, 1, 2 (LC1, X1, Z1)

Mémorial André Basset ... 1957. (Card 2)

CONTENTS—Continued.

Zuara nouns with special reference to those with consonant initial, by T. F. Mitchell.—*Am* et *zun(d)*, "comme," en berbère, par C. Pellat.—Du prétérit intensif en berbère, par A. Picard.—Le problème berbère des radicales faibles, par K. G. Prasse.—Sull'origine del nome Imâzighen, di T. Sarnelli.—L'article défini du berbère, par W. Vycichl.—Dilettantismus und Scharlatanerie und die Erforschung der Eingeborenensprache der Kanarischen Inseln, von D. J. Wölfel.

1. Berber languages. 2. Basset, André, 1895-1956.

AN
(Dewhurst, F.)

A **memorial**: Frederic E. Dewhurst, pastor of the University Congregational church of Chicago, Illinois. Chicago, Priv. print., 1907.

88 p. front. (port.) 19½cm.

1. Dewhurst, Frederic Eli, 1855-1906.

Festschrift.

Library of Congress 7-18575

AN
(Davidson, T.)

Memorials of Thomas Davidson, the wandering scholar; collected and ed. by William Knight. Boston [etc.] Ginn and co., 1907. xi, 241 p. illus. 21cm.

"Bibliography of Thomas Davidson's works," p. 235-241.

Festschrift

1. Davidson, Thomas, 1840-1900. I. Knight, William Angus, 1836-1916, ed.

N. Y. P. L.

D-15
5400

Mendelson, Wallace, *ed.*

Felix Frankfurter: a tribute. New York, Reynal, 1964.

viii, 242 p. 22 cm.

Bibliographical references included in "Notes" (p. 229-242)

CONTENTS.—Introduction, by W. Mendelson.—Presentation of American Bar Association medal, August 15, 1963.—The humanity of this man, by H. A. Murray.—A man for all seasons, by Sir H. Beale.—Felix Frankfurter at Oxford, by I. Berlin.—Felix Frankfurter, by J. Monnet.—Trips to Felix, by G. Kanin.—To gather meaning, not from reading the Constitution, but from reading life, by F. Biddle.—How

(Continued)

NN * R 10.64 e/3 OC PC, 1, 2 SL (LC1, X1, Z1)

MENDELSON, WALLACE, ed. Felix Frankfurter: a tribute. (Card 2)

Justice Frankfurter got his spasm, by J. Reston.—A fifty year friendship, by E. M. Morgan.—F. F. C. C. N. Y., by N. Phillips.—A mirror of friendship, by A. Meiklejohn.—Felix, by H. M. Ehrmann.—Felix long ago, by M. Lowenthal.—Felix Frankfurter at Harvard, by R. Pound.—Mr. Justice Frankfurter, by P. A. Freund.—Applied politics and the science of law: writings of the Harvard period, by A. M. Bickel.—Themes in United States legal history, by J. W. Hurst.—Law and politics, by A. MacLeish.

1. Frankfurter, Felix, 1882- 2. Law--U.S.--Addresses, essays.

F-10
6219

MENDOZA, Argentine Republic (City). Universidad nacional de Cuyo. Filosofía y letras, Facultad de.

Homenaje a Fritz Krüger. Mendoza, 1952-54.
2 v. illus., maps. 28cm.

Contributions in Spanish, German, Portuguese, Catalan, Italian or English.

Includes bibliographies.

1. Krüger, Fritz Otto, 1889- .
NN 1.62 e/B OS PC, 1 SL (LC1, X1, Z1) [I]

G-10
815

Menéndez y Pelayo, Marcelino, 1856–1912.

Facsímiles de trabajos escolares de Menéndez Pelayo. Con un estudio crítico del Dr. Gregorio Marañón. [Historia y presentación por Enrique Sánchez Reyes. 1. ed. Santander, Taller de Artes Gráficas de los Hnos. Bedia, 1959]
xv, 215 p. (p. 3-[184] facsims.) ports. 36 cm.

"Edición patrocinada por el Ministerio de Educación Nacional y costeada por el Banco de Santander en su I centenario."

Bibliography: p. 209–211.

I. Marañón, Gregoria, 1887- . II. Sánchez Reyes, Enrique.
NN*R 9.60 l/// OC, I, II PC, I, II SL (LC1, Z1, ~~X1~~)

3-MAS

Der MENSCH und die Künste. Festschrift für Heinrich Lützeler zum 60 Geburtstage. [Redaktionskomitee: Günter Bandmann, et al. 1. Aufl.] Düsseldorf, L. Schwann [1962] 508 p. plates (124 figs.), port. 25cm.

"Schriftenverzeichnis," p. 500-506; "Dissertationen unter Heinrich Lützeler," p. 507.

1. Lützeler, Heinrich, 1902- . 2. Art--Essays and misc. I. Bandmann, Günter, ed. II. Title: Festschrift für Heinrich Lützeler zum 60. Geburtstage.
NN R 3.63 a/ OC, I PC, 1, 2, I, II SL A, 1, 2, I, II (LC1, X1, Z1)
[I]

Write on slip words underlined below and class mark —
SEA

...Menyhárth Gáspár- emlékkönyv. Dolgozatok Menyhárth Gáspár egyetemi ny.r. tanár születésének 70. évfordulójára. Irták: kartársai. Szerkesztette: Túry Sándor Kornél... Szeged, 1938. 426 p. front. (port.) 25½cm. (Szegedin, Hungary. Tudományegyetem. Acta litterarum ac scientiarum Reg. universitatis Hung. Francisco-Josephinae. Sectio: jurídica-politica. tom. 13.)

"A. M. kir. Ferencz József-tudományegyetem és a Rothermere alap tamogatasval kiada. A. M. kir. Ferencz József-tudományegyetem barátainak egyesülete.
Bibliographical footnotes.

(Continued)

N. Y. P. L. March 28, 1939

...Menyhárth... (Card 2)

Contents.—Ajánlás.—Balás, P. E. Szerzői magánjogunk de lege ferenda.—Buza, László. A felkelök nemezetközi jogi helyzete és a spanyol polgárháborúba való "benemavatkozás".—Csekey, István. A magyar nemzetfogalom.—Ereky, István. A tárgyi jogról.—Heller, Erik. Anyagi jogellenesség és büntetöjogi reform.—Horváth, Barna. A szociológia elemei.—Polner, Ödön. A választás mint jogügylet.—v. Surányi-Unger, Tivadar. Müszaki haladás és gazdasági jólét.—Túry, S. K. Fokozott hatályú tulajdonfenntartás.

1. Menyhárth, Gáspár, 1868- . 2. Law—Essays and misc.
I. Túry, Sándor Kornél, ed. II. Ser.
N. Y. P. L. March 28, 1939

AN
(Edwards, A.)

El Mercurio, Santiago de Chile.

Don Agustín Edwards, M. C. (1878–1941); homenaje de "El Mercurio" al enterarse un año de su fallecimiento. Santiago de Chile: Imprenta universitaria, 1942. 193 p. front. 22cm.

246226B. 1. Edwards, Agustín, 1878–1941.
N. Y. P. L. October 28, 1943

OAP

METALLGESELLSCHAFT AKTIENGESELLSCHAFT, Frankfurt am Main.

Science and the economic order. [Frankfurt am Main, 1956] 248 p. 19cm.

Issued in celebration of the 75th anniversary of the Metallgesellschaft.

CONTENTS. — The influence of economic theory on economic policy, by E. von Beckerath. — The meaning and purpose of scientific research, by A. Butenandt. —The economic order and the law, by H. Dölle. — Uranium: the key to the revelation of the ultimately small and the release

(Continued)

NN**~~R 11~~.56 p/B OS PC, 1, 2 SL E, 1 ST, 1t, 2t (LC1, X1, Y1, ~~Z1~~)

METALLGESELLSCHAFT AKTIENGESELLSCHAFT, Frankfurt am Main. Science and the economic order. (Card 2)

of the infinitely great, by O. Hahn. — Humanism and technical precision, by W. R. P. Hartner. —Pure and applied research in atomic physics, by W. K. Heisenberg. —What is pure chemistry?, by R. Kuhn. — The disintegration of our concept of the world, by W. Schöllgen. — Can human relations be organised?, by H. Thielicke.

1. Science— Social and economic aspects. 2. Science-- Essays and misc. t. 1956.

OAP

METALLGESELLSCHAFT AKTIENGESELLSCHAFT, Frankfurt am Main.

Wissenschaft und Wirtschaft. [Festschrift zur Feier ihres 75 jährigen Bestehens] [Frankfurt am Main, 1956] 252 p. 19cm.

CONTENTS. — Über den Einfluss der Wirtschaftstheorie auf die Wirtschaftspolitik, von E. von Beckerath. — Sinn und Nutzen wissenschaftlicher Forschung, von A. Butenandt. — Wirtschaft und Recht, von H. Dölle. — Uran: Schlüssel zum Nachweis des Klein- sten und zur Entfesselung des

(Continued)

NN **R 10.56 p/ OS PC, 1, 2, 3 SL E, 2, 3 ST, 1t, 2t (LC1, X1, ~~Z1~~, Y1)

METALLGESELLSCHAFT AKTIENGESELLSCHAFT, Frankfurt am Main. Wissenschaft und Wirtschaft. (Card 2)

Grössten, von O. Hahn. -- Humanismus und Technische Präzision, von W.R. P. Hartner. -- Grundlagenforschung und angewandte Forschung in der Atomphysik, von W. K. Heisenberg. — Was ist reine Chemie? von R. Kuhn. — Der Zerfall unseres Weltbildes, von W. Schöllgen. — Sind menschliche Beziehungen organisierbar? von H. Thielicke.

1. Science-- Essays and misc. 2. Science-- Social and economic aspects. 3. Economics and the social sciences. t. 1956.

E-11
4224

METZ, FRIEDRICH, 1890-
Land und Leute; gesammelte Beiträge zur deutschen Landes- und Volksforschung. Stuttgart, W. Kohlhammer [1961] vii, 1099 p. illus., port. 24cm.

"Aus Anlass seines [i.e F. Metz's] 70. Geburtstages im Auftrag von Freunden und Schülern zusammengestellt und herausgegeben von E. Meynen und R. Oehme."
Includes bibliographies.

1. Germany--Geography. I. Meynen, Emil, ed.
II. Oehme, Ruthardt, ed. III. Oehme, Ruthardt.
NN R 2.62 g/ OC, I, II, IIIb+ PC, 1, I, II SL (LC1, X1, Z1)

ZDD

METZGER, BRUCE MANNING, comp.
Index of articles on the New Testament and the early church published in Festschriften. Philadelphia, Society of Biblical literature, 1951.
xv, 182 p. 23cm. (Journal of Biblical literature. Monograph series. v. 5.)

1. Bible. N. T. --Criticism--Bibl. 2. Church history--Undivided church, to 1054--Bibl. 3. Festschriften--Indexes. I. Series.

NN *X 2.56 f/ OC (OS) I PC, 1, 2, 3, I SL (U 1, LC1, X1, Z1)

E-11
8252

MEXICO. Antropología e historia, Instituto nacional de.
A Pedro Bosch-Gimpera en el septuagésimo aniversario de su nacimiento. [1. ed.] México, 1963. lxiv, 445 p. illus., plates, ports., maps. 25cm.

Contributions in Spanish, English, French, German, Italian, Portuguese or Catalan.
Bibliographical footnotes.
1. Bosch y Gimpera, Pedro, 1891- . 2. Archaeology--Addresses, essays, lectures. t. 1963
NN 11.63 a/ ODt EDt PC, 1, 2 SL (LC1, X1, Z1) [I]

HTC

MEXICO. Antropología e historia, Instituto nacional de.
Homenaje a Pablo Martínez del Río en el vigésimo-quinto aniversario de la primera edición de Los orígenes americanos. México, 1961. 520 p. illus. (part fold.) maps. 25cm.

Contributions in Spanish or English.
Includes bibliographies.

1. Martínez del Río, Pablo, 1892- . 2. Mexico--Archaeology. t. 1961
NN 3.63 a/ ODt EDt PC, 1, 2 SL AH, 1, 2 (LC1, X1, Z1)

WAF

Mexico (City). Universidad nacional.
Libro homenaje al profesor doctor Ignacio Chávez, en ocasión del XXV aniversario de su recepción profesional. México, Editado por la Univ. nacional autónoma, 1945. xxvi, 526 p. illus. 24cm.

Contributions in English or Spanish.
No. 81 of 500 copies.
Bibliography at end of each article.

538289B. 1. Chávez, Ignacio, 1897- . 2. Medicine—Essays and misc.
N. Y. P. L. August 30, 1950

YBX
(Caso)

MEXICO (CITY). Universidad nacional. Centro de estudios filosóficos.
Homenaje a Antonio Caso [por] Antonio Gómez Robledo [et al.] México, Editorial Stylo, 1947. 317 p. 25cm.

Bibliographical footnotes.
CONTENTS. --Prólogo, por A. Gómez Robledo. — Las mocedades de Caso, por J. Gaos. --Antonio Caso, pensador y moralista, por E. García Máynez. --Antonio Caso y el heroísmo filosófico, por O. Robles. -- Don Antonio Caso y las ideas contemporáneas en México, por P. Romanell. --Antonio Caso y la Mexicanidad, por L. Zea. --
(Continued)
NN** 1.55 g/ OS PC, 1 SL (Z1, LC1, X1) [I]

MEXICO (CITY). Universidad nacional. Centro de estudios filosóficos. Homenaje a Antonio Caso... (Card 2)

Caso, su concepto de la filosofía, por R. Moreno. --Las polémicas filosóficas de Antonio Caso, por J. Hernández Luna. --La biblioteca de Caso, por J. Gaos. --Antonio Caso visto desde la Universidad de Boston, por E. S. Brightman. --La filosofía de las ciencias según Antonio Caso, por D. García Bacca. --Antonio Caso y Émile Meyerson, por E. Uranga. --La estética de Antonio Caso, por S. Ramos. --La filosofía de la historia en Antonio Caso, por J. Manuel Terán. --La filosofía social de Antonio Caso, por L. Recaséns Siches.

1. Caso, Antonio, 1883-1946.

E-10
6049

Mexico. Courts. Suprema corte de justicia.
Homenaje de la Suprema Corte de Justicia de la Nación, en nombre del poder judicial de la federación, al Código de 1857 y a sus autores, los ilustres constituyentes. México, 1957.
xxi, 302 p. ports. 24 cm.
At head of title: 1957, año de la Constitución de 1857 y del pensamiento liberal mexicano.
Half title: Homenaje a la Constitución de 1857.
Includes bibliographies.
CONTENTS.—Relación de los CC. ministros que en diciembre de 1956 integraban la Suprema Corte de Justicia inamovible, según el orden de su designación.—Introducción.—Discurso pronunciado el 5 de febrero de 1957, por H. Medina, presidente de la Suprema Corte.—
(Continued)
NN R 8.58 m/ (OC) I, II, IIb, IIIODt EDt PC, 1, I, II, III SL (E) 1, I, II, III (LC1, X1, Z1)

Mexico. Courts. Suprema corte de justicia. Homenaje de la Suprema Corte de Justicia de la Nación ... 1957. (Card 2)

CONTENTS—Continued.

Colaboración del Lic. F. González de Cossío: Apuntes biográficos de los ministros de la Suprema Corte, 1856–1913. Presidentes de la Suprema Corte, 1856–1913. Ministros de la Suprema Corte que fueron constituyentes en 1856. Retratos de los presidentes de la Suprema Corte que adornan la antesala del pleno. Disposiciones que han regido la vida de la Suprema Corte, 1856–1913.—Colaboración del Lic. S Oñate: La primera sentencia de amparo, 1849. La causa de Roque Miranda, 1848. Circular del Lic. Ignacio L. Vallarta, sobre obediencia

(Continued)

Mexico. Courts. Suprema corte de justicia. Homenaje de la Suprema Corte de Justicia de la Nación ... 1957. (Card 3)

CONTENTS—Continued.

a las sentencias de amparo, 1868. Proyecto de Ley de amparo, 1879. Voto del Lic. Ezequiel Montes sobre suspensión de garantías. El amparo de Tavares: interpretación del artículo 16 constitucional, 1881. Discurso de don Justo Sierra sobre inamovilidad judicial, 1893.

1. AMPARO (LAW)--MEXICO I. González de Cossío, Francisco, ed. II. Oñate Salemme, Santiago, ed. III. Homenaje de la Suprema Corte de Justicia de la Nación ... al Código de 1857 y a sus autores. t. 1957.

MAS

Meyer, Erich, Oct. 29, 1897- *ed.*
Eine Gabe der Freunde für Carl Georg Heise zum 28.VI.1950. [Berlin, Gebr. Mann, 1950]

252 p. illus. (chiefly mount.) port. 26 cm.

Bibliographical footnotes.

CONTENTS.—Das Urteilen über zeitgenössische Kunst, von F. Ahlers-Hestermann.—Wiedersehen mit Bildern, von K. Scheffler.—Vom Umgang mit dem Holz, von T. Heuss.—Kunstgeschichte und Milieutheorie, von H. Keller.—Reliquie und Reliquiar im Mittelalter, von E. Meyer.—Landschaft der Ewigkeit, von R. Guardini.—Die Gestalt Giottos im Spiegel einer zeitgenössischen Urkunde, von W. Paatz.—Christus am Kreuz und der heilige Franziskus, von K.

(Continued on next card)

[1] Festschrift cat. A 51-1577

Meyer, Erich, Oct. 29, 1897- *ed.* Eine Gabe der Freunde ... [1950] (Card 2)

CONTENTS—Continued.

Bauch.—Raphaels Krönung des heiligen Nikolaus von Tolentino, von W. Schöne.—Die Capella Vasari und der Hochaltar in der Pieve von Arezzo, von C. A. Isermeyer.—Das Abendmahl am Naumburger Westlettner, von H. Deckert.—Der Gekreuzigte des Jacques de Baerze, von O. Goetz.—Bernt Notkes Triumphkreuz, von H. A. Gräbke.—Friedrichstadt, von H. Holtorf.—Nürnberg! Du vormals weltberühmte Stadt! Von L. Grote.—Die Sammlung des Konsuls Wagener als Kern der National-Galerie, von P. O. Rave.—Zwei Landschaften Friedrich Nerlys, von V. A. Dirksen.—Clemente Orozco, von A. Neumeyer.—Das Kölner Totenmal von Gerhard Marcks, von L. Reidemeister.

1. Art—Addresses, essays, lectures. 2. Heise, Carl Georg, 1890- I. Title.

A 51-1577

Harvard Univ. Library for Library of Congress [1]

E-11
5575

MICHEL, FRITZ, 1877-
Forst und Jagd im alten Erzstift Trier. Trier, Paulinus-Verlag, 1958. xviii, 270 p. illus., map, facsims. 24cm. (Schriftenreihe zur Trierer Landesgeschichte und Volkskunde. Bd. 4)

"... dem Verfasser... zu seinem 80. Geburtstag."
"Das Schrifttum... von Fritz Michel," p. xiv-xvii.
Bibliographical footnotes.

1. Forestry--Germany--Trier (Archdiocese). 2. Hunting--Germany--Trier (Archdiocese). 3. Trier, Germany (Archdiocese)--Hist. I. Series.

NN R 5.62 a/OC (OS)I PC, 1, 2, 3, I SL (LC1, X1, Z1)

D-12
521

MICHIGAN. Wayne state university, Detroit. English, Dept. of.
Studies in honor of John Wilcox, by members of the English dept., Wayne State university, edited by A. Dayle Wallace [and] Woodburn O. Ross. Detroit, Wayne State University Press, 1958. xiv, 269 p. port. 23cm.

Bibliographical references included in "Notes." Bibliography, p. viii-ix.

(Continued)

NN R 6.60 1/5(OC)I, II ODt EDt PC, 1, 2, I, II SL (LC1, X1, Z1) 4

MICHIGAN. Wayne state university, Detroit. English, Dept. of. Studies in honor of John Wilcox... (Card 2)

CONTENTS.--Foreword, by L. L. Hanawalt.--Heroic diction in The dream of the rood, by R. E. Diamond.--Jonson, Seneca, and "Mortimer," by L. Kirschbaum.--Chivalric themes in "Samson Agonistes," by R. Nash.--A reading of "Musicks duell," by W. G. Madsen.--"Absalom and Achitophel" as epic satire, by C. H. Cable.--An early defense of farce, by S. A. Golden.--Le Texier's early years in England, 1775-1779, by A. D. Wallace.--Playbills and programs: the story of a summer's quest, by R. W. Babcock.--City life in American drama, 1825-1860,

(Continued)

MICHIGAN. Wayne state university, Detroit. English, Dept. of. Studies in honor of John Wilcox... (Card 3)

by G. H. Blayney.--"Othello" transformed: Verdi's interpretation of Shakespeare, by H. M. Schueller.--Billy Budd as Moby Dick: an alternate reading, by V. Wagner.--The development of Frank Norris's philosophy, by A. L. Goldsmith.--John Galsworthy: aspects of an attitude, by W. O. Ross.--H. M. Tomlinson, essayist and traveller, by A. A. Gay.--A preliminary checklist of the periodical publications of Dorothy M. Richardson, by J. Prescott.--Rythm in Forster's A passage to India, by R. R. Werry.--Freud and the riddle of "Mrs.

(Continued)

MICHIGAN. Wayne state university, Detroit. English, Dept. of. Studies in honor of John Wilcox... (Card 4)

Dalloway," by K. Hollingsworth.--William Ellery Leonard: an appraisal, by C. E. Jorgenson.

1. Wilcox, John, 1887- . 2. English literature--Addresses, essays, lectures. I. Wallace, Alva Dayle, ed. II. Ross, Woodburn O., joint ed. t. 1958.

Copy only words underlined & classmark-- RKA

Middle Ages, Reformation, Volkskunde; Festschrift for John G. Kunstmann. Chapel Hill, University of North Carolina Press, 1959.

224 p. port. 23 cm. (North Carolina. University. Studies in the Germanic languages and literatures, no. 26)

Includes bibliographical references.

CONTENTS.—The ethos of the Waltharius, by G. F. Jones.—Prolegomena to an English translation of Waltharius, by E. H. Zeydel.—Notes on the French fabliaux, by U. T. Holmes, Jr.—Frauenlob's Bits

(Continued)

NN * 2.62 e/. OC (OD)I (ED)I PC, 1, 2, 3, I (LC1, X1, Z1) [I] 4

MIDDLE AGES, Reformation, Volkskunde... (Card 2)

of wisdom: fruits of his environment, by S. A. Gallacher.—Hermann Körner's Weltchronik, by C. F. Bayerschmidt.—The French versions of the Ancrene riwle, by J. H. Fisher.—King Alfonso's Virgin of Villa-Sirga, rival of St. James of Compostela, by J. E. Keller.—The foundation of Johannes Hueven de Arnhem for the College of Sorbonne (1452) by A. L. Gabriel.—Charles d'Orleans and medicine, by R. W. Linker.—The stage directions in Schernberg's Spiel von Frau Jutten, by J. E. Engel.—The Tristan romance in Hans Sachs' Meisterlieder, by E. Sobel.—The theologia Platonica in the religious thought of the

(Continued)

MIDDLE AGES, Reformation, Volkskunde... (Card 3)

German humanists, by L. W. Spitz.—On the source of an English thunder-treatise of the fifteenth century, by T. Silverstein.—Rudolph Agricola and Peter Schott, by M. A. Cowie and M. L. Cowie.—"Was mein Gott will, das gscheh' allzeit," by H. Motekat.—Mythological solution of crisis: a parallel between Luther's and Hitler's Germany, by J. Rysan.—Joseph Lang and his anthologies, by B. L. Ullman.—A North Carolina Himmelsbrief, by W. D. Hand.—"Art thou He who is to come ...?" By O. F. Jones.—Aspect as a prominent factor in the survival of the third weak conjugation in Old High German, by F. A. Raven.

(Continued)

MIDDLE AGES, Reformation, Volkskunde... (Card 4)

1. Kunstmann, John Gotthold, 1894- 2. Philology—Addresses, essays, lectures. 3. German literature—Addresses, essays, lectures. I. Series.

PMN

Mikrochemie; internationales Archiv für deren Gesamtgebiet. Festschrift zum 60. Geburtstag von Hofrat Prof. Dr. Fritz Pregl... Wien: E. Haim & Co., 1929. xii, 340 p. incl. tables. front. (port.), illus. 8°.

Bibliographical footnotes.

Mr. Moth.

470479A. 1. Microchemistry. I. Pregl, Fritz, 1869-
N. Y. P. L. April 30, 1930

PSR

MILLER, ROBERT LEE, 1920- , ed.
Papers in marine geology; Shepard commemorative volume. New York, Macmillan [1964] xx, 531 p. illus., port., maps, charts, 26cm.

Dedicated to Professor Francis Parker Shepard by his former students to commemorate his more than three decades of research and inquiry into the earth's vast water-covered third surface.

Includes bibliographies.

1. Ocean bottom. 2. Shepard, Francis Parker, 1897- . t. 1964
NN * R 7.64 a/ OC PC, 1, 2 SL ST, 1t, 2 (LC1, XI, Z1)

Copy only words underlined & classmark— RKA

MILTON Studies, in honor of Harris Francis Fletcher. Urbana, University of Illinois Press, 1961. p. 609-854 illus., port. 23cm. (Journal of English and Germanic Philology. v. 60, no. 4)

Bibliographical footnotes.
Bibliography of the writings of Harris Francis Fletcher, p. 847-854.

1. Fletcher, Harris Francis, 1892- 2. Milton, John.
NN 5.63 f/B OI (PC)1, 2 (LC3, X1, Z1)

MWE

Mimus und Logos; eine Festgabe für Carl Niessen. Emsdetten (Westf.), Verlag Lechte, 1952. xi,281 p. illus. 24cm.

Bibliographical footnotes.

1. Niessen, Carl, 1890- 2. Stage, 1926-

NN Schreiber

D-15
141

MINDERAA, P., ed.
Aandacht voor Cats bij zijn 300-ste sterfdag; studies naar aanleiding van de herdenking op 12 September 1960, op verzoek van het desbetreffende comité bijeengebracht door P. M. deraa. Zwolle, W. E. J. Tjeenk Willink, 1962. 200 p. illus., port., maps. 21cm. (Zwolse reeks van taal- en letterkundige studies, nr. 12)

(Continued)

NN R 3.64 p/ OC PC, 1, I SL (LC1, X1, Z1) 3

MINDERAA, P., ed. Aandacht voor Cats bij zijn 300-ste sterfdag... (Card 2)

Bibliographical footnotes.
CONTENTS.--Cats als moralist en dichter, door G. A. van Es.--Jacob Cats als staatsman, door L. W. G. Scholten.--Cats en Zuid-Nederland, door E. Rombauts.--Cats als Zeeuw, door P. J. Meertens.--Aantekeningen bij het proza van Cats, door W. A. P. Smit.--Cats in een Dordtse school? Door W. J. M. A. Asselbergs.--Jacob Cats voor het gericht van Potgieter en Huet, door G. Kuiper.--Een merkwaardige Cats-epigoon, Gillis Jacobsz. Quintijn, door P. Minderaa.--Jacob Cats en de landaanwinning, door S. J. Fockema

(Continued)

MINDERAA, P., ed. Aandacht voor Cats bij zijn 300-ste sterfdag... (Card 3)

Andreae.--De emblemata van Cats, door P. J. H. Vermeeren.--Cats' laatste refugium:" Sorghvliet," door A. Goekoop.

1. Cats, Jacob, 1577-1660. I. Title.

*MEC
(Simonsen, R.)

Mindeskrift om Rudolph Simonsen, udg. af en kreds af venner, 30. april 1949. København, R. Naver, 1949.
151, [1] p. illus., ports., music. 25 cm.

CONTENTS.—Humanisten, af T. A. Müller.—Rudolph Simonsen, af L. Moltesen.—Rudolph Simonsen og konservatoriet, af Ch. Christiansen.—Rudolph Simonsen som skabende personlighed, af F. Høffding.—Rudolph Simonsen som personlighed og menneske, af A. Rachlew.—Rudolph Simonsen som lærer, af H. D. Koppel.—Minder om Rudolph Simonsen fra "Ny musik" og folke-musikskolen, af J. Bentzon.—Rudolph Simonsen i nærbilleede, af E. B. Swing.—Glimt fra et lykkeligt menneskes liv, af E. Simonsen.—Mindetale over min far, 2. april 1947, af A. Simonsen.—Fortegnelse over kompositioner og litterær produktion, af E. Simonsen (p. 147-[152])

1. Simonsen, Rudolph, 1889-

(Z1) A 50-691

Minnesota. Univ. Libr. for Library of Congress [1]

E-11
3492

Minnesota. University.
Immigration and American history; essays in honor of Theodore C. Blegen, edited by Henry Steele Commager. Minneapolis, University of Minnesota Press [1961]
x, 166 p. port. 24 cm.
"Based on a conference at the University of Minnesota, January 29-30, 1960."
Bibliographical footnotes.
CONTENTS.—The study of immigration, by H. S. Commager.—Immigration in American life: a reappraisal, by O. Handlin.—Emigration and the image of America in Europe, by I. Semmingsen.—The

(Continued)
NN* R 10.61 g/H (OC)I ODt EDt PC, 1, 2, 3, 4, I SL
AH, I, 4, I (E)2, 3, I (LC1, X1, Z1)

SSD

Minnesota. University. *College of education.*
The changing educational world, 1905-1930; papers read on the occasion of the twenty-fifth anniversary of the College of education, University of Minnesota, edited by Alvin C. Eurich. Minneapolis, The University of Minnesota press, 1931.
xii, 311 p. diagrs. 24cm.
CONTENTS.—Education and the new world: Introduction, Twenty-five years, by M. E. Haggerty. Men and machines, by Stuart Chase. The revival of personality, by E. H. Lindley. New problems in education, by W. J. Cooper. Forces behind education in Europe, by Paul Dengler.—The university school of education: As an institution for the professional training of educational workers, by M. G. Neale. As a center for the
(Continued on next card)
31—9852
[31k5]

Mr. Math.

MINNESOTA. University. Immigration and American history... (Card 2)

stranger looks at the Yankee, by P. D. Jordan.—The immigrant in western fiction, by J. T. Flanagan.—Immigration as a world phenomenon, by C. C. Qualey.—The migration of ideas, by H. A. Pochmann.—The immigration theme in the framework of national groups, by F. D. Scott.—Prospects for materials in immigration studies, by C. C. Qualey.—New prospects in immigration studies, by C. J. Barry.—The saga of the immigrant, by T. C. Blegen.—About the authors.—Theodore C. Blegen: a bibliography (p. 157-161)

(Continued)

Minnesota. University. *College of education.* The changing educational world ... 1931. (Card 2)
CONTENTS—Continued.
development of a science of education, by C. H. Judd. As a source of educational leadership, by W. C. Bagley. As related to other divisions of the university, by M. E. Haggerty.—Educational trends: Vocational education in an industrial state, by A. B. Meredith. Educational trends in the state of Minnesota, by J. M. McConnell. Educational trends in a university, by L. D. Coffman. Process in city school administration during the past twenty-five years, by G. D. Strayer. Changing practices in the administration of the teaching personnel, by Fred Engelhardt. Trends in secondary school organization, by H. R. Douglass.—Research in secondary education, by H. R. Douglass.—Educational pioneering in Minnesota: The increasing professionalization of educa-
(Continued on next card)
31—9852
[31k5]

MINNESOTA. University. Immigration and American history... (Card 3)

1. Blegen, Theodore Christian, 1891- . 2. Emigration and immigration --U.S. 3. Emigrants and immigrants in literature. 4. United States in foreign opinion. I. Commager, Henry Steele, 1902- , ed. T. 1961

Minnesota. University. *College of education.* The changing educational world ... 1931. (Card 3)
CONTENTS—Continued.
tional workers, by F. H. Swift. The schools of Minnesota in the last quarter of the nineteenth century, by L. C. Lord. The beginnings of secondary education in Minnesota, by G. B. Aiton. Twenty-five years of development in elementary education, by W. E. Peik. Chronological outline of the development of public education in Minnesota, by Jean H. Alexander.—The College of education at the University of Minnesota: An address to the alumni, by M. E. Haggerty. The growth of the College of education, by V. H. Noll. Educating school administrators, by Fred Engelhardt. Training doctors of philosophy in education, by A. C. Eurich.
1. Education—Addresses, essays, lectures. 2. Education—Minnesota. I. Eurich, Alvin Christian, ed. II. Title.
31—9852
Library of Congress LB7.M5
~~Copy 2.~~
Copyright A 35731 [31k5] 370.4

SB p.v.1537

Minnesota. University.
The individual and liberal education; papers delivered at the dedication of Johnston hall, April 19-21, 1951. [Minneapolis] Pub. for the Social science research center of the Graduate school by the Univ. of Minnesota press [1952] x, 102 p. 23cm.
"Essays in honor of John Black Johnston."
CONTENTS.—Dedication address, by J. L. Morrill. Ideologies and the American way, by J. B. Wolf.—Ideological conflict and the liberal arts college, by C. J. Turck.—The clash of ideologies and the integrity of words, by H. N. Smith.—Science and the liberal tradition, by L. A. DuBridge.—The natural sciences and man, by Vannevar Bush.—The individual in liberal education, by T. R. McConnell.—The education of the ablest students, by Dael Wolfle.—The individual, the teacher and the curriculum, by J. E. Burchard.

1. Johnston, John Black, 1868- . I. Minnesota. University. Social science research center.
NN R 5.53 OD, I ED, I PC, 1, I SL (LC1, Z1, X1)

M-10
2184
v.12

MINOICA. Festschrift zum 80. Geburtstag von Johannes Sundwall. Hrsg. von Ernst Grumach. Berlin, Akademie-Verlag, 1958. viii, 465 p. illus. 25cm. (Deutsche Akademie der Wissenschaften, Berlin. Altertumswissenschaft, Sektion für. Schriften. 12)
Contributions chiefly in German, English or French.
Bibliographical footnotes.
"Verzeichnis der Schriften von Johannes Sundwall," p. [461]-465.
1. Sundwall, Johannes, 1877- 2. Minoan writing. 3. Mycenaean inscriptions. 4. Greece—Civilization, Minoan and Mycenaean. I. Grumach, Ernst, ed. II. Series.
NN R X 1.59 p/H OC, I (OS)II PC, 1, 2, 3, 4, I, II (LC1, X1, Z1)

SSD

Minnesota. University.
Trends in student personnel work; a collection of papers read at a conference sponsored by the Univ. of Minnesota to celebrate a quarter century of student personnel work and to honor Professor Donald G. Paterson. Ed. by E. G. Williamson. Minneapolis, Univ. of Minnesota Press [1949]
x, 417 p. 24 cm.
Includes bibliographies.

1. Personnel service in education. 2. Paterson, Donald Gildersleeve, 1892- I. Williamson, Edmund Griffith, 1900- ed. II. Title.
LB2343.M485 371.422 49—8555*
Library of Congress [49q15]

F-11
4108

MISCELÂNEA de estudos a Joaquim de Carvalho. [Edição do Manuel Montezuma de Carvalho. Figueira da Foz, Portugal, Biblioteca-Museu Joaquim de Carvalho; Distrubição: Publicações Europa-América] 1959-63] 9 v. in 2 (993 p.) ports. 26cm.
Text in Portuguese, Spanish, English, French or German.
(Continued)
NN R 4.68 p/LOC, I, IIIb+ (OS)II PC, 1, 2, 3, I, II SL (LC1, X1, Z1) 2

MISCELÂNEA de estudos a Joaquim de Carvalho. (Card 2)

Bibliographical footnotes.

1. Carvalho, Joaquim Martins Teixeira de, 1892-1958. 2. Portugal--Civilization--Addresses, essays, lectures. 3. Civilization--Addresses, essays, lectures. I. Carvalho, Manuel Montezuma, ed. II. Biblioteca-Museu Joaquim de Carvalho III. Carvalho, Manuel Montezuma de

---

D-19
910

Miscellanea. Essays by present and former students in the English Department of the University of Oslo. A tribute to Professor Kristian Smidt on the occasion of his fiftieth birthday 20 November 1966. Oslo, Universitetsforlaget, 1966.

135 p. 23 cm.

Bibliographical footnotes.

(Continued)

NN R 9.69 v/ OC PC, 1, 2, 3 SL (LC1, X1, Z1)

MISCELLANEA... (Card 2)

CONTENTS.—The importance of William Tyndale, by J. Stokkeland.—Christopher Marlowe's Doctor Faustus, by R. D. Haukelid.—On taking Shakespeare's comic characters seriously, by S. Henning.—The women in Julius Cæsar, by A. Midgaard.—A critical appreciation of Marvell's 'To his coy mistress,' by A. Despard.—Six poems by William Blake, by T. Obrestad.—The poet as a rebel: Blake's and Shelley's views of Promethean man, by H. Rønning.—Jane Austen: Facts, myths and misconceptions, by R. Nessheim.—The revival of Scott Fitzgerald criticism, by S. Ito.—Stephen Spender and the thirties, his political credo, by J. Forberg.—Der ingenting hender, to ganger, av J. E. Vold.—The use of literary allusions in Samuel Beck-

(Continued)

MISCELLANEA... (Card 3)

ett's Happy days, by O. M. Ellingsen.—Saul Bellow's Herzog: a further sophistication and a new naïveté, by E. Michelet.—Gender as a grammatical category in modern English, by S. Vargeid.—On the teaching of English pronunciation in Norway, by I. Moen.—The Chinese goes to a garden party, by A. Despard.—Time adverbials: Two levels of morphemic structure, by L. Houck.—The position of the Negro in the United States, by C. Lie.—Edmund Burke og naturretten, av L. R. Langslet.—The fastidious second generation of university historians, by G. Stang.

1. Smidt, Kristian. 2. English language. 3. English literature--Addresses, essays, lectures.

---

*GAH

Miscellanea bibliografica in memoria di Don Tommaso Accurti, a cura di Lamberto Donati. Roma, "Storia e letteratura," 1947. xi, 220 p. illus. 25cm.

"Questo libro, in edizione originale, costituisce il n.15 della serie Storia e letteratura."

CONTENTS.—Mercati, Giovanni. Da incunaboli a codici.—Albareda, Anselmo. Un incunabulo sconosciuto dello stampatore J. Luschner.—Campana, Augusto. Antonio Blado e Bartolomeo Platina.—Ceva Valla, Elena. Nota su alcuni incunaboli posseduti dalla Biblioteca Braidense di Milano.—Donati, Lamberto. Note empiriche sul libro illustrato.—Fava, Domenico. L'Esopo di Modena dell 1481 e Nicolò Jenson.—Galli, Giuseppe. Due ignote edizioni quattrocentine della "Corona della Beatissima Vergine Maria" di fra' Bernardino de' Busti.—Guarnaschelli, Teresa. Alfonso Fernandez da

(Continued)

N. Y. P. L. September 21, 1949

Miscellanea bibliografica in memoria di Don Tommaso Accurti... (Card 2)

Cordova e la prima stampa di Murcia.—Inguanez, Mauro. La prima edizione del Chronicon Casinense, Venezia 1513.—Mercati, Angelo. Rara edizione romana di una bolla di Bonifacio VIII sull'Università di Roma.—Mercati, Angelo. Un breve di Giulio III a tutela della filigrana di una Cartiera di Piòraco.—Moricca Caputi, Ada. Di alcuni opuscoli rari nella Biblioteca Casanatense.—Oliger, Livario. Intorno alla bibliografia francescana.—Santoro, Caterina. Due contratti di lavoro per l'arte della stampa a Milano.—Scaccia Scarafoni, Camillo. La più antica edizione della Grammatica Latina di Aldo Manuzio finora sconosciuta ai bibliografi.—Sorbelli, Albano. Lo "Specchio della prudenza" di Frate Beltrame da Ferrara (GW 3807) presunto incunabulo.—Vichi Santovito, Nella. Una correzione al Reichling ed alcune notizie sulla stampa di Cagli.

470188B. 1. Accurti, Tommaso, 1862–1946. 2. Bibliography—Addresses, essays, lectures. 2. Bibliography—Rarities. I. Donati, Lamberto, ed.

N. Y. P. L. September 21, 1949

MAP DIV.

MISCELLANEA FRANCESCANA.

Il P. Vincenzo Coronelli dei Frati minori conventuali, 1650-1718, nel III centenario della nascita. Roma, 1951. 525 p. illus., 11 plates, facsim. 25cm.

"Bibliografia coronelliana del III centenario," p. 473-490.

1. Coronelli, Marco Vincenzo, 1650-1718. 2. Map making—Italy, 17th-18th cent.

NN** 6.53 OC PC, 1, 2 SL MP, 1, 2 (LC1, Z1, X1)

ZLH

Miscellanea Francesco Ehrle; scritti di storia e paleografia, pubblicati sotto gli auspici di S. S. Pio XI, in occasione dell'ottantesimo natalizio dell' E.mo cardinale Francesco Ehrle... Roma: Biblioteca apostolica vaticana, 1924. 6 v. in 5. facsims., front. (port.), illus. (incl. maps, plans), plates, tables. 4°. (Studi e testi. [v.] 37–42.)

[v. 6.] Album.
"Pubblicazioni dell' E.mo Ehrle," v. 6, p. 17–28.

(Continued)

N. Y. P. L. September 14, 1928

Miscellanea Francesco Ehrle; scritti di storia... (Continued)

Bibliographical footnotes.

Contents: v. 1. Per la storia della teologia e della filosofia. v. 2. Per la storia di Roma e dei papi. v. 3. Per la storia ecclesiastica e civile dell' età di mezzo. v. 4. Paleografia e diplomatica. v. 5. Biblioteca ed Archivio vaticano. Biblioteche diverse. [v. 6.] Album.

1. Ehrle, Franz, 1845- . 2. Catholic Church, Roman—Hist.—Middle Ages. 3. Palaeography—Italy—Middle Ages. 4. Libraries—Italy—Middle Ages. 5. Ser.

N. Y. P. L. September 14, 1928

RBG
+

MISCELLANEA Giovanni Galbiati... Milano, U. Hoepli, 1951. 3 v. facsims., illus., plans. 30cm. (Fontes ambrosiani. 25-27)

Contributions in Italian, Latin, Greek, German, English and French. Bibliographies included.

1. Galbiati, Giovanni, 1881- . 2. Classical studies. 3. Oriental studies. 4. History, Ancient—Addresses, essays, lectures. I. Ser.

NN OC PC, 1, 2, 3, 4 SL O, 3 (LC1, Z1, X1)

NAC

Miscellanea Giovanni Mercati. Città del Vaticano, 1946.

6 v. illus., port., facsims., tables. 26 cm. (₍Vatican. Biblioteca vaticana₎ Studi e testi, 121-126)

CONTENTS.—v. 1. Bibbia. Letteratura cristiana antica.—v. 2. Letteratura medioevale.—v. 3. Letteratura e storia bizantina.—v. 4. Letteratura classica e umanistica.—v. 5. Storia ecclesiastica. Diritto.—v. 6. Paleografia. Bibliografia. Varia.

1. Mercati, Giovanni, Cardinal, 1866- 2. Theology—Collections. 3. Bibliography—Collections. 4. Paleography. 5. Literature—Addresses, essays, lectures. I. Series.

AC9.M5 47-29688*

Library of Congress ₍3₎ Mr Schreiner.

BAC

...Miscellanea historica in honorem Alberti de Meyer, Universitatis catholicae in oppido Lovaniensi iam annos XXV professoris. Louvain, Bibliothèque de l'Univ., Bureaux du "Recueil" [etc., etc.] 1946. xlii, 649 p. illus. 25cm. (Université de Louvain. Recueil de travaux d'histoire et de philologie. sér. 3, fasc. 22)

Contributions in French, Dutch or English.

Bibliographical footnotes.

604590B. 1. History—Addresses, essays, lectures. 2. Theology—Essays and misc. 3. Meyer, Albert de, 1887- 4. Church history—Addresses, essays, lectures. I. Ser.

BAC

Miscellanea historica in honorem Leonis van der Essen Universitatis catholicae in oppido Lovaniensi iam annos XXXV professoris... Brussel ₍etc.₎ Éditions universitaire, 1947. 2 v. illus. 25cm. (Université catholique, Louvain. Recueil de travaux publiés par les membres des conférences d'histoire et de philologie. sér. 3, fasc. 28-29)

Contributions in Flemish or French.

"Bibliographie du jubilaire," p. lx-lxx.

Bibliographical footnotes.

489729-30B. 1. History—Addresses, essays, lectures. 2. Netherlands—Hist.—Addresses, essays, lectures. 3. Belgium—Hist.—Addresses, essays, lectures. 4. Essen, Léon van der, 1883- . I. Ser.

N. Y. P. L. Festschrift October 26, 1949

3-MAS
+

MISCELLANEA I.Q. van Regteren Altena, 16/v/1969. Amsterdam, Scheltema & Holkema, 1969. viii, 406 p.(p. 242-399 plates) port. 32cm.

Festschrift.

Essays in English, Dutch, German or French with summaries in English of the Dutch.

"Lijst van publikaties van I.Q. van Regteren Altena," by E. van der Vossen-Delbrück: p. 236-240.

(Continued)

NN R 8.70 w/A OC PC,1,2,3 SL A,1,2,3 (LC1,X1,Z1) [I] 2

MISCELLANEA I.Q. van Regteren Altena... (Card 2)

Bibliographical footnotes.

1. Regteren Altena, Johan Quirijn van, 1899- . 2. Regteren Altena, Johan Quirijn van, 1899- --Bibl. 3. Art--Essays and misc.

RAE

Miscellanea J. Gessler. ₍Deurne₎ 1948. 2 v. illus. 28cm.

Contributions in Flemish or French.

No. 159 of 550 copies.

"Bibliographia Gessleriana, door Dr. Rob. Roemans," v. 1, p. 45-102.

496646-7B. 1. Philology—Addresses, essays, lectures. 2. Civilization, Medieval. 3. Gessler, Jean, 1878- .

N. Y. P. L. Festschrift October 3, 1949

RAE

Miscellanea linguistica in onore di Graziadio Ascoli. Torino: E. Loescher, 1901.

viii, 626pp., 1port. 4°

BWO

MISCELLANEA lucchese di studi storici e letterari in memoria di Salvatore Bongi. Lucca: Scuola tipografica Artigianelli, 1931. x*, li, 410 p. incl. front. ports. 28½cm.

"Bibliografia delle opere di Salvatore Bongi," p. xxxvii-li.

685352A. 1. Bongi, Salvatore, 1825-1899. 2. Lucca, Italy (city)—Hist.

Festschrift cwa

N. Y. P. L. February 15, 1934

F-10
4070

Miscellanea in onore di Roberto Cessi. Roma, Edizioni di Storia e letteratura, 1958.

3 v. illus., port., maps. 26 cm. (Storia e letteratura, 71-73)

"Bibliografia degli scritti di Roberto Cessi (1904-1957) a cura di Giampietro Tinazzo": v. 1, p. ₍xlv₎-lxxvii. Bibliographical footnotes.

1. Cessi, Roberto, 1885- . 2. Italy--Hist.--Addresses, essays, lectures.

NN * 8.60 m/J OC PC,1,2 SL (LC1, X1, Z1) [I]

Copy only words underlined & classmark — BTGR

Miscellanea philologica historica et archaeologica in honorem Huberti van de Weerd. Bruxelles, 1948. xxxv,594 p. illus.,plates, port.,maps. 26cm. (L'Antiquité classique. t. 17)

Bibliographical footnotes.

1. Weerd, Hubert van de, 1878-

NN R X 11.53 OC OI PC,1 (Z/1,LC2,X1)

Copy only words underlined
& Classmark-- MAK

MISCELLANEA pro arte: Hermann Schnitzler zur Vollendung des 60. Lebenjahres am 13. Januar 1965. [1. Aufl.] Düsseldorf, L. Schwann [1965]
358 p. illus., 186 plates. 26cm. (Schriften des pro arte Medii aevi. 1)

"Bibliographie Hermann Schnitzler," by A.v. Euw, p. 353-356.
Bibliographical footnotes.

1. Schnitzler, Hermann, 1905- . 2. Schnitzler, Hermann, 1905- --Bibl. 3. Art--Essays and misc.
I. Series.
NN R 2.67 1/r OC (OS)I PC, 1, 2, 3, I A, 1, 2, 3, I(LC1, X1, Z1)

L-10
7719
v.1

MISCELLANEA queriniana, a ricordo del II centenario della morte del cardinale Angelo Maria Querini. Brescia, Tipo-litografia Fratelli Geroldi, 1961.
xi, 359 p. illus., plates, ports. 25cm. (Brescia, Italy (City). Biblioteca civica queriniana. Studi queriniani. 1)

1. Quirini, Angelo Maria, cardinal, 1680-1755.
NN 12.65 e/g OI (PC)1 (LC1, X1, Z1)

---

*GAH
+

Miscellanea di scritti di bibliografia ed erudizione in memoria di Luigi Ferrari. Firenze, L.S. Olschki, 1952. viii, 534 p. illus., facsims. 33cm.

Includes bibliographies. Bibliographical footnotes.
Contents.—Luigi Ferrari, primi studi e uffici, di F. Pintor.—Uno scambio strano di qualche interesse per tre grandi biblioteche. Amici innominati
(Continued)
NN** X 7.55 j/j OC PC, 1, 2 SL (LC1, X1, Z1)

Miscellanea di scritti di bibliografia ed erudizione in memoria di Luigi Ferrari. (Card 2)

del Savile in Roma? di G. Card. Mercati.—L'attività di una tipografia lucchese nel settecento, di E. Amico Moneti.—Le edizioni romane di Francesco Minizio Calvo, di F. Barberi.—Un amico e un libro del Petrarca, di G. Billanovich.—Un Esopo volgare veneto, di V. Branca.—Biblioteche generali e biblioteche speciali nelle discussioni parlamentari, di V. Carini-Dainotti.--Il contributo di eruditi veneti alla pubblicazione dei "Rerum
(Continued)

Miscellanea di scritti di bibliografia ed erudizione in memoria di Luigi Ferrari. (Card 3)

Italicarum Scriptores", di E. Coen-Pirani.—La tipografia vicentina nel secolo XVI, di M. Cristofari.—Appunti di tecnica catalografica (la scheda d'autore per i cataloghi di musei e gallerie), di G. de Gregori.—Nota su Angelo Catone di Benevento, di T. de Marinis.—Marco Marulo traduttore di Dante, di C. Dionisotti.—Appunti di biblioiconologia, di L. Donati.—Oggetto e limite della storia giornalistica, di F. Fattorello.—I corali degli Olivetani di Bologna, di D. Fava.—La
(Continued)

Miscellanea di scritti di bibliografia ed erudizione in memoria di Luigi Ferrari. (Card 4)

metodologia bibliografica, verso una definizione del suo svolgimento, di G.E. Ferrari.—Le versioni latine medievali di Aristotele e dei suoi commentatori greci ed arabi nelle biblioteche delle Tre Venezie, di E. Franceschini.—Notizie e documenti inediti sul tipografo Antonio Carcano (1475-1525), di T. Gasparrini Leporace.—L'editore veneziano Michele Tramezino ed i suoi privilegi, di P.S. Leicht—Il carteggio inedito del legato
(Continued)

Miscellanea di scritti di bibliografia ed erudizione in memoria di Luigi Ferrari. (Card 5)

Araujo, di A.M. de Sánchez Rivero.—Un cardinale editore: Marcello Cervini, di P. Paschini.—Prime indagini sulla stampa padovana del cinquecento, di B. Saraceni Fantini.—An anatomical demonstration by Giovanni Lorenzo of Sassoferrato, 19 November 1519, by D.M. Schullian.—Precedenti storici di attuali questioni sociali, di G. Stendardo.—I manoscritti di Giulio Salvadori nella Biblioteca Vaticana, di N. Vian.—Les sources hagiographiques de S. Catherine de Sienne et le
(Continued)

Miscellanea di scritti di bibliografia ed erudizione in memoria di Luigi Ferrari. (Card 6)

Ms.Marciano Ital. CL.V.26, par M.H. Laurent.

1. Ferrari, Luigi. 2. Bibliography—Addresses, essays, lectures.

M-10
3702
no. 6

MISCELLANEA di storia Ligure in onore di Giorgio Falco [1. ed.] Milano, Feltrinelli [1962]
498 p. illus. 22cm. (Genoa (City). Università. Istituto di storia medievale e moderna. Fonti e studi. no. 6)

1. Liguria, Italy--Hist. 2. Falco, Giorgio.
NN R 10.63 g/g OC OI PC, 1, 2 (LC3, X1, Z1)

M-11
3954
v.1

Miscellanea Walter Matúri. Torino, G. Giappichelli, 1966.
526 p. illus. 26 cm. (Turin (City). Università. Lettere e filosofia, Facoltà di. Storia. v.1)
At head of title: Istituto di storia moderna e del Risorgimento.
Bibliographical footnotes.
Contents.—Un inedito di Walter Maturi: Il pensiero di Giuseppe de Maistre, di M. L. Pesante.—Un prelato italiano tra "ligueurs" e "politiques," di A. Lay.—Giannone e i suoi contemporanei: Lenglet
(Continued)
NN* 7.69 w/j OC, II (OS)I, III. IIIb* PC, 1, I, II, III (LC1, X1, Z1)
3

MISCELLANEA Walter Maturi. 1966. (Card 2)

du Fresnoy, Matteo Egizio, e Gregorio Grimaldi, di G. Ricuperati.—Gli anni '30 del Settecento, di F. Venturi.—Un misoneista tenace: il conte di Canale, di A. Ruata.—La composizione e le vicende editoriali del "Cours d'études" di Condillac, di L. Guerci.—Giuseppe Maria Galanti editore, di M. L. Perna.—Giuseppe Novolone, agronomo piemontese, di G. Torcellan.—Tra Russia e Piemonte, di N. Nada.—I salari edilizi a Torino dal 1815 al 1874, di G. Levi.—L'ambiente politico napoletano nell'esperienza giovanile di Arturo Labriola, di D. Marucco.—Sul concetto di "borghesia," verifica storica di un saggio crociano, di A. Garosci.—Bibliografia di Walter Maturi, a cura di N. Nada (p. [477]-508)

(Continued)

MISCELLANEA Walter Maturi. 1966. (Card 3)

1. Italy--Hist.--Addresses, essays, lectures. I. Series. II. Maturi, Walter. III. Turin (City). Università. Istituto di storia moderna e del risorgimento.

RIW

Miscellània Fabra; recull de treballs de lingüística catalana i romànica, dedicats a Pompeu Fabra pels seus amics i deixebles amb motiu del 75è aniversari de la seva naixença. Buenos Aires, "Coni," 1943. vii, 400 p. 24cm.

Colophon dated 1944.

"Advertiment" signed: Joan Coromines.

CONTENTS.—Aebischer, Paul. Autour de l'origine du nom de Catalogne.—Balaguer, P. B. Bastero i els orígens de la llengua catalana.—Cases-Carbó, Joaquim. La preposicio "amb" dins el textos antics.—Galí, Alexandre. L'alliberament de la frase.—Mas, J. G. "La colla del Carrer."—Alonso, Amado. Partición de las lenguas románicas de Occidente.—Bosch i Gimpera, P. Lingüística i etnología primitiva á Catalunya.—Coromines,

(Continued)

N. Y. P. L. February 6, 1945

Miscellània Fabra... (Continued)

Joan. Noms de lloc catalans d'origen germànic.—Entwistle, W. J. Remarks on the idealistic extensions of linguistic science.—Faraudo de Saint-Germain, L. Consideracions entorn d'un pla de glossari raonat de la llengua catalana medieval.—Gauchat, Louis. Homo non sapit.—Grandó, Carles. Vocabulari rossellonès.—Mateu i Llopis, F. Nòmina dels Sarraïns de les muntanyes del coll de Rates, del regne de València, en l'any 1409.—Salvador, Carles. Petit vocabulari de Benassal.—Spitzer, Leo. Étymologies catalanes et provençales.—Tallgren, Tuulio. Petites glanures de sémantique catalane.—Violant i Simorra, R. La terminología sobre l'individu en el flamisell.—Flores, L. P. Vocabulari valencià de l'art de la navegació i de la construcció naval.—Renat i Ferrís, G. Les e tòniques del Valencià.—Sagarra, Ferran de. De les llegendes o inscripcions sigil'lars.—Sanchis Guarner, M. Folklore geogràfic de la comarca d'Alcoi.

293648B. 1. Catalan language. 2. Fabra, Pompeu, 1868- I. Coromines, Joan.

N. Y. P. L. February 6, 1945

RDV

A **miscellany** of studies in Romance languages & literatures presented to Leon E. Kastner... Edited by Mary Williams and James A. de Rothschild. Cambridge [, Eng.]: W. Heffer & Sons, Ltd., 1932. xii, 576 p. 2 facsims., front. (port.) 25½cm.

Bibliographical footnotes.

Partial contents: ARNOLD, I. D. O. The Brut tradition in the English manuscripts. BRUGGER, E. "Pellande," "Galvoie" and "Arragoce" in the romance of Fergus. KING Edward's ring. CLAPTON, G. T. Carlyle and some early English critics of Baudelaire. CRUMP, P. E. Musset and Malibran. EGGLI, E. Talma à Londres en 1817. GARDNER, E. G. Imagination and memory in the psychology of Dante. MOORE, W. G. The evolution of a sixteenth-century satire. PEERS, E. A. The

(Continued)

N. Y. P. L. October 26, 1932

A **miscellany** of studies in Romance languages & literatures... (Card 2)

influence of Manzoni in Spain. BARTSCH, K. F., and G. PARIS. Correspondance de Karl Bartsch et Gaston Paris de 1865 à 1885. Troisième partie; 1871. SAURAT, D. Renouvier et Victor Hugo. BARLAAM and JOSAPHAT. Un frammento di un nuovo manoscritto dell'anonimo poema in antico francese di Barlaam e Josafat. TILLEY, A. A. The literary circle of Margaret of Navarre.

603115A. 1. Kastner, Leon Émile. 1878- 2. Romance philology. I. Rothschild, James Armand Edmond de, , editor. II. Williams, Mary, editor.

N. Y. P. L. October 26, 1932

Write on slip words underlined below and class mark — XAA

Mr. Justice Holmes on his ninetieth birthday. [Articles by Charles Evans Hughes and others.]

(Harvard law review. Norwood, 1931. 8°. v.44, p.677-798. port.)

Bibliography p.797-798.

form 100b [11-13-31 25m]

AN (Oud, P.)

Mr P. J. Oud, gezien door zijn tijdgenoten: N. Arkema...[en anderen.] Rotterdam, W. L. & J. Brusse, 1951. 302 p. illus. 25cm.

1. Oud, Pieter Jacobus, 1886-

NN

*L

Mittelalterliche Handschriften; paläographische, kunsthistorische, literarische und bibliotheksgeschichtliche Untersuchungen. Festgabe zum 60. Geburtstage von Hermann Degering... Leipzig: K. W. Hiersemann, 1926. vi, 327 p. 17 facsim. (1 col'd), front. (port.), illus. (music.) 4°.

Edited by Alois Bömer and Joachim Kirchner.

Contents: ABB, G. Von der verschollenen Bibliothek des Klosters Lehnin. BOECKLER, A. Beiträge zur romanischen Kölner Buchmalerei. BÖMER, A. Ein gotisches Prachtmissale Utrechtscher Herkunft in der Universitäts-Bibliothek Münster.

(Continued)

N. Y. P. L. September 9, 1927

Mittelalterliche Handschriften... (Continued)

CASPAR, E. Paläographisches zum Kanon des Eusebius. LE LIVRE DU PAUMIER. Le livre du paumier; ein Beitrag zur Kenntnis der altfranzösischen Mystik. COLLIJN, I. Kalendarium Munkalivense. FREITAG, A. Ein Band aus Luthers Erfurter Klosterbibliothek. GÖBER, W. Ein spätantiker Pergamentkodex des Dionysius Thrax. HESSEL, A. Mabillons Musterbibliothek. MICHAEL BLAUNPAYN. Eine mittellateinische Dichterfehde. HUSUNG, M. J. Aus der Zeit des Übergangs von der Handschrift zum Druck. KIRCHNER, J. Das Staveloter Evangeliar der Preussischen Staatsbibliothek. KÖHLER, W. Turonische Handschriften aus der Zeit Alkuins. LIETZMANN, H. Zur Datierung der Josuarolle. MONTEBAUR, J. Vinricus, episcopus placentinus. ROSENFELD, H. F. Die Berliner Parzivalfragmente. SCHUSTER, J. Secreta Salernitana und Gart der Ge-

(Continued)

N. Y. P. L. September 9, 1927

Mittelalterliche Handschriften... (Continued)

sundheit. Strauch, P. Rigaer Handschriftenfragmente. Strecker, K. Die zweite Beichte des Erzpoeten. Theele, J. Aus der Bibliothek des Kölner Kreuzbrüderklosters. Willems, J. F. Briefwisseling van Jan Frans Willems en Jakob Grimm. Walther, H. Kleine mittellateinische Dichtungen aus zwei Erfurter Handschriften. Wegener, H. Die deutschen Volkshandschriften des späten Mittelalters. Wolf, J. Zwei Tagelieder des 14. Jahrhunderts.

305057A. 1. Degering, Hermann, 1866– . 2. Manuscripts, Mediaeval. 3. Boemer, Alois, 1868– , editor. 4. Kirchner, Joachim, 1890– , jt. editor.
N. Y. P. L. September 9, 1927

L-10
2908
v. 3

Moberg, Carl Axel, 1915–
Studier i bottnisk stenålder I–V. Stockholm, I distribution Almqvist & Wiksell ₍1955₎ 137 p. illus., port., maps. 25cm. (Kungliga vitterhets-, historie- och antikvitetsakademien, Stockholm. Handlingar. Antikvariska serien. 3)

"Tillägnas minnet av Sigurd Dahlbäck."
Summary in German.
Bibliography, p. ₍135₎–137.

(Continued)

NN R X 1.60 OC(1b*) (OS)I PC,1,2,3,I (LC1,X1,Z1)

---

* QT

Μνῆμα. Sborník vydaný na pamět čtyřicitiletého učitelského působení Prof. Josefa Zubatého na universitě Karlově, 1885–1925. Praha: S podporou ministerstva školství a národní osvěty vydala Jednota českých filologů, 1926. 498 p. incl. tables. diagrs., front. (port.), map. 8°.

Bibliographical footnotes.

428745A. 1. No subject. 2. Zubatý, Josef, 1855– .
N. Y. P. L. March 31, 1930

Moberg, Carl Axel, 1915– . Studier i bottnisk stenålder I–V. Stockholm, I distribution... ₍1955₎ (Card 2)

Contents.—Lösfynd från boplatser vid Lansjärv.—Slutna fynd från Pääkölä.—Dubbelredskap från Övre Norrland.—Om nordbottniska radskap.—Problem i Östra Norrbottens stenålder.—Bilaga A: Redogörelse över petrografisk granskning (T. Eriksson).—Bilaga B: Rapport från Statens maskinprovningar beträffande undersökning av stenversktyg.

1. Dahbäck, Sigurd, 1866-1932. 2. Stone age—Bothnia, Gulf of. 3. Stone age—Sweden—Norrbotten. I. Series.

E-13
4899

Mnemeion Siro Solazzi. ₍A cura di Antonio Guarino e Mario Bretone₎ Napoli, Jovene ₍1964₎

549 p. 24 cm. (Biblioteca di Labeo, 1)

German, Italian, Spanish, or French.
Bibliographical footnotes.

1. Law, Roman--Addresses, essays, lectures. I. Solazzi, Siro, 1875-1957. II. Guarino, Antonio, ed. III. Bretone, Mario, ed. IV. Bretone, Mario.
NN * 4. 69 d/OC, I, Ib*, II, III, IVb* PC, I, I, II, III SL (LC1 X1, Z1)

D-19
8932

MODERN miscellany presented to Eugène Vinaver by pupils, colleagues and friends. Edited by T. E. Lawrenson, F. E. Sutcliffe and G. F. A. Gadoffre. [Manchester] Manchester university press; New York, Barnes & Noble [1969] xiii, 314 p. illus., port. 23cm.

English or French.
"Select bibliography of the works of Eugène Vinaver," p. ix-xiii.
Includes bibliographical references.

1. French literature--Addresses, essays, lectures. I. Vinaver, Eugène, 1899- II. Lawrenson, T. E., ed.
NN R 4. 70m/OC, I, II PC, 1, I, II SL (LC1, X1, Z1) [I]

3-MAH

Mnemosynon Theodor Wiegand; dargebracht von Joh. Fr. Crome, Hermann Gundert, Bruno Meyer, Werner Peek, Hans U. v. Schoenebeck, Otto Uenze, Joachim Werner. Mit 36 tafeln und 17 abbildungen im text. München, F. Bruckmann verlag, 1938.

2 p. l., 99, ₍1₎ p. illus., 36 pl. on 18 l. 30½ᶜᵐ.

"Johann Friedrich Crome ... ₍war₎ der urheber des planes und leiter seiner ausführung."—Geleitwort, signed: Georg Karo.
Bibliographical foot-notes.

Contents.—Karo, Georg. Geleitwort.—Gundert, Hermann. Der alte Pindar.—Peek, Werner. Metrische inschriften.—Uenze, Otto. Ein absolutes datum innerhalb des ablaufs der schnurkeramik.—Crome, J. F.

(Continued on next card)

A C 39-3008

₍2₎

Festschrift

MPW

Modernt svenskt glas; utveckling, teknik, form. Stockholm, Jonson & Winter ₍1943₎ 254 p. illus., maps. 27cm.

"Denna bok är utgiven i samband med Edward Halds 60-års dag."
"Professor Gregor Paulsson, huvudredaktör."

397015B. 1. Glassware, Swedish. 2. Hald, Edward, 1883– . I. Paulsson, Gregor, 1889– , ed.
N. Y. P. L. October 2, 1947

Festschrift

Mnemosynon Theodor Wiegand ... 1938. (Card 2)

Contents—Continued.

Löwenbilder des siebenten jahrhunderts.—Schoenebeck, H. U. v. Ein hellenistisches schalenornament.—Werner, Joachim. Italisches und koptisches bronzegeschirr des 6. und 7. jahrhunderts nordwärts der Alpen.—Meyer, Bruno. Das Goldene tor in Konstantinopel.

1. Wiegand, Theodor, 1864-1936. 2. Art—Addresses, essays, lectures. I. Crome, Johann Friedrich.

A C 39-3008

New York. Public library for Library of Congress ₍2₎

VYR

[MOLIN, GAETANO]
Memorie che possono servire alla vita di Vettor Pisani, nobile veneto ... In Venezia, Apresso A. Locatelli, 1767. xxvii, 366 p. (p. 364-366 advertisements) front. 21cm.

1. Pisani, Vettore, 1324-1380. 2. Navy, Italian—Venice. I. Title.

NN ** R 11.53 OC (1b), 1b, I PC, 1, 2, I SL (Z1, LC1, X1)

*MF

Moll, Adolf.
Das Schleswig-Holstein-Lied als Mittelpunkt der Heimatlieder im Befreiungskampf des Landes von dänischer Bedrückung. Eine Würdigung von Wort und Ton von Dr. Adolf Moll... ₍Hamburg: Alster-Verlag, 1936₎ 88 p. front. (ports.), illus. (music), plates (incl. facsim.) 21cm.

"Verein geborener Schleswig-Holsteiner zu Hamburg."
"Festschrift für die Einweihung der Chemnitz-Gedenktafel in Altona zur Erinnerung an die 88. Wiederkehr der Erhebung Schleswig-Holsteins am 24. März, 1848–1936."
"Quellen-Nachweis," p. 84–86.
With autograph of author.

911123A. 1. Songs, National—Germany—Schleswig-Holstein. 2. Chemnitz, Matthäus Friedrich, 1815–1870. I. Verein geborener Schleswig-Holsteiner zu Hamburg. II. Title.
N. Y. P. L. December 2, 1937

E-12
2564

MONTPELLIER, France. Université. Lettres, Faculté des.
Mirèio; mélanges pour le centenaire de Mireille. [Paris] Presses universitaires de France [1960]
ix, 234 p. 24cm. (ITS: Publications, 16)

Includes bibliographies.

1. Mistral, Frédéric, 1830-1914. Mirèio. I. Series.
NN 2.65 g/s OS,I PC,1,I SL (LC1,X1,Z1)

IVE

Monaghan, James, 1891–
This is Illinois, a pictorial history. Chicago, University of Chicago Press ₍1949₎
v, 211 p. (chiefly illus., ports., maps) 29 cm.
"Fiftieth anniversary publication of the Illinois State Historical Society."

1. Illinois—Hist.—Pictorial works. I. Title. Festschrift

F541.M85 977.30084 49-11864*

Library of Congress ₍15₎

F-11
3282

MORENO MENDIGUREN, ALFREDO.
Discurso pronunciado para presentar al Reverendo Padre Geraldo Protain, en la sociedad cultural "Insula," de Miraflores, Lima, Peru, el dia miercoles 16 de noviembre de 1960, quien pronuncio una conferencia sobre el tema: "El dilema de hoy: Catolicismo social o socialismo ateo." Lisboa; 1962. 19 l. 27cm.
(Continued)
NN R 8.67 g/ OC,1b+ PC,1,2 SL E,2 (LC1, X1,Z1)
2

TB

Money, trade, and economic growth. In honor of John Henry Williams. New York, The Macmillan Company, 1951. 343 p.

MORENO MENDIGUREN, ALFREDO. Discurso pronunciado para presentar al Reverendo Padre Geraldo Protain... (Card 2)

1. Protain, Geraldo. 2. Catholic church, Roman—Influence, Political and social—Peru.

* KP
(Dolmen)

MONTAGUE, JOHN, ed. and comp.
A tribute to Austin Clarke on his seventieth birthday, 9 May 1966. [Dublin] Dolmen editions [1966]
27(1) p. 1 illus., port. 28cm. (Dolmen editions, 4)

Compiled and edited by John Montague and Liam Miller.
One of 1000 copies printed.
"Distributed outside Ireland, except in Canada and the United States of America by Oxford university press and in America by Dufour
(Continued)
NN R 3.67 g/c OC,I PC,1,I SL R,1,I (RI 3,RS2,LC1,X1, Z1)
2

Write on slip words underlined below and class mark —
PEA

...Moritz von Rohr zum siebzigsten Geburtstag. Jena ₍C. Zeiss₎ 1938. 74 p. incl. diagrs. illus. (incl. charts, ports.) 21cm. (Zeiss Nachrichten. Sonderheft 3.)

Contributions by various authors.
"Schrifttumhinweise," p. 69.
CONTENTS.—Köhler, A. M. v. Rohrs Arbeiten auf dem Gebiet der Mikroskopie.—Albada, L. E. W. van. M. v. Rohr und die Stereoskopie.—König, Albert. Einige Veröffentlichungen von M. v. Rohr.—Boegehold, H. M. v. Rohr als Geschichtsforscher und Geschichtsschreiber der Optik.—Wandersleb, E. Moritz von Rohr in der photographischen Optik.—Merté, W. Die grundlegenden Arbeiten von M. v. Rohr

(Continued)

N. Y. P. L. May 29, 1942

MONTAGUE, JOHN, ed. and comp. A tribute to Austin Clarke on his seventieth birthday... 1966. (Card 2)

editions inc., Chester Springs, Pennsylvania."

1. Clarke, Austin, 1896- . I. Miller, Liam, joint ed. and comp.

...Moritz von Rohr zum siebzigsten Geburtstag. (Continued)

über den Verzeichnungsfehler und ihre Anwendung für photographische Objektive mit Vorder- oder Hinterblende.—Hartinger, H. M. v. Rohr, ein Förderer der ophthalmologischen Optik.

1. Rohr, Moritz von, 1868- 2. Microscope and microscopy—Hist. I. Ser.
N. Y. P. L. May 29, 1942

NNBC
(Sanctis)

Morra de Sanctis, Italy. Sanctis, Francesco de, Comitato per la celebrazione cinquantenaria della morte di.
Studii e ricordi desanctisiani; pubblicati a cura del Comitato irpino per la celebrazione cinquantenaria della morte di Francesco de Sanctis. (1883–1933). Avellino: Tip. Pergola, 1935. xviii, 436 p. incl. front. facsims., plates, ports. 25½cm.

CONTENTS.—Albeggiani, Ferdinando. Francesco de Sanctis e la dignità delle lettere.—Amatucci, A. G. La grammatica nel pensiero di F. de Sanctis (noterele di un grammatico).—Arcari, Paolo. Il tono del de Sanctis.—Bach, Giovanni. La letteratura tedesca in F. de Sanctis.—Biondolillo, Francesco. Dante e de Sanctis.—

(Continued)

N. Y. P. L. June 3, 1938

Morra de Sanctis, Italy. Sanctis, Francesco de, Comitato per la celebrazione cinquantenaria della morte di. Studii e ricordi desanctisiani... (Card 2)

Bosurgi, Domenico. L'idealismo patriottico di F. de Sanctis.—Bruno, Francesco. F. de Sanctis e la critica estetica.—Busetto, Natale. F. de Sanctis e la critica alfieriana. —Caccese, Francesco. F. de Sanctis nella vita politica.—Calò, Giovanni. F. de Sanctis educatore.—Capaldo, Luigi. Ricordi.—Cerreti, Alfonso. F. de Sanctis e la Calabria.—Coppola, Nunzio. Vittorio Imbriani e F. de Sanctis.—Cotone, Romualdo. La scuola di F. de Sanctis.—De Felice, Gaetano. F. de Sanctis intimo (cinquanta anni dalla morte del maestro).—Faelli, Emanuele. Il de Sanctis giornalista.—Gentile, Giovanni. Torniamo a de Sanctis.—Iamalio, Antonio. Il pensiero religioso di F. de Sanctis.—Janner, Arminio. La critica del de Sanctis e le nuove tendenze della scienza letteraria tedesca.

(Continued)

N. Y. P. L. June 3, 1938

Morra de Sanctis, Italy. Sanctis, Francesco de, Comitato per la celebrazione cinquantenaria della morte di. Studii e ricordi desanctisiani... (Card 3)

—Lo Parco, Francesco. Il Petrarca umanista e poeta latino. Dalla concorde esaltazione dei biografi e dei critici all'opposta concezione di F. de Sanctis.—Manfredi, Michele. Un discorso inedito di F. de Sanctis-aggiunta ai "Frammenti di scuola."—Marghieri, Alberto. La terza scuola. Nel ricordo dei tempi trascorsi.—Mazzoni, Guido. Ammonimenti di F. de Sanctis.—Patrizi Moleschott, Elsa. Le lezioni di F. de Sanctis a Zurigo nei Ricordi postumi di Jac Moleschott.—Pescatori, Salvatore. F. de Sanctis e Filippo Capone. Lettere da Torino (1853–1855).—Sgroi, Carmello. Motivi artistici nella "Giovinezza" di F. de Sanctis.—Sorbelli, Albano. Una lettera politica di F. de Sanctis a Ferdinando Martini.—Tarozzi, Giuseppe. Il critico artista (F. de Sanctis),

(Continued)

N. Y. P. L. June 3, 1938

Morra de Sanctis, Italy. Sanctis, Francesco de, Comitato per la celebrazione cinquantenaria della morte di. Studii e ricordi desanctisiani... (Card 4)

1883–1933.—Tedesco, Ettore. Reminiscenze irpine.—Testa, N. V. Il giornale intimo di F. de Sanctis.—Tilgher, Adriano. Sull'estetica di de Sanctis.—Toffanin, Giuseppe. De Sanctis e noi.—Tonelli, Luigi. Attualità del de Sanctis.—Trabalza, Ciro. Un maestro: F. de Sanctis. Nel cinquantenario della morte.—Zitarosa, G. R. De Sanctis e Napoli.

810035A. 1. Sanctis, Francesco de, 1818–1883. I. Title.
N. Y. P. L. June 3, 1938

NIC p.v.343

Morten Korch, 1898, 22. september, 1948. København, M. A. Korch, 1948. 105 p. illus. 22cm.

"Redigeret af Chr. Kirchhoff-Larsen."

1. Korch, Morten, 1876– . I. Kirchhoff-Larsen, Christian, 1880– , ed.
N. Y. P. L. March 31, 1950

D-16
6529

Moser, Hugo, *ed.*
Festschrift Josef Quint, anlässlich seines 65. Geburtstages überreicht. Hrsg. von Hugo Moser, Rudolf Schützeichel und Karl Stackmann. Bonn, E. Semmel, 1964.

. 306 p. map, port. 23 cm.

Erratum slip inserted.
"Bibliographie Josef Quint": p. [304]-306.
Bibliographical footnotes.

1. German literature--Addresses, essays, lectures. 2. Quint, Josef.
NN* 5.66 g/ OC PC,1,2 SL (LC1,X1,Z1) [I]

*PWZ
(Maimonides)

Moses Maimonides, 1135–1204; Anglo-Jewish papers in connection with the eighth centenary of his birth, edited by Rabbi Dr. I. Epstein... London: The Soncino Press [pref. 1935] vi, 248 p. 24cm.

"A bibliography of Maimonides," p. 228–248.
CONTENTS.—Preface, by the editor.—Moses Maimonides: a general estimate, by J. H. Hertz.—Maimonides' sources and his method, by Adolph Büchler.—Maimonides conception of the law and the ethical trend of his Halachah, by the editor.—The union of prophetism and philosophism in the thought of Maimonides, by R. V. Feldman.—Maimonides as physician and scientist, by W. M. Feldman.—Maimonides as Halachist, by I. Herzog.—The place of Maimonides' Mishneh Torah in the history and develop-

(Continued)

N. Y. P. L. July 2, 1936

Moses Maimonides, 1135–1204; Anglo-Jewish papers... (Card 2)

ment of the Halachah, by A. Marmorstein.—Philosophy as a duty, by Simon Rawidowicz.—Maimonides' conception of state and society, by E. Rosenthal.—Maimonides and England, by Cecil Roth.—Notes on some Rambam manuscripts, by D. S. Sassoon.—A bibliography of Maimonides, by J. I. Gorfinkle.

SCHIFF COLLECTION.

828203A. 1. Maimonides, Moses, 1135–1204. I. Epstein, Isidore, 1894– , ed.
N. Y. P. L. July 2, 1936

M-10
7581

MOSTHAF, WALTHER.
Die Württembergischen Industrie- und Handelskammern Stuttgart, Heilbronn, Reutlingen, Ulm, 1855-1955. Festschrift zum 100 jährigen Bestehen der Industrie- und Handelskammern Stuttgart, Heilbronn, Reutlingen, Ulm. Hrsg. von den Industrie- und Handelskammern, Stuttgart, Heilbronn, Reutlingen, Ulm. Stuttgart, 1955-62. 2 v. ports., facsim. 26cm.

(Continued)

NN R 1.64 f/ OC (1bo) (OD)Its (ED)Its PCs, 1s, Is SLs Es, 1s (LC1s, X1s, Z1)

MOSTHAF, WALTHER. Die Württembergischen Industrie- und Handelskammern Stuttgart, Heilbronn, Reutlingen, Ulm, 1855-1955. (Card 2)

Bd. 1-2.
Bd. 2 has subtitle: Festschrift zum 100 jährigen Bestehen der Industrie- und Handelskammer Stuttgart.
CONTENTS.--Bd. 1. Die Handels- und Gewerbekammern, 1855-1899. --Bd. 2. Die Handelskammern, 1900-1933.

1. Commerce--Assoc. and org.--Germany--Württemberg. I. Stuttgart. Industrie- und Handelskammer. t. 1955

D-11
533

MOT til fred; om europeisk samtid og framtid. Festskrift til Max Tau på 60-årsdagen 19. jan. 1957. [Redaktør: Reidar Huseby] Oslo, Aschehoug, 1957. 160 p. illus., port. 23cm.

1. Tau, Max, 1897- I. Huseby, Reidar, ed. II. Huseby, Reidar.
NN 5.58 p/~~X~~ OC, I, IIbo PC, 1, I SL (LC1, X1, ~~Z1~~, C1, Y1)

---

*EM. A161
v.127

MOULAERT, RAYMOND.
Notice sur Martin Lunssens, membre de l'Académie, né à Molenbeek Saint-Jean (Bruxelles) le 16 avril 1871, décédé à Bruxelles le 1er février 1944. (IN: Académie royale des sciences, des lettres et des beaux-arts, Brussels. Annuaire. Bruxelles. 19cm. [v.] 127. Notices biographiques, p. 3-13. port.)

"Œuvres musicales de Martin Lunssens," p. 12-13.

1. Lunssens, Martin, 1871-1944.
NN R 12. 61 m/~~B~~ (OC)Ib+ OI (MU)1 (LC2, X1, ~~Z1~~)

TAH

MOUNT HOLYOKE COLLEGE.
"Those having torches..." Economic essays in honor of Alzada Comstock, presented by her former students. Edited by Lucile Tomlinson Wessmann. South Hadley, Mass., 1954. 134 p. 23cm.

Includes bibliographies.
CONTENTS. --Alzada Comstock, by A. Hewes. --Britain's small shopkeepers, by W. M. Breed. --Family allowances in Great Britain, by M. H. Gillim. --Britain's trade 1945-1950: an example of socialist planning, by R. D. Hale. --Problems of French tax reform, by E. Harris. --The crisis in France, by F. C. Manning. --Postwar intra-European payments institutions, by M. J. Murphy. --Town finance in seventeenth century Plymouth, by
(Continued)
NN * R X 10.54 p/R (OC) I OS PC, 1, 2, 3, I, II SL E, 1, 2, 3, I, II (~~Z1~~, LC1, X1) [I]

MOUNT HOLYOKE COLLEGE. "Those having torches..." (Card 2)

M. S. Belcher. --Economic bases for power markets in the Pacific Northwest, by C. Colver. --Canal fever: the development of a Connecticut valley town, by E. T. Grasso. --Alexander Hamilton as a lieutenant of Robert Morris, by L. P. Mitchell. --Economic history reconsidered, by E. H. Sherrard. Innovation and consumption, by C. S. Bell. --Some observations on personal savings and life insurance savings, by E. S. Daniel. --Women in the professions 1870-1950, by J. M. Hooks. --Investment management: some tangibles and intangibles, by I. D. Pratt.

1. Economic history, 1700- 2. Economics--Essays and misc. 3. Comstock, Alzada Peckham, 1888- I. Wessmann, Lucile (Tomlinson), 1912- , ed. II. Title.

D-17
7107

Müller-Seidel, Walter, 1918- *ed.*
Formenwandel: Festschrift zum 65. Geburtstag von Paul Böckmann. [Hrsg. von Walter Müller-Seidel und Wolfgang Preisendanz. Hamburg] Hoffmann und Campe [1964]
519, [1] p. mounted port. 23 cm.
Includes bibliographical references.
CONTENTS.--Die Bedeutung des Paradiessteins im "Alexanderlied."

(Continued)

NN * R 10.67 1/A OC, I, II PC, 1, 2, 3, I, II SL (LC1, ~~X1~~, ~~Z1~~) [I]

MÜLLER-SEIDEL, WALTER, 1918- , ed.
Formenwandel... (Card 2)

von J. Quint.—Der heilsgeschichtliche Symbolgrund im "Gregorius" Hartmanns von Aue, von F. Tschirch.—Brunetto Latini als allegorischer Dichter, von H. R. Jauss.—Luther als Schriftsteller, von H. Bornkamm.—Andreas Gryphius und Johann Arndt, von H. H. Krummacher.—Hütte und Palast in der Dichtung des 18. Jahrhunderts, von H. Meyer.—Formen des idyllischen Menschenbildes, von F. Sengle.—Klopstocks Geburtstage, von D. W. Schumann.—Riccaut, die Sprache und das Spiel in Lessings Lustspiel "Minna von Barn-

(Continued)

MÜLLER-SEIDEL, WALTER, 1918- , ed.
Formenwandel... (Card 3)

helm," von F. Martini.—Die Kunst der Darstellung in Wielands "Oberon," von W. Preisendanz.—Die Sprache als Erzählform in Goethes "Werther," von V. Lange.—Zu Sinn und Form von Goethes "Unterhaltungen deutscher Ausgewanderten," von G. Fricke.—Schillers Kontroverse mit Bürger und ihr geschichtlicher Sinn, von W. Müller-Seidel.—Die Rede als dramatische Handlung, von K. A. Ott.—Ein Traum, was sonst? Von R. Pascal.—Immermanns "Münchhausen" und der Roman der Romantik, von B. von Wiese.—Sur le lyrisme de Platen, par C. David.—Trochäen bei Heinrich Heine, von L. L. Hammerich.—Die funktionale Strukturierung des "Traumspiels" von Strindberg, von H. Steffen.—Die Pathetik des heiligen Berstens und ihre Gestaltwandlung im Werk Gerhart Haupt-
(Continued)

MÜLLER-SEIDEL, WALTER, 1918- , ed.
Formenwandel... (Card 4)

manns, von R. C. Zimmermann.—Zur Polemik Georges und seines Kreises, von W. Kohlschmidt.—Eugen Gottlob Winklers "Gedenken an Trinakria," von W. Mauser.—Literarische Erneuerung, von P. M. Mitchell.—Verzeichnis der Schriften von Paul Böckmann (p. 511-[520])

1. Böckmann, Paul, 1899- . 2. German literature --Addresses, essays, lectures. 3. Literature--Addresses, essays, lectures. I. Preisendanz, Wolfgang, joint ed. II. Title.

MAMG
+

Münchener altertums-verein, e.V.
Alte kunstschätze aus Bayern; herausgegeben von Hubert Wilm. Festschrift zum 70 jährigen jubiläum des Münchener altertumsvereins e. v. von 1864/1934. Mit 66 abbildungen. Ulm-Donau, Verlag dr. Karl Höhn [°1934]
3 p. l., 9-88 p. incl. illus. (incl. facsims., coats of arms) plates. 30cm.
"Die bücher von Hubert Wilm": p. 87-88.
CONTENTS.—Geleitwort des schirmherrn des Münchener altertumsvereins.—Vorwort des herausgebers.—Buchheit, H. Stammbuchblätter des 16. jahrhunderts.—Feulner, A. Ein elfenbeinrelief von Permoser.—Kehrer, H. Altdorfers Alexanderschlacht.—Bernhart, M. Ein taufgro-
(Continued on next card)
A C 35-348
[2]

Münchener altertums-verein, e.V. Alte kunstschätze aus Bayern ... [°1934] (Card 2)

CONTENTS—Continued.

schen des 16. jahrhunderts.—Hofberger, K. Von frühen exlibris und alter gebrauchsgraphik.—Fuchs, L. F. Der bocksbeutel.—Hausladen, A. Kostbarkeiten aus der schatzkammer der Münchener residenz.—Pocci, F., graf von. Die Humpenburg.—Hofmann, F. Was drei romantische bilder erzählen.—Gröber, K. Alabasterplastik aus Mindelheim.—Peltzer, R. A. Sebastian Füll, ein vergessener Münchener kunstmäzen.—Wilm, H. Die kunstsammlung im schloss zu Berchtesgaden.—Roth, H. Ein nicht gehaltener trinkspruch beim 70 jährigen jubiläum des Münchener altertumsvereins.

1. Art, German—Bavaria. I. Wilm, Hubert, 1887- ed. II. Title.
A C 35-348
Title from N. Y. Pub. Libr. Printed by L. C.
[2]

D-15
5476

MÜNSTER, Germany. Universität. Institut für Genossenschaftswesen.
Gegenwartsprobleme genossenschaftlicher Selbsthilfe; Festschrift für Paul König. Hamburg, Edeka Verlagsgesellschaft, 1960. 353 p. illus., port. ; 21cm.

Bibliographical footnotes.

1. Co-operation, Commercial. 2. König, Paul.
NN 11.64 c/ OS PC, 1, 2 SL E, 1, 2 (LC1, X1, Z1)

C-13
967

MÜNSTER, Germany. Universität. Institut für Publizistik.
Publizistik im Dialog; Festgabe für Prof. Dr. Henk Prakke zur Vollendung seines 65. Lebensjahres, dargebracht von seinen Mitarbeitern und Schülern am Institut für Publizistik der Westfälischen Wilhelms-Universität Münster. Winfried B. Lerg, Michael Schmolke [und] Gerhard E. Stoll, Herausgeber Assen, Van Gorcum, 1965. vii, 160 p. illus., ports. 18cm. (Münsteraner Marginalien zur Publizistik. Nr. 7)
(Continued)
NN R 6.66 r/ (OC)I, IIIb+ OS, II PC, 1, 2, I, II SL (LC1, X1, Z1)
2

MÜNSTER, Germany. Universität. Institut für Publizistik. Publizistik im Dialog... (Card 2)

Includes bibliographies.

1. Prakke, H. J. 2. Journalism--Addresses, essays, lectures. I. Lerg, Winfried B., 1932- , ed. II. Series. III. Lerg, Winfried B., 1932- .

E-10
2884

MÜNSTER, GERMANY. Universität. Institut für Publizistik.
Publizistik als Wissenschaft; sieben Beiträge für Emil Dovifat. Emsdetten, Verlag Lechte, 1951. viii, 86 p. 24cm.

Includes bibliographies.
CONTENTS.--Emil Dovifat, der Mensch und das Werk, von K. d'Ester. --Publizistik als Wissenschaft, von W. Hagemann.--Die Macht der
(Continued)
NN * 6.57 j/p (OC)I OS PC, 1, 2, I SL (LC1, X1, Z1)

MÜNSTER, GERMANY. Universität. Institut für Publizistik. Publizistik als Wissenschaft... (Card 2)

öffentlichen Meinung, von K. Baschwitz.--Hebel als Feuilletonist, von W. Haacke.--Wege und Umwege zur Wissenschaft, von E. Stern-Rubarth.--Gedanken zum Fernsehen, von K. Wagenführ.--Das Berliner Institut für Publizistik, von F. Medebach.

1. Journalism--Addresses, essays, lectures. 2. Dovifat, Emil, 1890- I. Title.

E-13
5448

MUHLENBERG COLLEGE, Allentown, Pa.
Muhlenberg essays, in honor of the college centennial. [Allentown, Pa., 1968] xiv, 435 p. illus. 24cm.

Includes bibliographies.
CONTENTS.--Homily of Melito of Sardis on the Passover: notes and translation, by J. B. Renninger.--The language of Middleton's tragic vision, by H. L. Stenger, jr.--Evelyn, Swift and "violent friendship", by
(Continued)
NNR 6.69 v/L OS PC, 1 SL (LC1, X1, Z1) [I]

MUHLENBERG COLLEGE, Allentown Pa. Muhlenberg essays... (Card 2)

K. S. Van Eerde.--The Philadelphia merchants and British imperial policy, 1756-1766, by V. L. Johnson.--"A doing man": Stanhope in free Greece, 1823-1824, by E. W. Jenninson, jr.--Franco-German rapprochement, 1909-1911: reality of illusion: By J. S. Mortimer.--Jānis Rainis, poet and ecumenist, by Z. Ziedonis, jr.--Are dispositional properties different? By S. A. Shaw.--Anti-Semitism through theological silence: Bonhoeffer and the Nuremberg laws, by H. A. K. Staak.--Boxing as it's fought in American literature, by R. S. Graber.--The act of waiting in contemporary drama, by N. L. Vos.--Steroisomerism
(Continued)

MUHLENBERG COLLEGE, Allentown Pa. Muhlenberg essays... (Card 3)

and stereoselectivity: a case study from the field of alicyclic chemistry, by G. N. R. Smart.--John Dalton: color-blind chemist, by C. E. Mortimer. --One-lying-across, Lewis Henry Morgan: the birth of American ethnology, 1842-1851, by J. A. Grossman.--Botanists of the lower Lehigh valley, by R. L. Schaeffer, jr.--The role of intrinsics and extrinsics in job satisfaction, by F. J. McVeigh.--Liberal and conservative attitudes toward college: a survey of town-gown relationships in Allentown, Pennsylvania, by G. A. Lee.-- Marx's economic and
(Continued)

MUHLENBERG COLLEGE, Allentown Pa. Muhlenberg essays... (Card 4)

philosophic manuscripts of 1844: the ideological basic for Communist liberalization, by C. S. Bednar.--Crime and punishment in Soviet Russia, by P. B. Secor.--The Korean minority in postwar Japan, by S. S. Lee.

1. Civilization--Addresses, essays, lectures.

M-11
2552
Nr. 4

Mundart und Geschichte. Hrsg. von Maria Hornung. (Eberhard Kranzmayer zu seinem 70. Geburtstag am 15. Mai 1967 zugeeignet) [Illustriert] Graz, Wien, Köln, Böhlau in Kommission, 1967.
viii, 180 p. 28 cm. (Studien zur österreichisch-bairischen Dialektkunde, Nr. 4)
(Continued)
NN* R 7.70 e/ OC, I, II (OS)III, IV PC, 1, 2, I, II, III, IV (LC1, X1, Z1)
4

MUNDART und Geschichte. (Card 2)

At head of title: Österreichische Akademie der Wissenschaften.
"Anhang": vi, 19 p. front. inserted in pocket.

CONTENTS.—Über "gekoppelte" Lautgesetze, von O. Höfler.—Satzmorphologische Betrachtungen zur Alltags- und Dichtersprache, von B. Horacek.—Romanische Entlehnungen in der deutschen Sprachinselmundart von Pladen, von M. Hornung.—Von den Deutschen im alten Trient, von F. Huter.—Königs- und hochadelige Namen in Niederösterreich, von K. Lechner.—Zur Zeitstellung und Bedeutung des

(Continued)

MUNDART und Geschichte. (Card 3)

Kärntner Herzogstuhles, von G. Morro.—Zur Geschichte und Geographie der Kollektivbildungen im Bairisch-österreichischen, von E. Seidelmann.—Sprachkunst in der Mundart, von H. Seidler.—Zur Urkundensprache im Stift Klosterneuburg, von L. Strebl.—Die Bezeichnung "Feitel" <Taschenmesser> und ihre sinnverwandten Ausdrücke in den bairischen Mundarten Österreichs, von H. Tatzreiter.—Die Regel des Gegensatzes in H. C. Artmanns Dialektgedichten, von W. Welzig.—Verzeichnis der Schriften von Eberhard Kranzmayer, von H. Hornung (p. 1–10 of Anhang)

(Continued)

MUNDART und Geschichte. (Card 4)

1. German language--Dialects--Bavaria. 2. German language--Dialects--Austria. I. Hornung, Maria, ed. II. Kranzmayer, Eberhard. III. Akademie der Wissenschaften, Vienna. IV. Series.

ZEC

Munera studiosa, edited by Massey Hamilton Shepherd, jr., and Sherman Elbridge Johnson, with a preface by Henry Bradford Washburn. Cambridge, Mass., The Episcopal theological school, 1946.

ix, 182 p. front. (port.) 21cm.

MAVY
+
(Munich)

MUNICH. Bayerisches Nationalmuseum.
Kunst und Kunsthandwerk: Meisterwerke im Bayerischen Nationalmuseum, München; Festschrift zum hundertjährigen Bestehen des Museums, MDCCCLV-MCMLV. München, F. Bruckmann [1955] 82 p. illus., 187 plates (8 col.) 31cm.

Bibliography, p. 82.
I. Title.
NN ** R X 5.56 d/, OS PC, I SL A, I (LC1, X1, Z1)

G-10
2684

MUNNICHS, ANDRÉ FRANCOIS PIERRE HUBERT, 1912-
André Munnichs: Keuze uit zijn werk. 2. druk. 's-Hertogenbosch, 1968. 56 p. illus., ports. 32cm.

"Uitgegeven ter gelegenheid van Munnichs' zilveren jubileum als leraar aan het Stedelijk gymnasium van 's-Hertogenbosch."
Essays previously published in the Provincial Nordbrabantsch dagblad, 1945-1946.

1. Essays, Dutch.
NN R 2.70 w/ OC(1b+) PC, 1 SL (LC1, X1, Z1)

E-11
8589

MUNSHI at seventy-five; volume of articles on the various facets of Dr. K.M. Munshi by his contemporaries. Foreword by Rajendra Prasad. [Bombay, 1962] 175 p. ports. 25cm.

Sponsored by Dr. K. M. Munshi's 76th birthday celebrations committee.

1. Munshi, Kanialal Maneklal, 1887-
NN R 1.64 f/ OC PC, 1 SL O, 1 (LC1, X1, Z1)

E-11
6857

MURCIA, Spain (City). Universidad. Filosofía y letras, Facultad de.
Homenaje al profesor Cayetano de Mergelina. Murcia, 1962. 865 p. illus., port., map, facsims. 24cm.

Bibliographical footnotes.

1. Mergelina, Cayetano de. 2. Spain--Hist.--Addresses, essays, lectures.
NN R 5.63 p/ OS (1b) PC, 1, 2 SL (LC1, X1, Z1) [I]

---

*MGA

MUSA—MENS—MUSICI. Im Gedenken an Walther Vetter. Hrsg. vom Institut für Musikwissenschaft der Humboldt-Universität zu Berlin. [Schriftleitung: Heinz Wegener] Leipzig, Deutscher Verlag für Musik [1969] 471 p. music. 31cm.

Includes bibliographies and list of Vetter's works.
"Abbildungen," 15 p. of illus., inserted at end.

(Continued)

NN R 10.70 e/ OC, II (OS)I, Ibo PC, 1, 3, I, II SL MU, 1, 2, I, II (LC1, X1, Z1)

MUSA—MENS—MUSICI. (Card 2)

1. Vetter, Walther, 1891- . 2. Essays. 3. Music--Essays. I. Berlin. Universität. Institut für Musikwissenschaft. II. Wegener, Heinz, ed.

*MGA

Musik und Bild; Festschrift Max Seiffert zum siebzigsten Geburtstag in Verbindung mit Fachgenossen, Freunden und Schülern herausgegeben von Heinrich Besseler. Kassel: Der Bärenreiter-Verlag, 1938. 160 p. incl. geneal. table. front., illus. (incl. music), 38 pl. (incl. ports.) 27cm.

Bibliographical footnotes.

CONTENTS.—Schneider, Thekla. Das Werk Max Seifferts.—Steglich, Rudolf. Über die Wesensgemeinschaft von Musik und Bildkunst.—Moser, H. J. Die Symbolbeigaben des Musikerbildes.—Schünemann, Georg. Volksfeste und Volksmusik im alten Nürnberg.—Frotscher, Gotthold. Die Volksinstrumente auf Bildwerken des 16. und 17. Jahrhunderts.—Ehmann, Wilhelm. Das Musizierbild der deutschen Kantorei

(Continued)

N. Y. P. L. November 9, 1938

Musik und Bild . . . (Card 2)

im 16. Jahrhundert.—Fellerer, K. G. Musikalische Bilddarstellungen des 15./16. Jahrhunderts zu Freiburg im Üchtland.—Pietzsch, Gerhard. Dresdner Hoffeste vom 16.–18. Jahrhundert.—Schneider, Max. Ein Braunschweiger Freudenspiel aus dem Jahre 1648.—Schenk, Erich. Johann Theiles "Harmonischer Baum".—Miesner, Heinrich. Porträts aus dem Kreise Philipp Emanuel und Wilhelm Friedemann Bachs.—Vetter, Walther. Die musikalischen Wesensbestandteile in der Kunst Moritz von Schwinds.—Taut, Kurt. Aus einem Musikerstammbuch des 19. Jahrhunderts.—Müller-Blattau, Josef. Die musikalische Karikatur.—Blume, Friedrich. Musik, Anschauung und Sinnbild.—Besseler, Heinrich. Musik und Raum.

CARNEGIE CORP. OF NEW YORK.

962594A. 1. Music in art. 2. Music—Essays. 3. Seiffert, Max, 1868– . I. Besseler, Heinrich, 1900– , ed.

N. Y. P. L. November 9, 1938

---

* MG p.v.281

Musik-Blätter.

Richard Strauss zum 85. Geburtstag [von Roland Tenschert und Erik Werba. Wien, Gerlach & Wiedling, 1949] 44 p. ports., facsims., music. 21cm.

"Sondernummer."

"'Rosenkavalier'—Aufführungen in der Wiener Staatsoper," p. 39–44.

1. Strauss, Richard, 1864–1949. I. Tenschert, Roland, 1894– . II. Werba, Erik.

NN R 12.60 (OC)I,II,IIbo OS PC,1,I,II SL MU,1,I,II (LC1,X1,Z1)

---

*MGA

MUSIK als Gestalt und Erlebnis; Festschrift Walter Graf zum 65. Geburtstag. Wien, H. Böhlaus, 1970. 262 p. illus., music. 24cm. (Wiener musikwissenschaftliche Beiträge. Bd. 9)

Includes bibliographies.

1. Essays. 2. Music--Essays. 3. Ethnomusicology. 4. Graf, Walter. I. Series.

NN 4.71 d/ OC (OS)I PC, 2, 3, 4, I SL MU, 1, 3, 4, I (LC1, X1, Z1)

---

*MFSB (Rumania)

MUSIKVEREIN "HERMANIA", Sibiu, Rumania.

Aus der Geschichte des Musikvereins "Hermania," 1839-1939; Festschrift zu seiner Jahrhundertfeier, 21.-29. Mai 1939. Hermannstadt, Im Selbstverlag des Musikvereins "Hermania," 1939. 109 p. illus., ports., facsims. 24cm.

Cover title: 100 [i.e. Einhundert] Jahre Musikverein "Hermania."

Contributions by various authors.

1. Music--Rumania--Sibiu. 2. Rumania--Sibiu. 3. Programs.

NN * 2.65 e/ OS(1b) PC, 1 SL MU, 2, 3 (LC1, X1, Z1)

D-16
6707

MUTHESIUS, VOLKMAR.

Was ist, was will, was leistet der Markenverband? zum 60 jährigen Bestehen. Frankfurt am Main, F. Knapp [c1963] 45 p. 22cm.

1. Markenverband.

NN R 8.66 1/ OC PC,1 SL E,1 (LC1, X1, Z1)

D-20
962

Myths and symbols; studies in honor of Mircea Eliade. Edited by Joseph M. Kitagawa and Charles H. Long. With the collaboration of Gerald C. Brauer and Marshall G. S. Hodgson. Chicago, University of Chicago Press [1969]

438 p. port. 23 cm.

CONTENTS.—Nomina numina, by G. Tucci.—The superhuman personality of Buddha and its symbolism in the Mahâparinirânasûtra

(Continued)

NN*R 11.70 r/z OC, I, II, III, IVb* PC, 1, 2, I, II, III SL (LC1, X1, Z1)

4

Myths and symbols; studies in honor of Mircea Eliade. [1969] (Card 2)

of the Dharmaguptaka, by A. Bareau.—Indian varieties of art ritual, by S. Kramisch.—No time, great time, and profane time in Buddhism, by A. Wayman.—The problem of the doublesense as hermeneutic problem and as semantic problem, by P. Ricoeur.—Eliade and folklore, by M. Popescu.—The weighing of the soul, by S. G. F. Brandon.—God in African mythology, by E. G. Parrinder.—Speaking of place, by K. W. Bolle.—Silence and signification: a note on religion and modernity, by C. H. Long.—The three last voyages of Il'ja of Murom, by G. Dumézil.—On sin and punishment; some re-

(Continued)

Myths and symbols; studies in honor of Mircea Eliade. [1969] (Card 3)

marks concerning Biblical and Rabbinical ethics, by G. Scholem.—The death of Gayōmart, by G. Widengren.—Symbol of a symbol, by A. Brelich.—Sexual symbolism in the Śvetāśvatara Upanishad, by R. C. Zaehner.—Manasā, goddess of snakes; the Ṣaṣṭhī myth, by E. C. Dimock, Jr.—The passivity of language and the experience of nature; a study in the structure of the primitive mind, by W. Müller.—Ordeal by fire, by E. Benz.—Docetism; a peculiar theory about the ambivalence of the presence of the devine, by U. Bianchi.—A vanishing problem, by J. Duchesne-Guillemin.—Chains of being in

(Continued)

MYTHS and symbols; studies in honor of Mircea Eliade. [1969] (Card 4)

early Christianity, by R. M. Grant.—Hitotsu-mono; a human symbol of the Shinto kami, by I. Hori.—Ainu myth, by J. M. Kitagawa.—Drugs and ecstasy, by E. Jünger.—The literary work of Mircea Eliade, by V. Ierunca.—Authenticity and experience of time; remarks on Mircea Eliade's literary works, by G. Spaltmann.—The forest as Mandala; notes concerning a novel by Mircea Eliade, by V. Horia.—Time and destiny in the novels of Mircea Eliade, by G. Uscatescu.—Beginnings of a friendship, by E. M. Cioran.—Bibliography of Mircea Eliade (p. 417–433)

1. Mythology--Essays and misc. 2. Symbolism. I. Eliade, Mircea, 1907- . II. Kitagawa, Joseph Mitsuo, 1915- , ed. III. Long, Charles H., ed. IV. Long, Charles H.

*PBM p.v.1025
NADIA STEIN zum Gedenken. Haifa, 1962.
72 p. ports. 24cm.

Title page in Hebrew and German.
Text mainly in German, with contributions in English or Hebrew.
Bibliography, p. 68-70.

1. Stein, Nadja. 2. Israel (State)--Addresses, essays, lectures.
NN R 10.66 a/JOC PC,1,2 SL J,1,2 (LC1,X1,Z1)

---

* C-4 p.v.356
Några uppsatser till Gunnar Lundh på hans femtioårsdag den 15 mars 1946. Stockholm, Skolan för bokhantverk [1946]
33 p. 24cm.

No. 166 of 200 copies.

1. Lundh, Gunnar, 1896- . 2. Printing—Sweden, 20th cent. I. Stockholm. Skolan för bokhantverk. i. 1946.
NN R 2.54 OC (OD)Ii (ED)Ii PC,1,2,I SL (LC1,Z1,X1)

SOC
+
Nagy László emlékkönyv; a Magyar gyermektanulmányi társaság tizéves fordulója alkalmából a társaság megalapitójának tiszteletére kiadták munkatársai. Szerkesztette: Nógrády László... Budapest: Budapesti nyomda és lapkiadó részvénytársaság, 1913.
159 p. illus. (incl. charts), port. 32cm.

746837A. 1. Child study. 2. Nagy, László, 1857- . I. Nógrády, László, 1871- , ed. II. Magyar gyermektanulmányi és gyakorlati lélektani társaság, Budapest.
N. Y. P. L. August 5, 1935

E-11
2364
NAPLES (City) Università. Istituto di glottologia.
Ioanni Dominico Serra ex munere laeto inferiae. Raccolta di studi linguistici in onore di G. D. Serra. [Napoli] Libreria Liguori, 1959.

402 p. port., maps. 24 cm.

"Opere di G. D. Serra": p. [15]-24.

1. Serra, Giandomenico, 1885-1958. 2. Philology --Addresses, essays, lectures. 3. Romance philology.
I. Title.
NN * R X-4. 61 p// (OC)I OS(1b*) PC. 1, 2, 3, I SL (LC1, X1, Z1) [I]

Napp-Zinn, Anton Felix, 1899- , ed. EKP
...Kultur und Wirtschaft im rheinischen Raum; herausgegeben im Auftrag des Herrn Oberbürgermeisters der Stadt Mainz und der Rechts- und Wirtschaftswissenschaftlichen Fakultät der Johannes Gutenberg-Universität Mainz, von Prof. Dr. Anton Felix Napp-Zinn und Regierungsrat a. D. Michel Oppenheim. Mainz, Selbstverlag der Stadt [1949] 321 p. illus. 25cm.

At head of title: Festschrift zu Ehren des Herrn Geheimen Regierungsrates Dr. jur., Dr. phil., Dr. rer. pol. h.c. Christian Eckert...anlässlich der Vollendung seines 75. Lebensjahres.
No. 936 of 1000 copies printed.
Bibliographies included.

(Continued) Fest.

NN

Napp-Zinn, Anton Felix, 1899- , ed. ...Kultur und Wirtschaft im rheinischen Raum... (Card 2)

Contents.—Köln im November und Dezember 1918, von Leopold von Wiese.—Die fränkisch-angelsächsischen Beziehungen im 6. und 7. Jahrhundert, von Herbert Kühn.—Die Finanzen des Erzstiftes Mainz um das Jahr 1400, von A. P. Brück.—Versuche zur Beseitigung der Kriegsschäden in Mainz nach dem 30jährigen Krieg, von Michel Oppenheim.—Josef Görres' Heidelberger Vorlesungen von 1806 bis 1808, von Leo Just.—Das Vermächtnis der alten Kölner Universität, von O. H. Förster.—Ein Kreuznacher Münzfund aus dem Mittelalter, von Gustav Behrens.—Der Rheinische Münzverein, von Wilhelm Diepenbach.—Karl Wilhelm Becker, ein rheinischer Münzfälscher zu Anfang des 19. Jahrhunderts, von Thomas Würtenberger.—Die Königshalle in Lorsch und der frühkarolingische Monumentalstil, von Friedrich Gerke.—Ein gotisches Patrizierhaus in Mainz, von Fritz Arens.—Zur Umgebungsgestaltung der Dome von Köln, Mainz und Worms, von Werner Bornheim gen. Schilling.—Neue

(Continued)

NN

Napp-Zinn, Anton Felix, 1899- , ed. ...Kultur und Wirtschaft im rheinischen Raum... (Card 3)

Forschungen zur Baugeschichte der Oppenheimer Katharinenkirche, von Ernst Jungkenn.—Pläne zu einer Mainzer Residenz für Napoleon I., im Rahmen rheinischer Schlossprojekte des Barock, von Heinz Biehn.—Die Sonderbund-Ausstellung 1912 und die Galerie der Neuzeit des Wallraf-Richartz-Museums in Köln, von Josef Haubrich.—Naturrechtsgedanken in der Verfassung für Rheinland-Pfalz, von H. G. Isele.—Finanzausgleichsprobleme in Rheinland-Pfalz, von Robert Nöll.—Gebiet, Bevölkerung und Wirtschaft im Lande Rheinland-Pfalz nach dem zweiten Weltkrieg, von Albert Zwick.—Betriebsgrössen und wirtschaftliche Verhältnisse im pfälzischen und rheinhessischen Weinbau, von Otto Sartorius.—Der Lorbeer des Industriellen, von F. M. Illert.—Über das Werden und die Probleme der Lederindustrie, von Hermann Scotti.—Aus der Geschichte der ältesten deutschen Waggonfabrik, von Albert Kirnberger.

(Continued)

NN

Napp-Zinn, Anton Felix, 1899- , ed. ...Kultur und Wirtschaft im rheinischen Raum... (Card 4)

—Die Entwicklung der Eisenbahn im Raume Worms, von Hans Kleinschmidt.—Ein Jahrhundert Rheinverkehr, von A. F. Napp-Zinn.—Die Crédit-Mobilier-Idee in der Geschichte der rheinischen Banken, von Adolf Weber.—Betrachtungen über die deutsche und die niederländische Geldreform, von L. J. Zimmerman.

1. Eckert, Christian Lorenz Maria, 1874- . 2. Rhine province—Hist. 3. Rhine province—Civilization. 4. Economic history—Germany—Rhine province. I. Oppenheim, Michel, jt. ed. II. Mainz. Oberbürgermeister. III. Mainz. Universität. Rechts- und wirtschaftswissenschaftliche Fakultät. IV. Title.
NN

THN
Národní banka československá, Prague.
Zehn Jahre Čechoslovakische Nationalbank; die čechoslovakische Währung. Die Tätigkeit der Čechoslovakischen Nationalbank. Die Lage und Entwicklung der Nationalwirtschaft der Čechoslovakischen Republik. Festschrift. Herausgegeben von der Čechoslovakischen Nationalbank... Prag [Buchdruckerei "Orbis"] 1937. 542 p. illus. (incl. charts), 2 maps (incl. front.), plates, ports., tables. 19cm.

Various contributors.
Map forms front end paper.
"Fremdsprachige Publikationen über die Čechoslovakei," p. 539-542.

976190A. 1. Banks and banking—Czecho-Slovakia.
N. Y. P. L. January 30, 1939

RAE
Natalicivm Johannes Geffcken zum 70. geburtstag 2. mai 1931, gewidmet von freunden, kollegen und schülern; beiträge zur klassischen altertumskunde von Rudolf Helm [u. a.] ... Heidelberg, C. Winter, 1931.

4 p. l., 187, [1] p. 23½cm.

Contents.—Helm, R. Heidnisches und christliches bei spätlateinischen dichtern.—Hohl, E. Zu Hesiods Theogonie.—Körner, O. Zwei beiträge zum verständnis Homers.—Lange, G. Xenophons verhältnis zur rhetorik.—Lücken, G. von. Goethe und der Laokoon.—Overbeck, J. Einige bemerkungen zu ⟨Xenophons⟩ Κυνηγετικός.—Schmitt, A. Δικαιοσύνη θεοῦ.—Schwenn, F. Studien zu Hesiodos.—Weisgerber, L. Galatische sprachreste.—Wiggers, R. Die grosse natur. Ein beitrag zur Platonforschung.

1. Geffcken, Johannes, 1861- 2. Classical philology—Collections.

Library of Congress PA26.G4 32-8879
Festschrift
[2] 880.4

D-16
5098

Nash, Ogden, 1902–
The animal garden, a story. Drawings by Hilary Knight. New York, M. Evans; distributed in association with Lippincott, Philadelphia [1965]
1 v. (unpaged) illus. 21 cm.

Poem.

I. Knight, Hilary. II. Title.
NN * R 3.66 a/, OC, I, Ibo PC, I, II SL (PRI 1, LC1, X1, Z1)

XBN

NATIONALISM and internationalism: essays inscribed to Carlton J. H. Hayes. Edited by Edward Mead Earle. New York, Columbia university press [1951, c1950] xvii, 508 p. 24cm.

Bibliographical footnotes.
CONTENTS.—Cultural nationalism and the makings of fame, by J. Barzun.—A secret agent's advice on America, 1797, by F. S. Childs.—"Big Jim" Larkin: a footnote to nationalism, by J. D. Clarkson.—The heavy hand of Hegel, by C. W. Cole.—H. G. Wells, British patriot in search of a world state, by E. M. Earle.—National sentiment in Klopstock's
(Continued)
NN**R X 11.54 g/ OC, I PC, 1, 2, I SL E, 1, 2, I (Z/1, LC1, X1)

NATIONALISM and internationalism... (Card 2)

odes and Bardiete, by R. Ergang.—Arthur Young, British patriot, by J. G. Gazley.—French Jacobin nationalism and Spain, by B. F. Hyslop.—Nationalism and history in the Prussian elementary schools under William II, by W. C. Langsam.—The Swiss pattern for a federated Europe, by C. Muret.—Sir John Seeley, pragmatic historian in a nationalistic age, by T. P. Peardon.—The Habsburgs and public opinion in Lombardy-Venetia, 1814-1815, by R. J. Rath.—American thought and the Communist challenge, by G. T. Robinson.—Friedrich Naumann: a German view of power and nationalism, by W. O. Shanahan.—Hitler and the revival of
(Continued)

NATIONALISM and internationalism... (Card 3)

German colonialism, by M. E. Townsend.—The nationalism of Horace Greeley, by G. G. van Deusen.—Scandinavia and the rise of modern national consciousness, by J. H. Wuorinen.

1. Nationalism and nationality. 2. Hayes, Carlton Joseph Huntley, 1882– . I. Earle, Edward Mead, 1894– , ed.

3-MCF
M23.B5

Nasica (Augusto Majani) e la sua Bologna. Scritti di Bianconi, Cantoni, Cervellati, ... Spadolini. Bologna, Tamari, 1968.
135 p. illus. 24 cm.

Foreword signed Franca D'Attimis Maniago Majani.

1. Majani, Augusto, 1867– . 2. Bologna, Italy (City)--Intellectual life. I. Bianconi, Mario.
NN * 1.72 m/b OC, I, Ib* PC, 1, 2, I SL A, 1, 2, I PR, 1 (LC1, X1, Z1) B

NARF

National Press Club of Washington, *Washington, D. C.*
Dateline: Washington; the story of national affairs journalism in the life and times of the National Press Club. Edited by Cabell Phillips [and others] Garden City, N. Y., Doubleday, 1949.
vii, 307 p. illus., ports. 22 cm.
Written to commemorate the fortieth anniversary of the National Press Club.
CONTENTS.—An introductory note, by A. Krock.—Prehistory, by D. Aikman.—From such a bond, by S. Hart.—This is how it used to be, by B. N. Timmons.—The placid twenties, by F. Knebel.—"We interrupt this program," by T. F. Koop.—Moisture, a trace, by H. J. Dodge.—"And here we sit today!" By H. Morrow.—Tradesmen's entrance, by H. J. Dodge.—"Just one more, please," by H. L. Kany and
(Continued on next card)
49-11680*
[30]

National Press Club of Washington, *Washington, D. C.*
Dateline: Washington ... 1949. (Card 2)
CONTENTS—Continued.
W. C. Bourne.—Handouts, by B. Catton.—Autocrats of the breakfast table, by C. Phillips.—World War II, by L. C. Wilson.—Passed by censor, by G. Creel, B. Price, E. Davis, and W. A. Kinney.—The diplomatic correspondent, by W. R. Deuel.—Every day is election day, by F. C. Othman.—Coverage today, by T. L. Stokes.—Journalist and Journalese, by C. B. Jones.

1. Journalism—Washington, D. C. I. Phillips, Cabell B. H., ed. II. Title.
PN4899.W29N3 1949 071.53 49-11680*

Library of Congress [30]

TB

Nationaløkonomisk forening, Copenhagen.
Professor, dr. polit. Axel Nielsen, 30.december 1880—22.maj 1951. Udgivet af Nationaløkonomisk forening. København, Gyldendal, 1951. 260 p. port. 26cm.
"Nationaløkonomisk tidsskrift—89. binds tillægshefte."

1. Nielsen, Axel Eduard Hjorth, 1880–1951. 2. Economics, 1926– . Danish authors. I. Nationaløkonomisk tidsskrift.
NN R 3.53 OS, I PC, 1, 2, I SL E, 1, 2, I (LC1, Z1, X1)

F-10
6371

NATIONALE FORSCHUNGS- UND GEDENKSTÄTTEN DER KLASSISCHEN DEUTSCHEN LITERATUR, Weimar.
Die 75-Jahr-Feier der Goethe-Institute in Weimar 1960. [Weimar, 1960] 87 p. illus., ports. 29cm. (THEIR$. Jahresgabe)

Contributions by various authors.

1. Goethe- und Schiller- Archiv, Weimar. 2. Weimar, Germany. Goethe-National-Museum. I. Nationale Forschungs- und Gedenkstätten der klassischen deutschen Literatur, Weimar. Jahresgabe. i. [Title] Fünfundsiebzig-Jahr-Feier.
NN R 3.62 c/OS, I PC, 1, 2 SL (LC1, I1, X1, Z1) [NSCM]

TB

NATIONALØKONOMISK FORENING, Copenhagen.
Til Frederik Zeuthen, 9. sept. 1958. [Redigeret af Poul Milhøj, bistået af et redaktionsudvalg] København, 1958. 411 p. port. 24cm.

"Nationaløkonomisk tidsskrift--tillægshefte til 96. bind... 1958."

1. Economics--Essays and misc. 2. Zeuthen, Frederik, 1888– . I. Milhøj, Poul, ed. II. Nationaløkonomisk tidsskrift. III. Title.
NN X 1.60 t/ (OC)I, III OS, II PC, 1, 2, I, II, III SL E, 1, 2, I, II, III (LC1, X1, Z1)

Natur und Geist; Fritz Medicus zum siebzigsten Geburtstag, 23. April 1946. Mit Porträtskizze von Cuno Amiet. Erlenbach-Zürich, E. Rentsch, 1946. 240 p. 23cm.

"Dieses Werk, herausgegeben von Hans Barth und Walter Rüegg, ist...in einer einmaligen Auflage von 680 numerierten Exemplaren...hergestellt worden. Dieses Exemplar trägt die Nummer 32."

CONTENTS.—Gratulanten-Tafel.—Aster, Ernst von. Erasmus von Rotterdam.—Barth, Hans. Die Idee der Toleranz.—Betschart, Ildefons. Theophrastus Paracelsus in religiöser Schau.—Bréhier, Emile. D'une nouvelle orientation de la pensée philosophique en France?—Ebbinghaus, Julius. Über die gegenwärtige Lage der Geistes-

(Continued)

N. Y. P. L. September 24, 1947

Naturforskeren Johannes Schmidt, hans Liv og Ekspeditioner. Skildret af Venner og Medarbejdere. Redaktion: Øjvind Winge, Å. Vedel Tåning. København, Gyldendal, 1947. 187 p. illus. 26cm.

412548B. 1. Schmidt, Johannes, 1877–1933. 2. Biology, Marine and fresh-water. I. Winge, Øjvind, 1886– , ed. II. Tåning, Åge Vedel, 1890– , ed.
N. Y. P. L. November 24, 1947

Natur und Geist... (Card 2)

wissenschaften in Deutschland.—Häberlin, Paul. Prolegomenon zur Ethik.—Hoenigswald, Richard. Homunculus, eine Problemskizze zu Goethes "Faust."—Hoffmann, Ernst. Zur Begriffsbestimmung der christlichen Philosophie.—Liechti, Walter. Selbstbesinnung des technischen Menschen.—Marti, Fritz. Göttermacht und Gottesfreiheit.—Meylan, Louis. Pestalozzi et l'éducation à l'humanité.—Schmalenbach, Herman. Macht und Recht: Platons Absage an die Politik.—Tillich, Paul. Zwei Wege der Religionsphilosophie.—Verzeichnis der Veröffentlichungen von Fritz Medicus (p. ⌈231⌉–240).

399373B. 1. Philosophy—Essays and misc. 2. Medicus, Fritz, 1876– . I. Barth, Hans, ed. II. Rüegg, Walter, ed.
N. Y. P. L. September 24, 1947

Naturwissenschaftlicher Verein, Regensburg.
...Kepler-Festschrift... Teil 1– Regensburg: Druck der graphischen Kunstanstalt H. Schiele, 1930– v. diagrs., facsims., plates, ports., tables. 23cm. (Bericht des Naturwissenschaftlichen «früher zoologisch-mineralogischen» Vereins zu Regensburg. ⟨XIX. Heft für die Jahre 1928/1930⟩.)

Bibliographies included.

CONTENTS.—Teil 1. Johannes Kepler, der kaiserliche Mathematiker... Zur Erinnerung an seinen Todestag vor 300 Jahren; im Auftrage des Naturwissenschaftlichen Vereins zu Regensburg und des Historischen Vereins der Oberpfalz und von Regensburg herausgegeben von Prof. Dr. Karl Stöckl.

1. Kepler, Johann, 1571–1630. I. Stöckl, Karl, 1873– , editor. II. Historischer Verein von Oberpfalz und Regensburg. III. Title.
N. Y. P. L. October 3, 1934

NATURFORSCHENDE GESELLSCHAFT, Davos, Switzerland.
Festschrift für die 110. Jahresversammlung der Schweizerischen naturforschenden Gesellschaft in Davos. Basel, Kommissionsverlag B. Schwabe, 1929. 270 p. illus. 23cm.

Includes bibliographies.

1. Natural history--Addresses, essays, lectures. I. Schweizerische naturforschende Gesellschaft.

NN 6.64 a/ OS, I PC, 1, I SL (LC1, X1, Z1)

NAVICULA chiloniensis; studia philologa Felici Jacoby professori chiloniensi emerito octogenario oblata. Leiden, E. Brill, 1956. x, 215 p. port. 25cm.

Bibliographical footnotes.

CONTENTS. --Der homerische Ate-Begriff und Solons Musenelegie, von G. Müller. --Des erste Lied des Demodokos, von W. Marg. --Hesiods Prometheus (Theogonie V. 507-616), von F. Wehrli. --Herakliden und Mermnaden; von O. Seel. --Zwei Erzählungen des Lyders Xanthos, von H. Diller. --Die Komposition der pseudoxenophontischen Schrift

(Continued)

NN* *R 4.57 a/POC PC, 1, 2 SL (LC1, X1, Z1, Y1)

NATURFORSCHENDE GESELLSCHAFT, Lucerne, Switzerland.
Festschrift zur 131. Jahresversammlung der Schweizerischen naturforschenden Gesellschaft in Luzern. Hrsg. von der Naturforschenden Gesellschaft Luzern. [Luzern] 1951. xvi, 169 p. illus., maps. 23cm.

Bibliographies included.

CONTENTS. —Willkommgruss. —Luzerner Naturforscher: Franz Joseph Kaufmann, Hans Bachmann, Arnold Theiler, Wilhelm Amrein, Max Düggeli. —Wissenschaftliche. Abhandlungen: Florenelemente

(Continued)

NN 3.53 OS(1b) PC, 1 SL (LC1, Z1, X1)

NAVICULA chiloniensis... (Card 2)

vom Staat der Athener, von H. Haffter. --Inschriften von Didyma Nr. 217 v. 4, von R. Harder. --Obscaenus, von A. Thierfelder. --Zur Medea des Ennius, von O. Skutsch. --Catus oder Cato? Noch einmal der Titel von Varros Logistoricus, von H. Dahlmann. --Nachträge in Ciceros Brutus, von H. Fuchs. --Ein griechischer Historiker bei Sallust, von W. Theiler. --Der korykische Greis in Vergils Georgica (IV 116-148), von E. Burck. --Tibulls erste Liebeselegie? (III, 19), von U. Knoche. --Das Charakterbild Galbas bei Tacitus, von E. Koestermann. --"Bedeutend," von H.-J. Mette.

1. Jacoby, Felix, 1876- 2. Classical studies--Collections.

NATURFORSCHENDE GESELLSCHAFT, Lucerne, Switzerland.
Festschrift zur 131. Jahresversammlung... (Card 2)

und Pflanzenverbreitung im Entlebuch und in den angrenzenden Gebieten von Obwalden, von Josef Aregger. Die Bergstürze und Rutschungen bei Sörenberg und am Hilfernpass (Entlebuch), von Jos. Kopp. Aspekte moderner Limnologie, Mitteilung aus dem Hydrobiologischen Laboratorium in Kastanienbaum (Luzern), von R. A. Vollenweider.

1. Natural history—Addresses, essays, lectures.

NEAR EASTERN archaeology in the twentieth century; essays in honor of Nelson Glueck. Edited by James A. Sanders. [1st ed.] Garden City, N.Y., Doubleday, 1970. xxiv, 406 p. illus., maps, plans, port. 25cm.

Includes bibliographical references.

CONTENTS. --Foreword; "This is for a celebration..." by J.A. Sanders. --Preface; The mind of Nelson Glueck, by F. Bamberger. --

(Continued)

NN* S 7.71 d/ OC, I, II PC, 1, 2, 3, I, II SL J, 1, 3, I, II O, 2, 3, I, II (LC1, X1, Z1)

NEAR EASTERN archaeology in the twentieth century... (Card 2)

Introduction: The phenomenon of American archaeology in the Near East, by G.E. Wright. James Henry Breasted; the idea of an oriental institute, by J.A. Wilson. The phenomenon of Israeli archaeology, by W.F. Albright. On right and wrong uses of archaeology, by R. de Vaux.--The Bronze Age: The beginnings of urbanization in Canaan, by R. Amiran. Palestine in the early Bronze Age, by P.W. Lapp. The "Middle Bronze I" period in Syria and Palestine, by W.G. Dever. Northern Canaan and the Mari texts, by A. Malamat. The saltier of Atargatis reconsidered, by

(Continued)

NEAR EASTERN archaeology in the twentieth century... (Card 3)

M.H. Pope.--The Iron Age: Symbols of deities at Zinjirli, Carthage and Hazor, by Y. Yadin. Israelite Jerusalem, by K.M. Kenyon. New aspects of the Israelite occupation in the north, by Y. Aharoni. The Megiddo stables, a reassessment, by J.B. Pritchard. The scripts in Palestine and Transjordan in the Iron Age, by J. Naveh. Ammonite and Moabite seals, by N. Avigad.--The Persian period and beyond: The cave inscriptions from Khirbet Beit Lei, by F.M. Cross, Jr. New excavations at Sardis and

(Continued)

NEAR EASTERN archaeology in the twentieth century... (Card 4)

some problems of western Anatolian archaeology, by G.M.A. Hanfmann and J.C. Waldbaum. Another deity with Dolphins? By R.D. Barnett. Archaeology and Babylonian Jewry, by J. Neusner and J.Z. Smith. A sequence of pottery from Petra, by P.J. Parr. Bibliography of Nelson Glueck, by E.K. Vogel (p. [382]-394)

1. Palestine--Archaeology. 2. Orient--Archaeology. 3. Glueck, Nelson, 1900--Bibl. I. Glueck, Nelson, 1900- . II. Sanders, J.A., ed.

ZSH

Nedergaard, Paul, 1895- , ed.

Personalhistoriske, sognehistoriske og statistiske bidrag til en dansk præste og sognehistorie (kirkelig geografi), 1849–1949. Samlet og udgivet af Paul Nedergaard... ₍Bind₎ 1, hefte 2–8; ₍bind₎ 2, hefte 1–4. København, I kommission O. Lohse, 1951–52. 2 v. 26cm.

Issued in parts, 1950–52. Parts also numbered consecutively, Hefte 2–12.

CONTENTS.—1. København stift (med Færøerne, Grønland og udlandspræster).—2. Roskilde stift.

1. Den Danske folkekirke—Hist. 2. Den Danske folkekirke—Clergy. 3. Denmark—Churches.

NN 1.53 OC PC, 1, 2, 3 SL (C1, Z2, X1)

G-10
1060

NEL primo centenario della morte: Giovanni Battista Cavedalis, 1858-1958. [Redattore responsabile: Arrigo Sedran. Portogruaro, 1958] 57 p. illus., ports. 34cm.

Bibliography, p. 57.

1. Cavedalis, Giovanni Battista, 1794-1858. I. Sedrān, Arrigo, ed. II. Sedrān, Arrigo.

NN R 8.62 e/ OC, 1b, I, IIb+ PC, 1, I SL (LC1, X1, Z1)

D-17
4665

Nelly Sachs zu Ehren. Zum 75. Geburtstag am 10. Dezember 1966. Gedichte, Beiträge, Bibliographie. Hrsg. vom Suhrkamp Verlag. (Frankfurt a. M., Suhrkamp Verlag, 1966)

238 p. with illus. 1 front. 23 cm.

Bibliography of works by and about Nelly Sachs: p. 223-234.

1. Sachs, Nelly, 1891-

NN*R 7.67 1/ OC PC,1 SL (LC1,X1,Z1)

D-17
3868

Nerman, Ture, 1886-

Den vackraste visan ... och 79 andra dikter. Utg. till Ture Nermans åttioårsdag. Stockholm, Rabén & Sjögren, 1966.

140, (1) p. 21 cm.

I. Title.

NN*R 6.67 g/ OC PC, I SL (LC1,X1,Z1)

PPB

Nestlé and Anglo-Swiss holding company ltd.

Volume jubilaire en l'honneur de Monsieur Louis E. C. Dapples...président du Conseil d'administration de Nestlé and Anglo-Swiss holding company ltd., pour son soixante-dixième anniversaire. Vevey, 1937. 804 p. incl. tables. charts, plans, plates (part col'd, mounted), port. 25cm.

Bibliographies included.

CONTENTS.—Anderson, Sir Robert. Appreciation of Dr. L. Dapples' visit to Australia and New Zealand.—Ariyoshi, Chuichi. A message from Japan.—Conti, Ettore. L'opera di Luigi Dapples come uomo di banca.—Conway, Palen. A tribute to Louis Dapples, international banker.—Garnica, Pablo de. Gratitud.—Kurz, Her-

(Continued)

N. Y. P. L. March 15, 1938

Nestlé and Anglo-Swiss holding company ltd. Volume jubilaire en... (Card 2)

mann. Die Beziehungen von Herrn. Dr. h. c. Louis Dapples zur schweizerischen Finanzwirtschaft und persönliche Reminiscenzen.—Lamont, Thomas. A tribute to Mr. Louis Dapples.—Masson, Robert. M. Louis Dapples.—McKenna, Reginald. The banker in industry.—Reymond, Arnold. Le chef, ses qualités et son rôle dans la société.—Rist, Charles. Réflexions.—Rossier, Benjamin. Rôle de Monsieur Louis Dapples dans la Société Nestlé.—Sauerbruch, E. F. Brief an Herrn Louis Dapples.—Schulthess, Edmund. Die Rolle des Unternehmers in der schweizerischen Volkswirtschaft.—Simon, Charles. Insurance in Switzerland.—Stodola, Aurel. Eine Begegnung.—Cornil, Lucien. Considérations sur les antagonismes et les incompatibilités physiologiques des vitamines.—Dutoit, Paul. Sur quelques microdosages d'éléments

(Continued)

N. Y. P. L. March 15, 1938

Nestlé and Anglo-Swiss holding company ltd. Volume jubilaire en... (Card 3)

minéraux.—Feer, Emil. Die Sauermilcharten in der Nahrung der Völker und in der modernen Medizin.—Fleisch, Alfred. Le métabolisme intermédiaire des hydrates de carbone.—Frontali, Gino. Gli oli vegetali nell'alimentazione del lattante.—Garot, Lucien. La croissance pubérale.—Gigon, Alfred. Essais préliminaires de chromatographie du sérum sanguin.—Glanzmann, Eduard. Studien zur Selter-Swift-Feerschen Krankheit (Infantile Akrodynie).—Schmid-Ganz, Madelaine. Psychologische und pädagogische Probleme bei der Feerschen Krankheit.—Hochsinger, Karl. Zur Diagnose und Therapie der Wurmfortsatzentzündung im Kindesalter.—Jehle, Ludwig. Die Nierenbecken-Entzündung beim Säugling und Kleinkind.—Kay, H. D. A recent contribution to our knowledge of the biochemistry of milk secretion: the precursors in

(Continued)

N. Y. P. L. March 15, 1938

Nestlé and Anglo-Swiss holding company ltd. Volume jubilaire en... (Card 4)

blood of the milk constituents.—Lesné, Edmond. Le rôle du bacille bovin dans l'étiologie de la méningite tuberculeuse de l'enfant.—Marañon, Gregorio. Los factores endocrinos del hambre infantil.—Michaud, Louis. Rôle de la diététique dans l'hôpital.—Péhu, Maurice. Mongolisme et syphilis infantile.—Polonovski, Michel. Les glucides du lait.—Pritchard, Eric. Condensed milk in the scientific feeding of infants. —Reuss, August. Ist die Angst vor dem Kuhmilchkasein bei der künstlichen Ernährung des Säuglings begründet?—Rohmer, Paul. Du besoin en vitamines du nourrisson.—Schweigart, H. A. Eine Ernährungsbetrachtung zur Milch.—Stheeman, H. A. Die Boxenquarantäne im Juliana Kinderkrankenhaus in 's-Gravenhage.—Suñer Ordoñez, Enrique. Alimentación del niño en España.—Taillens, Jules. Com-

(Continued)

N. Y. P. L. March 15, 1938

Nestlé and Anglo-Swiss holding company ltd. Volume jubilaire en... (Card 5)

ment doit-on comprendre la construction et l'exploitation d'une pouponnière.—Zangger, Heinrich. Vitamin- und Hormonlage — als Grundlage von Verschiebungen besonderer Giftauswirkungen.—Contribution de la Société Nestlé. Nestlé, son passé — son présent.—Bakke, Arnold. L'huile de foie de morue et d'autres poissons.—Boca, César del. L'application des méthodes physico-chimiques à l'industrie alimentaire.—Huguenin, Gustav. Herstellung von Milchprodukten einst und heute.—Loertscher, Waldemar. Quelques remarques sur le dosage des vitamines.—Neukomm, Alexandre. Contribution à l'étude de la bactériothérapie lactique. Ferments lactiques et laits fermentés.—Rafn, Willy. Die Bedeutung der Wissenschaft und die Aufgaben des Chemikers in der Milchindustrie.—Streit, Hans. Über die Gewinnung und Kontrolle von Milch

(Continued)

N. Y. P. L. March 15, 1938

Nestlé and Anglo-Swiss holding company ltd. Volume jubilaire en... (Card 6)

für die Herstellung von Dauermilchprodukten.—Thöni, Johannes. Silofutter und Kondensmilchfabrikation.—Zbinden, Christian. Aperçu sur la constitution chimique et la synthèse des vitamines A, B^1, B^2, C.—Crocker, W. P. Methods used in the milk industry for the chemical and bacteriological control.—Qvam, Olaf. Kontrolle von Gummiringen.—Sparks, J. B. The crystallization of lactose.—Borgeaud, Pierre. Quelques problèmes de la chimie colloïdale des laits concentrés.—McNab, L. M. Manufacturing principles.—Alpers, Ernst. Reinheit und Normalisierung in der deutschen Schokoladenindustrie.

Bibliographies included.

931365A. 1. Dapples, Louis E. C., 1867–1937. 2. Milk. 3. Biochemistry.
N. Y. P. L. March 15, 1938

E–10
6542

Neuburg, Germany.

Neuburg, die junge Pfalz und ihre Fürsten; Festschrift zur 450-Jahr-Feier der Gründung des Fürstentums Neuburg, hrsg. im Auftrag der Stadt Neuburg an der Donau von Josef Heider. Neuburg an der Donau, 1955. 151 p. illus., maps, facsims. 25cm.

Various contributors.
Includes bibliographies.

1. Neuburg, Germany—Hist. I. Heider, Josef, ed. t. 1955.
NN R 6.59 (OC)I ODt EDt PC,1,I SL (LC1,X1,Z1)

XAH

Neuchâtel, Switzerland (City). Université. Faculté de droit et des sciences économiques.

Recueil de travaux offert à la Société suisse des juristes à l'occasion de sa 80ème Assemblée générale. Neuchâtel, 1946.

321 p. 24cm. (Mémoires de l'Université de Neuchâtel, 20)

Bibliographical footnotes.

L-10
8241
Heft 37

NEUE Beiträge zur deutschen Grammatik, Hugo Moser zum 60. Geburtstag gewidmet. Hrsg. von Ulrich Engel und Paul Grebe. Mannheim, Dudenverlag des Bibliographischen Instituts [1969] 128 p. 23cm. (Duden-Beiträge. Heft 37)

Includes bibliographical references.

(Continued)

NN 11.69 w/ OC, I, II, III, Vbo (OS)IV PC, 1, I, II, III, IV (LC1, X1, Z1)

2

NEUE Beiträge zur deutschen Grammatik... (Card 2)

1. German languages--Grammar. I. Engel, Ulrich, ed. II. Grebe, Paul, ed. III. Moser, Hugo. IV. Series. V. Engel, Ulrich.

Copy only words underlined & Classmark-- TB

NEUE Beiträge zur geschichtlichen Landeskunde Tirols. [Festschrift für Franz Huter anlässlich der Vollendung des 70. Lebensjahres. Dargebracht von Kollegen, Schülern und dem Verlag. Hrsg. und redigiert von Ernest Troger und Georg Zwanowetz] Innsbruck, Universitätsverlag Wagner, 1969. 2 v. (522 p.) illus., ports., maps (issued in pockets) 25cm. (Tiroler Wirtschaftsstudien, Folge 26)

(Continued)

NN R 7.71 w/ OC, II, III, IV (LC1, X1, Z1) (OD)I (ED)I PC, 1, I, II, III, IV

2

NEUE Beiträge zur geschichtlichen Landeskunde Tirols. (Card 2)

"Bibliographie Franz Huter," p. [513]-518. Includes bibliographies.

1. Tyrol--Hist. I. Series. II. Troger, Ernest, ed. III. Zwanowetz, Georg, ed. IV. Huter, Franz, 1899- .

3-MAH

NEUE Beiträge zur klassischen Altertumswissenschaft; Festschrift zum 60. Geburtstag von Bernhard Schweitzer, hrsg. von Reinhard Lullies. [Stuttgart] W. Kohlhammer [1954] 419 p. illus., 91 plates, (incl. facsims.) 26cm.

Bibliographic footnotes.
"Bibliographie Bernhard Schweitzer," p. 410-415.

1. Schweitzer, Bernhard, 1892- . 2. Art, Classical—Addresses, essays, lectures. I. Lullies, Reinhard, 1907- , ed.
NN**R 9.55 g/ OC, I PC, 1, 2, I SL A, 1, 2, I (LC1, X1, Z1)

L-10
3377
Bd. 21

Neue Beiträge zur südwestdeutschen Landesgeschichte; Festschrift für Max Miller, dargebracht von Freunden und Kollegen. ₍Redigiert von Werner Fleischhauer, Walter Grube und Paul Zinsmaier₎ Stuttgart, W. Kohlhammer, 1962. viii, 359 p. illus., ports, maps. 24cm. (Baden-Würtemberg. Geschichtliche Landeskunde, Kommission für. Veröffentlichungen. Reihe B: Forschungen. Bd. 21)

Bibliographical footnotes.

1. Miller, Max, Oct. 17, 1901- . 2. Germany, Southwestern—Hist.—Addresses, essays, lectures. I. Fleischhauer, Werner, 1903- , ed. II. Series.
NN R 4.64 OC,I (OD)II (ED)II PC,1,2,I,II (LC1,X1,Z1)
₍I₎

RAA
(Neueren)

Neusprachliche Studien; Festgabe Karl Luick zu seinem sechzigsten Geburtstage dargebracht von Freunden und Schülern... Marburg a. d. Lahn: N. G. Elwert, 1925. 279 p. port. 8°. (Die Neueren Sprachen. Beiheft. ₍Nr.₎ 6.)

Contents: Ettmayer, K. Zur Intonation der Romanen. Lach, R. Sprach- und Gesangsmelos im Englischen. Koziol, H. Zur Betonung im Wiener Deutsch. Brunner, K. Einige Dialektaufnahmen aus Lancashire. Sievers, E. Zu Cynewulf. Scripture, E. W. Das Wesen des Verses. Wild, F. Über die Verstechnik des Verfassers der me. Umdichtung von Boccaccios "De claris mulieribus." Holthausen, F. Zur Textkritik me. Romanzen. Funke, O. Zum Problem "Sprachkörper und Sprachfunktion." Zwierzina, K. Mhd. ait<aget. Zachrisson, R. E. Notes on

(Continued)

N. Y. P. L. January 29, 1929

TB

NEUE Beiträge zur Wirtschaftstheorie. Festschrift anlässlich des 70. Geburtstages von Hans Mayer, unter den auspizien von Luigi Einaudi... in Verbindung mit Jean Marchal... Theo Surányi-Unger... und Francesco Vito... Hrsg. von Alexander Mahr... Wien, Springer, 1949. vi, 445 p. 24cm.

541379B. 1. Economics, 1926- 2. Mayer, Hans. I. Mahr, Alexander, ed.

NN

Neusprachliche Studien... (Card 2)

the English pronunciation of Greek v and French oi in loan-words. Pogatscher, A. Altenglisch Grendel. Ekwall, E. On some old English charters. Meyer-Lübke, W. Vom Passivum. Strauss, O. Beiträge zur Syntax der im Codex Junius enthaltenen altenglischen Dichtungen. Förster, M. Die Weltzeitalter bei den Angelsachsen. Hittmair, R. Der Begriff der Arbeit bei Langland. Priebsch, R. Von der Beicht. Eichler, A. Shakespeares The Tempest als Hofaufführung. Winkler, E. Über ein Innsbrucker Exemplar der Erstausgabe des Don Quixote. Küchler, W. Malbrough s'en va-t-en guerre. Richter, H. Zur Selbstcharakteristik Lord Byrons. Brecht, W. Annette von Droste-Hülshoff. Karpf, F. Die neueren Sprachen an den österreichischen Bundeserziehungsanstalten.

1. Luick, Karl, 1865- . 2. Philology—Essays and misc. 3. Ser.
N. Y. P. L. January 29, 1929

YAR

Neue Münchener philosophische abhandlungen; herausgegeben von E. Heller und F. Löw. Leipzig, Johann Ambrosius Barth, 1933.

3 p. l., 259 p. 23ᶜᵐ.

"Alexander Pfänder zu seinem sechzigsten geburtstag gewidmet von freunden und schülern."—2d prelim. leaf.

Contents.—Geiger, M. Alexander Pfänders methodische stellung.—Schwarz, P. Über die oberste ontologische kategorie.—Stavenhagen, K. Charismatische persönlichkeitseinungen.—Celms, T. Lebensumgebung und lebensprojektion.—Beck, M. Problem der analogie zwischen seelischen und dinglichen qualitäten.—Spiegelberg, H. Sinn und recht der begründung in der axiologischen und praktischen philosophie.—Voigtländer, E. Bemerkungen zur psychologie der gesinnungen.—Löwenstein, K. Wunsch und wünschen.—Löw, F. Über die definition.—Specht, W. Die grenzen der biologischen erfassung der persönlichkeit.—Heller, E. Über die willenshandlung.

1. Philosophy—Addresses, essays, lectures. 2. Pfänder, Alexander, 1870- I. Heller, Ernst, ed. II. Löw, Friedrich, joint ed.
₍2₎ A C 35-940
Title from N. Y. Pub. Libr. Printed by L. C.

Copy only words underlined & classmark— * YIA

NEUTESTAMENTLICHE studien für Rudolf Bultmann zu seinem siebzigsten Geburtstag am 20. August 1954. 2. berichtigte Aufl. Berlin, A. Töpelmann, 1957. 304 p. port. 24cm. (Zeitschrift für die neutestamentliche Wissenschaft und die Kunde des Urchristentums. Beihefte. 21)

Bibliographical footnotes.

1. Bultmann, Rudolf Karl, 1884- 2. Bible. N. T.--Criticism, Textual literature. 4. Bible. N. T. -- 3. Bible. N. T. and Jewish Theology. I. Series.
NN * 8.65 p/, OC (OS)I PC, 1, 2, 3, 4, I I, 1, 3 (LC1, X1, Z1)

YEA

```
Neue psychologische Studien...
Bd.12¹
München,1934.                          8°.

  Contents:
  Bd.12¹. Klemm,O. and others,editors. Ganzheit
     und Struktur; Festschrift zum 60.Geburts-
     tage Felix Kreugers.                 1934.
```

F-11
6268

Neuzelle. Festschrift zum Jubiläum der Klostergründung vor 700 Jahren. 1268-1968. Hrsg. von Joachim Fait und Joachim Fritz. München, Zürich, Schnell u. Steiner, 1968.

135 p. with illus., 68 p. of illus., front. 30 cm.

Bibliographical footnotes.

1. Neuzelle, Germany (Cistercian monastery). 2. Art, Ecclesiastical --Germany--Neuzelle. I. Fait, Joachim, ed. II. Fritz, Joachim, ed. III. Fait, Joachim. IV. Fritz, Joachim.
NN * R 5.70 1/4OC, I, II, IIIb* IVb* PC, 1, 2, I, II SL A, 1, 2, I, II (LC1, X1, Z1)

Copy only words underlined & Classmark-- ZAA

NEUSNER, JACOB, ed.

Religions in antiquity; essays in memory of Erwin Ramsdell Goodenough. Leiden, E. J. Brill, 1968. x, 688 p. illus., port. 25cm. (Studies in the history of religions (Supplement to Numen), 14)

"A bibliography of the writings of Erwin Ramsdell Goodenough," p. [621]-632.

Bibliographical footnotes.

1. Religion, Comparative. 2. Bible--Essays and misc. lectures. 3. Judaism--Addresses, essays, lectures. 4. Judaism--Essays. I. Series. II. Goodenough, Erwin Ramsdell, 1893-1965.
NN R 8.69 k/ROC, II (OS)I PC, 1, 2, 3, I, II J, 4, II (LC1, X1, Z1)

SH

NEW directions in social work; edited by Cora Kasius. New York, Harper [1954] xxi, 258 p. port. 21cm.

"To Philip Klein, social worker, educator, scholar, on the occasion of his retirement from the New York school of social work, Columbia university, September 15, 1954."

Includes bibliographies.

CONTENTS. —Introduction, by C. Kasius. —Philip Klein, by G. Hamilton. —Guiding motives in social work, by M. A. Cannon. -- The responsibilites of a socially oriented profession, by H. L. Lurie. -- The people and their government by A. J. Altmeyer. —The changing functions

(Continued)

NN ** R 11.54 p/, OC, I PC, 1, 2, I SL E, 1, 2, I (LC1, X1)

NEW directions in social work... (Card 2)

of voluntary agencies, by L. B. Granger. — Professional implications of international social work developments, by J. M. Hoey. — Needs and problems of medical care, by M. M. Davis. — The financing of social welfare, by E. M. Burns. — Social work and social reform, by D. S. Howard. — Social work education: problems for the future, by H. R. Wright. — The nature of social work knowledge, by A. J. Kahn. — Concepts and methods in social work research, by H. S. Maas and M. Wolins. — The folklore of social work, by F. Sytz.

1. Social service. 2. Klein, Philip, 1889- I. Kasius, Cora, ed.

MA

NEW YORK UNIVERSITY. Institute of fine arts.
Essays in honor of Walter Friedlaender. Edited by Marsyas: Walter Cahn [and others] [New York] Distributed by J.J. Augustin, Locust Valley, N.Y., 1965. xiii, 194 p. plates, port. 29cm. (Marsyas; studies in the history of art. Supplement 2: a special volume)

Bibliographical footnotes.

1. Friedlaender, Walter F., 1873-1966. 2. Art--Essays and misc. I. Cahn, Walter, ed. II. Marsyas; a publication by the students of the Institute of fine arts, New York University. Supplement. III. Title.

NN R 12.68 k/(OC)Is, III OSs, IIs PCs, 1s, 2s, Is, IIs, III SLs As, 1s, 2s, Is, IIs, III (LC1s, X1s, Z1s) [I]

MA

NEW YORK UNIVERSITY. Institute of Fine Arts.
Essays in memory of Karl Lehmann, edited by Lucy Freeman Sandler. [New York] Distributed by J. J. Augustin, Locust Valley, N. Y., 1964.
395 p. illus.(part mounted),facsims.,maps,plans, plates,port. 29cm. (Marsyas; studies in the history of art. Supplement I: a special volume)
"Bibliography of the writings of Karl Lehmann": p.xi-xv.

(Continued)

NN R 10.67 e/ (OC)II, IIIb*,IV OS,I PC,1,2, 3,I,II,IV SL A,1,2, 3,I,II,IV (LC1,X1,Z1)

2

NEW YORK UNIVERSITY. Institute of Fine Arts.
Essays in memory of Karl Lehmann... (Card 2)

Bibliographical footnotes.
1. Lehmann, Karl, 1894-1960. 2. Lehmann, Karl, 1894-1960--Bibl. 3. Art--Essays and misc.
I. Marsyas; a publication by the students of the Institute of Fine Arts, New York University. Supplement. II. Sandler, Lucy Freeman, 1930- , ed. III. Sandler, Lucy Freeman, 1930- IV. Title.

---

*KP
(Lakeside)

NEWBERRY LIBRARY, Chicago.
Essays in history and literature presented by fellows of the Newberry library to Stanley Pargellis. Edited by Heinz Bluhm. Chicago, The Newberry library, 1965. viii, 231 p. illus., port., facsims. 27cm.

"Designed, printed and bound at The Lakeside press."
CONTENTS.--Stanley Pargellis: Newberry librarian, 1942-1962, by

(Continued)

NN R 11.67 r/ (OC)I OS, I PC, 1, I SL R, 1, I (RI 1, RS1, LC1, X1, Z1) [I]

3

NEWBERRY LIBRARY, Chicago. Essays in history and literature... 1965. (Card 2)

R. A. Billington.--A forgotten chronicle of early fifteenth-century Venice, by H. Baron.--Valla's Encomium of St. Thomas Aquinas and the humanist conception of Christian antiquity, by H. H. Gray.--The pride of Martin Luther, by H. Bluhm.--Ronsard and Belleforest on the origins of France, by B. L. O. Richter.--Three Spanish libraries of emblem books and compendia, by K. L. Selig.--The road to Esmeraldas: the failure of a Spanish conquest in the seventeenth century, by J. L. Phelan.--Paolo Sarpi's appraisal of

(Continued)

NEWBERRY LIBRARY, Chicago. Essays in history and literature... 1965. (Card 3)

James I, by J. L. Lievsay.--The influence of Thomas Ellwood upon Milton's epics, by J. M. Patrick.--Defoe's "Queries upon the foregoing act": a defense of civil liberty in South Carolina, by J. R. Moore.--The case of Swaine versus Drage: an eighteenth-century publishing mystery solved, by P. G. Adams.--Blake's Blake, by J. H. Hagstrum.--"The infernal Hazlitt," The New monthly magazine, and the Conversations of James Northcote, R. A., by H. M. Sikes.--The history of bibliography, by A. Taylor.--Theocracy and the individual, by S. Morison.--The writings of Stanley Pargellis, by D. W. Krummel (p. 221-231).

1. Pargellis, Stanley McCrory, 1898- . I. Bluhm, Heinz, ed.

AN
(Broun, H.)

Newspaper guild of New York.
Heywood Broun as he seemed to us, by John L. Lewis, Franklin P. Adams, Herbert Bayard Swope [and others] ... biographical commentaries by Morris Watson and Ernest L. Meyer. New York, N. Y., Published for the Newspaper guild of New York, by Random house, 1940.
48 p. incl. front. 28½cm.
"A stenographic record of the Heywood Broun memorial meeting which was held under the auspices of the Newspaper guild of New York at Manhattan center ... New York, on the evening of February 12, 1940."
"First edition."
1. Broun, Heywood Campbell, 1888-1939. I. Lewis, John Llewellyn, 1880- II. Adams, Franklin Pierce, 1881- III. Title.

Library of Congress PS3503.R76Z7 41-406
~~Copy 2.~~
Copyright [6] 920.5

YBX
(Hartmann)

NICOLAI HARTMANN; der Denker und sein Werk. Fünfzehn Abhandlungen mit einer Bibliographie, hrsg. von Heinz Heimsoeth and Robert Heiss. Göttingen, Vandenhoeck & Ruprecht, 1952. 312 p. ports. 25cm.

CONTENTS. — Das Ethos der Persönlichkeit, von Nicolai Hartmann. — Nicolai Hartmann, von Robert Heiss. — Das Echte im objektiven Geiste, von Eduard Spranger. — Das Individuum in der Geschichte. Untersuchung zur Geschichtsphilosophie von N. Hartmann and M. Scheler, von Ingetrud Pape. —Die Behandlung der Tugenden bei Nicolai Hartmann, von Otto Friedrich Bollnow. — Offene Problemgeschichte, von Helmuth Plessner. --

(Continued)

NN ** R X 6.54 OCs, Is, IIs PCs, 1, Is, IIs SLs (LC1s, Z1s, X1s)

NICOLAI HARTMANN; der Denker und sein Werk. (Card 2)

Nicolai Hartmann und die Marburger Schule, von Joseph Klein. — Die Wiedergeburt der Ontologie, von Hans Pichler. —Zur Geschichte der Kategorienlehre, von Heinz Heimsoeth. —Nicolai Hartmanns Kategorialanalyse und die Idee einer Strukturlogik, von Hermann Wein. — Kategorialanalyse und physikalische Grundlagenforschung, von Hans Joachim Höfert. —Die Stellung Nicolai Hartmannsin der neueren Naturphilosophie, von Eduard May. — Die Philosophie des Organischen im Werke von Nicolai Hartmann, von Max Hartmann. — Aporetik als philosophische Methode, von Gottfried Martin. — Klugheit und Weisheit. Diskussionsproteokolle aus dem Sommersemester 1933. — Bibliographie der Werke von und über

(Continued)

NICOLAI HARTMANN; der Denker und sein Werk. (Card 3)

Nicolai Hartmann einschliesslich der Ubersetzungen, von Theodor Ballauff. (p. 286-309).

1. Hartmann, Nicolai, 1882-1951. I. Heimsoeth, Heinz, 1886- , ed. II. Heiss, Robert, 1903- , ed.

E-11
8100

NIPPERDEY, HANS CARL, 1895- , ed.
Festschrift für Erich Molitor zum 75. Geburtstag 3. Oktober 1961. München, C. H. Beck, 1962.
viii, 438, [1] p. port. 24cm.

Bibliographical footnotes.
CONTENTS. — Zur Methode der Bestimmung von privatem und offentlichem Recht, von E. Wolf. —Grundrechte, und Privatrecht, von H. C. Nipperdey. —Das Arbeitsrecht als Kritik des Burgerlichen Rechts, von F. Brecher. —Mutterschutz und Sozialstaat, von
(Continued)

NN 10.63 g/$_{4}$OC PC,1,2,3,I SL E,1,2,3,I (LC1,X1,Z1) 3

RKK

Niederdeutsche studien; festschrift für Conrad Borchling. Neumünster in Holstein, Wachholtz [1932] 4 p.l., 366 p. front. (port.) fold. map, fold. tab. 24cm.

Added t.-p.: Niederdeutsche studien. Conrad Borchling zum 20. märz 1932, dargebracht von freunden und mitarbeitern und dem verleger.
CONTENTS.—Lauffer, Otto. Der uchtvogel.—Schröder, Edward. Altpaderbörnisches.—Rooth, Erik. Die sprachform der Merseburger quellen.—Lasch, Agathe. Die altsächsischen Psalmenfragmente.—Seip, D. A. Einige bemerkungen über den mnd. einfluss auf das altnorwegische.—Katara, Pekka. Die zwölf geistlichen jungfrauen.—Petsch, Robert. Der aufbau des Helmstädter Theophilus.—Rosenhagen, Gustav. Die Wolfenbütteler spiele und das spiel des Arnold von Immesen.—Schulte-Kemminghausen, Karl. Eberhard Tappes sammlung westfälischer und holländischer
(Continued)

NN*R 3.54 OC PC,1,2,3 SL (Z1, LC1, X1)

NIPPERDEY, HANS CARL, 1895- , ed. Festschrift für Erich Molitor zum 75. (Card 2)

F. Gamillscheg. —Das Arbeitsgesetzbuch und die Lehre vom Arbeitsverhältnis, von A. Nikisch. —Das suspendierte Arbeitsverhaltnis, von H. G. Isele. —Bestandsschutz und Vertragsinhaltsschutz im Lichte der Anderungskundigung, von E. Botticher. — Die autonome Rechtsetzung im Arbeitsrecht, von H. Galperin. —Die Auslegung der Tarifvertragsnormen, von W. Herschel. —Zur kollektiven Gestaltung der Einzelarbeitsverhaltnisse, von G. Hueck. —Kollektivmacht und Individualrechte im Berufsverbandswesen, von G. Schnoor. —Gesamtvertrage und Schiedsspruche im Kassenarztrecht, von G. Kuchenhoff. —
(Continued)

Niederdeutsche studien; festschrift für Conrad Borchling. Neumünster in Holstein, Wachholtz [1932] (Card 2)

sprichwörter.—Mackel, Emil. Die namenbildung im hochstift Hildesheim mit rücksicht auf die einzelnen stände.—Meyer-Benfey, Heinrich. "Maren."—Teske, Hans. Johann Hinrich Fehrs als novellist.—Wolff, Ludwig. Vom deutschen volksmärchen.—Nörrenberg, Erich. Zwei lautliche eigentümlichkeiten der emder mundart.—Martin, Bernhard. Page, pagenwimmel, pagenstecher und konsorten.—Suolahti, Hugo. Die hundstage.—Reincke, Heinrich. "Beede."—Mitzka, Walther. Das niederländische in Deutschland. —Muller, J. W. Nnl. On(ge)tijdig; ontijg, ont, onter.—Kloeke, G. G. Zum ingwäonismenproblem (mit einer karte)—Selmer, E. W. Die sylterfriesischen verschlusslaute.—Berendsohn, W. A. Hrólfssaga kraka und Beowulf-epos.

1. German language, Low. 2. German literature, Low—Hist. and crit. 3. Borchling, Conrad August Johann Carl, 1872-

---

NIPPERDEY, HANS CARL, 1895- , ed. Festschrift für Erich Molitor zum 75. (Card 3)

Uvertarifliche Löhne und Friedenspflicht, von F. Sitzler. —Sympathie-Massnahmen im Arbeitskampf, von G. A. Bulla. — Das Prinzip der absoluten Unzumutbarkeit bei der Amtsenthebung des Betriebs- und Personalrats oder eines Mitglieds, von H. Neumann-Duesberg. — Prozesshindernde Einreden im arbeitsgerichtlichen Verfahren, von K. Sieg. — Vier Fragen aus dem Schadensersatzrecht, von L. Schnorr von Carolsfeld. —Studien zum Recht des Grundstücksmaklers, von H. Krause. — Mangelhafte Gesellschafterbeschlusse bei der GmbH, von A. Hueck. — Bibliographie Erich Molitor, von K. Molitor (p. 429-[439]

1. Law--Addresses, essays, lectures. 2. Labor--Jurisp. --Germany. 3. Molitor, Erich, 1886- . I. Title.

---

*C p.v.4366

Niederösterreichischer gewerbe-verein, *Vienna.*
Festschrift, herausgegeben vom Niederösterreichischen gewerbeverein aus anlass seiner neunzigjährigen bestandfeier. Wien [Buchdruckerei Friedrich Jasper] 1929.

104 p. incl. front. ports. 31cm.

On cover: Festbeiträge aus anlass der neunzigjährigen bestandfeier, 1839–1929.

I. Title. II. Title: Festbeiträge aus anlass der neunzigjährigen bestandfeier.

36-15808
Festschrift

Library of Congress T3.N65 606.24361

QNN

The Non-human primates and human evolution. Arr. by James A. Gavan. In memory of Earnest Albert Hooton, 1887-1954. Detroit, Wayne university press, 1955. 134 p. illus., port., map, tables. 25cm.

These papers were first presented as a symposium at the annual meeting of the American association for the advancement of science, Boston, Dec. 27, 1953.
(Continued)

NN * R 7.55 s/s OC, I, IIIbo (OS)II PC,1,2, 3,I,II SL (LC1,X1, Z1)

L-10
5721
v.7

NILS AFZELIUS tryckta skrifter, 1917-1969; bibliografi utg. till 75-årsdagen 21 januari 1969. Stockholm, 1969. xiii, 29 p. 25cm. (Sweden. Kungliga biblioteket, Stockholm. Acta Bibliothecae regiae stockholmiensis. 7)

Edited by E. Andersson.

1. Afzelius, Nils, 1894- . --Bibl. I. Series. II. Andersson, Eva.
NN R 10.71 w/$_{4}$ OCs, IIs (OD)I (ED)I PCs, 1s, I, IIs (LC1s, X1s, Z1s)

The Non-human primates and human evolution. (Card 2)

They were published in the Sept. 1954 issue of Human biology.
Includes bibliographies.
Contents.—A dedication, by J.A. Gavan.—The importance of primate studies in anthropology, by E. Hooton.—Fossil primates in the New World, by G.L. Jepsen.—The geologic history of non-hominid primates in the Old World by B. Patterson. —Comparative anatomy of New World
(Continued)

The Non-human primates and human evolution. (Card 3)

primates and its bearing on the phylogeny of anthropoid apes and men, by G.E. Erikson.—Primate evolution from the viewpoint of comparative anatomy, by D.D. Davis.—A comparative functional analysis of primate skulls by the split-line technique, by N.C. Tappen.—Metric and morphologic variations in the dentition of the Liberian chimpanzee; comparisons with anthropoid and human dentitions, by E.L. Schuman and (Continued)

The Non-human primates and human evolution. (Card 4)

C.L. Brace.—Tentative generalizations on the grouping behavior of non-human primates, by C.R. Carpenter.—Problems of mental evolution in the primates, by H.W. Nissen.—The cultural capacity of chimpanzee, by K.J. Hayes and C. Hayes.—Closing remarks, by W.L. Straus, jr.

1. Primates. 2. Evolution. 3. Hooton, Earnest Albert, 1887-1954. I. Gavan, James A., ed. II. American association for the advancement of science. III. Gavan, James A.

AN (Faleide, E.)

Nordfjord hestealslag.
Festskrift til Elias Faleide på sytti-årsdagen — 10de oktober 1949. [Sandane] Nordfjord hestealslag [1949] 169 p. illus. 23cm.

Festschrift

532405B. 1. Faleide, Elias, 1879- —Norway. 2. Horse—Breeding and raising
N. Y. P. L. July 27, 1951

RAE

Nordiska studier tillegnade Adolf Noreen på hans 50-årsdag den 13 mars 1904 af studiekamrater och lärjungar. Uppsala, K. W. Appelberg, 1904. 492 p. 25cm.

1. Philology—Addresses, essays, lectures. 2. Noreen, Adolf Gotthard, 1854-1925.

NN

F-10
1795

NORDWESTDEUTSCHER VERBAND FÜR ALTERTUMSFORSCHUNG.
Zur Ur- und Frühgeschichte Nordwestdeutschlands; neue Untersuchungen aus dem Gebiete zwischen Ijssel und Ostsee. [Festschrift zum 70. Geburtstage von K. H. Jacob-Friesen] Im Namen von Freunden, Mitarbeitern und Schülern hrsg. von Peter Zylmann. Hildesheim, A. Lax, 1956. vii, 279 p. illus., 20 plates, ports., maps (4 in pocket) 26cm.

(Continued)

NN* 2. 58 g/ (OC)I,II OS(1b+) PC,1,2,I,II SL (LC1,X1,Z1)

NORDWESTDEUTSCHER VERBAND FÜR ALTERTUMSFORSCHUNG. Zur Ur- und Frühgeschichte Nordwestdeutschlands... (Card 2)

Includes bibliographies.
CONTENTS. — Karl Hermann Jacob-Friesen, Leben und Werk, von P. Zylmann. — Faustkeil, Handspitze und Schaber, von K. J. Narr. — Altpaläolithfunde von Beulshausen an der Leine, von W. Barner. —Die Untersuchung eines zerstörten Steingrabes in der Feldmark Buchholz-Buensen im Kreis Harburg, von W. Wegewitz. — Untersuchungen an zerstörten Megalithgräbern, von E. Schlicht. — Beobachtungen an Untergräbern der Einzelgrabkultur in Niedersachsen, von (Continued)

NORDWESTDEUTSCHER VERBAND FÜR ALTERTUMSFORSCHUNG. Zur Ur- und Frühgeschichte Nordwestdeutschlands... (Card 3)

W. D. Asmus. —Funde der mittleren Altsteinzeit aus der Weser bei Bremen, von H. Schwabedissen. — Zur Frage der Einheitlichkeit der Hünenbetten, von A. E. van Giffen. —Zwei jungbronzezeitliche Hortfunde aus Niedersachsen, von G. Jacob-Friesen. — Die Steinkreise von Hamburg-Ohlsdorf, von R. Schindler. — Gedanken zu einigen späten Wendelringen Mitteldeutschlands, von E. Sprockhoff. —Die Ripdorfstufe, von G. Schwantes. —Die römische Frauenkopfattache von (Continued)

NORDWESTDEUTSCHER VERBAND FÜR ALTERTUMSFORSCHUNG. Zur Ur- und Frühgeschichte Nordwestdeutschlands... (Card 4)

Luhmühlen, Kreis Harburg, und ihre Zeit, von H.-J. Eggers. — Hölzerne Gefässe aus dem Untergrunde von Einbeck und Breslau, von F. Geschwendt. —Beginn und Art der Durchführung der vorgeschichtlichen Landesaufnahme in Oldenburg, von W. Hartung und J. Pätzold. —Die älteste Nachricht über einen Urnenfriedhof im Regierungsbezirk Stade, von H. Gummel. —Die historische Entwicklung der Forschung, insbesondere der Wurten- oder Warfenforschung, im Küstengebiet der Nordsee, von W. Haarnagel. —Der Historische Verein für Niedersachsen und (Continued)

NORDWESTDEUTSCHER VERBAND FÜR ALTERTUMSFORSCHUNG. Zur Ur- und Frühgeschichte Nordwestdeutschlands... (Card 5)

die Urgeschichte, von G. Schnath. —Das Heimatmuseum als Spiegel und als Pflegestätte der Kultur, von W. Pessler.

1. Germany--Archaeology. 2. Jacob-Friesen, Karl Hermann, 1886- . I. Zylmann, Peter, ed. II. Title.

TB

Norges handelshøyskole, Bergen, Norway.
Festskrift til I. Wedervang på 60 årsdagen 21. juli 1951 fra kollegene ved Norges handelshøyskole. [Bergen, 1951] 263 p. port., maps. 26cm.

Added t.-p.: Studier i samfunnsøkonomi, bedriftsøkonomi, rettslære, historie, geografi, språk...
Three contributions in English.
Bibliographies included.

1. Economics, 1926- . Norwegian authors. 2. Philology—Addresses, essays, lectures. 3. Wedervang, Ingvar Brynhjulf, 1891-
N. Y. P. L. January 17, 1952

STR

Norges lærerinneforbund.
Den nye barneskole; festskrift til overlærer Anna Sethne i anledning av hennes 65-årsdag 25. september 1937. Oslo, Steenske forlag [1937]
173 p., 1 l. incl. illus. (incl. port.) tables, diagrs. 26 x 21cm.
Introduction signed: For styret for Norges lærerinneforbund, Herdis Holmboe, Thora Daae, Oline Holtmon, Maren Ingebretsen.
"Av dette festskrift er trykt fire hundre og fem og åtti nummererte salgs-eksemplarer hvorav dette er nr. 288."
CONTENTS.—Sørensen, Anna. Lärarpersonligheten.—Zilliacus, Laurin. En undersökning av skolelevers uppfattning av begreppet kollektiv fred.—Hertzberg, Johan. Litt om de krav en lærer bør stille til sig selv.—Kaper, Ernst. Svingende udvikling.—Kristvik, Erling. Striden millom gamal og ny skule.—Grenness, Otto. Noen oplysninger om Landstads
(Continued on next card)
A C 38-3373
[2]

Norges lærerinneforbund. Den nye barneskole ... [1937]
(Card 2)
CONTENTS—Continued.
reviderte kirkesalmebok.—Härner, Frida. Barnet, centrum i vår läraregärning.—Andrén, Thyra. Samarbeid mellem skole og hjem.—Arnesen, Katrine. Fra forsøksarbeidet ved sagene skole.—Skaard, Åse Gruda. Skulen og psykologien.—Ribsskog, B. Forhåndskarakterer og eksamenskarakterer ved lærerskolene.—Gierow, A. Några synpunkter på historieundervisningen.—Sjöholm, L. G. Historieundervisningens grundval.—Helgeby, Maren. Samlet undervisning i 2nen klasse.—Eng, Helga. Barn og bok.—Holtmon, Oline. Håndarbeidsundervisningen.—Petersen, Margrethe. Anna Sethne set med danske øjne.—Franck, Sofus. Mælkebøtten.
1. *Sethne, Anna (Johannson) 1872- 2. Education—Scandinavia. I. Title.
A C 38-3373
New York. Public library for Library of Congress [2]

3-MNK

NORSK GRAVØRMESTER FORENING.
Norsk gravørmester forening, 1911-1961. Utgitt til 50-års jubileet, 5. mai 1951 [sic]. [Utarb. av Halfdan Rui. Oslo, Kirstes boktrykkeri, 1961]
43,[4] p. facsims.,ports. 24cm.
350 copies printed.
"Gravorliste (utdrag av adressekalendere)," p. 39-[44]
Bibliography, p. [45]
1. Metal workers--Assoc. and org.--Norway. 2. Jewelers--Assoc.and org.--Norway. I. Rui, Halfdan, ed. II. Rui, Halfdan.
NN R 4.68 e/L (OC)I,IIb* OS(1b+) PC,1,2,I A,1,2, I E,1,2,I (LC1,X1,Z1)

MAM
+

Norsk kunstforskning i det tyvende århundre, redigert av Arne Nygård-Nilssen, Anders Bugge, Thor Kielland, Haakon Shetelig. [Oslo] Cammermeyers boghandel [1945] 411 p. illus. 30cm.
Half-title: Festskrift til Harry Fett, 1875—8. september—1945.
CONTENTS.—Nygård-Nilssen, Arne. Harry Fett.—Hougen, Bjørn. Oldtidskunst.—Kloster, Robert. Folkekunst.—Bugge, Anders. Arkitektur.—Lexow, E., og B. A. Frimannslund. Billedkunst.—Kielland, Thor, and E. S. Engelstad. Kunstindustri.—Krohn-Hansen, Thv., and Roar Hauglid. Stilhistorie og farveforskning.—Willoch, Sigurd. Fremmed kunst.—Østby, Leif. Verker av blandet innhold.—Sommerfelt, W. P. Harry Fetts forfatterskap (p. 340-377)—Bakken, H. Sund. Litteraturliste med register (p. 381-412)
476893B. 1. Fett, Harry Per, 1875- 2. Fett, Harry Per, 1875- —Bibl. 3. Art. 4. Art, Norwegian. 5. Art, Norwegian—Bibl. I. Nygård-Nilssen, Arne, 1899- , ed.
N. Y. P. L. June 23, 1950

F-10
2042
NORSK litteraturvitenskap i det 20 århundre; festskrift til Francis Bull på 70-årsdagen. Oslo, Gyldendal, 1957. 453 p. port. 27cm.
"Denne bok vil i form av biografier og selvbiografier gi et omriss av norsk litteraturforskning i tiden fra 1900 til midten av 1950-årene."
1. Norwegian literature--Hist. and crit., 20th cent. 2. Bull, Francis, 1887- . 3. Norway--Biog.
NN 3.58 g/ OC PC,1,2,3 SL (LC1,X1,Z1,C1,Y1)

E-12
9057
Northern geographical essays in honour of G. H. J. Daysh, edited by J. W. House. Newcastle-upon-Tyne, Oriel P., 1966 [i. e. 1967]
[20], 374 p. front. (port.) 2 plates, maps, tables, diagrs. 25 cm.
Includes bibliographical references.
(Continued)
NN * R 6.67 1/ OC,I PC,1,2,3,I SL E,1,2,3, I (LC1,X1,Z1)
2

NORTHERN geographical essays in honour of G.H.J. Daysh... (Card 2)
1. Daysh, George Henry John. 2. Regional planning--Gt.Br. 3. Regional planning. I. House, John William, ed.

F-11
787
NORTHWESTERN UNIVERSITY, Evanston Ill. Geography, Dept. of.
Malcolm Jarvis Proudfoot memorial volume. Evanston, Ill., 1957. v, 140 p. illus., port., maps. 28cm. (Northwestern university studies in geography, no. 2)
At head of title: The William and Marian Haas research fund.
Includes bibliographies.
1. Proudfoot, Malcolm Jarvis, 1907-1955. 2. Economics--Essays and misc. I. Series.
NN R 5.66 g/ OS,I PC,1,2,I SL E,1,2 (LC1,X1,Z1)

JLD
72-675
La Notion d'un Marché commun dans un processus d'intégration. Mélanges offerts à Rudolf Regul. Bruges, College of Europe, [Dijver, 11], 1969.
258 p. port., tables. 22 cm. (College of Europe, Bruges. Studies in contemporary European issues. 6)
English, French or German.
Bibliography: p. 111-114.
CONTENTS: Préface, par J. Rey.—Hommage, par H. Brugmans.—Widmung eines Schülers, von P. Pabst.—Europa und eine Weltentwicklungsstrategie, von J. Tinbergen.—Les stimulants au dé-
(Continued)
NN* 4.72 w/J OC (OS)I PC, 1,2,3,I SL E,1,2,3 (LC1, X1,Z1)
3

La NOTION d'un Marché commun dans un processus d'intégration. Mélanges offerts à Rudolf Regul. (Card 2)
veloppement, par A. Campolongo.—Les industries nouvelles et le Marché commun, par H. Aujac.—Interventions publiques en faveur de la recherche-développement et Marché commun, par P. Maillet.—Concentrations nationales ou intra-communautaires? par J. Chabert.—Economic integration and co-operation in a disintegrated world, by B. Fritsch.—Zusammenhalt der Gemeinschaft nach aussen, von W. Renner.—Monnaie européenne et processus d'intégration, par J. Denizet.—La nécessité, les possibilités et les limites d'une politique économique régionale communautaire, par N. Vanhove.—Probleme eines wettbewerbsorientierten Subventionsmodells für den

La NOTION d'un Marché commun dans un processus d'integration. Mélanges offerts à Rudolf Regul. (Card 3)

Steinkohlenbergbau der Gemeinschaft im Rahmen einer gemeinschaftlichen Energiepolitik, von O. Schumm.—Eingliederung der Landwirtschaft in die Wachstumswirtschaft des Gemeinsamen Marktes, von H.-B. Krohn.—Les pays européens face au développement de leur système d'enseignement, par J.-P. Jallade.—Pour un Marché commun de la recherche économique, par J.-P. Abraham.—Verzeichnis der Veröffentlichungen von Rudolf Regul.

1. European Economic Community. 2. Economic integration --Europe. 3. Regul, Rudolf. I. Series.

MNO
+

NOTRE DAME DE REIMS, France (Cathedral)
Tresor de la cathédrale de Reims. Photographié par A. Marguet & A. Dauphinot. Text par M. l'abbé Cerf. Dédié à Son éminence monseigneur le cardinal Th. Gousset. Paris, Veuve Berger-Levrault & fils, 1867. [9], 67 [i.e. 71] p. 88 mounted photos. 35cm.
No. 32 of 200 copies.
Dedication signed: A. Marguet; A. Dauphinot.

(Continued)

NN S 9.69 w/a(OC)I, II, IIbo, III, IIIbo OS PC, 1, 2, I, II, III SL A, 1, 2, I, II, III (LC1, X1, Z1)

2

NOTRE DAME DE REIMS, France (Cathedral). Tresor de la cathédrale de Reims. (Card 2)

Text comprises descriptive commentary to the illustrations.
Letterpress throughout.

1. Church plate--France--Paris. 2. Ecclesiastical vestments--France--Reims. I. Cerf, Charles. II. Marguet, A. III. Dauphinot, A.

---

* QPZ

NOWAK-ROMANOWICZ, ALINA.
Józef Elsner; zarys życia i twórczości. Katowice, Wydaw. "Śląsk," 1958. 55, [5] p. illus., ports., facsims., music. 22cm.

"Wykaz ważniejszych kompozycji i prac teoretycznych Elsnera," p. 55-[56]

1. Elsner, Josef Xaver, 1769-1854.
NN R 5.59 m/OC PC, 1 SL MU, 1 S, 1 (LCE 1, LC1, X1, Z1)

Copy only words underlined & classmark— BYV
+

NÚMERO comemorativo do IV centenário da morte de São Francisco Xavier. [Bastorá, Tip. Rangel, 1952] xii, 162 p. illus., ports (part col. mounted), fold. map. 25cm. (Instituto Vasco da Gama. Boletim. no. 69)

Bibliographical footnotes.

1. Francis Xavier, Saint, 1506-1552.

NN X 12.56 d/ OI (PC).1 (Z1, LC2, X1) [I]

Write on slip words underlined below and class mark— *DM

Numéro spécial consacré à Victor Hugo à l'occasion du cinquantenaire de sa mort. [Articles by Romain Rolland, Heinrich Mann, and others.]

(Europe. Paris, 1935. 1935, juin 15, p. 1-177. plates.)

form 400b [xi-6-33 25m]

D-12
5969

O. V. DE L. MILOSZ, 1877-1939. Paris, A. Silvaire [1959] 222 p. port., facsim. 23cm. (Collection Les lettres)

Letters and articles by various contributers, including a few letters by Milosz.
"Bibliographie des éditions originales," p. [213] -217. "Publications originales en periodiques," p. [218] -222.

1. Milosz, Oscar Vladislas, 1877-1939.
NN 8. 60 m/ OC PC, 1 SL S, 1 (LC1, X1, Z1)

---

*QW

O Zdeňku Nejedlém, stati a projevy k jeho sedmdesátinám [uspořadal V. Pekárek] Praha, Orbis, 1948. 296 p. port. 24cm.

"Spisy Zdeňka Nejedlého," p. 289-291.
Bibliography, p. 293-196.

1. Nejedlý, Zdeněk, 1878- . I. Pekárek, V., ed.

NN**Z 4.54 OC, I, Ib PC, 1, I SL S, 1, I (LC1, Z1, X1)

E-10
6587

OBERHESSISCHE GESELLSCHAFT FÜR NATUR- UND HEILKUNDE, Giessen.
Festschrift für W. J. Schmidt zum 70. Geburtstage 21. Februar 1954. Giessen, W. Schmitz, 1954. 225 p. illus., port. 24cm.

Appeared simultaneously as Bericht der Oberhessischen Gesellschaft für Natur- und Heilkunde zu Giessen, n. F., Naturwissenschaftliche Abt., Bd. 27, 1954.

(Continued)

NN 11. 58 g/ (OC)Ib+, I, Ib, II OS PC, 1, 2, I, II SL (LC1, X1, Z1)

OBERHESSISCHE GESELLSCHAFT FÜR NATUR- UND HEILKUNDE, Giessen. Festschrift für W. J. Schmidt zum 70. Geburtstage... (Card 2)

Includes bibliographies.
CONTENTS. — Ansprache bei der Festsitzung beider Abteilungen der Oberhessischen Gesellschaft aus Anlass des 70. Geburtstages von Professor Dr. W. J. Schmidt, von W. E. Ankel. — Die polarisationsoptischen Untersuchungen W. J. Schmidts und ihre Bedeutung für die Elektronenmikroskopie (Festrede), von L. H. Bretschneider. — Bedeutung und Möglichkeiten der Polarisationsmikroskopie in der Medizin, von H. P. Missmahl. — Zur Frage der vegetativen Steuerung

(Continued)

OBERHESSISCHE GESELLSCHAFT FÜR NATUR- UND HEILKUNDE, Giessen. Festschrift für W.J. Schmidt zum 70. Geburtstage... (Card 3)

zentralnervöser Funktionen, von E. Schuchardt. — Die Bedeutung des polarisierten Lichtes für die Knochenpathologie, dargestellt an Beispielen eigener Erfahrung, von M. Weber. — Die Natur und die Herkunft roter Lipochrome in der Klasse der Vögel, von O. Völker. — Zoologie in tierärzt lichen Studium und Beruf, von W. Schauder. --Studien über die Empfindlichkeit und die Genauigkeit der Chinalizarinmethode bei der Bestimmung kleinster Mengen Bor, von K. Scharrer und H. Kühn. — Die Feinstruktur des Kragens bei den Choanocyten der

(Continued)

OBERHESSISCHE GESELLSCHAFT FÜR NATUR- UND HEILKUNDE, Giessen. Festschrift für W.J. Schmidt zum 70. Geburtstage... (Card 4)

Spongilliden, von E.F. Kilian. — Beobachtungen am Hirnrelief der Aussenfläche des Schädels, am Endokranium und der Hirnform des südamerikanischen Nachtaffen Aotes, Ceboidea, von H. Hofer. — Zur Kenntnis des Feinbaues der Flottoblastenschalen von Plumatella repens (L.) und Cristatella mucedo Cuvier, von H. Lerner. — Eine Elytrenanomalie bei Carabus cancellatus Ill. und Versuche zu ihrer Entstehung an Carabus granulatus L., von H. Scherf. — Aur Systematik der Farben, insbesondere der Interferenz- farben, von S. Rösch. —

(Continued)

OBERHESSISCHE GESELLSCHAFT FÜR NATUR- UND HEILKUNDE, Giessen. Festschrift für W.J. Schmidt zum 70. Geburtstage... (Card 5)

Zement und Wurzelhaut menschlicher Zähne nach polarisationsoptischer Untersuchung, von A. Keil. —On hard wax secreted by Cereplastes and by the Madagascar lac insect, by S. Mahdihassan. —Praktische Anwendungen der Polarisationsmikroskopie in der Pflanzenanalyse (Pulveranalyse) von A. Czaja. —Arzt und Priester in Pergamon, von H. Erhard. — Polarisationsoptische Untersuchungen am Nierenparenchym, von H. Rollhäuser. —Die Vorbereitung der Kalkschalenbildung in den

(Continued)

OBERHESSISCHE GESELLSCHAFT FÜR NATUR- UND HEILKUNDE, Giessen. Festschrift für W.J. Schmidt zum 70. (Geburstage... (Card 6)

Cyprisstadien der Balaniden, von O. Kuhn und H. Fuchs. —Zum Wesen der sog. idiopathischen Haemosiderosis pulmonum, von G. Herzog. — Sekretorische Vorgänge in den Ganglienzellen der Netzhaut und ihre biologische Bedeutung, von H. Becher.

1. Schmidt, Wilhelm J., 1884- . 2. Biology--Addresses, essays, lectures. I. Völker, Otto, 1907- , ed. II. Title.

* PBN

Occident and Orient; being studies in Semitic philology and literature, Jewish history and philosophy and folklore in the widest sense. In honour of Haham Dr. M. Gaster's 80th birthday. Gaster anniversary volume, edited by Bruno Schindler...in collaboration with A. Marmorstein... London: Taylor's foreign press [1936] xviii, 570 p. illus., 8 pl. (incl. facsims., front. «port.») 25½cm.

Binder's title: Gaster anniversary volume.
"List of books and papers by Dr. M. Gaster, by Bruno Schindler," p. 21-36.
Bibliographical footnotes.

(Continued)

N. Y. P. L. June 16, 1937

Occident and Orient... (Card 2)

CONTENTS.—Schindler, B. Preface.—Schwarzfeld, M. Biographical sketch of Dr. Gaster's early days.—Bensusan, S. L. Moses Gaster.—Cartojan, N. Dr. M. Gaster's activity in the field of Roumanian language, literature and folk lore.—Schindler, B. List of books and papers of Dr. Gaster.—Adler, E. N. Jewish art.—Canney, M. A. Boats and ships in temples and tombs.—Cassuto, Umberto. Some poems of Joseph Sarphati.—Daiches, Samuel. Interpretation of Psalm CXVI.—Sola Pool, D. de. Saul Brown (Pardo), first known chazan in New York.—Driver, G. R. Confused Hebrew roots.—Drower, E. S. The Kaprana.—Duschinsky, C. May a woman be a shoheteth? —Eitrem, S. To pull by the hair.—Eisler, Robert. The Sadoqite Book of the New Covenant.—Elbogen, Ismar. Briefwechsel zwischen Leopold Zunz und Frederick D. Mocatta.—Gaster, T. H. A new Asianic language.—Gottheil, R. Some responsa of Maimonides.—Rosenbaum-Gruenfeld, Judith. A contribution towards the sources of

(Continued)

N. Y. P. L. June 16, 1937

Occident and Orient... (Card 3)

the Ma'ase Buch.—Grunwald, M. Beiträge zur Volkskunde und Kunstgeschichte.—Halliday, W. R. A modern Greek folk-tale from Samos.—Hasluck, M. An Albanian ballad on the assassination in 1389 of Sultan Murad I on Kosovo plain.—Heller, B. Beiträge zur Stoff-und Quellengeschichte des Ma'assebuchs.—Herford, R. T. Pirke Aboth.—Higger, Michael. The formation of the child.—Hyamson, A. M. Solomon da Costa and the British museum.—James, E. O. Ethical monotheism.—Jopson, N. B. Literary style in Judaeo-Spanish.—Kaminka, A. The meaning of some difficult passages in the Psalter.—Kaufmann, F. Kunst und Religion.—Kisch, Guido. The Jewry law of the "Sachsenspiegel."—Krappe, A. H. The birth of Eve.—Krauss, Samuel. Der richtige Sinn von "Schrecken in der Nacht."—Landau, J. L. The conflict between Judah and Ephraim.—Langdon, S. The liturgical series, "From the assembly wisdom is departed." —Langstadt, Erich. Zu Philos Begriff der Demokratie.—Lauterbach, J. Z. Unpublished

(Continued)

N. Y. P. L. June 16, 1937

Occident and Orient... (Card 4)

parts of the Yalkut ha-Makiri on Hosea and Micah.—Löw, Immanuel. Marmor.—Loewe, Herbert. Scholars, builders and peace.—Loewinger, S. Letters of Moses Gaster to Wilhelm Bacher.—Margoliouth, D. S. The date of Ben Sira.—Marmorstein, A. Comparisons between Greek and Jewish religious customs and popular usages.—Marx, Alexander. William Wright's letters to Moritz Steinschneider.—Morgenstern, Julian. The new year for kings.—Oesterley, W. O. E. Persian angelology and demonology.—Pettazzoni, R. Confession of sins in Hittite religion.—Rawidowicz, S. Moses Mendelssohn, the German and Jewish philosopher.—Rechnitz, W. Horace's prayer to Apollo Palatinus.—Roth, Cecil. The Jews in Minorca under British rule (1708–1781).—Schindler, Bruno. The dramatic character of the old Chinese harvest festival songs.—Scholem, G. David ben Abraham ha-laban — ein unbekannter jüdischer Mystiker.—

(Continued)

N. Y. P. L. June 16, 1937

Occident and Orient... (Card 5)

Stevenson, W. B. Pictorial numbers as used by poets and chroniclers.—Strauss, Bertha, and Bruno Strauss. Wer ist der "Mann von Stande?"—Ward, H. G. A Spanish legend in English literature.—Weinreich, Max. Form versus psychic function in Yiddish.—Wischnitzer-Bernstein, Rachel. Der Streiter des Herrn.—Yates, D. E. A Romani tale.—Gelber, L. N. Dr. M. Gaster's letters from the time of the Berlin congress, 1878.—Buechler, Adolph. Notes on the religious position of the 'Canaanite slave' a century before and after the destruction of the second temple.

SCHIFF COLLECTION.

881258A. 1. Essays, Jewish—Collections. 2. Gaster, Moses, 1856- . I. Schindler, Bruno, 1882- , ed. II. Marmorstein, Arthur, 1882-

N. Y. P. L. June 16, 1937

* MF

Ochsner, Martin.

Festschrift zur 125 jährigen Jubelfeier der Musikgesellschaft Concordia Einsiedeln, von Martin Ochsner. 1806–1931. Einsiedeln: Verlagsanstalt Benziger & Co., A.G.[, 1931.] 102 p. incl. tables. front., plates. 21cm.

"I. and II. Teil, zweite Auflage."
"Quellen," p. 3.

Festschrift

CARNEGIE CORPORATION OF NEW YORK.

648589A. 1. Music—Assoc. and org.—Switzerland—Einsiedeln. I. Title.

N. Y. P. L. July 14, 1933

SES

Öffentliche Hand und Wirtschaftsgestaltung; Beiträge zur Erkenntnis der Problematik gegenwärtiger Wirtschaftsgestaltung. Leipzig: G. A. Gloeckner, 1931. viii, 214 p. 25cm.

Added t.-p.: Festschrift für Kurt Wiedenfeld zum 60. Geburtstag...herausgegeben von Max Richard Behm.

CONTENTS.—Ursachen und Methoden des Staatseingriffs in die Kartellpreisbildung. Von B. Rogowsky.—Die Betriebstypen der freien und der gebundenen Wirtschaft. Von W. Mahlberg.—Die wirtschaftliche Bedeutung der Publizitätspflichten im neuen Aktienrechtsentwurf. Von E. Geldmacher.—Die Kontrolle der öffentlichen Unternehmungen. Von W. Adler.—Die Genossenschaftsidee in Staat und Wirtschaft. Von J. Kempkens.—Öffentliche Hand und Grundstücksverkehr. Von W. Ruscheweyh.

(Continued)

N. Y. P. L. September 10, 1934

Öffentliche Hand und Wirtschaftsgestaltung... (Card 2)

—Die öffentliche Energiewirtschaft und die Betätigung der öffentlichen Hand. Von E. Ledermann.—Die staatliche Exportförderungspolitik. Von G. Herrmann.—Die öffentliche Hand im Kreditverkehr. Von M. R. Behm.

686830A. 1. Wiedenfeld, Kurt, 1871- . 2. Industry and state—Germany. I. Behm, Max Richard, editor. II. Title: Festschrift für Kurt Wiedenfeld.
N. Y. P. L. September 10, 1934

D-14
1093

OEHLER, KLAUS, ed.
Einsichten; Gerhard Krüger, zum 60. Geburtstag. [Hrsg. Klaus Oehler und Richard Schaeffler] Frankfurt am Main, V. Klostermann [1962] 398 p. 22cm.

CONTENTS.--Tod und Unsterblichkeit, von W. Anz.--Zur Frage einer "philosophischen Theologie", von R. Bultmann.--Individuum und Kategorie, von W. Cramer.--Zur Problematik des Selbstverständnisses, (Continued)

NN R 3.63 e/;OC, I, IIbo, IIIbo PC, 1, 2, I SL (LC1, X1, Z1)
[I]

OEHLER, KLAUS, ed. Einsichten... (Card 2)

von H.-G. Gadamer.--Hiob, von K. Jaspers.--Der moderne Wahrheitsbegriff, von W. Kamlah.--Der Mensch als Thema der Geschichte, von H. Kuhn.--Hegels Aufhebung der christlichen Religion, von K. Löwith.--Philosophiegeschichte als Philosophie, von H. Lübbe.--Das aristotelische Argument: Ein Mensch zeugt einen Menschen, von K. Oehler.--Über die Wahrheit der platonischen Mythen, von J. Pieper.--Wahrheit und Geschichte, von R. Schaeffler.--Jesus Christus und die Geschichte nach der Offenbarung des Johannes, von H. Schlier.--Das Problem der absoluten

(Continued)

OEHLER, KLAUS, ed. Einsichten... (Card 3)

Reflexion, von W. Schulz.--Zu Mendelssohns "Sache Gottes oder die gerettete Vorsehung", von L. Strauss.--Kopernikus, Kepler, Galilei, von C.F. von Weizsäcker.--Verzeichnis der Werke von Gerhard Krüger.

1. Krüger, Gerhard, 1902- . 2. Philosophy--Addresses, essays, lectures. I. Schaeffler, Richard, joint ed. II. Oehler, Klaus. III. Schaeffler, Richard.

E-10
8332

ÖSTERREICH und die europäische Agrargemeinschaft. Festschrift für Dr. h.c. Ing. Vinzenz Schumy zum 80. Geburtstag. [Wien] Österreichischer Agrarverlag, 1958. 303 p. port. 24cm.

"Das Schrifttum von Dr. h.c. Ing. Vinzenz Schumy," p. 301-303.

1. Agriculture--Economics--Austria. 2. Agriculture--Economics--Europe. 3. Schumy, Vinzenz, 1878- .
NN R 7.59 m/ OC PC, 1, 2, 3 SL E, 1, 2, 3 (LC1, X1, Z1)

D-16
1202

ÖSTERREICHISCHE ZENTRAL-LANDWIRTSCHAFTSMESSE, Wels, Austria.
80 Jahre Österreichische Zentrallandwirtschaftsmesse Wels, Welser Volksfest, 1878-1958; Festschrift. [Zusammengestellt und verantwortlich für den Inhalt: G. Trathnigg und K. Holter. Wels, Werbe- und Presseabteilung, 1958] 63 p. illus., facsims. 21cm.

1. Agriculture--Exhibitions--Austria--Wels. I. Trathnigg, Gilbert, ed. II. Holter, Kurt. i.[Title] Achtzig
NN 4.66 p/ (OC)I, II OS (1b) PC, 1, I, II SL (LC1, X1, Z1)

VDE

ÖSTERREICHISCHER VEREIN FÜR VERMESSUNGSWESEN.
Festschrift Eduard Doležal; zum siebzigsten Geburtstage am 2. März 1932 gewidmet vom Österreichischen Verein für Vermessungswesen. Wien [1932?] xl, 198 p. illus., port. 26cm.

Includes bibliographies.
CONTENTS.--Zur Berechnung von Geoidundulationen aus Schwerkraftstörungen, von F. Ackerl.--Zur Fehlertheorie der Verbindungsgeraden geodätisch ermittelter Punkte, von A. Basch.--Die neuen Katastral- (Continued)

NN ** 7.56 j/ OC PC, 1, 2, I SL ST, 1, 2, I (LC1, X1, Z1)

ÖSTERREICHISCHER VEREIN FÜR VERMESSUNGSWESEN.
Festschrift Eduard Dolezal... (Card 2)

mappen Österreichs, von E. Demmler.--Über die Ausfüllung eines festen Rahmens durch Nadirtriangulation, von S. Finsterwalder.--Die Vorteile der gegenwärtigen Organisation des bundesstaatlichen Vermessungsdienstes, von A. Gromann.--Räumliches Rückwärtseinschneiden aus zwei Festpunkten, von A. Haerpfer.--Zur Ausgleichung nach der Methode des grössten Produktes nebst einem Beitrag zur Gewichtsverteilung, von E. Hellebrand.--Die Bestimmung der Geoidundulationen aus Schwerkraftwerten, von F. Hopfner.--Das Seitswärtseinschneiden im Raum, von J. Koppmair.--Die Aufsuchung und die Widerherstellung verlorengegangener trigonometrisch bestimmter Punkte, von K. Lego.-- (Continued)

ÖSTERREICHISCHER VEREIN FÜR VERMESSUNGSWESEN
Festschrift Eduard Dolezal... (Card 3)

Grenzpunktberechnung und rechnerische Ausschaltung grober Beobachtungsfehler im Strahlenmessverfahren, von K. Levasseur.--Eine Denkmalsaufnahme durch einfache Bildmessung, von H. Löschner.--Ermittlung der wahrscheinlichsten Punktlage aus Achsenabschnitten, von L. Maly.--Projekt einer Katastervermessung Spaniens mittels Luftphotogrammetrie, von F. Manek.--Die Bestimmung des Verhältnisses der Katastertriangulierung von Tirol zur Gradmessungstriangulierung, von H. Rohrer.--Über Schwerpunktbeziehungen bei einem fehlerzeigenden Vielecke, von R. Schumann.--Die "Aufgabe des unzugänglichen Abstandes" (Hansen-Problem) in vektoranalytischer Behandlung, von J. Sébor.--Der (Continued)

ÖSTERREICHISCHER VEREIN FÜR VERMESSUNGSWESEN
Festschrift Eduard Dolezal... (Card 4)

technische Grundgedanke photogrammetrischer, Seilaufnahmen, von F. Skrobanek. —Über die Ausgleichung unvollständiger Richtungssätze nach der Methode der Ausgleichung direkter Beobachtungen, von V. Theimer. — Der Abschlussfehler in langen Polygonzügen, von K. Ulbrich. —Über den sphärischen Exzess, von S. Wellisch. —Gemeinsame Bestimmung der Polhöhe φ und der Uhrkorrektion Δu mit Hilfe von Zenitdistanzen, von P. Werkmeister. —Grubengrenzen in alter Zeit, von P. Wilski. —Ergänzungsgeräte zu einem Feldtheodolit für Neuaufnahmszwecke, von K. Zaar. Bildpolygonierung bei gleichmässiger Nadirdistanz und Geländeneigung, von A. Buchholtz.

1. Surveying, 1932. 2. Dolezal, Eduard, 1862- . I. Title.

3-MAS
OETTINGER, KARL, ed.
Festschrift für Hans Sedlmayr [hrsg. von Karl Oettinger und Mohammed Rassem] München, C.H. Beck, 1902. 355 p. illus., plates. 24cm.

Contributions in German or Italian.
Bibliographical footnotes.
CONTENTS. —Die Irrealität des Kunstwerks, von H. Conrad-Martius. —Zur Ontogenese der Kunst, von H. Kuhn. —Arbeit oder Kunst, von M. Rassem. —Bemerkungen zur Bildhauerdarstellung des Nanni di Banco,
(Continued)

NN R 9.62 g/B OC, I PC, 1, 2, 3, I SL A, 1, 2, 3, I (LC1, X1, Z1)
[I] 3

OETTINGER, KARL, ed. Festschrift für Hans Sedlmayr... (Card 2)

von H. von Einem. —Gedanken zur Plastik, von E. Gradmann. —Sul concetto di tipologia architettonica, di G. C. Argan. —Über die kunstgeschichtlichen Begriffe Stil und Sprache, von W. Weidlé. — Bemerkungen zu den Begriffen Herrschaft und Legitimität, von O. Brunner. —Zur Herkunft der Heraldik, von O. Höfler. —Laube, Garten und Wald; zu einer Theorie der süddeutschen Sakralkunst, 1470-1520, von K. Oettingen. — Umrisse zur Geschichte der Ausstattung von St. Peter in Rom von Paul III bis Paul V, 1547-1606, von H. Siebenhüner. —Aus der Frühzeit der Wiener
(Continued)

OETTINGER, KARL, ed. Festschrift für Hans Sedlmayr... (Card 3)

Schule der Kunstgeschichte: Rudolf Eitelberger und Leo Thun, von T. von Borodajkewycz. —Verzeichnis der Schriften Hans Sedlmayrs.

1. Sedlmayr, Hans, 1896- . 2. Art--Essays and misc. 3. Sedlmayr, Hans --Bibl. I. Rassem, Mohammed, 1922- , joint ed.

---

*PBS
Offenbach am Main, Germany. Israelitische Religionsgemeinde.
...Max Dienemann zum 60. Geburtstag gewidmet vom Vorstand der Israelitischen Religionsgemeinde Offenbach am Main, unter Mitwirkung von Leo Baeck, Martin Buber, Ismar Elbogen ...[und anderen] Frankfurt am Main: J. Kauffmann, 1935. 102 p. pl. 23½cm.

Title in Hebrew at head of title.
CONTENTS.—Zur Einführung. Verzeichnis der Veröffentlichungen, von Siegfried Guggenheim.—Glauben, von Leo Baeck.—Gespräch um Gott, von Martin Buber.—Von den Anfängen der gottesdienstlichen Reform im deutschen Judentum, von Ismar El-

(Continued)

N. Y. P. L. March 10, 1939

Offenbach am Main, Germany. Israelitische Religionsgemeinde.
...Max Dienemann... (Card 2)

bogen.—Der Rest Israels, von Max Grünewald.—Eine Sederschüssel aus dem 16. Jahrhundert, von Bruno Italiener.—Aron Chorin, von Paul Lazarus.—Von der Eigenart der klassischen Handhabung des jüdischen Religionsgesetzes im Rheingebiet, von Sali Levi.—Gesetz und Freiheit, von C. G. Montefiore.—"Religionsgesetze" oder "jüdische Lebensform"? Von Caesar Seligmann.—Religionsgesetzliche und religionsphilosophische Frömmigkeit im Judentum, von Max Wiener.—Zur Interpretation des Propheten Habakuk, von Eugen Täubler.

972991A. 1. Dienemann, Max, 1875- . 2. Judaism. I. Title.
N. Y. P. L. March 10, 1939

YAR
OFFENER Horizont; Festschrift für Karl Jaspers [hrsg. von Klaus Piper] München, R. Piper [1953] 463 p. port. 25cm.

Includes bibliographies.
CONTENTS. —Die Gottesmörder, von A. Camus. —Die theologische Bestreitung des philosophischen Glaubens, von O. Hammelsbeck. — Wesenszüge des östlichen Denkens, von F. Hashimoto. —Das Problem der Autorität, von G. Krüger. —Philosophie und philosophische Logik bei Jaspers. Ihr Verhältnis zueinander, von E. Mayer. —Stücke aus einer "Geburt der Philosophie", von J. Ortega y Gasset. —Geschichte der
(Continued)

NN**R X 8.53 OC, I, Ib PC, I, 2, I SL (Z1, LC1, X1)

OFFENER Horizont... (Card 2)

Philosophie als kontinuierliche Schöpfung der Menschheit auf dem Wege der Kommunikation, von P. Ricoeur. —Wert und Grenze der Wissenschaft, von K. Rossmann. —Brief an Karl Jaspers, von R. Gaupp. — Psychopathologie und akademischer Unterricht, von H. W. Gruhle. — Pathologie des sozialen Kontaktes, von K. Kolle. —Existenzphilosophische Richtungen in der modernen Psychopathologie, von R. de Rosa. —Fünfzig Jahre Mendelforschung, von F. Oehlkers. —Um ein neues Bild vom Organismus, von A. Portmann. —Ideologie und Terror, von H. Arendt. —Der Kriegsdienst der Christen in der Kirche des Altertums, von H. v. Campenhausen. —Tragweite und Grenzen des politischen Handelns, von J. Hersch. — Die zweifache Krise, von
(Continued)

OFFENER Horizont... (Card 3)

G. Mann. —Über die Menschenverachtung, von H. Plessner. —Der Gestaltwandel des europäischen Unternehmers, von E. Salin. —Der Mensch und seine Wandlungen, von A. Weber. —Über die Sendung des Dichters, von S. Andres. —Philosophie, Dichtung und Humanität, von W. Kaufmann. —Das Frankfurter Goethemuseum, von E. Beutler. — Die antike Kunst in der modernen Welt, von L. Curtius. —Das Ereignis des Schönen, von G. Nebel. —Kunstkrise und Kunsterziehung, von E. Preetorius. —Anliegen und Gegenstand der Musik, von R. Oboussier. — Notizen über die Prosa von Karl Jaspers, von D. Sternberger. —Karl Jaspers als Lehrer, von J. Hersch. — Karl Jaspers' Lebensdaten. — Bibliographie der Werke und Schriften von Karl Jaspers, zusammengestellt von K. Rossmann.

1. Philosophy, 1901- . 2. Jaspers, Karl, 1883- . I. Piper, Klaus, ed.

F-10
3289
OG alle fugle :[s]junge--festskrift til Herman Wildenvey. Oslo, Gyldendal, 1957. xxii, 127 p. port. 28cm.

Issued on the 50th anniversary of the publication of Wildenvey's "Nyinger."
CONTENTS. --En kandidat til fredsprisen, av A. Bjerke. --[Dikt, av A. Hjertenæs Andersen et al.] --Nuet, evighetens tinde, av P. Holm.

1. Wildenvey, Herman, 1886- 2. Poetry, Norwegian--Collections
NN 7.58 a/V OC PC, 1, 2 SL (LC1, X1, Z1, Y1)

*OSL

OGURA, SHIMPEI, 1882-1944.
Chōsen gogaku shi. Kōno, Rokurō, hochū. Tokyo, Tōkō shoin, 1964. 1 v. (various pagings) illus. 22cm.

小倉進平. 朝鮮語学史.

Bibliographical footnotes.

1. Japanese literature--Philology. 2. Korean language. 3. Japanese literature--Bibl. I. Kōno, Rokurō.
NN R 11.65 e/ (OC)IboO SL O,1,2,3,I(LC1, X1, Z1)

MW p.v.245

Ohnsorg, Richard.
Fünfundsiebzig Jahre Hamburger Thalia-Theater, Vergangenheit und Gegenwart. Festschrift zum 9. November 1918. Mit zahlreichen Bildern früherer und jetziger Thalia-Theater-Künstler. Hamburg ⌊Broschek⌋ 1918. 116 p. illus., ports. 24cm.

1. Theatres—Germany—Hamburg.
NN** 2.57 OC(1bo) PC,1 SL (T2,Z1,LC1,X1)

AN (Norli,O.)

Olaf Norli; et festskrift. 1883—10. desember—1933. ⌊Oslo, Nikolai Olsens boktrykkeri, 1933⌋

119 p., 2 l. incl. front. (port.) facsim. 26½cm.

"Oplag: 250 eksemplarer."
"Dette festskrift er blitt til ved samarbeide mellem en del av Olaf Norlis venner som har funnet at åpningen av firmaet i 1883 var et så betydningsfullt ledd i den norske bokhandel- og forlagsvirksomhets utvikling at dagen burde minnes."

CONTENTS.—Ørjasæter, T. Rudningsmannen.—Hauff, N. S. En kjærlighetserklæring til bøkene.—M., O. Bak disken hos Jacob Dybwad.—"Verdens gang" 20. dec. 1883. Ny boghandel.—Thommessen, O. Kjære

(Continued on next card)

A C 34-3047

⌊2⌋

Olaf Norli; et festskrift ... ⌊1933⌋ (Card 2)

CONTENTS—Continued.

Olaf Norli.—Huseby, O. Attersyn og kringsja.—Haffner, H. J. Bokhandel i Oslo i 80 årene.—Rosendahl, H. "80-årene."—Sfinx ⌊pseud.⌋ Lekekameraten Olaf Norli.—Haavie-Thoresen, G. Utenfor den nye "Venstrebokhandelen" på Karl Johan.—Zozo ⌊pseud.⌋ Han som trykket Rifleringen.—Vogt, N. C. Oprøreren Olaf Norli.—Egge, P. Hvordan jeg kom til Norli.—Bojer, J. For firti år siden.—Dybwad, C. Norsk forlag i nittiårene.—Liestøl, K. Olaf Norli og den norske målreisingi.—Brinchmann, C. "Kringsjaa."—Duun, O. Ein idealist.—Eriksen, M. Skoleboksforleggeren.—Seip, D. A. Olaf Norli og studentene.—Falk, A. Olaf Norli og "For bygd og by".—Baardseth, T. En modig mann.—Myre, O. Den oprinnelige Olaf Norli.—Den første annonce.

1. Norli, Olaf, 1861- 2. Publishers and publishing—Norway.

A C 34-3047

Title from N. Y. Pub. Libr. Printed by L. C.

⌊2⌋

A p.v.574

Olav Duun; serprent av 60-årsheftet i Syn og segn. Oslo: Det Norske samlaget, 1936. 83 p. incl. front. illus. (incl. ports.) 21½cm.

Articles by Tore Ørjasæter, Ola Setrom, Henrik Rytter, and others.

1. Duun, Olav, 1876- . I. Syn og segn.
N. Y. P. L. February 15, 1938

D-19
3895

Olav H. Hauge. Ei bok til 60-årsdagen 18. august 1968. Redigert av Einer Bjorvand og Knut Johansen. Oslo, Noregs boklag, 1968.

183 p. illus., music 22 cm. (⌊Det norske studentersamfund⌋ Kulturutvalets skriftserie)

CONTENTS.—Kvardag, av O. H. Hauge.—Føreord, av E. Bjorvand og K. Johansen.—Møte med Olav H. Hauge, av T. Vesaas.—For Olav H. Hauge, av P.-H. Haugen.—Skor for tanken, av H. M. Vesaas.—

(Continued)

NN*R 12.69 v/ OC, I, II, IIIb* IVb* PC, 1, I, II SL (LC1, X1, Z1)

OLAV H. HAUGE. Ei bok til 60-årsdagen 18. august 1968. (Card 2)

Olav H. Hauge, av E. Økland.—Ein dag i Ulvik, av E. Bjorvand og K. Johansen.—Ein fri mann, eller Du er ein bra mann, Hauge, av E. Økland.—Ein diktar med vengefang, av B. Birkeland.—Olav H. Hauge, av T. Obrestad.—Heim til det framande, av A. Eggen.—Det går an å leve i hverdagen òg, av J. E. Vold.—Svarte krossar, av G. Tveitt.—Tone til diktet Svarte krossar, av G. Tveitt.—I aldehagen under bergfallet, av N. Hellesnes.—Europearen frå Ulvik, av W. Dahl.—Margnotatar i Olav H. Hauges dikting, av O. Hageberg.—I eit diktlandskap, av K. Ødegård.—To omsetjingar, av O. H. Hauge.—Olav H. Hauge og Bertolt Brecht, av G. Johannesen.—Tone til diktet

(Continued)

OLAV H. HAUGE. Ei bok til 60-årsdagen 18. august 1968. (Card 3)

Seljefløyta, av S. Olsen.—Austavind med dyre dropar, av A. M. Andersen.—Ein diktanalyse, av I. Stegane.—Eit vern mot draumen, av A. Kittang.

1. Hauge, Olav H. I. Bjorvand, Einar, ed. II. Johansen, Knut, ed. III. Bjorvand, Einar. IV. Johansen, Knut.

---

* C p.v.2048

Olav, Norges kronprins; festskrift i anledning av H. K. H. kronprins Olavs bryllup, Oslo 21. mars 1929. ⌊Oslo:⌋ A-S H. Erichsens forlag, 1929. 39 p. plates, ports. (1 mounted.) 4°.

Plates printed on both sides.

484492A. 1. Olav, crown prince of Norway, 1903-
N. Y. P. L. July 1, 1930

E-13
7204

OLD Norse literature and mythology; a symposium. Edited by Edgar C. Polomé. Austin, Published for the Dept. of Germanic languages of the University of Texas by University of Texas press [1969] xii, 347 p. 24cm.

The papers were written in honor of professor L. M. Hollander. Five of them were presented at the sixth Germanic languages symposium conducted by the Dept. of Germanic languages at the University of

(Continued)

NNR 1.70 r/ OC, I (OD)IIt (ED)IIt PC, 1, 2, 3, I, II SL (LC1, X1, Z1)

OLD Norse literature and mythology... (Card 2)

Texas,November 30 and December 1 and 2, 1964.
Biographical footnotes.
CONTENTS.--On translating from the Scandinavian, by E.Haugen. --Fact and fancy in the Vinland sagas, by E.Wahlgren.--Some observations on the influence of Tristrams saga ok Isöndar on Old Icelandic literature, by P.Schach.--The heroic pattern: Old Germanic helmets, Beowulf and Gettis saga, by A.M.Arent.--A contribution to the interpretation of skaldic poetry, Tmesis, by K.Reichardt.--On reflections of Germanic legal terminology and situation in Edda.--Fertility of beast and soil on Old Norse literature, by E.O.G.Turville-Petre.--Some

(Continued)

D-11
9727

OMAGGIO a Corrado Alvaro. [A cura di Carlo Bernari. Roma, 1957] 199 p. port. 21cm.

"Supplemento al Bollettino del Sindacato nazionale scrittori, N. 1-2, Serie 1957."
"Guida essenziale bio-bibliografica," p. [192]-196.

1. Alvaro, Corrado, 1895-1956. I. Sindacato nazionale scrittori. Bollettino. Supplemento. II. Bernari, Carlo, 1909- , ed.

NN R 9.60 m/ OC, II (OS)I PC, 1, I, II SL (LC1, X1, Z1)

OLD Norse literature and mythology... (Card 3)

comments on Voluspá, by E.C. Polomé.--Lee M.Hollander, a biographical sketch.--Lee M.Hollander, a Chronological bibliography.

1. Hollander, Lee Milton, 1880- . 2. Norse literature--Hist. and crit. 3. Mythology, Norse. I. Polomé, Edgar C., ed. II. Texas. University. Germanic languages, Dept. of. t.1969

D-12
7810

OMAGGIO a Husserl, saggi di Antonio Banfi [et al] A cura di Enzo Paci. [1. ed. Milano] Il Saggiatore [1960] 319 p. 22cm. (La cultura. v. 9)

Bibliography, p. 291-[316]
CONTENTS—Husserl sempre di nuovo, di E. Paci.—La fenomenologia e il compito del pensiero contemporaneo, di A. Banfi.—Una fonte remota della teoria husserliana dell'intenzionalità, di S. Vanni-Rovighi.—La filosofia come ontologia universale e le obiezioni del relativismo

(Continued)

NN R 12.60 g/ OC, I, II PC, 1, 2, I, II SL (LC1, X1, Z1)
[NSCM] 2

---

*IPE

OLDENBOURG, R., firm, Munich.
500 [i.e. Fünfhundert] Jahre Buch und Druck. [Die Herausgabe besorgte Horst Kliemann] München, 1940. 167 p. plates, port., map, facsims. 24cm.

CONTENTS.—Johann Gutenberg. von G. Birkenfeld.—Werden und Wesen, von J. Hohlfeld.—In Jena nach Goethes Tod, von R. Oldenbourg.—Bayerischer Buchhandel - grossdeutsch gesehen, von F. Oldenbourg.—Zur Geschichte des Münchner Buchwesens, von F.W. Niegisch.—Die ältesten Druckorte, von H. Kliemann.—Über die Deposition, das

(Continued)

NN**R X 2.55 g/ (OC)I OS(1b) PC, 1, I, II SL (Z1, LC1, X1)

OMAGGIO a Husserl... (Card 2)

scettico in Husserl, di G.D. Neri.—I paradossi dell'infinito nell'orizzonte fenomenologico, di E. Melandri.—La "filosofia come scienza rigorosa" e la critica fenomenologica del dogmatismo, di G. Semerari.—La fondazione trascendentale della logica in Husserl, di L. Lugarini.—Realtà e prassi in Husserl, di G. Pedroli.—Ego ed alter-ego nella "Krisis" di Husserl, di E. Filippini.—Fenomenologia e psicologia, di R. Pucci.—Di una posizione "storicamente" positiva rispetto alla fenomenologia di Husserl, di G. Guzzoni.

1. Husserl, Edmund, 1859-1938. 2. Phenomenalism. I. Paci, Enzo, 1911- , ed. II. Banfi, Antonio.

OLDENBOURG, R., firm, Munich. 500 [i.e. Fünfhundert]...
(Card 2)

Postulat und das Gautschen, von R. Schellhorn.—Das Wappen der Buchdrucker, von K.F. Bauer.—Die Buchdruckersprache, von W.G. Oschilewski.—Der Weg des Papiers, von A. Renker.—Lob und Schelte des Buches, von H. Kliemann.—Die deutsche Druckschrift, von K. Schottenloher.—Das Buchgewerbe in Zahlen.—Merkwürdigkeiten von A-Z, von H. Kliemann.

1. Printing—Hist. I. Kliemann, Horst, 1896- . ed. II. Title.

---

*MEC
(Montemezzi)

Omaggio a Italo Montemezzi a cura di Luigi Tretti e Lionello Fiumi. Verona [Ghidini & Fiorini] 1952 79 p. illus., ports., facsims. 24cm.

"'Numero unico' edito a cura del 'Comitato onoranze a Italo Montemezzi' in collaborazione con la rivista mensile 'Vita veronese'."

1. Montemezzi, Italo, 1875-1952. I. Fiumi, Lionello, 1894- , ed. II. Tretti Luigi, ed. III. Tretti, Luigi.

NN** 11.54 m/ OC, I, II, IIIbo PC, 1, I, II SL MU, 1, I, II (Z1, LC1, X1)

ZDC

Oluf Kolsrud in memoriam; kirkehistoriske studier samlet og utgitt til minne om forskeren og vennen Oluf Kolsrud... Oslo, Grøndahl & søn, 1946. 181 p. illus. 24cm.

604601B. 1. Church history. 2. Kolsrud, Nils Oluf, 1885-1945.
NN

E-10
3609

OPSTELLEN, door vrienden en collega's aangeboden aan Dr. F.K.H. Kossmann ter gelegenheid van zijn vijf en zestigste verjaardag en van zijn afscheid als bibliothecaris der gemeente Rotterdam. 's-Gravenhage, M.Nijhoff, 1953. viii, 264 p. port., facsims., music. 25cm.

CONTENTS.—Antwerpen vóór 1914, door L.Baekelmans.—Rondom Joachim Oudaan's Haagsche broedermoord', door L. Brummel.—Over enige boeken te Vianen gedrukt

(Continued)

NN R 11.59 c/ OC PC, 1, 2 SL (LC1, X1, Z1) [I]

OPSTELLEN... (Card 2)

tijdens het 'Voorspel', door H. de la Fontaine Verwey. --Rotterdamse boekverkopers uit de patriottentijd door H.C. Hazewinkel.--La cite des livres, door R. Jacobsen. --A(lgemeen) B(eschaafd) N(ederlands), door G. Kloeke. --Bodin, Althusius en Parker, door E. Kossmann.-- Erasmus-uitgaven A°. 1531 in het bezit van kanunnik Mr. Jan Dircsz. van der Haer te Gorkum, door M.E. Kronenberg.--Venusjankers, door C. Kruyskamp.--Een zedenbeeld uit het Rotterdam voor de opkomst van de wereldhaven, door W.F. Lichtenauer.--Enige

(Continued)

OPSTELLEN... (Card 3)

problemen met betrekking tot gedateerde Goudse handschriften, door G.I. lieftinck.--De compositie van de Walewein, door P. Minderaa.--De 'Verlichting' te Rotterdam, door O. Noordenbos.--"De paradox": een curiosum, door W. van Ravesteyn.--Een schimpdicht van Erasmus op Julius II, door C. Reedijk.--Het boek en 'Jezus onder de schriftgeleerden', door G. Schmook.--Boekselectieproblemen in de Amerikaanse public library, door P.J. van Swigchem. --Willem Pijper en Beethhoven, door W.H. Thijsse.--Op het spoor

(Continued)

OPSTELLEN... (Card 4)

van een onbekende postincunabel? Door F. de Tollenaere --De reprografie en het vermenigvuldigen van een geschreven tekst, door L.J. van der Wolk.--Overzicht der geschriften van Dr. F.K.H. Kossmann, bewerkt door J.C. Mazure.

1. Kossmann, Friedrich Karl Heinrich, 1893-
2. Bibliography--Addresses, essays, lectures.

F-10
5482

OPSTELLENBUNDEL ter huldiging van Prof. Dr. J. Wisselink hem aangeboden op 20 Oktober, 1960. Haarlem, De erven F. Bohn [1960] 275 p. illus. 28cm.

Bibliographical footnotes.

CONTENTS.--Het economisch instituut voor de textielindustrie, van J. Bulte en J. Bunt.--Structuur en functie van de katoenhandel in Nederland, van J. Bos.--De econoom en de jurist, van H.J.F. ten Cate.--

(Continued)

NN R 4.61 a/ OC PC, 1, 2, 3 SL E, 1, 2, 3 (LC1, X1, Z1)

4

OPSTELLENBUNDEL ter huldiging van Prof. Dr. J. Wisselink... (Card 2)

Kartellering, van G. Diephuis.--Production-control, van P.M.J. van Eekelen.--De problematiek van de investeringsbeslissing, van G. Elshof. --Eigendommelijkheden van het hoger onderwijs, van Ch. Glasz.--Het staatkundig aspect van de textielindustrie, van B.W. Kranenburg.-- De geschiedenis van het reizende katoenparlement, van W.T. Kroese.-- Marktontwikkeling voor textielproducten, van H.J. Kuhlmeyer.--De rol van de synthetica in het textielverbruik, van F.W. Meyer.--Termijnhandel en kostprijsberekening, van F.L. van Muiswinkel.--Voorkeurreeksen in verband met de keuze van de eenheid.

(Continued)

OPSTELLENBUNDEL ter huldiging van Prof. Dr. J. Wisselink... (Card 3)

van F.M. Oberstadt.--Pay-out periode, levensduur en rentabiliteit, van B. Pruijt.--Vezelverwerkingskunde, van H.L. Röder.--De voorgecalculeerde balans, van C.F. Scheffer.--Personeelsvraagstukken van de Twents-Gelderse textielindustrie gedurende dertig jaar, van A.L. van Schelven.-- Prof. Dr. J. Wisselink; zijn leven-- zijn werk, van Th. A. van der Spil.-- De anti-dumpingbepalingen van Havana Charter, van C.N.F. Swarttouw.-- Verkorting van de doorlooptijd? Van H. Thierry.--Internationale planning van investeringen? Van J. Tinbergen.--Zeven jaren katoenen garen in Nederland, van D.J. Wisselink.--Geschriften van Prof. Dr. J. Wisselink (p. [269]-273).--Naamlijst van gepromoveerden bij Prof. Dr. J. Wisselink.

(Continued)

OPSTELLENBUNDEL ter huldiging van Prof. Dr. J. Wisselink... (Card 4)

1. Textile trade and statistics--Netherlands. 2. Cotton--Trade and stat.--Netherlands. 3. Wisselink, J.

F-11
6744

Opus nobile. Festschrift zum 60. Geburtstag von Ulf Jantzen. Hrsg. von Peter Zazoff. (Mit 103 Bildern auf 30 Tafeln und 18 Textabbildungen.) Wiesbaden, F. Steiner, 1969.

190 p., 30 p. of illus. 29 cm.

Bibliographical footnotes.

1. Archaeology, Classical--Addresses, essays, lectures. 2. Art, Classical--Addresses, essays, lectures. I. Jantzen, Ulf. II. Zazoff, Peter, ed. III. Zazoff, Peter.

NN*R 1.70 e/ OC, I, II, IIIb* PC, 1, 2, I, II SL A, 2, I, II (LC1, X1, Z1)

* MG p.v.335

ORGELN, Organisten, Kantoren; Bilder und Profile aus drei Jahrhunderten Gemeindegesang und Kirchenmusik in der Lutherischen Pfarrkirche zu Hagen. Eine Festschrift hrsg. aus Anlass der Einweihung der neuen Ott-Orgel in der Johanniskirche am Sonntag Estomihi A.D. 1959, von Werner Gerber. [Hagen, 1959] 64 p. illus., ports., facsims. 21cm.

Bibliography, p. 64.

(Continued)

NN R X 9.66 p/c OC, I, Ibo PC, 1, 2, 4, 5, I SL MU, 1, 2, 3, 4, I (LC1, X1, Z1)

2

ORGELN, Organisten, Kantoren... (Card 2)

1. Cantors--Germany--Hagen. 2. Organists--Germany--Hagen
3. Organ--Germany--Hagen. 4. Church music--Germany--Hagen
5. Organ--Hist.--Germany--Hagen. I. Gerber, Werner.

*OAC

Oriental studies in honour of Cursetji Erachji Pavry; edited by Jal Dastur Cursetji Pavry, with a foreword by A. V. Williams Jackson. London: Oxford Univ. Press, 1933. xv, 503 p. front. (port.) 25cm.

Essays and researches on Oriental languages, literature, history, philosophy and art by seventy scholars from seventeen different countries.
One of 1000 copies printed.
"Bibliography of Dasturji Pavry's works," verso of p. xv.

703476A. 1. Pavry, Cursetji Erachji, 1859– . 2. Oriental studies—Collections. I. Pavry, Jal Dastur Cursetji, 1899– , editor.
N. Y. P. L. June 13, 1934

F-11
4793

ORRICK, ALLAN H., ed.
Nordica et anglica; studies in honor of Stefán Einarsson. The Hague, Mouton, 1968 [c1967]
196 p. illus., port. 27cm. (Janua linguarum; studia memoriae Nicolai van Wijk dedicata. Series major. 22)

CONTENTS.--Stefán Einarsson, by J.G. Allee.--The Franks casket and the date of Widsith, by K. Malone.--The Icelandic version of the Somniale Danielis, by E.O.G. Turville-Petre.--Six Old English Runic
(Continued)

NN R 11.68 1/$_{4}$OC, IIbo (OS)I PC, 1, 2, 3, I SL (LC1, X1, Z1)

---

*OAC

Oriental studies published in commemoration of the fortieth anniversary (1883–1923) of Paul Haupt as director of the Oriental seminary of the Johns Hopkins university, Baltimore, Md., under the editorial direction of Cyrus Adler ... and Aaron Ember ... Baltimore, The Johns Hopkins press; [etc., etc.] 1926.
lxx p., 1 l., 470 p., 1 l. front. (port.) illus. (2 mounted; incl. facsims.) 24½cm.
"Bibliography of Paul Haupt": p. [xxxiii]–lxx.
CONTENTS.—Old Testament and Judaica.—Assyriology.—Egyptology.—Semitica.

305881A- 1. *Haupt, Paul, 1858–1926. 2. Semitic philology—Collections. 3. Oriental philology—Collections. I. Adler, Cyrus, 1863– ed. II. Ember, Aaron, 1878–1926, joint ed.

27-6845

Library of Congress PJ3002.Z5H3
[5]

ORRICK, ALLAN H., ed. Nordica et anglica...
(Card 2)

inscriptions reconsidered, by K. Schneider.--"When wine is in, wit is out", by A. Taylor.--The first Polish versions of the Icelandic Eddas, by M. Schlauch.--On the pronounciation of Old Norse, by E. Haugen.--Wulfstan Cantor and Anglo-Saxon law, by D. Whitelock.--Some remarks on the language of the Magnus legend in the Orkneyinga saga, by D.A. Seip.--A study of diction and style in three Anglo-Saxon narrative poems, by A.G. Brodeur.-- A newly discovered runic stone from Västerljung, Södermanland, by B.F. Jansson.--The use of Hittite
(Continued)

---

*PBS

Orientalistische Studien; Fritz Hommel zum sechzigsten Geburtstag am 31. Juli 1914, gewidmet von Freunden, Kollegen und Schülern... Leipzig: J. C. Hinrichs, 1917–18. 2 v. in 1. front. (port.), illus., plates. 8°. (Vorderasiatische Gesellschaft, Berlin. Mitteil. Jahrg. 21-22.)
——— Second copy.

1. Hommel, Fritz, 1854– . 2. Assyriology. 3. Ser.
N. Y. P. L. November 19, 1928

ORRICK, ALLAN H., ed. Nordica et anglica...
(Card 3)

and Tocharian materials in Germanic etymologies, by G.S. Lane.--Icelandic parallels among the Northeastern Algonquians: a reconsideration, by S. Thompson.--Some remarks on learned and novelistic elements in the Icelandic sagas, by D.A. Strömbäck.--Post-consonantal l m n r and metrical practice in the Beowulf, by W.P. Lehmann.--Hans Hylen-a pioneer Norwegian translator of Icelandic poetry, by R. Beck.--The writings of Stefán Einarsson.
1. Einarsson, Stefán, 1897- 2. Icelandic literature--Addresses, essays, lectures. 3. Anglo-Saxon literature--Hist. and crit. I. Series. II. Orrick, Allan H.

TNK

ORKLA GRUBE-AKTIEBOLAG, Løkken, Norway.
Løkken verk; en norsk grube gjennom 300 år. [Løkken] 1954.
505 p. illus. (part col.) ports., maps. 26cm.

Half-title: Løkken kaabervaerk 1654.
Bibliography, p. 493.
CONTENTS. — Verkets historie i eldre tid: Løkken verk 1654-1904, av R. Støren. Verket, bygdene, byen, av A. Skrondal. Partisipantene i Løkken verk, av E. Hartmann. — Verkets utvikling under Orkla grube-aktiebolag: Merkantil utvikling 1904-1954, av H. P. [illegible]drup.
(Continued)

NN ** 4.55 p/$_{4}$ OS (1b) PC SL E (LC1, X1, Z1)

D-18
5071

Oschilewski, Walther Georg, 1904– *ed.*
Begegnungen: Arno Scholz, 60 Jahre alt; Glückwünsche und Würdigungen, dargeboten von Walther G. Oschilewski. Berlin-Grunewald, Arani [1964]
1 v. (unpaged) illus., ports. 22 x 23 cm.
Cover title: Arno Scholz.
Includes bibliography of Arno Scholz.

1. Scholz, Arno.
NN * R 10.68 1/$_{4}$ OC PC, 1 SL E, 1 (LC1, X1, Z1)

ORKLA GRUBE-AKTIEBOLAG, Løkken, Norway. Løkken verk; en norsk grube gjennom 300 år. (Card 2)

Teknisk utvikling ved gruben, av O. F. Borchgrevink. Transportvesen og kraftforsyning, av Th. A. Tangen. Smelteverket, av S. Aannerud. Sosiale og kulturelle forhold, av M. G. Jyssum. — Geologiske forhold: Løkkenfeltets geologi, av H. Carstens.

TB

Oskar Engländer; festschrift zur feier des 60. geburtstages gewidmet von fachkollegen, freunden und schülern. Brünn/Leipzig/Wien, Verlag Rudolf M. Rohrer [1937]
4 p. l., 354 p., 1 l. incl. tables. front. (port.) 24cm.
Cover-title: Festschrift für Oskar Engländer.
Bibliographical foot-notes.
CONTENTS.—Schranil, Rudolf. Vorwort.—Adler, Franz. Legislative and wirtschaft.—Amonn, Alfred. Grundfragen der konjunkturtheorie und krisenpolitik.—Baireuther, Otto. Arbeitsbeschaffung und ihre finanzierung.—Charmatz, Hans. Die geschichte der geldrechtlichen bestimmungen des österreichischen privatrechts.—Hoyer, Ernst. Währungsfragen im Codex juris canonici.—Kraus, Oskar. Einige bemerkungen zur allgemeinen rechtslehre.—Macek, Josef. Die kaufkraft des geldes in anderer beleuchtung.—Müller, Hugo. Das kapital als dritter
(Continued on next card)
A C 37-2313
[2]

Oskar Engländer; festschrift zur feier des 60. geburtstages ... ₍1937₎ (Card 2)

CONTENTS—Continued.

produktionsfaktor.—Peterka, Otto. Der kauf in den niederösterreichischen weistümern.—Röpke, Wilhelm. Versuch einer neufassung des quantitativen bevölkerungsproblems.—Schenk, H. G. Zur begründung und rechtspolitischen auswertung des gleichheitsgedankens.—Schranil, Rudolf. Das vereinbaren und verhandeln im steuerrecht.—Spitaler, Armin. Steuerrechtliche und betriebswirtschaftliche fragen im zusammenhang mit den währungsdevalvationen.—Stark, Werner. Währungsverträge.—Valina, František. Betrachtungen über wirtschaftsentwicklung und unternehmertätigkeit.—Weiss, F. X. Die gebühren im system der öffentlichen abgaben.—Ziegler, H. O. Statistisches zur berufsstruktur der Prager bevölkerung.—Stark, Werner. Der jubilar, lebensgeschichte, lehren und werke.

1. Engländer, Oskar, 1876–1937. 2. Economics—Addresses, essays, lectures.

A C 37-2313

New York. Public library for Library of Congress ₍2₎

F-11
1455

OSLEY, A.S., ed.
Calligraphy and palaeography; essays presented to Alfred Fairbank on his 70th birthday. [London] Faber & Faber [1965] 286 p. illus., plates, port., maps, facsims., diagrs. 26cm.

"Alfred Fairbank's opus" (p. 17-28) by R. McLean.
Includes bibliographies.

(Continued)

NN R 3.66 a/ OC, I, IIbo PC, 1, 2, 3, 4, I SL A, 1, 3, 4, I (LC1, X1, Z1)

2

OSLEY, A.S., ed. Calligraphy and palaeography... (Card 2)

1. Design, Calligraphic--Addresses, essays, lectures. 2. Paleography--Addresses, essays, lectures. 3. Lettering--Addresses, essays, lectures. 4. Fairbank, Alfred J. I. Title. II. Osley, A.S.

AN
+
(Abel, N)

OSLO. Universitet.
Festskrift ved hundredaarsjubilæet for Niels Henrik Abels fødsel. Kristiania, I kommission hos J. Dybwad, 1902. 1 v. (various pagings) illus., port., 6 facsims. 30cm.

Presentation copy to university librarian A. Kjær, signed by members of the jubilee committee, Fridtjof Nansen, chairman.

(Continued)

NN ** R X 9.55 p/s (OC) I, II OS PC, 1, I, II SL ST, 1, I, II (RA1, LC1, X1, Z1)

OSLO. Universitet. Festskrift ved hundredaarsjubilæet for Niels Henrik Abels fødsel. (Card 2)

Bibliography, p. [112] of the first section.
CONTENTS.-- Niels Henrik Abel, af B. Bjørnson. -- Historisk indledning, af E. Holst. -- Breve fra og til Abel. -- Breve om Abel. -- Oplysninger til brevene. -- Dokumenter angaaende Abel, ved C. Størmer. -- Oplysninger til dokumenterne. -- Abels studier og hans opdagelser, af L. Sylow.

1. Abel, Niels Henrik, 1802-1829. I. Abel, Niels Henrik, 1802-1829. Breve. II. Title.

---

* OAC

ØST og Vest; Afhandlinger tilegnede Professor Dr. phil. Arthur Christensen paa Halvfjerdsaarsdagen d. 9. Januar 1945 af nordiske Orientalister og Folkemindeforskere. [Redigeret af K. Barr og Hans Ellekilde] København, E. Munksgaard, 1945. 224 p. illus., port., map. 25cm.

CONTENTS. — Det Kongelige biblioteks origntalske haandskriftsamling, af S. Dahl. — Indoeuropaeiske sprog i det gamle Østturkestan, av S. Konow. — Khushhāl Khān; en afghansk nasjonaldikter, av G. Morgenstierne. — Hādjdjīābād-inskriften, av H. S. Nyberg. — Digtere som hof-

(Continued)

NN* R 9.57 c/ OC, I, II PC, 1, 2, I, II SL O, 1, 2, I, II (LC1, X1, Z1)
[I]

ØST og Vest... (Card 2)

diplomater, af J. Pedersen. — Sasanidisk tradition i Firdausis kongebog, af H. Andersen. — Chinggis Khans erobring af Persian efter de mongolske kilder, af K. Grønbech. — Qanaterne, Irans underjordiske vandingskanaler, af C. G. Feilberg. — Korresponderende skønhedspletter; Somadeva, Casanova, Lavater, af P. Tuxen. — Henvendelsen til guddommene i babyloniske hymner og bønner, af O. E. Ravn. — Principia Zarathustriaca, af K. Barr. — Några synpunkter på sagoforskning och filologi, av C. W. v. Sydow. — Den ungarske ridder i den irske skærsild, af L. L. Hammerich. — Ørvarod og kejser Mikael den 3. af Byzans, af A. Stender-Pedersen. — Gadetraditioner i Øst og Vest, af I. M. Boberg. — Heksene i Vemmelev kirke, af G. Knudsen. — Julegubben i Vinten, af H. Ellekilde.

1. Christensen, Arthur Emanuel, 1875-1945. 2. Oriental studies--Collections. I. Barr, Kaj, 1896- , ed. II. Ellekilde, Hans Lavrids, 1891- , ed.

L-10
4597
Bd. 8

OSTAFRIKANISCHE Studien; East African studies. Ernst Weigt zum 60. Geburtstag. Schriftleitung: Herfried Berger. Nürnberg, im Selbstverlag des Wirtschafts- und Sozialgeographischen Instituts der Friedrich-Alexander-Universität, 1968. 406 p. illus., maps. 25cm. (Nürnberger wirtschafts- und sozialgeographische Arbeiten. Bd. 8)

(Continued)

NN 1.70 v/L OC, II, III (OS)I PC, 1, I, II, III E, 1, I, II, III (LC1, X1, Z1)

2

OSTAFRIKANISCHE Studien... (Card 2)

Articles in German or English, with summaries in the other language.
Bibliographical footnotes.

1. Africa, East--Economic geography. I. Series. II. Berger, Herfried, ed. III. Weigt, Ernst.

D-11
2478

Ostdeutsche Akademie, Lüneburg.
Festschrift zur 725-Jahrfeier der Stadt Thorn und zur Übernahme der Patenschaft durch die 1000 Jährige Stadt Lüneburg. Lüneburg, Verlag Hoppe ₍1956₎ 39 p. illus. 21cm.

CONTENTS.—725 Jahre Thorner Geschichte, von H. Lohmeyer.—Kopernikus und die Entwicklung des abendländischen Denkens, von P. Jordan.—Die bedeutendsten Baudenkmäler und Werke der bildenden Kunst in Thorn, von K. Stachowitz.

1. Thorn, Poland. 2. Copernicus, Nicolaus, 1473–1543.
NN R X 7.59 OS PC, 1, 2 SL S, 1, 2 (LC1, X1, Z1)

Write on slip, name, year, vol., page of magazine and class mark — PAA

Oswald Redlich zugeeignet anlässlich der Feier seines siebzigsten Geburtstages.

(Vienna. Universitaet. Oesterreisches Institut für Geschichtsforschung. Mitteil. Wien,1929. 8°. Ergänzungsband 11,portrait preceding p.1.)

form 404a [vi-7-29 25m]

ØVERÅS, ASBJØRN, 1896- Frå virke og vitskap... (Card 2)

skulen gjera ghennom elevinstitusjonar til a fremja ei sosial innstilling og forståing hos elevane. --Stiklestadslaget; Olav Haraldsson og trønderne. --Ivar Aasen og Det Kgl. norske videnskabers selskab. --Bjørnstjerne Bjørnson og bøndene. --Bjørnson og Romsdal--Bjørnstjerne Bjørnsons religiøse syn fram til "Fritenkjaren": føresternad og framvokster. --Arne Garborg; tale 12. aug. 1951, da Garborgheimen vant opna. --Arne Bergsgård; minnetale i Det Kgl. norske videnskabers selskab 8. nov. 1954. --Hovudtale ved 800 arsjubileet til Trondheim katedralskole, 1952.

1. Essays, Norwegian. 2. Bjørnson, Bjørnstjerne, 1832-1910. 3. Education--Addresses, essays lectures.

L-10
4462
no. 6

OTTERBJÖRK, ROLAND, ed.
Personnamnsstudier 1964 tillägnade minnet av Ivar Modéer, 1904-1960. Stockholm, Almqvist & Wiksell [1965] 344 p. illus., port. 25cm. (Anthroponymica suecana. 6)

Summaries in English
Bibliographical footnotes.

1. Names, Swedish. 2. Modéer, Ivar, 1904-1960.
I. Series. II. Title.
NN 2.66 p/ OC, II (OS)I PC, 1, 2, I, II G, 1, I, II (LC1, X1, Z1)

C-13
7452

Øverland, Arnulf, 1889-
Sprog og usprog. [I anledning av Riksmålsforbundets 60-års jubileum] Oslo, Riksmålsforlaget, (Bokcentralen), [1967].
168 p. 18 cm.

1. Norwegian language. 2. Riksmålsforbundet.
NN*R 5.68 v/R OC PC, 1,2 SL (LC1,X1,Z1)

*HB

Otto Glauning zum 60. geburtstag. Festgabe aus wissenschaft und bibliothek. Leipzig, Verlag der offizin Richard Hadl, 1936-38. 2 v. facsims., front.(v.2), illus., plates, ports. 27cm.

"Die herausgabe besorgte Heinrich Schreiber."

For contents see official catalogue.

Copy only words underlined & Classmark-- RDTA

OVIEDO Y VALDÉS, GONZALO FERNÁNDEZ DE, 1478-1557.
De la natural hystoria de las Indias por Gonzalo Fernández de Oviedo. A facsimile edition issued in honor of Sterling A. Stoudemire. Chapel Hill, University of North Carolina press [1969] port., xvip., facsim. (108 p.), [109]-116 p. 23cm. (North Carolina. University. Studies in Romance languages and literatures, no. 85)
(Continued)
NN 3.70 m/ OC (OD)I (ED)I PC, 1, 2, 3, 4, 5, I AH, 1, 2 (LC1, X1, Z1)

2

NFD
(Bierbaum)

OTTO JULIUS BIERBAUM zum Gedächtnis. München, G. Müller, 1912. xiii, 269 p. illus., ports. 18cm.

1. Bierbaum, Otto Julius, 1865-1910.

NN**R 3.53 OC PC, 1 SL (LC1, Z1, X1)

OVIEDO Y VALDÉS, GONZALO FERNÁNDEZ DE, 1478-1557. De la natural hystoria de las Indias por Gonzalo Fernández de Oviedo. (Card 2)

Bibliography, p. xiii-xiv.

1. West Indies--Descr. and trav. to 1800. 2. Central America--Descr. and trav., to 1800. 3. Natural history--Central America. 4. Natural history--West Indies. 5. Stoudemire, Sterling Aubrey, 1902- I. Series.

E-10
1593

ØVERÅS, ASBJØRN, 1896-
Frå virke og vitskap; utvalde artiklar og talar utg. til 60-årsdagen den 4. april 1956. Oslo, Aschehoug, 1956. 175 p. ports. 26cm.

"Liste over noko av det som rektor, dr. philos. Asbjørn Øveras har skrivi," p. 170-175.
CONTENTS. --Tale til kongen ved 800 årsjubileet til Tronheim katedralskole, 27. juni, 1952. --Landsgymnas. --Elevane og skullen. --Kva kan
(Continued)
NN **1.57 j/ OC PC, 1, 2, 3 SL (LC1, X1, Z1, Y1)

Copy only words underlined & classmark-- CA

Oxford Historical Society.
Oxford studies presented to Daniel Callus. Oxford, Clarendon Press, 1964.
viii, 319 p. illus., port. 23 cm. (ITS; [Publications] n. s. v. 16)

Bibliographical footnotes.

CONTENTS. — Foreword, by R. W. Southern. — Northerners and southerners in the organization of the university to 1509, by A. B. Emden.—The halls and schools of medieval Oxford: an attempt at
(Continued)
NN*R 5.65 a/ OS, I PC, 1, 2, I (G)I (LC1, X1, Z1) [I]

OXFORD HISTORICAL SOCIETY. Oxford studies presented to Daniel Callus. (Card 2)

reconstruction, by W. A. Pantin.—Foreign Dominican students and professors at the Oxford Blackfriars, by W. A. Hinnebusch.—The curriculum of the Faculty of Canon Law at Oxford in the first half of the fourteenth century, by L. Boyle.—Oxford grammar masters in the Middle Ages, by R. W. Hunt.—Walter Burley, by C. Martin.—Roger Swyneshed, O. S. B., logician, natural philosopher, and theologian, by J. A. Weisheipl.—Wyclif's Postilla on the Old Testament and his Principium, by B. Smalley.—Medieval aftermath: Oxford logic and logicians of the seventeenth century, by I. Thomas.—Bibliography of the published writings of Daniel Callus (p. ₍318₎-319)

1. Oxford university--Hist. --Addresses, essays, lectures.
2. Callus, Daniel Angelo. I. Series.

---

*QT

50 let Edvarda Beneše; vzpomínky, svědectví, úvahy. ₍Praha, Vydala Československá obec legionářská ₍1934₎ 354 p. front. (port.) 21½cm.

On cover: II. vydání.

765577A. 1. Beneš, Edvard, 1884- . I. Československá obec legionářská.
N. Y. P. L. December 17, 1935

B-10
2732

PADRE GEMELLI, Psicologo; scritti di Leonardo Ancona [et. al.] Milano, Società Editrice Vita e Pensiero [1960] 189 p. 17cm. (Presente e avvenire dell'Università Cattolica, 4)

These essays were published in a special issue of Archivio di psicologia neurologia e psichiatria, fasc. 5-6, Sept.-Dec., 1959, which was dedicated to Agostino Gemelli.

1. Psychology--Addresses, essays, lectures. 2. Gemelli, Agostino, 1878-1959. I. Ancona, Leonardo
NN *R 1.65 p/6 OC, I PC, 1, 2, I SL (LC1, X1, Z1)

XAH

PADUA, Italy (City). Università. Giurisprudenza, Facoltà di.

Scritti giuridici in onore di Vincenzo Manzini. Padova, CEDAM, 1954. xxiv, 766 p. port. 25cm.

By various authors.

"Pubblicazioni di Vincenzo Manzini," p. [xv]-xxii.

1. Law—Addresses, essays, lectures. 2. Criminal law. 3. Manzini, Vincenzo, 1872- .
NN**R 3.56 g/v OS PC, 1, 2, 3 SL E, 2, 3 (LC1, X1, Z1)

AN
(Artigas, J.)

El País, Montevideo.

...Artigas; estudios publicados en "El País" como homenaje al jefe de los orientales en el centenario de su muerte, 1850–1950. Plan y dirección general de Edmundo M. Narancio. Prólogo de Gustavo Gallinal. Estudios de Carlos A. Maggi . . . ₍y otros₎ Ilustraciones de Emilio Cortinas. Montevideo, Colombino hnos., 1951. 331 p. illus., maps. 24cm. (Ediciones de "El País")

CONTENTS.—La banda oriental a fines del siglo XVIII y comienzos del XIX, por C. A. Maggi.—Artigas antes de 1811, por J. M. Traibel.—Síntesis de la actuación de Artigas entre 1811 y 1815, por M. Flores Mora.—Artigas y el primer sitio de Montevideo, por M. Blanca Paris y Q. Cabrera Piñón.—"La Redota" (el éxodo), por C. A.

(Continued)

NN R 4.53 (OC)I OS PC, 1, 2, I SL AH, 1, 2, I (PRI 1, LC1, Z1, X1)

El País, Montevideo. ...Artigas; estudios publicados en "El País" (Card 2)

Maggi.—El Congreso de abril, por Edmundo Favaro.—La formación de la Liga federal, por F. A. Arce.—El Congreso de oriente, por J. M. Traibel.—Síntesis de la actuación de Artigas entre 1816 y 1820, por M. Flores Mora.—El gobierno artiguista en la provincia oriental, por M. J. Ardao.—El reglamento de 1815, por E. M. Narancio.—Artigas, el directorio, el Congreso de Tucumán y la invasión portuguesa, por Edmundo Favaro.—Artigas como militar, por O. Antúnez Olivera.—Las campañas navales de Artigas, por Agustín Beraza.—La lucha contra el centralismo y el Tratado de Pilar, por A. Capillas de Castellanos.—La formación del ideario artiguista, por H. Gros

(Continued)

El País, Montevideo. ...Artigas; estudios publicados en "El País" (Card 3)

Espiell.—Trascendencia de los ideales y la acción de Artigas en la revolución argentina y americana, por Emilio Ravignani.—Los secretarios de Artigas, por M. Flores Mora.—Artigas y los indios, por E. Petit Muñoz.—Las banderas de Artigas, por Agustín Beraza.—Rasgos biográficos de Artigas en el Paraguay, por D. Hammerly Dupuy.—Valoración de Artigas, por E. Petit Muñoz.

1. Artigas, José, Gervasio, 1764-1850. 2. Uruguay—Hist.
I. Narancio, Edmundo M., ed.

F-10
5024

PALEOLOGICAL ASSOCIATION OF JAPAN.

New studies in ancient Eurasian history; essays presented to Józef Kostrzewski. Edited by Ryô-chû Umeda, with the assistance of Bun-ei Tsunoda. Osaka, 1955. 138 p. illus., ports., maps. 27cm.

"Reprinted from the Palaeologia, vol. IV, no. 3/4."

CONTENTS.--Seventy years life of Józef Kostrzewski, by K. Jażdżewski. --L'origine de l'art et l'art franco-cantabrique, par J. A. Mauduit. --A barrow of the Unetician culture in Łęki Male, district of Kościan.

(Continued)

NN R 10.60 p/ (OC)I, Ib, III OS, II PC, 1, 2, I, II, III SL O, 1, I, II, III S, 1, I, II, III (LC1, X1, Z1)

PALEOLOGICAL ASSOCIATION OF JAPAN. New studies in ancient Eurasian history... (Card 2)

by M. Kowiańska-Piaszykowa. --Polybios Exkurs über die oberitalienischen Kelten, von R. Stiehl. --Die Aufgabe der Kelten in Mitteleuropa und ihre kulturelle Erbschaft, von J. Filip. --Die Italiker, von G. O. Onorato. --Slawische Ethnogenesis von J. Eisner. --Urgeschichtliche Erkenntnisse zum eurasiatischen Viehzüchter-Nomadentum, von F. Hančar. --Neue Zuteilungen zur Münzprägung der Chioniten, von R. Gobl. --Scythians notes, by T. Sulimirski. --Der Schamanismus der Awaren. von A. Kollautz. --The problem of the ending of the ancient world, by B. Tsunoda. --Slavonic rite in Poland, by L. Koczy. --Bibliography of works by Professor Dr. Józef Kostrzewski (p. 107-137)

(Continued)

PALEOLOGICAL ASSOCIATION OF JAPAN. New studies in ancient Eurasian history... (Card 3)

1. Kostrzewski, Józef. 2. Civilization--Addresses, essays, lectures.
I. Umeda, Ryōchū, ed. II. Palaeologia. III. Title.

Ɛ-14
1895

Palme, Johan Henrik, 1841–1932.
Utveckling och idé. Henrik Palme intill grundandet av Stockholms intecknings garanti aktiebolag, skildrad i hans brev 1860–1869. En minnebok utg. genom Wilhelm Odelberg. Stockholm, Svenska intecknings garanti aktiebolaget, 1969.

xvi, 130, (1) p. illus. 25 cm.

Published on the occasion of the 100th anniversary of the founding of Svenska intecknings garanti AB.

(Continued)

NN*R 8.71 d/z OC(1b*), I (OS)II PC, 1, I, II SL E, 1, I, II (LC1, X1, Z1) 2

PALME, JOHAN HENRIK, 1841-1932. Utveckling och idé. (Card 2)

1. Svenska intecknings garanti AB. I. Odelberg, Wilhelm, ed. II. Svenska intecknings garanti AB.

BWV

Paolo Orsi (1859–1935) A cura dell' Archivio storico per la Calabria e la Lucania. Roma, 1935.

2 p. l., 488, [4] p. illus., XXII pl. (incl. ports.) 25cm.

Plate XIX accompanied by leaf with descriptive letterpress not included in the paging.
Bibliographical foot-notes.

CONTENTS.—Zanotti-Bianco, Umberto. Paolo Orsi.—Roberti, Giacomo. L'archeologia trentina.—Cafici, Corrado, e Cafici, Ippolito. Sicilia preistorica; il problema delle origini.—Levi, Doro. Traccie della civiltà micenea in Sicilia.—Aberg, Nils. Scavi preellenici in Calabria.—Crispo, C. F. I Siculi dell' Italia antichissima.—Ducati, Pericle. L'arte figurata greca di Sicilia e del Bruzio.—Marconi, Pirro. I templi della Sicilia e della Magna Grecia.—Oldfather, W. A. Gli scavi di Locri.—Zancani-Montuoro, Paola. Il giudizio di Persephone in un pinakion locrese.—Fuchs, Siegfried. Le arti minori.—Libertini, Guido. Romanità e avanzi

(Continued on next card)

A C 37-2031

[2]

Paolo Orsi (1859–1935) ... 1935. (Card 2)

CONTENTS—Continued.

romani della Sicilia.—Agnello, Giuseppe. La Sicilia sotterranea cristiana e la Sicilia bizantina.—Cappelli, Biagio. L'arte medioevale in Calabria.—Gagliardi, Enrico. Paolo Orsi numismatico.—Guarducci, Margherita. Il contributo agli studi epigrafici.—Randall MacIver, David. Il Museo di Siracusa.—Agati, Sebastiano. L'opera di restauro della Sopraintendenza di Siracusa.—U. Z. B. Paoli Orsi e la Società Magna Grecia.—Agnello, Giuseppe. Bibliografia completa delle opere di Paolo Orsi (p. [353]–482)—Indice dei nomi dei luoghi.

1. Orsi, Paolo, 1859–1935. 2. Orsi, Paolo, 1859–1935—Bibliography. 3. Sicily—Antiquities. 4. Italy—Antiquities. I. Archivio storico per la Calabria e la Lucania. II. Agnello, Giuseppe.

A C 37-2031

New York. Public library for Library of Congress [2]

AN
(Keogh, A.)

Papers in honor of Andrew Keogh, librarian of Yale university, by the staff of the library, 30 June 1938. New Haven, Priv. print., 1938.

ix, 492 p. illus., fold. plan, facsims. 24½cm.

CONTENTS.—There is honor in one's own country, by C. E. Rush.—The books sent from England by Jeremiah Dummer to Yale college, by Anne S. Pratt.—Notes on some Arabic manuscripts on curious subjects in the Yale university library, by Leon Nemoy.—Beginnings of printing in New Haven; from letters of Benjamin Franklin and James Parker. By Winnifred R. Reid.—Carlyle, Neuberg, and Frederick the Great, by Emily H. Hall.—Contribution to a bibliography of Francis Bacon; editions before 1700 in Yale libraries, by Dorothy F. Livingston and Mollie M. Patton, with the assistance of Florence E. Adams, R. G.

(Continued on next card)

38-16515

[5]

Papers in honor of Andrew Keogh ... 1938. (Card 2)

CONTENTS—Continued.

Stephens, and Dora H. Goldschmidt.—Bookplates of the Yale libraries, 1780–1846, by G. M. Troxell.—George Catlin's portraits of North American Indians, by Ruth R. Brown.—The philosophical apparatus of Yale college, by H. M. Fuller.—A Roger Sherman notebook, by D. G. Wing.—Letters to Sarah Storrow from Spain by Washington Irving, ed. by Barbara D. Simison.—A ledger-book (1771–1787) of William Ward, silversmith, by Emma H. E. Stephenson.—Historical notes on the catalogues and classifications of the Yale university library, by Anna M. Monrad, with the assistance of M. E. Vosburgh and Ragnhild F. Lühnenschloss.—A selection of Baskerville imprints in the Yale university library, described by Rebecca D. Townsend and Margaret Currier, with the assistance of Marcia M. Lutz.—A letter of Robert Burns, by Dorothea Bolton.—President Stiles's letter to Ebeling, by Dorothy W. Bridg-

(Continued on next card)

38-16515

[5]

Papers in honor of Andrew Keogh ... 1938. (Card 3)

CONTENTS—Continued.

water.—Thoreau's plan of a farm, by B. L. Hatch.—The "Trumbull manuscript collections" and early Connecticut libraries, by Malcolm Sills and Eleanor S. Upton.—An apparently unrecorded appearance of Gray's Elegy, 1751: an appendix to Stokes, by Michael Rothkrug.—American imprints and their donors in the Yale college library of 1742, by Margaret L. Johnson.—A Yale bibliophile in European book shops, by Zara J. Powers.—The list of books sent by Jeremiah Dummer, by Louise M. Bryant and Mary Patterson.

1. Yale university. Library. 2. Keogh, Andrew, 1869– I. Yale university. Library.

38-16515

Library of Congress Z733.Y18P

——— ~~Copy 2.~~

Copyright A119308 [5] [010.4] 027.77468

NNBC
(Papini)

Papini, settant'anni, 9 gennaio 1951. [Firenze] Vallecchi [1951] 162 p. illus. 21cm.

No. 35 of 100 copies with autograph of Papini.
"Notizie bibliografiche," p. 147–162.

581962B. 1. Papini, Giovanni, 1881–
N. Y. P. L. June 7, 1951

* C p.v.3844

Parahiba, Brazil (State). Estatística e publicidade, Departamento de.
...As homenagens da Paraíba á passagem do aniversário do presidente Vargas. João Pessôa, Paraíba, 1939. 16 p. illus., plates. 30½cm.

At head of title: Departamento de estatística e publicidade (Serviço de divulgação e publicidade).
Portrait on cover.
Includes ceremonies and addresses at the dedication of the Instituto de educação and other schools.

1. Education—Brazil—Parahiba, 20th cent. 2. Vargas, Getulio, pres. Brazil, 1884–
N. Y. P. L. May 14, 1942

*OEL

Paris. Université. Institut des études islamiques.
Mélanges offerts à William Marçais par l'Institut d'études islamiques de l'Université de Paris avec le concours du Centre national de la recherche scientifique, du gouvernement général de l'Algérie, de l'Institut des hautes études marocaines et de l'Institut des hautes études de Tunis. Paris, G.-P. Maisonneuve et cie, 1950. xiii,329 p. illus.,map. 28cm.
Bibliographical footnotes.
"Travaux de M. William Marçais," p. ix-xiii.

1. Arabic studies. 2. Marçais, William, 1872-
NYPL

E-11
1501

HET PAROOL, Amsterdam.
Gerritt Jan van Heuven Goedhart, bijdragen tot een biografie; met medewerking van Dag Hammarskjöld [et al.] samengesteld door S. Carmiggelt en Johan Winkler. Amsterdam, 1959. 126 p. illus., ports. 25cm.

1. Heuven Goedhart, Gerrit Jan van, 1901-1956. I. Carmiggelt, Simon, 1913- , ed. II. Winkler, Johan, 1898- , ed. III. Hammarskjöld, Dag, 1905- . IV. Title.
NN R 11. 60 m/ (OC)I, II, III, IV OS PC, 1, I, II, III SL E, 1, I, II, III (LC1, X1, Z1)

AE-10
1041

Παρρησία (Parrhesia. Fröhliche Zuversicht) Karl Barth, zum 80. Geburstag am 10. Mai 1966. Zürich, EVZ-Verlag (1966)

xii, 723 p. 1 port. 25 cm.

"Tabula gratulatoria": [9] p. inserted.
"Bibliographie zusammengestellt von Eberhard Busch": p. [700]-723.
Bibliographical footnotes.

1. Theology--Essays and misc. 2. Barth, Karl, 1886- --Bibl. I. Barth, Karl, 1886-
NN * R 1.69 l/J OC, I PC, 1, 2, I SL (LC1, X1, Z1)

---

*QV

PASTRNEK, FRANTIŠEK, 1853-1940, ed.
Jan Kollár, 1793-1852; sborník statí o životě, působení a literarní činnosti pěvce "Slávy dcery" na oslavu jeho stoletých narozenin red. Františka Pastrnka vydaly Český akademický spolek ve Vídni a Slovenský akademický spolok "Tatran" vo Viedni. Ve Vídni, Nákladem obou spolkoû, Tiskem J. Otty v Praze, 1893. 283 p. illus., ports., facsims. 26cm.

Contributions by various authors in Czech, Croat, Polish, Serbian, Slovak, Ukrainian, or Wendic.
1. Kollár, Jan, 1793-1852.
NN R 7. 65 a/b OC PC, 1 SL S, 1 (LC1, X1, Z1)

E-14
1819

Patterns of the life-world; essays in honor of John Wild. Edited by James M. Edie, Francis H. Parker [and] Calvin O. Schrag. Evanston, Northwestern University Press, 1970.

xi, 414 p. port. 24 cm. (Northwestern University studies in phenomenology & existential philosophy)

CONTENTS.—Insight, by F. H. Parker.—Why be uncritical about the life-world? By H. B. Veatch.—Homage to Saint Anselm, by R. Jordan.—Art and philosophy, by J. M. Anderson.—The phenomenon of world, by R. R. Ehman.—The life-world and its historical (Continued)

NN R 7. 71 w/z OC, I, II, III, IV PC, 1, 2, I, II, III, IV SL (LC1, X1, Z1)

2

PATTERNS of the life-world... (Card 2)
horizon, by C. O. Schrag.—The Lebenswelt as ground and as Leib in Husserl: somatology, psychology, sociology, by E. Paci.—Life-world and structures, by C. A. van Peursen.—The miser, by E. W. Straus.—Monetary value and personal value, by G. Schrader.—Individualisms, by W. L. McBride.—Sartre the individualist, by W. Desan.—The nature of social man, by M. Natanson.—The problem of the will and philosophical discourse, by P. Ricouer.--Structuralism and humanism, by M. Dufrenne.—The illusion of monolinear time, by N. Lawrence.—Can grammar be thought? By J. M. Edie.—The existentialist critique of objectivity, by S. J. Todes and H. L. Dreyfus.—Bibliography (p. 391-400)

1. Philosophy--Addresses, essays, lectures. 2. Phenomenalism--Addresses, essays, lectures. I. Wild, John Daniel, 1902- . II. Edie, James M., ed. III. Parker, Francis H., ed. IV. Schrag, Calvin O., ed.

---

*C-5 p.v. 214

PAUL ARÈNE, son centenaire, Sisteron, 27 juin 1943. [Cannes, 1944] 1 v. (unpaged) plate, ports., facsims. 27cm.

Cover title.
Chiefly speeches delivered at the centenary celebration for Paul Arène.

1. Arène, Paul Auguste, 1843-1896.
NN * * R 5. 56 J/P OC PC, 1 SL (LC1, X1, Z1)

---

* PXS

PAUL LAZARUS GEDENKBUCH.; Beiträge zur Würdigung der letzten Rabbinergeneration in Deutschland. Jerusalem, 1961. 160 p. port. 23cm.

Added t. p., introd. and table of contents in Hebrew.
CONTENTS.--Paul Lazarus--sein Leben und Wirken in Deutschland, von L. Baerwald.--Paul Lazarus in der Jugendarbeit, von H. Hahn.--Paul Lazarus in Israel, von M. Elk.--Aus einer Predigt, gehalten beim Abschied von der Gemeinde Wiesbaden von P. Lazarus--Bibliography of Publications by Paul Lazarus, by H. Lazarus-Yafeh (p. 42-51)--Etwas vom Judisch-Theolog- (Continued)

NN R 2. 64 p/ OC PC, 1, 2 SL J1, 2 (LC1, X1, Z1)

3

PAUL LAZARUS GEDENKBUCH... (Card 2)

ischen Seminar in Breslau, von K. Wilhelm.--Erinnerungen an meine Jahre als Feldrabbiner, von G. Salzberger.--Eine Krisis im rabbinischen Berufe und ihre Uberwindung, von M. Eschelbacher.--Der Rabbiner in der Kleingemeinde, von S. Ucko.--Jugendrabbiner in Frankfurt am Main, von H. Lemle.--N. A. Nobel als Prediger, von E. Simon.--Life and Work of B. Jacob, von E. I. Jacob.--Emil Cohn--fighter and poet, by B. Coh.--Schicksalsreiche Jahre im Saargebiet, von S. F. Rülf.--Leo Baeck--the last teacher of the Lehranstalt, by W. Hamburger.--Tradition and Traditions by M. Gruenewald. (Continued)

PAUL LAZARUS GEDENKBUCH... (Card 3)

As a German rabbi to America, by H. Frank.--Franz Rosenzweig in his student years, von N. N. Glatzer.--Franz Rosenzweig and the German rabbis, by I. Maybaum.

1. Lazarus, Paul, 1888-1951. 2. Rabbis--Germany.

L-10
6944
v. 4

PAUWELS, J. L.
Verzamelde opstellen aangeboden aande auteur ter gelegenheid van zijn 65 e verjaardag. Assen, Van Gorcum, 1965. 231 p. port., map. 25cm. (Studia theodisca. 4)

1. Dutch language--Dialects. I. Series.
NN R 12. 66 r/L OC (OS)I PC, 1, I (LC1, X1, Z1)

... **Peabody** studies in psychology, edited by Lyle H. Lanier ... Columbus, O., The American psychological association, The Ohio state university [1938]
iii, 237 p. incl. illus., diagrs., tables. front. (port.) 25cm. (Psychological monographs. v. 50, no. 5; whole no. 225)
"Peterson memorial number."
"Erratum" slip inserted between p. 176 and 177.
Bibliography at end of most of the studies.
CONTENTS.—Joseph Peterson.—Bibliography of the writings of Joseph Peterson, by L. H. Lanier (p. 5-11)—Does practice with inverting lenses make vision normal? By Joseph Peterson and J. K. Peterson.—Factors affecting speed in serial verbal reactions, by J. R. Stroop.—Maturity and learning ability, by W. W. Cruze.—The behavior of right and wrong responses during work and rest intervals, by Katherine Vickery.—Learn-
(Continued on next card)
39-13504
[7]

... **Peabody** studies in psychology ... [1938] (Card 2)
CONTENTS—Continued.
ing to generalize, by J. L. Graham.—Comparative studies of full and mixed blood North Dakota Indians, by C. W. Telford.—Comparative studies of certain mental disorders among whites and Negroes in Georgia during the decade 1923-32, by J. E. Greene.—The measurement of attitudes towards mathematics, by Euri B. Bolton.—A study of the interests of college students, by K. C. Garrison.—The relation of intelligence of college freshmen to parental occupation, by B. F. Haught.—The descriptive categories of psychology, by L. H. Lanier.

1. Peterson, Joseph, 1878-1935. 2. Psychology—Addresses, essays, lectures. I. Lanier, Lyle Hicks, 1903- ed.
39-13504
Library of Congress BF1.P8 vol. 50, no. 5
[7]
[(159.9082)] (150.82) [159.904] 150.4

D-11
3945
PEAKE, ARTHUR SAMUEL, 1865-1929.
Arthur Samuel Peake, 1865-1929; essays in commemoration, by Elsie Cann [and others] and selections from his writings. Edited by John T. Wilkinson. London, Epworth press [1958] 167 p. port. 23cm.

CONTENTS. — In commemoration: Arthur Samuel Peake: a retrospect, by H. G. Meecham. Oxford days, by W. F. Lofthouse. Manchester
(Continued)
NN R 11. 58 g/H OC, I, II, IIbo PC, 1, I, II SL (LC1, X1, Z1)

PEAKE, ARTHUR SAMUEL, 1865-1929. Arthur Samuel Peake, 1865-1929... (Card 2)
university, by T. W. Manson. Author and editor, by A. V. Murray. Ecumenical churchman, by J. T. Wilkinson. A layman's tribute, by A. B. Hillis. Impressions of an early student, by W. E. Farndale. In the study, by E. Cann. In the family circle, by L. S. Peake. —Excerpts from the writings of A. S. Peake: Critical: The legitimacy and necessity of Biblical criticism. The permanent results of Biblical criticism. History as a channel of revelation. Biblical: The teaching of Jeremiah. The teaching of the Epistle to the Hebrews. Theological: The Quintessence of
(Continued)

PEAKE, ARTHUR SAMUEL, 1865-1929. Arthur Samuel Peake, 1865-1929... (Card 3)
Paulinism. Ecclesiastical: The reunion of the Christian churches. -- Select bibliography (p. 161-167).

1. Bible--Essays and misc. I. Wilkinson, John Thomas, ed. II. Cann, Elsie.

D-14
3760
PENNSYLVANIA UNIVERSITY.
Studies in medieval literature. In honor of Professor Albert Croll Baugh. Edited by MacEdward Leach. Editorial committee: Frederick L. Jones [and others] Philadelphia, University of Pennsylvania Press [1961]
844 p. port. 22 cm.
Includes bibliographical references.
CONTENTS.—Biographical sketch of Albert Croll Baugh.—A partial list of the publications of Albert Croll Baugh (p. 11-18) — Was Chaucer a free thinker? by R. S. Loomis.—The development of the
(Continued)
NN*R 7. 63 g/R (OC)I OS PC, 1, 2, 3, I SL (LC1, X1, Z1)
[I]

PENNSYLVANIA UNIVERSITY. Studies in medieval literature. (Card 2)
Wife of Bath, by R. A. Pratt.—Chaucer's Retraction, a review of opinion, by J. D. Gordon.—From Gorgias to Troilus, by H. Craig.—Scene-division in Chaucer's Troilus and Criseyde, by F. L. Utley.—Wyclif, Langland, Gower, and the Pearl poet on the subject of aristocracy, by J. H. Fischer.—Remarques sur le prologue du Couronnement de Louis, v. 1-11, by J. Frappier.—The enfances of Tristan and English tradition, by H. Newstead.—The antecedents of Sir Orfeo, by J. B. Severs.—The buried lover escapes, by A. Taylor.—Middle English metrical romances and their audience, by K. Brunner.—The comic element in the Wakefield Noah, by H. H. Schless.—The conclusion of the
(Continued)

PENNSYLVANIA UNIVERSITY. Studies in medieval literature. (Card 3)
Perceval continuation in Bern ms. 113, by W. Roach.—Readings from folios 94 to 131, Ms. Cotton Vitellius Axv by K. Malone.—Some notes on Anglo-Saxon poetry, by F. P. Magoun, Jr.—A Middle English medical manuscript from Norwich, by C. F. Bühler.—A manuscript of the Chronicle of Mathieu d'Escouchy and Simon Greban's Epitaph for Charles VII of France, by S. C. Aston.

1. Literature--Hist. and crit., Middle Ages. 2. Baugh, Albert Croll, 1891- 3. English literature, Middle, 1100-1500--Addresses, essays, lectures. I. Leach, MacEdward, ed.

BAC
Persecution and liberty; essays in honor of George Lincoln Burr. New York, The Century co. [©1931]
xviii, 482 p. front. (port.) facsims. 24½cm. $5.00
"This edition is limited to five hundred copies of which this is no. 183."
Includes bibliographies.
CONTENTS.—Introduction, by J. F. Jameson.—The theory of persecution, by E. W. Nelson.—Hebrew history and historical method, by A. T. Olmstead.—Nugae palaeographicae, by E. A. Lowe.—A lost diploma of Otto III, by E. V. Moffett.—Social aspects of medieval heresy, by A. P. Evans.—The consent of the English lower clergy to taxation during the reign of Henry III, by W. E. Lunt.—The attitude of Erasmus toward toleration, by W. K. Ferguson.—Sebastian Castellio and the toleration controversy of the sixteenth century, by R. H. Bainton.—Lelio Sozzini's
(Continued on next card)
31-16384
[5]

Persecution and liberty ... [©1931] (Card 2)
CONTENTS—Continued.
confession of faith, by E. M. Hulme.—Vincenzo Maggi, a Protestant politician, by F. C. Church.—John de Feckenham and the Marian reaction, by A. H. Sweet.—The Colloquium heptaplomeres of Jean Bodin, by G. H. Sabine.—James I of England and the "Little Beagle" letters, by F. G. Marcham.—A seventeenth century humanitarian: Hermann Löher, by Lois O. Gibbons.—The first Earl of Shaftesbury, by Louise F. Brown.—Further considerations on the origins and nature of the enlightened despotism, by G. M. Dutcher.—The young Barère, by Leo Gershoy.—Early revolutionary newspapers, by G. G. Andrews.—The French revolution: conspiracy or circumstance? By L. R. Gottschalk.—Agitation against the slave trade in Rhode Island, 1784-1790, by Elizabeth Donnan.

1. Persecution. 2. Liberty. 3. Religious liberty. 4. History—Addresses, essays, lectures. 5. Burr, George Lincoln, 1857-
31-16384
Library of Congress D6.P4
~~Copy 2.~~
Copyright A 38947 [5] 904

D-12
7027

PERSPECTIVES in psychological theory: essays in honor of Heinz Werner. Edited by Bernard Kaplan and Seymour Wapner. New York, International Universities Press[1960] 384 p. illus. port. 23cm.

Includes bibliographies.

CONTENTS.—Introductory remarks, by B. Kaplan and S. Wapner.—The experiences of inner status, by S. Arieti.—The development of double function terms in children: an exploratory investigation, by S. E. Asch and H. Nerlove.—The functions of perceiving: new look retrospect, by J. S. Bruner and G. S. Klein.—A theoretical and experimental inquiry into concrete values and value systems, by T. Dembo.—Sensoritonic theory and the concept of self-realization, by K. Goldstein.—Why "Mama" and "Papa"? By R. Jakobson.—Selector-inte-

(Continued)

NN*R 11.60 s/ ; OC, I, II, IIIb* PC, 1, 2, I, II SL (LC1, X1) (Z1)

PERSPECTIVES in psychological theory... (Card 2)

grator mechanisms in behavior, by N. R. F. Maier.—Resistance to being rubricized, by A. H. Maslow.—Organism and quantity: a study of organic structure as a quantitative problem, by G. Murphy.—Psychoanalysis as a developmental psychology, by D. Rapaport.—Cognitive embeddedness in problem solving: a theoretical and experimental analysis, by M. Scheerer and M. D. Huling.—Instinctive behavior, maturation—experience and development, by T. C. Schneirla.—The problem of individuality in development, by H. A. Witkin.—Publications of Heinz Werner (p. [362]-374)

1. Psychology--Addresses, essays, lectures. 2. Werner, Heinz, 1890- . I. Wapner, Seymour, 1917- , ed. II. Kaplan, Bernard, ed. III. Kaplan, Bernard.

L–10
6353
Heft 12

Perst, Otto, ed.

Festschrift zum 60. Geburtstag von Karl August Eckhardt. Marburg, Trautvetter & Fischer, 1961. 310 p. illus., maps, fold. geneal. tables. 24cm. (Beiträge zur Geschichte der Werranlandschaft und ihrer Nachbargebiete. Heft 12)

Bibliographical footnotes.

CONTENTS.—Die Pfalz auf dem Ermschwerder Burgberg, von W. Görich.—Kaufungen und Kassel. Pfalz-Kloster-Stadt, von W. A. Eckhardt.—Kassel und das Stapelrecht der Stadt Münden, von R. Friderici.—Beiträge zur Geschichte der Befestigungen Han-

(Continued)

NN R 9.63 OC,Ibo (OS)I PC,1,2,3,I (LC1,X1,Z1)

Perst, Otto, ed. Festschrift... 1961... (Card 2)

noversch Mündens, von K. Brethauer.—Zur Geschichte der Ämter Ziegenberg und Ludwigstein, von A. Eckhardt.—Das Christophorusbild in der Kirche zu Kleinalmerode, von G. Ganssauge.—Ein Gutachten über Georg Witzel und seine Lehre, von G. Franz.—Das Beneficium Jacobinum in Eschwege von K. Holzapfel.—Ein unbekanntes Kopiar der Diede zum Fürstenstein, von W. E. Kellner.—Eine bedeutende hessische Beamtenfamilie aus dem Witzenhäuser Raum (Stammtafel Henkel), von E. Grimmell.—Die protestantische Pfarrkirche zu Oberrieden, von D. Grossmann.—"Der Stadtkämmerei lehnbar." Die Stadt Eschwege als Obereigentümerin von Grund und Boden im Ort und seiner Gemarkung, von O. Perst.—Vormärz und Revolution in den kurhessischen Landen "am Werra-Strom," von E. G. Franz.—Was erzählt der 'Prinz Rosa-Stramin'? Von F. Neumann.

1. Eckhardt, Karl August, 1901- . 2. Werra river and valley, Germany—Hist. 3. Hesse—Hist. I. Series. II. Perst, Otto.

E-11
8861

PETITE REVUE DES BIBLIOPHILES DAUPHINOIS. Numéro spécial en hommage à Stendhal. Grenoble, Impr. Allier, 1955. xv, 163 p. ports. 26cm.

Published also with title: Dans le sillage de Stendhal. Edited by Yves du Parc.

Bibliographical footnotes.

CONTENTS.--Hommage à Stendhal, par Y. du Parc.--Les oeuvres

(Continued)

NN 2.64 f/B (OC)I OS PC, 1, I SL (LC1, X1, Z1)

3

PETITE REVUE DES BIBLIOPHILES DAUPHINOIS. Numéro spécial en hommage à Stendhal... (Card 2)

non littéraires de Stendhal, par G. Letonnelier et Y. du Parc.--Une lettre inédite de Stendhal au chevalier Cobianchi, par A. Denier et Y. du Parc.--Une relation anglaise annotée par Stendhal des moeurs américaines vers 1830, par P. Vaillant.--Stendhal et Marseille: lettres consulaires, par Y. du Parc et A. Villard.--Il signor Lisimaco, chancelier de Stendhal, par Y. du Parc.--Sur un volume annoté par Stendhal, par V. del Litto.--Stendhal,

(Continued)

PETITE REVUE DES BIBLIOPHILES DAUPHINOIS. Numéro spécial en hommage à Stendhal. (Card 3)

Ernest Hébert et le prince Caetani, par Y. du Parc et A. Denier.

1. Beyle, Marie Henri, 1783-1842. I. Du Parc, Yves, ed. Dans le sillage de Stendhal.

3-MAR

Petrovics Elek emlekkönyv. Budapest: Kiadják az Országos magyar szépművészeti múzeum barátai és tisztviselői, 1934. 241 p. illus., plates, ports. 26cm.

Added t.-p.: Hommage à Alexis Petrovics. Budapest: Les amis et fonctionnaires du Musée hongrois des beaux-arts, 1934.

No. 216 of 300 copies printed.

"Versions des articles en langues étrangères [English, French, German or Italian]" p. 135–241.

CONTENTS.—Balógh, Jolán. Agostino di Duccio egy ismeretlen Madonnája.—Gombosi, György. A Márkustemplom porticusa.—Hekler, Antal. A Giustiniani Athena új megvilágitásban.—Hoffmann, Edith. A régi osztrák müvészet egy ismeretlen fontos emlékéről.—Meller, Simon. Antonio Pollaiuolo tervrajzai Francesco Sforza lovas-

(Continued)

N. Y. P. L. July 8, 1936

Petrovics Elek emlekkönyv. (Card 2)

szobrához.—Oroszlán, Zoltán. Szilenosz-szobrocskák a Szépművészeti múzeum antik terrakotta-gyüjteményében.—Péter, András. Két sienai trecento-rajz.—Pigler, Andor. Valerius Maximus és az újkori képzőművészetek.—Rózsaffy, Dezső. Az igazi Munkácsy.—Somogyi, József. A tell halafi ásatások jelentősége.—Szentiványi, Gyula. Szerelmey Miklós.—Takács, Zoltán. Sino-Hunnica.—Wilde, János. Néhány velencei női képmás a renaissance korából.—Zichy, István gróf. A Képes Krónika miniatürjei viselettörténeti szempontból.—Az Országos magyar szépművészeti múzeum néhány szerzeménye az utolsó húsz év alatt.

827882A. 1. Petrovics, Elek, 1873- . 2. Art—Essays and misc.
N. Y. P. L. July 8, 1936

F–10
296

Pfeddersheim, Germany.

1200 [i. e. Zwölfhundert] Jahre Pfeddersheim. Zum Tage der Wiederverleihung der Stadtrechte und zur Feier des Jubiläums am 22., 23. und 24. Mai 1954. [Pfeddersheim, 1954] 101 p. illus. 27cm.

"1200-Jahrfeier mit Wiederverleihung des Stadttitels am 22., 23. und 24. Mai 1954 und Kreisbauerntag [Festprogramm]" 24 p., inserted.

(Continued)

NN** 7.57 ODt EDt PC,1 SL (LC1,X1,Z1)

Pfeddersheim, Germany. 1200 ‹i. e. Zwölfhundert› Jahre Pfeddersheim . . . (Card 2)

CONTENTS.—Landschaft und Schicksal, von F. M. Illert.—Aus der Urgeschichte von Pfeddersheim, von W. Weiler.—1200Jährige Pfeddersheimer Geschichte, von W. Alter.—Volksschule und Berufsschule, von G. Friess.—Die evangelische Gemeinde Pfeddersheim, von K. Goebel.—Aus der Geschichte der katholischen Kirche und der Pfarrgemeinde, von J. Dürck.—Tatsachen und Gedanken zum Klima Pfeddersheim, von A. Cappel.—Pfeddersheims Landwirtschaft im Wandel der Zeiten, von J. Knab.—Zum Lob des Weines, von E. Meier.—Die Entwicklung von Handel, Handwerk und Gewerbe, von W. Scheuermann.—Die Enzinger Union Werke.—Die Johann Braun A. G.—Pfeddersheim in neuerer Zeit, von H. Haupt.—Die 1200 Jahrfeier Pfeddersheim, von E. Garst.

1. Pfeddersheim, Germany— Hist. t. 1954.

Philipp, Franz Adolf, *ed.*

In honour of Daryl Lindsay; essays and studies, edited by Franz Philipp and June Stewart. Melbourne, New York, Oxford University Press, 1964.

xxi, 246 p. plates, port. 28 cm.

Includes bibliographical references.

CONTENTS.—Daryl Lindsay: the man, by H. S. Newland.—The idea of a great gallery, by K. Clark.— On buying pictures for a public gallery, by T. Bodkin.—Some notes on museum directors and trustees, by W. S. Lewis.—The training of a gallery administrator, by

(Continued)

 3

PFEIFER, GOTTFRIED, 1901- , ed.

Heidelberg und die Rhein-Neckar-Lande. Festschrift zum 34. Deutschen Geographentag vom 4. bis 7. Juni 1963 in Heidelberg. Hrsg. von Gottfried Pfeifer, Hans Graul [und] Hermann Overbeck, Schriftleitung: Wendelin Klaer. Heidelberg, In Kommission Keyserche Verlagsbuchhandlung, 1963. 291 p. illus., maps (5 fold. part col., in pocket) 24cm.

(Continued)

 2

PHILIPP, FRANZ ADOLF, ed. In honour of Daryl Lindsay... (Card 2)

T. Sizer.—The building of a great gallery, by R. Boyd.—The Felton painter and a newly acquired Apulian comic vase by his hand, by A. D. Trendall.—Observations on the dating of two Chinese Buddhist figures, by L. B. Cox.—A portrait of a cardinal by El Greco, by A. G. Xydis.—The sources of "Hercules and Antaeus" by Rubens, by U. Hoff.—Poussin's "Crossing of the Red Sea," by F. Philipp.—Tiepolo's "The banquet of Cleopatra," by A. Morassi.—The eidetic and the borrowed image: an interpretation of Blake's Theory and practice of art, by J. Burke.—"The lock" as a theme in the work of John Con-

(Continued)

PFEIFER, GOTTFRIED, 1901- , ed: Heidelberg und die Rhein-Neckar-Lande. (Card 2)

Bibliographical footnotes.

1. Heidelberg. 2. Rhine valley--Historical geography. 3. Neckar river and valley--Historical geography. I. Deutscher Geographentag. 34th, Heidelberg, 1963. II. Graul, Hans, joint ed. III. Overbeck, Hermann, joint ed. IV. Graul, Hans.

PHILIPP, FRANZ ADOLF, ed. In honour of Daryl Lindsay... (Card 3)

stable, by W. G. Constable.—Two studies by Degas, by D. C. Rich.—Tom Roberts and Alfred Deakin, by R. M. Crawford.

1. Lindsay, Sir Daryl, 1890- . 2. Melbourne. National gallery of Victoria. 3. Museums--Administration. I. Stewart, June, joint ed. II. Title. III. Stewart, June. IV. Philipp, Franz Adolf.

The **Philadelphia Anthropological Society:** papers presented on its golden anniversary, edited by Jacob W. Gruber. New York, Distributed by Columbia University Press, 1967.

ix, 162 p. 25 cm. (Temple University publications)

"A day long session ... held at the University of Pennsylvania Museum on October 12, 1962."

Includes bibliographies.

CONTENTS.—Anthropology in Philadelphia, by A. I. Hallowell.—The American Philosophical Society in American anthropology, by J. F. Freeman.—The direction of physical anthropology, by H. L.

(Continued)

 2

PHILOLOGICA; the Malone anniversary studies, edited by Thomas A. Kirby and Henry Bosley Woolf. Baltimore, Johns Hopkins Press, 1949. x, 382 p. illus., port., maps. 24cm.

Includes bibliographical references. "List of the writings of Kemp Malone": p. 363-379.

558694B. 1. Malone, Kemp, 1889- 2. English language. 3. English literature, Middle, 1100-1500—Hist. and crit. 4. Anglo-Saxon literature —Hist. and crit. I. Woolf, Henry Bosley, 1910- II. Kirby, Thomas Austin, ed.

The PHILADELPHIA Anthropological Society: papers presented on its golden anniversary... (Card 2)

Shapiro.—The paleo-indian, by H. M. Wormington.—Mesoamerican archaeology, by G. F. Ekholm.—Arctic anthropology in America, by C. S. Chard.—Northern woodland ethnology, by F. Eggan.—A challenge for linguistics today, by W. L. Chafe.—Anthropology and the museum, by F. J. Dockstader.

1. American--Archaeology. 2. Indians, American--Anthropology. 3. Anthropology--Addresses, essays, lectures. I. Gruber, Jacob W., ed.

PHILOLOGICAL essays; studies in Old and Middle English language and literature, in honour of Herbert Dean Merritt. Edited by James L. Rosier. The Hague, Mouton, 1970. 203 p. ports. 27cm. (Janua linguarum; studia memoriae Nicolai van Wijk dedicata. Series major, 37)

Bibliographical footnotes.

CONTENTS.--Herbert Dean Meritt, by R. W. Ackermann.--Bibli-

(Continued)

 4

PHILOLOGICAL essays... (Card 2)

ography of the writings of Herbert Dean Meritt, compiled by F.C. Robinson and J.J. Quinn (p. [13]-15).--On the consonantal phonemes of Old English, by S.M. Kuhn.--Much and many, by A.H. Marckwardt.--Beowulf's old age, by J.C. Pope.--Destiny and the heroic warrior in Beowulf, by G.V. Smithers.--Death and transfiguration: Guthlac B, by J.L. Rosier.--Verse influences in Old English prose, by A. Campbell.--Lexicography and literary criticism, by F.C. Robinson.--The rhetorical lore of the Boceras in Byhrtferth's Manual, by J.J. Murphy.--The authorship of the account of King Edgar's establishment

(Continued)

PHILOLOGICAL essays... (Card 3)

of monasteries, by D. Whitelock.--Six words in the Blickling homilies, by R.L. Collins.--Some notes on the Liber scintillarum and its Old English gloss, by R. Derolez.--A.S. Napier, 1853-1916, by N. Ker.--The Venus of Alanus de Insulis and the Venus of Chaucer, by D.B. Loomis.--The tale of Gareth and the unity of Le Morte Darthur, by R.W. Ackerman.

(Continued)

PHILOLOGICAL essays... (Card 4)

1. Anglo-Saxon language--Addresses, essays, lectures. 2. Anglo-Saxon literature--Addresses, essays, lectures. 3. English language, Middle, 1100-1500--Addresses, essays, lectures. 4. English literature, Middle, 1100-1500--Addresses, essays, lectures. I. Meritt, Herbert Dean, 1904- II. Rosier, James L., ed. III. Series.

Write on slip words underlined below and class mark —

STG

Philological studies in honor of Walter Miller. Presented by former students upon his completion of fifty years of teaching. Edited by Rodney Potter Robinson... [Columbia: The Univ. of Missouri, 1936] 189 p. front. (port.), 12 facsims. 26½cm. (Missouri. University. The University of Missouri studies; a quarterly of research. v. 11, no. 3.)

Bibliographical footnotes.

Contents.—Foreword, by J. R. Angell.—The gymnasium in Ptolemaic Egypt, by T. A. Brady.—Romanos and the mystery play of the East, by Marjorie Carpenter.—Arts and crafts in the epics of Vergil, Lucan and Statius, by M. E. Folse.—Botanical refer-

(Continued)

N. Y. P. L. January 14, 1937

Philological studies in honor of Walter Miller... (Continued)

ences in Hemacandra, by H. M. Johnson.—The form of Varro's Menippean satires, by B. P. McCarthy.—The cicada, a note on Homer, Iliad III, 150 ff., by F. C. Murgotten.—The clausula, by L. J. Richardson.—The Hersfeldensis and the Fuldensis of Ammianus Marcellinus, by R. P. Robinson.—Manuscript no. 16 of the Michigan collection, by H. A. Saunders.—Publications by Walter Miller.

1. Classical studies. I. Miller, Walter, 1864- II. Robinson, Rodney Potter, 1890- , ed. III. Ser.

N. Y. P. L. January 14, 1937

Write on slip words underlined below and class mark —

RDTA

...**Philologisch**-philosophische Studien; Festschrift für Eduard Wechssler zum 19. Oktober, 1929. Jena: W. Gronau, 1929. 404 p. front. (port.) 8°. (Berliner Beiträge zur romanischen Philologie. Bd. 1.)

Verzeichnis der bis 1929 erschienenen Veröffentlichungen Eduard Wechsslers, von Bruno Rech, p. 1–5.

1. Wechssler, Eduard, 1869- . Bibl. 2. Wechssler, Eduard, 1869- ,

N. Y. P. L. March 25, 1931

RKE

Philologische studien; festgabe für Eduard Sievers zum 1. oktober, 1896. Halle a. S., M. Niemeyer, 1896.

vi, 441 p. 24cm.

Contents. — Etymologisch-kulturhistorisches. Von O. Schrader. — Wimmers runenlehre. Von G. Hempl. — Bemerkungen zu Cynewulfs Crist. Von A. S. Cook.—Zur textkritik der York plays. Von F. Holthausen.—Ueber eine zweifelhafte ausnahme der frühme. dehnung von a, e, o in offenen silben. Von E. E. Hale.—Das Merowingerepos und die fränkische heldensage. Von C. Voretzsch.—Der nominativ pluralis der a-deklination im althochdeutschen. Von G. Burchardi.—Das Hildebrandslied. Von F. Kauffmann.—Zur metrik Otfrids von Weissenburg. Von F. Saran.—Personennamen aus dem höfischen epos in Baiern. Von F. Panzer.—Zur sprache Veldekes. Von J. H. Kern.—Die episode vom raube der königin in Hartmanns Iwein. Von G. Rosenhagen.—Zur be-

(Continued on next card)

7—16269

[a28f1]

Philologische studien ... 1896. (Card 2)

Contents—Continued.

antwortung der frage nach den quellen von Wolframs Parzival. Von E. Wechssler.—Das verhältnis des Lorengel zum Lohengrin. Von E. Elster.—Die ältesten deutschen pilgerlieder. Von W. Mettin.—Notiz über einige elsässische bilderhandschriften aus dem ersten viertel des 15. jahrhunderts. Von R. Kautzsch.—Fauststudien. Von G. E. Karsten.—Die widmung von Georg Forsters 'Ansichten vom Niederrhein'. Von A. Leitzmann.—Die deminutiva in der Berner mundart. Von H. Stickelberger.—Die siebenbürgische vokalkürzung. Von A. Scheiner.—Ueber den schwerttanz der Siebenbürger Sachsen. Von O. Wittstock.—Zu den flurnamen. Von K. Bohnenberger.—Deutsche sprache und litteratur am Philanthropin zu Dessau (1775 bis 1793) Von K. Kehrbach—Eine populäre synonymik des 16. jahrhunderts. Von J. Meier.

1. Sievers, Eduard, 1850- 2. Germanic philology—Collections.

7—16269

Library of Congress PD25.P5

[a28f1]

RAE

Philologische Studien aus dem romanisch-germanischen Kulturkreise. Karl Voretzsch zum 60. Geburtstage und zum Gedenken an seine erste akademische Berufung vor 35 Jahren, dargebracht von M. Artigas, G. Baesecke, P. Barnils, Ph. A. Becker, J. Brüch, K. Christ, A. Griera, F. Krüger, G. Moldenhauer, W. Mulertt, K. Pietsch, G. Rohlfs, F. Saran, D. Scheludko, O. Schultz-Gora, E. Sievers, F. Specht, W. Suchier, A. Wallensköld, K. Warnke, K. Weber, B. Wiese, E. Winkler, Herausgegeben von B. Schädel

(Continued)

N. Y. P. L. November 19, 1928

Phililogische Studien aus dem romanisch-germanischen Kultur kreise... (Card 2)

und W. Mulertt. Halle an der Saale: M. Niemeyer, 1927. 543 p. facsims., map, plates. 8°.

366189A. 1. Voretzsch, Karl, 1867- . 2. Philology—Collections. 3. Schaedel, Bernhard A. O., 1878-1926, editor. 4. Mulertt, Werner, 1892- , editor.

N. Y. P. L. November 19, 1928

YBX
(Dewey)

The philosopher of the common man; essays in honor of John Dewey to celebrate his eightieth birthday. New York, G. P. Putnam's sons [°1940]

4 p. l., 7-228 p. 22cm.

CONTENTS. — Ratner, Sidney. Foreword.—Kallen, H. M. Freedom and education.—Murphy, A. E. Dewey's theory of the nature and function of philosophy.—Nagel, Ernest. Dewey's reconstruction of logical theory.—Barnes, A. C. Method in aesthetics.—Randall, J. H., jr. The religion of shared experience.—Hamilton, Walton. A Deweyesque mosaic.—Patterson, E. W. Pragmatism as a philosophy of law.—Hu, Shih. The political philosophy of instrumentalism.—Dewey, John. Creative democracy, the task before us.

1. Dewey, John, 1859-

40-8301

Library of Congress B945.D44P5
——— Copy 2.
Copyright [15] 191.9

YAM

Philosophia perennis; abhandlungen zu ihrer vergangenheit und gegenwart, herausgegeben von Fritz-Joachim von Rintelen. Regensburg, J. Habbel, 1930.

2 v. front. (port.) 24½cm.

Paged continuously.
Each volume has special t.-p.
"Festgabe Josef Geyser zum 60. geburtstag."
"Das schrifttum von Joseph Geyser": bd. II, p. [1199]-1201.

CONTENTS.—I. Abhandlungen über die geschichte der philosophie.—II. Abhandlungen zur systematischen philosophie.

1. Geyser, Joseph, 1869- 2. Philosophy—Addresses, essays, lectures. I. Rintelen, Fritz Joachim von, ed.

31-2275

Library of Congress B29.P45
Copyright A—Foreign 9622
[2] 104

E-11
9397

PHILOSOPHICAL essays dedicated to Gunnar Aspelin on the occasion of his sixty-fifth birthday 23rd of September 1963 [Edited by Helge Bratt and others] Lund, CWK Gleerup bokförlag [1963]
364 p. front. 24cm.

"Bibliography of writings published 1917-1962 by Gunnar Aspelin," p. [319]-364.

1. Aspelin, Gunnar, 1898- . 2. Philosophy--Addresses, essays, lectures.
I. Bratt, Helge, ed. II. Bratt, Helge.
NN R 4.64 f/ OC, I, IIbo PC, 1, 2, I SL (LC1, X1, Z1) [I]

YAR

Philosophical essays in honor of James Edwin Creighton, by former students in the Sage school of philosophy of Cornell university, in commemoration of twenty-five years' service as teacher and scholar. New York, The Macmillan company, 1917. xii p., 1 l., 356 p. 24½cm.

"Editor: George Holland Sabine."

1. Philosophy—Essays, and misc. 2. Creighton, James Edwin, 1861- I. Sabine, George Holland, ed.

YBX
(Husserl)

Philosophical essays in memory of Edmund Husserl, edited by Marvin Farber ... Cambridge, Mass., Pub. for the University of Buffalo by the Harvard university press, 1940.

viii, 332 p. front. (port.) diagrs. 23cm.

CONTENTS.—An approach to phenomenology, by Dorion Cairns.—Husserl's critique of psychologism, by John Wild.—The ideal of a presuppositionless philosophy, by Marvin Farber.—On the intentionality of consciousness, by Aron Gurwitsch.—The "reality-phenomenon" and reality, by Herbert Spiegelberg.—The phenomenological concept of "horizon", by Helmut Kuhn.—Phenomenology and logical empiricism, by Felix Kaufmann.—Phenomenology and the history of science, by Jacob Klein.—Phenomenology and the social sciences, by Alfred Schuetz. — Art and phenomenology, by Fritz Kaufmann.—The relation of science to philos-

(Continued on next card)

40-35634

[8]

Philosophical essays in memory of Edmund Husserl ... 1940. (Card 2)

CONTENTS—Continued.

ophy in the light of Husserl's thought, by L. O. Kattsoff.—Husserl and the social structure of immediacy, by Charles Hartshorne.—A materialist approach to Husserl's philosophy, by V. J. McGill.—Outline-sketch of a system of metaphysics, by W. E. Hocking.—Men and the law, by Gerhart Husserl.—The ghost of modality, by Hermann Weyl.—Supplement: Grundlegende untersuchungen zum phänomenologischen ursprung der räumlichkeit der natur, by Edmund Husserl.

1. *Husserl, Edmund, 1859-1938. 2. Phenomenology. I. Farber, Marvin, ed. II. *Husserl, Edmund, 1859-1938. Grundlegende untersuchungen zum phänomenologischen ursprung der räumlichkeit der natur.

40—35634

Library of Congress B29.P463
——— ——— Copy 2.
Copyright [a41i5] 104

YAR

PHILOSOPHICAL studies in honor of Ignatius Smith. Edited by John K. Ryan. Westminster, Md., Newman press, 1952. x, 316 p. port. 24cm.

CONTENTS. — Introduction, by J. K. Ryan. — The dialectical character of scientific knowledge, by J. M. Marling. — Thomistic philosophy and international society, by Gerald Benkert. — St. Thomas Aquinas's proofs of the existence of God presented in their chronological order, by J. A. Baisnée. — Ens et unum convertuntur, by Rudolf Allers. — Chance in Aristotle and Aquinas, by J. B. McAllister. — The Protestant philosophy of John Locke, by J. T. Noonan. — Lux in spiritualibus according to the mind of St. Thomas Aquinas, by F. X.

(Continued)

NN ** R 4.53 OC, I, Ib * PC, 1, 2, I SL (LC1, Z1, X1)

PHILOSOPHICAL studies in honor of Ignatius Smith... (Card 2)

Meehan. — Existence and the first principles according to St. Thomas Aquinas, by O. Bennett. — Scheler's transition from Catholicism to pantheism, by J. Collins. — Action does not change the agent, by J. A. McWilliams. — Toward a philosophy of economics, by W. J. Mc Donald. — The recognition of miracles, by A. B. Wolter. — Freedom in the philosophy of Kant, by J. R. Rosenberg. — The law of contracts and the natural law, by B. F. Brown. — The dynamics of moral conduct, by G. C. Reilly. — Number freedom, by E. A. Maziarz.

1. Smith, Ignatius, 1886- 2. Philosophy, 1901-
I. Ryan, John Kenneth, 1897- ed.
NN** R 4.53 OC, I, Ib* PC, 1, 2, I SL (LC1, Z1, X1)

E-12
2812

PHILOSOPHIE der Toleranz; Festschrift zum 65. Geburtstag von Konstantin Radakovic, überreicht von Mitarbeitern und Schülern. Graz, Leykam [1959] 88 p. 24cm.

Bibliographical footnotes. "Veröffentlichungen von Konstantin Radakovic," p. 86-87.

CONTENTS. — Vorwort eines Freundes, von L. Biró. — Über das Gute, von R. Freundlich. — Zur Frage: "Was ist ein

(Continued)

NN R 3.65 g/B OC, Ib+ PC, 1, 2 SL (LC1, X1, Z1)

PHILOSOPHIE der Toleranz... (Card 2)

Kunstwerk?" Von R. Haller. — Das Allgemeine und das Einzelne, von G. Jánoska. — Bemerkungen zur philosophischen Soziologie, von J. Jánoska-Bendl. — Zu Nietzsches Spinozadeutung, von J. Ohms. — Franz Michael Vierthalers "Geist der Sokratik," von K. Wolf.

1. Radakovic, Konstantin, 1894- . 2. Toleration.

D-14
1960

PHILOSOPHISCHE Aufsätze. Eduard Zeller zu seinem fünfzigjährigen Doctor-Jubiläum gewidmet. Leipzig, Zentral-Antiquariat der Deutschen Demokratischen Republik, 1962. 482 p. 23cm.

Reprint of 1887 edition.
Bibliographical footnotes.
CONTENTS.--Zählen und Messen erkenntnisstheoretisch betrachtet, von H. von Helmholtz.--Zur Würdigung Comte's und des Positivismus,
(Continued)

2

PHILOSOPHISCHE Aufsätze. (Card 2)

von R. Eucken.--Spinoza und die Scholastik, von J. Freudenthal.--Die herkulanische Biographie des Polemon, von T. Gomperz.--Das Symbol, von F. Vischer.--Zur Theorie des Syllogismus und der Induktion, von B. Erdmann.--Ueber die ältesten Philosophenschulen der Griechen, von H. Diels.--Ueber den Zahlbegriff, von L. Kronecker.--Alte Bittgänge; ein religionsgeschichtlicher Beitrag, von H. Usener.--Die Einbildungskraft des Dichters; Bausteine für eine Poetik, von W. Dilthey.

1. Zeller, Eduard, 1814-1908. 2. Philosophy--Addresses, essays, lectures. I. Germany (Democratic Republic, 1949-). Zentral-Antiquariat. t. 1962

BAL

Philosophy & history; essays presented to Ernst Cassirer. Edited by Raymond Klibansky and H. J. Paton. Oxford: Clarendon Press, 1936. xii, 360 p. facsims., illus., plates. 23cm.

"Edited with the support of the Warburg Institute, London."
Bibliographical footnotes.
CONTENTS.—A definition of the concept of history, by J. Huizinga.—The historicity of things, by S. Alexander.—History and philosophy, by L. Brunschvicg.—On the so-called identity of history and philosophy, by G. Calogero.—Religion, philosophy, and history, by C. C. J. Webb.—Concerning Christian philosophy, by É. Gilson.—Towards an anthropological philosophy, by B. Groethuysen.—The transcending of time in history, by G. Gentile.—Some ambiguities in discussions concerning time, by L. S. Stebbing.—The universal in the structure of historical knowledge, by T. Litt.—On the objectivity

(Continued)

N. Y. P. L. December 9, 1936

Philosophy & history... (Card 2)

of historical knowledge, by F. Medicus.—The formation of our history of philosophy, by É. Bréhier.—Platonism in Augustine's philosophy of history, by E. Hoffmann.—The Cartesian spirit and history, by L. Lévy-Bruhl.—Veritas filia temporis, by F. Saxl.—Et in Arcadia ego, by E. Panofsky.—Some points of contact between history and natural science, by E. Wind.—The philosophical significance of comparative semantics, by H. J. Pos.—Historiography, by F. Gundolf.—History as a system, by J. Ortega y Gasset.—The philosophic character of history, by R. Klibansky.—Bibliography of E. Cassirer's writings, by R. Klibansky and W. Solmitz.

854316A. 1. History—Philosophy. 2. Cassirer, Ernst, 1874- . I. Klibansky, Raymond, ed. II. Paton, Herbert James, 1887- , ed.
N. Y. P. L. December 9, 1936

RBG

Phyllobolia, für Peter Von der Mühll zum 60. Geburtstag am 1. August 1945, von Olof Gigon [et al.] Basel, B. Schwabe [1946]

288 p. port. 25 cm.
Bibliographical footnotes.
CONTENTS.—Der erhabene und der schlichte Stil in der poetisch-rhetorischen Theorie der Antike, von Fritz Wehrli.—Tacitus und die antike Schicksalslehre, von Willy Theiler.—Studien zu Platons Protagoras, von Olof Gigon.—Zu Gregor von Nazianz, von Bernhard Wyss.—Griechische Opferbräuche, von Karl Meuli.

1. Greek literature—Hist. & crit. 2. Tacitus, Cornelius. 3. Plato. Protagoras. 4. Gregorius Nazianzenus, Saint, Patriarch of Constantinople. 5. Rites and ceremonies—Greece. 6. Mühll, Peter von der, 1885- I. Gigon, Olof Alfred, 1912-

A 48-8828*

Harvard Univ. Library for Library of Congress [3]

PLB

PHYSICO-CHEMICAL SOCIETY OF JAPAN.
The review of physical chemistry of Japan; commemoration volume, dedicated to Prof. Shinkichi Horiba in celebration of his sixtieth birthday. [Kyoto] 1946. xvii, 157 p. illus., port. 26cm.

Cover-title.
"Bibliography of Professor Shinkichi Horiba," p. [iv]-xv.
CONTENTS. — Differential heat of sorption of vapor on active charcoal. I. Apparatus and method of measurement, by S. Tamaru and K. Sato.
(Continued)

PHYSICO-CHEMICAL SOCIETY OF JAPAN. The review of physical chemistry of Japan... (Card 2)

2. Result of measurements, by K. Sato. — Studies on organosols, II. Silver organosols obtained by a chemical method, by I. Yamakita. — Studies on organic peroxides, II. The decomposition of ethyl hydroperoxide catalysed by platinum sol, by S. Hasegawa. — The surface-chemical study of the solid to water, by S. Tutihasi. — Studies of colloidal catalysts by thermal analysis of reaction velocity, VII. On the permanent poisoning of catalysts, by E. Suito. — On the effects of surfaces upon the spontaneous ignition of
(Continued)

PHYSICO-CHEMICAL SOCIETY OF JAPAN. The review of physical chemistry of Japan... (Card 3)

the liquid fuels, by S. Ono. — Macropolymerization of ethylene, I. by S. Kodama, H. Tahara and I. Taniguti. —On the viscosity of pure liquid, by M. Tamura. — The induced photo-dichroism by infra-red rays, by J. Shidei, D. Yamamoto and Y. Kubo. — Some experiments about the oxygen and hydrogen reaction, KCl effect on the surface of steel, by T. Watanabe. — Ultra pressure, VIII. Material flow of attachments of high pressure apparatus, by R. Kiyama. —On the photochemical explosive
(Continued)

PHYSICO-CHEMICAL SOCIETY OF JAPAN. The review of physical chemistry of Japan... (Card 4)

reactions, I, by J. Osugi. —Inflammation of aluminum powder, by R. Goto and E. Suito. — On the structural change of mechanically pulverized iron powder due to the procedures of annealing, by H. Hirata, H. Fujihira and E. Fujii. — Studies on high pressure gaskets, by S. Uchida and Y. Suezawa. —Polymerisation of ethylene under high pressure, by T. Kume. —The photo-effect on serum albumin, chiefly on its viscosity and solubility, by N. Hayami. —A comparison of catalytic activities of some
(Continued)

PHYSICO-CHEMICAL SOCIETY OF JAPAN. The review of physical.chemistry of Japan... (Card 5)

solid salts in the recombination of hydrogen free atoms and hydroxyl free radicals, by M. Tamura and S. Shida. — A study of the recombination reactions of free atoms by the thermal analysis of Budde effect, II, by S. Shida. — Study on the selenium colloidal solution, by K. Juna. — Studies on the explosive reaction between hydrogren and oxygen, by K. Moriya. — Thermal decomposition of diethyl peroxide, by K. Moriya. — Methylol condensation of acetaldehyde, by S. Fujii.

1. Horiba, Shinkichi, 1886- 2. Chemistry, Physical and theoretical, 1946. I. Title.

TAH

I PIANI di sviluppo in Italia dal 1945 al 1960; studi in memoria del Prof. Jacopo Mazzei. Milano, A. Giuffrè, 1960. 361 p. 25cm. (Economia e storia. Biblioteca. 5)

CONTENTS. —Note biobibliografiche su Jacopo Mazzei, di M. R. Caroselli. —Studi italiani dal 1944 al 1960 sul problema della programmazione economica di A. Fiaccadori—Il dibattito politico sulla programmazione economica in Italia dal 1945 al 1960, di F. Sullo. —I provvedimenti per lo sviluppo della marina mercantile: 1947-1960, di F. Caffè. —Il piano settennale per incrementare l'occupazione mediante la costruzione di case

(Continued)

NN 10.62 a/L OC PC, 1, 2 SL E, 1, 2 (LC1, X1, Z1) 2

I PIANI di sviluppo in Italia dal 1945 al 1960... (Card 2)

operaie: 1949-1960, di S. Alberti. —I provvedimenti per il mezzogiorno: 1950-1960, di G. Nardi. —La riforma fondiaria: 1950-1960, di M. Bandini. —Il piano dodecennale per lo sviluppo dell'agricoltura: 1952-1960, di C. Bonato. —Formulazione originale e verifica storica dello schema Vanoni, di S. Lombardini. —Piano decennale per la scuola: 1958; di G. Medici.

1. Economic policy--Italy, 1945- . 2. Mazzei, Jacopo, 1892-1947.

E-11
9711

PINKNEY, DAVID H., ed.
A festschrift for Frederick B. Artz, edited by David H. Pinkney and Theodore Ropp. Durham, N.C., Duke University press, 1964. viii, 236 p. 25cm.

Bibliographical footnotes.
CONTENTS. --Frederick B. Artz: the man and the teacher, the historical scholar and critic, by T. Ropp and D. H. Pinkney. --Patronage, piety, and

(Continued)

NN *R 4. 64 p// OC, I PC, 1, 2, I, II SL (LC1, X1, Z1) 3

PINKNEY, DAVID H., ed. A festschrift for Frederick B. Artz... (Card 2)

and printing in sixteenth-century Europe, by R. M. Kingdom. --Nationalism and science, Sir Joseph Banks and the wars with France, by A. H. Dupree. --The myth of the French Revolution of 1830, by D. H. Pinkney. --The Wu-shih-shan incident of 1878, by E. C. Carlson. --A century of war and peace (1863-1963) by T. Ropp. --Two centuries of American interest in Turkey, by S. N. Fisher. --Carpetbaggers reconsidered, by R. N. Current. --The "freedom to control" in American business history, by R. Berthoff. -- Who burned the Reichstag? The present state of an old controversy, by R. E. Neil. --

(Continued)

PINKNEY, DAVID H., ed. A festschrift for Frederick B. Artz... (Card 3)

International control of the atom: roots of a policy, by O. E. Anderson, Jr. --Bibliography of the scholarly writings of Frederick B. Artz (p. [228]-232).

1. History, Modern--Addresses, essays, lectures. 2. Artz, Frederick Binkerd, 1894- I. Ropp, Theodore, 1911- joint ed. II. Title.

E-12
7564

Pinney, Edward L., *ed.*
Comparative politics and political theory; essays written in honor of Charles Baskervill Robson, edited by Edward L. Pinney. Chapel Hill, University of North Carolina Press [1966]

xiii, 215 p. illus., port. 24 cm.
Bibliographical footnotes.

(Continued)

NN* R 1, 67 g/ OC PC, 1, 2 SL E, 1, 2 (LC1, X1, Z1) 3

PINNEY, EDWARD L., ed. Comparative politics and political theory... (Card 2)

CONTENTS.—The myth of equality and the actualities, by R. McCleery.—The ideological orientation, by A. P. Grimes.—Beliefs: A neglected unit of analysis in comparative politics, by L. W. Milbrath.—Political culture and the idioms of political development, by D. D. Hughes and E. L. Pinney.—New dimensions of West German federalism, by T. Cole.—The integration of Latin America, by F. G. Gil and J. D. Martz.—Technological change and higher defense or-

(Continued)

PINNEY, EDWARD L., ed. Comparative politics and political theory... (Card 3)

ganization, by F. N. Cleaveland and R. H. Dawson.—Negro political participation in the South, by D. R. Matthews and J. W. Prothro.—Response set in political survey research on Costa Rican and Panamanian students, by D. R. Goldrich.

1. Robson, Charles B. 2. Political science--Addresses, essays, lectures.

FHR

Pirchegger, Hans, 1875–
...Ausgewählte Aufsätze; zum 75. Geburtstage Hans Pircheggers hrsg. vom Historischen Verein für Steiermark. Graz, Selbstverlag des Historischen Vereines für Steiermark, 1950. xi, 204 p. port. 23cm.

"Veröffentlichungen," p. 16–18.

1. Styria, Austria—Hist. I. Historischer Verein für Steiermark, Gratz.

N. Y. P. L. January 29, 1952

MA

PISA, Italy (City). Università. Istituto di storia dell'arte.
Studi in onore di Matteo Marangoni [nel suo ottantesimo compleanno] Pisa, 1957. Firenze, Vallecchi, 1957. xxviii, 332 p. 122 plates. 28cm. (Studi di storia dell'arte, v.8)
"Bibliografia di Matteo Marangoni, 1897-1957": p. 1-12.
Includes bibliographical references.

(Continued)

NN*R 10.68 v/L (OC)I OS PC,1,2,3,I SL A,1,2,3,I (LC1,X1,Z1) 2

PISA, Italy (City). Università. Istituto di storia dell'arte. Studi in onore di Matteo Marangoni ... (Card 2)

1. Art, Italian--Essays and misc. 2. Marangoni, Matteo, 1876- . 3. Marangoni, Matteo, 1876- .--Bibl. I. Title.

Write on slip words underlined below and class mark —
ZDB

Pisciculi; Studien zur Religion und Kultur des Altertums, Franz Joseph Dölger zum sechzigsten Geburtstage dargeboten von Freunden, Verehrern und Schülern. Herausgeber: Theodor Klauser und Adolf Rücker. Münster in Westfalen: Verlag Aschendorff, 1939. 350 p. front. (port.), illus., 8 pl. 25½cm. (Dölger, F. J. Antike und Christentum... Ergänzungsband 1.)

Bibliographical footnotes.
CONTENTS.—Tabula gratulatoria.—Alföldi, Andreas. Hoc signo victor eris; Beiträge zur Geschichte der Bekehrung Konstantins des Grossen.—Altaner, Berthold.

(Continued)

N. Y. P. L. May 20, 1940

Pisciculi; Studien zur Religion und Kultur des Altertums... 1939. (Card 2)

Augustinus und die griechische Sprache.—Beek, C. I. M. I. van Ostenderunt Cryfios.—Bickel, Ernst. Fiunt, non nascuntur christiani.—Bolkestein, Hendrik. Humanitas bei Lactantius.—Clemen, Carl. Tempel und Kult in Heirapolis.—Cumont, Franz. Les vents et les anges psychopompes.—Curtius, Ludwig. Zum Galliersarkophag im Museo Mussolini.—Dölger, Franz. Lachen wider den Tod.—Dyroff, Adolf. Zum Prolog des Johannes-Evangeliums.—Eitrem, Sam. Sonnenkäfer und Falke in der synkretistischen Magie.—Festugière, A. J. La création des âmes dans la Korè kosmou.—Herzog, Rudolf. Der Kampf um den Kult von Menuthis.—Hopfner, Theodor. Hekate-Selene-Artemis und Verwandte in den griechischen Zauberpapyri und auf den Fluchtafeln.—Kazarow, G. I. Ein neues Denkmal zum Kult der Donauländischen Reiter.—Kirsch,

(Continued)

N. Y. P. L. May 20, 1940

Pisciculi; Studien zur Religion und Kultur des Altertums... 1939. (Card 3)

J. P. Das Querschiff in den stadtrömischen christlichen Basiliken des Altertums.—Klauser, Theodor. Taufet in lebendigem Wasser!—Nock, A. D. Conversion and adolescence.—Pfister, Friedrich. Ekstasis.—Prümm, Karl. Zur Terminologie und zum Wesen der christlichen Neuheit bei Irenaeus.—Quasten, Johannes. Das Bild des Guten Hirten in den altchristlichen Baptisterien und in den Taufliturgien des Ostens und Westens.—Rücker, Adolf. Die Kreuzzeichen in der westsyrischen Messliturgie.—Schöne, Hermann. Ein Einbruch der antiken Logik und Textkritik in die altchristliche Theologie.—Styger, Paul. Heidnische und christliche Katakomben.—Waszink, J. H. Tertullians eschatologische Deutung der Siebenzahl.—Weigand, Edmund. Zu den ältesten abendländischen Darstellungen der Jungfrau und Märtyrin Katharina von

(Continued)

N. Y. P. L. May 20, 1940

Pisciculi; Studien zur Religion und Kultur des Altertums... 1939. (Card 4)

Alexandria.—Weinreich, Otto. Religiös-ethische Formen der Epipompe.—Wiesner, Joseph. Zum Hirsch in der Frühzeit.—Wikenhauser, Alfred. Die Traumgesichte des Neuen Testaments in religionsgeschichtlicher Sicht.—Bibliographia Doelgeriana Zusammengestellt von Karl Baus (p. ₍334₎-341)—Personen-, Wort- und Sachregister. Zusammengestellt von Karl Baus.

1. Dölger, Franz Joseph, 1879- . 2. Christianity—Essays and misc. 3. Classical studies. I. Klauser, Theodor, 1894- , ed. II. Rücker, Adolf, 1880- , ed.
N. Y. P. L. May 20, 1940

HKR
✚

La Plata.

La Plata a su fundador. ₍La Plata₎ Edicion de la municipalidad, 1939. 65 p. incl. front. facsim., illus., plans, plates (part col'd), ports. 31cm.

"Homenaje de la ciudad de La Plata a su fundador el doctor Dardo Rocha."
CONTENTS.—Berro, L. M. Prologo.—Villarino, María de. ₍Poems₎—Sánchez Reulet, Anibal. Historia y presentación de la ciudad.—Calabrese, Salvador. Cabezas al carbon.—La nueva capital, 1882–84. Fotografias retrospectivas.

Festsch

7699B. 1. La Plata (City). 2. La Plata (City)—Views. I. Rocha, Dardo, 1838–1921.
N. Y. P. L. August 15, 1940

F-11
3986

Poems addressed to Hugh MacDiarmid, and presented to him on his seventy-fifth birthday by John M. Bett ₍and others₎; preface by Sir Compton Mackenzie, edited with an introduction by Duncan Glen, drawings by Leonard Penrice. Preston (Lancs.), Akros Publications, 1967.

₍2₎, 67 p. front., illus. (ports.). 27 cm.

Limited ed. of 350 numbered and signed copies. No. 67.

(Continued)

NN * R 3.68 1/₍₎OC,I, II SL (LC1,X1,Z1,PRI Ibo,II,IIIb* PC,1,2,I, 2

POEMS addressed to Hugh MacDiarmid,.. (Card 2)

1. Grieve, Christopher Murray, 1892- . 2. Poetry, English--Collections. I. Bett, John M. II. Glen, Duncan, ed. III. Glen, Duncan.

Spencer Coll.
Ital. 1785

Poesie per l'ingresso solenne di Sua Eccellenza il signor Gio: Antonio Gabriel cavaliere, e cancellier grande. ₍Venezia, 1785?₎ 2 p.l., c f. incl. front. illus. 35cm. (4°.)

See: Morazzoni: Libro illustrato veneziano del settecento, 270, 81–82.
Illustrations: 108 copper engravings, comprising frontispiece after Novelli (which includes Gabriel's portrait and views of Italian cities, and is signed: App₍ress₎o Alessandri, e Scattaglia incisori), title-page with arms on verso, 12 borders (repeated to 100) and 5 tailpieces. For reproductions of frontispiece and title-page, *cf. Morazzoni 131.*
Binding (unsigned), by James Macdonald, Inc., New York, of half brown morocco with marbled paper sides.

Festschrift-

1. Gabriel, Giovanni Antonio—Poetry. 2. Poetry, Italian—Collections.
N. Y. P. L. January 7, 1949

Write on slip only words underlined and class mark —
Spencer Coll.
Ital. 1780

Poesie pel solenne ingresso di Sua Eccellenza il cavaliere Pietro Mocenigo alla dignità di procuratore di S. Marco. Venezia, Presso S. Occhi, 1780. 3 p.l., (i)vi–lxiv p., 1 l. illus. 26cm. (4°.)

Morazzoni: Libro illustrato veneziano del settecento, 274.
Edited by Pietro Berti. —*cf. dedication.*
Illustrations: 72 copper engravings, comprising title-page designed by Giovanni David, 16 borders (repeated to 64), 6 head- and tailpieces (some after P. A. Novelli,

(Continued)

N. Y. P. L. January 14, 1949

Poesie...di...Pietro Mocenigo... (Card 2)

some by Antonio Visentini) and colophon leaf after Novelli, all engraved in the establishment of Teodoro Viero. For reproductions, *cf. Morazzoni 99–100.* One engraved initial.
Bound with: Berti, Pietro. Pel solenne ingresso di...Pietro Mocenigo. ₍Venezia, 1780₎

1. Mocenigo, Pietro, b. ca. 1698— Poetry. 2. Poetry, Italian—Collections. I. Berti, Pietro, 1741–1813, ed.
N. Y. P. L. January 14, 1949

D-18
4877

Poesi og virkelighet. Festskrift til Emil Boysons 70-årsdag 4. september 1967. Redaktører: Asbjørn Aarnes, Aasmund Brynildsen, A. H. Winsnes. Oslo, Gyldendal, 1967.
149 p. port. 23 cm. 48.50 nkr
(N 67-36)
CONTENTS.—Et portrett av dikteren, av A. Aarnes.—Dikter, av A. Larsen.—Poesi og virkelighet, av A. Brynildsen.—Tre Boyson-studier, av E. Eggen.—En dikter ver grensen, av H. Wildenvey.—Poesiens hemmelighet, av A. Larsen.—En oplesers hilsen til Emil Boyson,

(Continued)

NN * 10.68 1/M OC PC,1 SL (LC1,X1,Z1) 2

POESI og virkelighet. (Card 2)

av L. Strømsted.—Ordet, av T. Ørjasæter.—Emil Boysons verden, av O. Solumsmoen.—Emil Boysons prosa, av A. Worren.—Brev til en ukjent, av J. Borgen.—Ekko Epitaf, av A. Eidslott.—Gjendikteren Emil Boyson, av L. Eckhoff.—En hilsen til Emil Boyson, av F. J. Billeskov Jansen.—Tegn og tydning, av P. Arneberg.—Her i den bitende kveld, av A. Brynildsen.—Emil Boysons poesi, av A. Aarnes.

1. Boyson, Emil, 1897-

---

* QP

POLAND. Bibljoteka narodowa, Warsaw.
Z zagadnień teorii i praktyki bibliotekarskiej; studia poświęcone pamięci Józefa Grycza. [Komitet redakcyjny: Bogdan Horodyski, redaktor naczelny et al. 1. wyd.] Wrocław, Zakład narodowy im. Ossolińskich, 1961.
427 p. port., facsims. 26cm.

Bibliographical footnotes.
CONTENTS.—Grycz, J. Dzienniczek z okresu powstania warszawskiego.—Horodyski, B. Józef Grycz.—Kurdybacha, E. Bibliografia drukowanych
(Continued)

NN 12.64 g/J (OC)I, II ODt EDt PC, 1, 2, I, II SL S, 1, 2, I, II (LCl, Xl, Zl) 3

POLAND. Bibljoteka narodowa, Warsaw. Z zagadnień teorii i praktyki bibliotekarskiej...
(Card 2)

prac artykułów i notatek J. Grycza.—Grycz, J. Polska polityka biblioteczna w latach powojennych.—Skwarnicki, M. Zarys rozwoju koncepcji i organizacji Biblioteki Narodowej w Warszawie, 1918-1954.—Baumgart, J. Struktura organizacyjna bibliotek naukowych.—Nagórska, L. Portrety czytelników-robotników w łódzkiej dzielnicy Chojny.—Dembowska, M. Bibliotekarstwo i bibliografia a dokumentacja.—Birkenmajer, A. Belgijski bibliofil Arseni Fasseau i jego związki z Polską.
(Continued)

POLAND. Bibljoteka narodowa, Warsaw. Z zagadnień teorii i praktyki bibliotekarskiej...
(Card 3)

1760-1777.—Rudnicka, J. Fragment biblioteki Lompy.—Korpała, J. Z dziejów miejskich bibliotek publicznych w Galicji.—Augustyniak, J. Nieznane fragmenty z historii Biblioteki publicznej w Łodzi.—Jasińska, S. Czy Jan z Sącza mógł być drukarzem poznańskim?—Chyczewska, A. Zasób drzeworytów ilustracyjnych i herbowych w XVI-wiecznych oficynach poznańskich.—Kłodzińska, K. Nieznane wydanie "Satyr" Marcina Bielskiego w Bibliotece Kórnickiej.—Budka, W. Papiernia w Poczesney.
1. Library science--Addresses, essays, lectures. 2. Libraries--Poland. I. Grycz, Józef. II. Horodyski, Bogdan, ed. t. 1961.

---

*C-3 p.v.1368

Policarpo Petrocchi ₍1852–1902₎ nel centenario della nascita e cinquantenario della morte. ₍Milano₎ A. Vallardi ₍1953₎
70 p. port. 22cm.

CONTENTS.—Policarpo Petrocchi nel centenario della nascita e cinquantenario della morte, discorso del prof. G. Bottiglioni.—La biografia di P. P. scritta da A. Gotti.—Ricordi di Alfonso Pisaneschi.—Spunti autobiografici di P. P. (Le ricordanze).—P. P. e la repubblica di Castello.—Il P. educatore (giudizio del maresciallo d'Italia E. Caviglia).—Giudizi politici di P. P.—Lo stile sintetico di P. P.—P. P. e l'accentazione della lingua italiana.—Opere e scritti di P. P. (p. 67–70)

1. Petrocchi, Policarpo, 1852–1902.
NN** X 2.57 OC PC,1 SL (Z1,LC1,X1)

TB

On political economy and econometrics; essays in honour of Oskar Lange. Warszawa, Polish Scientific Publishers ₍°1964₎
viii, 661 p. illus., port. 25 cm.
English, German, Italian, Russian or French with summaries in English.
Includes bibliographical references. "Bibliography of ₍Lange's₎ works, 1925–1963": p. 651–661.

1. Economics--Essays and misc. 2. Lange, Oscar Richard, 1904- .
NN* R 2.66 g/ OC PC, 1, 2 SL E, 1, 2 S, 1, 2 (LCl, Xl, Zl)

E-13
4679

POLITICS and experience; essays presented to Professor Michael Oakeshott on the occasion of his retirement, edited by Preston King and B.C. Parekh. Cambridge, Eng., University press, 1968. 424 p. port. 24cm.

CONTENTS. --The practical and the historical past, by W.H. Walsh.--Michael Oakeshott's theory of history, by W.H. Dray.--M. Oakeshott's philosophy of education, by R.S. Peters.--A case of identity, by M.M. Goldsmith.--Idealism, modern philosophy and politics, by W.H. Greenleaf.--Paradigms and political theories, by S.S. Wolin.--The
(Continued)

NN R 4.69 k/OC, I, II, IIIbo PC, 1, 2, I, II SL E, 1, 2, I, II (LCl, Xl, Zl) [I] 2

POLITICS and experience... (Card 2)

nature of political philosophy, B.C. Parekh.--Time, institutions and action, by J.G.A. Pocock.--Is there reason in tradition?, by S. Coleman.--Revolution, tradition and political continuity, by K.R. Minogue.--Essay on the kibbutzim of Israel, by D. Krook.--An ideological fallacy, by P. King.--John Adams and Doctor Johnson, by D. Davie.--Bibliography of works by M. Oakeshott, by W.H. Greenleaf.

1. Political science--Addresses, essays, lectures. 2. Oakeshott, Michael Joseph, 1901- . I. King, Preston, 1936- ed. II. Parekh, B.C., ed. III. Parekh, B.C.

F-11
2220

POLLIN, BURTON RALPH, ed.
Toward excellence in education; writings in honor of Dr. Morris Meister. [New York] Bronx community college, 1966. 128 p. illus., ports. 28cm.

CONTENTS. --A chronicle of service. --The Bronx high school of science. --Bronx community college. --Science education. --Sights and insights in education. --Morris Meister, the man. --From the pen of Dr. Meister.

1. Meister, Morris, 1895- . 2. Science--Study and teaching--U. S. --N. Y. --New York. t. 1966.

NN R 12. 66 r/L OC PC, 1, 2 SL ST, 1, 2t (LC1, X1, Z1)

---

*QO

Polskie towarzystwo filologiczne, Lemberg. Oddział poznański.
Munera philologica, Ludovico Ćwikliński bis sena lustra professoria claudenti ab amicis collegis discipulis oblata. Posnaniae: Liber editus cura Circuli Posnan. Societatis philologae Polonorum, 1936. xi, 483 p. plates, port. 24cm.

Contributions in French, German, Italian, Latin or Polish.

PARTIAL CONTENTS.—Cybulski, Étienne. Le "Carmen saeculare" d'Horace mis en musique par Philidor.—Seliga, Stanislaus. Tertullianus et Cyprianus de feminarum moribus pravis.—Sajdak, Ioannes. De codicibus Vergilianis in bibliotheca Cornicensi asservatis.—Birkenmajer, Józef. Epitafjum Bolesława Chrobrego.—Hahn, Wiktor. Motywy klasyczne w tragedji o polskim Scilurusie Jana Jurkowskiego.—Bruchnalski,

(Continued)

N. Y. P. L. August 27, 1937

Polskie towarzystwo filologiczne, Lemberg. Oddział poznański.
Munera philologica... (Card 2)

Wilhelm. Piękna kobieta w poezji Kochanowskiego.—Pilch, Stanisław. Czem była Ligja w zamiarze Sienkiewicza.—Dembiński, Bronisław. L'amitié franco-polonaise (1791).

886764A. 1. Ćwikliński, Ludwik, 1853- . 2. Latin literature—Hist. and crit. 3. Greek literature—Hist. and crit. I. Title.

N. Y. P. L. August 27, 1937

VFB

Polytechnic institute of Brooklyn.
Reissner anniversary volume; contributions to applied mechanics. Edited by the staff of the Department of aeronautical engineering and applied mechanics of the Polytechnic institute of Brooklyn. Ann Arbor, Mich., J. W. Edwards [1949] viii, 493 p. illus. 24cm.

"H. J. Reissner's scientific publications," p. 5-12.

605899B. 1. Mechanics, Applied. 2. Reissner, Hans Jakob, 1874- . I. Title.

NN

Copy only words underlined & classmark— VEA

DEN POLYTEKNISKE LÆREANSTALT, Copenhagen. Laboratoriet for bygningsteknik.
Festskrift til professor Anker Engelund. Kobenhavn, 1959. 234 p. illus., port., diagrs. 26cm. (ITS: Meddelelse. nr. 10)

At head of title: Laboratoriet for bygningsteknik, Danmarks tekniske hojskole....

Includes bibliographies.

CONTENTS. --Omprofessor Engelund som ingeniør, forsker og

(Continued)

NN X 7. 65 s/ (OC)II, 2b+ (LC1, X1) (Z1) OS, I PC, 1, 2, I, II ST, 1t, 2, I, II

DEN POLYTEKNISKE LÆREANSTALT, Copenhagen. Laboratoriet for bygningsteknik. Festskrift til professor Anker Engelund...(Card 2)

lærer, af P.M. Frandsen. --The measurement of pressure between an infinitely rigid wall and a compressible medium, by V. Askegaard. --Bending of conical shells of uniform thickness and of cylindrical shells of uniform or non-uniform thickness, by T. Brondum-Nielsen. --Eksempel på undersøgelse af risteværk efter plasticitetsteorien, af C. Dyrbye. --Bond testing of reinforcing bars, by A. Efsen. --Pæleværkers sikkerhed mod brud, af F. Engelund. --
(Continued)

DEN POLYTEKNISKE LÆREANSTALT, Copenhagen. Laboratoriet for bygningsteknik. Festskrift til professor Anker Engelund...(Card 3)

Om søjler, af P.M. Frandsen. --Murværks styrke, af O. Glarboe. --Elastisk halvrum begrænset af en stiv plade med cirkulært stempel, af S. Gravesen. --Stabilitet af søjler med variabelt trærsnit, af I.G. Hannemann. --Tilnærmet beregning af flangemomenterne i en parabeldrager med V-gitter, af J. Brinch Hansen. --On dynametre, af P. Lange Hansen. --Behavioristic models representing hysteresis in structural joints, by L.S. Jacobsen. --Nogle
(Continued)

DEN POLYTEKNISKE LAEREANSTALT, Copenhagen. Laboratoriet for bygningsteknik. Festskrift til professor Anker Engelund...(Card 4)

formler for laveste svingningstal ved bøjningssvingninger, af K.W. Johansen. --Trækkilen indflydelse pa jernbetons snitspændinger og deformationer, af H. Krenchel. --Bemærkninger om trærfordeling, af N.C. Larsen og I.G. Hannemann. --Artificial roughness in coastal engineering, by H. Lundgren. --Særlige bropillekonstruktioner ved Fredrikstadbroen, af C. Ostenfeld. --Betonsøjlers bæreevne, af E. Poulsen. --Stangpolygoners stabilitet, af B.J. Rambøll. --Centralt belastede sojler med variabelt
(Continued)

DEN POLYTEKNISKE LAEREANSTALT, Copenhagen. Laboratoriet for bygningsteknik. Festskrift til professor Anker Engelund...(Card 5)

tværsnit, påvirkede over proportionalitetsgrænsen, af B. Højlund Rasmussen.

1. Engineering--Addresses, essays, lectures. 2. Engelund, Anker, 1889- I. Series. II. Title. t. 1959.

Copy only words underlined & classmark-- VEA

DEN POLYTEKNISKE LÆREANSTALT, Copenhagen. Laboratoriet for bygningsteknik.
Festskrift til professor P.M. Frandsen. København, 1950. 116 p. port. 26cm. (ITS: Meddelelse. nr. 1)

Includes bibliographies.

CONTENTS.-- Professor P.M. Frandsen som ingeniør, videnskabsmand og lærer, af A. Engelund. --Belastningsfordeling ved buebroer med afstivningsdrager, af M. Folmer Andersen. --Influenslinier for lige stænger med variabelt inertimoment, af A. Efsen. --Dimensionering af bøjningspåvirkede søjler, af I.G. Hannemann. --Om differensligninger,
(Continued)

NN X 8. 65 s/B (OC)II OS, I PC, 1, 2, I, II ST, 1t, 2, I, II (LC1, X1, Z1)

DEN POLYTEKNISKE LÆREANSTALT, Copenhagen. Laboratoriet for bygningsteknik. Festskrift til professor P.M.Frandsen... (Card 2)

af K.W.Johansen.--Ekscentrisk belastede søjler, af J. Nielsen.--Forspændte betonbeholderes statiske forhold, af C. Ostenfeld.--Momenter i søjler med bjælkebelastning, af B.J.Rambøll.--Stabilitet af søjler med variabølt inertimoment, af B. Hojlund Rasmussen.--Sidestabilitet af gitterdragerès trykflange, af T.Brøndum-Nielsen.

1. Engineering--Addresses, essays, lectures. 2. Frandsen, Peter Marius, 1880- I. Series. II. Title. t.1950.

AN (Derouet, L.)

Portugal. Imprensa nacional, Lisbon. A Pensionista.

À memória de Luís Derouet; palavras justas. Homenagem por iniciativa de A Pensionista, cooperativa do pessoal da Imprensa nacional de Lisboa. Lisboa: Imprensa nacional, 1928. xvi, 263 p. front., plates, ports. 29½cm.

Contributions by various authors.

156029B. 1. Derouet, Luís, d. 1927.
N. Y. P. L. September 25, 1942

A p.v.290

Pontificia accademia delle science — Nuovi Lincei, Rome.

Al Rev. padre Giovanni Hagen S. I., direttore della Specola vaticana, la Pontificia accademia delle scienze a festeggiare il compimento dei suoi LXXX anni. [Roma, 1927.] 54 p. front. (port.), illus. 8°.

408461A. 1. Hagen, John George, 1847- .
N. Y. P. L. May 3, 1929

OAI

PORTUGAL. Missões geográficas e de investigações do ultramar, Junta das.

Estudos científicos oferecidos em homenagem ao Prof. doutor J. Carrington da Costa por ocasião do seu 70°. aniversário, abril de 1961. Lisboa, Junta de investigações do ultramar, 1962. xxvii, 747 p. illus., port., maps. 26cm.

"Bibliografia do Prof. J. Carrington da Costa," p. xxi-xxvii.

1. Science--Essays and misc. 2. Costa, João Carrington Simões da, 1891- I. Title. t. 1962.

NN 10.63 p/ (OC) 2b, I ODt EDt PC, 1, 2, I SL ST, 1t, 2, I (LC1, X1, Z1)

AN (Hostos, E.)

Porto Rico. Hostos, Eugenio María de, Commission for the celebration of the centenary of the birth of.

...America y Hostos; coleccion de ensayos acerca de Eugenio Maria de Hostos, recogidos y publicados por la Comision pro celebracion del centenario del natalicio de Eugenio Maria de Hostos. Habana, Cuba: Cultural, s. a. [1939] 391 p. facsims., plates, ports. 24½cm.

At head of title: Edicion conmemorativa del gobierno de Puerto Rico. 1839-1939.

(Continued)

N. Y. P. L. June 17, 1940

E-12 3522

Pound, Roscoe, 1870-1964, *ed.*

Perspectives of law; essays for Austin Wakeman Scott. Edited by Roscoe Pound, Erwin N. Griswold [and] Arthur E. Sutherland. [1st ed.] Boston, Little, Brown, 1964.

xx, 386 p. ports. 24 cm.

Bibliographical footnotes.

CONTENTS.—A letter from Mr. Justice Frankfurter.—Preface.—Autobiographical letter from Professor Scott.—Conflict of interest in Massachusetts, by R. Braucher.—Oral contracts to provide by will and the choice-of-law process: some notes on Bernkrant, by D. F.

(Continued)

NN * R 6.65 e/ OC PC, 1, 2 SL E, 2 (LC1, X1, Z1)

Porto Rico. Hostos, Eugenio María de, Commission for the celebration of the centenary of the birth of. ...America y Hostos ... (Card 2)

CONTENTS.—Comisiones del centenario de Hostos.—Eugenio María de Hostos. Noticia biográfica.—Eugenio María de Hostos, por Máximo Gómez.—Cómo ve Gabriela Mistral a Hostos.—Discurso pronunciado por Emilio del Toro.—Crítica y estilo literarios en Eugenio María de Hostos, por J. A. Balseiro.—Hostos juzgado por los norteamericanos.—Hostos y la naturaleza de América, por Concha Meléndez.—Eugenio María de Hostos (1839-1903), por R. Blanco-Fombona.—Hostos, por C. A. Torres.—La sociología de Hostos, por Pedro Henríquez Ureña.—Hostos político, por A. S. Pedreira.—La moral social de Eugenio María de Hostos, por Pedro de Alba.—La filosofía moral de Eugenio María de Hostos, por Antonio Caso.—Hostos, aconteci-

(Continued)

N. Y. P. L. June 17, 1940

POUND, ROSCOE, 1870-1964, ed. Perspectives of law... (Card 2)

Cavers.—A system of judicial notice based on fairness and convenience, by K. C. Davis.—Influence of the Abbé de Mably and of Le Mercier de la Rivière on American constitutional ideas concerning the Republic and judicial review, by M. Franklin.—The house of law, by R. Graveson.—Vested and contingent remainders: a premature requiem for distinctions between conditions precedent and subsequent, by E. C. Halbach, Jr.—The first American reform of civil procedure, by G. L. Haskins.—Reflections on the executory accord, by H. C. Havighurst.—Perpetuities: cy pres on the march, by W. B. Leach.—The strange destiny of trusts, by P. LePaulle.—Incompletely consti-

(Continued

Porto Rico. Hostos, Eugenio María de, Commission for the celebration of the centenary of the birth of. ...America y Hostos ... (Card 3)

miento de América, por Mauricio Magdaleno.—Las ideas pedagógicas de Hostos, por Camila Henríquez Ureña.—Esencia ideológica de Hostos, por J. A. Fránquiz.—El libro de Hostos sobre "Derecho constitucional," por Adolfo Posada.—La muerte de Hostos, por Francisco Henríquez y Carvajal.—Complemento biográfico y bibliografía.—Bibliografía hostosiana, trabajos referentes a Hostos.

33520B. 1. Hostos y Bonilla, Eugenio María de, 1839-1903. I. Title.
N. Y. P. L. June 17, 1940

POUND, ROSCOE, 1870-1964, ed. Perspectives of law... (Card 3)

States as suitors in interstate litigation in the Supreme Court, by W. G. Rice.—"Result-orientation" and appellate judgment, by J. Stone.—Blackstone after two centuries, by A. E. Sutherland.—From some colleagues and sometime students.

tuted trusts, by R. H. Maudsley.—Constitutional interpretation: the obligation to respect the text, by M. H. Merrill.—Some reflections on the function of the confidential relationship doctrine in the law of trusts, by R. A. Newman.—The king can do no wrong, by R. Pound.—

1. Law--Addresses, essays, lectures. 2. Scott, Austin Wakeman, 1884- .

MA
+

Pour Daniel-Henry Kahnweiler. [Ouvrage établie sous la direction de Werner Spies] New York, G. Wittenborn [1965]

311 p. illus. (part mounted) facsims. (part mounted) 8 plates (7 col.) ports. 30 cm.

On spine: Pour Kahnweiler.
The contributions, in French, German, English or Swedish, include poems, plays and 22 mounted facsims. of letters to Kahnweiler with their transcriptions.

(Continued)

NN* R 11.66 g/c OC, I, II, IIIb* PC, 1, 2, 3, I, II SL A, 1, 2, 3, I, II (LC1, X1, Z1) 2

POUR Daniel-Henry Kahnweiler. (Card 2)

"Bibliographie: Daniel-Henry Kahnweiler, compiled by Lucy R. Lippard": p. 287-295.
Bibliographical references included in "Notes" (p. 206-301)

1. Kahnweiler, Daniel Henry, 1884- . 2. Kahnweiler, Daniel Henry, 1884- --Bibl. 3. Art--Essays and misc. I. Spies, Werner, ed. II. Title: Pour Kahnweiler. III. Spies, Werner.

L-10
783
Bd. 1

PRAGER Festgabe für Theodor Mayer; neu hrsg. von Rudolf Schreiber. Freilassing, O. Müller, 1953. 288 p. illus., port. 24cm. (Forschungen zur Geschichte und Landeskunde der Sudetenländer. Bd. 1)

"Neudruck nach dem einzigen erhaltenen Widmungsstück."
Bibliographical footnotes.
CONTENTS. — Das Eisenacher Diplom als Kunstwerk, von A. Blaschka. —
(Continued)

NN R X 2.58 g/3 OC, II, IIIb* (OS)I PC, 1, I, II S, 1, I, II (Z1, LC1, X1)

PRAGER Festgabe für Theodor Mayer... (Card 2)

Freiherr vom Stein im Exil in Prag-Brünn, von A. Ernstberger. —Ursachen und Wege der Rezeption des Römischen Rechtes in Böhmen und Mähren, von O. Peterka. — Karlstein, von G. Pirchan. — Terra Bohemiae, regnum Bohemiae, corona Bohemiae, von J. Prochno. —Das Stammbuch der Prager Fischniederlage 1600-1679, von R. Schreiber. — Über eine böhmische Schöffenspruchsammlung in der Lemberger Staatsbibliothek, von W. Weizsäcker. — Kaiser Josef II und der Kardinalprotektor der deutschen Reichskirche F. Herzan Reichsgraf von Harras, von E. Winter. — Die Ursprünge der Primisliden, von W. Wostry. —Die Anfänge der Lehrkanzel
(Continued)

PRAGER Festgabe für Theodor Mayer... (Card 3)

für historische Hilfswissenschaften an der Prager Universität, von H. Zatschek.

1. Mayer, Theodor, 1883- . I. Series. II. Schreiber, Rudolf, 1907- , ed. III. Schreiber, Rudolf, 1907- .

AN
(Masaryk, T.)

Prager Presse.
Masaryk; Staatsmann und Denker. Prag: "Orbis", 1930. 250 p. 21cm.

"Die in diesem Bande enthaltenen Beiträge sind zum ersten Male in den Sondernummern erschienen, die die "Prager Presse" zum 75. und zum 80. Geburtstag des Präsidenten Masaryk am 7. März 1925 und 1930 herausgegeben hat."

24588B. 1. Masaryk, Tomás Garrigue, pres. Czecho-Slovakia, 1850-1937. I. Title.
N. Y. P. L. December 7, 1939

E-12
6223

PRAM, CHRISTEN.
Kopibøker fra reiser i Norge, 1804-06. Utgitt som festskrift til Sigurd Grieg på 70-årsdagen 22. august 1964. Lillehammer, 1964. vii, 272 p. map. 24cm. (De Sandvigske samlinger, Lillehammer, Norway. Kildeskriftserie. nr. 1)

1. Grieg, Sigurd, 1894- . 2. Norway--Descr. and trav., 1800-1900. I. Series.
NN R 6.66 a/, OC (OS)I PC, 1, 2, I SL (LC1, X1, Z1)

E-11
8711

PREDÖHL, ANDREAS, 1893- , ed.
Verkehr; mit Ideen und Erfahrung in die Zukunft. [Festgabe für Hans-Christoph Seebohm] Berlin, Duncker & Humblot [1963] 217 p. illus., port. 24cm.

CONTENTS. --Hans-Christoph Seebohm; Persönlichkeit und Wirken, von R. Fischer. --Verkehrspolitik, heute von E. Salin. --Verkehr als Aufgabe, von O. Most. --Weltwirtschaft und Verkehr, von A. Predöhl. --Verkehrstechnik heute und morgen, von P. Koessler. --Die Deutsche
(Continued)

NN R 1.64 f/B OC PC, 1, 2, 3 SL E, 1, 2, 3 (LC1, X1, Z1) 3

PREDÖHL, ANDREAS, 1893- , ed. Verkehr...
(Card 2)

Bundesbahn und die Zukunft, von H. M. Oeftering. --Die Binnenschiffahrt im Umbruch, von W. Geile. --Der gewerbliche Strassenverkehr von G. Geiger. --Die Lage der deutschen Seeschiffahrt, von R. Stödter. --Die deutsche Luftfahrt von H. J. Abs. --Die Rationalisierungsbewegung im Speditions- und Lagereigewerbe, von W. M. Rademacher. --Technische Probleme des modernen Strassenbaus, von A. Böhringer. --Die Binnenwasserstrassen in der Bundesrepublik Deutschland, von K. Förster. --
(Continued)

PREDÖHL, ANDREAS, 1893- , ed. Verkehr...
(Card 3)

Verkehrsprobleme und Meteorologie, von H. Flohn. --Die Eisenbahn heute und morgen, von E. Grassmann.

1. Traffic--Germany. 2. Transportation--Social and economic relations--Germany. 3. Seebohm, Hans Christoph.

E-11
4321

PRETE, SESTO, ed.
Didascaliæ; studies in honor of Anselm M. Albareda, prefect of the Vatican library. Presented by a group of American scholars. New York, B.M. Rosenthal[1961] xiv, 530 p. facsims., music. 25cm.

One of 500 copies printed.
Bibliographical footnotes.
CONTENTS.--The three earliest Vitae of St. Galganus, by R. Arbesmann.
(Continued)

NN R 8.62 c/ OC PC, 1, 2 SL (LC1, X1, Z1) [I]

PRETE, SESTO, ed. Didascaliæ.... (Card 2)

--Hadoardus and the manuscripts of classical authors from Corbie by B. Bischoff.--The structure of Sallust's Historiæ, by H. Bloch.--A medieval treatment of Hero's Theorem on the area of a triangle in terms of its sides, by M. Clagett.--Additional question on Aristotle's Physics, by Siger of Brabant or his school, by C.J. Ermatinger.--The defense of Europe in the Renaissance period, by O. Halecki.--Cardinal Domenico Grimani, Questio de intensione et remissione qualitatis: A commentary on the tractate of that title by Richard Suiseth (Calculator), by P. Kibre.--Sebastiano Salvini, a Florentine humanist
(Continued)

PRETE, SESTO, ed. Didascaliae.... (Card 3)

and theologian, and a member of Marsilio Ficino's Platonic academy, by P.O. Kristeller.--The gestures of prayer in papal iconography of the thirteenth and early fourteenth centuries, by G.B. Ladner.--Greek symptoms in a sixth-century manuscript of St. Augustine and in a group of Latin legal manuscripts, by E.A. Lowe.--Gomez versus the Spanish college at Bologna, by B. Marti.--A note on Gregory of Nyssa's Commentary on the Song of Solomon, homily IV, by H. Musurillo.--The Bibliotheca Albana Urbinas as represented in the library of the Catholic university of America, by B.M.
(Continued)

PRETE, SESTO, ed. Didascaliæ... (Card 4)

Peebles.--The Vossianus latinus III and the arrangement of the works of Ausonius, by S. Prete.--Copernicus' Quotation from Sophocles, by E. Rosen.--Urgentibus imperii fatis (Tac. Germ. 33), by W. Schmid.--Aristotle's word for "matter", by F. Solmsen.--Notes on Leo Tuscus' translation of the liturgy of St. John Chrysostom, by A. Strittmatter.--Manuscripts of Michael Scot's Liber introductorius, by L. Thorndike.--Achilles Statius' manuscripts of Tibullus, by B.L. Ullman.--The unknown author of the Libri Carolini, by L. Wallach.--Four music books at Washington from the pontificate of Benedict XIII, by F.J. Witty.
1. Albareda, Anselmo María, 1892- 2. Bibliography--Addresses, essays, lectures.

MVS
+

Preussischer Protektorenverband.
50 Jahre Schülerrudern; Festschrift des Preussischen Protektorenverbandes, Jahrbuch 1930–31. Kiel: Kunstdruck- und Verlagsbüro, 1931. 254 p. illus. (incl. ports.) 30cm.

Bibliography, p. 245–252.

600307A. 1. Rowing—Germany. I. Title.
N.Y.P.L. September 27, 1932

AN
(Bernadotte, O.)

PRINS OSCAR BERNADOTTE, en minnesbok av 32 författare. Under redaktion av Bo Bengtson och Hugo Cedergren. Uppsala, J. A. Lindblad [1953] 191 p. illus., ports. 23cm.

1. Bernadotte, Oscar, prins, 1859-1953. I. Bengtson, Bo, ed. II. Cedergren, Hugo, ed.

NN** R X 4.54 OC, I, II, IIbo PC, 1, I, II SL (LC1, X1, X1)

E-11
3397

PRO EXCOLENDO IURE PATRIO.
Pro excolendo iure patrio, 1761-1961. Gröningen, J.B. Wolters, 1961. 212 p. illus., facsims. 24cm.

Contributions by W.W. Feith, and others.
Bibliographical footnotes.

1. Law--Assoc. and org.--Netherland--Groningen. 2. Law--Netherlands--Groningen. I. Feith, Willem Wolter, 1889-
NN R 10.61 a/ (OC)I, Ib OS(Ib) PC, 1, 2, I SL (LC1, X1, Z1)

TIV

PROBLEME des Finanz- und Steuerrechts; Festschrift für Ottmar Bühler, hrsg. von Armin Spitaler. Köln, O. Schmidt [1954] 294 p. port. 24cm.

CONTENTS.—Begrüssung Prof. Dr. jur. Ottmar Bühlers zum 70. Geburtstag, von H.C. Nipperdey.—Gemeindeabgabenrecht in der Entwicklung, von P. Eising.—Pensionslasten und bedingte Lasten bei der Einheitswertfeststellung des Betriebsvermögens, von B. Gübbels.—Einkommensteuerliche Probleme bei der Veräusserung von unverzinslichen Baudarlehen, von K. Heintges.—Der Steuererfindungsgeist von Bund und
(Continued)

NN** R 5.56 a/ OC, I PC, 1, 2, I SL E, 1, 2, I (LC1, X1, Z1)

PROBLEME des Finanz- und Steuerrechts... (Card 2)

Ländern seit Inkrafttreten des Grundgesetzes—seine verfassungsrechtlichen Grenzen, von H. Meilicke.—Der Grundsatz der Gleichmässigkeit der Besteuerung—sein Inhalt und seine Grenzen, von H. Paulick.—Unzulässigkeit einer ländermässigen Staffelung der Steueranteile des Bundes nach Art. 106 Abs. 3 GG, von H. Peters.— Die gegenseitige Annäherung der Steuersysteme der Kulturstaaten, von A. Spitaler.—Grundsätzliches zur Frage des Missbrauchs von Formen und Gestaltungsmöglichkeiten im Steuerrecht, von G. Thoma.—Die wirtschaftliche Betrachtungsweise im Steuerrecht, von
(Continued)

PROBLEME des Finanz- und Steuerrechts... (Card 3)

H. v. Wallis.—Verzeichnis der Schriften Prof. Dr. jur. Ottmar Bühlers, von G. Felix (p. 279-294).

1. Taxation—Jurisp.—Germany, 1954. 2. Bühler, Ottmar, 1884- I. Spitaler, Armin, ed.

PAH

Probleme der modernen Physik; Arnold Sommerfeld zum 60. Geburtstage gewidmet von seinen Schülern... Herausgegeben von P. Debye... Leipzig: S. Hirzel, 1928. viii, 221 p. incl. tables. diagrs., illus. 8°.

Bibliographical footnotes.

409571A. 1. Sommerfeld, Arnold Johannes Wilhelm, 1868- . 2. Physics—Collected essays. 3. Debye, Peter, 1884- , editor.
N. Y. P. L. June 4, 1929

TIE

Problemi di finanza fascista, saggi di R. Bachi, V. Bompani, C. Bresciani Turroni [ed altri] ... Bologna, N. Zanichelli, 1937.

3 p.l., 344 p., 2 l. diagrs. 24cm.

Festschrift 1937

TID

Probleme der öffentlichen Finanzen und der Währung; Festgabe für Eugen Grossmann. Zürich, Polygraphischer Verlag, 1949. xiv, 317 p. port. 24cm.

Contributions in German or French by Alfred Amonn and others.
Bibliographical footnotes.
"Publikationen von Eugen Grossmann," p. 303-307.

524351B. 1. Finance. 2. Finance—Switzerland. 3. Money, 1933- 4. Money—Switzerland. 5. Grossmann, Eugen, 1879-
N. Y. P. L. June 23, 1950

PBE

PROBLEMS of continuum mechanics; contributions in honor of the seventieth birthday of N.I. Muskhelishvili, 16th February 1961. English edition. [Editor: J.R.M. Radok] Philadelphia, Society for industrial and applied mathematics, 1961. xx, 601 p. illus., port. 25cm.

Issued also in Russian edition by the Academy of sciences, U.S.S.R., G.K. Mikhailov, ed.

(Continued)

NN R 9.61 g4 OC. I (OS)II, III PC, 1, 2, I, II, III SL S, 2, III ST, lt, 2, I, II, III (LC1, X1, Z1)

2

TAH

Problemi economici dall'antichità ad oggi; studi in onore del prof. Vittorio Franchini nel 75° compleanno. Milano, Giuffrè, 1959.

389 p. port. 24 cm. (Biblioteca della rivista "Economia e storia," 1)

Bibliographical footnotes.

CONTENTS.—Presentazione, di A. Fanfani.—Note biografiche e pubblicazioni di Vittorio Franchini (p. [3]-7)—Senso e problemi dell'economia antica, di A. Petino.—La vita economica dell'antica Grecia secondo l'Iliade, di A. Fanfani.—Considerazione sociale del lavoro nel mondo romano, di F. M. de Robertis.—Uno sguardo al mercato dei panni di lana a Pisa nella seconda metà del Trecento, di F. Melis.—

(Continued)

NN 8.61 g/5 OC (OS)I, II PC, 1, 2, I SL E, 1, 2, I (LC1, X1, Z1)
[NSCM]

3

PROBLEMS of continuum mechanics... (Card 2)

1. Mechanics--Addresses, essays, lectures. 2. Muskhelishvili, Nikolaĭ Ivanovich, 1891- . I. Radok, J.R.M., ed. II. Society for industrial and applied mathematics. III. Akademiya nauk. t. 1961

PROBLEMI economici dall'antichità ad oggi... 1959. (Card 2)

Aspetti dell'organizzazione corporativa in Perugia nel XIV secolo, di G. Mira.—Provvedimenti annonari dello Stato pontificio, di A. Lodolini.—Le grance dell'Ospedale della Scala in Siena, di G. Cecchini.—Spedale scuola e chiesa in popolazioni rurali del secc. XVI-XVII, di I. Imberciadori.—Statistica e "scienza economica" in alcuni scrittori del XVI-XVII secolo, di G. Barbieri.—Compagnie "de negotio" veronesi agli inizi del Seicento, di M. Lecce.—Trasporti transalpini in Piemonte nel sec. XVII, di M. Abrate.—Il Muratori e le origini dell'idea di assistenza, di C. Curcio.—L'introduzione delle risaie in Romagna, di L. dal

(Continued)

TB

Problems of economic dynamics and planning; essays in honour of Michał Kalecki. Warszawa, PWN-Polish Scientific Publishers [°1964]

viii, 494 p. port. 25 cm.

Contributions in English, French, German, or Russian; English summaries for papers in other languages.
"Bibliography of [Kalecki's] works, 1927-1963": p. 481-494.

1. Kalecki, Michał. 2. Economics--Essays and misc. 3. Economic policy--Addresses, essays, lectures.
NN * R 9.65 e/ OC PC, 1, 2, 3 SL E, 1, 2, 3 (LC1, X1, Z1)

PROBLEMI economici dall'antichità ad oggi... 1959. (Card 3)

Pane.—Agostino Bassi sull'agricoltura lodigiana (1808) di M. Romani.—Le ultime corporazioni di arti e mestieri (sec. XIX) di E. Lodolini.—Cooperazione e mutualità nella storia economica, di O. Fantini.—Recenti studi sul capitalismo, di M. R. Caroselli.—Realizzazioni della Cassa per il Mezzogiorno ed effetti di esse, di G. Pescatore.—Confrontazione e coordinamento delle politiche valutarie e monetarie dei paesi della Comunità europea, di G. U. Papi.

1. Economic history. 2. Franchini, Vittorio, 1884- . I. Economia e storia. II. Economia e storia. Biblioteca.

---

*PDB

Proclamation and presence; Old Testament essays in honour of Gwynne Henton Davies. Edited by John I. Durham & J. R. Porter. Richmond, John Knox Press [1970]

xx, 315 p. port. 23 cm.

Includes bibliographical references.

CONTENTS.—Gwynne Henton Davies; a biographical appreciation.—A bibliography of the writings of Gwynne Henton Davies.—Old Testament hermeneutics. The limits of Old Testament interpre-

(Continued)

NN*R 8.71 m/s OC, I, II, III, IVb* PC, 1, I, II, III SL J, 1, I, II, III (LC1, X1, Z1)

3

PROCLAMATION and presence ... [1970]
(Card 2)

tation, by N. W. Porteous.—The Hexateuch. What de wo know about Moses? By G. Widengren. — The revelation of the divine name YHWH, by R. de Vaux. — The Deuteronomic legislator; a proto-Rabbinic type, by J. Weingreen.—Gilgal or Shechem? By O. Eissfeldt. — The succession of Joshua, by J. R. Porter. — The former prophets and the latter prophets. All the King's horses? By D. R. Ap-Thomas.—Elijah at Horeb; reflections on I Kings 19.9–18, by E. Würthwein.—Prophet and covenant: observations on the exegesis of Isaiah, by W. Eichrodt.—Jeremiah's complaints: liturgy or expres-

(Continued)

PROCLAMATION and presence ... [1970]
(Card 3)

sions of personal distress? By J. Bright.—Baruch the scribe, by J. Muilenberg.—Shiloh, the customary laws and the return of the ancient kings, by H. Cazelles.—The Psalms. Psalm 23 and the household of faith, by A. R. Johnson.—שלום and the presence of God, by J. I. Durham.

1. Bible. O.T.--Criticism. I. Davies, Gwynne Henton, 1906- . ed. II. Durham, John I., 1933- . ed. III. Porter, Joshua Roy, 1933- . ed. IV. Durham, John I,

Copy only words underlined
& classmark— TAA

PROFESSOR, dr. polit. Axel Nielsen; 30. december 1880-22. maj 1951, udgivet af Nationaløkonomisk forening. København, 1951. 260 p. illus., port. 26cm. (Nationaløkonomisk tidsskrift, bind 89, tillaegsheft)

1. Nielsen, Axel Eduard Hjorth, 1880-1951. 2. Economics, 1926- — Danish authors.

NN R 6.53 OI (PC)1, 2 (E)1, 2 (LC3, Z1, X1)

SB

Professor Ghurye felicitation volume, edited by K. M. Kapadia; issued under the auspices of Ghurye 60th birthday celebration committee. Bombay, Popular book depot [1954] xxiv, 283 p. port. 26cm.

Includes bibliographies.
Contents.—The energy theory of cultural development, by L.A. White.—A note on "Status," by J.H. Marshall.—The science of social change, by C.
(Continued)

NN ** R X 4.55 s/v OC, I,IIboO PC,1,2,I SL E,1,2,I (LC1,X1,Z1)

Professor Ghurye felicitation volume... (Card 2)

C. Zimmerman.—The "Heimat," in the light of ecology, by L. von Wiese.—The common factor in aboriginal and European settlement in Australia, by A.P. Elkin.—Sociology in Turkey, by H.Z. Ulken.—Tragedy and transcendence of tribal altruism, by P.A. Sorokin.—Sociology in a new frame of reference: man, symbol and society, by R. Mukerjee.—Observations on the nature of economic change in underdeveloped countries, by A. Borne.—Some
(Continued)

Professor Ghurye felicitation volume... (Card 3)

aspects of the ideology of industrial sociology, by Y.Dadabhoy.—Social work education, by M.S. Gore.—The impact of industrialization in West Africa, by K.A. Busia.—Towards an integration of the social sciences, by L.J. Lebret.—Sociology as a science, by W.F. Ogburn.—Fertility of early years of marriage in India, by D.G. Mandelbaum.—Social change in rural Maharashtra, by N.G. Chapekar.—The Asrama system, by A.S. Altekar.—The hypergamy of the Patidars, by D.F. Pocock.—Caste and race, by D. N. Majumdar.—Division
(Continued)

Professor Ghurye felicitation volume... (Card 4)

of India into linguistic states, by B.S. Guha.—Social research by D.P. Mukerji.—A brief note on Ayyappa, the South Indian deity, by M.N. Srinivas.—Some aspects of Yaksha cult in ancient India, by Motichandra.—A note on the change in the caste, by I.P. Desai and Y.B. Damle.—Iconography of Vayu and Vayu-worshippers in Gujarat, by M.R. Majmudar.
1. Ghurye, Govind Sadashiv. 2. Sociology—Addresses, essays, lectures. I. Kapadia, K. M., ed. II. Kapadia, K. M.

*OHO

PROF. M. HIRIYANNA commemoration volume. Editors: N. Sivarama Sastri [and] G. Hanumantha Rao. Mysore, Prof. M. Hiriyanna commemoration volume committee [1952] xxvi, 272 p. port. 22cm.

Biographical sketch, p. [xiii]-xxi.
"Bibliography of Prof. Hiriyanna's writings, by N. Sivarama Sastry," p. [xxii]-xxvi.
1. Indic literature—Hist. and crit. 2. Philosophy, Indian. 3. Hiriyanna, Maisūru.
NN**R 8.54 OC PC,1,2, 3 SL O,1,2,3 (Z1,LC1,X1) [I]

* OM

PROFESSOR POURE DAVOUD memorial volume. Bombay, Iran league 1951. 1 v. illus., port. 23cm.

Vol. 2.
CONTENTS. — v. 2. Papers on Zoroastrian and Iranian subjects [in English and French]

1. Poure Davoud, Ebrahim, 1886- 2. Persia—Civilization. 3. Zoroastrianism. I. Iran league, Bombay.

NN ** R 12.53 OC (OS) I PC, 1, 2, 3, I SL O, 1, 2, 3, I (LC1, Z1, X1)

Copy only words underlined
& classmark —GMA

Professori Einar W. Juvalle, hänen 7.1.1952 täyttäessään 60 vuotta. [Turku, 1951] 597 p. illus., port. 22cm. (Turun historiallinen arkisto. [n:o] 11)

Summaries in German.
Bibliographical footnotes.

1. Finland—Hist.—Addresses, essays, lectures.
2. Juvalle, Einar W.

NN R 9.53 (OC)2bo OI (PC)1,2 (LC3,Z1,X1)

AN
(Verheyden, P.)
Prosper Verheyden gehuldigd ter gelegenheid van zijn zeventigsten verjaardag 23 October 1943. Antwerpen, De Nederlandsche boekhandel [1943] 338 p. illus. 25cm.

"Uitgegeven...door...Willy Godenne, Luc Indestege en Bert Pelckmans."
No. 309 of 400 copies printed.
"Bibliographie Prosper Verheyden," p. [323]-334.

420162B. 1. Verheyden, Prosper, 1873-
N. Y. P. L. Festschrift ed. February 25, 1948

AF-10
29
PROVINZIAL-LANDWIRTSCHAFTS-VEREIN, Bremervörde, Germany.
Festschrift zur 50jährigen Jubelfeier des Provinzial-Landwirtschafts-Vereines zur Bremervörde (Regierungsbezirk Stade). Stade, Druck und Kommissionsverlag von A. Pockwitz, 1885. xix, 584 p. illus., fold. col. maps, diagrs., tables. 26cm.

1. Agriculture—Germany—Stade. 2. Stade, Germany—Hist.
3. Agriculture—Economics—Germany—Stade.

NN R 5.57 p/ OS (1b) PC, 1, 2, 3 SL E, 3 (LC1, X1, Z1)

E-10
3192
PROTESTANTISCHES GYMNASIUM, Strasbourg.
Festschrift zur Feier des 350 jährigen Bestehens des Protestantischen Gymnasiums zu Strassburg. Hrsg. von der Lehrerschaft des Protestantischen Gymnasiums. Strassburg, J. H. E. Heitz, 1888. 2 v. in 1. illus., maps. 25cm.

Bibliographical footnotes.

(Continued)

NN R 9.57 a/ (OC)I OS(1b) PC, 1, I SL (LC1, X1, Z1) [I]

L-10
6322
Bd. 4
PROVINZIALINSTITUT FÜR WESTFÄLISCHE LANDES- UND VOLKSKUNDE, Münster. Historische Kommission
Dona westfalica; Georg Schreiber zum 80. Geburtstag dargebracht. Münster in Westfalen, Aschendorffsche Verlagsbuchhandlung [1963] 392 p. plates. 25cm.
(ITS: Schriften. [Bd.] 4)

Contributions in German or Dutch.
Bibliographical footnotes.

(Continued)

NN R 7.65 p/ OS, I PC, 1, 2, I (LC1, X1, Z1) [I]

PROTESTANTISCHES GYMNASIUM, Strasbourg.
Festschrift zur Feier des 350 jährigen Bestehens ... (Card 2)

CONTENTS.—T. 1. Zum Gedächtnis Johannes Sturms, von H. Veil. Das Gründungsjahr des Strassburger Gymnasiums (1538-1539), von K. Engel. M. Samuel Gloner, ein Strassburger Lehrerbild aus den Zeiten des Dreissigjährigen Krieges, von R. Reuss. Ueber die älteren hebräischen Steine im Elsass, von J. Euting. Die französische Sprache in Strassburg bis zu ihrer Aufnahme in den Lehrplan des Protestantischen Gymnasiums, von C. Zwilling. Zur Strassburger Schulkomödie, von J. Crüger. Christoph Thomas Walliser, von A. Bähre. Die Gebäude des alten und des

(Continued)

PROVINZIALINSTITUT FÜR WESTFÄLISCHE LANDES- UND VOLKSKUNDE, Münster. Historische Kommission. Dona westfalcia... (Card 2)

CONTENTS.--Een onbekende Passio S. Wilgefortis, door W. J. Alberts. --Kurfürst-Fürstbischof Clemens August als Jagd-und Bauherr im Hümmling (Clemenswerth), von M. Braubach. --Die rheinisch-westfälischen Wirtschaftsbiographien, von W. Däbritz. --Die Attribute des hlg. Patroclus, von W.-H. Deus. --Über das Priesterzeugnis im friesischen Recht, von W. Ebel. --Die Jesuiten in Wiedenbrück, von F. Flaskamp. --Die Klosteranlage der Prämonstratenser in Varlar, von L. Frohne. --Unbekannte Klausen und Klöster

(Continued)

PROTESTANTISCHES GYMNASIUM, Strasbpurg.
Festschrift zur Feier des 350 jährigen Bestehens... (Card 3)

neuen Strassburger Gymnasiums (1538-1888), von E. Salomon.—T. 2. Beziehungen auf Tagesereignisse und polemische Aeusserungen in Horazens Satiren, chronologisch verwertet, von H. Schröder. Ueber ein Problem der Raumgeometrie der Anzahl, von L. Göring. Adversaria critica in Malalae chronographiam, scripsit M. Erdmann. Beitrag zur Ethnographie Madagaskars mit besonderer Berücksichtigung der Vazimba, von H. Schnakenberg. Unsere Vogesenseen, von H. Hergesell und E. Rudolph.

(Continued)

PROVINZIALINSTITUT FÜR WESTFÄLISCHE LANDES- UND VOLKSKUNDE, Münster. Historische Kommission. Dona westfalcia... (Card 3)

in Westfalen, von A. K. Hömberg. --Berichte des 9. Jahrhunderts über Wunder am Grabe der heiligen Pusinna in Herford, von C. Honselmann. --Das Kreuzherrenkloster Falkenhagen, von E. Kittel. --Die Kirchenvisitation vom Jahre 1650 im Fürstentum Minden, von L. Koechling. --Der Einzug des Fürstbischofs Franz Wilhelm von Osnabrück als Gesandter beim Friedenskongress in Münster, von H. Lahrkamp. --Missalhandschriften aus dem Bistum Münster, von E. Lengeling. -- Die deutsch Zentrumspartei

(Continued)

PROTESTANTISCHES GYMNASIUM, Strasbourg.
Festschrift zur Feier des 350 jährigen Bestehens... (Card 4)

Die Tiefenverhältnisse und die Bodenbeschaffenheit des mittleren Teils des Ostatlantischen Ozeans, von R. Langenbeck. Animadversiones criticae ad rerum scriptores graecos, scriptores graecos, scripsit L. K. Enthoven. Die Kapitulation zwischen Kaiser Karl V. und Papst Paul III. gegen die deutschen Protestanten (1546), von P. Kannengiesser. Der Infinitiv im Ostromir'schen Evangelium, von T. Forssmann.

1. Education, Secondary--Strasbourg. I. Title.

PROVINZIALINSTITUT FÜR WESTFÄLISCHE LANDES - UND VOLKSKUNDE, Münster. Historische Kommission. Dona westfalcia... (Card 4)

zwischen November-Revolution und Weimarer Nationalversammlung, von R. Morsey. --Die Professoren Dr. Harpprecht und Dr. Schöpff von der juristischen Fakultät Tübingen und der Prozess "Jud Süss", von H. Schnee. --Zur Geschichte der Gegenreformation im Mündungsgebiet von Ruhr, Lenne und Volme, von O. Schnettler. --Die Legation des Kardinals Nikolaus von Kues in Deutschland und ihre Bedeutung für Westfalen, von A. Schröer. --Die Herforder Fraterherren als Vertreter spätmittelalterlicher Frömmigkeit in Westfalen, von R Stupperich. --Ein Kirchenverzeichnis für den münsterischen Archidiakonat Friesland 1500 p. von G. Theuerkauf. --Die Beziehungen der Osnabrücker Augustiner

(Continued)

PROVINZIALINSTITUT FÜR WESTFÄLISCHE LANDES- UND VOLKSKUNDE, Münster. Historische Kommission. Dona westfalica... (Card 5)

zum Bistum und zur Stadt Münster, von K. Zuhorn.

1. Schreiber, Georg, 1882- 2. Church history--Germany--Westphalia
I. Series.

D-16
2187

PRUNTY, MERLE C., ed.
Festschrift: Clarence F. Jones. Edited by Merle C. Prunty. Evanston, Ill., 1962. 172 p. illus., port., maps. 20cm. (Northwestern university studies in geography. no. 6)

Bibliographical footnotes.

1. Jones, Clarence Fielden, 1893. 2. Latin America--Geography.
3. Geography, Economic I. Series. II. Prunty, Merle C.
NN 7.66 p/c OC, IIbo (OS)I PC, 1, 2, 3, I SL AH, 1, 2 E, 3 (LC1, X1, Z1)

PTB

Prussia. Geologische Landesanstalt.
...Beyschlag-Festband; in den Sitzungen der Anstalt von den wissenschaftlichen Beamten vom Januar bis April 1926 gehaltene Vorträge... Herausgegeben von der Preussischen geologischen Landesanstalt. Berlin, 1926. 97 p. illus. (incl. charts), mounted port. 4°. (Its: Sitzungsberichte. Heft 1.)

Mr. Moth

1. Beyschlag, Franz Heinrich August, 1856- . 2. Geology—Essays and misc. 3. Ser.
N. Y. P. L. January 9, 1928

---

* HSD
(Berlin)

Prussia. Koenigliche Bibliothek, Berlin.
Fuenfzehn Jahre Königliche und Staatsbibliothek. Dem scheidenden Generaldirektor Exz. Adolf von Harnack zum 31. März 1921 überreicht von den wissenschaftlichen Beamten der Preussischen Staatsbibliothek. Berlin: Preussische Staatsbibliothek, 1921. vi, 285 p. facsims., front., illus., plates. sq. 4°.

Bibliographical footnotes.
Partial contents: Voulliéme, E. H. Die Inkunabelsammlung. Haebler, K. Ramon Lull und seine Schule. Christ, K. Ältere Drucke volkstümlicher italienischer Dichtung in der Preussischen Staatsbibliothek. Paalzow, H. Ein unbekanntes Werk

(Continued)

N. Y. P. L. June 8, 1931

Prussia. Koenigliche Bibliothek, Berlin: Fuenfzehn Jahre Königliche und Staatsbibliothek... (Continued)

des Abtes de Rancé. Degering, H. Das Prümer Evangeliar (Ms. lat. theol. fol. 733) in Berlin. Kirchner, J. Die Berliner Gregoriusfragmente. Lindau, H. R. D. Gustav Freytag und Heinrich von Sybel. Crous, E. Die Bücherzeichen (Exlibris) in den Wiegendrucken der Staatsbibliothek. Haebler, K. Der Gesamtkatalog der Wiegendrucke.

478793A. 1. Libraries, Government —Germany—Berlin. 2. Harnack, Adolf von, 1851–1930.
N. Y. P. L. June 8, 1931

YEK

PSYCHOANALYSIS and culture; essays in honor of Géza Róheim. Editors: George B. Wilbur [and] Warner Muensterberger; editorial board: Henry A. Bunker [and others]; assistant editor: Lottie M. Maury. New York, International universities press [c1951] xii, 462 p. illus., port. 24cm.

"Dedicated to Géza Róheim on the occasion of his sixtieth birthday September 12, 1951."

"Bibliography of Géza Róhem's writings," p. 453-462.

1. Psychoanalysis. 2. Psychology, Social. 3. Roheim, Géza.
I. Münsterberger, Werner, 1913- , ed. II. Wilbur, George B , ed.
NN * R 7.53 OC, I, II, IIb PC, 1, 2, 3, I, II SL E, 2, I, II (LC1, Z1, X1) [I]

YED

Psychologischer club, *Zürich.*
Die kulturelle bedeutung der komplexen psychologie, herausgegeben vom Psychologischen club Zürich, mit einem porträt und 5 tafeln. Berlin, J. Springer, 1935.
vii, 625, [1] p. front., v pl. (ports., facsims.) on 4 l. 25½cm.
"Festschrift zum 60. geburtstag von C. G. Jung."
Contents.—C. G. Jung zum 60. geburtstag.—Einführung in die grundlagen der komplexen psychologie, von Toni Wolff.—Die geschichte vom indischen könig mit dem leichnam, von Heinrich Zimmer.—Chinesische kontemplationen: 1. Zu Richard Wilhelms gedächtnis. Die redaktion. 2. Das wasser als mythisches ereignis chinesischen lebens, von Erwin Rousselle.—Remarques sur l'initiation des medicine men, par L. Lévy-Bruhl.—Die indo-arische lehre vom selbste im vergleich mit Kants lehre

(Continued on next card)

36-21047

[2]

Psychologischer club, *Zürich.* Die kulturelle bedeutung der komplexen psychologie ... 1935. (Card 2)
Contents—Continued.

vom intelligiblen subjekt, von J. W. Hauer.—Ideendialektik und lebensdialektik. Das gegensatzproblem bei Hegel und bei Jung, von Fr. Seifert.—Analytische psychologie und religionsforschung, von Adolf Keller.—Die analytische psychologie als weg zum verständnis der mystik, von Ivar Alm.—Selbstbesinnung; eine philosophische meditation, von B. Wyscheslavzeff.—Betrachtungen über die symbolik der pyramiden, von H. H. Baumann.—Moderne physik—moderne psychologie, von C. A. Meier.—Analytical psychology and poetry, by Leonard Bacon.—Analytical psychology and the art of teaching, by W. H. Durham.—Analytical psychology and the English mind, by H. G. Baynes.—La psychologie

(Continued on next card)

36-21047

[2]

Psychologischer club, *Zürich.* Die kulturelle bedeutung der komplexen psychologie ... 1935. (Card 3)
Contents—Continued.

de l'inconscient et l'esprit français, par Y. Le Lay.—Die institution als ordnendes prinzip, von G. R. Heyer.—Über die psychologischen grenzen der dramatischen gestaltung, von H. E. Fierz.—Frauen als weckerinnen seelischen lebens, von Linda Fierz.—Vom werdegang des inneren menschen, von Ida Bianchi.—C. G. Jung in seiner handschrift, von Gertrud Gilli.—Streiflichter über C. G. Jungs geburts-horoskop, von Alice von Morawitz-Cadio.—Ein paar jugenderinnerungen, von Albert Oeri.—Individuation, schuld und entscheidung. Über die grenzen der psychologie, von Hans Trüb.—Bildnis der persönlichkeit im rahmen des gegenseitigen sich kennenlernens, von Emil Medtner.—Lebenslauf.—Schriften von C. G. Jung (p. 619–624)—Mitarbeiter.
1. Psychology—Collections. 2. Jung, Carl Gustav, 1875- I. Title.
36-21047

Library of Congress BF23.P7
Copyright A—Foreign 30122
[2] [159.904] 150.4

E-10
6847

PUERTO RICO. UNIVERSITY.
Homenaje a Juan Ramón Jiménez. San Juan, Ediciones de la Universidad de Puerto Rico, 1956. [i.e. 1957] 67 p. illus., port. 24cm.

"J.R.J. Tres selecciones de Platero y yo y un poema... Dibujo de Rafael Alvarez Ortega..." p. [59]-67.

1. Jiménez, Juan Ramón, 1881- I. Title. t. 1957.
NN R X 12.58 p/c (OC)I ODt EDt PC, 1 SL (PRI 1, LC1, X1, Z1)

Write on slip words underlined and class mark- **NAA**

Pushkin; homage by Marxist critics; translated from the Russian by Bernard Guilbert Guerney, edited by Irving D. W. Talmadge. New York, Critics group, 1937.

104 p. $20\frac{1}{2}^{cm}$. (*On cover:* Critics group series, no. 4)

"Chronology. <Principal works of Alexander Pushkin ... listed in order of probable date of composition. Outstanding English renderings are noted.>": p. 6.

CONTENTS.—Pushkin: an appraisal, by Maxim Gorky ⌈*pseud.*⌉—The heritage of Pushkin, by A. Zeitlin. — Pushkin as critic, by A. Lunacharsky.— Pushkin's road to realism, by I. Vinogradov.

1. Pushkin, Aleksandr Sergfeevich, 1799–1837. I. Pfeshkov, Aleksfeï Maksimovich, 1868–1936. II. Tseitlin, Aleksandr Grigor'evich, 1901– III. Lunacharskii, Anatolii Vasil'evich, 1875–1933. IV. Vinogradov, Ivan Arkhipovich. V. Guerney, Bernard Guilbert, tr. VI. Talmadge, Irving D. W., ed.

39–30801

Library of Congress PG3356.A1P82

⌈3⌉ 928.917

---

* C-3 p.v. 761

PUTTING knowledge to work, 1942-1952; a tribute to Datus C. Smith, jr. on the occasion of his tenth anniversary as director of Princeton university press. Princeton, N.J., 1952. 89 p. illus. 21cm.

CONTENTS.—Foreword, by J.P. Boyde.—In the social sciences, by J.D. Brown.—In the arts, by C.R. Morey.—In literature and language, by D.A. Stauffer.—In history and philosophy, by J.R. Strayer.—In

(Continued)

NN**R X 1.56 g/ OC PC, 1, 2, I SL (Z 1, LC1, X1)

dd

PUTTING knowledge to work, 1942-1952... (Card 2)

the sciences, by H.S. Taylor.—Bibliography, 1942-1952 (p. 71-89)

1. Smith, Datus C. 2. Princeton university press. I. Title.

dd

RAE

Quantulacumque; studies presented to Kirsopp Lake by pupils, colleagues and friends, edited by Robert P. Casey, Silva Lake, and Agnes K. Lake. London ⌈etc.⌉ Christophers ⌈©1937⌉

viii, 367 p. plates, plans, facsims. (part fold.) 26^{cm}.

CONTENTS.—Biographical note, by G. K. Lake.—The sibyl and bottle imps, by Campbell Bonner.—A political treatise of the early French renaissance, by J. M. Potter.—The Tertia philosophia of Guillaume de Conches and the authorship of the Moralium dogma philosophorum, by Theodore Silverstein.—Reflections on a synagogue inscription (Isaiah 66) by B. D. Erdmans.—Dionys von Alexandrien und die Libyer, by H.-G. Opitz.—Aux origines de l'architecture chrétienne, by L. H. Vincent.—The early Muslim sects, by William Thomson.—Der begriff des klassischen in der religionswissenschaft, by Joachim Wach.—Rebuttal, a submerged motive in the Gospels, by H. J. Cadbury.—Some remarks

(Continued on next card)

38–17329

⌈3⌉

Quantulacumque; studies presented to Kirsopp Lake by pupils ... ⌈©1937⌉ (Card 3)

CONTENTS—Continued.

Agnes K. Lake.—A sellisternium on the Parthenon frieze? By Lily R. Taylor.—Crisis in Ezekiel research, by George Dahl.—The Edessene origin of the Odes of Solomon, by J. de Zwaan.—Midrash in the books of Samuel, by R. H. Pfeiffer.—*Χριστός*, by C. C. Torrey.—The Codex cavensis, by E. A. Lowe.—A redating of two important uncial manuscripts of the Gospels, Codex zacynthius and Codex cyprius, by W. H. P. Hatch.—Ein blatt aus einer antiken weltchronik, by Hans Lietzmann.—Portions of an Old-Latin text of Saint Matthew's Gospel, by A. Souter.—Notes on the text of the Georgian and Armenian Gospels, by R. P. Blake.—A note on Greek ciphers, by Silva Lake.

1. Theology—Collections. 2. Philology—Collections. 3. Bible. Manuscripts. 4. Lake, Kirsopp, 1872– I. Casey, Robert Pierce, 1897– ed. II. Lake, Mrs. Silva (Tipple) 1898– joint ed. III. Lake, Agnes Kirsopp, joint ed.

Library of Congress BL25.Q3 38–17329

~~Copy 2.~~

Copyright A 119164 ⌈3⌉ 204

Quantulacumque; studies presented to Kirsopp Lake by pupils ... ⌈©1937⌉ (Card 2)

CONTENTS—Continued.

on formgeschichtliche methode, by R. P. Casey.—The date of Peter's confession, by M. S. Enslin.—The sources of Mark, by Norman Huffman.—Three notes on Saint Paul's journeys in Asia Minor, by T. R. S. Broughton.—Paul in the Agora, by Suzanne Halstead.—Some notes on the Chester Beatty Gospels and Acts, by F. G. Kenyon.—Codices 157, 1071, and the Caesarean text, by B. H. Streeter.—A third century papyrus of Matthew and Acts, by H. A. Sanders.—P 50. Two selections from Acts, by C. H. Kraeling.—Que vaut notre texte des Évangiles? By Hubert Pernot.—A misdated New Testament manuscript: Athos, Laura B. 26 (146) by E. C. Colwell.—Remarks on the Prophetologion, by Carsten Höeg and Günther Zuntz.—Literal mystery in Hellenistic Judaism, by E. R. Goodenough.—The supplicatio and Graecus ritus, by

(Continued on next card)

38–17329

⌈3⌉

WZX

The Queen's book of the Red cross, with a message from Her Majesty the queen and contributions by fifty British authors and artists, in aid of the Lord Mayor of London's fund for the Red cross and the Order of St. John of Jerusalem. ⌈London⌉ Hodder and Stoughton ⌈1939⌉

3 p. l., 5–255 p. front. (port.) plates (part col.) facsim. (music) $25\frac{1}{2}^{cm}$.

"First printed November 1939."
Prefatory letter of the Queen is a facsimile reproduction.

1. English literature (Collections) I. Elizabeth, queen consort of George VI, 1900– II. Red cross. Gt. Brit. British Red cross society. III. Malta, Knights of, in England.

40–5696

Library of Congress PR1149.Q38 1939

~~Copy 2.~~

Copyright A ad int. 25795 ⌈3⌉ 820.822

---

* PBN
(Breuer)

Rabbi Samson Raphael Hirsch Publications Society, *New York.*

עטרת צבי Jubilee volume presented in honor of the eightieth birthday of Rabbi Dr. Joseph Breuer. ⌈Edited by Marc Breuer and Jacob Breuer⌉ New York, P. Feldheim, 1962.

xx. 264. 56 p. illus., ports. 24 cm.
Title transliterated: Ateret Tsvi.
English or Hebrew.
"Bibliography of the writings of ... Joseph Breuer": p. xv–xx.

(Continued)

NN R 5.65 g/ (OC)Ib*, I, II, IIIb* OS(Ib) PC, 1, 2, 3, I, II
SL J, 1, 4, 5, I, II (LC1, X1, Z1)

4

Rabbi Samson Raphael Hirsch Publications Society, *New York.* עטרת צבי Jubilee volume ... 1962. (Card 2)

Bibliographical footnotes.

CONTENTS.—From the writings of Rabbi Dr. Joseph Breuer: High Holidays. Tashlich. Kol nidrei. The longing of the Seder Night. Faith. Towards worlds to come. Eretz Yisroel and the Golah. Youth in the kehilla. "German Jewishness." Dedication address.—From the heritage of Rabbi Samson Raphael Hirsch: The source, by I. Breuer. Rabbi S. R. Hirsch as a pioneer of Judaism in Eretz Yisroel and in the Diaspora, by S. Ehrmann. Taamei hamitzvoth in the Jewish legal philosophy of Rabbi S. R. Hirsch, by I. Grunfeld. The educational work of Rabbi S. R. Hirsch: Jewish schools in Western Europe, by M. Elias. The Frankfurt Yeshiva, by E. Posen.—

(Continued)

Rabbi Samson Raphael Hirsch Publications Society, *New York.* עטרת צבי Jubilee volume ... 1962. (Card 3)

Essays on Jewish thought: Zionism and the Sabbath mincha prayer, by R. Breuer. Women through the ages, by H. Meyer-Breuer. Comparative Jewish chronology, by S. Schwab. The actuality of Jewish philosophy, by E. Munk. Ashkenasi and Sephardi pronunciation, by E. Ehrentreu. Cardinal point and color schemes in Jewish symbolism, by P. Forchheimer. On the astronomical aspects of twilight in halakha, by L. Levy. —מכתבי יד של הרה"ג שמשון רפאל הירש זצוק"ל.—דברי הלכת, מאת ש. ז. ברייער.—בסוגי' דהזמנה מילתא היא, מאת ש. ברויאר.—על התיסדות קהלות חדשות לענין לא תתגודדו, מאת י. י. וויינברג.—בית המקדש והמשכן, מאת י. מרצבך.—הפראה מלאכותית, מאת מ. פינדלינג.

(Continued)

RABBI SAMSON RAPHAEL HIRSCH PUBLICATIONS SOCIETY, New York. עטרת צבי Jubilee volume... (Card 4)

1. Breuer, Joseph, 1882- . 2. Judaism--Addresses, essays, lectures. 3. Jews--Hist.--Addresses, essays, lectures. 4. Judaism--Essays. 5. History--Addresses, essays, lectures. I. Breuer, Marc, ed. II. Breuer, Jacob, ed. III. Breuer, Marc, ed.

---

* PBM p.v.689

Rada židovskych náboženských obcí v zemích české a moravsko-slezské.

Jewish studies; essays in honour of the Very Reverend Dr. Gustav Sicher, chief rabbi of Prague. ⌊Published at the occasion of the 75th birthday of the chief Rabbi. Edited by Rudolf Iltis⌋ Prague, Council of Jewish religious communities ⌊1955⌋ 111 p. illus., port. 21cm.

Bibliographical footnotes.

(Continued)

NN**R 3.58 (OC)1bo,I,IIbo OS PC,1,2,I SL J,1,3,I (LC1,X1,Z1)

Rada židovskych náboženských obcí v zemích české a moravsko-slezské. Jewish studies... (Card 2)

CONTENTS.—Concept of work in the Jewish faith, by G. Sicher.—The celebration of a great birthday, by B. Farkaš.—The literary work of Gustav Sicher, by M. Bič.—Weapons of mass destruction and our religion, by E. Katz.—The life of our religious communities, by E. Davidovič.—The social work of Jewish religious communities, by R. Iltis.—Jews in literature of the Czech lands, by P. Eisner.—The old-new synagogue—in the steps of Josef Mánes, by H. Volavková.—The unity of the new covenant—the unity of brethren, by S. Segert, translated from the Czech.—Musil, Madian and the mountain of the law, by G. Hart.—The State Jewish museum in Prague, by H. Volavková.—From the archives of the State Jewish museum, by O. Muneles.—At the end of the trail, by J. Weil.

1. Sicher, Gustav. 2. Jews in Czechoslovakia. 3. Czechoslovakia. I. Iltis, Rudolf, ed. II. Iltis, Rudolf.

YAR

Radhakrishnan; comparative studies in philosophy presented in honour of his sixtieth birthday. Editorial board: The Very Rev. W. R. Inge... ⌊and others⌋ London, G. Allen and Unwin ⌊1951⌋ 408 p. port. 22cm.

"Bibliography," p. 25-26.

Festschrift

1. Radhakrishnan, Sir Sarvepalli, 1888- . 2. Philosophy, 1901- . I. Inge, William Ralph, 1860- , ed.

N. Y. P. L.

E-13
2816

RAGNHILD, HATTON, ed.

William III and Louis XIV; essays 1680-1720 by and for Mark A. Thomson. Edited by Ragnhild Hatton and J. S. Bromley. With an introductory memoir by Sir George Clark. [Toronto] University of Toronto press, 1968. x,332 p. port. 25cm.

Bibliographical footnotes.

CONTENTS.--Introduction: Mark Alméras Thomson (1903-62), by Sir G. Clark.--'Maxims of (Continued)

NN R 7.68 e/A OC,I,II PC,1,2,3,I,II,III SL (LC1,X1,Z1)

4

RAGNHILD, HATTON, ed. William III and Louis XIV... (Card 2)

state' in Louis XIV's foreign policy in the 1680s, by A. Lossky.--Louis XIV and William III, 1689-97, by M. A. Thomson.--William III and the Brest fleet in the Nine years war, by A. N. Ryan.--Gratifications and foreign policy, by R. Hatton.--The interception of posts in Celle, 1694-1700, by S. P. Oakley.--The English newspapers from 1695 to 1702, by E. S. de Beer. --Parliament and foreign policy, 1689- (Continued)

RAGNHILD, HATTON, ed. William III and Louis XIV... (Card 3)

1714, by M. A. Thomson.--Louis XIV and the origins of the war of the Spanish succession, by M. A. Thomson. --Some Zeeland privateering instructions, by J. S. Bromley.--Louis XIV and the Grand alliance, 1705-10, by M. A. Thomson.--King and minister, by J. C. Rule.--The safeguarding of the protestant succession, 1702-18, by M. A. Thomson.--The protestant succession, April 1713-September 1715, by J. H. Shennan. --Self-determination and collective security as factors in English and French (Continued)

RAGNHILD, HATTON, ed. William III and Louis XIV... (Card 4)

foreign policy, 1689-1718, by M. A. Thomson.--Parliament and the treaty of quadruple alliance, by G. C. Gibbs.--The writings of Mark A. Thomson, by I. R. Christie (p. [306]-317).

1. Thomson, Mark Alméras. 2. Great Britain--Hist.--William and Mary, 1689-1702. 3. France--Hist.--Louis XIV, 1643-1715. I. Thomson, Mark Alméras. II. Bromley, J. S., joint ed. III. Title.

E-11
8721

RAHNER, HUGO, ed.

Perennitas; Beiträge zur christlichen Archäologie und Kunst zur Geschichte der Literatur, der Liturgie und des Mönchtums, sowie zur Philosophie des Rechts und zur politischen Philosophie. P. Thomas Michels OSB zum 70. Geburtstag, hrsg. von Hugo Rahner und Emmanuel von Severus. Münster, Verlag Aschendorff [1963] xxiii, 734 p. port. 25cm.

(Continued)

NN 3.64 p/ OC, I, III, IVbo (OS)II PC, 1, 2, I, II, III SL (LC1, X1, Z1) [I]

2

RAHNER, HUGO, ed. Perennitas... (Card 2)

(Beiträge zur Geschichte des alten Mönchtums und des Benediktinerordens. Supplementband. 2)

Contributions in German, English or French.

Bibliographical footnotes.

1. Michels, Thomas, 1892- 2. Civilization--Addresses, essays, lectures. I. Severus, Emmanuel von, joint ed. II. Series. III. Title. IV. Severus, Emmanuel von.

E-13
8259

Rakowski, Franz, *comp.*
Die öffentliche Bibliothek. Auftrag und Verwirklichung. (Wilhelm Schmitz-Veltin, dem Direktor der Stadtbücherei Duisburg, zum 60. Geburtstag.) Beiträge zu einer Diskussion zusammengestellt von Franz Rakowski. Berlin, Deutscher Büchereiverband, 1968.
160 p. 25cm.

Includes bibliographies.

(Continued)
NN*R 10. 70 w/S OC, I, Ib*, IIb* PC, 1, 2, I SL (LC1, X1, Z1)

RAKOWSKI, FRANZ, comp. Die öffentliche Bibliothek. (Card 2)

1. Libraries, Public--Addresses, essays, lectures. 2. Libraries--Germany. I. Schmitz-Veltin, Wilhelm, 1907- . II. Rakowski, Franz.

---

* QYN p.v.264

Rakstu vainags profesoram Jāzepam Vītolam, 1863-1933. [Rīgā] A. Gulbis [1933] 113 p. front. (port.), illus. (music.) 20cm. (Added t.-p.: Filosofijas un reliģijas zinātnu b-ba... Reliģiski-filosofiski raksti. 4.)

CONTENTS.—Zīverte-Zālīte, Milda. Jāzeps Vītols (1863.-1933.).—Dāle, P. Cēlais skaistums un jūtu dziļums mūzikā un reliģijā.—Maldonis, Vold. Kādēļ latvieši dzied?—Kundziņš, K. Garīgā dziesma kristiānisma sākumos.—Menšings, Gustavs. Dziesma reliģijas pasaulē.—Bencingers, J. Dziesmu cikls par Jahves kalpu.

1. Vītols, Jāzeps, 1863- . I. Zīverte-Zālīte, Milda.
N. Y. P. L. April 22, 1938

SSD

Ramalinga Reddy ṣaṣṭyabdapūrti commemoration volume. Waltair, South India, Andhra university [1940] 2 v. illus., ports. 25cm.

Includes bibliographies.
Contents.—Pt.1. Sciences.—Pt.2. Humanities.

1. Reddy, Sir C Ramalinga. 2. Science—Essays and misc. 3. Essays, English—Hindu authors. I. Andhra university. t.1940.
NN**R X 1.55 a/ OC (OS)I PC,1,2,3,I
SL 0,1,3,I ST,2t,I (LC1,X1,Z1)

E-11
6692

RANDZONEN menschlichen Verhaltens; Beiträge zur Psychiatrie und Neurologie; Festschrift zum fünfundsechzigsten Geburtstag von Prof. Dr. Hans Bürger-Prinz. Stuttgart, Enke, 1962. 262 p. illus., port. 25cm.

Includes bibliographies.
CONTENTS.-- Der Bogen des Philoktet, von V.-E.V. Gebsattel.--Asyle, von A. Gehlen--Das Problem des Nonkonformismus bei David
(Continued)

NN R 3.63 f/s OC PC, 1, 2 SL (LC1, X1, Z1)

RANDZONEN menschlichen Verhaltens... (Card 2)

Riesman, von H. Schelsky.--Der Arzt als Berater im Spannungsfeld der Pädagogik, von F.-G. v. Stockert.--Wandlungen, Möglichkeiten und Grenzen der klinisch-psychiatrischen Exploration, von H. Jacob.--Das ärztliche Ethos in Grenzsituationen, von G. Schorch.--Zur systematischen Klassifikation des Schwachsinns, von H. Büssow.--Dyskinetische Störungen und Kraftfahrtauglichkeit, von F. Stucke und W. Müller-Jensen.--Über halluzinatorische Alterpsychosen, von E.A. Franke.--Über die Depravation bei Süchtigen, von O. Schrappe.--Rechtssicherheit oder Verkehrssicherheit-- der Sachverständige zwischen
(Continued)

RANDZONEN menschlichen Verhaltens... (Card 3)

den Entscheidungen, von H. Lewrenz.--Zum Problem der Psychogenie, von U. Spiegelberg.--Bewusstsein und morphologisches Substrat, von H. J. Colmant.--Über das Beschäftigungssyndrom, von J. M. Burchard.--Über Spieler, von W. Rasch.--Über Verhältnisblödsinn, von H. Albrecht.--Verzweiflung, von H. J. Bochnik.--Über seltene Suchtformen, von F. J. M. Winzenried.--Zur Psychologie des Aussenseiters, von H. Giese und J. Hansen.--Am Faden der Gewohnheit, von P.A. Fischer.
1. Bürger-Prinz, Hans, 1897- 2. Psychiatry--Addresses, essays, lectures.

L-10
9624

RANGANATHAN festschrift. Bombay, New York, Asia pub. house [1965-67] 2 v. plates. 25cm. (Ranganathan series in library science. 14-15)

Vol. 2 is also Bengal library association. English series 3.
CONTENTS.--v.1. Library science today, papers contributed on the 71st birthday of Dr. S. R. Ranganathan; ed. by P. N. Kaula.--v.2. An essay in personal bibliography, a bibliography of the writings on and by Dr. S. R. Ranganathan [by] A. K. Das Gupta.
(Continued)
NN R 4.70 e/ OC, I, II (OS)III PC, 1, 2, 3, I, II, III SL (LC1, X1, Z1) [I]

RANGANATHAN festschrift. (Card 2)

1. Ranganathan, Shiyali Ramamrita, 1892- . 2. Ranganathan, Shiyali Ramamrita, 1892- --Bibl. 3. Library science--Addresses, essays, lectures. I. Kaula, Prithvi Nath, ed. Library science today. II. Dasgupta, Ajit Kumar. An essay in personal bibliography. III. Series.

SDC
+

RAO, C. RADAKRISHNA, ed.
Contributions to statistics; presented to Professor P.C. Mahalanobis on the occasion of his 70th birthday. Edited by C.R. Rao in collaboration with D.B. Lahire [and others] Oxford, New York, Pergamon press [1963] 528 p. illus. 29cm.

Includes bibliographies.

1. Statistics--Methods. 2. Mahalanobis, Prasanta Chandra. t.1963
NN R 3.66 a/c OC PC, 1, 2 SL E, 1, 2 ST, 1t, 2 (LC1, X1, Z1)

E-14
1520

The Rarer action; essays in honor of Francis Fergusson. Edited by Alan Cheuse and Richard Koffler. New Brunswick, N. J., Rutgers University Press [°1970]

xviii, 384 p. illus. 24 cm.

Contents.—Tribute by Allen Tate.—Memoir by R. W. B. Lewis.—Ibsen, Shaw, Brecht: three stages, by E. Bentley.—"This mist, my friend, is mystical": place and time in Elizabethan plays, by M. Charney.—The political theater, by N. Chiaromonte.—Untuning the Othello music: Iago as stage villain, by S. E. Hyman.—Euripidean

(Continued)

NN*R 7.71 w/ OC,I,II,III,IVb*, Vb* PC,1,I,II,III SL (LC1, X1, Z1)

The RARER action... (Card 2)

comedy, by B. Knox.—Actuals: a look into performance theory, by R. Schechner.—Leaves from an Asian diary, by S. Barr.—Dante's Purgatorio as elegy, by E. D. Blodgett.—Unamuno's romantic tragedy, by P. Pastras.—Fairfax versus Wiffen: Tasso's Clorinda in Elizabethan and in romantic garb, by G. Cambon.—Eyesight and vision: forms of the imagination in Coleridge and Novalis, by R. Freedman.—Writing as imitation: observations on the literary process, by P. Fussell, Jr.—Bilingualism and the problems of translation, by E. Kahler.—The poetry of Zbigniew Herbert, by S. Miller.—"That sweet man, John Clare," by R. Pinsky.—Paradiso, Canto XXXIII, by J. Ciardi.—The place of forms, by R. Fitzgerald.—Dostoevsky and Russian populism, by J. Frank.—Emerson,

(Continued)

The RARER action... (Card 3)

Vico, and history, by J. O. McCormick.—On the resemblances between science and religion, by H. Nemerov.—Myth and discovery, by J. Wright.—A list of the writings of Francis Fergusson, by R. Ellenwood (p. 373-384)

1. Literature--Addresses, essays, lectures. I. Fergusson, Francis, II. Cheuse, Alan, ed. III. Koffler, Richard, ed. IV. Cheuse, Alan. V. Koffler, Richard.

C-12
5390

RAUMER, KURT VON, 1900-
Freiherr vom Stein; Reden und Aufsätze. [Zum 60. Geburtstag von Kurt von Raumer am 15. Dezember 1960 hrsg. von Heinz Gollwitzer und Rudolf Vierhaus] Münster Westf., Aschendorff [1961] 268 p. port. 20cm.

1. Stein, Heinrich Friedrich Karl, Freiherr vom und zum, 1757-1831. I. Gollwitzer, Heinz, ed. II. Vierhaus, Rudolf, ed.

NN R 2.64 j/ OC, I, II PC, 1, I, II SL E, 1, I, II (LC1, X1, Z1)

MAC

RAVE, PAUL ORTWIN, 1893-
Kunstgeschichte in Festschriften; allgemeine Bibliographie kunstwissenschaftlicher Abhandlungen in den bis 1960 erschienenen Festschriften, von Paul Ortwin Rave unter Mitarbeit von Barbara Stein. Berlin, Gebr. Mann, 1962. 314 p. 26cm.

1. Art--Hist.--Bibl. 2. Festschriften--Bibl. I. Stein, Barbara.

NN R 12.63 p/ OC, I, Ibo PC, 1, 2, I SL A, 1, 2, I (LC1, X1, Z1)

PAV

RECENT research in molecular beams; a collection of papers dedicated to Otto Stern on the occasion of his seventieth birthday. New York, Academic Press, 1959. 190 p. diagrs., tables. 24cm.

Edited by Immanuel Estermann.
Includes bibliographies.
CONTENTS.--Molecular beam research in Hamburg, 1922-33, by I. Estermann.--Molecular and atomic beams at Berkeley, by W. A.

(Continued)

NN*R 1.60 l/ OC, I PC, 1, 2, I SL ST, 1, 2t, I (LC1, X1, Z1)

RECENT research in molecular beams... (Card 2)

Nierenberg.--Velocity distributions in potassium molecular beams, by P. M. Marcus and J. H. McFee.--Electron magnetic moment and atomic magnetism, by V. W. Hughes.--Hyperfine structure measurements in the metastable 2S state of hydrogenic atoms, by P. Kusch.--Shapes of molecular beam resonances, by N. F. Ramsey.--Comparison of methods for the determination of nuclear spin as applied to radioactive nuclei, by V. W. Cohen.--Molecular scattering at the solid surface, by F. C. Hurlbut.--Some applications of molecular beam techniques to chemistry, by S. Datz and E. H. Taylor.--A Stern-Gerlach experiment on polarized neutrons, by J. E. Sherwood, T. E. Stephenson, and S. Bernstein.

(Continued)

RECENT research in molecular beams... (Card 3)

1. Stern, Otto, 1888- . 2. Molecular beams. I. Estermann, Immanuel, 1900- , ed. t. 1959.

E-10
3908

RECHTSFRAGEN der internationalen Organisation; Festschrift für Hans Wehberg, zu seinem 70. Geburtstag; hrsg. von Walter Schätzel und Hans-Jürgen Schlochauer. Frankfurt am Main, V. Klostermann [c1956] 408 p. port. 24cm.

Contributions in German, French, or English.
CONTENTS.—Lebensgeschichte und Zeitgeschichte, von M. Huber.—Die internationalen Organisationen und ihre Funktionen im inneren

(Continued)

NN I.58 g/ OC, I, II PC, 1, 2, 3, I, II SL E, 1, 2, 3, I, II (LC1, X1, Z1, Y1)

RECHTSFRAGEN der internationalen Organisation... (Card 2)

Tätigkeitsgebiet der Staaten, von R. Ago.—L'application du principe représentatif dans les organisations internationales, par Baron F. M. van Asbeck.—Grundfragen der kollektiven Sicherheit, von R. L. Bindschedler.—Le "Concert européen" au XIXe siècle, par M. Bourquin.—Die Balkan-Allianz und das internationale Recht, von D. S. Constantopoulos.—Supranational, von Jonkheer W. J. M. van Eysinga.—Landesrechtliche Begriffe im Völkerrecht, von P. Guggenheim.—The binding character of the provisional measures of protection indicated by the International court of justice, by E. L. Hambro.— Ein Beitrag zum Problem der

(Continued)

RECHTSFRAGEN der internationalen Organisation...
(Card 3)

Macht im "klassischen" und im "neuen" Völkerrecht, von F. A. Freiherr von der Heydte. —Contiguity as a title to territorial sovereignty, by H. Kelsen. —Das Haager Abkommen zum Schutze von Kulturgütern im Falle bewaffneter Zusammenstösse vom 14. Mai 1954, von H. Kraus. — Zum Problem der Behandlung der nationalen Frage durch internationale Organisation, von R. Laun. —Beiträge des "Institut de droit international" zu den Problemen der internationalen Organisation bis 1914, von A. N. Makarov. —Internationale Organisation und Staatsverfassung, von H. Mosler. —Internationale Organisationen mit Hoheitsrechten, von F. Münch. —Le phénomène juridique de dédoublement
(Continued)

RECHTSFRAGEN der internationalen Organisation...
(Card 4)

fonctionnel, par G. A. J. Scelle. —Die Universalität der Weltorganisation, von W. Schätzel. —Zur Frage der Rechtsnatur der Europäischen Gemeinschaft für Kohle und Stahl, von H.-J. Schlochauer. —Les résolutions de l'Institut de droit international sur les amendements à apporter au Statut de la Cour internationale de justice, par J. Spiropoulos. —Zum Problem der völkerrechtlichen Grundnorm, von A. Verdross. —L'interdiction du recours à la force dans l'organisation internationale, par C. de Visscher. — Verzeichnis der wissenschaftlichen Monographien und Abhandlungen von Professor Hans Wehberg. p. [404]-408.
(Continued)

RECHTSFRAGEN der internationalen Organisation...
(Card 5)

1. Federation, International, 1939- . 2. Law, International--Addresses, essays, lectures. 3. Wehberg, Hans, 1885- . I. Schaetzel, Walter, 1890- , ed. II. Schlochauer, Hans Juergen, ed.

SE

Rechtsidee und Staatsgedanke; Beiträge zur Rechtsphilosophie und zur politischen Ideengeschichte. Festgabe für Julius Binder, in Verbindung mit Ernst Mayer und Max Wundt herausgegeben von Karl Larenz... Berlin: Junker und Dünnhaupt, 1930. vii, 263 p. front. (port.) 8°.

Mr. Moth.

560622A. 1. Binder, Julius, 1870- . 2. Law—Philosophy. 3. Political science—Hist., 1750- . I. Larenz, Karl, 1903- , editor. II. Mayer, Ernst, 1862- . III. Wundt, Max W. Aug., 1879- .
N. Y. P. L. January 21, 1932

3-MAK

Recueil d'études dédiées à la mémoire de N. P. Kondakov. Archéologie. Histoire de l'art. Études byzantines. Prague: "Seminarium Kondakovianum," 1926. xliv, 298 p. illus., plates, port. f°.

Added t.-p. in Russian.
Bibliographical footnotes.

Mr. Moth.

1. Kondakov, Nikodim Pavlovich, 1844-1925. 2. Archaeology. 3. Art —Essays and misc. 4. Civilization—Byzantine Empire. 5. Kondakov, Nikodim Pavlovich, 1844-1925—Bibl.
N. Y. P. L. June 24, 1929

RFB

Recueil de mémoires philologiques présenté à monsieur Gaston Paris ... par ses élèves suédois le 9 août 1889 à l'occasion de son cinquantième anniversaire. Stockholm, Imprimerie centrale, 1889.

4 p. l., 260 p., 1 l. 2 fold. tab., diagr. 23cm.

CONTENTS.—Quelques remarques sur l'amuïssement de l'r finale en français, par H. Andersson.—Exemples de r adventice dans des mots français, par S.-F. Eurén.—Sur quelques cas de labialisation en français, par P.-A. Geijer.—Observations sur les composés espagnols du type aliablerto, par A. W. Munthe.—Romance de la tierra, chanson populaire asturienne, pub. par A. W. Munthe.—Classification des manuscrits des Enfances Vivien, par A. Nordfelt.—La philologie française au temps jadis ... par

(Continued on next card)

11—2608 [a34b1]

Festschrift

Recueil de mémoires philologiques ... 1889. (Card 2)

CONTENTS—Continued.

C. Wahlund. (Reprints of Guillaume Rabot's "Oratio de gente et lingva francica, Witebergæ, 1572" and of the first chapter of "Recherches historiques sur les obstacles qu'on eut à surmonter, pour épurer la langue française [par Edmond Codier] Paris, 1806")—Les débuts du style français, par J. Vising.—Un chapitre de phonétique andalouse, par F. Wulff.

1. Paris, Gaston Bruno Paulin, 1839-1903. 2. Romance philology—Collections.

Library of Congress PC14.P2 11—2608 [a34b1]

D-11
4490

REES, WILHELM, 1888-
Kleine Spätlese [Festschrift zum 70. Geburtstag von Dr. Wilhelm Rees am 23. Januar 1958] Remscheid, Kulturamt der Stadt [1958] 93 p. illus. port. 21cm.

Selections from the author's works.

1. Essays, German. I. Remscheid, Germany. Kulturamt. t. 1958.
NN R 12. 58 1/ OC (OD)It (ED)It PC, 1, I SL (LC1, X1, Z1)

*MEC
(Engle, C.)

Reese, Gustave, 1899- *ed.*
A birthday offering to [Carl Engel] compiled and edited by Gustave Reese. New York, G. Schirmer, inc., 1943.
viii, 233 p. front., illus. (music) plates (incl. ports.) 3 facsim. on 1 l. 23½cm.

Name of Carl Engel represented on title-page by musical device.
Includes music.
"Privately printed in a limited and numbered edition of three hundred copies. No. 142."

CONTENTS.—Congratulatory message, by Herbert Putnam.—Portrait of Carl Engel, by John Erskine.—Carl Engel, librarian, by Harold Spivacke.—An American composer: Carl Engel, by Norman Peterkin.—Selected list of works by Carl Engel (p. 23-26).—Boston days (1909-1922): some Engeliana, by P. L. Atherton.—Ad Bibinem cum me rogaret

(Continued on next card)

43—13484 [43c1] Cd.

Reese, Gustave, 1899- *ed.* A birthday offering to [Carl Engel] ... 1943. (Card 2)

CONTENTS—Continued.

ad cenam (for four voices) by Samuel Barber.—From the correspondence of Harold Bauer and O. G. Sonneck.—Van Swieten or Constanze? By Nathan Broder.—The literary taste of Richard and Cosima Wagner, by Gladys Burch.—Four unpublished letters of Georg Friedrich Händel, by J. M. Coopersmith.—Themes from words and names, by H. T. David.—Tributum ad Angelum, a fugal fantasia (for piano) by Carl Deis.—Henry Gilbert: nonconformist, by Olin Downes.—The gentle art of editing a musical magazine, a letter, by Alfred Einstein.—Extract from "Views and reviews" (for voice and piano) by Anis Fuleihan.—Two conflicting theories of international copyright protection, by Francis Gilbert.—The specialist and the all-round man, by P. A. Grainger.—The composer as thinker, by Felix Greissle.—Thomas Mace and his tattle de

(Continued on next card)

43—13484 [43c1]

Reese, Gustave, 1899- *ed.* A birthday offering to ⌈Carl Engel⌉ ... 1943. (Card 3)

CONTENTS—Continued.

moy, by Otto Kinkeldey.—The formation of the lyric stage at the confluence of renaissance and baroque, by P. H. Láng.—From the correspondence of Charles Martin Loeffler.—The feasts of Plato and Pushkin, by Arthur Lourié.—Thoughts on the translation of vocal texts, by Arthur Mendel.—Recollections of Leopold Godowsky, by Isidor Philipp.—More about the namesake, by Gustave Reese.—J. C. Engel and the Kroll opera, by Curt Sachs.—Birthday canons (for three voices) by Arnold Schoenberg.—Three-score set (for piano) by William Schuman.—Amy Lowell and music, by Willis Wager.—The Wa-Wan press: an adventure in musical idealism, by E. N. Waters.

1. Engel, Carl, 1883- 2. Music—Addresses, essays, lectures. 3. Musicians. I. Title.

Library of Congress ML55.E5R4 43—13484

⌈43c1⌉ 780.4

Copy only words underlined & classmark-- RKA

REICHERT, HERBERT WILLIAM, 1917- , ed.
Studies in Arthur Schnitzler; centennial commemorative volume, edited by Herbert W. Reichert and Herman Salinger. Chapel Hill, University of North Carolina press [1963] 116 p. 23cm. (North Carolina. University. Studies in the Germanic languages and literatures, no. 42)

Contributions in German or English.

(Continued)

NN R 3.64 g/⁊ OC,I (OD)II (ED)II PC,1,I,II (LC1,X1, Z1)

2

E-12
3644

REESE, WILLIAM LEWIS, 1921- , ed.
Process and divinity; the Hartshorne festschrift. Philosophical essays presented to Charles Hartshorne and edited by William L. Reese & Eugene Freeman. LaSalle, Ill., Open Court Pub. Co., 1964.

ix, 633 p. 24 cm.

Appendices (p. ⌈579⌉-609): A. Published writings of Charles Hartshorne, compiled by Mrs. C. Hartshorne.—B. Bibliography of writings by and about Alfred North Whitehead in languages other than English, compiled by G. L. Kline.

(Continued)

NN * R 6.65 e/⁊ OC, I PC, 1, 2, 3, I SL (LC1, X1, Z1)

2

REICHERT, HERBERT WILLIAM, 1917- , ed.
Studies in Arthur Schnitzler... (Card 2)

Includes bibliographies.

CONTENTS. — Arthur Schnitzlers unveröffentlichte Tragikomödie, von K. Bergel. —Schnitzler in französischer Sicht, von J. H. Dayag. — The meaning of death in Schnitzler's work, by L. B. Foltin. —The image of the Austrian in Arthur Schnitzler's writings, by R. A. Kann. — An interpretation of Die Weissagung, by R. H. Lawson. —Arthur Schnitzler und der junge Hoffmannsthal, von W. H. Perl. — Nietzsche and Schnitzler, by H. W. Reichert. —Observations on Schnitzler's narrative techniques in the short novel, by R. D. Spector.

1. Schnitzler, Arthur, 1862-1931. I. Salinger, Herman, 1905- , joint ed. II. Series.

REESE, WILLIAM LEWIS, 1921- , ed. Process and divinity... (Card 2)

1. Philosophy--Addresses, essays, lectures. 2. Whitehead, Alfred North, 1861-1947. 3. Hartshorne, Charles, 1897- . I. Freeman, Eugene, joint ed.

SIO

Reichsverband der deutschen landwirtschaftlichen Genossenschaften-Raiffeisen-e. V.
F.W.Raiffeisen zum Gedächtnis. Neuwied am Rhein: Druck: Genossenschaftsdruckerei Raiffeisen, g.b.H., 1938. vii, 227 p. front. (port.), illus. (charts), plates. 27½cm.

Festschrift

---

*POR

Reform Judaism; essays by Hebrew Union College alumni. Cincinnati, Hebrew Union College Press ⌈°1949⌉

xii, 288 p. 25 cm.

CONTENTS.—Introd., by B. J. Bamberger.—Rethinking the liberal faith, by L. A. Olan.—New trends in reform Jewish thought, by J. L. Liebman.—Reform Judaism and prayer, by S. B. Freehof.—Conservative and reconstructionist Judaism as seen by a reform rabbi, by B. D. Cohon.—The religion of the Jewish veteran, by M. Lieberman.—Where are our youth? By N. A. Perilman.—Reform Judaism and Zionism: A Zionist interpretation, by L. Fram. A non-Zionist interpretation, by D. H. Wice.—The changing functions of the synagogue and the rabbi, by A. J. Feldman.—Reform Jewish practice, by J. D. Schwarz.—What has liberal Judaism to offer America? By E. W. Leipziger.—Reform Judaism and world Jewry, by M. Reichler.

1. Jews—Religion—Reform movements.

BM197.R39 296 Fest. 50-2207

Library of Congress ⌈10⌉

MTE
✚

Reinecke Festschrift; zum 75. Geburtstag von Paul Reinecke am 25. September 1947. Hrsg. von Gustav Behrens und Joachim Werner. Mainz, E. Schneider, 1950. vii, 180 p. illus., 43 pl. 30cm.

Bibliographical footnotes.

608117B. 1. Archaeology. 2. Reinecke, Paul, 1872- . I. Behrens, Gustav, 1884- , ed. II. Werner, Joachim, 1909- , ed.

N. Y. P. L. November 21, 1951

TAH

Reformer och försvar; en bok till Per Edvin Sköld på 60-årsdagen. Stockholm, Tidens förlag [1951] xiv, 197 p. front. 24cm.

1. Economic history—Sweden. 2. Defense—Sweden. 3. Sköld, Per Edvin, 1891-

WS

NN

MCK
N138.R3

REINHOLD NÄGELE: Bilder aus fünf Jahrzehnten; Stimmen der Freunde. Eingeleitet von Otto Rombach. Mit einem Grusswort von Theodor Heuss und Beiträgen von Hugo Borst [et al.] Konstanz, J. Thorbecke [1962] 105 p. illus. (part col.) 26cm.

1. Nägele, Reinhold, 1884- . I. Rombach, Otto, 1904- .

NN R 6.63 g/⁊ OC, I PC, 1, I SL A, 1, I B (LC1, X1, Z1)

YAR

Reiningerkreis, Vienna.
Philosophie der Wirklichkeitsnähe. Festschrift zum 80. Geburtstag Robert Reiningers (28. September 1949) Wien, A. Sexl, 1949. 279 p. 24cm.

"Eine Denkausgabe des Reiningerkreises." —*Foreword.*
"Gesamtverzeichnis der Veröffentlichungen Robert Reiningers," p. 278-279.

526617B. 1. Reininger, Robert, 1869- . 2. Philosophy—Essays and misc.
N. Y. P. L. July 27, 1950

Copy only words underlined
& Classmark-- EAM

REIS, HANS.
Konkordat und Kirchenvertrag in der Staatsverfassung. Willi Geiger zum befohrstehenden 60. Geburtstag am 22. Mai 1969 in steter Dankbarkeit und Verehrung. (IN: Jahrbuch des öffentlichen Rechtes der Gegenwart. Tübingen. 25cm. N.F., Bd.17(1968) p.[165]-394)

Bibliography, p. [165]-181.

1. Church and state. 2. Constitutions.
NN R 9.69 r/ OC(1bo) OI PC, 1, 2 E, 1, 2 (LC1, X1, Z1)

NCB

Renaissance studies in honor of Hardin Craig. Edited by Baldwin Maxwell, W. D. Briggs, Francis R. Johnson [and] E. N. S. Thompson. Stanford University, Calif., Stanford university press; [etc., etc., 1941]
viii, 339 p. front. (port.) 23½cm.
"A reprint of the Philological quarterly, xx, iii (July, 1941)."—p. [iv]
CONTENTS.—Hardin Craig, by Rudolf Kirk.—The York play of Christ led up to Calvary (Play xxxiv) by M. G. Frampton.—The miracle play: notes and queries, by G. R. Coffman.—Some aspects of Italian humanism, by B. L. Ullman.—Fortune in the tragedies of Giraldi Cintio, by A. H. Gilbert.—Fracastoro and the imagination, by M. W. Bundy.—Current English translations of The praise of folly, by H. H. Hudson.—The proverb "The black ox has not trod on his foot" in renaissance literature, by Archer Taylor.—Aspects of Spenser's vocabulary, by F. M. Padel-

(Continued on next card)

A 43-985
[10]

Renaissance studies in honor of Hardin Craig ... [1941] (Card 2)

CONTENTS—Continued.

ford.—The neo-Platonic ladder in Spenser's Amoretti, by Edwin Casady.—Greene's Panther, by J. L. Lievsay.—Backgrounds for Marlowe's atheist lecture, by P. H. Kocher.—The taming of a shrew, by H. D. Gray.—The two angrey women of Abington and Wily beguiled, by Baldwin Maxwell.—Aims of a popular Elizabethan dramatist, by G. F. Reynolds.—The fall of Icarus, by J. W. Ashton.—Shakespeare's Rape of Lucrece, by E. P. Kuhl.—Perseus purloins Pegasus, by T. W. Baldwin.—Two notes on Shakespeare, by G. C. Taylor.—Shakespeare's use of his sources, by V. K. Whitaker.—Shakespeare as a critic, by H. T. Price.—The mind's construction in the face, by Carroll Camden.—That undiscovered country, by Madeleine Doran.—Comedy in the court masque: a study of Ben Jonson's contribution, by T. M. Parrott.—John Ford and

(Continued on next card)

A 43-985
[10]

Renaissance studies in honor of Hardin Craig ... [1941] (Card 3)

CONTENTS—Continued.

Elizabethan tragedy, by G. F. Sensabaugh.—Richard Hooker among the controversialists, by E. N. S. Thompson.—The myth of John Donne the Rake, by A. R. Benham.—A protest against the term conceit, by G. R. Potter.—The themes of pre-existence and infancy in The retreate, by M. Y. Hughes.—A note on two words in Milton's History of Muscovia, by Harris Fletcher.—Grundtvig on Paradise lost, by Kemp Malone.—The English religious restoration, 1660-1665, by H. G. Plum.—Bibliography of the writings of Hardin Craig, by F. R. Johnson (p. [335]-339)

1. Craig, Hardin, 1875- 2. English literature—Early modern (to 1700)—Hist. & crit. 3. Renaissance. I. Maxwell, Baldwin, 1893- ed. II. Briggs, William Dinsmore, joint ed. III. Johnson, Francis Rarick, 1901- joint ed. IV. Thompson, Elbert Nevius Sebring, 1877- joint ed.

A 43-985

New York. Public library
for Library of Congress [10]

F-10
7293

RENARD, MARCEL, ed.
Hommages à Albert Grenier. Bruxelles, Latomous, 1962. 3 v.(xiv, 1665 p.) illus., port., maps. 26cm. (Collection Latomus. v.58)

Contributions in French, English, German, Italian or Spanish.
Bibliographical footnotes.

1. Grenier, Albert, 1878-1961. 2. Archaeology--Addresses, essays, lectures. 3. Art, Classical--Addresses, essays, lectures. I. Series.
NN 2.63 p/ OC (OS)I PC, 1, 2, 3, I SL A, 3 (LC1, X1, Z1) [I]

F-10
9530

RENARD, MARCEL, ed.
Hommages à Jean Bayet, édités par Marcel Renard et Robert Schilling. Bruxelles, Latomus, 1964. xv, 751 p. plates, port. 26cm. (Collection Latomus. v. 70)

Text in French or German.
Bibliographical footnotes.

1. Bayet, Jean, 1892- . 2. Classical studies--Collections. I. Schilling. Robert, 1913- , joint ed. II. Series.
NN 12.64 g/ OC, I (OS)II PC, 1, 2, I, II SL (LC1, X1, Z1) [I]

QEI

[**Rennes,** France. **Université**]
Mélanges dédiés au professeur Lucien Daniel... Université de Rennes, 19 décembre 1936. [Rennes: Imprimeries Oberthur, 1936] xii, 495 p. front. (port.), illus. (incl. charts), 40 [i. e. 42] pl., tables. 27½cm.

"Cet ouvrage a été tiré à 250 exemplaires...no. 114."
Bibliography at end of each article.
CONTENTS.—Abbayes, H. des. Contribution à l'étude du narcisse des iles Glénans (Finistère) II. Morphologie des chromosomes somatiques.—Bethaut, M. Note sur les différents parasites ou accidents de végétation des blés tendres au Maroc (campagne 1935-1936).—Chadefaud, M. Les constituants du protoplasme et la classification

(Continued)

918984A. 1. Botany. 2. Daniel, Lucien Louis, 1856- . I. Title.
N. Y. P. L. January 7, 1938

[**Rennes,** France. **Université**] Mélanges dédiés au professeur Lucien Daniel... (Card 2)

générale des êtres vivants.—Chalaud, G. La multiplication végétative chez Scapania subalpina (Nees) Dum.—Chermezon, H. Comparaison entre les flores cypérologiques de quelques régions de l'Afrique tropicale.—Chevalier, Aug. Notes historiques et biologiques sur quelques arbres et arbustes du district armorico-ligérien.—Chouard, P. Sur la polarité et les facteurs de la formation de bourgeons et de racines dans des boutures de feuilles.—Costantin, J. Faits plaidant en faveur de l'hérédité des caractères acquis.—Courcelle, R. M. Lucien Daniel et son œuvre botanique dans le département de la Mayenne.—Dufrénoy, J. Modifications pathologiques du système vascuolaire des cellules végétales.—Gain, E. Recherches sur la résistance des pailles des céréales à la traction.—Guéguen, Ed. L'amidon floridéen chez Furcellaria fastigiata; ses variations saisonnières.—Hochreutiner, B. P. G. La valeur relative des groupes systématiques.—

(Continued)

N. Y. P. L. January 7, 1938

[**Rennes,** France. **Université**] Mélanges dédiés au professeur Lucien Daniel... (Card 3)

Houlbert, C. L'œuvre pomologique du professeur L. Daniel.—Labbé, A. Ontogenèse d'un instinct chez une araignée.—Lallemand, Mme S. Influence de l'hydratation de graines de légumineuses sur l'effet toxique de diverses solutions.—Lefèvre, M. Phytoplancton de quelques étangs de l'ouest de la France.—Le Roux, J. Le problème de la relativité d'après les idées de Poincaré.—Malcuit, G. Contributions à l'étude phytosociologique du littoral normand; la végétation halophile de l'estuaire de la Dives.—Maresquelle, H.-J. Quelques observations sur les phénomènes d'inhibition d'origine cécidogène.—Meslin, R. Les Hutchinsia de la flore normande, à propos d'une nouvelle station de l'H. procumbens Desv. à Coutainville.—Miège, E. Sur le mode d'apparition de diverses espèces dans la descendance de deux hybrides interspécifiques de Triticum.—Moreau, F. et Moruzi, Mlle C. Les "chimères" des champignons.—Nicolas, G. L'amélioration du blé dans le sud-ouest de la France.—Pesson, P. La mutation "mopse"

(Continued)

N. Y. P. L. January 7, 1938

⌊Rennes, France. Université⌋ Mélanges dédiés au professeur Lucien Daniel... (Card 4)

chez Perca fluviatilis L.—Picquenard, Ch. Observations sur les réactions de la flore des montagnes vis-à-vis du climat bas-breton.—Poisson, R. Sur un Enmycète nouveau: Smittium arvernense n. g., n. sp., parasite intestinal de larves de Smittia sp. (Diptères chironomides), et description d'une nouvelle espèce du genre Stachylina Lég. et Gauth. 1932. Quelques observations biologiques et morphologiques sur Ceresa bubalus (Fab.) insecte hémiptère-homoptère de la famille des Membracides, d'origine américaine.—Popesco, C.-T. La similitude des mouvements ondulatoires de la circulation et de la sédimentation de la matière morte et vivante dans la nature. L'œuvre scientifique du professeur Lucien Daniel.—Prat, H. Sur la correspondance entre la structure des pousses de pins et les cycles saisonniers.—Ripert, J. De l'examen botanique des plantes servant aux études de chimie végétale.—Seyot, P. Agaricus Danieli.—Tison, A. Sur quelques anomalies de chatons femelles d'Ephedra.—Werner, R.-G. Esquisse sur la répartition phytogéographique des lichens océaniques du Maroc.

N. Y. P. L. January 7, 1938

D-18
2989

The Responsibility of power; historical essays in honor of Hajo Holborn. Edited by Leonard Krieger and Fritz Stern. ⌊1st ed.⌋ Garden City, N. Y., Doubleday, 1967.

xiv, 464 p. port. 22 cm.

Bibliographical footnotes.

(Continued)

NN*R 7.68 e/⁄₄OC,I,II, SL E,2,3,I,II,III III PC,1,2,3,I,II,III (LC1,X1,Z1) [I] 4

The RESPONSIBILITY of power... (Card 2)

CONTENTS.—Power and responsibility; the historical assumptions, by L. Krieger.—Machiavelli; the art of politics and the paradox of power, by H. H. Gray.—The responsibilities of power according to Erasmus of Rotterdam, by R. H. Bainton.—Sebastian Castellio on the power of the Christian prince, by H. R. Guggisberg.—Richelieu, by D. Gerhard.—The nature of political power according to Louis XIV, by A. Lossky.—Friedrich Schiller and the problems of power, by G. A. Craig.—1848, by T. S. Hamerow.—Juridical and political responsibi-

(Continued)

The RESPONSIBILITY of power... (Card 3)

lity in nineteenth-century Germany, by O. Pflanze.—Burckhardt's Renaissance; between responsibility and power, by P. Gay.—Power and responsibility; Otto Hintze's place in German historiography, by W. M. Simon.—Freedom and power in history, by W. Kaegi.—Politics in a new key: Schönerer, by C. E. Schorske.—Bethmann Hollweg and the war: the limits of responsibility, by F. Stern.—Domestic causes of the First World War, by A. J. Mayer.—Naumann and Rathenau; their paths to the Weimar Republic, by H. C. Meyer.—Friedrich Ebert and the German Revolution of 1918, by R. N. Hunt.—Lenin and power, by H. L. Roberts.—Neville Chamberlain and Munich; two aspects of power, by W. E. Scott.—Reinhold Niebuhr; prophet in politics, by J. H. Nichols.—Limits of American internationalism, 1941–45, by J. M. Blum.—Political power and academic responsibility;

(Continued)

The RESPONSIBILITY of power... (Card 4)

reflections on Friedrich Meinecke's Drei Generationen deutscher Gelehrtenpolitik, by F. Gilbert.—The conditions of revolutionary power, by O. Kirchheimer.—The responsibility of science, by H. Marcuse.

1. History, Modern—Addresses, essays, lectures. 2. Force (Political and social science, etc.) 3. Power, Philosophy of. I. Holborn, Hajo, 1902- II. Krieger, Leonard, ed. III. Stern, Fritz, 1926- , ed.

Mus. Res.
*MN p.v. 25

Le RETOUR de Nantes. Parodies nouvelles... A Paris, Chez Mme. Boivin, Mr. LeClerc, et Mr. Duval, 1738. 5 p. 19cm.

Unacc. melodies.

CONTENTS.--Menuet de Castor et Pollux.--Air de Castor et Pollux.--Air nouveau de Mr. C.

(Continued)

NNR7.70 w/⁄₄OC,I SL MUg, 1g.2g.1g (MUS6, MUR1, DC2, LC1,X1,Z1) 2

Le RETOUR de Nantes. (Card 2)

THE OTTO KINKELDEY MEMORIAL COLLECTION

1. Songs, French--Collections. 2. Parodies--Songs. I. Rameau, Jean Philippe, 1683-1764. Castor et Pollux.

YBX
(Descartes)

Revue philosophique de la France et de l'étranger. Descartes, par Ch. Adam, E. Bréhier, L. Brunschvicg ... ⌊e. a.⌋ Recueil publié par "La Revue philosophique" à l'occasion du troisième centenaire du "Discours de la méthode". Paris, Librairie Félix Alcan, 1937.

2 p. l., 372 p., 2 l. diagrs. 25[cm].

Bibliographical foot-notes.

CONTENTS.—Adam, C. Descartes; ses trois notions fondamentales.—Bréhier, E. La création des vérités éternelles dans le système de Descartes.—Brunschvicg, L. Note sur l'épistémologie cartésienne.—

(Continued on next card)

A C 37-3163

⌊2⌋

Festschrift

Revue philosophique de la France et de l'étranger. Descartes ... 1937. (Card 2)

CONTENTS—Continued.

Jaspers, K. La pensée de Descartes et la philosophie.—Koyré, A. La loi de la chute des corps; Galilée et Descartes.—Lachièze-Roy, P. Réflexions sur le cercle cartésien.—Laird, J. L'influence de Descartes sur la philosophie anglaise du XVIIe siècle.—Laporte, J. La connaissance de l'étendue chez Descartes.—Rivaud, A. Remarques sur le mécanisme cartésien.—Robinson, L. Le "cogito" cartésien et l'origine de l'idéalisme moderne.—Schrecker, P. La méthode cartésienne et la logique.—Schuhl, P.-M. Un souvenir cartésien dans les "Pensées" de la reine Christine.—Wahl, J. Notes sur Descartes.

1. Descartes, René, 1596–1650. I. Adam, Charles, 1837-

A C 37-3163

New York. Public library
for Library of Congress ⌊2⌋

TB

Rheinisch-Westfälisches Institut für Wirtschaftsforschung, Essen, Germany.

Beiträge zur Wirtschaftsforschung; Festgabe für Walther Däbritz. Beiträge von: Fritz Baade...[und anderen] Essen, Rheinisch-Westfälisches Institut für Wirtschaftsforschung, 1951. 358 p. port. 23cm.

Bibliographical footnotes.

1. Däbritz, Walther, 1881- 2. Economics, 1926- —German and Austrian authors.

NN

AN
RHODES, DENNIS E (Hutton, E.)
The writings of Edward Hutton; a bibliographical tribute compiled and presented to Edward Hutton on his eightieth birthday by his friend, Dennis E. Rhodes. London, Hollis & Carter, 1955. 64 p. illus., port. 22cm.

1. Hutton, Edward, 1875- —Bibl.
NN**R 11.55 g/ OC(1bo) PC, 1 SL (LC1, X1, Z1)

NPE
Ribera y Tarragó, Julián, 1858–
...Disertaciones y opúsculos; edición colectiva que en su jubilación del profesorado le ofrecen sus discípulos y amigos (1887–1927), con una introducción de Miguel Asín Palacios... Madrid: E. Maestre, 1928. 2 v. front. (port.) 8°.

Bibliographical footnotes.

MrMoth.

1. Spanish literature—Collected works. 2. Arabs in Spain. 3. Asín Palacios, Miguel, 1871–
N. Y. P. L. June 21, 1929

Copy only words underlined
& Classmark-- TB
RICH, ARTHUR.
Aufrisse; Vorarbeiten zum sozialethischen Denken. [Herausgeber: Hans ten Doornkaat Koolman] Zürich, Zwingli Verlag [1970] 247 p. 24cm. (Zürich (City). Universität. Institut für Sozialethik. Veröffentlichungen. Bd. 4)

Essays collected in honor of the author's 60th birthday.
Bibliographical footnotes.

(Continued)
NN R 5.71 m/e OC, II (OS)I PC, I, I, II E, I, I, II (LC1, X1, Z1)

2

RICH, ARTHUR. Aufrisse; Vorarbeiten zum sozialethischen Denken. (Card 2)

PARTIAL CONTENTS.--Das Judenproblem.--Zwingli.--Berdiajew.--Pascal.--Paulus.--Publikationen von Arthur Rich (p. 237-247)

1. Ethics, Social. I. Series. II. Doornkaat Koolman, Hans ten, 1917- , ed.

---

* MFSB
(Germany)
Riedel-Verein, Leipzig.
Der Riedel-Verein zu Leipzig: eine Denkschrift zur Feier seines fünfzigjährigen Bestehens, herausgegeben von Dr. Albert Göhler. Leipzig: Im Selbstverlag des Vereins, 1904. 161 p. front., ports. 25cm.

CONTENTS.—Die Programme der vom Riedel-Verein veranstalteten Konzerte.—Die Programme der akademischen Konzerte von Professor Dr. Hermann Kretzschmar.—Das Leben Carl Riedels.—Die Geschichte des Riedel-Vereins.—Verzeichnis der Mitglieder und Gäste des Riedel-Vereins.—Register zu den Programmen des Riedel-Vereins.—Verzeichnis der Orte, an denen der Riedel-Verein Aufführungen veranstaltete.

406695. 1. Riedel, Carl, 1827–1888. I. Göhler, Albert, 1879–1914, ed.
N. Y. P. L. *Card revised* October 22, 1941

Copy only words underlined
& classmark-- TB
RIES, JOSEF, ed.
Betriebswirtschaftliche Planung in industriellen Unternehmungen; hrsg. von Josef Ries und Gert v. Kortzfleisch. [Festgabe für Theodor Beste] Berlin, Duncker & Humblot [1959] 209 p. tables, port. 24cm. (Cologne. Universität. Industrieseminar. Abhandlungen. Heft 10)

CONTENTS.—Zum Wesen der betriebswirtschaftlichen Planung, von G. v. Kortzfleisch.—Gedanken zur mineralölwirtschaftlichen
(Continued)
NN R 4.62 g/B OC, I (OS)II PC, 1, 2, I, II E, 1, 2, I, II (LC1, X1, Z1)

3

RIES, JOSEF, ed. Betriebswirtschaftliche Planung in industriellen Unternehmungen... (Card 2)

Absatzplanung, von J. Wibbe.--Mathematische Grundlagen für die Arbeitszeitplanung, von G. Struckmann.—Die Disposition in der Schallplattenindustrie, von G. Hundertmark.—Die Bedeutung elektronischer Rechenanlagen für die betriebliche Planung, von H. Fryburg.—Der Einfluss des Titers in den Planungen der Chemieindustrie, von H. Rüschenpöhler.—Risiko und Kostenplanung, von H. Schönnenbeck.—Kontrolle des Ausbringens durch Planung, dargestellt am Beispiel eines Kaltbandwerkes, von S. Büchner.—Die Planung der Innenrevision, H. v. Kortzfleisch.— Betriebswirtschaftliche
(Continued)

RIES, JOSEF, ed. Betriebswirtschaftliche Planung in industriellen Unternehmungen... (Card 3)

Steuerplanung, von H. Schockenhoff.—Der Finanzplan in einem Unternehmen mit langfristiger Auftragsabwicklung, von E. Feuerbaum.—Die Planung des Zukunftserfolges bei der Bewertung der Unternehmung als Ganzem, von H. Bergner.

1. Management--Addresses, essays, lectures. 2. Beste, Theodor, 1894. I. Kortzfleisch, Gert von, joint ed. II. Series.

E-11
9486
RIESNER, DIETER, ed.
Festschrift für Walter Hübner, hrsg. von Dieter Riesner und Helmut Gneuss. [Berlin] E. Schmidt [1964] xii, 339 p. port., facsims. 24cm.

Contributions in German or English.
Bibliographical footnotes.
CONTENTS.--Problems and limits of textual emendation, by B. von Lindheim.--Textkritisches zum Wilhelmslied, von G. Reichenkron.--
(Continued)
NN 4.64 e/ OC, I, IIbo PC, 1, 2, I SL (LC1, X1, Z1) [I]

4

RIESNER, DIETER, ed. Festschrift für Walter Hübner... (Card 2)

Zur Methode einer bedeutungsgeschichtlichen Untersuchung, von W. Winter.--Eine englische Ausspracheliste des späten XVII. Jahrhunderts, von R. Kaiser.--Das Shaw Alphabet und das Initial teaching alphabet, von G. Scherer.--Zu den englischen Wörtern in einem französischen Gebrauchswörterbuch, von R. Rohr.--Einige Handwerke in der ae. Dichtung und in zeitgenössischen Inschriften, von K.R. Grinda.--Englands Bibliotheken im Mittelalter und ihr Untergang, von H. Gneuss.--Vergil in England, von R. Sühnel.--Tragik und Komik in Chaucers Troilus and
(Continued)

RIESNER, DIETER, ed. Festschrift für Walter Hübner... (Card 3)

Criseyde, von W. Erzgräber.--Gavin Douglas' Aeneis-Übersetzung, von H. Käsmann.--Englische Beiträge zur Erforschung romanischer Epistolar-Literatur der Renaissance und Frühklassik, von F. Neubert.--Due Theatralik der Tugend in Miltons Comus, von T.A. Riese.--Die Ankunft in der neuen Welt, von H. Galinsky.--Zur Namengebung bei Defoe, von R. Gerber.--Hawthornes Briefe über The old manse, von A. Weber.--"The test of death and night"; Pose und bewältigte Wirklichkeit in Whitmans Leaves of grass, von K. Poenicke.--Kunst- prosa in der Werkstatt: Hardys

(Continued)

RIESNER, DIETER, ed. Festschrift für Walter Hübner... (Card 4)

The mayor of Casterbridge 1884-1912, von D. Riesner.--Zwischen Laugharne und Llaregyb; zur Entstehungsgeschichte von Dylan Thomas' Under milk wood, von H. Meller.

1. Hübner, Walter, 1884- . 2. English literature--Addresses, essays, lectures. I. Gneuss, Helmut, joint ed. II. Riesner, Dieter.

---

*R-Econ. 71-51

The RIGHTS of Americans; what they are, what they should be. Essays commemorating the 50th anniversary of the American civil liberties union. Edited by Norman Dorsen. [1st ed.] New York, Pantheon books [1971] xxi, 679 p. 25cm.

1. Civil rights--U.S. I. American civil liberties union. II. Dorsen, Norman, ed.

NN S 8.71 w/OC, II (OS)I PC, 1, I, II SL E, 1, I, II (LC1, X1, Z1)

NNBC (Bertola)

RIMINI, ITALY.

Studi su Aurelio Bertola nel II centenario della nascita (1953). Bologna, Steb [1953] ix, 319 p. illus. 24cm.

Bibliographical footnotes.

CONTENTS.—Aurelio De' Giorgi Bertola, di F. Flora.—Il "diario svizzero" del Bertola (1787), di Baldini.—Lettere del Bertola

(Continued)

NN **11.55 f/ ODt EDt PC, I, I SL (LC1, Z1, X1)

RIMINI, ITALY. Studi su Aurelio Bertola nel II centenario della nascita... (Card 2)

al cardinale Garampi, di A. Campana.—Note sul pensiero storico di Aurelio Bertola, di F. Catalano.—Lettere inedite del Bertola a Leonhard Meister, di F. Chiappelli.—Il viaggio renano del Bertola, di F. Del Beccaro.—Aurelio De' Giorgi Bertola filosofo della storia, di E. Di Carlo.—Dodici lettere inedite di Aurelio De'Giorgi Bertola nella Biblioteca civica di Bergamo, di G. Gervasoni.—La critica di Aurelio Bertola di B. Maier.—Aurelio Bertola "letterato alla moda del secolo XVIII", di G. Natali.—Il Bertola e la sua filosofia della

(Continued)

RIMINI, ITALY. Studi su Aurelio Bertola nel II centenario della nascita... (Card 3)

storia, di G. Semprini.—Liriche inedite e rare di Aurelio Bertola, di A. Servolini.—Lettere inedite di Salomone Gessner ad Aurelio Bertola e l'idillio di Ticofilo in morte di Aronte, di L. Servolini.—Le opere a stampa di Aurelio Bertola. Saggio bibliografico di G. Pecci.

1. Bertola, Aurelio de' Giorgi, 1753-1798. I. Title. t. 1953.

BWW

[Rinaudo, Costanzo,] 1847- , editor.

Emanuele Filiberto. Torino: S. Lattes & c.[, 1928.] xxxii, 477 p. incl. mounted front. (port.), mounted plans, mounted plates. facsims. (part mounted), tables (1 geneal.). 4°.

On cover: IV centenario di Emanuele Filiberto e X anniversario della vittoria, Torino MCMXXVIII, anno VI.

Introduction signed: C. Rinaudo.

Articles by Alberto Caviglia, Pietro Maravigna, Arturo Segre and others.

Bibliographical footnotes.

1. Emmanuel Philibert, duke of Savoy, 1528–1580. 2. Piedmont, Italy—Hist., 1550–1580. 3. Title.

N. Y. P. L. August 26, 1929

E-12 9720

Ritter, Gerhard A., ed.

Faktoren der politischen Entscheidung; Festgabe für Ernst Fraenkel zum 65. Geburtstag, hrsg. von Gerhard A. Ritter und Gilbert Ziebura. Berlin, De Gruyter, 1963.

x, 451 p. port. 24 cm.

Bibliographical footnotes.

CONTENTS.—Politics, ethics, religion and law, by H. Kelsen.—Die Masstäbe der politischen Entscheidung, von O. H. v. d. Gablentz.—Zum Begriff des politischen Stils, von A. Bergstraesser.—Faktoren

(Continued)

NN * R 8.67 1/ OC, I PC, 1, 2, 3, I, II SL E, 1, 2, 3, I (LC1, X1, Z1)

3

RITTER, GERHARD A., ed. Faktoren der politischen Entscheidung... (Card 2)

nationalsozialistischen Herrschaftsdenkens, von W. Scheffler.—Über Entscheidungen und Formen des politischen Widerstandes in Deutschland, von G. Schulz.—Kritische Betrachtungen über den Primat der Aussenpolitik, von K. D. Bracher.—Staatsräson und Ideologie in den sowjetisch-chinesischen Beziehungen, von R. Löwenthal.—Oberbefehl und Regierung in der neueren Geschichte, von H. Herzfeld.—Anfänge des deutschen Parlamentarismus, von G. Ziebura.—Baker v. Carr: policy decision und der Supreme Court, von K. Loewenstein.—Bureaucracy and interest groups in the decision-making process of the Fifth Republic, by H. W. Ehrmann.—Die

(Continued)

RITTER, GERHARD A., ed. Faktoren der politischen Entscheidung... (Card 3)

Kontrolle von Regierung und Verwaltung in Grossbritannien, von G. A. Ritter.—Rechtliche Garantien der innergewerkschaftlichen Demokratie, von O. Kahn-Freund.—Plebiszitäre Demokratie und Staatsverträge, von H. Huber.—Die Volksbefragung in der Schweiz, von M. Imboden.—Zur Rolle der Führungspartei in einigen jungen Staaten Afrikas, von F. Ansprenger.

1. Government—Addresses, essays, lectures.
2. Political science—Addresses, essays, lectures.
3. Fraenkel, Ernst, 1898 1898- .
I. Ziebura, Gilbert, joint ed. II. Title.

E-10
6240

RITTER, GERHARD, 1888-
Lebendige Vergangenheit; Beiträge zur historisch-politischen Selbstbesinnung. Zum 70. Geburtstage des Verfassers hrsg. von Freunden und Schülern. München, R. Oldenbourg, 1958. 331 p. port. 24cm.

CONTENTS. --Ursprung und Wesen der Menschenrechte. --Vom Ursprung des Einparteienstaates in Europa. --Allgemeiner Charakter und geschichtliche Grundlagen des politischen Parteiwesens in Deutschland. --Stein und der

(Continued)

NN R X 9.58 d//OC, I PC, 1, I SL (LC1, X1, Z1, Y1)

RITTER, GERHARD, 1888- . Lebendige Vergangenheit ... (Card 2)

Geist des älteren deutschen Liberalismus. --Grossdeutsch und Kleindeutsch im 19. Jahrhundert. --Geschichtliche Erfahrungen deutscher Kolonialpolitik. --Das politische Problem des Militarismus in Deutschland. --Die Wehrmacht und der politische Widerstand gegen Hitler. --Das Rätsel Russland. --Zur Problematik gegenwärtiger Geschichtsschreibung. --Die Idee der Universität und das öffentliche Leben. --Nachweis der Entstehung und früherer Druckorte der Aufsätze. --Verzeichnis der Schriften von Gerhard Ritter 1910-1958 (p. [315]-331)

1. Germany--Hist. --Addresses, essays, lectures. I. Title.

NCC
(Fergusson)

ROBERT FERGUSSON, 1750-1774; essays by various hands to commemorate the bicentenary of his birthday, ed. by Sydney Goodsir Smith. Foreword by Sir Herbert Grierson. [London] Nelson [1952] xiii, 216 p. illus. 19cm.

CONTENTS. -- To Robert Fergusson, by Robert Garioch. -- Introductory: Robert Fergusson, his life, his death and his work, by S. G. Smith. -- Robert Fergusson: direct poetry and the Scottish genius, by Hugh MacDiarmid. -- The making of a poet: some notes on Fergusson's educational backgrounds, by Douglas Young . Fergusson and Ruddiman's magazine, by

(Continued)

NN R 2.53 OC, I PC, 1, I SL (LC1, Z1, X1)

ROBERT FERGUSSON, 1750-1774; essays by various hands to commemorate the bicentenary of his birthday... (Card 2)

J. W. Oliver. -- Tradition and Robert Fergusson, by John Spiers. -- Fergusson and Stevenson, by J. B. Caird. --Fergusson's language: Braid Scots then and now, by A. D. Mackie. -- A note on the bibliography and 'Lives' of Robert Fergusson, by Alexander Law. -- The Scottish folk-song tradition in Ramsay, Fergusson and Burns, by William Montgomerie. -- Letter to Robert Fergusson, by Alexander Scott. -- In the High street, Edinburgh, by Maurice Lindsay.

1. Fergusson, Robert, 1750- 1774. I. Smith, Sydney Goodsir, 1915- , ed.

AN
(Holland-Martin, R.)

Robert Holland-Martin, a symposium, ed. by Eleanor Adlard. London, F. Muller [1947]

110 p. plates, ports., facsim. 22 cm.

CONTENTS.—Prelude, by F. E. Hutchinson.—R. H. M. at home, by two of his sons.—Life in the Cotswolds, by Eleanor Adlard.—R. H. M. as antiquarian, by Sir Frederic Kenyon.—The excavation of the iron age camp on Bredon Hill, by Thalassa C. Hencken.—An architect's reminiscences of R. H. M., by Sir Herbert Baker.—Treasure hunting, by W. G. Constable.—R. H. M. as travelling companion, by C. H. St. J. Hornby.—At the sign of the grasshopper, by R. V. Buxton.—The Southern Railway, by Eric Gore-Browne.—R. H. M. and the Territorial Army, by P. R. Simner.—R. H. M. and the Fishmongers Company, by C. N. Hooper.

1. Holland-Martin, Robert Martin, 1872-1944. I. Adlard, Eleanor, ed.

CT788.H735R6 923.342 48-14731*
Library of Congress [1]

AN
(Gorham, R.)

Robert Stetson Gorham, born June 28, 1863, died June 18, 1913. Boston, Press of Geo. H. Ellis co., 1915.

31 p. front. (port.) 24cm.

CONTENTS.—Address of Rev. Julian C. Jaynes, West Newton, June 21, 1913.—Proceedings of the Boston bar association.

1. Gorham, Robert Stetson, 1863-1913. I. Jaynes, Julian Clifford, 1854-1922. II. Bar association of the city of Boston.

39-2726
Library of Congress [2]

E-12
9070

Robertson, D B *ed.*
Voluntary associations, a study of groups in free societies; essays in honor of James Luther Adams. Edited by D. B. Robertson. Richmond, John Knox Press [1966]

448 p. port. 24 cm.

Bibliographical references in "Notes and acknowledgments," p. [396]-434.

(Continued)

NN*R 6.67 g/OC PC, 1,2,3,4 SL (LC1, X1, Z1)

Robertson, D B *ed.* Voluntary associations ... [1966] (Card 2)

CONTENTS.—The nature of voluntary associations, by K. Hertz.—Associational thought in early Calvinism, by F. S. Carney.—The religious background of the idea of a loyal opposition, by G. H. Williams.—The meaning of "church" in Anabaptism and Roman Catholicism: past and present, by M. Novak.—Hobbe's theory of associations in the seventeenth-century milieu, by D. B. Robertson.—The voluntary principle in religion and religious freedom in America, by

(Continued)

Robertson, D B *ed.* Voluntary associations ... [1966] (Card 3)

R. T. Handy.—The political theory of voluntary association in early nineteenth-century German liberal thought, by G. G. Iggers.—Rauschenbusch's view of the church as a dynamic voluntary association, by D. E. Smucker.—A note on creative freedom and the state in the social philosophy of Nicolas Berdyaev, by D. E. Sturm.—Missionary societies and the development of other forms of associations in India, by R. W. Taylor.—The communauté de travail: experimentation in integral association, by V. H. Fletcher.—"The politics of mass society": significance for the churches, by W. A. Pitcher.—A new pattern of community, by F. H. Littell.—The crisis of the congregation:

(Continued)

ROBERTSON, D B ed. Voluntary associations... [1966] (Card 4)

a debate, by G. Fackre.—The voluntary church: a moral appraisal, by J. M. Gustafson.—SANE as a voluntary organization, by H. A. Jack.—James Luther Adams: a biographical and intellectual sketch, by M. L. Stackhouse.—Voluntary associations as a key to history, by J. D. Hunt.—A bibliography of the writings of James Luther Adams, by R. B. Potter.

1. Sociology, Christian--Addresses, essays, lectures. 2. Religion--Essays and misc. 3. Societies. 4. Adams, James Luther, 1901- .

D-14
9005

ROBINSON, KENNETH, 1914- , ed.
Essays in imperial government presented to Margery Perham, by Kenneth Robinson and Frederick Madden. Oxford, B. Blackwell, 1963. viii, 293 p. port. 23cm.

Bibliography, p. [289]-293.
CONTENTS.--Some origins and purposes in the formation of British colonial government, by F. Madden.--British imperialism in the late eighteenth century, by D. Fieldhouse.--Indirect rule in Northern (Continued)

NN R 2.64 p/ OC, I PC, 1, 2, 3, I SL E, 1, 2, 3, I (LC1, X1, Z1)

ROBINSON, KENNETH, 1914- , ed. Essays in imperial government presented to Margery Perham... (Card 2)

Nigeria, 1906-1911, by M. Bull.--Native administration in the West Central Cameroons, 1902-1954, by E. Chilver.--Imperial paternalism: the representation of African interests in the Kenya Legislative Council by G. Bennet.--Economic policy and the Kenya settlers, 1945-1948, by M. McWilliam.--The dilemma of local government in Africa, by B. K. Lucas.--The application of soviet nationality theory to Africa in soviet writing, by M. Holdsworth.--Self-government reconsidered by J. Plamenatz.--Constitutional autochthony, and the transfer of power, by K. Robinson.

1. Colonies and colonization, British--Govt. 2. Imperialism--Gt. Br. 3. Perham, Margery Freda, 1896- I. Madden, Frederick, joint ed.

D-18
5471

Robinson, Oliver.
I dream in Irish. Boston, Branden Press [1967]
199 p. 22 cm.

"Stories in honor of Raymond Woodbury Pence and his fifty years of teaching creative writing at DePauw University."

I. Pence, Raymond Woodbury, 1885- . II. Title.
NN * R 11.68 l/ OC, I PC, I, II SL (LC1, X1, Z1)

*QP

ROCZNIK Kasprowiczowski. Poznań, Nakładem Zarządu miejskiego w Poznaniu, 1938. 1 v. illus., ports. 26cm.

Tom 2.
One of 500 copies printed.
Includes bibliographical references.

1. Kasprowicz, Jan, 1860-1926.
NN 11.66 r/ OC PC, I SL S, I (LC1, X1, Z1)

D-16
3025

ROGGE, JOACHIM, ed.
Johannes Calvin 1509-1564. Eine Gabe zu seinem 400. Todestag. Berlin, Evangelische Verlagsanstalt [1963] 170 p. illus. 22cm.

1. Calvin, Jean, 1509-1564. I. Rogge, Joachim.
NN * R 10.65 s/ OC, Ib* PC, 1 SL (LC1, X1, Z1)

RDV

Rohlfs, Gerhard, 1892-
An den Quellen der romanischen Sprachen; vermischte Beiträge zur romanischen Sprachgeschichte und Volkskunde. Halle (Saale), M. Niemeyer, 1952. xi, 286 p. maps. 22cm.

"Diesem Buche ist eine Tabula gratulatoria zum sechzigsten Geburtstage von Gerhard Rohlfs beigegeben und ein Verzeichnis seiner Schriften, zusammengestellt von Liselotte Bihl." (Continued)

NN**R 10.53 OC, I, Ibo PC, 1, I SL (Z/1, LC1, X1)

Rohlfs, Gerhard, 1892- An den Quellen der romanischen Sprachen... (Card 2)

Some items in French or Italian.
Bibliographical footnotes.

1. Romance philology—Addresses, essays, lectures. I. Bihl, Liselotte.

RDV

Romanica; Festschrift. Prof. Dr. Fritz Neubert, Berlin, zum 60. Geburtstag am 2. Juli 1946. Hrsg. von Prof. Dr. Rudolf Brummer... Berlin, Stundenglas-Verlag, 1948. 286 p. port. 21cm.

593054B. 1. Neubert, Fritz, 1886- . 2. Romance philology. I. Brummer, Rudolf, ed.
N. Y. P. L. October 10, 1951

D-17
5822

Rombach, Heinrich, *ed.*
Die Frage nach dem Menschen. Aufriss einer philosophischen Anthropologie. Festschrift für Max Müller zum 60. Geburtstag. Freiburg, München, Alber (1966)
402 p. 1 front. 22 cm.

Bibliographical footnotes.

1. Anthropology, Philosophical—Addresses, essays, lectures. 2. Müller, Max, 1906- . I. Title.
NN*R 8.67 a/ OC PC, 1, 2, SL (LC1, X1, Z1)

TB

Rome (City). **Università.** Giurisprudenza, Facoltà di.
Studi in memoria di Guglielmo Masci, per gli auspici della Facoltà giuridica dell'Università di Roma. Milano, Dott. A. Giuffrè, 1943. 2 v. 25cm.

"Pubblicazioni del prof. Guglielmo Masci," v. 1, p. v-xi.

581632-3B. 1. Economics, 1925- —Italian authors. 2. Masci, Guglielmo, 1889- .
N. Y. P. L. December 20, 1951

TC

ROME (City) Università. Istituto di economia e finanza.
Contributi in omaggio di Giuseppe Ugo Papi. Milano. Giuffrè [1964] vi,712 p. port. 25cm.

Includes bibliographical references.
CONTENTS.--L'"absorption approach" e l'analisi degli effetti della svalutazione sulla bilancia dei pagamenti, di M. Amendola.--In tema di distinzione tra "vincolo" e "coazione" nell'economia della finanza pubblica, di P. (Continued)

NN*R 7.68 e/A (OC)I OS PC,1,I SL E,1,I (LC1,X1,Z1)

ROME (City) Università. Istituto di economia e finanza. Contributi in omaggio di Giuseppe Ugo Papi. (Card 2)

Armani.--La politica economica nel sistema di analisi "al livello soggettivo, di F. Caffè.--Innovazione tecnologica, condotta dell'oligopolista ed effetti sul prezzo di mercato, di G. Campa.--Oligopolio differenziato e processo di sviluppo, di G. Caravale. --Premesse teoriche allo studio dell'investimento pubblico, di D. Cavalieri.--Intorno agli incentivi fiscali per una politica di sviluppo economico, di C. Cosciani.--Su alcuni (Continued)

ROME (City) Università. Istituto di economia e finanza. Contributi in omaggio di Giuseppe Ugo Papi. (Card 3)

effetti economici dell'imposizione dei plusvalori patrimoniali, di A. Cristofaro.--Nesso costituzionale tra imposizione e spesa pubblica, di N. d'Amati.--Riflessioni in tema di progresso tecnico, tempo libero e programmazione, di G. della Porta.--Un idea fondamentale nel campo della metodologia economica, di V. del Punta.--Il mito dell'eguaglianza del prezzo dei fattori fra paesi, di C. Fiaccavento.--L'influenza del comportamento del pubblico sulla creazione di liquidità, di A. (Continued)

ROME (City) Università. Istituto di economia e finanza. Contributi in omaggio di Giuseppe Ugo Papi. (Card 4)

Gambino.--Rapporti fra espansione finanziaria e livello dei prezzi nei sistemi economici moderni, di G. Gera.--Economie di scala e sviluppo economico, di L. Izzo.--Capacità di importazione, stabilizzazione e struttura nei paesi sottosviluppati, di V. Marrama. --Indagini e considerazioni sul sistema tributario italiano in realazione al principio costituzionale della imposizione progressiva di C. Mezzacapo.--Appunti sulla misura della sensibilità congiunturale delle imposte, (Continued)

ROME (City) Università. Istituto di economia e finanza. Contributi in omaggio di Giuseppe Ugo Papi. (Card 5)

di A. Pedone.--Emissioni obbligazionarie estere sui mercati europei, di C. Segrè.--La funzione di una teoria del consumo nell'analisi economica, di L. Spaventa.--L'impresa pubblica nel quadro dell'azione economica dello Stato, di G. Stammati.--L'onore del debito pubblico e le generazioni future, di A. Tramontana.--Bibliografia di Guiseppe Ugo Papi (p. [693]-709)
1. Economics--Essays and misc. I. Papi, Giuseppe Ugo, 1893-

E-10
5957

ROME (City) UNIVERSITA. Istituto di filosofia.
Medioevo e Rinascimento; studi in onore di Bruno Nardi. Firenze, Sansoni [1955] 2 v. (x, 932 p.) port., facsims. 20cm. (ITS: Pubblicazioni, 1-2)

Articles in Italian, French, English, German, or Latin.
Scritti di Bruno Nardi": v. 2, p. [905]-927.
Bibliographical footnotes.

1. Literature—Hist. and crit., Middle Ages. 2. Renaissance—Addresses, essays, lectures. 3. Nardi, Bruno. I. Series. II. Title.
NN * X 8. 58 d/JOS, I PC, 1, 2, 3, I, II SL (LC1, X1, Z1) [I]

TB

ROME (City). Università. Istituto di statistica.
Studi in onore di Corrado Gini. [Roma] Istituto di statistica della Facoltà di scienze statistiche demografiche et attuariali [1960] 2 v. 24cm.

Contributions in Italian, English, French, German or Spanish.
Bibliographical footnotes.
CONTENTS.--v. 1. Contributi alla metodologia statistica. Contributi alla Statistica economica.--v. 2. Contributi alla demografia. Contributi alla sociologia.

1. Gini, Corrado, 1884- 2. Social sciences--Addresses, essays, lectures. I. Title.
NN 5. 63 f/ (OC)I OS PC, 1, 2, I SL E, 1, 2, I (LC1, X1, Z1)

Copy only words underlined & classmark-- * OAA

ROME (City). Università. Scuola orientale.
A Francesco Gabrieli; studi orientalistici offerti nel sessantesimo compleanno dai suoi colleghi e discepoli Roma, G. Bardi, 1964. xxviii, 360 p. illus. 25cm. (ITS: Studi. v. 5)

Bibliographical footnotes. "Bibliografia degli scritti di Francesco Gabrieli, " p. [xiii]-xxviii.
1. Gabrieli, Francesco, 1904- 2. Oriental studies--Collections. I. Series.
NN 4. 65 p/JOS, I PC, 1, 2, I O, 1, 2, I (LC1, X1, Z1)

NCE

Rose window: a tribute offered to St. Bartholomew's hospital by twenty-five authors, with a foreword by the Lord Horder ... London, Toronto, W. Heinemann ltd. [1939]
xii, 385 p. illus. 20cm.
"First published 1939."
"Printed ... at the Windmill press, Kingswood, Surrey."
CONTENTS.—Dedicatory poem, by Humbert Wolfe.—Stories, sketches & essays: Last day of summer, by Marjorie Bowen. Luke, by Ann Bridge. Glamour, by Vera Brittain. On letter-writing, by Susan Ertz. Ninety-nine—out! By St. John Ervine. The doctor's husband, by Eric Linklater. The canary waistcoat, by A. G. MacDonell. The great mistake, by André Maurois. Prologue to an unfinished novel, by J. B. Priestley. Doctor v. astrologer; and Mr. William Blake, by Helen Simpson. Mrs. Broadbent, senr., by G. B. Stern. The three priests—a chap-
(Continued on next card)
40-7758
[3]

Festschrift

Rose window ... [1939] (Card 2)
CONTENTS—Continued.
ter from The bright pavilions, by Hugh Walpole.—Poems: Nature's daring, by Edmund Blunden. Kind Johnny, by A. E. Coppard. Hospital, by Walter De La Mare. The spotted flycatcher, by Lord Dunsany. The blackbird in the town, by O. St. J. Gogarty. Three Stuart songs, by Radclyffe Hall. Two passages from the Georgics of Virgil (translation) by C. D. Lewis. A mystery, by Eden Phillpotts. Aged 70, by Sylvia T. Warner.—Plays: Star chamber, by Noel Coward. The last of Casanova, by George Preedy. Vigil, by Emlyn Williams.—Editor's note, by L'Estrange Fawcett.—Epilogue, by the treasurer of St. Bartholomew's hospital.

1. English literature—20th cent. 2. English literature (Collections) 3. London. St. Bartholomew's hospital. I. Horder, Thomas Jeeves Horder, baron, 1871- II. Fawcett, L'Estrange, ed.

Library of Congress PR1149.R65 1939 40-7758
Copyright A ad int. 25841 [3] 828.910822

* C-5 pv. 276

ROSENBAUM, ALFRED, 1861-
August Sauer; ein bibliographischer Versuch. Prag, Verlag der Gesellschaft deutscher Bücherfreunde in Böhmen [1925] 63 p. 28cm.

"Dieses Buch wurde... als Festgabe für August Sauer zu dessen 70. Geburtstag am 12. Oktober 1925 in 300 Exemplaren... gedruckt." Nr. 67.

1. Sauer, August, 1855-1926--Bibl.
NN* * 4.57 c/ℓ OC PC, 1 SL (LC1, X1, Z1)

D-14
4061

ROSENBERG, ALFONS, ed.
Wanderwege. Festgabe zum 60. Geburtstag von Ida Friederike Görres. Zürich, Thomas-Verlag [c1961] 204 p. 22cm.

CONTENTS.--Ein Freundesbrief, von M. Hörhammer.--Ein Zeugnis des Dankes für lange Strecken eines gemeinsamen Weges, von B. zu Münster.--Panoramische Betrachtung, von A. Rosenberg.--Herausgegriffen, von W. Bergengruen.--Der alte Friedhof in Freiburg, von E. W. Stiefvater.--
(Continued)

NN R 7.63 p/r OC PC, 1, 2 SL (LC1, X1, Z1)

2

ROSENBERG, ALFONS, ed. Wanderwege. (Card 2)

Ir Kint lag vor ihr Ougen val..., von B. Herzog.--Aus der Zeit der frommen kleinen Höfe, von F. zu Sayn-Wittgenstein.--Die Predigt, von H. Asmussen.--Wandlung der Ehe, von J. von Graevenitz--Von der Dummheit, von C. Menck.--Der Christ und die nichtchristliche Welt, von A. Böhm.--Das "Gebot" der Liebe unter den anderen Geboten, von K. Rahner.--Die Grenzen der Freiheit und die Verantwortung des Menschen, von G. Siewerth.--Könige und Priester, von E. von Kuehnelt-Leddihn.--Lebensexperiment für Morgen, von E. Fl. Winter.--Bibliography (p. 203-204)

1. Görres, Ida Friederike (Coudenhove), 1901-
2. Religion--Essays and misc.

C-14
1010

Rosenstock-Huessy, Eugen, 1888-
Ja und Nein; autobiographische Fragmente. Aus Anlass des 80. Geburtstages des Autors im Auftrag der seinen Namen tragenden Gesellschaft hrsg. von Georg Müller. Heidelberg, L. Schneider, 1968.

180, [4] p. 19 cm.

"Lieferbare Schriften von Eugen Rosenstock-Huessy": p. [181]-[184]

1. Essays, German. I. Müller, Georg, 1893- ed.
NN*R 8.69 w/a OC, I PC, 1, I SL (LC1, X1, Z1)

E-12
6270

ROSOVSKY, HENRY, ed.
Industrialization in two systems; essays in honor of Alexander Gerschenkron by a group of his students. New York, J. Wiley [1966] ix, 289 p. 24cm.

Bibliographical footnotes.

CONTENTS.--The mechanization of reaping in the ante-bellum Midwest, by P. A. David.--The common school revival: fact or fancy, by A. Fishlow.--No safety in numbers: some pitfalls of historical
(Continued)

NN R 6.66 l/d OC PC, 1, 2, 3 SL E, 1, 2, 3 (LC1, X1, Z1)

2

ROSOVSKY, HENRY, ed. Industrialization in two systems... (Card 2)

statistics, by G. Ohlin.--Japan's transition to modern economic growth, 1868-1885, by H. Rosovsky.--The relative decline of the British steel industry, 1880-1913, by P. Temin.--The economics of overtaking and surpassing, by J. S. Berliner.--On the theory of economic administration, by R. W. Campbell.--Gold and the sword: money in the Soviet command economy, by G. Grossman.--Foreign trade behavior of centrally planned economies, by F. D. Holzman.--Pressure and planning in the Soviet economy, by H. S. Levine.

1. Gerschenkron, Alexander. 2. Industrialism. 3. Economic policy--Addresses, essays, lectures.

Write on slip words underlined below and class mark—
*QCB

Rossiĭskaya akademiya istorii material'noĭ kul'tury, St. Petersburg.
...Recueil d'études historiques sur les formations de la société pré-capitaliste. Moscou [etc.] Les Éditions de l'état, Section sociale et économique, 1933. 679 p. illus., plates, port. 27cm. (Its: Известия. Выпуск 100.)

At head of title: XLV. En l'honneur de N. J. Marr.

Russian t.-p.: Из истории докапиталистических формаций; сборник статей к сорокапятилетию научной деятельности Н. Я. Марра. Москва [etc.] ОГИЗ, 1933.

Text in Russian; table of contents in Russian, French, English, and German.

(Continued)

N. Y. P. L. November 25, 1936

Rossiĭskaya akademiya istorii material'noĭ kul'tury, St. Petersburg.
...Recueil d'études... (Card 2)

CONTENTS.—The thing as a historical source, by F. V. Kiparisov.—Material culture and mentality, by I. I. Meščaninov.—Science at a higher level, by Š. Čakvetadze.—The new linguistics and the Finno-Ugrian studies, by M. J. Palvadre.—Totemism problems, by S. N. Bykovskij.—Genetical problems of the history of society before the formation of social classes, by M. P. Žakov.—Collectors and hunters of the Capsien, by P. P. Efimenko.—Cults of ancient Siberia, by V. V. Holmsten.—Elements of 'heaven' in material monuments, by A. A. Miller.—The Indo-German question archaeologically resolved, by E. G. Kričevskij.—Hut-burials, by P. S. Rykov.—The most ancient traces of cattle-breeding in the Baikal region, by G. P. Sosnovskij.—N. J. Marr on Etruscans, by B. L. Bogaiewsky.—The cult of "horse" in the Kama region, by M. G. Khudjakov.—Semantics of the Karasu steles, by S. V. Kiseljov.—The dog-bird, Senmurv and Paskud, by K. V. Trever.—Comparative methods in the history of

(Continued)

N. Y. P. L. November 25, 1936

Rossiĭskaya akademiya istorii material'noĭ kul'tury, St. Petersburg.
...Recueil d'études... (Card 3)

material culture, by T. S. Passek.—The struggle of classes and the fall of the antique society, by S. I. Kovaljov.—Happy cities, by S. A. Žebeljov.—Helots and plebeians, by V. V. Struve.—The fortifications of Olbia as a historical source, by S. I. Kapošina.—On Sarmatian language, by X. M. Kolobova.—Semantics of Homerical names, by M. S. Altman.—Origins of western feudalism, by A. G. Prigožin.—The genesis of feudalism in ancient Russia, by M. M. Cvibak.—The main contradiction of the feudal society, by E. K. Nekrasova.—Patriarchal organization of the Tu-gju in the VIII century, by A. N. Bernštam.—Stages of the ideological evolution of the Goths, by L. A. Maculevič.—Inscriptions and marks on the swords of Dneprostroj, by V. I. Ravdonikas.—Origins of the basilica-type, by F. I. Šmit.—Temple ruins of Baš-garni, by K. K. Romanov.—The Kremlin of Rostov, by N. N. Voronin.

712581A. 1. Marr, Nikolaĭ Yakovlevich, 1864–1934. 2. History—Addresses, essays, lectures. I. Title: Iz istorii dokapitalisticheskikh formatziĭ.
N. Y. P. L. November 25, 1936

---

* R-BAE

ROUNDS, DOROTHY.
Articles on antiquity in Festschriften, an index; the ancient Near East, the Old Testament, Greece, Rome, Roman law, Byzantium. Cambridge, Harvard University Press, 1962. 560 p. 28cm.

1. History, Ancient--Bibl. 2. Bible. O. T.--Bibl. 3. Law, Roman--Bibl. 4. Byzantine Empire--Bibl. 5. Festschriften--Indexes.

NN*R 12.62 g/w OC(1b*) PC, 1, 2, 3, 4, 5 SL MR, 1, 2, 3, 4, 5 *R, 1, 2, 3, 4, 5 (LC1, X1, Z1)

F-11
7655

ROWE, J.G., ed.
Florilegium historiale. Essays presented to Wallace K. Ferguson, J.G. Rowe, W.H. Stockdale editors. [Toronto] University of Toronto press [c1971] xiii, 401 p. port., music, coat of arms. 26cm.

Includes bibliographical references.
CONTENTS.--The Italian view of Renaissance Italy, by D. Hay.--Petrarch: his inner struggles and the humanistic discovery of man's
(Continued)
NNR 4.71 d/a OC, I, II, IIIbo, IVbo PC, 1, 2, 3, I, II SL (LC1, X1, Z1) 4

ROWE, J.G., ed. Florilegium historiale. (Card 2)

nature, by H. Baron.--A little-known letter of Erasmus and the date of his encounter with Reuchlin, by P.O. Kristeller.--De modis disputandi: the apologetic works of Erasmus, by M.P. Gilmore.--Jacques Lefèvre d'Etaples and the medieval Christian mystics, by E.F. Rice.--"By little and little"; the early Tudor humanists on the development of man, by A.B. Ferguson.--Atropos-Mors; observations on a rare early humanist image, by M. Meiss.--A music book for Anne Boleyn, by E.E. Lowinsky.--The enlargement of the great council of Venice, by F.C. Lane.--Biondo, Sabellico, and the beginnings of Venetian
(Continued)

ROWE, J.G., ed. Florilegium historiale. (Card 3)

official historiography, by F. Gilbert.--An essay on the quest for identity in the early Italian Renaissance, by M.B. Becker.--Notes on the word stato in Florence before Machiavelli, by N. Rubinstein.--Bonds, coercion, and fear; Henry VII and the peerage, by J.R. Lander.--Incitement to violence? English divines on the theme of war, 1578-1631, by J.R. Hale.--The principal writings of Wallace K. Ferguson, p. [400]-401.
(Continued)

ROWE, J.G., ed. Florilegium historiale. (Card 4)

1. History--Addresses, essays, lectures. 2. Renaissance--Addresses, essays, lectures. 3. Ferguson, Wallace Klippert, 1902- . I. Stockdale, W.H., joint ed. II. Title. III. Rowe, J.G. IV. Stockdale, W.H.

NCC
(Jones)

Royal Asiatic society of Bengal, Calcutta.
Sir William Jones. Bicentenary of his birth; commemoration volume, 1746-1946. Calcutta, Royal Asiatic soc. of Bengal, 1948. xi, 173 p. illus. 26cm.

562106B. 1. Jones, Sir William, 1746-1794. 2. India—Civilization.
N. Y. P. L. June 21, 1951

OXE

Royal Astronomical Society, *London*.
The earth today; a collection of papers dedicated to Sir Harold Jeffreys by some of his students and colleagues on the occasion of his 70th birthday. [Edited by A. H. Cook and T. F. Gaskell] London, Published by the Royal Astronomical Society and distributed by Interscience Publishers, New York [1961]
xi, 404 p. illus., port., charts, diagrs., tables. 26 cm.
Originally published as a special issue (v. 4) of the Geophysical journal.
Includes bibliographies.
(Continued)
NN* R 1.63 g/: (OC)I, II, IIIb* OS PC, 1, 2, I, II SL ST, 1, 2, I, II (LC1, X1, Z1) 2

ROYAL ASTRONOMICAL SOCIETY, London. The earth today... (Card 2)

1. Jeffreys, Sir Harold, 1891- . 2. Earth, 1961. I. Cook, Alan H., ed. II. Gaskell, Thomas Frohock, ed. III. Cook, Alan H.

PXX

Royal society of South Africa.
...Robert Broom commemorative volume. Ed. ...by Alex L. Du Toit. Capetown, The soc., 1948. 257 p. illus. 25cm.

At head of title: Special publication of the Royal society of South Africa.
"Bibliography of R. Broom," p. 244-256.

601762B. 1. Broom, Robert, 1866-1951. 2. Vertebrata, Fossil—Africa. 3. Evolution. I. Du Toit, Alexander Logie, 1878-1948, ed.
N. Y. P. L. January 8, 1952

C-12
302

RUCKSCHAU und Ausblick; Jakob Hegner zum achtzigsten Geburtstag. [Hrsg. von Hans M. Jürgensmeyer] Köln, J. Hegner [1962] 245, [1] p. illus., ports. facsims. 19cm.

CONTENTS.--Auftrag des Verlegers, von R. Schneider.--Entdecker und Mittler, von R. Grosche.--Laudatio auf Jakob Hegner, von R. Hagelstange.— Jakob Hegner, der Buchgestalter, von G. K. Schauer.-- Dem Freunde, von R. Seewald.--An Jakob Hegner, von K. Wolff.--Der Turm
(Continued)
NN 4.62 p/n OC, I, IIbo PC, 1, 2, 3, I SL (LC1, X1, Z1) [I] 3

RUCKSCHAU und Ausblick... (Card 2)

der Standhaftigkeit, von E. Schaper.--Stellte Dein Wort sich ein, so verschlang ich es; zu Martin Bubers Bibelübersetzung, von W. Nigg.--Sum theologischen Gespräch um Karl Barth, von H. Urs von Balthasar.--Die Kiefer, von P. Claudel.--An Sabinus Fuscus aus Tirol; Einladung zum Betrachten der himmlischen Dinge, von J. Blade.--Jacob Balde und die Ode "An Sabinus Fuscus," von M. Wehrli.--Julien Green und de Aporien des Bildes, von K. A. Horst.--Der Ubeltäter, von J. Green.--Theater und Wirklichkeit, von S. von Radecki.--Eine faule Sache, von B. Marshall.--Schattenbeschwörung, Tagebuchnotizen auf Capri, von W.Helwig.--Die Freiheit in Gott; zum Verständnis der Hegelschen Dialektik,
(Continued)

RUCKSCHAU und Ausblick... (Card 3)

von B. Lakebrink. --Aus dem Tagebuch einer Asienreise, von J. Overhoff. --Die letzte Nacht des Malchus ben Levi, von E. Schaper. --Briefe zus Frankreich, von R. Schneider. --Patmos, die Insel der Offenbarung, von H. Dallmayr. -Die Demostration, von J. Rfiber. --Die Bücher des Verlages Jakob Hegner (p. [227-246])

1. Hegner, Jakob, 1882- 2. Essays, German 3. German literature --Collections. I. Jürgensmeyer, Hans M., ed. II. Jürgensmeyer, Hans M

Write on slip, name, vol., page of magazine and class mark — GEA

Rudbecks-Studier. Festskrift...

(Upplands fornminnesförenings, Uppsala. Tidskrift. Uppsala,1930. 4°. Häfte 44, Bilaga,p.1-337. illus.,ports.)

form 400a [11-13-30 25m]

AN (Rudbeck, O.)

Rudbecks-studier; festskrift vid Uppsala universitetets minnesfest till högtidlighållande av 300-årsminnet av Olof Rudbeck d. ä:s födelse. Uppsala: Almqvist & Wiksells boktryckeri-aktiebolag, 1930. 337 p. front. (port.), illus. (incl. facsims., music, plans.) 27½cm.

Bibliographical footnotes.

Contents: Herdin, K. W. Olof Rudbeck d. ä:s födelse och tidigare ungdom. Almgren, O. Disasagans innebörd. En Rudbeckshypotes i nutida belysning. Rudbeck, J. Olof Rudbeck d. ä:s porträtt. Nelson, A. Rudbeckens fåfänga. Wiklund, K. B. Olof Rudbeck d. ä. och lapptrummorna. Hult, O. T. Några ord om det Rudbeckska "kejsarsnittet." Hahr, A. Olof Rudbeck d. ä. som arkitekt. Moberg, C. A.

(Continued)

N. Y. P. L. April 28, 1933

Rudbecks-studier; festskrift vid Uppsala universitetets minnesfest... (Card 2)

Olof Rudbeck d. ä. och musiken. Lönnberg, E. De Rudbeckska fågelbilderna och deras betydelse. Lindqvist, S. Olof Rudbeck d. ä. som fältarkeolog. Nordström, J. De yverbornes ö. Bidrag til Atlanticans förhistoria.

630647A. 1. Rudbeck, Olof, 1630?-1702. I. Upsala. Universitet.

N. Y. P. L. April 28, 1933

D-13 1569

RUDOLF, KARL, 1886- , ed.

Custos quid de nocte? Österreichisches Geistesleben seit der Jahrhundertwende. [Michael Pfliegler zur Vollendung seines 70. Lebensjahres von Schülern und Freunden dargeboten] Hrsg. von Karl Rudolf und Leopold Lentner. Wien, Verlag Herder [1961] 388 p. 23cm.

Includes bibliographies.

(Continued)

NN R 8. 61 v/ OC(1b)I PC, 1, 2, I SL (LC1, X1, Z1) [I]

3

RUDOLF, KARL, 1886- , ed. Custos quid de nocte? (Card 2)

CONTENTS. --1918, eine Zeitenwende? von A. Wandruszka.--Niederösterreich und Wien, von K. Lechner. --Die politisch-geographische Lage Österreichs nach 1918, von E. Lendl. --Irrationalismus und Intuitionismus, von W. Keilbach. --Glaube und Einsicht, von J. Liener. --Wien und das Erbe Sigmund Freuds, von V. E. Frankl. --Das Bildungsideal einst und jetzt, von K. Wolf. --Michael Pfliegler, Leben und Werk, von F. M. Kampfhammer. --Jugend zwischen den Kriegen, von A. Böhm. --Das Phänomen des religiösen Sozialismus, von A. Burghardt. --Vom statischen zum dynamischen Erziehungs- und Bildungsbegriff, von L. Lentner. --Die Neulandschule, von L. Leitmaier. -- Erziehungsprobleme der

(Continued)

RUDOLF, KARL, 1886- , ed. Custos quid de nocte? (Card 3)

Gegenwart, von H. Asperger. --Gedanken eines Christen zum modernen Staat, von J. Scholswohl. --Die neue Katechetik, von G. Hansemann. --Die liturgische Bewegung, von J. E. Mayer. --Bibelbewegung, von A. Stöger. --Die Heilsnotwendigkeit der Predigt, von E. Hesse. --Grossstadtseelsorge heute, von A. Dolezal. --Das Dorf vor neuen Aufgaben, von M. Stur. --Die Sendung der österreichischen Stifte, von H. Tausch. --Schrifttum Michael Pflieglers, von E. Hanel.

1. Pfliegler, Michael, 1891- . 2. Austria--Intellectual life. 20th cent. I. Lentner, Leopold, joint ed.

NFD (Kassner)

RUDOLF KASSNER zum achtzigsten Geburtstag; Gedenkbuch, hrsg. von A. Cl. Kensik und D. Bodmer. [Erlenbach] E. Rentsch [1953] 250 p. port. 23cm.

Letters, articles and poems by various authors, in German, French or Italian.

"Die Moral der Musik (1905)," a review by Hermann, Graf Keyserling, p. 129-137.

(Continued)

NN **R X 3. 56 f/4 OCs, I, II PCs, 1s, Is, IIs SLs (MU) 2s (LC1s X1s, Z1)

RUDOLF KASSNER zum achtzigsten Geburtstag... (Card 2)

"Verzeichnis der Werke Rudolf Kassners," p. 243-248.

1. Kassner, Rudolf, 1873- 2. Kassner, Rudolf, 1873- . Die Moral der Musik. I. Kensik, A. Cl. ed. II. Bodmer, D., ed.

A p.v.751

Rudolf Maria Holzapfel zum Gedächtnis... Basel: B. Schwabe & Co., 1930. 46 p. 2 ports. (incl. front.) 25cm.

Contents.—Vorbemerkung.—Zur Gedenkfeier für R. M. Holzapfel, von Romain Rolland.—Eine Begegnung mit Holzapfel, von Hugo Debrunner.—Après sa mort, par Christian Sénéchal.—Der Mensch und das Werk, von Wladimir Astrow.—Das Leben Rudolf Maria Holzapfels, von Hans Zbinden.—Ein Wort des Dankes, von Hans Rhyn.—Mein Nachbar, von Ernst Oser.

1. Holzapfel, Rudolf Maria, 1874-1930.

N. Y. P. L. July 17, 1942

Write on slip, name, year, vol., page of magazine and class mark— BA +

Rudolf Meringer Gewidmet.

(Woerter und Sachen. Heidelberg,1929. 4°. Festband 12,Heft 1,p.1-160.)

form 144a [viii-10-28 25m]

RUPPERT, KARL, ed. Zum Standost der Sozialgeographie. (Card 2)

Bibliographical footnotes.

1. Geography, Economic--Addresses, essays, lectures. 2. Anthropogeography--Addresses, essays, lectures. 3. Hartke, Wolfgang. I. Series.

Write on slip words underlined below and class mark — RAA

Rudolf Thurneysen zur Vollendung des 70. Lebensjahres am 14. März 1927 gewidmet von Schülern, Freunden und Kollegen. [Berlin, etc.: W. de Gruyter & Co., 1927] iv, 416 p. charts, port. 23cm. (Indogermanische Forschungen. Bd. 45.)

Bibliographical footnotes.

374780A. 1. Thurneysen, Rudolf, 1857- . Festschrift
N. Y. P. L. November 6, 1939

PKI

Ruska, Julius Ferdinand, 1867– , editor.
Studien zur Geschichte der Chemie; Festgabe Edmund O. v. Lippmann zum siebzigsten Geburtstage; dargebracht aus Nah und Fern, und im Auftrage der Deutschen Gesellschaft für Geschichte der Medizin und der Naturwissenschaften, herausgegeben von Julius Ruska... Berlin: J. Springer, 1927. vi, 242 p. front. (port.) 4°.

Alc Moth

1. Lippmann, Edmund Oskar von, 1857– . 2. Chemistry—Hist. 3. Alchemy. 4. Deutsche Gesellschaft für Geschichte der Medizin und der Naturwissenschaften.
N. Y. P. L. October 11, 1927

E-12
8859

Ruf und Antwort; Festgabe für Emil Fuchs zum 90. Geburtstag. Leipzig, Koehler & Amelang [1964]

575 p. 24 cm.

Includes bibliographies.

1. Fuchs, Emil, 1874- 2. Theology—Essays and misc.
NN * R 5.67 1/ OC PC, 1,2 SL (LC1,X1,Z1)

WAF p.v.386

Russian medical society of New York, inc.
Fifteenth anniversary bulletin of the Russian medical society of New York, September, 1939. Юбилейный сборник Общества российских врачей г. Нью Иорка (1924–1939). Dedicated to the memory of Dr. Michael J. Kamensky. Посвящается памяти д-ра Михаила Яковлевича Каменского. Benjamin O. Alpern, editor. New York, N. Y.: The Russian medical soc. of New York, inc. [1939] 113 p. incl. tables. illus. (incl. ports.) 25½cm.

Cover-title.

(Continued)

N. Y. P. L. Festschrift October 22, 1940

NIE

Runer og rids, festskrift til Lis Jacobsen, 29. januar 1952. [København] Rosenkilde og Bagger [1952] xix,205 p. illus. 30cm.

"Bibliografi, ved Grete Jacobsen og Karl Martin Nielsen," p. 185-204.

1. Jacobsen, Lis (Rubin), 1882- . 2. Runic inscriptions—Denmark. 3. Danish language. 4. Scandinavia—Hist.—Addresses, essays, lectures.
NN

Russian medical society of New York, inc. Fifteenth anniversary bulletin... (Continued)

Contributions and summaries in Russian or English.
Bibliographies included.

1. Kamenski, Mikhail Yakovlevich, 1862–1938. 2. Medicine—Essays and misc. I. Alpern, Benjamin Ovsievitz, 1888– , ed. II. Title. III. Title: Yubileinyĭ sbornik Obshchestva rossiĭskikh vracheĭ.
N. Y. P. L. October 22, 1940

M-11
2420
Bd.4

RUPPERT, KARL, ed.
Zum Standost der Sozialgeographie. Wolfgang Hartke zum 60. Geburtstag. Kallmünz, M. Lassleben, 1968. 207 p. port., maps (part fold., issued in pocket). 30cm. (Münchner Studien zur Sozial- und Wirtschaftsgeographie. Bd. 4)

(Continued)

NN 11.68 k/A OC (OS)I PC, 1, 2, 3, I E, 1, 2, 3, I (LC1, X1, Z1) 2

ITC

RUTMAN, DARRETT BRUCE, 1929-
The Old Dominion; essays for Thomas Perkins Abernethy, edited by Darrett B. Rutman. Charlottesville, University Press of Virginia [1964]
x, 200 p. 24 cm.
Bibliographical footnotes.
CONTENTS.—The Virginia Company and its military regime, by D. B. Rutman.—Virginia and the Cherokees: Indian policy from Spotswood to Dinwiddie, by W. S. Robinson.—The War of Jenkins' Ear, by F. L. Berkeley, Jr.—The rise and decline of the Virginia aristocracy in the eighteenth century: the Nelsons, by E. G. Evans.—

(Continued)

NN*R 3.65 g/ OC PC, 1, 2 SL AH, 1, 2 (LC1, X1, Z1)
[I] 2

RUTMAN, DARRETT BRUCE, 1929- The Old Dominion... (Card 2)

The fat major of the F. H. C., by Carson.—Two men on a tax: Richard Henry Lee, Archibald Ritchie, and the Stamp act, by J. C. Matthews.—Letters from Norfolk: Scottish merchants view the Revolutionary crisis, by W. M. Dabney.—Weights, measures, and mercantilism: the inspection of exports in Virginia, 1742–1820, by N. B. Jones.—Depredations in Virginia during the Revolution, by E. Cometti.—Virginia's "critical period," by A. Schaffer.—The formation of the Virginia Historical Society, by W. M. E. Rachal.

1. Virginia—Hist.—Addresses, essays, lectures. 2. Abernethy, Thomas Perkins, 1890-

---

SSMC

Sächsische technische Hochschule, Dresden.
Ein Jahrhundert Sächsische technische Hochschule, 1828–1928. Festschrift zur Jahrhundertfeier, 4. bis 6. Juni 1928. Überreicht von Rektor und Senat. [Dresden, 1928] 222 p. illus. 26cm.

209961B. 1. Education, Industrial and technical—Indiv. inst.—Germany—Dresden.
N. Y. P. L. April 9, 1943

E-13
177

RYNNE, ETIENNE, ed.
North Munster studies; essays in commemoration of Monsignor Michael Moloney. Limerick, Thomond archaeological society, 1967. xvi,535 p. illus., maps. 25cm.

Includes bibliographies.
1. Moloney, M. 2. Ireland--Archaeology--Addresses, essays, lectures.
I. Rynne, Etienne.
NN R 10.67 p/ OC,Ibo PC,1,2 SL (LC1,X1,Z1)
[I]

MCO
+
T16.S1

SAGE, KAY, 1898- , comp.
Yves Tanguy. Un recueil de ses œuvres. A summary of his works. New York, P. Matisse, 1963. 230 p. illus. (part col.) ports. (1 mounted col.) plates (part col.) facsims. 30cm.

French and English.
CONTENTS. —Avant-dire, par K. Sage Tanguy. — La maison d'Yves Tanguy, par A. Breton. — Yves Tanguy, par P. Eluard. —
(Continued)
NN R 5.64 g/ OC PC,1 SL A,1 B (LC1,X1,Z1) 2

Copy only words underlined & classmark—
RIG

SACHE. Ort und Wort; Jakob Jud zum sechzigsten Geburtstag, 12. Januar 1942. Genève, E. Droz, 1943. xix, 839 p. illus., port., maps (part col. fold.) 26cm. (Romanica helvetica. v. 20)

Articles in German, French or Italian
Includes bibliographies.

1. Jud, Jakob, 1882-1952. 2. Philology--Addresses, essays, lectures. 3. Civilization--Addresses, essays, lectures. I. Ser.

NN **R X 3.57 j/ OC PC, 1, 2, 3 (U1, LC1, X1, Z1) [I]

SAGE, KAY, 1898- , comp. Yves Tanguy. (Card 2)

Chronologie, par L. R. Lippard. — Catalogue illustrée des œuvres d'Yves Tanguy. —Bibliographie illustrée, par B. Karpel et M. Poupard-Lieussou (p. 193-223)

1. Tanguy, Yves, 1900-1955.

L-11
409
Nr. 1

SACHS, WOLFGANG, 1899- , ed.
Lebensversicherungstechnisches Wörterbuch: Deutsch, Englisch, Französisch, Italienisch, Spanisch. 2. Aufl. Zusammengestellt und durchgesehen von C. Brandau [et al.] Hrsg. von W. Sachs und G. Drudè. Karlsruhe, Verlag Versicherungswirtschaft, 1964. 308 p. 25cm. (Deutsche Gesellschaft für Versicherungsmathematik Deutscher Aktuarverein. Sonderveröffentlichung. Nr. 1)
(Continued)
NN R 9.66 l/ OC(IbWWG)I, IIIbo (OS)II PC,1,2,I,II E,1,I,II (LC1,X1) 2

F-10
5691

SAINT-WILLIBRORD, ECHTERNACH, Luxemburg (Benedictine abbey).
Willibrordus; Echternacher Festschrift zur XII. Jahrhundertfeier des Todes des heiligen Willibrord. Hrsg. von Nikolaus Goetzinger. Mit einem Geleitwort Seiner Exzellenz Monsignore Dr. Josef Philippe und einem Vorwort des Unterrichtsministers Dr. Nikolaus Margue. [2. unveränderte Aufl.] Luxemburg, Verlag der St. Paulus-Druckerei, 1940 [i.e. 1958]
(Continued)
NN R 6.61 e/ (OC)I OS PC,1,I SL (LC1,X1,Z1) 2

SACHS, WOLFGANG, 1899- , ed.
Lebensversicherungstechnisches Wörterbuch... (Card 2)

Title page in each language; title in English: Dictionary of actuarial and life insurance terms.

1. Insurance, Life--Dictionaries. 2. Dictionaries, Polyglot. I. Drudè, G., joint ed. II. Series. III. Drudè, G.

SAINT-WILLIBRORD, ECHTERNACH, Luxemburg (Benedictine abbey). Willibrordus... (Card 2)

420, xxiii p. 74 plates (incl. ports.), music, plans. 28cm.

Added t.p. in French.
Prefatory material in French and German.
Contributions in German, French, or Dutch.

1. Willibrord, Saint, bp. of Utrecht, d. 738. I. Goetzinger, Nikolaus, ed.

Copy only words underlined
& classmark-- BGEA

ST. XAVIER'S COLLEGE, Bombay. Indian historical research institute.
Indica; the Indian historical research institute silver jubilee commemoration volume. Bombay, 1953. xvi, 414 p. illus., plates, ports. 25cm. (St. Xavier's college, Bombay. Indian historical research institute. Studies in Indian history. no. 18)

Bibliographical footnotes.

1. Indic studies--Collections. I. Series. II. Title.
NN**R 1.57 g/ (OC)II OS, I PC, 1, I, II O, 1, I, II (LC1, X1, Z1)

SEB

[Salin, Edgar] 1892- ed.
Synopsis. [Festgabe für] Alfred Weber, 30.VII.1868–30.VII.1948. Heidelberg, L. Schneider [1948]

788 p. mounted illus. 24 cm.

~~Inserted are [8] p. addressed Hochverehrter Herr Jubilar and signed by editor and publisher.~~
Bibliographical footnotes.

1. Weber, Alfred, 1868– 2. Social sciences—Addresses, essays, lectures. I. Title.

A 50-3185

Harvard Univ. Library for Library of Congress [1] Festschrift

---

FKY

SALLINGER, RICHARD.
Graz im Jahre 1809; Festschrift aus Anlass der Enthüllung des Hackher-Denkmales auf dem Schlossberge zu Graz. Über Anregung des Historischen Vereines für Steiermark verfasst von Richard Sallinger. Graz, U. Moser's Buchhandlung (J. Meyerhoff), 1909. vi, 568 p. illus., ports. 24cm.

1. Gratz, Austria—Hist. 2. Napoleonic wars, 1803-1815—Campaigns, 1809. 3. Hackher zu Hart, Franz Xaver, Freiherr von, 1764-1837. I. Historischer Verein für Steiermark, Gratz. II. Title.
NN** R X 9.54 OC(1bo)3b, II (OS)I PC, 1, 2, 3, I, II SL (Z1, LC1, X1)

---

* C–5 p.v.94

Salzburger Wissenschaftswochen. 1st, 1939.
...Festschrift. Verzeichnis der Vorlesungen. Verzeichnis der Dozenten. [Leipzig, 1939] 20 l. illus. (part col.) 31cm.

At head of title: Salzburger Wissenschaftswochen; veranstaltet vom Reichsministerium für Wissenschaft, Erziehung und Volksbildung sowie von der Forschungs- und Lehrgemeinschaft "Das Ahnenerbe."
"Diese Festschrift ist vom Generalsekretariat der 'Salzburger Wissenschaftswochen' herausgegeben."
CONTENTS.—Spitzenleistungen der Wissenschaft, von Rudolf Mentzel.—Salzburg, ein Sinnbild, von Walther Wüst.—Deutsche Wissenschaft in Salzburg, von Friedrich Rainer.—Das grössere Deutschland, von Erna Blaas.—Die Erneuerung akademischer,

(Continued)

NN 1.53 (OD)I (ED)I OS PC, 1, 2, I SL ST, 2, I (LC1, Z1, X1)

Salzburger Wissenschaftswochen. 1st, 1939. ...Festschrift. Verzeichnis der Vorlesungen. Verzeichnis der Dozenten. (Card 2)

Tradition in Salzburg, von Walter Del-Negro.—Germanenkunde als europäischer Beitrag, von J. O. Plassmann.—Geist und Geburt, von Josef Weinheber.—Der Staat der Athener, aus der Rede des Perikles für die Gefallenen.—Nicht vom Brote allein, von Josef Weinheber.—Rom und die germanische Welt, von Siegfried Fuchs.—Das geistige Bollwerk, von Julius Sylvester.—Der neue Tag, von Bruno Brehm.—Der Stadt Saltzburg, aus der Topographia Germaniae des Matthaeus Merian.—Am Grenzkamm, von Robert Hohlbaum.—Bei den Puppenspielern, von Herbert Hassenkamp.—Wir waren Saat, von Robert Hohlbaum.

1. Germany—Civilization. 2. Science—Hist.—Germany. I. Germany. Wissenschaft, Erziehung und Volksbildung, Ministerium für.

---

*OHM

Samaddar, Jogindranath, editor.
Sir Asutosh memorial volume. Patna: J. N. Samaddar, 1926–1928. 2 parts in 1 v. col'd front., ports. 8°.

Bibliographical footnotes.

409094A. 1. Mookerjee, Sir Asutosh Saraswati, 1864-1924. 2. Orientalia—Collections. 3. Title.
N. Y. P. L. August 28, 1929

Mr. Moth.

M-10
8233
v. 1

SAMFUNDET FOR SVENSK FOLKLIVSFORSKNING, Stockholm.
Årsskrift 1948; utg. under redaktion av Sigurd Erixon. Stockholm, Redaktionen för Liv och folkkultur i distribution, 1948. 157 p. illus., ports. 26cm. (Liv och folkkultur. v. 1)

Published also with title: Till en örtagårdsmästare, festskrift, tillägnad J. G. Löwgren 11.8.1948.

(Continued)

NN R 7.63 p/ (OC)1b+, I, III OS, II, IV PC, 1, 2, I, II, III, IV E, 2, I, III, IV (LC1, X1, Z1) [I] 3

SAMFUNDET FÖR SVENSK FOLKLIVSFORSKNING, Stockholm. Årsskrift 1948... (Card 2)
Bibliographical footnotes.
CONTENTS.--Löwgreniana: Med rötterna i hembygdens jord, av S. Erixon. En gärning i den enskilda familjepensioneringens tjänst, av A. Wigert. Pour les quatre-vingts ans du docteur J. G. Löwgren, par L. Maury. Studenthemmet i Paris, av G. Forssius. J. G. Löwgren och Frankrike, av A. Engblom. Institut Tessin i Paris, av G. W. Lundberg. J. G. Löwgren och Baltiska stiftelsen, av A. Schück. Samfundet för svensk folklivsforskning, av S. Erixon. En resa i det befriade Normandie, av M. Bouvier. --Örtagårdsmästarens tack: Blommor och människor, av

(Continued)

SAMFUNDET FÖR SVENSK FOLKLIVSFORSKNING, Stockholm. Årsskrift 1948... (Card 3)

J. G. Löwgren. --Från vetenskapens skördefält: Rävens fiskafänge, av G. Tillander. Bårarydsbonaden, av N. Strömbom. Sömnadsindustrien, av G. Grenander-Nyberg. Svenska årder, av S. Erixon.

1. Löwgren, John Gustaf, 1868-1953. 2. Swedes in France. I. Erixon, Sigurd Emanuel, 1888- , ed. II. Series. III. Till en örtagårdsmästare; festskrift, tillägnad J. G. Löwgren 11.8.1948. IV. Samfundet för svensk folklivsforskning, Stockholm. Till en örtagårdsmästare; festskrift, tillägnad J. G. Löwgren 11-8. 1948.

M-10
8233
v. 5

SAMFUNDET FÖR SVENSK FOLKLIVSFORSKNING, Stockholm.
Studier och översikter tillägnade C. A. Wicander den 13 augusti 1952. [av Samfundet för svensk folklivsforskning och Institutet för folklivsforskning] Stockholm, Institutet för folklivsforskning, i distribution [1952] 152 p. illus., ports., maps. 26cm. (Liv och folkkultur. v. 5)

(Continued)

NN 7.63 p/ (OC)III OS, I, II PC, 1, I, II, III (LC1, X1, Z1) [I] 2

SAMFUNDET FOR SVENSK FOLKLIVSFORSKNING, Stockholm. Studier och översikter tillägnade ... (Card 2)

Smfundet för svensk folklivsforskning. Skrifter. 9
Includes bibliographies.

1. Wicander, Carl August, 1885- I. Series. II. Institutet för folklivsforskning, Stockholm. III. Title.

SANDNER, GERHARD, ed. Kulturraumprobleme aus Ostmitteleuropa und Asien... (Card 3)

urkundlichen Zeugnisse für die deutsche Bauernsiedlung in Schlesien, von H. Appelt. —Zum schlesischen Dorfkretscham, von, J.J. Menzel. — Formen der Flachsbearbeitung in Ost- und Westpreussen, von E. Riemann. —Zum Problem der ländlichen Überbevölkerung und der Verstädterung in Polen, von W. Wöhlke. —Hochmittelalterliche Siedlungsverlegungen in Kärnten, von H. Paschinger. —Der Grundriss von Stambul, von R. Stewig. —Die Versalzung und Versumpfung der pakistanischen Indusebene, von H. Blume.

1. Europe, Central--Economic geography. 2. Europe, Central--Historical geography. 3. Asia--Economic geography. 4. Schlenger, Herbert. I. Series. II. Title.

MA
+

SAMUEL H. KRESS FOUNDATION, New York. Studies in the history of art, dedicated to William E. Suida on his eightieth birthday. London, Phaidon press, 1959. 402 p. col. front, illus., port. 32cm.

Contributions in English, Italian, German, French, Spanish or Portuguese.
"Bibliography of the writings of William E. Suida," p. 395-402.

1. Suida, William Emil, 1877- . 2. Suida, William Emil, 1877- --Bibl. 3. Art--Essays and misc. I. Title.
NN R 9. 59 t/ (OC)I OS PC, 1, 2, 3, I SL A, 1, 2, 3, I (LC1, X1, Z1)
[I]

D-12
4512

SANKT GABRIEL, Mödling, Austria (Mission house of the Society of the Divine word)
Festschrift zum 50jährigen Bestandsjubiläum des Missionshauses St. Gabriel, Wien-Mödling. Wien-Mödling, Druck der Missionsdruckerei St. Gabriel, 1939.

578 p. plates, facsims. 23 cm. (Sankt Gabrieler Studien, 8)
Includes bibliographies.

1. Catholic church, Roman--Addresses, essays, lectures
2. Religion--Addresses, essays, lectures
NN * 7.60 p/ OS PC, 1, 2 SL (LC1, X1, Z1)

---

* MEC
(Scheidt)

... Samuel Scheidt; Festschrift aus Anlass des 350. Geburtstages, 1587–1937. Im Auftrage des Oberbürgermeisters herausgegeben vom Kulturamt der Händelstadt Halle. Wolfenbüttel ⌊etc.⌋ G. Kallmeyer, 1937. 52 p. incl. geneal. table. front. (port.), illus. (facsim.), 2 pl. 24cm. (Schriftenreihe des Händelhauses in Halle; Veröffentlichungen aus dem Musikleben Mitteldeutschlands. Heft 2.)

"Literatur," p. 33.
Contents.—Vorwort.—Samuel Scheidt; ein Gedenkwort, von Arnold Schering.—Samuel Scheidt und das hallische Musikleben seiner Zeit, von Walter Serauky.—Scheidt und Halle; eine Studie über die Zusammenhänge von Erb- und Bildungskräften, von Rolf Hünicken.—Zcheidt-Gedenktag 1937 der Stadt Halle; Veranstaltungsplan.

1. Scheidt, Samuel, 1587–1654. I. Ser. Festschrift
N. Y. P. L. April 28, 1939

---

* ET
S236.a.99, no.41

Santiago de Chile. Universidad de Chile.
...Homenaje a Rubén Darío... ⌊Santiago⌋ Univ. de Chile, 1941. 512 p. illus. 28cm. (Its: Anales. ser. 3, año 99, no. 41.)

Contents.—Rubén Darío y la Universidad de Chile.—Halmar, Augusto d'. Rubén Darío y los americanos en Paris.—Ghiraldo, Alberto. En la tumba de Rubén Darío.—Saavedra Molina, Julio. Rubén Darío y Sarah Bernhardt.—Orrego Vicuña, Eugenio. El alba de oro.—Balmaceda Toro, Pedro. Los "Abrojos" de Rubén Darío.—Darío, Rubén. Antología chilena.

1. Darío, Rubén, 1867–1916. I. Title. II. Ser. Festschrift
N. Y. P. L. February 25, 1943

Copy only words underlined
& classmark-- KAA

SANDNER, GERHARD, ed.
Kulturraumprobleme aus Ostmitteleuropa und Asien. [Herbert Schlenger zum 60. Geburtstag 10.4.1964] Kiel, Im Selbstverlag des Geographischen Instituts der Universität Kiel, 1964. 245 p. illus., port. maps (part fold.) 24cm. (Kiel, Germany. Universität. Geographisches Institut. Schriften. Bd. 23)

Includes bibliographies.

(Continued)
NN 1.66 a/ OC, II (OS)I PC, 1, 2, 3, 4, I, II E, 1, 3, 4, II, O, 3, II (LC1, X1, Z1)
3

E-11
1044

SANTIAGO DE COMPOSTELA, Spain. Universidad.
Colección de estudios en homenaje al profesor Camilo Barcia Trelles, en sus bodas de plata de catedrático de derecho internacional. Santiago, 1945.

393 p. illus., ports. 25 cm.
"Número extraordinario del Boletín universitario."
Spanish, English, or Portuguese.
Bibliography: p. 14–15. Bibliographical footnotes.

1. Law, International--Addresses, essays, lectures. 2. Law--Addresses, essays, lectures. 3. Barcia Trelles, Camilo, 1888- I. Santiago de Compostela, Spain. Universidad. Boletín.
NN*R 9.60 s/ OS, I PC, 1, 2, 3 I SL E, 1, 3, I (LC1, X1, Z1)

SANDNER, GERHARD, ed. Kulturraumprobleme aus Ostmitteleuropa und Asien... (Card 2)

CONTENTS.—Herbert Schlenger zum 60. Geburtstag. Verzeichnis der Schriften von Herbert Schlenger. Von G. Sander.—Reliktzonen und moderne Gebiete in der bäuerlichen Sachkultur der Neuzeit, von G. Wiegelmann.—Beschreibende und genetische Typologie in der ostmitteleuropäischen Siedelformenforschung, von W. Czajka.—Landgewinnung im deutschen Osten durch Waldrodung und Moorkultivierung, von W. Hubatsch.—Schlesien im Geschichtsbild der Deutschen, von L. Petry.—Die ältesten
(Continued)

E-11
3221

SANTIAGO DE COMPOSTELA, Spain. Universidad.
Estudios jurídico-sociales, homenaje al profesor Luis Legaz y Lacambra. [Santiago de Compostela, 1960] 2 v. (1330 p.) port. 25cm.

Contributions chiefly in Spanish, some in English, German, Italian or French.
Bibliographical footnotes.
1. Law--Philosophy. 2. Law, International--Addresses, essays, lectures. 3. Sociology of law--Addresses, essays, lectures. 4. Law--Addresses, essays, lectures. 5. Legaz y Lacambra, Luis.
NN R 8. 61 e/ OS PC, 1, 2, 3, 4, 5 SL E, 1, 2, 3, 5 (LC1, X1, Z1)

* C-5 p.v.124

Santifaller, Leo, 1890-

...Das Institut für österreichische Geschichtsforschung; Festgabe zur Feier des zweihundertjährigen Bestandes des Wiener Haus-, Hof- und Staatsarchivs. Wien, Universum, 1950. 164 p. 26cm. (Veröffentlichungen des Instituts für österreichische Geschichtsforschung. Bd. 11)

"Literatur über das Institut für österreichische Geschichtsforschung in Wien," p. 11-12.

1. Institut für österreichische Geschichtsforschung, Vienna. 2. Austria. Haus-, Hof- und Staatsarchiv. 3. Austria—Hist.—Sources—Bibl. I. Ser.
NN R 5.53 OC PC, 1, 2, 3 SL (LC1, Z1, X1)

Copy only words underlined
& classmark— XAA

SAO PAULO, BRAZIL (City). UNIVERSIDADE. Direito, Faculdade de.

Fasciculo em honra do professor Waldemar Ferreira, no. 25º año de seu ensinamento. São Paulo, Emprêsa grafica da" Revista des Tribunais, 1950. 459 p. tables, port. 24cm. (IN: São Paulo, Brazil (City). Universidade. Direito, Faculdade de Revista. São Paulo. 24cm. v.45)

CONTENTS. — Professor Waldemar Ferreira. — A aula inaugural deo curso de direito comercial de professor Waldemar Ferreira. — A obra juri-
(Continued)
NN R X 11.57 p/ (OC)1b OS OI PC, 1, 2 (Z1, LC3, X1)

SAO PAULO, BRAZIL (City). UNIVERSIDADE. Direito, Faculdade de. Fasciculo em honra do professor Waldemar Ferreira... (Card 2)

dica do professor Waldemar Ferreira. — Usufruto de acoes, de partes e de quotas sociais, por B. de. Magalhaes. — L'imitazione servile come atto di concorenza sleale, por M. Rotondi. — Naturaleza de la sentencia de segunda instancia, por E. J. Couture. — La familia: concepto y elementos, por E.D. de Guijarro. — Derechos, funciones y libertades, por J.C. Rébora. — Atos de comércio e contractos administrativos, por R.C. Lima. — Waldemar Ferreira e a evolucao doutrinal do direito mercantil, por A. Martins Filho. — Politica criminal sem preocupacoes
(Continued)

SAO PAULO, BRAZIL (City). UNIVERSIDADE. Direito, Faculadade de. Fasciculo em honra do professor Waldemar Ferreira... (Card 3)

metafisicas, por N. Azevedo. — Do registo deo resumo do balanco no diario das sociedaddes comerciais, por S.S. de Faria. — A universidade medieval, por A. Correia. — Feijó e o Kantismo, por M. Reale. — Trabalhos de tecelões, por A. Almeida Junior. — A prova do erro no casamento romano e o casamento putativo, por G. Sciascia. — Da teoria do juros no código comercial, por H. Estrella. — A história de direito nos cursos juridicos do Brasil, por W. Ferreira. — Extracto do relatório do secretario da Faculdade de direito, referente ao ano de 1950.

1. Ferreira, Waldemar. 2. Law — Addresses, essays, lectures.

D-13
4553

SARKISSIAN, ARSHAG OHAN, 1905- , ed.
Studies in diplomatic history and historiography in honour of G.P. Gooch. [London] Longmans [1961] xiii, 393 p. 23cm.

CONTENTS.--History by team-work, by A.J. Toynbee.--Paradiplomacy, by R. Butler.--L'affaire Dreyfus dans la diplomatie française, by M. Baumont.--Concert diplomacy and the Armenias, 1890-1897, by
(Continued)
NN R 4.62 e/ OC, I PC, 1, 2, I SL (LC1, X1, Z1) [I]

4

SARKISSIAN, ARSHAG OHAN, 1905- , ed. Studies in diplomatic history and historiography... (Card 2)

A.O. Sarkissian.--Obligations by treaty: their place in British foreign policy, 1898-1914, by L.M. Penson.--The House-Bernstorff conversations in perspective, by C. Seymour.--Totalitarian approaches to diplomatic negotiation, by G.A. Craig.--Eden's mission to Rome on the eve of the Italo-Ethiopian conflict, by M. Toscano.--Hungary's declaration of war on the U.S.S.R. in 1941, by C.A. Macartney.--Action: his training, methods and intellectual system, by H. Butterfield.--Bismarck as a dramatist, by W.L. Langer.-- Bismarck and Bucher: the 'Letter
(Continued)

SARKISSIAN, ARSHAG OHAN, 1905- , ed. Studies in diplomatic history and historiography... (Card 3)

of instructions' of June 1870, by L.D. Steefel.--Bismarck and Beaconsfield, by W.N. Medlicott.--Holstein as Bismarck's critic, by E. Eyck.--Stresemann and Adenauer: two great leaders of German democracy in times of crisis, by F.E. Hirsch.--Scandinavian preventive wars in the 1650s, by H. Koht.--Historical appreciations of the Holland Regent regime, by P. Geyl.--Les relations franco-allemandes de 1871 à 1914: esquisse d'un programme de recherches, by P. Renouvin.--The relation of
(Continued)

SARKISSIAN, ARSHAG OHAN, 1905- , ed. Studies in diplomatic history and historiography... (Card 4)

public opinion and foreign affairs before and during the First World war, by B.E. Schmitt.--The political attitude of the German army, 1900-1944: from obedience to revolt, by G. Ritter.--The German resistance in its international aspects, by H. Rothfels.--Europe and the wider world in the nineteenth and twentieth centuries, by G. Barraclough.--Published works of George Peabody Gooch, 1898-1960, by F.E. Hirsch.

Bibliographical footnotes.

1. History--Addresses, essays, lectures. 2. Gooch, George Peabody, 1873- . I. Title.

RBG

SATURA, Früchte aus der antiken Welt; Otto Weinreich zum 13. März 1951 dargebracht. Baden-Baden, Verlag für Kunst und Wissenschaft, 1952. 182 p. plates. 25cm.

Bibliographical footnotes.

CONTENTS. —Carmen gratulatorium, von H. Weller. —Ein persischer Feueraltar aus Kappadokien, von K. Bittel. —Der Namensatz, von F. Focke. —Antigone-Interpretationen, von W. Jens. —Zur Bildungsweise einiger lateinischer Götternamen, von H. Krahe. — Fatum, fors, fortuna und Verwandtes im Geschichtsdenken des Tacitus, von J. Kroymann. —Eudoxos von Knidos und die Lehre vom unbewegten
(Continued)
NN**R 8.54 OC PC, 1, 2 SL (Z1, LC1, X1) [I]

SATURA, Früchte aus der antiken Welt... (Card 2)

Beweger, von W. Schadewaldt. —Abecedarium und elementum, von E. Sittig. —Timaios und Philistos, von K.F. Stroheker. —Die Tochter des Grosskönigs und Pausanias, Alexander, Caracalla, von J. Vogt.

1. Classical studies. 2. Weinreich, Otto, 1886-

E-11
4592

Sauerländischer Gebirgsverein. Abteilung Dortmund e. V.
Festschrift zum Jubiläums- und Herbstfest 1960. 1890–1960. [Verantwortlich für den Inhalt: Gustav Stockenberg] Dortmund [F. W. Ruhfus, 1960] 72 p. 25cm.

Cover subtitle: 7 [i. e. sieben] Jahrzehnte an Mensch und Heimat.

1. Stockenberg, Gustav, ed.
NN R 12.62 (OC)I OS PC,I SL (LC1,X1,Z1)

Write on slip only words underlined and classmark—
EAA

Saxe-Weimar-Eisenach. Landesbibliothek, Weimar.
Aus der Geschichte der Landesbibliothek zu Weimar und ihrer Sammlungen. Festschrift zur Feier ihres 250 jahrigen Bestehens und zur 175 jahrigen Wiederkehr ihres Einzuges ins Grüne Schloss. Herausgegeben von Hermann Blumenthal... Jena, G. Fischer, 1941. xii, 210 p. illus. 22cm. (Verein für thüringische Geschichte und Altertumskunde. Zeitschrift. N. F. Supplementheft 23.)

Contents.—Der Bau.—Aus der Geschichte der bibliothek.—Aus den Sammlungen der Bibliothek.

1. Libraries—Germany—Weimar. I. Blumenthal, Hermann, ed. II. Ser.
N. Y. P. L. December 13, 1946

E-10
3098

SAXONY. Landesbibliothek, Dresden.
Sächsische Landesbibliothek Dresden, 1556-1956; Festschrift zum 400-jährigen Bestehen. [Hrsg. von Karl Assmann und Mitarbeitern] Leipzig, O. Harrassowitz, 1956. vi, 298 p. plates (part col.) map. 25cm.

CONTENTS. — Die Landesbibliotheken gestern, heute und morgen, von H. Kunze. — Die Anfänge der Sächsischen Landesbibliothek, von K. Assmann. — Die Sächsische Landesbibliothek von 1945 bis 1955; Zerstörung,
(Continued)

NN* R 8.57 g/(OC)I, IIb* ODt EDt PC, 1, I SL (LC1, X1, Z1)

SAXONY. Landesbibliothek, Dresden. Sächsische Landesbibliothek Dresden, 1556-1956... (Card 2)

Wiederaufbau und gegenwärtiger Stand der Arbeit, von K. Assmann. -- Aus der täglichen Arbeit der Sächsischen Landesbibliothek, von J. Pepino. — Der Dresdner Fachkatalog, von B. Burgemeister. —Die Richtlinien für den Schlagwortkatalog der Sächsischen Landesbibliothek, von H. Trepter. — Die Handschriftenabteilung, von M. Kremer. —Die Kartenabteilung, von H. Pfeifer. —Die Musikabteilung, von L. Willi. —Die übrigen Sondersammlungen, von H. Deckert. —Das neue Buchmuseum der Sächsischen Landesbibliothek, von H. Deckert [et al.] — Bibliographie zur Geschichte der Sächsischen Landesbibliothek,
(Continued)

SAXONY. Landesbibliothek, Dresden. Sächsische Landesbibliothek Dresden, 1556-1956... (Card 3)

von C. Alschner und M. Bundesmann (p. [207]-279).

1. Libraries, Government--Germany--Dresden. I. Assmann, Karl, 1890- , ed. II. Assmann, Karl, 1890- . t. 1956.

---

*QDY

Sbornik... Сборникъ статей учениковъ профессора барона Виктора Романовича Розена ко дню двадцатипятилѣтія его первой лекціи, 13-го ноября 1872–1897. Санктпетербургъ: тип. Императорской академіи наукъ, 1897. 363 p. incl. tables. facsims. 27½cm.

Text partly in Armenian, Arabic, Georgian and Hebrew.
No. 105 of 260 copies printed.

Contents.—Хафизи-Абру и его сочиненія. В. Бартольда.—Примѣты и повѣрія тюрковъ Китайскаго Туркестана, касающіяся явленій природы. Н. Катанова.—Гіератическій папирусъ изъ кол-
(Continued)

N. Y. P. L. January 17, 1935

Sbornik... Сборникъ... (Continued)

лекціи В. Голенищева, содержащій отчетъ о путешествіи Уну-Амона въ Финикію. В. Голенищева.—Объ одномъ изъ источниковъ ат-Табарія. Н. Мѣдникова.—Хитонъ Господень въ книжныхъ легендахъ армянъ, грузинъ и сирійцевъ. Н. Марра.—Толкованіе Танхума изъ Іерусалима на книгу пророка Іоны. П. Коковцова.—Выдержки изъ дивана Нагиби. Бар. Д. Гинцбурга.—О персидской прозаической версіи "Книги Синдбада." Сергѣя Ольденбурга.—Сказаніе о пророкѣ Салихѣ. (Изъ Кысасу-ль-Энбія Рубгузи.) П.
(Continued)

N. Y. P. L. January 17, 1935

Sbornik... Сборникъ... (Continued)

Меліоранскаго.—Примѣненіе системы фикһа въ арабской грамматикѣ. А. Шмидта.—Омаръ Хайямъ и "странствующія" четверостишія. В. Жуковскаго.

SCHIFF COLLECTION.

508649. 1. Oriental studies. 2. Rosen, Viktor Romanovich, baron, 1849–1908.
N. Y. P. L. *Revised* January 17, 1935

Copy only words underlined & classmark—
*QVA

SBORNÍK FILOZOFICKEJ FAKULTY UNIVERZITY Komenského. [1. wyd.] Bratislava, Slovenské pedagogické nakl., 1964. 385 p. illus., port, maps. 25cm. (Bratislava, Czechoslovakia. Univerzita. Filozofická fakulta. Sborník. Historica. roč. 15 (1964))

"... Branislav Varsik. K šest'desiatym narodeninám dňa 5 marca 1964."
Contributions in Slovak, Czech, or Russian.
Table of contents also in Russian, German, French, and English.
(Continued)

NN R 10.65 l/p OI (PC)1, 2 (S)1, 2 (LC1, X1, Z1)

Copy only words underlined & classmark—

SBORNIK FILOZOFICKEJ FAKULTY UNIVERZITY Komenskeho. (Card 2)

Summaries in Russian, German, or Italian.
Includes bibliographical references.
"Bibliografia prác ... Branislava Varsika," p. 379-385.

1. Varsik, Branislav, 1904- . 2. Slovakia--Hist.--Addresses, essays, lectures.

*QT
Sborník k sedmdesátým narozeninám Karla B. Mádla. Praha, J. Štenc, 1929. 265 p. illus. 27cm.

"Bibliografický přehled literární činnosti Karla Mádla v oboru výtvarných umění," p. 257–265.

W.S.

609896B. 1. Mádl, Karel Boromejský, 1859– . 2. Art, Bohemian.
N. Y. P. L. January 15, 1952

---

*QV
Sborník prací filologických dvornimu radovi professoru Josefu Královi k šedesátým narozeninám... V Praze, B. Stýblo, 1913. xi, 313 p. illus., map. 25cm.

Bibliography, p. 307–313.

Fest.

600693B. 1. Philology—Addresses, essays, lectures. 2. Král, Josef, 1853–1917.
N. Y. P. L. February 7, 1952

---

*QT
SBORNÍK prací k poctě šedesátých narozenin Františka Weyra, 25. iv. 1939. Praha, Orbis [1939] 300 p. 25cm. (Sbírka spisů pravnických a narodohospodářských. sv. 95)

1. Weyr, František, 1879- 2. Law—Addresses, essays, lectures. 3. Economics, 1926- —Czech authors. I. Ser.

NN 11.52 OC PC,1,2,3 SL E,1,3 S,1,2,3 (LC1,Z1,X1)

---

*QT
Sborník prací věnovaných profesoru dru Václavu Tillovi k šedesátým narozeninám, 1867–1927. Pořádali Jiří Polívka, Jan Frček, Jiří Ježek a Jiří Horák. Vydala Národopisná společnost československá v Praze. Praha: "Obris," 1927. 271 p. front. (port.), illus. (music.) 8°.

Added t.-p. in French.
Résumés in French.
Bibliography, p. 241–266.

Mr Moth

479805A. 1. No subject. I. Tille, Václav, 1867– . II. Polívka, Jiří, 1858– , editor. III. Frček, Jan, jt. editor. IV. Ježek, Jiří, 1901– , jt. editor. V. Horák, Jiří, 1884– , jt. editor.
N. Y. P. L. June 25, 1930

MZE p.v.22
Schaakgenootschap "Discendo Discimus," The Hague.
Ter herdenking aan het zestigjarig bestaan van het Schaakgenootschap "Discendo Discimus," 1852–1912. ['s-Gravenhage: V. H. Koch & Knuttel, 1912] 94 p. illus., ports. 24cm.

Festschrift

FRANK J. MARSHALL CHESS COLL.
775264A. 1. Chess—Netherlands. 2. Chess—Clubs.
N. Y. P. L. September 23, 1935

L-11
3895
SCHADEWALDT, WOLFGANG, 1900-
Hellas und Hesperien. Gesammelte Schriften zur Antike und zur neueren Literatur in 2 Bänden. (Zum 70. Geburtstag von Wolfgang Schadewaldt am 15. März 1970. 2., neugestaltete und vermehrte Ausg. Unter Mitarb. von Klaus Bartels, hrsg. von Reinhard Thurow und Ernst Zinn.) Zürich, Stuttgart, Artemis-Verlag [1970] 2 v. illus., plates. 23cm.

(Continued)
NN R 12.71 e/t OCs,Is,IIs PCs, 1s,2s,Is,IIs SLs (LC1s,X1s,Z1s) 2

SCHADEWALDT, WOLFGANG, 1900- Hellas und Hesperien. (Card 2)

Includes bibliographical references.
CONTENTS.--Bd. 1. Zur Antike.--Bd. 2. Antike und Gegenwart.

1. Classical studies--Collections. 2. Greek literature--Foreign influence of. I. Thurow, Reinhard, ed. II. Zinn, Ernst, ed.

GDWX
Schaffhausen, Switzerland (Canton).
[i.e. 450 Vierhundertfünfzig]-Jahrfeier des Standes Schaffhausen; offizielle Feier des Schaffhauser Volkes, 10.-12. Aug. 1951. Text: Heinrich Bächtold. Schaffhausen, Lempen & Cie., 1952. 72 p. plates. 21cm.

Various contributors.
1. Schaffhausen, Switzerland (City)--Centennial celebrations, etc. I. Title. II. Bächtold, Heinrich, ed. i. 1952.
NN**X 2.54 (OC)I,II, IIb ODi EDi PC,1,I,II SL (Z1,LC1,X1)

GDWX
Schaffhausen, Switzerland (City).
Festschrift der Stadt Schaffhausen zur Bundesfeier, 1901. Im Auftrage des Stadtrates der Stadt Schaffhausen hrsg. vom Historisch-antiquarischen Verein. Schaffhausen, Kühn, 1901. 1 v. (various pagings.) illus., ports., map. 26cm.

Part of illustrative matter in pocket.
CONTENTS.—Schaffhausen und die Eidgenossenschaft bis zum ewigen Bunde von 1501, von K. Heking.—Die Stadt Schaffhausen zur Zeit ihres Eintritts in den Schweizerbund, von C. U. Bächtold.—Wie die Stadt Schaffhausen ihre Landschaft erwarb, von C. U. Bächtold.—Schaffhauser Künstler, von C. H. Vogler.—Schaffhauser Gelehrte und Staatsmänner, von R. Lang.—Die Entwicklung der Industrie der Stadt Schaffhausen, von H. Pfister.

I. Historischer Verein des Kantons Schaffhausen. II. Schaffhausen, Switzerland (City). Stadtrat. i. 1901.
NN R 4.53 ODi, IIi, EDi, IIi (OS)I PC, I, II SL (LC1,Z1,X1)

Copy only words underlined & Classmark-- TB
SCHAGEN, F. VAN, ed.
Essays in honour of Professor Jac. P. Thijsse on the occasion of his retirement as professor of comprehensive planning of the Institute of social studies on July 8, 1966. The Hague, Mouton, 1967. 175 p. port., maps. 23cm. (Institute of social studies, The Hague. Publications. Series minor. 14)

Includes bibliographies.

(Continued)
NN R 1.69 e/μ OC, Ib+, IIbo (OS)I PC, 1, 2, I E, 2, I (LC1, X1, Z1) 2

SCHAGEN, F. VAN, ed. Essays in honor of Professor Jac. P. Thijsse on the occasion of his retirement as professor of comprehensive planning of the Institute of social studies on July 8. 1966. (Card 2)

Includes bibliographies.

1. Thijsse, Jacobus Pieter, 1896- 2. Economic policy--Addresses, essays, lectures. I. Series. II. Schagen, F. van.

Copy only words underlined & classmark-- QOA

SCHAPERA, ISAAC, 1905- , ed. Studies in kinship and marriage. Dedicated to Brenda Z. Seligman on her 80th birthday; with a foreword by E.E. Evans-Pritchard. London, 1963. vi, 113 p. 26cm. (Royal Antropological institute of Great Britain and Ireland. Occasional papers. no. 16)

Includes bibliographies.

CONTENTS.--Some Zande texts, by E.E. Evans-Pritchard.--Bilateral descent groups: an operational viewpoint, by R. Firth.--Unilineal fact or fiction: an analysis of the composition of kingroups among the Yakö, by (Continued)

NN R 12.64 c/B OCs (OS)I PCs, 1s, 2s, 3s, I Es, 1s, 2s, 3s (LC1s, X1s, Z1s) 2

Copy only words underlined & classmark--

SCHAPERA, ISAAC, 1905- , ed. Studies in kinship and marriage. (Card 2)

D. Forde.--The submerged descent line' in Ashanti, by M. Fortes.--Did the Wild Veddas have matrilineal clans? By E. Leach.--Dinka representations of the relations between the sexes, by G. Lienhardt.--Kinship and inheritance, by Lord Raglan.--Agnatic marriage in Tswana royal families, by I. Schapera.

1. Family, Primitive. 2. Marriage, Primitive. 3. Society, Primitive. I. Series.

E-13
7280

SCHARFF, ALEXANDER, 1904-
Schleswig-Holstein in der deutschen und nordeuropäischen Geschichte; gesammelte Aufsätze. Hrsg. von Manfred Jessen-Klingenberg. Stuttgart, E. Klett [1969] 187 p. 24cm. (Kieler historische Studien. Bd. 6)

Festschrift.
List of works, p. 273-286.

(Continued)

NN R 1.70 l/ROC (OS)I PC, 1, 2, I SL (LC1, X1, Z1) 2

SCHARFF, ALEXANDER, 1904- . Schleswig-Holstein in der deutschen und nordeuropäischen Geschichte... (Card 2)

Includes bibliography.

1. Schleswig-Holstein question. 2. Schleswig-Holstein--Hist. I. Series.

E-12
3927

SCHENK-DANZINGER, LOTTE, ed.
Gegenwartsprobleme der Entwicklungpsychologie; Festschrift für Charlotte Bühler, hrsg. von Lotte Schenk-Danzinger [und] Hans Thomae. Göttingen, Verlag für Psychologie [1963] 210 p. port. 24cm.

Includes summaries.
Includes bibliographies.
CONTENTS.--Die Grundideen und die theoretischen Fragestellungen in Charlotte Bühlers Lebens- werk, von L. Schenk-Danzin- (Continued)

NN R 5.66 r/ OC(lb)I PC, 1, 2, I SL (LC1, X1, Z1) 4

SCHENK-DANZINGER, LOTTE, ed. Gegenwartsprobleme der Entwicklungspsychologie... (Card 2)

ger.--Veröffentlichungen, von Charlotte Bühler.--Dominant concerns in the life cycle, by R.J. Havighurst.--Croissance et structure psychiques, par R. Dellaert.--Konflikt und Lebensalter, von H. Thomae u. U. Lehr.--Notes on innocent cognition, by A.H. Maslow.--Wandlungen des Denkens im Lebenslauf, von W. Fischel.--Vom Zeiterlebnis des alten Menschen, von A.L. Vischer.--Über normale und krankhafte Änderungen der mütterlichen Beziehung zum Kinde, von D.A. van (Continued)

SCHENK-DANZINGER, LOTTE, ed. Gegenwartsprobleme der Entwicklungspsychologie... (Card 3)

Krevelen.--"The happiest day of my life" as judged by Junior school children, by M.L. Kellmer Pringle.--Finger-mouth-contact in relation to feeding and weaning in early childhood, by A.G. Skard and A. Brekstad.--Geschwisterkonstellation und Persönlichkeitsreifung, von A. M. Däumling.--Untersuchungen zur Entwicklung des visuellen Wahrnehmens, von R. Bergius.--Die unterschiedlichen Erfolgschancen von Schulanfängern in verschie- denen Schulklassen, von H. (Continued)

SCHENK-DANZINGER, LOTTE, ed. Gegenwartsprobleme der Entwicklungspsychologie... (Card 4)

Hetzer.--Aus empirischen Untersuchungen über Vorbilder heutiger Jugendlicher, von W. Jaide.--Beobachtungen über die seelische Entwicklung Debiler in Pubertät und Adoleszenz, von H. Wegener.--Entwicklungspsychologische Probleme der Reifungsgestörten, von H. Hoff u. W. Spiel.--Group psychotherapy in adolescents, by E. A. D. E. Carp.--Selbsthypnose und Persönlichkeitsentwicklung, von J.H. Schultz.--Inculcation in psychotherapy, by E. Ziskind.

1. Psychology, Genetic. 2. Bühler, Charlotte Bertha (Malachowski), 1893- I. Thomae, Hans, joint ed.

Copy only words underlined & classmark-- STG

SCHILLER 1759/1959; commemorative American studies edited by John R. Frey. Urbana, University of Illinois press, 1959. vii, 213 p. 26cm. (Illinois. University. University of Illinois studies in language and literature. v. 46)

Bibliographical footnotes.
CONTENTS.--Antike Götterwelt in Wielands und in Schillers Sicht, von M. Gerhard.--Schiller, Winckelmann, and the myth (Continued)

NN * X 11. 59 a/+ OC, II, IIIbo (OD)I (ED)I PC, 1, I, II (LC1, X1, Z1)

SCHILLER 1759/1959... (Card 2)

of Greece, by H. Hatfield. —Schillers Philosophie der Existenz, von H. Jaeger. —Schiller's Indian threnody, by H. Jantz. —Schuldverwicklung in Schillers Dramen, von F. W. Kaufmann. —Zum Problem der "Erschütterung" in Schillers Dichtung und Gedankenwelt, von H. Rehder. —Schiller's "treacherous signs," by O. Seidlin. —Chorus and choral function in Schiller, by W. Silz. —Oedipus Tyrannus and Die Braut von Messina, by H. Weigand. —American Schiller literature; a bibliography, by J. R. Frey (p. 203-213).

1. Schiller, J. C. F. von. I. Series. II. Frey, John R., ed. III. Frey, John R.

E-12
5401

Schlösser, Anselm, ed.
Shakespeare-Jubiläum 1964; Festschrift zu Ehren des 400. Geburtstages William Shakespeares und des 100jährigen Bestehens der Deutschen Shakespeare-Gesellschaft, hrsg. im Namen der Gesellschaft von Anselm Schlösser. Weimar, H. Böhlaus Nachfolger, 1964.
213 p. illus., facsims., ports. 25 cm.
Bibliographical footnotes.

NN* R 3.66 g/ OC PC, 1, 2 (Continued) SL (LC1, X1, Z1)

E-11
3584

SCHIMMELPFENNIG, HEINZ, ed.
Grundsatzfragen der sozialen Unfallversicherung; Festschrift für Dr. Herbert Lauterbach zum 60. Geburtstag. [Berlin]E. Schmidt [1961] 358 p. 24cm.

Contributions by various authors.
Bibliographical footnotes.

1. Insurance, Accident--Germany. 2. Lauterbach, Herbert. I. Schimmelpfennig, Heinz.
NN R 11.61 p/ OC, 2bo, Ibo PC, 1, 2 SL E, 1, 2 (LC1, X1, Z1)

SCHLÖSSER, ANSELM, ed. Shakespeare-Jubiläum 1964... (Card 2)

CONTENTS.—Hundert Jahre Deutsche Shakespeare-Gesellschaft, von M. Lehnert.—Sonett 107 von W. Shakespeare, übers. von G. Regis.—Über meine Hamlet-Inszenierung, von G. von Wangenheim.— Shakespeares Volkstümlichkeit, von R. Weimann.—Richard II, von A. Schlösser.—Die Bedeutung der Romanzen Shakespeares, von W. Martin.—Aus dem Übersetzungswerk von R. Schaller.—Von meiner Begegnung mit Shakespeare, von O. Lang.—Die Partnerbeziehungen in Shakespeares Dramen, von A.-G. Kuckhoff.—Shakespeare und Händel, von J. Rudolph.

1. Shakespeare, William--Celebrations, 1964. 2. Deutsche Shakespeare Gesellschaft.

E-13
8173

Schlegel, Wolfgang, 1912-
150 [Hundertfünfzig] Jahre Landkreis Kusel. Beiträge zur Verwaltungs- und Wirtschaftsgeschichte von 1818-1968. Festschrift zum 150jährigen Bestehen des Landkreises Kusel. Von Wolfgang Schlegel [und] Albert Zink. Hrsg. vom Landkreis Kusel. Otterbach-Kaiserslautern, Arbogast (1968).
x, 230 p. with 10 illus., col. map. 24 cm.
Bibliographical footnotes.

NN*R 4.70 m/OC, I, IIIb* (OD)IIt (ED)IIt PC, 1, 2, I, II (Continued) E, 1, 2, I (LC1, X1) SL (Z1)

C-11
66

SCHLUETER, HERBERT, 1906-
Signor Anselmo; drei Erzählungen. [Zum fünfzigsten Geburtstage des Novellisten hrsg. von seinem Jugendfreunde Hellmut Draws-Tychsen] Diessen vor München, J. C. Huber [1957] 114 p. port. 19cm.

400 copies printed.
CONTENTS. —Ein Brief des Herausgebers anstelle von Geleitworten. —Signor Anselmo. —Erstes Abenteuer. —Der Deserteur.
I. Title.
NN R 2.59 p/ OC PC, I SL (LC1, X1, Z1)

SCHLEGEL, WOLFGANG, 1912- 150 [Hundertfünfzig] Jahre Landkreis Kusel. (Card 2)

1. Kusel, Germany--Govt. 2. Economic history--Germany--Kusel. I. Zink, Albert, joint author. II. Kusel, Germany. III. Zink, Albert. t. 1968.

K-10
4561
Bd. 2

SCHMIDT-EBHAUSEN, F. HEINZ, ed.
Festschrift für Alfons Perlick zum 65. Geburtstag am 13. Juni 1960, dargebracht von Freunden und Schülern; hrsg. von F. Heinz Schmidt-Ebhausen unter Mitarbeit von Eva-Maria Unsel. Dortmund, 1960.
233 p. port., fold. maps. 21cm. (Kommission für Volkskunde der Heimatvertrieben. Schriftenreihe. Bd. 2)
1. Perlick, Alfons. 2. Folk lore--Addresses, essays, lectures.
NN R 2.65 a/k OC OI PC, 1, 2 (LC1, X1, Z1) [I]

TB p.v.2015

Schleiffer, Hedwig, 1899-
Index to economic history essays in Festschriften, 1900-1950 [by] Hedwig Schleiffer and Ruth Crandall; with a pref. by Arthur H. Cole. Cambridge, A. H. Cole; distributed by Harvard University Press, 1953.
68 p. 28 cm.

1.Economic history--Bibl. 2.Economics--Hist.--Bibl. 3.Social conditions--Hist.--Bibl. 4.Festschriften--Indexes. I.Crandall, Ruth, 1893- , joint author.
NN * R X 2.56 OC (Ib*)I, Ib PC, 1, 2, 3, 4, I SL E, 1, 2, 3, I (LC1, X1, Z1)

THN
+

Schmidt (Karl) Bankgeschäft.
125 [i.e. Hundertfünfundzwanzig] Jahre Karl Schmidt Bankgeschäft, 1828-1953; eine Festschrift... Hof/Saale, 1953. 58 p. illus., plates, ports., map. 33cm.

1. Banks and banking—Germany—Wunsiedel. 2. Bank buildings—Germany—Wunsiedel. I. Title.
NN** R X 10.53 (OC)I, Ib OS PC, 1 SL A, 2 E, 1 (LC1, Z1, X1)

L-10
2596

SCHMITT, LUDWIG ERICH, ed.
Deutsche Wortforschung in europäischen Bezügen, Untersuchungen zum Deutschen Wortatlas. Giessen, W. Schmitz, 1958-68. 5 v. illus., maps. 24cm.

Bd. 1-5.
Vol. 1 forms Beiträge zur deutschen Philologie Bd. 19-23.
Vol. 2 is Festschrift for Walther Mitzka; vol. 4, for Luise Berthold.
Bibliographical footnotes.

(Continued)

NN R 12.71 m/s OCs, II (OS)Is PCs, 1s, 2s, Is, II SLs (LC1s, X1s, Z2)

2

SCHMITT, LUDWIG ERICH, ed. Deutsche Wortforschung in europäischen Bezügen... (Card 2)

1. German language--Semantics. 2. Language--Geographical distribution--Germany. I. Series: Beiträge zur deutschen Philologie. Bd. 19-23. II. Title.

L-11
2513

SCHMITT, LUDWIG ERICH, ed.
Germanische Dialektologie. Festschrift für Walther Mitzka zum 80. Geburtstag. Wiesbaden, F. Steiner, 1968. 1v. maps. 25cm. (Zeitschrift für Mundartforschung. Beiheft. n.F. Nr. 5)

[Bd.] 1.
Includes bibliographies.
CONTENTS.--Bd. 1. Alemannische Mundartforschung, von S. Sonderegger. Bairische

(Continued)

NN 2.69 e/s OC (OS)I PC, 1, 2, I SL (LC1, X1, Z1) [I]

2

SCHMITT, LUDWIG ERICH, ed. Germanische Dialektologie. (Card 2)

Mundartforschung, von R. Freudenberg. Westmitteldeutsche Mundartforschung, von H. Friebertshäuser. Ostmitteldeutsche Dialektologie, von W. Putschke. Niederdeutsche Mundartforschung der Stammlande, von J. Hartig und G. Keseling. Zur Geschichte der niederländischen Dialektologie, von J. Goossens. Afrikaanse Mundartforschung, von S.A. Louw. Die Erforschung der jiddischen Sprache, von H. P. Althaus. Friesische Dialektologie, von N. Århammar.
1. Mitzka, Walter, 1888- 2. German language--Dialects. I. Series.

L-10
9718
Heft 2

SCHMITZ, CARL A., ed.
Festschrift Alfred Bühler, hrsg. von Carl A. Schmitz und Robert Wildhaber. Basel, Pharos-Verlag H. Schwabe, 1965. 466 p. illus., plates, port., maps., music. 25cm. (Basler Beiträge zur Geographie und Ethnologie. Ethnologische Reihe. Heft 2)

Includes bibliographical references.
1. Bühler, Alfred, 1900- 2. Ethnology--Essays and misc. I. Wildhaber, Robert, 1902- joint ed. II. Series.
NN R 11.66 a/s OC, I (OS)II PC, 1, 2, I, II A, 1, I (LC1, X1, Z1) [I]

D-11
4682

SCHNEIDER, GOTTLOB, 1835-1912.
Gothaer Gedenkbuch; des Gothaer Wegweisers 3. umgearb. und verm. Aufl. Gotha, Stollberg, 1906. 2 v. illus., ports. 21cm.

Bd. 2. has title: Gothaer Gedenkbuch und Heimat-Erinnrungen au Dorf und Stadt.
Bd. 2 has imprint: Leipzig-Gohlis, B. Volger, 1909.
1. Gotha, Germany (City)--Biog. 2. Gotha, Germany (City)--Guidebooks, 1906.
NN R X 12.58 a/s OC(1b) PC, 1, 2 SL (LC1, X1, Z1)

PLD

Schneider, Walter, *Dr. chem., Zürich, ed.*
Essays in co-ordination chemistry, dedicated to Gerold Schwarzenbach on his 60th birthday, 15 March 1964, edited by W. Schneider, G. Anderegg [and] R. Gut. Basel, Birkhäuser Verlag, 1964.

805 p. illus., port. 25 cm. (Experientia; Monatsschrift für das gesamte Gebiet der Naturwissenschaft. Supplementum.9)
English or German.
Includes bibliographies.
1. Coordination compounds. 2. Schwarzenbach, Gerold, 1904- t. 1964. I. Series.
NN * R 1.65 e/s OC (OS)I PC, 1, 2, I SL ST, 1t, 2, I (LC1, X1, Z1)

---

*MEC
(Strecke)

SCHODROCK, KARL, ed.
Gerhard Strecke [zum fünfundsiebzigsten Geburtstag am 13. Dezember 1965] Würzburg, Verlag Kulturwerk Schlesien, 1965. 30,[4] p. port. 24cm. (Schriftenreihe Kulturwerk Schlesien)

Contains "Werkverzeichnis" (p. 14-28) and facsim. of a song in ms.: Ich geh durch die dunklen Gassen; music by Strecke, words by Eichendorff (p. [31-34])
1. Strecke, Gerhard. 1890- 2. Songs, German. I. Strecke, Gerhard, 1890- Lieder, op. 81 Ich geh durch die dunklen Gassen. II. Strecke, Gerhard, 1890-
NN 11.68 e/s OC, I, IIb+ (OAF1) PC, 1 SL MU, 1, 2g, Ig (MUD1, LC1, X1, Z1)

---

*KF
1966

SCHOLDERER, VICTOR, 1880-
...Fifty essays in fifteenth- and sixteenth-century bibliography. Edited by Dennis E. Rhodes. Amsterdam, Menno Hertzberger & co., 1966. 302 p. facsims., port. 29cm.

Published to mark the author's 85th birthday (1965).
Bibliography: p. 15-29.
1. Printing--Hist., 15th cent. 2. Printing--Hist., 16th cent. 3. Incunabula--Addresses, essays, lectures. I. Rhodes, Dennis E., ed.
NN R 12.67 r/s OC, I PC, 1, 2, 3, I SL R, 1, 2, 3, I (RI 1, LC1, X1, Z1) [I]

M-10
2277
Bd. 3

Schottenloher, Otto, ed.
Bayern Staat und Kirche, Land und Reich; Forschungen zur bayerischen Geschichte vornehmlich im 19. Jahrhundert. Wilhelm Winkler zum Gedächtnis, hrsg. von den staatlichen Archiven Bayerns. München, K. Zink [1959?] 509 p. port. 25cm. (Archiv und Wissenschaft. Bd. 3)

1. Bavaria—Hist.—Addresses, essays, lectures. 2. Church and state—Germany—Bavaria. 3. Winkler, Wilhelm, 1893–1958 I. Series.
NN R 5.62 OC,3b (OD)I (ED)I PC,1,2,3,I E,2,3 (LC1,X1,Z1)

AC-10
270

SCHRAG, J.L., firm, publishers, Nuremberg.
J.L. Schrag-Verlag 1810-1960. Die Veröffentlichungen 1910-1960. Nürnberg, 1960. xxvi, 38 p. mounted illus. (incl. ports). 20cm.

NN 7.61 g/ OS PC SL (LC1, X1, Z1)

C-12
9610

SCHREIBEN ist Leben; zum 70. Geburtstag von Friedrich Sieburg am 18. Mai 1963. Stuttgart, Deutsche Verlags-Anstalt [1963] 57 p. illus., ports., facsim. 19cm.

CONTENTS.--Friedrich Sieburg, von K.A. Horst.--Autobiographisches, von F. Sieburg.

I. Sieburg, Friedrich, 1893- . II. Horst, Karl August.
NN R 7.66 e/ OC, I, II, IIb* PC, I, II SL (LC1, X1, Z1)

---

*MEC
(Reger)

SCHREIBER, OTTMAR, 1906- ed.
Max Reger. Zum 50. Todestag am 11. Mai 1966. Eine Gedenkschrift. Hrsg. von Ottmar Schreiber und Gerd Sievers. Bonn, Hannover, Hamburg, München, Dümmler (1966)

217 p. front. 21 cm. (Max-Reger- Institut, Bonn, Germany. Veröffentlichungen. Heft 4)

Bibliographical footnotes. (Continued)
NN* 4.68 v/ OC, II (OS)I PC, 1, I, II SL
MU, 1, I, II (LC1, X1, Z1) 2

SCHREIBER, OTTMAR, 1906- ed. Max Reger.
(Card 2)

CONTENTS.—Max Reger—Leben und künstlerische Erscheinung, von G. Bagler.—Max Reger in München, von H. Niemann.—Max Regers geistliche Musik, von O. Söhngen.—Max Reger als Komponist katholischer Kirchenmusik, von A. Becker.—Max Regers Violinsonate op. 72, von H. Rösner.—Regers Klarinettenquintett op. 146, von K. Dorfmüller. — Reger-Gesamtausgabe — Entstehungsgeschichte, von G. Sievers.

1. Reger, Max, 1873-1916. I. Series.
II. Sievers, Gerd, joint ed.

APD

Schröder, Edward, 1858-
Deutsche namenkunde; gesammelte aufsätze zur kunde deutscher personen- und ortsnamen von Edward Schröder. Festgabe seiner freunde und schüler zum 80. geburtstag. Mit einem bildnis. Göttingen, Vandenhoeck & Ruprecht, 1938.

11*, 342 p. front. (port.) 26cm.

Bibliographical foot-notes.

1. Names, Personal—Germany. 2. Names, Geographical—Germany. I. Title. II. Title: Festgabe seiner freunde und schüler zum 80. geburtstag (Edward Schröders)

Northwestern univ. Library for Library of Congress A C 39-3351 (2)

D-16
7182

SCHRÖDER, KARL HEINZ, ed.
Studien zur südwestdeutschen Landeskunde. Festschrift zu Ehren von Friedrich Huttenlocher anlässlich seines 70. Geburtstages. Bad Godesberg, Bundesanstalt für Landeskunde und Raumforschung, 1963. xxx, 476 p. illus., port., maps(part in pocket (as issued)) 22cm.

Pages 1-476 reprinted from Beiträge zur deutschen Landeskunde, Bd. 31.
Includes bibliographies.
1. Huttenlocher, Friedrich. 2. Würtemberg-Baden--Geography.
NN 6.66 1/ OC PC, 1, 2 SL (LC1, X1, Z1)

E-11
4881

SCHRÖDER, WERNER, 1914- , ed.
Festschrift für Ludwig Wolff zum 70. Geburtstag. Neumünster, K. Wachholtz, 1962. 374 p. illus., port., maps, facsim. 24cm.

Contributions in German and English.
Bibliographical footnotes.
1. Wolff, Ludwig, 1892- . 2. Germanic literature--Addresses, essays, lectures. 3. Germanic languages--Addresses, essays, lectures. I. Schröder, Werner, 1914-
NN R 9.62 a/ OC, IbKG PC, 1, 2, 3 SL (LC1, X1, Z1) [I]

E-11
7092

SCHÜRER, WILHELM, ed.
Hestia, 1960/61; Beiträge zur Würdigung und Weitergabe des Werkes von Ludwig Klages, 10. Dezember 1872-29. Juli 1956. [Bonn, In Kommission bei H. Bouvier, 1960] 115 p. illus., port. 24cm.

"Werke von Ludwig Klages": p. 114-115.

1. Klages, Ludwig, 1872-1956. 2. Philosophy--Addresses, essays, lectures. 3. Psychology--Addresses, essays, lectures. I. Title. II. Schürer, Wilhelm.
NN * R 12.63 f/ OC, IIb* PC, 1, 2, 3, I SL (LC1, X1, Z1)

E-12
9499

Schützeichel, Rudolf, *ed.*
Namenforschung; Festschrift für Adolf Bach zum 75. Geburtstag am 31. Januar, 1965. Hrsg. von Rudolf Schützeichel und Matthias Zender. Heidelberg, C. Winter, 1965.

494 p. facsims., maps (part fold.) 25 cm.
Bibliographical footnotes.

(Continued)
NN * R 8.67 1/ OC, I PC, 1, 2, 3, 4, I, II SL
(LC1, X1, Z1) 2

SCHÜTZEICHEL, RUDOLF, ed. Namenforschung...
(Card 2)

1. Names, Germanic. 2. Geography--Names, Germanic
3. Germanic languages--Etymology. 4. Bach, Adolf, 1890- . I. Zender, Matthias, joint ed.
II. Title.

AVGI
(Schulthess)

SCHULTHESS, HANS, 1872-
Die Familie Schulthess von Zürich; Festschrift zur Feier des einhundert fünfzigjährigen Bestehens der Schulthess'schen Familienstiftung, von Hans Schulthess. Zürich, Schulthess, 1908. iv, 121 p. illus., plates, fold. geneal. tables. 30cm.

Bibliography, p. 115-116.

1. Schulthess family. I. Schulthess'sche Familienstiftung.

NN R 2. 71 b/z OC (OS)I, Ib+ PC, 1, I SL G, 1, I (LC1, X1, Z1)

MTE

Schumacher-Festschrift zum 70. Geburtstag Karl Schumachers, 14. Oktober, 1930; herausgegeben von der Direktion des Römisch-Germanischen Zentral-Museums in Mainz... Mainz: In Kommission bei L. Wilckens, 1930. vi, 370 p. illus. (incl. maps, plans), 48 pl. (part col'd.) 4°.

Includes bibliographies.

Contents: Ledroit, J. Karl Schumacher. Seger, H. Die Anfänge des Dreiperioden-Systems. Schrohe, H. Aus der Frühzeit der römischen Altertumswissenschaft in Mainz. Finke, H. Mainzer antiquarische Briefe vor hundert Jahren. Deecke, W. Zur Entstehung der Deckschichten über ur- und frühgeschichtlichen Fundstätten Südwestdeutschlands. Curschmann, J. Die älteste Besiedlung der Gemarkung Buden-

(Continued)

N. Y. P. L. June 29, 1931

Schumacher-Festschrift zum 70. Geburtstag Karl Schumachers ... (Card 2)

heim bei Mainz. Gutmann, K. S. Der Kaiserstuhl in ur- und frühgeschichtlicher Zeit. Kraft, G. Siedlungskundliche Fragen in Oberbaden. Wagner, F. Zur vorrömischen Besiedlung des bayerischen Alpengebietes. Petzsch, W. Die Besiedlung Rügens in vorgeschichtlicher Zeit. Frickhinger, E. Hallstatt- und latènezeitliche Hausgrundrisse aus dem Ries. Kiekebusch, A. Die vorgeschichtliche Siedlung von Lüdersdorf, Kreis Teltow. Loeschcke, S. Vorrömische Funde aus Trier. Hörmann, K. Vorgeschichtliche Leichendörrung. Hock, G. Ein Beitrag zur vorgeschichtlichen Technik. Schröder, E. Harug, harah in Ortsnamen. Schmidtgen, O. Nachweise einer paläolithischen Besiedlung im engeren Gebiet des Mainzer Beckens. Reinerth, H. Die Besiedlung des Bodensees zur mittleren Steinzeit. Birkner, F. Hirschgeweihgeräte aus der

(Continued)

N. Y. P. L. June 29, 1931

Schumacher-Festschrift zum 70. Geburtstag Karl Schumachers ... (Card 3)

Rheinpfalz. Kupka, P. L. B. Zur Systematik der Grosssteingräber des nordischen Kulturkreises. Reinecke, P. Die Bedeutung der Kupferbergwerke der Ostalpen für die Bronzezeit Mitteleuropas. Merhart, G. von. Urnengrab mit Peschierafibel aus Nordtirol. Sprockhoff, E. Formenkreise der jüngeren Bronzezeit in Norddeutschland. Günther, A. Die ältere und mittlere Bronzezeit im Neuwieder Becken. Jacob-Friesen, K. H. Die Lanzenspitzen vom Lüneburger Typus. Gummel, H. Tongefässe aus der jüngeren Bronze- und ältesten Eisenzeit im Museum der Stadt Osnabrück. Bersu, G. Fünf Mittel-La-Téne-Häuser vom Goldberg, O.-A. Neresheim, Wttbg. Langewiesche, F. Die Wallburg Babilonie. Rademacher, C. Germanisches La-Tène im Kölner Gebiet. Steiner, P. Eine vorgeschichtliche Plateaufeste im Trevererland. Behn, F. Zur

(Continued)

N. Y. P. L. June 29, 1931

Schumacher-Festschrift zum 70. Geburtstag Karl Schumachers ... (Card 4)

ersten germanischen Besiedelung Starkenburgs. Schuchhardt, C. Die Schulenburg bei Cotzofeni und andere dakische Burgen. Jacobsthal, P. Keltische Grabpfeiler aus Glanum. Lammerer, A. Olérdola, eine iberische Felsenfeste in Katalonien. Lippold, G. Korinthische Salbgefässe. Zahn, R. Zur hellenistischen Schmuckkunst. Herzog, R. Epigramm der Kinderstatue eines Lysippos in Kos. Klenk, H. Barditus. Jacobi, H. Der keltische Schlüssel und der Schlüssel der Penelope. Neugebauer, K. A. Aus der Werkstatt eines griechischen Toreuten in Ägypten. Hofmann, H. Die stadtrömische Haartracht an den Bildnissen italischer und provinzialer Grabsteine. Krüger, E. Matres Parcae im Treverergebiet. Keune, J. B. Colonia Treverorum. Gündel, F. Ein neues frührömisches Erdlager bei Heddernheim. Sprater, F. Römische Tongewinnung in

(Continued)

N. Y. P. L. June 29, 1931

Schumacher-Festschrift zum 70. Geburtstag Karl Schumachers ... (Card 5)

der Pfalz. Kutsch, F. Eine Mainzer Bildhauerwerkstätte claudischer Zeit. Feigel, A. Der Bronzekopf eines jugendlichen Satyr. Jahn, M. Ein frühkaiserzeitlicher Prunksporn von der Donaugrenze. Behrens, G. Spätrömische Kerbschnittschnallen. Fremersdorf, F. Die Herstellung der Diatreta. Oxé, A. Barocke Reliefkeramik aus Tiberius' Zeit. Knorr, R. Verzierte Sigillata des 1. Jahrhunderts mit Töpfernamen. Unverzagt, W. Römisches Dolium mit Biermaische aus Alzey. Schwantes, G. Eine römische Kasserolle aus dem unteren Wesergebiet. Schulz, W. Mitteldeutsch-südwestdeutsche Beziehungen in der spätrömischen Germanenkultur. Kunkel, O. Vier neue römische Funde in Pommern. Volbach, F. W. Spätantike und frühmittelalterliche Elfenbeinarbeiten aus dem Rheinland und ihre Beziehungen zu Ägypten. Schmidt, L.

(Continued)

N. Y. P. L. June 29, 1931

Schumacher-Festschrift zum 70. Geburtstag Karl Schumachers ... (Card 6)

Zur Geschichte der Krimgoten. Bierbaum, G. Zwei langobardische Gräber von Dresden-Nickern. Kühn, H. Die Fibeln mit ausgezackter Kopfplatte. Baum, J. Zu den Hornhauser Steinen. Goessler, P. Von den württembergischen Landgräben. Kessler, P. T. Technische Beobachtungen an der Mainzer Adlerfibel. Berichtigungen und Nachträge. Verzeichnis der Mitarbeiter.

526851A. 1. Schumacher, Karl, 1860- . 2. Archaeology. I. Roemisch-Germanisches Central-Museum, Mainz.

N. Y. P. L. June 29, 1931

---

*MP
(German)

SCHUMANN, ROBERT, 1810-1856.
[MYRTHEN]
Myrthen; Liederkreis von Göthe [et al.] für Gesang und Pianoforte von Robert Schumann. Op. 25. Leipzig, F. Kistner [1840] Pl. no. 1290-1291, 1293-1294. 4 v. in 1. 35cm.

For voice and piano.
1st ed.

(Continued)

NN S 5. 70 r/c OC (OAF1) SL MUg, 1g, 2g, Ig (LC1, X1, Z1, MUD7)

SCHUMANN, ROBERT, 1810-1856. [MYRTHEN]
Myrthen... (Card 2)

THE OTTO KINKELDEY MEMORIAL COLLECTION

1. Songs, German. 2. Song cycles. I. Title.

E-10
9421

Der SCHUTZ des privaten Eigentums im Ausland; Festschrift für Hermann Janssen zum 60. Geburtstag, hrsg. von Fritz Kränzlin und H.E.A. Müller. Heidelberg, Verlagsgesellschaft "Recht und Wirtschaft" [1958]
232 p. port. 25 cm.

Bibliography, p. 225-227.

Contents.—Die Behandlung des deutschen Privatvermögens in den Vereinigten Staaten nach dem ersten und zweiten Weltkrieg von H.W. Baade.—Probleme der enteignungsrechtlichen Spaltgesellschaft, von G. Beitzke.—Grenzen der Auswirkung des besatzungsrechtlichen Be-

(Continued)

NN * R 1. 60 m/e OC, 2b, I, II, IIIb*, IVb* PC, 1, 2, I, II SL E, 1, 2, I, II (LC1, X1, Z1)

Der SCHUTZ des privaten Eigentums im Ausland...
(Card 2)

CONTENTS—Continued.

schlagnahmerechts in Deutschland auf deutsches Auslandsvermögen, von O. Böhmer.—Die Auslandsenteignung im englischen internationalen Privatrecht, von E. J. Cohn.—Zur internationalen Doppelbesteuerung, von G. Gast.—Behandlung des deutschen Vermögens in Schweden, von J. Hepner.—Konfiskatorische Eingriffe in private Auslandsschuldverhältnisse durch die Friedensverträge von 1947, von F. Kränzlin.—Wechsel der Staatsangehörigkeit und Eigentumsschutz im Kriege (Der Fall Nottebohm) von E. Langen.—Das Eigentumsrecht in Italien und seine Begrenzung mit besonderem Hinweis auf Auslandsinvestitionen, von C. Piola Caselli.—Betrachtungen über die Sozialisierung des argentinischen Privatrechtes, von H. Rastalsky.—

(Continued)

Der SCHUTZ des privaten Eigentums
im Ausland... (Card 3)

CONTENTS—Continued.

Zur Auslegung des Interalliierten Reparationsabkommens vom 14. 1. 1946, von U. Scheuner.—Zur Frage der Rechtsanwendung im internationalen Rechtsverkehr, von D. J. Schottelius.—Die sowjetische Beurteilung der Rechtsprechung des Westens über die sowjetischen Nationalisierungsmassnahmen, von E. Schütte.—Eigentumsschutz durch Resolutionen internationaler Organisationen, von I. Seidl-Hohenveldern.—Die Freigabe des deutschen Vermögens in der Schweiz im Lichte des deutschen Verfassungsrechts, von K. E. Thomä.

1. Property--Alien holdings. 2. Janssen, Hermann, 1897- . I. Kränzlin, Fritz, ed. II. Müller, Heinrich E. A., joint ed. III. Kränzlin, Fritz. IV. Müller, Heinrich E. A.

D-17
5859

SCHUTZ, WALTER J., ed.

Aus der Schule der Diplomatie; Beiträge zu Aussenpolitik, Recht, Kultur, Menschenführung. [Festschrift zum 70. Geburtstag von Peter H. Pfeiffer. Zusammenstellung und Bearbeitung: Walter J. Schütz] Düsseldorf, Econ-Verlag [1965]

712 p. port. 23 cm.

Includes bibliographies.

(Continued)

NN * R 8.67 1/-OC,I, E,1,2,3,4,I (LC1,X1, 4b* PC,1,2,3,4,I SL Z1)

2

SCHUTZ, WALTER J., ed. Aus der Schule der Diplomatie... (Card 2)

1. Diplomatic service--Germany. 2. Germany--For. rel., 1945- . 3. World politics, 1945- 4. Pfeiffer, Peter H., 1895- . I. Title.

EAG

Schwarz, Klaus, *ed.*

Strena praehistorica; Festgabe zum 60. Geburtstag von Martin Jahn, hrsg. im Namen seiner Schüler. Zugleich gewidmet der Tagung für Vorgeschichte in Halle/Saale 1948 anlässlich des 125 jährigen Bestehens des Landesmuseums. Halle/Saale, M. Niemeyer, 1948.

253 p. illus., port., maps (part fold.) 24 cm.

Bibliographical footnotes.

CONTENTS.—Lagen die Siedlungen der linearbandkeramischen Kultur Mitteldeutschlands in waldfreien oder in bewaldeten Landschaften? Von K. Schwarz.—Die neuen Funde der Glockenbecherkultur im Lande Sachsen-Anhalt, von F. Schlette.—Untersuchungen am Menhir

(Continued on next card)

W.S.

A 50-931

[3]

Schwarz, Klaus, *ed.* Strena praehistorica ... 1948.
(Card 2)

CONTENTS—Continued.

von Benzingerode, von J. Pätzold.—Die seltsamen Schicksale einiger Oberlausitzer Bronzegegenstände und deren Stellung im Rahmen der bronzezeitlichen Geschichte, von G. Smolla.—Typische Formen der jüngsten Bronzezeit Oberschlesiens, von C. Zettler.—Späthallstättische Kulturströmungen im Ostalpenraum, von C. Pescheck.—Alte und neue Grabfunde der Hausurnenkultur Mitteldeutschlands, von W. Hoffmann.—Ein provinzial-römisches Bronzegeschirrdepot aus dem Elbtal bei Grieben, Kr. Stendal, von K. H. Otto.—Das karolingische Hamburg und die Probleme der frühgeschichtlichen Städteforschung Niedersachsens, von R. Schindler.

1. Germany—Antiq. 2. Jahn, Martin, 1888- I. Title.

A 50-931

Harvard Univ. Library
for Library of Congress [3]

A p.v.245, no.1

Schwedentum an deutschen Universitäten; Gedenkschrift für Dr. Wolrad Eigenbrodt, weil. Lektor der schwedischen Sprache an der Universität Jena, herausgegeben von seinen Schülern und Freunden. Jena: G. Neuenhahn, 1922. 50 p. front. (port.) 8°.

"Geleitwort" signed: Rudolf Eucken.

1. Eigenbrodt, Wolrad, 1860-1921. 2. Eucken, Rudolf Christof, 1846-1926.

N. Y. P. L. July 15, 1927

D-13
6916

SCHWEDISCHE Volkskund, Quellen, Forschung, Ergebnisse; Festschrift für Sigfrid Svensson zum Sechzigsten Geburtstag am 1. Juni 1961. [Redaktion: Gösta Berg et al. [ins Deutsche übertragen von Christiane Bæhncke-Sjöberg] Stockholm, Almqvist & Wiksell [1961] 511 p. illus., maps. 22cm.

Includes bibliographies.

CONTENTS.—Die Erforschung der schwedischen Volkskultur, von

(Continued)

NN R 6.62 g/-OC,I PC,1, 2,3,I SL (LC1,X1,Z1)

3

SCHWEDISCHE Volkskund... (Card 2)

G. Berg.—Der gegenwärtige Stand der schwedischen Volkskunde, von J. Granlund.—Der religions- und kirchengeschichtliche Hintergrund der schwedischen Volkskultur, von H. Pleijel.—Der sozialgeschichtliche Hintergrund der schwedischen Volkskultur, von J. Rosén.—Kulturgrenzen und Kulturwege, von S. O. Jansson.—Dörfer und Flurstrukturen, von S. Erixon.—Soziale Organisation, von A. Eskeröd.—Bodenbau, von R. Jirlow.—Viehhaltung, von A. Sandklef.—Pferde, von M. Szabó.—Jagd, von S. Lagercrantz.—Fischerei, von O. Hasslöf.—Handwerk, von B. Bengtsson.—Handel, von B. Hanssen.—Bauweise und Inneneinrichtung, von G. von Schoultz.—Kleidung, von A.-M. Nylén.—Kost, von B. Egardt.—Jahresfeste, Arbeitsfeste, Kalender, von J.-O. Swahn.—Der Festkreis

(Continued)

SCHWEDISCHE Volkskund... (Card 3)

des Lebens, von N.-A. Bringeus.—Volksglaube, von C.-M. Edsman.—Marchen und Sage, von A.B. Rooth.—Volkslied, von B.R. Jonsson.

1. Svensson, Sigfrid, 1901- . 2. Folk lore--Sweden. 3. Sweden--Civilization. I. Berg, Gösta, 1903- , ed.

TAH

Schweizerische Gesellschaft für Statistik und Volkswirtschaft.
Schweizerische Wirtschaftsfragen; Festgabe für Fritz Mangold herausgegeben von der Schweizerischen Gesellschaft für Statistik und Volkswirtschaft. Basel: Helbig & Lichtenhahn, 1941. 339 p. front. (port.) 24cm.

CONTENTS.—Anrede.—Statistik und Wirtschaftspolitik, von Carl Brüschweiler.—Steuerenlastungskämpfe in der Schweiz, von Eugen Grossmann.—Die mineralischen Rohstoffe der Schweiz und ihre Gewinnungsmöglichkeiten, von Ernst Gutzwiller.—Kriegsgewinne, von Camille Higy.—Gegenwarts- und Zukunftsaufgaben der schweizerischen Agrarpolitik, von Oskar Howald.—Grundzüge einer schweizerischen Schiffahrtspolitik, von Nicolas Jaquet.—Die Entwicklung der kantonalen und kommunalen

(Continued)

N. Y. P. L. Festschrift March 11, 1942

Schweizerische Gesellschaft für Statistik und Volkswirtschaft.
Schweizerische Wirtschaftsfragen... (Card 2)

Statistik, von O. H. Jenny.—Probleme schweizerischer Bankpolitik, von Theo Keller.—Wissenschaffer und Unternehmer, von E. H. Mahler.—Das Konditionenkartell, von Fritz Marbach.—Les rapports réciproques entre l'émigration industrielle et l'exportation suisses sous l'action de la politique douanière étrangère (1925–1939), par Albert Masnata.—Trois économistes genevois et la révision du Pacte fédéral de 1815, par W. E. Rappard.—Eigentumsgarantie und Volkswirtschaft, von Erwin Ruck.—Der Merkantilismus, von Manuel Saitzew.—Von der Sozialpolitik zum Recht auf Arbeit, von Edgar Salin.—Bemerkungen zur Kriegswirtschaftspolitik, von V. F. Wagner.—Anrede ehemaliger Schüler.—Bibliographie (p. 327–335).

159111B. 1. Economic history—Switzerland. 2. Mangold, Fritz, 1872— —Bibl. I. Title. 3. Mangold, Fritz, 1872–
N. Y. P. L. March 11, 1942

F-10
207

SCHWEIZERISCHER BUCHDRUCKER-VEREIN.
Jubiläumsschrift zum fünfundsiebzigjährigen Bestehen des Schweizerischen Buchdruckervereins, 1869-1944; Beiträge zur Geschichte des Buchdrucks in der Schweiz. Zürich, 1944. 203 p. facsims. 30cm.

Added t.p. in French.
CONTENTS. —Die wirtschaftliche und kulturelle Bedeutung des Buchdrucks in der Schweiz, von P. Leemann-van Elck. —Buchdruck

(Continued)

NN**R 10.56 d/a OS PC,1 SL (RIB1, LC1, X1, Z1)

SCHWEIZERISCHER BUCHDRUCKER-VEREIN. Jubiläumsschrift zum fünfundsiebzigjährigen Bestehen des Schweizerischen Buchdruckervereins... (Card 2)

und Buchdrucker als Mittler geistiger Entwicklungen, von A. Hoefliger. —Beispiele schweizerischer Druckkunst aus fünf Jahrhunderten. —Politique tarifaire de la Société suisse des maîtres imprimeurs, par T. Eberhard. —Prinzipal und Gehilfe im Buchdruckgewerbe, von H. Marti. —Protokoll der Gründung des SBV. --Verzeichnis der Abbildungen. --Literatur-Nachweis (p. 201-203)
1. Printing—Switzerland—Hist.

F-10
5015

Schweizerischer Fremdenverkehrsverband.
Fremdenverkehr in Theorie und Praxis; Festschrift für Walter Hunziker [zum 60. Geburtstag, dargebracht vom Schweizerischen Fremdenverkehrsverband und der Schweizer Reisekasse. Bern, Verbandsdruckerei, 1959]
208 p. port., diagrs. 27 cm.
Bibliography: p. 107-108. Bibliographical footnotes.
CONTENTS. — Sozialtourismus: sein Ursprung und der schweizerische Weg, von W. Abplanalp.—Les perspectives de l'intégration européenne et le tourisme, par G. Bauer. — Betriebswirtschaftliche Ordnungsprobleme der Fremdenverkehrsbetriebe, von P. Bernecker.—Probleme und Aufgaben des Gastwirtschaftsgewerbes, von V. Egger.—Les réseaux européens et le tourisme social, von E. Fallet.—Professor Hunziker und das Seminar für Fremdenverkehr an der Handels-Hoch-

(Continued)

NN*R X 10.60 g/A OS, I, Ib PC, I, 2, I SL E, I, 2, I (LC1, X1, Z1) 2

Schweizerischer Fremdenverkehrsverband. Fremdenverkehr in Theorie und Praxis ... [1959] (Card 2)
CONTENTS—Continued.
schule St. Gallen, von T. Keller.—Wirtschafts- und Fremdenverkehrsprobleme der Entwicklungsländer, dargestellt am Beispiel Tunesiens, von K. Krapf.—Fremdenverkehr in der modernen Arbeitsgesellschaft, von J. Leugger.—Transport and tourism, by L. Lickorish.—Evoluzione della politica turistica in Italia, di A. Mariotti.—Die touristische Konsumfunktion Deutschlands 1924–1957, von G. Menges.—Organisationsprobleme der Fremdenverkehrspolitik, von K. Morgenroth.—A propos de quelques principes de planification touristique, par V. Planque.—Konsumfunktion und Konsumentenverhalten im Tourismus, von H. Sauermann.—Stagnation oder traditionsbewusster Fortschritt in der schweizerischen Hotellerie? von F. Seiler. — Die Heilbäder der Schweiz, von A. Schirmer. — Eine theoretische Untersuchung der Marktstruktur des Beherbergungswesens, von H. Todt.
1. Tourist industry—Addresses, essays, lectures. 2. Hunziker, Walter, 1899- . I. Schweizer Reisekasse.

TAK

Schweizerischer Fremdenverkehrsverband.
Gegenwarts- und Zukunftsprobleme des schweizerischen Fremdenverkehrs; Festgabe für Hermann Seiler, hrsg. vom Schweizerischen Fremdenverkehrsverband. Zürich, Buchdruckerei AG. vormals J. Rüegg Söhne, 1946. 175 p. illus. 23cm.

401179B. 1. Tourist industry—Switzerland. 2. Seiler, Hermann, 1876- . I. Title.
N. Y. P. L. June 3, 1948

---

*PXR

SCHWEIZERISCHER ISRAELITISCHER GEMEINDEBUND.
Festschrift zum 50 jährigen Bestehen, 1904-1954. [Zürich, 1954] 334 p. illus. 22cm.

Two articles in French.
CONTENTS. —50 Jahre Gemeindebund, von L. Littmann. —Jüdische soziale Arbeit und Flüchtlingshilfe in der Schweiz, von O. H. Heim. —Abwehr und Aufklärung, von G. Guggenheim. —Die Juden in der Schweiz im Spiegel der Bevölkerungsstatistik, von H. Guth. —Die erblosen Vermögen in der Schweiz und das Völkerrecht, von P. Guggenheim. —Die ältesten jüdischen Familien in Lengnau und Endingen, von F. Guggenheim-Grünberg.

(Continued)

NN** R 7.54 OC PC, 1 SL J, 2 (LC1, Z1, X1)

SCHWEIZERISCHER ISRAELITISCHER GEMEINDEBUND. Festschrift zum 50 jährigen Bestehen, 1904-1954. (Card 2)

—Fragen jüdischer Kulturarbeit in der Schweiz, von H. L. Goldschmidt. —Jüdische Erziehung in der Diaspora, von E. J. Messinger. —Die jüdische Frau in moderner Zeit, von C. Wohlmann-Meyer. —Les rapports spirituels entre l'Etat d'Israël et la Diaspora, par A. Safran. —Aus meinem Leben, von D. Farbstein. —Erinnerungen eines Baslers an den ersten Zionistenkongress, von M. Cohn. —Spitteler und der Geist der hebräischen Sprache, von J. Fränkel. —Aus Gesprächen mit Karl Joël, von A. Weil. Jeremia—Prophet des Unglücks und Tröster des Volkes, von Z. Taubes. —Die Friedensbotschaft der Propheten, M. Susman. —Franz Kafka und das Judentum,

(Continued)

SCHWEIZERISCHER ISRAELITISCHER GEMEINDEBUND. Festschrift zum 50 jährigen Bestehen, 1904-1954. (Card 3)

von F. Strich. —Profession de foi, par E. Fleg. —Gemeinde und Gemeinschaft. Die älteste jüdische Bettagspredigt, von L. Rothschild. —Die jüdischen Gemeinden, Organisationen und Institutionen in der Schweiz.

1. Jews in Switzerland—Assoc. and org. 2. Switzerland—Assoc. and org.

D-10
4578

SCHWEIZERISCHER METALL- UND UHRENARBEITERVERBAND.

Festgabe für Nationalrat Dr. h.c. Konrad Ilg, Präsident des Schweizerischen Metall- und Uhrenarbeiterverbandes, zum siebzigsten Geburtstag am 25. Januar 1947, dargebracht von Freunden und Mitarbeitern. [Bern, 1947] 269 p. port. 23cm.

CONTENTS. -- Zum Geleit, von R. Grimm. —Die Kreditschöp-
(Continued)

NN R 6.57 d/b (OC)1b+, I OS PC, 1, 2, I SL E, 1, 2, I (LC1, X1, Z1)

SCHWEIZERISCHER METALL- UND UHRENARBEITERVERBAND. Festgabe für Nationalrat Dr. h.c. Konrad Ilg... (Card 2)

fung der Handelsbanken und das Postulat der Verstaatlichung des Kredits, von F. Marbach. —Die Entwicklung der Lohntheorie, von A. Amonn. —Die Arbeiterschaft, die Demokratie und die Freiheitsrechte, von V. Gawronski. —Gedanken zur Aussenhandelspolitik der Schweiz im zweiten Weltkrieg, von H. Schaffner. —Arbeitgeber und Arbeitnehmer in der schweizerischen Maschinen- und Metallindustrie, von E. Dübi. —Über die Erziehung des Nachwuchses und die Weiterbildung der Arbeiter in der Maschinenindustrie, von H. Ambühl. --Vermenschlichung der Gewerkschaftsarbeit, von
(Continued)

SCHWEIZERISCHER METALL- UND UHRENARBEITERVERBAND. Festgabe für Nationalrat Dr. h.c. Konrad Ilg... (Card 3)

E. Ernst. —Die Einstellung der Arbeiterschaft zum Wohnungsproblem, von E. Reinhard. —Konrad Ilg und der Schweiz. Metall- und Uhrenarbeiterverband, von J. Uhlmann. —Wandlungen, von A. Steiner. —La paix du travail: un moyen et non un but, par E. Giroud. —Démocratie syndicale, par A. Grädel. --Metallarbeiter berichten über ihre Erfahrungen: Ein kleiner Rückblick, von F. Saam. Was einst begonnen wurde, von J. Valli. Erfahrungen, von O. Frieden. --Vom Ethischen im Kollektivvertragswesen, von P. Bratschi. —Aus meinen Erinnerungen, von
(Continued)

SCHWEIZERISCHER METALL- UND UHRENARBEITERVERBAND. Festgabe für Nationalrat Dr. h.c. Konrad Ilg... (Card 4)

J. Kjerböl. —La Fédération internationale des ouvriers sur métaux, par L. Chevalme. —Widmung eines Ausländers und eines Freundes, von L. Evans.

1. Ilg, Konrad, 1877- . 2. Economics--Essays and misc. I. Title.

Schweizerisches Bauernsekretariat. VPE

Stand der Forschung auf dem Gebiete der Wirtschaftslehre des Landbaues. Recherches dans le domaine de l'économie rurale. Hrsg. vom Schweizerischen Bauernsekretariat Brugg. Brugg, Effingerhof [1951] 392 p. port. 23cm.

"Festschrift zum 80. Geburtstag von Professor Dr. phil. und Dr. h. c. Ernst Laur, Ing. Agr. ETH."

606357B. 1. Agriculture—Economics. 2. Agriculture—Economics—Switzerland. 3. Laur, Ernst Ferdinand, 1871-

N. Y. P. L. October 25, 1951

E-11
4378

SCHWINGE, ERICH, 1903- , ed.

Festgabe für Heinrich Herrfahrdt zum 70. Geburtstag. Marburg, N.G. Elwert, 1961. 212 p. port. 25cm.

Bibliographical footnotes.

CONTENTS.--Der Streit um die Wirtschaftsverfassung der Bundesrepublik, von P. Erlinghagen.--Beamter und Politik, von H.-U. Evers.--Grenzen der politischen Entschliessungsfreiheit des Bundeskanzlers und der
(Continued)

NN R 3.62 e/½ OC PC, 1, 2, 3 SL E, 1, 2, 3 (LC1, X1, Z1)

3

SCHWINGE, ERICH, 1903- , ed. Festgabe für Heinrich Herrfahrdt zum 70. Geburtstag. (Card 2)

Bundesminister, von K.H. Friauf.--Die gegenseitige Treupflicht des Bundes und der Länder auf Gebieten des Finanzwesens, von H. Görg.--Richter und Ankläger, von K.A. Hall.--Die Repräsentation des Volkes, von W. Hamel.--Die politische Betätigung des Richters, von E. W. Hanack.--Betrieb und Unternehmen in der Wirtschaftsordnung der Bundesrepublik und der Sowjetischen Besatzungszone, von K. Pleyer.--Gedanken über das Verhältnis von Universität und Demokratie,
(Continued)

SCHWINGE, ERICH, 1903- , ed. Festgabe für Heinrich Herrfahrdt zum 70. Geburtstag. (Card 3)

von R. Reinhardt.--Das Jus sanguinis der ehelichen Mutter, von W. Schätzel.--Der Wissenschaftler und die Freiheit der Meinungsäusserung, von E. Schwinge.--Zum Begriff des Schuldverhältnisses, von E. Wolf.

1. Germany--Govt., 1945- . 2. Economic history--Germany, 1945- . 3. Herrfahrdt, Heinrich, 1890-

OAC

SCIENCE, medicine and history; essays on the evolution of scientific thought and medical practice, written in honour of Charles Singer. Collected and edited by E. Ashworth Underwood. London, New York, Oxford university press, 1953. 2 v. illus., ports, map. 27cm.

Contributions chiefly in English, some in French, and one in Italian. Includes bibliographies.

"A bibliography of the published writings of Charles Singer, compiled by E. Ashworth Underwood," v. 2, p. [555]-581.

J. S. BILLINGS MEM. COLL.

1. Science—Hist. 2. Medicine—Hist. 3. Singer, Charles Joseph, 1876- . I. Underwood, Edgar Ashworth, ed.

NN**R6.54 OC, I, Ib PC, 1, 2, 3, I SL ST, 1, 3, I (Z1, LC1, X1)

OAP

Science in the university, by members of the faculties of the University of California. Berkeley and Los Angeles, University of California press, 1944.

x p., 1 l., 332 p. illus. (incl. maps) plates, tables, diagrs. (1 double) 24cm.

"Published in commemoration of the seventy-fifth anniversary of the founding of the University of California."
"References" throughout.

CONTENTS.—Driving back the dark, by R. G. Aitken.—Cosmic rays: report of recent progress, 1936-1941, by J. R. Oppenheimer.—Molecular forces and solubility, by J. H. Hildebrand.—The chemistry of the amino acids and proteins, by C. L. A. Schmidt.—The task of the organic chemist, by G. R. Robertson.—What makes the barometric pressure rise or fall? By Jakob Bjerknes.—The California current, by H. U. Sverdrup.—Evo-

(Continued on next card)

A 44-3156

[3]

Science in the university ... 1944. (Card 2)

CONTENTS—Continued.

lution of a Sierran landscape, by W. C. Putnam.—Subsidence and elevation in the Los Angeles region, by U. S. Grant.—A modern conception of living material, by O. L. Sponsler.—On some facts pertinent to the theory of the gene, by R. B. Goldschmidt.—Longevity in organisms, by C. B. Lipman.—The study of the sea and its relation to man, by C. E. ZoBell.—Trees and history, by R. W. Chaney.—Ornithology of the looking glass, by Loye Miller.—General aspects of the study of plant nutrition, by D. R. Hoagland.—Physiology as an independent science, by J. M. D. Olmsted.—The contribution of psychology, by Knight Dunlap.—Life, morals, and Huxley's "Evolution and ethics," by S. J. Holmes.

1. Science—Collected works. I. California. University.

A 44-3156

California. Univ. Libr.
for Library of Congress ⌊3⌋

OAI

Scientific papers presented to Max Born...on his retirement from the Tait chair of natural philosophy in the University of Edinburgh. With a bibliography. Edinburgh, Oliver and Boyd [1953] vi,94 p. port. 23cm.

Text in English, French or German.

Contents.—Geomagnetism and the ionosphere, by Sir E. Appleton.—A discussion of certain remarks by Einstein on Born's probability interpretation of the ψ-function, by D. Bohm.—L'interprétation de la

(Continued)

NN**R 6.54 OC PC,1,3 SL ST,2,3 (LC1,Z1,X1)

Scientific papers presented to Max Born... (Card 2)

mécanique ondulatoire à l'aide d'ondes à régions singulières, by L. de Broglie.—On the classification of partial differential equations, by R. Courant.—Elementare Überlegungen zur Interpretation der Grundlagen der Quanten-Mechanik, by A. Einstein.—Der Begriff der Wahrscheinlichkeit in der Phylogenie, by P. Jordan.—The thermal theory of constant-pressure deflagration for first-order global reactions,by T. v. Kármán and S. S. Penner.—Probability in classical

(Continued)

Scientific papers presented to Max Born... (Card 3)

and quantum theory, by A. Landé.—The general theory of relativity and wave mechanics, by E. Schrödinger.—A simple example for the legitimate passage from complex numbers to numbers of an arbitrary field, by H. Weyl.—Bibliography (p.81-94).

1. Science—Essays and misc. 2. Science—Essays and misc., 1953. 3. Born, Max, 1882- .

D-10
2605

Scripta amicorum; Sewed Sjöholm på femtioarsdagen. ⌊Redaktör: Rune Lindström; teckningar: Dagmar Lodén, Rune Lindström och Kjell Löwenadler. Falun⌋ 1954. 46 p. illus. music. 21cm.

"Tryckt i 250 numrerade ex, varav detta är nr. 150."

CONTENTS.—Den gyllene legenden om den Heliga Katarina av Alexandria, av R. Lindström.—Kring en visa, av Lille Bror Söderlundh.—De gustibus, av K. Löwenadler.—Näktergalen och nötskrikan, av G. Lodhammar.—Liten historik om det textila trycket, av P. Jobs.

1. Sjöholm, Sewed, 1904- . 2. Catharine, Saint, of Alexandria. Legend. 3. Aesthetics. 4. Textile printing—Hist. 5. Blomberg, Harry, 1893-1950. I. Lindström, Rune, 1916- , ed.
NN**R 3.58 OC(1b) PC,1,2,3,4, 5,I SL A,3,4,I (LC1,X1,Z1)

E-10
8251

SCRITTI di diritto internazionale in onore di Tomaso Perassi. Milano, A. Giuffrè, 1957. 2 v. port. 25cm.

Contributions in Italian, French, English or German.
"Pubblicazioni di Tomaso Perassi," v. 1, p.[ix]-xvi.

1. Perassi, Tomaso, 1886- . 2. Law, International--Addresses, essays, lectures.
NN R 7. 59 t/(OC(1b+) PC, 1, 2 SL E, 1, 2 (LC1, X1, Z1)

E-13
5598

Scritti in memoria di Antonino Giuffrè. Milano, Giuffrè, 1967.

4 v. plates, port. 24 cm.

Bibliographical footnotes.

CONTENTS.—1. Rievocazioni, filosofia e storia del diritto, diritto romano, storia delle idee.—2. Diritto civile, diritto commerciale, diritto comparato, diritto del lavoro, diritto agrario, diritto processuale civile.—3. Diritto amministrativo e costituzionale, diritto ecclesiastico, diritto tributario.—4. Diritto e procedura penale, diritto della navigazione, diritto internazionale, scienze economiche.

1. Law--Addresses, essays, lectures. 2. Law--Italy.
I. Giuffrè Antonio, 1902-
NN * R 6.69 c/ OC,I, Ib* PC, 1, 2, I SL E, 1, 2, I (LC1, X1, Z1)

---

*PBN

Scritti in memoria di Leone Carpi; saggi sull'ebraismo italiano, a cura di Daniel Carpi, Attilio Milano ⌊ed⌋ Alexander Rofé. Milano, Fondazione Sally Mayer, 1967.

319, 160 p. illus., facsims., port. 24 cm.

"ספר זכרון לאריה ליאונה קארפי; קובץ מחקרים לתולדות היהודים באיטליה"
(160 p. at end) has special t. p.

"Scritti di Leone Carpi": p. 29-31 (1st group)
Bibliographical footnotes.

(Continued)

NN * R 7.68 1/R OC,I PC,1,2,I SL J,1,3,I (LC1,X1,Z1)

2

SCRITTI in memoria di Leone Carpi... (Card 2)

1. Carpi, Leone, 1887-1964. 2. Jews in Italy. 3. Italy--Hist.
I. Carpi, Daniel, ed.

JFF
71-75

Scritti in memoria di W. Cesarini Sforza. Milano, A. Giuffrè, 1968.

860 p. port. 26cm.

Italian, Spanish or French.
Bibliographical footnotes.

1. Law--Philosophy--Addresses, essays, lectures. 2. Law--Addresses, essays, lectures. I. Cesarini Sforza, Widar, conte, 1886- .
NN*R 5. 71 m/z OC, I PC, 1, 2, I SL (LC1, X1, Z1)

3-MAH

Scritti in onore di Bartolomeo Nogara, raccolti in occasione del suo LXX anno. Città del Vaticano, 1937.

xiii p., 1 l., 542 p., 2 l. front. (port.) illus. (incl. facsim., plans) LXXVI pl. (incl. facsim., plan) diagrs. 32½cm.

"Pubblicazioni di Bartolomeo Nogara": p. [ix]–xiii.

CONTENTS.—Albizzati, C. Due intagli d'arte italica.—Bianchi Bandinelli, R. Un "pocolom" anepigrafe del Museo di Tarquinia.—Boëthius, A. Appunti sul carattere razionale e sull' importanza dell' architettura domestica di Roma imperiale.—Buonamici, G. La formula onomastica nell' iscrizione tarquiniese di Laris Pulenas.—Calderini, A. Nuovi documenti per lo studio del censimento romano d'Egitto.—Carcopino, J. Sur un passage d'une lettre de Cicéron.—Cecchelli, C. "Exagia" inediti con figure di tre imperatori.—Cesano, S. L. Bronzetto etrusco inedito a rovescio liscio.—Cumont, F. Mithra en Étrurie.—Curtius, L. Thalia.—Seta, A. della. Iscrizioni tirreniche di Lemno.—Sanctis, G. de. La dittatura di Caere.— Devoto, G. Il Pantheon umbro.—Ducati, P.

(Continued on next card)

A C 38–307 Revised

[r38c2]

Scritti in onore di Bartolomeo Nogara ... 1937. (Card 2)

CONTENTS—Continued.

Bucrani e festoni.—Ferri, S. Scultori peregrini a Emèrita: Demetrios.—Giglioli, G. Q. Testa fittile veiente del tempio dell' Appollo.—Guarducci, G. Velchanos—Volcanus.—Kirsch, G. P. Il transetto nella basilica cristiana antica.—Langlotz, E. Eine metope des Nemesistempels in Rhamnus.—Leopold, H. M. R. Elementi indigeni nel corredo della tomba Regolini-Galassi.—Lippold, G. Athenion.—Loewy, E. Tazza vulcente del Museo Gregoriano.—Mâle, É. La mosaïque de l'église de S. Stefano Rotondo, à Rome.—Mercati, ~~Card.~~ G. Una visita a Cilli del 1487.—Mercklin, E. von. Etruskischer bronzelöwe in der Ermitage.—Messerschmidt, F. Tomba Querciola I bei Tarquinia.—Minto, A. Le stele arcaiche volterrane.—Muñoz, A. Francesco Borromini nei lavori della Fabbrica di San Pietro (con documenti inediti)—Neuge-

(Continued on next card)

A C 38–307

[2]

Scritti in onore di Bartolomeo Nogara ... 1937. (Card 3)

CONTENTS—Continued.

bauer, K. A. Perseus, Gorgo und Apollon.—Pace, B. Elementi di tecnica indigena nella fortificazione greca dell' Eurialo.—Pallottino, M. Nomi etruschi di città.—Paribeni, R. Figurina italica di bronzo.—Pernier, L. Statuetta di Ercole da Sinalunga.—Piganiol, A. Le papyrus de Servius Tullius.—Richter, G. M. A. Perspective, ancient, mediaeval and renaissance.—Rodenwaldt, G. Zum sarkophag der Helena.—Romanelli, P. Cippo vulcente già della collezione Guglielmi ed ora nel Museo nazionale tarquiniense.—Rumpf, A. Ein fragment im Museo Chiaramonti.—Säflund, G. Unveröffentlichte antike steinmetzzeichen und monogramme aus Unteritalien und Sizilien mit besonderer berücksichtigung der stadtmauer von Tyndaris.—Serafini, C. Saggio intorno alle monete e medaglioni antichi ritrovati nelle catacombe di Panfilo sulla

(Continued on next card)

A C 38–307

[2]

Scritti in onore di Bartolomeo Nogara ... 1937. (Card 4)

CONTENTS—Continued.

via Salaria Vetus in Roma.—Silvagni, A. Intorno alle due sillogi medievali di iscrizioni cristiane milanesi.—Sittig, E. Germanenspuren auf etruskischen inschriften.—Strong, E. Sulle tracce della lupa romana (progetto di studio)—Toesca, P. Dell' urnetta argentea di S. Nazaro a Milano.—Van Buren, A. W. Saggi critici su testi letterari a contenuto archeologico.—Wilpert, G. Le pitture della "confessio" sotto la basilica dei Ss. Giovanni e Paolo.

1. Nogara, Bartolomeo, 1868– 2. Art, Greco-Roman—Addresses, essays, lectures. 3. Classical antiquities—Addresses, essays, lectures.

A C 38–307

Columbia univ. Library
for Library of Congress

[2]

Copy only words underlined
& classmark— TAA

SCRITTI in onore di Camillo de Franceschi. [Trieste] Università di Trieste, 1951. 329 p. port. 25cm.
(Trieste. (City). Università. Annali. v. 21, sez. 1, suppl.)

"Vol. 1º del Centro studi per la storia del risorgimento."

CONTENTS.—Camillo de Franceschi, di A. Gentile.—Bibliografia degli scritti a stampa di Camillo de Franceschi (a cura di A. Gentile).—Camillo de Franceschi storico dell' Istria, di G. Rossi Sabatini.—Intorno alla cultura classica nella Trieste dell' ottocento, di P. Tremoli.—L'interpretazione del medioevo nella storiografia triestina dell

(Continued)

NN R X 5.54 OC, 1b OI PC, 1 (LC2, ~~X1~~, X1) [I]

SCRITTI in onore di Camillo de Franceschi. (Card 2)

ottocento, di G. Rossi Sabatini.—Intorno al cosmopolitismo triestino: le memorie di Giovanni Guglielmo Sartorio, di G. Cervani.—L'unità ed il problema adriatico (1911-1920), di E. Apih.—Una protesta della Borsa mercantile di Trieste (1789), di E. Apih.—Intorno ad alcuni riflessi del problema triestino nella letteratura e nella pubblicistica tedesca locale del primo '900, di I. Laurenti Cervani.—I pittore Giuseppe Gatteri padre e Lorenzo Scarabelotto, di L. Amodeo.

1. Franceschi, Camillo de, 1868-

SLE

Scritti in onore di Enrico Ferri per il cinquantesimo anno di suo insegnamento universitario, R. Università di Roma, 1879–1929. Torino: Unione tipografico-editrice torinese, 1929. 526 p. incl. tables. diagrs., port. 4°.

Articles by Enrico Altavilla, Gustav Aschaffenburg, Agostino Berenini and others. Bibliographical footnotes.

460707A. 1. Ferri, Enrico, 1856– 1929. 2. Criminology. 3. Criminal law.
N. Y. P. L. March 31, 1930

SLE

Scritti in onore del prof. Ugo Conti per il trentesimo anno di ordinariato, 1902–1932. Città di Castello, Tipografia dell' "Unione arti grafiche", 1932.

420 p. port. 25cm.

CONTENTS.—Comitato per le onoranze.—Elenco degli aderenti.—Lettere di adesione.—Sabatini, G. Ugo Conti.—Amelio, M. d.' Piazza san Pietro e la legge penale.—Cuboni, G. Della cittadinanza italiana secondo il Cod. pen.—Semo, G. de. Rapporti giuridici collettivi nel diritto corporativo italiano.—Neymark, E. Influence du chômage sur la criminalité.—Sabatini, G. Il reato progressivo nel sistema delle deroghe al concorso di reati.—Sensini, G. Intorno al cosi' detto "libero arbitrio."—Tejera, D. Los robos en que la victima entrega lo deseado por el delincuente.—Rappaport, E. S. "Delicta juris gentium" nella nuova legislazione criminale

(Continued on next card)

36–3889

[2]

Scritti in onore del prof. Ugo Conti ... 1932. (Card 2)

CONTENTS—Continued.

polacca.—Vieites, M. A. El adulterio ya no constituye delito en Cuba.—Pozzolini, A. Talune chiose non inutili in tema d'imputabilità penale.—Fornasari di Verce, E. Sui rapporti di frequenza della criminalità.—Brugi, B. L'opera degli antichi giureconsulti italiani e il diritto penale.—Cassinelli, B. Sulla definizione giuridica della falsa iscrizione come legittimo di un figlio naturale.—Carnevale, E. I fattori sociali della lotta contro il delitto.—Palazzo, G. A. L'appello incidentale del pubblico ministero.—Rende, D. Intorno al delitto di omicidio preterintenzionale (art. 584 e 586 C. p.).—Penso, G. Il concetto del "consenso" nel nuovo Codice penale (art. 50 e 579).—Saldana, Q. Les limites du pragmatisme pénale.—Heller, E. Le misure di sicurezza in sostituzione o complemento delle pene.—Santoro, A. Il concetto delle circostanze di reato.—Maggiore, G. Il risarcimento dei danni non patrimoniali e la pretesa forza espansiva dell' articolo 185 Codice penale.—Longhi, S. Solidarietà

(Continued on next card)

36–3889

[2]

Scritti in onore del prof. Ugo Conti ... 1932. (Card 3)

CONTENTS—Continued.

antiterroristica.—Carton de Wiart, H. Le travail en commun pour l'unification du droit pénal.—Zanobini, G. Pubblici ufficiali e incaricati di servizi pubblici nel nuovo Codice penale.—Carlo, E. di. Un teorico della ragion di stato: Scipione di Castro.—Thót, L. Sulla scienza di diritto penale orientale.—Marciano, G. Colpa con previsione e dolo eventuale.—Mocci, M. "Cittadino" e "straniero" dinanzi alla "legge penale" dello stato-nazione.—Angioni, M. Il problema della causalità materiale (art. 40 e 41 Cod. pen.).—Albini, G. Quaesitor Minos.—Stella Maranca, F. Intorno al fr. 7 pr. Dig. "De bonis damnat." (48, 20).—Rubeis, R. de. Lo agente provocatore nella partecipazione al reato secondo il novello Codice penale.

1. Conti, Ugo, conte. 1864– 2. Law—Collections. 3. Law—Italy—Collections. 4. Criminal law—Collections.

36–3889

Library of Congress [2] 347.04

*IC

Scritti di paleografia e diplomatica in onore di Vincenzo Federici. Firenze, L. S. Olschki, 1944. x, 381 p. illus., 34 pl. 26cm.

Contributions in Italian, German or Latin.
Bibliographical footnotes.

Festschrift

424329B. 1. Paleography, Italian. 2. Federici, Vincenzo, 1871– .
N. Y. P. L. October 28, 1949

MA

SCRITTI di storia dell'arte in onore di Mario Salmi. Roma, De Luca, 1961-63. 3 v. illus., port. 27cm.

Vol. 1 edited by V. Martinelli; v. 2-3, by Filippa M. Aliberti.
Papers in Italian, French, English, or German.

1. Salmi, Mario, 1889- . 2. Art--Essays and misc. I. Martinelli, Valentino, ed. II. Aliberti, Filippa M., ed. III. Aliberti, Filippa M.
NN R 2.64 f/b OC, I, II, IIIbo PC, 1, 2, I, II SL A, 1, 2, I, II (LC1, X1, Z1)
[I]

L-11
801
v.19

Scritti per il XL ⌊i. e. quarantesimo⌋ della morte di P. E. Bensa. Milano, A. Giuffrè, 1969. 276 p. port., plate. 25cm. (Genoa (City). Università. Giurisprudenza, Facoltà di. Collana degli annali. 19)

Includes bibliographical references.

CONTENTS.—La figura e l'opera di P. E. Bensa: Ricordi biografici, di P. E. Bensa, di G. B. Cereseto.—P. E. Bensa scrittore e maestro, di R. Luzzato.—In memoria di P. E. Bensa, di G. Del Vecchio.—

(Continued)

NN* 8.71 w/b OC, II, IIb* (OS)I PC, 1, 2, I, II E, 1, 2, II (LC1, X1, Z1) 3.

BWD

Scritti storici in onore di Camillo Manfroni nel XL anno di insegnamento. Padova: A. Draghi, 1925. xxvi, 456 p., front. (port.), plates. 4°.

List of author's works, p. ⌊xi⌋-⌊xviii.
Bibliographical footnotes.

1. Manfroni, Camillo, 1863– . 2. Manfroni, Camillo, 1863– —Bibl.
N. Y. P. L. February 23, 1927

SCRITTI per il XL [i. e. quarantesimo] della morte di P. E. Bensa. (Card 2)

Università di ieri, di C. Cereti.—Professori e maestri (nel ricordo di P. E. Bensa), di A. Piola.—L'omaggio scientifico: Azione civile e processo penale (prospettive de iure condendo), di V. Andrioli.—Crisi delle istituzioni e pianificazione, di L. Bagolini.—Due citazioni del Codex Iustinianus nella Historia tripartita di Cassiodoro, di F. De Marini Avonzo.—I protecting and indemnity clubs, di S. Ferrarini.—Un errore pendolare: l'accusatore giudice e il giudice accusatore, di G. Foschini.—Prefazione ad un corso di diritto romano sulle servitù prediali, di G. Grosso.—Postille e repliche critiche sull'onus probandi, di G. Longo.—Note intorno all'art. 544 del Code civil, di S. Rodotà.—Società di persone tra società di capitali, di S. Satta.—Un caso di obbligazioni naturali nel diritto civile italiano

(Continued)

F-10
5133

SCRITTI vari dedicati a Marino Parenti per il suo sessantesimo anniversario [a cura di Giovanni Semerano] Firenze, Sansoni, 1960. 272 p. illus., ports. 26cm. (Biblioteca bibliografica italica. Contributi alla Biblioteca bibliografica italica. 23)

"Bibliographia di Marino Parenti," p. [261]-267.

1. Parenti, Marino, 1900- . I. Series. II. Semerano, Giovanni, ed. III. Semerano, Giovanni.
NN X 5.61 s/P OC, II, IIIbo (OS)I PC, 1, I, II SL (LC1, X1, Z1)
[I]

SCRITTI per il XL [i. e. quarantesimo] della morte di P. E. Bensa. (Card 3)

(art. 770 comma 2° cod. civ. e art. 64 l. fall.), di G. Scherillo.—La Scuola dell'esegesi e la sua diffusione in Italia, di G. Tarello.

1. Law--Italy. 2. Law--Addresses, essays, lectures. I. Series. II. Bensa, Paolo Emilio, 1858- 1928.

SLL

Searchlights on delinquency; new psychoanalytic studies dedicated to Professor August Aichhorn on the occasion of his seventieth birthday, July 27, 1948. Managing editor: K. R. Eissler; chairman of the editorial board: Paul Federn. New York, International Universities Press ⌊1949⌋

xiii, 456 p. port. 24 cm.

Includes "References." "Bibliography of August Aichhorn's writings": p. 455–456.

1. Psychoanalysis. 2. Crime and criminals. 3. Aichhorn, August, 1878– I. Eissler, Kurt R., 1908– ed.

BF173.A575 132.6 49-7622*
Festschrift cd
Library of Congress ⌊15⌋

C-12
6738

SCRITTI in ricordo di Vincenzo Capruzzi (30, VII, 1895- 3, V, 1958) a cura di Nino Ruppi. Bari, Grafiche Cressalti, 1959. 93 p. port. 20cm.

CONTENTS:--La morte, di M. Viterbo. --L'uomo vivo, di N. Ruppi. --Il poeta, di P. Cafaro. --L'autore di teatro, di G. Luongo. --Il pubblicista di C. Savonarola. --Il letterato, di G. Savelli. --L'uomo di pensiero, di E. Pappacena. --Il critico, di C. Turi. --L'avvocato, di C. Russo-Frattasi. --Aspetti di vita, di S. La Sorsa.

1. Capruzzi, Vincenzo. I. Ruppi, Nino , ed.
NN R 5.65 1/s OC, I PC, 1, I SL (LC1, X1, Z1)

---

*M

. . . Seashore commemorative number ⌊of the⌋ University of Iowa studies in psychology no. 12; edited by Walter R. Miles and Daniel Starch . . . Princeton, N. J. ⌊etc.⌋ Published for the Amer. psychological assoc. by Psychological review co. ⌊1928⌋ 223 p. illus. (incl. charts, music), 2 pl., port. 24½cm. (Psychological monographs. v. 39, no. 2.)

At head of title: . . . Psychological review publications . . .
References at end of most of the chapters.
CONTENTS.—Carl Emil Seashore.—A complete annotated bibliography of the writings of Carl Emil Seashore, by J. E. Bathurst and R. D. Sinclair.—Ten volumes of Iowa

(Continued)

N. Y. P. L. July 10, 1949

... **Seashore** commemorative number... (Card 2)

studies in psychology; reviewed by M. C. W. Kemmerer.—A comparative study of the performances of stutterers and normal speakers in mirror tracing, by L. E. Travis.—Stanford motor skills unit, by R. H. Seashore.—The sense of direction in mental imagery, by C. I. Erickson.—The Iowa State college reasoning test, by T. F. Vance.—Vestibular sensitivity to intermittent passive rotation of the body, by R. C. Travis.—Iowa placement examinations; a new departure in mental measurement, by G. D. Stoddard.—Seashore's plan of sectioning on the basis of ability as a motivation device, by H. J. Arnold.—Successful teaching, by R. W. Tallman.—Some aspects to be considered in the organization of a first course in psychology, by A. R. Lauer.—The determination of a general factor in research ability of college students, by F. O. Smith.—What is the voice vibrato? by Milton Metfessel.—Seashore measures of musical talent, by H. M. Stanton.—

(Continued)

N. Y. P. L. July 10, 1940

... **Seashore** commemorative number... (Card 3)

Five studies of the music tests, by E. A. Gaw.—Correlation between intelligence and musical talent among university students, by G. C. Fracker and V. M. Howard.—The aesthetic attitude in music, by Max Schoen.—A measure of art talent, by N. C. Meier.—The first vocal vibrations in the attack in singing, by F. A. Stevens and W. R. Miles.

YEA
(Psychological)
——— ——— Second copy.

1. Seashore, Carl Emil, 1866– 2. Seashore, Carl Emil, 1866– —Bibl. 3. Singing. 4. Musical ability—Testing. 5. Psychology, Physiological. 6. Education—Psychology. I. Miles, Walter Richard, 1885– ed. II. Starch, Daniel, 1883– , ed. III. Ser. IV. Ser.: Iowa.

N. Y. P. L. July 10, 1940

TB

SECONDS mélanges d'économie politique et sociale offerts à Edgard Milhaud. Thème: L'économie collective. Liège, Éditions du C.I.R.I.E.C., 1960. 300 p. illus., port. 21cm.

An edition in German was published under title Festschrift Edgard Milhaud. Ökonomische und sozialpolitische Themen zur Gemeinwirtschaft.

Works of Milhaud: p. [49]-53. Includes bibliographical references.

CONTENTS:-- Esquisse d'un portrait et d'un hommage, par C.-H. Barbier.--Aspects de la vie et de l'oeuvre d'Edgard Milhaud, par

(Continued)

NN * 7.63 f/ OC PC, 1, 2 SL E, 1, 2 (LC1, X1, Z1) 3

SECONDS mélanges d'économie politique et sociale offerts à Edgard Milhaud. (Card 2)

A. Baeyens.--Hommage au Professeur Edgard Milhaud, initiateur de la section autrichienne du C.I.R.I.E.C., par K. Pröbsting.--Le sous-développement. La nation en voie de se faire et les moyens de l'economie collective, par F. Perroux. -- Politique économique des petites unités, par G. Weisser. -- L'idéal commumautaire: quelques réinterprétations, par W.H.G. Armytage.--Les nationalisations et l'Etat en France, par P. Ramadier.--Relations entre plans économiques et plans scientifiques, par

(Continued)

SECONDS mélanges d'économie politique et sociale offerts à Edgard Milhaud. (Card 3)

A. Angelopoulos.--Le mot et la doctrine dans le développement de la pensée économique, par J. Weiller.-- Réflexions sur le statut des organismes parastataux et des entreprises publiques en Belgique, par A. Buttgenbach.-- Les postulats de la "nouvelle économie du bien-être" en relation avec la vente au coût marginal dans les entreprises d'utilité publique, par G. Stefani.--Structure et importance de l'economie collective en Suisse, par A. Rieder.--Explications sur la doctrine coopérative, par P. Lambert.

1. Economics--Essays and misc. 2. Milhaud, Edgard, 1873- .

D-18
5959

Security and reduced tension. On the occasion of the 70th birthday of General <ret.> Adolf Heusinger. (Translated by Barry Jones). (Köln, Markus) 1967.

79 p. front. 23 cm.

CONTENTS.—Adolf Heusinger, soldier in the "contradiction" of history, by H. Herzfeld.—The chief of the operations section, by P. Young.—The first inspector-general of the Bundeswehr, by U. de Maizière.—In the service to the cause of peace and security, by L. Norstad.—In the international field.—A fruitful exchange of views, by

(Continued)

NN*R 2.69 v/ OC PC, 1 SL (LC1, X1) (Z1) 2

SECURITY and reduced tension. (Card 2)

A. Beaufre.—Security and reduced tension, by A. Heusinger.—Orders in contradiction, by R. Pirk.

1. Heusinger, Adolf, 1897-

AN
(Handel-Mazzetti, E.)

Seibertz, Paul, 1877– , editor.

Enrica von Handel-Mazzettis Persönlichkeit, Werk und Bedeutung, gemeinsam mit Adolf Buder, Anton Dörrer... bearbeitet und herausgegeben von Paul Siebertz. München: J. Kösel & F. Pustet[, cop. 1930]. front., illus. (incl. facsims, ports.) 8°.

567552A. 1. Handel-Mazzetti, Enrica Ludovica Maria, Freiin von, 1871– . I. Buder, Adolf. II. Doerrer, Anton, 1887– .

N. Y. P. L. March 16, 1932

E-11
8881

SEIDENFUS, HELLMUTH STEFAN, ed.

Beiträge zur Verkehrstheorie und Verkehrspolitik; [Festgabe für Paul Berkenkopf zur Vollendung seines 70. Lebensjahres am 17. September 1961, dargebracht von Kollegen und Schülern] Düsseldorf, Verlag Handelsblatt, 1961. 181 p. port. 25cm.

Bibliographical footnotes.

CONTENTS. — Pragmatische Verkehrspolitik und Liberalisierungstendenzen

(Continued)

NN R 2.64 g/B OC PC,1,2,I SL E,1,2,I (LC1,X1,Z1) 3

SEIDENFUS, HELLMUTH STEFAN, ed. Beiträge zur Verkehrstheorie und Verkehrspolitik... (Card 2)

in der Verkehrswitschaft, von A. Predöhl. —Möglichkeiten einer marktwirtschaftlichen Ordnung des Verkehrs, von H.-R. Meyer. — Staatsplanung und Marktwirtschaft, von E. Welter. —Verkehrspreise und ihre Veröffentlichung im Rahmen des Grenzkostenprinzips, von A. Löw. — Betrachtungen zur Entwicklung der Eisenbahn in Mitteldeutschland, von E. Frohne. — Der Bau der Jauntalbahn—Verkehrsgestaltung in einem österreichischen Grenzlande, von M. Schantl. — Zur Frage der Wirtschaftlichkeit des Strassenausbaues, von P. Koessler. —Kurzstrecken-luftverkehr in Europa — Stand

(Continued)

SEIDENFUS, HELLMUTH STEFAN, ed. Beiträge zur Verkehrstheorie und Verkehrspolitik... (Card 3)

und Entwicklungsaussichten, von V. Porger. —Der europäische Personenluftverkehr und seine Knotenpunkte, von E.-A. Eversmeyer. — Gedanken zur Stellung der deutschen Seehäfen in der Europäischen Wirtschaftsgemeinschaft, von L. Jolmes. — "Social Costs" in der Verkehrswirtschaft, von H. St. Seidenfus. —Notwendigkeit und Aufgaben einer Betriebswirtschaftslehre der Verkehrsbetriebe, von W. Böttger. — Zur Philosophie des Verkehrs, von F. Niessen.

1. Transportation--Social and economic relations. 2. Berkenkopf, Paul. I. Title.

NITC

Selskab for nordisk Filologi.

Fra Rask til Wimmer; otte Foredrag om Modersmaalsforskere i det 19. Aarhundrede, udgivne af Selskab for nordisk Filologi. København: Gyldendal, 1937. 146 p. illus. (ports.) 24½cm.

"Selskabets 25-aars Dag [feijres] med Udsendelse av dette Skrift." — *Forord.*
"Kronologisk Oversigt over de i Foredragene nævnte sprogvidenskabelige Arbejder," p. [135]–141.
CONTENTS.—Forord, af Paul Diderichsen.—Rasmus Rask, af Poul Andersen.—Christian Molbech og Jakob Hornemann Bredsdorff, af Jørgen Glahder.—Israel Levin, af Aage Hansen.—Folmer Dyrlund, af Kristen Møller.—Edwin Jessen, af Viggo Brøndal.—K. J. Lyngby, af Anders Bjerrum.—Ludvig F. A. Wimmer, af Johs. Brøndum-Nielsen.—P. K. Thorsen og hans Samtid, af Marius Kristensen.

957500A. 1. Danish language—Hist. 2. Philologists—Denmark. I. Diderichsen, Paul, ed. II. Title.
N. Y. P. L. September 20, 1938

GHX

SEKSTEN Århusrids. Tilegnede Svend Unmack Larsen, 23. september 1953. Aarhus, Universitetsforlaget, 1953. 360 p. illus., ports., maps. 27cm.

Includes bibliographies.
CONTENTS. —Af den jydske operas forhistorie, af G. Albeck. — Højene på Vorbjerg banke, af H. Andersen. —Sønderjyder i Århus gennem 250 år, af Å. Bonde. —Et bytingsvidne, af J. Clausen. —M.P. Bruun-politikeren bag gadenavnet, af V. Dybdahl. —Omkring møller A. S. Weis og hans hustru, af K. Elkjær. —Socialdemokratiet og den kommunale lønpolitik 1900 til verdenskrigens slutning, af
(Continued)

NN** X 9.54 OC (2b) PC,1,2 SL (Z1, LC1, X1)
[I]

NPV

Semana de Bello, Caracas, 1951.

Primer libro de la Semana de Bello en Caracas, 25 de noviembre—1º de diciembre de 1951. Caracas, Ediciones del Ministerio de educación, Dirección de cultura y bellas artes, 1952. xvii,371 p. illus., ports., facsims. (Biblioteca venezolana de cultura; colección "Andres Bello")

Partial Contents.—Premio nacional "Andres Bello."—Conferencias y discursos.—Articulos publicados con ocasión de la "Semana de Bello."—Catalogo de la
(Continued)

NN** 5.54 (OD)I (ED)I OSs PCs,1s,I SLs AH,1,I (U 1,LC1s,Z1s,X1s)

SEKSTEN Århusrids. (Card 2)

A. Jørgensen. —Købmand i Århus Abraham Lewis, af F. H. Lauridsen. — Ole Rømers triduum i det 18. århundredes astronomi, af A. V. Nielsen. — Dialekt, jargon og vulgærsprog i Århus, af N. Å. Nielsen. —Lektor Sveinbjørn Sveinbjørnsson, af O. Olesen. —Fr. Sneedorff-Birch, en digters tragedie, af E. Sejr. —Å-ets historie, af P. Skautrup. —Bidrag til urmageriets historie i Århus, af H. Søgaard. —Jydsk natur gennem sidste halvsekel, af H. M. Thamdrup. —Musikpioneren Arthur Allin, af E. Winkel.

1. Aarhus, Denmark. 2. Larsen, Svend Unmack, 1893-

Semana de Bello, Caracas, 1951. Primer libro de la Semana de Bello en Caracas... (Card 2)

exposición bibliográfica e iconográfica de Bello. "Referencias bio-bibliográficas de los autores," p. [359]-366.

1. Bello, Andrés, 1781-1865. I. Series.

---

*PBS

Sellin-Festschrift. Beiträge zur Religionsgeschichte und Archäologie Palästinas. Ernst Sellin zum 60. Geburtstage dargebracht ... Leipzig: A. Deichert, 1927. 156 p. front. (port.) 8°.

Bibliographical footnotes.
Contents: ALBRIGHT, W. F. Egypt and Palestine in the Third Millennium B.C. ALT, A. Das System der Stammesgrenzen im Buche Josua. CASPARI, W. Textkritische Beleuchtung eines Ausgangspunktes der Auseinandersetzungen über das Deuteronomium. DÜRR, L. Zur Frage nach der Einheit von Ps. 19. GALLING, K. Der Bautypus des Palasttores im Alten Testament und das Palasttor von Sichem. GRESSMANN, H. Der Festbecher. HEHN, J. יצר "bilden," "formen" im Alten Testa-

(Continued)

360431A Mr. Math.
N. Y. P. L. April 12, 1928

F-10
7326

SENCKENBERGISCHE NATURFORSCHENDE GESELLSCHAFT, Frankfurt am Main.

Festschrift zur Erinnerung an die Eröffnung des neuerbauten Museums der Senckenbergischen naturforschenden Gesellschaft zu Frankfurt am Main am 13. Oktober 1907. Frankfurt a. M., Druck von Gebr. Knauer, 1907. 75 p. 12 plates. 27cm.

Contributions by various authors.

1.Natural history--Germany--Frankfurt am Main. Museums and collections

NN R 1.63 c/ OS PC,1 SL (LC1, X1, Z1)

Sellin-Festschrift. Beiträge zur Religionsgeschichte und Archäologie Palästinas... (Continued)

ment. HERRMANN, J. Das zehnte Gebot. JIRKU, A. Zur Götterwelt Palästinas und Syriens. KITTEL, R. Die Religion der Achämeniden. PRASCHNIKER, C. Bronzenes Köpfchen im Landesmuseum zu Klagenfurt. SACHSSE, E. 'Ānī als Ehrenbezeichnung in inschriftlicher Beleuchtung. SCHMIDT, H. Hosea 6, 1–6. SEEBERG, E. Zum Problem der pneumatischen Exegese. STAERK, W. Noch einmal das Problem Deuteronomiums. STEUERNAGEL, C. Zum Verständnis von Ps. 51.

1. Bible, O. T.—Essays and misc. 2. Palestine—Archaeology. 3. Sellin, Ernst Fr. M., 1867–
N. Y. P. L. April 12, 1928

D-20
7420

Sense and sensibility in twentieth-century writing; a gathering in memory of William Van O'Connor. Edited by Brom Weber. With a pref. by Harry T. Moore. Carbondale, Southern Illinois University Press [1970]

xvi, 174 p. 22 cm. (Crosscurrents/modern critiques)
Includes bibliographical references.

(Continued)

NN*R 7.71 e/ OC, I, II PC, 1, 2, 3, I, II SL (LC1, X1, Z1)
3.

SENSE and sensibility in twentieth-century writing...
(Card 2)

CONTENTS.—The state and future of criticism: The continuing need for criticism, by M. Krieger. The double truth of modern poetic criticism, by E. Miner.—Writers of Europe and Africa: John Fowles's The magus, by M. Bradbury. An African tragedy of hubris; Thomas Mofolo's Chaka, by A. Gérard. Demonic strategies; The birthday party, and The firebugs, by R. B. Heilman.—American writers: The upward path; notes on the work of Katherine Anne Porter, by H. Baker.. The way to read Gatsby, by R. Foster. Mark Twain among

(Continued)

SENSE and sensibility in twentieth-century writing...
(Card 3)

the malefactors, by L. Leary. The Pisan cantos, the form of survival, by W. Sutton.—Poetry and fiction, materials for criticism: How distant, by P. Larkin. Indomitable city, London 1943–1946, by V. d. S. Pinto. Cockfight in Milo, by K. Shapiro. On the heights of grief, That old new year, and, Who'll be like you? By L. Unger. Bad year, bad war; New Year's card, by R. P. Warren. A centenary ode inscribed to Little Crow, leader of the Sioux rebellion in Minnesota, Northern pike, A way to make a living, and, A summer memory in the crowded city, by J. Wright.

1. Literature--Hist. and crit., 20th cent. 2. Literature, American--Collections. 3. Literature, English--Collections. I. O'Connor, William Van, 1915-1966. II. Weber, Brom, 1917- , ed.

SENZ, JOSEF, ed.
Festschrift für Friedrich Lotz. München, Verlag des Südostdeutschen Kulturwerks München, 1962.
122 p. port., facsims. 24cm. (Südostdeutsches Kulturwerk. Arbeitsgemeinschaft Donauschwäbischer Lehrer. Schriftenreihe. Bd. 2)

Includes bibliographical references.

1. Lotz, Friedrich, 1890- . 2. Germans in Europe, Eastern.

SERAPHIM, HANS JÜRGEN, 1899- , ed.
Studien zu Wohnungswirtschaft und Städtebau; Gedachtnisschrift fur Otto Kamper. [Bearb. von Jurgen Heuer] Koln-Braunsfeld, R. Muller, 1963. 232 p. port. 25cm.

Bibliography, p. 220-225.

CONTENTS. --Zum Geleit, von J. Fischer-Dieskau. --Difficile est satiram non scribere! Von O. Kämper. --Wohnungsbaufinanzierung,
(Continued)

 3

SERAPHIM, HANS JÜRGEN, 1899- , ed. Studien zu Wohnungswirtschaft und Städtebau... (Card 2)

Ideologie oder Utopie? Von O. v. Nell-Breuning. --Abbau oder Umbau der Subventionierung im Wohnungsbau, von H. Jaschinski. --Der volks- und betriebswirtschaftliche Problematik der Abschreibung bei Wohnungsunternehmen, von K. Schneider. --Ausländische Bodenkreditsysteme, von L. Kühne-Büning. --Zur Finanzierung des städtebaulichen Sanierung in England, von H. J. Seraphim und J. Heuer. --Die Finanzierung künftieger Sanierungsmassnahmen im Städtebau, von N. Cremer.
(Continued)

SERAPHIM, HANS JÜRGEN, 1899- , ed. Studien zu Wohnungswirtschaft und Städtebau...(Card 3)

1. Cities--Plans--Addresses, essays, lectures. 2. Housing--Addresses, essays, lectures. I. Heuer, Jürgen, joint ed. II. Heuer, Jürgen.

SERTA monacensia Franz Babinger zum 15. Januar 1951 als Festgruss dargebracht. Hrsg. von Hans Joachim Kissling und Alois Schmaus. Leiden, E. J. Brill, 1952. 244 p. port., facsims. 25cm.

Bibliographical footnotes.

CONTENTS. -- Schriftenverzeichnis Franz Babinger. -- Philanthropenos. Das Belisar-Leid der Palaiologenzeit, von H. G. Beck. -- Altkirchenslavisch praprodb "Purpur," von P. Diels. -- Der
(Continued)

SERTA monacensia Franz Babinger zum 15. Januar 1951... (Card 2)

Vertrag des Sultans Qalā'ūn von Ägypten mit dem Kaiser Michael VIII. Palaiologos," von F. Dölger. -- Zur orientalischen Namenkunde: Maria, Moses, Aaron von I. Hösl. -- Šaʿban Veli und die Šaʿbānijje, von H. J. Kissling. -- Zur Aussprache des Türkischen, von E. Koschmieder. -- Über Krankheitsdämonen im Volksglauben der Balkanslaven, von W. Lettenbauer. — Abdülhak Şinasi Hisar's "Vollmondnächte am
(Continued)

SERTA monacensia Franz Babinger zum 15. Januar 1951... (Card 3)
Bosporus," von F. von Rummel. -- Beiträge zur südslavischen Epenforschung, von A. Schmaus. -- Mā rā'ahū illā biund Verwandtes, von A. Spitaler. — Die Visitationsreise des Erzbischofs Marino Bizzi, von G. Stadtmüller. -- Die Bücherei des Orientalisten Johann Albrecht Widmanstetter, von H. Striedl.

1. Babinger, Franz Carl Heinrich, 1891- 2. Philology--Addresses, essays, lectures. 3. Oriental studies--Collections. 4. Slavonic studies --Collections. I. Kissling, Hans Joachim, ed. II. Schmaus, Alois, ed. III. Kissling, Hans Joachim. IV. Schmaus, Alois.

SERTA Eusebiana; miscellanea philologica. [Genova] Istituto di filologia classica, 1958.
124 p. illus., port. 28cm. (Genoa (City). Università. Istituto di filologia classica. Pubblicazioni. 11)

1. Eusebio, Federico, 1852-1913. 2. Osco-Umbrian dialects. 3. Xenophon. Apologia Socratis. 4. Papyri--Collections--Italy--Genoa. I. Series.

*QT

ŠESTÁK, ANTONÍN, ed.
Sborník prací věnovany památce profesora dra P.M. Haškovce. Pořádali Ant. Šesták a Ant. Dokoupil. [Brno] Kroužek brněnských romanistů při Jednotě českých filologů, odbočka v Brně [1936]
411 p. port. 25cm.

At head of title: Melanges P.M. Haškovec.
Added t.p. in French.
Contributions in Czech, French, German, Italian, or Russian.
(Continued)

NN 1.65 c/ OC(1b)I, IIbo PC, 1, 2, 3, I SL S, 1, 2, 3, I
(LC1, X1, Z1)

2

SETTLEMENT & encounter; geographical studies presented to Sir Grenfell Price... (Card 2)

CONTENTS.—Sir Grenfell Price: an appreciation, by A. Marshall.—The spread of settlement in South Australia, by M. Williams.—Climate and man in Northwestern Queensland, by F. H. Bauer.—A changing Aboriginal population, by F. Gale.—Apartheid: background, problems and prospects, by R. K. Hefford.—Problems of vegetation change in western Viti Levu, Fiji, by G. R. Cochrane.—Jet age medical geography, by B. Maegraith.—Some non-nutritive functions of food in New Guinea, by D. Lea.—Australia

(Continued)

ŠESTÁK, ANTONÍN, ed. Sborník prací věnovany památce profesora dra P.M. Haškovce. (Card 2)

"Al Liška: Bibliografický soupis literární činnosti profesora P.M. Haškovce," p. 347-407.
Bibliographical footnotes.

1. French literature--Addresses, essays, lectures. 2. French language--Addresses, essays, lectures. 3. Haškovec, Miroslav Prokop, 1876-1935. I. Dokoupil, Ant., joint ed. II. Dokoupil, Ant.

SETTLEMENT & encounter; geographical studies presented to Sir Grenfell Price... (Card 3)

in New Guinea; none so blind, by D. Howlett.—A macrogeography of Western imperialism: some morphologies of moving frontiers of political control, by D. W. Meinig.—A bibliography of the work of Sir Grenfell Price.

1. Geography--Addresses, essays, lectures. I. Price, Sir Archibald Grenfell, 1892- . II. Gale, Fay, ed. III. Lawton, Graham Henry, ed. IV. Lawton, Graham Henry.

Copy only words underlined
& classmark-- RRA

SETALA, EMIL NESTOR, 1864-1935.
Memoria saecularis E.N. Setälä, 27.II. 1964. Helsinki, Suomalais-ugrilainen seura, 1964. 1 v. (various pagings) port. 26cm. (Suomalais-ugrilainen seura, Helsingfors. Suomalais-ugrilaisen seuran toimituksia, 135)

Text in Finnish, French or German.
CONTENTS.--P. Ravila: E.N. Setälä kielentutkijana (Les travaux linguistiques d'E.N. Setälä).-- S. Haltsonen: L'oeuvre
(Continued)

NN 1.65 e/ OC, II, III (OS)I PC, 1, 2, 3, 4, I, II, III (LC1, X1, Z1)

NCB

The seventeenth century; studies in the history of English thought and literature from Bacon to Pope, by Richard Foster Jones and others writing in his honor. Stanford, Calif., Stanford univ. press [1951] viii, 392 p. illus. 24cm.

"Essays by Richard Foster Jones," p. 10-160; "A bibliography of the published writings of Richard Foster Jones," p. 161-164.
Bibliographical footnotes.

1. English literature—Hist. and crit., 17th cent. I. Jones, Richard Foster, 1886- .
N. Y. P. L. February 28, 1952

SETALA, EMIL NESTOR, 1864-1935. Memoria saecularis E.N. Setälä, 27.II. 1964. (Card 2)

d'E.N. Setälä.--E.N. Setälä: Valittuja tutkielmia (Etudes choisies).--E.N. Setälän vatjalaismuistiinpanot (Les notes d'E.N. Setälä sur la langue vote).--E.N. Setälän kirjeitä Antti Jalavalle vuosilta 1888-1889 (Lettres écrites par E.N. Setälä à Antti Jalava en 1888-1889).

1. Finno-Ugrian languages--Addresses, essays, lectures. 2. Setälä, Emil Nestor, 1864-1935. 3. Letters, Finnish. 4. Jalava, Antti, 1846-1909. I. Series. II. Ravila, Paavo Ilmari, 1902- . III. Title.

Seventeenth century studies presented to Sir Herbert Grierson. Oxford, The Clarendon press, 1938.
xv, 415, [1] p. front. (port.) 5 pl. on 4 l. 23cm.
Preface signed: J. Dover Wilson.
CONTENTS.—Rekenschap, voor Sir Herbert Grierson, by P. C. Boutens.—Bacon and the defence of learning, by Geoffrey Bullough.—Bacon's part in the intellectual movement of his time, by Rudolf Metz.—A French précieux lyrist of the early seventeenth century: Pierre Motin, by T. B. Rudmose-Brown.—King James the First of England as poet and political writer, by C. J. Sisson.—Donne and love poetry in the seventeenth century, by C. S. Lewis.—The love poetry of John Donne, a reply to Mr. C. S. Lewis, by Joan Bennett.—Joost van den Vondel, by A. J. Barnouw.—An apology for Mr. Hobbes, by A. E. Taylor.—George Herbert, by F. E. Hutchinson.—Calderón and the Spanish religious theatre of the seventeenth century, by J. B. Trend.—A note on Milton's imagery and rhythm,
(Continued on next card)
38—10219
[39k5]

D-20
3718

Settlement & encounter; geographical studies presented to Sir Grenfell Price, edited by Fay Gale and Graham H. Lawton. Melbourne, New York, Oxford University Press, 1969.
251 p. illus., diagrs., maps, tables. 23cm.
Includes bibliographies.
(Continued)

NN*R 4.71 m/ OC, I, II, III, IVb* PC, 1, I, II, III SL
(LC1, X1, Z1)

3

Seventeenth century studies presented to Sir Herbert Grierson ... 1938. (Card 2)

CONTENTS—Continued.
by Laurence Binyon.—Milton and Poussin, by Mario Praz.—Milton and the English epic tradition, by E. M. W. Tillyard.—A note on two odes of Cowley, by T. S. Eliot.—Henry Vaughan and the theme of infancy, by L. C. Martin.—Pascal in debate, by H. F. Stewart.—Corneille and Dryden as dramatic critics, by Pierre Legouis.—The limits of Locke's rationalism, by R. I. Aaron.—English architecture during the seventeenth century, by H. S. Goodhart-Rendel.—Leibniz and the fitness of things, by L. J. Russell.—Words and music: some obiter dicta, by D. F. Tovey.—Phalaris and Phalarism, by H. W. Garrod.—The turn of the century, by Basil Willey.—A list of Sir Herbert Grierson's publications, 1906-37 (p. [395]-403)—Index.
1. Literature, Modern — 17th cent. — Hist. & crit. 2. English literature—Early modern (to 1700)—Hist. & crit. 3. Seventeenth century. 4. Grierson, Sir Herbert John Clifford, 1866- I. Wilson, John Dover, 1881-
Library of Congress PN741.S4 38—10219
[39k5] 820.4

E-13
9903

The Shaken realist; essays in modern literature in honor of Frederick J. Hoffman. Edited by Melvin J. Friedman and John B. Vickery. Baton Rouge, Louisiana State University Press [1970]

xxvi, 344 p. port. 24 cm.

CONTENTS.—Preface, by J. B. Vickery.—Introduction: the achievement of Frederick Hoffman, by M. J. Friedman.—The modern tradition, figures and texts: The silence of Ernest Hemingway, by I. Hassan. A sketchbook of the artist in his thirty-fourth year; William Carlos Williams' Kora in hell: improvisations, by S. Paul. The

(Continued)

NN*R 11.70 m/OC, I, II, III PC, 1, I, II, III SL (LC1, X1, Z1)

The SHAKEN realist ... (Card 2)

wanderer and the dance: William Carlos Williams' early poetics, by J. N. Riddel. Murder in the cathedral: the limits of drama and the freedom of vision, by M. Krieger. Virginia Woolf's All Souls' Day: the omniscient narrator in Mrs. Dalloway, by J. H. Miller. Some notes on the technique of Man's fate, by M. J. Friedman.—The growing edge, themes and motifs: The inferno of the moderns, by O. W. Vickery. The impact of French symbolism on modern American poetry, by H. M. Block. Mythopoesis and modern literature, by J. B. Vickery. The "conscience" of the new literature, by N. A. Scott, Jr.—The contemporary scene, talents and directions: The unspeakable peacock: apocalypse in Flannery O'Conner, by L. Casper.

(Continued)

The SHAKEN realist ... (Card 3)

Mr. Kell and Mr. Burgess: inside and outside Mr. Enderby, by C. G. and A. C. Hoffmann. The second major subwar: four novels by Vance Bourjaily, by J. M. Muste.—A bibliography of the writings of Frederick J. Hoffmann (1909–1967), by P. R. Yanella (p. 327–344).

1. Literature--Addresses, essays, lectures. I. Hoffman, Frederick John. II. Friedman, Melvin J., ed. III. Vickery, John B., ed.

---

*NCV

Shakespeare-Studien; Festschrift für Heinrich Mutschmann, zum 65. Geburtstag überreicht von den Herausgebern Walther Fischer und Karl Wentersdorf. Marburg, N. G. Elwert, 1951. 208 p. 21cm.

CONTENTS.—Structural analysis of "Troilus and Cressida," by T. W. Baldwin.—"It is a sword of Spain, the Isebrookes temper," by K. Brunner.—Shakespeare und die Frage der Raumbühne, von F. Budde.—Shakespeare and Elizabethan psychology, by H. Craig.—Scene tempo in Macbeth, by J. W. Draper.—Zur Frage der Staatsauffassung in Shakespeares Königsdramen, von W. Fischer.—"Richard II." als Drama der

(Continued)

NN 3.53 OC, I, II PC, 1, 2, I, II SL (LC1, Z1, X1)

Shakespeare-Studien... (Card 2)

Wende, von H. Jensen.—Ist Shakespeares Stil barock? Von W. Freiherr Kleinschmit von Lengefeld.—Über Sir Laurence Olivier's "Hamlet"-Film, von H. Klitscher.—The metamorphosis of Sir John Falstaff, by S. A. Nock.—Shakespeares Stilkritik in den Sonetten, von W. Schmidt-Hidding.—Der "Spectateur" und sein Shakespeare-Bild, 1714–1726, von K. Schreinert.—Shakespearean chronology and the metrical tests, by K. Wentersdorf.—Wort und dramatische Existenz, von H. O. Wilde.—Verzeichnis der Schriften von Heinrich Mutschmann. (p. 207–208)

1. Shakespeare, William—Commentaries and criticism. 2. Mutschmann, Heinrich, 1885– . I. Fischer, Walther Paul, 1889– , ed. II. Wentersdorf, Karl, ed.

PAH

SHALIT, AMOS DE, 1926- , ed.
Preludes in theoretical physics; in honor of V.F. Weisskopf, edited by A. De-Shalit, H. Feshbach [and] L. Van Hove. Amsterdam, North-Holland pub. co.; New York, Wiley, 1966. x, 351 p. illus., port. 23cm.

Includes bibliographies.

1. Physics--Addresses, essays, lectures. 2. Weisskopf, Viktor, 1908- t. 1966.

NN R 4.66 r/c OC PC, 1, 2 SL ST, 1t, 2 (LC1, X1, Z1)

SEB

Shannon, Jasper Berry, 1903– *ed.*
The study of comparative government, an appraisal of contemporary trends; essays written in honor of Frederic Austin Ogg. New York, Appleton-Century-Crofts [1949]

viii, 338 p. 25 cm.

Bibliographical footnotes.

CONTENTS.—American democracy—after war, by F. A. Ogg.—World federation, by N. L. Hill.—The British Labor Party, by C. A. M. Ewing.—Prospects of democracy in Germany, by W. Ebenstein.—Japanese government under the 1946 Constitution, by A. Fernbach.—Latin America comes of age: an interpretation, by R. H. Fitzgibbon.—Dual federalism in Canada, Australia and the United States, by W. Mendelson.—Some new forms of democratic participation in Ameri-

(Continued on next card)

50-5140

[20]

Shannon, Jasper Berry, 1903– *ed.* The study of comparative government ... [1949] (Card 2)

CONTENTS—Continued.

can government, by J. D. Lewis.—Regional government and administration, by L. S. Greene.—Trends in rural local government, by R. Parks.—Trends in city government, by W. Young.—The executive, by E. S. Wengert.—Training for public service, by E. L. Johnson.—Political parties in transition, by C. W. Smith, Jr.—News communication and world affairs, by R. D. Nafziger.—The study of political leadership, by J. B. Shannon.

1. Ogg, Frederic Austin, 1878– 2. Political science—Addresses, essays, lectures.

JF51.S48 320.4 50-5140

Library of Congress [20]

SSD p.v.542

Sheldon, Henry Davidson, 1874– , ed.
De Busk memorial essays, edited by Henry Davidson Sheldon. Eugene, Ore.: Univ. of Oregon [1937] 68 p. front. (port.) 23cm.

"Bibliography of the writings of Dr. B. W. De Busk," p. 63.

Festschrift

1. De Busk, Burchard Woodson, 1877–1936. 2. De Busk, Burchard Woodson, 1877–1936—Bibl. 3. Education—Psychology.

N. Y. P. L. December 6, 1938

E-12
7693

Shock, Nathan Wetherill, 1906– *ed.*
Perspectives in experimental gerontology; a festschrift for Doctor F. Verzár, compiled and edited by Nathan W. Shock, with the assistance of F. Bourliere, H. von Hahn [and] D. Schlettwein-Gsell. Springfield, Ill., Thomas [1966]

x, 409 p. illus. 24 cm.

Includes bibliographies.

1. Aged--Addresses, essays, lectures. 2. Verzar, Frigyes, 1886- .

NN* R 1.67 g/c OC PC, 1, 2 SL E, 1, 2 (LC1, X1, Z1)

D-18
7037

Sicherheit und Entspannung. Zum 70. Geburtstag von General a. D. Adolf Heusinger, 4. August 1967. (Köln, Markus-Verlagsgesellschaft, 1967.)

79 p., front. 23 cm.

CONTENTS.—Adolf Heusinger, Soldat im "Widerstreit" der Geschichte, von H. Herzfeld.—Der Chef der Operationsabteilung, von P. Young.—Der erste Generalinspekteur, von U. de Maizière.—Im Dienst für die Sache des Friedens und der Sicherheit, von L. Norstad.—Auf internationalem Feld.—Ein fruchtbarer Meinungsau-

(Continued)

NN*R 3.69 v/ OC PC,1,2,3 SL E,3 (LC1,X1,Z1)

2

SICHERHEIT und Entspannung. (Card 2)

stausch, von A. Beaufre.—Sicherheit und Entspannung, von Heusinger.—"Befehl im Widerstreit," von R. Pirk.

1. Heusinger, Adolf, 1897- . 2. World war, 1939-1945--Germany. 3. North Atlantic Treaty Organization.

TPQ

Siebenbrot, Willy.

Die Braunschweigische Staatseisenbahn. Zur Jahrhundertfeier der ersten deutschen Staatsbahn Braunschweig-Wolfenbüttel herausgegeben von der Reichsbahndirektion Hannover, bearbeitet von W. Siebenbrot... Braunschweig: E. Appelhans & Co. [1938] 112 p. incl. mounted port. mounted illus. (incl. charts.) 25cm.

On cover: 1838-1938.

Festschrift.

987153A. 1. Braunschweigische Staatseisenbahn. I. Germany. Reichseisenbahndirektion, Hanover.

N. Y. P. L. January 4, 1940

E-13
3523

SIEBER, MARC, ed.

Discordia concors; Festgabe für Edgar Bonjour zu seinem siebzigsten Geburtstag am 21. August 1968. Basel, Helbing & Lichtenhahn [1968] 2 v.(797 p.) plates. 25cm.

Text in German, English or French.
Bibliographical footnotes.

1. Civilization--Addresses, essays, lectures. 2. Switzerland--Hist.--Addresses, essays, lectures. I. Bonjour, Edgar, 1898-

NN R 11.68 1/ OC,I PC,1,2, I SL (LC1,X1,Z1) [I]

E-10
6517

Siebzig Jahresringe; eine kleine Schrift für Martin Christensen, verfasst von Freunden und Mitarbeitern. Hamburg, 1954. 34 p. mounted port. 25cm.

PARTIAL CONTENTS.—Das Vermächtnis des R. [i. e. N.] F. S. Grundtvig, von R. Buchwald.—Werk und Persönlichkeit. "Der zweite Verlag," 1932-1950 [von I. Tönnies]—Genüssliches (eine sekto-, vino-, librologische Studie bei Gelegenheit, von zwei Klassiker-Ausgaben des Standard-Verlags) [von K. Balser]

1. Christensen, Martin. 2. Publishers and publishing—Germany. 3. Grundtvig, Nicolai Frederik Severin, 1783-1872. 4. Wine in literature.

NN**R 7.59 OC,1bo PC,1,2,3,4 SL (LC1,X1,Z1)

MWES
(Nestriepke, S.)

SIEGFRIED NESTRIEPKE; Leben und Leistung, hrsg. von Walther G. Oschilewski. Berlin, Arani [1955] 65 p. illus., ports. 19cm. (Kopfe der Zeit)

Half-title: Siegfried Nestriepke zum siebzigsten Geburtstag, Glückwünsche und Würdigungen dargeboten von Freunde und Weggefährten.

CONTENTS. --Mann und Werk sind eins, von C. Tesch. --Ein aufrechter Demokrat, von O. Suhr. --Aufgehen in der Sache, von A. Grimme. --Dank und Gruss der deutschen Gewerkschaften, von W. Freitag. --Kameradschaft

(Continued)

NN* * R X 10.56 a/ OC,I PC,1, I SL E,1,I (T2,LC1,X1,Z1,Y1)

SIEGFRIED NESTRIEPKE... (Card 2)

des Geistes, von J. Tiburtius. --Er schuf den Grund, auf dem wir bauen, von K. Landsberg. --Auf rechter Bahn, von M. Brauer. --Im Emanzipationskampf der Angestellten und Beamten, von H. Lüdemann. --Wissen und Kunstverstand, von H. Knudsen. --Unbeirrbar und glaubensfest, von O. F. Schuh. -- Mehr sein als scheinen, von A. Horlitz. --Ein Proteus der Volksbühne, von K. Raeck. --Aus alten Tagen erklingt ein Lied, von W. Fleischer. --Siegfried Nestriepke-Leben und Leistung, von W. G. Oschilewski. --Siegfried-Nestriepke-Bibliographie (p. 62-65).

1. Nestriepke, Siegfried, 1885- I. Oschilewski, Walther Georg, 1904- , ed.

E-13
7870

Sigfred Pedersen i digt og hverdag. København, Forlaget Børge Binderup (D. B. K.) 1969.

95 p., 8 plates. 25 cm.

CONTENTS.—Forord, af T. Kristensen.—Min barndoms Sigfred, af L. Pedersen.—Studentertiden—og senere, af O. Strange Petersen.—Tårnet, af H. Scherfig.—Mine 14 år med Sigfred, af B. Bovin.—Kun polske zloty, af J. Vibe.—Sigfred som jeg kendte ham, af Lunde-Christensen.—Visevennen Sigfred, af E. Jensen.—Shakspilleren, Sigfred, af J. Allen.—Sigfred, min ven, af B. Binderup.—De urolige år—og de sidste, af S. Biering.—En ny og ikke særlig sørgelig vise om mig selv, af S. Pedersen.

1. Pedersen, Sigfred, 1903- 1967.

NN*R 4.70 v/ OC PC,1 SL (LC1,X1,Z1)

---

*ITE
*

Silfverstolpe, Gunnar Mascoll, 1893-

Bokbindare i Stockholm, 1630-1930. Festskrift på uppdrag av Bokbindare-mästare-föreningen i Stockholm, utarbetad av Gunnar Mascoll Silfverstolpe. Stockholm: P. A. Norstedt & söners förlag, 1930. 242 p. facsims., plates, ports. f°.

513993A. 1. Bookbinding—Sweden. I. Bokbindare-mästare-föreningen i Stockholm.

N. Y. P. L. March 4, 1931

Copy only words underlined & classmark— BVA

SILLOGE bizantina, in onore di Silvio Giuseppe Mercati. Roma, 1957. xxiii, 426 p. plates. 25cm. (Studi bizantini e neoellenici. v. 9)

Bibliography, p. [ix]-xxiii.

1. Mercati, Silvio Giuseppe.

NN R 7.59 t/ OC OI PC,1 (LC2,X1,Z1)

REA

Silloge linguistica dedicata alla memoria di Graziadio Isaia Ascoli nel primo centenario della nascita.

(Archivio glottologico italiano. Torino,1929. 4°. v.22-23,p.i-xlvii,1-690. port.)

Biographical sketch,p.ix-xxvii.

form 406a [11-13-30 25m]

RAE

Silloge linguistica, dedicata alla memoria di Graziadio Isaia Ascoli, nel primo centenario della nascita. Torino: G. Chiantore, 1929. xlvii, 690 p. front. (port.), map. 4°.

Bibliographical footnotes.

526005A. 1. Ascoli, Graziadio Isaia, 1829–1907. 2. Philology —Collections.
N. Y. P. L. June 27, 1931

E-14
1309

Silvae; Festschrift für Ernst Zinn zum 60. Geburtstag. Dargebracht von Kollegen, Schülern und Mitarbeitern. [Herausgabe: Michael von Albrecht und Eberhard Heck] Tübingen, M. Niemeyer, 1970. 313 p. illus., mounted port. 24cm.

Bibliography of E. Zinn's works: p. [305]–313.
Includes bibliographical references.

(Continued)

NN*R 5. 71 w/℄ OC, I, II, III PC, 1, I, II, III SL (LC1, X1, Z1)
[I]

SILVAE; Festschrift für Ernst Zinn zum 60. (Card 2)

CONTENTS.—Zur Tragik von Vergils Turnusgestalt, von M. von Albrecht.—Die Statue des L. Accius im Tempel der Camenen, von H. Cancik.—Manumissio, von J. Eberle.—Bemerkungen zu Pindars 10. olympischer Ode, von H. Erbse.—Bemerkungen eines Grazisten zum Text des Plautus, von K. Gaiser.—Nike, von U. Hausmann.—Iuventa-iuventas-iuventus in der römischen Dichtung, von E. Heck.—Porzellan, von H. Hommel.—Zum Humanismus Fritz Reuters, von L. Huber.—Cicero und Sallust über den Neubau des Staates unter Caesars Diktatur, von J. Kroymann.—Apotheose und Unsterblichkeit in Ovids Metamorphosen, von G. Lieberg.—Formen der Textbehandlung in Kommentar des Marius Victorinus zum Galaterbrief, von A. Locher.—Historisches Wissen und Allegorese, von K.-H.

(Continued)

SILVAE; Festschrift für Ernst Zinn zum 60. (Card 3)

Lütcke.—Rudolf Borschardts Epilegomena zu Homeros und Homer, von U. Ott.—Zu Ciceros Rede für A. Caecina, von R. Rau.—Die Tränen des Helden, von R. Rieks.—Wort und Sache im Denken Goethes, von W. Schadewaldt.—Iuvenalis saturae XVI fragmentum nuperrime repertum, von H. C. Schnur.—Die Schlacht bei Bedriacum, von E.-R. Schwinge.—Zu den ersten Begegnungen der Germanen mit dem spätantiken Bildungsgedanken, von K. F. Stroheker.—Musikalischer Rhythmus und Metrik, von H. Vocke.—Zur Bedeutung und Anordnung von Philoden Fragment I 24 Kemke über das ästhetische Massenurteil, von G. Wille.—Seele und Zahl in Platons Phaidon, von J. Wippern.—Zur griechischen Grammatik des Konrad Celtis, von D. Wuttke.—

(Continued)

SILVAE; Festschrift für Ernst Zinn zum 60. (Card 4)

1. Classical studies--Collections. I. Zinn, Ernst. II. Albrecht, Michael von, ed. III. Heck, Eberhard, ed.

PBT

Silver, Daniel Jeremy, *ed.*
In the time of harvest, essays in honor of Abba Hillel Silver on the occasion of his 70th birthday. Board of editors: Solomon B. Freehof [and others] New York, Macmillan [1963]

viii, 450 p. port. 26 cm.

"A bibliography of the writings of Abba Hillel Silver": p. [90]–120.
Bibliographical footnotes.

(Continued)

NN*R 10. 63 g/k OC, IIb* PC, 1, 2, 3, I SL J, 1, 4, 5, I, IIb* (LC1, X1, Z1) [I]

SILVER, DANIEL JEREMY, ed. In the time of harvest... (Card 2)

1. Silver, Abba Hillel, 1893- 2. Judaism—Addresses, essays, lectures. 3. Jews—Hist.—Addresses, essays, lectures.
4. Judaism--Essays. 5. History--Addresses, essays, lectures. I. Title. II. Silver, Daniel Jeremy.

AN
(Bolívar, S.)

Simón Bolívar; síntesis panorámica de la vida del grande hombre. Edición conmemorativa del primer centenario del traslado de sus restos a Caracas... Caracas: Impresores Unidos, 1942. 356 p. illus. (part col'd.) 27cm.

"Compilador: Félix R. Fragachán."

249227B. 1. Bolivar, Simón, 1783–1830. I. Fragachán, Félix R., comp.
N. Y. P. L. October 27, 1943

D-14
8299

SIMON, WERNER, 1900- , ed.
Festgabe für Ulrich Pretzel, zum 65. Geburtstag dargebracht von Freunden und Schülern. Hrsg. von Werner Simon, Wolfgang Bachofer [und] Wolfgang Dittmann. [Berlin] E. Schmidt [1963] xix, 436 p. port. 23cm.

Bibliographical footnotes.

1. Pretzel, Ulrich. 2. German literature--Addresses, essays, lectures. I. Title.

NN R 2. 64 a/B OC(Ib)I PC, 1, 2, I SL (LC1, X1, Z1) [I]

M-10
3922
no.6

SIMPOSIUM en homenaje a Humboldt. Lima [1960] 278 p. illus., ports., fold. maps. 26cm. (IN: Lima (City). Universidad mayor de San Marcos. Instituto de geografía. Revista. Lima. no. 6)

1. Humboldt, Alexander, Freiherr von, 1769-1859. 2. South America--Descr. and trav., 1800-1850. 3. Natural history--Addresses, essays, lectures.
NN R 10.65 1/B OI (PC)1, 2, 3 (AH) 1, 2 (LC1, X1, Z1)

A p.v.795

Síntesis biográfica del profesor doctor Don Teófilo Fuentes Róbles en sus bodas de oro profesionales; homenaje de sus ex-discipulos. Guayaquil: Impr. i talleres municipales, 1942. x, 172 p. illus. 19cm.

1. Fuentes Róbles, Teófilo, 1869-
N. Y. P. L. December 28, 1943

D-20
1426

SINGAM, S. DURAI RAJA.
Tribute to Tunku Abdul Rahman; on his 60th birthday, February 8th, 1963. Foreword by the Hon'ble Tun Abdul Razak Al-Haj. [Kuala Lumpur, 1963] 140 p. illus., ports. 21cm.

1. Abdul Rahman, Tunku, 1903-
NN*R 6.71 w/s OC PC,1 SL O,1 (LC1, X1, Z1)

PTI

...Sir Douglas Mawson anniversary volume; contributions to geology in honour of Professor Sir Douglas Mawson's 70th birthday anniversary presented by colleagues, friends and pupils. Editors: M. F. Glaessner [and] E. A. Rudd. Adelaide, University of Adelaide, 1952. ix, 224 p. illus., maps. 25cm.

At head of title: The University of Adelaide.
Includes bibliographies.
CONTENTS.—Mount Fitton talc as a possible source of forsterite refractories, by A. R. Alderman.—The transformation of quartzite by migmatization at Mount Fitton, South Australia, by D. R. Bowes.—Pleistocene glaciation in the Kosciusko region, by W. R. Browne.—Soil nodules and their significance, by W. H. Bryan.—A note on glauconitic minerals of low refractive index from Lower Tertiary beds in South

(Continued)

NN R 4.53 OC, I, II (OS)III PC, 1, 2, I, II, III SL ST, 1, 2, I, II, III (LC1, Z1, X1)

*OAC

SINO-JAPONICA; Festschrift André Wedemeyer zum 80. Geburtstag. [Hrsg. von Helga Steininger, Hans Steininger und Ulrich Unger] Leipzig, O. Harrassowitz, 1956. 245 p. illus., port., maps, facsims. 25cm.

Bibliographical footnotes.
CONTENTS.—Jagdmagie in alten China, von W. Böttger.—Die ursprüngliche Bedeutung der Ausdrücke chün-tse und hsiao-jen, von E. Erkes.—Der geistige Umbruch Japans in seiner Auswirkung auf die Sprachreform, von A. Fröschle-Firnmann.—Das Heikyoku, von J. Glaubitz.—Bodhidharma und

(Continued)

NN R 4.57 d/P OC, I, II, III, IVbo, Vbo, VIbo PC, 1, 2, 3, I, II, III SL O, 1, 2, 3, I, II, III (LC1, X1, Z1, Y1)

...Sir Douglas Mawson anniversary volume... (Card 2)

Australia and Victoria, by W. B. Dallwitz.—Geology of Port Moresby, Papua, by M. F. Glaessner.—The Wood's Point dyke swarm, Victoria, by E. S. Hills.—The determination of the extinction angle in monoclinic pyroxenes and amphiboles, by A. W. Kleeman.—The thermal metamorphism of coal seams, by C. E. Marshall.—South-west Yilgarnia, by R. T. Prider.—Sedimentation in the Adelaide geosyncline and the formation of the Continental Terrace, by R. C. Sprigg.—Uraninite from Rum jungle and Fergusson river, Northern Territory, by F. L. Stillwell.—Nepheline paragneses, by C. E. Tilley.—Diastrophism and correlation, by L. K. Ward.—Stratigraphic correlations by petrographic methods applied to artesian bores in the Lake Frome area, by A. W. G. Whittle.—The charnockite problem in Australia, by A. F. Wilson.

1. Geology—Addresses, essays, lectures. 2. Mawson, Sir Douglas, 1882- . I. Glaessner, Martin F., ed. II. Rudd, E. A., ed. III. Adelaide university.

SINO-JAPONICA... (Card 2)

Wu-Di von Liang, von W. Gundert.—Chinas polyglottes Schrifttum, von E. Haenisch.—Wegbericht aus den Jahren U-tatsu, von H. Hammitzsch.—Das 82. Kapitel des Schï-gi, von F. Jäger.—Die Erwählung zwischen Gott und König in Agypten, von S. Morenz.—Die Verschwörung des Yui Shôsetsu, von M. Ramming.—Mount Everest, das Namensproblem, von J. Schubert.—Der heilige Herrscher, sein Tao und sein praktisches Tun, von H. Steininger.—Der Tennô-Gedanke in einigen Liedern des Manôshû, von H. Steininger.—Zur Deutung der Formel X 則 X 集 , von U. Unger.—A lost ballad by Po Chü-i, by A. Wiley.—Die Manyō-gana der Silbe /na/, von G. Wenck.

(Continued)

D-14
9768

SIR Gordon Gordon-Taylor [1878-1960]. In memoriam. London, Middlesex hospital medical committee, private circulation [1962] 64 p. ports. 23cm.

Reprints of tributes from papers and journals.
Bibliography, p. 59-64.

1. Gordon-Taylor, Sir Gordon.
NN R 3.64 g/s OC PC,1 SL (LC1, X1, Z1)

SINO-JAPONICA... (Card 3)

1. Wedemeyer, André, 1875- . 2. Chinese studies--Collections. 3. Japanese studies--Collections. I. Steininger, Helga, ed. II. Steininger, Hans, ed. III. Unger, Ulrich, ed. IV. Steininger, Helga. V. Steininger, Hans. VI. Unger, Ulrich.

D-19
8744

Det Siste ord blir aldri sagt. Tre enere og en avis. Av Ingvar Molaug, Per Thomsen, Alfred Hauge [m. fl.] Ved Stavanger Aftenblads 75 års jubileum. Illustrert av Henry Imsland. Oslo, Cappelen, 1968.
198 p. 23 cm.

1. Journalists--Norway. 2. Oftedal family. I. Molaug, Ingvar, 1907- II. Stavanger aftenblad.
NN*R 5.70 m/A OC,I (OS)II PC, 1, 2, I, II SL G, 2, I, II (PRI1, LC1, X1, Z1)

* C p.v.2131

Skal, Georg von, editor.
Das deutsche Rote Kreuz; seine Geschichte, Organisation und Tätigkeit. Festschrift, zumsammengestellt von Georg von Skal... ⌊New York: S. R. Bursch, 1916.⌋ 46 p. illus. 4°.

542186A. 1. Red Cross. Germany.
N. Y. P. L. August 5, 1931

APB p.v.50

Slægten Høgsberg gennem 300 aar. Holstebro, Thomsen, 1948. 32 p. 24cm.

Preface signed: Thorvald Høgsberg, Karl Høgsberg.

1. Høgsberg family. I. Høgsberg, Thorvald, 1895– , ed. II. Høgsberg, Karl, 1919– , ed.
NN 1.53 OC, I, II PC, 1, I, II SL G, 1, I, II (LC1, Z1, X1)

---

* QW

SLOVENSKÁ AKADEMIA VIED, Bratislava, Czechoslovakia. Historický ústav.
K počiatkom slovenského národného obrodenia; sborník štúdií Historického ústavu SAV pri príležitosti 200 ročného jubilea narodenia Antona Bernoláka. ⌊Vedecký redaktor: Ján Tibenský. 1. vyd.⌋ Bratislava, Vydavateľstvo Slovenskej akadémie vied. 1964.
477 p. 25 cm.
Bibliographical footnotes.
CONTENTS.—Holotík, Ľ. Bernolákovské hnutie v slovenskom národnom obrodení.—Špiesz, A. Rozvoj kapitalistických vzťahov
(Continued)

NN* R 6.65 g/ (OC)I, II OS PC, 1, 2, 3, I, II SL S, 1, 2, 3, I, II (LC1, X1, Z1)

5

SLOVENSKÁ AKADEMIA VIED, Bratislava, Czechoslovakia. Historický ústav. K počiatkom slovenského národného obrodenia... (Card 2)

na Slovensku na konci 18. a na začiatku 19. storočia—objektívna báza pre vznik slovenského národného obrodenia.—Hučko, J. K charakteristike vlasteneckej inteligencie v prvej fáze slovenského národného obrodenia so zreteľom na jej sociálne zloženie a pôvod.—Tibenský, J. Historická podmienenosť a spoločenská báza vzniku bernolákovského hnutia.—Sášký, L. Bratislavský generálny seminár a bernolákovské hnutie.—Maťovčík, A. Anton Bernolák.—Habovštiaková, K. Bernolákovo jazykovědné dielo.—Krajčovič, R. Hlavné fázy formovania kultúrnej západoslovenčiny.—Miškovič, A. Organizácia, činnosť a význam Slovenského učeného tovarišstva.—Bálent, B. K organizácii

(Continued)

SLOVENSKÁ AKADEMIA VIED, Bratislava, Czechoslovakia. Historický ústav. K počiatkom slovenského národného obrodenia... (Card 3)

a vydavateľskej činnosti Slovenského učeného tovarišstva.—Simončič, J. Trnava a počiatky bernolákovského hnutia.—Eliáš, M. K činnosti pobočného stánku Slovenského učeného tovarišstva v Nitre.—Bakoš, M. Poézia u bernlákovcov pred Hollým.—Vyvíjalová, M. Bernolákovci a stúpenci bibličtiny v rokoch 1790–1830.—Čaplovič, J. Bratislavské lýceum a slovenské národné obrodenie 1780–1830.—Bokes, F. Bratislava 1780–1830 — hlavné stredisko slovenského národného života.—Považan, J. Juraj Palkovič a jeho miesto v bernolákovskom hnutí.—Marčok, V. Vytváranie kultúrno-národných centier na strednom Slovensku v rokoch 1780–1830.—Sedlák, I. Príspevok k počiatkom

(Continued)

SLOVENSKÁ AKADEMIA VIED, Bratislava, Czechoslovakia. Historický ústav. K počiatkom slovenského národného obrodenia... (Card 4)

slovenského národného obrodenia na východnom Slovensku.—Michalcová-Cesnaková, M. Počiatky slovenského obrodeneckého divadla.—Novotný, J. Ke vzájemnému vztahu českých buditelů a bernolákovců v období národního obrození.—Butvin, J. Snahy o jednotnú kulturno-politickú platformu v slovenskom národnom hnutí v rokoch 1825–1848.—Jóna, E. Vplyv bernoláčtiny a benolákovcov na štúrovskú spisovnú normu.

(Continued)

SLOVENSKÁ AKADEMIA VIED, Bratislava, Czechoslovakia. Historicky ústav. K počiatkom slovenského národného obrodenia... (Card 5)

1. Slovakia--Hist.--Addresses, essays, lectures. 2. Slovak language--Addresses, essays, lectures. 3. Bernolak, Anton, 1762-1813. I. Tibenský, Jan, ed. II. Title.

Copy only words underlined & classmark-- * QLA

SLOVENSKA AKADEMIJA ZNANOSTI IN UMETNOSTI, Ljubljana, Yugoslavia.
Brodarjev zbornik, serta Broclariana. Ljubljana, 1962-63. 574 p. illus., maps. 25cm. (Arheoloski vestnik; acta archaeologica. v. 13-14)

Contitbutions in French, German, Italian or Sebo-Croatian, with summaries in English, French, German, Italian or Serbo-Croatian.
"Bibliografija profesorja Srečka Brodarja," p. 13-18.
Includes bibliographies.
1. Brodar, Srečko, 1893- . 2. Archaeology--Addresses, essays, lectures. I. Title.
NN 2.64 g/r (OC)Ib+, I OS OI PC, 1, 2, I S, 1, 2, I (LC1, X1, Z1)

---

* QL +

SLOVENSKA AKADEMIJA ZNANOSTI IN UMETNOSTI, Ljubljana, Yugoslavia.
Poslanica predsedniku Slovenske akademije znanosti in umetnosti dr.-ju Franu Ramovšu ob šestdesetletnici 14. septembra 1950. [Ljubljana, 1950] xvi l. 35cm.

1. Ramovš, Franc, 1890-

NN** R 12.53 OS PC, 1 SL S, 1 (LC1, Z1, X1)

---

*QL

Slovenska matica v Ljubljani.
Kopitarjeva spomenica, vredil Josip Marn. V Ljubljani, Matica slovenska, 1880. v, 188 p. plates, facsim. (fold.) 22cm.

Bibliographical footnotes.
"Zapisek manjših spiskov Kopitarjevih," p. 107-111.
Contents.—Jernej Kopitar, spisal J. Navratil.—K. Kopitar in sedanja slovenska slovnica, spisal P. L. Hrovat.—Slovnice slovenske, spisal Julij Kleinmayr.—Tri prošnje Kopitarjeve l. 1809.—
(Continued)
NN**R X 6 54 (OC)I, II, IIIbo8 OS PC, 1, I, II SL S, 1, I, II (LC1, Z1, X1)

Slovenska matica v Ljubljani. Kopitarjeva spomenica, ... (Card 2)

J. Kopitar pa dr. J. Zupan, po njegovih pismih posnel J. Marn.—Patriotische Phantasien eines Slaven, spisal J. Kopitar.—SS.Cyrillus et Methodius, spisal J. Kopitar.—Slavorum cisdanubianorum historiae conspectus chronologicus usque ad obitum S. Methodii (Glag. Cloz. LXXVI). Poslovenil z lastnimi ocompar'. P. L. Hrovat.—Kopitar sprožitelj slovenske kmetijske "Pratike", zapisal J. Bleiweis.—Kopitar pa Pypin in Kolár,

(Continued)

Slovenska matica v Ljubljani. Kopitarjeva spomenica, ... (Card 3)

sestavil J. Marn.—Slavnost Kopitarjeva v nedeljo dné 22. avg. 1880.

1. Slovenian language—Hist. and crit. I. Marn, Josip, ed. II. Kopitar, Bartholomej, 1780-1844. III. Marn, Josip.

---

*Q p.v.515

Slovenská umelecká beseda, Bratislava, Czecho-Slovakia. Literárný odbor.

Sborník Josefa Gregora-Tajovského, vydaný bol k jeho 50. narodeninám ako tretí zväzok knižnice Literárneho odboru Umeleckej besedy slovenskej "Vel'ká Morava" za podpory Ministerstva školstva a národnej osvety a redakciou dra Fr. Tichého, dra Franka Wollmana a dra L. N. Zvěřinu. ꞁV Bratislave: Vytlačené v Slovenskej kníhtlačiarni, 1925ꞁ 111 p. 18½cm. (On cover: Vel'ka Morava...sv. 3.)

(Continued)

N. Y. P. L. Festschrift. January 31, 1941

Slovenská umelecká beseda, Bratislava, Czecho-Slovakia. Literárný odbor. Sborník... (Card 2)

Contributions by various authors.
"Bibliografia diela Jozefa Gregora-Tajovského", p. 107-111.

1. Gregor-Tajovský, Josef, 1874- , ed. II. Wollman, Frank, ed. . I. Tichý, František, 1886- III. Zvěřina, L. N., 1891- , ed. IV. Title.

N. Y. P. L. January 31, 1941

---

*QW +

SLOVENSKO Masarykovi, sostavil Dr. Jozef Rudinský. Praha. Vyd. pod protektorátom slovenskej odbočky československej národnej rady v Bratislave, Literárne-vedecké nakl. V. Tilkovského, 1930. plates, ports. 269 p. 30cm.

By various authors.

1. Masaryk, Tomás Garrigue, pres. Czecho-Slovakia, 1850-1937. I. Národní rada československá. II. Rudinsky, Joseph, ed.

NN**R 8.53 OC,II (OS)I PC,1,I,II SL S,1,I,II (Z/,LC1, XI)

E-13 2310

Smeetsbundel. Opstellen aangeboden aan Prof. Dr. M. J. H. Smeets ter gelegenheid van zijn afscheid als hoogleraar aan de Katholieke Hogeschool te Tilburg. Deventer, Æ. E. Kluwer, 1967.

396 p. port. 24 cm.

Bibliographical footnotes.

CONTENTS.—Vijftien jaar discussie over een belasting van privé-

(Continued)

NN * R 5.68 1/R OC,I PC,1, 2,I SL E,1,2,I (LC1,X1, Z1) 4

SMEETSBUNDEL. 1967. (Card 2)

vermogenswinsten, door K. V. Antal.—Goodwill bij inbreng, door D. Brüll.—Het begrip gestort kapitaal, door J. H. Christiaanse.—Belastingbeginselen, door J. G. Detiger.—Voordeel verwachten, voordeel beogen, door H. J. Doedens.—Verleden, heden en toekomst van de benadering der optierechten voor de belastingen wegens nalatenschappen en schenkingen in Nederland, door H. A. Drielsma.—De overeenkomst onder bezwarende titel van art. 27 van de Registratiewet 1917, door P. L. Dijk.—Wie geniet het inkomen? door J. E. A. M. van Dijck.—Schending van het recht als grond voor cassatie in belastingzaken, door Ch. P. A. Geppaart.—Vermogenswinst-

(Continued)

SMEETSBUNDEL. 1967. (Card 3)

belasting op kunstvoorwerpen, door H. J. Hellema.—De belastingunificatie van 1805, door H. J. Hofstra.—Concentratie van ondernemingen, door M. V. M. van Leeuwe.—Een kritische beschouwing over de Successiewet 1956 en de noodzaak van een algehele herziening dezer wet, door G. Meijling.—Rechtvaardigheid en doelmatigheid van belastingheffing naar draagkracht, door W. F. Nederstigt.—De rechtsonzekerheid ... geprezen, door L. J. M. Nouwen.—Over accijnzen, door J. Reugebrink.—Internationale belastingverdeling en verlangens inzake belastingobject of tariefstructuur bij de vennootschapsbelasting, door B. Schendstok.—De verkrijging krachtens erfrecht, door H. Schutteväer.—De grondbeginselen van de vermogensbelasting, door

(Continued)

SMEETSBUNDEL. 1967. (Card 4)

J. van Soest.—Welke factoren bepalen de veranderingen in het niveau en de structuur van de belastingen in de 19e en 20e eeuw? door Th. A. Stevers.—De rekkelijkheid in de fiscale jaarwinstbepaling, door P. Vinke.—Moorse wortel der omzettax, door TJ. S. Visser.

1. Taxation--Jurisp.--Netherlands. 2. Law--Netherlands. I. Smeets, M.J.H.

E-13 491

SMITH, ROBERT SIDNEY, 1904- , ed.

Economic systems and public policy; essays in honor of Calvin Bryce Hoover. Edited by Robert S. Smith and Frank T. de Vyver. Durham, N.C., Duke university press, 1966. xix, 274 p. illus. 25cm.

Bibliographical footnotes.

CONTENTS.--Introduction, J. J. Spengler.--Economic freedom and public policy, by C. L. Allen.--Systems of thought and economic

(Continued)

NN R 11.67 c/J OC, I, IIbo PC, 1, 2, I SL E, 1, 2, I (LC1, X1, Z1) 3

SMITH, ROBERT SIDNEY, 1904- , ed. Economic systems and public policy... (Card 2)

systems by R. Brandis.--The concept and the classification of economic systems, by H.M. Oliver.--The government and the central bank in a free society, by L.S. Silk.--The pursuit of full employment, by J.M. Kreps and C.H. Kreps.--The demonstration effect, savings, and Southern economic development, by J.C.T. Taylor.--The financing of capital formation in the United States and Soviet Russia, by J.J. O'Leary.--A neo-classical interpretation of the withering of the Soviet state, by F.M. Gottheil.--German recovery: a study in economic planning, by R. Havens.

(Continued)

Copy only words underlined & Classmark-- TB

The Social anthropology of Latin America; essays in honor of Ralph Leon Beals. Edited by Walter Goldschmidt & Harry Hoijer. Los Angeles, Latin American Center, University of California, 1970.

xi, 309 p. 25 cm. (Latin American studies, v. 14)
Includes bibliographies.

NN*R 3.72 e/ OC, II, III, IV IV AH, 1, 2, 3, II, III, IV E, 1, II, (OD)I (ED)I PC, 1, 2, 3, I, II, III, III, IV (LC1, X1, Z1) (Continued) 4

SMITH, ROBERT SIDNEY, 1904- , ed. Economic systems and public policy... (Card 3)

--Agricultural policy in the Central American Common Market by R.S. Smith.--The transfer of economic ideas in the Commonwealth, by C.D. Goodwin.

1. Hoover, Calvin Bryce, 1897- . 2. Economic policy--Addresses, essays, lectures. I. Vyver, Frank T. de, joint ed. II. Vyver, Frank T. de.

The SOCIAL anthropology of Latin America; essays in honor of Ralph Leon Beals. (Card 2)

CONTENTS.—Tarascan folk religion, Christian or pagan? By P. Carrasco.—Indian acculturation in Nayarit: the Cora response to mestizoization, by T. B. Hinton.—Bonds of laughter among the Tarahumara Indians: a rethinking of joking relationship theory, by J. G. Kennedy.—A web of land: differential acculturation in southern Oaxaca, by B. N. Litzler.—Labor migration and family structure in the Tlaxcala-Pueblan area, Mexico, by H. A. Nutini and T. D. Murphy.—Contrasting forms of nativism among the Mayos and

(Continued)

MTE

So live the works of men; seventieth anniversary volume honoring Edgar Lee Hewett, edited by Donald D. Brand and Fred E. Harvey. Albuquerque, N. M. ⌊Printed by the University of New Mexico press⌋ 1939.

162 p., 1 l., 163–232 p., 1 l., 233–366 p. front. (port.) illus. (incl. plans) xxxv pl. on 22 l. 28ᶜᵐ.

Plates XIX–XXVII are accompanied by explanatory letterpress, which is printed on rectos facing plates XIX, XX, XXV–XXVI, and at the foot of plates XXI–XXIV, XXVII.

"Six hundred copies of which this is no.469."

Includes bibliographies.

CONTENTS.—Edgar Lee Hewett: his biography and writings to date, by L. B. Bloom.—Hewett, the realist, by A. S. Riggs.—A half century of achievement, by P. A. F. Walter, sr.—Ceramics and chronology in the Near East, by W. F. Albright.—The horse in American Indian culture,

(Continued on next card)

39–28088

⌊4⌋ Festschrift

The SOCIAL anthropology of Latin America; essays in honor of Ralph Leon Beals. (Card 3)

Yaquis of Sonora, Mexico, by E. H. Spicer.—Urbanization and a traditional market system, by R. Waterbury.—A survey of provincial power structure in Guatemala, by R. N. Adams.—Panajachel a generation later, by S. Tax and R. Hinshaw.—Cultural evolution in South America, by J. H. Steward.—Ethnicity and social mobility in Chancay Valley, Peru, by L. C. Faron.—Stratification and pluralism in the Bolivian Yungas, by M. B. Léons.—The mechanisms of culture change, by K. H. Schwerin.—Goajiro kinship and the eiruku cycle, by J. Wilbert.

(Continued)

So live the works of men ... 1939. (Card 2)

CONTENTS—Continued.

by H. B. Alexander.—Notes on the geography and archaeology of Zape, Durango, by D. D. Brand.—Anthropology and education, by Lyman Bryson.—Early days in Utah, by Byron Cummings.—The poetry of Indian songs, by Frances Densmore.—Early racial fusion in eastern Mediterranean lands, by H. R. Fairclough.—An outline of Pueblo government, by R. G. Fisher.—Anthropological miscellany: 1. Chainfern and maidenhair, adornment materials of northwestern California basketry. 2. Kiowa memories of the northland, by J. P. Harrington.—New applications of tree ring analysis, by Florence M. Hawley.—The mollusca of New Mexico and Arizona, by Junius Henderson.—A square kiva at Hawikuh, by F. W. Hodge.—Anthropological and archaeological riches in the far Northwest, by Aleš Hrdlička.—Notes on the archaeology of the Babícora district, Chihuahua, by A. V. Kidder.—Some ancient records from Babylonia, by C. S. Knopf.—A word on philology, by H. N. von Koerber.—

(Continued on next card)

39–28088

⌊4⌋

The SOCIAL anthropology of Latin America; essays in honor of Ralph Leon Beals. (Card 4)

1. Latin America--Soc. condit. 2. Indians, American--Social life. 3. Beals, Ralph Leon, 1901- --Bibl. I. Series. II. Beals, Ralph Leon, 1901- III. Goldschmidt, Walter Rochs, 1913- ed. IV. Hoijer, Harry, 1904- ed.

So live the works of men ... 1939. (Card 3)

CONTENTS—Continued.

Aeneas as a hero, by L. E. Lord.—Archaeology as a science, by R. V. Magoffin.—Southern mound cultures in the light of recent explorations, by W. K. Moorehead.—Recent epigraphic discoveries at the ruins of Copan, Honduras, by S. G. Morley.—Indian petroglyphs from the western plains, by E. B. Renaud.—The development of a unit-type dwelling, by F. H. H. Roberts, jr.—Mongolian epics (diary leaves), by Nicholas Roerich.—The empire of the Inkas, by J. C. Tello.

1. Hewett, Edgar Lee, 1865– 2. Archaeology—Addresses, essays, lectures. I. Brand, Donald Dilworth, 1905– ed. II. Harvey, Fred E., 1895– joint ed.

39–28088

Library of Congress CC65.S6

——— ~~Copy 2.~~

Copyright A 126350 ⌊4⌋ 570.4

QOV

Social structure; studies presented to A. R. Radcliffe-Brown. Ed. by Meyer Fortes. Oxford, Clarendon press, 1949. xiv, 232 p. illus. 23cm.

"Bibliography," p. 224-225. "Bibliography of Professor A. R. Radcliffe-Brown," p. 226-228.

CONTENTS.—A methodology for the study of social class, by W. L. Warner.—Character formation and diachronic theory, by M. Mead.—Bali: the value system of a steady state, by G. Bateson.—Time and social structure: an Ashanti case study, by M. Fortes.—Nuer rules of exogamy and incest, by E. E. Evans-Pritchard.—The Tswana conception of incest, by I. Schapera.—The Hopi and the lineage principle, by F. Eggan.—The role of the sexes in Wiko circumcision ceremonies, by M. Gluckman.—Authority and public opinion in Tikopia, by R. Firth.—Government chiefs in New Guinea, by H. I. Hogbin.—American military government, by J. F. Embree.

543829B. 1. Radcliffe-Brown, Alfred Reginald, 1881- . 2. Society, Primitive. I. Fortes, Meyer, ed.

N. Y. P. L. November 3, 1950

TAH

Socialism, capitalism and economic growth: essays presented to Maurice Dobb; edited by C. H. Feinstein. London, Cambridge U. P., 1967.

x, 367 p. front. (port.), tables, diagrs. 24 cm.

"A bibliography of the works of Maurice Dobb" (p. 351-360)

(Continued)

NN • R 6.68 1/R OC, I PC, 1, 2, 3, I SL E, 1, 2, 3, I (LC1, X1, Z1)

SOCIALISM, capitalism and economic growth... (Card 2)

1. Economic development--Addresses, essays, lectures.
2. Economic policy--Addresses, essays, lectures. 3. Dobb, Maurice Herbert, 1900- . I. Feinstein, C.H., ed.

AN (Bolívar, S.)

Sociedad bolivariana del Perú.

...Homenaje a Bolívar; selección por Pedro Ugarteche. Lima, 1942. 316 p. port. 19cm.

At head of title: Sociedad bolivariana del Perú.

209034B. 1. Bolívar, Simón, 1783-1830. I. Ugarteche, Pedro, 1902- , ed. II. Title.
N. Y. P. L. March 25, 1943

NPB

Sociedad de Menéndez y Pelayo, *Santander, Spain.*

... Homenaje a d. Miguel Artigas en conmemoración de su nombramiento de director de la Biblioteca nacional: estudios de investigación ... Edición del Boletín de la Biblioteca de Menéndez Pelayo. Santander, 1931–32.

2 v. illus. (incl. ports., maps, plans, facsims., coats of arms) pl. 25cm.
Cover-title.
At head of title: Sociedad de Menéndez Pelayo.
T.-p. reads: Boletín de la Biblioteca Menéndez y Pelayo. Número extraordinario en homenaje a d. Miguel Artigas ... Artes gráficas, viuda de F. Fons.
"Publicaciones de Miguel Artigas": v. 1, p. [xiii]–xvi.
1. Artigas y Ferrando, Miguel, 1887- 2. Spanish literature—Hist. & crit. 3. Spain—Hist.—Addresses, essays, lectures. I. Santander, Spain. Biblioteca Menéndez y Pelayo. Boletín. II. Title.

34-9729

Library of Congress PQ6004.A7 [2] 860.4

MTE

Sociedade Martins Sarmento, *Guimarães, Portugal.*

Homenagem a Martins Sarmento; miscelánea de estudios em honra do investigador vimaranense. No centenário do seu nascimento (1833–1933) Guimarães (Portugal) Edição da Sociedade Martins Sarmento, subsidiada pelo Ministério da instrução pública e pela Junta de educação nacional, 1933.

3 p. l., 477 p., 2 l. illus. (incl. ports., music) pl., 2 fold. maps, plan, facsims., fold. geneal. tab., diagrs. 30cm.

Bibliographical foot-notes.

CONTENTS.—I. Dedicatória.—II. Autógrafo (fac-simile) do ex.mo ministro da instrução pública.—III. Estudios em honra de Martins Sarmento: ALEMANHA. Kraft, G. Feuersteinbeile westlicher form in

(Continued on next card)

A C 35-720

[3]

Sociedade Martins Sarmento, *Guimarães, Portugal.* Homenagem a Martins Sarmento ... 1933. (Card 2)

CONTENTS—Continued.

Baden. Kühn, H. Westgotische durchbruchschnallen. Richthofen, B., frhr. von. Zur bearbeitung der vorgeschichtlichen und neueren kleinen rundbauten der Pyrenäenhalbinsel. Schulten, A. Segeda. Wickert, L. De nonnullis miliariis bracarensibus. Wilke, G. Die bestattung in bauchlage und verwandte bräuche. Zeiss, H. Spätrömische stempelverzierte keramik aus Portugal und Spanien. BÉLGICA. Siret, L. Origen y significación de las corridas de toros. ESPANHA. Bosch-Gimpera, P. Los Celtas en Portugal y sus caminos. Bouza-Brey, F. Máscaras galegas de origen prehistórico. Cabré Aguiló, J., y Cabré Herreros, María de la Encarnación. La espada de antenas tipo Alcácer-do-Sal y su evolución en la necrópoli de La Osera, Chamartín de la Sierra, Avila. Cuevillas, F. L. A área xeográfica de cultura norte dos castros. Gómez-

(Continued on next card)

A C 35-720

[3]

Sociedade Martins Sarmento, *Guimarães, Portugal.* Homenagem a Martins Sarmento ... 1933. (Card 3)

CONTENTS—Continued.

Moreno, M. La cerámica primitiva ibérica. Martínez Santa-Olalla, J. Monumentos funerários célticos; as "pedras formosas" e as estelas em forma de casa. Mélida, J. R. Idolos lusitanos de hueso. Morán, C. Salamanca en la prehistoria. Pérez de Barradas, J. Necrópolis visigótica de Daganzo de Arriba (Madrid) Pericot, L. La representación serpentiforme de la Citania de Troña (Galicia) Risco, V. Notas en col do culto do lume na Galiza. Taracena Aguirre, B. Tribus celtibericas; "Pelendones". Vega del Sella, Conde de la. Asturienses, capsienses y vascos. FRANÇA. Bégouen, Comte. Affutoirs pour pointes d'os en France et en Portugal. Breuil, H. Moule à figurine humaine schématique de l'Oural. Favret, P. M. La hache gardienne des tombeaux à l'époque néolithique en Champagne. Grenier, A. La Voie régordane

(Continued on next card)

A C 35-720

[3]

Sociedade Martins Sarmento, *Guimarães, Portugal.* Homenagem a Martins Sarmento ... 1933. (Card 4)

CONTENTS—Continued.

et Mercure. Joleaud, L. Le rôle des coquillages marins fossiles et actuels dans la magie berbère. Lantier, R. Les dieux orientaux dans la Péninsule ibérique. Linckenheld, E. Observations sur les sièges primitifs des Senons cisalpins. Luquet, G. H. Gravures rupestres de Villadesuso. Octobon, Comdt. Les gravures du Puy de Lacan et leurs relations avec les figurations anthropomorphes. INGLATERRA. Oswald, F. Un indice présumable de la présence de la huitième légion en Angleterre. Prestage, E. Portugal: a pioneer of Christianity. Radford, C. A. R. The culture of southwestern Britain in the early iron age. Leeds, E. T. A. milestone in western archaeology. POLÓNIA. Kostrzewski, J. Four à minerai datant du I. s. après J.-C. découvert à Mechlin, arrondt. de Srem, en Grande Pologne. PORTUGAL. Almeida,

(Continued on next card)

A C 35-720

[3]

Sociedade Martins Sarmento, *Guimarães, Portugal.* Homenagem a Martins Sarmento ... 1933. (Card 5)

CONTENTS—Continued.

E. d'. A mocidade literária de Sarmento. Alves, F. M. Bragança e o dr. Francisco Martins Sarmento. Alves Pereira, F. Os vestíbulos das habitações citanienses. Athayde, A. Ossadas prè-históricas da gruta dos Refugidos. Baião, A. O Arquivo do estado português no princípio da nossa nacionalidade; teria permanecido em Guimarães? Basto, C. Canto do cisne. Cardozo, M. Dr. Francisco Martins Sarmento; esbôço bio-bibliográfico. Carvalho, J. de. Sôbre a autenticidade dos sermões de fr. João Xira. Chaves, L. Notas etnográficas colhidas na obra de Martins Sarmento. Fontes, J. Figuras rupestres astrais no santuário prè-histórico do Gião (Arcos-de-Valdevez) Girão, A. de Amorim. Sepulturas antropomórficas abertas em rocha. Jalhay, E. Uma nova hipótese sôbre a utilização da indústria lítica de tipo asturiense. Leite

(Continued on next card)

A C 35-720

[3]

Sociedade Martins Sarmento, *Guimarães, Portugal.* Homenagem a Martins Sarmento ... 1933. (Card 6)

CONTENTS—Continued.

de Vasconcellos, J. Lápide lusitano-romana da Arruda-dos-Vinhos. Magalhães Basto, A. de. Algumas páginas inéditas de Fernão Lopes? Magalhães Lima, J. de. Francisco Martins Sarmento: o seu legado e o seu carácter. Mendes Corrêa, A. A. Valencianos e Portugueses. Monteiro, M. Um génio tutelar. Paço, A. do. Vaso de bôrdo horizontal, de Vila-Fria. Pina, L. de. Notas para a prè-história vimaranense. Pinho, J. de. Considerações sôbre a religiosidade dos citanienses de Briteiros e Sabroso. Rodrigues, J. M. O Périplo de Hanão e o seu primeiro comentador. Sampaio, G. Côro das maçadeiras. Santos Graça, A. A crença do Pòveiro nas "almas penadas". Santos Júnior, J. R. dos. A cerâmica campaniforme de Mairos (Trás-os-Montes) Serpa Pinto, R. de. O castro de Sendim, Felgueiras. Sousa Machado, J. de. Casa da

(Continued on next card)

A C 35-720

[3]

Sociedade Martins Sarmento, *Guimarães, Portugal.* Homenagem a Martins Sarmento ... 1933. (Card 7)

CONTENTS—Continued.

Ponte, em S. Salvador de Briteiros; árvore de costado até aos terceiros avós. Souto, A. A "Pelagia insula" de Festus Avienus. Viera Braga, A. Influência de s. Tiago da Galiza em Portugal. Vitorino, P. Um discipulo de Sequeira. Xavier da Costa, L. Páginas da "História resumida das belas-artes em Portugal no século XVIII". ROMÉNIA. Plopsor, C. S. Nicolaescu. Les Celtes en Olténie. SUISSA. Deonna, W. Un ex-voto délien: la pivoine. Pittard, E., et Wietrzykowska, J. La grandeur du trou occipital en fonction de la capacité cranienne.

1. Archaeology—Addresses, essays, lectures. 2. *Martins Sarmento, Francisco, 1833–1899. I. Portugal. Ministério da instrução pública. II. Portugal. Junta de educação nacional. III. Title.

A C 35-720

Title from N. Y. Pub. Libr. Printed by L. C.

[3]

SOCIETÀ ARCHEOLOGICA COMENSE. [Origines] Raccolta di scritti in onore di Mons. Giovanni Baserga (Card 3)

1. Baserga, Giovanni. 2. Europe—Archaeology. I. Laviosa Zambotti, Pia. I Balcani e l'Italia nella preistoria.

3-MCQ
M24.S6

Sociedade nacional de belas-artes, Lisbon.
Livro da homenagem ao grande pintor José Malhôa realizada, com a exposição das suas obras, na Sociedade nacional de belas-artes em junho de 1928. Com 100 reproduções de obras do mestre e mais 3 ilustrações. Lisboa [Imp. Libanio da Silva] 1928. 216 p. incl. plates. front., ports. 26cm.

100594B. 1. Paintings, Portuguese. 2. Malhôa, José, 1854– I. Title.
N. Y. P. L. August 26, 1941

E-10
6054

SOCIETÀ SICILIANA PER LA STORIA PATRIA, Palermo.
Studi medievali in onore di Antonino de Stefano. Palermo [1956] xxiv, 585 p. port. facsims. 25cm.

Articles by various authors, chiefly in Italian, with several contributions in French, German, Spanish or Catalan.
"Bibliografia di Antonino de Stefano," p. [xi] - xii.

1. Stefano, Antonino de. 2. Middle Ages--Hist.--Addresses, essays, lectures.
NN 8.58 m/P OS PC, 1, 2 SL (LC1, X1, Z1, Y1) [I]

E-10
6498

Società archeologica comense.
... Raccolta di scritti in onore di Antonio Giussani. Milano, U. Hoepli, 1944.

xxxi, 358 p., 1 l. plates (part fold.) port., fold. map, plans (part fold.) facsims., diagrs. 25cm.

Half-title: Munera.
"Bibliografia delle pubblicazioni dell' ing. Antonio Giussani": p. [xvii]–xxxi.

1. GIUSSANI, ANTONIO 2. ITALY--ARCHAEOLOGY
3. ART, ITALIAN I. Munera
NN * 11.58 m/P OS PC, 1, 2, 3, I SL A, 3, I (LC1, X1, Z1) [I]

E-10
506

SOCIETÀ DI STORIA PATRIA PER LA SICILIA ORIENTALE.
Miscellanea di studi sicelioti ed italioti in onore di Paolo Orsi. Catanai, V. Giannotta [1921] v, 432p. illus., ports. 25cm. (ITS: Pubblicazione)

Bibliographical footnotes.

1. Orsi, Paolo, 1859-1935. 2. Sicily--Hist.--Addresses, essays, lectures. 3. Sicily--Archaeology. I. Società di storia patria per la Sicilia orientale. Pubblicazione.
NN 10.58 m/J OS(1b)I PC, 1, 2, 3 SL (LC1, X1, Z1)
[I, NSCM]

BTE

SOCIETÀ ARCHEOLOGICA COMENSE.
[Origines] Raccolta di scritti in onore di Mons. Giovanni Baserga. Como, Tip. editrice A. Noseda, 1954. 469 p. illus., plates, port., maps. 25cm.

"Bibliografia della pubblicazioni di Mons. Dott. Giovanni Baserga," p. 1-7.

CONTENTS. --Mons. Giovanni Baserga, di A. Calderini. --Cuestiones sobre al alfabeto y lengua de los Iberos, di. A. Beltran. --Tombe galliche a Esino Lario, di M. Bertolone. --Acondicionamiento de las cuevas con arte rupestre, para efectos de (Continued)

NN * * 3.55 p/ (OC) I OS PC. 1, 2, I SL (LC1, X1, Z1)

E-11
3599

SOCIETÀ DI STUDI GEOGRAFICI, Florence.
Studi geografici pubblicati in onore del Prof. Renato Biasutti. Supplemento al volume LXV. (1958) della Rivista geografica italiana. Firenze, La Nuova Italia, 1958. 354 p. illus., maps. 25cm.

1. Georgraphy--Addresses, essays, lectures. 2. Biasutti, Renato, 1878- . I. Rivista geografica italiana.
NN 2.62 g/J OS, I PC, I, 2, I SL (LC1, X1, Z1)

SOCIETÀ ARCHEOLOGICA COMENSE. [Origines] Raccolta di scritti in onore di Mons. Giovanni Baserga (Card 2)

conservacion, di A. F. De Aviles. --Panzer-Studie, von G. v. Merhart--La station micoquienne de Saint-Plancart, di L. Méroc. --L'elmo di bronzo di Oppeano nella irradiazione occidentale dell'arte atestina, di A. Minto. --Stazione Arginate-Praebenacci, di R. Pittioni. --Le Isole Pontine e il commercio di ossidiana nel continente durante il neo-eneolitico, di A. M. Radmilli. --Contributi di recenti ricerche paletnologiche in Italia, di F. Rittatore. --Esame tecnologico della spada tipo La Tène III di Ésino Lario, di C. Storti ed E. Mariani. --Fibeln aus Aquileia, von J Werner. --I Balcani e l'Italia nella preistoria, di P. Laviosa Zambotti.
(Continued)

E-11
3025

SOCIETAS STUDIOSORUM REFORMATORUM.
Vier glazen; gedenkboek 1886-1961. [Delft? 1961] 410 p. illus., ports. 25cm.

Includes bibliographical references.
CONTENTS. --Societas studiosorum reformatorum. --Christen in deze tijd. --Venster op de wereld. --Toekomstverwachting.

1. Societies, Religious--Netherlands. 2. Christianity--Essays and misc.
NN R 8.61 a/R OS(1b) PC, 1, 2 SL (LC1, X1, Z1)

MTE

SOCIETAT CATALANA D'ESTUDIS HISTÒRICS.
Miscel·lània Puig i Cadafalch; recull d'estudis d'arqueologia, d'història de l'art i d'història oferts a Josep Puig i Cadafalch. Barcelona, Institut d'estudis catalans, 1951. 1 v. illus., port. 26cm.

Vol. 1.
Title-page of v. 1 dated 1947-1951.
Bibliographical footnotes.

1. Puig i Cadafalch, José, 1869- . 2. Archaeology—Addresses, essays, lectures. 3. Art—History. 4. History—Addresses, essays, lectures. I. Institut d'estudis catalans, Barcelona. II. Title.
NN** X 8.54 (OC)II OS(1b), I PC, 1, 2, 3, 4, I, II SL A, 3, I, II (Z1, LC1, X1) [I]

MAR p.v.1046

Société des amis de Gustave Courbet.
Hommage à Gustave Courbet. [Besançon] Les Amis de Gustave Courbet, 1948. 27 l. illus. 25cm.

No. 330 of 750 copies.

Festschrift

1. Courbet, Gustave, 1819–1877. I. Title.
N. Y. P. L. January 8, 1951

QEN

Societatea română de ştiinţe, Bucharest.
Hommage au professeur E. C. Teodoresco. Bucuresti: Institut de arte grafice şi editură "Marvan", s.a.r., 1937. 240 p. incl. diagrs., tables. illus. (incl. charts), plates (1 col'd), port. 23½cm.

"Ce livre a été publié par les soins de la 'Société roumaine des sciences'."
Bibliography at end of most of the chapters.
CONTENTS.—Colin, H. La corrélation des caractères et la sélection. Le cas de la betterave.—Dufour, Léon. Monsieur E. C. Teodoresco et la Laboratoire de biologie végétale de Fontainebleu.—Guilliermond, A. Remarques sur la coloration vitale des cellules épidermiques des écailles d'Allium Cepa par le vert Janus et par les violets de Dahlia et de méthyle.—Michel-Durand, E. Le métabolisme du phosphore dans les

(Continued)

N. Y. P. L. December 23, 1938

OAP

Société française des électriciens, Paris.
A propos du centenaire des découvertes de Michel Faraday, 1831–1931. Paris: Société française des électriciens[, 1932]. 244 p. incl. pl., port. illus. 27cm.

Cover-title.
Plate printed on both sides; facsim. on recto.
On back: Tome 2, no. 23 bis. Bulletin de la Société française des électriciens. Novembre, 1932.

Festschrift.

637160A. 1. Faraday, Michael, 1791–1867. 2. Science—Essays and misc. 3. Electromagnetism. I. Title.
N. Y. P. L. June 27, 1933

Societatea română de ştiinţe, Bucharest. Hommage au professeur E. C. Teodoresco... (Card 2)

feuilles caduques sur la fin de la végétation.—Molliard, Marin. Rendement et croissance des plantes vertes en fonction de la teneur de l'atmosphère en gaz carbonique.—Davy de Virville, Ad. Observations sur la température des végétaux en altitude dans les Pyrénées.—Maige, Albert. Les aspects de la chloroplastogénèse dans les cellules de la pomme de terre et du lis.—Alexandri, A. V. La mosaïque de Solanum melongena L. en Roumanie.—Grintzesco, Jean. Observations écologiques sur les plantes alpines et leurs migrations.—Ionesco, M. A. La larve de Cephennium carnicum Reitter (Coleoptera). Étude morphologique.—Iuracec, A. La variation de l'acidité actuelle du liquide nutritif dans les cultures de l'Aspergillus niger. L'influence de la température et du zinc.—Moreau, Fernand, and C. Moruzi. Sur l'existence de "souches neutres"

(Continued)

N. Y. P. L. December 23, 1938

PMB

SOCIETY FOR ANALYTICAL CHEMISTRY.
Analytical chemistry, 1962; the proceedings of the international symposium held at Birmingham University (U.K.) April, 1962, in honor of Fritz Feigl, to commemorate his 70th birthday. Edited by Philip W. West, A.M.G. Macdonald, and T.S. West. Amsterdam, New York, Elsevier Pub. Co., 1963. x, 411 p. diagrs., tables. 25cm.

Organized by its Midlands section.

(Continued)

NN * R 11.64 j/ (OC)I OS, II PC, 1, 2, 3, I, II SL ST, 1, 2, 3, I, II (LC1, X1, Z1) 2

Societatea română de ştiinţe, Bucharest. Hommage au professeur E. C. Teodoresco... (Card 3)

chez les Ascomycètes du genre Neurospora.—Oescu, C. V. Quelques folles-avoines de Roumanie.—Popa, G. T., and F. G. Popa. The flying-reflex in pigeon.—Popescu, Ştefan. Anomalies chez les plantes cultivées.—Rayss, T. Contributions à la connaissance des Urédinées de Palestine.—Sălăgeanu, N. Sur la nutrition chez les Rhinanthacées.—Sandu-Ville, C. Essais de stimulation de la végétation par l'acide cyanhydrique.—Săvulescu, Tr. Uredineae novae Romaniae.—Stănescu, P. P. Wilting and drying out of Sedum Telephium L. in various environmental conditions.—Steopoe, I. Observations cytologiques sur l'ovogénèse du Dytique.

963535A. 1. Teodorescu, Emanuel Const., 1866- . 2. Botany, Economic.
N. Y. P. L. December 23, 1938

SOCIETY FOR ANALYTICAL CHEMISTRY. Analytical chemistry, 1962... (Card 2)

Includes bibliographies.

1. Chemistry--Congresses, Internat., 1962. 2. Chemistry, Analytical, 1963. 3. Feigl, Fritz, 1891- . I. West, Philip William, 1913- ed. II. Title: International Feigl anniversary symposium on analytical chemistry.

E-10
6195

Société des amis d'Albert Thomas.
Albert Thomas vivant, un grand citoyen du monde: études, témoignages, souvenirs. [Genève, 1957] xvi, 337 p. illus., ports. 25 cm.

"Publié ... à l'occasion de la célébration du vingt-cinquième anniversaire de la mort ... d'Albert Thomas."
Bibliographical footnotes.

1. THOMAS, ALBERT ARISTIDE, 1878-1932

NN* R 9.58 d/ OS(1b*) PC, 1 SL E, 1 (LC1, X1, Z1)

E-11
6940

SOCIETY OF ARCHIVISTS (Great Britain)
Essays in memory of Sir Hilary Jenkinson; edited by Albert E.J. Hollaender. Chichester, Sussex, Printed by Moore and Tillyer, 1962. 189 p. illus., port. 25cm.

Bibliographical footnotes.
CONTENTS.--The archivist; Latin verses, by G.H. Fowler.--The building of the Public record office, by R. H. Ellis.--Some early seals at

(Continued)

NN R 5.63 p/ (OC)I, IIbo OS PC, 1, 2, I SL E, 1, 2, I (LC1, X1, Z1) [I] 3

SOCIETY OF ARCHIVISTS (Great Britain) Essays in memory of Sir Hilary Jenkinson... (Card 2)

Arundel castle, by F. W. Steer. --The study of palaeography and sigillography in England: Sir Hilary Jenkinson's contribution, by P. T. V. M. Chaplais. --The fine art of destruction, by W. K. Lamb. --The development of local archive service in England, by E. Ralph. --The British records association and the modern archive movement, by M. F. Bond. --Administration of the archives of the British transport commission, by L. C. Johnson. --Business archives; a survey of developments in Great Britain, the United States of America and in Australia, by D. S. Macmillan. --An analysis of (Continued)

---

*PDG

Society for Old Testament study.
Studies in Old Testament prophecy, presented to Professor Theodore H. Robinson...by the Society for Old Testament study on his sixty-fifth birthday, August 9th, 1946. Ed. by H. H. Rowley. Edinburgh, T. & T. Clark, 1950. xi, 206 p. 22cm.

"A bibliography of the writings of Theodore Henry Robinson," p. 201-206.

1. Robinson, Theodore Henry, 1881- . 2. Bible. O. T. Prophets—Criticism. I. Rowley, Harold Henry, 1890- , ed. II. Title.
N. Y. P. L.

SOCIETY OF ARCHIVISTS (Great Britain) Essays in memory of Sir Hilary Jenkinson... (Card 3)

Jenkinson's Manual of archive administration in the light of Australian experience, by L. Maclean. --Jenkinson and Jamaica, by C. V. Black. --Archivist itinerant; Jenkinson in wartime Italy, by H. E. Bell. --The education of an archivist, by R. Irwin.

1. Jenkinson, Sir Hilary. 2. Archives. I. Hollaender, Albert E. J., ed. II. Hollaender, Albert E. J.

CBA

Some modern historians of Britain; essays in honor of R. L. Schuyler, by some of his former students at Columbia university, ed. by Herman Ausubel, J. Bartlet Brebner and Erling M. Hunt. New York, Dryden press, 1951. xiv,384 p. 22cm.

Bibliographical footnotes.

1. Historians, British. 2. Great Britain—Hist.—Historiography. 3. Schuyler, Robert Livingston,1883- I. Ausubel, Herman, ed.
NN*

---

*PDB

Society for Old Testament Study.
Promise and fulfilment; essays presented to Professor S. H. Hooke in celebration of his ninetieth birthday, 21st January, 1964, by members of the Society for Old Testament Study, and others. Edited by F. F. Bruce. Edinburgh, T. & T. Clark [°1963]
vii, 214 p. port. 23 cm.
Bibliographical footnotes.
CONTENTS.—Samuel Henry Hooke: a personal appreciation, by W. R. Matthews.—Old Testament theology and its methods, by A. A. Anderson.—The propaganda factor in some ancient Near Eastern cosmogonies, by S. G. F. Brandon.—Promise and fulfilment in Paul's presentation of Jesus, by F. F. Bruce.—The ark in the Psalms, by G. H. Davies.—Sacred numbers and round figures, by G. R. Driver.—
(Continued)

NN * R 3.65 c/ȝ (OC)I OS PC, 1, 2, SL 3, I, II J, 1, 2, 3, I, II (LC1, X1, Z1)

E-13
8864

Some pathways in twentieth-century history; essays in honor of Reginald Charles McGrane. Edited by Daniel R. Beaver. Detroit, published for the University of Cincinnati by Wayne State University Press, 1969.
313 p. port. 24 cm.

CONTENTS.—Introduction, by W. C. Langsam.—Editor's preface, by D. R. Beaver.—Reginald Charles McGrane, by H. R. Stevens.—"A fair field and no favor": The structure of informal empire, by T.
(Continued)

NN*R 6. 70 r/ OC, I, II PC, 1, I, II SL (LC1, X1, Z1)

Society for Old Testament Study. Promise and fulfilment ... [°1963]
CONTENTS—Continued.
Inspiration: poetical and divine, by A. M. Farrer.—The Arabic background of the book of Job, by A. Guillaume.—The Old Testament and some aspects of New Testament Christology, by A. J. B. Higgins.—Kingship as communication and accommodation, by N. Q. King.—The Pentateuch and the triennial lectionary cycle: an examination of a recent theory, by J. R. Porter.—Time in the Old Testament, by N. H. Snaith.—Exposition in the Old Testament and in rabbinical literature, by J. Weingreen.—Royal ideology and the Testaments of the Twelve Patriarchs, by G. Widengren.—Principal works of Professor S. H. Hooke (p. 213-214)

(Continued)

Some pathways in twentieth-century history ... 1969. (Card 2)

McCormick.—William Howard Taft and the Ohio endorsement issue, 1906-1908, by A. D. Sumberg.—George W. Goethals and the problem of military supply, by D. R. Beaver.—The British Labour Party and the Paris settlement, by H. R. Winkler.—Leopold Amery: Man against the stars in the courses, by C. W. Vogel.—An illusion that shaped history: New light on the history and historiography of American peace efforts before Munich, by F. L. Loewenheim.—The American arsenal policy in World War II: a retrospective view, by
(Continued)

SOCIETY FOR OLD TESTAMENT STUDY. Promise and fulfilment... (Card 3)

1. Bible. O. T.--Criticism. 2. Hooke, Samuel Henry, 1874- 3. Bible. N. T. and Jewish literature. I. Bruce, F. F., ed. II. Title.

SOME pathways in twentieth-century history... 1969. (Card 3)

R. M. Leighton.—Yalta viewed from Tehran, by W. M. Franklin.—Reginald Charles McGrane: A selected bibliography, compiled by H. R. Stevens (p. 263-266)—Notes (p. 267-301)

1. History, Modern, 20th cent. I. McGrane, Reginald Charles, 1889-1967. II. Beaver, Daniel R., ed.

E-11
9132

SOMERS, GERALD G., ed.
Labor, management, and social policy; essays in the John R. Commons tradition. Madison, University of Wisconsin press, 1963. xiv, 303 p. mounted port. 24cm.

Includes bibliographies.

1. Labor economics. 2. Labor--U.S. 3. Commons, John Rogers, 1862-1945. I. Somers, Gerald G.
NN R 3.64 f/$\mathcal{B}$ OC, Ibo PC, 1, 2, 3 SL E, 1, 2, 3 (LC1, X1, Z1)

---

*PAM

Soncino-gesellschaft der freunde des jüdischen buches e. v., *Berlin.*
Festschrift für Aron Freimann zum 60. geburtstage; herausgegeben von Alexander Marx und Herrmann Meyer ... Dargebracht von der Soncino-gesellschaft der freunde des jüdischen buches e. v., Berlin. Berlin, 1935.
173, [3] p. illus. (map, facsim.) mounted port. 32cm.
In double columns.
CONTENTS.—Emmrich, Hanna. Aron Friemann-bibliographie.—Cassuto, Umberto. Manoscritti ebraici della R. Biblioteca laurenziana in Firenze.—Blondheim, D. S. Liste des manuscrits de l'Arouk de Nathan bar Yehiel.—Freimann, Jakob. Eine handschrift der "Simane or sarua" aus dem jahre 1408.—Horovitz, Jakob. Aus der Oxforder handschrift des Josif Omez.—Scholem, Gerhard. Einige kabbalistische handschriften
(Continued on next card)
A 40-549
[2]

Festschrift

Soncino-gesellschaft der freunde des jüdischen buches e. v., *Berlin.* Festschrift für Aron Freimann ... 1935. (Card 2)

CONTENTS—Continued.
im Britischen museum.—Alting, Jacob. The Hebrew letters of Jacob Alting, communicated by George Alexander Kohut.—Wischnitzer-Bernstein, Rahel. Der Siddur der Altstädtischen synagoge in Rzeszow.—Marx, Alexander. Ein verschollener pergamentdruck Riva di Trento 1560.—Cowley, A. E. Ein Soncino-druck aus Kairo 1566.—C., M. Zur geschichte des hebräischen buchdruckes in Russland und Polen.—Brilling, Bernhard. Die jüdische buchdruckerei in Auras (Niederschlesien)—Bamberger, S. Wandsbeker druckperiode des Israel ben Abraham 1726-1733.—Bibliographisches verzeichnis der hebräischen drucke in Wandsbek 1726-1733.—Trennungsstrich, fragezeichen und ausrufungszeichen im hebräischen buchdruck.—Weinryb, S. B. Berliner jüdischer kalen-
(Continued on next card)
A 40-549
[2]

Soncino-gesellschaft der freunde des jüdischen buches e. v., *Berlin.* Festschrift für Aron Freimann ... 1935. (Card 3)

CONTENTS—Continued.
der.—Simonsen, D. Eine sammlung polemischer und apologetischer literatur.—Freimann, Alfred. Zur bibliographie der hebräischen Responsen des Maimonides.—Krauss, Samuel. Zur literatur der Siddurim.—Cohen, Boaz. A list of authors of responsa printed in the פחד יצחק.—Schwarz, A. Z. Ein vorschlag.—Bloch, Joshua. An early Hebrew translation of the Book of common prayer..—Schapiro, Israel. Schiller und Goethe im hebräischen, eine bibliographie.—Italiener, Bruno. Isak B. Secharjah, ein jüdischer lederschnittkünstler des 15. jahrhunderts.—Marmorstein, Alexander. Zum wortlaut der Keduschah.—Agnon, S. J. Eine hübsche geschichte von meinem gebetbuch.

1. Freimann, Aron, 1871- 2. Jewish literature—Bibliography. I. Marx, Alexander, 1878- ed. II. Meyer, Herrmann, ed.
A 40-549
New York. Public library for Library of Congress [2]

Write on slip words underlined below and class mark — *DF

Sonderheft für Egon Erwin Kisch der am 29. IV. 1935 fünfzig Jahre alt wurde. [Articles by Pierre Merin, Karl Schmückle and others.]

(Neue deutsche Blätter. Prag, 1935. Jahr 2, p.257-287.)

form 400b [xi-6-33 25m]

AN
(Mannerheim, C.)

Sotainvaliidien veljesliitto.
C. G. Mannerheim, suomen marsalkka. Toimituskunta: V. A. M. Karikoski, H. Kekoni, A. E. Martola. [Helsinki] Kivi, Sotainvaliidien veljesliitto [1951]
334 p. illus., maps. 30cm.

1. Mannerheim, Carl Gustaf Emil, friherre, 1867-1951. I. Karikoski, Väinö Adolf Mathias, 1899- , ed. II. Title.
NN

NAB

SOUTH ATLANTIC MODERN LANGUAGE ASSOCIATION.
South Atlantic studies for Sturgis E. Leavitt, edited by Thomas B. Stroup and Sterling A. Stoudemire. Washington, D. C., Scarecrow press, 1953. 215 p. port. 22cm.

Includes bibliographies.
CONTENTS.—Vita.—Defense against neo-barbarism, by L. B. Wright. -- Pitas payas, by L. G. Moffat.—Criticism of La Araucana by Ercilla's contemporaries, by P. T. Manchester.—Bird names in Spanish, by U. T. Holmes, jr.—Two early Quechua-Spanish dictionaries and American Spanish pronunciation, by D. L. Canfield.—Lope de Vega and the common
(Continued)
NN ** R 4.54 (OC) I, Ib, II, III OS PC, 1, 2, I, II, III SL (LC1, Z1, X1) [1]

SOUTH ATLANTIC MODERN LANGUAGE ASSOCIATION. South Atlantic studies for Sturgis E. Leavitt. (Card 2)

man, by F. Hayes.—The literary sources of El castigo del penséque of Tirso de Molina, by G. E. Wade.—Resources for research in Latin-American literature in Southern libraries, by L. S. Thompson.—Some aspects of Spanish American fiction, by J. A. Crow.--Mariano Azuela: a summing up, 1873-1952, by J. E. Englekirk.—Concepts of genteel conversation in the French Renaissance, by W. L. Wiley.—The critical appreciation of Greek literature in the French Renaissance, by L. C. Stevens.—Machiavelli as poet, by A. Gilbert.--Echoing verse endings in Paradise lost, by A. Oras.—An interpretation of A psalm of life with reference to
(Continued)

SOUTH ATLANTIC MODERN LANGUAGE ASSOCIATION. South Atlantic studies for Sturgis E. Leavitt. (Card 3)

Manrique's Coplas, by R. S. Ward.—A note on Borrow's bookish dialogue, by J. E. Tilford, jr.—The mosaic technique in the novel, by E. W. Parks.

1. Leavitt, Sturgis Elleno, 1888- 2. Literature—Hist. and crit. I. Stroup, Thomas B., ed. II. Stoudemire, Sterling Aubrey, 1902- , ed. III. Title.

VBA p.v.1642
SOUTH HOLLAND. Gedeputeerde staten.
Het Zuid-Hollandse waterschapsrecht 1946-1954. [Te Alphen aan den Rijn, N. Samson, 1954] 1 v. (various pagings) fold. map. 24cm.

Presented by the Gedeputeerde staten van Zuid-Holland to Mr. G. J. C. Schilthuis on his 70th birthday, published by the Zuidhollandse waterschapsrecht.
CONTENTS.—Voorword, door L. A. Kesper.--De bestuurlijke zijde van het beleid, door D. Ormel.--Het belang van een goede waterschapszorg uit
(Continued)
NN ** R 10.57 v/ (OC)II ODt EDt (OS)I, Ib PC, 1, 2, 3, I, II SL (E)1, 2, 3, I, II ST, 1, 2, 3, I, II (LC1, X1, Z1)

SOUTH HOLLAND. Gedeputeerde staten. Het Zuid-Hollandse waterschapsrecht 1946-1954. (Card 2)

technisch oogpunt, door J. L. Klein. --Waterschappen en landbouw, door F. Hellinga. --Waterschapsrecht in beweging, door C. H. F. Polak.

1. WATERWAYS--JURISP.--NETHERLANDS, 1954
2. WATER--JURISP.--NETHERLANDS, 1954
3. DIKES--JURISP.--NETHERLANDS, 1954 I. Zuidhollandse waterschapsbond
II. Het Zuid-Hollandse waterschapsrecht 1946-1954. t. 1954

AN
(Bainville, J.)

Le souvenir de Jacques Bainville. Paris, "Les Amis des beaux livres" [1936]

8 p. l., 189, [1] p., 1 l. incl. facsim. front. (port.) 25½cm.

"Il a été tiré de cet ouvrage pour les membres de la société de bibliophiles 'Les amis des beaux livres': 130 exemplaires ... 25 exemplaires ... réservés au Cercle d'études Jacques Bainville de Marseille; 375 exemplaires numérotés ... et quelques exemplaires de présent. Exemplaire nº 150."

Introductions by Léon Daudet and Henri Massis, director of La Revue universelle.

"Ont collaboré à cet ouvrage: Henry Bordeaux ... Abel Bonnard ... André Bellessort ... [et 50 d'autres]"—7th prelim. leaf.

Reprinted, with a few additions, from La Revue universelle, t. 64, no. 23. Original title: Hommage à Jacques Bainville.

1. Bainville, Jacques, 1879–1936. I. *Daudet, Léon, 1867– II. Massis, Henri, 1886– III. Amis des beaux livres, Paris.

A C 37-140. Festschrift

New York. Public library for Library of Congress [2]

---

* MN p.v. 15

SOUVENIRS de Fanny Cerrito; trois airs de danse pour le piano-forte, avec le violin ou le flûte ad libitum dansé par Mª Cerrito pendant l'automne de l'année 1843. Rome, J. Briaschi & J. Maneschi [1843?] 8 p. 36cm.

Colored port. of Fanny Cerrito on cover.

CONTENTS. —Saragosse. —Caciuka. —Masurka [par] Laner [sic].

1. Dances (Piano). 2. Dances (Violin and piano). 3. Dances (Flute and piano).
NN 8.63 g/r OC SL MUg, 1g, 2g, 3g (LC1, X1, Z1)

TAH

SOVANI, N. V., ed.
Changing India; essays in honour of Professor D. R. Gadgil. Edited by N. V. Sovani [and] V. M. Dandekar. Bombay, New York, Asia Pub. House [1961] x, 356 p. illus., port. 23cm.

Bibliographical footnotes.

1. Economic history--India, 1945- . 2. India--Soc. condit. 3. Gadgil, Dhananjaya Ramchandra. I. Dandekar, V. M., joint ed.
NN*R 12.63 g/r OC, I PC, 1, 2, 3, I SL E, 1, 2, 3, I O, 2, 3, I (LC1, X1, Z1)

D-10
5240

SOZIALPOLITIK, Arbeits- und Sozialrecht; Festschrift für Friedrich Sitzler zu seinem 75. Geburtstag. Hrsg. von Hans Constantin Paulsen [et al.] Stuttgart, Forkel, 1956. 448 p. port. 21cm.

Bibliographical footnotes.

1. Legislation, Social. 2. Labor--Jurisp. 3. Sitzler, Friedrich. I. Paulsen, Hans Constantin, ed. II. Paulsen, Hans Constantin.
NN R 7.57 d/r OC, I, IIbo PC, 1, 2, 3, I SL E, 1, 2, 3, I (LC1, X1, Z1, Y1)

E-11
113

SOZIALREFORM und Sozialrecht; Beiträge zum Arbeits- und Sozialversicherungsrecht und zur Sozialpolitik. Festschrift für Walter Bogs, hrsg. von Kurt Jantz, Horst Neuman-Duesberg [und] Dieter Schewe. Berlin, Duncker & Humblot [1959]

439 p. port. 21 cm.

Bibliographical footnotes.

1. Bogs, Walter, 1899- . 2. Social policy--Addresses, essays, lectures. 3. Labor--Jurisp. 4. Insurance, Workmen's--Jurisp.
I. Jantz, Kurt, ed.
NN * R 4.60 m/r OC, Ib+, I PC, 1, 2, 3, 4, I SL E, 1, 2, 3, 4, I (LC1, X1, Z1)

SB

Soziologische Forschung in unserer Zeit; ein Sammelwerk, Leopold von Wiese zum 75. Geburtstag. Hrsg. von Karl Gustav Specht. Köln [etc.] Westdeutscher Verlag [1951] 349 p. diagr. 24cm.

Bibliographies included.

1. Sociology, 1945- . 2. Wiese und Kaiserswaldau, Leopold Max Wather, 1876- . I. Specht, Karl Gustav, ed.
NN* 1.53 OC, I PC, 1, 2, I SL E, 1, 2, I (LC1, Z1, X1)

SB

Soziologische Studien zur Politik, Wirtschaft und Kultur der Gegenwart; Alfred Weber gewidmet. Potsdam: A. Protte[, 1930]. 305 p. front. (mounted port.) 8°.

Contents: Lederer, E. Durch die Wirklichkeit zur politischen Idee. Brinkmann, C. Die Integration des amerikanischen Staatswesens. Salz, A. Die irrationale Grundlage der kapitalistischen Wirtschafts- und Gesellschaftsordnung. Marschak, J. Zur modernen Interessendifferenzierung. Haubach, T. Die Generationenfrage und der Sozialismus. Goverts, H. Wahlverfahren und lebendige Demokratie in Deutschland. Petzet, W. Die Paradoxie des Revolutionärs. Eckardt, H. von. Die Depossedierung des Führers und die politische Praxis des Kollektivs. Lütkens, C. Demokratie und öffentliche Meinung in den Vereinigten Staaten. Lütkens, G. Staat und Aussenpolitik.

(Continued)

N. Y. P. L. April 7, 1931

Soziologische Studien zur Politik, Wirtschaft und Kultur der Gegenwart... (Card 2)

Clauss, M. Erziehung der Nation zum Reich. Rohan, K. A. P. Inventar der politischen Grundhaltungen im modernen Europa. Ziegler, H. O. Zur Souveränität der Nation. Reiner, P. Ueber die kulturpolitische Bedeutung der Freien Erziehungsgemeinschaften in Deutschland. Mitgau, H. Grundlagen des sozialen Aufstieges. Ungern-Sternberg, L. von. Der Geist der modernen chinesischen Jugend. Preetorius, E. Das Problem der Qualität.

516177A. 1. Weber, Alfred, 1868- . 2. Sociology—Essays and misc.
N. Y. P. L. April 7, 1931

---

*PBN
(Millás Vallicrosa)

SPAIN. Investigaciones científicas, Consejo superior de.
Homenaje a Millás-Vallicrosa. Barcelona, 1954-56. 2 v. illus., port. 26cm.

Contributions in various languages.
Includes bibliographies.

1. Millás i Vallicrosa, José María, 1897- . 2. Semitic studies. I. Title. t. 1954.
NN R 1.63 e/r (OC)I ODt EDt PC, 1, 2, I SL J, 1, 2, I O, 1, 2, I (LC1, X1, Z1) [I]

Copy only words underlined & classmark— HCA

SPAIN. Investigaciones científicas, Consejo superior de. Instituto Gonzalo Fernández de Oviedo. [Homenaje a Fernández de Oviedo. Madrid, 1957] [391]-705 p. illus. 24cm. (Revista de Indias. Año 17, no. 69/70)

CONTENTS. --Rasgos del semblante espiritual de Gonzalo Fernández de Oviedo, por J. Pérez de Tudela Bueso. --Fernández de Oviedo, etnólogo, por M. Ballesteros Gaibrois. --Fernández de Oviedo y el conocimiento del mar del Sur, por R. Ferrando. -- El indio americano y su (Continued)

NN R 8.59 t/ ODt EDt OI PC, 1 AH, 1 (LC2, X1, Z1)

SPAIN. Investigaciones científicas, Consejo superior de. Instituto Gonzalo Fernández de Oviedo. [Homenaje a Fernández de Oviedo. (Card 2)

cicunstancia en la obra de Fernández de Oviedo, por J. Z. Vázquez. --Gonzalo Fernández de Oviedo y Valdés, veedor de Tierra Firme, por E.J. Castillero R. --La historia natural en Fernández de Oviedo, por E. Alvarez López. --Contribuciones para una biografía de Gonzalo Fernández de Oviedo, por J. de la Peña y Cámara.

1. Oviedo y Valdés, Gonzalo Fernández de, 1478-1557. t. 1957.

RG

SPAIN. Investigaciones científicas, Consejo superior de. Patronato Marcelino Menédez y Pelayo. Estudios dedicados a Menéndez Pidal. Madrid, 1950-62. 7 v. in 8. illus., ports., maps (part fold.) facsims. 26cm.

Most contributions in Spanish: some in English, German, Italian, or French.

Bibliographical footnotes accompany most contributions.

1. Spanish language--Addresses, essays, lectures. 2. Spanish literature--Addresses, essays, lectures. 3. Spain--Hist. --Addresses, essays, lectures. 4. Menéndez Pidal, Ramón, 1869- . I. Title. t. 1950

NN 11.63 g/ (OC)Is ODts EDts PCs, 1s, 2s, 3s, 4s, Is SLs (LC1s, X1s, Z1)

AD-10
760

Der SPANNUNGSBOGEN; Festgabe für Paul Tillich zum 75. Geburtstag [Hrsg. von Karl Hennig] Stuttgart, Evangelisches Verlagswerk [1961] 186 p. 23cm.

CONTENTS. --Paul Tillich-- Wanderer zwischen zwei Welten, von H. Thielicke. --Paul Tillichs philosophische Theologie, W. Weischedel. --Uber das "Gloria Patri" von W. Stählin. --Vom Gebrauch neuer Begriffe in der Theologie, von U. Neuenschwander. --Was heisst "natürliche Offenbarung"? Von T. Siegfried. --Theologie-Fachwissen oder Grundwissen? (Continued)

NN R 2.64 p/ OC, I, IIbo PC, 1, 2, I SL (LC1, X1, Z1) 2

Der SPANNUNGSBOGEN... (Card 2)

Von E. Heimann. --Über eine dritte Kraft, von A. Löwe. --Über die deutschen Juden, von M. Horkheimer. --Paul Tillichs Bedeutung für das amerikanische Geistesleben, von H. Lilje. --Paul Tillich: Leben und Werk, von K. Hennig.

1. Tillich, Paul, 1886- 2. Theology--Addresses, essays, lectures. I. Hennig, Karl, ed. II. Hennig, Karl.

E-11
9120

SPECHT, KARL GUSTAV, ed.
Studium Sociale; Ergebnisse sozialwissenschaftlicher Forschung der Gegenwart. [Karl Valentin Müller zugeeiguet] Hrsg. von Karl Gustav Specht, Hans Georg Rasch [und] Hans Hofbauer. Köln, Westdeutscher Verlag [1963] xvi, 835 p. port. 25cm.

Contributions in German, English, French, Italian or Spanish.
Includes bibliographies.

1. Mueller, Karl Valentin. 2. Social sciences--Addresses, essays, lectures. I. Title.

NN R 3.64 a/ OC, I PC, 1, 2, I SL E, 1, 2, I (LC1, X1, Z1)

E-12
602

SPECIAL SCIENCES ASSOCIATION, Madras.
Anthropology on the march; recent studies of Indian beliefs, attitudes and social institutions, edited by Bala Ratnam, general secretary, Social sciences association. Madras, The Book centre [1963] xvi, 390 p. illus., ports. 25cm.

Includes bibliographies.
Issued for the centenary of the birth of L. K. Ananthakrishna Iyer. (Continued)

NN R 7.64 a/ (OC)I, IIb* OS PC, 1, 2, 3, 4, I SL O, 1, 2, 3, I (LC1, X1, Z1) 2

SPECIAL SCIENCES ASSOCIATION, Madras. Anthropology on the march. (Card 2)

1. India--Civilization. 2. India--Native races. 3. Ananta Krishna Ayyar, L. K., 1864-1937. 4. Anthropology--India. I. Ratnam, Bala, ed. II. Ratnam, Bala.

E-11
7071

SPEGG, HANS LUDWIG, ed.
Unterwegs mit Rolf Italiaander; Begegnungen, Betrachtungen, Bibliographie. [Zum 50. Geburtstag von Rolf Italiaander] Hamburg, Freie Akademie der Künste [1963] 142 p. illus., ports. 24cm.

1. Italiaander, Rolf, 1913- . I. Freie, Akademie der Künste, Hamburg. II. Spegg, Hans Ludwig.

NN R 2.64 a/ OC, IIbo (OS)I PC, 1, I SL (LC1, X1, Z1)

YBG

Spinoza-festschrift; herausgegeben von Siegfried Hessing, zum 300. geburtstage Benedict Spinozas (1632–1932) ... Heidelberg, Carl Winter [°1933]
xvi, 222, [2] p. ports. 24½cm.

"Das werk wurde in eintausend handnummerierten exemplaren gedruckt. Dieses exemplar trägt die nummer 404."

CONTENTS.—Einleitung.—Hessing, S. Salve Spinoza!—Brucar, J. Spinoza und die ewigkeit der seele.—Buber, M. Spinoza und die chassidische botschaft.—Droop, F. Fünf szenen aus dem leben Spinozas.—Dubnow, S. Die gestalt.—Gebhardt, C. Der gotische Jude.—Gherasim, V. Die bedeutung der affektenlehre Spinozas.—Grunwald, M. Der lebensphilosoph Spinoza.—Hessing, S. Die glückseligkeit des freien menschen.—Klatzkin, J. Der missverstandene.—Klausner, J. Der jüdische charakter der lehre Spinozas.—Marcianu, M. Ein bekennt-
(Continued on next card)

A C 33-3181

[2]

Spinoza-festschrift; herausgegeben von Siegfried Hessing ...
[c1933] (Card 2)

CONTENTS—Continued.

nis.—Myslicki, I. Spinoza und das ideal des menschen.—Niemirower, I. Spinozaverehrung eines nichtspinozisten.—Petrovici, I. Eine Spinoza huldigung.—Rolland, R. Der lichtstrahl Spinozas.—Sass, K. Spinozas Bibelkritik und Gottesbegriff.—Siegel, C. Vom grundlegenden dualismus in Spinozas system.—Sokolow, N. Der Jude Spinoza.—Zweig, A. Der schriftsteller Spinoza.—Äusserungen von: Alfred Einstein, Sigmund Freud und Jakob Wassermann.

1. Spinoza, Benedictus de, 1632–1677. I. Hessing, Siegfried, 1903– ed.

A C 33–3181

Title from N. Y. Pub. Libr. Printed by L. C.

[2]

NFD
(Spitteler)

Spitteler, Carl, 1845–1924.
Carl Spitteler, Leben und Dichtung. Zum 100. Geburtstag, 24. April 1945. Zürich, Verein Gute Schriften [1945] 107 p. port. 20cm.

Edited by Alfred Specker. — *cf Zum Geleit.*
"Literaturangaben," p. 105–107.

430946B. I. Specker, Alfred, ed.
N. Y. P. L.

Festschrift

November 29, 1951

---

* Q p.v.1906

SPOLEK RODÁKŮ A PŘÁTEL MĚSTA TURNOVA A OKOLÍ, Prague.
Václav Fortunát Durych [K 150. výročí úmrtí vydal s podporou ministerstva informací a osvěty Spolek rodáků a přátel města Turnova a okolí v Praze. Uspořádal a předmluvu napsal Jindřich Dlouhý] [Praha] 1952. 56 p. illus., facsims. 21cm.

(Continued)

NN* * R X 3.59 m/L (OC)Ib, I (OD)IIt (ED)IIt, OS(Ib)
PC, 1, I, II SL S, 1, I, II (LC1, X1, Z1)

SPOLEK RODÁKŮ A PŘÁTEL MĚSTA TURNOVA A OKOLÍ, Prague. Václav Fortunát Durych... (Card 2)

CONTENTS. --Vaníček, J. Václav Fortunát Durych (Životopisny nástin.) --Durychová, M. Vědecká činnost Václava Fortunáta Durycha. --Vaníček, J. Výňatky z Durychovy korespondenee. -- Eysselt-Klimpěly K. "Nikoli nejmenší." --Kinsky, K. Kult památky P. Fortunáta Durycha. --Marek, A. Řeč při svěccní Durychova pomníku v Turnově.

1. Durych, Vaclav Fortunat, 1735-1802. I. Dlouhy, Jindrich, ed. II. Czechoslovakia, Ministerstvo informaci a osvety. t. 1952. i. informaci.

---

* QKK

SPOMEN-Knjiga iz Bosne. Uredio Ivan Saric. Odobrio Ordinarijat vrhbosanski. Zagreb, Nakl. Kaptola vrhbasanskoga, 1901. 227 p. illus., ports. 35cm.

"Biskupu Josipu Jurju Strossmayeru u spomen petdesetgodisnjice njegova biskupovanja, 1850-1900."
Includes bibliographies.
CONTENTS. — Dio 1. U slavu Josipu Jurju Strossmayeru, o zlatnom njegov biskupskom jubileu: 8. rujna 1850-8. rujna 1900. —dio 2. Bosanska biskupija do turskoga gospodstva. —dio 3. Katolicka crkva u Bosni. — dio 4. Stolna crkvu u Djakvu.

(Continued)

NN * X 10.54 OC, II, IIIb* (OS) I, Ib* PC, 1, 2, 3, I, II SL S, 1, 2, 3, I, II (LC1, Z1, X1)

SPOMEN-Knjiga iz Bosne. Uredio Ivan Saric... (Card 2)

1. Strossmayer, Josip Juraj, bp. of Diakovo, 1815-1905. 2. Catholic church, Roman--Bosnia and Herzegovina. 3. Cathedrals--Yugoslavia--Djakovo. I. Sarajevo, Yugoslavia (Archdiocese). Ordinarijat. II. Saric, Ivan, abp. 1871- ed. III. Saric, Ivan, abp. 1871-

---

E-13
7112

SPRACHE und Politik; Festgabe für Dolf Sternberger zum sechzigsten Geburtstag. Hrsg. von Carl-Joachim Friedrich und Benno Reifenberg. [Redaktion: Udo Bermbach und Peter Haungs] Heidelberg, L. Schneider [1968] 545 p. 24cm.

"Auswahlbibliographie" (a list of works by A. Sternberger): p. [537]-545.

(Continued)

NN*R 12.69 r/L OC, I, II, III PC, 1, I, II, III SL E, 1, I, II, III (LC1, X1, Z1) [I]

2

SPRACHE und Politik... (Card 2)

1. Political science--Addresses, essays, lectures. I. Sternberger, Dolf, 1907- . II. Friedrich, Carl Joachim, 1901- ed. III. Reifenberg, Benno, 1892- ed.

D-12
6650

SRI AUROBINDO MANDIR, Calcutta.
Loving homage. [Collection of the main speeches delivered on the occasion of the anniversary celebrations of the Mother's 80th birthday] Calcutta [1958] 386 p. port. 22cm.

Text in English or in French and English.
CONTENTS. --The divine Mother, by N. K. Gupta. --Presidential address, by R. R. Diwakar. --The Mother, by H. K. Niyogi. --The shape of things to

(Continued)

NN 10.60 p/L OS (Ib) PC, 1, 2 SL O, 1, 2 (LC1, X1, Z1)

3

SRI AUROBINDO MANDIR, Calcutta. Loving homage. (Card 2)

come as envisaged by Sri Aurobindo, by S. K. Maitra. --Sri Aurobindo or the future of philosophy, by K. C. Varadachari. --The Mother and the concept of divine Shakti, by H. Chaudhuri. --Shankara and Sri Aurobindo, by J. N. Chubb. --The universal mother in Sino-Indian culture, by Tan Yun Shan. --Sri Aurobindo & the Mother on dreams, by N. K. Das Gupta. --Science and its fulfilment, by M. Venkataraman. --The mother's sadhana for the earth, by Rishabhchand. --Sri Aurobindo's Savitri, by S. Iyengar. --The literary genius of the Mother, by K. Prasad. --Sri Aurobindo as a dramatist, by S. C. Sarkar. --Interviews in Japan, by V. K. Gokak. --Subjectivism and the ideal social order, by J. Mohanty. --Sri Aurobindo &

(Continued)

SRI AUROBINDO MANDIR, Calcutta. Loving homage. (Card 3)

the Indian freedom movement, by P.C. Chakravarty. --The gospel of beauty, by R.F. Piper. --Revival of the Veda, by R. Vaidyanathaswamy. --Lettre pour Mère, par G. Monod Herzen. --Les grands problèmes sociaux de notre temps, par F. Challaye. --L'allégorie de l'homme divin, par A. Niel. Pour le 21 février 1958, par C.F. Baron. --Two visions, by S.M.

1. The Mother associate of Sri Aurobindo Ghose. 2. Ghose, Aurobindo, 1872-1950. i. Aurobindo.

D-19
3349

Staat und Gesellschaft. Festgabe für Günther Küchenhoff zum 60. Geburtstag am 21. August 1967. Hrsg. von Franz Mayer. Göttingen, Schwartz, 1967.

x, 375 p., port. 23 cm.

"Aus den Schriften von Günther Küchenhoff": p. [365]-370. Bibliographical footnotes.

1. Law--Addresses, essays, lectures. I. Küchenhoff, Günther. II. Mayer, Franz, 1920- ed. III. Mayer, Franz, 1920- .
NN*R 11.69 w/ OC, I, II, IIIb PC, 1, I, II SL E, 1, I, II (LC1, X1, Z1)

SES

Staat und Wirtschaft; Beiträge zum Problem der Einwirkung des Staates auf die Wirtschaft. Festgabe zum 70. Geburtstag von Hans Nawiasky. Einsiedeln [etc.] Benziger Verlag [1950] xxiv, 309 p. port. 23cm.

"Veröffentlichungen von Professor Dr. Hans Nawiasky; zusammengestellt von Willi Geiger," p. 297-309.

565645B. 1. Industry and state. 2. Nawiasky, Hans, 1880–
N. Y. P. L. January 31, 1951

---

* MF p.v.10, no.9

Staatliche Musikschule, Weimar.

Festschrift zur Feier des fünfzigjährigen Bestehens der Staatlichen Musikschule zu Weimar (24. Juni 1922). [Weimar: Panses Verlag G.m.b.H., 1922.] 64 p. facsims., front., plates. 8°.

"Verzeichnis der Lehrer von 1872-1922," p. 51-53.
Cover-title.

1. Music—Conservatories. JUILLIARD FOUNDATION FUND. Germany—Weimar.
N. Y. P. L. October 18, 1928

SEB

Staatswetenschappelijke opstellen, aangeboden aan Prof. Mr R. Kranenburg, bij zijn aftreden als hoogleraar aan de Rijksuniversiteit te Leiden, door zijn oud-leerlingen. Alphen aan den Rijn, N. Samsom [1948] 301 p. port. 24cm.

CONTENTS.—Mok, S. Marsilius van Padua.—Meulen, J. van der. Sir John Eliot.—Vandervelden, Jos. Vondel's rechts-metaphysiek.—Kisch, I. Proeve van een typologie der rechtstheorieën.—Simons, D. Recht en rechtsbewustzijn in den bezettingstijd.—Polak, M. V. Pluralistische staatsleer.—Praag, M. M. van. De idee der democratie.—Kramer, H. L. M. Actuele problemen der Nederlandse democratie.—Veld, J. in 't. Doelmatigheid in de bestuursinrichting.—Nerée tot Babberich, M. F. F. A. de.

(Continued)

N. Y. P. L. November 23, 1949

Staatswetenschappelijke opstellen... (Card 2)

Kroon en Kamer, overwicht of evenwicht?—Bijvoet, F. A. De ontwikkeling van de financieele verhouding tusschen het rijk en de gemeenten vanaf 1865 tot 1946.—Houten, J. N. van den. Souvereiniteit en nationale autonomie.—Nord, H. R. Statengemeenschap en internationale regeering.—Kranenburg, B. W. De Uno en het machtenevenwicht.—Bibliografie van de geschriften van Prof. Mr R. Kranenburg (p. [294]-301)

491236B. 1. Kranenburg, Roelof, 1880- . 2. Law, Internat., 1914- . 3. Law—Essays and misc. 4. Political science, 1918- .
N. Y. P. L. November 23, 1949

E-11
2428

STABILE Preise in wachsender Wirtschaft; das Inflationsproblem. Erich Schneider zum 60. Geburtstag, hrsg. von Gottfried Bombach. Mit Beiträgen von John Åkerman [et al.] Tübingen, J.C.B. Mohr, 1960. x, 274 p. illus., port. 24cm.

Bibliographical footnotes.

CONTENTS. --An institutional approach to the problem of inflation, by J. Åkerman. --A chapter of the history of monetary theory and policy,

(Continued)

NN R 4.61 p/ OC, I PC, 1, 2, I SL E, 1, 2, I (LC1, X1, Z1)

STABILE Preise in wachsender Wirtschaft... (Cont.)

by J. Pedersen. --Politique monétaire Belge et inflation, par L. H. Dupriez. -- Inflation und Inflationsbekämpfung in Österreich seit 1945, von W. Weber und K. Socher. --Vers une "economie fine," par J. Rueff. --Geldinflation. Nachfrageinflation, Kosteninflation, von G. Haberler. --The infra effect of investments, by R. Frisch. --Economic models for the explanation of inflation, by J. Tinbergen. --Über die Wirkung der Zinspolitik auf die Güterpreise, von J. Niehans. --Geldwertstabilisierung bei Vollbeschäftigung, von C. Föhl. --On some factors causing inflation, by. G. U. Papi. --Inflation in dynamic theory, by R. Harrod. -- Inflation and growth, by A. H. Hansen. --Ursachen der Nach- kriegsinflation und Probleme der

(Continued)

STABILE Preise in wachsender Wirtschaft. (Cont.)

Inflationsbekämpfung, von G. Bombach. --Built-in flexibility and economic growth, by A. T. Peacock. --Finanzpolitische Massnahmen zur Inflationsverhinderung, von H. Haller. --The problem of inflation in developing countries: Chile, a case study, by B. Kragh.

1. Inflation and deflation--Addresses, essays, lectures. 2. Schneider, Erich, 1900- I. Bombach, Gottfried, ed.

---

* MF

Stadtmusik Solothurn.

Festschrift zur Feier des 75jährigen Bestehens der Stadtmusik Solothurn, 1845–1920. Solothurn: Zepfel'sche Buchdruckerei A.-G., 1920. 165 p. incl. tables. front., plates, ports. 21cm.

"Vorwort" signed: Der Berichterstatter, A. Dietler.

645218A. 1. Music—Assoc. and org.—Switzerland—Solothurn. I. Dietler, A. II. Title. JUILLIARD FOUNDATION FUND.
N. Y. P. L. August 11, 1933

EAS

STÄDTEWESEN und Bürgertum als geschichtliche Kräfte; Gedächtnisschrift für Fritz Rörig. Hrsg. von A. von Brandt und W. Koppe. Lübeck, M. Schmidt-Römhild, 1953. 560 p. port. 29cm.

Bibliography, p. 535-560.

1. Cities--Germany, Middle Ages. 2. Lübeck--Hist. 3. Rörig, Fritz, 1882-1952. I. Brandt, A., von, ed. II. Koppe, Wilhelm, ed.

NN ** X 8.53 OC, I, II PC, 1, 2, 3, I, II SL E, 1, 3, I, II (Z1, LC1, X1)

TLS

Der stand und die nächste zukunft der konjunkturforschung. Festschrift für Arthur Spiethoff. Beiträge von Aftalion/Åkerman/Altschul [u. a.] Mit einem vorwort von Joseph Schumpeter. München, Duncker & Humblot, 1933.

viii, 320 p. port. 24cm.

Articles in German, French, Italian or English.

Festschrift.

1. Spiethoff, Arthur August Caspar, 1873- 2. Business cycles. [2. Economic cycles]

Agr 33-810

Library, U. S. Dept. of Agriculture 280St2 [HB3711]

[2]

F-10
6386

STÄDTISCHE SPARKASSE, Stuttgart.

75 Jahre Stuttgart; Beiträge zu seiner Kultur- und Wirtschaftsgeschichte. Festschrift zum 75 jährigen Bestehen der Städtischen Sparkasse Stuttgart. Hrsg. von der Städt. Sparkasse und Städt. Girokasse Stuttgart. [Stuttgart, 1961?] 291 p. plates (part col.) 30cm.

"Den kulturellen Teil verfasste Professor Hermann Missenharter. Den wirtschaftlichen Teil... Hans Georg Müller-Payer [et al.]"

(Continued)

NN R 3.62 g/ (OC)II OS(I)b)I, Ibo PC, I, 2, 3, I, II SL E, 2, 3, I, II (LC1, X1, Z1, [1])

2

STÄDTISCHE SPARKASSE, Stuttgart. 75 Jahre Stuttgart... (Card 2)

1. Stuttgart--Hist. 2. Banks and banking, Savings--Germany--Stuttgart. 3. Economic history--Germany--Stuttgart. I. Städtische Girokasse, Stuttgart. II. Missenharter, Hermann. i. [Title] Fünfundsiebzig.

STALLYBRASS, OLIVER, ed.

D-18
8984

Aspects of E. M. Forster; essays and recollections written for his ninetieth birthday 1st January 1969 by John Arlott [and others] [London] E. Arnold [1969] viii, 195 p. port. 22cm.

Bibliography, p. [177]-178.

1. Forster, Edward Morgan, 1879- . I. Arlott, John. II. Stallybrass, Oliver. III. Title.

NN R 4.69 k/OC, I, IIbo, III PC, 1, I, III SL (LC1, X1, Z1)

RAE

Stand und Aufgaben der Sprachwissenschaft; Festschrift für Wilhelm Streitberg, von J. Friedrich, J. B. Hofmann, W. Horn ... [und Anderen.] Heidelberg: C. Winter, 1924. xix, 683 p. 8°.

List of works by Wilhelm Streitberg, p. vii-xix.

Mr Moth

312448A. 1. Streitberg, Wilhelm, 1864-1925. 2. Streitberg, Wilhelm, 1864-1925—Bibl.

N. Y. P. L. September 26, 1927

---

* QR

STANISŁAW IGNACY WITKIEWICZ, człowiek i twórca; księga pamiątkowa pod redakcją Tadeusza Kotarbińskiego i Jerzego Eugeniusza Płomieńskiego. [Wyd. 1. Warszawa] Państwowy instytut wydawniczy [1957] 406 p. port. 25cm.

CONTENTS.—Płomieński, J. E. Rozważania nad twórczością St. Ign. Witkiewicza.—Kotarbiński, T. Filozofia St. I. Witkiewicza.—Szuman, S. Niektóre aspekty i zagadnienia dramatu St. I. Witkiewicza "Szewcy".—Wallis, M. St. I. Witkiewicz jako teoretyk malarstwa.—

(Continued)

NN R 6.59 g/ OC, I, II PC, I, I, II SL S, I, I, II (LCE 1, LC1, X1, Z1)

STANISŁAW IGNACY WITKIEWICZ, człowiek i twórca... (Card 2)

Miller, J. N. Teoria czystej formy w teatrze.—Miłosz, C. Grancie sztuki.—Leszczynski, J. Filozof metafizycznego niepokoju.—Piechal, M. St. I. Witkiewicz jako powieściopisarz.—Winkler, K. Twórczość plastyczna St. I. Witkiewicza.—Ingarden, R. Wspomnienie o St. I. Witkiewiczu.—Płomieński, J. E. Polski pontifex maximus katastrofizmu.—Rytard, J. M. Witkacy, czyli O życiu po drugiej stronie rozpaczy.—Tatarkiewicz, W. Wspomnienie o St. I. Witkiewiczu.—Kasprowiczowa, M. Niedzielne popołudnie z Witkiewiczem na Harendzie.—Koziebrodzka, I. S. R. Urywek z pamiętnika. —Birula-Białynicki, T.

(Continued)

STANISŁAW IGNACY WITKIEWICZ, człowiek i twórca... (Card 3)

Fragmenty wspomnień o St. Ign. Witkiewiczu.—Jasiński, R. Witkacy.—Winkler, K. Wspomnienie o Witkacym.—Roguska-Cybulska, J. Witkacy w oczach Zakopanego.—Witkiewicz, J. Życiorys St. I. Witkiewicza.—Grzegorczyk, P. Dzieło pisarskie St. I. Witkiewicza; próba bibliografii (p. 351-[393])

1. Witkiewicz, Stanisław Ignacy, 1885-1939. I. Kotarbiński, Tadeusz, 1886- , ed. II. Płomieński, Jerzy Eugeniusz, ed.

E-13
6342

STATE and local tax problems. Edited by Harry L. Johnson. Knoxville, University of Tennessee Press [1969] xiii, 190 p. 24cm.

Issued as a Festschrift in honor of Dr. Charles P. White.

Bibliographical footnotes.

CONTENTS.--Financing a viable federalism, by J. M. Buchanan.--Reform of property tax systems: substance or semantics, by A.D. Lynn.--Property tax problems confronting state and local governments, by A.P.

(Continued)

NN *R 9.69 r/ OC, I, II, IIb* PC, 1, 2, 3, I, II SL E, 1, 2, 3, I, II (LC1, X1, Z1)

3

STATE and local tax problems... (Card 2)

Becker.--Recent developments in property taxation in Florida: a case study, by C.H. Donovan.--The politics and economics of intergovernmental fiscal relations: Federal grants, tax credits, and revenue sharing, by D.S. Wright.--The property tax case for Federal tax sharing, by D. Netzer. Ways the Federal Government may strengthen state and local financing, by J. Shannon.--Fiscal outlook for state and local government, by E.M. Watters.--Economic criteria for sound State debt financing, by W.D. Ross and J.M. Bonin.--New dimensions of the capitalization of earnings in

(Continued)

STATE and local tax problems... (Card 3)

appraising public utility property, by J.W. Martin.--Local service charges: theory and practice, by M.Z. Kafoglis.

1. Taxation--U.S.--States. 2. Taxation, Local--U.S. 3. Intergovernmental tax relations-- U.S. I. Johnson, Harry Lee, ed. II. White, Charles Pressley, 1896- . III. Johnson, Harry Lee.

SDHK

Die statistik in Deutschland nach ihrem heutigen stand. Friedrich Zahn zum 70. geburtstage am 8. januar 1939 als ehrengabe dargebracht von L. Achner, A. Agthe, O. Barbarino (u. a.) ... Herausgegeben von Friedrich Burgdörfer. Berlin, P. Schmidt, 1940.

2 v. illus. (facsim.) tables, diagrs. 25cm.

Each volume has also added t.-p.
Paged continuously.
"Schrifttum" at end of some of the papers. Bibliographical foot-notes.

1. Statistics. 2. Germany—Stat. 3. Zahn, Friedrich, 1869- I. Burgdörfer, Friedrich, 1890- ed.

A 41-4249

Harvard univ. Library
for Library of Congress (2)

SDC

STATISTISCHE VEREINIGUNG, Cologne.
Beiträge zu Gegenwartsproblemen der Angewandten Statistik; Festgabe für Prof. Dr. Jakob Breuer. Köln, Westdeutscher Verlag, 1960. 134 p. illus. 24cm.

Bibliographical footnotes.
CONTENTS.--Über die Begriffe des Mittelwertes und der Streuung, von K. Dörge.--Sterblichkeitsbeobachtungen bei Risiken, mit erhöhtem Blutdruck oder Erktankungen des Herzmuskels in der Lebensversicherung, von

(Continued)

NN R 3.66 p/&OSs PCs, 1s, 2s SLs Es, 1s, 2s STs, 1ts (LC1s, X1s, Z1s [i]) 3

STATISTISCHE VEREINIGUNG, Cologne. Beiträge zu Gegenwartsproblemen der Angewandten Statistik... (Card 2)

J. Gugumus.--Internationaler Vergleich der Kaufkraft des Lohnes mit Hilfe von Regressions- und Korrelationsrechnung, von L. Karus-Daiber.--Vereinfachung von Sequential-Plänen durch gleiche Entscheidungsrisiken, von H. Karus.--Über die Theorie der Abschreibungen, von G. Otto.--Die Ausschaltung der unterschiedlichen Länge der Berichtszeiträume bei nichtlinearer Verteilung der Ereignisse, von H. van Radenborgh.--Einige Problems statistischer Verfahrensweisen in der Sozialforschung, von E.A. Scheuch.--Statistics in den USA, von H.H. Statwald.--

(Continued)

STATISTISCHE VEREINIGUNG, Cologne. Beiträge zu Gegenwartsproblemen der Angewandten Statistik... (Card 3)

Über Toleranzen bei zusammengestzten Massenfabrikaten, von F. Stöcker.

1. Statistics--Methods. 2. Breuer, Jakob. t. 1960 i. subs for S-V-, Köln.

---

*PBN

STEINBERG, ARON ZAKHAROVICH, ed.
Simon Dubnow, the man and his work; a memorial volume on the occasion of the centenary of his birth (1860-1960). Paris, French section of the World Jewish congress, 1963. 256 p. 25cm.

Contributions in English, French, Hebrew, Italian and Yiddish.
CONTENTS.--La vie de Simon Dubnov, par S. Erlich-Dubnov.--World dimensions of Jewish history, by S.W. Baron.--On Dubnow's conception of Jewish history, by M. Ginsberg.--History, sociology and

(Continued)

NN S 2.64 a/& OC (OS)I, Ib PC, 1, 2, I, II SL J, 1, 3, I, II (LC1, X1, Z1) 4

STEINBERG, ARON ZAKHAROVICH, ed. Simon Dubnow... (Card 2)

ideology, by N. Rotenstreich.--Dubnov: sa methode et son accomplissement (en hébreu), par R. Mahler.--Dubnow's autonomism and his "Letters on old and new Judaism, by J. Lestschinsky.--Migration problems in Dubnow's theory of Jewish nationalism, by A. Tartakower.--Dubnow's assessment of the reform movement of German Jewry, by I. Maybaum.--Moses Mendelssohn and his followers in Dubnows presentation, by H.I. Bach.--Dubnow's presentation of Sephardi Jewry, by H.J. Zimmels.--

(Continued)

STEINBERG, ARON ZAKHAROVICH, ed. Simon Dubnow ... (Card 3)

Simon Dubnow and the history of political Zionism, by J. Fraenkel.--L'Attitude de Dubnow envers l'hébreu et yiddich (en Yiddich), par S. Auerbach.--Come Dubnow ha trattato la storia dell'ebraismo italiano, da D. Lattes.--The historian of Russian Jewry, by S. Levenberg.--Dubnow on Anglo-Jewish history, by V.D. Lipman.--Simon Dubnows Darstellung des Deutschen Judentums, von H. Levin Goldschmidt.--L'Appréciation de la Révolution française e du premier empire dans l'oeuvre de Dubnov, par A. Neher.--L'Autobibliographie de Simon Dubnov (p. 225-251).--

(Continued)

STEINBERG, ARON ZAKHAROVICH, ed. Simon Dubnow ... (Card 4)

Supplementary list of books by Simon Dubnow which appeared after 1939 (p. 254-255).

1. Dubnow, Semen Markovich, 1860-1941. 2. Jews--Hist.--Addresses, essays, lectures. 3. History--Addresses, essays, lectures. I. World Jewish congress. French section. II. Title.

F-10
3789

Steinby, Torsten, 1908–
På Gianicolo: vänskrift till Amos Anderson. [Helsingfors, 1958]

134 p. illus., col. plate, col. port. 27 cm.

1. Rome (City)--Descr., 1900- . 2. Anderson, Amos, 1878- . 3. Institutum Romanum Finlandiae. I. Title.
NN*R 9.59 1/- OC, I PC, 1, 2, 3, I SL (SR1, LC1, X1, Z1)

MFC

Stenger, Erich, 1878–
Die Geschichte der Kleinbildkamera bis zur Leica. Hrsg. von den Optischen Werken Ernst Leitz, Wetzlar, aus Anlass ihres hundertjährigen Firmen-Jubiläums. [Frankfurt am Main, Umschau-Verlag] 1949.

76 p. illus., ports. 30 cm.
Bibliography: p. 71-74.

1. Leitz (Ernst) GmbH. 2. Cameras.

TR260.S7 771.31 50-26997
Library of Congress [3]

E-13
5287

Steinen, Wolfram von den, 1892-1967.
Menschen im Mittelalter. Gesammelte Forschungen, Betrachtungen, Bilder. (Festgabe zum 75. Lebensjahr.) Hrsg. von Peter von Moos. Bern, München, Francke, (1967).

358 p. 24 cm.

Bibliography of the author's works: p. 335-345.

1. Latin literature, Neo-Latin --Hist. and crit. I. Moos, Peter von, ed.
NN*R 5.69 v/4 OC, I PC, 1, I SL (LC1, X1, Z1)

MAH

Stephanos; Theodor Wiegand zum 60. geburtstag von freunden und verehrern dargebracht. Berlin, Schoetz & Parrhysius, 1924. 17 p. incl. illus., pl. xv pl. (part col.) 41cm.

"Diese festschrift ist gedruckt in fünfhundert exemplaren...nr. 4."
Issued in portfolio.

1. Wiegand, Theodor, 1864-1936. 2. Art, Greek.
NN*R 3.54 OC PC, 1, 2 SL A, 1, 2 (Z1, LC1, X1)

AF-10
17

STEINER, BRÜDER, firm, Vienna.
75 [i.e. Fünfundsiebzig] Jahre Brüder Steiner; die Geschichte eines Wiener Hauses [Festschrift] [Wien, 1956] [30] p. illus. (part col.), ports., col. map. 26cm.

NN **R X 1.57 d/b OS(1b) PC SL E (LC1, X1, Z1, Y1)

---

*IIV

Stier, Friedrich.
Das Verlagshaus Gustav Fischer in Jena; Festschrift zum 75 jährigen Jubiläum 1. Januar 1953. [Jena] 1953. vii, 134 p. illus., ports., facsim. 24cm.

Includes bibliography.
Contents.—Rückblick auf die Geschichte und die Anfänge des Verlages von Gustav Fischer.—Der Verleger Gustav Adolf Fischer (1878-1946).—Tätigkeit des Verlages von 1928-1952.—Der Verlag und seine Mitarbeiter— Personenverzeichnis.
1. Fischer (Gustav) Verlag, Jena.
NN**R 4.54 OC (OS)1b PC, 1 SL (LC1, Z1, X1)

MCF
(Buonarroti)

Steinmann, Ernst, 1866–
Michelangelo im Spiegel seiner Zeit, von Ernst Steinmann. Leipzig[: Poeschel & Trepte], 1930. 112 p. 6 facsims., front. (port.), 26 pl. 4°. (Roemische Forschungen der Bibliotheca Hertziana. [Bd. 8.])

no. 273 of 410 copies printed.
Festschrift in honor of Theodor Lewald.

515000A. 1. Buonarroti, Michel Angelo, 1475-1564. I. Ser.
N. Y. P. L. April 22, 1931

AN
(Bodmer, J.)

Stiftung von Schnyder von Wartensee, Zürich.
Johann Jakob Bodmer Denkschrift zum CC. Geburtstag (19. Juli 1898). Veranlasst vom Lesezirkel Hottingen und herausgegeben von der Stiftung von Schnyder von Wartensee. Zürich: Commissionsverlag von A. Müller, 1900. xii, 418 p. facsims., front., illus. (incl. ports.) 24½ cm. [Its: Schriften. Nr. 10]

Bibliographies included.

954368A

Write on slip words underlined below and class mark—
SHA

Die Stellung der Wohlfahrtspflege zur Wirtschaft, zum Staat und zum Menschen; Bericht über den 41. Deutschen Fürsorgetag in Berlin am 26. und 27. November 1930 anlässlich der 50-Jahr-Feier des Deutschen Vereins für öffentliche und private Fürsorge. Karlsruhe i. B.: G. Braun, 1931. 116 p. 8°. (Deutscher Verein für öffentliche und private Fürsorge. Schriften. Heft 122.)

Contents: Eröffnungsrede des Vorsitzenden. Begrüssungsreden. LUPPE, DR. "Die gegenseitigen Beziehungen von Wirtschaft und Wohlfahrtspflege." MUTHESIUS, DR. "Kollektivverantwortung und Einzelveranwortung in der Wohlfahrtspflege." POLLIGKEIT, DR. "Die Bedeutung der Persönlichkeit in der Wohlfahrtspflege." BÄUMER, DR. "Die sozialpädagogische Aufgabe in der Jugendwohlfahrtspflege." Aussprache zum letzten Referat.

1. Charities—German. I. Ser.
N. Y. P. L. November 14, 1931

STT
(Stockholm)

Stockholm. Högskolan.
Stockholms högskola under Sven Tunbergs rektorat; minnesskrift tillägnad professor, juris och filiosofie doktor Sven Tunberg vid hans avgång från rektorsämbetet den 31 december 1949. Stockholm, P. A. Norstedt & söner [1949] xxvi, 280 p. illus. 25cm.

584827B. 1. Tunberg, Sven August Daniel, 1882–
N. Y. P. L. February 7, 1952

XAH
STOCKHOLM. Högskolan. Stats- och rättsvetenskapliga fakulteten.
Festskrift tillägnad professor juris och filosofie doktor Nils Herlitz vid hans avgång från professorsämbetet, den 30 juni 1955. [Stockholm, Norstedt, 1955]
xii, 472, [1] p. port. 24cm.

Text chiefly in Swedish, one contribution each in Danish and Norwegian.
CONTENTS.--Till frågan om rättsvetenskapens gränser, av I. Agge.--Statskalenderns historiska föregångare (1728-1823), av J. E. Almquist.--
(Continued)
NN**11.56 p/b (OC)I OS PC, 1,2,I SL (LC1, X1, Z1)

STOCKHOLM. Högskolan. Stats- och rättsvetenskapliga fakulteten. Festskrift tillägnad professor juris och filosofie doktor Nils Herlitz ... (Card 2)

Folketingets ombudsmand, av P. Andersen.--"Realisme" og "idealisme" i nordisk rettsvitenskap, av F. Castberg.--Om tvångsöverlåtelsen av de tidigare tyskägda varumärkena, av G. Eberstein.-- Ett fullmaktsstadgande i successionsordningen, av E. Fahlbeck.--FN, freden och säkerheten, av T. Gihl.--Några utvecklingslinjer i internationell luftfartslagstiftning, av K. Grönfors.--Några ord om processförutsättningar och processhinder, av Å. Hassler.--Om upplysningsplikt och ansvarsbegränsning i försäkringsrätten,
(Continued)

STOCKHOLM. Högskolan. Stats- och rättsvetenskapliga fakulteten. Festskrift tillägnad professor juris och filosofie doktor Nils Herlitz... (Card 3)

av J. Hellner.--Om pensionsutfästelser till arbetstagare i enskild tjänst, av H. Hessler.--Rättskontinuitetens problem i Sverige 1809 sett i belysning av den rena rättsläran, av F. Lagerroth.--Administrativ och judiciell prövning på det industriella rättsskyddets område, av S. Ljungman.--Radiomonopolet i Finland, av V. Merikoski.--Några reflexioner om utländska aktiebolags rättsställning i Sverige, av H. Nial.--Om resning i förvaltningsmål, av G. Petrén.--Domaren som lag- tolkare, av F. Schmidt.--
(Continued)

STOCKHOLM. Högskolan. Stats- och rättsvetenskapliga fakulteten. Festskrift tillägnad professor juris och filosofie doktor Nils Herlitz... (Card 4)

Regeringsrätten och den medborgerliga rättssäkerheten, av H. G. F. Sundberg.--Legalitet och teleologisk metod i straffrätten, av H. Thornstedt.--Om skadebringande engeskaper, av L. Vahlén.--Införsel och förmånsrätt, av L. Welamson.--Om maktenöver skatter, avgifter och pålagor enligt 1809 års regeringsform, av O. Westerberg.--Förteckning över professor Herlitz' skrifter 1907-1954, av G. Bodman (p. 450-[473]

1. Law--Addresses, essays, lectures. 2. Herlitz, Nils, 1888- I. Title.

*MEC (Forsell)
Stockholm. Kungliga operan.
Boken om John Forsell; utgiven av Operan på John Forsells 70-årsdag den 6 nov. 1938. Stockholm: P. A. Norstedt & söner [1938] 112 p. front., illus., 56 pl. (incl. facsims., ports.) on 28 l. 25½cm.

"Redaktör: Folke Gustavson."
CONTENTS.—Förord.—John Forsell 70 år, av Arthur Engberg.—John Forsell som barn, av Anna Söderblom.—En käck officer, av Herb. Brenguiér.—John Forsell som sångare, av Hjalmar Meissner.—Selma Lagerlöf om John Forsell.—Ett minne för livet, av Emile Stiebel.—Björn Björnson hyllar John Forsell.—John Forsell som scenisk konstnär, av Gerda Lundequist.—Sven Hedin hyllar John Forsell.—John
(Continued)
N. Y. P. L. August 15, 1940

Stockholm. Kungliga operan. Boken om John Forsell... (Card 2)

Forsell som motspelare, av Davida Hesse.—Med John Forsell på konsertestraden, av Märtha Ohlson.—John Forsell — charmören, av Pauline Brunius.—Leo Blech hyllar John Forsell.—"Mästersångaren" sedd från "operadiket," av O. F. Wennberg.—John Forsell — operachefen, av Ragnar Hyltén-Cavallius.—Aino Ackté hyllar John Forsell.—John Forsell och skolungdomen, av Alarik Klefbeck.—Hans von Stedingk hyllar John Forsell.—John Forsell och pressen, av Erik Ljungberger.—Georg Høeberg hyllar John Forsell.—Operachefens arbetsdag, av Folke Gustavson; Operachefens arbetsdag, texten till bildserien.—Till John Forsell, av Anders de Wahl.—John Forsell i karikatyrens skrattspegel, av Hjalmar Eneroth.—Ett knippe biografiskt.—John Forsells roller på Kungl. teatern, en tabell av Arne Lindenbaum.

24820B. 1. Forsell, John, 1868- . 2. Opera—Sweden—Stockholm. I. Gustavson, Folke, ed.
N. Y. P. L. August 15, 1940

MNE +++
Stockholm. Nationalmuseum.
...Kunglig prakt från barok och rokoko; teckningar till beställningar för det svenska hovet. Företal av Erik Wettergren, förklarande text av Carl Hernmarck, Torsten Lenk och Åke Setterwall; redaktion, Carl Hernmarck och Runar Strandberg. Malmö, J. Kroon [1948] 159 p. illus., plates(part col.) 46cm. (Nationalmusei Handteckningssamling. 5)

(Continued)
NN

Stockholm. Nationalmuseum. ...Kunglig prakt från barok och rokoko... (Card 2)

Summary in French.
No. 242 of 300 copies.
"Litteraturförteckning," p. 155-156.

1. Art industries and trade—Sweden. 2. Drawings—Collections—Sweden—Stockholm. I. Hernmarck, Carl, 1901- , ed. II. Strandberg, Runar, ed. III. Ser.
NN

MA
STOCKHOLM. Nationalmuseum.
Opuscula in honorem C. Hernmarck, 27. 12. 1966. Stockholm [1967?] 299 p. illus., facsims., plates, ports. 29cm. (Stockholm. Nationalmuseum. Skriftserie. nr. 15)
Dedicatory letter signed Carl Nordenfalk.
Includes bibliographies.
CONTENTS.--Altere Quellen zur Kenntnis der Goldschmiedetechnik, von B. Bengtsson. Le service de
(Continued)
NN 7.68 v/A (OC)II,III OS,I PC,1,2,3,I,II,III SL A,1,2,3,I,II,III (LC1, X1, Z1) [I] 4

STOCKHOLM. Nationalmuseum. Opuscula in honorem C. Hernmarck, 27. 12. 1966. (Card 2)

toilette français de Hedvig Sofia, par G. Boesen. Lundberg and Ljungberg; give and take in the ceramic industry of the 18th century, by R. Charleston. A 'Bizarre' silk, by A. Geijer. Old Japanese lacquer and japanning in Sweden, by B. Gyllensvärd. Feuilles d'acanthe; deux sculpteurs royaux, par R. Hauglid. The Gustavian Vasa Sheaf, by M. Lagerquist. Silver furniture in Holland, by T.H. Lunsingh Scheurleer. Ein Augsburger Silberaltärchen in Prag, von T. Müller. Noch einmal:
(Continued)

STOCKHOLM. Nationalmuseum. Opuscula in honorem
C. Hernmarck, 27. 12. 1966. (Card 3)

Georg Schweiggers Gustav Adolf-Darstellung von 1633, von L.L. Möller. Nattier - Tocqué et vice-versa, par E. Kai Sass. Bemerkungen zu den von Vilém Juza entdeckten Werken Ignaz Günthers in Mähren, von A. Schönberger. Signed French furniture in the Swedish Royal Collection, by A. Setterwall. A possible source for the practice of mounting French furniture with Sèvres porcelain, by F.J.B. Watson. Contribution a l'étude de la manufacture de la Savonnerie d'après les collections de
(Continued)

---

*ZP-425
Film Reproduction

STONA, MARIE, ed.
Ludwig Jacobowski im Lichte des Lebens. Mit Beitragen von Hermann Friedrich [et al.] Buchschmuck von Hirzel. Breslau, Schlesische Verlags. Anstalt [1901] 157 p. illus. 19cm.

Film reproduction. Negative.
CONTENTS.--Ludwig Jacobowski's Leben, von H. Friedrich.--Mondscheinfahrt, von P. Remer.--Jacobowski's Lyrik, von R.M. Werner.--
(Continued)

NN R 5.65 e/s OC(1bo)I, Ibo, II PC, 1, I, II SL J, 1, I, II (PRI1, UM1, LC1, X1, Z1)

2

STOCKHOLM. Nationalmuseum. Opuscula in honorem
C. Hernmarck, 27. 12. 1966. (Card 4)

Suede, par P. Verlet. Le demeure de Cronström à Paris, par R.A. Weigert. A Roman mosaic, by E. Zahle. Printed works by Carl Hernmarck, 1927-1966; bibliography, compiled by G. Osterman. Tabula gratulatoria.
1. Hernmarck, Carl, 1901- . 2. Hernmarck, Carl, 1901- --Bibl. 3. Art--Essays and misc. I. Series. II. Nordenfalk, Carl, 1907- . III.Title.

STONA, MARIE, ed. Ludwig Jacobowski im Lichte des Lebens. (Card 2)

In Deiner Sonne, von H. Ehlen.--Loki, von R. Steiner.--Am Weltenende, von A.K.T. Tielo.--Laune und Ideal in Jacobowski's Drama, von O. Reuter.--Früh genug, von T. Lingen.--Ludwig Jacobowski, von G. Brandes.--Ludwig Jacobowski's volksthümliche Bestrebungen, von A.K.T. Tielo.--An Ludwig Jacobowski, von A. Ritter.--Erinnerungen, von M. Stona.--Mailied, von M. Boelitz.

Schiff Coll.

1. Jacobowski, Ludwig, 1868- 1900. I. Friedrich, Hermann. II. Title.

MNR

Stockholm. Nordiska museet.
Smycken i svensk ägo. Stockholm, Nordiska museet [1952] 226 p. illus. 21cm.

"Juvelerare och guldarbetare i Sverige 1520-1850. Av Kersti Holmquist," p. 198-224.
"Litteratur," p. 225-226.

1. Jewelry, Swedish. 2. Gold-smiths—Sweden. 3. Jewelers—Sweden. I. Title.
NN 1.53 (OC)I OS PC, 1, 2, 3 SL A, 1, 2, 3 (LC1, Z2, X1)

Copy only words underlined & classmark— *MA

STOUTZ, EDMOND DE.
Paul Müller zum 60. Geburtstag (19. Juni) (IN: Schweizerische Musikzeitung. Zürich. 25cm. Jahrg. 98, [Heft]6(1 Juni 1958) p. 241-246. music.)

"An die Toten, 'Ist denn dies alles,'" for voice and piano, by Paul Müller, facsimile of autographed ms., p. 243.
List of Paul Müller's works, p. 245-246.

1. Müller, Paul, 1898- . I. Müller, Paul, 1898- . An die Toten.
NN R 6. 59 m/ OI (PC)1 (MU)1, Ig (MUS2, LC2, X1, Z1)

TAH

Stolberg, Germany. Industrie- und Handelskammer.
Aus Vergangenheit und Gegenwart; wirtschaftlichen Geschehens im Bezirk der Industrie- und Handelskammer für die Kreise Aachen-Land, Düren und Jülich zu Stolberg (Rhl.). Festschrift der Kammer auf Anlass ihres 75 jährigen Bestehens, April 1925. Aachen, Ruelle Accidenzdruckerei u. Lith. Anst. [1926?] plates (part col.), ports., fold. col. maps, tables. 26cm.

(Continued)

NN••R 11.56 /r ODts SLs (E)1s,2s,3s,4s EDts PCs,1s,2s,3s,4s (LC1s,X1s,Z1)

MVV
+

Strandblomster; en bukett överräckt till Sven Salén med anledning av hans sextioårsdag den 7 november 1950. [Stockholm] Förlags ab. Fågel blå [1950] 156 p. illus.,maps. 31cm.

Contents.—Ballad om Sven Gustaf Salén, av E. Taube.—Kallt sommarhav, av S. Siwertz.—Den sista skötbåten, av E. Selin.—Vid El lago de Atitlán, av K. Jungstedt.—Den förnämsta tra-
(Continued)

NN** 6.53 OC PC,1, 2 SL MU,3[g] (MUS2, LC1,Z1,X1)

Stolberg, Germany. Industrie- und Handelskammer.
Aus Vergangenheit und Gegenwart wirtschaftlichen Geschehens ... (Card 2)

1. Economic history—Germany—Aix-la-Chapelle. 2. Economic history—Germany—Dueren. 3. Economic history—Germany—Jülich. 4. Economic history—Germany—Stolberg. t.1926.

Strandblomster... (Card 2)

ditionen, av T. Rinman.—Att resa med lastbåt, av S. Barthel.—Vi seglade med sexor, av H. Ramsey.—Ledung, av G. Hafström.—Hamnstycke, av E. Asklund.—Robinson Cruxoe på Vinga, av E. Taube.—En gammal sjömansvisa, av N. Jonsson [unaccompanied melody with words]—Tre skärgardsdikter, av E. Malm.—Passagerarnas vals av Hadell, Norlén, Olrog, Pim-Pim och Sundblad [song with piano accompaniment]—A la matelote, av A. Liedholm.—Entonnarseglingen 1950, av T. Höglund.— Ingvar den vittfarne,
(Continued)

Strandblomster... (Card 3)

av A. Schück.—De rodde över Ingaröfjärden, av E. Jonson.

1. Salén, Sven, 1890- . 2. Sea life—Sweden. 3. Sea songs, Swedish.

F-11
2152

STRIEDL, HANS, ed.
Buch und Welt; Festschrift für Gustav Hofmann, zum 65. Geburtstag dargebracht. [Im Auftrag der Bayerischen Staatsbibliothek hrsg. von Hans Striedl und Joachim Wieder] Wiesbaden, O. Harrassowitz, 1965. xxvi, 532 p. illus., facsims., col. plates, port. 26cm.

"Verzeichnis der Schriften von Gustav Hofmann, 1930-1964": p. 1-5.
(Continued)

NN * R 11. 66 r/d OC, 2b*, I, IIb*, III PC, 1, 2, I, III SL (LC1, X1, Z1) [1]

D-20
1469

STREETEN, PAUL, ed.
Unfashionable economics; essays in honour of Lord Balogh. London, Weidenfeld and Nicolson [1970] xviii, 379 p. diagrs. 23cm.

Includes bibliographical references.

1. Economics--Essays and misc. I. Balogh, Thomas.
NNR 12. 70 d/z OC, I PC, 1, I SL E, 1, I (LC1, X1, Z1)

STRIEDL, HANS, ed. Buch und Welt... (Card 2)

German, French, Spanish, or English.
Includes bibliographies.

1. Library science--Addresses, essays, lectures. 2. Hofmann, Gustav, 1900- . I. Wieder, Joachim, joint ed. II. Striedl, Hans. III. Title.

E-10
3189

STRENA anglica; Otto Ritter zum 80. Geburtstag am 9. Januar 1956. Hrsg. von Gerhard Dietrich und Fritz W. Schulze. Halle (Saale) M. Niemeyer, 1956. vii, 263 p. illus., port. 25cm.

CONTENTS. --Die Akzentverhältnisse im Englischen bei Adverb und Präposition in Verbindung mit einem Verb und Verwandtes, von G. Dietrich. --Untersuchungen über das R und die Vokalentwicklung vor R im heutigen amerikanischen English, von K. Wittig. --Gedanken zu
(Continued)

NN R 7. 57 g/g OC, I, Ib, II, IIb PC, 1, 2, I, II SL (LC1, X1, Z1, Y1)

SB

Strijdenskracht door wetensmacht; opstellen aangeboden aan S. de Wolff ter gelegenheid van zijn 60e verjaardag. Amsterdam: N. v. De Arbeiderspers, 1938. 306 p. incl. tables. illus. (charts), port. 24½cm.

Contributions in Dutch or German.
CONTENTS.—Wijk, J. v. d. Inleiding.—Ravesteyn, W. van. De stand van het Marxisme.—Jong, L. de. Zur Erkenntnistheorie des "Kapitals".—Sinzheimer, Hugo. Das Transformationsproblem in der Soziologie des Rechts.—Gerhard, A. H. Marxisme en levenshouding.—Goes, F. van der. De Parijsche Kommune als proletarische diktatuur.—Valkhoff, J. Marx en Engels over de klassen en de klassentegenstellingen in de maatschappij.—Mendels, M. Revolutie met en zonder R.—Spier, J. De wet der grote getallen.—Vos, H. Over de levensduur van machines en gebruiksgoederen.—
(Continued)

N. Y. P. L. August 24, 1939

STRENA anglica... (Card 2)

Kyd's "Spanish tragedie", von K. Wittig. —Topos und commonplace, von E. Mertner. —Wordsworthian and Coleridgian texts (1784-1822) mostly unidentified or displaced, by R. W. Schulze. --Bibliographie der Veröffentlichungen Otto Ritters, von R. Koch.

1. English language--Addresses, essays, lectures. 2. Ritter, Otto, 1876- . I. Dietrich, Gerhard, 1900- , ed. II. Schulze, Fritz W., 1921- , ed.

Strijdenskracht door wetensmacht... (Card 2)

Woestijne, W. J. van de. Enkele opmerkingen over "forced saving".—Tinbergen, J. Vertragingsgolven en levensduurgolven.—Mendelsohn, K. Charakter und Probleme des neuen Konjunkturcyclus.—Wijk, J. v. d. Inkomensverdeling en conjunctuur.—Gulden, Tees. Conjunctuur en echtscheiding.—Verwey-Jonker, Hilda. Konjunktuur en oorlog.—Zwalf, M. De internationale vakbeweging in de spiegel der conjunctuur.—Velde, J. J. van der. Goodwill en zijne factoren.—Wiedijk, P. Een vergeten figuur: Bernard Nieuwentijt M.D.—Barmes, D. De Amerikaanse vakbeweging en de "doctrine of conspiracy". Polak, Henri. Eigendomsrecht, natuur- en stedenschoon.—Wolff, Leo de. Evenredige vertegenwoordiging en districtenstelsel.—Roode, J. J. de. De nationale en de internationale gedachte.—Ankersmit, J. F. De politieke betekenis van het Zionisme.

1560B. 1. Socialism—Hist. 2. Communism—Hist. 3. Economics. 4. Statistics. 5. Accounting and bookkeeping. 6. Business cycles. 7. Law. 8. Zionism. 9. Wolff, Sam de, 1878-
N. Y. P. L. August 24, 1939

Copy only words underlined & Classmark-- DR

Strenae; estudios de filología e historia dedicados al profesor Manuel García Blanco. Salamanca [Universidad de Salamanca] 1962.

490 p. illus. 25 cm. (Acta salmanticensia. Serie de filosofía y letras, t.16, [no.1])

Bibliography, p. [473]-487.

1. Spanish language--Addresses, essays, lectures. 2. Spain--Hist.--Addresses, essays, lectures. 3. Garcia Blanco, Manuel. I. Series.
NN * R 2. 67 1/ OC (OS)I PC, 1, 2, 3, I (LC1, X1, Z1)

D-10
8894

A STUBBORN faith; papers on Old Testament and related subjects presented to honor William Andrew Irwin, edited by Edward C. Hobbs. Dallas, Southern Methodist university press, 1956. vii, 170 p. 21cm.

Includes bibliographies.
CONTENTS. —The fable in the ancient Near East, by R. J. Williams. —The Exodus and Apocalyptic, by G. Edwards. —The question of coregencies among the Hebrew kings, by E. R. Thiele. —The "Enthronement of Yahweh"
(Continued)

NN*R 2. 58 g/P OC, I, IIbo PC, 1, 2, I SL J, 1, 2, I (LC1, X1, Z1)

A STUBBORN faith... (Card 2)

psalms, by W. S. McCullough. —Some further observations concerning the strophic structure of Hebrew poetry, by C.F. Kraft. —Jeremiah's vision of the almond rod, by W. G. Williams. —Some historical perspective, by H. G. May. —Notes on the present state of the textual criticism of the Judean biblical cave scrolls, by H. M. Orlinsky. —The service of God, by R. B. Y. Scott. —Identifying the distinctive features of early Christianity, by W. A. Beardslee. —A different approach to the writing of commentaries on the synoptic Gospels, by E. C. Hobbs. --Publication of William Andrew Irwin.

1. Bible. O. T. --Criticism. 2. Irwin, William Andrew, 1884-
I. Hobbs, Edward C., ed. II. Hobbs, Edward C.

E-11
9716

STUDENTENE fra 1935, biografiske opplysninger, artikler og statistikk, samlet til 25-års jubileet september 1960. Redaksjon: Erling Welle-Strand[et al.] Oslo, Bokkomiteen for Studentene fra 1935 [1960] 510 p. illus., ports. 25cm.

1. Oslo. Universitet--Students. 2. Students--Norway. 3. Norway--Biog. I. Welle-Strand, Erling, 1916- , ed.
NN R 4.64 f/ OC, I PC, 1, 2, 3, I SL RC, 3 (LC1, X1, Z1)

BWS

Studi aquileiesi offerti il 7 ottobre 1953 a Giovanni Brusin nel suo 70. compleanno. Aquileia, Associazione nazionale per Aquileia, 1953. xxv,456 p. illus., port. facsim. 25cm.

Contributions in Italian or German.
Bibliographical footnotes.
"Pubblicazioni del prof. Giovanni Brusin," p. ix-xiv.
1. Aquileia, Italy— Archaeology. 2. Art, Roman—Italy—Aquileia. 3. Brusin, Giovanni. I. Associazione nazionale per Aquileia.
NN**X 10.54 OC (OS)I, Ib PC,1,2,3,I SL A,2,I (Z1,LC1,X1) [I]

---

*GAH

Studi di bibliografia e di argomento romano, in memoria di Luigi de Gregori [compilato a cura di Cristina Arcamone Barletta] Roma, Fratelli Palombi [1949] 418 p. illus., ports., facsims. 28cm.

Bibliographical footnotes.
CONTENTS.—Pref. di G. Arcamone.—Luigi de Gregori, F. Barberi.—Opere di Luigi de Gregori (p. 32–39)—La Bibbia di Borso, d'A. Baldini.—Di due recenti acquisti della Biblioteca nazionale braidense di Milano, di M. Buonanno-Schellembrid.— Osservazioni sullo stampatore Nicolò Brenta da Varenna, d'A. Campana.—Padre Bresciani a Roma, di Ceccarius.—Sulla legislazione italiana relativa al deposito degli stampati, di G. de Gregori.—Di alcuni agionimi e gentilizi nella toponomastica min-

(Continued)

NN*R 6.54 OC, I PC, 1, 2, 3, I SL (Z1, LC1, X1)

Studi di bibliografia e di argomento romano... [1949] (Card 2)

turnese, d'A. de Santis.—Meditationes Johannis de Turrecremata, di L. Donati.—Scrittorii conventuali ferraresi del Quattrocento, di D. Fava.—Per la Bibliografia del teatro italiano in Vienna, di L. Ferrari.—L'ordinamento della voce "Roma" nel catalogo per soggetti, d'I. Fraschetti-Santinelli.—Il volume di L. de Gregori sulle Piante di Roma, di C. Galassi-Paluzzi.—La collezione Busuttil della Biblioteca romana Sarti, di C. Garinei-Canori.—Gigi Zanazzo e le sue opere edite ed inedite alla Biblioteca angelica, di T. Gnoli.—Note sulla raccolta dei manoscritti della Biblioteca nazionale di Napoli, di G. Guerrieri.—Spunti romani in Lodovico Pepòreo, di L. Huetter.—Note di tecnica e specializzazione bibliotecaria, d'E. Jahier.—Osservazioni sugli autografi delle "Epistolae ad Thyrrenum" di Giano Nicio Eritreo, di G. Incisa della Rocchetta.—Scrittori e miniatori di codici nei loro rapporti cogli scolari bolognesi nella seconda metà del sec. XIII, di P. S. Leicht.—La vera storia di un presunto cimelio cinquecentesco (Il cosiddetto torchio della Biblioteca medicea orientale) di T. Lodi.—Bernini

(Continued)

Studi di bibliografia e di argomento romano... [1949] (Card 3)

regista e scenografo, di V. Mariani.—La Biblioteca Landau-Finaly, d'A. Mondolfo.—Le stampe del Goltzius nella Biblioteca casantense di Roma, di L. Moricca.—Appunti su alcuni incunaboli casanatensi, d'A. Moricca-Caputi.—L'Europa francese e il marchese Caraccioli, d'A. Muñoz.—Il più antico codice della Biblioteca casantense, di G. Muzzioli.—La nuova sistemazione della Biblioteca di archeologia e storia dell'arte (problemi di una moderna biblioteca specializzata) di L. Olivieri-Sangiacomo.—Senza la cupola, la Sapienza, d'E. Re.—La collezione romana della Biblioteca nazionale centrale di Roma, di N. Santovito-Vichi.—La grammatica di Sulpizio Verolano in un incunabulo ignoto ai bibliografi, di C. Scaccia-Scarafoni.—Il padre Tommaso Masetti ultimo prefetto della Casanatense, d'I. Taurisano.—Un gesuita in esilio, di P. P. Trompeo.—La cultura in Roma nei secoli X–XII, di R. Valentini.

1. Bibliography—Collections. 2. Gregori, Luigi de, 1874–1947. 3. Libraries—Italy. I. Arcamone Barletta, Cristina, ed.

F-11
2982

STUDI di bibliografia e di storia in onore di Tammaro de Marinis. [Verona, Stamperia Valdonega] 1964 4 v. plates, ports, facsims. 30cm.

Italian, French, English, German; or Catalan; part of documentary material in Latin.
"Bibliografia di Tammaro de Marinis, a cura di Romeo De Maio, v.1, p. xxxi-xxxviii."

(Continued)

NN * R 6.67 p/L OC PC, 1,2 SL (RS1,LC1,X1, Z1) [I]

2

STUDI di bibliografia e di storia in onore di Tammaro de Marinis. (Card 2)

Includes bibliographical references.

J.S. BILLINGS MEM. COLL.

1. Bibliography--Addresses, essays, lectures. 2. Marinis, Tammaro de, 1879-

---

D-15
7550

STUDI sulla letteratura dell'ottocento in onore di Pietro Paolo Trompeo [a cura di Giovanni Macchia e Glauco Natoli. Napoli, Edizioni scientifiche italiane, 1959. 561 p. 22cm. (Collana di saggi. 20)

Bibliografia degli scritti di Pietro Paolo Trompeo, p. [1]-43.

1. Trompeo, Pietro Paolo, 1886- 2. Literature--Hist. and crit., 19th cent. I. Macchia, Giovanni, ed.
NN R 1.65 a/ OC, I PC, 1, 2, I (LC1, X1, Z1) SL

Copy only words underlined & classmark— RDTA

STUDI di letteratura, storia e filosofia in onore di Bruno Revel. Firenze, L.S. Olschki, 1965. xx, 662 p. port. 26cm. (Archivum romanicum. Biblioteca. Serie 1, v. 74)

In Italian or French.
Bibliographical footnotes.

1. Revel, Bruno, 1895- . 2. French literature--Addresses, essays, lectures. 3. Philosophy--Addresses, essays, lectures. I. Series.
NN 1.66 a/ OC (OS)I PC, 1, 2, 3, I (LC1, X1, Z1) [I]

* ZAN-2398
v. 9

STUDI in memoria di Mons. Cesare Dotta. Milano, 1955. 239 p. illus., port. 25cm. (Archivio ambrosiano. [v.] 9)

Microfilm.

Bibliographical footnotes.

PARTIAL CONTENTS.--Catechismi liturgici carolingi a Milano, di P. Borella.--L'evoluzione delle feste di precetto a Milano, dal secolo XIV al XX, di E. Cattaneo.--La storia como scienza e il (Continued)

NN R 10.68 p/A OC, 1b+ (OS)I PC, 1, 2, I (LC1, X1, Z1, UM1) 2

STUDI in memoria di Mons. (Card 2)

relativismo contemporaneo, di U. Pellegrino.-- Quesiti di sacerdoti ambrosiani nell'epistolario rosminiano, di G. Radice.

1. Dotta, Cesare, 1882-1953. 2. Catholic church, Roman--Addresses, essays, lectures. I. Series.

* BR. C13
v. 21

STUDI offerti al prof. B. R. Motzo per il suo LXX genetliaco. [Cagliari] Università di Cagliari, 1953. 2 v. illus. 26cm. (Cagliari, Italy. Università. Lettere e filosofia, Facoltà di. Annali. v. 21)

CONTENTS.--1. Storia: Bronzetti nuragici di Terralba (Cagliari), di G. Lilliu. In margine alle storia dell'ultima guerra in Libia, di G. Pesce. Θαυριακός, di L. Lana.. L'amministrazione della Sardegna nel I secolo d. C., di P. Meloni. Intorno a la grande epigrafe del Nemrud-Dagh ed Antioco I di Commagene, di M. Carcangiu (Continued)

NN R X 12.57 v/A OC OI PC, 1 (LC2, X1, Z1)

STUDI offerti al prof. B. R. Motzo per il suo LXX genetliaco. (Card 2)

Pidello. Le memorie di Augusto in Appiano Illyr. 14-28, di A. Migheli. Inviati barcellonesi a Napoli presso Alfonso il Magnanimo, di A. Boscolo. Due complessi normativi regi inediti sul governo della Sardegna (1686 e 1755), di F. Loddo-Canepa. La feudalità e il patriziato nel Piemonte di Carlo Emanuele II (1663-1675), di L. Bulferetti. Feofan Prokopovic, di F. Venturi.--2. Filosofia e letteratura: Il problema della storia nella filosofia di B. Croce, di C. Motzo Dentice di Accadia. Mostri e simboli nell'Inferno dantesco, di C. Grabher. Le intentiones rerum, di R. Lazzarini. Particolari influssi di Andrea Cappellano (Continued)

STUDI offerti al prof. B. R. Motzo per il suo LXX genetliaco. (Card 3)

sul Boccaccio, di C. Grabher. Sulle "Lettere a Milena" di Franz Kafka, di R. Paoli. L'illuminismo nell'opera filosofica di Volney, di G. Solinas. Su alcuni aspetti della cultura fiorentina nel tardo rinascimento, di L. Fratta. Definizione operativa dei concetti di sostanza e di tabula rasa in J. Locke, di A. Pala. Il "Pentamerone" di Giambattista Basile, di P. Sarrubo. Analisi di alcune interpretazioni moderne di Zenone d'Elea, di G. Struglia.

1. Motzo, Bacchisio Raimondo, 1883-

E-11
7522

Studi in onore di Achille Donato Giannini. Milano, Giuffrè, 1961.

xii, 1128 p. 25 cm.

Italian, Spanish, French, or German.
Bibliographical footnotes.

1. Taxation--Jurisp.--Addresses, essays, lectures. 2. Law--Addresses, essays, lectures. 3. Giannini, Achille Donato, 1888- .

NN*R 7.63 g/A OC PC, 1, 2, 3 SL E, 1, 3 (LC1, X1, Z1)

L-10
8744

STUDI in onore di Amintore Fanfani. Milano, Giuffrè, 1962. 3 v. plates, ports., maps (part fold., part col.) diagrs., facsims. 25cm.

[Vol.] 3, 5-6

Italian, German, French, English, Portuguese, or Spanish.

Some articles have documentary appendixes in Latin.

Bibliographical footnotes.

CONTENTS.--3. Medioevo.--5. Evi moderno e contemporaneo.--6. Evo contemporaneo.

1. Fanfani, Amintore. 2. Economics--Essays and misc. 3. Economic history--Italy

NN *R 4.65 p/A OC PC, 1, 2, 3 SL E, 1, 2, 3 (LC1, X1, Z1)

JFF
70-68

Studi in onore di Antonio Segni. Milano, A. Giuffrè, 1967.

4 v. port. 26cm. (Pubblicazioni della Facoltà di giurisprudenza dell'Università di Roma, 28-31)

Italian, French, German, or Spanish.
Bibliographical footnotes.

1. Law--Addresses, essays, lectures. 2. Law--Italy. I. Segni, Antonio, 1891-

NN* 1.71 m/A OC, I PC, 1, 2, I SL (LC1, X1, Z1)

E-10
5404

Studi in onore di Armando Sapori. Milano, Istituto editoriale cisalpino [1957]

2 v. (lvii, 1491 p.) port. 25 cm.

Contributions in various languages.
"Scritti di Armando Sapori": v. 1, p. xxxix-lvii. Bibliographical footnotes.

1. COMMERCE--HIST. 2. COMMERCE--ITALY 3. SAPORI, ARMANDO, 1892-

NN* R 5.58 1/A OC PC, 1, 2, 3 SL E, 1, 2, 3 (LC1, X1, Z1)

L-10
7075
v. 2

STUDI in onore di Carlo Pellegrini. [Torino] Società editrice internazionale [1963] xxxix, 846 p. ports. 25cm. (Biblioteca di studi francesi. 2)

Contributions in Italian, French or English.

Includes bibliographies.

"Bibliografia degli scritti di Carlo Pellegrini, a cura di Dina Lanfredini," p. [ix]-xxxix.

1. Pellegrini, Carlo, 1889- . 2. French literature--Addresses, essays, lectures. I. Series.

NN R 4.65 e/B OC (OS)I PC, 1, 2, I (LC1, X1, Z1) [I]

Studi in onore di Gino Luzzatto. Milano, Dott. A. Giuffrè, 1949–50. 4 v. in 3. port. 26cm.

Contributions in Italian, English or French.
"Scritti di Gino Luzzatto," v. 1, p. ix–xx.

610117-19B. 1. Luzzatto, Gino. 2. Economic history. 3. Economic history—Italy. 4. Italy—Hist.— Addresses, essays, lectures.
NN

STUDI in onore di Luigi Castiglioni. Firenze, Sansoni [1960] 2 v. (xxxvi, 1143 p.) 24cm.

Latin, Italian, German, English, French, or Greek.
"Bibliografia degli scritti di Luigi Castiglioni": v. 1, p. [xiii]-xxxvi.
Bibliographical footnotes.

1. Castiglioni, Luigi, 1882- 2. Classical studies--Collections.
NN 10. 64 a/ᵇOC PC, 1, 2 SL (LC1, X1, Z1) [I]

Copy only words underlined
& Classmark-- RDTA

STUDI in onore di Italo Siciliano. Firenze, L. S. Olschki, 1966. 2 v. (1238 p.) port. 26cm. (Archivum romanicum. Biblioteca. Serie 1, v. 86)

1. Siciliano, Italo, 1895- . 2. French literature--Addresses, essays, lectures. I. Series.
NN 3. 67 r/L OC (OS)I PC, 1, 2, I (LC1, X1, Z1)

STUDI in onore di Luisa Banti. Roma, "L'Erma" di Bretschneider, 1965. xvii, 355 p. illus., plates, port. 27cm.

Contributions in Italian, English, French or German.
"Bibliografia di Luisa Banti," p. [xi]-xvii.
Bibliographical footnotes.

1. Banti, Luisa.
NN S 10. 69 r/ᴿOC PC, 1 SL A, 1 (LC1, X1, Z1) [I]

STUDI in onore di Lorenzo Bianchi. Bologna, Zanichelli, editore [1960] xiv, 507 p. port. 24cm.

Contributions in Italian, German and Latin.
Bibliographical footnotes.
CONTENTS.--Nuovi documenti sul soggiorno di Sordello alla corte di Raimondo Berengario V di Provenza, di M. Boni.--Vergnügen; Vorläufiges zur Geschichte von Wort und Wert im 18. Jahrhundert, von H. O. Burger.--
(Continued)

NN 8. 61 p/ᴾOC PC, 1, 2 SL (LC1, X1, Z1) [I]

3

Studi in onore di Pietro Bonfante nel XL anno d' insegnamento. v. 1- Milano: Fratelli Treves, 1930- v. illus. (facsims.), 2 ports. (incl. front.) 4°.

"Raccolta a nome del... 'Comitato per le onoranze a Pietro Bonfante.'"—v. 1, p. [vii, xix.]

1. Bonfante, Pietro, 1864- . 2. Law, Roman. I. Comitato per le onoranze a Pietro Bonfante, Milan.
N. Y. P. L. March 4, 1931

STUDI in onore di Lorenzo Bianchi. (Cont.)

L'espressionismo tedesco; un problema di metodo critico, di P. Chiarini.--L'allegoria della nave, di C. del Grande.--Die italienische Canzonette und das deutsche Lied im Ausgang des XVI. Jahrhunderts, von W. Dürr.--Dal "l'Arnaldo da Brescia di G. B. Niccolini a The waste land di T. S. Eliot per il tramite di W. D. Howells, di C. Izzo.--Rüdeger von Bechelaren; sinossi di un problema filologico, di L. Lun.--Novalisiana, di G. Necco.--Loci propertiani, di E. Pàsoli.--Un sacerdote dell'assoluto: G. Benn, di M. Penna. --La codificazione della legislazione del lavoro in Somalia, di F. Pergolesi.--Fonti e lingua del Laureolus di Giovanni Pascoli, di G. B. Pighi.--Ein Versuch
(Continued)

Studi in onore del professore Salvatore Ortu Carboni. [Roma: Tip. del Senato] 1935. xxvii, 259 p. incl. diagrs. front. (port.) 25½cm.

Bibliographical footnotes.
CONTENTS.—Parole del senatore Mattia Moresco.—Un maestro.—L'ultima lezione del prof. S. Ortu Carboni.—Ambroso, Luigi. La dinamica della circolazione.—Bonferroni, C. E. Il calcolo delle assicurazioni su gruppi di teste.—Chessa, Federico. I rischi del credito e la loro eliminazione.—Alvise, Pietro d'. Le partite di giro nei conti preventivi e consuntivi delle amministrazioni pubbliche italiane.—Vecchio, Ettore del. Sul premio naturale.—Dettori, Giovanni. Del benessere economico in relazione alla dinamica della popolazione.—Falchi, A. L'oggettività del mondo sociale.—Fasiani,

(Continued)

Festschrift.

N. Y. P. L. August 27, 1937

STUDI in onore di Lorenzo Bianchi. (Cont.)

im Dienste der Weltliteratur-Idee: Goethes Übersetzung von Manzonis Ode "Il cinque maggio," von H. Rüdiger.--Rosen, Veilchen und Ginster: Leopardi und die Blumenmotiv-Tradition, von H. L. Scheel.--Kleists "Verhöre", van H. Singer.--Dichtung und Bildung bei Goethe, von E. Thurnher.--I drammi storici di Laszló Németh, di E. Várady.--Eine Brieffolge von Ricarda Huch, von V. Wittowski.

1. Bianchi, Lorenzo, 1889- 2. Literature--Addresses, essays, lectures.

Studi in onore del professore Salvatore Ortu Carboni. (Card 2)

Mauro. Imposta e rischio.—Griziotti, Benvenuto. Sui metodi d'ammortamento del debito pubblico.—Insolera, Filadelfo. Previdenze popolari e politica demografica.—Lenzi, Enrico. Assicurazioni sulla vita a premio periodico ed ammortamenti.—Loria, Gino. Eulero o i neo-pitagorici? (Una questione di priorità).—Medolaghi, Paolo. Controlli tecnici dell'assicurazione obbligatoria per la invalidità e la vecchiaia.—Noli, A. C. Di una forma nuova di ammortamento progressivo di prestito a interesse variabile.—Togliatti, E. G. Alcune osservazioni intorno ad una particolare superficie di 5° ordine.

857048A. 1. Ortu Carboni, Salvatore, 1859- . 2. Economics, Mathematical. 3. Insurance, Life—Mathematics.
N. Y. P. L. August 27, 1937

XAP

Studi in onore di Salvatore Riccobono nel XL anno del suo insegnamento ... Palermo, Arti grafiche G. Castiglia, 1936.

4 v. port. 26cm.

"Indice delle fonti citate nel quattro volumi": v. 4, p. [529]-605.
Bibliographical foot-notes.

1. Riccobono, Salvatore, 1864- 2. Law—Addresses, essays, lectures. 3. Roman law—Addresses, essays, lectures.

A C 37-1022

Princeton univ. Library for Library of Congress [2]

STUDI di paleografia... (Card 3)

principi longobardi di Benevento, di Capua e di Salerno nella tradizione beneventana, di F. Bartoloni. —Ricerche sulla pecia nei codici del "Digestum vetus," di G. Battelli. —Studi sul passaggio dal manoscritto allo stampato: la decorazione degli incunabuli italiani, di L. Donati. —Le B "a pance à droite" dans l'ancienne cursive romaine et les origines du B minuscule, par R. Marichal.

1. Manaresi, Cesare, 1880- . 2. Middle Ages—Hist.—Addresses, essays, lectures.

---

*ZAN-1799
Film Reproduction
ser. 4, v. 1

STUDI in onore di Ugo Enrico Paoli. Firenze, F. Le Monnier, 1956. xix, 782 p. illus., plates, port. 25cm. (Florence (City). Università. Lettere e filosofia, Facoltà di. Pubblicazioni. ser. 4, v. 1)

Film reproduction. Positive.
English, French, German or Italian.

1. Classical studies—Collections. 2. Paoli, Ugo Enrico, 1884- . I. Series.
NN R X 5.67 r/ OC (OS)I PC,1,2,I (UM1,LC1,X1,Z1)

D-16
6073

STUDI e scritti in onore di Mario Vecchioni pel 15.° anno della sua attività letteraria. [Cuneo? 1964] 142 p. 21cm. (Collana Orsa maggiore. n. 3)

"Bibliografia di Mario Vecchioni," p. 13-21.

1. Vecchioni, Mario. I. Orsa maggiore. Collana. II. Collana Orsa maggiore.
NN 7.66 1/ OC (OS)I, II PC, 1 SL (LC1, X1, Z1) [SID, NSCM]

E-12
1001

STUDI in onore di Vittorio Lugli e Diego Valeri. Venezia, N. Pozza, 1961. 2 v. (lxxxvi, 1015 p.) group port. 25cm.

Vol. 2: Collana di varia critica, v. 16.
Italian, French, or German.
"Bibliografia degli scritti di Vittorio Lugli e Diego Valeri [a cura di C. Cordiè]": v. 1, p. [xvii]-lxxviii. Bibliographical footnotes.

1. Lugli, Vittorio, 1885- 2. Valeri, Diego, 1887- 3. Literature--Addresses, essays, lectures.
NN * R 9.64 a/ OC PC, 1, 2, 3 SL (LC1, X1, Z1) [I]

Copy only words underlined & classmark—
MAA

STUDI di storia dell'arte; raccolta di saggi dedicati a Roberto Longhi in occasione del suo settantesimo compleanno. Firenze, Sansoni [1962] 503 p. 241 plates (12 col.) 27cm. (Arte antica e moderna. n. 13-16 (1961))

Articles in Italian, English or French.
Bibliographical footnotes.

1. Longhi, Roberto, 1820- 2. Painting, Italian--Addresses, essays, lectures.
NN 3.66 1/ OC OI A, 1, 2 (LC1, X1, Z1) [I]

BTH

STUDI di paleografia, diplomatica, storia e araldica in onore di Cesare Manaresi. Milano, A. Giuffrè, 1953. xxiii, 363 p. illus. 25cm.

Contributions in French, German or Italian.
"Elenco della pubblicazioni di Cesare Manaresi," p. [xv]-xix.
Bibliographical footnotes.
CONTENTS.—Aggiunta agli "Atti del comune di Milano fino all'anno MCCXVI," di G. P. Bognetti. —Einige Bemerkungen zur Erforschung des frühmittelalterlichen Heiligenkultes in der Schweiz, von A. Bruckner.—Du renouvellement des titres détruits au declin du moyen (Continued)

NN**R X 2.54 OC PC, 1, 2 SL (Z1, LC1, X1) [I]

E-10
6894

STUDI di storia medievale e moderna in onore di Ettore Rota, a c. di P. Vaccari e P. F. Palumbo. Roma, Edizioni del lavoro, 1958. xvi, 610 p. 25cm. (Biblioteca storica. 3)

Bibliographical footnotes.
CONTENTS.—Bibliografia di Ettore Rota (p. [ix]-xvi). —La crisi del III secolo e l'avvio alla ripresa agricola in Italia, di F. M. De Robertis. —La concezione della storia in Ticonio, di A. Quacquarelli. —La Gallia (Continued)

NN X 12.58 a/ OC, I, II (OS) III PC, 1, 2, I, II, III SL (LC1, X1, Z1)

STUDI di paleografia... (Card 2)

âge, par A. de Bouard. —I sigilli dei comuni italiani nel medio evo e nell'età moderna, di G. C. Bascapè. —Il "Secreti secretorum pseudoaristotelici de physiognomia caput" nella versione di Filippo Tripolitano in un codice della capitolare monzese, di L. Cazzaniga. —Tabularium principis, di G. Cencetti. —Una "descrizione" del Cairo di Guglielmo Postel, di A. Codazzi. —La brique de Villaviciosa de Cordoba, par J. Mallon. —Silvestro II e Gerusalemme, di C. G. Mor. —Il patriziato piacentino nell'età del principato (Considerazioni di storia giuridica, sociale e statistica), di E. Nasalli Rocca. —Le sottoscrizioni dei signori di Canossa, di C. Santoro. — I diplomi dei (Continued)

STUDI di storia medievale e moderna in onore di Ettore Rota. (Card 2)

precarolingia, di P. Vaccari. —Due note intorno alla concezione dell'autorità imperiale al tempo di Carlo Magno, di G. Soranzo. —Gervasio da Tilbury maresciallo del Regno di Arles, di M. Abrate. —Lineamenti di una storia della cavalleria, di G. Fasoli. —La tradizione guelfa in Italia durante il pontificato di Benedetto XII, di G. Tabacco. —Sulla politica orientale di Clemente VI, di F. Giunta. —Intorno a Nicola Scillacio umanista siciliano del sec. XV, studente e professore a Pavia, di A. De Stefano. —Enrico Caterino Davila e la "Storia delle guerre civili di Francia," di G. Spini. —Oldenbarnevelt & Maurizio d'Orange, di R. Belvederi. —La forma aristocratica di governo (Continued)

STUDI di storia medievale e moderna in onore di Ettore Rota. (Card 3)

nel dottrinarismo politico italiano del seicento, di R. de Mattei. --Il problema italiano nella politica europea del settecento: Alberoni, di F. Valsecchi. --Una biografia inedita dell'abate Alberoni, di E. Nasalli Rocca. --Il commercio lombardo davanti ai problemi creati dalla guerra di successione di Spagna, di A. Visconti. --Un diario ai margini del Congresso di Vienna, di L. Bulferetti. --Interessi e problemi sociali nel pensiero italiano della Restaurazione (1815-1830), di C. Curcio. --Borghesia e spirito borghese in Italia nei secoli XVIII e XIX, di V. Titone. --La riunione del Landtagprussiano nei dispacci dei ministri sardo e napoletano

(Continued)

STUDI di storia medievale e moderna in onore di Ettore Rota. (Card 4)

a Berlino (febbraio-luglio 1847), di F. Curato. --Carlo Rigotti incaricato d'affari del governo provvisorio della Lombardia a Ferrara e a Bologna, di L. Marchetti. --Il generale Eusebio Baba nelle sue carte inedite del 1848-49, di P. Pieri. --Origine dei protettorati di Obbia e della Migiurtinia, di C. Giglio. --Per una storia dei partiti nel mondo moderno, di G. Vaccari.

1. Rota, Ettore, 1883- . 2. Europe--Hist.--Addresses, essays, lectures. I. Palumbo, Pier Fausto, ed. II. Vaccari, Pietro, 1880- , ed. III. Series.

L-10
4340
v.1-2

STUDI storici in onore di Francesco Loddo Canepa Firenze, G.C. Sansoni [1959] 2 v. illus., port. 24cm. (Regia deputazione di storia patria per la Sardegna. Biblioteca. v.1-2)

Contributions in Italian, Spanish, French or English.
Includes bibliographical references.
"Elenco delle pubblicazioni di e su Francesco Loddo Canepa," v.1, p. [xi]-xxvii.

1. Sardinia--Hist.--Addresses, essays, lectures. 2. Loddo-Canepa, Francesco. I. Series.

NN R 4.61 e/ OC (OS)I PC, 1, 2, I (LC1, X1, Z1)

E-10
6331
v.1

STUDI storici in onore di Gioacchino Volpe per il suo 80° compleanno. Firenze, G.C. Sansoni [1958] 2 v. (1158 p.) port. 24cm. (Biblioteca storica Sansoni. Nuova ser. v. 31-32)

Bibliographical footnotes.

1. Volpe, Gioacchino, 1876- . 2. Italy--Hist.--Addresses, essays, lectures. I. Series.

NN R X 1.59 g/ OC (OS)I PC, 1, 2, I (LC1, X1, Z1)
[I]

NNBC
(Grossi)

Studi su Tommaso Grossi, pubblicati in occasione del centenario della morte. [Milano] Comune di Milano, 1953. 243 p. port. 22cm.

"Di questo volume... sono stati impressi 500 esemplari per l'edizione originale. 116."
Includes bibliographies.
Contents.--Tommaso Grossi e il suo tempo di M. Marcazzan.--La poesia milanese di Tommaso Grossi,

(Continued)

NN** 4.55 f/ OC (OD)It (ED)It PC,1,I
SL (LC1,Z1,X1)

Studi su Tommaso Grossi... (Card 2)

di L. Medici.--Il Grossi editore del Porta, di D. Isella.--I rapporti Grossi-Manzoni e il romanzo storico, di M. L. Giartosio de Courten."--Tommaso Grossi e le idee politiche e religiose del suo tempo di L. Ambrosoli.--Saggio bibliografico sulle edizioni di Tommaso Grossi, di G. Soldati.

1. Grossi, Tommaso, 1791-1853. I. Milan (City). t. 1953.

Write on slip only words underlined and classmark: YAG

Studia Albertina; Festschrift für Bernhard Geyer zum 70. Geburtstage. Hrsg. von Dr. Heinrich Ostlender. Münster, Westf., Aschendorff, 1952. 471 p. plates. 24cm. (Beiträge zur Geschichte der Philosophie des Mittelalters. Supplementband 4)

Bibliographies included.
CONTENTS.—Die Autographe Alberts des Grossen, von H. Ostlender.—Das Uppsalenser Albertusautograph, von F. Stegmüller.—Albertus-Magnus-Fragmente in Schweden, von T. Schmid.—Das zeitliche Verhältnis der Summa De incarnatione zu dem

(Continued)

NN 4.53 OC, II (OS)I PC, 1, 2, I, II (LC1, Z1, X1)

Studia Albertina; Festschrift für Bernhard Geyer... 1952. (Card 2)

dritten Buche des Sentenzenkommentars Alberts des Grossen, von I. Backes.—Der Geist als höherer Teil der Seele nach Albert dem Grossen, von A. J. Backes.—Bemerkungen zur Ehelehre des hl. Albertus Magnus, von H. Doms.—Die Behandlung der Tugend der Keuschheit im Schrifttum Alberts des Grossen, von C. Feckes.—Um die Quaestiones de animalibus Alberts des Grossen, von E. Filthaut.—Principium Biblicum Alberti Magni, ed. A. Fries.—En marge de l'explication du "Credo" par Saint Albert le Grand, par J. de Ghellinck.—Zur Frage der anfangslosen und zeitlichen Schöpfung bei Albert dem Grossen, von J. Hansen.—Die ursprüngliche Einteilung des Sentenzenkommentars Alberts des Grossen, von A. Hiedl.—Das Person-Problem bei Albertus Magnus, von A. Hufnagel.—Albertus Magnus und die Erdkunde, von K. Klauck.—Eucharistia als Bona Gratia, von A. Kolping.—Die Lehre von der Auferstehung der

(Continued)

Studia Albertina; Festschrift für Bernhard Geyer... 1952. (Card 3)

Toten nach Albertus Magnus, von W. Kübel.—Die frühscholastischen Vorarbeiten zum Kommentar Alberts des Grossen zu 3 dist. 38 a.6, von A. M. Landgraf.—Die Bedeutung Alberts des Grossen für die Aufrollung der fundamentaltheologischen Frage, von A. Lang.—Die biblischen Vorbilder von Taufe und Eucharistie nach der Summa De sacramentis Alberts des Grossen, von A. Ohlmeyer.—Alberts des Grossen Lehre vom Wesen des Weihesakramentes, von J. M. Overbeck.—Die Wirkursächlichkeit der Sakramente nachdem Sentenzenkommentar Alberts des Grossen, von H. Weisweiler. —Zum Fortleben Alberts des Grossen bei Heymerich von Kamp und Nikolaus von Kues, von R. Haubst.—Albert-Ehrungen in zwei Jahrzehnten, von A. Walz.

1. Geyer, Bernhard, 1880- . 2. Albertus Magnus, Saint, bp. of Ratisbon, 1193?–1280. I. Series. II. Ostlender, Heinrich, ed.

• OO

Studia altaica; Festschrift für Nikolaus Poppe zum 60. Geburtstag am 8. August 1957. Wiesbaden, O. Harrassowitz, 1957.
189 p. port. 26 cm. (Ural-altaische Bibliothek. 5)

Bibliographical footnotes.
CONTENTS.—Nikolaus Poppe zum 60. Geburtstag, von O. Pritsak.—Ayayqa tegimlig, von P. Aalto.—Einige Bemerkungen zum Kolophon des Geschichtswerkes Erdeni-yin Tobči von Sayang-Sečen, von C. R. Bawden.—Noms de la "Chèvre" en Turc et en Mongol, par L. Bazin.—

(Continued)

NN* R X 1.65 g/ OC (OS)I PC, 1, 2, 3, I SL O, 1, 2, 3, I
S, 3 (LC1, X1, Z1)

STUDIA altaica; Festschrift für Nikolaus Poppe zum 60.
(Card 2)

The Turkish Y and related sounds, by G. Clauson.—Der Numerus nach Zahlwörtern im Mandschu, von G. Doerfer.—Zur Charakteristik der islamischen mittelasiatisch-türkischen Literatursprache, von J. Eckmann.—Oirat-Chinese tribute relations, 1408–1446, by D. M. Farquhar.—[illegible] in Yüan-ch'ao Mi-shih, by S. Hattori.—Zur Entstehungsgeschichte der mongolischen Kandjur-Redaktion der Ligdan Khan-Zeit, 1628–1629, von W. Heissig.—Über die Herkunft einiger unregelmässiger Imperativformen der mandschurischen Verben, von J. Ikegami.—The question of Nicodemus, by F. D. Lessing.—Zum

(Continued)

STUDIA altaica; Festschrift für Nikolaus Poppe zum 60
(Card 3)

lexikalischen Bestand der aralo-kaspischen Sprachen, von K. H. Menges.—Note sur le culte du Vieillard blanc chez les Ordos, par A. Mostaert.—Evet, Evet Ki and Geyise, by C. S. Mundy.—Vergleichende Betrachtung der Kasus-Suffixe im Altjapanischen, von S. Murayama.—On some phonological developments in the Kharachin dialect, by M. Nomura.—Tschuwaschische Pluralsuffixe, von O. Pritsak.—Einiges über den Ursprung der Wörter für Messing, von M. Räsänen.—The city of Urga in the Manchu period, by R. A. Rupen.—Some notes on *Jou-jan*, by G. Uchida.—A note on the migration of the Uriangkhai, by H. Wilhelm.—Nikolaus Poppe Bibliographie, von J. R. Krueger und O. Pritsak (p. [177]–188)

(Continued)

STUDIA altaica; Festschrift für Nikolaus Poppe zum 60.
(Card 4

1. Ural-Altaic languages. 2. Ural-Altaic tribes. 3. Poppe, Nikolaĭ Nikolayevich, 1897- . I. Series.

MTI

STUDIA archaeologica Gerardo van Hoorn oblata (Studia van Hoorn). Leiden, E. J. Brill, 1951. 114 p. illus. 24cm.

"Tabula scriptorum potiorum Gerardi van Hoorn," p. 110-114.

CONTENTS.—Vollgraff, W. Le théatre d'Argos.—Byvanck, A. W. La chronologie de Praxitèle.—Roes, Anne. Une fibule étrusque du Musée de Dijon.—Essen, C. C. van. Due statue di giovani togati del Vaticano.—Haspels, C. H. E. Lions.—Beyen, H. G. The workshops of the "fourth style" at Pompeii and its neighbourhood.—Jongkees, J. H. On price inscriptions on Greek vases.—Groot, J. C. de. Quelques fragments de calices en terre sigillée du Musée d'Utrecht.— Aken, A. R. A. van. Some aspects of nymphaea in Pompeii, Herculaneum and Ostia.— Vermaseren, M. J. The miraculous birth of Mithras.

1. Hoorn, G. van. 2. Archaeology, Classical.

NN 3.53 OC PC, 1, 2 SL A, 1, 2 (LC1, Z1, X1)

---

* QR

STUDIA z dziejów kultury polskiej; ksiazka zbiorowa. Warszawa, Gebethner i Wolff [1949] 616 p. 25cm.

Various contributors.

"Redaktorzy: Henryk Barycz i Jan Hulewicz."

Originally announced as a festschrift to honor Stanisław Kot cf. Kwartalnik historyczny, rocznik 54, 1947, cover.

1. Poland—Civilization. 2. Kot, Stanisław, 1885- I. Barycz, Henryk, ed.

NN R X 3.55 p/ OCs, Is PCs, 1s, 2, Is SLs Ss, 1s, 2, Is (LC1s, X1s, Z1)

Write on slip words underlined below and class mark- RKA

Studia germanica tillägnade Ernst Albin Kock den 6 december 1934. Lund, C. W. K. Gleerup; [etc., etc., 1934]

6 p. l., 462 p. front. (port.) VII maps. 24½cm. (*Half-title:* Lunder germanistische forschungen, hrsg. von Erik Rooth. 1)

Contributions in Swedish, Danish, Norwegian, English, German, or French.

1. Germanic philology—Collections. 2. Kock, Ernst Albin, 1864-

35-35042

Library of Congress PD26.K7

[2] 439.04

L-10
8434

STUDIA Gratiana, post octava Decreti Sæcularia auctore Consilio commemorationi Gratianæ instruenda edita. Curantibus Ios. Forchielli [et] Alph. M. Stickler. [Bologna] Apud Institutum iuridicum Universitatis studiorum Bononiensis, 1953-68. 14 v. illus., facsims. 25cm.

[Vol.] 1-14.

Vols. 4-14. have imprint: Bononiæ, Institutum Gratianum.

(Continued)

NN R 10.70 d/ OCs, Is, IIs, IIIs PCs, 1s, 2s, Is, IIs, IIIs SLs (LC1s, X1s, Z1s)

2

STUDIA Gratiana, post octava Decreti... (Card 2)

Title varies slightly.

Text in Italian, French, English or German.

Vol. 1-14: "Collectanea Stephan Kuttner."

Bibliographical footnotes.

1. Gratianus, fl. 12th cent. 2. Canon and ecclesiastical law. I. Forchielli, Giuseppe, ed. II. Stickler, Alfonso Maria, 1910- ed. III. Kuttner, Stephan Georg, 1907-

---

*QR

Studia historyczne ku czi Stanisława Kutrzeby... Kraków, Nakładem komitetu, 1938. 2 v. illus., maps. 26cm.

"Bibliografia prac Stanisława Kutrzeby," v. 1, p. ix-xxxiii.

1. Poland—Hist.—Addresses, essays, lectures.
2. Kutrzeba, Stanisław, 1876-1946.

NN 10.54 OC PC, 1, 2 SL S, 1, 2 (Z, X, LC1, X1)

Copy only words underlined & classmark— * OAC

STUDIA Indologica. Festschrift für Willibald Kirfel zur Vollendung seines 70. Lebensjahres. Hrsg. von Otto Spies. [Bonn] Selbstverlag des Orientalischen Seminars der Universität Bonn, 1955. 375 p. port. 22cm. (Bonner orientalistische Studien. Neue Ser. Bd. 3)

Bibliographical footnotes.

CONTENTS.--Der Stupa des Kṣemaṃkara, von L. Alsdorf.--An Interpretation of ṚV 10.109, by B. Bhawe.--Interpolationen in Pāṇini's Aṣṭād-

(Continued)

NN X 12.59 p/ OC, I (OS)II PC, 1, 2, I, II O, 1, 2, I, II (LC1, X1, Z1)

STUDIA Indologica. (Card 2)

hyāyi, von R. Birwé. --Il P. Calmette e le sue conoscenze indologiche, di Della Casa. --Candramati und sein Daśapadārthaśastram, von F. Frauwallner. -- Das Gleichnis in der Vedānta-Philosophie, von von Glasenapp. -- Der Sanskrit-Text von Nāgārjuna's Pratītyasamutpādahṛdayakārikā, von V. V. Gokhale. --Purohita, von J. Gonda. --Einige Bemerkungen zur Zahlensymbolik und zum Animismus im botanischen System des Jaina-Kanon, von J. F. Kohl. --Rigvedic loanwords, by F. B. J. Kuiper. --Zarathustras Priesterlohn, von H. Lommel. --Ein Abriss der Waffenkunde, von H. Losch. --Das Problem indo-germanischer Altertümlichkeiten im Mittelindischen, von M. Mayrhofer. (Continued)

STUDIA Indologica. (Card 3)

-- Von fabelhaften Glücksländern, von V. Pisani. --Studies in the Jaiminīya Brāhmaṇa, by Raghu Vira and Lokesh Chandra. --Über die ethische Idealgestalt des Rāma, von W. Ruben. --150 Strophen Niryukti, von W. Schubring. -- Türkisches Sprachgut im Hindūstānī, von O. Spies. --Fonti sanscrite di materia medica, di M. Vallauri. --Beil und Lauch, von W. Wüst.

1. Indic studies--Collections. 2. Kirfel, Willibald, 1885- . I. Spies, Otto, 1901- , ed. II. Series.

Copy only words underlined & classmark— *QPA

STUDIA nad książka poświęcone pamięci Kazimierza Piekarskiego. Wrocław, Wydawn. Zakładu Narodowego im. Ossolińskich, 1951. 393 p. illus., ports., map, facsims. 26cm. (Książka w dawnej kulturze polskiej. 1)
Edited by Kazimierz Budzyk and Alodia Gryczowa.
Bibliographical footnotes.
CONTENTS. — Nota biograficzna. —Borowy, W. Wspomnienie. — Wegner, J. Wspomnienie o pracy naukowej Kazimierza Piekarskiego w Łowickim. —Gryczowa, A. Dzieło Kazimierza Piekarskiego. —Mikulski, T. Historia literatury wobec zagadnień ksiegoznawstwa. — Muszkowski, J. (Continued)

STUDIA nad ksiazka poswiecone pamieci Kazimierza Piekarskiego. (Card 2)

Książka jako zjawisko społeczne. — Birkenmajer, A. W sprawie rejestracji i katalogowania opraw zabytkowych. — Budzyk, K. Bibliografia dzieł prawniczych Bartłomieja Groickiego, wiek XVI. —Budka, W. Papiernia w Młodziejowicach. — Birkenmajer, A. Rodowód krakowskiego Plateana. -- Chwalewik, E. Jan Filipowicz, rytownik i drukarz. — Lisowski, S. Do dziejów Biblioteki Zygmunta Augusta. —Brahmer, M. O bibliotece Pinocciích. — Mikulski, T. Kniaźnin w Bibliotece Załuskich. —Reychman, J. Zbiory orientaliów w Polsce XVIII w. —Horodyski, B. Zarys dziejów Biblioteki Ord. Zamojskiej. —Krzyzanowski, J. O artyźmie "Kazań Świetokrzyskich." (Continued)

STUDIA nad ksiazka poświecone pamieci Kazimierza Piekarskiego. (Card 3)

skich." —Badecki, K. Bartłomieja Zimorowicza "Żywot Kozaków Lisowskich." —Ameisenowa, Z. Nieznany wzór złotniczy z xv w. Bibliotece Jagiellońskiej. —Olszewicz, B. Wzmianki o mapach Bernarda Wapowskiego w listach z r. 1529. — Lipska, H. Bibliografia prac Kazimierza Piekarskiego (p. [377]-393)

1. Piekarski, Kazimierz. 2. Bibliography—Addresses, essays, lectures. 3. Libraries—Addresses, essays, lectures. I. Budzyk, Kazimierz, ed. II. Kawecka, Alodja, ed. III. Series.

* QA

STUDIA linguistica in honorem Thaddaei Lehr-Spławiński. [Komitet redakcyjny Tadeusz Milewski, Jan Safarewicz, Franciszek Sławski. 1. wyd. Warszawa] Państwowe wydawn. naukowe [1963] 512 p. port., maps. 25cm.

Contributions in Bulgarian, Czech, English, French, German, Polish, Russian, Serbo-Croatian, Slovak, or Slovenian.
"Bibliografia prac Tadeusza Lehra-Spławińskiego za lata 1951-1961," p. [7]-18.
(Continued)

2

STUDIA linguistica in honorem Thaddaei Lehr-Spławiński. (Card 2)

Bibliographical footnotes.

1. Lehr-Spławiński, Tadeusz, 1891-1965. 2. Slavonic languages--Addresses, essays, lectures. I. Milewski, Tadeusz, ed.

ZEC

Studia mediaevalia in honorem admodum Reverendi Patris Raymundi Josephi Martin, Ordinis Praedicatorum s. theologiae magistri LXXum natalem diem agentis. Brugis Flandrorum, De Tempel [1948]
xvi, 540 p. port. 26 cm.
Bibliographical footnotes.
CONTENTS.—Levensschets van Raymond J. Martin, door B. L. van Helmond.—L'œuvre scientifique de Raymond J. Martin, par G. de Brie et S. Brounts.—Bibliographie du R. P. Martin (p. [27]-37)—Iuventus, gravitas, senectus, par J. de Ghellinck.—Sur la doctrine eucharistique d'Hériger de Lobbes, par J. Lebon.—The introductions to the "Artes" in the twelfth century, by R. W. Hunt.—Die anonyme Verteidigungsschrift der Lehre Gilberts von Poitiers im Cod. Vat. 561 und ihr Verfasser Canonicus Adhemar von Saint-Ruf in Valence (um

(Continued on next card)
Festschrift file A 50-657
[2]

Studia mediaevalia in honorem admodum Reverendi Patris Raymundi Josephi Martin ... [1948] (Card 2)
CONTENTS—Continued.
1180) von Fr. Pelster.—Une tradition spéciale du texte des "Sententiae divinae paginae," par O. Lottin.—Frühscholastische Abkürzungen der Sentenzen des Lombarden, von A. M. Landgraf.—L' "Explanatio symboli" de Raymond Martin, par F. Cavallera.—Die handschriftliche Verbreitung der Werke Alberts des Grossen als Maszstab seines Einflusses, von B. Geyer.—Les "Quaestiones" de Thomas de Buckingham, par M.-D. Chenu.—The "Tabulae super Originalia Patrum" of Robert Kilwardby, by D.-A. Callus.—Date de quelques commentaires de saint Thomas d'Aquin sur Aristote (De Interpretatione, De Anima, Metaphysica) par A. Mansion.—Notre premier jugement d'existence selon saint Thomas d'Aquin, par R. Garrigou-Lagrange.—Analyse et synthèse dans l'œuvre de saint Thomas, par L.-M. Régis.—Le problème

(Continued on next card)
A 50-657
[2]

Studia mediaevalia in honorem admodum Reverendi Patris Raymundi Josephi Martin ... [1948] (Card 3)
CONTENTS—Continued.
de l'existence de Dieu dans le "Scriptum super Sententiis" de saint Thomas, par F. van Steenberghen.—Die Zielsetzung der "Divina commedia," von H. Ostlender.—Jean Sarrazin, "traducteur" de Scot Erigène, par G. Théry.—De Sententiënkommentaar (Cod. Brugen. 491) van de Gentse lektor Philip o. p. (1302-4), door G. Meersseman.—Der Belgische Thomist Johannes Tinctoris († 1469) und die Entstehung des Kommentars zur "Summa theologiae" des Hl. Thomas von Aquin, von M. Grabmann.—Les anciens manuscrits de la Bibliothèque métropolitaine de Zagreb, par C. Balić.—Boekenbezit en boekengebruik bij de Dominikanen in de dertiende eeuw, door St. Axters.—Die Dominikaner an der Universität Trier, von G. Löhr.
1. Martin, Raymond Marie, Father, 1878-

A 50-657

Harvard Univ. Library
for Library of Congress [2]

M-10
9639
no.3

STUDIA palaeometallurgica in honorem Ernesti Preuschen. Wien, F. Deuticke, 1958. 155 p. illus., port., maps (1 fold.) diagrs., profiles, tables. 26cm. (Archaeologia austriaca. Beiheft, 3)

Archiv für ur- und frühgeschichtliche Bergbauforschung. Nr. 12. Includes bibliographies.

(Continued)

NN * X 3.65 e/4 OC (OS)I PC, 1, 2, I ST, 1, 2 (LC1, X1, Z1) 3

STUDIA palaeometallurgica in honorem Ernesti Preuschen. (Card 2)

CONTENTS.--Spektralanalytische Untersuchungen von Bleifunden aus Kärntner Ausgrabungen, von M. Brandenstein und E. Schroll.--Researches upon prehistoric copper metallurgy in England, by H.H. Coghlan.--Beiträge zur Metallurgie des Kupfers in der Urzeit, von F. Czedik-Eysenberg.--Das Gebiet der alten Goldwäscherei am Klieningbach bei Wiesenau, Kärnten, von O.M. Friedrich.--Die ur- und frühgeschichtliche Bergbauforschung in Niederösterreich, von F. Hampl und R.J. Mayrhofer.--Grabfunde der Urnenfelderkultur aus dem

(Continued)

STUDIA palaeometallurgica in honorem Ernesti Preuschen. (Card 3)

salzburgischen Pinzgau, von M. Hell.--Das jungsteinzeitliche Hornsteinbergwerk Mauer bei Wien, von F. Kirnbauer.--Der Schmelzplatz Nr. 13 des Bergbaugebietes Jochberg bei Kitzbühel, Tirol. Neue Schmelzplätze im Bergbaugebiet Jochberg bei Kitzbühel, Tirol. Zum Erzeugungsgebiet der bronzezeitlichen Sichelnadeln (mit Spektralanalysen von H. Neuninger) von R. Pittioni --Der hl. Prokop als Bergbaupatron Böhmens, von L. Schmidt.--Neue pollenanalytische Untersuchungen aus dem Gebiet des Mitterberger Kupferbergbaues, von E. Sitte-Lürzer.

1. Preuschen, Ernst. 2. Metallurgy--Hist. I. Series.

L-10
4469

STUDIA philologica; homenaje ofrecido a Dámaso Alonso por sus amigos y discípulos con ocasión de su 60° aniversario. Madrid, Editorial Gredos, 1960. 1 v. facsims. 25cm.

[Tomo] 1.
Contributions in Spanish, French or Portuguese.
Bibliographical footnotes.

1. Alonso, Dámaso, 1898- . 2. Romance philology.

NN R 3.61 x/ OC PC, 1, 2 SL (LC1, X1, Z1) [I]

F-10
5235

STUDIA philologica et litteraria in honorem L. Spitzer; ediderunt A.G. Hatcher [et] K.L. Selig. Bern, Francke [c1958] 430 p. illus., port., facsims. 28cm.

Contributions in English, French, German, Italian or Spanish.
Bibliographical footnotes.

1. Spitzer, Leo, 1887- . 2. Philology--Addresses, essays, lectures. I. Hatcher, Anna Granville, 1905- ed. II. Selig, Karl Ludwig, 1926- , ed. III. Selig, Karl Ludwig, 1926- .

NN R 2.61 m/o OC, I, II, IIIbDAS PC, 1, 2, I, II SL (LC1, X1, Z1) [I]

* OVC

STUDIA Serica Bernhard Karlgren dedicata. Sinological studies dedicated to Bernhard Karlgren on his seventieth birthday, October fifth, 1959. Edenda curaverunt: Søren Egerod et Else Glahn. Copenhagen, E. Munksgaard [1959] viii, 282 p. illus., port., maps. 26cm.

Bibliographical footnotes.
CONTENTS.—Ambiguity in Chinese, by Yuen Ren Chao.—The Chinese cosmic magic known as watching for the ethers,

(Continued)

NN* 8.60 g/# OC, I, II, IIIb* PC, 1, 2, I, II SL O, 1, 2, I, II (LC1, X1, Z1) 4

STUDIA Serica Bernhard Karlgren dedicata. (Card 2)

by D. Bodde.—A sampling of Chungshan Hakka, by S. Egerod.—Tibetan Glo-ba-'dring, by Li Fang-Kuei.—Some characteristics of parallel prose, by J.R. Hightower.—A note on the Szech'uanese dialects, by G. Malmqvist.—The Chinese colonization of Fukien until the end of T'ang, by H. Bielenstein.—"Tunguse"-"Pomback," von A.J. Joki.—Liao-chai chi-i by P'u Sung-ling, by J. Průšek.—Things Chinese, from the 17th and 18th centuries, by M. Boyer.—Structure and meaning of the rite called the bath of the Buddha according to

(Continued)

STUDIA Serica Bernhard Karlgren dedicata. (Card 3)

Tibetan and Chinese sources, by F.D. Lessing.—Notes on the Tun-Huang Pien-Wên Chi, by A. Waley.—Fei, wei and certain related words, by E.G. Pulleyblank.—A note on Ode 220, by G.A. Kennedy.—The meaning of hsing-ming, by H.G. Creel.—Ancient and archaic Chinese in the grammatonomic perspective, by P.A. Boodberg.—The ethnic name Hun, by O.J. Maenchen-Helfen.—The Shuo-wen dictionary as a source for ancient Chinese law, by A.F.P. Hulsewé.—Han "hill censers," by H.H. Dubs.—The China

(Continued)

STUDIA Serica Bernhard Karlgren dedicata. (Card 4)

illustrata romanisation, by W. Simon.—Parrots in medieval China, by E.H. Schafer.

1. Chinese studies--Collections. 2. Karlgren, Bernhard, 1889- . I. Glahn, Else, ed. II. Egerod, Søren, ed. III. Glahn, Else.

L-10
4379
Bd. 2-3

STUDIEN zur älteren Geschichte Osteuropas. Graz, H. Böhlaus Nachf., 1956-59. 2 v. port., facsims. 25cm. (Wiener Archiv für Geschichte des Slawentums und Osteuropa. Bd. 2-3)

Some articles in vol. 1 in English.
Bibliographical footnotes.

(Continued)

NN X 12.61 e/# OC, I, III (OS)II PC, 1, 2, 3, I, II, III S, 1, 2, 3, I, II, III (LC1, X1, Z1) 2

STUDIEN zur älteren Geschichte Osteuropas. (Card 2)

CONTENTS.--T. 1. Festschrift für Heinrich Felix Schmid, redigiert von G. Stökl.--T. 2. Festgabe zur Fünfzig-Jahr-Feier des Instituts für osteuropäische Geschichte und Südostforschung der Universität Wien, redigiert von H. F. Schmid.

1. Europe, Eastern--Hist.--Addresses, essays, lectures. 2. Schmid, Heinrich Felix, 1896- . 3. Vienna. Universität. Institut für osteuropäische Geschichte und Südostforschung. I. Schmid, Heinrich Felix, 1896- , ed. II. Series. III. Stökl, Günther, 1916- , ed.

Studien zur geschichte und kultur des Nahen und Fernen Ostens; Paul Kahle zum 60. geburtstag überreicht von freunden und schülern aus dem kreise des Orientalischen seminars der Universität Bonn, herausgegeben von W. Heffening und W. Kirfel. Leiden, E. J. Brill, 1935.

viii, 231 p. front. (port.) 25½cm.

CONTENTS.—Schott, A. Wann entstand das Gilgamesch-epos?—Edelmann, R. Zur geschichte der Masora.—Horst, F. Der diebstahl im Alten Testament.—Peters, C. Beitrag zur textgeschichtlichen überlieferung von Ex. 32, 18.—Sperber, A. Probleme einer edition der Septuaginta.—Engberding, H. Nachhall altchristlicher liturgischer akklamationen in den ṣelāvāthā der ostsyrischen liturgie.—Atiya, A. S. A fourteenth century fatwā on the status of Christians in the Mamlūk

(Continued on next card)

A C 35-2678

[3]

Studien zur geschichte und kultur des Nahen und Fernen Ostens ... 1935. (Card 2)

CONTENTS—Continued.

empire.—Dietrich, E. L. Lehrer und schüler im Kairiner ordensleben des 16. jahrhunderts.—Frick, H. Der begriff des prophetischen in Islamkunde und theologie.—Fück, J. W. Spuren des zindīqtums in der islamischen tradition.—Heffening, W. Zum aufbau der islamischen rechtswerke.—Levy, K. Lá'bät elḥôtā. Ein tunesisches schattenspiel.—Mostafa, M. Ḫāirbāj, "Sultān Laila".—Röder, K. Über glasierte irdenware und chinesisches porzellan in islamischen ländern.—Spies, O. al-Muġulṭā'ī's spezialwerk über "Märtyrer der liebe".—Hilgenberg, L. Die anschauungen von den konstitutionstypen in der medizin Altindiens und unserer zeit.—Kirfel, W. Vom steinkult in Indien.—Losch, H. Totenwiedererweckungsgeschichten in Indien.—Matsumoto, T. Suvikrānta-

(Continued on next card)

A C 35-2678

[3]

Studien zur geschichte und kultur des Nahen und Fernen Ostens ... 1935. (Card 3)

CONTENTS—Continued.

vikrāmi-prajñāpāramitā, Ānadaparivartaḥ.—Kressler, O. Kantan no makura. Ein spezifisch chinesisches formprinzip und die beiden gegentypen seiner verwertung in der mitteljapanischen literatur.—Pippon, T. Shôtoku Taishi Jû shichi jô kempô—Die 17 verfassungsartikel Shôtoku Taishi's und eine japanische interpretation.—Schmitt, E. Verwendungen pulverisierten porzellans in der chinesischen medizin.—Wang, K. Musikalische beziehungen zwischen China und dem Westen im laufe der jahrtausende.—Korn, K. Paul Kahle's schriften.

1. Kahle, Paul, 1875- 2. Bible. O. T.—Criticism, interpretation, etc. 3. Mohammedanism. 4. India—Civilization. 5. Civilization, Oriental. 6. Bible—Criticism, interpretation, etc.—O. T. I. Heffening, Willi, 1894- ed. II. Kirfel, Willibald, 1885- joint ed.

A C 35-2678

Title from Columbia Univ. Printed by L. C.

[3]

Write on slip words underlined below and class mark- YAG

Studien zur geschichte der philosophie. Festgabe zum 60. geburtstag Clemens Baeumker gewidmet von seinen schülern und freunden ... Mit einem bildnis von Clemens Baeumker. Münster i. W., Aschendorff, 1913.

viii, 491 p. port., 25cm. (*Added t.-p.:* Beiträge zur geschichte der philosophie des mittelalters ... Supplementband [Nr. 1])

CONTENTS.—Das verhältnis von αισθησις und δόξα in dem abschnitt 151e–187a von Platons Theaitet, von J. Geyser.—Zur lehre des Aristoteles von der ewigkeit Gottes, von G. Wunderle.—Die unterscheidung von wesenheit und dasein in der arabischen philosophie, von M. Wittmann.—Neues zur modustheorie des Abu Háschim (933†), von. M. Horten.—Psychologische definitionen aus dem "Grossen buche des nutzens", von 'Abdallàh ibn al-Faḍl (11. jahrh.), aus dem arabischen übers. von G. Graf.—Dialectique et dogme aux xe–xiie siècles, par J. de Ghellinck.—Die stellung Abaelards in der universalienfrage nach neuen handschriftlichen

(Continued on next card)

14—6020

[s27f1]

Studien zur geschichte der philosophie ... 1913. (Card 2)

CONTENTS—Continued.

texten, von B. Geyer.—Philosophiegeschichtliche bemerkungen über die dem Alexander von Hales zugeschriebene Summa de virtutibus, von P. Minges.—Metaphysische begriffe des Bartholomaeus Anglicus, von A. Schneider.—Die metaphysik des Thomas von York († ca. 1260) von M. Grabmann.—Die ästhetik Bonaventuras, von E. Lutz.—Die lehre vom naturrecht bei Bonaventura, von L. Baur.—Zum thomistischen wahrheitsbegriff, von M. Baumgartner.—De regimine principum des hl. Thomas von Aquin, von J. A. Endres.—Der einfluss des willens und der tugend auf die wahrheit und sicherheit des gewissens; studie nach dem hl. Thomas von Aquin, von O. Renz.—L'intellectualisme de Godefroid de Fontaines d'après le Quodlibet VI, q. 15, von M. de Wulf.—Der intellectus agens bei Roger Baco, von O. Keicher.—Wilhelm von Ware über das menschliche erkennen; ein beitrag zur geschichte des kampfes zwischen dem Augustinismus und dem Aristotelismus im 13. jahrhun-

(Continued on next card)

14—6020

[29g1]

Studien zur geschichte der philosophie ... 1913. (Card 3)

CONTENTS—Continued.

dert, von A. Daniels.—Über Albertus von Sachsen, von A. Dyroff.—Heinrich Susos bedeutung als philosoph, von S. Hahn.—Un écrit de Vincent d'Aggsbach contre Gerson, par E. Vansteenberghe.—El primo libro de filosofia impreso en el Nuevo Mundo, von P. Blanco Soto.—Das wahrheitsproblem bei Kant, von T. Steinbüchel.—Fichtiana, von G. Bülow.—Zum begriff des absoluten in der neuern englischen philosophie, von F. Nauen.—Die philosophie der werte bei Wilhelm Windelband und Heinrich Rickert, von J. Fischer.—Erkenntniskritik und Gotteserkenntnis mit besonderer berücksichtigung von Vaihingers als-ob-philosophie, von E. Krebs.

1. Philosophy—Collected works. 2. Philosophy, Medieval—Hist. 3. Baeumker, Clemens, 1853–1924.

Library of Congress B720.B4 14—6020

[a27f1]

STUDIEN zur Kunst des Oberrheins: Festschrift für Werner Noack. Konstanz, J. Thorbecke [1959]
175 p. illus., 3 col. plates. 25cm.

CONTENTS.--Keltische Motive auf alemannischen Mittelaltermünzen, von F. Wielandt.--Das Freiburger Einzelblatt- der Rest eines Musterbuches der Stauferzeit? Von O. Homburger.--Ein wiedergefundener romanischer Sandsteinkopf im Historischen Museum Basel, von H. Reinhardt.--Ein Vortragekreuz aus dem 14. Jahrhundert, von L. Ehret.--Die Propheten am Oktogon des Freiburger Münstertürmes, von, I. und

(Continued)

NN R 6.59 1/ OC, 1bo PC, 1, 2, 3, SL A, 1, 2, 3 (LC1, X1, Z1)

STUDIEN zur Kunst des Oberrheins... (Card 2)

R. Oertel.--Die Wandgemälde der Augustinerkirche in Konstanz, von C. Altgraf zu Salm.--Zwei Neuerwerbungen des Augustinermuseums, von H. Gombert.--Bildnisse von Martin Schongauer, von K. Bauch.--Zur "Madonna im Rosenhag" im Isabella Steward Gardner Museum in Boston, von K. Martin.--Zu Schongauers "Heiligem Antonius" von L. Fischel.--Eine kleine Schnitzfigur aus der Nachfolge des Nicolaus Gerhaert, von W. Paatz.--Ein wiedergefundenes Fragment zu einem Glasgemälde in Oberehnheim, von E. Schulze-Battmann.--Ein Gemälde aus Dürers Wanderzeit? Von A. Stange.-- Zwei Werke des Sixt von

(Continued)

STUDIEN zur Kunst des Oberrheins... (Card 3)

Staufen, von M. Meier.--Holbeins "Christus in der Grabnische", von W. Ueberwasser.--Ein Freiburger Kristallpokal in Graz, von A. Legner.--Einige manieristische Bilder in Freiburg, von I. Schroth.--Paul Egells Bauplastik am Mannheimer Neckartor, von E. Zimmermann.--Das Fürstenbergische Jagdschloss auf der "Länge", von J. L. Wohleb.--Eine Vision des Rheingrabens im Jahre 1934, von G. Schmidt.--Der Ottheinrichsbau als Ausstellungsforum, von G. Poensgen.--Bibliographie Werner Noack.

1. Noack, Werner. 2. Art, German--Rhine valley. 3. Art, Swiss.

* MGA
(Adler)

Studien zur Musikgeschichte; Festschrift für Guido Adler zum 75. Geburtstag. Wien: Universal-Edition, A. G., 1930. 224 p. facsims. (incl. music), front. (port.), illus. (music.) 4°.

Bibliographical footnotes.

Contents: Vorwort. Dent, E. J. The universal aspect of musical history. Hornbostle, E. M. v. Gestaltpsychologisches zur Stilkritik. Closson, E. Une nouvelle série de hautbois égyptiens antiques. Cesari, G. Tre tavole di strumenti in un "Boezio" del X secolo. Wagner, P. Zur mittelalterlichen Tonartenlehre. Krohn, I. Der tonale Charakter gregorianischer Rezitative. Jachimecki, Z. Symbolismus in der Motivik des ersten gregorianischen Credo. Ludwig, F. Über den Entstehungsort der grossen "Notre Dame-Handschriften." Handschin, J. Der

(Continued)

N. Y. P. L. October 14, 1931

Studien zur Musikgeschichte... (Continued)

Organum-Traktat von Montpellier. Nef, K. Gesang und Instrumentenspiel bei den Troubadours. Anglès, H. Gacian Reyneau am Königshof zu Barcelona in der Zeit von 139- bis 1429. Pirro, A. Musiciens allemands et auditeurs français au temps des rois Charles V et Charles VI. Borren, C. van den. Le madrigalisme avant le madrigal. Moser, H. J. Eine Trienter Orgeltabulatur aus Hofhaimers Zeit. Orel, D. Stilarten der Mehrstimmigkeit des 15. und 16. Jahrhunderts in Böhmen. Müller-Blattau, J. Wach auff, mein hort! Studie zur deutschen Liedkunst des 15. Jahrhunderts. Gombosi, O. Ghizeghem und Compère; zur Stilgeschichte der burgundischen Chanson. Kroyer, T. Zur Chiavettenfrage. Trend, J. B. Spanish madrigals and madrigal-texts. Einstein, A. Annibale Padoanos Madrigalbuch. Jeppesen, K. Wann entstand die Marcellus-Messe? Ursprung, O. Die Chorord-

(Continued)

N. Y. P. L. October 14, 1931

Studien zur Musikgeschichte... (Continued)

nung von 1616 am Dom zu Augsburg. Schering, A. Zur Entstehungsgeschichte des Orchesterallegros. Tessier, A. Une pièce inédite de Froberger Prunières, H. Le page de Dassoucy. Nettl, P. Kaiser Leopold als deutscher Liedkomponist. Koczirz, A. Über die Fingernageltechnik bei Saiteninstrumenten. St. Foix, G. de. Le dernier quatuor de Mozart. Heuss, A. Wie verhält es sich mit den Taktstrichen in dem Zauberflöten-Duett: Bei Männern, welche Liebe fühlen? Lorenz, A. Das Relativitätsprinzip in den musikalischen Formen. Altmann, W. Die Streichquintette Dittersdorfs. Prod'homme, J. G. Beethoven et Pleyel. Mantuani, J. Ein Kapitel über die Musikpflege Laibachs zur Zeit Schuberts. Waltershausen, H. W. v. Der stilistische Dualismus in der Musik des 19. Jahrhunderts. Werner, T. W. Der Roman "Anton Reiser" als musikgeschichtliche Quelle. Engel, C. O. G. Sonneck: Ein Charakterbild. Verzeichnis der gedruckten Werke und Abhandlungen von Guido Adler.

546619A. 1. Adler, Guido, 1855- . 2. Music—Essays.
N. Y. P. L. October 14, 1931

RAE p.v.327

...**Studien** zur Sprach- und Kulturgeschichte. Festschrift zu Ehren von Josef Schatz. Innsbruck, Wagner, 1948. 100 p. 25cm. (Schlern-Schriften. 57)

"Bisherige Veröffentlichungen von Josef Schatz," p. 99–100.

1. Schatz, Josef, 1884- . 2. Germanic languages—Collections.
I. Ser.
N. Y. P. L. March 23, 1951

E-11
2430

STUDIEN zur Textgeschichte und Textkritik [Günther Jachmann zur fünfzigsten Wiederkehr seiner Promotion gewidmet] Hrsg. von Hellfried Dahlmann und Reinhold Merkelbach. Köln, Westdeutscher Verlag [1959] 307 p. 25cm.

Bibliographical footnotes.

Contents.—Zum Text der Vögel des Aristophanes, von E. Fraenkel.—Eine Korruptel in der Überlieferung des Lukan, von B. Axelson.—Bemerkungen zu Varros Menippea Tithonus, περὶ γήρως von H. Dahlmann.—Eine Schauspielerinterpolation in der Sophokleischen Elektra, von A. Dihle.—Verderbnisse im Petrontext, von H. Fuchs.—Tereus in den Vögeln des Aristophanes, von L. Koenen.—Die Mahnung an Memmius im ersten Prooemium des Lukrez, von J. Kroll.—Adver-

(Continued)

NN* R .4.61 g// OC, I, II PC, 1, 2, I, II SL (LC1, X1, Z/1)

STUDIEN zur Textgeschichte und Textkritik...
(Card 2)

saria philologica, di S. Mariotti.—Annotazioni critiche a Cratino, di B. Marzullo.—Kritische Beiträge, von R. Merkelbach.—Zu Anthol. Lat. 102 R.[2], von F. Munari.—Problems, hypotheses and theories on the history of the text of Ausonius, by S. Prete.—Nuvole non recitate e Nuvole recitate, di C. F. Russo.— Ein christlicher Heroidenbrief des sechsten Jahrhunderts. (Zur spätantiken Traditionsgeschichte elegischer Motive und Junkturen) von W. Schmid.—Textprobleme im zehnten Buch der Platonischen Nomoi, von F. Solmsen.—Liebesgespräch und Pastourelle, von W. Theiler.—Die Überlieferung der Metzer Alexanderepitome, von P. H. Thomas.—Tre noterelle, di S. Timpanaro.

1. Classical literature—Criticism, Textual. 2. Jachmann, Günther, 1887- . I. Dahlmann, Hellfried, 1905- , ed. II. Merkelbach, Reinhold, ed.

---

* OAC

Studier tilegnede Professor, Dr. Phil. & Theol. Frants Buhl i Anledning hans 75 Aars Fødselsdag den 6 September 1925 af Fagfæller og Elever. Redigeret af Johannes Jacobsen. København: V. Pios Boghandel, 1925. 265 p. 8°.

One of 600 copies printed.

—— —— Second copy.

1. Buhl, Frants, 1850- . 2. Jacobsen, Johannes Christian, 1862- , editor.
N. Y. P. L. January 7, 1927

NIVC

Studier tilegnede Verner Dahlerup paa Femoghalvfjerdsaarsdagen, den 31. Oktober 1934; udgivet af Danske Folkemaal, og Sprog og Kultur. Aarhus: Universitetsforlaget [etc., etc.] 1934. 256 p. illus. (facsim.) 23½cm.

Contents.—Aakjær, Svend. Hilla, Hleiðra og Skjalf.—Andersen, Harry. Johannes V. Jensens Oversættelse af Egils Saga.—Andersen, Poul. Nogle Fejl i Rask's Lydopfattelse.—Bjerregaard, N. P. Nogle Stedsadverbiers Brug i Ømmersysselsk.—Brøndum-Nielsen, Johs. Om middelalderlig Ned skrivning efter Diktat.—Diderichsen, Paul. Om Brugen af det sammenfattende þa i østnordisk Lovsprog.—Glahder, Jørgen. Genitiv paa -es i dansk.—Haislund, Niels. Abstrakter og Konkreter og Artikelbrug på engelsk.—Hald, Kristian. Om Personnavnene i de danske Møntindskrifter.—Hansen, Aage. Om

(Continued)

N. Y. P. L. July 9, 1937

Studier tilegnede Verner Dahlerup paa Femoghalvfjerdsaarsdagen... (Card 2)

Lydutviklinger i Sammensætninger.—Hansen, H. P. Bleg-Blegjord-Blegkorn.—Jensen, K. B. Knud Hertugs Tilnavn.—Jespersen, Otto. Gruppegenitiv på dansk.—Juul-Jensen, H. Om den lexikalske Udnyttelse af Efterleddet i Sammensætninger.—Jørgensen, Peter. Om Nasalindskud i Fremmedord.—Knudsen, Gunnar. Præpositioner i bornholmske Bebyggelsesnavne.—Knudsen, Regnar. Vi og Vis i Stednavne.—Kristensen, K. L. Svundet og svindende fra et Folkemaal.—Kristensen, Marius. Abstrakte og konkrete Verber i Folkemålene.—Kroman, Erik. Et Par senmiddelalderlige Haandskrifter fra Skovkloster.—Lollesgaard, Johs. Fremmed og hjemligt i Ordforraadet i Schousbølles Saxo-Oversættelse.—Møller, Christen. Et Dialektdigt i sproglig Belysning. —Møller, Kristen. Nogle forstærkende Adverbialforbindelser i Dansk.—Nielsen, K. M.

(Continued)

N. Y. P. L. July 9, 1937

Studier tilegnede Verner Dahlerup paa Femoghalvfjerdsaarsdagen... (Card 3)

Et Lovhaandskrift og dets Forlæg.—Oxenvad, Erik. Om nogle upersonlige Konstruktioner i Dansk.—Raae, Ellen. En Fugls Navne i Folkemaalene.—Rehling, Erik. Om Brug af passiv på dansk.—Rohmann, Aage. Det bornholmske Fadervor.—Sandfeld, Kr. Paa godt og ondt.—Skautrup, Peter. Fylling på Sandemænd.—Skov, Gunnar. Et af Peder Laales "dunkle" Ordsprog.—Widding, Ole. Bemærkninger til Neckels dialektale Inddeling af de ældste islandske Håndskrifter.

795794A. 1. Dahlerup, Verner, 1859- . 2. Danish language. I. Danske Folkemaal. II. Sprog og Kultur.
N. Y. P. L. July 9, 1937

Write on slip only words underlined and classmark:

NIMA

Studier tillägnade Anton Blanck den 29 december 1946. Uppsala, 1946. xii, 373 p. port. 26cm. (Svenska litteratursällskapet, Upsala. Skrifter. 30)

1. Literature—Hist. and crit. 2. Blanck, Anton, 1881– . I. Ser.
NN

Write on slip words underlined below and class mark—

NIAC

Studier tillägnade Axel Kock. Lund: C. W. K. Gleerup, 1929. 575 p. 8°. (Arkiv för nordisk filologi. Ny följd. v. 40, tilläggsband.)

1. Kock, Axel, 1851– . 2. Philology—Collections. I. Ser.
N. Y. P. L. December 16, 1931

GFD

Studier tillägnade Curt Weibull den 19 augusti 1946. [Göteborg, 1946] 356 p. 25cm.

Fest.

404158B. 1. Weibull, Curt Hugo Johannes, 1886– . 2. Sweden—Hist.—Addresses, essays, lectures.
N. Y. P. L. June 28, 1951

YAR

Studier tillägnade Efraim Liljeqvist den 24 september, 1930; utgivna av Gunnar Aspelin och Elof Åkesson. Del –2. Lund: A.-b. skånska centraltryckeriet, –1930. 1 v. 25½cm.

"250 numrerade exemplar...detta är n:r 208."

(Continued)

Festschrift.

N. Y. P. L. September 20, 1943

Studier tillägnade Efraim Liljeqvist den 24 september, 1930... (Card 2)

Contents.—
bd. 2. Ramul, K. Kant, Husserl und die Psychologie als Wissenschaft. Lagerborg, R. Om det medvetna, det psykiska, det intentionella. Eriksen, R. Drift og vilje. Åhlberg, A. Lustkänslornas roll i handlingslivet. Kuhr, V. Die Welten des Künstlers und des Wissenschaftlers. Schjelderup, H. K. Psykologisk analyse av et tilfælde av tungetale. Hegge, T. G. Effects of remedial reading in supposedly feebleminded children. Freudenthal, G. Något om den teoretiska pedagogikens betydelse för lärarens utbildning. Ingvar, S. Om nervösa organsjukdomar. Vaihinger, H. Ist die Philosophie des Als-Ob religionsfeindlich? Gustavson, J. Max Schelers religionsfilosofi. Några grundlinjer. Cullberg, J. Till frågan om mystiken såsom religiös

(Continued)

N. Y. P. L. September 20, 1943

Studier tillägnade Efraim Liljeqvist den 24 september, 1930... (Card 3)

erfarenhetsform. Hensel, P. Causalität und Wunder. Pfannenstill, M. Några tankar om skuld och skuldkänsla. Eidem, E. Paulus amicus. Wallerius, A. Clemens Alexandrinus om tro och vetande. Hall, B. R. Dubbelnaturen i Örebro mötes beslut 1529. Petri, L. Till belysning av John Nelson Darbys teologi. Schwarz, H. Zur Metaphysik der Gemeinschaftsformen. Haralds, H. Den organiska statsläran. Landtman, G. Rousseaus sociala vision och verkligheten. Dam, A. World-peace through education. Jaederholm, G. A. Ett transatlantiskt universitet och dess pedagogiska fakultet. En skiss i akademisk organisation och administration. Wulff, B. E. V. Bidrag till en bibliografi över Efraim Liljeqvists tryckta skrifter.

1. Liljeqvist, Efraim, 1865– . 2. Liljequist, Efraim, 1865– —Bibl. 3. Philosophy—Essays and misc. I. Aspelin, Gunnar, ed. II. Åkesson, Elof, ed.
N. Y. P. L. September 20, 1943

3-MAS

Studier tillägnade Henrik Cornell på sextioårsdagen. Stockholm, 1950. 271 p. illus. 22cm.

Contributions in Danish, French, German, Italian or Swedish.

1. Cornell, Henrik, 1890- . 2. Art—Essays and misc.

NN OC PC,1,2 SL A,1,2 (LC1,Z1,X1)

NAB

Studies, aangeboden aan Prof. Dr Gerard Brom. [Commissie van redactie: L. C. Michels et al.] Utrecht, Dekker & Van de Vegt, 1952. xx,246 p. port.,facsim. 26cm.

Contents.—Inleidend woord, door L. C. Michels.—Bibliografie (p. ix-xx).—Enrica von Handel-Mazzetti, von E. Alker.—Folkloristische thema's bij Gezelle, door F. Baur.—Schilder-, teken- en graveerkunst von Blank Zuid-Afrika vóór 1900, door D. Bax.—Le machiavélisme de Pierre Charron, par J. (Continued)

NN*X 10.54 t/ OC,I PC, 1,2,3,I SL (Z/1,LC1,X1)
[I]

Studies, aangeboden aan Prof. Dr Gerard Brom. ... 1952. (Card 2)

Dagens.—De Roomse Vondelschool, door A. van Duinkerken.—Over stijl-ontwikkeling in the Middelleeuwen, door G. J. Hoogewerff.—De huidige stand van de Nederlandse Protestantse kerkgeschiedenis, door J. Lindeboom.—Van voorjaar tot voorjaar; over de poëzie van Gabriël Smit, door K. Meeuwesse.—Prof. Dr. Brom als apologeet, door W. [illegible]et.—Het Romeinse verhoor van Petrus Codde, door O. F. M. Polman.—Lentetij der Nederlanden, door D. Roggen.—Uit het elfde hoofdstuk van (Continued)

Studies, aangeboden aan Prof. Dr Gerard Brom. ... 1952. (Card 3)

Max Havelaar: de Japanse steenhouwer, door P. Sobry.—Die Bedeutung der allegemeinen Religionswissenschaft für Theologie und Seelsorge, von J.P.Steffes.—De studie van de Middeleeuwse beeldhouwkunst der Nederlanden, door J.J.M. Timmers.—Voorkeur en tegenzin bij de studie van de Nederlandse litteratuurgeschiedenis, door C.G.N. de Vooys.—De godsdienstige denkbeelden van Jan van der Noot in zijn Keulsche periode, door J. Wille.

1. Literature—Hist. and crit. 2. Religion—Essays and misc. 3. Brom, Gerard, 1882- I. Michels, L C ,ed.

F-11
5968

Studies in ancient Europe; essays presented to Stuart Piggott; edited by J. M. Coles and D. D. A. Simpson. Leicester, Leicester U. P., 1968. 367 p. illus., maps, port. 30cm

Includes bibliographical references.

CONTENTS.--Ancient man in Europe, by J.M.Coles.--A preliminary study of the early neolithic and latest mesolithic blade industries in southern and central Europe, by R. Tringham.--Some aspects of ovicaprid and pig breeding in neolithic England.--Easterton of (Continued)

NN*R 11.69 r/μOC, I, II, IIIb*, IVb* PC, 1, 2, 3, I, II SL
(MU)4 (LC1, X1, Z1) 3

MA
+

STUDIES in art and literature for Belle da Costa Greene. Edited by Dorothy Miner. Princeton, N.J., Princeton university press, 1954. xviii, 502 p. illus., port., facsims. 31cm.

Bibliographical footnotes.

1. Greene, Belle da Costa, d. 1950. 2. Art—Essays and misc. 3. Literature—Hist. and crit. 4. Illustration of books. I. Miner, Dorothy, Eugenia, ed.

NN*R X 8.54 OC, I PC, 1, 2, 3, I SL A, 1, 2, I PR, 1, 4, I
(Z1, LC1, X1) [I]

STUDIES in ancient Europe... (Card 2)

Roseisle: a forgotten site in Moray, by I.C.Walker.--The stone implement trade in third-millenium Scotland, by P.R.Ritchie.--Jet sliders in late neolithic Britain, by I.McInnes.--Stone mace-heads and the latest neolithic cultures of the British Isles, by F.Roe.--Scottish dagger graves, by A.S.Henshall.--Food vessels: associations and chronology, by D.D.A. Simpson.--Fenland rapiers, by B.A.V.Trump.--Iron age enclosures in the Cologne basin, by I.Scollar.--Massive armlets in the North British Iron age, by M.Simpson.-- Shafts, pits, wells-

(Continued)

ZDC

Studies in early Christianity, edited by Shirley Jackson Case, presented to Frank Chamberlin Porter and Benjamin Wisner Bacon by friends and fellow-teachers in America and Europe. New York & London, The Century co. [°1928]

ix, 467 p. front. (2 port.) 23cm. $4.50

"Publications of Frank Chamberlin Porter": p. 440–443; "Publications of Benjamin Wisner Bacon": p. 443–457.

CONTENTS.—The limitations of the historical method, by E. F. Scott.—The text of the Gospels, by K. Lake.—The casual use of ἵνα, by A. T. Robertson.—Vom reinen wort Gottes und vom Lukas-prolog, by E. von Dobschütz.—A primitive tradition in Mark, by B. S. Easton.—The literary structure of the Gospel of Mark, by H. B. Carré.—Prolegomena to a new study of John the Baptist, by C. R. Bowen.—John the Baptist and Jesus, by E. W. Parsons.—'O τέκτων, by C. C. McCown.—Jesus on (Continued on next card)

369445A 28-10979
[5]

STUDIES in ancient Europe... (Card 3)

sanctuaries of Belgic Britons? by A.Ross.--Hanging bowls, by E.Fowler.--Grass-marked pottery in Cornwall, by C.Thomas.--Problems and non-problems in palaeo-organology: a musical miscellany, by J.V.S.Megaw.

1. Archaeology--Addresses, essays, lectures. 2. Europe--Archaeology--Addresses, essays, lectures. 3. Pigott, Stuart. 4. Instruments. I. Coles, John M., ed. II. Simpson, Derek Douglas Alexander, ed. III. Coles, John M. IV. Simpson, Derek Douglas Alexander.

Studies in early Christianity ... [°1928] (Card 2)

CONTENTS—Continued.

sins, by J. Moffatt.—Jesus und der geist nach synoptischer überlieferung, by H. Windisch.—Method in studying Jesus' social teaching, by F. C. Grant.—Outcroppings of the Jewish Messianic hope, by C. C. Torrey.—The rise of Christian Messianism, by S. J. Case.—The Pauline idea of forgiveness, by W. H. P. Hatch.—The Epistle to the Romans and Jewish Christianity, by J. H. Ropes.—Concurrent phases of Paul's religion, by H. J. Cadbury.—Some economic and social conditions of Asia Minor affecting the expansion of Christianity, by S. Dickey.—Bemerkungen zum zweiten Klemensbrief, by G. Krüger.

1. Porter, Frank Chamberlin, 1859– 2. Bacon, Benjamin Wisner, 1860– 3. Christianity—Addresses, essays, lectures. 4. Bible. N.T.—Criticism, interpretation, etc. 5. Church history—Primitive and early church. I. Case, Shirley Jackson, 1872– ed.

Library of Congress BR50.S83 28-10979
~~Copy 2.~~
Copyright A 1074010 [5]

Write on slip words underlined and class mark- HBA

... Studies in the anthropology of Oceania and Asia, presented in memory of Roland Burrage Dixon, by James M. Andrews, IV, Gordon T. Bowles, Carleton S. Coon [and others] ... edited by Carleton S. Coon and James M. Andrews, IV. Cambridge, Mass., The Museum, 1943.

xiv, 220 p. incl. illus. (incl. maps) tables, diagr. front. (port.) plates. 27cm. (Harvard university. Peabody museum of archaeology and ethnology. Papers, v. 20.)

"Bibliography of Roland Burrage Dixon, prepared by Miss Constance Ashenden": p. xii–xiv. "References cited" at end of most of the articles.

CONTENTS.—Physical differentiation in Polynesia, by H. L. Shapiro.—Polynesian stone remains, by K. P. Emory.—Two unique petroglyphs in the Marquesas which point to Easter Island and Malaysia, by E. S. C. Handy.—The gods of Rennell Island, by Gordon MacGregor.—The racial (Continued on next card)

44-2765
[15]

*MFBH

Studies in eighteenth-century music: a tribute to Karl Geiringer on his seventieth birthday; edited by H. C. Robbins Landon in collaboration with Roger E. Chapman. London, Allen & Unwin, 1970.

3–425 p., plate. music, port. 25 cm.

"A selected bibliography of the works of Karl Geiringer in honour of his seventieth birthday, compiled by Martin A. Silver": p. [407]–419.

(Continued)

NN*R 11.71 w/λOC, I, II, III PC, 2, 5, 6, I, II, III SL MU, 1,
3, 4, I, II, III (LC1, X1, Z1) [I] 2

... Studies in the anthropology of Oceania and Asia ... 1943. (Card 2)

CONTENTS—Continued.

elements of Melanesia, by W. W. Howells.—The horomorun concepts of southern Bougainville: a study in comparative religion, by D. L. Oliver.—Notes on northeast Australian totemism, by R. L. Sharp.—Culture sequences in Madagascar, by Ralph Linton.—Linguistic and racial aspects of the Munda problem, by G. T. Bowles.—Evolutionary trends in body build: data from Thailand (Siam) by J. M. Andrews, IV.—Physical types among the Japanese, by F. S. Hulse.—The prone burials of Anyang, by Li Chi.—Observations on the bronze age in the Yenisei valley, Siberia, by J. H. Gaul.—Southern Arabia, a problem for the future, by C. S. Coon.

1. Dixon, Roland Burrage, 1875–1934. 2. Ethnology—Oceanica. 3. Ethnology—Asia. I. Coon, Carleton Stevens, 1904– ed. II. Andrews, James Madison, 1905– joint ed. III. Ashenden, Constance.

44-2765
Library of Congress E51.H337 vol. 20
~~Copy 2.~~ GN662.S75
[15] (572.897) 572.99

STUDIES in eighteenth-century music; a tribute to Karl Geiringer on his seventieth birthday... (Card 2)

1. Essays. 2. Music--Essays. 3. History and criticism, 1600-1750. 4. History and criticism, 1750-1800. 5. Music--Hist. and crit.--Baroque, 1600-1750. 6. Music--Hist. and crit.--Classical, 1750-1800. I. Geiringer, Karl, 1899- . II. Landon, H.C. Robbins, ed. III. Chapman, Roger Eddington, 1916- , ed.

Copy only words underlined
& classmark— STG

STUDIES in English honoring George Wesley Whiting by members of the Department of English. Houston, Tex., Rice institute, 1957. viii, 146 p. port. 23cm. (Rice institue, Houston, Tex. The Rice institute Pamphlets. v. 44, no. 1)

Bibliographical footnotes.

CONTENTS.--Spenser's "Little fish, that men call Remora," by C. Camden.--Phonetic discrimination of Middle English dialects, by J. E. Conner.--The light and the dark; imagery and thematic development in Conrad's Heart of darkness, by W. S. Dowden.--Edwin Booth.

1. Whiting, George Wesley. 2. English literature--Addresses, essays, lectures.

NN 12.64 p/ OC OI PC, 1, 2 (LC1, X1, Z1)

D-11
8704

STUDIES in the English Renaissance drama, in memory of Karl Julius Holzknecht. Edited by Josephine W. Bennett, Oscar Cargill [and] Vernon Hall, jr. New York, New York university press, 1959. xxvi, 368 p. port. 23cm.

Bibliographical footnotes.

CONTENTS.--A medieval survival in Elizabethan punctuation, by

(Continued)

NN R 8.59 m/J OC, I PC, 1, 2, I SL (LC1, X1, Z1) [I]

Copy only words underlined
& classmark— NCB

STUDIES in English language and literature, presented to Karl Brunner on the occasion of his seventieth birthday. Edited by Siegfried Korninger. Wien, W. Braumüller [1957] x, 290 p. port. 25cm. (Wiener Beitraege zur englischen Philologie. Bd. 65)

Bibliographical footnotes.

CONTENTS.—The secretary of the duke of Norfolk and the first Italian grammar in England, by S. Baldi.—Sir Richard Fanshawe and Guarini, by G. Bullough.—Stoicism in Shakespeare... and elsewhere, by L. Eckhoff.—Spanische Sprachbücher in elisabethanischen England,

(Continued)

NN X 5.58 e/b OC, I, IIIbo (OS)I PC, 1, 2, 3, I, II (LC1, X1, Z1, Y1)

STUDIES in the English Renaissance drama... (Card 2)

A.C. Baugh.--Enter citizens, by M. Black.--The death of Hamlet: a study in plot and character, by F. Bowers.--Revised Elizabethan quartos: an attempt to form a class, by H. Craig.--Robert Walker's editions of Shakespeare, by G. E. Dawson.--James I, Bacon, Middleton and the making of the Peacemaker, by R. Dunlap.--Anthony Munday, by M. Eccles.--Julius Caesar: a play without political bias, by V. Hall, jr.--The mystery of Perkin Warbeck, by A. Harbage.--Troilus divided, by R. C. Harrier--The tragic hero in early Elizabethan drama, by S. F. Johnson.--A quip from

(Continued)

STUDIES in English language and literature... (Card 2)

von O. Funke.—Transpositionen aus Shaekespeare's King Lear in Thomas Hardy's Return of the native, von K. Hammerle.—The dedication of Tudor and Stuart plays, by V. B. Heltzel.—Edward Brerewoods Enqviries, von S. Korninger.—Zur Aussprache des Englischen im 18. und 19. Jahrhundert, von H. Koziol.—E. A. Poe und Alfred Kubin; zwei künstlerische Gestalter des Grauens, von H. H. Kühnelt.—The contention and 2 Henry VI, by J. G. McManaway.—Réflexions sur la genèse de la "forme progressive", par F. Mossé.—Of Jane Austen's use of expanded verbal forms, by E. Raybould.—Der neue Othello, von L. L. Schücking.—Moral, Sex und Euphemismus im neusten Englisch, von H. Spies.—W. B. Yeats und Oscar Wildes "Ballad of Reading Gaol", von R. Stamm.

(Continued)

STUDIES in the English Renaissance drama... (Card 3)

Tom Nashe, by D. J. McGinn.--Heywood's sources for the main plot of A woman killed with kindness, W. F. McNeir.-- The acting in university comedy of early seventeenth century England, by L. J. Mills.--Evidence for dating Marlowe's Tragedy of Dido, by T. M. Pearce.--Mucedorus, most popular Elizabethan play? by G. F. Reynolds.--Then I denie you starres: a reading of Romeo and Juliet, by I. Ribner.--A chaste maid in Cheapside and Middleton's city comedy, by S. Schoenbaum.--Song in Jonson's comedy: a gloss on Volpone, by F. W. Sternfeld.--Clarendon and

(Continued)

STUDIES in English language and literature... (Card 3)

—Die Erzählsituation und die umschriebenen Zeitformen, von F. Stanzel.—Studien zu Marlowe's Tamburlaine, von F. Wild.—The language of Milton, by C. L. Wrenn.—Wartime English, by R. W. Zandvoort.—Bibliographie der Veröffentlichungen von Karl Brunner, von K. Lumpi.

1. English literature--Addresses, essays, lectures. 2. English language--Addresses, essays, lectures. 3. Brunner, Karl, 1887- . I. Series. II. Korninger, Siegfried, ed. III. Korninger, Siegfried.

STUDIES in the English Renaissance drama... (Card 4)

Ben Jonson as witnesses for the Earl of Pembroke's character, by D. Taylor, jr.--Falstaff, clown and man, by E. C. Wilson.

1. Holzknecht, Karl Julius. 2. Drama, English--Hist. and crit., 1500-1642. I. Bennett, Josephine Waters, ed.

RNB

Studies in English philology; a miscellany in honor of Frederick Klaeber, edited by Kemp Malone ... and Martin B. Ruud ... Minneapolis, The University of Minnesota press, 1929.

x, 486 p. front. (port.) facsims. 24cm.

"A bibliography of the works of Frederick Klaeber [by] Stefan Einarsson": p. 477-485.

1. English philology—Collections. 2. Klaeber, Friedrich, 1863- . I. Malone, Kemp, ed. II. Ruud, Martin Brown, joint ed.

29-24223

——Copy 2.

Library of Congress PE26.K6

Copyright A 14090 [5]

OAP

Studies and essays in the history of science and learning offered in homage to George Sarton on the occasion of his sixtieth birthday, 31 August 1944. Ed. by M. F. Ashley Montagu. New York, Schuman [1946?]

xiv, 594 p., 2 l. illus., ports. 24 cm.

1. Science—Addresses, essays, lectures. 2. Science—Hist. 3. Sarton, George, 1884- I. Ashley-Montagu, Montague Francis, 1905- ed.

Med 47—1299

U. S. Army medical library for Library of Congress [Q171S033 1946] [17f5]

OEG

Studies and essays presented to R. Courant on his 60th birthday, Jan. 8, 1948. New York, Interscience Publishers [1948]

470 p. diagrs. 25 cm.

1. Mathematics—Collected works. 2. Courant, Richard, 1888-

QA3.S85 510.4 48-5885*

Library of Congress [10]

Studies in French language... (Card 2)

words, by P. Barbier.—Proust and Hardy: incidence or coincidence, by L. A. Bisson.—Napoléon et ses admiratrices britanniques, by J. Deschamps.—A semantic group in Alpine romance, by W. D. Elcock.—A bibliography of eighteenth-century translations of Voltaire, by H. B. Evans (p. 48-62)—Guillaume d'Angleterre, by E. A. Francis.—A contemporary dramatist: René Bruyez, by H. J. Hunt.—Brûlé de plus de feux... by R. C. Knight.—An Anglo-French collection of books in the Royal Malta Library, by F. Mackenzie.—Théophile Gautier et le dandysme esthétique, by J. M. Milner.—Textual problems of the Lai de l'ombre, by J. Orr.—Goethe's autobiography and Rousseau's Confessions, by R. Pascal.—Une amitié entre honnêtes gens, le comte Roger de Bussy-Rabutin, 'Libertin,' et le père René Rapin, jésuite, by E. Pichler.—

(Continued)

N. Y. P. L. January 15, 1952

E-10
5944

STUDIES in folklore in honor of Distinguished service professor Stith Thompson. Edited by W. Edson Richmond. Bloomington, Indiana university press, 1957. xv, 270 p. port. music. 24cm. (Indiana. University. Indiana university publications. Folklore series. no. 9)

Bibliographical references included in "Notes."

CONTENTS.--Foreword: biographical sketch of Stith Thompson.--The brave tailor in Danish tradition, by L. Bødker.--The sisters and the troll:

(Continued)

NN X 12.58 m/P OC, II, IIIbo (OD)I (ED)I PC, 1, 2, I, II SL (LC1, X1, Z1, Y1) [I]

Studies in French language... (Card 3)

Variant readings to three Anglo-Norman poems, by M. K. Pope.—Grammar, grimoire, glamour, gomerel, by T. B. W. Reid.—A note on Taine's conception of the English mind, by F. C. Roe.—Pascal and Brunschvicg, by D. Saurat.—Leconte de Lisle and Robert Burns, by A. L. Sells.—Pontigny, by H. F. Stewart.—Two French attempts to invade England during the Hundred Years' War, by G. Templeman.—Ernest Renan and Alfred Loisy, by H. G. Wood.—A problem of influences: Taine and the Goncourt brothers, by J. S. Wood.

1. French language. 2. French literature—Hist. and crit. 3. Ritchie, Robert Lindsay Graeme, 1800- 4. Great Britain—Invasions—Attempts and projects, 1385-1386. I. Birmingham University, Birmingham, Eng. Arts, Faculty of.

N. Y. P. L. January 15, 1952

STUDIES in folklore in honor of Distinguished service professor Stith Thompson. (Card 2)

notes to a folktale, by R. T. Christiansen.--Celtic tales from Cape Breton, by M. Leach.--A medieval story and its Irish version, by J. Szövérffy.--The emergence myth in native North America, by E. Wheeler-Voegelin and R. W. Moore.--Hugh Miller, pioneer Scottish folklorist, by R. M. Dorson.--Classifying performance in the study of verbal folklore, by W. H. Jansen.--Folklore in the novels of Thomas Deloney, by W. E. Roberts.--Toward a statistical contingency method in folklore research, by T. A. Sebeok.--Toward a definition of formal style, with examples from Shawnee, by C. F. Voegelin and J. Yegerlehner.-- A miscellany of tune notes, by S. P. Bayard.--Some Norwegian contributions to a Danish ballad,

(Continued)

RFB

Studies in French language and mediæval literature, presented to Professor Mildred K. Pope, by pupils, colleagues and friends. [Manchester] Manchester university press, 1939.

xiv, 429, [1] p. front. (port.) pl., facsims., diagrs. 25½cm. (*Half-title:* Publications of the University of Manchester, no. CCLXVIII)

"A list of the published writings of Professor M. K. Pope": p. xiii-xiv.

1. French philology—Collections. 2. French literature—Old French—Hist. & crit. 3. Literature, Medieval. 4. Pope, Mildred Katharine, 1872-

41-641

Library of Congress PC2026.P6S7

Copy 2. [5] 440.4

STUDIES in folklore in honor of Distinguished service professor Stith Thompson. (Card 3)

by W. E. Richmond.--Abraham Lincoln's when Adam was created, by F. L. Utley.--American analogues of the couvade, by W. D. Hand.--The paganism of the Norsemen, by N. Lid.--The feast of Saint Martin in Ireland, by S. Ó Súilleabháin.--Proverbial materials in Edward Eggleston, the Hoosier schoolmaster, by A. Taylor.

1. Folk lore--Addresses, essays, lectures. 2. Thompson, Stith, 1885- I. Series. II. Richmond, W. Edson, ed. III. Richmond, W. Edson.

D-18
5681

STUDIES in French literature, presented to H. W. Lawton by colleagues, pupils and friends. Edited by J. C. Ireson, I. D. McFarlane and Garnet Rees. New York, Barnes R. Noble [1968] 335 p. port. 23cm.

Includes bibliographical references.

CONTENTS.--Introd. by R. W. Ladborough.--H. W. Lawton bibliography.--Seventeenth-century tragedy, by H. T. Barnwell.--La

(Continued)

NN R 12.68 e/ OC, I, II, III PC, 1, 2, I, II, III SL (LC1, X1, Z1) [I]

2

RFB

Studies in French language, literature, and history, presented to R. L. Græme Ritchie. [General editors, on behalf of the Faculty of Arts of the University of Birmingham: Fraser Mackenzie, R. C. Knight and J. M. Milner] Cambridge [Eng.] University Press, 1949. xvi, 259 p. port. 23cm.

Includes bibliographies.

CONTENTS.—Foreword, by J. J. Milne.—Selected publications of R. L. G. Ritchie (p. xv-xvi)—Sainte-Beuve's Tableau de la poésie française au XVIe siècle and Cary's Early French poets, by I. D. O. Arnold.—On the origin and history of three French

(Continued)

Festschrift

N. Y. P. L. January 15, 1952

STUDIES in French literature... (Card 2)

femme pauvre and feminine mythology, by E. Beaumont.--Le grand mystère de Jésus, by M. Blaess.--The early history of the essai title in France and Britain, by A. M. Boase.--Le théâtre de Marcel Aymé.--Knowledge and belief in Pascal's Apology, by J. Cruickshank.--Molière and his reasoners, by R. Fargher.--Some popular scientific myths in Rabelais: a possible source, by K. H. Francis.--Towards a theory of the symbolist theatre, by J. C. Ireson.--Suite à une observation de Maffai sur l'esprit poétique' de Ronsard, by B. Juden.--A Festschrift of 1855: Baudelaire and the Hommage à C. F. Denecourt, by F. W. Leakey.-- Narrative and the drama in

(Continued)

STUDIES in French literature... (Card 3)

medieval France, by W. H. Lyons.--George Buchanan and France, by I. D. McFarlane.--Clément Marot and literary history, by C. A. Mayer.--Rabelais, Thaumaste and the king's great matter, by R. Murphy.--Nature in Apollinaire's Alcools, by G. Rees.--Shakespearean performances in Paris in 1827-8, by M. Shaw.--The concept of fate in the tragedies of Racine, by J. P. Short.

1. French literature--Addresses, essays, lectures. 2. Lawton, Harold Walter. I. Ireson, J. C., ed. II. McFarlane, Ian Dalrymple, ed. III. Rees, Garnet, ed.

Copy only words underlined
& Classmark-- RKA

STUDIES in German literature of the nineteenth and twentieth centuries; Festschrift for Frederic E. Coenen. Edited by Siegfried Mews. Foreword: Werner P. Friedrich. Chapel Hill, University of North Carolina press, 1970. xix, 250 p. port. 23cm. (North Carolina. University. Studies in the Germanic languages and literatures. no. 67)

Includes bibliographical references.

1. German literature--Addresses, essays, lectures. I. Coenen, Frederic Edward. II. Mews, Siegfried, 1933- , ed. III. Series. IV. Mews, Siegfried, 1933-

---

Studies in honor of Basil L. Gildersleeve. Baltimore: Johns Hopkins Pr., 1902. ix, 517 pp. 8°.

Festschrift

Studies in honor of DeWitt T. Starnes. Edited by Thomas P. Harrison ⌊and others⌋ Austin. ⌊Published for the University of Texas by the Humanities Research Center, 1967⌋

295 p. 24 cm.

Includes bibliographies.

CONTENTS.—De Witt T. Starnes, by J. Sledd.—Publications of De Witt T. Starnes, 1921-1965.—Errors and Marprelate, by T. W. Baldwin.—Shakespeare's gaudy: the method of The rape of Lucrece, by R. L. Montgomery.—Richard II to Henry V: a closer view, by L. F.

(Continued)

STUDIES in honor of DeWitt T. Starnes. (Card 2)

Dean.—Death in victory: Shakespeare's tragic reconciliations, by F. Bowers.—Shakespeare and the all-inclusive law of nature, by H. Craig.—The political import and the first two audiences of Gorboduc, by E. W. Talbert.—"Excerpta quaedam per A. W. adolescentem" by J. G. McManaway.—A quatrain version of the trental of St. Gregory, by W. A. Ringler, Jr.—"The wonderful yeere," by C. Camden.—Richard Whytford and his work, by H. White.—Herrick's "Rex Tragicus," by D. C. Allen.—"Idea" titles in John Milton's Milieu, by W. J. Ong.—"Devils to adore for deities," by M. Y. Hughes.—Plato's Ion, comic and serious, by A. H. Gilbert.—Wise men's counters, fool's money: a preface to a study of diction, by A. Norman.

(Continued)

STUDIES in honor of DeWitt T. Starnes. (Card 3)

1. English literature--Addresses, essays, lectures.
2. Starnes, DeWitt Talmadge, 1888-1967.
I. Harrison, Thomas Perrin, 1897- ,ed.

Studies in honor of Hermann Collitz...presented by a group of his pupils and friends on the occasion of his seventy-fifth birthday, February 4, 1930. Baltimore, Md.: The Johns Hopkins Press, 1930. xii, 331 p. front. (port.) 8°.

Printed in Germany.
Bibliographical footnotes.
Contents: Tabula gratulatoria. G. L. FIELD. To Professor Collitz. C. WIGHT. To Professor Collitz. Biographical sketch. Bibliography of Professor Collitz' writings. E. H. STURTEVANT. Neuter pronouns referring to words of different gender or number. F. EDGERTON. Dialectic phonetics in the Veda. T. MICHELSON. Linguistic miscellany.

(Continued)

N. Y. P. L. September 16, 1930

Studies in honor of Hermann Collitz... (Card 2)

G. M. BOLLING. A matter of semantics. E. SIEVERS. Zur Duenosinschrift. T. FRANK. On the name of Lucretius Carus. J. T. HATFIELD. Aeneid, II, 557. E. PROKOSCH. The Germanic vowel shift and the origin of mutation. L. BLOOMFIELD. Salic litus. E. H. SEHRT. Der Genitiv Plural auf -Ē im gothischen. A. M. STURTEVANT. Gothic syntactical notes. S. H. CROSS. Scandinavian-Polish relations in the late tenth century. C. N. GOULD. Blótnaut. H. PIPPING. Hávamál 136. E. E. ERICSON. The use of old English swa in negative clauses. S. H. KROESCH. Change of meaning by analogy. T. STARCK. Der Wortschatz des Ahd. J. L. CAMPION. Randglossen zum Moriz von Craon. J. GOEBEL. Kleine Beiträge zur Textkritik und Erklärung von "Des Minnesangs Frühling." J. L. KELLOGG. The phonetic and morphological settings of the Middle High German clipt preterits. D. B. SHUMWAY. Old preterites of the first ablaut

(Continued)

N. Y. P. L. September 16, 1930

Studies in honor of Hermann Collitz... (Card 3)

class in the 1671 Wittenberg revision of the Lutheran Bible. A. TAYLOR. "Der Rihter und der Teufel." W. G. HOWARD. A view of Lessing. A. W. PORTERFIELD. Repetitions as an element in Lessing's works. W. KURRELMEYER. Wielands Briefwechsel mit Johannes Gottfried Gurlitt. B. J. VOS. A letter of Goethe. E. FEISE. Rhythm and melody as parodistic means in Heine's Unterwelt. A. B. BENSON. Swedish witchcraft and the Mathers. K. Malone. Anglist and Anglicist. L. POUND. The etmology of stir 'prison.'

492330A. 1. Collitz, Hermann, 1855- . 2. Language.
N. Y. P. L. September 16, 1930

Studies in honor of John Albrecht Walz. Lancaster, Pa. ⌊The Lancaster press, inc.⌋ 1941.

4 p. l., 335 p. front. (port.) 23½cm.

"Studies ... written by former graduate students of Professor Walz at Harvard university. On the occasion of his seventieth birthday and his presidency of the Modern language association of America, they are herewith presented."—4th prelim. leaf.

Bibliographical foot-notes.

CONTENTS.—Niclas Müller, German-American poet and patriot, by P. A. Shelley.—"Zwischen pfingsten und Strassburg," by Archer Taylor.—A note on Kleist and Kant, by I. S. Stamm.—Goethe's Auf dem see, by Walter Silz.—Notes on Walther's use of können and mögen, by R-M. S. Heffner.—English loan words in Pennsylvania German, by A. F. Buf-

(Continued on next card)

42-9685

⌊8⌋

Studies in honor of John Albrecht Walz ... 1941. (Card 2)

CONTENTS—Continued.

fington.—Werther in America, by O. W. Long.—George Henry Calvert, admirer of Goethe, by H. W. Pfund. Calvert bibliography (p. 159-161)—Early Danish and Swedish writers on native history, by C. F. Barnason.—Functional burdening of stressed vowels in German, by W. F. Twaddell.—Goethe's Lila as a fragment of the great confession, by T. K. Brown, jr.—Art and reality, by F. O. Nolte.—Abstractions as forms of address in fifteenth century German, by G. J. Metcalf.—Stifter and the Biedermeier crisis, by Alan Holske.—Mittelhochdeutsche jägerwörter vom hund, by W. P. von Schmertzing.—Publications of John Albrecht Walz, prepared by P. A. Shelley (p. 329-335)

1. Walz, John Albrecht, 1871- 2. German literature—Addresses, essays, lectures. 3. Germanic philology—Collections.

Library of Congress PT30.W28 42-9685

[8] 830.4

E-13
8936

STUDIES in honor of Samuel Montefiore Waxman. Edited by Herbert H. Golden. Boston, Boston university press, 1969. ix, 263 p. ports. 25cm.

In English or Spanish.

"Bibliography of the writings of Samuel Montefiore Waxman, p. 15-18."

Includes bibliographies.

CONTENTS.--A personal tribute to a dear friend, by P. Lelo de Moura.--Anent Romain Rolland, by J.H. Powers.--André Suarès

(Continued)

NN R 6.70 1/OC, I, II PC, 1, I, II SL (LC1, X1, Z1) [I]

STUDIES in honor of Samuel Montefiore Waxman. (Card 2)

and Villiers de l'Isle-Adam, by S.D. Braun.--Remarks on a famous letter of Paul Cézanne and the making of a twentieth-century myth, by G. Levitine.--A note on artistic interdependence, by W.M. Jewell.--The French influence on the writings of A. Hamilton Gibbs, by J.P. Gibbs.--Some Old French words in current English, by C.P. Merlino.--The independent theater in Vienna against the background of German naturalism, by J.H. Dayag.--Dramatic suspense and dialogue in the Inferno, by A.J.

(Continued)

STUDIES in honor of Samuel Montefiore Waxman. (Card 3)

de Vito.--Giulio Bertoni and the aesthetic factor in linguistics, by H.H. Golden.--Three poems of Machado in context, by M.P. Young.--García Lorca's basic affirmation in Poet in New York, by J. Devlin.--The theater of Jacinto Grau, by S.O. Simches.--Gironella and Hemingway; novelists of the Spanish Civil war, by R.L. Sheehan.--Current trends in Spanish education, by I.E. Avery.--The Harvard Council on Hispano-American studies, by S.E. Leavitt.--Hacia el humor de Sarmiento, by R. Lida.--Society and the novel in Spanish America, by S. Lipp.--The

(Continued)

STUDIES in honor of Samuel Montefiore Waxman. (Card 4)

Argentine theater and Florencio Sánchez, by R. Richardson.--The New Christians and the Brazilian sentiment of alienation, by J.S. Mazzone.

1. Romance literature--Addresses, essays, lectures. I. Waxman, Samuel Montefiore, 1885- . II. Golden, Herbert Hershel, 1919- , ed.

E-10
6880

STUDIES in honor of T. W. Baldwin; edited by Don Cameron Allen. Urbana, University of Illinois press, 1958. 276 p. illus., facsims. 25cm.

Bibliographical footnotes.

CONTENTS.—Introduction, by D. C. Allen.—Criticism of Elizabethan dramatic texts, by H. Craig.—Old-spelling editions of dramatic texts, by F. Bowers.—Humor and satire in Heywood's epigrams, by R. A. Milligan.—The blatant beast, by L. Hotson.—The origin of the euphuistic novel and its significance for Shakespeare, by L. Borinski.—The earliest (?) printing of Sir Thomas More's two epigrams to John Holt, by H. Fletcher.—Spenser's scholarly script and "right writing," by R. M. Smith.—King Leir and King Lear: an examination of the two plays, by R. A. Law.—Susanna and the elders in sixteenth-century drama, by M. T. Herrick.—Marlowe and Greene:

(Continued)

NN* R 2.59 g/ OC, I PC, 1, 2, I SL (LC1, Z1, X1)

STUDIES in honor of T. W. Baldwin... (Card 2)

CONTENTS—Continued.

a note on their relations as dramatic artists, by U. Ellis-Fermor.—Shakespeare's prologues and epilogues, by C. Leech.—Giles Fletcher and the Catholics, by A. Holaday.—Conjectures on The London prodigal, by B. Maxwell.—Izaak Walton and the arte of angling, 1577, by M. S. Goldman.—Milton and Olaus Magnus, by J. E. Hankins.—That unnecessary shell of Milton's world, by H. F. Robins.—"Our vegetable love": Marvell and Burton, by R. Putney.—The problem of Brutus: an eighteenth-century solution, by G. B. Evans.—Milton's celestial battle and the theogonies, by M. Y. Hughes.—George Bernard Shaw and Shakespeare's Cymbeline, by R. Stamm.—A bibliography of the scholarly writings of Thomas Whitfield Baldwin, by J. H. Smith (p. 267-276)

1. ENGLISH LITERATURE--ADDRESSES, ESSAYS, LECTURES
2. BALDWIN, THOMAS WHITFIELD, 1890- I. Allen, Don Cameron, 1904- , ed.

QGF

STUDIES honoring Trevor Kincaid. Seattle, University of Washington Press, 1950. iii, 167 p. illus., ports. 26cm.

Includes bibliographies. "Publications of Trevor Kincaid": p. 6-7.

CONTENTS.—Trevor Kincaid, by M. H. Hatch.—An account of the life of Orson Bennett Johnson, by M. H. Hatch.—The Young Naturalists' Society (1879 1905) by M. H. Hatch.— A comparative study of the thyroid follicle, by S. E. Johnson.— The genotype and systematic position of Sporadogenerina Cushman (Foraminifera, Polymorphinidae) by D. L. Frizzell.—Review of thirteen genera of South American fishes in the subfamilies Cynodontinae, Hepsetinae, and Characinae,

(Continued)

NN*R 11.52 OC, I PC, 1, 2 SL (LC1, Z1, X1)

STUDIES honoring Trevor Kincaid... (Card 2)

with the description of a new Cyrtocharax, by L. P. Schultz.—Early life history and larval development of some Puget Sound echinoderms, by M. W. Johnson and L. T. Johnson.—Some monogenetic trematodes of Puget Sound fishes, by K. Bonham.—Methods for the study and cultivation of Protozoa, by V. Tartar.—Conopisthine spiders (Theridiidae) from Peru and Ecuador, by H. Exline.—Some remarks on the blood volume of fish, by A. W. Martin.

594982B. 1. Kincaid, Trevor, 1872- . 2. Zoology—Addresses, essays, lectures. I. Hatch, Melville Harrison, 1898- ed.

---

*EA
S659
v.137

STUDIES in invertebrate morphology; published in honor of Dr. Robert Evans Snodgrass on the occasion of his eighty-fourth birthday, July 5, 1959. Washington, Smithsonian institution, 1959. v, 416 p. illus., plates, ports. 24cm. (Smithsonian institution. Smithsonian miscellaneous collections. v.137)

Includes bibliographies.

(Continued)

NN R 9.62 e/s OC OI (PC)1, 2 (LC3, X1, Z1)

4

STUDIES in invertebrate morphology... (Card 2)

CONTENTS.--Robert Evans Snodgrass, insect anatomist and morphologist, by E.B. Thurman.--Bibliography of R.E. Snodgrass between the years 1896 and 1958, by E.B. Thurman.--Contributions to the problem of eye pigmentation in insects; studied by means of intergeneric organ transplantations in Diptera, by D. Bodenstein.--The structure and some aspects of development of the onychophoran head, by F.H. Butt.--The external anatomy of the South American semiaquatic grasshopper Marellia remipes Uvarov (Acridoidea, Pauliniidae), by C.S. Carbonell.--The first leg segments in the Crustacea malecostraca and the insects, by F. Carpentier and J. Barlet.-- Spinasternal musculature in

(Continued)

STUDIES in invertebrate morphology... (Card 3)

certain insect orders, by L.E. Chadwick.--The nerves and muscles of the proboscis of the blow fly Phormia regina Meigen in relation to feeding responses, by V.G. Dethier.--Morphology of the larval head of some Chironomidae (Diptera, Nematocera), by F.J. Gouin.--The problems of "morphological adaptation" in insects, by G. Grandi.--The shaping of the egg strings in the copepods, by P. Heegaard.--Mechanism of feeding in Hemiptera, by M.A.H. Qadri.--Studies on the molecular organization of insect cuticle, by A.G. Richards and R.L. Pipa.--Metachemogenesis--postemergence biochemical maturation in insects, by

(Continued)

STUDIES in invertebrate morphology... (Card 4)

M. Rockstein.--A physiological approach to the relation between prey and predator, by K.D. Roeder.--The cervicothoracic nervous system of a grasshopper, by J.B. Schmitt.--Notes on the mesothoracic musculature of Diptera, by J. Smart.--The metathoracic musculature of Crymodes devastator (Brace) (Noctuidae) with special reference to the tympanic organ, by A.E. Treat.--The phylogenetic significance of entognathy in entognathous apterygotes, by S.L. Tuxen.

1. Snodgrass, Robert Evans, 1875- . 2. Invertebrates.

---

*PA

Studies in Jewish bibliography and related subjects, in memory of Abraham Solomon Freidus (1867–1923) ... New York, The Alexander Kohut memorial foundation, 1929.

cxxx, 518 p., 2 l., קנט p. front. ~~(port.) 2 pl., 2 port.~~, facsims. 25½cm.

Printed in Austria.

On cover: Distributed by the Jewish division, New York public library.

Preface by the Freidus memorial committee, Louis Ginzberg, chairman.

Contributions in Hebrew, forming the second part of the volume, have title: יד ושם לזכר אברהם זלמן פריידוס. קבוצת מאמרים וחקירות בספרות ישראל מאת ידידיו מוקיריו וחבריו למדע ... ניו יארק, הוצאת המוסד לזכר אלכסנדר קאהוט, תר"צ.

"Freidusiana, a list of writings by and about A. S. Freidus": p. [xi]–xxii.

(Continued on next card)

30—22543

[31f3]

Studies in Jewish bibliography ... 1929. (Card 2)

"The classification of Jewish literature in the New York public library, by J. Bloch": p. [l]–lxxvii.

"Jewish customs, a list of works compiled by A. S. Freidus, prepared for publication by D. C. Haskell": p. [lxxviii]–cxxx.

CONTENTS.—[pt. I] Bernheimer, C. The library of the Talmud Torah at Leghorn.—Enelow, H. G. Isaac Belinfante, an 18th century bibliophile.—Adler, E. N. A bibliography of the writings of Adolf Neubauer (1832–1907).—Freimann, A. Das einteilungssystem der Judaica in der Stadtbibliothek Frankfurt a. M.—Kohut, G. A. Steinschneideriana.—Krauss, S. Merkwürdige Siddurim.—Lauterbach, J. Z. Abbreviations and their solutions.—Reider, J. Non-Jewish motives in the ornament of early Hebrew books.—Roth, C. A seventeenth century library and trousseau.—Schwarz, A. Z. Nikolsburger hebräische handschriften.—Schapiro, I.

(Continued on next card)

30—22543

[31f3]

Studies in Jewish bibliography ... 1929. (Card 3)

CONTENTS—Continued

Bibliography of Hebrew translations of English works.—Cohen, B. Nehemiah Brüll (1843–1891) [with bibliography of his works].—Marx, A. The polemical manuscripts in the library of the Jewish theological seminary of America.—Wolfson, H. A. Isaac ibn Shem-Tob's unknown commentaries on the Physics and his other unknown works.—Simonsen, D. Über die vorlage des ספר האשכול.—Kohler, M. J. Some new light on the Dreyfus case.—Yarmolinsky, A. The wandering Jew.—Kinkeldey, O. A Jewish dancing master of the renaissance (Guglielmo Ebreo) [with bibliography].—Markon, I. Bemerkungen zum bericht des R. Jakob Emden über die Wilnaer flüchtlinge im XVII. jahrhundert.—Goldstein, I. Ritual questions.—Idelsohn, A. Z. Collections of and literature on synagogue song.—Levias, C. Who were the Amorites?—Blau, L. Zur Massora.—

(Continued on next card)

30—22543

[31f3]

Studies in Jewish bibliography ... 1929. (Card 4)

CONTENTS—Continued

Black, G. F. The beginnings of the study of Hebrew in Scotland.—Eames, W. On the use of Hebrew types in English America before 1735.—Ginzberg, L. Die Haggada bei den kirchenvätern.—[pt. II]

י. ראווידזאן. לקט מכתבים מחכמי ישראל לשח"ה.—ד. תאכשטיין. שרידים מפנקסו של רבי
יעקב יושע בעל פני יהושע.—ג. ש. ליבאוויטש. השארת הנפש על ידי הספרים.—ש"ב. שוארצ־
בערג. שיאור וקש. רשימת ספריו, הוצאותיו ומאמריו.—ד. ילין. השם הערבי לספר הגלוי
לר' סעדיה גאון.—ש. בארון. תשבה בשפה איטלקית מאת ר' אברהם גראציאנו.—י. ריבקינד,
אליה מורפורגו מסייעו של ויזל במלחמת ההשכלה.

(Continued on next card)

30—22543

[31f3]

Studies in Jewish bibliography ... 1929. (Card 5)

1. Freidus, Abraham Solomon, 1867–1923. 2. Freidus, Abraham Solomon, 1867–1923—Bibl. 3. Jews—Bibl. 4. Hebrew literature—Bibl. 5. Classification—Books—Judaica and Hebraica. 6. Bibliography—Collections. I. Alexander Kohut memorial foundation, New York. II. Ginzberg, Louis, 1873- III. Bloch, Joshua. IV. Freidus, Abraham Solomon, 1867–1923. V. Haskell, Daniel Carl, 1883- ed. VI. Title: Jewish bibliography, Studies in. VII. Hebrew title (transliterated): Yad we-shem.

Library of Congress Z6368.S93 30—22543

[31f3] [013.296] 016.296

E-12
8594

Studies in language and literature in honor of Margaret Schlauch. Editorial committee: Mieczysław Brahmer, Stanisław Helsztyński [and] Julian Krzyżanowski. Warszawa, Polish Scientific Publishers [1966]

486 p. port. 25 cm.

Bibliographical footnotes.

(Continued)

NN*R 4.67 g/AOC,I PC, 1,2,3,I SL (LC1,X1, Z1)

2

STUDIES in language and literature in honor of Margaret Schlauch. (Card 2)

1. Schlauch, Margaret, 1898- . 2. English literature--Addresses, essays, lectures. 3. English language-- Addresses, essays, lectures. I. Brahmer, Mieczysław, ed.

E-10
6719

STUDIES in the literature of the Augustan age, essays collected in honor of Arthur Ellicott Case; edited by Richard C. Boys. Ann Arbor, Distributed for the Augustan reprint society by G. Wahr pub. co., 1952. ix, 367 p. port. 24cm.

Bibliographical footnotes.

CONTENTS. —A note in defence of satire, by L. I. Bredvold. — The beggar's opera, by B. H. Bronson. — The authenticity of

(Continued)

NN R 12.58 g/p OC, I PC, 1, 2, I SL (LC1, X1, Z1)

STUDIES in the literature of the Augustan age... (Card 2)

Anna Seward's published correspondence, by J. L. Clifford. — Suggestions toward a genealogy of "The man of feeling", by R. S. Crane. —The nature of Dr. Johnson's rationalism, by J. H. Hagstrum. — Thomas Warton and the eighteenth century dilemma, by R. D. Havens. — The purpose of Dryden's "Annus Mirabilis", by E. N. Hooker. — The originality of "Absalom and Achitophel," by R. F. Jones. — The influence of Bernard Mandeville, by F. B. Kaye. — Jonathan Swift, by L. A. Landa. — Epistolary technique in Richardson's novels, by A. McKillop.— The muse of satire,

(Continued)

STUDIES in the literature of the Augustan age... (Card 3)

by M. Mack. — The search for English literary documents, by J. M. Osborn. —Situational satire: a commentary on the method of Swift, by R. Quintana. —Fielding's "Amelia": an interpretation, by G. Sherburn. — Rules and English critics of the epic, 1650-1800, by H. T. Swedenberg. — One relation of rhyme to reason: Alexander Pope, by W. K. Wimsatt, jr. — The art collection of a virtuoso in eighteenth century England, by H. B. Wright and H. C. Montgomery. —Arthur Ellicott Case: Biographical note, by T. Banks. A checklist of the writings of Arthur E. Case, by .

(Continued)

STUDIES in the literature of the Augustan age... (Card 4)

A. Mizener (p. 344). —New attributions to Pope: by A. E. Case, with a reply by N. Ault.

1. Case, Arthur Ellicott, 1894-1946. 2. English literature--Addresses, essays, lectures. I. Boys, Richard Charles, 1912- , ed.

CO
(London)

STUDIES in London history, presented to Philip Edmund Jones. Edited by A. E. J. Hollaender and William Kellaway. [London] Hodder and Stoughton [1969] 509 p. illus., port. 25cm.

Bibliographical footnotes.

CONTENTS. --P. E. J. by A. E. J. Hollaender. --The pre-Norman bridge of London, by M. B. Honeybourne. --Books at St. Paul's Cathedral before 1313 by N. R. Ker. --The coroner in medieval by W. Kellaway.

(Continued)

NN R 3.70 e/ OC, I, II, III PC, 1, 2, I, II, III SL E, 2, I, II, III G, 1, I, II, III (LC1, X1, Z1)

STUDIES in London history... (Card 2)

--The mayor's household before 1600, by B. R. Masters. --A fourteenth-century law book of London interest, by M. Weinbaum. --Craftsmen and the economy of London in the fourteenth century, by E. M. Veale. "Les Bones gentes de la merceye de Londres": a study of the membership of the medieval Mercers' company, by J. M. Imray. --The Collectors of customs in London under Richard II, by O. Coleman. --Richard Whithington: the man behind the myth, by C. M. Barron. --Aliens in and around London in the fifteenth century, by S. L. Thrupp. --A Source-book for Stow? by M. Holmes. --Sir Henry James of Smarden,

(Continued)

STUDIES in London history... (Card 3)

Kent, and Clerkenwell, Recusant (c. 1559-1625), by H. Bowler. --London Puritans and Scotch fifth columnists: a mid-seventeenth-century phenomenon, by V. Pearl. --The city loans on the hearth tax, 1664-1668, by C. A. F. Meekings. --Socio-economic status and occupations in the city of London at the end of the seventeenth century, by D. V. Glass. --Places of worship in London about 1738, by E. S. de Beer. --Eighteenth-century London shipping, by R. C. Davis. --Roman Catholics in London 1850-1865, by K. G. T. McDonnell. --Holloway prison as the city of London's house of correction, 1852-1877, by W. M. Stern

(Continued)

STUDIES in London history... (Card 4)

--List of writings by P. E. Jones, comp. by B. R. Masters.

1. London--Hist. 2. London--Soc. condit. I. Jones, Phillip E. II. Hollaender, Albert E. J. III. Kellaway, William.

OEG

Studies in mathematical analysis and related topics; essays in honor of George Pólya. Edited by Gabor Szegő [and others. Contributors: Lars V. Ahlfors, and others] Stanford, Stanford University Press, 1962.

xxi, 447 p. port., diagrs. 25 cm. (Stanford studies in mathematics and statistics, 4)

English, German, or French.
"Publications of George Pólya": p. xiii-xxi.
Includes bibliographies.

1. Mathematics--Addresses, essays, lectures. 2. Pólya, György, 1887- I. Szegő, Gábor, 1895- , ed. II. Series. t. 1962

NN*R 4.63 f/ OC, I (OS)II PC, 1, 2, I, II SL (E)II ST, 1t, 2, I (LC1, X1, Z1)

OEG

STUDIES in mathematics and mechanics, presented to Richard von Mises by friends, colleagues, and pupils. New York, Academic press, 1954. ix, 353 p. port., diagrs. 24cm.

Includes bibliographies.

1. Mathematics—Addresses, essays, lectures. 2. Mechanics, 1954. 3. Mises, Richard, Edler von, 1883-1953. t. 1954.

NN*X 3.55 g/ OC PC, 1, 2, 3 SL ST, 1t, 2, 3 (LC1, X1, Z1)

Copy only words underlined & classmark— RAA

Studies in memory of Frank Martindale Webster by Robert M. Schmitz [and others] of the Dept. of English, Washington university. Saint Louis, 1951. 24cm. (Washington university studies, New series: language and literature. no. 20)

Contents.—In deference to David Hume, by R.M. Schmitz.—Leigh Hunt's Shakespeare: A "Romantic" concept, by G.D. Stout.—Jeffrey, Marmion, and Scott, by A.M. Buchan.—The frustrated opposition: (Continued)

NN R X 3.55 j/ OC,2b (OS)I PC,1,2,I (Z1, LC3,X1) [I]

Copy only words underlined & classmark— RAA

Studies in memory of Frank Martindale Webster by Robert M. Schmitz [and others] of the Dept. of English, Washington university. (Card 2)

Burke, Barré, and their audiences, by D.C. Bryant.—The first public address of George W. Cable, Southern liberal, by G.A. Cardwell.—Linguistic equations for the study of Indo-European culture, by V. Jelinek

1. Essays, American. 2. Webster, Frank Martindale, 1882-1949. I. Series.

*PBN

Studies in mysticism and religion, presented to Gershom G. Scholem on his seventieth birthday by pupils, colleagues and friends. [Edited by E. E. Urbach, R. J. Zwi Werblowsky and Ch. Wirszubski] Jerusalem, Magnes Press, Hebrew University, 1967. 387,235 p. port. 25cm.

Hebrew section, 235 p. at end, has special t. p.

(Continued)

NN * R 6.70 1/LOC, I, II, III, IV PC, 1, 3, I, II, III, IV SL J, 2, 4, I, II, III, IV (LC1, X1, Z1) 2

STUDIES in mysticism and religion... (Card 2)

Some articles in French, some in German.
Bibliography of Gershom G. Scholem, p. 199-235 (2d group).
Bibliographical footnotes.

1. Mysticism, Jewish. 2. Mysticism. 3. Judaism--Addresses, essays, lectures. 4. Judaism--Essays. I. Scholem, Gershom Gerhard, 1897- II. Urbach, Efraim E., ed. III. Werblowsky, Raphael Jehudah Zwi, 1924- , ed. IV. Wirszubski, Chaim, 1915- , ed.

F-11
6739

STUDIES in Old English literature in honor of Arthur G. Brodeur. Edited by Stanley B. Greenfield. [Eugene, Ore.] University of Oregon books, 1963. vii, 272 p. port. 27cm.

"Arthur Gilchrist Brodeur bibliography," p. vi-vii.
Bibliographical footnotes.
CONTENTS.--Aspects of microcosm and macrocosm in Old English literature, by J. E. Cross.--Maldon and the (Continued)

NN R 1.70 1/LOC, I, II PC, 1, I, II SL (LC1, X1, Z1) 3

STUDIES in Old English literature in honor of Arthur G. Brodeur. (Card 2)

Oláfsdrápa, by J.B. Bessinger.--Patristics and Old English literature, by M.W. Bloomfield.--The singer looks at his sources, by R.P. Creed.--Byrhtnoth and Hildebrand, by R.W.V. Elliott.--The Christian perspective in Beowulf, by M.E. Goldsmith.--Beowulf and epic tragedy, by S.B. Greenfield.--Two English Frauenlieder, by K. Malone.--Two Anglo-Saxon harps, by C.L. Wrenn.--The Beowulf poet and the tragic muse, by A. Bonjour.--Haethenra Hyht in Beowulf, by E.G. Stanley.--Strange sauce from Worcester, by H. D. Meritt.-- (Continued)

STUDIES in Old English literature in honor of Arthur G. Brodeur. (Card 3)

"He that will not when he may; when he will shall have nay," by A. Taylor.--Episcopal magnificence in the eleventh century, by D. Bethurum.--The subjectivity of the style of Beowulf, by G. Storms.--The fall of man in Genesis B and the Mystère d'Adam, by R. Woolf.--"Hygelac" and "Hygd" by R.E. Kaske.--The flood narrative in the Junius manuscript and in Baltic literature, by F.L. Utley.--The edged teeth, by F.G. Cassidy.--The heroic oath in Beowulf, the Chanson de Roland and the Nibelungenlied, by A. Renoir.

1. Anglo-Saxon literature--Addresses, essays, lectures. I. Greenfield, Stanley B., ed. II. Brodeur, Arthur Gilchrist, 1888-

3-MAI

Studies over de kerkelijke en kunstgeschiedenis van West-Vlaanderen, opgedragen aan Z. E. H. Michiel English. Brugge, Uitgeverij de Tempel, 1952. xl,455 p. illus. 22cm.

Bibliography, p. x-xxii.
1.Art, Ecclesiastical--Belgium--West Flanders. 2.Church history--Belgium--West Flanders--Sources. 3.English, Michiel,1885-

NN 12.52 OC PC,1, 2,3 SL A,2 (LC,1, Z1,X1)

MAS

STUDIES presented to David Moore Robinson on his seventieth birthday. Edited by George E. Mylonas. Saint Louis, Washington university, 1951-53. 2 v. illus., plates., ports. 28cm.

Contributions in English, French, German, Italian or Spanish.
Vol. 2, edited by G. E. Mylonas and Doris Raymond.
Writtings of David Moore Robinson, 1904-1950, v. 1, p. xxii-xliii, and other bibliographies.

1. Art, Classical. 2. Sculpture, Classical. 3. Robinson, David Moore, 1880- . 4. Classical studies. I. Mylonas, George Emmanuel, 1898- , ed. II. Raymond, Doris, ed.

NN**R X 6.53 OCs, Is, II, IIb PCs, Is, 2s, 3s, 4, Is, II SLs As, Is, 2s, 3s, Is, II (LC1, Z1, X1)

L-11
3930
no.1

STUDIES presented to Robert B. Lees by his students. Edited by Jerrold M. Sadock [and] Anthony L. Vanek. Edmonton, Champaign, Linguistic research, inc. [c1970] xvii, 312 p. 23cm. (Papers in linguistics. Monograph series. 1)

"Publications of Robert B. Lees," p. xiii-xv.
Includes bibliographies.

(Continued)

NN 7.71 d/LOC, I, II, III, Vbo, VIbo (OS)IV PC, 1, 2, I, II, III, IV (LC1, X1, Z1) 4

STUDIES presented to Robert B. Lees by his students. (Card 2)

CONTENTS.--Problems of polarity in counterfactuals, by C.L. Baker.--Do so: do + adverb, by L.F. Bouton.--Domains of phonological rule application, by C. Cheng.--Rule ordering and apparent irregularities in the Turkish aorist verb, by J.F. Foster.--Does meaning grow on trees? By M. Gallagher.--Lithuanian third person future, by M.J. Kenstowicz.--Vowel elision in Tonkawa and derivational constraints by C.W. Kisseberth.--English question intonation, by R.W.

(Continued)

STUDIES presented to Robert B. Lees by his students. (Card 3)

Langacker.--Two proposals about Japanese polite expressions, by S. Makino.--The root modal: can it be transitive? By F.J. Newmeyer.--Some basic rules of Portuguese phonology, by B. Saciuk.--Whimperatives, by J.M. Sadock.--Focus on focus: propositional generative grammar, by M. Saltarelli--Grammatical formatives: some basic notions, by A.L. Vanek.--Stress assignment in Spanish, by B.E. Willis.

(Continued)

STUDIES presented to Robert B. Lees by his students. (Card 4)

1. Philology--Addresses, essays, lectures. 2. Language--Addresses, essays, lectures. I. Lees, Robert B. II. Sadock, Jerrold M., ed. III. Vanek, Anthony L., ed. IV. Series. V. Sadock, Jerrold M. VI. Vanek, Anthony L.

F-10
1965

STUDIES presented to Sir Hilary Jenkinson. Edited by J. Conway Davies. London, New York, Oxford University Press, 1957. xxx, 494 p. port., facsims. 26cm.

Bibliographical footnotes.

CONTENTS.—Memoir of Sir Hilary Jenkinson.—Italian archives, by H.E. Bell.—Medieval ordination lists in the English Episcopal registers, by H.S. Bennett.—"The treasury" of the later twelfth century, by R.A. Brown.—The "private" hundred before the Norman Conquest, by H.M. Cam.—The Chancery of Guyenne, 1289-1453, by P. Chaplais.—The Memoranda rolls of the Exchequer to 1307, by J.C. Davies.—

(Continued)

NN* R 5.58 e/ OC, I PC, 1, 2, 3, I SL (LC1, X1, Z1) [I] 3

STUDIES presented to Sir Hilary Jenkinson. (Card 2)

Ely Almonry boys and choristers in the later Middle Ages, by S. Evans.—Articles of Almayne, by A.A.E. Hollaender.—The Public Record Office, by C. Johnson.—William Worcester, a preliminary survey by K.B. McFarlane.—The Pipe roll order of 12 February 1270, by C.A.F. Meekings.—The medieval shire house (Domus vicecomitis) by M.H. Mills.—Sortilegium in English homiletic literature of the fourteenth century, by G.R. Owst.—University of London Library ms. 278, Robert Gloucester's chronicle, by J.H.P. Pafford.—The Union and the Tests, by T.F.T. Plucknett.—The early history of the Admiralty Record Office, by R.B. Pugh.—The Founder's statutes of King's College, Cambridge, by J. Saltmarsh.—Wreck rolls of Leiston Abbey, by B. Schofield.—The

(Continued)

STUDIES presented to Sir Hilary Jenkinson. (Card 3)

preparation and issue of instruments under seal in the Duchy of Lancaster, by R. Somerville.—The collectors of the customs at Newcastle-upon-Tyne in the reign of Richard II, by A. Steel.—Background for a bishop, by G.S. Thomson.—The mission of Thomas Wilkes to the United Provinces in 1590, by R.B. Wernham.—Sir Henry Spelman and the Royal Commission on Fees, 1622-40, by J.S. Wilson.—The solemn entry of Mary Tudor to Montreuil-sur-Mer in 1514, by F. Wormald.—A bibliography of the writings of Sir Hilary Jenkinson, by R. Ellis (p. [480]-494).

1. Jenkinson, Sir Hilary. 2. Middle Ages--Hist.--Addresses, essays, lectures. 3. Great Britain--Hist.--Addresses, essays, lectures. I. Davies, James Conway, ed.

YED

Studies in psychology, contributed by colleagues and former students of Edward Bradford Titchener. Worcester, Mass., L.N. Wilson, 1917. 1 p. l., 337 p. front. (port.) illus. 23½cm.

Bibliographical foot-notes.

1. Psychology.-Essays and misc. 2. Titchener, Edward Bradford, 1867- .

KAT

Studies in regional consciousness and environment; essays presented to H. J. Fleure...edited by Iorwerth C. Peate... [Oxford:] Oxford Univ. Press, 1930. xii, 220 p. incl. diagrs., tables. front., illus. (incl. charts), maps, plans, plates. 8°.

Some plates printed on both sides.
Includes bibliographies.
Contents: Fleming, R. M. An outline of some factors in the development of Russia, with special reference to European Russia. Laidler, F. F. Notes on the limits of certain cultures in Spain. Evans, E. E. The Pyrenees: a geographical interpretation of their rôle in human times. Sayce, R. U. The transport ox and the ox-wagon in Natal. Garrard, L. Sociographs of the Kolymans, Andamanese, and

(Continued)

N. Y. P. L. October 20, 1930

Studies in regional consciousness and environment... (Card 2)

Palaungs. Jones, S. J. The typology and distribution of perforated stone axes in Europe and South-West Asia. Harris, S. Settlements and field systems in Germany. Wilcox, H. A. A map of the prehistoric woodlands and marshlands of England. Pelham, R. A. The foreign trade of the Cinque Ports during the year 1307-8. Hauck, H. The influence of geographical factors on the French elections of 1928. Pugh, W. J. A contribution to the geology of Central Wales. Peate, I. C. Some Welsh wood-turners and their trade. Bowen, E. G. A clinical study of miners' phthisis in relation to the geographical and racial features of the Cardiganshire lead-mining area. Flattely, F. W. The biology of Cestodes, with special reference to the genus Moniezia. Stephenson, T. A. Science and the sea.

488241A. 1. Fleure, Herbert John, 1877- . 2. Geography. 3. Anthropo-geography. I. Peate, Iorwerth Cyfeiliog, editor.
N. Y. P. L. October 20, 1930

MA
+

STUDIES in Renaissance & Baroque art presented to Anthony Blunt on his 60th birthday. London, New York, Phaidon, 1967. xi,268 p. illus., plate (port.),maps,plans,facsims. 32cm.

Contributions in English, French and German. Edited by M. Kitson and J. Shearman.
"The writings of Anthony Blunt, compiled by Elsa Scheerer": p. 257-268.

(Continued)

NN R 4.68 e/ OC,I,Ib+, II PC,1,2,3,4,I,II SL A,1,2,3,4,I,II (LC1,X1, Z1) [I] 2

STUDIES in Renaissance & Baroque art presented to Anthony Blunt on his 60th birthday. (Card 2)

Bibliographical footnotes.

1. Blunt, Sir Anthony, 1907- . 2. Blunt, Sir Anthony, 1907- .--Bibl. 3. Art, Renaissance 4. Art, Baroque. I. Kitson, Michael. II. Shearman, John K. G.

STUDIES in Russian and Polish literature in honor of Wacław Lednicki. (Card 2)

oldest Polish Carmen patrium, by J. Krzyzanowski. --A definition of the emotion of grief, by J. Mersereau, jr. --The confession of Epiphany, a Muscovite visionary, by S.A. Zenkovsky. --Dans quelle mesure Derzhavin est-il un baroque? Par C. Backvis. --Sull elemento lirico-autobiografico nell'Evgenij Onegin di Puškin, di E. lo Gatto. --The Conclusion of Pushkin's Queen of spades, by J. T. Shaw. --Two slavic poets at the czar's court, by M. Giergielewicz. --A duel of improvisations, by W. Weintraub. --The theme of crime and punishment in Słowacki's

(Continued)

TAH

Studies in Roman economic and social history in honor of Allan Chester Johnson; ed. by P. R. Coleman-Norton with the assistance of F. C. Bourne and J. V. A. Fine. Princeton, Princeton univ. press, 1951. xiii,373 p. illus. 23cm.

Bibliographical footnotes.

1. Economic history—Rome. 2. Johnson, Allan Chester, 1881- I. Coleman-Norton, Paul Robinson, ed.

NN*R OC,I PC,1,2,I SL E,1,2,I (SR1,Z1,LC1,X1)

STUDIES in Russian and Polish literature in honor of Wacław Lednicki. (Card 3)

poetry, by Z. Folejewski. --Turgenev in England, 1850-1950, by D. Davie. --A re-examination of Ostrovsky's character Lyubim Tortsov, by A. Kaspin. --The narrator in Dostoevsky's Notes from the house of the dead, by R. L. Jackson. --Aksin'ia Astakhova of The quiet Don, by X. Gasiorowska. --Sense and nonsense about Doctor Zhivago, by G. Struve.

1. Russian literature--Addresses, essays, lectures. 2. Polish literature--Addresses, essays, lectures. 3. Lednicki, Wacław, 1891- . I. Folejewski, Zbigniew, 1910- , ed. II. Series.

D-12
163

STUDIES in the Roman law of sale. Dedicated to the memory of Francis De Zulueta. Oxford, Clarendon Press, 1959. xi, 195 p. 23cm.

Edited by David Daube.
Bibliography, p.[ix]-xi.
CONTENTS. --Sale and hire, by A. M. Prichard. --Certainty of price, by D. Daube. --Laesis enormis: the Roman-Dutch story, by R. W. M. Dias. --An arrangement concerning shortage of measure, and pacts

(Continued)

NN*R 10. 59 t/b OC, I PC, 1, 2, I SL E, 1, 2, I (LC1, X1, Z1)

NAFD

Studies in speech and drama, in honor of Alexander M. Drummond. Ithaca, N. Y., Cornell university press, 1944.
viii, 472 p. front. (port.) illus. (map) 23½cm.
Bibliographical references included in "Notes" (at end of each essay except the first)
CONTENTS.—Alexander M. Drummond, by H. H. Hudson.—Musical drama as a union of all the arts, by H. D. Albright.—Stanislavski and the idea, by Edwin Duerr.—Expression in stage scenery, by Barnard Hewitt.—Color music, by W. H. Stainton.—Senecan influence in Gorboduc, by M. T. Herrick.—Some plays in the repertories of the patent houses, by A. L. Woehl.—Actors and audiences in eighteenth-century London, by William Angus.—The stage Yankee, by J. W. Curvin.—The realism in romanticism: Hugo and Wordsworth, by Leland Schubert.—Henry Irving, 1870–1890, by E. J. West.—The Meininger: an evaluation, by Joel Trapido.—The challenge of Ibsen: a study in critical contradic-

(Continued on next card)

44-9025

[5]

STUDIES in the Roman law of sale. (Card 2)

in general, by P. W. Duff. --Sale of wine, by R. Yaron. --Eviction in Roman and English law, by R. Powell. --Dicta promissive, by J.K. B.M. Nicholas. --Medieval discussions of the buyer's actions for physical defects, by P.G. Stein. --Implied warranty against latent defects in Roman and English law, by A. Rogerson. --The history of the aedilitian actions from Roman to Roman-Dutch law, by A. M. Honoré. --Celsus: sale and the passage of property, by J. A. C. Thomas. --Celsus: sale and conditional gift, by D. E. C. Yale.

1. Sales--Jurisp., Roman. 2. Zulueta, Francis M. de, 1853-1937. I. Daube, David, ed.

Studies in speech and drama ... 1944. (Card 2)

CONTENTS—Continued.
tions, by Ross Scanlan.—Arnold Bennett and the drama, by Argus Tresidder.—The dialectal significance of the non-phonemic low-back vowel variants before R, by C. K. Thomas.—The pronunciation of monosyllabic form-words in American English, by L. S. Hultzén.—The meaning of dispositio, by R. H. Wagner.—The decay of eloquence at Rome in the first century, by Harry Caplan.—Compendium rhetorices by Erasmus: a translation, by H. H. Hudson.—The listener on eloquence, 1750–1800, by H. F. Harding.—Edmund Burke's conversation, by D. C. Bryant.—God's dramatist, by C. H. King.—The style of Robert G. Ingersoll, by W. M. Parrish.—On analogy: re-definition and some implications, by K. R. Wallace.—Contemporary theories of public opinion, by W. E. Utterback.—The forensic mind, by Richard Murphy.
1. Drummond, Alexander Magnus, 1884– 2. Oratory—Addresses, essays, lectures. 3. Drama—Addresses, essays, lectures. 4. Theater—Addresses, essays, lectures.

44-9025

Library of Congress PN4012.D7
[5] 808.2

---

*QD

STUDIES in Russian and Polish literature in honor of Wacław Lednicki. Edited by Zbigniew Folejewski [and others] 's-Gravenhage, Mouton, 1962. 250 p. front. 25cm. (Slavistic printings and reprintings. 27)

Contributions in English, French or Italian.
Bibliographical footnotes.
CONTENTS. --Bibliography of Wacław Lednicki's works. --Back to the

(Continued)

NN R 10. 62 e/ OC, I (OS)II PC, 1, 2, 3, I, II SL S, 1, 2, 3, I, II (LC1, X1, Z1) [I]

3

RAE

Studies for William A. Read; a miscellany presented by some of his colleagues and friends, edited by Nathaniel M. Caffee and Thomas A. Kirby. University, La., Louisiana state university press, 1940.
x, 338 p. front. (port.) illus. (map) 23½cm.
"Bibliography of William A. Read": p. vi-viii.
CONTENTS.—Language: The naming of women by the continental Germans, by H. R. Woolf. Some notes on place-names in middle English writings, by E. Ekwall. The French of Chaucer's Prioress, by T. A. Kirby. Mittelenglische verse vom deutschen Niederrhein, by H. M. Flasdieck. Shakespeare's name and origin, by J. Hoops. Thomas Jefferson, linguistic liberal, by A. C. Baugh. American English today, by L. Pound. Some notes on consonant pronunciation in the South, by N. M. Caffee. The phonemes of current English, by K. Malone. Mourning and morning, by H. Kurath. An unpublished song of the troubador

(Continued on next card)

40—12303

[41d2]

Studies for William A. Read ... 1940. (Card 2)

CONTENTS—Continued.

Aimeric de Pégulhan, by W. P. Shepard. Zur palatalisierung im romanischen, by E. Gamillscheg.—Literature: Shakespeare's melancholy, by J. E. Uhler. The Epitaphium Damonis in the stream of the classical lament, by W. A. Montgomery. Ambrose Philip's Humfrey, duke of Gloucester: a study in eighteenth-century adaptation, by A. J. Bryan. The sentimentalism of Goldsmith's Good-natured man, by R. B. Heilman. The psychological basis of literary periods, by M. Förster. The rise of nationalism in American literature, by E. Bradsher. Reading taste in Louisiana, 1830–60, by W. Patrick. Hawthorne's methods of using his source materials, by A. Turner. An unpublished letter by Longfellow to a German correspondent, by W. Fischer. The ninth door of propaganda, by R. Smith. The first description of an Indian tribe in the territory of the present United States, by J. R. Swanton.

1. Read, William Alexander, 1869– 2. Philology—Collections. I. Caffee, Nathaniel Montier, ed. II. Kirby, Thomas Austin, joint ed.

Library of Congress P26.R35 40—12303
——— Copy 2.
Copyright [41d2] 404

VDYR

Stuhlinger, Ernst, *ed.*

Astronautical engineering and science, from Peenemünde to planetary space. Honoring the fiftieth birthday of Wernher von Braun. Written by his former and present associates in Peenemünde, Fort Bliss, Huntsville, and Cape Canaveral. Edited by Ernst Stuhlinger [and others] New York, McGraw-Hill [1963]

xviii, 394 p. illus., ports., tables. 24 cm.

Includes bibliographies. "A bibliography of works by Wernher von Braun": p. [377]–383.

1. Braun, Wernher von. 2. Astronautics--Addresses, essays, lectures. I. Stuhlinger, Ernst. t. 1963

NN*R 10.63 g/ OC,Ib* PC,1,2 SL ST,1,2I (LC1,X1,Z1)

VPW

STYRIA, AUSTRIA. Landeskammer für Land- und Forstwirtschaft.

Festschrift zum 25 jährigen Gründungsjubiläum der Landeskammer für Land- und Forstwirtschaft in Steiermark. [Verfasst von Otto Holzinger] Graz, 1954. 247 p. illus.,ports. 25cm.

1. Agriculture—Govt. depts. and officials—Austria—Styria. I. Holzinger, Otto. t. 1954.

NN**R X 2.56 j/ (OC) I,Ibo ODt(1b) EDt PC,1, I SL (E)1,I (LC1,X1, Z1)

---

* MG p.v.136

Sudetendeutsche Bruckner-Festtage, Usti and Litoměřice, Czecho-Slovakia, 1936.

Festschrift zu den anlässlich des 40. Todestages Anton Bruckners in der Zeit vom 22. Okt. – 22 Nov. 1936 in Aussig und Leitmeritz stattfindenden sudetendeutschen Bruckner-Festtagen. [Leitmeritz: Selbstverlag der Deutschen Bruckner-Gemeinde, 1936?] 62 p. illus. (port.) 23cm.

Cover-title.
Includes programmes and articles about Bruckner.

1. Bruckner, Anton, 1824-1896. 2. Musical festivals. I. Deutsche Bruckner-Gemeinde, Litoměřice, Czecho-Slovakia. Festschrift.

N. Y. P. L. October 20, 1939

M-10
5411
Bd. 16

SÜDOSTDEUTSCHE HISTORISCHE KOMMISSION.

Gedenkschrift für Harold Steinacker, 1875-1965. München, R. Oldenbourg, 1966. vii, 367 p. port. 24cm. (ITS: Buchreihe. Bd. 16)

Bibliographical footnotes.

CONTENTS.--Harold Steinacker 26. Mai 1875-29. Jänner 1965, von T. Mayer.--Idee und Wirklichkeit der Nationalität in Südosteuropa, von (Continued)

NN R 2.67 r/ OS,I PC,1,I (LC1,X1,Z1) 5

SÜDOSTDEUTSCHE HISTORISCHE KOMMISSION.
Gedenkschrift für Harold Steinacker...
(Card 2)

H. Steinacker.--Harold Steinackers Briefwechsel mit Albert Graf Apponyi, 1914-1915, von F. Huter.--Hospites Theutonici. Rechtsprobleme der deutschen Südostsiedlung, von H. Zimmermann.--Die mittelalterliche deutsche Besiedlung in Krain, von B. Saria.--Zisterziensergotik im Fürstentum Moldau [1487 bis 1582) von J. Lehner.--Die niederungarischen Bergstädte als Kriegsschauplatz, von G. Probszt.--Beiträge zur Mercyschen (Continued)

SÜDOSTDEUTSCHE HISTORISCHE KOMMISSION.
Gedenkschrift für Harold Steinacker...
(Card 3)

Besiedlung des Banats, von L. M. Weifert.--Die frühtheresianische Kolonisation des Banats, 1740-1762, von F. Lotz.--Schicksale des Pestalozzismus im ungarischen Raum, von O. Folberth.--Graf Stephan Széchenyi über die Nationalitäten in Ungarn, von M. Weidlein.--Der Wandel in der Bevölkerungszahl sowie in der nationalen und konfessionallen Bevölkerungsstruktur des heutigen Südburgenlandes in der Zeit von der Durchführung der kanonischen Visitation des Stefan Kazó, 1697-1698, bis (Continued)

SÜDOSTDEUTSCHE HISTORISCHE KOMMISSION.
Gedenkschrift für Harold Steinacker...
(Card 4)

zur österreichischen Volkszählung 1961, von J. K. Homma.--Habsburgs Wehrmacht im Spiegel des Nationalitätenproblems 1815 bis 1918, von R. Kiszling.--Ungarisches Militär vor dem Ersten Weltkrieg in Tirol, von O. Gschliesser.--Die Beteilung der magyarischen Protestanten an der Revolution, 1848-1849, von F. Walter.--Erzherzog Franz Ferdinand und Tirol, von H. Kramer.--Die ungarländische Deutschtumsfrage im Spiegel der (Continued)

SÜDOSTDEUTSCHE HISTORISCHE KOMMISSION.
Gedenkschrift für Harold Steinacker...
(Card 5)

diplomatischen Gespräche zwischen Budapest und Berlin, von H. Beyer.--Die Gassennamen des Ofner Berglandes (Ungarn) im deutschen Volksmund, von E. Bonomi.--Verzeichnis der Arbeiten von Harold Steinacker, von W. Neumann.

1. Steinacker, Harold, 1875-1965. I. Series.

K-10
4857
Heft 1

SÜDOSTDEUTSCHES KULTURWERK.

Festgabe Harold Steinacker zum 26. Mai 1955. München, 1957. 30 p. ports. 21cm. (ITS: Veröffentlichungen. Reihe D: Kleine Südostreihe. Heft 1)

Cover title.

1. Steinacker, Harold, 1875- I. Series.

NN R 10.65 1/ OS,I PC,1,I (E)I (S)I (LC1,X1,Z1)

K-10
4857
Heft 2

SÜDOSTDEUTSCHES KULTURWERK.
Gedenkschrift für Fritz Valjavec, 1909-1960. München, 1963. 39 p. port. 21cm. (ITS: Veröffentlichungen. Reihe D: Kleine Südostreihe. Heft 2)

1. Valjavec, Fritz. I. Series.
NN R 10.65 1/ OS, I PC, I, I (E)I (S)I (LC1, X1, Z1)

L-10
6939
Bd. 2

SÜDOSTEUROPA-GESELLSCHAFT, Munich.
Wirtschaft und Gesellschaft Südosteuropas; Gedenkschrift für Wilhelm Gülich. [Redaktion: Gerhard Teich und Leonore Hennig]. München, Südosteuropa-Verlagsgesellschaft, 1961. ix, 600 p. port., maps (part fold.), tables (part fold.) 25cm. (Südosteuropa-Schriften. Bd. 2)

CONTENTS.--Wilhelm Gülich als Wissenschaftler und Politiker, von J.W. Mannhardt.--Wirtschafts- politik und weltwirtschaftliche (Continued)

NN R 3.66 g/ (OC)Is, IIs, IIIs, IV, Es, Is, 2s, 3s, Is, IIs, IIIs, IV OSs, IV PCs, Is, 2s, 3s, Is, IIs, IIIs, Ss, Is, 2s, 3s, Is, IIs, IIIs, IV (LC1s, X1s, Z1s)

SÜDOSTEUROPA-GESELLSCHAFT, Munich. Wirtschaft und Gesellschaft Südosteuropas... (Card 2)

Verflechtung Südosteuropas, von H. Gross.--Die Wirtschaftsbeziehungen der Südosteuropastaaten zur Bundesrepublik Deutschland und zur sogenannten DDR, von B. Kiesewetter.--Der Südosten in der Welternährungswirtschaft, von H. Wilbrandt und H. Ruthenberg.--Grundlagen der Verkehrsbeziehungen Deutschlands und Österreichs zu Südosteuropa, von K. Wessely.--Der Binnenschiffsverkehr der Südoststaaten, von K. Förster.--Die östlichen und westlichen Planungsmethoden für Entwicklungspläne, von B. Knall.--Staatsverfassungstendenzen der Südoststaaten seit 1945, von F. Ronneberger.-- (Continued)

SÜDOSTEUROPA-GESELLSCHAFT, Munich. Wirtschaft und Gesellschaft Südosteuropas... (Card 3)

Die Verstädterung in Südosteuropa und ihre sozialen und wirtschaftlichen Auswirkungen, von W. Krallert.--Der Panslawismus als politische Idee in Südosteuropa im 19. und 20. Jahrhundert, von J. Matl.--München und Südosteuropa, von E. Turczynski.--Bestand und Lage des Deutschtums in Südosteuropa, von F.H. Riedl.--Ungarns Sozialpolitik seit 1945, von O. Liess.--Über die rechtliche Stellung der Religionsgemeinschaften in Jugoslawien und dessen Kirchenpolitik, von R. Trofenik.--Die langfristigen Tendenzen in der regionalen Orientierung des Aussenhandels Jugoslawiens, (Continued)

SÜDOSTEUROPA-GESELLSCHAFT, Munich. Wirtschaft und Gesellschaft Südosteuropas... (Card 4)

von V. Pertot.--Die Probleme der Zahlungsbilanz und die aussenwirtschaftliche Integration Griechenlands, von D. Delivanis.--Schrifttumsverzeichnisse (p. 562-577).

1. Economic history--Balkan peninsula. 2. Economic history--Europe, Eastern. 3. Gülich, Wilhelm, 1895-1960. I. Teich, Gerhard, ed. II. Hennig, Leonore, 1920- , ed. III. Title. IV. Series.

E-11
9263

SUID-AFRIKAANSE AKADEMIE VIR WETENSKAP EN KUNS.
Taalkundige opstelle van oud-studente aan prof. dr. T.H. LeRoux, ter geleentheid van sy tagtigste verjaarsdag 18 Maart 1963, met biografiese aantekeninge en biografie. Kaapstad, HAUM [1963] 154 p. illus., port. 24cm.

CONTENTS.--Die gebruik van vreemde woorde, deur L.W. Hiemstra.--Enkele gedagtes oor die agtergrond en natuurbeskouing in "Van den vos (Continued)

NN R 3.64 e/ OS PC, 1, 2 SL (LC1, X1, Z1, NWA1)

3

SUID-AFRIKAANSE AKADEMIE VIR WETENSKAP EN KUNS. Taalkundige opstelle van oud-studente aan prof. dr. T.H. LeRoux... (Card 2)

Reinaerde", deur J.A.E. Leue.--Afrikaanse spraakgebiede, deur S.A. Louw.--Die variasie b/p, d/t, g/x, v/f in Afrikaans, deur M.J. Posthumus.--Die Afrikaans van die Angolaboere, deur S. Strydom.--Die Afrikaanse vaktaal, deur H.J. Terblanche.--Die tweeklanke en verkleinwoorde by Van Riebeeck, deur H.J.J.M. van der Merwe.--'n Bladsy uit die ontstaansgeskiedenis van Afrikaans as skryftaal, deur H.M. van der Westhuysen.--Die taal van die wetenskap en die tegniek, deur (Continued)

SUID-AFRIKAANSE AKADEMIE VIR WETENSKAP EN KUNS. Taalkundige opstelle van oud-studente aan prof. dr. T.H. LeRoux... (Card 3)

M.S. van Zyl.--Biografiese aantekeninge: Prof. dr. T.H. LeRoux.--Chronologiese bibliografie (p. 151-154).

1. Afrikaans language. 2. Le Roux, Thomas Hugo, 1883- .

XAH

Suomalainen lakimiesyhdistys.
Juhlajulkaisu Kaarlo Juho Ståhlberg, 1865·28/1·1945. [Helsinki] Suomalainen lakimiesyhdistys [1945] 559 p. port. 26cm.

Three contributions in Swedish, the rest in Finnish.

491932B. 1. Ståhlberg, Kaarlo Juho, pres. Finland, 1865- 2. Finland—Govt. 3. Government, Local—Finland. 4. Law—Essays and misc. I. Title.
N. Y. P. L. June 21, 1950

Write on slip only words underlined and classmark:
RRA

Suomalais-ugrilainen seura, Helsingfors.
Commentationes fenno-ugricae in honorem Y. H. Toivonen, sexagenarii die xix mensis Ianuarii anno MCML... Helsinki, 1950. iv, 391 p. illus. 25cm. (Suomalais-ugrilainen seura, Helsingfors. Suomalais-ugrilaisen seuran toimituksia. 98)

Contributions in English, French or German.
CONTENTS.—Aalto, Pentti. Some South-Mongolian proverbs.—Beke, Ödön. Ung. *innen, annan, honnan.*—Bergsland, Knut. Remarques sur les pronoms démonstratifs lapons.—Fuchs, D. R. Ostj. *kēl* 'Wort' und 'Strick'.—Hakulinen, Lauri. Bedeutungsgeschichtliches.—Hämäläinen, Albert. Der hl. Stephan, der Apostel der Syrjänen.—
(Continued)

NN 4.53 OS, I PC, 1, 2, I O, 1, 2, I S, 1, 2, I (LC1, Z1, X1)

Suomalais-ugrilainen seura, Helsingfors. Commentationes fenno-ugricae... (Card 2)

Itkonen, Erkki. Das Perfekt des Partizips im Lappischen.—Itkonen, T. I. Ostjakisch-lappische Wortvergleichungen.—Joki, A. J. Eine samojedische Benennung des Bären.—Kalima, Jalo. Zur ungarischen Etymologi.—Kiparsky. V. Russ. Терский (берег) altruss. Тьрѣ 'Ostküste der Kolahalbinsel' <finn. Tyrjä (nicht Turja!) —Lagercrantz, Eliel. Die Primitivismen arktischer Sprachen im Lichte der Entwicklungspsychologie.—Lakó, György. Zur Frage des permischen Prosekutivs und Transitivs.—Lehtisalo, T. Etymologien.—Lewy, Ernst. Wortbedeutung, Wortdeutung.—Liimola, Matti. Etymologische Bemerkungen.—Mägiste, J. Fi.-estn. *nuha, noha, nohu, nuhu, nohi* 'Schnupfen' und est. *päri* 'Schafbock' und die ostseefi. onomatopoetischen Nomina auf *-ä, -a* und (estn.) *-i*.—Naert, Pierre. Note préliminaire sur

(Continued)

Suomalais-ugrilainen seura, Helsingfors. Commentationes fenno-ugricae... (Card 3)

l'aspect en zyriane.—Nesheim, Asbjörn. On the question of consonant combinations in Finno-Ugrian.—Nielsen, Konrad. A curious word in earlier Lapp dictionaries.—Posti, Lauri. Remarks on the treatment of Proto-Finnic *s* in Karelian and Veps.—Ramstedt, G. J. Das deverbale Nomen auf *-m* in den altaischen Sprachen.—Rapola, Martti. Das finnische *kuri* in der älteren Schriftsprache.—Raun, Alo. Zur ursprünglichen Bedeutung der Korrelation *je—desto*—im Finnisch-Ugrischen.—Ravila, Paavo. Zur Geschichte der Deklination der Personalpronomina in den uralischen Sprachen.—Räsänen, Martti. Beiträge zu den altaisch-slavischen Berührungen.—Sebeok, T. A. The importance of areal linguistics in Uralic studies.—Tunkelo, E. A. Das finnische *ahava* bzw. *ahva*.—Vilkuna, Kustaa. Über die obugrischen und samojedischen Pfeile und Köcher.

1. Finno-Ugrian languages. 2. Toivonen, Yrjö Henrik, 1890- . I. Series.

Write on slip only words underlined and class mark —
RAA

Suomalais-ugrilainen seuran, Helsingfors.

Juhlakirja Yrjö Wichmannin kuusikymmenenvuotipäiväksi... Helsinki, 1928. 471 p. port. 25cm. (Suomalais-ugrilainen seuran, Helsingfors. Suomalais-ugrilaisen seuran toimituksia. 58.)

Contributions in English, Finnish or German, with German summaries of some of the articles in Finnish.

CONTENTS.—Airila, Martti. Yksipersoonaisina käytetyt verbit.—Donner, Kai. Samojedische Benennungen der Russen.—Holmberg-Harva, Uno. Petsamonmaan kolttain

(Continued)

N. Y. P. L. March 18, 1948

Suomalais-ugrilainen seuran, Helsingfors. Juhlakirja Yrjö Wichmannin kuusikymmenenvuotipäiväksi... (Card 2)

pyhät paikat.—Itkonen, T. I. Lappalais-suomalaisia sanavertailuja. II.—Kalima, Jalo. Karjalais-vepsäläisestä Vapahtajan nimityksestä. — " — Referat des Obigen.—Kannisto, Artturi. Zur Etymologie des Völkernamens Ostjake.—Karsten, T. E. Entlehnung oder Urverwandtschaft oder Zufall?—Kettunen, Lauri. Suomen ts:n astevaihtelu.—Krohn, Ilmari. Melodien der Permier.—Krohn, Kaarle. Zaubermacht des Gesanges. Statistisch-geographische Untersuchung.—Lagercrantz, Eliel. Eine lappische Melodie aus Varanger.—Lehtisalo, T. Uralische Etymologien.—Mansikka, V. J. Zur altostslavischen Totenklage.—Mark, Julius. Zum längeren I. Infinitiv im Finnischen.—Mikkola, J. J. Liivinkielisiä kirjeitä A. J. Sjögrenille vv. 1851-53.—Niemi, A. R. Sampojakso.—Ramstedt, G. J. Remarks on the Korean language.—Rapola, Martti. Tuomas Rajaleniuksen saneet »hywäsäns» ja »hyywästäns».—Räsänen, Martti. Ostt-

(Continued)

N. Y. P. L. March 18, 1948

Suomalais-ugrilainen seuran, Helsingfors. Juhlakirja Yrjö Wichmannin kuusikymmenenvuotipäiväksi... (Card 3)

scher. k z r-pijambar.—Salminen, Väinö. Suomalaista kansanrunoutta 1700-luvun alkupuoliskolta.—Schmidt, Gustav. Über verbale Stammbildung in der sog. tschetschenischen Gruppe der kaukasischen Sprachen.—Setälä, E. N. Tehdas. — " — Deutsches Referat.—Sirelius, U. T. Die syrjänische Wohnung in ihren verschiedenen Entwicklungsstadien. Eine vergleichende Untersuchung.—Tallgren, A. M. Miniaturbogenfutteral aus Ostrussland.—Toivonen, Y. H. Über Alter und Entwicklung des Ackerbaus bei den finnisch-ugrischen Völkern.—Tunkelo, E. A. Pari balttilaiperäiseltä näyttävää suomen sanaa.—Uotila, T. E. Eräs suomen monikon genetiivin muodostus.—Väisänen, A. O. Das Zupfinstrument Gusli bei den Wolgavölkern.—Äimä, F. Etymologisia lisiä.—Öhmann, Emil. Ungelöste Aufgaben der Fennistik.

1. Wichmann, Yrjö Jooseppi, 1868–1932. 2. Slavonic languages. 3. Finnish-Ugrian languages. I. Title. II. Ser.

N. Y. P. L. March 18, 1948

Write on slip only words underlined and class mark —
RAA

Suomalais-ugrilainen seura, Helsingfors.

Kieli- ja kansatieteellisiä tutkielmia. Juhlakirja professori E. N. Setälän kuusikymmenvuotispäiväksi 27/11 1924... Helsinki, 1924. 386 p. port. 25cm. (Suomalais-ugrilainen seura, Helsingfors. Suomalais-ugrilaisen seuran toimituksia. 52.)

Contributions in English, Finnish or German.

CONTENTS.—Aarne, Antti. Muuan saduntutkimuksen merkkiteos.—Airila, M. Kielellisten ilmiöiden perustelemisesta.—Anttila, Aarne. Varhaisimpia ranskalaisia tietoja Suomesta ja suomalaisista.—Donner, Kai. Zur Vertretung der Konsonantenverbindung

(Continued)

N. Y. P. L. March 19, 1948

Suomalais-ugrilainen seura, Helsingfors. Kieli- ja kansatieteellisiä tutkielmia... (Card 2)

nasal + homorganer Klusil im Tschaja-Dialekt des Ostjak-Samojedischen.—Holma, Harri. Hatten die Assyrer und Babylonier eine besondere Bezeichnung für "Lunge"?—Holmberg, Uno. Doppelfrucht im Volksglauben.—Jaakkola, Jalmari. Pakanallisiin kulttitarkoituksiin "vihitystä" maasta Suomessa.—Kalima, Jalo. Etymologische Miszellen.—Kannisto, Artturi. Etymologische Bemerkungen.—Koskimies, A. V. Huomioita suomenkielen uudissanaston alalta.—Krohn, Kaarle. Das Lazarusthema in der finnisch-estnischen Volksdichtung.—Laurosela, Jussi. Etelä-Pohjanmaan murteen svarabhaktivokaalit.—Lehtisalo, T. Zu den samojedisch-arischen Beziehungen.—Mansikka, V. J. Itkujen Tuonela.—Mark, Julius. Mrd. *inks* 'Schabhobel, Schabmesser' und mrd. *jonks*

(Continued)

N. Y. P. L. March 19, 1948

Suomalais-ugrilainen seura, Helsingfors. Kieli- ja kansatieteellisiä tutkielmia... (Card 3)

'Bogen, Pfeilbogen'.—Mikkola, J. J. Zur Etymologie von ung. *könyv* und slav. *kъnjiga*.—Penttillä, Aarni. Zur Erklärung des syrjänischen Ausdrucks: ťšoja voka 'Schwester und Bruder'.—Ramstedt, G. J. Die Verneinung in den altaischen Sprachen. Eine semasiologische Studie.—Rapola, Martti. Suomenkielen *us-, üs-* loppuiset ominaisuudennimet.—Rudnev, A. A Buriat epic.—Räsänen, Martti. Tscheremissische Zeit- und Massbestimmungen.—Saarimmaa, E. A. Minna Canthin kielestä.—Silander, Alpo. Snellmanin ja Suomettaren välinen oikeakielisyykiista.—Sirelius, U. T. Eräs keisarillinen lahjoituskirja.—Tallgren, A. M. Viron keskisestä rautakaudesta.

1. Setäla, Emil Nestor, 1864–1935. 2. Finnish-Ugrian languages. I. Title. II. Ser.

N. Y. P. L. March 19, 1948

SST

SUOMEN kansanopistot ja niiden työntekijät, 1.1. 1955. Finlands folkhögskolor och deras arbetare. [Toimitus kunta: Heikki Hosia et al. Helsingissä, 1955] 567 p. illus., ports. 22cm.

Text in Finnish or Swedish.

Published by Suomen kansanopistoyhdistys (Finlands folkhögskoleförening).

"Opettajamatrikeli. Lärarmatrikel," p. [373]-557.

(Continued)

NN **R X 4. 57 p/ OC, I, III, III SL E, 1, I, II, III RC, 1, 2, 3 IVbo (OS)II, IIb PC, 1, 2, 3, I, II, (LC1, X1, Z1)

SUOMEN kansanopistot ja niiden työntekijät...
(Cont.)

1. People's high schools—Finland. 2. Teachers—Finland. 3. Finland--Biog. I. Hosia, Heikki, ed. II. Suomen kansanopistoyhdistys. III. Title: Finlands folkhögskolor och de ras arbetare. IV. Hosia, Heikki.

ZDC

Suomen kirkkohistoriallinen seura, Helsingfors.
Xenia Ruuthiana; professori emerito Martino Ruuth praesidi promotorique suo. III kal. novembr. MCMXLV pio gratoque animo dedicavit Societas historiae ecclesiasticae fennica. [Helsinki, 1945] xiv, 391 p. port. 23cm. (Suomen kirkkohistoriallisen seuran toimituksia. 47)

Contributions chiefly in Finnish, two in Swedish.

1. Church history—Addresses, essays, lectures. 2. Ruuth, Martti, 1870- . I. Title.
NN R 5.53 (OC)I OS PC, 1, 2 SL (LC1, Z1, X1)

SUOMEN MAATALOUSTIETEELLINEN SEURA. Juhlajulkaisu Artturi I. Virtasen 6-vuotispäivän kunniaksi... (Card 5)

An improved processing of sausage by means of bacterial pure cultures. -- Kreula, M. On the contents of butyric acid and butyric acid bacteria in silage.

1. Virtanen, Artturi Ilmari, 1895- . 2. Agriculture--Research.

Copy only words underlined & classmark-- VPA

SUOMEN MAATALOUSTIETEELLINEN SEURA.
Juhlajulkaisu Artturi I. Virtasen 60-vuotispäivän kunniaksi. Jubilee issue in honour of the 60th birthday of Artturi I. Virtanen. Hämeenlinna, A. A. Karisto, 1955. 243 p. illus., port. 25cm. (Suomen maataloustieteellisen seura. Julkaisuja. 83)

Articles in Finnish or English, a few in Finnish and English. Summaries in English, German or Finnish.
Includes bibliographies.

(Continued)

NN** R 12. 57 v/ OS PC, 1, 2 OI (LC1, X1, Z1)

D-16
1790

SUOMEN NAISJÄRJESTÖJEN KESKUSLIITTO.
50 vuotta, Suomen naisten yhteistyötä, 50 ar, Finlands kvinnors samarbete; Suomen naisjärjestöjen keskusliiton ja sen jäsenjärjestöjen tomintaa 1911-1961, Finlands kvinnoorganisationers centralförbunds medlemsorganisationers verksamhet ar 1911-1961. [Helsinki, 1961] 192 p. illus., ports. 22cm.

Text in Finnish with summary in Swedish.
I. [Title] Viisikymmenta.
NN R 6.66 1/ OS PC SL E (LC1, X1, Z1[1])

SUOMEN MAATALOUSTIETEELLINEN SEURA. Juhlajulkaisu Artturi I. Virtasen 60-vuotispäivän kunniaksi... (Card 2)

CONTENTS. --Rosenqvist, G. L. Artturi I. Virtanen maanviljelijänä ja karjankasvattajana. --Peltola, E. Artturi I. Virtanen Suomen meijeritalouden kehittäjänä. --Kaila, A. Studies on the colorimetric determination of phosphorus in soil extracts. --Pohjakallio, O. & Vaartaja, O. & Antila, S. Frost resistance of potato tubers. --Koivisto, E. Meijerivoin hintojen kausivaihtelusta. --Roine, P. & Wichmann, K. & Vihavainen, L. Askorbiinihapon määristä ja säilyvyydestä eri perunalajikkeissa. --Aikkinen, L. Inspection of silage in Finland. --Ervi, L. O. &
(Continued)

MWEG
(Stockholm)

Svanberg, Johannes, 1852–1918.
Kungl. teatrarne under ett halft sekel 1860–1910, personalhistoriska anteckningar af Johannes Svanberg... [Stockholm, Nordisk familjeboks förlagsaktiebolag (i distribution) [1917– 2 v. in 1. front. 22cm.

1. Theatres—Sweden—Stockholm. 2. Actors and acting, Swedish.
NN*R 5.54 OC PC, 1, 2 SL (T3, Z1, LC1, X1)

SUOMEN MAATALOUSTIETEELLINEN SEURA. Juhlajulkaisu Artturi I. Virtasen 60-vuotispäivän kunniaksi... (Card 3)

Hanioja, P. & Kivinen, E. Mesimarjan (Rubus arcticus L.) marjontaa koskevia tutkimuksia. --Paloheimo, L. & Herkola, E. & Mäkelä, A. Studies on the composition of cow's milk. --Pesola, V. A. Protein content of field pea seeds as a varietal character. --Saarinen, P. On the nutritional factors affecting the level of volatile fatty acids in cow's peripheral blood. --Ylimäki, A. On the effectiveness of penta- and tetrachloronitrobenzenes on clover rot (Sclerotinia trifoliorum Erikks.)--Jamalainen, E. A. Fusarium species causing plant diseases in Finland. --Poijärvi,
(Continued)

F-10
6692

SVARDFEJARE och själamord; en festskrift till Malmö nation 1962. [Redaktion: Jan Thulin och Hans Ruin. Malmö] Allhem [1962] 236, iii p. illus., ports. 27cm.

CONTENTS. --Storm och stiltje i cerebrum; några reflexioner angående tänkandets fysiologiska bakgrund, av G. Ehrensvärd. --Skvallret som skön konst och själamord, av H. Hanson. --Mellan skökan och mor; akademiskt sexualliv från åttiotalet till första världskriget, av D. Hjorth. --Den öppna handen och den slutna, av H. Ruin. --Slutstrofen till Aniara,
(Continued)

NN R 7.65 1/. OC, I, II, IVbo (OS)III, IIIb PC, 1, I, II, III SL (LC1, X1, Z1) [I] 3

SUOMEN MAATALOUSTIETEELLINEN SEURA. Juhlajulkaisu Artturi I. Virtasen 60-vuotispäivän kunniaksi... (Card 4)

I. AIV-, Calcifor- ja Kofa-menetelmän vertailukokeita. --Vartiovaara, U. & Lampila, M. & Saarenmaa, H. Enrichment culture and animal inoculation experiments regarding the efficiency of the intestinal cellulose-decomposing bacteria of the horse. --Valle, O. Untersuchungen zur Sicherung der Bestäubung von Rotklee. --Suomalainen, P. & Pillgren, A.-M. On the thiaminase activity of fish and some other animals and on the preservation of thiaminase in silage made from fish. --Niinivaara, F. P. & Durchman, E. & Vartiovaara, U.
(Continued)

SVARDFEJARE och själamord... (Card 2)

version II, av H. Martinson. --Solens söner; om Navaho-indianerna, deras myter, riter och sändmålning, av H. Lang. --Hotellbrand i Horsagårde, av F. Nilsson Piraten. --Guldbägare, bronsharnesk och andra fynd i Dendrá, av P. Åström. --Antecknat vid garderobsstädning, av B. Strömstedt. --Råttor, möss och annat smått i Malmö före Roskildefreden; plock ur bouppteckningar, av E. Bager. --En svärdfejarefamilj i Malmö och ett svärdfejarhus, av E. Fischer. --Lösaktigheten i världshistorien, dropp från vetandets kran; ur ett radioföredrag, av A. Sten. --Ett uteslutet

(Continued)

SVARDFEJARE och själamord... (Card 3)

kapitel ur "Den gröna draken", av B. Widerberg. --Annu en sommar, Bokskogen i juli; två miniatyrer, av A. Osterling. --Min generation och filosofien, av G. Aspelin. --Några blad ur Malmö stads teaterannaler, av A. Bergstrand. --Minnen från staden inom broarna, av H. Dhejne. --Skaldernas Malmö, av G. Jönsson. --Malmö i konsten, av M. Nanne-Brahammar. --Victoria Benedictsson i Malmö, av K. E. Rosengren. --Musikaliskt hwarjehanda, av B. Widerberg.

1. Essays, Swedish. I. Thulin, Jan. II. Ruin, Hans, 1891- ed. III. Lund, Sweden. Universitet. Malmö nation. IV. Thulin, Jan.

L-10
5721
Nr. 9

SVEN RINMAN tryckta skrifter 1922-1969; bibliografi utg. till 65-årsdagen 1 april 1970 [Utarb. av Anders Hedvall] Stockholm, 1970. xiii, 56 p. 25cm. (Sweden. Kungliga biblioteket, Stockholm. Acta Bibliotheca regiae Stockholmiensis. Nr. 9)

1. Rinman, Sven, 1905- . --Bibl. I. Series. II. Hedvall, Anders, ed.

NN 7.71 e/J OC, II (OD)I (ED)I PC, 1, I, II (LC1, X1, Z1)

BTGP

Svensk-italienska föreningen.
Festskrift tillägnad Axel Boëthius den 18 juli 1949 av Svensk-italienska föreningen. Göteborg, 1949. 173 p. illus. 28cm.

Contributions in Swedish, with summaries in Italian; 1 article in Italian.
"Förteckning över Axel Boëthius' av trycket utgivna skrifter, av S. Hallbert." p. 157-173.

537433B. 1. Boëthius, Axel, 1889- . 2. Archaeology, Classical. I. Hallberg, Seth Severin, 1886- .
N. Y. P. L. September 15, 1950

XAD

Svensk juristtidning.
Festskrift tillägnad hans excellens riksmarskalken, juris doktor Birger Ekeberg den 10 augusti 1950. [Stockholm, 1950] 602 p. port. 25cm.

"Utgiven av Svensk juristtidning."
"Forteckning över Birger Ekebergs skrifter, 1904-1950," p. 591-602.

1. Law—Addresses, essays, lectures. 2. Ekeberg, Lars Birger, 1880-

NN

MTE
+

SVENSKA ARKEOLOGISKA SAMFUNDET.
Arkeologiska forskningar och fynd; studier utgivna med anledning av H. M. Konung Gustaf VI Adolfs sjuttioårsdag 11.11. 1952. Stockholm [1952] 462, [3] p. illus., maps. 31cm.

Bibliographical references in "Noter," p. 447-463.

1. Archaeology—Addresses essays, lectures. 2. Sweden—Archaeology. 3. Gustavus VI, king of Sweden, 1882- I. Title.

NN **R 4.53 (OC)I OS(1b) PC, 1, 2, 3, I SL (LC1, Z1, X1)

G-10
1263

SVENSKA ARKEOLOGISKA SAMFUNDET.
Proxima Thule, Sverige och Europa under forntid och medeltid; hyllningsskrift till H. M. Konungen den 11. november 1962. [Redaktör: Per Gustaf Hamberg. Stockholm, Norstedt, 1962] 238 p. illus. (part col.), maps. 31cm.

Includes bibliographies.

(Continued)

NN 3.63 f/s (OC)I, II OS PC, 1, 2, I, II SL (LC1, X1, Z1) [I] 3

SVENSKA ARKEOLOGISKA SAMFUNDET. Proxima Thule... (Card 2)

CONTENTS. --Sveriges äldsta kontakt med Västeuropa, av B. Salomonsson. --Stenkammargravar i Sverige och deras europeiska bakgrund, av L. Kaelas. --Fångstfolk, herdar och bönder i stenålderns Sverige, av M. Stenberger. --Den osynliga gudomen, av B. Almgren. --Ett svenskt praktfynd med sydeuropeiska bronser, av B. Stjernquist. --Skatten från Havors fornborg, av E. Nylén. --Lovö-bor med kontinentala förbindelser på 400-talet, av G. Arwidsson. --Handel på nordliga vägar under Järnåldern, av M. Biörnstad. --Helgö, en internationell handelsplats, av W. Holmqvist. --Sverige och Östern under vikingatiden,

(Continued)

SVENSKA ARKEOLOGISKA SAMFUNDET. Proxima Thule... (Card 3)

av H. Arbman. --Guldet i Norden under senmedeltiden, av N. L. Rasmusson. --Lunds första domkyrka? Av R. Blomqvist. --Romanska målningar i Torpa kyrka i Rekarne, av A. Andersson. --Vadstena kungsgård och kloster, av I. Anderson och B. Berthelson. --Kungabilder i svenska laghandskrifter, av P. G. Hamberg.

1. Gustavus VI, king of Sweden, 1882- . 2. Sweden--Archaeology. I. Title. II. Hamberg, Per Gustaf, ed.

NIC

SVENSKA litteratursällskapet i Finland. Festskrift tillägnad Gunnar Castrén den 27 december 1938. Helsingfors, 1938. 425 p. port. 25cm. (Svenska litteratursällskapet i Finland Skrifter. 271)

1. Scandinavian literature—Hist. and crit. 2. Literature—Hist. and crit. 3. Castrén, Gunnar, 1878- I. Title. II. Ser.

NN R 5.53 (OC) I OS PC, 1, 2, 3, I SL (LC1, Z1, X1) [I]

GM

Svenska litteratursällskapet i Finland.
Historiska uppsatser tillegnade Magnus Gottfrid Schybergson på hans sextioårsdag den 26 november 1911. Helsingfors, 1911. 242 p. illus., ports. 23cm. (Svenska litteratursällskapet i Finland. Skrifter. 100)

Contents.—Finska uttalanden om Mikael Speranskys fall, af C. v. Bonsdorff.—En konflikt mellan generalguvernör Steinheil och de ryska regeringsmyndigherterna, af T. Hartman.—Den kateketiska

(Continued)

NN** 1.54 OS PC, 1, 2 SL (U 1, LC1, Z1, X1)

Svenska litteratursallskapet i Finland.
Historiska uppsartser tillegnade Magnus Gottfrid Schybergson... (Card 2)

undervisningen i Åbo stift vid 19: de seklets ingång, af G. Nikander.—Handelsförhållandena i Finland under Gustavianska tiden, af J.Qvist.—Tillkomsten av universitetets huvudbyggnad, af T. Carpelan.—Pehr Kalm och biskopsvalet i Åbo 1776, af P. Nordmann.—Gustaf Filip Creutz' Lettre sur l'Espagne,

(Continued)

NIZ

Svenska litteratursällskapet i Finland.
Zacharias Topelius hundraårsminne; festskrift den 14 januari 1918. Helsingfors, 1918. 289 p. ports., facsim. 26cm. (Svenska litteratursällskapet i Finland. Skrifter. 137)

Contents.—Vid Topelius-jubileet, af S. Lagerlöf.—Finlands romantiker, af F. Vetterlund.—Z. Topelii psalmdiktning, af V. T. Rosenqvist.—Zachris Topelius bland västfinnar, af M. G. Schybergson.—Topelius som historiker, af B. Estlander.—Fältskärns

(Continued)

NN** 1.54 OS PC,1 SL (U 1,LC1,Z1,X1)

Svenska litteratursallskapet i Finland.
Historiska uppsatser tillegnade Magnus Gottfrid Schybergson... (Card 3)

af A. Hultin.—Språkfragan i Finska deputationen vid riksdagen år 1746-1747, af A. Mickwitz.—Finska porträtt från 1600-talet, af K. K. Meinander.—Populära föreställningar om Gustaf II Adolf i trettioariga krigets flygskrifts litteratur, af G. Rein litteratur, af G. Rein.—Finlands storfurstliga krona, af G. Granfelt.— Stämningen i Sverige

(Continued)

Svenska litteratursällskapet i Finland. Zacharias Topelius hundraårsminne... (Card 2)

Regina i dramatisk omklädnad, af A. Hultin.—Porträtt av Zacharias Topelius, af K. K. Meinander.—Topelius' fosterländska lyrik, af G. Castrén.—Sagan om björken och stjärnan, af E. Lagus.—Z. Topelius' projekt till Finlands flagga.

1. Topelius, Zakarias, 1818-1898. I. Ser.

NN** 1.54 OS PC,1 SL (U 1,LC1,Z1,X1)

Svenska litteratursallskapet i Finland.
Historiska uppsatser tillegnade Magnus Gottfrid Schybergson... (Card 4)

inför 1788 års krig, bedömd af en fransman, af A. Söderhjelm.—De finska medeltidsbiskoparnes besök vid den påfliga kurian, af P.O.v.Törne.—Några ord om de äldsta danska medeltidsannaler, som innehalla uppgifter om tågen till Finland 1191 och 1202, af J.W.Ruuth.—Om den nyaste ståndpubkten i etrusker frågan, af J. Sundwall.
1. Finland—Hist.—Addresses, essays, lectures. 2. Schybergson, Magnus Gottfrid, 1851-1925.

QMS

Svenska naturskyddsföreningen.
Festskrift tillägnad Erik Rosenberg på 50-årsdagen 19 52. Utgiven av Svenska naturskyddsföreningen. Stockholm [1952] 109 p. illus. 22cm.

"Redaktör: Kai Curry-Lindahl."

1. Birds—Sweden. 2. Rosenberg, Erik, 1902- . I. Curry-Lindahl, Kai, 1917- , ed.
NN 1.53 (OC)I OS PC,1,2,I SL (LC1,Z1,X1)

NIZ

SVENSKA LITTERATURSÄLLSKAPET I FINLAND.
Johan Ludvig Runebergs hundraårsminne. Festskrift den 5 februari 1904. Helsingfors, 1904. 441 p. ports., music. 26cm. (Svenska litteratursällskapet i Finland. Skrifter. 62)

Contributions in Swedish, German and Danish.
CONTENTS. — Den gamle knekten och Fänrik Stal, af C. G. Estlander. — Der Dichter und sein Volk, af R. Eucken. — Til erindring om Johan Ludvig Runeberg, af L. Dietrichson. — Om ordställningen hos Runeberg, af F. Gustafsson. —Runeberg och Sverige, af E. Wrangel. —Runeberg in Deutschland, af W. Eigenbrodt. —Runeberg og Danmark, af J. Clausen. --

(Continued)

NN ** 1.54 OS PC,1 SL MU,1,II (U1,Z1,LC1,X1)

VLT
+

Svenska pappersbruksföreningen.
Molæ chartariæ Suecanæ. Svenska pappersbruksföreningens tjugufemårsskrift. Stockholm, 1923. 2 v. diagrs., plans, plates, illus., ports. 4°.

One of 1000 copies printed.
Plates printed on both sides.

1. Paper—Hist.—Sweden.
N. Y. P. L. April 13, 1928

SVENSKA LITTERATURSÄLLSKAPET I FINLAND. Johan Ludvig Runebergs hundraarsminne. (Card 2)

J. L. Runeberg i den bildande konsten, af J. Ahrenberg. — Porträtt af Johan Ludvig Runeberg, af K. K. Meinander. — Om Runebergs arbeten i finsk öfversättning, af O. Grotenfelt. -- Om musiken till Runebergs dikter, af K. Flodin. — Björneborgarnes marsch, af E. Lagus. — Runebergs insats i arbetet för åstadkommande af en ny svensk psalmbok i Finland, af V. T. Rosenqvist.

1. Runeberg, Johan Ludvig, 1804-1877. I. Ser. II. Title: Björneborgarnes marsch.

PRN

Svenska sällskapet för antropologi och geografi, Stockholm.
Glaciers and climate; geophysical and geomorphological essays dedicated to Hans W:son Ahlmann, 14 November 1949. [Stockholm, 1949] 383 p. illus., maps. 25cm. (Geografiska annaler. Häfte 1–2, 1949)

Contributions in English, French or German.
Includes bibliographies.

1. Glaciers. 2. Glaciers, 1949. 3. Climate. 4. Climate, 1949. 5. Ahlmann, Hans Wilhelmson, 1889-
NN** 4.53 OS PC,1,3,5 SL ST,2,4,5 (LC1,Z1,X1)

KAA

Svenska sällskapet för antropologi och geografi, Stockholm.
Hyllningsskrift tillägnad Sven Hedin på hans 70-årsdag den 19 febr. 1935... Stockholm: Generalstabens litografiska anstalt [1935] xvi, 668 p. charts, illus., maps, plates (part col'd), ports. 25½cm.

"I serie med Geografiska annaler 1935, utgivna av Svenska sällskapet för antropologi och geografi, årg. XVII, 1935."
Bibliographies included.

830517A. 1. Hedin, Sven Anders, 1865– . 2. Geography—Addresses, essays, lectures. I. Geografiska annaler. II. Title.
N. Y. P. L. July 10, 1936

NARA

Svenska tidningsutgivareföreningen, Stockholm.
...50 år. Minnesskrift utgiven med anledning av föreningens femtioårsjubileum den 31 maj 1948. [Stockholm, 1948] 251 p. illus. 26cm.

464018B.
N. Y. P. L. February 10, 1949

E-11
2786

SVERIGES SOCIALDEMOKRATISKA ARBETAREPARTI.
Idé och handling [av] Tage Erlander [et al. Till Ernst Wigforss på 80-årsdagen den 24 januari 1961] Stockholm, Tiden [1960] 220 p. port. 24cm.

"Det är både för partiet och förlaget en stor glädje att...få överräcka denna hyllningsskrift."

(Continued)

NN R X 6.61 e/ (OC)I, III (OS)II PC, 1, 2, I, II, III SL
E, 1, 2, I, II, III (LC1, X1, Z1)

2.

SVERIGES SOCIALDEMOKRATISKA ARBETAREPARTI.
Idé och handling... (Card 2)

1. Wigforss, Ernst Johannes, 1881- . 2. Socialism--Sweden.
I. Erlander, Tage, 1901- . II. Tidens förlag, Stockholm.
III. Title.

SFC

Sveriges socialdemokratiska arbetareparti.
Människan och samhället, en bok till Tage Erlander på 50-årsdagen. Stockholm, Socialdemokratiska partistyrelsen, Tidens förlag [1951] xx, 245 p. port. 24cm.

WS

NN 1. Erlander, Tage, 1901- . 2. Socialism—Sweden. I. Title.

SNF

Sveriges socialdemokratiska kvinnoförbund.
Socialdemokratisk kvinnogärning; festskrift i anledning av Disa Västbergs 60-årsdag den 17 maj 1951. [Stockholm] Sveriges socialdemokratiska kvinnoförbund, Tidens förlag [1951] 253 p. port. 24cm.

1. Västberg, Disa (Ögren), 1891- . 2. Woman and socialism.
I. Title.
NN

VWE

Sweden. Försvarsstaben. Krigshistoriska avdelningen.
Krigshistoriska studier tillägnade Olof Ribbing av vänner och medarbetare vid Försvarsstabens Krigshistoriska avdelning. Stockholm, 1950. 144 p. illus. 26cm.

"Litteratur," p. 136–137.
CONTENTS.—En återblick, av Ejnar Nordfeldt.—Olof Ribbing, arbetsledare och vetenskapsman, av Måns Mannerfelt.—Rostocksberättelsen och spelet om Skåne 1360, av Arne Stade.—Wallensteins stridsplan vid Lützen, av Gunnar Nordström.—Till kuppen mot Prag 1648, Trettioåriga krigets dramatiska slutakt, av Erik Zeeh.—Lennart Torstensons personliga krigsbyte från slaget vid Leipzig 1642, av Ludvig

(Continued)

NN

IKC

Sweden. Försvarsstaben. Krigshistoriska avdelningen. Krigshistoriska studier tillägnade Olof Ribbing av vänner och medarbetare vid... (Card 2)

Hammarskiöld.—Krig och konst i Prag 1648, av Carl-Fredrik Palmstierna.—De nordiska väpnade neutralitetsförbunden, av Ernst Bergman.—Den "franska" kartan över löpgravarna vid Fredriksten, av Nils Strömbom.—"Polarräven," en tysk anfallsplan mot Sverige under andra världskriget, av Ernst Jungstedt.—Något om teknik i sjökriget, av A. F. E:son Scholander.

NN 1. Military arts and science—Hist. 2. Ribbing, Olof, 1887-

---

G-10
1890

SWEDEN. Riksbokslutsbyrån.
Rikshuvudboken av år 1623, presenterad av Per V. A. Hanner; tillägnad Oskar Sillén. [Stockholm, Förlags ab Affärsekonomi, 1952] 32 p.(p.10-32 facsim.) 36cm.

Summary of introd. in English.
No. 274 of 500 copies printed.
Bibliography, p. 9.

1. Finance--Sweden. 2. Sillén, Oskar.
I. Hanner, Per V. A., ed. t. 1952.
NN R 7.66 l/4 (OC)I ODt EDt PC, 1, 2, I SL(E)1, 2, I (LC1, X1, Z1)

NBC

Sweezy, Paul Marlor, 1910- *ed.* (Matthiessen)
F. O. Matthiessen, 1902–1950; a collective portrait. Edited by Paul M. Sweezy and Leo Huberman. New York, Schuman [1950]
xii, 154 p. ports. 22 cm.
"Originally published as the October, 1950, issue of ... Monthly review."
CONTENTS.—The education of a socialist, by F. O. Matthiessen.—Of crime and punishment, by F. O. Matthiessen.—The teacher, by L. Marx.—The making of an American scholar, by B. Bowron.—American Renaissance, by H. N. Smith.—Labor and political activities, by P. M. Sweezy.—Notes for a character study, by J. Rackliffe.—Statements, by H. Baker [and others]—A preliminary bibliography of F. O. Matthiessen (p. 148–154)

1. Matthiessen, Francis Otto, 1902–1950. I. Huberman, Leo, 1903– joint ed.
PN75.M3S9 928.1 50–58262
Library of Congress [7] festschrift

3-MQWE

Swensen, Wilhelm, 1894-
Kulturbilder fra Grenland og Telemark. Utgitt som festskrift til sekstiårsdagen, 2. august 1954. [Oslo] Norsk folkemuseum [1954] 201,[3] p. illus., port.,plans. 24cm.

"Et utvalg av artikler...opprinnelig skrevet for dagspressen...og emnene er
(Continued)

NN ** R X 10.55 s/D OC (OS)I PC,1, I SL A,1,I (LC1, X1,Z1)

Swensen, Wilhelm, 1894- . Kulturbilder fra Grenland og Telemark. (Card 2)

begrenset til Skiensfjorden og Telemarksbygdene."
Bibliographical references included in "Noter" (p. 197-[202])

1. Architecture—Norway—Telemark. I. Oslo. Norsk folkemuseum.

STT

Symbola litteraria; hyllningsskrift till Uppsala universitet vid jubelfesten 1927 från universitets-bibliotekets tjänstemän och universitetets boktryckare Almqvist & Wiksells boktryckeri-a.-b. Uppsala: Almqvist & Wiksells boktryckeri-a.-b., 1927. 305 p. 4°. (Uppsala. Universitet. Biblioteket. Acta Bibliothecae R. universitatis Upsaliensis. v. 2.)

367794A Mr. Moth

1. Upsala. Universitet. 2. Ser.
N. Y. P. L. June 13, 1928

RBG

Symbola philologorum Bonnensium in honorem Friderici Ritschelii collecta. Lipsiae, 1864-67. 8°.

1.Classical studies. 2.Ritschl, Friedrich Wilhelm.

---

* OCS

Symbolae ad iura Orientis antiqui pertinentes Paulo Koschaker dedicatae quas adiuvante Th. Folkers, ediderunt J. Friedrich, J. G. Lautner, J. Miles eq. Leiden: E. J. Brill, 1939. 246 p. illus., plates, port. 25cm. (Added t.-p.: Studia et documenta ad iura Orientis antiqui pertinentia... v. 2.)

Bibliographical footnotes.
CONTENTS.—Friedrich, J. Zu einigen umstrittenen Paragraphen der hethitischen Gesetze.—Furlani, G. La corresponsabilità familiare presso gli Hittiti.—Güterbock, H. G. Das Siegeln bei den Hethitern.—Korošec, V. Das Eigentum an Haustieren nach dem hethitischen Gesetzbuch.—Kraus, F. R. Die sumerische Entsprechung der Phrase Ana ittišu.—Pohl, A. Zu einer Klausel altsumerischer Rechtsurkunden.—Driver, G. R.,

(Continued)

N. Y. P. L. Festschrift April 18, 1940

Symbolae ad iura Orientis antiqui pertinentes Paulo Koschaker ... (Card 2)

and Sir John Miles. Code of Hammurabi, §§ 117–119.—Lautner, J. G. Rechtsverhältnisse an Grenzmauern.—Ungnad, A. Die Formulare für die altbabylonische Personenmiete.—Gadd, C. J. Text of the "Babylonian Seisachtheia".—Scheil, V. Fraternité et solidarité à Suse, au temps de Sirukduh.—Hrozný, B. Ueber eine unveröffentlichte Urkunde vom Kültepe (ca. 2000 v. Chr.).—Dossin, G. Un cas d'ordalie par le dieu fleuve d'après une lettre de Mari.—Thureau-Dangin, F. Sur des étiquettes de paniers à tablettes provenant de Mâri.—David, M. Zur Verfügung eines Nichtberechtigten nach den mittel-assyrischen "Gesetzesfragmenten".—Speiser, E. A. Gleanings from the Billa texts.—Böhl, F. M. Th. Die Tochter des Königs Nabonid.—San Nicolò, M. Ein Urteil des königlichen Gerichtes in Babylon aus der Zeit des Nabonid.—Weiss-

(Continued)

N. Y. P. L. April 18, 1940

Symbolae ad iura Orientis antiqui pertinentes Paulo Koschaker ... (Card 3)

bach, F. H. Die elamische Uebersetzung der Daiwa-Inschrift.—Von Soden, W. Nominalformen und juristische Begriffsbildung im Akkadischen: die Nominalform "Qutullā".—Boyer, G. Supur X kima kunnukkišu.—Landsberger, B. Die babylonischen termini für Gesetz und Recht.—Van Proosdij, B. A. Zum sogenannten orientalischen Despotismus.—Liste der Werke Paul Koschakers zur orientalischen Rechtsgeschichte (p. ⌊242⌋–246).

25984B. 1. Law, Oriental. 2. Law—Hittites. 3. Law—Assyria and Babylonia. 4. Koschaker, Paul, 1879- . I. Folkers, Th. II. Friedrich, Johannes, 1893- , ed. III. Lautner, Julius Georg, 1896- , ed. IV. Miles, Sir John Charles, 1870- , ed. V. Ser.
N. Y. P. L. April 18, 1940

E-13
7906

Symbolae iuridicae et historicae Martino David dedicatae. Ediderunt J. A. Ankum, R. Feenstra ⌊et⌋ W. F. Leemans. Leiden, E. J. Brill, 1968.

2 v. port. 25 cm.

Dutch, English, French, German or Italian.
"Bibliographie der Geschriften van Martin David" p. ⌊ix⌋-xvi.
CONTENTS.—t. 1. Ius Romanum.—t. 2. Iura orientalis antiqui.

(Continued)

NN*R 4.70 w/μOC, I, II, IIIb* PC, 1, 2, 3, I, II SL O, 2, I, II (LC1, X1, Z1)

2

SYMBOLAE iuridicae et historicae Martino David dedicatae. (Card 2)

1. Law, Roman. 2. Law, Oriental. 3. Law--Hist., Ancient. I. David, Martin, 1898- . II. Ankum, J.A., ed. III. Ankum, J. A.

XAN

Symbolae ad jus et historiam antiquitatis pertinentes Julio Christiano van Oven dedicatae (Symbolae van Oven) quas ediderent M. David, B. A. van Groningen ⌊et⌋ E. M. Meijers... Leiden, E. J. Brill, 1946. viii, 410 p. port. 25cm.

Bibliographical footnotes.
CONTENTS.—Buck, A. de. La littérature et la politique sous la douzième dynastie égyptienne.—Proosdij, B. A. van. Šar mēšarim, titre des rois babyloniens comme législateurs.—Léemans, W. F. Kidinnu, un symbole de droit divin babylonien.—Böhl, F. M. T. Een schuldvordering uit de regeering van Darius I met een Arameesch bijschrift.—Thiel, J. H. Solon en de tyrannis.—Byvanck, A. W. Le procès de Phidias. —Groningen, B. A. van. Mantithée contre Mantithée.—Buriks, A. A. Papyrus de

(Continued)

Festschrift

N. Y. P. L. December 27, 1950

Symbolae ad jus et historiam antiquitatis... (Card 2)

Leyde, dénonçant un vol.—Visser, E. A petition to Queen Cleopatra.—Leeman-de Ridder, A. Requête concernant une vente de terrains.—Peremans, W. Sur la titulature aulique en Égypte au IIe et Ier siècle av. J.-C.—Wegener, E. P. The βουλευταί of the μητροπόλεις in Roman Egypt.—Menkman, A. The edict of Valerius Eudaimon, prefect of Egypt.—Verdam, P. J. St.-Paul et un serf fugitif.—David, M. The treaties between Rome and Carthage and their significance for our knowledge of Roman international law.—Polak, J. M. The Roman conception of the inviolability of the house.—Hermesdorf, B. H. D. Enkele aanteekeningen bij een Romeinschrechtelijke dingtaal (G. IV 16).—Jonkers, E. J. A few reflections on the background of Augustus's laws to increase the birth-rate.—Roos, A. G. Nero and the Christians.—Visscher,

(Continued)

N. Y. P. L. December 27, 1950

AN
(Furuseth, A.)

A Symposium on Andrew Furuseth. New Bedford, Mass., Darwin Press [1948]

233 p. illus., ports., map. 24 cm.

Comp. by S. B. Axtell.

1. Furuseth, Andrew, 1854-1938. 2. Merchant seamen—U. S. I. Axtell, Silas Blake, 1885- comp.

HD8073.F8S9 923.373 49-9391*

Library of Congress [3]

Festschrift.

Symbolae ad jus et historiam antiquitatis... (Card 3)

F. de. L'extension du régime de la noxalité aux délits prévus par la lex Aguilia.—Schulz, F. The manuscripts of the Collatio legum mosaicarum et romanarum.—Duyvendak, N. Restraining regulations for Roman officials in the Roman province.—Scheltema, H. J. The Nomoi of Iulianus of Ascalon.—Fischer, H. F. W. D. Les doctrines des romanistes du moyen âge sur l'acquisition de la possession et de la propriété par l'intermédiaire d'un mandataire.—Meyers, E. M. La réalité et la personnalité dans le droit du nord de la France et dans le droit anglais.—Eysinga, W. J. M. van. Quelques observations sur Grotius et le droit romain.

529670B. 1. Oven, Julius Christiaan van, 1881- . 2. Law—Hist. 3. History, Ancient—Addresses, essays, lectures. I. David, Martin, 1898-

N. Y. P. L. December 27, 1950

E-10
8274

Syntactica und Stilistica; Festschrift für Ernst Gamillscheg zum 70. Geburtstag, 28 Oktober 1957. «In verbindung mit Mario Wandruszka und Julius Wilhelm hrsg. von Günter Reichenkron» Tübingen, M. Niemeyer, 1957. 699 p. 24cm.

Chiefly in German, some articles in French or English and one in Catalan.

Bibliographical footnotes.

(Continued)

NNR 7.59 p/λ OC, I PC, 1, 2, I SL (LC1, X1, Z1)

Copy only words underlined & classmark—
*QPA

SYMBOLAE linguisticae in honorem Georgii Kuryłowicz. [Komitet redakcyjny: Adam Heinz et al. 1. wyd.] Wrocław, Zakład narodowy im. Ossolińskich, 1965. 394 p. port. 25cm. (Polska akademia nauk, Warsaw. Oddział w Krakowie. Komisja językoznawstwa. Prace. nr. 5)

Contributions in English, French, German, Polish, Russian and Serbo-Croatian.

Includes bibliographical references.

1. Philology--Addresses, essays, lectures. 2. Kuryłowicz, Jerzy, 1895- I. Series. II. Heinz, Adam, ed.

NN 3.66 r/dl OC, II (OS)I PC, 1, 2, I, II S, 1, 2, I, II (LC1, X1, Z1)

SYNTACTICA und Stilistica... (Card 2)

1. GAMILLSCHEG, ERNST, 1887-
2. PHILOLOGY—ADDRESSES, ESSAYS, LECTURES
I. Reichenkron, Günter, ed.

RAE

Symbolae philologicae O. A. Danielsson octogenario dicatae. Upsaliae: A.-B. Lundequistska bokhandeln, 1932. 390 p. front. (port.), plates. 24½cm.

No. 216 of 400 copies printed.
"Hoc volumen edendum curavit Axel Nelson."
Contributions in Italian, German, Swedish, Latin, French or English.

Festschrift

691962A. 1. Danielsson, Olof August, 1852-1933. 2. Philology—Addresses, essays, lectures. I. Nelson, Axel Herman, 1880- , editor.

N. Y. P. L. April 13, 1934

D-13
1593

SYNTAGMA Friburgense; historische Studien Hermann Aubin dargebracht zum 70. Geburtstag am 23.12. 1955. Lindau, J. Thorbecke [1956] 359 p. plates, port. 22cm. (Kopernikuskreis. Schriften. Bd. 1)

Bibliographical footnotes.

CONTENTS.--Jakob Villinger, Grossschatzmeister Kaiser Maximilians, von C. Bauer.--Das mittelalterliche Konstanz, von F. Beyerle.--Die Ostpolitik Kaiser Ottos II. von M. Hellmann.--Die Völker Osteuropas im Urteil Herders, von E. Keyser.--Zürichtal und Schaba, zwei Schweizer

(Continued)

NN R X 8.61 p/ρ OC (OS)I PC, 1, 2, I SL (LC1, X1, Z1) 3

E-11
154

Symbolae Verzijl, présentées au professeur J. H. W. Verzijl à l'occasion de son LXX-ième anniversaire. La Haye, M. Nijhoff, 1958.

viii, 453 p. port. 25 cm.

Contributions in French, English or Dutch.

"Bibliographie de l'œuvre de J. H. W. Verzijl (mise à jour jusqu'au 31 janvier 1958)": p. [431]-453.

Bibliographical footnotes.

1. Law, International--Addresses, essays, lectures. 2. Verzijl, Jan Hendrick Willem, 1888- .

NN*R 4.60 l/// OC PC, 1, 2 SL E, 1, 2 (LC1, X1, Z1)

SYNTAGMA Friburgense... (Card 2)

Bauerndörfer im Schwarzmeergebiet, von J. Künzig.--Die Bezeichnung für Stadt im Slavischen, von H. Ludat.--Preussisch-russiche Verhandlungen um einen europäischen Sicherheitspakt im Zeichen der Heiligen Allianz, von W. Markert.--Burgund und der preussische Ordensstaat, von E. Maschke.--Wesenszüge der sudetendeutschen Kulturlandschaft, von F. Metz.--Der Reichslandfriede vom 20.8.1467, von I. Most.--Die internationale Wirksamkeit slawischer und magyarischer Musiker vor 1600, von W. Salmen.--Fouqué, Heimatvertriebener und Wahlschlesier, von E. von Schickfus.--Die Ehescheidung Heinrichs VIII. als europäischer Rechtsfall, von

(Continued)

SYNTAGMA Friburgense... (Card 3)

H. Thieme. --Zur Bibliotheksgeschichte Revals im 16. und 17. Jahrhundert, von H. Weiss. — "Huden" und "Hüten", von W. Weizsäcker. --Über die sogenannten nationalen Schulen der osteuropäischen Musik, von W. Wiora. --Calvins Einwirken auf die Reformation in Polen-Litauen, von E. W. Zeeden.

1. History, Modern--Addresses, essays, lectures. 2. Aubin, Hermann, 1885- I. Series.

E-13
6784

Synteleia: Vincenzo Arangio-Ruiz. ₍A cura di Antonio Guarino e Luigi Labruna₎ Napoli, Jovene ₍1964₎

2 v. (xxvii, 1285 p.) ports. 24 cm. (Biblioteca di Labeo, 2)

Italian, French, Spanish, English, or German.
"Scritti di Vincenzo Arangio-Ruiz": v. 1, p. ₍xix₎-xxvii.
Bibliographical footnotes.

1. Law—Addresses, essays, lectures. I. Arangio-Ruiz, Vincenzo, 1884-1964. II. Guarino, Antonio, ed. III. Labruna, Luigi, ed. IV. Labruna, Luigi.

NN* 11.69 r/$_{M}$OC, I, II, III, (LC1, X1, Z1) IVb* PC, 1, I, II, III SL

D-16
1218

SYRACUSE UNIVERSITY. Maxwell graduate school of citizenship and public affairs.
Public affairs education and the university; a symposium on the occasion of the installation of Stephen Kemp Bailey as fourth Dean of the Maxwell Graduate School of Citizenship and Public Affairs of Syracuse University, June 14, 1962. Edited by Gerard J. Mangone. [Syracuse, N.Y., 1963]
(Continued)

NN * R 5.66 1/ (OC)I (LC1, X1, Z1) OS PC, 1, 2, 3, I SL E, 2, I

2

SYRACUSE UNIVERSITY. Maxwell graduate school of citizenship and public affairs. Public affairs education and the university... (Card 2)

ix, 132 p. plates. 21cm.

Cover title.
Bibliographical footnotes.

1. Education, Higher--Addresses, essays, lectures. --U.S. 3. Bailey, 2. Education Public service Stephen Kemp. I. Mangone, Gerard J., ed.

---

*QR

SZKOŁA GŁÓWNA SŁUŻBY ZAGRANICZNEJ, Warsaw.
Księga pamiątkowa ku czci Juliana Makowskiego z okazji 50-lecia pracy naukowej. [Komitet redakcyjny Tadeusz Cieślak, Ludwik Gelberg, Wojciech Morawiecki. Warszawa] Państwowe wydawn. naukowe [1957] 278 p. port. 24cm.

Includes bibliographies.
CONTENTS. --Julian Makowski-uczony, pedagog, dyplomata. --Babiński, L. "Responsa et consultationes juris" w zakresie prawa międzynarodowego na Pomorzu Zachodnim do połwy wieku
(Continued)

NN 3.65 c/B (OC)I OS(1b) (LCE1, LC1, X1, Z1) PC, 1, 2, I SL E, 1, 2, I S, 1, 2, I

4

SZKOŁA GŁÓWNA SŁUŻBY ZAGRANICZNEJ, Warsaw.
Księga pamiątkowa ku czci Juliana Makowskiego z okazji 50-lecia pracy naukowej. (Card 2)

XVIII. --Balicki, J. Sygnafariuseze laotańskiego układu rozejmowego. --Berezowski, C. Niektóre zagadnienia uznania międzynarodowego. --Bierzanek, R. Poczatki nietykalności poselskiej. --Boratyński, S. Zagadnienie baz wojskowych na konferencji moskiewskiej (1943). --Bramson, A. Z zagadnień prawnych granicy nad Odrą i Nysa. --Cieślak, T. Studia Tomasza Dreznera nad prawem porównawczym. --Gelberg, L. Z problematyki umów miedzynarodowych. --Libera, K. Przywilej nietykalności archiwum konsularnego i nietykalność placówki
(Continued)

SZKOŁA GŁÓWNA SŁUŻBY ZAGRANICZNEJ, Warsaw.
Księga pamiątkowa ku czci Juliana Makowskiego z okazji 50-lecia pracy naukowej. (Card 3)

konsularnej. --Machowski, J. Prawne aspekty działalności ludzkiej w przestrzeni pozaatmosferycznej. --Morawiecki, W. Skład organów i procedura głosowania Międzynarodowej agencji energii atomowej. --Nahlik, S. Zagadnienie międzynarodowej ochrony dzieł sztuki w czasie pokoju. --Winiarski, B. Kilka uwag o rzekomym "forum prorogatum" w prawie międzynarodowym. --Zaorski R. Rozstrzyganie sporów miedzynarodowych w sprawach ochrony zasobów bibliogicznych morza
(Continued)

SZKOŁA GŁÓWNA SŁUŻBY ZAGRANICZNEJ, Warsaw.
Księga pamiątkowa ku czci Juliana Makowskiego z okazji 50-lecia pracy naukowej. (Card 4)

pełnego. --Ważniejsze opublikowane prace prof. Juliana Makowskiego. (p. [277]-278)

1. Makowski, Juljan, 1875- 2. Law, International--Addresses, essays, lectures. I. Cieślak, Tadeusz, ed.

---

* C p.v.3581

Tacuarembo, Uruguay.
Centenario de Tacuarembó; revista oficial que conmemora sus cien años de vida departamental. 1837...1937. ₍San Fructuoso? 1937₎ 58 l. illus. (incl. ports.) 22 x 24cm.

Printed in double and triple columns.
Advertisements interspersed.
"Monografía de Tacuarembó; datos tomados del libro editado por el padre Jaime Ros," l. 5-16.

1. Tacuarembo, Uruguay. I. Ros, Jaime.
N. Y. P. L. January 2, 1940

D-17
3332

Tambimuttu, Thurairajah, 1915- *ed.*
Festschrift for Marianne Moore's seventy seventh birthday, by various hands. Edited by Tambimuttu. ₍New York₎ Tambimuttu & Mass, 1964.

117 p. illus. 23 cm.

1. Moore, Marianne, 1887- . I. Moore, Marianne, 1887- . II. Tambimuttu, Thurairajah, 1915-
NN * R 5.67 1/ OC, I, IIb* PC, 1, I SL (LC1, X1, Z1)

* PBN

... **Tanulmányok** Dr. **Blau Lajos** (1861–1936). A Ferenc József országos rabbiképző intézet néhai igazgatójának emlékére. Tisztelői, kartársai és tanítványai közreműködésével szerkesztették: Dr. Hevesi Simon, Dr. Guttmann Mihály, Dr. Lőwinger Sámuel. Budapest, 1938. 351, 194 p. illus. 23cm.

Added t.-p. in Hebrew; second paging in Hebrew.

CONTENTS.—Hevesi, Simon. Blau Lajos.—Wertheimer, Adolf. Emlékezés Dr. Blau Lajosra.—Kiss, Arnold. Blau Lajos emlékezete.—Löw, Immánuel. Blau Lajos. —Kecskeméti, Lipot. Blau Lajos és Sokolow Náhum.—Katona, József. Blau Lajos, ahogy a tanitvány láthatta.—Barát, Endre. A rekter úr.—Bakonyi, József. Blau Lajos irodalmi munkássága élte utolsó éveiben (1926–1936).—Bakonyi, László. A kongresszusi zsidó hitközségek statisztikája.—Bernstein, Béla. A zsidokérdés 1848 előtt.

(Continued)

N. Y. P. L. December 7, 1943

... **Tanulmányok** Dr. **Blau Lajos** (1861–1936)... (Card 2)

—Csetényi, Imre. A negyvenes évek liberális sajtoja és a zsidókérdes.—Deutsch, Gábor. Igehirdetés.—Farkas, József. Néhány szőjaték magyarázata a Bibliából, a talmudikus és későbbi vallasos irodalomból.—Fokos, David. A Szentirásnak ègy helyéhez.—Goldberger, Izidor. A tatatóvárosi zsidóság története.—Groszmann, Zsigmond. A pesti zsidóság második nemzedéke.—Guttmann, Henrik. Párhuzamok Szt. Ágoston műveiből a zsidó hagyomány Ádám-legendáihoz.—Jakab, Jenó. Hillél babilóniai tanulmányairól.—Krausz, Sámuel. Az Aruch completum segitő emberei.—Lányi, György. Micha József Lebensohn és a felvilágosodás kora.—Munkácsi, Ernó. Miniatürművészet Itália könyvtáraiban. Héber kódexek.—Scheiber, Sándor. Keleti hagyományok a nyelvek keletkezéséről.—Vajda, György. Ali ben Rabban al-Tabari néhány zsoltáridézetéről.—Weisz, Pál. "A bölcseség hét pillére" és a Biblia.—Winkler, Ernóné. Zsidó lakodalmi szokások Máramarosszigeten.—Zsoldos, Jenő. A felvilágosadas német-zsidó irói a harmincas évek magyar irodalmában.—Fúggelek.

(Continued)

N. Y. P. L. December 7, 1943

... **Tanulmányok** Dr. **Blau Lajos** (1861–1936)... (Card 3)

Blau Lajos. Fosztat városa, Maimonides múködésének szinhelye. Carlo Bernheimer: Die hebräischen Handschriften der Ambrosiana in Milano. Irodalmi szemle.—Landau, J. L. Blau Lajos emlékezete.—Lówinger, Sámuel. Dr Blau Lajos élete és irodalmi munkásságo.—Klein Sámuel. A Tóra a prófétàk írásaiban.—Guttmann, Mihály. Az ujabb zsidó tudományos irodalomról.—Marmorstein, Artúr. Agádikus kutatások.—Goldberger, Izidor. Az amorák száma.—Hoffer, Ármin. A hat misnarend neve.—Büchler, Adolf. R. Simon ben Gamliél és R. Jochanan b. Zakkaj körlevelei.—Maarsen, J. "Keren Ha-pukh".—Patai, Rafael. A kékbibor.—Libowitz, N. S. Luzzato könyvdrámái és à Zohar.—Fleischer, J. L. Ábr. ibn Ezra irodalmi tevékenysége Lucca városában.

195571B. 1. Blau, Ludwig, 1861–1936. I. Hevesi, Simon, 1868–1943, ed. II. Guttmann, Michael, 1872– , jt. ed. III. Loewinger, Samuel.

N. Y. P. L. December 7, 1943

* MGS
(Austrian)

TANZ und Brauch; aus der musikalischen Volksüberlieferung Kärntens [Roman Maier zur Vollendung seines 75. Lebensjahres dargebracht] Klafenfurt, Verlag des Landesmuseums für Kärnten, 1959. 176 p. illus., port., music. 24cm. (Kärntner Museumsschriften, 19)

Includes music.
Includes bibliographies.

1. Dancing--Austria--Carinthia. 2. Maier, Roman, 1884- . I. Series.

NN X 11.60 p/⁄ OC, 2b+ (OS)I PC, 1, 2, I SL MU, 1, 2 (LC1, X1, Z1)

NAC p.v.1420

Tarjei Vesaas; serprent av 50-årsheftet i Syn og segn. Oslo, Det Norske samlaget, 1947. 115 p. illus. 21cm.

1. Vesaas, Tarjei, 1897- . I. Syn og segn.

N. Y. P. L. February 28, 1952

Copy only words underlined
& classmark— *HA

TAUBE, GURLI ELISA (WESTGREN), friherrinna, 1890-
Svensk festskriftsbibliografi, åren 1891-1925. Uppsala, Appelbergs boktr., 1954. 168 p. 25cm. (Svenska bibliotekariesamfundet, Skriftserie, 2)

1. Festschriften—Bibl. 2. Festschriften—Indexes. I. Series.

NN *X 5.57 p/⁄ OC (1b) (OS)I PC, 1, 2, I RC, 1, 2 (U1, LC1, X1, Z2)

D-14
6254

TAUBE, OTTO VON, 1879-
Otto, Freiherr von Taube, Goldene Tage [Auswahl. Herausgabe besorgte Herbert M. Schönfeld. Starnberg, 1959] 37 p. 22cm.

Poems.
"Dieser Sonderdruck wurde vom Starnberger Kunstkreis Buzentaur als dessen fünfte Veröffentlichung, aus Anlass des 80. Geburtstages des Dichters am 21. Juni 1959."

(Continued)

NN S 10.63 g/⁄ OC, I, IIIbo PC, I, II SL (LC1, X1, Z1) 2

TAUBE, OTTO VON, 1879- . Otto, Freiherr von Taube... (Card 2)

"Subskriptionsliste" (8 p.), inserted.

I. Schönfeld, Herbert M., ed. II. Title. III. Schönfeld, Herbert M.

VBA
+

Technische Hochschule, Breslau.
Festschrift der Technischen Hochschule Breslau zur Feier ihres 25jährigen Bestehens, 1910–1935; ein Bericht über ihre Entwicklung und wissenschaftliche Beiträge aus ihrem Kreise. Breslau: W. G. Korn [1935] 538 p. incl. diagrs., tables. illus. (incl. plans), port. 30½cm.

823910A. 1. Industrial arts. 2. Education, Industrial and technical—Indiv. inst.—Germany—Breslau. I. Title.

N. Y. P. L. July 28, 1936

SSMC

TECHNISCHE HOCHSCHULE, Hanover.
100 Jahre Technische Hochschule Hannover; Festschrift zur Hundertjahrfeier am 15. Juni 1931; herausgegeben im Auftrage von Rektor und Senat. [Hannover: Druck Göhmannische Buchdruckerei, 1931] 394 p. illus. 26cm.

730474A. 1. No subject.

N. Y. P. L. February 1, 1935

Technische Hochschule, Karlsruhe.
Festschrift anlaesslich des 100jährigen Bestehens der Technischen Hochschule Fridericiana zu Karlsruhe. Karlsruhe: C. F. Müller, 1925. iv, 542 p. incl. tables. col'd diagrs., illus. (incl. plans), ports. 4°.

On cover: 1825–1925.
Includes bibliographies.
Contents: SCHNABEL, F. Die Anfänge des technischen Hochschulwesens. BALDUS, R. Die Gestalt eines im Fluge frei herabhängenden, beschwerten Drahtes. HEUN, K. Grundlagen der modernen Mechanik. KRAZER, A. Die Konvergenz der allgemeinen pfach unendlichen Thetareihe. SANDEN, K. v. und A. STAUS. Der

(Continued)

N. Y. P. L. September 12, 1930

Technische Hochschule, Karlsruhe: Festschrift anlaesslich des 100jährigen Bestehens... (Card 2)

kreisrunde Überfall als Messwehr. BREUER, S. Über die irreduzibelen auflösbaren Gleichungen fünften Grades. SCHLEICHER, F. Über Kreisplatten auf elastischer Unterlage. WELLSTEIN, J. Isotrope Drehungen und Schraubungen. BRAUER, T. Idealistischer Ökonomismus. WULZINGER, K. Die Piruz-Moschee zu Milas. HOLTZMANN, F. Zur Frage der Lungentuberkulose der Staubarbeiter, namentlich der Sandsteinhauer. AMMANN, O. Oberbauuntersuchungen im Institut für Strassen- und Eisenbahnwesen. GABER, E. Vereinfachung in der Gewölbeberechnung. HÖPFNER, K. Das Siedlungswesen, das Stadtbauwesen und der Städtebau als Sondergebiete der Ingenieurwissenschaft und des Ingenieurwesens. NÄBAUER, M. Ein Zielfernrohr ohne materielle Bildmarke. PROBST, E. Untersuchungen über den Einfluss

(Continued)

N. Y. P. L. September 12, 1930

Technische Hochschule, Karlsruhe: Festschrift anlaesslich des 100jährigen Bestehens... (Card 3)

wiederholter Belastungen auf Elasticität und Festigkeit von Beton und Eisenbeton. REHBOCK, T. Die Bekämpfung der Sohlen-Auskolkung bei Wehren durch Zahnschwellen. GRIMM, F. Grundlagen für die Beurteilung von Eisenbahnsicherungslagen. RITZMANN, F. Arbeitsaufsicht. BÖSS, P. Untersuchungen über zeiflich veränderliche Wasserbewegungen in offenen Gerinnen. BRAUER, E. Rollfedergetriebe. LINDNER, G. Berechnung der beim Lochen auftretenden Schubspannungen. NUSSELT, W. Die Wärmeübertragung an Wasser im Rohr. SPANNHAKE, W. Die Leistungsaufnahme einer parallelkränzigen Zentrifugalpumpe mit radialen Schaufeln. BADER, H. G. Beitrag zur Theorie des Segelns. MAYER, R. Versuche über die ebene Biegung gekrümmter Stäbe. TEICHMÜLLER, J. Die Bedeutung des Zapfen- und Stäbchensehens in der Photometrie und in der Lichttechnik allgemein. THOMA,

(Continued)

N. Y. P. L. September 12, 1930

Technische Hochschule, Karlsruhe: Festschrift anlaesslich des 100jährigen Bestehens... (Card 4)

H. Sicherheit und Wirtschaftlichkeit der elektrischen Fernkraftübertragung. HAUSRATH, H. Eine Kompensationsmethode für Mittelfrequenzen. BREDIG, G. Asymmetrische Synthese durch Katalysatoren als Modell der Fermentwirkung. FREUDENBERG, K. Über den Zusammenhang der Gerbstoffe mit den Pflanzenfarbstoffen. GOLDSCHMIDT, S. Über einige theoretische Fragen der organischen Chemie. ELÖD, E. Zur Theorie der Färbervorgänge. GÖHRINGER, A. Die Ursachen von gesetzmässigabnormen Flussgefällen... HENGLEIN, M. Die Blei-Zinkerzlagerstätte von Bleibach im Elztal. KÖGEL, G. Das integrale Farbbild. KOENIG, A. Über die Bildung von Formaldehyd aus Wassergas in der elektrischen Glimmentladung. ZSCHIMMER, E. Zur Erkenntniskritik der technischen Wissenschaft.

480421A. 1. Science—Essays and misc. I. Title.
N. Y. P. L. September 12, 1930

TEN afscheid van Dr. J. Waterink, hoogleraar, 1926-1961. Wageningen, Uitg. voor het Comité Afscheid Professor Waterink door Gebr. zomer en Keuning [1961] 82 p. port., diagrs. 24cm.

Bibliography, p. 75-76.
CONTENTS.--Principe en gezag in de hedendaagse psychologie en paedagogiek; afscheidscollege, door J. Waterink.--Professor Dr. J. Waterink, een levensschets, door H. R. Wijngaarden.--De psychologie

(Continued)

NN R 3.65 c/_ OC PC, 1, 2 SL (LC1, X1, Z1)

TEN afscheid van Dr. J. Waterink... (Card 2)

ten dienste van een veranderende industriële situatie, door R. W. van der Giessen.--Tendenties in de kinderpsychologie, door J. de Wit.--Bibliografie Prof. Dr. J. Waterink (p. 77-82)

1. Waterink, Jan, 1890- 2. Psychology--Addresses, essays, lectures.

TEUBER, OSCAR, 1852-1901.
Fünfzig Jahr' in Lied und That! Festschrift zur Feier des fünfzigjährigen Bestandes des Wiener Männergesangvereines. Wien, Verlag des Wiener Männergesangvereines, 1893. 77 p. 28cm.

1. Wiener Männergesangverein.
NN R 6.57 g/B OC PC, 1 SL MU, 1 (LC1, X1, Z1)

That soueraine light; essays in honor of Edmund Spenser, 1552–1952. Ed. by William R. Mueller and Don Cameron Allen. Baltimore, Johns Hopkins press, 1952. 133 p. 23cm.

CONTENTS.—The facade of morality, by J. W. Saunders.—"Eterne in mutabilite": the unified world of "The fairie queene," by K. Williams.—Spenser and Ireland, by R. Jenkins.—The truancy of Calidore, by J. C. Maxwell.—The theological structure of the "Fairie queene," Book I, by V. K. Whitaker.—"In these XII books severally handled and discoursed," by W. J. B. Owen.—The degredation of the Red cross knight, by K. Neill.—Spenser and the Countess of Leicester, by C. E. Mounts.—The pictorial element in Spenser's poetry, by R. Gottfried.

1. Spenser, Edmund, 1552?–1599. I. Mueller, William R., ed. II. Allen, Don Cameron, 1904– , ed.
NN R 6.53 OC, I, II PC, 1, I, II (LC1, Z1, X1)

THEATER, Wahrheit und Wirklichkeit; Freundesgabe zum sechzigsten Geburtstag von Kurt Hirschfeld am 10. März 1962. Zürich, Verlag Oprecht [1962] 183 p. illus., port., facsim. 20cm.

1. Hirschfeld, Kurt, March 10, 1902- . 2. Stage--Switzerland. 3. Stage--Addresses, essays, lectures.
NN 12.64 e/ OC, 1b PC, 1, 2, 3 SL T, 1, 2, 3 (LC1, X1, Z1)

THEN and now; Quaker essays, historical and contemporary, by friends of Henry Joel Cadbury, on his completion of twenty-two years as chairman of the American Friends Service Committee. Edited by Anna Brinton. Philadelphia, University of Pennsylvania Press [1960] 352 p. illus., port. 22cm.

Includes bibliography.
1. Friends, Society of. 2. Cadbury, Henry Joel, 1883- . I. Brinton, Anna (Cox), ed.
NN * R 4.61 e/ OC, I PC, 1, 2, I SL (LC1, X1, Z1)

Theodor Kroyer-Festschrift zum sechzigsten Geburtstage am 9. September 1933. Überreicht von Freunden und Schülern. Herausgegeben von Hermann Zenck, Helmut Schultz [und] Walter Gerstenberg. Regensburg: G. Bosse, 1933. 182 p. incl. front. (mounted port.), tables. facsim., illus. (music.) 24½cm.

CONTENTS.—Gerstenberg, W. Eine Neumenhandschrift in der Dombibliothek zu Köln.—Wolf, J. L'arte des biscanto misurato secondo el maestro Jacopo da Bologna.—Birtner, H. Renaissance und Klassik in der Musik.—Cauchie, M. La pureté des modes dans la musique vocale franco-belge du début du XVIe siècle.—Higini, A. Die spanische Liedkunst im 15. und am Anfang des 16. Jahrhunderts.—Jeppesen, K. Ein venezianisches

(Continued)

N. Y. P. L. September 17, 1935

Theodor Kroyer-Festschrift zum sechzigsten Geburtstage... (Card 2)

Laudenmanuskript.—Schwartz, R. Zum Formproblem der Frottole Petruccis.—Zenck, H. Nicola Vicentinos L'antica musica (1555).—Halbig, H. Eine handschriftliche Lautentabulatur des Giacomo Gorzanis.—Cesari, G. L'archivo musicale di S. Barbara in Mantova ed una messa di Guglielmo Gonzaga.—Werner, T. W. Archivalische Nachrichten und Dokumente zur Kenntnis der Familie Schildt.—Schneider, M. Zum Weihnachtsoratorium von Heinrich Schütz.—Moser, H. J. Eine Augsburger Liederschule im Mittelbarock.—Ursprung, O. Stilvollendung.—Bücken, E. Zur Frage des Stilverfalls.—Schultz, H. Das Orchester als Ausleseprinzip.

CARNEGIE CORPORATION OF NEW YORK.

749221A. 1. Kroyer, Theodor, 1873– . 2. Music—Essays. I. Zenck, Hermann, ed. II. Schultz, Helmut, ed. III. Gerstenberg, Walter, ed.

N. Y. P. L. September 17, 1935

THEODOR MAYER und der Konstanzer Arbeitskreis. Theodor Mayer zum 80. Geburtstag. [Konstanz] Druckerei und Verlagsanstalt Konstanz [1963] 58 p. port. 24cm.

CONTENTS.--Theodor Mayer und der Konstanzer Arbeitskreis, von W. Schlesinger.--Verzeichnis der bisher veröffentlichten Protokolle des Konstanzer Arbeitskreises für mittelalterliche Geschichte, von R. Wais.--Verzeichnis der Vortragenden beim Konstanzer Arbeitskreis, von R. Wais.

(Continued)

NN R 5.66 g/ OC, I, Ibo, II PC, 1, 2, I, II SL (LC1, X1, Z1)

THEODOR MAYER und der Konstanzer Arbeitskreis. (Cont.)

1. Mayer, Theodor, 1883- . 2. Konstanzer Arbeitskreis für mittelalterliche Geschichte. I. Wais, Reinhard. II. Schlesinger, Walter, 1908- .

THÉODORE LAURENT, 1863-1953; l'industriel, l'homme. Paris, 1955. 173 p. illus., plates, ports. 26cm.

"Albert Decaris.. réalisa les gravures au burin, Pierre Guyénot.. dessina les sanguines et peignit les aquarelles."

1. Laurent, Theodore, 1863-1953. 2. Compagnie des forges et aciéries de la marine et d'Homécourt.

NN* * 7.57 c/ OC, Ib+ PC, 1, 2 SL E, 1, 2 (PRE1, LC1, X1, Z1)

Theodore von Kármán anniversary volume; contributions to applied mechanics and related subjects, by the friends of Theodore Kármán on his sixtieth birthday. [Pasadena, Cal., 1941] xv, 337 p. front. (port.), illus. 28½cm.

Reproduced from typewritten copy; t.-p. and cover printed.
Includes bibliographies.

CONTENTS.—Theodore von Kármán; an appreciation [by C. B. Millikan]—Some definite integrals occurring in aerodynamics, by H. Bateman.—On the geometry of streamlining, by M. M. Munk.—Dimensional analysis and similitude in mechanics, by J. C. Hunsaker.—Impulse and momentum in an infinite fluid, by Theodore Theodorsen.—Coriolis and the energy principle in hydraulics, by B. A. Bakhmeteff.—The influ-

(Continued)

N. Y. P. L. May 4, 1942

Theodore von Kármán anniversary volume... (Card 2)

ence of bottom topography on ocean currents, by H. U. Sverdrup.—Ionization as a factor in fluid mechanics, by W. F. Durand.—Isotropic turbulence in theory and experiment, by H. L. Dryden.—The intrinsic theory of elastic shells and plates, by J. L. Synge and W. Z. Chien.—The compressibility of solids under extreme pressures, by F. D. Murnaghan.—Hydrodynamics and the structure of stellar systems, by F. Zwicky.—On the elastic distortion of a cylindrical hole by a localized hydrostatic pressure, by H. M. Westergaard.—On the absorption of sound waves in suspensions and emulsions, by P. S. Epstein.—On a method for the solution of boundary-value problems, by R. Courant.—The engineering treatment of ring or wheel problems, by Karl Arnstein.—On the five-dimensional representation of gravitation and electricity, by A. Einstein, V. Bargmann and P. G. Bergmann.—The forced vibrations of tie-rods, by S. Timo-

(Continued)

N. Y. P. L. May 4, 1942

Theodore von Kármán anniversary volume... (Card 3)

shenko.—A note on the effect of the wind-tunnel size on pitching moments, by Th. Troller.—The creep of metals under various stress conditions, by A. Nádai.—On the minimum buckling load for spherical shells, by K. O. Friedrichs.—The theory of flow through centrifugal pumps, by William Bollay.—The ideal performance of curved-lattice fans, by F. L. Wattendorf.—Stress concentrations due to elliptical discontinuities in plates under edge forces, by L. H. Donnell.—On lubrication flow with periodic distribution between prescribed boundaries, by Hans Reissner.—Some remarks on the laws of turbulent motion in tubes, by R. v. Mises.—Stress pattern crazing, by W. B. Klemperer.

172399B. 1. Kármán, Theodore von, 1881– 2. Mechanics, Applied.

N. Y. P. L. May 4, 1942

Aus **Theologie** und Philosophie. Festschrift für Fritz Tillmann zu seinem 75. Geburtstag (1. November 1949). Hrsg. von Theodor Steinbüchel† und Theodor Müncker. Düsseldorf, Patmos-Verlag [1950] 615 p. port. 24cm.

Bibliography at end of most chapters.

602575B. 1. Theology—Essays and misc. 2. Ethics, Christian. 3. Tillmann, Fritz, 1874– . I. Steinbüchel, Theodor, 1888– , ed. II. Müncker, Theodor, 1887– , ed.

N. Y. P. L. January 15, 1952

Theologische Abhandlungen; Carl von Weizsäcker zu seinem siebzigsten Geburtstage, 11. December 1892, gewidmet von Adolf Harnack, Emil Schürer [und anderen]... Freiburg i. B.: J. C. B. Mohr, 1892. 352 p. 24cm.

CONTENTS.—Die Briefe des römischen Klerus aus der Zeit der Sedisvacanz im Jahre 250. Von A. Harnack.—Die Prophetin Isabel in Thyatira. Offenb. Joh. 2 20. Von E. Schürer.—Die Katechese der alten Kirche. Von H. J. Holtzmann.—Das Interesse des apostolischen Zeitalters an der evangelischen Geschichte. Von Hermann Freiherr von Soden.—Gedankengang und Grundgedanke des ersten Johannesbriefs. Von T. Häring.—Die Perle. Aus der Geschichte eines Bildes. Von H. Usener.—Zur Geschichte der Abendmahlsfeier in der ältesten Kirche. Von A. Jülicher.—Das Ver-

(Continued)

N. Y. P. L. September 20, 1943

Theologische Abhandlungen; Carl von Weizsäcker... (Card 2)

hältniss der Paulinischen Schriften zur Sapientia Salomonis. Von E. Grafe.—Der Umschwung in der Lehre von der Busse während des 12. Jahrhunderts. Von K. Müller. —Die urchristliche Ueberlieferung und das Neue Testament. Von C. F. G. Heinrici.

239546B. 1. Theology. 2. Weizsäcker, Karl Heinrich von, 1822–1899.
N. Y. P. L. September 20, 1943

ZEC

Theologische Studien. Herrn Wirkl. Oberkonsistorialrath Professor D. Bernhard Weiss zu seinem 70. Geburtstage dargebracht von C. R. Gregory, Ad. Harnack, M. W. Jacobus ₍und anderen₎ Göttingen: Vanderhoeck & Ruprecht, 1897. 357 p. 24cm.

Contents.—Harnack, Adolf. Ein jüngst entdeckter Auferstehungsbericht.—Jacobus, M. W. The citation Ephesians 5:14 as affecting the Paulinity of the Epistle.—Koffmane, G. Ist Luther Verfasser einer Schrift, welche das Komma Johanneum behandelt?—Kühl, Ernst. Zur paulinischen Theodicee.—Resch, Alfred. Τὰ Λόγια Ἰησοῦ = חברי ישוע Ein Beitrag zur synoptischen Evangelienforschung.—Ritschl, Otto. Schleiermachers Theorie von der Frömmigkeit.—Weiss, Johannes. Beiträge zur Paulinischen Rhetorik.—Zimmer, Friedrich. I Thess. 2:3–8 erklärt.—Gregory, C. R.

(Continued)

N. Y. P. L. November 30, 1943

Theologische Studien... (Card 2)

Die Kleinschrifthandschriften des Neuen Testamentes.—Titius, A. Das Verhältnis der Herrnworte im Markusevangelium zu den Logia des Matthäus.—Sieffert, Fr. Die Entwicklungslienie der paulinischen Gesetzeslehre nach den vier Hauptbriefen des Apostels.

239548B. 1. Theology. 2. Weiss, Bernhard, 1827–1918.
N. Y. P. L. November 30, 1943

ZEC

Theology and modern life; essays in honor of Harris Franklin Rall, edited by Paul Arthur Schilpp. Chicago, New York, Willett, Clark & company, 1940.

x p., 1 l., 297 p. front. (port.) 20½cm.

Bibliographical references in "Notes" at end of most of the chapters.

Contents.—Harris Franklin Rall, by I. G. Whitchurch.—Our immortality, by S. S. Cohon.—The significance of critical study of the Gospels for religious thought today, by F. C. Grant.—The Christian doctrine of man, by A. C. Knudson.—Facing the problem of evil, by F. J. McConnell.—The realistic movement in religious philosophy, by E. W. Lyman.—The meaning of rational faith, by P. A. Schilpp.—Interpreting the religious situation, by I. G. Whitchurch.—The kingdom of God and the life of today, by C. C. McCown.—The church and social optimism, by Shailer Mathews.—The church, the truth, and society, by E. S. Brightman.—Let the church be the church! By E. F. Tittle.—Bibliography of the writings of Harris Franklin Rall (p. 285–297)

1. Theology—Addresses, essays, lectures. 2. Rall, Harris Franklin, 1870– I. Schilpp, Paul Arthur, 1897– ed.

Library of Congress BT10.T53 40–8892
~~Copy 2.~~
Copyright ₍12₎ 204

E-13
4064

Theoretische und institutionelle Grundlagen der Wirtschaftspolitik. Theodor Wessels zum 65. Geburtstag. Mit Beiträgen von Hans Albert ₍u. a.₎ Berlin, Duncker u. Humblot (1967).

xiv, 464 p. front. 24 cm. (Quaestiones oeconomicae, Bd. 1)

Includes bibliographies.

(Continued)

NN • 1.69 1/₍ OC PC, 1, I, II SL E, 1, I, II (LC1, X1, Z1)

THEORETISCHE und institutionelle Grundlagen der Wirtschaftspolitik. (Card 2)

Contents.—Ökonomische Theorien und wirtschaftspolitisches Handeln, von C. Watrin.—Zielbestimmung für die Wirtschaftspolitik in der pluralistischen Gesellschaft, von H. K. Schneider.—Politische Ökonomie und rationale Politik, von H. Albert.—Der Begriff "normal" in den öko-technischen Handlungslehren, dargestellt an der Arbeitswissenschaft, von H. J. Wallraff.—Quasimonopole und Pseudomonopole, von G. Gäfgen.—Workable Competition als wettbewerbspolitisches Konzept, von E. Hoppmann.—Zur wettbewerbspolitischen Bedeutung der Markttransparenz, von A. Woll.—Investitionen und

(Continued)

THEORETISCHE und institutionelle Grundlagen der Wirtschaftspolitik. (Card 3)

technischer Fortschritt in der neueren Wachstumstheorie und die Problematik wirtschaftspolitischer Rezepte, von H. Walter.—Strukturwandel und harmonisches Wachstum, von M. Neumann.—Profite, externe Vorteile und wirtschaftliche Entwicklung, von H.-G. Krüsselberg.—Die Bedeutung der Faktorausstattung für die Struktur des Aussenhandels, von K. Rose.—Wirtschaftspolitische Leitbilder der Entwicklungsländer, von W. Kraus.—Der Sachverständigenrat, von

(Continued)

THEORETISCHE und institutionelle Grundlagen der Wirtschaftspolitik. (Card 4)

W. Bauer.—Kritische Anmerkungen zur jüngsten Konjunkturdiskussion, von H. Besters.—Importierte Inflation als Problem der Wirtschaftspolitik, von R. Rettig.—Wechselkursänderungen und Zahlungsbilanzausgleich, von H. Luckenbach.—Geldtheoretische und finanztechnische Aspekte der Rentendynamik, von W. Schreiber.—Verzeichnis der Schriften von Theodor Wessels (p. ₍451₎–457)

1. Economic policy--Addresses, essays, lectures. I. Wessels, Theodor, 1902- . II. Albert, Hans.

NRC

THESAURISMATA; Festschrift für Ida Kapp zum 70. Geburtstag, hrsg. von Otto Hiltbrunner, Hildegard Kornhardt [und] Franz Tietze. München [Aus-ferung: C.H. Beck] 1954. 168 p. 21cm.

Bibliographical footnotes.

CONTENTS. --Caesar und sein Glück, von W.H. Friedrich. --Ὅπερ σαφεστάτη πίστις, von K. von Fritz. --Lancicula satura, von P. Geissler. --Dicta Scipionis, von O. Hiltbrunner. --Restitutio

(Continued)

NN ** 4.56 d/b OC, 2bo, I, II, III PC, 1, 2, I, II, III SL (LC1, X1, Z1)

THESAURISMATA... (Card 2)

in integrum bei Terenz, von H. Kornhardt. --Der Cod. Feschianus Heinsii zu Ovids Ep. ex Ponto, von G. Meyer. --Morgendämmerung, von R. Pfeiffer. --Zur Geschichte vom Gastmahl der Sieben Weisen, von B. Snell. --Noch einmal die Dichter der Ilias, von W. Theiler. --Zur attractio inversa im Lateinischen, von F. Tietze.

1. Classical studies—Collections. 2. Kapp, Ida. I. Hiltbrunner, Otto, ed. II. Kornhardt, Hildegard, ed. III. Tietze, Franz, 1909- , ed.

THIERBACH, HANS, ed.
Adolf Grabowsky; Leben und Werk. Dem Altmeister der politischen Wissenschaften als-Fest- und Dankesgabe gewidmet. Köln, C. Heymann, 1963. viii, 232 p. port. 22cm.

Bibliography, p. 203-232.

1. Grabowsky, Adolf, 1880- .
NN R 12.63 g/r OC PC,1 SL E,1 (LC1,X1,Z1)

This ministry, the contribution of Henry Sloane Coffin ... New York, C. Scribner's sons, 1945.
vi p., 1 l., 128 p. port. 21cm.
"Essays ... presented ... on the occasion of Doctor Coffin's retirement from the presidency of Union theological seminary."—Foreword.
"Reinhold Niebuhr, editor."
CONTENTS.—Parish minister, by M. P. Noyes.—Theological educator, by H. P. Van Dusen.—Leader of liberal Presbyterianism, by R. H. Nichols.—Preacher, by W. R. Bowie.—Liturgist and hymnologist, by W. P. Merrill.—Exponent of social Christianity, by J. C. Bennett.—Religious leader in colleges, by C. W. Gilkey.—Member of the Yale corporation: I, by J. R. Angell. II, by Charles Seymour.—Theologian and church statesman, by Reinhold Niebuhr.
1. Coffin, Henry Sloane, 1877- I. Niebuhr, Reinhold, 1892- ed.
46-917
Library of Congress • BX9225.C624T5
Festschrift
[5] 922.573

Write on slip, name, year, vol., page of magazine and class mark— NAA

This number of Modern philology is dedicated by the University of Chicago press, by the editors and by colleagues and pupils to Francis Asbury Wood.

(Modern philology. Chicago, 1929. 8°. v.26, May, p.i-vii, 385-497. front.port.)

form 400a [viii-10-28 25m]

Thomas, Daniel H ed.
Guide to the diplomatic archives of Western Europe. Edited by Daniel H. Thomas and Lynn M. Case. Philadelphia, University of Pennsylvania Press [1959]
xii, 389 p. 22 cm.
Published in honor of William E. Lingelbach.
Includes bibliographies.
CONTENTS.—Austria, by A. J. May.—Belgium, by D. H. Thomas.—Denmark, by W. Westergaard.—France, by V. Confer.—Germany, by R. J. Sontag.—Great Britain, by K. Eubank.—Italy, by M. L. Shay.—The Netherlands, by D. P. M. Graswinckel.—Norway, by F. J. Sherriff.—Portugal, by M. Cardozo.—Spain, by L. G. Canedo.—Sweden, by F. J. Sherriff.—Switzerland, by L. M. Case.—Vatican
(Continued)
NN*R 7.59 t/ OC, I, IIb* PC, 1, 2, I SL E, 1, I (LC1, X1, Z1)

Thomas, Daniel H ed. Guide to the diplomatic archives of Western Europe. [1959] (Card 2)
CONTENTS—Continued.
City, by N. Summers.—Bavaria, by O. J. Hale.—The League of Nations and the United Nations, by R. Claus.—Public opinion and foreign affairs, by J. J. Mathews and L. M. Case.—Unesco, by R. H. Heindel.

1. ARCHIVES—EUROPE 2. EUROPE—HIST.—SOURCES—BIBL.
I. Case, Lynn Marshall, 1903- , joint ed. II. Thomas, Daniel H.

Thomas, David Winton, 1901- , ed.
Archaeology and Old Testament study: jubilee volume of the Society for Old Testament Study, 1917-1967, edited by D. Winton Thomas. Oxford, Clarendon P., 1967.
xxxvii, 493 p. 20 plates, maps, plans. 22½ cm.

Includes bibliographies.

1. Bible. O.T.--Archaeology. I. Society for Old Testament study.
NN * R 11.68 l/l OC (OS)I PC,1,I SL J,1,I (LC1,Z1,X1)

THOMAS, DAVID WINTON, 1901- , ed.
Hebrew and Semitic studies. Presented to Godfrey Rolles Driver... in celebration of his seventieth birthday, 20 August 1962. Edited by D. Winton Thomas and W.D. McHardy. Oxford, Clarendon press, 1963. vi, 206 p. illus., port. 24cm.

CONTENTS.--Godfrey Rolles Driver.--Archaic survivals in the text of Canticles, by W.F. Albright.-- A Syro-hexaplar text of the
(Continued)
NN R 4.66 k/l OCs, Is PCs, 1s, 2s, 3s, Is SL Js, 1s, 2s, 3s, Is Os, 2s, 3s, Is (LC1s, X1s, Z1s)
3

THOMAS, DAVID WINTON, 1901- ,ed. Hebrew and Semitic studies. (Card 2)

Song of Hannah: I Samuel ii, 1-10, by P.A.H. De Boer.--A new list of so-called "Ben Naftali" manuscripts, by A. Diez-Macho.--Un ostracon araméen inédit d'Éléphantine, by A. Dupont-Sommer.--The second lamentation for Ur, by C.J. Gadd.--"Roots below and fruit above" and related matters, by H.L. Ginsberg.--Abraham of Ur, by C.H. Gordon.--On the so-called infinitivus absolutus in Hebrew, by E. Hammershaimb. שחל by S. Mowinckel.--The origin of the subdivisions of Semitic, by C. Rabin.--Notes on the Aramaic of the Genesis Apocryphon, by H.H. Rowley.--Jesaja xv-xvi, by
(Continued)

THOMAS, DAVID WINTON, 1901- ,ed. Hebrew and Semitic studies. (Card 3)

W. Rudolph.--Le qayl en Arabie méridionale préislamique, by G. Ryckmans.--Compound tenses containing the verb "be" in Semitic and Egyptian, by T.W. Thacker.--Die Vokabel-Varianten der O-Rezension im griechischen Sirach, by J. Ziegler.--Select bibliography of the writings of Godfrey Rolles Driver (p. [191]-206)

1. Bible. O.T.--Criticism. 2. Semitic studies. 3. Driver, Godfrey Rolles, 1892- . I. McHardy, W.D., joint ed.

THORS, CARL-ERIC, ed.
Studier tillägnade Rolf Pipping den 1 juni 1949. Helsingfors [Svenska litteratursällskapet i Finland] 1949. 108 p. 24cm.

Bibliographical footnotes.
CONTENTS.--Got. andhruskan och andsitan, av T. Johannisson.--Plácitúsdrápa, av D.A. Seip.--Norr. vilmögom Hávamál 134, av E. Hummelstedt.--Til Gammelnorsk homiliebok, av T. Knudsen.--Skeppare,
(Continued)
NN 6.64 e/b OC, II (OS)I PC, 1, 2, I, II SL (LC1, X1, Z1) [I]
2

THORS, CARL-ERIC, ed. Studier tillägnade Rolf Pipping den 1 juni 1949. (Card 2)

en syntaktisk studie, av I. Modéer.--Till frågan om uppkomsten av uttryckstypen "din stackare," av K.G. Ljunggren.--En Bellmanstolkning och en dialektal ljudutveckling, av N. Lindqvist.--Några språkformer i Reyncke Fosz 1621, av O. Ahlbäck.--Nogle exempler på brugen af Du och De i nutidsdansk, av L. Jacobsen.--Det uppländska sockennamnet Alunda, av J. Sahlgren.--Svinönamnen i Finland, av E. Anthoni.--Räckhals, en namnstudie, av C.-E. Thors.

1. Pipping, Rolf, 1889- . 2. Scandinavian languages. I. Svenska litteratursällskapet i Finland. II. Title.

E-10
7196

THORSTEIN VEBLEN: a critical reappraisal; lectures and essays commemorating the hundredth anniversary of Veblen's birth. Edited by Douglas F. Dowd. Ithaca, N.Y., Cornell University Press [1958] xii, 328 p. 24cm.

Bibliographical footnotes.

CONTENTS. — Preface, by D.F. Dowd. — The sources and impact of Veblen's thought, by J. Dorfman. —Veblen, then and now, by

(Continued)

NN* R .3. 59 g/⫲ OC, I, IIb* PC, 1, I SL E, 1, I (LC1, X1, Z1)

THORSTEIN VEBLEN: a critical reappraisal... (Card 2)

W. Hamilton. —Veblen's theory of instincts reconsidered, by C. E. Ayres. — Idle curiosity, by N. Kaplan. —On the scope and method of economics, by M.A. Copeland. —Veblen's critique of the orthodox economic tradition, by L. Nabers. —The cycle theories of Veblen and Keynes today, by M.D. Brockie. —Veblen and Marx, by F.G. Hill. -- Veblen's theory of economic growth, by A.G. Gruchy. —Veblen on American capitalism, by P.M. Sweezy. — The place of corporation finance in Veblen's economics, by J.B. Dirlam. —Veblen, Hoxie, and

(Continued)

THORSTEIN VEBLEN: a critical reappraisal... (Card 3)

American labor, by L. Fishman. —The ideology of the engineers, by P. Morrison. —Veblen's view of cultural evolution, by M.W. Watkins. — The case of the new countries, by C. Goodrich. —Technology and social change: Japan and the Soviet Union, by D.F. Dowd. — Veblen's macroinstitutionalism, by G.W. Zinke. — Bibliography of Veblen's writings, by J. Dorfman (p. 319-326).

1. Veblen, Thorstein, 1857-1929. I. Dowd, Douglas Fitzgerald, 1919- , ed. II. Dowd, Douglas Fitzgerald, 1919- .

D-19
7123

Tieto ja mielikuvitus. Professori Irma Rantavaaran juhlakirja. 4. 5. 1968. [Toimituskunta: Maija Lehtonen ym.] Helsinki, Otava [1969]

214 p. front. 21 cm.

Summaries in French.

CONTENTS.—Kirjallisuus ja yhteiskunta, kirj. D. Daiches.—Runouden Kieli, kirj. C. Brooks.—Dombey ja Poika, kirj. F. R. Leavis.—

(Continued)

NN*R 2. 70 v/L OC PC, 1, 2, 3 SL (LC1, X1, Z1)

2

TIETO ja mielikuvitus. (Card 2)

Fiktion kysymyksiä, kirj. A. Kinnunen.—Kirjallisten fiktioiden kuvaamisesta ja tulkitsemisesta, kirj. J. Wrede.—Minna Canth kaunokirjallisuuden arvostelijana, kirj. H. Kannila.—Toiston merkityksestä Otto Mannisen Säkeiden tyylissä, kirj. M. Lehtonen.—Siljon toinen linja ja Hellaakoski, kirj. K. Marjanen.—Modernismi ja itämaat, kirj. R. Koskimies.—Varhaiset kapinoitsijat. John Fordin näytelmä "Tis pity she's a whore," kirj. I. Niemi.—Ensimmäinen teatteriperinteemme, kirj. T. Tiusanen.—Groteski näyttämötyyli nykyaikaisen elämäntunteen ilmaisijana, kirj. A. Kivimaa.

1. Finnish literature--Addresses, essays, lectures. 2. Literature, Modern--Addresses, essays, lectures. 3. Rantavaara, Irma Irene, 1908-

---

AN
(Falkberget, J.)

Til Johan Falkberget på 60-årsdagen; redigert av Fredrik Paasche. Oslo, Forlagt av H. Aschehoug & co. (W. Nygaard) 1939.

3 p. l., 252 p. incl. pl. front. (port.) facsim. 25cm.

CONTENTS. — Braaten, Oskar. Johan Falkberget. — Scott, Gabriel. Johan Falkberget på sekstiårs dagen [dikt] — Jensen, Johannes V. Johan Falkberget.—Nerman, Ture. Till Johan Falkberget [dikt]—Døhl, Einar. "Mod lys og grav"; debutbok og programskrift.—Luihn, Otto. Falkberget og den unge arbeiderrørsla.—Grepp, Rachel. Mennesket og vennen.—Johnson, Eyvind. Till Johan Falkberget [dikt]—Stauning, Th. En hilsen fra Danmark.—Øisang, Ole. Dikteren, politikeren og idealisten.—Nygaardsvold, Johan. Hilsen.—Ström, Fredrik. Sagan om den stolliga gumman och gruvpojken. — Hovden, Anders. Johan Falkberget.—Kvikne, Olav. Bergmannen og journalisten.—Strømmevold, O. Viddens sønn— —.—Pedersen, Jens. Kobbersmeden [dikt] — Paulson,

(Continued on next card)

A C 40-2421

[2]

Til Johan Falkberget ... 1939. (Card 2)

CONTENTS—Continued.

Andreas. Over vidden til grubene.—Matthis, Henry Peter. Røros i litteraturhistorien.—Haugbøll, Charles. Hilsen.—Hedenvind-Eriksson, Gustav. Et litet minne på din sextioårsdag.—Bornebusch, Arne. Örnen vid Rugelsjön; några anspråkslösa ord om den härlige diktaren och strålande människan Johan Falkberget.—Fett, Harry. Glück auf!—Av en bergstadpreken.—Duun, Olav. I Falkbergetlande.—Ørjaseter, Tore. Til Johan Falkberget [dikt]—Undset, Sigrid. Hilsen.—Borgen, Johan. Hilsen.—Krokann, Inge. Helsing til Johan Falkberget.—Vesaas, Tarjei. Hilsen. — Bojer, Johan. Hilsen til Johan Falkberget. — Egge, Peter. Takk til Johan Falkberget. — Wall, Annie. Hilsen. — Rytter, Henrik. Helsing til Johan Falkberget [dikt] — Normann, Regine. Hilsen. — Ansen, Arne Paasche. Mannen som hadde tid—.—Christiansen, Sigurd. Hilsen.—Balstad, Stein. Personlige minner om Johan Falkberget. — Anker, Nina Roll. Hilsen.—Bregendahl, Marie. En tak til Johan Falk-

(Continued on next card)

A C 40-2421

[2]

Til Johan Falkberget ... 1939. (Card 3)

CONTENTS—Continued.

berget. — Dalgard, Olav. Johan Falkberget. — Beyer, Harald. Noen grunndrag hos forfatteren av "Christianus Sextus".—Ring, Barbra. En stjerne i hjertet.—Floden, Halvor. Helsing [dikt]—Fangen, Ronald. Hilsen.—Kirk, Hans. Hilsen.—Søiberg, Harry. Johan Falkberget.—Meyer, Håkon. Den fjerde nattevakt.—Øverås, Asbjørn. Ei helsing frå Trøndelag; og litt om dei fremste åndelege fedrane til diktaren.—Hoffmann, Kai. Hilsen.—Gravlund, Thorkild. Hilsen.—Brøgger, A. W. Med "Christianus Sextus" til Hellas. — Stiernstedt, Marika. Nattvandraren [dikt]—Koch, Martin. Vikingar och köpmän; till vännen Johan Falkberget på hans 60-års dag.—Kielland, Eugenia. Korrektur.—Thesen, Rolv. Kjære Johan Falkberget.—Debes, Inge. En hilsen fra de unge år. — Sørensen, Henrik. [Tegning] — Paasche, Fredrik. Johan Falkberget og "Christianus Sextus" (1936)

1. *Falkberget, Johan, 1879- I. *Paasche, Fredrik, 1886- ed.

A C 40-2421

New York. Public library for Library of Congress [2]

D-19
4719

Tilegnet Carl Hj. Borgstrøm. Et festskrift på 60-årsdagen 12. 10. 1969 fra hans elever. Oslo, Universitetsforlaget, 1969.

142 p. diagrs. 23 cm.

Includes bibliographical references.

CONTENTS.—The semivowels of Icelandic, by H. Benediktsson.—Case grammar and the preposition med in standard colloquial Norwegian, by T. Fretheim.—Notes on a problem of Maaori syntax, by

(Continued)

NN * R 4. 71 b/á OC PC, 1, 2 SL (LC1, X1, Z1)

2.

TILEGNET Carl Hj. Borgstrøm. (Card 2)

M. Haslev.—Case and gender in Proto-Indo-European, by E. Hovdhaugen.—Gibt es ein bleiben-Passiv im heutigen Deutsch? Von O. Leirbukt.—Hethitisch lahhuwai: mykenisch lewotrokhowoi usw. von F. O. Lindeman.—The problem of neutralization in phonology, by O. Lorentz.—The analysis of reference in Eskimo and the computer, by J. Mey.—Stress rules in English and Norwegian, by I. Moen.—"Word tones" in Welsh? By M. Oftedal.—Nok en gang om alveolarene, av G. D. Rinnan.—Einiges über di Geschicte des isländischen Vokalsystems, von T. Skomedal.

1. Philology--Addresses, essays, lectures.
2. Borgström, Carl Hjalmar, 1909- .

3-MAS
+

Tilegnet Mogens Koch. Udg. i anledning af Mogens Kochs 70 års fødselsdag 2. marts 1968 under redaktion af Axel Thygesen. København (Nyt Nordisk Forlag) 1968.

354 p. illus., maps, plans. 31cm.

Includes bibliographies.

1. Koch, Mogens. 2. Architecture--Addresses, essays, lectures. 3. Design--Addresses, essays, lectures.
NN° 10. 69 v/ OC PC, 1, 2, 3 SL A, 1, 2, 3 (LC1, X1, Z1)

SIO

Till Axel Gjöres på sextioårsdagen, 11 november 1949. [Stockholm] KF:s bokförlag [etc., 1949] 264 p. port. 24cm.

Festschrift

558181B. 1. Gjöres, Axel, 1889- . 2. Co-operation.
N. Y. P. L. January 15, 1951

VBA

Till Erland Borglund den 6 augusti 1954 [Redaktion: Josef Andersson, L. Gottfrid Sjöholm, Holger Torger. Göteborg, Handelstryckeriet, 1954] 199 p. illus., ports. 25cm.

1. Borglund, Erland, 1894- 2. Industrial arts--Sweden. 3. Sloyd--Sweden. 4. Occupational therapy--Sweden. I. Andersson. Josef, ed. t. 1954.
NN ** X 3.55 d/e OC, 1b, I PC, 1, 2, 3, 4, I SL A, 3, I ST, 2t, 3t, I (Z1, LC1, X1)

ZDC

Till Gustaf Aulén, 19 15/5 39. [Stockholm: Svenska kyrkans diakonistyrelses bokförlag, 1939] 413 p. 24½cm.

CONTENTS.—Eidem, Erling. Cantate Domino.—Bohlin, Torsten. Den kristna ångern.—Boström, Folke. Om "förandringarna" i troslärorna.—Briem, Efraim. Till omvändelsens psykologi.—Brilioth, Yngve. Birgitta som religiös personlighet.—Bring, Ragnar. Kring uppgörelsen mellan Erasmus och Luther.—Cullberg, John. Kyrkan och teologien.—Fridrichsen, Anton. Människosonen och Israel.—Holmquist, Hjalmar. Från regeringsformen till Rosenius.—Holmström, Folke. Guds rike och historiens värld.—Johansson, Axel. Anteckningar till Waldenströms teologi.—Josefson, Ruben. Andreas Knös om Voltaire och encyklopedisterna.—Kjöllerström, Sven. Laurentius Petris De officiis.—Lindblom, Joh. I vilken mening bör termen "Guds rike"

(Continued)

Festschrift.

N. Y. P. L. July 29, 1940

Till Gustaf Aulén... (Card 2)

brukas inom teologien?—Lindroth, H. A. Till frågan om uppenbarelse och historia.—Ljunggren, Gustaf. Luther och barndopet.—Newman, Ernst. Den "kritiska" perioden i svensk homiletik.—Nygren, Anders. Simul iustus et peccator hos Augustinus och Luther.—Odeberg, Hugo. Hellenism och judendom.—Olsson, Herbert. Det dubbla necessitas-begreppet i skolastiken och Luthers kritik därav.—Pleijel, Hilding. Luthers inställning til Confessio Augustana.—Rosén, Hugo. Gudsuppenbararen eller Frälsaren.—Sjöstrand, Arvid. Den ekumeniska rörelsens teologiska grundproblem.—Gierow, Krister. Bibliografi över biskop Gustaf Auléns skrifter, 1906–1938 (p. [364]–413).

54987B. 1. Aulén, Gustaf Emanuel Hildebrand, 1879- . 2. Aulén, Gustaf Emanuel Hildebrand, 1879- —Bibl. 3. Christianity—Essays and misc.
N. Y. P. L. July 29, 1940

SST

Till Gustaf Carne på femtioårsdagen den 21 oktober 1938 med hyllning och lyckönskan. [Malmö: Lundgrens söners boktr., 1938] 120 p. incl. tables. front. (port.), illus. (facsims.), col'd plates. 27½cm.

CONTENTS.—Bengtsson, Arvid. Stilblommor.—Bergquist, Sixten. Metod och material i språkkurserna.—Bergström, Carl. Latinet som skolämne.—Björkheden, Filip. Sveriges jordbruk under det sista halvseklet.—Cromnow, Einar. Kvalitetsmärke för elektriska installationer.—Ehlefors, Gunnar. "Fel av annat slag."—Gaddén, Gunnar. Gammal och ny kritik av affärsspråket.—Hanström, Bertil. Resa till Anholt.—Kökeritz, Helge. Stenografipedagogiska rön.—Lundmark, Knut. Stjärnhimlens anblick.—Noreen, Erik. Jöns Budde och den svenska Bibeln.—Norlind, Wilhelm. Om felkate-

(Continued)

N. Y. P. L. November 18, 1940

Till Gustaf Carne... (Card 2)

gorier i latinska översättningsuppgifter.—Ohlsson, Alfr.—Återblick på tillkomsten av Hermodshuset.—Rodenstam, Sten. Hermods, folkets eget lyceum.—Runquist, C. G. Den Stora pyramiden och dess talmystik.—Thornberg, Marta. Hermodsannonsen förr och nu.—Welander, Viktor. Dialektbenämningar på arbetsvagnen och dess delar.

74010B. 1. Schools, Correspondence—Sweden—Malmö. 2. Carne, Gustaf, 1888-
N. Y. P. L. November 18, 1940

E-12
4151

TILL Per Ahlberg världsspråkstankens svenske banbrytare på femtioårsdagen den 21 November 1914. A Per Ahlberg la sueda pioniro dil mondolinguala ideo en lua 50: a aniversario la 21. Novembro 1914. Stockholm. A.-B. Sandbergs bokhandel [1914] 143 p. port. 25cm.

Text mostly in Ido or Swedish.
Small paper edition.

1. Ahlberg, P. 2. Ido--Books in. Mrs. Dave H. Morris collection
NN R 6. 66 r/ OC PC, 1, 2 SL (LC1, X1, Z2)

IVE

TINGLEY, DONALD FRED, 1922- , ed.
Essays in Illinois history, in honor of Glenn Huron Seymour. Carbondale, Published for Eastern Illinois university by Southern Illinois university press [1968] xi, 167 p. 23cm.

Bibliography included in "Notes," p. 135-157.
CONTENTS.--Anti-intellectualism on the Illinois frontier, by D.F. Tingley.--Lincoln's particular freind, by L.M. Hamand.--John P. Altgeld, promoter of higher education in Illinois, by

(Continued)

NN R 7.68 l/ OC, I, Ib+ PC, 1, I SL AH, 1, I (LC1, X1, Z1) [I]

TINGLEY, DONALD FRED, 1922- , ed. Essays in Illinois history... (Card 2)

N. Thorburn.--Urban immigrant lawmakers and progressive reform in Illinois, by J.D. Buenker.--John H. Walker, labor leader from Illinois, by J.H. Keiser.--Harold Ickes and Hiram Johnson in the presidential primary of 1924, by R.E. Hennings.--Unemployment in Illinois during the Great Depression, by D.J. Maurer.

1. Illinois--Hist.--Addresses, essays, lectures. I. Seymour, Glenn Huron, 1901-

---

TIRYAKIAN, EDWARD A., ed. Sociological theory... (Card 3)

1. Sorokin, Pitirim Aleksandrovich, 1889- 2. Sociology--Addresses, essays, lectures.

TAH

TIROLER Wirtschaft in Vergangenheit und Gegenwart; Festgabe zur 100- Jahrfeier der Tiroler Handelskammer... Innsbruck, Universitäts-Verlag Wagner, 1951. 3 v. illus., ports., fold. maps. 25cm. (Schlern-Schriften. 77-79)

Includes bibliographies.

CONTENTS. —Bd. 1. Beiträge zur Wirtschafts- und Sozialgeschichte Tirols, geleitet von H. Gerhardinger und F. Huter. —Bd. 2. Kammergeschichte, geleitet von H. Gerhardinger, F. Egert und F. Huter. —Bd. 3. Die gewerbliche Wirtschaft in Tirol, Tatsachen und Probleme, (Continued)

NN** X 6.54 OCs, IIs, IIIs, (OS)Is PCs, Is, Is, IIs, IIIs, IV, LCIs, XIs) IV, V, VIIbo (OD)VIIs (ED)VIIs V, VIs SLs Es, Is (U1, Z1s,

---

*MGA

TISCHLER, HANS, ed.
Essays in musicology; a birthday offering for Willi Apel. [Bloomington] School of music, Indiana university [1968] v,191 p. music. 25cm.

Articles in English, German or French.
Includes bibliographies.

1. Essays. 2. Music—Essays. 3. Apel, Willi, 1893-
NNR 7.68 e/OC PC,2,3 SL MU,1,3 (LC1,X1,Z1)

TIROLER Wirtschaft in Vergangenheit und Gegenwart... (Card 2)

von A. Günther.

1. Economic history—Austria—Tyrol. I. Series. II. Gerhardinger, Hermann, comp. III. Huter, Franz, comp. IV. Egert, Franz, comp. V. Günther, Adolf, 1881- comp. VI. Tyrol. Kammer für Handel, Gewerbe und Industrie, Innsbruck. VII. Egert, Franz. t. 1951.

Copy only words underlined & classmark-- *QVA

Tlustý, Vojtěch.
Dialektické rozpory a jejich zákonitosti; studie z marxistické filosofie. Prof. L. Svobodovi k šedesátinám. Praha, Universita Karlova, 1962.

163 p. 25 cm. (Universita karlova, Prague. Acta Universitatis Carolinae. Philosophica et historica. Monographia. 1)

"1. vydání."

(Continued)

NN*R 1.65 g/k OC(Ib*) (OS)I PC, 1, 2, 3, I E, 1 S, 1, 2, 3, I (LC1, X1, Z1)

2

E-12
1678

Tiryakian, Edward A *ed*
Sociological theory, values, and sociocultural change; essays in honor of Pitirim A. Sorokin. [New York] Free Press of Glencoe [1963]
xv, 302 p. port. 24 cm.
Includes bibliographical references.
CONTENTS.—Preface, by E. A. Tiryakian.—Lessons from Sorokin, by A. K. Davis.—Some problems for a unified theory of human nature, by M. J. Levy, Jr.—Christianity and modern industrial society, by T. Parsons.—Sociological dilemmas: five paradoxes of institutionalization, by T. F. O'Dea.—Sociological ambivalence, by R. K. Merton

(Continued)

NN* R 11.64 g/ OC PC, 1, 2 SL E, 1, 2 (LC1, X1, Z1)

TLUSTÝ, VOJTĚCH. Dialektické rozpory a jejich zákonitosti... (Card 2)

Tables of contents and summaries in Russian and German.
Bibliographical footnotes.

1. Materialism, Dialectical or historical. 2. Contradiction (Logic). 3. Svoboda, Ludvík. I. Series.

TIRYAKIAN, EDWARD A., ed. Sociological theory... (Card 2)

and E. Barber.—Is American business becoming professionalized? Analysis of a social ideology, by B. Barber.—Conditions for the realization of values remote in time, by W. Firey.—The temporal structure of organizations, by W. E. Moore.—Social structure and the multiplicity of times, by G. Gurvitch.—Social change and social systems, by C. P. Loomis.—Some reflections on the nature of cultural integration and change, by F. R. Kluckhohn.—Convergence of the major human family systems during the space age, by C. C. Zimmerman.—Don Luigi Sturzo's sociological theory, by N. S. Timasheff.—Disjunctive processes in an academic milieu, by L. Wilson.—Bibliography of Pitirim A. Sorokin (p. 295-302)

(Continued)

D-11
9938

TO Dr. Albert Schweitzer; a festschrift commemorating his 80th birthday from a few of his friends. Evanston, Ill., 1955. 178 p. 22cm.
Edited by H.A. Jack.
CONTENTS. --Salutations: Dr. Schweitzer's one answer to the problem of the many, by J.S. Bixler. A realist of the Spirit, by M. Buber. The belief of Schweitzer in the power of the Spirit, by F. Buri. To Albert Schweitzer, by A. Chakravarty. An elephant in ebony, by C.C. Chesterman. The point about Schweitzer, by N. Cousins. Out of inner necessity, by A. Einstein. Philosophical learning and (Continued)

NN * R 10.59 m/OC, I PC, 1, I SL (LC1, X1) (Z1)

TO Dr. Albert Schweitzer... (Card 2)

medical science, by N. A. Gillespie. Memories and meditations: 1935-55, by L. Goldschmid. The pattern of prestige by G. Heard. Dear Albert Schweitzer, by T. Heuss. "The lion who laughs"--and weeps, by A. A. Hunter. Lieber Bruder Albert! By L. Mayer. Albert Schweitzer: reform, revolution, regeneration! by G. B. Oxnam. For whom religion is a reality, by S. Radhakrishnan. Albert Schweitzer, by M. Ratter. Reverence for life: an interpretation, by G. Seaver. Albert Schweitzer, humanitarian, by E. Skillings. An emissary of Western civilization, by

(Continued)

TO Dr. Albert Schweitzer... (Card 3)

A. E. Stevenson. The answer of Albert Schweitzer to the search for the historical Jesus, by M. Werner. On the hill of Adalinanongo, by A Wildikann. Homage, by P. Casals and J. Nehru. --Recent writings: The problem of ethics in the evolution of human thought. The H-bomb. Peace. --Bibliography (p. 161-174)--A chronological biography.

1. Schweitzer, Albert, 1875- . I. Jack, Homer Alexander, ed.

---

*KF
1946

To Doctor R. Essays here collected and published in honor of the seventieth birthday of Dr. A.S.W.R Philadelphia, 1946. 301 p. 24½cm.

D-16
6279

Toomla, Jaan, *ed.*

Vaateid Vilde elusse; lühiuurimusi Eduard Vilde 100. aasta sünnipäeva puhul. Tallinn, Kirjastus "Eesti Raamat," 1965.

303, [1] p. 21 cm.

"Eduard Vilde teoste ja väljaannete register": p. 301-[304] Bibliographical footnotes.

1. Vilde, Eduard. 2. Vilde, Eduard--Bibl.

NN * R 1.69 1/4 OC PC, 1, 2 SL (LC1, X1, Z1)

D-17
2674

TOPSÖE-JENSEN, HELGE GOTTLIEB, 1896-

H.C. Andersen og andre studier. Utg. som festskrift i anledning af forfatterens halvfjerdsaarsdag 15. december 1966. Odense, Odense bys museer, 1966. 436 p. 23cm. (Fynske studier. vol. 6)

Bibliographical references included in "Henvisninger og noter", p.[401]-420.

1. Andersen, Hans Christian, 1805-1875. I. Series.

NN 4.67 1/A OC (OS)I PC,1,I (A)I (G)I (LC1,X1,Z1)

C-14
3737

Tora Dahl, 9/6 1966. Stockholm, Tiden, 1966.

118, (1) p. illus. 20cm.

"Denna bok har tryckts i en numrerad bibliofilupplaga om 300 exemplar. Detta exemplar har nummer 191."

CONTENTS.—Villan, av E. Asklund.—Tack, av K. och T. Aurell.—Toras ögon, av A. Bergstrand.—Dikt för att finna en riktning, av L. Bäckström.—Uppvaknandets rop, av S. Carlson.—Albumblad, av J. Edfelt.—Dröm med svarta och vita fåglar, av M. Ekström.—Latona, av R. Enckell.—Liten Torabild, av J. Fridegård.—Böckernas öden, av

(Continued)

NN * R 4.71 b/4 OC, I PC, 1, I SL (LC1, X1, Z1)

2.

TORA DAHL, 9/6 1966. (Card 2)

F. Fridell.—Kräftor, av C.-E. af Geijerstam.—Makt, myt och skapelsesaga, av G. Gunnarson.—Böckerna om Gunborg, av R. Halldén.—Min barndoms jular, av I. Hedenius.—Översättning av Chaim Nachman Bialik: Det skall ske då I finnen, av V. Heyman.—Översättning av en dikt av Nelly Sachs, av O. Lagercrantz.—Dagen väntar, av E. Lindstedt.—Stycken, av A. Lundkvist.—Kårar, av H. Martinson.—Pojken från Jante, av C.-E. Nordberg.—Mysteriet finns i det synliga, av B. Runeborg.—En afton på Parkvägen 10, av K. Vennberg.—Till Tora, av M. Wine.

1. Swedish literature--Collections. I. Dahl, Tora, 1886-.

TO

Toronto University.

Essays in transportation in honour of W. T. Jackman, edited by H. A. Innis, with a foreword by the Hon. and Rev. H. J. Cody. Toronto, Can., The University of Toronto press, 1941.

TB(Political) viii p., 1 l., 165 p., 1 l. illus. (map) diagr. 23½cm. [Political economy series, no. 11]

CONTENTS.—Introduction, by Alexander Brady.—Nationalism and internationalism on Canadian waterways, by G. P. de T. Glazebrook.—Some comparisons in Canadian and American railway finance, by H. E. Dougall.—Principal international and interterritorial class-rate structures of North America, by F. L. Barton.—Some basic problems in the

(Continued on next card)

42-14169

[6]

Fest.

Toronto University. Essays in transportation in honour of W. T. Jackman ... 1941. (Card 2)

CONTENTS—Continued.

public regulation of transportation, by G. L. Wilson.—Transportation and Canadian agriculture, by W. M. Drummond.—Some problems of urban transportation, by N. D. Wilson.—An aspect of the British railways act, 1921, by W. G. Scott.—Recent developments in balance of international payments statistics, by Herbert Marshall.—Publications of W. T. Jackman (p. 159-162)—Index.

1. Jackman, William T., 1871- 2. Transportation—Addresses, essays, lectures. I. Innis, Harold Adams, 1894- ed.

42-14169

Library of Congress HE152.T6

[6] 385.04

AN
(Bohlin, T.)

Torsten Bohlin, en minnes- och vänbok. 2. uppl. Stockholm, Svenska kyrkans diakonistyrelses bokförlag [1951] 382 p. illus. 20cm.

"Redigerad av Gert Borgenstierna, Nils Karlström [och] Gustaf Risberg."

Festschrift

576573B. 1. Bohlin, Torsten Bernhard, 1889-1950. I. Borgenstierna, Gert, 1911- , ed.

N. Y. P. L. June 14, 1951

YAR

Totuutta etsimässä; tutkielmia henkitieteiden alalta. Toimittaneet Urpo Harva ₍ja₎ Aarre Tuompo. Porvoo, Helsinki, W. Söderström ₍1951₎ 257 p. illus. 22cm.

"Professori J. E. Salomaalle hänen 60-vuotispäivänään 19. IV. 1951 omistavat tämän juhlajulkaisun oppilaina ja ystävinä."
Bibliographies included.

1. Salomaa, Jalmar Edvard, 1891- . 2. Philosophy, 1901- . I. Harva, Urpo, ed. II. Tuompo, Aarre, ed.
NN 1.53 OC, I, II PC, 1, 2, I, II SL (LC1, X1, Z1)

---

*QR

Towarzystwo geograficzne we Lwowie.
Zbiór prac poświęcony przez Towarzystwo geograficzne we Lwowie Eugenjuszowi Romerowi w 40-lecie jego twórczości naukowej. Redaktor H. Arctowski. Lwów ₍Nakładem Tow. geograficznego we Lwowie₎ 1934. xxxii, 643 p. incl. tables. front. (port.), illus. (incl. charts), maps, pl. 25½cm.

Contributions in Czech, English, French, German, Italian, or Polish.
Bibliographies included.

830173A. 1. Geography—Addresses, essays, lectures. 2. Geology—Addresses, essays, lectures. 3. Ethnology—Essays and misc. 4. Romer, Eugenjusz, 1871- . I. Arctowski, Henryk, 1871- , ed. II. Title.
N. Y. P. L. July 10, 1936

---

*QOB

Towarzystwo przyjaciół nauki i sztuki w Gdańsku.
Krzysztof Celestyn Mrongowjusz, 1764–1855; księga pamiątkowa pod redakcją dra Władysława Pniewskiego. Gdańsk: Towarzystwo przyjaciół nauki i sztuki w Gdańsku, 1933. 378 p. illus. (facsims.), pl., port. 24cm.

"Bibljografja wydawnictw i rękopisów Mrongowjusza," p. 77–87; "Źródła," p. 87–93.
CONTENTS.—Pniewski, Władysław. Krzysztof Celestyn Mrongowjusz. Żywot i dzieła. Korespondencja Mrongowjusza.—Słoński, Stanisław. Mrongowjusz jako gramatyk.—Michejda, Karol. Postyla Mrongowjusza.—Kawecka, Alodja. Pieśnioksiąg Mrongowjusza.—Wojtkowski, Andrzej. Gustaw Gizewjusz i jego listy do Józefa Łukaszewicza,

(Continued)

N. Y. P. L. August 27, 1937

Towarzystwo przyjaciół nauki i sztuki w Gdańsku. Krzysztof Celestyn Mrongowjusz... (Card 2)

Andrzeja Niegolewskiego i Edwarda Raczyńskiego.—Mocarski, Zygmunt. Nieznany exlibris Gizewjusza.—Kantak, Kamil. Starania bernardynów polskich o odzyskanie konwentu (gimnazjum) gdańskiego.— Mańkowski, Alfons. Bibljografja polskich druków gdańskich od r. 1800 do r. 1918.

895882A. 1. Mrongovius, Krzysztof Celestyn, 1764–1855. 2. Polish language. I. Pniewski, Władysław, ed. II. Title.
N. Y. P. L. August 27, 1937

TIK

Tractatus tributarii, opstellen op belastinggebied aangeboden aan Prof. Dr. P. J. A. Adriani, ter gelegenheid van zijn afscheid als hoogleraar aan de Universiteit van Amsterdam. Haarlem, H. D. Tjeenk Willink, 1949. ix,251 p. port. 24cm.

Contents.—Belastingen als rechtsbegrip, door E. M. Meijers.—Tributum, door J. C. van Oven.—Voorlopers van de draagkracht-heffingen, door M. J. H. Smeets.—De ontwikkeling van de Belgische inkomstenbelasting in de XIXe en XXe eeuw, door

(Continued)

NN R X 10.53 OC PC, 1,2 SL E,1,2 (Z1,LC1, X1)

Tractatus tributarii... (Card 2)

J. van Houtte.—Lo sviluppo dell'imposta sul reddito in Italia, del B. Griziotti (met Nederlandse vertaling van J. P. Croin).—Le développement de l'impôt sur le revenu en France, de 1914 à 1918, par L. Trotabas.—Notariaat en belastingrecht, door A. Pitlo.—De functie van de gemeente in het huidige staatsbestel, gezien in het licht van de financiële verhouding tussen rijk en gemeenten, door M. J. Prinsen.—Enkele opmerkingen over de fiscale betekenis van de internationale verhouding tussen moeder- en

(Continued)

Tractatus tributarii... (Card 3)

dochtermaatschappijen, door J. H. T. Schipper.—Die Rechtsprechung des schweizerischen Bundesgerichts betreffend Doppelbesteuerung und ihre Bedeutung für das internationale Steuerrecht, von E. Blumenstein.—Internationale vraagstukken bij de heffing van belastingen wegens nalatenschappen, door H. Schuttevaer.—De invloed van de belastingsheffing op het internationale kapitaalverkeer, door B. Schendstok.—Publicaties van Prof. Dr P. J. A. Adriani, door A. van Keulen c.-n., J. W. Kal en J. van Hoorn, jr. (p. 224-251)

1. Taxation. 2. Adriani, P J A

D-16
7278

TRADE, growth, and the balance of payments; essays in honor of Gottfried Haberler, by Robert E. Baldwin [and others] Chicago, Rand McNally, 1965. viii,267 p. diagrs. 23cm.

Bibliographical footnotes.
CONTENTS.--Optimal trade intervention in the presence of domestic distortions, by H. G. Johnson.--Equalization by trade of the interest rate along with the real wage, by P. A.

(Continued)

NN R 6.66 1/Z OC, I PC, 1, 2,3, I SL E, 1, 2, 3, I (LC1, X1, Z1)

3
A

TRADE, growth, and the balance of payments... (Card 2)

Samuelson.--On the equivalence of tariffs and quotas, by J. Bhagwati.--Tariff-cutting techniques in the Kennedy Round, by R.E. Baldwin.--Some aspects of policies for freer trade, by B. Ohlin.--"Vent for surplus" models of trade and growth, by R.E. Caves.--International, national, regional, and local industries, by J. Tinbergen.--The multiplier if imports are for investments, by W.F. Stolper.--Trade, speculation, and the forward exchange rate, by P.B. Kenen.--

(Continued)

B

TRADE, growth, and the balance of payments... (Card 3)

Monetary stability as a precondition for economic integration, by R. Kamitz.--Adjustment, compensatory correction, and financing of imbalances in international payments, by F. Machlup.--Interest rates and the balance of payments: an analysis of the Swiss experience, by J. Niehans.--Germany's persistent balance-of-payments disequilibrium, by C.P. Kindleberger.--Competition and growth: the lesson of the United States balance of payments, by E. Sohmen.

1. Haberler, Gottfried, 1900- 2. Commerce, Foreign. 1945- . 3. Balance of payments. I. Baldwin, Robert E.

C

D-12
2390

TRADISJON og fornyelse; festskrift til A.H. Winsnes på syttiårsdagen, 25. okt. 1959. Oslo, Aschehoug, 1959. xv, 307 p. port. 22cm.

CONTENTS.—Platons øyeblikks-filosofi eller Dialogen Parmenides' 3. hypotese, av E.A. Wyller.—Gresk og israelittisk historiesyn, av T. Roman.—Lukrets, dikter og filosof, av E. Skard.—Amor og Psyche—elskoven og sjelen, av H.P. L'Orange.—Augustins liv og laere, av P. Dietrichson.—Thomas Aquinas' syn pa naturvitenskapene, av (Continued)

NN R 2.60 g/P OC PC, 1, 2 SL (LC1, X1, Z1) [I]

TRADISJON og fornyelse... (Card 2)

D. Føllesdal.—Mester Eckehart, av Aa. Brynildsen.—Renessanse-humanistene og "humanitas," av P. Svendsen.—Striden mellom de gamle og de nye, av A. Aarnes.—Harmonitanken i Schillers filosofiske avhandlinger, av O. Koppang.—Grunntrekk i Wilhelm von Humboldts sprogfilosofi av I. Dal.—Noen bemerkninger til Dostojevskijs Storinkvisitoren, av E. Krag.—Speculum og analogi i Peer Gynt, av M. Blekastad.—Om pakt-begrepet i "Kristin Lavransdatter," av D. Haakonsen.—Subjektivitet og sanning, av H. Skjervheim.—Refleksjoner om helhetssyn, sannhet og kunnskap, av A. Næss.—I tid og rum, av A. Øverland.
1. Winsnes, Andreas Hofgaard, 1889- . 2. Philosophy--Addresses, essays, lectures.

* PXS

TRAMER, HANS, ed.
In zwei Welten; Siegfried Moses zum fünfundsiebzigsten Geburtstag. Tel-Aviv, Verlag Bitaon, 1962. 650 p.; 22 p. port. 25cm.

Added t.p. in Hebrew.
Contributions mainly in German with an article in English and a section in Hebrew.
Issued by Irgun olej merkas Europa.
(Continued)

NN R 5.63 p/B OC, II (OS)I PC, 1, 3, I, II SL J, 2, 3, I, II (LC1, X1, Z1) 2

TRAMER, HANS, ed. In zwei Welten... (Card 2)

Bibliographical footnotes.

1. Jews in Germany--Hist.--Addresses, essays, lectures. 2. Germany--Hist.--Addresses, essays, lectures. 3. Moses, Siegfried, 1887- I. Irgun olej merkas Europa II. Title.

*PBS

TRAMER, HANS, ed.
Robert Weltsch zum 70. Geburtstag, 20. Juni 1961, von seinen Freunden [hrsg. von Hans Tramer und Kurt Loewenstein. Tel-Aviv, Irgun Olej merkas Europa, Verlag Bitaon, 1961] 219 p. illus., ports. 25cm.

Bibliographical footnotes.
CONTENTS.--Die Entwicklungslehre im Gedankengebäude von Rav Kook, von H. Bergman.--Motive in der Politik, von F. Weltsch.--Von der Zionssehnsucht zum politischen Zionismus, von A. Bein.--Unverschuldete (Continued)

NN R 2.64 f/ OC, I (OS)II PC, 1, 2, I, II SL J, 1, 3, I, II (LC1, X1, Z1) [I] 3

TRAMER, HANS, ed. Robert Weltsch zum 70. (Card 2)

Verschollenheit und unverdienter Ruhm, von D. Baumgardt.--Vom Geschichtswert der Predigt, von K. Wilhelm--Historiker und Publizist, von K. Loewenstein.--Über die Grundlagen der Demokratie, von M. Keren.--Rückblick auf eine gemeinsame Jugend, von H. Kohn.--Auf dem Jenaer Delegiertentag, von K. Blumenfeld.--Prag, Jerusalem, London, von G. Schocken.--Awodat-am, von S. Adler-Rudel.--Wertungen und Umwertungen, von E.G. Reichmann.--Die Dreivölkerstadt Prag, von (Continued)

TRAMER, HANS, ed. Robert Weltsch zum 70. (Card 3)

H. Tramer.--Funktion des Geistes in der Geschichte, von M. Buber.--Zwei Perioden, von S. Moses.--In Sorge um die kostbarste Erbschaft, von E. Kahler.--Skepsis aus Glauben, von E. Simon.--Der noble Gegner, von A. Wiener.--Abwägend und überlegen, von F.S. Brodnitz.--Observations on the family, by M. Gruenewald.

1. Weltsch, Robert. 2. Essays, Jewish, in German--Collections. 3. Essays, in German--Collections. I. Loewenstein, Kurt, joint ed. II. Hitachduth olej Germania we olej Austria.

*PDA

TRANSLATING & understanding the Old Testament; essays in honor of Herbert Gordon May. Edited by Harry Thomas Frank and William L. Reed. Nashville [Tenn.] Abingdon Press [1970] 351 p. illus. 25cm.

Includes bibliographical references.
CONTENTS.--The Standard Bible Committee, by L.A. Weigle.--The terminology of adversity in Jeremiah, by J. Mullenburg.--The (Continued)

NN*S 2.71 e/C OC, I, II, III SL J, 1, 2, I, II, III (LC1, X1, Z1) PC, 1, 2, I, II, III 3

TRANSLATING & understanding the Old Testament... (Card 2)

participle of the immediate future and other matters pertaining to correct translation of the Old Testament, by W.F. Stinespring.--Some remarks concerning and suggested by Jeremiah 43: 1-7, by P.A.H. de Boer.--The literary category of the Book of Jonah, by M. Burrows.--The settlement of the Israelites in Southern Palestine and the origins of the Tribe of Judah, by R. de Vaux.--Israel: Amphictyony: 'AM; KĀHĀL; EDĀH, by G.W. Anderson.--Were there an ancient historical credo in Israel and an independent Sinai tradition? By J.P. Hyatt.--The Arabian genealogies in the Book of Genesis, by (Continued)

TRANSLATING & understanding the Old Testament... (Card 3)

F. V. Winnett.--Midianite donkey caravans, by W. F. Albright.--Nationalism-universalism and internationalism in ancient Israel, by H.M. Orlinsky.--The significance of cosmology in the ancient Near East, by W. Harrelson.--The geography of monotheism, by D. Baly.--Historical knowledge and revelation, by G. E. Wright.--Form and content: a hermeneutical application, by R. L. Hicks.--Incense altars, by N. Glueck.
1. Bible. O.T.--Essays and misc. 2. May, Herbert Gordon, 1904---Bibl. I. Frank, Harry Thomas, ed. II. Reed, William LaForest, 1912- , ed. III. May, Herbert Gordon, 1904- .

D-18
7488

Transzendenz als Erfahrung. Beitrag und Widerhall. Festschrift zum 70. Geburtstag von Graf Dürckheim. (Hrsg. von Maria Hippius) Weilheim/Obb., Barth (1966)

513 p. 23 cm.

Bibliography: p. 506-509.

(Continued)

NN R 3.69 v/a OC, I, IIb PC, 1, 2, 3, I SL (LC1, X1, Z1) 2

TRANSZENDENZ als Erfahrung. (Card 2)

1. Transcendentalism. 2. Psychology--Addresses, essays, lectures. 3. Dürckheim-Montmartin, Karl Friedrich, Graf von, 1896- . I. Hippius, Maria Theresia Winterer, ed. II. Hippius, Maria Theresia Winterer.

D-15
8513

TREVOR ROPER, HUGH REDWALD, ed.
Essays in British history, presented to Sir Keith Feiling; with a foreword by Lord David Cecil. London, Macmillan; New York, St. Martin's press, 1964. x, 305 p. port., maps. 23cm.

Includes bibliographies.

CONTENTS.--Wansdyke and the origin of Wessex, by J. N. L. Myres.--Before Wolsey, by W. A. Pantin.--Thomas Brouns, bishop

(Continued)

NN R 3.65 c/B OC PC, 1, 2 SL (LC1, X1, Z1) [I] 2

TREVOR ROPER, HUGH REDWALD, ed. Essays in British history... (Card 2)

of Norwich, 1436-45, by E. F. Jacob.--The fast sermons of the Long Parliament, by H. R. Trevor-Roper.--Arthur Onslow and party politics, by J. Steven Watson.--The imperial machinery of the younger Pitt, by A. F. McC. Madden.--Lord Brougham and the conservatives, by E. G. Collieu.--The rise of Disraeli, by R. Blake.--The Prince Consort and ministerial politics 1856-9, by C. H. Stuart.--The White mutiny, by M. Maclagan.--A bibliography of the writings of Sir Keith Feiling (p. 303-305)

1. Feiling, Sir Keith Grahame, 1884- 2. Great Britain--Hist.--Addresses, essays, lectures.

F-10
8315

A TRIBUTE to Basil O'Connor on the occasion of his seventieth birthday. Dr. Milton S. Eisenhower, Miss Helen Hayes [and] Brigadier General David Sarnoff, co-charimen. The Waldorf-Astoria, New York City, January 11th, 1962. [New York City? 1962] 47 p. ports. 26cm.

1. O'Connor, Basil, 1892- . I. Eisenhower, Milton Stover.

NN R 12.63 j/ OC, I PC, 1, I SL (LC1, X1, Z1)

AN
+
(Mangkoe Nagoro VII)

HET triwindoe-gedenkboek Mangkoe Nagoro VII. Soerakarta, Uitgegeven vanwege het Comité voor het triwindoe-gedenkboek, 1939. xx, 290 p. illus. (part col.) 32cm.

Text in Balinese, Ductch, English, French, German, Javanese or Malay.

1. Mangkoe Nagoro VII. 2. Java—Civilization. I. Comité voor het triwindoe-gedenkboek Mangkoe Nagoro VII.

NN ** R 4.54 OC, Ib (OS) I, Ib PC, 1, 2, I SL O, 1, 2, I (LC1, Z1, X1)

K-10
3138
Heft 11

TROLL, CARL, 1899-
Ökologische Landschaftsforschung und vergleichende Hochgebirgsforschung. Wiesbaden, F. Steiner [1966] 366 p. illus., plates, maps (part col.) 24cm. (Erdkundliches Wissen; Schriftenfolge für Forschung und Praxis, Heft 11)

Special t. p.: Carl Troll, Ausgewählte Beiträge I, zusammengestellt und gewidmet Carl Troll zum 65. Geburtstag von seinen

(Continued)

NN 10.66 r/ OC (OS)I PC, 1, 2, I (LC1, X1, Z1) 2

TROLL, CARL, 1899- Ökologische Landschaftsforschung und vergleichende Hochgebirgsforschung. (Card 2)

Kollegen und Mitarbeitern.
Bibliographical footnotes.

1. Mountains. 2. Botany--Geographical distribution. I. Series.

D-12
4511

Tromsø, Norway. Tromsø museum.
Generalregister over de av Tromsø museum 1872–1947 utgitte avhandlinger. Trondheim, J. Christiansens boktr., 1948. 30 p. 23cm.

At head of title: Tillegg til Tromsø museums 75 års-beretning.
Indexes chiefly its Aarshefter and Skrifter.

I. Tromsø, Norway. Tromsø museum. Skrifter. (Indexes). II. Tromsø, Norway. Tromsø museum. Tromsø museums aarshefter. (Indexes).

NN*R 4.61 OS, I, II PC, I, II SL (LC1, X1, Z1)

IKG
(Conn.:10th inf.)

TRUMBULL, HENRY CLAY, 1830-1903.
The knightly soldier: a biography of Major Henry Ward Camp, tenth Conn. vols. 6.ed., rev. Boston, Noyes, Holmes, 1871. 335, 14 p. illus., port. 20cm.

1. Camp, Henry Ward, 1839-1864. 2. Connecticut infantry, 10th regt., 1861-1865. 3. United States--Hist.--Civil war--Personal narratives. 4. United States--Hist.--Civil war--Military--Regt. hist.--Conn. inf.--10th. i. Subs. for main entry, 1830-1930.

NN R 7.66 a/ OCs PCs, 1s, 2s, 3s, 4 SLs AHs, 1s, 2s, 3s, 4 (LC1s, X1s, Z1s, [i])

L-10
1965

TUCUMÁN, Argentine Republic (City). UNIVERSIDAD. Filosofía y letras, Facultad de.
Estudios de historia de la filosofía en homenaje al profesor Rodolfo Mondolfo con motivo del quincuagesimo aniversario de su doctorado. [Tucumán] 1957. 1 v. 24cm.

Fasc. 1.
Bibliographical footnotes.
1. Philosophy--Addresses, essays, lectures. 2. Mondolfo, Rodolfo, 1877- . I. Title.
NN 9.58 e/P (OC)I OS PC, 1, 2, I SL (LC1, X1, Z1, Y1) [I]

BWW
+

Turin. Università.
Studi pubblicati dalla Regia università di Torino nel IV centenario della nascità di Emanuele Filiberto. 8 luglio 1928. Torino: Villarboito F. & figli, 1928. viii, 498 p. illus. (incl. facsims.), ports. sq. 4°.

Bibliographical footnotes.
Contents: Prefazione del rettore. PIVANO, S. Emanuele Filiberto e le Università di Mondovì e di Torino. CHIAUDANO, M. I lettori dell'Università di Torino ai tempi di Emanuele Filiberto. GIACOSA, P. La medicina in Piemonte nel secolo XVI. VIDARI, G. La fondazione di Collegi dei Gesuiti negli stati del duca Emanuele Filiberto. VENTURI, L. Emanuele Filiberto e l'arte figurativa. PEANO, G. Gio. Francesco Peve-

(Continued)

N. Y. P. L. August 14, 1930

E-10
988

Tübingen. Universität.
Deutscher Osten und slawischer Westen, Tübinger Vorträge hrsg. von Hans Rothfels und Werner Markert. [Hermann Aubin zum 70. Geburtstage, 23. Dezember 1955] Tübingen, J. C. B. Mohr, 1955. 127 p. 24cm. (Tübinger Studien zur Geschichte und Politik. nr. 4)

Includes bibliographies.
CONTENTS.—Zur Einführung, Eröffnungsansprache von H. Rothfels.—Das erste Scheitern des Nationalstaats in Ost-Mittel-Europa 1848/49, von H. Rothfels.—Volkstumsprobleme der deutschen Sprachinseln in Ost- und Südosteuropa, von H. Moser.—Die germanisch-slavischen Beziehungen im Lichte der Sprachwissen-
(Continued)

NN**X 7.57 (OC)I,II,IV OS,III PC,1,2,I,II,III,IV SL (LC1,X1,Z1,Y1)

Turin. Università: Studi pubblicati dalla Regia università di Torino... (Card 2)

rone ed altri matematici piemontesi ai tempi di Emanuele Filiberto. MATTIROLO, O. L'opera del duca Emanuele Filiberto in favore della "Botanica" e della "Agricoltura." MASCARELLI, L. Chimica ed alchimia nei rapporti con Emanuele Filiberto. SEGRE, A. Emanuele Filiberto, agricoltura, industria, commercio, banca, miniere. RUFFINI, F. Matteo Gribaldi Mofa, Antonio Govea e lo studio generale di Mondovì. BERTONI, G. Margherita duchessa di Savoia e la poesia francese. STAMPINI, E. Monsregalensia et Taurinensia. CIAN, V. Le lettere e la coltura letteraria in Piemonte nell'età di Emanuele Filiberto. PATETTA, F. Di Niccolò Balbo prof. di diritto nella Università di Torino e del Memoriale al duca Emanuele Filiberto che gli è falsamente attribuito. TORRI, L. Quattro sonetti musicati per le nozze e in onore di Emanuele Filiberto e Mar-

(Continued)

N. Y. P. L. August 14, 1930

Tübingen. Universität. Deutscher Osten und slawischer Westen (Card 2)

schaft, von H. Wissemann.—Schlesischer Barock, von D. Frey.—Danzig—ein Kulturzentrum im deutschen Osten, von W. Drost.—Die deutsche Musik und der Osten, von W. Gerstenberg.—Der Osten zwischen Nationaldemokratie und Sowjetföderation, von W. Markert.—Agrargesellschaft und Industriegesellschaft in Ostmitteleuropa, von W. Conze.—Die Kirchen in den Ländern Ostmitteleuropas, von B. Stasiewski.—Ostmitteleuropa im deutschen Geschichtsbewusstsein, von E. Lemberg.
1. Germany, Eastern. 2. Aubin, Hermann, 1885- . I. Markert, Werner, 1905- , ed. II. Rothfels, Hans, 1891- , ed. III. Series.

IV. Title.

Turin. Università: Studi pubblicati dalla Regia università di Torino... (Card 3)

gherita di Francia. STAMPINI, E. Testo dei diplomi di laurea honoris causa conferiti alle LL. AA. RR. Emanuele Filiberto di Savoia duca di Aosta e Luigi Amedeo di Savoia duca degli Abruzzi.

475972A. 1. Emmanuel Philibert, duke of Savoy, 1528-1580. 2. Piedmont.
N. Y. P. L. August 14, 1930

E-11
6434

TÜBINGEN. Universität. Geographisches Institut.
Hermann von Wissmann-Festschrift; hrsg. von Adolf Leidlmair. Tübingen, Im Selbstverlag des Geographischen Instituts der Universität Tübingen, 1962. 384 p. illus., maps (1 fold.) 24cm.

Includes bibliographies.

1. Geography--Addresses, essays, lectures. 2. Wissmann, Hermann Sedan von, 1895- I. Leidlmair, Adolf, ed.
NN 2.63 p/(J) (OC)I OS PC, 1, 2, I SL (LC1, X1, Z1) [I]

AN
(Lister)

Turner, Arthur Logan, editor.
Joseph, Baron Lister, centenary volume, 1827-1927; edited for the Lister Centenary Committee of the British Medical Association, by A. Logan Turner... Edinburgh: Oliver and Boyd, 1927. xv, 182 p. front., illus. (facsim.), plates, ports. 8°.

Mr. Moth

347250A. 1. Lister, Joseph Lister, 1st baron, 1827-1912. 2. Antisepsis.
N. Y. P. L. February 17, 1928

* ZAN-T 1072
Film Reproduction
v. 1

Turin (City). Università. Istituto di scienze politiche.
Studi in memoria di Gioele Solari dei discepoli Felice Balbo [et al.] Torino, Edizioni Ramella, 1954. 534 p. port. 23cm. (ITS: Pubblicazioni. v. 1)

Film reproduction. Positive.
Bibliographical footnotes.

1. Solari, Gioele, 1872-1952. 2. Political science—Addresses, essays, lectures. I. Series.
NN R 12.63 OS,I PC,1,2,I E,1,2,I (UM1,LC1,X1,Z1)

* C p.v.2286

Turnverein Mannheim von 1846.
Festschrift zum 75jährigen Bestehen des Turnverein Mannheim von 1846, verfasst von Prof. K. Selzle. [Mannheim, 1921.] 48 p. incl. tables. illus. (incl. plan, ports.) 8°.

Festschrift

588721A. 1. Gymnastics—Assoc. and org.—Germany—Mannheim. I. Selzle, K.
N. Y. P. L. June 22, 1932

Copy only words underlined
& classmark— GMA

TURUN HISTORIALLINEN YHDISTYS, Turku, Finland.
Professori Einar W. Juvalle hänen 7.1.1952 täyttäessään 60 vuotta. [Turku, 1951] 597 p. illus., port., map. 22cm. (Turun historiallinen arkisto. [n:o] 11)

German summaries.
CONTENTS. —Aaltonen, E. Muutoksia maaseudun oloissa suuren murroksen ajoilta. —Ekko, P. O. Varsinais-Suomen kirkkojen symbolinen kuva-aines. —Haavio, M. Johannes Messeniuksen papereissa säilyneitä varhaishistoriamme aineksia. —Jaakkola, J. Suomen ensimmäinen piispa. —Jutikkala, E. Vuoden 1697 kansallisonnettomuus, sen tuhot ja väistämismahdollisuudet. —Juva, K. Piirteitä Suomen kansan lukuharrastuksesta 1820-

(Continued)

NN** R 9.57 c/b (OC)I OS OI PC, 1, 2, I (ZI, LC4, XI)

TURUN HISTORIALLINEN YHDISTYS, Turku, Finland.
Professori Einar W. Juvalle... (Card 2)

1850-luvuilla. —Juva, M. Valvojan ryhmän syntyhistoria. —Jäntere, K. Naantalin valtiopäiväedustus ajanjaksona 1719-1800. —Kaukoranta, T. Mitä olivat vanhat lukumiehet? —Korhonen, A. Hakkapeliittamajuri ilmiantajana. —Laurikkala, S. Perukirjan laatijoista Varsinais-Suomen maaseudulla 1700-luvulla. —Livola, U. Miten kansakoulu otettiin vastaan Varsinais-Suomessa. —Maliniemi, A. Elias Brenner kirjojen keräilijänä. —Mäntylä, R. A. Venäjän vallan alkupuolella ratkaistu kysymys Suomen luterilaisen kansalaisen oikeudesta mennä avioliittoon luterilaista uskoa tunnustamattoman kanssa. —Numminen, P. Cicero ja roomalainen elämäntyyli. —Oja, A. Virrentekijä ja kirkonrakentaja Kustaa Stenman. —Paasivirta, J. Kysymys Suomen autonomian oikeusperusteista (Erikoisesti silmällä pitäen J. V. Snellmanin ja J. Ph. Palménin kesken käytyä polemiikkia). —Perälä, T. Friedrich von Hardenbergin valtio-opilliset ajatukset. —Perälä, V. Kasvatusta ja herätystä. —Renvall, P. Piirteitä suomalaisen maaseudun

---

TURUN HISTORIALLINEN YHDISTYS, Turku, Finland.
Professori Einar W. Juvalle... (Card 3)

herläämisestä. —Rytkönen, A. "Lehtiä jatkuvasta rikosromaanista". —Sainio, M. Vanhan virsikirjah maailmankuvasta. —Vilkuna, K. Muinaisrunojen Kainuu ja Suomi. —Wirilander, K. Armeijan lomaoloja 1700-luvulla. —Virtanen, E. A. Varsinais-Suomen sarkajako. —Virtanen, V. Turun työ-ja ojennuslaitoksen sekä rangaistusvankilan perustamisvaiheet vv. 1839-1863.

1. Juva, Einar Wilhelm, 1892- . 2. Finland--Hist.--Addresses, essays, lectures. I. Title.

TB

25 economic essays, in English, German and Scandinavian languages, in honour of Erik Lindahl, 21 November, 1956. Stockholm, Ekonomisk Tidskrift, 1956. 412 p. illus., group port. 25cm.

CONTENTS: —Om aggregation av produktionsfunktioner, av R. Bentzel. —Några synpunkter på penningteoriens doktrinhistoria, av E. Dahmén. —Macroeconomics and linear programming, by R. Frisch. —Ligninger vs. identiteter i økonomisk makroteori, av T. Haavelmo. —Selfdetermination

(Continued)

NN R 2.58 g/c OC PC, 1, 2 SL E, 1, 2 (LC1, X1, Z1, C1, Y1)
[I]

---

25 economic essays, in English, German and Scandinavian languages... (Card 2)

and economic assistance for underdeveloped countries, by D. Hammarskjöld. —On wage-drift. A problem of money-wage dynamics, by B. Hansen & G. Rehn. —Methods of dynamic analysis, by J. R. Hicks. —Några synpunkter på bostadsbyggandet som konjunkturpolitiskt instrument, by A. Johansson. —Ekonomiska prognoser och statistik, by K. Kock. —En not om inflationen i Bolivia, Chile och Paraguay, by B. Kragh. —Wicksell och gränsproduktivitetsläran, av K. G. Landgren. —Some results of an investigation of the gross domestic product of Sweden

(Continued)

---

25 economic essays, in English, German and Scandinavian languages... (Card 3)

for the period 1861-1951, by O. Lindahl. —En not om ekonomisk handlingsteori, av J. G Lindgren. —Stability problems in the Australian economy. Some comparisons with Sweden, by E. Lundberg. —The research work of the Secretariat of the Economic commission for Europe, by G. Myrdal. —Tre kritiska år (1841-43) i den svenska silvermyntfotens historia, av H. E. Pipping. —Zur Frage der Multiplikatorwirkung eines ausgeglichenen Budgets; von E. Schneider. —Om reglering av jordbruksarrenden efter prisindex, av G. W. Silverstolpe. —Capital

(Continued)

---

25 economic essays, in English, German and Scandinavian languages... (Card 4)

accumulation and national wealth in an expanding economy, by I. Svennilson. —On the transactions demand for money, by R. Turvey. —Villfarelsenes skole, av J. Vogt. —Penningvardeförsämring och beskattning, av C. Welinder. —Regnemaskinen og mennesket, af F. Zeuthen. —Marginal productivity with different agricultural products, by G. Åkerman. —The cumulative process, by J. Åkerman.

1. Lindahl, Erik Robert, 1891- . 2. Economics--Essays and misc.

NGO

Tymbos für Wilhelm Ahlmann; ein Gedenkbuch, hrsg. von seinen Freunden. Berlin, W. de Gruyter & Co., 1951. xii, 326 p. illus. 24cm.

Bibliographies included.

Festscrift cd.

586831B. 1. Ahlmann, Wilhelm, 1895–1944. 2. Sociology, 1945– . 3. Philosophy, 1900–
N. Y. P. L. September 24, 1951

D-16
8012

Tymieniecka, Anna Teresa, ed.
Contributions to logic and methodology in honor of J. M. Bocheński. Edited by Anna-Teresa Tymieniecka in collaboration with Charles Parsons. Amsterdam, North-Holland Pub. Co., 1965.

xviii, 326 p. port. 23 cm.

Title on spine: Logic and methodology.

(Continued)

NN* R 8.66 g/c OC PC, 1, 2, 3 SL S, 3 (LC1, X1, Z1)
[I]

TYMIENIECKA, ANNA TERESA, ed. Contributions to logic and methodology in honor of J. M. Bocheński. (Card 2)

English, French, or German.
Includes bibliographies.

CONTENTS.—Scientific publications of J. M. Bocheński (p. [ix]-xviii)—Betrachtungen zum Sequenzen-Kalkul, by P. Bernays.—Remarks on inferential deduction, by H. B. Curry.—Marginalia on Gentzen's Sequenzen-Kalküle, by H. Leblanc.—A modal logic with eight modalities, by S. McCall.--Zur Syllogistik strikt partikulärer Urteile, by A. Menne.—Banks ab omni naevo vindicatus, by E. W. Beth.—

(Continued)

TYMIENIECKA, ANNA TERESA, ed. Contributions to logic and methodology in honor of J.M. Bocheński. (Card 3)

Method and logic in presocratic explanation, by J. Stannard.—Pseudo-Scotus on the soundness of consequentiae, by B. Mates.—The later history of the pons asinorum, by I. Thomas.—Reification, quotation, and nominalization, by J. F. Staal.—Annex: Einige linguistische Bemerkungen zum vorstehenden Thema, by P. Hartmann.—On the logic of preference and choice, by H. S. Houthakker.—Sense, denotation, and the context of sentences, by F. R. Barbo.—Leibniz's law in belief context, by R. M. Chisholm.—Conjectural inference and phenomenological analysis, by A. T. Tymieniecka.—On ontology and the province of logic: some critical remarks, by R. M. Martin.—Réflexions sur la méthode

(Continued)

TYMIENIECKA, ANNA TERESA, ed. Contributions to logic and methodology in honor of J.M. Bocheński. (Card 4)

de Teilhard de Chardin, by N. M. Luyten.—N. A. Vasil'ev and the development of many-valued logics, by G. L. Kline.

1. Logic—Addresses, essays, lectures. 2. Methodology—Addresses, essays, lectures. 3. Bocheński, Innocentius M., 1902-

---

TMF

TYÖNTUTKIJAIN KILTA R. Y.

Bernhard Wuolle 75-vuotias. [Helsinki, 1951] 130 p. illus., port. 21cm.

Includes bibliographies.

CONTENTS. —Professori Kustaa Bernhard Wuolle 75-vuotias, Työntutkijain killan kiltaneuvosto. —Tuotantotoiminnan rakenteen vaikutuksesta teollisen yrityksen toimintaan, E. M. Niini.—Dynaamisen kentän teoria organisaatiotutkimuksen pohjana, O. Oksala. —Työntutkimuksen

(Continued)

NN**R 3.56 f/ (OC) I OS PC, 1, 2, I SL E, 1, 2, I ST, 1, 2, I (LC1, X1, Z1)

TYÖNTUTKIJAIN KILTA R. Y. Bernhard Wuolle 75-vuotias. (Card 2)

kehityskysymksiä, A. Pukkila. —Sekavalmisteisen konepajan työntutkimus-organisaatio. E. Ilmonen. —Palkkaustavoista monikonekäytössä, J. Ruutu. —MTM-menetelmän mukaiset standardiajat, E. Lampen. —Työnluokituksen soveltamismahdollisuuksista, P. Wuorenjuuri. —Työntutkimustoiminnasta ja työsuhteiden hoitamisesta, P. Riikkala.

1. Wuolle, Bernhard, 1876- . 2. Management, 1931- . I. Title.

---

*KP
(Typophiles)

The TYPOPHILES, New York.

Recalling Peter: The life and times of Peter Beilenson and his Peter Pauper press. New York, The Typophiles, 1964. 86 p., 1 l. illus., port., facsims. 19cm. (Typophile chap books, 40)

"Seven hundred copies printed for subscribers, contributors, and friends of Peter Beilenson."

"Printed by Joseph Blumenthal at the Spiral press, New York."

(Continued)

NN R 12.65 e/ (OC)II, III OS, I PC, 1, 2, I, II, III SL R, 1, 2, I, II, III (RI 2, RS1, LC1, X1, Z1)

2

The TYPOPHILES, New York. Recalling Peter... 1964. (Card 2)

"Edited by Paul A. Bennett, with a checklist by David M. Glixon."

1. Beilenson, Peter, 1905-1962. 2. Peter Pauper press, Mount Vernon, N.Y. I. Series. II. Bennett, Paul Arthur, 1897- , ed. III. Glixon, David M., comp.

VQW

TYROL. Landesforstinspektion.

Tiroler Waldwirtschaft. Festschrift zum 100-jährigen Bestehen des Reichsforstgesetzes in Tirol. Innsbruck, Universitätsverlag Wagner, 1954. 263 p. illus., maps (part fold.) 24cm. (Schlern-Schriften. 125)

Includes bibliographies.

CONTENTS. — Die forstlichen Verhältnisse im Lande Tirol, ein Überblick, von F. Dietrich. —Zum hundertjährigen Bestande des Österreichischen Forstgesetzes, von F. Schmid. —

(Continued)

NN**12.55 g/ ODt(lb) EDt (OS)I PC, I, I SL (U1, LC1, X1, Z1)

TYROL. Landesforstinspektion. Tiroler Waldwirtschaft. (Card 2)

Das Forstgesetz vom 3. Dezember 1852, RGBl. Nr. 250. — Aufruf des k. k. Statthalters Karl Fürst Lobkowitz an die Gemeinden Tirols und Vorarlbergs von 17. Juni 1865. —Die Edelrassen des Tiroler Waldes und ihr Holz, von R. F. Wieser. —Die künstliche Verjüngung im Nichtstaatswald Tirols, von R. Kirschner. —Der Gemeindewald des Pitztales und seiner Nachbargemeinden, von H. Figala. — Forstschutz und Forstgesetz (Tiroler Forstschutzfragen), von E. Schimitschek. — Arbeiten auf dem Gebiete des Forstschutzes und der Forstentomologie im Rahmen der Landesforstinspektion für Tirol in

(Continued)

TYROL. Landesforstinspektion. Tiroler Waldwirtschaft. (Card 3)

den Jahren 1945 bis 1953, von E. Jahn. —25 Jahre Forsteinrichtung im Tiroler Gemeinde- und Gemeinschaftswald, von N. Mair. —Beispiel eines freiwilligen Zusammenschlusses von Teilwaldberechtigten zu einer Waldwirtschaftsgemeinschaft in der Gemeinde Silz, von N. Mair. — Holzbringung und Forstaufschliessung in Tirol, von J. Mederer. —Die Erschliessung des Madautales, von H. Lorenz. — 70 Jahre Waldaufseherkurs Rotholz, von F. Dietrich. —Der Stand der Forstarbeiterausbildung in Tirol, von H. Scheiring. — Der Forstverein für Tirol und Vorarlberg, von R. Happak.

(Continued)

TYROL. Landesforstinspektion. Tiroler Waldwirtschaft. (Card 4)

1. Forestry—Austria—Tyrol. I. Series. t. 1954.

NABM

Überlieferung und Gestaltung. Festgabe für Theophil Spoerri zum sechzigsten Geburtstag, am 10. Juni, 1950. Zürich, Speer-Verlag [1950] 206 p. 22cm.

Contributions (with bibliography) in German, French or Italian.
"Tabula gratulatoria," 6 l. inserted.

573246B. 1. Spoerri, Theophil, 1890- . 2. Wolfram von Eschenbach, 12th cent. 3. Pascal, Blaise, 1623-1662. 4. Diderot, Denis, 1713-1784. Le père de famille. 5. Voltaire, François Marie Arouet de, 1694-1778. 6. Lessing, Gotthold Ephraim, 1729-1781. Minna von Barnhelm. 7. Manzoni, Alessandro, 1785-1873. 8. Italian literature—Hist. and crit., 19th cent. 9. Renard, Jules, 1864-1910. 10. Valéry, Paul Ambroise, 1871-1945. 11. Leger, Alexis Saint-Léger, 1889- .
N. Y. P. L. July 27, 1951

ULRICH, HANS, ed. Strukturwandlungen der Unternehmung... (Card 2)

CONTENTS.--Emil Gsell zum 70. Geburtstag, von H. Ulrich.--Der Unternehmer vor neuen Aufgaben, von C. Gasser.--Unternehmung und Markt, von H. Weinhold-Stünzi.--Die Unternehmung als soziales System, von C. Lattmann.--Der Strukturwandel in der Faktorkombination der industriellen Produktion als Folge des technischen Fortschritts, von H. Böhrs.--Führungs- und Organisationsprobleme multinationaler Unternehmungen, von F. Trechsel.--Tradition und Fortschritt; Strukturfragen im schweizerischen Bankwesen, von H. R. Wuffli.--Strukturwandlungen der Versicherungsunternehmung, von M. Grossmann.--Strukturwand-

(Continued)

GHX

Uhrskov, Anders, 1881- , ed.
Hillerødbogen, udgivet af Hillerød Byraad. Redigeret af Anders Uhrskov. [Hillerød] Boghandlerne i Hillerød, 1948. 549 p. illus. 26cm.

Bibliography included in "Noter," p. 505-525.
CONTENTS.—Frederiksborg; Det nationalhistoriske museum paa Frederiksborg, af O. Andrup.—Haver og lystanlæg, af J. Paulsen.—Nordsjællandsk folkemuseum; Grundtvigs højskole; Luthersk missionsforenings højskole, af A. Uhrskov.—Statens forsøgsmejeri, af H. Jensen.—Bystyre og byliv, af A. Uhrskov.—Den sociale forsorg

(Continued)

NN R 3.53 OC (OD)I (ED)I PC, 1, I SL (LC1, Z1, X1)

ULRICH, HANS, ed. Strukturwandlungen der Unternehmung... (Card 3)

lungen der Fremdenverkehrsunternehmung, von W. Hunziker.--Die Verkehrswirtschaft an einem Wendepunkt, von C. Kaspar.--Wandlungen in der Struktur der Gewerbebetriebe, von A. Gutersohn.--System der Unternehmungsplanung und -kontrolle, von W. Hill.--Forschungs- und Entwicklungspolitik, von H. Siegwart.--Finanzielle Entscheidung und Risiko, von B. Lutz.--Wandlungen der betrieblichen Risikopolitik, von P. Steinlin.--Die Gestaltung der Unternehmungsorganisation zur Bewältigung neuer Aufgaben, von R. Staerkle.--Die psycho-sozialen Grundlagen und Auswirkungen der Neuerung in der Unternehmung, von C. Lattmann.--Die Anwendung quantitativer Methoden zum

(Continued)

Uhrskov, Anders, 1881- , ed. Hillerødbogen... (Card 2)

i Hillerød, af P. Balsløw.—Hillerød bys historie indtil 1864, af V. Hermansen.—Vange, veje og huse, af J. Steenberg.—Hillerødsholm. Det kgl. Frederiksborgske stutteri, af J. Paulsen.—Hillerøds i litteraturen, af E. Thomsen.—Hillerøds fremtid, af P. Bredsdorff og A. M. Sørensen.—Bag fremt'dens slør, af C. F. Raaschou.

493416B. 1. Hilleröd, Denmark—Descr. and trav. I. Hilleröd, Denmark. Byraadet.

ULRICH, HANS, ed. Strukturwandlungen der Unternehmung... (Card 4)

Lösen von Unternehmungsproblemen, von E. Soom--Die Information der Öffentlichkeit durch die Unternehmung, von E. Bossard.--Probleme der Forschung in der Betriebswirtschaftslehre, von W. Ganz.--Konzept einer Unternehmungsführungslehre, von H. Ulrich.--Wege zu einer Pädagogik der Betriebswirtschaftslehre, von R. Dubs.--Veröffentlichungen von Emil Gsell.

1. Management--Addresses, essays, lectures. 2. Business--Organization and management. I. Series. II. Ganz-Keppeler, Vera, joint ed. III. Ganz-Keppeler, Vera. IV. Gsell, Emil.

Copy only words underlined
& classmark-- *QGAA

UKRAYINS'KYĬ NAUKOVYĬ INSTYTUT, Berlin.
Prof. Michael Hruschewskyj, sein Leben und sein Wirken (1866-1934); Vorträge des Ukrainischen wissenschaftlichen Institutes anlässlich der Todesfeier an der Friedrich-Wilhelms-Universität zu Berlin. Berlin, Im Verlage der Gesellschaft der Freund des Ukrainischen wissenschaftlichen Institutes, 1935. 48 p. 21cm. (Beiträge zur Ukrainekunde. Heft 3)

1. Hrushevs'kyĭ, Mykhaĭlo, 1866-1934. I. Series.
NN 5.65 a/c OS, I PC, 1, I S, 1, I (LC1, X1, Z1)

F-11
6068

UNDER, MARIE.
Ääremail. [Stockholm] Vaba Eesti [1963] 118 p. illus. 26cm.

Published in honor of author's 80th birthday.
Illustrated by H. Talvik; front. is original etching.
No. 143 of 300 numbered copies printed.

1. Poetry, Esthonian. I. Title.
NN R 3.70 w/c OC PC, 1, I SL (PRET1, PRI 1, LC1, X1, Z1)

L-11
249
Bd. 7

ULRICH, HANS, ed.
Strukturwandlungen der Unternehmung. Festschrift zum 70. Geburtstag von Prof. Dr. Emil Gsell. Hans Ulrich [und] Vera Ganz-Keppeler, Herausgeber. Bern, P. Haupt [1969] xvi, 315 p. diagrs., port. 25cm. (Schriftenreihe "Führung und Organisation der Unternehmung". 7)

Bibliographical footnotes.

(Continued)

NN R 9.69 r/c OC, II, IIIbo, IV (OS)I PC, 1, 2, I, II, IV E, 1, 2, I, II, IV (LC1, X1, Z1)

4

NIC p.v.238

Unge Lyrikeres Vers til Tak for Johannes Jørgensens "Vers," og hvad ellers fulgte, fra 24-8-1887 til 24-8-1937. Under Redaktion og med Indledning af Arne Hall Jensen. København: A. Jensen, 1937. 63 p. illus. 22cm.

Cover-title: Til Johannes Jørgensen i Anledning af 50-Aarsdagen for Udsendelsen af "Vers"... Tegninger af Ebbe Sadolin. Bidrag af: Peter Andreasen, J. Anker-Paulsen, Finnur Erlendsson... [og 14 andre]

1. Jørgensen, Johannes, 1866- . 2. Poetry, Danish. I. Jensen, Arne Hall, ed.
N. Y. P. L. November 9, 1938

*PXT

Union österreichischer Juden.
Festschrift zur Feier des 50 jährigen Bestandes der Union österreichischer Juden. Wien: Union österreichischer Juden, 1937. 143 p. 22cm.

171757B. 1. Jews in Austria. 2. Societies, Jewish—Austria.
N. Y. P. L. September 28, 1942

---

* Z-942
Film Reproduction

UNITED STATES. Letterman army hospital, San Francisco.
Diamond jubilee, 1898-1958; 60 years of medical service. San Francisco, 1958. 11 p. illus., ports.

Film reproduction. Negative.
Fog horn, v. 18, no. 7 (Dec. 2, 1958)

1. Military hospitals--U. S. --Calif. --San Francisco. t. 1958.
NN R 2.61 p/J ODt EDt PC, 1 SL (UM1, LC1, X1, Z1)

---

*QP

UNITED NATIONS EDUCATIONAL, SCIENTIFIC AND CULTURAL ORGANIZATION.
Adam Mickiewicz. 1798-1855; in commemoration of the centenary of his death. [Paris, 1955] x, 295 p. illus., ports. 20cm.

CONTENTS.--A brief sketch of the life of Adam Mickiewicz.--Essays: Introduction to the life and work of Adam Mickiewicz, by J. Parandowski. Adam Mickiewicz and European romanticism, by J. Fabre. Mickiewicz in Russia, by S. Sovietov. Adam Mickiewicz in France: professor and social
(Continued)

NN* 4.56 a/b ODt EDt PC, 1 SL S, 1 (LC1, X1, Z1)

NPD

Universidad central de España, Madrid. — Filosofía y letras, Facultad de.
Estudios eruditos in memoriam de Adolfo Bonilla y San Martín (1875–1926), con un prólogo de Jacinto Benavente, publícalos la Facultad de filosofía y letras de la Universidad central en homenaje a su ilustre ex decano. Tomo 1– Madrid: Viuda e hijos de J. Ratés, 1927– v. front. (port.), illus. (facsim.) 4°.

Mr. Mott

1. Spanish literature—Hist. and crit. 2. Bonilla y San Martín, Adolfo, 1875–1926. 3. Title.
N. Y. P. L. October 27, 1928

UNITED NATIONS EDUCATIONAL, SCIENTIFIC AND CULTURAL ORGANIZATION. Adam Mickiewicz... (Card 2)

philosopher, by M. Leroy. Adam Mickiewicz and Italy, by G. Maver. Mickiewicz and the literature of the western and southern Slavs, by K. Krejči. Poland in Pan Tadeusz, by J. Kleiner.--Selections from Mickiewicz' writings.--Tributes by contemporaries of Mickiewicz.--Principal translations of Mickiewicz' works.

1. Mickiewicz, Adam, 1798-1855. t. 1955.

Copy only words underlined & classmark— STZ
(Panama)

UNIVERSIDAD. Panamá.
Edición especial en homenaje al Dr. José Dolores Moscote. Panamá 1958. 406 p. 23cm. (IN: Universidad. Panamá. no. 37)

1. Moscote, José Dolores, 1879-1956 2. Education--Panama.
NN 10.65 1/ OI (PC)1, 2 (E)2 (LC1, X1, Z1)

TAK

UNITED PLANTERS' ASSOCIATION OF SOUTHERN INDIA.
UPASI, 1893-1953. Coonoor [1953] xiv, 452 p. illus., ports. 23cm.

A souvenir volume, by various contributors, commemorating the Diamond jubilee general meeting.

1. Plantations—India. 2. Plantation life—India—South. I. Speer, S. G., ed.
NN**R X 4.54 (OC)I, Ibo OS, (Ib) PC, 1, 2, I SL E, 1, 2, I O, 1, 2, I (Z1, LC1, X1)

Write on slip words underlined below and class mark — XAA

Università cattolica del Sacro Cuore, Milan.
Raccolta di scritti di diritto pubblico in onore di Giovanni Vacchelli. Milano: Soc. editrice "Vita e pensiero," 1938. xi, 527 p. front. (port.) 25½cm. (Its: Pubblicazioni. Serie seconda: Scienze giuridiche. v. 58.)

Bibliographical footnotes.
CONTENTS.—Gemelli, Agostino. Prefazione.—Vacchelli, Giovanni. Per un nuovo indirizzo nella scienza del diritto pubblico.—Ambrosini, Gaspare. La natura giuridica dell'Africa orientale italiana.—Barillari, Michele. L'indirizzo psicologico nel diritto pubblico.—Bodda, Pietro. La potestà normativa del capo del governo.—Borsi, Umberto. La cittadinanza e la sudditanza coloniale italiana nella più recente legislazione.—
(Continued)

N. Y. P. L. July 22, 1938

---

*C-5 p.v.109

United States. Army. 5th mobile radio broadcasting company.
The Fifth mobile radio broadcasting company. [Bad Nauheim, 1945] 61 l. illus. 29cm.

Clyde E. Shives, editor.

1. World war, 1939-1945—Regt. hist.—U.S.—5th mobile radio broadcasting company. 2. World war, 1939-1945—Radio.

NN 1.53 OD ED PC, 1,2 SL AH,1 (LC1, Z1, X1)

Università cattolica del Sacro Cuore, Milan. Raccolta di scritti di diritto... (Card 2)

Cammeo, Federico. Gli immobili per destinazione nella legislazione sulle belle arti.—Chimienti, Pietro. Le formazioni giuridiche spontanee ed il diritto pubblico fascista.—Crosa, Emilio. Osservazioni sulla rappresentanza politica.—Alessio, Francesco d'. Concetto, obietto e natura del diritto finanziario.—Francesco, G. M. de. Persone giuridiche pubbliche e loro classificazione.—Valles, Arnaldo de. Il contraddittorio nel giudizio amministrativo.—Donati, Donato. Sulla posizione costituzionale della corona nel governo monarchico presidenziale.—Forti, Ugo. Gli statuti dei consorzi provinciali antitubercolari.—Guicciardi, Enrico. L'abrogazione degli atti amministrativi.—Jemolo, C. A. Osservazioni in tema di annullamenti di nomine.—Lucifredi, Roberto. Inammissibilità di un esercizio "ex post" della funzione consultiva.—Marchi,
(Continued)

N. Y. P. L. July 22, 1938

Università cattolica del Sacro Cuore, Milan. Raccolta di scritti di diritto... (Card 3)

Teodosio. Sul carattere rigido o flessibile della costituzione italiana.—Orlando, V. E. Il processo del Kaiser.—Panunzio, Sergio. L'ente politico.—Pergolesi, Ferruccio. Osservazioni sul sistema gradualistico delle fonti normative.—Raggi, Luigi. Ancora sul concetto di demanialità.—Ranelletti, Oreste. La giurisdizione delle acque pubbliche.—Rapisardi-Mirabelli, Andrea. Su i concetti d'amministrazione internazionale e di diritto internazionale amministrativo.—Romano, Santi. Osservazioni sulla invalidità successiva degli atti amministrativi.—Rovelli, Francesco. Lo sviamento di potere.—Salemi, Giovanni. Sulla natura giuridica delle sentenze collettive.—Vuoli, Romeo. La rappresentanza politica del Senato del regno.

1. Vacchelli, Giovanni. 2. Law, Administrative. 3. Law, Constitutional. I. Title. II. Ser.
N. Y. P. L. July 22, 1938

YBX
(Malebranche)

Università cattolica del Sacro Cuore, Milan. Filosofia, Facoltà di. ...Malebranche nel terzo centenario della nascita. Pubblicazione a cura della Facoltà di filosofia dell'Università cattolica del Sacro Cuore. Milano: Soc. editrice "Vita e pensiero", 1938. xiv, 380 p. front. (port.) 25½cm.

At head of title: Rivista di filosofia neo-scolastica. Supplemento speciale al volume 30. Settembre 1938.

CONTENTS.—Gemelli, Agostino. Introduzione.—Tavecchio, Piera. La spiritualità berulliana e la filosofia di Malebranche.—Ceriani, Grazioso. Il concetto metafisico di

(Continued)

N. Y. P. L. April 7, 1939

Università cattolica del Sacro Cuore, Milan. Filosofia, Facoltà di. ...Malebranche... (Card 2)

realtà in Nicola Malebranche.—Amerio, Romano. I teoremi della causalità inefficace nella metafisica di Malebranche.—Mazzantini, Carlo. Intorno alle dottrine gnoseologiche di Malebranche.—Giacon, Carlo. La cosmologia di Malebranche.—Noce, Augusto del. La veracità divina e i rapporti di ragione e fede nella filosofia di Malebranche.—Oddone, Andrea. Libertà umana e grazia divina nelle dottrine del Malebranche.—Pelloux, Luigi. Il valore religioso delle "Méditations chrétiennes."—Noce, Augusto del. Note sulla critica malebranchiana.—Rotta, Paolo. Il platonismo nel Malebranche.—Casotti, Mario. Malebranche nello sviluppo della pedagogia cris-

(Continued)

N. Y. P. L. April 7, 1939

Università cattolica del Sacro Cuore, Milan. Filosofia, Facoltà di. ...Malebranche... (Card 3)

tiana moderna.—Bontadini, Gustavo. Il fenomenismo razionalistico da Cartesio a Malebranche.—Vigorelli, Giancarlo. Variazioni su Malebranche: Malebranche e Montaigne.—Bo, Carlo. Malebranche e Pascal.—Verme, M. E. dal. Di alcuni rapporti fra Malebranche e Hume.—Sasso, Antonio dal. Malebranche e l'illuminismo.—Lantrua, Antonio. Malebranche ed il pensiero italiano dal Vico al Rosmini.—Noce, Augusto del. Bibliografia malebranchiana.

88991A. 1. Malebranche, Nicolas, 1638-1715. 2. Descartes, René, 1595-1650. 3. Montaigne, Michel Eyquem de, 1533-1592. 4. Pascal, Blaise, 1623-1662. 5. Hume, David, 1711-1776. 6. Malebranche, Nicolas, 1638-1715—Bibl. I. Rivista di filosofia neo-scolastica. II. Title.
N. Y. P. L. April 7, 1939

E-11
2881

UNIVERSITÉ D'AIX-MARSEILLE. Lettres et sciences humaines, Faculté des.
Hommage au doyen Étienne Gros. [Gap, 1959]
278 p. port. 25cm.

Bibliographical footnotes.

1. Gros, Étienne. 2. Literature--Addresses, essays, lectures.
NN 8.61 g/(P OS PC, 1, 2 SL (LC1, X1, Z1) [I]

E-12
2444

UNIVERSITE CATHOLIQUE, Louvain.
Études etrusco-italiques; melanges pour le 25e anniversaire de la chaire d'Etruscologie à l'Universite de Louvain. Louvain, Bureaux du recueil, Bibliotheque de l'Universite, 1963. 325 p. illus., 27 plates. 25cm. (ITS: Recueil de travaux d'histoire et de philologie. Ser. 4, fasc. 31)

Bibliography, p. 317-319.
Bibliographical footnotes.

1. Etruscans. 2. Etruria--Archaeology. I. Series.
NN 2.65 c/ OS, I PC, 1, 2, I SL (LC1, X1, Z1)

F-10
7527

UNIVERSITÉ CATHOLIQUE, Louvain.
Scrinium Lovaniense; mélanges historiques [pour] Étienne van Cauwenbergh. Louvain, Bibliothèque de l'Université, Bureau du recueil, 1961. 688 p. illus. (part fold.), ports, geneal. tables. 26cm. (ITS: Recueil de travaux d'histoire et de philologie. sér. 4, fasc. 24)

Contributions in French and Flemish.
Bibliographical footnotes.

1. Cauwenbergh, Étienne van, 1890- . 2. Civilization--Addresses, essays, lectures. 3. Belgium--Civilization--Addresses, essays, lectures. I. Series.
NN 4.63 p/J OS, I PC, 1, 2, 3, I SL (LC1, X1, Z1) [I]

AN
(Mercier, D.)

Université catholique, Louvain. Institut Supérieur de philosophie (École Saint Thomas d'Aquin).
Le cardinal Mercier, fondateur de l'Institut supérieur de philosophie à l'Université de Louvain; la commémoration du centenaire de sa naissance, 1851-1951. Louvain, Publications universitaires de Louvain [1952] 105 p. plates. 30cm.

Text in French, Flemish, Latin or English.
1. Mercier, Désiré Félicien François Joseph, cardinal, 1851-1926. I. Title.
NN** 2.54 (OC)I OS PC,1,I SL (LC1,Z1,X1)

TB

Ünnepi dolgozatok Balás Károly és Heller Farkas születésének 60. évfordulója alkalmából; szerkesztették Laky Dezső és v. Surányi-Unger Tivadar. Budapest, Gergely R. könyvkereskedésének kiadása, 1937.
496 p. front. (ports.) tables (part fold.) 25½cm.
Bibliographical foot-notes.

CONTENTS.—Balás Károly irodalmi munkássága.—Heller Farkas irodalmi munkássága.—Andreich Jenő. Szükség van-e az árelmélet kiépítésére?—Bene Lajos. Pénzügytani vonatkozások a magyar városok háztartási statisztikájában.—Boér Elek. Töke ès tökeképződés.—Dékány István. A társadalom természete és a szociálpolitika négy tipusa.—Erödi-Harrach Béla. A strukturális szemlélet alkalmazása a társadalmi gazdaságtanban.—Fellner Frigyes. A világgazdasági válság

(Continued on next card)

A C 38-3488

[3]

Ünnepi dolgozatok Balás Károly és Heller Farkas ... 1937. (Card 2)

CONTENTS—Continued.

hatása a közlekedésre.—Guóthfalvy-Dorner Zoltán. A gazdasági szervezés alapkérdései.—Hantos Elemér. Az új ipari forradalom.—Ihrig Károly. A szövetkezeti járadék.—Kádas Kálmán. Gazdasági törvényszerüségek—matematikai összefüggések.—Laky Dezső. Csonka-Magyarország népének halandóságáról.—Mattyasovszky Miklós. Jogi személyek a földbirtokpolitikában.—Mórotz Kálmán. Váltóárfolyam és produktivitás.—Nagy Dénes. Az univerzalizmus gazdasági kategóriái.—Navratil Ákos. Magángazdasági vonatkozások és szempontok a közgazdaságtanban.—Neubauer Gyula. A tökéletes gazdaság.—Neumann Károly. A közlekedési eszközök fejlődésének kedvezötlen gazdasági ha-

(Continued on next card)

A C 38-3488

[3]

Ünnepi dolgozatok Balás Károly és Heller Farkas ... 1937. (Card 3)

CONTENTS—Continued.

tásai.—Surányi-Unger Tivadar. Áralakulás és árszabályozás.—Schweng Loránd. Dinamikus mezőgazdasági politika.—Szádeczky-Kardoss Tibor. Adóztatás és nemzeti jövedelem.—Szigeti Gyula. A fizetési mérleg egyensúlybantartásának kérdése a háború útáni Magyarországon.—Theiss Ede. Az oekonometria főbb szempontjai és problémái.—Varga István. A drágaság kérdéséről.—Zelovich László. A spekuláció szerepe a közgazdaságban.

1. Balás, Károly, 1877- 2. *Heller, Farkas, 1877- 3. Balás, Károly, 1877- —Bibliography. 4. *Heller, Farkas, 1877- —Bibliography. 5. Economics—Addresses, essays, lectures. I. Laky, Dezső, 1887- ed. II. Surányi-Unger, Theo, ed.

A C 38-3488

New York. Public library for Library of Congress ⌜8⌝

TB

Ünnepi dolgozatok Navratil Ákos születésének 60-ik és egyetemi tanári kinevezésének 30-ik évfordulója alkalmából...közreműködésével Kenéz Béla, Judik József ⌜és⌝ Varga István. Budapest: Gergely R. könyvkereskedésének kiadása, 1935. 472 p. front. (port.) 26cm.

"Navratil Ákos irodalmi munkássága, 1896–1935," p. ⌜10⌝–14.

CONTENTS.—Kenéz, Béla. Előszó.—Navratil Ákos irodalmi munkássága, 1896–1935.—Balás, Károly. A vámok és az egyedárușágok jövedelemeloszlásbeli hatása pénzügytani szempontból.—Balogh, Tamás. Gazdaságpolitika és közgazdaságtan a válságban.—Boér, Elek. A naturál- és reálgazdaság pénzgazdasági jelentőségéről.—Csizik, Béla. Id. Wekerle Sándor és Magyarország pénzügyei.—Fellner, Frigyes. A földbirtok-megoszlás állami irányítása figyelemmel a magyar földbirtokviszonyokra.—

(Continued)

N. Y. P. L. January 31, 1939

Ünnepi dolgozatok Navratil... (Card 2)

Hantos, Elemér. A világpiac változásai a világháború után.—Hegedüs, Lóránt. Kossuth Lajos vámpolitikája.—Heller, Farkas. A gazdasági liberalismus elmélete és bírálata. —Judik, József. A világgazdasági válság és a fizetési mérlegek.—Kuncz, Ödön. A rochdale-i elvek és a szövetkezet jogi fogalmának körülirása.—Mattyasovszky, Miklós. Világháboru és közgazdaságtan.—Moór, Gyula. A gazdasági élet és a jogi rend.—Kisléghi, N. D. Mandeville meséje a méhekről.—Neubauer, Gyula. Világválság és gazdaságelmélet.—Rostás, László. A mezőgazdaság helyzetének alakulása, mint konjunkturatényező.—Schneller, Károly. A magyar mezőgazdasági termelés átalakitása, különös tekintettel a beavatkozás módjára és társadalompolitikai jelentőségére.—Surányi-Unger, Tivadar. A magyar gazdaságpolitika heteronóm céljainak ujabb fejlődése.—Szász, Lajos. Az adóztatási lehetőség határáról.—Varga, István. A közgazdaságtan elhatárolása az u. n. segédtudományaitól.

972622A. 1. Navratil, Ákos, 1875- . 2. Navratil, Ákos, 1875- —Bibl. 3. Economics—Essays and misc. I. Kenéz, Béla, 1874- , ed. II. Judik, József, ed. III. Varga, István, ed.

N. Y. P. L. January 31, 1939

JFD
71-535

Unser kompliziertes Steuersystem. Beiträge von Clemens A⌜ugust⌝ Andreae ⌜u. a.⌝ Volkmar Muthesius z. 70. Geburtstag am 19. März 1970. Frankfurt a. M., F. Knapp (1970).

92 p. with 1 illus. 22 cm.

Includes bibliographical references.

CONTENTS.—Einleitung, von P. Muthesius.—Zur Steuerreform in Norwegen, von C. A. Andreae.—Steuerpolitik der offenen Hände? von F. Dietz.—Unser kompliziertes Steuersystem, von H. Freders-

(Continued)

NN*R 5. 71 m/ℓ OC, I, II PC, 1, I, II SL E, 1, I, II (LC1, X1, Z1)

2

Unser kompliziertes Steuersystem. (1970). (Card 2)

dorf.—Entschleierung der Sozialsubventionen—Entkomplizierung des Steuersystems, von W. Frickhöffer.—Über den Nutzen von Steuerreformen, von E. Schneider.—Die Disziplin im Steuerverkehr ist besser als im Strassenverkehr, von H. Schulze-Borges.—Das Steuersystem—ein wenig geketzert, von G. Siara.—Man muss auch rechnen, von F. Silcher.—Eine freundschaftliche Entgegnung, von H. Troeger.

1. Taxation--Germany. I. Andreae, Clemens August. II. Muthesius, Volkmar.

C-13
883

UNTERFRANKEN im 19. Jahrhundert. Festschrift, mit dem Festvortrag des bayerischen Ministerpräsidenten Alfons Goppel, und Beiträgen von Erich Carell [et al.] Würzburg, H. Stürtz, 1965. 316 p. illus., ports. 19cm. (Mainfränkische Heimatkunde. Bd. 13)

Includes bibliographies.

1. Franconia, Lower--Civilization. 2. Bavaria--Govt. I. Series. II. Goppel, Alfons. III. Carell, Erich, 1905-

NN R 2.66 p/ OC, II, IIbo, III (OS)I PC, 1, 2, I, II, III (LC1, X1, Z1)

TG

Die UNTERNEHMUNG im Markt; Festschrift für Wilhelm Rieger zu seinem 75. Geburtstag. Stuttgart, W. Kohlhammer, 1953. 322 p. port. 24cm.

Bibliographical footnotes.

CONTENTS. —Die Wirtschaftsgeschichte des Kapitals und die Lehrgeschichte des Kapitalbegriffs, von C. Brinkmann. —Der Kapitalbegriff und die neuere Theorie, von E. Preiser. —Kapitalwirtschaft und Kapitalrechnung, von H. Linhardt. —Kapital, Kapitalbildung und Kapitalertrag im System der gesamtwirtschaftlichen Rechnung, von .

(Continued)

NN**R X 8.53 OC PC, 1, 2 SL E, 1, 2 (Z/1, LC1, X1)

Die UNTERNEHMUNG im Markt... (Card 2)

H. Haller. —Umlaufgeschwindigkeit als Phänomen, von W. Vershofen. —Probleme um das Eigenkapital der Kreditbanken, von C. Eisfeld. —Unternehmer und Manager als persönliche Träger der Kapitalwirtschaft, von G. Bergler. —Das Kapital als steuerliche Bemessungsgrundlage, von E. Lohmann. —Lenkung und Privatwirtschaft, von H. Peter. —Wirtschaftlichkeit und Wirtschaftlichkeitsmessung, von E. H. Sieber. —Die Reserven der Unternehmung, von A. Walther. —Marktpreis und Kosten, von J. Fettel. —Die Kreditüberwachungsprüfung unter Berücksichtigung des functionellen Wertes, von K. Berger. —The origin of profit and the relationship between profit and wages.

(Continued)

Die UNTERNEHMUNG im Markt... (Card 3)

by A. Kokkalis. —Entwicklung und Bestimmung des Begriffes Liquidität, von K. Hellmann. —Über den Bilanzinhalt (zugleich eine kritische Betrachtung gegenwärtiger Bilanzierungsbestimmungen), von H. Pries. —Über die Anwendbarkeit der Mathematik in den Wirtschaftswissenschaften, von P. Scherpf.

1. Corporations—Finance. 2. Rieger, Wilhelm, 1878-

GFZE

Uppländsk bygd; en samling studier tillägnade Wera von Essen på hennes femtioårsdag den 3 februari 1940. ⌜Stockholm⌝ Nordisk rotogravyr ⌜1940⌝

252 p. incl. illus., plates (1 mounted col.) port., plans. 26 x 21½cm.

"Rättelser" slip inserted.

"Denna festskrift är utgiven av Disastiftelsen i Upsala och utarbetad i samråd med flera av friherrinnan Wera v. Essens vänner utom och inom stiftelsen. Redaktör: Nils Alenius."

"1300 exemplar, därav en bibliofilupplaga om 300 numrerade exemplar.."

Bibliography at end of some of the articles.

CONTENTS.—Åreporten på Salsta, av Sigurd Curman.—Helig mark, av Andreas Lindblom.—Skoklosters trädgård, av Erik Lundberg.—Resan till Valhall, av Oscar Almgren.—Salstaherrarnas kyrkliga donationer, av

(Continued on next card)

41-21210

⌜2⌝

Uppländsk bygd ... [1940] (Card 2)

CONTENTS—Continued.

Gerda Boëthius.—Rännverkssmidet vid Österby och Vattholma bruk under 1500-talet, av Carl Sahlin. — Uppländsk knuttimring, av Nils Alenius. — Salstaherrarnas kor i Uppsala domkyrka, av Mats Åmark.—Benkammen från Rönnängen, av Gunnar Ekholm.—Bielkesamlingen i Skoklosters bibliotek, av O. Walde.—Katarina Jagellonicas gravvård i Uppsala domkyrka, av August Hahr.—Runstenen vid Skokloster—en bildsten från Vendeltid, av Bertil Almgren.—"Sic oculos, sic ora ferebat," av Axel L. Romdahl.—Skokloster—ett hem, av Åke Stavenow.—Gustav II Adolfs och Maria Eleonoras biläggersäng, av Åke Setterwall.—Flasta mur—äldsta kyrkan i Sko, av Nils Sundquist.—Textilinventering, av Mattis Hörlén.—Drottning Disas blomma, av Rutger Sernander.

1. Essen, Wera Irene (Lagercrantz) friherrinna von, 1890- 2. Uppland, Sweden. I. Alenius, Nils, ed. II. Disastiftelsen, Uppsala.

UPSALA, Sweden. Universitet. Juridiska fakulteten. Festskrift tillägnad Halvar Sundberg. (Card 2)

CONTENTS.--Remiss till allmänheten, en laghistorisk studie, av E. Anners.--Några synpunkter på sparandets dynamik, av R. Bentzel.--Det juridiska ansvaret för rättskränkningar i rundradioprogram, av S. Bergström.--Forskningsprogram för folkrätten? Av P.O. Boldings.--Svenska medborgares skydd i utlandet, en fråga om förhållandet mellan den enskilde och det allmänna, av. H. Eek.--Tillämpningen av RB 31:11 st. 1 bilmål, av P.O. Ekelöf.--Kring regeringsformens 150-årsminne, av E. Fahlbeck.--

(Continued)

Uppsala, Sweden. **Universitet.** *Geografiska institutionen.*

Geografiska studier tillägnade John Frödin den 16 april 1944. [Redaktörer: Gerd Enequist och Filip Hjulström] Uppsala, Appelbergs boktr., 1944.

viii, 500 p. illus., port., maps (part fold. in pocket) plans. 25 cm. (Its Geographica, nr. 15)

Bibliographies at end of some chapters.

CONTENTS.—Bynstudier i Luleå skärgård, av Gerd Enequist.—Norra Sveriges sågverksindustri i början av 1800-talet, av Harald Wik.—Den äldsta fasta bosättningen i Norrbottens läns lappmarker, av Gunnar Hoppe.—Något om den gamla skogsrenskötseln i Arvidsjaurs socken, av Israel Ruong.—Några drag ur skogslapparnas äldre kulturgeografi, av Filip Hultblad.—Massupphöjningens betydelse för höjdgränser i Skanderna och Alperna, av Erik Ljungner.—Enköpingsåsen

(Continued on next card)

UPSALA, Sweden. Universitet. Juridiska fakulteten. Festskrift tillägnad Halvar Sundberg. (Card 3)

Om riksdagsarbete, strödda iakttagelser och reflexioner, av N. Herlitz.--Några spörsmal om tillsyn över stiftelser, av H. Hessler.--Riksbankens investeringsvillkor och bolagsbildning i utlandet, av L. Hjemer.--Kvalifikationsproblemtet i den internationella privaträtten; en strid om pavens skägg, en gåta för mindre begåvade--eller vad? Av P. Hult.--Synpunkter pa den svenska penninglagstiftningen, av E. Lindahl.--Jämförande rättsvetenskap, synpunkter och riktlinjer, av. A. Malmström.--Reflexioner kring några kriminalpolitiska problem, av H. Munktell.--

(Continued)

Uppsala, Sweden. **Universitet.** *Geografiska institutionen.* Geografiska studier tillägnade John Frödin den 16 april 1944 ... 1944. (Card 2)

CONTENTS—Continued.

mellan Mälaren och Dalälven, av Sten Rudberg.—Södra Kallberget, en byfäbod i Västerdalarna, av Olle Veirulf.—Fäbodbebyggelsen i Finland, av Helmer Smeds.—Östergötland under mitten av 1600-talet, av Johannes Öster.—Bebyggelsens vertikala fördelning inom Asundenområdet, av Gunnar Lindgren.—1749 års ekinventering i Östergötland, av Robert Pettersson.—Uppsalaasen; karta med beskrivning, av Filip Hjulström.—Om förhållandet mellan virkestillgång och virkeskonsumtion inom den norduppländska bergshanteringen under 1600-talets första kvartessekel, av Gustaf Uhr.—Schering Rosenhane, av

(Continued on next card)

UPSALA, Sweden. Universitet. Juridiska fakulteten. Festskrift tillägnad Halvar Sundberg. (Card 4)

Skadestånd i offentlig verksamhet, några kommentarer till ett aktuellt betänkande (SOU 1958:43) av G. Petrén.--Några reflexioner agående rättssäkerheten i den moderna kriminalrättsskipningen, av I. Strahl.--Laglighetsprövning och lämplighetsprövning, av H. Strömberg.--Condictio indebiti i offentlig rätt, av O. Westerberg.

1. Sundberg, Halvar Gustaf Fredrik, 1894- . 2. Social sciences--Addresses, essays, lectures. 3. Law--Addresses, essays, lectures. I. Series. II. Title.

Uppsala, Sweden. **Universitet.** *Geografiska institutionen.* Geografiska studier tillägnade John Frödin den 16 april 1944 ... 1944. (Card 3)

CONTENTS—Continued.

Torsten Lagerstedt.—Stadsgeografiska studier över Uppsala, av Ivar Ekstedt [et al.]—Inledningsforelesning for nye geografistuderande ved Universitetet i Oslo 6. oktober 1943, av Fridtjov Isachsen.

1. Frödin, John, 1879- 2. Geography—Addresses, essays, lectures. I. Enequist, Gerd Margareta, 1903- ed. II. Title. (Series)

Upsala. Universitet. Bibliotek.

Uppsala universitets biblioteks minneskrift, 1621–1921; med bidrag av bibliotekets forna och nuvarande tjänstemän. Uppsala: Almqvist & Wiksells boktryckeri-a.-b., 1921. ix, 622 p. front., illus. (incl. facsims., ports.), col'd pl. 27cm. (Upsala. Universitet. Bibliotek. Acta Bibliothecae R. Universitatis Upsaliensis. v. 1.)

Bibliographical footnotes.

CONTENTS.—Annerstedt, C. Förteckning å Upsala universitetsbiblioteks ledare jämte korta upplysningar rörande deras verksamhet.—Rooth, E. Die mittelalterlichen

(Continued)

UPSALA, Sweden. Universitet. Juridiska fakulteten. Festskrift tillägnad Halvar Sundberg. Papers dedicated to Halvar Sundberg. Uppsala, Lundequistska bokhandeln [1959] 425 p. 25cm. (Upsala, Sweden. Universitet. Upsala universitets årsskrift. 1959:9)

Summaries in English.
Bibliographical footnotes.

(Continued)

Upsala. Universitet. Bibliotek: Uppsala universitets biblioteks minneskrift, 1621–1921... (Card 2)

deutschen Handschriften einschliesslich der lateinischen mit deutschen Bestandteilen der Universitätsbibliothek zu Uppsala.—Collijn, I. Paul Grijs, Uppsalas förste boktryckare, 1510–1519.—Nelson, A. Peder Swarts Gensvar 1558. Ett bidrag till kännedomen om 1500-talets svenska politiska litteratur.—Colliander, E. Ein Unikum aus der niederländischen Reformationszeit in der Universitätsbibliothek zu Uppsala.—Walde, O. En svensk boksamlare från Vasatiden. Hogenskild Bielke och hans bibliotek.—Högberg, P. Une édition rarissime du Roman de la rose dans la Bibliothèque de l'Université royale d'Uppsala.—Lewenhaupt, E. Rosenhaneska handskriftssamlingen i Uppsala universitetsbibliotek.—Heyman, H. J. Stiernhielms skrifter om mått och vikt.—Grape, A. Riksråd — språkforskare. Med anledning av ett par

(Continued)

Upsala. Universitet. Bibliotek: Uppsala universitets biblioteks minneskrift, 1621–1921... (Card 3)

nyfunna brottstycken av Bengt Skyttes etymologiska verk.—Andersson, A. Några rangfrågor vid Uppsala universitet vid tiden för Erik Benzelius d. y:s utnämning till bibliotekarie.—Rudbeck, G. Uppsala universitetsbiblioteks exlibris.—Döbeln, E. von. Björkholms-samlingen i Uppsala universitetsbibliotek. Några ord om von Döbelnska släktarkivet.—Hulth, J. M. Uppsala universitetsbiblioteks förvärv av Linneanska originalmanuskript.—Bring, S. E. Uppsala universitetsbiblioteks bytesförbindelser. Några anteckningar om deras uppkomst och utveckling.—Lundgren, H. En Uppsala-bibliotekets donator och dennes biblioteksplaner.—Ågren, S. Om Nordinska handskriftssamlingen i Uppsala universitetsbibliotek.—Carlsson, A. B. Jonas Hallenbergs anteckningar och samlingar till Gustaf II Adolfs historia i Uppsala universitetsbiblio-

(Continued)

N. Y. P. L. October 20, 1933

Upsala. Universitet. Bibliotek: Uppsala universitets biblioteks minneskrift, 1621–1921... (Card 4)

tek.—Taube, N. E., friherre. Några ord om utländska kartor i Uppsala universitetsbibliotek.—Uggla, A. H. Uppsala universitetsbiblioteks samling av nyisländsk litteratur.—Ekholm, G. Om Uppsala universitetsbiblioteks handteckningssamling.—Samzelius, J. L. De utländska tidskrifterna vid Uppsala universitet.—Stjernberg, C. W. Domkapitelsavhandlingar efter 1890. Jämte tilläg och rättelser till Aks. Josephson, Avhandlingar ock program (1855-1890); bibliografi.

644419A. 1. No subject. I. Ser.
N. Y. P. L. October 20, 1933

E-11
2761

URBAN, GEORG, ed.
Philipp Melanchthon, 1497-1560, Gedenkschrift zum 400. Todestag des Reformators 19. April 1560/1960, mit 90 Abbildungen und einem Bericht über die Gedenkfeiern in Bretten als Anhang. [2. erweiterte Aufl.] Bretten, Melanchthonverein, 1960. 224 p. illus., ports. 24cm.

Includes bibliographies.
1. Melanchthon, Philipp, 1497-1560. I. Melanchthonverein, Bretten, Germany. II. Urban, Georg.
NN R 6.61 e/4 OC, IIbo (OS)I, Ib PC, 1, I SL (LC1, X1, Z1)

L-10
5733
v.4

UTRECHT (City). Rijksuniversiteit. Instituut voor vergelijkend literatuuronderzoek.
Miscellanea litteraria in commemorationem primi decennii Instituti edita. Groningen, J. B. Wolters, 1959.
184 p. 24 cm. (Studia litteraria rheno-traiectina. v. 4)
CONTENTS.--Magisches in der Struktur des germanischen Zauberspruches, von H. H. Braches.—Historie, roman en historische roman, door J. C. Brandt Corstius.—Art for art's sake and form and matter, by O. de Deugd.—Drei Kontrafakurten zu Carmina burana, 79, 85 und 157, von J. A. Huisman.—Einiges zu den stofflichen Grundlagen der Walthersage, von A. van der Lee.—Petronianum, door L. P.

(Continued)

NN * 2.65 e/J OS, I PC, 1, I (LC1, X1, Z1)

2

UTRECHT (City). Rijksuniversiteit. Instituut voor vergelijkend literatuuronderzoek. Miscellanea litteraria in commemorationem primi decennii Instituti edita. (Card 2)

Rank.—Opitz als vertaler van Nederlandse sonnetten, door W. A. P. Smit.—Der Enkel des Königs Armenios und die Gregorsage, von H. Sparnaay.—Van het kind, dat Jezus te eten gaf, door J. W. Steenbeel.--Die Magie der Zahlen, von H.P.H. Teesing.--Tweemaal Frankrijk-Nederland, door C.A. Zaalberg.

1. Literature--Addresses, essays, lectures. I. Series.

APC

VALKO, WILLIAM G.
The illustrated who's who in reigning royalty; a history of contemporary monarchial systems. Philadelphia, Pa., Community press, 1969. 263 p. ports. 18cm. (A Vasilikon publication)

Bibliography, p. 259-262.

1. Kings and rulers--Geneal. 2. Royal houses. I. A Vasilikon publication. II. Title.
NN 2.70 w/J OC(1bo) (OS)I PC, 1, 2, II SL E, 2, II G, 1, 2, II (LC1, X1, Z1) [NSCM]

L-11
606

VALLADOLID, Spain (City). Universidad. Filosofía y letras, Facultad de.
Homenaje al Excmo. Sr. Dr. D. Emilio Alarcos García. Valladolid, 1965. 1 v. port. 25cm.

[Tomo] 1.
Half-title: Homenaje al profesor Alarcos.
Bibliographical footnotes.
CONTENTS.--[t.] 1. Seleccion antologica de sus escritos.

1. Alarcos García, Emilio. 2. Spanish language--Addresses, essay, lectures. 3. Spanish literature--Addresses, essays, lectures. I. Alarcos García, Emilio
NN R 10.66 p/ (OC)I OS PC, 1, 2, 3, I SL (LC1, X1, Z1)

C-14
4777

Vän med böcker. En bok till Brita von Zweigbergk 31/3 1970. ₍Kalmar, Stadsbiblioteket (distr.)₎, 1970.
185, (1) p. illus. 19 cm.
Includes bibliographical references.
CONTENTS. — Folkbiblioteket i utbildningssamhället, av R. Arnling.—Dominikanerna i medeltidens Kalmar, av B. Brisman.—Något om Pierre Loti och om hans plats i litteraturen, av P. G. Ekström.—Den globala svältens biologi, av B. Forsman.—Havet och ön, av M. Friberg.—"Jag har läst igenom Era småbitar," av B. Hallvik.—

(Continued)

NN * R 3.71 b/Z OC PC, 1, 2 SL (LC1, X1, Z1)

2

VÄN med böcker. En bok till Brita von Zweigbergk 31/3 1970. (Card 2)

Stangnelius i tonspråk, av M. Hofrén.—Språkvård, språkfördärv, av N. Holmberg.—Läsning i en gammal bibliotekskatalog, av E. E. Lundgren.—Biblioteksförbunden, ett stycke bibliotekshistoria, av T. Olsoni.—Sinclairsvisan och dess roll i öländskt byliv, av G. Palm s: r.—"Kalmar landskansli i Södra Vi", av A. Sandberg.—Stan, av E. Skillius.—Penu proverbiale och dess författare, av H. Wibling.—Vardagsmänniskan och boken, av E. Wulff.

1. Zweigbergk, Brita von, 1905- . 2. Literature--Addresses, essays, lectures.

NRC

Varia variorum; Festgabe für Karl Reinhardt, dargebracht von Freunden und Schülern zum 14. Februar 1951. Münster [etc.] Böhlau-Verlag, 1952.
280 p. port. 25cm.

"Verzeichnis der Schriften Karl Reinhardts," p.[281-282]

1. Classical studies. 2. Reinhardt, Karl, 1886-
NN OC PC,1,2 SL (LC1, Z1, X1)

VATICAN. Archivio vaticano.
Miscellanea archivistica Angelo Mercati. Città del Vaticano, Biblioteca apostolica vaticana, 1952.
xxvii, 462 p. port., facsims. 26cm. (Studi e testi. [v.] 165)

Includes bibliographies.
CONTENTS.—Problèmes archivistiques d'aujourd'hui et de demain, par C. Samaran. — Gli archivi e il progresso delle scienze sociali, di C. Gini. —Intérêt et importance des Archives vaticanes pour l'histoire économique du moyen âge spécialement du XIVe siècle, par y. Renouard. —Paolo Kehr e le ricerche archivistiche per l'Italia pontificia, par
(Continued)

VATICAN. Archivio vaticano. Miscellanea archivistica Angelo Mercati. (Card 2)

W. Holtzmann.—Die archivalischen Quellen der "Hierarchia catholica," von R. Ritzler.—Annotationes zu den Registern Urbans IV, von F. Boch. —Minutes of papal letters (1316-1317) by G. Barraclough.—Poggio-Autographen kurialer Herkunft, von K. A. Fink.—L'inventaire de la Chambre Apostolique de 1440, par L. M. Bååth.—Suppliques originales adressées au Cardinal-Légat Carlo Carafa (1557-1558) par C. Tihon.—El archivo de la S. congregación de negotios ecclesiásticos extraordinarios y la encíclica de León XII sobre la revolución hispano-americana por P. de Leturia.—Die mittelalterlichen Papsturkunden im Stiftsarchiv
(Continued)

VATICAN. Archivio vaticano. Miscellanea archivistica Angelo Mercati. (Card 3)

Einsiedeln von R. Henggeler.—La tradizione archivistica di Montecassino, di T. Leccisotti.—Cenni sull'archivio capitolare di Reggio Emilia, di L. Tondelli.—Perdita e ricuperi del diplomatico Farnesiano, di R. Filangieri di Candida.—Listes bénéficiales en France et enregistrement des titres de bénéfices, par J. de Font-Reaulx.—Los archivos de la Embajada de España cerca de la Santa Sede, por J. M. Pou y Martí.—Das Oesterreichische Staatsarchiv, von L. Santifaller.—Archive developments in England 1925-1950, by H. Jenkinson.—The college and university archives in the United States, by E. Posner.—Per una "Guida storica degli Archivi ecclesiastici" di A. Panella.—I registri vaticani e le loro provenienze originarie, di M. Giusti.

VATICAN. Archivio vaticano. Miscellanea archivistica Angelo Mercati. (Card 4)

1. Mercati, Angelo, 1870- 2. Archives. I. Series. II. Title.

Vatican. *Biblioteca vaticana.*
Collectanea Vaticana in honorem Anselmi M. Card. Albareda a Bibliotheca Apostolica edita. Città del Vaticano, Biblioteca aspostolica vaticana, 1962.
2 v. facsims., plates. 26 cm. (Studi e testi, 219-220)
Italian, Spanish, French, German, or English.
Bibliographical footnotes.

1. Albareda, Anselmo Maria, Cardinal, 1892- I. Series. II. Title.

25 [i. e. Veinticinco] estudios de folklore; homenaje a Vicente T. Mendoza y Virginia Rodríguez Rivera. [1. ed.] México, 1971. 394 p. illus. 24cm. (Mexico (City). Universidad nacional. Instituto de investigaciones estéticas. Estudios de folklore, 4)

Includes bibliographies.
CONTENTS: Dos investigadores ejemplares en el folklore: Vicente T. Mendoza y doña Virginia Rodríguez Rivera, por F. Anaya
(Continued)

25 [i.e. VEINTICINCO] estudios de folklore... (Card 2)

Monroy.—Biobibliografía del profesor Vicente T. Mendoza, por G. Moedano Navarro (p. 23-55)—Biografía de la profesora Virginia Rodríguez Rivera, por G. Moedano Navarro (p. 57-72)—Imagen popular de lo jurídico, por J. Castillo Farreras.—Os componentes do folclore brasileiro, por M. Diégues Júnior.—El grupo folk como grupo marginal, por J. Martínez Ríos.—Esbozo de una axiología del folklore, por J. de J. Montoya Briones.—Martina Chapanay, un personaje legendario, por S. Chertudi.—Da poesia popular narrativa no Brasil, por L. da Camara Cascudo.—Cantos de Navidad en lengua
(Continued)

25 [i.e. VEINTICINCO] estudios de folklore... (Card 3)

náhuatl, por M. León-Portilla.—El dueto Sandoval y el corrido de don Vicente T. Mendoza, por G. Moedano N.—Romance y corrido, por C. Díaz y de Ovando.—Romances y corridos del Soconusco, por C. Navarrete.—Folklore e historia: dos cantares de la frontera del norte, por A. Paredes.—La música afro-venezolana, por L. F. Ramón y Rivera.—Notas sobre los textiles indígenas de Guatemala, por L. de Jongh Osborne.—La vivienda rural en Venezuela, por M. Acosta Saignes.—As pastôras do Natal, por E. Carneiro.—Las cofradías rurales y sus aspectos folklóricos, por E. de la Torre Villar.—Una misa del niño en mi barrio, por D. Guevara.—Fiesta
(Continued)

25 [i.e. VEINTICINCO] estudios de folklore... (Card 4)

de las almas, por P. de Carvalho-Neto.—Gestures in an American detective story, by A. Taylor.—Les gestes humains, par A. Marinus.—La capa; glosa médico-romántica, de sus dichos y refranes, por A. Castillo de Lucas.—Juegos infantiles tradicionales en el Perú, por E. Romero de Valle.

1. Folk lore--Addresses, essays, lectures. 2. Mendoza, Vicente T., 1894-1964. 3. Rodríguez Rivera, Virginia. I. Series. II. Mendoza, Vicente T., 1894-1964. III. Rodríguez Rivera, Virginia.

VEJLE AMTS HISTORISKE SAMFUND.
Jelling, det gamle kongesæde; Vejle amts historiske samfunds festskrift, 1905 -- 6. jan. -- 1955. [Redaktionsudvalg: Arnold Hansen, Niels Jacobsen og Jakob Jakobsen] København, Munksgaard, 1955. 206 p. illus., ports., plans. 27cm.

Half title: Vejle amts aarbog, festskrift 1955.
Text in Danish, one contribution in Swedish.
(Continued)

VEJLE AMTS HISTORISKE SAMFUND. Jelling... (Card 2)

CONTENTS. --Vejle amts historiske samfund i de første halvtreds aar, af R. Mortensen. --Stiftamtmand Vilhelm Bardenfleth, Vejle amts historiske samfunds første formand, af V. Topsøe. --Uppsala Jellings ømegn, af N. Jacobsen.

1. Societies, Historical--Denmark--Vejle. 2. Bardenfleth, Vilhelm, 1850-1933. 3. Jelling, Denmark--Archaeology. 4. Upsala, Sweden--Archaeology. 5. Runic inscriptions--Denmark--Jelling. I. Title. II. Hansen, Arnold, ed. III. Hansen, Arnold.

---

*QYN

Veltījums izglītības ministram un profesoram dr. h. c. Augustam Tentelim, 23. XI. 1876. – 23. XI. 1936. Rediģējis T. Zeids. Rīgā: Ramaves apgāds, 1936. 227 p. incl. tables. front. (port.), illus. (incl. facsims.) 26cm.

Bibliographical footnotes.

CONTENTS.—Zeids, T. De vita patriae atque scientiae dedicata; Profesora Augusta Tenteļa iespiestie darbi.—Ķiķauka, P. Vai divas Hērodota kļūdas?—Lukstiņš, Ģ. Romula un Rema problēma un tās atrisinājuma mēģinājumi.—Ģinters, V. Daugmales pilskalna jātnieka figūra.—Biļķins, V. Kuršu uzbrukums Rīgai.—Švābe, A. Kuršu līgumi.—Malvess, R. Livonijas chronista Dionizija Fabricija avoti.—Dunsdorfs, E. Vidzemes zviedru laiku finances.—Straubergs, J., and T. Zeids. Daži jauni dokumenti par Juri Manceli.—Augstkalns, A. Latviešu fragmenti 17. g. s. beigu Liepājas aktīs.—

(Continued)

N. Y. P. L. March 22, 1938

Veltījums izglītības ministram un profesoram... (Card 2)

Grīnbergs, V. Precēšanās ierobežojumi Kurzemes dzimtcilvēkiem.—Melander, T. Kāds 1682. gada laimes vēlējums latviešu valodā.—Straubergs, K. Uzruna Jānim Sobjeskim Grodņā.—Vippers, R. Augusta Ludvika Šlōcera domas par dzimtbūšanu Vidzemē.—Altements, A. Vidzemes dzimtzemnieku bēgļu gūstišana XVIII gadsimteņa pēdējā ceturksnī.—Karlsons, Ž. Daži momenti no literārajām cīņām ap dzimtbūšanu un zemnieku jautājumu XVIII g. s. beigās un XIX g. s. sākumā.—Ābers, B. Vidzemes zemnieku brīvlaišana un 1819. gada 26. marta likums.—Bērziņš, J. Bēŗu ierašas Mārcienas apkaimē.—Altements, A. Dokumenti par 1870. g. petīciju Vidzemes latviešu politisko tiesību jautājumā.

925498A. 1. Tentelis, Augusts, 1876– . I. Zeids, Teodors, ed.

N. Y. P. L. March 22, 1938

---

*C–4 p.v.302

Venice (City).

...Vincenzo Coronelli nel terzo centenario dalla nascita. Venezia, C. Ferrari, 1950. 74 p. 24cm.

CONTENTS.—Almagià, Roberto. Vincenzo Coronelli; discorso celebrativo tenuto in Palazzo ducale il 21 maggio 1950.—Gallo, Rodolfo. Vincenzo Coronelli e la repubblica di Venezia.—Catalogo delle opere di Vincenzo Coronelli esposte nalla Galleria dell' Ala napoleonica.

1. Coronelli, Marco Vincenzo, 1650-1718.

NN 2.53 OD ED PC, 1 SL ST, 1 (LC1, Z1, X1)

D-15
2675

VERBAND FÜR ARBEITSSTUDIEN-- REFA- e. V.

Arbeitsstudium heute und morgen; Festschrift zum 70. Geburtstag von Prof. Dr. -Ing E. Bramesfeld. Berlin, Beuth-Vertrieb, 1963. 222 p. illus. 22cm.

Includes bibliographies.

1. Bramesfeld, Erwin. 2. Management--Addresses, essays, lectures, etc. 3. Work measurement

NN R 7.64 p/$ OS PC, 1, 2, 3 SL E, 1, 2, 3 (LC1, X1, Z1)

AF-10
426

VERBAND BERLINER KAUFLEUTE DER KOLONIALWAREN-BRANCHE.

Festschrift zum 60 jährigen Jubiläum des Verbandes Berliner Kaufleute der Kolonialwarenbranche e. V., gegründet 1870. [Berlin] 1930. 67 p. (p. 49-67 advertisements) illus., ports. 30cm.

Cover title: 60 [i. e. Sechzig] Jahre Verband Berliner Kaufleute...

1. Commerce--Assoc. and org. --Germany--Berlin.

NN 2.65 c/ OS(1b) PC, 1 SL E, 1 (LC1, X1, Z1)

F-11
861

VERBAND VON FABRIKANTEN-VEREINEN IM REGIERUNGSBEZIRK ARNSBERG UND BENACHBARTEN BEZIRKEN.

Festschrift, April 1929, des Verbandes von Fabrikanten-Vereinen im Regierungsbezirk Arnsberg und in benachbarten Bezirken, Sitz Iserlohn: Sozialpolitisches und Wirtschaftliches aus Vergangenheit und Gegenwart der südwestfälischen und oberbergischen Eisen- und Metallindustrie. [Iserlohn, 1929] 147 p. illus., ports. 27cm.

(Continued)

NN R 9.66 1/c OS(1b) PC, 1, 2, 3 SL E, 1, 2, 3 ST, 1t (LC1, X1, Z1)

VERBAND VON FABRIKANTEN-VEREINEN IM REGIERUNGSBEZIRK ARNSBERG UND BENACHBARTEN BEZIRKEN. Festschrift... (Card 2)

Cover title reads: Festschrift, 25 Jahre...

CONTENTS. --Die Geschichte des Verbandes, von Dr. Klute. --Streifzüge durch die Geschichte von Lohn und Arbeitszeit in der Mark, von H. F. Thomée. --Iserlohner sozialpolitische Begebenheiten aus dem Jahre 1848, von O. Clewing. --Geschichtliches aus der Arbeiter-Bewegung im unteren Lenneťal, von L. Sachs. --Technisches und Sozialpolitisches aus der Geschichte der märkischen Drahtindustrie, von O. H. Dönner. --Die Iserlohner Nadelindustrie, von H. Kirchoff

(Continued)

VERBAND VON FABRIKANTEN-VEREINEN IM REGIERUNGSBEZIRK ARNSBERG UND BENACHBARTEN BEZIRKEN. Festschrift... (Card 3)

--Die Entwicklung der Lüdenscheider Industrie, von P. Gautzsch. --Olper Blechfabrikation in früherer Zeit, von J. Sion. --Die Industrie des Wirtschaftsgebietes von Plettenberg und Umgegend, von E. Langenbach. --Entwicklung der oberbergischen Eisen- und Metallindustrie, von E. Habermas.

1. Industrial arts--Assoc. and org. --Germany--Westphalia. 2. Labor--Germany--Westphalia. 3. Industries--Germany--Westphalia. t. 1929.

F-10
3971

Verband der Geistig Schaffenden Österreichs.

Zehn Jahre Verband der Geistig Schaffenden Österreichs; eine Festschrift. [Wien, 1956?] 23 p. (p. 19-23 advertisements) 30cm.

Cover title.

CONTENTS.—Zehn Jahre Verband der Geistig Schaffenden Österreichs, ein Dezennium Bewährung, von E. Ludwig.—Licht und Schatten: Im Kampf gegen die mate-

(Continued)

NN**R X 6.60 OS PC, 1 SL (LC1, X1, Z1)

Verband der Geistig Schaffenden Österreichs. Zehn Jahre Verband der Geistig Schaffenden Österreichs... 1956? (Card 2)

rielle und geistige Nivellierung, von A. S.—Schicksal eines Standes — Schicksal eines Landes, von F. Wallisch.—Dienst an Europa — Dienst an Österreich, von E. Ludwig.—999 Worte österreichisch oder der blinde Fleck, von H. Weigel.—Der Weg aus der Vergangenheit in die Zukunft, von J. Seifert.—Wo steht der Dichter heute? Von F. Braun.—Das österreichische Musikleben 1945–1955, von E. Werba.—So sehen sie uns.—Die Situation des Ärztestandes und der österreichischen Medizin, von H. Hoff.—Zehn Jahre Theater in Österreich, von F. Schreyvogl.—Der Geistig Schaffende und die Wirklichkeit, von K. M. Bründl.

1. Austria—Civilization, 20th cent.

Verband der jüdischen Kantoren im Königreiche Jugoslavien. Festschrift zu Ehren des Herrn Oberkantors David Meisel, anlässlich des Jubiläums seiner 25. jährigen Amtstätigkeit in Karlovac. Herausgegeben vom Verbande der jüdischen Kantoren in Königreiche Jugoslavien. Zagreb: T. A. Engel, 1931. 23 p. port. 30cm.

CONTENTS.—Oberkantor David Meisel, von Josef Rendi.—In honorem David Meisel, von Heinrich Fischer.—Die Kantorenbildungsanstalt des Israelitischen Proseminars in Brünn, von Josef Heller.—Zum 25 Jährigen Amstjubiläum des Herrn

(Continued)

N. Y. P. L. December 13, 1940

Verband der jüdischen Kantoren im Königreiche Jugoslavien. Festschrift... (Card 2)

Oberkantors David Meisel, von Isidor Lowit.—Ein Wahres Ehrenfest, von Josef Grob.—Die Vorbildung des Kantors, von Magnus Davidsohn.—Bor'chu und Hammelech, von Arno Nadel.—Der blinde Chasan Chone, von Aron Kašicky.—Dem Verdienste seine Krone, von Armin Wilkowitsch.—David Meisel als Vorkämpfer, von Jakob Lamm.—Ein unerlässliches Postulat im Judentume, von A. Stoessler.—Das Wunder des Bestandes Israels und der "Scheliach Zibbur", von Josef Schon.

1. Meisel, David, 1885–
N. Y. P. L. December 13, 1940

Verband der Lithographen und Steindrucker. Festschrift zum 150. Geburtstag des Erfinders der Lithographie Alois Senefelder. Karlsruhe[, 1921]. 8 l. illus. (incl. facsim., ports.) f°.

Cover-title.

1. Senefelder, Alois, 1771–1834. 2. Lithography—Hist.
N. Y. P. L. April 23, 1929

Verein für Geographie und Statistik, Frankfurt am Main. Festschrift zur Hundertjahrfeier des Vereins für Geographie und Statistik zu Frankfurt am Main, 9. Dezember 1836—9. Dezember 1936... Im Auftrage des Vorstandes herausgegeben von Dr. Wolfgang Hartke. Frankfurt am Main: Verlag der Geographischen Verlagsanstalt L. Ravenstein A. G., 1936. xii, 438 p. incl. tables. charts, front., illus., plans, plates, ports. 30½cm.

Six charts in pocket.
"Literaturverzeichnis," p. 99–100 and bibliographical footnotes.

(Continued)

N. Y. P. L. September 20, 1937

Verein für Geographie und Statistik, Frankfurt am Main. Festschrift... (Card 2)

CONTENTS.—Gley, Werner. Grundriss und Wachstum der Stadt Frankfurt a. M. Eine stadtgeographische und statistische Untersuchung.—Siebert, Jürgen. Die Landschaften des rhein-mainischen Kerngebietes.—Wagner, Julius. Die vorgeschichtliche Urlandschaft als Lebensraum mit besonderer Berücksichtigung des Rhein-Main-Gebietes.—Böhler, Jakob. Die Bevölkerungsverhältnisse in der Pfalz und Rheinhessen mit Randgebieten.—Hannemann, Max. Morphologische Untersuchungen im hessischen Bergland.—Overbeck, Hermann. Standortsfragen in der Industriegeographie am Beispiel der Warndtgrenze erläutert.—Krebs, Norbert. Die Verteilung der Kulturen in Deutschland.

(Continued)

N. Y. P. L. September 20, 1937

Verein für Geographie und Statistik, Frankfurt am Main. Festschrift... (Card 3)

—Schultze, J. H. Geomorphologische Forschungen in Neugriechenland.—Maull, Otto. Die Bestimmung der Tropen am Beispiel Amerikas.—Schrepfer, Hans. Ergebnisse geographischer Beobachtungen in einigen Landschaften Neufundlands auf Grund einer Reise im Spätsommer und Frühherbst 1932.—Kühn, Franz. Die Cordilleren-Landschaft in Südmendoza (Argentinien).

881746A. 1. No subject. I. Hartke, Wolfgang, ed. II. Title.
N. Y. P. L. September 20, 1937

Verein für Geschichte und Altertumskunde, Frankfurt am Main. Festschrift zur Feier des 25jährigen Bestehens des Städtischen historischen Museums in Frankfurt am Main, dem Historischen Museum dargebracht vom Verein für Geschichte und Alterthumskunde. Frankfurt am Main: Druck von Gebrüder Knauer, 1903. 198 p. illus., plates. 31½cm.

CONTENTS. — Die städtischen Sammlungen in reichs- und freistädtischer Zeit 1691–1866. Von Rudolf Jung.—Die Gründung des Städtischen historischen Museums und des Vereines für dasselbe im Jahre 1877. Von Otto Donner-von Richter.—Ergebnisse und Aufgaben der Heddernheimer Lokalforschung. Von Georg Wolff.—Römische Terracot-

(Continued)

N. Y. P. L. January 26, 1940

Verein für Geschichte und Altertumskunde, Frankfurt am Main. Festschrift zur Feier des 25jährigen Bestehens... (Card 2)

ten aus unserer Umgegend im Historischen Museum. Von Alexander Riese.—Das römische Villengebäude bei der Güntersburg und die Bornburg. Von C. L. Thomas.—Der Kachelofen in Frankfurt. Von Otto Lauffer.—Das Frankfurter Zinngiessergewerbe und seine Blüthezeit im 18. Jahrhundert. Von Alexander Dietz.—Frankfurter Medailleure im 16. Jahrhundert. Von Julius Cahn.

30948B. 1. Museums, Historical—Germany—Frankfurt-am-Main. I. Title.
N. Y. P. L. January 26, 1940

Verein schweizerischer Centralheizungs-Industrieller. ...Zum 25jährigen Bestehen. Publication à l'occasion du 25e anniversaire. 1906–1931. [Zürich, 1932.] 195 p. incl. diagrs. illus. (incl. charts, plans.) 29½cm.

Some articles are in German and French; others, in German only.

723244A. 1. Heating. 2. Heating, Central station.
N. Y. P. L. October 2, 1934

Verein Schweizerischer Lithographiebesitzer, *Bern.*

Die Lithographie in der Schweiz und die verwandten Techniken: Tiefdruck, Lichtdruck, Chemigraphie. ₍Festschrift zum 50 jährigen Bestehen des Vereins Schweizerischer Lithographiebesitzer, 1894–1944₎ Zürich, Orell Füssli ₍1944₎

356 p. illus. (part col.) plates (part col.) ports., col. maps. 31 cm.

"Literatur zur Lithographie in der Schweiz im 19. Jahrhundert": p. 351.

1. Lithography—Switzerland. 2. Lithography. 3. Printing—Hist.—Switzerland. 4. Printing—Specimens. 5. Art in advertising.

A 43-5686*

Harvard Univ. Library for Library of Congress ₍2₎

Festschrift

Verein zur Wahrung der Interessen der chemischen Industrie Deutschlands, Berlin.

...Ausgewaehlte Kapitel aus der chemisch-industriellen Wirtschaftspolitik, 1877–1927, überreicht der 50 jährigen Hauptversammlung vom Geschäftsführer Dr. C. Ungewitter. Berlin₍: O. Elsner₎, 1927. 489 p. incl. tables. ports. 4°.

"Festschrift...aus Anlass des 50 jährigen Jubiläums des Vereins zur Wahrung der Interessen der chemischen Industrie Deutschlands." —*Pref.*

Pref. signed: Hans Blankenstein.

375031A. 1. Chemical industries—Germany. 2. Commerce—Treaties—Germany, 1877–1927. 3. Chemicals—Tariff—Germany. 4. Ungewitter, Claus.

N. Y. P. L. October 6, 1928

VERENIGING VOOR TECHNISCH ONDERWIJS.

Uit de typografische kruidtuin; een bundel grafisch allerlei herdrukt bij het vijftig-jarig bestaan van de afdeling typografie van de eerste technische school te 's-Gravenhage. ['s-Gravenhage] 1962. 100 p. illus. 23cm.

CONTENTS.--Van minnaars en dwazen in boekenland, door F. Kerdijk. --Sint Jan voor de Latijnse poort, door F. Kerdijk.--

(Continued)

NN R 2.65 e/s (OC)I OS(1b) PC, 1, I SL (LC1, X1, Z1)

2

VERENIGING VOOR TECHNISCH ONDERWIJS. Uit de typografische kruidtuin... (Card 2)

Legende Boec van den Houte.--Drukkers in Venetië, door F. Kerdijk.--Afbeelding en verbeelding uit de zetkast, door D. Dooijes.--Cervantes, door E. de Baumont.--Het zetfoutenduiveltje, door B. Kruitwagen.

1. Printing--Addresses, essays, lectures. I. Title.

Verfassungsrecht und Verfassungswirklichkeit. Festschrift für Hans Huber zum 60. Geburtstag, 24. Mai 1961, dargebracht von Freunden, Kollegen, Schülern und vom Verlag. Bern, Verlag Stämpfli, 1961.

246 p. port. 24 cm.

In German or French.

Bibliographical footnotes.

(Continued)

NN*R 3.63 g/ OC PC, 1, 2, 3 SL E, 1, 2, 3 (LC1, X1, Z1)

3

VERFASSUNGSRECHT und Verfassungswirklichkeit... 1961 (Card 2)

CONTENTS.—Finanzverwaltung und Rechtsstaat, von W. Antoniolli.—Die richterliche Kontrollfunktion im westdeutschen Verfassungsgefüge, von O. Bachof.—L'évolution du droit budgétaire genevois, par M. Battelli.—Verfassung und Verwaltung in der Schweiz, von R. Bäumlin.—Principe et limites de la liberté doctrinale des pasteurs de l'Église nationale vaudoise, par M. Bridel.—Die politische Verantwortlichkeit der Regierung im schweizerischen Staatsrecht, von K. Eichenberger.—Normenkontrolle und Verfassungsinterpretation, von M. Imboden.—Von der klassischen Dreiteilung zur umfassenden

(Continued)

VERFASSUNGSRECHT und Verfassungswirklichkeit... 1961. (Card 3)

Gewaltenteilung, von W. Kägi.—Die aufsehende Gewalt, von H. Marti.—Die Wertordnung der schweizerischen Bundesverfassung, von H. Nef.—Verwaltung ohne gesetzliche Ermächtigung? Von H. Peters.—Das repräsentative Prinzip in der modernen Demokratie, von U. Scheuner.

1. Switzerland--Constitutional law--Addresses, essays, lectures. 2. Germany--Constitutional law--Addresses, essays, lectures. 3. Huber, Hans, 1901-

---

Verzamelde opstellen, geschreven door oud-leerlingen van Professor Dr J. H. Scholte. Amsterdam, J. M. Meulenhoff, 1947. 364 p. front. 24cm.

PARTIAL CONTENTS.—Zeeman, D. J. C. Die erste Fortsetzung zu Rudolf von Ems' Weltchronik.—Absil, T. E. La divina commedia en Faust.—Stockum, T. C. van. Storm om Alkestis.—Theissen, E. W. De reiniging van Orestes.—Meyer, H. Nietzsches Bildungsphilister und der Philister der Goethezeit.—Perquin, N. Die Lüge in Grillparzers "Weh' dem der lügt".—Winkler, Joh. Ds M. P. Hasebroek.—Heberle, J. A. J. Slauerhoff en Reinhold Schneider.—Hommes, T. Het onderwijs in Indië.

cd.

440940B. 1. Scholte, Jan Hendrik, 1874- . 2. Philology—Addresses, essays, lectures. 3. Sagas—Hist. and crit. 4. Goethe, Johann Wolfgang von.

N. Y. P. L. June 17, 1948

...**Verzameling** van opstellen door oud-leerlingen en bevriende vakgenooten opgedragen aan Mgr. Prof. Dr. Jos. Schrijnen, bij gelegenheid van zijn zestigsten verjaardag, 2 mei 1929. Nijmegen: N. V. Dekker & van de Vegt₍, 1929₎. xxvii, 926 p. front. (port.), maps, plates. 4°.

At head of title: Donum natalicum Schrijnen.

534226A. 1. Schrijnen, Josef C. F. H., 1869- . 2. Philology—Collections.

N. Y. P. L. December 16, 1931

VI

Vyer; essäer och artiklar ur tidningen Vi, tillägnade Anders Örne i urval av Nils Thedin. [Vinjetter av Georg Lagerstedt. Stockholm] Rabén & Sjögren [1953] 255 p. illus. 20cm.

1. Essays, Swedish—Collections. 2. Örne, Anders Emanuel, 1881- . I. Thedin, Nils, 1911- , ed.

NN**R X 4.54 (OC)I OS PC, 1, 2, I SL (PR1, Z4, LC1, X1)

* PWZ
(Weisgal)

VICTOR, EDWARD, ed.
Meyer Weisgal at seventy; an anthology. London, Weidenfeld and Nicolson [1966] xii, 216 p. ports. 23cm.

1. Weisgal, Meyer Wolfe, 1894-
NN R 6.66 g/ OC PC,1 SL J,1 (LC1,X1,Z1)

...Vida y pensamiento de Martí... (Card 2)

Martí, escritor; la españolidad literaria de José Martí, por Juan Marinello. Martí viajero, por Salvador Massip. Aspectos de la crítica literaria en Martí, por J. A. Portuondo. Martí, los clásicos y la enseñanza humanística, por Manuel Bisbé. Martí, crítico de arte, por Félix Lizaso. Martí y el espiritualismo, por Raquel Catalá. Notas sobre conferenciantes.—v. 2. Martí y el derecho, por Eduardo Le Riverend Brusone. Martí, periodista, por Gonzalo de Quesada y Miranda. Martí y el teatro, por Francisco Ichaso. Martí, conspirador y revolucionario, por Gerardo Castellanos G. Las ideas económicas de Martí, por Felipe de Pazos y Roque. La capacidad de magisterio en Martí, por Medardo Vitier. Introducción al estudio de las ideas sociales de Martí, por J. A. Portuondo. Martí, orador, por Salvador García Agüero. Martí, poeta, y su influencia innovadora en la poesía de América, por A. I. Augier. Martí y las razas, por Fernando Ortiz. La república de Martí, por Emilio Roig de Leuchsenring. Notas sobre conferenciantes.

1. Martí, José Julian, 1853-1895. I. Havana (City). II. Ser.
N. Y. P. L. June 28, 1946

NHC
(Vriesland)

Victor, het boek der vrienden; een literaire parade ter ere van Victor E. van Vriesland. Amsterdam, "De Spiegel," 1947. 160 p. 28cm.

Festschrift ed.

441367B. 1. Vriesland, Victor Emanuel van, 1892-
N. Y. P. L. December 15, 1948

Copy only words underlined
& Classmark-- KBV

VÍDALÍN, ARNGRIMUR THORKILSSON.
Den tredie part af det saa kaldede Gamle og Nye Grønlands beskrivelse. København, 1971. 125 p. 24cm. (Gronlandske Selskab. Skrifter. 21)

Published by the Grønlandske selskab on the occasion of 250 years since H. Egedes voyage to Greenland with the introduction and commentaries by F. Gad.

1. Egede, Hans Poulsen, 1686-1758. 2. Greenland--Descr. and trav., to 1800. I. Gad, Finn, 1911- , ed.
NN R 8. 72 n/ OC(1b+)I OI PC,1,2,I AH,2,I (LC1,X1,Z1)

SSD

Victoria university college, Wellington, N. Z.
The university and the community; essays in honour of Thomas Alexander Hunter. Wellington, Victoria university college, 1946. vii, 302 p. front. 23cm.

"Preface" signed: Ernest Beaglehole.
CONTENTS.—A knight's progress, by F. A. De la Mare.—Psychology & child guidance, by Ernest Beaglehole.—Psychology & the human problems of industry, by L. S. Hearnshaw.—The sciences of man & the Maori, by I. L. G. Sutherland.—History & the New Zealander, by J. C. Beaglehole.—Educational research in New Zealand, by H. C.

(Continued)

N. Y. P. L. June 19, 1947

AN
(Renaudot)

...La vie de Théophraste Renaudot, par ******** Paris: Gallimard, 1929. 221 p. front. (port.) 12°. (Vies des hommes illustres. no.42)

"Les membres du Jury Renaudot ont décidé de rendre hommage à leur patron... chacun d'eux ayant écrit un des dix chapitres qui la composent."
Bibliography, p.[219-]221.

482945A. 1.Renaudot, Théophraste,1584-1653. I.Ser.

Victoria university college, Wellington, N. Z. The university and the community... (Card 2)

McQueen.—Law & the University, by I. D. Campbell.—The Court of appeal's own prior decision, by R. O. McGechan.—The University, the civil service & democracy, by Leslie Lipson.—The study of mathematics, by J. T. Campbell.—Geology in the middle University district, by C. A. Cotton.—Biology in New Zealand, by L. R. Richardson.—Botany in review, by I. V. Newman.—Administration in the University: a critical review.—'Tommy': a personal memoir.

390733B. 1. Hunter, Thomas Alexander, 1876- 2. Colleges and universities—New Zealand. 3. Science—Hist.—New Zealand. 4. New Zealand—Hist. 5. Education—Addresses, essays, lectures. I. Beaglehole, Ernest, 1906- , ed. II. Title.
N. Y. P. L. June 19, 1947

E-11
3380

VIEBROCK, HELMUT, ed.
Festschrift zum 75. Geburtstag von Theodor Spira, hrsg. von H. Viebrock und W. Erzgräber. Heidelberg, C. Winter, 1961. 405 p. illus., port. 25cm.

Chiefly in German, a few articles in English.
Bibliographical footnotes.

1. Spira, Theodor, 1885- 2. English literature--Addresses, essays, lectures. I. Erzgräber, Willi, joint ed.
NN R 4. 65 p/ OC,I PC,1,2,I SL (LC1,X1,Z1) [I]

Write on slip only words underlined and classmark —
HOB

...**Vida** y pensamiento de Martí; homenaje de la ciudad de la Habana en el cincuentenario de la fundación del Partido revolucionario cubano, 1892–1942... [Habana] Municipio de la Habana, 1942. 2 v. 23cm. (Colección histórica cubana y americana. [no.] 4.)

CONTENTS.—v. 1. Nota preliminar, por Emilio Roig de Leuchsenring. Humanidad de Martí, por M. I. Méndez. Americanismo en Martí, por Enrique Gay-Calbó. Martí y la filosofía, por Miguel Jorrín. Teoría martiana del partido político, por Julio Le Riverend Brusone. Martí y las religiones, por Emilio Roig de Leuchsenring. Sobre

(Continued)

N. Y. P. L. June 28, 1946

Write on slip only words underlined and classmark:
BAA

Vienna. Universität. Institut für Völkerkunde.
...Kultur und Sprache... Wien, Verlag Herold, 1952. 511 p. illus., maps. 23cm. ("Wiener Beiträge zur Kulturgeschichte und Linguistik". Bd. 9)

"Ein Festband dem 4. Internationalen Kongress für Anthropologie und Ethnologie."
On cover: Herausgegeben von Wilhelm Koppers unter Mitwirkung von Robert Heine-Geldern und Josef Haekel.
Bibliography included.
CONTENTS.—Koppers, W. Der historische Gedanke in Ethnologie und Prähistorie.

(Continued)

NN 4.53 (OC)II OS,I PC,1,2, I,II (LC1,X1,Z1)

Vienna. Universität. Institut für Völkerkunde. ...Kultur und Sprache...1952. (Card 2)

—Closs, A. Das Versenkungsopfer.—Fürer-Haimendorf, C. von. The cult of Ayak among the Kolams of Hyderabad.—Haékel, J. Die Vorstellung vom Zweiten Ich in den amerikanischen Hochkulturen.—Slawik, A. Zum Problem des Bärenfestes der Ainu und Giljaken.—Fuchs, S. The social organization of the Gond in Eastern Mandla.—Graf, W. Zur Individualforschung in der Musikethnologie.— Hohenwart-Gerlachstein, A. Zur "Geschwisterehe" im alten Ägypten.—Meister, R. Anfänge und Frühformen der Erziehung.—Schmidt, W. Ehe und Familie im vermännlichten Mutterrecht.—Drobec, E. Heilkunde bei den Eingeborenen Australiens.—Feriz, H. Die Harndiagnostik in der indianischen Volksmedizin.—Heine-Geldern, R. Some problems of migration in the Pacific.—Bulck, V. van. Existe-t-il une langue des Pygmées en Afrique Centrale?—

(Continued)

Vienna. Universität. Institut für Völkerkunde. ...Kultur und Sprache...1952. (Card 3)

Havers, W. Das indogermanische Enklisengesetz in den Orationen des Missale Romanum.—Locker, E. Dévelopement et décomposition du type des langues indo-europeenes.—Schebesta, P. Das Problem der Pygmäensprache.—Wurm, S. Sind Türksprachen Tonsprachen?—Hančar, F. Stand und historische Bedeutung der Pferdezucht Mittelasiens im ersten Jahrtausend v. Chr.—Jettmar, K. Zum Problem der tungusischen "Urheimat."

1. Ethnology—Essays and misc. 2. Philology—Addresses, essays, lectures. I. Series. II. Koppers, Wilhelm, 1886- , ed.

D-10
4559

VIENNA. UNIVERSITÄT. Institut für Völkerkunde.
Die Wiener Schule der Völkerkunde. The Vienna school of ethnology. Festschrift anlässlich des 25-jährigen Bestandes des Institutes für Völkerkunde der Universität Wien (1929-1954). Herausgeber: J. Haeckel, A. Hohenwart-Gerlaehstein und A. Slawik. Horn, Austria, F. Berger, 1956. viii, 568 p. 21 illus., 11 plates, 2 maps. 23cm.

Contributions in German, English, French, or Italian.

(Continued)

NN X 7.57 c/o (OC)I, II, IIb, III, IVb+ OS PC, 1, I, II, III SL (LC1, X1, Z1, Y1) [I]

VIENNA. UNIVERSITÄT. Institut für Völkerkunde. Die Wiener Schule der Völkerkunde... (Card 2)

Includes bibliographies.

1. Ethnology--Addresses, essays, lectures. I. Haekel, Josef, ed. II. Hohenwart-Gerlachstein, Anna, ed. III. Slawik, Alexander, ed. IV. Haekel, Josef.

E-12
7201

VIERHAUS, RUDOLF, ed.
Dauer und Wandel der Geschichte; Aspekte europäischer Vergangenheit. Festgabe für Kurt von Raumer zum 15. Dezember 1965. Hrsg. von Rudolf Vierhaus und Manfred Botzenhart. Münster, Aschendorff [1966] 554 p. illus., plates, port. 24cm. (Neue münstersche Beiträge zur Geschichtsforschung. Bd. 9)

Bibliographical footnotes.

(Continued)

NN R 12.66 r/o OC, II, IIbo (OS)I PC, 1, 2, I, II, IV SL (LC1, X1, Z1) [I]

VIERHAUS, RUDOLF, ed. Dauer und Wandel der Geschichte... (Card 2)

CONTENTS.--Möglichkeiten und Grenzen der Geschichtswissenschaft in der Gegenwart, von R. Wittram.--Der Staatsbau des Prinzipats im Spiegel römischer Reichsarchitektur, von H.E. Stier.--Politische und asketische Aspekte der Christianisierung, von K. Hauck.--Tiere und Heilige, von A. Nitschke.--Isokrates, Erasmus und die Institutio principis christiani, von O. Herding.--Sebastian Franck und das münsterische Täufertum, von R. Stupperich.--Über frühneuzeitliche Städtetypen, von H. Stoob.-- Wartenberg, Chigi und Knöringen im Jahre 1645, von K. Repgen.--Probleme des

(Continued)

VIERHAUS, RUDOLF, ed. Dauer und Wandel der Geschichte... (Card 3)

dänischen Frühabsolutismus, von D. Gerhard.--Fortschritt und Beharrung in der österreichischen Geschichte, von A. Wandruszka.--Andreas Schlüter, von W. Hager.--Träger und Vermittler romanischer Kultur im Deutschland des 18. Jahrhunderts, von M. Braubach.--Ständewesen und Staatsverwaltung im Deutschland im späten 18. Jahrhundert, von R. Vierhaus.--Wirtschaftliche und soziale Auswirkungen der Säkularisation in Deutschland, von R. Morsey.--Stein und Goethe, zu ihren, von A.H. von Wallthor.--Ludwig Vincke und Therese vom Stein, von J. Bauermann.--Eine Aufzeichnung Zar Nikolaij's I für seinen

(Continued)

VIERHAUS, RUDOLF, ed. Dauer und Wandel der Geschichte... (Card 4)

Sohn, von M. Hellmann.--Die Stiehlschen Regulative, von K.E. Jeismann.--Ranke und Karl der Grosse, von A. Borst.--Zur Auffassung der Mittelalterlichen Kaiserpolitik im 19. Jahrhundert, von H. Gollwitzer.--Zur Flamenpolitik des I. Weltkrieges, von F. Petri.--Das hinterlassene Werk des Parlamentarischen Untersuchungsausschusses, von W. Hahlweg.

1. Raumer, Kurt von, 1900- . 2. Europe--Hist.--Addresses, essays, lectures. I. Series. II. Botzenhart, Manfred, joint ed. III. Botzenhart, Manfred. IV. Title.

E-10
306

VIKTOR VON WEIZSÄCKER; Arzt im Irrsal der Zeit.
Eine Freundesgabe zum siebzigsten Geburtstag am 21. 4. 1956 [Hrsg. von Paul Vogel] Göttingen, Vandenhoeck & Ruprecht [1956] 326 p. port. 25cm.

CONTENTS.—Die Kreatur, von M. Buber.—Das Verhältnis des Arztes Weizsäcker zur Theologie und das der Theologen zu Weizsäckers Medizin, von H. Ehrenberg.—Gestaltkreis und Komplementarität, von C.F. von Weizsäcker.—Die Einheit von Leib und Seele in der theologischen Anthro-

(Continued)

NN ** X 8.56 j/o OC, I, Ib PC, 1, 2, I SL (LC1, X1, Z1)

VIKTOR VON WEIZSÄCKER; Arzt im Irrsal der Zeit. (Card 2)

pologie und in der anthropologischen Medizin, von R. Siebeck.—Begegnung und Interpretation in ärztlicher Sicht, von C. Oehme.—Der Allgemeinzustand des Schwerkranken, von H. Plügge.—Die Kuckucksterz; eine anthropologische Studie, von R. Bilz.—Herakleitos von Ephesos schreibt an Parmenides von Elea, von E. Rosenstock-Huessy.—Psychologie des Hausarztes, von F.J.J. Buytendijk.—Neurosen und Psychosen als soziale Phänomene, von A. -Mitscherlich.—Hierarchie und Führungsfeld in der Psychobiologie, von G.-R. Heyer.—Grundfragen der klinischen Neurologie, von P. Vogel.— Der Begriff Reaktion in

(Continued)

VIKTOR VON WEIZSÄCKER; Arzt im Irrsal der Zeit. (Card 3)

Neurologie und Psychiatrie, von A. P. Auersperg und J. Weibel. —Die kombinatorische Leistung des binokularen Sehens, von P. Christian. — Zur funktionalen Analyse der Echolalie, von A. Derwort. —Nachgehende ärztliche Fürsorge bei Hirnverletzten, von E. Wiesenhütter. —Anthropologische Medizin in der inneren Klinik, von W. Kütemeyer. —Vom Wesen der Phthise, von H. Huebschmann. —Über Sterbeangst bei vegetativen Störungen, von W. F. Seemann. —Über Fridtjof Nansen, von K. Hansen. —Natur und Geist;" eine Besprechung der lebenserinnerungen Viktor von Weizsäckers, von H. Ruffin. — Bibliographie der Schriften von Viktor von Weizsäcker, von C. von Weizsäcker (p. [318]-326).

(Continued)

E-12
2102

VINTERLANDBRUKSSKULENS ELEVLAG.
Vinterlandbruksskulens elevlag; festskrift, 50 år. Redaktør: Tønnes Mauland. Stavanger, Gjøstein boktr. 1961. 55 p. illus., ports. 24cm.

1. Agriculture--Education--Institutions--Norway--Jæren. 2. Farmers--Norway. I. Mauland, Tønnes, ed. II. Mauland, Tønnes

NN 5. 65 p/s (OC)I, IIbo OS(1b*) PC, 1, 2, I SL (LC1, X1, Z1)

VIKTOR VON WEIZSÄCKER; Arzt im Irrsal der Zeit. (Card 4)

1. Weizsäcker, Viktor von. 2. Medicine—Addresses, essays, lectures. I. Vogel, Paul, 1900- , ed.

NBP

Virginia. University.
...English studies in honor of James Southall Wilson. Charlottesville, 1951. 298 p. port. 23cm. (Virginia. University. University of Virginia studies. v.5)

1. Wilson, James Southall, 1880- 2. English literature--Hist.and crit. 3. American literature--Hist.and crit. I. Bowers, Fredson Thayer, ed. II. Series.

NN 11.52. (OC)I (OD)Ii (ED)II PC 1,2,3,I,II SL (LC1,Z1,X1)

---

* KB
1546

Villalón, Cristóbal de, 16th cent.
Una obra de derecho mercantil del siglo XVI. El Vallisoletano Cristobal de Villalon y su Prouechofo [sic] tratado de cambios y contrataciones de mercaderes y reprouacion de usura. Reproduccion en fotogr963abado. Homenaje de la Facultad de derecho de la Universidad de Valladolid y con motivo de su jubilacion al catedratico de derecho mercantil...Sr. Dr. D. Jose Maria Gonzalez de

(Continued)

N. Y. P. L. April 30, 1948

YBX

VISION & action, essays in honor of Horace M. Kallen on his 70th birthday. Edited by Sidney Ratner. New Brunswick, Rutgers university press, 1953. xvii, 277 p. port. 22cm.

CONTENTS. — Academic freedom re-visited, by T. V. Smith. — Human rights under the United Nations Charter, by B. V. Cohen. —The absolute, the experimental method, and Horace Kallen, by P. H. Douglas. —Some tame reflections on some wild facts, by J. Frank. — Some central themes in Horace Kallen's philosophy, by S. Ratner. — Cultural relativism and standards, by G. Boas. — The philosophy of democracy as a philosophy of history, by S. Hook. — The rational imperatives, by C. I. Lewis. — From Poe to Valéry, by T. S. Eliot. -- Events and the future, by

(Continued)

NN * R 12.53 OC, I PC, 1, 2, I SL (LC1, Z1, X1)

Villalón, Cristóbal de, 16th cent. Una obra de derecho mercantil del siglo XVI... 1546. (Card 2)
Echávarri y Vivanco... [Valladolid, Imprenta castellana, 1945] 24 p., facsim. (47 l.), 119–279 p. 25cm.

Reproduced from the original of the 1546 edition in the library of the Colegio de Santa Cruz, Valladolid, with reproduction of the t.-p. of the 1542 edition in place of the 1546 t.-p. (wanting in the original); without reproduction of sig. F_{3-4} (wanting in the original?), of sig. F_{11} (blank) and of sig. G^{18} (Tratado de la confesión, with a second colophon).

"Los capitulos estan glosados por discipulos esclarecidos del homenajeado."

"Obras publicadas por...Echávarri y Vivanco," p. 273–277.

See: Salvá 4038. See: Gallardo 4582. See: Alcocer y Martínez 135.

(Continued)

N. Y. P. L. April 30, 1948

VISON & action... (Card 2)

J. Dewey. — Teleological explanation and teleological systems, by E. Nagel. —Ch'an (Zen) Buddhism in China, by Hu Shih. — Reconsideration of the origin and nature of perception, by A. Ames, Jr. — Horace M. Kallen: a bibliography (p. 275-277)

1. Philosophy, 1901- 2. Kallen, Horace Meyer, 1882- I. Ratner, Sidney, ed.

Villalón, Cristóbal de, 16th cent. Una obra de derecho mercantil del siglo XVI... 1546. (Card 3)

Colophon of original, sig. F_{11}^{b}: ...Jmpresso enla...villa de Ualladolid...enla officina de Francisco Fernandez de cordoua impressor. Acabosse en .15. dias del mes d'Agosto...1546.

Collation of original: liij [i. e. 50] f., 14 l. Leaf 2 at end blank, several folios wrongly numbered.

433766B. 1. Commerce—Jurisp. 2. Interest—Jurisp. 3. González de Echávarri y Vivanco, José María, 1875- . I. Valladolid, Spain (City). Universidad. Derecho y ciencias sociales, Facultad de.

N. Y. P. L. April 30, 1948

AN
(Plesman, A.)

De Vliegende Hollander; in memoriam Dr Albert Plesman. [Samensteller Chr. K. Werkman] Baarn, Wereldvenster, 1954. 175 p. illus. 23cm.

Text in Dutch, English, French or German.

1. Plesman, Albert, 1889-1953. I. Werkman, Chr. K , ed.

NN**R X 9.54 OC,1b,I, Ib PC,1,I SL ST,1,I (Z1,LC1,X1)

*QL
+

Vodnikov spomenik. Na svitlo dal Etbin Henrik Costa. V Ljubljani, Natisnila I. Žl. Kleinmayr in F. Bamberg, 1859. xi,268,[6] p. port. facsim. 30cm.

Added t.-p. in German.
Preface in Slovenian and German, with articles and poems either in Slovenian or German.
"Krajnska," chorus (TTBB) or one voice with piano
(Continued)

NN** X 10.53 OC,1b,I IIb PC,1,2,I SL
(MU)IIg S,1,2,I,II (MUS, 1 LC1,Z1,X1)

Vodnikov spomenik. Na svitlo dal Etbin Henrik Costa... (Card 2)

accompaniment, op. 51, by Kamillo Maschek, p. [273-274]
Contents.—razdělek 1. Spisi o Vodnikovem življenji in znaňajnosti njegovi.—razdělek 2. Izbor slovenskih in Krajnskih pisateljev.
1. Vodnik, Valentin, 1758-1819. 2. Slovenian literature—Collections. I. Costa, Ethbin Heinrich. II. Maschek, Kamillo. Krajnska.

D-12
6839

VOGT, JOSEPH, 1895-
Orbis; ausgewählte Schriften zur Geschichte des Altertums [Zum fünfundsechzigsten Geburtstag von Joseph Vogt am 23. Juni 1960 hrsg. von Fritz Taeger und Karl Christ] Freiburg, Herder [1960] 400 p. 23cm.

Bibliographical footnotes
"Schriftenverzeichnis," p. 381-390.
(Continued)

NN 10.60 g/ OC,I,II PC, 1,I,II SL (LC1,X1,Z1)

VOGT, JOSEPH, 1895- . Orbis... (Card 2)

1. History, Ancient--Addresses, essays, lectures. I. Taeger, Fritz, 1894- , ed. II. Christ, Karl, 1878- , ed.

ZBIE

...Volk und Heimat; Festschrift für Viktor von Geramb. Graz [etc.] A. Pustet [1949] 320 p. illus. 21cm.

At head of title: Hanns Koren. Leopold Kretzenbacher.
Includes music.

Festschrift

505415B. 1. Geramb, Viktor, Ritter von, 1884- . 2. Folk lore—Austria. 3. Folk art, Austrian. I. Koren, Hanns, ed. II. Kretzenbacher, Leopold, ed.
N. Y. P. L. January 6, 1950

* C-6 p.v.25

Volksbank Wien, Hietzing-Penzing.
Festschrift anlässlich des 25 jähr. Bestandes der Volksbank Wien, Hietzing-Penzing, 1925–1950. [Wien, 1950] 20 p. ports. 30cm.

1. Banks and banking—Austria—Vienna.
NN 1.53 OS PC,I SL E,I (LC1,Z1,X1)

E-12
1647

VOLKSHOCHSCHULE, Landeck, Austria.
Bildner, Planer und Poeten im Oberen Inntal; Festschrift der Volkshochschule Landeck anlässlich des 300. Geburtstages Jakob Prandtauer's, geleitet von Hermann Kuprian. Innsbruck, Universitätsverlag Wagner, 1960. xvi, 330 p. plates, music. 24cm. (Schlern-Schriften. 214)

1. Prandtauer, Jakob, d. 1726. 2. Tyrol--Civilization--Addresses, essays, lectures. 3. German literature--Austria--Collections I. Kuprian, Hermann, ed. II. Series.
NN 3.65 p/s (OC)I OS (1b), II PC, 1, 2, 3, I, II SL A, 1, I (LC1, X1, Z1) [I]

ZBG

...Volkskundliche Ernte; Hugo Hepding dargebracht am 7. September 1938 von seinen Freunden. Giessen: Münchowsche Universitäts-Druckerei O. Kindt GmbH, 1938. 273 p. 24½cm. (Giessener Beiträge zur deutschen Philologie... 60.)

Contents.—Au, Hans v. d. Der Bajessmann, ein Spessarter Volkstanz.—Becker, Albert. Politik und Volkstum.—Berthold, Luise. Sprachliche Niederschläge absinkenden Hexenglaubens.—Fritzsche, R. A. ἀνώνυμον.—Frölich, Karl. Begriff und Aufgabenkreis der rechtlichen Volkskunde.—Götze, Alfred. Der Name Hepding.—Gundel, Wilhelm. Zur Herkunft unserer Wochentagsnamen.—Helm, Karl. Notfeuer.—Hoffmann, Wilhelm. Volkstümliche Neck- und Schwankdichtung in Rheinland und Hessen.—Jacoby, Adolf. Die Sage vom verlorenen Kind in der Schatzhöhle.—Koch, Georg. Arndt, Goethe und die Ursprünge der deutschen Volkskunde.—Lauf-

(Continued)

N. Y. P. L. February 27, 1939

...Volkskundliche Ernte... (Card 2)

fer, Otto. Die Hexe als Zaunreiterin.—Lehnert, Georg. Zauber und Astrologie in den erhaltenen römischen Deklamationen.—Mackensen, Lutz. Zu Riehls Novellenwerk.—Martin, Bernhard. Erntegatter am Bauernwagen in Oberhessen und Waldeck.—Marzell, Heinrich. Segen und Zauberformeln aus einem österreichischen Rossarzneibuch des 16. Jahrhunderts.—Maurer, Friedrich. Zur Geschichte der Nasalierungen vor Reibelaut.—Mössinger, Friedrich. Vom Weihnachtsbaum im Hessischen.—Ohrt, Ferdinand. Merseburg und Lindisfarne.—Spamer, Adolf. Himmelsbriefe der deutschen Mystik.—Stammler, Wolfgang. Atzmann.—Stroh, Fritz. Das Lied der hessischen Landgänger.—Süss, Wilhelm. Der heilige Hieronymus und die Formen seiner Polemik.—Taylor, Archer. A seventeenth-century collection of biblical riddles.—Wagner, Kurt. Formen der Volkserzählung.—Lehnert, Georg. Verzeichnis der Schriften von Hugo Hepding.

978738A. 1. Hepding, Hugo, 1878- . 2. Folk lore. 3. Folk lore—Germany. I. Ser.
N. Y. P. L. February 27, 1939

Write on slip words underlined below and class mark—
STL

Volksschule und Lehrerbildung, 1832–1932; Festschrift zur Jahrhundertfeier, herausgegeben vom Erziehungsrate des Kantons Zürich. Bearbeitet von G. Guggenbühl, Alfred Mantel, Heinrich Gubler, Hans Kreis und Emil Gassmann. Zürich: Erziehungsdirektion, 1933. x, 720 p. plates, ports., table. 25cm. (Zürich «Canton». Erziehungswesens, Direktion des. Die zürcherischen Schulen seit der Regeneration der 1830er Jahre. v. 1.)

"Quellennachweis," p. 691–714.

(Continued)

Festschrift

N. Y. P. L. October 23, 1940

Volksschule und Lehrerbildung, 1832–1932... (Card 2)

CONTENTS.—Hundert Jahre zürcherischer Volksherrschaft. Zeiträume und Hauptströmungen, von J. G. Guggenbühl.—Die zürcherische Volksschule vor dem Ustertag, von Alfred Mantel.—Die zürcherische Volksschule von 1831 bis 1845, von Heinrich Gubler.—Die zürcherische Volksschule von 1845 bis 1872, von Hans Kreis.—Die zürcherische Volksschule und die ihr angegliederten Bildungs- und Wohlfahrtseinrichtungen von 1872 bis 1932, von Emil Gassmann.

71834B. 1. Education—Switzerland—Zürich (Canton). 2. Teachers—Training—Switzerland—Zürich (Canton). I. Gassmann, Emil, 1878- . II. Gubler, Heinrich, 1877- . III. Guggenbühl, Johann Gottfried, 1888- . IV. Kreis, Hans, 1885- . V. Mantel-Ross, Alfred, 1881- .
N. Y. P. L. October 23, 1940

VOLLANS, ROBERT FRANKS, ed. Libraries for the people... (Card 2)

Collison.--The Library association, by D. D. Haslam.--International federation of library associations, by A. Thompson.--Anglo-Scandinavian conferences, by R. D. Rates.--British public library service, by F. M. Gardner.--Library development in Australia, by J. Metcalfe.--"Chance to read" in New Zealand, by G. T. Alley.--Danish public libraries after 1945, by E. A. Jensen.--Public libraries in Norway, by A. Andreassen.--Public libraries in Sweden, by B. Hjelmqvist.--Finnish public libraries since World war II, by H. Kannila.-- Dutch public libraries, by G. A.

(Continued)

SB

Volkstum und Kulturpolitik; eine Sammlung von Aufsätzen. Gewidmet Georg Schreiber zum fünfzigsten Geburtstag. Herausgegeben von H. Konen...und J. P. Steffes. Köln: Gilde-Verlag G.m.b.H., 1932. xi, 620 p. 25½cm.

"Bibliographie Georg Schreiber," p. 606–610.

Festschrift

692484A. 1. Schreiber, Georg, 1882- . 2. Political science, 1918- . 3. Germany—Civilization. I. Konen, Heinrich Mathias, 1874- , editor. II. Steffes, Johann Peter, 1885- , editor.
N. Y. P. L. March 27, 1934

VOLLANS, ROBERT FRANKS, ed. Libraries for the people... (Card 3)

van Riemsdijk.--Public library system of West Germany since 1945, by R. Joerden.--Public library U.S.A., by L. Shores.

1. McColvin, Lionel Roy, 1896- . 2. Libraries, Public. 3. Libraries--Assoc. and org. I. Library association. II. Title. III. Vollans, Robert F.

SFC p.v.279

Volkswacht, Breslau.
Grundsätzliches zum Tageskampf; Festgabe für Eduard Bernstein dargebracht von Mitarbeitern der Breslauer "Volkswacht". [Breslau: Volkswacht G.m.b.H., 1925] 94 p. front. (port.) 22½cm.

CONTENTS.—Eduard Bernstein, dem Fünfundsiebzigjährigen.—Löbe, Paul. Eduard Bernstein als Breslauer Abgeordneter.—Olberg, Paul. Aus der Geschichte des russischen Sozialismus.—Marck, Siegfr. Philosophie des Revisionismus.—Neisser, Hans. Die Idee des Klassenkampfes.—Landauer, Carl. Die Sozialisierung als Konsequenz

(Continued)

Festschrift

N. Y. P. L. August 15, 1940

Copy only words underlined & classmark— BVA

Volume dedicated to John Davidson Beazley. [London. Society for the promotion of Hellenic studies, 1951. xiv, 279 p. 47 plates 29cm. (Journal of Hellenic studies, v. 71)

Includes bibliographies.
"A list of the published writings of John Davidson Beazley. Oxford, Clarendon press, 1951" (27 p. port.) inserted.
1. Beazley, John Davidson, 1885-

NN 3.55 d/e OI (PC)1 (LC2 X1, Z1)

Volkswacht, Breslau. Grundsätzliches zum Tageskampf... (Card 2)

des demokratischen Staatsgedankens.—Eckstein, Ernst. Mehr Demokratie!—Grumbkow, Waldemar v. Sozialismus und Pazifismus.—Ganzenmüller, Wilhelm. Schulerziehung zur Friedensgesinnung.—Koitz, Heinrich. Amerikas Wege zur Befriedung der Welt.—Birnbaum, Immanuel. Internationaler Syndikalismus.

1. Bernstein, Eduard, 1850-1932. 2. Socialism, 1923–1933. I. Title.
N. Y. P. L. August 15, 1940

Write on slip words underlined below and class mark— *CAA

Volume dédié à l'ancien éditeur du Monde oriental, M. le professeur K.V. Zetterstéen.

(Monde oriental. Uppsala, 1931. 4°. v.25, p.i-xii, 1-327. port.)

form 400b [11-13-31 25m]

D-16
8943

VOLLANS, ROBERT FRANKS, ed.
Libraries for the people; international studies in librarianship in honour of Lionel R. McColvin. Edited by Robert F. Vollans. [London] Library association, 1968. xiii, 265 p. illus. 21cm.

Includes bibliographies.
CONTENTS.--My father, by K. R. McColvin.--McColvin, the librarian, by R. F. Vollans.--L. R. McColvin: a bibliography, by R. L.

(Continued)

NN S 5.69 y/2 OC, II, IIIbo (OS)I PC, 1, 2, 3, I, II SL (LC1, X1, Z1) 3

Write on slip words underlined below and class mark— *OHN

A volume of Eastern and Indian studies, presented to Professor F. W. Thomas...on his 72nd birth-day, 21st March, 1939; edited by S. M. Katre...and P. K. Gode... Bombay, India: Karnatak pub. house [1939] xxxii, 318 p. incl. tables. facsim., plates, port. 26cm. (New Indian antiquary. Extra series. [v.] 1.)

Bibliographical footnotes.
CONTENTS.—Katre, S. M. Foreword.—Randle, H. N. Dr. Thomas. Bibliography of the published philological writings of Prof. F. W. Thomas.—Bailey, H. W. Khotanese names.—Bapat, P. V. Middha and Middhavādins.—Belvalkar, S. K. The

(Continued)

Festschrift

N. Y. P. L. August 20, 1941

A volume of Eastern and Indian studies . . . (Card 2)

cosmographical episode in Mahābhārata and Padmapurāṇa.—Bhandarkar, D. R. Brahmanic revival.—Bhattacharyya, B. The ten Avatāras and their birthdates.—Bloch, Jules. Emprunts dravidiens a l'aryen moyen.—Carpani, E. G. Il termine Saṁkalpa.—Chakravarty, Chintaharan. Propitiatory rites for warding off the evils of old age.—Coedès, G. La plus ancienne inscription en langue Cham.—De, S. K. Sanskrit literature under the Sena kings of Bengal.—Debrunner, Albert. Zwei altindische Probleme.—Dikshitar, V. R. R. A note on cow veneration in ancient India.—Edgerton, Franklin. Kauśika and the Atharva Veda.—Emeneau, M. B. Toda menstruation practices.—Ghosh, J. C. The donated land of the Nadhanpur grant of Bhāskaravarman of Kāmarūpa.—Gode, P. K. Āpadeva, the author of Mīmāṁsānyāyaprakāśa and Mahāmahopādhyāya Āpadeva, the author of the Adhikaraṇacandrikā and the

(Continued)

N. Y. P. L. August 20, 1941

A volume of Eastern and Indian studies . . . (Card 3)

Smṛticandrikā — Are they identical?—Gonda, J. The meaning of the word Alaṁkāra.—Jagan Nath. The Kaumudīmahotsava as a historical play.—Jha, Ganganath. Magnetism as explained by Śāntarakṣita, a Buddhist writer of the eighth century.—Johnston, E. H. On some difficulties of the Kaṭha Upaniṣad.—Kane, P. V. The Mahābhārata verses and very ancient Dharmasūtras and other works.—Kanga, M. F. E. The age of Yaṣts.—Katre, S. M. Two middle Indo-Aryan words.—Kibe, M. V. Inhabitants of the country around Rāvaṇa's Laṅkā in Amarkantak.—Konow, Sten. A Śaka name of Mazār-tāgh.—Marchal, H. The flying (quivering) flame in the decorations of the Far East.—Mirashi, V. V. Vāmadeva, an early Kalacuri king.—Nagaraja Rao, P. God in Dvaita Vedanta.—Oertel, Hans. The genitivus personae with verbs of eating . . and accepting . . . in Vedic prose.—Pisani, V. The rise of the

(Continued)

N. Y. P. L. August 20, 1941

A volume of Eastern and Indian studies . . . (Card 4)

Mahābharāta.—Renou, Louis. L'hymne aus Aśvin de l'Ādiparvan.—Ruben, Walter. On the original text of the Kṛṣṇa-Epic.—Saksena, Baburam. A Hindi version of the story of the Kharaputta-Jātaka.—Saletore, B. A. Did Tuḷuva revolt after the battle of Rākṣasa-Tangadi?—Saletore, R. N. Relations between the Girāssias and the Marāṭhās.—Sankaran, C. R. Postulation of two probable degrees of abstraction in the primitive Indo-European tongue in the light of compound accentuation.—Sastri, S. S. The Saviśeṣābheda theory.—Scherman, L. Der Schnitter und die Erleuchtung Buddhas.—Sheth, H. C. The spurious in Kauṭilya's Arthaśāstra.—Shamasastri, R. Indra's wars with Śambara.—Sankar, K. G. The age of Srī Saṅkarācārya.—Sarma, B. N. K. Śrī Vyāsarāya Svāmin (1478–1539).—Sharma, H. D. Nidānacintāmaṇi, a commentary on the Aṣṭāṅgahṛdaya of Vāgbhaṭā.—Sircar, D. C. King Sātakarṇi of

(Continued)

N. Y. P. L. August 20, 1941

A volume of Eastern and Indian studies . . . (Card 5)

the Sanchi inscription.—Sukthankar, V. S. The Nala episode and the Rāmāyaṇa.—Sarup, Lakshman. The problem of textual criticism of the Nirukta.—Ayyangar, S. K. The great Siva image at Elephanta.—Raghavacharya, E. V. V. Ācāryaparamparā of Western Sanskritists.

1. India. 2. Thomas, Frederick William, 1867– I. Katre, Sumitra R. M. R., ed. II. Gode, P. K., ed. III. Ser.

N. Y. P. L. August 20, 1941

Copy only words underlined
& classmark — YEA

...Volume jubilaire offert en hommage à Henri Piéron. Paris, Presses universitaires de France, 1951. xvi,718 p. illus. 23cm. (L'Année psychologique. Année 50)

At head of title: Bibliothèque de philosophie contemporaine...

Contributions by various authors in French or English.

(Continued)

NN R 5.53 OC PC,1, 2 (LC1,Z1,X1)

...Volume jubilaire... (Card 2)

1. éd.
"Liste des principaux ouvrages publiés par Henri Piéron," p.xv-xvi.

1. Piéron, Henri, 1881- . 2. Psychology, 1936- . I. Ser.

OEG

. . . A volume of studies on the history of mathematics and the history of science; presented to David Eugene Smith on his 76th birthday (Jan. 21, 1936). Edited by George Sarton, with the cooperation of Prof. R. C. Archibald . . . Miss B. M. Frick . . . Dr. A. Pogo . . . Bruges (Belgium): The Saint Catherine Press Ltd. [1936] 777 p. incl. diagrs., tables. facsims., illus., plates. 25½cm. (Osiris. v. 1.)

Cover-title: The David Eugene Smith presentation volume.

Contents.—Frick, B. M. Bibliography of the historical writings of David Eugene Smith; The David Eugene Smith mathematical library.—Archibald, R. C. Unpublished letters of James Joseph Sylvester and other new information concerning his life and

(Continued)

N. Y. P. L. August 28, 1936

. . . A volume of studies on the history of mathematics and the history of science . . . (Card 2)

work.—Barnes, S. B. The editing of early learned journals.—Boatner, C. H. Certain unpublished letters from French scientists of the revolutionary period taken from the files of Joseph Lakanal.—Bortolotti, Ettore. L'algebra nella storia e nella preistoria della scienza.—Coolidge, J. L. Origins of analytic geometry.—Darby, G. O. S. The mysterious Abolays.—Funkhouser, H. G. A note on a tenth century graph.—Gandz, Solomon. The sources of Al-Khowārizmī's algebra.—Getman, F. H. Samuel Morey, a pioneer of science in America.—Ginzburg, Benjamin. The scientific value of the Copernican induction.—Hellman, C. D. Legendre and the French reform of weights and measures.—Hornberger, Theodore. Samuel Lee (1625–91).—Ionides, S. A. Cæsar's astronomy by Peter Apian.—Johnson, F. R. The influence of Thomas Digges on the progress of modern astronomy in XVIth-century England.—Karpinski, L. C. The first

(Continued)

N. Y. P. L. August 28, 1936

. . . A volume of studies on the history of mathematics and the history of science . . . (Card 3)

printed arithmetic of Spain.—Loria, Gino. Michel Chasles e la teoria delle sezzione coniche.—Millás i Vallicrosa, J. Una obra astronomica desconocida de Johannes Avendaut Hispanus.—Mitchell, U. G., and M. Strain. The number *e*.—Pelseneer, J. Une lettre inédite de Newton à Pepys.—Pogo, Alexander. Three unpublished calendars from Asyut.—Sanford, Vera. François Legendre, arithméticien.—Sarton, George. Montucla.—Sergescu, P. Les mathématiques dans le Journal des savants; première période, 1661–1701.—Simons, L. G. Short stories in colonial geometry.—Singh, A. N. On the use of series in Hindu mathematics.—Thorndike, Lynn. Coelestinus' summary of Nicolas Oresme on marvels.—Tropfke, J. Die Siebeneckabhandlung des Archimedes.—Uvanovic, Daniel. The Indian prelude to European mathematics.—Vyver, A. van de. Les plus anciennes traductions latines médiévales de

(Continued)

N. Y. P. L. August 28, 1936

. . . A volume of studies on the history of mathematics and the history of science . . . (Card 4)

traités d'astronomie et d'astrologie.—Vetter, Quido. Quatre notes sur les mathématiques babyloniennes.—Vogel, Kurt. Bemerkungen zu den quadratischen Gleichungen der babylonischen Mathematik.—Vollgraff, J. A. Snellius' notes on the reflection and refraction of rays.—Walker, H. M. An unpublished hydraulic experiment of Roberval, 1668.—Wiener, P. P. The tradition behind Galileo's methodology.—Zinner, Ernst. Die Tafeln von Toledo.

842099A. 1. Smith, David Eugene, 1860– . 2. Science—Essays and misc. 3. Mathematics—Addresses, essays, lectures. I. Sarton, George Alfred Léon, 1884– , ed. II. Archibald, Raymond Clare, 1875– . III. Frick, Bertha Margaret, 1894- . IV. Pogo, Alexander. V. Ser.

N. Y. P. L. August 28, 1936

D-10
9850
VOM Bonner Grundgesetz zur gesamtdeutschen Verfassung; Festschrift zum 75. Geburtstag von Hans Nawiasky; hrsg. von Theodor Maunz. München, Isar Verlag, 1956. 446 p. 23cm.

CONTENTS. — Die Funktionsnachfolge und das Problem der staatsrechtlichen Kontinuität, von U. Scheuner. — Deutschland als Rechtsbegriff, von W. Wengler. — Die Wiedervereinigung Deutschlands und der deutsche Föderalismus, von T. Ellwein. — Die Wesensverschiedenheit der Akte des Herrschens und das Problem der Gewaltenteilung, von H. Jahrreiss. (Continued)

NN *R 4. 58 p/T OC, I PC, 1, 2, 3, I SL E, 1, 2, 3, I (LC1, X1, Z1)

VOM Bonner Grundgesetz zur gesamtdeutschen Verfassung... (Card 2)

— Das Subsidiaritätsprinzip als Grundlage der vertikalen Gewaltenteilung, von A. Süsterhenn. — Grundrechte und Zivilrechtsprechung, von G. Dürig. — Aufgaben, Wesen und Grenzen der Verfassungsgerichtsbarkeit, von J. Wintrich. — Zur Reform des Bundesverfassungsgesetzes, von W. Geiger. — Die Grundlagen unserer föderativen Staatsordnung, von H. Ritter von Lex. — Zu den föderalistischen Aspekten der "Auswärtigen Gewalt," von F. Berber. — Gesetzgebung und Verwaltung in deutschen Verfassungen, von T. Maunz. — Die Kulturverwaltung im Verhältnis von Bund und Ländern, (Continued)

VOM Bonner Grundgesetz zur gesamtdeutschen Verfassung... (Card 3)

von H. Wenke. — Die Finanzverfassung der Bundesrepublik und Artikel 107 des Grundgesetzes, von W. Seuffert. — Eigentumspolitische Probleme unserer Wirtschaftsverfassung, von W. Gebauer. — Parlamentarismus in Deutschland und in Frankreich, von F. A. Freiherr von der Heydte. — Zur Kandidatenaufstellung für freie demokratische Wahlen, von H. Peters. — Die Neugliederung des Bundesgebietes nach Art. 29 des Grundgesetzes, von R. Jæger. — Ist der Betrieb des Rundfunks im heutigen Deutschland öffentliche Verwaltung? Von W. Apelt. — Einfluss des Staates auf die öffentliche Meinung, von (Continued)

VOM Bonner. Grundgesetz zur gesamtdeutschen Verfassung... (Card 4)

O. H. Leiling. — Hat die Gleichstellung der Vertriebenen mit Inländern in Art. 116 I GG kollisionsrechtlichen Gehlat? Von M. Ferid. — Von den Begrenzungen der Staatsgewalt, von R. Zorn. — Zusammenstellung der Veröffentlichungen von Prof. Dr. Hans Nawiasky, von H. F. Zacher (p. 431-446)

1. Law, Constitutional—Germany. 2. German reunification question (1949-) 3. Nawiasky, Hans, 1880- I. Maunz, Theodor, 1901- , ed.

AN
(Bäumer, G.)
VOM Gestern zum Morgen; eine Gabe für Gertrud Bäumer. Berlin, H. Bott [1933] 231 p. 24cm.

CONTENTS. — Gertrud Bäumer, von M. Weber. — Geltung und Stellung der Frau in der menschlichen Gesellschaft, von L. Kühn. — Von der Erziehung zum Menschen, von E. Meyn von Westenholz. — Von der Lehrerin, von H. Lion. — Rede an junge Mädchen, von I. Seidel. — Gertrud Bäumer in der Frauenbewegung, von E. Beckmann. — Vom Wesen des Politischen, von E. Ulich-Beil. — Friedrich Naumann und sein Kreis, von T. Heuss. — Der politische Liberalismus, von W. Goetz. — (Continued)

NN**R 3. 54 OC PC, 1, 2 SL (Z1, LC1, X1) [I]

VOM Gestern zum Morgen... (Card 2)

Fronterlebnis und Wiederaufbau, von J. C. Hinrichs. — Der Weg der Jugend zur Nation, von R. F. Frhr. v. Feilitzsch. — Staat und Wirtschaft, von G. Kessler. — Der Mensch und die Technik, von F. Meyer zu Schwabedissen. — Spannung und Ausgleich im Volksleben, von M. Baum. — Die deutsche Landschaft, von J. Schaffner. — Landschaft und Mensch, von D. von Velsen. — Ein Strauss wird gemalt, von H. Voigt-Diederichs. — Bildende Kunst als Zeitausdruck, von W. Riezler. — Das lyrische Gedicht als bildende Kraft, von E. Wolff. — Von Harnack bis zu den Deutschen Christen, von O. Piper. — Die Welt annehmen, von M. Buber. — Du—über—mir, von G. Bäumer.

1. Bäumer, Gertrud, 1873- . 2. Essays, German.

*GAH
Von büchern und bibliotheken, dem ersten direktor der Preussischen staatsbibliothek geheimen regierungsrat dr. phil. Ernst Kuhnert als abschiedsgabe dargebracht von seinen freunden und mitarbeitern, hrsg. von Gustav Abb. Berlin, Verlag von Struppe & Winckler, 1928.

ix, 332 p., 1 l. front., plates (incl. facsims.) port., tables, diagr. $26\frac{1}{2}$cm.

Geleitwort signed: Hugo Andres Krüss.

1. Bibliography—Collections. 2. Kuhnert, Ernst, 1862- 3. Books. 4. Libraries—Germany. I. Abb, Gustav, 1886- ed.

Library of Congress Z1009.V94 28-30860
[3]

*ZB-103
Film Reproduction
VON deutscher Tonkunst, Festschrift zu Peter Raabes 70. Geburtstag, in Gemeinschaft mit dreiundzwanzig Fachgenossen hrsg. von Alfred Morgenroth. Leipzig, C.F. Peters [c1942] 247 p. port, music. 26cm.

Film reproduction. Positive.
CONTENTS.--Peter Raabe und sein Weg, von A. Morgenroth.-- (Continued)

NN R & 62 e/\# OC, I, IIbo PC, 1, 3, I SL MU, 1, 2, I (MUF1, UM1, Z1, LC1, X1)

VON deutscher Tonkunst, Festschrift zu Peter Raabes 70. Geburtstag... (Card 2)

Musik als Ausdruck ihrer Zeit, von W. Egk.--Hausmusik, von E. Preussner.--Musik und Musikwissenschaft, von J. Wolf.--Ton und Wort, von R. Hohlbaum.--Tonkunst und Bildkunst, ihr Wesen, ihre Wirkung, von E. Preetorius.--Musikpolitik.--Musiksoziologie.--Musikdramaturgie, Begriffsbestimmungen und Zielsetzungen, von W. Berten.--Bekenntnis zu Ludwig van Beethoven, von E. Ney.--Zu Beethovens Schicksalsidee, von L. Schiedermair.--Carl Maria von Weber in Berlin. Sein erster Besuch im Jahre 1812, von G. Schünemann.--Bachs Kunst der (Continued)

VON deutscher Tonkunst, Festschrift zu Peter Raabes 70. Geburtstag... (Card 3)

Bearbeitung, dargestellt am Tripelkonzert a-moll, von H. Boettcher.--Zur älteren Musikgeschichte des Burgenlandes, von H.J. Moser.--Verschollene Kompositionen Franz Liszts, von F. Schnapp.--Intuition und Werktreue als Grundlagen der Interpretation, von W. Gieseking.--Über die Kunst der Improvisation in der Musik, von J. Haas.--Die Zeitmassbestimmungen der beiden Fassungen von Bruckners 1. Symphonie, von S. von Hausegger.--Die Bach-Interpretation im Wandel der Anschauungen, von H. Boell.--Grundlage einer deutschen Klavierlehre, (Continued)

VON deutscher Tonkunst, Festschrift zu Peter Raabes 70. Geburtstag... (Card 4)

von C.A. Martienssen. --Das Legato des deutschen Sängers, von P. Lohmann. --Der Musiker. Beruf und Lebensformen, von H. Engel. --Berufsfreudiger Orchesternachwuchs, von F. Stein. --Neue Musikerberufe, von P. Oberborbeck. --Künstlerische Probleme im Alltag des Geigers, von M. Strub. --Mein erstes Frontkonzert (1916), von W. Kempff. --Anhang: Veröffentlichungen Peter Raabes (p. 237). Zeitgenössische Werke, die Raabe als Dirigent herausgestellt hat. Peter Raabes Vortragsthemen. Verzeichnis der Städte, in denen Raabe gewirkt hat.

1. Raabe, Peter, 1872-1945. 2. Essays. 3. Music--Essays. I. Morgenroth, Alfred, ed. II. Morgenroth, Alfred.

Von der Steuer in der Demokratie ... [1946] (Card 2)

CONTENTS—Continued.

rung der eigenössischen Wehrsteuer.—Camille Higy. Die berufliche Ausbildung der höheren Steuerbeamten.—Alfred Amonn. Demokratie und finanzwirtschaftliche Entscheidungen. — Irene Blumenstein. Veröffentlichungen von Prof. Dr. Ernst Blumenstein (p. [229]-243)

1. Blumenstein, Ernst, 1876- —Addresses, essays, lectures. 2. Taxation—Switzerland. 3. Taxation. I. Im Hof, Adolf, 1876- ed.

HJ2861.V6 336.2 47-24477*

Library of Congress [2]

TE

Von land und kultur; beiträge zur geschichte des mitteldeutschen ostens in gemeinsamer arbeit mit Wolfgang Ebert, Walter Franke, Hermann Heimpel [u. a.] ... zum 70. geburtstag Rudolf Kötzschkes, herausgegeben von Werner Emmerich. Leipzig, Bibliographisches institut a. g., 1937.

254 p. front. (port.) maps (1 double) 25cm.

CONTENTS. — Die arbeiten Rudolf Kötzschkes, zusammengestellt von Herbert Helbig.—Tackenberg, Kurt. Beiträge zur landschafts- und siedlungskunde der sächsischen vorzeit.—Helbig, Herbert. Völkerbewegungen und kulturströmungen im grenzland Oberlausitz in vorgeschichtlicher und frühdeutscher zeit.—Radig, Werner. Sachsens gaue als burgwalllandschaften.—Schlesinger, Walter. Burgen und burgbezirke, beobachtungen im mitteldeutschen osten.—Ebert, Wolfgang. Mitteldeutsch-

(Continued on next card)

38-31500

[3]

SFC

Voor vrijheid en socialisme; gedenkboek van het Sneevliet herdenkingscomité. Onder redactie van M. Perthus. Rotterdam, Druk: "Gramo," 1953. 195 p. illus.,ports. 25cm.

Contents.—Marx-Lenin-Luxemburg-front.—Henk Sneevliet.—Ab Menist.—Willem Dolleman.—Jan Edel.—Cor Gerritsen.—Jan Koeslag.—Jan Schriefer.—.—Rein Witteveen.—De Revolutionnair

(Continued)

NN**R 12.55 j/ OC, 2b,I,IIbo PC,1,2,I SL E,1,2,I (LC1,X1,Z1)

Von land und kultur ... 1937. (Card 2)

CONTENTS—Continued.

land und der deutsche osten, gedanken über ein heimatgeschichtliches problem.—Emmerich, Werner. Bemerkungen zur besiedlung des Fichtelgebirges und seiner vorlande.—Leipoldt, Johannes. Wesen und wandlungen der saupenverfassung im amte Meissen.—Heimpel, Hermann. Aus der vorgeschichte des königtums Ruprechts von der Pfalz.—Kretzschmar, Hellmut. Die anfänge des geheimen rates in Sachsen.—Franke, R. W. Der pennalismus auf der Universität Leipzig.—Schultze, Werner. Forderungen an eine bildkunde zur sächsischen geschichte.

1. Kötzschke, Rudolf, 1867- 2. Saxony — Historical geography. 3. Thuringia — Historical geography. 4. Saxony — Hist. — To 1423. 5. Cities and towns—Saxony. 6. Cities and towns—Thuringia. 7. Kötzschke, Rudolf, 1867- —Bibl. I. Emmerich, Werner, ed.

38-31500

Library of Congress DD801.S322V6
Copyright A—Foreign 37195
[3] 943.2004

Voor vrijheid en socialisme... (Card 2)

socialistische arbeiders partij.—R.S.A.P.—lied.—Het Nationaal arbeids secretariaat.—Herinneringen.—Artikelen van Sneevliet.—Namenregister.—Verklaring bij de foto's.—Comité van aanbeveling Sneevlietherdenking.—Sneevliet herdenkingscomité.

1. Socialism—Netherlands. 2. Sneevliet, Henk, 1883-1942. I. Perthus, Max, ed. II. Perthus, Max.

TIN

Von der Steuer in der Demokratie; Festschrift zum 70. Geburtstag von Prof. Dr. Ernst Blumenstein am 23. Oktober 1946. Zürich, Polygraphischer Verlag [1946] 243 p. port. 23cm.

Festschrift cd

441363B. 1. Taxation—Switzerland. 2. Blumenstein, Ernst, 1876-
N. Y. P. L. May 25, 1948

E-10
4674

VORDERASIATISCHE Studien; Festschrift für Prof. Dr. Viktor Christian, gewidmet von Kollegen und Schülern zum 70. Geburtstag. Hrsg. von Kurt Schubert in Verbindung mit Johannes Botterweck und Johann Knobloch. Wien [Verlag Notring der wissenschaftlichen Verbände Österreichs] 1956. 120 p. 24cm.

CONTENTS. Viktor Christian und die Anthropologische Gesellschaft in

(Continued)

NN 7.58 d/J OC, I, II PC, 1, 2, 3, I SL J, 3, I O, 1, 2, I (LC1, X1, Z1)

TIN

Von der Steuer in der Demokratie, Festschrift zum 70. Geburtstag von Prof. Dr. Ernst Blumenstein am 23. Oktober 1946 [Hrsg. von A. Im Hof] Zürich, Polygraphischer Verlag [1946]

243 p. port. 23cm.

CONTENTS.—Jacob Wackernagel. Die Aufgabe der Steuerrechtswissenschaft.—Eugen Grossmann. Der Standort der Erbschaftssteuer im Föderativstaate.—Ernst Wyss. Gesetzmässige Verwaltung der Bundessteuern.—C. A. Halbeisen. Der steuerrechtliche Wohnsitz.—Joseph Kaufmann. Geschäfts- und Privatvermögen.—Walter Geering. Von Treu und Glauben im Steuerrecht.—Charles Perret. Der Steuererlass auf dem Gebiete der direkten Bundessteuern.—Joseph Henggeler. Pauschalie-

(Continued on next card)

47-24477*

[2]

VORDERASIATISCHE Studien... (Card 2)

Wien, von J. Weninger. --Ludwig v. Rauter und sein verschollenes Reisebuch (1567/71), von F. Babinger. --Zur Eigenart der chronistischen Davidgeschichte, von J. Botterweck. --Verschollene Sprachen in Vorderasien und der österreichische Beitrag zu ihrer Entzifferung, von W. Brandenstein. --Die neue Gnosisforschung im Lichte der koptischen Handschriften von Chenoboskion, von R. Haardt. --Die altsüdarabischen Monatsnamen, von M. Höfner. --Zum Problem des Verhältnisses der Sekte von Chirbet Qumran zu den Essenern, von H.-J. Kandler. --Hethitische Etymologien, von J. Knobloch. --Der Glaube

(Continued)

VORDERASIATISCHE Studien... (Card 3)

an die Auferstehung der Toten in den Gathas, von F. König. —Die Hymnen von Chirbet Qumran (1 Q T), von G. Molin. —"Wahrheit" als theologischer Terminus in den Qumran-Texten, von F. Nötscher. —Die ersten beiden Kolumnen der Kriegsrolle von Chirbet Qumran, von K. Schubert. —Beiträge zum Verständnis der neuassyrischen Briefe über die Ersatzkönigsriten, von F. v. Soden—Amarna-Gedanken in einem Sargtext, von G. Thausing. —Amts- und Privatarchive aus mittelassyrischer Zeit, von E. Weidner.

1. Christian, Viktor, 1885- . 2. Oriental studies—Collections. 3. Dead sea scrolls. I. Schubert, Kurt, 1923- , ed. II. Title: Vorderasiatische Studien.

VRAGEN en geven. Uitg. ter gelegenheid van het 40-jarig jubileum van de Stichting Centraal Archief... (Card 2)

goede doel anno 1965, door J. T. M. de Vreeze.—De coördinatie tussen het praktische werk van de landelijk collecterende instellingen, door J. C. Margadant.—Verslag van het Congres.

1. Charities--Netherlands. I. Stichting Centraal Archief en Inlichtingenbureau inzake het Inzamelingswezen.

MWES
(Bildt, P.)

VOSS, KARL, ed.
Paul Bildt, ein Schauspieler in seinen Verwandlungen. Beiträge von Paul Altenberg [et al. Starnberg] J. Keller [1963] 116 p. (chiefly illus., ports.) 29cm.

2 phonodiscs issued with above in *LMYS.28-29.

1. Bildt, Paul, 1885- . I. Voss, Karl.
NN R 6.64 e/ OC, 1b+, Ibo PC, 1 SL T, 1 (LC1, X1, Z1)

E-12
3825

VRIENDENKRING VAN HET PERSONEEL DER DRUKKERIJ HET VOLK.
Stijn Streuvels, 3 oktober, 1871-1956. [Gent] 1956. 1 v. (unpaged) illus., ports. 25cm.

Includes "Streuvels' werken."

1. Lateur, Frank, 1871-1956.
NN R X 5.66 r/ OS(1b+) PC, 1 SL (LC1, X1, Z1)

3-MQWE

Voss, Knud.
Herregården Hindsgavl. [Af] Knud Voss og Frantz Wendt. København, Foreningen Norden, 1969.
87 p. illus., map, plans, port. 25cm.
Commissioned by Foreningen Norden on the occasion of its 50th anniversary.
Bibliographical references included in "Noter." (p. 77-81)

(Continued)
NN*R 2.72 m/o OC, I (OS)II PC, 1, 2, 3, I, II SL A, 1, 2, 3, I, II (LC1, X1) (Z1)

2

VBA p.v. 1196

Waard, D de, ed.
Sporen der ijstijd; nieuwe bijdragen over de glaciale geologie van Nederland, opgedragen aan P. van der Lijn ter ere van zijn tachtigste geboortedag. Zutphen, Thieme, 1950.
110 p. illus., port., maps, profiles. 24 cm.
Some of the articles have summaries in English.
"Lijst der geschriften van P. van der Lijn, 1917-1949": p. [13]-15.

1. Lijn, P. van der, 1870- 2. Glacial epoch—Collected works. 3. Geology, Stratigraphic—Pleistocene—Collected works. 4. Geology—Netherlands—Collected works.

A 51-786
Yale Univ. Library for Library of Congress [1]

VOSS, KNUD. Herregården Hindsgavl. (Card 2)

1. Hindsgavl, Denmark (Manor) 2. Architecture, Domestic--Denmark--Hindsgavl (Manor) 3. Middelfart, Denmark. I. Wendt, Frantz Wilhelm, 1905- . II. Norden, dansk Forening For nordisk samarbejde.

SDG
+

Die Wahl zum 2. deutschen Bundestag am 6. September 1953. Stuttgart, W. Kohlhammer [1954]
1 v. col. fold map, tables. 30cm. (Germany. Federal republic, 1949-). Statistisches Bundesamt. Statistik der Bundesrepublik Deutschland. Bd. 100)

Heft 1.
Contents.—Heft 1. Allgemeine Wahlergebnisse nach Ländern und Wahlkreisen.
1. Germany—Elections—Stat., 1953.
NN 4.55 d/ OI (PC)1 (S)1 (Z1, LC1, X1)

D-18
6038

Vragen en geven. Uitg. ter gelegenheid van het 40-jarig jubileum van de Stichting Centraal Archief en Inlichtingenbureau inzake het Inzamelingswezen. Alphen aan de Rijn, N. Samson, 1966.
76 p. with illus. 21 cm.

CONTENTS.—Het Centraal Archief en het verleden, door J. W. Noteboom.—Plaats en taak van de gemeenten tussen de sociale instellingen het publiek in een veranderende maatschappij, door A. P. Korthals Altes.—Een beschouwing over vragen en geven voor het

(Continued)
NN * R 1.69 1/c OC (OS)I PC, 1, I SL E, 1, I (LC1, X1, Z1)

2

AE-10
1028

WAKSMAN, SELMAN ABRAHAM, 1888-
Scientific contributions of Selman A Waksman; selected articles published in honor of his 80th birthday, July 22, 1968. Edited by H. Boyd Woodruff. New Brunswick, N.J., Rutgers university press [1968] xx, 391 p. illus., ports. 25cm.

1. Micro-organisms. I. Woodruff, H. Boyd, ed. II. Woodruff, H. Boyd.
NN R 10.68 1/c OC, I, IIbo PC, 1, I SL (LC1, X1, Z1)

D-16
4493

WALKER, PINKNEY C., ed.
Essays in monetary policy in honor of Elmer Wood. Columbia, Mo., University of Missouri press [1965] 135 p. port. 23cm.

CONTENTS.--Confessions of a central banker, by K.R. Bopp.--International central banking, by L.V. Chandler.--Monetary and fiscal policy in the 1950's and 1960's, by S.E. Harris.--The changing functions of monetary policy, by W.A. Morton.--Fact and fiction in central banking, by C.E. Walker.

1. Banks and banking, Central--Addresses, essays, lectures. 2. Money, Managed--U.S. 3. Wood, Elmer. I. Walker, Pinkney C.

NN R 1.66 p/ OC, Ibo PC, 1, 2, 3 SL E, 1, 2, 3 (LC1, X1, Z1)

RAA

Washington university, *St. Louis.*
Studies in honor of Frederick W. Shipley, by his colleagues ... St. Louis, 1942.
xi, 314 p. front. (port.) 24½cm. (Washington university studies. New series. Language and literature, no. 14)

CONTENTS.—Frederick William Shipley, by G. R. Throop.—A constitutional doctrine re-examined, by Donald McFayden.—The use of fire in Greek and Roman love magic, by Eugene Tavenner.—Thucydides and the causes of the Peloponnesian war, by T. S. Duncan.—Prehistoric Macedonia, by G. E. Mylonas.—Classical "Ariels," by Otto Brendel.—An Aesopic allusion in the Roman d'Alexandre, by Bateman Edwards.—The poetic theories of Minturno, by Bernard Weinberg.—Pereda's real-

(Continued on next card)

42-19118

[5]

E-12
6611

WALLACH, LUITPOLD, ed.
The classical tradition; literary and historical studies in honor of Harry Caplan. Edited by Luitpold Wallach. Ithaca, N.Y., Cornell university press 1966. xv, 606 p. illus., port. 24cm.

Bibliographical footnotes.

1. Caplan, Harry, 1896- 2. Classical studies--Collections.

NN R 9.66 1/ OC PC, 1, 2 SL (LC1, X1, Z1) [I]

Washington university, *St. Louis.* Studies in honor of Frederick W. Shipley ... 1942. (Card 2)

CONTENTS—Continued.

ism: his style, by Sherman Eoff.—Early English and American critics of French symbolism, by B. A. Morrissette.—Bibliographical data on Diderot, by Herbert Dieckmann.—Rosencrantz and Guildenstern, by W. R. Mackenzie.—The contemporary reception of Edmund Burke's speaking, by D. C. Bryant.—The moral sense of simplicity, by R. F. Jones.—Imitation as an aesthetic norm, by F. O. Nolte.—Immediacy: its nature and value, by C. E. Cory.

1. Shipley, Frederick William, 1871- I. Title.

42-19118

Library of Congress AS36.W29

[5] 041

A p.v.702

Walther Burckhardt, 1871–1939. [Zürich: Polygraphischer Verlag A. G., 1939] 51 p. port. 23cm.

Cover-title.
CONTENTS.—Ansprache des Rektors Dr. Theo Guhl bei der Bestattungsfeier, 19. Oktober 1939. Ansprache von Bundesrichter Dr. E. Kirchhofer bei der Bestattungsfeier, 19. Oktober 1939.—Professor Walther Burckhardt und die Rechtswissenschaft. Von Prof. Dr. A. Homberger.—Über Walther Burckhardt's wissenschaftliches Werk. Von Bundesrichter Dr. Hans Huber.—Verzeichnis der Werke und Schriften von Prof. Walther Burckhardt [von Dr. Helene Pfander] (p. 39–51).

1. Burckhardt, Walther, 1871–1939. 2. Burckhardt, Walther, 1871–1939—Bibl. I. Pfander, Helene.
N. Y. P. L. February 11, 1941

F-10
9278

WATT, JOHN A., ed.
Medieval studies presented to Aubrey Gwynn, S.J.; edited by J.A. Watt, J.B. Morrall [and] F.X. Martin. Dublin, Printed by C.O. Lochlainn, 1961. xi, 509 p. port. 2 maps (1 fold.) facsims. 26cm.

Bibliographical footnotes.
"The historical writings of Reverend Professor Aubrey Gwynn, S.J.," p. [502]-509.

(Continued)

NN * R 10.64 p/8 OC, I, IIb* PC, 1, 2, I SL (LC1, X1, Z1) [I] 2

---

* QO

Warsaw. Uniwersytet.
Księga pamiątkowa celem uczczenia 350-ej rocznicy założenia Uniwersytetu Stefana Batorego w Wilnie. Warszawa: Staraniem Uniwersytetu warszawskiego, 1931. 411 p. illus. 25½cm.

CONTENTS.—Handelsman, Marceli. Możliwości i konieczności w procesie historycznym.—Jabłczyński, Kazimierz. Kinetyka koagulacji suspensoidów.—Jarra, Eugenjusz. Aron Aleksander Olizarowski jako filozof prawa.—Karwacki, Leon. Saprofityzm prątków gruźliczych.—Korduba, Miron. Ukazy jugenheimskie.—Krzywicki, Ludwik. Pilkalnia w Gabryeliszkach.—Pieńkowski, S. K. Dusza i jej siedlisko w świetle badań neurologicznych lat ostatnich.—Przychocki, Gustaw. Charakterystyka tragedji

(Continued)

N. Y. P. L. January 3, 1941

WATT, JOHN A., ed. Medieval studies presented to Aubrey Gwynn... (Card 2)

1. Gwynn, Aubrey Osborn. 2. Middle Ages--Hist.--Addresses, essays, lectures. I. Title. II. Watt, John A.

Warsaw. Uniwersytet. Księga pamiątkowa... (Card 2)

rzymskiej epoki republikańskiej.—Rafacz, Józef. Adopcja w Polsce XVI wieku.—Słoński, Stanisław. Funkcje prefiksu werbalnego O-/OB- w języku staro-słowiańskim.—Szlagowski, Antoni, bp. Ojciec Zadżumionych w świetle biblji.—Ujejski, Józef. Ballady Tomasza Zana.—Wierzuchowski, Mieczysław. O śródżylnym przyswajaniu cukrów.

83812B. 1. No subject. I. Uniwersytet Stefana Batorego w Wilnie. II. Title.
N. Y. P. L. January 3, 1941

E-11
8710

WECZERKA, HUGO, ed.
Rossica externa; Studien zum 15.-17. Jahrhundert. Festgabe für Paul Johansen zum 60. Geburtstag. Marburg, N.G. Elwert, 1963. viii, 196 p. illus., port. 24cm.

Bibliographical footnotes.
CONTENTS.--Schnitzereien am Novgorodfahrer-Gestühl zu Stralsund als Beitrag zum Russlandbild hansischer Bürger im 14. und 15. Jahrhundert, von

(Continued)

NN R 2.64 p/ OC PC, 1, 2 SL S, 1, 2 (LC1, X1, Z1) [I] 2

WECZERKA, HUGO, ed. Rossica externa... (Card 2)

P. Heinsius. --Russland im Spiegel der livländischen Schonnen Hysthorie von 1508, von F. Benninghoven. --Der finnländische Bischof Paul Juusten und seine Mission in Russland, von R. Dencker. --Die niederen Stände im Moskauer Reich in der Sicht deutscher Russlandberichte des 16. Jahrhunderts, von E. Harder-von Gersdorff. --Denninge, von G. Hatz. --"Kayserliche grossmächtigkeit"; Titularfragen bei den Verhandlungen zwischen Kaiser und Zar, 1661/62, von K. Meyer. --Sebastian Glavinich und seine Schilderung des Moskowitischen Reiches, von H. Weczerka. --Eine Beschreibung Moskaus durch den Kurländer Jakob Reutenfels, von F. -K. Proehl.

1. Johansen, Paul. 2. Russia--Hist. --Addresses, essays, lectures.

L-10
4597
Bd. 5

WEIGT, ERNST, ed.
Angewandte Geographie; Festschrift für Professor Dr. Erwin Scheu zur Vollendung des 80. Lebensjahres, besorgt von Ernst Weigt. Nürnberg, Wirtschafts- und sozialgeographisches Institut der Friedrich-Alexander Universität, 1966. 223 p. diagrs., maps. 24cm. (Nürnberger wirtschafts- und sozialgeographische Arbeiten. Bd. 5)
(Continued)

NN 10.66 r/ OC (OS)I PC,1, 2,I E,1,2,I (LC1,X1,Z1)

5

BYC

WEERKLANK op het werk van Jan Romein; liber amicorum [onder redactie van het werkcomité: H. J. Pos, voorzitter] Amsterdam, Wereld-bibliotheek, 1953. 227 p. port. 24cm.

Includes bibliographies.

CONTENTS. — Een moeilijke kwestie in verband met Croce's voorstelling van de vooruitgang, door C. Antoni. —Essentials of history, by R. F. Beerling. — Sentences, ideal entities and classes, by W. Cerf. — Wij zaten wachtende als in een kring, door N. A. Donkersloot. — Het begrip feit in geschiedenis en rechtswetenschap, door H. R. Hoetink. — Die teoretiese geskiedenis en de Suid-Afrikaanse historiografie, deur R. Hugo. — Over
(Continued)

NN ** R X 2.54 OC,I PC, 1,2,I SL (LC1,Z1,X1)

WEIGT, ERNST, ed. Angewandte Geographie... (Card 2)

Includes bibliographies.

CONTENTS. --Angewandte Geographie-aus meinem Leben, von E. Scheu. --Angewandte Geographie, Begriff und Entwicklungsstand im Lichte des Schrifttums, von E. Weigt. --Möglichkeiten und Grenzen der angewandten Geographie, von A. Kühn. --Angewandte Geographie-Raumwirtschaftliche Modelle, von W. Christaller. --Die Ausbildung des Diplom-Geographen für die angewandte Geographie, von H. Uhlig. --Die angewandte Geographie in Wirtschaft und Verwaltung,
(Continued)

WEERKLANK op het werk van Jan Romein... (Card 2)

enkele trekken van het Amerikaanse volkskarakter, door T. J. G. Locher. — Pia Fraus bij Plato, door D. Loenen. —Die Problematik des Verhältnisses von Ordnung und Freiheit bei Rousseau und im genuinen Marxismus, von A. von Martin. — Sabetai Rephael in Hamburg, door J. Meijer. — Dammen en dijken in Frankisch Nederland, door J. F. Niermeyer. — D'Alembert's inleiding tot de 'Encyclopedie,' door O. Noordenbos. — Over de verhouding van geschiedenis en geschiedwetenschap, door H. J. Pos. —Van Douglas tot Aptheker: de geboorte ener geschiedschrijving, door J. Presser. — Zakelijkheid en zekerheid in de Indonesische geschiedschrijving, door
(Continued)

WEIGT, ERNST, ed. Angewandte Geographie... (Card 3)

von E. W. Hübschmann. --Aufgaben der Geographie in der Kartographie, von F. Hölzel. --Aufbau, Arbeitsmethoden und Aufgaben der Zentralstelle für angewandte Geographie am Instituto de tierras y colonización in Costa Rica, von G. Sandner. --Über die Bedeutung von Geographie und Landeskenntnis bei der Vorbereitung wirtschaftlicher Entscheidungen und bei langfristigen Planungen in Entwicklungsländern, von E. Wirth. --Kahn die zunehmende Gebirgsentvölkerung des Apennins zur Wiederbewaldung führen?, von F. Tichy. --Das Entstehen und der
(Continued)

WEERKLANK op het werk van Jan Romein... (Card 3)

G. J. Resink. —Het 'klassieke'in het dichterschap van Henriette Roland Holst, door A. Romein-Verschoor. — Entre deux chaises? Non, par K. Schmidt-Phiseldeck. — Sulpiz Boisseree en zijn betekenis voor de ontwikkeling der kunstgeschiedenis als historische wetenschap, door H. Schulte Nordholt. — De betekenis van Helvetius, door J. Suys. — History and humaneness, by R. E. Turner. -- Aspecten van taalgebruik, door V. E. van Vriesland. —Het contrapunt in de samenleving, door W. F. Wertheim. —Het beeld van Filips van de Elzas, door H. van Werveke.

1. History-- Addresses, essays, lectures. 2. Romein, Jan Marius, 1893- I. Pos, Hendrik Josephus, 1898- , ed.

WEIGT, ERNST, ed. Angewandte Geographie... (Card 4)

Ausbau zentraler Orte und ihrer Netze an Beispielen aus Portugiesisch Guinea und Südwest-Angola, von J. Matznetter. --Grundlagen und Entwicklungsmöglichkeiten der afghanischen Volkswirtschaft, von G. Voppel. --Die Gründung einer Stahlbau-Firma im Iran, von K. -H. Hottes. --Zur Frage der Autobahntrassierung im unteren Eisacktal, von W. Rutz. --Versuch der Analyse des Ausländerfremdenverkehrs in der Bundesrepublik Deutschland im Jahre 1964, von R. Bauer. --Der Strukturwandel im fränkischen Weinbau seit 1950, von H. -H.
(Continued)

QOI

Weidenreich, Franz, 1873–1948.
The shorter anthropological papers of Franz Weidenreich published in the period 1939–1948; a memorial volume, comp. by S. L. Washburn [and] Davida Wolffson... New York, Viking fund [pref. 1949] vii, 267 p. illus. 23cm.

"Bibliography," p. 257–267.

582285B. 1. Man, Prehistoric. 2. Evolution. I. Washburn, S. L., ed. II. Wolffson, Davida, ed.
N. Y. P. L. June 28, 1951

WEIGT, ERNST, ed. Angewandte Geographie... (Card 5)

Kopp. --Der Raum Ingolstadt als neuer Raffineriestandort, von H. Schall. --Stadtgeographische Fragestellungen und Flächennutzungsplan am Beispiel von München, von K. Ganser. --Der Grossraum Nürnberg-Versuch einer Abgrenzung durch den Personenverkehr, von W. Pöllath. --Wissenschaftliche Arbeiten von Erwin Scheu.

1. Scheu, Erwin, 1886- . 2. Geography, Economic. I. Series.

E-12
5172

WEINHEIMER VERBAND ALTER CORPSSTUDENTEN.

100 Jahre Weinheimer Senioren-Convent; Festschrift zum hundertjährigen Bestehen des Weinheimer Senioren-Convents. Zusammengestellt und hrsg. vom Vorstand des Weinheimer Verbandes alter Corpsstudenten, in Zusammenarbeit mit der historischen Kommission des WVAC. Bochum [Druck: Laupenmühlen & Dierichs] 1963. 177 p. illus., ports. 25cm.

1. Weinheimer Senioren-Convent. I. [Title] Hundert
NN R 2.66 p/ OS (1b+) PC, 1 SL (LC1, [I], X1, Z4)

NPB

Wellesley college. Spanish dept.

Estudios hispánicos; homenaje a Archer M. Huntington. Wellesley, Mass., 1952. xi,620 p. port., facsims. 23cm.

Essays in Spanish, English, Portuguese, French or German.

Bibliographical footnotes.

—— —— Anejo único. Un recuerdo de juventud, por Ramón Menéndez Pidal. Wellesley, Mass., 1952. 13 p. 23cm.

Bound with above. (Continued)

NN** X 2.54 (OC)I, II OS PC,1,2,I,II SL (LC1,Z1,X1)

Wellesley college. Spanish dept. Estudios hispánicos... (Card 2)

1. Huntington, Archer Milton, 1870- . 2. Spanish literature—Hist. and crit. I. Menéndez Pidal, Ramón, 1869- . II. Title.

NAB

Weltliteratur; Festgabe für Fritz Strich zum 70. Geburtstag, in Verbindung mit Walter Henzen hrsg. von Walter Muschg und Emil Staiger. Bern, Francke, 1952. 183 p. port. 24cm.

Contents.—Geleitwort, von W. Henzen.—Tabula gratulatoria.—Der Geist des Barocktheaters, von R. Alewyn.—Philologie der Weltliteratur, von E. Auerbach.—Die Entfaltung der Weltliteratur als Prozess, von A. Carlsson.—Dichtertypen, von W. Muschg.—Probleme des Musikalischen in der Sprache, von R. Peacock.— (Continued)

NN**R X 11.53 OC,I,II PC,1,2,I,II SL (Z1,LC1, X1)

Weltliteratur... (Card 2)

Zur Theorie der Dichtung bei Coleridge im Hinblick auf Goethe, von E. L. Stahl.—Das Spätboot. Zu C. F. Meyers Lyrik, von E. Staiger.—Die deutsche Literatur und die Krise der europäischen Kultur, von K. Viëtor.—Modern romantic criticism, by L. A. Willoughby.—Bibliographie der Werke von Fritz Strich, zusammengestellt von G. Strich-Sattler (p. 177-183).

1. Literature—Hist. and crit. 2. Strich, Fritz, 1882- I. Muschg, Walter, 1898- , ed. II. Staiger, Emil, 1908- , ed.

TB

Weltwirtschaftliche studiengesellschaft.

Weltwirtschaftsdämmerung. Festschrift zum 10jährigen bestehen des Weltwirtschafts-instituts der Handels-hochschule Leipzig. Herausgeber: generalmajor a. d. prof. dr. Karl Haushofer ... und prof. dr. Walther Vogel ... Überreicht von der Weltwirtschaftlichen studiengesellschaft. Stuttgart, W. Kohlhammer, 1934.

143, [1] p. 2 port. 27½cm.

CONTENTS.—Geleitwort, von dr. Mevert, vorsitzendem der Weltwirtschaftlichen studiengesellschaft.—I. Wissenschaftlicher teil: Weltwirtschaftsdämmerung. Weltwirtschafts-dämmerung, von graf P. Teleki. Die Vereinigten Staaten am scheidewege, von dr. W. Notz. Weltwirt-

(Continued on next card)

A C 37-60

[2]

Weltwirtschaftliche studiengesellschaft. Weltwirtschaftsdämmerung ... 1934. (Card 2)

CONTENTS—Continued.

schafts-problematik des augenblicks, von dr. E. Quesada. Werdegang und wesen des fünfjahresplanes, von dr. B. Brutzkus. Indo-pazifische rückschlags-dynamik, von dr. K. Haushofer. Weltwirtschaft und kolonialwirtschaft, von dr. Seitz. Alte und neue ideale des kolonialpolitischen denkens, von dr. E. Egner. Weltwirtschaftskrise und welteisenbahnkrise, von B. v. Enderes. Das Saargebiet in der französischen wirtschaft, von dr. H. Röchling. Die bilanz des staatlich-völkischen lebensraumes, von dr. W. Vogel. Autarkie und nationalwirtschaft, von dr. K. Thalheim. Weltwirtschaft und nationale kulturpolitik, von dr. F. Thierfelder.—II. Die tätigkeit des Weltwirtschafts-instituts. Was lei-

(Continued on next card)

A C 37-60

[2]

Weltwirtschaftliche studiengesellschaft. Weltwirtschaftsdämmerung ... 1934. (Card 3)

CONTENTS—Continued.

stet das Weltwirtschafts-institut? Von dr. F. Grautoff. Gutachtensammlung über die bedeutung des Weltwirtschafts-instituts. Kuratorium und Beirat. Redner des Weltwirtschafts-instituts 1924–1934. Verzeichnis der weltwirtschaftlichen von prof. dr. Ernst Schultze herausgegebenen schriftenreihen. Verzeichnis der weltwirtschaftlichen diplom-arbeiten an der Handels-hochschule Leipzig 1924–1934.

1. Economic conditions—1918- —Addresses, essays, lectures. 2. Leipzig. Handels-hochschule. Weltwirtschafts-institut. I. Haushofer, Karl, 1869- ed. II. Vogel, Walther, 1880- joint ed. III. Title.

A C 37-60

N. Y. Public library
for Library of Congress [2]

D-16
7085

WENIG, OTTO, ed.

Freundesgabe für Viktor Burr. Bonn, H. Bouvier, 1966. 115 p. 23cm. (Bonner Beiträge zur Bibliotheks- und Bücherkunde. Bd. 15)

Bibliographical footnotes.

CONTENTS.--Über die allegorische Dichtung in Indien, Iran und im Abendlande, von W. Kirfel.--Lydische Adelskämpfe, von H. Herter.--Quintus Septimus Florens Tertullianus zum Soldatendienst, von A. Rölli.--Zum Kampf um das Sein in der Philosophie der Gegenwart, von V. Rüfner.

1. Burr, Viktor, 1906- . 2. Classical studies--Collections. I. Series.

NN R 7.66 r/ OC (OD)I (ED)I PC, 1, 2, I SL (LC1, X1, Z1)

D-16
6638

WENIG, OTTO, ed.

Wege zur Buchwissenschaft. [Viktor Burr zur Vollendung des 60. Lebensjahres] Bonn, H. Bouvier, 1966. 416 p. 23cm. (Bonner Beiträge zur Bibliotheks- und Bücherkinde. Bd. 14)

Bibliographical footnotes.

CONTENTS.--ΚΕΦΑΛΙΣ ΒΙΒΛΙΟΥ (Kephalis bibliou), von T. Schäfer.--Bemerkungen zum voralexandrinischen Buchwesen, von I. Ooms.--Von alten Siegburger Büchern, von M. Mittler.--Die Ellwanger Litanei, von W. Irtenkauf.--Das Mirakel von Bolsena in der Bonner Hanschrift

(Continued)

NN 5.66 p/ OC (OD)I (ED)I PC, 1, 2, I SL (LC1, X1, Z1)

3

WENIG, OTTO, ed. Wege zur Buchwissenschaft. (Card 2)

S 291, von A. Becker. -Hermann Schaaffhausen, von H. Fremerey-Dohna. -Autographeninterpretation, von O. Wenig. Bemerkungen zu den ältesten Drucken des Konstanzer Breviers, von H. Tüchle. -Zur Basler Ausgabe des Sentenzenkommentars Alberts des Grossen von Jahre 1506, von A. Hiedl. -Michael Wecklein, ein Theologe der Aufklärung als Bibliothekar an der Universitäts-Bibliothek Bonn 1818-1828, von H. Hegel. --Die Direktoren der Universitätsbibliothek Bonn, von R. Mummendey. --Die Universitäts-Bibliothek Bonn, Abt. Landwirt- schaft, von W. Göcke. --

(Continued)

WENIG, OTTO, ed. Wege zur Buchwissenschaft. (Card 3)

Die Bibliothek des Bundesministeriums für Wirtschaft, von E. Richter. --Unterirdisches Schrifttum im Rheinland in den Tagen des Vormärz, von H. Neu. -Jean Pauls Verhältnis zum Buch, von G. Soffke. -Von der Notwendigkeit und Möglichkeit einer allgemeinen Buchwissenschaft, von H. Grundmann.

1. Burr, Viktor, 1906- 2. Bibliography--Addresses, essays, lectures. I. Series.

E-12
8950

Wenke, Hans, 1903- *ed.*
Festschrift zur Eröffnung der Universität Bochum. Hrsg. von Hans Wenke und Joachim H. Knoll. Bochum, F. Kamp, 1965.

394 p. illus., maps (part fold., part col.) plans, port. 24 cm.

Includes bibliographies.

1. Ruhr Universität, Bochum, Germany. I. Knoll, Joachim H., ed.

NN*R 5.67 g/ OC,I PC,1,I SL (LC1,X1, Z1)

D-15
8334

WENZEL, FRITZ, 1910- ,ed.
Geographie, Geschichte, Pädagogik; Festschrift für Walther Maas zum 60. Geburtstag am 9. Juni 1961. Göttingen, E. Goltze, 1961. xv, 258 p. illus. 22cm.

Contributions in English, French or German.
Includes bibliographies.
"Arbeiten von Walther Maas," p. 223-250.

1. Maas, Walther Gerhard Eduard, 1901- . 2. Geography--Addresses, essays, lectures.

NN R 10.65 1/β OC PC, 1, 2 SL (LC1, X1, Z1)

E-10
1030

Das WERCK der Bücher: von der Wirksamkeit des Buches in Vergangenheit und Gegenwart; eine Festschrift für Horst Kliemann zu seinem 60. Geburtstag hrsg. von Fritz Hodeige. Freiburg, Rombach, 1956. 359 p. illus., port. 24cm.

CONTENTS. --Biographicum, von L. Schneider. --Begegnungen, von H. Bott. --Buch und Buchhandel im Jahre 1896, von B. Hack. --Zitate und ihre Schicksale, von H. Widmann. --Von der Würde bibliographischer

(Continued)

NN **R 12.56 a/P OC, I, IIbo PC, 1, 2, I SL (LC1, X1, Z1, Y1)
[1]

Das WERCK der Bücher. (Card 2)

Arbeit, von H. W. Eppelsheimer. --Zur Geschichte und zur heutigen Rolle des gebundenen Ladenpreises, von H. Loeb. --Wenn die Konjunktur abfällt--Zur Strukturänderung im Buchhandel, von T. Dengler. --Der Schätzungswert bei Fachzeitschriften, von G. Ruprecht. --Ausblicke auf eine verbesserte Statistik der Buchproduktion, von E. Umlauff. --Internationales Urheberrecht, von H. Kleine. --Die "Rechte" an der Zeitschrift, von W. Bappert. --Der Privatdruck im Rechtsleben, von H. G. Hauffe. --Die Frau im Buchgewerbe, von A. Meiner. --Geld und Geldeswert, von H. R. Altenhein. --Über einige Formen des Bucherfolges in der Trivialliteratur wie in der

(Continued)

Das WERCK der Bücher. (Card 3)

Belletristik, von F. Hodeige. --Der Antiquar, von B. Wendt. --Ernst Schulz, 8. Oktober 1897 bis 19. Dezember 1944, von H. Koch. --Buch und Kulturstil, von H. Rössler. --Historikerbiblio hetheken, von G. Franz. --Gutenbergs Aachener Heiltumsspiegel, von K. Köster. --Der Buchillustrator Josef Hegenbarth, von S. Taubert. --Architektur und Typographie, von G. K. Schauer. --Horst Kliemann: die Schriften und Aufsätze, 1915-1956.

1. Kliemann, Horst, 1896- . 2. Booksellers and book trade--Addresses, essays, lectures. I. Hodeige, Fritz, ed. II. Hodeige, Fritz.

AN
(Wergeland, H.)

Wergelandia; studier tilegnet Dr. Rolv Laache på hans 50-års dag 19 november 1936. Oslo: J. G. Tanum, 1936. 161 p. incl. tables. illus. (plans), plates. 22cm.

"Trykt i 600 eksemplarer."

CONTENTS.—Bødtker, K. E. Eidsvoll prestegård i Wergelandstiden.—Høigaard, Einar. Hvad protokoller i Oslo Katedralskoles arkiv kan fortelle om Henrik Wergeland.—Skard, Sigmund. Henrik Wergeland og europeisk millomalder.—Amundsen, Leiv. Horats-minnelser i "Digte, første ring."—Seip, D. A. En kampsituasjon i Henrik Wergelands liv.—Eitrem, H. Omkring "Norges fjelde. Paa Egeberg."—Olsen, Magnus. Henrik Wergeland og Dynna-stenen.—Svendsen, H. B. Et brev fra Mauritz Hansen til Henrik Wergeland.—Tunold, Solveig. Wergelands-manuskripter i Universitetsbiblioteket.

893648A. 1. Wergeland, Henrik Arnold, 1808-1845. I. Laache, Rolv, 1886- , ed.
N. Y. P. L. August 19, 1937

MA

Das WERK des Künstlers; Studien zur Ikonographie und Formgeschichte Hubert Schrade zum 60. Geburtstag dargebracht von Kollegen und Schülern. [Hrsg. von Hans Fegers] Stuttgart, W. Kohlhammer [1960] 366 p. illus. 27cm.

Bibliographical footnotes.

CONTENTS. — Der griechische Tempel, von H. G. Evers. —Textbelege zum islamischen Bilderverbot, von R. Paret. —Die Ahnen der dritten Kirche von Cluny, von H. Sedlmayer. — Vorbemerkungen zu einer

(Continued)

NN R 7.61 g/ OC, I, IIbo PC, 1, 2, I SL A, 1, 2, I (LC1, X1, Z1)

Das WERK des Künstlers... (Card 2)

Formengrammatik der vegetabilischen Grundmotive romanischer Kapitelldekoration, von G. Weise. — Über die Bedeutung der Jakobsleiter von Erwitte, von F. Holländer. — Der Wandmalerei-Zyklus im Querschiff von St. Chef, von R. Storz. —Die Geigerlegende des Volto Santo und ihre antike Herkunft, von D. de Chapeaurouge. —Ad infantiam Christi, von H. Wenzel. — Albizzo di Piero, von M. Wundram. — Beiträge Leonardo da Vincis zum Städtebau, von J. H. Schmidt. —Über einige Zeichnungen Grünewalds und Dürers von G. Scheja. —Eine Handzeichnungsgruppe aus der Rembrandtwerkstatt

(Continued)

Das WERK des Künstlers... (Card 3)

um 1655, von W. Drost. —Guarinis Theatinerfassade in Messina, von W. Hager. —Drei Passionsbilder von Franz Anton von Leydensdorff, von K. Mugdan. —Porträt eines Kunstsammlers: Karl II. August von Pfalz-Zweibrücken, von M. Schrecklinger. —Medaillenentwürfe von Peter Anton von Verschaffelt, von A. Stemper. —Die Anfänge der Miniaturmalerei von Heinrich Friedrich Füger, von W. Fleischhauer. —Baudelaire und der belgische Barock, von W. Drost. — Hans von Marées und Paul Cézanne, von H. Fegers. —Die Patrozinien südwestdeutscher Kastellkirchen, von H. Martin-Decker-Hauff. —Verzeichnis der Veröffentlichungen von Hubert Schrade (p. 363-366).

AN
(Mitchell, W.)

Wesley Clair Mitchell: the economic scientist, ed. by Arthur F. Burns. New York, National bureau of economic research, 1952. viii,387 p. ports. 24cm. (National bureau of economic research. Publications. no. 53)

Various contributors.

"List of publications by Wesley C. Mitchell," p. 343-366; "Some writings about Wesley C. Mitchell," p. 367-374.

1. Mitchell, Wesley Clair, 1874-1948.
I. Burns, Arthur Frank, 1904- , ed.
NN OC,I PC,1,I SL E,1,I (LC1,Z1,X1)

Das WERK des Künstlers... (Card 4)

I. Schrade, Hubert, 1900- . 2. Art--Essays and misc. I. Fegers, Hans, ed. II. Fegers, Hans.

K-10
3808
Bd.20

WESTERMANN, HARRY.

Rechtsprobleme der Genossenschaften. [Professor Dr. Harry Westermann zum 60. Geburtstag am 6. April 1969, gewidmet von den Direktoren und Mitarbeitern des Instituts für Genossenschaftswesen der Westfälischen Wilhelms-Universität Münster. Karlsruhe, C.F. Müller, 1969. 179 p. port. 23cm. (Münster, Germany. Universität. Institut für Genossenschaftswesen. Quellen und

(Continued)

NN 10.69 r/ OC (OS)I PC, 1, I E, 1, I (LC1, X1, Z1) 2

E-13
8031

Werk—Typ—Situation. Studien zu poetologischen Bedingungen in der älteren deutschen Literatur. (Herausgeber: Ingeborg Glier u. a.) Stuttgart, Metzler, 1969.

ix, 381 p. 24 cm.

Issued in honor of Hugo Kuhn.

Bibliographical footnotes.

1. German literature, Middle High--Addresses, essays, lectures. I. Kuhn, Hugo. II. Glier, Ingeborg, ed. III. Glier, Ingeborg.
NN*R 4.70 r/ OC, I, II, IIIb* PC, 1, I, II SL (LC1, X1, Z1)

WESTERMANN, HARRY. Rechtsprobleme der Genossenschaften... (Card 2)

Studien. Bd. 20)

Collection of the author's essays.

"Professor Westermann und sein Werk: Jahrzehnte der Entwicklung im deutschen Genossenschaftsrecht," von F. Schmitz-Herscheidt, p. 1-11.

Bibliographical footnotes.

1. Co-operation--Jurisp.--Germany. I. Series.

Copy only words underlined & classmark— ELB

WERNER, JOACHIM, 1909- , ed.

Aus Bayerns Frühzeit; Friedrich Wagner zum 75. Geburtstag. Für die Kommission für bayerische Landesgeschichte hrsg. München, C.H. Beck, 1962.

vi, 406 p. illus., plates, port., maps (part fold. 1 issued in pocket) 26cm. (Schriftenreihe zur bayerischen Landesgeschichte, Bd. 62)

Bibliographical footnotes.

1. Wagner, Friedrich, 1887- . 2. Bavaria--Archaeology. I. Series.
NN 6.64 e/B OC (OS)I PC, 1, 2, I (LC1, X1, Z1) [I]

EKI

Westfaelische Studien; Beiträge zur Geschichte der Wissenschaft, Kunst und Literatur in Westfalen; Alois Bömer zum 60. Geburtstag gewidmet... Leipzig: K. W. Hiersemann, 1928. vi, 312 p. incl. tables. facsims., front. (port.), illus. (map, music.) 4°.

Dedication signed: Die Herausgeber, Hermann Degering, Walter Menn.
Bibliographical footnotes.
Contents: BAHLMANN, P. Eine Anweisung zur Kinderlehre im Münsterlande aus dem Jahre 1613. BAUERMANN, J. Die Gründungsurkunde des Klosters Abdinghof in Paderborn. BEHREND, F. Höxter-Corvey in Geschichte, Sage und Dichtung. BOECKLER,

(Continued)

N. Y. P. L. June 21, 1929

Write on slip words underlined and classmark —TB

Wesley Clair Mitchell, the economic scientist, ed. by Arthur F. Burns. New York, National bureau of economic research, 1952. viii,387 p. ports. 24cm. (National bureau of economic research. Publications. no. 53)

Various contributors.

"List of publications by Wesley C. Mitchell," p. 343-366. "Some writings about Wesley C. Mitchell," p. 367-374.

1. Mitchell, Wesley Clair, 1874-1948.
I. Burns, Arthur Frank, 1904- , ed. II. Ser.
NN OC,I PC,1,I,II E,1,I,II (LC1,Z1,X1)

Westfaelische Studien... (Card 2)

A. Corveyer Buchmalerei unter Einwirkung Wibalds von Stablo. DEGERING, H. Theophilus presbiter qui et Rugerus. DEUTSCH, J. Die Handschrift des Weseler Stadtrechts ... FUCHS, W. Was sind und was leisten juristische Theorien. GEISBERG, M. Der Ingenieur J. L. M. Gröninger. GRIMME, H. Die Buchstabendubletten im Sinai-Alphabet. HUSUNG, M. J. Joseph Niesert. JANSEN, H. Der Westfale August Stramm als Hauptvertreter des dichterischen Frühexpressionismus. JUCHHOFF, R. Johann und Konrad von Paderborn. KREYENBORG, H. Proben einer ungedruckten Übertragung arabischer Sprüche und Sinngedichte von Friedrich Rückert. LOEFFLER, K. Die Corveyer Schlossbibliothek. MENN, W. Der Oberpräsident v. Vincke und die Aufhebung der Universität Münster. OHLY, K. Das Inkunabelverzeichnis Bernhards von Mallinckrodt. PHILIPPI, F. Gemeine Marken. SCHMITZ-KALLENBERG, L. Ein in Vergessenheit geratener Druck

(Continued)

N. Y. P. L. June 21, 1929

Westfaelische Studien... (Card 3)

einer Papsturkundenlehre aus dem 18. Jahrhundert. SCHOENE, H. Palimpsestblaetter des Protevangelium Jacobi in Cesena. SCHULTE-KEMMINGHAUS, K. Aus dem westfälischen Freundeskreise der Brüder Grimm. SCHULZ, E. G. H. Immermanns Übersetzung aus Dante. SCHWERING, J. Die politische Dichtung der Westfalen während des 19. Jahrhunderts. SMEND, F. Zur Kenntnis des Musikers Fortunato Santini. WEGENER, H. Das Gebetbuch der Johanna von Bocholt. ZIMMERMANN, H. Luther-Bibeln des 16. Jahrhunderts in der Universitätsbibliothek zu Münster in W.

408596A. 1. Boemer, Alois, 1868- , editor. 2. Degering, Hermann, 1866- , editor. 3. Menn, Walter, 1890- ,
N. Y. P. L. June 21, 1929

WETENSCHAPPELIJKE bijdragen door leerlingen van Dr. D. H. Th. Vollenhoven... (Card 2)

en Protarchos in Plato's Philèbos 36C-44A, door A. W. Begeman. —Het betoog in Augustinus' Contra academicos III, VII, 15-XX, 43, door A. P. Muys. — De beginselen van Mr J. J. L. van der Brugghen als achtergrond van het conflict met Mr G. Groen van Prinsterer, door H. de Jongste. —Historisme en antihistorisme, door M. C. Smit. —Jaspers' kijk op de geschiedenis en op onze levenspraktijk, door H. van Riessen. —Apologetisch existentialisme, door S. J. Popma. —Heidegger's wijsbegeerte van het zijn, door S. U. Zuidema.

1. Vollenhoven, Dirk Hendrik Theodor, 1892- 2. Philosophy—Addresses, essays, lectures. 3. Theology—Essays and misc. I. Zuidema, S. U., ed. II. Zuidema, S. U.

---

*MGA

Westrup, *Sir* **Jack Allan, 1904-**
Essays presented to Egon Wellesz. edited by Jack Westrup. London, Oxford U. P., 1966.
viii, 188 p. front. (port.) illus. (music) plates, tables. 29 cm. 90/-
(B 66-22099)
Bibliographical footnotes.
CONTENTS.—The rediscovery of Byzantine music, by H. W. J. Tillyard.—Byzantine composers in MS. Athens 2406, by M. Velimirović.—
(Continued)

NN * R 7.67 1/ OC PC, 1,3 SL MU,2,3,4,5 3
(LC1,X1,Z1) [I]

A p.v.713

Where is there another? A memorial to Paul Y. Anderson: Death of a fighter, by Freda Kirchwey; Paul Y. Anderson, by Oswald Garrison Villard; Great reporter, valiant crusader, by Marguerite Young; with selections from the Nation, 1937-38, by Paul Y. Anderson. Norman, Okl., Cooperative books, 1939.

52 p. 21cm. (*On cover:* Cooperative books. ser. I, no. 4)

1. Anderson, Paul Y., 1893-1938. I. Kirchwey, Freda. II. Villard, Oswald Garrison, 1872- III. Young, Marguerite.

40-6623

Library of Congress PN4874.A53W5
——— Copy 2.
Copyright AA 319502 [4] 920.5

WESTRUP, Sir JACK ALLAN, 1904- . Essays presented to Egon Wellesz... (Card 2)

The genesis of the liturgical sanctus, by E. Werner.—Sakraler Gesang und Musik in den Schriften Gregors des Grossen, von H. Anglès.—The problem of the old Roman chant, by P. Peacock.—'De glorioso officio ... dignitate Apostolica ...' (Amalarius): Zum Aufbau der Gross-Alleluia in den Päpstlichen Ostervespern, von J. Smits van Waesberghe.—Les chants de la Missa Greca de Saint-Denis, par M. Huglo.—Essai analytique sur la formation de l'Octoéchos latin, par J. Chailley.—An English liquescent neume, by J. D. Bergsagel.—A hitherto unpublished letter of Claudio Monteverdi, by A. Rosen-

(Continued)

E-13
3354

WHITE, HAYDEN V., ed.
The uses of history; essays in intellectual and social history, presented to William J. Bossenbrook. With a foreword by Alfred H. Kelly. Detroit, Wayne state university press, 1968. 285 p. port. 24cm.

Includes bibliographies.
CONTENTS.--Adam Smith and the philosophy of anti-
(Continued)

NN R 10.68 v/L OC, IIbo PC,1,2,I SL
(LC1,X1,Z1) 3

WESTRUP, Sir JACK ALLAN, 1904- . Essays presented to Egon Wellesz... (Card 3)

thal.—Il Tamerlano de Giuseppe Clemente Bonomi, par D. Cvetko.—Expression and revision in Gluck's Orfeo and Alceste, by F. W. Sternfeld.—Vincenzo Righinis Oper Alcide al Bivio, von H. Federhofer.—Wagnerian elements in pre-Wagnerian opera, by H. F. Redlich.—Bizet's La jolie fille de Perth, by J. Westrup.—The operas of Serov, by G. Abraham.

1. Music—Essays. 2. Essays. 3. Wellesz, Egon, 1885- . 4. Chant (Plain, Gregorian, etc.) 5. Operas.

WHITE, HAYDEN V., ed. The uses of history... (Card 2)

history, by J. Weiss.--Towards a disolution of the ontological argument, by A.C. Danto.--Romanticism, historicism, realism, by H. V. White.--History and humanity: the Proudhonian vision, by A. Noland.--Hintze and the legacy of Ranke, by M. Covensky.--Objections to metaphysics, by J. Cobitz.--The term expressionism in the visual arts, by V. H. Miesel.--Karl Löwith's anti- historicism, by B. Riesterer.--Antonio Gramsci: Marxism and
(Continued)

YAR

WETENSCHAPPELIJKE bijdragen door leerlingen van Dr. D. H. Th. Vollenhoven; aangeboden ter gelegenheid van zijn 25-jarig hoogleraarschap aan de Vrije universiteit, gebundeld door S. U. Zuidema, met een opdracht van K. J. Popma. Franeker, T. Wever, 1951. 244 p. port. 24cm.

CONTENTS. —Enkele lijnen in de ontwikkeling der taaltheorie, door P. A. Verburg. — De wijsbegeerte der wetsidee en de paedagogiek, door L. van Klinken. — Teologiese, wysgerige en vakwetenskaplike etiek, door L. H. Stoker. —Enige algemene beschouwingen, gegrond op de betekenis van het hart in het Oude Testament, door F. H. von Meyenfeldt. — "Prof. Vollenhoven's Significance for reformed apologetics, by C. van Til. —De norm voor ons geloven, door J. M. Spier. —Heraclitus' inleiding in de wijsbegeerte, door K. J. Popma. —De posities van Sokratès
(Continued)

NN * * X 10. 54 OC, I, IIbo PC, 1, 2, 3, I SL (LC1, Z1, X1)

WHITE, HAYDEN V., ed. The uses of history... (Card 3)

the Italian intellecutal tradition, by J. Cammett.--Traditional Chinese historiography and local histories, by E.H.Pritchard.--From principle to principal: restoration and emperorship in Japan, by H.D. Harootunian.--National development and the evolution of the legal-rational bureaucracy: the prefectural governor in Japan, 1868-1945, by B. Silberman.
1.History--Addresses, essays, lectures.
2.Bossenbrook,William John, 1897- .
I.Title. II.White, Hayden V.

E-12
1746

White, Robert W., ed.
The study of lives; essays on personality in honor of Henry A. Murray. Edited by Robert W. White, assisted by Katherine F. Bruner. New York, Atherton Press, 1963.
xxi, 442 p. 24 cm. (The Atherton Press behavioral science series)
CONTENTS.—Growth and change in personality: The freeing and acting out of impulse in late adolescence, by N. Sanford. Inburn, an American Ishmael, by K. Keniston. Sense of interpersonal competence, by R. W. White. The harlequin complex, by D. C. McClelland.—Procedures and variables for studying personality: The method of self-confrontation, by G. S. Nielsen. Somerset Maugham, a thematic analysis of ten short stories, by L. Bellak. Psychodynamic and sociocultural factors related to intolerance of ambiguity, by A. Davids. The coping functions of the ego mechanisms, by T. C. Kroeber. Orientations toward death; a vital aspect of the study of lives,
(Continued)

*R 11.64 c/ OC PC, 1, 2, 3 SL (LC1, X1, Z1)

White, Robert W., ed. The study of lives ...
1963. (Card 2)
CONTENTS—Continued.
by E. S. Shneidman.—Creative processes in personality: Diffusion, integration, and enduring attention in the creative process, by F. Barron. Creativity and images of the self, by D. W. MacKinnon. Explorations in typology, by M. I. Stein. The reconstruction of the individual and of the collective past, by F. Wyatt.—Values in personality: Personal values in the study of lives, by M. B. Smith. Albert Camus, personality as creative struggle, by R. N. Wilson. Two influences on Freud's scientific thought, by R. R. Holt. Left and right: a basic dimension of ideology and personality, by S. Tomkins. The Golden rule and the cycle of life, by E. H. Erikson.—Bibliography of Henry A. Murray (p. [429]-434)

1. Murray, Henry Alexander, 1893- 2. Personality. 3. Psychology--Addresses, essays, lectures

---

D-16
5187

Whitehead, Frederick, *ed.*
Medieval miscellany, presented to Eugène Vinaver by pupils, colleagues and friends. Edited by F. Whitehead, A. H. Diverres and F. E. Sutcliffe. [Manchester] Manchester University Press; New York, Barnes & Noble [1965]
xv, 365 p. geneal. table. port. 23 cm.
English or French.
Includes bibliographies.
CONTENTS.—Select bibliography of the works of Eugène Vinaver
(Continued)

NN*R 3.66 g/ OC, Ib* PC, 1, 2, 3 SL (LC1, X1, Z1)
[I]

Whitehead, Frederick, *ed.* Medieval miscellany ... [1965]
(Card 2)

(p. xiii-xv)—'Luf-daungere' by W. R. J. Barron.—The scribal process, by B. Blakey.—Konrad von Würzburg's verse Novellen, by D. M. Blamires.—Part III of the Turin version of Guiron le Courtois, by F. Bogdanow.—The downfall of the Templars and a letter in their defence, by C. R. Cheney.—The romantic hero of the twelfth century, by J. P. Collas.—The geography of Britain in Froissart's Meliador, by A. H. Diverres.—An instance of cyclical recurrence in French literary history, by A. Ewert.—The theme of fortune in the writings of Alain Chartier, by J. M. Ferrier.—A comment on Chevrefoil, by E. A.

Whitehead, Frederick, *ed.* Medieval miscellany ... [1965]
(Card 3)

Francis.—The narrative function of irony in Troilus and Criseyde, by I. L. Gordon.—Syntactical features common to Girart de Roussillon and Béroul's Tristan, by W. M. Hackett.—The giants (Inferno, XXXI), by E. F. Jacob.—King Arthur in the first part of the prose Lancelot, by E. M. Kennedy.—The dedication of Guillaume d'Angleterre, by M. D. Legge.—The literary originality of Galeran de Bretagne, by F. Lyons.—The description of Hell in the Spanish Libro de Alexandre, by I. Michael.—The Spanish Mester de Clerecía and its intended public: concerning the validity as evidence of passages of direct address to the audience, by G. B. Gybbon-Monypenny.—A fifteenth-cen-

---

WHITEHEAD, FREDERICK, ed. Medieval miscellany...
[1965] (Card 4)

tury copyist and his patron, by C. E. Pickford.—On the text of the Tristran of Beroul, by T. B. W. Reid.—Villon et Jean de Bueil (d'un exemple à un mythe), by R. L. Wagner.—The composition of Diu Krône: Heinrich von dem Türlin's narrative technique, by R. E. Wallbank.—Yvain's wooing, by F. Whitehead.—The Tristan of Béroul, by G. Whitteridge.

1. Literature--Hist. and crit., Middle Ages. 2. Middle Ages--Hist.--Addresses, essays, lectures. 3. Vinaver, Eugene, 1899- I. Whitehead, Frederick.

D-18
6650

WHITTLESAY, CHARLES RAYMOND, 1900- , ed.
Essays in money and banking, in honour of R. S. Sayers, edited by C. R. Whittlesey and J. S. G. Wilson. Oxford, Clarendon press, 1968. x, 327 p. port. 23cm.
Bibliographical footnotes.
CONTENTS.--1. Bank rate, money rates, and the treasury-bill rate, by R. F. G. Alford.--2. Rules of the game of international adjustment? by A. I. Bloomfield.--3. Some issues in federal reserve discount policy, by L. V. Chandler.--4. The transfer problem: formal
(Continued)

NN R 1.69 k/l OC, I, II PC, 1, 2, I, II SL E, 1, 2, I, II (LC1, X1, Z1)

WHITTLESAY, CHARLES RAYMOND, 1900- , ed.
Essays in money and banking... (Card 2)

elegance or historical realism, by F. W. Fetter.--5. Regularities and irregularities in monetary economics, by L. Harris.--6. Problems of balance-of-payments adjustment in the modern world, by H. G. Johnson.--7. The relative growth of commercial banks, by E. P. Neufeld.--8. An African monetary perspective, by W. T. Newlyn.--9. Gold reserves, banking reserves, and the Baring crisis of 1890, by L. S. Pressnell.--10. Banking ratios past and present, by J. E. Wadsworth.--11. Rules, discretion, and central bankers, by C. R. Whittlesey.--12. The evolution of the Sterling
(Continued)

WHITTLESAY, CHARLES RAYMOND, 1900- , ed.
Essays in money and banking... (Card 3)

system, by D. Williams.--13. The art of developing a capital market, by J. S. G. Wilson.

1. Money, 1933- . 2. Banks and banking, 1918- . I. Wilson, John Stuart Gladstone, 1916- , joint ed. II. Sayers, Richard Sidney.

---

*PXS

WIENER LIBRARY, London.
On the track of tyranny; essays presented by the Wiener library to Leonard G. Montefiore, O.B.E. on the occasion of his seventieth birthday. Edited by Max Beloff. London, Published for the Wiener library by Vallentine, Mitchell [1960] xi, 232 p. port. 23cm.

Contributions in English, French or German.
(Continued)

NN R 1.62 e/ (OC)I OS PC, 1, 2, 3, 4, I SL E, 2, I J, 4, 5, I (LC1, X1, Z1) [I]

WIENER LIBRARY, London. On the track of tyranny...
(Card 2)

Includes bibliographies.

CONTENTS.--Plebiszit und Machtergreifung; eine kritische Analyse der nationalsozialistischen Wahlpolitik, 1933-34, von K.D. Bracher.--Goebbels and his newspaper Der Angriff, by E. Bramsted.--Is it possible to write contemporary history? by A. Bullock.--War-time activities of the SS-Ahnenerbe, by F.T. Epstein.--The Karaites under Nazi rule, by P. Friedman.--Germany and the Spanish Civil war, by J. Joll.--Jews and non-Jews in Nazi-occupied Holland, by L. de Jong.--Die Wiener Library
(Continued)

WIENER LIBRARY, London. On the track of tyranny...
(Card 3)

und die Zeitgeschichte, von P. Kluke.--Lois de Nuremberg et Lois de Vichy; du racisme intégral au racisme de compromis, par L. Poliakov.--The study of contemporary history as a political and moral duty, by E.G. Reichmann.--Quelques apercus sur les origines du nazisme hitlérien, par E. Vermeil.--Untersuchungen zum Widerhall des deutschen Kirchenkampfes in England, 1933-38, von A. Wiener.

1. Jews in Germany--Anti-Semitism. 2. Fascism--Germany. 3. History, Modern--Historiography. 4. Montefiore, Leonard G. 5. Germany--Anti-Semitism. I. Beloff, Max, 1913- , ed.

F-10
7792

WIESENHÜTTER, ECKART, ed.
Werden und Handeln. Mit Beiträgen von A. Prinz Auersperg [et al.] Stuttgart, Hippokrates-Verlag [1963] 537 p. illus., port. 28cm.

"V. E. Freiherr von Gebsattel zum 80. Geburtstag."

1. Gebsattel, Victor Emil, Freiherr von, 1883- . 2. Psychiatry--Addresses, essays, lectures. 3. Psychology--Addresses, essays, lectures.
NN R 7.63 f/ OC, 1bWiW PC, 1, 2, 3 SL (LC1, X1, Z1) [I]

AD-10
792

WIKGREN, ALLEN PAUL, 1906- , ed.
Early Christian origins; studies in honor of Harold R. Willoughby. Chicago, Quadrangle Books, 1961. 160 p. illus. 22cm.

Includes bibliography.

CONTENTS.--The genealogies of Jesus, by R.T. Hood.--Jesus as theologian, by A. Barnett.--Seek and you will find, by C.H. Kraeling.--The Resurrection in the early church, by R. Branton.--The historical
(Continued)
NN * R 4.64 e/ OC PC, 1, 2, 3, 4 SL (LC1, X1, Z1) [I]

2

WIKGREN, ALLEN PAUL, 1906- , ed. Early Christian origins... (Card 2)

Paul, by F.C. Grant.--Hellenistic elements in I Corinthians, by R.M. Grant.--Social factors in early Christian eschatology, by A.N. Wilder.--The black one, by S.V. McCasland.--Christianity in Sardis, by S.E. Johnson.--Early Christian asceticism, by M.M. Deems.--The sins of Hermas, by K.W. Clark.--Josephus and the marriage customs of the Essenes, by H.R. Moehring.--The origin of texttypes of New Testament manuscripts, by E.C. Colwell.--History and Scripture, by A. Wikgren.

1. Willoughby, Harold Rideout, 1890- . 2. Christianity--Origin. 3. Jesus Christ--Historicity. 4. Church history--Primitive church, to 325.

---

*CA

The Wilder quarter-century book. A collection of original papers dedicated to... B.G. Wilder at the close of his twenty-fifth year of service in Cornell University (1868-1893) by some of his former students. Ithaca, N.Y.: Comstock Pub. Co., 1893. vi, 493 pp., illus., 1 map, 27 pl., 1 port. 8°.

Gift of B.G. Wilder.

Wilder, Burt Green.

E-12
9680

WILGUS, D.K., ed.
Folklore international; essays in traditional literature, belief and custom in honor of Wayland Debs Hand. Edited by D.K. Wilgus with the assistance of Carol Sommer. Hatboro, Pa., Folklore associates, 1967. xiv, 259 p. 24cm.

1. Hand, Wayland Debs, 1907- . 2. Folklore--Addresses, essays, lectures.
NN R 8.67 l/ OC PC, 1, 2 SL (LC1, X1, Z1)

---

*C-4 p. v. 257

WILHELM HOFFMANN zum fünfzigsten Geburtstag am 21. April 1951. [Bebenhausen, 1951] 79 p. 25cm.

Cover-title: Glückwunsch aus Bebenhausen.

"Als Privatdruck in 300 Exemplaren hergestellt."

"Carl Keidel: Entwurf und Ausführung."

CONTENTS.—Beissner, Friedrich. Aus Rilkes Vergers [French with German translation]—Beck, Adolf. Hölderlin und das Stift im November 1789.—Kolschlig-Wiem, Irene. Ein Altersbildnis Hölderlins von Louise Keller.—Autenrieth, Johanne. Kleine Funde in mittelalterlichen
(Continued)
NN OC, I, Ib PC, 1, 2, I, II SL (LC1, Z1, X1)

WILHELM HOFFMANN zum fünfzigsten Geburtstag am 21. April 1951.
(Card 2)

Handschriften aus dem Bodenseegebiet.—Killy, Walther. Weltordnung im Märchen.—Kelletat, Alfred. Mörike in Bebenhausen.—Kohler, Maria. Aufsätze und Schriften Wilhelm Hoffmanns.

1. German literature—Hist. and crit. 2. Hoffmann, Wilhelm, 1901. I. Keidel, Carl, ed. II. Title: Glückwunsch aus Bebenhausen.

NN OC, I, Ib PC, 1, 2, I, II SL (LC1, Z1, X1)

---

* MEC
(Peterson-Berger)

Wilhelm Peterson-Berger festskrift den 27 februari 1937. [Stockholm] Natur och kultur [1937] 302 p. illus. (music), plates, 11 ports. (incl. front.) 26cm.

"Denna festskrift är redigerad av Ernst Arbman, Gösta Morin, Sten Beite, Einar Rosenborg."

"Bibliografi över Wilhelm Peterson-Bergers verk, av Telemak Fredbärj," p. [237]–302.

CONTENTS.—Det svenska, av Bo Bergman.—Wilhelm Peterson-Berger som kulturpersonlighet, av Olof Rabenius.—Wilhelm Peterson-Berger som instrumental tondiktare, av Sten Beite.—Wilhelm Peterson-Berger i sina dramer, av Ivan Oljelund.—Ran, Arnljot, Domedagsprofeterna, Adils och Elisiv, av Curt Berg.—Vi jämtar och Arnljot, av J. A. Selander.—Peterson-Berger och Frösöspelen, av H. G. Pihl.—Jungsein ist alles! P.-B. als europäische Kulturpersönlichkeit, av Friedrich Ege.—Wilhelm Peterson-Bergers
(Continued)

N. Y. P. L. January 18, 1938

Wilhelm Peterson-Berger festskrift... (Card 2)

romanser, av F. H. Törnblom.—Inför Wilhelm Peterson-Bergers körer och kantater, av Johannes Norrby.—Något om folktonen i Wilhelm Peterson-Bergers musik, av Gottfrid Berg.—Några studier i Peterson-Bergers harmoniska stil, av S. E. Svensson.—Musikuppfostraren P.-B., av Torsten Fogelqvist.—Wilhelm Peterson-Berger som musikskriftställare, av Bertil Carlberg.—Ordstudier i Wilhelm Peterson-Bergers kritiker, av R. G. Berg.—Peterson-Berger i Jämtland, av E. W. Olson (Eveo).—Minnen från ungdomsliv och färdestig, av Lennart Wahlberg.

Carnegie Corp. of New York.

911119A. 1. Peterson-Berger, Ernst Gottfrid, 1891- , ed. I. Arbman, Wilhelm, 1867- . II. Morin, Gösta, 1900- , ed. III. Beite, Sten, 1897- , ed. IV. Rosenberg, Einar, 1882- , ed. V. Fredbärj, Telemak.
N. Y. P. L. January 18, 1938

E-13
6193

WILLIAM BLAKE; essays for S. Foster Damon. Edited by Alvin H. Rosenfeld. Providence, Brown University Press, 1969. xlvi,498 p. 31 plates. 24cm.

On cover: Essays for S. Foster Damon.
On-spine: William Blake.
Includes Bibliographical references.
CONTENTS.--S. Foster Damon, the New England voice, by M. Cowley.--S. Foster Damon; a bibliography, by E. D. Costa and E. C. Wescott.--Blake and the post- modern, by H. Adams.--
(Continued)

NN *R 9.69 r/a OC,I,II,IIIb* PC, I,I,I SL A,I,I,II (LC1,X1,Z1) 3

E-13
2635

Wilhelm von Humboldt 1767-1967. Erbe, Gegenwart, Zukunft. Beiträge vorgelegt von der Humboldt-Universität zu Berlin anlässlich der Feier des zweihundertsten Geburtstages ihres Gründers. (Hrsg. von Werner Hartke und Henny Maskolat.) Halle <Saale> Niemeyer, 1967.

242 p. front. 25 cm. (Beiträge zur Geschichte der Humboldt-Universität)

Includes bibliographical references.

(Continued)

NN * R 7.68 1/R OC (OS)I,II PC,1,I SL ST,1,I (LC1,X1, Z1) [NSCM] 2

WILLIAM BLAKE; essays for S. Foster Damon...
(Card 2)

The visionary cinema of romantic poetry, by H. Bloom.--Blake's Miltonic moment, by H. Fisch.--Blake and the progress of poesy, by G. H. Hartman.--Blake and Shelley; beyond the uroboros, by D. Hughes.--William Blake and D. H. Lawrence, by V. de Sola Pinto.--The evolution of Blake's large color prints of 1795, by M. Butlin.--Blakes's 1795 color prints; an interpretation, by A.T. Kostelanetz.--Blake's Night thoughts; an exploration of the fallen world, by M.D. Paley.--The thunder of Egypt, by A.S. Roe.--Blake and the kabbalah, by A.A. Ansari.--Blake's reading of the book of Job, by N. Frye.--The divine tetrad in Blake's Jerusalem, by G. M. Harper.-- Visions in the darksom air; as-
(Continued)

WILHELM VON HUMBOLDT, 1767-1967. Erbe, Gengenwart, Zukunft. (Card 2)

1. Humboldt, Wilhelm, Freiherr von, 1767-1835. I. Berlin. Universität. II. Beiträge zur Geschichte der Humboldt-Universität.

WILLIAM BLAKE; essays for S. Foster Damon...
(Card 3)

pects of Blake's Biblical symbolism, by P. Miner.--Materia prima in a page of Blake's Vala, by P. Nanavutty.--Negative sources in Blake, by M. K. Nurmi.--Blake's verbal technique, by R.F. Gleckner.--Two flowers in the garden of experience, by J.E. Grant.--The fly, by J.H. Hagstrum.--A note on Blake's unfettered verse, by K. Raine.--A temporary report on texts of Blake, by D.V. Erdman.--The William Blake Trust, by G. Keynes.

1. Blake, William, 1757-1827. I. Rosenfeld, Alvin Hirsch, ed. II. Damon, Samuel Foster, 1893- . III. Rosenfeld, Alvin Hirsch.

BZAP

[Wilkinson, I G G]
87th heavy anti-aircraft regiment royal artillery, 1939-1945. Newcastle upon Tyne, Mann & son [1950] 55 p. 22cm.

"Foreword" signed: I.G.G. Wilkinson.

1. World war, 1939-1945—Regt. hist.—Gt.Br.— 87th heavy anti-aircraft regiment.

NN LB

HBC

A WILLIAM CAMERON TOWNSEND en el vigésimoquinto aniversario del Instituto lingüístico de Verano. México, 1961. xiv, 694 p. illus., port., maps(1 fold.) 24cm.

In Spanish or English.
Bibliographical footnotes.

1. Townsend, William Cameron, 1896- 2. Indians, S.A. 3. Indians, Mexican

NN R 8.63 p/ OC PC,1,2,3 SL AH,1,2,3 (LC1,X1,Z1) [I]

E-10
4056

WILLARD PARKER BUTLER, 1857-1935. [Compiled by Franklin Butler Kirkbride and Otto Carl Wierum. New York?] Priv. print., 1936. 81 p. port. 24cm.

Foreword: signed: F.B.K., O.C.W.
"The edition is limited to 175 copies, of which this copy is number 27."

1. Butler, Willard Parker, 1857-1935. I. Kirkbride, Frank Butler, 1867- comp.
NN* R X 10.57 a/POC,I PC,1, I SL (LC1,X1,Z1)

---

*HB

William Warner Bishop; a tribute, 1941, edited by Harry Miller Lydenberg and Andrew Keogh. New Haven, Yale university press; London, H. Milford, Oxford university press, 1941.

vi, 204 p. front. (port.) 24½cm.

Contents.—William Warner Bishop, by F. P. Keppel.—Reflections from Ingonish, by Herbert Putnam.—William Warner Bishop, by H. M. Lydenberg.—Rinaldo Rinaldini (Capo brigante) and George Washington, by J. C. Bay.—The Federation of library associations, by A. C. de Breycha-Vauthier.—Some rare Americana, by I. G. A. Collijn.—Monsieur William Warner Bishop et la Fédération internationale des associations de bibliothécaires, by Marcel Godet.—Book divisions in Greek and Latin literature, by Sir F. G. Kenyon.—The Yale library in 1742, by Andrew

(Continued on next card)

41-12521
[8]

William Warner Bishop ... 1941. (Card 2)

CONTENTS—Continued.

Keogh.—Palm leaf books, by Otto Kinkeldey.—Sir Henry Ellis in France, by G. R. Lomer.—Some trends in research libraries, by K. D. Metcalf.—De Bibliotheca neerlandica manuscripta de Vreese in Leiden, by T. P. Sevensma.—The preparation of a main index for the Vatican library manuscripts, by Eugene, cardinal Tisserant.—Optima in library service for the South by 1950, by L. R. Wilson.

1. Bishop, William Warner, 1871- 2. Bibliography—Collections. 3. Libraries—Addresses, essays, lectures. I. Lydenberg, Harry Miller, 1874- ed. II. Keogh, Andrew, 1869- joint ed.

Library of Congress Z1009.Z3B638 41-12521

[8] 020.4

MGO
(Riemenschneider)

Der WINDSHEIMER Zwölfbotenaltar von Tilman Riemenschneider im Kurpfälzischen Museum zu Heidelberg; Beiträge zu seiner Geschichte und Deutung, hrsg. von Georg Poensgen. [München] Deutscher Kunstverlag, 1955. 161 p. 136 illus., col. front. 26cm. (Heidelberger kunstgeschichtliche Abhandlungen. n. F. Sonderband)

(Continued)

NN ** R 5. 56 s/P OC, II (OS)I PC, 1, 2, I, II SL A, 1, 2, I, II (U1, LC1, X1, Z1)

Der WINDSHEIMER Zwölfbotenaltar von Tilman Riemenschneider im Kurpfälzischen Museum zu Heidelberg... (Card 2)

"Festgabe zum 75. Geburtstag von Karl Lohmeyer."
Includes bibliographical references.
CONTENTS. -Der Altar und seine Geschichte, von G. Poensgen. - Zeitliche Stellung und Bedeutung des Altars im Werke Riemenschneiders, von K. Mugdan. -Zur Ikonographie des Altars, von E. M. Vetter. -Tilmann Riemenschneider als Zeichner, von J. Bier. -Anhang: Zur Rekonstruktion des Windsheimer Altars, von M. Kantner. Zur Deutung der Wappen, von O. Neubecker. 1. Riemenschneider, Tilmann, d. 1531. 2. Lohmeyer, Karl, 1878- . I. Series. II. Poensgen, Georg, ed.

MTE

Winther-festskrift; til købmand Jens Winther paa 75-aarsdagen. 1863–16. december–1938. Mit deutschen zusammenfassungen. København, Ejnar Munksgaard, 1938.
207 p. incl. illus., port., maps. 20cm.
Redaktion: Hans Norling-Christensen, Peter V. Glob.
Bibliographical notes at the end of most of the chapters.
CONTENTS. — Forssander, J. E. Den spetsnackiga flintyxan. — Glob, Peter V. Stenredskaber fra bronzealderen.—Vifot, B.-M. Svensk Lausitzkeramik.—Arbman, H. Mälardalen som kulturcentrum under yngsta bronsåldern.—Riismøller, Peter. En urnegravplads fra ældre jernalder i Lille Vildmose. — Norling-Christensen, H. Skrøbeshave-fundet. Et gravfund fra romersk jærnalder med romersk importgods.—Marstrander, Sverre. En gravplass fra folkevandringstid ved Evje Nikkelverk i Setesdalen.—Gjessing, Gutorm. En "nordlandsbåt" fra jernalderen.
1. Winther, Jens, 1863- 2. Scandinavia—Antiquities. I. Norling-Christensen, Hans, 1909- ed. II. Glob, Peter Vilhelm, 1911- ed.

A C 39-3178

Columbia univ. Library for Library of Congress [2]

E-10
2806

WIR erlebten Rudolf Steiner; Erinnerungen seiner Schüler. [Herausgeber: M.J. Krück v. Poturzyn. 2. Aufl.] Stuttgart, Verlag Freies Geistesleben, 1957. 274 p. ports. 24cm.

1. Steiner, Rudolf, 1861-1925. I. Krück, Maria Josepha (von Fischer-Poturzyn), 1896- , ed.
NN R 5.57 d/P OC, I PC, 1, I SL (LC1, X1, Z1, Y1)

MA

WIR FINGEN einfach an; Arbeiten und Aufsätze von Freunden und Schülern um Richard Riemerschmid zu dessen 85. Geburtstag gesammelt und hrsg. von Heinz Thiersch. München, R. Pflaum [1953] 127 p. illus., ports. facsims. 32cm.

1. Riemerschmid, Richard. 2. Art—Essays and misc. I. Thiersch, Heinz, ed.

NN ** R X 3. 54 OC, Ibo, I, Ib PC, 1, 2, I SL A, 1, 2, I (LC1, Z1, X1)

D-12
2788

WIRKENDES, Sorgendes Dasein; Begegnungen mit Adolf Grimme, hrsg. von Walter G. Oschilewski. Berlin-Grunewald, Arani [1959] 192 p. ports. 22cm.
"Gruss der Freunde und Weggefährten zum siebzigsten Geburstag am 31 Dezember 1959."
"Adolf-Grimme-Bibliographie," p. 145-178.

1. Grimme, Adolf, 1889- . I. Oschilewski, Walther Georg, 1904- . ed
NN R 4.60 c/P OC, I PC, 1 I SL (LC1, X1, Z1)

BAC

Wirtschaft und kultur; festschrift zum 70. geburtstag von Alfons Dopsch, gearbeitet [!] von Gian Piero Bognetti ... Helen M. Cam ... Alexander Domanovsky ... [u. a.] Baden bei Wien, Leipzig, R. M. Rohrer verlag [c1938]
x, 696 p. 24½cm.
CONTENTS.—Naumann, Hans. Die magische seite des altgermanischen königtums und ihr fortwirken in christlicher zeit.—Hohenlohe-Schillingsfürst, Constantin. Salvo jure ecclesiae possidere.— Patzelt, Erna. Die kontinuitätsfrage.—Lennard, Reginald. From Roman Britain to Anglo-Saxon England.—Mickwitz, Gunnar. Der verkehr auf dem westlichen Mittelmeer um 600 n. Chr.—Mal, Josef. Karantanisches Kroatien.—Sánchez-Albornoz, Claudio. La caballería visigoda.—Bognetti, G. P. Arimannie e guariganghe.—Uyehara, Senroku. Gefolgschaft und vasallität im Fränkischen reiche und in Japan.—Schröder, Edward. Landes-
(Continued on next card)

A C 38-3339

[3]

Wirtschaft und kultur; festschrift zum 70. geburtstag von Alfons Dopsch ... [c1938] (Card 2)

CONTENTS—Continued.

art, kultur und wirtschaft nach dem zeugnis der französischen ortsnamen.—Cam, H. M. The early burgesses of Cambridge in relation to the surrounding countryside.—Hauptmann, Ludmil. Colonus, barschalk und freimann.—Wopfner, Hermann. Beiträge zur bevölkerungsgeschichte der österreichischen länder.—Kötzschke, Rudolf. Hufe und hufenordnung in mitteldeutschen fluranlagen.—Törne, P. O. von. Die älteste besteuerung in Schweden.—Johnsen, O. A. Die wirtschaftlichen grundlagen des ältesten Norwegischen staates.—Hóman, Bálint. Stephan der Heilige.—Wojciechowski, Zygmunt. Usque in vurta fluvium.—Dungern, Otto von. Königsgericht und reichsfürstenrat zur zeit kaiser Lothars III.—Goetz, Walter. Die entstehung der italienischen nationalität.—Thompson, J. W. Serfdom in the medieval Campagna.—Powicke, F. M. Observations on the English freeholder in the thirteenth century.—
(Continued on next card)

A C 38-3339

[3]

Wirtschaft und kultur; festschrift zum 70. geburtstag von Alfons Dopsch ... [c1938] (Card 3)

CONTENTS—Continued.

Leicht, P. S. Note sull' economia friulana al principio del secolo XIII.—Haller, Johannes. Die überlieferung der annalen Lamperts von Hersfeld.—Validi, A. Z. Über die bevölkerungsdichte Zentralasiens im mittelalter.—Lukinich, Imre. Zur frage der besiedlung des Waagtales.—Domanovszky, Alexander. Zur geschichte der gutsherrschaft in Ungarn.—Zycha, Adolf. Vom durchgang der arbeitsfreiheit durch die grundherrschaft.—Nabholz, Hans. Der kampf der Schweizerbauern um autonomie und befreiung von den grundlasten.—Koht, Halvdan. Vereinigte königreiche des späteren mittelalters.—Lauffer, Otto. Ausstattung nach stand und rang.—Huizinga, Johan. Ruyers und poyers.—Mitteis, Heinrich. Rechtsgeschichte und machtgeschichte.—Künssberg, Eberhard von. Rechtserinnerung und vergessenes recht.—Fehr, Hans. Die gerechte vergeltung im diesseits und jenseits.—Ussani, Vincenzo.
(Continued on next card)

A C 38-3339

[3]

Wirtschaft und kultur; festschrift zum 70. geburtstag von Alfons Dopsch ... [c1938] (Card 4)

CONTENTS—Continued.

I viaggi di Virgilio nel sotterra.—Sayous, A. E. L'adaptation des méthodes commerciales et des institutions économiques des pays chrétiens de la Méditerranée occidentale en Amérique pendant la première moitié du xvie siècle.—Temperley, Harald. Austria and the Peace of Paris, 1855–1856.—Lhéritier, Michel. La coopération intellectuelle avant le siècle des nationalités.—Peterka, Otto. Die Prager universität in der böhmischen geschichte.—Norvin, William. Aus der werdezeit der römischen geschichte von Barthold Georg Niebuhr.—Handelsman, Marcely. Die frühmittelalterlichen forschungen der Warschauer schule.—Halecki, Oskar von. Kulturgeschichte und geschichtsphilosophie.

1. Dopsch, Alfons, 1868– 2. Europe—Civilization. 3. Civilization, Medieval. 4. Economic conditions. 5. Constitutional history. I. Bognetti, Gian Piero.

A C 38-3339

No. Carolina. Univ. Libr. for Library of Congress D101.2.W5 [3]

TB

WIRTSCHAFTLICHE Entwicklung und soziale Ordnung [hrsg. von] Lagler-Messner, mit Beiträgen von L. Adamovich [et al.] Wien, Herold [1952] 456 p. port., diagrs., tables. 24cm.

"Ferdinand Degenfeld-Schonburg zum 70. Geburtstag gewidmet."
Includes bibliographies.

1. Degenfeld-Schonburg, Ferdinand, Graf von, 1882- 2. Economics, 1926- —German and Austrian authors. I. Messner, Johannes, 1891- ed. II. Lagler, Ernst, ed.

NN ** Z X 12.53 OC, I, II PC, 1, 2, I, II SL E, 1, 2, I, II (LC1, Z1, X1)

TB

WIRTSCHAFTS-FRAGEN der freien Welt. Hrsg. von Erwin von Beckerath, Fritz W. Meyer [und] Alfred Müller-Armack. [Zum 60. Geburtstag von Bundeswirtschaftsminister Ludwig Erhard] Frankfurt a.M., F. Knapp [c1957] xi, 633 p. illus., mounted port., maps. 25cm.

Bibliographical footnotes.

1. Economics--Essays and misc. 2. Erhard, Ludwig. I. Beckerath, Erwin von, 1889- , ed. II. Meyer, Fritz W., ed. III. Müller-Armack, Alfred, 1901- , ed.

NN * R 7.57 d/ OC, I, II, III PC, 1, 2, I, II, III SL E, 1, 2, I, II, III (LC1, X1, Z1)

TAH

WIRTSCHAFTSHISTORISCHER VEREIN ZU KOELN, e. V.

Europa, Erbe und Auftrag; eine Festschrift für Bruno Kuske zum 29. Juni 1951. Mit Beiträgen von V. Agartz... [und anderen] Hrsg. im Auftrage des Wirtschafts-Historischen Vereins an der Universität Köln e. V. ... [Köln] Kölner Universitätsverlag, 1951. 240 p. port. 24cm.

"Schrifttum von Bruno Kuske, zusammengestellt von Dipl. -Kfm. Marga Limper," p. 235-240.

1. Kuske, Bruno, 1876- 2. Economic history, 1918- I. Title.

NNR (OC)I OS PC, 1, 2 SL E, 1, 2 (LC1, Z1, X1)

E-13
6554

Wirtschaftsprüfer im Dienst der Wirtschaft. Festschrift für Ernst Knorr. Hrsg. von Erwin Pougin und Klaus von Wysocki. Düsseldorf, Verlagsbuchhandlung des Instituts der Wirtschaftsprüfer, 1968.

x, 452 p., port. 24cm.

CONTENTS.—Das Bild des Vergleichsverwalters, von H. Papke.—Die Gläubigerautonomie als Grundprinzip der Vergleichsordnung, von C. R. Wellmann.—Der fehlerhafte Vergleichsvorschlag, von J. Mohrbutter.—Die Übernahme von Handelsgeschäften und Mitglied-

(Continued)

NN*R 10.69 r/L OC, I, Ib*, II, III, IVb* PC, 1, 2, 3, I, II, III SL E, 1, 2, 3, I, II, III (LC1, X1, Z1)

Wirtschaftsprüfer im Dienst der Wirtschaft. 1968. (Card 2)

schaften an Personengesellschaften durch den Testamentsvollstrecker, von W. Schumacher.—Die Rechnungslegung der Aktiengesellschaft während der Abwicklung (§270 AktG 1965), von K. H. Forster.—Wirtschaftsprüfer und Rechtsberatung, von P. Möhring.—Netzplantechnik und Jahresabschlussprüfung, von H. Münstermann.—Zur Bedeutung der Grundsätze ordnungsmässiger Abschlussprüfung, von E. Spieth.—Grundlagen und Aufgaben der Bauwirtschaftsprüfung, von S. Eichhorn.—Das Rechnungswesen als Führungsinstrument, von E. Keysers.—Die Rechnungslegungsvorschriften des neuen Aktiengesetzes als Grundsätze ordnungsmässiger Buchführung, von E. Pougin.—Das Stabilitätsgesetz als Schrittmacher des rechts- und wirtschaftswissenschaftlichen Zusam-

(Continued)

Wirtschaftsprüfer im Dienst der Wirtschaft. 1968. (Card 3)

menwirkens, von G. Greitemann.—Steuern bei der Bewertung von Unternehmen, von F. J. Friedrich.—Kapital- und Gewinnanteil bei der GmbH & Co., von H. Krollmann.—Das deutsche Krankenhauswesen, von W. Adam.—Bedeutung und Probleme privater Krankenanstalten, von W. Landerer.—Die Schadenausgleichspflicht des Krankenhausträgers gegenüber dem angestellten Krankenhausarzt aus dem Gesichtspunkt der gefahren- oder schadensgeneigten Tätigkeit, von W. Uhlenbruck.—Die Bedeutung des betriebswirtschaftlichen Hochschulstudiums im Rahmen der Ausbildung zum Wirtschaftsprüfer, von K. v. Wysocki—Gedanken zu einer Reform der Fachprüfung zum Wirtschaftsprüfer, von W. Dieterich.—Zur

(Continued)

WIRTSCHAFTSPRÜFER im Dienst der Wirtschaft... (Card 4)

Ausbildung und Weiterbildung im Wirtschaftsprüferberuf, von E. Potthoff.—Veröffentlichungen von Ernst Knorr.

1. Accounting and bookkeeping for corporations--Germany. 2. Auditing. 3. Management consultants--Germany. I. Knorr, Ernst, 1898- II. Pougin, Erwin, ed. III. Wysocki, Klaus von, joint ed. IV. Pougin, Erwin.

TB

WIRTSCHAFTSTHEORIE und Wirtschaftspolitik; Festschrift für Alfred Amonn zum 70. Geburtstag, hrsg. von Valentin F. Wagner und Fritz Marbach. Bern, Francke, 1953. 371 p. port. 24cm.

Bibliographies included in "Anmerkungen."

CONTENTS.—Tabula gratulatoria.—Subjektivismus in der sozialökonomischen Theorie, Seine Grenzen und Relativität, von O. von Zwiedineck-Südenhorst.—Sozialökonomische und steuerpolitische Anschauungen von Jean-Jacques Rousseau, von H. Schorer.—Zur Frage der Rechenbarkeit des subjektiven Wertes. Eine Lösungsmöglichkeit für ein altes, immer noch offenes Problem der ökonomischen Grundlagenforschung, von H. Meyer.

(Continued)

NN ** R X 10.53 OC, I, II PC, 1, 2, I, II SL E, 1, 2, I, II (Z1, LC1, X1)

WIRTSCHAFTSTHEORIE und Wirtschaftspolitik... (Card 2)

—Unternehmungswirtschaftliche Grundlagen für volkswirtschaftliche Massnahmen, von A. Walther.—Kreditschöpfung und Geldschöpfung, von E. Kellenberger.—Beitrag zur Kontroverse um den Monopolbegriff, von F. Marbach.—Zur Psychologie der nationalökonomischen Erkenntnis, von E. Böhler.—Quantitätstheorie und Geldpolitik, von V. F. Wagner.—Zum Begriff der Sozialpolitik, von M. Weber.—Das Landhandwerk in der alten Schweiz. Anwendungsprobleme der Wirtschaftstheorie in Soziologie und Wirtschaftsgeschichte, von E. J. Walter.—Von der Stabilität zur Flexibilität der Wechselkurse. Eine dogmengeschichtliche Studie, von A. Bosshardt.—Bemerkungen zum gegenwärtigen Stand der

(Continued)

WIRTSCHAFTSTHEORIE und Wirtschaftspolitik... (Card 3)

Konjunkturtheorie, von G. Haberler. --When is a problem of economic policy solvable? By O. Morgenstern. --Betrachtung einiger Konjunkturmechanismen, von H. Böhi. -- Theorie und Praxis in der Verkehrspolitik, von H. R. Meyer. --Nationalökonomie und Soziologie, von W. A. Jöhr. -- Die Bedeutung der Notenbankbilanzgewinne und-verluste bei Änderungen des Wechselkurses, von H. Sieber. -- Neomerkantilismus in der Zahlungsbilanzpolitik, von E. Küng. --Entwicklung und Stand der Theorie von Keynes, von H. G. Bieri.

1. Economics, 1926- --Swiss authors. 2. Amonn, Alfred, 1883- I. Wagner, Valentin Fritz, 1895- , ed. II. Marbach, Fritz, 1892- , ed.

TB

Wirtschaftstheorie und Wirtschaftspolitik; eine Sammlung von Abhandlungen unter Mitarbeit von Erich Carell...[und anderen] hrsg. von Alfred Kruse. Berlin, Duncker & Humblot [1951] 364 p. port. 25cm.

Half-title: Festgabe für Adolf Weber...zur Vollendung seines 75. Lebensjahres am 29. Dezember 1951, dargebracht von habilitierten Schülern und Münchener Kollegen.

"Schriften von Adolf Weber," p. 357-364.

1. Weber, Adolf, 1876- 2. Economics, 1926- German and Austrian authors. I. Kruse, Alfred, 1912-

NN

YBX (James)

Wisconsin. University.

William James, the man and the thinker; addresses delivered at the University of Wisconsin in celebration of the centenary of his birth, by Max C. Otto [and others] ... with introductions by George C. Sellery and Clarence A. Dykstra. Madison, The University of Wisconsin press, 1942.

5 p. l., 3-147 p. front. (port.) 22cm.

Bibliographical references included in "Notes" (p. [143]-147)

CONTENTS.—William James and Wisconsin, by G. C. Sellery.—The distinctive philosophy of William James, by M. C. Otto.—William James, man and philosopher, by D. S. Miller.—William James and psychoanalysis, by Norman Cameron.—The William James centenary dinner: Introductory remarks, by C. A. Dykstra. William James and the world today,

(Continued on next card)

43-52550

[15]

Wisconsin. University. William James ... 1942. (Card 2)

CONTENTS—Continued.

by John Dewey, read by Carl Boegholt. William James in the American tradition, by B. H. Bode.—The Sunday service: William James as religious thinker, by J. S. Bixler.

1. James, William, 1842-1910. I. Otto, Max Carl, 1876-

43-52550

Library of Congress B945.J24W5

[15] 191.9

D-14
4086

Die WISSENSCHAFT von deutscher Sprache und Dichtung:Methoden, Probleme, Aufgaben. [Festschrift für Friedrich Maurer zum 65. Geburtstag am 5. Januar 1963. Hrsg. von Siegfried Gutenbrunner, et al.] Stuttgart, E. Klett [1963] xvi, 518 p. port., fold. maps. 22cm.

Bibliographical footnotes.

1. Maurer, Friedrich, 1898- . 2. German language--Addresses, essays, lectures. 3. German literature --Addresses, essays, lectures. I. Gutenbrunner, Siegfried, ed.

NN R 7.63 a/rOC, I PC, 1, 2, 3, I SL (LC1, X1, Z1) [I]

F-11
3975

Wissenschaft und Praxis. Festschrift zum zwanzigjährigen Bestehen des Westdeutschen Verlages. Köln u. Opladen, Westdeutscher Verlag, 1967.

391 p. 26 cm.

Includes bibliographical references.

CONTENTS.—Forschungspolitik in der Industriegesellschaft, von L. Brandt.—Regierungslehre als praktische Wissenschaft, von T. Ellwein.—Der Politikwissenschaftler als Berater der politischen Praxis, von O. Stammer.—Medien der Massenkommunikation und rationale

(Continued)

NN * R 3.68 1/ OC (OS)I Ib* PC,1,I SL E,1,I (LC1,X1,Z1) 3

WISSENSCHAFT und Praxis. (Card 2)

Politik, von F. A. Hermens.—Gesellschaftslehre und Kulturwandel, von L. von Wiese. — Zeitbewusstsein und sozialer Wandel, von R. König.—Zu einer Theorie der Planung, von F. H. Tenbruck.—Zur Kritik der Betriebsklima-Forschung, von F. Fürstenberg.—Berufsanalyse und Berufsprognostik in der Berufsberatung, von F. Molle.—

Abstraktionsgrad und Realitätswert der Wirtschaftstheorie, von S. Klatt. — Wirtschaftswachstum und technischer Fortschritt, von T. Wessels.—Währungspolitisches Instrumentarium und aktuelle Währungspolitik, von R. Nöll v. d. Nahmer. — Theoretisches und praktisches Denken in der Unternehmensrechnung, von D. Schneider.—Von

(Continued)

WISSENSCHAFT und Praxis. (Card 3)

den Anfängen der Marktforschungslehre und von ihrem Verhältnis zur Betriebswirtschaftslehre, von E. Schäfer.—Stand und Entwicklungstendenzen der Unternehmensforschung in Deutschland, von H. Albach.—Mitbestimmung als organisatorisches Problem in der Unternehmenswirtschaft, von K. Hax.—Dynamische Bilanz; Grundlagen, Weiterenwicklung und Bedeutung in der neuesten Bilanzdiskussion, von H. Münstermann.—Kybernetische Probleme im Industriebetrieb, von A. Adam.—Die Überwindung der Ungewissheit, von G. Menges.

1. Social sciences--Addresses, essays, lectures. I. Westdeutscher Verlag.

ZDTH

Wissenschaftliche Festgabe zum zwölfhundertjährigen Jubiläum des heiligen Korbinian. Hrsg. von D. Dr. Joseph Schlecht... München, A. Huber, 1924. xvi, 551 p. illus., map. 26cm.

Bibliographical footnotes.

1. Corbinianus, Saint, bp. of Freising, d. ca. 730. 2. Church history—Germany—Freising. I. Schlecht, Joseph, 1857-1925, ed.

N. Y. P. L.

---

*C-3 p.v.170

Woel, Cai Mogens, 1895-

...Bibliografisk fortegnelse over Soyas arbejder, 1911-1946. København, Uhlman, 1946. 108 p. 21cm.

1. Soya, Carl Erik, 1896- —Bibl.

NN R 3.53 OC PC,1 SL (LC1,Z1,X1)

G-10
1734
WOHNUNGSAKTIENGESELLSCHAFT, Linz, Austria.
25 Jahre Wohnungsaktiengesellschaft Linz, [Für den Inhalt verantwortlich Albert Schöpf. Linz, 1963]
143 p. illus., ports. 33cm.

1. Building and loan associations--Austria--Linz. 2. Housing--Austria. I. [Title] Fünfundzwanzig.
NN R 5.66 r/ OS PC, 1, 2 SL E, 1, 2 (LC1, X1, Z1 [I])

NCC
(Wordsworth)
Wordsworth and Coleridge; studies in honor of George McLean Harper; edited by Earl Leslie Griggs ... an appreciation by J. Duncan Spaeth; a bibliography by Evelyn Griggs. Princeton, Princeton university press, 1939.
viii, 254 p. 23½cm.
"First edition."
CONTENTS.—pt. I. Some remarks on the composition of the Lyrical ballads of 1798, by Émile Legouis. Solitude, silence, and loneliness in the poetry of Wordsworth, by R. D. Havens. Wordsworth's conception of the esthetic experience, by O. J. Campbell. The tragic flaw in Wordsworth's philosophy, by N. P. Stallknecht. Wordsworth and his daughter's marriage, by Ernest de Selincourt. An imitation of Wordsworth, by L. N. Broughton. Helen Maria Williams and the French revolution, by M. R. Adams. Anna Seward and the romantic poets: a study in taste,
(Continued on next card)
39-16345
[4]

AE-10
484
WOLF, ERNST, 1902- , ed.
Zwischenstation; Festschrift für Karl Kupisch zum 60. Geburtstag. Hrsg. in Verbindung mit Helmut Gollwitzer und Joachim Hoppe von Ernst Wolf. München, C. Kaiser, 1963. 302 p. 24cm.

Bibliographical footnotes.
CONTENTS. –Überlegungen zum Zweiten vatikanischen Konzil, von K. Barth. –Die Inspirierten-Gemeinde zu Berlin, von W. Delius. –Thesen und Anmerkungen zum exegetischen Paulusverständnis
(Continued)
NN R 4.64 a/ OC PC, 1, 2 SL (LC1, X1, Z1)
3

Wordsworth and Coleridge; studies in honor of George McLean Harper ... 1939. (Card 2)
CONTENTS—Continued.
by S. H. Monk. Samuel Taylor Coleridge discovers the Lake country, by the Rev. G. H. B. Coleridge. Coleridge's "Preface" to Christabel, by B. R. McElderry, jr. An early defense of Christabel, by E. L. Griggs. Coleridge on the sublime, by C. DeW. Thorpe. Coleridge in Germany (1799) by Edith J. Morley.—pt. II. Professor Harper: an appreciation, by J. D. Spaeth. Bibliography of the works of George McLean Harper (p. [244]-247) by Evelyn Griggs.
1. Wordsworth, William, 1770-1850. 2. Coleridge, Samuel Taylor, 1772-1834. 3. Williams, Helen Maria, 1762-1827. 4. Seward, Anna, 1742-1809. 5. Harper, George McLean, 1863- I. Griggs, Earl Leslie, 1899- ed. II. Spaeth, John Duncan Ernst, 1868- III. Griggs, Evelyn.
39-16345
Library of Congress PR5881.W8
~~Copy 2.~~
Copyright A 130100 [4] 821.71

WOLF, ERNST, 1902- , ed. Zwischenstation...
(Card 2)

des Pelagius, von H.H. Esser. –Vom Problem der Milieuseelsorge, von M. Fischer. –Christlicher Glaube im atomaren Zeitalter, von M. Geiger. –Was ist des Deutschen Vaterland heute? Von G. Giese. –Humanismus zwischen West und Ost, von H. Gollwitzer. –Die Sprache der Kundgebungen der Bekennenden Kirche, von G. Harder. –Die verweltlichte Kirche und der verchristlichte Staat, von J. Hoppe. –Die letzte Redaktion des Markusevangeliums, von M. Karnetzki. –"Die Juden unter uns!" über Karl Kupischs Beitrag zur Judenfrage, von F.-W. Marquardt. –Erwägungen zur
(Continued)

*OGC
The WORLD of Islam; studies in honour of Philip K. Hitti, edited by James Kritzeck and R. Bayly Winder. London, Macmillan; New York, St. Martin's press, 1959. viii, 372 p. illus., port. 23cm.

Bibliographical footnotes.
CONTENTS.--Philip K. Hitti, by the editors.--A bibliography of works by Philip K. Hitti (p. 10-37).--The meaning of amānīy(a) in Sūrah 2:73, by A. Guillaume.--Some similarities and differences between Christianity and
(Continued)
NN R 2.60 t/ OC, I, II, IIIbo PC, 1, 2, I, II SL O, 1, 2, I, II (LC1, X1, Z1)

WOLF, ERNST, 1902- , ed. Zwischenstation...
(Card 3)

Geschichtsschreibung des Kirchenkampfes, von W. Niemöller. –Alttestamentliche Theologie und israelitisch-jüdische Religionsgeschichte, von R. Rendtorff. –Zur Ideengeschichte des Sozialismus, von H.-J. Schoeps. –Gerhart Hauptmann, von H. Urner. –Vom Geheimnis der Geschichte, von H. Vogel. –Vergegenwärtigung der Geschichte in den Psalmen, von C. Westermann. –Johannes Bugenhagen und die "Ordnung der Gemeinde," von W. Wolf.

1. Kupisch, Karl. 2. Christianity--Essays and misc.

The WORLD of Islam... (Card 2)

Islam, by W.C. Smith.--ʿUrf and law in Islam, by F.J. Ziadeh.--The head upon the knees, by R. Mach and J.H. Marks.--On the patriciate of Imru'-al-Qays, by I. Kawar.--Some new light on the history of Kirmān in the first century of the Hijrah, by G.C. Miles.--al-Mushatta, Baghdād, and Wāsit, by O. Grabar.--The Arabic palimpsests of Mount Sinai, by A.S. Atiya.--Some biographical and bibliographical notes on al-Hakīm al-Tirmidhi, by N.L. Heer.--Ridwān the maligned, by R.W. Crawford.--Ibn-Rushd's Defence of philosophy, by G.F. Hourani.--Ibn-al-Tiqtaqa and the fall of Baghdād, by J. Kritzeck.--A fourteenth-century
(Continued)

F-11
1651
WOLGAST, Germany. Rat.
Festschrift zur 700-Jahrfeier der Stadt Wolgast vom 5. bis 14. Juli 1957. [Wolgast, 1957] 134 p. illus. (part col.) maps, facsims. 30cm.

1. Wolgast, Germany--Hist. 2. Economic history--Germany--Wolgast. 3. Architecture--Germany--Wolgast. t. 1957.
NN 7.66 p/ ODt (1b+) EDt PC, 1, 2 SL A, 3 (E)2 (LC1, X1, Z1)

The WORLD of Islam... (Card 3)

view of language, by T.B. Irving.--Abu-al-Duhūr, the Ruwalah 'Utfah, by J. Jabbur.--Islamic philately as an ancillary discipline, by H.W. Hazard.--Ideological influences in the Arab revolt, by C.E. Dawn.--Arab unity, by H.W. Glidden.--The Turko-Iraqi frontier and the Assyrians, by J. Joseph.--Islamic literature in post-war Iran, by Y. Armajani.--Education in al-Bahrayn, by R.B. Winder.--Lebanon, "land of light", by N.A. Faris.--Americans from the Arab world, by M. Berger.

1. Hitti, Philip Khūri, 1886- . 2. Islamic studies--Collections. I. Kritzeck, James, ed. II. Winder, Richard Bayly, 1920- , ed. III. Kritzeck, James.

ZSB

World Lutheranism of today; a tribute to Anders Nygren, 15 November 1950. Stockholm, Svenska kyrkans diakonistyrelses bokförlag [etc., etc., 1950] xxxii, 438 p. port. 24cm.

Added t.-p. in German: Welt-Lutherthum von heute...
Contributions in English, French or German.

608890B. 1. Evangelical Lutheran church. 2. Nygren, Anders, bp., 1890- . I. Title: Welt-Lutherthum von heute.
N. Y. P. L. November 21, 1951

Copy only words underlined & Classmark-- TB

WORLD, nations, and groups in development. A series of three lectures delivered on the occasion of the tenth anniversary of the Institute of social studies, The Hague, October 1962, by Peter Kuenstler, M.T. Ramzi [and] J. Tinbergen. The Hague, Mouton, 1963. 55 p. 19cm. (Institute of social studies, The Hague. Publications. Series minor. v. 2)

Bibliographical footnotes.

(Continued)

NN 7.66 1/d OC, I (OS)II PC, 1, 2, I, II E, 1, 2, I, II (LC1, X1, Z1)

2

WORLD, nations, and groups in development. (Card 2)

CONTENTS.--Individuals, groups, and communities, by P. Kuenstler.--Problems of national development: a viewpoint of public administration, by M.T. Ramzi.-A world development policy, by J. Tinbergen.

1. Economic development--Addresses, essays, lectures. 2. Social policy--Addresses, essays, lectures. I. Kuenstler, Peter, 1919- . II. Series.

---

*POR

WORLD UNION FOR PROGRESSIVE JUDAISM.
Aspects of progressive Jewish thought. With an introd. by Israel I. Mattuck. London, V. Gollancz, 1954. 158 p. 21cm.

"Dedicated to Rabbi Dr. Leo Baeck, president of the World union for progressive Judaism, in honor of his 80th birthday, 23rd May 1953."
CONTENTS.--Introduction, by I.I. Mattuck.--The attitude to the Bible, by J. Morgenstern.--The relation of progressive Judaism to rabbinic Judaism, by I. Bettan.—The prophetic element in progressive Judaism, by

(Continued)

NN R X 8.57 j/P(OC)I, II OS PC, 1, 3, I, II SL J, 2, 3, I, II (LC1, X1, Z1)

WORLD UNION FOR PROGRESSIVE JUDAISM. Aspects of progressive Jewish thought. (Card 2)

S.H. Blank.—Progressive Jewish liturgy, by S.B. Freehof.—The missionary idea, by I.I. Mattuck.—Fundamental concepts of progressive Judaism, by S.S. Cohon.—The present task, by M.N. Eisendrath.—The social teaching, by A. Cronbach.—The conception of prayer, by L.H. Montagu.—The mystical element, by A.C. Zaoui.—The attitude to psychology, by R. Assagioli.—The attitude to the State of Israel and Jewish nationalism, by B.L.Q. Henriques.—The national conception of Judaism, by M. Elk.—The religious situation in Israel, by M.C. Weiler.—Faith and reason, by S.H. Bergman.—Biblical archaeology and progressive Judaism, by N. Glueck.

1. Judaism--Reform. 2. Reform. 3. Baeck, Leo, 1873- I. Mattuck, Israel Isidor. II. Title.

AE-10
1149

Wort und Welt. Festgabe für Prof. D. Erich Hertzsch anlässlich der Vollendung seines 65. Lebensjahres. (Herausgeber: Manfred Weise.) Berlin, Evangelische Verlagsanstalt (1968).

335 p. with front. 24 cm.

Bibliographical references included in "Anmerkungen" at the end of each article.

1. Theology--Collections. I. Hertzsch, Erich.
II. Weise, Manfred, ed.

NN* 1.70 w/J OC, I, II PC, 1, I, II SL (LC1, X1, Z1)

E-11
2405

WORTE und Werte; Bruno Markwardt zum 60. Geburtstag. Hrsg. von Gustav Erdmann und Alfons Eichstaedt. Berlin, W. de Gruyter, 1961.
xvi, 498 p. port., maps, facsim. 25cm.

Contributions in German and English.
Bibliographical footnotes.

1. Markwardt, Bruno, 1899- . 2. Literature--Addresses, essays, lectures. I. Erdmann, Gustav, ed. II. Eichstaedt, Alfons, ed.
III. Erdmann, Gustav. IV. Eichstaedt, Alfons.

NN R 5.61 e/POC, Ib*, I, II, IIIbo, IVbo PC, 1, 2, I, II SL (LC1, X1, Z1) [I]

---

* PDB

Wright, George Ernest, 1909- *ed.*
The Bible and the ancient Near East; essays in honor of William Foxwell Albright. [1st ed.] Garden City, N. Y., Doubleday [1961]

409 p. illus., port. 25 cm.

"Bibliography of W. F. Albright": p. [363]-389. Includes bibliographical references.

1. Bible. O.T.--Criticism. 2. Near East--Hist.--Addresses, essays, lectures. 3. Albright, William Foxwell, 1891- I. Title.

NN R 1.63 g/ OC PC, 1, 2, 3, I SL J, 1, 2, 3, I O, 2, 3, I (LC1, X1, Z1)

HBC

Wright, Muriel Hazel, 1889-
A guide to the Indian tribes of Oklahoma... Norman, University of Oklahoma press [1951] xvii, 300 p. illus., maps. 24cm. (Civilization of the American Indian. vol. 33)

1. ed.
"Complete list of suggested readings," p. 270-273. "Bibliography," p. 274-285.

1. Indians, N. A.—Reg. areas—Oklahoma.
NN

NBC
(Bianco)

Writing and criticism; a book for Margery Bianco, ed. by Anne Carroll Moore and Bertha Mahony Miller, decorated by Valenti Angelo. Boston, Horn book co., 1951. xii, 93 p. port. 23cm.

1. Bianco, Margery (Williams), 1880-1944. I. Moore, Anne Carroll, 1871- , ed. II. Mahony, Bertha E., jt. ed.
N. Y. P. L. January 15, 1952

WROCŁAWSKIE TOWARZYSTWO NAUKOWE.
Pamięci Jerzego Kowalskiego; przemówienia wygłoszone na Akademii żałobnej w dniu 29 kwietnia 1948 roku oraz na posiedzeniu Wydziału nauk filologicznych Wrocławskiego towarzystwa naukowego w dniu 6 lutego 1948 roku. Wrocław, Nakł. Wrocławskiego towarzystwa naukowego, 1948. 24 p. port. 25cm.

Bibliographical footnotes.

1. KOWALSKI, JERZY, 1893-

NN * * R 12.57 v/✓OS PC, 1 SL S, 1 (Z1, LC1, X1)

WÜRTTEMBERGISCHE BIBEL-ANSTALT, Stuttgart.
Festschrift zum dritten Halb-Jahrhundert. [Stuttgart] 1962. 62 p. illus., ports. 24cm.

1. Bible societies--Germany--Stuttgart.
NN R 6.64 a/✓ OS PC, 1 SL (LC1, X1, Z1)

WÜRTENBERGER, THOMAS, ed.
Existenz und Ordnung; Festschrift für Erik Wolf zum 60. Geburtstag. [Hrsg. von Thomas Würtenberger, Werner Maihofer und Alexander Hollerbach] Frankfurt am Main, V. Klostermann [1962] 502 p. 24cm.

Contributions in German, French or English.
Bibliographical footnotes.

(Continued)

NN R 1.63 f/ OC, I, II PC, 1, 2, 3, I, II SL (LC1, X1, Z1)
[I]

Wuerzburg, Germany. Universitaet.
Aus der Vergangenheit der Universität Würzburg. Festschrift zum 350 Jährigen Bestehen der Universität, im Auftrage von Rektor und Senat herausgegeben von Max Buchner... Berlin: J. Springer, 1932. viii, 799 p. incl. front., tables. 3 pl. 28cm.

Two plates printed on both sides.
Bibliographies included.

628913A. 1. Wuerzburg, Germany. Universität—Hist. I. Buchner, Max, 1881- , editor.
N. Y. P. L. March 20, 1933

WÜRTENBERGER, THOMAS, ed. Existenz und Ordnung... (Card 2)

CONTENTS.--Von der Taufe des Johannes zur Taufe auf den Namen Jesu, von K. Barth.--Christliche Freiheit für die "freie Welt", von E. Wolf.--Réalité sociale et théologie du droit, par J. Ellul.--Über den Begriff des "Ius divinum" im katholischen Verständnis, von K. Rahner.--Das Altestenamt im Aufbau der evangelischen Kirchenverfassung, von G. Wendt.--Evangelisches Kirchenrecht und staatliches Eherecht in Deutschland, von H. Liermann.--Zur Problematik der bedingten Taufe, von A. Hollerbach.--Soziale Fragen in der alten Kirche, von A. Ehrhardt.--Calvinistische Elemente in der kurpfälzischen Kirchenordnung von 1563, von E. W. Zeeden.--
(Continued)

WÜRZBURG, Germany. Universität. Rechts- und Staatswissenschaftliche Fakultät.
Festschrift der Rechts- und staatswissenschaftlichen Fakultät der Julius-Macimilians-Universität Würzburg zum 75. Geburtstag von Hermann Nottarp. Im Auftrage der Fakultät hrsg. von Paul Mikat. Karlsruhe, C.F. Müller, 1961. 330 p. port. 24cm.

Half-title: Festschrift Hermann Nottarp.

(Continued)

NN R 9.64 e/✓ (OC)I, IIb* OS(1b*) PC, 1, 2, 3, I SL E, 2, 3, I (LC1, X1, Z1)

WÜRTENBERGER, THOMAS, ed. Existenz und Ordnung... (Card 3)

Kants These über das Sein, von M. Heidegger.--Konkrete Existenz; Versuch über die philosophische Grundlagen der Politik, von M. Müller.--Two questions about law, by A. Passerin d'Entrèves.--Zur Unterscheidung von Recht und Unrecht, von F. von Hippel.--Vom rechtschaffenen Gewissen, von T. Würtenberger.--Gesetz und Recht, von A. Kaufmann.--Vom Sinn des hypothetischen juristischen Urteils, von K. Engisch.--Die juristische Sekunde, von F. Wieacker.--Über das Misslingen, von K. A. Hall.--Aufbau und Stallung des bedingten Vorsatzes im Verbrechensbegriff, von H.-H. Jescheck.--Schriftenverzeichnis
(Continued)

WÜRZBURG, Germany. Universität. Rechts- und Staatswissenschaftliche Fakultät. Festschrift der Rechts... (Card 2)

Bibliographical footnotes.
CONTENTS.--Der Deutsche Bund und die Zivilgesetzgebung, von F. Laufke.--Rechtsvergleichendes zur Haftung des Warenherstellers und Lieferanten gegenüber Dritten, von W. Lorenz.--Zur Pfändung und Verpfändung des mit der Auflassung entstehenden Sogenannten dinglichen Anwartschaftsrechts, von M. Ronke.--Zu den Einwilligungen der Annahme an Kindes Statt, von A. Kränzlein.-- Der entgeltliche Erbverzicht,

(Continued)

WÜRTENBERGER, THOMAS, ed. Existenz und Ordnung... (Card 4)

Erik Wolf.

1. Philosophy--Addresses, essays, lectures. 2. Theology--Essays and misc. 3. Wolf, Erik, 1902- I. Maihofer, Werner , joint ed. II. Hollerbach, Alexander , joint ed.

WÜRZBURG, Germany. Universität. Rechts- und Staatswissenschaftliche Fakultät. Festschrift der Rechts... (Card 3)

von H. Lange.--Über rechtsbegriffe Gedanken zur Grenze rechtlicher Begriffsbildung, von W. Sax.--Ist Strafschärfung bei Rückfall berechtigt? Von U. Stock.--Die Haftung des Arbeitgebers für Sachschäden des Arbeitnehmers im Betriebe bei gefährlicher Arbeit, von G. Küchenhoff.--Die Anfänge der Verwaltungsgerichtsbarkeit in Bayern, von R. Schiedermair.--Das Verfassungsrechtliche Gebot der gesetzlichen Ermächtigung, von F. Mayer.--Grundfragen des staatlichen Kirchenaustrittsrechtes,

(Continued)

WÜRZBURG, Germany. Universität. Rechts- und Staatswissenschaftliche Fakultät. Festschrift der Rechts... (Card 4)

von P. Mikat. --Das Selbstbestimmungsrecht in der Theorie Karl Renners, von H. Raschhofer. --Die Problematik des militärischen Objekts, von Friedrich August Freiherr von der Heydte. --Sozialpolitik im dritten Bundestag, von A. Franz. --Freiheit und gesellschaftlicher Fortschritt, von F. P. Schneider. --Das System vertraglich gesetzter Wechselkurse und die Unterbewertung der D-Mark, von E. Carell. --Die Anwendung des Territorialitätsprinzips auf reine Exportkartelle im GWB als

(Continued)

WÜRZBURG, Germany. Universität. Rechts- und Staatswissenschaftliche Fakultät. Festschrift der Rechts... (Card 5)

volkswirtschaftliches Problem, von E. Hoppmann. --Wirtschaftspolitische Ziele und möglichkeiten der Raumordnung, von F. Huhle. --Der wirtschaftliche Charakter der Passivseite der Bilanz, von H. Ruchti. --Die Problematik der Kostenrechnung in Handelsbetrieben, von P. Nowak.

1. Law--Addresses, essays, lectures. 2. Social sciences--Addresses, essays, lectures. 3. Nottarp, Hermann, 1886- . I. Mikat, Paul, 1924- , ed. II. Mikat, Paul, 1924- .

E-11
2823

WUPPERTAL, Germany. Stadtbücherei.
Ausfahrt und Landung; Festgabe für Bibliotheksdirektor Dr. Wolfgang van der Briele zum 65. Geburtstag am 16. Mai 1959. Wuppertal, J. H. Born, 1960. 156 p. illus., ports., facsims. 25cm.

Includes bibliographical references.
CONTENTS. --W. van der Briele und die geschichtliche Entwicklung der Wuppertaler Bibliotheken, von W. Springmann. --Die literarische Fälschung des Thomas J. Wise, von R. Juchhoff. --

(Continued)

NN R 6. 61 m/ (OC)Ib+ ODt EDt PC, 1 SL (LC1, X1, Z1) 3

WUPPERTAL, Germany. Stadbücherei. Ausfahrt und Landung... (Card 2)

Kinderausgaben der Grimmschen Märchen; eine bibliothekarische Besinnung auf deren Grundsätze, von J. Langfeldt. --Dürer-Erinnerungen in Josef Führichs Illustrationen zu "Der wilde Jäger" von G. A. Bürger, von H. Wille --Historischer Versuch zur Theorie der Kunstkritik, von A. H. Fink. --Streiflichter zur Bergischen Dynastengeschichte, von M. -L. Baum. --Altenberg in der Romantik von Caspar Scheuren, von K. Eckert. --Friedrich Engels als Wuppertaler, von G. Werner. --Gerhard Tersteegen schreibt an Joh. Engelbert Evertsen, von K. Göbel. -- Briefe eines gefallenen

(Continued)

WUPPERTAL, Germany. Stadbücherei. Ausfahrt und Landung... (Card 3)

Wuppertaler Bibliothekars, von A. Krefting. --Bibliographie der Schriften W. van der Brieles, p. 153-156.

1. Briele, Wolfgang van der, 1894- . t. 1960.

E-12
3993

WYER, SAMUEL S., 1879-
Man's shift from muscle to mechanical power. Prepared for Fuel-power-transportation educational foundation. Columbus, O., Fuel-power-transportation educational foundation [1930] 30 p. 24cm.

Cover title.
"Preliminary page proofs—June 26, 1930."
"Universal language needs," p. 20
Bibliographical footnotes.

(Continued)

NN R 6.66 a/ OC PC, 1, 2 SL E, 1-ST, 2t (LC1, X1, Z1) 2

WYER, SAMUEL S., 1879- . Man's shift from muscle to mechanical power. (Card 2)

Mrs. Dave H. Morris Collection.

1. Economic history--U.S., 1873- 2. Power (Mechanics)--U.S. t. 1930

NRF

Xenia Bonnensia; Festschrift zum fünfundsiebzigjährigen Bestehen des Philologischen Vereins und Bonner Kreises. Bonn: F. Cohen, 1929. 167 p. 8°.

Bibliographical footnotes.
Contents: OPPERMANN, H. Die Einheit der vorsophistischen Philosophie. BÜLOW, P. Ein vielgesungener Asklepiospaean. HERTER, H. Kallimachos und Homer. BRINKMANN, H. Zum Ursprung des liturgischen Spieles. RING, W. Gustav Böningers "Festungstid."

487660A. 1. Philologischer Verein und Bonner Kreis, Bonn.
N. Y. P. L. September 25, 1930

VIB

Yale university. Engineering, School of. Department of metallurgy. Yale metallurgical alumni.
Champion Herbert Mathewson, sixtieth birthday, October 7, 1941; an appreciation of him as teacher and friend. A book of technical papers written by former students of Dr. Mathewson, and containing biographical and other information ... New Haven, Conn.: The Yale metallurgical alumni at Hammond laboratory, Yale univ., 1941. xxxi, 184 p. incl. diagrs., front. (port.) illus. 23½cm.

"Publications of Champion Herbert Mathewson," p. xvii-xix.
"References," at end of chapters.

161867B. 1. Mathewson, Champion Herbert, 1881- 2. Metallurgy, 1941. 3. Metallography, 1941. I. Title.
N. Y. P. L. October 2, 1942

---

*PDA

YEHEZKEL KAUFMANN jubilee volume; studies in Bible and Jewish religion dedicated to Yehezkel Kaufmann on the occasion of his seventieth birthday, edited by Menahem Haran. Jerusalem, Magnes press, the Hebrew university, 1960. 114 p.; xii, 158 p. port. 25cm.

Added t. p. and section in Hebrew.

(Continued)

NN R 6.61 e/5 OC, I, IIbo PC, 1, 2, 4, I SL J, 1, 3, 4, I, IIbo (LC1, X1, Z1) 4

YEHEZKEL KAUFMANN jubilee volume... (Card 2)

Bibliographical footnotes.

CONTENTS.--Some postulates of Biblical criminal law, by. M. Greenberg.--Leviticus and the critics, by E.A. Speiser.--David the dancer, by C.H. Gordon.--Studies in Hosea 1-3, by H.L. Ginsberg.--The date of Ezra's mission to Jerusalem, by J. Bright.--Introduction to rabbinic ethics, by M. Kadushin.--Hebrew section: Professor Yehezkel Kaufmann, by I.L. Seeligmann.--Bibliography of Yehezkel Kaufmann's writings.--The south-western border of the Promised land, by Y.M. Grintz.--The symbolical significance of the complex of ritual acts performed

(Continued)

YEHEZKEL KAUFMANN jubilee volume... (Card 3)

inside the Israelite shrine, by M. Haran.--The ceremony of bringing the first fruits, by Y. Gutmann.--The ransom of half shekel, by J. Liver.--The northern limit of David's kingdom, by A. Biram.--The historical background of Hosea's prophecies, by H. Tadmor.--The dependence of Deuteronomy upon the Wisdom literature, by M. Weinfeld.--Elucidation of Prov. 9:1, by N.H. Tur-Sinai.--On an alleged gnostic element in Mishna Hagiga ii, 1, by S.E. Loewenstamm.--Studies in rabbinic views concerning Divine Providence, by E. E. Urbach.--The ban in Mari and in

(Continued)

YEHEZKEL KAUFMANN jubilee volume... (Card 4)

the Bible, by A. Malamat.

1. Bible. O.T.--Essays and misc. 2. Judaism--Addresses, essays, lectures. 3. Judaism--Essays. 4. Kaufman, Ezekiel, 1889- . I. Haran, Menahem, ed. II. Haran, Menahem.

G-10
1894

YOUTHS' art and culture circle, Bombay. Nicholas Roerich, memorial volume. Bombay [1948?] 49 p. illus. (part col.), ports. 32cm. (Y.A.C.C. news & activities bulletin)

Cover title.

1. Roerich, Nikolai Konstantinovich, 1874-1947. I. Gupta, Ram Chandra, ed.

NN R 10.66 r/c (OC)I OS PC,1, I SL A,1,I O,1,I S,1,I (LC1,X1, Z1)

---

*QT

Z dějin východní Evropy a slovanstva. Sborník věnovaný Jaroslavu Bidlovi, profesoru Karlovy university, k šedesátým narozeninám. Uspořádali Miloš Weingart, Josef Dobiáš, Milada Paulová. Praha: A. Bečková, 1928. xv, 512 p. incl. plan. front. (port.), plates. 4°.

Plates printed on both sides.
Résumés in French and German.
Table of contents in Bohemian and French.
Bibliography, p. v-xv.

535701A. 1. No subject. I. Bidlo, Jaroslav, 1868- . II. Weingart, Miloš, 1890- , editor. III. Dobiáš, Josef, 1888- , jt. editor. IV. Paulová, Milada, 1891- , jt. editor.
N. Y. P. L. October 6, 1931

---

*QO

...Z zagadnień kulturalno-literackich Wschodu i Zachodu. Prof. F. Baldensperger, prof. G. Bertoni, prof. J. Benešić... [i inni] Kraków [etc.] Gebethner i Wolff, 1933/34. xlvii, 358 p. port. 24cm. (Prace Polskiego towarzystwa dla badań Europy wschodniej i Bliskiego Wschodu...nr. IV.)

"Marjanowi Zdziechowskiemu... IV tom swoich 'Prac' poświęca Polskie towarzystwo dla badań Europy wschodniej i Bliskiego Wschodu."
Articles in Polish, Bulgarian, Croatian, English, French, German, Russian or Ukrainian.
Bibliographies included.
"Bibljografja prac Marjana Zdziechowskiego," p. [xl]-xlvii.

881165A. 1. Zdziechowski, Marjan, 1861- . 2. Literature—Hist. and crit. 3. Slavonic literature—Hist. and crit. I. Baldensperger, Fernand, 1871- . II. Bertoni, Giulio, 1878- . III. Benešić, Julije. IV. Ser.
N. Y. P. L. July 14, 1937

RAX p.v.9

ZAMENHOF, LUDWIK, 1859-1917.
An international language: the problem and its solution (esenco kaj estonteco de la ideo de lingvo internacia) Esperanto text by Unuel [pseud.] Translated from "Fundamenta krestomatio" by Alfred E. Wackrill. London, "Review of reviews" off. [1920?] 51, 51 p. 19cm.

Esperanto and English on opposite pages.

1. Esperanto. 2. Esperanto--Books in. I. Wackrill, Alfred E., tr. i. Subs. for Zamenhot.

NN R 11.66 a/c OCs,I PC,1s, 2s,Is SLs (LC1s,[i],X1s,Z1s)

Copy only words underlined & classmark— FHC

ZATSCHEK, HEINZ.
Aus der Geschichte des Wiener Handwerks während des Dreissigjährigen Krieges; eine soziologische Studie. (IN: Verein für Geschichte der Stadt Wien. Jahrbuch. Wien. Bd. 9 (1951). p. 28-74)

At head of title: Rudolf Geyer zum sechzigsten Geburtstag.

1. Bakers and bakeries—Austria—Vienna.

NN R 4.53 OI (PC)1,2 (LC3,Z1,X1)

---

*QKK

Zbornik naučnih radova Ferdi Šišiću povodom šezdesetgodišnjice života, 1869–1929, posvećuju prijatelji, štovatelji i učenici. Uredio: Grga Novak. Zagreb: Tiskara C. Albrecht [1929] xvi, 676 p. illus. 25½cm.

Imperfect: p. vii–xii wanting.
Added t.-p.: Šišićev zbornik. Mélanges Šišić.
Contributions in Croatian, Serbian, Bulgarian, Polish, Bohemian, Russian, French, German, English, and Hungarian.
All articles except those in French, German and English have resumés in French or German.
"Bibliografija Ferde Šišića, 1892–1929," p. vii–xvi.

613351A. 1. Šišić, Ferdo, 1869- . I. Novak, Grga, 1888- , ed.
N. Y. P. L. August 5, 1935

---

*QKK

ZBORNIK u proslavu petstogodišnjice rođenja Marka Marulića, 1450-1950. Zagreb, 1950. 345 p. illus. 24cm. (Djela Jugoslavenske akademije znanosti i umjetnosti. Knjiga 39)

"Latinske pjesme Marka Marulića, preveo Nikola Šop." p. 5-23.
"Bibliography." p. 316-345.

1. Marulić, Marko, 1450-1524. I. Ser.

NN R 10.52 OC PC,1 SL S, 1 (LC1,Z1,X1)

AN
(Zdarsky, M.)
Zdarsky. Festschrift zum 80. Geburtstage des Begründers der alpinen Skifahrweise, 25. Februar 1936; ein Beitrag zur Geschichte und Lehre des Alpenschneelaufes, unter Mitwirkung zahlreicher Fachleute bearbeitet von Prof. Dr. Erwin Mehl... Wien [etc.] Deutscher Verlag für Jugend und Volk Gesellschaft m.b.H. [1936] 207 p. incl. diagrs., front. (port.) illus. (incl. facsims.) 22½cm.

"Schrifttum," p. 197–203.

846104A. 1. Zdarsky, Mathias, 1856- . 2. Ski-running. I. Mehl, Erwin, ed.
N. Y. P. L. September 15, 1936

---

*XMT-125
10 [i.e. ZEHN] Jahre Österreichische Theatergemeinde. (Wien [1966]) 22 p. 24cm.

Microfiche (neg.) 1 sheet. 11 x 15cm. (NYPL FSN: 9365)

1. Stage--Austria. 2. Stage--Austria, 20th cent. I. Österreichische Theatergemeinde.
NN*R 10.72 m/ OC (OS)I, Ib* PC, 1, I SL T, 2, I (LC1, X1, Z1)
(UMI)

D-19
7157
Zeichen der Freundschaft. Eine Gabe zum 70. Geburtstag von Wilhelm Fredemann. Mit Beiträgen von Waldemar Augustiny [u. a.] Frankfurt a. M., Verlag Das Viergespann (1967).
46 p. with illus. 21 cm.

Bibliography of works by W. Fredemann: p. [48]

1. Fredemann, Wilhelm, 1897- I. Augustiny, Waldemar, 1897-
NN * R 6.70 d/ OC, I PC, 1, I SL (LC1, X1, Z1)

E-13
7111
ZEIT und Geschichte; Dankesgabe an Rudolf Bultmann zum 80. Geburtstag. Im Auftrage der Alten Marburger und in Zusammenarbeit mit Hartwig Thyen hrsg. von Erich Dinkler. Tübinger, J.C.B. Mohr, 1964. xi, 749 p. port. 24cm.

Contributions in German or English.
Bibliographical footnotes.

1. Theology--Collections. I. Bultmann, Rudolf Karl, 1884- II. Dinkler, Erich, ed. III. Thyen, Hartwig, ed.
NNR 12.69 r/ OC, I, II, III PC, 1, I, II, III SL (LC1, X1, Z1) [I]

RAE
ZEIT und Stunde; Ludwig von Ficker zum 75. Geburtstag gewidmet. Hrsg. von Ignaz Zangerle. Stuttgart, O. Müller [1955] 222 p. port. 24cm.

CONTENTS. —Widmung, von G. von Le Fort. —Hölderlins Hymne "Der Frieden, " oder von der Schuld der Väter, von E. Wasmuth. —Gott sprach: Es werde Licht! Von P. Schlier. —Priester und Dichter, von K. Rahner. —Das Auferlegte, von C. Levant. —Schicksal der Sprache, von H. Hornstein. —Immer gleiche Stimme, von L. Sertorius. —Perspektiven des zeitgenössischen Romans, von I. Zangerle. — Der Hass Welt, von W. Warnach.
(Continued)
NN * *R 9.56 d/ OC, I PC, 1, 2, I SL (LC1, X1, Z1) [I]

ZEIT und Stunde... (Card 2)

—Zeit und Sprache, von W. Kraft. —Das Wort "deutsch, " von E. Steinacker. —Fallendes Feuer, von H. Schinagl. —Engelslegende von Mariae Empfängis, von G. Haffner-Theiner. —Beiläufiges aus Briefen, von H. Kestranek. —Zu später Stunde, von C. Busta. —Wandel des Zeitlichen, von F. Slovencik. —Ausblick der Erkenntlichkeit, von I. Zangerle. —An den Mond, von H. Schlier.

1. Ficker, Ludwig, 1880- . 2. Philology—Addresses, essays, lectures. I. Zangerle, Ignaz, ed.

E-11
7943
ZEITEL, GERHARD, ed.
Konjunkturelle Stabilität als wirtschaftspolitische Aufgabe, hrsg. von Gerhard Zeitel und Jürgen Pahlke. Tübingen, J.C.B. Mohr, 1962. 170 p. 24cm

Published on the occasion of Woldemor Koch's 60th birthday.
Bibliographical footnotes.
CONTENTS.--Über die Wechselbeziehungen von Unternehmungskonzentration und Konjunktur, von D. Pohmer.--Preis- und Quotenkartelle im Konjunkturverlauf, von U. Willeke.--Beziehungen
(Continued)
NN R 9.63 f/ OC, I PC, 1, 2, 3, I, II SL E, 1, 2, 3, I, II (LC1, X1, Z1)
3

ZEITEL, GERHARD, ed. Konjunkturelle Stabilität als wirtschaftspolitische Aufgabe... (Card 2)

zwischen der konjunkturpolitischen Zielsetzung und anderen Aufgaben der Finanzpolitik sowie den politischen Gegebenheiten von J. Pählke--Haushaltsgestaltung und Konjunktur, von G. Ollenburg.--Geldpolitik, Finanzpolitik und konjunkturelle Stabilität, von R. Schilcher.--Über die Wirksamkeit der Zinspolitik bei freier Konvertibilität der Währungen von W. Blochowitz.--Devisenüberschüsse--Geldpolitik--Konjunkturstabilisierung, von R. Pohl.--Internationale Währungsreserven, nationale Konjunkturpolitik und zwischenstaatliche Währungsordnung, von G. Zeitel.--Entwicklungshilfe und Konjunkturstabilisierung, von
(Continued)

ZEITEL, GERHARD, ed. Konjunkturelle Stabilität als wirtschaftspolitische Aufgabe... (Card 3)

D. Lorenz.--Kreislauftheorie und Konjunkturzyklus, von U. Schleehauf.

1. Business--Cycles. 2. Economic policy, 1945- . 3. Koch, Woldemar, 1902- . I. Pahlke, Jürgen, joint ed. II. Title.

E-11
3607
Zemanek, Karl, *ed.*
Völkerrecht und rechtliches Weltbild. Festschrift für Alfred Verdross. Hrsg. von F. A. Frhr. v. d. Heydte [et al.] Wien, Springer, 1960.
345 p. port. 24 cm.
Bibliographical footnotes.
CONTENTS.—Alfred Verdross.--Leben und Werk, von S. Verosta.—Zur Entwicklung der modernen Völkerrechtswissenschaft an der Wiener Juristenfakultät, von W. M. Plöchl.—Nachbarrecht und Wassernutzung, von J. Andrassy.—Zum Problem der Grundnorm, von R. L. Bindschedler.—Betrachtungen zur Erneuerung des Malteser-Ordens, von A. C. Breycha-Vauthier.—The incidental jurisdiction of the International Court of Justice as compulsory jurisdiction, by
(Continued)
NN * R 11.61 p/ OC, I. II (LC1, X1, Z1) * PC, 1, 2, I, II SL E, 1, 2, I,
4

Zemanek, Karl, *ed.* Völkerrecht und rechtliches Weltbild ... 1960. (Card 2)

H. W. Briggs.—Die Erklärung der Menschenrechte im Licht der Geschichte, von F. Castberg.—Die Entmilitarisierung und Neutralisierung der Ålandinseln, von E. Castrén.—Der sogenannte automatische Vorbehalt der inneren Angelegenheiten gegenüber der Anerkennung der obligatorischen Gerichtsbarkeit des Internationalen Gerichtshofes in seiner neuesten Gerichtspraxis, von P. Guggenheim.—Das Prinzip der guten Nachbarschaft im Völkerrecht, von F. A. Frhr. v. d. Heydte.—International law and human communication, by B. Horvath.—Vom Geltungsgrund des Rechts, von H. Kelsen.—The law of outer space—its beginnings, by J. L. Kunz.—Völkerrechtliche Sicherheit, von L. Legaz y Lacambra. — Gemeinwohl und Naturrecht bei Cicero, von T. Mayer-Maly.—Die Frage der rechtlichen Grundnorm, von L. Pitamic.—De-facto-Staatsangehörigkeit und De-facto-Staaten-

(Continued)

Zemanek, Karl, *ed.* Völkerrecht und rechtliches Weltbild ... 1960. (Card 3)

losigkeit, von W. Schätzel.—Die Rechtsetzungsbefugnis internationaler Gemeinschaften, von U. Scheuner.—Legal effects of illegal war, by G. Schwarzenberger.—Die Rolle der Rechtsvergleichung im Völkerrecht, von I. Seidl-Hohenveldern. — L'uniformité des régimes politiques au sein des ligues et confédérations grecques à l'époque classique, par G. Ténékidès. — Staatsräson und Völkerrecht in der Zeit Karls v., von A. Truyol y Serra.—The role of international law in international relations, by G. I. Tunkin.—Der Grundsatz der Vertragstreue, von H. Wehberg.—Über das dualistische Denken in der Völkerrechtswissenschaft, von K. Zemanek.—Verzeichnis der wissenschaftlichen Veröffentlichungen von Alfred Verdross, von H. Scheuba (p. [339]–345)

(Continued)

ZEMANEK, KARL, ed. Völkerrecht und rechtliches Weltbild... 1960. (Card 4)

1. Law, International--Addresses, essays, lectures. 2. Verdross, Alfred, Edler von, 1890- I. Heydte, Friedrich, Aug. Freiherr von der, ed. II. Title. III. Zemanek, Karl.

NHP

Zestig! Gedenkboek ter eere van Hendrik van Tichelen (1883–6 maart–1943) Hoogstraten, Moderne uitgeverij, 1943.

423 p. incl. front., illus., plates, ports. 27cm.

Includes music of six songs.
"Bibliografie": p. 58. "Gebundeld werk van Hendrik van Tichelen": p. [59]–61.

1. Education—Addresses, essays, lectures. 2. Juvenile literature—Hist. & crit. 3. Tichelen, Hendrik van, 1883–

AC16.T5 A F 47–4028

New York. Public library for Library of Congress [3]†

---

* ZAN–* Q159
Film Reproduction
no. 15

Zeszyt XV, specjalny, z okazji 30-lecia pracy naukowej Andrzeja Grodka. Warszawa, Szkoła głowna planowania i statystyki, 1959. xiii, 357 p. port. 24cm. (Szkoła głowna planowania i statystyki, Warsaw. Zeszyty naukowe. zesz. 15)

Film reproduction. Negative.
Bibliographical footnotes.
Contents.—Andrzej Grodek: człowiek, naukowiec, pedagog.—Bibliografia prac prof. dr. Andrzeja Grodka, 1927–1959, p. vi–xiii.—Kostrowicka, I. Z problematyki rozwoju kapitalizmu w rolnictwie Królestwa Polskiego przed uwłaszczeniem chłopów. Tomaszewski, J. Gospodarka drobnotowarowa w Polsce międzywojennej.—Landau, Z. Pierwsza polska pożyczka emisyjma w Stanach Zjednoczonych.—Jasiczek, S. Kapitał

(Continued)

NN R 6.62 OI (PC)1,2 (E)1,2 (S)1,2 (UM1,LC3,X1,Z1)

Zeszyt XV, specjalny, z okaszji 30–lecia pracy naukowej Andrzeja Grodka... (Card 2)

francuski w przemyśle górniczohutniczym. Zagłębia Dąbrowskiego, 1870–1914.—Cieplewski, J. Poglądy na kwestię robotniczą przedstawicieli oficjalnej katolickiej myśli, społecznej w Polsce lat 1918–1930.—Beczkiewicz, Z. O charakterze socjalistycznych poglądów Stanisława Worcella.—Uniejewska, H. Poglądy społeczno-ekonomiczne Ludwika Królikowskiego.—Święcicki, M. Związki zawodowe i izby pracy w ustawach i projektach ustaw z lat 1918–1939.—Lipiński, E. Ceny a koszty krańcowe.—Wakar, A. Handel socjalistyczny.—Romaniuk, K. Czynnik demograficzny w planowaniu procesu reprodukcji.—Szturm de Sztrem, E. Struktura społeczeństw ludzkich według wieku chronologicznego i fizjologicznego.—Sadowski, W. O problemie optymalnych decyzji.—Kwejt, J. Sprawa teorii przedsiębiorstwa.—Secomski, K. O nie-

(Continued)

Zeszyt XV, specjalny, z okaszji 30–lecia pracy naukowej Andrzeja Grodka... (Card 3)

których problemach rozwoju gospodarczego w latach 1959–65.—Koźmiński, L. Kierunki i możliwości unowocześnienia handlu detalicznego w Polsce.—Filipowicz, Z. Koncepcja ekonomiczno-społeczna organizacji wypoczynku.—Dąbrowski, E. Pedagogika gospodarcza.—Strzelecki, E. W sprawie społecznego kierunku nauczania w szkole.—Skrzywan, S. W sprawie kadr kierowniczych rachunkowści.

1. Grodek, Andrzej. 2. Economic history—Poland.

---

*QYN

ZINAĪDAS LAZDAS PIEMIŅAS FONDS.
Zinaida Lazda; dzejnieces piemiņai veltīts rakstu krājums. Sakārtojuši Valdemārs Kārkliņš un Kārlis Rabācs. [Chicago, 1963] 422 p. illus., ports. 22cm.

1. Lazda, Zinaīda, 1902-1957. I. Kārkliņš, Valdemārs, ed. II. Rabācs, Kārlis, 1905- , ed.
NN R 12.63 e/ (OC)I, II OS PC, 1, I, II SL S, 1, I, II (LC1, X1, Z1)

E-12
4391

Zinsli, Paul, *ed.*
Sprachleben der Schweiz; Sprachwissenschaft, Namenforschung, Volkskunde. Hrsg. von Paul Zinsli [et al.] Bern, Francke, 1963.

xvi, 340 p. illus., port., maps. 25 cm.

"Dieser Band ist Prof. Dr. Rudolf Hotzenköcherle zum 60. Geburtstag gewidmet."
Bibliographical footnotes.

(Continued)

NN * R 10.65 e/ OC PC, 1, 2, 3 SL (LC1, X1, Z1)

ZINSLI, PAUL, ed. Sprachleben der Schweiz... (Card 2)

Contents. — Die viersprachige Schweiz im Atlas der schweizerischen Volkskunde, von R. Weiss.—Die althochdeutsche Schweiz, von S. Sonderegger.—Zur Stellung des Schweizerdeutschen im Alemannischen, von E. E. Müller.—Phonologie und Dialekteinteilung, von W. G. Moulton.—Ein Lautwandel der Gegenwart, von R. Trüb.—Formenspaltung in der schweizerdeutschen Adjektivflexion, von K. Meyer.—Über Relativpronomen im Schweizerdeutschen, von P. Dalcher.—Wortpaare vom Typus *recken: strecken* im Schweizerdeutschen, von H. Wanner.—Schweizerisch Unterbruch, von W. Henzen.—Die Formen der Andrede im älteren Schweizerdeutschen, von H. Trümpy.—

(Continued)

ZINSLI, PAUL, ed. Sprachleben der Schweiz...
(Card 3)

Zur Physiologie der rätoromanischen Affrikaten *tsch* und *tg* (*ch*) von R. Brunner.—Zur Morphologie und Syntax des Verbum *avé* in den Mundarten der italienischen Schweiz, von F. Spiess.—Seidenraupenzucht in Ligornetto um 1920, von P. Scheuermeier.—Ornavasso, von K. Huber. — Romanisches Wortgut in der Sprache der Oberwalliser Weinbauern, von E. Schüle.—Die Wand, von F. Gysling.—Das Ortsnamenbild zwischen Zürich- und Walensee als Zeugnis für die Sprachgrenze im 7. und 8. Jahrhundert, von B. Boesch.—Zur Schichtung der thurgauischen Ortsnamen, von O. Bandle. — Prolegomena zum St. Galler Namenbuch, von G. Hilty.—Die mittelalterliche Walserwan-

(Continued)

ZINSLI, PAUL, ed. Sprachleben der Schweiz...
(Card 4)

derung in Flurnamenspuren, von P. Zinsli.—*Haiaho*, von M. Szadrowsky.—Bibliographie der wissenschaftlichen Publikationen von Rudolf Hotzenköcherle (bis 1962) von S. Sonderegger und R. Hinderling.

1. Hotzenkocherle, Rudolf. 2. German language--Dialects--Switzerland. 3. Geography--Names--Switzerland.

---

*PWZ
(Rashi)

Zionist organization. Argentine Republic. Comité de homenaje a Raschi.

Raschi, Rabi Salomón Isaki, glosador de la Biblia y del Talmud, 1040–1940. Traducción del idisch de Salomón Resnick. Buenos Aires: Comité de homenaje a Raschi, 1941. 395 p. 24cm.

"Editado por el Comité de homenaje a Raschi, bajo los auspicios de la Federación sionista argentina."

194812B. 1. Rashi, 1040–1105. I. Resnick, Salomón, tr.
N. Y. P. L. January 22, 1943

---

*PBM p.v.492

Zionist organization. South Africa.

In tribute to Dr. Chaim Weizmann on the occasion of his 70th birthday, 27th November, 1944. Comp. by Z. Infeld... Johannesburg, Information and organisation dept. of the S. A. Zionist federation [1944] 28 p. port. 25cm.

1. Weizmann, Chaim, 1874– . I. Infeld, Zvi Harry.
N. Y. P. L. February 17, 1948

---

* MGA

Zoltano Kodály, octogenario sacrum. **Budapest, Akadémiai** Kiadó, 1962.

309 p. illus., facsims., music, port. 25 cm.

"Zoltán Kodálys Werke": p. [11]–48.

Contributions in various languages.

1. Kodály, Zoltán, 1882- . 2. Kodaly, Zoltan--Bibl. 3. Music--Essays. 4. Essays.
NN R 8.65 g/ OC (OAF 1) PC,1,3 SL MU,1,2,4 (LC1, X1, Z1)

TAH

ZORN, WOLFGANG.
Sechs Jahrhunderte schwäbische Wirtschaft. 125 Jahre Industrie- und Handelskammer Augsburg. Beiträge zur Geschichte der Wirtschaft im bayerischen Regierungsbezirk schwaben, von Wolfgang Zorn [und] Leonhard Hillenbrand. [Augsburg, Industrie- und Handelskammer] 1969. xiii,464 p. illus.(part col.),ports.,fold. col. maps,facsims. 25cm.

(Continued)

NN R 7.70 v/rOC,I, IIIbo (OD)IIt (ED)IIt
PC,1,I,II SL E,1,I (LC1,X1,Z1) 2

ZORN, WOLFGANG. Sechs Jahrhunderte schwäbische Wirtschaft. (Card 2)

Half-title: Schwäbische Wirtschaft; Jubiläumsschrift der Industrie- und Handelskammer Augsburg.
Bibliography, p. 451-452.

1. Economic history--Germany--Swabia. I. Hillenbrand, Leonhard, joint author. II. Augsburg, Germany. Industrie- und Handelskammer. III. Hillenbrand, Leonhard. t. 1969.

L-10
6939
Bd.4

ZOTSCHEW, THEODOR, 1916- , ed.
Wirtschaftswissenschaftliche Südosteuropa-Forschung; Grundlagen und Erkenntnisse [Hermann Gross zum 60. Geburtstag] München, Südosteuropa-Verlagsgesellschaft, 1963. 362 p. 25cm. (Südosteuropa. Bd.4)

CONTENTS.--Hermann Gross, von R. Vogel.--Wandlungen im Verständnis Südosteuropas, von F. Ronneberger.--Wirtschaftliche

(Continued)

NN R 6.64 e/ OC, IIb+ (OS)I PC, 1, 2, I E, 1, 2 (S)I (LC1, X1, Z1) 4

ZOTSCHEW, THEODOR, 1916- , ed. Wirtschaftswissenschaftliche Südosteuropa-Forschung...
(Card 2)

Entwicklung und gegenseitige Handelsbeziehungen der südosteuropäischen Staaten, von T. Zotschew.--Die Auseinandersetzung zwischen dem Sowjet- und Reformkommunismus, von B. Meissner.--Balkanpakt und Ostpolitik, von G. W. Strobel.--Der Mitteleuropäische Wirtschaftstag, von F. Glück.--Die Beurteilung und Bewertung von Entwicklungsplänen und ihre Erfolgsmessung, von B. Knall.--Industrieforschung in einzel- und gesamtwirtschaftlicher Sicht, von J. Meier.--KIEL, eines der

(Continued)

ZOTSCHEW, THEODOR, 1916- , ed. Wirtschaftswissenschaftliche Südosteuropa-Forschung...
(Card 3)

ostwissenschaftlichen Zentren in der Bundesrepublik, von J. Hacker.--Anleitung zu wirtschaftswissenschaftlichen Arbeiten, von G. Savelsberg.--Bibliographie der Bibliographien Südosteuropas, von G. Teich.--Die gesellschaftlichen Organisationen Polens und ihre Veröffentlichungen, von E. Pohlhausen.--Katalog wirtschafts- und sozialwissenschaftlicher Zeitschriften sowie anderer Periodika aus den ostmittel- und südosteuropäischen Ländern, von E. Pohlhausen und G. Teich.--Das Schrifttum

(Continued)

ZOTSCHEW, THEODOR, 1916- , ed. Wirtschafts-wissenschaftliche Südosteuropa-Forschung... (Card 4)

von Hermann Gross, von H. Güllch-Bielenberg (p. 343-350)

1. Gross, Hermann, 1903- . 2. Economic history--Balkan peninsula. I. Series. II. Zotschew, Theodor, 1916- .

YFX

Zürich (City). Universität.
Vom Krieg und vom Frieden; Festschrift der Universität Zürich zum siebzigsten Geburtstag von Max Huber. Zürich, Schulthess & Co., 1944. 323 p. illus. 25cm.

443584B. 1. Huber, Max, 1874- . 2. War and peace—Hist. of the peace movement. 3. Law, Internat.—Hist. 4. Medicine—Social and economic aspects. 5. War. I. Title.
N. Y. P. L. October 29, 1948

STL

Zürich (Canton). Erziehungswesens, Direktion des.
Die zürcherischen Schulen seit der Regeneration der 1830er Jahre; Festschrift zur Jahrhundertfeier, herausgegeben vom Erziehungsrate des Kantons Zürich... Bd. 3. Zürich: Verlag der Erziehungsdirektion, 1933. 1 v. charts, plates, ports., tables. 25cm.

CONTENTS.—

(Continued)

1. Education—Switzerland—Zürich (Canton).
N. Y. P. L. November 22, 1939

TB

Zürich (City) Universität. *Rechts- und staatswissenschaftliche fakultät.*
Festgabe Fritz Fleiner zum siebzigsten geburtstag am 24. januar 1937 dargebracht von der Rechts- und staatswissenschaftlichen fakultät der Universität Zürich. Zürich, Polygraphischer verlag a.-g. [1937]
432 p. front. (mounted port.) 22½cm.
"Der für diese festgabe bestimmte beitrag 'Grundsätze des gewährleistungsrechts' von prof. dr. Julius Lautner erscheint im einvernehmen mit dem verfasser aus technischen gründen separat im gleichen verlag."—p. 10.
Bibliographical foot-notes.

(Continued on next card)

A C 37-2154
[3]

Festschrift

Zürich (Canton). Erziehungswesens, Direktion des. Die zürcherischen Schulen seit der Regeneration der 1830er Jahre... (Card 2)

Bd. 3. Die Universität Zürich, 1833-1933, und ihre Vorläufer... Bearbeitet von Ernst Gagliardi, Hans Nabholz und Jean Strohl.

N. Y. P. L. November 22, 1939

Zürich (City) Universität. *Rechts- und staatswissenschaftliche fakultät.* Festgabe Fritz Fleiner ... [1937] (Card 2)

CONTENTS.—Schindler, Dietrich. Schiedsgerichtsbarkeit und friedenswahrung.—Giacometti, Zaccaria. Verfassungsrecht und verfassungspraxis.—Egger, August. Ueber scheinehen.—Mutzner, Paul. Der zeitliche geltungsbereich des Bundesgesetzes über die nutzbarmachung der wasserkräfte.—Hug, Walther. Die rechtliche organisation der öffentlichen unternehmen von kanton und gemeinde.—Herold, Hans. Verwaltungsrecht im mittelalter.—Oftinger, Karl. Die haftung des bürgen für die gesetzlichen folgen eines verschuldens oder verzugs des hauptschuldners.—Hafter, Ernst. Wirtschaftsspionage und wirtschaftsverrat.—Fritzsche, Hans. Studiosus juris J. J. Blumer von Glarus.—Pfen-

(Continued on next card)

A C 37-2154
[3]

VDE

Zürich (City). Schweizerische Landesausstellung. Fachgruppe "Vermessung, Grundbuch und Karte."
Vermessung, Grundbuch und Karte; Festschrift zur Schweizerischen Landesausstellung in Zürich 1939. Zürich, Verlag des Schweizerischen Geometervereins [1941?] 287 p. illus., maps. 26cm.

"Vorwort" signed: Für das Fachgruppenkomitee "Vermessung, Grundbuch und Karte." Der Vizepräsident: S. Bertschmann.

Festschrift

433202B. 1. Topographical surveying. 2. Map making—Switzerland. 3. Geodesy—Instruments and apparatus, 1939. I. Title.
N. Y. P. L. October 11, 1948

Zürich (City) Universität. *Rechts- und staatswissenschaftliche fakultät.* Festgabe Fritz Fleiner ... [1937] (Card 3)

CONTENTS—Continued.

ninger, H. F. Liberalismus und strafrecht.—Raschle, Hans. Zivilprozesssache und verwaltungsstreitsache im aargauischen rechtsgang.—Grossmann, Eugen. Die kunst der besteuerung.—Saitzew, Manuel. Der interventionismus.—Büchner, Richard. Wirtschaftspolitik als wissenschaft. Gygax, Paul. Die finanzielle kriegsbereitschaft der Schweiz.—Higy, Camille. Die Bundesfinanzreform und Artikel 42 lit. f. der Bundesverfassung.—Weber, Karl. Zur soziologie der zeitung.

1. Fleiner, Fritz, 1867- 2. Economics—Addresses, essays, lectures. 3. Switzerland—Economic conditions. 4. Finance—Switzerland. I. Title.

A C 37-2154

New York. Public library for Library of Congress [3]

STN
+

Zürich (city). Universität.
Universität Zürich; festschrift des Regierungsrates zur einweihung der neubauten. 18. april 1914. Zürich, Orell Füssli [1914?]
2 p. l., 208 p. front. (port.) illus. (incl. plans) plates. 31cm.

Festschrift.

I. Title: Festschrift.

20—21111

Library of Congress LF5039.5.A5 1914
[30b1]

---

* IDS p.v.265

Zum 70. Geburtstage Ferdinand Schreys, den 19. Juli, 1920. Festschrift. Berlin: W. Reh, 1920. 24 p. 8°.

Contents: BÖHR, O. Ferdinand Schrey. AMSEL, G. Nicht nur Stenograph. JOHNEN, C. Von Gabelsberger zur vereinfachten Stenographie, System Schrey. MANTZEL, A. Über den Anteil Ferdinand Schreys an der Entstehung des Einigungssystems. LIEDLOFF, A. Ferdinand Schrey und die Redeschrift. HARTMANN, S. Zur Reform der Kurzschrift.

Mr. Moth

BRIDGE SHORTHAND COLL.

415217A. 1. Schrey, Ferdinand, 1850- .
N. Y. P. L. June 14, 1929

PSO

Zur Geographie der deutschen Alpen; Professor Dr. Robert Sieger zum 60. Geburtstage gewidmet von Freunden und Schülern; herausgegeben vom Deutsch-akadem. Geographenverein Graz. Wien: L. W. Seidel & Sohn, 1924. 234 p. incl. diagrs., tables. front. (port.), illus. 4°.

Bibliographical footnotes.

Contents: Widmung. SÖLCH, J. Alte Flächensysteme im Ostmurischen Randgebirge Steiermarks. AIGNER, A. Vorzeitformen in den ostalpinen Zentralketten. HERITSCH, F. Die Kare der Koralpe. KRÖPFL, K. Die Grenzen des hochstämmigen

(Continued)

N. Y. P. L. July 16, 1927

Zur Geographie der deutschen Alpen... (Continued)

Holzwuchses im Koralpengebiete. SCHARFETTER, R. Die Grenzen der Pflanzenvereine. SPREITZER, H. Der Almnomadismus des Klagenfurter Beckens. PASCHINGER, V. Versuch einer landschaftlichen Gliederung Kärntens. WUTTE, M. Alte deutsche Berg- und Flussnamen in den Karawanken. PENCK, A. Mittenwald. KREBS, N. Todtnauberg. PIRCHEGGER, H. Beitraege zu einer geschichtlichen Statistik der steirischen Städte und Märkte. SIDARITSCH, M. Die steirischen Städte und Märkte in vergleichend-geographischer Darstellung. SELLINGER, T. Die Strassendichte von Graz. KURKA, G. Das Wachstum städtischer Siedlungstypen Österreichs. STÖCKL, R. Die Karte der Bevölkerungsverteilung. HEIDERICH, F. Geographisch-methodische Streiflichter. MAREK, R. Südslavien.

1. Alps, Austrian. 2. Sieger, Robert, 1864- . 3. Graz. Universitaet. Deutsch-akademischer Geographenverein.

N. Y. P. L. July 16, 1927

E-10
8180

ZUR Geschichte und Problematik der Demokratie; Festgabe für Hans Herzfeld, Ord. Professor der Neueren Geschichte an der Freien Universität Berlin anlässlich seines fünfundsechzigsten Geburtstages am 22. Juni 1957. [Hrsg. von Wilhelm Berges und Carl Hinrichs] Berlin, Duncker & Humblot [1958] 693 p. port. 24cm.

Bibliographical footnotes.

1. Herzfeld, Hans, 1892- . 2. Democracy. I. Berges, Wilhelm, ed. II. Hinrichs, Carl, 1900- , ed.

NN 4.59 1/J OC, I, II PC, 1, 2, I, II SL E, 1, 2, I, II (LC1, X1, Z1)

D-16
4352

ZUR Geschichte von Volkskunde und Mundartforschung in Württemberg. Helmut Dölker zum 60. Geburtstag. Tübingen, Tübinger Vereinigung für Volkskunde [1964] 317 p. ports., facsims. 21cm. (Volksleben. Bd. 5)

Includes bibliographies.

Edited by Hermann Bausinger.

CONTENTS. --Johann Christoph von Schmid, von M. Blümcke. --Friedrich David Gräter, von D. Narr. --Ludwig Uhland, von H. Moser. --

(Continued)

NN 1.66 a/c OC, II (OS)I PC, 1, 2, 3, I, II SL (LC1, X1, Z1)

2

ZUR Geschichte von Volkskunde und Mundartforschung in Württemberg. (Card 2)

Adelbert von Keller, von M. Walker. --Ernst Meier, von H. Bausinger. --Michael Richard Buck, von R. Schenda. --Anton Birlinger, von R. Schenda. --Paul Beck, von K. Schaaf. --Hermann Fischer, von A. Ruoff. --Karl Haag, von R. Mehne. --Karl Bohnenberger, von U. Engel. --Rudolf Kapff, von H. Schwedt. --Heinrich Höhn, von I. Hampp. --Josef Karlmann Brechenmacher, von W. Müller. --August Lämmle, von H. U. Roller. --Günter Groschopf, von H. Schick. --Erika Kohler, von M. Scharfe.

1. Dölker, Helmut. 2. Folk lore--Study and teaching--Germany--Würtemberg. 3. German language--Dialects--Swabia. I. Series. II. Bausinger, Hermann, ed.

D-20
3352

Zwischen Stadtmitte und Stadtregion; Berichte und Gedanken: Rudolf Hillebrecht zum 60. Geburtstag. Hrsg. von der Deutschen Akademie für Städtebau und Landesplanung. Stuttgart, K. Krämer, [1970]

188 p. illus., maps, plans. 28 cm. (Beiträge zur Umweltplanung)

Includes bibliographies.

CONTENTS.—Zum Geleit, von H. Koch.—Einige Gedanken zu aktuellen Fragen des Städtebaues, von E. Hruska.—Das Gebiet

(Continued)

NN* 3.71 d/J OC, I (OS)II PC, 1, 2, I, II SL E, 1, 2, I, II (LC1, X1, Z1)

3

ZWISCHEN Stadtmitte und Stadtregion... (Card 2)

Hamburg, von W. Wortmann.—Die City, von K.-D. Ebert.—Hamburg und Toronto, von H. Blumenfeld.—Stadtmitte im Wandel, von F. zur Nedden.—Stadtregion—Regionalstadt, von R. Wurzer.—Die City; Objekt der Gesellschaftspolitik, von F. Rosenberg.—Stadtentwicklung als staatspolitische Aufgabe, von C. G. Schöning.—Arbeitszeit und Städtebau, von F. Tamms.—Im Vorraum und im Nachraum der Planung, von C. Farenholtz.—Zur Rolle des Soziologen in der Planung, von E. Spiegel.—Überlegungen zu einem Konzept der empirischen Stadtforschung, von O. Boustedt.—Das Theater; Element der Stadtmitte, von W. Kallmorgen.—Struktur und Gestalt im Städtebau, von G. Albers.

(Continued)

ZWISCHEN Stadtmitte und Stadtregion... (Card 3)

1. Cities--German. 2. Cities--Plans--Addresses, essays, lectures. I. Hillebrecht, Rudolf. II. Deutsche Akademie für Städtebau und Landesplanung.